# ENCYCLOPEDIA OF COMPUTER SCIENCE

# ENCYCLOPEDIA OF COMPUTER SCIENCE

FIRST EDITION

ANTHONY RALSTON, Editor
CHESTER L. MEEK, Assistant Editor

VNR VAN NOSTRAND REINHOLD COMPANY
NEW YORK CINCINNATI ATLANTA DALLAS SAN FRANCISCO
LONDON TORONTO MELBOURNE

Van Nostrand Reinhold Company Regional Offices:
New York Cincinnati Atlanta Dallas San Francisco

Van Nostrand Reinhold Company International Offices:
London Toronto Melbourne



Library of Congress Catalog Card Number: 78-7312
ISBN: 0-442-80321-4



Manufactured in the United States of America

Published in the United States of America
135 West 50th Street, New York, NY 10020

Published simultaneously in Canada by Van Nostrand Reinhold Ltd.

15 14 13 12 11 10 9 8

Library of Congress Cataloging in Publication Data

Main entry under title:

Encyclopedia of computer science.

Includes bibliographical references and index.
1. Computers--Dictionaries. 2. Electronic data processing--Dictionaries. 3. Information science--Dictionaries. I. Ralston, Anthony. II. Meek, Chester L., 1941-
QA76.15.E48 1978 001.6'4'03 78-7312
ISBN 0-442-80321-4

# CONTENTS

# EDITORIAL BOARD



# CONTRIBUTORS

John N. Ackley, *Digital Computer Controls, Inc.*
A. K. Agrawala, *University of Maryland*
Suad Alagić, *Univerzitet U. Sarajevu*
Saul Amarel, *Rutgers University*
J. K. Amsbaugh, *Sun Oil Co.*
Isaac L. Auerbach, *Auerbach Corporation*
Algirdas Avižienis, *University of California at Los Angeles*
Charles W. Bachman, *Honeywell Corp.*
G. David Baer, *Computer Task Group, Inc.*
Jean-Loup Baer, *University of Washington*
D. W. Barron, *University of Southampton, U.K.*
F. L. Bauer, *Technischen Universität, Munich*
John M. Bennett, *University of Sydney.*
Gilbert R. Berglass, *State University of New York at Buffalo*
John C. G. Boot, *State University of New York at Buffalo*
A. D. Booth, *Lakehead University*
K. H. V. Booth, *Lakehead University*
Susan Brewer, *Honeywell Corp.*
Peter J. Brown, *University of Kent, U.K.*
William F. Brown, *Ball State University*
G. Edward Bryan, *Xerox Corp.*
Janusz A. Brzozowski, *University of Waterloo*
W. Buchholz, *IBM Corp.*
Sander Buchman, *IBM Corp.*
R. A. Buckingham, *University of London*
John Case, *State University of New York at Buffalo*
Robert P. Cerveny, *State University of New York at Buffalo*
Ned Chapin, *InfoSci, Inc.*
W. J. Cody, *Argonne National Laboratory*
Samuel D. Conte, *Purdue University*
James W. Cooley, *IBM Corp.*
David C. Cooper, *University of London*
Joseph F. Cunningham, *Boca Raton, Fla.*
B. Garland Cupp, *McDonnell-Douglas Automation Co.*

## CONTRIBUTORS

Charles H. Davidson, *University of Wisconsin*
Dorothy E. Denning, *Purdue University*
Peter J. Denning, *Purdue University*
George D. Detlefsen, *General Electric Co.*
J. K. Dixon, *Naval Research Laboratory*
T. A. Dolotta, *Bell Laboratories*
Philip H. Dorn, *Dorn Computer Consultants*
A. S. Douglas, *London Sch. of Economics & Polit. Science*
Michael A. Duggan, *University of Texas*

Patricia James Eberlein, *State University of New York at Buffalo*
Richard H. Eckhouse, Jr., *Digital Equipment Corp.*
Carl Engelman, *The MITRE Corp.*
Kurt Enslein, *Genesee Computer Center, Inc.*

B. R. Faden, *North American Rockwell*
Jerome A. Feldman, *University of Rochester*
Nicholas V. Findler, *State University of New York at Buffalo*
Aaron Finerman, *State University of New York at Stony Brook*
Clive B. Finkelstein, *IBM Australia*
Patrick C. Fischer, *Pennsylvania State University*
Dennis A. Fletcher, *D. A. Fletcher & Associates*
Ivan Flores, *Baruch College, CUNY*
Michael J. Flynn, *Stanford University*
Caxton C. Foster, *University of Massachusetts*
Mark A. Franklin, *Washington University*
David N. Freeman, *Ketron, Inc.*
Gideon Frieder, *State University of New York at Buffalo*
Samuel H. Fuller, *Carnegie Mellon University*

Bernard A. Galler, *University of Michigan*
W. Morven Gentleman, *University of Waterloo*
Bruce Gilchrist, *Columbia University*
Amos N. Gileadi, *University of Massachusetts*
Stanley Gill *(deceased)*
George Glaser, *Consultant*
Jonathan Goldstine, *Pennsylvania State University*
Robert H. Gonter, *University of Massachusetts*
C. C. Gotlieb, *University of Toronto*
Thomas S. Grier, *Burroughs Corp.*
Michael D. Grigoriadis, *IBM Corp.*
Ralph E. Griswold, *University of Arizona*
Fred Gruenberger, *California State University at Northridge*
Mark Halpern, *Tymshare, Inc.*
John W. Hamblen, *University of Missouri at Rolla*
R. W. Hamming, *Naval Postgraduate School*
Fred H. Harris, *University of Chicago*
Robert V. Head, *Consultant*
L. B. Heilprin, *University of Maryland*

Herbert Hellerman, *State University of New York at Binghamton*
Harry A. Helm, *Defense Communications Agency*
Gabor T. Herman, *State University of New York at Buffalo*
I. T. Ho, *IBM Corp.*
Richard C. Holt, *University of Toronto*
John E. Hopcroft, *Cornell University*
J. N. P. Hume, *University of Toronto*
E. Gerald Hurst, Jr., *University of Pennsylvania*
Harry D. Huskey, *University of California at Santa Cruz*
S. R. Hyde, *Joint Speech Research Unit, U.K.*

R. V. Jacobson, *Chemical Bank, New York*
Charles V. Jones, *York University*
T. L. Jones, *Howard University*

Laveen N. Kanal, *University of Maryland*
Arthur I. Karshmer, *University of Massachusetts*
Ronald H. Kay, *IBM Corp.*
Kenneth M. Kempner, *National Institutes of Health*
Robin H. Kerr, *General Electric Co.*
Michael J. Kessler, *Control Data Corp.*
Peter T. Kirstein, *University of London*
Kenneth E. Knight, *University of Texas*
Robert R. Korfhage, *Southern Methodist University*
David J. Kuck, *University of Illinois*
Shan S. Kuo, *University of New Hampshire*

Börje Langefors, *University of Stockholm*
Duncan H. Lawrie, *University of Illinois*
Charles L. Lawson, *California Institute of Technology*
John A. N. Lee, *Virginia Polytechnic Institute*
R. P. Leinius, *Union Carbide Corp.*
Arthur Llewelyn, *Computer-Aided Design Centre, Cambridge, U.K.*
Keith R. London, *Keith London Ltd., U.K.*
Harold Lorin, *IBM Corp.*
Col. William F. Luebbert, *U.S. Military Academy*
Daniel H. Lufkin, *Consultant*

George Marsaglia, *McGill University*
Francis F. Martin, *Consultant*
Johannes J. Martin, *Virginia Polytechnic Institute*
Francis Parkash Mathur, *Wayne State University*
David W. Matula, *Southern Methodist University*
Michael M. Maynard, *Sperry Rand Corp.*
Davis B. McCarn, *National Library of Medicine*
John McCarthy, *Stanford University*
Edward J. McCluskey, *Stanford University*
Daniel D. McCracken, *Consultant*
John M. McKinney, *University of Cincinnati*

John C. McPherson, *Amagansett, New York*
C. L. Meek, *Andco, Inc.*
Albert R. Meyer, *Massachusetts Institute of Technology*
Benjamin Mittman, *Northwestern University*
Georgia Mollenhoff, *Journalist*
Calvin N. Mooers, *Rockford Research, Inc.*
Bruce C. Moore, *Louisiana State University*
G. J. Morris, *International Computers, Ltd.*
Philip M. Morse, *Massachusetts Institute of Technology*
François Muller, *United Nations*
Jean E. Musinski, *Cornell University*
J. Necas, *Prague, Czechoslovakia*
Roger M. Needham, *University of Cambridge, U.K.*
Allen Newell, *Carnegie-Mellon University*
Carol M. Newton, *University of California at Los Angeles*
Jerre D. Noe, *University of Washington*

T. William Olle, *Consultant*

Leonard J. Palmer, *Palmer Data Corporation*
Donn B. Parker, *Stanford Research Institute*
Azaria Paz, *Technion-Israel Institute of Technology*
Trevor Pearcey, *Caulfield Institute of Technology, Australia*
C. R. Pearson, *Georgia Institute of Technology*
Milton Pine, *Caulfield Institute of Technology, Australia*
Seymour V. Pollack, *Washington University*
Michael J. F. Poulsen, *IBM Australia*
C. E. Price, *Union Carbide Corp.*

Anthony Ralston, *State University of New York at Buffalo*
Brian Randell, *University of Newcastle upon Tyne*
Bertram Raphael, *Stanford Research Institute*
Edwin D. Reilly, Jr., *State University of New York at Albany*
Lee Revens (deceased)
John R. Rice, *Purdue University*
Frederic N. Ris, *IBM Corp.*
Saul Rosen, *Purdue University*
Azriel Rosenfeld, *University of Maryland*
Robert F. Rosin, *Bell Laboratories*
Paul Roth, *National Bureau of Standards*
B. C. Rowe, *Polytechnic of North London*
Arthur I. Rubin, *Electronic Associates Inc.*

Harry J. Saal, *IBM Corp.*
Arto Salomaa, *University of Aarhus, Denmark*
David Salomon, *San Diego State University*
Gerard Salton, *Cornell University*
Jean E. Sammet, *IBM Corp.*
Adel S. Sedra, *University of Toronto*
Sally Yeates Sedelow, *University of Kansas*
Eugene Shapiro, *IBM Corp.*
Ben Shneiderman, *University of Maryland*
Herbert A. Simon, *Carnegie-Mellon University*
James R. Slagle, *Naval Research Laboratory*
Vladimir Slamecka, *Georgia Institute of Technology*
Alvy Ray Smith, III, *Xerox Corp.*
Cecil L. Smith, *Louisiana State University*
I. A. Smith, *State University of New York at Binghamton*
Kenneth C. Smith, *University of Toronto*
John S. Sobolewski, *University of Washington*
Fred A. Stahl, *Columbia University*
Elizabeth Luebbert Stoll, *Santa Clara, Calif.*
T. B. Steel, *Equitable Life Assurance Society*
Theodor D. Sterling, *Simon Fraser University*
Jon C. Strauss, *University of Pennsylvania*
Robert W. Taylor, *University of Massachusetts*
Daniel Teichroew, *University of Michigan*
Thilo Tilemann, *University of Cologne*
Anthony L. Torrance, *McKinsey & Company, Inc.*
Henry S. Tropp, *Humboldt State University, California*
D. C. Tsichritzis, *University of Toronto*

Andries van Dam, *Brown University*
R. H. VanDenburg, Jr., *Southern Bank and Trust Co.*

W. M. Waite, *University of Colorado*
Charles H. Warlick, *University of Texas*
Peter Wegner, *Brown University*
Eric A. Weiss, *Sun Company*
Anne H. Werkheiser, *The MITRE Corp.*
Milton R. Wessel, *Attorney*
Gio Wiederhold, *University of California at San Francisco*
Maurice V. Wilkes, *University of Cambridge, U.K.*
James H. Wilkinson, *National Physical Laboratory, U.K.*
D. Wotschke, *Pennsylvania State University*

Stephen S. Yau, *Northwestern University*
David M. Young, *University of Texas*

H. Zemanek, *IBM Austria*
Karl L. Zinn, *University of Michigan*
Stanley Zionts, *State University of New York at Buffalo*
Albert L. Zobrist, *University of Arizona*

# PREFACE

When the idea of an Encyclopedia of Computer Science was first proposed to me almost five years ago, I embraced it eagerly. I believed, then, and believe even more strongly now, that computer science has come sufficiently of age as a discipline that it is appropriate and necessary to produce—in breadth and in depth—a snapshot of it (for, after all, a snapshot is what an encyclopedia is). Equally important is a belief that such a snapshot will have value not just for the moment but for some considerable number of years. The discovery and development of new knowledge and techniques and the discarding of the old are still rapid in computer science and technology, at least in relation to other scientific and technical disciplines. But the pace is no longer so breakneck as it was in the 1950s and 1960s when a computer system became obsolete every two or three years; the effective and useful life of an encyclopedia of computer science today, like that of a computer system, should be measured in terms of half-decades or more. Moreover, while parts of any encyclopedia become obsolete after a time, this one contains a major proportion of material which will continue to be of reference value for many years to come.

Five years ago the scope of, as well as the need for, this encyclopedia seemed sufficiently clear that I believed this volume could be efficiently and expeditiously developed. How naive I was! Despite a long and relatively broad association with book publishing, I underestimated the scientific, administrative, and production complexities of a project as large as this one. But, if the result has taken longer to achieve than I anticipated, I do not regret the effort. Editing an encyclopedia like this one is an education itself in one's own discipline. And I value considerably the contacts with the members of the Editorial Board, all eminent computer scientists whose advice has much improved the quality of this volume, and with the over 200 authors of articles, all of whom I love, even the most recalcitrant and prima donnaish of them!

Anthony Ralston

*February, 1976*

*Note*

The Editor and Publisher would appreciate an indication from readers of how future editions of this Encyclopedia could be improved. What additional subjects need to be covered? Which articles need improvement? Any such comments or notification of errors found should be sent to Petrocelli/Charter, 641 Lexington Avenue, New York, New York 10022.

# EDITOR'S FOREWORD

An encyclopedia has one main purpose—to be a reference work for the layman or the non-specialist who needs elaboration of a subject in which he is not expert. The implication of "basic" is that an encyclopedia, while it should attempt to be comprehensive in *breadth* of coverage, cannot be comprehensive in the *depth* with which it treats most topics. An encyclopedia should, however (and this one does), direct the reader to information at the next level of depth through cross-references to other articles and bibliographic references.

What constitutes breadth of coverage is always a difficult question and especially so for computer science. As a new discipline that has evolved over the past three decades, and which is still changing rather rapidly, its boundaries are blurred. This is complicated further because there is no general agreement among computer scientists or technologists about whether certain areas are or are not part of computer science.

The choice of specific subject matter for this encyclopedia has been necessarily a personal one by the Editor, modulated by the Assistant Editor, the Editorial Board, and by the practical problems of finding authors to write particular articles. My hope is that, while inevitably there will be quibbles about the inclusion of certain topics, little or nothing of major importance has been omitted.

An encyclopedia is *not* a handbook, which is normally intended only for practitioners in the subject area or for professional users of the subject area knowledge. Neither is it a *dictionary* nor a *glossary*.

Articles in this encyclopedia normally contain definitions of the article titles, but even the shortest articles also contain explanatory information to broaden and deepen the reader's understanding. Long articles contain historical and survey information in order in integrate the subject matter and put it into perspective. Overall, it is a basic reference to computer science as well as a broad picture of the discipline, its history, and its directions.

**Organization**

The organization of this volume is on an alphabetic basis according to the first word of each article title. Titles have been chosen in such a way that the first word is the one most likely to be selected by the reader searching for a given topic. In addition, main cross-references have been provided when more than one word in a title might reasonably be referenced. These cross-references are also used to refer to important subjects that are included in longer, more general articles rather than as separate articles.

Three additional aids to the reader have been provided. The first is the CROSS-REFERENCES at the beginning of each article, which list titles of other articles and names of terms used which may be unfamiliar to the reader.

The APPENDIXES at the back of the book constitute the second aid. These include lists of abbreviations, acronyms, special notation and terminology, as well as some useful numerical tables.

The third aid is the INDEX. In a dictionary or glossary, all terms appear as entries, but in an encyclopedia only the most important terms are used as article titles or even main cross-references. Without an Index the location of much important information would be left to the ingenuity of the reader. In fact, the Index contains *all* terms that should appear in a *dictionary* of computer science. In addition, it contains entries that would not normally appear in a dictionary, such as references to subcategories. The encyclopedia user who searches among the article titles unsuccessfully will find the Index invaluable in locating specific information. In addition, the Index will often provide pointers to unfamiliar terms.

**Using the Encyclopedia**

Even a rapidly developing discipline such as computer science exhibits some coherent internal structure. We have been guided in the development of this encyclopedia by our perception of this structure. Five articles cover broad disciplinary subject matter:

Computer Science
Data Processing
Information Science
Information Processing
Symbol Manipulation

The remaining articles may be grouped under ten headings:

I. *Software*
II. *Hardware*
III. *Computer Systems*
IV. *Basic Terminology*
V. *Theory*
VI. *Mathematics for Computer Science*
VII. *Applications*
VIII. *Management, Societal, Economic, and Legal Aspects*
IX. *Professional and Educational Aspects*
X. *History*

To aid the user in grasping the overall taxonomy of computer science, a CLASSIFICATION OF ARTICLES precedes the main body of the Encyclopedia. It includes *all* article titles, except those five designated above as broad disciplinary subject matter, as well as some additional headings. All headings that are not article titles are preceded by an asterisk (*). The CLASSIFICATION OF ARTICLES will enable most readers who wish to concentrate on a particular area of computer science to find a list of relevant articles. In addition, the following lists provide useful groupings of articles not adequately reflected in the CLASSIFICATION.

*1. Basic Disciplinary Areas of Computer Science.* As an academic discipline, computer science is well established and its basic content is fairly clear. The article "Education in Computing Science" overviews the subject matter of the curricula at the graduate and undergraduate levels. Topics considered to be major subdisciplines of computer science and (or) which form the subject matter of one or more college courses are listed below. As in the CLASSIFICATION OF ARTICLES, italicized titles are for grouping purposes only and do not refer to actual articles.

(a) *Software and Programming-Related:* Programming Languages; Language Processors; Operating Systems; Machine and Assembly Language Programming; Procedure-Oriented Languages; Data Structures; Files; Programming Linguistics; Structured Programming.

(b) *Hardware-Related*: Computer Architecture; Computer Circuitry; Logic Design; Microprogramming.

(c) *Computer Systems*: Computer Networks; Information Systems; Management Information Systems; Time Sharing.

(d) *Theory*: Algorithms, Analysis of; Algorithms, Theory of; Computational Complexity; Formal Languages.

(e) *Mathematics of Computer Science*: Automata Theory; Numerical Analysis; Sequential Machines.

(f) *Applications*: Artificial Intelligence; Computer-Assisted Learning and Teaching; Computer Graphics; Image and Picture Processing; Information Retrieval; Pattern Recognition; Simulation.

*2. Scientific Computing and Applications.* The following categories contain major articles relating specifically to the use of computers in science and technology, and to articles on applications in science and technology.

(a) *Software and Programming-Related*: Algebraic Manipulation Languages; Mathematical Software; Problem-Oriented Languages; Simulation: Languages.

(b) *Applications*: Computer-Aided Design; Computer Graphics; Control Applications; Engineering Applications; Image and Picture Processing; Medical Applications; Pattern Recognition; Scientific Applications; Simulation: Principles; Speech Recognition; Text-Editing Systems.

This list is not exhaustive, since other articles also contain topics relevant to scientific-technical applications. Conversely, most of the articles listed above contain material applicable to other areas.

*3. Administrative and Business Data Processing*: The following major articles are related specifically to the use of computers for administration and business and to articles on applications in these areas.

(a) *Software and Programming-Related*: Access Methods; Data Base and Data Base Management; Data Security; Decision Table Languages; Files; Nonprocedural Languages; Software Packages.

(b) *Applications*: Administrative-Business Applications; Credit Applications; Information Systems; Management Information Systems; Planning Applications; Sorting.

Important aspects of these articles are relevant beyond administrative and business data processing.

The foregoing lists and the Classification of Articles that follows have been especially designed to guide curriculum development, to satisfy the requirements of the computer specialist outside his/her areas of expertise, to direct the readings of lay persons who may wish to become familiar with particular aspects of computer science, or to guide readers in following a self-study regime.

It would be pretentious to claim that the Encyclopedia will be "all things to all people," but I am confident that it will fill a much-needed basic reference in the field of computer science.

ANTHONY RALSTON

# CLASSIFICATION OF ARTICLES

(Note: This classification list includes all article titles except the five designated as broad disciplinary subjects: All headings that are not article titles are preceded by an asterisk.)

## I SOFTWARE

PROGRAMMING LANGUAGES
- Algebraic Manipulation Languages
- Associative Languages
- Authoring Languages and Systems
- Command and Job Control Languages
- Decision Tables: Languages
- List-Processing Languages
  - Garbage Collection
- Macrolanguages
- Nonprocedural Languages
- Problem-Oriented Languages
- Procedure-Oriented Languages: Survey of
  - Algol 68
  - Extensible Language
  - Pascal
- Simulation: Languages
- String Processing Languages

*SYSTEMS SOFTWARE
- Assemblers
- Input-Output Control Systems
- Interpreter
- Language Processors
  - Arithmetic Scan
  - Binding Time
  - Compatibility
  - Compile and Run Time
  - Compiler, Incremental
  - Compiler, Syntax-Directed
  - Load-and-Go Compiler
  - Reentrant Program
  - Side Effect
- Macroinstruction
- Operating Systems
  - Bootstrap
  - Buffer
  - Deadlock
  - Linkage Editor
  - Loader
  - Nucleus
  - Overhead

## CLASSIFICATION OF ARTICLES

## IV *BASIC TERMINOLOGY

### *PROGRAMMING-RELATED

- Algorithm
  - Markov Algorithm
  - Parallel Algorithm
- Flowchart
  - Block Diagram
  - Flow Diagram
  - System Chart
- Heuristics
- Identifier
- Iteration
- Job
- Label
- Lists and List Processing
  - String
- Masking
- Program
  - Subroutine
- Recursion
- Stored Program Concept
- Task

### *GENERAL

- Automation
- Cybernetics
- Errors
  - Errors, Absolute and Relative
- *Jargon
  - Bug
  - Fix
  - GIGO
  - Glitch
  - Kludge
  - Ping-Pong
- Models

## V *THEORY

- Algorithms, Analysis of
- Algorithms, Theory of
- Computability
- Computational Complexity
- Decidability
- Formal Languages
  - Backus-Naur Form
  - Meta Character

## VI *MATHEMATICS FOR COMPUTER SCIENCE

CODES
- ASCII
- Baudot Code
- Binary-Coded Decimal, Natural
- EBCDIC
- Error-Correcting Codes

OPERATIONS RESEARCH
- Mathematical Programming
- Simplex Method

GRAPH THEORY

LAMBDA CALCULUS

## VII *APPLICATIONS

*COMPUTER SCIENCE APPLICATIONS
- Artificial Intelligence
  - Theorem Proving
- Computer Graphics
  - Cursor
  - Joystick
  - Lightpen
  - Pictures, Basic Structure
  - Rand Tablet
- Image and Picture Processing
- Information Retrieval
  - Current Awareness Systems
  - Keyword-in-Context (KWIC) Index
  - Medlars-Medline
- Pattern Recognition
  - Perceptron
- Sorting
  - Sort-Merge Packages

*OTHER APPLICATIONS
- Administrative-Business Applications
  - Exception Reporting
  - Management Information Systems
- Arts Applications
- Computer-Aided Design
- Control Applications
- Credit System Applications
- Cryptography, Computers in
- Economic Applications
- Engineering Applications

## IX *PROFESSIONAL AND EDUCATIONAL ASPECTS

COMPUTER-ASSISTED LEARNING AND TEACHING
- Computer-Assisted Instruction (CAI)
- Computer-Managed Instruction (CMI)

EDUCATION IN COMPUTING SCIENCE

HIGHER EDUCATION, COMPUTERS IN

LITERATURE IN COMPUTING

COMPUTER USER GROUPS
- CUBE
- GUIDE
- Joint Users Group (JUG)
- SHARE
- USE
- VIM

*COMPUTER SOCIETIES
- American Federation of Information Processing Societies (AFIPS)
- American Society for Information Science (ASIS)
- Association for Educational Data Systems (AEDS)
- Association for Computing Machinery (ACM)
- Association Francaise pour la Cybernetique, Economique et Technique (AFCET)
- British Computer Society (BCS)
- Conference on Data Systems Languages (CODASYL)
- Data Processing Management Association (DPMA)
- Institute for Certification of Computer Professionals (ICCP)
- Institute of Electrical and Electronic Engineers—Computer Society (IEEE-CS)
- Intergovernmental Bureau for Informatics (IBI)
- International Federation of Automatic Control (IFAC)
- International Association for Analog Computation
- International Federation for Information Processing (IFIP)
- Society for Computer Simulation (SCS)
- Society for Industrial and Applied Mathematics (SIAM)

## X *HISTORY

DIGITAL COMPUTERS: EARLY, and ORIGINS
- *Computers
  - Atlas
  - EDSAC
  - EDVAC
  - ENIAC

# A

**ACM.** *See* ASSOCIATION FOR COMPUTING MACHINERY.

**AEDS.** *See* ASSOCIATION FOR EDUCATIONAL DATA SYSTEMS.

**AFCET.** *See* ASSOCIATION FRANÇAISE POUR LA CYBERNETIQUE, ECONOMIQUE ET TECHNIQUE.

**AFIPS.** *See* AMERICAN FEDERATION OF INFORMATION PROCESSING SOCIETIES.

**APL.** *See* PROCEDURE-ORIENTED LANGUAGES.

**APT.** *See* PROBLEM-ORIENTED LANGUAGES.

**ASIS.** *See* AMERICAN SOCIETY FOR INFORMATION SCIENCE.

## ACCESS METHODS

For articles on related subjects *see* DATA BASE AND DATA BASE MANAGEMENT; FILES; HASHING; KEY; and RECORD.

An access method is a technique of accessing data that has been placed in some kind of storage. This term was derived from the earlier term "access time," which concerned the speed with which data could be located on a storage device. The use of the term "access method" became popular in about 1964–1965 when it was used by IBM in connection with OS/360. Although the term implies a way of getting to data that is already stored, it is primarily a way of storing data under circumstances that also dictate the way it is to be subsequently accessed.

In a typical situation a choice of such access methods is available, and one method must normally be chosen for each file. For the purposes of this article, a *file* is defined as a collection of records usually, but not necessarily, all of the same type (hence, the occasional term "file access method"). An access method is therefore a property of a file whose essential purpose is to instruct how the file is to be stored. There may then be several ways of accessing or retrieving the records in the file.

**Classes of Access Methods.** If a file is stored on a device such as magnetic tape, then the only type of access available is pure sequential access, in which a search is made starting from the beginning of the file. Thus, the concept of an access method really became of interest only with the advent of direct access devices such as disks and drums. On such devices, data may be accessed directly by the address, or location, of the data on the device. Direct access of this kind is rare because the precise location of a data record in a storage device is seldom known to the software system that desires the access. It is necessary, therefore, to have available indirect methods for accessing data.

Indirect methods may be classified (1) as sequential, in which there is some type of search through a sequence of records (but generally not a complete search that starts from the first record and proceeds through the whole file), or (2) as nonsequential, in which the desired record is located without such a search. A common nonsequential method is based on the use of an index and is usually called "Index Sequential Access Method" (ISAM). Other common nonsequential access methods use key transformation techniques and are usually referred to as "randomizing" or "hashing" techniques.

**Index Sequential Access Method.** If an index is used, then some extra storage space is required to hold the index. In ISAM, one or more items in the record type are chosen as the ISAM "key." If the file has in fact two or more record types, then the ISAM key must be an item or items to be found in all record types.

The index then consists of an ordered sequence of the values of the ISAM key in the collection of records that are initially stored using this access method. Associated with each value is a list of addresses or pointers to the records, which have this value as their prime key. As an example, consider a file of records, each containing data about an employee in a company. Each employee has an employee number that distinguishes him from all other employees in the company. In other words, no two employees have the same employee number. One item in each record type would be the employee number and if this file of employee data is to be stored as an ISAM file, this item would most probably be chosen as the ISAM prime key. This means that it would always be possible to retrieve an employee record from the file if the employee number is known. As indicated above, the file is assumed to be stored on some kind of direct access storage such as disk or drum.

Typically with an ISAM file indexed on a single key in this way, the index could be used for updating. In other words, if the file contains 10,000 records and it is necessary to update 25 of these, then the index can be used to access the 25 records separately without unnecessarily accessing the other 9,975, as would be necessary if the file were stored on tape or if it were stored on disk without an index being available for use. If a new record is added to the file, then the ISAM index is automatically updated by the indexing mechanism to include the new employee number and the address of the employee record containing it in the file.

In view of the fact that ISAM is often used for very long files containing possibly hundreds of thousands of records, the index table itself may become quite long. In the most simple case, it would be necessary first to scan this long index table for a value when it was necessary to find a record having this value. One way of alleviating this problem is to associate with a group of key values a single address or pointer to the beginning of a block of records which contains the records with these key values. This block would then be searched either sequentially or by binary search to find the record with the desired key. If the blocks are not large, this does not introduce serious inefficiency. Moreover, this scheme has the advantage of facilitating insertions into, and deletions from, the file if the blocks are set up initially with extra locations.

If, however, the blocks are small, the index table may still be quite long. Therefore, the idea of a hierarchy of indexes (Table 1) has evolved to expe-

**Table 1.** A Hierarchical Block-Oriented Index.

| Index Level 1 | Index Level 2 | Block Number | Block Starting Address |
|---|---|---|---|
| | 00000-00713 | 1 | 46217 |
| | 00718-01426 | 2 | 46337 |
| | . | . | . |
| 00000-08756 | . | . | . |
| | . | . | . |
| | 07823-08756 | 10 | 47395 |
| . | | | |
| . | | | |
| . | 41063-42217 | 41 | 50362 |
| | . | . | . |
| 41063-52071 | . | . | . |
| | . | . | . |
| | 49278-50593 | 49 | 51612 |
| | 50614-52071 | 50 | 51738 |
| | . | . | |
| | . | . | |
| | . | . | |

dite the process of finding a value in an index table. For example, suppose an employee file with 10,000 records has employee numbers in the range 00000–99999. To retrieve the record for employee number 49,731, the first level would be searched until the fifth entry (41063–52071) was found, and then the second level would be searched until the ninth entry (49278–50593) was found, which would be substantially more efficient than searching through 49 entries of a single level index. The key 49731 is in block 49, with a starting address (usually on a disk) of 51612. The addresses starting with 51612 would then be searched sequentially for the record with key 49731. While the 100 blocks hold an average of 100 employee records each, the blocks generally contain more than 100 locations. This allows change and growth of the file before it must be reorganized and the index table updated.

There are many different approaches to using indexes in file access, as well as other access methods that do not involve indexes. Acronyms for some of these (e.g., VSAM, Virtual Sequential Access Method; QSAM, Queued Sequential Access Method) have arisen from IBM operating system terminology.

**Access Methods Using Key Transformation.** In this class of access methods, no index is maintained as in the other class. Instead, to decide where in storage to place the record, the value of the key is used as input to some algorithm that is designed to produce as output an address in storage. This address is not normally a physical address, in the sense of stipulating exactly which physical location in direct access storage will be used. It is usually a logical address within some area, or extent, or realm (all these words are in common use).

An example of the simplest algorithm is the following: Assume the space in which the records are to be stored is divided into $N$ equal sized "pages," each of which can store some number $M$ of records. It is necessary for $N$ to be a prime number for the algorithm to be effective. If the value of the chosen key is divided by $N$, then the result will be

$$\frac{\text{Key value}}{N} = I + R$$

where $I$ is the integral part of the quotient and $R$ is the remainder. Then $R$ identifies the page in which the record is to be stored.

When more than $M$ key values randomize (or hash) to the same value, which is a possibility with almost all such algorithms, then provision must be made to store the additional values in some kind of overflow area (perhaps on a different storage medium). When the record is to be retrieved from storage, the same algorithm is used to obtain the page from the key value. Locating the record in the page may then be by sequential or binary search or by a further indexing or key transformation technique, depending upon the number of records stored in each page.

The fact that these algorithms distribute the records somewhat randomly throughout the available space accounts for the fact that the approach is sometimes called a "random access" method. The fact that the bits in the key value are sometimes jumbled up, or "hashed," by the algorithm in order to produce the address accounts for the term "hashing."

**Application to Data Base Management.** In many present-day host-language data base systems the term "access method" is simply not used. The reason for this is that the records are stored in the data base and there are often many different ways of accessing each. The term "access method," as indicated, implies both a way of storage and a way of retrieval. There can, of course, be only one way in which any given record type is stored, and this has recently been called its "location mode." In view of the unfortunate ambiguity of the word "locate," which means both to find and to place, the term "storage mode" would have been a better choice.

REFERENCES

1971. Lefkovitz, D. *File Structures for On-Line Systems*. New York: Spartan-Macmillan.

1971. Davis, G. B. *Introduction to Electronic Computers*. New York: McGraw-Hill.

T. W. OLLE

# ACCESS TIME

For articles on related subjects *see* DIRECT ACCESS; LATENCY; and MEMORY: Auxiliary.

Direct access devices require varying times to position a read/write head over a particular record. In the case of a moving-head disk drive, this involves positioning the "comb" (head assembly, as in Fig. 1)

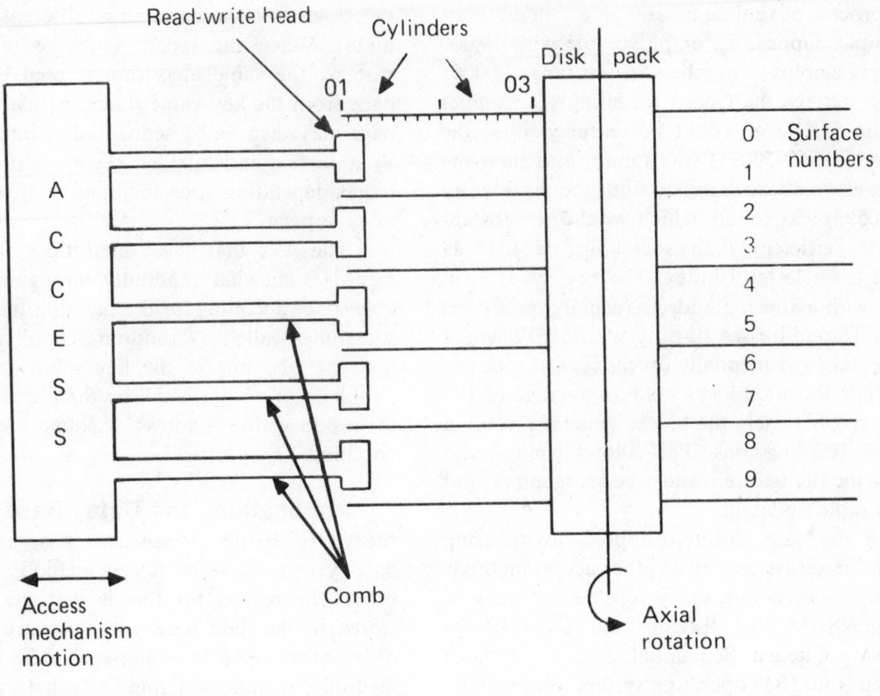


**Fig. 1.** Side view of typical disk drive.

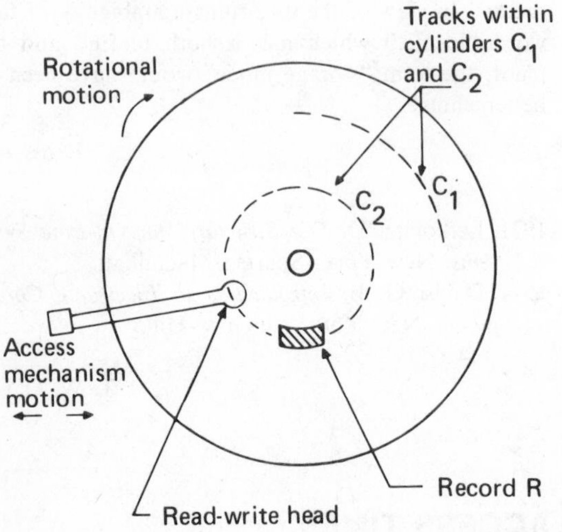


**Fig. 2.** Top view of typical disk drive.

to the designated cylinder, plus rotation of the selected track to the desired record. Comb-movement times for a typical medium-sized disk drive are shown in Fig. 3.

"Access time" is the sum of comb-movement and rotational times to reach a particular record. There is a different access time for each record retrieved at random from a disk drive, since it is necessary to move from cylinder $C_1$ to cylinder $C_2$ (Fig. 2), then await rotational positioning of record R. Generally of interest are *maximum access time* for a particular device (135 ms for the disk drive of Fig. 2), *average access time* (60 ms for this particular drive), and *minimum access time* (25 ms—the time to move the comb to an adjacent cylinder). The latter is also called "track-to-track access time."

Average access time is an important parameter for analytical planning of a real-time computer application, e.g., an on-line inquiry system. Minimum access time is more important for sequential usage of disk drives. The dominant component of delay for sequential retrieval of records from a disk drive is the average time for a half-rotation (12.5 ms for the drive described in Figs. 1 and 2).

During the past 15 years, rotational speeds for disk drives have improved very little: 2400 rpm is typical, equivalent to 25 ms per rotation. Bit densities per track have increased fivefold in this same period, so that average transfer speeds have increased even if track-to-track access times have not diminished. During this period, average access times have been halved, as a result of a widespread changeover from hydraulic actuators to "voice coil"

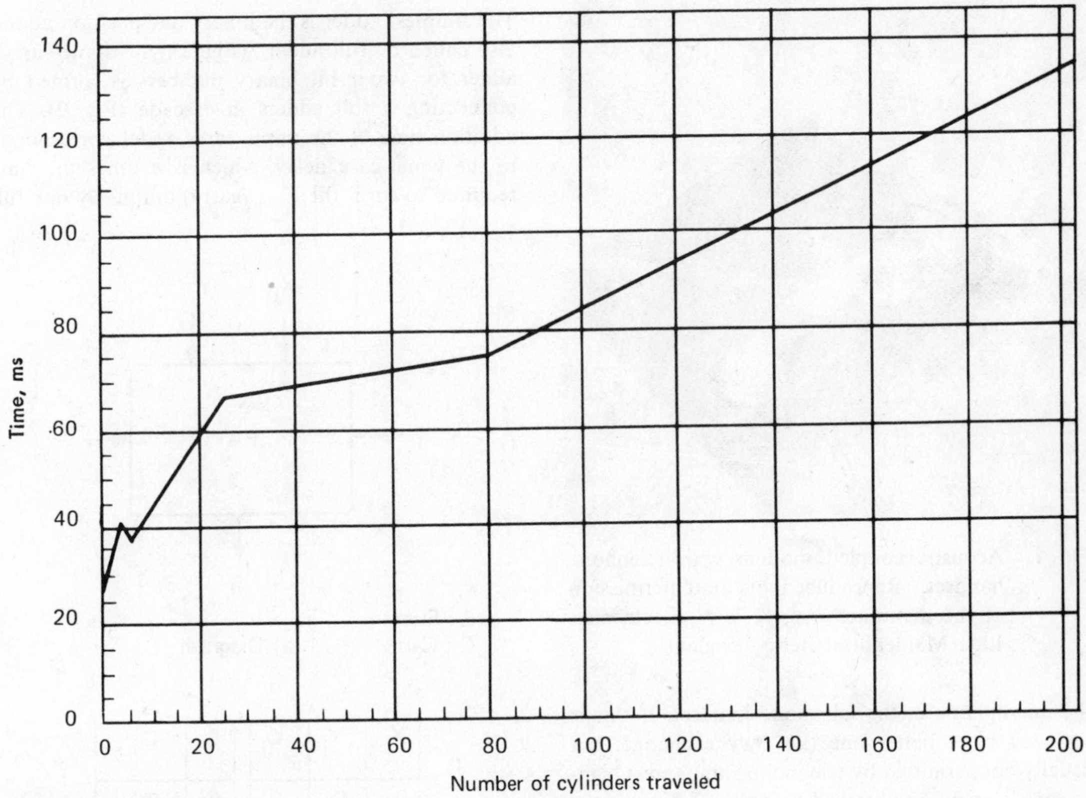


**Fig. 3.** Comb-movement times for typical disk drive.

actuators for moving the comb mechanism.

For a drum, average access time is a half-revolution and maximum access time is a full revolution, since drum heads are typically fixed over the data areas. Average access times for drums are 5 to 10 ms.

For magnetic card and similar mass storage systems, average access times depend on movement of the medium to a read/write head. Typical average access times for magnetic card devices are 1 sec and maximum access times are 2 to 4 sec. For tape-cartridge mass storage systems, average access time is approximately 15 sec and minimum access time to a new cartridge is approximately 12 sec.

D. N. Freeman

**ACCOUNTING, COMPUTER.** *See* Computer Accounting and Resource Control.

## ACOUSTIC COUPLER

For article on related subject *see* Modem.

An acoustic coupler (see Fig. 1) is a modem in which the coupling between a computer processor or terminal device and the communications line (almost always the telephone network) is acoustic rather than electric. The output of an acoustic coupler is an audible sound, which is applied directly to the telephone mouthpiece; in the reverse direction, the telephone earpiece is applied to a microphone in the modem. The advantage of an acoustically coupled modem is that almost any telephone handset can be used, and the modem is truly portable. The disadvantage is that the acoustic coupling can be noisy and may limit the speed of operation of the device; acoustically coupled modems are seldom used at data speeds above 300 bps (bits per second). With electric coupling, speeds of 1,200 bps or even 4,800 bps can be achieved with low error rates on switched telephone lines. The limiting component is usually

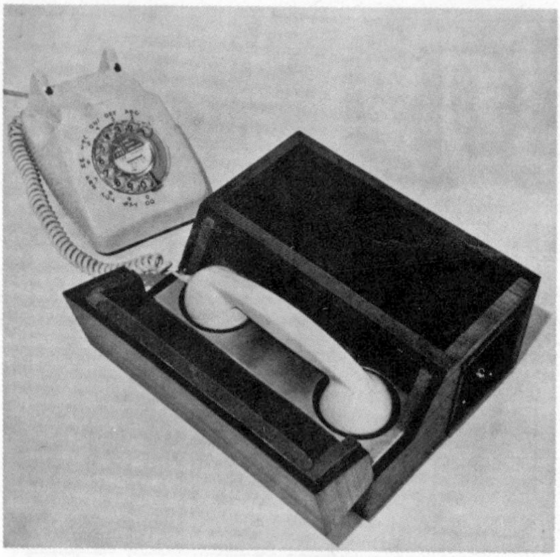

**Fig. 1.** Acoustic coupled modem with telephone handset. (Reproduced by kind permission of the manufacturers, K & N Electronics, Ltd., Maidenhead Berks, England.)

the microphone in the telephone handset. If this is replaced by a better one (an easy exchange, but usually not permitted by telephone companies) higher speeds could be obtained reliably.

P. T. KIRSTEIN

## ADDER

For articles on related subjects *see* ARITHMETIC, COMPUTER; and ARITHMETIC-LOGIC UNIT.

The adder is a logic circuit that forms the sum of two or more numbers represented in digital form. The simplest adder is the binary one-position adder, also called a "full adder" (Fig. 1). A "ripple-carry" adder for two *n*-bit binary numbers is formed by connecting *n* full adders in cascade (Fig. 2). The addition time of the ripple-carry adder corresponds to the worst-case delay, which is *n* times the time required to form the $C_{i+1}$ (carry) output by one full

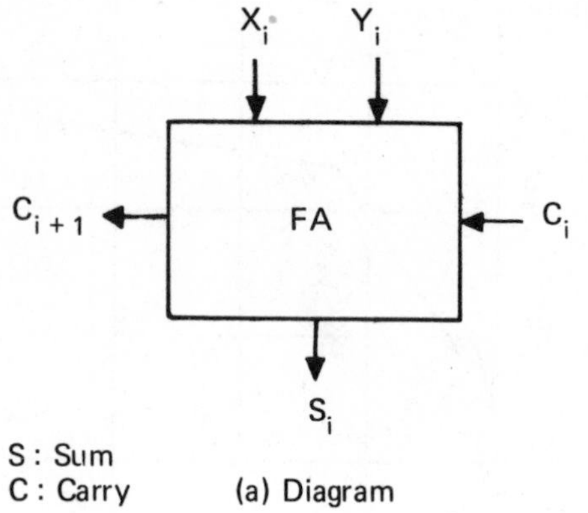


(a) Diagram

| $X_i$ | $Y_i$ | $C_i$ | $S_i$ | $C_{i+1}$ |
|---|---|---|---|---|
| 0 | 0 | 0 | 0 | 0 |
| 0 | 0 | 1 | 1 | 0 |
| 0 | 1 | 0 | 1 | 0 |
| 0 | 1 | 1 | 0 | 1 |
| 1 | 0 | 0 | 1 | 0 |
| 1 | 0 | 1 | 0 | 1 |
| 1 | 1 | 0 | 0 | 1 |
| 1 | 1 | 1 | 1 | 1 |

(b) Truth table

**Fig. 1.** The binary full adder (FA).

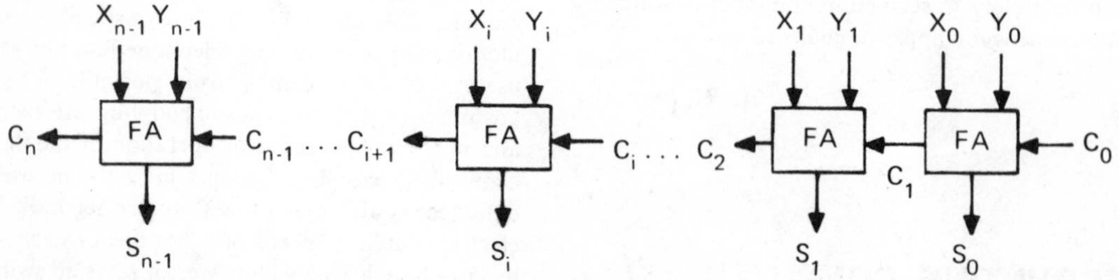


**Fig. 2.** Binary ripple-carry adder.

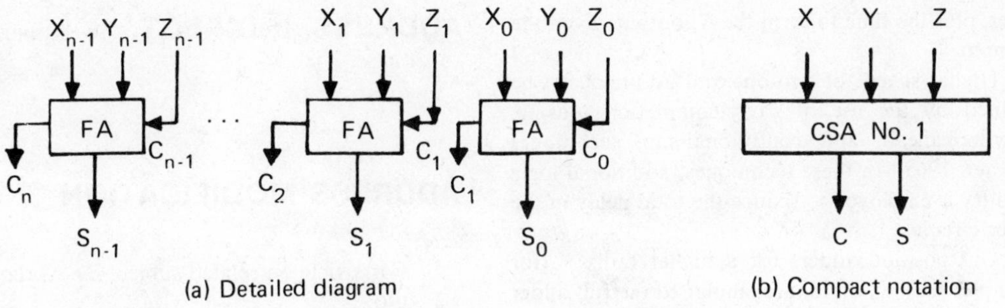


**Fig. 3.** Three-operand binary carry-save adder.

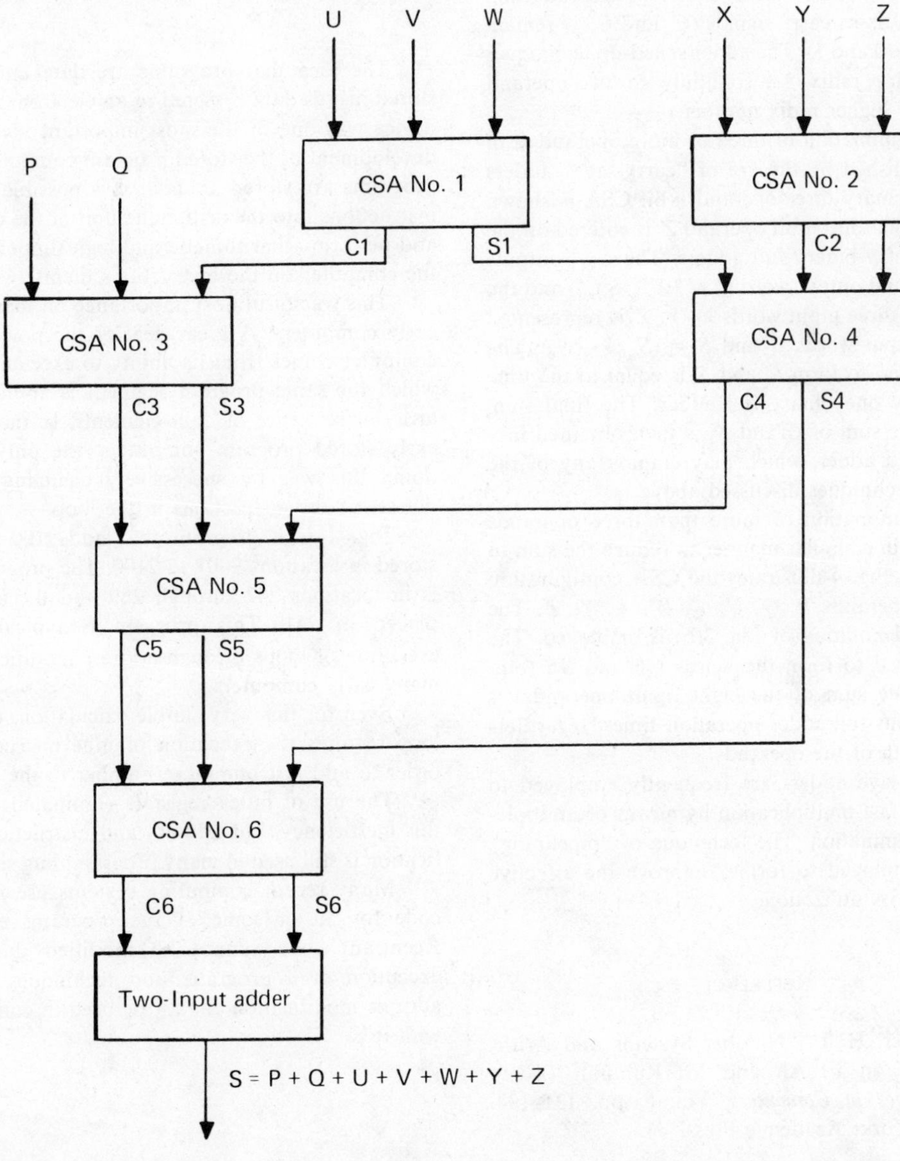


**Fig. 4.** CSA summation of eight operands.

adder, plus the time to form the $S_i$ output, given the $C_i$ input.

Higher speeds of two-operand addition can be attained by the use of carry-completion sensing, carry-lookahead, and conditional-sum techniques (Garner, 1965). In these techniques, additional logic circuitry is employed to reduce the total delay in the adder circuits.

One-position adders for a higher radix $r$ (for example, 4, 8, 10, or 16) are similar to the full adder of Fig. 1. The digits $X_i$ and $Y_i$ assume values 0 to $r - 1$, and they are represented by two or more logic variables. The truth table describes the addition table for radix $r$; carry signals ($C_i$ and $C_{i+1}$) remain two-valued (0 and 1). The adder speed-up techniques discussed for radix 2 also apply to two-operand addition of higher radix numbers.

Fast summation of three or more operands can be accomplished by the use of "carry-save" adders (CSA). A binary three-operand $n$-bit CSA is shown in Fig. 3. The third $n$-bit operand $Z$ is entered on the $C_i$ inputs of $n$ binary full adders. The $C_{i+1}$ outputs form a second output word $C = (C_n \cdots C_1)$ and the sum of the three input words $X$, $Y$, $Z$ is represented by two output words $C$ and $S = (S_{n-1} \cdots S_0)$. The time required to form $C$ and $S$ is equal to the time required by one binary full adder. The final sum, which is the sum of $C$ and $S$, is then obtained in a two-operand adder, which may employ any of the speed-up techniques discussed above.

The summation of more than three operands uses CSAs in a similar manner to reduce the sum to two words. Fig. 4 illustrates the CSA configuration for eight operands $P$, $Q$, $U$, $V$, $W$, $X$, $Y$, $Z$. The abbreviated notation of Fig. 3(b) is employed. The time required to form the words $C6$ and $S6$ (representing the sum of the eight input operands) is equal to four full-adder operation times, regardless of the length of the operands.

Carry-save adders are frequently employed to implement fast multiplication by means of multiple-operand summation. The technique of "pipelining" may be employed to further improve the effective speed of CSA utilization.

### Reference

1965. Garner, H. L. "Number Systems and Arithmetic," in F. Alt and M. Rubinoff (Eds.), *Advances in Computers*, Vol. 6, pp. 131–194. New York: Academic Press.

A. Avižienis

## ADDRESS, INDIRECT. *See* Indirect Address.

## ADDRESS MODIFICATION

For article on related subject *see* Addressing.

For articles on related terms *see* Index Register; and Reentrant Program.

The idea that programs are data and can be stored just as data is stored in an electronic memory device was one of the most important ideas in the development of the stored program computer. When programs are stored as data, it is possible to bring instructions into the arithmetic unit of the computer and perform all arithmetic and logical operations of the computer on the instructions themselves.

This was of utmost importance on many of the early computers. A great deal of the power of the computer comes from its ability to execute loops in which the same program segment is applied to an array or sequence of data elements. In most of the early stored program computers, the only way of doing this was by successively changing the addresses of the instructions in the loop.

Fig. 1 is a program that adds 100 numbers stored in locations 2001 to 2100. The program itself is in locations 242 through 259 and the answer is placed in 241. This program is typical of the execution of loops through address modification on many early computers.

Even for this very simple calculation, the main loop requires the execution of nine instructions in order to add just one more number to the sum.

The use of index registers eliminated much of this inefficiency, but address and instruction modification is still used in many programming situations.

Many recent computing systems use reentrant code for all or some of the programs executed. Reentrant code cannot be modified during the execution of a program, and techniques such as address modification cannot be used in conjunction with it.

S. Rosen

| Location | Instruction | Comment |
|---|---|---|
| 241 | | (Location of ultimate result) |
| 242 | FETCH 259 | Initialize sum to zero (242 begins program) |
| 243 | STORE 241 | |
| 244 | FETCH 256 | Initialize location 250 |
| 245 | STORE 250 | |
| 246 | FETCH 250 | Modify address in 250 to add next number (Main Loop begins) |
| 247 | ADD 257 | |
| 248 | STORE 250 | |
| 249 | FETCH 241 | Do the addition (Instruction in location 250 is the one modified; the contents of this location before execution of the program are irrelevant. It is initialized by the instruction in location 245.) |
| 250 | [ADD 2000 + n] | |
| 251 | STORE 241 | |
| 252 | FETCH 250 | Check if all numbers have been added |
| 253 | SUBTRACT 258 | |
| 254 | BRANCH ON NEG 246 | (Main Loop ends) |
| 255 | JUMP OUT | |
| 256 | ADD 2000 | Constants used by the program. Note: some of the constants look like instructions. |
| 257 | 000 000 001 | |
| 258 | ADD 2100 | |
| 259 | 000 000 000 | |

**Fig. 1.** Use of address modification in a simple program on an early computer.

# ADDRESSING

For articles on related subjects *see* MACHINE INSTRUCTION SET; STORAGE ALLOCATION; and STORAGE ORGANIZATION.

For articles on related terms *see* BASE REGISTER; GENERAL REGISTER; INDEX REGISTER; INDIRECT ADDRESS; OVERLAY; and VIRTUAL MEMORY.

## BASIC TERMINOLOGY AND HARDWARE CONCEPTS

A typical computer instruction must indicate not only the operation to be performed but also the location of one or more operands, the location where the result of the computation is to be deposited, and, sometimes, the location where the next instruction is to be found. Of course, in certain kinds of instructions such as those involved in decision making, there may be no computational operands but only a determination of the next instruction to be executed. Normally, however, all parts of the instruction are either explicitly or implicitly given. We will first consider the hardware techniques by which an address (or location) in the computer may be specified. In what follows, we shall consider primarily storage in which each location has associated with it a sequentially assigned address. An alternative method of determining a desired storage location will be considered briefly in the later section "Content-Addressable Storage."

Historically and presently, computer hardware allows addresses to be specified in a variety of ways. The most straightforward approach would be to put the entire address directly into the instruction, representing a specific location of a word or part of a word in storage. Thus, on the IBM 650, an early decimal computer, the 2-digit operation code, and the two 4-digit addresses, representing the location of the data and the location of the next instruction, respectively, were represented in the instruction itself. (It should be noted that, on modern computers, except for the case of decision-making instructions, the address of the next instruction is virtually always taken implicitly to be the location after that of the instruction being executed.) The operation code in the 650 (as on modern computers) implied the location of one of the operands and the location of the result.

| Op Code | Data Address | Next Inst. Address |
|---|---|---|
| 2 digit | 4 digit | 4 digit |

For example, the operation code AU (add to upper) implied that the upper half of the accumulator register was one of the operands, along with the explicitly named operand, and the result was to remain in the upper half of the accumulator.

As the amount of storage increases, however, and the number of digits (either binary or decimal) needed to represent an address becomes large relative to the size of the instruction, it becomes clear that it is no longer feasible to represent an entire address each time it occurs in an instruction. This is especially true when the address part of an instruction must be able to accommodate the largest possible storage that might be attached to a particular model of computer, even though an individual installation might only have a small part of that storage. In such cases the addresses actually occurring use only a small portion of that part of the instruction set aside for addresses. The remaining portion must always contain zeros, representing a waste of a valuable resource.

Several hardware devices have been and are employed to obtain, from one of a small number of larger registers, most of the information needed to specify an address, with the instruction itself containing only the information needed to complete the address. A number of these methods were employed in the Control Data Corp. (CDC) 160 and 160A computers, early small machines that started out with 4,096 12-bit words of storage. In the CDC 160, which dates back to 1959, six bits were used for the operation code, while the other six bits (with only 64 possible values) were used in the determination of an address. By choosing an appropriate operation code, the address would be interpreted to be in one of five modes: direct address (d); indirect address (i); relative address forward (f), and backward (b); and no address (n).

The direct addressing mode (d-mode) corresponds to the IBM 650 situation discussed above in that the address referred to a 12-bit operand in one of the first 64 words of storage.

Relative addressing provided for operand addresses and jump addresses that were near the storage location containing the current instruction. In relative addressing forward (f), the six-bit address portion was added to the current contents of the program control register P. (This register held the full 12-bit address of the current instruction.) The new value was then used for obtaining the operand, or used to jump to one of the 63 addresses forward from the address holding the instruction that was being executed. For relative addressing backward (b), the operand or jump address was obtained by subtracting the six-bit address from the current contents of P.

In the no-address mode (n), which is usually now referred to as the "immediate" mode, the six-bit address part was not treated as an address, but as a constant to be used in the actual computation. Indirect addressing is considered below in a more general context.

In the CDC 160A, seven banks of 4,096 words each were added to the storage, thus complicating the specification of an address. The modes of addressing already available were retained, but several three-bit registers were added to contain the number of the bank (0–7) in which a designated address would be found, and different operations referred to different bank registers. Additional operations were provided so that the programmer could set the values of these registers as necessary. This later machine also provided for two-word instructions, in which the second word might be a 12-bit immediate operand as well.

**Indirect Addressing.** One way to address a memory larger than the address part of an instruction allows is to have the instruction address point to another address that stores the operand address. This facility, called "indirect addressing," was available on the CDC 160 and is available on most contemporary computers. Fig. 1 illustrates this situation on a hypothetical 16-bit computer with a 7-bit instruction field and a 9-bit address field that permits the direct addressing of only 512 ($=2^9$) memory locations.

Indirect addressing can be used to address a memory of up to 65,536 words. In the example in Fig. 1, the program has placed the operand address 021326 (where we express addresses in octal for convenience) at a specific address (125) in the first 512 words of memory. If the instruction is, for example, an "add indirect" instruction, the address 125 is interpreted as an indirect address or pointer to the actual operand at location 021326. The address stored at 125 (namely, 021326) becomes the *effective address*.

Some systems allow multilevel indirect addressing. Thus, the number stored at 021326 may have a bit set that indicates that it, itself, is an indirect address that points to another location which contains the operand address. Indirect addressing may be combined in various ways with the use of index registers to produce complex addressing chains.

**Index Registers.** The concept of an index register, sometimes called a "tally register" or "base register" (see below), grew out of the B-line or B-register introduced on some of the earliest computers developed in England at the University of Manchester. This represented a major advance in computer design. Index registers are hardware reg-

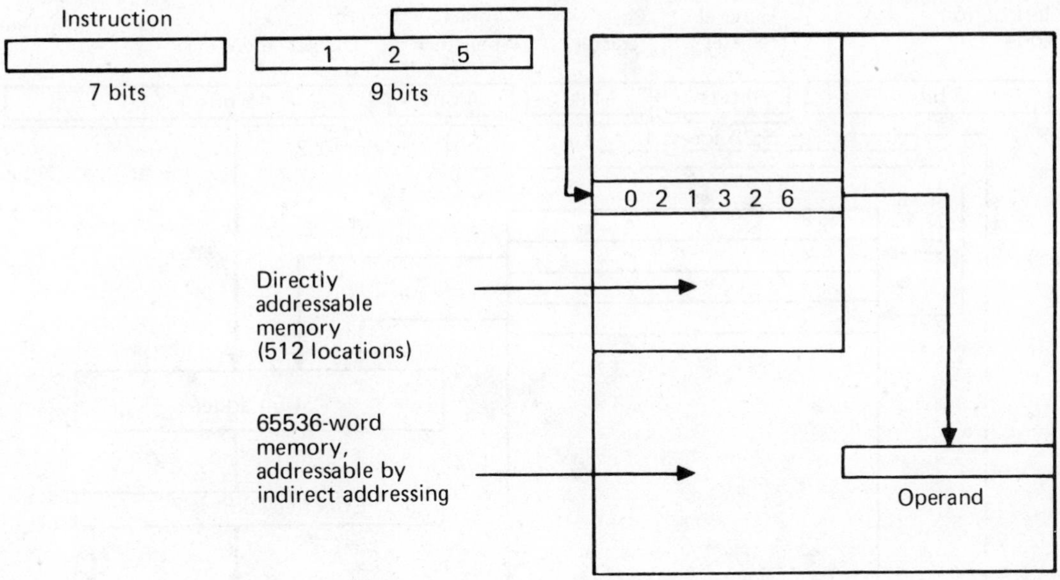


**Fig. 1.** Extension of addressing through indirect addressing.

isters that can be set, incremented, tested, etc., by machine instructions. Each instruction contains an indication as to whether its address is to be added to (or subtracted from) the contents of a designated index register to form the effective address. One of the main purposes, as suggested by the name, was to allow the effective address to be used as an index into a set of contiguous storage registers, commonly referred to as a "vector." Without changing the part of the address which was in the instruction itself, one could refer to one after another of the contiguous registers, merely by changing the contents of the index register successively. This replaced the more time- and space-consuming sequence of instructions which would normally put an instruction containing an address into an arithmetic register, modify it by ordinary addition, and then store it back to replace its former value. (This modified instruction was then executed, and it would refer to a different storage location.)

The use of index registers eliminated the need for modification of the instruction itself by allowing the index register to be modified by special instructions added to the computer for that purpose. With the advent of newer systems in which more than one task may be executing the same instructions at the same time, it has become very important that instructions not be modified during execution, since the modification by one task might be inappropriate for another task executing the same set of instructions.

**General Registers.** The use of variable-length instructions has also become much more widespread in recent years. The IBM System/360 or 370, for example, uses instructions that may take one, two, or three half-words for their representation. In the System/360 or 370, 16 *general registers* are provided, each capable of acting as an arithmetic register, a base register for relative addressing, or as an index register. (The fact that one cannot tell by looking at one of these registers whether its contents represents an ordinary number or an address has sometimes led to other problems, but this degree of flexibility is very useful.) An instruction might refer only to one or two of these registers, in which case only four bits would be needed in the instruction for each one, and it could fit in a half-word (16 bits).

A full-word instruction could accommodate one reference to a general register (4 bits) and a reference to a storage address. The latter could be a combination of a base register (4 bits), an index register designation (4 bits), and a 12-bit displacement, which could be used as a local offset from the contents of the base register. Fig. 2 illustrates the determination of an effective address from a System/360 or 370 instruction.

**Relocation Registers.** Many computers have one or more hardware relocation registers, which aid in the implementation and running of multiprogramming systems. An example is the CDC 6000 series. A number of different programs may be

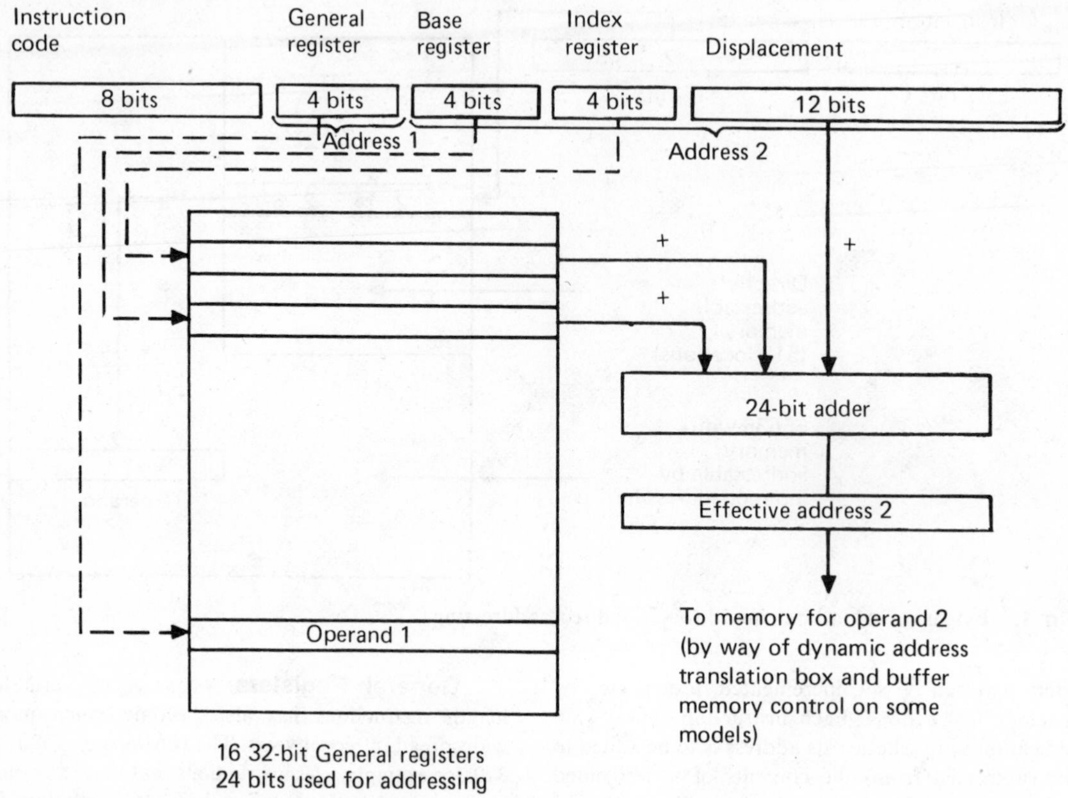


**Fig. 2.** Effective address calculation on IBM 360 and 370.

in the computer memory, each occupying a contiguous area. Thus, program A might occupy the area from 40,000 to 67,777, but this program (as well as all other programs in memory) is written and loaded into memory as if the area it occupies actually has the addresses 0 to 27,777. When program A is given control, the address 40,000 is stored in the hardware relocation register, and this constant is automatically added to all memory reference addresses while program A is running. The program could have been loaded anywhere else in memory, and can be loaded into different areas at different times. It will always produce the correct memory addresses, since all addressing is automatically made relative to the starting address of the area into which the program has been loaded.

In computers of this type, another hardware register will contain the "field length" or program size. Any attempt to reference beyond the area occupied by the program will be trapped, and an error condition will be signaled.

In a machine with two relocation registers, like the Univac 1108, a program may consist of two segments: for example, a program segment and a data segment, which can be placed independently anywhere in memory. The starting addresses of each of the two segments are placed in the two relocation registers, and every effective address has an associated bit that specifies which relocation register is to be added.

A relocation register is quite different in nature from an index register or a register used as a base for relative addressing. The relocation register is a special hardware register whose contents can be accessed and changed only through the use of privileged instructions under control of the operating system.

**Content-Addressable Storage.** Content-addressable or associative memories are quite different in concept from the more conventionally addressed memories described above. In a content-addressable memory the data item itself contains a key, usually in a specified field. This key is, in effect, the address of the item. The key may be the whole data item itself. The desired data item is located by means of an examination of all relevant keys. This could be done by software in a computer system with conventional memory addressing, but it would be quite slow.

In an associative or content-addressable memory, comparison circuits are used to provide a hardware-assisted and presumably very fast search through all data items to find the one that is addressed. Small memories of this type have been used to speed up address translation in virtual memory systems. Larger systems in which all addressing is associative have been proposed and some experimental models have been built.

The use of content-addressable memory was very expensive in terms of earlier technologies, but may prove practical with modern large-scale integration (LSI) technology. There are a number of important application areas in which associative memories would be very useful. The reader is referred to Hanlon (1966) for more information in this area.

B. A. GALLER AND S. ROSEN

## SOFTWARE ASPECTS

Corresponding to each hardware aspect of addressing there must be one or more techniques by which the programmer specifies addresses in his program.

**Absolute Addressing.** In the earliest and most elementary programming systems a programmer would assign instructions and data to locations in memory, and instructions would refer to absolute locations in memory. Thus, using a decimal computer for convenience, a programmer might write

```
267    ADD    3256
```

and, as a result of the eventual loading process, the instruction ADD 3256 would appear in location 267. It was the responsibility of the programmer to make sure that the appropriate data word was in location 3256 at the time the program was to be run. These are absolute addresses in that 267 always represents the same physical location in memory and 3256 similarly represents a specific physical location.

**Relative Addressing.** Some of the first advances in programming involved permitting the programmer to write programs or parts of programs without having to be aware of the absolute physical locations in which the instructions and data were to be stored. One of the early approaches to this goal was by way of regional or relative programming. A programmer, or several programmers, might decide that the program would be divided into a number of regions, A, B, C, D, etc. Addresses would then be relative to the start of a region. A programmer might write

```
A5    ADD    B15
```

to specify that an instruction located in the fifth location in region A is to add (to the accumulator) the data located in the fifteenth location in region B. A translator and loader would eventually take all regional addresses and convert them into absolute addresses.

There are a number of important advantages to this procedure. The programmer does not have to make arbitrary decisions about how large the regions are going to be. Separate sections of the program can be written independently, and unexpected or undesirable interactions can be avoided.

**Symbolic Addressing.** It was a relatively short step from regional addressing to free symbolic addressing. In the typical assembly system the programmer may write

```
INCR    ADD    ALPHA
```

and leave it up to an assembler to decide where the instruction INCR is to be placed. Somewhere else in his program he would have a data item named ALPHA.

**Indirect Addressing.** In a computer that allows indirect addressing, the programmer typically indicates an indirect address by adding a character, such as *, to the absolute or symbolic address. Thus,

```
INCR    ADD    ALPHA*
```

would indicate that the effective address is not ALPHA but is in the location specified by ALPHA.

**Indexing.** If an index register is to be used in calculating an effective address, this is normally specified following the instruction address. For example,

```
ADD    A,4
```

indicates that the contents of index register 4 is to be

added (subtracted on some computers) to A to determine the effective address. Indexing can be combined with indirect addressing so that

```
ADD    A*,4
```

would specify the effective address as the sum of the contents of location A and index register 4.

**Higher-Level Languages.** The development of higher-level programming languages has relieved the programmer of the responsibility for many aspects of memory management. However, that responsibility must reside somewhere: Either the programmer or the language processor and operating system must take on the responsibility for allocating space for instructions and data and for producing the programs that make appropriate use of the addressing structure of the computer. The software features of addressing discussed in this article are therefore mainly of interest to the assembly language programmer. The programmer who writes in a higher-level language such as Fortran or Cobol usually does not have to be aware of the details of memory addressing in the computer on which his program will run, but he may be sure that the Fortran or Cobol compiler is very much aware of these details, and usually expends a great deal of effort to take advantage of the memory-addressing hardware features provided on the computer.

S. ROSEN

## VIRTUAL MEMORY

**Overlays.** Many programs are too long to fit into the space in main memory that can be allocated to them at run time. In a uniprogramming system this will be true when the amount of space required by the program is greater than the total memory available to problem programs. In a multiprogramming system it may be true because the amount of space that is needed is more than the operating system is willing to allocate to this particular program. In either case, it becomes necessary to break the program up into sections, segments, or overlays so that the entire program need not be in main memory at the same time. The term "folding" has sometimes been used for this process.

In many systems the programmer has the responsibility for breaking his program into overlays and for providing the loading instructions that bring necessary overlays into main memory as they are needed. Many software systems provide aids to overlay planning. The user can name his overlays so that all symbolic addresses in an overlay will be automatically tagged with a special identifier that indicates which overlay they belong to.

A loader or linkage editor creates an object program organized as a set of overlays and a root segment containing information about the overlay structure. The root segment is loaded into main memory along with the segments needed to get the program started. Any reference to a symbolic address in a segment that is not in main memory causes a call on the supervisor to load the required segment, overlaying other segments if necessary.

There have been a number of efforts to produce software systems that provide automatic folding of programs. In such systems a programmer would write a program as if there were enough main memory to contain the whole program, and the software system would organize the program into overlays to fit the actual amount of storage that would be available. Efforts to produce software systems of this type date back to the earliest computers, but none has been particularly successful.

Most workers in the field feel that hardware assistance of some kind is necessary. Such hardware assistance is provided in the so-called virtual memory systems that first made their appearance around 1959 and which are becoming increasingly popular in the 1970s.

**The Atlas System.** The Atlas computer was probably the first virtual memory system. Its designers called it a single-level storage system. The idea was that a programmer would program as if all available memory were on a single level and directly addressable, whereas in fact memory was on two levels. In the Atlas the two levels were drum and core.

A program for the Atlas could be written as if it were to run in a homogeneous memory consisting of $2^{20}$ = 1,048,576 words. Memory was organized into *pages* of $2^9$ = 512 words each. The physical core memory might consist only of 32 or 64 such pages. However, the "address space" (i.e., the addresses that a user could address) consisted of $2^{11}$ = 2,048 such pages. Thus, an address in the Atlas consisted of an 11-bit page number and a 9-bit number indicating the location within the page.

A hardware page-address register is associated with each physical page (or "page frame," as it is sometimes called). A typical running program might consist of 50 pages, of which 20 pages at a particular time would be located in core memory and the other 30 located on the drum.

Each page of the program represents a set of 512 consecutive addresses with the same page number (i.e., the same 11 leftmost bits). The program page number is kept in the page address register of the physical page that is occupied by that program page. Thus, any program (or logical) page may occupy any physical page, and it may occupy different physical pages at different times during the running of the program.

Assume now (see Fig. 3) that the next instruction to be executed refers to an operand whose address (in octal) is 0231443. This is a reference to location 443 in page 231. Note that core memory of the machine contains nowhere near 231 pages, and there are only 50 pages in the program being executed. The programmer does not have to confine his program to the first 50 pages or to any contiguous block of 50 pages. He can use any areas in virtual memory that are convenient. Thus, the programmer does not have to know beforehand how long his code areas and his data areas are going to be. He can break his program up into segments and place the segments far enough apart in virtual memory so that he will be sure that their memory allocations will not overlap. There is no point at all to scattering a program at random over a large virtual memory; in fact, such programs will usually perform very inefficiently. One wants a very large virtual memory in order to be able to assign areas, whose ultimate size is not necessarily known in advance, to program and data modules that do not overlap and that form the structural units of a program. The segmented, two-dimensional virtual memories discussed below were introduced to make this type of modular programming more automatic and more convenient.

The page address registers form an associative or content-addressable memory. They are subject to a very rapid hardware scan to determine if one of them is page 231. If it is (say, if page 231 is in physical page 12, as in Fig. 3), then the operand sought is in physical location 12443, and the operand is fetched from that location. If, on the other hand, page 231 of this program is not in core memory, it must be fetched from the drum. An interrupt occurs, and the operating system initiates a transfer of that

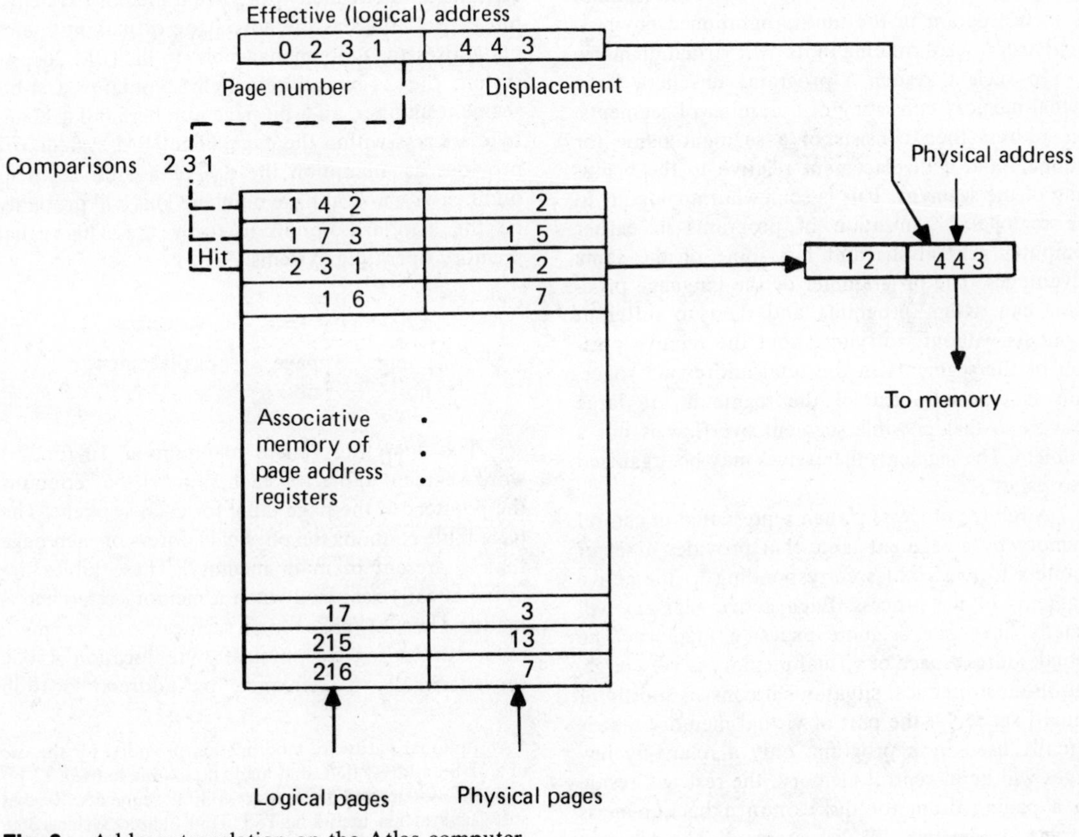


**Fig. 3.** Address translation on the Atlas computer.

page from drum into core. Assume that physical page 16 is available. The supervisor will cause program page 231 to be loaded into physical page 16, and will place the number 231 in the corresponding page address register. It then returns control to the program, which tries again to access an operand in virtual location 231443. This time it finds logical page 231 in physical page 16 and translates the address 231443 to 16443.

**Segments and Pages.** The Atlas system is an example of a one-dimensional or single segment virtual memory system. The programmer or the language processor must provide symbolic or absolute addresses in the one-dimensional virtual memory. Many of the classical storage allocation problems remain, although they are helped considerably by the fact that the virtual memory is much larger than the actual central memory of the computer on which the program is run.

From the point of view of program organization there are a number of advantages to a two-dimensional organization of virtual memory. Although two-dimensional virtual memory systems usually are multiprogrammed systems, it is convenient to think of each program in the multiprogrammed environment as if it were running in its own virtual memory.

In such a system a program runs in a large virtual memory consisting of a number of segments. An address then consists of a segment name (or number) and a displacement relative to the beginning of the segment. This is somewhat analogous to the regional organization of programs in earlier computer generations and has some of the same advantages. The programmer or the language processor can assign programs and data to different segments without worrying about the relative position of the segments in the total addressing space. This is especially true if the segments are large enough so that possible segment overflow is not a problem. The segments themselves may be organized into pages.

A job (or process) is then represented in central memory by a segment table that provides a set of pointers to page tables corresponding to the active segments of the process. Each active segment will usually have one or more pages in memory. The actual address space or virtual memory is very large, and in most practical situations it consists mostly of unused space. Of the part of virtual memory that is actually used by a program, only a relatively few pages will be in central memory; the rest will reside on a paging drum (or disk) or in a backup mass storage system (usually disk storage). The segment may serve as a unit of sharing among programs. The same segment (i.e., a pointer to the same page table) may appear in several segment tables that correspond to several jobs that are simultaneously active. The possibility of sharing segments was one of the strong motivations for the development of the segmented virtual memory systems.

The first and perhaps the only complete implementation of this type of virtual memory system was attempted in the Multics system developed at M.I.T. on the General Electric (now Honeywell) 645 computer. The actual addressing and address translation scheme used is too complicated to be discussed here. The reader is referred to Organick (1972).

**IBM Virtual Memory Systems.** The IBM 360/67 in 1965, and later the IBM 370 series in 1972, have popularized some of the concepts of virtual memory. In the standard 360/67 hardware systems the virtual memory associated with a process consists of 16 segments, and a segment consists of 256 pages, each of which has 4096 bytes. The relatively small size of the virtual memory loses some of the advantages associated with virtual memory systems, but it probably has the advantage of making memory addressing more manageable. In the IBM 360/67 system the 24-bit address field* contains a 4-bit segment number, an 8-bit page number, and a 12-bit byte address within the page. (The IBM system 370 provides as an option the use of a 5-bit segment number with a 7-bit page number. This will probably be the standard option used by the 370 virtual memory operating systems.)

| segment no. | page no. | displacement |
| --- | --- | --- |

The operating system maintains a 16- (or 32-) word segment table for each process that contains the pointers to the page table for each segment. The page table contains the physical address of each page that is present in main memory. These tables are automatically searched when a memory reference is made. Thus, if page 4 of segment 6 is in main memory starting at physical byte location 15000 (hexadecimal), a reference to address location

* An optional hardware modification provided for the use of a 32-bit address field that made it possible to use a 12-bit segment system and thus address 4096 segments. Several software systems, including TSS (Time Shared System) 360, took advantage of this extended addressing capability.

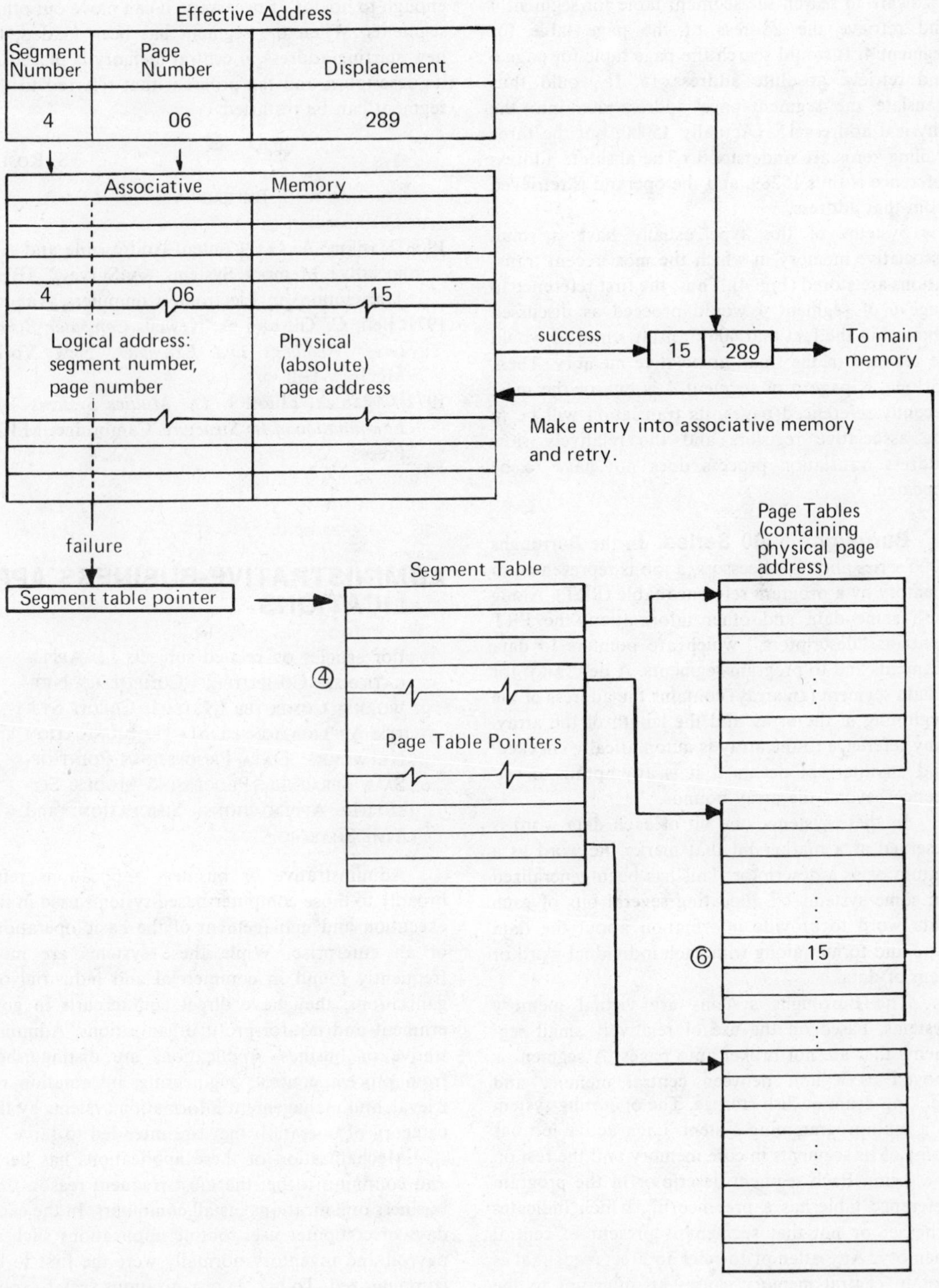


**Fig. 4.** Address translation on a virtual memory machine (IBM 360/67).

406289 would cause the dynamic address translation hardware to search the segment table for segment 4 and retrieve the address of the page table for segment 4. It would search the page table for page 6 and retrieve absolute address 15. It would thus translate the segment/page address 406 into the physical address 15. (Actually 15000, but the three trailing zeros are understood.) The absolute address reference is thus 15289, and the operand is retrieved from that address.

Systems of this type usually have a small associative memory in which the most recent translations are stored (Fig. 4). Thus, the first reference to page 6 of segment 4 would proceed as discussed above, but the fact that 406 translates into 15 would be retained in the small associative memory. Then, so long as page 6 of segment 4 is one of the most recently referenced pages, its translation will be in the associative registers and the relatively slow address translation process does not have to be repeated.

**Burroughs 5000 Series.** In the Burroughs 5000 series and its successors, a job is represented in memory by a program reference table (PRT). Along with some data and other information, the PRT contains "descriptors," which are pointers to data segments and to program segments. A descriptor for a data segment (an array) contains the address of the beginning of the array and the length of the array. Any reference to the array is automatically checked, and an interrupt occurs if it is attempting to reference beyond the array bounds.

In these systems, one bit of each data word is reserved as a marker bit that marks the word as a datum or as a descriptor. This has been generalized on some systems by allocating several bits of each data word to provide information about the data type and format along with each individual word or item of data.

The Burroughs systems are virtual memory systems, based on the use of relatively small segments that are not broken into pages. A segment is moved as a unit between central memory and backing drum or disk storage. The operating system is a multiprogramming system. Each active job has some of its segments in core memory and the rest on the drum. Each segment descriptor in the program reference table has a presence bit, which indicates whether or not that segment is present in central memory. Any attempt to refer to a segment that is not in central memory causes an interrupt to the supervisor, requesting that that segment be loaded. The supervisor can load the segment into any available contiguous area of memory that is large enough to hold it. If necessary, it can move out other segments. When the segment has been loaded, its new starting address in central memory is placed in its descriptor, and the program that referred to the segment can be restarted.

S. Rosen

References

1966. Hanlon, A. G. "Content-Addressible and Associative Memory Systems—A Survey," IEEE Transactions in Electronic Computers, August.

1971. Bell, C. G., and A. Newell. *Computer Structures: Readings and Examples.* New York: McGraw-Hill.

1972. Organick, Elliott I. *The Multics Systems—An Examination of Its Structure.* Cambridge: M.I.T. Press.

## ADMINISTRATIVE-BUSINESS APPLICATIONS

For articles on related subjects *see* Applications, Computer; Computer Networks; Computer Systems; Credit System Applications; Data Communication Networks; Data Processing; Point-of-Sale Terminal; Processing Modes; Scientific Applications; Simulation; and Time Sharing.

Administrative or business applications refer broadly to those computer-based systems used in the execution and management of the basic operations of an enterprise. While these systems are most frequently found in commercial and industrial organizations, they have direct counterparts in government and not-for-profit organizations. Administrative or business applications are distinguished from process control, engineering, information retrieval, and management information systems by the category of operation they are intended to serve.

Mechanization of these applications has been, and continues to be, the most frequent reason that business organizations install computers. In the early days of computer use, routine applications such as payroll and inventory normally were the first to be computerized. Today, as organizations seek to solve more difficult business problems and to gain control over broader and more closely integrated areas of their operations, highly complex computer applications are being undertaken. For example, distribution management systems are being developed to integrate finished goods inventory control, warehousing, and transportation, and new order-entry systems do the same for requirements planning, production scheduling, and sales analysis. Whereas the high cost of early computers limited their installation to large organizations, the extension of the minicomputer's capability—beyond its previously scientific or process control orientation—is making it possible for thousands of small organizations to computerize their operations.

This article describes the evolution of administrative and business applications over the past 20 years and discusses specific applications that have been and are being computerized in each of the four major areas of business and administrative operations. Finally, the References at the end of the article list sources of additional information about such systems.

**Evolution of Administrative and Business Applications.** In order to establish a frame of reference for reviewing specific systems, this section outlines briefly how such systems have evolved, and why, over the past 20 years.

EARLY SYSTEMS. When the first computers were installed in commercial and industrial organizations in the 1950s, they were most often used to automate office functions such as payroll, invoicing, and inventory accounting. This was a logical step in the evolution of these activities, for several reasons:

1. These activities were well understood and reasonably well documented as a result of existing accounting and auditing requirements, both of which made computerization easy.

2. The precomputer step-by-step method of carrying out these activities suited the capabilities of early computers, which could only process information serially from card files or magnetic tape. Moreover, in many cases these activities were already being processed on punched card equipment, making them easy to convert to a computer.

3. Computerization of these functions was readily justified by clerical staff reduction and by savings brought about by replacing more expensive punched card equipment.

These early computer systems processed data in batches; i.e., they executed one program at a time and handled transactions one by one after they had been sorted into numerical sequence. In general, they were simply more efficient electronic outgrowths of the punched card systems that were initially installed in the early 1930s. In spite of their greater speed and capability, they still retained many limitations of their predecessors: They required substantial manual intervention and their impact was confined to narrow functional areas of business. The applications they processed were similarly limited in scope.

ADVANCES IN SYSTEMS. Many of the administrative and business applications that are commonly processed on computers today differ greatly from the earlier accounting-oriented applications. Notably, they are *broader in scope*: Whereas early applications dealt with a single activity, current systems frequently consist of several integrated subsystems covering a broad segment of the business.

They are *more responsive*: Early systems performed simple calculations, printed out 100% of the transactions they processed, and were run usually at fixed intervals (weekly or monthly). Today's systems perform complex calculations, screen results so that only those that exceed a range of acceptable performance are printed out or displayed, and do so daily or even hourly, with the result that important information is made available in time for corrective action to be taken.

They *serve many more users*: Initially, an employee who wanted to run a computer program did so at a computer center, or he sent his job to the center to be processed. Now, through easy-to-use terminals, computers can be accessed by large numbers of users who may be close by or thousands of miles away.

They *offer a variety of new benefits*: Traditionally, reduction of clerical costs was the primary benefit anticipated from automation of administrative or business functions. Today, computerized applications have the potential to provide information that can result in a wide range of benefits, from significantly improved customer service to tighter managerial control over major segments of the organization.

Some of the commercial systems in use today illustrate these advances. For example, by means of a Touch-Tone telephone or a small remote terminal, an airline reservation clerk can call upon a central computer to check a customer's credit rating; the computer can notify him in a matter of seconds whether the credit card is stolen or the account is delinquent. Similarly, the sales clerk in a local store can be connected to a computer by telephone and can be told by computer-produced voice response

EXAMPLE: CONVERSATIONAL ORDER ENTRY

| QUESTION: COMPUTER GENERATED DISPLAY | RESPONSE BY TERMINAL OPERATOR |
|---|---|
| ORDER ENTRY OE<br>ORDER STATUS INQUIRY OS<br>PAYMENT POSTING PP<br>(etc.) | OE |
| CUSTOMER NAME OR NUMBER | SF5190 (or) SMITH DATA PROCESSING |
| SMITH DATA PROCESSING CO<br>ATTEN P.J. ANTHONY<br>635 JACKSON ST<br>LOS ANGELES CA 96402<br>SHIP VIA CF<br>IS THIS CORRECT? | C (correct) |
| ENTER MACHINE NUMBER, QUANTITY | 129, 1 |
| SPECIFY (1 AND 2 REQUIRED, 3 AND 4 OPTIONAL)<br>1. VOLTAGE (AC, 1-PHASE, 60 CYCLE)<br>A LOCKING PLUG, 115V #9880<br>B LOCKING PLUG, 208V #9884<br>C NON-LOCKING PLUG, 115V #9881<br>D NON-LOCKING PLUG, 208V #9885<br>2. CHARACTER ARRANGEMENT A11<br>3. ACOUSTIC COVER FOR CARD TRANSPORT (FIELD INSTALLABLE) #9014<br>4. CARD I/O ATTACHMENT #9619 | 9882, A11, 9014 |
| 9882 INVALID FEATURE NUMBER, REENTER CORRECT VOLTAGE AND PLUG | 9880 |
| FEATURE 9014 - FACTORY OR FIELD INSTALLED? | FACTORY |
| SPECIAL FEATURES<br>NOTE: MAXIMUM COMBINATIONS ARE INDICATED BY X IN VERTICAL COLUMNS<br>ACCUMULATOR #1020 XXXX<br>ACCUMULATE PROGRAM LEVELS #1025 XXXX<br>AUXILIARY STORAGE #1201 X<br>CARD I/O ATTACHMENT #7503  X<br>INTERPRET #4601   X<br>FEED, VARIABLE LENGTH #3950    X<br>PRODUCTION STATISTICS #4802 XXXX<br>SELF CHECK NUMBER MOD 10 #7061 X XX | 1020, 1025, 4802, 7061 |
| RPQ'S? (special engineering) | NO |
| DELIVERY REQUESTED | MAY 29, 1974 |
| ADDITIONAL REMARKS? | CALL MR. ANTHONY BEFORE DELIVERY TO RESERVE FREIGHT ELEVATOR |
| MORE ADDITIONAL REMARKS? | NO |
| END OF ORDER ENTRY PROCEDURE? | YES |
| ORDER ENTRY OE<br>ORDER STATUS INQUIRY OS<br>PAYMENT POSTING PP<br>(etc.) | |

**Exhibit 1**

whether a product requested by a customer is available, where it is located, and when it will be shipped. In a third example, manufacturers can install computers for conversational order entry. Instead of writing or typing out all detailed specifications about a machine to be ordered, the terminal operator tells the computer he wants to enter an order for a specific model of machine. The computer then asks a series of questions about the order, which the operator answers in turn. When the dialog is completed, the full specifications are recorded in the computer ready for matching with production and shipping schedules. Exhibit 1 illustrates the type of dialog that takes place between terminal operator and computer in conversational order entry.

FOUR STAGES OF EVOLUTION. The evolution of administrative and business systems to their current status has followed the expanding hardware and software capabilities of the computer. Exhibit 3 describes four broad stages of computer development and the application characteristics that correspond to those stages. Briefly:

1. *Basic batch* is the least complex level of computer processing. At this level, application systems are normally made up of small programs that are run through the computer one by one and which can process transactions only from sequential files.

2. *Expanded batch* programs perform complex computations and produce reports that analyze performance, not just report it as in basic batch systems.

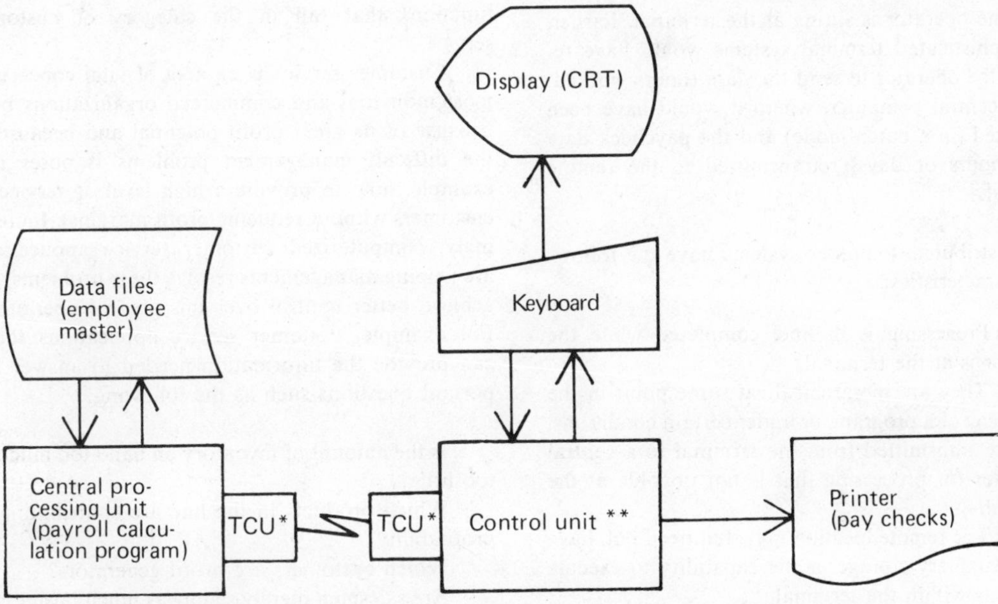


* – Transmission control unit.
** – Contains arithmetic, logic, and primary storage units. Auxiliary storage (e.g. disk unit) would be attached to and controlled by this unit also.

| CENTRAL (COMPUTER) SITE | REMOTE (TERMINAL) LOCATION |
|---|---|
| 1. Receive data from remote location | 1. Input payroll data (e.g. hours worked by job class) needed for central computer payroll calculation |
| 2. Calculate payroll using programs and data files (e.g. employee master) located at central site | 2. Control Unit edit of data, operator correction of invalid or incomplete data |
| 3. Update payroll files | 3. Transmit to central site computer |
| 4. Transmit payroll data to remote location | 4. Receive payroll data from central site computer, format and print pay checks |

**Exhibit 2**

Larger programs, further automation of manual functions, and a small capability for processing transactions that occur in random sequence are characteristics that distinguish expanded batch from basic batch systems.

3. *On-line inquiry* application systems result from adding to expanded batch systems the capability to immediately access, by terminal, any record that is stored in the disk files attached to the computer. Processing of transactions that are not in numerical sequence is also possible at this higher level of systems complexity.

4. *Distributed computing* systems consist of combinations of large central computers, data communications networks, and remote terminals that enable terminal operators located remotely from the central computer to carry out complete operations. For example, an employee's paycheck can be prepared while the operator is sitting at the terminal. Earlier, less sophisticated terminal systems would have required the operator to send the data (hours worked) to the central computer, where it would have been processed (in a batch mode) and the paycheck data later (hours or days) retransmitted to the remote terminal.

Distributed computer systems have the following characteristics:

(a) Processing is in line, completed while the operator is at the terminal.

(b) They are hierarchical; at some point in the processing of a program, or under certain conditions, data are transmitted from the terminal to a central computer for processing that is not possible at the terminal.

(c) The remote location may, but need not, have either auxiliary storage or the capability to execute programs within the terminal.

Exhibit 2 illustrates a distributed computing system used in payroll processing. The mode of processing is in line, with the terminal operator keying in the data required by the central site computer program, correcting errors caught by the terminal edit program, and transmitting the data to the central site computer. The central computer calculates the payroll and retransmits paycheck data to the remote terminal, where it is printed.

Exhibit 3 illustrates that as the computer's capabilities have progressed from basic batch processing to on-line inquiry and distributed computing, commercial applications have also advanced from relatively simple, low-cost, narrow impact groups of programs to highly complex, expensive, and far-reaching systems.

The remainder of this article will discuss the four major types of administrative and business applications: customer service, manufacturing, accounting and finance, and payroll and personnel. To aid in reading the exhibit that accompanies each of these four sections, customer service will be reviewed in detail, while the remaining three categories will be discussed less extensively.

**Customer Service Systems.** Customer service systems relate to the interaction between an organization and its customers. Processing orders, keeping track of inventory available to meet customer demand, collecting accounts receivable, and analyzing sales transactions are representative of the functions that fall in the category of customer service.

Customer service is an area of vital concern in most industrial and commercial organizations both because of its great profit potential and because of the difficult management problems it poses (for example, how to provide a high level of service to customers without reducing profit margins). Increasingly, computerized customer service applications are helping managements resolve these problems and achieve better control over this area of operations. For example, customer service applications today can provide the information needed to answer important questions such as the following:

Is the amount of inventory on hand too much or too little?

Which products in the line are contributing to profitability?

Which customers are profit generators?

Are salesmen merely selling as much business as they can, or are they selling profitable business?

Is the level of accounts receivable too high?

Are bad debt write-offs above industry norms? Are they increasing?

Although some of the earliest business computer applications were related to customer service, only very recently have computer capabilities advanced to the point where large-scale improvements in this area of business operations are possible. Today, many of the most sophisticated and expensive computer systems being installed in commercial and industrial organizations are in customer service. In addition, industry sources estimate that one-third of the computers installed throughout the world pro-

## EVOLUTION OF ADMINISTRATIVE AND BUSINESS SYSTEMS

| Application Characteristics | Least Complex → | | | → Most Complex |
|---|---|---|---|---|
| Category of hardware system | Basic Batch - electronic unit record plus magnetic tape | Expanded Batch - electronic unit record, magnetic tape, small-capacity disk storage | On-Line Inquiry - electronic unit record, larger disks, typewriter, and CRT terminals | Distributed Computing - large disks, remote terminals (mini-computers, CRTs), data communications devices |
| Cost to develop an application system | Less than $50,000 | —— increasing to → | | $000,000's to millions |
| Time required for development | Several man months | —— increasing to → | | Several man years (2-5 plus) |
| Degree of integration with other application systems | Low - normally 1 department served | More than 1 department served | Several departments served | High - many departments served |
| Degree of difficulty of development and implementation | Simple - mostly internal to data processing department | Relatively simple - some technical problems | Relatively difficult - operational problems in implementation | Difficult - often large operational as well as technical problems |
| Criticality of computerized system to departmental operation | Low - manual backup always possible | Medium - manual backup usually possible | Medium - manual backup difficult | High - manual backup almost impossible |
| Organization level at which commitment needed for development and implementation success | Manager of department requesting the system | Manager of department requesting the system | Vice president | President, top managing executive |
| Type of benefit | Clerical savings | Primarily clerical savings, some improvement in management control | Improved customer service, improved management control | Cost reductions, improved service, improved management control |
| Magnitude of benefit | Small, but demonstrable and immediate | —— increasing to → | | Large, difficult to quantify in advance, gained over time |
| Amount of user participation required in systems development | Limited, generally not critical | Needed in design phases | Needed in all phases | Extensive, critical to project success |
| Amount of user participation required in systems operation | None | Limited to coding of input data | Moderate - for inquiry operation | Extensive, user runs the system from terminals |
| Response time of system to user request for information | Week(s)-days | Days | Minutes - seconds | Minutes - seconds |
| Historical time frame of first systems | Early 1950s | Mid-1950s | Late 1950s | Late 1960s |

**Exhibit 3**

cess customer service applications—another indication of their importance.

Exhibit 4 lists the applications that make up the customer service group and illustrates how sophistication and complexity increase as computer capabilities progress from basic batch to distributed computing.

BASIC BATCH. In most organizations, automation of customer service applications began at a relatively low level of complexity; i.e., in the form of basic batch systems. Despite their lack of sophistication, such systems were often able to produce important benefits.

The second column of Exhibit 4 describes the types of customer service applications typically executed in a basic batch mode. In this mode, the computer performs a number of calculating and record-keeping functions formerly performed manually. In order processing, for example, after the information about an order is entered into the computer (via key-punched cards or magnetic tapes or disks), the computer prepares shipping notices, warehousing picking lists, and later invoices showing items shipped and back ordered, price and discount amounts, and shipping, taxes, and other charges. After an order is processed, the same records that were used to prepare invoices can be sorted and rerun to generate weekly stock status reports showing beginning balance, amounts received, shipped, back ordered and on order, and balance on hand. The same records can be sorted again and processed to produce sales analysis reports listing sales volume by product, customer, and salesman; and finally, the records can be used to prepare aged trial balances and accounts receivable statements. Exhibit 5 illustrates examples of an aged statement and trial balance.

Despite their low level of complexity, basic batch customer service systems can be very successful. In many instances the introduction of such systems has permitted sizable reductions in clerical staffs. In almost all instances, organizations have benefited from faster processing and more accurate, up-to-date, and complete records about inventory levels, sales transactions, and accounts receivable status. With this information, managements have been better able to answer many of their basic questions about product movement, customer purchases, and sales force effectiveness.

EXPANDED BATCH. The desires to perform more sophisticated analyses and to further reduce manual intervention in processing customer service functions were the forces that led many organizations to reprogram their basic batch systems into systems of greater complexity and capability. This second stage of customer service systems development is described in Exhibit 4 under the column headed Expanded Batch.

Many operations that were manual in the basic batch environment, such as credit checking, release of back orders, and handling of special billing instructions are automated in expanded batch customer service systems. Order entry, which was normally carried out by key-punching cards in the basic batch mode, is automated in numerous systems by the use of OMR (optical mark reading) and OCR (optical character recognition) order documents, which are filled out by the salesmen at the time the orders are taken and are then fed directly into the computer for processing. Rate and routing tables are frequently computerized, making calculation of freight charges and preparation of transportation documents possible. Computer printing of collection follow-up letters further reduces manual intervention.

In the basic batch mode, computerized sales analysis consisted merely of breakdowns of sales volume by customer, product, and salesman. In expanded batch systems, as historical sales records and product cost information are made part of computer files, comparative analyses can be made of current versus historical sales volume and profitability by customer, product, and salesman. Exhibit 6 shows examples of such reports. In addition, inventory systems are expanded to include programs for statistical sales forecasting and for the calculation and reporting of economic order quantities (EOQ) to aid inventory managers. Inventory levels are determined on the basis of current and historical sales records, price, and cost data, enabling many organizations to reduce investment in inventory without sacrificing customer service.

ON-LINE INQUIRY. By the mid- to late 1960s, many organizations had developed comprehensive expanded batch customer service systems. The data files of these systems contained detailed information about many aspects of the customer service function; however, the information was not readily available because it was usually stored on a reel of magnetic tape located in a library away from the computer. Obtaining information from these data files to answer unscheduled requests (e.g., What is the balance on hand of a certain part in inventory?) took hours to accomplish and was a costly, disruptive operation.

On-line inquiry systems resolve the problem of inaccessibility by keeping primary data files (about customers, products, and orders) continuously

**CUSTOMER SERVICE SYSTEMS**

| | Least Complex → | | | → Most Complex |
|---|---|---|---|---|
| **Application** | **Basic Batch** | **Expanded Batch** | **On-Line Inquiry** | **Distributed Computing** |
| Order Processing | – Preparation of billing documents<br>• Warehouse picking lists<br>• Customer invoices | – Automated order entry<br>• OCR (optical character recognition)<br>• OMR (optical mark recognition)<br>– Order editing<br>– Computation of freight charges<br>– Handling of invoicing exceptions | – Credit checking<br>– Stock availability checking<br>– Order status checking | – Conversational order entry<br>– Multiple location stock availability checking<br>– Automatic order transmission to shipping warehouse<br>– On-line invoicing |
| Inventory - Finished Goods | – Weekly stock status reporting | – Daily exception reporting<br>– Sales forecasting<br>– Simple EOQ calculations | – Stock status inquiry handling | – Continuous updating of inventory records<br>– Multiple location balancing of stock<br>– Complex EOQ calculations |
| Accounts Receivable | – Preparation of aged trial balances and monthly statements | – Preparation of follow-up letters | – Account status inquiry handling | – On-line cash posting and account maintenance<br>– Automated scheduling of follow-up activities |
| Sales Analysis | – Breakdown of sales volume - by product, customer, and salesman | – Analysis of sales profitability by product, customer, and salesman | | |

Note: System component features listed in one column will be found where applicable (though not listed again) in all columns to the right (e.g., order processing application feature "order editing" under "expanded batch" will be part of "on-line inquiry" and "distributed computing" systems)

**Exhibit 4**

AGED TRIAL BALANCE

PAGE 1

DATE 7/17/74

| CUST NO. | CUSTOMER NAME | TELEPHONE NUMBER | LAST PAY MO | DA | YR | CREDIT LIMIT | TOTAL OUTSTANDING | CURRENT AMOUNT | OVERDUE ACCOUNTS 30 DAYS | 60 DAYS | 90 & OVER |
|---|---|---|---|---|---|---|---|---|---|---|---|
| 108 | ALLEN & CO | 415-378-1089 | 2 | 16 | 74 | $15,000 | $ 7,296.35 | $ 6,919.77 | $ 376.58 | | |
| 165 | ANDERSON AUTO SUPPLY | 408-286-6741 | 1 | 28 | 74 | 2,500 | 1,665.49 | 1,665.49 | | | |
| 178 | ANDREWS AND SONS INC | 408-262-2074 | 2 | 05 | 74 | 750 | 146.64 | | | $ 146.64 | |
| 189 | ARGONAUT ENGINEERING | 415-867-2506 | 12 | 27 | 73 | 2,000 | 3,125.41 | 2,111.30 | 611.54 | 312.13 | $ 90.44 |
| 247 | BERKLEY PAPER CO | 408-251-4189 | 2 | 21 | 74 | 6,300 | 5,289.00 | 1,185.50 | 2,652.45 | 1,400.06 | 51.00 |
| 252 | BEST DISTRIBUTION CO | 408-296-1667 | 10 | 06 | 73 | 1,000 | 765.44 | 3.25 | | | 762.19 |
| | FINAL TOTALS | | | | | | $36,241.33* | $21,085.31* | $5,601.57* | $3,831.82* | $998.63* |

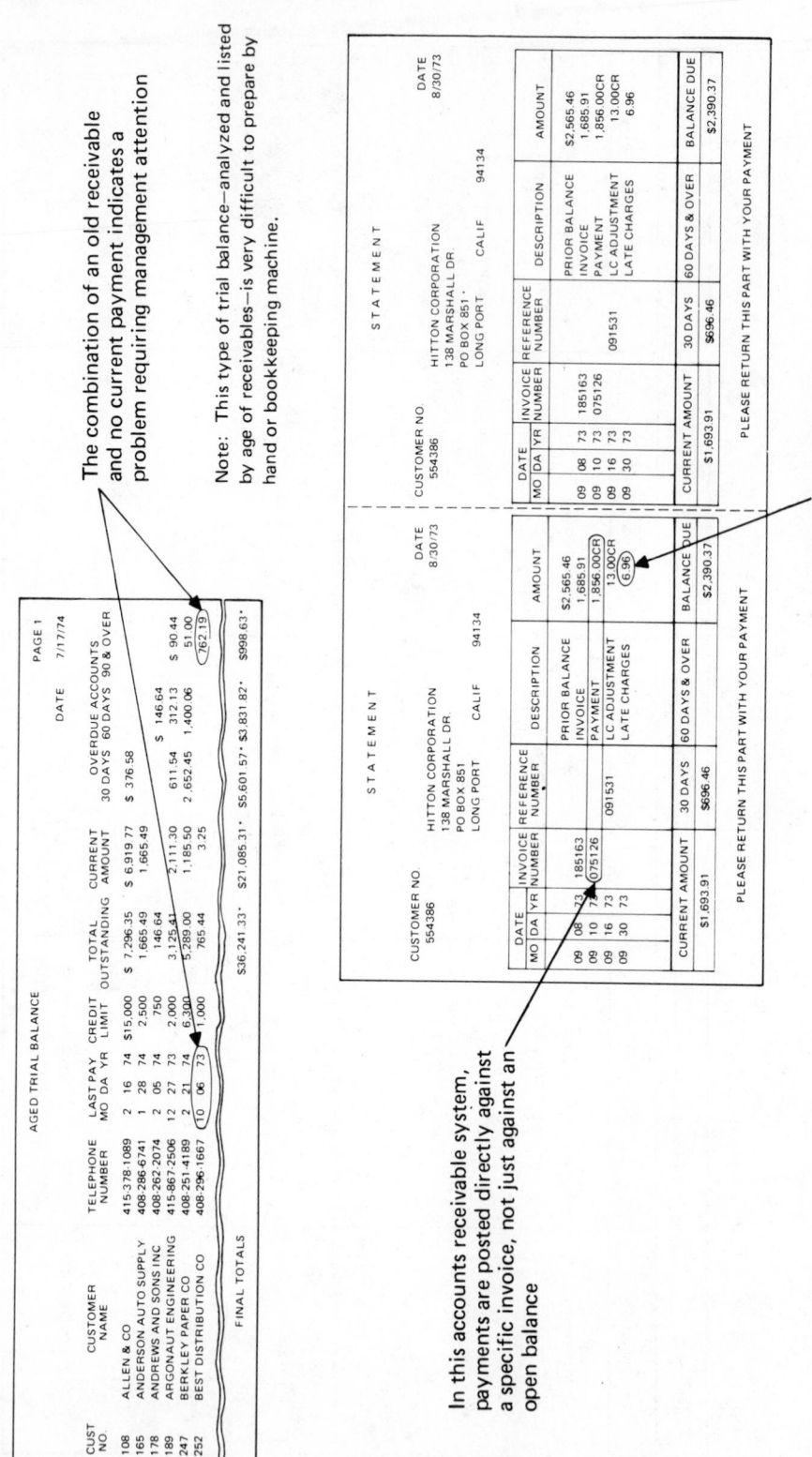

The combination of an old receivable and no current payment indicates a problem requiring management attention

Note: This type of trial balance—analyzed and listed by age of receivables—is very difficult to prepare by hand or bookkeeping machine.

STATEMENT

CUSTOMER NO. 554386

HITTON CORPORATION
138 MARSHALL DR.
PO BOX 851
LONG PORT CALIF 94134

DATE 8/30/73

| DATE MO | DA | YR | INVOICE NUMBER | REFERENCE NUMBER | DESCRIPTION | AMOUNT |
|---|---|---|---|---|---|---|
| | | | | | PRIOR BALANCE | $2,565.46 |
| 09 | 08 | 73 | 185163 | | INVOICE | 1,685.91 |
| 09 | 10 | 73 | 075126 | | PAYMENT | 1,856.00CR |
| 09 | 16 | 73 | | 091531 | LC ADJUSTMENT | 13.00CR |
| 09 | 30 | 73 | | | LATE CHARGES | 6.96 |

| CURRENT AMOUNT | 30 DAYS | 60 DAYS & OVER | BALANCE DUE |
|---|---|---|---|
| $1,693.91 | $696.46 | | $2,390.37 |

PLEASE RETURN THIS PART WITH YOUR PAYMENT

STATEMENT

CUSTOMER NO. 554386

HITTON CORPORATION
138 MARSHALL DR.
PO BOX 851
LONG PORT CALIF 94134

DATE 8/30/73

| DATE MO | DA | YR | INVOICE NUMBER | REFERENCE NUMBER | DESCRIPTION | AMOUNT |
|---|---|---|---|---|---|---|
| | | | | | PRIOR BALANCE | $2,565.46 |
| 09 | 08 | 73 | 185163 | | INVOICE | 1,685.91 |
| 09 | 10 | 73 | 075126 | | PAYMENT | 1,856.00CR |
| 09 | 16 | 73 | | 091531 | LC ADJUSTMENT | 13.00CR |
| 09 | 30 | 73 | | | LATE CHARGES | 6.96 |

| CURRENT AMOUNT | 30 DAYS | 60 DAYS & OVER | BALANCE DUE |
|---|---|---|---|
| $1,693.91 | $696.46 | | $2,390.37 |

PLEASE RETURN THIS PART WITH YOUR PAYMENT

In this accounts receivable system, payments are posted directly against a specific invoice, not just against an open balance

Computed automatically, based on overdue balance

**Exhibit 5.** Aged trial balance and statement.

COMPARATIVE ANALYSIS OF SALES BY ITEM

PERIOD ENDING 10/31/74 PAGE 12

| ITEM NO. | DESCRIPTION | CURR. PERIOD QUAN. THIS YR | CURR. PERIOD QUAN. LAST YR | PCT CHG | YTD QUANTITY THIS YR | YTD QUANTITY LAST YR | PCT CHG |
|---|---|---|---|---|---|---|---|
| 824634 | D20068 OVERHAUL GASKET | 10 | 14 | 29– | 90 | 98 | 8– |
| 624832 | 17D0011 BELT DYNAMIC FAN | 190 | 150 | 27 | 1,820 | 1,905 | 4– |
| 624901 | DMK6448 HUB ASSEMBLY J2 | 1– | 8 | 120– | 18 | 18 | 0 |

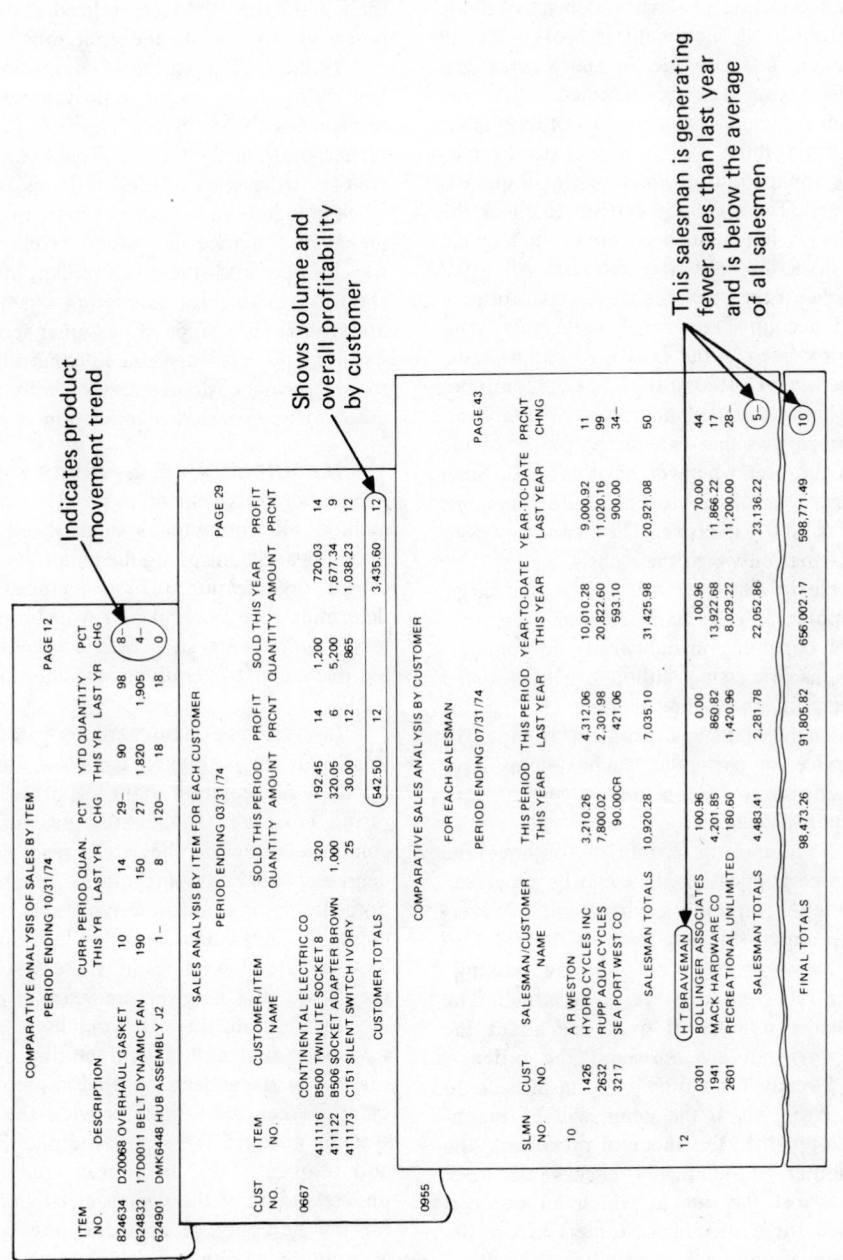

Indicates product movement trend

SALES ANALYSIS BY ITEM FOR EACH CUSTOMER

PERIOD ENDING 03/31/74 PAGE 29

| CUST NO. | ITEM NO. | CUSTOMER/ITEM NAME | SOLD THIS PERIOD QUANTITY | SOLD THIS PERIOD AMOUNT | PROFIT PRCNT | SOLD THIS YEAR QUANTITY | SOLD THIS YEAR AMOUNT | PROFIT PRCNT |
|---|---|---|---|---|---|---|---|---|
| 0667 | | CONTINENTAL ELECTRIC CO | | | | | | |
| | 411116 | B500 TWINLITE SOCKET 8 | 320 | 192.45 | 14 | 1,200 | 720.03 | 14 |
| | 411122 | B506 SOCKET ADAPTER BROWN | 1,000 | 320.05 | 6 | 5,200 | 1,677.34 | 9 |
| | 411173 | C151 SILENT SWITCH IVORY | 25 | 30.00 | 12 | 865 | 1,038.23 | 12 |
| | | CUSTOMER TOTALS | | 542.50 | 12 | | 3,435.60 | 12 |
| 0955 | | | | | | | | |

Shows volume and overall profitability by customer

COMPARATIVE SALES ANALYSIS BY CUSTOMER

FOR EACH SALESMAN

PERIOD ENDING 07/31/74 PAGE 43

| SLMN NO. | CUST NO. | SALESMAN/CUSTOMER NAME | THIS PERIOD THIS YEAR | THIS PERIOD LAST YEAR | YEAR-TO-DATE THIS YEAR | YEAR-TO-DATE LAST YEAR | PRCNT CHNG |
|---|---|---|---|---|---|---|---|
| 10 | | A R WESTON | | | | | |
| | 1426 | HYDRO CYCLES INC | 3,210.26 | 4,312.06 | 10,010.28 | 9,000.92 | 11 |
| | 2632 | RUPP AQUA CYCLES | 7,800.02 | 2,301.98 | 20,822.60 | 11,020.16 | 99 |
| | 3217 | SEA PORT WEST CO | 90.00CR | 421.06 | 593.10 | 900.00 | 34– |
| | | SALESMAN TOTALS | 10,920.28 | 7,035.10 | 31,425.98 | 20,921.08 | 50 |
| 12 | | H T BRAVEMAN | | | | | |
| | 0301 | BOLLINGER ASSOCIATES | 100.96 | 0.00 | 100.96 | 70.00 | 44 |
| | 1941 | MACK HARDWARE CO | 4,201.85 | 860.82 | 13,922.68 | 11,866.22 | 17 |
| | 2601 | RECREATIONAL UNLIMITED | 180.60 | 1,420.96 | 8,029.22 | 11,200.00 | 28– |
| | | SALESMAN TOTALS | 4,483.41 | 2,281.78 | 22,052.86 | 23,136.22 | 5– |
| | | FINAL TOTALS | 98,473.26 | 91,805.82 | 656,002.17 | 598,771.49 | 10 |

This salesman is generating fewer sales than last year and is below the average of all salesmen

**Exhibit 6.** Sales analysis reports.

mounted on disk drives attached to the computer. As a result, the data needed to answer questions are always available to operators of typewriter or CRT (cathode ray tube) terminals connected to the computer. The introduction of such systems has made possible a number of significant improvements in customer service. For example, in many cases customer inquiries can now be handled while the customer is on the telephone, not hours or days later.

The fourth column of Exhibit 4 lists the customer service applications in which on-line inquiry is most often used. These include systems to check the status of various items, such as credit in a given account or stock levels in a warehouse. All other customer service programs, such as preparation of invoices and accounts receivable statements, continue to be processed in the expanded batch mode.

DISTRIBUTED COMPUTING. Today, computer systems are being installed in industrial and commercial organizations that extend the power of the computer to the user wherever he is located. Such systems—known as distributed computing systems—are complex and expensive. They can, however, offer benefits that outweigh their costs.

Being able to distribute the power of a large, central computer among many remote users is a relatively new capability in industrial and commercial applications processing, although it has existed for some time in the form of time sharing for mathematical and statistical problem solving. In customer service, in particular, such systems have permitted major improvements in management, control, and responsiveness.

The fifth column in Exhibit 4 outlines the customer service applications that can be processed in a distributed computing environment. Conversational order entry (the top item in the column) implies that the clerk enters an order by "talking" with the central computer via a terminal. The computer asks a number of questions about the order, and when all are answered the order is complete and ready for automatic transmission to the location from which the items will be manufactured or shipped. In this mode of processing, the central computer automatically checks all stock locations (not just the one at which an order is normally filled for a specific customer) before declaring an item out of stock. And when an order is shipped, the computer notifies the order clerk, who completes the order-processing cycle by preparing the invoice at his terminal.

Distributed computing systems are complex. They may take years to design and may cost hundreds of thousands (and sometimes millions) of dollars to install. They require large central computers, complex software, and normally involve extensive communication and terminal networks. Nevertheless, they can be significantly less expensive than a number of decentralized stand-alone computers installed to do the same jobs.

In addition, distributed computing systems can help bring about major improvements in customer service. Such systems can significantly reduce order turnaround time. They can provide information that enables order clerks to locate items that are out of stock in their own locations. They can help inventory managers balance inventory levels across many warehouses, and they can make information instantly available for answering customer inquiries about the entire range of customer service activities. Exhibit 7 depicts a distributed computing orientation to processing customer service activities in a geographically dispersed organization.

**Manufacturing Systems.** Manufacturing applications (also known as production applications) include all computer systems used to assist in planning and controlling the manufacturing function of an organization. These include systems that determine raw material and work-in-process inventory requirements, help plan production schedules, aid dispatching operations, and monitor work-order status.

Because the manufacturing process in many organizations is highly complex, involving large numbers of people in many departments, manufacturing computer applications are also necessarily complex. In general, they are characterized by a high degree of subsystem integration, making the tasks of both developing and modifying such systems much more difficult than in other administrative and business areas. As a result, these systems are often very costly and may require years to develop.

In addition, there is normally a high degree of risk associated with manufacturing systems. Their success is dependent on their acceptance by the plant workers who must provide the data for the systems and use the system output. Problems can, and frequently do, arise from employees' lack of understanding of the system or lack of appreciation for the necessity of providing the computer with accurate, complete, timely information.

On the other hand, a very high potential benefit is generally associated with manufacturing systems. Since the manufacturing operation often accounts for the largest portion of product cost, even small improvements in its utilization of resources can generate large profits. Reduction of work-in-process

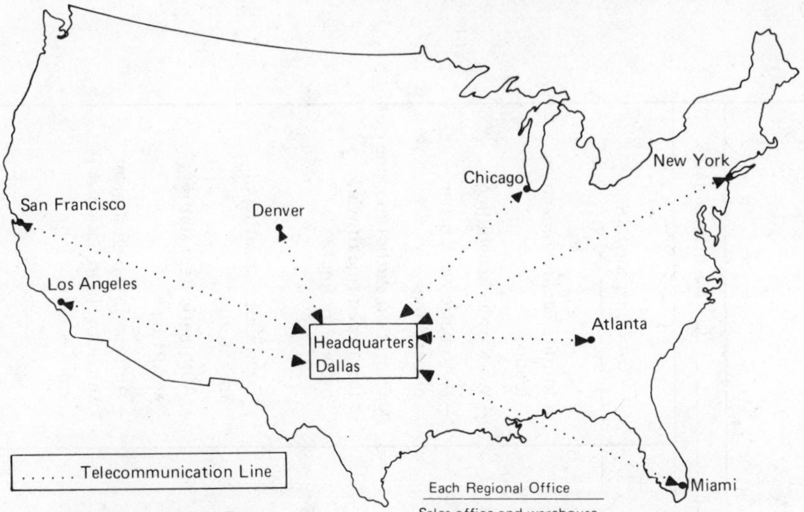


Headquarters – Dallas, Texas

- Manufacturing and principal warehouse
- Staff functions (e.g., inventory planning for all warehouses)
- Central computer and master files
- Communication network control
- All programming personnel
- Process weekly and monthly programs (e.g., sales analysis); transmit to regional offices

Each Regional Office

- Sales office and warehouse
- Terminal(s) connected to headquarters computer
- Process all routine customer service activities
  - Order entry and invoicing
  - Inventory status inquiry
  - Cash (payment) posting
  - Order status inquiry
- Terminal query of headquarters computer for data needed in daily activities (e.g., inventory status of a part in nonlocal warehouses)
- Transmission of summary data to headquarters

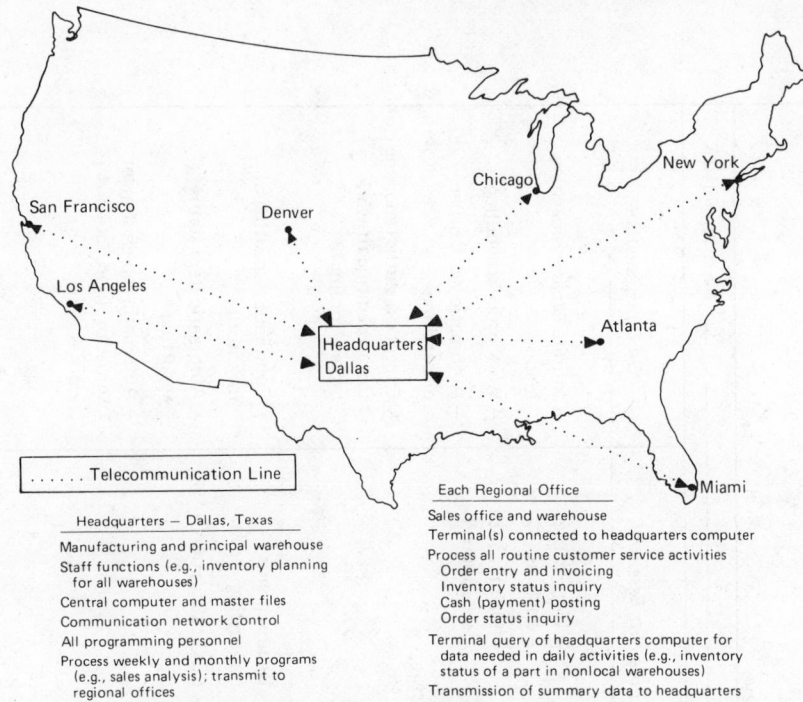

**Exhibit 7.** Distributed computing—customer service.

inventory, elimination of duplicate parts, shortening of production-planning cycles, and order status information that permits the identification and expediting of behind-schedule orders are some of the benefits that are gained from computerized manufacturing systems.

Exhibit 8 describes the kinds of manufacturing applications used in systems environments of increasing complexity. A prerequisite for manufacturing application systems is an item-coding system that can be used for all subsystems of inventory, bills of materials, engineering changes, and purchasing records. At the simplest stage, inventory accounting systems are implemented, followed by requirements generation (bill of materials explosion) and physical inventory systems.

Up to this point, manufacturing applications are normally used to assist in staff planning and control operations. The next state in the evolution of manufacturing systems, that of preparing work orders used to dispatch jobs, is the first time that the system directly affects the plant worker. Work center analysis helps identify bottlenecks in manufacturing by preparing reports for each work center that show production (actual versus standard), downtime, and backlog.

At the most complex level, the manufacturing computer system calculates work-order schedules and, via terminals located on the plant floor, records the completion of one job, dispatches the next, and notifies management of all behind-schedule orders.

**Accounting and Finance Systems.** Historically, operations such as accounts payable, cost accounting, and financial statement preparation were among the first to be automated, via punched-card systems in the 1930s and 1940s and on computers in the 1950s and 1960s. As in payroll procedures, these functions are largely routine, making them relatively easy to automate. The benefits offered by such applications traditionally have been in the form of clerical cost reduction, and although they have not normally led to dramatic increases in profitability, they have produced sufficiently large dollar savings to more than justify their computerization.

In spite of the traditional nature of accounting and finance applications, several sophisticated, high-benefit systems are being implemented in this administrative and business area. Cash management, financial modeling, and advanced purchasing systems are three examples of the new interest in accounting and finance applications.

In large, diversified, or widely dispersed organizations, the management of cash resources is a difficult job, yet one that has a large impact on profitability. Failure to invest temporarily available cash, premature payment of obligations, or short-

**MANUFACTURING SYSTEMS**

| Application | Least Complex → | | | Most Complex |
|---|---|---|---|---|
| | | | *On-Line Not Essential* ← | → *On Line Essential* |
| Production Planning and Control | | – Work order preparation (manual dispatch)<br>– Engineering specification file maintenance<br>– Work order status reporting | – Work center analysis<br>– Maintenance scheduling | – Infinite capacity machine loading<br>– Work order scheduling<br>– Automatic work order dispatching<br>– Exception status reporting (for expediting of work orders, tooling) |
| Inventory | – Weekly stock status reporting with daily activity listings<br>– Item catalog preparation<br>– ABC analysis (distribution by value)<br>– Net return analysis | – "Where used" reporting<br>– Requirements reporting (low-level bill of materials explosion)<br>– Time series requirements reporting<br>– Listing of procurement requirements<br>– Cycle count physical inventory accounting | – Requirements forecasting<br>– EOQ calculation | – Continuous updating of inventory<br>– Automatic item status reporting<br>– Automatic replenishment initiation (purchase orders, work orders) |

**Exhibit 8**

## ACCOUNTING – FINANCE SYSTEMS

| Application | Least Complex ⟶ | | | Most Complex |
|---|---|---|---|---|
| General Accounting | – Cost record keeping | – Cost accounting - comparison to standards or projected amounts<br>– Budgetary accounting<br>– Daily exception reporting | | – Cost estimating |
| Accounts Payable - A/P | – Preparation of A/P registers<br>– Check processing<br>– Check reconciliation<br>– A/P distribution | | | |
| Purchasing | | – Vendor analysis - volume of purchases<br>– Purchase order preparation and follow-up | – Vendor analysis - quality, reliability, price, etc.<br>– Derivation of economic purchase quantities (EPQs) | – Make-or-buy analysis |
| Finance | | – Financial statements preparation | – Requirements planning - e.g., cash management system<br>– Maintenance of stockholder records | – Analysis of financial proposals |

Note: None of the application systems listed requires on-line or distributed computing capability.

**Exhibit 9**

sighted investment programs that force an organization to borrow at high rates, all result in less than optimal use of financial resources. In an attempt to avoid these problems, many large organizations are using their computers to help collect, analyze, and report data about cash requirements and reserves. The benefits of such systems include less frequent and smaller short-term loans (a result of being able to project needs over longer periods of time), lower rate loans (a result of being able to forecast needs and investigate multiple sources of debt financing), and higher returns on short-term investments (a result of being able to project how long funds should remain invested).

Financial analysis of proposals is a second area where computers are playing an increasingly important role. Relatively straightforward simulation models enable the financial manager or analyst to generate pro forma statements that show the financial impact of different proposals, such as adding a new product to a current line or opening a new warehouse. The advantage of such models is that many possible outcomes can be evaluated in the time that one or two could be calculated by hand.

Advanced purchasing systems are a third area of current interest. Computer-based systems monitor data about price and quantity discounts, product quality (from product acceptance statistics) and reliability, and speed of delivery. On the basis of these data, computer programs calculate vendor rankings and economic-purchase quantities (EPQS) for individual items and store product information that helps buyers evaluate vendor performance and negotiate favorable contracts with suppliers.

Exhibit 9 lists many of the traditional accounting and finance applications as well as those of high current interest. In addition to those already described, make-or-buy analysis applications in manufacturing companies and computer-based systems for cost estimating are indicative of the trend toward more complex but also higher benefit applications in the accounting and finance area.

**Payroll and Personnel Systems.** Payroll and personnel systems constitute a fourth important category of administrative and business applications. This category includes all applications dealing in some way with the management and costs of an organization's human resources. The direct benefits of such systems are often less significant (in tangible dollar terms) than other categories of administrative and business systems.

Historically, the payroll function was often the first administrative operation to be computerized. The highly repetitive nature of the job, with its well-defined rules of computation, made it a logical target for automation, particularly since large numbers of clerical personnel—and hence high clerical costs—were required to perform the function manually. Moreover, by the early 1950s the payroll function in many instances had already been mechanized on punched-card equipment; thus, once an organization installed a computer, it was a relatively simple matter to convert the existing payroll system to the computer (with magnetic tape storage for data files rather than the trays of punched cards used with the former system).

In general, payroll applications have undergone no major changes over the past several years other than in the type of equipment used (e.g., from magnetic tape to disk files for storing data records). An example of one of the few relatively new applications is a computer-based system that simulates the effect of proposed changes in compensation packages. For example, such systems can make it much easier for an organization to evaluate the cost of proposed programs, such as granting a 6.5% across-the-board salary increase or giving an extra holiday to all employees.

In contrast to the relatively few advances in payroll applications, a number of new application systems have been developed in personnel management. In an attempt to cope with rising demands for various kinds of information about employees, many organizations have created computerized personnel systems. These systems are designed to answer requests for information from persons within the organization (e.g., how many employees have not taken their annual vacation this year?) and from outside agencies (e.g., what is the percentage of minority employees in clerical, supervisory, management, and executive positions?). Organizations are also using their personnel data files to monitor and evaluate the effectiveness of personnel management practices. For example, in cases where an organization has a "pay for performance" philosophy, computers help monitor the program by printing out correlations of performance rating and position within salary range. Other programs check to see if all employees are receiving their performance appraisals at the intervals prescribed by the organization.

In organizations with large numbers of employees or wide-ranging skill requirements, data banks containing information about employees' skills and experience have been computerized. When a specific skill mix is needed for an unfilled position, the computer performs a skills search to identify

**PAYROLL – PERSONNEL SYSTEMS**

| Application | Least Complex ——→ | | | Most Complex |
|---|---|---|---|---|
| Payroll | – Calculation of net payroll from manually calculated gross<br>– Preparation of payroll register<br>– Check processing<br>– Production of required reports (FICA, etc.) | – Attendance accounting<br>– Calculation of net payroll from "hours worked"<br>– Preparation of labor distribution reports | – Evaluation of proposed changes in compensation package | |
| Personnel | | – Automation of basic personnel file<br>– Preparation of scheduled reports, e.g.,<br>• Seniority<br>• Vacation | – Salary analysis<br>– Preparation of performance appraisal notices<br>– High-potential employee tracking system<br>– Preparation of unscheduled reports (using a generalized information retrieval system) | – Skills inventory accounting (skills search)<br>– Manpower planning analyses<br>*– On-line payroll/personnel record maintenance at location of employee (e.g., plant) |

Note: Other than the system identified with the asterisk, none of the application systems requires on-line or distributed computing capability

**Exhibit 10**

(and print out the names of) those who meet the qualifications. These systems are often very costly to establish and keep up to date, and some organizations have discontinued them after finding that their use frequency did not justify their expense.

Exhibit 10 describes the range of payroll and personnel applications systems that are found today in industrial, commercial, and governmental organizations.

REFERENCES

1966. Dearden, John. *Computers in Business Management.* Homewood, Ill.: Dow Jones-Irwin. (Hardware and software fundamentals, management problems of computer systems, mathematical programming, and future impact of computers in management.)

1968. Boutell, Wayne S. *Computer-Oriented Business Systems.* Englewood Cliffs, N.J.: Prentice-Hall. (Basic forms of application systems (e.g., batch), data processing department organization, introduction to hardware and software.)

1968. Heany, D. F. *Development of Information Systems.* New York: Ronald Press. (History of computer use in business data processing; projections about future use; begin at page 373.)

1969. Orlicky, Joseph. *The Successful Computer System.* New York: McGraw-Hill. (Application systems development.)

1970. Humphrey, Sturt, and Ronald Yearsley. *Computers for Management.* New York: American Elsevier. (Computer applications in business; e.g., marketing.)

1970. Krauss, Leonard I. *Computer-Based Management Information Systems.* New York: American Management Association. (Management-oriented treatment of concept, development, and implementation of management information system.)

1971. Smith, Leighton F. *An Executive Briefing on the Control of Computers.* Park Ridge, Ill.: Data Processing Management Association. (Development and management of computer systems —analogy to factory operation.)

G. GLASER AND A. L. TORRANCE

## ADVANCED RESEARCH PROJECTS AGENCY. 
*See* ARPA NETWORK.

## AIKEN, HOWARD

For articles on related subjects *see* DIGITAL COMPUTERS, Early; MARK I; and WATSON, THOMAS, SR.

Howard Hathaway Aiken was born March 8, 1900, in Hoboken, N.J., and died March 14, 1973, in St. Louis, Missouri. He grew up in Indianapolis, Indiana, where he attended Arsenal Technical High School while working 12 hours a night at the Indianapolis Light and Heat Company. Upon graduation he went to work for the Madison (Wisconsin) Gas Company, a position that allowed him to go to the University of Wisconsin. He received his B.A. degree in 1923 and was immediately promoted to chief engineer at Madison Gas.

In 1935 he returned to school, first at the University of Chicago and then at Harvard. His doctoral thesis at Harvard, resulting in a Ph.D. in 1939, was on the theory of space charge conduction. The research required laborious calculations of nonlinear differential equations. This experience led him to investigate the possibility of performing these types of calculations with machine assistance. His thoughts on this subject led him in 1937 to circulate a memo entitled, "Proposed Automatic Calculating Machine" (reprinted in *Spectrum*, August 1964, pp. 62–69).

Harvard was not the most likely environment to get support for this type of research. Fortunately, Harvard professors Ted Brown (Business) and Harlow Shapley (Astronomy) were impressed with his work, and both knew of the interest of Thomas Watson Sr. in projects of this nature. With their encouragement, and the knowledge that IBM had the necessary technology, Aiken approached Watson. A contract was signed in 1939 whereby IBM, with financial support from the U.S. Navy, would build the Automatic Sequence Controlled Calculator (Harvard Mark I). The machine was running in 1944, and Aiken and Grace Hopper described it in a paper in *Electrical Engineering* (Vol. 65, 1946, pp. 384–391, 449–454, 522–528).

The Mark I was followed by the Mark II (a relay machine built for the Naval Proving Ground at Dahlgren and completed in 1946), the Mark III (an electronic machine, also for Dahlgren, completed in 1950), and the Mark IV (an electronic machine built for and delivered to the Air Force in 1952). With the completion of Mark IV, Aiken got out of the business of building computers.

**Fig. 1.** Howard Aiken

It is difficult to evaluate precisely the impact of Aiken's series of machines and the Harvard Computation Laboratory which he founded. Fortunately, the documents are available to anyone interested. One need only look at the log books of the computation lab for this period to see the worldwide range of people who visited the laboratory. Another source of Aiken's work is the many publications in the "Annals of the Harvard Computation Laboratory" series. The Harvard catalog also provides clear evidence of the existence of courses in "computer science" a decade before the emergence of this program at most universities.

In 1947 and again in 1949 Aiken organized symposia on large-scale digital devices at Harvard. Programs from both meetings strongly reflect his hand and his philosophy at that time. Perhaps his most profound impact was in the environment he created at Harvard, which enabled the University to become a vital training ground for many people who are outstanding in the field today. A perusal of those who did their doctoral dissertations under his direction is an excellent example of this impact.

Aiken retired from Harvard in 1961 and moved to Fort Lauderdale, Florida, where he formed Aiken Industries. He also joined the faculty of the University of Miami as Distinguished Professor of Information Technology. In this latter position, he helped the University develop a computer science program and design a computing center.

His honors are much too numerous to mention in detail. They include honorary degrees (University of Wisconsin, Wayne State University, and Technische Hochsule, Darmstadt), prizes (Rochlitz Prize, Edison Medal of IEEE, the John Price Award of the Franklin Institute) as well as medals from both the United States (Air Force and Navy for distinguished service) and foreign governments (Sweden, Belgium, France, and Spain).

Howard Aiken felt that he had to be continuously involved in challenging endeavors in order to stay alive both physically and intellectually. His career is a document of that creed. Some of his detractors accused him of living in the past, but nothing could be further from the truth. He was a man of rare vision, whose insights have had a profound effect on the entire computing profession.

REFERENCES

1947. *Anon.* "Howard Hathaway Aiken," *Current Biography*, pp. 5–7.

1973. Oettinger, Anthony G. "Howard Aiken," *Communications of the ACM*, May, pp. 298–299.

H. S. TROPP

## ALGEBRA, BOOLEAN. *See* BOOLEAN ALGEBRA.

## ALGEBRAIC MANIPULATION LANGUAGES

For articles on related subjects *see* ARTIFICIAL INTELLIGENCE; LIST PROCESSING LANGUAGES; NUMERICAL ANALYSIS; and SYMBOL MANIPULATION.

For articles on related terms *see* PORTABILITY; and TREE.

Algebraic manipulation languages comprise a family dedicated to a single application area, the symbolic computations of applied mathematical analysis. A number of names have been suggested and employed to refer to this field. Among the most common are Symbol Manipulation, Formula Manipulation, Nonnumerical Programming, and Algebraic Manipulation. There are obvious objections to each of these. We are choosing the last for the title in spite of the lack of connection of many of the applications with any contemporary use of the word "algebra"; in fact, the title "Algebraic Manipulation" would seem a much better choice to denote the systems that have been developed for such computations as the determination of the lattice of subgroups of a given finite group. Our choice is meant only as a recognition of custom, the term, "algebraic manipulation" being prevalent in current usage.

The solution of analytic problems by means of symbolic computation was, of course, much more common before the advent of high-speed digital computers. The incredible power of these machines brought numerical techniques into dominance as, by far, the most practical approach to general scientific computation. The current search for mechanical assistance in symbolic computation is usually predicated on a desirability for analytic results deriving from their capacity to reveal the structural dependence of problem solutions on problem parameters. If we are to take this argument seriously, then we are forced to the conclusion that our efforts to date have been only partially successful. There have certainly been quite a few useful and impressive computations performed by current systems. Nonetheless, an all too common occurrence is the display of a single computed expression that occupies many pages of line-print output. It is difficult to see how such enormous expressions really contribute to the user's comprehension of the structure of the solution. Nor does it suffice to shrug off the result as due to the nature of the problem posed. Means must be found for the more intelligible presentation of analytic results, and this challenge remains as open today as it was in the first days of Formac, the first widely distributed algebraic manipulation language.

There are, of course, other quite realistic reasons for the pursuit of symbolic solutions by means of algebraic manipulation systems. For instance, even if—as is usually the case—numerical results are required, the preliminary analytic solution of the problem in terms of symbolic parameters might well prove a more economical route to a family of parameter-dependent numerical solutions. Of equal importance is another phenomenon coming recently into greater recognition (see Horowitz, 1972). This is the fact that—particularly since so many of the more modern algebraic manipulation systems provide an infinite precision integer arithmetic capability—such systems can often be employed for the solution of scientific problems that are so numerically ill-conditioned as to defy solution by conventional numerical techniques.

It might help the unfamiliar reader if we first present a pair of examples of the types of computations that the systems we shall discuss are designed to handle. The first, a famous benchmark problem of the late 1960s, is the so-called $F$ and $G$ series. Like so many of the early examples of nonnumerical computation, it derives from astronomy. Two sequences, $F_i$ and $G_i$, are determined by the recurrence relations

$$F_i = \dot{F}_{i-1} - \mu G_{i-1}$$

and

$$G_i = F_{i-1} + \dot{G}_{i-1},$$

where the dot represents total differentiation (with respect to "time"); and $F_0 = 1$, $G_0 = 0$, $\dot{\mu} = -3\mu\sigma$, $\dot{\sigma} = \epsilon - 2\sigma^2$, and $\dot{\epsilon} = -\sigma(\mu + 2\epsilon)$.

These equations are sufficient to determine $F_i$ and $G_i$ as polynomials in $\epsilon$, $\mu$, and $\sigma$; some results that might be generated by an algebraic manipulation system are summarized in Fig. 1.

This problem was so popular precisely because it was within the province of all systems. All, one way or another, could accept polynomials and all could differentiate. Furthermore, one can get to $F_{12}$ and $G_{12}$ (12 is clearly magical!) with the coefficients remaining within the single word integer precision of a 36-bit arithmetical word machine.

Before turning to more specific issues, we would like to cite one more example to illustrate a different species of capability within the repertoire of a few current systems. What we would like to demonstrate is an example of a complex mathematical procedure for which these more ambitious systems have more expertise than the average user. We will choose our example from the most popular such domain, indefinite integration. If we were to ask one of these systems to integrate the expression in Fig. 2(a), we would get as an answer the expression of Fig. 2(b).

The two-dimensional typewriter-generated display of the expressions in Figs. 2(a) and 2(b) is typical of those provided by some of the more advanced systems.

These two examples should serve to introduce two of the three areas that have dominated algebraic manipulation research in the past decade, simplification and integration. The third, the analysis of algorithms for seminumeric (polynomial) computation, is too technical for discussion here.

$$F_0 = 1$$

$$G_0 = 0$$

$$F_1 = 0$$

$$G_1 = 1$$

$$F_2 = -MU$$

$$G_2 = 0$$

$$F_3 = 3*SIG*MU$$

$$G_3 = -MU$$

$$F_4 = -15*SIG^2*MU + 3*EPS*MU + MU^2$$

$$G_4 = 6*SIG*MU$$

$$\vdots$$

$$F_{12} = -13749310575*SIG^{10}*MU + SIG^8*(29462808375*EPS*MU + 9820936125*MU^2)$$
$$- SIG^6*(1331512182O*EPS*MU^2 + 21709437750*EPS^2*MU + 1640268630*MU^3)$$
$$+ \ldots + 2031*EPS*MU^5 + 9823275*EPS^5*MU + 9951525*EPS^4*MU^2$$
$$+ 2480958*EPS^3*MU^3 + 164610*EPS^2*MU^4 + MU^6$$

$$G_{12} = 6547290750*SIG^9*MU - SIG^7*(12405393000*EPS*MU + 3308104800*MU^2)$$
$$+ \ldots + SIG*(355608*EPS*MU^4 + 98232750*EPS^4*MU$$
$$+ 60350400*EPS^3*MU^2 + 9227196*EPS^2*MU^3 + 2046*MU^5)$$

**Fig. 1**

```
              7    6    5    4
             X  + X  + X  + X  + 1
         ------------------------------
          8    7    6    4    3    2
         X  + X  + X  + X  + X  + X


      1                  2                        1                       2X + 1
  - --- + 1/2*LOG(X  + X + 1) - ---------ARCTAN(---------)
      X                                       SQRT(3)                 SQRT(3)
  +
     1/4*LOG(X⁴ + 1) - LOG(X)
```

**Fig. 2**

**Simplification.** The theoretical situation here is a bit muddy. We are, of course, on firm ground as long as our system is dedicated to the manipulation of a class of mathematical objects; e.g., polynomials, rational functions or truncated power, Fourier or Poisson series, which admit a canonical representation. Many systems are so dedicated while others often include rather self-contained packages for these seminumerical computations. A typical tiny example of the automatic simplification facilities offered by such systems would be the transformation of the expression.

$$\frac{A(X + A)/(1 - X * A)^2 + 1/(1 - X * A)}{1 + [(X + A)^2/(1 - X * A)^2]}$$

into

$$\frac{1}{X^2 + 1}$$

This is not to suggest that these systems have no problems in giving the user sufficient control over the form in which his answers are presented, in choosing and implementing efficient representations and algorithms—this is, in fact, probably the most active and contentious research area in algebraic manipulation today—or in avoiding the practical pitfalls [e.g., the forcing of the binomial expansion of $(x + y)^{1000}$] associated with too heavy reliance on canonical forms. We are only emphasizing the facts that as long as the domain possesses a canonical form, it can always be decided by very simple means whether two of its objects are equivalent, and that as we pass to more complex domains, the equivalence of two expressions may be undecidable by any means.

Most of the general-purpose simplification programs that have been implemented to date rely on some well-ordering of the admissible expressions, which allows for rapid checks for combinations or cancellations in complex sums or products, provided the equivalences can be recognized. Such an algorithm is usually augmented by a collection of disparate facts, such as $\cos(0) = 1$ or $e^{\log(x)} = x$, which are to be applied as local transformations. Applied recursively, such rules can easily find such simplifications as the reduction to zero of

$$y[\exp(\log(\cos(0)x + \sin(0))] - xy.$$

What capacity for global transformations (e.g., simplification via the familiar trigonometric identities) might exist is usually in the form of allowance for user-defined transformations to be applied interpretively and disastrously inefficiently.

While there have been a number of interesting though isolated theoretical results on the reduction of certain wider classes of algebraic expressions to canonical forms, they have had remarkably little effect on the design of systems for the simplification of broad spectra of mathematical expressions. A few partial exceptions to this are the work of Moses (1969) on the implementation of algorithms due to Risch for the integration of certain classes of elementary functions, the RADCAN facility of MACSYMA, and some simplication algorithms recently implemented within REDUCE (see later section "Systems"). Typical of such transformations would be the replacement of

$$\frac{\log(A^{2X} + 2A^X + 1)}{\log(A^X + 1)}$$

by 2.

**Integration.** Probably no problem in algebraic manipulation has excited more lay interest and is in more demand during demonstrations than indefinite integration. We will discuss only the history of indefinite integration of elementary functions and defer on both definite integration and the more general question of the integration of differential equations, even though some programs exist for these problems.

The first program written to attack the problem of symbolic integration was Slagle's thesis, SAINT. To this day, this program is the purest example of the application of classical tree-pruning, backtracking, artificial intelligence techniques to algebraic manipulation. It was an awesome achievement, especially considering its date—1961; and it contained features, especially its semantic pattern-matching facility, which addressed areas that remain difficult today.

Nonetheless, the basic artificial intelligence approach was soon to be abandoned as the path to symbolic integration. The next relevant program was that of Manove et al., (1968), written as part of the MATHLAB system for the integration of rational functions, a well-defined domain of integrands for which an algorithmic attack was available. This program was also important in that it contained the first complete implementation of an algorithm for the factorization of multivariate polynomials over the integers. It led, too, to an interesting algorithm for the inverse Laplace transform of rational functions, also implemented for MATHLAB and sharing a great deal of code with the integration algorithm. This program dates from 1964 to 1966.

By the end of 1967, Moses had completed the thesis version of his symbolic integration program, SIN. This program far excelled SAINT in both breadth of success and speed of solution. It comprised a three-step sequential attack:

1. Determine if the integrand can be expressed as a constant multiple of an expression of the form $f(u(x))u'(x)$, where $f$ is a member of an extremely narrow class of functions whose antiderivatives are known. If so, the solution is immediate.

2. If the integrand cannot be so expressed, the program passes into a "bag of tricks" stage similar to SAINT except that no backtracking ever takes place. The program is able, employing a semantic pattern-matching facility (again like SAINT), to classify each problem into *one* (quite unlike SAINT) of a finite number (eleven) of categories; e.g., trigonometric, rational function, rational function of logarithms, etc. For each such category, the program continues the analysis, finally settling on exactly one trick, which might or might not work. While still heuristic, this second stage really contained a great deal of practical knowledge about integration. It employed as a subroutine, and was deeply dependent upon, the rational function integration program of Manove, Bloom, and Engelman. For example, if SIN were asked to integrate $\int x^2 \sin^{-1}(x)\, dx$, it would classify this problem as "Method 9, rational times arctrigonometric" and perform an integration by parts, yielding

$$\frac{x^3 \sin^{-1}(x)}{3} - \frac{1}{3}\int \frac{x^3\, dx}{(1-x^2)^{1/2}}.$$

This would bring it to

$$\int \frac{x^3\, dx}{(1-x^2)^{1/2}}.$$

SIN would classify this problem as "Method 4, binomial-Chebyshev" and substitute $y$ for $x^2$, yielding

$$\frac{1}{2}\int \frac{y\, dy}{(1-y)^{1/2}},$$

followed immediately by the substitution of $z^2$ for $1-y$, yielding

$$-\int (1-z^2)\, dz.$$

The problem is now $\int (1-z^2)\, dz$. This is a polynomial, a trivial case of a rational function. The next call, this time to the MATHLAB package (Method 8), is the last, yielding

$$\int (1-z^2)\, dz = z - \frac{z^3}{3}.$$

Finally, SIN must unwind its stack by a series of inverse substitutions, which yield the final answer:

$$\int x^2 \sin^{-1}(x)\, dx = \tfrac{1}{3}x^3 \sin^{-1}(x) + \tfrac{1}{3}(1-x^2)^{1/2} - \tfrac{1}{9}(1-x^2)^{3/2}.$$

3. The third stage (entered only when the first two have failed) contained, in addition to integration by parts, a powerful heuristic method, called EDGE (for EDucated GuEss) based on a reasonable guess as to the possible form of the integral. It was, in some ways, a precursor to the algorithmic solution to the problem of integration of elementary functions, soon to be discovered by Risch in the 1968–1970 period.

The Risch method represents the final passage of the problem of symbolic integration from heuristic methods to algorithmic ones. It is, in its greatest generality, dependent on results from algebraic geometry and is certainly beyond any reasonable discussion here. We should like to point out, though, that it probably represents the most deeply recursive application known of the idea of "undetermined coefficients." Some parts have been implemented by Moses, but at this time the general case defies our capability to analyze its complexity.

**Systems.** We prefer the word "system" to "language" partly because the concern here, as with most application-oriented situations, tends not to be with the questions most frequently in the fore during discussions of general-purpose computer languages (e.g., syntax, control mechanisms, variable bindings, macrofacilities), but more on the semantics of the computational machinery provided. Can it integrate? What functions? Definite and indefinite? Facilities of this sort, by necessity, accrete to form a lumpy porridge that no self-respecting "language" designer would acknowledge. At times, the only reasonable way to determine the usefulness of such a facility with respect to a given problem is by experimentation. Another reason for our preference of the word "system" is that so many of the extralinguistic features, the display programs, the file management, the editors, and the libraries are so applications oriented.

We will soon list some of the major systems along with capsule descriptions that can serve only as a source of first impressions for those who might be shopping. Anyone seriously interested should, as a more meaningful introduction to the field, obtain a copy of the Proceedings of the Second Symposium on Symbolic and Algebraic Manipulation (Petrick, 1971), which is still remarkably *au courant*. We will use it as a universal reference for contemporary systems, both for description of facilities and as a source of contacts from whom the various systems may be obtained. In reference to this last point, the reader should understand that, while the various systems vary enormously as to their portability, it is the desire of most of the authors to provide the widest possible user community for their programs and therefore most systems are available (usually source code as well as binary program) to all. In those few cases where our understanding is otherwise, we will note it below.

What questions would we expect a user to ask before choosing a system? While they must obviously depend on the anticipated application, the following certainly must be among the most common:

1. Is it available to me? Is it well documented? How much effort is involved in my setting it up and learning to use it?

2. What data types are available? Does it provide variable precision integer (rational) arithmetic? Does it admit only, say, polynomials or can it simplify general mathematical expressions? Differential equations? Matrices? Tensors?

3. What transformations are delivered with the system? Are arithmetic, substitution, simplification, and differentiation sufficient for my problems, or do I need more advanced features such as polynomial factorization, matrix inversion, integration, or Laplace transforms?

4. How efficient is the system for my problem domain? Am I likely to lose because the intermediate expressions swell to the point of destroying the computation? Would another system be much faster or fit better within the space allotted by my facility?

5. Can I edit my expressions? Can I easily obtain equivalent but more revelatory forms for the answers? Who is boss?

6. Will the system provide legible two-dimensional displays of my expressions? Does it operate interactively so that I can decide what to do next on the basis of what has happened? Does it provide good file management for the support of continuing computation?

7. Does the system come with a useful library of symbolic routines? Can the formulas generated be compiled as numerical programs?

It would be too confusing to list the systems in some arbitrary (e.g., chronological) order. To introduce a little sense into the listing, we will group them according to a single characteristic: their internal data representations. We mean this only in the broadest possible sense; i.e., while we will ask whether a system is, say, restricted to canonically represented polynomials, we will not go into the question of *which* canonical representation. Our choice of criterion is quite likely biased by our experience as systems designers, but it is extremely important from a user's viewpoint, too, and in fact is probably the most decisive single factor in determining what the system can and cannot do for him. We will establish four categories and place each system within one. In some cases the choices are borderline, but no real harm can ensue should our choice be different from the one the system's authors would have made. The four categories are discussed below.

*Seminumerical.* The name "seminumerical" is borrowed from Knuth. These systems are constructed to manipulate data from rigid classes of mathematical objects possessing strictly canonical forms. The classes most generally treated are multivariate polynomials, rational functions, and truncated power series. However, sometimes other classes, such as Laurent series or trigonometric series, are accepted. The operations performed by these systems are generally closed with respect to the domain. So, for example, one should expect a rational function system to differentiate—since the derivative of a rational function is rational—but not, in general, to integrate or perform inverse Laplace transforms, since these lead to logarithmic and exponential results, respectively. These systems have very little to do with "symbolic" computation and are in fact much closer to being very powerful arithmetic facilities. Hence the name.

*Ghost.* These systems appear externally to manipulate quite general mathematical expressions, but appear internally to be functioning with canonically represented data, much like the seminumerical systems. When their services are sufficient, they can represent quite intelligent compromises, providing limited but often adequate manipulation of general expressions with the efficiency normally associated with seminumerical systems.

*Symbolic.* These systems admit the most general species of mathematical expressions, usually representing them as quite general tree structures. While it is precisely this generality that allows for the provision of such features as user-defined pattern replacements, this characteristic often makes the system inadequate for performing certain tasks because it fails to provide some quite commonly required special machinery, such as a reasonably efficient algorithm for the greatest common divisor of two polynomials. This particular lacuna is in fact the reason that purely "symbolic" simplifiers are so poor at division.

*Hybrid.* These are generally the most ambitious systems, accepting the broadest spectrum of mathematical expressions in general but possessing, in addition, special representations and special algorithms for particular special classes of expressions. Typical of a hybrid is a symbolic system that possesses, for use when appropriate, a special package for the manipulation of multivariate rational functions over the integers. An excellent example of the potential of such systems is the MATHLAB program for the automatic solution of linear differential equations with constant coefficients. The method of solution involves the computation of both direct and inverse Laplace transforms. It is approximately true that the general symbolic features are used for the initial pattern-matching problem classification, the canonical rational function package for the inverse Laplace transforms, and both for the direct transforms.

Seminumerical Systems. We will omit discussion of, as probably outside the interests of our general reader, a number of very special purpose systems that fall within this category. We feel compelled, however, to mention the system of Deprit, Henrard, and Rom, which is constructed basically for a single computation—the reproduction and extension of the DeLaunay lunar theory expansion. This splendid achievement probably represents a mechanical computation on an order of magnitude greater in size than any achieved by earlier researchers.

*ALTRAN (Petrick, 1971; pp. 153–157).* Developed at Bell Labs out of its predecessor ALPAK system, ALTRAN is perhaps the most typical of seminumerical systems. It provides precisely for the arithmetic (through greatest common divisors, but not factorization) of multivariate rational functions over the integers and truncated power series. It is written in Fortran, but a few primitives must be hand coded. Its authors see this as a method of achieving portability while making no untoward sacrifice of efficiency.

*SAC-1 (Petrick, 1971; pp. 144–152).* This is a large system of Fortran subroutines, callable from Fortran, for the manipulation of multivariate rational functions with (infinite precision) integer coefficients. This implementation does have some unfortunate consequences for SAC-1 programming in that, unlike most other systems that create an applications-oriented environment, the burden of Fortran accounting is on the user. The excerpt in

```
 IMPLICIT INTEGER (A-Z)
 LOGICAL LASTIN
 DIMENSION  Z(30), ZZ(30), ZPWR(30, 3), DZ(30), DDZ(30),
1    ABCD(4), PARTL(15)
 COMMON     /TR1/  AVAIL, STAK, RECORD(72)
1           /TR2/  SYMLST
 COMMON    /PMODE/  KMPRES
 COMMON /EPSLON/  ECODE, EPSNAM, EPSLST, ELAST, ETAIL
 COMMON /PROBLM/  ZPWR, DZ,DDZ,PARTL, ZAZB, DZADZ28, ZDOZAD, DZDZ3
1  , PFOOCT, SOTOTL, OTHERZ, OTHER1, DENOM, LIMIT, LVDUMP, N, ABCD
2  , MAXLIM, L1, L2, L3, L4, L5, L8, L12, L24, L48, LM4, LM12, LM24
 COMMON   /EXTRA/  RESERV
 EQUIVALENCE  (ZPWR(1,1),Z(1)), (ZPWR(1,2),ZZ(1)),
1     (ZPWR(1,3),ZZZ(1)),
2     (ABCD(1),A), (ABCD(2),B), (ABCD(3),C), (ABCD(4),D),
3     (PARTL(15),P4L2), (PARTL(4),P4L8), (PARTL(8),P4L12),
4     (PARTL(3),P4L24), (PARTL(10),P4L48),
5     (PARTL(12),P3LI), (PARTL(9),P3L4), (PARTL(1),P3L12),
6     PARTL(6),P3L24)
 DATA  INPUT, OUTPUT /5, 6/
 CALL CATCHR(-1)
```

**Fig. 3**

Fig. 3 from a SAC-1 program exhibits this unnaturalness. Note that the users' concern is as much with type declarations and space allocations as with the mathematics. Algorithms supplied include those for rational function arithmetic, polynomial factorization, the solution of simultaneous linear equations, and one that returns (only) the rational part of the integral of a rational function.

This system is important, not only for itself but also for the focus it has provided for the prolific school centered around G. E. Collins at the University of Wisconsin for the study of seminumeric algorithms. A series of Ph.D. dissertations has produced not only many new algorithms but also the majority of the worst-case analyses of such algorithms that we possess today.

*CAMAL (Petrick, pp. 134–143).* On the borderline of being classified as a ghost system, this highly efficient physics-oriented system is probably not exportable beyond the Titan machine in Cambridge. It contains seminumeric modules for the arithmetic of polynomials (not rational functions), truncated power series, and trigonometric series with polynomial coefficients. It differs from almost all other systems we will mention in that the burden for the "garbage collection" of the space occupied by those intermediate expressions that are no longer needed in the execution of a program is placed on the user rather than being supplied automatically by the system. CAMAL has been credited with a number of computational successes, particularly in celestial mechanics and general relativity.

*SYMBAL (Engeli, 1970).* Restricted to polynomials, rational functions, and truncated power series, this system is distinguished primarily by its elegant Algol-like syntax. Engeli provides many extremely concise programming examples.

Fig. 4 exhibits a sample of the code and a few lines of output for the computation of the Legendre polynomials.

GHOST SYSTEMS

*REDUCE 2 (Petrick, 1971; pp. 128–133).* Starting from a canonical form suited to multivariate polynomials, REDUCE 2 extends itself by a variety of means to the manipulation of quite general mathematical expressions, relying on the polynomial procedures for basic simplification. It is quite different from seminumerical programs in its support of a (rather constrained) user-defined pattern replacement facility and of a 1½-dimensional (exponents raised, but no nice two-dimensional (2-D) fractions like those in Fig. 2) mathematical display program.

A REDUCE program for computing the $F$ and $G$ series mentioned at the beginning of this article would look like Fig. 5.

The REDUCE 2 system supplies, in addition to its general-purpose routines, a significant facility specialized to the multilinear algebra associated with high-energy physics. This part of the system has proved extremely successful, with numerous published physics papers citing it as the computational vehicle.

*IAM (Petrick, 1971; pp. 115–127).* This is a remarkably ambitious system, considering its basic dependence on a single canonical data representation. Included are a number of advanced facilities generally associated with hybrid systems (e.g., polynomial factorization), a SIN-like indefinite integration program, and good 2-D output. This is a proprietary program; i.e., the binary program is available for a fee; the source code is not. The system is receiving minimal support at this time.

```
begin

      P:= {0:1, X, 25:};                        (Sets P0(X) = 1, P1(X) = X)
      for   I:= 2:25 do                         (Calculates P2(X) to (P25(X))
            P[I]:= (2*I-1)/I*X*P[I-1]- (I-1)/I*P[I-2];

end

      P       := {0:25:};
      P[2]    := - 1/2 + 3/2 * X ↑ 2;
      P[3]    := - 3/2 * X - 5/2 * X ↑ 3;
      .
      .
      .
      P[25] := 16900975/4194304*X - ...
```

**Fig. 4**

```
    DEPS← -SIG*(MU+2*EPS)$
    DMU←-3*MU*SIG$
    DSIG←EPS-2*SIG↑2$
    F←1$
    G←Ø$
FOR 1←1 STEP 1 UNTIL 12 DO
BEGIN
    F1←-MU*G + DEPS*DF(F,EPS) + DMU*DF(F,MU) + DSIG*DF(F,SIG)$
    WRITE "F(",I,")←",F1;
    G1←F + DEPS*DF(G,EPS) + DMU*DF(G,MU) + DSIG*DF(G,SIG)$
    WRITE "G(",I,")←",G1;
    F←F1$
    G←G1$
END;
```

**Fig. 5**

```
*TYPE EQA; TYPE EQB; TYPE EQC

              12 A L + 15 B L + 2Ø C L + 2Ø
   EQA:  A = -----------------------------
                         6Ø

              1Ø A L + 12 B L + 15 C L + 15
   EQB:  B = -----------------------------
                         6Ø

              3Ø A L + 35 B L + 42 C L + 42
   EQC:  C = -----------------------------
                         21Ø

*SOLVE EQA FOR B
*ELIMINATE B FROM EQB
*ELIMINATE B FROM EQC
*SOLVE EQB FOR C
*ELIMINATE C FROM EQC
*SOLVE EQC FOR A

*TYPE A

              -1575 L + 126ØØØ
   A:  -----------------------------
         3        2
        L -414Ø L -2268ØØ L + 378ØØØ

*ELIMINATE A FROM EQA
*ELIMINATE A FROM EQB
*SOLVE EQA FOR C
*ELIMINATE C FROM EQB
*SOLVE EQB FOR B
*TYPE B

               21ØØ L + 945ØØ
   B:  -----------------------------
         3        2
        L -414Ø L   -2268ØØ L + 378ØØØ

*ELIMINATE B FROM EQA
*SOLVE EQA FOR C
*TYPE C

            2
          -L   + 351Ø L + 756ØØ
   C:  -----------------------------
         3         2
        L   -414Ø L   -2268ØØ L + 378ØØØ
```

**Fig. 6**

As an example of the conceptual level of this system, we present in Fig. 6 the conversation accompanying the symbolic solution of three simultaneous linear equations.

*ALADIN (Petrick, 1971; pp. 90–99).* This system uses the MATHLAB rational function package (Manove et al.) for simplification. Its primary contribution is its display program, which employs the graphical capabilities of the IBM 2250 for the creation of high-quality (approaching textlike) two-dimensional presentations of mathematical expressions. It also supports the use of a lightpen for subexpression selection.

SYMBOLIC SYSTEMS. We should mention first a sequence of three early programs for the simplification of general symbolic mathematical expressions represented as prefix-notation tree structures. The first, at M.I.T., was due to Hart, and the other two were due to Wooldridge and Korsvold at Stanford. The latter has survived in current usage as a result of its incorporation, subject to modification, into the MATHLAB, MACSYMA, and SCRATCHPAD systems.

In the mid-1960s there appeared two systems, Formula Algol and FAMOUS, which, while dedicated to the symbolic manipulation of mathematical expressions, presented the user with almost no built-in automatic simplification facilities. This was due, at least in the case of FAMOUS, to a conscious decision that, since the "simplicity" of an expression is surely context-dependent, it should be reasonable to present the user with *complete* control over the simplification process. That is, the user should be compelled to define all transformations, rather than, as with most systems, be permitted simply to switch on and off the transformations supplied by the system architects. No system of this species has ever solved the inherent efficiency problems to the extent that it could serve more than didactic purposes. Probably neither Formula Algol nor FAMOUS could be revived today.

Another lost symbolic system of importance is the Symbolic Mathematical Laboratory of W. A. Martin. This system provided high-quality 2-D graphics on a DEC-340 display and was also the first to employ a lightpen for subexpression selection. In some ways, it represented a degree of interaction that has not been duplicated by any subsequent system. Nor were its innovative internal programming techniques restricted to its graphics facilities. Of particular interest is the use of hash coding for subexpression matching (Petrick, 1971; pp. 305–310).

The best known, purely symbolic systems are, of course, Formac and its current version PL/I-Formac (Petrick, 1971; pp. 105–114). Formac was the first widely available general-purpose algebraic manipulation system and served for a period to define the field. Certainly, there was a time when one could have safely made the statement that the majority of *all* mechanical symbolic mathematical computations had been done within Formac. The practical success of these systems, in spite of their rigidity with respect to user modifications and their lack of any seminumerical facilities for rational function computations, is probably due to the overall intelligence of the facilities that were provided. Above all, they were certainly sufficient to support the dominant application area of truncated power series expansion. Current support is minimal.

HYBRID SYSTEMS

*MATHLAB (Petrick, 1971; pp. 29–41).* This system is distributed currently for on-line operation on the DEC system-10 (PDP-10) computer, although subsystems have been converted to run on IBM and CDC machines. This was the first heavyweight hybrid system passing data freely between a general-purpose simplification package and a powerful rational function package. Marred by the lack of a number of practical necessities, this system is probably most important for its computational innovations. These include the first complete program for the factorization of multivariate polynomials over the integers, and consequently for the partial fraction expansion of rational functions; for the integration of rational functions; for the inverse Laplace transform of rational functions; for the solution of linear differential equations with constant coefficients; and for the solution of equations via polynomial factorization. In addition it contains CHARYBDIS, the first program for the two-dimensional display of mathematical expressions on typewriter-like devices (Teletypes, alphanumeric displays, line-printer, etc.). Its dedication to an on-line environment led to an interesting command structure and a number of convenient core-oriented and disk-oriented bookkeeping facilities.

As a first example of the facilities of this system, we should like to return to the preceding example, introduced in our discussion of the IAM system, of the symbolic solution of simultaneous linear equations. Because of the still higher conceptual level of MATHLAB, at least with respect to this problem, the entire conversation would be condensed into the single instruction:

```
'SIMSOLVE ('EQA, 'EQB, 'EQC, A, B, C)$
```

The output would be almost identical.

A further demonstration of the expertise of this system is provided in Fig. 7 by the conversation representing the solution (controlled by the machine, not the user) of the differential equation representing the motion of a velocity-damped spring. The lines starting with "#" are those typed by the user.

*MACSYMA (Petrick, 1971; pp. 58–75).* In many ways a descendant of MATHLAB, this leviathan of the field possesses enough sheer code to approach an order of magnitude dominance over many other systems. It can do just about anything any other system can do, with the obvious exception of certain very specialized capabilities, such as the REDUCE high energy physics machinery. Furthermore, considerable attention has been devoted recently to insure that it concedes little in efficiency to less general systems.

It is impossible to summarize here its facilities, ranging as they do from extremely flexible user control over the form in which rational functions are presented to a semantic pattern-matching facility that, at least, if taken together with SCHATCHEN (Moses, 1969), serves to define the state of the art. Features such as programs for the manipulation of polynomials over the Gaussian integers or the best extant program for the computation of symbolic limits (Petrick, 458–464) are almost lost in the enormity of this first system to approach the goal of an algebraic manipulation facility.

As an example of the power of MACSYMA, we return a third time to the symbolic solution of the simultaneous linear equations. Again, as in the case of MATHLAB, a single instruction will suffice:

```
SOLVE ([EQA, EQB, EQC], [A, B, C]).
```

Again, the output is almost identical. What is different here is that the instruction is at a still higher

```
DSS:DERIV(X,T,2)=-K*X-A*DERIV(X,T)$

  2
D X             D X
--- = (- K)X - A---
  2             DT
DT

#'LDESOLVE('DSS,X,T)$
NEED INITIAL CONDITIONS
#ASK$
X(Ø) =
#L$
X'(Ø) =
#Ø$

IS THE EXPRESSION

          2
  4K - A
---------
    4

TO BE CONSIDERED POSITIVE NEGATIVE OR ZERO?
#POSITIVE$

      A
  - ---T                                                          2
      2                    2                     SIN(1/2*SQRT(4K -A )T)
E        (L*COS(1/2*SQRT(4K -A )T) + L*A-----------------------)
                                                            2
                                                  SQRT(4K - A )
```

**Fig. 7**

level, since the instruction SOLVE is more generic and the *program* must classify the problem as the solution of simultaneous *linear* equations. Chosen to exemplify the many expert facilities possessed uniquely by this system, the following example is given for the computation of the residue of a meromorphic function. The command is

RESIDUE (SIN (A*X)/X**4, X, 0, 4).

The answer is $-A^3/6$.

At present the only reasonable route of access to MACSYMA is through the ARPA network (Arpanet). This is due primarily to the complexity of the system, but is also a result of its author's reluctance to distribute source code.

*SCRATCHPAD (Petrick, 1971; pp. 42–58).* This most eclectic of systems derives most of its considerable computational powers from the direct accretion of code from such sources as (especially) REDUCE, MATHLAB (including CHARYBDIS), SIN, Korsvold's simplification program, and Martin's graphical display programs.

An important innovation of this system is its highly expressive and succinct syntax, which not only allows the user an especially wide class of natural notational devices but also provides him with the means of extending them himself. As an example of this naturalness, we would like to return to the succinct definition of the Legendre polynomials presented in connection with SYMBAL (see Fig. 4) and now present the SCRATCHPAD version:

$p\langle 0\rangle = 1$
$p\langle 1\rangle = x$
$p\langle i\rangle = (2*i-1)/i*x*p\langle i-1\rangle - (i-1)/i*p\langle i-2\rangle,$
$\quad i$ in (3,4, . . .)
$i$ in (0,1, . . ., 25) $p\langle i\rangle$

The last line invokes the actual computation and printing of the results.

Another unique feature of this system is, as a result of its commitment to interactive problem solving, the preservation of enough information to allow the user to return not only (as with several systems) to old results, but also to past *states*.

The system is actively in current use only at the IBM T.J. Watson Research Center.

It is important to acknowledge the enormous debt algebraic manipulation owes to the invention and development of the symbolic list processing language Lisp. Among the systems mentioned in this article, those written in Lisp include SAINT, MATHLAB, SIN, REDUCE, ALADIN, the simplification programs of Hart, Wooldridge, and Korsvold MACSYMA, FAMOUS, Martin's Symbolic Laboratory, SCHATCHEN, SCRATCHPAD, and CHARYBDIS.

### References

1968. Manove, M., S. Bloom, and C. Engelman. "Rational Functions in MATHLAB." In D. G. Bobrow (Ed.), *Symbolic Manipulation Languages and Techniques.* North Holland, Amsterdam.

1969. Moses, J. "Symbolic Integration, MAC-TR-47, Project MAC," M.I.T.

1970. Engeli, Max E. "SYMBAL, Summary + Examples." Zurich: FIDES Union Fiduciaire.

1971. Petrick, S. R. (Ed.). *Proc. Second Symposium Symbolic and Algebraic Manipulation, Los Angeles.* Available from Association for Computing Machinery, New York.

1972. Horowitz, Ellis. "The Application of Symbolic Mathematics to a Singular Perturbation Problem," *Proc. ACM Annual Conf.*, Boston.

C. Engelman

# ALGOL 68

For articles on related subjects *see* Pascal; Procedure-Oriented Languages; and Programming Languages.

For articles on related terms *see* Block Structure; and Identifier.

Algol 68 is a language designed by a working group (WG 2.1) of the International Federation for Information Processing (IFIP) in order to provide a general-purpose programming language that would be suitable for communicating algorithms, executing them efficiently on different computers, and teaching computer science. Even though Algol 68 is a successor of Algol 60, it is a completely new language, different from Algol 60 in many essential aspects. Its design reflects the 1968 understanding of a number of fundamental concepts of programming languages and computer science.

Algol 68 has great expressive power and yet a very elegant and interesting basic structure. It features five primitive types (called "modes") of values: **bool** (boolean), **char** (character), **int** (integer), **real** and **format**; and five rules for constructing new modes from the already defined ones. So, for example, values of mode [ ] **real** are one-dimensional arrays or *multiple values* of reals. Values of mode **struct** ([ ] **char** *name,* **bool** *sex,* **int** *age*) are personal records or *structured values*. Values of mode **union (real, int)** are either reals or integers, but no value of this mode can be both of mode **real** and **int**. *References* are values that refer (point) to other values. For example, values of mode **ref** [ ] **char** are references to one-dimensional arrays of characters. Values of mode **proc (int, real) bool** are *routines* (i.e., procedures) that take two arguments of respective modes **int** and **real** and return a value of mode **bool**.

Since references and routines are values, they can be manipulated like any other values. In particular, they can be passed as parameters in procedure calls. Because of this it is possible to achieve the effects of three types of procedure calls found in other programming languages: call by value, call by name, and call by reference. So, for example, values of mode **proc (ref [ ] char, int) int** are routines with the first formal parameter called by reference.

Different sorts of declarations (for example, array declarations and switch declarations) found in other programming languages are captured in the *identity declaration* of Algol 68. This concept is also the basis of the parameter-passing mechanism; it allows construction of an infinite number of new modes from the already defined ones and permits declaration of arithmetic and logical operators and their priorities.

The identity declaration and the concept of a reference clarify the distinction between a variable and a constant. An identity declaration in a program defines the value possessed by the identifier that appears in the declaration. This value may be a reference to another value, in which case the identifier is declared as a variable. An example of an initialized (i.e., one that includes assignment) declaration of that sort is **real** *x: = 3.14,* which gives rise to the following scheme:

identifier $x \rightarrow$ reference to a real value $\rightarrow$ 3.14.

The effect of a standard assignment statement is achieved by making the reference possessed by the identifier refer to the value specified in the statement. This is not possible if the value possessed by an identifier is not a reference, i.e., if this intermediate link is not present. In that case the identity declaration establishes the identifier as a constant, which can be changed only by redeclaring it. An example of a declaration that establishes *pi* as a constant 3.14 is **real** *pi* = *3.14*, which gives rise to the following scheme:

identifier *pi* $\rightarrow$ 3.14.

This careful distinction permits, in particular, the definition of constant and variable procedures. For example, the declaration **proc** *f* = (**real** *x*, **real** *y*) **real**: $(x + y)/2 - sqrt(x \times y)$ establishes *f* as a constant, as opposed to **proc** *f*: = (**real** *x*, **real** *y*) **real**: $(x + y)/2 - sqrt(x \times y)$, which defines a variable procedure. In the latter case we can, at another point in the program, assign some other value of mode **proc (real, real) real** to *f*; for example, we can write *f*: = (**real** *x*,**real** *y*) **real:** $(x + y)/2$.

A number of standard statements are available in Algol 68: assignment, e.g., *x*: = $(a + b)/2$; repetitive, e.g., **for** *i* **from** 2 **to** *n* **do** *f*: = $f \times i$; **go to**, e.g., **go to** *loop*; conditional, e.g., **if** $x \geq y$ **then go to** *label* **else go to** *end* **fi**, etc. In addition to the conventional serial statement execution, it is possible to specify parallel or *collateral* execution. In the latter case, execution of statements is merged in time in a way to be specified by the implementation. Parallel programming facilities in Algol 68 include elementary means of control or synchronization of collateral execution. These are language-defined values called "semaphores."

The Algol 60 concept of a block appears in a more general form in Algol 68 as a *range*. An example of a range is a sequence of declarations and statements placed between generalized parentheses. Examples of pairs of these parentheses are **begin** and **end, if** and **then, then** and **else, else** and **fi**, etc. References possessed by the identifiers declared in a range may be local to that range. Since the hardware representation of a reference is a memory location, storage is allocated dynamically to local variables; i.e., storage for local variables of a range is deallocated when leaving that range. In addition to these stack-controlled values, Algol 68 also has values whose lifetime does not fit into the last-in-first-out principle of a stack. Values of this sort are stored in a randomly organized memory region called the *heap*.

REFERENCES

1969. van Wijngaarden, A., et al. "Report on the Algorithmic Language ALGOL 68." Springer-Verlag *Numerische Mathematik, 14.*

1971. Lindsey, C. H., and S. G. van der Meulen. *Informal Introduction to ALGOL 68.* Amsterdam: North-Holland.

S. ALAGIĆ

# ALGORITHM

For articles on related subjects *see* ALGORITHMS, ANALYSIS OF; ALGORITHMS, THEORY OF; ERRORS; ERROR ANALYSIS; MARKOV ALGORITHM; PARALLEL ALGORITHM; PROGRAM CORRECTNESS, PROOF OF; SCHEDULING ALGORITHM; and TURING MACHINE.

In discussing problem solving, we presuppose both a problem and a device to be used in solving the problem. The problem may be mathematical or nonmathematical in nature, simple or complex. The basic requirements for a well-posed problem are that (1) the known information is clearly specified; (2) the solution is specified to the extent that it can be determined when the problem has been solved; and (3) the problem does not change during its attempted solution. The second requirement does not mean that the solution to the problem is known a priori, but only that we can determine when we have reached the solution. For example, in some numerical problems we obtain repeated approximations to the answer, terminating the solution process when two successive approximations are "sufficiently close" together. We can specify in the problem statement the exact meaning of "sufficiently close," without knowing the exact answer. The device to be used for problem solution may be man or machine, or a combination of the two.

**Definition.** Given both the problem and the device, an *algorithm* is the precise characterization of a method of solving the problem, presented in a language comprehensible to the device. In particular, an algorithm is characterized by these properties:

1. Application of the algorithm to a particular input set or problem description results in a finite sequence of actions.

2. The sequence of actions has a unique initial action.

3. Each action in the sequence has a unique successor.

4. The sequence terminates with either a solution to the problem, or a statement that the problem is insoluble.

We illustrate these concepts with an example: "Find the square root of the real number $x$." As it is stated, this problem is algorithmically either trivial or unsolvable, owing to the irrationality of most square roots. If we accept "$\sqrt{2}$" as the square root of 2, for example, the solution is trivial: The answer is the square root sign ($\sqrt{\ }$) concatenated with the input. In SNOBOL, the entire algorithm is

```
OUTPUT = '√' INPUT
END
```

However, if we want a decimal expression, then the square root of 2 can never be exactly calculated. Hence, the requirement of a finite number of actions is violated.

A modified statement of the problem is more suited to our purposes. "Find the positive square root, to four decimal places, of the real number $x$." This statement has three useful properties:

1. It explicitly names the *positive* square root as the desired one, whereas the earlier statement left that quality ambiguous.

2. It eliminates the string "$\sqrt{x}$" as a problem solution.

3. By stating "four decimal places" (or any other fixed number of places), it provides a test for termination.

A possible method of solution is

(a) Choose a number $y$ and compute $y^2$.

(b) If $|y^2 - x| < 5 \times 10^{-5}$, the solution is $y$; if not, return to step (a).

This method fails to be an algorithm, since no procedure is specified for choosing either the initial value $y$ or subsequent values. Moreover, even if there is a solution, there is no guarantee that this method will find it.

Now consider another method:

1. Let $y = 1$.

2. Compute $y^2$.

3. If $|y^2 - x| < 5 \times 10^{-5}$, the solution is $y$, HALT; if not, go to step 4.

4. Replace $y$ by $((x/y) + y)/2$; go to step 2. (This procedure is a special case of a general technique known as the Newton-Raphson technique.)

This method has the precise definition of each step required of an algorithm. Moreover, whenever applied to a nonnegative real number $x$, the method will produce the proper solution in a finite number of steps. However, whenever applied to a negative number, the method will endlessly recompute $y$ without recognizing the futility of the task. This is typical of a class of methods called *semi-algorithms*: They will halt in a finite number of steps if the problem posed has a solution, but will not necessarily halt if there is no solution.

To transform the given method into an algorithm, two things must be done:

(a) Add a step, (0); if $x < 0$, there is no solution; HALT; and

(b) Rewrite the given method in a language suitable for the proposed device. (For English-speaking people, the given language is satisfactory; for a computer, a programming language must be used. For example, the following algorithm in Basic is suitable for computers utilizing that language, with the data set {3, 107, 1, 0, −4}.)

```
 10 READ X
 20 IF X<0 THEN 80
 30 LET Y = 1
 40 LET Z = Y↑2
 50 IF ABS (X-Z) < 0.00005 THEN 100
 60 Y = ((X/Y)+Y)/2
 70 GO TO 40
 80 PRINT "THERE IS NO SOLUTION FOR " X "."
 90 GO TO 10
100 PRINT "THE SQUARE ROOT OF " X " IS " Y "."
105 GO TO 10
110 DATA 3
111 DATA 107
112 DATA 1
113 DATA 0
114 DATA -4
120 END
```

Note that statements 110 through 114 specify the data set to be used with the algorithm and are not part of the algorithm itself. If the algorithm is applied to this particular data set, the result will be

```
THE SQUARE ROOT OF 3      IS 1.73205 .
THE SQUARE ROOT OF 107    IS 10.3441 .
THE SQUARE ROOT OF 1      IS 1 .
THE SQUARE ROOT OF 0      IS 3.90625E-3 .
THERE IS NO SOLUTION FOR -4  .
```

**Significance of Algorithms.** While the concept of an algorithm is useful in crystallizing the informal notation of a "method of solution" for a problem, it has a much deeper significance. Whereas it was at one time assumed that any properly stated mathematical problem was solvable, mathematicians in the 1920s began to question this, asking what precisely it meant to say that we could "solve a problem" or "compute a function." Several important areas of mathematics have resulted from attempts to answer these questions, including the theory of Turing machines and the theory of algorithms. All the concepts proposed proved to be equivalent: Any problem that is solvable according to one concept is solvable according to all other concepts. Thus, while the algorithm, properly formalized, may not be the only way to solve problems, it appears to be essentially the only way that the human intellect in its present stage of development can comprehend.

**Quality Judgments on Algorithms.** Any computer program is at least a semi-algorithm, and any program that always halts is an algorithm. (Of course it may not solve the problem for which the programmer intended it.) Given a solvable problem, there are many algorithms (programs) to solve it, not all of equal quality. The primary practical criteria by which the quality of an algorithm is judged are time and memory requirements, accuracy of solution, and generality. To cite an extreme example, since a properly defined game of chess has only a finite number of possible moves, there exists an algorithm to determine the "perfect" chess game. Simply examine all possible move sequences, in some specified order. Unfortunately, the time required to execute any algorithm based on this idea is measured in billions of years, even at today's computer speeds. The memory requirements for such an algorithm are similarly overbearing.

On a more practical plane, several numerical methods for solving problems fail to yield satisfactory algorithms because the rate of convergence is so slow that thousands or millions of iterations may be needed to determine the answer. For other numerical methods, rounding or truncation errors may accumulate so rapidly that they destroy the answer.

There is often a trade-off in time and memory requirements, which must be settled pragmatically. The simplest case of this arises in the computation and repeated use of a complicated function. If the computation of each function value is sufficiently complex, then in repeated usage much time may be saved by precomputing a table of values and using table lookup techniques. However, such a table may require sufficient additional memory space that this becomes a critical factor. Thus, one may have to sacrifice some speed to stay within available memory bounds.

The accuracy of an algorithm is a characteristic often more closely related to time than to memory requirements. For example, the square root algorithm previously presented is not very accurate. (It yields 0.00390625 as the square root of zero.) Its accuracy may be improved by changing the test constant in line 50, at the cost of a longer run time. Further improvement may be obtained from the corresponding algorithm in double-precision Fortran, at a cost of both run time and additional memory space. In each case the basic algorithmic concept is unchanged.

Altering the basic algorithmic concept may provide an improved algorithm to accomplish a given task. For example, three multiplications and two additions are required to evaluate the quadratic expression $ax^2 + bx + c$ in the order $((ax^2) + (bx)) + c$. Changing the concept of the evaluation algorithm to $(((ax) + b)x) + c$ eliminates one multiplication, resulting in a more efficient process. This will improve the speed of solution of the problem, and probably also improve the accuracy of the result.

The remaining important characteristic of an algorithm is its generality. While there are occasions when an algorithm is needed to solve a single isolated problem, more often algorithms are designed to handle a range of input data. Generality, like accuracy, is often attained at the cost of speed and memory requirements. A general polynomial root finder is more costly in both time and storage than an algorithm for extracting the roots of a quadratic equation. But the increased generality may justify the cost. This is a pragmatic decision. In another example, an information retrieval system based on a free vocabulary is generally more expensive to design and operate than one based on a fixed or coded vocabulary. But the difference in utility may far outweigh the additional cost burden.

R. R. KORFHAGE

## ALGORITHM, MARKOV. *See* MARKOV ALGORITHM.

## ALGORITHM, PARALLEL. *See* PARALLEL ALGORITHM.

## ALGORITHM, SCHEDULING. *See* SCHEDULING ALGORITHM.

## ALGORITHMS, ANALYSIS OF

For articles on related subjects *see* ALGORITHM; ALGORITHMS, THEORY OF; COMPUTATIONAL COMPLEXITY; ITERATION; and RECURSION.

For article on related term *see* GRAPH THEORY.

The analysis of algorithms can be partitioned into two areas: algorithm complexity and problem complexity. The former is concerned with consideration of a specific algorithm for a problem and the analysis of its behavior with respect to the amount of memory space, time, or other resource used. The latter is concerned with the class of all algorithms for a particular problem and the determination of the minimum requirements of the problem with respect to space and time or other resources. Such analyses are second in importance only to the determination of the correctness of an algorithm. They provide the means to choose intelligently and improve algorithms.

Contrary to one's intuition, the advent of the electronic computer has made the efficiency of algorithms a topic of utmost concern. One might suspect that as the speed of computers increases, the effects of the efficiency of the algorithms decrease. Actually, just the opposite is true. The reason for this is that the asymptotic behavior of the algorithm becomes more important, as we will now illustrate.

With a problem we associate an integer, which we call the size of the problem. For example, the size of a matrix multiplication problem is the dimension of the matrix, the size of a graph problem is the number of edges, etc. The growth rate of the execution time of the algorithm is determined as a function of the size of the problem. The limiting behavior of the growth rate is called the asymptotic growth rate. For example, the asymptotic behavior of the function $17 + 5n + 2n^2$ is $2n^2$, since, for sufficiently large $n$, $2n^2$ approximates $17 + 5n + 2n^2$ to arbitrary accuracy. For $n = 100$, the lower-order terms account for less than 3%.

In performing a hand computation, the size of the problem is small, and consequently the asymptotic growth rate is unimportant. On such small problems most algorithms perform reasonably well. However, on a high-speed computer, the problem size normally encountered is large and the asymptotic growth rate becomes important. Given two algorithms with growth rates $n^2$ and $2^n$, for problems up to size 6, the difference in execution times is never more than a factor of 2. However, with a computer, a problem of size 100 might be encountered. In this case, the $n^2$ algorithm is easily executed, whereas the $2^n$ algorithm would require centuries to compute. This example illustrates why in the past ten years a tremendous effort has been devoted to analysis of algorithms.

**Algorithm Complexity.** Space and time are the most important considerations of algorithm complexity. Since both are limited, it is advisable to determine how much space and time an algorithm requires. An algorithm that requires relatively little memory space for execution may have a greater running time than another algorithm that requires more space, while both algorithms may provide a solution to the same problem. Thus, there is frequently a trade-off between space and time.

As an example of a space-time trade-off, consider an algorithm that requires the storage of an undirected graph. (An undirected graph is a set $V$ of $n$ vertices, $V = \{v_1, v_2, \ldots, v_n\}$, and a set $E$ of edges, where an edge is an unordered pair of vertices.) The algorithm stores the graph as an $n \times n$ connection matrix $A$, where

$$a_{ij} = \begin{cases} 1 & \text{if } (v_i,v_j) \text{ is an edge in } E; \\ 0 & \text{otherwise.} \end{cases}$$

This requires $n^2$ words of memory, regardless of the number of edges. Assume that the algorithm is used only for planar graphs. (A planar graph is an undirected graph that can be drawn on a plane surface so that no edges intersect.)

Let $G$ be a planar graph with $p$ vertices. Then $G$ can be represented in the computer by a linked list of $n$ vertices where the data structure for each vertex $v_i$ is a linked list of all vertices adjacent to $v_i$. Since each edge $(v_i,v_j)$ of $G$ is stored twice ($v_j$ is on the list of vertices adjacent to $v_i$, and $v_i$ is on the list of vertices adjacent to $v_j$), the memory required to store the list representation of $G$ is proportional to the number of edges. For planar graphs it can be shown that the number of edges is bounded by $3n - 6$, where $n$ is the number of vertices. Thus, the memory required is bounded by $C \times n$, where $C$ is a constant, rather than the $n^2$ that was required for the connection matrix representation. If the algorithm is required to determine if vertex $v_i$ is connected to vertex $v_j$, then a trade-off between space and time occurs, since only one operation is needed with the connection matrix representation, whereas the list representation requires searching the entire list of vertices adjacent to $v_i$ to see if $v_j$ is on the list.

A *frequency analysis* of an algorithm reveals the number of times certain parts of the algorithm are executed. Such an analysis indicates which parts of the algorithm consume large quantities of time and hence where efforts should be directed toward improving the algorithm. For example, the following section of Fortran-like code calculates

$$\sum_{i=1}^{N+1} a_i x^{i-1}$$

and stores the result in $T$.

```
       DIMENSION S(N), A(N + 1)
       DO 10 I = 1,N
 1     Y = 1.0                   N
       DO 20 J = 1,I
 2     Y = Y * X                 N(N-1)/2
20     CONTINUE
 3     S(I) = A(I + 1)*Y         N
10     CONTINUE
 4     T = A(1)                  1
       DO 30 I = 1,N
 5     T = T + S(I)              N
30     CONTINUE
```

The program is poorly written and just about every statement can be changed to decrease the amount of time required. To the right of each assignment statement is the number of times it is executed. As $N$ increases, the program spends proportionately more and more time executing statement 2 than it does for statements 1, 3, 4, or 5. Thus, it is really futile to try to improve the program by decreasing the time spent executing the latter statements without first decreasing the time spent executing statement 2. The portion of the program containing statement 2 can be improved by using Horner's rule for polynomial evaluation. Again, the number of times each assignment statement is executed is given at its right.

```
       DIMENSION A(N + 1)
 1     T = A(N + 1)              1
       DO 10 I = 1,N
 2     T = T*X + A(N + 1 - I)    N
10     CONTINUE
```

To determine the actual execution time of an algorithm in seconds requires a knowledge of the operation times for each instruction of the computer on which the algorithm is to be executed and how the compiler generates code. In order to avoid becoming involved in the specific details of operation of a particular computer, it is customary to find upper and lower bounds $c_1$ and $c_2$ such that the execution time of every instruction is between $c_1$ and $c_2$. Then the execution time of an algorithm can be estimated from a count of the number of operations that are executed. This frees the analysis of the algorithm from peculiarities of individual computers.

Frequently the time required by an algorithm is data dependent. In this case one of two types of analyses is possible. The first is called the "worst-case analysis," in which that set of data of given size requiring the most work is determined and the behavior of the algorithm is analyzed for that specific set of data. The other alternative is to assume a probability distribution for the possible input data and compute the distribution of the execution time as a function of the input distribution. Usually, this computation is so difficult that only the expected or average execution time as a function of size is computed. This is called the "average case analysis."

**Problem Complexity.** In problem complexity we are concerned with analyzing a problem rather than an algorithm. The analysis provides us with lower bounds on the amount of time and space required for a solution to the problem, independent of the algorithm used. The lower bounds may be either "worst case" or "average case" bounds. These lower bounds can serve as an indication of how well an algorithm fits the problem and whether it can be improved. For example, such an analysis shows that any algorithm that evaluates an arbitrary $n$-degree polynomial represented by its coefficients requires at least $n$ multiplications and $n$ additions. Thus, Horner's rule (given above) cannot be improved upon.

On the other hand, an analysis of matrix multiplication gives a lower bound of order $n^2$ operations for multiplying two matrices of dimension $n$. The usual matrix multiplication algorithm has an asymptotic growth rate of order $n^3$. Thus, there is substantial interest in trying either to find a better lower bound or to improve on the current matrix multiplication algorithms. At the current state of knowledge the fastest algorithm has an asymptotic growth rate of order $n^{2.81}$, and thus there is a large gap between the best-known lower bound and the performance of the best-known algorithm.

In problem analysis, it is often important to consider the frequency of occurrence of a specific operation. The reason for this is that reducing the number of occurrences of a specific operation can lead to a recursive algorithm with a lower asymptotic growth rate. Consider multiplying two $n$-digit numbers, where $n$ is a power of 2. The usual algorithm learned in elementary school requires on the order of $n^2$ operations. A recursive method of multiplying two $n$-digit numbers $x$ and $y$ is to write $x = a10^{n/2} + b$ and $y = c10^{n/2} + d$, where $a$, $b$, $c$, and $d$ are $n/2$-digit numbers. Compute $ab$, $cd$, and $ad + bc$. Then

$$xy = ab10^n + (ad + bc)10^{n/2} + cd.$$

The problem of computing $xy$ is reduced to the problem of computing $ab$, $cd$, and $ad + bc$, which are computed by the three multiplications $ab$, $cd$, and $(a + c)(b + d)$. The formula $ad + bc$ is obtained by $(a + c)(b + d) - ad - cd$. Let $T(n)$ be the time to compute the product of two $n$-digit numbers. Then $T(n) \simeq 3T(n/2) + kn$, where the $3T(n/2)$ is the time to compute the three multiplications, $k$ is a nonnegative constant, and $kn$ is the time to compute the necessary sums. Successively applying the formula above to each product, we obtain

$$\begin{aligned} T(n) &\simeq kn(1 + (3/2) + (3/2)^2 + \cdots + (3/2)^{\log_2 n}) \\ &\simeq 3kn^{\log_2 3} \simeq 3kn^{1.58}. \end{aligned}$$

The asymptotic growth rate is of order $n^{1.58}$ rather than the $n^2$ of the more elementary method. The important observation is that in computing $ab$, $cd$, and $ad + bc$, the number of multiplications was reduced from four to three at the expense of increasing the number of additions from one to four. The reason for doing this is that the exponent in the asymptotic growth rate is affected by the number of multiplications, whereas the number of additions affects only the constant.

A major difficulty with problem analysis is that it is concerned with the class of all algorithms for a given problem. One no longer can postulate a computer with a given structure and operation set. Instead, one must envision an abstract computer that is sufficiently general to encompass any physically implementable algorithm. The difficulties involved are of such magnitude that one is forced to obtain bounds for certain limited classes of programs. For example, sorting $n$ integers can be shown to require $n \log n$ operations if restricted to the class of algorithm that sorts by binary comparisons. This follows from the simple information theoretic argument that there are $n!$ possible permutations of $n$ items, and each comparison can at best divide the set of possible permutations by a factor of 2. Since the asymptotic growth rate of $\log(n!)$ is $n \log n$, it takes at least $n \log n$ comparisons to determine uniquely the actual permutation. Of course, if one sorts by some method other than by comparisons (radix sort, for example), then the bound is no longer valid.

A typical assumption for a class of programs might be that the computation uses only the arithmetic operations of addition, subtraction, multiplication, and division. When this is done, it is necessary to specify the underlying algebraic structure. For example, the complexity of computing an algebraic expression may depend on whether the underlying structure is the rational, real, or complex number system.

One of the most powerful techniques for establishing results of this nature is due to Winograd, who showed that any algorithm for computing the product of an arbitrary vector $X$ times a matrix $A$ requires a number of multiplications at least as great as the number of nondependent columns of $A$. It immediately follows from this result that Horner's rule evaluates arbitrary $n$-degree polynomials with the minimum number of multiplications. Let $X = (x^n, x^{n-1}, \cdots, x, 1)$ and let $A = (a_{n+1}, a_n, \cdots, a_1)^T$. Then

$$XA = \sum_{i=1}^{n+1} a_i x^{i-1}.$$

$X$ has $n$ nondependent columns, which implies that $n$ multiplications are required. The result requires that the algorithm evaluate any polynomial, given its coefficients. Specific polynomials can often be evaluated with fewer multiplications. Similarly, if the polynomial is specified by parameters other than its coefficients, a saving in the number of multiplications is possible.

The one facet of problem complexity that is probably the most intriguing is the lack of nontrivial lower bounds for various problems. Almost all known lower bounds are either linear in the size of the problem or have been obtained by restricting the classes of algorithms. The notable exceptions are lower bounds obtained by the diagonalization techniques of recursive function theory. One of the major goals of computer scientists working in the analysis of algorithms is to close the gap in our knowledge of problem complexity. Hopefully, the next decade will provide powerful new tools in the area or startling improvements in the efficiency of algorithms.

REFERENCE

1968, 1969, 1973, Knuth, D. E. *The Art of Computer Programming*, vols. 1, 2, 3. Reading, Mass.: Addison-Wesley.

J. E. HOPCROFT AND J. E. MUSINSKI

## ALGORITHMS, THEORY OF

For articles on related subjects *see* ALGORITHM; ALGORITHMS, ANALYSIS OF; COMPUTABILITY; COMPUTATIONAL COMPLEXITY; DECIDABILITY; FORMAL LANGUAGES; and TURING MACHINE.
For article on related term *see* PROCEDURE.

The meaning of the word "algorithm," like the meaning of most other words commonly used in the English language, is somewhat vague. In order to have a *theory of algorithms*, we need a mathematically precise definition of an algorithm. However, in giving such a precise definition, we run the risk of not reflecting exactly the intuitive notion behind the word. The finding of a mathematically precise replacement of the notion of algorithm was the earliest problem in the theory of algorithms. Many authors have tried to capture the essence of the intuitive notion of an algorithm. We give four examples.

*Hermes (1965).* "An algorithm is a general procedure such that for any appropriate question the answer can be obtained by the use of a simple computation according to a specified method. . . . [A] general procedure [is] a process, the execution of which is clearly specified to the smallest details."

*Minsky (1967).* " . . . an effective procedure is a set of rules which tell us, from moment to moment, precisely how to behave."

*Rogers (1967).* " . . . an algorithm is a clerical (i.e., deterministic, bookkeeping) procedure which can be applied to any of a certain class of symbolic *inputs* and which will eventually yield, for each such input, a corresponding symbolic *output*."

*Hopcroft and Ullman (1969).* "A *procedure* is a finite sequence of instructions that can be mechanically carried out, such as a computer program. . . . A procedure which always terminates is called an *algorithm*."

Note that what Hermes calls a "general procedure" is what Minsky calls an "effective procedure" is what Hopcroft and Ullman call a "procedure." Other terms are also used in the literature, and some authors use the word "algorithm" to denote any procedure whatsoever. In the remainder of this article the Hopcroft and Ullman terminology will be used.

An important fact to note is that the notion of a procedure cannot be divorced from the environment in which it operates. What may be a procedure in certain situations, may not be considered a procedure in other situations. For example, the instructions of a computer program are not usually understood by most people. Alternatively, the description of a chess game that appears in a newspaper is a perfectly clear algorithm for a chess player who wants to reproduce the game, but it is quite meaningless to people who do not play chess. Thus, when we talk about a procedure as a finite sequence of instructions, we assume that whoever is supposed to carry out those instructions, be it man or machine, understands them in the same way as whoever gave those instructions.

Another sense in which the environment influences the notions of procedure and algorithm is indicated by the following examples. If the instruction requires us to take the integral part of the square root of a number, such an instruction can be carried out if we are dealing with positive integers only, but it cannot always be carried out if we are dealing with both positive and negative integers. Thus, the same set of instructions may or may not be a procedure, depending on the subset of integers for which it is intended. Alternatively, we can easily give a procedure that, given an integer $x$, keeps subtracting 1 until 0 is reached and then stops. Such a procedure will be an algorithm if we intend to use it for positive integers only, but it will not be an algorithm if we also intend to apply it to negative integers.

The recognition of whether or not a sequence of instructions is a procedure or an algorithm is a subjective affair. No precise theory can be built on the vague definitions given above. In trying to build a precise theory, one must examine the situations in which the notion of algorithm is used. In the theory of computation, one is mainly concerned with algorithms that are used either for computing functions or for deciding predicates.

A *function* $f$ with domain $D$ and range $R$ is a definite correspondence by which there is associated with each element $x$ of the domain $D$ (referred to as the "argument") a single element $f(x)$ of the range $R$ (called the "value"). The function $f$ is said to be "computable" (in the intuitive sense) if there exists an algorithm which, for any given $x$ in $D$, provides us with the value $f(x)$.

A *predicate* $P$ with domain $D$ is a property of the elements of $D$, which each particular element of $D$ either has or does not have. If $x$ in $D$ has the property $P$, we say that $P(x)$ is true; otherwise, we say that $P(x)$ is false. The predicate $P$ is said to be *decidable* (in the intuitive sense) if there exists an algorithm which, for any given $x$ in $D$, provides us with a definite answer to the question of whether or not $P(x)$ is true.

The computability of functions and the decidability of predicates are very closely related notions because we can associate with each predicate $P$ a function $f$ with range $\{0,1\}$ such that, for all $x$ in the common domain $D$ of $P$ and $f$, $f(x) = 0$ if $P(x)$ is true and $f(x) = 1$ if $P(x)$ is false. Clearly, $P$ is decidable if and only if $f$ is computable. For this reason we will hereafter restrict our attention to the computability of functions.

A further restriction customary in the theory of algorithms is to consider only functions whose domain and range are both the set of nonnegative integers. This is reasonable, since in those situations where the notion of a procedure makes any sense at all, it is usually possible to *represent* elements of the domain and the range by nonnegative integers. For example, if the domain comprises pairs of nonnegative integers, as in the case with an arithmetic function of two arguments, we can represent the pair $(a, b)$, by the number $2^a3^b$ in an effective one-to-one fashion. If the domain comprises strings of symbols over an alphabet of 15 letters, we can consider the letters to be nonzero hexadecimal digits, and assign that nonnegative integer to a string that is denoted by the string in the hexadecimal notation. The device of representing elements of a set $D$ by nonnegative integers is referred to as "arithmetization" or "Gödel numbering," after the logician K. Gödel, who used it to prove the undecidability of certain predicates about formal logic. From now on we will be exclusively concerned with functions whose domain and range are subsets of the set of nonnegative integers.

In order to show that a certain function is computable, it is sufficient to give an algorithm that computes it. But without a precise definition of an algorithm, all such demonstrations are open to question. The situation is even more uncertain if we want to show that a given function is uncomputable, i.e., that no algorithm whatsoever computes it. In order to avoid such uncertainty, we need a mathematically precise definition of a computable function.

It is clear from the way in which algorithms are discussed above that for a proper algorithm we ought to be able to construct a machine that carries out the instructions of the algorithm. One possible way of making precise the concept of a computable function is to define an appropriate type of machine, and then define a function to be computable if and only if it can be computed by such a machine. This has indeed been done. The machine usually used for this purpose is the so-called Turing machine. This simple device has a tape and a read-write head, together with a control that may be in one of finitely many states. The tape is used to represent numbers. A function $f$ is called computable if there exists a Turing machine that, given a tape representing an argument $x$, eventually halts with the tape representing the value $f(x)$. Since a precise definition of a Turing machine can be given, the notion of a computable function has become a precise mathematical notion.

The question arises whether or not it is indeed the case that a function is computable in the intuitive sense if and only if it is computable by a Turing machine. The claim that this is true is usually referred to as "Church's thesis" (sometimes as Turing's thesis). Such a claim can never be "proved," since one of the two notions whose equivalence is claimed is mathematically imprecise. However, there are many convincing arguments in support of Church's thesis, and an overwhelming majority of workers in the theory of algorithms accept its validity. One of the strongest arguments in support of Church's thesis is the fact that all of the many diverse attempts at precisely defining the concept of computable function have ended up with defining exactly the same set of functions.

Given a precise definition of a computable function, it is now possible to show for particular functions that they are computable. Conversely, it becomes possible to prove that certain functions are not computable. We will give two examples.

*Example 1.* Consider the following problem. Give an algorithm that, for any Turing machine, decides whether or not the machine eventually stops if it is started on an empty tape. This problem is called the "blank-tape halting problem." The required algorithm would be considered a *solution* of the problem. A proof that there is no such algorithm would be said to show the (effective) *unsolvability* of the problem.

The blank-tape halting problem is in fact unsolvable. This is proved by rephrasing the problem into a problem about the computability of a function, as follows: Turing machines can be Gödel-numbered in an effective manner; i.e., there exists an algorithm which for any Turing machine will give its Gödel number. Furthermore, this can be done in such a way that every nonnegative integer is the Gödel number of some Turing machine. Let $f$ be the function defined as follows:

$$f(x) = \begin{cases} 0 & \text{if } n \text{ is the Gödel number of a Turing machine that eventually stops if started on the blank tape;} \\ 1 & \text{otherwise.} \end{cases}$$

It is easy to see that $f$ is computable if and only if the blank-tape halting problem is solvable. The unsolvability of the blank-tape halting problem is proved by showing that the assumption that $f$ is computable leads to a contradiction.

*Example 2.* Our second example indicates that there are unsolvable problems in classical mathematics. The following problem is known as "Hilbert's tenth problem" (after the German mathematician David Hilbert, 1862–1943):

> Given a diophantine equation [an equation of the form $E = 0$, where $E$ is a polynomial with integer coefficients; e.g., $xy^2 - 2x^2 + 3 = 0$] with any variables, give a procedure with which it is possible to decide after a finite number of operations whether or not the equation has a solution in integers.

Although this problem was stated by Hilbert in 1900 (long before there was such a thing as a theory of algorithms), it has only been recently that the Russian mathematician I. Matiajasevitch has shown it to be unsolvable.

That there are clearly defined problems, like the two given above, that cannot be solved by any computer-like device is probably the most striking aspect of the theory of algorithms. A whole superstructure has been built on such results, and there are methods to find out not only whether something is uncomputable, but also how badly it is uncomputable (see Rogers, 1967).

A typical question that one may ask is the following: Suppose we had a device which, for any given Turing machine, told us whether or not the Turing machine will eventually stop on the blank tape. Can we write an "algorithm" that makes use of this device and solves Hilbert's tenth problem? It has been known for some time that such an "algorithm" exists. In this sense, Hilbert's tenth problem is *reducible* to the blank-tape halting problem. It is the proof that the reverse is also true which gave us the unsolvability of Hilbert's tenth problem. Two problems that are both reducible to the other are said to be "equivalent." Most of the theory of algorithms has, until recently, concerned itself with questions of the reducibility and equivalence of various unsolvable problems.

In recent years a new trend has developed. Much of the activity in the theory of algorithms began to concern itself with computable functions, decidable predicates, and solvable problems. Questions about the nature of the algorithms, the type of devices that can be used for the computation, and about the difficulty or complexity of the computation have been investigated and are discussed in other articles.

### References

1965. Hermes, H. *Enumerability, Decidability, Computability*. Berlin, Germany: Springer Verlag.

1967. Minsky, M. *Computation: Finite and Infinite Machines*. Englewood Cliffs, N.J.: Prentice-Hall.

1967. Rogers. H. *Theory of Recursive Functions and Effective Computability*. New York: McGraw-Hill.

1969. Hopcroft, J. E., and J. D. Ullman. *Formal Languages and Their Relation to Automata*. Reading, Mass.: Addison-Wesley.

G. T. Herman

## ALLOCATION, STORAGE. *See* STORAGE ALLOCATION.

*See* STORAGE ALLOCATION.

## AMERICAN FEDERATION OF IN-INFORMATION PROCESSING SOCIETIES (AFIPS)

For articles on related terms *see* AMERICAN SOCIETY FOR INFORMATION SCIENCE; ASSOCIATION FOR COMPUTING MACHINERY; ASSOCIATION FOR EDUCATIONAL DATA SYSTEMS; INTERNATIONAL FEDERATION FOR INFORMATION PROCESSING; INSTITUTE OF ELECTRICAL AND ELECTRONIC ENGINEERS —COMPUTER SOCIETY; and SOCIETY FOR INDUSTRIAL AND APPLIED MATHEMATICS.

**Purpose.** The American Federation of Information Processing Societies is a national federation of professional societies established to represent the member societies on an international level and for the advancement and diffusion of knowledge of the information processing sciences. Toward the latter end it engages in appropriate literary and scientific activities. High on the list of its original goals was the provision of a complete, responsible, and effective public information program for the information processing community, and AFIPS has performed this function primarily and most effectively through sponsorship of the Spring and Fall Joint Computer Conferences, which as of June 1973 were merged into an annual National Computer Conference. AFIPS represents the United States in a variety of international information processing activities, including IFIP (International Federation for Information Processing). AFIPS acts as national spokesman for the information processing community in matters dealing with or affected by computing, data processing, and related sciences.

**How Established.** AFIPS was organized as an unincorporated society on May 10, 1961. It was the outgrowth of the National Joint Computer Committee, which had been established ten years earlier to sponsor the Joint Computer Conferences. The AFIPS founding societies were the American Institute of Electrical Engineers, Institute of Radio Engineers (which later merged into the Institute of Electrical and Electronic Engineers), and the Association for Computing Machinery.

The presidents who have held office in the National Joint Computer Committee and AFIPS are

Morton M. Astrahan, 1956–1958
Harry H. Goode, 1959–1960
Willis Ware, 1961–1962
J. D. Madden, 1963
Edwin L. Harder, 1964–1965
Bruce Gilchrist, 1966–1967
Paul Armer, 1968
Richard I. Tanaka, 1969–1970
Keith W. Uncapher, 1971
Walter L. Anderson, 1972
George Glaser, 1973–1975
Anthony Ralston, 1975–

**Organizational Structure.** There are two classes of AFIPS participation: member societies, which have a principal interest in computers and information processing, and affiliated societies, which, although not principally concerned with computers and information processing, do have a major interest in this field. A minimum membership of 1,500 is required for admission to either class of membership.

In 1975 the 15 constituent societies of AFIPS were

- The Association for Computing Machinery, Inc. (ACM)
- The Institute of Electrical & Electronics Engineers, Inc. (IEEE)
- Data Processing Management Association (DPMA)
- Society for Computer Simulation (SCS)—formerly Simulation Councils, Inc. (SCI)
- The American Society for Information Science (ASIS)
- Association for Computational Linguistics (ACL)
- Society for Information Display (SID)
- Special Libraries Association (SLA)
- The American Institute of Certified Public Accountants (AICPA)
- American Statistical Association (ASA)
- Society for Industrial and Applied Mathematics (SIAM)
- American Institute of Aeronautics and Astronautics (AIAA)
- Instrument Society of America (ISA)
- Association for Educational Data Systems (AEDS)
- Institute of Internal Auditors (IIA)

The Federation is managed by its Board of Directors. Each member society has one to three directors, depending on size; each affiliated society has one director. The President is the principal officer of the Federation and the Executive Director is the senior paid officer. Other AFIPS officers include a vice-president, secretary, and treasurer. Meetings of the Board of Directors are held at least once a year to elect member and associate member societies, to act on constitutional amendments, and to conduct other pertinent business.

The headquarters of AFIPS is located at 210 Summit Avenue, Montvale, New Jersey 07645.

**Technical Program.** The chief contribution of AFIPS to the professional community has been made through its sponsorship each year of both Spring and Fall Joint Computer Conferences, which offered technical sessions in the widest possible spectrum of subjects, and an accompanying exhibit of the latest equipment and literature relevant to the information sciences. In 1973 these conferences were replaced by an annual National Computer Conference, which continues to provide both the professional community and the interested public with the latest information regarding developments in the field of information technology. AFIPS also sponsors small meetings and workshops on specialized topics. Several of these have resulted in publications.

The Harry Goode Memorial Award was authorized in 1964, and since that time has been presented annually to an individual in recognition of outstanding achievement in the field of information processing. The recipients of this award are

Howard Hathaway Aiken, 1964
George Robert Stibitz and Konrad Zuse, 1965
J. Presper Eckert and John William Mauchly, 1966
Samuel Nathan Alexander, 1967
Maurice Vincent Wilkes, 1968
Alston Scott Householder, 1969
Grace Murray Hopper, 1970
Allen Newell, 1971
Seymour R. Cray, 1972
(No award, 1973)
Edsger W. Dijkstra, 1974.

The AFIPS Press publishes proceedings of annual conferences and other publications of interest to its members and to the lay public, and is also the distributor of IFIP publications in the United States.

I. L. AUERBACH

## AMERICAN SOCIETY FOR INFORMATION SCIENCE (ASIS)

For article on related subject *see* AMERICAN FEDERATION OF INFORMATION PROCESSING SOCIETIES.

**Purpose.** The American Society for Information Science is a not-for-profit professional association organized for scientific, literary, and educational purposes, and dedicated to the creation, organization, dissemination, and application of knowledge concerning information and its transfer, with particular emphasis on the applications of modern technologies in these areas.

An auxiliary purpose of the Society is to provide its members with a variety of channels of communication within and outside the profession, including meetings and publications, and with a service organization to help them in their professional development and advancement.

**How Established.** ASIS was founded on March 13, 1937, as the American Documentation Institute (ADI) when Watson Davis, director of Science Service (which was operated out of the National Academy) and one of the first Americans to become interested in documentation as a separate field of endeavor, invited approximately 35 documentalist colleagues to meet with him at the National Academy of Sciences. ADI was made up of individuals nominated by and representing affiliated scientific and professional societies, foundations, and government agencies, of which there were 68 in 1937. In 1952, the bylaws were amended to admit individual as well as institutional members. By vote of the membership on Jan. 1, 1968, the name was changed to American Society for Information Science, to indicate its concern with all aspects of the information-transfer process.

The following individuals have held the office of president:

Watson Davis, 1937–1943
Keyes D. Metcalf, 1944
Waldo G. Leland, 1945
Watson Davis, 1946
Waldo G. Leland, 1947
Vernon D. Tate, 1948–1949
Luther H. Evans, 1950–1952
E. Eugene Miller, 1953
Milton O. Lee, 1954
Scott Adams, 1955

Joseph Hilsenrath, 1956
James W. Perry, 1957
Herman H. Henkle, 1958
Karl F. Heumann, 1959
Cloyd Dake Gull, 1960
Gerald J. Sophar, 1961
Claire K. Schultz, 1962
Robert M. Hayes, 1963
Hans Peter Luhn, 1964
Laurence B. Heilprin, 1964–1965
Harold Borko, 1966
Bernard M. Fry, 1967
Robert S. Taylor, 1968
Joseph Becker, 1969
Charles P. Bourne, 1970
Pauline Atherton, 1971
Robert J. Kyle, 1972
John Sherrod, 1973
Herbert S. White, 1974
Dale Baker, 1975
Melvin S. Day, 1976

**Organizational Structure.** The ASIS Council, the governing body of the Society, is composed of 15 individuals: Thirteen hold office by election; the other two are ex officio.

The Council meets four times a year, in January, April, July, and during the Annual Meeting in the last quarter of the year. ASIS membership now totals nearly 4,000 individuals (including about 500 students) and more than 50 institutions.

ASIS has chartered 15 Special Interest Groups (SIGs) which provide those members with similar professional specialties the opportunity to exchange ideas and information about current and specialized developments. Special Interest Groups include the following areas:

Arts and Humanities
Automated Language Processing
Behavioral and Social Sciences
Biological and Chemical Information Systems
Classification Research
Costs, Budgeting, and Economics
Education for Information Science
Foundations of Information Science
Information Analysis Centers
Library Automation and Networks
Non-Print Media
Reprographic Technology
Selective Dissemination of Information
Technology, Information, and Society
User On-Line Interaction

The headquarters of ASIS is located at 1140 Connecticut Avenue, N.W., Suite 804, Washington, D. C. 20036. Telephone: 202-659-3644.

**Technical Program.** The technical and professional activities of ASIS extend from the work of the 15 Special Interest Groups and the 30 chapters to such activities on the national scale as operating the ERIC Clearinghouse on Library and Information Sciences, operating a Placement Service, and conducting a distinguished lecturer series.

Annual awards are presented for the Best Information Sciences Book, the Best Publication by an ASIS chapter or Special Interest Group, the Best Paper Published in the *Journal of the American Society for Information Science*, the Outstanding Information Sciences Movie, the Best ASIS Student Member Paper, and the Award of Merit, which is presented to a member of the profession who is deemed to have made a noteworthy contribution to the field of information science. Recipients of the Award of Merit are:

Hans Peter Luhn (posthumously), 1964
Charles P. Bourne, 1965
Mortimer Taube (posthumously), 1966
Robert A. Fairthorne, 1967
Carlos A. Cuadra, 1968
Cyril W. Cleverdon, 1970
Jerrold Orne, 1971
Phyllis Richmond, 1972
Jesse Shera, 1973
Manfred Kochen, 1974

ASIS publications include:

*Journal of the American Society for Information Science*
*ASIS Newsletter*
*Handbook and Directory*
*Annual Review of Information Science & Technology*
*Cumulative Index to the Annual Review of Information Science and Technology*, Volumes 1–7
Key Papers in Information Science
*Directory of Educational Programs in Information Science*, 1972–1973
*Proceedings of the ASIS Annual Meeting*

I. L. AUERBACH

## AMERICAN STANDARD CODE FOR INFORMATION INTERCHANGE.

*See* ASCII.

## ANALOG COMPUTERS

For articles on related subjects *see* DIFFERENTIAL ANALYZER; DIGITAL COMPUTERS; DIGITAL TO ANALOG CONVERTERS; HYBRID COMPUTERS; NUMERICAL ANALYSIS; SIMULATION; and SPECIAL PURPOSE COMPUTERS.

For articles on related terms *see* INTERRUPT; and REGISTER.

### BACKGROUND

The history of the analog computer goes back to antiquity, when tax maps were first reported as being used for assessments and surveying. However, this article is confined to the analog computer as it evolved in the period from World War II to the present time. (For those interested in the history of the analog computer from antiquity to World War II, the reader is referred to an excellent article by J. Roedel, 1955.)

Between World Wars I and II, much work was done in developing the mechanical differential analyzer, a close relative of the modern analog computer. Simultaneous equation solvers and harmonic analyzers of many types appeared in the 1920s and 1930s. Special computers in the form of network analyzers for the simulation of power networks appeared around 1925. The network analyzer is a passive element analog. A scale model of the particular network to be studied is made with resistors, capacitors, and inductors. The early network analyzers could be used only to investigate steady-state problems, i.e., voltage drops along lines, possible current flow in lines, etc. The more recent network analyzers can be used to investigate transient conditions during faults or switching on networks. These may be considered true general-purpose computers.

George H. Philbrick worked on an all-electronic analog computer in the mid-1930s and is credited by many to have first used feedback amplifier theory to develop the operational amplifier (see Holst, 1971). He envisioned the analog computer as an electronic model of the system to be studied. Independently of and shortly after Philbrick's first work, the Bell Telephone Laboratories developed the M-9 Gun Director under the impetus of the then impending World War II. The M-9 computer was a union of electronic analog computation and the mechanical differential analyzer. The first published work seems to have been handbooks accompanying the M-9 Director.

Following World War II, J. B. Russell of Columbia University brought the electronic circuitry used in the M-9 Gun Director to the attention of J. Ragazzini and others. Basing their work on the operational amplifier used in the M-9 Gun Director, Ragazzini, Randall, and Russell (1947) built an all-electronic d-c analog computer.

Immediately thereafter, several companies designed and developed analog computers for their own use and for sale to others. In 1948, Reeves Instrument Co., under a Navy contract, built the forerunner of the first commercially available analog computer.

Many companies have entered and left the analog computing field since its birth in 1948. The principal manufacturers of general purpose analog computing equipment today are Electronic Associates, Inc., Systron-Donner, Inc., Applied Dynamics Corp., Telefunken, and Hitachi.

### TYPES OF ANALOG COMPUTERS

Fig. 1 shows the classification system used to characterize analog computers. The two main branches of analog computers are direct (special purpose) and indirect (general-purpose) computers, as shown in the figure.

DIRECT ANALOG COMPUTER. Direct analog computers are used in the solution of so-called field problems, e.g., conductive and convective heat transfer, fluid flow, and structures. The equations for these types of problems are partial differential equations. A "thermal analyzer" is an example of a direct analog computer that can be used in the solution of parabolic and elliptic type equations such as

$$\frac{\partial^2\phi}{\partial x^2} = k\frac{\partial\phi}{\partial t}; \qquad \frac{\partial^2\phi}{\partial x^2} = 0$$

This type of computer has resistors and capacitors (and units that compute the fourth power of $x$ for radiation studies). For the hyperbolic equation $\partial^2\phi/\partial x^2 = k(\partial^2\phi/\partial t^2)$, which describes structures, vibrating membranes, beams, etc., one might use a similar computer that has resistors, capacitors, inductors, and transformers. Both types are relatively

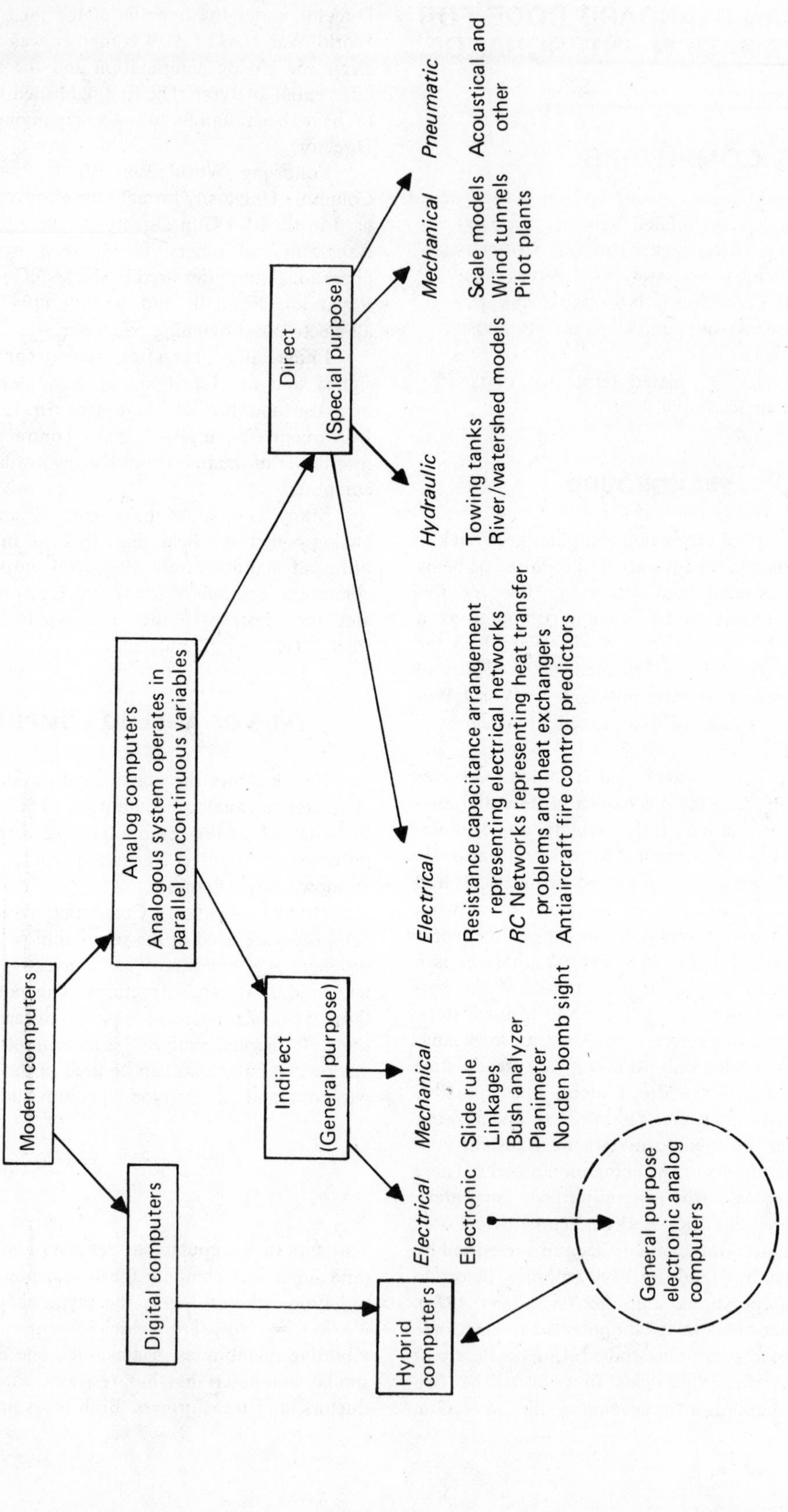


**Fig. 1.** Types of analog computers

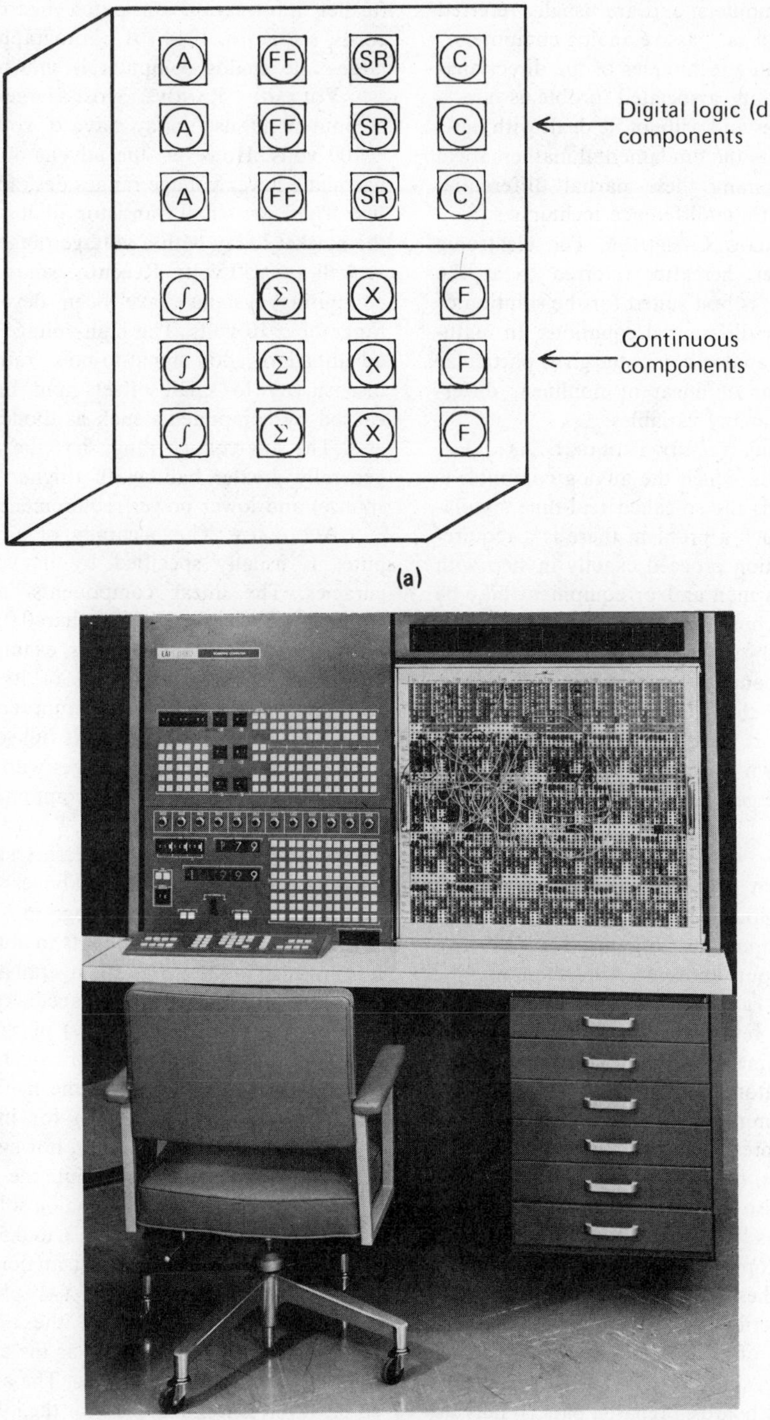


(a)

(b)

**Fig. 2.** Hybrid computers. (a) Analog computer with continuous and discrete components organized in parallel fashion. (b) Modern analog computing system, EAI Model 680.

special-purpose computers, and are usually referred to in the analog field as "passive analog computers."

The programming techniques of the direct analog computer and its associated problems are a subject in themselves and will not be dealt with here, except to remark that the fundamental mathematical theory of programming these partial differential equations involves finite-difference techniques.

INDIRECT ANALOG COMPUTER. The electronic differential analyzer, hereafter referred to as the "analog computer," is best suited for the solution of systems of ordinary differential equations. In mathematical terms the analog computer gives particular solutions to systems of linear or nonlinear differential equations of many variables.

COMBINED DIRECT AND INDIRECT ANALOGS. One area of study in which the analog computer is particularly useful is the so-called real-time simulation problem. In such a problem there is a requirement that the solution proceed exactly in step with real time because a man and/or equipment may be part of the overall computing loop. Such simulations allow realistic hardware testing as well as training and evaluation of complex "man-machine" systems. In these instances there is a combination of the direct analog (man is the direct analog of man, and hardware is its own best direct analog) and the indirect analog (the general-purpose analog computer).

**The Modern Analog Computer.** The modern analog computer consists of a large number of individual components, organized in such a manner that the inputs and outputs of these may be interconnected by a programmer-user. Fig. 2(a) shows a schematic representation of a computer as seen by a programmer. The main continuous components are integrators, represented in the figure by the symbol $\int$; summers, represented by $\Sigma$; multipliers/dividers, represented by $\times$; and arbitrary function generators, represented by F. The modern analog computer also contains a number of discrete components such as "and" gates, represented in the figure by A; flip-flops, FF; shift registers, SR; and counters, C. (All these components, and other elements, will be described later in more detail.) The inputs and outputs of all elements are brought to a central patch bay, into which removable patch boards (or problem boards, prepatch panels) may be inserted. In turn, the patch boards are patched or plugged by the programmer, using patch cords (or plugs). These cords and plugs, when inserted, essentially specify the interconnections of the analog components to solve a particular problem. (For further information on patch boards and patch cords, see Korn, 1964.) A photograph of a modern large-scale analog computer is shown in Fig. 2(b).

VOLTAGE RANGES. Most large-scale analog computers in use today have a voltage range of $\pm 100$ volts. However, the advent of the transistor has made lower voltage ranges desirable and attractive. There are small transistor analog computers on the market today with a voltage range of $\pm 20$ volts as well as $\pm 50$ volts. Recently, some medium-scale computing systems have been developed with a range of $\pm 10$ volts. The high-voltage range has the advantage of good signal-to-noise ratio and relative insensitivity to small offsets and biases that are caused by components such as diodes (in multipliers). The low-voltage range has the advantages of generally greater bandwidth (higher frequency response) and lower power requirements.

ACCURACY. The accuracy of an analog computer is usually specified by its component accuracies. The linear components in high-quality computers have errors of less than 0.01% of value or full scale, as appropriate. For example, a resistor may have an error of 0.01% of its value, but a multiplier has a fixed minimum error, which is usually stated as a percent of its full-scale output. In the latter case, the error changes with the output of the multiplier. The nonlinear components may have errors of 0.02% of full scale. Lower quality computers may have component errors as much as ten times larger than those given above.

Since a typical analog program requires the use of many computing components to obtain a solution, it is not easy to state what the overall accuracy of the solution will be. The overall accuracy depends not only on the quality (accuracy) of the components used, but also on the manner in which they are used (the program), as well as on the method of formulating the problem (analysis) for insertion in an analog computer. One can say, however, that if best practices are used throughout the programming process, the overall error of analog solutions to large problems is on the order of 0.1% to 0.5%, for the best quality computers. Since most analog solution outputs consist of recordings on $X$-$Y$ plotters or strip-chart time-history recorders, the analog solution accuracy is of the same order as the accuracy of the usual output recording devices. The analog computer, however, is well matched for the job it is intended to perform, since it is used almost exclusively for the solution of engineering and scientific problems in which much of the input data is empirically determined, generally to less accuracy than the analog computer solutions thereto. For a detailed discussion of error analysis of analog programs, see Hausner (1971).

CAPACITY. Modern self-contained analog computers may have any capacity, from the very smallest sold today (such as ten amplifiers and ten potentiometers) to the largest capacities currently being sold as single units, which have a capacity generally measured as 250–300 amplifiers, 200–300 potentiometers, 60 multipliers, 20—40 function generators, and significant quantities of digital logic devices such as comparators, flip-flops, "and" gates, "one-shots," shift registers, and counters. If a larger capacity than that available in a single unit is required in a single problem, then two or more units may be connected together to form a single, large, analog computing system. Analog computing systems containing more than 1,000 amplifiers have been successfully assembled.

A rapidly growing use of analog computers is occurring as a major portion of a hybrid computer. Hybrid computation generally enlarges the equivalent capacity of the analog part of the system by a factor of about 2. This is due to the mix of high-frequency and low-frequency parts of a problem. If a hybrid computer problem were put on an all-analog machine, it would usually require at least twice as much analog equipment as that required in the hybrid solution.

MULTISPEED OPERATION. Most modern analog computers are equipped with controls to allow instantaneous change of the speed of solution. The solution time for a large set of simultaneous nonlinear differential algebraic equations may be as short as 1 ms or as long as 100 sec by appropriate manipulation of controls. With proper programming, analog solutions can be made to last for several hours.

## BASIC OPERATIONS

In an analog computer circuit for investigating the behavior of a physical system, only a few of the operational amplifiers will be used as integrators; many others will be used as "summers," "inverters," or "high-gain amplifiers." In modern equipment, about 30% of the amplifiers are able to perform all of the functions mentioned above, 45% are able to perform all operations except the integrating operation, and 25% are able to perform only the simple inverting operation. For these different arrangements the operational amplifiers are known as combination, summing, or inverting amplifiers, respectively.

## BASIC CONCEPTS

### THE OPERATIONAL AMPLIFIER

1. *General.* The operational amplifier is the basic component in the analog computer. It can be used in a "summing mode" to perform the operations of inversion, summation, and multiplication by a constant. It can also be used in an "integrating mode" to integrate a voltage or the sum of a number of voltages. The change from one mode of operation to another is determined by the feedback element around the amplifier.

2. *The Fundamental Relationship.* To understand the basic operations performed by the amplifier, consider the block diagram in Fig. 3. Associated with the high-gain amplifier are the input and feedback networks, having impedances of $Z_i$ and $Z_f$, respectively. Now let the voltages at the input, the output, and the amplifier grid be $V_i$, $V_0$, and $E$, respectively. Using Kirchoff's and Ohm's laws, we may write

$$\frac{V_0 - E}{Z_f} + \frac{V_i - E}{Z_i} = i_g \qquad (1)$$

where $i_g$ is the grid current. By definition

$$\frac{V_0}{E} = -A \qquad (2)$$

where $-A$ is the amplifier gain, and $A$ is usually greater than $10^4$.

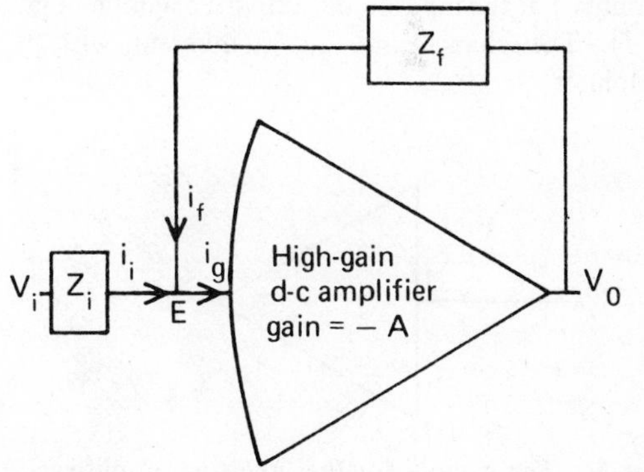


**Fig. 3.** Block diagram of an operational amplifier.

A further property of the high-gain amplifier is that the current $i_g$ is at least a factor of $10^4$ smaller than $i_i$, so that $i_g$ can be set equal to zero; consequently, $E$ is a voltage that is much smaller (by at least a factor of $10^4$) than either $V_i$ or $V_0$, so that $E \simeq 0$. Then

$$\frac{V_0}{V_i} = -\frac{Z_f}{Z_i} \tag{3}$$

*This is the fundamental relationship in analog computation.* The output voltage will not be affected by the internal characteristics of the amplifier; it will be governed by, and its accuracy will be dependent upon, the accuracy of the input and feedback elements.

(a) Inversion. When both $Z_i$ and $Z_f$ are resistors, the amplifier output will be a constant times the input voltage. If both are equal, the constant is unity and we have an inverter, as shown in Fig. 4.

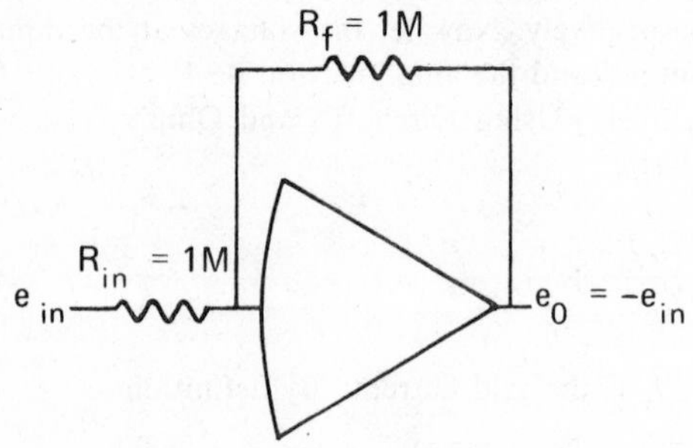


**Fig. 4.** The inverting amplifier (M = megohm).

To represent an inverter on computer circuit diagrams, the symbol shown in Fig. 5 is used. Fig. 5 is the "shorthand notation" for Fig. 4. Note that the number 1 at the input to the amplifier signifies a gain of 1. The change in sign is inherent with the amplifier.

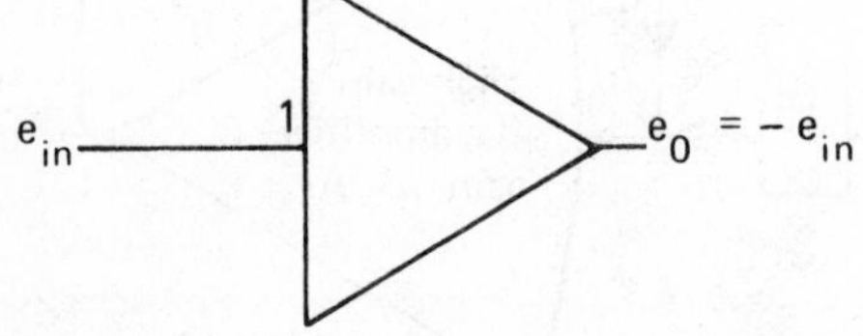


**Fig. 5.** The symbol for the inverting amplifier.

(b) Summation. If several input resistors are connected to a summing point SJ at the grid of an amplifier and voltages are applied to them, as shown in Fig. 6, then (owing to the fact that the grid voltage of the amplifier is effectively at zero potential) no single input will interfere with any other input, and their effects on the output will be independent of one another. It is easily derived, then, that

$$e_0 = -\left(\frac{R_f}{R_1}e_1 + \frac{R_f}{R_2}e_2 + \frac{R_f}{R_3}e_3 + \cdots + \frac{R_f}{R_n}e_n\right) \tag{4}$$

The resulting output is therefore minus the sum of the input voltages, each multiplied by a constant depending upon the ratio of the resistors involved.

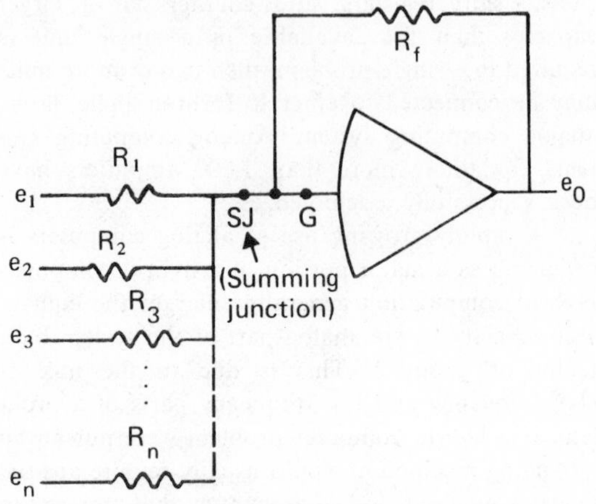


**Fig. 6.** The summing amplifier.

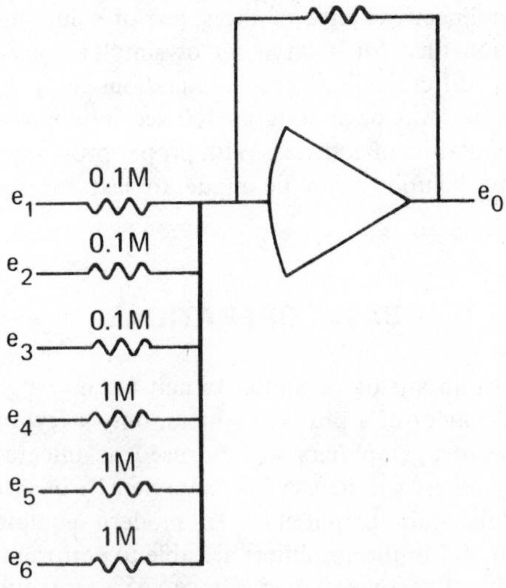


**Fig. 7.** Example of a summing amplifier.

From experience it was found that the most convenient values for the input resistors are 1 M (1 megohm) and 0.1M for 100-volt computers. The resistors are correspondingly smaller on lower voltage computers. A typical summing amplifier with three 1 M and three 0.1 M resistors is shown in Fig. 7. These give gains of 1 and 10, as shown on the symbol for the summing amplifier in Fig. 8.

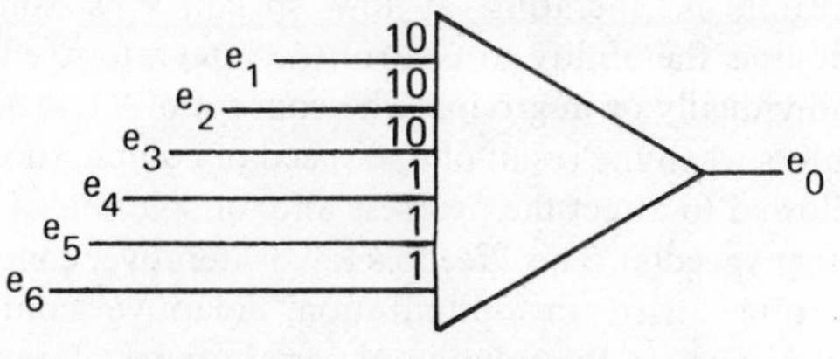


**Fig. 8.** Symbol for the summing amplifier.

(c) Integration with Respect to Time. Integration of an input voltage is obtained if a capacitor is substituted as the feedback component (Fig. 9).

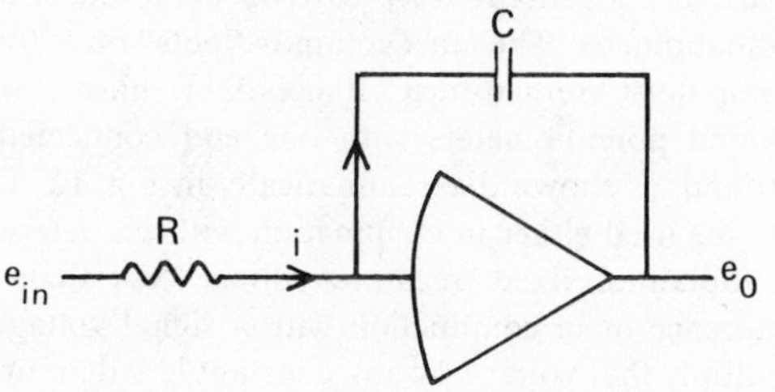


**Fig. 9.** Operational amplifier with capacitor feedback and resistor input.

Since the grid current $i_g$ is zero, the current $i$ through the input resistor $R$ must pass through the feedback capacitor $C$, and will produce a potential difference between output and grid of the amplifier. Thus, in Fig. 9,

$$i = \frac{e_i}{R} \tag{5}$$

and

$$e_0 = \frac{q}{C} = -\int_0^t \frac{1}{C} i\, dt, \tag{6}$$

where $q$ = charge on the capacitor and $C$ = capacitance. Thus,

$$e_0 = -\frac{1}{RC} \int_0^t e_i dt. \tag{7}$$

Alternatively, using operational notation for the impedances,

$$\frac{e_0}{e_i} = -\frac{Z_f}{Z_i} = -\frac{1}{RCp},$$

where $p = d/dt$. Therefore,

$$e_0 = -\frac{1}{RC} \int_0^t e_i dt.$$

Note that the proportionality factor $RC$ is actually a time constant which, if we make $R$ = 1M and $C$ = 1$\mu$f (i.e., a time constant of 1 sec), will produce an integration rate of 1 volt/sec when $e_i$ is equal to 1 volt.

Modern analog computers are equipped with integrators that have a variety of selectable time constants. The range of time constants normally encountered is from 10 sec (for very slow real-time solutions) to 100 $\mu$s (for very fast iterative and/or repetitive solutions).

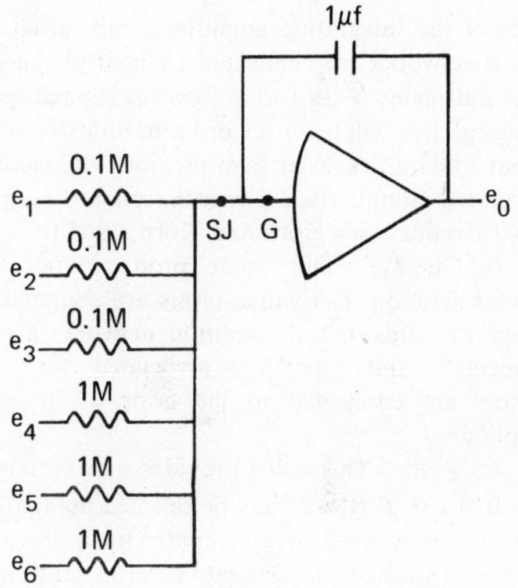


**Fig. 10** A typical integrating amplifier.

Several inputs may be connected to produce the integral of the sum of a number of voltages. Figs. 10 and 11 show a typical integrating amplifier and its equivalent symbol. There is also an input terminal for inserting independent initial conditions on each integrator.

### Control Modes

1. *Ordinary Modes*

(a) Reset. This mode produces a solution at $t = 0$. All derivative terms are disconnected from the

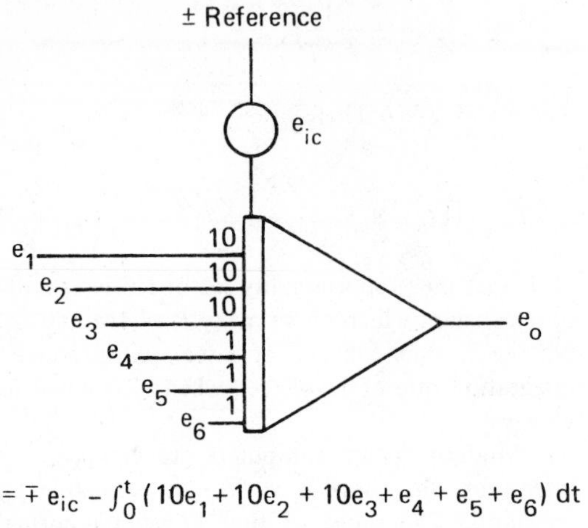


**Fig. 11.** The symbol for the integrating amplifier of Fig. 10, including the initial condition.

grids of the integrating amplifiers, and initial condition networks are connected by control relays or electronic gates. With 1-$\mu$f integrating capacitors, the charging time will be of the order of milliseconds, or about 1,000 times faster than previous *RC* feedback integrated circuits (IC). (For a thorough description of IC circuitry, see Korn and Korn, 1964.)

(b) Operate. This mode produces the time-variant solution. Derivative terms are connected to integrator grids, initial condition networks are disconnected, and capacitors associated with integrators are connected to the grids of integrator amplifiers.

(c) Hold. This mode provides a stationary solution at $t = T$ (HOLD may be selected manually by operator or selected by a computer for a previously defined value of $t$). Derivative terms and initial condition networks are disconnected from the integrators, capacitors remaining associated with integrators.

2. *Repetitive Operation.* In this mode all integrators are switched or cycled automatically from reset-to-operate to reset-to-operate, etc. This mode is usually associated with high solution speeds, of the order of milliseconds in duration, and with the solution displayed on an oscilloscope. When such is the case, the user will obtain the impression that a solution is obtained "instantaneously." However, it is not necessary that high solution speeds be associated with repetitive operation. All that is required is the automatic cycling of the computer between the reset and operate modes for predetermined lengths of time.

3. *Iterative Operation.* This mode may appear to be similar to the repetitive mode, but it differs from it in several respects. In iterative operation there are usually at least two, sometimes more, speeds of operation. For example, one portion of the computer may be operating at a high speed while another portion is operating at low speed. This simply requires the ability to control the integrators, either individually or in groups. The concept of "iteration" enters when the result of one speed of computation is allowed to affect the progress and/or solution of the other speed(s). This "feedback," or iterative, concept is often used in optimization, adaptive control, prediction, in the solution of certain types of partial differential equations, and in boundary value problems.

### Multiplication by a Constant

1. *Potentiometers.* Multiplication by a positive constant less than unity can be achieved with a potentiometer. The most common "pots" on 100-volt computers are ten-turn, 30,000-ohm, linear, wire-wound potentiometers with one end connected to ground, as shown diagrammatically in Fig. 12. They can be used either in conjunction with the reference to obtain a fixed accurate voltage less than the reference or in conjunction with a signal voltage to multiply that voltage by any constant less than unity. For example, if +100 volts is applied to the high end of the pot as shown in Fig. 12, the output at the wiper will be $k$ times 100 volts, where $k = R_1/R_T$ (neglecting the effect of external loading).

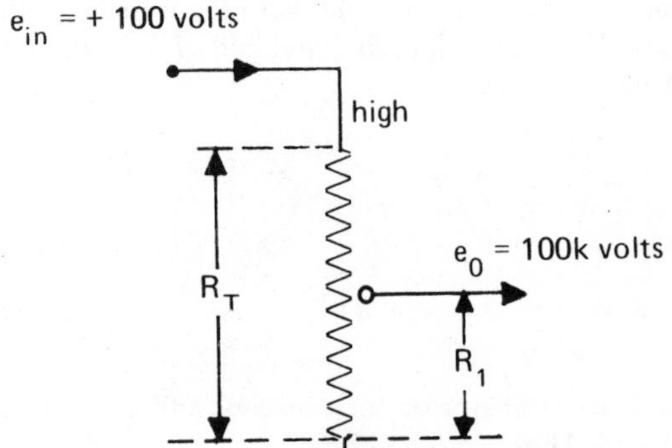


**Fig. 12.** Schematic of a potentiometer shown with +100 volts connected to the input side to give an output at the wiper of +100$k$ volts, where $k = R_1/R_T$.

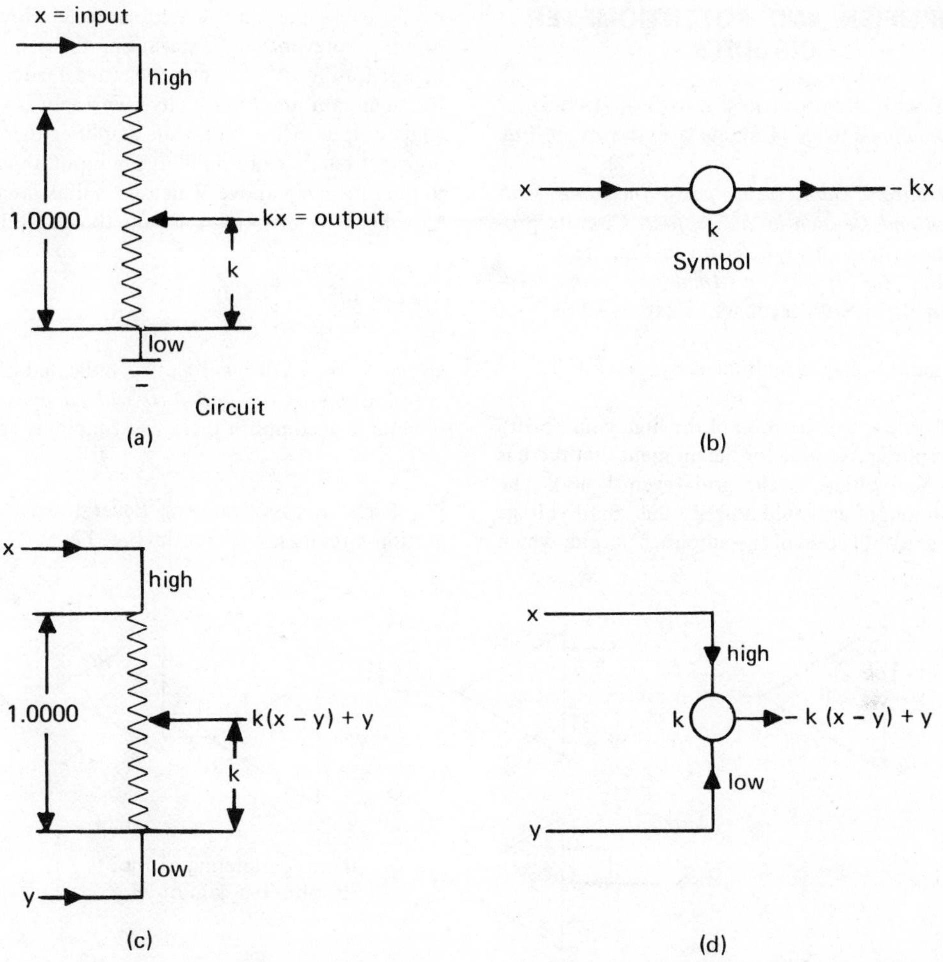


**Fig. 13.** Here, (b) is the symbolic representation of the attentuator shown schematically in (a); (d) is the symbol used to represent the ungrounded attentuator shown schematically in (c).

(a) The Potentiometer Symbol. Two forms of potentiometer or, as it is sometimes called, attenuator units are shown in Fig. 13; both electric circuits and analog programming symbols are shown.

(b) Pot-Set Mode. In order to set pots to their proper values under true load conditions, a special control mode called "pot set" is supplied in most analog computers. In this mode, the SJ (input resistors) are disconnected from the grid of the operating amplifier (see Figs. 6 and 10), and the SJ are grounded. Under these conditions, there will be no inputs to the amplifiers that could cause an amplifier overload while a pot is being set, for in order to set a pot a reference must be applied to its input terminal. Note that the load seen by the pot is the same as under normal operation, for in normal operation the grid voltage $E$ is so small that it can be considered to be the same as if it were at ground potential, the potential at which the summing junction is held during "pot set."

2. *Digital Coefficient Attenuators (DCA).* This component is a hybridized version of a potentiometer that permits very rapid setting of coefficient values, under digital computer control, in less than 10 $\mu$s. This unit is also known as a digital-to-analog multiplier (DAM) in some versions.

## AMPLIFIER AND POTENTIOMETER CIRCUITS

ADDITION, SUBTRACTION, AND SIGN INVERSION

1. *Amplifiers Only*. Circuits are shown in Fig. 14.

2. *Arbitrary Gains (using pots), Including Multiplication and Division by a Constant.* Circuits providing these functions are shown in Fig. 15.

3. *Rule for High-Gain Amplifiers with Feedback.* High gain with feedback is expressed as

$$\Sigma \text{ input voltages multiplied by gains} = 0$$

This rule is true because of the high gain ($>10^8$) of the amplifier. Assume for the moment that there is a small net voltage at the grid (even 1 mv). The high-gain amplifier would amplify this small voltage to more than full scale of the amplifier output, which would cause the amplifier to saturate. However, in order to prevent this saturation, there must be a compensating or balancing negative feedback from the high-gain amplifier to its own input, so that for some output of the high-gain amplifier there will be an exact balance or "null" at the input, thus leading to the rule given above. This rule is illustrated in Fig. 15, where, by invoking the rule above, we have

$$ax + 10by + \frac{e_0}{K} = 0 \qquad (8)$$

so that $e_0 = -K(ax + 10by)$, as indicated in Fig. 15.

4. *Gains of 0.5 and 0.10 without Pots.* Special circuits to accomplish these two functions are shown in Fig. 16.

INTEGRATION CIRCUITS. Several types of integration circuits are shown in Fig. 17.

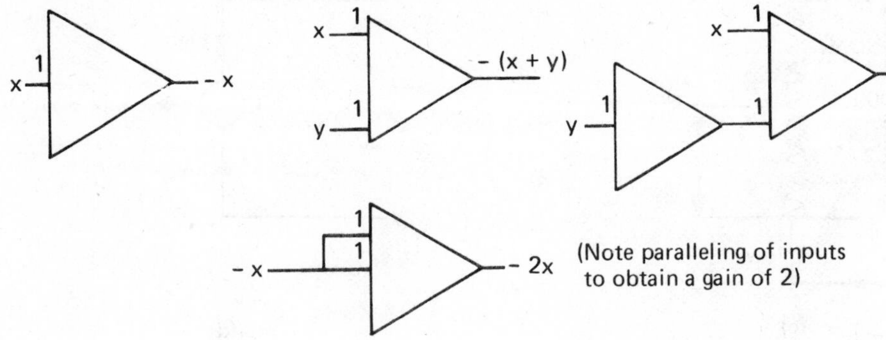


Fig. 14

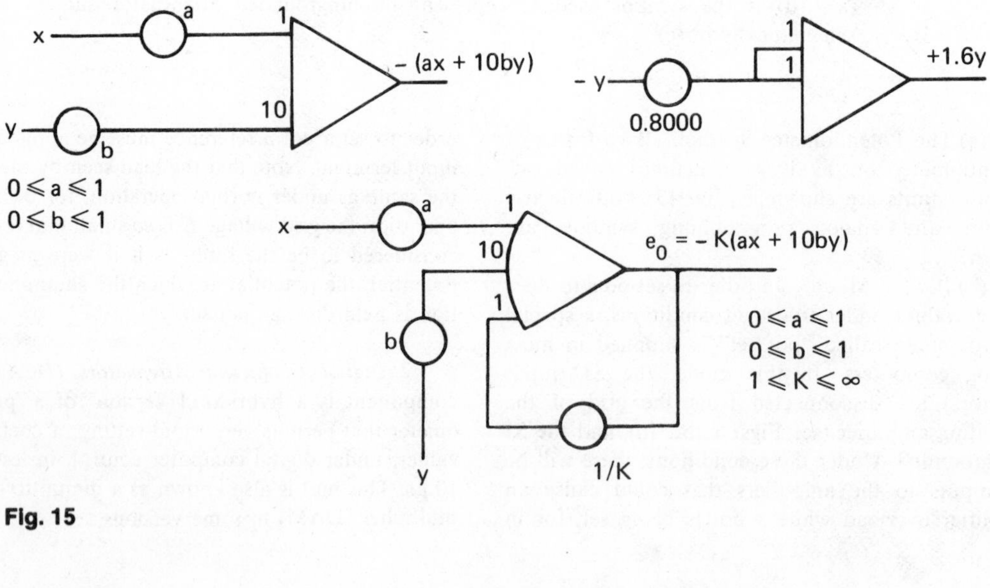


Fig. 15

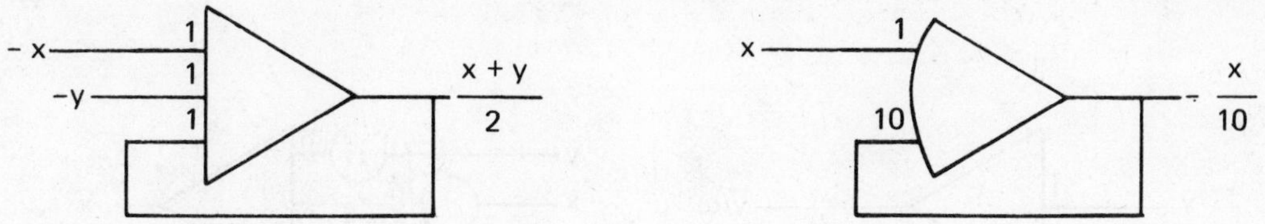


**Fig. 16**

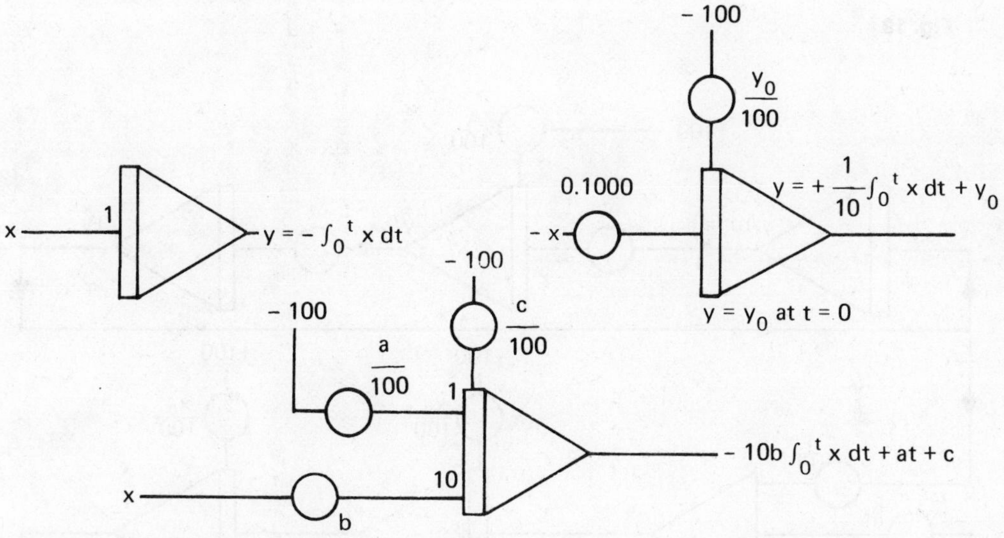


**Fig. 17.** Integration circuits.

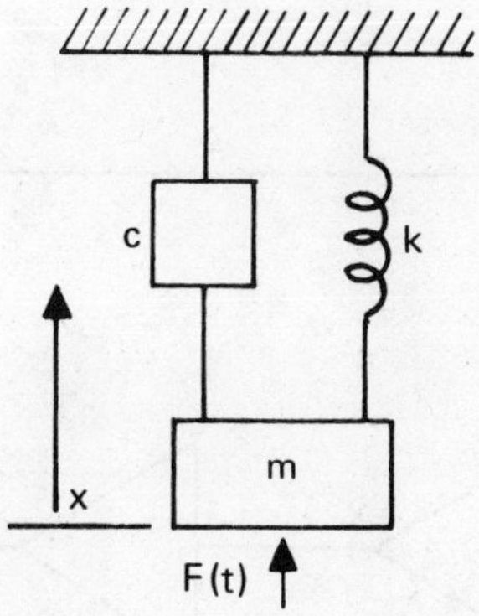


**Fig. 18**

**Application to Linear Differential Equations.** While the analog computer is most useful in solving complex, nonlinear differential equations, it is instructive to consider a linear differential equation example to learn how it is programmed.

THE BOOTSTRAP METHOD. Consider a mechanical system with a sinusoidal forcing function

$$F(t) = y(t) = A \sin \omega t, \tag{9}$$

where $y(t)$ is read $y$ (of $t$), acting on a body of mass $m$ which is restrained by a spring of stiffness $k$, and a "velocity type" damper with damping constant $c$. This system is shown in Fig. 18.

If $x$ is the displacement of the body from its equilibrium position, the forces acting upon the body may be written as follows:

External force $= F(t) = y$,
Spring force $= -Kx$,
Damping force $= -c(\text{velocity}) = -c(dx/dt)$.

The equations to be solved are

$$m\frac{d^2x}{dt^2} + c\frac{dx}{dt} + kx = y(t) \tag{10}$$

and

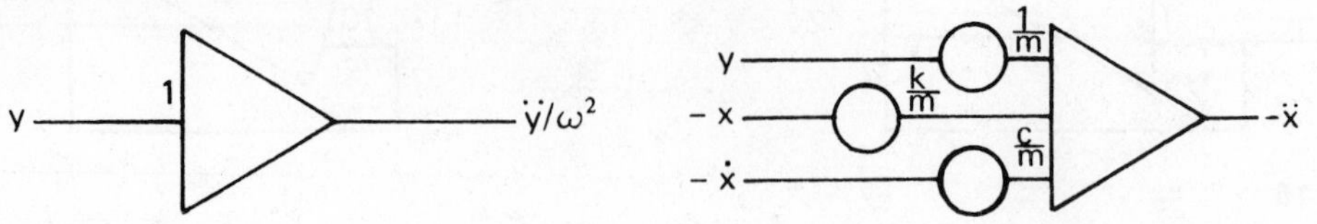


**Fig. 19**

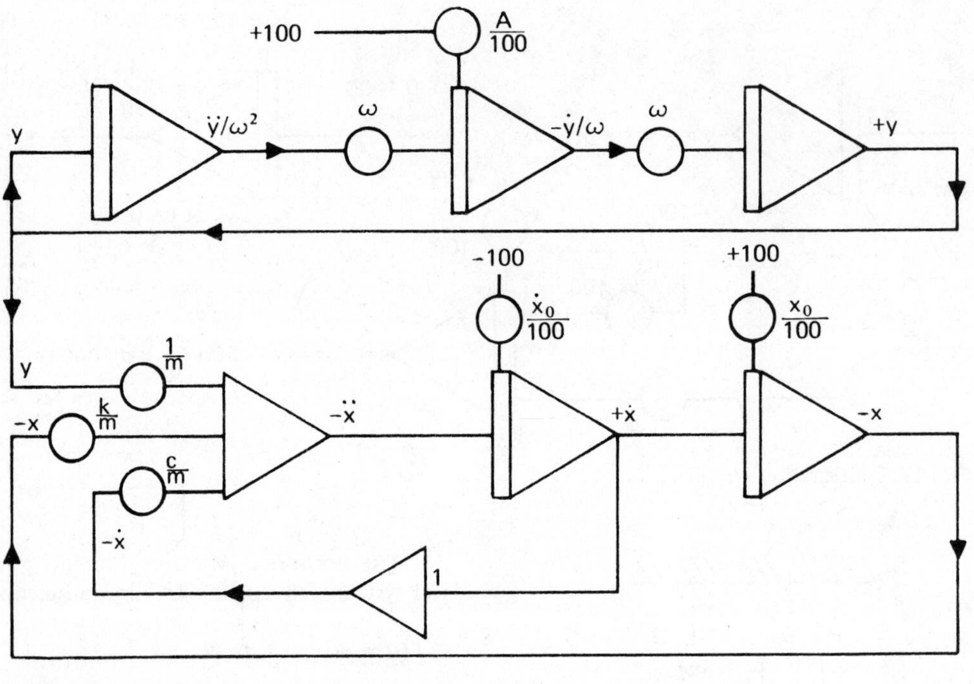


**Fig. 20**

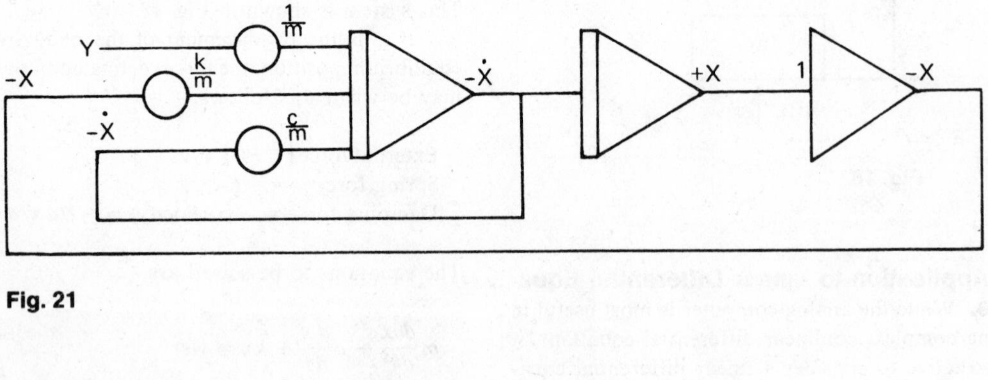


**Fig. 21**

$$\frac{d^2y}{dt^2} + \omega^2 y = 0 \qquad (11)$$

The solution to Eq. 11 is the desired sinusoid.

The bootstrap method assumes that the terms for generating the highest-order derivatives of each variable are available. To execute the bootstrap method, the equations are rewritten in the form

$$\ddot{x} = -\frac{c}{m}\dot{x} - \frac{k}{m}x + \frac{y}{m} \qquad (12)$$

$$\frac{\ddot{y}}{\omega^2} = -y \qquad (13)$$

where

$$\ddot{x} = \frac{d^2x}{dt^2}; \quad \ddot{y} = \frac{d^2y}{dt^2}; \quad \dot{x} = \frac{dx}{dt}, \text{ etc.}$$

The symbolic analog computer diagram for Eqs. 12 and 13 is shown in Fig. 19.

Using the necessary summers, integrators, inverters, and pots, the inputs to the derivatives are generated and the diagram of Fig. 19 becomes that of Fig. 20.

The initial condition for $-y/\omega$ is obtained from

$$-\frac{1}{\omega}\frac{d}{dt}(A \sin \omega t) \text{ at } t = 0 \qquad (14)$$

An alternative method is to sum the acceleration terms for $\ddot{x}$ directly into the $\dot{x}$ integrator. This saves one summing amplifier, as shown in Fig. 21. The $y$ circuit remains the same, since no saving of amplifiers would occur in that circuit.

## NONLINEAR OPERATIONS

### Multiplication and Division of Variables

Types of Multipliers. There have been three major types of multipliers in common use on analog computers. These are the servomultiplier, the time-division multiplier, and the quarter-square multiplier. The servomultiplier (Huskey and G. A. Korn, 1962) is the oldest type and consists essentially of a servo-driven pot where the input to the servo is one variable, the input to the pot is the other variable of the product, and the output of the pot is the desired product. Because of the inherent frequency limitation of the servomechanical arrangement and the generally low reliability of such a device, these have been eliminated from modern computers.

The time-division multiplier (see Korn and Korn, 1964; Huskey and G. A. Korn, 1962) is essentially an electronic device for producing a train of rectangular pulses whose height is proportional to one variable and whose width is proportional to the second variable of the desired product. The actual product is obtained by averaging the area of the output train of pulses. The use of this type of multiplier has been restricted because of the inherent compromise that one must make between static (d-c) accuracy and wide bandwidth (dynamic accuracy). Indeed, the development of the high-accuracy, quarter-square multiplier with favorable static and dynamic accuracies has virtually eliminated the time-division multiplier. There are other types of multipliers, such as the logarithmic multiplier, the Hall effect multiplier, and triangular integration multipliers, which are used only under special circumstances and then usually not in a general-purpose computer.

The Quarter-Square Multiplier. This all-electronic multiplier gives the best accuracy, reliability, and frequency response of any general-purpose multiplier. Its fundamental operation is derived from the relation

$$\tfrac{1}{4}(X + Y)^2 - \tfrac{1}{4}(X - Y)^2 = XY. \qquad (15)$$

For example, quarter-square multiplication could be mechanized as shown in Fig. 22. The boxes marked FG are function generators (described in the next section), which here have the property of producing the square of the input variable.

General-purpose analog computers have quarter-square multipliers with fixed squaring networks that can be used for either one product or two squares. Here we adopt the convention that the multiplier has all the necessary hardware and therefore can be regarded as a "black box." The symbol for diagrams is shown in Fig. 23.

Squaring. Squaring is accomplished by connecting the same variable to both inputs of a multiplier, as shown in Fig. 24.

Division and Square Root by Use of Implicit Arithmetic. A nonlinear component may be used in the feedback loop around high-gain amplifiers to perform the inverse of the operation that the component performs in the forward loop configuration. The most frequent use of this technique is in division and square root circuits with multipliers.

1. *Square Root.* Refer to Fig. 25. Let

$$\epsilon = X - Z^2 \qquad (16)$$

and assume that, for a high-gain amplifier, the

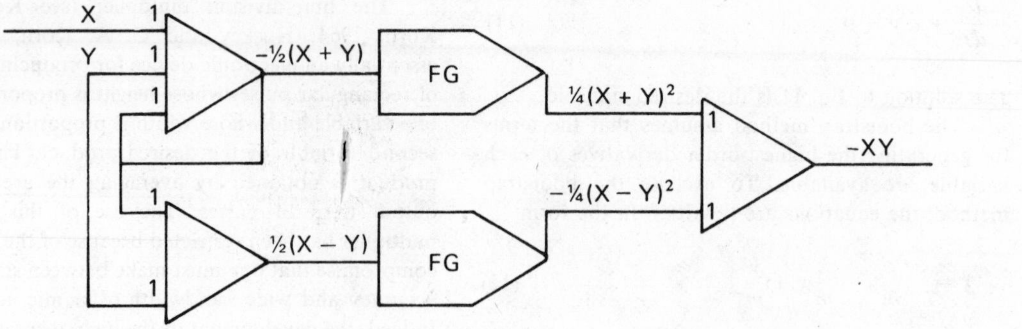


**Fig. 22** Quarter-square multiplication.

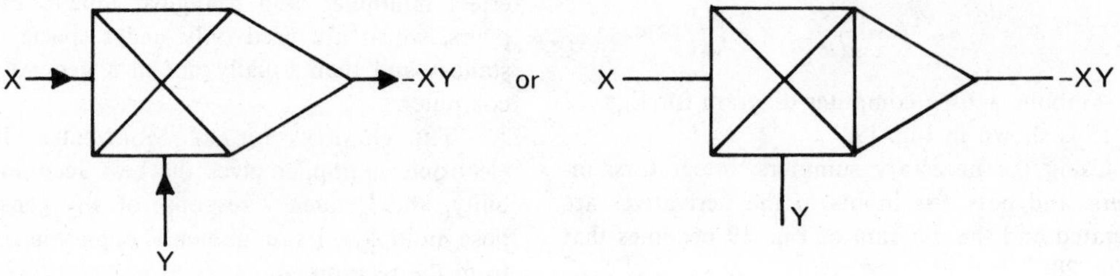


**Fig. 23.** Multiplier symbol (note the sign inversion).

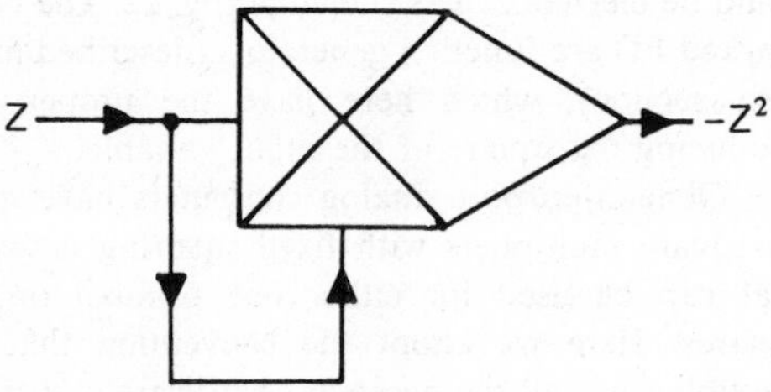


**Fig. 24.** Squaring circuit.

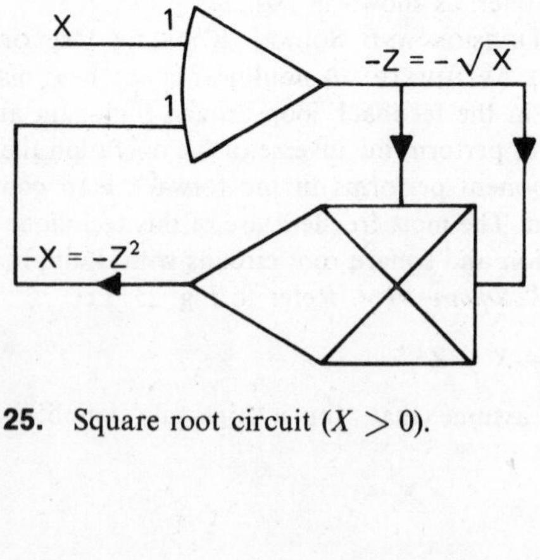


**Fig. 25.** Square root circuit ($X > 0$).

output is related to the input grid voltage

$$Z = A\epsilon \tag{17}$$

where $A > 10^8$. Eliminating $\epsilon$,

$$X - Z^2 = \frac{Z}{A} \simeq 0. \tag{18}$$

Therefore,

$$Z = (X)^{1/2}. \tag{19}$$

For stability, the feedback loop must have an odd number of inversions of the signal so that the sum of the currents through the input resistors to the amplifier grid is equal to zero ($\epsilon$). It is this rule that allows the determination of the sign of the output, which would otherwise be indeterminate.

Note that a squaring device has the property of acting as a sign changer for only one sign of the input variable. In analog multipliers there is usually a built-in sign inversion, as described previously under "Amplifier and Potentiometer Circuits," so that analog squarers act as sign inverters for positive inputs only. Consequently, in the square root circuit the squarer counts for zero inversions, since when $Z$ is negative the output $-Z^2$ is also negative. The one inversion in the circuit is the high-gain amplifier producing $-Z = -(X)^{1/2}$.

Note also that the circuit is stable only for $X > 0$. For values of $X < 0$, an additional inverter must be placed in the feedback loop, and the output of the high-gain amplifier becomes $+Z = (-X)^{1/2}$.

Since modern analog computers have provision for automatically converting a multiplier to a square root circuit, a convenient symbol to use is shown in Fig. 26.

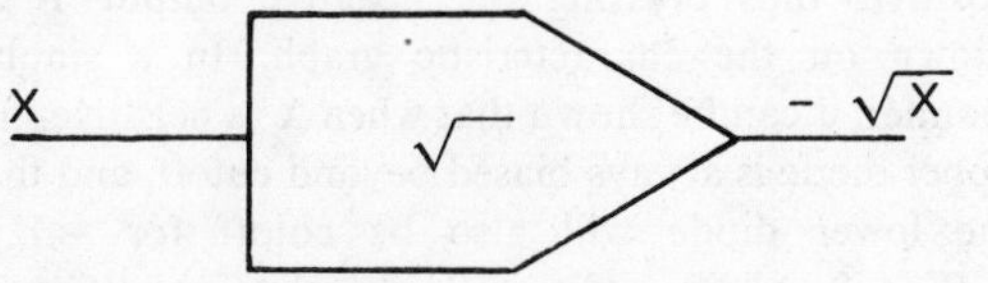


**Fig. 26.** Symbol for square root circuit.

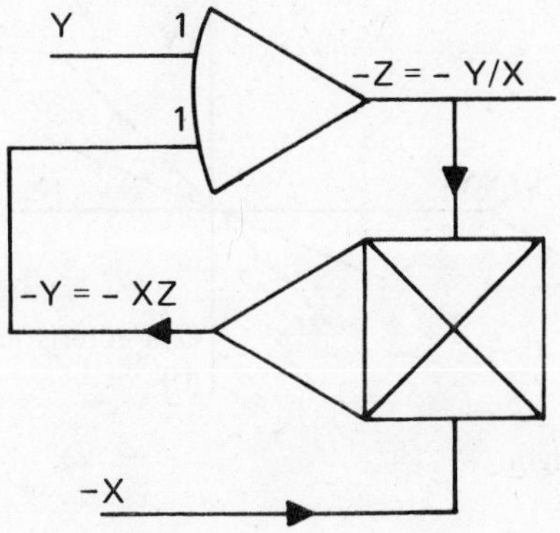


**Fig. 27.** Division circuit ($X > 0$).

2. *Division Circuit.* Similarly, for division (Fig. 27), let

$$\epsilon = Y - XZ, \qquad Z = A\epsilon,$$
$$Y - XZ = Z/A \simeq 0, \qquad Z = Y/X.$$

Note that $X$ must be positive but that $Y$ can be of either sign. Also note that the negative of $X$ must be brought to the multiplier terminal in order to satisfy the stability rule described above for the square root circuit.

Since modern analog computers have provision for automatically converting a multiplier to a divider, a convenient symbol to use is shown in Fig. 28.

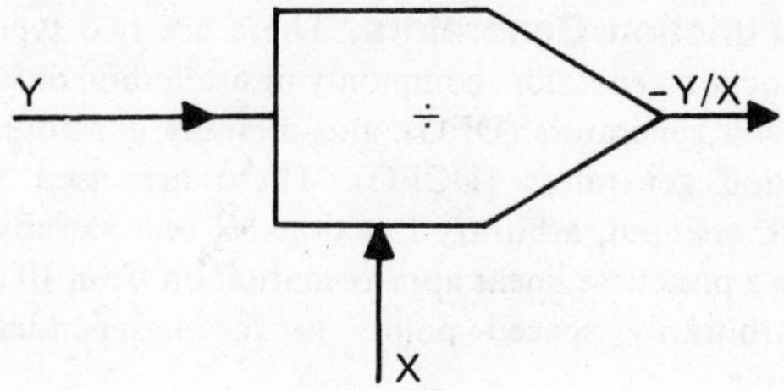


**Fig. 28.** Symbol for divider.

Special Multiplier Hookups. Some modern multipliers have provisions for obtaining special sign-sensitive squares and square roots, which are important in fluid flow phenomena. As an example, take the case of the flow of fluid through an orifice, which is proportional to the square root of the pressure drop across the orifice. If the reverse flow is to take place, it is necessary to implement the equation

$$Q = \text{sign}(\Delta P)\,(\Delta P)^{1/2} \tag{20}$$

Similarly, drag forces acting on bodies moving through fluids are generally proportional to the square of the relative velocity between body and fluid, and are opposite in sign to the direction of motion. It is necessary to implement the equation

$$C_{\text{drag}} = -\text{sign}\,(V) \cdot V^2. \tag{21}$$

By a simple patch change on modern analog computers, the two operations exemplified by Eqs. 20 and 21 are directly implemented without requiring any special logic-switching operations. Since these are direct analog outputs, convenient symbols may be used as shown in Fig. 29. Note that the two special multiplier hookups in Fig. 29 apply only to squaring and square rooting.

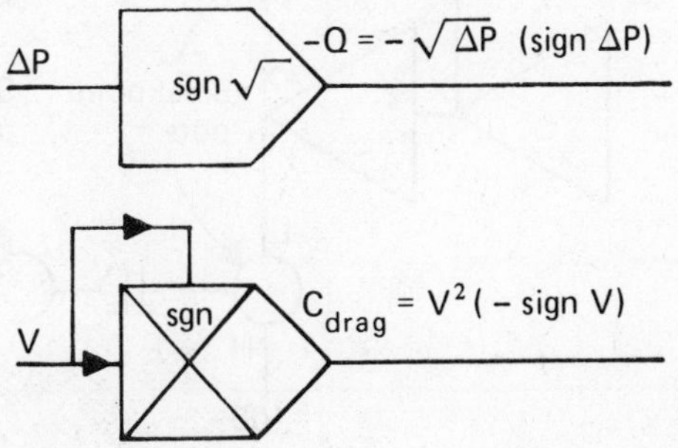


**Fig. 29.** Other convenient nonlinear programming symbols.

**Function Generators.** There are two types of function generators commonly in use today, diode function generators (DFG), and digitally controlled function generators (DCFG). These are used to insert, or input, arbitrary functions of one variable, using a piecewise linear approximation on from 10 to 20 arbitrarily spaced points in the independent variable.

THE DIODE FUNCTION GENERATOR. This component, which has been available since 1955, accomplishes the FG operation by the circuitry shown in Fig. 30, using the techniques discussed in the next section, "Simulation of Discontinuities."

By modifying the dead space circuit (refer to the later discussion "Simulation Discontinuities"), having both signs of the input and reference voltages available, one can choose "breakpoints and slopes" at will, as shown in Fig. 31.

The circuit works as follows: If $X$ is positive, the lower diode is biased beyond cutoff (rendered nonconducting = open circuit) so that only the upper diode circuit can contribute. In the region $0 \leq X \leq$ b.p. (where b.p. is the breakpoint setting of the upper b.p. pot), the upper diode is also biased beyond cutoff so that there is no input to the $y$ amplifier (both input diodes are on open circuit). This is also shown in the characteristic graph of $Y$ versus $X$ in Fig. 31(b); i.e., there is no output $Y$ between zero and the breakpoint. Now, when $X$ is positive and greater than the upper breakpoint, the output of the upper b.p. pot will be positive, increasing linearly with $X$ from a zero value when $X$ is at the breakpoint value; see Fig. 13(d). The slope of the output characteristic will be determined by the slope pot. Note that the input to the $Y$ amplifier is positive, thus creating the negative output $Y$ as shown on the characteristic graph. In a similar manner, it can be shown that when $X$ is negative, the upper diode is always biased beyond cutoff, and that the lower diode will also be cutoff for $-$ b.p. $\leq X \leq 0$, where $-$b.p. is the breakpoint setting of the lower b.p. pot. At this point the analysis of the

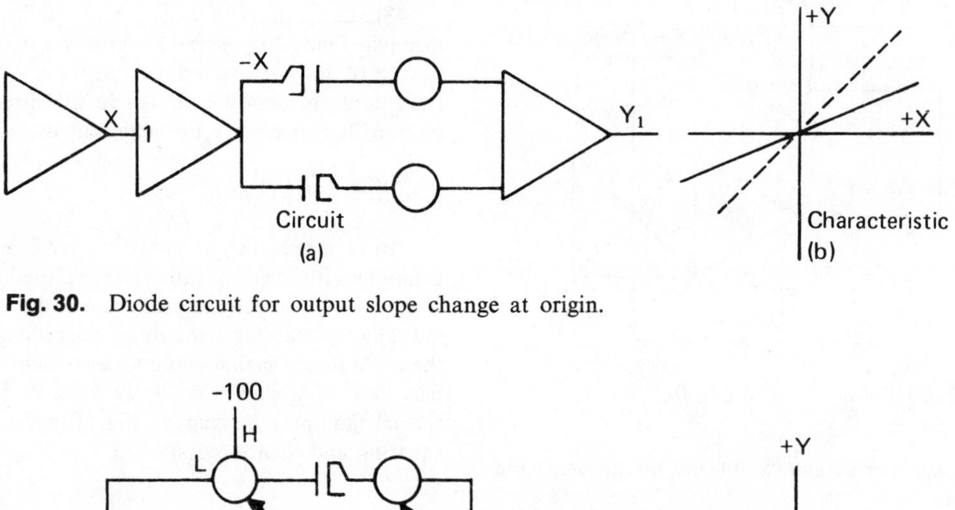


**Fig. 30.** Diode circuit for output slope change at origin.

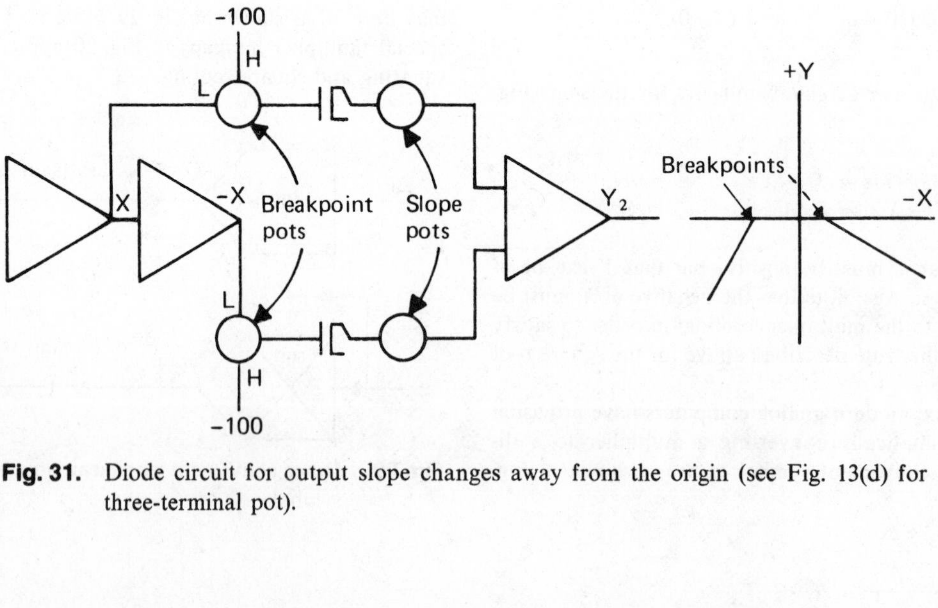


**Fig. 31.** Diode circuit for output slope changes away from the origin (see Fig. 13(d) for three-terminal pot).

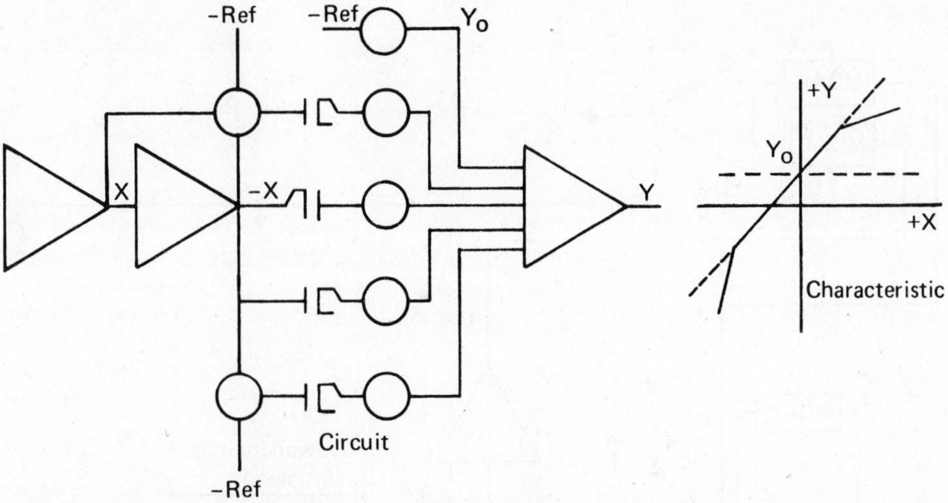


**Fig. 32.** Complete DFG circuits, including bias pot $Y_0$.

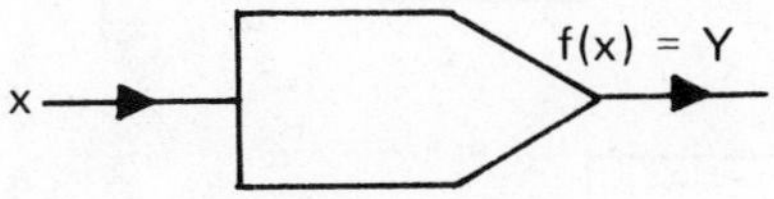


**Fig. 33** Function generator symbol.

lower circuit is identical to the upper circuit, since $-X$, the input to the lower circuit, is now a positive voltage.

To obtain positive output values $Y$ [in the upper two quadrants of Fig. 31(b)], it is only necessary to reverse the polarity of the diode connection while at the same time changing the polarity of the reference voltage on the corresponding breakpoint pot.

By combining the two circuits in Figs. 30–31, we have a circuit that produces an output function $Y(X)$; i.e., a superposition of the two functions. A coefficient pot from the negative reference voltage is added so that $Y_0 \neq 0$ (see Fig. 32). By extension of this technique, straightline segment approximations are obtained for a wide variety of arbitrary functions. The symbol for an arbitrary function generator of one variable is shown in Fig. 33.

THE DIGITALLY CONTROLLED FUNCTION GENERATOR. The digitally controlled function generator (DCFG) is a hybrid computing device, now supplied as a fully self-contained unit in existing analog computers. It consists of a small, high-speed core memory (to contain the function data points) and multiplying digital-to-analog converters, organized as shown in Fig. 34.

The function $f(x)$, to be generated, is computed by a linear interpolation between function values $f(x_i)$ and $f(x_{i+1})$, where $x_i$ is a general "breakpoint" value. The number of breakpoints is typically 16, and they can be unequally spaced.

If $x$ is the independent (input) variable, then

$$\Delta x = \frac{x - x_i}{x_{i+1} - x_i} \tag{22}$$

is the normalized value of $x$ in the interval $[x_i, x_{i+1}]$. The equation used to generate $f(x)$ is then

$$f(x) = \Delta x\, f(x_{i+1}) + (1 - \Delta x) f(x_i). \tag{23}$$

In Fig. 34 the independent variable $-x$ (at the lower left) is summed with a digital-to-analog converter (DAC) containing $x_i$, and is divided by a multiplying DAC (MDAC) containing $x_{i+1} - x_i$. The output of this circuit is $\Delta x$, defined in Eq. 22. The output $\Delta x$ is subtracted from the reference, forming $1 - \Delta x$, and both $\Delta x$ and $1 - \Delta x$ are fed to the MDAC (at top of figure) containing $f(x_{i+1})$ and $f(x_i)$, respectively, thus forming the output $f(x)$.

The control and logic for changing the digital data in the DAC and MDAC are shown in the lower right of Fig. 34. Here, $\Delta x$ enters two comparators (see later section, "The Analog Comparator"), one sensing when $\Delta x$ is less than zero, the other sensing when $\Delta x$ is greater than the reference. Both logic outputs are connected to priority interrupt lines in the processor containing the digital data $f(x_i)$ and $x_i$, $i = 1$ to $n$.

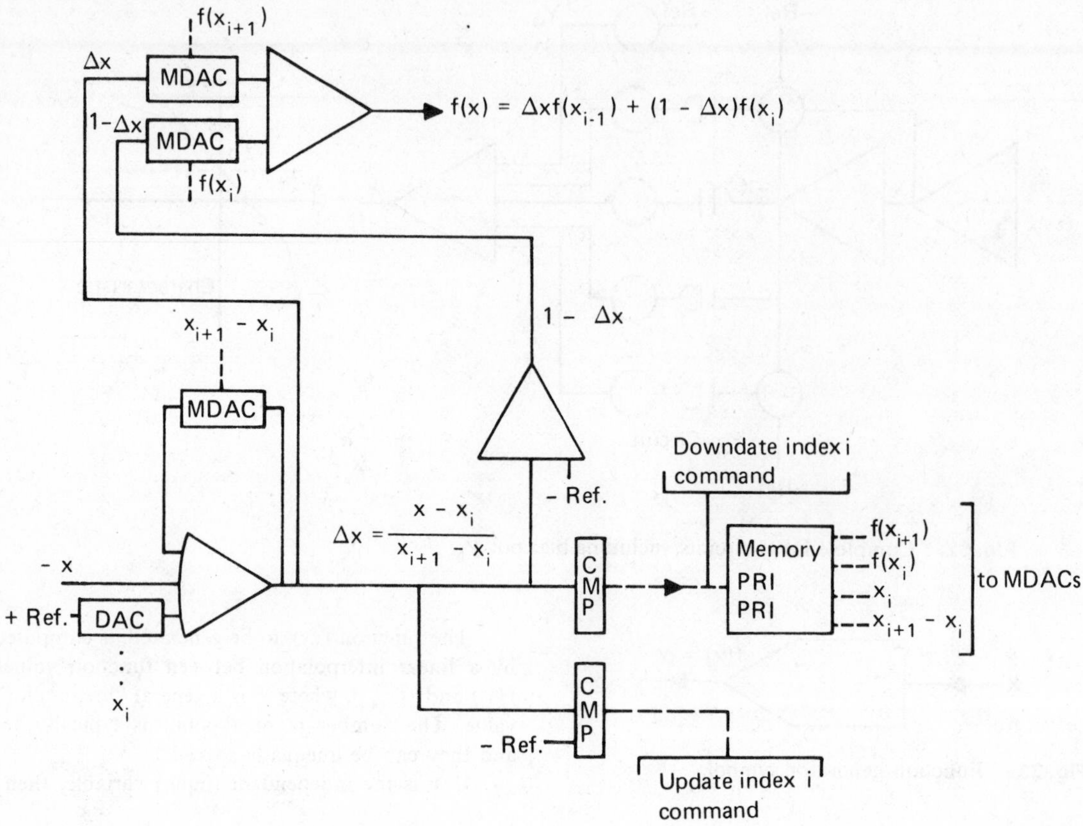

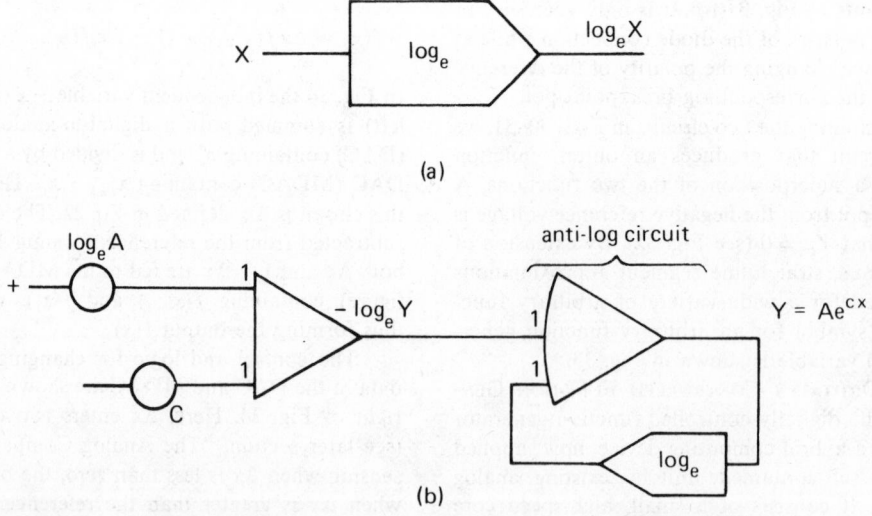


**Fig. 34.** Digitally controlled function generator.

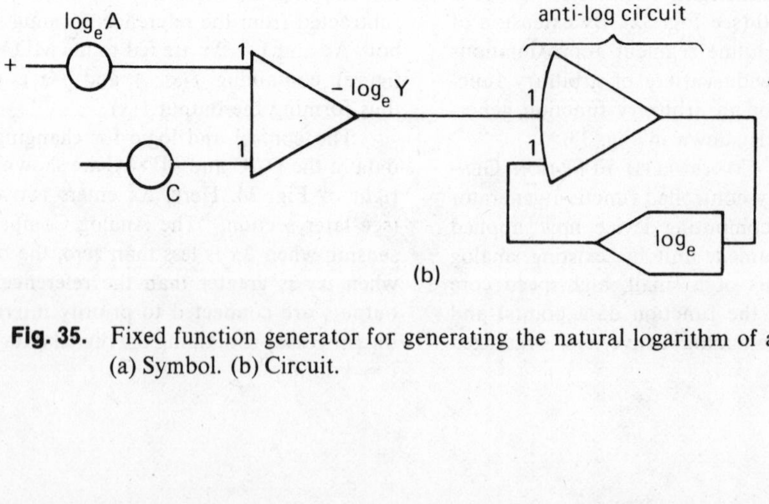


**Fig. 35.** Fixed function generator for generating the natural logarithm of a variable. (a) Symbol. (b) Circuit.

One comparator triggers a downdate of the index $i$ and the other triggers an update of the index $i$. Whenever a trigger occurs, the appropriate values of $x_i$, $x_{i+1} - x_i$, $f(x_i)$, and $f(x_{i+1})$ are transferred within a few memory-cycle times to the appropriate DAC and MDAC, thus allowing the circuit generating $f(x)$ to be correct in all intervals $x_{i+1} - x_i$.

SPECIAL FUNCTION GENERATORS (FIXED-FUNCTION GENERATORS). Certain functions such as exponentials, sines and cosines, squares, and cubes recur so often in engineering and scientific studies that it has been found useful to build fixed-function generators for these operations.

1. *Exponential Log Generator.* Perhaps the most flexible method for generating an exponential is to use a fixed-function generator from which any exponential can be generated. The symbol for such a device is shown in Fig. 35. Using this device, it is possible to generate any exponential by employing the logarithm generator in the feedback of a high-gain amplifier, thus obtaining the inverse operation (or antilog). (This is analogous to using a multiplier in the feedback of a high-gain amplifier to obtain division.)

For example, to generate the exponential $Ae^{cx}$, where $A$ and $c$ are constants and $x$ is a variable, let $y = Ae^{cx}$. Then

$$\log_e y = \log_e A + cx. \tag{24}$$

The circuit for forming the $\log_e y$ from Eq. 24 is shown in Fig. 35(b). Inserting this sum into a high-gain amplifier, which has a $\log_e$ generator in its feedback path, will take the antilog of the input, thus producing the desired output $y$.

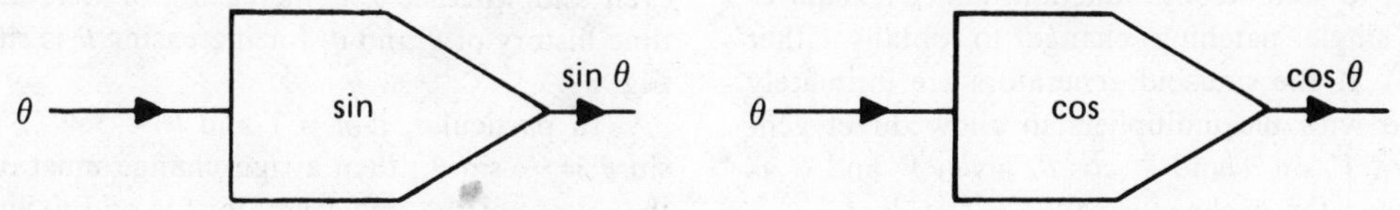


**Fig. 36.** The sin/cos generators.

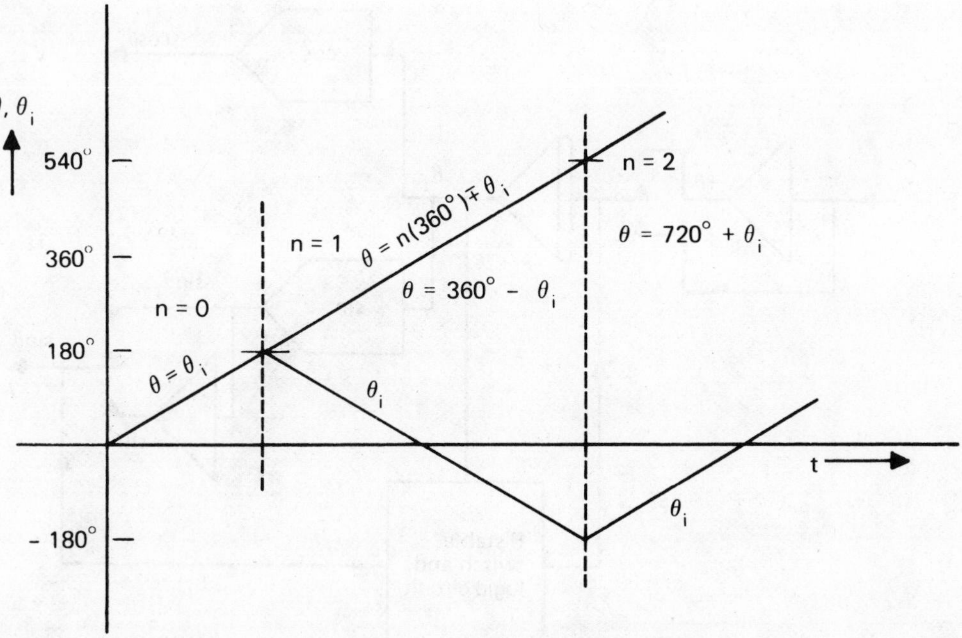


**Fig. 37.** Time history showing $\theta$ and $\theta_i$ with switching occurring at $\theta = 180°$ and $\theta = 540°$.

2. *The Resolver (Sine-Cosine Generator).* A resolver is actually a combination of computing elements, including provisions for generating sin $\theta$ and cos $\theta$, given $\theta$ as an input, and also allowing for the multiplication of both sin $\theta$ and cos $\theta$ by any other variable $V$, thereby generating $V$ cos $\theta$. This device is an outgrowth of servomultiplying technology, wherein it was a relatively simple matter to change a linear pot to a sine or cosine pot (padded-pot technique) and (by applying $\pm V$ to the endpoints of the padded pot) to obtain $V$ sin $\theta$ and $V$ cos $\theta$. Modern computers, however, usually have a fixed (electronic) function generator to generate either the sine or the cosine function. This is shown symbolically in Fig. 36.

It is, of course, still possible to combine the preceding operation with electronic multipliers to obtain $V$ sin $\theta$ and $V$ cos $\theta$. If one merely has a sine or cosine generator, then it is termed a "sinusoid" generator to include both functions (since it requires only a single patching change to obtain either function). If the sinusoid generators are intimately packaged with the multipliers to allow direct generation of $V$ sin $\theta$ and $V$ cos $\theta$, given $V$ and $\theta$ as inputs, then the package is called a "resolver."

(a) Rate Resolver. A rate resolver allows the insertion of $\dot{\theta}$, instead of $\theta$, into a resolver input terminal, and sin $\theta$ and cos $\theta$ will be automatically produced. This is simply accomplished by inclusion of an integrator within the resolver package, which will integrate $\dot{\theta}$ and produce $\theta$.

(b) Continuous Rate Resolver. The normal allowed range of input to the sinusoid generator (SG) is $\pm 180$ deg. If $\theta$ should go larger than this—as, for example, in continuous rolling and/or tumbling—then a switch is incorporated on the rate input, which changes the sign of the $\theta$ input to the resolver integrator whenever $|\theta_i|$ reaches 180 deg. At the same time, the sign of sin $\theta$ is changed. This follows from the relations

$$\theta = n\,(360°) \pm \theta_i, \qquad |\theta_i| < 180°,$$
$$\sin\theta = \pm \sin\theta_i, \qquad \cos\theta = \cos\theta_i,$$
$$\text{Input to SG} = \theta_i,$$

where $n = \pm 0, 1, 2,$ etc.

The $\pm$ signs depend upon whether $n$ is odd or even and whether $\theta$ is increasing or decreasing. A time history of $\theta$ and $\theta_i$ for increasing $\theta$ is shown in Fig. 37.

In particular, if $n = 1$ and $\theta = 360° - \theta_i$ and sin $\theta = -$ sin $\theta_i$, then a sign change must occur at the output of the sine generator for odd $n$. Similarly, when $\theta = 360° - \theta_i$, then cos $\theta = \theta_i$, which is correct for all $n$. The circuit is shown in Fig. 38.

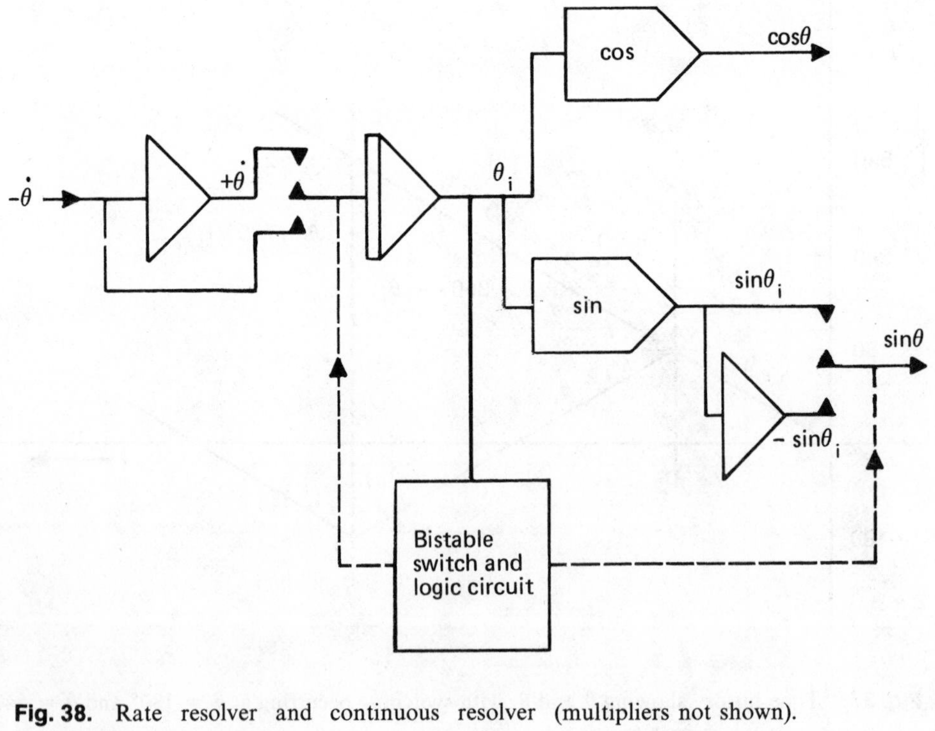


**Fig. 38.** Rate resolver and continuous resolver (multipliers not shown).

(c) Polar Resolution. The object here is, given the $x$ and $y$ components of a vector (or a complex variable), to find $R$, the magnitude of the vector, and $\theta$, the angle that the vector makes with the $X$-axis. This is accomplished by forming the error equation $\epsilon = x \sin\theta - y \cos\theta$, which, as can be seen from the geometry of the relationships among $x$, $y$, and $\theta$ as shown in Fig. 39, is zero only when $\theta$ is the correct angle. In these circumstances—i.e., when an implicit algebraic relationship must be satisfied by a dependent variable $\theta$—given the independent variables $x$ and $y$, a mathematical method exists, called the "method of steepest descent" (see Hausner, 1971), which defines a stable formula for the generation of the time derivative of the dependent variable as follows:

$$\frac{d\theta}{dt} = -k\epsilon\frac{\partial\epsilon}{\partial\theta}, \tag{25}$$

where $\epsilon$ is as defined above and $k$ is an arbitrary constant. From the definition of $\epsilon$ we derive

$$\frac{\partial\epsilon}{\partial\theta} = x\cos\theta + y\sin\theta. \tag{26}$$

From the geometry of Fig. 39, we see that $x\cos\theta + y\sin\theta = R$, so that $\partial\epsilon/\partial\theta = R$. Substituting the last expression into the original equation for $d\theta/dt$, we obtain $d\theta/dt = -k\epsilon R$. The circuit for obtaining $R$ and $\theta$ from $x$ and $y$ is shown in Fig. 40.

(d) Polar Resolution Circuit. For fastest response in this circuit, $k$ should be made as large as loop stability will permit. This is usually a value between 1,000 and 10,000. Such large gains are obtained by using small capacitors for the integrator feedback (0.01 $\mu$f or smaller).

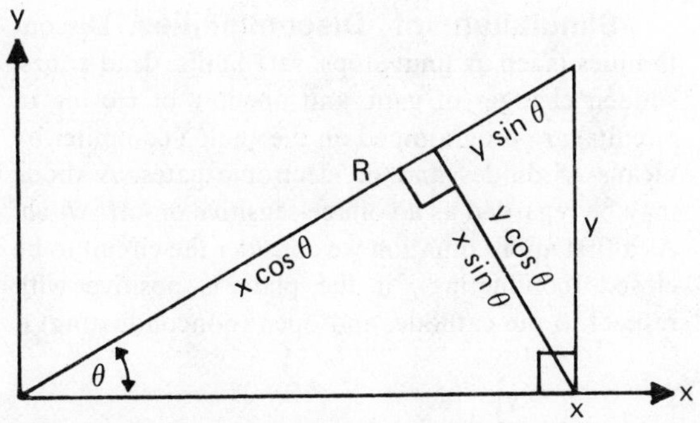


**Fig. 39** Polar resolution geometry.

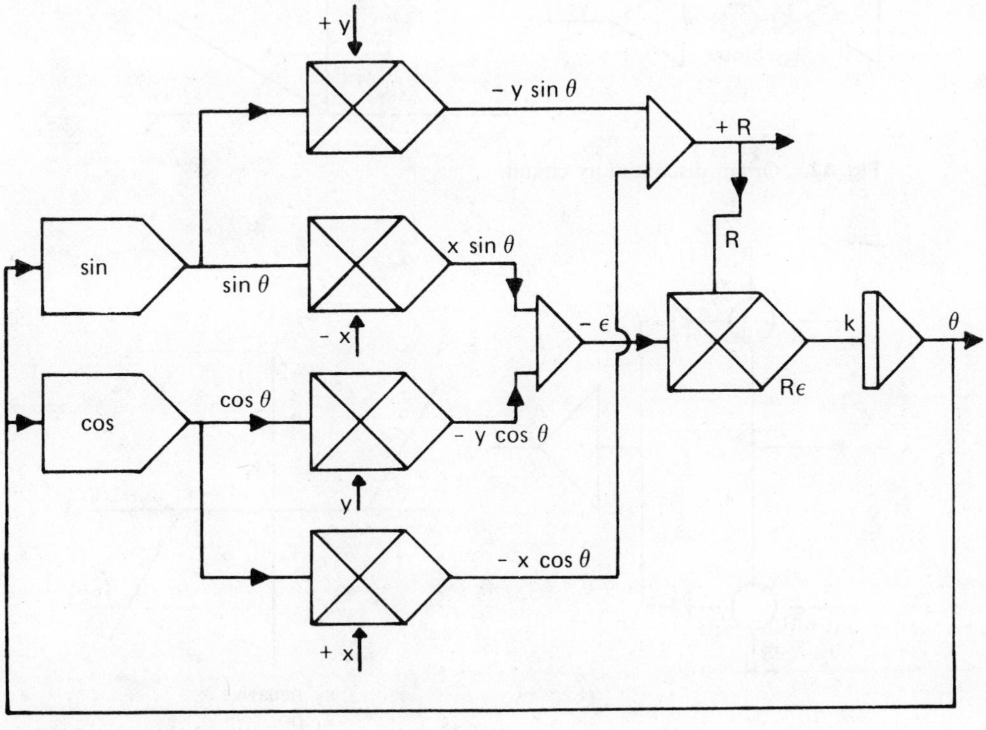


**Fig. 40.** Polar resolution circuit.

3. *$X^3$ and $X^4$ Generators.* These are similar in operation to the previously discussed special generators, differing only in the output function. The programming symbols are shown in Fig. 41.

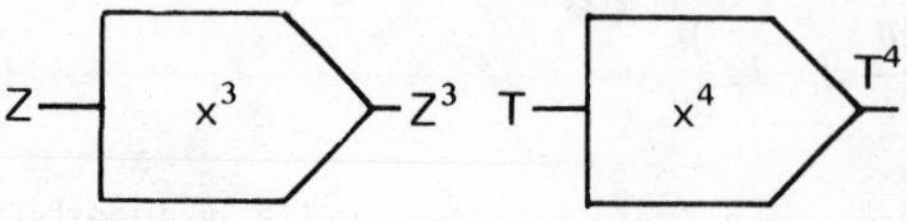


**Fig. 41.** Programming symbols for $X^3$ and $X^4$ units.

The $X^4$ generator is particularly useful in heat radiation studies.

FUNCTIONS OF MORE THAN ONE VARIABLE. Most analog programmers must resort to some mathematical juggling or simplification of functions in order to be able to insert multivariable functions on an analog computer. For example, a function $F(x,y)$, may sometimes be expressed as the sum or product of two functions of one variable, such as

$$f_1(x,y) = g_1(x) + h_1(y),$$

or

$$f_2(x,y) = g_2(x)h_2(y) + \text{similar terms.}$$

More details on purely analog techniques for multivariable function generation may be found in Hausner (1971), and Huskey and G. A. Korn (1962). There exists a general method for handling the generation of functions of any arbitrary number of variables, but it requires a hybrid computer. This is essentially an extension of the method described for the DCFG.

**Simulation of Discontinuities.** Discontinuities (such as limit stops, rate limits, dead zones, sudden changes of gain, and opening or closing of circuits) are programmed on the analog computer by means of diodes and/or electronic gates. A diode may be regarded as a voltage-sensitive on-off switch. As a first approximation we consider the circuit to be closed (conducting), if the plate is positive with respect to the cathode, and open (nonconducting) if

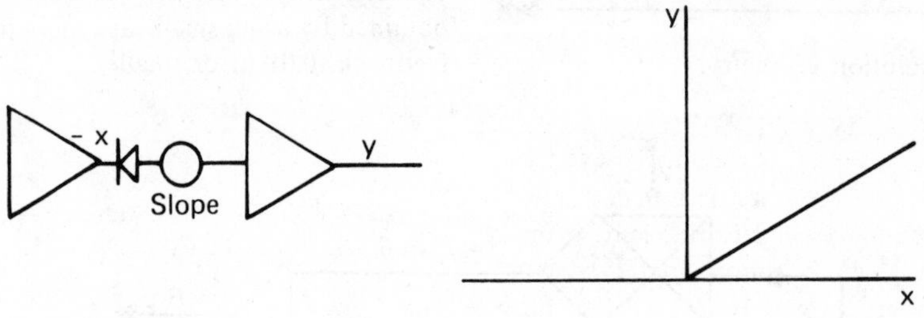


**Fig. 42.** Origin discontinuity circuit.

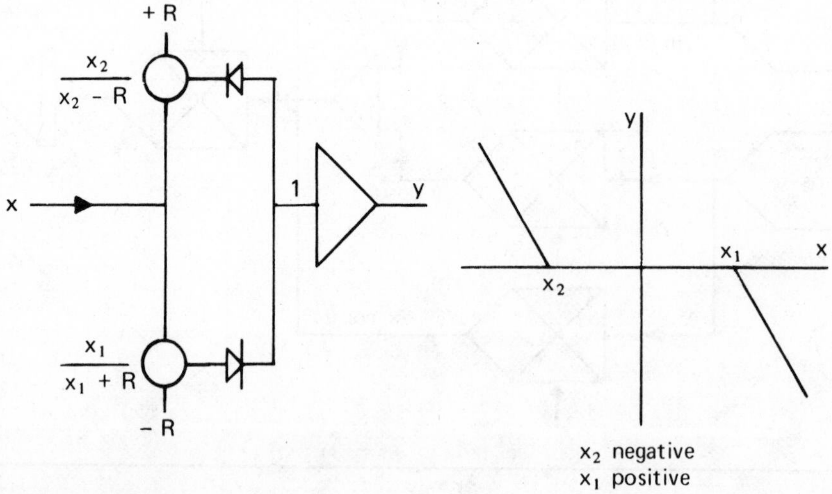


**Fig. 43.** Dead-space circuit.

the plate is negative with respect to the cathode. A simple circuit for introducing a discontinuity at the origin is shown in Fig. 42.

In the circuit shown in Fig. 42, $-X$ is connected to the cathode of the diode and the plate is connected to a pot. When $-X$ is negative, the cathode of the diode is negative with respect to the plate, so the diode conducts and produces a positive output through the inversion of the $Y$-amplifier. When $-X$ is positive, the diode is rendered in the nonconducting state, and $Y = 0$. The circuit characteristic is shown to the right of the circuit diagram. This circuit is also called a nonnegative limiter (i.e., $Y$ is constrained to positive values only). By reversing the diode, one can make a nonpositive limiter. The circuit in Fig. 42 can be considered to have a breakpoint at zero (a discontinuity in the derivative of the output occurs when $X = 0$). The discontinuity in the output can be made to occur at any arbitrary value of $X$, as in the "dead-space" circuit shown in Fig. 43; see Fig. 13(d). Notice that the discontinuity occurs at other than $X = 0$.

A group of common diode circuits with their input-output characteristics is shown in Fig. 44.

## DIGITAL LOGIC OPERATIONS

**The Analog Comparator.** The analog comparator has been a fundamental component of the analog computer from its inception. In the past it was intimately associated with a relay such that the comparator output drove the relay arm to one of two sets of contacts. Actually, the analog comparator is a true hybrid device, since it accepts analog inputs (usually two) and produces a digital logic level output (either a binary "1" or a binary "0"). The symbol is shown in Fig. 45.

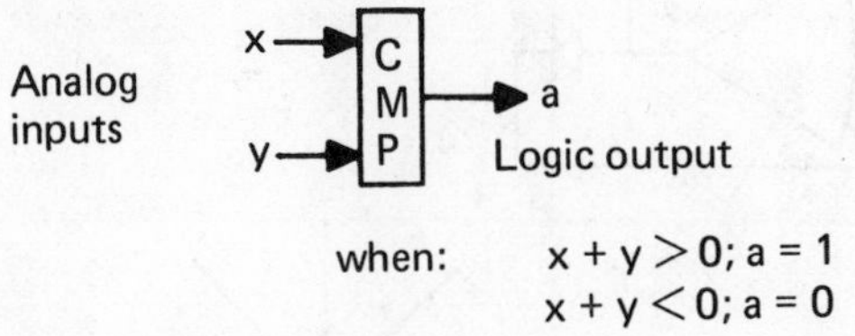


**Fig. 45.** Analog comparator symbol.

If one of the two analog inputs is a constant voltage (as, for example, a reference voltage multiplied by a constant coefficient), then the output of the comparator shows when the other variable is greater than or less than a particular constant value.

The output of the comparator can be used to control the analog computer to drive electronic gates or as inputs to other digital logic components, to sense lines, control lines, interrupt lines, or priority interrupt lines of digital computers.

**General-Purpose Digital Logic Modules.** It may seem strange to include a section on true general-purpose digital logic components with material on analog computers, but analog programmers have always made use of digital logic in the normal course of obtaining a solution to a problem.

Not many years ago, general-purpose digital logic modules were not available, so the manufacturers of analog equipment did not supply such modules. The programmer, however, by using comparators, relays, diodes, limiters, and amplifiers, was usually able to "simulate" digital logic. This "logic" was asynchronous, and operated in parallel, so that outputs of all logic components were available to the programmer at all times. At present, analog manufacturers include a good supply of digital logic modules as part of the normal computing complement of the analog computer. These modules are patched one to another, just as analog components are, and operate in parallel and simultaneously, as analog components do. In view of the last statement, one may consider such logic modules to be discrete analog components.

The most common types of logic modules used with analog computers are flip-flops, "and" gates, "or" gates, "one shots" (or "pulsers," or "time delays," or "monostables"), and combinations of these elements to produce "exclusive or" circuits (or "modulo 2 adder," or "ring sum"), up-and-down counters, and shift registers.

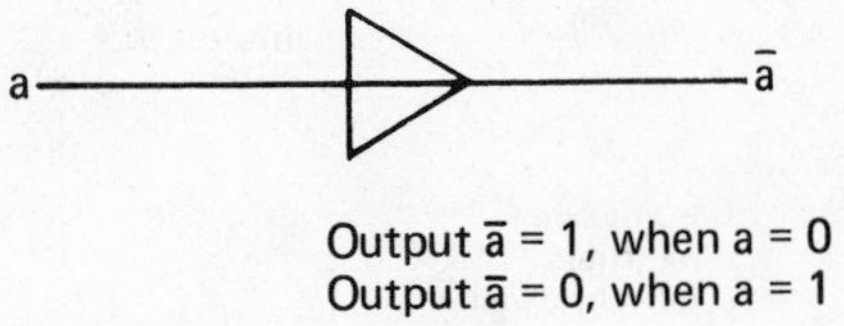


**Fig. 46.** Digital inverter symbol.

Associated with the logic modules is the concept of a digital inverter, shown in Fig. 46. A table of symbols and functions of common digital logic modules is shown in Fig. 47.

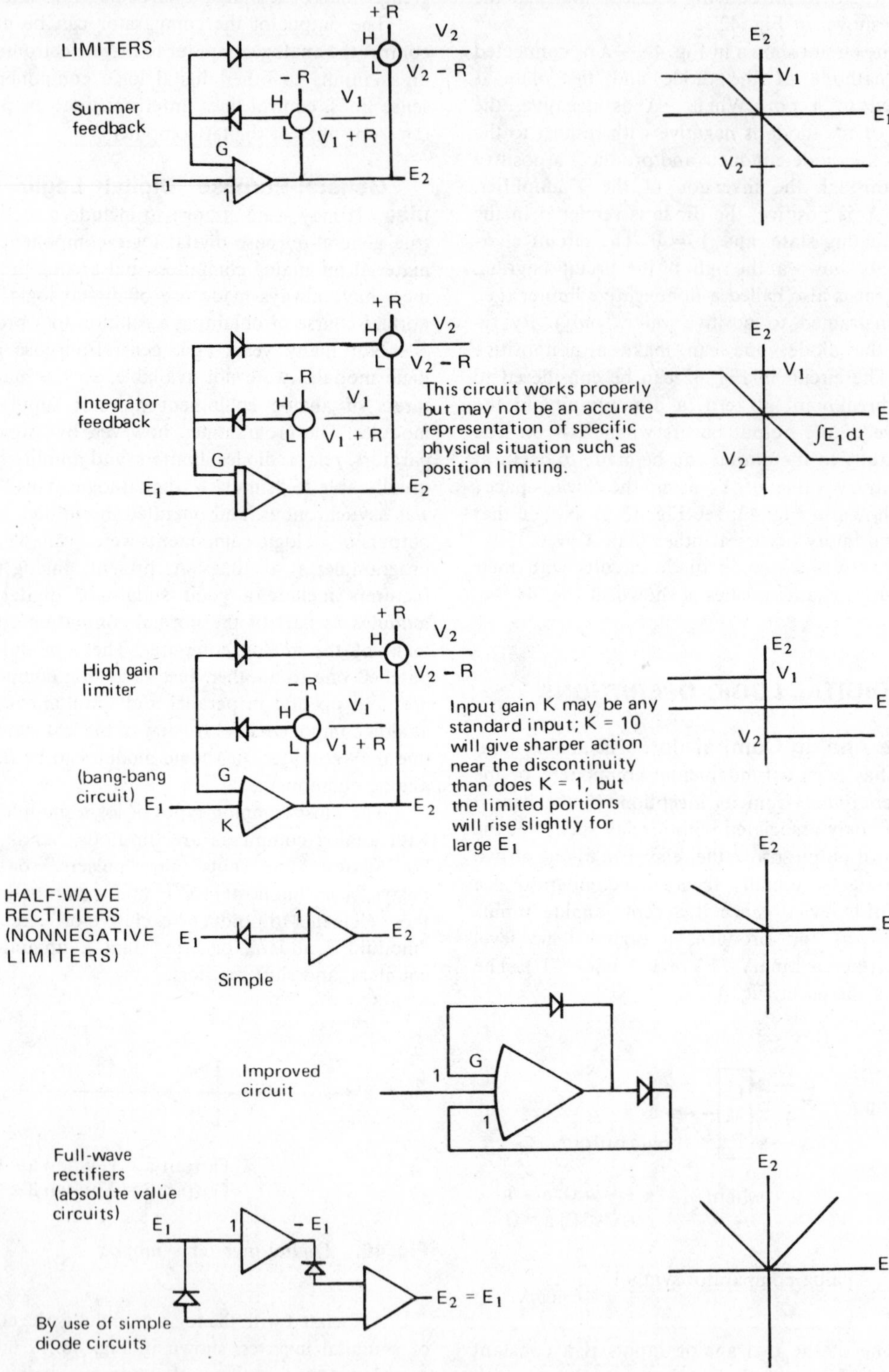


**Fig. 44.** Common diode circuits.

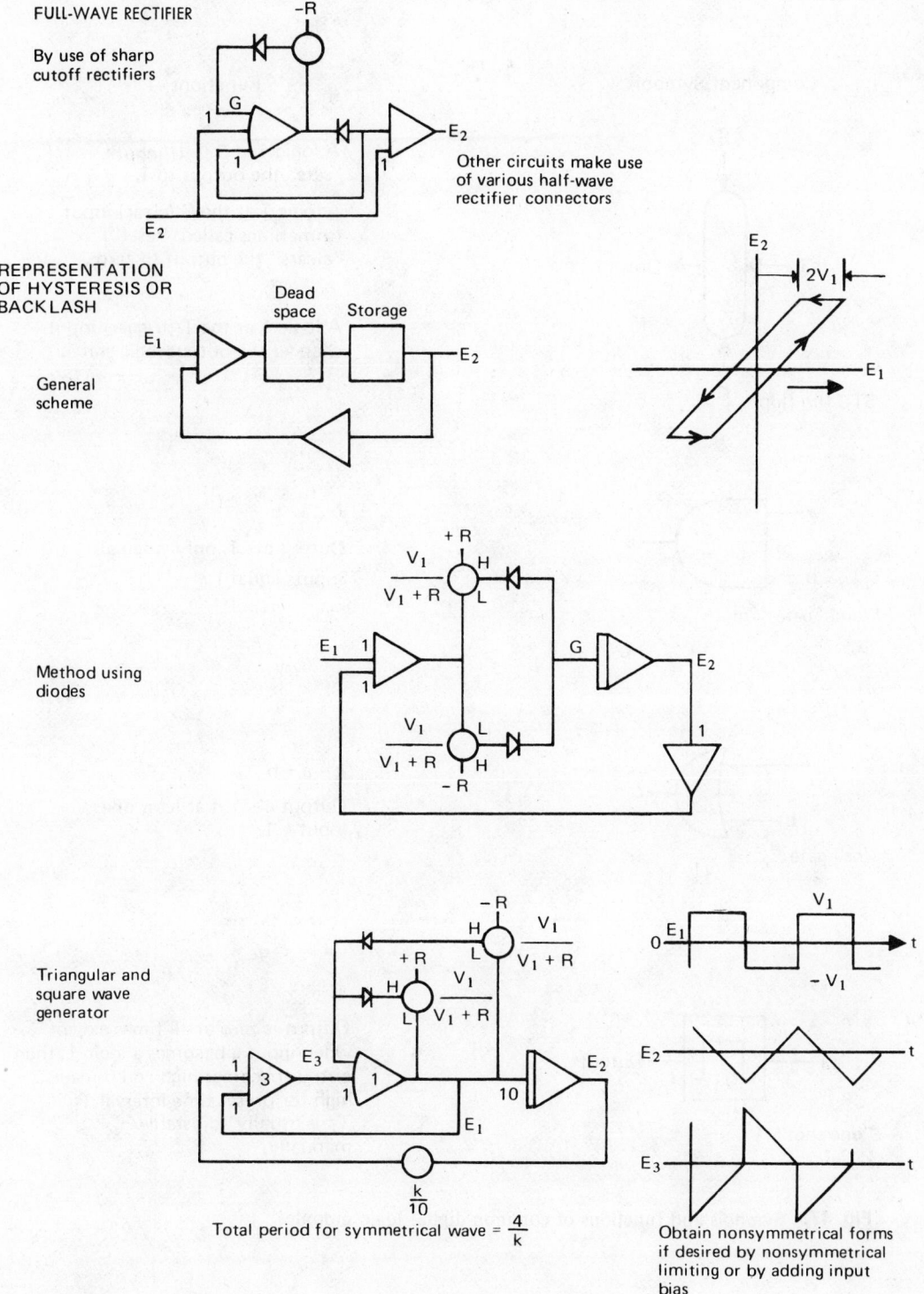

FULL-WAVE RECTIFIER

By use of sharp cutoff rectifiers

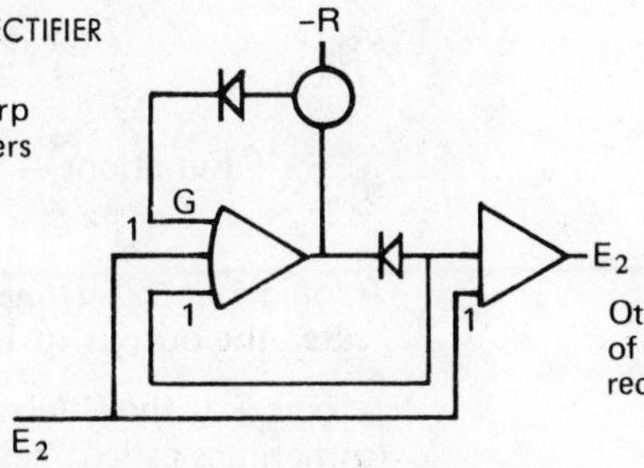


Other circuits make use of various half-wave rectifier connectors

REPRESENTATION OF HYSTERESIS OR BACKLASH

General scheme

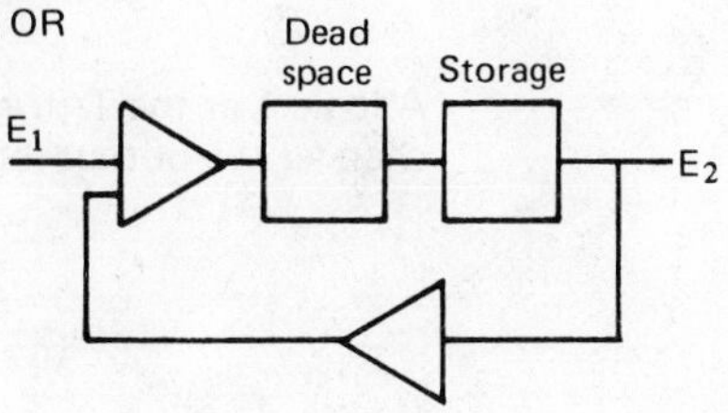


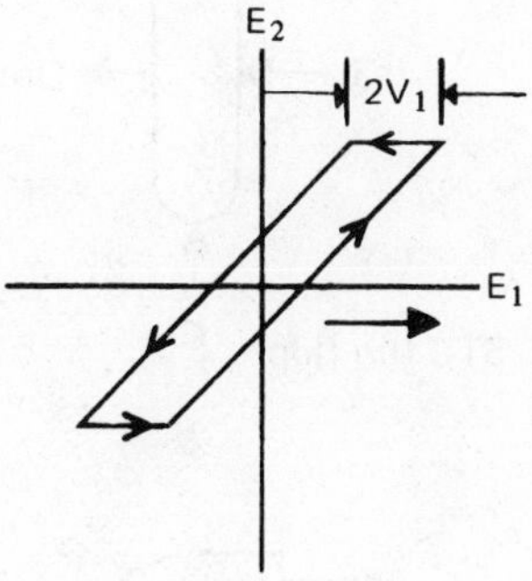


Method using diodes

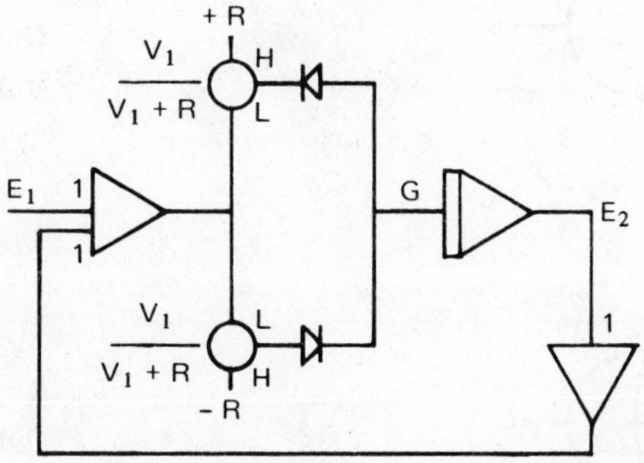


Triangular and square wave generator

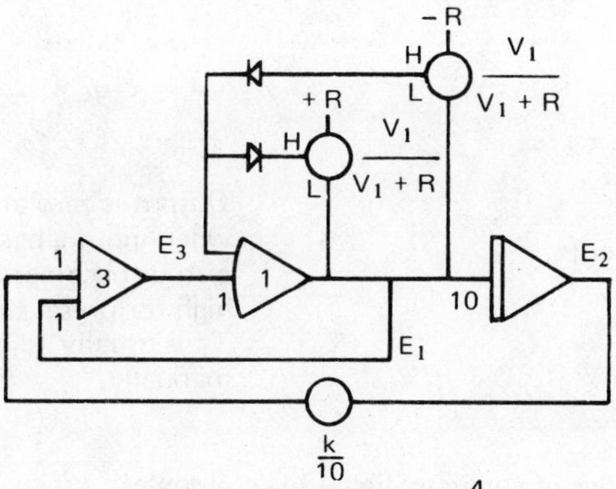


Total period for symmetrical wave = $\frac{4}{k}$

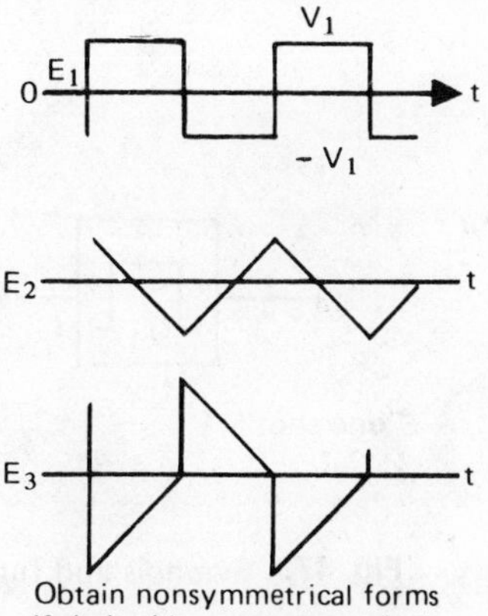


Obtain nonsymmetrical forms if desired by nonsymmetrical limiting or by adding input bias

Component Symbols | Functions

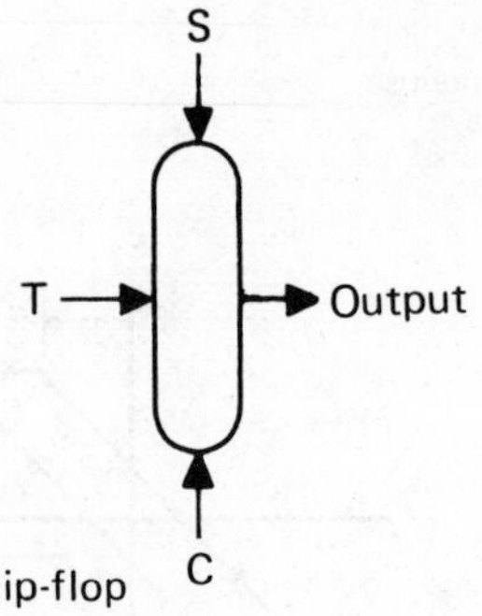


STC flip-flop

A logic 1 at S (set) input "sets" the output to 1.

A logic 1 at the C (clear) input (sometimes called "reset") "clears" the output to zero.

A logic 1 at the T (trigger) input changes the output logic state.

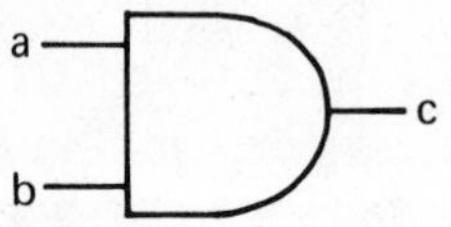


"and" gate

$c = a \cdot b$

Output c = 1, only when all inputs equal 1.

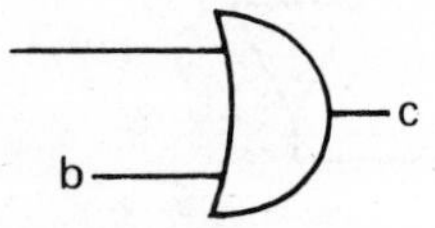


"or" gate

$c = a + b$

Output c = 1 if at least one input = 1.

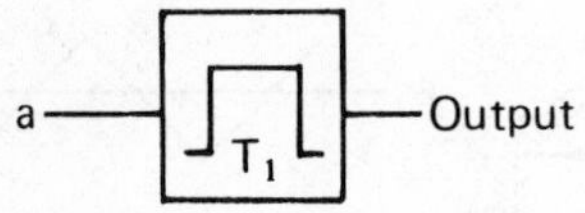


"one shot"

Output is zero at all times except when input a becomes a logic 1; then output becomes high and remains high for preset time interval $T_i$. $T_1$ is usually adjustable manually.

**Fig. 47.** Symbols and functions of common digital logic modules.

## OUTPUT EQUIPMENT

The classical analog output is a multichannel voltage–time recorder. The usual recorders associated with modern analog computers are eight channels wide, write rectangularly, and have adjustable voltage scales and chart speeds. As many variable outputs as desired may be recorded simultaneously, provided one has a sufficient number of recorders. The results produced are called "time histories." The accuracy is good to about 0.25% of the voltage range at which one is recording, and the bandwidth is about 100 Hz.

For wider bandwidth recording, an optical recorder (oscillograph) or some form of magnetic tape recorder must be used.

To obtain $X-Y$ graphs (for example, pressure vs. flow), where any variable $Y$ is plotted as a function of any other variable $X$ (as distinct from plotting $X$ and $Y$ as functions of time), an $X-Y$ "plotter" is used. These may have graph paper from as small as 8½ by 11 in. to as large as 45 by 60 in. The typical $X-Y$ plotter is rather slow, having a useful bandwidth of under 5 Hz. The larger plotters are usually restricted to 1 Hz or slower. Accuracy may be good to about 0.1% of the voltage range at which one is plotting.

Many analog computers are equipped with digital line printers that can print at rates of three to ten lines per second. A "line" consists of the voltage value (converted to four- or five-place decimal digital format) plus sign, plus the address of the analog component being "read" or printed. Hybrid computers can increase this speed considerably by using high speed conversion equipment. With high-speed analog-to-digital conversion directly linked to a digital core memory, one can obtain rates of 100,000 "lines" per second. All digital outputs are usually accurate to four decimal places (0.01% of full scale). Since all outputs of the analog computer are continuous voltages, they may also be used to drive voltmeters, ammeters, oscilloscopes, servos, etc., allowing one an infinite variety of output displays.

## PROGRAMMING

**Amplitude Scaling.** Differential and/or algebraic equations, in order to be mechanized on the analog computer, must first be converted to voltage equations. A scale factor, or volts per physical unit ratio, must be chosen for all the dependent variables. Scale factors are chosen from estimated ranges of the problem variables. These estimates are usually "educated guesses," derived from the engineer's experience in his field. If the first estimates prove to be poor, scale factors can be changed at the computer.

Having determined the amplitude scale factors, the problem variables in the mathematical equations are replaced by the voltages or machine units representing them, and adjustments are made to the coefficients throughout the equations in order to maintain equality.

The equations are thus changed into voltage or machine unit equations from which a computer circuit diagram can be drawn.

**Time Scaling.** With the all-electronic, high-speed analog computers available today, extremely high solution speeds (as short as several milliseconds) as well as very slow solutions (lasting several hours) can be obtained with the same computer. The choice of the solution time is largely dependent on factors external to the computer, such as the method of recording or displaying the solution, the need for tying into real hardware (hence the necessity of operating in "real time"), or the desire to display results to a "man in the loop," etc. A time-scale change is defined by the equation $T = \beta t$, where $T$ is machine time, $t$ is original problem time, and $\beta$ is the time scale factor and has the units of machine time/original problem time.

In order to slow down a problem (i.e., to cause machine time to be larger than original problem time), $\beta$ is made greater than unity; to speed up a problem (i.e., to cause machine time to be smaller than original problem time), $\beta$ is made less than unity.

An objective of time scaling is to change computer time with respect to original problem time, but without causing a change in the original equations, without giving rise to new definitions of derivatives, and without changing any amplitude scaling. For details on how to program an analog computer, see Hausner (1971) or Huskey and G. A. Korn (1962).

## MATHEMATICAL APPLICATIONS

It is well known that the analog computer can solve nonlinear, ordinary differential equations, and therefore it is typically used in engineering design and real-time simulation. For up-to-date applications to the various engineering and science disciplines, the reader is referred to the publication *Simulation*. What is not too well known is that the analog computer can be used effectively to solve a variety of other mathematical equations, and can also be used for analog data analysis. For example, algebraic equations, both linear and nonlinear, are readily solvable. Problems in complex variables are likewise amenable to solution by the analog computer (see Hausner, 1971). These types of problems, while amenable to analog solution, are not of major importance to analog computation. Partial differential equations (PDE) and statistical applications, on the other hand, are of importance in the analog field. For a comprehensive discussion of the solution of the PDE by analog techniques the reader is referred to Hausner (1971), while for statistical applications the reader is referred to the section "Random Process Studies" in Huskey and G. A. Korn (1962).

References

1947. Ragazzini, J., R. H. Randall, and F. A. Russell. "Analysis of Problems in Dynamics by Electronic Circuits," *Proc. IRE*, Vol. 35, pp. 444–452.

1955. Rodel, J. In H. M. Paynter (Ed.). *Palimpsest on the Electric Analog Art*. George H. Philbrick Researches, pp. 27–47.

1962. Huskey, H., and G. A. Korn. *Computer Handbook*. New York: McGraw-Hill.

*Simulation*, published since 1963 by Simulation Councils, Inc., La Jolla, Calif. (Describes current analog and hybrid computer work.)

1964. Korn, G. A., and T. M. Korn. *Electronic Analog and Hybrid Computers*. New York: McGraw-Hill.

1971. Hausner, A. *Analog & Hybrid Computer Programming*. Englewood Cliffs, N. J.: Prentice-Hall.

1971. Holst, P. A. "A Note of History," *Simulation*, Vol. 17, No. 3, September, pp. 131–135.

A. I. Rubin

## ANALOG TO DIGITAL CONVERTERS.

*See* Digital to Analog Converters.

## APPLICATIONS OF COMPUTERS.

*See* Administrative-Business Applications; Arts Applications; Control Applications; Credit System Applications; Economic Applications; Engineering Applications; Humanities Applications; Medical Applications; Planning, Computer Applications in; Real Time Applications; Scientific Applications; Social Science Applications; and Statistical Applications.

## APPLICATIONS PROGRAMMING

For articles on related subjects *see* Programming Languages; and Systems Programming.

For articles on related terms *see* Access Methods; Data Base and Data Base Management; Sort-Merge Package; and Subroutine.

Applications programs are the programs that are written to solve specific problems, to produce specific reports, to update specific files. The programming languages that are mostly used in applications programming are Fortran for scientific applications and Cobol for data processing applications. Special Report Program Generator (RPG) languages are used on small data processing computers, and languages like Basic and APL are used extensively in time-sharing systems. The language PL/I was introduced by IBM in the hope that it would prove attractive over almost the entire spectrum of applications programming and might eventually supersede both Fortran and Cobol. The resulting language uniformity would have many advantages, but the impact of PL/I has not been very great. Fortran and Cobol remain the standard applications programming languages.

The ultimate aim of all software is to make it possible for the applications programmer to perform his job well and to write programs that produce results and make effective and efficient use of the computing system. Applications programs make use of subroutine libraries and special packages such as sort-merge systems and data access and data management systems. Most well-designed operating systems provide the applications programmer with special tools for analyzing and debugging his programs.

There are very large applications systems such as airline reservations systems and on-line banking and merchandising systems in which many considerations of systems programming and of applications programming are intermixed.

S. Rosen

**APPROXIMATION.** *See* CHEBYSHEV APPROXIMATION; and LEAST SQUARES APPROXIMATION.

## APPROXIMATION THEORY

For articles on related subjects *see* CHEBYSHEV APPROXIMATION; LEAST SQUARES APPROXIMATION; and NUMERICAL ANALYSIS.

Approximation theory concerns the following problem: Given a function $f(x)$ defined for $x$ in a prescribed set $X$, a family of functions $G$, and a metric $d(f,g)$ (a mathematical prescription for measuring the distance between two functions), determine a function $g(x)$ in $G$ which is "close" to $f(x)$ for $x$ in $X$. For computer applications, $f(x)$ is typically a continuous function of one real variable, $X$ is a real interval, $G$ is a family of polynomials or of rational functions (ratios of polynomials), and the metric is either a least squares metric

$$d_2(f,g,w) = \int_X [f(x) - g(x)]^2 w(x)\,dx,$$

or the Chebyshev metric

$$d_\infty(f,g,w) = \max_X |[f(x) - g(x)]w(x)|,$$

where $w(x)$ is a weight function. For the Chebyshev metric, the weight is usually either $w(x) = 1$ or $w(x) = 1/f(x)$, where $f(x)$ is assumed not to vanish for $x$ in $X$. This latter weighting is most useful when $f(x)$ varies considerably in magnitude across the interval $X$. Basic theorems examine the existence, uniqueness, and characterization of $g(x)$, sometimes in very abstract settings. In this article we will concentrate on the Chebyshev metric, which is more important than the least squares metric in the generation of approximations to functions to be used on a computer.

Let $f(x)$ be defined and continuous over a finite real interval $X$. The theoretical justification for using the Chebyshev metric (with $w(x) = 1$) is the Weierstrass approximation theorem, which asserts the existence of real polynomials that are arbitrarily close to $f(x)$ over the entire interval $X$. These polynomials are often obtained by appropriately truncating an infinite power series expansion of the function,

$$f(x) = \Sigma_{k=0}^{\infty} a_k x^k,$$

provided the series converges to $f(x)$ over $X$, i.e., provided that for any fixed value of $x$ in $X$ and any $\epsilon > 0$, there is an integer $N$ such that all partial sums

$$s_n(x) = \Sigma_{k=0}^{N} a_k x^k, \qquad n > N$$

differ from $f(x)$ by less than $\epsilon$. Such expansions are unique whenever they exist.

Some of the more important methods for generating series expansions are based upon the analytic properties of the function. Let $f(x)$ be continuous and have continuous derivatives of all orders at some point $x_0$ in X. Then the *Taylor series* expansion of $f(x)$ about $x_0$ is given by

$$f(x) = \sum_{k=0}^{\infty} a_k (x - x_0)^k$$

$$a_k = f^{(k)}(x_0)/k! = \frac{1}{k!}\frac{d^k f(x)}{dx^k}\bigg|_{x=x_0}.$$

Since this expansion is based upon a detailed knowledge of the function at $x_0$, the Taylor polynomials $g_n(x)$ of degree $n$, obtained by truncating the series, approximate $f(x)$ well for small $|x - x_0|$, but the error $f(x) - g_n(x)$ typically grows monotonically in magnitude with increasing $|x - x_0|$. Frequently $\max_X |f(x) - g_n(x)|$ occurs at one of the boundaries of $X$. For example, Fig. 1 shows the error associated with the fourth-degree Taylor polynomial approximation to $e^x$ over $[-1,1]$, where the Taylor series is

$$e^x = 1 + x + \frac{x^2}{2} + \frac{x^3}{6} + \frac{x^4}{24} + \cdots + \frac{x^n}{n!} + \cdots.$$

A function $f(x)$ has a pole of finite integer order $n$ at $x_0$ whenever the Taylor series for $(x - x_0)^m f(x)$ exists for $m = n$, but fails to exist for smaller integer values of $M$. The *Laurent series* is then given by $(x - x_0)^{-n}$ times the Taylor series for $(x - x_0)^n f(x)$. As an example, the Laurent series for $\csc(x)$, which has an isolated pole of order 1 at $x = 0$, is

$$\csc(x) = \frac{1}{x} + \frac{x}{6} + \frac{7x^3}{360} + \frac{31x^5}{15{,}120} + \cdots,$$

which converges for $|x| < \pi$. When the function

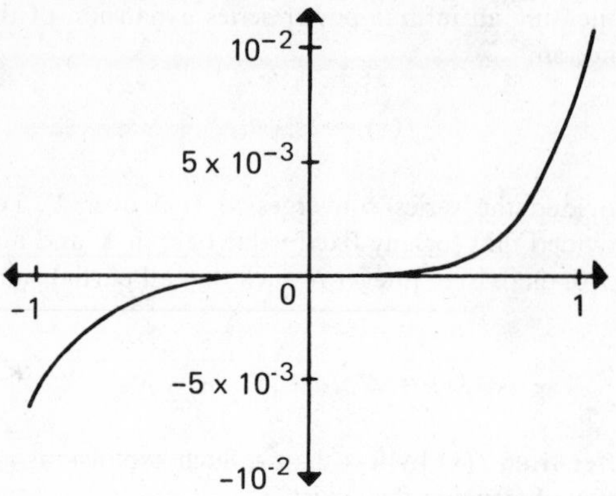


**Fig. 1.** Error $e^x - g_4(x)$, $g_4(x) = 1 + x + (x^2/2!) + (x^3/3!) + (x^4/4!)$ for approximation over $[-1,1]$ by fourth degree Taylor polynomial.

has an isolated pole of infinite order, the Laurent series takes the form

$$f(x) = \Sigma_{k=-\infty}^{\infty} a_k x^k,$$

where the derivation of the coefficients $a_k$ generally involves methods from the theory of functions of a complex variable. The expansion

$$\arctan(x) = \frac{\pi}{2} - \frac{1}{x} + \frac{1}{3x^3} - \frac{1}{5x^5} + \cdots,$$

valid for $|x| > 1$, is of this type. Truncation of Laurent series leads to rational approximations for $f(x)$.

If the interval $X$ is semi-infinite, $X = [b,\infty)$, $b > 0$, a divergent *asymptotic expansion* of $f(x)$,

$$f(x) \sim \Sigma_{k=0}^{\infty} a_k x^{-k},$$

may yield useful rational approximations to $f(x)$ even though it does not converge to $f(x)$ for any finite value of $x$. Let $s_n(x) = \Sigma_{k=0}^{n} a_k x^{-k}$ be the partial sum of the asymptotic series. Then, for any fixed value of $x$, there is an $n$ which minimizes the error $|f(x) - s_n(x)|$. For fixed $n$, and $x$ sufficiently large, the error can be made as small as desired. Thus, for a particular $\epsilon > 0$, it is usually possible to choose first an $n$ and then an $X$ (i.e., $a,b$) so that $s_n(x)$ approximates $f(x)$ to within $\epsilon$ over $X$ in the Chebyshev metric. The derivation of an asymptotic series is often a difficult task involving advanced mathematical tools. As with power series, the expansions are unique.

If the Taylor series expansion for $f(x)$ exists, then the *Padé table* for $f(x)$ is the array of rational approximations

$$R_{mn}(x) = \frac{p_0 + p_1 x + \cdots + p_m x^m}{1 + q_1 x + \cdots + q_n x^n},$$

characterized by the property that the power series expansion of $R_{mn}(x)$ is identical to the Taylor series expansion through terms in $x^{m+n}$. The entries $R_{mo}(x)$ are the Taylor polynomials, and the entries $R_{00}(x)$, $R_{01}(x)$, $R_{11}(x)$, ... along the main diagonal are the successive convergents of a Stieltjes continued fraction, or *S-fraction*, expansion of $f(x)$.

$$f(x) = \cfrac{a_0}{1 - \cfrac{a_1 x}{1 - \cfrac{a_2 x}{\ddots}}}$$

These latter elements are often better approximations to $f(x)$ than are the Taylor polynomials of degree $m + n$. All elements of the Padé table agree with $f(x)$ exactly at the point of expansion, but $f(x) - R_{mn}(x)$ tends to grow as $x$ moves away from that point. As an example, the S-fraction expansion of $e^x$ is

$$e^x = \cfrac{1}{1 - \cfrac{x}{1 + \cfrac{x/2}{1 - \cfrac{x/6}{1 + \cfrac{x/6}{\ddots}}}}}$$

The corresponding Padé approximation $R_{22}(x)$ is obtained by truncating the S-fraction to just the terms given above, and is

$$R_{22}(x) = \frac{12 + 6x + x^2}{12 - 6x + x^2}$$

Fig. 2 shows the error $e^x - R_{22}(x)$ over the interval $[-1,1]$. Note that the maximum error is less than half of that associated with the fourth-degree Taylor polynomial.

By sacrificing accuracy in the neighborhood of the point of expansion, it is possible to distribute the error over the interval of approximation and to

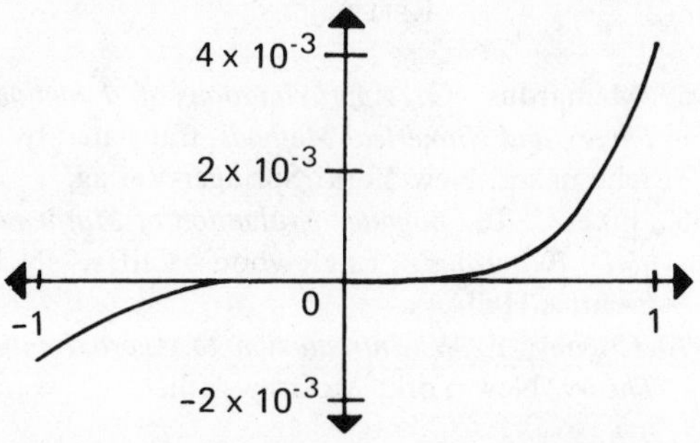


**Fig. 2.** Error $e^x - R_{22}(x)$ for approximation over $[-1,1]$ by Padé element.

obtain better approximations to $f(x)$ over $X$ in the sense of the Chebyshev metric. The rational Chebyshev, or minimax, approximation to $f(x)$ of degree $(m,n)$ is that rational function $R^*_{mn}(x)$, which minimizes $d(f,R_{mn},w)$. Basic theorems assert that such an $R^*_{mn}(x)$ exists, is unique, and is characterized by the error $[f(x) - R^*_{mn}(x)]w(x)$ achieving its maximum magnitude with alternating sign a prescribed number of times as $x$ moves across the interval $X$. The determination of $R^*_{mn}(x)$ is not easy, but the characterization theorem leads to algorithms, such as the Remes algorithm, for computing approximations close to $R^*_{mn}(x)$.

The Chebyshev polynomials

$$T_n(x) = 2^{1-n}\cos(n\cos^{-1}x), \quad -1 \leq x \leq 1,$$

are instrumental in the generation of near-minimax polynomial approximations. If $f(x)$ is continuous and sufficiently smooth, then

$$f(x) = \tfrac{1}{2}a_0T_0(x) + \textstyle\sum_{k=1}^{\infty} a_kT_k(x), \qquad -1 \leq x \leq 1,$$

where

$$a_k = \frac{2}{\pi}\int_{-1}^{1}\frac{f(x)T_k(x)}{(1-x^2)^{1/2}}dx,$$

is the *Chebyshev polynomial expansion* of $f(x)$. (This is related to the *Fourier series* for $f(x)$ by the change of variable $w = \cos^{-1}x$). The partial sums of this expansion are the best polynomial approximations to $f(x)$ for the metric $d_2[f,g, 1/(1-x^2)^{1/2}]$ and are very close to the minimax polynomial approximation to $f(x)$ in most cases. As an example, the coefficients in the Chebyshev series expansion for $e^x$ are $a_k = 2I_k(1)$, where the $I_k$ are modified Bessel functions. Truncation of this series after five terms leads to the approximation

$$g(x) = 1.000045 + 0.997308x + 0.499197x^2 + 0.177347x^3 + 0.043794x^4$$

for the interval $[-1,1]$. The maximum error associated with this approximation is only about one-twentieth of that associated with the fourth-degree Taylor polynomial (see Fig. 3).

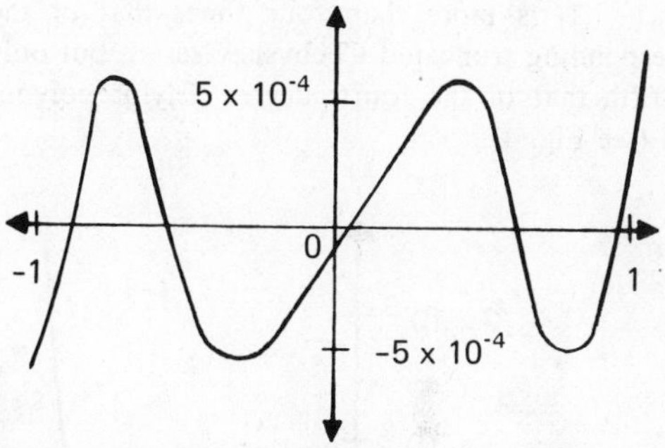


**Fig. 3.** Error $e^x - \Sigma_{k=0}^{4} a_kT_k(x)$ for approximation over $[-1,1]$ by truncated Chebyshev series.

Legendre, Jacobi, Hermite, Laguerre, and Gegenbauer polynomials are other important families of polynomials similarly associated with particular choices of weights and intervals in least squares approximation. Since power series expansions are unique, the expansion of $f(x)$ in polynomials from any of these families can be formally obtained by replacing each $x^k$ in the power series by its exact representation in polynomials of the family and then collecting terms. This "rearrangement" of the power series may alter the convergence of the series so that the new series converges for a larger (or smaller) interval than the original series.

Lanczos' telescoping, or economizing, process is similar to this rearrangement process. Starting from a truncated power series, such as a Taylor polynomial, over the interval $[-1,1]$, the degree of the polynomial is lowered by successively replacing the highest-order term $x^n$ by the polynomial

$$P_{n-1}(x) = x^n - 2^{1-n}T_n(x),$$

which is the minimax approximation to $x^n$ by a polynomial of degree less than $n$. The approximation error introduced at each step tends to distribute the cumulative error over the interval of approximation so that the polynomials in the resulting sequence tend to be better approximations to $f(x)$ than the corresponding truncations of the original power series, but they are not as good as those obtained by truncating the Chebyshev polynomial expansion. For example, the approximation

$$g(x) = 1 + 0.997396x + 0.5x^2 + 0.177083x^3 + 0.041667x^4$$

to $e^x$ is obtained by truncating the Taylor series after six terms and replacing $x^5$ by $P_4(x) = (20x^3 - 5x)/16$. The corresponding maximum error over $[-1,1]$ is more than four times that of the corresponding truncated Chebyshev series, but only one-fifth that of the fourth-degree Taylor polynomial (see Fig. 4).

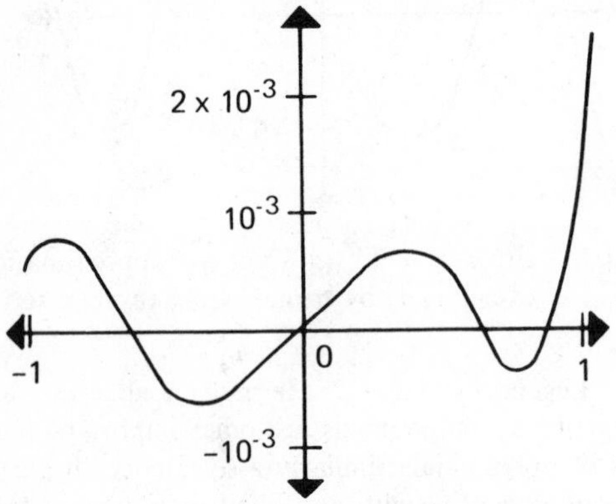


**Fig. 4.** Error $e^x - g(x)$ for approximation over $[-1,1]$ by fifth-degree Taylor polynomial telescoped to fourth degree.

An extensive theory of approximation exists for functions of a complex variable and for multivariate functions (functions of two or more real variables). The theory relies heavily upon convergent or asymptotic power series and continued fraction expansions. The Taylor and Laurent series and the Padé table extend to the complex case directly. While the theory of minimax approximation generalizes to these functions, the generalizations are not very useful (e.g., uniqueness is lost in the multivariate case) and reliable algorithms for generating the approximations do not exist. Except for certain elementary functions, direct approximations to complex or multivariate functions are not often used in computer applications. Instead, indirect evaluation methods based upon recurrence relations, differential equations, etc., are used.

REFERENCES

1967. Meinardus, G. *Approximation of Functions: Theory and Numerical Methods*, translated by L. Schumaker. New York: Springer-Verlag.

1968. Fike, C. T. *Computer Evaluation of Mathematical Functions.* Englewood Cliffs, N.J.: Prentice-Hall.

1970. Cheney, E. W. *Introduction to Approximation Theory.* New York: McGraw-Hill.

W. J. CODY

## ARCHITECTURE, COMPUTER. *See* COMPUTER ARCHITECTURE.

## ARGUMENT

For articles on related subjects *see* DATA TYPE; MACROINSTRUCTION; PROCEDURE; SUBPROGRAM, CALLING; and SUBROUTINE.

In strict analogy to mathematics, where an argument of a function is the value of a variable used to evaluate the function, an argument in computing is a value supplied to a procedure, a subroutine, or a macroinstruction which is required in order to evaluate the procedure, subroutine, or macro. Another term used interchangeably with argument is "parameter."

Two different kinds of arguments need to be distinguished: "dummy" or "formal" arguments, and "actual" or "calling" arguments. A dummy argument is an argument used in the definition of a procedure or macro; an actual argument is that which is substituted when the procedure or macro is invoked. For example, Fig. 1 displays a Fortran SUBROUTINE subprogram to compute the solution of a quadratic equation.

$$ax^2 + bx + c = 0.$$

The variables A, B, C, MODE, X1, and X2 in Fig. 1 are all dummy arguments. If this subroutine were to be used to compute the roots of

$$10.7X^2 + (R1 + 6.23)X + S*S = 0 \quad (1)$$

where R1 and S are variables appearing elsewhere in

```
      SUBROUTINE QUAD (A,B,C,MODE,X1, X2)
      DISC = B*B - 4.0*A*C
      IF(DISC.LT.0.) GO TO 3
C PROGRAM IGNORES CASE A = 0
C MODE PARAMETER SET TO 0 IF ROOTS ARE
C     REAL AND TO 1 IF THEY ARE COMPLEX
      MODE = 0
C TWO REAL ROOTS COMPUTED SO AS TO
C     AVOID DIFFERENCE OF TWO NEARLY
C     EQUAL QUANTITIES
      IF(B.LE.0) GO TO 5
         X1 = -B - SQRT (DISC)
         GO TO 7
5        X1 = -B + SQRT (DISC)
7     X2 = C/(X1*A)
      RETURN
3     MODE = 1
      X1 = B/(2.0*A)
      X2 = SQRT (-DISC)/(2.0*A)
      RETURN
      END
```

**Fig. 1.** Quadratic equation subprogram.

the program, the statement

```
CALL QUAD (10.7, R1 + 6.23, S*S, J, Y, Z)
```

might be given. Each argument in the CALL statement is an actual argument, i.e., the argument that will be associated with the dummy arguments in the subroutine definition. Thus, when QUAD is executed in response to CALL,

- The values used for A, B, and C will be, respectively, 10.7, R1 + 6.23, and S*S, with the latter two being evaluated using the current main program values for R1 and S.
- The variable J in the main program will be set equal to the value of MODE in the subprogram.
- The main program variables Y and Z will contain the results of the solution of Eq. (1) after execution of QUAD.

Formal arguments are always required to be identifiers, but, as the example above indicates, actual arguments may be identifiers or numbers or arithmetic expressions. Most languages allow great generality in the form of the actual arguments, although there may be requirements that the calling arguments have the same "type" or "mode" as the formal arguments (i.e., a real calling argument if the formal argument denotes a real variable).

Subprogram arguments may also be classified as "input" or "output" arguments, with the former denoting arguments provided to the subprogram and the latter the arguments that convey results back to the main program. In the example given in Fig. 1, A, B, and C are input arguments and MODE, X1, and X2 are output arguments. Sometimes an argument may be both an input and output argument; for example, when a procedure to compute the next prime number receives as input the variable P denoting the current prime number and returns the value of the next prime number to P. Sometimes the arguments of a subprogram may be *implicit*; i.e., they are not stated explicitly in the statement heading the subprogram. This happens in block-structured languages when a procedure in a subblock uses variables global to that block. It happens in Fortran when arguments are held in so-called COMMON storage that is accessible and known by both the main program and the subprogram.

REFERENCE

1971. Ralston, A. *An Introduction to Programming and Computer Science*. New York: McGraw-Hill.

A. RALSTON

## ARITHMETIC.

*See* INTERVAL ARITHMETIC; and SIGNIFICANCE ARITHMETIC.

## ARITHMETIC, COMPUTER

For articles on related subjects *see* COMPLEMENT; NUMBERS AND NUMBER SYSTEMS; PRECISION; ROUNDOFF ERROR; SIGNIFICANCE ARITHMETIC; and SIGNIFICANT DIGIT.

For article on related term *see* WORD LENGTH, VARIABLE.

The earliest electronic computers were developed in the late 1940s to fill a need for fast arithmetic engines that could solve a variety of problems, many of them military. Although computers, as general symbol manipulators, now solve many problems that do not involve arithmetic computation, numerical calculations are still of vital importance in computer applications. Therefore, how computers perform arithmetic and, in particular, how computer arithmetic differs from ordinary hand computation are topics that should be understood by anyone who uses computers.

**Storage of Numbers in Computers.** In most computers, a single number occupies a single memory unit (in *word*-oriented memories) or a fixed number of memory units (in *character* or *byte*-oriented memories; e.g., four bytes in IBM 360–370 series computers), which are usually called a "word" or "full word." Such numbers are sometimes called "single precision" numbers in contrast to double precision numbers, which are used when additional accuracy is required and which occupy twice the memory space of single precision numbers (e.g., eight bytes in IBM 360–370 computers). (Years ago, some computers—epitomized by the IBM 1400 series and the IBM 1620—had *variable* word lengths and therefore could handle variable length numbers. Few such computers are still in use.)

A given number may be stored in one of two modes: *fixed point* or *floating point*. Fig. 1(a) illustrates the storage of .15625 as a fixed-point number in a word-oriented computer memory with 36 bits per word. (Throughout this article, numbers in the text will be decimal numbers and those illustrated in computer storage will be binary.) Two points are worth noting about this example:

1. The left-hand bit (S) in Fig. 1 represents the sign of the number, 0 for + and 1 for −. (Hereafter in this article we will, for convenience, use only positive numbers in examples. Storage of negative numbers can be either in absolute value and sign form or in complement form.)

2. The binary point (i.e., the "decimal" or *radix* point) is assumed to be at the left end of the number; hence the name "fixed-point" numbers. All computers must embody an assumption on the invariant location of the binary point in fixed-point numbers. In most computers this assumption (used throughout this article) is the one shown in Fig. 1. However, some computers (e.g., CDC 6000 series) assume the binary point to be at the right-hand end of the number.

Hardware for storing and manipulating numbers in fixed-point form was the only kind available in early computers, but handling them and doing arithmetic with them created major problems:

1. How could numbers with magnitudes of 1 or greater be handled? The answer to this is that such numbers can be stored as fixed-point numbers but the programmer must be aware of and keep track of the implicit location of the radix point as such numbers are used in computations. Thus, 57.8125 could be stored as shown in Fig. 1(b).

2. More significant are the problems with numbers whose implicit radix points are in different positions. How could these be added, subtracted, multiplied, and divided? As a simple example, consider adding the numbers in Figs. 1(a) and 1(b). Before this can be done by adding the contents of the words, bit by bit, one of the numbers must be shifted relative to the other. The process of such shifting and the associated problem of choosing the location of the implicit binary point for numbers before they are stored is called "scaling." The difficulty and tediousness of scaling for all but the simplest computations led to the introduction of floating-point hardware capabilities, which are now used for the vast majority of all numerical computation on computers.

*Floating-point* numbers are more than the solution to the above problems because they also allow computations where the range of the magnitude of the numbers is very large, larger than can be handled with fixed-point numbers except with great diffi-

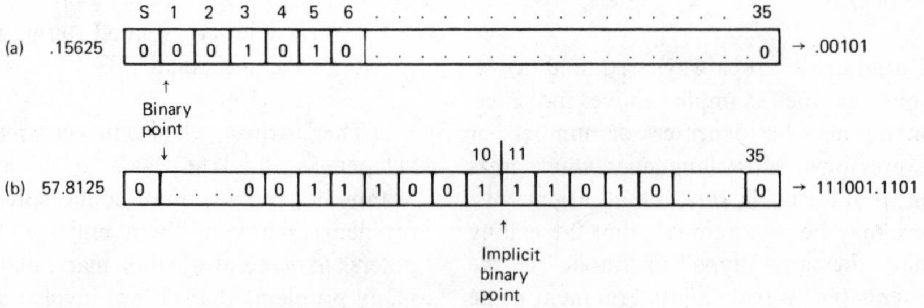


**Fig. 1.** Fixed-point numbers.

culty. Floating-point representation of numbers corresponds very closely to what is usually called "scientific notation"; that is, each number is represented as the product of a normal number with a radix point and an integral power of the radix. Thus, for example, the number of Fig. 1(b) might be expressed in scientific notation as

$$.578125 \times 10^2$$

with the .578125 being called the "fractional" part and the 2 the "exponent" part; or, borrowing from logarithmic terminology, the mantissa and characteristic, respectively. This notation is called "floating point" in computer arithmetic because the radix point of the entire number (57.8125 in Part (b) of Fig. 1) is not fixed but can "float," depending upon the value of the exponent.

In order to store such numbers in memory units of the same length as single precision fixed-point numbers, separate portions of each unit must be assigned to the fractional part and the exponent part. Standard ways of doing this in computers having a 36-bit word memory and four 8-bit bytes to a word (like the IBM 360–370 computers) are shown in Figs. 2(a) and 2(b) for the number $.578125 \times 10^2$. The following comments pertain to these figures.

1. A notation sometimes used for the number in Fig. 2(a) is (8,27), indicating 8 bits for the exponent part and 27 for the fractional part. Similarly, the number in Fig. 2(b) is a (7,24) number.

2. As with fixed-point numbers, the binary point of the fractional part is always assumed to be in the same place, usually at the left end, as in Fig. 2, but sometimes at the right-hand end (in which case the "fractional part" is an integer). The sign bit S always represents the sign of the fractional part.

3. Exponents may be positive or negative, but since the sign bit denotes the sign of the fractional part, the sign of the exponent must be handled by a special mechanism. One possibility would be to let bit 1 denote the sign of the exponent, but a much more common technique is to use "excess-n" notation. In Fig. 2(a) the 8 exponent bits can represent binary integers from 0 to $2^8 - 1 = 255$. If the desired exponent is $X$ and the exponent part stored in bits 1 to 8 is $Y$, then $Y = X + 128$ is said to be an excess-128 exponent. Thus, true exponents $X$ from $-128$ to $+127$ can be represented by values of $Y$ from 0 to 255. Therefore it is necessary only for the arithmetic unit of the computer to interpret correctly the excess-128 exponent.

4. In IBM 360–370 computers the exponent is considered to be an excess-64 binary number, which is interpreted as a power of 16 because many of the internal operations of this series of computers are hexadecimally oriented. Thus, the exponent shown in Fig. 2(b) is interpreted as $16^1$.

5. The range of exponents in the (8,27) case is from $2^{-128}$ to $2^{+127}$, or from about $10^{-38}$ to $10^{+38}$. In the (7,24) hexadecimal case, the range is from $16^{-64}$ to $16^{63}$, or from about $10^{-77}$ to $10^{+76}$. On CDC 6000 series computers, which use an (11,48) binary format with the mantissa radix point at the right, the range is from about $10^{-294}$ to $10^{322}$. Even so, this range is not always adequate, as pointed out in the discussion on overflow in the next section.

The floating-point number in Fig. 2(a) is said to be *normalized* because the most significant bit in its fractional part (bit 9) is nonzero. Similarly, the floating-point number in Fig. 2(b) is normalized in a hexadecimal sense because the first hexadecimal digit in the fractional part (0011 = hexadecimal 3) is nonzero. Most computers automatically create normalized numbers as the result of floating-point arithmetic operations because in this way the maximum number of significant bits are retained. Some computers allow the programmer to choose whether the result should be normalized or unnormalized. One school of thought believes that leaving results unnormalized gives a better picture of the true accuracy of the retained result.

Double precision floating-point numbers occupy two words, or twice the number of bytes, as single precision numbers. Two formats for these numbers

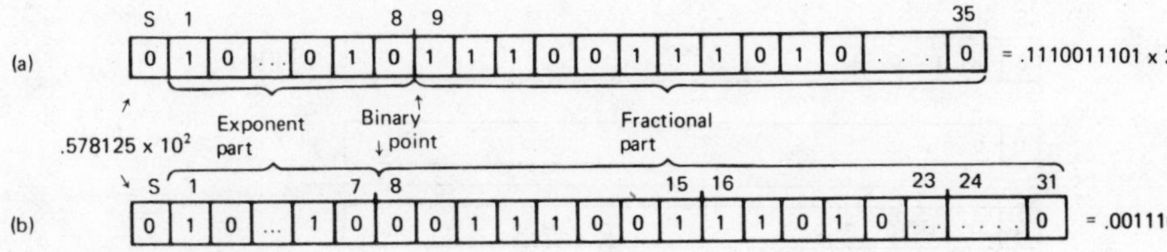


**Fig. 2.** Floating-point numbers.

are in use, with the first format below being more common today:

| S | EXP | FRACT. PART | | FRACTIONAL PART |
|---|---|---|---|---|

where the second fractional part is just an extension of the first and

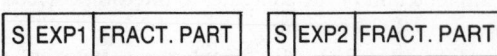

| S | EXP1 | FRACT. PART | | S | EXP2 | FRACT. PART |
|---|---|---|---|---|---|---|

where the second fractional part is an extension of the first, but where EXP2 is less than EXP1 by the number of bits in each fractional part and both halves have the same sign.

**Arithmetic, Fixed-Point.** The actual mechanics of fixed-point arithmetic are essentially those of ordinary binary arithmetic, given the restriction that negative numbers are generally stored and manipulated in some complement form. However, some aspects of fixed-point arithmetic on computers need to be considered explicitly. In the following examples we assume that fixed-point numbers are binary fractions of magnitude less than 1 (i.e., binary point at the left).

The only snare for the unwary in fixed-point addition and subtraction is the phenomenon known as "overflow." Since not only the two operands but also the result in addition and subtraction must be less than 1 in magnitude, a result greater than this will not be handled correctly, as illustrated in Fig. 3. Overflow occurs when bit 1 has a carry-out. In some computers this carry-out is discarded; in others, as shown in Fig. 3, it replaces the sign bit, resulting in the example shown in a spurious negative number. In any case, the result is incorrect; normally this is indicated by setting an internal switch which the programmer can test, using a *branch on overflow* instruction.

Overflow cannot occur in fixed-point multiplication, since the product of two factors less than 1 in magnitude is also less than 1. But the multiplication of two $n$-bit factors results in a 2-$n$ bit product, which cannot be accommodated in an $n$-bit accumulator register in the arithmetic unit. Normally, the least significant $n$ bits are placed in a second register, called the "multiplier-quotient (or MQ) register," as shown in Fig. 4, in which for convenience we have assumed the word length to be only five bits. If the programmer wishes to retain the full $2n$-bit product, he may do so, but usually only the most significant $n$ bits are retained after rounding, as shown in Fig. 4.

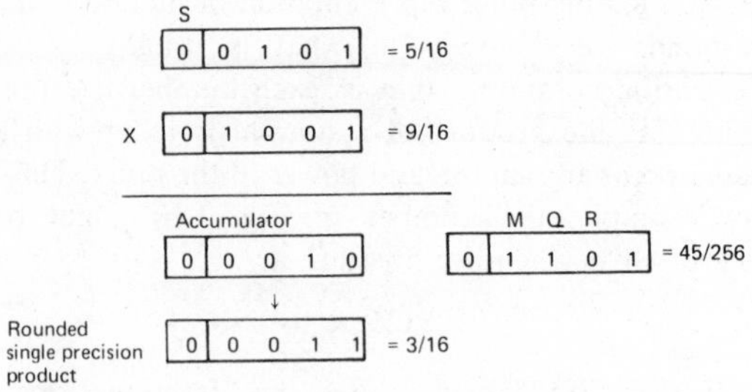


**Fig. 4.** Fixed-point multiplication.

As with addition and subtraction, division can result in overflow if the dividend has magnitude greater than the divisor. Such an overflow, often called a "divide check," is ordinarily tested by the programmer with an instruction separate from that used to test additive or subtractive overflow.

The dividend in fixed-point division can usually be double length (or precision), occupying both the accumulator and MQ registers. The single precision quotient is commonly placed in the MQ register and the remainder is placed in the accumulator, as illustrated in Fig. 5.

In actual practice the great majority of fixed-point arithmetic operations are normally performed on integer quantities in higher-level language programs. Appropriate adjustments must be made when the computer assumes that the radix point is at the left-hand end of the number. However, the higher-level language programmer need not be concerned about this, since the higher-level language processor performs all the necessary manipulations. Fig. 6 illustrates what would actually happen in our hy-

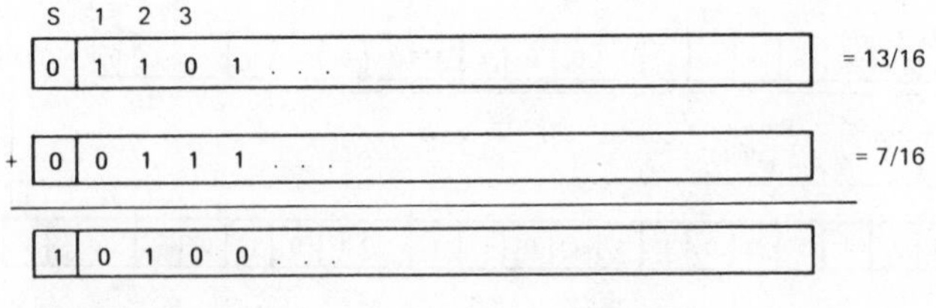


**Fig. 3.** Overflow in fixed-point numbers.

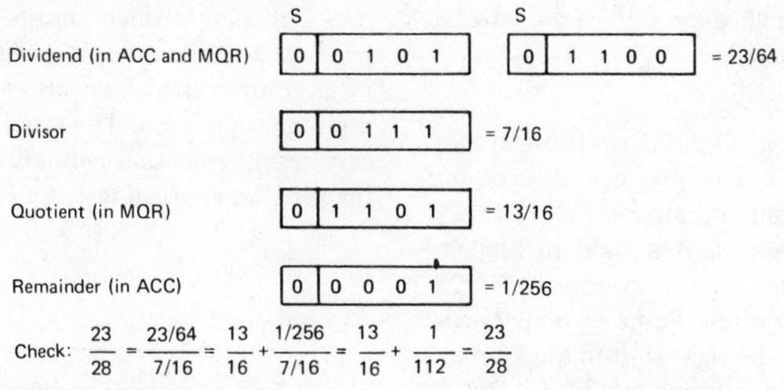


**Fig. 5.** Fixed-point division.

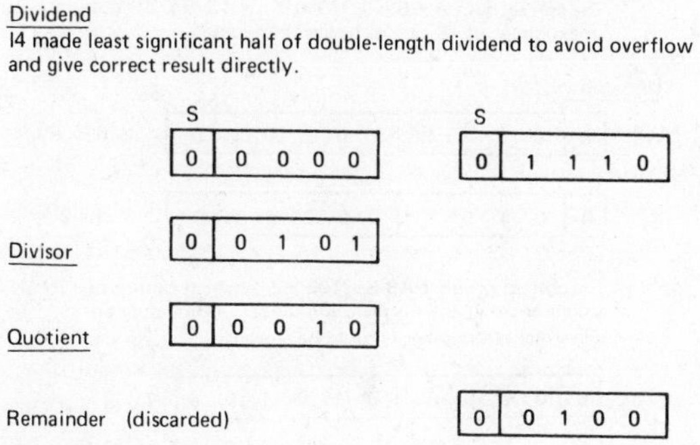


**Fig. 6.** Integer division in Fortran.

pothetical four-bit plus-sign computer in executing the Fortran statement

I = 14/5

to give the result 2, since remainders are discarded in Fortran integer division.

**Arithmetic, Floating Point.** The most difficult operations in floating-point arithmetic are addition and subtraction. A (simplified) algorithm for floating-point addition is the following: Let the two numbers to be added be $A$ and $B$, and let $C$ be the result. Let the exponent and fractional parts be denoted by $E_a$, $E_b$ and $E_c$ and $F_a$, $F_b$ and $F_c$, respectively.

STEP 1. Set $E_c$ = the larger of $E_a$ and $E_b$. Assume in what follows that $E_a \geq E_b$.

STEP 2. *Shift right.* Shift $F_b$ to the right $E_a - E_b$ places (which has the effect of giving $F_a$ and $F_b$ the same exponent).

STEP 3. *Add.* Set $F_c = F_a + F_b$

STEP 4. *Normalize.* Shift $F_c$ to make 1 its most significant digit and adjust $E_c$ accordingly. This algorithm is illustrated in Fig. 7, assuming a hypothetical computer with a four-bit excess-8 exponent and a six-bit fractional part.

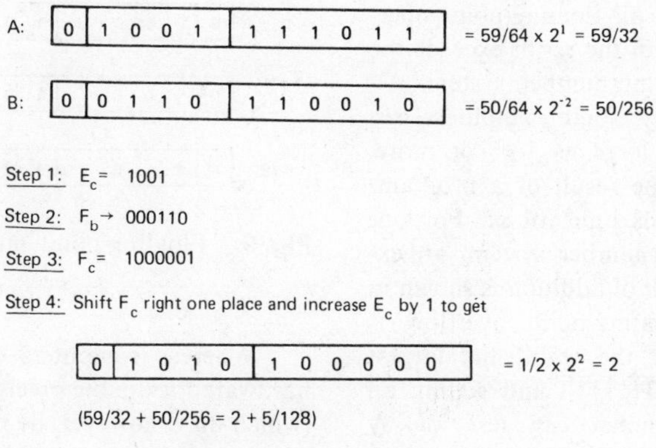


**Fig. 7.** Floating-point addition.

In proceeding through these four steps, several points should be considered:

1. Step 3 may result in a kind of overflow in that the two six-bit operands may produce a seven-bit result. But no error results because the "overflow" bit is always retained and shifted right in Step 4.

2. The final computer result is in error by 5/128 with respect to the true result. Some error is inevitable in general because the right shift in Step 2 may cause the loss of some significant bits of $F_b$. But if the final fractional part were 100001 instead of 100000, C would equal 2 + 1/16, in which case the error would be 3/128 instead of 5/128. Many floating-point add algorithms would, in fact, achieve this result by *rounding* $F_c$ after Step 3 (by adding 1 in the seventh position) before performing Step 4.

3. Many computers have machine instruction sets that allow the machine or assembly language programmer to choose either normalized or unnormalized floating-point operations (i.e., with or without Step 4, except that when a right shift is required, it is always performed). The higher-level language programmer has no such options. Normalized floating-point operations are almost always used in higher-level language processors.

4. Floating-point subtraction or floating-point addition of numbers with different signs may result in a normalization that requires a left shift of $F_c$. In some computers the arithmetic unit will have retained the bits shifted right in Step 2, and these will now be shifted left to avoid the loss of precision that would be caused if zeros were inserted at the right. Other computers (e.g., the IBM 360–370 series) retain a single *guard digit* (a hexadecimal, not a binary digit, in IBM 360–370) on the right, which can be shifted left during normalization.

Overflow can occur in all floating-point operations when the magnitude of the result exceeds the capacity of the floating-point number system. Although, as noted previously, some computers can accommodate numbers as large as $10^{300}$ or more, overflow—particularly as the result of a programming error—is by no means unheard of. For our hypothetical floating-point number system, an example of overflow as a result of addition is shown in Fig. 8. The result of floating-point overflow is handled either by making the result the largest number possible (0 | 1111 | 111111) and setting an indicator that the programmer can test, or by stopping the computation with an appropriate error message.

*Underflow*, which results from the attempt to produce a nonzero result too small (in magnitude) to be accommodated, can also result from any floating-point operation. The usual result is to generate a zero result; sometimes an indicator is also set, which the programmer can test. An example is given in Fig. 8.

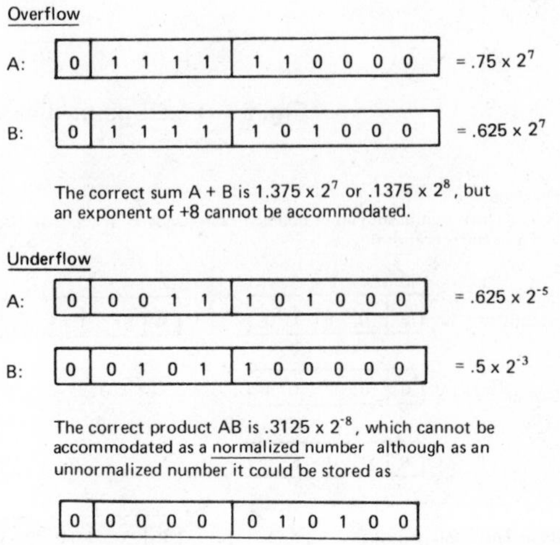


**Fig. 8.** Floating-point overflow and underflow.

Floating-point multiplication and division only require performing the appropriate action on the fractional parts, rounding the results, adding (for multiplication) or subtracting (for division) the exponents, and then normalizing if necessary. Examples are shown in Fig. 9.

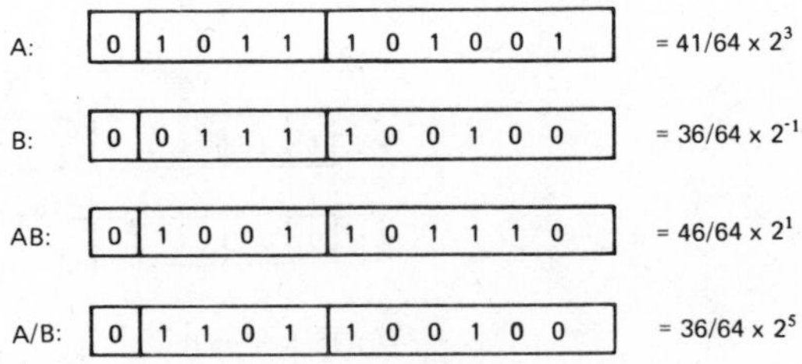


**Fig. 9.** Floating-point multiplication and division.

Whereas computers do not normally provide hardware for double precision fixed-point arithmetic (which may, however, be programmed), hardware is often provided for double precision floating-point arithmetic. The details, however, do not differ sufficiently from those of single precision arithmetic to merit inclusion here. A comprehensive discussion of floating-point arithmetic is found in Sterbenz (1974).

**Computer Arithmetic and Real Arithmetic.** Two groups of common laws of arithmetic on the real-number system are:

1. *Associative Laws*
   Addition: $a + (b + c) = (a + b) + c$
   Multiplication: $a \cdot (b \cdot c) = (a \cdot b) \cdot c$

2. *Distributive Law*:

$$a \cdot (b + c) = a \cdot b + a \cdot c$$

The truth of these laws depends in part on the denseness of the real numbers on the number line or, equivalently, on the ability of numbers to have arbitrarily large numbers of digits. Due to the finiteness of computer arithmetic, these laws are not generally satisfied on computers, although the commutative laws for addition,

$$a + b = b + a$$

and for multiplication,

$$a \cdot b = b \cdot a$$

are generally satisfied. The failure of the associative and distributive laws to be satisfied affects relatively few computations, but on occasion such failure can be crucial. For a further discussion of this see Ralston (1971).

### References

1963, Flores, I. *The Logic of Computer Arithmetic*. Englewood Cliffs, N.J.: Prentice-Hall.

1969. Knuth, D. E. "Seminumerical Algorithms," in *The Art of Computer Programming*, vol. 2. Reading, Mass.: Addison-Wesley. (This book is *the* reference on the algorithms by which computer arithmetic is performed.)

1971. Ralston, A. *Introduction to Programming and Computer Science*. New York: McGraw-Hill.

1974. Sterbenz, P. H. *Floating-Point Computation*. Englewood Cliffs, N.J.: Prentice-Hall.

A. Ralston

# ARITHMETIC-LOGIC UNIT

For articles on related subjects *see* Adder; Arithmetic, Computer; Boolean Algebra; Codes; Machine Instruction Set; Numbers and Number Systems; Operand; Register; and Shifting.
For articles on related terms *see* Algorithm; Multiprocessing; Stack; and Word Length, Variable.

The ALU is a functional part of the digital computer which carries out arithmetic and logic operations on machine words that represent the operands. It is usually considered to be a part of the central processing unit (CPU). In some computer systems, separate units exist for arithmetic operations (the arithmetic unit, AU) and for logic operations (the logic unit, LU).

Many computers contain more than one AU. For example, a separate Index AU is frequently employed to perform addition or subtraction operations on address parts of instructions for the purpose of indexing, boundary tests for memory protection, etc. Large computer systems employ separate AUs for different classes of algorithms; for example, the IBM System 360, Model 91, contains a fixed-point AU and a floating-point AU. Multiprocessor systems contain several identical ALUs; for example, the ILLIAC IV contains 64 identical ALUs with associated memory modules.

A complete discussion of an ALU must describe its three fundamental attributes:

1. Operands and results.
2. Functional organization.
3. Algorithms.

**Operands and Results.** Two kinds of ALU organizations can be distinguished with respect to the length of machine words. In machines with *fixed* word length, all words consist of the same number of bits. In machines with variable word length, one byte is the shortest machine word; a typical length of one byte is eight bits. Longer machine words consist of some integral number of bytes.

The operands and results of the ALU are machine words of two kinds: *arithmetic words*, which represent numerical values in digital form, and *logic words*, which represent arbitrary sets of digitally encoded symbols.

Arithmetic words consist of strings of digits. Conventional radix $r$ number representations allow

$r$ values for one digit: 0, 1, . . ., $r - 1$. Practical design considerations have limited the choice of radices to the values 2, 4, 8, 10, and 16. The value of every digit is represented by a set of bits. Radices 2, 4, 8, and 16 employ binary numbers having length of 1, 2, 3, and 4 bits, respectively, to represent the values of one digit. Radix-10 digit values are usually represented by four or five bits. Most commonly used are the four-bit BCD (binary coded decimal) and excess-3, and the five-bit biquinary encodings.

Two methods have been employed to represent negative numbers. In the sign-and-magnitude form, a separate *sign bit* is attached to the string of digits to represent the + and − signs. (Usually 0 represents the +, and 1 represents the − sign.) In the true-and-complement form, the negative value $-x$ is represented as the complement with respect to $A$ of the value $x$; i.e.,

$$-x \text{ is represented by } A - x$$

Two values of $A$ are used in ALUs: $A = r^{n+1}$ and $A = r^{n+1} - 1$, when $x$ is represented by $n$ digits in the sign-and-magnitude form. An illustration for radix 10 and radix 2 and $n = 4$ is given below.

| Sign and Magnitude | $A = 10^5 - 1$ (9s complement) | $A = 10^5$ (10s complement) |
|---|---|---|
| +4902 | 04902 | 04902 |
| −4902 | 95097 | 95098 |
| | $A = 2^5 - 1$ (1s complement) | $A = 2^5$ (2s complement) |
| +1010 | 01010 | 01010 |
| −1010 | 10101 | 10110 |

The use of complements to represent negative values makes it possible to replace the subtraction algorithm in an ALU by a complementation followed by an addition modulo $A$.

Other important properties of operands and results are (Avižienis, 1972):

1. Location of the radix point.
2. Use of multiple-precision representations.
3. Use of floating-point forms.
4. Explicit designation of the number of significant digits in a representation.
5. Encoding in error-detecting (or error-correcting) codes.

The use of nonconventional number representations in computers as a means to increase the speed of arithmetic has been proposed. Extensive studies have been made of *residue* number systems (Svoboda, 1962) and of *signed-digit* number systems (Avižienis and Tung, 1970); however, they have not yet reached practical application in ALU design.

Logic words that serve as operands represent alphanumeric information and are subject only to logic algorithms that are applied to individual bits of the operands. These algorithms are (1) negation for one operand, and (2) the 16 two-variable logic operations for corresponding bits of two operands.

**Functional Organization and Algorithms of an ALU.** An ALU consists of three types of functional parts: storage registers, operation circuits, and sequencing circuits, as shown in Fig. 1. The inputs and outputs of the ALU are connected to other functional units of the computer, such as the main memory, the program execution control unit, and input/output devices. A bus is most frequently used as the means of connection. In some cases the ALU may be connected to two or more busses within the computer system.

The input information received by the ALU consists of operands, operation codes, and format codes. The operands are machine words that represent numeric or alphanumeric information in the

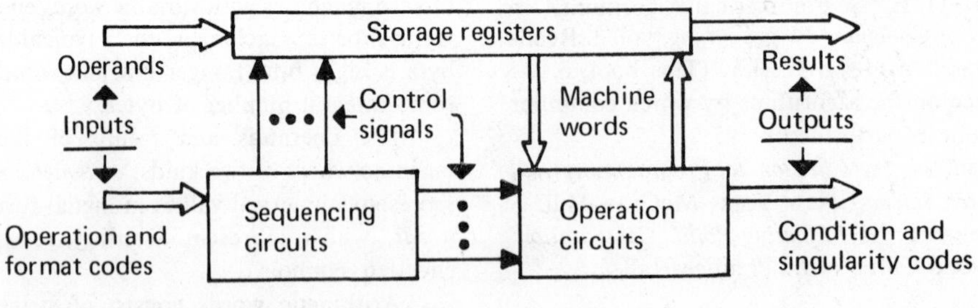


**Fig. 1.** Functions of an ALU.

form of a string of binary digits (bits). The operation code identifies one operation from the set of available arithmetic and logic operations, and also designates the location (within local storage) of the operands and of the results. The designation of operands is omitted in ALUs with limited local storage; for example, an ADD operation code in a single-accumulator ALU always means the addition of the incoming operand to the operand in the accumulator register and storage of the sum in the accumulator. The format code is used when the ALU can operate on more than one type of operand; for example, the ADD operation can be specified either for fixed-point or for floating-point operands. Often the operation code and the format code are represented by a single set of bits.

The output information delivered by the ALU consists of results, condition codes, and singularity codes. The results are machine words generated by the specified operations and stored in the local storage registers. The condition codes are bits or sets of bits that identify specific conditions associated with a result, such as that the value of the result is positive, negative, zero; that the result consists of all zeros, all ones, etc. The singularity codes indicate that the specified operation does not yield a representable result. Examples of singularities are: "overflow," i.e., the value of the result exceeds the allowed range; attempted division by zero; excessive loss of precision in floating-point operations; error caused by a logic fault, etc. Singularity codes usually set a flip-flop in the machine status word.

Internally, the ALU is composed of storage registers, logic circuits that perform arithmetic and logic algorithms, and logic circuits that control the sequence of gating operations within the ALU. The diagram of a simple ALU is shown in Fig. 2.

The ALU contains three registers: the operand register, OPR; the accumulator register, ACC; and the multiplier-quotient register, MQR. Each register contains one machine word, i.e., for a machine word length of *n* bits, the register consists of *n* flip-flops.

The gating of words into the ALU registers and from the registers into the operation circuits or out of the ALU is controlled by the sequencing logic (SL), which applies a sequence of gate-enabling signals to the gates $G_i$ of Fig. 2. Each sequence corresponds to one of the algorithms provided within

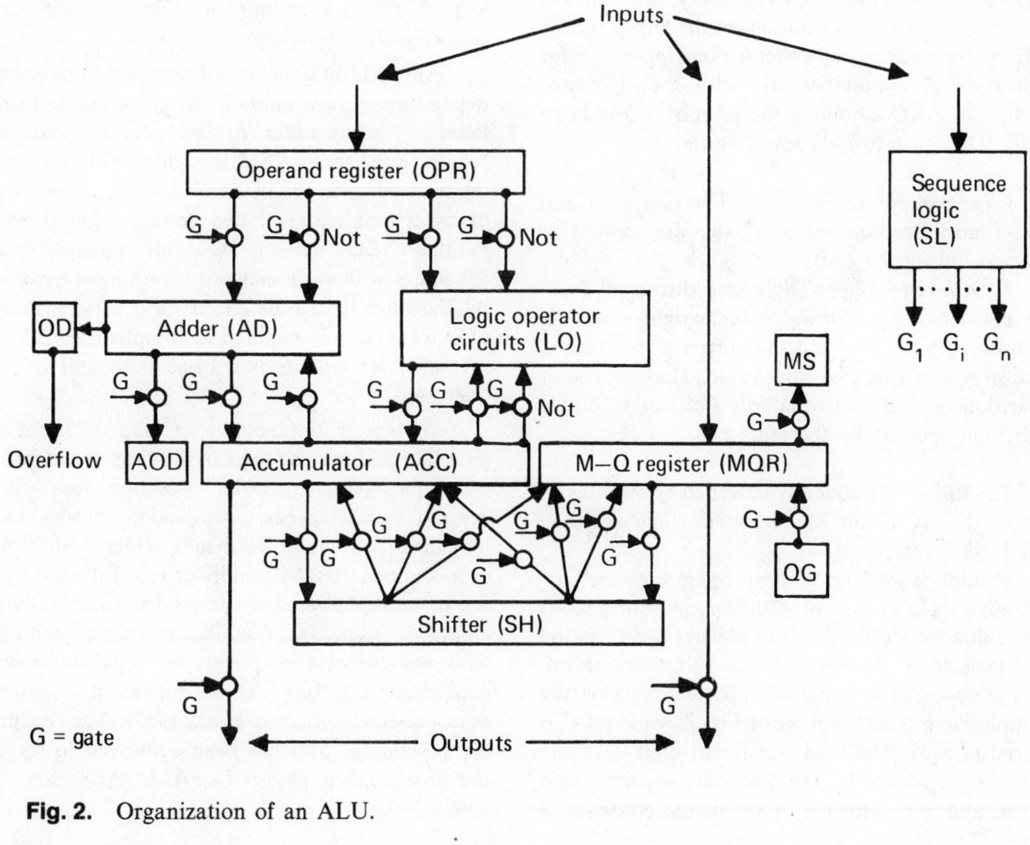


**Fig. 2.** Organization of an ALU.

the ALU. The sequencing logic is implemented either in "hard wired" form, using counters and decoding circuits, or by means of a microprogrammed control unit. The sequence of gating signals is initiated by the receipt of the operation and format codes in the ALU.

The operation circuits consist of the adder (AD), the shifter (SH), and the logic operator circuits (LO). The adder forms the sum of the numbers in OPR and ACC and returns it to the ACC. When the length of the sum exceeds the standard word length, the overflow detection (OD) circuit issues an overflow singularity code, and the excess digit of the sum is placed into an overflow digit position (AOD) which is located at the left end of the ACC. Subtraction is usually implemented as complementation of the subtrahend in OPR, followed by its addition to the minuend in ACC. A subtractor may be used instead of an adder in Fig. 2; in this case, subtraction is carried out directly, and addition is implemented as the complementation of the addend in OPR followed by its subtraction from the augend in ACC.

The SH circuits perform left-shift and right-shift operations on the words in ACC and MQR. A single-shift operation displaces every digit in the register to the adjacent position on the left or on the right. Shifts are specified either for one register or for both registers simultaneously, with the rightmost position of ACC adjoining the leftmost position of MQR. There are two classes of shifts:

1. *Circular (or Logic) Shifts*. The rightmost and the leftmost positions of a register are treated as adjacent during the shift.
2. *Arithmetic Shifts*. Digits are discarded from end positions; e.g., during a single right shift, the rightmost digit is lost and the leftmost position is filled in with a specified digit value. The purpose of an arithmetic shift is to multiply (left) or to divide (right) the operand by the radix $r$.

The shifter is frequently designed as an integral part of the ACC and MQ registers; they are then called "shift registers."

Multiplication and division operations are carried out as a sequence of additions or subtractions and arithmetic shifts. The MQ register serves as the third register for these operations. In multiplication, the multiplicand $x$ is placed into OP register, the multiplier $y$ into MQ register of Fig. 2, while ACC is cleared to zero. The least significant digit $y_0$ of the multiplier is sensed by the multiplier sensing (MS) circuit, and $x$ is added $y_0$ times to the contents of ACC. Then ACC and MQ registers are arithmetically shifted one position to the right, and the next multiplier digit, $y_1$, is sensed by the MS circuit. After all $n$ digits of $y$ have been sensed, the double-length product $xy$ is located in ACC and MQ registers. A round-off operation is needed to reduce the product to single-word length.

To perform division, the dividend is placed into ACC. If the dividend is of double length, MQ register receives its less significant half. The divisor is placed into OP register, and division is carried out as a sequence of trial subtractions and left arithmetic shifts. Quotient digits are generated one at a time in the quotient generation (QG) circuit and inserted at the right end of the MQ register after each shift, beginning with the most significant quotient digit, $q_{n-1}$. After $n$ steps, the quotient is located in MQ register and the remainder in the ACC register.

The logic operator LO circuits perform the specified logic operation on pairs of bits in corresponding storage positions $a_i$ of ACC and $x_i$ of OP registers. The bits of the result are returned to ACC. The usual set of operations includes NOT (one bit: $\bar{a}_i$ or $\bar{x}_i$), AND ($a_i \wedge x_i$), OR ($a_i \vee x_i$), EXCLUSIVE-OR ($a_i \oplus x_i$), EQUIVALENCE ($a_i \equiv x_i$), NAND ($\bar{a}_i \vee \bar{x}_i$) and NOR ($\bar{a}_i \wedge \bar{x}_i$); sometimes all 16 two-variable logic operations are provided.

An ALU may be serial, byte-serial, or parallel, depending on how many digits are processed simultaneously in the adder (or logic operator) circuits of Fig. 2. In the serial ALU, the adder adds one pair of digits at once; in the byte-serial ALU, it adds a pair of bytes (consisting of two or more digits); in the parallel ALU, it adds two full machine words. Machines with variable word length have byte-serial ALUs, since the words consist of a varying number of bytes. The time required to complete one addition in the adder circuits is a basic time unit of ALU operation.

The speed of execution of the algorithms in a parallel ALU may be increased by the use of various techniques (Garner, 1965). Addition speed is increased by use of carry-completion sensing, carry-lookahead, or conditional-sum adders. Multiplication is accelerated by multiplier recoding and by the use of multiple-operand carry-save adders. Division employs redundant quotient recoding techniques with approximate estimates, or quadratic convergence which utilizes fast multiplication to generate the quotient (Anderson et al., 1967). The technique of "pipelining" also has been employed to increase the effective throughput of an ALU (Anderson et al., 1967).

The use of more storage registers within the ALU increases the speed of computing by reducing the number of memory accesses. Therefore, 8, 16, or more ALU registers are often used instead of the three registers shown in Fig. 2; each register may perform the function of ACC, OP, or MQ registers. Several ALU registers may be used to hold a *stack* of ALU operands and results.

Some ALUs provide a more extensive set of algorithms, including square root, complex arithmetic, trigonometric functions, etc. Such ALUs are most often found in special-purpose computers.

REFERENCES

1962. Svoboda, A. "The Numerical System of Residual Classes," in *Digital Information Processors*. New York: Interscience, pp. 543–574.

1965. Garner, H. L. "Number Systems and Arithmetic," in F. L. Alt (Ed.), *Advances in Computers*, vol. 6. New York Academic Press, pp. 131–194.

1967. Anderson, S. F., J. G. Earle, R. E. Goldschmidt, D. M. Powers. "The IBM System/360 Model 91: Floating-Point Execution Unit," *IBM Journal of Research and Development*, vol. 11, No. 1 (January), pp. 34–53.

1970. Avižienis A., and C. Tung. "A Universal Arithmetic Building Element (ABE) and Design Methods for Arithmetic Processors," *IEEE Trans. Comput.*, vol. C-19, No. 8 (August) pp. 733–745.

1972. Avižienis, A. "Digital Computer Arithmetic: A Unified Algorithmic Specification," in *Computers and Automata*. Brooklyn, N. Y.: Polytechnic Institute, pp. 509–525.

A. AVIŽIENIS

## ARITHMETIC SCAN

For articles on related subjects *see* LANGUAGE PROCESSORS; POLISH NOTATION; and PRECEDENCE.

In the process of compilation into machine executable code of a program written in a higher-level language, the procedure for examining arithmetic expressions and determining the order of execution of the operators is often referred to as the "arithmetic scan." Since arithmetic expressions are well formed in that they possess regular properties related to the operands and the operators, many specialized parsing or scanning techniques have been developed. One possible, but impractical, technique is to require the programmer to write arithmetic expressions in fully parenthesized notation (i.e., parentheses must be placed around each pair of operands and its associated operator) so as to obviate the need for knowledge about the relationships between operators in determining the order in which the operations are to be performed.

Most commonly used are transformational systems, which convert the normal infix form (i.e., the form in which the operator is placed between its operands) to a Polish form in which there exists no parentheses and the order of execution of the operators is specified by their positioning. Such a system is needed because of the difficulty of associating operands with operators in infix notation. As an example, consider the Fortran expression

$$(A * X + B)/(C * X + D) \qquad (1)$$

which, because of the *precedence* relations among Fortran arithmetic operators, is to be interpreted in fully parenthesized notation, as

$$(((A*X)+B)/((C*X)+D)) \qquad (2)$$

By use of an algorithm (see Ralston, 1971), which scans across the string in expression (1) from left to right just once, this string can be converted to the Polish postfix string

$$AX*B+CX*D-/ \qquad (3)$$

which, without a need for parentheses or precedence relations, has only the interpretation of expression (2). With one more single scan across the string, it can be compiled into machine code.

The arithmetic scan described above is a special case of a general syntactic analyzer that uses precedence relationships.

REFERENCES

1971. Ralston, A. *An Introduction to Programming and Computer Science*. New York: McGraw-Hill.

J. A. N. LEE AND A. RALSTON

## ARPA NETWORK

For articles on related subjects *see* COMPUTER NETWORKS; DATA COMMUNICATIONS; INTERFACE MESSAGE PROCESSOR; and TELEPROCESSING SYSTEMS.
For article on related term *see* HOST SYSTEM.

In 1968 the Advanced Research Projects Agency (ARPA) of the U.S. Department of Defense embarked on a project to implement a nationwide computer network, called the ARPA network, or simply ARPANET. This network allows a large number of dissimilar computers, called "hosts," to communicate with each other. The major goals of the network are to

1. Permit computer resource sharing whereby programs, data, storage, special purpose hardware, etc., can be shared among many computers and users.
2. Develop highly reliable and economic digital communications.
3. Permit access to unique and powerful facilities that are economically feasible only when widely shared.

In late 1975 the network consisted of about 60 nodes and was expanding at the rate of about one node every three months.

**Fig. 1.** A terminal interface message processor.

**Network Properties.** Each host is connected to the network via a small local computer called the Interface Message Processor (IMP), shown in Fig. 1. Each IMP in turn is connected to several other IMPs via 50 kilobit/sec communication lines. Terminal IMPs (TIPs) with flexible terminal-handling capabilities are also available to provide a wide variety of terminals direct access to the network. Fig. 2 shows the geographic and logical maps of the network plus the computers at each node, and Table 1 shows the site abbreviations. Note that the network is multiconnected; i.e., more than one path exists between any pair of nodes. The topology was selected to provide good response times and high reliability, and have good growth potential while keeping costs to a minimum.

Message switching rather than circuit switching is used to establish communication between nodes. In a circuit-switched network, the source and destination are connected by a dedicated communication path established at the beginning of the connection and broken only at the end. In a message-switched system such as ARPANET, no dedicated path exists. Instead, a source host or terminal passes its message, including a destination address, to its local IMP or TIP. The message is then passed from IMP to IMP until it finally arrives at its destination. The choice of the path is determined dynamically. Each IMP forwards the message on the path it determines best to assure prompt delivery, taking into account the network loading and failures. The current design allows variable length messages of up to 8095 bits. To improve transit times, the IMPs partition messages into 1024-bit packets and send them one after the other. Since more than one path exists between any two hosts, it is thus possible that the individual packets of a given message actually travel by different paths, depending upon the loading at that particular time.

Three steps have been taken to insure reliability. These include a multiconnected network, a 24-bit cyclic redundancy check, and an IMP that is ruggedly constructed for protection against external environmental conditions. The cyclic check is used for error detection, with correction by retransmission. This reduces transmission errors to less than one bit in $10^{12}$. Because of the multiconnections between IMPs, a single line failure will not isolate a node, nor will it prevent the flow of messages through the network. At least two adjacent line failures or an IMP failure are required to isolate a node. Once again, this will not prevent all other nodes from using the net.

The capacity of the network is the throughput rate at which saturation occurs, and is a function of the topology and capacity of the transmission lines, the distribution of traffic, and the average size of blocks being sent. The capacity can be easily improved by adding additional lines or upgrading some lines from 50 to 230.4 kilobits/sec (TELPAK C channel). To enable interaction, the target is that the transit time from any node to any other node for a 1000-bit packet should be less than 0.5 sec, with an average of 0.2 sec.

**Special Network Centers.** In any distributed system such as the ARPANET, it is difficult to detect failures quickly. For this reason, a special Network Control Center (NCC) has been established at Bolt, Beranek, and Newman to continuously monitor line or IMP failures and the volumes of host and line traffic. The IMPs are also equipped with automatic reloading facilities. This enables the NCC to reload any IMP with a copy of the operating program in case of revisions or an IMP memory crash.

There is also a Network Information Center (NIC) at Stanford Research Institute. This is a powerful on-line system, implemented on a PDP-10 computer, to provide ARPANET users with information on hardware and software resources available at each node of the network.

**The Future of ARPANET.** ARPANET has proved that message-switched networks are well adapted to interconnection of diverse computers and terminals. Since the network is operational and growing, it is conceivable that it will shift from a government-supported research and development activity to some national service organization. During its development, many vital questions concerning large computer resource-sharing networks have been answered. Nevertheless, technical improvements in the existing network will continue.

Projects currently under way include the development of IMPs capable of coping with data rates in excess of 1 million bits/sec and a study of the feasibility of using satellite communication channels. Problems include the type of operational procedures large networks should follow and the way in which programs and widely different operating systems should communicate with each other. Answers to

**Table 1.** Site Abbreviations

| | |
|---|---|
| ABERDEEN | Aberdeen Research and Development Center |
| AMES | NASA Ames Research Center |
| ARPA | Advanced Research Projects Agency |
| BBN | Bolt, Beranek, and Newman |
| BELVOIR | Fort Belvoir, USAMERDC |
| CASE | Case Western Reserve University |
| CCA | Computer Corporation of America |
| CMU | Carnegie-Mellon University |
| DOCB | Department of Commerce, Boulder |
| ETAC | Environmental Technical Applications Center, USAF |
| FNWC | Fleet Numerical Weather Center |
| GWC | Global Weather Center |
| HARVARD | Harvard University |
| HAWAII | University of Hawaii |
| ILLINOIS | University of Illinois |
| LBL | Lawrence Berkeley Laboratory |
| LLL | Lawrence Livermore Laboratory |
| LINCOLN | MIT Lincoln Laboratory |
| LONDON | University College, London |
| MIT-IPC | Massachusetts Inst. of Technology, Inf. Proc. Services |
| MIT-MAC | Massachusetts Inst. of Technology, Project MAC |
| MITRE | MITRE Corporation |
| MOFFET | Moffet Field, USAF |
| NBS | National Bureau of Standards |
| NCC | Network Control Center at BBN |
| NORSAR | Norwegian Seismic Array |
| RADC | Rome Air Development Center |
| RAND | Rand Corporation |
| RML | Range Measurement Lab., Patrick AF Base |
| RUTGERS | Rutgers University |
| SCRL | Special Communication Research Laboratory |
| SDAC | Seismic Data Array Center |
| SDC | Systems Development Corporation |
| SRI | Stanford Research Institute |
| STANFORD | Stanford University |
| TYMSHARE | Tymshare Corporation |
| UCLA | University of California at Los Angeles |
| UCSB | University of California at Santa Barbara |
| UCSD | University of California at San Diego |
| UNIVAC | Univac Corporation |
| USC | University of Southern California |
| USC-ISI | University of Southern California, Infor. Sciences Inst. |
| WPAFB | Wright Patterson AF Base |
| XEROX | Xerox Corporation |

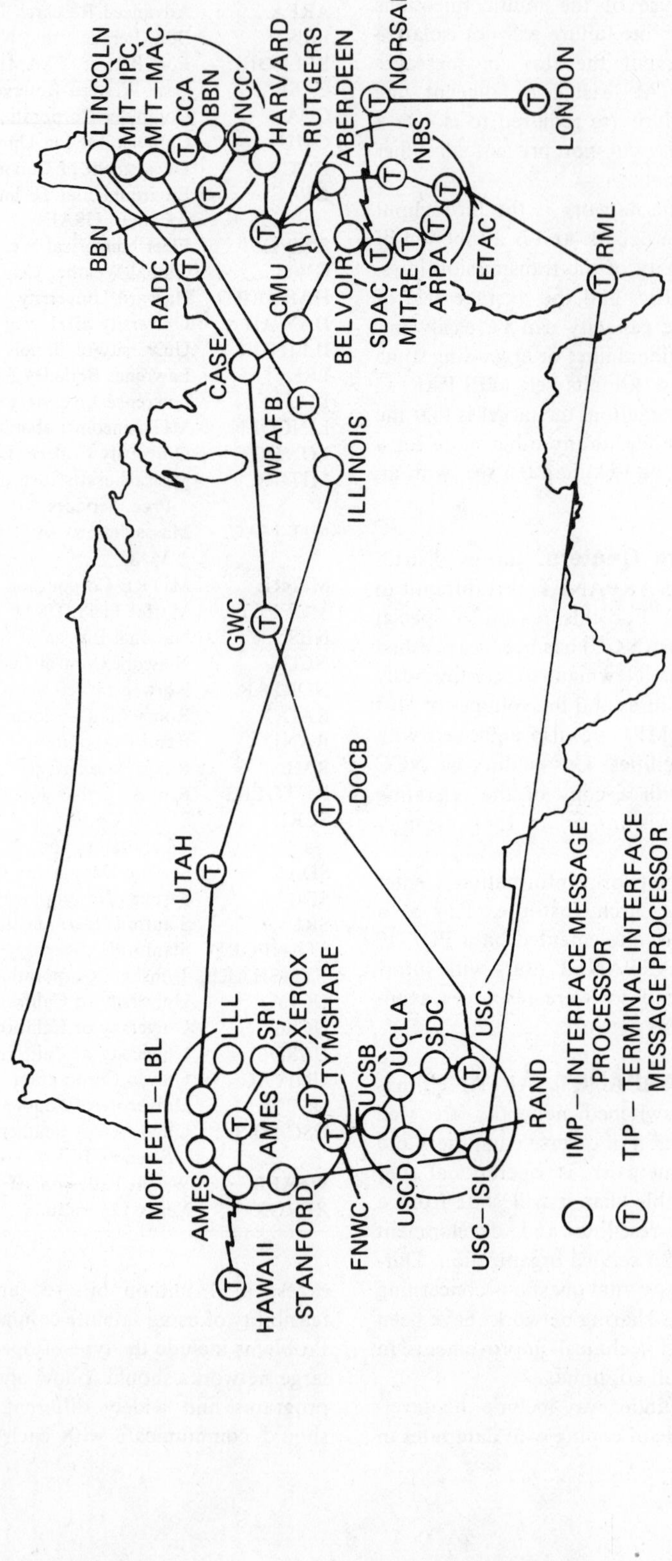
BBN
LINCOLN
MIT–IPC
MIT–MAC
CCA
BBN
NCC
HARVARD
RUTGERS
ABERDEEN
NORSAR
LONDON
NBS
RADC
CMU
BELVOIR
SDAC
MITRE
ARPA
ETAC
RML
CASE
WPAFB
ILLINOIS
GWC
DOCB
UTAH
MOFFETT–LBL
LLL
SRI
XEROX
TYMSHARE
AMES
AMES
HAWAII
STANFORD
FNWC
UCSB
UCLA
SDC
USC
RAND
USCD
USC–ISI
T
IMP – INTERFACE MESSAGE PROCESSOR
TIP – TERMINAL INTERFACE MESSAGE PROCESSOR

(a)

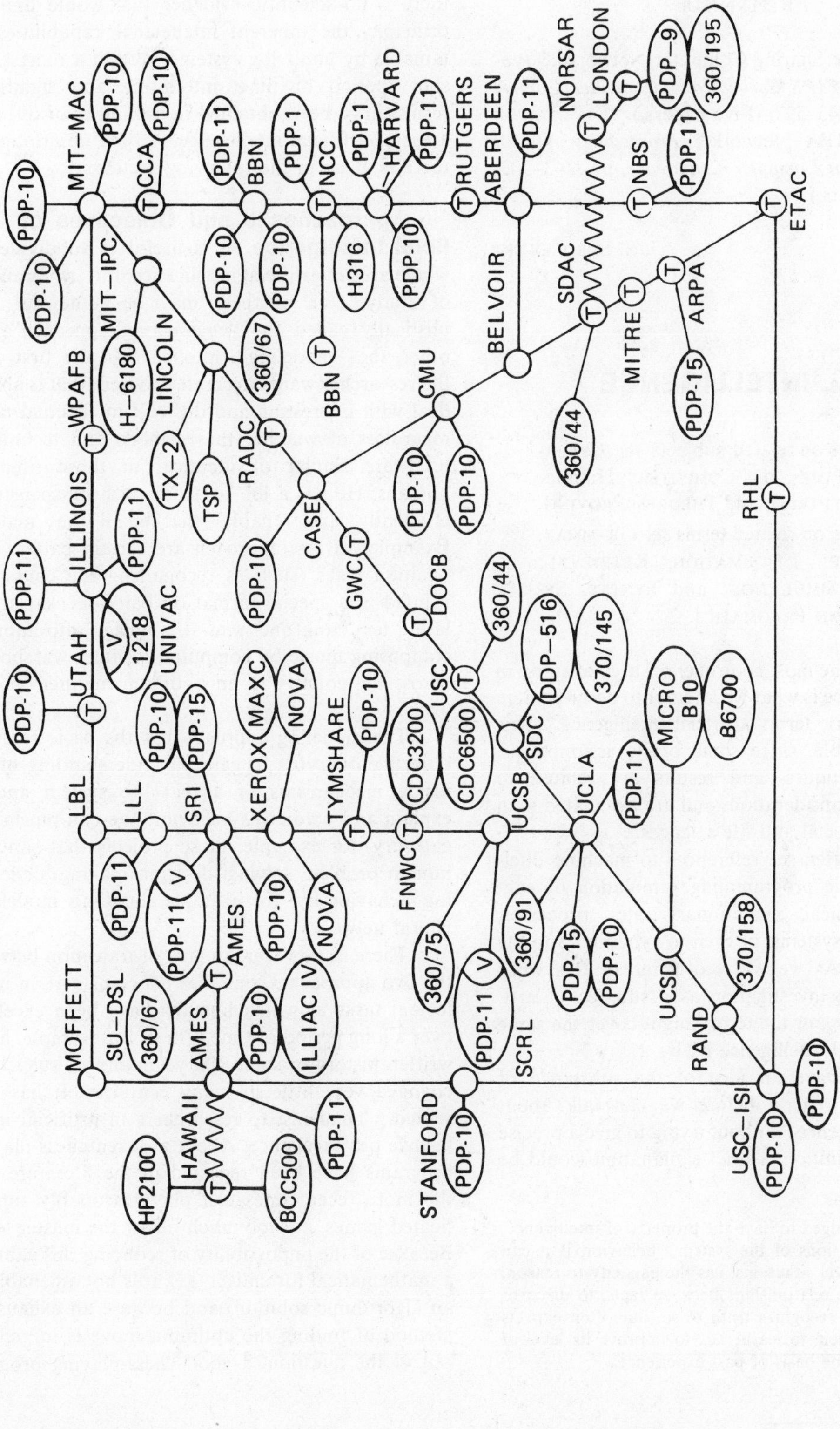


(b)

**Fig. 2.** Geographical (a) and logical (b) maps of the ARPA network issued by Bolt Beranek and Newman Inc.

these problems will lead to the improved use of computers.

REFERENCES

1970. "Resource Sharing Computer Networks," *Proceedings AFIPS Spring Joint Computer Conference*, pp. 543–597. (Five papers.)

1972. "The ARPA Network," *Proceedings AFIPS Spring Joint Computer Conference*, pp. 243–303. (Five papers.)

J. S. SOBOLEWSKI

## ARTIFICIAL INTELLIGENCE

For articles on related subjects *see* CYBERNETICS; GAMES ON COMPUTERS; HEURISTICS; PERCEPTRON; and THEOREM PROVING. For articles on related terms *see* GRAMMAR, REDUCTIVE; INFORMATION RETRIEVAL; MODELS; SIMULATION; and SYNTAX, SEMANTICS AND PRAGMATICS.

Probably the most controversial area of study in computer science is what we attempt to describe here under the generic term "artificial intelligence." This is understandable, since some of its assumptions, methods, techniques, and results are related to philosophical considerations and are associated with the nonexact social and life sciences.

One can often see references to machine intelligence, heuristic programming, simulation of cognitive, biophysical, evolutionary, etc., processes, self-organizing systems, or even to cybernetics in the same context. As we will see, some of this work could represent investigation as a subarea of artificial intelligence, or the terms might cover the same area as artificial intelligence itself.

We must have an idea of the substance of intelligence in general before we can talk about artificial intelligence. Without trying to give a precise and formal definition, a brief explanation would be that

> ... a system is judged to have the property of intelligence, based on observations of the system's behavior, if it can adapt itself to novel situations, has the capacity to reason, to understand the relationships between facts, to discover meanings, and to recognize truth. Also, one often expects an intelligent system to learn; i.e., to improve its level of performance on the basis of past experiences.

This loose but suggestive definition might be applied to nonliving systems or artifacts as well as to humans and animals. In fact, it must be stated that there is no scientific evidence that would limit, in principle, the inherent intellectual capabilities attainable by nonliving systems. Within a remarkably short period of time, interesting and significant results have been obtained in a number of different areas of artificial intelligence. A brief description of these is given in the following sections.

**Approaches to and Objectives of Artificial Intelligence.** It is useful to subdivide the whole area of artificial intelligence into two branches of study. One of these may be somewhat simplistically called the "engineering approach"; the other, the "modeling approach." In the first case, the researcher wants to create a system that is able to deal with interesting and difficult intellectual tasks, regardless of whether the methods and techniques used are similar or identical to those used by humans. He has a job to accomplish inexpensively, efficiently, and reliably—that is all that matters. Examples of this approach are certain pattern recognition tasks (such as recognizing the characters printed in a special format on bank checks), translating text from one natural language into another, composing music by computer, locating warehouses across the country in an optimum manner, and so on.

The modeling approach has the basic research objective of trying to gain an understanding of the inside mechanisms of a real life system and to explain and predict its behavior. We can put in this category, for example, those projects that simulate human problem solving, decision making, or learning behavior by, for example, building models of neural networks.

There is, however, an area of transition between the two approaches, one that concerns certain intellectual tasks at which humans have been excellent over a long period of time. Chess, for example, has a written history of some 400 years and its rules have changed very little in many centuries. It has presented a challenge to researchers in artificial intelligence par excellence. About a dozen chess-playing programs have been reported in the literature and the more recent ones can play reasonably sophisticated games, not too much below the master level. Because of the impossibility of reducing this game to a mathematical formalism (i.e., it is not amenable to an algorithmic solution) and because an exhaustive method of finding the optimum move is in general out of the question, a good chess-playing program has to incorporate so-called heuristics. These are based on loosely formulated rules of thumb that are occasionally referred to as "insight," "intuition," or simply "experience."

In other words, the knowledge of how humans perform certain tasks is indispensable to and must be incorporated into those programs whose main objective is to accomplish these intellectual tasks as well as possible.

We can now briefly enumerate the three basic motivations for research in artificial intelligence:

1. To replace human intelligence because the latter is expensive, scarce, and often less than reliable.
2. To establish theories of human intelligence in the form of simulation models.
3. To assess the capabilities of presently available software and hardware, and to point to lines of development for future programming languages and computer systems.

**Three Fundamental Problems.** In the following discussion a large number of study areas will be outlined. Three problems are common among all these areas and it is therefore advisable to examine them briefly at this stage.

Problem of Representation. The selection and design of representation is a central issue in programming in general. How a particular task is translated into information structures and information processes inside the computer may render the solution of the task efficient and effective, or so cumbersome that it is prohibitively unwieldy.

One of the long-term objectives of artificial intelligence research is to automate the processes that make the decision on a particular representation after the specification of the task has been given, possibly in natural language. At present, however, the information structures and processes are chosen ad hoc and are assumed to be quasi-optimum for the task at hand. This task dependence in representation has obvious shortcomings.

Generality versus Efficiency. Human intelligence is multipurpose by nature. The majority of projects in the study of artificial intelligence have, however, resulted in somewhat narrow and single-minded programs whose efficiency is reasonably high. As soon as the range of applicability of a program increases, its level of complexity rises, but its efficiency in solving individual problems drops.

Again, a long-term objective is to write highly efficient programs of "universal" applicability. A plausible avenue to this goal is via learning programs that can initially tackle simple problems and gradually acquire more and more power for a larger number of, and more difficult, problems. Also, a reasonable level of success has already been achieved with programs that subdivide a large and difficult task into smaller, possibly known ones. This technique has to be developed further.

Problem of Search. It is often the case that one can write a program that generates potential solutions to a problem, tests them, and, hopefully, sometimes discovers the right ones. With nontrivial problems, however, the "solution space" is very large, for practical purposes infinite, and there can be no exhaustive search performed. It has been, for example, estimated that in order to find the best possible starting move in chess, the machine would have to evaluate $10^{120}$ game positions. It has also been pointed out that if a computer consisting of all the elementary particles in the universe could be constructed and run with the speed of light, the current estimate of the age of the universe would not have been long enough to find the best first move according to the exhaustive search strategy.

It would therefore be a good idea to direct the search process by detecting relative improvements as the program moves around in the domain of all potential solutions. Heuristic rules should be built in or, in a more sophisticated manner, automatically generated by the program to recognize the structure of the search space and thereby cut down the computing time and memory requirements. Although many efficient search techniques have been developed in various studies in artificial intelligence, there is a great need for further work in this area.

Finally, it should be noted in a nonapologetic manner that the area discussed, like the majority of the branches of computer science, has a predominantly experimental flavor. Although more and more theoretical foundation is being developed in several directions, the basic motive of experimentation is likely to prevail in the foreseeable future.

**Research Topics in Artificial Intelligence.** Mechanical and electromechanical toys have been built for a long time to demonstrate certain goal-oriented behavior. More recent ones (by Shannon, MacKay, Ashby, etc.) have shown certain *cybernetic* principles involving negative feedback concerning, for example, the recharge state of their batteries. The robot projects currently pursued at Stanford University, Stanford Research Institute (see Fig. 1), M.I.T., and various Japanese and British laboratories, go well beyond them in sophistication. The robots not only can perceive visual stimuli via

**Fig. 1.** "Shakey," a robot project of the Artificial Intelligence Center of Stanford University.

television cameras but are also equipped with tactile receptors and some effectors to move, for example, wooden blocks around. The controlling computer may communicate with the robot via cables or radio signals, or the robot may carry the computer along its adventurous path.

These projects aim at integrating the many piecemeal results of artificial intelligence research, from theorem proving to pattern recognition and picture processing, from learning and problem-solving techniques to natural language processing and to question-answering systems. Beyond the interest in basic research, workers in this field hope to make use of their results in planetary or underwater exploration and in areas where human access is difficult or impossible.

Simulation of neurological and physiological phenomena often consists of building a computer model of a network of (idealized) nerve cells. These networks are self-adaptive; i.e., they can be trained to recognize audio and visual patterns by changing certain parametric values or the interconnections between them. One of the most remarkable of these experiments was made by Rochester, Holland, Haibt, and Duda to test Hebb's verbally described theory of neural cell assembly. They discovered some flaws in the assumptions, and after making some extensions of the model, they were able to show the learning capability of the network.

Rosenblatt and his coworkers investigated a class of random nets of neuron-like elements, called "perceptrons." Their mathematical analysis was recently extended by Minsky and Papert. The EEG-like output of permanently connected nonlinear elements was demonstrated by Farley. Wooldridge and Broadbent tried in various studies to describe the activity of the brain in terms of electric circuitry.

Another idea of somewhat limited success by Fogel and others was to simulate the evolution of intelligence from its most primitive beginnings via mutations and natural selection.

Several projects have simulated robots in environments of varying complexity (Doran, Toda, Findler, and Allan). Planning and search behavior have been interesting aspects of these works. The problems of heuristic search have often formed the basis of some abstract investigations (Sandewall, Pohl, Nielsson), sometimes in connection with the special task of the Graph Traverser (Michie, Doran, Marsh, Ross). Techniques of tree search are of primary interest in game playing and theorem-proving programs.

The simulation of cognitive processes will now be discussed in some detail. (Affective processes involving motivation, ambition, etc., have been considered by Simon, Findler, and others.) The basic tenet here is that man's complex behavior can be analyzed and broken down into elementary symbol manipulation processes. The computer can be programmed in terms of these elementary building blocks to perform the same information-processing tasks that humans do. The computer program, representing a psychological theory of various behavioral phenomena, becomes a convenient vehicle to determine objectively the implications of the model. The need for precise formulation in the program leaves no room for vagueness, ambiguity, and lack of rigor. A comparison with experimental data may lead to modifications in the model until the researcher is satisfied that he has constructed a sufficient theory. According to Newell and Simon, human thinking can be explained in information processing terms without waiting for a theory of the underlying neurological mechanisms.

An often used technique for finding out about the details of human thought processes is to make the experimental subject utter the reasons behind every step of his activity verbally into a tape recorder ("thinking aloud"). A detailed analysis of these "protocols" would lead to a flowchart of the subject's behavior. (Newell and his students have obtained promising results in trying to automate the process of analysis.) The flowchart is then translated into a program, several variants of which can be run to simulate different individuals.

Three classical pieces of work along these lines were produced by Newell, Shaw, and Simon. The first one, the *Logic Theorist*, is a heuristic theorem-proving program for the first-order predicate calculus. Its original version could prove 38 of the 52 theorems in Chapter 2 of Whitehead and Russell's *Principia Mathematica*.

The second work, the *General Problem Solver* (GPS), has been able to separate to a significant extent problem-solving techniques and task environments. The so-called means-ends analysis lies at the center of the program. It goes as follows: The present and the desired objects are given ("object" in the most general sense of the word). GPS discovers the difference between them and tries to find an operator (i.e., a transformation) relevant to this difference. If successful, the task is accomplished. Otherwise, it attempts to bridge over the much too large difference by creating objects in between the present and the desired objects. In this recursive manner, either it produces a sequence of operators that is the solution of the problem or it reports failure. The latter may also be due to the fact that the program has exceeded the prespecified time limit or has run out of memory. This basic paradigm of problem solving has penetrated many projects, including the Newell, Shaw, Simon chess program, which is the third piece of work referred to above.

Concept learning has been the target of several simulation models (Hunt, Holland, Johnson, Baker, and others). The behavior of these programs reflects the attribute and rule-learning characteristics of humans. The detection of temporal sequences implies an understanding of event generation in order to predict future members of the sequence. Simon and Kotovsky, Abrahams et al., D. S. Williams, and others have written programs to simulate humans in these tasks. The first of this kind of program was in fact Feldman's *Binary Choice Model*, which reproduced even the idiosyncratic behavior of several individuals.

The elementary perceiver and memorizer (EPAM) by Feigenbaum and Simon (1963) represents a theory of human memory and models the learning of associated nonsense syllables, a standard psychological test. It reproduces the increasing discriminative ability, retroactive inhibition, stimulus generalization, response oscillation, and other phenomena usually pinpointed and analyzed by psychologists conducting tests on experimental subjects.

Two other complex information-processing models also have an aspect of practical applicability. Tonge has written a heuristic program that balances factory assembly lines (to keep idle time of machines minimum or throughput maximum), and Clarkson's simulated financial advisor selects a quasi-optimum portfolio for investors.

In his study of human decision making under uncertainty and risk, Findler experimented with and simulated subjects that optimized certain state variables by selected control-variable values in a dynamic task environment. In a later work, Findler, Klein, and their students studied the generation and utilization of heuristic rules within the framework of the card game poker.

Evans' program is able to discover geometrical analogy between line drawings. Although formula-manipulating languages are outside the domain of this article, the heuristic formal integration programs of Slagle and Moses must be mentioned here.

Another program of great potential applicability is by Feigenbaum, Lederberg, and others, called the "heuristic dendral," which discovers the most likely molecular configuration of certain chemical compounds on the basis of spectroscopic data and built-in chemical knowledge. F. A. Miller constructed a practical heuristic regression analysis program that improves with experience in a particular problem.

Individual belief systems have been simulated by Abelson and Carrol. Colby has worked on computer models of neurotic patients. Weizenbaum's ELIZA program can imitate a certain type of psychiatric interviewer.

McCarthy and his students proposed a system called "Advice Taker," which is more formal than GPS but has similar objectives in making "common sense" deductions from facts. Interpersonal interactions were modeled by Gullahorn and Gullahorn, following Homan's sociological theory. McWhinney studied and simulated human communication network experiments.

Loehlin worked on a program that reproduced individuals' likes and dislikes, depending on a complex, interacting set of attributes. Findler and McKinzie wrote programs to simulate demographical processes, and to build and query complex kinship structures from primitive input information.

Research on intelligent question-answering programs has become very popular in the past few years. These programs not only retrieve information stored in the computer memory but also make logical inferences and (may) ask the user for more information in case of ambiguity. Bobrow's STUDENT, for example, solves high school algebra problems stated in much restricted English. Simmons and his coworkers have produced several question-answering systems of varying sophistication, from which the Protosynthex projects ought to be singled out for their very large data base.

The basis of most of these projects is a *semantic network*, which consists of concept nodes connected by association links. Raphael's Semantic Information Retrieval program, Coles' Picture Language Machine, Black's Deductive Question-Answering System, and Quillian's Semantic Memory and Teachable Language Comprehender must be mentioned in this context. The problems of grammar of natural languages have been tackled by modern theories of syntax (by Chomsky and others) reasonably successfully, but *meaning* has eluded satisfactory treatment. Semantics has been shown to be the central problem in the study of language. One needs to think of the resolution of ambiguities only to appreciate the importance of it. Machine translation is unlikely to reach a significantly higher level of success until computer programs can exhibit understanding in the full sense of the word. Winograd's work in this area shows great promise. His system, which does not separate syntax and semantics, simulates a robot that follows instructions given in an interestingly rich subset of English that reasons, that asks questions of and provides answers to an interactive user about the small universe of wooden blocks of different colors and sizes. Information retrieval has become an endeavor in its own right. Many of its techniques, however, are closely related to those used in the area under discussion.

Interesting work is going on in automatic speech recognition and synthesis (Reddy, Hill, Vincens, and others). A task force has been set up to specify the work to be accomplished in the next five years. This refers to the vocabulary size of recognizable words, the quality and number of different speakers, the tolerable error rate, etc.

**Final Comments.** We have given a necessarily cursory overview of the major research areas in artificial intelligence. Some topics were deliberately left out, such as game playing, pattern recognition, image and picture processing, computer assisted instructions, augmentation of human intellect, computer-aided design, management information systems, social science and humanities applications, language translation, arts and medical applications, each of which is closely related to and overlapping our interest and is discussed in other articles in this volume.

Two more issues should be discussed here briefly. First, one often hears the statement of the skeptic: "A computer can only do what it is told to do." If this is so—and no computer professional has ever doubted the plain truth of this saying—how can we expect intelligence to emerge from our machines if they simply follow our instructions? The answer lies in the interpretation of the statement. Admittedly, computers execute the orders in a program step by step. However, with every nontrivial program (and we are talking about extremely complex hierarchies of programs), its creator does not know what the intermediate or final results will turn out to be. There is no way of telling how a program will behave under any of a large, possibly infinite number of conditions it will be exposed to. The situation is not dissimilar to the case in which the parents and teachers of a child cannot, with any certitude, foretell how he will act later in his life, given the hereditary, educational, and environmental information up to a certain point in time. Learning programs, although still somewhat in their infancy, often outperform the persons who wrote them.

The other side of the coin can be seen when a particular program that exhibits some high-level intellectual capability is described in terms of the elementary processes on which it has been built. Then our respect for the program suddenly drops because, as Minsky puts it, the problem is "explained away." Thus, many people will no longer consider that particular task to require intelligence. Human thinking may meet with this fate sometime, too.

The second issue is called the "superhuman fallacy." Many projects in artificial intelligence receive a paternalistic, deprecatory criticism: "Well, that computer-composed music is pretty awful"; or, "It is all right to prove those theorems in Euclidean geometry but the machine surely could not have *invented* Euclidean geometry"; and so on. Let us ask, however, how many Mozarts, Euclids, Einsteins, or Shakespeares have there been? We find only one of each, and each has been the descendant of the generation after generation development of human intelligence. We must compare this with only 15 years' progress in artificial intelligence research and development to obtain an approximate perspective.

### Suggested Readings

The literature in artificial intelligence is naturally scattered over many books, conference proceedings, and journals. The following provides a first approximation to the most important subset of relevant literature and contains discussions of or references to almost all the projects discussed in this article.

#### Books

1967–1972. Meltzer, B., and D. Michie (Eds.). Articles by N. L. Collins and D. Michie; E. Dale and D. Michie; D. Michie; B. Meltzer and D. Michie; B. Meltzer and D. Michie in *Machine Intelligence*. Edinburgh, Great Britain: Edinburgh University Press. (These are collections of most relevant papers presented at one of a series of annual workshops. So far, seven volumes have been published.)

1968. Minsky, M. (Ed.). *Semantic Information Processing*. Cambridge, Mass.: M.I.T. Press. (This is a collection of Ph.D. theses plus contributions by Minsky and McCarthy.)

1971. Findler, N. V., and B. Meltzer (Eds.). "Artificial Intelligence and Heuristic Programming." Edinburgh, Great Britain: Edinburgh University Press. (This is the *Proceedings of the First Advanced Study Institute on Artificial Intelligence and Heuristic Programming*, with 14 contributions.)

1971. Feigenbaum, E. A., and J.Feldman. *Computers and Thought*. New York: McGraw-Hill. (Contains some classical contributions to the area up to 1962.)

1971. Slagle, J. R. *Artificial Intelligence—The Heuristic Programming Approach*. New York: McGraw-Hill. (This is a more up-to-date introductory survey of the main research projects.)

1974. Jackson, P. C., Jr. *Introduction to Artificial Intelligence*. New York: Petrocelli/Charter. (This is a rather comprehensive description of research projects in artificial intelligence and in areas closely related to it.)

#### Conferences

There were two *International Joint Conferences on Artificial Intelligence*, the first in Washington, D.C., 1969 and the second in London, England, 1971. The proceedings are full of excellent modern papers.

The *Proceedings of the IFIP Congresses* (Paris, 1959; Munich, 1962; New York, 1965; Edinburgh, 1968; Ljubljana, 1971) contain several interesting contributions to the field. Similarly, the yearly *Spring* and *Fall Joint Computer Conferences*, and the annual *ACM National Conferences* always publish papers in artificial intelligence in their respective proceedings. There are many other meetings in related areas every year—it is impossible to list them here.

#### Journals

*International Journal of Man-Machine Studies, Information Sciences, International Journal of Computer and Information Sciences, Artificial Intelligence, Behavioral Science, ACM Communications and Journal, Computer Journal, Kybernetik, Cybernetica, IEEE Transactions on Computers, Systems Science and Cybernetics, Information and Control,* etc.

#### Surveys

Of the many survey papers of varying age, three are singled out.

1961. Minsky, M. "Steps toward Artificial Intelligence," *Proc. IRE*, Vol. 49, pp. 8–30. (Reprinted in the book edited by Feigenbaum and Feldman, 1971.)

1963. Newell, A., and H. A. Simon. "Computers in Psychology," in Luce, Bush, and Galanter (Eds.), *Handbook of Mathematical Psychology*, Vol. I. New York: Wiley.

1968. Hunt, E. B. "Computer Simulation: Artificial Intelligence Studies and Their Relevance to Psychology," *Annual Rev. of Psych.*, Vol. 19, pp. 135–168.

N. V. Findler

# ARTS APPLICATIONS

For articles on related subjects *see* COMPUTER GRAPHICS; HUMANITIES APPLICATIONS; IMAGE AND PICTURE PROCESSING; INFORMATION RETRIEVAL; and PATTERN RECOGNITION.

For article on related term *see* DATA BANK.

As is the case with computer applications in the humanities, computer applications in the arts (painting, sculpture, film making, music, and dance) include the use of data banks in pattern recognition (analysis) and pattern generation (synthesis).

**Data Banks in the Arts.** Just as libraries have traditionally served as data banks for the verbally oriented humanities, museums have traditionally served as data banks for the nonverbally oriented humanities. Efforts to use the computer to make museum collections more accessible to users have resulted in the development of a number of data bank projects for museums. Examples of such projects are GIPSY (*G*eneral *I*nformation *P*rocessing *Sy*stem), used to record ethnographic museum specimens in Oklahoma, Missouri, and Arizona; GIS (*G*eneral *I*nformation *S*ystem), used in the FLORA N. A. program, a large-scale, centralized data bank designed to collect, analyze, maintain, and disseminate diverse kinds of information about the plants of North America; GRIPHOS (*G*eneral *R*etrieval and *I*nformation *P*rocessing for *H*umanities *O*riented *S*tudies), used by the Museum Computer Network, an organization of several dozen museums and related organizations, primarily to record art objects and archeological data; SELGEM (*Sel*f-*Ge*nerating *M*aster), used to record specimen inventories of mammals, conodont types, foraminifera, nematodes, crustacea, and other collections; and TAXIR (*Tax*onomic *I*nformation *R*etrieval), used primarily for the storage and retrieval of biological specimen data (see Chenhall et al., 1972).

In the United States, the development of these systems has promoted the formation of a museum data bank coordinating committee (Chenhall et al., 1972), among whose functions are the following:

1. To develop comparative descriptions of the general information systems that are presently available so that a potential new user would have an objective basis for deciding which system was most appropriate to his needs.

2. To serve as a clearing house of data categories and minimal standard recording conventions for all museum data banks, so that data recorded in one of the systems will be compatible with that recorded in other systems. Standard recording conventions would be recommended only for such categories as dates, proper names, etc., or when requested by a representative body of scholars for a particular discipline.

3. To serve as a central point for the communication of information to and from other data bank organizations around the world.

4. To coordinate the development of programs for the conversion of data from one system to another.

5. At a later date, when sufficient information has been gathered in data banks across the country (U.S.), to coordinate or contract for the synthesis of actual data for specific disciplines on a regional or national basis.

These goals of the committee indicate the problems attendant in the use of massive data banks.

Other types of information banks necessary for pattern recognition and pattern generation in the arts include bibliographies, special-purpose catalogs, musical scores in computer-accessible form, and rules for combining elements and artifacts.

An example of a bibliographical project that includes abstracts as well as the standard author, title, etc., reference information is the *Répertoire International de la Littérature Musicale* (RILM). This computer-based information bank currently references scholarly publications on music from the year 1967 onward. After production problems are solved, the plan is to move backward from the year 1967 (while, of course, continuing to keep up with current publications) so as to provide in time a comprehensive computer data bank on publications in music (see Brook, 1967). An example of a special purpose catalog (in music) is that proposed for French chansons, which would include a listing of all manuscript and printed sources for chansons, musical incipits (notes at the beginning of the chansons), a melodic index, and other relevant information (see Hudson, 1970).

Information banks consisting of musical scores are requisite for pattern recognition studies focused on either a particular composer or a musical genre. No extensive data bank of musical scores has yet been provided, primarily because of the input problem. To date, almost all computer scores that have been put into computer-accessible form have been translated into Teletype keyboard characters using either the Ford-Columbia system of transcription (DARMS) developed by Stefan Bauer-Mengelberg of the State University of New York at Binghamton or the Plaine and Easie Code (see Brook and Gould, 1964), or systems developed by various individual scholars for their own specific research needs.

An alternative to transcribing musical scores into keyboard characters is the use of graphic input devices. One such experiment displays (on a cathode-ray tube) a musical staff as well as conventional notation for musical notes, pauses, and other standard music symbols. The scholar may then select the appropriate symbols and place them as desired on the music staff. Although this system has been proposed for music editing, it is clear that such an approach could be used to input scores, once some of the limitations (e.g., the availability of upward stems only) of the experimental system were eliminated (Cantor, 1971). The use of graphic input devices has also been advocated for data bank information necessary to computer generation of music.

An approach devised somewhat earlier than the one mentioned above considered the cathode-ray tube display as a grid across which the composer could draw graphlike lines to indicate amplitude, frequency, note duration, and so on (Mathews and Rosler, 1969). Because this particular graphic input system did not use common music notation, the user had to learn a notational system in order to input his data. Thus, the only presumed advantage of this system over transcription into keypunch characters would be the greater speed with which data could be input.

Another important type of data bank for both pattern recognition and generation in music is digitized sound. Breaking down musical acoustical signals into digitized form as well as using the digitized form to generate acoustical signals requires an analog-to-digital and digital-to-analog converter system with a speed sufficient for 20,000 to 50,000 samples per second and a quantization accuracy of from 10 to 13 bits. As is the case for speech, storage of digitized music poses space requirements that are sometimes a seriously limiting factor on the scope of the research being undertaken (Beauchamp, 1967).

**Pattern Recognition.** Pattern recognition projects focused upon painting and sculpture are almost nonexistent. Thus far, fine arts museum information banks consist of listings of artists, works of art, dates when created, perhaps the date of acquisition by a given museum, and other comparable detail. Although there is a strong interest in providing content information (e.g., physical objects represented in a painting; the colors used in a painting), there is at present little effort to make such information available as part of computer-accessible information banks. Conceivably there will be some effort to hand-code such information, but any such encoding, albeit useful, will be prone to the subjective responses and lapses of any given encoder. It seems likely that in time (whether measured in years or decades is not yet clear), pattern recognition efforts currently being pursued in other areas (e.g., aerial photography, artificial intelligence research on robots, character recognition) will be used to facilitate input of information concerning museum holdings.

Current work on identification of two- and three-dimensional objects, on methods of locating and following edges so as to identify objects, and on the use of regional analysis rather than edge delineation to describe objects is all obviously relevant to pattern recognition of paintings, sculpture, and other objects in museums (Guzman, 1968; Rosenfeld, 1969 a,b). A recent dissertation by Lawrence Krakauer, M.I.T., on computer analysis of visual properties of curved objects uses digitized photographs of apples, oranges, peaches, Bartlett pears, and sweet pears as data banks. Mathematical and statistical techniques are then used to identify and describe parameters related to shape (e.g., stems, protrusions, stem hollows) and texture (visual texture and tactile texture) so as to describe and discriminate among the types of fruit being analyzed.

The determination of characteristics sufficient to identify a few known artifacts is hardly comparable to digitizing and then describing the artifacts in even the smallest of museums. It also should be noted that the work on the fruit entailed only black and white images, although the addition of color apparently poses no serious additional problems. It may be that it will be many years, if ever, before it is feasible and practical to try to map categories such as boat or vase (let alone Etruscan vase as opposed to Grecian vase) onto parameters indicating shape (such as eccentricity), or texture, or alignment of edges, or whatever indicators emerge from digitized representations of artifacts. Nonetheless, we may expect the parameters that do emerge easily from such digitized representations will in themselves provide useful categories for the art historian or student of style and content in painting and sculpture.

In contrast to painting and sculpture, pattern recognition in music is a very active research area. Pattern recognition involving digitized acoustical signals faces the storage problem mentioned earlier. For example, an effort to analyze tones produced by a range of musical instruments used a hardware configuration that did not permit adequate continuous transfer of digitized analog samples to magnetic tape. As a result, only core storage was available in this particular configuration and (using 29,952 samples per second at a sample rate of 30 kc) the maximum length of sound that could be digitized was 0.997 sec. This block of information could, of course, then be transferred to tape and a new 0.997 sec of acoustic signal could be stored and transferred. These blocks of data were characterized and graphed to show time-variant spectral information (Beauchamp, 1969).

In general, work on digitized music can deal with such parameters as frequency or pitch, amplitude, timbre, tone, and phase. When storage and processing speed problems are solved, there will probably be music information banks consisting of digitized music as performed, rather than, or in addition to, its appearance in a printed score. If and when such data banks are available, it may well be—analogously to possibilities for museum artifacts—that the parameters used for characterizing music will not all be mapped onto the traditional symbols of a printed score. In the case of music, as well as in spoken and written language, what could eventuate is a parallel development involving, on the one hand, graphic pattern recognition devices and, on the other, acoustic pattern recognition techniques.

Much pattern recognition in music has depended upon information banks consisting of musical scores. Representation systems, such as the Plaine and Easie Code or DARMS, permit the scholar to encode in keypunch characters all the symbols in a written score. Written scores permit studies of styles of individual composers as well as groups of composers. Written scores cannot be used for studies of interpretations of a given work by conductors or performing artists; digitized acoustical recordings might have to be used for pattern recognition of this type.

Computer-accessible music scores have been used for work on questions of harmony, of composer identification, of particular themes or motives within the works of a particular composer, and for ethnomusicology. Many of these studies concentrate upon pitch and combinations of pitches, although other information such as duration of notes, amplitude of notes, and various frequency distributions of notes is obviously available from music scores. For example, studies concerned with harmony depend upon chords and patterns of chords, which are described in terms of the pitches of the individual tones combined into chords (Fuller, 1970; Jackson, 1970). A study of motif, or musical theme, again looks at the pitch of notes and combination of pitches into chords, but it is also concerned with changes of dynamics and tempo (Fiore, 1970). Studies of dynamics and tempo imply analyzing information concerning the amplitude (loudness-softness) with which the individual notes or chords are played and analyzing information about the duration of individual notes or chords. One project explicitly directed toward composer identification was concerned with root progression, which is a study of the way chords are connected—again, a study emphasizing pitch (Youngblood, 1970).

Work in ethnomusicology is directed toward describing the music of a particular culture or, sometimes, comparing the musical habits of a number of cultures (Lieberman, 1970; Suchoff, 1970). A project directed toward analyzing Japanese music concentrated upon fixed melodies (F.M.) and variations on the F.M. achieved through its rendition by different instruments and through elaborations played on still other instruments. Once this data was encoded, the computer was used to sort out and derive statistical summaries of the data (Lieberman, 1970). It should be noted that implicit in the pitch of any given tone is not only its location relative to any given octave but also the octave in which it actually occurs (e.g., an A in the octave above middle C).

Pattern recognition in dance is of considerable interest because the dance notation systems that do exist are relatively little used (Noll, 1967a). Hence, dances exist principally in the heads of choreographers and the dancers, and often a particular dance vanishes when its originating dance company breaks up or a choreographer passes from the scene. In the context of a discussion of generating dance movements by computer (Fig. 1), it has been pointed out by Noll (1967a) that specifying human movement in any detail is exceedingly complicated:

> ... obtaining the equations for as simple a motion as walking would be formidable. A better attack on this problem might be for the computer itself to analyze human motion using devices which have just become available for converting pictorial data into machine digestable data. A library of basic movements could be built within the computer, and particular movements could then be put together at will.

As should be apparent from the earlier discussion of painting and sculpture, the pattern recog-

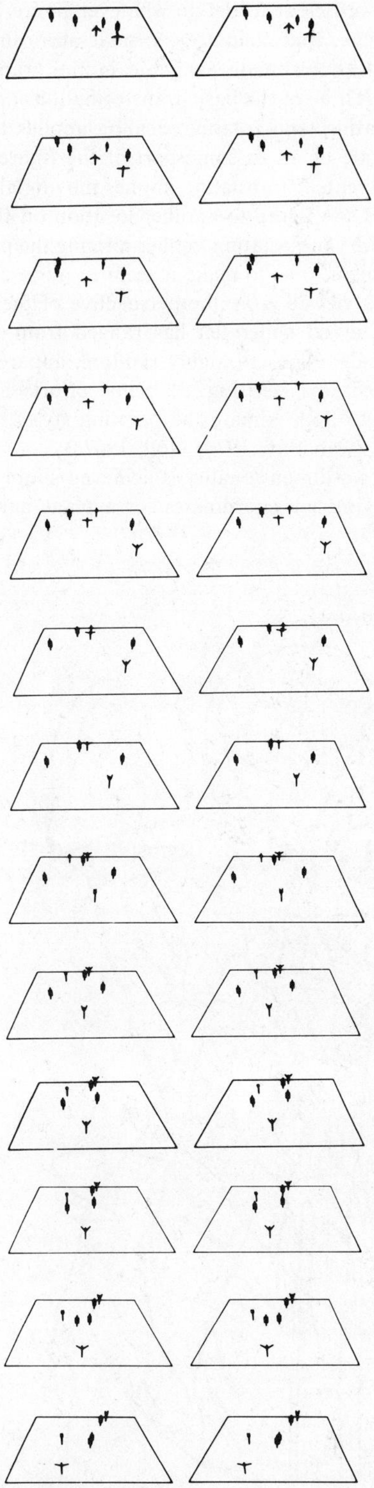

Fig. 1. Computer-generated ballet. Courtesy of A. Michael Noll.

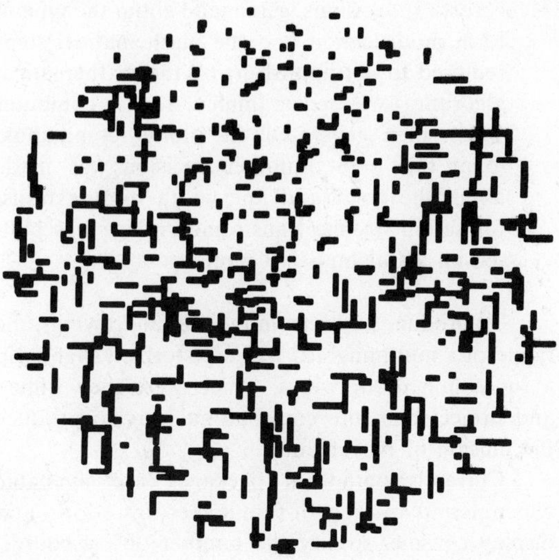

Fig. 2. Computer composition with lines. Courtesy of A. Michael Noll. (© AMN 1965.)

nition problems implied by this approach are complex. Walking entails the angles of legs, feet, and other parts of the body, which are changing through time (see Fig. 2). As it is possible to imagine in the cases of painting, sculpture, and music that other than traditional parameters may be useful for pattern recognition, so, too, may be the parameters other than those to which the dancer is accustomed. Thus, the preparation of information banks to be used for pattern recognition that could take the place of or provide the stimulus for dance notation would seem to imply a mapping of whatever parameters are best for the digitized information onto those that are best for the dancer.

**Pattern Generation.** In contrast to computer-based pattern analysis, pattern generation in painting and sculpture and its allied field, film making, is firmly established. Computer-generated paintings and films in two, three, and even four dimensions have been produced. Output media have ranged from computer printers to cathode-ray tubes, and input media from punched cards to lightpens. One early approach (Csuri and Shaffer, 1968) which resulted in a so-called sine curve man and a prize winning film, *Hummingbird*, used the following technique:

(1) an artistic drawing was made with line segments of points of the subject matter to be used; (2) a drawing was digitized line by line with the resulting coordinates punched into

cards; (3) decisions were made about the type of form modification and the mathematical steps required to accomplish it; (4) the mathematical algorithm was programmed for a computer which then generated the plotter commands; (5) at this point, another decision was made about the color and line width for the transformation; (6) the transformed image was plotted on a Calcomp 563 plotter.

To produce a film from individual drawings, the figure of a hummingbird was transformed slightly in a succession of drawings, which were then filmed and projected in the conventional way to produce the illusion of movement.

Currently, graphics packages are available which permit an artist or film maker to sit down at a display console, specify the number of *x-y* coordinates sufficient to define whatever figure he wishes to create, and then transform it according to the specifications made available in the graphics program. Three of the basic transformations are scaling, translating, and rotating. Scaling implies modifying the scale of all or some part of the figure that has been created; translating implies moving all or some part of the figure to another location on the output medium; and rotating implies altering the position of the object so as to make it seem to move around an axis as viewed from the perspective of the artist.

The art generated has ranged from very geometrical designs to highly random, apparently chaotic patterns (see Fig. 3). Some efforts have been made to approximate the painting styles of human artists (Canaday, 1970; Noll, 1967c).

Two-dimensionality is achieved simply through specifying *x-y* coordinates for a plane surface. Ac-

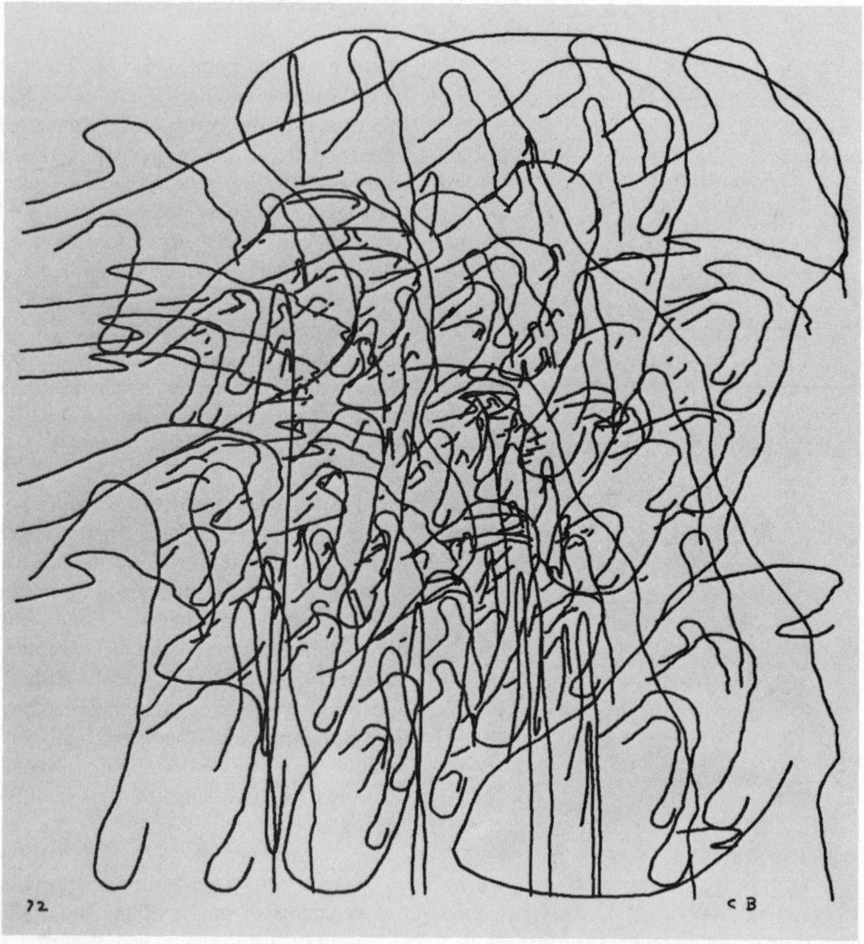


**Fig. 3.** Contained contour II. Courtesy of Colette and Charles Bangert.

cording to Noll (1967b), a three-dimensional

> ... perspective drawing is produced by choosing a point (representing the eye and formally called the station point) from which the object is viewed. The picture plane is then inserted between the object and station point, and projection lines are drawn from the object to the station point. The points of intersection of these projection lines with the picture plane are joined together to produce the perspective drawing.

Four-dimensional objects can be specified mathematically and produced by mathematical formulas analogous to those used for two-dimensional perspectives of three-dimensional objects. Although it is impossible to see a four-dimensional object, the three-dimensional (and, in turn, two-dimensional) projection of the four-dimensional object produces effects that differ from conventional two- and three-dimensional artifacts. It has been noted that "the programs and mathematical techniques for four-dimensional projections and rotations are quite general and can easily be extended to even higher dimensions" (Noll, 1967b).

A number of programming languages have been especially designed for the artist and film maker. Kenneth Knowlton and his associates at Bell Laboratories, Murray Hill, N. J., have developed three such languages: Beflix, Tarps, and Explor.

Beflix, a film-making language in Fortran IV, provides drafting operations that draw rectangles, straight lines, arcs, other curves, and alphanumeric characters, as well as operations concerning the content of rectangular areas, the specification of the projection grid, operations related to elements labeled bugs (not to be confused with the undesirable bugs that occur in many computer programs), and miscellaneous operations having to do with output, debugging, etc. Tarps is a two-dimensional alphanumeric raster picture system for the production of designs, diagrams, and textures, usually for movies. Tarps contains operations such as ZOOM, which progressively enlarges the image by an integral factor; ESPEZOOM, which gives a clockwise (right) or counterclockwise (left) spiraling zoom; and SYM, which produces an enlarging kaleidoscope image.

Explor—a generator of images from *ex*plicit *p*atterns, *l*ocal *o*perations, and *r*andomness—is a system for computer generation of still or moving images from explicitly defined patterns, local operations, and randomness. Explor produces output images comprising rectangular arrays (240 by 340) of black, white, and "twinkling" dots. Among its intended scientific and artistic applications are the "production of stimuli for visual experiments, the depiction of visual 'phosphors' such as moving checkerboards and stripes, and picture processing." This system may also be used to simulate a "variety of two-dimensional processes and mechanisms, such as crystal growth and etching, neural (e.g., retinal) nets, random walk, diffusion, and iterative arrays of logic modules."

Explor is a macrolanguage with sets of instructions for picture output, for changing the internal array, for defining patterns, for flow of control, and for instruction modification. It provides facilities for specifying periodic and/or random applications of its operations, and flexible means of specifying uniform or locality-dependent translation of internal symbols. Another approach to programming languages for the artist permits the artist to define his own vocabulary, built on an REL (rapidly extensible language) support system, as he creates his art (Thompson et al., 1969).

The use of the computer for sculpture is ordinarily to use graphic facilities, such as those already described for painting and film making, to display a range of design possibilities and perspectives for proposed sculpture. Programs that produce paper tapes, which in turn are used to drive milling machines that actually produce artifacts, have also been designed (Mallary, 1969).

**Music.** Computer-generated music produces either scores, which are then performed, or music for which the acoustic properties are specified and which is then synthesized by a digital-to-analog converter.

Musicomp is a compositional programming language that provides techniques for generating original musical scores as well as for synthesizing music (Hiller, 1969). An adaptable language that can be changed and expanded according to need, Musicomp consists of three basic parts: system regulatory routines, compositional and analytical subroutines, and sound synthesis routines. The latter "are not actual synthesis programs but rather routines that prepare and organize data that serve as input to sound-generating programs." Among Musicomp's compositional subroutines are a subroutine for choice of a rhythmic mode; a subroutine that provides choice of a range of pitches and then of a specific pitch from within this range; a subroutine that controls the melodic range rule (in a single line a limit such as an octave is imposed on melodic motion); and others. The routines provide for the generation of phrases and their imitations and permutations; generation of all the permutations of the given role of *n* items; generation of similar rhythmic data from more than one instrument for any length of time; and generation of dynamics indications in playing styles according to serial processes. Musicomp can be used in conjunction with Fortran.

Output of musical scores either uses standard printer conventions that can then be translated onto regular music staffs, a cathode-ray tube configuration such as that described earlier in terms of input of musical scores, or a plotter to draw a score. In one such program written for a Calcomp plotter, the notation makes use of a select set of symbols already available in the Calcomp library (triangles, circles, lines, and so on). The "language of the scores is given by the distribution, size, and position of symbols on each page of the scores; in effect, each page is a plot of dynamic level versus time. Once the performer is provided with a short introductory explanation of the notation, he is able to perform directly from the score" (Hiller, 1970).

Computer-generated scores have ranged from music that is highly random in character to music that is intended to approximate some aspects of the style of a given composer or musical genre. In fact, in the course of some experiments, a range from greater to less randomness is apparent (Moorer, 1972). Analysis of church hymns (Brooks et al., 1957), using Markovian analysis, resulted in simulated hymns with considerable randomness when low-order probabilities (probabilities of orders 1 through 8 were assigned in this experiment) were used. The use of high-order probabilities produced parts of original hymns connected together. The *Illiac Suite*, one of the best known early computer compositions, was a string quartet comprising rhythms, chosen at random, and melodies constructed according to some rules of classical harmony and counterpoint. Another computer-generated composition, *Sonoriferous Loops*, written for instrumental ensemble and tape, used four parameters: pitch, register, rhythmic unit, and rhythmic mode. Rhythmic modes (basic metrical patterns) and rhythmic units within those modes were chosen in accord with assigned probability distributions; probability distributions that differed for each instrument and for different parts of the composition were also used to make choices between rest or play and for octave registers (Hiller, 1970). A recent effort to generate scores for western popular music (Moorer, 1972) proceeded according to the following sequence:

> . . . the overall form of the piece is chosen first, the chords are chosen second, and the melody, last. . . . the choice of chords before melody is to avoid the problem of deciding what chords should go with a given melody. The problem is reversed and simplified to constraining some number of the prospective melody notes to lie in the chord. The overall structure is similarly chosen first, to prevent attempting to derive the structure from the melody. . . . The overall structure is decided upon by first choosing two numbers, the number of major groups and the number of minor groups. Each of these numbers is constrained to be a power of two times the number of beats per measure, a parameter supplied by the operator. The total piece length is then the product of the number of major groups times the number of minor groups times the number of beats per minor group.

Two parameters implicit in some of the choices made in experiments with computer-generated music are the periodicity of the melodic line and the consonance and/or dissonance implied by the structures of chords. Periodicity implies the repetition and transformation of melodic groups. Consonance and dissonance are subjective matters, but some combinations of notes such as a perfect fifth or a major third are considered to be more consonant than others (Moorer, 1972). Another statement on consonance and dissonance notes that "tones are most dissonant when their frequencies are separated by a particular fraction of a critical bandwidth and are consonant when their frequencies coincide or are separated by more than a critical bandwidth" (Pierce and Mathews, 1969). This statement continues by noting that partials "not crowded too close together at high frequencies" can be pleasing or consonant.

Composers who use the computer to synthesize sound rather than to produce musical scores are concerned with many of the same elements, although they are parameterized according to acoustic categories rather than graphic symbols. The composer using sound synthesis must be concerned with amplitudes, frequencies, amplitude modulation rate, and waveform specification. According to one set of specifications, the digital-analog converters used in music synthesis must be capable of converting 12 to 14 bit words at a rate of 40,000 per second. "The long word length ensures adequate dynamic range and the high rate, a sufficiently broad frequency response" (Freedman, 1969). Additionally, for pleasant sound, the computer equipment must have adequate block transfer rates between auxiliary storage and main memory so that there will be continuous reproduction of sound without breaks.

Because electronically synthesized sound lacks some of the variability to which the human ear is accustomed, composers who are generating sound electronically have concerns with which those who are generating scores are not troubled. For example, electronically sustained tones seem to provide a constant stimulus that may fatigue the ear. To achieve a more pleasing timbre, it has been suggested (Roberts, 1969) that any one of the following techniques might be used: "(1) control of the amplitude envelope: crescendo, diminuendo, exponential decay, and so on; (2) variation of the pitch—vibrato or glissando; (3) variation of wave form." Roberts also notes that "another feature of electronic tone that the listener finds distressing, or at least unnatural, is that quality is independent of loudness. ... It is, of course, easy to correct this feature by introducing deliberate nonlinearities into the computer-simulated oscillators."

As is the case with computer-generated art, the field of computer-generated music is very extensive and cannot be done full justice in an article of this length. For a useful survey of music composed with the computer, the reader is referred to Hiller (1970).

**Dance.** Computer-generated dance is in a much more embryonic state. One experiment used the computer to specify the number of dancers on the stage at any given time and to indicate the positions they would occupy on that stage throughout the period of time they were on stage (Sagasti and Page, 1970). Another experiment (Noll, 1967a) used a computer display to delineate the spatial and arm movements of a group of dancers on stage. The difficulties encountered in pattern analysis for the dance also obtain for pattern generation. That is, specifying the intricacies of movements entailed by dance is exceedingly complicated and, as yet, beyond the reach of any current experiment.

### References


1957. Brooks, F. P., A. L. Hopkins, P. G. Newmann, and W. V., Wright. "An Experiment in Musical Composition," *IRE Trans. Electronic Computers*, EC-Vol. 6, No. 1, September, pp. 175–182.

1964. Brook, Barry, and Murray Gould. *Notating Music with Ordinary Typewriter Characters: A Plaine and Easie Code System for Musicke.* Flushing, N. Y.: Queens College of the City University of New York.

1967. ———. "Music Bibliography and the Computer." In Gerald Lefkoff (Ed.), *Computer Applications in Music.* Morgantown: West Virginia University Library, pp. 9–27.

1967a. Noll, Michael. "Choreography and Computers," *Dance Magazine*, January.

1967b. ———. "Computers and the Visual Arts," *Design and Planning*, No. 2, Hastings House Publications, Inc.

1967c. ———. "The Digital Computer as a Creative Medium," *IEEE Spectrum*, Vol. 4, No. 10, October, pp. 89–95.

1968. Csuri, Charles, and James Shaffer: "Art, Computers and Mathematics," *AFIPS—Conference Proceedings*, Vol. 33. Wayne, Pa.: MDI Publications, pp. 1293–1298.

1968. Guzman, Adolfo. "Decomposition of a Visual Scene into Three-Dimensional Bodies," *AFIPS —Conference Proceedings*, Vol. 33, pt. 1. Wayne, Pa.: MDI Publications, pp. 291–304.

1969. Beauchamp, James W. "A Computer System for Time-Variant Harmonic Analysis and Synthesis of Musical Tones." In Heinz von Foerster and James W. Beauchamp (Eds.), *Music by Computers.* New York: John Wiley, pp. 19–62.

1969. Freedman, M. David. "On-Line Generation of Sound." In Heinz von Foerster and James Beauchamp (Eds.), *Music by Computers.* New York: John Wiley, pp. 13–18.

1969. Hiller, Lejaren. "Some Compositional Techniques Involving the Use of Computers." In Heinz von Foerster and James W. Beauchamp (Eds.), *Music by Computers.* New York: John Wiley, pp. 71–83.

1969. Mallary, Robert. "Computer Sculpture: Six Levels of Cybernetics," *Art Forum*, May, pp. 29–35.

1969. Mathews, M. B., and L. Rosler. "Graphical Language for the Scores of Computer-Generated Sounds." In Heinz von Foerster and James W. Beauchamp (Eds.), *Music by Computers.* New York: John Wiley, pp. 84–114.

1969. Pierce, J. R., and M. V. Mathews. "Control of Consonance and Dissonance with Nonharmonic Overtones." In Heinz von Foerster and James W. Beauchamp (Eds.), *Music by Computers.* New York: John Wiley, pp. 63–68.

1969. Roberts, Arthur. "Some New Developments in Computer-Generated Music." In Heinz von Foerster and James W. Beauchamp (Eds.), *Music by Computers.* New York: John Wiley, pp. 63–68.

1969a. Rosenfeld, Azriel. *Picture Processing by Computer.* New York: Academic Press.

1969b. ———. "Picture Processing by Computer," *Computing Surveys*, Vol. 1, No. 3, September, pp. 146–176.

1969. Thompson, F. B., P. C. Lockeman, B. H. Dostert, and R. S. Deverill. "REL: A Rapidly Extensible Language System," *Proceedings 24th National ACM Conference*, August, Vol. 24.

1970. Canaday, John. "Less Art, More Computer, Please." *The New York Times*, Aug. 30, Section D, p. 19.

1970. Fiore, Mary E. "Webern's Use of Motive in the Piano Variations." In H. B. Lincoln (Ed.), *The Computer and Music*. Ithaca, N.Y.: Cornell University Press, pp. 115–122..

1970. Fuller, Ramon. "Toward a Theory of Webernian Harmony, Via Analysis with a Digital Computer." In H. B. Lincoln (Ed.), *The Computer and Music*. Ithaca, N.Y.: Cornell University Press, pp. 123–131.

1970. Hiller, Lejaren. "Music Composed with Computers—A Historical Survey." In H. B. Lincoln (Ed.), *The Computer and Music*. Ithaca, N.Y.: Cornell University Press, pp. 49–96.

1970. Hudson, Barton. "Toward a Comprehensive French Chanson Catalogue." In H. B. Lincoln (Ed.), *The Computer and Music*. Ithaca, N.Y.: Cornell University Press, pp. 277–287.

1970. Jackson, Roland. "Harmony Before and After 1910: A Computer Comparison." In H. B. Lincoln (Ed.), *The Computer and Music*. Ithaca, N.Y.: Cornell University Press, pp. 132–146.

1970. Lieberman, Fredric. "Computer-Aided Analysis of Japanese Music." In H. B. Lincoln (Ed.), *The Computer and Music*. Ithaca, N.Y.: Cornell University Press, pp. 181–192.

1970. Sagasti, Francisco, and William Page. "Computer Choreography: An Experiment on the Interaction Between Dance and the Computer," *Computer Studies in the Humanities and Verbal Behavior*, Vol. 3, No. 1, January, pp. 46–49.

1970. Sedelow, Sally Yeates. "The Computer in the Humanities and Fine Arts," *Computing Surveys*, Vol. 2, No. 2, June, pp. 89–110.

1970. Suchoff, Benjamin. "Computer-Oriented Comparative Musicology," In H. B. Lincoln (Ed.), *The Computer and Music*. Ithaca, N.Y.: Cornell University Press, pp. 193–206.

1970. Youngblood, Joseph. "Root Progressions and Composer Identification." In H. B. Lincoln (Ed.), *The Computer and Music*. Ithaca, N.Y.: Cornell University Press, pp. 172–180.

1971. Cantor, Dawn. "A Computer Program That Accepts Common Musical Notation," *Computers and the Humanities*, Vol. 6, No. 2, November, pp. 103–109.

1971. Whitney, John H. "A Computer Art for the Video Picture Wall," *Proceedings: International Federation for Information Processing*, August.

1972. Chenhall, Robert G., et al. *Report of Museum Data Bank Study Group*. Hershey, Pa., March 27–28. (Available from Dr. Chenhall, Margaret Woodbury Strong Museum, Rochester, N.Y.)

1972. Moorer, James Anderson. "Music and Computer Composition." *Communications of the ACM*, Vol. 15, No. 2, February, pp. 104–113.

S. A. SEDELOW

## ASCII

For articles on related subjects *see* CODES; and EBCDIC.

The American Standard Code for Information Interchange (ASCII) is a seven-bit code also known as the USA Standard Code for Information Interchange (USASCII).

Because eight-bit codes are much more common on computers than seven-bit codes, ASCII is commonly embedded in an eight-bit code, ASCII-8, which is shown as Exhibit 1. This arrangement shows the 128 ($=2^7$) possible combinations for the seven-bit USASCII code. The leftmost four bits (or first hexadecimal digit) of the eight-bit code are shown as column heads across the top and the rightmost four bits (or second hexadecimal digit) are listed on the side. Thus, for example, we have

| Character | Code | |
|---|---|---|
| | Binary | Hexadecimal |
| 4 | 01010100 | 5 4 |
| Y | 10111001 | B 9 |
| c | 11100011 | E 3 |
| = | 01011101 | 5 D |

The meanings of the control characters and special graphic characters are shown below the illustraction.

I. FLORES

## ASSEMBLERS

For articles on related subjects *see* INDEX REGISTER; LANGUAGE PROCESSORS; LINKAGE EDITOR; LOADER; MACHINE AND ASSEMBLY LANGUAGE PROGRAMMING; MACROINSTRUCTION; OPERAND; and OPERATION CODE.

For articles on related terms *see* EDSAC; IBM 360–370 SERIES; and READ-ONLY STORE.

| Bit positions 4, 3, 2, 1 | Second Hexadecimal Digit | 00 | | | | 01 | | | | 10 | | | | 11 | | | |
|---|---|---|---|---|---|---|---|---|---|---|---|---|---|---|---|---|---|
| | | 00 | 01 | 10 | 11 | 00 | 01 | 10 | 11 | 00 | 01 | 10 | 11 | 00 | 01 | 10 | 11 |
| | | 0 | 1 | 2 | 3 | 4 | 5 | 6 | 7 | 8 | 9 | A | B | C | D | E | F |
| 0000 | 0 | NUL | DLE | | | SP | 0 | | | | | @ | P | | | ` | p |
| 0001 | 1 | SOH | DC1 | | | ! | 1 | | | | | A | Q | | | a | q |
| 0010 | 2 | STX | DC2 | | | " | 2 | | | | | B | R | | | b | r |
| 0011 | 3 | ETX | DC3 | | | # | 3 | | | | | C | S | | | c | s |
| 0100 | 4 | EOT | DC4 | | | $ | 4 | | | | | D | T | | | d | t |
| 0101 | 5 | ENQ | NAK | | | % | 5 | | | | | E | U | | | e | u |
| 0110 | 6 | ACK | SYN | | | & | 6 | | | | | F | V | | | f | v |
| 0111 | 7 | BEL | ETB | | | ' | 7 | | | | | G | W | | | g | w |
| 1000 | 8 | BS | CAN | | | ( | 8 | | | | | H | X | | | h | x |
| 1001 | 9 | HT | EM | | | ) | 9 | | | | | I | Y | | | i | y |
| 1010 | A | LF | SUB | | | * | : | | | | | J | Z | | | j | z |
| 1011 | B | VT | ESC | | | + | ; | | | | | K | [ | | | k | { |
| 1100 | C | FF | FS | | | , | < | | | | | L | \ | | | l | ¦ |
| 1101 | D | CR | GS | | | - | = | | | | | M | ] | | | m | } |
| 1110 | E | SO | RS | | | . | > | | | | | N | ^ | | | n | ~ |
| 1111 | F | SI | US | | | / | ? | | | | | O | _ | | | o | DEL |

Bit Positions 8, 7 — Bit Positions 6, 5 — First Hexadecimal Digit

Control Character Representations

| | | | |
|---|---|---|---|
| NUL | Null | DLE | Data Link Escape (CC) |
| SOH | Start of Heading (CC) | DC1 | Device Control 1 |
| STX | Start of Text (CC) | DC2 | Device Control 2 |
| ETX | End of Text (CC) | DC3 | Device Control 3 |
| EOT | End of Transmission (CC) | DC4 | Device Control 4 |
| ENQ | Enquiry (CC) | NAK | Negative Acknowledge (CC) |
| ACK | Acknowledge (CC) | SYN | Synchronous Idle (CC) |
| BEL | Bell | ETB | End of Transmission Block (CC) |
| BS | Backspace (FE) | CAN | Cancel |
| HT | Horizontal Tabulation (FE) | EM | End of Medium |
| LF | Line Feed (FE) | SUB | Substitute |
| VT | Vertical Tabulation (FE) | ESC | Escape |
| FF | Form Feed (FE) | FS | File Separator (IS) |
| CR | Carriage Return (FE) | GS | Group Separator (IS) |
| SO | Shift Out | RS | Record Separator (IS) |
| SI | Shift In | US | Unit Separator (IS) |
| | | DEL | Delete |
| (CC) | Communication Control | | |
| (FE) | Format Effector | | |
| (IS) | Information Separator | | |

Special Graphic Characters

| | | | |
|---|---|---|---|
| SP | Space | < | Less Than |
| ! | Exclamation Point | = | Equals |
| \| | Logical OR | > | Greater Than |
| " | Quotation Marks | ? | Question Mark |
| # | Number Sign | @ | Commercial At |
| $ | Dollar Sign | [ | Opening Bracket |
| % | Percent | \ | Reverse Slant |
| & | Ampersand | ] | Closing Bracket |
| ' | Apostrophe | ^ | Circumflex |
| ( | Opening Parenthesis | ¬ | Logical NOT |
| ) | Closing Parenthesis | _ | Underline |
| * | Asterisk | ` | Grave Accent |
| + | Plus | { | Opening Brace |
| , | Comma | ¦ | Vertical Line (This graphic is stylized to distinguish it from Logical OR) |
| - | Hyphen (Minus) | | |
| . | Period (Decimal Point) | | |
| / | Slant | } | Closing Brace |
| : | Colon | ~ | Tilde |
| ; | Semicolon | | |

**Exhibit 1** ASCII-8

An assembler (contraction for assembly program) is a program that facilitates the preparation of programs at the machine language level by taking symbolic representations of individual (instruction or data) words and converting them into a form (binary or byte) suitable for input to a linker or loader. It permits the use of mnemonic names for function codes, allows symbolic names to be assigned to storage locations, provides facilities for address arithmetic in terms of such symbolic names, and (usually) enables the user to write numerical constants to various bases in a variety of forms.

An alternative, more abstract definition is as follows: An *assembly language* is a programming language in which the basic set of operations includes the operation codes of the machine, and whose data structure maps directly onto the store and registers of the machine. An assembler is a compiler for an assembly language.

Either of these definitions leads to the informal description often used, namely, that an assembler is a way of writing symbolic programs that allows the programmer full access to all the facilities of the real machine. (By contrast, higher-level languages such as Fortran and PL/I provide an abstract machine that conceals some of the facilities available in the real machine.)

**History.** The term "assembly subroutine" for a routine that assembles a master routine and a number of subroutines into a single program was used in the first book about programming digital computers (Wilkes, Wheeler, and Gill, 1951) in connection with the EDSAC computer. Indeed, EDSAC had a rudimentary assembler called Initial Orders, which allowed the user to write machine instructions consisting of a single alphabetic-letter instruction code, a decimal address, and a terminating letter, which caused one of 12 preset quantities to be added to the address at assembly time. (The Initial Orders were implemented in a kind of read-only store consisting of a wired telephone uniselector.)

Although the use of a symbolic representation of machine language programs now seems so obviously desirable as not to be worth discussing, this was not always so. A dichotomy of view existed right from the start in England, with the EDSAC group advocating a measure of symbolic programming, which was derided by the binary faction at Manchester (MARK I). This controversy is exemplified by the following quotation from Wilkes (1956),

> ... the utility or otherwise of elaborate conversion schemes is at present a matter of some controversy ... there are ... people who will have nothing to do with any form of conversion. They believe that the programmer does best to write his orders in a form as near as possible to that which they will take inside the machine.

Probably the first assembler in the sense used in this article was SOAP (Symbolic Optimizer and Assembly Program) on the IBM 650 computer in the mid-1950s. However, the symbolic assembly features of SOAP were not its main feature (the 650 was a decimal computer anyway, which removed some of the difficulties of direct machine language coding). The 650 had a magnetic drum memory and an instruction code in which each instruction specified the address of its successor. For maximum efficiency, instructions had to be placed on the drum in positions such that the execution of each instruction overlapped as far as possible the time for the drum to rotate to the next instruction position, thus minimizing the latency time waiting for instructions. Such minimum-access coding involved a very difficult optimizing process, and it was this that SOAP achieved.

The most significant event in the history of assemblers was the Symbolic Assembly Program (SAP) for the IBM 704. The original SAP assembler (UASAP) was written by programmers at United Aircraft Corporation and was distributed by the SHARE organization. SAP set the external form of an assembly language that was to be a model for all its successors, and which persists almost unchanged to the present day. On later versions of the 700 series computers, SAP was replaced by FAP (Fortran Assembly Program).

**Facilities.** A typical machine instruction consists of an operation code, an address, and one or more register fields. The address may refer to a data area or to another instruction (e.g., the destination of a transfer of control). A SAP-like assembler provides a fixed set of (usually mnemonic) function codes and an open-ended set of programmer-defined symbols for use in address parts. Such address symbols may be defined explicitly or (in the case of jump destinations) implicitly by attaching them as labels to particular instructions. Although a symbol stands for an address, the assembler cannot convert label symbols directly into addresses, since the address in storage into which a particular instruction will be loaded is not known at assembly time. (It is finally determined only when a number of routines are combined together to form a complete program.) The difficulty is resolved by recording as the value of the label symbol the displacement of the instruction in question from the beginning of the code for the subroutine, and marking it in the assembler output as a relative or relocatable value, to be adjusted later by the linker or loader.

Thus, SAP introduced the basic structure of a symbolic instruction as being made up of three fields:

1. *Location* (possibly blank). A symbol placed here takes as its value the address of the register in which the corresponding instruction will be stored: Thus it serves as a label by which the instruction can be referenced by other instructions.
2. *Operation code.* The symbol here is one of a fixed repertoire of operation-code symbols
3. *Operand.* This field is usually made up of a number of subfields, reflecting the address/register structure of the computer. The subfields may be simple integer constants or may be expressions made up of symbols (representing addresses), constants, and simple arithmetic operations (usually plus and minus). Alternatively, a literal operand may be supplied: The assembler will store this and substitute the appropriate address in the instruction.

The following fragment of SAP coding illustrates this structure:

```
        TRA  ALPHA
        LOC  16385
ALPHA   CLA  BETA
        STO  DELTA
SYMB    FAD  =3.14159
        SXO  STMB-2,4
        STO  SYMT
```

Each instruction in this example is made up of three fields: location (label), operation code, and address. The operation codes are mnemonic, e.g., TRA = transfer control, CLA = clear accumulator, FAD = floating add, etc. The address fields show the various possible constructions. In the first line the address is a symbol ALPHA, as yet undefined. (It appears as a label on a later instruction.) In line 2 the address is explicit, and in lines 3 and 4 symbols (presumably defined elsewhere in the program of which this fragment forms a part) are used. Line 5 illustrates the use of a literal operand: the "equals" indicates that the 3.14159 following is the actual value to be loaded by the FAD, not the address of the operand. The next line illustrates a more complex address: It is a two-field form in which the first component is a store address and the second component identifies an index register to be used; in this example the store address is specified as an expression.

The following excerpt of OS/370 assembler code for the IBM System/370 computers, whose purpose is to sum 13 numbers, shows how little things have changed in ten years:

```
      L    3, =F'0'     CLEAR REGISTER
      L    5, =F'0'     USING LITERAL
      LH   4, =H'14'    LOAD REGISTER
      B    BCNT         ENTER LOOP
BNTER AH   5,STZ(3)     INDEX STZ BY REG 3
      AH   3, =H'2'     INCREMENT INDEX
BCNT  BCT  4,BNTER      BRANCH ON COUNT
*
      ST   5,BSUM
STZ   DC   H'15,225,1,52,10,48,76,42,88,26,14,4,32'
BSUM  DC   F'0'
```

The three-field format is still used, though the mnemonics have changed. With the exception of the branch (B) order, which has a label as its address, the address field is made up of a register designator and a second field, which in these examples is either a symbolic store address or a literal. (For certain instructions it might be another register designator.)

Literals are introduced by "equals," but now include a type code (F = full word, H = half-word). Indexing (modification) is illustrated in the line starting BNTER, and finally there are specifications of a number of constants introduced by the DC (Define Constant) pseudo-operation. The comments on the right are the part of the programmer's documentation of the program. To explain the program a bit more fully we note that the "14" in the third instruction is one more than the number of numbers to be added. The first AH instruction adds the contents of STZ plus register 3 to register 5, thus forming the sum. The next AH instruction increases the contents of register 3 by 2 so that the next number in the STZ list will be picked up by the previous instruction. The BCT instruction subtracts 1 from register 4 and transfers to BNTER as long as register 4 is positive. After 13 numbers have been added, register 4 becomes 0 and the sum is stored in BSUM.

**Pseudo-Operations.** Another important feature of assemblers, again first introduced in SAP, is the pseudo-operation. Its primary use is to convey information to the assembler about the way it is to deal with the program: In this respect it resembles the control combinations of the EDSAC Initial Orders. A secondary use of pseudo-instructions is to deal with constructions (e.g., numerical constants) that do not conform to the operation-code/address structure. The name "pseudo-operation" arises from the use of the operation-code field to specify the action that is to take place.

Important uses of pseudo-operations are in defining and manipulating symbols and in the allocation of storage. For example, the SAP pseudo-operation BSS reserves an area of storage and sets the address of the start of the area as the value of a symbol (so that the area can be referenced symbolically by other instructions). More precisely,

*symbol* BSS *integer-constant*

will reserve a block of storage of length *integer-constant* registers, and set the address of the first register as the value of *symbol.*

Other pseudo-operations allow explicit setting of symbol values; thus,

*symbol* SET *expression*

will set the *symbol* to the value given by the *expression* (which must consist of constants and/or previously defined symbols), and

*symbol-1* SYN *symbol-2*

will give *symbol-2* the same value as *symbol-1* (i.e., they become synonyms).

Another group of pseudo-operations is concerned with the cross-referencing between separately assembled pieces of code; thus

*symbol* COMMON *n*

defines the value of *symbol* as the address of a block of *n* registers in the COMMON area, and ENTRY is used to define the entry point(s) to a subroutine.

Numerical constants are also dealt with by pseudo-instructions. In SAP, pseudo-operations OCT, DEC were provided, the "operand" field for these consisting of a list of constants in octal or decimal notation, respectively, and the constants being converted into binary by the assembler. The pseudo-operation BCD allowed decimal constants to be converted to binary-coded decimal (packed decimal) format. In assembler code for the IBM 370, there is only a slight change: A single pseudo-operation DC (Define Constant) is followed by a list of constants, each of which is preceded by a format code to specify the type of conversion to be carried out.

**Conditional assembly.** A feature of many assemblers is the ability to selectively assemble pieces of program: This is particularly useful in package programs that have to provide a large number of options. In its simplest form this facility is provided by a pseudo-instruction that controls the assembly of the immediately following instruction. For example, there might be an operation IFT (if-true) such that

IFT *symbol*-1 *relation symbol*-2

will cause the next instruction to be assembled only if the relation between the symbols is true. The obvious converse IFF (if-false) will usually be provided also.

In more recent assemblers a more elaborate facility of assembly-time jumps and labels is provided. Typically, assembly-time labels (or sequence symbols) are preceded by a period and appear in the label field. However, they are ignored by the assembler except in the context of two new pseudo-instructions AGO and AIF. (The mnemonics are derived from "assembler GOTO" and "assembler IF") Let .ss be a sequence symbol; then

AGO .SS

causes assembly to be continued from the line in which the symbol .ss appears in the label field (usually, this must be a forward jump), and

AIF (*symbol-1 relation symbol-2*) .SS

causes assembly to be continued from the line labeled .ss if the condition is true; otherwise, assembly continues with the next line of code, as usual.

**Listings.** An assembler usually provides a variety of information about the program that it has assembled. Besides details of any obvious errors such as incorrect syntax or multiple definition of symbols, the following may be provided:

1. Listing of symbolic instructions side by side with generated binary or binary-symbolic code.
2. Table of symbols defined in a routine, with or without their values.
3. Table of symbols used in a routine.
4. Cross-reference table: for each symbol defined, its name, value, and a list of all the instructions that reference it.

The form of the listing is generally controlled by one or more pseudo-operations; for example:

```
LIST FULL
LIST NONE
LIST SYMBOLS
etc.
```

Other common pseudo-operations are EJECT, which causes a page feed on the printer at the point in the listing where it occurs, and SPACE *n*, which causes a spacing of *n* blank lines in the listing. The listing corresponding to the program fragment for the IBM System/370 (given in the section "Facilities") is shown in Fig. 1.

**Macro Assemblers.** An important attribute of an assembler is the ability to define and use macros. It often happens that a certain pattern of orders occurs in several places in a program with only minor variations. This is particularly the case if there is a common operation that requires several machine orders for its execution; for example, the calling sequence for a call of another routine. Thus,

```
LOC      OBJECT CODE        ADDR1   ADDR2   ST#  NAME    OP    OPERANDS
 .
 .
 .
00000C   5830  2030                 00038     8          L     3, =F'0'      CLEAR REGISTER
000010   5850  2030                 00038     9          L     5, =F'0'      USING LITERAL
000014   4840  2034                 00030    10          LH    4, =H'14"     LOAD REGISTER
000018   47F0  2010                 00024    11          B     BCNT          ENTER LOOP
00001C   4A53  2038                 00040    12   BNTER  AH    5,STZ(3)      INDEX STZ BY REG 3
000020   4A30  2036                 0003B    13          AH    3, =H'2'      INCREMENT INDEX
000024   4640  2014                 0001C    14   BCNT   BCT   4,BNTER       BRANCH ON COUNT
000028   5050  2054                 0005C    15          ST    5,BSUM        STORE SUM
                                             16   *
000040   000F00E100010034  }                 17   STZ    DC    H'15,225,1,52,10,48,76,42,88,26,14,4,32'
000048   000A00300046002A  } (Hexadecimal equivalents
000050   0058001A000E0004  }  of 13 numbers)
000058   0020              <-
00005A   0000 <- (Filler needed to align next instruction properly)
00005C   00000000                            18   BSUM   DC    F'0'
```

The LOC column shows the address of each instruction relative to the beginning of the program. The OBJECT CODE columns show the contents of the instructions as they will appear in memory. The ADDR1 (not used in this example) and ADDR2 columns give the effective addresses of the operands. Thus, assuming general register 2 holds the value 8, 2030 has the effective value 8 + 30 = 38. The ST# column is a sequential line number for the programmer's convenience. Note that columns to left of ST# are all given in hexadecimal.

**Fig. 1.** Example of Listing from System/370 Assembler.

to call the routine SUB with parameters A and B, it might be necessary to write

```
LDX 4,*
TFR SUB
NOP A
NOP B
```

(The first instruction loads into register 4 the address of itself; i.e., its location in store. From this the subroutine can compute the return address to resume operation of the main program after the calling sequence. The parameters A and B are assumed to be addresses, and have been placed as the address parts of two no-operation [i.e., null] instructions.) Evidently, it would be convenient for the programmer to be able to write

```
CALL   SUB,A,B
```

and have the calling sequence generated for him. The advantages of this approach are threefold. The programmer writes less; his program is more readable; and if at some future stage the calling sequence is changed, a change at one place in the program will insure that all CALLs are changed without the need to alter each one individually.

(In SAP the CALL macro was built into the system, and was described as a pseudo-operation. This usage of the term "pseudo-operation" is no longer current.) A macro assembler allows the programmer to define macroinstructions as sequences of ordinary instructions, and provides a means of inserting variable information in the generated sequences.

**The Working of the Assembler.** The "classic" assembler takes a routine (or subprogram) and converts it into binary symbolic form for subsequent processing by a linkage editor. The conversion is accomplished in two passes (i.e., the source program is scanned twice). The basic strategy is very simple. The first pass through the source program collects all the symbol definitions into a symbol table, and the second pass converts the program to binary symbolic form, using the definitions collected in the first pass. (The merit of a separate pass to collect symbol definitions is that it obviates the tricky situation that arises if an occurrence of a symbol has to be processed before the symbol has been defined.)

Although the program is scanned twice, only in the crudest systems is the physical source material read twice. If the assembler is reading directly from cards, then the source material can be copied onto magnetic tape or disk during the first pass, and so preserved for the second pass. In the environment of modern operating systems, the assembler will in any case read card images from tape or disk on the first pass. A good assembler may encode the information read in the first pass into a form that allows a more efficient second pass.

During the second pass, the assembler will have to recognize three sorts of quantities: absolute quantities, relocatable quantities, and references to externally defined symbols. In the simplest case, all relocatable quantities are expressed relative to an origin at the beginning of the routine. The assembler therefore has to categorize the symbols as it builds up the symbol table, and then check for illegal combinations in expressions. (For example, it is meaningless to add two relocatable symbols, though their difference may be a respectable absolute quantity.) The exact form of the output from the assembler depends on the linkage editor. Typically, the assembler might produce the following output:

| | |
|---|---|
| Header | Name of routine, |
| RLB | Relocatable binary section: Consists of binary symbolic code and relocation information, |
| Definition table | Definitions of global symbols defined in the routine (i.e., symbols that will be referenced in other routines). |
| Use table | Details of use of global and COMMON symbols in the routine (i.e., symbols used here but defined elsewhere). |

The *definition table* carries information about symbols defined in this routine which are to have a global meaning. Since these may be absolute or relative, the table must carry this information as well as the value. In the case of a relative symbol the value is relative to the beginning of the routine.

The *use table* is more complex, since it records all occurrences of global symbols within the routine. Its exact form will depend on the facilities provided by the assembler—in particular the circumstances in which global symbols can be used. (If multiplication of global symbols is allowed, an additional table, the *product use table*, is also required.)

If multiple location counters are used, an extra block must be output giving the amount of space used by the routine relative to each location counter. Each relocatable item will carry with it an indication of the relevant location counter.

**Meta Assemblers.** Assemblers for different machines have much in common. They organize symbol tables, evaluate expressions, and generate binary words from a number of symbolic fields. The idea of a meta assembler is to provide a system with these general capabilities, together with a means of describing (in machine-independent form) the assembly rules for a particular machine. The meta assembler accepts this description and then functions apparently as a normal assembler.

The idea of a meta assembler originated with Ferguson (1966), who produced the only published paper on the subject. The ideas described in the paper were utilized in the Metasymbol assembler for the SDS 900 series, in the Sleuth 11 and Utmost assemblers for the Univac 1107/8, and in the Meta system for the CDC 3300. An important feature of these systems (which is usually glossed over in their descriptions) is that the syntax of the input to a meta assembler is fixed. The meaning of the symbolic information can be defined by the user, but he cannot change the syntax. Thus, although it is possible in using a meta assembler to write an assembler for most machines, it is not possible to mimic an existing assembler. (This is one of the many differences between a meta assembler and a compiler-compiler.)

The essentially new features of a meta assembler are (1) the provision of compile-time procedures and functions, and (2) a mechanism whereby the programmer can define binary output formats and cause such binary output to be generated.

Superficially, the input to a meta assembler looks like input to any assembler; each line has three fields—label, operation, and operand. The label is optional: If there is a symbol in this field, it is assigned a value equal to the current location-counter value. The operation may be the name of a built-in system operation, in which case it is no different from a pseudo-operation in a conventional assembler. If the operation is not the name of a built-in operation, it is assumed to be the name of a programmer-defined procedure, which will be obeyed, taking the operand field as an argument.

This procedure may have the effect of generating some code, or may just perform housekeeping operations such as entering items in a table. It should be particularly noted that the procedure is obeyed during assembly. It is in many ways comparable to a macro, but instead of textual substitution we obey a piece of program *written in assembly language*. This may itself contain calls to other procedures.

The operand field contains an expression, or group of expressions, made up of symbols and/or constants. (A group of expressions separated by commas is called a set; these can be nested in the operand field.) These expressions are evaluated by the system in the same way that a normal assembler evaluates its address field. Unlike a normal assembler, the expressions may contain calls to user-defined functions.

Included in the built-in procedures are GEN and GENB, which output the values of the operand set as a sequence of words or bytes, respectively, and FORM, which allows the user to define a named template for binary output. Thus,

```
INSTR   FORM 6, 3, 15
```

defines (for a 24-bit word machine) a template made up of 3 fields consisting of 6, 3, and 15 bits, and attaches the name INSTR to this template (FORM is a built-in operation that generates named templates for later use). Suppose that subsequent to the definition of INSTR, we write

```
INSTR   LDA, 7, ALPHA + 1
```

(Here INSTR is in the operation field, and the operand field is a set of three expressions.) This will cause the three elements of the operand set to be evaluated, truncated, and concatenated to form a 24-bit binary output word. (Note that this technique would allow the operation code of an instruction to be written as an expression!)

More elaborate constructions allow the operation code mnemonics of a conventional assembler to be defined as the names of multiple-entry points to a procedure using FORM to generate instruction words. In this way, and using procedures to produce the required effect for pseudo-instructions, a "conventional" assembler image can be built up.

**"Higher-Level" Assemblers.** At this point we should perhaps ask the question, "why are assemblers still used?" Higher-level languages are adequate for many problems, but one needs to resort to assembly language if it is desired to have a close control over storage allocation and to have direct control over the machine's internal registers. Thus, assembly language finds its main use in the writing of operating systems and similar system software. In order to have direct control at the internal register level, an assembly language program is necessarily written at a fine level of detail, with each instruction representing a single primitive operation. An unfortunate effect of working at this level of detail is that programs are rarely as perspicuous as programs written in a higher-level language can be; it is impossible to write an assembly language program that displays clearly the structure of the underlying algorithm.

Recently there has been a development in the direction of "higher-level" or "Algol-like" assembly languages that attempt to combine fine control over machine registers and store with a structure that reflects the overall structure of the program; for example, repetition loops, conditional statements, and functions and procedures. The facilities provided in such a language must correspond fairly closely to the actual hardware. For example, we cannot include anything that depends on dynamic storage allocation if the underlying hardware does not provide such facilities. (Put another way, the compiler for an Algol-like assembly language cannot assume the existence of a "run-time system". Every source statement except a procedure call must compile into open code.) The precise facilities provided in a system will depend on the particular machine, but will typically include the following:

1. Symbolic names (identifiers) with associated types. The types will correspond to the storage units manipulated by the machine instructions; for example, on the IBM System/370 they would include byte, short integer, integer, real, and long real.
2. Reserved identifiers for machine registers. A synonym facility may also be provided to associate other names with registers.
3. Block structure, giving scopes to identifiers.
4. Conditional and compound statements.
5. One-dimensional arrays, but not multidimensional arrays (these cannot be accessed by simple indexing on most machines).
6. Procedures and functions. (Usually only one parameter will be possible, and the calling mechanism will be the Fortran call-by-address. This corresponds to passing the parameter as an address in an accumulator or general-purpose register.)
7. Simple expressions (but nothing involving temporary storage; all operators are of equal prece-

dence and evaluation is by a simple left-to-right scan).

8. Provision for including basic assembly language (e.g., for input operations).

The first higher-level assembler was the PL/360 system described by Wirth (1968) in a classic paper. As its name implies, it was designed for the IBM System 360 machines. An Algol-like assembler for a small machine has been developed at the National Physical Laboratory in the United Kingdom; called PL516, it is designed for the Honeywell DDP516.

REFERENCES

1951. Wilkes, M. V., D. J. Wheeler, and S. Gill. *The Preparation of Programs for an Electronic Digital Computer*. Cambridge, Mass.: Addison-Wesley

1956. Wilkes, M. V. *Automatic Digital Computers*. London: Methuen & Co.

1966. Ferguson, D. E. "The Evolution of the Meta-Assembly Program," *Commun. Assoc. Comput. Mach.*, vol. 9, p. 190.

1968. Wirth, N. "PL/360, A Programming Language for the 360 Computers," *J. Assoc. Comput. Mach.*, vol. 15, p. 37.

1971. Flores, I. *Assemblers and BAL*. Englewood Cliffs, N.J.: Prentice-Hall.

1972. Barron, D. W. *Assemblers and Loaders*, 2d ed. New York: American-Elsevier, 1972.

D. W. BARRON

## ASSEMBLY LANGUAGE. *See* MACHINE AND ASSEMBLY LANGUAGE PROGRAMMING.

## ASSOCIATION FOR COMPUTING MACHINERY (ACM)

For article on related subject *see* AMERICAN FEDERATION OF INFORMATION PROCESSING SOCIETIES.

**Purpose.** The Association for Computing Machinery is the largest scientific, educational, and technical society of the computing community. Founded in 1947, the Association is dedicated to the development of information processing as a discipline, and to the responsible use of computers in an increasing diversity of applications.

The purposes of the Association are: (1) To advance the sciences and arts of information processing, including but not restricted to the study, design, development, construction, and application of modern machinery, computing techniques and appropriate languages for general information processing, storage, retrieval, and processing of data of all kinds and the automatic control and simulation of processes. (2) To promote the free interchange of information about the sciences and arts of information processing, both among specialists and among the public in the best scientific and professional tradition. (3) To develop and maintain the integrity and competence of individuals engaged in the practices of the sciences and arts of information processing.

**How Established.** ACM was founded at Columbia University on Sept. 15, 1947, as the Eastern Association for Computing Machinery. A constitution and bylaws were adopted in September 1949. ACM was incorporated in Delaware in December 1954. The following have held the office of ACM president:

J. H. Curtiss, 1947
John W. Mauchly, 1948–1950
Franz L. Alt, 1950–1952
Samuel B. Williams, 1952–1954
Alston S. Householder, 1954–1956
John W. Carr III, 1956–1958
Richard W. Hamming, 1958–1960
Harry D. Huskey, 1960–1962
Alan J. Perlis, 1962–1964
George E. Forsythe, 1964–1966
Anthony Oettinger, 1966–1968
Bernard A. Galler, 1968–1970
Walter M. Carlson, 1970–1972
Anthony Ralston, 1972–1974
Jean E. Sammet, 1974–

**Organizational Structure.** The Association is organized into 12 regions, 11 covering the United States and Canada, and one encompassing western Europe. Each region is represented in the Council of the ACM (the elected governing body) by a regional representative. With an additional six members-at-large and the ex officio members (president, past-president, vice-president, secretary, treasurer, chairman of the Publications Board, and chairman of the Board of Special Interest Groups and Committees), the full Council comprises 25 members.

Each geographic region is subdivided into local chapters and student chapters. Presently there are approximately 100 local chapters and 125 student chapters.

The four classes of ACM membership and their qualifications are:

MEMBER—must subscribe to the purposes of the Association and have attained professional stature by demonstrating intellectual competence and ethical conduct in the arts and sciences of information processing.

ASSOCIATE—must subscribe to the purposes of the Association, but is ineligible for Member status.

STUDENT—full-time registrant at an accredited educational institution.

INSTITUTIONAL—institutions that subscribe to the purposes of the Association.

Total membership is about 30,000. The headquarters of ACM are located at 1133 Avenue of the Americas, New York, New York 10036.

**Technical Program.** The major organizational units of ACM devoted to technical activities of its members are the Special Interest Groups (SIGs) and Special Interest Committees (SICs). The SIGs and SICs operate as semiautonomous bodies within ACM for the advancement of activities in the following subject areas: Automata and Computability Theory; Computer Architecture; Artificial Intelligence, Business Data Processing; Biomedical Computing; Computers and the Physically Handicapped; Computers and Society; Data Communications; Computer Systems Installation Management; Computer Personnel Research; Computer Science Education; Computer Uses in Education; Design Automation; File Description and Translation; Computer Graphics; Information Retrieval; Language Analysis and Studies in the Humanities; Mathematical Programming; Measurement and Evaluation; Microprogramming; Numerical Mathematics; Operating Systems; Programming Languages; Symbolic and Algebraic Manipulation; Digital Simulation; Social and Behavioral Science Computing; University Computing Centers.

The National Lecturership Series was instituted in 1961 to enrich chapter activities by providing acknowledged specialists in various aspects of computing and its application. In 1966 ACM established the Turing Award, given annually to an individual selected for his contributions of a technical nature made to the computing community. The award carries an honorarium of $1,000. The recipients to date have been: Alan J. Perlis, Maurice V. Wilkes, R. W. Hamming, Marvin Minsky, J. H. Wilkinson, John McCarthy, Edsger W. Dijkstra, Charles W. Bachman, Donald E. Knuth, and (jointly) Allen Newell and Herbert A. Simon.

In 1970 the Distinguished Service Award was instituted. Its recipients have been Franz Alt, J. Donald Madden, George E. Forsythe, William Atchison, and John W. Carr III. A Programming Systems and Language Paper Award was established in 1969. In 1971, in conjunction with the twenty-fifth anniversary of the invention of the modern digital computer, ACM established the Grace Murray Hopper Award, to be given annually to the outstanding young computer professional of the year as nominated by ACM. To qualify, candidates must have been 30 years or younger at the time the qualifying contribution was made. The first award was to Donald E. Knuth.

The ACM publishes five major periodicals: *Journal of the Association for Computing Machinery* (1954, a quarterly) is devoted to highly technical papers of lasting value reporting on research and advances in the computing sciences. *Communications of the ACM* (1958, a monthly) publishes technical papers and timely articles on topics of interest to the computing profession. *Computing Reviews* (1960, a monthly) comprehensively covers the literature on computing and its applications. (A *Bibliography of Computing Literature*, keyed to *Computing Reviews*, but including additional materials, is published annually.) *Computing Surveys* (1969, a quarterly) presents comprehensive survey coverage of the state-of-the-art in the various areas of computing science and business data processing. *Transactions on Mathematical Software* (1975, a quarterly) publishes theoretical and applied articles on mathematical software as well as algorithms for computers.

ACM holds an annual conference that stresses technical programs and publishes a proceedings of the papers presented. ACM sponsors the annual Computer Science Conference, which is devoted mainly to brief reports of current research. ACM is a founding member of the American Federation of Information Processing Societies and participates in the annual National Computer Conference. In addition, the Special Interest groups and other subunits sponsor numerous technical symposia and meetings in North America and Europe.

I. L. AUERBACH

## ASSOCIATION FOR EDUCATIONAL DATA SYSTEMS (AEDS)

For article on related subject *see* AMERICAN FEDERATION OF INFORMATION PROCESSING SOCIETIES.

The Association for Educational Data Systems (AEDS) is a private, not-for-profit educational corporation founded and incorporated in Florida in 1962 by a group of professional educators and technical specialists oriented in educational applications.

The purpose of AEDS is to provide a forum for the exchange of ideas and information about the relationship of modern technology to modern education. Its objectives are:

- To provide a national association for educational data systems and encourage and assist the establishment of associations for educational data systems.
- To provide for sharing and exchanging ideas, techniques, materials, and procedures for use in modern educational data processing.
- To promote general recognition of the vital professional role played by the educational data processing specialist in a modern school system and the high level of competence required for this role.
- To promote and encourage appropriate use of electronic data processing and computing equipment and techniques for the improvement of education.
- To cooperate with manufacturers, distributors, and operators of educational data processing equipment and supplies in establishing and maintaining proper technical standards, and in meeting new needs for specialized devices and systems.
- To encourage and advise concerning research relating to educational data processing.

The following have served as presidents of the Association:

Robert Gates, 1962–1963
John Caffrey, 1963–1964
Don D. Bushnell, 1964–1965
C. Taylor Whittier, 1965–1966
John W. Sullivan, 1966–1967
Ernest Anderson, 1967–1968
John W. Hamblen, 1968–1969
Ralph Van Dusseldorp, 1969–1970
L. Everett Yarbrough, 1970–1971
Sylvia Charp, 1971–1972
Russell E. Weitz, 1972–1973
James Augustine, Jr., 1973–1975
Thomas McConnell, 1975–

The headquarters of AEDS is located at 1201 Sixteenth Street, N. W., Washington, D. C. 20036.

AEDS conducts an annual meeting dedicated to general and technical sessions on educational data processing.

The following publications are included in the membership fee: *AEDS Monitor*—a monthly publication giving current information about educational data processing; and *AEDS Journal*—a quarterly publication containing technical information about the development and specific applications of educational data processing.

I. L. AUERBACH

## ASSOCIATION FRANÇAISE POUR LA CYBERNETIQUE ECONOMIQUE ET TECHNIQUE (AFCET)

For article on related subject *see* INTERNATIONAL FEDERATION OF INFORMATION PROCESSING.

**Purpose.** AFCET endeavors to bring together French scientists, engineers, users, and manufacturers working and interested in data processing, automation, and operational research, as well as in measurement and applied mathematics.

**How Established.** The organization was established in 1969 as a result of the amalgamation of: AFIRO (Association Française d'Informatique et de Recherche Operationnelle), AFRA (Association Française de Regulation et d'Automatisme), and AFIC (Association Française d'Instrumentation et de Controle). The merger was due to the relation between measurement and instrumentation as well as the relation of operational research to automation and data processing. The presidents of AFCET since 1969 have been

R. Mercier, 1969
J. Csech, 1970–1971
F. Genuys, 1972–1973
L. Guilysse, 1974

**Organizational Structure.** AFCET has 4,000 members at present. In addition, about 300 industrial companies are registered with AFCET and pay a much higher contribution than do members. The Association has various independent sections, each headed by a chairman. These include: AT—Automatique; CI—Composants Instrumentation; IG—Informatique de Gestion; SI—Systemes et Machines Informatiques; MA—Mathematiques; RO—Recherche Operationnelle; and AP—Applications Scientifiques et Industrielles. Its headquarters is located at Universite Paris IX Dauphine, 75775 Paris Cedex 16, France.

**Technical Program.** The sections organize seminars regularly (for 150 to 300 persons) on current subjects. Every year, AFCET holds a congress on data processing or on other subjects closely connected with its activities. It also participates and organizes international symposia such as the Fifth IMEKO Congress, Versailles 1970; the First IFAC/IFIP Symposium on Traffic Control, Versailles 1970; and the Fifth IFAC World Congress on Automatic Control, Paris 1972.

**Publications.** The Association issues four official publications:

*Rairo* (Revue Française d'Automatique, d'Informatique et de Recherche Operationnelle), published, in four series of three issues each, per year. This review contains reports of a very high level on the work done in laboratories and research institutes, Ph. D. theses, etc.

*Automatisme,* published in ten issues per year; covers industrial applications of automatic control and computer systems.

*Informatique de Gestion,* published in ten issues during the year; treats administrative data processing systems and computers.

*Mesures,* published in ten issues over the year; covers measurement, instrumentation, and components.

I. L. AUERBACH

# ASSOCIATIVE LANGUAGES

For articles on related subjects *see* ARTIFICIAL INTELLIGENCE; INFORMATION AND DATA; INFORMATION RETRIEVAL; LIST PROCESSING LANGUAGES; LISTS AND LIST PROCESSING; PROGRAMMING LANGUAGES; and STRING PROCESSING LANGUAGES.
For article on related term *see* HASHING.

Associative language research has been motivated by two considerations. The languages might be useful in associative computers or could simply be a better way of stating algorithms. Applications have been suggested or carried out in essentially all nonnumerical problems and in a few special numerical ones such as sparse matrix calculations.

The essential fact about an associative memory is that it does not rely on explicit addresses. A reference to information contained in a memory cell is specified by a partial description of its contents. All cells in the memory which meet the specification are referred to by the statement. A conventional coordinate-addressed memory can be thought of as a special case in the following way: Each cell of the associative memory will be a pair consisting of a conventional cell and its address:

| Associative cell: | address | conventional cell |
|---|---|---|

To access a cell in this special associative memory, one specifies the contents of one particular part (the address field) of a cell. In the general associative memory a cell can be accessed by specifying the contents of any part of the cell.

The following example may help point out the importance of this seemingly minor difference. Suppose one were to store the contents of a telephone directory in a computer memory. There are several ways in which the data could be organized so that the telephone number of a given person could be found fairly quickly. However, the problem of going from a telephone number to its owner is rather difficult. One could, of course, enter a second directory ordered by numbers rather than names, but this entails representing the same information twice in the memory. There are several other possibilities, but all lead to compromises between inefficiency in time and inefficiency in storage. In an associative memory either question could be answered in one memory access and without any redundant information being stored in the memory.

This example is so clear and striking that it should be suspect. First of all, it is often the case that one person has several telephone numbers or that several people are listed for the same number. This is the so-called multiple-hit situation and is at the root of many of the problems encountered in using associative memories. Many other difficulties arise in the design of hardware associative memories.

## ASSOCIATIVE LANGUAGES

There is even a theoretical basis for questioning the inherent practicality of a hardware associative memory. However, the idea of referring to information by a partial specification of its contents is intriguing and has found its way into a number of programming systems.

Let us consider the behavior of an associative memory each of whose cells contains an ordered 3-tuple:

3-element associative cell: | a | o | v |

written $a \cdot o \equiv v$. The symbols $a$, $o$, and $v$ can be thought of as mnemonics for attribute, object, and value.

The elements of the 3-tuple are drawn from a universe of items; a 3-tuple of items is an association. Typical associations might be

father • john doe ≡ don doe
end • line ≡ point

If a universe of associations were stored in an associative memory, any partial specification should lead to retrieval. Letting $x$, $z$ represent unspecified positions in an association, Table 1 enumerates the partial specifications (forms) possible in a 3-element associative memory.

**Table 1**

| Form Name | Form | Example | Interpretation |
|---|---|---|---|
| F0 | $a \cdot o \equiv v$ | son • john ≡ don | The association itself, if in memory |
| F1 | $a \cdot o \equiv x$ | son • john ≡ $x$ | Sons of john |
| F2 | $a \cdot x \equiv v$ | son • $x$ ≡ don | Father of don |
| F3 | $x \cdot o \equiv v$ | $x$ • john ≡ don | Relation of john to don |
| F4 | $a \cdot x \equiv z$ | son • $x$ ≡ $z$ | All father-son pairs |
| F5 | $x \cdot z \equiv v$ | $x$ • $z$ ≡ don | All associations with don as third component |
| F6 | $x \cdot o \equiv z$ | $x$ • john ≡ $z$ | All associations with john as second component |

Alternatively, Table 1 can be viewed as a generalization of the property list features of languages such as Lisp and IPL-V, and of the records (structures) features of languages such as Algol 68, Simula, and PL/I. In all these systems there are provisions for directly treating forms F0 and F1 and handling F3 and F6 fairly efficiently. The associative languages treat the association symmetrically and attempt to process efficiently all the forms of Table 1.

The basic operations on the universe of associations are entry, removal, and retrieval. Typically,

MAKE father • tom ≡ bill

will place the new association in the universe if it is not already there. Similarly,

ERASE father • ANY ≡ bill

will erase all associations that match the specification.

The heart of any associative system is its retrieval capability. One problem is that a retrieval statement is, in general, multiple-valued. This has led to the inclusion of *sets* in several systems and to statements like sons ← son • john, which assigns to *sons* all the sons of john.

Another technique is to have iteration statements ranging over all values; e.g.:

**foreach** $x$ **suchthat** son • $x$ ≡ don **do** • • •

The situation becomes much more complicated when there are several unspecified elements in a retrieval request. For example, consider

**foreach** $x,y,z$ **suchthat**
father • $x$ ≡ $y$ and father • $y$ ≡ $z$ **do** (1)
**make** granddad • $x$ ≡ $z$.

Statement (1) requires solving for three variables. It is clearly inadequate to solve for each variable independently; the system must form an assignment of items that satisfies the associative context. For example, if the associations of the universe were

father • tom ≡ bill
father • pete ≡ tom
father • bill ≡ don
father • george ≡ clyde

statement (1) would yield assignments

$(x,y,z)$ = (tom , bill , don)
$(x,y,z)$ = (pete , tom , bill)

and after the execution of statement (1) the universe would also contain the associations

granddad • tom ≡ don
granddad • pete ≡ bill

Treating statements like this requires a system to make use of intermediate structures and a fairly sophisticated interpreter. It should be noted that *no associative processing hardware has been suggested which can directly solve the general case of the problem above.* Statement (1) also suggests yet another way to view associative languages—as a generalization of pattern matching systems (e.g., SNOBOL) to move complex structures. If we picture an association as a labeled arrow in a graph, e.g.,

$$\text{john} \xrightarrow{\text{son}} \text{don}$$

the associative language is a graph-matching system.

Most associative languages incorporate the concepts described above, but differ in other ways. One natural extension is to drop the restriction to triples. Most of the research on *n*-ary relations has been done in work oriented toward information retrieval (Codd, 1970). Although there is no clear demarcation, the following points generally separate the two fields. Associative languages are designed to (1) be used by programmer, (2) respond in fractional seconds, (3) have their data base fit in secondary storage. Information retrieval presupposes very large files, naive users and a somewhat slower response. There is currently no known mechanism for efficiently handling all the forms analogous to Table 1 for *n*-ary relations.

One problem that is common to information retrieval and associative languages is the question of how much deduction to incorporate. For example, one probably wants a system to use the fact that "bigger" is transitive in retrieval. Tramp (Ash and Sibley, 1968), for example, incorporates a few simple deduction rules. The problem is where to stop; one could incorporate many such rules or even a general theorem prover. At this point, the associative retrieval problem becomes part of artificial intelligence. In fact, all the new AI languages (Sussman and McDermott, 1972) incorporate associative retrieval features, including mechanisms for retrieving implied relations.

There has been quite a bit of work on the problem of efficiently implementing associative languages. Most systems employ a combination of hash-coding (Feldman and Rovner, 1969) and list-processing techniques. This work overlaps similar studies in data structures and information retrieval. A related problem is to retrieve compound requests (like statement 1) efficiently; one should not, for example, find all males and then select only those over 7 feet tall. Some work has been done along these lines, but much more could be done.

### References

1968. Ash, W. L., and E. H. Sibley. "TRAMP: An Interpretive Associative Processor with Deductive Capabilities," *Proc. ACM 23rd National Conference*, pp. 143–156.

1969. Feldman, J. A., and P. D. Rovner, "An ALGOL-Based Associative Language," *Communications of the ACM*, Vol. 12, No. 8, pp. 439–449.

1970. Codd, E. F. "A Relational Model of Data for Large Shared Data Banks," *Communications of the ACM*, Vol. 13, No. 6, June, pp. 377–387.

1971. Findler, N. V., J. L. Pfaltz, and H. J. Bernstein. *Four High-Level Extensions of FORTRAN IV: SLIP, AMPPL II, TREETRAN, and SYMBOLANG*, Part II. New York: Spartan Books.

1972. Sussman, G. J., and D. V. McDermott. "From PLANNER to CONNIVER—A Genetic Approach," *Proc. AFIPS Fall Joint Computer Conference*, Vol. 41, Part II, pp. 1171–1179.

J. Feldman

## ASSOCIATIVE MEMORY

For articles on related subjects *see* Addressing; Cache Memory; and Memory: Main.
For article on related term *see* Atlas.

Data in an associative memory (Lewin, 1972) or content-addressable memory is not accessed by address as in conventional memory. Rather than being identified by the name of its location, it is identified from properties of its own value. To retrieve a word from associative store, a search key (or descriptor) must be presented which represents particular values of all or some of the bits of the word. This key is compared in parallel with the corresponding lock or tag bits of all stored words, and all words matching this key are signaled to be available. If the key is loose, with few attributes, it will access many words. The memory might indicate the number of such words and would in any case normally provide each of these in turn for examination. The order in which they are presented is usually related to their order in physical storage and tells nothing of their value. Once available, each word can be used or, if not wanted, flagged (by a change of a single search bit) so that succeeding words can be retrieved.

It is obvious that associative search can be fairly complex if the search key has few elements and the association is loose. A limiting case is that in which at most one occurrence of a search key match exists. This is the case in the use of associative stores between levels in a memory hierarchy where the associative store is a scratch pad notating the existence of a copy of a record in the next higher-level store. Such is also the use of associative storage in cache memory management.

Various attempts have been made to build associative processors in which the main memory is partially or completely associative (Lewin, 1972). In this case each memory word, in addition to match or equality logic on each bit, has other facilities such as "greater than" detection.

Fig. 1 illustrates the logical structure of an associative store, showing the possibility of search inputs ("don't care") whose value results in a positive match independent of the bit stored in the associative memory. In practice, such a store may be implemented using magnetic core or integrated circuit technology. In addition to the associative search mechanism, the memory is usually equipped with conventional read/write facilities (not shown in Fig. 1).

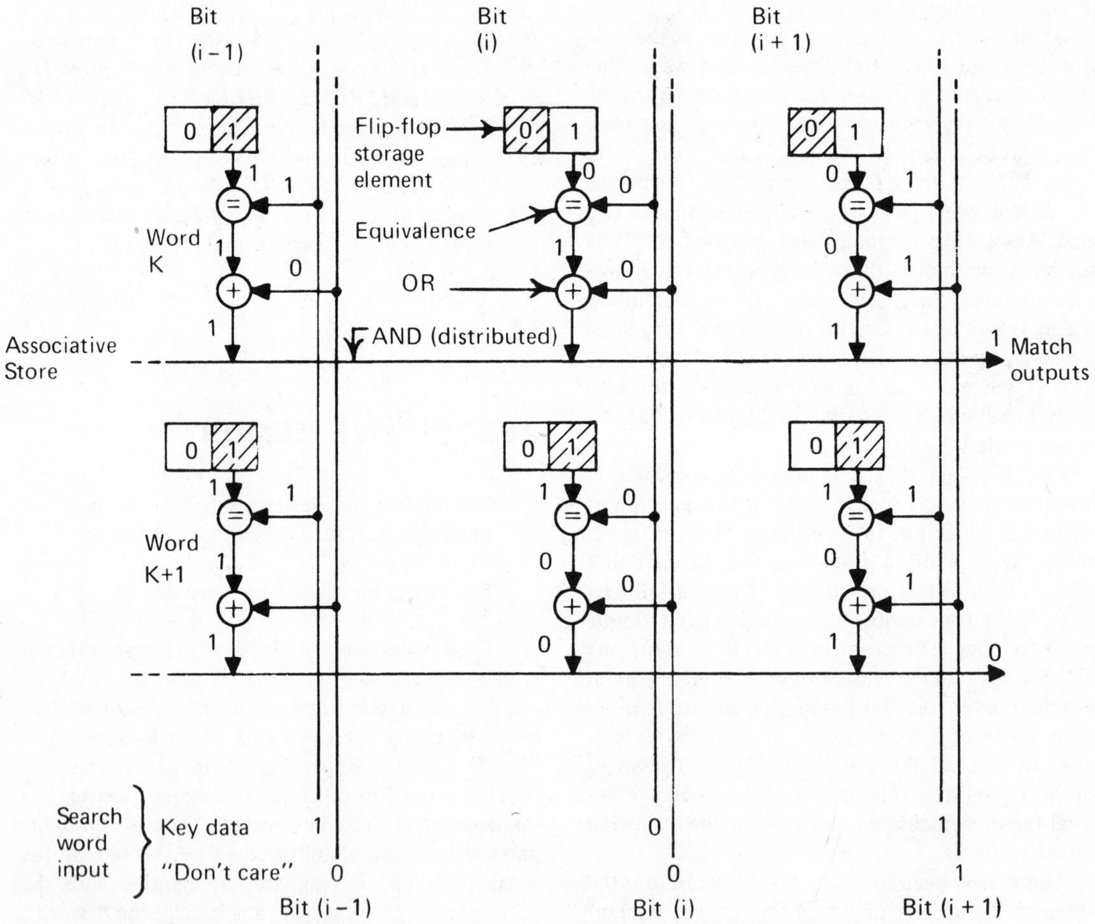


**Fig. 1.** Schematic of an associative store of two words of three bits each being accessed by match on two bits and by "don't care" on one.

A flip-flop is shown as the basic storage element and is shaded to indicate its current state. An equivalence circuit (denoted by =) is used to make the comparison with the search key. An additional OR circuit (denoted by +) per bit allows the use of a "don't care" search condition. The output from each bit is combined in an AND, represented by the horizontal line on the figure. A match output is 1 if and only if the stored data and key data bits match everywhere that "don't care" inputs are zero. Fig. 1 shows a match between a stored value of (1,0,0) and a search key of (1,0,X), where X indicates the "don't care" condition.

One important application of associative storage is in paging memory management. In such systems, of which the Atlas computer was an early major example, a relatively small, fast, main store is used in conjunction with a slow, large bulk or backup store. Each memory is divided into blocks or pages whose size may vary typically from 64 to 1,024 words. The small main memory will hold a small number of these, say 8 to 32, while the bulk store may have a capacity of thousands of pages. Data is transferred between main and backup store in page-size quantities. When the central processor requires a new word of information, high-order bits of its address are checked against appropriate bits of an associative page-address store in order to ascertain the existence in main memory of the word sought. If the page is already present, the associative store provides additional bits, giving its location in main store. If not present, related central processing unit (CPU) activity is halted while the page-memory access mechanism establishes a main store page location whose contents are returned to backup storage, after which this area of main store is refilled with the required new page.

A paging organization utilizing an associative page lookup is shown in Fig. 2. In this example a backup store of 1,024 pages of 64 words each is

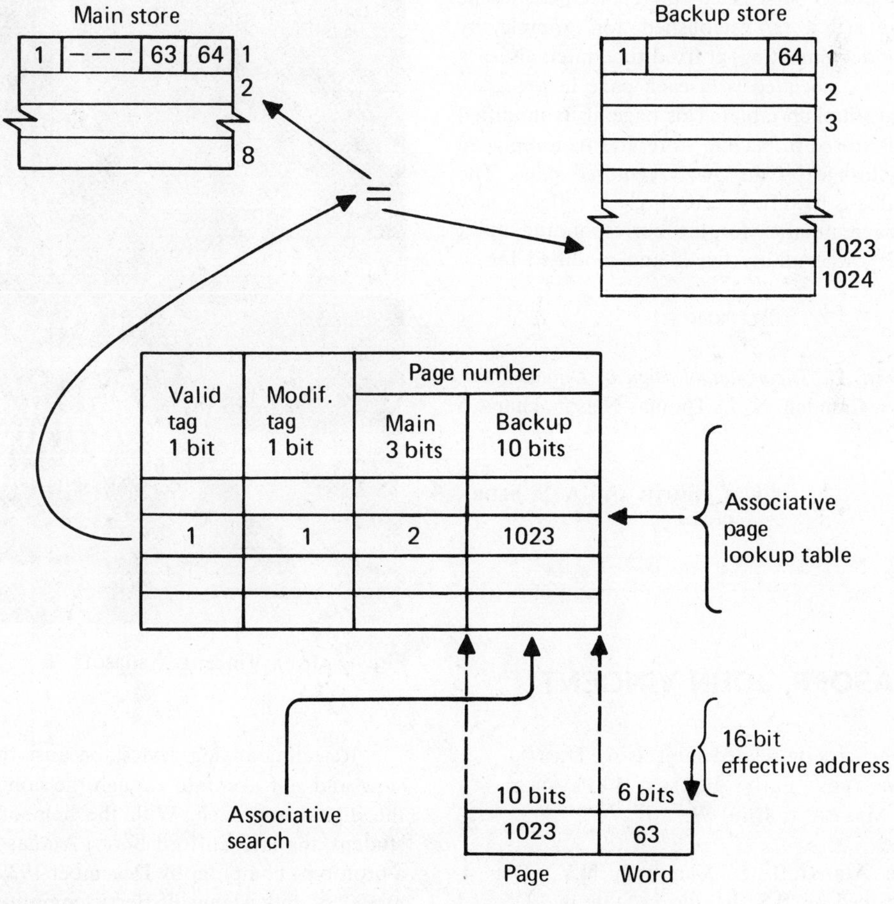


**Fig. 2.** A paging organization using an associative lookup table.

illustrated. The main store has a capacity of 8 pages of 64 words. An associative page lookup table of 4 words of 15 bits each is used to maintain order. In use, the upper 10 bits or page address of the effective address (1023) from the CPU is compared associatively with ten-bit page number in the associative store. If a match occurs, 5 bits are provided (3, 1, 1), giving the page location in main store (2) as well as two data integrity tags (1, 1). The valid tag indicates that the data in main store is a valid copy of that in backup store. The modified tag indicates that the data in main store has been modified by the CPU and is therefore not the same as in backup storage.

The result in the preceding example is that the word sought, number 63 from page 1023, is present at page 2, word 63 of the main store, that it is valid, and may differ from its image in backup store. Had the desired page not been in main store, one page of main store would have been selected for replacement, ideally one whose valid tag was zero, indicating it to be no longer needed. If all valid tags were 1, a page would be selected for replacement whose recent use is low (as established, for example, by automatic decrementing, at fixed time intervals, of a use counter associated with each page in the associative page-lookup table). This page, if its modified tag is 1, is stored in backup store and then replaced in main storage by the newly required page. The lookup table is modified accordingly to reflect a new backup page number for the corresponding main store page with validity tag 1, and modified tag 0.

REFERENCE

1972. Lewin, D. *Theory and Design of Digital Computers*. Camden, N. J.: Thomas Nelson, chaps. 6 and 9.

K. C. SMITH AND A. S. SEDRA

## ATANASOFF, JOHN VINCENT

For articles on related subjects *see* DIGITAL COMPUTERS: Early; ECKERT, J. PRESPER; and MAUCHLY, JOHN W.

John Atanasoff (b. Hamilton, N.Y., Oct. 4, 1903) received his B.S. at Florida State in 1925 and his M.S. at Iowa State in 1926.

Impeded by the cumbersome solving of large systems of equations and other complex calculations while working on his Ph.D. (Wisconsin, 1930, in math-physics), Atanasoff dismantled desk calculators in an attempt to adapt them and increase their computational capabilities. After receiving his doctorate, he returned to Iowa State in 1930, where he remained until 1945 as a professor in mathematics and (later) in physics. During his tenure there, he revamped an IBM punched card machine in another attempt to speed tedious calculations for his graduate students.

**Fig. 1.** John Vincent Atanasoff

Rejecting analog devices because they were too slow and not accurate enough, he concentrated on the digital approach. With the help of a graduate student, the late Clifford Berry, Atanasoff had built a prototype computer by December 1939. A working model of the Atanasoff-Berry computer was completed in 1942. It was a serial, binary, electromechanical machine, and employed various new techniques that Atanasoff had invented, including novel uses of logic circuitry and a regenerative memory.

Atanasoff did not understand completely the extent of the contribution he had made to the advancement of technology and did not anticipate the wide use of computers. IBM and Remington Rand rejected Atanasoff's overtures, and Iowa State —not fully realizing the potential importance of his computer—failed to obtain patent rights. Discouraged by his own attempts to obtain a patent, Atanasoff gave up. He spent the rest of his professional career in various governmental and industrial jobs, including the presidency of two companies he founded, Ordnance Engineering Corporation and Cybernetics, Inc. For his work with the Naval Ordnance Laboratory during World War II, he received the U.S. Naval Distinguished Service Award in 1945.

Only very recently has Atanasoff achieved recognition as one of the fathers of the digital computer. In a patent infringement suit filed in 1973 by Sperry-Rand against Honeywell, there was testimony by Atanasoff and others concerning the development of the first electronic computer, the ENIAC, by John Mauchly and J. Presper Eckert of the Moore School of Electrical Engineering at the University of Pennsylvania between 1942 and 1946. The decision in this case by Federal District Judge Earl R. Larson concluded that Eckert and Mauchly had derived some of their ideas from Atanasoff, partly as a result of a visit Mauchly made to Atanasoff at Iowa State in 1941.

G. MOLLENHOFF

## ATLAS

For article on related subject *see* DIGITAL COMPUTERS: Contemporary and Future.

The Atlas computer was the third in a series of early computers designed in the United Kingdom by a team under T. M. Kilburn in the Department of Electrical Engineering, University of Manchester, in association with Ferranti Ltd. (later ICT Ltd.). Previous systems were the Ferranti Mark I and Ferranti Mark II (Mercury).

Design of Atlas began in 1958, and ultimately three systems, known as Atlas 1, were constructed and installed at the University of Manchester (1962), University of London (1963), and the Atlas Laboratory, Chilton (1963). All were operated until the early 1970s with the Chilton machine being the last to be switched off in March, 1973.

In many respects, Atlas led the way in design of an integrated computer system, combining many novel hardware features with an advanced software operating system. Among the new concepts that Atlas successfully introduced to the computer world were multiprogramming, onel-level store, and paging. It was the first major system designed for multiprogramming and was provided with a composite memory, consisting of ferrite cores and magnetic drums linked by program to provide the user with a one-level store. This was achieved by a paging system in which page switching was controlled by a simple learning program, or swapping algorithm. There was also a wire-mesh/ferrite rod (hairbrush) memory of 8,000 words to hold the supervisor. The standard word length was 48 bits, equivalent to one single-address instruction with two modifiers and allowing for up to $2^{20}$ addresses; 128 index registers were provided. Instructions were normally executed at an average rate of 0.5 ms, about a hundred times faster than the Mercury computer.

The magnetic tape system used 1-in. tapes, although standard 0.5-in. tapes could also be used. Magnetic disks were not standard, but were fitted later to the Manchester and Chilton machines. Multiple I/O channels provided for both paper-tape and punched-card peripherals as well as line printers.

Other features of the supervisor program, which was produced by a small team under D. J. Howarth (1961–1962, 1962) were the facilities for scheduling and streaming of jobs, automatic control of peripherals, detailed job accounting, and a sophisticated level of operator control. It was normal, with some discretion in selecting the job mix, to obtain 60–80% effective use of the CPU.

A modified version of Atlas, known as Atlas 2, was produced with increased core memory and no magnetic drums (thereby dispensing with paging), the prototype being the Titan computer at the University of Cambridge, which was taken out of service at the end of 1973. Two others in this series were installed: one at the Atomic Weapons Research Establishment, Aldermaston, and one at the Computer-Aided Design Centre, Cambridge. The latter was still in use in 1974.

Although technical and economic reasons, partly due to advances in component manufacture, prevented the Atlas computers from achieving commercial success, they represent an important landmark in the development of advanced computer systems.

REFERENCES

1961–1962. Howarth, D. J., R. B. Payne, and F. H. Sumner. "The Manchester University Atlas Operating System; Part II, Users' Description," *Computer J.*, Vol. 4. pp. 226–229.

1962. Howarth, D. J., P. D. Jones, and M. T. Wyld. "The Atlas Scheduling System," *Computer J.*, Vol. 5. pp. 238–244.

1961–1962. Kilburn, T., D. J. Howarth, R. B. Payne, and F. H. Sumner. The Manchester University Atlas Operating System; Part I, Internal Organisation," *Computer J.*, Vol. 4, pp. 222–225.

1962. Kilburn, T. D., B. G. Edwards, M. J. Lanigan, and F. H. Sumner. "One-Level Storage System," *IRE Trans.*, EC-11, Vol. 2. pp. 223–235.

R. A. BUCKINGHAM

# AUDIO RESPONSE TERMINAL

For articles on related subjects *see* DATA COMMUNICATIONS; INPUT-OUTPUT DEVICES; and TERMINALS.

Audio response terminals allow data to be entered into a computer through a keyboard similar to a typewriter terminal. However, the output from the computer is in the form of a spoken (audio) reply. This spoken reply is generated by an audio response unit attached to the computer.

**Audio Response Units.** Basically, there are two techniques that allow a computer to generate a spoken reply. The first technique is to synthesize human speech by the generation of signals and frequencies similar to that produced in speech. Such a device is the IBM 7772 audio response unit (Fig. 1). The other technique is based upon the prerecording on a magnetic drum or disk of words spoken by humans, similar to the use of magnetic tape in home tape recorders. In this case the audio response unit is able to select a number of prerecorded words from the drum or disk, and transmit these one at a time along a telephone line to an audio response terminal, so constructing a meaningful sentence or message. The IBM 7770 audio response unit uses this technique (Fig. 1). With this unit, the number of words that may be prerecorded is limited by the size of the drum. Such audio response units have a limited vocabulary, but are fully capable of providing meaningful responses when used for specific applications. The appropriate words relating to the particular applications are prerecorded on the drum, generally during manufacture of the unit.

Thus, audio response units allow a computer to respond to a question with a spoken reply in whatever language required and, in the case of the 7770, in any accent, using either a male or female voice as prerecorded on the drum.

Devices suitable for use as audio response terminals include Touch-Tone telephones and portable audio terminals.

THE TOUCH-TONE TELEPHONE AS A TERMINAL. The Touch-Tone telephone (Fig. 2), which uses buttons rather than a dial, is now widely in use. The depression of a particular button creates a tone of an audio frequency that can be transmitted along a telephone line. Each button generates a specific tone, so that each tone can be interpreted as a particular number.

As a computer input device, Touch-Tone telephones are very economical and readily available. However, they are generally limited only to numeric information, plus one or two other special keys or buttons. The general-purpose Touch-Tone telephone does not have the ability to enter alphabetic information. Similarly, the only medium available for output is an audio response in the human speech frequency.

The advent of audio response units provided a means whereby the Touch-Tone telephone could be used both as an input device and an output device. Thus, any Touch-Tone telephone may be used as a computer terminal by first dialing the number of the computer, after which a telephone operator answers the call and connects into the computer the appropriate transmission line used by the telephone. Alternatively, the computer may itself automatically answer the call and connect itself to the appropriate transmission line.

After the call has been established, the numeric keyboard on the Touch-Tone telephone may be used to enter information to the computer—for example, an inquiry requesting the stock availability of specific products. The audio response unit accepts the various tones transmitted along the telephone line and converts these into digital signals representing

**Fig. 1.** IBM 7770 (left) and IBM 7772 (right) audio response units.

**Fig. 2.** Touch-Tone telephone, which may be used as an audio response terminal for numeric input.

the appropriate numeric value. At this stage, the message received from the Touch-Tone telephone is in exactly the same form in the computer as it would come from a card reader or a typewriter terminal, for example. Consequently, the computer can access the appropriate files, determine the necessary response to the question received from the terminal, and prepare that response for transmission back to the telephone.

However, while the various letters making up the words comprising the reply are transmitted directly to other terminals after translating those letters into the appropriate terminal code, with audio response terminals the process is slightly different. In this case (particularly with the IBM 7770 audio response unit) the response constructed by the computer is a series of addresses rather than words. These addresses indicate the location on drum of the appropriate word to be read and transmitted along the telephone line. The audio response unit recognizes each of these addresses, reads the appropriate words from the specified drum location, and plays back that word on the telephone line, after which it is transmitted to the telephone receiver. As each subsequent word is accessed by the audio response unit, the words combine to form a spoken reply to the request entered by the Touch-Tone terminal.

PORTABLE AUDIO TERMINALS. Portable terminals, designed to increase the capabilities of audio

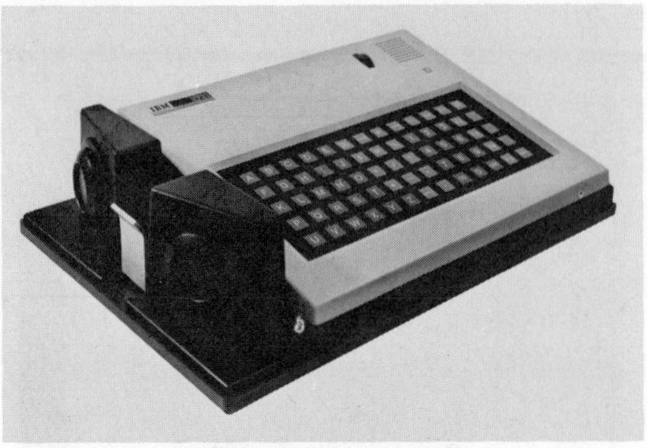

**Fig. 3.** IBM 2721 portable audio terminal used for alphanumeric input.

response terminals by providing a full typewriter keyboard with alphabetic, numeric, and special character keys, are now available (Fig. 3). These terminals attach to a normal telephone handset, using an acoustic coupler, by placing the handset in a receptacle in the terminal. Thus, signals generated by the keyboard can be transmitted through the mouthpiece of the telephone to the computer, and a spoken response can be received through the telephone receiver and amplified by the terminal if necessary.

Such terminals may weigh as little as 10 lb. (Fig. 3) and can be carried in a small case that contains all necessary batteries and connectors for operation. The terminal can be moved from point to point, and yet is able to enter both alphabetic and numeric information from any telephone, regardless of whether that telephone has Touch-Tone keys or a dial.

Thus, this kind of terminal is particularly suited for applications requiring considerable mobility, such as a representative traveling to various customers. In this case, the representative may take orders for goods from the customer and then use his portable audio terminal to transmit that order directly to the computer. He can use the customer's telephone on his own premises, dial the computer, and then enter the order through the keyboard. The computer is able to access appropriate files to determine the stock availability, for example, of the goods ordered and give a spoken response indicating the acceptance or rejection of the order.

AUDIO TERMINALS USED FOR DATA ENTRY. While audio response terminals have mainly been used in an inquiry environment, they are also suited for use as data entry devices. Because of their low cost and ready availability, such terminals can be used to capture data at its point of origin and transmit that data directly to the computer. In this way the need for any data transcription is bypassed. Certainly, no hard copy or visual display of the computer response is practical. However, as data is keyed on the terminal and transmitted to the computer, that data can be immediately edited and validated, accessing any computer files that may be necessary to determine the accuracy and reasonableness of the information received. If the data passes the appropriate validation tests, the computer can transmit a spoken response such as "accepted." However, if an error is detected in the data, the computer can transmit a spoken error message, such as "invalid product number—please reenter," or "only quantity of xxxx in stock—enter A to accept or C to cancel."

**The Future.** While the use of computers for spoken responses to queries is a practical and useful proposition today, at present the use of the human voice for input of data directly into a computer is not a commercial proposition. Although experimental devices have been developed to recognize certain words spoken by a limited number of people, the various intonations, accents, and use of language in the human voice makes audio input a vastly more difficult job than audio output. Nevertheless, the time may come when we can pose questions to a computer in a spoken voice and receive a spoken reply.

C. B. FINKELSTEIN

## AUTHORING LANGUAGES AND SYSTEMS

For articles on related subjects *see* COMPUTER-ASSISTED INSTRUCTION; COMPUTER ASSISTED LEARNING AND TEACHING; COMPUTER-MANAGED INSTRUCTION; and PROGRAMMING LANGUAGES.

Considerable attention has been given to providing a convenient programming language for the use of authors of computer-based learning materials. However, obtaining a single, ideal language is a fiction; different uses require different capabilities, which are not conveniently provided within a single language and its associated processor. Furthermore, most users want to learn only those parts of the language and system which are necessary to accomplish a particular set of purposes.

The specific programming language used by an author is not so significant for effective computer-based instruction as are three other factors. With what notation does the author describe for himself and others the substance and procedures of his computer-based instruction? By what means are these ideas and notes reliably transcribed into an executing computer program? How efficiently does the computer operate on this program and related data bases to deliver instruction or provide adjunct learning activities?

One concept of authoring languages and systems is represented in Fig. 1. The designer of material assembles information and opinion about what is needed, working with students and others who should know of the problems and resources (steps 1 through 3). The designer may work with a language or notation devised especially for the topic and objectives (step 4), delegating to the machine or technical assistants the determination of minor details (step 5). Separation of the content of instruction from the description of program logic makes curriculum development less costly. Various steps in the translation may be handled by humans or by ma-

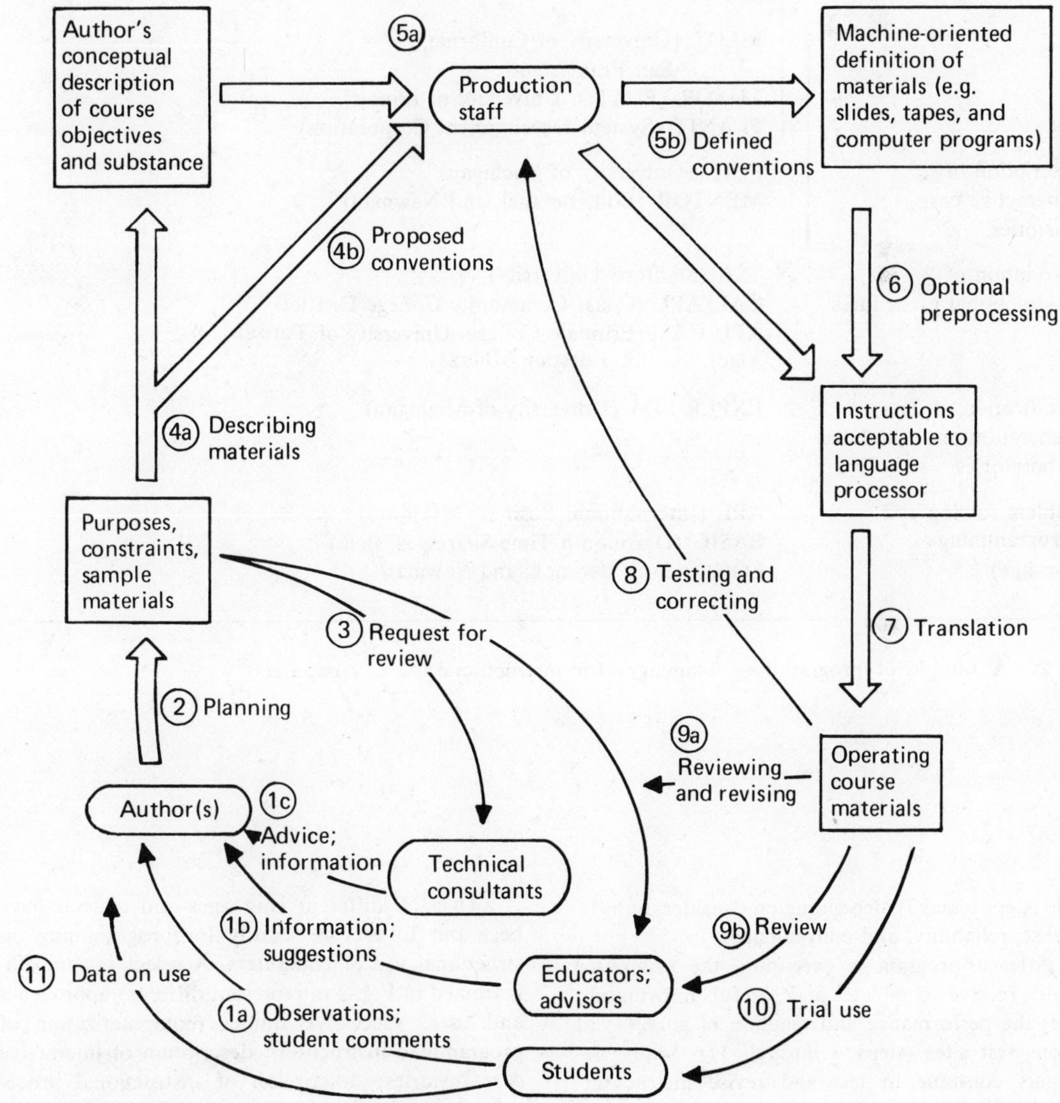


**Fig. 1.** One representation of authoring activity.

| | |
|---|---|
| Description of successive frames | COPI (Univac) |
| | COURSEWRITER (International Business Machines) |
| | IDF (Hewlett-Packard) |
| | CAN (Ontario Institute for Studies in Education) |
| | SCHOLAR-TEACH (Digital) |
| | PILOT (University of California, San Francisco) |
| | TUTOR (PLATO, University of Illinois) |
| | PLANIT (System Development Corporation) |
| Description of interactive case histories | FOIL (University of Michigan) |
| | MENTOR (Bolt, Beranek and Newman) |
| Description of instructional procedures | TSA (Stanford University) |
| | CAL/APL (Coast Community College District) |
| | APL/CAT (Erindale College, University of Toronto |
| | Algol, Snobol, Fortran, others |
| Specification of data generation and simulated laboratories | EXPER SIM (University of Michigan) |
| Problem solving and programming (on-line) | APL (International Business Machines) |
| | BASIC (Dartmouth Time-Sharing System) |
| | LOGO (Bolt, Beranek, and Newman) |

**Fig. 2.** A sample of programming languages for instructional use of computers.

chine (steps 6 and 7), depending on considerations of expense, reliability, and convenience.

After a program is executing, the originator should receive complete and useful information about the performance and reaction of students at various test sites (steps 9 through 11). Many developers continue to test and revise instruction-related computer programs over a long period of time.

Over 50 different languages and dialects have been put to use specifically for programming instructional use of computers. A select set are diagrammed in Fig. 2 to represent different approaches and uses: successive frames. (computerization of programmed instruction); description of interactive case histories; description of instructional procedures; specification of data generation and simulated laboratories; problem solving and programming.

| *Program Statements* | *Description of Directive* |
| --- | --- |
| GENERAL: "Proceed with investigation." | [type out message within quotation marks for the student to read; "GENERAL" labels this block of the program] |
| ACCEPT | [accept directive from student and execute statements which are indented below] |
| IF /suspects/ (REPORT 1) | [if the student mentioned "suspects" execute (1) or (2) indented below] |
| 1) "Wife, brother and partner." | [first time, type message marked (1)] |
| 2) "No new suspects." | [all other times, type message marked (2)] |
| IF /lab, rifle, glass, pipe/ | [if he mentioned any of these, execute the following] |
| IF ALL REPORTS, GO TO LAB | [only if he has requested all reports, defined elsewhere, process his request for a laboratory test] |
| "I advise you to check reports first." | [if he has not requested all reports, advise him accordingly] |
| IF /interrogate/ | |
| IF ALL LAB, GO TO INTERR | [if all lab tests have been requested, process his request for interrogation] |
| "I advise you request lab tests first." | [otherwise, advise ... ] |
| ... | |
| ... | |
| "I don't understand." | [if nothing is recognized in his directive let him know and wait for another directive] |
| LAB "This is the lab." | |
| IF /glass/ (GLASS) | [if he mentioned the "glass" set GLASS switch] |
| IF WIFE | [and if he has already interrogated the wife] |
| "Glass contained arsenic." | [type damaging evidence] |
| 1) "Prints belong to the wife." | [otherwise type (1) the first time] |
| 2) "Nothing new." | [type (2) all other times] |
| ... | |
| ... | |
| "What is it you want?" | [if no lab test request is recognized, type query] |
| ACCEPT | [accept directive] |
| TO LAB + 1 | [go back to process a second directive relating to the lab] |

**Fig. 3.** Sample of a notation suited for exercises in information gathering and diagnosis (interactive case histories). A sample conversation of this program is given on p. 269.

Information about these and many other languages can be obtained from secondary sources (Zinn, 1971; Bode and Dutting, 1974).

A sample of program code for an interactive "case history" is given in Fig. 3. The annotations in the right column point out the means by which the author specifies contingencies conveniently in the interaction between user and program. The example is adapted from a Mystery problem programmed in the Mentor language; both were developed at Bolt, Beranek, and Newman.

Any language appears simple and convenient when it is used for the specific purpose for which it was designed to be convenient. The great diversity of instructional uses of computers repeatedly forces specific-purpose languages into situations for which they were not designed.

REFERENCES

1971. Zinn, Karl L. "Requirements for Programming Languages in Computer-Based Instructional Systems." Paris: Organization for Economic Cooperation and Development.

1974. Bode, Arndt, and Martin Dutting. "Computer-Assisted Instruction: Problems, Languages, Systems, and Documentation" (translated from the German and edited by Karl L. Zinn). Ann Arbor: EXTEND Publications.

K. L. ZINN

**AUTOMATA.** *See* CELLULAR AUTOMATA; and PROBABILISTIC AUTOMATA.

## AUTOMATA THEORY

For articles on related subjects *see* ALGORITHM; CELLULAR AUTOMATA; FORMAL LANGUAGES; PERCEPTRON; PROBABILISTIC AUTOMATA; SEQUENTIAL MACHINES; and TURING MACHINE.

For articles on related terms *see* CONCATENATION; and PROGRAM.

**Introduction and Definitions.** Automata theory is a mathematical discipline concerned with the invention and study of mathematically abstract, idealized machines called "automata." These automata are usually abstractions of information processing devices, such as computers, rather than of devices that move about, such as mechanical toys or automobiles.

This article gives a short and informal survey of the major classes of automata that automata theorists have heretofore seen fit to study, and indicates the primary respective motivations (from the point of view of computer science) for the study of these classes of automata.

For the most part, the automata discussed here process strings of symbols from some finite alphabet of symbols. Let $A$ be any alphabet (finite set of symbols). For example, $A$ might be $\{a,b,c, \cdots, z\}$ or $\{0,1\}$. We write $A^*$ to mean the set of *all* finite strings of symbols chosen from $A$. If $A$ is $\{a,b,c, \cdots, z\}$, then $A^*$ contains strings representing English words, such as "cat" and "mouse," along with nonsense strings such as "czzxyh". If $A$ is $\{0,1\}$, then $A^*$ contains the strings representing the nonnegative integers in binary notation $(0,1,10,11,100, \cdots)$ and also these same strings but with extra zeros on the left (e.g., 00010).

Automata generally perform one (or both) of two symbol-processing tasks. They compute partial functions from $X^*$ to $Y^*$ for some finite alphabets $X$ and $Y$ or they *recognize* languages over some alphabet $X$.

A *partial function* from $X^*$ to $Y^*$ is a correspondence between some subset of $X^*$ and the set $Y^*$ that associates with each element of the subset of $X^*$ a unique element in $Y^*$. For example, let $X = Y = \{0,1\}$ and let the subset of $X^*$ be the elements $x$ of $X^*$ such that $x$ begins with 1 or consists of a single 0. If $f$ associates with $x$ the string in $Y^*$ that denotes the binary number representing two times the binary number represented by $x$, then $f$ is a partial function from $X^*$ to $Y^*$.

We say roughly that an automaton $\alpha$ *computes* a partial function $f$ from $X^*$ to $Y^*$ when, if $\alpha$ is given any input $x$ in $X^*$ such that $f(x)$ is defined, $\alpha$ eventually produces an output $y \in Y^*$ such that $f(x) = y$, and, otherwise, $\alpha$ produces no output. Automata usually receive their inputs on a linear or one-dimensional tape, which they are capable of reading one symbol at a time. The manner in which they read symbols on an input tape (left to right, back and forth, with or without changing symbols, etc.) depends on the particular class of automata under consideration. Automata for computing partial functions produce their output on a tape (perhaps the input tape, perhaps a different tape) in a manner also prescribed by the particular class of automata under consideration.

A *language* over an alphabet $X$ is just a subset of $X^*$. For example, if $X = \{a,b,c,\cdots,z\}$, then $\{a, aa, aaa, \cdots\}$ and $\{x \in X^* \mid x$ is a word in the English language$\}$ are both languages over $X$.

We say that an automaton $\alpha$ *recognizes* a language $L$ over $X$ when $\alpha$ reads an input $x \in X^*$ on its input tape in the manner of automata of its type; then, if $x \in L$, $\alpha$ eventually performs some particular act of recognition such as halting, emptying a particular auxiliary tape, or getting into some special internal state; whereas, if $x \notin L$, $\alpha$ never performs such an act of recognition. Exactly what constitutes an act of recognition depends on the particular class of automata under consideration.

It is presumably clear why it is of interest to computer scientists to study automata that compute (partial) functions, since computer science is the computation business. Among the interesting questions to ask are whether some function is or is not computable by some representative of a particular class of automata and, if it is computable, how efficiently (with respect to some mathematically precise measure of efficiency) can it be so computed.

We motivate the study of automata that recognize languages by some examples. Let $X$ be the set of allowable symbols for some programming language $P$. Include in $X$ the necessary punctuation symbols and the blank symbol. Let $L = \{x \in X^* \mid x$ is a valid program of $P\}$. In the process of compiling from $P$ into some other language, it is useful to (among other things) *recognize* the valid programs of $P$ as being valid. Automata theory gives some insight into the sort of computing ability that may be required to recognize valid programs. For example, *pushdown automata* (to be defined below) are capable of recognizing the valid syntactic classes of all (and only) Algol-like languages.

Automatic theorem proving, a subarea of artificial intelligence, is also concerned with language recognition. The language to be recognized is the set of propositions derivable from some set of axioms. Automatic theorem proving has been applied to discover new mathematical theorems, to question-answering systems, and to robotics.

**Types of Automata.** Most (but not all) types of automata are special cases of the Turing machine (see Fig. 1). Turing machines may be operated either to recognize or to compute partial functions. Very roughly, a Turing machine is a finite-state deterministic device with read and/or write heads (which read and/or write one symbol at a time) attached to one or more tapes. "Finite state" means that the number of distinguishable internal configurations of the device is finite, and "deterministic" means that the next state of the device and its subsequent action (writing or motion) on the tapes is completely determined by its current state and the symbols it is currently reading on its tapes.

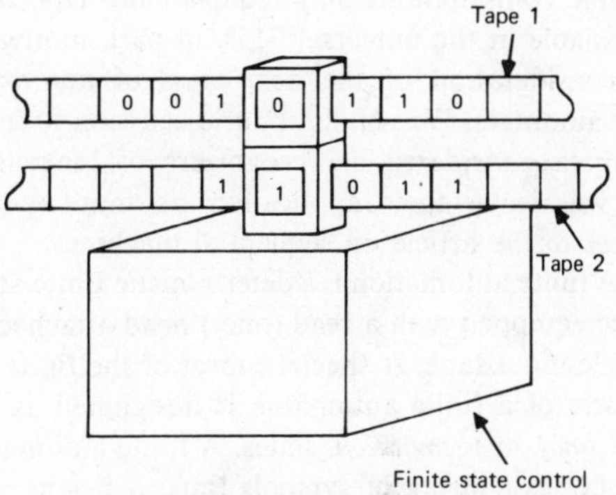


**Fig. 1.** A two-tape Turing machine. Each tape is scanned by a single read/write head. Tape 1 contains the string of nonblank symbols 0010110, with the underlined 0 currently being read. Tape 2 contains 11011, with the underlined 1 being currently read. If the tapes can move only in one direction, the same diagram would depict a two-tape automaton.

Turing machines were first introduced independently by Turing and Post in 1936 to give a precise mathematical definition of *effective procedure*. There is considerable evidence that the partial functions computed by (languages recognized by) Turing machines are exactly those computed (recognized) by informal effective procedures or algorithms. Any computation or recognition problem for which there is a known informal algorithm can be handled by a Turing machine. Turing machines with many (in general, $n$-dimensional) tapes and read/write heads can compute and recognize *no more* than can Turing machines with a single one-dimensional tape and single read/write head, although they may compute and recognize more efficiently.

Attempts to define effective procedures in terms of automata more closely resembling modern electronic stored-program digital computers have led to the unlimited register machines of Shepherdson and

Sturgis and to the *random-access* stored-program machines of Elgot and Robinson. These machines can be shown to compute the same partial functions (recognize the same languages) computed by Turing machines.

Turing machines model the most general sort of computation processes, in part by virtue of their ability to move about freely on their tapes without fear of running out of tape. In general no a priori bound can be set on the amount of tape a Turing machine computation will require. Some Turing machine computations may require more tape than is available in the universe! This, in part, motivates our consideration of the next class of automata, finite automata. We will limit our discussion to finite automata considered as recognizers of languages, and will leave their application as input/output devices to the article on sequential machines.

A finite automation is a deterministic finite-state device equipped with a read (only) head attached to a single input tape. A special subset of the finite set of states of a finite automaton is designated as the set of *final*, or *recognition*, states. A finite automaton $\alpha$ processes a string of symbols thus: $\alpha$ begins in a special initial, or start, state and automatically reads the symbols of $x$ (on its tape) from left to right, changing its states in a manner depending only on its previous state and the symbol just read. If, after the last (rightmost) symbol of $x$ is read, $\alpha$ goes into a final state, $\alpha$ recognizes $x$; otherwise, $\alpha$ does not recognize $x$. Let $A = \{0,1\}$. It is possible, for example, to design a finite automaton $\alpha$ such that $\alpha$ recognizes $L = \{x \in A^* \mid x$ ends in two consecutive 1s and does not contain two consecutive 0s$\}$. See Fig. 2. On the other hand, it can be shown that *no* finite automaton can recognize $L' = \{x \in A^* \mid x$ consists of a consecutive string of $n$-squared 1s for some positive integer $n\}$. As might be expected, however, a Turing machine can be designed to recognize $L'$.

In Fig. 2 the circles represent the different states of $\alpha_0$ and the number inside each circle is a name for the state that circle represents. Hence, 0 is the start state of $\alpha_0$ and 4 is its only final state. An arrow (labeled with an alphabet symbol) from one state to another means that if $\alpha_0$ is in the first state while scanning the alphabet symbol that labels the arrow, then it goes next into the second state. For example, if $\alpha_0$ is in state 1 scanning a 0, it goes next into state 2; whereas, if it is in state 1 scanning a 1, it goes next into state 3. If $\alpha_0$ is given the input string 010111, beginning in state 0, the successive states into which it is thereafter driven are (in order) 1,3,1,3,4,4. Since 4 is a final state, $\alpha_0$ (correctly) recognizes the input string 010111. If $\alpha_0$ is given 10011, beginning in state 0, the successive states into which it is thereafter driven are (in order) 3,1,2,2,2. Since 2 is *not* a final state, $\alpha_0$ (correctly) fails to recognize 10011.

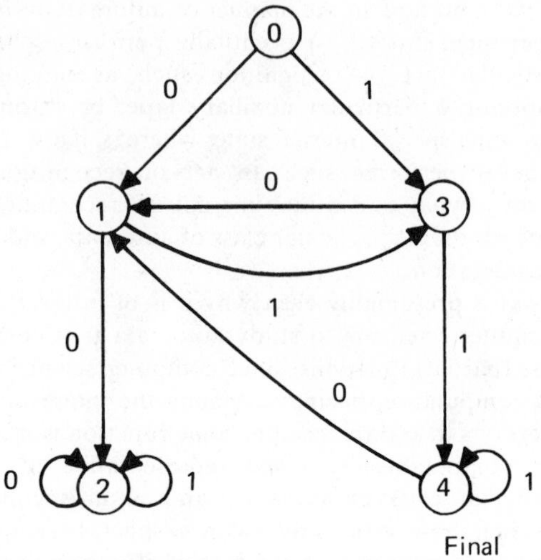


**Fig. 2.** The state diagram of a finite-state automaton for recognizing $\{x \in \{0,1\}^* \mid x$ ends in two consecutive 1s and does not contain two consecutive 0s$\}$.

A nondeterministic finite automaton is a device just like a finite automaton except that the next state is not completely determined by the current state and symbol read. Instead, a set of next *possible* states is so determined. A nondeterministic finite automaton $\alpha$ may be thought of as processing a string of symbols $x$, just like an ordinary finite automaton except that it has to be run over again several times so that each of the different possible state-change behaviors is eventually realized. One should imagine there being a separate, deterministic control device C which runs $\alpha$ and completely determines $\alpha$'s *actual* state-change behavior each time it is run. There are but finitely many different possible state-change behaviors for $\alpha$ processing $x$, and C simply systematically runs $\alpha$ first one way, then another, then another, etc., until all possibilities have been exhausted.

A finite automaton $\alpha$ *recognizes* $x$ just in case at least one of the possible ways of running $\alpha$ on input $x$ results in getting $\alpha$ into a final state after the last symbol of $x$ has been read (see Fig. 3).

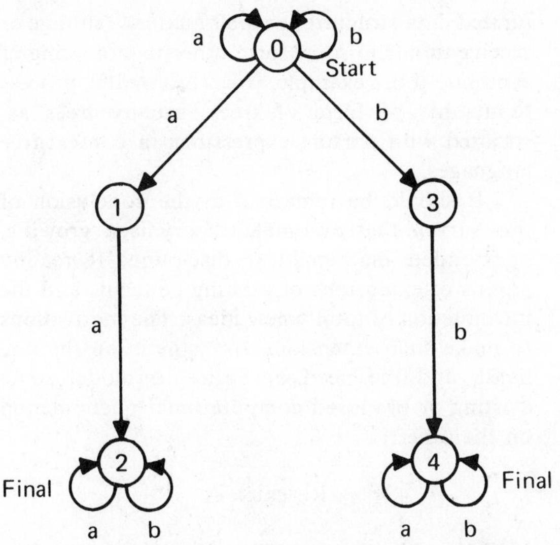


**Fig. 3.** The state diagram of a nondeterministic finite-state automaton $\alpha_1$ for recognizing $\{x \in \{a,b\}* \mid x$ contains two consecutive *a*'s or two consecutive *b*'s (or both)$\}$.

In Fig. 3, $\alpha_1$ is nondeterministic because (for example, from state 0, if it is scanning *a*) it can go into either state 0 or state 1 next. From state 1, if it is scanning *b*, it "jams," since the set of next possible states is empty. If $\alpha_1$ is given the input string *abababba*, beginning in state 0, one possible succession of states is (in order) 0,0,0,0,0,0,0,1. Here, 1 is not one of the final states, so this way of running $\alpha_1$ does not lead to recognition. Another possible succession of states is (in order) 0,0,0,1, jam. Another is 1, jam. However, 0,0,0,0,0,3,4,4 is still another possible succession of states. Since 4 *is* a final state, $\alpha_1$ (correctly) recognizes *abababba*. It is easy to check that if $\alpha_1$ is given *babababab*, beginning in state 0, then *none* of the possible ways of running $\alpha_1$ leads to a final state; hence, $\alpha_1$ (correctly) does *not* recognize *babababab*.

Interestingly (and perhaps unexpectedly), it can be shown that nondeterministic finite automata recognize exactly the same class of languages as ordinary finite automata. Turing machine recognizers that operate nondeterministically can also be defined, but they cannot recognize more languages than can ordinary Turing machines. For nondeterministic Turing machine recognizers, as well as for some of the other nondeterministic devices to be discussed below, some of the different possible ways to process a given string *x* may take infinitely many steps. For such devices it is convenient to imagine the separate, deterministic control device C as operating in a parallel mode.

In addition to ordinary and nondeterministic automata, a variety of automata called "probabilistic" automata have been studied. A probability of occurrence is assigned to each of the possible next states in a probabilistic automaton.

In 1943 McCulloch and Pitts introduced nets of formalized neurons and showed (in essence) that such neural nets could realize the state-change behavior of any finite automaton. These nets were composed of synchronized elements, each capable of realizing some boolean function such as AND, OR, or NOT. It has been suggested that von Neumann had these networks in mind when he established his logical design for digital computers. In 1948, von Neumann added to the computational and logical questions of automata theory by introducing new questions pertaining to construction and self-replication of automata. The iterated arrays of interconnected finite automata which he introduced have also been used to study pattern processing for patterns of symbols, including (but not restricted to) one-dimensional strings of symbols.

Automata theory, especially finite automata theory, impinges on both mathematical systems theory and modern algebra. In mathematical systems theory, one is interested in the problem of which, (if any) input sequences will drive an automaton to some desired internal state. In modern algebra one can study the relations between semigroups and automata. For example, certain decomposition theorems in group theory give information about decomposition of automata into particularly simple component automata.

A *linear-bounded* automaton is a nondeterministic, one-tape Turing machine whose read/write head is restricted to move only on the section of tape initially containing the input. Special end markers are placed on each side of an input string to prevent the tape head from leaving this restricted section of tape. A form of deterministic linear-bounded automata was first studied by Myhill in an attempt to find models of computation more realistic than the completely general Turing machines, but less restricted than the finite automata. Later it was shown that linear-bounded automata recognize all (and only) the *context-sensitive* languages, an important and natural class of languages more restricted than the languages recognizable by Turing machines but more general than the *context-free* languages. It is an open question whether the linear-bounded automata can recognize more languages than the deterministic linear-bounded automata.

A *pushdown* automaton is a nondeterministic finite automaton with a special sort of auxiliary tape called a "pushdown store." A pushdown store is a tape quite like the stack of plates found on a spring in cafeterias. It is a "Last In–First Out" store. A special read/write head always scans the top symbol on the pushdown store. The pushdown store is initially loaded with a single special START symbol. The top symbol can be replaced by any finite string of symbols (stack of plates), including the empty string of symbols. Replacing the top symbol by the empty string has the effect of completely removing the top symbol and setting the read/write head to scan the next symbol down. The read (only) head on the input tape reads one symbol at a time from left to right, just as in a finite automaton, except that it is allowed (if desired) to stop scanning the input tape momentarily while only the pushdown store is operated.

Pushdown automata recognize a string $x$ by one of two conventions. Either $x$ is recognized by the device as it gets into one of its final states or by the pushdown store as it empties just after the rightmost symbol of $x$ is read. The class of languages recognized by emptying the pushdown store is the same as that recognized by final states. Let $A = \{0,1\}$. For $x \in A^*$, let $x^R$ be $x$ written backwards. For example, $001110^R$ is 011100. $L = \{x \in A^* \mid x$ is of the form $w$ followed by $w^R$ for some $w \in A^*\}$ is recognizable by a suitable pushdown automaton; however, $L$ is *not* recognizable by any finite automaton or even by any deterministic pushdown automaton. Pushdown automata recognize all (and only) the context-free (or equivalently, Algol-like) languages.

Many variations on a slight generalization of pushdown automata have been studied. A *stack* automaton is just like a pushdown automaton except that the read (only) head of the input tape is allowed to move both ways (but not off the section of tape containing the input) and the read/write head on the pushdown store is allowed to scan the entire pushdown list in a READ ONLY mode. The class of languages recognized by stack automata is intermediate between context-sensitive and Turing-machine recognizable.

Many other types of automata that have been and could be studied employ some other sort of limited data structure for their auxiliary storage or receive inputs in some form other than a string of symbols. For example, *tree* automata process inputs in the form of trees, usually trees associated with parsing expressions in context-free languages.

It should be remarked at the conclusion of this survey that automata theory is a growing, open-ended mathematical discipline. It readily admits of extensions of existing concepts and the introduction of totally new ideas. The motivations to make such extensions are esthetic on the one hand, and the need or desire to model some existing or proposed computational phenomenon on the other.

References

1966. Von Neumann, J. *Theory of Self-Reproducing Automata* (edited and completed by A. W. Burks). Urbana: University of Illinois Press.

1967. Minsky, M. *Computation: Finite and Infinite Machines.* Englewood Cliffs, N.J.: Prentice-Hall.

1969. Arbib, M. A. *Theories of Abstract Automata.* Englewood Cliffs, N.J.: Prentice-Hall.

1969. Hopcroft, J. E., and J. D. Ullman. *Formal Languages and Their Relation to Automata.* Reading, Mass.: Addison-Wesley.

1969. Minsky, M., and S. Papert. *Perceptrons.* Cambridge, Mass.: M.I.T. Press.

1973. Bobrow, L. S., and M. A. Arbib. *Discrete Mathematics: Applied Algebra for Computer and Information Science.* Philadelphia: W. B. Saunders.

1973. Engeler, E. *Introduction to the Theory of Computation.* New York: Academic Press.

J. Case

## AUTOMATION

For articles on related subjects *see* Communications and Computers; Computer Networks; Computers and Society; Control Applications; Digital Computers; and Time Sharing.

For articles on related terms *see* Information Science; Minicomputers; Operations Research; Optical Character

READERS; SIMULATION; TERMINALS; and COMMUNICATION CONTROL UNIT.

**Concept of Automation.** The concept of automation includes five main functions:

1. Collection of information through data collection equipment.
2. Communication between man-machine, man-man, and machine-machine, through generating and regulating the flow of data collected.
3. Computation with the information, such as data logging, data analysis, and data processing with the help of mathematical formulations.
4. Control of operations, both human and mechanical, on the basis of information analysis.
5. Logical coordination among the preceding four functions.

In order to describe the different functions of automation, the following key words might be used:

- Information *collection* function: based on measuring devices of physical (time, length, weight, temperature, etc.) and chemical properties (concentration, color, etc.), counting devices, reading devices (optical character reading) and data preparation.
- Information *communication* function: based on data communication, computer networks, using different types of languages for communicating data within man-machine systems (problem-oriented languages).
- *Computation* function: based on information processing, data processing, data management.
- Operation *control* function: based on process control, process simulation, cybernetic features (feedback and feed-forward control), distributed control.
- *Coordination* function: based on management information systems, computer-aided instruction, operations research, and model building.

The automation concept is thus not limited to a given production process or a given service but is linked to a host of human activities. Attempts have been made to define certain degrees of automation; as a rule these apply to the labor intensive aspect of a given manufacturing industry. However, no general method for assessing automation in its broad sense has yet been developed.

In the absence of a general statistical framework for assessing the diffusion of automation in the different sectors of the economy, the number of computers used in a given sector will indicate, to a certain extent, the progress made in automating its activities. There are, of course, many industrial processes or services that can be considered highly automatic without having to rely on computing facilities, especially when information processing is not critical to fulfillment of the process or service. This is especially true for specialized small-scale industries and service centers (e.g., precision instrument assembling and automatic vending machine centers) where physical communication, information flow, and data processing are of minor importance in the total activities. However, for those production processes and services that require a large, complex organization, and a relatively large amount of information processing (and the general trend is a continuing shift in this direction as a consequence of large-scale, multinational manufacturing and services), the use of computers becomes increasingly critical with regard to automating these activities. In other words, the more an activity increases in volume and importance, the more the criterion of computer utilization, as an indicator of the degree of automation, becomes relevant.

According to available statistics on computer utilization, the largest share of computers is used in the metal-working industry, including both mechanical and electrical engineering (20%); banking, insurance, administration, research and development, and computing centers each account for 10% of the computer market. The chemical and food industries and trade and transport each account for 5% of the market, and the remaining 10% is distributed between other industrial sectors and services. See Table 1.

The main functions of the computer are financial applications (30%) production control (20%), market studies (15%), distribution (15%), research and development (10%), and coordination (10%). See Table 2.

The aim of automation, in its broad sense, is thus to enhance human capabilities, both manual and intellectual, in order to meet the increasing complexity of the human way of life. In the future, emphasis will be laid on a global approach to solve problems facing the manufacturing and servicing activities that result from the interaction of technological, economical, and social forces. Such a global approach is only possible if the relevant information is adequately collected, rapidly and correctly diffused, and logically processed in order to serve as guidelines for controlling and coordinating forces.

**Table 1.** Distribution of Computers in the Different Economic Sectors (U.S., %).

| | |
|---|---|
| Industry | 40 |
| Banking and insurance | 20 |
| Administration | 7 |
| Transport | 7 |
| Processing services | 6 |
| Research | 5 |
| Public services | 5 |
| Miscellaneous | 10 |

**Table 2.** Main Functions of Computer Utilization (U.S., approx. %).

| | |
|---|---|
| Financial applications (payroll, etc.) | 30 |
| Production control | 20 |
| Market surveys | 15 |
| Distribution | 15 |
| Research and development | 10 |
| Coordination, scheduling, forecasting | 10 |

## Current State of Automation

TECHNOLOGICAL DEVELOPMENT. The progress of automation is a result of scientific research and technical development in the following main sectors:

- Electronics industries (primarily for information collection).
- Telecommunication equipment industries (primarily for information flow).
- Computing equipment industries (primarily for information processing).
- Industrial control industries (primarily for process control).
- Management services (primarily for coordinating activities).

The most striking technical achievements in these sectors in the past years are the following:

1. In the electronics industries, almost any type of physical or chemical value can be measured by highly reliable sensors, based essentially on the progress made in solid state electronics, resulting in miniaturization and high reliability of semiconductors and integrated circuits.

2. In the telecommunication equipment industries, outstanding achievements have been made in large-scale systems such as the worldwide communication network through satellites and the intercontinental computer networks. The development of transmission control units, especially as regards data concentrators and message switchers in conjunction with the development of numerous computer terminals, has greatly enhanced the possibilities for information flow in time and in space.

3. In the computing equipment industries great developments have been made both in hardware and in software. Minicomputers and supercomputers have increased the equipment range, the former being more or less tied into the communication equipment and linked to data preparation and data reduction devices and used to control various peripheral equipment. The development of time sharing has led to the proliferation of computer terminals and has made possible the efficient use of supercomputers. Optical character reading and the use of packaged programs have facilitated the utilization of computers in a great variety of nonmanufacturing activities such as wholesale and resale trade, and personal services.

4. In the industrial control industries, which include electrical measuring instruments, engineering and scientific instruments, measuring and controlling instruments, automatic temperature controls and optical instruments, the reliability and miniaturization of the equipment, by using integrated circuits as well as the direct link of the equipment onto a computer (direct digital computer control), are the most outstanding development features.

5. In the field of management services, research in information science, management science, operations research, and software management has permitted greater insight into computer aided manufacturing and servicing, thus increasing the efficiency of computer utilization and automatic control. But, above all, the spread of automation has resulted in a systematic collection of the basic information of a large number of industries and services that will be used not only for running the production process (or service) itself but also for analyzing the prospective development of the processes or services, through simulation techniques and long-range planning analysis.

So far, there are about 500 packaged programs on the market which are readily available to users for commercial, scientific, and management applications. Their number will rapidly increase in the near future.

In the coming years the pace of technological progress and technological change will be significantly increased through the greater acquisition, dissemination, and application of scientific and technical knowledge, mainly thanks to automation

**Fig. 1.** IBM System/7, an automated laboratory aid.

and computer techniques. It is generally assumed that the rate of development and diffusion of technological innovations introduced during the post-World War II period (1945–1960) was twice the rate for those introduced during the post-World War I period (1920–1940) and three times the rate for innovations introduced during the early part of the century (1890–1920).

Not only the pace of technological progress and change but also its diffusion from advanced technological sectors into less developed industries will increase in the future. This accelerated generation and transfer of technology will speed the rate of economic growth. As a consequence, management will become more future-oriented and planning-minded in order to remain at the vanguard of development. This requires adequate information processing, in which the computer will play a dominant role in the future. The efficient use of computers in education and management might thus be considered as the dominant criterion for coping with the pace of technological progress.

Economic Change. Four main characteristics of computer applications explain their rapid growth rate in all industries and services:

1. They are time-saving, thus influencing productivity directly.
2. They have a very large capacity for data handling, thus making possible the accurate control of large-scale systems.
3. They can work on many different applications at the same time, thus permitting a perfect integration of data processing, handling, and distribution of information without delay.
4. The computer programs developed for general-purpose applications, and which are readily available in program libraries, can be adapted to specific requirements. Therefore they permit a rapid introduction of computer technology into a large variety of industries and services.

The development of many traditional industries and the creation of many new industries and services were thus only made possible through the introduction of computer-based automation. Large nuclear powerplants, for instance, as well as the present air transport system, would be impossible to operate

**Table 3.** Forecast of the Economic Development of Industries Related to Automation (U.S.)

| | 1970 | | | 1975 | 1980 |
|---|---|---|---|---|---|
| (1) Industry and Sector | (2) Value of Shipments, billion $ | (3) Number of Establishments | (4) Number of Employees (1,000) | (5) Expected Value of Shipments, billion $ | (6) Expected Value of Shipments, billion $ |
| Electric equipment and components | 22.5 | — | — | | |
| Consumer products | 3.0 | 350 | 140 | 30 | 45 |
| Telephone and telegraph | 4.0 | 90 | 170 | 4.5 | 6.0 |
| Electronic equipment | 8.5 | 640 | 330 | 6.5 | 10.5 |
| Electronic components | 5.5 | 1400 | 340 | 11.5 | 17.5 |
| Research and development | 1.0 | — | — | 6.5 | 7.5 |
| Instrumentation (measurement, | | | | 1.0 | 1.0 |
| analysis, control) | 5.5 | — | — | | |
| Electric measuring devices | 1.5 | 540 | 70 | 7.5 | 10.0 |
| Engineering and scientific | | | | 2.0 | 3.0 |
| instruments | 1.2 | 680 | 70 | | |
| Measuring and controlling | | | | 2.0 | 2.5 |
| equipment | 1.5 | 660 | 70 | 2.0 | 2.5 |
| Automatic temperature control | 0.5 | 100 | 40 | 1.0 | 1.5 |
| Optical instruments | 0.5 | 300 | 20 | 1.0 | 1.0 |
| Office and computing machinery | 5.0 | 600 | 190 | 9.5 | 13 |
| Typewriters | 0.5 | — | — | 0.6 | 0.7 |
| Electronic computing equipment | 3.8 | — | — | 7.5 | 10.5 |
| Calculating and accounting machinery | 0.5 | — | — | 1.0 | 1.5 |
| Office machinery | 0.5 | — | — | 0.5 | 0.5 |
| Communication equipment | | | | | |
| Domestic telephones | 20* | 2000 | 970 | 30* | 50* |
| Domestic telegraph | 0.5* | | | 0.5* | 1.0* |
| Radio broadcasting | 1.0* | 4** | 75 | 1.5* | 2.0* |
| TV broadcasting | 3.0* | 4** | 60 | 4.5* | 6.5* |

* Revenues.
** Nationwide networks.

SOURCE: "U.S. Industrial Outlook 1972 with Projections to 1980," U.S. Department of Commerce, Washington, D.C.

without the assistance of computer control. It can thus be said that a substantial part of the development of the American economy, both in volume of production as well as in quality of production, is virtually due to computer applications. It is expected in the near future that in all modern enterprises, the collecting, processing, and distributing of information through computers will increase in volume and in quality, with a direct beneficial effect on production costs and productivity.

The economic impact of automation is felt both in the field of capital spending for equipment and in the pattern of production and product range. The purchase of capital goods related to automation increased significantly in recent years and still shows a significant growth rate in the United States. See Table 3. Many new industries have been created in order to produce a wide selection of compatible automatic equipment that can be used in a great variety of combinations to meet any specific need.

For example, the computing equipment industry has developed about 250 central computing systems, about 150 varieties each of memory storage and magnetic tape systems, and about 100 different card punch and printer systems. Thus, a great combination of computing equipment is possible to allow optimum selection to meet a variety of needs.

By 1980 it is expected that about $100 billion worth of electronic equipment will be used in the world, of which almost 60% will be used in industry, over 20% in research and development, and the remaining 20% or less for consumer durables.

The production pattern is, of course, steadily adapting itself to the potentialities of automation equipment, especially with regard to the optimum number and size of equipment and its required output, to enable automatic equipment to be applied efficiently. Automation generally widens the possible range of plant and equipment size, mainly toward larger units, but sometimes also toward smaller units, especially when it permits the replacement of batch-type processes by continuous-flow processes.

Product range is also significantly influenced by the introduction of automation equipment, both in quality and quantity of the products. Product quality is closely checked for its reliability and its service life, and new products are being marketed at a much faster rate than before. Production costs are more predictable and less influenced by physical production factors, since labor costs influence production rate and production flow to a lesser degree.

The service sector is especially becoming increasingly engaged in automation applications. Many data management institutes offer computer-aided bookkeeping services as well as access to specific data banks for information retrieval. These "computing utilities" already have a $2 billion turnover and present a growth rate of about 25% per year. In the United States a large computer manufacturer runs a computing center, grouping over 100 large-scale computers with almost 100 regional offices throughout the country. Another manufacturer has established a time-sharing system to which over 40,000 customers have access. About 400 organizations are thus engaged in this market, and an Association of the Data Processing Service Organization (ADAPSO) has been created.

The best example of the possiblities offered today in telecommunication services is the world network of communication satellites. In transport services, computer-controlled flight reservation systems, as practiced by all the major airline companies, are characteristic of the potentialities in traffic organization and control. Finally, with respect to retail sales, it may suffice to indicate the tremendous growth of automatic vending machines for food, drink, stamps, tickets, etc.

Although the rate of development and diffusion is increasing, the elapsed time from the basic technical discovery of technological innovations to the point where economic changes become evident is relatively long. Almost without exception, those technological innovations that will have a significant impact on the economy and on society during the next five years have already been introduced as commercial products or processes. This is especially so for automated equipment, which will not change radically in essence, but rather in a qualitative manner such as decrease in specific cost and in maintenance, increase in numbers, capacity, speed, and reliability. The economic development of those branches of the industry related to automation will certainly be bright (Table 3).

Also, new industries will emerge as a result of technological change, and diversified services will become available in the economy. Automation will check the self-induced information explosion and paperwork through progress made in data reduction and in computer output on microfilm (COM). A new industry of knowledge will emerge and *information cost* will have to be considered just as carefully as traditional capital, material, and labor costs in the total cost of production. The profit margin will have to be calculated, not only to give a return on the invested capital and to remunerate labor, but also to forecast the technological risk, which will be increasingly important in the industries of the future. The automation-oriented industries will soon reach the level of such basic industries as automobile, petroleum, chemical, and steel. (See Table 4.)

Besides the development of automation in industrial production and in the service sector, a large field of activity is also gradually opening in the management activities. This will be brought about by the introduction of integrated information, computation, and communication systems that will be necessary to apply automation advantageously. The advantages of automation in this sector result from the increased rapidity in the flow of information and in decision making, compact information, and regularity of information, which are necessary in the rapidly changing industrial world. The convergence of political systems will result in a greater interdependence of nations and in a rapid development of multinational corporations and organizations. A prerequisite for this development will be the establishment of international information transfer and processing through automated equipment. For example, General Electric has recently put into operation an international computer system network linking over 300 cities worldwide.

Adequate management techniques and accurate production forecasting will reduce more and more the amplitudes of the economic business cycles and will thus contribute significantly to a balanced economic growth.

The Social Impact. With a rapidly changing economy made possible by automation, significant changes in many fields are taking place in the work environment and all these within the period of an individual's lifetime. The increase of labor productivity through automation and technological change

**Table 4.** Comparison of U.S. Industrial Corporations (1971).

| Activity | Company | Total assets (*A*), in billion $ | Operating revenues (*R*), sales, in billion $ | Manpower (*M*), in thousand hr | $R_1 = A/M$ in thousand $ | $R_2 = R/M$ in thousand $ |
|---|---|---|---|---|---|---|
| 1. Automobile | General Motors | 18.0 | 28.0 | 733 | 23 | 36 |
| | Ford | 10.5 | 16.0 | 433 | 24 | 37 |
| 2. Petroleum | Standard Oil | 20.0 | 18.7 | 143 | 140 | 130 |
| | Mobil Oil | 8.5 | 8.2 | 75 | 110 | 110 |
| 3. Steel industry | U.S. Steel | 6.4 | 4.9 | 183 | 35 | 27 |
| | Bethlehem Steel | 3.4 | 2.9 | 115 | 30 | 25 |
| 4. Chemical industry | Dupont | 3.9 | 3.8 | 106 | 37 | 36 |
| | Union Carbide | 3.5 | 3.0 | 99 | 35 | 30 |
| 5. Electrical engineering industry | General Electric | 6.8 | 9.4 | 363 | 19 | 26 |
| | Westinghouse | 3.5 | 4.6 | 180 | 19 | 25 |
| 6. Electronic engineering industry | ITT | 7.6 | 7.3 | 398 | 19 | 18 |
| | RCA | 3.0 | 3.7 | 118 | 25 | 31 |
| 7. Computer (and related) industry | IBM | 9.5 | 8.2 | 265 | 36 | 31 |
| | Honeywell | 2.1 | 1.9 | 94 | 22 | 20 |
| 8. Retail services | Sears Roebuck | 8.3 | 10.0 | 365 | 23 | 27 |
| | Penney | 1.9 | 4.8 | 162 | 12 | 30 |
| 9. Telecommunication services | American Telephone and Telegraph | 54.0 | 18.5 | 776 | 70 | 24 |
| | General Telephone and Electronics | 9.0 | 3.8 | 173 | 52 | 22 |
| 10. Transportation services | Penn Central | 4.6 | 1.7 | 82 | 56 | 21 |
| | TWA | 1.4 | 1.2 | 58 | 24 | 21 |

*Notes:* Based on two largest companies in each field of activity. $R_1$ = assets per employee. $R_2$ = revenues per employee.

SOURCE: *Fortune*, June 1972.

results in a shift in the demand for manpower, both in number and in work qualifications. Increased productivity has more impact on employment in industry than in areas of increasing demand for services. Clerical rather than service functions of office workers will be more affected by technological change. The need for professional, scientific, and technical personnel grows at a faster rate than the total labor force, and these personnel require continuing training or retraining to keep their qualifications up to date.

Unemployment will not necessarily result from automation, but there is a real threat of unemployment in those industries that have not kept abreast of technical development and which are bound to go out of business unless they adopt to more efficient operation. Technological unemployment is a temporary situation for a certain number of individuals who did not make a timely change from a traditional activity to a modern one. A person who is thus temporarily out of a job can be compared to the traveler who changes trains to take a new direction but who unfortunately misses the connection. A later train will surely arrive, but until it does, the traveler has to sit in the waiting room. Compare this situation with that of a traveler on a train shunted onto a dead-end track because it missed the technological crossing and had no other place to go.

Many solutions have been put forward to reduce technological unemployment in the short term; their intent is to reduce the number of people who have missed the train, as well as to reduce the waiting time. Basically, efforts have to be made in two directions: better information and better retraining of the work force while on a job; and better information and better planning with respect to alternative activities.

Here, again, automation will provide part of the answer to improve the situation through better information processing and information transmission, on the one hand, and on the other hand, through improving the training or retraining facilities (audiovisual means of learning, computer-aided training, etc.).

While at the beginning of the century the main shift in manpower was from agriculture to manu-

**Table 5.** Change in Share of Total Employment by Sector, 1950–1970.

| Country | Agriculture | Industry Total | Industry Manufacturing | Services |
|---|---|---|---|---|
| United States | − 7.8 | − 0.5 | +0.2 | + 8.3 |
| Canada | −15.1 | − 4.4 | −3.7 | +19.5 |
| France | −11.8 | + 3.1 | +1.5 | + 8.8 |
| Federal Republic of Germany | −13.1 | + 5.9 | +6.7 | + 7.2 |
| Italy | −25.1 | +13.1 | +8.5 | +11.9 |
| Japan | −26.2 | +12.1 | +9.7 | +14.1 |
| United Kingdom | − 2.5 | − 1.7 | +0.3 | + 4.2 |
| Sweden | −14.8 | − 0.2 | −2.9 | +15.0 |

SOURCE: Bureau of Labor Statistics, Washington, D.C.

facturing industries, automation and technological change has brought about a shift of manpower from manufacturing industries into services. See Table 5. Also, working-hour schedules are becoming less and less rigid and the work content physically less strenuous. The number of wage earners (paid per hour of work) will decrease continuously, whereas the number of employees (paid per month) will increase correspondingly. These in turn will contribute to the stabilization of the economy, thanks to more stable purchasing power.

Hierarchic management systems are no longer adapted to modern production techniques, and computer utilization in management techniques make them obsolete. Participative management and motivated management methods are being increasingly used in industry and services. Training and retraining of personnel and permanent education programs permit the working force to keep abreast of technological knowledge.

Technical progress involves new methods of utilizing the labor force, especially as a result of the new quantitative, structural, and technical training requirements that workers must meet because of increasing automation. These labor-force plans must provide for the following requirements:

1. Meeting labor-force requirements in relation to the economic changes in the branches of industry (short-term adjustments).
2. Determining the change in the prospective structure of the labor force on the basis of the present occupational pattern (long-term adjustments).
3. Determining the general prospective trend of the population and the demands made on the educational system (structural change).

Because of the universal nature of information processing, which is applicable to a great many of the activities in industry and administration, broad instructional programs for dissemination of automation techniques must be incorporated into educational curricula.

The introduction and development of automation in developing countries can be expected to help overcome the handicaps created by the scarcity of skilled labor for industrial production, thus intensifying the pace of industrialization, widening and consolidating intersectoral relationships (agriculture, manufacturing, services), and increasing the rate of economic growth.

REFERENCES

1970. International Institute of Labour Studies. "Employment Problems of Automation and Advanced Technology—An International Perspective." Geneva, Switzerland.

1971. International Labour Organisation. "Automation: Some Classification and Measurement Problems." Geneva, Switzerland.

1971. United Nations. "Economic and Social Aspects of Automation." U.N. Economic Commission for Europe, Sales No. 4. E. 70. II. E. 16. Geneva, Switzerland.

1972. U.S. Dept. of Commerce. "U.S. Industrial Outlook 1972 with Projections to 1980." Washington, D.C.: U.S. Government Printing Office.

F. MULLER

**AUXILIARY MEMORY.** *See* MEMORY: Auxiliary.

# B

**BCD.** *See* BINARY CODED DECIMAL, NATURAL.

**BCS.** *See* BRITISH COMPUTER SOCIETY.

## BABBAGE, CHARLES

For articles on related subjects *see* DIGITAL COMPUTERS: History; and STORED PROGRAM CONCEPT.

Charles Babbage was born in Totnes, Devonshire, on Dec. 26, 1791. He was educated privately and went up to Cambridge in 1810. At that time, Cambridge education was strongly oriented toward mathematics and there was intense competition for high honors in the Mathematical Tripos. Babbage, however, soon discovered that Newton's ideas still dominated the Cambridge curriculum, whereas he had been exposed to, and was much drawn toward, the type of mathematics then receiving attention on the Continent. He did not, therefore, compete for honors. Nevertheless, he acquired a high mathematical reputation which increased with the years, so much so that in 1828 he was appointed Lucasian Professor, a position that Newton himself had held many years before. The stipend in Babbage's time

**Fig. 1.** Charles Babbage. *Courtesy of New York Public Library.*

was only £80 to £90 per annum. He did not reside in Cambridge nor lecture there, though he performed some of the other duties of the Professorship, such as examining for the Smith's Prize.

It was while still a student that Babbage began to work on the difference engine, a device intended to mechanize the production of the final values in a mathematical table from the widely spaced pivotal values that are first computed. It would also produce a stereotype mold, ready for the printer, thus eliminating one source of error. Babbage's own attempt at implementing the difference engine failed, in spite of financial support from the British government. The soundness of his ideas was, however, demonstrated by the fact that an independent implementation by George and Edward Sheutz, who had read of Babbage's ideas, was successful.

In a long life, Babbage turned his attention to many subjects, including mathematics, railroads, lighthouses, economics, the ophthalmoscope, politics, and public controversies of various kinds. But the dominating interest of his life was calculating machinery, and his claim to fame is through his work on the analytical engine, which was to have been an automatically sequenced, general-purpose calculating machine. Here he was profoundly original. He published some of his ideas and others have come down to us in his manuscript notebooks. The real breakthrough came in 1834 and the years immediately following, but Babbage continued to work on the subject for the remainder of his life.

Babbage's thoughts on the analytical engine were entirely in mechanical terms, with no suggestion, even in later years, that electricity might be called in aid. The analytical engine was to be decimal, although Babbage considered other scales of notation. Numbers were to be stored on wheels, with ten distinguishable positions, and transferred by a system of racks to a central *mill*, or processor, where all arithmetic would be performed. He had in mind a storage capacity for a thousand numbers of 50 decimal digits. He studied exhaustively a wide variety of schemes for performing the four operations of arithmetic and he invented the idea of anticipatory carry, which is much faster than carrying successively from one stage to another. He also knew about hoarding carry, by which a whole series of additions could be performed with one carrying operation at the end.

The sequencing of the analytical engine was to have been fully automatic, but not, of course, on what we would now call the stored-program principle. Punched cards of the type used in a Jacquard loom were to be adopted both for sequencing and for the input of numbers. Babbage proposed to have two sets of sequencing cards, one for controlling the mill and one for controlling the store; these would be separately stepped and would not necessarily move together.

Babbage never arrived at the idea of instructions containing both an operation part and an address part, nor at the formal concept of a program that we have today. Lady Lovelace, the daughter of Lord Byron, in notes to a translation that she made of a paper describing some of Babbage's ideas, published by Ménabréa in French in 1842, gives what at first sight appears to be a program along modern lines for computing Bernoulli numbers. This gives the arithmetic operations in detail, but does not contain anything corresponding to the conditional jump instructions in a modern program; after the main loop there is simply the sentence: "Here follows a repetition of operations 13 to 23."

Babbage's notebooks show him struggling with various ideas for handling the repetition of parts of a calculation, and although he sketched out many schemes that would have worked satisfactorily, one feels that he never arrived at one that entirely pleased him. For subsequencing within an operation he proposed to use drums with fixed studs, on the barrel-organ principle. It is odd that in his published writings there is no hint of the range and originality of his thoughts on the important matter of sequencing. Lady Lovelace has left us in her debt for the translation and notes referred to above, but there has been a tendency to exaggerate her importance in the Babbage saga.

Although he had workmen in his employ until the end of his life, Babbage failed to implement the analytical engine. We must conclude, as did some of his contemporaries, that he was temperamentally incapable of carrying a project through. Unfortunately, this time, there was no Sheutz to take up his ideas, and it may well be that the ultimate development of automatic calculating machinery was delayed by the aura of failure that surrounded Babbage's work. His detailed design studies lay buried in his unpublished notebooks and were forgotten. Of his genius, however, no one who has studied his work will have any doubt.

Babbage died in London on Oct. 18, 1871. His youngest son, Henry, who had spent most of his life in various military and civil appointments in India, did what he could to carry on his father's work, and published a collection of papers relating to it. The eldest son, Herschel, migrated in 1851 to South Australia, where he became a prominent member of the colony.

REFERENCES

1889. Babbage, H. P. (Ed.). *Babbage's Calculating Engines*. London.
1961. Morrison, P., and E. Morrison (Eds.). *Charles Babbage and His Calculating Engines*. New York: Dover.
1968. Babbage, C. *Passages from the Life of a Philosopher*. London, 1864; facsimile edition, London: Dawson's.
1971. Wilkes, M. V. "Babbage as a Computer Pioneer," Report of the Babbage Memorial Meeting, British Computer Society.

M. V. WILKES

## BACKTRACKING

For articles on related subjects *see* ALGORITHM; and HEURISTICS.

Often problems occur for which the only possible (or known) method of solution is by a search through the space of (perhaps a very large number) all possible solutions. In such cases it is important to attempt possible solutions systematically, eliminating potential solutions as quickly as possible, and never retrying a potential solution that has already been tried. The backtracking technique achieves these aims.

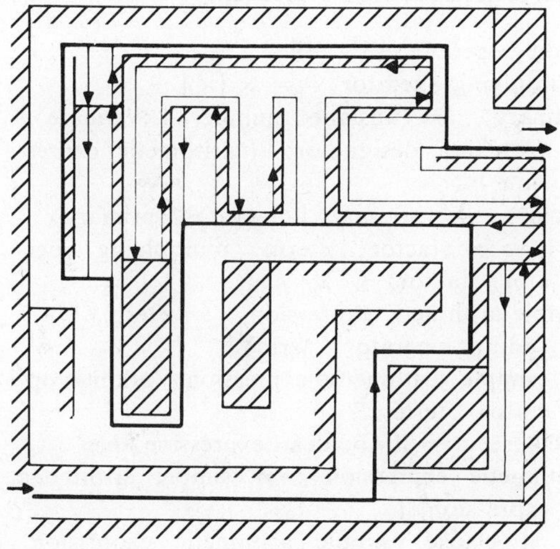

**Fig. 1**

Two examples will suffice to explain backtracking. Fig. 1 shows a simple maze. Our systematic technique to find a path through the maze is to always keep to the right until a dead end is reached, then *backtrack* until an alternate path is found, again keep to the right, etc. The dark line shows the path through the maze, the light lines show the other paths traversed in finding this path.

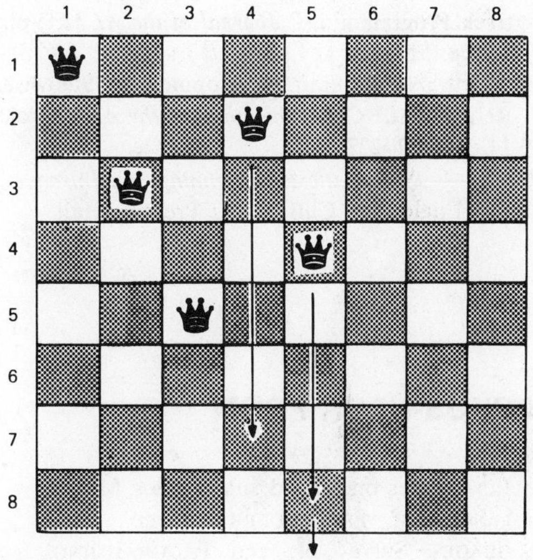


**Fig. 2**

Fig. 2 shows a chessboard at a stage in an attempt to solve the 8-Queen's problem in which eight queens are to be placed on a chessboard so that no two are in the same row or column or on the same diagonal. Our technique begins by placing a queen in the first column on the first row (1,1). The next queen is then placed in the second column on the first possible square, the third (3,2). Then subsequent queens are placed on (5,3), (2,4), and (4,5) as shown in Fig. 2. But with this arrangement no queen can be placed in column 6, so we *backtrack* to column 5 and move the queen to (5,8), again try but fail to place a queen in column 6, backtrack to column 5 but then, since we are already in row 8, backtrack again to column 4, move the queen on (2,4) to (7,4), etc. Eventually we find the first of 92 solutions, 12 of which are really distinct, that is, not related to others by some type of symmetry, at (1,1), (5,2), (8,3), (6,4), (3,5), (7,6), (2,7), (4,8). This method of solving the 8-Queen's problem can be easily and efficiently programmed for a computer (see Wirth, 1971).

Other areas in which backtracking is a commonly employed and useful technique are in the parsing process in the compilation of a higher level programming language, theorem-proving and game-playing programs, and generally those tasks whose search domain is "ill structured." A formal description of backtracking is found in Golomb and Baumert (1965).

REFERENCES

1965. Golomb, S. W., and L. D. Baumert. "Backtrack Programming," *Journal of the ACM*, Vol. 12, pp. 517–524.
1971. Wirth, N. "Program Development by Stepwise Refinement," *Communications of the ACM*, Vol. 14, pp. 221–227.
1973. ———. *Systematic Programming: An Introduction*. Englewood Cliffs, N.J.: Prentice-Hall.

A. RALSTON

# BACKUS-NAUR FORM

For articles on related subjects *see* METALANGUAGE; PROCEDURE-ORIENTED LANGUAGES, Survey of; and PROGRAMMING LANGUAGES.
For articles on related terms *see* RECURSION; and SYNTAX, SEMANTICS AND PRAGMATICS.

The Backus-Naur form, named after John W. Backus of the United States and Peter Naur of Denmark, and usually written BNF, is the best-known example of a *metalanguage*; i.e., one that syntactically describes a programming language. Using BNF it is possible to specify which sequences of symbols constitute a syntactically valid program in a given language. (The question of *semantics*—i.e., what such valid strings of symbols mean—must be specified separately.) A discussion of the basic concepts of BNF follows.

A *metalinguistic variable* (or metavariable), also called a *syntactic unit*, is one whose values are strings of symbols chosen from among the symbols permitted in the given language. Metalinguistic variables are enclosed in brackets (⟨ ⟩) for clarity and to distinguish them from symbols in the language itself. The symbol : : = is used to indicate metalinguistic equivalence; a vertical bar ( | ) is used to indicate that a choice is to be made among the items so indicated; and concatenation (linking together in a series) is indicated simply by juxtaposing the elements to be concatenated.

For an example, here is how the definition of an Algol integer is built up: First, we have a definition of what a digit is, according to the usual meaning:

⟨digit⟩ : : = 0 | 1 | 2 | 3 | 4 | 5 | 6 | 7 | 8 | 9.

Next we have a statement that an unsigned integer consists either of a single digit or an unsigned integer followed by another digit:

⟨unsigned integer⟩ : : = ⟨digit⟩ |
⟨unsigned integer⟩ ⟨digit⟩

This definition may be applied *recursively* to build up unsigned integers of any length whatever. If there were to be a limit on the number of digits, it would have to be stated separately in conjunction with each particular implementation. (The Algol language contains no such limitation, but all computer implementations must, of course, have some limitation.) Finally, the definition of an integer is completed by noting that it may be preceded by a plus sign, a minus sign, or neither:

⟨integer⟩ : : = ⟨unsigned integer⟩ |
+ ⟨unsigned integer⟩ | − ⟨unsigned integer⟩

For a second example, suppose that the metalinguistic variables ⟨unsigned number⟩, ⟨variable⟩, ⟨function designator⟩, and ⟨boolean expression⟩ have all been defined earlier, with usual meanings, and that the up-pointing arrow stands for exponentiation. Here, then, is the complete definition of an Algol arithmetic expression:

⟨adding operator⟩ : : = + | −
⟨multiplying operator⟩ : : = × | / | ÷
⟨primary⟩ : : = ⟨unsigned number⟩ | ⟨variable⟩ | ⟨function designator⟩ | (⟨arithmetic expression⟩)
⟨factor⟩ : : = ⟨primary⟩ | ⟨factor⟩ ↑ ⟨primary⟩
⟨term⟩ : : = ⟨factor⟩ | ⟨term⟩ ⟨multiplying operator⟩ ⟨factor⟩
⟨simple arithmetic expression⟩ : : = ⟨term⟩ |
⟨adding operator⟩ ⟨term⟩ |
⟨simple arithmetic expression⟩ ⟨adding operator⟩ ⟨term⟩
⟨if clause⟩ : : = **if** ⟨boolean expression⟩**then**
⟨arithmetic expression⟩ : : = ⟨simple arithmetic expression⟩ |
⟨if clause⟩ ⟨simple arithmetic expression⟩ **else** ⟨arithmetic expression⟩

It is no error that the third definition contains ⟨arithmetic expression⟩, enclosed in parentheses, even though it is an arithmetic expression that we are trying to define. This also is a matter of recursive definition, and simply says in this case that one choice for a ⟨primary⟩ is just any ⟨arithmetic expression⟩ enclosed in parentheses.

The words **if**, **then**, and **else**, since they are not enclosed in the meta-linguistic brackets, stand for themselves; they are elements of the Algol language and are defined elsewhere in the complete Algol language definition.

Almost any programming language can be defined in BNF, but somewhat different meta languages have been used with the major procedure-oriented languages other than Algol.

REFERENCE

1969. Sammet, Jean E. *Programming Languages: History and Fundamentals*. Englewood Cliffs, N.J.: Prentice-Hall (Chap. 2, sec. 6).

D. D. McCRACKEN

# BANDWIDTH

For articles on related subjects *see* COMMUNICATIONS AND COMPUTERS; and DATA COMMUNICATIONS.

The bandwidth of a communication network is a measure of the range of frequencies it can transmit at or near maximum power levels. As an example, consider a normal telephone system, which is an analog communication network normally designed to carry voice traffic in the frequency range 300–3400 Hz. Thus the equipment in the telephone exchange collects incoming data from the sound spectrum and arranges to attenuate sharply the signals outside that part of the spectrum. But even within that range there is further attenuation as the signals propagate through the telephone network, since the power of signals passing through the telephone transmission system is reduced. A typical measurement on the U.S. telephone network of attenuation is shown in Fig. 1, which indicates that somewhere below 300 Hz and above 3–4K Hz, the attenuation rises very rapidly. The range of frequencies in which the power level stays at above one-half its peak value (the so-called 3 *db* points) is the *nominal bandwidth* of the circuit. This is typically 3K Hz in a switched telephone line.

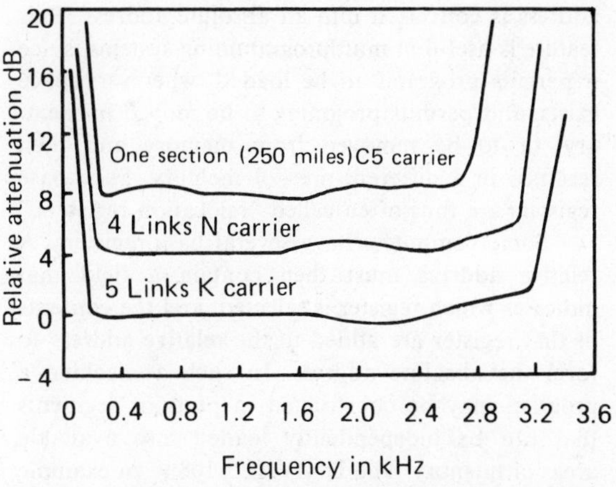


**Fig. 1.** Attentuation for frequency division multiplexing (FDM) systems. (reproduced from *Communication-Networks for Computers* by D. W. Davies and D. L. A. Barber. New York: Wiley, 1973, Fig. 2.16.)

P. T. KIRSTEIN

# BASE REGISTER

For article on related subject *see* ADDRESSING.

For article on related term *see* IBM 360-370 SERIES.

A base register is used in addressing a computer memory. In a computer that uses base registers, the effective address (i.e., the address field of the instruction, possibly modified by indexing and indirect addressing) is a relative address. The actual memory address used is determined by adding this relative address to the contents of one or more base registers.

The Control Data Cyber 70 series is an example of a computer system that uses a single base register. Every program is written as if it were meant to run in a single memory area, starting at location 0. The program may in fact be loaded starting at any memory location. When the program is run, the operating system places the address of the first word of the program in the base register. The content of the base register is automatically added to every memory reference address, and thus every relative address is converted into an absolute address. This feature is useful in multiprogramming systems, since it permits programs to be loaded wherever space exists, and permits programs to be moved in memory, or to be removed from memory and then resumed in a different area of memory. Such base registers are thus often called "relocation registers."

Some computers have several base registers. A relative address must then contain a field that indicates which register is selected, and the contents of that register are added to the relative address to form the absolute address. In such a machine a program may be constructed in parts or segments that can be independently loaded into available areas of memory. The UNIVAC 1108 is an example of a machine with two base registers. The Multics machine (Honeywell GE645) is an example of a machine with four base registers.

The term "base register" is sometimes used more or less interchangeably with the term "index register." Thus, the IBM 360 and 370 have 16 general registers, each of which provides a 24-bit base address to which the 12-bit address field (displacement) in an instruction is added to produce the effective address. These registers can be, and usually are, loaded by and stored in the programs that use them. It is conceptually better to think of them as index registers and to limit the use of the term "base register" to system registers that are not accessible to the programs whose addresses they modify.

S. ROSEN

**BASIC.** *See* PROCEDURE-ORIENTED LANGUAGES.

## BAUD

For articles on related subjects *see* BAUDOT CODE; and CHANNEL.

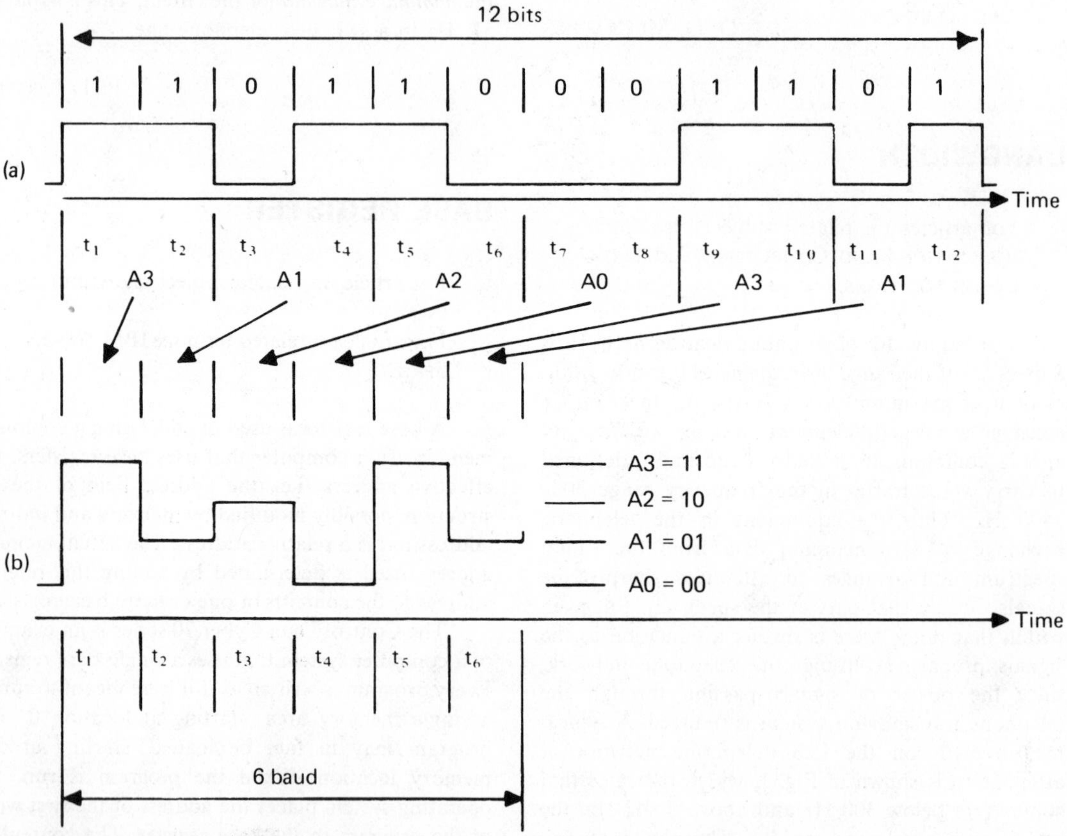


**Fig. 1.** Relationship between baud and bits per second. Each combination of two bits is encoded as one of four possible amplitudes, hence, one baud is equal to two bits per second.

A baud is a unit of signaling speed and refers to the number of times the state (or condition) of a line changes per second. It is the reciprocal of the length (in seconds) of the shortest element in the signaling code. Historically, it is a contraction of the surname of the Frenchman J. M. E. Baudot, whose five-bit code was adopted by the French telegraph system in 1877. By contrast, a bit is the smallest unit of information in a binary system. The baud rate is therefore equal to the bit rate only if each signal element represents one bit of information.

The relationship between bauds and bits per second is illustrated in Fig. 1, where amplitude is used as a coding method. In this particular case, there are four line conditions, one for each of the four combinations of two bits. Each line change signal element is therefore represented by two bits and, if we can have one line change in 1 ms, the baud rate is 1,000, whereas the bit rate is actually 2,000 bits per second. Similarly, if the signals are coded into eight possible states, one line condition could represent three bits and one baud would then equal three bits per second and so on.

Unfortunately, in much of today's literature, the terms "baud" and "bits per second" are used synonymously. This is correct in cases where pure two-state signaling is used, as in Fig. 1(a), but is incorrect in general. For this reason, the term "baud" is gradually being replaced by "bits per second," since the latter is independent of the coding method and truly represents the information rate.

J. S. SOBOLEWSKI

## BAUDOT CODE

For articles on related subjects *see* BAUD; CODES; and ERROR CORRECTING CODE.

The Baudot code, also known as the International Telegraph Code No. 1, is named after its inventor, J. M. E. Baudot (1845–1903). It was invented about 1880, and by the 1950s it had become one of the standards for international telegraph communication.

Baudot is a fixed character-length code in which each character is represented by five binary digits. The 5-digit character length allows for only 32 unique combinations, not enough to represent the 26 letters of the alphabet, the 10 digits, and the punctuation characters needed for telegraph messages. This problem of digit limitation is solved by defining two unique shift-control characters, and interpreting all subsequent characters in terms of the last shift-control character received. The shift-control characters are called "letter shift" and "figure shift". This arrangement is very similar to that of a shift-lock key on a typewriter, i.e., once the shift lock has been depressed, all subsequent characters are typed in the same shift.

Using the technique of two unique shift characters, a 5-bit code can then represent 62 characters. However, in the Baudot code the total number of characters is less than this because other control characters such as "line feed" and "carriage return" are given unique representations.

**Table 1.** Baudot Code Characters.

| *Letters* | | *Figures* |
|---|---|---|
| A | 10 000 | 1 |
| B | 00 110 | 8 |
| C | 10 110 | 9 |
| D | 11 110 | Ø |
| E | 01 000 | 2 |
| F | 01 110 | NA |
| G | 01 010 | 7 |
| H | 11 010 | + |
| I | 01 100 | NA |
| J | 10 010 | 6 |
| K | 10 011 | ( |
| L | 11 011 | = |
| M | 01 011 | ) |
| N | 01 111 | NA |
| O | 11 100 | 5 |
| P | 11 111 | % |
| Q | 10 111 | / |
| R | 00 111 | – |
| S | 00 101 | . |
| T | 10 101 | NA |
| U | 10 100 | 4 |
| V | 11 101 | ' |
| W | 01 101 | ? |
| X | 01 001 | , |
| Y | 00 100 | 3 |
| Z | 11 001 | : |
| LS | 00 001 | LS |
| FS | 00 010 | FS |
| CR | 11 000 | CR |
| LF | 10 001 | LF |
| ER | 00 011 | ER |
| NA | 00 000 | NA |

*Symbols:* LS = Letter Shift, FS = Figure Shift, CR = Carriage Return, LF = Line Feed, ER = Error, NA = Not Assigned, Space = LS or FS.

The Baudot code does not have the capability of detecting errors because all combinations of the five bits are valid characters within the code. During transmission, therefore, a character can be transformed into another character by the loss or gain of one or more bits. Particularly harmful is an error in a shift-control character because all characters after the transformed shift-control character up to the next shift-control character would be interpreted in the wrong shift. For example, in the message PAY 810 DOLLARS, if the "figure shift" character between the PAY and the 810 were transformed into, say, a J (i.e., 00010 to 10010), then the message would be received as PAYJBAD DOLLARS (see Table 1 for letter-shift, figure-shift equivalents). In order to alleviate this problem, telegraph systems frequently retransmit at the end of the message all figures that occur in the message.

The five-level code most used today is the International Telegraph Code No. 2 (Murray code), invented about 20 years after the Baudot code. In computer manufacturer's literature, there is some confusion concerning the use of the term "baudot code." It is sometimes used to apply to all five-level codes and is frequently applied to International Telegraph Code No. 2.

G. D. DETLEFSEN AND R. H. KERR

## BENCHMARK

For articles on related subjects *see* GROSCH'S LAW; and PERFORMANCE OF COMPUTERS.

Benchmarks are standardized computer programs used to test the processing power of different computers. They specify the input data, the computations to be performed, and the output formats very rigidly while leaving the details as to how the calculation is to be performed flexible enough to allow the individual advantages of a particular computer being tested to be maximized. (See Sharpe, 1969.)

Auerbach Information, Inc., who have been providing benchmark comparisons since 1962 in their "Standard EDP Reports," uses five general benchmark programs to compare computers: (1) a generalized file processing problem, (2) a random access file processing problem, (3) a sorting problem, (4) a matrix inversion problem, and (5) a generalized mathematical problem. This is probably the longest running series of benchmark programs and allows general comparison between machines over a considerable time frame.

If the user has a specific type of problem that will account for a large percentage of the use of his machine, he can run more specific benchmark problems to evaluate various manufacturers' products.

Benchmark programs are one way by which machine characteristics can be compared. Alternatively, a user may specify a set of instructions and compare machines on the basis of how well they perform this instruction mix. This allows comparison among machines regardless of programming language, hardware construction, etc.

Benchmark programs may either be actually run or their performance may be calculated from the manufacturer's published data on the characteristics of the computer. Either form of comparison may be useful in evaluating computers.

Benchmarks are used by computer purchasers to determine what machine is best for their particular use in terms of both speed and cost. However, benchmarks alone cannot be used for this purpose, since most large, general-purpose computers will be used to handle a wide class of problems whose frequency will be unpredictable before purchase. Thus, in addition to benchmarks, other evaluations, subjective and objective, will enter into the decision of what computer to obtain.

One example of another objective comparison is the computer power versus cost formula developed by Knight and Cerveny in the article Performance of Computers, which allows very general comparisons both by power/cost and by year.

REFERENCE

1969. Sharpe, W. F. *The Economics of Computers.* New York: Columbia University Press, pp. 308–312.

K. E. KNIGHT AND R. P. CERVENY

## BINARY CODED DECIMAL, NATURAL

For article on related subject *see* CODES.

Natural binary-coded decimal (NBCD) is a particular binary-coded decimal (BCD) code that is itself often called BCD. It is "natural" because it uses the first ten binary numbers in sequence to represent the digits 0 through 9 (see Table 1).

**Table 1.** NBCD Code.

| *Digit* | *NBCD Combination* |
|---|---|
| 0 | 0000 |
| 1 | 0001 |
| 2 | 0010 |
| 3 | 0011 |
| 4 | 0100 |
| 5 | 0101 |
| 6 | 0110 |
| 7 | 0111 |
| 8 | 1000 |
| 9 | 1001 |

Since 9 is represented by 1001, NBCD is a four-bit code. Moreover, it is a weighted code, since the four bits, left to right, correspond to weights of 8, 4, 2, and 1. Thus, 0110 represents a decimal 6.

Six possible four-bit combinations (1010, 1011, 1100, 1101, 1110, 1111) are not part of the code and are called "forbidden" combinations.

I. FLORES

# BINARY SEARCH

For articles on related subjects *see* COLLATING SEQUENCE; KEY; SORTING; and TABLE LOOKUP.

Binary search is a quick method for searching an ordered, dense list (i.e., every cell of the list contains a record) for a particular record by successively looking at one half of the list in which the record is known to be.

A record is recognized by a field, called its "key." We assume that the list is ordered with respect to the collating sequence of its keys.

There are several ways to find a specific record identified only by its key. The simplest, but longest, is the sequential search, in which cells of the list are searched in the physical order as they appear in the list. Binary search considerably reduces the time required to find a desired record.

To present the basic idea of binary search, we introduce the idea of a "fence cell" or simply a fence that divides a list into two equal or nearly equal parts. Examining the key of the fence record will tell us which half of the list contains the desired record. A fence is set up for the half-list that contains the record and then the quarter-list that contains the record is determined. From the quarter-list we determine an eighth-list and so forth. The actions of binary search then consist of three phases:

1. Dividing a list or sublist into two fairly equal parts by defining a fence.
2. Examining the fence to determine which half to use next.
3. Determining when our search is finished.

To present the details of the mathematics of binary search, we define the parameters:

$S$ = address of the starting point of the list in memory.
$N$ = length of the list in number of cells.
$C$ = size of each cell in bytes or words, or other appropriate units.
$K$ = key of the record sought.
$f_i$ = ordinal number in the list of the $i$th fence.
$F_i$ = address of the $i$th fence.
$n_i$ = number of items in the $i$th sublist with $n_0 = N$.

To begin the binary search we calculate

$$f_1 = [n_0/2] + 1, \tag{1}$$

where the square brackets denote the integer less than or equal to the number contained within them. Then

$$F_1 = S + C(f_1 - 1). \tag{2}$$

To find $F_2$, we must determine in which half of the list the desired record is contained. Denote by $(F_1)_K$ the key in cell $F_1$. Then, either (a) $K = (F_1)_K$, in which case the search is finished; or (b) $K < (F_1)_K$, in which case the lower sublist is used and

$$n_1 = \left[\frac{n_0}{2}\right] \qquad f_2 = f_1 - \left[\frac{n_1}{2}\right]; \tag{3}$$

or (c), $K > (F_1)_K$, in which case the upper sublist is used and

$$n_1 = n_0 - 1 - \left[\frac{n_0}{2}\right] \qquad f_2 = f_1 + \left[\frac{n_1}{2}\right] + 1 \tag{4}$$

The difference in the equations for $f_2$ is to insure that the lower half-list is always the same length or one greater in length than the upper half-list. In any case,

$$F_2 = S + C(f_2 - 1), \quad (5)$$

and then we proceed to find $F_3, F_4, \ldots$ by a similar procedure, using

$$f_{i+1} = f_i - \left[\frac{n_i}{2}\right] \text{ or } f_i + \left[\frac{n_i}{2}\right] + 1,$$
$$F_{i+1} = S + C(f_{i+1} - 1), \quad (6)$$
$$n_{i+1} = \left[\frac{n_i}{2}\right] \text{ or } n_i - 1 - \left[\frac{n_i}{2}\right].$$

At some point $K$ must equal $(F_i)_K$ and the search is finished; otherwise, the desired record is not in the list. The latter case is automatically discovered when $n_i = 1$ and the key does not match $K$.

Fig. 1 illustrates the binary search procedure for the case $N = 28$ and where the record sought is in cell 11. For convenience we assume $S = C = 1$. Using the foregoing equations, we have

$$f_1 = F_1 = 15, \quad n_1 = 14,$$
$$f_2 = F_2 = 8, \quad n_2 = 6,$$
$$f_3 = F_3 = 12, \quad n_3 = 3,$$
$$f_4 = F_4 = 10, \quad n_4 = 1,$$
$$f_5 = F_5 = 11,$$

at which point we have found the desired record.

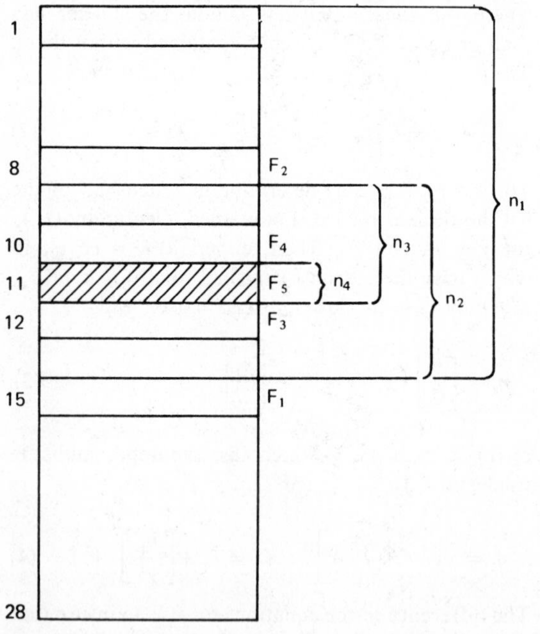


**Fig. 1.** Binary search.

The efficiency of a search procedure can be judged according to the number of "looks" it takes to find the desired record. In the case of binary search, the action proceeds by continuously dividing successive sublists in half. This is a logarithmic process, using 2 as a base. It is not hard to see that the largest number of looks required to find the desired item is given as

$$L = [\log_2 N] + 1. \quad (7)$$

In the preceding example, $[\log_2 28] + 1 = 5$. Often it will not take this many looks because one of the fences that we examined along the way will actually contain the record sought. If we call $\overline{L}$ the average number of looks, where $L$ is the maximum number of looks, then this average number is such that

$$L - 1 < \overline{L} \leq L. \quad (8)$$

REFERENCE

1970. Flores, Ivan. *Data Structures and Management.* Englewood Cliffs, N.J. Prentice-Hall, pp. 71–75.

I. FLORES

# BINDING TIME

For articles on related subjects *see* ASSEMBLERS; and LANGUAGE PROCESSORS.

Binding time refers to the instant when a symbolic expression in a computer program is reduced to a form directly interpretable by the hardware. For example, a symbolic expression given to a translator is progressively bound as that translator does its work. Normally binding time refers to that moment when the symbol or expression concerned has been reduced to a bit pattern in a fixed location in the storage device concerned. But binding time can also refer to an intermediate point in this process if the context in which it is used makes this clear. For example, the translator under discussion may leave certain symbols incompletely bound, letting a linking loader complete the job. Used in such a context, binding time can mean the point at which that translator has gone as far in binding the symbol as it can.

Binding time is often used with reference to the allocation of storage in higher level language programs. For example, in Fortran the binding time for all storage allocation is at compilation or loading time. In other languages like Algol or PL/I, data is dynamically created and erased while a program is executing so that the binding time for much storage allocation is at run time.

In general the later something is bound the more flexibility it provides for the programmer but the harder it is for the computer to deal with. Binding sometimes takes place progressively as happens when a language processor binds various parts of an expression at different stages of the translation process. The rate at which binding takes place, and the moment when it has taken place completely, are important design considerations for all sorts of software. Early binding means efficiency, with character strings replaced by addresses and expressions by binary numbers. For the same reasons, it means loss of debugging information and the ability to optimize by recognizing identical constants, common subexpressions and the like. Broadly speaking, the history of software development is the history of ever-later binding time, as user convenience is given more attention and efficiency left to faster hardware and specialized translators that are employed only after all debugging is done.

Some translators have attempted to put the question of binding time, to some degree, in the users' hands. One, at least (Strachey, 1968) has gone all the way for experimental purposes, letting the user specify the rate at which each of his symbols is to be bound.

REFERENCES

1968. Strachey, C. "A General Purpose Macro Generator," *The Computer Journal*, Vol. 8, pp. 225–241.

1968. Wegner, P. *Programming Languages, Information Structures and Machine Organization*. New York: McGraw-Hill Book Company.

M. HALPERN

# BIOMEDICINE, COMPUTER GRAPHICS IN

For articles on related subjects *see* COMPUTER GRAPHICS; and MEDICAL APPLICATIONS.

For many years, investigators of complex biological models have welcomed interactive graphics. When their problems taxed conventional analog computers, they contrived various devices to extend their capabilities and were among the early developers and users of hybrid computers. Interaction and a graphics display were among design criteria for the LINC, whose development for biological laboratory computing was supported by the National Institutes of Health (NIH). Around 1965, Levinthal's rotating molecules drew attention to the power of major digital graphics (Levinthal, 1966). Soon several research centers extended the demonstration of this power to a variety of biomedical applications. Further applications, NIH-supported development of graphics systems software and low-cost hardware, and commercial advances have recently culminated in cost-effective graphics hardware and software resources that can and should advance rapidly throughout the biomedical domain.

This brief review is necessarily incomplete and will select projects that illustrate important categories of biomedical graphics applications.

Complex *three-dimensional structures* (3-D) abound in biology. The sensation of three-dimensionality and variety of perspectives provided by dynamic graphical presentations have been unprecedentedly effective in revealing atom-rich planes and suggesting active structures in biological molecules (Levinthal, 1966). Z-brightening, which increases the plotting intensity of portions of the structure "nearer" to the observer, enhances the three-dimensional sensation in viewing rotating displays. Interaction facilitates exploration of van der Waals limitations on rotations of molecular substructures, investigations of adding substituents, and a variety of visualizations from basic carbon skeletons to complete structures highlighting certain atoms. Valuable insights concerning embryonic evolution of the nervous system are being derived from graphically supported 3-D reconstructions from microscopic serial sections. Development of craniofacial structures and the mechanics of limb motion also are subjects of graphics-supported investigations.

Early expectations of full automation in diagnostic radiology and other areas of biomedical *image analysis* underestimated skills of the trained eye. Many projects foundered at the level of feature perception or location of regions of interest. Interactive graphics permits such obstacles to be bypassed. An observer approximately indicates chromosomes in overlapping spreads, leaving tasks of precise delineation, measurement, and classification

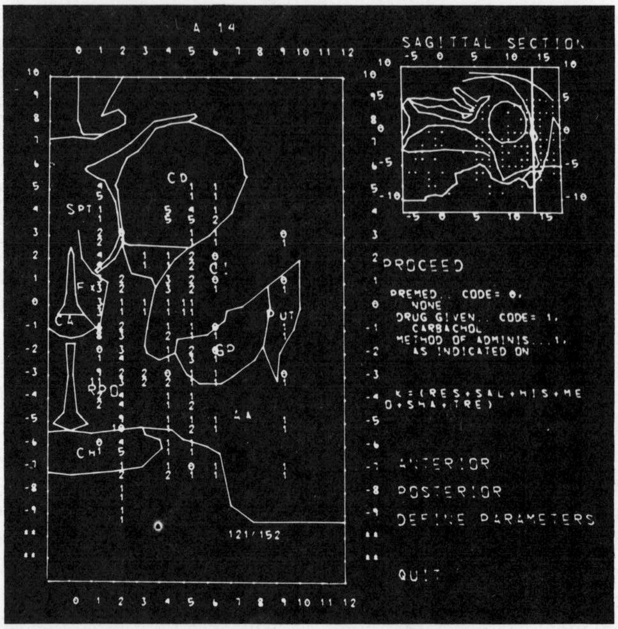


**Fig. 1.** Relating retrieved data to meaningful structures. A boolean combination of physiological and behavioral responses is related to sites of the brain where a given pharmacological agent has been injected. The notation $\frac{3}{4}$ means that the combination occurred three times, for four injections at the site.

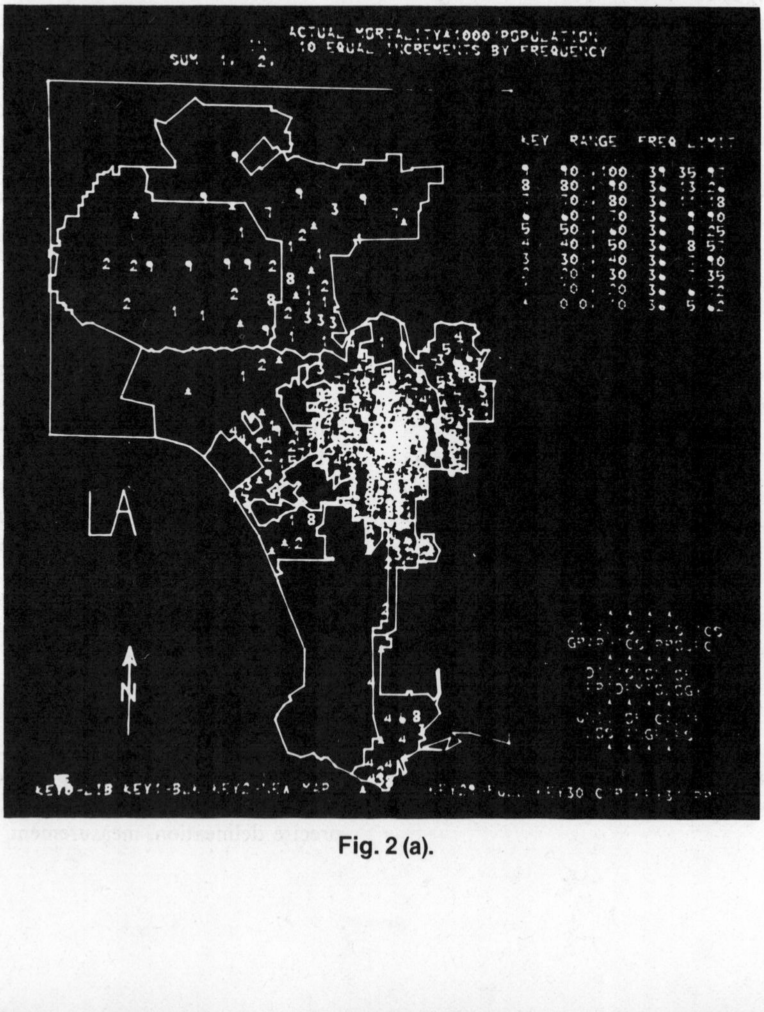


**Fig. 2 (a).**

to the machine (Neurath et al., 1966). The machine performs texture analysis for areas he indicates in a chest X-ray. The observer promptly reroutes when a rib or artifact entices edge tracking away from the heart in a sequence of radiographs used to study volume changes in normal and abnormal beating hearts. Gray-level video representations of the original X-ray films are back-projected onto the graphics screen for later application.

The power of interactive graphics finds full expression in *biological modeling* (Newton, 1972). Realistic mathematical description and productive investigation of difficult models encountered in biology and medicine demand high levels of analytical skill and biomedical knowledge. Few people are trained to provide both, and even a variety of biomedical experts may be required for some problems. Properly designed graphics displays can communicate with these various scientists, providing further characterizations of underlying mathematical structures or biological assumptions as needed. Investigation of complex models is made tractable by techniques that monitor inconsistencies and otherwise facilitate model specification, as well as by meaningful multivariate displays during computation. Intuitive guidance of model exploration can result in substantial economies; the observer often can terminate a run well before the foreseeable stopping rules required in batch processing would take effect.

**Fig. 2.** (a) Demographic variables from the census tract can be associated with variables related to the incidence of heart disease in Los Angeles County. (b) User can zoom for closer study of neighborhoods.

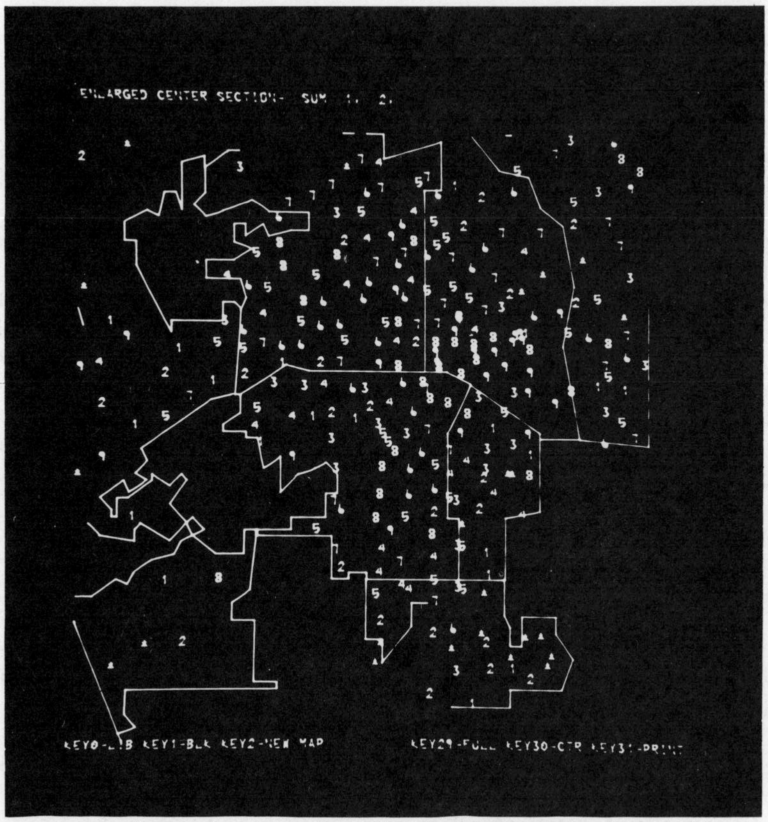


**Fig. 2 (b).**

Rand's BIOMOD system supports models that guide the treatment of leukemia and instruct medical students in fluid therapy (Groner et al., 1971). Others support exploration of multiagent strategies in cancer therapy and of realistic epidemiological models that incorporate timely features such as school busing and regional disparities in housing. After clarifying how diseases such as emphysema cause misinterpretation of certain conventional pulmonary function tests, a City of Hope internist directed his graphics model to the development of improved tests. Simpler graphics models of metabolic compartment analysis, enzyme kinetics, and community health care aid instruction.

*Data examination* in a rapidly evolving science is apt to emphasize hypothesis discovery; both physiological signals and data bases encountered in clinical studies are characteristically complex and noisy. Thus, the need to infuse human intuition and pattern perception into the analysis of biomedical data has motivated the development of a variety of interactive graphics programs for data exploration. Statistical programs range from novel approaches to profile analysis, to interactive graphics implementation of conventional time-series, regression, or discriminant function analyses. To specify retrieval, lightpen selection from branching menus or composition of boolean conditions from lists of descriptors provide an effective natural-language interface to biomedical investigators. Most important are meaningful displays of the retrieved information. The relationship of pharmacological action to anatomical neural pathways has been facilitated by research data summaries superimposed on a three-dimensional brain map, the sites of injection of pharmacological agents being known (Sheu et al., (1969) (see Fig. 1). The Los Angeles Heart Study data have been examined in conjunction with census demographic data, superimposed on a map of Los Angeles County, displayed in entirety or zoomed to any area (see Fig. 2.).

Interactive graphics data analysis has been directed to *designing economical patient-monitoring systems*. Alternative digital processing algorithms or simulated analog circuit designs operate upon physiological signals recorded from a large number of patients. The statistician/engineer and physician join in determining which works best and in hypothesizing how it might be improved. A cost-effective digital algorithm for monitoring electrocardiograms of coronary patients has resulted, as has inexpensive bedside analog circuitry for obstetrical monitoring.

Two additional examples of direct *medical applications* should be noted: In radiation treatment planning, sources of radiation and interposed materials must be deployed to maximize dose delivered throughout the tumor and to minimize its effect on critical organs. Computation of dose distribution is complicated by tissue inhomogeneities, such as bone and air-filled lungs. The Programmed Console, an early graphics minicomputer turnkey system for exploring treatment alternatives, was an immediate success (Holmes, 1970). More versatile and powerful supports now are provided by remote graphics terminals that access major computers by dial-up telephone lines. Low-cost graphics would be welcomed to make more readable displays that superimpose the patient's anatomical diagram, dose-distribution contour plots, and related numerical data.

The computer itself is therapist in Colby's approach to treating nonspeaking autistic children, who reject humans but tend to be fascinated by machines (Smith et al., 1972). As they operate his responsive graphics-audio system, their progress toward speech is catalyzed to the extent that most soon can be hopefully referred back to previously unsuccessful conventional therapy.

## References

1966. Levinthal, C. "Molecular Model-Building by Computer," *Scientific American*, Vol. 214:42.

1966. Neurath, P. W., et al. "Human Chromosome Analysis by Computer—An Optical Pattern Recognition Problem," *Ann. N. Y. Acad. Sci.*, Vol 128, pp. 1013–1028.

1969. Sheu, Y., et al. "Topographic Information Retrieval in Neuropharmacology by Using Graphic Display," *Proc. of 24th Annual Conference of the Assoc. Comput. Mach.*, pp. 485–489.

1970. Holmes, W. F. "External Beam Treatment-Planning with the Programmed Console," *Radiology*, Vol. 94, pp. 391–400.

1971. Groner, G. F., et al. *BIOMOD-An Interactive Computer Graphics System for Modeling*. The Rand Corporation, R-617-NIH (July).

1972. Newton, C. M. "Planning Radiotherapeutic Strategy," *Proc. San Diego Biomedical Symposium*, Vol. 11, pp. 189–203.

1972. Smith, D. C., et al. "Automated Therapy for Non-Speaking Autistic Children," *Proc. Spring Joint Computer Conference*, Vol. 40, pp. 1101–1106.

C. M. Newton

## BLOCK AND BLOCKING

For article on related subject *see* MEMORY: Auxiliary.

For articles on related terms *see* CHANNEL; and DATA STRUCTURES.

The term "block" is synonymous with "physical record": a sequence of words or characters written contiguously by a computer on an external storage medium. Typically, one block is written each time a WRITE command is executed by an I/O channel (or equivalent I/O facility). Analogously, one block is read from an external medium each time that a READ command is executed by the channel.

"Block" is distinguished from "logical record" as follows: A block is defined by the physical characteristics and constraints of the external storage medium, whereas a logical record is defined by a particular data structure in a processing program. Logical records (often shortened to "records," although this term is also loosely used for "blocks") are aggregates of data such as bits, numbers, and character strings, which are naturally and conveniently transmitted at one time from the main storage of a computer to an external medium. One type of data aggregate is a "master record," comprising all attributes associated with a member of some population.

Blocks typically contain several logical records when written onto magnetic media such as drums, tape drives, and disk drives. The size of a block is chosen to take into account the software characteristics of a system (e.g., buffer size) and the hardware characteristics of the external medium (so as to avoid too much starting or stopping when reading or writing tape). In the case of fixed-length blocks, the standard format is as shown in Fig. 1. For fixed-length logical records, the number of records per block is called the "blocking factor." For many computers (e.g., current IBM models), variable-length logical records are formatted into blocks, as shown in Fig. 2. Fig. 3 shows how large logical

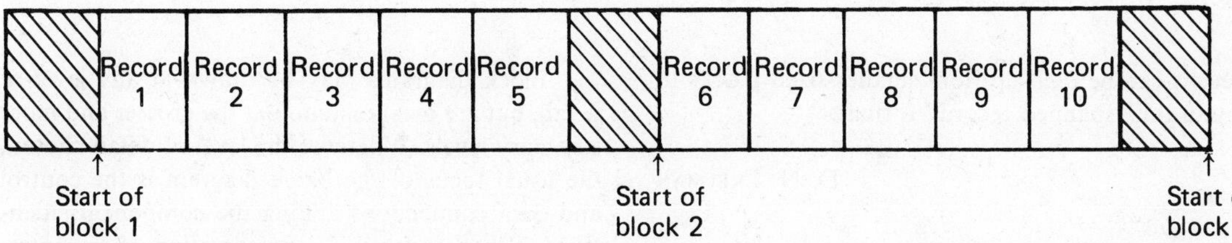


**Fig. 1.** Fixed-length blocks: blocking factor = 5; all records have same length; block length = 5 × (record length).

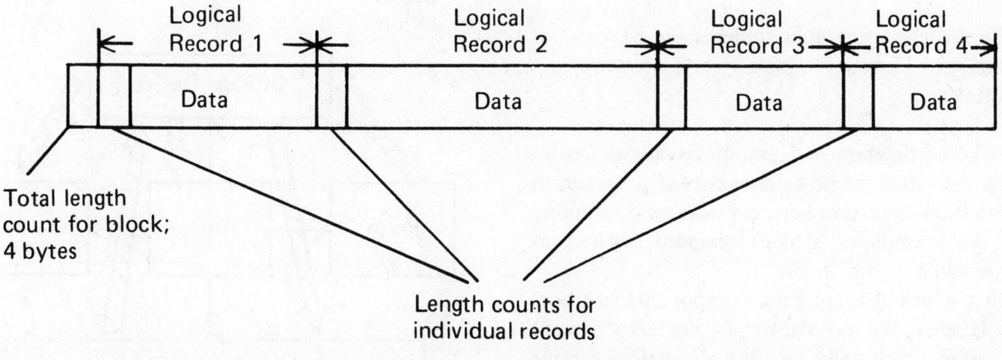


**Fig. 2.** Variable-block lengths (no logical record larger than one physical block): blocking factor, variable; block length = 4 + [(length of record-1) + 4] + [(length of record-2) + 4] + . . .

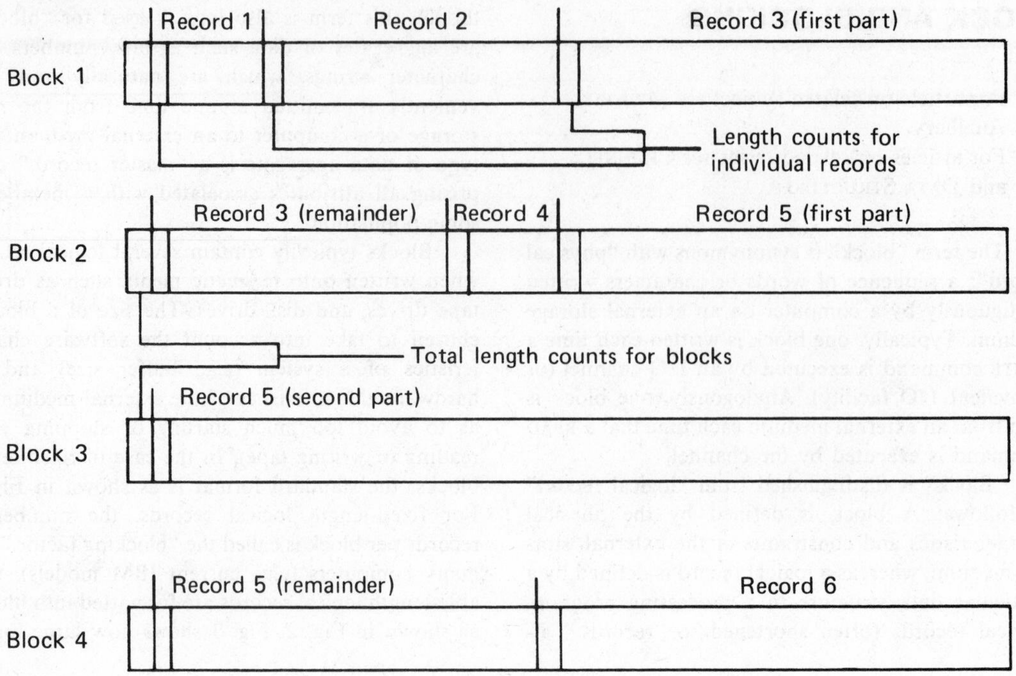


**Fig. 3.** Variable-length blocks (logical records may be larger than physical blocks).

records can be built up from smaller-sized blocks to obtain the "spanned record" format.

D. N. FREEMAN

# BLOCK DIAGRAM

For articles on related subjects *see* FLOWCHART; FLOW DIAGRAM; and SYSTEM CHART.

A block diagram is a graphic means of representing the functions or components of a system in order to show the control or data connections among them. An example of a block diagram for a computer is given in Fig. 1.

In a block diagram, the components are normally labeled, but no attempt is made to present them either pictorially or dimensionally. Simple rectangles or circles are common. Lines or arrows generally indicate the operational directions of the control or data connections.

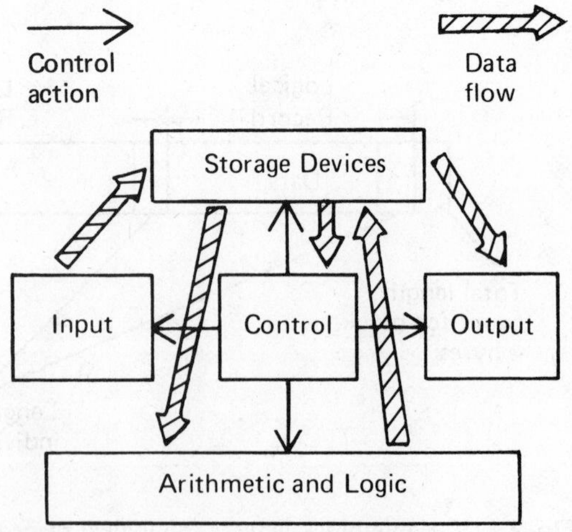


**Fig. 1.** Block diagram of a computer.

Block diagrams may be drawn at any level of detail, but are most common at the grosser and more summary levels. Whatever the level of detail chosen, the usual focus of the block diagram is the control and data connections among the components identified. When a detailed representation of the interactions among components or circuit elements is needed, the usual practice is to draw logic diagrams, functional diagrams, or circuit diagrams instead of block diagrams.

In the early days of the computer field, the term "block diagram" was also used as a synonym for flowchart. That practice is rarely followed today now that flowcharts have become more specialized in function.

N. CHAPIN

# BLOCK STRUCTURE

For articles on related subjects *see* PROCEDURE-ORIENTED LANGUAGES; and PROGRAMMING LANGUAGES.

For articles on related terms *see* PROCEDURE; SIDE EFFECT; and STACK.

Block structure is one of the most powerful conceptual tools employed by the programmer. When used judiciously it can help transform a large, unwieldy program into a disciplined, well-structured, and easy-to-understand piece of code.

Because of the important functions it performs, block structure (first introduced in Algol 60) is found in one guise or another in practically all procedural languages developed after 1960.

After a brief look at the functions performed by block structure, from the programmer's perspective, we take a careful look at the syntax, semantics, and run-time implementations of the Algol 60 block structure.

**The Programmer's View of Block Structure.** From the programmer's point of view, block structure performs two major control functions:

1. It groups a sequence of statements into a single "compound" statement.
2. It allows explicit control by the programmer over the scope of the variables he uses.

Groupings imply two things: First, we can reference a compound statement and use it wherever a single statement can be used (e.g., as the object of a loop). Therefore, we can think of a sequence of statements as a single entity and thus simplify the process of program construction. Second, we can decompose any large, unwieldy program into a disciplined nest of blocks, since a block may contain other blocks as components. This is perhaps the most important use of the block from the programmer's angle, for it allows him to construct his program in hierarchical fashion, which often results in increased program clarity and elegance.

Scope of variables implies three things: First, the ability to control dynamically (i.e., at run time) the allocation and freeing of storage. In particular, since the dimensions of all arrays, declared within the block are determined upon entry into a block, they may vary from invocation to invocation; second, the creation of a current context (environment), independent of all previous contexts, upon entry to a block, since locally allocated storage is freed upon exiting from a block. Third, since local variables do not have global side effects (such as assignment), the programmer can control the local logical complexity of the data objects referenced.

| Block Structure | Without Block Structure |
|---|---|
| <pre>real a, b, x, y, z;<br>  .<br>  .<br>  .<br>if a ≥ b then<br>  begin<br>    real temp;<br>    temp :=x;<br>    x:=y;<br>    y:=z;<br>    z:=temp;<br>  end<br>else<br>  begin<br>    real temp;<br>    temp :=z;<br>    z:=y;<br>    y:=x;<br>    x:=temp;<br>  end</pre> | <pre>real a, b, x, y, z, temp;<br>  .<br>  .<br>  .<br>temp :=x;<br>if a < b then go to L1;<br>    x:=y;<br>    y:=z;<br>    z:=temp;<br>    go to L2;<br>L1:x:=z;<br>    z:=y;<br>    y:=temp;<br>L2:</pre> |

**Fig. 1.** A program with and without block structure.

In order to appreciate the importance of block structure, let us look at a trivial piece of code in Algol 60 in its blocked and unblocked versions (See Fig. 1). In the overall structure of Fig. 1, a selection between two computations is readily visible in the block-structured version, but is rather obscure at first glance in the unblocked version, which in addition incurs the creation of three additional identifiers.

**Using Block Structure in Programs.** The material given in this section has been adapted from Wegner (1971).

DECLARATIONS. In most block-structured languages a program is also a block. A block in turn is a list of declarations called the "block head," followed by a list of statements called the "block body" enclosed within the brackets **begin** ... **end**. The rules of Algol 60 state that all identifiers (e.g., names of variables) used within a block have to be declared in its block head. Furthermore, *identifiers can be used only within the block in which they have been declared.* This block is their "scope" and they are said to be "local" to it.

In addition to scalar variables of types, **boolean**, **integer**, and **real**, arrays of each of these data types and procedures may also be declared in the block head. Each time a block is activated [discussed below], the expressions for the array bounds are newly computed, thereby allowing the aforementioned variable array bounds. Procedures may be of the statement type—returning no value (i.e., an extension of the Fortran subroutine concept)—or they may be of the function type, in which case they return a single value to their point of invocation. Both types of procedures may assign new values to any number of nonlocal variables. They are then said to have a side effect. Function type procedures have a type associated with the values they return.

SCOPE RULES AND INITIALIZATION. As mentioned above, a block body is a sequence of statements and a block is a particular kind of statement. Therefore, blocks may be nested to any depth. This design has several consequences:

1. Although an identifier may be used only to name one object in a block, the same identifier may be used to name different objects in different blocks.

2. At run time, whenever a block is entered a new copy of all the variables declared in its block head is created. This set of objects (collectively known as the activation record of the block) defines a particular instance of the block in time. The activation records comply with a strict stack discipline of first-in-first-out (see next section). Therefore, if an identifier is declared in an outer block as well as in the currently active block, only the currently declared identifier may be referenced.

3. Labels in front of blocks may be implicitly declared (as in our example below). Since blocks may be entered only from their block head, a major design decision is how to treat goto's. Two basic

```
B1: begin real a, b, x;
    procedure P(x,y);
      real x,y;

        BP: begin real a;
            ...
            y:=x+a;
            ...
            end

    B2: begin real b, c;
            ...
            P(a,b);
            ...
        end;
end
```

B1's block head consists of the declarations of a, b, x as real variables and the procedure P(x,y) and its block body.

B1's block body is the block B2 in which we find among others the procedure statement [or procedure call] P(a,b). x and y are its formal parameters and a and b are its actual parameters.

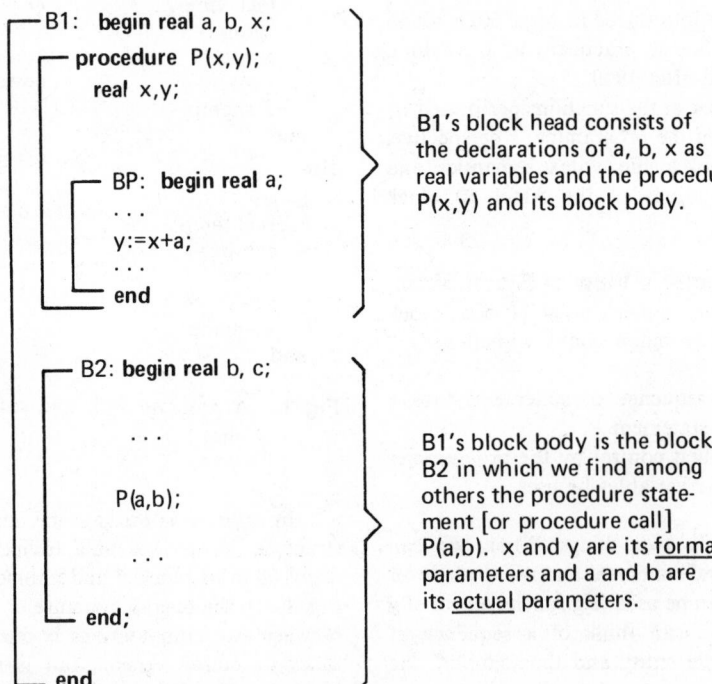

**Fig. 2.** Procedures in block structure.

strategies may be employed: (1) The conservative strategy is not to allow goto's to the middle of the block, thereby maintaining the stacklike discipline of Algol 60; (2) the liberal strategy is to assume that all information pertaining to the state of a computation at a particular statement in the program is carried in the label of that statement. This results in a rather interesting but error-prone language design.

Identifiers of type **procedure** are said to be "initialized" to the value of their body. They cannot be redefined at run time. All other identifiers are "uninitialized" and must be explicitly assigned a value via the execution of an assignment statement.

To summarize, let us look at the example in Fig. 2. Note that the identifier *b* is declared once in the B1 block and again in the B2 block. Thus, P(*a,b*) refers to the local declaration of *b* which is created upon entering the B2 block. Also, *a* in BP has scope BP and is a local variable used in computing P(*a,b*).

**Theoretical Models of Block Structure Execution.** The descriptions and examples in this section are from Wegner (1971).

Several models have been suggested for describing the run-time execution of programs written in block-structured languages. We will look at two of them: the stack model proposed by Dijkstra (1967) and the contour model developed by Johnson (1971).

The *stack model*, SM = (P,C,S), consists of

P: a program component, which remains unchanged throughout the execution of the program.

C: a control component, consisting of two pointers: an instruction pointer **ip**, pointing to the current instruction, and an environment pointer **ep**, pointing to the current environment.

S: a stack of activation records containing all the data the program operates on.

In terms of the preceding example, we have the following in Fig. 3: At the time instant modeled, execution is at statement $b: = x + a$, within block BP. Previously, blocks P, B2, and B1 have been properly entered.

Using our model, we can follow the execution of block B1 and its contained blocks by setting the **ip** = 1 and **ep** = null and taking a sequence of snapshots of our model as the computation proceeds in time. The snapshots should be taken after any of the following actions has taken place: block entry or block exit; procedure call or procedure return.

The model works as follows: When **ip** points to statement BP, which is a block, then an activation record is created (consisting of sufficient memory locations for storing the values of all the identifiers declared in BP) and placed on top of the stack S. Next, the **ip** is pointed to the first statement in B1 and the **ep** is pointed to the first location of the newly created activation record. Upon exiting from BP, the current activation record is deleted from S; **ep** is pointed to the next lower activation in S; and **ip** is pointed to the next statement in sequence. Analogous processes occur upon procedure call and procedure return.

Since the stack and contour models are similar in many ways, only those features unique to the contour model are described in the following discussion. The *contour model*, CM = (P,C,D), consists of

P: the program component, represented by a two-dimensional picture in which the nesting of blocks and procedures is denoted by the contours enclosing the statements of the block.

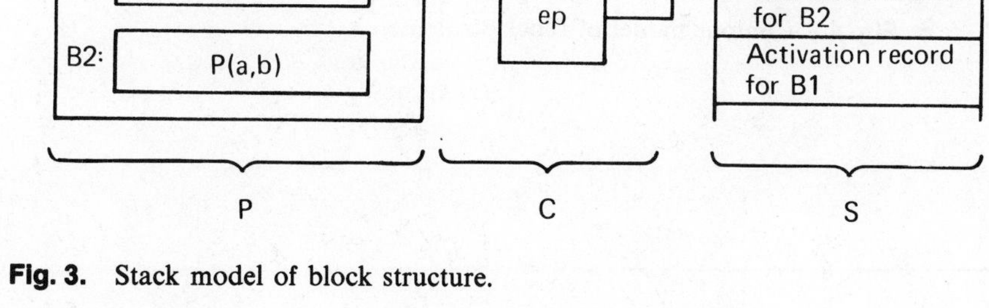

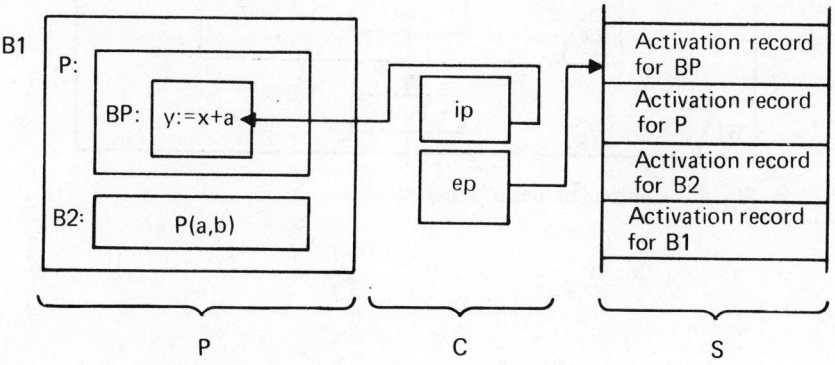


**Fig. 3.** Stack model of block structure.

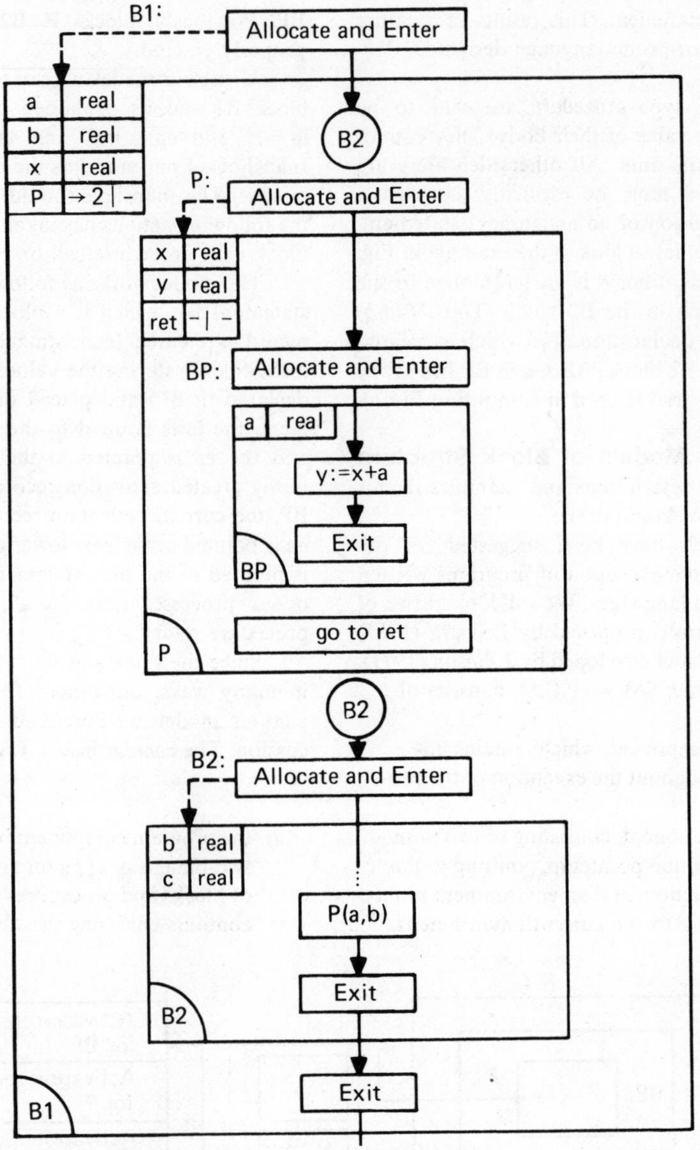


**Fig. 4.** Contour model of block structure.

D: the data component, represented by a nesting of activation records enclosed in their respective contours.

C: the control component, represented by the symbol $\pi$ (for processor) drawn inside the contour of the current activation record.

The symbol $\pi$ points to the value of the current **ip**, but the **ep** is implicit because it is bound by the innermost contour.

The contour model of our sample program is given in Fig. 4. Instead of explicit block entry and exit, the contour model employs the instructions *allocate and enter* and *exit*, respectively. To enter a block or a procedure, the *allocate and enter* employs an *identifier definition template* of the block to create the proper activation record. An *exit* instruction is inserted at the end of each block. Likewise, each procedure has a label-valued variable, represented by the symbol "ret," which is initialized at entry time to a return label. (This procedure is analogous to the one employed by most current machine languages to implement the subroutine feature.)

Snapshots of execution states are represented by contour diagrams. Upon entering block B1 the diagram is as shown in Fig. 5. The cells *a,b,x* are uninitialized, while the cell P is initialized to **ip** = 2, the location where P(*x,y*) is defined and the **ep** arrow points to the contour in which P(*x,y*) is declared.

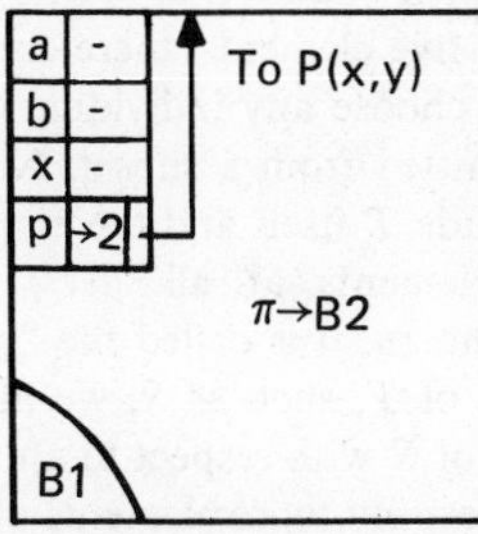


**Fig. 5.** Contour diagram snapshot of execution state.

The major advantage of the contour model is that the two-dimensional contour diagrams used to represent snapshots of the execution show explicitly the run-time identifier-accessing relation. They do not, however, give a direct representation of the order in which activation records are entered and exited. That is the strength of the stack model.

REFERENCES

1964. Randell, B., and L. S. Russell. *ALGOL 60 Implementation*. New York: Academic Press.

1967. Dijkstra, E. W. "Recursive Programming." In S. Rosen (Ed.) *Programming Systems and Languages*. New York: McGraw-Hill.

1967. Ekman, T., and C. E. Froberg. *Introduction to ALGOL 60*. London: Oxford University Press. (This book contains the complete text of the revised ALGOL 60 report by Naur et al., as well as a beautiful discussion of the control and data structures of ALGOL 60.)

1968. Wegner, P. *Programming Languages, Information Structures and Machine Organization*. New York: McGraw-Hill.

1971. —. "Structured Model Building in Computer Science." Providence, R. I.: Brown University, Dept. of Applied Mathematics.

1971. Johnson, J. B. "The Contour Model of Block Structured Processes," in J. T. Tou and P. Wegner (Eds.), *Proceedings of a Symposium in Programming Languages*. Gainsville: University of Florida, pp. 55–82.

A. N. GILEADI

## BNF. *See* BACKUS-NAUR FORM.

## BOOLE, GEORGE

For article on related subject *see* BOOLEAN ALGEBRA.

George Boole (b. Lincoln, England, 1815; d. Cork, Ireland, 1864) was one of those rarities in an era of increasing specialization: the self-taught man who followed his own path to the penetration of territory untouched by his contemporaries. Due to the family's sparse financial resource, Boole's formal education was limited to elementary school and a short stint in a commercial school. Beyond this he was almost totally self-educated.

Boole's first scientific publication was an address on Newton to mark the presentation of a bust of Newton to the Mechanics Institution in Lincoln. In 1840 he wrote his first paper for the *Cambridge Mathematical Journal*. In 1849, despite his lack of formal training, he was appointed to a professorship of mathematics in the newly established Queen's College, Cork, Ireland.

During his career he published approximately fifty scientific papers, two textbooks (on differential equations, 1859; and finite differences, 1860), and his two famous volumes on mathematical logic (see references). In 1844 the Royal Society awarded him a medal for his papers on differential operators, and in 1857 they elected him a Fellow. He was married in 1855 to Mary Everest, a niece of Sir George Everest after whom Mount Everest was named.

Although Boole made significant contributions in a number of areas of mathematics, his immortality stems from his two works that gave decisive impetus to the need to express logical concepts in mathematical form: "The Mathematical Analysis of Logic, Being an Essay Towards a Calculus of Deductive Reasoning" (1847) and "An Investigation of the Laws of Thought, on Which are Founded the Mathematical Theories of Logic and Probability" (1854). Through these works he truly became the founder of modern symbolic logic. He reduced logic to a propositional calculus, now called boolean algebra, which was extremely simple and perhaps too strongly based upon classical logic.

Under the influence of his work, a school of symbolic logic evolved, which made a determined effort to unify logic and mathematics. As is usual, the impact of this effort was not realized until the latter part of the nineteenth century. Although de Morgan and Jevons expounded on his work during Boole's lifetime, it remained for Frege, Peano, and C.S. Peirce to relight the torch that finally led to the "Principia Mathematica" (1910–1913) of Russell and Whitehead.

Boole's discovery that the symbolism of algebra could be used in logic has had wide impact in the twentieth century. Today, boolean algebra is important not only in logic but also in the theory of probability, the theory of lattices, the geometry of sets, and information theory. It has also led to the design of electronic computers through the interpretation of boolean combinations of sets as switching circuits. For example, the logical sum of two sets corresponds to a circuit with two switches in parallel and the logical product corresponds to a pair of switches in series.

REFERENCE

1970. Broadbent, T. A. A., "George Boole." In *Dictionary of Scientific Biography*, vol. II, pp. 293–298. New York: Scribners. (This is an outstanding biography with an excellent bibliography of both primary and secondary sources.)

H. TROPP

# BOOLEAN ALGEBRA

For articles on related subjects *see* ARITHMETIC, COMPUTER; and LOGIC DESIGN.
For related biographical information *see* BOOLE, GEORGE.

The concept of a boolean algebra was first proposed by the English mathematician George Boole in 1847. Since that time, Boole's original conception has been extensively developed and refined by algebraists and logicians. The relationships among boolean algebra, set algebra, logic, and binary arithmetic have given boolean algebras a central role in the development of electronic digital computers.

**Set Algebras.** The most intuitive development of boolean algebras arises from the concept of a set algebra. Let $S = \{a,b,c\}$ and $T = \{a,b,c,d,e\}$ be two sets consisting of three and five elements, respectively. We say that $S$ is a "subset" of $T$, since every element of $S$ (namely, $a$, $b$, and $c$) belongs to $T$. Since $T$ has five elements, there are $2^5$ subsets of $T$, for we may choose any individual element to be included or omitted from a subset. Note that these 32 subsets include $T$ itself and the empty set, which contains no elements at all. If $T$ contains all elements of concern, it is called the "universal set." Given a subset of $T$, such as $S$, we may define the "complement" of $S$ with respect to a universal set $T$ to consist of precisely those elements of $T$ which are not included in the given subset. Thus, $S$ as above defined has as its complement (with respect to $T$) $\overline{S} = \{d,e\}$. The "union" of any two sets (subsets of a given set) consists of those elements that are in one or the other or in both given sets; the "intersection" of two sets consists of those elements that are in both given sets. We use the symbol $\cup$ to denote the union, and $\cap$ to denote the intersection of two sets. For example, if $B = \{b,d,e\}$, then $B \cup S = \{a,b,c,d,e\}$, and $B \cap S = \{b\}$.

While other set operations may be defined, the operations of complementation, union, and intersection are of primary interest to us. A boolean algebra is a finite or infinite set of elements together with three operations—negation, addition, and multiplication—that correspond to the set operations of complementation, union, and intersection, respectively. Among the elements of a boolean algebra are two distinguished elements: 0, corresponding to the empty set; and 1, corresponding to the universal set. For any given element $a$ of a boolean algebra, there is a unique complement $a'$ with the property that $a + a' = 1$ and $aa' = 0$. Boolean addition and multiplication are associative and commutative, as are ordinary addition and multiplication, but otherwise have somewhat different properties. The principal properties are given in Table 1, where $a$, $b$, and $c$ are any elements of a boolean algebra.

**Table 1**

| | |
|---|---|
| Distributivity: | $a(b + c) = ab + ac$ |
| | $a + (bc) = (a + b)(a + c)$ |
| Idempotency: | $a + a = a$ |
| | $aa = a$ |
| Absorption laws: | $a + ab = a$ |
| | $a(a + b) = a$ |
| DeMorgan's laws: | $(a + b)' = a'b'$ |
| | $(ab)' = a' + b'$ |

Since a finite set of $n$ elements has exactly $2^n$ subsets, and it can be shown that the finite boolean algebras are precisely the finite set algebras, each finite boolean algebra consists of exactly $2^n$ elements for some integer $n$. For example, the set algebra for the set $T$ defined above corresponds to a boolean algebra of 32 elements. Tables 2 and 3 define the boolean operations for boolean algebras of two and four elements, respectively.

**Table 2.** Two elements.

| $a + b$ | 0 | 1 | $a \cdot b$ | 0 | 1 | $a$ | $a'$ |
|---|---|---|---|---|---|---|---|
| 0 | 0 | 1 | 0 | 0 | 0 | 0 | 1 |
| 1 | 1 | 1 | 1 | 0 | 1 | 1 | 0 |

**Table 3.** Four elements.

| $a + b$ | 0 | $p$ | $p'$ | 1 | $a \cdot b$ | 0 | $p$ | $p'$ | 1 | $a$ | $a'$ |
|---|---|---|---|---|---|---|---|---|---|---|---|
| 0 | 0 | $p$ | $p'$ | 1 | 0 | 0 | 0 | 0 | 0 | 0 | 1 |
| $p$ | $p$ | $p$ | 1 | 1 | $p$ | 0 | $p$ | 0 | $p$ | $p$ | $p'$ |
| $p'$ | $p'$ | 1 | $p'$ | 1 | $p'$ | 0 | 0 | $p'$ | $p'$ | $p'$ | $p$ |
| 1 | 1 | 1 | 1 | 1 | 1 | 0 | $p$ | $p'$ | 1 | 1 | 0 |

While it is possible to use a different symbol to denote each element of a boolean algebra, it is often more useful to represent the $2^n$ elements of a finite boolean algebra by binary vectors having $n$ components. With such a representation the operations of the boolean algebra are accomplished componentwise by considering each component as an independent two-element boolean algebra. This corresponds to representing subsets of a finite set by binary vectors. For example, since the set $T$ has five elements, we may represent its subsets by five-component binary vectors, each component denoting an element of the set $T$. A numeral 1 in the $i$th component of the vector denotes the inclusion of the $i$th element of that particular subset; a 0 denotes its exclusion. Thus, the subset $S = \{a,b,c\}$ has the binary vector representation $\{1,1,1,0,0\}$. The set operations become boolean operations on the components of the vectors. This representation of sets, and the correspondence to boolean or logical operations, is very useful in information retrieval. Because of it, sets of document and query characteristics may be easily and rapidly matched.

**Elementary Logic.** In information retrieval work, and in identifying boolean algebras as set algebras, we find that various logical connectives, such as "and," "or," and "not," recur frequently. Thus, it is not surprising to find that the two-element boolean algebra can be identified with elementary logic or propositional calculus. A "proposition" is a statement that can be said to be either true or false. We will denote propositions by letters such as $p$, $q$, and $r$.

The connectives or operators "and" and "or" combine two such propositions into a new one. If we consider two propositions, $p$ and $q$, each may, independently of the other, assume the value true (T) or false (F). Hence, together the ordered pair $\langle p,q\rangle$ may assume $2 \cdot 2 = 4$ combinations of truth values: $\langle T,T\rangle$, $\langle T,F\rangle$, $\langle F,T\rangle$, and $\langle F,F\rangle$. If $\circ$ denotes a binary operator, then $p \circ q$ may assume either (T) or (F) independently for each of these four T-F combinations. Thus we can define $2^4 = 16$ distinct binary logical operators, as shown in Table 4. Of the 16 binary logical operators that can be defined, 5 are commonly used and are more than sufficient to define the remaining operators.

**Table 4**

| $p$ | $q$ | 1 | 2 | 3 | 4 | 5 | 6 | 7 | 8 | 9 | 10 | 11 | 12 | 13 | 14 | 15 | 16 |
|---|---|---|---|---|---|---|---|---|---|---|---|---|---|---|---|---|---|
| T | T | T | T | T | T | T | T | T | T | F | F | F | F | F | F | F | F |
| T | F | T | T | T | T | F | F | F | F | T | T | T | T | F | F | F | F |
| F | T | T | T | F | F | T | T | F | F | T | T | F | F | T | T | F | F |
| F | F | T | F | T | F | T | F | T | F | T | F | T | F | T | F | T | F |

The "negation" or "not" operation, $\sim p$, is defined to form a proposition that is true precisely when the proposition $p$ is false, and false whenever $p$ is true. If we equate the truth values "true" and "false" with the boolean values 1 and 0, respectively, then we find that negation corresponds to boolean complementation. That is, $\sim p$ replaces the value "true" with "false," and vice versa, just as $p$ replaces the value "1" with "0," and vice versa. (In Table 4, column 13 is $\sim p$.)

The logical "conjunction" or "and," $p \wedge q$, forms a proposition that is true precisely when both $p$ and $q$ are true, and false otherwise. This corresponds to the boolean operation of multiplication, with the boolean expression $pq$ having the value 1 if and only if both $p$ and $q$ have as value the 1. (See Table 4, column 8.)

In ordinary usage the word "or" has two distinct meanings, referred to as the "inclusive or" and the "exclusive or." In the inclusive sense, the statement "$p$ or $q$" is true if $p$ or $q$ or both are true; in the exclusive sense, the same statement is true if either $p$ or $q$, but not both, are true. The logical "disjunction" or "or," $p \vee q$, is defined to be the inclusive "or." That is, $p \vee q$ is true precisely when at least one of the statements $p$ and $q$ is true. Thus, this operation corresponds to boolean addition as we have defined it. (See Table 4, column 2.)

The exclusive "or," $p \not\equiv q$, is commonly called "inequivalence," since it defines a proposition that is true precisely when $p$ and $q$ have opposite or inequivalent truth values. This corresponds to any of several more complex boolean operations such as $pq' + p'q$, and $(p + q)(pq)'$. (See Table 4, column 10.)

The remaining conventional logical operator is the "conditional" or "implication," $p \supset q$, corresponding to the statement "if $p$ then $q$." The conditional proposition $p \supset q$ takes the value "false" if $p$ is true and $q$ is false, and takes the value "true" otherwise. Thus, it corresponds to the boolean operation $p' + q$. Note that if $p$ is false, then $p \supset q$ is true, regardless of the value of $q$. This corresponds to the statement that one can prove anything ($q$, whether true or false) from a false hypothesis ($p$). (See Table 4, column 5.)

While the logical operators that we have defined suffice to define all logical operators, it is only necessary to use two of the above operators, namely, negation, and one of the operators conjunction, disjunction, or conditional. However, of importance to computer design is the fact that we can define all logical operators in terms of one basic operator, either the "nand" or the "nor" operator. These are the negation of the conjunction and disjunction operators, respectively. That is, the "nand" operator defines a statement, $p \mid q$, which has the value "false" precisely when both $p$ and $q$ are true, and the value "true" otherwise. The "nor" operator defines a statement, $p \downarrow q$, which has the value "true" precisely when both $p$ and $q$ are false, and the value "false" otherwise. (See Table 4, columns 9 and 15.)

**Truth Tables.** A truth table gives the truth values of a logical expression for each combination of the truth values of its variables. Thus, for a logical expression in $n$ variables, the truth table contains $2^n$ lines, one for each combination of truth values of its variables. Since the truth value of an expression is determined from the truth values of various subexpressions, the truth table may be given in an extended form, which explicitly lists all subexpressions, a standard form in which the subexpressions are not separately listed and a condensed form in which the lines of the table are compressed by indicating the truth value of certain critical subexpressions. Tables 5 through 7 illustrate these three forms of truth table for the logical expression $(p \equiv q) \supset \sim(((p \vee \sim r) \wedge (\sim p \vee q)) \supset r)$.

In each of these three tables the truth values for the given expression are in the boxed column. In the

**Table 5**

| $p\ q\ r$ | (1) $p \equiv q$ | (2) $p \vee \sim r$ | (3) $\sim p \vee q$ | (4) (2)$\wedge$(3) | (5) (4)$\supset r$ | (6) $\sim$(5) | Expression (1)$\supset$(6) |
|---|---|---|---|---|---|---|---|
| T T T | T | T | T | T | T | F | F |
| T T F | T | T | T | T | F | T | T |
| T F T | F | T | F | F | T | F | T |
| T F F | F | T | F | F | T | F | T |
| F T T | F | F | T | F | T | F | T |
| F T F | F | T | T | T | F | T | T |
| F F T | T | F | T | F | T | F | F |
| F F F | T | T | T | T | F | T | T |

**Table 6**

| $p$ $q$ $r$ | $(p\equiv q)$ | $\supset$ | $\sim$ | $(((p\vee\sim r)\wedge(\sim p\vee q))\supset r)$ | | | |
|---|---|---|---|---|---|---|---|
| T T T | T | F | F | T | T | T | T |
| T T F | T | T | T | T | T | T | F |
| T F T | F | T | F | T | F | F | T |
| T F F | F | T | F | T | F | F | T |
| F T T | F | T | F | F | F | T | T |
| F T F | F | T | T | T | T | T | F |
| F F T | T | F | F | F | F | T | T |
| F F F | T | T | T | T | T | T | F |

**Table 7**

| $p$ $q$ $r$ | $(p\equiv q)$ | $\supset$ | $\sim$ | $(((p\vee\sim r)\wedge(\sim p\vee q)\supset r$ | | | |
|---|---|---|---|---|---|---|---|
| T F – | F | T | – | – | – | – | – |
| F T – | F | T | – | – | – | – | – |
| F – F | – | T | T | T | T | T | F |
| – T F | – | T | T | T | T | T | F |
| T T T | T | F | F | – | – | – | T |
| F F T | T | F | F | – | – | – | T |

condensed form, Table 7, each line of the table may represent one or more lines of the uncondensed table. For example, the first line of Table 7 represents the two lines TFT and TFF of the uncondensed table. In this particular example, the line FTF is represented three times, namely, in lines 2, 3, and 4 of the Table 7. Also in the condensed table, the dashes represent values that are immaterial and hence do not need to be calculated. For example, in the first line of Table 7, since $p \equiv q$ is false, we know that the entire expression has the value "true," regardless of the value of the remaining portion of the expression.

The truth table for an unknown logical function can be used to generate an expression for that function. The expression thus generated is called a "disjunctive normal form" or, in boolean algebra, a "sum of products form." The development of this expression is illustrated in Table 8. For each line of the table wherein the unknown function has the value "true," an expression is formed by taking the conjunction of all variables that are true in that line and the negations of all variables that are false in that line. The expression for the function $f$ is then the disjunction of all expressions formed for the single lines. In Table 8, $f$ is given in this form, and in the corresponding boolean algebra form, as well as in a shorter form developed by direct inspection of the function values. (Equivalence, $\equiv$, is defined by column 7 of Table 4.)

The development of the disjunctive normal form shows that the logical operators conjunction,

**Table 8**

| $p$ $q$ $r$ | $f(p,q,r)$ | Generated expression |
|---|---|---|
| T T T | F | – |
| T T F | T | $p\wedge q\wedge\sim r$ |
| T F T | T | $p\wedge\sim q\wedge r$ |
| T F F | F | – |
| F T T | T | $\sim p\wedge q\wedge r$ |
| F T F | F | – |
| F F T | F | – |
| F F F | T | $\sim p\wedge\sim q\wedge\sim r$ |

$$f(p,q,r) = (p\wedge q\wedge\sim r)\vee(p\wedge\sim q\wedge r)\vee(\sim p\wedge q\wedge r)\vee(\sim p\wedge\sim q\wedge\sim r)$$
$$f(p,q,r) = pqr' + pq'r + p'qr + p'q'r'$$
$$f(p,q,r) = p\equiv(q\not\equiv r)$$

**Table 9**

| | $\wedge,\sim$ | $\vee,\sim$ |
|---|---|---|
| $\sim p$ | $\sim p$ | $\sim p$ |
| $p\wedge q$ | $p\wedge q$ | $\sim(\sim p\vee\sim q)$ |
| $p\vee q$ | $\sim(\sim p\wedge\sim q)$ | $p\vee q$ |
| $p\supset q$ | $\sim(p\wedge\sim q)$ | $\sim p\vee q$ |
| $p\equiv q$ | $\sim(\sim(p\wedge q)\wedge\sim(\sim p\wedge\sim q))$ | $\sim(p\vee q)\vee\sim(\sim p\vee\sim q)$ |

**Table 10**

| | $\mid$ | $\downarrow$ |
|---|---|---|
| $\sim p$ | $p\mid p$ | $p\downarrow p$ |
| $p\wedge q$ | $(p\mid q)\mid(p\mid q)$ | $(p\downarrow p)\downarrow(q\downarrow q)$ |
| $p\vee q$ | $(p\mid p)\mid(q\mid q)$ | $(p\downarrow q)\downarrow(p\downarrow q)$ |

disjunction, and negation are sufficient to develop an expression for any logical function. Furthermore, we may use DeMorgan's laws to transform conjunctions to disjunctions, or vice versa. Thus, as we previously asserted, any logical function can be developed from the operators negation and either conjunction or disjunction. Table 9 shows the development of the five common logical operators in terms of these two minimal combinations of operators. In turn, Table 10 shows the development of negation, conjunction, and disjunction in terms of both the "nand" and the "nor" operators, thus indicating that every logical operator can be defined in terms of either one of these latter two operators.

**Computer Arithmetic.** The identification of the logical constants $T$ and $F$ with the boolean constants 1 and 0, respectively, leads to the development of the arithmetic properties of the computer in terms of its logical or boolean operators. In binary arithmetic, the multiplication of bits is exactly the same as boolean multiplication: The product of two bits is 1 if and only if both bits are 1. However, the addition of two bits is quite different from boolean addition. This is apparent, since in boolean arithmetic $1 + 1 = 1$, while in binary arithmetic $1 + 1 = 10$.

We also observe that in binary arithmetic the sum bit is 1 if and only if one, but not both, summands have the value 1, while the carry bit is 1 if and only if both summands have the value 1. Thus, we can compute the sum bit by using the logical inequivalence (exclusive or) operation, and the carry bit by using the logical conjunction, or boolean multiplication operation. Finally, we observe that, since the negative of an integer is normally represented in the computer by a complementary bit pattern (1's complement), arithmetic negation can be accomplished by logical negation, or boolean complementation, with slight modification if 2's-complement arithmetic is used.

**Logical Design.** Logical design of a computer is the development of computer circuitry to perform the desired functions for the particular machine. It is necessary that the circuitry be accurate and reliable, and desirable that it be relatively simple so that it is inexpensive and easy to maintain. While logical design must include consideration of timing problems and the various electromechanical attachments to the computer, the heart of the problem resides in the development of logical circuitry to perform the desired functions.

Of the various devices designed to systematize study of the logic, the Venn diagram or Karnaugh map is particularly simple and highly effective for functions of 2, 3, 4, or 5 variables. However, the use of this device becomes increasingly difficult as the number of variables increases beyond five. The classical Venn diagram consists of a rectangle representing the universe, containing a circle or other simple closed curve for each variable represented. The interpretation is that within the circle the given variable has the value 1, while outside it has the value 0. These circles are arranged in such a way as to include all possible combination of 1's and 0's for the variables. The Venn diagram for a 3-variable problem is given in Fig. 1, with the various regions labeled in Fig. 1(a) and certain regions shaded to represent the boolean function $pq + pr + p'r$ in Fig. 1(b). In this form the Venn diagram is relatively ineffective for logical analysis. The varying shapes of the regions cause some difficulty in visualizing possible combinations of these regions, particularly if four or more variables are involved.

The Karnaugh map is a practical modification of the Venn diagram, with each region of the diagram represented by a square within a larger rectangle. The Karnaugh maps for 2-, 3-, and 4-variable problems are given in Fig. 2. The region represented by each square is determined by the product of the letters on the edges of the rectangle. For example, the square marked $A$ in the 4-variable rectangle represents the region $pq'rs$. To represent a boolean function, say $pq + pr + q'r$, on a Karnaugh map, first expand each term of the functions to include all variables present:

$$
\begin{aligned}
pq + pr + q'r
&= pq \cdot 1 + p \cdot 1 \cdot r + 1 \cdot q'r \\
&= pq(r + r') + p(q + q')r + (p + p')q'r \\
&= pqr + pqr' + pqr + pq'r + pq'r + p'q'r \\
&= pqr + pqr' + pq'r + p'q'r .
\end{aligned}
$$

Then mark each square corresponding to a term in the expanded expression.

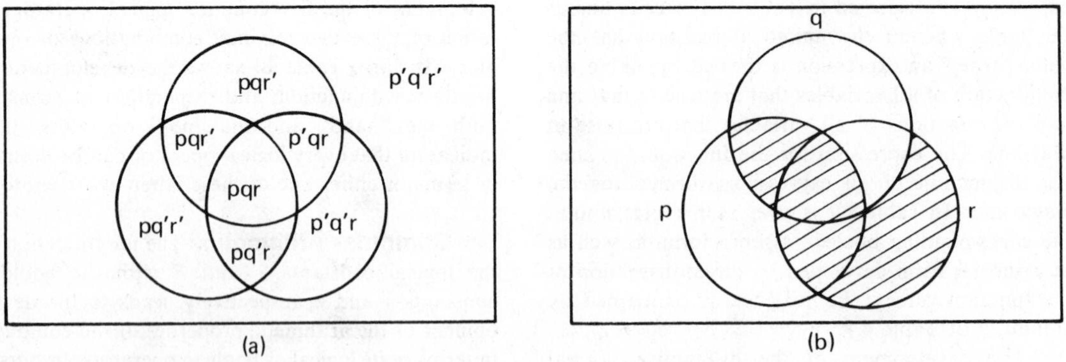


**Fig. 1.** Venn diagram.

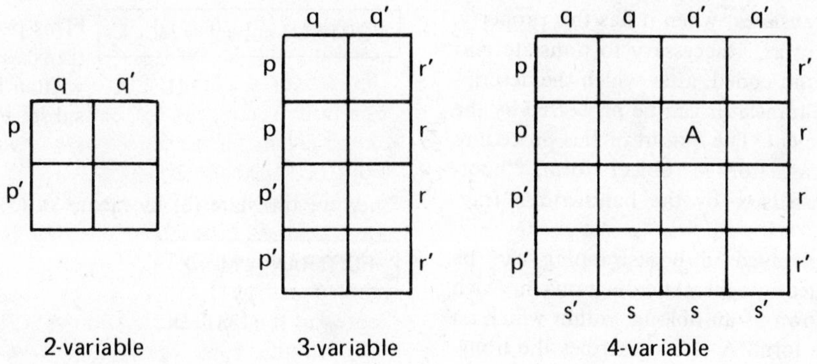


**Fig. 2.** Karnaugh maps.

Thus, the boolean function $pq + pr + q'r$ is represented by the squares marked "1" in Fig. 3, while 0's fill those squares not included in the representation. Note that $pq + q'r$ is also represented by the same four marked squares, and hence is equivalent to the given function. It is also possible to label a square $d$, denoting "don't care," if the value of that square is irrelevant to the particular function being represented.

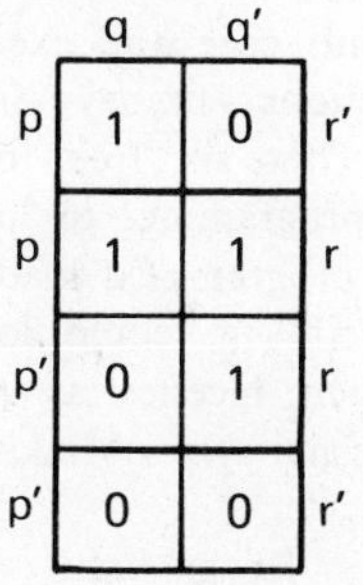


**Fig. 3.** Karnaugh map for $pq$ plus $pr$ plus $q'r$.

**Minimization of Boolean Functions.** In the interest of economy it is often desirable to use the simplest possible expression for a boolean function in the design of computer circuitry. For example, since the expression $pq + pr + q'r$ is equivalent to the expression $pq + q'r$ in the sense that these expressions have the same value for given argument values, the former expression should be replaced by the latter whenever it occurs in a given circuit design. The determination of the simplest expression equivalent to a given one is known as "minimization." Minimization is understood to be with respect to a given function form, such as the sum of products form, since a change in permissible operators often permits one to find an expression that is simpler yet. Karnaugh maps and a variety of algebraic or geometrical algorithms have been used to accomplish boolean function minimization.

REFERENCES

1965. McCluskey, E. J. *Introduction to the Theory of Switching Circuits*. New York: McGraw-Hill.

1966. Korfhage, R. R. *Logic and Algorithms*. New York: Wiley.

1970. Mendelson, E. "Theory and Problems of Boolean Algebra and Switching Circuits." In *Schaum's Outline Theories*. New York: McGraw-Hill.

1972. Peatman, J. D. *The Design of Digital Systems*. New York: McGraw-Hill.

R. R. KORFHAGE

# BOOTSTRAP

For article on related subject *see* MACHINE AND ASSEMBLY LANGUAGE PROGRAMMING.
For articles on related terms *see* LANGUAGE PROCESSORS; and LOADER.

Using some already running part of a language processor as a tool to get the rest of it running more easily (or using such a processor to get itself running on another machine without entirely rewriting it) is the programming counterpart of the apocryphal feat of lifting oneself by one's own bootstraps. These shortcuts are possible when the translator can be written using only a small but well-defined subset of the language it translates; when it has this property, only so much of it as is necessary to translate that subset need be hand coded, after which the description of the whole translator can be processed by the handwritten fragment. The output of this procedure is the whole translator in object form, "bootstrapped" into existence by the handwritten fragment of itself.

The steps involved in bootstrapping can be usefully represented by schematic diagrams in which a translator is shown as an oblong, within which an expression of the form 'A → B' describes the translation it performs. The language in which the translator has been, or is to be, written is noted as a kind of subscript outside the oblong. For example, the representation in this notation of a Fortran compiler producing machine language (ML) code for computer X, and itself existing as an ML program for X, is

| Fortran → ML 'X' |
|---|

ML 'X' (1)

Note that if the subscript is a machine language, the translator in question is running on a real machine and can be used immediately; if the subscript is a higher-level language, the translator is so far merely a source-language file that must itself be translated before it can be used to translate another source-language program. Given an immediately usable translator, the question of whether it can translate a given program is answered by matching the language in which the potential processee is written against part 'A' of the potential processor's 'A → B' formula. If they are identical, or the former is a subset of the latter, the desired translation is feasible. In the notation (1) example, if the processee is a Fortran source program, it can be translated.

If we postulate that there exists some proper subset of the Fortran language in which a Fortran compiler can be written, the steps involved in bootstrapping into existence a Fortran compiler for and on machine X can be outlined in our notation. We must handwrite two programs:

| FORTRAN → ML 'X' |
|---|

Fortran Subset

[This program written in the Fortran subset will translate any Fortran program to ML 'X'.]

(2)

| FORTRAN subset → ML 'X' |
|---|

ML 'X'

[This program will translate any program written in the Fortran subset into ML 'X'.]

(3)

Then we translate (2) by means of (3), yielding

| FORTRAN → ML 'X' |
|---|

ML 'X' (4)

which is the required product—a full Fortran-to-ML 'X' compiler running on machine X.

The question of when this approach is better than that of coding the desired product directly [as in notation (1)] is a complex one; some of the considerations involved are discussed in Halpern (1965).

"Bootstrapping" is used also to describe the process whereby a programmed loader, whose job it is to load other pieces of software into a machine, gets itself in. This task, which at first glance seems to threaten infinite regression, is made possible by a miniloader built into the hardware. In a typical example, the computer will offer the operator the ability to load into core and execute some small number of instructions—six, say—simply by pushing a console button. These six "free" instructions would be used by the programmer to load and transfer control to a full programmed loader, which, when thus "bootstrapped" in, could load any desired program with such niceties as check sums, relocation, and external symbol linking.

### Reference

1965. Halpern, M. "Machine Independence: Its Technology and Economics," *CACM*, Vol. 8, No. 12 (December), pp. 782–785.

M. Halpern

## BREAKPOINT

For articles on related subjects *see* Computer, Using a; Debugging; and Diagnostics.

A breakpoint is a position in a program at which the programmer has arranged for normal execution to be interrupted so that some type of external intervention can occur. This usually is associated with the debugging process in that the intervening activity is designed to provide status information and/or diagnostic data relative to the progress of the program up to that point. For example, the programmer may select one or more strategic places in the program where he would like to see a dump (i.e., a copy of the contents) of pertinent storage locations to assess the correctness of intermediate results.

In some systems the action at a breakpoint is performed automatically by a software component (an instruction inserted in the program for this purpose). For example, the programmer writing in PL/I for the IBM 360/370 series has direct access to a dump routine, with normal processing resuming after its completion. Accordingly, the breakpoint is set up like any other subroutine call:

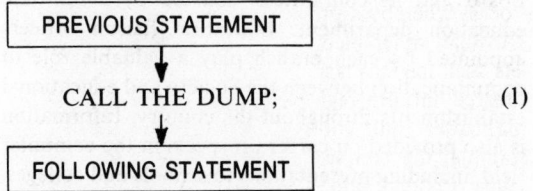

PREVIOUS STATEMENT

CALL THE DUMP; (1)

FOLLOWING STATEMENT

In other types of breakpoints, the external action must be performed by an operator. Under these circumstances the action is independent of the user's program so that it is necessary for the operator to reactivate the program manually. An example of such a facility is seen in some dialects of Fortran, where one may write

PAUSE message (2)

with the result that the program will halt and the message associated with the particular PAUSE statement will be displayed. Prior to the resumption of processing (which is done manually), the operator may interject the appropriate action. Whatever their form, the statements that create the breakpoint are retained until the programmer has identified and corrected the difficulties. Conversely, breakpoints may be created anew when unanticipated troubles develop in a seemingly operational program.

Additional types of breakpoints may be set up in conjunction with hardware. These facilities generally take the form of bistable switches, which may be set externally and tested by special statements within the program. Thus, the position of one of the switches may determine whether or not the program will halt at some point, to be restarted manually after some action is taken by the operator. Accordingly, that switch may be "on" during a debugging run; for normal execution, the switch is left in the "off" position, in which case the program will execute without interruption.

S. V. Pollack

# BRITISH COMPUTER SOCIETY (BCS)

For article on related subject *see* International Federation of Information Processing.

The British Computer Society (BCS) was formed in September 1957 with the following main objectives;

1. To further the development and use of computational machinery, and the techniques related thereto.
2. To facilitate the exchange of information and views, and to inform public opinion on the subject.
3. To hold conferences and meetings for the reading of papers and delivery of lectures.
4. To publish information for the benefit of members.
5. To organize and conduct examinations, for members and others, in subjects requiring a knowledge of or otherwise in any way concerning the development and use of computational machinery and the techniques related thereto, and in any allied subjects.

A number of interested people, who foresaw the vital importance of computers to the community, met during the early 1950's to initiate lectures on different aspects of computing science and to discuss the problems of its application to industrial and commercial work. These conferees were, on the one hand, people with scientific and engineering interests, and on the other, members of the London Computer Group, which represented industry and commerce. As a result of these meetings, the British Computer Society, a company limited by guarantee, was formed on Oct. 14, 1957.

At a special meeting in May 1968, the Society decided to become a fully professional body. To this end, the Society has introduced examinations (held annually in April each year since 1969); adopted a Code of Conduct (February 1971); and produced a Code of Good Practice (January 1973).

The following have held the office of BCS president:

Professor M.V. Wilkes, 1957–1960
Sir Frank Yates, 1960–1961
D.W. Hooper, Esq., 1961–1962
R.L. Michaelson, Esq., 1962–1963
Sir Edward Playfair, 1963–1965
Sir Maurice Banks, 1965–1966
Earl of Mountbatten of Burma, 1966–1967
Dr. S. Gill, M.A., Ph.D., 1967–1968
B.Z. de Ferranti, M.A., C.Eng., 1968–1969
The Earl of Halsbury, 1969–1970
A. d'Agapeyeff, Esq., 1970–1971
Professor A.S. Douglas, 1971–1972
G.J. Morris, Esq., 1972–1973
R.A. Barrington, Esq., 1973–1974
E.L. Willey, Esq., 1974–1975
C.P. Marks, Esq., 1975–

**Organizational Structure.** The British Computer Society is run by a Council, which consists of 47 members: 18 elected; 12 from the branches of the BCS; and 17 others, including officers, students, and specialist group representatives. The Council, which meets quarterly, operates through boards and committees. The main boards are the Membership Board, the Technical Board, the Education Board, and Branch Board.

**Membership.** The membership and education boards work in close collaboration to set the standards of experience and education required for Membership in the British Computer Society. The membership structure of the Society allows seven classifications, as follows:

FELLOW. Fellowship is by election from the Member grade. The minimum requirements are that Fellows must be over 30 and have eight years' experience in computing, five in a responsible position.

MEMBER. Applicants must be over 25, have passed (or have been exempted from) BCS Parts I and II, and have five years' experience in computing, or have seven years' experience.

LICENTIATE. Licentiates must be over 21, have passed (or been exempted from) BCS Parts I and II, but not both, and have three years' experience in computing.

ASSOCIATE. This is a holding grade by people who have passed Part I and are taking Part II. They remain as Associate until they have the required three years experience for Licentiate grade or five years for Member grade.

AFFILIATE. This grade is for those who do not wish to become fully professional members of the BCS. This is also a grade for those with less than seven years' experience who will shortly be applying for transfer to higher grades, without having to take examinations.

STUDENT. A student must be over 17 years of age. He remains a student until he passes Part I of the BCS examinations, when he is eligible to become an Associate.

INSTITUTIONAL AFFILIATE. This grade accommodates corporate bodies, companies, educational institutions, societies, etc.

**Education.** The responsibility for the Society's educational activities lies with the Education Board and its committees, assisted by a full-time education department. Education liaison officers appointed by each branch play a valuable role in communication between the Society and educational establishments throughout the country. Information is also provided on career prospects in the computer field, including presentations to schools and colleges.

The Society has played, and is sustaining, an important part in encouraging the spread of computer knowledge through its Schools Committee, which consists of people from education administration, from the teaching profession and industry, and the Group for Computer Education, also affiliated with the Society. The Group, with a membership of 2,700—comprising secondary school teachers, college lecturers, and training officers from industry—has an international reputation through the publication of its quarterly bulletin, *Computer Education*; almost a quarter of its membership is drawn from abroad.

The Society plays a major role in setting and maintaining standards, at many levels of competence, by its representation on the advisory committees of national examining and educational bodies.

The work of the Society's members, individually or as government representatives, in international organizations concerned with education, places it at the international center of computer education circles.

The Society's annual publication, *The Educational Yearbook*, is the definitive work of reference for computer education and is international in its coverage.

**The Society Examination.** The Society's examination, set in two parts, is designed to assess the candidate's understanding of the underlying principles of the discipline, his ability to reason and to evaluate information, and his capacity for application of his knowledge to the solution of both practical and theoretical problems.

The Part I examination, set at the level of the Higher National Diploma, requires candidates to take two compulsory papers covering the general knowledge that all computer professionals should have, together with two papers from a number of widely defined areas of more specialized computer knowledge (computer technology, programming, data processing, analysis and design of systems, computational methods, and analog and hybrid computing). The Part II examination, set at the level of a university honors degree, requires candidates to take two papers in one area and one paper in a second, more specialized, area than those defined for Part I (digital computer technology, systems programming, data processing and information systems, advanced programming theory, data processing management, numerical analysis, and hybrid computing).

**Branch Activities.** There are 35 branches in the United Kingdom, one in Hong Kong, and one in Zambia. The branches, staffed entirely by volunteers, arrange programs of lectures and visits to installations.

**Technical Activities.** The Society is actively engaged in formulating and expressing professional viewpoints on a variety of subjects of importance. This is a primary responsibility of the Technical Division and its specialist committees.

In addition to its technical work in the United Kingdom, the Technical Board coordinates the work of its representatives on the IFIP technical committees and working groups and on the International Standards Organization. The Technical Board also coordinates the work of its 37 specialist groups, which study aspects of computer science ranging from advanced programming to urban planning.

**Publications.** In addition to the publications mentioned above, the Society has three other major publications. The *Computer Journal* is published quarterly. It contains articles and papers on scientific, business, and commercial subjects related to computers, together with reviews of the most important books and other publications in the field. The *Computer Bulletin* is also published quarterly and contains articles of a more general, tutorial nature than those in the *Journal.* The weekly *Computing* is published for the Society by Haymarket Publishing Group and contains news of the European computer industry and articles of a general nature on computer applications. It is the main communications link between the Council and the members of the Society, and carries reports of branches and specialist groups as well as advance notice of all the Society's activities.

Along with these publications are the reports of the proceedings of the Society's many specialized conferences, together with authoritative handbooks such as *Code of Good Practice, Privacy and the Computer—Steps to Practicality,* and *Character Recognition,* all published by the Society.

**Conferences.** The Society, in conjunction with its partners, presents a number of conferences of interest to the computing fraternity and conducts techniques Workshops on a number of specialized subjects. It also provides a number of highly specialized conferences on such subjects as Codasyl and Relational Data Base concepts.

I. L. AUERBACH

# BUFFER

For article on related subject *see* INPUT-OUTPUT CONTROL SYSTEM.
For article on related term *see* FIFO-LIFO.

A buffer is an area of storage which temporarily holds data that will be subsequently delivered to a processor or input/output (I/O) transducer. Buffers exist as an integral part of many transducers; e.g., bits arriving serially over a telephone line are collected in a buffer before the appropriate teleprinter character is activated. Similarly, the bits representing a given keyboard stroke remain in a buffer while being serialized for transmission. Since the buffer is an integral part of the transducer, it is usually dedicated to the transducer and not shared with any other device.

Buffers are also used in conjunction with the input/output control system (IOCS) to hold the data which is the object of various I/O commands. In this case, the buffer is usually a portion of main storage and is often dynamically allocated and freed by software. In either case, a buffer exists in order to

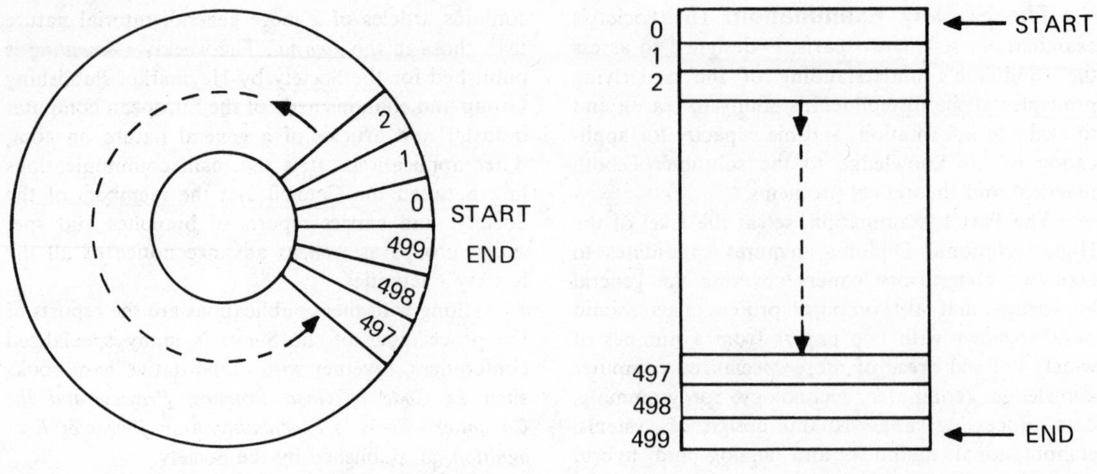


**Fig. 1.** Circular buffer organization shown logically (left) and as it actually appears in memory (right).

accommodate the different rates at which data is produced or consumed by the processor or transducers involved.

In a typical situation, a processor will be capable of producing data three orders of magnitude faster than a transducer can accept it. In order to make most efficient use of the processor, the data will be placed in a buffer and its location made known to the transducer. The transducer then proceeds to empty the buffer while the processor is freed for other work.

Various buffering techniques have evolved in IOCS. These techniques can be analyzed according to the policy used for (1) receiving data from the producer and (2) delivering data to the consumer.

When receiving data, two techniques are common: (1) a pool of buffers and (2) circular buffering. With the buffer-pooling technique a number of buffers are available to the IOCS. Usually, each buffer is large enough to hold the single physical record that is being transferred. When a record is produced, a buffer is taken from the pool and used to hold the data. Data is then consumed on a first-in, first-out basis, and when all data in a buffer has been transmitted, the buffer is returned to the pool.

Circular buffering, in contrast, typically uses a single buffer, usually larger than a single physical record. The basic strategy is to give the appearance that the buffer is organized in a circle, with data "wrapping around" as shown in Fig. 1. This appearance of circular organization is accomplished by using two pointers, IN and OUT, associated with the buffer; the starting and ending addresses of the buffer (START and END) are also known. Initially, START = IN = OUT. Data received from the producer fills the buffer, starting from START and incrementing the pointer IN. The consumer takes data from the buffer, incrementing the pointer OUT (and taking care not to go past IN-1). When the last word of the buffer has been filled (IN = END), then IN is reset to START and subsequent data will wrap around to the start of the buffer.

Similarly, when OUT reaches END, it is reset to START and also wraps around. Clearly, the following restrictions hold:

1. If IN > OUT, then OUT must not become greater than IN-1.

2. If OUT > IN, then IN must not become greater than OUT-1.

If either of these two conditions is violated, then the consumer is trying to access data that has not been produced, *or* the producer is attempting to store over data that has not yet been consumed.

Data is delivered to the consumer either by moving it to a storage area provided by the consumer or by providing the consumer with a pointer to the data in the buffer. In the latter case, the consumer will frequently provide the IOCS with additional space, which becomes the new buffer. Such a technique is often called "exchange buffering."

R. W. Taylor

## BUG

For articles on related subjects *see* DEBUGGING; and GLITCH.

A "bug" is an error in either the mechanics or the logic of a computer program. The term arose during World War II, in connection with electronic testing, as an outgrowth of "debug" which was a synonym for "troubleshoot". The earliest computer programmers, who were frequently the designers and builders of the computers, transferred the term to its present usage.

Most mechanical bugs can be detected during the translation from the symbolic languages that programmers use into the (binary) language which is eventually executed. For example, the proper symbolic code for addition on many machines is ADA ("add to accumulator"). If the programmer mistakenly writes ADD, this bug will be detected, an error message will be printed, and execution of the program will be halted, since the attempted operation code is illegal.

A bug is also created, and a more serious one, if the programmer writes the legal code SBA ("subtract from accumulator") when he meant to write ADA. This is a logical bug, and no coding system can catch such an error.

Properly speaking, the elimination of the first type of bug is the process of debugging, whereas the detection and elimination of the second type is the process of program testing. Program bugs can be so extremely subtle that they may resist great efforts to eliminate them. It is commonly accepted that all very large computer programs (such as compilers) have bugs remaining in them. The number of possible paths through a large computer program is enormous, and it is physically impossible to explore all of them. The single path containing a bug may not be followed in actual production runs for a long time (if ever) after the program has been certified as correct by its author or others.

F. GRUENBERGER

**BUSINESS DATA PROCESSING.** *See* ADMINISTRATIVE-BUSINESS APPLICATIONS.

# C

**CAD.** *See* COMPUTER-AIDED DESIGN.

**CAI.** *See* COMPUTER-ASSISTED INSTRUCTION.

**CMI.** *See* COMPUTER-MANAGED INSTRUCTION.

**CPU.** *See* CENTRAL PROCESSING UNIT.

**CPM.** *See* PERT/CPM.

## CACHE MEMORY

For articles on related subjects *see* ASSOCIATIVE MEMORY; MEMORY: Main; and STORAGE HIERARCHY.

Cache memory is a mechanism interposed in the memory hierarchy between main memory and the CPU to improve effective memory transfer rates and accordingly raise processor speeds. The name refers to the fact that the mechanism is essentially hidden and appears transparent to the user, who is aware only of an apparently higher speed large main memory. The cache memory is implemented in high-speed semiconductor technology, often with an associative address selection, whereas the main memory may be either core or semiconductor.

The cache concept anticipates the likely reuse of an organized temporary copy of data in main storage which has been recently used by the CPU. The concept is further extended to include data that is adjacent to data that has been used. Accordingly, it is usual to transfer several words from main store to the cache even though the immediate need is for only one word. If the required word is included in a stream of sequential instructions, it is likely that subsequent words will also be used; if these are retrieved with the required first word, repeated accesses to main memory will be unnecessary.

When used in conjunction with a cache store, the main memory is equipped to provide several words in address sequence when one of them is required. By this means the memory data-transfer rate can be very high. It remains for the cache memory organization to make adequate use of such multiword transfers.

When a request originates in the CPU for a new word, whether it be data or instruction, a check is made to see if it is already in the cache. If present, it is used directly; if not, a new access to main memory must be made. Since the cache is of limited size (16K bytes in the IBM 360/85), space must often be sought to accommodate the new information. An algorithm based on history of use is used to identify the least necessary words for overwriting. Since the data in main memory is updated each time the CPU writes into the cache (a process called "store-through"), no data is lost in the overwriting process.

The search in the cache for the next word is made using an associative address store conceptually in the same way as for a general paging organization. In this associative search, the target word address is compared with stored addresses of words in the cache. The result of a match is the location in the cache of the desired word. No match initiates the main storage access process.

A general problem of updating of the cache and main store exists if, as is usual, the CPU and I/O do not both use the cache. This arises because, under these conditions, two versions of a variable might exist in two corresponding locations in cache and main store. Global and local solutions exist. The global solution is, as usual in a memory hierarchy, to restrict processing to blocks of data that are static with respect to I/O transfers; this insures that only consistent data is treated. This may be arranged by periodic programmed checking of flagged memory locations, modified by initiation and subsequent completion of I/O transfers. The second local solution is to insure that CPU modified data in cache is returned quickly and automatically to main store, as is done in the IBM 360/85.

K. C. Smith and A. S. Sedra

# CALCULATOR, DESK

For articles on related subjects *see* Calculator, Electronic; and Digital Computers.
For related biographical information *see* Leibniz, G. W.; and Pascal, Blaise.

Man's needs for aids to calculation obviously began as soon as he began to count, assuming that human memories in those days were as bad as they are today. He used his fingers and perhaps toes (they were at least visible), and cut notches in a stick when a permanent record was required.

It was a natural development to replace fingers by small pebbles that would slide in a groove carved in a piece of wood. Such an elementary abacus was simplified when the pebbles were replaced by beads sliding on a wire or slim rod. There is good evidence that the abacus was invented prior to 500 B.C.

**Fig. 1.** A Chinese abacus. (Courtesy Science Museum, London. British Crown copyright.)

The simplest abacus has either ten or nine beads on each wire, and the number system is obvious. In most modern forms of abacus (Chinese), the wire is divided into two parts and the coding system is essentially biquinary in that there are five beads below the division and two above. In the Japanese abacus, four beads are below and one above. The upper bead designates whether the rod represents more or less than 5; the lower one, whether 0 to 4 or 6 to 9.

Visitors to the Far East will know that the abacus is still a common form of desk calculator and is used with great dexterity and speed. It has been reported that a competition held in 1946 between an abacus and an electric calculator was (with human assistance!) easily won by the operator of the abacus.

The invention of anything resembling today's desk calculator had to await the development of a system of decimal notation as we know it today, and this did not occur until as late as the sixteenth century. One of the earliest aids was Napier's "bones" (about 1620), which effectively had multiplication tables written out on strips of bone or wood. Napier also invented logarithms. These greatly assisted in arithmetic calculation, at the cost of some accuracy, and are the basis of slide rule operations.

The mechanical calculator was first invented by Pascal, about 1640, and depended on linking a toothed gear wheel to a shaft and an arrangement for a "carry" from one wheel to its left-hand neighbor when the original wheel passed from 9 to 0. The accumulation gear wheels were driven by other

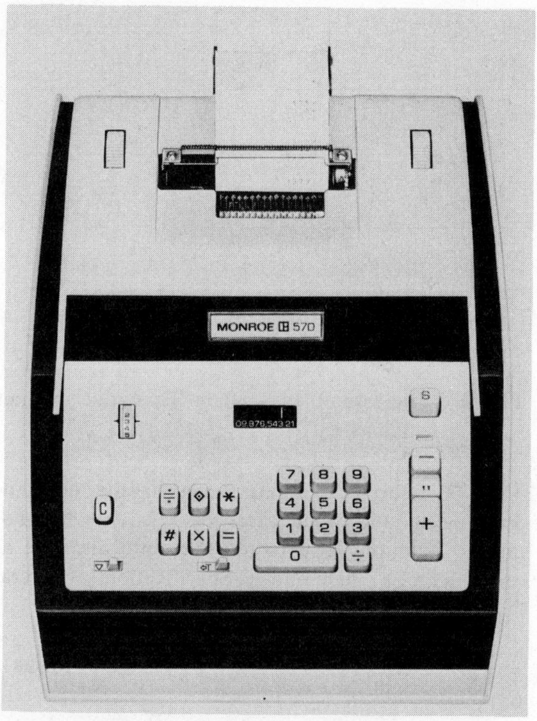


**Fig. 2.** The Monroe desk calculator with printed tally tape output.

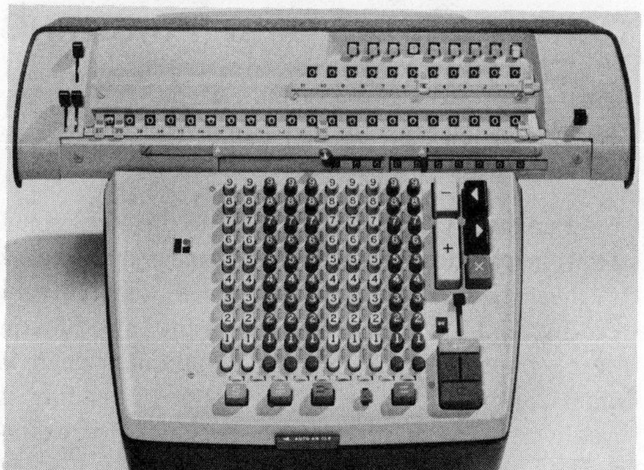

**Fig. 3.** The electromechanical Monroe 6F-212 calculator with output displayed but not printed (an obsolete model).

toothed wheels, set to represent a desired number and driven by a rotating hand crank. Such calculators, and they still exist today, were essentially adders and subtractors in which multiplication and division was performed by repeated additions and subtractions. In the 1670s Leibniz invented a much more complicated gearing arrangement by which a machine could multiply directly, but this found little common application.

The twentieth century has seen a wide variety of desk calculators, all basically operating on a principle similar to that of Pascal's machine but with varying degrees of sophistication and aids to convenience. Input numbers may be set by moving selector levers to designated positions or, in some cases, by a simple keyboard. Operation may either be manual or electrical, and results are usually shown in plain figures on dials read through small windows (Fig. 2). There are also simple adding and listing machines that print results on a roll of tally tape (Fig. 3). Well-known manufacturers' names include Monroe, Marchant, Brunsvega, Facit, and a host of others.

G. J. MORRIS

# CALCULATOR, ELECTRONIC

For articles on related subjects *see* CALCULATOR, DESK; and INTEGRATED CIRCUITRY.

Until the early 1960s desk calculators were essentially mechanical in operation, driven either by hand or an electric motor. They were bulky, usually fairly heavy, and certainly not easy to carry about. At their fastest, they took about a third- to a half-second to add a pair of numbers.

By the late 1940s technologists had found how electronics could be applied to computation, and by 1960 electronic computers were in wide use. The earliest models relied on the electronic tube as the basis of their circuitry, and therefore the machines were large. A significant reduction in size of the second generation of computers was made possible when the transistor replaced the tube. Circuits were, however, still far too big to use them in the construction of a desk-size calculator.

The solution to the problem was found in a by-product of the United States space research program. More than anything else, devices to be used in space vehicles had to be small and light, and vast amounts of development money were spent in search of ways and means of achieving this. One result was the microintegrated circuit, a method of compacting many electronic components and complicated circuitry in a very small space.

Transistors and other components in integrated circuits (IC) depend for their operation on minute chemical differences between adjacent parts of a tiny flake of silicon. In the early days, a suitably treated wafer of silicon was chopped up to make many individual transistors. The major breakthrough to IC design was a process of making the desired interconnection between the components on the silicon wafer itself, and so reduce size and, even more important, cost.

These circuits are really tiny. An IC chip less than a quarter-inch square may contain over 7,000 interconnected transistors, together with diodes and other components. Such a massive array of electronic power in a small package (see Fig. 1) enabled designers of the desk calculator to replace mechanical parts with electronic components, and at one swoop reduce size and weight, greatly increase speed, and obtain silent operation.

The earliest electronic calculators appeared about 1962, and they have poured onto the market in great numbers since 1970. As production of the circuits and of the calculators themselves has rocketed, so prices have tumbled. In a very short time manufacturers have produced a bewildering array of machines from which to choose. The simplest models are already so cheap that a growing number of students use them to do homework.

Some electronic calculators are intended for desk use, but since 1970 numerous hand models have been available, some as small as a pack of cigarettes and easily carried in a pocket. Scientists, engineers, and mathematicians, as well as accountants and businessmen, use them extensively because their small size (Fig. 2) makes them extremely convenient. In these pocket calculators, numbers are entered by tapping a sequence of digitally marked keys; the desired arithmetic operation is ordered by tapping other keys marked with +, −, ×, ÷, =, etc. Some models often cope automatically with decimal points. Results are usually shown in clear figures, using some form of lighted display. More elaborate hand-held machines are equipped with small auxiliary memory capabilities, can handle constant multipliers, and some cases can evaluate trigonometric functions, square roots, reciprocals, etc., at the touch of a single button. Specifications of several models can include simple printing facilities.

**Fig. 1.** The Monroe 1920 desktop electronic calculator.

**Fig. 2.** The assembled Sinclair "Executive" pocket calculator.

G. J. Morris

**CARD.** *See* IBM Card; and Ninety-Column Card.

## CARD READING AND PUNCHING TECHNIQUES

For articles on related subjects *see* IBM Card; and Input-Output Devices.

Punched card reading used to be performed electromechanically by sensing pins or reading brushes. The need for higher speed, reliability in reading, and lower cost resulted in the introduction of the photoelectrical reading technique, which is widely applied now. High reliability of reading is usually secured by checking techniques, for example:

1. A dual read station.
2. Echo (in which the data transmitted is returned to the point from which it was sent and compared with original data).
3. Validity.
4. Parity.
5. Single-access clutch.
6. Column strobe count.
7. Light/dark probe.

Usually a combination of these types of checks is used. Cards with readings that do not match are generally sent to a secondary stacker. In present-day readers the scanning of a card is usually performed by columns (often referred to as "serial scanning") as opposed to the previously used scanning by rows (also called "parallel scanning").

Fig. 1 shows the principle of the photoelectrical reading technique. The reading of a card is performed at a dual read station consisting of two vertical columns of 12 photodiodes each and 2 gating diodes, located at each side of the read diode columns (these last two diodes are not shown in Fig. 1). Spacing between read diode columns is equal to that of one card column. Vertical spacing between diodes is 0.25 in. and the diodes span the 12 information rows of the card.

The two gating diodes are located between the horizontal rows of read diodes in such a way that they always see the solid portions of the punched card. Hence, these diodes are triggered only by the leading or by the trailing edge of the card.

All read station photodiodes are covered by a mask that contains rectangular holes, which are slightly narrower than the width of the punched card holes. Masking slots covering gating diodes 1 and 2 are smaller than those used for read diodes. The smaller dimension allows for a minute card skew or the possibility of slight disorientation between the information holes contained in the punched card.

The photodiode exciter source is a 28-volt, incandescent lamp. Light rays from the lamp are directed toward a periscopic mirror element, where the reflective surface at the upper end directs light rays downward, through the optical glass, to strike the second reflective surface at the lower end. Parallel light rays are emitted from the edge of the glass and mirror element. The periscopic system distributes the light evenly over the 3-in. read station area.

When the punched card reaches the dual read station, parallel light rays pass through the information holes of the card and strike the corresponding read diodes. At the peak of the light transmission, timing circuits transmit a read gate probe, which permits information contained in the first card column to be recorded in the primary read register. Hence, each 12-bit column of the punch card is read in character serial mode. Once read and recorded, the first card column is read again by the second group of read diodes. This operation is performed in sequence for each column of the card. If any two information groups do not correspond, in the automatic mode of operation, a compare error signal is transmitted to the computer, and the computer may return a gate command signal to channel the card into a secondary tray. In the manual mode of operation, the compare error signal acts as a gate command to channel the card into the secondary receiving tray.

Card punching is performed at the punch station of a card punch. The punch station consists of a punch matrix and punch dies with punch mag-

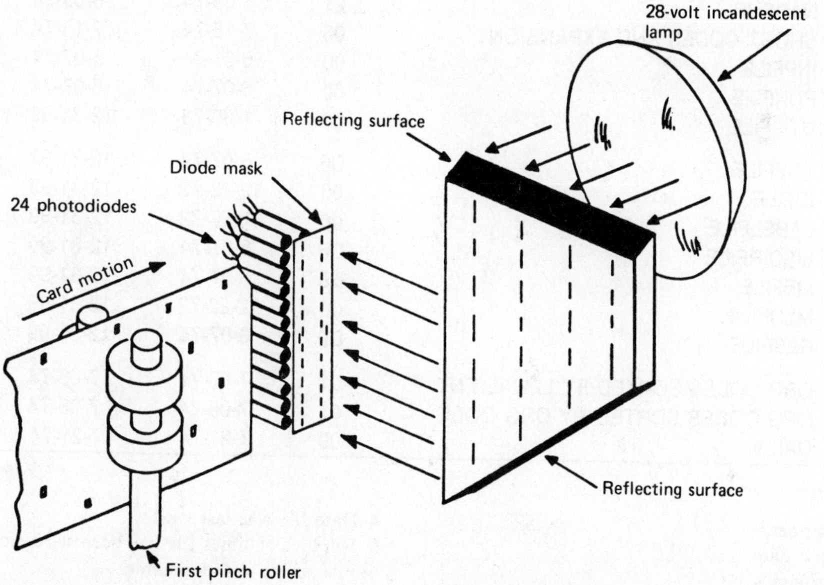


**Fig. 1.** The principle of a photoelectrical reading technique as used by Control Data Corp. in its CDC 405 high-speed card reader.

nets. A punch matrix has 80 holes corresponding with the 80 punching positions in a punch row of an 80-column card (if the punching is performed by rows) or it has 12 holes corresponding with the 12 punching positions of a punch column in an 80-column card (if the punching is performed by columns). The 80- or 12-punch dies are positioned upright with respect to the holes in the punch matrix.

Each punch die has its assigned punch magnet. These are set by the electronic image of the output information to be punched in the card. When activated, the punch die moves against the hole in the punch matrix, thus causing the punching of all data relative to a row (or column) of a card that is being moved (by rows or by columns) between the punch dies and the punch matrix.

The check of correct punching is generally performed by a "read-after-punch" verification, echo, check on punching dies activated, and validity. Other error-checking capabilities generally built into the card punch include card synchronization and row-by-row hole-counting parity checking.

J. Necas

# CATALOG

For articles on related subjects *see* Files; and Memory: Auxiliary.

A catalog is a file, usually stored on some auxiliary storage medium, which contains an ordered list of names and other pertinent information on all files stored permanently in the computer system. In

**FILE DIRECTORY LISTING**

| 15 | | 1 | 2 | 3 | 4 |
|---|---|---|---|---|---|
| OWNER | FILE NAME | ED | C-DATE | E-DATE | L-DATE |
| JOB | GATHER-FILE | 00 | 7-19-74 | 12-31-99 | 7-19-74 |
| JOB | GATHERFILE | 01 | 7-09-74 | 12-31-99 | 7-19-74 |
| MSOS | FILE 54 | 00 | 7-19-74 | 7-19-74 | 7-21-74 |
| MSOS | FILE 55 | 00 | 6-07-74 | 6-07-74 | 7-21-74 |
| MSOS | FILE 56 | 00 | 7-19-74 | 7-19-74 | 7-21-74 |
| MSOS | L-MSIO | 00 | 12-22-72 | 12-31-99 | 7-21-74 |
| NAD | NADSUB | 21 | 6-03-74 | 6-03-74 | 7-19-74 |
| NADS | SHORT CODES AND EXPANSION | 00 | 7-18-74 | 7-18-74 | 7-19-74 |
| PPR | INPFILE | 00 | 6-07-74 | 6-07-74 | 7-21-74 |
| PPR | PUNFILE | 00 | 6-07-74 | 6-07-74 | 7-21-74 |
| PPR | UTILFILE | 00 | 1-30-73 | 12-31-99 | 7-21-74 |
| RTS | ABSFILE | D6 | 6-07-74 | 12-31-99 | 6-07-74 |
| RTS | IDFILE | 00 | 12-22-72 | 12-31-99 | 5-02-73 |
| RTS | LABELFILE | 00 | 12-22-72 | 12-31-99 | 5-02-73 |
| RTS | LIBDIRFILE | D6 | 6-07-74 | 12-31-99 | 6-07-74 |
| RTS | LIBFILE | D6 | 6-07-74 | 12-31-99 | 6-07-74 |
| RTS | MSDFILE | 00 | 12-22-72 | 12-31-99 | 10-20-72 |
| RTS | RESFILE | D6 | 6-07-74 | 12-31-99 | 6-07-74 |
| TABLE | ORG CODES SORTED BY LEGAL ENT | 01 | 7-06-74 | 7-06-74 | 7-11-74 |
| TABLE | ORG CODES SORTED BY ORG CODE | 01 | 7-06-74 | 7-06-74 | 7-11-74 |
| TLOG | DAILY | 00 | 7-21-74 | 7-21-74 | 7-21-74 |

*Explanatory Notes*

**1** Edition number.
**2** File creation date.
**3** Expiration date.
**4** Date file was last used.
**5** Number of times file has been used since creation.
**6** File size in disk segments.

**Fig. 1.** Example of an excerpt from a catalog. For purposes of finding a file, the file name consists of *owner, file name,* and *edition* for uniqueness.

addition to the name of the file (e.g., "1974-EARNINGS-RECORDS"), the catalog record may contain the creation date, an edition (or version) number, and a proposed (or assumed) expiration date. Normally it must contain the size of the file, the location of the file in storage (where the file has been stored on what device), and it will often maintain some usage measures such as number of accesses since creation, and date of last access, etc.

The catalog contains information on files stored on permanently mounted auxiliary storage units such as disks and drums. It also contains information on files stored on magnetic tape or on removable disk packs. When a tape or disk pack file is requested by a program, the information in the catalog together with other information is used by the operating system to determine if the file requested is available on line or if a tape or disk pack must be obtained and mounted. In the latter case, appropriate instructions for the operator are issued at the computer console.

Files are stored permanently and cataloged when it is anticipated that they will be used repeatedly. In addition to data files, both source programs and object programs are often cataloged, the former so that they can be easily modified and the latter to enable repeated use without reloading the program from cards.

Fig. 1 contains an excerpt from a typical catalog of files showing the files stored on a particular disk pack.

The file catalog is also known by various other names among which the following are most common:

File Directory (as in Fig. 1)
File Name Table
Volume Table of Contents (for files on a

| 5 USE CT | 6 F-SIZE | 7 B-SIZE | 8 BLK CT | 9 SEG CT | 10 SEG | 11 DT | 12 DN | 13 LSL | 14 SL |
|---|---|---|---|---|---|---|---|---|---|
| 3 | 20 | 256 | 1 | 1 | 1 | 854 | 8541 | 13792 | 20 |
| 39 | 20 | 256 | 13 | 1 | 1 | 854 | 8541 | 4736 | 20 |
| 294 | 50 | 480 | 282 | 1 | 1 | 854 | 8541 | 3216 | 50 |
| 8664 | 50 | 480 | 282 | 1 | 1 | 854 | 8541 | 22240 | 50 |
| 8665 | 80 | 960 | 277 | 1 | 1 | 854 | 8541 | 24640 | 80 |
| 14307 | 10 | 10240 | 4 | 1 | 1 | 854 | 8541 | 18640 | 10 |
| 217 | 3 | 960 | 9 | 1 | 1 | 854 | 8541 | 23520 | 3 |
| 8 | 6 | 504 | 43 | 1 | 1 | 854 | 8541 | 21568 | 6 |
| 445 | 50 | 1024 | 400 | 1 | 1 | 854 | 8541 | 25920 | 50 |
| 445 | 50 | 1024 | 240 | 1 | 1 | 854 | 8541 | 23040 | 30 |
| 2680 | 10 | 1024 | 0 | 1 | 1 | 854 | 8541 | 19808 | 10 |
| 1 | 92 | 4 | 1462 | 1 | 1 | 854 | 8541 | 30960 | 92 |
| 1 | 4 | 480 | 1 | 2 | 1 | 854 | 8541 | 240 | 2 |
| 0 | 40 | 392 | 36 | 2 | 1 | 854 | 8541 | 32 | 13 |
| 1 | 3 | 500 | 17 | 1 | 1 | 854 | 8541 | 13744 | 3 |
| 1 | 241 | 960 | 962 | 1 | 1 | 854 | 8541 | 5072 | 241 |
| 1 | 50 | 4 | 10 | 1 | 1 | 854 | 8541 | 272 | 50 |
| 1 | 7 | 4 | 111 | 1 | 1 | 854 | 8541 | 19232 | 7 |
| 6 | 2 | 256 | 6 | 1 | 1 | 854 | 8541 | 32432 | 2 |
| 3 | 2 | 256 | 6 | 1 | 1 | 854 | 8541 | 13712 | 2 |
| 40 | 20 | 46 | 38 | 1 | 1 | 854 | 8541 | 19344 | 20 |

**7** Block size in characters.
**8** Block count, number of blocks in file.
**9** Segment count; number of segments into which file is divided.
**10** Segment number stored at this location.
**11** Type model of disk device on which file is stored.
**12** Device number.
**13** Lowest segment location is track number on disk where this segment of file starts.
**14** Length of this segment.
**15** Since two people may use the same file name, an additional name is attached, giving the owner's name. In these cases the owner is the name of a package of programs (or system) which uses that file.

particular pack)
Permanent File Directory

C. L. MEEK

# CELLULAR AUTOMATA

For article on related subject *see* AUTOMATA THEORY.
For article on related term *see* PATTERN RECOGNITION.

A cellular automaton is a theoretical model of a parallel computer, subject to various restrictions to make formal investigation of its computing powers tractable. All versions of the model share these properties: Each is an interconnection of identical cells, where a cell is a model of a computer with finite memory—i.e., a finite-state machine. Each cell computes an output from inputs it receives from a finite set of cells, forming its neighborhood, and possibly from an external source.

All cells compute one output simultaneously and each cell computes an output at each tick of a clock, i.e., after each unit time step. The output of a cell is distributed to its neighborhood and possibly to an external receiver.

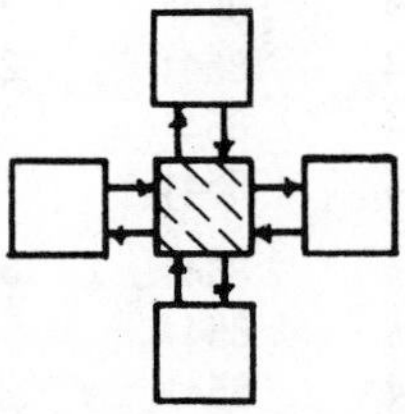

**Fig. 1.** A cell (hatched) and its neighborhood.

A version of the cellular automaton model exists for each set of choices in the following dichotomies: an infinite or a finite number of cells; a uniform interconnection scheme (all cells have neighborhoods of the same shape, e.g., that in Fig. 1) or a nonuniform scheme (Fig. 2); deterministic or nondeterministic cells (a choice of one output value at each unit time step or one of several values chosen randomly); the absence or presence of an external input (output), and in the case of an external input (output) the automaton is connected to all cells or to only a subset; Moore-type or Mealy-type cells (unit

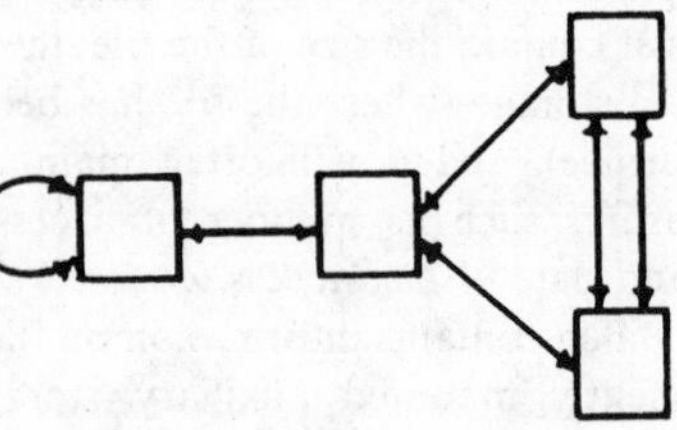

**Fig. 2.** A cellular automaton with nonuniform neighborhood.

time steps allowed or not allowed, respectively between inputs and the associated output); a static or dynamic interconnection scheme (neighborhood does or does not remain fixed in time). Some of the names associated with one or more of these versions are cellular automaton, tessellation automaton, modular computer, iterative automaton, intelligent graph, Lindenmayer system, and cellular network.

The first version of the cellular automaton, historically, was the cellular space obtained by selecting the first choice in each dichotomy above, but with no external input or output. It can be visualized in two dimensions as an infinite chessboard, each square representing a cell. It has been used to prove the existence of nontrivial self-reproducing machines, is capable of computing any computable function with only three states per cell and the four nearest cells as the neighborhood (Fig. 1), and can exhibit Garden of Eden configurations; i.e., patterns of cell states at one time, which can never arise in a given cellular space except at time zero. If an external input is assumed distributed to each cell, then the cellular space becomes what is usually called a "tessellation" space.

The cellular automaton is obtained from the cellular space by admitting only a finite, connected set of cells on the chessboard (Fig. 3). A cell with a neighbor missing has a special boundary signal substituted instead. The cellular automaton is particularly useful as a pattern recognizer, where the pattern comprises the states of the cells at time zero, especially if nondeterministic cells are allowed. A famous problem for the (deterministic) cellular automaton, the Firing Squad problem, calls each cell a soldier with one of them as the general—i.e., all cells but one are "off" initially—and asks if all soldiers can begin firing simultaneously by going into the

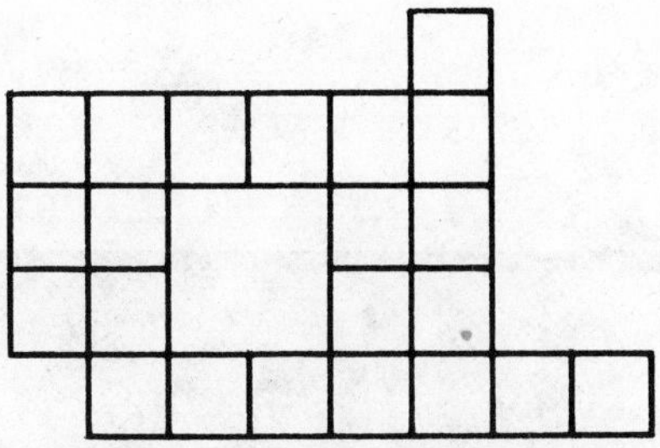

**Fig. 3.** A cellular automaton with uniform neighborhood of Fig. 1 assumed.

same state. The Firing Squad theorem, which solves this problem, guarantees an affirmative answer.

The Firing Squad theorem remains valid even when a nonuniform interconnection scheme is allowed. Thus, another version of the cellular automaton, the graphical cellular automaton (Fig. 2), requires only that the number of neighbors be fixed, not that they be in any fixed geometric relationship with a cell. They have been shown to be more powerful than the uniformly interconnected cellular automata.

The final type of cellular automaton to be mentioned, the dynamic cellular automaton, or Lindenmayer system, allows a cell to divide into daughter cells—regardless of the position of that cell in the initial array of cells—and allows the disappearance, or death, of cells. This version, with its dynamic interconnection scheme, is of interest to theoretical biologists as a model for the growth and development of living things.

If instantaneous communication is made possible between any two cells, by allowing Mealy-type cells, then each of the versions mentioned above gives rise to another. This class of cellular automata types is not well understood, although it is perhaps of the most interest in practical computing.

### References

1961. Hennie, F. C., III. *Iterative Arrays and Logical Circuits*. New York: M.I.T. Press and Wiley.

1968. *Cellular Automata*, ACM Monograph Series. New York: Academic Press.

1970. Burks, A. W. (Ed.). *Essays on Cellular Automata*. Urbana: University of Illinois Press.

1971. Gardner, M. "On Cellular Automata, Self-Reproduction, the Garden of Eden, and the Game 'Life'". Mathematical Games Department, *Scientific American*, vol. 224, pp. 112–117.

A. R. SMITH

# CENTRAL PROCESSING UNIT (CPU)

For articles on related subjects *see* ARITHMETIC-LOGIC UNIT; DIGITAL COMPUTERS; MEMORY: Main; and STORED PROGRAM CONCEPT.
For article on related term *see* OPERATING SYSTEMS.

Although we still talk about "computers," some believe that the term "data processing system" is more descriptive of what is found in the normal computer room. The stress is on the term "system," implying that the modern computer consists of a selection of units of various types, all interconnected and functioning harmoniously with one another under central control. Most of the units in a system are called "peripheral" devices and serve either as the means of feeding raw data or file data into the system or of receiving results or updated files from the system.

The term "peripheral" conjures up a vision in which these units surround others, which serve as the focal point or center of the system (although this is rarely true physically). The name "central processor," or central processing unit (CPU), is used to describe elements that carry out a variety of essential data manipulations and controlling tasks at the heart of the computer.

Probably the most obvious element is the one required to carry out arithmetic and other operations on data, which is usually called the "arithmetic unit." It is designed to operate on a pair of numbers and carry out on them the processes of addition, subtraction, multiplication, and division. It can compare numbers and determine whether one is the greater or whether both are equal. These operations are carried out at very high speeds; even the slowest computers can do at least 10,000 such operations in a second, and the really fast "number crunchers" handle as many as 12 million.

The other obvious element is the control unit, required to supervise the functioning of the machine as a whole, calling into operation the various units as required by the program. It receives the program instructions one by one in sequence, interprets them, and sends appropriate control signals to the various units. It acts in many ways as a very sophisticated telephone switchboard operator, making interconnections between various parts of the system. When the control unit recognizes special signals (for example, that the result of a subtraction is negative), it

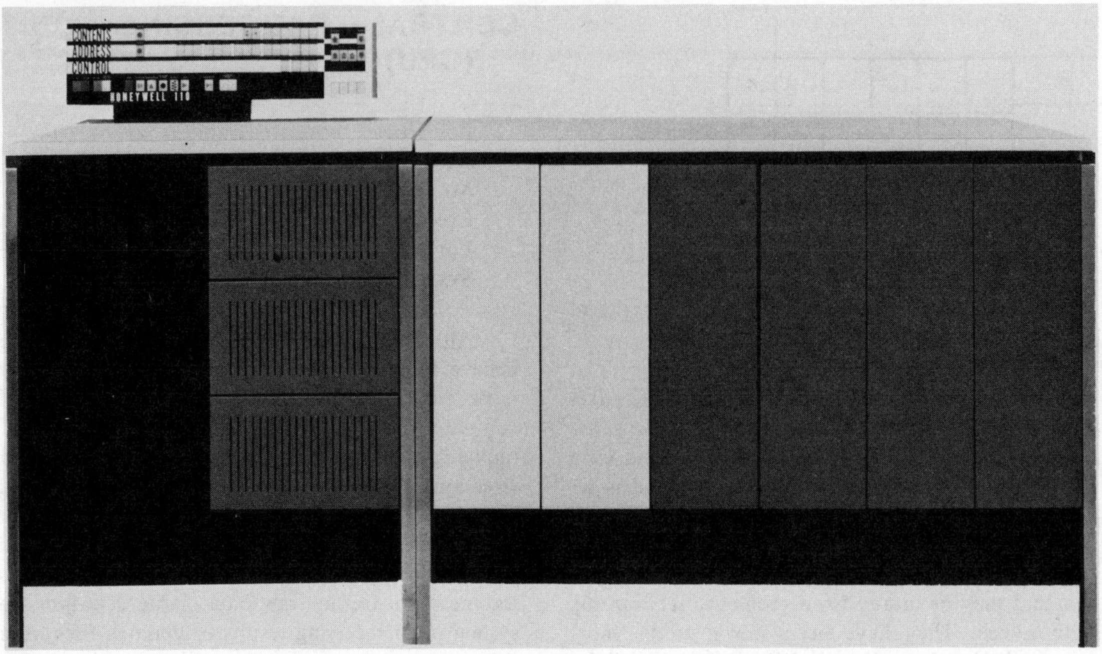


**Fig. 1.** Central processing unit of Honeywell 110 system.

can depart from the strict sequence of program instructions and jump to a different part of the program which is designed to deal with those circumstances.

Both the arithmetic unit and control unit depend heavily on the third main part of the central processor (Fig. 1), the main or central storage (or memory) unit. The arithmetic unit needs numbers on which to operate and needs to store intermediate results at some place until the end of the calculation. The control unit needs program instructions in rapid succession. Both data and instructions are held in memory. The program for a given job is read into memory from an input unit or auxiliary storage device as part of the setting-up procedure for the job. Data flows into memory from such devices as card readers and magnetic tape or disk units, and is manipulated while in storage to produce results that are output, for example, to a printer.

Memory is also used to store a complex of programs known as the "operating system"; this system is designed to supervise the total operation of the computer in as efficient a method as possible. These programs function in some ways analogous to "traffic controllers" as they have to monitor the flow of data around the computer, giving some streams right of way over others, opening up clearways for top priority messages, looking out for emergency signals, and generally keeping things flowing smoothly.

The central processing unit is aptly named. It is very much at the center of computer activity, and it completes a massive amount of processing work both directly to produce the desired results and generally to supervise the efficient operation of the computer system as a whole.

G. J. Morris

## CHAIN. *See* Overlay.

## CHANNEL

For articles on related subjects *see* Buffer; Communication Control Unit; Data Communications; Interrupt; Input-Output Devices; Memory: Auxiliary; and Multiplexing.
For articles on related terms *see* Lockout; Privileged Instruction; and Register.

**Early Design.** In the design of early computing systems it was usual to provide for only a minimum of input and output devices, such as paper tape or card readers and punches, and perhaps a line printer or teleprinter. All these peripherals were essentially slow. In such cases data could be transferred to and from the peripheral, character by character, and each unit had its special input or output line. Normally, data transferred between an I/O device and the store passed through the CPU. Later it was found necessary to provide many I/O devices. With the advent of magnetic tape units, a much faster device with a short crisis time (i.e., a need to be serviced very quickly if data was not to be lost), multicharacter block transfers became necessary.

In all cases, however, it was necessary to provide some indication of the status of the I/O device in use, such as "ready" or "busy." If a busy status of the device called upon was detected, the program usually had to stop and wait for the unit to become available again.

The need for block transfers to devices with short crisis times and the avoidance of delays due to unsuitable peripheral conditions led to the use of buffered peripherals and the development of continuously operating channels communicating directly with the store instead of through the CPU.

**Autonomous Channel Operation.** The eventual availability of fast buffered block peripherals such as magnetic tape and buffered peripherals such as card units and line printers called for the fast transfer of data to and from peripherals. If these transfers were controlled by the CPU, much time would be lost by the CPU, especially as character transfer was slow compared with other CPU operations. It follows that methods of autonomous transfer were needed. In these methods a whole block of data is transferred rapidly, word by word, to and from the main store, the cycles of the storage time taken for the word transfer being stolen from those available to the CPU. This usually causes only a slight hesitation of the CPU, whose storage cycle time of a 1–2 $\mu$s should be compared with that of magnetic tape unit, which usually operates at a rate of about 60 $\mu$s per word.

To facilitate block transfers directly between the store and the peripheral units, a controller called a "data channel" was introduced. There may be more than one channel. A data channel unit is essentially a small special-purpose computer. The CPU sends to the channel the length of the block of the continuous storage words to be transferred and the number of those words to be transferred. The channel initiates the transfer, if possible; i.e., if the channel is not already busy and the channel equipment is available and ready to operate.

Usually the transfer from store to channel unit is in words, but the channel usually divides the words into a number of fields (or bytes), each of between 6 and 12 bits, suitable for acceptance by the peripheral unit controller and the peripheral itself. Then each byte is sent in turn, usually starting at the leftmost or the most significant byte. As a word is transferred to and from the store, the word count (the number of words still to be transferred) is decremented and the address incremented until the word count becomes zero after all data has been transferred.

In the case in which there is more than one channel, the channels are connected at the CPU end via a scanner device which may be called a "communication unit." The communication unit polls the various data channels in turn, and when a word is ready it is transferred, the data channel providing the address to store in or from which data is to be provided,and then providing or receiving the word. This scanning may be done sufficiently rapidly to avoid any crisis times, e.g., with magnetic tapes. The communication unit has direct access to the store and activates the input to the output from store. In some cases, the communication unit scans the channels in a defined order of priority. A communications unit may handle about eight channels.

The channels are connected to peripheral unit controllers. These may further break down the channel byte into units that can be handled by the actual I/O peripheral, e.g., a six- to eight-bit byte. The peripheral unit controller may not actually activate the output peripheral until its internal buffer has been filled by the channel, nor may it activate the input channel until its buffer has been filled by the peripheral device.

It is common for a read or write instruction relating to channel operations to be in two or more parts, since it is usually impossible to provide all data for the specification of the operation in one instruction word. Thus, the first part will specify and initiate the action of reading or writing, will give the address to which transfer will be made in the case of the rejection of the operation for any reason, and will contain the address of a "control word." The control word contains the length and head address of the block to be transferred and is that information which is actually passed to the channel unit. It is also possible to allow a sequence of data blocks to be transferred by providing a sequence or chain of control words that are sent one after another to the channel.

The control word also provides a function code that specifies and provides for certain types of variation of the normal mode of transfer of data such as skipping, reading, or writing zeros or terminating transfers, before or after the specified number of words indicated in the control word. However, the transfer of data is by no means the only function performed by a channel unit, for it may receive a variety of special orders from the CPU, such as channel and equipment selection and channel and equipment status inquiry.

**Channel Capacity.** The rate at which a channel can transmit data to or from an I/O device, or to or from main storage, is the channel capacity. This is usually given in bytes or kilobytes per second. The channel capacity must, of course, be great enough to service the fastest I/O device connected to it.

Computer manuals and channel specifications usually give figures for data transfer rates under the assumptions of ideal conditions. Actual data transmission rates are usually below these. If the channel hardware and the CPU hardware use the same registers, the channel may have to wait on the CPU for available registers (and vice versa), thus affecting transfer rates in a manner that cannot be determined a priori. The maximum rates given for discrete channels will also be lowered by the operation of other channels.

Since multiplexer or selector channels are essentially independent computers controlling I/O, they will, of course, have their transfer rates affected by the way they are programmed. If the data is entered into a contiguous area of storage, the rate of data transmission will be greater than if it is entered into a noncontiguous set of areas, where all sorts of addresses must be computed and the CPU notified as to which storage area is being affected. This use of noncontiguous memory for a data set is known as "data chaining." Of course, with data chaining, more areas of conflict with the CPU are possible, slowing either data transmission or processing.

**Channel Command.** A computer program is made up of a set of instructions that are decoded and executed by the CPU. Channel commands are instructions that are decoded and executed by the I/O channels. A series of commands in sequence constitute a channel program. Commands are stored in the main storage just as though they were instructions. They are fetched from main storage and are common to all I/O devices, but modifier bits are used to specify device-dependent conditions. The modifier bits of the command may also be used to order the I/O device to execute certain functions that are not involved in data transfer, such as tape rewinding.

During its execution of a program the CPU will initiate I/O operations. A command will specify a channel, a device, and an operation to be performed, and perhaps a storage area to be used, and perhaps also some memory protection information about the storage area involved. All this information may appear in the command word, or the command may tell the channel in which locations in memory to seek the necessary information. Upon receipt of this information, the multiplexer channel will attempt to select the desired device by sending the device address to all I/O units (including controllers) attached to the channel. A unit that recognizes its address connects itself logically to the channel. Once the connection is made, the channel will send the executable command to the I/O device. The device will respond to the channel, indicating if it can execute the command. The channel will then make this information available to the CPU.

The I/O operation involving data transfer to or from a series of noncontiguous memory locations may involve a series of channel commands. Termination of an I/O operation involves channel-end and device-end conditions. These conditions are brought to the attention of the CPU via interrupts or programmed interrogation of the I/O device. The channel-end condition occurs when the data transmission is completed. The channel is considered busy until this condition is accepted by the CPU. The device-end signal is given when the I/O device has terminated execution of the operation. The device remains unavailable until it is cleared by the CPU.

**Lockout, Cycle Steal, Hesitation.** The memory of a computer cannot be accessed continuously, but only at specific points in time. The time elapsed between two consecutive points in time that the memory may be accessed by the processor or an I/O channel is known as a "memory cycle." The reason that the memory cannot be accessed continuously is that during a read/write operation, the information is not available, and some time must elapse before it is available again. Most memory cycle times are measured in microseconds or nanoseconds.

The CPU is essentially involved in processing the data that is in main memory while the channels are concerned with the flow of data between I/O

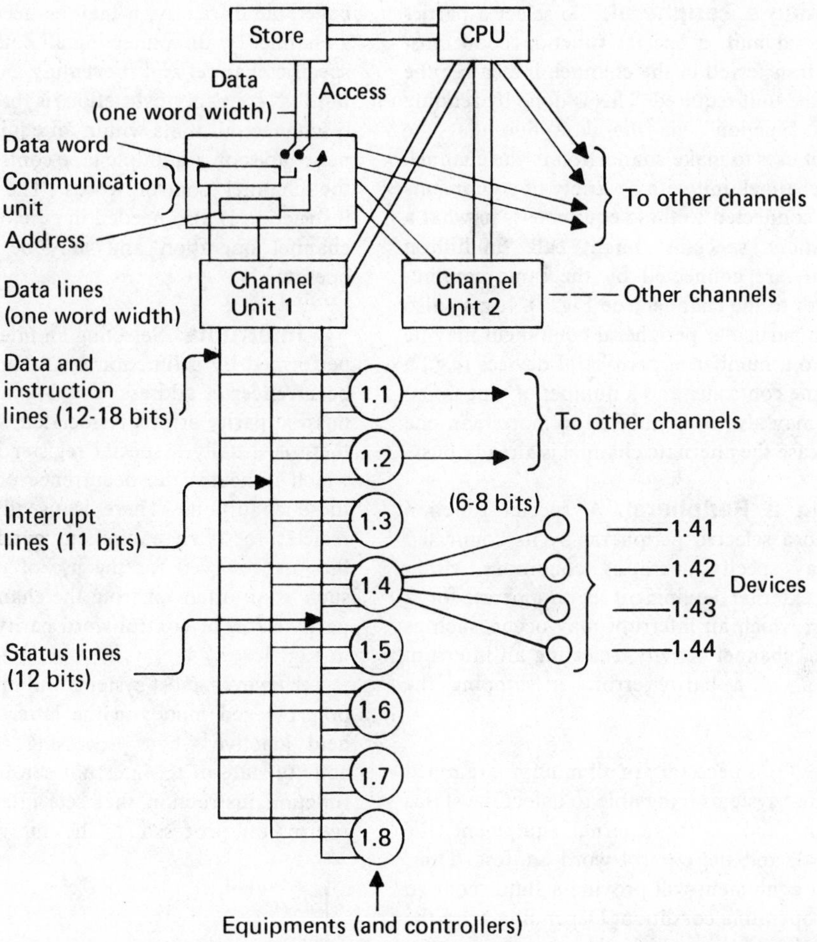


**Fig. 1.** Selector channel organization.

devices and main memory. Main memory is a high-speed data store, whereas peripherals are comparatively low-speed data stores. The channels and the CPU are busy moving data into and out of main memory. A source of conflict arises if they both need access to data at the same time. Since memory behaves the same way, whether the source or destination of the data is the I/O channels or the CPU, some method is needed to resolve the conflict.

Suppose another request for memory access is initiated by another channel while a memory cycle is going on. Since all requests must eventually be granted, but some more quickly than others, a priority system must be set up. It is the comparatively slow I/O devices, rather than the high-speed CPU, that must have their requests answered first. A tape speeding under the read head must give up its data before the next data passes the read head; otherwise the data will be lost. The moving I/O devices must always have open space to accept more data and cannot be concerned with memory access problems. The CPU, on the other hand, goes from one stable state to another. Once the information is in its registers, it can wait. This will slow the processing, but will not lose any information. Therefore, a priority lock up is set up whereby the CPU is locked out from access to memory at the instant that the channels want to access the memory.

The memory cycle during which the channels have access to memory and the CPU is locked out is known as a "cycle steal," i.e., the channels have stolen the cycle from the CPU. For that cycle the CPU must stop and wait until it can access the memory again. This is known as "hesitation."

**Selecting a Peripheral.** To select a particular peripheral unit, a special function code must initially be transferred to the channel, indicating the identity of the unit required. This is done by sending a "connect function" via the data line that the selected unit uses to make connection to the channel. Usually, a channel unit with a variety of equipments attached is connected to these equipments in what a communications specialist might call "multidrop manner"; all are connected by the same communication path to the channel (see Fig. 1). It may also occur that a particular peripheral equipment may be connected to a number of peripheral devices (e.g., a magnetic tape controller and a number of tape units) and that it may also be connected to more than one channel in case the alternate channel is already busy.

**Setting a Peripheral.** A special function code sent to a selected peripheral by its connected channel may specify operating conditions within which the external equipment is to operate or a condition in which an interrupt may occur, such as stopping the channel activity, selecting an interrupt on detection of a parity error, or stopping the operation.

**Status.** It is necessary in all multiprogrammed or time-shared systems to be able to detect the status of a channel and of the external equipment, the control word, and the control word address. Thus, the external equipment will provide a status code to indicate its operating condition. Depending upon the kind of equipment to which the channel is connected, certain bits in the code indicate that a parity error is present, or that a read or write is in progress, or that the operation is complete. Other codes in the status instruction cause the current data address and the word count to be sent to the CPU and/or the current control word address to be sent to other CPU registers.

In this way it is possible to detect not only the progress of a transfer and the chaining of control words but also a complex status, e.g., an empty card hopper, a card jam, empty line-printer paper, or a magnetic tape condition.

Detection of a busy channel or equipment status may be used appropriately to transfer control to a different program until a further interrupt recalls attention to the channel and its user program. An example is shown in Fig. 1 for one particular type of coding (e.g., CDC 3600).

**Clear Channel.** When initiating a program, or starting from a dead-stop condition or a recoverable difficulty, it may be necessary (1) to clear a channel by disconnecting all equipments from the specific channel and preventing any communication until a connect instruction is provided; or (2) to disconnect all units within an equipment (e.g., magnetic tapes on a multiple tape controller) and to clear the channel control words. The CLEAR CHANNEL instruction is also needed in case of difficulty with a channel operation and may be initiated by the operator.

**Interrupts.** Selecting an interrupt condition is performed by a function instruction that can select occurrences of address, and data and channel transmission parity errors. Associated with each channel, there is usually a special register in a channel unit which indicates the occurrence of one or more of these conditions. There is usually one bit in the register for each equipment condition. Additional bits are reserved for the use of the channel itself, such as an interrupt from the channel, channel data parity error, or control-word parity errors, as shown in Fig. 1.

However, most systems will operate in a normal or privileged mode; in the latter all interrupts are held inactive when processing an interrupt. The activity state of an interrupt can be set by a special function instruction that sets interrupts active and returns the processor to the unprivileged state. The

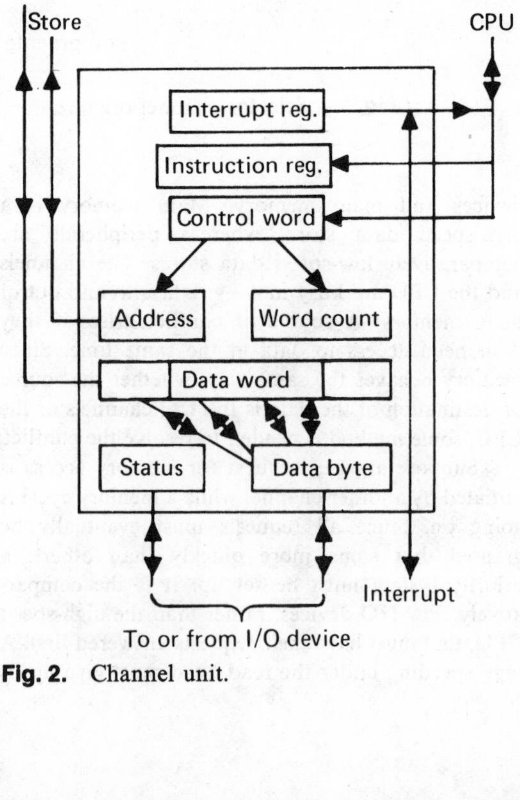


**Fig. 2.** Channel unit.

privileged status is automatically set on the detection of an interrupt when in normal state.

The structure of a channel unit is illustrated in Fig. 2. This shows the channel interrupt register, which indicates the conditions of the interrupt itself; the instruction register of the instruction which is received from the CPU; the control word, which gives the address and the number of words to be transferred; and the data word assembly registers, from which the data is to be sent from store. In addition to this, there is the status register, which is used to indicate the status of the connected unit or the channel.

**Selector and Multiplexer Channels.** Channels provide the ability to read, write, and compute concurrently. Each channel is essentially a small independent computer that responds to its own set of commands. The channel governs the flow of information between computer memory and the external world.

The two types of channels available are known as selector and multiplexer channels. High-speed I/O devices such as magnetic tapes, drums, and disks are usually connected to selector channels, while multiplexer channels usually have low-speed devices (card readers, line printers, teleprinters, paper tape readers) connected to them.

Numerous low-speed I/O devices connected to a multiplexer channel, may operate essentially simultaneously, their data being interleaved and directed to the proper locations in memory. Should high-speed I/O equipment be attached to a multiplexer channel, only one device will be able to operate at a time because of the high transmission rates and short crisis times. The multiplexer channel is then said to be operating in "burst" mode. Selector channels always operate in burst mode. Usually, the operation of either type of channel does not inhibit processing.

A selector channel transmits information to memory from one I/O device at a time. A multiplexer channel may transmit information to memory from many I/O devices in an interleaved fashion. A selector channel will contain the information connecting the desired I/O device to an address in memory, a word count, and all other necessary information within the channel itself. Since a multiplexer channel may have as many as 256 subchannels (connections between peripherals and the main memory), a table is set up in memory with the information necessary to each subchannel. During the actual transmission the information is in the multiplexer channel and is shuttled back and forth between multiplexer channel and main memory. Most computer manufacturers have this "table" area of memory set up so that it can be accessed only by the supervisory program, and not by the applications programmers. It is possible to access the memory for each subchannel transmission because memory access time is measured in microseconds, whereas access time of the slow I/O devices connected to a multiplexer channel is measured in milliseconds. It is therefore unnecessary to keep the control information for each subchannel in the channel between data transfers. A symbolic block diagram differentiating multiplexer and selector channels is shown in Fig. 3.

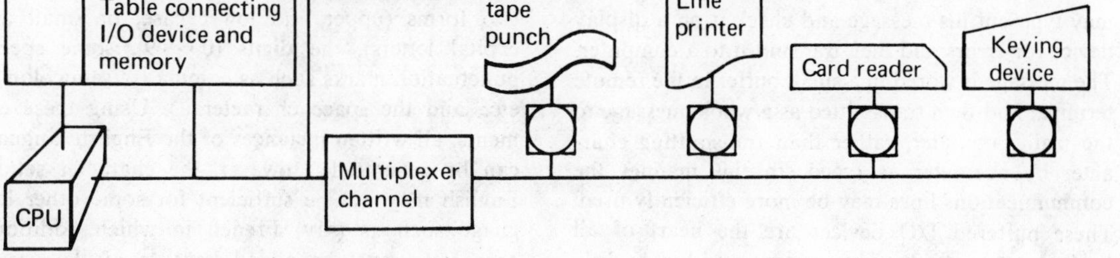

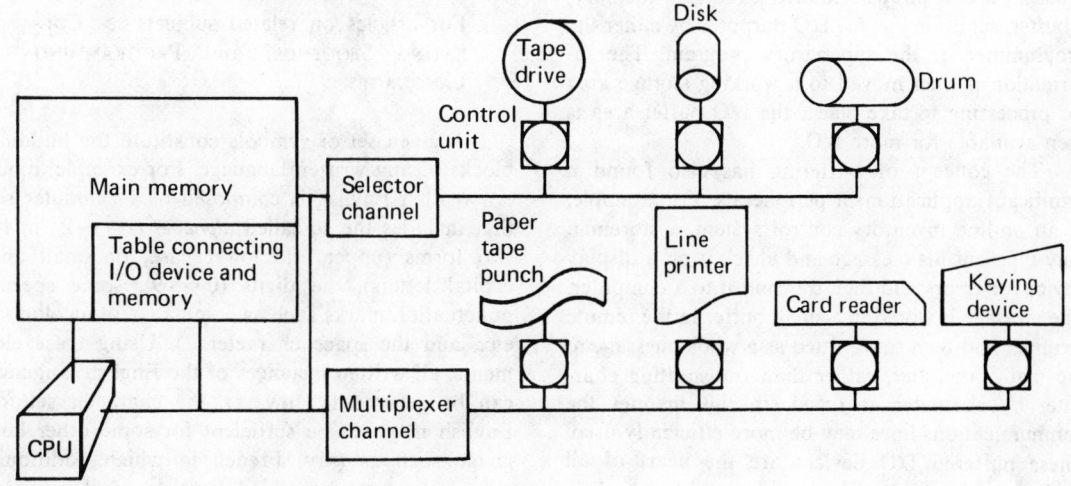


**Fig. 3.** A selector and a multiplexer channel.

**Communication Channels.** Some channels may be devoted to communication between store or processor and a number of remote terminals. These terminals may be of the interactive type or of the batch type. In either case the channel makes connection via a multiplexer channel, and thence (usually) via public transmission lines of specified bandwidth prescribed by the data carrier organization. The communication outlets from the multiplexer are made via "data sets," which pass the data between the multiplexer and the transmission lines and convert signals to frequency modulation or otherwise adapt them to the communication line. Communication may be in one direction only (i.e., in "simplex" or "half-duplex" form, in which transmission may take place in either direction at any one time), or in "duplex" (needing four wires instead of two) in which transmission can pass in both directions at the same time.

**Buffering.** Buffering is used to gather information at a time when it is not needed so that the information will be available for processing when it is needed. An early use of buffering was to overlap I/O and CPU operations. For example, an I/O operation is initiated to read a block of data into memory. While the channels are controlling this operation, the CPU may go merrily on its way processing with available cycles. When the CPU needs the information from memory, it will be available and the CPU need not wait for the data.

Care must be taken during programming to see that the I/O is completed by the time the CPU needs the buffered information, and also that just enough information goes into each block of memory. Sometimes all I/O is directed toward a block of memory, a buffer, set aside just for I/O purposes by either the programmer or the supervisory program. The information is then moved to a working storage area for processing to take place; the I/O buffer area is then available for more I/O.

The concept of buffering has also found a significant application in peripherals. For example, in an on-line inventory control system, a storeman may type out his message and check it on a display device for errors and then transmit it to a computer. The message is stored in a small buffer in the remote terminal and then transmitted as a whole message to the main computer, rather than transmitting character by character as typed. In this manner the communications lines may be more efficiently used. These buffered I/O devices are the heart of all keying systems such as key-to-tape and key-to-disk. A card reader will have some buffer memory so that the whole card may be read, stored, and then transmitted rather than read and transmitted one character at a time. Shrewd manipulation of buffers will greatly enhance the efficiency of its associated processing equipment by making necessary information available at the appropriate moment.

**Current Trends.** It is apparent that the complete function required of a channel allowing for multiprogramming and time sharing far exceeds those of simply reading and writing data. It is therefore becoming more common for channel units actually to be small programmed processors or minicomputers. This easily allows the extension of the channel functions; moreover, a greater variety of conditions can be specified by software design at a later stage of development. In this way a large CPU may be in charge of many small independent processors. This is one of the main design features of the CDC Cyber series of computers.

It is also becoming more common to provide a channel with an intermediary large buffer store to which the block may be rapidly transferred from the main store (e.g., at a 40 Mc rate), and from there transferred to the peripheral equipment connected to the buffer, at a slower rate appropriate to the equipment, while under the control of a small programmed processor.

T. Pearcey and M. Pine

## CHARACTER SET

For articles on related subjects *see* Collating Sequence; and Programming Languages.

A given set of symbols constitute the building blocks of any written language. For example, modern written English is composed of a character set that includes the so-called *alphabet* (A · · · Z) in its two forms (upper and lower case, or small and capital letters), the digits (0 · · · 9), some special punctuation marks such as comma (,), semicolon (;) etc., and the space character ( ). Using these elements, all written instances of the English language can be generated. However, the character set for English may not be sufficient for some other language such as (say) French in which additional characters must be added because of the use of accents.

Each computer language has its own character set which defines the set of characters that may be used in writing programs in that language. Table 1 gives the character sets of some common languages. PL/I has two possible character sets because it was designed at just the time when the IBM 026 keypunch (which had been the standard card-punching device and whose keyboard was limited to 48 characters) was being replaced by the IBM 029 keypunch, which allowed a larger character set, more convenient for writing programs in higher-level languages (but which has no provision for lower-case letters). As indicated in Table 1, implementations of a language in a particular computer may not allow certain characters or may allow characters in addition to the officially defined ones.

Most of the characters in the character sets of higher-level languages have their usual meanings. But this is not always the case for the *special characters*, those which are neither letters nor digits. For example:

- * denotes multiplication
- = generally denotes *replacement* of the quantity on the left by the quantity on the right

**Table 1.** Character Sets of Fortran, PL/I, Cobol

| Characters | Fortran | PL/I, 48-char. set | PL/I, 60-char. set | Cobol |
|---|---|---|---|---|
| A,B,C, . . .,Y,Z | X | X | X | X |
| 0,1,2, . . .,8,9 | X | X | X | X |
| = + − * / ) ( , . $ | | | | |
| blank | X | X | X | X |
| ′ | Z | X | X | X |
| @ # % : & . − ? ¬ | | | X | |
| ; > < | | | X | Y |

*Notes:*

X indicates character is part of character set.
Y indicates character is part of character set, but is not allowed at many installations.
Z indicates character is not part of character set, but often is allowed.

One language whose character set is markedly different from all other higher-level languages is APL (*A Programming Language*) developed by Kenneth Iverson. APL contains many special symbols which serve as special *operations*. Some of these are shown in Table 2. In addition, APL defines many operators as a combination of two symbols from the character set. These are produced in practice by striking one key of a typewriter (with a special keyboard), backspacing, and then striking a second key.

Various codes have been developed to enable the characters used in higher-level languages to be represented by combinations of bits in a single 8-bit byte. Of particular note are the ASCII and EBCDIC codes.

**Table 2.** Some Special Characters in APL

| Character | Name | Definition | Example (result of operator given under it) |
|---|---|---|---|
| ι | Index | ιA generates indices in ascending order, starting from 1 to A | ι6<br>1 2 3 4 5 6 |
| ⌈ | Ceiling | ⌈B is the least integer greater than or equal to B | ⌈14.7<br>15 |
| ⌊ | Floor | ⌊C is the greatest integer less than or equal to C | ⌊−5.9<br>−6 |
| ○ | Pi times | ○D multiplies D by $\pi$ | ○3<br>9.424777962 |
| ! | Generalized factorial | !E is the factorial of E when E is a positive integer (and the gamma funtion of E + 1 otherwise) | !7<br>5040 |

REFERENCES

1970. Ralston, A. *An Introduction to Programming and Computer Science*. New York: McGraw-Hill.

1972. Pakin, S. *APL/360 Reference Manual*. Chicago: Science Research Associates.


J. A. N. LEE AND A. RALSTON

# CHEBYSHEV APPROXIMATION

For articles on related subjects *see* APPROXIMATION THEORY; LEAST-SQUARES APPROXIMATION; and NUMERICAL ANALYSIS.

Many computations on computers require the calculation of values of one or more functions such as square roots, sines, cosines, logarithms, exponentials, and other elementary functions or more complicated functions such as Bessel functions. Since computers can only perform the operations of arithmetic, these functions cannot be evaluated directly, but must be *approximated* by some other functions that can be evaluated arithmetically. For example, a common method for computing the square root of a number $A$ is the following application of the Newton-Raphson method:

$$x_{i+1} = \frac{1}{2}\left(x_i + \frac{A}{x_i}\right) \qquad i = 0,1,2,3,\ldots \quad x_0 = A$$

It can be shown that $x_i$ gets arbitrarily close to $A$ as $i \to \infty$. For example, let $A = 2$. Then

$$x_0 = 2$$
$$x_1 = 1.5$$
$$x_2 = 1.41666\cdots$$
$$x_3 = 1.414215\cdots$$

while $\sqrt{2} = 1.414213\ \ldots.$

The general problem we wish to consider here is: Given a function $f(x)$ and an interval $[a,b]$ on which we wish to approximate $f(x)$, find an approximation to $f(x)$ on this interval—which can be computed arithmetically—of minimum error. But what do we mean by minimum error? In many problems in mathematics this would mean minimum least squares error over the interval. But in approximating functions for computers we are more usually interested in minimizing the maximum error on the interval, for then the user of the approximation always knows that the worst possible case is as favorable as it can be. Rigorously stated, we wish to find an approximation $R(x)$ which has the property that

$$r = \max_{[a,b]} |f(x) - R(x)|$$

is smaller than for any other approximation. Such a *minimum–maximum error approximation*, or *minimax* approximation, is usually called a "Chebyshev approximation" after the great Russian mathematician P. L. Chebyshev (1821–1894), whose name is transliterated from the Russian in a variety of other ways (e.g., Tchebycheff).

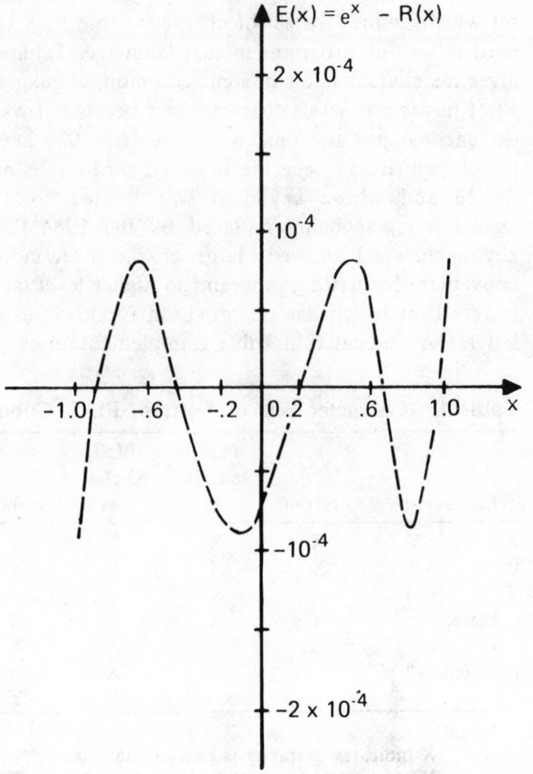


**Fig. 1.** Error in Chebyshev approximation to $e^x$ on $[-1,1]$ as a ratio of two quadratics.

The question remains of what form $R(x)$ should have. If it is to be evaluated arithmetically, then the most general function it can be is a *rational function*, i.e., the ratio of two polynomials. For example, the Chebyshev approximation to the exponential function $e^x$ on the interval $[-1, 1]$, which is the ratio of two quadratic polynomials, is given by

$$R(x) = \frac{1.00007255 + 0.50863618X + 0.08582937x^2}{1.0 - 0.49109193x + 0.07770847x^2}$$

for which $r = 0.86899 \times 10^{-4}$. The error, $E(x) = e^x - R(x)$, is shown in Fig. 1. It exhibits the characteristic property of Chebyshev approximations of alternating between its greatest and least values twice more than the sum of the degrees of numerator and denominator of $R(x)$ or, in the example above, $2 + 2 + 2 = 6$ times.

REFERENCE

1965. Ralston, A. *A First Course in Numerical Analysis.* New York: McGraw-Hill.

A. RALSTON

## CHECKPOINT AND RESTART

For articles on related subjects *see* COMPUTER, USING A; and DEBUGGING.

A designated place in a program at which normal processing is interrupted specifically to preserve the status information necessary to allow resumption of processing at some arbitrary time in the future is called a "checkpoint."

The primary purpose of a checkpoint is to avoid repeating the execution of a program from its beginning, should an error or malfunction occur somewhere in the middle of processing. This is especially effective in runs involving several hours of machine time. For such situations it is often appropriate to set up checkpoints at a number of strategic places in the program, either with all checkpoint information being saved, or by using a less conservative system in which the information captured at the most recent checkpoint replaces (overwrites) the previous set. Then, should difficulties arise, it is possible to take corrective action and resume processing from the last checkpoint, rather than starting over. Since the manipulations associated with checkpoint/restart procedures can consume substantial amounts of time and storage, it is possible to have situations in which it is more economical to avoid checkpoints. This capability is implemented by means of a procedure (often termed a "checkpoint routine") that captures the status of the program at the particular instant when it stopped and copies it onto an auxiliary storage medium. This data includes the contents of the special registers, storage locations associated with the program, and other information relating to the status of input/output devices. Later on, another procedure (a restart routine) can reset the system to resume processing by reading in and restoring the checkpoint information.

In many systems the checkpoint and restart routines are prepackaged software components accessible to the higher level language programmer via ordinary CALL statements. These facilities usually include numerous options that allow the programmer to exercise some control over the type of information gathered, the form in which it is stored, and the circumstances under which the restart is to proceed.

The introduction of complex operating systems has prompted an expansion in the use of checkpoint-restart procedures beyond the context of insurance against malfunctions. Depending on the strategy implemented in a particular system, it may be decided to interrupt a particular run, releasing its storage for other purposes with the intent of resuming that run at some later (presumably more propitious) time. In order to handle that type of procedure without the user's involvement, the checkpoint/restart process must become completely automated.

S. V. POLLACK

**CIRCUITRY.** *See* COMPUTER CIRCUITRY; and INTEGRATED CIRCUITRY.

**CLOSE AND OPEN A FILE.** *See* OPEN AND CLOSE A FILE.

**CLOSED SHOP.** *See* OPEN SHOP.

**CMI.** *See* COMPUTER-MANAGED INSTRUCTION.

**COBOL.** *See* PROCEDURE-ORIENTED LANGUAGES; PROCEDURE-ORIENTED LANGUAGES, PROGRAMMING IN.

**CODASYL.** *See* CONFERENCE ON DATA SYSTEMS LANGUAGES.

# CODES

For articles on related subjects *see* BINARY CODED DECIMAL, NATURAL; ERROR CORRECTING CODE.
For articles on related terms *see* ASCII; COLLATING SEQUENCE; COMPLEMENT; EBCDIC; HOLLERITH, HERMAN; and PARITY.

A code is a correspondence between a symbol of an alphabet (e.g., our alphabet of letters) and a number of digits of a number system (e.g., six bits for base 2). To be more precise, the mathematician would say that a code is a couple, which might be represented as $\Gamma(\Sigma, \Pi)$. Here, $\Sigma$ is the symbol space and the $\Pi$ are numeric combinations. Suppose that $S$ is some symbol in the symbol space $\Sigma$ and $P$ is one of the permutations of the digits in a numeric counting system $\Pi$. We might say "$S$ is mapped into $P$" or that "$S$ is represented by $P$," using the following symbols:

$$S \rightarrow P \quad \text{or} \quad S \equiv P. \tag{1}$$

I prefer to call $P$ a "combination." Since $P$ consists of $n$ digits, it can be written as

$$P = P_1P_2P_3 \cdots P_n, \tag{2}$$

where $P_i$ is any digit of the counting system with base $B$; i.e.,

$$P_i = 0,1,2,\ldots, \text{or } B - 1. \tag{3}$$

To make this more concrete, let us examine the case where the symbol space $\Sigma_A$ consists of letters of the alphabet. Let each combination $P$ consist of two decimal digits, $B = 10$ and $n = 2$. A very simple code might assign numbers consecutively to the letters so that we would have

$$A \equiv 01, \quad B \equiv 02, \quad C \equiv 03, \ldots, Z \equiv 26. \tag{4}$$

It is convenient here to introduce the number operator $\nu$, whose action is to find the number of elements in a set. Notice for our example that

$$\nu\Sigma_A = 26 \quad \text{and} \quad \nu\Pi = 100 \tag{5}$$

Since there are many more permutations than there are symbols in the symbol space, it is customary to find many permutations that go unassigned. These are sometimes called "forbidden combinations."

**Need.** Data is an abstraction of information in the real world. People keep this information in the form of symbols. The computer stores information in the various hardware elements that constitute it. Elements have been designed which have two or more states. An element such as the Nixie tube has ten states. But by far the most common, least expensive, and most efficient element is the *bistable device*; it has only two stable states. For the computer to represent information, it must be structured so that the devices used in the computer can accommodate it. Since there are not enough states in a single bistable device to represent each symbol as a human being uses it, the symbols are represented by a combination of these settings, by a combination of some codes.

It might seem initially that any representation of a symbol would do. This is not so. The design of a code usually must take into account the following requirements:

1. The original order relations that apply to the symbols within the symbol space should apply to the relation between combinations in the code.
2. Operations applied to the symbols should have analogous operations, which—when defined upon the combinations—produce a corresponding result.
3. The representation should be efficient (to minimize the number of combinations that go to waste) and the digit string should not be too long.

**Decimal Codes.** A decimal code provides a representation for the decimal numbers. The codes of interest to us use the base 2. Hence, these are called "binary coded decimal codes" (BCDs). To summarize their characteristics

$$\nu\Sigma_D = 10, \quad B = 2 \quad n \geq 4. \tag{6}$$

Note that these codes can be four bits or more. There are many useful codes that consist of more than four bits, and it is an error to believe that BCDs are *all* four bits; they are not.

There are several means for associating the symbols with combinations:

1. *Weighted codes* assign different weights to each bit in the combination as discussed shortly.

2. *Transition rules* may be created to indicate how the code for the successor number is created from the code for any given number.

3. Finally, there is the explicit assignment, where no rule as such exists.

As an example of a random BCD we have

$$0 = 111000, \quad 1 = 101010, \quad 2 \equiv 110011, \quad \text{etc.} \tag{7}$$

## Four-Bit BCDs

WEIGHTED CODES. Let us label the bits of the combination that represents a decimal digit. Unlike Expression (2), where the subscripts go from left to right, we will now order the subscripts 1 through 4 in reverse, going from right to left. Thus, if $D$ is a decimal digit, then we have

$$D \equiv b_4b_3b_2b_1. \tag{8}$$

A weighted code associates a weight with each bit and might be stated symbolically as

$$b_i \longleftrightarrow W_i \qquad i = 1 \text{ to } 4 \tag{9}$$

The requirement of the weighted code can be stated in the form of an algorithm: Multiply each bit by its weight and then total these. The total must be equal in value to the digit. Stated symbolically, we have

$$D = \sum_{1}^{4} b_iW_i = b_4W_4 + b_3W_3 + b_2W_2 + b_1W_1 \tag{10}$$

Some restrictions arise in setting up the weights:

1. For each digit to be encoded, there must be a combination of bits and their corresponding weights, whose total—using Expression (10)—is equal to the value of the digit.

2. When two combinations exist which, when substituted into Expression (10), yield the same digit, $D$, then another rule must be provided to decide which combination will be used.

*8421 Code.* The weighted 8421 code is illustrated in Table 1. From left to right, weights 8, 4, 2, and 1 are assigned to the bits that make up the combination. When the bits are set to 0 or 1, the resulting number is shown in the left column of the table.

| | Table 1 | Table 2 | Table 3 | Table 4 |
|---|---|---|---|---|
| Weights | 8 4 2 1 | 7 4 2 1 | 7 4 2–1 | Excess-3 |
| Digits | Code | Code | Code | Code |
| 0 | 0 0 0 0 | 0 0 0 0 | 0 0 0 0 | 0 0 1 1 |
| 1 | 0 0 0 1 | 0 0 0 1 | 0 0 1 1 | 0 1 0 0 |
| 2 | 0 0 1 0 | 0 0 1 0 | 0 0 1 0 | 0 1 0 1 |
| 3 | 0 0 1 1 | 0 0 1 1 | 0 1 0 1 | 0 1 1 0 |
| 4 | 0 1 0 0 | 0 1 0 0 | 0 1 0 0 | 0 1 1 1 |
| 5 | 0 1 0 1 | 0 1 0 1 | 0 1 1 1 | 1 0 0 0 |
| 6 | 0 1 1 0 | 0 1 1 0 | 1 0 0 1 (0110) | 1 0 0 1 |
| 7 | 0 1 1 1 | 1 0 0 0 (0111) | 1 0 0 0 | 1 0 1 0 |
| 8 | 1 0 0 0 | 1 0 0 1 | 1 0 1 1 | 1 0 1 1 |
| 9 | 1 0 0 1 | 1 0 1 0 | 1 0 1 0 | 1 1 0 0 |
| *(A) | 1 0 1 0 | 1 0 1 1 | 1 1 0 1 | 1 1 0 1 |
| *(B) | 1 0 1 1 | 1 1 0 0 | 1 1 0 0 | 1 1 1 0 |
| *(C) | 1 1 0 0 | 1 1 0 1 | 1 1 1 1 | 1 1 1 1 |
| *(D) | 1 1 0 1 | 1 1 1 0 | ----- | ---- |
| *(E) | 1 1 1 0 | 1 1 1 1 | ----- | ----- |
| *(F) | 1 1 1 1 | ---- | ----- | ----- |

* Forbidden combinations.

The six entries at the bottom of the table provide values 10 through 15. Of course there are no digits to correspond to these values in the decimal system. Hence, these combinations are forbidden. If these occur, the computer should signal an error.

Note that these combinations would be legal if the base for our system were 16. Hence, we will return to this table when we discuss the hexadecimal (base 16) system.

Finally note that the sequence of combinations for the 8421 code is the same sequence in which these binary numbers occur in the binary counting system. The binary counting system has been called the "natural" counting system in the literature. Hence, the appellation *natural binary coded decimal*, or simply NBCD for the code of Table 1.

*7421 Code.* Table 2 presents the 7421 code. Again there are six forbidden combinations. The bits that constitute each combination are calculated so that Expression (10) will yield the digit value.

A problem arises for encoding the digit 7. There are two combinations, 1000 and 0111, both of which yield the value 7. An auxiliary rule is required to settle this difficulty: Use the combination with the least number of 1's in it (i.e., 1000).

*742–1 Code.* The code for these weights is presented in Table 3. It illustrates that one or more of the weights may be negative as long as the weights fulfill the requirement that all digit values must be created. This time we find that there are two combinations that yield the digit value 6. Since both have the same number of 1's, we choose the combination with the 1 in the least significant place.

*XS 3 Code.* To show that not all codes require weights explicitly, we examine the XS 3 (excess 3) code presented in Table 4. The rule for generating this code requires that we use the NBCD code for a digit, call it $n_D$, and add the binary number 0011 (i.e., 3 in decimal) to it:

$$D \equiv n_D + 0011 \tag{11}$$

What use would there be for this code? It has two advantages:

1. No proper combination consists of all zeros; therefore no combination will be mistaken for a null transmission.
2. It is a self-complementing code.

A self-complementing code is very valuable because it possesses this quality: The combination for the complement of a digit is the complement of the combination for that digit. The complement of a number is needed when we do subtraction by addition and complementation. For decimal arithmetic this requires that we subtract the value of the digit from 9. In our binary code the complement of a combination $b_D$ is taken with respect to the largest valued combination; for a four-bit code, this would be 1111. Then, our definition for a self-complementing code is one for which the following holds:

$$9 - D \equiv 1111 - b_D \tag{12}$$

As an example of how XS 3 fulfills this requirement, we have

$$2 \equiv 0101, \quad 9 - 2 = 7,$$
$$1111 - 0101 = 1010, \quad 7 \equiv 1010 \tag{13}$$

## Natural Binary Coded Hexadecimal.

This code (NBCH) is what others have called simply the "hexadecimal code." Programmers normally deal with NBCH using bytes. The byte consists of eight bits or two halves, each consisting of four bits. If the combination for each half has a different symbol to represent it, then this simplifies the description. The binary values with decimal equivalent between 10 and 15 have been assigned the upper case letters *A* through *F* as shown in Table 1 in parentheses. Thus, the programmer can describe the byte consisting of 10110101 in hexadecimal as B5.

| | Table 5 2-out-of-5 Code | Table 6 Biquinary Code | Table 7 MBQ Code | Table 8 Gray Code |
|---|---|---|---|---|
| Weights | 74210 | 50 43210 | 5421 | |
| Digits | | | | |
| 0 | 11000 | 01 00001 | 0000 | 0000 |
| 1 | 00011 | 01 00010 | 0001 | 0001 |
| 2 | 00101 | 01 00100 | 0010 | 1001 |
| 3 | 00110 | 01 01000 | 0011 | 1101 |
| 4 | 01001 | 01 10000 | 0100 | 0101 |
| 5 | 01010 | 10 00001 | 1000 | 0111 |
| 6 | 01100 | 10 00010 | 1001 | 1111 |
| 7 | 10001 | 10 00100 | 1010 | 1011 |
| 8 | 10010 | 10 01000 | 1011 | 0011 |
| 9 | 10100 | 10 10000 | 1100 | 0010 |
| 10 | ---- | ------- | ---- | 1010 |
| 11 | ---- | ------- | ---- | 1110 |
| 12 | ---- | ------- | ---- | 0110 |
| 13 | ---- | ------- | ---- | 0100 |
| 14 | ---- | ------- | ---- | 1100 |
| 15 | ---- | ------- | ---- | 1000 |

## Other BCDs.

If we do not restrict ourselves to four-bit BCDs, we can provide one or more of the following advantages:

1. Error detection.
2. Simplicity of combination construction.
3. Simplicity of implementation in hardware.

*2-out-of-5 Code.* The 2-out-of-5 code provides the first advantage and is illustrated in Table 5. Every five-bit combination that represents a digit contains exactly two 1's. Since there are ten such permutations, this works out well. To assign each combination, we establish a set of five pseudo-weights. One of these weights, $W_1$, is 0, and the bit corresponding to this weight, $b_1$, should be set to 1 when the value of the digit being encoded corresponds to one of the nonzero weights; this is true for the digits 1, 2, 4, and 7. The weights work out for all digit values except 0; this digit uses bits with weights 7 and 4, which obviously do not sum to 0; hence, the term "pseudo-weights."

*Biquinary.* The biquinary code is a seven-bit code using exactly two 1's; it is illustrated in Table 6. One of the 1's is chosen from the left two bits; the other is chosen from the right five bits. The weights are used as would be expected. This code provides error detection whenever more than one "1" appears in either half of a combination, and also provides a logical progression from one combination to the next, which is useful for implementing arithmetic.

*MBQ Code.* The modified biquinary code (MBQ), illustrated in Table 7, is derived from biquinary by replacing the first two bits by a single bit, and the last five bits (which represent 0, 1, 2, 3, or 4) by three bits, which represent them in NBCD.

*Gray Code.* The Gray code, invented and patented by F. Gray, was developed to fill a particular requirement. Many of the devices designed to read information into the computer depended on the mechanical position of a shaft. Attached to the shaft was an encoder that produced electromechanical or optical signals corresponding to the shaft rotation. This created a transition problem. From Table 1 it is clear that the combination for 7 is 0111 and that for 8 is 1000. As the shaft rotated, the apparatus for reading out the position could not be depended upon to change simultaneously in each bit position. Thus, totally erroneous readings occurred. If $b_4$ goes to 1 before the other bits change in going from 7 to 8, the output would be read as 15.

To overcome the transition difficulty, a code was devised whereby successive combinations changed in exactly one-bit position only, as shown in Table 8. The Gray code is not the only one that does this, but it has long been a standby. The length of each combination $L$ is a function of the number ($N$) of discrete shaft positions to be encoded, as given by the formula

$$2^{L-1} < N \leq 2^L \quad (14)$$

Fig. 1 displays a code disk for the Gray code of Table 8, which indicates the change of one bit at a time.

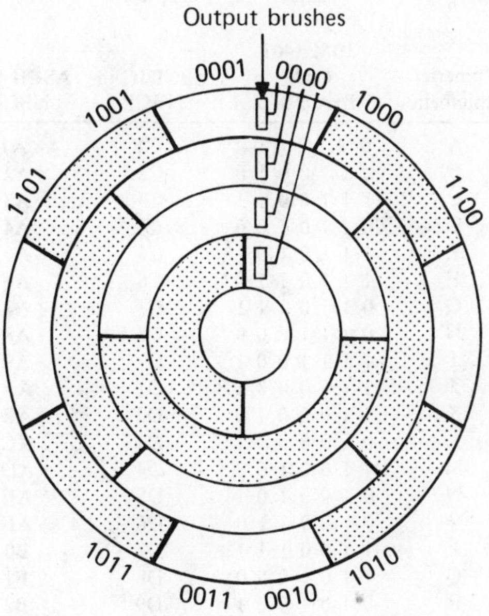

**Fig. 1.** The Gray code disk for Table 8.

**Full Alphabet.** Thus far we have restricted our symbol set Σ to decimal numerals. As computers went from infancy to early childhood, it was obvious they could be applied to accounting problems in which alphabetic output is mandatory, and where we encounter the following classes of symbols:

1. Letters: the alphabet from A to Z.
2. Numerals 0 through 9 (which we have already examined).
3. Punctuation.
4. Special symbols, which include &, @, $.

The question arose of how large or how small the symbol space should be. With six bits we can encode 64 symbols. Since most printers today have a 48-character set, why should we want more?

Perhaps the manufacturers have convinced industry that eight bits are really necessary because they need to represent lower-case letters, special symbols, control characters, and space to accommodate future requirements. This argument seems unconvincing. An estimated 30% inefficiency has been introduced into computers because of this standardization.

*Hollerith.* The Hollerith card code for IBM cards (which enables each column in the card to represent alphabetic, numeric, or symbolic information) is discussed in the article IBM Card.

*IBM 1401.* When the second generation IBM 1401 computer was developed, it was intended to replace electronic accounting machines that rely entirely on punched cards. Therefore, as expected, the code used in the 1401 computers, as given in Table 9, corresponds closely to the Hollerith code. We note the following:

1. Digit bits 1 through 9 in the 8421 columns are given by NCBD, but 0 is represented by 1010.
2. The bits $B$ and $A$ represent the three zone punches 12, 11, and 0 as follows: $BA = 11$ for 12, $= 10$ for 11, $= 01$ for 0, and $= 00$ for no zone punch.
3. The $C$ bit is the check bit (or parity bit,

| | Table 9 | Table 10 | Table 11 |
|---|---|---|---|
| Numeric/ Alphabetic | IBM 1401 Code C B A 8 4 2 1 | EBCDIC in NBCH | ASCII-8 in NBCH |
| A | 0 1 1 0 0 0 1 | C1 | A1 |
| B | 0 1 1 0 0 1 0 | C2 | A2 |
| C | 1 1 1 0 0 1 1 | C3 | A3 |
| D | 0 1 1 0 1 0 0 | C4 | A4 |
| E | 1 1 1 0 1 0 1 | C5 | A5 |
| F | 1 1 1 0 1 1 0 | C6 | A6 |
| G | 0 1 1 0 1 1 1 | C7 | A7 |
| H | 0 1 1 1 0 0 0 | C8 | A8 |
| I | 1 1 1 1 0 0 1 | C9 | A9 |
| J | 1 1 0 0 0 0 1 | D1 | AA |
| K | 1 1 0 0 0 1 0 | D2 | AB |
| L | 0 1 0 0 0 1 1 | D3 | AC |
| M | 1 1 0 0 1 0 0 | D4 | AD |
| N | 0 1 0 0 1 0 1 | D5 | AE |
| O | 0 1 0 0 1 1 0 | D6 | AF |
| P | 1 1 0 0 1 1 1 | D7 | B0 |
| Q | 1 1 0 1 0 0 0 | D8 | B1 |
| R | 0 1 0 1 0 0 1 | D9 | B2 |
| S | 1 0 1 0 0 1 0 | E2 | B3 |
| T | 0 0 1 0 0 1 1 | E3 | B4 |
| U | 1 0 1 0 1 0 0 | E4 | B5 |
| V | 0 0 1 0 1 0 1 | E5 | B6 |
| W | 0 0 1 0 1 1 0 | E6 | B7 |
| X | 1 0 1 0 1 1 1 | E7 | B8 |
| Y | 1 0 1 1 0 0 0 | E8 | B9 |
| Z | 0 0 1 1 0 0 1 | E9 | BA |
| 0 | 1 0 0 1 0 1 0 | F0 | 50 |
| 1 | 0 0 0 0 0 0 1 | F1 | 51 |
| 2 | 0 0 0 0 0 1 0 | F2 | 52 |
| 3 | 1 0 0 0 0 1 1 | F3 | 53 |
| 4 | 0 0 0 0 1 0 0 | F4 | 54 |
| 5 | 1 0 0 0 1 0 1 | F5 | 55 |
| 6 | 1 0 0 0 1 1 0 | F6 | 56 |
| 7 | 0 0 0 0 1 1 1 | F7 | 57 |
| 8 | 0 0 0 1 0 0 0 | F8 | 58 |
| 9 | 1 0 0 1 0 0 1 | F9 | 59 |

which is discussed in the following section, "Error Detection and Correction").

There are many other six-bit codes that are characteristic of the machine that employs them. They are generally listed in an appendix of the programmer's manual for the machine.

*EBCDIC.* The Extended Binary Coded Decimal Interchange Code (EBCDIC) is an eight-bit code developed by IBM and is available on all IBM 360 and IBM 370 computers. In fact, it is the only code used with the IBM 370. NBCH may be used to convey each combination, as shown in Table 10. Thus, *A* is represented by *C*1, which in turn means 11000001. A more complete discussion of EBCDIC appears elsewhere in this encyclopedia.

*ASCII.* The American Standard Code for Information Interchange (ASCII) is actually a seven-bit code. To make it an eight-bit code, it has been embedded into ASCII-8, a comparable eight-bit code. Table 11 displays the encoding of the important characters—letters and numerals. A more complete discussion is found elsewhere in this book.

*Contrast.* There is no clear superiority of either EBCDIC and ASCII-8, but there is an important difference. The collating sequence for EBCDIC has the numerals follow the letters; for ASCII-8, the reverse is true. Hence, documents coded and sorted under one system would be in a different order than if they were coded and sorted by the other.

**Error Detection and Correction.** In the case of biquinary, we have seen how a code can be constructed with error detection properties. This is helpful, and even necessary, in many situations, such as:

1. Information is transmitted from one site to another along lines where noise or other signal distortion might occur.
2. The data is recorded on a medium that is not impervious to noise so that 1's may get lost and be read as 0's, or 0's may be interpreted as 1's because of noise.
3. Devices within the computer may become faulty and create or destroy information.

*Parity.* The simplest means for detecting errors is to attach an extra bit to each combination of the code, called a "parity" bit. This bit is set to 0 or 1, according to the scheme used: For *odd* parity, the total number of 1's, including the parity bit, must be odd; for *even* parity, the total number of 1's, including the parity bit, must be 0 or even. An example of the use of an odd parity bit (also called a "check" bit), labeled *C*, is shown in Table 9. There are two phases in the use of the parity bit: creation and checking.

In the *creation phase*, the combination is examined and a parity bit is created so that the number of 1's in the total combination is proper. Now the combination can be transmitted from one place inside or outside the computer to another place. When it arrives there, the checking action follows. Circuitry similar to that for parity creation examines the combination exclusive of the parity bit as though it were creating that parity bit. If this developed bit and the accompanying parity bit coincide, a *single* bit error could not have occurred, and the information is accepted.

**Other Codes.** Many different kinds of computers have been built, and there are almost as many types of codes as there are computers. Further, some peripheral devices have their own codes. Magnetic tape usually uses the same code as that employed in the computer proper, but because magnetic tape is used for transmitting at densities and speeds approaching the limit of engineering capability, these devices are prone to error. A parity bit is added for each character of information. Thus, we find seven-track and nine-track tapes used with characters represented by six-bit and eight-bit codes, respectively, with the addition of a parity bit.

Punched paper tape devices that employ five-, six-, seven-, or eight-bit codes are available. The codes are usually peculiar to these devices.

Most typewriter consoles use a printing head that looks much like a golf ball. The head can tilt and rotate to get the proper character into position to strike the paper. To tell this golf ball at what angle to tilt and what angle to rotate, a *Tilt/Rotate code* (T/R) has been developed. Characters transmitted to the type mechanism in EBCDIC must be converted to the T/R code to activate the mechanism properly. It is interesting to note that when the operator presses a key on such a typewriter, he produces a character coded in the paper-tape transmission code. This is normally converted into EBCDIC for transmission to the computer; it is also translated into the T/R code to energize the print ball. The operator can verify that both translations have occurred successfully, since the key struck produces only a code character; it prints the character he wants only if the code and two translations of the code are all correct.

REFERENCE

1961. Peterson, W. W. *Error Correcting Codes*. Cambridge, Mass.: M.I.T. Press.

I. FLORES

## CODE, ERROR CORRECTING. *See* ERROR CORRECTING CODE.

## COGO. *See* PROBLEM-ORIENTED LANGUAGES.

## COLLATING SEQUENCE

For articles on related subjects *see* SORTING; and TABLE LOOKUP.
For articles on related terms *see ASCII; EBCDIC;* and KEY.

The American National Standard *Vocabulary for Information Processing* defines collating sequence as:

> An ordering assigned to a set of *items*, such that any two sets in that assigned order can be *collated.*

Collating, in the computer processing sense, derives from punched-card processing in which two decks of punched cards ordered in the same sequence on the same *key* are merged together (or collated), using a card collating machine. (The essence of the merging or collating methodology is explained elsewhere in this volume in the discussion of the merge search technique for table lookup).

Collating is often necessary in data processing applications; a good example is the collating of a set of updated records into a master file (or set) of records. This requires that both sets of records be ordered or sorted on a key in the same sequence (ascending or descending). This is illustrated by the following example of collating two sets into one, using a person's social security number as a key.

Set 1 (Updates)

| Key | Action |
|---|---|
| 408-44-6083 | Add |
| 414-22-3598 | Delete |
| 414-36-1776 | Add |

| Set 2 (Master) |
|---|
| 222-22-2222 |
| 333-33-3333 |
| 414-22-3598 |

| Set 3 (New Master after Collating and Updating) |
|---|
| 222-22-2222 |
| 333-33-3333 |
| 408-44-6083 |
| 414-36-1776 |

In the example given, a social security number (a supposedly unique identity number which is often used in the United States for identifying each person) is the key, and these numbers are collated in ascending numerical sequence.

In a general sense, a *collating sequence* must be considered when assigning codes to the various characters to be represented in a computing system in order that collating may also be done in non-numerical keys. For example, consider the ordering or sequence for this set of characters:

A, X, 2, 7, a, b, ?, /, #

It must be determined in what order the various graphic characters of the set are to take. The preceding characters would order as follows, using two common character representation schemes.

| ASCII (7 bit) | | IBM EBCDIC (8 bit) | |
|---|---|---|---|
| Character | Code | Character | Code |
| # | 010 0011 | / | 0110 0001 |
| / | 010 1111 | ? | 0110 1111 |
| 2 | 011 0010 | # | 0111 1011 |
| 7 | 011 0111 | a | 1000 0001 |
| ? | 011 1111 | b | 1000 0010 |
| A | 100 0001 | A | 1100 0001 |
| X | 101 1000 | X | 1110 0111 |
| a | 110 0001 | 2 | 1111 0010 |
| b | 110 0010 | 7 | 1111 0111 |

Of course alphabetization is achieved by ordering the binary codes representing the alphabetic characters. Also, codes representing the numbers should order properly, but the decision as to whether alphabetic characters should collate before or after numbers is somewhat arbitrary. The collating sequence for special characters is also an arbitrary choice, and various schemes are found in practice. ASCII (American Standard Code for Information Interchange) and EBCDIC (Extended Binary Coded Decimal Interchange Code) are perhaps the codes most often encountered, and the characters they represent will have a collating sequence corresponding to the value of the binary number code assigned to each character, as may be inferred from the tables in the articles on ASCII and EBCDIC.

When multiple characters are used to constitute a key for an item, the keys will collate in accordance with the composite character codes. For example, the name JOHNSON collates before JONES because the key representing JOHNSON has a lower value than the key for JONES. When EBCDIC codes are used, the keys for JOHNSON and JONES appear as follows (using a ten-character maximum length, left-justified key):

| Name | Key (in Hexadecimal) |
|---|---|
| JOHNSON | D1 D6 C8 D5 E2 D6 D5 40 40 40 |
| JONES | D1 D6 D5 C5 E2 40 40 40 40 40 |

Note that hexadecimal 40 (binary 0100 0000) represents a blank—the character used to pad out the key.

C. E. PRICE

## COMIT. *See* STRING PROCESSING LANGUAGES

## COMMAND AND JOB CONTROL LANGUAGES

For articles on related subjects *see* CATALOG; JOB; INPUT-OUTPUT DEVICES; LANGUAGE PROCESSORS; LINKAGE EDITOR; TERMINALS; and TIME SHARING.
For articles on related terms *see* CENTRAL PROCESSING UNIT; MULTIPROGRAMMING; OBJECT PROGRAM; OPERATING SYSTEMS; and SOURCE PROGRAM.

A command language (CL) or a job control language (JCL) is a language in which users of a data processing system (DPS) describe the requirement of their tasks (or job) to that system. Most data processing systems operate under the control of an operating system (OS). (Operating systems are also referred to as “monitors”, “supervisors”, and “command systems”.) The operating system is the prime interface between a DPS and its users. The users interact with a DPS via the command or job control language of its operating system. The term “command language” is most often used when speaking of a time-sharing or interactive DPS, while “job control language” is used primarily in relation to batch processing systems. Here, we will use the term “command language” to mean *both* CL and JCL.

More specifically, users of data processing systems employ the command language to:

1. Identify themselves to the system for security and accounting purposes, and, in some instances, to inform the DPS which data files and file catalogs are to be used in processing their respective tasks.

2. Inform the DPS about the particular resources required by their tasks (e.g., amounts of primary and secondary storage, language translator(s) to be used, expected amount of central processor time for each task).

3. Specify input/output (I/O) devices required by their tasks (e.g., magnetic tapes, disks, line printer, plotter), and define the manner in which the information is or should be organized (or formatted) on these devices.

4. Specify what action the DPS should take in exceptional cases (e.g., errors in programs, missing or incorrect input data, I/O device malfunctions).

In batch systems, CL statements also separate the task(s) of each user from the tasks of other users which are in the same batch of tasks (also known as a "job stream") to be executed by the DPS.

**Batch Command Languages.** Early batch DPSs had no operating systems and were capable of executing only one task at a time. As a result, users of these systems controlled the execution of their respective tasks themselves; while the DPS was executing their tasks, such users often acted as operators of the DPS, and controlled the operation of the entire system. As data processing systems grew in complexity (and therefore in cost), this mode of operation became no longer economically feasible. Simple operating systems were developed to allow the DPS to sequence automatically the various user's tasks through the system. These early, simple batch operating systems executed one task at a time, either to completion or until some error made it impossible to continue a task [Rosin (1969); Jardine (1975); Barron (1971, chap. 9)]. In the latter case, the operating system would usually give the user (via a printed report) some rudimentary indication of what went wrong, and would then immediately proceed to the next user's task. The user had only a very limited ability to affect the behavior of the operating system. The system simply sequenced various user's tasks through the DPS, giving up on any task that did not behave exactly according to the user's (and the system's) expectations.

These batch operating systems utilized the DPS more efficiently, but at the price of increasing the overhead on the user's time: They forced the users to work in a much more formal and regulated fashion, sometimes with large delays (turnaround time) between the time a job was submitted by the user and the time when the user received the corresponding output.

Because of the large cost of DPSs, further attempts at making their use more efficient and at increasing their throughput resulted in the development of multiprogramming operating systems, which allow several independent tasks to use the DPS simultaneously. Thus, one task may be performing calculations while a second task may be reading a magnetic tape; a third, reading cards; etc. In addition, such concurrently executing tasks can, for instance, access the same disk unit (each task, of course, using only those portions of the disk which the operating system has assigned to that task) or specify that their output is to be printed on the same printer (in which case, the output of each task is saved by the operating system on some secondary storage device (e.g., a disk) and then printed when the printer becomes available). This mode of operation requires the users to inform the operating system about the specific resources which their tasks require.

This evolution of multiprogramming has had several notable effects:

1. Use of the DPS became more efficient.

2. Users were forced to state explicitly (and a priori) the resource requirements of their tasks. Users must state these requirements in a formal way, through the facilities of the command language, as opposed to remembering them, writing them on pieces of paper as "instructions to the operator," or coding them directly into their programs. Users can no longer assume that each user task has total control of the DPS.

3. It became possible for users to state their requirements in a more abstract fashion. Thus, one can say, for instance, that a task requires *three tape drives*, and the operating system chooses the actual tape drives to be used each time that this task is executed. This tends to minimize the interference between various user tasks, and allows a DPS to continue operating even when some of its resources (e.g., a tape drive) are unavailable because of failure or other reasons. In this fashion, a certain amount of independence from the actual physical configuration of the DPS is achieved.

Thus, with the passage of time, it became necessary for users to be able to state their requirements to the operating system in a more and more rigorous and detailed fashion. Simultaneously, the complexity of user tasks grew. Users want operating systems to take care of exceptional conditions (e.g., errors in input data) automatically without necessarily giving up on their tasks. To accomplish this, operating systems have to be able to make decisions based on what happens to a task while it is executing, and therefore command languages have to allow the user to state the rules and conditions for making these decisions.

As a result, the complexity of the user's interface (i.e., the CL) with the operating system has grown to accommodate these needs. As additional capabilities became needed in CLs, they were added, often in purely ad hoc ways, resulting in CLs that are very flexible and powerful, but also very complex, difficult to learn, unnatural to use, nonsystematic, and very often needlessly so [IBM (1972); Brown (1970); Barron and Jackson (1972)].

This increase in complexity has had several results:

1. The need, in most big data processing centers, for one or more (often full-time) "CL experts."

2. The development of procedure capabilities in CLs; these facilities allow a user to invoke, in a relatively simple fashion, a set of complex CL statements (i.e., a CL procedure) which that user, another user, or, more often, a "CL expert" has developed and has "debugged," and which is stored in the DPS under a specific name.

3. The emergence of research aimed at developing the theory and design of more general, systematic, simpler, and easier to use CLs [Dolotta and Irvine (1969); SHARE (1972); Gram and Hertweck (1975)].

4. The recent emergence of attempts at standardizing CLs. The purpose of such standardization is to make CLs less machine-dependent, just as was done with several programming languages (e.g., Fortran, Cobol). In this context, see the concluding section below.

5. The increasing appeal to many users of timesharing DPSs; this is due to the fact that, in addition to some other important factors, these systems very often tend to have CLs that are easier to learn and to use than the more traditional batch DPSs. We will return to this point below.

The part of the operating system which interprets the user's CL statements is often referred to as a "command language interpreter." The cards on which CL statements are punched are called "control cards." In order to give the reader a better understanding of a contemporary batch CL, we show in Fig. 1 a very simple job deck, the purpose of which is to compile, link edit, and execute (under the operating system known as OS/VS2 [IBM, 1972]), a Fortran source program.

The first card of the deck gives the name of the job (SAMPLE), the user's account number (1234) and name (JOHNDOE), and the priority class (K) which the user is requesting for this job. The second card indicates that the cataloged (prestored) CL procedure FORTCLG (for Fortran Compile, Link edit, and Go; i.e., execute) is to be executed. (Fig. 2 is a listing of FORTCLG.) The third card in Fig. 1 is a Data Definition card (DD), and it indicates that the Fortran source program is next in the deck. After the Fortran source program comes another DD card indicating that the data cards required by the program during the execution (GO) job step are next in the deck. After the data cards comes an end-

```
//SAMPLE   JOB 1234,JOHNDOE,CLASS=K                                00000010
//JOBDECK EXEC FORTCLG                                             00000020
//FORT.SYSIN DD *                                                  00000030
 ...
 ...
 ...The Fortran source program to be compiled goes here.
 ...
 ...
//GO.SYSIN DD *                                                    00001000
 ...
 ...
 ...Data cards for the above Fortran program go here.
 ...
 ...
/*                                                                 00009000
//                                                                 00009999
```

**Fig. 1.** Example of a simple IBM OS/VS2 job deck.

of-data card (/*) and and end-of-job card (//). In large decks, all the cards are usually numbered so that a deck can be put back into proper order should it be dropped or otherwise shuffled.

When the DPS (in this case, an IBM System/370 operating under OS/VS2) reads this deck, it verifies that the account number given on the first (JOB) card is a valid one, and then stores the job until a time when all the resources required for the first job step are available. The cataloged procedure FORTCLG (shown in Fig. 2) controls the execution of the job. We will not explain this procedure in detail. We do observe, however, that it consists of 20 cards (the first three cards and the last card are simply comments, which the operating system ignores). Procedure FORTCLG invokes two prestored programs: IEYFORT for the FORT, Fortran compilation, step; and IEWLF440 for the LKED, link editing, step. For each job step, a number of additional files are specified by various, rather complex Data Definition (DD) statements, and various "default parameters" are set. These parameters specify various choices which the user can override, such as the amount of secondary storage space allocated to a specific file. Three of the statements (those starting on cards 50, 100, and 140) have to be continued on additional cards because of their length.

The first job step (FORT) compiles the Fortran source program (which follows card 30 in the deck shown in Fig. 1) into an object deck. If no errors are detected by the compiler, the second job step (LKED) link edits (combines) into a load module that object deck with other (already existing) programs required by that object deck. If this operation is successful, the load module is "loaded" (i.e., read) into the DPS main memory by the third job step (GO), and the user's program begins its execution, during which it presumably reads the data cards that follow card 1000 in the deck of Fig. 1.

Each job step produces output, which is stored on magnetic tape or disk. Some of that output is of a temporary nature and is discarded at the end of the job step. Other output (e.g., the object program) may be used by subsequent steps; still other output may be retained on disk or tape, as requested by the user, for subsequent use by other jobs. Finally, some output is usually returned, at a later time, to the user in the form of printouts and card decks.

Should any of the job steps run into some difficulty (e.g., errors in the source program), the printed output for that job step will so inform the user (occasionally in a rather cryptic fashion); and,

```
//*          -------------------------------------------------------------------- 00000010
//*          FORTCLG - FORTRAN COMPILE, LINK, AND EXECUTE.                        00000020
//*          -------------------------------------------------------------------- 00000030
//           PROC DECK=NODECK,SOURCE=,MAP=NOMAP,LOAD=LOAD,LIST=NOLIST             00000040
//FORT       EXEC PGM=IEYFORT,REGION=100K,                                        00000050
//                PARM='&DECK,&SOURCE,&MAP,&LOAD,&LIST'                           00000060
//SYSPRINT     DD SYSOUT=A                                                        00000070
//SYSPUNCH     DD SYSOUT=B                                                        00000080
//SYSLIN       DD UNIT=SYSDA,SPACE=(CYL,(1,1)),DISP=(,PASS)                       00000090
//LKED       EXEC PGM=IEWLF440 ,COND=(4,LT,FORT),REGION=96K,                      00000100
//                PARM=(XREF,LIST,LET)                                            00000110
//SYSLIB       DD DSN=&&FORTLIB1,DISP=(SHR,PASS)                                  00000120
//             DD DSN=&&FORTLIB2,DISP=(SHR,PASS)                                  00000130
//SYSLMOD      DD DSN=&&GOSET(GO),DISP=(,PASS),UNIT=SYSDA,                        00000140
//                SPACE=(CYL,(1,1,1))                                             00000150
//SYSPRINT     DD SYSOUT=A                                                        00000160
//SYSUT1       DD DSN=&&SYSUT1,UNIT=SYSSQ,SPACE=(1024,(100,50),,,ROUND)           00000170
//SYSLIN       DD DSN=*.FORT.SYSLIN,DISP=(OLD,DELETE)                             00000180
//             DD DDNAME=SYSIN                                                    00000190
//GO         EXEC PGM=*.LKED.SYSLMOD,COND=((4,LT,FORT),(4,LT,LKED))               00000200
//FT05F001     DD DDNAME=SYSIN                                                    00000210
//FT06F001     DD SYSOUT=A                                                        00000220
//FT07F001     DD SYSOUT=B                                                        00000230
//*          -------------------------------------------------------------------- 00000240
```

**Fig. 2.** Example of a simple IBM OS/VS2 cataloged procedure.

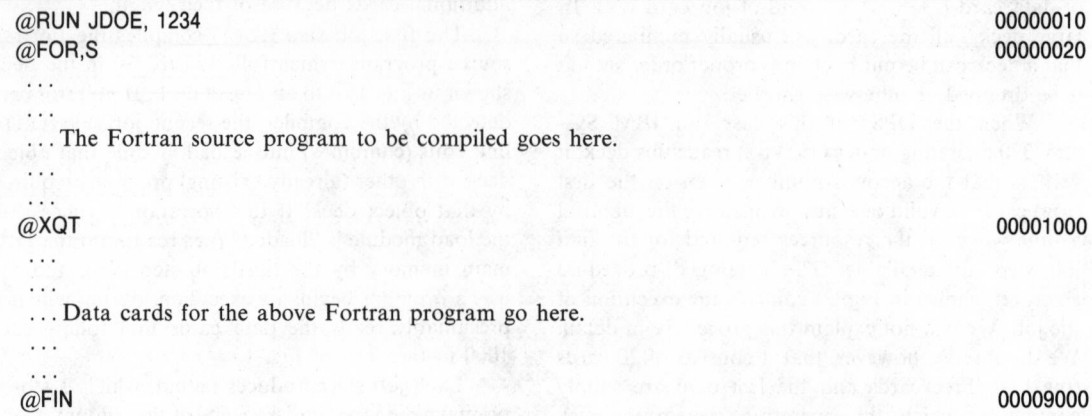

```
@RUN JDOE, 1234                                              00000010
@FOR,S                                                       00000020
...
...
...The Fortran source program to be compiled goes here.
...
...
@XQT                                                         00001000
...
...
...Data cards for the above Fortran program go here.
...
...
@FIN                                                         00009000
```

**Fig. 3.** Example of a simple UNIVAC EXEC-8 job deck.

at least in the example of Figs. 1 and 2, the job will be terminated at the end of that job step.

The reader should be warned that the OS/VS2 command language is probably the most complex CL in wide use today, and is very difficult to use. Barron and Jackson (1972) have said: "It is a language in which the articulate can speak powerful words of wisdom, but fluency is at the end of a long hard road." Many other batch CLs are significantly simpler, but also somewhat less flexible and versatile. The EXEC-8 CL, used on UNIVAC 1100 series of computers (UNIVAC, 1974), is an example of such a CL.

Fig. 3 shows an EXEC-8 job deck that is functionally quite analogous to the OS/VS2 deck of Fig. 1. The first (@RUN) card identifies the user (JDOE) and his account (1234). The second (@FOR) card requests the Fortran compilation of the immediately following Fortran source deck, and also requests a "short" (s) listing of that program. Card 1000 (@XQT) requests the execution of the just-compiled Fortran program, assuming that the compilation is error-free; the data for that execution follow the @XQT card. The @FIN card signals the end of the job.

**Time-Sharing Command Languages.** Command languages meant to be used in a time-sharing or interactive mode are usually very much simpler than batch command languages. There are several reasons for this:

1. In a time-sharing mode the user most often types in a single CL statement at a time, observes the results of that statement, and then decides what to do next. Thus, the user does not have to decide and explicitly state a priori what the system is to do under *all* possible conditions; he or she can make these decisions implicitly while interacting with the DPS.

2. The users interact directly and in real time with the DPS, as opposed to having to utilize the DPS through operators who submit their tasks.

3. Users of a time-sharing DPS are often geographically isolated from that DPS (e.g., by working at home). Under such conditions, simplicity and ease of use of the CL is a very important factor (Dolotta and Irvine, 1969).

4. Since CL statements are usually typed every time they are to be executed (as opposed to being punched on a cards that can be reused many times), it is vitally important that they be simple and short.

5. The DPS can guide the user by printing "prompting messages," thus making it less necessary for the user to remember all the details of the CL.

As a result, a great deal more attention has been paid to date to the human engineering aspects of time-sharing CLs than to that of batch CLs. In addition, time-sharing CLs and DPSs have a number of the better facilities found in batch systems. Thus, in many time-sharing CLs it is possible to construct and save cataloged command procedures for repeated use. In time-sharing DPSs, there is virtually no use made of card decks; all users' data files and programs are stored on line. Editing programs are usually provided in a DPS to allow users to conveniently create, examine, and modify their on-line files of programs and data.

We will again use an example to give the flavor of a modern time-sharing CL [Ritchie and Thompson (1974)]. Fig. 4 is a *verbatim* record of a short

```
login: janedoe
Password:
12/13/74 - System off the air after 19:00 for preventive maintenance!
% date
Fri Dec 13 18:48:24 EST 1974
% ed quad.f
1752
/Cong/
    54      format ('Conjugate roots; real  = ',1pg16.6,' imag. = ',1pg16.6)
s/g/j/p
    54      format ('Conjugate roots; real = ',1pg16.6,' imag. = ',1pg16.6)

w
1752
q
% fc quad.f
% mv a.out quad
% quad

Please enter the values of a, b, and c:
1 -2 1
a =      1.00000     b =    -2.00000     c =     1.00000
Double real root; root =      1.00000

Please enter the values of a, b, and c:
1e4 2e3 3e2
a =      10000.0     b =     2000.00     c =     300.000
Conjugate roots; real =    -0.100000    imag. =      0.141421

Please enter the values of a, b, and c:
,,-6.25
a =      0.00000     b =     0.00000     c =    -6.25000
==> Coefficients imply that   -6.25000      = 0   (?!)

Please enter the values of a, b, and c:
1,,-6.25
a =      1.00000     b =     0.00000     c =    -6.25000
Two real roots; first =      2.50000     second =    -2.50000

Please enter the values of a, b, and c:
1.667e-3 6.375e+5
a =      1.667000e-03 b =     637500.     c =     0.00000
Two real roots; first = 0 second =    -3.824236e+08

Please enter the values of a, b, and c:

a =      0.00000     b =     0.00000     c =     0.00000
All coefficients are zero. Program terminated.

% date
Fri Dec 13 18:51:07 EST 1974
%
```

**Fig. 4.** A short terminal session with a time-sharing DPS.

```
c   quad.f - interactive Fortran program to solve quadratic equations of
c   the form: a*x**2 + b*x + c = 0; the following cases are considered:
c            if a≠0 & c≠0              = => general case              (500);
c            if a≠0 & c=0              = => roots are 0 and -b/a      (400);
c            if a=0 & b≠0              = => only root is -c/b         (300);
c            if a=0 & b=0 & c≠0        = => input error               (200);
c            if a=0 & b=0 & c=0        = => terminate program.
 100     write (6,10)
   10      format (/,'Please enter the values of a, b, and c:')
         read (5,12) a, b, c
   12      format (3g16.6)
         write (6,14) a, b, c
   14      format ('a = ',1pg16.6,' b = ',1pg16.6,' c = ',1pg16.6)
         if (a .ne. 0.0 .and. c .ne. 0.0) goto 500
           if (a .ne. 0.0) goto 400
             if (b .ne. 0.0) goto 300
               if (c .ne. 0.0) goto 200
                 write (6,18)
   18              format ('All coefficients are zero. Program terminated.',/)
                 stop
 200           write (6,20) c
   20            format ('= => Coefficients imply that ',1pg16.6,' = 0 (?!)')
               goto 100
 300         x = -c/b
             write (6,30) x
   30          format ('Single real root; root = ',1pg16.6)
             goto 100
 400       x = -b/a
           write (6,40) x
             format ('Two real roots; first = 0 second = ',1pg16.6)
           goto 100
c                   General case (a and c are both nonzero)
 500     x = -b/(2.0*a)
         disc = b**2 - 4.0*a*c
         srdisc = sqrt(abs(disc))/(2.0*a)
         if (disc .gt. 0.0) goto 560
           if (disc .lt. 0.0) goto 540
             write (6,52) x
   52          format ('Double real root; root = ',1pg16.6)
             goto 100
 540       write (6,54) x, srdisc
   54        format ('Congugate roots; real = ',1pg16.6,' imag. = ',1pg16.6)
           goto 100
 560     x1 = x + srdisc
         x2 = x - srdisc
         write (6,56) x1, x2
   56      format ('Two real roots; first = ',1pg16.6,' second = ',1pg16.6)
         goto 100
         end
```

**Fig. 5.** A simple Fortran source program (adapted from Kernighan and Plauger, 1974).

"terminal session" with such a system; *except that*, for ease of understanding, we have underlined everything that was typed by the user. The purpose of this session is, again, to compile and execute an already existing Fortran program.

As soon as the user has dialed-up the DPS from a terminal, the system asks for a "login" code, which the user types (*janedoe*). The system then asks for the user's secret password to make sure that the user is indeed the person who is authorized to log into the system with the code *janedoe*; at this point, the DPS also turns off the printing mechanism of the terminal, thus preserving the secrecy of the password by making it invisible. Once the user has entered the correct password, the printing is turned back on, and the user is informed, via a "message of the day," that the system will be unavailable after 7 P.M. The percent sign (%) is a system-prompting message, or "prompt," for the next command. The user asks for the *date* (knowing that this will cause the system to print both the date and the time). Observing that there is still in excess of 11 minutes before the system is to shut down, the user continues with the substance of the session.

The next command indicates that the user wishes to edit (*ed*) a Fortran source program that is stored in an on-line file called *quad.f*, the contents of which are shown in Fig. 5. The system reads this file and acknowledges the request by printing the number of characters in that file (*1752*). (Note that, unlike most batch systems, most interactive systems accept both upper and lower-case input; this is possible because most interactive terminals (unlike card punches) can type in both upper and lower case.) The user asks the editing program (the "editor") to find a source statement that contains the letters *Cong*; the system prints that line; the user corrects the typographical mistake by substituting (*s*), the first occurrence of the letter *g* by the letter *j* and printing (*p*) the corrected line. Satisfied with the result, the user writes out (*w*) the modified program onto on-line storage; the system reports that the length of the file is still 1752 characters. The user then quits (*q*) using the editor; the system prompts for the next command via the percent sign. The user asks that the just-modified file be compiled by the Fortran compiler (*fc*); the compiler, having found no errors, causes the system to make a load module from the resulting object program (leaving that load module in a file called, by convention, *a.out*), and then to prompt for the next command. The user moves (*mv*) the load module *a.out* to a file called *quad* (so that it will not be overwritten next time she or he uses the compiler); and then, simply by typing the name of that module (*quad*), causes it to be executed.

At this point, the compiled Fortran program begins interacting with the user. The purpose of this program is to solve quadratic equations of the form $ax^2 + bx + c = 0$, given the values of the coefficients $a$, $b$, and $c$. The program prompts the user for the first set of coefficients, which the user types in. The program "echoes" the values of the coefficients ($a$ = 1.00000 . . .), prints the type of the solution and the value of the root (1.00000), and prompts for the next set of coefficients. The user solves three more equations, making a mistake on the second one of these, and thus having to do it over. Note that if the user does not supply the values of one or more coefficients, then these coefficients are automatically set to zero. Furthermore, the Fortran program assumes that it is to terminate itself if all three coefficients are zero (see the three lines immediately above statement 200 in Fig. 5). Therefore, the user terminates the program by simply typing an empty (blank) line. At this point, the system prompts for the next command. The user asks again for the time, discovers that the session lasted a bit under 3 minutes, and instead of entering another command, turns off the terminal, thus disconnecting it from the DPS.

**General Observations.** Unlike programming languages (e.g., Fortran), command languages available for various computer vendors' DPSs have very little in common with each other; for example, as can be deduced from Figs. 1 and 3, there is no compatibility between IBM OS/VS2 CL and UNIVAC EXEC-8 CL. In fact, even the terminology used to describe the various CL facilities is different between the two. Therefore, while it is relatively easy to convert a Fortran program from one of these systems to the other, the conversion of the corresponding CL statements is very difficult. This situation leads to a great deal of inefficiency, and is a very unfortunate one.

It is becoming more and more common to provide both batch and time-sharing services on the same DPS. Users of some of these systems [IBM (1970), IBM (1972)] often are faced with the need to learn two CLs if they wish to use the system in both modes. Furthermore, since the two CLs in such a system must coexist (e.g., be able to access the same files), both tend to be less than optimal for their respective tasks. For historical reasons, in such a situation the time-sharing CL usually "lives under" the batch CL and must adjust to it, acquiring in the process many of the undesirable characteristics of its "parent" (IBM, 1970).

On the other hand, because the state-of-the-art in the area of CL design and implementation is still relatively rudimentary, it is not clear that attempts at standardizing CLs (OSCLTG, 1975) are desirable at this time. It is conceivable that such premature standardization of CLs might in fact slow down progress in this area.

Nonetheless, it is likely that CLs in the future will be designed in more systematic ways and with more attention being paid to human engineering factors than has been the case in the past.

### References

1969. Dolotta, T. A., and C. A. Irvine, "Proposal for a Time-Sharing Command Structure," *Information Processing* Vol. 68, pp. 493–498. Amsterdam: North Holland Publishing.

1969. Rosin, R. F. "Supervisory and Monitor Systems," *Computing Surveys*, Vol. 1, No. 1, pp. 37–54.

1970. Brown, G. D. *System/360 Job Control Language*. New York: John Wiley.

1970. Data Processing Division, IBM Corp. *IBM System/360 Operating System: Time-Sharing Option Command Language Reference*. Form GC28-6732. White Plains, N.Y.: IBM.

1971. Barron, D. W. *Computer Operating Systems*. London: Chapman and Hall; New York: Barnes and Noble.

1972. Barron, D. W., and I. R. Jackson. "The Evolution of Job Control Languages," *Software—Practice & Experience*, Vol. 2, No. 2, pp. 143–164.

1972. Data Processing Division, IBM Corp. *OS/VS JCL Reference*. Form GC28-0618. White Plains, N.Y.: IBM.

1972. SHARE Inc. "Command Language Position Paper." SSD No. 221, Serial No. C-5647, April 15, 1972; also SSD No. 226, Serial No. C-5715, Sept. 25, 1972. Chicago, Ill.

1974. Kernighan, B. W., and P. J. Plauger. *The Elements of Programming Style*. New York: McGraw-Hill.

1974. Ritchie, D. M., and K. Thompson. "The UNIX Time-Sharing System," *Communications of the ACM*, Vol. 17, No. 1, pp. 365–375.

1974. UNIVAC DIVISION, Sperry Rand Corp. *UNIVAC 1100 Series Operating System Programmer Reference*. Form UP-4144, Rev. 3. Blue Bell, Pa.

1975. Gram, C., and F. R. Hertweck. "Command Languages: Design Considerations and Basic Concepts," in C. Unger (Ed.), *Command Languages*. Amsterdam: North Holland; New York: American Elsevier, pp. 43–69.

1975. Jardine, D. A. "The Structure of Operating System Control Languages," in C. Unger (Ed.), in *Command Languages*. Amsterdam: North Holland; New York: American Elsevier, pp. 27–42.

1975. OSCLTG. "The Operating Systems Command Language Task Group Technical Report," in C. Unger (Ed.), *Command Languages*, Amsterdam: North Holland; New York: American Elsevier, pp. 353–388.

T. A. Dolotta

# COMMUNICATION CONTROL UNIT

For articles on related subjects *see* Channel; Data Communications; Data Communication Networks; Front End; Multiplexing; Teleprocessing Systems; and Terminals.

Modern large-scale computers generally have the capability of accepting data or jobs originating from remote terminals or computers. This necessitates some form of a data communication network to transmit the data. Such a network consists of a set of nodes connected by a set of links as shown in Fig. 1. The nodes may be the host computer(s), terminals or some type of communication control units, while the links are the communication channels, which are usually private or switched lines leased from a common carrier. Because transmission over these lines is generally analog, while the signals at the nodes must be digital, data sets are used to provide the interface between node and link.

The name "Communication Control Unit" is vague. It may include such units as message switchers, remote terminal controllers, concentrators, front-end communication controllers, or simple multiplexers. The latter are usually hardwired units, while the first four may be hardwired or programmable, in which case they are computers programmed to perform various communication-oriented tasks. Such computers are referred to as "communication processors." The main function of these controllers is to increase the efficiency and decrease the cost of the total network.

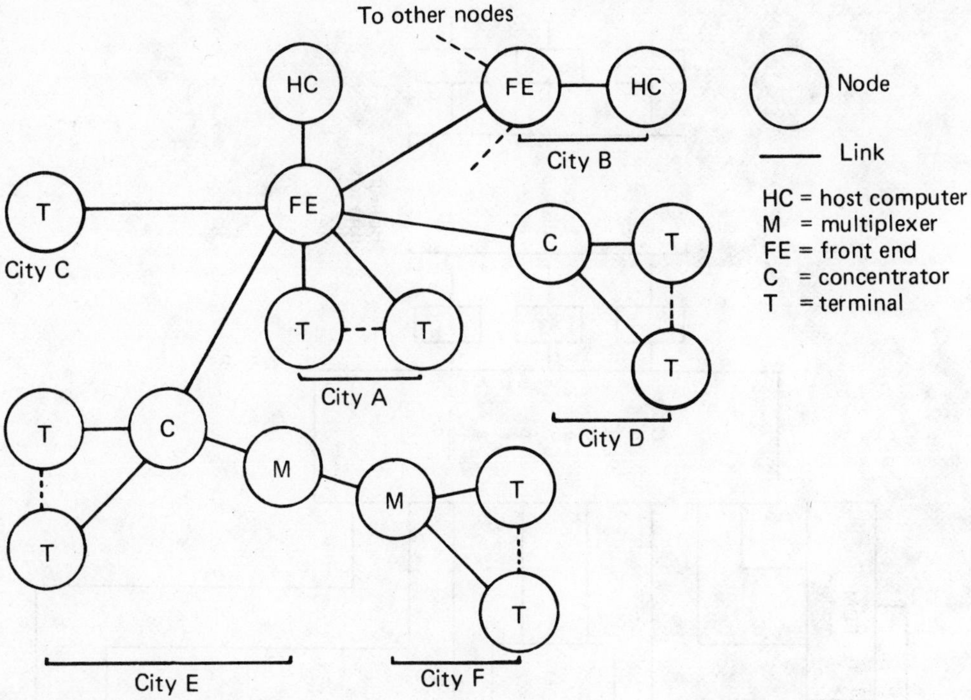


**Fig. 1.** Example of a data communication network.

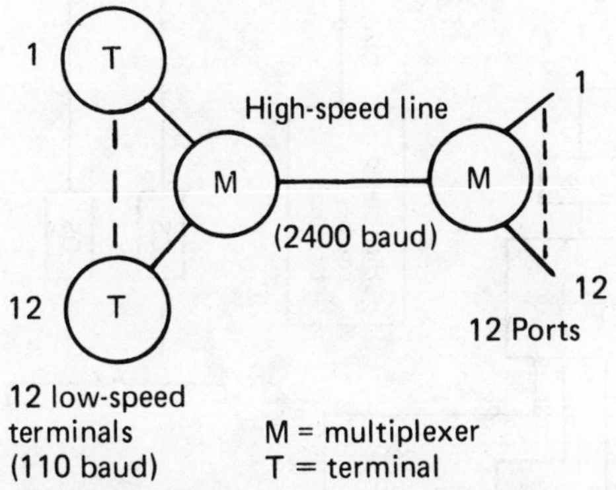


**Fig. 2.** Example of the use of multiplexer.

**Multiplexers.** Multiplexing permits the transmission of several lower-bandwidth data streams over a single higher-bandwidth line, as shown in Fig. 2. There are two basic techniques: frequency division multiplexing (FDM) and time division multiplexing (TDM). FDM divides the frequency spectrum of a line into several smaller frequency bands. Data from terminals is sent over these smaller bands by frequency-shift keying. At the receiving end, the various frequency bands will be reconverted into their original data by means of bandpass filters. TDM is very similar to the action of a commutator. Each terminal is sampled one by one for one "bit time" in round-robin fashion, and the samples are assembled into a serial data stream. At the receiving end the serial stream is disassembled and the data is routed to the correct terminal or computer port.

Multiplexers are usually simple hardwired units. Their main use is in reducing line costs through reduction of the number of lines needed to handle remote terminals.

**Concentrators.** The term "concentrator" is usually reserved for a small computer programmed to perform the task of a multiplexer. In practice, terminals do not transmit or receive data at maximum bit rates over sustained periods of time. Since the FDMs and TDMs have no buffering, they must be capable of handling data under worst-case conditions, that is, at maximum bit rates. Because of its stored program flexibility and buffering capability, a concentrator can pack the higher-speed line to its maximum capacity. This allows the concentrator to multiplex more low-speed lines onto a given line having a higher speed than an FDM or TDM system. The buffering absorbs the peak loads, while occasionally sustained peak loads can be accommodated by software. This may be done by tem-

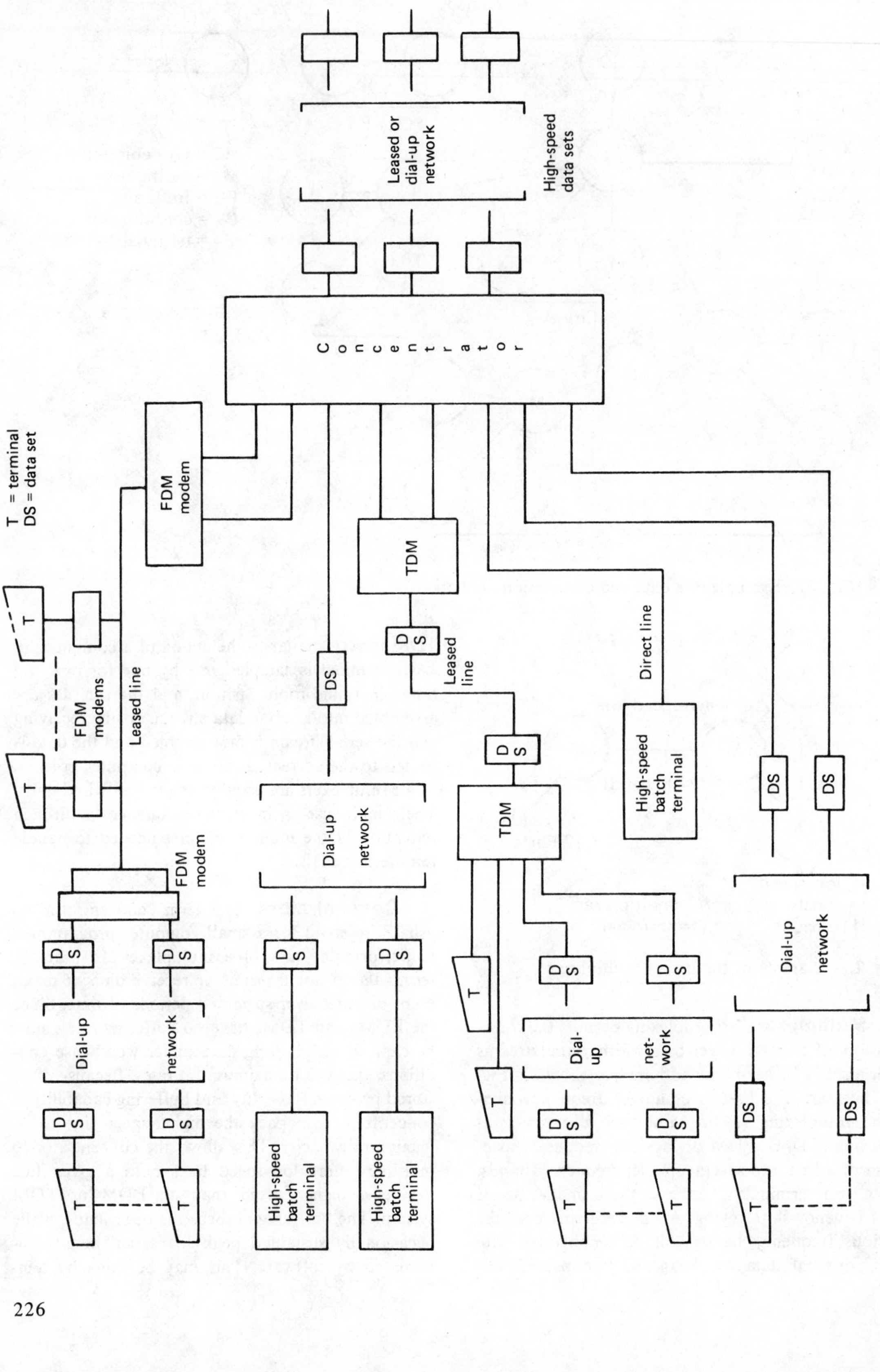


**Fig. 3.** A concentrator supporting a large variety of local and remote terminals.

porarily inhibiting transmission to some terminals or sending a command to a terminal to reduce its transmission.

Even though a concentrator is more expensive than a simple multiplexer, it can be far more efficient. Moreover, it can be programmed to perform additional tasks such as control of local terminals, code conversion, line polling, error detection, and other control functions at no additional hardware cost. Furthermore, interfaces may be built to enable it to accept data from a far wider range of local or remote equipment than could a conventional hardwired multiplexer.

Fig. 3 shows a concentrator accepting data from a number of terminals of various types and concentrating it onto three high-speed lines. The terminals are connected to the concentrator by dial-up, leased or direct lines as in the case of the local high-speed batch terminal. Notice the flexibility afforded by the TDM and the FDM. The former supports local and dial-up terminals at the remote end. The FDM modem may also support local or dial-up terminals. Furthermore, the leased line may pass through several cities, each of which may have a "drop" to a terminal. Such use of leased lines is known as "multidropping."

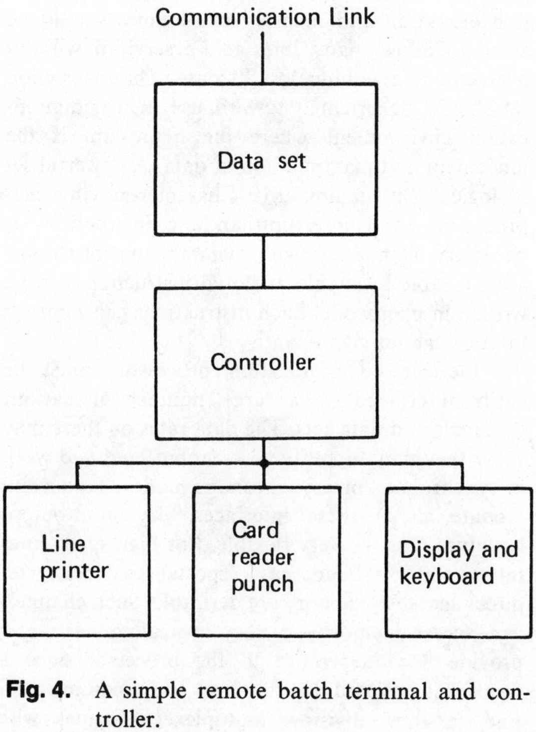


**Fig. 4.** A simple remote batch terminal and controller.

**Remote Terminal Controllers.** Some types of remote terminals require sophisticated controllers. An example is a bank of several CRT terminals or a remote batch-processing station consisting of a line printer and card reader/punch, as shown in Fig. 4. Again, such controllers may be hardwired or programmable. The latter are becoming more attractive because of their flexibility. Thus, they may be programmed to emulate IBM, CDC, or UNIVAC batch-processing stations merely by a program change. Their use as "intelligent terminals" is also becoming popular.

**Front-End Communication Controllers.** These provide the interface between the main computer and the communication network, as shown in Fig. 5. In the past these were hardwired, and consequently the mechanism of data transfer for the various terminals, error control, and data set control required a large amount of host computer resources in the form of CPU time and core space. These hardwired controllers are often called "transmission control units." A programmable unit is usually referred to as a front end processor or simply as the front end. Programmable front ends are becoming more and more popular because they are usually lower in cost and provide far better performance. Many of the functions (such as code conversion, message assembly, and editing) that were previously handled by the host computer may now be pro-

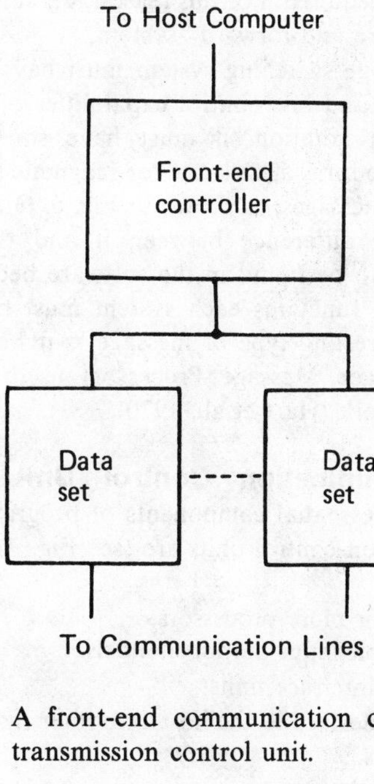


**Fig. 5.** A front-end communication controller or transmission control unit.

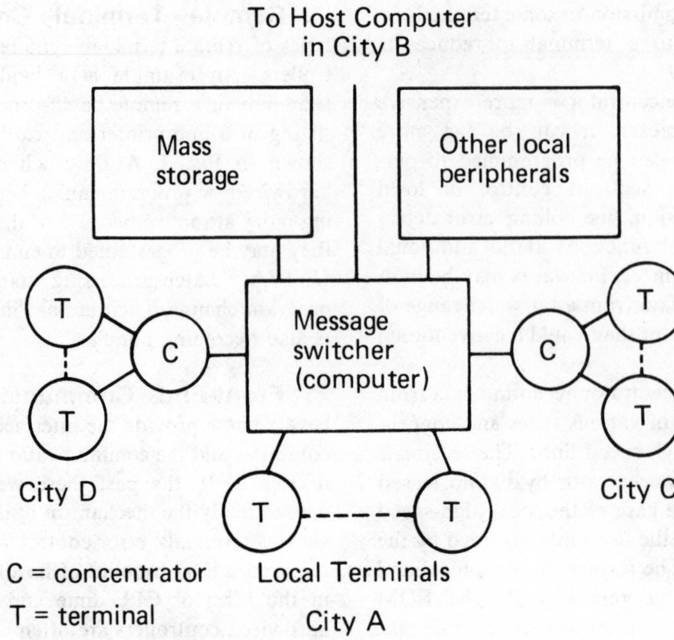


**Fig. 6** A simple message-switching system.

grammed and handled by the front end. Overhead on the main system is thus reduced.

**Message Switchers.** A message switching system essentially accepts data from a large number of terminals, stores it, and then forwards it to other terminals as required. For this reason it is sometimes called a "store and forward" system.

A message switching system must have all the input-output and line control capabilities of a concentrator. In addition, it must have some mass storage in the form of disk and/or magnetic tape for the various messages, as shown in Fig. 6. Otherwise, the essential difference between it and the concentrator is to be found in the software because of the different functions each system must perform.

An interesting type of message switcher is the IMP (Interface Message Processor) used on the ARPA network (Hart et al., 1970).

**Communication Control Unit Hardware.** The essential components of programmable communcation control units are (see Fig. 7):

1. One or more processors.
2. Flexible input-output channels.
3. Line interface units.
4. An interface to the host computer in the case of front ends.

The processor is a small stored program computer with data channels. The memory should be large enough to store the required program and provide adequate buffering for all lines. The instruction execution and memory cycle times should be small to allow many lines to be serviced without overruns, i.e., without loss of data. The instruction set should be oriented toward use in a communication environment where the main aim is the movement and manipulation of data. A powerful set of logical, bit manipulative, character-moving, list-processing, and interrupt-handling instructions is necessary. Computers with dynamic control storage are desirable to enable "tailored instructions" to be written in microcode. Such instructions can improve the throughput significantly.

Flexible communication processors must be easily interfaced to a large number of various terminals and data sets. The data rates on these may vary; they may be buffered or unbuffered and work in synchronous or asynchronous modes. To accommodate all of these interfaces, the input-output structure must be very flexible. For high-speed lines (above 40,000 baud, say), special channels with direct access to memory are desirable. Such channels can access memory on a cycle-stealing basis and provide no interference to the processor once a transfer is initiated. For the low- and medium-speed line, a time division multiplexer channel with maskable multilevel interrupts and short interrupt response times is desirable. The address and status of the interrupt-causing device should be available quickly, and branching to the routine servicing the interrupt should be rapid. This may be accomplished by automatic swapping of current and new "program status words" that reflect the location of the instruction to be executed, the condition code, and the state of the interrupt masks. Several such program status words should be provided, one for each type of interrupt. The handshaking on the high- and low-speed bus should be as simple as possible to ease the design of the various interfaces to terminals and data sets (modems).

The interface units link the channels with the terminals or data sets terminating the communication lines. A general-purpose interface should be speed-independent and handle synchronous or asynchronous transmission. Because of the wide variety of speeds, this is not always possible. To simplify hardware, two or three different types of interface units are usually built, each optimized for a given speed range. Control of data sets and terminals is done by hardware or software, usually the latter. The hardware inputs data-set status and outputs control signals. The software senses this status, interprets it, and outputs appropriate control signals. The processing is small but the flexibility is high, since any changes in equipment may be accommodated by appropriate changes in software. This makes the interface equipment independent and prolongs the usability of the system.

Since transmission between nodes is usually serial by bit, while on the bus it is parallel, the interface must perform the necessary conversion (character assembly and disassembly). This also may be done by software or hardware. Assembly by software results in a very cheap interface, since the characters are actually assembled in core, but the software overhead is high. This overhead is greatly reduced when hardware conversion or sampling is used. When the hardware has assembled or disassembled a character, an interrupt is generated and the computer fetches this character or sends the next one for disassembly. This technique is always used for high-speed lines and, considering the current

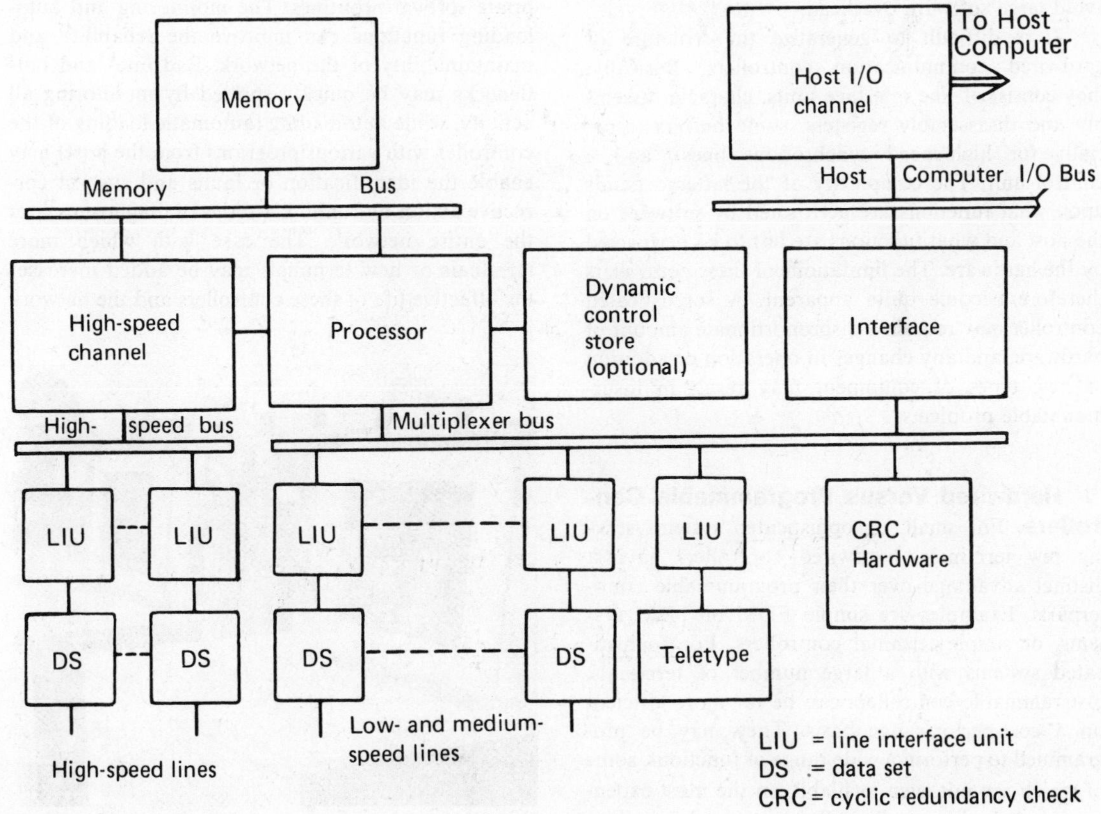


**Fig. 7.** Block diagram of a programmable front end.

prices of circuits, it is economical even for a large number of low-speed lines.

An interface to the host computer is required for front ends. A multiple address or a single address interface may be used. In a multiple address interface, each address corresponds to a terminal. In a single address interface, the address corresponds to the front end. In the single address case, as characters are passed between the front end and the host, they must be accompanied by an "address field" specifying the terminal to or from which they are coming. With a modest number of terminals, multiple address interfaces are more common. As the number of terminals becomes very large, the single address interface will become more popular.

A simple, programmable front end is shown in the block diagram of Fig. 7. Other types of programmable controllers would be similar, but they would not require the interface to the host. Note the Cyclic Redundancy Check (CRC) hardware in Fig. 7. Error control is very important in these systems; consequently, some form of error detection is usually included. If a cyclic code is used, evaluating the CRC characters by hardware is very common to avoid large software overhead.

It is difficult to generalize the structure of hardwired communication controllers. Basically, they consist of line interface units, character assembly and disassembly registers, some buffers (especially for high-speed synchronous lines), and a control unit. The complexity of the latter depends upon what functions are performed by software on the host and what functions are left to be performed by the hardware. The limitations of these controllers therefore become quite apparent. A sophisticated controller may require a disproportionate amount of hardware, and any changes in operation or addition of new types of equipment may result in insurmountable problems.

**Hardwired Versus Programmable Controllers.** For small, unsophisticated systems serving few terminals, hardwired controllers have a distinct advantage over their programmable counterparts. Examples are simple FDM or TDM systems, or simple terminal controllers. For sophisticated systems with a large number of terminals, programmable controllers can be far more efficient on a cost-performance basis. They may be programmed to perform a wide range of functions, some of which are not even available on the most expensive hardwired controllers. Some of these functions include:

1. Line polling and control.
2. Adaptive line-speed control.
3. Code conversion.
4. Message assembly and editing.
5. Error control.
6. Data compression.
7. Simple syntax checking.
8. Automatic loading of network programs from the host.
9. Line monitoring.
10. Buffering and concentrating.
11. Message recording.
12. Message answering and routing.

These functions, and many more, relieve the host, allowing it more time for data processing. It should be remembered, however, that as more of these functions are performed by the controller, the fewer lines it can handle.

Besides relief of the host, there are other indirect advantages to programmable controllers. One of these is terminal independency. A terminal not supported by the host may be made to appear like another terminal that is supported by having appropriate software routines. The monitoring and autoloading functions can improve the reliability and maintainability of the network. Bad lines and bottlenecks may be quickly spotted by monitoring all activity, while autoloading (automatic loading of the controller with various programs from the host) may enable the identification of faults and suggest corrective action by running a series of diagnostics over the entire network. The ease with which more terminals or new terminals may be added increases the effective life of these controllers and the network

**Fig. 8.** IBM 3704 transmission control units.

as a whole. This, together with the relief provided to the host, also enables the latter to have a longer useful life.

Although the above advantages make programmable controllers very attractive, they have not been around long enough for their capabilities to be fully assessed and exploited. One reason for this is that the operating system on the host has been oriented, in the past, toward hardwired controllers. This will change rapidly in the years to come.

**Future Trends and Conclusions.** The advent of independent data channels and multiprogramming enabled computers to support simultaneously many remote terminals. This resulted in the development of data communication networks, requiring several different types of communication control units. In the past these tended to be hardwired. As the networks grew, these controllers became very costly and imposed large overhead on the host. This, together with decreasing costs of small computers, led to the development of programmable controllers, which are more flexible and can be programmed to perform a wide variety of functions at lower cost. Thus, a single programmable controller could simultaneously be a terminal controller for some local terminals and a concentrator or message switcher for some of the remotes. Such flexibility will result (in some cases it already has) in announcements of new programmable controllers neatly integrated with the network and the host computer. The new teleprocessing systems will reflect this change. They will be simpler and will greatly improve the efficiency of the host.


REFERENCES

1970. Heart, F. E., et al."The Interface Message Processor for the ARPA Computer Network," *AFIPS Conference Proceedings*, Spring Joint Computer Conference, pp. 551–567.

1971. Sobolewski, J. S. "Programmable Communication Processors,"*First International Conference on Computer Communication*, Washington, D.C., October, pp. 380–389.

1972. Ball, C. J. "Communications and the Minicomputer,"*Computer*, September, pp. 13–21.


J. S. SOBOLEWSKI

**COMMUNICATIONS.** *See* DATA COMMUNICATION NETWORKS; and DATA COMMUNICATIONS.

## COMMUNICATIONS AND COMPUTERS

For articles on related subjects *see* ARPA NETWORK; COMMUNICATION CONTROL UNIT; COMPUTER NETWORKS; DATA COMMUNICATIONS; and PACKET SWITCHING.
For articles on related terms *see* BLOCK DIAGRAM; and STORED PROGRAM CONCEPT.

The first truly automatic digital computers were a direct outgrowth of the telecommunications switching art, using electromechanical components common to telephone central offices. Today the situation is reversed, with the computer imposing the new requirements and technology on telecommunications, and on switches in particular. In this article we consider the utilization of computers within communications networks.

Computers are predominantly used in communications networks as switches, or to control switches. In the first case, which is restricted to data communications, the computers are the switching nodes of the network. The interconnections and line capacities are determined by the geographical distributions of the message traffic. Each switching computer accepts messages from data terminals or other computers and records it in transient memory, where it is held until a communications channel is available to the computer serving the message destination. Multiple addressing is possible for any message. This type of switching is known as "store and forward," or "message," switching. In the second case, the computer controls equipment (commonly called the "matrix") that makes a metallic connection between origin and destination. The subscriber then uses the end-to-end communication channel capacity to transmit his information, either voice or data. (Today, voice traffic predominates.) There are also computers used as communication front ends, concentrators, etc., but these are auxiliary to the dominant roles above.

**Computers in Message Switching.** Fig. 1 shows the main functional elements of a typical message switch. Incoming messages are buffered in the incoming line buffers. These buffers need provide only relatively limited storage to accommodate small delays in the availability of the main processor, which must share its capacity with many other assigned tasks. The message is placed in memory, and the address portion of the message (also known as the "leader") is extracted. Depending upon the sophistication of the system, the address may be in a language that closely resembles English for the convenience of the user or close to machine language for more automated data systems. In any case, the computer can provide many service features such as inserting multiple addresses from an abbreviated code word and a standard list, giving priorities to authorized messages, permanent storage for record, and code conversion for different terminals where one terminal might use an older 5-bit per character code and the other a modern 8-bit per character code. Upon completion of the required processing the messages are outputted to the selected trunk via a small output buffer. Obviously not all messages will require the same processing time, and the size of the buffers and the message handling capacity are highly dependent upon processing rate. To design a switch properly requires knowledge of the theory of stochastic processes and "birth-death" processes in particular (Feller, 1967).

The analysis of switch performance must proceed from basic assumptions about the statistics of the messages the switch is being asked to process. The most commonly made assumptions are: The messages arrive at random and their distribution function is Poisson, with some average arrival rate $\lambda$; the switch completion rate is also random, with an exponential distribution function and an average completion rate $\mu$. Using these assumptions, which many years of telephone traffic engineering have shown to be remarkably accurate, the following formulas can be derived (Hillier and Lieberman, 1967):

1. Expected input queue plus traffic in process length, $L$.
2. Expected input queue length, $L_q$.
3. Expected waiting time in system, $W$.
4. Expected waiting time in input queue, $W_q$.

$$L = \frac{\lambda}{\mu - \lambda} \tag{1}$$

$$L_q = \frac{\lambda^2}{\mu(\mu - \lambda)} \tag{2}$$

$$W = \frac{1}{\mu - \lambda} \tag{3}$$

$$W_q = \frac{\lambda}{\mu(\mu - \lambda)} \tag{4}$$

Much of the behavior of the computer in message switching applications can be explained in terms of Eqs. 1–4. Note that as the message-arrival rates (or requests for service) approach the completion rates, the queue lengths and waiting times approach infinity. In actual service the system will saturate and messages will be lost or denied access to the system. For a given traffic capability the hardware and software must be capable of supporting a

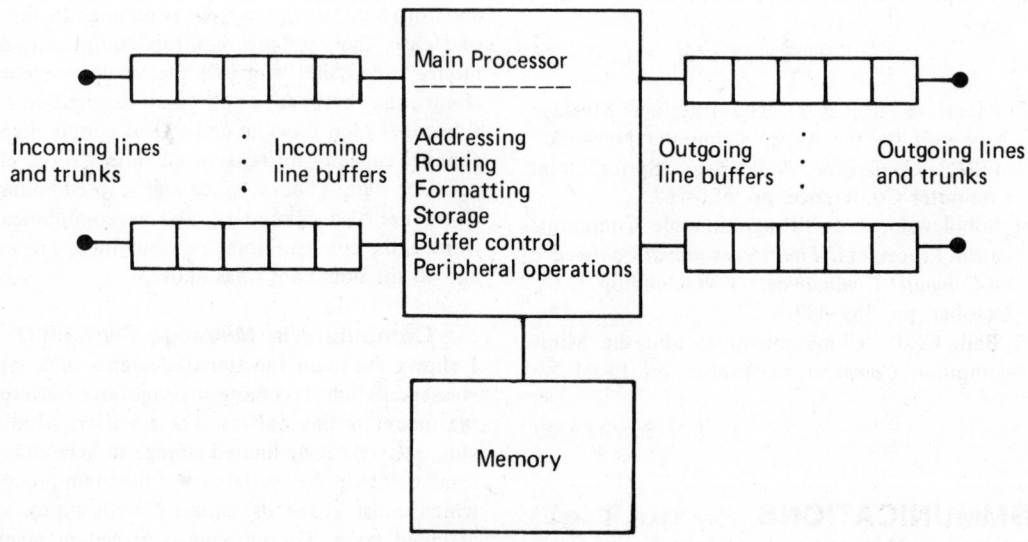

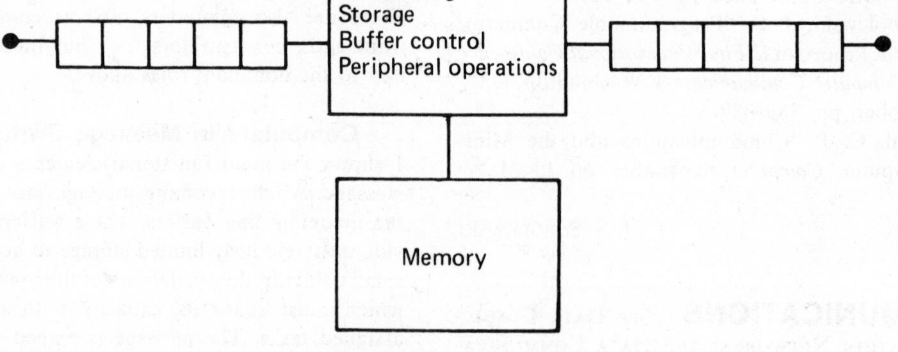


**FIG. 1.** Functional block diagram of typical message switch.

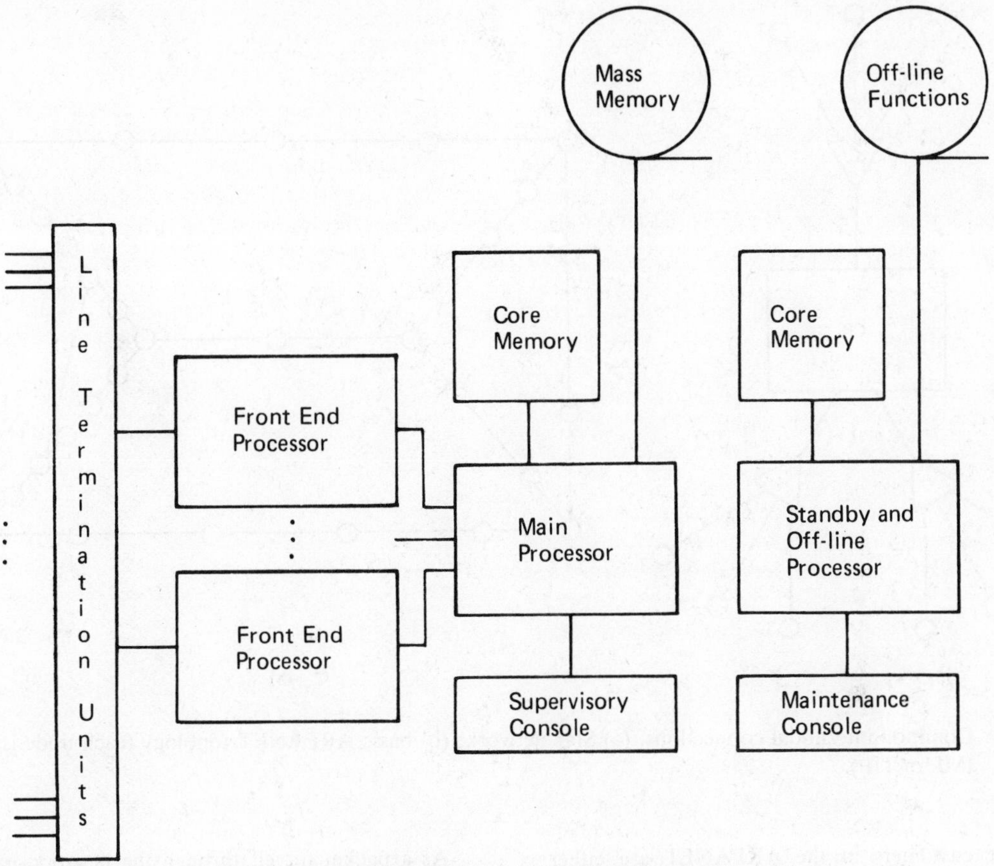


**Fig. 2.** Hardware functional block diagram of large message switch.

completion rate of about twice the expected arrival rate to provide adequate performance margins. Higher completion rates increase performance by increasingly smaller marginal improvements. Any rate lower than about 1.25 times the arrival rate is subject to overload by small fluctuations. In communications applications where the computer is an essential element in providing network service, practically all such applications are queueing systems of one form or another, and Eqs. 1–4 will at the least estimate their expected performance.

Fig. 2 shows a simplified hardware block diagram of a typical large-scale message switch. It should be noted that the complete switch is usually made up of more than one computer, and in fact is a true multiprocessor. In addition to the minicomputers performing line buffering, there are duplicate main processors, one being used as standby and to provide peripheral off-line computation. This is a common practice in switches of this size. In such a system, speed of service will vary, depending upon the distribution and type of traffic and the topology of the network.

Fig. 3 shows some of the possible internodal connections in common use. Figure 3(a) is a star configuration with the message switch (CP) at the center and user terminals (C, concentrator; T, terminal) connected to it. This configuration is typically used with a large computer complex at the node and for messages of reasonably large size. However, large numbers of short messages can badly overload the computer. But this is precisely the type of traffic generated by users accessing computers in an interactive, time-sharing mode and by much computer to computer traffic. Furthermore, fast network response times of the order of 0.5 sec are imperative. Fig. 3(b) is the general topology of the ARPANET developed by the Advanced Research Project Agency of the Department of Defense to handle such traffic. As such, it represents the largest and most advanced use of computers in communications today.

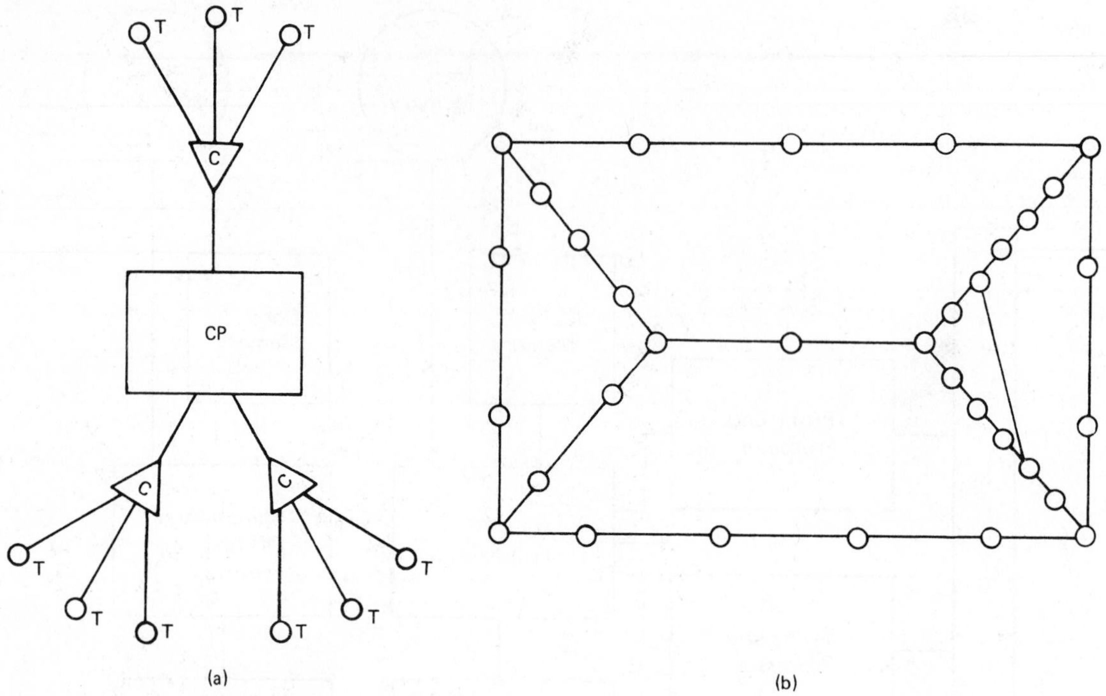


**Fig. 3.** Common internodal connections. (a) Star network; (b) basic ARPANET topology (each node is an IMP or TIP).

The customers in the ARPANET are either computers (called "hosts" in the network terminology) or terminals. Host computers access the network through an Interface Message Processor (IMP) which is a general-purpose minicomputer. Terminals access the network through either a Terminal Interface Processor (TIP) or a local host computer. Thus, at every node there is a message-switching computer. Note that the network topology is a set of interconnecting loops. Since the transmission links are bidirectional, there is a minimum of two separate routes between any two nodes, which increases reliability. Because of the statistics of the input traffic, the average message size is small. However, no matter what the size of the offered message, the IMP breaks it into small *packets* of approximately 1000 bits maximum size. Each packet becomes a small message in itself, to which the IMP appends addressing and other information for network use (e.g., linkage information for reassembly of multipacket messages and error control bits). The maximum throughput of an IMP, where throughput is defined as the sum of the message bits entering and leaving the IMP each second, is approximately 700 kilobits per second.

As a packet travels through the network, each node stores it until it receives from the next node an acknowledgment that the packet has been received correctly. The route a packet follows is not determined in advance. At each node the IMP will select a minimum delay route to the destination. This requires that each IMP have a knowledge of the queue lengths at every other node. The information is stored in routing tables, which are dynamically updated approximately twice a second. Route selection is thus by table lookup. Since routing is adaptive, packets in a multipacket message may travel by different paths and arrive at the destination out of sequence, which necessitates linkage information in the packet header.

As a result of this innovative use of computers, very impressive operational results have been achieved. Trans-network delays have been of the order of tens of milliseconds (depending on message lengths), well under the desired 0.5 sec. Reliability has been brought to a high point, and the cost per megabit transmitted is lower than any other method except mailing a computer tape.

The ARPANET has incorporated a satellite link between the network in the continental United

States and Hawaii. Because of the much longer propagation delay, standard packet-operating procedures have had to be modified, using essentially the same fundamental techniques that have proved their efficiency for satellite links.

Today the most expensive part of a communication network is the cost of the lines. With the cost of minicomputers being rapidly reduced, very substantial savings can be effected by using the computers to concentrate the traffic at a point close to the originating terminals. Advantage is taken of the statistics of the incoming traffic to increase the utilization of the long-haul lines by buffering and sophisticated operating procedures. Concentrator requirements, which once posed a rather large design effort, now are fulfilled by off-the-shelf minicomputers.

The final major application of computers in communications is in the circuit switch, the classical telephone central office. Fig. 4 is a functional block diagram of a typical circuit switch. The switching matrix is the element that actually makes the circuit connection between subscribers. It is a highly specialized device, either electromechanical or (today) solid state. The computer task is to control the action of the matrix. Status of the lines and trunks (such as line busy, idle), changes in state (requests for service, etc.), and control signals (dial signals, multifrequency tone signals) are monitored by line-scanning equipment at a rate sufficiently high to insure that every line is scanned sufficiently often so that no information is lost. This information is then transferred to the computer, which assembles it, interprets it, decides what must be done, and then causes the control elements of the matrix to execute the required action.

A typical sequence of actions for the computer upon detecting a request for service ("off hook") would be (1) to look in memory for an idle path to a dial tone generator and order the matrix to connect the path, (2) upon receiving dial pulses to assemble them, (3) to decide whether the call is local or not, etc. A moment's consideration of the complexities involved in making even a crosstown call will

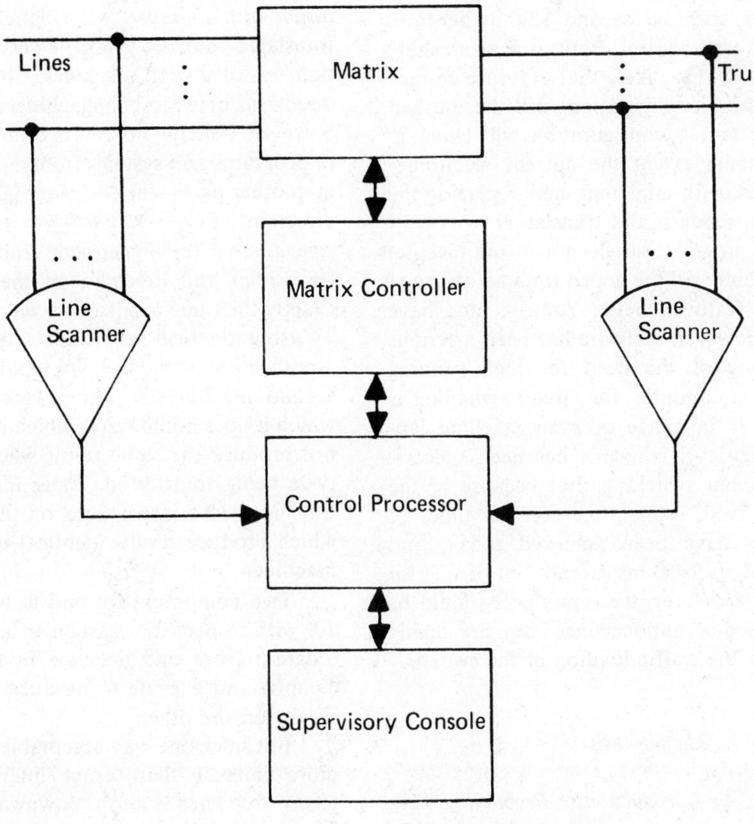


**Fig. 4.** Block diagram of a stored program circuit switch.

indicate why such a very large number of sequences of actions must be performed. However, because each action is the result of a fixed logical sequence of decisions, the digital computer is ideally suited to the job of controlling the switching center.

The computational load imposed upon the computer is twofold. First there are a large number of highly repetitive, fast response computations associated with status monitoring; e.g., line scanning. The logical level of these tasks is low, but the repetition rate is high and to a large extent independent of the number of calls in the switch. Secondly, the other tasks require a much higher level of logical decision making: routing, addressing, path hunting, etc. These tasks are highly call-dependent. In many successful systems the same computer handles both loads. However, even though each individual status monitoring action requires negligible computation, the high repetition rate and large numbers (up to 10,000 lines to be scanned in 100 ms in a large machine) of interrupts imposes a severe overhead load on the computer. For this reason the modern trend is toward the use of multiprocessors, with one processor performing the repetitive fast response chores and the second the higher-level decisions and overall control. Both processors share a common memory. It is likely that in future designs the multiprocessor configuration will be pushed further and the switch configuration will come to reassemble to some extent the current electromechanical switches, with minicomputers replacing the various markers, senders, and translators.

The stored program has been a mixed blessing for circuit switching. All the hoped for advantages of flexibility, new features, better control, etc., have been realized. However, software has been a serious problem. Because of the need for high running efficiency, all programming for circuit switching is done in assembly language or even machine language. No higher-level language has been successfully used in circuit switching. But because of the efficiencies achieved, cross-office connect times of 100 to 200 ms have been achieved today, and connect times of 10 to 50 ms are not out of line for the near future. However, these numbers should be regarded with some caution, since they are highly dependent upon the traffic loading of the switch.

### References

1967. Feller, W., *An Introduction to Probability Theory and Its Applications*, vol. 1, 2d ed. New York: Wiley.

1967. Hillier, F. S., and G. J. Lieberman. *Introduction to Operations Research*. San Francisco: Holden Day.

H. A. Helm

## COMPATIBILITY

For articles on related subjects *see* Emulation; Machine Instruction Set; Memory: Auxiliary; Object Program; Simulation: Principles; Software; and Source Program.

Compatibility is a term applied to both hardware and software systems to describe the ease with which a computer program running on one machine may be made to run on another machine. Hardware compatibility is achieved through similarity of instruction sets (or the ability to simulate similarity of instruction sets), whereas software compatibility deals with the use of a language that can be translated into the (perhaps very different) instruction sets of several machines. Compatibility in both directions between two machines is rarely of interest, however. Usually, interest is centered on the transfer of programs and systems from a particular computer to another particular computer (and only in that one direction). Two computers are said to be *hardware compatible* if the object code from one machine can be loaded and executed on the other to produce exactly the same results. One way of achieving this is by using identical instruction sets in both machines. Another way is the use of special instructions in the second machine so that it recognizes instructions which it does not have (or which it does have but will not produce the same result when executed) in the code being transferred. These instructions are then translated into instructions on the second machine, which produce results identical to those of the first machine.

Two computers are said to be *software compatible* with respect to a particular language if a source program from one machine in that language will compile and execute to produce acceptably similar results on the other.

But since one-way acceptable compatibility is of more interest than exact intercompatibility, the terms "upward" and "downward" compatibility have come into common use. *Upward compatibility* refers to the amount of similarity of a newer, bigger, or better (hence, upward) computer compared to that of a smaller one, but this applies only to the transfer of programs *from* the older one *to* the newer one. Similarly, "downward" compatibility refers to the transfer from the newer one to the older one.

Upward compatibility refers not only to computers with respect to the programs that run on them, but also to the data that they accept and operate on. For example, a computer software system is said to be upward compatible if identical data will produce identical results on a more recent (hence, upward) version as on an older version, even though the newer version may also accept additional forms of data. The term "identical" in this context is somewhat utopian because it almost never is realized in practice.

Manufacturers have historically extolled upward compatibility as an improvement of their small machines extended to their own larger machines, while minimizing any compatibility (especially upward) between their machines and those of their competition. However, they have been quick to point out the upward compatibility of their equipment as compared with that of the competition. In fact, computing equipment and compilers of particular manufacturers have been deliberately designed so that programs running on competitive equipment can be easily converted to run on their systems. Conversely, equipment and systems have also been designed to maximize the difficulty of converting programs so that they cannot be run on competing equipment or systems. The result has been that true compatibility is almost never achieved between equipment from different manufacturers.

Hardware component compatibility is another area where competitive practices have been counterproductive. Since many peripheral devices are hooked to the computer by a relatively small number of cables (usually with a plug, in fact), so-called plug-to-plug compatible peripherals have been developed by some competitive firms. Their practice is to purchase, say, a tape drive, find out how it works (spending only a fraction of the original development costs), and build one that works exactly the same (and even has identical plugs on the ends of the cables) as the original, but which can be profitably marketed at a much lower price than the original. Thus, potential customers exist wherever the original equipment was installed.

Manufacturers have developed several defenses against these practices. Probably the most compelling deterrent is refusal to provide a maintenance contract on a system in which parts have been supplied by a competitor. The implication of this policy is, of course, that maintenance will be done by the hour (rather than on a flat-fee basis, as is usual with most contracts) and that sufficient service time will be spent to offset most of the user's savings earned by installing competitive equipment. This substitution practice has been declared illegal in several cases, and has been rendered less effective recently by the mass conversion (where price advantages show) to plug-to-plug compatible peripherals by the federal government (by far the largest owner and lessor of equipment in the computer world). It has also been countered by the original designers, who have designed peripheral equipment wherein the most expensive part (called the "controller") is integrated (wired directly) into the central processor, leaving only the relatively less expensive mechanical part of the device to be a target for substitution by plug-to-plug compatible replacement.

Although integrated equipment serves to deter replication of parts by competitors, this approach has run into legal complication. In a recent landmark suit, IBM was held to be indulging in monopolistic practices by implementing this integration, despite the fact that the plaintiff in the case, Telex, was found guilty of stealing trade secrets when it built a plug-to-plug device (with controller) that made interchange possible. The verdict against IBM was later overturned on appeal, and was then settled by the litigants on terms favorable to IBM before reaching the U.S. Supreme Court. This result is expected to have far-reaching effects throughout the computing industry.

C. L. MEEK

## COMPILE AND RUN TIME

For articles on related subjects *see* LANGUAGE PROCESSORS; OBJECT PROGRAM; and PROCEDURE-ORIENTED LANGUAGES, PROGRAMMING IN.

The complete process of running a program that has been written in a higher-level language such as Fortran or Cobol is accomplished in two steps:

1. Translation of the source program as written by the programmer into a machine executable form (a process commonly referred to as "compilation").

2. Execution of the generated form; i.e., the *running* of the compiled or *object* program.

To distinguish between certain actions that may occur during one or another of these phases, the period of compilation is known as the "compile time" and the succeeding period as the "run time." In the usual compile and execute system, these two phases are distinct and may be temporally separated. In fact, the running of a program may be accomplished many times without the need for the recompilation of the program, provided the compiled code is saved on tape, disk, or (occasionally) punched cards. In an interpretive system, however, the two phases are intertwined, since execution of each piece of source program follows immediately after its "compilation".

Typically, errors in a program are related to compile time or run time. Where the error is an error of language (i.e., incorrect syntax such as a missing parenthesis), then the system is capable of recognizing this at compilation time; on the other hand, errors in logic or arithmetic (i.e., semantic errors) are normally discovered (if at all) at run time. Some sophisticated language processor systems allow the programmer to use certain facilities called compile-time and run-time facilities. As an example of the latter, some systems allow the programmer to specify the format of his input data and output results at run time rather than in the source program.

J. A. N. LEE

**COMPILER.** *See* COMPILER, INCREMENTAL; COMPILER, SYNTAX-DIRECTED; LANGUAGE PROCESSORS; and LOAD-AND-GO COMPILER.

## COMPILER, INCREMENTAL

For articles on related subjects *see* COMPILER, SYNTAX-DIRECTED; and TIME SHARING.

The advent of conversational time-sharing systems, in which the problem-solving process invokes a dialog between the user at a terminal and a remote computer, has led to the development of various compiling techniques that can be of particular benefit to the time-sharing user. One of these is *incremental* compiling in which the compiler generates code for a statement, or group of statements, which is independent of the code generated for other statements.

Provided the language statements entered by the user are ordered in a standard fashion, the compilation process is closely related to that used in batch-processing operations. On the other hand, if the user is permitted to present the statements in any order, such as specifying array dimensions following the usage of an array element in a statement, then more sophisticated techniques of compilation are required. In any case, the advantage of incremental compiling to the user is that he may compile and test parts of his program as he "composes" it at the terminal rather than being required to postpone the debugging process until the entire program has been written.

J. A. N. LEE

## COMPILER, SYNTAX-DIRECTED

For articles on related subjects *see* COMPILER, INCREMENTAL; GRAMMAR, GENERATIVE; and LANGUAGE PROCESSORS.

A syntax-directed compiler (sometimes called a "syntax-oriented" compiler) is a general-purpose compiler that will service a family of languages by providing the syntactic rules for language analysis in the form of data, typically in tabular form, rather than building the specific parsing algorithm for a particular language into the compiler. In this manner, a single processor can be used for the compilation of many differing languages, provided only that the syntactic rules of each language can be expressed in the required format of the data. Table 1 is an example of a part of a simplified syntax table that might be used by a syntax-directed compiler. To see how such a table is used, consider the entries 2.0–2.3. If the compiler is searching for the construct TERM, line 2.0 says that if it finds a factor (FT) without a following (successor) construct, this is acceptable (OK) but, if not, there is the alternate 2.1, which states that a factor followed by a multiply operator (2.2) followed by another factor (2.3) is OK, but that any other alternate fails. A syntax table, therefore, acts like a series of small programs. Note in particular that the syntax can be changed merely by changing entries in the table. For example, to allow a term to have the form FT ÷ FT where ÷ indicates division by integers, the "fail" in line 2.3

**Table 1.** Part of a syntax table

| Language Construct | Index | Name | Successor | Alternate |
|---|---|---|---|---|
| Arithmetic | 1.0 | TE | 1.1 | Fail |
| expression (AE) | 1.1 | AO | 1.2 | Fail |
| | 1.2 | TE | OK | Fail |
| Term (TE) | 2.0 | FT | OK | 2.1 |
| | 2.1 | FT | 2.2 | Fail |
| | 2.2 | MO | 2.3 | Fail |
| | 2.3 | FT | OK | Fail |
| Factor (FT) | 3.0 | PR | OK | 3.1 |
| | 3.1 | PR | 3.2 | Fail |
| | 3.2 | EO | 3.3 | Fail |
| | 3.3 | PR | OK | Fail |
| Primary (PR) | 4.0 | CO | OK | Fail |
| | 4.1 | UA | OK | Fail |
| Exponentiation operator (EO) | 5.0 | ** | OK | Fail |
| Add operator (AO) | 6.0 | + | OK | 6.1 |
| | 6.1 | − | OK | Fail |
| Multiply operator (MO) | 7.0 | * | OK | 7.1 |
| | 7.1 | / | OK | Fail |

could be replaced by "2.4" and lines "2.4–2.6" would contain the entries for FT, ÷ and FT.

Syntax-directed compilers also form the basis for a compiler-compiler, which is a specialized processor that generates compilers (McKeeman, 1970).

REFERENCES

1966. Ingerman, P. Z. *A Syntax Oriented Translator.* New York: Academic Press.

1970. McKeeman, W. M. *A Compiler Generator.* Englewood Cliffs, N.J.: Prentice-Hall.

J. A. N. LEE AND A. RALSTON

# COMPLEMENT

For articles on related subjects *see* ARITHMETIC, COMPUTER; and NUMBERS AND NUMBER SYSTEMS.

In ordinary arithmetic we represent negative numbers by a minus sign followed by the absolute value (i.e., magnitude) of the number (e.g., −6.42). In computers we can represent negative numbers this way also, and sometimes this is actually done, but more often a "complement" representation is used. Even when the sign-magnitude representation is used, the hardware of the computer normally will include a complementer to assist in carrying out the various arithmetic operations.

To motivate the need for complements or complementers, consider the addition of two numbers expressed in sign-magnitude form. Before the operation can be carried out, the signs of the numbers must be compared. If they are the same, the two numbers can be added; if they are different, the smaller in magnitude must be subtracted from the larger and the correct sign appended to the result. As we will see, the use of complements avoids much of this complication.

**Definitions.** There are two kinds of complements, *radix* complements and *diminished radix* complements, where "radix" refers to the base of the number system being used. Let $x$ be a positive number in the decimal system. Then the diminished 10's complement of $x$, which we denote by $\bar{x}$ and which is generally called the "9's complement," is formed by subtracting every digit of $x$ from 9. Thus, if $x = 426.3091$, $\bar{x} = 573.6908$. The 10's complement $\tilde{x}$ is defined as the result of adding 1 in the least significant place of $\bar{x}$ or, equivalently, as the result of subtracting $x$ from $10^n$, where $n$ is such that the 1 in $10^n$ is one place to the left of the most significant digit of $x$. Using the above example, $\tilde{x} = 573.6909 = 1000.0000 - 426.3091$. Both the quantities $\bar{x}$ and $\tilde{x}$ are thus representations of the quantity $-x$.

The other complements of practical importance are those in the radix 2, or binary, system. If $x$ is now a positive binary number, then its "1's complement" $\bar{x}$ is formed by changing all 0's in $x$ to 1's and 1's to zeros (i. e., subtracting all bits of $x$ from 1) and the "2's complement" $x$ is formed by adding 1 in the least significant place of $\bar{x}$ or, equivalently, subtracting $x$ from $2^n$ with $n$ chosen as above. Thus, if $x = 10.1101$, then $\bar{x} = 01.0010$ and $\tilde{x} = 01.0011 = 100.0000 - 10.1101$.

**Properties of Complements.** The useful properties of complements in computers are best illustrated using the binary system. For illustrative purposes consider a computer where the numbers on which arithmetic operations are to be performed each have eight bits, the first of which denotes the sign (0 for plus, 1 for minus) and the other seven bits are, for convenience, assumed to represent an integer. If the sign is negative, let us assume the integer is in the 2's complement form. Then, to add two such numbers, we need only treat them as eight-bit positive integers (i.e., treat the sign as another bit of the number), add them, and discard any carry to the left of the eighth position (see Fig. 1). Thus, we are able to ignore both the sign and relative magnitudes of the two numbers. With negative numbers in the 1's complement form, there is the slight additional complication that carries to the left of the eighth position must be added into the first (i.e., least significant) position (see Fig. 2).

Let $x = 00001000$ (decimal 8)
$y = 00010101$ (decimal 21)
Then $\tilde{x} = 11111000$ (decimal −8)
$\tilde{y} = 11101011$ (decimal −21)

Then
$$\begin{array}{rr} x + \tilde{y} = & 00001000 \\ & +\underline{11101011} \\ & 11110011 \end{array}$$
which is the 2's complement of 13 in decimal (00001101 in binary); and
$$\begin{array}{rr} \tilde{x} + \tilde{y} = & 11111000 \\ & +\underline{11101011} \\ & 11100011 \end{array}$$
which is the 2's complement of 29 in decimal (00011101 in binary).

**Fig. 1.** Addition of numbers using 2's complements.

Let $x = 00001000$
$y = 00010101$
$\bar{x} = 11110111$
$\bar{y} = 11101010$

Then
$$\begin{array}{rr} x + \bar{y} = & 00001000 \\ & +\underline{11101010} \\ & 11110010 \end{array}$$
which is the 1's complement of 13 in decimal (00001101 in binary); and
$$\begin{array}{rr} \bar{x} + \bar{y} = & 11110111 \\ & +\underline{11101010} \\ & 111100001 \\ & \llcorner\!\longrightarrow 1 \\ & 11100010 \end{array}$$
which is the 1's complement of 29 in decimal (00011101 in binary).

**Fig. 2.** Additions of numbers using 1's complements.

Both results given above are rather easily proved by writing complemented numbers as $2^n$ minus the corresponding positive number (minus 1 for 1's complements).

One interesting property of the 1's complement form is the existence of two zeros, one with a positive sign and one with a negative sign. This follows because the 1's complement of 00000000 is 11111111. With 2's complements, however, there is only one zero, since the 2's complement of 0000 0000 is 10000 0000, which has nine bits. In 2's complement representation, 1111 1111 is the complement of 00000001. The existence of two zeros can be used with advantage in some contexts, but requires a somewhat more difficult test to determine if a number is zero than would otherwise be the case.

Since 1's complements are generated merely by changing 0's to 1's, and vice versa, it is very easy to build a circuit to generate the 1's complement of a

Let $x = 00001000$
$y = 00010101$

Then $x - y$ is found by first forming

$\bar{y} = 11101010$

and then adding $x + \bar{y}$, as in Fig. 2, to get 11110010, which is the 1's complement of 13 in decimal.

**Fig. 3.** Subtraction using 1's complements

number. It is somewhat more difficult, but not very hard, to build a circuit to generate 2's complements. Therefore, it is easy to perform subtraction by first complementing the minuend and then adding (see Fig. 3). This means it is not necessary to have a hardware subtracter if there is a hardware adder and a complementer. It is for this reason that computers rarely have subtracters.

For performing multiplication and division, there are no direct advantages to the complement form and some disadvantages. However, the adjustments to algorithms for multiplying or dividing two positive numbers to allow them to handle operands in complement form are not major. Alternatively, negative operands in multiplication or division can first be complemented and then the appropriate sign can be appended at the end.

Most modern computers store negative numbers in either 1's or 2's complement form. Which of the two forms to choose depends upon some rather subtle and by no means conclusive considerations concerning the details of computer circuitry. Even in those rather rare cases when negative numbers are stored in sign-magnitude form, it is usual to have a complementer in the arithmetic unit for use in performing arithmetic operations involving negative numbers or subtraction.

A. RALSTON

## COMPLEXITY.

*See* COMPUTATIONAL COMPLEXITY.

## COMPUTABILITY

For articles on related subjects *see* ALGORITHMS, THEORY OF; and DECIDABILITY.
For article on related term *see* ALGORITHM.

"Computability" is a property of *functions*. A function $f$ with domain $D$ and range $R$ is a definite correspondence by which there is associated with each element $x$ of the domain $D$ (referred to as the "argument") a single element $f(x)$ of the range $R$ (called the "value"). The function $f$ is said to be computable if there exists an algorithm that, for any given $x$ in $D$, provides the value of $f(x)$.

For example, consider the function $g$, whose domain $D$ is the set of all pairs of positive integers and whose range $R$ is the set of positive integers, and which is defined as

$$g(a,b) = \text{the greatest common divisor of } a \text{ and } b.$$

This function is computable by the well-known Euclidean algorithm (Knuth, 1968).

The above definition is lacking rigor for the following reasons:

1. It is not explained in what form the argument $x$ in $D$ is "given." In particular, this part of the definition makes sense only if elements of $D$ are in some way finitely describable. Thus, the notion of computability, as described above, makes no sense for a function $f$ whose domain is the set of real numbers.
2. The notion of an algorithm is not precise.
3. It is not explained in what sense the algorithm provides us with the value of $f(x)$.

How the notion of computability of a function can be made mathematically rigorous is explained in the article, ALGORITHMS, THEORY OF.

REFERENCE

1968. Knuth, D. "The Art of Computer Programming," in Vol. 1, *Fundamental Algorithms*. Reading, Mass.: Addison-Wesley.

G. T. HERMAN

## COMPUTATIONAL COMPLEXITY

For articles on related subjects *see* ALGORITHMS, THEORY OF; and TURING MACHINE.
For articles on related terms *see* FAST FOURIER TRANSFORM; FORMAL LANGUAGES; and MATHEMATICAL PROGRAMMING.

The complexity of computations must have been an issue since the time counting came to play a role in human culture. Current widespread use of modern digital computers has substantially increased the importance of questions about the difficulty of computational problems.

Obvious and familiar algorithms are continually being replaced by more efficient ones as programmers and mathematicians gain more sophistication in computing methods. The aim of the study of computational complexity is to develop techniques for discovering better algorithms and to explain why some computational tasks are difficult, no matter what algorithm is applied to them.

**The Computational Complexity of Multiplying Integers.** Computing the product of two integers is an example of an apparently simple problem whose computational complexity turns out to hold some surprises.

One natural way to measure the difficulty or computational complexity of multiplication is to count the number of basic operations on digits —such as reading or writing a digit, adding two digits, or multiplying two digits—required to multiply two integers. The usual grade-school method for computing the product of any two $n$ digit integers requires each digit of the multiplier to be multiplied by each digit of the multiplicand, so the number of basic digital operations required is proportional to $n^2$.

In contrast, the sum of two $n$ digit numbers, again using the familiar grade-school algorithm for addition, can be calculated with a number of digital operations proportional to $n$. This latter algorithm is surely close to optimal, since proportional $n$ operations are necessary just to read the numbers to be added.

Experience with these simple arithmetic algorithms suggests that multiplying is harder than adding; adding is even used as a subprocess in grade-school multiplication. While this operation is well suited for calculation with pencil and paper, and may also have a certain nostalgic appeal, the grade-school multiplication algorithm is far from the most efficient algorithm now known. Over the past decade a succession of faster methods have been discovered, culminating in a method that requires only proportional $n \cdot \log n \cdot \log \log n$ digital operations. This fast method is based on an algorithm known as the "Fast Fourier Transform," which itself performs in $n \cdot \log n$ operations—a computation which, like multiplication, at first sight seems to require $n^2$ operations.

There is no record of fast multiplication methods having been discovered earlier than 1962. Considering how many of history's greatest mathematicians were also prodigious calculators, it is remarkable that fast multiplication should be such a recent discovery. (One explanation might be that the bookkeeping details involved in some of the highly optimized methods are too complicated for hand calculation and demand the patient reliability of computing machines.)

Whether multiplication really is harder than addition is still unknown. There is no reason to suppose that the best way to multiply has already been discovered, and it may be that multiplication of $n$ digit numbers can be performed in proportional $n$ operations. On the other hand, if the most efficient method presently known is the best, proving that it is will be an interesting mathematical challenge. Theoretical results about computational complexity reveal the possibility that there might not even *be* a best way to multiply!

**The Mathematical Theory of Computational Complexity.** The theory of computational complexity provides a mathematical framework for studying all algorithms that accomplish any computational task. A difficulty faced by this study is that, for any computable mathematical function (of which multiplication is only one of the simplest examples), there are an infinite number of different ways to compute it. Anyone with a bit of programming experience will realize that there is endless variety possible in programs for any given task; this observation can actually be proved as one of the elementary theorems of the mathematical theory.

Mathematical theory begins with the notion of an algorithm or program that computes a function $f(x)$ on the integers: Given any input integer $x$, the algorithm is applied and yields as output the integer $f(x)$. Algorithms can be defined rigorously as being programs for simple models of computers such as Turing machines. The general properties of algorithms and computable functions have been studied by mathematicians for nearly 40 years, and it is generally agreed that anything which could reasonably be regarded as an algorithm can be carried out by a Turing machine.

The time required by an algorithm $A$ depends on the input to which $A$ is applied. The complexity of $A$ is therefore defined to be the function $T_A(x)$ equal to the number of basic steps required by algorithm $A$ applied to input $x$. Actually, the number of steps is just one measure of complexity and other measures, such as amount of storage space or number of memory accesses, may also be used.

Two axioms characterize most of the basic properties of complexity measures:

1. $T_A(x)$ is finite if and only if algorithm $A$ applied to input $x$ eventually halts and gives an output. (In other words, an algorithm halts if and

only if it halts after a finite number of steps.)

2. There is an algorithm which, given as inputs any integers $x$ and $y$ and any algorithm $A$, will determine whether or not $T_A(x) = y$. (Given $x$, $y$, and $A$, one can simulate $A$ applied to $x$ for exactly $y$ steps and see whether $A$ halts on the last step.)

These straightforward axioms are enough to imply, for example, that there are computable functions which cannot be computed rapidly by any algorithm, and that more functions can be computed if more time is allowed. They also imply a much less obvious fact, known as the "Speed-up Theorem": There is a computable function $f$ with the property that given any algorithm $A$ which computes $f$, there is another algorithm $B$ which computes $f$ "much faster" than $A$. "Much faster" is interpreted by choosing any rapidly growing computable function such as $2^w$; then, according to the speed-up theorem, there is a function $f$ such that if $A$ is any algorithm for $f$, there is always another algorithm $B$ for $f$ such that $2^{T_B(x)} \leq T_A(x)$ for all large integers $x$. Thus, algorithm $B$ requires at most the logarithm of the time required by $A$.

Of course, since $B$ is itself an algorithm for $f$, there must be another algorithm $C$ for $f$ which requires only the logarithm of the time for $B$, and so on. Clearly, there is no single most efficient way to compute such an $f$.

Also, notice that $f$ must be hopelessly difficult to compute even though it has faster and faster programs. Each program for $f$ must require more than $2^x$, and more than $2^{2^x}$, and so on, steps for all large inputs $x$; otherwise, the program could only be "sped-up" by an exponential a fixed number of times before "hitting bottom," after which it could not be sped up further.

These conclusions may seem to violate intuition, but they follow inevitably for any model of computer with any reasonable notion of computational step. The speed-up theorem is proved using "diagonal" arguments similar to those used in the theory of algorithms to establish the existence of undecidable problems.

**Inherently Complex Computation Problems.** The first uncontrived examples of functions with computational properties similar to those predicted by the speed-up theorem were discovered in 1972. Dozens of examples have now been discovered, mainly in the areas of mechanical theorem proving and automata theory.

A mechanical theorem-proving problem of this type is to determine whether sentences written in the standard notation of mathematical logic express true statements about addition of integers. In this notation, a statement such as "not every integer is divisible by 3" could be expressed by writing

$$\sim \forall x \, \exists y \, [y + y + y = x],$$

which literally is read "it is false that, for every integer $x$, there exists an integer $y$ such that $y + y + y = x$." This statement, of course, is true. The statement "for every integer $x$ it is false that $x + x = x$," which would be written

$$\forall x \, [\sim(x + x = x)],$$

is not true, since $0 + 0 = 0$.

Although not all theorems about integers can be proved automatically, the additive properties of integers are simple enough so that all sentences of this kind can be proved true or false by a mechanical procedure. One can design an algorithm which, given as input any sentence about integer addition, will correctly produce the output "True" or "False."

An efficient procedure of this kind would yield other efficient procedures for linear and integer programming problems and a variety of similar optimization problems with immediate practical applications, since these mathematical programming problems involve only additive properties of integers. Sentences about integer addition turn out to have enough expressive power that, if one hypothesized that their truth could be decided quickly, it would follow that *any* problem decidable within $2^{2^n}$ steps could also be decided quickly. Abstract complexity theory rules out the latter possibility, and it follows that any algorithm which decides the truth of sentences about integer addition must eventually, when applied to sentences of length $n$, use more than $2^{2^n}$ basic digital operations. The values of $2^{2^n}$ become astronomical for $n \geq 6$; any correct procedure for solving this computational problem would rapidly exhaust the resources of the known universe.

Reducibility Among Problems. Computational problems that appear to be complex arise in nearly every engineering and scientific discipline. A rich variety of problems in areas such as operations research, computer design, data manipulation, graph theory, and mathematical logic cannot be efficiently solved by any known procedure, but present mathematical knowledge leaves open the possibility of efficient solutions for them.

There seem to be so many kinds of computational problems that, even should many of them prove to be inherently difficult, they might be difficult for different reasons. For example, each of the following different problems can be solved by algorithms, using a number of steps that is an exponential function of the "size" of the problem, while none of them are known to be solvable by algorithms using only a polynomial number of steps:

1. Given the distances between $n$ cities, find the shortest "traveling salesman" route which visits each city exactly once.
2. Given an arbitrary map, determine whether the countries can be colored, using only three colors so that all adjacent countries have different colors.
3. Given a circuit built of gated logic, find the smallest equivalent circuit.
4. Given a truth-functional formula, determine whether it is identically true.
5. Given a record of mutual friendships among $n$ people, find the largest group of them such that every pair of people in the group are friends.
6. Given a set of linear arrays stored in a computer memory, find a subset of them which fills a given block of memory as fully as possible.

Despite their apparent differences, these problems are virtually the same from a computational point of view. Each one is "efficiently reducible" to any other in the sense that an efficient algorithm for any one of them could be used as a subroutine in the design of an efficient algorithm for any of the others. If one of these problems can be solved in polynomial time, then all can; and if they really are hard, they surely are all hard for the same reason.

Other groups of problems—such as matrix multiplication, finding paths in graphs, and parsing context-free languages—can also be intimately related by efficiently reducing one to another. The most efficient known parser for general context-free languages was discovered only in January 1974 by reducing this problem to the problem of computing matrix products (for which a fast algorithm has been known for a few years).

The discovery of efficient reducibilities is beginning to bring intellectual order to the diversity of computational problems by coalescing dozens of problems into a few basic ones.

Concrete Problems. Special computational problems like sorting, evaluating polynomials, or approximating roots of rational functions have led to the formulation of special classes of algorithms for which precise bounds on difficulty can be proved.

For sorting problems a natural class of algorithms involves comparisons between elements as the only basic operation. The maximum among $n$ elements, for example, can be found with only $n - 1$ comparisons in an obvious way. Since each of the $n - 1$ elements other than the maximum must have been determined to be the smaller of two compared elements, any comparison algorithm for finding the maximum must require this many comparisons. Completely sorting $n$ elements can be accomplished with little more than $n \cdot \log n$ comparisons, and a simple counting argument shows that this many comparisons are necessary. Finally, finding the median (middle element) seems at first to require a full sorting, but an extremely clever new algorithm does the job in only $3n$ comparisons; at least $7n/4$ are known to be necessary.

A natural complexity measure for the problem of evaluating a polynomial is the number of arithmetic operations (additions, subtractions, multiplications, and divisions) required. Horner's rule is a classical trick for factoring a polynomial of degree $n$ so that only $n$ multiplications are required to evaluate the polynomial at any given point. Better methods have been discovered which require only half this many multiplications, and the latter number can be shown by algebraic arguments to be necessary in general.

**Conclusions.** Proving lower bounds on complexity of computation is essential for a thorough understanding of the potential power of computing devices. When efficient algorithms for some computational problem are provably impossible, the proof can provide important clues for reformulating or specializing the problem so that efficient methods can be found. Proofs of impossibility, of course, also save time and brainpower that might otherwise be spent futilely. It is remarkable that in many cases it is possible to prove such lower bounds.

The mathematical analysis required to prove that an algorithm is optimal can also lead to the happy discovery of a still better algorithm. Some of the fast algorithms mentioned in this article, as well as several others for such problems as matrix multiplication, finding paths in graphs, testing graphs for planarity, and evaluating integer polynomials, were found after the failure of attempts to verify that known algorithms were the best possible.

Research on computational complexity has just begun, but already it has explained why some computations are hard and some are easy.

### References

1968, 1969, 1973. Knuth, D. *The Art of Computer Programming,* Vol. I, II, and III. Reading, Mass.: Addison-Wesley.

1973. Borodin, A. "Computational Complexity: Theory and Practice," in A. Aho (Ed.), *Currents in the Theory of Computing*. Englewood Cliffs, N.J.: Prentice-Hall, pp. 35–89.

A. R. MEYER

## COMPUTATIONAL LINGUISTICS.

*See* PROGRAMMING LINGUISTICS.

## COMPUTER, USING A

For articles on related subjects *see* DEBUGGING; DIAGNOSTICS; DOCUMENTATION; FLOWCHART; and PROCEDURE-ORIENTED LANGUAGES.

For articles on related terms *see* ADMINISTRATIVE-BUSINESS APPLICATIONS; ALGORITHM; DECISION TABLES; INFORMATION RETRIEVAL; and SYSTEM CHART.

Using a computer means getting it to do some desired piece of information processing: give an answer; store some information; show some fact, condition, or trend; control a process; produce a product. In some cases these desires are expressed to the computer in the form of a program directly by the end user, the one who wants the answer. In other situations, most of the programming has been done for him by the designer of the communication system, and he can concentrate on describing the specific data and desired output. In almost all cases, he is buffered from the computer by a "use facilitator," known variously as a programmer, systems analyst, or systems programmer, who works behind the scenes to prepare the programs and operating systems that simplify the problem of communication for the end user.

Let us consider three situations described by the phrase "using a computer," but which in each case has a quite different meaning:

A. *An engineer "uses" a computer to solve a mathematical problem.*

*Meaning:* The engineer writes and runs his own program, using a higher-level language, say, Fortran.

B. *A court officer "uses" a computer to find out whether an arrested man requesting bail has a criminal record.*

*Meaning:* He sits at a terminal attached to the computer and enters the necessary descriptive information; the desired record is displayed on the screen for him.

C. *A company "uses" a computer to handle its accounts, financial records, billing, payroll, and inventory.*

*Meaning:* The staff of the data processing department design and implement an integrated processing system, into which transactions are entered as they occur; it handles normal operations, makes routine decisions, and in response to inquiry makes information available to management to help them make better informed decisions.

CASE A: SINGLE PROBLEM SOLUTION; PROGRAM WRITTEN BY THE END USER. The first task of the person setting out to solve a problem is too often overlooked, or too hastily skimmed over: the necessity for acquiring a thorough understanding of the problem, including what is known, what is wanted, and what additional information may be needed.

Furthermore, since the computer must always be told what to do, the data supplied is usually not enough to describe the problem to the computer. In most cases, the computer must also be told how to solve it, by having spelled out to it the computational steps to be followed to reach the solution. Most common computer languages are therefore "procedure-oriented," i.e., designed to express this procedure to the computer.

Therefore, the next step for the problem solver must be to select a method that he feels will work in the present situation, and then to go about developing an algorithm that is an accurate and detailed description of the procedure to be followed, including rules for what to do in all possible situations that may develop.

To assist him in visualizing this procedure, he will usually draw flowcharts, ranging from the very general overall view to the explicit detailing of all steps to be followed. The flowcharts have two advantages over either a narrative description or the higher-level language program itself: Whole processes involving many steps may be summarized in a single block; and the graphic nature of the flowchart, with branches labeled according to various choices and conditions, and with arrows leading from step to step, enables the designer to see at a glance what follows what.

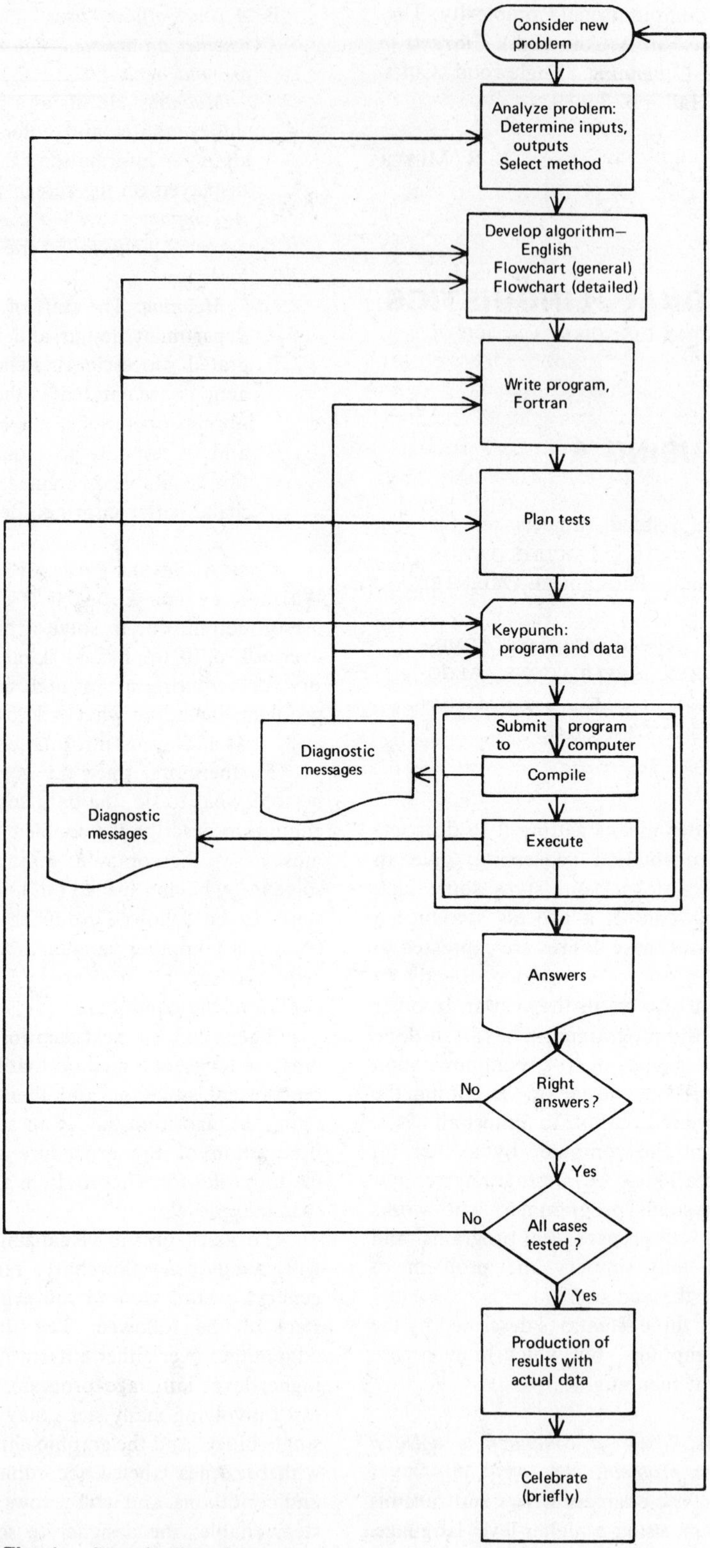


**Fig. 1.** Sample flowchart.

As a sample of a flowchart representation of an algorithm, Fig. 1 illustrates the procedure currently being described. Once the flowchart has been completely laid out, both in general terms and with some of the processes expanded, the programmer must then translate the algorithm from flowchart form, using arrows and general English phrases, into a language that can be accepted and understood by the computer. For scientific and engineering work, most likely this language will be Fortran (formula translator). Operation blocks resulting in the assignment of initial values or the calculation of new values are generally converted into series of assignment statements capable of expressing a wide variety of mathematical operations; loops and iterations are most conveniently handled by DO statements, which control repetition and incrementing, and branch points by IF statements, which test the data or various intermediate values.

As his program is being developed, a wise programmer makes plans for the inclusion of enough tests to satisfy him that the instructions are stated correctly, that the values calculated are indeed the ones he intends, and that the method works satisfactorily for the range of values with which he is concerned. These tests may involve calculating by hand the first few values or those corresponding to some special cases, examining the output values at a series of known checkpoints, or using additional mathematical or physical properties such as check sums or the constancy of certain relationships.

Furthermore, he should be realistic enough to realize that in spite of all such efforts, there will likely be logical errors and residual bugs that will never show up until certain special circumstances or numerical values occur. He can provide some further protection by building into his program some additional tests and traps, sometimes called "error exits." These may require input data to pass certain consistency and plausibility checks, may test whether certain immediate results are within a reasonable range, or may make back calculations, with the answers arrived at, to see whether they do indeed satisfy the initial equations. Failure at any of these points will then cause the program to terminate with appropriate warning messages.

In any case, these tests should be planned in advance and incorporated in the program from the very beginning. Although it is a truism that complex programs are never completely debugged, enough different cases should be chosen and sufficient variety of data selected for testing to assure some reasonable confidence in the reliability of the answers produced by the program.

Eventually, he feels that his program is complete. However, a sheet of programming statements, no matter how neatly hand-lettered or typed, is not as yet accepted as input by most computers, and the program must be converted to machine-readable form before it can be submitted to the machine. In most cases this is done by keypunching the program into cards, one statement to a card. Since this process, like most human operations involving routine work, almost invariably produces errors, it is advisable to verify the card deck, once punched, either by repunching on a verifier or by listing the deck to produce a printed page and comparing this with the original.

In addition to the program, the data (numerical values to be used by the program) must also be punched, as well as the control cards peculiar to the computer system being used. These control cards contain the identification of the programmer, accounting information (who is to get charged for the run), and other instructions to the operator, whether it be a human or an operating system.

Now, at last, with his deck containing control cards, program, and data, the programmer is ready to do battle with the machine. By one means or another the programmer submits his job, either by placing the cards in the card reader and pushing the button, or by giving the deck through a window to an input clerk. Depending upon the philosophy, efficiency, and busyness of the shop, and on the size of job and priority of the programmer, the turnaround time (time until he gets back a response from the computer) may vary from a few seconds to many hours.

What happens when the program is read into the computer? It must be remembered that Fortran (like other higher-level languages), the language in which the program is written, is not the native language of the computer. Its native language consists of a very primitive set of basic operations wired into the machine, each of which can accomplish only one small step or test one condition. Furthermore, when programming in the machine's language, the programmer must keep very careful track of exactly where every number is stored at any time. Fortran, on the other hand, is an intermediate or higher-level language and is much easier for people to use because they can express operations in symbols and phrases that are much closer to the way they normally describe their work. But the only way the computer can understand a Fortran program is first to have it translated into the corresponding series of machine-language instructions, and then execute

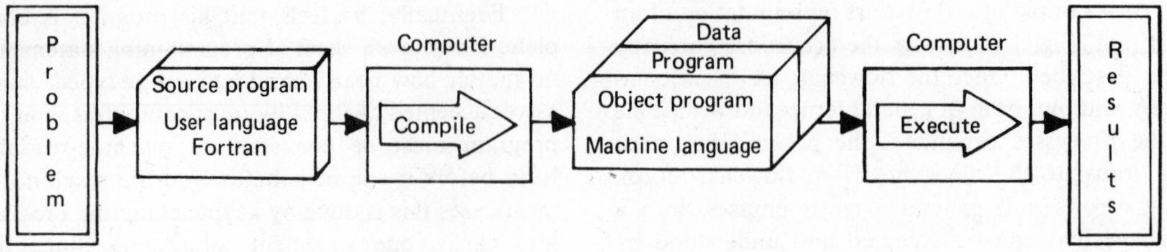


**Fig. 2.** Translation of Fortran to machine language. (From Davidson & Koenig, *Computers,* Wiley, 1967)

those. The saving feature of this process is that the translation from Fortran to machine language can be carried out by the machine itself, using an automatic translating program called a *compiler*. The process, then, undergone by the program when it is submitted to the computer can be depicted as in Fig. 2.

When the output finally is returned to the user, including the computer printout together with the original deck, the problem solver looks to see how far his program has progressed and examines the nature of the output. Human beings being what they are, it is extremely unlikely that satisfactory answers will be produced the first time, and it is usual to make from two or three to a great many iterations of this procedure, tracking down and fixing errors in the program, before the programmer is finally satisfied and the answers obtained are accepted as the ones desired.

In rare cases, our problem solver may be quite sure his program will never be needed again and may throw it away, once he has obtained his answers. More commonly, however, it will be needed for a series of runs, either by himself or by others, and it can either go directly into production or be filed in the program library. In either case, it must be properly documented while its structure and usage are still fresh.

*Example (Case A): Engineer Solving a Mathematical Problem*

Problem: Solution of quadratic equation

$$Ax^2 + Bx + C = 0.$$

Inputs: Several sets of three coefficients: $A$, $B$, and $C$.

Outputs desired: Two values of $x$ representing the roots for each $A$, $B$, and $C$.

Method: Quadratic formula:

$$x = \frac{-B \pm \sqrt{B^2 - 4AC}}{2A}.$$

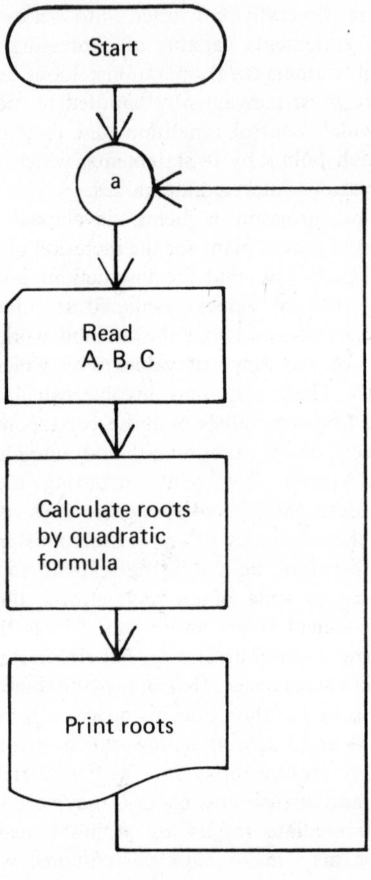


**Fig. 3.** Flowchart for Version 1.

This first flowchart is shown as Fig. 3. Such a flowchart can be converted into a Fortran program (Fig. 4) to carry out the various steps indicated. Test data can be easily generated by choosing special roots and working backward to determine the coefficients of the corresponding quadratic equations. For example, the roots

$$x_1 = 1 \qquad x_2 = 2$$

```
Program
    1  READ, A, B, C
       PRINT, A, B, C
       D = B*B - 4*A*C
       S = SQRT(D)
       X1 = (-B + S)/(2*A)
       X2 = (-B - S)/(2*A)
       PRINT, X1, X2
       GO TO 1
       END
Data
       1    -3    2
       1     5    6
       1     1    1
Results
       1.0000    -3.0000    2.0000
       2.0000     1.0000
       1.0000     5.0000    6.0000
      -2.0000    -3.0000
       1.0000     1.0000    1.0000
ERROR IN *MAIN* AT STMT. NO. 00001 + 03 LINES:
   SQRT OR DSQRT OF A NEGATIVE NUMBER
ABORT
```

**Fig. 4.** Program for Version 1.

can easily be shown to lead to the equation

$$x^2 - 3x + 2 = 0,$$

for which the coefficients are

$$A = 1, \quad B = -3, \quad C = 2.$$

However, the unwary engineer who implements this simple flowchart, even though he checks it out with some valid test cases such as the set above, is in for some rude surpries if he tries it out on real data.

To begin with, this method finds only real roots; if for a given set of coefficients the discriminant $D$ comes out negative, then the program will be asking for the square root of a negative quantity. In most Fortran implementations this will cause the job to be thrown off the machine, usually with a comment as to just what error occurred. (Unfortunately, some Fortran compilers may make an assumption about what you might have *meant* to say rather than what you did say, make an adjustment such as taking the absolute value of $D$, and then proceed with never a warning!) The solution is for the programmer, then, to insert a test statement before the square root step, testing the sign of the discriminant himself so that he can specify what he wants done if it turns out to be negative. If it is, then the roots are complex, and can be expressed as

$$x_1 = \frac{-B}{2A} + i\,\frac{\sqrt{4AC - B^2}}{2A},$$

$$x_2 = \frac{-B}{2A} - i\,\frac{\sqrt{4AC - B^2}}{2A}.$$

He can then incorporate these two procedures into one flowchart, shown as Fig. 5.

This procedure will lead to a program (Fig 6) that will handle many more cases than before, but it still will not correctly handle all cases that may be encountered. Suppose, due either to the nature of the equation or to a keypunching mistake, a set of coefficients is encountered in which $A = 0$ but both $B$ and $C$ are nonzero. When the step is reached in which the computer is asked to divide by zero, the program will again stop. Once again, the engineer programmer can insert another statement in his program, testing whether or not $A = 0$. If it does, then the equation reduces to a simple linear one:

$$Bx + C = 0,$$

which has the solution

$$x = -C/B,$$

provided, of course, $A$ and $B$ are not both zero! To be completely sure, he should also test for this, for if both $A$ and $B$ are zero, the equation reduces to $C = 0$, which is either a contradiction (if $C \neq 0$) or a useless truism (if also $C = 0$).

A complete algorithm for handling all these situations can be represented then by the final flowchart and its program (Figs. 7 and 8, respectively).

CASE B: INFORMATION RETRIEVAL VIA A TERMINAL. If an information storage and retrieval system such as a CORI (criminal offender record information) file is well designed, one need know nothing about computers or programming languages to use it. One needs only be taught a few simple steps such as the following:

1. *Sign on:* activate the terminal, establish communication with the computer.

2. *Identify:* give user name, number, password, or other security information.

3. *Select:* identify the file from which information is desired.

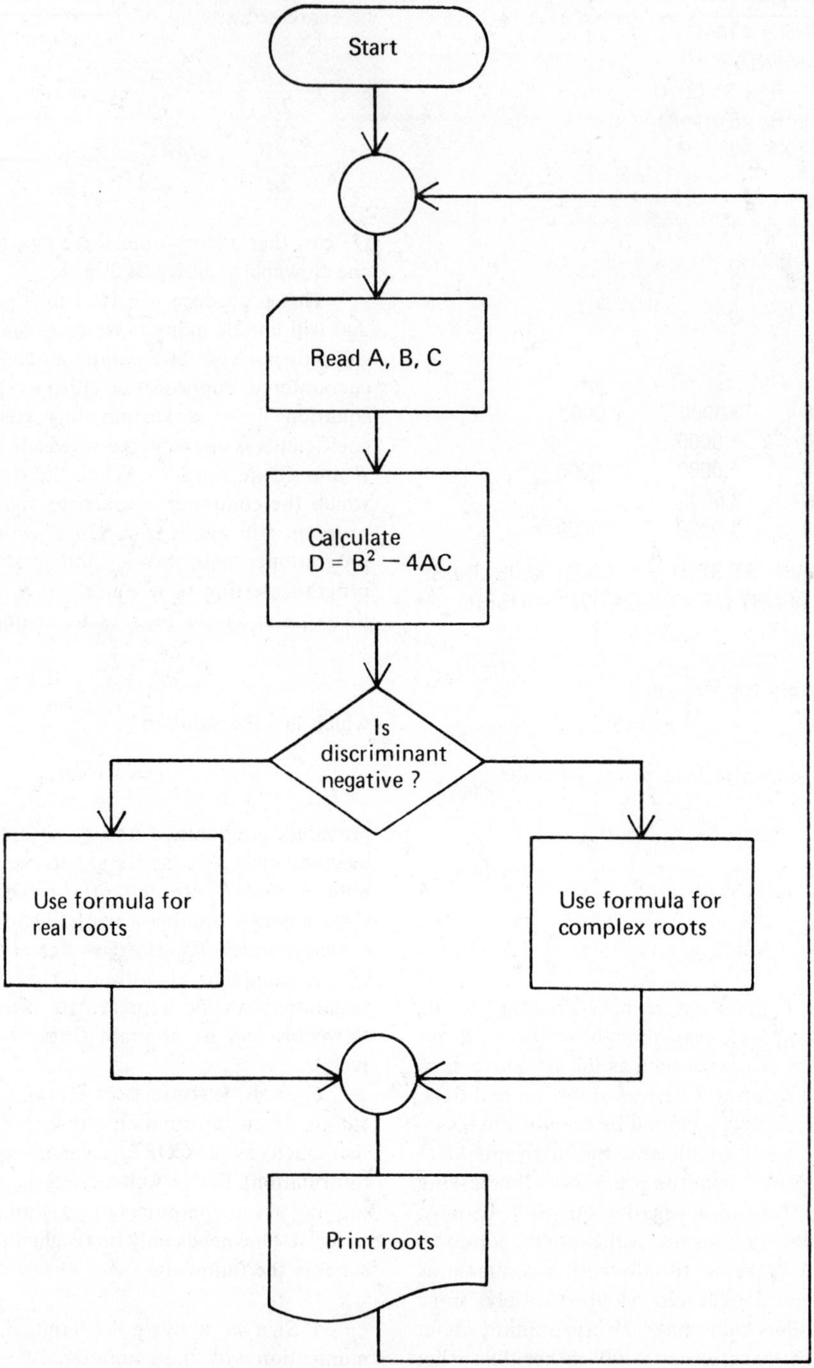


**Fig. 5.** Flowchart for Version 2.

Program

```
1  READ, A, B, C
   PRINT, A, B, C
   D = B*B - 4*A*C
   IF(D .LT. 0)  GO TO 2
   S = SQRT(D)
   X1 = (-B + S)/(2*A)
   X2 = (-B - S)/(2*A)
   PRINT, X1, X2
   GO TO 1
2  S = SQRT(-D)
   RR = -B(2*A)
   RI1 = S/(2*A)
   RI2 = -S/(2*A)
   PRINT, RR, RI1
   PRINT, RR, RI2
   GO TO 1
   END
```

Data

```
   1   -3    2
   1    5    6
   1    1    1
   0    3   12
```

Results

```
   1.0000          -3.0000          2.0000
   2.0000           1.0000
   1.0000           5.0000          6.0000
  -2.0000          -3.0000
   1.0000           1.0000          1.0000
  -5.0000E-01       8.6603E-01
  -5.0000E-01      -8.6603E-01
   0.0000           3.0000         12.0000
ERROR IN *MAIN* AT STMT. NO. 00001 + 05 LINES:
   DIVISION BY ZERO
ABORT
```

**Fig. 6.** Program for Version 2.

4. *Specify:* give the identification information (name, Social Security number, or fingerprint classification) of the individual whose record is desired.

5. *Get answer:* read the desired information from the display screen.

In many such systems, use is made still simpler by having the computer prompt the user through asking questions and indicating the nature and form of the next piece of information needed.

CASE C: DESIGN AND IMPLEMENTATION OF A COMPLEX BUSINESS DATA PROCESSING SYSTEM. Compiler writers who supply the language translators, and even the systems analysts who design complex information processing systems, are not end users of a computer, but end-use facilitators. It is their job to build programs whereby others less knowledgeable about the computer can nevertheless use it to get their various tasks done. In principle, the program designer's task is similar to that of the engineer in Case A, but its greater complexity makes it different on several counts.

For one thing, the operations of the business to be computerized need to be studied in far greater detail, and a thorough understanding of the whole process must be gained. At the same time, an awareness of the potential impact of the computer must be kept uppermost in mind. "How are things done now?" is an important question, but it must not become all-important. A much better way to phrase the question is, "Now that we have the computer, how *should* we run our business?"

The study of the overall process of information flow must include answers to such questions as:

- What are the fundamental (inherent) inputs?
- What other inputs are necessary?
- What outputs are wanted:
  - Summary reports?
  - Exception reports?
  - Answers to enquiries?
- How should the data base (files) be designed?
- What transactions take place?
- What are the impacts of every transaction?
- When are each of these processes carried out:
  - Immediately upon occurrence of the transaction?
  - Periodically?
  - When triggered by some other event?

It may be noted that in such a data processing system, the files and the flow of data into and out of these files are of much greater concern than the computational operations. This is indeed true of data processing in general, and hence the computational algorithm is often secondary here.

Once the flow of information is properly laid out—using lists, decision tables, flowcharts, systems charts, or even some specially designed problem statement language—the remainder of the process can proceed much as with the single problem solution. The program is written (often by several individuals, each working on assigned sections, so that consistency of nomenclature and the intercommunication between the sections become particularly important), punched, and debugged, as before. The testing process also is more complex,

## COMPUTER, USING A

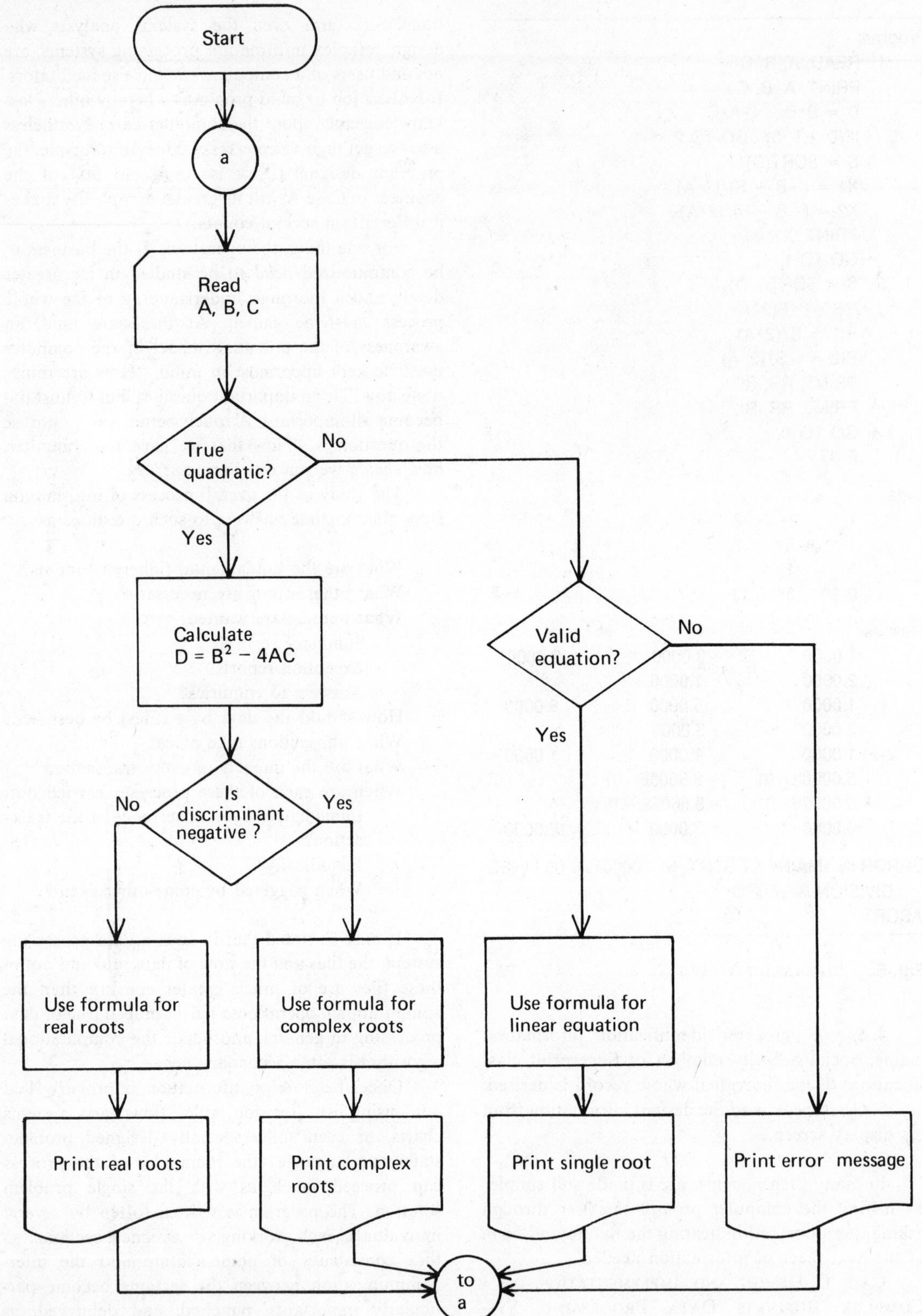


**Fig. 7.** Flowchart for Version 3.

```
Program
         WRITE(6,10)
       1 READ, A, B, C
         IF(A .NE. 0)  GO TO 2
         IF(B .EQ. 0)  GO TO 7
C
C  EQUATION IS LINEAR
C
         ROOT = -C/B
         WRITE(6,11) A, B, C, ROOT
         GO TO 1
C
C  ERROR
C
       7 WRITE(6,16) A, B, C
         GO TO 1
C
C  TEST DISCRIMINANT
C
       2 D = B*B - 4*A*C
         IF(D .LT. 0)  GO TO 4
C
C  EQUATION HAS TWO REAL ROOTS
C
         S = SQRT(D)
         ROOT1 = (-B + S)/(2*A)
         ROOT2 = (-B - S)/(2*A)
         WRITE(6,12) A, B, C
         WRITE(6,13) ROOT1, ROOT2
         GO TO 1
C
C  EQUATION HAS TWO COMPLEX ROOTS
C
       4 S = SQRT(-D)
         RR = -B/(2*A)
         RI = -S(2*A)
         WRITE(6,14) A, B, C
         WRITE(6,15) RR, RI
         GO TO 1
   10    FORMAT(6X,'A',6X,'B',8X,'C'/1X,3('  -------'))
   11    FORMAT(3F9.2,'  IS A LINEAR EQUATION'/
      *         36X,'ROOT = ',1PE11.4/)
   12    FORMAT(3F9.2,'  HAS TWO REAL ROOTS')
   13    FORMAT(38X,'R1 = ',1PE11.4/38X,'R2 = ',1PE11.4/)
   14    FORMAT(3F9.2,'  HAS TWO COMPLEX ROOTS')
   15    FORMAT(36X,'REAL = ',1PE11,4/)
      *         31X,'IMAGINARY = ',1PE11.4/)
   16    FORMAT(3F9.2,'  NO EQUATION')
         END
Data
   1   -3    2
   1    5    6
   1    1    1
   0    3   12
   0    0   12
Results
     A       B       C
  ------  ------  ------
  1.00   -3.00    2.00  HAS TWO REAL ROOTS
                                  R1 =  2.0000E+00
                                  R2 =  1.0000E+00
  1.00    5.00    6.00  HAS TWO REAL ROOTS
                                  R1 = -2.0000E+00
                                  R2 = -3.0000E+00
  1.00    1.00    1.00  HAS TWO COMPLEX ROOTS
                                REAL = -5.0000E-01
                           IMAGINARY =  8.6603E-01
  0.00    3.00   12.00  IS A LINEAR EQUATION
                                ROOT = -4.0000E+00
  0.00    0.00   12.00  NO EQUATION
```

**Fig. 8.** Program for Version 3.

frequently involving independent testing of each process at a time, followed by simultaneous testing of various sections working together, and then of the complete system, making sure to test it under expected full-load conditions. Even when it appears to be ready, it has been found highly advisable to plan a concurrent operation of the old system and the new for a transition period. Essential to the system at any stage are backup files and restart procedures, so that when (not if) something goes wrong, only a small amount of the most recent processing is lost and, with a minimum of redoing, all records can be completely restored.

In the data processing system case it is even more essential than in the earlier case that complete documentation, explanation, and instructions for operation be prepared. Not only is it necessary for employees unfamiliar with either the program or the computer to use the system and to supply the daily inputs it must have, but managers, accountants, and tax investigators must all be able to gain a clear picture of how it operates, what it does, and what the meanings and validity of the results are.

Properly designed, built, tested, explained, and trained for, such a computer information processing system can be "used" by a great many people for a long time to carry out the operations of the company faster, more accurately, and more efficiently, and above all to provide management with more meaningful information about how to run the company.

C. H. DAVIDSON

# COMPUTER ACCOUNTING AND RESOURCE CONTROL

For articles on related terms *see* ADMINISTRATIVE-BUSINESS APPLICATIONS; COMPUTING CENTER; COMPUTING SYSTEMS; COMPUTING UTILITY; DATA SECURITY; FILES; and OPERATING SYSTEMS: Contemporary, Features of.
For articles on related terms *see* COMMAND AND JOB CONTROL LANGUAGES; and INTERVAL TIMER.

As computer/software systems have developed, there has been a corresponding need to develop an accounting system for the resources of the system. As with any accounting system, the goal of this capability must be to charge the user for the cost of services rendered to him in such a fashion that he is motivated to evaluate the benefits of those services. The implications of this statement are that not only must there be charges rendered for these services but that also there must be means of preventing unauthorized use of the system. Furthermore, the resources used by any one user must be limited in order to prevent him from degrading the total effective services offered.

Accountability is important both to the computing center staff and to its users. In order to perform their duties as financial planners for the center, the administrators require some form of an accounting system. Such a system may be expected to yield statistics on hardware utilization and individual spending. These statistics can then be used to form the monthly and yearly reports submitted by the administrator(s) to whom the staff reports.

The completely automated accounting and resource control system—

Provides minute details concerning both hardware and software utilization along with job statistics on account spending.

Prevents unauthorized users from utilizing hardware and software facilities for which they have not received permission.

Prevents users from exceeding their allocated funds or other account limits.

Enforces job limitations on such things as page or line limits, computer time, core size, and permanent files.

Assists the operating system in providing more effective control of the resources (main memory, auxiliary memory, peripheral devices, etc.) of the system.

## Development of Accounting and Resource Control Systems

EARLY COMPUTER SYSTEMS. Since early computer systems consisted of hardware with little or no software support, automated accounting was almost nonexistent. The accounting that did exist was done by user sign-up sheets, time clocks, or a flat-rate charge per computer run.

The idea of basing charges on the value of resources used was not very important either. Because the entire computer was dedicated to the current user, there was little reason to charge less if the program used only half of memory or no tapes, etc. Besides, the hardware could not usually support an accounting system because there was no hardware-readable clock and it was often not practical for the machine operator to type in the date and time for each job logged on the machine.

EARLY AUTOMATED ACCOUNTING SYSTEMS. As Rosin (1969) points out, the first accounting systems were often nothing more than system logs produced by the "on-line" printing facility. Since the purpose of such a log was to record the use of major system components, the log was more useful for measuring system behavior than for actual user accounting.

Some systems were enhanced by a hardware-readable clock, which made it possible to log the time along with the system component in use. However, the content of each entry in the log was a function of the sophistication of the resident monitor and often provided only such information as log-on and log-off time. Thus, user accounting was still based on total machine time used, with the hardware clock now providing a more accurate method for recording that time.

EXECUTIVE SYSTEMS AND AUTOMATED ACCOUNTING. With the introduction of channels and interrupts, the establishment of resident monitors or supervisors became an accepted fact. These supervisors were complex routines that could process interrupts, software requests, and a new language called the "command" language. Thus, the computer user could communicate with the system via command language control cards that provided such information as name and account number, job limitations on time, pages, and cards to be used, and special resources (tapes, plotter, etc.) required.

Utilizing the hardware clock, most user interactions with the system were recorded, detailing what commands the system had received. The purpose of the accounting system was to monitor the individual user's interaction with the system and not simply the system performance.

Still, until the introduction of disk files, it was not feasible to verify each user's identification against some master file of valid users. Nor was it possible to determine user limits as to funds available, privileges, etc. Instead, accounting information was collected on magnetic tape or punched cards for later processing on an after-the-fact basis.

Disk Files. The introduction of disk files added another step in automated accounting. Although not truly a random access storage device, a disk file was sufficiently fast to provide for an on-line verification of valid user identification. The accounting files could be permanent or resident files in the system, available only to the supervisor and the accounting system (i.e., privileged).

The accounting system could record each job transition or step, print out job charges at the completion of a job, and accumulate monthly statistics. By maintaining the accounting information in an on-line fashion, users could be prevented from using more than their current funds or exceeding their current account limits.

Multiprogramming and Time Sharing. The more recent advances in computer hardware/software—namely, multiprogramming and time sharing —have produced the greatest impact on automated accounting. Because these advantages have made it feasible to allocate and share the multiple resources of a computing system, it is possible to have multiple users on the system at the same time. And as Nielsen (1968, p. 522) points out:

> ... in order to allocate the resources of the entire system so as to maximize the utilization of these resources, it is necessary to have not just an array of prices, but an array of flexible or adjustable prices that are responsive to demand. In other words, services as well as computer resources must be taken into consideration."

For each user of the system, the accounting system must know (1) who is responsible for the charges, (2) what type of service this user is entitled to (and with what constraints), (3) what resources have been allocated to the user, and (4) what price schedule applies. Further, the pricing structure must allow the user to easily estimate and predict his costs, and should require only small amounts of system resources for the accounting.

Unbundling and Proprietary Software. With unbundling and time sharing has come new problems in automated accounting. Where it was previously possible to simply charge the proprietary system user for computer time used, more complex multiuser systems have made it possible to allow one user to provide service to another. The result is that users are billed by both the computing center (for hardware use, expendable supplies, etc.) and other users (for proprietary software use). Thus, the accounting system must be cognizant of the use of such proprietary software and should, in fact, allow some "higher-order" user to suballocate to another user some of the resources under his control. For instance, it should be possible for one user to develop and maintain a subsystem, fully consistent with the operating and accounting systems, which bills the individual users for actual resources used (both hardware and software).

Another example might be the course instructor who allocates fixed amounts of time or money to each student in his course in such a fashion that no student can use more than his share. Obviously, the person responsible for the account must be able to reallocate the resources without exceeding the total allotted to him. In addition, he should be able to place limits, which may not be uniform, on each student account so that special projects may use extra core or disk space, special hardware, etc.

Since some software can be charged only on a "value received" or transaction basis (such as ledger entries in an accounting system, or students scheduled in an automated scheduling system), the accounting system must be flexible in terms of the algorithm used to calculate actual charges.

**Costs of an Automated Accounting System and Charges Levied.** The costs of an automated accounting system are directly a function of the resources used to gather and maintain the accounting information. In order that the overhead of collecting the information not interfere with normal system operation, the charges themselves must reflect the unique characteristics of the system. Normally, charges are based on such things as:

1. CPU time.
2. Memory time.

3. Connect time and/or port cost.
4. I/O operations performed.
5. Physical I/O units used:
   (a) Cards read/punched.
   (b) Lines printed.
   (c) Magnetic tapes mounted.
   (d) File space used.

However, these charges must relate to the characteristics of the operating system if they are to be easily collected. They should also relate to the allocation scheme for the resources if they are to be fairly levied (i.e., disk space should not be charged on a bit or character basis if it is allocated on a track or sector basis).

An on-line system where each user has an active account, although costly in terms of disk space required, allows the accounting system to—

1. Encumber funds on a per-job basis so as to prevent negative spending.
2. Set dynamic limits on controlled privileges as a function of time, geographic entry point, and system load.
3. Maintain flexible and dynamic pricing with actual cost information available to users on demand.
4. Maintain up-to-the-minute accounting for each user and periodically inform users of their accumulated computer resource utilization.

As described, automated systems can be fairly costly. However, the benefits provided both to the computing center operations staff (e.g., current resource use, system load, operating difficulties, etc.) and to the users (e.g., current pricing structure, resources available, job flow, etc.) generally outweigh the costs. Indeed, by knowing the state of the computing system, both operators and users are able to optimize their interaction with it so as to increase its effective utilization.

REFERENCES

1968. Nielsen, N. R. "Flexible Pricing: An Approach to the Allocation of Computer Resources," *Proceedings of the Spring Joint Computer Conference*, pp. 521–531.

1969. Rosin, R. F. "Supervisory and Monitor Systems," *Computing Surveys*, Vol. 1, pp. 37–54.

R. H. ECKHOUSE

# COMPUTER-AIDED DESIGN

For articles on related subjects *see* COMPUTER GRAPHICS; IMAGE AND PICTURE PROCESSING; INPUT-OUTPUT DEVICES; LIGHTPEN; TERMINALS; and TIME SHARING.

Design is that creative activity which translates ideas into tangible reality. Engineering design has as its aim the production of specifications to allow manufacture to proceed and satisfactorily meet requirements.

Computer-aided design (CAD) concerns the utilization of computer systems for the purpose of design and communication of design information. The individual techniques used are not necessarily unique to CAD, but the particular combinations of computer system characteristics necessary for the full realization of CAD warrant special attention as a field of computer application. Design (and here we imply not just engineering design but any analogous activity that has as its objectives the output of manufacturing or construction information) may be considered on two quite distinct levels: first as a process of manipulating, analyzing, and assessing information (often of a geometric kind) in order to select options and optimize some performance characteristics against a given specification; and second, as a process of planning and information exchange between various organizations or parts of an organization in order to assemble and utilize the necessary design and manufacturing information in an optimum fashion. The first viewpoint emphasizes the special techniques of man/computer interaction that are sometimes taken to be synonymous with CAD, while the second viewpoint highlights the economically more significant factors of overall computer system design for effective information exchange.

Special-purpose analog computers were perhaps the first true design aids in that they provided models of systems, which could then be refined by experimentation, an analog not only of the system but of the mental processes of the designer. Design aids in the form of analysis programs were among the first uses of digital computers, and with the addition of output plotters they provided the ability to generate and visalize geometric information. The term computer-aided design became recognized following the work at M.I.T. in the late 1950s on the SAGE system and on multiaccess computing, which produced, respectively, the computer-driven cathode-ray tube display and the time-sharing computer systems that made interactive computing possible at an economic cost.

The special power of interactive graphical displays lies in the iterative nature of design, normally a slow process bedeviled by lack of information. The interactive terminal permits many design options to be explored in a short time, and the addition of high-speed graphical visualization provides a means of data compression in a form familiar to the designer—a graph, diagram, or drawing. The lightpen as a means of input is also essentially a data compression device and is replaced as appropriate by keyboard commands, joystick movements, programmed function buttons, or stylus movements.

Time sharing has led to a massive growth in the use of multiaccess computers for both interactive and remote-batch processing in engineering, since it has made possible on-line working and interactive computing, if required, at reasonable cost. However, from the point of view of CAD, it is the multiaccess nature of the operating system and not the time sharing that is primarily significant, because it allows multiple access to files of information and so provides the essential basis for integrated information systems.

The multiple use of large computer systems made possible by time sharing in turn made feasible the development of advanced software, both at system and application levels. The linking of computers through data communications is a continuation of the trend that also favors the increased application of CAD through dedicated interactive graphics processors forming "terminals" in such a network. The two main aspects of CAD—interactive design optimization and large-scale information processing—may thus be functionally separated while remaining part of an integrated operational system.

**Special Equipment.** There is on the market a wide range of printing terminals, of graphics terminals (particularly storage tube types), and of various sorts of add-on plotters to terminals attached to the ends of telephone lines. Some of these have been available for some time, and are generally well known. The ubiquitous Teletype hardly needs any description; in recent years a number of improvements have been made to this type of device, usually accompanied by a corresponding increase in price. A number of manufacturers have made available a plotting addition to the Teletype terminal. In most cases, this is driven by interposing a control box between the Teletype and the telephone line, so that a character stream from the computer is diverted to the plotter on appropriate occasions.

What has become popular in the last few years is the graphics terminal based on the storage-tube technique. Using a direct-view storage tube, a number of manufacturers have produced terminals on which may be displayed either alphanumeric or graphical information. At least one model is now available for less than $5,000, and is capable of presenting a very clear line definition so that a complex picture may be painted on the screen. Storage tubes do have the disadvantage of not showing up particularly well in high ambient lighting conditions, and the erasure of chosen elements on the screen cannot be achieved except by clearing the screen and starting again. However, for certain applications they have proved to be more than adequate in real use and in many instances have become the equipment of choice. More recently, inexpensive terminals based on a conventional television display have made an appearance. Although for the present these are somewhat lacking in line definition, they can be seen in bright light, and the screen can be quite large.

An important development is the recent availability of the refreshed display terminal driven by a minicomputer, interfaced in turn to a communications line. These terminals are a development from the classical approach to computer graphics, except that they are very much cheaper, much more compact, and more restricted in the facilities they offer. The communications interface is asynchronous, so it looks to the host computer more like a conventional terminal. The absence of flashing lights is a relief, and the whole setup is small enough to stand on or sit next to a desk.

It is not within the scope of this article to discuss in any detail the pros and cons of any particular terminal. However, it is possible to point out one or two deficiencies in current ways of working. Much of the terminal equipment in use at the present time has been developed by specialist manufacturers who can be only partially concerned with the design problems to be solved. On the other hand, a clear understanding of what is needed to adopt CAD methods is still beyond the grasp of most computer system designers. It is hardly surprising that the exposure of available hardware to real design problems has shown some shortcomings in what is available.

An example is the simple storage-tube terminal used at the end of a telephone line. This is now commonly used for design work, fulfilling a dual role as an alphanumeric terminal and a graphic display. A difficulty that emerges when trying to use such a device in a real-life application is that the alphanumeric information tends to get mixed up with the pictorial content, and a muddle ensues. The penalty incurred in avoiding the muddle is to clear the screen and to withstand another response-time delay. A frequently expressed desire is to be able to turn a hard copy device on and off, line by line, instead of having to deal with the contents of the whole screen. A solution to these problems seems to be in the development of a storage-tube terminal with an additional printing unit.

Finally, the use of powerful plotter systems should not be overlooked. These hardly come in the category of terminals for CAD, but do form an important ancillary to them. They can provide a very useful cover for the obvious deficiencies of a storage-tube terminal in the production of final accurate drawings, provided the graphics software facilities in the computer are correctly and rationally organized.

**Computer System Aspects.** Much of the early work in CAD was achieved by the use of dedicated computer power. Leaving aside for the moment the general-purpose computing done for engineering purposes, much of this early work was associated with graphic systems in which the display screen is directly refreshed from a stand-alone computer. The user sits in front of the display screen, which fulfills the function of an output device, while a variety of input devices may be available to the designer, such as lightpens, tracker balls, graphical tablets, and so forth. These systems can be highly interactive, giving the designer an almost instantaneous response to many of his demands. Much of the hardware has had an expensive air about it, and some of the display systems have been capable of manipulating pictures on the screen by means of hardware. Fundamental problems of picture manipulation include windowing and the rotation of three-dimensional wire diagrams. Windowing allows the user to display a small part of a large picture within finite screen bounds in two-dimensions, that is, in the $X$- and $Y$-dimensions, all parts of the picture outside these bounds being suppressed. Scissoring, or clipping, allows the user to control a three-dimensional display in the $Z$-dimension. Rotation, windowing, and even perspective projection have all been implemented as hardware options on some displays.

The designers' ability to input free-form information, as with Sutherland's Sketchpad and other similar devices, is an important element in computer-aided design. Three-dimensional flexibility is required, but this awaits a new breakthrough in equipment.

The disadvantage with the stand-alone graphics approach to CAD has been the expense. The capital cost of the equipment has been high and beyond the means of any but large organizations. Consequently, much of the pioneer work in CAD has been accomplished in university environments and in the larger companies. The advent of the simple storage tube meant that attempts had been made to run design processes on more conventional computer systems. In particular, the nature of the design program is that it has the characteristics of being rather large and yet spends a great deal of its time waiting for human intervention. On the face of it, it would appear to be a good candidate for running in a multiaccess system, and successful attempts have been made in this area. However, there remains the class of truly interactive design requirements that cannot successfully run in a multiaccess system, which is inevitably under management pressure to be optimized in revenue terms rather than in response terms. What may be required is a new design of multiaccess systems in which multiprocessor configurations are available to designers. In this way, each designer would have full private use of his individual processor whenever he is logged in. At the time of writing, attempts are being made to devise practicable systems along these lines, and it could be that this will be one of the major developments in the history of CAD.

**Software Aspects.** Perhaps the most important criterion in the design of software systems for CAD is portability. The cost of developing software tools and applications programs is often large in relation to the obvious economic benefits. In other words, the advantages of the CAD approach over manual methods are usually to be seen in terms of lead time to the finished product, rather than any direct reduction in costs. Consequently, it is of great importance that a software system developed on any particular type of hardware should be arranged in such a way that its use is not confined. Therefore most practical approaches in the applications area have been based on the use of Fortran as the prime language, although many software systems have been much more parochial in nature.

It is now of importance that software systems which have been in full and regular use in general- and special-purpose centers should be re-created in such a way that useful software facilities can be made available on computing systems other than those on which they have been developed. This requires a sensitivity by software writers to the need for using intermediate-level assembly systems and languages, which have been little used so far despite the many enthusiastic beginnings. One of the problems in this area is that the writing of graphics subsystems requires the use of a language that compiles very efficient code and yet which has a full range of arithmetic capabilities for matrix manipulation and the like. This dual requirement could account for the many individual and divisive approaches that have been made.

**Applications.** All CAD applications utilize in varying degrees the three special computer system facilities of interaction, graphical visualization, and large-scale data communication. It can be argued that purely analytic or algorithmic design methods are possible and do not constitute CAD, but in practice it is generally found that such methods can be adopted only in restricted circumstances and that any attempt to produce a comprehensive design/manufacturing system leads to the adoption of CAD techniques.

The classic application areas of printed circuit and integrated circuit design, structural design optimization, and graphical part programming for numerical control machining were explored in an aerospace industry context in the 1960s and have now been highly developed. In such industries the complexity of design and the large work load have always put a premium on computer aids, and although the general approach adopted is relevant to other industries and applications, the specific solutions need to be modified to allow for different economic circumstances. In particular, it has not been found possible until recently to justify extensive use of dedicated graphic display processors although some pilot-scale installations have been used and have proved cost effective.

The developments that have recently taken place in types of display terminals, plotters, communication equipment, auxiliary storage (including cassette tape and disks), and in minicomputers means that, in contrast to the situation that obtained in the 1950s and 1960s, it is now possible to analyze an application requirement in detail and obtain computing facilities to suit, either from a specialized center or in house, or in combination. As a con-

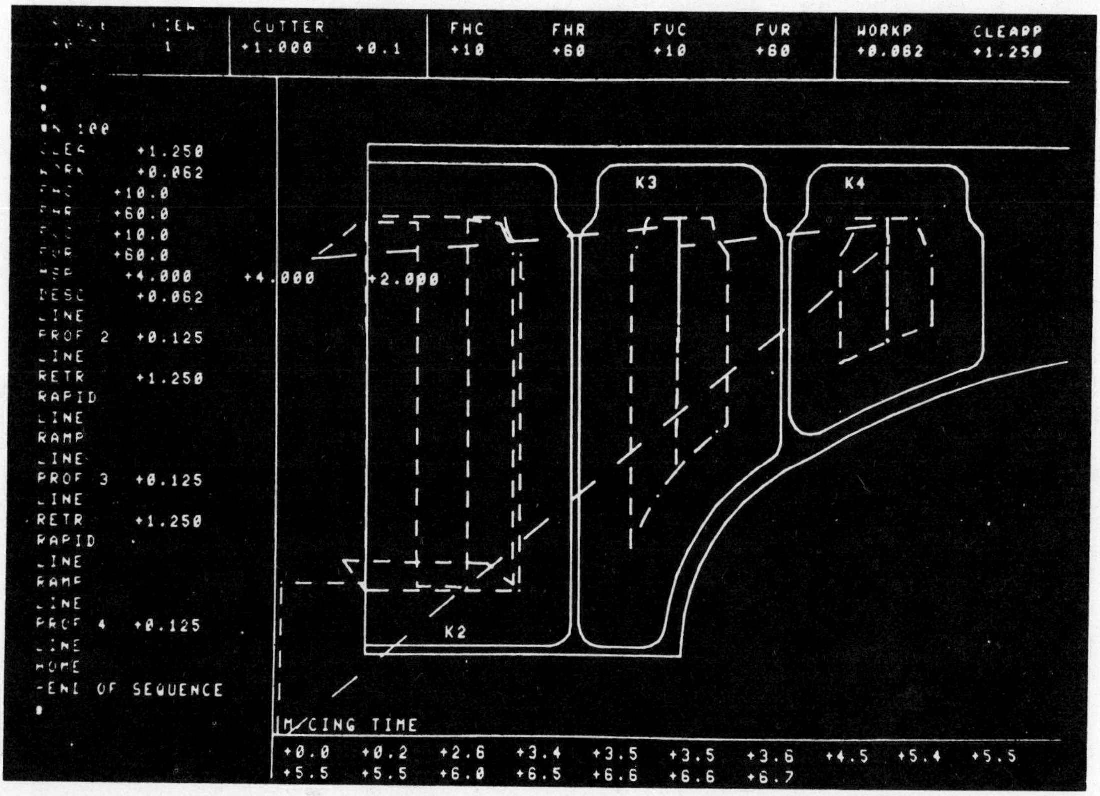


**Fig. 1.** Graphical numerical control programming taken from a storage-tube display.

sequence, even classic applications like printed circuit board and graphical numerical control programming can be reoptimized in terms of cost, performance, and convenience. Fig. 1 illustrates graphical numerical control programming, using a low-cost storage tube terminal with a software system suitable for desk use on a free-standing minicomputer system. The same developments in time-shared computer systems and lower-cost equipment have made CAD more widely available in all fields of engineering and design.

The interactive use of computers through CAD is frequently aimed at design optimization. Optimum structural design becomes possible through on-line display of graphed output from analysis programs (Fig. 2). In the construction industry, increasing use is being made of computer-produced drawings for engineering purposes and halftone representations for environmental evaluation (Fig. 3). The design of buildings provides fertile ground for CAD, since design optimization to meet user requirements within the many constraints of site, cost, and materials is a complex process. Yet, with the development of coordinated dimensioning systems and component standardization, it becomes possible to consider completely integrated "architectural" CAD systems. At the conceptual design stage, layouts and relationships may be explored quickly; during design realization, interactive methods permit optimization of structure and layout with visualization at each stage (Fig. 4); and in an integrated design system, data processing may be invoked on a large scale,

**Fig. 3.** Halftone representations for environmental evaluation taken from a refresh tube display.

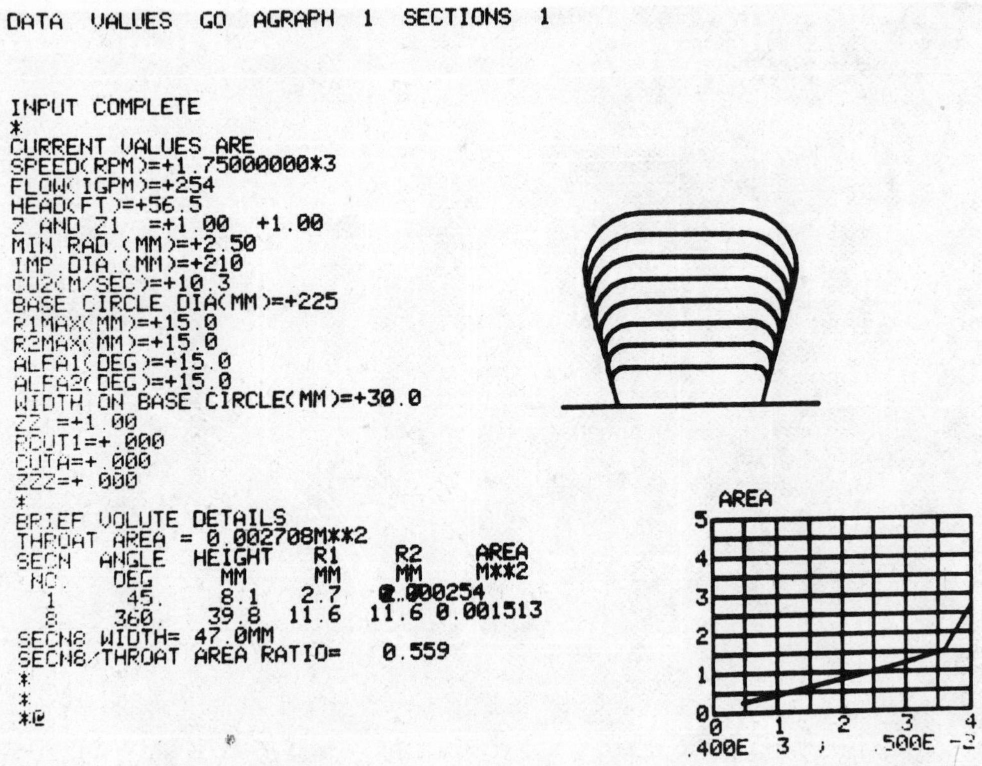


**Fig. 2.** On-line display of graphic output from analysis programs taken from a storage-tube display.

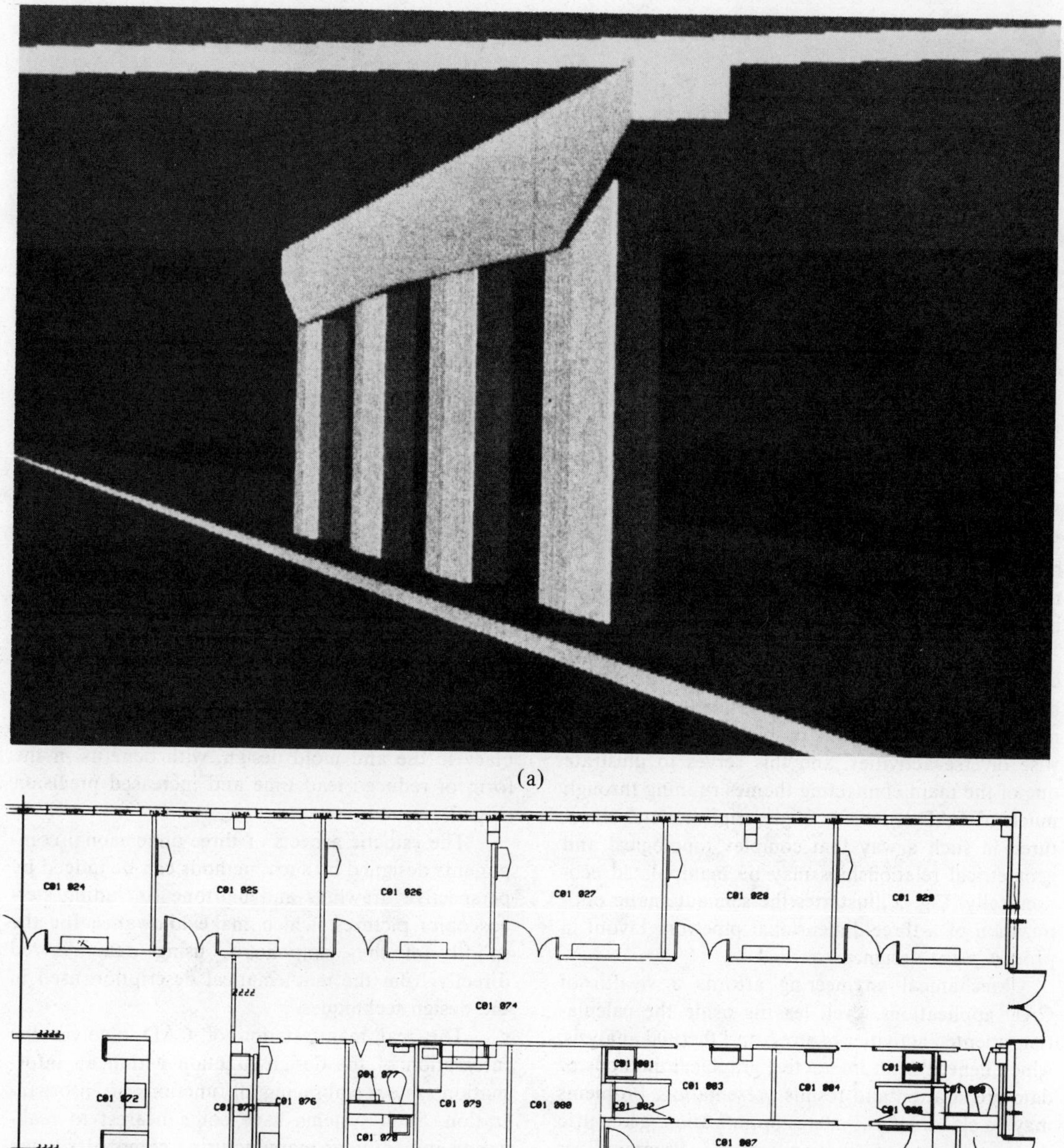

(a)

(b)

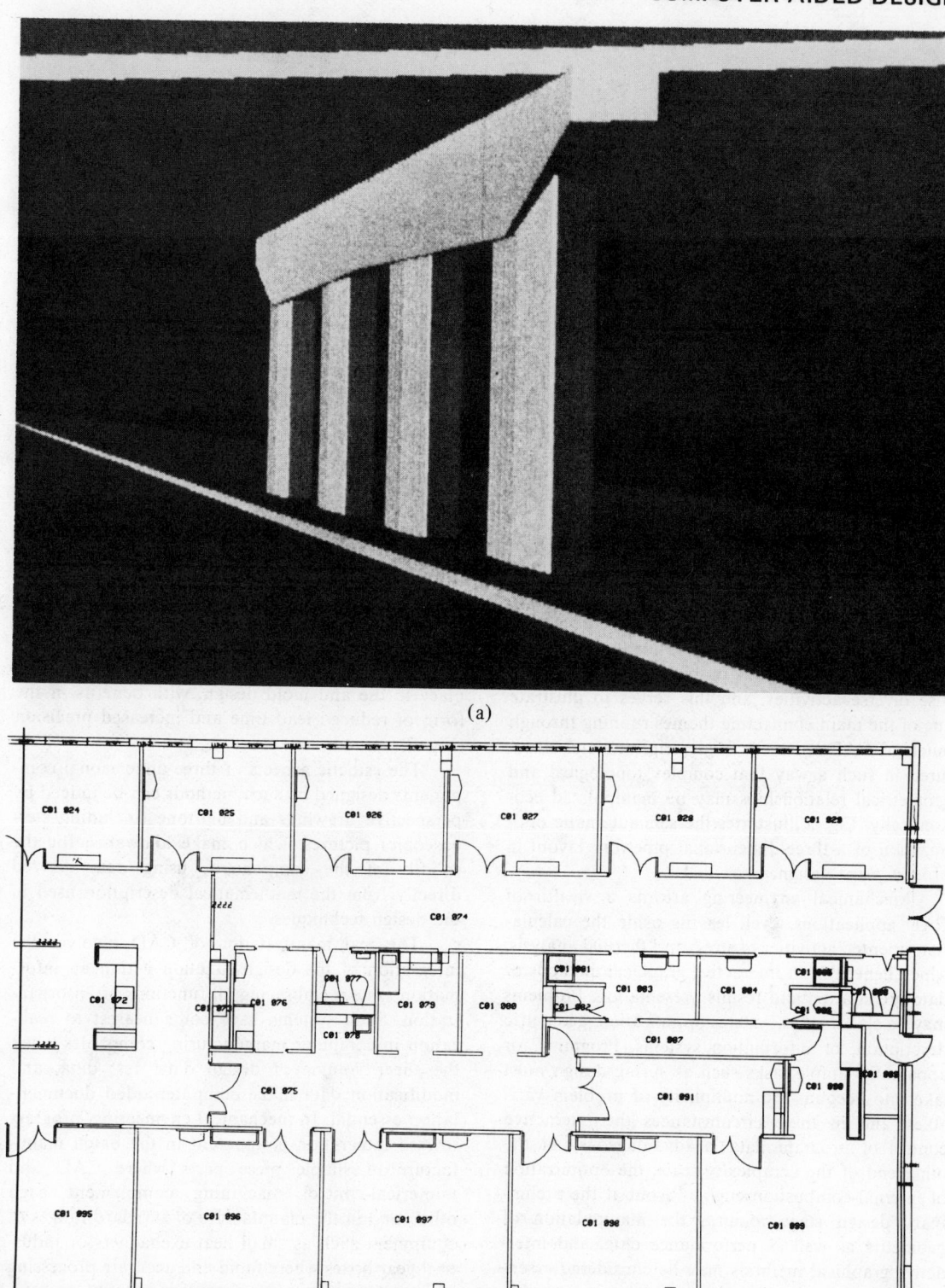

**Fig. 4.** (a) Structure; (b) composition showing architectural visualization of structure and layout.

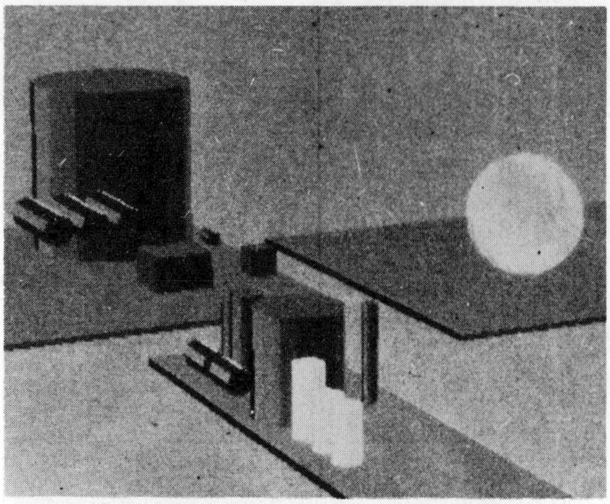

**Fig. 5.** Three-dimensional pipework layout in chemical plant design.

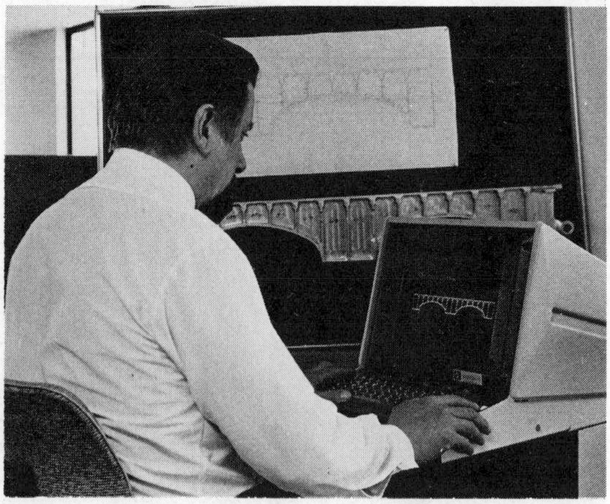

**Fig. 6.** Designs of engineering components.

both to utilize stored data on components and methods and to generate quantitative construction information.

Optimization of layout of components and their connections is a common requirement in circuit boards, architecture, and process plants. There are many related topological problems in these otherwise diverse activities, and this serves to illustrate one of the main connecting themes running through much of CAD—the use of descriptive data, structured in such a way that complex topological and geometrical relationships may be manipulated economically. Fig. 5 illustrates the semiautomatic optimization of a three-dimensional pipework layout in process plant design.

Mechanical engineering affords a wealth of CAD applications, even leaving aside the calculation-oriented activities of stress and thermal analysis, which benefit from interactive graphical methods of data preparation and results presentation. Problems may be classified as systems optimization, geometric description, or information systems. Programs for apparently simple tasks such as spring design must take into account the multiplicity of problem variables, and in these circumstances the interactive control of program data is advantageous. At the other end of the complexity scale, the optimization of internal-combustion engine layout at the preliminary design stage requires the manipulation of geometric as well as performance data, and interactive graphical methods may be considered essential to a full exploration of options in a reasonably short time.

Very many engineering components are two-dimensional in nature, and the ability to describe and manipulate profiles via the display screen makes possible both the drafting and part programming of components (Fig. 6) and the computer-aided design of press tools. Three-dimensional geometry manipulation is among the more difficult design and manufacturing problems, and the use of either curve fitting or analytical surface geometry is finding a place in die and mold design, with benefits in the form of reduced lead time and increased precision (Fig. 7).

The esthetic aspects of three-dimensional components designed by such methods can be judged by perspective drawings and halftone (including stereoscopic) pictures, which make allowance for the solidity of the components, using data derived directly from the mathematical description used in the design techniques.

The real manifestation of CAD involves the integration of the design function within an information system embracing all functions of an organization. Such systems have come nearest to realization in computer manufacturing companies when the sheer volume of design data, test data, and modification data make computer-aided documentation essential. In mechanical engineering, progress toward integration is apparent in the batch manufacture of simple piece parts where CAD and numerical-control machining complement each other, and in the manufacture of standard ranges of equipment such as small heat exchangers or industrial gear boxes where rapid and accurate processing of documentation is a prime requirement.

The ultimate manifestation of CAD will carry this integration process a stage further and provide a system able to examine total design options, i.e.,

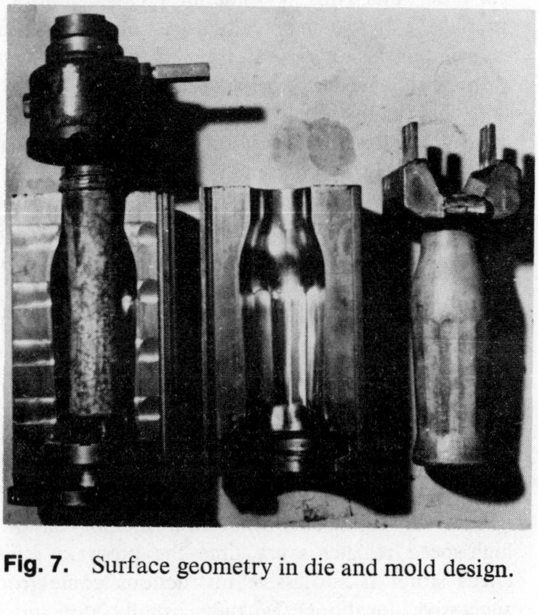

**Fig. 7.** Surface geometry in die and mold design.

trade-offs not just between design and manufacturing but also in service, use, and reliability. As technology progresses, this need will extend to an examination at the design stage of the balance of benefits to the community. The CAD system must therefore be arranged to take account of this to allow such participation.

REFERENCES

1967. Gruenberger, F. (Ed.). *Computer Graphics—Utility–Product–Art.* Washington, D.C.: Thompson Book Co.

1970. Furman, T. T. (Ed.). *Uses of Computers in Engineering Design.* London: E U P.

1970. Wolfendale, E. *C. A. D. Techniques.* London: Butterworths.

1973. Hyman, A. *The Computer in Design.* London: Studio Vista.

1973. Vlietstra, J., and R. F. Wielinga (Eds.). *Computer-Aided Design.* Amsterdam: North Holland.

A. I. LLEWELYN

## COMPUTER ARCHITECTURE

For articles on related subjects *see* ADDRESSING; ARITHMETIC-LOGIC UNIT; CHANNEL; DATA COMMUNICATIONS: INPUT-OUTPUT DEVICES; INTERRUPT; MEMORY: Auxiliary; MEMORY: Main; OPERATING SYSTEMS; SOFTWARE; and SUPER-COMPUTERS.

For articles on related terms *see* CACHE MEMORY; CONTENTION; CONTROL DATA CORPORATION 6000 SERIES; CPU; and VON NEUMANN MACHINE.

Computer architecture embraces the art and science of assembling logical elements into a computing device. As normally conceived, a computer architect accepts from a logical designer units such as adders, stacks, memory modules, and tape drives; puts them together so that they form a computer; and turns this over to a systems programmer, who then constructs an operating system for the machine. This should not be construed as being a passive role. The computer architect is responsible for (and, indeed, is almost the only one in a position to accomplish) the ideas interchanged between the two groups. He must bring software problems to the attention of the hardware types and hardware potentialities to the attention of the software types.

There are five fundamental components in any particular machine design. These are input/output, storage, communication, control, and processing. These are the five basic units of the simplest

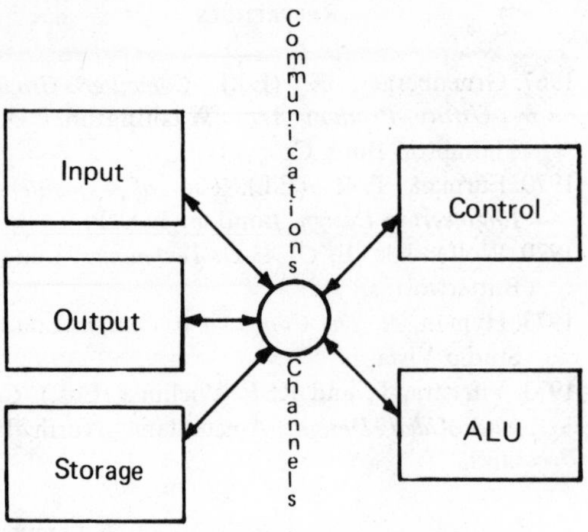


**Fig. 1.** Basic elements of every computer.

computer, as shown in Fig. 1. The devices on the left correspond to the "tape," the channel corresponds to the "head," and the units on the right correspond to the control mechanism of a Turing machine.

For reasons of cost and/or performance, various of these basic units are elaborated in different ways in extant machines. We will discuss the separate units and their complications one by one.

**Input-Output.** Although it is only through the input and output (I/O) devices that one can "converse" with a computer, surprisingly little attention has been paid to them architecturally. What *has* happened is that a separate channel has been provided between the I/O devices and the main storage device. Over this channel, information can flow into and out of the computer without tying up the arithmetic-logic unit (ALU) or the control unit. This requires that the storage units have more than one port (see below). The "channel" connecting I/O with storage has enough intelligence to be able to assemble and disassemble words, count how many units of information have been transferred, remember which I/O unit it is talking with, and where in main storage the information should go or come from; and finally, in some of the more sophisticated channels, it knows where to look to find more work to do when the present transfer is completed (chained I/O). Some of the larger machines may have several independent I/O channels capable of working simultaneously.

**Storage.** In addition to more or less continual technological advances, there are two basically architectural methods of improving storage device cost/performance.

The first of these has to do with overlap of references. In the earliest machines, and even today in the less expensive machines, only one storage reference could be going on at a time. That is, there was only one memory address register and one memory buffer register. In modern large machines, main storage is broken up into several separate blocks. Some subset of bits in the address are used to determine which block is being addressed, and the remaining bits are used to determine which word within the block is wanted. Since the blocks are independent, each with its own address and buffer register, it is possible to have as many storage references in progress as there are blocks. In theory then, for the price of a few extra registers, we can speed up storage access by a factor of $N$ if there are $N$ separate blocks of storage. In practice, of course, a program will often want a second thing from a given storage block before the first reference is completed. This is called "memory contention," and the more often it happens, the less benefit is obtained from dividing storage into blocks. Some contemporary computers use the high-order two or three or four bits of the address to select the block, some use the low-order bits (this is sometimes called "storage interlace"), and some actually use a couple of bits at each end of the address. All three methods have their proponents and disparagers.

The other basically architectural method of improving storage/cost performance can be given the general name of "paging." It involves a hierarchy of storage devices with two or more levels: one level fast but expensive; the other cheaper but slower. The idea is to get the data and instructions you are going to be wanting in the near future into the few fast words of storage you have purchased and keep the bulk of your program and data on the large, slow "backing store.". If you are sufficiently clever about this, the user is deluded into believing that you have lots of "quite fast" storage for a price very near that of your competitor's slow storage. Perhaps the simplest example of this "paging" strategy is to fetch up several adjacent words from memory into a high-speed register every time the program references store. If successive instructions come from successive locations (as they usually do), or if successively required items of data come from adjacent locations, then one has the next instruction or datum right on tap in high-speed registers when needed and only, say, one reference out of four or eight (depending on how "wide" a fetch is made) needs to go down into main storage, while three out of four or seven out of eight run at a speed dictated by the register access time rather than by the main store access time.

The next stage in this approach is to provide a moderately large number of high-speed storage locations. This has been called a "cache." On FETCH the CPU looks first in the cache for an operand or instruction, and only upon failure to find it there does it look in main memory (Fig. 2). Deposits (writes) are usually organized as a "write through" into main store so that main store always contains a valid up-to-date copy of all data. That is, information to be deposited is written into both the cache and the appropriate cell of main storage. Transfers of blocks of words between main store and the cache are performed strictly by hardware without software intervention. With appropriate fetching and assignment strategies, hit ratios (the probability of finding an item in the cache) as high as 0.8 have been observed.

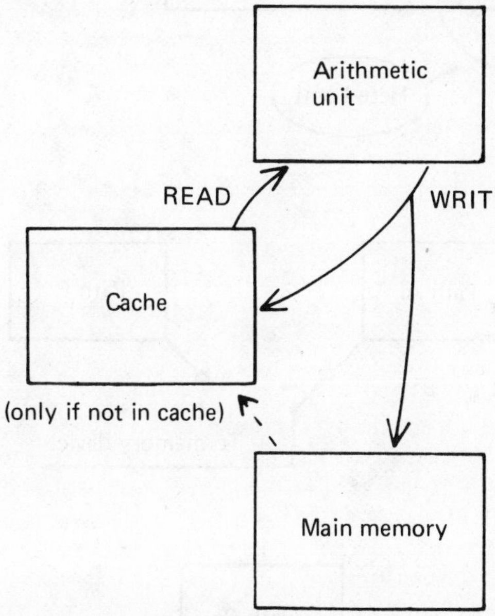


**Fig. 2.** Operation of reads and writes in a machine with cache memory.

The third stage in using a storage hierarchy is to swap programs and data between main store and a cyclically accessible device such as a disk or a drum. This is called "paging." Items are fetched up into main store as required, a page at a time. About 1,000 words seems to be a standard amount to transfer, although several other page sizes have been used or proposed. Since drum store is very much slower than most main stores, write-through is not done, and the current contents of an area of main storage must be preserved (assuming they have been changed since coming up from drum) before new information is written into that area. The decision on which area of storage to overwrite is called the "page turning strategy" and is beyond the scope of this article. When a program references a nonresident datum or instruction, a "page fault" is said to occur and an interruption is raised, giving control of the processor to a portion of the operating system which then handles the matter via software. This technique of loading pages only as they are requested is called "demand paging." When loadings are specified in advance of reference to them, the technique is best called "overlaying."

**Communication.** Within a computer, data and information must be transferred from one place to another. In Fig. 1 the simple communication channel shown moves all information from one point to another under the direction of the control unit. In larger machines, communication becomes substantially more complicated.

We will define an "aggressive" device as one that can initiate a request for communication with another device; the device that honors that request we will call the "passive" device. If only the control unit can be aggressive, then it must periodically "poll" the input/output devices to see if any of them has anything to say. If I/O devices can also be aggressive, they may generate interrupts, which temporarily command the attention of the CPU in order to process the input or output and to ready further work for the device or channel.

Consider first the case where there is more than one peripheral device to be handled. Two principal modes of communication have been employed. The first of these is called a "radial selector" or a private-line arrangement.

In a private-line arrangement, each I/O device has a set of lines between it and the CPU for its own private use. The advantage of this scheme is that if a device is free, it is guaranteed that the pathway leading to it is also available. The disadvantage is that of high initial fixed cost for the decoding and driving of many sets of lines, even if only a few of them have peripherals attached.

Most contemporary machines use the other type of communication scheme called the party line, broadcast mode, daisy chain, or unibus (Fig. 3). The basic idea of this scheme is that one pathway connects the CPU to all peripheral devices. The active device (say, the CPU) broadcasts to all passive devices the name of the unit it wishes to communicate with. This unit, recognizing its own name, in

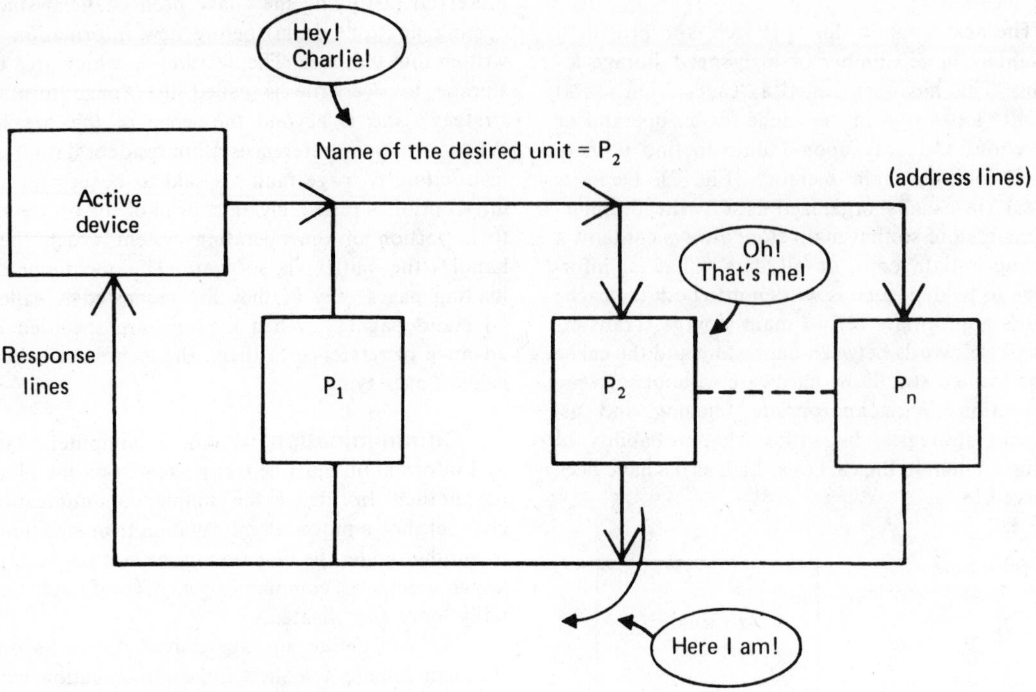


**Fig. 3.** Party-line selection.

effect holds up its hand, saying "Here!," and the dialog then ensues. The obvious problem here is that when one pair of devices is communicating, no other conversations can take place. Partial remedy may be had by keeping the occupancy of the "highway" short in duration. If this is not sufficient, more than one pathway may be installed, each called a "channel." Some devices may then be connected on each channel and some may be connected on more than one channel. For example, if several devices are connected to both of two channels, then any two of them may be active at a given time. The advantage of this approach is that only when a new device is attached to the computer need a "name recognizer" be purchased.

When the attention of a device (CPU, memory, or even a channel) may be requested over several pathways, a "contention resolver" is required. That is, the device must give its attention to one pathway and (temporarily, at least) ignore all others. Such a resolver is often found in memory units that allow access from more than one CPU or from a CPU and an I/O channel. Sometimes this unit is called a "scanner." Two basic strategies are employed for the resolution of contention. The first is called "round robin." Suppose there are three pathways, *A*, *B*, and *C*, connected to a memory (Fig. 4). *A* is examined to see if it needs service. If it does, it receives it. If it does not, or when the service is completed, the scanner examines *B*. Then it examines *C*, and then back to *A* and around the circle once again. If there are *N* pathways, each one is guaranteed at least $(1/N)$th of the memory cycles. No pathway gets

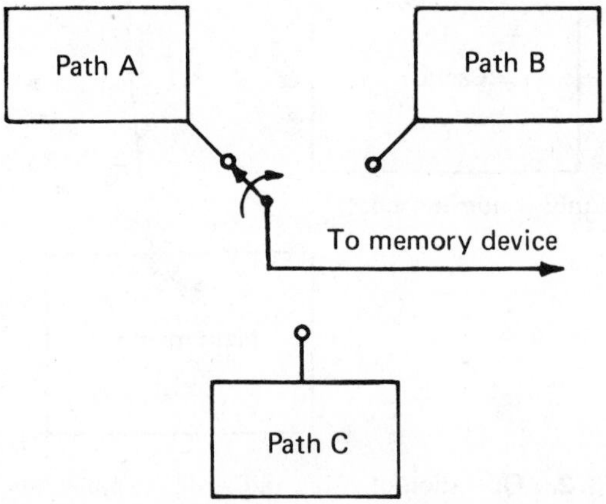


**Fig. 4.** A round-robin type of contention resolver. Service is offered to paths A,B,C,A,B,C,A, etc.

better service than any other and all are treated equally.

The other basic scanning method is called the "resetting scanner." After servicing a pathway, the scanner looks at the list, starting over again from the beginning. Only if pathways *A* and *B* are both idle will *C* be able to get into memory. This gives pathways early in the scanning sequence priority over those later in the sequence. Such priority is extremely useful for impatient devices such as drums or tapes, where data may be lost forever; at least, it may cause severe inconvenience if the device does not get attention within a short time after demanding it.

**Control.** The control unit of a computer is charged with fetching and decoding instructions and then computing the addresses of required operands and fetching them. Finally it must select which portion of the ALU will be required to perform the instructions and transmit the required data to it. In order to speed up this process, the technique of "instruction lookahead" has been employed. To begin with, the control unit is designed to "fetch ahead"—i.e., whenever the path to memory is available and there are less than *n* unexecuted instructions on hand: Go get some more. This may be accomplished by (1) packing two or four instructions into each word and fetching up single words; (2) fetching up four words at a time, each with one or more instructions; (3) keeping a file of the eight most recent instruction word fetches and going there for the instruction in preference to main memory. Once more than one as-yet-unexecuted instruction is on hand (in the control unit), it becomes possible to start working on them before their "turn" actually comes up. (The obvious danger, of course, is that because of branching their turn may *never* come up.) We fetch instruction $i$ while we are decoding $i - 1$, while we are simultaneously (in independent hardware) computing the effective addresses of $i - 2$ while we are actually executing $i - 3$.

Provided the execution of none of these instructions modifies other instructions in the stream (this is reasonable for reentrant coding) and provided none of the instructions references registers that other instructions are in the process of changing (this is somewhat less safe), and provided none of the instructions in the stream changes the flow of control (i.e., are branches)—and this last is ridiculous; approximately one out of every four or five instructions executed has been found to be a branch—then instruction lookahead is worthwhile, but even if some of or all these provisos are not satisfied, instruction lookahead may still be useful.

One way to avoid the problems of interacting instructions described above and to realize the potential of instruction lookahead is to take successive instructions from different, independent programs. This is perhaps the ultimate in multiprogramming in which one instruction from a program stream gets executed before moving on to the next program. The Honeywell 800 and the peripheral processors of the Control Data CDC-6600 do exactly this. This approach does not help get a particular job done quicker; it "merely" increases the throughput of the computer by having several jobs running at once.

**Arithmetic-Logic Units.** The part of the machine in which arithmetic and logical operations are actually carried out is called the ALU. Two schemes for speeding up an ALU have been used. Both depend on instruction lookahead to provide several instructions to work on at the same time, and consequently both suffer degraded performance when lookahead does. These methods are called "pipelining" and "division of labor." In both methods we try to increase the number of instructions being completed per second by increasing the number going on simultaneously. Pipelining may be likened to an assembly line, whereas "division of labor" might be thought to be similar to a job shop operation. In the first type, a part of the hardware unit does a little bit for instruction $i + 1$ just as an automobile assembly line puts an automobile together a bit at a time. Sometimes a pipeline may have as many as 20 or 30 stages and be capable of processing that many separate instructions. One instruction may take half a microsecond to pass *through* the pipeline, but the pipeline can *accept* another new instruction every 25 ns.

The other method of speeding up an ALU is to design specialized units dedicated to performing particular tasks rather than having general-purpose units. Thus, we may find a boolean unit, a floating-point multiplier and divider, a floating-point add/subtract unit, a fixed-point arithmetic unit, and others. These are sometimes called "functional" units. The IBM 370/195 and the CDC CYBER 73 both have multiple functional units. Of course a designer may combine pipelining with multiple units and have several pipelines—either a general-purpose type as does the CDC-STAR or a special-purpose type.

Several recent studies have shown that even when given as much hardware as might be desired, the interaction of instruction streams and the interdependency of successive data references limit the average number of instructions that may be executed simultaneously (from a single program) to somewhat less than two (Riseman and Foster, 1972).

**Other Designs.** Several other ways of designing computers exist, besides the way described above. The best known such design is the "array" type of computer and the earliest example of this approach is the machine of Unger (1958). Two contemporary examples of array-type machines are the ILLIAC IV built at the University of Illinois and the STARAN computer built by Goodyear Aerospace Corporation. An array machine is characterized as one having many pieces of data being simultaneously processed by one program. STARAN has the further interesting property that its memory is content-addressable.

The other major variation in computer design is due to von Neumann and is called a "tessellated automaton" or a Holland machine, after John Holland who described a definitive version of the type. In this type of machine an unbounded, usually planar, array of cells each hold (and are capable of executing) an instruction. A program is a collection of physically adjacent cells, with one or more of them "active," i.e., currently executing its instruction. Holland's contribution was to show that arbitrarily many programs could be simultaneously active in such a machine. Von Neumann showed that a program could be written which reproduced itself. No physical embodiments of tessellated machines of any appreciable size (more than 100 cells) have yet been constructed, nor are there present plans to build any.

A computer with more than one processor is sometimes called a "multiprocessor." Depending on how the work load and job functions are divided among the several processors, one can have a master/slave configuration, a front-end/back-end configuration, a "first among equals" organization, or an each-man-for-himself type of chaos.

When the number of connected processors exceeds some small integer, people begin to speak of parallel processing. Clearly, ILLIAC IV and STARAN are of this type. Not nearly so clear is whether a machine like a CDC 6500 with two central processors and ten peripheral processors should be called a parallel processor. Usually it is not, but it does meet the normal criteria.

### References

1958. Unger, S. H. "A Computer Oriented Toward Spatial Problems," *Proc. IRE* (October), pp. 1744–1750.

1970. Foster, Caxton C. *Computer Architecture*. New York: Van Nostrand-Reinhold.

1971. Bell, C. Gordon, and Allen Newell. *Computer Structures: Readings and Examples*. New York: McGraw-Hill.

1972. Riseman, E., and C. Foster. "The Inhibition of Potential Parallelism by Conditional Jumps," *IEEE Trans. on Electronic Computers*, Vol. C-21, No. 12 (December), pp. 1405–1411.

C. C. Foster

## COMPUTER-ASSISTED INSTRUCTION (CAI)

For articles on related subjects *see* Computer-Assisted Learning and Teaching; and Computer-Managed Instruction.

Computer-assisted instruction (CAI) refers to the use of computers to present drills, practice exercises, and tutorial sequences to the student, and perhaps to engage the student in a dialog about the substance of the instruction. A CAI (tutorial) dialog is achieved between computer program and student when the responses derived from the program are highly responsive to the questions, answers, and directives given by the student, while at the same time the dialog advances the goals and means established by the author of the curriculum materials.

CAI is only one part of computer assistance in the processes of learning and teaching. It has proved successful where the goals of instruction are clearly defined, achievement of those goals is highly valued by the organization providing instruction, the substance of instruction is suited to automated delivery, and the student is lacking important skills, background, or motivation for self-instruction via less expensive media. Research studies tend to show advantages for CAI in terms of shorter learning times and improved performance. Inhibitors to operational use include high costs of delivery systems and curriculum development, conflicts between individualized instruction and current educational practices, and commitment of most of the computing resources available in schools to instructional use for education about computers. A comprehensive analysis of CAI effectiveness, along with other media for instruction, is given by Jamison, Suppes, and Wells (1974).

**Major Demonstration Projects.** A group of engineers and educators in the Computer-based Education Research Laboratory at the University of Illinois, Urbana, have designed a computing system (PLATO IV) especially for effective and efficient teaching. It is a large system intended to provide instructional computing to over 1,000 simultaneous users throughout the University and also a number of other colleges and schools in Illinois. The design includes notable advances in the technology for display and special arrangements for efficient communications through broadband channels of the telephone system. University faculty are authoring computer-based curriculum materials for many subject areas and at various levels of education.

Stanford University has operated a CAI system that distributes instructional computing to a number of centers throughout the country. It is a large-scale service operation using long-distance telephone communications, clusters of terminals, and some stand-alone computer systems. The remote centers are usually associated with elementary school demonstration projects and special education institutions. The service operation is conducted in parallel with an extensive program of research and development at the Institute for Mathematical Studies in the Social Sciences, Stanford University. Curriculum materials have been prepared for young children (elementary school math and reading), learners with special difficulties (for example, the deaf), and certain university courses (especially second-language learning and logic).

TICCIT (Time-shared, Interactive, Computer-Controlled Informational Television) is a name given to systems being developed by the Mitre Corpora-

| | |
|---|---|
| James Smith was found unconscious under suspicious circumstances. You are the Scotland Yard Inspector. Proceed with your investigation. | |
| WHO ARE THE SUSPECTS? | The program recognizes "suspects" and provides the stored response. |
| The wife, brother and partner presently are considered the suspects. | |
| WHAT IS THE MEDICAL REPORT? | "medical" is recognized. |
| The victim is in a coma. He has wounds on his head and symptoms of poisoning are evident. | |
| GIVE ME THE CONSTABLE'S REPORT. | "constable" is recognized. |
| A glass was found next to the victim's bed, and a bottle labeled poison in the closet. The window has a bullet hole in it. A bloody pipe wrench was found in the shed. | |
| I WANT TO INTERROGATE THE WIFE. | The program recognizes "interrogate" but will not permit exploration of that branch until another one has been fully explored. |
| I advise you request the lab tests first. | |
| LAB TESTS | |
| This is the lab. What is it you want? | |
| WHAT DO YOU FIND ON THE GLASS? | After the wife has been interrogated this branch of the program will release more incriminating information. |
| This is the lab. Fingerprints found which match those of the wife. | |
| MEDICAL REPORT | "medical" is recognized a second time. |
| No change in the condition of the victim. | |
| ANY NEW SUSPECTS? | The program includes a "stack" of replies for some directives so that on subsequent requests for information a fresh reply is given. |
| No new suspects. | |

**Fig. 1.** Sample of CAI learning exercise (exerpted from Bolt, Beranek, and Newman program).

tion in McLean, Virginia. The first version of an instructional system is designed especially for use in a small college. It is based on a medium-sized computer system and video technology to obtain low-cost operation with about 100 simultaneous users. The hardware and software design has been coordinated with the development of instructional materials, which are very carefully prepared according to certain rules of effective instruction. The first set of materials is being prepared by instructional design teams at Brigham Young University in Utah to provide basic remedial instruction in mathematical and language skills at small colleges.

The list of schools and colleges pursuing interesting development programs is very long. One of the long-standing operations combining development and applications is in the Philadelphia public schools. Activities there, under the direction of Sylvia Charp, include a wide range of CAI along with many other uses of computing in the instructional program.

**Sample of Tutorial Dialog.** Fig. 1 is an example of CAI taken from a student learning exercise in gathering information and making decisions. As a demonstration, it requires no specific content knowledge; the application of this computer teaching strategy is common in physics, chemistry, biology, and medical diagnosis where knowledge of the subject is essential to success in the exercise. The computer program guides the student in the exploration of a tree of possibilities, some of which lead to the solution of a simulated problem through reports, laboratory tests, and direct interrogation.

**Areas of Application.** CAI materials have been prepared for many subjects, from accounting to zoology, and from preschool through adult education. One representation of the curriculum datum base is provided by Hoye and Wang (1973). Many more materials can be found in selected discipline areas by consulting teaching publications or professional committees associated with mathematics, physics, chemistry, biology, geography, political science, history, business, engineering, law, and medicine, among others.

REFERENCES

1973. Hoye, Robert E., and Anastasia C. Wang (Eds.). *Index to Computer Based Learning.* Englewood Cliffs, N.J.: Educational Technology Publications.

1974. Jamison, Dean, Patrick Suppes, and Stuart Wells. "The Effectiveness of Alternative Instructional Media: A Survey," *Review of Educational Research* (AERA), Vol. 44, No. 1, pp. 1–67.

K. L. ZINN

## COMPUTER-ASSISTED LEARNING AND TEACHING

For articles on related subjects *see* AUTHORING LANGUAGES AND SYSTEMS; COMPUTER-ASSISTED INSTRUCTION; COMPUTER-MANAGED INSTRUCTION; and NETWORKS FOR INSTRUCTION.

For articles on related terms *see* EXTENSIBLE LANGUAGES; INFORMATION PROCESSING; SIMULATION; and SPEECH RECOGNITION.

The impact of computers on teaching and learning activities at all levels of education is considerable and the extent of use is increasing rapidly. Current uses in post-secondary education are quite varied. A medical student practices diagnosis and prescription on a wide variety of hypothetical patients simulated by computer programs. A senior engineering student using computer assistance solves problems in road design which ten years ago were not approached until after two years of experience on the job. A sophomore in computer science develops a program to help his professor of chemistry evaluate the effectiveness of questions on a multiple-choice quiz. A freshman in general psychology directs a computer-based information system to assemble a complete bibliography on the relation between achievement motivation and college grades, which is as current as the journals received by his professor. A laboratory technician tests himself on newly acquired skills, using a terminal on a hospital information system.

Computing is also quite visible in education outside colleges and universities. A high school science student applies wildlife management practices to a computer simulation of the American bison herds that were slaughtered in the 1800s. An English literature student programs a computer to generate poetry. A child in the fifth grade explores mathematics by writing computer programs that draw spirals or solve mazes. A bedridden second grader practices addition problems "spoken" by a computer over the telephone; the computer checks the answers that the student enters on the Touchtone telephone buttons; or, in some experimental systems, the student simply speaks the answer into the telephone to be "recognized" by the computer. A high school dropout improves language skills using a computer program made available on a community television cable system.

When the computer system is appropriate for educational uses and the programs are properly written, the learner should find the assistance to be: responsive to his needs; patient and not punitive while he learns; accurate in assessment of answers and problem solutions; individualized in a useful way; realistic in the presentation of training or testing situations; and helpful with many information processing tasks. Teachers find computer assistance valuable for keeping accurate records, summarizing data, projecting student-learning difficulties, assembling individualized tests, and retrieving information about films or other learning resources. Authors of textbooks and other learning materials use computers to draw figures, to animate motion picture sequences, or to keep track of the introduction and frequency of occurrence of concepts throughout a text. Researchers record and analyze data, build models of student learning and performance, and administer experiments on methods of instruction. Administrators use computers for keeping records, planning, scheduling, allocating resources, and processing data.

These applications and many others are described in a rapidly growing literature. The single most comprehensive publication is the proceedings of an international school (Zinn et al., 1973), which also includes a list of many other sources, both

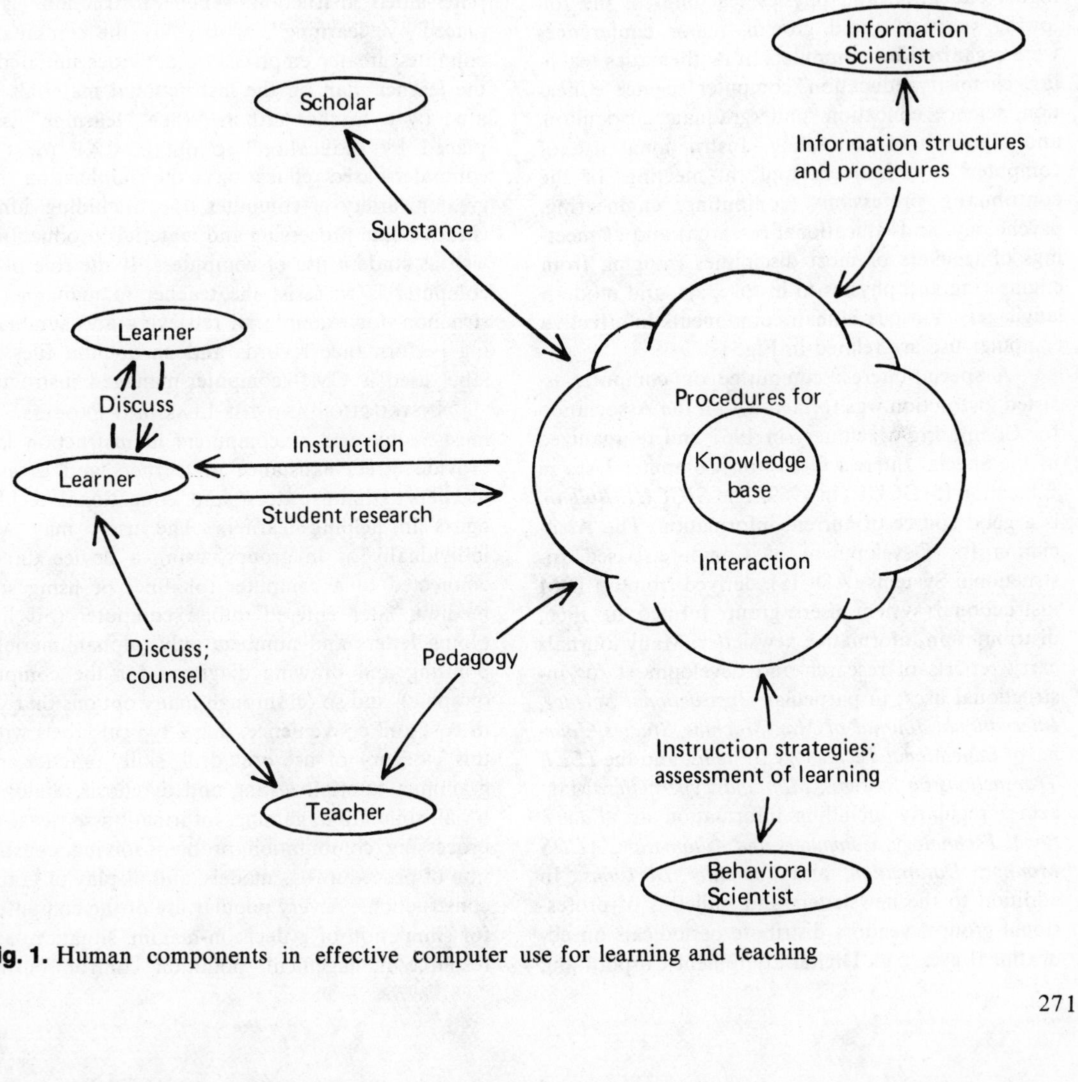


**Fig. 1.** Human components in effective computer use for learning and teaching

introductory and highly technical. An important guide for computer use in higher education is the report of a RAND Corporation study for the Carnegie Commission on Higher Education (Levien, 1972). The *Annual Review of Information Science and Technology* carries a scholarly review every three to five years (Silberman and Filep, 1968; Vinsonhaler and Moon, 1973).

Use of the computer as a tool for problem solving in education began in graduate schools about 1955, and a few years later moved into the classroom with the initiation of curriculum development projects in engineering and sciences. Computer use as a teaching machine dates from 1958; early developments took place at IBM's Watson Research Center, System Development Corporation, and the University of Illinois Coordinated Science Laboratory. The topic of computers in education became popular for meetings in 1965; separate conferences were held on computers in American education, higher education and physics teaching. In the following years of rapid growth, major conferences were organized for computers in mathematics teaching, chemistry education, computer science education, science education, undergraduate curriculum, and high school counseling. Instructional use of computers is a frequent topic at meetings of the contributing professions (computing, engineering, psychology, and educational research) and at meetings of teachers of most disciplines (ranging from engineering and physics to history, art, and modern languages). Various human components in effective computer use are related in Fig. 1.

A special-interest committee on computer-assisted instruction was formed within the Association for Computing Machinery in 1967 and reorganized as the Special Interest Group on Computer Uses in Education (SIGCUE) in 1969. The *SIGCUE Bulletin* is a good source of current information. The Association for Development of Computer-Based Instructional Systems (ADCIS), derived from an IBM instructional system users group formed in 1966, distributes an informative newsletter. Many journals carry reports of research and development for instructional uses; in particular: *Instructional Science, International Journal of Man-Machine Studies, Journal of Educational Technology Systems*, and the *IEEE Transactions on Systems, Man and Cybernetics*. Magazines regularly including information are *Educational Technology, Computers and Automation, AEDS Monitor, Datamation,* and *Computer Decisions*. In addition to the newsletters and bulletins of professional groups, vendors distribute periodicals on educational uses, e.g., Digital Equipment Corporation, Hewlett-Packard Company, and Wang Laboratories.

**Kind of Use.** Computer assistance with learning and teaching has been described by many different phrases. One could follow the word "computer" with two terms, one from each of the following lists:

| | |
|---|---|
| -aided | training |
| -assisted | instruction |
| -augmented | learning |
| -based | teaching |
| -extended | education |
| -managed | |
| -mediated | |
| -monitored | |
| -related | |
| uses in | |

The most common label has been CAI: computer-aided instruction. When "instruction" is replaced by "learning", as in CAL, the combination connotes greater emphasis on activities initiated by the learner than on the instructional materials created by a teacher-author. When "learning" is replaced by "education" to obtain CAE (or CBE, computer-based education), the implication is a greater variety of computer uses, including administrative data processing and materials production as well as student use of computers. If the role of the computer is to assist the teacher in managing instruction, for example, in retrieving and summarizing performance records and curriculum files, the label used is CMI: computer-managed instruction.

Instruction and the Learning Process. The most visible use of computers in instruction is to provide direct assistance to learners and to assist teachers, administrators, and educational technologists in helping learners. The users may work individually or in groups, using a device directly connected to a computer (on line) or using some medium later entered into a computer (off line), typing letters and numbers only (alphanumeric) or pointing and drawing diagrams for the computer (graphic), and so on through many options that vary in cost and convenience. Some typical labels within this category of use are: drill, skills practice, programmed tutorial, testing and diagnosis, dialog tutorial, simulation, gaming, information retrieval and processing, computation, problem solving, construction of procedures as models, and display of graphic constructions. A very popular use of the computer is for simulation of a decision-making situation, as in resource management, pollution control, business marketing, or medical testing. For example, college economics students study the history of a hypothetical national economy (similar to that for the United States), prescribe actions such as changing the prime interest rate, and observe the consequences for unemployment, inflation, and other indicators. Time is much compressed in the hypothetical situation, and real-world complexities are abstracted for easier study.

MANAGEMENT OF INSTRUCTION RESOURCES AND PROCESS. Computer aids help teachers to supervise the instructional process, and similar assistance is provided directly to students without intervention of teachers and managers. Information management services are readily extended to potential users of learning resources outside traditional educational institutions. The essential information in the various files for management of instructional resources concerns student performance, learning materials, desired outcomes, job opportunities, and student interests. For example, a student obtains information from the computer about his achievement and then compares his own performance, interests, and goals with averages recorded for all similar students using the information system. After interpreting the information provided, the student uses the computer further to locate and retrieve suitable learning aids from a large file keyed to goals, learning difficulties, job opportunities, and interests.

PREPARATION AND DISPLAY OF MATERIALS. Materials may be generated in "real time," i.e., as needed by a student in a seminar or by a teacher during a lecture. Text and problems also may be assembled by computer in advance of scheduled use so that individualized materials may be distributed at less expense than through on-line computing. Computers assist writers of materials in many ways —for example: procedures for generating films and graphs; on-line trial of materials under development; procedures for automatically editing and analyzing text materials for new uses, and information structures for representing new organizations of knowledge; hierarchies of instructional objectives; and libraries of learning materials. New technologies are changing the work of technicians and teachers in developing educational materials and media. Machines handle much of the routine in drafting graphics and editing film.

OTHER USES OF INFORMATION PROCESSING. Those planning instructional uses also attend to the educational implications of computers in administration (accounting, scheduling, planning, etc.) and in research (institutional, sociological, psychological, instructional, etc.), and to the practice of various computer-related vocations in science, technology, management, banking, production, retailing, etc. The last area is especially important because of needs for preservice training. For example, most large retailing operations use computing heavily in many areas, and employees with some sensible background in computing have a better chance of coming to terms with computer assistance on the job. Indeed, a general literacy about computing and information processing may be essential in the age of informatics. Educated persons should have sufficient knowledge about the practices of automated information processing to exercise on occasion effective control over the machines and data files with which they must deal.

## Means And Goals

DIVERSITY OF RESOURCES. Many different kinds of computer and software systems are being used by research and development projects today; a few are being marketed for operational use. Some small machines can be used by one or a few students (Fig. 2) at a time to access stored programs (usually drills or simulations) or to write simple computer programs. Slightly larger systems dedicated in a similar way to interactive instruction have been programmed for simultaneous use by as few as 4 and as many as 40 students. Larger systems in operation now can handle up to 200 students accessing a variety of programs. The PLATO system at the University of Illinois has been planned for up to

**Fig. 2.** Two students study science with aid of a computer in Project LOCAL, one of the first to bring computing into the schools for student use.

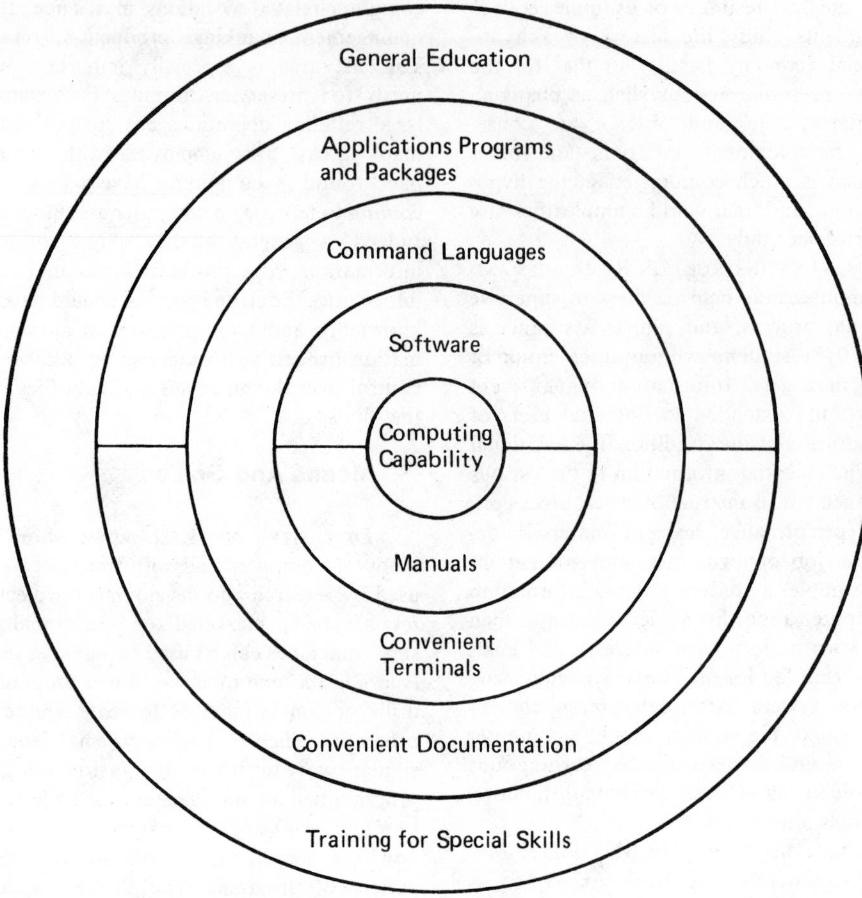


**Fig. 3.** A perspective on software and services for users.

4,000 simultaneous users and diverse applications: self-instruction, self-testing, simulation, gaming, and problem solving. Many of the multipurpose computer systems serving general user communities at colleges and universities include instructional applications among other uses for research and administration. Examples can be found at Dartmouth College, Massachusetts Institute of Technology, Carnegie-Mellon University, the University of Michigan, and Stanford University, to name only a few.

Programming languages and systems (software) exhibit even more diversity than the computing equipment (hardware). More than 40 languages and dialects have been developed specifically for programming conversational instruction, although many programs have been written in general-purpose languages such as Fortran, PL/I, and Basic. Different kinds of users have distinguishable requirements: students, instructors, authors, instructional researchers, administrators, and computer programmers working on convenience programs for any of the other users. The characteristics of different subject areas also necessitate different language features. Authoring languages and systems are described in a separate article. Fig. 3 summarizes a perspective on software and services for users; a set of concentric circles represents successive levels of access for users approaching the core of computing capability. Fig. 4 represents the perspective of the user at the center.

Instructional materials (sometimes called "courseware") have been written in almost all subject areas and for many age levels, including preschool reading, elementary school science laboratory, intermediate school social studies games, high school biology laboratory, college mathematics, introductory German, physics, chemistry laboratory, and professional school exercises in business management, medical diagnosis, architectural planning, and many others. While some of the materials use

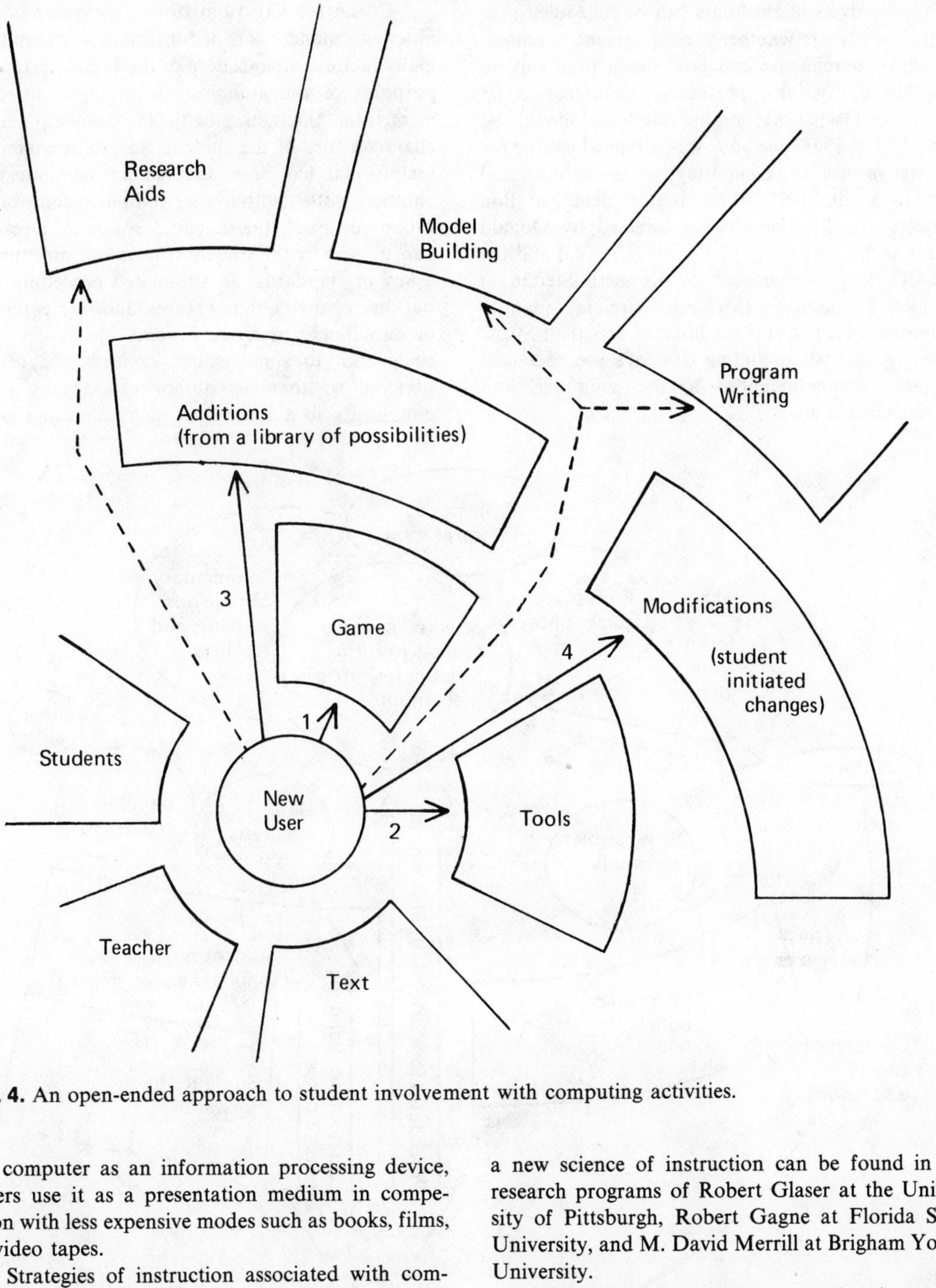


**Fig. 4.** An open-ended approach to student involvement with computing activities.

the computer as an information processing device, others use it as a presentation medium in competition with less expensive modes such as books, films, or video tapes.

Strategies of instruction associated with computer use (the name "teachware" has been proposed) are at an early stage of development. Guidelines for writing instruction-related computer programs have been derived from psychological and educational research, but most developers work from a "common sense" analysis and by trial and error. Some basis for a new science of instruction can be found in the research programs of Robert Glaser at the University of Pittsburgh, Robert Gagne at Florida State University, and M. David Merrill at Brigham Young University.

The costs of using various operational or experimental computer instruction systems and languages vary considerably. Figures reported by manufacturers and research projects range from $0.15 to $30.00 per student per hour. Some of the differences can be attributed to variations in assumptions about how many effective student hours can be scheduled in a month or a year; whether the equipment is rented, leased, or purchased; and how much time will be spent in utility jobs, preventive maintenance, or repair; and what accounting methods should be used. About $3.00 per hour was a typical charge for interactive use of computing within educational institutions in 1975. Two major demonstration projects, the PLATO Project directed by Donald Bitzer at the University of Illinois (Urbana) and the TICCIT Project managed by Kenneth Stetten at MITRE Corporation (McLean, Virginia), plan to achieve a cost per student hour of less than $0.50, covering all costs including student's use of a user terminal, communications to the computer, and curriculum materials.

COMPUTER CONTRIBUTIONS. The value of computer assistance for self-instruction depends on many factors: organization of the subject matter, the purposes of the author or institution, convenient means for interacting with the subject, and the characteristics of the student. Self-study material in text format has been adapted for computer presentation, with the following computer contributions proposed: First, the machine evaluates a response constructed by the student (the author must provide a key or standard); an automated procedure prints out discrepancies, tallies scores, and selects remedial or enrichment material. Second, the machine conceals and, to some extent, controls the teaching material so that the author can specify greater complexity in a strategy of instruction and assume

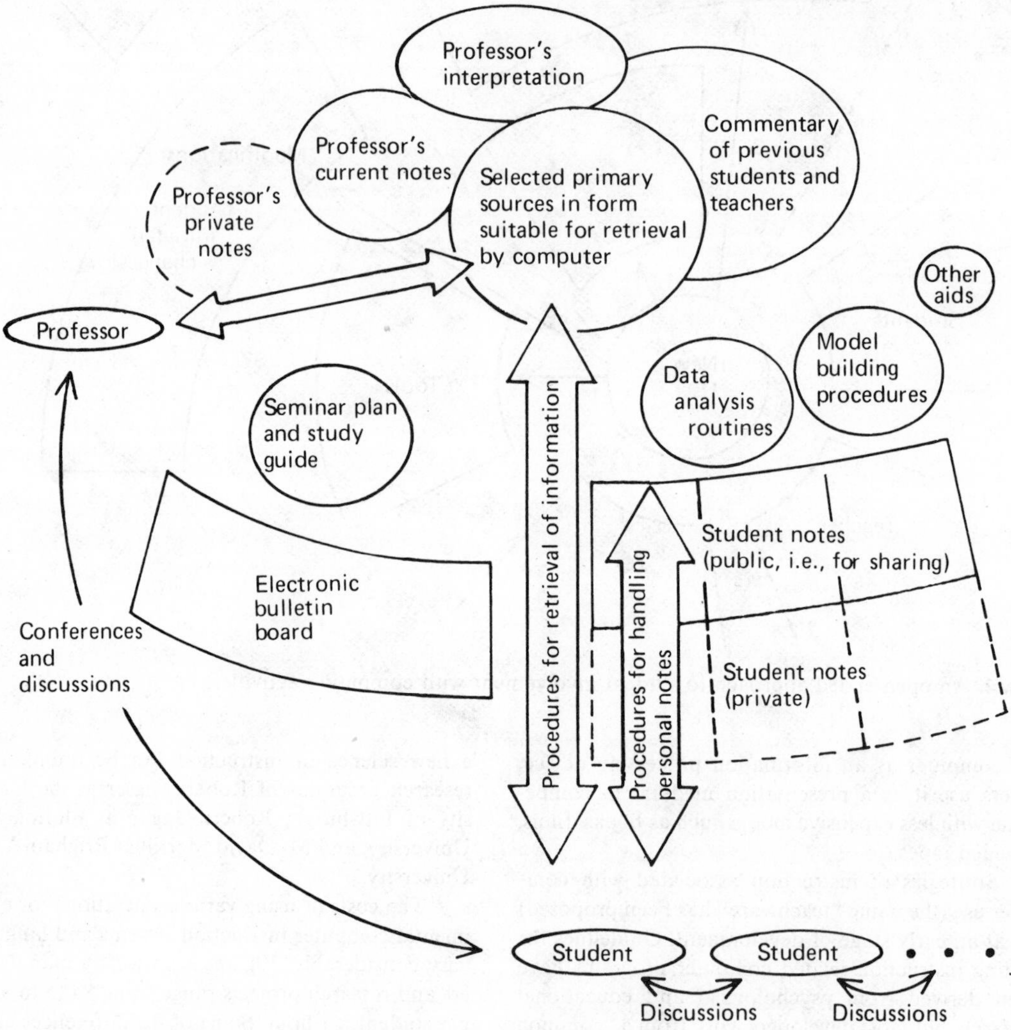


**Fig. 5.** A dynamic information system for scholar and learner.

more accuracy in its execution than is possible when the student is expected to find his way though the branching instructions in the pages of a large booklet (the scrambled text format for programmed instruction). Third, the computer carries out operations specified by the student, who uses a simple programming language or computer-aided design system. Fourth, the author or researcher obtains detailed data on student performance (and perhaps attitude) along with a convenient summarization of student accomplishment ready for interpretation. Fifth, the author is able to modify his text on the basis of student use and prepare alternative versions with relative ease.

Prepackaged self-instruction can be replaced by a dynamic information system that serves as a common working ground for a scholar and a learner; they share a computer-based, primary-source "textbook," continually updated by the scholar and occasionally annotated by each student who uses it (Fig. 5). Prototype systems have been demonstrated: HYPERTEXT was conceived by Theodor Nelson (then at Vassar College) and implemented by Andries van Dam and others at Brown University; and SPIRES was designed by Edwin Parker and others at Stanford. In a similar way, an automated information system helps a learner and teacher share a common working environment for hypothesis testing. The environment is sometimes artificial, as in computer simulation of physical and social processes (e.g., a model of evolution), and sometimes real in the sense of actual data from experiments (e.g., election returns or radiation measures). Increased access to information processing tools is perhaps the most important contribution of computers to instruction and learning. Many such activities, perhaps not called computer-assisted instruction, demonstrate viable alternatives to strictly specified instructional strategies for computer use. For example, students in sociology retrieve and summarize information obtained from large-scale surveys and test hypotheses that might never have been conceived by those who executed and reported the survey. Students in physics test lens designs according to a detailed model of aberrations and corrections, perhaps finding variations on standard lens designs which better serve a particular photographic or instrumentation purpose.

Whatever the technique or philosophy of computer use, the extent of use will ultimately be determined by judgments of appropriateness by subject experts, effectiveness observed from records of student performance, and costs that must be met by administrators of schools or training programs. Costs may be reduced and quality of instruction improved through computer aids for preparation and revision of material, self-modifying strategies of instruction, and automatic assembly of additional teaching samples or testing situations.

Some of the limitations imposed by present computer technology involve high cost and unreliability of processing lengthy verbal constructions, and inability to interpret bodily gestures or vocal intonations. Computing costs are decreasing even while capabilities are increasing, but one of the most difficult problems remaining is lack of organization of the subject matter. Somehow, human teachers manage to be reasonably successful in spite of vague goals and material poorly organized for learning; instructional computing (and educational technology in general) seems to require specific text materials and clear guidelines (prepared by curriculum experts) for successful use.

## Major Approaches

EDUCATIONAL TECHNOLOGY. Educational technology and instructional psychology have been the main sources of one kind of development activity. IBM's Coursewriter programming language, one of the earliest languages for authors of computer-based lessons, characterizes this first approach to computer use. The software has built into it an implicit logic of instruction, requiring the author to fit text and key words into the following pattern: (1) the computer program presents information to the student; (2) the computer program then asks a question and waits for a response from the student; (3) the program scans a short textual response and classifies the response as right or wrong according to key words identified within it; and (4) if the student's response matches an anticipated wrong answer, the program displays a corrective hint, and if nothing was recognized, it offers a general hint. Many instances of this approach can be characterized as the computerization of programmed instruction. Careful development of a total curriculum for elementary school mathematics and reading was carried out by teams of authors at Stanford University directed by Patrick Suppes and Richard Atkinson. The same approach has been used at the University of Texas for college mathematics, at Pennsylvania State University for education methods courses, and at the U.S. Naval Academy for college physics.

In some curriculum development projects the content has been assembled in files separate from the logic of the computer program (the strategy of instruction). Elements of the curriculum can thereby be varied without rewriting many lines of instructions to the computer, and different strategies can be tried on the same file of learning materials. This arrangement helps the instructional psychologist give full attention to the design of effective instructional strategies and helps the subject expert avoid the distraction of programming procedures. In fact, this approach is generally pursued by a team, with each member contributing different expertise. Authoring teams organized by C. Victor Bunderson at Brigham Young University are working on materials for community college courses in mathematics and English for the TICCIT system under development by Mitre Corporation.

Problems faced by the educational technology approach to computer use result from the high cost of the computer as a primary medium for exposition of learning materials, the difficulties of accurately identifying unconstrained input (text, algebraic expressions, drawings, spoken expression, etc.), and the lack of a well-developed theory of instruction. These and other obstructions to more widespread use of computers for instruction have been discussed in a report by Anastasio and Morgan (1972).

DISCIPLINES AND CURRICULUM. Discipline-oriented use of the computer has until recently been pursued by many institutions quite separately from the educational technology developments. Dartmouth College provides a prime instance of spreading computer uses throughout a college curriculum. The University of California at Irvine uses computing extensively in physics courses. Six annual conferences have been held on the topic of computers in the undergraduate curriculum; the sites have been the University of Iowa (1970), Dartmouth College (1971), Georgia Institute of Technology (1972), the Claremont Colleges (1973), Washington State University (1974), and Texas Christian University (1975). Regional computing services, conferences, and newsletters have been established to serve the needs of colleges throughout a region. In contrast to the educational technology approach, the teacher as subject expert in the discipline approach assumes the central role in determining computer use, creating materials, and persuading colleagues to use them. Computing activity is likely to include more student initiative in solving problems and more problem-orienting program packages than does expository material. Student use of simulation and modeling tools is favored; one goal is to adapt the scholar's research tools to student use.

The discipline approach to computer use has many problems; among them are: sparse user documentation for instruction-related computing activities that are worthy of widespread use; lack of economic and professional incentives for the production and dissemination of programs and related materials; and difficult procedures for review and validation of programs. The National Science Foundation has sponsored a consortium of regional computing services (called CONDUIT) to explore solutions to these problems. Publications and program exchange activities with a discipline orientation are being pursued within professional societies.

COMPUTING AND INFORMATION SCIENCES. Some researchers suggest that major advances in instructional use of computers will occur through significant developments in artificial intelligence, natural language processing, speech recognition, and extensible programming languages. Although information scientists typically are more interested in their own disciplines and related research topics than in educational techniques and practice, the tools developed may be useful to others. The results of computer science research may be an important source of suitable models for instruction strategies, information structures, and representations of knowledge. The work of a dozen computer science projects is referenced in a summary of directions for research and development on computers in the instructional process (Zinn, 1972). Projects giving particular attention to educational applications are located at the Massachusetts Institute of Technology, Bolt, Beranek, and Newman, Carnegie-Mellon University, the University of Texas, California Institute of Technology, and Stanford University. In addition to the tools to be borrowed from computing and information sciences, new models of human learning and information processing may be obtained.

The information science approach has not yet produced many operational systems. Development of techniques and materials is very costly and time consuming; the resulting applications are expensive in execution with students; skill in use of the specialized techniques is not easily acquired by persons outside computer science. Nevertheless, the projects based in computing and information sciences continue to provide important indicators of future resources which may be essential to success of computers in education. Furthermore, a project at the University of Illinois directed by Jurg Nievergelt has adapted ideas from computing and information sciences for economical execution so that the computer-based materials can be used by over 2,000 students per semester in a set of introductory courses. Because the courses are in computer science, the authors combine a detailed knowledge of the specialized techniques with considerable experience in teaching the subject.

COMPUTING TECHNOLOGY, ENGINEERING, AND "COMMON SENSE". A fourth category includes all other approaches, particularly those characterized by the engineering of a helpful technology, perhaps involving some combination of the first three approaches. Engineers at the Computer-Based Educational Research Laboratory, University of Illinois, designed and built a computer-based education system (PLATO, Fig. 6) which is intended to be convenient for: educational technologists presenting programmed instruction, instructional psychologists conducting research on teaching and learning, professors preparing a computer presentation of a lecture or laboratory, and computer specialists building information processing aids for learning and scholarly work. Specialists in computers and education at Bolt, Beranek, and Newman (led by Wallace Feurzeig) and the Massachusetts Institute of Technology (notably, Seymour Papert) have devised various programming languages (Mentor, Telcomp, Stringcomp, and Logo) and equipment (computer-controlled "turtle," music player, etc.) for computer-related learning activities.

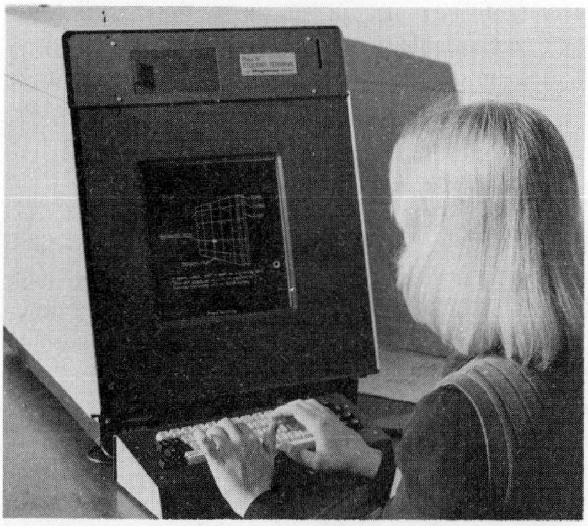

**Fig. 6.** Student terminal used with the PLATO computer-based education system, which includes a flat panel on which characters and line drawings are combined with rear projection of color images. (Courtesy of Computer-Based Education Research Laboratory, University of Illinois.)

Two other groups evidence a similar philosophy but offer different approaches to creative student work: the Soloworks Project directed by Thomas Dwyer at the University of Pittsburg and the Learning Research Group directed by Allen Kay at the Palo Alto Research Center of Xerox Corporation. In each case, children write simple programs for controlling robots, drawing and animating pictures, generating speech and music, and the like. Their interest in enhancing such capabilities motivates a new approach to mathematics and heuristics in which programming languages provide a powerful conceptual framework. The M.I.T. group has given particular attention to teaching children how to think, reason, and solve problems. These projects and others having an engineering approach are described in the proceedings of the World Conference on Computer Education (Scheepmaker and Zinn, 1971).

**Trends.** A major trend in the design of computer-based exercises is a shift from programmer to learner control. The designer of the exercise invests less effort in a careful diagnosis and prescription accomplished by some automated instructional strategy, and instead provides information from which the student can derive his own diagnosis from alternative interpretations and guidance. The student can assemble prescriptions specific to his own situation.

Increased use of graphics is seen in many projects. Pictures are an important component of the learning process, and computer-drawn pictures can add to the responsive uses of computing. For many topics the picture is a valuable way of representing complex relationships derived by the computer.

Computer-based education systems and designers of materials are providing an increasing variety of functions for the user. More attention is being given to interaction between student and computer program, not simply to provide a quick reply to some question, but to increase the actual responsiveness of the system to the particular input. The SCHOLAR system designed by the late Jaime Carbonell at Bolt, Beranek, and Newman is a prime instance. Machine responses are increasingly dependent upon the commands and questions and answers constructed by the student, and the lessons are designed in a way that helps the student respond to information provided by the computer.

A very important trend concerns the role of the machine from the perspective of the individual using it. The teacher is now more likely to see computer-managed instruction as an aid to human management than as a replacement for it. Learners view the machine more as an aid to learning than as a drill master.

Naturalness of communication between learner and system is being improved day by day. Computer-based learning exercises are achieving increased relevance for the subject being studied, and the nomenclature and conventions that have to be learned in order to use the system tend to be essential to the study of the topics rather than peculiar to the requirement of the computer as a medium of presentation.

Although these advances may be quite impressive to observers of educational research and development, dissemination of sound practices throughout educational systems will be a long time coming. The influence of the new technology within education will, as usual, lag behind the impact of the new technology on society.

### References

1968. Silberman, Harry F., and Robert T. Filep. "Information Systems Applications in Education," in Carlos A. Cuadra (Ed.), *Annual Review of Information Science and Technology*, Vol. 3. Chicago: Encyclopaedia Britannica, Inc., pp. 357–395.

1971. Scheepmaker, Bob, and Karl L. Zinn (Eds.). *IFIP World Conference on Computer Education 1970*. Amsterdam: International Federation of Information Processing.

1972. Anastasio, Ernest J., and Judith S. Morgan. *Factors Inhibiting the Use of Computers in Instruction*. Princeton, N.J.: EDUCOM (Interuniversity Communications Council, Inc.)

1972. Levien, Roger E. *The Emerging Technology: Instructional Uses of the Computer in Higher Education*. New York: McGraw-Hill.

1972. Zinn, Karl L. "Computers in the Instructional Process: Directions for Research and Development," *Communications of the ACM*, Vol. 15, No. 7 (July), pp. 648–651.

1973. Vinsonhaler, John, and Robert Moon. "Information Systems Applications in Education," *Annual Review of Information Science and Technology*, Vol. 8. Chicago: Encyclopaedia Britannica, Inc.

1974. Zinn, Karl L., Mario Refice, and Aldo Romano (Eds.). *Computers in the Instructional Process: Report of an International School*. Ann Arbor: EXTEND Publications.

K. L. ZINN

# COMPUTER CIRCUITRY

For articles on related subjects *see* GENERATIONS, COMPUTER; and INTEGRATED CIRCUITRY.

For articles on related terms *see* ADDERS; BINARY CODED DECIMAL, NATURAL; ENIAC; MARK I; SEQUENTIAL MACHINES; and SHIFTING.

Although the development of digital computers can be traced back to Charles Babbage, who conceived a mechanical machine with toothed wheels to perform arithmetic processes, electrical principles were first utilized in a computer through electromechanical relays by the Bell Telephone Laboratories in 1940. The first general-purpose computer with relays was the Harvard Mark I which was jointly developed by International Business Machines Corporation (IBM) and Harvard University in 1944 (Huskey and Korn, 1962). The first electronic computer implemented by vacuum tubes was ENIAC, built in 1945 at the University of Pennsylvania for the U.S. Army to solve ballistic problems. In this article, we will survey the circuits (and their general characteristics) used in various generations of computers, present some commonly used computer circuits, and discuss the trend of future computer circuitry.

**Circuitry in Various Generations of Computers.** Modern digital computers contain thousands of logic circuits for their arithmetical and logical operations and for their control of data flow, all composed of only a few different kinds of elementary circuits. Through boolean algebra manipulations, any complex logic function can be reduced to three primary operations: AND, OR, and INVERT operations. In the AND operation—also called "logical multiplication" (or "product") or "intersection"—the output will be up or in a high-voltage position if and only if all the inputs are up. In the OR operation—also called "logical sum" (or "sum") or "union"—the output will be up if one or more of its inputs are up. In the INVERT operation—also called "negation," "complementation," or "NOT" operation—a logic circuit has only a single input. Its output will be up only when the input is down, or vice versa. A set of logic circuits capable of performing these three logical operations is said to be *functionally complete*. There are two other well-known functionally complete sets (Kohavi, 1970;

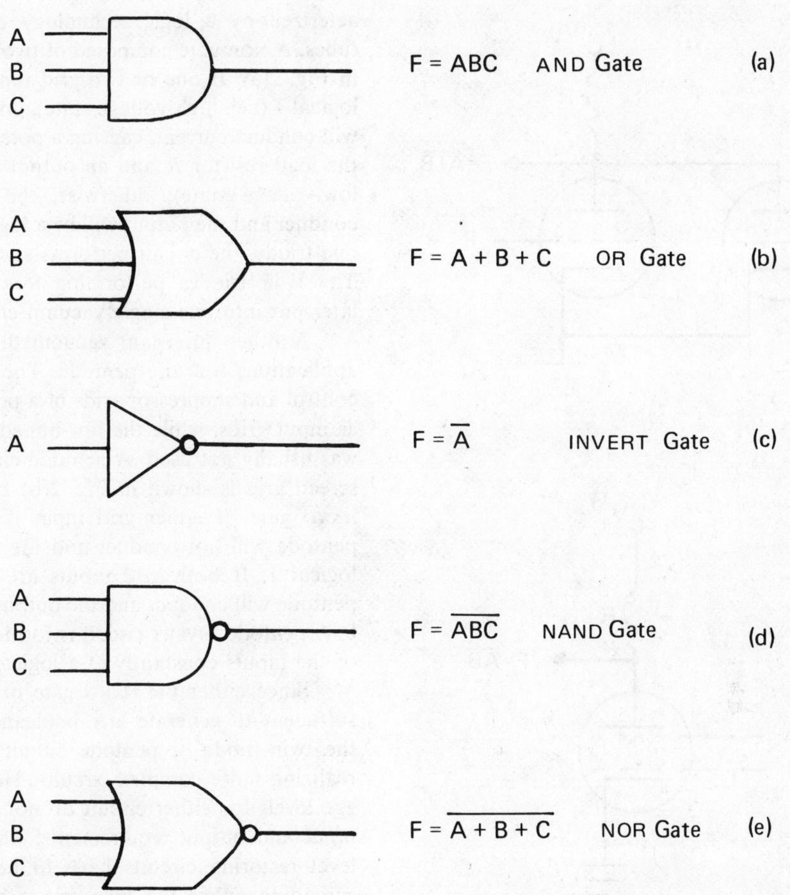


**Fig. 1.** Logic symbols.

Torng, 1972). One consists of only the NAND circuit which is actually an AND circuit with its output inverted. The other consists of only the NOR circuit which is an OR circuit with its output inverted. With either circuit, all logical functions of a modern digital computer system can be implemented. The AND, OR, INVERT, NAND, and NOR circuits are shown symbolically in Fig. 1. A circuit performing any of these basic operations is usually referred to as a "gate."

Over the years, logic circuit configurations and the technologies to produce them—as well as the architecture, complexity, software sophistication, and computing performance of computers—have gone through an enormous evolutionary process. So striking has this evolution been that computers are universally classified according to the concept of generation. Although there is not always general agreement among those in the computer community, a computer generation has been widely defined in terms of the logic technology and the structure of the active logic devices. The *first generation* computers used vacuum tubes, mostly triodes and pentodes, and spanned the years from approximately 1945 to 1958. The *second generation* computers used transistors, starting about 1958 and ending about 1965. Since about 1965, computers have contained integrated circuit versions of transistor circuits and have commonly been called *third generation* computers. The *fourth generation* computers have yet to be clearly defined, but they will probably use medium or large-scale integration circuits extensively. Thus, several logic circuits will be described here according to the computer generations with which they are most closely associated. Actual implementation of interesting logic circuits will also be presented.

FIRST-GENERATION COMPUTERS. The first-generation electronic computers were primarily char-

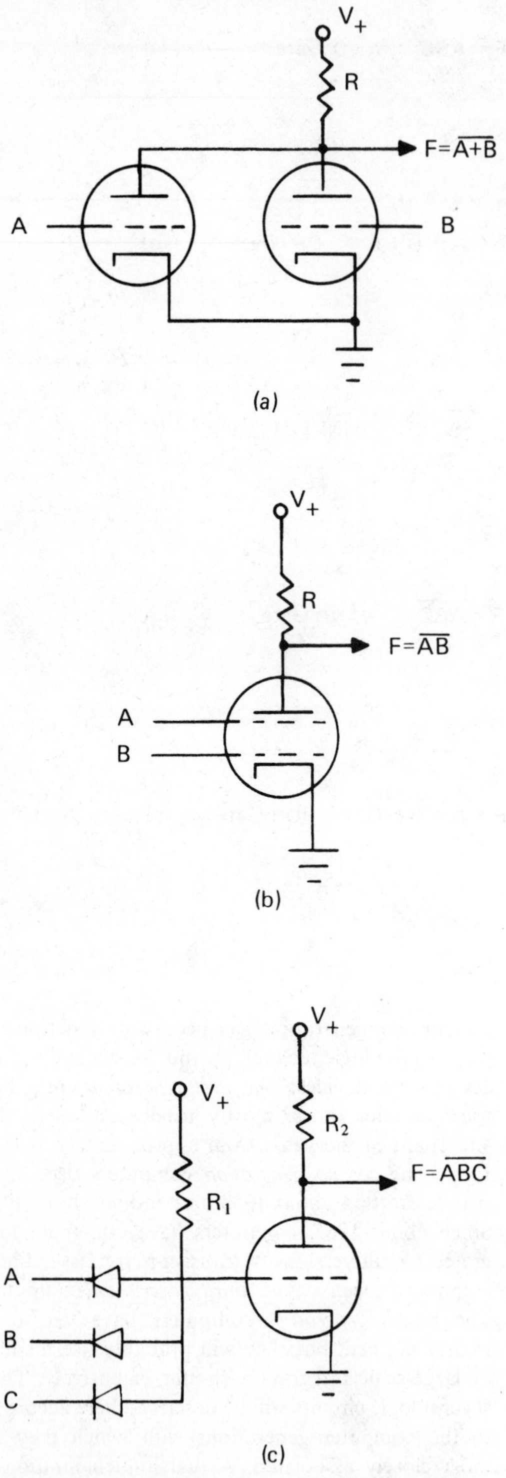


**Fig. 2.** First-generation circuits. (a) NOR gate; (b) NAND gate; (c) INVERTER.

acterized by a logic technology utilizing vacuum tubes. A NOR gate composed of two triodes is shown in Fig. 2(a). If one or two grid inputs ($A,B$) are at logical 1 (i.e., high-voltage state), one or both triodes will conduct current, causing a potential drop across the load resistor $R$ and an output of logical 0 (i.e., low-voltage state); otherwise, the triode will not conduct and the output will be a logical 1. With only one triode, the circuit performs an INVERT function. The twin triodes performing NOR functions were later put into one single vacuum chamber.

Another important vacuum tube for computer applications was the pentode. The high-impedance control and suppressor grids of a pentode were used as input grids, while the low-impedance screen grid was usually not used. A pentode circuit without the screen grid is shown in Fig. 2(b) and behaves as a NAND gate. If either grid input is a logical 0, the pentode will not conduct and the output will be a logical 1. If both grid inputs are a logical 1, the pentode will conduct and the output will be a logical 0. A pentode INVERT circuit is formed by setting one of the inputs constantly at a logical 1.

Since either the NAND gate or the NOR gate is sufficient to generate any boolean function, either the twin-triode or pentode circuit is sufficient for realizing more complex circuits. However, the voltage levels for either circuit do not have compatible input and output requirements. Therefore, voltage-level restoring circuits have to be introduced for cascading either the twin triode or pentode logic circuits. A resistance-voltage divider circuit can be used for voltage-level restoring, but resistor tolerances may introduce imprecise logical levels.

Besides the high cost, computer circuits using vacuum tubes had other shortcomings. Vacuum tubes were limited by their large physical size, which introduced substantial transmission delays. Power consumption was high, so that cooling requirements were also high. Furthermore, they had a rather limited lifetime and a gradual deterioration property, which restricted the practical size of a system that could be seriously contemplated. Consequently, the complexity of the first-generation computers was quite limited. ENIAC contained approximately 18,000 vacuum tubes and was the largest vacuum tube computer ever attempted. With so many vacuum tubes, reliability was quite poor.

A major advance in this technology was the practical application of germanium diodes as logic gates to reduce the required number of vacuum tubes. For example, a multi-input NAND gate could be formed from a multi-input diode AND gate followed by a triode or a pentode INVERT circuit as shown in Fig. 2(c), and thus replace an equivalent circuit requiring several vacuum tubes. The Whirlwind I computer (1951) built by Massachusetts Institute of Technology had a speed of 20,000 operations per second, the fastest computer of its time. This computer required only 5,000 vacuum tubes, mostly pentodes, but there were 11,000 diodes. The IBM 701 computer (1953) had 4,000 vacuum tubes, mostly twin triodes, and 13,000 germanium diodes.

SECOND-GENERATION COMPUTERS. The logic circuits used in second-generation computers were primarily discrete circuits using transistors. Although invented in 1948, the transistor required a decade of development effort before it became a superior alternative to vacuum tubes. Transistors are faster, smaller, more reliable, and dissipate less power than vacuum tubes. A faster operating device results in greater computing power. A smaller device with less power dissipation permits greater packaging density with shorter interconnections, which reduce stray reactance and a shortening of transmission delays. A more reliable device permits a larger and more complex computer to be successfully built.

There are many ways and configurations to implement logic circuits with semiconductor diodes, resistors, and transistors. The transistors in this second generation were primarily bipolar transistors, which means that carriers of both polarities, electrons and holes, are involved to form the total current. No single transistor configuration was superior to all others in all respects. Some of the more important attributes of a logic circuit include speed, fan-in/fan-out capability, noise immunity, noise-generation/stabilization properties, operating temperature range, power dissipation, and cost. The more widely used types of circuits include RTL (resistor-transistor logic), DTL (diode-transistor logic), TTL (transistor-transistor logic), and ECTL (emitter-coupled transistor logic), which are shown in Fig. 3.

*RTL (Resistor-Transistor Logic).* The basic RTL circuit is shown in Fig. 3(a). The RTL circuit is a simple and inexpensive logic circuit. Resistors $R_1$, $R_2$, and $R_3$ form an OR gate. The transistor $T$ along with its load resistor $R_4$ forms the amplifier-inverter section of the circuit in a manner similar to the triode shown in Fig. 2(c). The RTL circuit is therefore a NOR gate and is relatively slow.

*DTL (Diode-Transistor Logic).* The basic DTL circuit is shown in Fig. 3(b). Speed, fan-out capability, noise immunity, and power dissipation are good. When one or more of the inputs $(A,B,C)$ are at logical 0, or low-voltage state, current will flow from $V_+$ through resistor $R_1$ into the inputs. Point $P$ as well as $Q$ will be in a low-voltage position. The transistor will be off and the output $F$ will assume a high-voltage, or logical 1, state. Only when all inputs are in logical 1, or high-voltage, state will the current then be directed to flow through $R_1$, two diodes in series, and $R_3$ into $V_-$. Point $Q$ will now be at a higher voltage level to turn on the transistor. Current will now be allowed to flow through the transistor, and the output $F$ will assume a low-voltage, or logical 0, state. The two diodes in series are used in order to get the correct voltage level at point $Q$. The output can go to logical 0 state only when all inputs are logical 1. The DTL circuit, therefore, performs a NAND function.

*TTL (Transistor-Transistor Logic).* The basic TTL circuit is shown in Fig. 3(c). The circuit is also a NAND gate and is capable of significantly higher speed operation than the RTL and DTL circuits. When either input $A$ or input $B$, or both, are at logical 0 state, there will be sufficient base-to-emitter voltage difference so that either $T_1$ or $T_2$, or both, will be turned on. Point $P$, which connects to the collectors of both transistors, will assume a low-voltage state to turn off $T_3$. There will be "on" current flowing through $R_2$ and the output will be high, or at logical 1. When and only when both inputs $A$ and $B$ are high, both transistors $T_1$ and $T_2$ will be "off" and point $P$ can return to a higher voltage level to turn on $T_3$. Output $F$ will come to a low-voltage state when $T_3$ is "on" and current flows through $R_2$.

*ECTL (Emitter-Coupled Transistor Logic).* The basic ECTL circuit is shown in Fig. 3(d) and is potentially the fastest transistor logic circuit available. All the transistors in ECTL operate in a nonsaturating mode in order to attain high speeds. The emitter current passing through $R_3$ is essentially constant with the current passing through $R_1$ when any of the inputs is a logical 1 or passing through $R_2$ when every input is a logical 0. Transistor $T_4$ establishes the reference voltage for the logical 0 and logical 1 states of the input transistors $T_1$, $T_2$, and $T_3$. The input transistors in combination with the reference transistor act as a differential amplifier having good common mode rejection of power-supply line noises. Also, both a NOR output $\bar{F}$ and an OR output $F$ are available, yielding complementary gating functions respectively.

Typical second-generation computers using these circuits include the IBM 7000 series (first delivery 1960) and Burrough B200 series (first delivery 1961).

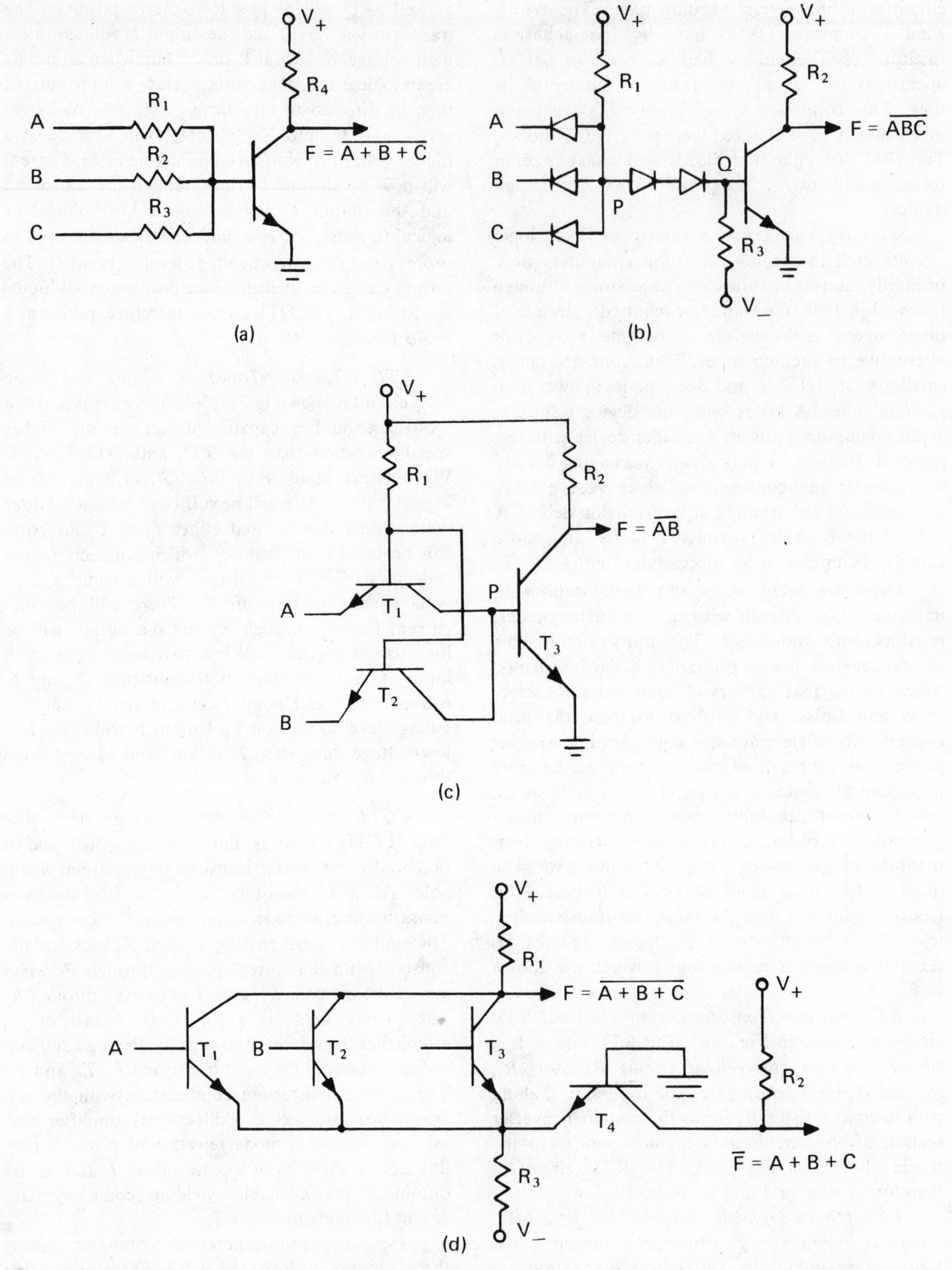


**Fig. 3.** Second-generation logic circuits. (a) RTL circuit; (b) DTL circuit; (c) TTL circuit; (d) ECTL circuit.

THIRD-GENERATION COMPUTERS. A computer using vacuum tubes was considered a first-generation computer, and one using transistors was considered a second-generation computer. However, the distinction between second- and third-generation computers is not so clear-cut. Those manufacturers using integrated circuits tend to believe that the use of integrated circuit (IC) technology should be the criterion for distinguishing third- from second-generation computers. On the other hand, those manufacturers still using discrete component technology tend to believe that performance would be a better measure. Thus, Control Data Corporation 6000 series computers, which were implemented by discrete component circuits, should certainly be classified as third-generation computers, according to their performance. Furthermore, the IBM 360 family of computers is considered third-generation, although it utilizes hybrid circuit technology that is partially integrated circuit technology and partially discrete device technology. Nevertheless, from the computer circuitry point of view, integrated circuit technology will be used to define a third-generation computer whether the circuitry is fully or only partially integrated.

The logic circuits used in a third-generation computer have the same basic circuit configuration as those in second-generation computers. In integrated circuits, the transistors, diodes, and resistors are all fabricated simultaneously on a silicon wafer. Cost differentiation among these devices, which is of utmost importance in discrete components, is not significant in integrated circuits. TTL circuits and ECTL circuits, which use more transistors, can be fabricated at about the same cost as RTL or DTL circuits. Consequently, the integrated circuit versions of logic circuits tend to have more transistors, are more complex, and have better performance at lower cost.

*Hybrid DTL.* The IBM 360 family of computers (first delivery 1965) used hybrid circuits. One aspect of this design is that the transistors and diodes were encapsulated in a protective layer of glass so that a hermetic seal was unnecessary. Resistors are fabricated as thin-film devices and metallization patterns make the substrate interconnections. The logic substrate contains a DTL circuit, which is given in Fig. 4. Basically, the circuit is still a NAND gate when $A$, $B$, and $C$ are used. The $X$ input lead is called an "expander" and serves to connect additional diodes that may be added to increase fan-in. The $R$ input lead permits an OR coupling circuit to be added to the logical operations of the circuit. Some of the advantages of this technology are better quality and reliability for both active and passive components, high component density, and high-speed performance.

*Integrated TTL.* The integrated version of TTL

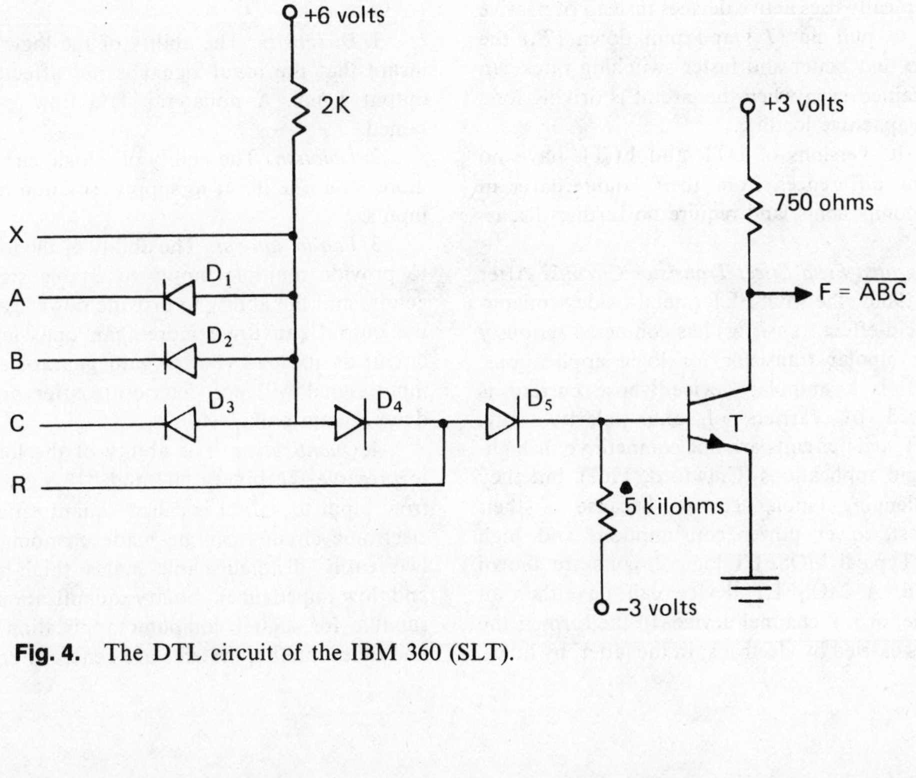


**Fig. 4.** The DTL circuit of the IBM 360 (SLT).

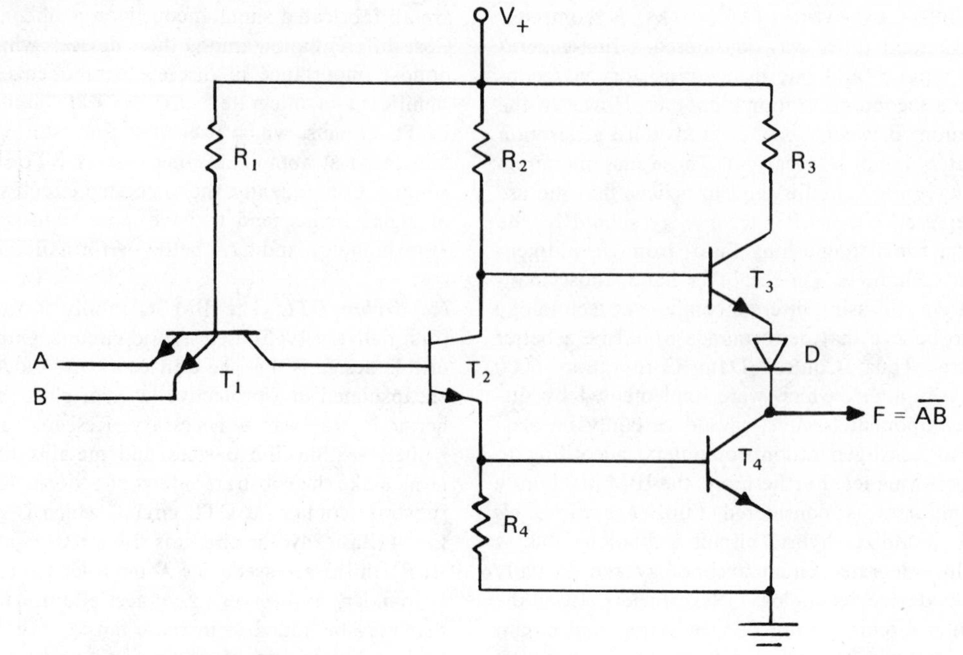


**Fig. 5.** An integrated TTL circuit.

shown in Fig. 5 is quite different from the discrete component TTL shown in Fig. 3(c). The input transistors $T_1$ and $T_2$ in Fig. 3(c) are combined into a single transistor with double emitters. The output circuit typically uses active devices instead of passive resistors to pull up ($T_3$) and pull down ($T_4$) the output so that better and faster switching rates can be maintained even when the circuit is driving long lines of capacitive loading.

The IC versions of DTL and ECTL have no significant differences from their counterparts in discrete components, and require no further discussion.

*Integrated Field-Effect Transistor Circuits.* After the mid-1960s, the MOSFET (metal-oxide-semiconductor field-effect transistor) has competed seriously with the bipolar transistor for logic applications. MOSFET is a unipolar device whose current is transported by carriers of one polarity only. MOSFET logic circuits are not competitive in high-speed logic applications (Crawford, 1967), but they are challenging bipolar circuits because of their lower cost, lower power consumption, and high density. Typical MOSFET logic circuits are shown in Fig. 6. A MOSFET device can be either an N-channel or a P-channel device. In the former, the current is carried by electrons; in the latter, by holes.

**General Characteristics of Various Types of Computer Circuitry.** All electronic logic circuits have certain characteristics (Lo, 1967) in common:

1. *Directivity.* The ability of the logic circuit to insure that the input signal is not affected by the output signal. A unilateral data flow is thus obtained.

2. *Isolation.* The ability of a logic circuit having more than one input to supply isolation among the inputs.

3. *Fan-in, fan-out.* The ability of the logic circuit to provide multiple inputs to enable signal interaction, and the ability to provide power gain so that the output can drive more than one similar logic circuit as its load. Power gain guarantees that an input signal will not deteriorate after propagating down a data path.

4. *Quantization.* The ability of the logic circuit to preserve the binary "0" and "1" signals distinct from input to output is called "quantization." Since electronic circuits can be made economically with two easily distinguishable states (high-impedance and low-impedance), binary quantization is most suitable for digital computer application. Decimal and other number systems are generally represented

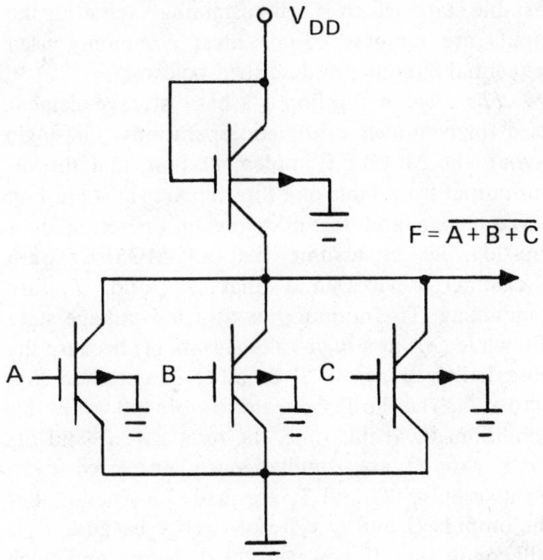


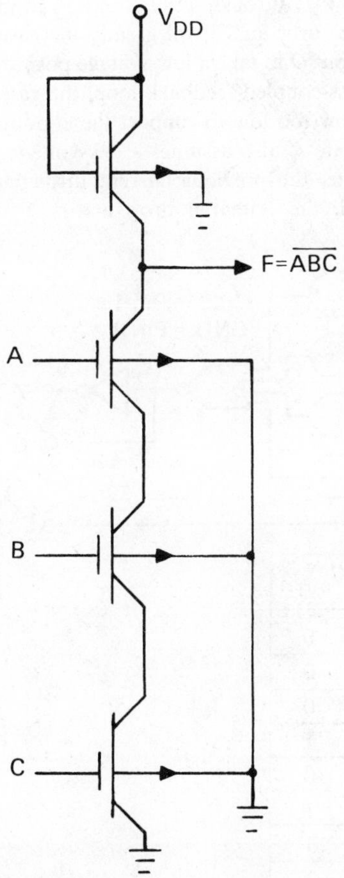


**Fig. 6.** MOSFET NOR and NAND circuits.

by a binary-coded form, such as BCD (binary-coded decimal).

The four general characteristics of logic circuits listed above can best be explained further with a typical logic circuit such as the DTL shown in Fig. 3(b). The property of directivity specifies that the output $F$ is controlled by the inputs $A$, $B$, $C$, but not vice versa. This property is achieved through the characteristic of the transistor. Its base controls the "on" or "off" of the transistor as well as the voltage level at the output $F$. The output, however, does not control the base voltage.

The property of isolation specifies that a voltage swing of any one input, such as $A$, has no effect on the other inputs, such as $B$ and $C$. Between input $A$ and input $B$ are two back-to-back diodes. No matter which way $A$ swings with respect to $B$, one of these two diodes will be reverse-biased. Therefore, input $B$ is isolated from, and will not respond to, the swing of input $A$. Obviously, the isolation between $A$ and $C$ works the same way.

The fan-in of the DTL circuit shown in Fig. 3(b) is three, i.e., the number of inputs driving the output. The ability to support fan-in is essential for performing the AND, OR, NAND, or NOR functions. The fan-out of a DTL circuit refers to how many similar DTL circuits can be driven from the output point $F$ of this circuit. This fan-out number is limited by the total current that is allowed to flow through the transistor without appreciably raising the voltage level of $F$. The total current includes that from $V_+$ flowing through $R_4$ and those from the driven DTLs.

The property of quantization in DTL circuits refers to the fact that the voltage swing at the output $F$ with any allowable fan-out should be the same as the voltage swing of the inputs. The quantization is obtained by properly designing the three resistors with the two voltage supplies of the DTL circuits.

**Some Commonly Used Computer Circuitry.** Computer circuitry can be divided into combinational circuits and sequential circuits. We will discuss them separately.

COMBINATIONAL CIRCUITS. A combinational circuit is a logic circuit whose output is determined solely by the states of its present inputs and is independent of the states of its previous inputs. Commonly used combinational circuits include majority logic, comparators, adders, and decoders. They are built from the basic logic gates shown in Fig. 1. Most of them are available in either bipolar or MOSFET integrated circuit modules from most semiconductor manufacturers. Some typical examples of combinational circuits quoted from semiconductor manufacturers' data sheets are described below.

*Full Adder.* A binary full adder will add two binary bit inputs ($A$ and $B$) and a previous carry bit ($C_{in\ 1}$). The outputs will be a sum bit $S_1$ and a carry bit $C_{out\ 1}$. The logic block diagram and the truth table are shown in Fig. 7.

*BCD-to-Decimal Decoder.* This circuit decodes a four-bit BCD (binary-coded-decimal) input to select one of ten outputs. The selected output is in the logical "0" state, and all the other outputs are in the logical "1" state. The logic layout and the truth table are shown in Fig. 8.

Many other combinational circuits available commercially are implemented by various technologies. The reader is referred to the data sheets or catalogs of the numerous semiconductor manufacturers.

SEQUENTIAL CIRCUITS. Logic circuits that can store digital information are classified as sequential circuits. In contrast to that of a combinational circuit, the output of a sequential circuit depends not only on the present input state, but also on the previous input states. From the circuitry point of view, a sequential circuit is different from a combinational circuit in that it has feedback paths that connect the outputs back to the inputs with proper phasing, time delay, and power gain. The feedback loops enable the sequential circuit to have a stable state, which is self-sustaining even after the inputs are removed. Some most commonly used sequential circuits are described below.

*Flip-Flop.* A flip-flop is a basic storage element used for computer arithmetic operations. The logic layout, the MOSFET implementation, and the input-output truth table of a flip-flop are shown in Fig. 9. To understand the principle of operation of a flip-flop, let us assume that all MOSFETs are N-channel devices and that $T_1$ and $T_2$ are conducting. The output $Q$ is at a low-voltage state (0), while $\bar{Q}$ is at a high-voltage state (1) because the potential drop across $T_1$ is much larger than that across $T_3$. The flip-flop is said to store a 0 under this condition. If, at this time, the reset gate $R$ and the clock gate $C$ are simultaneously energized by a positive pulse, $T_5$ and $T_6$ are made conducting, but the outputs $Q$ and $\bar{Q}$ will not change because $T_1$ is still conducting. If, however, the set gate $S$ and clock gate $C$ are energized instead, $T_7$ and $T_8$ will start to conduct. Current can now flow from the source voltage $V_{DD}$ through $T_3$, $T_7$, and $T_8$ to ground. The potential drop in $T_3$ will greatly increase and force the output $\bar{Q}$ to take a low-voltage position. Through the cross-coupled feedback loop, the gate voltage of $T_2$ is now too low to support the conduction of $T_2$. Since gate $R$ also assumes a low-voltage position at this time, the previous current through $T_1$ is now blocked, the potential drop across $T_1$ is reduced

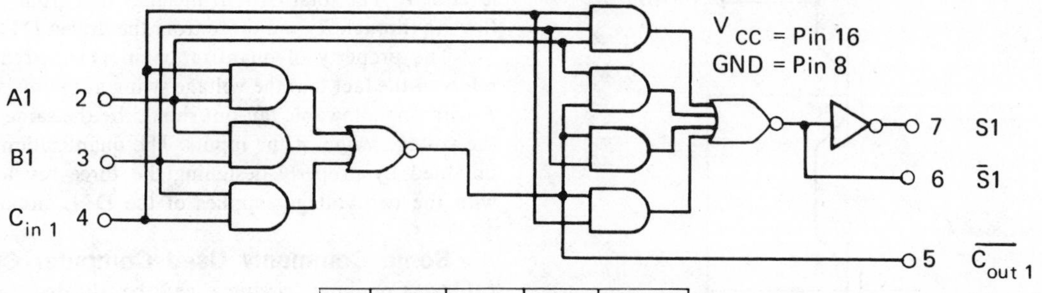

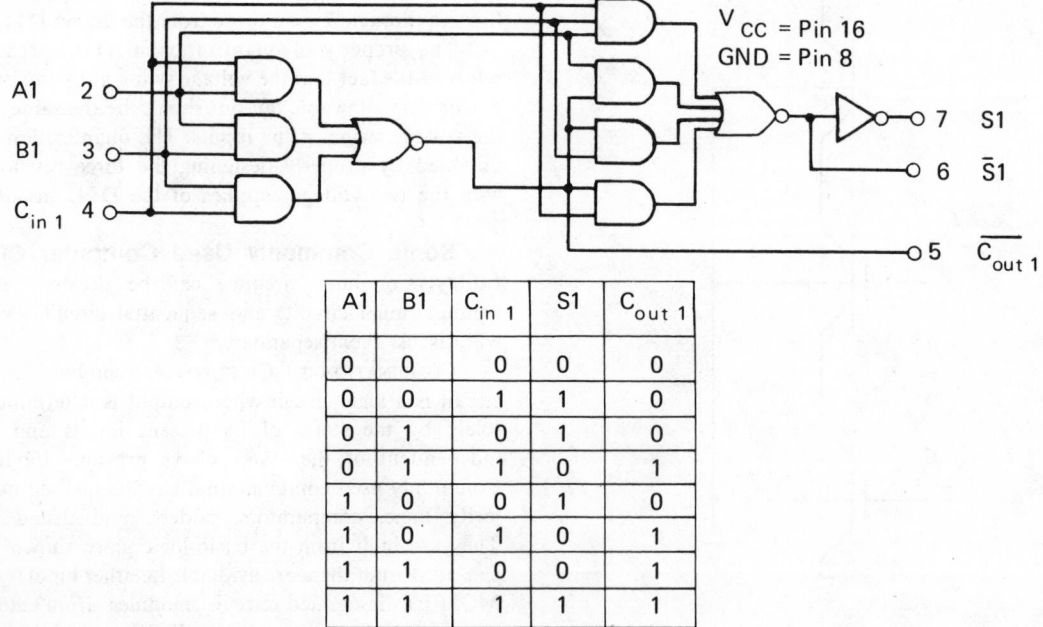

| A1 | B1 | $C_{in\ 1}$ | S1 | $C_{out\ 1}$ |
|---|---|---|---|---|
| 0 | 0 | 0 | 0 | 0 |
| 0 | 0 | 1 | 1 | 0 |
| 0 | 1 | 0 | 1 | 0 |
| 0 | 1 | 1 | 0 | 1 |
| 1 | 0 | 0 | 1 | 0 |
| 1 | 0 | 1 | 0 | 1 |
| 1 | 1 | 0 | 0 | 1 |
| 1 | 1 | 1 | 1 | 1 |

**Fig. 7.** Dual full adder.

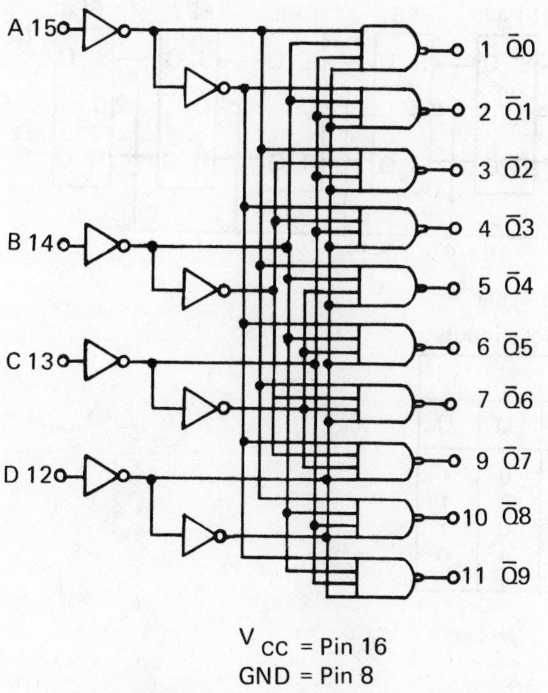


| Inputs | | | | Outputs | | | | | | | | | |
|---|---|---|---|---|---|---|---|---|---|---|---|---|---|
| D | C | B | A | $\overline{Q9}$ | $\overline{Q8}$ | $\overline{Q7}$ | $\overline{Q6}$ | $\overline{Q5}$ | $\overline{Q4}$ | $\overline{Q3}$ | $\overline{Q2}$ | $\overline{Q1}$ | $\overline{Q0}$ |
| 0 | 0 | 0 | 0 | 1 | 1 | 1 | 1 | 1 | 1 | 1 | 1 | 1 | 0 |
| 0 | 0 | 0 | 1 | 1 | 1 | 1 | 1 | 1 | 1 | 1 | 1 | 0 | 1 |
| 0 | 0 | 1 | 0 | 1 | 1 | 1 | 1 | 1 | 1 | 1 | 0 | 1 | 1 |
| 0 | 0 | 1 | 1 | 1 | 1 | 1 | 1 | 1 | 1 | 0 | 1 | 1 | 1 |
| 0 | 1 | 0 | 0 | 1 | 1 | 1 | 1 | 1 | 0 | 1 | 1 | 1 | 1 |
| 0 | 1 | 0 | 1 | 1 | 1 | 1 | 1 | 0 | 1 | 1 | 1 | 1 | 1 |
| 0 | 1 | 1 | 0 | 1 | 1 | 1 | 0 | 1 | 1 | 1 | 1 | 1 | 1 |
| 0 | 1 | 1 | 1 | 1 | 1 | 0 | 1 | 1 | 1 | 1 | 1 | 1 | 1 |
| 1 | 0 | 0 | 0 | 1 | 0 | 1 | 1 | 1 | 1 | 1 | 1 | 1 | 1 |
| 1 | 0 | 0 | 1 | 0 | 1 | 1 | 1 | 1 | 1 | 1 | 1 | 1 | 1 |
| 1 | 0 | 1 | 0 | 1 | 1 | 1 | 1 | 1 | 1 | 1 | 1 | 1 | 1 |
| 1 | 0 | 1 | 1 | 1 | 1 | 1 | 1 | 1 | 1 | 1 | 1 | 1 | 1 |
| 1 | 1 | 0 | 0 | 1 | 1 | 1 | 1 | 1 | 1 | 1 | 1 | 1 | 1 |
| 1 | 1 | 0 | 1 | 1 | 1 | 1 | 1 | 1 | 1 | 1 | 1 | 1 | 1 |
| 1 | 1 | 1 | 0 | 1 | 1 | 1 | 1 | 1 | 1 | 1 | 1 | 1 | 1 |
| 1 | 1 | 1 | 1 | 1 | 1 | 1 | 1 | 1 | 1 | 1 | 1 | 1 | 1 |

**Fig. 8.** BCD to decimal decoder.

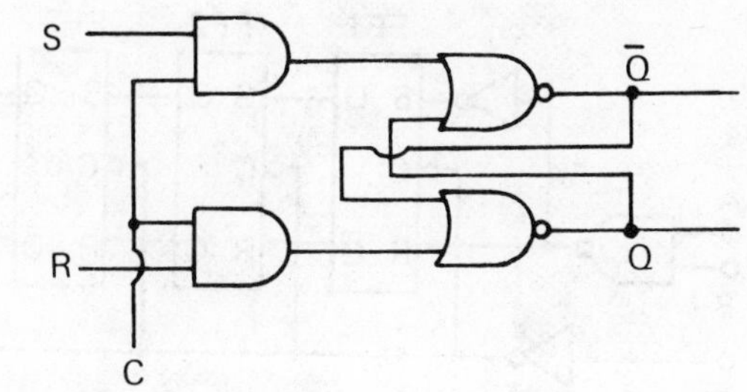


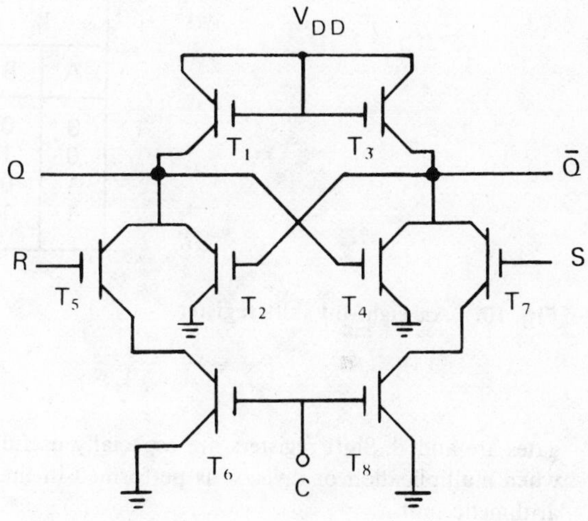


Truth Table

| C | R | S | Q | $\overline{Q}$ |
|---|---|---|---|---|
| 1 | 0 | 1 | 1 | 0 |
| 1 | 1 | 0 | 0 | 1 |
| 1 | 0 | 0 | Previous state | |
| 0 | 0 | 1 | " | " |
| 0 | 1 | 0 | " | " |
| 0 | 0 | 0 | " | " |

**Fig. 9.** The logic layout, the truth table, and MOSFET implementation of a flip-flop.

greatly, and the output $Q$ is raised to a high-voltage or 1 level. An examination of the truth table shows that the stored information will not be disturbed by either $S$ or $R$ when $C$ stays low. When $C$ is energized, the flip-flop can be set to 1 by energizing $S$, and reset to 0 by energizing $R$.

*Shift Registers.* Shift registers may be formed from a series of flip-flop circuits. A typical shift register is shown in Fig. 10, where the clock signal is connected to all the flip-flops. At each clock pulse, one bit of information will be written into the flip-flop FF1 from inputs $A$ and $B$. At the next clock pulse, this bit will move to the flip-flop FF2 while a new bit is being written into FF1. Bidirectional shifting is possible when some additional control

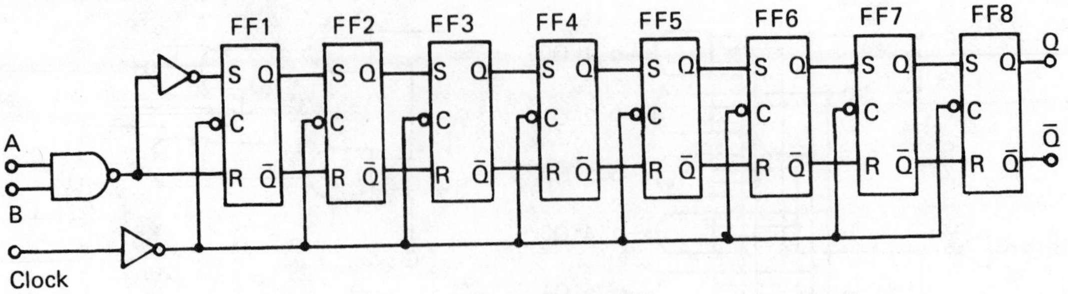


Truth Table
Synchronous Inputs

| $t_n$ | | $t_{n+8}$ | |
|---|---|---|---|
| A | B | Q | $\bar{Q}$ |
| 0 | 0 | 0 | 1 |
| 0 | 1 | 0 | 1 |
| 1 | 0 | 0 | 1 |
| 1 | 1 | 1 | 0 |

**Fig. 10.** An eight-bit shift register.

gates are added. Shift registers are especially useful when multiplication or division is performed in the arithmetic unit.

**Future Computer Circuitry.** The definition of a fourth-generation computer has not yet been well defined. One thing being generally agreed upon is that it will probably use large-scale integration (LSI) extensively. The logic circuit configuration in the fourth-generation LSI could be basically the same as those used in the third-generation computer. The LSI circuits could be either in bipolar or in MOSFET technology. As mentioned before, bipolar LSI will outperform MOSFET LSI in speed, but suffer from less density and higher power dissipation.

Through LSI, the number of chips and modules in a system can be reduced greatly. Besides cost reduction and reliability improvement, performance can be improved from reduced wire delay. However, LSI also creates such problems as (1) sizable design and initial tooling cost, (2) decreased yield with increased chip size, (3) excessive heat generation, (4) more complex debugging and testing, and (5) the limitation of the number of input/output (I/O) connection terminals.

In small-scale integration (SSI) and medium-scale integration (MSI), with circuit count roughly

**Fig. 11.** Photomicrograph of a silicon field-effect transistor, about 100$\mu$ on a side and 1$\mu$ wide. (Courtesy of IBM.)

less than 10 and 100, respectively, air cooling is generally adequate for heat removal. In LSI, designers may be forced to choose between low-power circuits or a sophisticated cooling system. In SSI, and even in MSI, many nodes are accessible for debugging and testing. In LSI, however, the number of accessible nodes is greatly reduced, and testing can become quite complicated. When chip size is doubled to accommodate more circuits, the peripheral area, which accommodates the I/O connection terminals, is increased only 40%. This problem may become a limiting factor in LSI logic circuit chip design.

LSI logic circuit chips can be roughly divided into four groups:

1. Custom chips designed for a specific single application.
2. Master chips having a given number of circuits and I/O connection terminals, and designers have some flexibility in interconnecting some of or all the circuits to perform certain functions, such as the universal logic circuits.
3. Array chips featuring, generally, READ ONLY memory arrays to perform certain specific functions.
4. Functional chips that perform predesigned functions such as those offered by manufacturers in their catalog.

Most LSI chips are presently being used in electronic calculators or minicomputers. For example, an eight-bit parallel central processing unit has been placed on a single chip marketed by Intel. An arithmetic logic unit, an accumulator-register-counter stack, an instruction decoding and control unit, a timing unit, and an I/O unit are all built into this single chip.

Another type of LSI chip that may have important impact on future computer circuitry has so-called *dynamic logic*. In all the logic circuits discussed previously, information (logical 1 or 0) is represented by a steady-state voltage level. This level is usually maintained by a steady-state current that causes power dissipation and generates heat. In dynamic logic, logic states are represented by charging or discharging a capacitor, without steady-state current. Power consumption will be greatly reduced. Since dynamic logic does not require resistors and since high-ohmage resistors demand a large silicon area, the circuit density of dynamic logic in LSI is substantially higher than that of other logics. Dynamic logic usually performs logical functions through four-phase clocks and is slower than other logics in general. Four-Phase Systems, Inc., has adopted dynamic logic in their IV/70 systems.

The future LSI will probably evolve from the present LSI. Two possible trends of the future LSI may be seen in the example of Intel processor chips: (1) LSI will contain logic, memory, and control in a single chip to perform as a complete system; and (2) LSI will be built as a collection of proven functions to ease the testing problem.

REFERENCES

1962. Huskey, H. D., and G. A. Korn. *Computer Handbook*. New York: McGraw-Hill, chap. 20.
1967. Crawford, R. H. *MOSFET in Circuit Design*. New York: McGraw-Hill, chap. 1.
1967. Lo, A. W. *Introduction to Digital Electronics*. Reading Mass.: Addison-Wesley, chaps. 1 and 2.
1970. Kohavi, Z. *Switching and Finite Automata Theory*. New York: McGraw-Hill.
1972. Torng, H. C. *Switching Circuits, Theory and Logic*. Reading, Mass.: Addison-Wesley.

S. S. YAU AND I. T. HO

## COMPUTER GENERATIONS. *See*

GENERATIONS, COMPUTER.

## COMPUTER GRAPHICS

For articles on related subjects *see* COMPUTER-AIDED DESIGN; CURSOR; DATA STRUCTURES; INPUT-OUTPUT DEVICES; JOYSTICK; LIGHTPEN; PICTURES, BASIC STRUCTURE; RAND TABLET; TERMINALS; and TIME SHARING.
For articles on related terms *see* BUFFER; FILES; MODELS; PERT/CPM; and RING.

Computer graphics (graphics) may be defined as the input, construction, storage, retrieval, manipulation, alteration, and analysis of pictorial data. Computer graphics in general includes both off-line *input* of drawings and photographs via scanners, digitizers, or pattern-recognition devices, and *output* of drawings on paper or (micro) film via plotters and film recorders. *Interactive* graphics is a term used to emphasize man-machine dialog, which takes place in real-time using an on-line display console with manual input (interaction) devices (Fig. 1).

Among such input devices are the alphanumeric and function keyboards for typing text and activating pre-programmed subroutines, respectively,

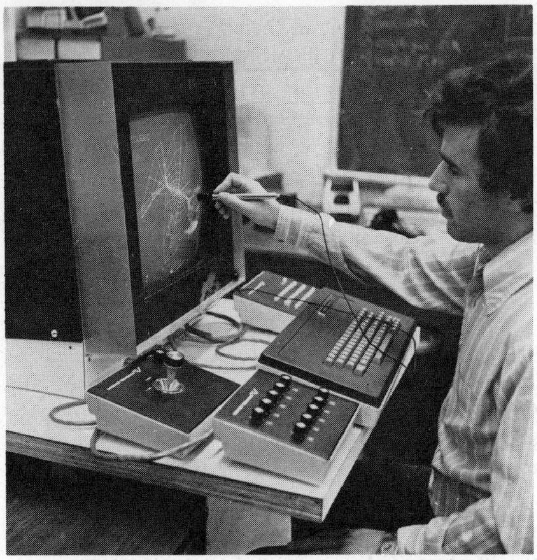

**Fig. 1.** A Vector General graphics display console showing a lightpen pointing to a picture on the display screen, the function keyboard (lower left), the alphanumeric keyboard (lower center), joystick (right center above alphanumeric keyboard) and potentiometer controls (lower right). The Display Processing Unit, which is the hardware controlling the display, is under the table.

and the lightpen and data tablet for identifying and entering graphic information by means of pointing and drawing.

The scope of this survey article is restricted to interactive graphics (called "graphics" in what follows), and therefore excludes scene analysis and pattern recognition, image processing and enhancement, computer animation, etc., which are covered elsewhere in this encyclopedia. Newman and Sproull (1973) discuss the technology surveyed here in far greater detail, and a good overview of applications and current trends is available (IEEE, 1974).

For various technological and historical reasons, most of today's graphics concerns line drawings (so-called wire-frame representations) of two- and three-dimensional abstractions such as electronic and mechanical circuits; structural components of buildings, cars, ships, and planes; chemical diagrams; functional plots of mathematical formulas; and flowcharts. In addition to line-drawing graphics, we are now beginning to see an increase in interest in on-line manipulation of solid pictures with gray scale, color, and hidden line/surface representations of three-dimensional scenes (Sutherland, Sproull, and Schumacker, 1974).

HISTORICAL OVERVIEW. Line-drawing graphics started with the two display consoles on Whirlwind I, one maintaining a user screen and the other feeding a computer-controlled camera as a precursor of today's film recorders. The Sage tactical air defense system in 1955 had a multiconsole, multiuser display configuration with human feedback entering the system via lightpens that had pointing capability, toggle switches, and alphanumeric and function keyboards. Ivan Sutherland and his associates at the M.I.T. Lincoln Laboratories introduced and popularized most of the fundamental notions of graphics (still in use today) with their cleverly named, seminal SKETCHPAD system (Sutherland, 1963) on the TX-2 computer. Since the early 1960s there has been commercial development, with DEC, IBM, and (later) Tektronix supplying most of the hardware, and big industry such as General Motors and Lockheed as the pioneers in designing large-scale systems software and applications programs for the new hardware.

Today, after more than ten years, however, the field is still in its infancy, with many unfulfilled promises. Graphics as the appealing "window into the computer" has been oversold on the one hand, and has been forced to cope with many legitimate but somewhat unforeseen problems on the other hand. Among these problems are very expensive, nonstandardized display hardware with inadequate, nonstandardized software; insufficient realization of, and accounting for, the cost of central computer hardware and software resources to support the display terminal and its application programs; and the difficulty and cost of implementing sophisticated large-scale applications programs (typically of the CAD variety; see Prince, 1971), very few of which have turned out to be cost-effective.

Only recently have we begun to see the long desired emphasis on simple, straightforward, and cost-effective applications via widespread use of truly low-cost graphics terminals. These are typically storage tubes or refreshed displays driven by small minicomputers costing less than $10,000 and programmed via a user-oriented subroutine package (typically embedded in Fortran). Indeed, device-independent graphic subroutine packages and languages are finally emerging to allow the user/programmer to concentrate on his application rather than on the peculiarities of his display or input devices. Similarly, the gap between "soft copy" on the display and "hard copy" prints is being closed by display-connected printout devices or plotters driven from the same program that builds pictures for the display. Given the much greater availability of reasonably priced hardware and easily used software, the long awaited era of man-machine symbiosis may finally have arrived.

APPLICATION AREAS. The following list, although admittedly far from comprehensive, gives at least an idea of the areas of use to which graphics has already been put.

- Verification drawings of numerical control tapes
- Weather maps
- Contour maps
- Exploration maps for petroleum and mining
- Ship, aircraft, missile, and satellite course plotting
- Cartography, including oceonographic charts
- PERT network drawings
- Flight test and engine performance graphs
- Telemetry data plotting
- Highway cut and fill
- Research and engineering data reduction
- Temperature and pressure drawing
- Fourier analysis
- Antenna scatter display
- Optical ray tracing
- Calibration curves
- Mathematical studies function analysis
- Kinetic analysis
- Route layout simulation
- Reservoir sizing
- Power spectrum displays
- Quality control displays
- Oil production maps
- Cockpit and aircraft landing visibility studies
- Wave research drawings
- Pattern layout (clothing, metal)
- Layout drawings, printed and integrated circuits
- Layout drawings, petroleum and chemical processes
- Pole, line, and distribution drawings, electrical utilities
- Computer animation in science and entertainment
- Electrical, mechanical, structural, and civil engineering drawings
- Drafting and schematic and dimensioned drawings
- Subdivision and construction layouts
- Computer-aided design systems
- Models of human organs and physiological systems
- Architectural and planning designs
- Computer-aided instruction via graphical output and simulation

CLASSES OF GRAPHICS APPLICATION PROGRAMS. The areas listed above can be categorized in a variety of ways. An obvious one is based on the type of picture generated: for example, whether two- or three-dimensional, or whether portraying an abstract or a real entity (such as a four-dimensional mathematical object or an idealized electronic circuit versus a perspective drawing of a house). A categorization that is less drawing-oriented and more programming-oriented divides the application areas into three reasonably distinct ones in a spectrum, based on the amount of man/machine interaction that they exhibit.

*Interactive plotting* describes probably three-quarters of graphics application programs. (*Note:* The term "application program" denotes the totality of the software system, including the graphics programs that produce the pictures, the interrupt handlers, the analysis routines, the data base routines, etc., as described in the next section). The display console is used simply to "browse" through output of computational processes, typically in the form of a graph prepared by the host computer. Little interaction is required except for the real-time display of successive frames on operator command, and simple "menu selection" (i.e., via labeled function key or lightpen identification of a command name displayed in a control area on the screen) to direct the browsing or further computation. Such applications as computer-assisted instruction and command and control operations fit into this category of primarily predefined pictures.

*Design drafting* describes the much more demanding and elaborate preparation of complex schematics and blueprints, typically those of industry. In these applications, an operator constructs a highly detailed drawing on line, using a variety of interaction devices and programming techniques. Facilities are required for replicating basic figures, achieving exact size and placement of components, making lines of specified length, width, or angle to previously defined lines, satisfying varying geometric and topological constraints between components of the drawing, etc.

One primary difference between these first two classes of graphics lies in the amount of effort the operator contributes, with interactive design drafting requiring far more responsibility for the eventual result. In interactive plotting, the computation is of central importance and the drawing is typically secondary. A second difference is that design drawings tend to have structure, i.e., to be hierarchies or networks (interconnected assemblies) of mechanical or electrical components. These components must be transformed (translated, rotated, scaled, projected in standard engineering views, etc.) and edited (inserted, deleted, reconnected, and reconfigured) at the console.

If, in addition to nontrivial layout, the applications program involves significant computation on the picture and its components (transient analysis or stress analysis, for example), we speak of the third and most complex category, that of *interactive design*. In addition to a pictorial datum base, or data structure, that defines where all the picture components fit on the picture and also specifies their geometric characteristics, an *applications datum base* is now needed to describe the electrical, mechanical, and other properties of the components in a form suitable for access and manipulation by the analysis program. This datum base must naturally also be editable and accessible by the interactive user.

Relatively long (multisecond) responses from the host computer may suffice for interactive plotting, since the user may look at one complete display (frame) for quite a few seconds before requesting the next or recomputing to produce the next. Such delays are intolerable in design drafting and interactive design, however, because the user may spend the entire console session manipulating and altering perhaps only a few pictures in a cyclic "design, view-results, redesign" process. Furthermore, human factors play an essential role in making graphics-based interactive design a palatable substitute for pencil-and-paper methodology. For example, being able to zoom smoothly in and out on a large drawing and display the detail part in a user-defined window is a necessary feature for overcoming the limitations of a small, low-resolution console screen (see the section on Windowing). Another human-factor criterion to be considered is that the program must be constructed in such a way that a novice user should not be overwhelmed by too many details when he is still in the learning phase; this is only one aspect of "user-friendliness."

**Review of Graphics Technology.** The purpose of this section is to describe in very general terms the various hardware and software components of a graphics system. Terms and nomenclature are introduced by example.

HARDWARE. Fig. 2 symbolizes the major hardware components with which the applications programmer and user deal directly or indirectly. (*Note:* The term "*user*" may denote either the application programmer who writes the graphic programs or the end user, who may be the noncomputer-oriented problem solver or draftsman. To avoid confusion, user in this article will mean end user.) A user's only contact with the configuration is confined to the display surface for viewing the picture (the output function) and to the manual input devices for creating and altering the picture and controlling the analysis program (the input function). All other hardware should ideally be of no concern to him.

For purposes of discussion, the display console is assumed to be attached via an I/O channel (as is any other peripheral) to a computer in which the graphics program is executed. In the display console, a buffer stores the set of display commands (called the "display file," display program, or buffer program) that defines the picture. This display file is directly executed by the *display controller* (also called display processor or display processing unit), in the same way that an ordinary program is executed by a CPU.

The display processing unit (DPU) decodes each command and causes the numeric description of the position of points and lines on the display surface to be transformed into analog movements of the electron beam in a cathode-ray tube (CRT), similar to that in a home television receiver. Phosphors in the screen surface emit light when stimulated by this moving electron beam. The phosphor's light output decays typically in tens of milliseconds, so the DPU on most displays must loop through the display file 30 to 60 times per second in order to restimulate the phosphor and provide a flicker-free image. This periodic refreshing of the screen is quite similar to what is done in a TV monitor by a 60-frame-per-second interlaced TV signal. If too much information is contained in the display file, the beam cannot move around in the time available for each frame, and the image will flicker.

The display file, or DPU program, as described above is oriented primarily toward specifying output of pictures on the screen. Where is the specification of the handling of user input? The typical DPU simply passes interrupts from programmed function keys, lightpens, etc., to a low level CPU interrupt-handling module in the operating system, which in turn passes control to an applications program to

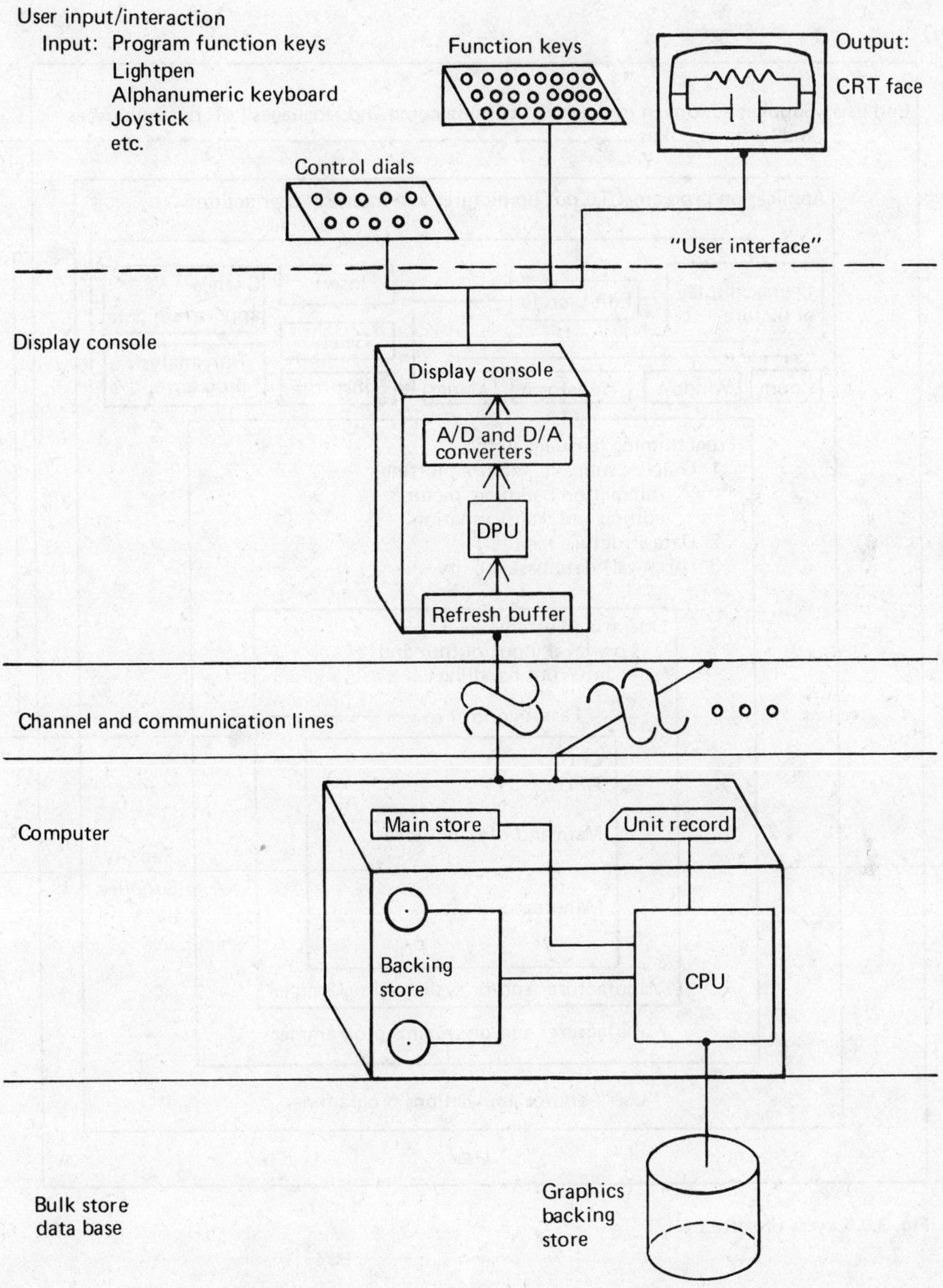


**Fig. 2.** Hardware view of configuration.

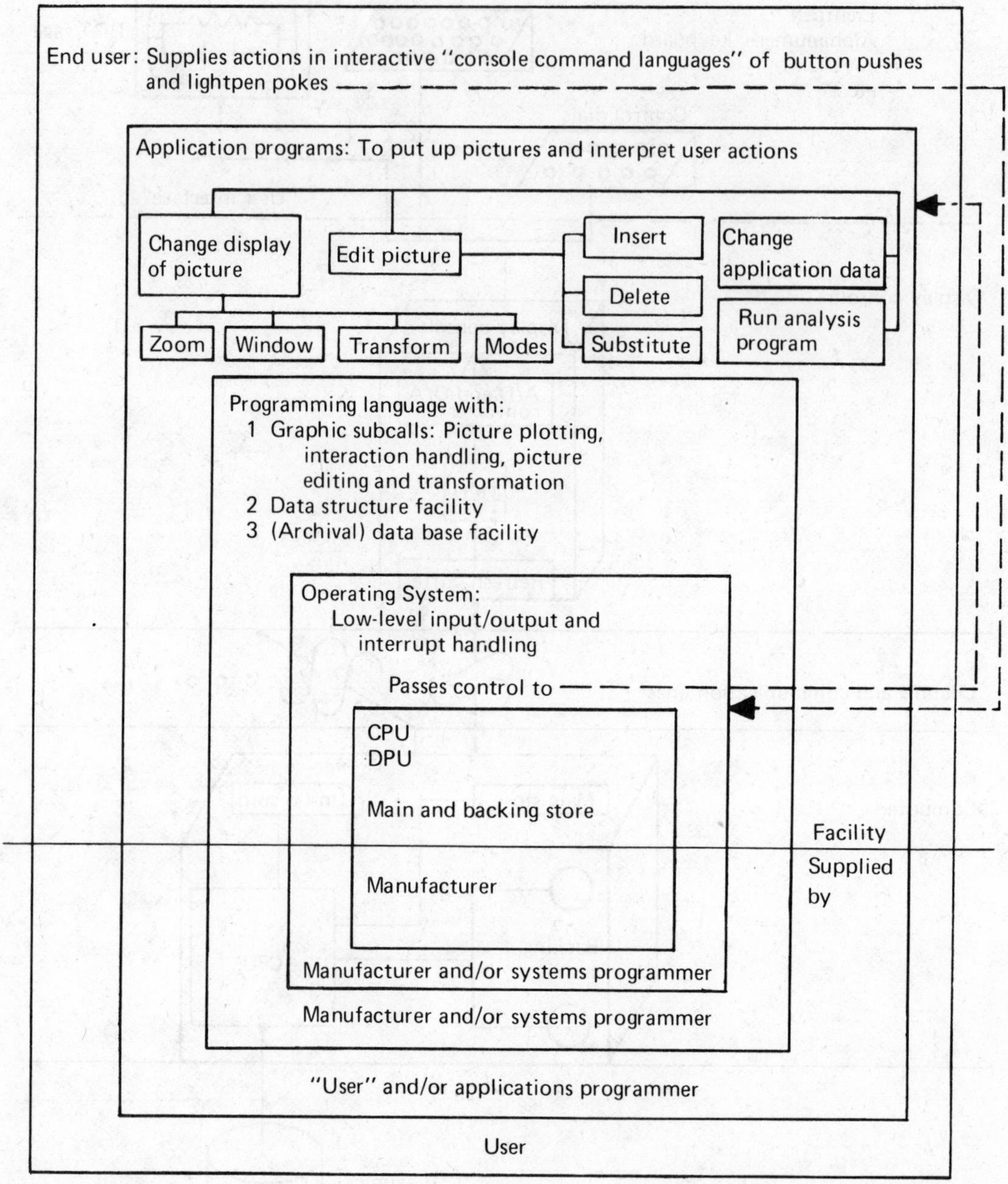


**Fig. 3.** Layers of software.

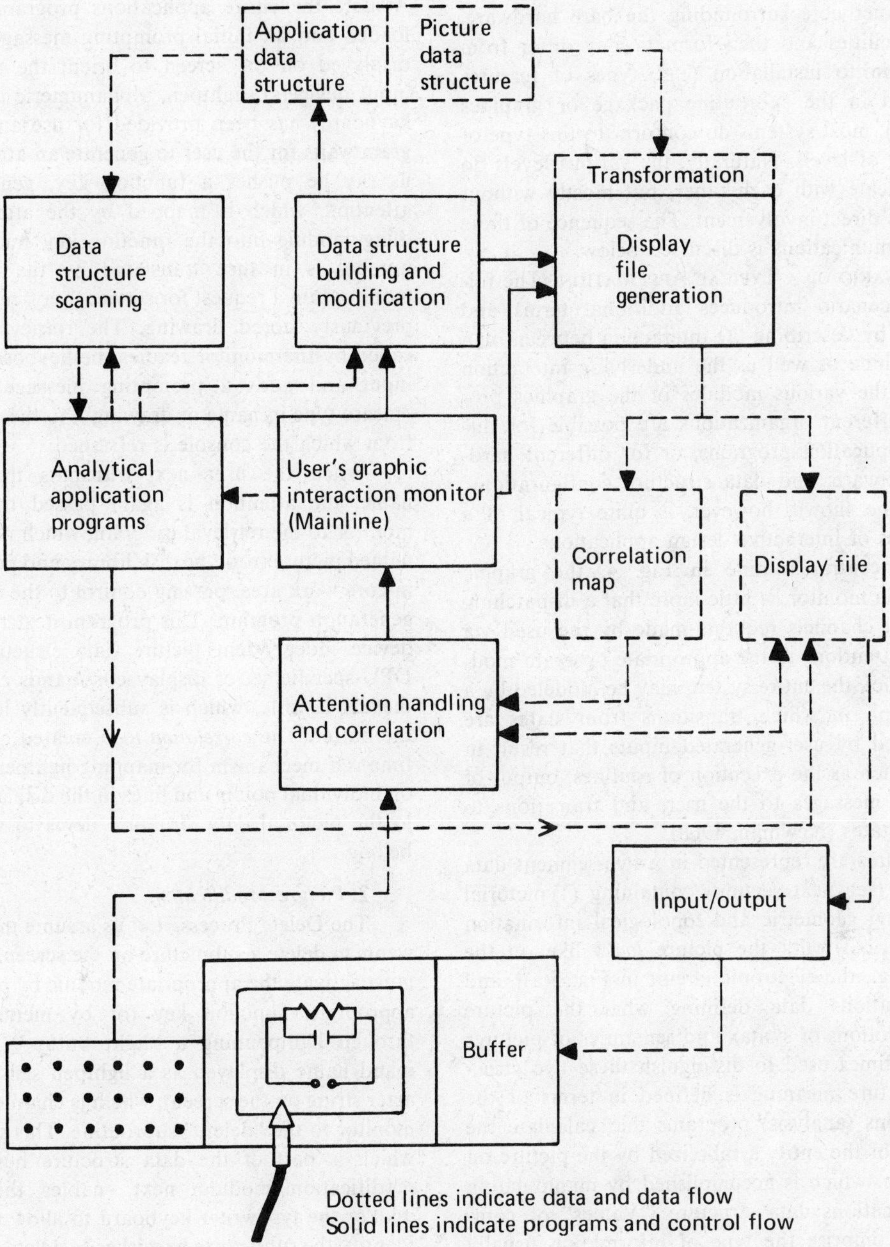


**Fig. 4.** Interrelationship among main software elements and data structure.

service that *attention* at a logical level.

SOFTWARE. The software point of view is shown in Fig. 3 as a series of shells or layers progressing from the level that the user deals with directly down to the inner core surrounding the bare hardware. While facilities and their formats may differ from installation to installation (e.g., types of features supported in the subroutine package or graphics language), most systems do conform to this type of hierarchy of levels. Naturally, the various levels do communicate with each other, but mostly without the user's direct involvement. The sequence of these intercommunications is discussed below.

SCENARIO OF A TYPICAL APPLICATION. The following scenario introduces additional terms and concepts by describing the interaction between man and machine as well as the underlying interaction between the various modules of the graphics program. Different organizations are possible for different application programs, or for different hardware, software, and data structure configurations; the scheme shown, however, is quite typical of a large class of interactive design applications.

The central routine in Fig. 4, the graphic interaction monitor, is little more that a dispatching table that channels requests made by the used via graphic attentions to the appropriate program modules. In fact, the entire system may be modeled by a state graph in which transitions from states are determined by user-generated inputs that result in actions such as the execution of routines, output of feedback messages to the user, and transitions to internal states (Newman, 1968).

Pictures are represented in a two-segment data structure (see next section) containing (1) pictorial data giving geometric and topological information that describes what the picture *looks* like on the screen [e.g., the electronic circuit in Fig. 5(a)], and (2) applications data defining what the picture means. Notions of syntax and semantics of pictures are sometimes used to distinguish these two structures. Picture meaning is defined in terms of the applications (analysis) programs that calculate the behavior of the entity symbolized by the picture on the screen, which is accomplished by manipulating the applications data structure. "Values" of components comprise the type of information usually stored in the application data structure. Naturally, some applications programs concentrate on geometry (e.g., mechanical structures), whereas others are virtually independent of geometry (e.g., topology, and not geometry, is important in network and circuit synthesis). In any case, picture display and picture analysis usually take place at different times and usually alternate, as described below.

1. *Picture Display*. This involves reduction of the picture data structure to a viewable display file. Assume the entire applications program has been loaded and an initial prompting message has been displayed on the screen to orient the user. Some input device(s) (lightpen, alphanumeric or function keyboard) has been provided for use and the program waits for the user to generate an attention. Let us say he pushes a function key, generating an attention, which is mapped by the attention-handling module into the function key number. This number is in turn translated by the interaction monitor into a request for service—say, retrieval of a previously stored drawing. The retrieval program called by the monitor readies the keyboard for new input and adds a prompting message (such as, "please type in name of drawing") to the display file from which the console is refreshed.

When the user next transmits the typed-in name, the attention is again passed through the monitor to the retrieval program, which retrieves the named picture from the disk library and puts it in the in-core work area, passing control to the display-file generation program. This program next reduces the device independent picture data structure into a DPU-specific set of display commands constituting the display file, which is subsequently loaded into the buffer. The *correlation map* created at the same time is a mechanism for mapping lightpen "detects" on individual points and lines in the display file back to the pictorial data structure items to which they belong.

2. *Picture Modification*.

The Delete Process. Let us assume that the user wants to delete a subpicture on the screen. Again, he must activate the appropriate module by pushing the appropriate function key (or by menu selection through lightpenning a "light button"—the command name displayed as a lightpen sensitive character string on the screen), which is channeled by the monitor to the "delete" subroutine. This subroutine, which is part of the data structure building and modification module, next enables the lightpen and/or the typewriter keyboard to allow the user to identify the subpicture he wishes to delete. If the user points at (a line on) a resistor, the attention handling and correlation routine determines which pictorial data structure item has been identified, deletes the data structure representation of that particular resistor, and calls the display file generator to update the display file in place or to replace the previous display file in the buffer.

In order to prevent the user from inadvertently deleting the wrong part of the data structure (in case of incorrect specification or a change of mind), a properly human-factored program would not go through the above procedure until a "soft-delete" had been tried out by the user. This process updates the display file by inserting a branch around the display code of the item to be deleted; it then prompts the user to ask him if that result was the one desired. If he accepts (another pass through the attention handler and the monitor), the above data structure and display file update is done.

Note that in the typical cycle that takes place while the display is being refreshed, the monitor waits for the attention handler to report the occurrence of a user-instigated attention. When the attention is received, it passes control to a subroutine, which initiates a sequence of intelligence-gathering operations from the user. As soon as the user has specified sufficient information, his initially designated subroutine carries out its task and waits for approval. It is this *attention-driven dialog* that makes graphics programs quite different from ordinary batch programs (and from other interactive programs, for that matter).

An additional feature of the delete process is that it tends to cause a "deletion ripple" in the data structure. For example, if an endpoint of a line is deleted, the user probably also expects the line to disappear, since it is no longer well defined. The line, in turn, might have been used in a constraint relation with other picture parts, or it might be labeled, causing additional updating of the data structure and display file. If a node in a network were to be deleted, the user might similarly want to delete all components attached to that node. The utility of the "soft-delete" procedure with its option for allowing the effects of an operation to be undone ("reverted") should be obvious at this point.

The Analysis Process. In Fig. 4 the display file generation step is purposely drawn symmetric to data structure scanning. Both scan the data structure in order to extract information, the former being primarily geometric pictorial information, the latter being topological and applications data. As another typical scenario, therefore, assume that the user has finished construction of his picture. To invoke an analysis program, he pushes an appropriate function key. The monitor transfers control to the data structure scanning program, which examines the part of the data structure that contains parameters such as physical dimensions and properties necessary for analysis. The data values are extracted and passed to the analysis program, which may display feedback to the user in the form of graphed results; it may also allow the user to identify elements of the picture with his pointing device in order to get a display of appropriate parameters at the point indicated. At this time, a cycle of redesign usually takes place in which the user modifies the picture in order to submit it for re-analysis.

Note the preponderance of data structure operations; very little output is displayed on the console without first involving data structure scanning, manipulation, and reduction. While this phenomenon is not necessarily unique to graphics, three key characteristics of graphics programs do make them differ. First, and most obviously, the hardware driven by programs is distinct in terms of its capabilities and instruction repertoire. Second, in addition to the normal data types such as characters and numbers, programs deal with points, lines, subpictures, and other geometric notions. Finally, along with other interactive programs, graphics programs spend most of their time waiting for the user to drive them; flow of control is more accurately modeled by the state graph than by straight-line, branched, or even looped-flow graphs used for batch programs.

Despite these differences, most of the code in graphics programs does not, in fact, deal with producing pictures or fielding interrupts. In common with most other (interactive) programs, the bulk of graphics applications programs is concerned with command-language parsing and interpretation; data structure manipulation, computation, and analysis; space management for main and backing store, etc. It is therefore fair to say that in addition to the obvious differences, graphics programs require all the normal concerns that any other nontrivial program induces.

Summary of Required Software. As shown in Fig. 3, software support required for writing graphics systems such as the one described above must include many facilities. Among these are those for describing the layout of pictures (picture-plotting software), decoding user input (attention-handling software) and subsequent picture transformations, alterations, and manipulations (picture-editing software). Additionally, the scenario showed the need for main-store data structure handling software and backing-store data base handling software. (Data structures and transformations are discussed in more detail in the last two sections.)

The exact nature of these facilities differs from installation to installation. The most common form of support is a graphic subroutine package, typically embedded in Fortran, which provides picture plotting and some amount of transformational capability, and adequate attention handling. Graphical languages or extensions of existing languages such as Fortran or PL/I with graphical constructs have been noticeably less successful and are not commercially available.

**Role of Data and Storage Structure in Graphics.** Manipulating (as opposed to merely plotting) pictures requires a conceptualization, or modeling, of the picture, which goes beyond a literal point-and-line representation. The totality of geometric and topological data, including the hierarchy of picture parts and associations between them, constitute a model of the picture referred to above as the pictorial data structure. This machine-independent data structure must naturally be encoded in digital storage in a machine-specific storage structure. Thus, "the storage structure ... is the image of the data structures in some computer memory" (D'Imperior, 1969). The storage structure should lend itself readily to displaying the picture, manipulating and transforming the picture at the console, and causing analysis routines to be applied to (parts of) the picture.

Sutherland's interactive SKETCHPAD established full ring structures as canonical storage structures for "master/instance" definitions of picture/subpicture hierarchies (see "Classes of Structures" below). Since that time (1963), hardware suppliers have for the most part ignored the data-structure/storage-structure aspect of graphics because the problems of implementing a data/storage structure package are far more difficult than those of providing graph-plotting subroutines or even graphic attention-handling subroutines. Only the latter have been provided, typically within a Fortran environment in which it is not natural and often inefficient for the user to implement the data/storage structures himself (primarily due to the lack of pointer and structure variables in Fortran). Most installations, having realized that the largest part of a comprehensive interactive design program deals not with picture plotting but with data structure manipulation, have been forced to implement their own data structure support, primarily in assembly language (Gray, 1967). The SLIP subroutine package for Fortran (Weizenbaum, 1963) has been used occasionally, and a few installations have embedded graphics support in PL/I, which does provide most basic data structure facilities. Other installations (frequently university graphics laboratories) have used derivatives of Bell Lab's Low-Level Linked List Language ($L^6$; Knowlton, 1964) to provide a reasonable compromise between efficiency of code produced and machine independence of the source language.

Classes of Data Structures. The simplest type of storage structure required is that for displaying primitive pictures made up of consecutive

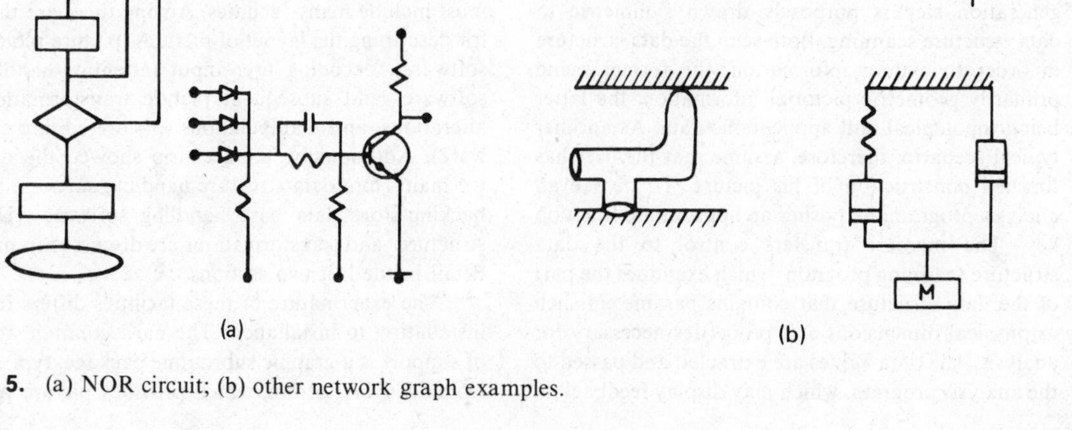

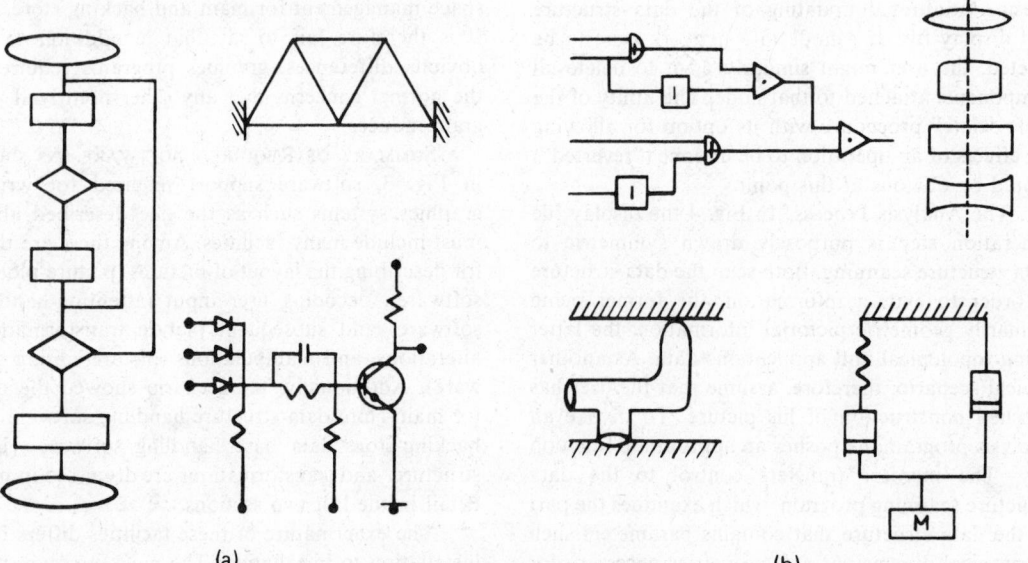


**Fig. 5.** (a) NOR circuit; (b) other network graph examples.

points and lines, say, for plotting purposes. In this case, a pair of arrays, one for points and one for lines, is all that is required. Most pictures have more structure, requiring minimally some facility for collecting logically related *picture atoms* (points, lines, characters) in a group and naming this group so it can be manipulated as a unit (to be deleted, moved on the screen, made sensitive or insensitive to the lightpen, etc.). Ordinary data graphs and many mechanical and structural drawings, for example, require no additional facilities.

Sutherland handled a very common class of more complex pictures that could be called "network graphs" (Fig. 5). These are two-or three-dimensional configurations in which discrete pictures are connected to others in a network, and are typically decomposable into a hierarchy of lower-level subpictures.

In the typical "bottom-up" interactive construction of a subpicture hierarchy (e.g., electric circuit design), components are gathered into subassemblies, which in turn are used in higher-level assemblies; in the "top down" method (e.g., flow charting), loose (macro) descriptions are iteratively refined and expanded into subassemblies of more detailed (micro) boxes. The "NOR" circuit of Fig. 5(a), for example, can be constructed bottom up as a hierarchy, as shown in the "parts explosion" of Fig. 6. Practically, one would not build up such an electric circuit starting at the low level shown here for illustration purposes, but would start at the level of primitive electrical components such as resistors and transistors. Note that the tree form of the data structure is not strictly accurate in that some of the nodes are duplicated.

The data structure use of a subpicture in a given picture closely parallels the programming use of a subroutine in a higher-level routine. The original data structure definition is called the "master," and its invocation is known as an "instance" of the master. The "subroutine" parameters, encoded with each instance portion of the storage structure for the total calling picture, consist of the geometric parameters that determine position, orientation, and scale of the subpicture within the calling picture. Often, such parameters are collected in a matrix called the "transformation" matrix (see concluding section). As with program subroutines, the advantage of using subpictures with transformation matrices is the space saved by not duplicating the definition.

A Practical Example. Figs. 7 through 9 represent the data and storage structures of a very large (greater than 700K bytes) applications program in engineering design. The 3DPDP (Strauss, 1969), a three-dimensional piping-design program, allows the user to lay out a three-dimensional piping configuration in on-line stereo mode or in any one of the three "engineering views." The configuration may then be analyzed for flexibility under thermal loading.

The data structure is that of a typical network: The circles (Fig. 7) called "tangent intersections" (TINs), represent the nodes of the network, and the straight-line piping segments (tangents), the "bends," and the "anchors" form the components of

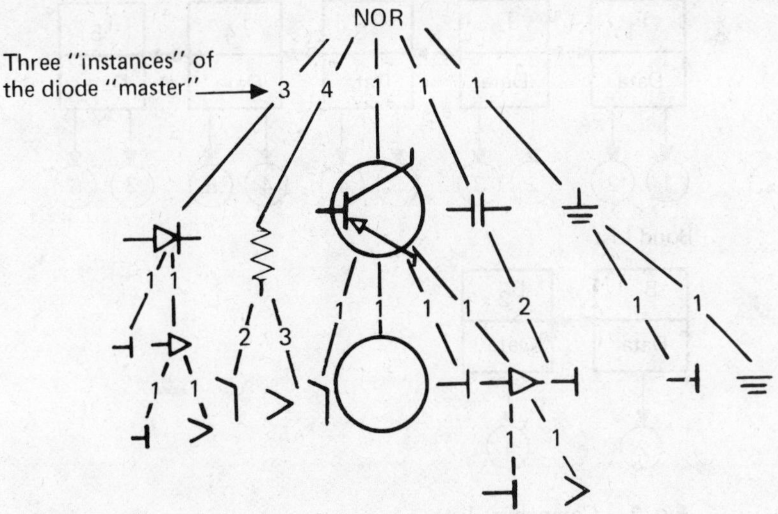


**Fig. 6.** Hierarchial representation of NOR.

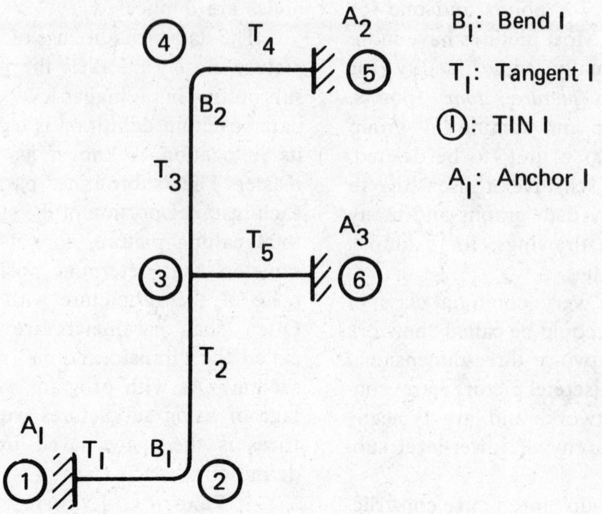


**Fig. 7.** Tangent intersections.

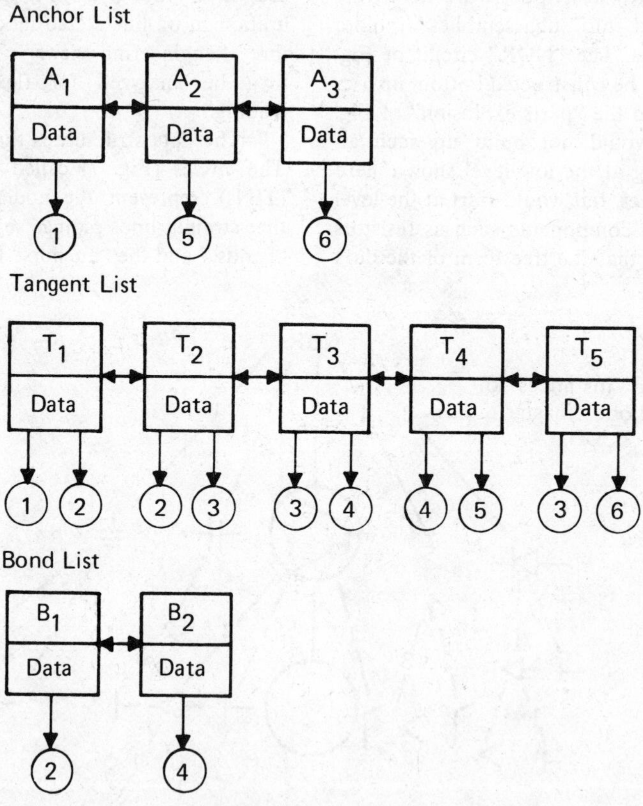


**Fig. 8.** Component lists.

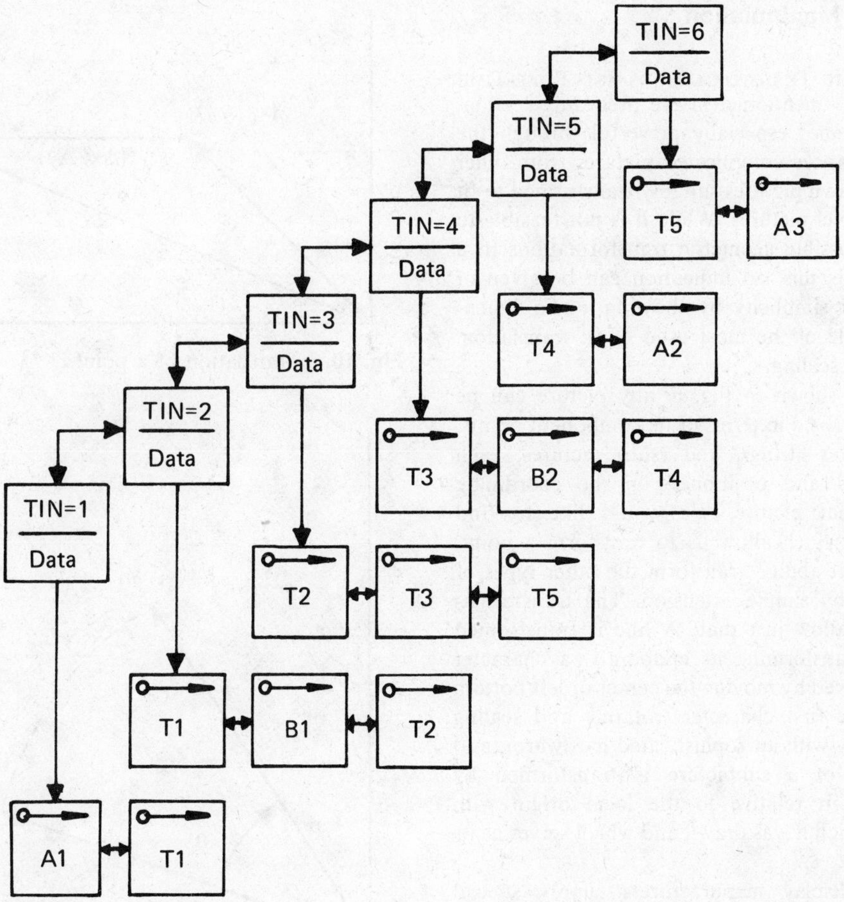


**Fig. 9.** TIN list.

the network. For purposes of display and for the analysis program, the designer found it useful to maintain lists of each of the three types of components (Fig. 8). The storage structure is a two-way linked list of blocks that contain an identifier, a string of physical properties, and finally one or two pointers to the nodes of the network to which the particular component is attached. The topology and geometry of the network are captured in the tangent intersection list (TIN list, Fig. 9), which is again encoded as a two-way linked list of blocks. Each block contains an identifier for the node, a string of physical properties, and a pointer to a two-way linked sublist. Each block on the sublist consists of the name of a component attached to the particular node, with a pointer indicating its location.

As an example of a data structure process, consider the method by which a user obtains results from the flexibility analysis program pertaining to the components attached to a given anchor. Assume that anchor A3 has been pointed at by the user with a lightpen. The A3 block on the anchor list (Fig. 8) is accessed via the correlation map, a pointer to node 6 is obtained, and the node 6 block on the TIN list (Fig. 9) is retrieved. Its sublist shows that tangent T5 is attached, and the proper values may be obtained from the analysis program. (Another method might be to have the analysis program store an explicit network connection matrix.)

Note that this simplified storage structure does not allow for picture/subpicture hierarchies, nor for cementing sections of large piping diagrams together. While the first facility is easily implemented by enriching the data structure with a tree hierarchy similar to that of Fig. 6, the second requires a hardware or software paging facility (van Dam, 1972).

### Picture Manipulation

GEOMETRIC TRANSFORMATIONS AND REAL-TIME DYNAMICS. As mentioned in the preceding section, graphics becomes especially powerful through the ability to compose complicated pictures from other previously drawn pictures suitably transformed to fit into higher-level pictures. While it is not feasible to discuss all possible geometric transformations in a survey such as this, an indication can be given of their inherent simplicity by showing a two-dimensional example of the most used ones: translation, rotation, and scaling.

First, as shown in Fig. 6, any picture can be recursively defined in terms of its component points, lines, character strings, and (sub) pictures, each suitably sized and positioned on the coordinate system of that picture. We would like to find formulations which allow us to transform a point, and given that ability, transform the other types of components by simple extension. The transformations below allow just that: A line is transformed simply by transforming its endpoints; a character (string) is moved by moving the center or left bottom corner of the first character (rotating and scaling may be tricky without sophisticated hardware); and an instance of a subpicture is transformed by transforming it relative to the local origin with respect to which it was drawn and which serves as its "handle."

Many display manufacturers supply special hardware to carry out the transformations summarized below. Some even provide the ability to combine the basic transformations with windowing and perspective mapping, thereby allowing very complicated picture manipulations to proceed in real time as the user twists knobs, dials, and joysticks, and "flies around" or "inside" his picture world. If hardware is not available for real-time dynamics, software simulation may still provide useful and interesting effects.

First, to move a point, add $x$- and $y$-translation factors to the $x$- and $y$-components of the coordinate pair describing the point. To move a line, move both endpoints by the same factor. Thus, in Fig. 10, to move $(x_0,y_0)$ by $(\Delta x,\Delta y)$:

$$\begin{bmatrix} x_0 \\ y_0 \end{bmatrix} + \begin{bmatrix} \Delta x \\ \Delta y \end{bmatrix} = \begin{bmatrix} x_1 \\ y_1 \end{bmatrix}$$

Second, to rotate a point about the center (origin) of the coordinate axes (the $z$-axis, in effect), rotate the vector with the beginning point at the origin and the endpoint at the desired point. Thus, in

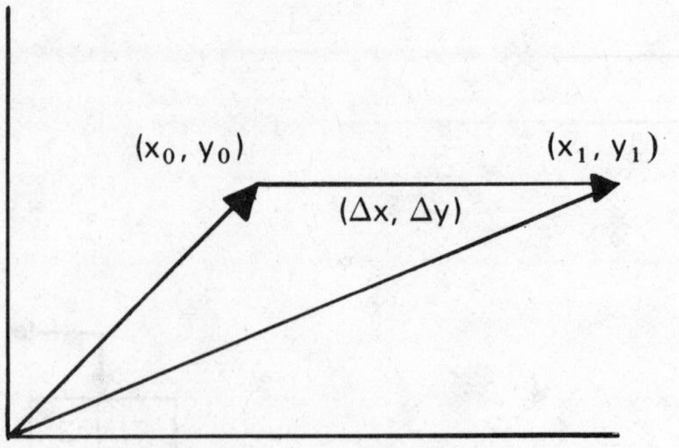


**Fig. 10.** Translation of a point.

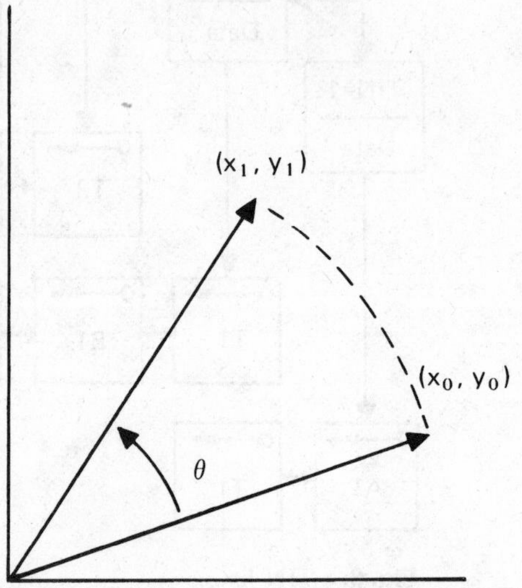


**Fig. 11.** Rotation of a point about origin.

Fig. 11, to rotate $(x_0,y_0)$ about the origin by $\theta$ degrees, use the matrix multiplication.

$$\begin{bmatrix} \cos\theta & -\sin\theta \\ +\sin\theta & \cos\theta \end{bmatrix} \begin{bmatrix} x_0 \\ y_0 \end{bmatrix} = \begin{bmatrix} x_1 \\ y_1 \end{bmatrix}$$

If we were to rotate the point about any other center of rotation, or were to rotate a line about either of its endpoints, we would have a slightly more difficult problem. Since the rotation formula allows us to rotate only about the origin, we could rotate about an arbitrary point only if we first moved it down to the origin. This is simply a well-known mathematical trick for reducing a given problem to a previously solved one. Thus, to rotate line $L_1$ (Fig. 12) about $P_1$, we translate $P_1$ to the origin, then apply the rotation matrix, and then put $P_1$ back where it belongs. In a similar manner we can rotate an entire subpicture

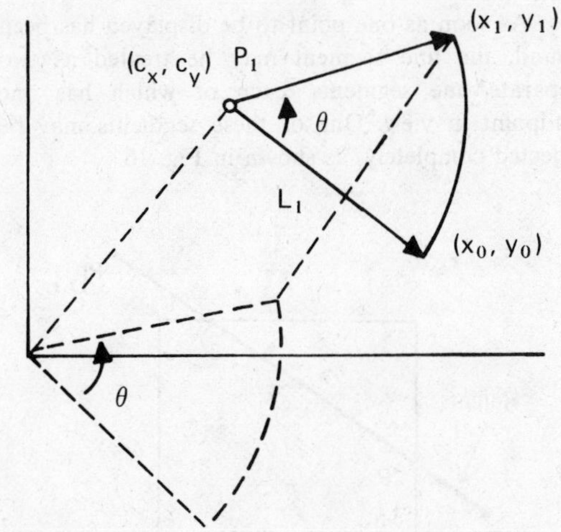


**Fig. 12.** Rotation about arbitrary centers.

instance about its local origin (rather than the picture origin) by translating, rotating, and "untranslating" all the individual picture components. Naturally, all these calculations may be simplified by "solving" these matrix and vector operations beforehand, i.e., reducing them to simple equations for the endpoints. Thus, in Fig 12, rotating $L_1$ about $P_1$ by $\theta$ degrees:

$$\begin{bmatrix} \cos\theta & -\sin\theta \\ \sin\theta & \cos\theta \end{bmatrix} \left( \begin{bmatrix} x_0 \\ y_0 \end{bmatrix} - \begin{bmatrix} c_x \\ c_y \end{bmatrix} \right) + \begin{bmatrix} c_x \\ c_y \end{bmatrix} = \begin{bmatrix} x_1 \\ y_1 \end{bmatrix}$$

To scale a line (scaling a point doesn't really make sense), we multiply the *x*- and *y*-components of its endpoints by *x*- and *y*-scale factors. Thus, in Fig. 13, scaling by different amounts in *x* and *y* ($L_1$ by $(A, B)$):

$$\begin{bmatrix} A & 0 \\ 0 & B \end{bmatrix} \begin{bmatrix} x_0 \\ y_0 \end{bmatrix} = \begin{bmatrix} x_1 \\ y_1 \end{bmatrix}$$

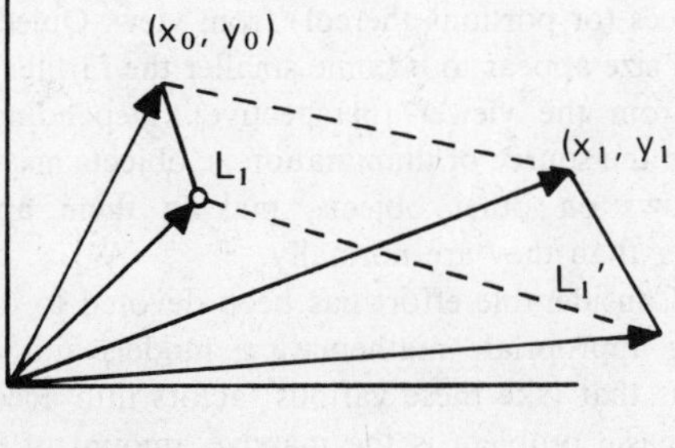


**Fig. 13.** Scaling.

Note that, in general, this will have the effect of moving the line as well. If we want a given point on the line to stay in place, a compensating translation must be applied. As with rotation, an entire subpicture instance (i.e., all its components) may be scaled about its local origin, by moving the local origin to the picture origin, scaling as desired, and moving it back. If scaling about axes inclined with respect to the picture axes is desired, the local axes should be translated down to the origin rotated to be parallel to the picture axes, scaled, unrotated, and then untranslated (Fig. 14).

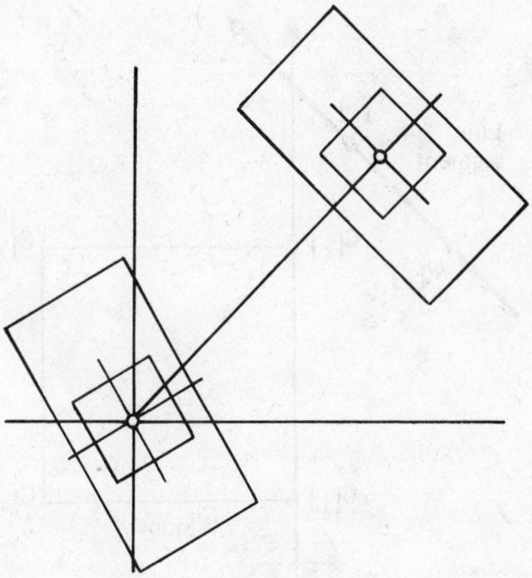

**Fig. 14.** Scaling about arbitrary axes.

WINDOWING. Since large drawings of the type typically found in engineering applications cannot fit in their entirety on small display screens, we can either compress them to fit—and thereby obscure details and induce clutter—or we can display only a portion of the total drawing. The portion to be displayed is usually indicated by the user by placing a rectangular window on the compressed version of the drawing on the screen, and the hardware or software will then "clip" ("scissor") off any points, lines, and characters that fall outside the window. The operation may be performed repeatedly to achieve any desired degree of magnification.

A two-dimensional window is usually defined by a maximum and minimum value for *x* and *y*, or by a center of the window and maximum relative *x*- and *y*-values. Simple subtractions or comparisons suffice to find out whether or not a point is in view.

For lines, the algorithm should allow any part of a line within the window to be displayed. If both endpoints lie in view, the line may be trivially accepted. If one of the endpoints lies in view, finding the other point is easy enough, and at least a portion of the line lies in the window. However, if both points are out of view, further tests must be made, since the line could be wholly outside or could cut the window. One method for deciding which case applies is to solve analytically for points of intersection of the line containing the line segment with the lines forming the edges of the window (Fig. 15).

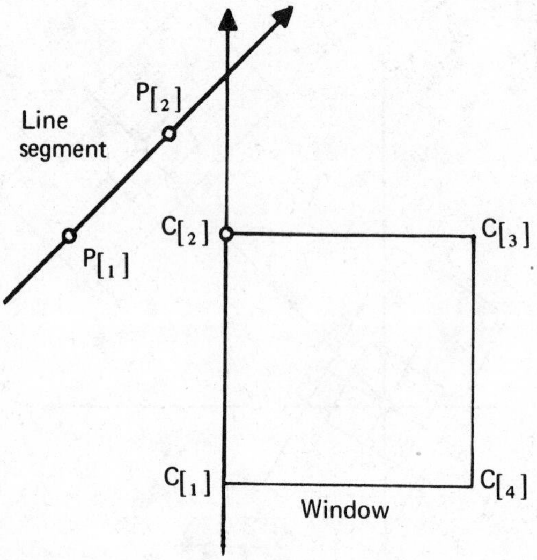


**Fig. 15.** Windowing.

Using notation from linear algebra, the equation of a line can be expressed in parametric form such that points of the form

$$X = tX[1] + (1 - t)X[2]$$

for real $t$ are on the infinite line through the points $X[1]$ and $X[2]$. When $t$ is restricted to the interval [0,1], the point is on the directed-line segment from $X[2]$ to $X[1]$. The problem can therefore be stated as finding parameters $t$ and $s$ such that

$$tP[1] + (1 - t)P[2] = sC[1] + (1 - s)C[2]$$

If both $t$ and $s$ are between 0 and 1, then the point of intersection is both: between $P[1]$ and $P[2]$ (so it actually lies on the line segment), and between $C[1]$ and $C[2]$ (so it is in view in the window).

As soon as one point to be displayed has been found, the line segment may be treated as two separate line segments, each of which has one endpoint in view. One of these segments may be rejected completely, as shown in Fig. 16.

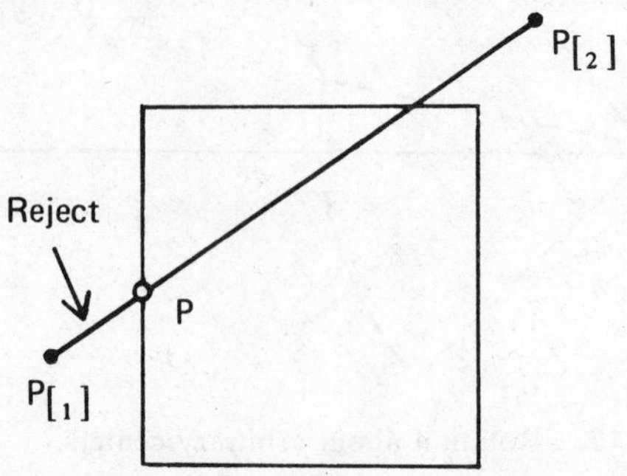


**Fig. 16.** Windowing: rejection of line segment.

To augment this straightforward analytical solution, special-purpose hardware has been built using various digital or analog methods for performing the window operation in real-time (Sproul and Sutherland, 1968). Both in hardware and software implementations, much effort is expended in accepting or rejecting the trivial cases (elements wholly inside or outside the window).

Enhancing the Illusion of Reality. The computer-generated scenes shown thus far in this article are not meant to be realistic; they are diagrammatic and symbolic in nature and are simple to draw. Presenting a realistic reproduction of a complex three-dimensional scene is several orders of magnitude more complex. First, line drawings themselves are often inadequate: We do not view real objects as sequences of lines but rather as various surfaces, some of which are connected one to another. Surfaces have color, texture, and light reflectance and transmittance properties. A solid surface close to the viewer can hide more distant surfaces (or portions thereof) from view. Objects of equal size appear to become smaller the farther they are from the viewer (perspective). Depending on where the source of illumination is, objects may cast shadows on other objects, making them appear darker than they are normally.

Considerable effort has been devoted to developing appropriate mathematical models and algorithms that take these various factors into account. The basic problem is the massive amount of computation required to transform a mathematical model into a picture. Current research efforts are thus directed as much toward improved algorithms as toward increased realism. A few of the faster algorithms to remove hidden lines and surfaces and do shading have been partially implemented in special-purpose hardware (Sutherland, Sproul, and Schumacker, 1974).

The applicability of this work to interactive computer graphics lies in the areas of design, simulation, and animation. It is easy to conceive of an automotive designer using pictures like Fig. 16 to view his current efforts from many directions. In simulation, we want to achieve effects such as the presentation of a realistic road scene in a driving simulator, or a realistic airport scene in a flight trainer. The making of animated movies for entertainment or for scientific, mathematical, and medical modeling is another area needing realism.

**A Sampling of Other Configurations and Technologies.** The display system organization shown in Fig. 2 is not the only one in use, but is probably the most widespread. Another kind of organization is the satellite graphics system. The display processor is connected to a small computer, which is in turn connected to the large host computer. The graphics system and application programs are distributed between the two computers, which may be separated by many miles. Motivations for such systems include placing the graphics terminal where the user is, not necessarily where the computer is, to provide fast response to simple user actions and to unburden the host CPU of some processing work (van Dam, 1974).

Another variation on the basic system organization is the use of a rectangular raster (TV) scan to present a picture. A line of a given length and orientation would not be drawn by a single continuous deflection of the CRT's beam, but by turning the beam on for each point of the sequential raster scan corresponding to a point on the line. This technique is attractive because TV technology is far less expensive than the random-scan deflection mechanism. The disadvantage of it is that an image must be broken down into a series of on/off commands, to be applied as the beam sweeps its scan down the screen. This is usually a time-consuming, relatively low resolution process, although a few special-purpose processors are able to do it as quickly as the image is displayed.

Raster-scan technology is especially applicable to many of the current hidden-line/hidden-surface algorithms. It also adapts nicely to conventional video-mixing techniques.

Other variations use the direct-view storage tube (DVST) and the plasma display panel. The DVST stores the electron beam drawn picture in a dielectric mesh in which the cathode-ray tube phosphor is embedded, and therefore obviates cyclical refreshing of the DPU from a stored display file. DVST consoles therefore can display an unlimited amount of information, but do not lend themselves to selective erasure of portions of the screen, nor are they as fast as ordinary cathode-ray tubes.

Plasma panels are solid-state matrices of individually $XY$-addressable picture elements (60 elements per inch is a typical resolution available today) that also exhibit memory. The panels are flat, can display color or superimposed static information from slides, and unlike cathode-ray tube devices, are easily batch-fabricated in various sizes.

**Graphics Progress.** Graphics has suffered in the past decade from a preoccupation with its fascinating and still rapidly evolving technology and hardware; too little attention has been paid to cost-effective, possibly even mundane, applications programs, and to making life easy for the ordinary user. Fortunately, this trend is changing, and we can look forward to some of the promises of graphics (such as ease of use, naturalness, and ready availability) finally becoming fullfilled. A cardinal rule, obvious but nonetheless often overlooked with unpleasant consequences, is that only simple things are simple to do (e.g., graph output of computational processes). Sophisticated interactive design systems take considerable amounts of people, hardware, and software resources, and should therefore not be underestimated. Despite the visual wizardry, there is no magic in computer graphics.

## References

1963. Sutherland, I. E. "SKETCHPAD," *Proceedings of AFIPS 1963 SJCC*, Vol. 23.

1963. Weizenbaum, J. "Symmetric List Processor," *Communications of the ACM*, Vol. 6, No. 9.

1964. Knowlton, K. C. "A Programmer's Description of $L^6$," *Communications of the ACM*, Vol. 9, No. 8.

1967. Gray, J. C. "Compound Data Structure for Computer-Aided Design—A Survey," *Proceedings 22nd ACM National Conference.*

1968. Newman, W. M. "A System for Interactive Graphical Programming," *Proceedings of AFIPS 1968 SJCC*, Vol. 32.

1968. Sproull, R. F., and I. E. Sutherland, "A Clipping Divider," *Proceedings of AFIPS 1968 FJCC*, Vol. 33-1.

1969. D'Imperior, M. "Data Structures and Their Representation in Storage," *Annual Review in Automatic Programming*, No. 5. New York: Pergamon.

1969. Strauss, C. M. "3DPDP—A Three-Dimensional Piping Design Program," Ph.D. Thesis, Brown University, Providence, R.I. (June).

1971. Prince, M. D. *Interactive Graphics for Computer-Aided Design*. Reading, Mass.: Addison-Wesley.

1972. van Dam, A. "Some Implementation Issues Relating to Data Structures for Interactive Graphics," *International Journal of Computer and Information Sciences* (August).

1973. Newman, W. M., and R. F. Sproull, *Principles of Interactive Computer Graphics*. New York: McGraw-Hill.

1974. Institute of Electronic and Electrical Engineers. "Special Issue on Computer Graphics," *IEEE Proceedings* (April).

1974. Resch, R. D., "Portfolio of Shaded Computer Images." Special Issue on Computer Graphics, *IEEE Proceedings* (April).

1974. Sutherland, I. E., R. F. Sproull, and R. Schumacker, "A Characterization of Ten Hidden-Surface Algorithms," *ACM Computing Surveys* (March).

1974. van Dam, A., G. M. Stabler, and R. J. Harrington, "Intelligent Satellites for Interactive Graphics." Special Issue on Computer Graphics, *IEEE Proceedings* (April).

A. van Dam

## COMPUTER-MANAGED INSTRUCTION (CMI)

For articles on related subjects *see* Computer-Assisted Learning and Teaching; and Computer-Assisted Instruction.

Computer-managed instruction (CMI) refers to the use of computer assistance in testing, diagnosing, prescribing, grading, and record keeping. Some writers prefer "computer-aided management of instruction" in order to emphasize computer assistance *to* the human teacher or counselor, in contrast with management *by* the computer.

Computer assistance has been made available in many ways to those managing instruction, including aids for students managing their own instruction. The teacher of a large class finds assistance in scoring tests, keeping records, checking on which students need what kind of work, and computing grades. A manager of a self-instruction group uses the computer to obtain summary records showing where each student stands. A student or teacher may call upon the computer files and procedures to generate a test at random but according to set rules. The procedure may select from an item pool and plug in variations on standard question forms to obtain the specific test items so they appear fresh each time. Computer-based information systems are used by students and teachers to locate instructional materials in various media according to needs, interests, and the limitations of course time and instructional budget.

Major projects using the computer for assistance in the management of instruction are located in Pittsburgh (Learning Research and Development Center), Philadelphia (Research for Better Schools), Palo Alto (Project PLAN of the American Institute for Research), and the Medical School at Ohio State University (Columbus). Each successful program is based on a large amount of curricular materials, probably in modular form, and a convenient testing and record-handling system. The arguments for CMI instead of CAI include: lower cost of operation, since students spend less time at computer terminals; more flexibility in learning formats, since students are referred to materials in a variety of media and learning settings apart from the computer; lower cost of development, since existing materials can be used for instruction. CMI and CAI may be used together; the management aids associated with CMI can refer the student to selected exercises that are presented by the computer (CAI) as well as to many others that do not benefit from presentation in the computer medium.

### Reference

1971. Baker, Frank B. "Computer-Based Management Systems; A First Look," *Review of Educational Research*. [AERA] Vol. 41, No. 1. pp. 51–71.

K. L. Zinn

# COMPUTER NETWORKS

For articles on related subjects *see* ARPA Network; Communications and Computers; Computer Systems; Computing Economics: Acquisition and Operation; Data Communication Networks; Data Communications; Multiplexing; Packet Switching; Terminals; and Time Sharing.

For articles on related terms *see* Hardware Monitors; Minicomputers; and Remote Job Entry.

The term "computer networks" has been used to describe situations in which:

1. Geographically remote terminals and RJE stations are connected to a central computer.
2. Geographically remote smaller computers are used for minor editing tasks and to transfer input to magnetic tape and from magnetic tape to output printers and plotters. Magnetic tapes are transferred by post or messenger between smaller machines and a central computer.
3. A central computing unit has connections to smaller machines with specialized functions, which provide it with services such as storage (and associated file management) and communication facilities (such as message concentration); in the case of small machines used for graphics, the central unit is used for major computing tasks.
4. Independent major computing systems ("hosts"), possibly in addition to the above, communicate with one another, and share resources such as hardware, programs or data (Fig. 1).

Computer networks should not be confused with information networks, a term usually applied to systems for the sharing of library resources. However, it is clear that, particularly with the growth of computerized printing (which provides text in machine-readable form—e.g., on magnetic tape—as a byproduct), a growing source of loading for computer networks will be their use as information networks.

The fourth definition of computer networks —resource-sharing networks of machines of comparable power—is coming to be the more widely accepted one. As an indication of the recent growth of activity in this area, a bibliography published by

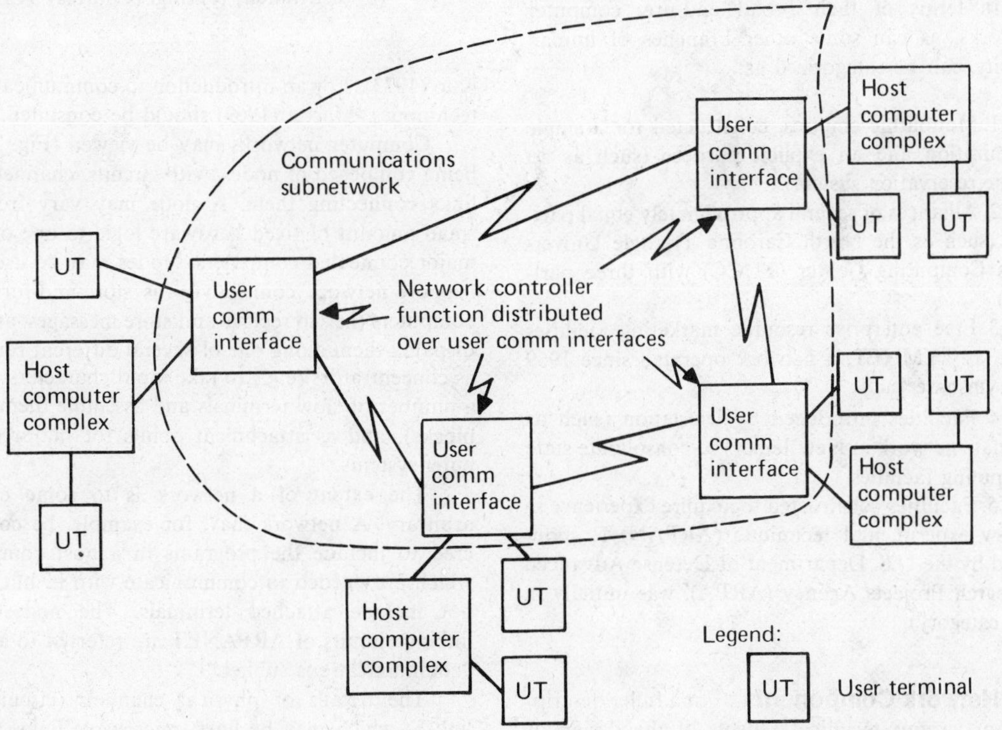


**Fig. 1.** Computer network. (Courtesy IEEE.)

the National Bureau of Standards (Blanc et al. 1973) lists over 500 citations relating to resource-sharing networks, nearly all of which were developed in the past decade.

The rate at which computer networks are now proliferating throughout the world indicates that they are becoming a powerful force in both the public and private sectors, both nationally and internationally. This upsurge of activity, which is of recent origin, may be ascribed to three main technological trends:

1. The greatly increased reliability of computers, which makes possible the implementation of complex systems that would have been unworkable a decade ago.
2. The availability of low-priced minicomputers suitable for carrying out most of the functions required to operate a network, with a minimum of change to the operating systems of the major connected computers (these operating systems are large, complex, and not designed to provide the quick interrupts needed for communications work).
3. Major changes in communications technology, which are reflected in a corresponding reduction of communication costs.

In terms of their broad end-use, computer networks, as can some other branches of human activity, can be categorized as:

1. Monolithic empires, constructed for a single organization and an explicit purpose (such as an airline reservation system).
2. Alliances of several approximately equal partners (such as the North Carolina Triangle Universities Computing Center (TUCC) with three partners).
3. Free enterprise resource marketing facilities (such as TYMNET, a network operated since 1969 by Tymshare Inc.).
4. Facilities introduced by legislation (such as the state network in New Jersey) to consolidate state computing facilities.
5. Facilities constructed to acquire experience in a new experimental technique (ARPANET, sponsored by the U.S. Department of Defense Advanced Research Projects Agency (ARPA), was initially in this category).

**Network Components.** For a fuller description of various technical aspects of the design of networks, the reader is referred to Abramson and Kuo (1973). For an introduction to communications techniques, Martin (1969) should be consulted.

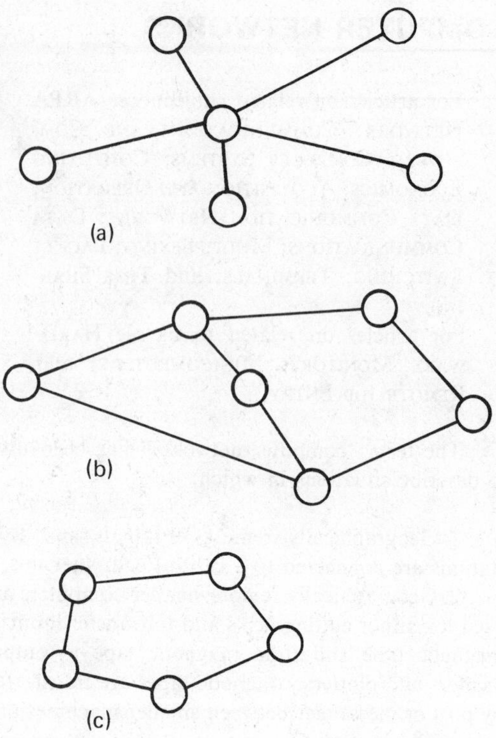


**Fig. 2.** Alternate network configurations: (a) star; (b) distributed; (c) ring. (Courtesy IEEE.)

Computer networks may be viewed (Fig. 2) as being composed of nodes, with circuits, channels, or links connecting them. A node may vary from a small amount of fixed hardware logic to one of the major connected computers. Nodes may be used to support network connectivity as store-and-forward computers (i.e., to receive and store messages, and to dispatch them along one of several different routes), as concentrators (e.g., to take input characters from a number of slow terminals and assemble them into blocks), and as attachment points for major computer systems.

The extent of a network is to some extent arbitrary. A network may, for example, be considered to include the programs in a host computer which are needed to communicate with it, but does not include attached terminals. The nodes and linking circuits of ARPANET are referred to as the "communications subnet."

The details of physical channels (circuits or links)—which may be lines, microwave links, radio links, cable TV installations, or satellites—are of little consequence from the point of view of computer networks. The relevant parameters of a channel are its maximum data rate, its error characteristics, and its directional limitations. The setup characteristics are also important information if a point-to-point circuit is not always dedicated to a network. This information may include the signaling mechanism and delays for circuit setup and breaking.

Commonly available speeds vary from 60 to 300 bps (bits per second), suitable for supporting a slow-speed terminal, through voice-grade line speeds of 2,000 to 4,800 bps (or higher) to $5 \times 10^4$ bps, the speed currently used by ARPANET. Higher speeds are available if required—systems to carry several gigabits per second (a gigabit equals $10^9$ bits, a volume equivalent of the Encyclopaedia Britannica) —are under development.

Requirements for data transmission arising in connection with computer networks are typically burst-oriented, with transmission from terminals or computers for a short period at a specified rate, and long time gaps with no transmission at all. Standard communications techniques (frequency division multiplexing, FDM; or time division multiplexing, TDM) make better use of available bandwidths by allocating smaller bandwidths or time slots to individual subchannels, but make no use of the burst characteristics of the data. If a channel is connected to one subchannel only when that subchannel is active, an address being added to indicate the source (available from timing considerations with FDM and TDM), more efficient use will be made of the channel; this approach is referred to as asynchronous time-division multiplexing (ATDM).

Since it would not be economic for every node (or its equivalent) to be connected to every other node with which communication may be desired, transmission is usually routed through a number of intermediate nodes. In a typical case, these nodes are minicomputers and the connecting links are leased lines. Messages with suitable header information and error checks are passed from one node to another on a store-and-forward basis, the route being chosen according to loading or fault conditions by the minicomputers or by separate machines with control and monitoring responsibilities. Because messages are variable in length, problems arise in selecting sizes for buffer storage, and so it is usual to break a message into fixed length segments called "packets." These packets are transmitted on a store-and-forward basis and, with some networks, may go to their destination by different routes if changes occur in the loading of the links. Typical packet sizes are between 1,000 and 2,000 bits for text, with an additional 100 bits for header information.

Packets are checked after passage through each link (an acknowledgment being returned to the sending node if correct), are reassembled in correct order at the destination, and passed on to the relevant process in the host computer to which they are addressed.

When nodes are allowed to compete for a channel, there may be a clash; in this case the check sums will not tally, no acknowledgment will be sent, and retransmission may be arranged to occur after a delay, which is different for each node so that a second clash is unlikely. The ALOHA system at the University of Hawaii uses a single radio channel in this way. The efficiency of this method can be raised considerably by introducing a reservation system in which a number of time slots may be reserved, one of these being subdivided into smaller slots that convey information about reservation requests to all user stations so that each station will know the position of the next free time slot.

At the time of this writing, there is still considerable controversy as to the extent to which packet-switching techniques should replace message-switching techniques or the more conventional circuit-switching techniques, in which a path is established from host to host by a dialing operation or its equivalent. For example, the British Post Office, although it has currently embarked on the construction of a network to evaluate the practicability of packet switching, has stated on several occasions that evidence of the practicability and viability of the packet mode of working is not sufficient to justify planning it as the main basis for any public service. Clearly, the "best" solution depends on the mix of message lengths involved, and the position is complicated by the trend toward digital transmission for general telecommunication usage.

**Network Configurations.** With the simplest network [Fig. 2(a)], a star network, all communication between the points of the star must take place through a central node. If this node is inoperable, the network cannot function.

Networks with alternative routings between nodes are referred to as "distributed" networks [Fig. 2(b)]. The reliability of a network may be assessed (Abramson and Kuo, 1973) by determining the number of nodes or links that must be inoperative before the network becomes disconnected, i.e., before there ceases to be at least one path between any sender and any receiver (apart from the removed nodes).

A further design consideration is the maximum delay in a network. This delay (which is, for example, a half-second for individual packets in the case of the ARPA network) may vary according to the end-use of the data and the loading. However, once it has been specified, it is an important parameter: A network should be designed so as to achieve it for stated loadings at a minimum cost.

One structure [Fig. 2(c)] that has particular advantages is the loop or ring network structure (Farber and Larson, 1972). This structure lends itself to a TDM technique in which a node with a message for another node places packets in empty slots as they appear, and copies messages addressed to it as they are passed around the ring. When a message originating at a node is returned to it, it is checked to insure that it has been received and that it has not been corrupted, and is then replaced by a vacant slot.

NETWORK MONITORING. A detailed knowledge of network traffic is essential for network planning and operation, and node computers should contain suitable monitoring programs to make this possible. Hardware monitors operating under computer control can supplement these software monitors. The General Electric network monitor system (Wedburgh and Hauschild, 1974) is relevant, as is recent work at the University of Waterloo (Morgan et al., 1974).

**Economics.** It is difficult to make definite statements now about the relative economics of networks except for those constructed for special purposes (such as airline reservation systems). However a number of commerical systems (e.g., TYMNET, Honeywell, and Cybernet) marketing facilities under a single management are clearly commercially viable.

Roberts (1974) has given some interesting figures concerning the economics of ARPANET. He advances arguments to show that work carried out through the network in 1973 would have cost about three times as much had equivalent local computing power been used, and that the difference more than offsets the annual cost of the network, even though at the time the network was only about 20% loaded.

Roberts draws some interesting conclusions about long-term trends. He points out that computing costs are being reduced by a factor of 10 every five years, as are satellite communication costs, whereas conventional land-line costs (which control the cost of transmission from ground stations to city centers) are reducing at the much lower rate of a factor of 10 every 22 years. These line costs would represent 80% of network costs by 1980 were it not for the anticipated introduction of higher transmission frequencies, which are likely to eliminate the need for land lines by making possible the direct satellite communication to city centers. (This situation already applies with experimental stations that form part of the Pacific Educational Computer Network being constructed under the aegis of the University of Hawaii. There, ground stations each cost as little as several thousands of dollars.)

**Management Problems.** To make resources available through a computer network, a user must

1. Make arrangements for accounts at each host computer system.
2. Know the control language for each host.
3. Learn the peculiarities of network protocols (i.e., network management information provided in headers such as destinations and lengths of messages) as implemented by each host.
4. Determine what help facilities (if any) exist at each host and how to use them.
5. Determine who at each site can assist with systems problems and how to establish contact with him.
6. Determine how to get data and/or programs to and from the serving site.
7. Learn how to use the resources of the remote site.

It is small wonder that the average user is deterred from making the best use of resources available to him. Clearly, there is a strong case for brokers who know what is available and will help the potential user, acting as retailers of computing power available to them through the network on a wholesale basis and as liaison links for strengthening help facilities obtainable through the network itself. REX, a resource location and acquisition service offered by the Mitre Corporation (Benoit and Graf-Webster, 1974), is an example of this type of advisory service. It concerns the resources of ARPANET, and is offered through the network itself, permitting terminal users to converse interactively with it.

In the United States, the problem of funding network management has been facilitated by a decision made in November 1973 to approve the establishment of commercial "value added" communication networks (Doll, 1974). Operators of these networks would obtain raw bandwidth from common carriers such as AT&T, and "repackage" it, using minicomputers for leasing to the ultimate user.

Protocols and Standards. Protocols within a network must be standard so that nodes can function in a uniform manner; much of this information, because it is concerned only with the mechanics of packaging, will be supplied by the communications computers. Moreover, some additional information may be required by individual processes, and this may vary from one installation to another, particularly with a heterogeneous network (i.e., one that has as hosts different computers that are not compatible with one another).

Transmitting information from one network to another with a different protocol and packet length presents special problems, and the use of a special internetwork processor (a "gateway" machine) for the express purpose of reformatting messages and changing to new protocols has been proposed. An IFIP Technical Committee Working Group (WG6.1) is currently formulating guidelines for internetwork protocols, on which future standards may be based.

The field of data transmission has so far been the subject of over 50 standards and international recommendations laid down by major United States and international standards organizations (ANSI, EIA, ISO and CCITT) (10).

**Some Typical Networks.** The following examples of general-purpose networks are selected as illustrative rather than exhaustive. ARPANET is described elsewhere in this encyclopedia.

MERIT, an educational computer network, links machines at Michigan State University (CDC 6500), University of Michigan (IBM 360/67), and Wayne State University (IBM 360/67) through small communications processors. Bandwidths of links can be varied dynamically by providing each communications computer with four modems and call-up facilities.

CSIRONET is a network constructed by CSIRO in Australia, primarily to provide a research computing service for its own use. Its principal machine is a CDC 7600, with a Cyber 172 as a front-end processor. It is a star network, with terminals connected to six PDPlls, which serve as computers at nodes. At four of these centers, CDC 3200s provide RJE facilities.

TYMNET is a distributed network operated for profit by a major time-sharing company, Tymshare Inc. Currently, it has over 10,000 interactive users in 70 cities throughout the United States and Europe. It contains 100 communications nodes (Varian 620s), operating in a "store and forward" mode.

CYCLADES is a general-purpose distributed computer network constructed under the sponsorship of the French government. With 16 host computers, it uses a distributed five-node packet-switching communications subnetwork CIGALE, with MITRA-15 minicomputers as nodes.

EPSS, the experimental packet-switching service being constructed by the British Post Office, will have nodes in three major cities with 48Kbps duplicated links between them. The nodes are being designed to handle 60 character-at-a-time inputs and 62 packet-at-a-time inputs at various speeds, and consist of similar modular units (Ferranti ARGUS 700Es), each handling about a third of the connected lines at each node and interconnected through fast store-to-store links, and provided with similar backup arrangements.

### References

1969. Martin, J. *Telecommunications and the Computer*. Englewood Cliffs, N.J.: Prentice-Hall.

1972. Farber, D. J., and K. C. Larson. "The System Architecture of the Distributed Computer System," *Proc. of the Symposium on Computer Networks,* the Polytechinic Institute of Brooklyn (April).

1973. Abramson, N., and F. F. Kuo (Eds.). *Computer-Communications Networks*. Englewood Cliffs, N.J.: Prentice-Hall.

1973. Blanc, R. P., I. W. Cotton, T. N. Pyke, Jr., and S. W. Watkins. *Annotated Bibliography of the Literature on Resource Sharing Computer Networks,* NBS Publication 384 (September).

1974. Benoit, J. W., and Erika Graf-Webster. "REX—A Resource Location and Acquisition Service for the ARPA Network." Washington, D.C.: The Mitre Corporation (January).

1974. Doll, D. R. "Telecommunications Turbulence and the Computer Network Evolution," *Computer*, Vol. 7, No. 2, pp. 13–22.

1974. Morgan, D. E., W. Banks, W. Colvin, and D. Sutton. "A Performance Measurement System for Computer Networks," *Proc. of IFIP 74*. Amsterdam: North Holland Publishing Co., pp. 29–33.

1974. Roberts, L. G. "Data by the Packet," *Spectrum*, Vol. 11, No. 2, pp. 46–51.

1974. Schutz, G. C., and G. E. Clark. "Data Communications Standards," *Computer*, Vol. 7, No. 2, pp. 32–41.

1974. Wedberg, G. H., and L. W. Hauschild. "The General Electric Network Monitor System," *Proc. of IFIP 74.* Amsterdam: North Holland Publishing Co.

J. M. BENNETT

# COMPUTER SCIENCE

For articles on related subjects *see* DATA PROCESSING; INFORMATION PROCESSING; INFORMATION SCIENCE; and SYMBOL MANIPULATION.

For articles on related terms *see* ALGORITHMS, ANALYSIS OF; ARTIFICIAL INTELLIGENCE; AUTOMATA THEORY; COMPUTER ARCHITECTURE; COMPUTER GRAPHICS; COMPUTER SYSTEMS; FORMAL LANGUAGES; INFORMATION RETRIEVAL; LOGIC DESIGN; NUMERICAL ANALYSIS; OPERATING SYSTEMS; PROGRAMMING LANGUAGES; SIMULATION; and UTILITY PROGRAM.

Computer science is concerned with information processes, with the information structures and procedures that enter into representations of such processes, and with their implementation in information processing systems. It is also concerned with relationships between information processes and classes of tasks that give rise to them.

**The Domain of Computer Science.** Even though the domain of discourse in computer science includes both man-made and natural information processes, the main effort in the discipline is now directed to *man-made* processes and to information processing systems that are designed to achieve desired goals (i.e., machines). The reason for this lies in the phenomenal growth of the computer field, its rapid penetration into almost all aspects of contemporary life, and the resulting pressure to bring some order into what is being done in the field, to educate the people behind the computing machines and to provide intellectual guidance for new developments in computer designs and applications. Thus, the bulk of empirical material currently available to computer science consists of systems, processes, and operational experience that grew in the computer field during the past quarter-century. Clearly, the empirical corpus in the science is not stationary. It is growing with new development in the computer field. Some of these developments are themselves stimulated by the ongoing activities in computer science.

The main objects of study in computer science today are the digital computer and the phenomena surrounding it. Work in the discipline is focused on the structure and operation of computer systems, on the principles that underlie their design and programming, on effective methods for their use in different classes of information processing tasks, and on theoretical characterizations of their properties and limitations. Also, a substantial effort is directed into explorations and experimentation with new computer systems and with new domains of intellectual activity where computers can be applied.

The central role of the digital computer in the discipline is due to its near-universality as an information processing machine. With enough memory capacity, a digital computer provides the basis for modeling any information processing system, provided the task to be performed by the system can be specified in some rigorous manner. If its specification is possible, then the task can be represented in the form of a program that can be stored in the computer memory. Thus, the stored program digital computer enables us to represent conveniently and implement (run) any information process. It provides a methodologically adequate, as well as a realistic, basis for the exploration and study of a great variety of concepts, schemes, and techniques of information processing.

There exist in nature information processes that are of great interest to computer science (e.g., perceptual and cognitive processes in man, and cellular processes that are controlled by genetic information). An understanding of these processes is intrinsically important, and it promises to enrich the pool of basic concepts and schemes that are available to computer science. In turn, application of the current approaches and techniques of the discipline to cognitive psychology and to biosciences promises to result in important insights into natural information processes. To date, most of the work on these processes has proceeded either by modeling them in digital computers and studying these models experimentally, or by using existing theoretical models in computer science (e.g., in automata theory) for the analysis of certain properties of these processes. There is still little contribution from the study of natural information systems to the design and use of computing machines, or to the development of theoretical concepts in computer science.

**Scope and Nature of Activities in Computer Science.** The subject matter of computer science can be broadly divided into two parts. The first part covers information processing tasks, procedures for handling them, and a variety of related representations. The second part is mainly concerned with a variety of structures, mechanisms, and schemes for processing information. From the point of view of the practitioner in the computer field, the first part corresponds to computer applications, and the second corresponds to computer systems. There are significant connections between the two parts. Indeed, it is a major goal of computer science to elucidate the relationships between application areas and computer systems.

Computer applications can be broadly subdivided into *numerical* applications and *nonnumerical* applications. Work in numerical applications is mainly oriented toward problems and procedures where numerical data are dominant, such as problems in the areas of numerical analysis, optimization, and simulation. These areas are important branches of computer science. Work in nonnumerical applications is primarily concerned with processes involving nonnumerical data such as representations of problems, programs, symbolic expressions, language, relational structures, and graphic objects. Branches of computer science with major activities in nonnumerical applications are artificial intelligence, information storage and retrieval, combinatorial processes, language processing, symbol manipulation, and graphics.

Computer systems can be partitioned into *software* systems and *hardware* systems. The emphasis of work in software systems is on machine-level representations of programs and associated data, on schemes for controlling program execution, and on programs for handling computer languages and for managing computer operations. Branches of computer science with major concern in software systems are programming languages and processors, operating systems, and utility programs and programming techniques. The emerging branch of computer architecture is concerned with software systems as well as with hardware systems. Other major branches of computer science with a main focus on hardware systems are machine organization and logical design.

Generally, applications-oriented activities in computer science are also concerned with related systems problems; e.g., with higher-level languages and with their computer implementation. Similarly, systems-oriented activities are also concerned with the task environments (e.g., classes of applications and modes of man-machine interaction) in which the systems operate.

We can identify two major types of activities in computer science:

1. Building conceptual frameworks for understanding the available empirical material in the discipline, via an active search for unifying principles, general methods, and theories.
2. Exploring new computer systems and applications in the light of new concepts and theories.

The first type of activity is analytic in nature; the second is oriented toward synthesis, experimentation, and probing for new empirical knowledge. A continuous interaction between these activities is essential for a vigorous rate of progress in the discipline. The situation is analogous to the interaction between theoretical and experimental work in any rapidly developing natural science.

At present, the theoretical underpinnings of computer science are at an early stage of development. In some areas, theoretical work is mainly oriented toward bringing elementary order into a rapidly accumulating mass of experience, via the introduction of broad conceptual frameworks and analytic methodologies. In a few areas, theoretical work is concentrating on comprehensive analysis of specific classes of phenomena for which formal models exist. Branches of computer science involved in this type of work are theory of computation, automata theory, theory of formal languages, and switching theory. In general, theoretical work in computer science has been diffused over a large number of fairly narrow phenomena. Much of this work has not yet had an appreciable impact on the complex problems of systems and applications that are encountered in the computer field. There is a growing concern, however, with the development of unifying principles and models that are appropriate for understanding and guiding the major constructive and experimental activities in the field. The emerging work in the new area of analysis of algorithms (which includes important approaches to the study of computational complexity) promises to contribute significant theoretical insights into problems that are in the mainstream of the computer field. As computer science continues to grow, theoretical work in the discipline is also likely to grow, not only in relative volume to the other activities in the discipline, but also in relevance to the significant problems in the domain of computer science.

Experimental work in computer science requires extensive use of computers, and it often stimulates new developments in computer design and utilization. Typical experimental activities may involve the development and evaluation of a new computer language or the testing of a procedure for a new class of problem. Theoretical work in the discipline relies on several branches of mathematics and logic. A typical theoretical problem may focus on the characterization of a class of computer procedures (e.g., procedures for sorting data), the analysis of their structure, and the establishment of bounds on the storage space and time that they require for execution. The objects of study in this example are computer procedures and their properties. The theoretical treatment of these objects is conducted within mathematical systems that provide the analytical framework needed to obtain the desired insights and specific results. Just as mathematics is used in chemistry (say, to develop theories of certain chemical processes), mathematics and logic are used in computer science to study information processes.

**Relationships Between Computer Science and Other Disciplines.** The bond between computer science and mathematics is stronger than the normal bond between mathematics and the theoretical component of a science. Computer science and mathematics have a common concern with formalism, symbolic structures, and their properties. Both put emphasis on general methods and problem-solving tools that can be used in a great variety of situations. There are subjects, such as numerical analysis, that are being studied in both disciplines. These are some of the reasons why computer science is widely considered a *mathematical science*.

Computer science is also considered an *engineering science*. The structure of a computer system consists of physical components (the hardware) in the form of electronic or electromechanical building blocks for switching, storage and communication of information, and programs (the software) for managing the operation of the hardware. In the logical design, and the system design of a computer system, the designer is concerned with the choice of hardware and software building blocks, and with their local and global organization in the light of given operational goals for the overall system. These design activities have strong points of contact with work in electrical engineering and in the emerging field of software engineering. They are also important subjects of study in computer science.

Every transition from the specification of an information processing task to a system for implementing the task involves a design process. In many cases, these processes are highly complex, and their effectiveness is strongly dependent on the availability of appropriate methodologies and techniques that may be used to guide and support them. This is one of the reasons why computer science is concerned with methodologies of systems analysis and synthesis and with general tools for design. This concern is shared not only with engineering, but also with other decision-oriented disciplines such as business administration and institutional planning. There is a more fundamental reason for a close coupling between computer science and a science of design. It comes from the concern of computer science with the information processes of problem solving and goal-directed decision making, which are at the core of design. Processes of this type are objects of study in artifical intelligence, a branch of computer science.

Several other disciplines are recognized as having domains of interest which overlap with computer science. One of these is library science. The problems of organizing and managing knowledge, and of designing systems for its storage and retrieval (in the form of documents or facts), are shared between computer science and library science. The activities at the interface between these two disciplines are often identified as part of information science. The main concern of information science is with processes of communication, storage, management, and utilization of information in large data base systems. Thus, the domain of information science is included in the broader domain of computer science.

Another discipline whose domain of interest overlaps with computer science is linguistics, which shares with computer science a concern with language and communication. The study of linguistic processes, and of related phenomena of "understanding," establishes a special bond between computer science and psychology. Psychological research in information processing models of cognition, perception, and other mental functions has a substantial overlap with work in computer science.

The study of certain theoretical questions about processes of reasoning by computer (performing deductions, forming hypotheses, using knowledge effectively in problem-solving processes) is beginning to create points of contact between certain parts of philosophy (logic, epistemology, methodology) and computer science.

The development of computer science has been strongly stimulated by demands for the application of computers in a wide variety of new areas. The challenges created by new computer applications, and the constructive attempts to meet them, are important factors in the growth of computer science. The exploratory activity in the discipline, as it interacts with other disciplines in the development of computer applications, results both in a better understanding of the power and limitations of current knowledge in the computer field, and in the identification of new problems of information processing that require further study. At a more practical level, the exploratory work on computer applications is contributing to the solution of significant problems in various disciplines that could not be approached without the introduction of computer methods.

There is a large "surface of contact" between computer science and the disciplines where new computer applications are being developed. Virtually all disciplines are involved in this contact. The nature of the contact is similar to the relationship between mathematics and the physical sciences; this relationship involves the representation of scientific problems in mathematical systems wherein the problems can be studied and solved. In the case of computer science, the contact involves the representation of knowledge and problems of a discipline in forms that are acceptable to computers, and the development of computer methods for the effective handling of these problems. Since computers can be made to represent and manipulate problems of enormous variety and complexity, it is likely that the extent of fruitful contact between computer science and other disciplines will be much larger than the contact between mathematics and the "mathematics utilizing" disciplines. In particular, it is likely that the role played by computer science in behavioral and social sciences, the professions, and the humanities will be similar to that played by mathematics in the growth of the physical sciences.

An important application for computers, which is of special interest to computer science, is in the design of more powerful, efficient, and easy-to-use computer systems. The use of computers in the study of computers and in their improvement is a powerful means for gaining the knowledge and insights that computer science seeks, while at the same time the field is being bootstrapped.

From the previous discussion it can be seen that computer science has two types of interface with other disciplines: The first type is characterized by a *shared concern* with subjects of study that are of intrinsic interest to computer science. Here there is an area of overlap between work in computer science and work in other disciplines. Mathematics and electrical engineering have this type of interface with computer science. To a lesser extent, such an interface exists between computer science and the decision-oriented disciplines (e.g., business administration; institutional planning), library science, linguistics, psychology, and philosophy. The second type of interface includes disciplines in which new computer applications are being explored. The main role of computer science in these activities is *to support* and enhance work in a discipline. Practically all disciplines that involve some kind of intellectual activity have this type of interface with computer science.

**The Internal Structure of Computer Science.** The pattern of relationships between computer science and other disciplines is likely to change as the internal structure of activities in computer science continues to change. While the overall structure of the discipline is beginning to attain considerable stability, its detailed internal structure is less stable, and the relative emphasis that various subdisciplines are receiving is still far from stabilized.

The conception, formulation, computer implementation, analysis, and evaluation of procedures (algorithms) for a broad variety of problems constitute a major part of the activities in computer science. Closely associated with these activities are efforts to develop schemes, means, and tools for building and executing procedures—such as languages, major principles for structuring procedures, programming mechanisms, computer organizations, and design aids to facilitate these efforts. In addition, a significant amount of effort is directed to the design of advanced systems—software and hardware. All these activities have important connections with several theoretical efforts in the field, some in application areas and others in the analysis of algorithms, in formal languages, automata theory, switching theory, and systems analysis.

An outline of the major areas of study in computer science (and some of the major relationships among them) is presented next.

1. *Representations in Computer Language of Problems, Data, and Procedures in Various Application Areas.* The main problems in this area are to find solution methods for classes of problems in different domains of application, and to formulate them in a suitable computer language. As mentioned previously, the two major families of applications in the discipline are numerical and nonnumerical applications.

2. *Theory of Computation and Analysis of Algorithms.* Work in this area is concerned with computability, recursive functions and properties of classes of procedures (algorithms) such as complexity, validity, and equivalence. It is related to work in (1).

3. *Higher-Level Languages for Various Applica-*

*tion Areas, Schemes for Structuring Data and Procedures, Language Descriptions, and Translation Schemes*. Work in this area is central to the facilitation of man-machine communication and it has a strong impact on computer applications. It is related to work in computer design and also to work in (1).

4. *Machine-Level Languages, Storage Schemes, and Programming Mechanisms*. This area is concerned with the art of programming computer hardware. It interfaces with (3) and to a lesser extent with (1), and also with (5).

5. *System Organization Schemes, Executive and Control Mechanisms, and Computer Design Processes*. Theoretical activities related to this area are system analysis and simulation (at the hardware/software configuration level), automata and switching theory (at the logical design level), and theory of digital circuits and devices (at the machine component level). This area is strongly related to professional activities in computer system design.

6. *Theory of Formal Languages, Automata Theory, and Switching Theory*. Theoretical activities in these areas are concerned with properties of computer languages, computer mechanisms and their realizations. They are related to work in (2), (3), and (5).

Computer science is a young and rapidly expanding discipline. In a period of less than 15 years, it has succeeded in establishing its distinct identity in universities and in laboratories throughout the world. One of its recognized roles is to provide the intellectual guidance needed for the understanding and development of the computer field. Another role, which is likely to grow in significance in the coming years, is to contribute to an understanding of the impact of computers on other disciplines and on society in general.

References

1968. National Academy of Sciences. "The Mathematical Sciences: A Report," Publication 1681. Washington, D.C.

1969. Hamming, R. W. "One Man's View of Computer Science," 1968 ACM Turing Lecture, *Journal of the ACM,* Vol. 16, No. 1 (January), p. 5.

1970. Wegner, P. "Three Computer Cultures-Computer Technology, Computer Mathematics, and Computer Science," in Walter Freiberger (Ed.), *Advances in Computers*, Vol. 10. New York: Academic Press.

1971. Amarel, S. "Computer Science; A Conceptual Framework for Curriculum Planning," *Communications of the ACM*, Vol. 14, No. 6 (June).

S. Amarel

## COMPUTER SCIENCE EDUCATION. 

*See* Education in Computing Science.

## COMPUTER SECURITY. 

*See* Crime and Computer Security; Data Security; and Security of Computer Installations, Physical.

## COMPUTER SYSTEMS

For articles on related subjects *see* Arithmetic-Logic Unit; Central Processing Unit; Channel; Communications and Computers; Computing Center; Computer Networks; Information Systems; Input-Output Devices; Interrupt; Memory: Main; Memory: Auxiliary; Operating Systems; Processing Modes; Software; and Storage Hierarchy.

For articles on related terms *see* Applications Programming; Compiler; Data Base and Data Base Management; Data Structures; Emulation; Loader; Microprogramming; Multiprogramming; Object Program; Source Program; Systems Programming; Time Sharing; and Utility Program.

A modern computer system is one of the most complex and wonderful achievements of mankind. Its complexity is indicated by the fact that the equipment of a single computer may easily contain over a million identifiable parts, all working together at very high speeds and with remarkable reliability.

As with any complex configuration, it is helpful to consider a computer system as composed of subsystems, each made up of various major components. Because it is more easily visualized, we will begin with a description of the equipment or *hardware* subsystem and then proceed to consider the programming, or *software*, subsystem. Finally, we

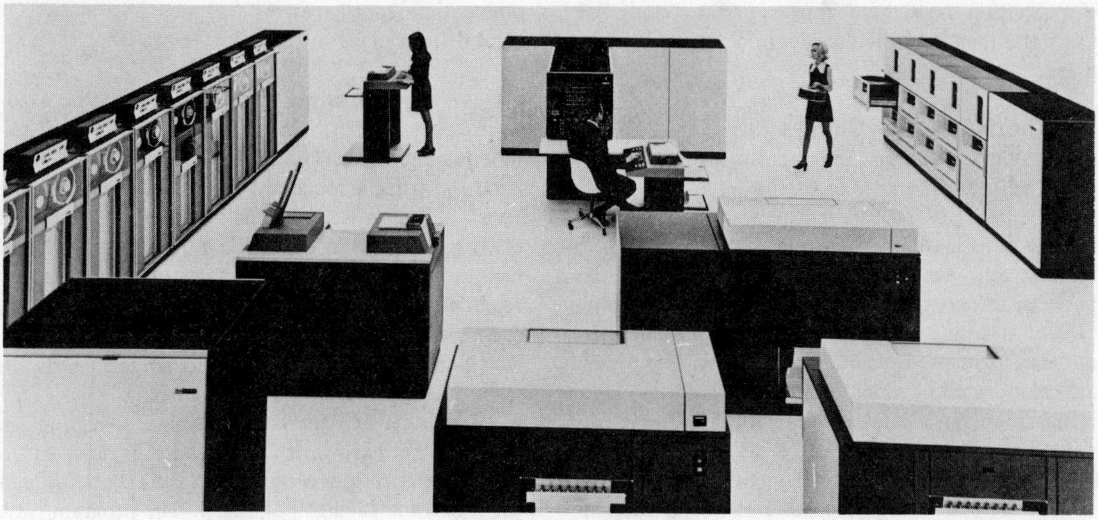

**Fig. 1.** An IBM 370/155 computer system.

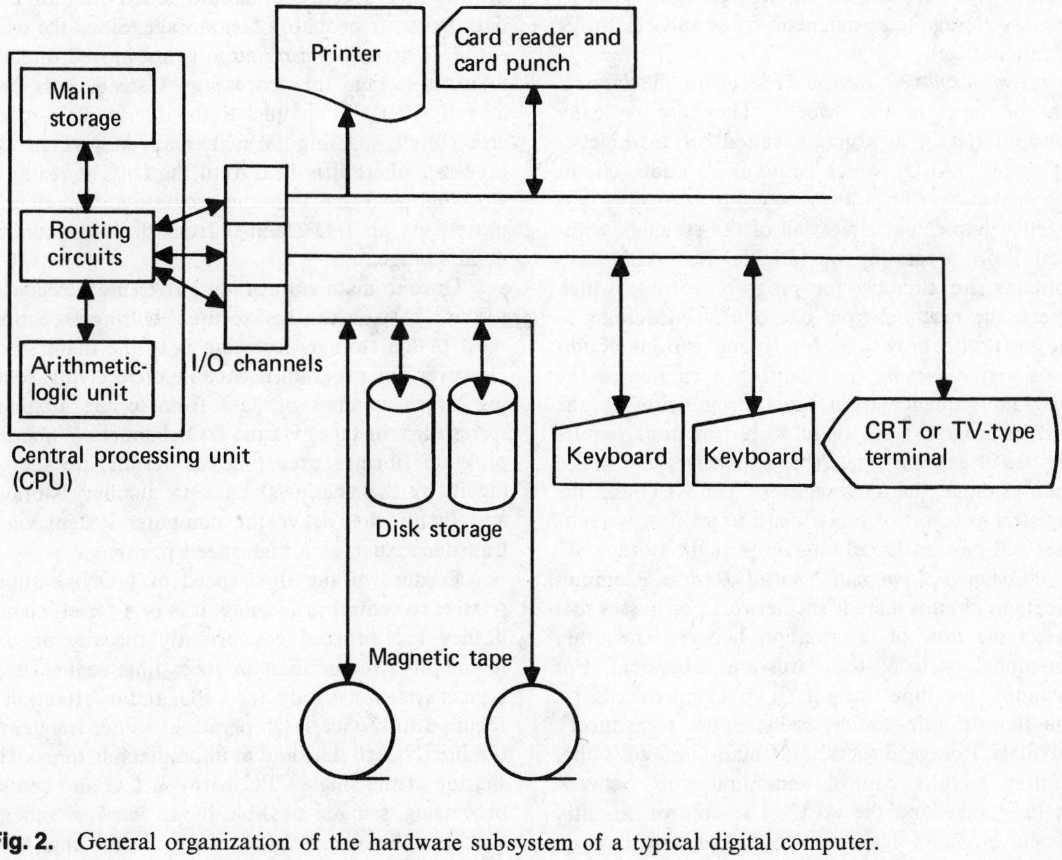


**Fig. 2.** General organization of the hardware subsystem of a typical digital computer.

will interpret how these appear first to computer users and then describe the programs created by the users.

**The Hardware Subsystem.** Fig. 2 shows the major hardware components. These can be classified into a number of categories:

*Transducers.* These are hardware devices that change information from one physical form to another and hence serve as communication links between the computer and its environment. Examples of transducers are card readers, graphics terminals, high-speed printers, typewriter terminals, and plotters, all of which transform human-readable information into an electrical form suitable for computer processing (or vice versa).

*Storage Devices.* These devices in a computer system store not only its data but its instructions (programs) as well. Storage devices come in many sizes, speeds, and costs. They range from the extremely cheap and slow (e.g., punched cards) to devices whose speed make them suitable as on-line (i.e., directly connected to the computer) auxiliary storage devices (e.g., magnetic tapes, disks, and drums). There are also devices fast enough for use as primary storage (e.g., magnetic cores and electronic circuit storage).

*Transformation Devices.* These are the circuits that do most of the "work." They are typically concentrated in a structure called an "arithmetic-logic unit" (ALU), which contains an adder circuit augmented by shift and other control features that together implement almost all of the system's arithmetic and processing operations. The ALU also contains the circuitry for program control which directs the machine from one of its instructions to the next with provisions for testing various conditions and *branching* (i.e., causing a change in the program sequence from strict progression in the written program). All these ALU functions require the use of extremely fast (but expensive, and hence small) storage, the ALU registers. The ALU uses the registers as a sort of scratch pad to jot down results that will be transferred later to primary storage.

*Communication and Control Devices.* Communications circuits include the networks or busses that direct the flow of information between the other functional parts of the hardware subsystem. For instance, the input/output (I/O) channels control the flow of information between the transducers, auxiliary storage devices, and main storage. Other routing circuits control communication between main storage and the ALU. The control circuitry generates timing signals in various complex arrangements that specify at what times information is moved from place to place in the system.

Another classification scheme divides the hardware subsystem into internal components and external components. The internal components are the ALU, with its associated registers and routing circuits, and main storage. The "internal computer" is often referred to as the CPU (although sometimes just the ALU registers and routing circuits are regarded as the CPU). All other hardware devices are part of the *peripheral*, or I/O, *subsystem.*

Now that we have introduced the hardware components of a computer system, how do they work together? Let us trace the path of a program through the hardware. The reader is advised to follow the description by tracing the events through the paths and facilities of Fig. 1. The program (say, as a deck of punched cards) must first be physically translated into electric-signal form, which is done by the card reader, a transducer device. To be executed, the program must be in the main storage, since this is usually the only store available to the CPU. Both the main store and CPU are very fast devices. To keep up with their speed, they should be fed program and data from a reasonably fast storage. Since the card reader is slow, its information is not moved directly to main storage for processing. Instead, it is first moved by an I/O channel to the intermediate-speed disk (briefly passing through main storage in the process), where it is held until the CPU is ready to work on it. At that time the program and its data is moved via an I/O channel from the disk store to main storage.

Once in main storage, the program is accessible to the CPU and can be executed. During execution, most of the storage accessing is to the main store. However, the program is capable of receiving/sending larger volumes of data from/to the auxiliary stores (disk or tape) via the I/O channels. When the program finishes executing, its results are moved (again by the channels) back to auxiliary storage, and finally they leave the computer system via a transducer such as a high-speed printer.

Because of the slow speed of I/O operations relative to central processing, it is best for efficiency if they can proceed concurrently (usually on different jobs) rather than in strict time sequence. A typical system has only one CPU, and its attention is required to service I/O operations rather frequently but briefly each time and at unpredictable times. The sharing of the single CPU between I/O and central processing is made possible by an *interrupt* scheme that permits channels to suspend ongoing CPU operations, give the required brief service to I/O or other external requests, and then return to what it was doing.

This completes the general explanation of how the hardware system components interact, but a few fundamental questions still remain. How does the computer system "know" when to transfer information, what information is required, where should it be stored? As we will see, this guidance is supplied by the second subsystem, the software.

**The Software Subsystem.** Unlike the hardware components, we can't point to a specific physical object and say, "this is a part of the software subsystem." The software simply isn't composed of physical devices; it is composed of *programs* and certain *data structures*. The programs include those that the computer users write, which are generically called *application programs*. Another category of programs, of primary interest to us now, is called *system programs*, the purpose of which is to give all programmers convenient ways to manage and control the hardware, software, and stored data.

During the time that a user's program is being processed, it makes requests for stored data, executes instructions that process the data, and generally controls at least a portion of the computer system's hardware resources. Hence, while a user's program is being executed, it is a part of the active software subsystem.

The next portion of the software that we consider is the *operating system*. Unlike applications programs, it is a permanent part of the computer system. Its function is to control the execution of the other resources in the system. The operating system is a collection of interrelated system programs. These can be classified into three groups.

*Control Programs*. Typical examples are: a reader-interpreter program that reads input from a transducer, translates certain control and scheduling information, and stores the program on auxiliary storage (disk); and a scheduler program that determines which job the computer system should service next. Once the scheduler has selected the next job, its program is placed under the control of an initiator/terminator program, which obtains the resources (such as main storage) necessary for the execution of the program, starts it up, and "cleans up" after it has been completed. During execution, the job delivers its output to a disk. Later, a system "writer" program moves the output to a printer for delivery in human-readable form.

*Installation (or manufacturer) Supplied Programs for User Convenience*. These programs fall into various categories: first there are *translators*, like *compilers*, which are programs that translate user-written programs from the *source language* used by the programmer into a language the machine can execute. Second are *loader* programs that place the translated programs into main storage in a form that the computer system can execute. Third are *utilities*, which are programs that perform frequently required tasks such as sorting and merging two or more lists, moving large masses of data from one place to another within the system, etc.

*System Data-Management Programs*. These programs keep track of what is in the system and where it is located, and use various means to store and access the data efficiently. For instance, when a user's program calls for data, the data-management programs locate and fetch the data to the requesting program. For every data collection (file or data set), data-management programs record who is permitted to use the data, who is currently using it, what is being done with it, whether or not the data should be retained in the system after the job ends, etc.

The third part of the software subsystem comprises the *installation libraries*. These contain data and programs that are useful to a wide spectrum of users. What is specifically contained in the libraries will vary from installation to installation; a manufacturing company's library would probably contain an up-to-date inventory of its products, a list of recent orders, etc. An airline reservation system's library would probably contain a schedule of all flights with arrival and departure times, destinations, flight numbers, number of vacant seats on each flight, etc.

System software is designed in many sizes and complexities. A modern computer system that allows *multiprogramming* (more than a single program executing concurrently) or *time sharing* (several users interacting with the system at typewriter or TV-type terminals at human reaction times) would have a software subsystem that contained all the features previously discussed, and probably some others. However, in a less sophisticated computer system, a good deal of what we have described as software functions is done by human intervention (either by the operator or by the user himself).

We have described a computer system as a collection of two interrelating subsystems, hardware and software. There are, however, certain aspects of the system that do not fall into either subsystem; an example is a *microprogram*, which has been termed "firmware." Microprogramming, as the name implies, is a type of programming. Microprograms directly control the sequencing of computer circuits at the detailed level of the single instruction. Organizing the control hardware in a microprogrammed structure rather than as wired circuitry has several advantages. First is economy of circuitry if the machine must have complex instructions. A second advantage is that it is possible, by microprogramming, to produce an *emulator*, i.e., a set of microprograms that makes a given machine have the same appearance to a programmer as some other machine! This permits the same machine to run programs written for either itself or the machine it is emulating at reasonable efficiency. Yet another advantage is to produce faster operations for the special functions that are microprogrammed rather than programmed in the usual manner. There are, however, some negative aspects of microprogramming, such as the highly specialized knowledge needed and the great tedium of writing microprograms. Also, although microprograms are faster than doing the same functions with software, they are slower than using wired control circuitry.

**The User's View of the Computer System.** Let us now imagine that we are the users of a large, modern computer system. How does this system appear to us? Our first problem is gaining access to the system. First, we must arrange with the computer personnel to issue an *account number* to us. This will be used in a number of ways; for example, to keep track of our use of computer time and resources so that we (or our employer) may be charged our fair share of the system's cost. When we have an account number, we can attempt to interact with the computer system. To do this, we must write a program in one of the many languages available in our particular system. Let us assume that we have written a Fortran program, punched it on a deck of cards, appended a deck of data cards that the program is to process, and are ready to submit the entire deck to the computer system. We then take our deck and surround it with some "job control cards." These tell the operating system our account number, the language our program is written in, and other information the system requires. We put a rubber band around the entire deck, which is now called a "job," take it to the computer center, and submit it to a computer operator. We then wait until the computer operator returns the deck and its associated printed output.

But wait, you say, what happened to the CPU, main storage, I/O devices, etc., that you were talking about before? Amazingly, almost the entire computer system, with all its functional characteristics, can be ignored by the average computer user (however, all this will reappear when we see how the computer system appears to our Fortran program). To the average computer user, the entire physical computer system may be regarded as a "black box" into which he submits his input (program) and from which he receives his results (output).

The user, however, does perceive something extremely important about a computer system. The entire computer system (hardware and software) is itself but a subsystem of a much larger system that is the environment in which the user works. This includes the computer operator, the policies of the computer center in scheduling and billing of jobs, etc.

**Program View of a Computer System.** Once the user leaves his program with the computer operator, how does the program interact with the system? First the program is placed in a card reader (a transducer), the card reader moves the information punched on the card deck to an auxiliary storage device (such as a disk) where it is stored by the reader-interpreter system program. The reader-interpreter is concerned primarily with the information contained on the job-control cards. Accounting information is placed in a file that will later be used to compute the individual user's bill. More importantly, from the point of view of the computer system, information describing various scheduling parameters is placed in a set of tables. These tables are scanned by the scheduler, which is another system program, to determine which job should be executed next. The tables contain all the information the scheduler needs to construct a relative priority ordering of all the programs waiting for service. When the scheduler determines that it is time for the user's program to be executed, the following events take place:

1. The control of the program is passed to another operating system routine, the initiator-terminator. This program scans the job-control card information supplied, determines from it that the program is written in Fortran, and hence must be translated into a language the computer can execute (machine language). The initiator-terminator calls for the Fortran compiler (the program that performs the translation) and then starts it executing. The Fortran compiler, using the program as input data, produces a machine-language translation. In the

course of the translation process, the compiler will call on various other programs in the operating system for help in doing tasks such as allocating temporary auxiliary storage space. When the Fortran compiler finishes the translation, it stores the resulting machine-language program (often called an "object module") on auxiliary storage, and then notifies the initiator-terminator that it is finished. The initiator-terminator releases the space the Fortran compiler occupied in main storage, and then calls another operating system program, the loader.

2. The loader does some necessary processing on the object module and brings it into main storage so its execution can begin. As the program executes, it will interact with various operating system programs that fetch the data it requires, supply the program with any auxiliary storage it requires, etc. When the program finishes executing, it signals the initiator-terminator. The program's output is stored on auxiliary storage. The initiator-terminator "cleans up" after the program and supplies the operating system's "writer" program with the program's output. The writer moves the output information to a high-speed printer. The computer operator then "bursts" (separates) the output and returns it with the punched-card job deck.

**Summary.** To summarize, a computer system is best considered as a collection of resources consisting of two broad classes, hardware and software. Work for the system consists of *jobs*, which are programs and their data prepared by programmers. Both hardware and software are managed by a carefully designed collection of system programs called an "operating" system, which controls the flow of jobs through the system, furnishes services such as language translation, and provides various utilities.

A computer system, through its large capacity storage, can serve as a repository for procedures (programs) that can be shared productively by members of an industrial or educational community.

REFERENCES

1971. Bell, C. G., and A. Newell. *Computer Structures, Readings and Examples.* New York: McGraw-Hill.

1973. Hellerman, H. *Digital Computer System Principles*, 2d ed. New York: McGraw-Hill.

H. HELLERMAN AND I. A. SMITH

# COMPUTER USER GROUPS

For article on related subject *see* MANUFACTURERS, COMPUTER.
For articles on related terms *see* CUBE; GUIDE; JOINT USERS GROUP (JUG); SHARE; and UNIVAC SCIENTIFIC EXCHANGE (USE).

This brief history of the rise, maturation, and old age of computer user groups represents a sociological textbook example of any volunteer organizational entity. After arising from a need and developing into a forceful activist group, a gradual decline has ensued as administrative paralysis set in. Computer user groups began because the manufacturers only barely understood how to support what they produced; by the mid-1960s the need was greatly reduced, and at the present time there is almost no need at all.

**History.** The precise origin in 1955 of the first user group, SHARE, is obscure. Prior to 1955, users of the IBM 701 in the Los Angeles area had worked cooperatively on PACT-I, a primitive automatic programming system. While working on PACT-IA for the forthcoming IBM 704, the users felt an urgent need to create a united front against a proposed IBM assembler, since it was far short of being as useful as it should have been. A meeting was hastily called, and the first formal user group meeting was held in a basement room at the RAND Corporation's headquarters in Santa Monica, California, during the week of August 22, 1955 (see Armer, 1956).

Installations represented were a fitting cross section of the large-scale, scientifically oriented computer community of that era. There was one government agency, NSA (National Security Agency), three government-sponsored research establishments (RAND, Los Alamos, and Livermore), eight aerospace organizations (Boeing, Curtis-Wright, Hughes, North American, United Aircraft and three Lockheed divisions), three industrial giants (General Electric, General Motors, and Standard Oil of California), and IBM (Steel, 1956).

Just a few months after the founding of SHARE, a group of IBM users of commercial computers, recognizing the idea of a user group, banded together to found GUIDE. Today this organization, whose membership requirements roughly parallel those of SHARE, far exceeds all others in head count, activity, and energy. Other early SHARE "spin-offs" included users of Control

Data equipment, the GE 600 line, and Philco Transac equipment. Of these user groups, only VIM (the CDC 6000 series) survives. From this beginning, a regular alphabet army of similar organizations has emerged; for example, COMMON, DECUS, HUG, USE, CUBE, SEAS, TAG, ECHO, DUA, CSSHARE, and the IVY LEAGUE. Each merger reduces the count; each new industry entrant increases the count. There is even a group of groups, JUG (Joint Users Group), although not all user groups are represented in it. A number of large groups are specifically unrepresented because of attempts by manufacturer employees to pretend to represent users.

**Purposes.** In an era before software was sold, a fundamental purpose of a user group was the swapping of home-grown software. Before manufacturers supplied subroutines, users had little but their own ingenuity on which to rely for the countless routines necessary to keep a system running. Such routines as a memory dump from Phillips Petroleum, an internal Sort from UCLA, an assembly program from United Aircraft, Bessel function subroutines from General Electric, and a CRT package from General Motors, all crossed and recrossed the country, spread by word of mouth and the SHARE library, founded and operated by Ben Faden of North American Rockwell Corporation.

It was not beyond the pale for a user group to generate the specifications and do most of the implementation for an entire operating system. One such example was SOS, the SHARE operating system, which was implemented for the IBM 709 and later for the IBM 7090. But the increasing complexity of today's systems has made it virtually impossible for a loosely organized, volunteer association to successfully implement large projects. To survive, user-group purposes had to be altered. The current SHARE purpose is stated in the group's by-laws as " ... to foster the development, free exchange and public dissemination of research data pertaining to SHARE computers ... in the best scientific tradition." It implies that the group now exists to generate a climate for the exchange of data rather than for the original creation of new data.

Despite this disclaimer of innovative objectives, the general view is that the user groups have become little more than underpowered lobbying forces, attempting with only marginal success to translate user needs into product specifications. Instead of the aggressive developmental attitudes of the late 1950s and early 1960s, the groups now display reactive and defensive tendencies.

**Membership.** Membership in user groups is generally confined to those installations that have installed or have on order the specific hardware, program, or service which the group is organized to market. However, groups such as CDC's VIM relax this requirement of eligibility to permit at least attendance at meetings by all who express interest in the "system." Although the relaxation of the rule is attractive, since it invites extended participation, this broader membership base may lead to more emphasis on sales prospects than on the interests of real customers for those groups under tight control by their vendor. This, then, is a sales device, a perversion of the reasons why users organize.

Membership counts vary widely, from as few as 50 or less to as many as the 1,100 or more installations now members of GUIDE, the IBM commercial users' group. Retaining membership requires little more than a declaration of interest, although a few of the more formal groups require representation at one meeting every year or two.

One still unsolved problem is that of the bona fide nature of an application for membership. With the industry's reluctance to release sales data, a user group has almost no way to verify that the statements on the application are genuine. It has not been unknown for a paper company, with no resources, to join a user group before its corporate certificate of incorporation was placed on file.

**Legal Status.** An often-used greeting at user-group meetings is: "Fellow Conspirators!" The legal status of user groups is vague; while no group intentionally frames a conspiracy to control the market, from time to time some of the groups have been on thin ice. The exact status of user-groups is questionable and will doubtless remain undefined, since nobody really is very interested in testing the matter in court.

A few user groups have incorporated to obtain the protections of corporate law for their officers. While accusations of secret societies and cabals have been made, no outsider has yet taken the matter seriously enough to use the courts to obtain entry, although in one case it was actually contemplated. From a tax viewpoint, a user group ought to be a not-for-profit, tax-exempt organization of a scientific and/or educational nature; unfortunately, the U.S. Internal Revenue Service (IRS) does not agree with this position. IRS rulings are rarely clear-cut, but the point of contention appears to be the restrictive nature of the membership rules. The IRS emphasized this point in taking action to withdraw the 501(c)(3) tax exemption from one user group, although this has not been generally applied to all user groups.

**Practices.** A first visit to a user-group meeting is equivalent to an introduction to a three-ring circus—exciting, stimulating, confusing, and almost overwhelming. Activity swirls from early in the morning to late at night; 20 meetings may be running in parallel; social events continue into the "wee" hours; and small knots of uptight people are seen huddling in corridors, engaging in apparently strategic planning. Actually, what is happening consists of small, face-to-face technical confrontations; limited-size working parties planning implementation and specification priorities; medium- to large-sized groups listening to technical presentations, with a minimum of interaction; and formal assemblies that are likely to be hearing sales pitches of the "you'll love it when you get it" variety, a term originated by Carl Reynolds of IBM at a SHARE meeting.

If a representative is to be more than a listener, he must learn to match his installation's needs with the information dispensed, which is not always easy because meeting agendas are usually broad in scope. He must seek out the intimate, unlisted (but critical) meetings that are held at odd hours, and to do this he must have experience. There is a whole class of "nonmeetings," which offers a convenient way for a vendor to try out ideas, avoid premature disclosures, and sidestep internal politics. An example is the 1970 CUBE meeting in St. Louis, where certain key Burroughs users "did not meet" in a hotel room with Burroughs management and technical people. From that meeting came the B-6700 PL/I compiler effort.

From a user's viewpoint, the happiest situation is the one in which the technical people meet quietly and engage in dialog with the product development team. More often, however, users find themselves faced with a marketing representative who can speak technical jargon but who exhibits considerable skill at sidestepping issues, avoiding promises, and evading commitments. When users and developers are not subjected to such routines, the relationship is mutually satisfactory. However, manufacturers generally try to avoid this situation. Vendors have nightmares about permitting development teams to make implementation decisions based on technical issues. Current development costs are so high that even the smallest implementation decision may require lengthy examination from the marketing viewpoint. What needs to be answered is always the same question: "If this is implemented, do we either avoid the loss of some account or gain the sale of additional hardware?"

**Accomplishments.** What is actually accomplished by user groups? The record is erratic, and it appears that the group effectiveness curve is dipping sharply. What was once a viable entity that created new compiler languages, operating systems, and applications packages has today become a patch-and-fix and complaint exchange, with little creative activity. The vastness of today's systems, the size of the vendors, the difficulties of sustaining voluntary action against full-time workers, and the rising expenses involved have all combined to squeeze the user group's effectiveness.

As a result, a handful of dedicated people working part time are gradually being subordinated to paid professionals. The user has almost no opportunity today to alter significantly the primary thrust of product developmental efforts; those lines are set by marketing requirements, competitive timings, and product life cycles. All the user group can do is perform minor cosmetic surgery on the specifications, detect and note the gross functional errors, and flag the basic implementation faults when the product is released to the field.

Does the user group have any lasting effect? Is there a positive return on the investment of time and money by the user community? Most outside observers doubt it. One critic has stated that all user groups ought to be dissolved six months after the first machine of its series has been installed; at that time its problems will either have been fixed or will never be fixed, no matter how long the system is out. Although the future seems technically bleak, there is no reason to conclude that these unique groups will quietly fade away. The façade of effectiveness, the pretense of working together, the sales value to the manufacturers, and the social amenities make it far too pleasant an experience for any abrupt termination. As with so many formal institutions whose time has passed, the body continues to expand and look alive, even though the soul and spirit have long since departed.

References

1956. Armer, Paul. "SHARE—An Eulogy to Cooperative Effort," RAND Report P-969 (October).

1956. Steel, T. B. *SHARE Reference Manual*, p. 0.1–01.

P. Dorn

# COMPUTER UTILITY

For articles on related subjects *see* ARPA NETWORK; COMMUNICATIONS AND COMPUTERS; COMPUTER NETWORKS; COMPUTER SYSTEMS; DATA BASE AND DATA BASE MANAGEMENT; and TIME SHARING.

The expression "computer utility" has come into use by analogy with other public utilities such as those that supply water and electricity. These utilities provide, often for metered payment, a public service almost everywhere. Electricity is delivered to one's home and one may use it for general purposes, provided the bill is paid. The analogy is made between electric power and computing power; the intent is to make computing power or capacity available to all comers at their convenience and for their purposes, provided they pay for it. The usual means envisaged for providing this service is the use of terminals such as teletypewriters connected to a computer by telephone lines.

Early experiments that led to the idea of the computer utility emphasized the provision of scientific calculating power for people who were (more or less) skilled at computer use. The great value of the prepackaged program for the untrained customer was in a sense an accidental discovery, and it is this which leads to the vision of the computer utility as a provider of all kinds of services to all kinds of people. Household bookkeeping, personal records of all kinds, public inquiry services (even access to an encyclopedia such as this via a computer rather than a book on a shelf) are all among the facilities that have been suggested for computer utilities.

The analogy with other utility services must not be pushed too far. For physical reasons, many public utilities are provided on a local monopoly basis; insofar as a computer service can be considered a utility at all, its classification as such depends on its coordination with telecommunication facilities, which are themselves usually provided as a public utility. (For this reason, however, government regulation of computer utilities is an important subject of discussion, particularly in the United States.) Furthermore, for most public utilities, there is little difficulty in insuring that one customer's activities will not interfere with another customer's getting what he pays for. The electricity user, for example, needs no personal equipment located in the power station, and the power station contains no equipment dedicated solely to his personal use. Moreover, the power channel from the user's equipment to the power station is very narrow and may readily be controlled (e.g., by a fuse). In the provision of computing power, by contrast, the computer is from time to time recognizably doing a particular customer's work, and there is a possibility of interference between one customer's work and another's. This interference may be caused either from sheer overloading of the machine (taking so much of its capacity that too little is left to give good service to others) or more indirectly as a result of accident or sabotage by altering another customer's data or programs.

These points lead to a number of requirements for a computer utility, each of which will be introduced briefly and then discussed in more detail. First is the requirement for very adequate and reliable *protection.* It is necessary that a computation done on behalf of one user will in no way alter another's material or have access to it illegitimately. Neither can one user's computation be allowed to affect noticeably the performance of the system as a whole, i.e., the rate at which it does work for others.

The second requirement is *reliability.* A computer utility as ordinarily conceived must be able to store a user's information and to give it up on request, as well as just being able to do computations. The system will not be used unless customers can trust it to retain information reliably and permanently, even if there are occasional failures of equipment. A customer will not pay to have his computations wrongly executed or his information mislaid. He is not interested in the mechanisms for insuring this, but he is interested in their effectiveness.

The preceding two requirements may be regarded as basic. No computer utility will have the confidence of its users unless they are satisfied that these requirements have been adequately met. Equally, no computer utility will make money for its proprietor unless customers are prepared to use the system in sufficiently large volume. To insure that they will do so, it is necessary to meet several other requirements, which, although the economic motivation for meeting them may be just as strong, should be recognized as being in a different class.

The first of these is generally termed *programming generality.* This is a name for a means to an end, the end being that it should be easy to make successive or joint use of possibly a considerable number of pieces of program without getting into enormous difficulty over the process of connecting them together. At one level, it should be possible to put together without difficulty a package for maintaining a data base about sewerage connections in a town, together with a package for drawing maps. At another level, it should be possible to plug together a subroutine for working out square roots with any mathematical program.

The second requirement in this class is for *predictability of performance.* A computer utility will be unattractive to its customers if the cost of a particular use is unclear, even if a similar use was made yesterday, or if elapsed time needed to perform the work is not definite. The utility must be predictable in both performance aspects.

A third requirement, which is worth mentioning at this point, although it is a requirement that bears more on the provider of the system than on the user, is that computing power of the system be readily enhanceable. It must be possible for the vendor of computing power via a computer utility to provide additional computing power when it is needed, without undue disturbance to his existing customers. He must be able to enhance the equipment used without either shutting the service down for a while or changing the way in which the computer has to be used.

All user and provider requirements present considerable challenge to a computer utility, and the remainder of this article will say a few words about each in turn.

**Protection.** If in a computer utility it were required to provide only brute computing power for service of a user, it would be sufficient to provide protection that insured that the work done for a particular user could not directly interfere with work being done for any other user or with the mechanisms that provide the entire service. However, it is usual to think of the user of a computer utility having available to him, possibly for a fee, a considerable number of programs. The proprietary nature of these programs must be protected if the owner of them is going to put them out for service.

Accordingly, protection systems must permit users to have access to programs without copying them, and programs must exist that will automatically and safely bill their users on every occasion. It must not be possible for a user to call a proprietary subsystem in such a way that it does the work for him without billing him properly. It must also be possible for the owner of a program or subsystem to stipulate which other customers of the utility may use it. Similar remarks apply to stored data bases.

Thus, it is evident that customer protection requires more than the simple encapsulation of the activities of a particular user while he is engaged in them. The imposition by the owner of a program or specific data of protection restrictions should be implementable by that owner directly, without his having to request the proprietors of the computer utility to do it for him. If this requirement is not met, the administrative burden is likely to impede effective exploitation of computer service. It would not be appropriate here to discuss at length the detailed techniques for effecting the protection required. The references give some pointers.

**Reliability.** Reliability of information storage poses very high technical requirements. If a system is to be trusted by users to retain their information indefinitely, it must be capable of providing a much higher degree of integrity than most users would ordinarily consider applying to data themselves in a more direct way. A user of an ordinary computer system will take steps to keep backup copies of his information, in proportion to the value he places upon it and to the difficulty (which only he knows) of recomputing it. He may be prepared to take a risk sometimes, but he will be most displeased if an automatic system assumes that prerogative. Keeping backup information of very diverse sorts for different people on a really large scale is a problem not yet solved. It is made more difficult by a reasonable desire on the part of the utility to provide the degree of safety that a user is prepared to pay for, no more and no less.

It is a question of policy whether the integrity system should protect the user against his own mistakes rather than against errors by the utility itself. This involves the relation between backup storage and performance failure—no matter how caused—and cheap archival storage for deliberate use. Although the two functions are logically quite distinct, the physical media used (usually magnetic tapes) are the same, and the required data organizations are at least similar. It is to some extent an open question how far the two functions can be given a common implementation.

Reliability is an area heavily dependent on the currently available storage technology, in which elaborate systems are very likely to become obsolete as technology progresses. Simple systems are, however, likely to be severely restrictive. For example, a very simple approach is to permit a user to request preservation of his material on magnetic tape centrally, or to permit him to request its preservation locally on a (simpler) tape driven directly from his terminal. However, this works only if there is a solid distinction between the material belonging to the system (automatically preserved) and material belonging to users (their own responsibility). Since one of the most attractive attributes of computer utilities is the sharing of material, this distinction is not admissible. Reliability could be severely questioned if something went wrong with shared material and the utility had to appeal to the proprietor for a backup copy. Both the owner and the user of shared material must have confidence in the integrity of the central system. Current approaches to these problems depend on automatic means of recovering reserve copies when either the system or the user notices that there is something wrong, so that the worst experience of the user will be a slight delay in his work. Ideally, recovering a data file should be as easy as redialing an abortive phone call.

**Programming Generality.** Programming generality places requirements on languages and system structure. It is commonplace to find that programs exist for doing the kind of calculation one wants, but that either they will not fit into the rest of one's program structure or will require an inconvenient (for the intended purpose) data organization. These problems lead to heavy and unnecessary programming costs. The avoidance or partial avoidance of such problems requires that there be discipline and convention in the entire structure of system and user programs. It is not clear to what extent this can be reconciled either with efficiency or with the possibility of progress. Programmers will have to be as disciplined as the installers of new telephone offices, and some way will have to be found to avoid a large investment in obsolete systems.

**Predictability of Performance.** Predictability of performance depends upon the existence of surplus capacity and a sufficient number of simultaneous users so that no single user's work will require a substantial portion of the capability of the system. Today, the number of users of multiple-access computer systems is so limited that even an isolated individual will have an effect; compare the few thousand customers of a computer system with the few million of a reasonably large electric company. Compare the minimal surplus capacity in most computer systems with the thousands of megawatts held in reserve in, say, the generating system of the United Kingdom—remembering that the comparative basis is not just one of proportionality but also one related to the demands of individuals. In this area there is hope, however, of progress. Prices of processing units are rapidly falling, and it should become possible to hold adequate reserves without incurring short-term economic problems. It is not yet so clear that this will also be possible for mechanical components such as disk stores for files, but the trends are favorable.

These points are clearly related to the matter of easy capacity enhancement. Only if components subject to capacity strain can be easily augmented will load reserve be maintained. To some extent this is possible with most current system designs. However, if we consider a computer to be an assemblage of processors, memories, channels, and peripherals, with as much mutual interconnection as required, then eventually a computer utility will come to consist of more than one CPU. Unless, as seems unlikely, the structure of computers becomes stable over longer periods than is now usual, the differences between early and late models will cause problems in the service given. Again, the analogy with other utilities is strained: The 1963 and 1973 electric generator models produce very similar 60-cycle alternating current, whereas 1963 and 1973 computer facilities are vastly different.

**State-of-the-Art.** Where are we in relation to the status of computer utilities as compared to other utilities? Early time-sharing systems, of a type intended to have a community of users rather than a mere collection (the M.I.T. Compatible Time-Sharing System (CTSS), the Cambridge Multiple-Access System), made a good start in this direction. The more recent developments of Multics (M.I.T.–Honeywell) place it as near as any existing system to actually being labeled a computer utility. Problems of scale still remain, however, and it is not quite clear when or whether market forces will promote the developments needed. There is, after all, competition: Minicomputers are becoming very cheap, and it may turn out that this low-cost computing power will seem more attractive than the higher cost of sharing programs, data, and power, the central theme of a computer utility. It would be contrary to experience in other developments in industrial society that the minicomputer would win out (rather like a cottage industry supplanting U.S. Steel), but it could happen.

References

1969. Lampson, B. W. "Dynamic Protection Structures," *AFIPS Conf. Proc*, Vol. 35.

1972. Organick, E. I. *The Multics System: An Examination of Its Structure*. Cambridge, Mass.: M.I.T. Press.

1972. Wilkes, M. V. *Time Sharing Computer Systems*, 2d ed. New York: American Elsevier.

R. M. NEEDHAM

# COMPUTERS. *See* ANALOG COMPUTERS; COMMUNICATION AND COMPUTERS; DIGITAL COMPUTERS; HYBRID COMPUTERS; MICROCOMPUTER; MINICOMPUTERS; SPECIAL-PURPOSE COMPUTERS; and SUPERCOMPUTERS.

# COMPUTERS, HISTORY OF. *See* DIGITAL COMPUTERS: History of; and MANUFACTURERS, COMPUTER.

# COMPUTERS, MAINTENANCE. *See* MAINTENANCE OF COMPUTERS.

# COMPUTERS, MULTIPLE ADDRESS

For articles on related subjects *see* ADDRESSING; INDEX REGISTER; INDIRECT ADDRESS; and MACHINE INSTRUCTION SET.

For articles on related terms *see* CONTROL DATA CORPORATION 6000 SERIES; GENERAL REGISTER; and IBM 360-370 SERIES.

Each arithmetic instruction in a computer may be thought of as having four addresses, two *sources* for the data operands, one *destination* for the result, and the *location* of the next instruction. Functionally, therefore, we may write an arithmetic instruction as

$$F(s_1,s_2,d)l, \qquad (1)$$

where $F$ is the arithmetic function to be performed, $s_1$ and $s_2$ are the source addresses, $d$ is the destination address, and $l$ is the location of the next instruction. Historically, computers have differed considerably in the way in which these four addresses were expressed explicitly and implicitly (as well as on such matters as the use of base registers, index registers, and indirect addressing).

Some very early computers, notably EDVAC and SWAC, were *four-address* computers in that each of the four addresses in Expression (1) above appeared explicitly in each arithmetic instruction. In a *three-address* computer, early examples of which were NORC and CADAC, the address $l$ of the next instruction is implicitly the next instruction in sequence. This convention is essentially universal in all modern computers; except for conditional or unconditional jump instructions, which change or may change the normal sequencing of instructions, the next instruction is the one physically following the current one in main memory.

An attractive aspect of three- and four-address computers in the early days when hardware was very expensive was that there was no need for an *accumulator* to hold operands and results. In this context it is interesting to note that the most notable current example of a three-address computer is the Control Data 6000 series, which is a multiple accumulator system in which all three addresses refer to accumulators.

There have been two kinds of *two-address* computers. One is epitomized by the IBM 650, one of the most widely used computers of the 1950s. In this computer, one of the source addresses and the destination address were both implicitly assumed to be the accumulator in the arithmetic unit. Thus, the form of an arithmetic instruction was

$$F(s_1)l.$$

Earlier versions of this type of machine included the HEC, based on work by Booth at Birkbeck College, London, and the Elliot 400 series.

On the 650 the main memory was a magnetic drum. Optimized programming required that the address $l$ be located on the drum such that it was just coming under the reading heads when the preceding instruction execution was completed. For the programmer to arrange this himself was quite tedious; therefore automatic optimization was a feature of assemblers for the 650, of which the best known was SOAP. Such optimization normally resulted in a factor of 2 to 3 in speed over arranging the instructions sequentially on the drum.

The other type of two-address computer is best represented by the IBM 360–370 series, in which $s_1$ is a *general register*, $s_2$ is either a general register or a location in main memory, $d$ is implicitly $s_1$, and $l$ is implicitly the next instruction in sequence. Thus, an instruction has the form

$$F(s_1,s_2).$$

The earliest working example of this type of machine was the Ferranti Mark I, built at Manchester University in 1950.

Until the advent of general registers, which serve in effect as multiple accumulators, *one-address* computers were the most common type. In these an instruction has the form

$$F(s_1),$$

with the accumulator serving as both $s_2$ and $d$ and $l$ being taken as the next instruction in sequence.

A. S. DOUGLAS

# COMPUTERS AND SOCIETY

For articles on related subjects *see* AUTOMATION; COPYRIGHTS AND PATENTS, COMPUTER ASPECTS OF; CRIME AND COMPUTER SECURITY; DATA BANK; DATA SECURITY; and PERSONNEL IN COMPUTERS.

Any application of computers in the public sector could illustrate how computers affect the way society operates. As examples of such applications, computers are used to process social security payments, help administer hospitals, maintain lists of persons wanted by law enforcement, and aid in the drafting of legislation. In principle, the operational procedures followed in such applications stem from policies, requirements, and guidelines laid down by the agencies and institutions within which the computers are used. But any means that greatly facilitates (or inhibits) the realization of certain ends can become important in determining whether these ends will be adopted as goals. Thus, in practice, the fact that computers are such powerful instruments for information processing leads to a blurring of the distinction between cause and effect in certain situations where they are used. For example, a national policy of basing security in old age on the distribution of monthly benefits, which are calculated from lifetime earnings, can be adopted only when there is a prompt, reliable method of distributing payments, and a method of automatically dealing with the enormous volume of transactions generated through payrolls.

By the same token it is natural to ask whether the fact that computers make it easier to store and disseminate information about people does not lead both private organizations and public authorities to collect more personal information and be less careful in controlling its distribution. We are thus led to examine how computers may be affecting our major institutions and social structures, not merely how effectiveness is altered by the presence of computers, but—more importantly—how computers influence the goals and very nature of societal structures and groupings. The study of computers and society, then, includes an analysis of how computers influence the operation, shape, and especially the goals of political, social, and cultural systems. To put the subject in perspective it is necessary to recognize that computers function in the larger area of automation and that automation is only one—although a key one—of several major technological forces that are reshaping society. Other key technological developments are occurring, for example, in transportation/communications (jet air travel, space flight, cable TV, satellite transmission) and in biology/medicine (contraceptives, transplants, drug experimentation, genetic engineering).

In this article the effects of computers on three systems are considered: the labor force, the individual, and the political system. Other articles in this encyclopedia discuss the effects on the educational system, on the health care delivery system, and the legal system. For additional reading see the references at the end of this article.

**Computers and Employment.** To understand the relation between computers and employment, it is useful to briefly review the earlier history of automation and employment. Along with the benefits of the industrial revolution which originated in Europe during the nineteenth century, there were widespread harmful effects, including serious displacement of labor because of the introduction of machines, and concentrated urban pollution due to the uncontrolled production of waste products. The unemployment gave rise to such events as the riots of the Luddites, who in 1811 and 1812 broke into factories and smashed machines, and the writings of Samuel Butler, who in 1872 published *Erewhon*, a novel about a utopia, in which all machines were banished because only in this way could society be certain that machines would not eventually take over control.

Computers (more precisely, data processors) are the instruments by which automation is put into effect in offices. As soon as electronic data processing equipment materialized, the possibilities of technological displacement—which manual (blue collar) workers had been experiencing for over a century—became real for clerical (white collar) workers. In 1950 Norbert Wiener published *The Human Use of Human Beings*, which was largely a plea that computers not be allowed to cause distressing unemployment.

A noticeable result of automation is that it brought about a change in the *composition* of the labor force. During the late nineteenth century and the first half of the twentieth century, as more sophisticated automatic machines were invented and put into use, there was a steady decline in the industrial countries of the number of workers engaged in farming, textile production, and mining (primary industries), but an increase in the number engaged in manufacturing (the secondary industries). This shift was accompanied and made possible by a continual increase in productivity (i.e., the output per man-hour). Thus, sufficient goods were produced in primary industries even though population increased, the demand for goods rose, and the work force declined. The increase in demand is important, for it is this factor that has allowed total employment to increase (although there have been large fluctuations in particular industries) in the face of automation and increased productivity.

Computers, which in the United States started to appear in significant numbers in the late 1950s, have been accompanied by still another major change in the composition of the labor force. There has been a shift to what is called the post-industrial society, i.e., from blue-collar to white-collar jobs, and to service-producing (or tertiary) employment as performed by clerks, government employees, managers, sales personnel, professionals, etc. This is illustrated in Fig. 1, where it can be seen that service and white-collar employment rose from 45.3 to 61.8% between 1947 and 1971, while blue-collar workers declined from 40.7 to 34.4% of the labor force. The role of computers in this change, particularly the extent to which computers have contributed to unemployment, has been the subject of detailed studies in many of the industrialized countries of western Europe. The conclusions are very similar to those reached earlier about automation in general, and are summarized by a statement in a report published by the International Labour Office: "For various reasons, the introduction of automation in offices has thus far not resulted in a decline in the general level of employment for office workers." (See the list below for some of these reasons.)

In spite of these conclusions it is impossible to be complacent about the long-term effects of automation and computers on employment. Sometimes, as occurred in the typesetting industry, computers gain general acceptance within a very few

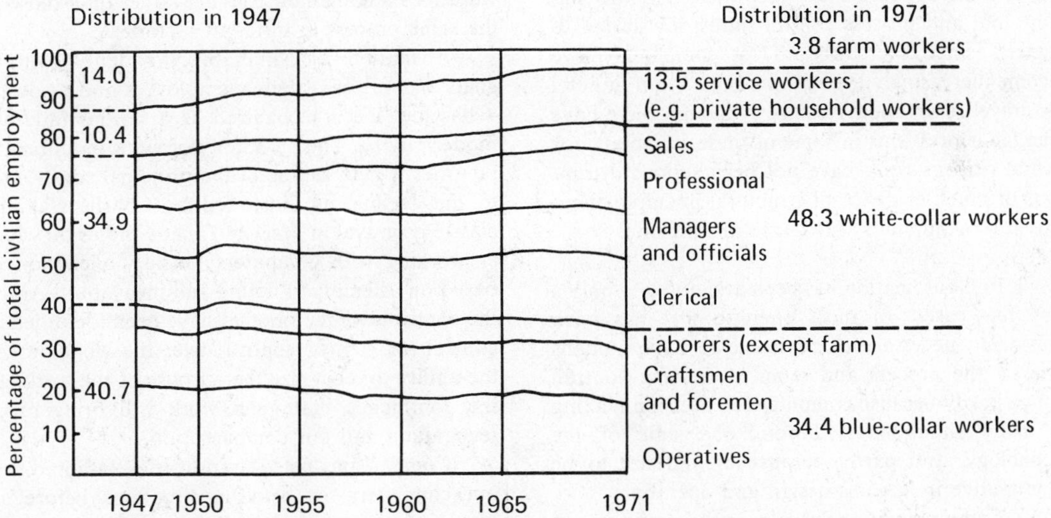


**Fig. 1.** Change in distribution of employment by major occupation group. Note: Statistics for 1947–1964 and 1964–1971 are based on somewhat different sets of occupational data (e.g., changes in the lower age limit for inclusion into the labor force). Similarly, the statistics for 1971 are not strictly comparable with earlier years. However, the changes have no significant effect. For 1964, the discrepancy was approximately 0.3 in the major classifications (e.g., white collar, etc.) and the two sets of statistics were averaged.

years, and the result is technological displacement and hardship for those with the specialized skills of that industry. Also, there are unanswered questions about how computers affect attitudes toward employment, in particular whether they increase the *alienation* of workers from their jobs, a major problem accompanying automation. Finally, if the increases in productivity are projected far enough (several decades), the question arises whether the decline in the work week will eventually result in greatly increased leisure time for a large fraction of the labor force and, if this does happen, whether society is equal to the challenge of making good use of increased leisure time.

During the recession that occurred in the early 1960s, when unemployment was relatively high in several countries, including the United States, some critics contended that the main obstacle to full employment was not lack of demand but rather the effect of *structural* factors brought on by automation. By this it was meant that the attributes of the labor force (education levels, skills, mobility, distribution in age, sex, etc.) were not matched to job needs. There are many examples of how automation (and computers) suddenly makes old skills obsolete and places great demands on new ones. In the United States during the early 1960s, insurance companies converted from punched card processing to computers; in the middle 1960s, airline reservation systems converted to computers, and the machine tool and process control industries started to convert; since the early 1970s, computers have become increasingly evident in banking and in hotel and travel reservation systems. Although there have been labor problems in some of these situations, for several reasons there have not been serious disruptions or much evidence of structural unemployment caused by computers. These reasons include:

1. Full automation has been attempted in only a very few cases. In most operations it has been considered necessary or advisable to have humans monitor the process and retain overriding control. This is partly because computerized decision making in many situations is beyond the state of the technology, and partly because of a desire to be conservative in systems design and operation.

2. Computerization usually requires years of planning, especially where service cannot be interrupted during installation. This allows time to adopt measures that will minimize the effect on employment. Both large companies and unions, because of earlier experiences with mechanization and automation, have come to recognize the need for such measures. These include advance notice of intentions, retraining programs, early retirement plans, compensatory payments, etc.

3. Very often computers are not brought in to save labor cost, but to achieve improved accuracy, better resource utilization, or simply to do a job that cannot be done without them. In certain cases (e.g., reservation systems), humans are needed to interface with customers; in others, both office and factory, decreases in direct labor are compensated by increased needs for indirect labor (e.g., computer maintenance, keypunching, etc.)

It is an open question whether on the whole, the introduction of computers tends to produce a net gain or reduction in the skill requirements for jobs. (Skill requirements must be distinguished from educational qualifications that might be imposed for a job but which are not essential for its accomplishment.) Studies show that in certain operations (e.g., demand deposit accounting), significantly increased skill levels are needed; in others (e.g., plant operation for electric utilities), less skill is needed. A man tending a numerically controlled machine tool may have a more routine job, with less opportunity to exercise control, than he would have for the same job if it were nonautomated. In general, the net changes in skill levels (taking both direct and indirect labor into account) are not large, and the variations among industries are larger than those for the same process in different factories.

Alienation—i.e., an inability to identify with the goals and values of fellow employees and associates —has long been recognized as a serious failure of modern living. The monotony of work in automated factories is held as one of the principal contributors to this feeling, as illustrated by Charlie Chaplin's classic portrayal in *Modern Times*. Studies on whether working with computers furthers alienation are based on attempts to define and measure it. Among the contributive factors that have been identified are control (or lack of control) over the work process, the ability to recognize the purpose of the work, and the confidence that good work will bring proper recognition and fair compensation.

Comparisons between industries with and without computers, or between situations before and after a computer is installed, reveal (as with the debate on skill levels) that the question is complex, with some evidence that the alienation resulting from computers is less than that found in other automated processes. Workers in computer-related jobs see their work as requiring greater responsibility, more accuracy, and more exacting deadlines. But often they also feel that middle supervisory positions have been eliminated and that their chances for promotion have therefore been reduced. It is a question whether such decreases in alienation will continue as the novelty and prestige of working with computers wears off. If eventually the attitudes become like those found on assembly lines, then the means being sought to reduce or compensate for boredom and alienation in those situations will also have to be applied to computer-based jobs. These measures include providing increased job benefits, redesigning the work environment so that the job becomes more interesting (this may involve putting together work teams), and developing compensating leisure activities.

Most of the people in most of the world must concentrate their full energies on acquiring the necessities of food and shelter for themselves and their families, and therefore it may seem unrealistic to be concerned with the problem of what to do with leisure time. But eventually the population of the world must stabilize; the finite limits to resources mean that the per capita consumption of material goods will also have to reach a limit, and if the rise in productivity experienced over the past century continues, man will have more and more time to spend on activities other than work. (Of course the demand for services—medical, educational, recreational, etc. —could grow without corresponding increase in requirements for material goods.)

In the United States the average work week has been decreasing about 3 hours each week every decade since 1890; at its present level it averages 37 hours. Extrapolations of the trend suggest that by the year 2000 the working year could go down to as little as 1,100 hours, which could take various forms: e.g., 27 full time (=37.5 hours) work-weeks per year, 50 short (3 day) weeks per year, or full time work-weeks for the whole year, with retirement at age 40.

Leisure is not to be equated with time free of work—the unemployed do not have leisure, nor is leisure the time spent in queueing for recreational services or job retraining. How people spend their leisure is highly dependent on social class, educational level, financial assets, nationality, and age. Working classes tend to use their extra time in relatively unstructured ways; working around the house, watching TV, relaxing with their families; professional groups, which on the average have less leisure, are more interested in activities such as music or participation in discussions; sports and travel are of interest to all groups. Educational institutions are playing an increasingly important role, as shown by enrollments in part-time degree programs, in nondegree courses (photography, gardening, language study). However, fundamental questions remain as to whether society can adapt to large increases in leisure time.

Some sociologists (e.g., Erich Fromm, David Reisman) feel that the work ethic is deeply ingrained, doubt whether leisure can be satisfying unless work is satisfying, and see the need to integrate the two activities within a common framework. But studies also show that industrial workers do not consider work to be their central interest, nor are their social relations based on their work. Computers, representing an advanced state in the mechanization and automation of work, are undoubtedly bringing nearer the time when large elements of society will have to come to grips with the problems of increased leisure. The answers to these problems will have to be found within a very broad context involving the structure and goals of society.

**Computers and the Individual.** Until quite recently, computers were expensive devices, accessible mainly to large corporations, governments, and institutions. In important ways, their use affects the lives of individuals. The effect that has been the subject of the most intense inquiry is the relation between computers and privacy. Interest in this stemmed from a series of U.S. congressional hearings on the gathering of information about private individuals. The hearings revealed that—aided by newly developed electronic devices for eavesdropping, surveillance, and personality testing—many agencies, both private and public, had enormously increased their activities in gathering personal information about employees and competitors. (Eventually, laws were passed to limit such surveillance and wire tapping.) When in 1965 the Bureau of the Budget proposed establishing a Federal Data Center to preserve economic data, this was viewed as a threat to individual freedom. Although the proposal was rejected, the Congressional hearings initiated (in the United States and subsequently in many other countries) a fundamental review of how data banks containing personal records (e.g., on credit, health, crime, educational performance), and more particularly computerized data banks, affect the rights of individuals.The concerns centered on a number of points:

1. Often, individuals are not aware that information about them is being collected. Even when they know about the existence of an information file, only very rarely is there an opportunity to see the records, challenge misrepresentations, and have mis-

takes corrected. These practices persist in spite of the fact that records gathered for insurance, financial, or medical purposes can contain opinions based only on hearsay, and in spite of frequent errors with many computerized billing systems.

2. The existence of the computer and the availability of mass storage encourage the collection of unnecessary data, particularly by governments. Further, there is the feeling that the computer is unforgetting and unforgiving, and instances of youthful indiscretions, misdemeanors, and delinquent payments are kept for times much longer than can be justified.

3. Records about an individual are passed about too freely. The existence of terminals and remote job entry makes it easy to disseminate medical reports, credit ratings, court actions, and school records, and the computerized files on which such records are kept are not adequately protected against unauthorized access.

Although measures have been put forward in some jurisdictions about certain types of information processing in response to these concerns, there are many reasons why progress is slow. First, it is very difficult, especially in countries where the common law is the basis of the legal system, to define a general right to privacy. Such a right inevitably conflicts to some degree with freedom of speech and freedom of the press, two very jealously guarded freedoms. Thus, in 1967, the Freedom of Information Act (U.S. Code, V15, Para. 552; suppl. III 1965-1967) was passed in the United States to insure access of information that should be open in the public interest.

Second, personal information is essential for the conduct of many of the functions of government and business. Government must collect such information, for example, to issue driver's licenses and welfare payments or a license to operate a prepaid medical scheme; businesses are entitled to data that allows them to establish credit ratings. Even more data is needed for planning (e.g., schools or housing developments) and for research, particularly in the social sciences.

Third, it is difficult to distinguish legitimate needs for information from excessive demands for unrequired data. There is a legal requirement to provide census data, but for every census it has been necessary to review what should be collected. Consent of the person providing the data is a useful concept, but it is not always easy to decide when consent is freely given (consider the case of a student or a welfare recipient). In any case, certain information should be regarded as matters of public record.

Fourth, as noted above, the concept of privacy is so strongly intertwined with other legal rights that any laws about it have to be carefully built into the existing legal framework. In countries where there are federal systems (the United States, Canada, Australia, West Germany), this can be particularly difficult because jurisdiction is divided between the levels of government. Moreover, when laws are passed, it is necessary to recognize that computerized data banks are not the only repository of personal information. If protection is to be effective, all other, more traditional, systems must also be considered.

These difficulties notwithstanding, a number of legal steps have been taken to strengthen the rights of privacy in the presence of the computer. Most common has been the enactment of laws regarding credit data banks (e.g., in the United States, the Fair Credit Reporting Act, 1969). These laws have usually established the right of persons to see their records, and have required mechanisms for correcting mistakes. Generally, it has been recognized that the *security* of data is a responsibility quite distinct from the protection of privacy. To an increasing degree, computer systems are incorporating both hardware and software devices to insure that unauthorized persons cannot gain access to confidential data. In some places (e.g., the State of Hesse in Germany), an ombudsman has been appointed to rule on disputes where computerized data banks are involved; in 1973, Sweden adopted a law that had been proposed in many places, one requiring that data banks containing personal information be licensed and that they follow laid-down procedures in their operations.

What has failed to emerge is the definition of a general right of privacy based on the notion that an individual has certain rights or ownership of the data about himself. Even more important is the slow progress in making a right to privacy effective (except, perhaps, in the case of credit data banks). The most difficult areas are undoubtedly those involving national security or crime records, for in these cases exceptions have to be made in relaxing certain safeguards that might be mandatory in other situations (e.g., not recording hearsay information).

The inquiries, debates, and studies about computers and privacy are still continuing (NAS, 1972). There is some consensus that progress will have to be made along the lines of working out procedures appropriate to each of the areas for which personal records are kept (employment, health, education, police). Most important is the recognition that data bank issues are not primarily technological, but rather administrative, political, and legal, and that they arise out of changes in the relationships among individuals and organizations. For these reasons, the main protective measures will have to be based on those long-established legal procedures or "due processes" on which all individual rights are founded: well-defined practices, rulings in open courts, and opportunities for challenging and reviewing decisions.

Quite aside from the issue of privacy are other aspects of the relationships among computers and individuals, which are being carefully reexamined. As computers become more and more used in administrative processing, questions arise whether (from the point of view of the individual) computer-based procedures are better or worse than the earlier manually based systems. Computers are installed for a variety of reasons, the most important of which are to achieve economy of operation and resource management, to speed up procedures, and to carry out certain operations that could not be done otherwise. It does not automatically follow that benefits accrue to the individual who is involved in the procedures. Is a computerized system of paying insurance claims, for example, as fair to an individual as one in which he deals exclusively with people? Is the claims form simpler? Is there equal opportunity for appealing a ruling? Is payment as fast? Is he made aware of all the consequences of presenting a claim?

As computers become more and more involved in the dealing between individuals on one hand, and governments and business on the other, it becomes increasingly important that there be answers to such questions. There are aspects of systems that operate even beyond fairness and promptness. Can systems be made to respond in a "human" rather than machinelike fashion? The properties of a system that seems human, or humane, are not altogether clear, but one might look for politeness, an ability to deal with special cases, and a value placed on satisfying the people involved. Human bureaucracies have long predated computers, and world history and world literature are full of instances of societies where rulers and administrators have had no regard for the sensitivities of those who live under their rule. But the question is: Are present-day computer based administrative procedures better or worse (from the point of view of the individual) than the systems they have replaced, and are computerized systems as satisfactory as they can be? As a particular sub-question, how much human presence is needed in a computer-based system so that it will be an acceptable substitute for personal relationship?

These questions are only beginning to be asked, and the responses have not yet influenced the design of new systems. But the more broadly phrased question, whether technology is benefiting the individual, has been asked for some time. In fact, this is the dominant theme of modern inquiry, and there is a wide divergence in the answers and beliefs of those who have addressed themselves to it.

There is an articulate school of technology critics (among them are Herbert Marcuse, Lewis Mumford, and Jacques Ellul), whose adherents feel that the industrialization and urbanization that have resulted from technology have turned out to be disasters. They reason that technological growth has become an end in itself, altogether removed from its original purpose of providing man with the goods and services to better himself socially. They see man as having become preoccupied with techniques and toolmaking, and in so doing has lost sight of humanistic values. The computer is regarded as an especially serious threat, for its use depends on factors such as calculability, precision, and efficiency and these essentials necessarily dominate.

Others who have attempted to assess the role of technology in society have also seen the influence on human values as detrimental, but they are less pessimistic of the relation and are more ready to believe that control can be exercised over technological developments (Erich Fromm, Jacob Bronowski, Marshall McLuhan, and Alvin Toffler are in this group). Recognizing that the rapid rate of technological change has led to challenges to the authority of religion, the family, and the state, as well as simultaneous desire for security and stability on the one hand and for innovation and mobility on the other, they do not concede that such value conflicts are necessarily bad. They argue that good planning can lead to an integration of conflicting values and that technology, far from being inconsistent with human goals, can lead to reemphasis of these goals.

If we interpret this general argument in terms of computers, it is obvious that computers can be used to let individuals choose color and style when purchasing a car, or to find a donor with the right type of blood. But can they help in allowing people to make important choices in life (e.g., in determining how and by whom they are governed, in choosing what they work at or where they live)? Can they help in reducing the universal threats of war, pollution, and overpopulation? When approached in these terms, it is obvious that computers represent but one set of forces acting upon individuals. Depending on one's philosophical outlook and degree of optimism, either one of two philosophies is acceptable: One can believe (1) that computers represent the latest of the technological forces acting to reduce choice and limit the activities of human beings; or (2) computers offer new possibilities in dealing with large populations so that attention to individual needs is a practicability and not just an ideal.

**Computers in Organizational Structures and in the Political Process.** Individuals and societal groups are the limiting members of a large number of organizational units that constitute society and interact with each other in various ways. As other examples of units, we might consider a government that comprises its electorate; the different entities of government at municipal, state, and federal levels; the functional departments within a company in the private sector; and citizen-action groups interested in the environment or civil liberties. Each unit arrives at a size, creates its own modus operandi, and acquires a sphere of influence that depends on its function and which determines its effectiveness. Computers today are altering the effectiveness of these different units and are leading to changes in the balance of powers or political relationships among them.

Computers play a role in determining the balance of powers because they are such powerful instruments for gathering, organizing, and disseminating information. Sociologists and political scientists have come to recognize that information is a new source of power, complementing the traditional sources of land and capital. The possession, distribution, and utilization of information is seen as a new major activity comprising what has been called the "knowledge industries." Many people are engaged in these industries: scientists, engineers, mathematicians, librarians, teachers, reporters, planners, management consultants, etc. Computers and computer personnel form only a part of the information-gathering activity, but they are an important part because information processing is the central function of a computer and many participants in knowledge industries use computers in their respective specialties. The fact that computers are used by librarians for information retrieval, by teachers in computer-assisted instruction, by lawyers looking for a legal precedent, or by politicians compiling lists of possible campaign donors is, of course, important, for all of these activities illustrate how the effectiveness of information gathering is enhanced. Beyond this direct benefit are indirect effects whereby the presence of computers in some way alters the climate in which things are happening. As already demonstrated in the case of employment and privacy, these indirect or secondary effects may, in the long run, be more important than the primary ones.

One question that might be asked about the political effects of computers is whether those who work with computers (programmers, analysts, system designers) have acquired an unusual or undue amount of power because of their expertise. The answer seems to be that they have not. One reason is that the politicians, administrators, and civil servants who exercise power can do so only by learning to make use of specialists like lawyers, engineers, and accountants; computer experts represent one more group that has to be managed. Another reason is that, in spite of promises and plans, there has been a noticeable lack of success in producing management decisions by computerized systems or in system design of complicated operations involving many people and functions. The result is that there has been no usurpation of management authority or decision-making powers, either by computers or by the people who work with computers. This situation is similar to the position of United States scientists in the decades of the 1950s and 1960s. In spite of very heavy concentration on (and expenditure for) electronics, nuclear technology, and space programs, an examination of the record shows that the key decisions were made by politicians on political grounds, acting at times on and at other times against the advice given by technical experts.

Large organizations exhibit structure, and of the many possible structural forms two basic ones can be identified. The first is a *centralized* mode in which each subunit (except the headquarters) reports to a single unit above it in the hierarchy. This corresponds to the mathematical concept of a tree, with the headquarters as root. The second structural mode is *decentralized* in that each subunit may be connected to any of or all other units. This corresponds to a graph. For any complex organization in the public or private sector, decisions have to be made, regardless of whether the centralized or decentralized mode dominates, and there may be a continual shift between the powers of the headquarters and those of the subordinates. There are extensive arguments to support either mode of structure, but basically the current philosophy is that centralization allows a better overview and better control of the whole system and offers better opportunities for taking advantage of "economies of scale"—the economic thesis that it is cheaper to manufacture things in large quantities. By contrast, decentralized organizations have an advantage in that control of the operation is closer to the end-user, so that service is likely to be faster and more responsive to user needs.

We can now ask the question whether computers favor or discourage centralized control. Early computers were large and expensive, and large-scale operations were usually needed to justify an installation, so that in this sense they favored centralization. More recently, as costs of hardware have come down, and time-sharing, remote job entry, and computer communications have become more common, it is becoming increasingly economic to run a decentralized computer system. This means that computer systems can be designed for either centralized or decentralized organization, and the decision on which structure to adopt (or which mode is to dominate) can be made on the basis of management philosophy rather than purely technical considerations. The trend to computer networks and distributed data bases is in effect influencing a trend toward decentralized organizational structures.

The factor that is becoming centrally important in determining how computers redistribute power is *access* to computer data and understanding of what can be done with computerized information systems. This is not quite the same thing as ownership of a computer. There probably was a time when ownership of a computer center conferred a certain amount of authority and prestige to its owner; for example, a government department that ran a computer center could formulate plans and influence decisions because it had sole access to special expertise. But with the great increase in the number of computers, the emergence of computer utilities, and the growth of minicomputers and time sharing, there are no marked advantages to be had from owning hardware. (There may, in fact, be some disadvantages because it is more difficult to adapt to new technology.) What benefits there are from computers, are derived from building up data bases along with systems and routines for extracting and processing the data, preparing reports and plans, and being able to present the results effectively.

Many in the industry feel that, to maintain a balance of power, computers must be made easily accessible not only to governments and large organizations, but to small unstructured groups and to individuals as well. But it is not enough to place a computer at the disposal of a community group, a body of students, or a citizens' action committee. If the computer is to be used for a purpose other than routine accounting and data processing, it is necessary to build up software and especially large data bases on broad subjects such as housing, recreational facilities, zoning by-laws, and employment registries. Systems of this type are not only expensive, but are also close to the limit of present-day technical capability, especially if they are expected to respond to general queries in a language close to English, a desirable feature if they are to be used by untrained persons.

The most interesting possibilities for broadening the accessibility to computer-based systems are anticipated from developments in cable TV and computer communications. It is technically feasible to have terminals that can accept data from the home and be switched to different receiving centers. Based on this, a great many specialized services could be provided in the home-message exchange: shopping; meter reading; computer-assisted instruction; participation in surveys, debates, voting, etc. The home terminal would act as a localized access point to service centers and to information centers such as schools and libraries. At the same time, the system would augment and extend the functions of establishing contacts between groups and disseminating ideas and proposals, functions now carried out to a large extent by newspapers, radio, and commercial TV.

How multiple-purpose, two-way computer communications will evolve, depends among other things on economic considerations of whether a fair rate structure will be offered to users, manufacturers, purveyors of services, and to the general public. If the systems can be even partly realized, they could introduce a new major technological force for change in society. Some have expressed concern about the instabilities that might result if too rapid a response rate were built into the political system. If it were easy to conduct nationwide polls, what effect would this have when legislation on the elimination of capital punishment was being considered? Elected politicians have dual roles: They are expected to act in accord with the wishes of their electorates, but they are also supposedly chosen to represent their constituency in accord with their judgment and experience, which requires them to vote on issues after carefully weighing all the relevant arguments.

The question of political responsiveness is another illustration of the employment and privacy quandary. Computers, in common with other major technological developments have the effect of heightening certain issues that confront society. In some cases (e.g., centralization versus decentralization), computers can probably be used with equal effect to achieve either of two opposing goals. In other cases (e.g., employment), if it is desired to realize the economic benefits of using computers, the secondary effects are less manageable. In all of the many places where computers affect issues, technological changes are forcing reexamination of values and goals. The success in resolving the issues will be dependent on the success in integrating value conflicts.


REFERENCES

1950. Wiener, Norbert. *The Human Use of Human Beings.* Boston: Houghton Mifflin.

1968. International Labour Office. *Labour and Automation,* Bull.7. Geneva.

1971. Westin, A. (Ed.). *Information Technology in a Democracy.* Cambridge, Mass.: Harvard University Press.

1972. National Academy of Sciences. *Data Banks in a Free Society.* New York: Quadrangle Books.

1973. Gotlieb, C. C., and A. Borodin. *Social Issues in Computing.* New York: Academic Press.

1973. Parkman, R. *The Cybernetic Society.* New York: Pergamon.

1973. U.S. Department of Health, Education, and Welfare, Secretary's Advisory Committee on Automated Personal Data Systems. *Records, Computers, and the Rights of Citizens,* DHEW Publ. No. (05). Washington, D.C.: U.S. Government Superintendent of Documents, pp. 73–94.


C. C. GOTLIEB

# COMPUTING CENTER

For articles on related subjects *see* APPLICATIONS PROGRAMMING; DATA PROCESSING; DATA SECURITY; OPEN SHOP; OPERATING SYSTEMS; PROCESSING MODES; PROGRAM LIBRARIES; SECURITY OF COMPUTER INSTALLATIONS, PHYSICAL; SERVICE BUREAUS, DATA PROCESSING; and SYSTEMS PROGRAMMING.

For articles on related terms *see* ADMINISTRATIVE-BUSINESS APPLICATIONS; FILES; MULTIPROGRAMMING; and SPOOLING.

A computing center provides computer services to a variety of users through the operation of computer and auxiliary hardware, and through ancillary services provided by its staff. A not-for-profit service center usually provides such services *at cost* to its *users*; but a for-profit center does so with the intention, at least, of making a profit from providing services to its *customers.* Since there is little distinction between the two centers other than pricing and the label used for the consumers of their services, we will deal with the computing center as a service center with users.

**Services.** The extent to which the users participate in the operation of the center determines its staffing and organization. At one extreme is the completely *closed shop,* wherein the users supply only the initial specifications for the computations to be carried out or the reports to be provided. Thereafter, they supply only the new data and/or current information used to bring files up to date and satisfy requests to supply computed output or reports according to those specifications. This closed-shop organization requires that all skills and equipment required to provide its services be supplied by the computing center.

At the other extreme is the completely *open shop,* wherein the users supply the initial specifications, convert them into computer programs, supply the current information, convert it into machine-readable form, and operate the computer to obtain the desired results. This arrangement requires only that the computing center supply the computer, the manuals on how to use it, some supplies, and heat and light. Most centers today are nearer the former than the latter, but many maintain closed-shop machine operation while providing both open- and closed-shop programming, as mentioned below.

Fundamentally, there are three services provided by a computing center, each usually offered with some degree of open-shop organization. The most obvious service is *machine operation.* This skill is not learned in a few minutes for any computer, and is acquired only after lengthy training on large sophisticated machines. For this and a variety of other reasons, as explained later, all but the smallest computing centers offer only closed-shop machine operation for the majority of their operating hours. Some provide open-shop (or partial open shop) operation during restricted hours or on weekends, but these are in the clear minority.

Perhaps the next most obvious service required is *programming and system analysis.* This service is most easily and conveniently provided on both an open- and closed-shop basis. Those users who wish to do their own analyses or write their own programs may do so, and those who wish to have them designed and written by the computing center staff (and can afford to pay for this service) may also be satisfied. Since (from the computing center's point of view) there are two kinds of programming, those services are usually divided into two departments: systems programming and applications programming.

The least obvious service provided is that of data control, scheduling, and quality control. This service deals with the inspection of the incoming information for completeness and timeliness, with scheduling the machine operation for applications whose current information and files are ready for processing, and with inspection and dispatching of output reports and updated files from applications that have been processed.

MACHINE OPERATION. In the smallest computing centers, or otherwise in those which provide the greatest degree of open-shop programming, open-shop machine operation is fairly common. Frequently, a machine operator is available to run the machine for some applications, to train prospective open-shop operators, and to assist with the machine operation of some aspects of other applications. Almost inevitably, however, as the work load of the center increases, open-shop machine operation is the first service to be restricted or eliminated.

One of the most compelling reasons for a restriction in open-shop operation is the security of the data files. As long as data files are small or easily replaced, little attention needs to be paid to their security. When files become large enough to be stored on some medium that must be kept at the computing center, however, the possibility that they could be destroyed or inspected (either inadvertently or deliberately) by another user arises. To the extent that either of the above is undesirable or costly, the cost of closed-shop operation can (and almost always does) become more attractive to the center owners.

As might be expected, open-shop operation frequently gives rise to inefficient use of the computer. In a new installation where there are not sufficient applications yet programmed, such inefficiency is of no particular moment. However, even if file security does not materialize as a problem, inefficient use of the computer may compel the introduction of closed-shop operation to escape the alternative requirement of a faster machine. In such cases the cost of operators is almost always the much more attractive alternative.

Machine operation varies in the amount of skill required, from nominal on small machines with simple or nonexistent operating systems to very substantial on large, fast machines with sophisticated operating systems. Since the operating system is supposed to speed up operation of the machine by providing a smooth transition from one application to the next (called "job-to-job transition"), operators must be trained in the language and procedures of the operating system.

The operating system and the operator must communicate about the running of some applications. This is accomplished via the operator's console, usually a display screen with a keyboard or a typewriter (most commonly the latter). The operating system sends messages to the computer, indicating operator intervention is required. For example, if the card reader jams or tears a card, thus inhibiting its action, it usually indicates a "turned-off" state to the operating system when the system issues a request to read a card. Upon noting the card reader in a turned-off state (either due to a jam or a partial power failure, or whatever), the operating system would issue a message to the operator, indicating the condition. Once the problem had been cleared, the operator would need to know what characters should be keyed into the console to indicate the back-to-normal condition.

Of course, in very simple computers, the communication is much more simple-minded. The computer issues the request to read a card and then just waits until the information is transmitted. If the card reader is jammed or turned off, then everything comes to a standstill until the problem is rectified. The difficulty with this situation is that some training is required for the operator to notice that the machine is waiting longer than usual for some operation, and then to know where to look to find out what it is waiting for, and finally how to fix it. Since the largest and fastest machines can perform millions of operations per second, their operating systems will typically be designed to note the fault, issue a message to the operator, and carry on with whatever can be done without the use of the faulty component.

SYSTEMS PROGRAMMING. Systems programming deals with the writing and maintenance of programs that are part of the computer operating system. The amount of systems programming skill required in a computing center is dependent probably as much on its management philosophy as on its size (an obvious factor). Most general-purpose computers are made available by their manufacturers complete with operating systems. The earliest machines had none or only very rudimentary operating systems, whereas modern machines have very sophisticated operating systems. These operating systems (or just systems) are designed for use by a typical installation and provide for installation-set parameters to be varied to meet a given installation's needs.

For example, one parameter in most operating systems is the number of files that will be maintained on permanent mass-storage media (e.g., rotating magnetic disks). This parameter is important because space must be allocated to catalog all the attributes of each file (such as its name and number of records it contains). Since these are permanent files, these names must be stored somewhere for ready access by the operating system. It will not do, for instance, to store the catalog of file names on a tape that the operator must fetch and mount every time one of these files is referred to or altered. On the contrary, this catalog (often called the "file name table") must be kept in main memory or on a mass-storage device. The point is that some large installations with very large numbers of files will have to allocate much space to store file-name tables, whereas a small installation will not wish to tie up a lot of valuable space for only a small file-name table.

Many such installation parameters are set to help tailor the operating system to fit a variety of needs. Often, however, the operating system, even with all of its parameters set, still falls short of the installation's needs. The usual case is that it can meet most needs, but meets some critical need only marginally or with low efficiency. For example, a computing center whose purpose is to run applications that simulate nuclear reactors will typically run a few very long jobs (on the order of hours of running time each) in a day. On the other hand, a programming school might run a very large number of very small jobs (each taking only a second or two to run). Even with a well-designed operating system, its machine accounting functions (to keep track of which jobs used what amounts of computer time) are unlikely to be adequate for both installations. In such a case the installation management must decide between the costs of inadequate or inefficient operating system performance in the accounting area, and the costs of systems programming talent to modify the operating system to meet its specific needs.

This decision is not nearly as simple to make as it seems on the surface. Since the computer manufacturer provides the operating system with the computer, and since such systems are made up of very sophisticated programs (even for relatively rudimentary systems), they are almost never fully debugged. Accordingly, the manufacturer provides software support (or operating system maintenance) to fix the bugs as they crop up.

Since the manufacturer has a support group of systems programmers, he is the target of many requests for improvements and enhancements to parts of the system that perform their published tasks properly. These requests for improvements come from the installations using the equipment and from the manufacturer's own sales organization, which recognizes that it could sell more machines if the operating system had more or better capability in certain areas. Regardless, if an installation does not make any changes in the operating system it receives from the manufacturer, it can expect a much more sympathetic hearing if the system supposedly fails to perform in some area. Just as in manufactured goods, the manufacturer feels much less compelled to support a device that has been "tampered" with (even by competent people) than he would for one that is still in its delivery state.

Principally for this reason, systems programming tends to be an all-or-nothing proposition. Either a shop has no systems programming talent or it has enough to become completely familiar with and substantially provide overall support for its operating systems.

The argument for no systems programming talent is that the costs of inefficiency or incapacity in some areas are less than the costs of learning about and maintaining an operating system. The opposite point of view is that if the operating system needs work that the manufacturer is not inclined to supply, then work on many marginal areas may as well be done too. This is usually the policy of the larger shops with specialized work loads not encountered by most users of the equipment. Systems programming, because of the relatively high level of sophistication of the programs, is usually staffed with the more experienced programmers. For this reason the systems programming function often serves as a consulting function to the applications programming staff, as well as performing the functions mentioned above.

APPLICATIONS PROGRAMMING. Applications programming is concerned with the writing and maintenance of programs that accept as input the information supplied by the users and possibly combine it with information on file to produce output for the user. In that context, applications programming is at the heart of the purpose of a computing center: making machines do what people want. As mentioned above, this service is the one most likely to be a mixture of open and closed shop. In a bank, for example, it is very likely to be a closed-shop function. The people for whom reports will be written will not be expected to have much programming proficiency. In an engineering or research department or at a university, however, frequently the users will have had computer programming training. This, combined with the nature of the reports, often results in more open-shop programming in the latter than in the former.

Frequently, the nature of the output is all-important, however, and mandates a closed-shop approach. For example, a report to be prepared for reading by many users on the basis of data submitted by many users will not usually be a good candidate for open-shop programming. Such a report should probably be programmed by some central function (such as the computing center) with the needs and interests of all users in mind. On the other hand, a program to calculate some pump-flow rates for the only piping engineer in the department would probably be a good candidate to be written under open-shop programming conditions. In that case, since the engineer would likely be the only user, the instructions on how to prepare the input data might never be formalized (i.e., documented), a frequent result in open-shop programming environments.

Sometimes, the nature of the programming itself dictates the need for an open or closed-shop applications programming approach. Simple programs usually have still simpler specifications. Often, however, very complex experimental procedures, for example, can be specified only to the extent that they can be coded into programs. In such cases, especially when the procedures are not well defined, the trained user himself can code the programs about as easily as he can specify exactly what must be done. In that case, one whole step—fraught with communications problems and potential errors—can be eliminated from the programming process by using an open-shop arrangement.

Data Control, Quality Control and Scheduling. Once again, the extent of this service is determined by the extent of open-shop practices at the installation. Clearly, in a fully open-shop (programming and operating) arrangement, users will provide their own data, validate and control it themselves, schedule their use of the machine to coincide with the availability of the latest data, and check their own reports. In that case, no service of this sort needs to be offered by the computing center. On the other hand, in a fully closed shop, a great deal of data handling prior to the production run will often be required. Thereafter, if the reporting system is complex, or if many reports are routed to several destinations, staff must be provided by the computing center to handle all those chores.

For example, in an application where man-hours are accumulated and posted for a department each week, somebody has to verify that each man submitted a time card. All the time cards must be checked to see that employee numbers are correct, that legitimate charge numbers were used, and that the hours charged are reasonable. Some of this checking can be done using computer programs that compare those numbers to sets of numbers on file. But that does not verify that a man used the correct numbers, only that he used legitimate numbers —numbers that are permissible to use. Some parts of the checking are best done in the department. For instance, in a department with large fluctuations in manpower, somebody familiar with everyone present might most efficiently check that a time card was collected from each man.

Keeping track of what has been received and processed by the computing center can be done only by the computing center staff. This service may be divided into two categories: checking that the center processes all the data it receives and checking that it receives all the data sent by the using department. Obviously, it will do little good to check that every man in a department submits a time card if the computing center cannot determine if it got all the time cards. Accordingly, much of the checking about amounts of data is handled by both the user and by the computing center. Then, before a production run is made, either on a special or periodic schedule, the user and computing center reconcile their separate control records to be sure there is agreement. Frequently, for example, in an application such as the time-card system, both the center and the user keep a written record with batch numbers, numbers of time cards, and total man-hours in each batch. The user counts the cards and totals the hours manually before sending the time cards to the computing center for processing. Upon receipt of the cards, the computing center punches the information into tab cards or some other machine-readable form. Such recording equipment sometimes accumulates card counts and total hours as the data is recorded. More commonly, a special computer program is used to read each batch of time cards, count the number of entries, total the hours, and verify that legitimate numbers are used, etc. Inspection of the counts and totals verifies (or contradicts) the manual counts and totals sent by the user. Once these are reconciled, the production run can be made.

Concern that all the information received is properly processed lies exclusively with the computing center. Typically, when each batch is added to the master file, a report is generated to display the total number of entries and total number of hours (using again the preceding example) on file at the start of the run, added as a result of the run, and on file at the end of the run. In addition to file-labeling and checking by the programs, a manual record is frequently kept to show counts and totals before and after every run made to add time cards to the file. In that way, in the case of reruns, when file-label checking sometimes needs to be bypassed, files can still be checked for completeness. Curiously, one of the biggest headaches in the data control area is not in making sure that all data has been added to the file, but that it has not been added more than once. This occurs most frequently when a file is updated with bad information, requiring a rerun.

Since the references in all the programs are to the latest file when one is updated, care must be taken in the case of a rerun to update the second-from-latest file. Further care must be taken to destroy the former latest file so it will not be confused with the one produced by the rerun. Every installation manager has aged visibly when, while walking through the machine room in such a situation involving novice operators, he sees two files, both labeled "latest." For these reasons, several generations of files are kept on hand at all times: the latest, the one before that (from which the latest was made), the one before that, and so on. Typically, four such copies are kept as backup to the latest file, but fewer are kept in applications not prone to error, and more are kept (up to six or eight) on applications subject to high error rates or many updates in a short time period. The shorter the period, the more backups are required. For example, three update runs, all in the same shift, all performed by the same operator may be handled incorrectly. If all the backups were created using the same bad technique, the file would be in danger of being wiped out (destroyed or rendered useless for purposes of making an update run).

Notice that each time a file is brought up to date (or updated), an entirely new copy of the file is made, in which the new information has been added. At the end of such an update run, the old file is intact, exactly as it was prior to the run, and the new copy contains everything from the preceding file plus all the new material. On the surface, this may seem extravagant, especially when compared to manual file maintenance. Imagine the cost to copy an entire file of letters everytime a new one was added to the file! But it would certainly insure that there would be adequate copies of the correspondence.

In computing, the cost of updating is nearly negligible by contrast. If the file is kept on tape, for example, a new copy can be made as each record is read, in substantially the same time as that required to simply read the file. Since there are always at least two tape drives available, the updated tape can contain a copy of the preceding generation of the file at substantially zero cost. This technique insures against operator, equipment, and program failure, since it allows for reproducibility of any update run. All that is needed to re-create any edition (or generation) of the file is the previous edition and the new material that was added. Contrast that with the case where the new edition is created by reading the old edition up to the end and then adding the new material to the end of the old file, thus making it the new one. Such a practice is not reproducible because the "end" of the old information is no longer identifiable. Accepted practice is to keep enough previous generations of files on hand so that any operator, equipment, or program error can be detected and corrected (by running the reproducible run that re-creates the faulty generation), all before either the backup or current information is discarded.

Occasionally, of course, errors are not detected in time, especially programming errors that introduce subtle errors into the files at each update. In such cases, files need to be regenerated from scratch. For this reason, current data is often stored for very long periods of times. Such a practice is called "archiving," wherein either the cards themselves, microfilm images, or separate files on magnetic tape are stored in case it is necessary to go back to a version of the file beyond the usual backup period. To reduce the incidence of having to regenerate a file from scratch, sometimes year-end or quarter-end copies are stored separate from the usual backups. In addition, hard-copy reports are sometimes used as a starting point in the case where all file information is destroyed. At any rate, even though the data control function is supposed to keep these problems from occurring in the first place, it must be aware of how best to detect and recoup any foul-ups well before the last good copy of the file is retired.

**Kinds of Computing Centers.** Computing centers provide service to a variety of constituents, using a variety of equipment and personnel configurations. We have already seen that the degree to which open-shop practice is allowed determines to a large extent the amount and kinds of services supplied by a center. The character of the work load also determines what levels of which services must be provided, but to a relatively smaller extent than the degree of open-shop practice. Some work loads lend themselves much more easily to a high degree of open shop than do others. Principally, computing work load (and hence the installations that cater to them) can be categorized into two categories: batch (including remote job entry) and time sharing. Historically, the first general-purpose computers were batch machines. In that kind of computing, jobs are processed in serial fashion, one after the other. Each job has exclusive use of the computer and all its peripheral devices (card reader, punch, magnetic-tape drives, disk drives, etc.) during the time it is being executed.

Until the mid-1960s, batch was by far the most common arrangement. But even the most casual observer will note that a batch arrangement makes very inefficient use of some resources most of the time. Consider, for example, the small job consisting of a program and some data on cards that produce a report on the printer, which is simply an exact listing of the information in the cards. Such a program is called a "card-to-print program," and if it is generalized to provide headings and optional spacing and other information, it is called a "card-to-print utility." At any rate, such a program does not use either tape or disk storage equipment. If the listing is short, of course, storage is not of much consequence, but if the listing is long, the tape and disk equipment are wasted for a long period of time. Similarly, the main memory of most machines is much larger and much faster than required for a card-to-print application, and presumably the arithmetic unit would be used only for counting line spacing, for page numbering, etc. Therefore, as faster computers were installed, ways had to be found to improve the efficiency of the computer use.

One fairly early solution was tape-oriented batch systems with two computers: the main computer and a smaller machine. All tape drives in such a system are wired to the main computer. At least one, and sometimes two, of them are also switchable to the smaller machine, to which the card reader, punch, and printer are also attached. Input jobs are loaded onto tape by the smaller machine from cards. The tape is then rewound and switched to the main computer, which is programmed to read that tape for all card input. Another tape drive is used by the main machine to write out all output destined for the printer and the card punch. After a batch of jobs has been run, that output tape is rewound and switched to the smaller machine to be read and listed and/or punched. Using this technique, processing times on the main computer are speeded up, but time is required to load a batch of jobs to tape. Of course, the first job cannot be started until the last job is loaded on and the tape rewound and switched to the main computer.

This apparent paradox of a reduction in service (i.e., longer turnaround) with faster processing led to a search for a solution that allowed the latter without the penalty of the former. A number of schemes were developed, including the use of common disk files and two computers hooked together so that one could stoke the other's memory directly (called variously "direct-coupled systems" and "attached support processors"). These methods preserved the batch nature of a main machine and improved both efficiency and turnaround by providing faster transfer of information in and out of the main computer and by reducing the waiting time of information in the input and output streams. But the main computer efficiency was still low, and turnaround far from the instantaneous ideal. With a great deal of oversimplification, what was needed was a main computer that had a large enough memory to hold several jobs, and enough random access mass storage to hold files for all those jobs being processed, including one holding card input and printer output for each job.

Some overhead in switching from job to job is required, of course, and the operating system must be much more sophisticated if it is to keep track of what portions of memory are in use and by what jobs (especially since jobs are finishing and new ones starting all the time), and what files are in use in what positions and by what jobs. This arrangement might be referred to as a sort of simultaneous batch, but it is called "multiprogramming" (more than one program in execution at once), in fact. Although computer efficiency is greatly improved, turnaround is still far from instantaneous. Since there are only a few card readers and printers on such systems, and since it is desirable to have input and output on disk or tape whenever possible (so it can be read and written faster), a job cannot be a candidate to start until all of it is on disk, nor can its output be started on the printer until all of it has been written out to the output file (called the "output queue"). If there were many input/output devices, one could be associated with each job. Then the execution of that job could be carried out piecemeal as the input was available and as any output could be printed. In this arrangement, with typewriter-like devices for input and output, we have time sharing.

**Kinds of Computing Center Applications.** Early in the history of computing, and until about the mid-1960s, computers tended to be more specialized in the kinds of applications they could handle. Some of those machines were designed and built to meet the needs of commercial and industrial accounting and record keeping. These applications require fast, reliable input-output devices of large capacity but with relatively small main memory and unsophisticated arithmetic capability. Records are usually processed sequentially one at a time, as when writing paychecks for one man after another. In contrast, for engineering and scientific problem solving, machines were developed with an emphasis on their arithmetic units rather than on their input-output devices. In fact, since most scientific problems used relatively small amounts of data and produced limited amounts of output—but required extensive main memory space to store both the relatively large number of programmed instructions and all the intermediate numbers in the calculation—such machines were normally equipped with the slower (and therefore less expensive) input-output devices.

Until the mid-1960s, the two kinds of machines were much more distinct than today's machines. Scientific machines were characterized by slow peripheral equipment, large memories, and sophisticated arithmetic instruction sets. Their arithmetic instructions often included floating-point instructions, a feature almost never required in accounting and record keeping because answers need be computed only to the nearest cent. Commercial machines, on the other hand, were characterized by relatively limited instruction sets.

Accordingly, computing centers tended to be divided along the same lines. Programming and operating staff who understood the need of commercial users for fast reliable access to large files of information were required for the commerical or data processing centers; and technically trained programming staff who could converse with and understand the requirements of engineers and scientists were required for the scientific and university centers. In recent years, however, an increasing need by scientists and engineers for exceptional amounts of very high speed calculations has coincided with the expansion by the commercial users into much more sophisticated record keeping (involving a greater need for better arithmetic performance) and an increasing requirement by the engineers and scientists in their applications for large amounts of data, particularly input data. Thus, the distinction between what was known as scientific computing and administrative data processing has become blurred. The result is that the machines of today

**Fig. 1.** Computer room at Computing Center, State University of New York at Buffalo, showing parts of Control Data 6400 computer used for education and research computing, and also the UNIVAC 1106 computer used for administrative data processing.

need many fast, reliable peripheral devices with plenty of mass storage and main computers with large memory capacity and sophisticated instruction sets.

Floating-point instructions are available as an option on almost all machines, memory can be added in incremental banks of a few thousand words, and peripheral devices with a wide range of speeds and capacities can be attached. Accordingly, computing centers are becoming more diversified, although many of the specialty shops still exist, especially for the commercial users. In a large firm, for example, where an early machine installed for record keeping in the early 1960s was found to be inadequate to meet the increasing computing needs of the engineering and research departments after about the mid-1960s, it was likely to be replaced with a machine suitable for both kinds of applications. Thus, new equipment can be configured to meet present and anticipated needs, through modular design and flexible financing, and configurations can be kept constantly in flux, changing to meet current needs. With this increasing flexibility in the equipment, many computing centers are also amply staffed to meet the needs of their users.

**Physical Characteristics.** Depending on the amounts and kinds of services provided, a typical computing center consists of a computer room (or machine room), a data preparation/dispatching area, a file-storage area, and offices for the personnel arranged in some logical manner. The machine room is about a third of the space (with wide variations between installations), and usually has a raised (or false) floor. This floor, usually tiled with 2 by 2 ft panels, rests on 8–14 inch pedestals above the main slab. Air conditioning and heating ducts force air under these panels, and power and control cables are also housed there. The (usually) cooled air and the cables come up through holes cut in the panels, often under the equipment modules, thus allowing each module to stand free of encumbrance by cabling or ductwork. In large systems, chilled-water piping is also housed under the panels and is hooked to the equipment through similar holes in the panels.

The machine room is usually heated and cooled, using equipment that is separated from all other areas of the center. This is done primarily because of the control nightmare that is generated by heat produced by the equipment, and also as a fire safety measure. Even in moderately cold climates, more heat is produced by the equipment in a computer room than is needed to keep the room at a comfortable temperature. Humidity also must be regulated much more rigidly for reliable operation of the machine than is required for human comfort. Usually, the absolute values of temperature and humidity are not nearly as important to regulate as are their fluctuations from one side of the machine to the other. Once set in the human comfort zone, tolerances are relatively narrow, and are typically narrower for larger machines than for smaller ones. As computers are made faster and their components become smaller, the heat-dissipation problem stays about the same. The faster equipment requires narrower tolerances because of the increasing importance of timing electronic speeds in conductors at certain temperatures; the smaller components produce less heat and require shorter wires to connect them, but this does not mitigate the problem.

The data preparation/dispatching area varies from a front counter in the input-output clerk's office, in a small installation, to several rooms in a large organization for input preparation of data, keypunching, file checking and scheduling of input; and for rows, bins, and counters for dispatching output, checking updated files, and preparing the files for storage. The file-storage area is usually separated from the machine room, for security and fire protection, but is close to the equipment with which it is used (tape storage near the tape drives; disk-pack storage near disk drives, etc.).

**Pricing.** Pricing of computing services in the early days of computing was a relatively easy task. Each job required exclusive use of the entire main processor and all peripheral equipment for a certain length of time. Virtually every job ran in exactly the same length of time if rerun with the same data. Managers simply divided total costs plus margin for a period by the number of production hours they could expect to run the machine during that period. This calculation produced a rate in dollars per hour of running time, one that appeared fair to the user because it was reproducible and he could control the running time by varying the amount of data he submitted and by specifying (or writing) programs that were more or less efficient in processing those amounts of data. Program and system development could also be fairly easily priced in dollars per man-hour for various levels of talent. Until the advent of time sharing and multiprogramming, pricing was one aspect of computing that was a fairly conventional procedure. Many other types of services were subject to the same pricing criteria. For example, printing is much like computing in that regard. The user can control the price of his work by controlling the quality of paper used, the number of copies to be made, and by using or avoiding special ink colors, etc., but he cannot control the speed or width of the printing press. If a press runs at 100 copies per minute and is 10 inches wide, he may not expect a reduction in price if his copy is only 8½ inches wide. Similarly, a computer user may not have required all available memory to run his job, but since he required exclusive use of the computer facility, the supplier's costs were not decreased.

When time sharing and multiprogramming became available, however, the user could expect that any memory not needed by his program might reasonably be sold to another customer. Hence, pricing in many centers has been subject to a great deal of controversy. The problem in multiprogramming arrangements is complicated by the fact that many measures of usage are not reproducible. For example, if a job writes a disk file, in some multiprogrammed systems the file may be written in either a large number of small blocks or a smaller number of large blocks, depending on how busy the system is (how much space is available for accumulation of large blocks, and how busy the disk storage device is). Therefore, as a result of the variability in the size of blocks that are accumulated before writing, the job can use a variable amount of computing time between writing each block. This, in turn, determines the amount of time the job spends taking up memory. The job may run in, say, 1 minute on an otherwise empty machine, and use 3 seconds of processor time during that minute (the rest being taken up by the writing out of the information on the disk file).

In a busy machine two effects are noticeable: There is less space for large blocks, so more time is spent writing a larger number of the smaller blocks; and the processor does not switch back to a particular job with any predictable regularity, since there is virtually no way to control whatever other jobs are running concurrently. The effect of both is to extend the amount of time that the job spends in main memory to perhaps 5 or 10 minutes. It still requires the same 3 seconds of processor time (because it still does exactly the steps it did before), but now they are spread over, say, 5 minutes. That is five times as long as it would take on an otherwise idle machine. In the case of pricing based on usage, this job should cost more when run on a busy machine (because it ties up memory and disk-file space longer, requires more overhead to write more blocks, and uses more overhead because it uses the processor more often, due to the reduced block sizes). In the case of pricing based on service, this job should cost less because the turnaround time is worse.

Computing centers that are service centers (as opposed to profit centers) price their services on the basis of either service or cost. Few of the special arguments that apply to computing are not applicable to many other services within a corporate, university, or government environment. There is a paradoxical apparent simplicity but persistent overruns (with even the most competent staff) require extra attention, no matter what the pricing scheme, to insure that the processing that can be handled most profitably by the computer is what is processed. For example, if the service center that is newly installed must recover all costs from services rendered, it would have a high rate and an under utilized system. The well-heeled departments could use its services, but those not so well off (and who might be able to use the machine more profitably) could not afford the rates. The computer would be standing idle part of the time, and departments (which could use it to produce considerably more return than the incremental cost to have it running) would be doing without it. On the other hand, a computing center whose costs are fully absorbed into overhead, will be processing the unpopular chores for user departments (not necessarily the profitable ones). Since the users cannot control the costs of computing, they might as well have the computing center do whatever work the using department would like to farm out. As in any service, either pricing method has its drawbacks. The problem is further complicated by the difficulty in allocating costs in multiprogrammed and time-sharing systems. The services are a little easier to identify, but much harder to price. All things considered, computing center pricing presents about the same problem as that of any centralized service.

C. L. MEEK

## COMPUTING ECONOMICS: ACQUISITION AND OPERATION

For articles on related subjects *see* ADMINISTRATIVE-BUSINESS APPLICATIONS; COMPUTER ACCOUNTING AND RESOURCE CONTROL; COMPUTING CENTER; GROSCH'S LAW; HARDWARE MONITOR; and PERFORMANCE MEASUREMENT AND EVALUATION.

For articles on related terms *see* BENCHMARK; FEASIBILITY STUDY; THROUGHPUT; and TURNAROUND TIME.

**Introduction of Computers in Organizations.** Computers do not interface readily with the economic and managerial structure of an organization. Originally, computers were brought in to solve specific technological or organizational problems. For instance, accounting departments used them for payroll operations. Research and development departments used them for scientific calculations. Finally, they were utilized on production lines for process control. In this environment it is relatively easy to introduce a computer. A particular well-defined problem needs solution, and if the computer can provide a better solution than was previously available, then it is perfectly acceptable.

Advances in hardware technology and software systems have had a tremendous impact, not only on the numbers of computers used, but also on the manner in which they are used. Man-machine communication has become easier. Complex computer systems can be utilized by the end-users without the intervention of computer specialists. Typical examples are airline reservation systems, where the clerks interrogate the computer directly; or inventory control systems, which often bring the computer into direct contact with the salesman. In these cases computers are not introduced to solve a specific well-defined problem, but rather to improve the way an organization functions. As a result, computers affect the basic structure and principles of an organization.

Most organizations have vast amounts of data. To a large extent, data handling was previously considered to be secondary to people, money, and products in an organization, but the data in modern organizations has increased so much in quantity and complexity that it currently represents a major asset and problem. Data manipulation and information flow are critical in the management of an organization. Computers play a key role in storing, retrieving, and manipulating pertinent data, and therefore they are essential in the operation of the organization.

Computers should be introduced with special care, since they can considerably alter the information flow and decision-making process. Feasibility and systems studies are required before even deciding to install a computer, and these studies should consider first the most important problems of the company. Computers should not be used to implement current policies and organization. A new structure of the company is sometimes needed, not to accommodate the peculiarities of computers, but rather to increase their effectiveness and to help achieve the goals of the organization. In fact, the introduction of computers is used sometimes as an excuse to effect far-reaching changes in the organization of a company.

**Acquisition.** After the decision is reached to introduce computers, there are many alternatives to consider. First, there is the choice between using a service bureau or obtaining one's own equipment. If the organization acquires its own computer, then there is a choice of leasing, renting, or buying the system. The organization can operate the computer itself, or it can have an independent company manage the installation. It is very difficult to decide which option best suits the needs of the organization. Some considerations are economic (Sharpe, 1969). In addition, there are many related factors such as level of support, manufacturer's reputation, local dealership, and available software.

The hardware must be evaluated in relation to the organization's needs. A processor cannot be chosen on its own merits, but must be selected for its compatibility and efficiency in the whole computer system with all attached peripherals. The processor speed can be estimated using instruction mixes, kernel programs, benchmarks, and synthetic programs (Sharpe, 1969). However, most of the expense in a standard installation is in the peripheral devices. Their performance with respect to the system must be established. There is usually a choice of acquiring peripheral devices and storage modules from the CPU manufacturer or from independent manufacturers. Site preparation (e.g., buildings) should not be overlooked; it can be as expensive as the computer hardware.

An organization acquires a computer to provide some services in a cost-effective manner. The hardware does not give these services directly. Most of the services are implemented by complicated software, such as operating systems, data base management systems, and applications systems. Hence, the organization should be extremely interested in the software that the system provides. Very often, computer manufacturers provide software free, or for a standard fee. In addition, many independent software companies sell their own software separately. The user may choose to develop his own software, but such a decision should be made carefully, since software is very expensive to build and to maintain.

The acquisition problem is getting increasingly difficult. It is not a question of choosing a particular machine, nor is it solely a question of buying the fastest machine per dollar. Rather, it is to provide a combined hardware and software system that best suits the organization because it provides the needed services in a cost-effective manner. Even after the equipment is installed, new requirements for additional equipment and special software continually arise. In a typical installation the budget is allocated as follows: 25% hardware, 20% software, 25% personnel, 10% supplies, and 10% site maintenance, with a 10% contingency allowance for constantly rising software and personnel costs.

The investment in a computer installation is of such magnitude that the system should be allowed to evolve. The old approach of scrapping the old system and buying a new one is becoming less feasible with time, mainly because of software conversion costs. In addition, the cost of organizational upheaval caused by conversion can be prohibitive. For these reasons, evolution of systems is likely to prevail in the future.

**Performance Monitoring.** There are three main measures of system performance. First, *throughput* measures the amount of work that the system can perform. Second, *turnaround time* measures the amount of elapsed time for a job to go through the system. Third, *availability* measures the portion of each day that a system can do useful work. These measures are user-oriented in that they relate to the amount and quality of service the user obtains from the computer system. There are other internal measures of efficiency that do not concern the user. These measures are tools to help technicians increase the effectiveness of the hardware and software facilities.

The most widely used tools for performance evaluation are hardware and software monitors. Monitors are used to collect a wide variety of data concerning a system's operation. Hardware monitors are units appended to the original system, and software monitors consist of small routines that are invoked in different parts of the system to take measurements. The data collected by monitors can be analyzed to estimate the system's effectiveness.

The problem of data reduction is considerable. Monitors provide vast amounts of data that have little meaning unless they are reduced and interpreted correctly. For that purpose a deep understanding is needed of the system's functions and organization. Theoretical models can provide some insight on what to measure and how to interpret the results of performance monitoring.

Performance monitoring provides the indicators that measure how effectively the system's resources are being used. These indicators can be used in two ways to increase the effectiveness of the system. First, the configuration of the system can be changed. That is, new equipment and/or programs are acquired and incorporated into the system to eliminate some of the problems detected by performance monitoring. Second, the load of user requests can be modified to better fit the available resources. One way to manipulate the load is to alter the price scale of services. The situation is analogous to any resource available in the economy. Economic indicators establish the state of the market. Then the rate of production is adjusted by manufacturers and the rate of consumption is controlled by pricing.

**Pricing.** Computers and their related facilities start out as free resources in most organizations. People are not accustomed to them and therefore need a strong incentive to use them. In universities they are often introduced as educational and research tools with large discounts. In companies they are included under general overhead expenditures.

Recently, people are becoming more accustomed to computers as man-machine communication becomes more flexible. This has led to an increased demand for computer-related resources. The demand for larger and better facilities is increasing at a faster rate than the price of hardware components is decreasing. As a result, computer systems are getting expensive, both to acquire and operate. Computer systems cannot, therefore, operate as a free resource. Their use and abuse will either force spiraling costs or require a set of arbitrary rules concerning their usage in an organization. It is better to control their use by pricing schemes.

There is no obvious scale by which computer users should be charged. They can be charged according to the basic resources they consume, such as processor time and memory space. Alternatively, they can be charged for services rendered, such as number of transactions processed. The quality of service, (e.g., fast turnaround) is also very important and may contribute to the cost. One of the main problems of any pricing scheme is balancing the work load. Users expect the same charge for the same computation. However, the amount of resources consumed during a computation may vary widely, depending on how busy the system is. For instance, a computation running during peak period will usually generate more overhead in the system than one running during an idle period. In addition, resources have inherently more value during peak periods, since more computations are competing to acquire them. The manager of the computer center must find a pricing scheme that discourages use during peak periods, but which does not lead to inflation of the price paid for a computation.

Ideally, one can think of a computer system as an environment completely controlled by pricing, as in a free-enterprise system. For instance, the compiler buys processor time and memory, and charges for cards compiled. Such an environment is probably undesirable, not to mention that the overhead incurred will be prohibitive. There are still some computations that have to be heavily subsidized. A typical case is computer time used for instruction in universities. The computer center itself needs resources to improve and maintain the computer facility. Nevertheless, computer facilities should be treated as scarce resources. They are both valuable and costly.

REFERENCES

1969. Sharpe, W. F. *The Economics of Computers*. New York: Columbia University Press.

1973. Gotlieb, C. C., and A. Borodin. *Some Issues in Computing*. New York: Academic Press.

D. TSICHRITZIS

# CONCATENATION

For article on related subject *see* STRING PROCESSING LANGUAGES.
For articles on related terms *see* FILES; and MACROINSTRUCTION.

Concatenation is an operation wherein a number of conceptually related components are linked together to form a larger, organizationally similar entity.

In the context of string processing, concatenation refers specifically to the synthesis of longer character strings from shorter ones. In PL/I, for example, the string concatenation operation is indicated by a double vertical bar (||) so that if W1 = 'CON', W2 = 'CAT', W3 = 'ION', then W4 = W1 || W2 || 'ENAT' || W3 is the title of this article. This kind of notation is generally used in higher-level languages.

Though still within the same general context of string construction, concatenation also is used to refer to a specific technique in defining macroinstructions, where a particular type of symbol may be a character string consisting of fixed and variable segments. When such a macroinstruction is used in a program, an appropriate string constant, given in the specifications, is concatenated with the fixed portion of the symbol during the macroexpansion process to form a complete syntactic component.

Within the general framework of files and file processing, concatenation refers to the operation of creating a collection of data by linking together several smaller collections. The resulting concatenated data set then can be processed as a single collection without relinquishing the individual identities of its components.

S. V. POLLACK AND T. E. STERLING

# CONDITIONING

For article on related subject *see* DATA COMMUNICATIONS: General Principles.

Conditioning is the term used to describe the improvements made in the signaling characteristics of leased telephone lines over those in the normal switched telephone network.

When a telephone connection is leased between two points, restrictions on the frequencies that can be transmitted over the switched network because of attenuation and related problems no longer apply. Since a leased line uses the *same path* continually, it is possible to put in special *equalizing filters* to insure that its attenuations and related parameters have much squarer wave characteristics than can be guaranteed on switched connections. It is this equalization that is called "conditioning." Standards are published of the characteristics the telephone company guarantees for lines to various degrees of conditioning (for which there is an extra charge). In such leased lines, it is also usual to have two pairs of connections to the nearest exchange (a so-called four-wire line) so that the full bandwidth can be used simultaneously in the two directions. Over the inter-exchange links, the conversations always go on different channels, but between the local exchange and the subscriber, the two directions of conversation share a normal switched telephone line.

Although the conditioning of a leased telephone line will considerably improve its characteristics, there will be time variations in the characteristics of the line. For this reason, the modems in high-performance data transmission systems will themselves add a further (variable) amount of equalization by use of adaptive digital filters. These enable (currently) switched telephone lines to be used at up to 4.8K bits per second (bps) and leased telephone lines at up to 9.6K bps. When higher speeds of data transmission are desired, it is possible to put in special lines that connect straight to the primary group in the telephone exchange and use 12 or more telephone channels. By these means, 48K Hz or even wider bandwidth can be used with appropriately high data rates of 50K bps or even higher.

P. T. KIRSTEIN

## CONFERENCE ON DATA SYSTEMS LANGUAGES (CODASYL)

For articles on related subjects *see* DATA BASE AND DATA BASE MANAGEMENT; PROCEDURE-ORIENTED LANGUAGES; and STANDARDS.

CODASYL is a volunteer organization consisting of professional computing personnel from the computing industry and from computing-systems user organizations. It was formed in 1958 to attempt to standardize the languages used in computer programs and thus to permit such programs to be "machine independent." Initially, it was the purpose of CODASYL to choose and "standardize" a common programming language from among the numerous "common programming languages" being promulgated at that time, mostly by computer hardware suppliers. A CODASYL task force, organized in 1958 to work on the technical aspects of this objective, found it impossible to achieve acceptance of any language as a standard and equally impossible to integrate features of one language with another. Therefore, this task force published a new common language in 1960, called Cobol (Common Business Oriented Language). Initially, the only suppliers to accept Cobol were UNIVAC and RCA. The U.S. Department of Defense, one of the original contributors to the "standardization" purpose and an organization with a candidate for the common language, Aimaco (Air Material Command Optimum), thereupon made Cobol mandatory for all suppliers of computing hardware and software who were bidding on defense procurements. This economic pressure resulted in persuading other suppliers to adopt Cobol also.

Experience gained with the initial language resulted in the publication of an improved version of Cobol in 1961. Another version, called "Cobol 61 Extended," was published in 1962, and additional features and enhancements have been added to the language almost every year since then. Cobol compilers were generally provided with all computer equipment from 1962 on. Cobol was adopted as an American standard by ANSI in 1968.

The CODASYL organization consists of: (1) an Executive Committee, (2) a Programming Languages Committee, and (3) a Systems Committee. The current CODASYL organization has evolved over the years from other organizational concepts that gave recognition to the separate interests of the hardware suppliers versus the users, as well as the short-range issues versus the long-range developments. As the Cobol language achieved acceptance, the disparity between the interests of the manufacturers of computers and the users of computers, which had to be recognized in the early existence of CODASYL, began to disappear, and the current organization evolved.

The Programming Languages Committee of CODASYL accepts comments and proposals for changes to Cobol from any competent source, reviews these proposals, modifies them, and publishes the resultant actions in a "periodic" Cobol *Journal of Development*, and approximately bi-annually publishes an updated version of the Cobol specifications.

Other CODASYL publications include "An Information Algebra," "Decision Tables (D-Tab)," and a "Data Base Task Group Report." The latter presents the features of various data base techniques and makes a comparison of the principal characteristics of each and the variance among them.

More recently, CODASYL has prepared specifications for a proposed concept of data base management and for language characteristics which would permit interaction with the data base management system from other programming languages such as Cobol, Fortran, and PL/I. Acceptance or finalization of both these principles will be time consuming, but when achieved they will presumably provide the same basis for standardization as the initial specifications for Cobol provided for standardization across a variety of then existing machine-oriented standard languages.

J. F. CUNNINGHAM

# CONSTANTS

For articles on related subjects *see* ARITHMETIC, COMPUTER; LABEL; NUMBERS AND NUMBER SYSTEMS; PROCEDURE-ORIENTED LANGUAGES; and PROGRAMMING LANGUAGES.

For articles on related terms *see* BOOLEAN ALGEBRA; and STRING.

In computing, a *constant* is a value in a calculation which remains unchanged during the calculation. There are a variety of different types of constants discussed in this article—numerical, character, logical, location, and figurative constants. While it is fundamental to many aspects of a computer's internal operation that the basic reference to an item of information is by its location or address, it is more convenient to refer to constants by their values, since these are intrinsically meaningful in an algorithm. Consequently, all higher-level languages and their translators are structured to allow the inclusion of actual values, specified directly in the program rather than being read by the program as data or produced by explicit computations. Whatever mechanisms may be required to reconcile these syntactic facilities with the processor's basic address orientation are embedded in the language translator, beyond the operating range of most users and therefore "invisible" to them.

The spectrum of items that may be expressed as direct literal values transcends the numerical quantities traditionally associated with the idea of a "constant." Depending on the scope and orientation of a particular language, a variety of nonnumeric constants also are recognized and handled. Some of these serve as data items, while others may provide operational information for the program.

**Numerical Constants.** In most instances the user need give little thought to the inclusion of numerical constants in higher-level language statements. For many languages, their specification closely resembles conventional mathematical notation, with the compiler taking care of any necessary conversion to internal representation. Thus, the constants in the familiar distance formula

$$S = v_0 t + 0.5at^2$$

require no special form for specification in equivalent higher-level language statements:

| | |
|---|---|
| (Fortran, Basic) | `S = VO*T + 0.5*A*T**2` |
| (Algol) | `S = VO*T + 0.5*A*T↑2;` |
| (PL/I) | `S = VO*T + 0.5*A*T**2;` |
| (Cobol) | `COMPUTE S = VO*T + 0.5*A*T**2.` |

A number of languages recognize an alternative representation for numerical constants. This form, similar to scientific notation, is particularly useful for expressing very large or very small values. Instead of writing long strings of zeros to establish a number's order of magnitude, the same value may be designated more concisely by showing only the significant digits in some convenient form, supplemented by an appropriate exponent value to adjust the scale. For instance, in languages like Basic, Fortran, and PL/I, the constant 0.00000513 can be expressed alternatively as 5.13E−06, 0.513E−5, or even 51.3E−7. (In Algol, the E is sometimes replaced by an apostrophe so that the exponential representation in that language would be 5.13′−6; other notations are also in use).

PL/I accepts numerical constants specified in binary form. The use of a B immediately after the rightmost digit of a string of 1's and 0's identifies that constant as being to the base 2. Thus, the constant in the assignment statement N = 11010.011B represents the binary value $11010.011_2$ (whose decimal equivalent is 26.375).

In certain areas of application, the manipulation of complex numbers plays an important role such that several languages include directly appropriate computational capabilities. Accordingly, there are provisions for defining complex variables and specifying complex numerical constants. Strictly speaking, there is no specific form reserved for complex constants per se. Rather, those languages accepting such data deal with complex numbers as combinations of real and imaginary components. In Fortran, for example, the statement COMPLEX A, B defines variable names A and B as being associated with complex numbers and instigates appropriate storage allocation. Now, supposing one wished to assign a value of $2.7 + 3.6i$ to A. The required statement would have the form A = (2.7,3.6), thereby causing the compiler to treat the two arguments as the real and imaginary components, respectively, of complex variable A. Along the same lines, then, the statement B = 4.4 * A − (1.0,−0.8) would produce the calculations $4.4(2.7 + 3.6i) - (1 - 0.8i)$, with the final result (equivalent to $10.88 - 15.04i$) being placed in B. PL/I uses the specific form *b*I for imaginary constants, so that the equivalent statements would be written as follows:

```
DECLARE (A, B) COMPLEX;
A = 2.7 + 3.6I;
B = 4.4 * A - (1-0.8I);
```

**Character String Constants.** Growing insight into computers' capabilities, coupled with developing human ability to identify and describe a widening variety of "computable" algorithms, have produced numerous important applications involving the processing of nonnumeric data. In response, special string-handling languages have been developed and more general higher-level languages have been equipped with facilities to synthesize and decompose character strings, search them in response to arbitrarily complex criteria, and perform a variety of other manipulations. An elemental aspect of these facilities is the recognition of constant values consisting of arbitrary combinations of letters, digits, and other symbols completely analogous to the treatment of numerical constants.

The syntactic approach generally followed in many languages is to bracket a character string constant by special delimiters, thereby identifying that string as a data item and distinguishing it from other strings whose usage is fundamentally different (e.g., names of variables). For example, the PL/I statement DECLARE ESTRING CHARACTER (7); defines a variable named ESTRING, associating that name with a string capable of accommodating seven characters. Then, the assignment statement ESTRING = 'EEEEEEE'; fills the seven places with EEEEEEE (an E string if I ever saw one!). Note that the apostrophes are not part of the actual character string; they serve merely to define its extent. Distinction of an apostrophe that is an intrinsic part of a character string constant from one serving as a delimiter is handled by specifying a double apostrophe for each one to be shown. Thus, a constant consisting of the five characters CAN'T is indicated as 'CAN''T'. The languages Cobol, Snobol, and some dialects of Fortran and Algol also use the apostrophe as a character string delimiter, while other Algol implementations recognize strings bracketed by '(' and ')'.

**Logical Constants.** The construction and representation of decision mechanisms in higher level languages often are facilitated by the availability of vehicles for specifying logical conditions, i.e., expressions describing situations whose outcome is either "true" or "false." A number of languages offer such facilities in terms of logical variables supported by operations that allow the synthesis of arbitrarily complex boolean combinations. When embedded in a program, these expressions can form the basis for dynamically selecting one of two alternative actions. Accordingly, such variables are inherently bistable, limited by definition to one of two possible values. Hence, the standard repertoire of logical constants is similarly restricted.

Logical variables are accommodated in Fortran and Algol (where they are known as boolean variables). Both compilers recognize the literal strings TRUE and FALSE as part of their respective vocabularies. Thus, in each of the examples listed here, the names V1 and V2 are declared to be associated with true-or-false types of variables. (Some versions of Fortran recognize the symbols .T. and .F..) Once this association has been defined, the assignment of one or the other alternative logical constant is straightforward. Conversion to the corresponding internal form used by the particular compiler is automatic so that evaluation of the expression proceeds without further intervention by the programmer.

| *Fortran* | *Algol* |
|---|---|
| LOGICAL V1,V2 | **boolean** V1,V2; |
| V1 = .TRUE. | V1: = **true**; |

PL/I's analogous facility is part of a more general structure for handling multiplicities of such variables, each of which independently may assume a value of "true" or "false." Such variables, which may of be arbitrary length, are called *bit strings*. In this context a logical variable is a string having a length of one bit and the two logical constants have the forms '1'B and '0'B representing true and false, respectively. Then, the PL/I equivalent of the statements shown above for Fortran and Algol would be

```
DECLARE (V1,V2) BIT(1);
V1 = '1'B;
```

**Location Constants.** When working in a higher-level language, the programmer relinquishes direct knowledge and control of the storage locations from which the program is executed. Moreover, there is no reason to expect that those locations will be invariant from one run to the next. Yet, there are countless occasions requiring explicit references to specific statements, so that some vehicle must be provided through the language to give the programmer the opportunity to obtain unerring access to any part of the program. This is done by allowing him to attach a distinctive *label* to a statement, thereby establishing an identity that is fixed within the context of the program and is impervious to its eventual location in storage. In this sense, such labels are constants and references to them are direct. Fortran and Basic, for example, allow the use of labels that resemble numerical constants but which are distinguishable by their contextual position. Thus, the assignment statement

```
22     X = 25.4 * Y ** 2
```

is equipped with the *label constant* 22 so that, at some other point in the procedure, one could write GO TO 22, thereby specifying a fixed directive to continue the processing from a particular point. Other languages differ with regard to the allowable construction of labels, but their use as constants still persists.

Extension of this idea of a location constant is seen in languages like PL/I and Algol, where label constants are constructed from alphanumeric characters, as are variable names. These languages allow components that act as location variables in that they may assume different "values" at various points during the execution of a program. For instance, the PL/I statement DECLARE PLACE LABEL; establishes a variable named PLACE whose "value" at any given time designates a particular statement in the program. This value is defined, conventionally, by an ordinary assignment statement. Thus, PLACE = THERE; defines a specific spot in the program, represented by the location constant THERE. Then, a reference to PLACE, e.g., GO TO PLACE; implies a reference to the statement with label THERE. Later on, it is possible to set PLACE to a different location constant, with the result that the same reference to PLACE now will lead to some other particular point in the program.

**Figurative Constants.** There are special types of constants that represent fixed and unambiguous values but which are unlike the other types discussed heretofore in that they are not designated by their literal values. Because their usage is particularly common, these fixed quantities are indicated by permanent parts of the language vocabulary. Such constants, known as "figurative constants," are provided as conveniences to enhance the "naturalness" of higher-level language statements. Cobol includes several such constants. For instance, a given variable may be set to a value of zero by any of the following statements:

```
MOVE ZERO TO X.
MOVE ZEROS TO X.
MOVE ZEROES TO X.
```

in which ZERO, ZEROS, and ZEROES are figurative constants. Similarly, the character string B may be filled with blanks by either of the Cobol statements MOVE BLANKS TO B. and MOVE SPACES TO B.

The Snobol language has another type of figurative constant to provide apparent visibility for nothing. This constant, NULL, refers to the absence of any numbers, letters, or any other items. For example, a character string named Y can be emptied (depleted and, in an operational sense, reduced to a length of zero characters) by the statement Y = NULL. An alternative form to accomplish the same thing, namely, Y = is not much more mysterious in the overall context of the language. However, there are many more complex situations in which the explicit appearance of something for nothing is very helpful in clarifying the nature and intent of intricate string-processing constructions.

### Reference

1969. Sammet, J. *Programming Languages: History and Fundamentals.* Englewood Cliffs, N.J.: Prentice-Hall. (See especially Section III.4.)

S. V. Pollack

## CONTENTION

For articles on related subjects *see* Communications and Computers; Lockout; Multiprocessing; and Multiprogramming.
For article on related term *see* Buffer.

Originally, the term "contention" was used to describe a communication system where the terminals, or lines, were competing for a circuit and the first one to find it free obtained it. This concept can be generalized to the case of multiple users (jobs, tasks, processes) competing for sharable resources (processors, channels, devices). For example, in a multiprogramming system, two jobs may simultaneously require the use of tape drives, thus possibly exceeding the capacity of the installation. This overflow situation would lead to contention delays, since one job would have to be put temporarily in a waiting state. Another example can be found in the case of a multiprocessing system where a process can be split into several tasks and the number of tasks ready to be processed in parallel is larger than the number of available processors.

Contention is solved by using priority schemes; the simplest one is a first-come-first-serve strategy. However, all processes contending for a resource must be remembered so that they will, in turn, be able to use it. This implies the presence of queues, or buffers, associated with each sharable resource.

J-L. BAER

# CONTROL APPLICATIONS

For articles on related subjects *see* ANALOG COMPUTERS; DIGITAL TO ANALOG CONVERTERS; MINICOMPUTERS; REAL TIME APPLICATIONS; and SPECIAL PURPOSE COMPUTERS.

For articles on related terms *see* ALGORITHM; ASSOCIATIVE MEMORY; BLOCK DIAGRAM; and MODELS.

The history of automatic control traces back thousands of years to the water clock used by the Egyptians in the third century B.C. This early clock consisted of a jar from which water escaped at a controlled rate. The level of the water in the jar indicated the time of day. Only since the Industrial Revolution, however, has there been a conscious effort by man to analyze elements of his environment and to control them automatically.

By 1950 there was a unified body of knowledge called "feedback control theory," which could be used to analyze and control the performance of complex devices and processes. The development at that time of the digital computer, capable of making hundreds of thousands of computations and logical decisions in 1 second, introduced a powerful new tool for solving conventional control problems. Furthermore, it uncovered many new theoretical and applied research problems for control theorists and engineers.

Although the full potential of the digital computer as a control tool has not yet been realized, its use in a wide variety of control applications is growing rapidly.

In the remainder of this article, we will explain what is meant by the term "automatic control" and discuss the role of the digital computer in the solution of control problems.

As the term "control" implies, in every control problem there is a system (which may be a device, a process, or some phenomenon) with associated *output* or *controlled* variables that are to be forced to satisfy certain constraints. Typically, output variables cannot be adjusted freely; instead, they depend in an indirect way on another set of variables that can be adjusted. The variables in this second set are termed "input" or "manipulated" variables.

The nature of the dependence of the output variables on the input variables is very often complex and cannot be determined precisely. However, the relationship that exists between the two sets of variables can often be approximated by a set of differential (or difference) equations, which is referred to as the "mathematical model" of the "system." We will represent this model, with its input and output variables by a block diagram, illustrated in Fig. 1.

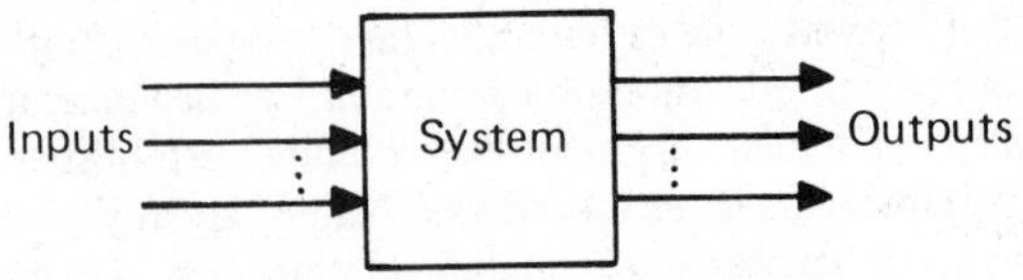


**Fig. 1.** Block diagram of model of system.

It may be that a given system performs very well as is. On the other hand, it may display unfavorable characteristics such as instability, sensitivity to parameter changes, slowness of response, or inefficient operation. Control theory embraces the problems of developing suitable mathematical models, determining system characteristics from the mathematical models and altering those characteristics when they are unacceptable.

Consider, as an example of a practical control problem, a lawn mower with a small internal combustion engine and a speed-control lever connected to a butterfly valve in the carburetor. The butterfly valve regulates the flow of fuel into the cylinder.

In control terms (Fig. 2), the output of this system is the engine speed $S_e$. With a constant load applied to the engine, the engine speed is determined

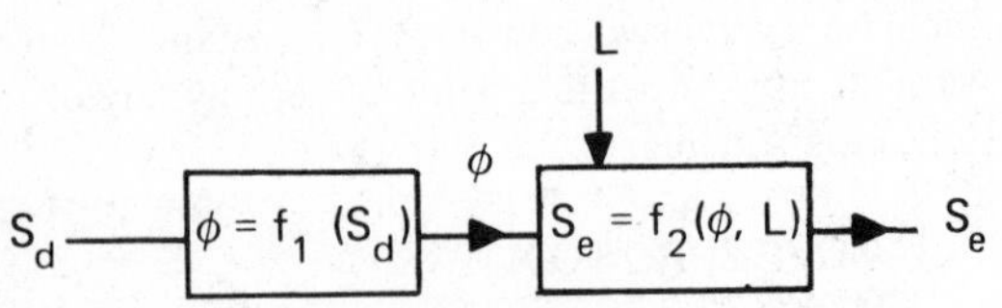


**Fig. 2.** Lawn mower model.

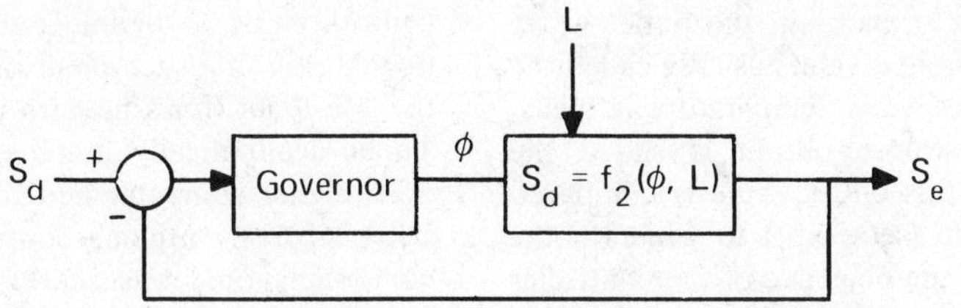


**Fig. 3.** Lawn mower model with feedback control.

by the angle $\phi$ of the butterfly valve in the carburetor. The angle $\phi$ is a function of the desired speed $S_d$, which is considered to be the system input and is set by the operator with the speed-control lever.

The problem with this system is that the speed of the engine ($S_e$) in actual operation is determined by the angle $\phi$ and the load $L$ on the engine. With $\phi$ held constant, an increase in the load will cause a decrease in engine speed. Consequently, if one attempts to use this machine to mow a lawn that is uneven and has thick patches of grass, he will find that the speed-control lever must be frequently adjusted to keep the engine running at a constant speed.

An intuitively simple solution to this problem (Fig. 3) utilizes *feedback control* to make the system less sensitive to load changes. Here the angle $\phi$ is forced mechanically to be a function of $S_d$, the desired engine speed, and $S_e$, the actual engine speed. The control scheme works in the following manner: With the use of springs, levers, and balanced weights, the engine speed $S_e$ is continuously measured and used to change the angle $\phi$ in proportion to the engine speed error $S_d - S_e$. As a consequence, an increase in the desired speed (caused by the operator) or a decrease in actual speed (caused by an increase in the load on the engine) results in an increase in fuel flow to the cylinder. This action tends to reduce the engine-speed error to zero. The mechanism that measures engine speed and makes the angle correction is called a "governor."

Many other examples of automatic control problems, like the one discussed above, have simple solutions that can be implemented at a low cost. On the other hand, there are many complex automatic control problems requiring sophisticated control schemes that cannot be easily implemented with mechanical devices or with simple electronic feedback circuits. It is in the solution of these problems that the digital computer is most effective.

We will now discuss several areas of control where the computer is being utilized. In each of these areas the motivation or justification for computer control is one or more of the following: More flexible control, improved product quality, greater safety, greater precision, more efficient operation, or a savings in manpower or equipment.

**Process Control.** Process control is the term given to the automatic control of industrial processes such as paper machines, blast furnaces, chemical plants, electric power generating stations, sewage treatment plants, and the like. The typical digital process control system may be expected to achieve either one or a combination of the following objectives:

1. Make the necessary adjustments so that the process recovers from upsets and disturbances in the most expeditious manner.
2. Determine the level of process operation that achieves the maximum economic return on investment.

The second objective is in reality an optimization problem, but in order to implement successfully the optimum conditions, a necessary prerequisite is an effective plant control system.

To illustrate these two types of objectives, suppose we consider the simple hot-water heater in Fig. 4. As shown, the control system admits steam at

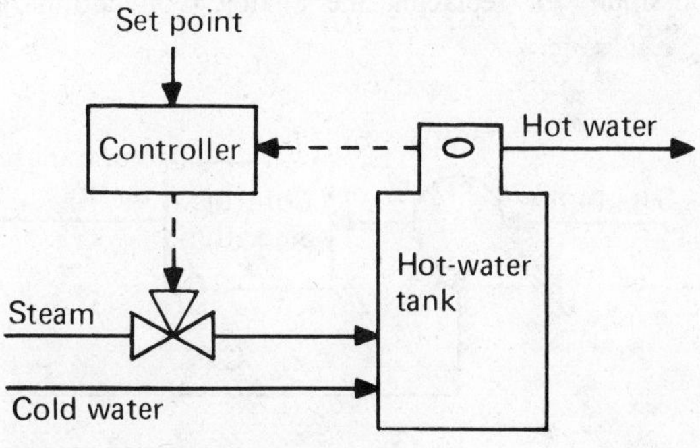


**Fig. 4.** Hot-water heater.

the proper rate so as to maintain the outlet water temperature at some desired value, usually called the "set point." The outlet water temperature is measured by the *sensor*, whose output is called the "feedback variable"; this outlet value is compared with the desired value (set point) to generate the error signal. In effect, the objective of the controller is to drive the error signal to zero. In so doing, the controller generates a signal, referred to as the "manipulated variable," which in this example determines the opening of the steam valve and therefore the amount of steam flow.

The relationships between the elements in the system are best illustrated by the block diagram in Fig. 5. The process consists of the hot-water tank, which is subject to two inputs. One input is the steam flow. The second input is the water flow through the tank, referred to as an "upset" or "disturbance," since changes in this flow affect the outlet temperature. These two inputs determine the flow of water from the tank and the temperature of the water; the latter is to be regulated by the control system, and is called the "controlled variable." Its value is measured by the sensor and fed back to the comparator to generate the error signal. On receiving this signal, the control algorithm generates a signal to the actuator, which in this case is a steam valve. The valve then adjusts the flow of steam into the vessel. The elements in Fig. 5 are arranged in a loop, and the system is frequently referred to as a "control loop."

In all loops in older industrial plants and in many loops in newer plants, the comparator and control algorithm are implemented in a hardware unit known as a "controller." In effect, this unit is a special-purpose analog computer, with the computing elements being either pneumatic, electronic, or occasionally hydraulic. This unit continuously monitors the feedback variable and set point, and generates adjustments to the steam valve in a continuous fashion.

With the appearance of digital computers, the possibility of replacing the analog (conventional) controllers by a digital control system was investigated; the first such plant installation appeared in the late 1950s (for a modern installation, see Fig. 6). To be economically feasible, a single general-purpose digital computer had to assume the responsibility of conventional controllers. Therefore, the computer's time was shared among many control loops. In effect, the computer services the loops in turn, i.e., computes the error signal, performs the algorithm computations, and proceeds to the next loop. The time between servicings for a given loop is referred to as the "sampling time," which is not necessarily the same for all loops. The use of digital computers in this fashion is called "direct digital control" (DDC).

In digital control, the output (the signal to the steam valve in Fig. 4) is usually computed from the error signal ($e_n$ is the error at sampling time $n$) by an equation (the control algorithm) containing three terms:

1. A proportional term, $K_c e_n$, where $K_c$ is a constant, the "proportional gain."
2. A summation or integral term, $(T/T_i)\Sigma_{i=0}^{n} e_i$, where $T_i$ is a constant, the "reset time," and $T$ is the sampling time.
3. A difference or derivative term, $T_d(e_n - e_{n-1})/T$, where $T_d$ is a constant, the derivative time.

The output of the controller is simply the sum of the values of these three terms. The proper values of $K_c$, $T_i$, and $T_d$ depend upon the process being controlled, and the adjustment of these constants to their proper values is a procedure known as "tuning." Although other control algorithms have been proposed, over 90% of the control loops in industry use this three-term, or proportional integral derivative (PID), algorithm. In some control loops the derivative term is omitted, leaving the two-term, or proportional integral (PI) algorithm.

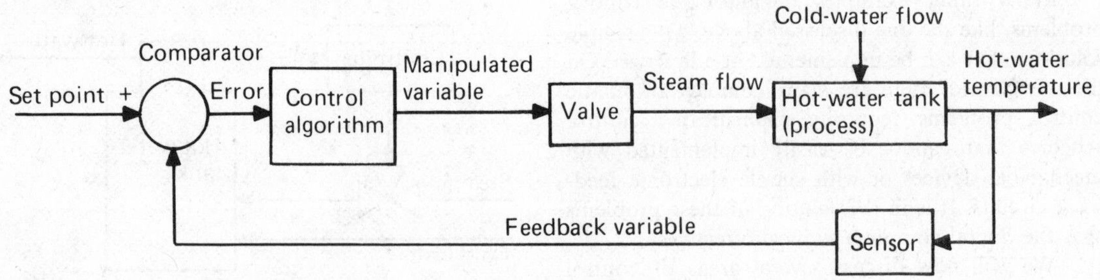


**Fig. 5.** Control loop.

**Fig. 6.** An IBM System/7 running in a process control environment.

The control system in Fig. 4 must perform satisfactorily for two somewhat different control problems. To illustrate, suppose the system is functioning in a large hotel. Each time a guest opens or closes the hot-water faucet in his room, he changes the flow of water through the tank. Suppose he also opens the cold-water valve. This effectively admits more cold water into the system, which tends to lower the outlet water temperature. However, the control system detects this change, and admits more steam to compensate. In this case, the control system is trying to maintain the controlled variable at the set point in face of upsets. This is the *regulator problem.*

To illustrate the second problem, suppose the hotel manager is unusually responsive to criticism from the guests so that each time a guest complains about the water being either too hot or too cold, he either raises or lowers the set point to the controller. If he raises the set point, the control system must respond by increasing the flow of steam so that the outlet temperature will increase. This control is the *servo problem.* The three-term algorithm previously described works well for both types of problems.

The current trend is to use minicomputers in most industrial direct digital-control systems. However, particularly in the chemical and petrochemical industry, direct digital control of the total plant has frequently not proved to be economically attractive. The conventional controller is relatively inexpensive compared to even small digital systems, and performs the three-term algorithm computation quite well. However, the digital computer is able to perform other services (e.g., feedback variable compensation, such as correcting flow measurements for temperature effects). In these cases, the flexibility and computational capabilities of the digital computer make it more attractive than conventional controllers. In many plants, those loops requiring this capability are implemented digitally and the others are implemented conventionally.

To illustrate the optimizing control problem mentioned previously, suppose we have a hot-water heater in which the heat source may be either steam, electricity, gas, or combinations of the three, as shown in Fig. 7. In this situation, the control system must choose which heat system to use. The choice should depend on which source can produce the hot water at the least cost. Any one of the three sources

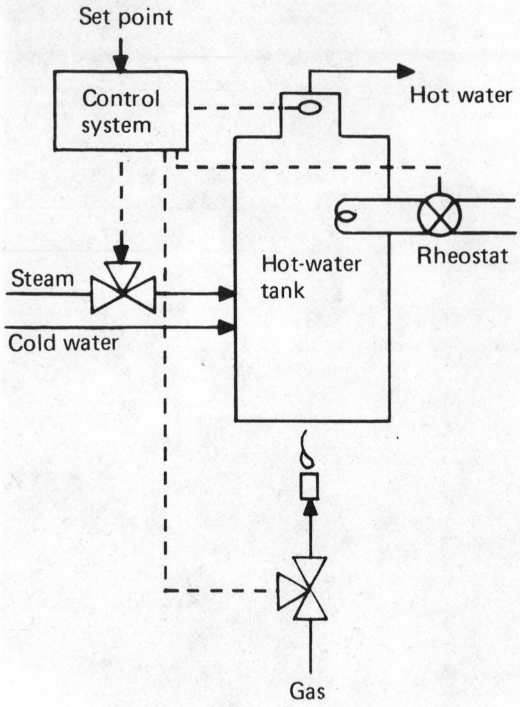


**Fig. 7.** Optimizing control problem.

or a combination of all may be chosen. A combination may be necessary if, for example, a limit (constraint) is imposed on the amount of heat available from one source. Changing demands from night to day, changing availabilities of energy, changing cost of energy (electricity is often cheaper for industrial use during the hours after midnight), and similar factors require that the optimum requirements be recomputed on a frequent basis.

In many industrial systems, the output of the optimizing control system in Fig. 7 would not be set directly by the valves but would be determined by the values of the flows. In case of the steam flow, for example, a separate control loop must be installed to sense the volume or pressure of the steam flow and adjust the valve automatically to produce the flow specified by the optimizing control system. In this case, the optimizing control system is frequently referred to as a "supervisory control system."

**Traffic Control.** The control of traffic, both in airways and on roadways, is becoming a critical problem. Projection of traffic volume into future years indicates that the present means of control is not a satisfactory long-term solution. Although air and ground traffic share the common goal of increasing the volume of traffic flow, the two problems have different natures.

Control of air traffic in and out of airports is now, as it has been in the past, the responsibility of air traffic controllers; these people from the air traffic control center monitor traffic data and give takeoff and landing instructions to aircraft pilots. The volume of controlled traffic through an airport is limited to the maximum number of aircraft that air traffic controllers can safely handle. This maximum number depends to a great degree on the form and extent of information available to the controller.

In the early years of air traffic control, the standard "real time" information available to the controller consisted of a flight schedule, aircraft position and altitude communicated from each pilot by radio, and an overall view of close-range traffic movement shown on a radar screen.

As the volume of traffic increased over the years, the need for more sophisticated systems for gathering, processing, and displaying flight information grew accordingly. The past decade has seen a major effort to utilize the computer and other electronic devices to develop a data handling system capable of meeting the requirements of air traffic control today and in years to come, although much needs yet to be done in this direction.

In England the first stage of a national air traffic control program, named *Mediator*, has been introduced (Editor, *Wireless World*, 1971). This system incorporates primary radar, together with a secondary radar facility that works with those aircraft equipped with transponders. These radar signals are processed by computer and distributed to graphics display units, which provide air traffic controllers with aircraft identification and route codes superimposed on the primary radar display. Altitude display is also provided for those aircraft equipped with altimeter telemetry.

The second stage of *Mediator* calls for the inclusion of a flight-plan processing system that will notify controllers of any aircraft which deviates from its flight plan or is flying a collision course.

Although systems like *Mediator* are effective, it is estimated that a maximum number of 300 aircraft can be tracked and identified using a conventional processor which must retrieve a word from memory before it can be used in logical operations. However, the number of aircraft expected to be under terminal control of large airports by the year 1980 is 1,500. Now in the experimental stage are two computers with *associative processors* (Editor, *Electronics*, 1970; Eddey, 1970), which have logic circuits at every word, or even at every bit location in memory. An

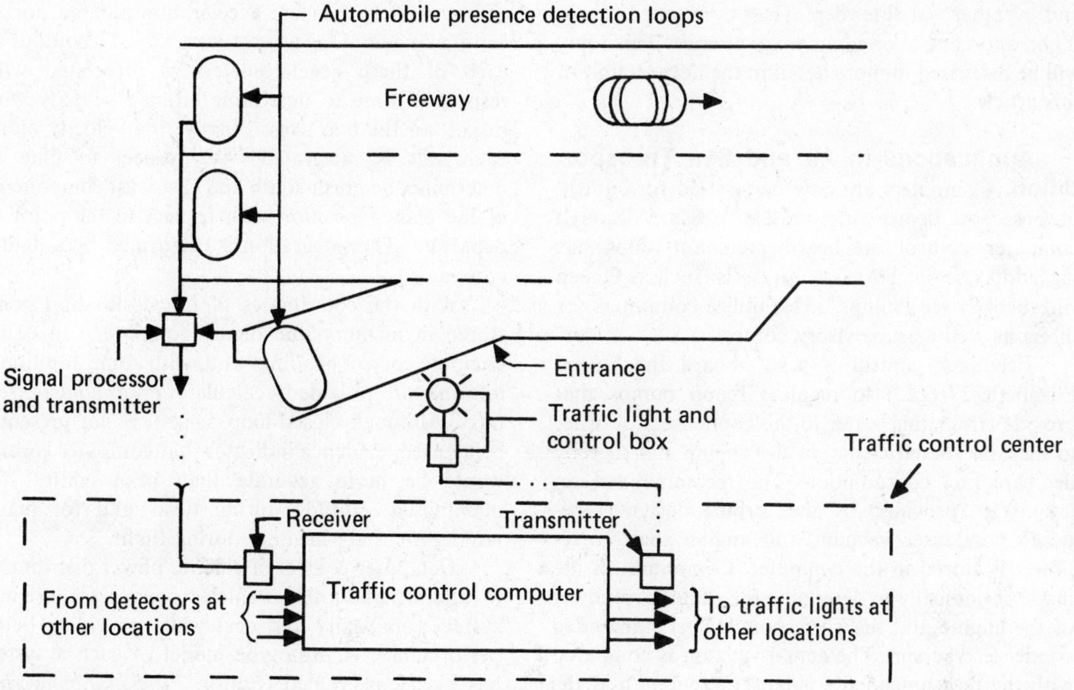


**Fig. 8.** Freeway traffic control.

exact match search of all bits in memory can be performed by these processors in 100 to 300 ns. With such speeds, it appears that these processors will be capable of monitoring a large number of aircraft and identifying those that are traveling on collision courses.

Ideally, one would like to have a computer monitor traffic data and compute, for each aircraft, an optimum route to be traveled. However, because so many lives depend on air traffic control, highly reliable equipment together with backup systems and fail-safe procedures must be developed before closed-loop computer control can be employed.

Control of traffic on the freeways and surface roads of large cities is another problem that is receiving increased attention. Unlike air traffic control, the traffic routes are fixed, and the only means of control are traffic lights and possibly roadside messages to automoble drivers.

In London (Holland, 1969), a computerized traffic control program has been in operation for some time and has increased traffic volume considerably. Detectors in the streets provide traffic flow data, which is processed by a central computer to determine optimum sequencing of traffic lights.

In Los Angeles, California, presence detectors have been installed on freeways to gather data for the development of mathematical models of freeway traffic as well as algorithms for parameter estimation, incidence detection, and flow optimization during times of peak loads and abnormal conditions, as illustrated in Fig. 8. After models and control schemes have been worked out, the loop will be closed and the computer will implement control schemes by regulating the flow of traffic at freeway entrance ramps.

**Defense Applications.** The early development of the electronic digital computer was within a military framework. Computer control is still used extensively in the armed services today but, compared to applications in industry and other commercial enterprises, the justification for its use is less dependent on economic considerations.

Although the details of most defense systems are classified, it is obviously true that the firing of many offensive and defensive weapons is performed under the control (either direct or supervisory) of a computer. Many applications that were initially developed within the defense department are now being used commercially. Automatic flight control with the use of inertial navigation, for example, was first developed to control the flight of ballistic missiles and is now being used for communications and weather satellite deployment, manned space flight, and control of commercial aircraft. This topic will be discussed in more detail in the next section of this article.

**Applications in Air and Sea Transportation.** Computers are now being used for control purposes on board air and sea vessels. Although computer control on board merchant ships has lagged its use on shore, some vessels (such as Queen Elizabeth 2; see Phillips, 1971) utilize computers for direct as well as supervisory control.

Feedback control is used aboard the Queen Elizabeth 2 (*QE2*) to regulate scoop pumps that provide circulating water to the condensers in order to increase the efficiency of the engine and thereby decrease fuel consumption. The recommended relationship (provided by the turbine designer) between condenser vacuum and engine shaft-horsepower is stored in the computer. Computations are made periodically to determine the shaft horsepower of the engine and the corresponding recommended condenser vacuum. The actual vacuum is compared with the recommended condenser vacuum, and the change in vane angle of the scoop pump necessary to give the recommended vacuum is computed. Finally, the computer sends a signal to an actuator to make the correct change in vane angle.

The computer in the *QE2* is also utilized for supervisory control to calculate the recommended power output, engine speed, and shaft speed of the ship over the route to be traveled. To accomplish this, the desired route is divided into as many as 20 sections. Over each section, wind speed and direction as well as ship's course are assumed constant. The calculations are based on weather reports and forecasts, the ship's load, and scheduled arrival time.

Plans are being made to have the computer control on a daily basis the generation of fresh water according to predicted usage. Scheduled stops would be considered to insure that fresh-water tanks are full when the ship stops and the evaporators are shut down.

In addition to its use on the ground for air traffic control, as discussed previously, the digital computer is being used on board commercial aircraft for control purposes, such as flight control and control of power distribution.

The Boeing 747 is equipped with an inertial navigation system, a compact version of systems used to control the flight of missiles and space vehicles. Gyroscopes are used to hold a platform in a fixed, level position with respect to true north. Two accelerometers placed on this platform continuously and accurately measure acceleration along a north-south axis and along an east-west axis. The output of each of these accelerometers is integrated with respect to time to determine aircraft velocity with respect to the two axes. Finally, the velocity along each axis is integrated with respect to time to determine the north-south and east-west components of the plane's position with respect to the point of departure. The integration is performed by a digital computer.

With the coordinates of the destination point stored in memory, the digital computer can easily compute correct headings and, with some additional information provided, calculate pilot control settings. Although closed-loop control is not presently being used, evidence indicates that computer control would be more accurate than pilot control for maintaining altitude during turns and for maintaining a correct heading during flight.

Computer control of electric power distribution in aircraft and other vehicles promises to reduce system complexity and cost while providing better performance. A prototype model of such a system has been constructed (Editor, *Product Engineering*, 1970). In this system (Fig. 9), a central digital computer controls the action of remote hybrid electronic power controllers that are located at load centers and which perform the switching. Load control and sequencing is under command of the central computer, which can be programmed to perform automatic self check-out, startup, and shutdown sequencing, and load shedding on a priority basis when generating capacity is reduced.

**Numerical Control.** In the manufacture of parts for such products as appliances, automobiles, airplanes, and the like, fabrication of the part is effected by such devices as milling and routing machines, rotary tables, lathe grinders, boring machines, flame cutters, drilling machines, and benders. When using any of these machines, some type of control mechanism is necessary to insure that the finished part meets specifications.

In the early manufacturing plants, such control was performed by a human operator. This mode of control was relatively expensive, and the consistency with which the resulting part met specifications was relatively low, especially for parts requiring extensive milling. With the development of the automotive industry, machines were designed with preset tool guides, automatic part holding and locating features, automatic feed systems, and the like. These machines, referred to as "fixed" or "Detroit automation," were designed to produce a specific part.

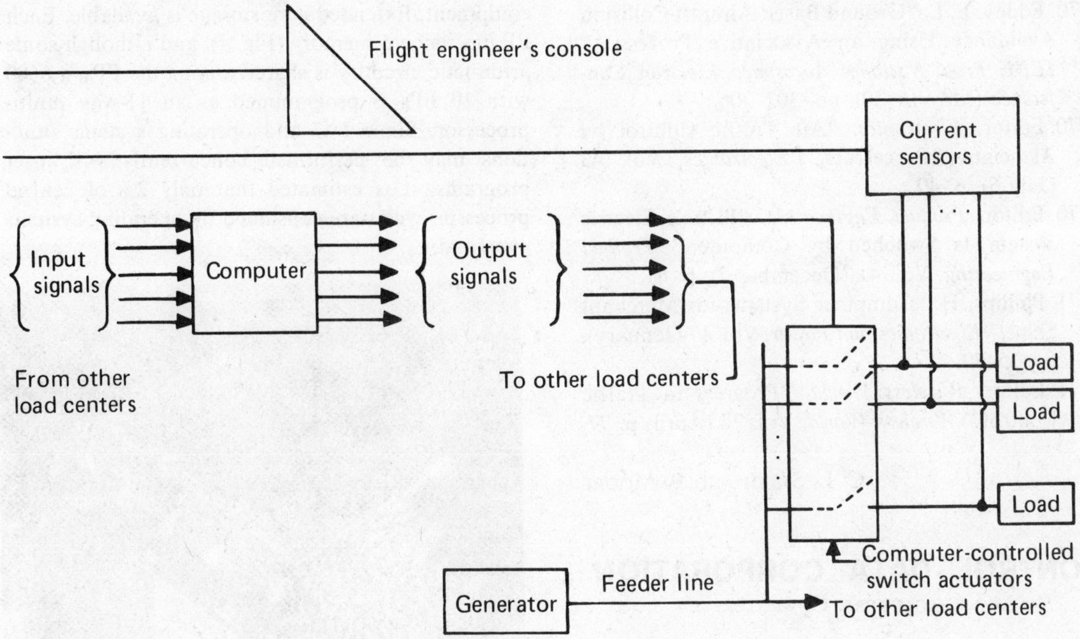


**Fig. 9.** Control of aircraft power distribution.

Although part changes frequently required major mill modifications, this was no great obstacle because of the large quantities of each part produced in the automotive industry.

Many major industries, such as the aircraft industry, must fabricate parts in considerably smaller quantities. In these applications the mill should have the flexibility to produce a variety of parts with a relatively short changeover time. The milling machines generally have capabilities such as positioning the part in either the two- or three-dimensional coordinate system, rotating the part as in a lathe, positioning a cutter as in a drill, and the like. When the instructions that specify the positioning, movement, and other machine operations are in the form of numbers, the machine is a candidate for numerical control.

The control of the machines by numerical control can be classified in two types: point-to-point control and contouring control. In point-to-point control, the route by which the tool moves from point A to point B is immaterial except that, among other considerations, the movement must be sufficiently precise so that the tool does not strike the part. Drilling multiple holes in a part is an example of this type of control. In contouring control, milling is usually done along a path, which must be controlled at every point. This type of control is the more demanding.

Basically, an order for a part generally includes a drawing of the part and some additional explanatory information. From this data, the plant must produce the part. The steps are frequently as follows:

1. The dimensions and other pertinent data of the part are punched onto cards.

2. These cards constitute the input to computer programs that provide a generalized milling and positioning format.

3. The resulting data is then entered into a post-processor program, specific to the machine being used, to produce the numerical control instructions, usually in the form of a punched paper tape.

4. This paper tape is mounted on a paper-tape reader at the machine to provide direct instructions to the machine.

To convert from manufacturing one part to the next, the mill operator need change only the paper tape and make the usually minor modifications on the mill. To facilitate this changeover, many machines have selectable tools, e.g., multiple drill heads mounted on a turret.

### References

1969. Holland, Ted. "London's Computerized Traffic," *Engineering*, Vol. 207 (March 7), pp. 374–375.

1970. Eddey, E. E. "Ground Based Aircraft Collision Avoidance Using an Associative Processor," *IEEE Proc. National Aerospace Electron Conference* (May 18–20), pp. 302–306.
1970. Editor, *Electronics*. "Air Traffic Control by Associative Processors," *Electronics*, Vol. 43 (July 6), p. 40.
1970. Editor, *Product Engineering*. "Plane's Electric System Is Switched by Computer," *Product Engineering*, Vol. 41 (December 7), p. 61.
1971. Phillips, H. "Computer Systems for Merchant Ships," *Electronics and Power*, Vol. 17 (January), pp. 35–39.
1971. Editor, *Wireless World*. "Progress in Traffic Control," *Wireless World*, Vol. 77 (April) p. 77.

C. L. SMITH AND B. MOORE

# CONTROL DATA CORPORATION.

*See* MANUFACTURERS, COMPUTER.

# CONTROL DATA CORPORATION 6000 SERIES

For articles on related subjects *see* MANUFACTURERS, COMPUTER; and SUPERCOMPUTERS.
For articles on related terms *see* CENTRAL PROCESSING UNIT; INTERLEAVING; MULTIPROCESSING; MULTIPROGRAMMING; PARITY; REGISTER; and STACK.

The Control Data 6000 series consists of the CDC 6600 and its variants. The 6600 was designed to provide high-speed arithmetic capability for large scientific applications, particularly solutions of very large systems of linear and nonlinear equations. The 6600 was both innovative and successful. The innovation lay in an architecture that employed an unprecedented degree of concurrency. The success was such that from the time the first 6600 was delivered in 1964 until about 1970, the CDC 6000 series dominated the large-scale scientific market. These machines were deservedly called the "biggest and most powerful in the world."

A CDC 6600 has been described (Bell and Newell, 1971) as a "network computer"; it consists of a central memory (CM), a central processor (CP), a set of peripheral processors (PPs), and peripheral equipment. Extended core storage is available. Each PP has its own memory (Fig. 1), and although some arithmetic circuitry is shared among the PPs, a 6600 with 10 PPs is programmed as an 11-way multiprocessor. Since I/O and operating systems functions may be performed concurrently with user programs, it is estimated that only 2% of central processor cycles are consumed by operating-systems overhead.

**Fig. 1.** The CDC 6000 memory unit.

The basis of the 6600 central processor architecture is "functional parallelism" (Thornton, 1970). It is achieved by the use of several functional units plus support facilities. In a typical central processor program, at least two or three functional units will be in operation simultaneously. Instructions from memory are first loaded automatically into a high-speed scratchpad memory (the "instruction stack"). Instructions are saved in the stack so that under some circumstances a program loop can be held, and the program can loop within the stack at high speed without requiring central memory references for instructions. The unit and register reservation control, or "Scoreboard," schedules instructions and the functional units, taking an instruction from the stack whenever a unit is free.

The 6600 is able to add two 18-bit quantities in 300 ns, to add two floating-point numbers in 400 ns with 14-place precision, and to multiply two floating-point numbers in 1$\mu$s. Since these operations use different functional units, they may be performed simultaneously. It is estimated (Grishman, 1971) that the processing unit of the 6600 typically executes about three million instructions per second. There are no interrupts in the usual sense.

The maximum memory of a 6600 consists of 131,072 sixty-bit words. The memory is divided into 32 *banks* with *low-bit interleaving* so that consecutive addresses are assigned to consecutive banks and references to consecutive addresses may be overlapped. Protection is by base-and-bounds registers not addressable by the programmer, and relocatability is such that programs may be freely moved about in memory in order to solve the storage-fragmentation problem of multiprogramming.

The other members of the CDC 6000 series are the 6400, 6500, and 6700. The 6400 is a slower and simpler version of the 6600, with a "unified arithmetic" unit instead of the ten functional units, and no instruction stack. The 6500 and the 6700 are dual processors, the first consisting of two 6400 processors and the second of one 6400 and one 6600.

In spite of the undoubted success of the 6000 architecture, some criticisms can be made. Floating-point round is performed *before* rather than after normalization, in contravention of the principles of numerical analysis. The subroutine-jump instruction stores into memory, thus making reentrant code difficult to implement. Fixed-point overflow is not detected. One's-complement arithmetic presents some problems, particularly in the handling of the two representations for zero. There is no parity checking on memory, making intermittent memory failures difficult to diagnose.

**Fig. 2.** A Control Data Cyber 70 system, a modern version of a 6000 series system.

In 1969 the Control Data Corporation introduced the 7600 system, which is about five or six times faster than the 6600. The 7600 is similar in organization to the 6000 series, but it uses faster circuitry, a faster memory, and a large backing store (magnetic core) in addition to the usual core memory directly addressable by the processor. Memory parity checking has been introduced. In the 1970s, the 6000 series and the 7600 were reintroduced as the Cyber 70 series (Fig. 2). The organization is again basically the same, the chief enhancement being a COMPARE AND MOVE instruction, which allows for rapid character manipulation. This addition makes the Cyber 70 line attractive, not only to the scientific community, but to the business community as well.

REFERENCES

1970. Thornton, J. E. *Design of a Computer: The Control Data 6000.* Glenview, Ill.: Scott, Foresman.

1971. Bell, C. G., and A. Newell. *Computer Structures: Readings and Examples.* New York: McGraw-Hill.

1971. Grishman, R. *Assembly Language Programming for the Control Data* 6000 Series. New York: Algorithmics Press.

A. H. WERKHEISER

# CONTROL POINT

For article on related subject *see* MICROPROGRAMMING.

For article on related term *see* REGISTER.

The hardware locations at which the output of the instruction decoder of the processor activates the input to and output from specific registers as well as the operational resources of the system (adders, shifters, etc.) are called the "control points." The control points basically determine intercycle register-to-register communications. For each register in the processor there are a fixed number of other registers to which data may be transmitted in one cycle. For each such possibility, a separate AND circuit is placed on the output of each bit of the source register, with the entry into the destination register being collected from all possible sources by an OR circuit.

Data may be communicated from one register to another directly or through some operational network (adder/shifter, etc.). Transmission to such a network must also be selected; the output of the network has a similar set of gates for each possible destination. In a typical system there must be control points corresponding to each bit of every register for each possible intercycle destination of that register and for each bit of each operational network that may be used in a cycle.

For example, consider a 32-bit computer with eight registers. Assume that each register can communicate with three other registers in one cycle. The number of control points required for register communication would therefore be $3 \times 8 \times 32$, or 768. In addition, assume the machine has three execution resources, each of whose 32-bit outputs can be gated to one of four registers. This would account for an additional $3 \times 4 \times 32$, or 384, control points. Of course there are additional control points for the selection of a particular function within a designated resource. This might account for 100 more control points. Thus, there is a total of somewhat over 1200 control points, which must be established for each cycle by the output of the instruction decoder (the control function). Fortunately, in most computer design situations, many of these control points are not independent. For example, one may not gate bit 7 of register 4 to another register, but one may gate the entire contents of register 7 to its destination register. Since only one line is required to control such multiple control points, the total number of outputs required can be significantly reduced. These outputs are then referred to as "independent control points." For the hypothetical system described, there might be anywhere from 50 to 200 independent control points, depending upon the variety of instructions in the vocabulary of the system.

M. J. Flynn

# CONTROLLED VARIABLE

For articles on related subjects *see* Iteration; and Procedure-Oriented Languages, Programming in.

The term "controlled variable" is used for the variable that is controlled to take on a specific set of values in an iterative structure in a programming language. The number of values in this set determines or partially determines how many times the statements in the iteration are executed. For example, in the Algol statement

**for** i: = 1 **step** 2 **until** j, j*j **while** $k<$m, 6, v, x*y **do begin** (iteration statements) **end**

$i$ is the controlled variable. Its values—1,3,5 . . . as long as $i < j$, then $j^2$ as long as $k < m$, and then the three values $6,v,x*y$—are taken on successively each time the statements in the iteration are executed. Only the value $j^2$ may be taken on by $i$ during more than one execution of the iteration statements; this value will be retained as long as $l < m$ (where $l$ or $m$, or both, will be changed by the iteration statements). For this reason the sequence of values of $i$ only partially determines the number of iterations. By contrast, in the Fortran structure

```
DO 212 I=1, 13, 3
```
(iteration statements, with last one labeled 212),

The variable $I$ takes on the values 1,4,7,10,13, once only, each time during the execution of the iteration statements, and thus the number of iterations is determined in advance.

Of course it must be noted that a statement in the set of iteration statements can itself terminate the iteration by (for example) transferring control to a statement outside the so-called **for**-loop in Algol or the DO-loop in Fortran. In this case the iteration terminates before the controlled variable has taken on all its values. Good programming practice, however, requires that such transfers be avoided if at all possible; usually, they can be in languages with a **while** structure, such as in Algol.

A. Ralston

# COPYRIGHTS AND PATENTS, COMPUTER ASPECTS OF

For articles on related subjects *see* Legal Protection of Software; and Proprietary Program.
For article on related term *see* Information Systems.

Patents and copyrights can be defined as legal devices, incorporating a bundle of intangible, proprietary rights and privileges granted to the authors of certain literary or other "written" expressions for limited times or to inventors of devices or manufacturing processes. They invest the applicant with the exclusive right to license others to make, publish, vend, and use copies of those original expressions in the case of copyright (Nimmer, 1974), and the right to exclude others from making, vending, or using an invention in the instance of patent. It should be noted that a patent does not necessarily give the inventor a restrictive right to "practice" his invention himself; it grants only the privilege to exclude or allow others to construct and market on his, the patent holder's, terms (Bowman, 1973). Similarly, although it is possible that the copyright holder may not be able to copy or perform his own work or to prevent others from utilizing his creation without his permission, only he can license others to utilize the work.

Thus, we can say that the limited rights granted the copyright holder and the patentee are exclusionary rather than permissive. The questions thus faced for the computer professional tend to be recursive: What effect does copyright and patent have upon his input and output data; and what effect does copyright and patent have upon his programs and algorithms (Duggan, 1972)?

To answer these questions, it is helpful if one begins by analyzing the purpose served by copyright and patent. In Anglo-American jurisdictions, it is clear that the purpose is to obtain certain public benefits so as "to encourage people to devote themselves to intellectual and artistic creation." The primary end is not to reward the individual author or inventor, or those who invest in the exploitation of those creative expressions, but rather to grant a limited monopoly as a means of promoting "the progress of science and the useful arts" (U.S. Constitution, Art. I, Sec. 8, I. 8).

## Means of Copyright and Patent Protection

COPYRIGHTS. It is useful to note that there are now three separate schemes of rewarding authors, subsumed under the notion of copyright. First and foremost, the federal government by positive federal legislation can provide substance to the bare bones of the constitutional grant. Although the federal government enforces some aspects of copyright directly, through its criminal and customs sanctions, the main right given by federal statute is the right to pursue nonlicensed users of protected material; i.e., federal law allows "bounty hunting" for infringers and admits contests in federal courts.

The remedies accruing to the successful plaintiff can be quite satisfactory, since he is able to claim costs of litigation, actual damages suffered, and the profits realized by the defendant, as well as punitive or exemplary penalties awarded by the court where appropriate. In addition, the infringing products may be impounded while the infringement action is pending, and once the infringement has been judicially determined, they may be destroyed.

If actual damages sustained or profits on the infringement cannot be proved or shown to exist, the trial court may in its discretion award statutory damages "in lieu of actual damages and profits." These damages, if awarded, must be set between a \$250 minimum and a \$5,000 maximum, with the maximum suspended in certain circumstances.

In addition to damages and injunctive relief, the successful copyright plaintiff may also be entitled to full costs of the suit as well as a reasonable attorney's fee. On the other hand, a successful defendant may also recoup costs and a reasonable attorney's fee.

However, in order to obtain these federal rights, one must comply with certain rigid requirements. These are that the work be published (1) with a mandatory notice, (2) in proper form, and (3) in the proper place. The required notice consists of the word "Copyright" or "Copyr.," or the symbol ©, accompanied by the name of the proprietary owner. If the work is a sound recording or a printed literary, musical, or dramatic work, the year of publication must also be included. If a computer program is considered a printed literary work, it would also require the "year" portion of the notice. If a work is considered a book or other printed publication, the notice must be placed on the title page or the page immediately following the title page. Determination of the "title page" of a computer program, even of one utilizing a virtual memory schemata, might prove vexatious. Failure to comply with each and every requirement, generally speaking, will place the published work in the public domain. And once a copyright is lost by failure to comply with these conditions, it may not be regained.

Federal statutory copyright of a published work is obtained by publication with proper notice of copyright, and the subsequent registration and deposit of copies (2) of the work with the Register of Copyrights, Copyright Office. Although this procedure has great significance, it does not create the copyright but merely records it. However, it should be noted that recording and deposit of copies of the published work does not require legal skills and is easily accomplished by direct application to the Copyright Office with the necessary fee (\$6.00 in 1976).

Although of lesser importance than federal statutory copyright, two other protection systems should also be mentioned: that afforded unpublished works (the so-called *common law* copyright) and that provided by state legislation, concurrently with federal protection.

Protection for unpublished works, even though based upon general common-law notions as well as state statutes, gives the owner the right to prevent unauthorized copying, printing, vending, publishing of an initial copy, making other versions of the work, performing, and recording the work; i.e., the rights are at least co-extensive with those under the federal copyright statute. Further, if a work is ineligible for statutory copyright because it is not a "writing," it may still receive protection under this co-extensive theory. However, many observers have theorized that the so-called *common law* copyright is in reality a species of tort law directed against those who unfairly appropriate values created by another.

In a recent case (*Goldstein v. California*, 412 U.S. 546, 1973) the Supreme Court enunciated the principle that states possess concurrent jurisdiction with the federal government as long as state legislation does not conflict with federal legislation; i.e., the states may protect those works for which Congress has failed to provide protection unless Congress has deliberately excluded them. This decision contrasts strongly with earlier decisions in patent law wherein the Supreme Court totally voided the concept of unfair competition ("copying") as conflicting with the exclusive jurisdiction of federal law over *patentable* subject matter.

**Patents.** In contrast to the copyright species of protection where the federal government essentially performs only the ministerial functions of recording and registering works for which protection is sought, an applicant must be the first to achieve a given result before patent protection can be obtained. The Patent Office, to whom an application is made, undertakes a rigorous search of the particular field and grants a patent only if the inventor's claim to be first is verified. Further, unlike copyright, the subject matter of patent is quite limited, including devices, processes, and compositions of matter, but excluding such discoveries as laws of nature, mathematical formulas, or business plans. If the discovery is to be given patent protection, it must not only be novel and useful, but must also be nonobvious to one skilled in the art.

The patent grant is exclusively a civil "bounty" license, with no federal criminal sanctions, and only limited customs barriers. However, it grants the patentee exclusivity for 17 years; i.e., other persons or companies may not replicate the patent holder's discovery even though they do so independently without access to his invention.

Since the patent search for prior discoveries is particularly arcane, it is doubtful that an inventor could adequately describe his invention without recourse to extremely specialized (and relatively expensive) legal assistance. Further, there is a substantial delay between the time that an application is submitted to the Patent Office and the final determination by it as to whether a patent should be granted. Then, too, the "hunting license" that the Patent Office grants is not treated with extreme respect by many courts; e.g., in one circuit court, not a single patent has been found valid in almost a decade; overall, less than 50% of all challenged patents are upheld on appeal.

At the present time it is arguable whether the states may enact patent-type legislation to protect discoveries that are not subsumed under federal standards. In 1964, the Supreme Court ruled that state laws which clash with the objectives of federal patent laws would not be allowed to exist (*Sears Roebuck v. Stiffel*, 376 U.S. 225: state laws prohibiting the copying and marketing of unpatented articles were unconstitutional). However, in 1974, the Supreme Court held that state laws which provided an *alternative* means of legal protection to federal patent statutes were constitutional (*Kewanee Oil Co. v. Bicron Corp.*, 94 S.Ct. 1879: state trade-secret laws which preclude illicit copying but not independent discovery or "reverse engineering" were not necessarily preempted by federal patent laws).

**Copyright and Patent Protection for Computer Programs.** In 1964, the Copyright Office announced somewhat reluctantly that it would accept computer programs for registration; however, it clearly indicated that whether a program is a "writing of an author" was a doubtful question.

Notwithstanding these substantial doubts, almost all purveyors of software have chosen to copyright at least part of their program libraries. IBM Circular 120–2083–1 (Rel. 1969) gives detailed instructions to its personnel regarding the procedures involved in licensable programs that are to be copyrighted (Bigelow, 1975).

On the other hand, the Supreme Court ruled in 1972 that computer programs were not patentable (*Gottshalk v. Benson*, 409 U.S. 63). However, the Court of Customs and Patent Appeals has indicated that it considers this decision not applicable to all computer programs, just those in which the algorithm seems to be exclusively mathematical in nature. Whether this narrow interpretation in the Supreme Court decision is justified is at best arguable.

Although computer programs may not be patentable, it is also possible that the courts might decide that programs are not "writings," thus leaving them without any statutory or common-law protection whatsoever. A discussion of the rationale behind this caveat is beyond the scope of this article; however, the possibility of such a "no-man's land" for computer programs should not be dismissed out of hand (Galbi, 1972).

Although no state has yet given explicit copyright statutory recognition to computer programs, unlike the sound recording ("tape and record piracy") field, one should recognize that such enactments could be legislated if a need should be manifested.

Even if computer programs are properly the subject of copyright protection, the extent of that protection may be somewhat limited; e.g., it probably would not extend to the ideas embedded in the program nor to the techniques used in developing or making the program, but only to the format. Even in that case, it is possible that the protection would not extend to the use of the program within the computer but only to the copying of the program for resale to others (Duggan, 1972).

Similarly, if Congress should grant patentlike protection to computer programs, as IBM has advocated (Bigelow, 1972), it is possible that the protection would not extend to the concepts or new principles, but only to the specific series of executable instructions deposited with the Patent Office.

**Copyrighted Material as Data for a Computer-Based Information System.** Here the problem faced by the computer user is the converse of that posed earlier, in that he wishes to use someone else's copyrighted material in his own information system without the copyright owner's permission (Duggan, 1972, p. 82). There are no legal precedents on which to base freedom of use, and in view of the uncertainty that the Supreme Court has interjected by its *Goldstein* decision (*Goldstein v. California*, 1973), any attempt to reason by analogy is at best most hazardous.

Nimmer (1971, §141) points out that there are two elements that must be established if a plaintiff is to be successful in obtaining relief from the defendant's activities: (1) ownership of the copyright by the plaintiff; and (2) "copying" by the defendant.

Assuming that these two elements can be proved where necessary ("copying" usually will be proved circumstantially by showing access and substantial similarity), then the infringer may be able to demonstrate that his "copying" was justified, most notably under the equitable and nonstatutory doctrine of "fair use." The issue of fair use is probably the most awkward and troublesome in the whole field of copyright. Among the elements felt to be applicable in determining whether a particular "copying" is not actionable are: (1) extent and relative value of the copyrighted material and the effects upon distribution; (2) nature and objects of selections made; (3) degree to which the copying prejudices the sale or profits of the original works, etc. Nimmer (1971, §145) argues for a rather simple "litmus" test: Does the "copying" diminish or prejudice the potential *sale* of the plaintiff's work? Another author (McDonald, 1962) has given a "golden rule" description of fair use: "Take not from others to such an extent and in such a manner that you would be resentful if they so took from you."

In one recent case on this subject (*Williams & Wilkins v. United States* 95 S.Ct. 1344 (1975); judgement of Court of Claims upheld by equally divided court) the court did not hold in favor of the plaintiff's claim that copying activities at the National Library of Medicine had infringed its copyrights. However, this case gives little clue to the boundaries of fair use in current library practice in copying particular articles for substantial distribution upon reader request. However, one may still conclude that *at present* inclusion of copyrighted material within a computer-based full or partial text information retrieval (IR) system would constitute fair use, due to *present* technological and economic realities; i.e., because computer-based IR systems are substantially more expensive than manual alternatives relative to the cost of reproducing the data. Depending on changes in technology, this may not continue to be the case (Duggan, 1972, pp. 82-83).

**Conclusions.** Although copyrights and patents have had no measurable effect upon computer developments, the lack of firm guidelines as to what can and cannot be done to protect programs, as well as to incorporate protected material in a data base, has lent a substantial degree of legal uncertainty to this industry. It does not appear reasonable to assume that this uncertainty will soon be dispelled, even if Congress enacts the long-awaited Copyright Revision Bill. Instead, it seems quite likely that this "product of censorship, guild monopoly, trade regulation statutes and misunderstanding" (Patterson,

1968) will continue to cause legal debate and operative uncertainty.


REFERENCES

1962. McDonald, J. "Non-Infringing Uses," *Bulletin Copyright Society*, Vol. 9, Nos. 466, 467.

1968. Patterson, L. R. *Copyright in Historical Perspective*. Nashville, Tenn.: Vanderbilt University Press, p. 229.

1972. Bigelow, R. *Computer Law Service*, Appendix 4-5a. Chicago: Callaghan and Co.

1972. Duggan, M. A. "Viewpoint of the Computer Scientist," in A. Kent and H. Lancour, *Copyright: Current Viewpoints on History, Laws, Legislation*. New York: R. R. Bowker, pp. 66–103.

1972. Galbi, E. W. "Copyright and Unfair Competition Law as Applied to the Protection of Computer Programming," in R. Bigelow, *Computer Law Service*, §4-3, Art. 1. (For a contrary view.)

1973. Bowman, W. S., Jr. *Patent and Antitrust Law: A Legal and Economic Appraisal*. Chicago: University of Chicago Press, p. 2.

1974. Nimmer, M. B. *Nimmer on Copyright*. 2 vol. New York: Mathew Bender, §§100, 141.

1975. Bigelow, R. *Computer Law Service*, Appendix 4-36. Chicago: Callaghan and Co.


M. A. DUGGAN

# COROUTINE

For articles on related subjects *see* SUBROUTINE; and PROCEDURE.
For articles on related terms *see* BUFFER; COMPILER; and OPERATING SYSTEMS.

A coroutine, like a subroutine, is a kind of program module. A program module consists of (1) a fixed part (such as instructions in a computer language) that is the same for all instances of execution of the module, and (2) a variable part (such as data and control information) that may vary with different instances of execution. This variable part is called an "activation record," and clearly there is a different activation record for each instance of execution.

A coroutine differs from a subroutine in that the lifetime of a particular activation record is independent of the time when control enters or leaves the module. Moreover, the activation record of a coroutine maintains a local instruction counter so that, whenever control enters the module, execution begins at the point where it stopped when control last left that particular instance of execution.

These features facilitate quasi-parallel execution. Given a group of coroutines, the execution of each proceeds essentially independently of the rest, subject only to explicit synchronization requests. Execution is only quasi-parallel, rather than actually being parallel, in that only one processor is envisioned (this also avoids timing problems). When a coroutine is selected for dispatch and execution begun, it continues to execute until control is explicitly relinquished by some natural break, whereupon some other coroutine is selected for dispatch.

This kind of quasi-parallel execution is extremely useful when writing programs that consist of several cooperating processes. This arises in discrete event simulation, and also in other event-driven activities such as in a computer operating system or in a multiphase compiler.

For example, the original application of coroutines was to a multiphase compiler. Each phase was written as a coroutine, and the output buffer of one phase was the input buffer of the next. Once given control, a phase would run until its input buffer was exhausted or its output buffer was full, and then would yield control to another phase. In this way the phases ran in quasi-parallel, subject only to the constraint that input for a phase be available, or that output be consumed by a subsequent phase. This unconventional implementation controls buffer size, permitting the use of in-core buffers and resulting in faster compilation.

M. GENTLEMAN

# COURSEWRITER. 

*See* AUTHORING LANGUAGES AND SYSTEMS.

# CREDIT SYSTEM APPLICATIONS

For articles on related subjects *see* ADMINISTRATIVE-BUSINESS APPLICATIONS; and POINT-OF-SALE TERMINAL.

In early Greece and Rome, and even up through the Industrial Revolution, a creditor did not need a computer to furnish him with information about a potential debtor. He was already familiar with the applicant's character, his ability to repay the debt, and the type of collateral available to secure the debt. Today, with hundreds of millions of credit cards in existence and billions of credit transactions occurring annually, most credit systems require the use of a modern, high-speed computer.

Following the introduction of oil company credit cards in the late 1930s, their use soon became widespread, making personal knowledge of potential debtors virtually impossible. Current estimates of the number of credit cards in existence in the United States range from 100 to 300 million cards. Any attempt to handle this number of credit accounts without the use of large, high-speed computers would certainly have met with economic failure. Other types of credit systems for bonds and mortgages are also being computerized, but their absolute volumes are small compared with the number of transactions processed through credit cards. Today, most banks will process small consumer loans only through a bank credit card account. In general, a credit card can be used to purchase almost all retail goods.

**Computers and Credit Systems.** An effective credit system must be concerned with the entire spectrum of credit activities: credit approval, sale authorization, billing, dunning, and collection.

CREDIT APPROVAL. The credit process usually begins when a person files a written application on which he states his name, address, telephone number, employment history and job statistics, bank references, and names of other creditors. An example of a credit card application is shown in Fig. 1. In evaluating the application, the creditor often uses a technique called "point scoring," i.e., assigning a numeric value, depending upon the applicant's response, to each item of information requested. The score or sum total of all points assigned to a particular application is then compared with predetermined values to decide whether to extend credit. Each credit-issuing company that uses a point-scoring technique will include the categories, variables, and assigned scores it has found to be most significant to its own operation.

After data from an application is entered into a computer, points are assigned by an evaluation program. The score for an application is compared with predetermined values to determine what action to take. Sophisticated computer programs have been developed to analyze past experiences, using particular techniques, and to recommend future changes in an attempt to reduce the cost of selling on credit. It would be very difficult to process the large number of credit card applications today without such a technique.

In developing the account number to be assigned to an applicant, the use of a check digit is usually employed. The computer creates the check digit by using the first N − 1 digits of the account number as input to a check-digit generation routine. The resulting calculations produce a single, unique digit, which becomes the last digit of the account number. An example of the "mod 10" technique for generating check digits is given in Fig. 2. The oil company credit card displayed utilizes an 11-digit account number, with the first ten digits (123 456 789 0) being the actual account number and the eleventh digit (3) being the check digit. In order to generate the check digit, using the "mod 10" technique, we start from the low-order position and work toward the high order (from right to left). First, we multiply the odd-position numbers by 2, carrying and adding where appropriate:

$$
\begin{array}{ll}
0 \times 2 = 0 & \\
8 \times 2 = 16 & \text{(carry 1)} \\
6 \times 2 = 12 + 1 & \text{(carry 1)} \\
4 \times 2 = 8 + 1 & \\
2 \times 2 = 4 &
\end{array}
$$

We now divide each result by 10 and sum the remainders;

$$0 + 6 + 3 + 9 + 4 = 22.$$

Next we sum the even-position digits (from left to right):

$$1 + 3 + 5 + 7 + 9 = 25,$$

and sum the two results:

$$22 + 25 = 47$$

The number that must be added to make this result evenly divisible by 10 is the check digit; in this instance it is the digit 3 (47 + 3 = 50). The use of a check digit helps reduce errors in the transcription of account numbers.

SALE AUTHORIZATION. After credit has been approved and a credit limit has been established, each sale above the preset dollar amount must be authorized. The authorization process determines whether the potential purchaser is actually allowed to make purchases on the account, whether the

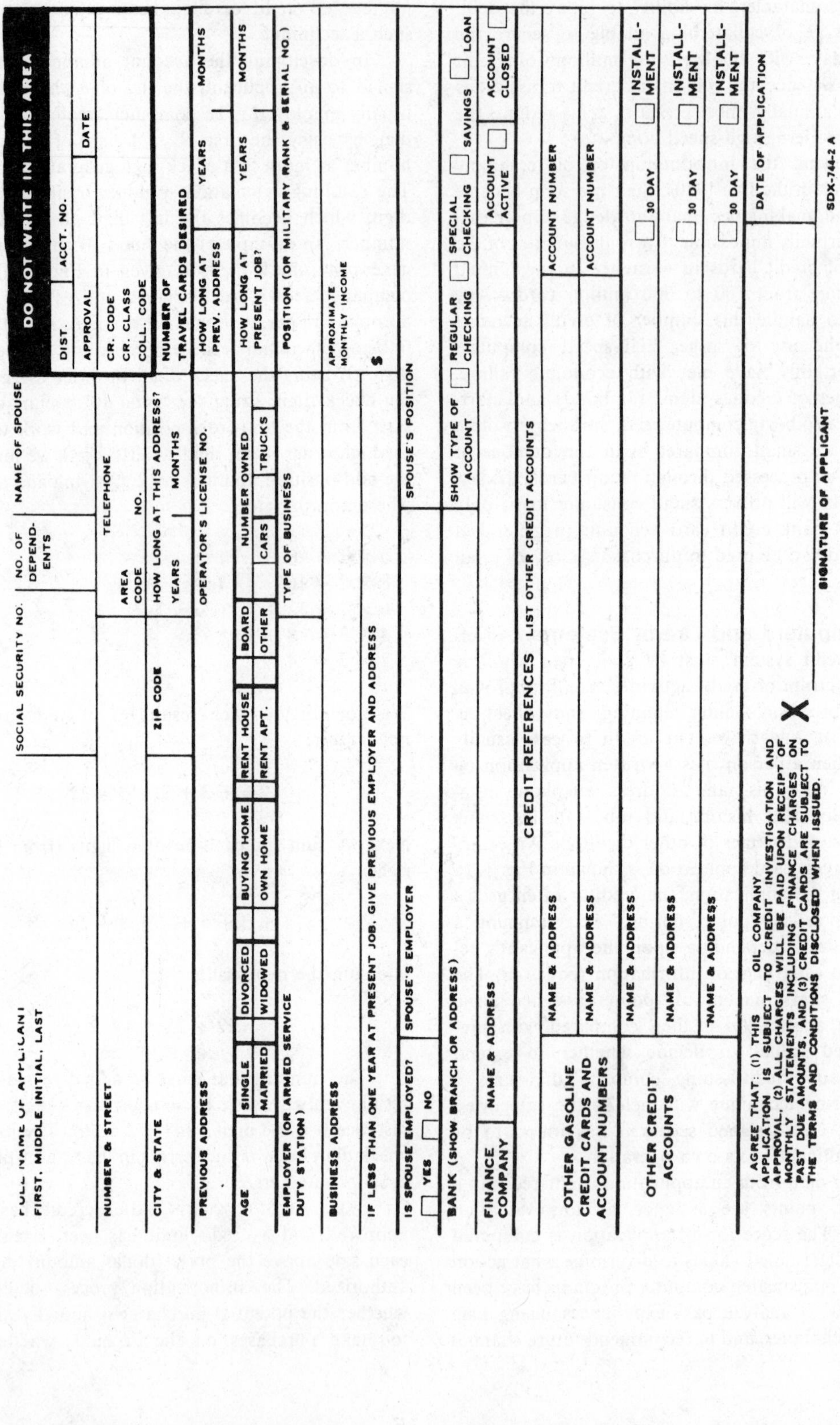
FULL NAME OF APPLICANT FIRST, MIDDLE INITIAL, LAST
SOCIAL SECURITY NO.
NO. OF DEPEND-ENTS
NAME OF SPOUSE
DO NOT WRITE IN THIS AREA
DIST.
APPROVAL
ACCT. NO.
DATE
CR. CODE
CR. CLASS
COLL. CODE
NUMBER & STREET
TELEPHONE
AREA CODE
NO.
CITY & STATE
ZIP CODE
HOW LONG AT THIS ADDRESS? YEARS MONTHS
NUMBER OF TRAVEL CARDS DESIRED
PREVIOUS ADDRESS
OPERATOR'S LICENSE NO.
HOW LONG AT PREV. ADDRESS YEARS MONTHS
AGE
SINGLE
MARRIED
DIVORCED
WIDOWED
BUYING HOME
OWN HOME
RENT HOUSE
RENT APT.
BOARD
OTHER
NUMBER OWNED
CARS
TRUCKS
HOW LONG AT PRESENT JOB? YEARS MONTHS
EMPLOYER (OR ARMED SERVICE DUTY STATION)
TYPE OF BUSINESS
POSITION (OR MILITARY RANK & SERIAL NO.)
BUSINESS ADDRESS
APPROXIMATE MONTHLY INCOME
$
IF LESS THAN ONE YEAR AT PRESENT JOB, GIVE PREVIOUS EMPLOYER AND ADDRESS
IS SPOUSE EMPLOYED? YES NO
SPOUSE'S EMPLOYER
SPOUSE'S POSITION
BANK (SHOW BRANCH OR ADDRESS)
SHOW TYPE OF ACCOUNT
REGULAR CHECKING
SPECIAL CHECKING
SAVINGS
LOAN
ACCOUNT ACTIVE
ACCOUNT CLOSED
FINANCE COMPANY
NAME & ADDRESS
CREDIT REFERENCES
LIST OTHER CREDIT ACCOUNTS
OTHER GASOLINE CREDIT CARDS AND ACCOUNT NUMBERS
NAME & ADDRESS
ACCOUNT NUMBER
NAME & ADDRESS
ACCOUNT NUMBER
OTHER CREDIT ACCOUNTS
NAME & ADDRESS
30 DAY
INSTALL-MENT
NAME & ADDRESS
30 DAY
INSTALL-MENT
NAME & ADDRESS
30 DAY
INSTALL-MENT
I AGREE THAT: (1) THIS OIL COMPANY APPLICATION IS SUBJECT TO CREDIT INVESTIGATION AND APPROVAL, (2) ALL CHARGES WILL BE PAID UPON RECEIPT OF MONTHLY STATEMENTS INCLUDING FINANCE CHARGES ON PAST DUE AMOUNTS, AND (3) CREDIT CARDS ARE SUBJECT TO THE TERMS AND CONDITIONS DISCLOSED WHEN ISSUED.
X
SIGNATURE OF APPLICANT
DATE OF APPLICATION
SDX-744-2 A

**Fig. 1.** Typical credit card application.

account has exceeded its credit limit, and the payment history for previous purchases.

**Fig. 2.** Mod 10 method of generating credit card identification digits.

Computers are playing an increasing role in the area of sales authorization, and several service bureaus now provide sales authorization services. When contacting a bureau, a merchant subscribing to such a service might communicate directly with the computer by means of his terminal or by phone with a person who has access to the computer. The merchant provides the customer's account number, the amount of the potential sale, and his own location and identification number for service-billing purposes. The sales information is then evaluated according to information in the customer's file, and the sale is approved or rejected. Of course the merchant has the final say and can override the computer's suggestion, but experience shows this is rarely done.

If a high-speed computer is used, the entire authorization process can be accomplished in less than a minute—often within a few seconds—depending on the technique used for communicating with the computer.

Several of the larger credit card-issuing companies are now applying a dark strip of magnetic recording material on the back of their credit cards, similar to those used by San Francisco's Bay Area Rapid Transit system (BART) on their commuter tickets. When the magnetic data strip is used in conjunction with point-of-sale terminals (i.e., a cash register type of terminal connected to the authorization computer), the credit-available field of the data strip can be decremented each time the customer makes a purchase. Many banks now use this technique to make cash available to depositors after banking hours. Both the American Bankers Association (ABA) and the International Air Transportation Association (IATA) have developed standards for recording data on the strip.

Billing. The billing data may be captured automatically at the time of the transaction, such as when making a credit-card telephone call or when purchasing merchandise at large department stores. These systems generally use the descriptive billing method, in which only an itemized list of charges is sent to the customer for billing purposes.

In systems where copies of the original sales slips are returned to the customer with his bill (country club billing), such as gasoline or food purchases on credit cards, the sales data is usually entered subsequent to the sale. Country club billing systems often use a special-purpose computer with optical character readers to read the sales data from the sales ticket and sort the tickets for return to the customer.

Dunning and Collection. This final phase of the credit process occurs only when a debtor is delinquent in his payment. A computer-processed analysis of all active accounts will single out those accounts for which required payment was not received within the specified time period. Depending on the size of the balance due and the amount of time the account is past due, an appropriate dunning letter can be selected from those stored in the computer's memory, printed, and then sent to the customer. After the proper series of dunning letters has been sent, the account can be flagged for personal review or for collection procedures.

As a result of the Truth in Lending Act (passed in 1972), billing, dunning, and collection procedures have become increasingly more complicated. Where a large number of accounts are involved, it would be impossible to determine and report the interest paid by each customer without the capabilities of a modern computer.

**A Typical Computerized Credit Card System.** A credit card system is a large data base system, typified by a large number of accounts, random access storage, and strictly specified formats for inputting data and generating output reports. Although real time inquiry into the file is usually available, inputting of data, file updating, and printing of invoices and statistical reports are usually done in a batch mode on a scheduled basis.

The basic functions performed by different credit card systems are very similar; however, there has been little sharing or purchasing of existing credit management packages. Each company has tended to develop and write its own in-house credit system, most often using Cobol and a machine language to handle the inquiry portion of the application.

As an example, we consider a typical credit card system used by a petroleum company to process its credit card sales, which handles about five million accounts. At the service station level, it requires a dollar-amount imprinter capable of transferring the customer data from the credit card and printing the dollar amount of the sale on the basic three-part paper sales document. The sales tickets are processed in one location, where the data is captured and entered automatically into the computer system through magnetic tape. The tape is created by a computer with optical capabilities for reading the imprinted information from the paper sales ticket. At the initial reading, the customer's account number and the dollar amount of the sale is sprayed in ink, using a unique recording code consisting of vertical lines and spaces, onto the back of the ticket to assist later in sorting.

Since all accounts are not billed on the same day of the month, the sales tickets are stored in a vault until a customer's cycle is billed. Cycle billing is used to level the daily processing time required by the system and to provide a more favorable cash flow situation.

After being billed, a customer is requested to return a portion of the bill with his payment. The payment is sent to a post office lock box, where collections are gathered and processed by the credit card company itself or by a bank, which charges a service fee.

In processing the payments, the amount of the check must be compared with the amount on the returned portion of the bill. Any discrepancy, either shortage or overpayment, requires additional handling and processing time. The checks must be encoded with the magnetic ink characters representing the amount for which the customer's check is drawn. The sum of the checks deposited is compared with the sum of the returned portion of the bills, to keep the system in balance.

For a system of about five million gasoline credit card accounts, between one $1 and $2 million per day must be processed and applied to the appropriate customers' accounts in order to keep the master file current. A staff of 75 customer service representatives is needed to process customer inquiries concerning bills, payments, and special charges, and to handle the collection of delinquent accounts. The work of the service representatives is supported by 25 CRT terminals capable of inquiring into the computer's customer file, 10 microfilm readers to examine past history files, and 20 clerical and typing assistants.

Names and address changes to the file, special handling of certain accounts, and entering data from sales tickets that could not be read automatically by the retina requires another 40 data entry operators. These operators use key-to-disk, key-to-tape, and keypunch machines to enter the data into the computer's mass storage.

The main processing computer is a third-generation computer and has 512K bytes of memory, 1¼ billion bytes of random access storage, 9 tape drives, 2 card readers, 1 card punch, 35 CRT terminals, and 3 high-speed printers. It rents for $60,000 per month and requires two operators per shift. In total, the credit system costs $20 million per year, of which $4 to $8 million is charged to bad debts and fraud, $1.5 million represents postage costs, and the remainder is overhead and payroll cost of the 400 people required to perform its various functions.

REFERENCES

1972. Hendrickson, Robert A. *The Cashless Society*. New York: Dodd, Mead & Company.

1971. Whiteside, Conon D. *EDP Systems for Credit Management*. New York: Wiley-Interscience.

J. K. AMSBAUGH

# CRIME AND COMPUTER SECURITY

For articles on related subjects *see* COMPUTERS AND SOCIETY; DATA SECURITY; and SECURITY OF COMPUTER INSTALLATIONS, PHYSICAL.

For articles on related term *see* DATA COMMUNICATION NETWORKS.

The need for security measures to protect computers and their contents was recognized from the beginnings of computer usage for classified government projects and data. This was easily accomplished for early batch-operated computers that were made to perform one job completely before going to the next.

Problems arose when technical advances allowed the sharing of resources by more than one job at a time, on-line storing of data from job to job, and on-line servicing of more than one user at a time. At the same time, computers were being used for more purposes where the possibilities for unauthorized or antisocial acts could result in gain, and errors could result in serious losses. Losses from errors were real, and resulted in the need to control access to computers, access to stored data, and access by one program into the memory space assigned to another.

Techniques were developed to protect the computer facilities, use secret passwords and authorization tables for access to computers and data files, and provide programs and hardware features to partition memory. This seemed to control the error problem, but limitations in completeness of computer security became evident when the possibilities of intentional unauthorized acts were considered.

The first computer-related act involving criminal prosecution occurred in 1964. A programmer in Texas stole his employer's computer programs, worth $5 million, and was convicted and served a five-year prison sentence (Texas v. Hancock). The first federal crime involving the use of a computer occurred in 1966 when a programmer in a bank put a change in a program to ignore his checking account when checking for overdrafts (U.S. v. Bennett). In 1968 an accountant was caught after embezzling $1 million over a six-year period, and was convicted and sentenced to ten years in prison. He used a computer to simulate the operation of his company to assist in regulating his peculations to avoid detection (California v. Mansfield). The first crime of stealing a program, held as a trade secret, from the memory of a computer through a remote terminal and telephone circuit occurred in 1971 (California v. Ward).

Broadening the concept of computer crime to any kind of act associated with computers where the victims suffered or could have suffered losses, or where the perpetrator experienced or could have experienced gain, provides a more all-inclusive perspective on the computer security problem. The number of such recorded acts has increased from 8 in 1969 to 23, 47, and 39 occurring respectively in each subsequent year.

A collection and study of 160 reported cases (Parker et al. 1973) produced valuable facts for developing more effective computer security. In the cases studied, it was found that computers play four roles:

1. *Subject*: Acts such as vandalism or unauthorized usage attack computers or their contents.

2. *Unique environment*: This refers to acts involving computer programs and data in computer-readable form.

3. *Tool*: The computer is used to plan or carry out a crime.

4. *Symbol*: Fraudulent acts, deceit, or intimidation are charged as due directly to the use of computers, such as in false advertising of computer dating services or abusive dunning of consumers for unpaid bills.

The population of potential perpetrators tends to be in computer-related occupations, for these are the only people with the necessary skills, access, and knowledge to perform the acts. Perpetrators in other occupations need the help of computer people to accomplish their ends. In fact, one study comparing computer- and noncomputer-related bank embezzlements bears this out. Collusion was present in one-third of the computer-related cases and in less than 4% of the other cases.

Perpetrators are generally young, energetic, highly motivated, intelligent people. In some cases, their acts deviate in only small ways from accepted practices of the perpetrators' associates. The Robin Hood syndrome is common: rationalizing acts against organizations, but believing acts against individuals to be immoral. This is combined with the vending machine syndrome—the challenge in the game of beating the machine and the absence of established ethical standards in the new computer-related occupations. A personal philosophy conducive to unauthorized acts and to criminal acts is created.

Assets subject to loss in computer-related acts are different enough from those in previous manual systems to confound the legal profession, the auditors, and traditional security people. Computer programs and data files represent entirely new types of assets—assets that are being subjected to theft, fraud, unauthorized use, and use in extortion. Data stored magnetically and electronically are compact, volatile, only indirectly accessible, and highly time-dependent in value compared to paper-based data in previous manual systems. This produces a different environment for the criminal and offers real possibilities for effective protective measures because of the more structured and controlled environment in computers. In fact, a contest is in progress between the criminal and security organizations when computers are used to penetrate the crime-prone environments. It also appears that the stakes are high; losses noted among the reported computer-related crime cases are ten times higher than in comparable noncomputer related crime.

A practical objective of security (Parker et al., 1973) is to reduce the number of potential perpetrators to as few people as possible. Technical methods to accomplish this include partitioning computer memory, imposing authorization requirements on use of programs and access of programs to stored data, using cryptographic techniques, and identifying people and outside processes attempting to gain entry to the system. Important principles imposed on the security design of such systems include the following:

1. *Absence of design secrecy*: Assume the potential attackers will know as much about the system and its security features as do its designers.
2. *Least privilege*: Provide no more privilege to a process within the system or to users of the system than is necessary to allow them to adequately accomplish their authorized purposes.
3. *Compartmentalization*: Minimize the penetration and subversion of other processes when one process is penetrated or subverted.
4. *Threat monitoring*: Provide detection mechanisms for all anticipated penetration and subversion methods, and produce a reporting facility for monitoring and auditing.
5. *Secure kernel*: Isolate the security processes from the system with minimal and formal interfaces to the system.
6. *Auditability*: Structure security processes to allow complete auditing for integrity.
7. *Permissive authorization*: Base authorization on permission to use any system function rather than exclusion from selected functions for all system activity.
8. *Acceptability*: Make security restrictions acceptable to personnel.

A computer system will be no more secure than its environment or the procedures used in its operation and maintenance. Adequate controls over physical access must be established, and sufficient administrative procedures and discipline in maintaining them must be imposed. Commonly accepted practices include manually or automatically guarded doors; coded badges to identify a wearer's authorized access area; separate performance and dual control of sensitive functions; preemployment, in-depth screening of staff; posting appropriate warning signs; and control and labeling of valuable materials and media. Operational security audits should be made periodically, and backup copies of sensitive programs and data should be stored in safe places. Assignments of security responsibility should be made and a contingency plan drawn up and made readily available. Error recovery and computer restart procedures should be formalized.

These security precautions should be present in any computer facility where possible threats that could result in losses, injuries, or damage are present. In the future, many security activities traditionally performed by people should be automated. However, technological methods are necessary, but not sufficient. Current computer systems cannot be sufficiently patched up—except in special cases and at high cost. No comprehensive technological solution is at hand (and none is expected for some years) so that entirely new computer systems will have security included as a design criterion from the beginning. Even if such a solution is found, computers will still be vulnerable to a few systems maintenance people with sufficient skills, knowledge, and access. However, this limited accessibility would be a vast improvement over the present situation, in which large numbers of computer users have the capacity to subvert computers at both the system and application levels, as substantiated by actual experience.

The use of computers in data communication networks poses a new problem for security. Input and output functions are dispersed to remote terminals in relatively informal and isolated environments, making it especially difficult to identify the authorized terminals and terminal users, and to protect data transmission paths. However, these problems should be solvable in the same time frame as other computer security problems.

### References

1967. Ware, W. H. "Security and Privacy in Computer Systems," *AFIPS Proc.*, Spring Joint Computer Conference.

1970. Smigel, E., and H. Ross. *Crimes Against Bureaucracy*, Van Nostrand Reinhold.

1973. Anderson, J. P. "Computer Technology Planning Study," U.S. Air Force, ESD-TR-73-51, Vol. 1.

1973. Parker, D. B., S. Nycum, and S. Oura. "Computer Abuse," Stanford Research Institute, Menlo Park, Calif. NSF Grant No. GI-37226 (October).

D. B. Parker

**CRITICAL PATH METHOD.** *See* PERT/CPM.

## CRYPTOGRAPHY, COMPUTERS IN

For article on related subject *see* CODES.

Cryptography is the science that deals with the concealment of information in messages for the purpose of making them secret. It is distinguished from steganography, which deals with the concealment of the very existence of secret messages. The alteration, or encryption, of a message is a transformation from the original form of the message into a form that is unintelligible to anyone who does not possess some converting information, called the "key." It is generally assumed that both the original message and its encrypted form, or cryptogram, are composed of sequences of discrete symbols.

There are two distinct methods by which the transformation of a message into a cryptogram may be accomplished: *codes* and *ciphers*. Codes are distinguished by the fact that the basic units of the message to be encoded are selected on the basis of meaningful sequences of symbols, the number of symbols chosen per unit being variable. For example, the basic units for encoding may be the individual words or perhaps even phrases of the message. Ciphers are characterized by the fact that the basic unit of encipherment is always the same. For example, one may encipher single symbols, or possibly groups of symbols of a fixed length.

There are two basic ways in which a message may be enciphered into a cryptogram: by *substitution* or *transposition*. As an example of simple substitution encipherment, consider the following key, or *cipher*, on the symbols of the English alphabet:

| | |
|---|---|
| Message Symbol: | ABCDEFGHIJKLMNOPQRSTUVWXYZ |
| Cryptogram Symbol: | ORGANIZEDBCFHJKLMPQSTUVWXY |

The message BUY GOLD TOMORROW would have the cryptogram RTX ZKFA SKHKPPKV. Each symbol of the message is substituted by its corresponding cryptogram symbol according to the above key.

A well-known transposition encipherment is the rail-fence transposition, in which the message symbols are arranged in one order and the cryptogram is composed by selecting the same symbols in different order; thus

B Y O D O O R W
U G L T M R O

would have the cryptogram BYODOORWUGLTMRO.

The process of enciphering a message may be a very complex combination of these basic transformations, thereby making *cryptanalysis*, the task of determining the original message without the aid of the key extremely difficult indeed. A *cryptanalyst*, the person who attempts to break or solve the cryptogram through cryptanalysis, will take measurements of the cryptogram, using such techniques as single-symbol frequency distribution (the number of occurrences of each distinct symbol) or contact variety (the number of distinct symbols a given symbol precedes or follows).

Many times, the great speed of modern computers is used to help the cryptanalyst in this arduous task, since the value of the information contained in the cryptogram is usually quite substantial. Computers have also been used to actually construct cryptograms but more likely than not this task will be accomplished by specialized devices.

In recent years, cryptography has been employed to protect sensitive information contained in computer systems (e.g., on disk or magnetic tape) from being used by unauthorized personnel. Due to the secrecy surrounding the development of both cryptographic techniques and cryptanalysis there has not been much written about the subject. For a historical account of cryptography, the reader is referred to Kahn (1967). A mathematical treatment can be found in Shannon (1949). The development of cryptographic techniques for computers is given in Krishnamurthy (1970).

### REFERENCES

1949. Shannon, C. E. "Communication Theory of Secrecy Systems," *Bell System Technical Journal*, Vol. 28, No. 4 (October), pp. 656–715.

1967. Kahn, D. *The Codebreakers*. New York: Macmillan.

1970. Krishnamurthy, C. V. "Computer Cryptographic Techniques for Processing and Storage of Confidential Information," *International Journal of Control*, Vol. 12, No. 5, pp. 753–761.

F. STAHL

## CUBE

For article on related subject *see* COMPUTER USER GROUPS.

CUBE is the official organization of the users of Burroughs computers. The name "CUBE" is an acronym derived from *C*ooperating *U*sers of *B*urroughs *E*quipment.

The present association was formed in 1962 through the merger of two earlier organizations of Burroughs computer users, CUE and DUO. These two predecessor groups had comprised the users of Burroughs B220 and B205 (Datatron) systems, respectively. The advent in the early 1960s of such computers as the B200 and B5000 prompted the merger and assured that a single association would serve the needs of all Burroughs computer users.

In 1971, CUBE was incorporated as a nonprofit association with the full name of CUBE, Incorporated. Currently, membership in CUBE is open to users of the B1700 or larger computers. These include the B300/B500, the B2700 through B4700 series, and the B5500, B6700, and B7700 systems. At the beginning of 1974, CUBE members represented approximately 700 installations. CUBE membership is international in scope.

CUBE meetings, which last for 3½ days, are regularly held twice each year. One of these conferences is typically held in the eastern part of the United States, and the other is usually scheduled for a western city.

The basic structure of CUBE centers around hardware-oriented subgroups (B1700, Medium Systems, B6700, etc.), each having its own elected officers. The semi-annual meetings consist of a series of technical sessions, user panels, workshops, etc., for each subgroup. The sessions are planned by the subgroup officers, and the topics are selected to be of current interest to the members and to be in accord with CUBE's purpose of providing a communications forum for the users of Burroughs computers.

The subgroup sessions are augmented by a series of industry-oriented Common Interest Group meetings whose programs are of special interest to Burroughs users from the financial, manufacturing, hospital, education, government, etc., sectors.

The communication emphasis within CUBE includes not only the sharing of ideas among users, but also the communicating to Burroughs of user sentiment on industry trends, future needs, and current products. Formal, two-way communication procedures have been established to facilitate this aspect of CUBE meetings.

Users of future Burroughs computers are assured of an opportunity to organize themselves into a subgroup within CUBE by procedural mechanisms already present in the bylaws of CUBE.

More information about CUBE may be obtained by writing to the CUBE secretary, Burroughs Corporation, P.O. Box 418, Detroit, Michigan 48232.

The presidents of CUBE have been:

Vic Whittier, Dow Chemical Co., 1962–1963
Rusty Langenfeld, Northern Natural Gas Co., 1963–1964
John Lynn, NASA, 1964–1965
Bill Macomber, Harvard Trust Co., 1965–1966
Pete Jensen, Georgia Institute of Technology, 1966–1967
David Guest, Young & Rubicam, International, 1967–1968
Henry Bowlden, Westinghouse Electric Corp., 1968–1969
John Dorosk, Financial Computer Services, 1969–1970
Bill Eichelberger, University of Denver, 1970–1971
Bob Steffens, Michigan National Bank, 1971–1972
Henri Berce, Marathon Oil Co., 1972–1973
Henry Carter, United Data Centers, 1973–1974

T. S. GRIER

# CURRENT AWARENESS SYSTEMS

For articles on related subjects *see* INFORMATION RETRIEVAL; and MEDLARS-MEDLINE.

A current awareness system is a system for notifying users on a periodic basis of the acquisition of information (usually literature) by a central file or library, which should be of specific interest to the user. Such systems are designed to respond to the problems of search selectivity and timeliness by carrying out information searches, using only small files of selected documents. User queries, or *interest profiles*, are typically stored on a permanent basis, to be processed periodically against small files of documents that might be newly received at a given information center. Users are notified on a weekly or monthly basis of new acquisitions that match their interest profiles. Under ideal conditions, such systems for the selective dissemination of information (SDI) are able to retrieve information exactly tailored to meet the specific, possibly changing, needs of each user, while supplying the output directly on a periodic and dependable basis.

The rapid development of selective dissemination services is due to two main factors: First, SDI services are much less expensive to implement than on-demand searches because there is no need to include in the document collections the backlog information covering many years in the past. Second, the existence of the many distribution services of magnetic tape data bases—normally containing titles, citations, and sometimes index terms and abstracts of published articles and research—insures the availability of the needed input data on a regular basis. Normally, the producers of the tape data bases sell the SDI services directly on their own account, or they make the document tapes available to third parties, who in turn provide the dissemination services. Ideally, a given organization might process data bases in many different subject areas and in many languages, thereby rendering flexible services to a large and heterogeneous user population. SDI services are implemented in all areas of applied science and engineering, and in many of the natural and social sciences as well.

It has been conjectured that a flexible SDI service may be the answer to the inefficiencies now inherent in the normal publication system, in which each published item carries high publication costs and minimal readership. An improved, more economical system might then eliminate bound-volume journals entirely and restrict certain types of books to library use, while providing at the same time an efficient distribution of individual articles and citations that are tailored to specific user populations. In view of the difficulties that still arise in the design of effective dissemination services, and considering the problems that would result for the publishing industry from such a drastic change of publishing standards, such developments may appear to be premature. They must, however, be considered seriously for the not-too-distant future.

A flowchart outlining a typical SDI service is shown in Fig. 1. Specific SDI features are as follows:

1. *Universal features*: utilization of user feedback; automatic or manual profile revision; option for hard copy of abstract and/or full text; and system evaluation.

2. *Optional features*: use of free text (title or abstract) search; use of multilingual thesaurus; searching of multiple data bases; incorporation of preprinted in addition to published information; incorporation of citation, author, or institution alert; and special distribution to designated recipients.

It should be noted that, to improve services at a later time, nearly all SDI services include feedback provisions that utilize user opinions about the effectiveness of the search output. Specifically, response cards are often included with the output sent to the

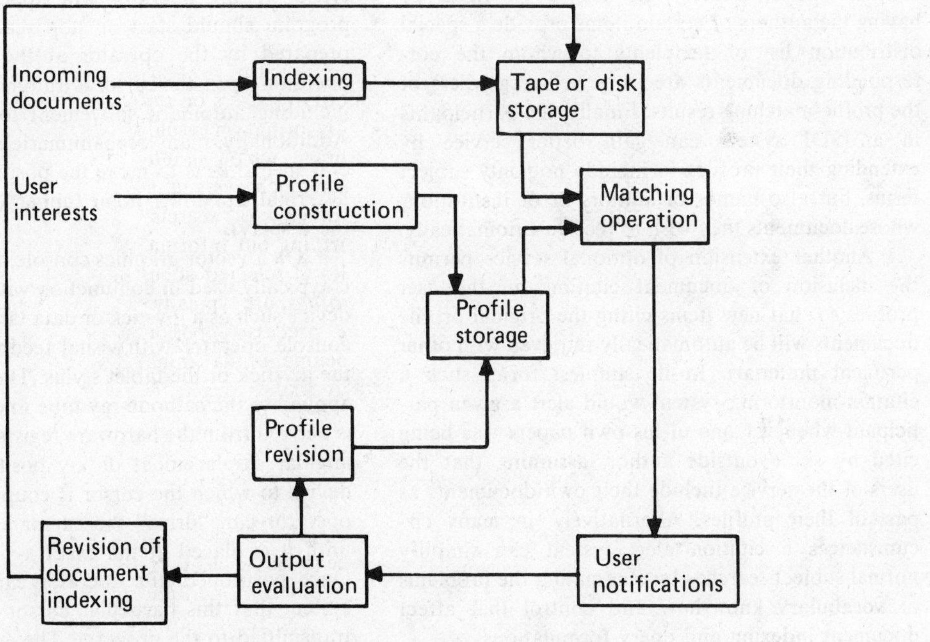


**Fig. 1.** Typical simplified selective dissemination service.

user population to enable the recipients to return information concerning the retrieved materials. Direct assessments of usefulness are sometimes wanted for each retrieved citation; alternatively, the return cards representing user requests for hard copies of certain retrieved documents are automatically taken by the system operators as an expression of approbation on the users' part.

In either case, the user profile statement may be updated, often manually, by reinforcing or increasing the weight of profile terms that match terms included in retrieved items designated as relevant by the users. Profile terms included in documents identified as nonrelevant may be similarly demoted or decreased in weight. Occasionally, the document indexing may be also changed as a function of user judgment. The corresponding feedback paths are indicated in Fig. 1.

The feedback feature is particularly useful in a research environment where user interests may change fairly rapidly. The profiles can then be adjusted little by little as the users express satisfaction or dissatisfaction with the materials obtained from the retrieval service.

Among the useful optional SDI features is the possibility of including in the distribution service those documents in preprint form or other items that are not intended for eventual formal publication. This option provides the means for bypassing the normal publication process and for avoiding publication delays. Delays can also be avoided by having the authors of certain items provide a special distribution list of recipients to whom the corresponding documents are to be sent regardless of the profile-matching results. Finally, the participants in an SDI system can gain better service by extending their profiles to include not only subject terms, but also names of authors or of institutions whose documents they wish to receive automatically.

Another extension of optional service permits the inclusion of document citations in the user profiles so that new items citing the original profile documents will be automatically retrieved with other pertinent materials. In its simplest form, such a citation-monitoring system would alert a given participant whenever one of his own papers was being cited by some outside author, assuming that the users of the service include their own documents as part of their profiles. Alternatively, in many circumstances a citation alert system can simplify normal subject searches by eliminating the problems of vocabulary know-how and control that affect document indexing and query formulations.

An evaluation of SDI services shows that a large proportion of the materials retrieved for the user population is indeed germane to user interests. However, complaints arise because of the large volume of output continually delivered by the services. Even if the proportion of relevant items is fairly high, users receiving 30 or 40 citations every week may eventually tire of the system and revert to on-demand searches that furnish output only when specific requests for service are made.

G. SALTON

## CURSOR

For articles on related subjects *see* COMPUTER GRAPHICS; JOYSTICK; and RAND TABLET.

A cursor is a special character or symbol on a soft copy (display) terminal, which is used by an interactive program as a pointer or attention-focusing device to allow communication and interaction between the console operator and the program. On alphanumeric displays, for example, a (blinking) underscore or overscore character (or an inverted v, called a "caret") may be used by the program or the hardware to indicate where the next character to be typed by the operator will appear or where the program should start or stop reading the message prepared by the operator at the console. As the operator types, the cursor is automatically advanced, including automatic movement to successive lines. Additionally, many alphanumeric displays have several special keys to move the position of the cursor: left, right, up, down, home (upper left-hand corner of the display).

On a vector-graphics console, the cursor symbol is typically used in conjunction with a manual input device such as a joystick or data tablet to provide the console operator with visual feedback as he moves the joystick or the tablet stylus. The beam deflection applied to the cathode-ray tube to display the cursor is derived from the hardware registers that record the angular displacement or x-y position of the input device to which the cursor is coupled. In effect, the operator can "drive" the cursor around the screen until it is placed at the exact x-y location desired. Once positioned, the operator can indicate to the system that this particular cursor position is to be transmitted to the program. The cursor x-y position can then be used by the program either to provide raw x-y *drawing* input data or to be compared against x-y positions of information already on the screen for identification purposes (thereby providing a substitute for identification by lightpen *picking*).

A. VAN DAM

# CYBERNETICS

For articles on related subjects *see* AUTOMATION; and CONTROL APPLICATIONS.
For article on related term *see* WIENER, NORBERT A.

Cybernetics is a science founded in the 1940s by a group of scientists and engineers led by N. Wiener and A. Rosenblueth, who coined the word "cybernetics" (from Greek: pilot, steersman, governor) to designate the science of "control and communication in the animal and the machine" (Wiener, 1948). This definition still expresses the substantial content of cybernetics, although there is a broad spectrum of current interpretations (Drozin et al., 1973).

Cybernetic concepts cluster around three related component concepts: systems (animal or machine), communication between systems, and regulation or self-regulation of systems. Since the first two are common to nearly all fields of knowledge, it is the third component, regulation, that distinguishes the discipline. Cybernetics is the science of regulation and control—purposive regulation for adaptive system survival (Beer, 1966).

Cybernetics borrows ubiquitously from other sciences. Borrowing from mathematical concepts, cybernetics concerns all conceivable *sets* of systems (Ashby, 1970); and from physical and psychological concepts, it "deals with all forms of behaviour in so far as they are regular, or determinate, or reproducible" (Ashby, 1970, p. 1). However, to be of practical interest, cybernetic systems have two properties: (1) some aspect must provide observable data over a period of time (the "protocol," Ashby, 1970, p. 88); (2) from the protocol it must be possible to infer some stable configuration or regularity in transformation of states. Without observable regularity in transformation, a system is said to be unconstrained. Without constraint, it is unpredictable; if it becomes unstable, it cannot be restored to stability or is uncontrollable. For regulation, a system must show some regularity.

Time is the principal cybernetic variable, while "variety" is the principal dependent variable. Variety is quantitatively measured by the logarithm (usually base 2) of the number of discriminations that an observer (or a sensing system) can make relative to a system (Ashby, 1968, p. 124). For example, in the phrase "take care" the variety is $\log_2 6 = 2.51$ bits if the system is the set of distinguishably different letters; $\log_2 2 = 1$ bit if the system is the set of words; and $\log_2 1 = 0$ if the system is the message considered as a unit. Because variety is based on discrimination of differences, it measures equally well all psychophysical or higher cognitive discriminations (Heilprin, 1973). For example the variety in five psychophysically discriminated shades of green is $\log_2 5 = 2.25$ bits, the same as the variety in a decision process from a choice of five abstract alternatives.

The real significance of variety lies not in its absolute amount, but in the possibility of its increase or decrease. We increase sensory variety when we gather data, decrease it when we summarize, compress, abstract. Both processes are necessary for cognition. However, "lower" cognitive processes are associated with data gathering or increase in concrete sensory variety, whereas "higher" cognitive processes are associated with data condensation, abstraction, or decrease in concrete variety.

When the variety shown by a system under one set of conditions is less than that shown by the system under another set of conditions, the relation between the two sets of variety is a *constraint* (Ashby, 1968, p. 127). For example, suppose two couples (A and B, or four voters) can each vote independently R or D. Then the number of distinguishably different outcomes is $2^4 = 16$ and the variety is $\log_2 16 = 4$ bits. If, however, Mr. A always defers to Mrs. A's judgment and votes the same as Mrs. A, the number of different outcomes is 8 and the variety shown $\log_2 8 = 3$ bits. If, further, Mr. and Mrs. B always vote R, then the variety in the outcomes is $\log_2 2 = 1$ bit. The progressive decrease in variety from 4 bits to 3 to 1 corresponds to increase in constraint on the system showing the variety. Returning to the requirement for regulation —that there must exist some constraint in order to predict the behavior of a system—it is apparent that to regulate a system is to impose a constraint on its variety.

The cybernetics of constrained and unconstrained sets was advanced by the insight of Wiener (1948) who said that "the transmission of information is impossible save as a transmission of alternatives," and by Shannon's observation that "the significant aspect is that the actual message is *selected from a set* of possible messages" (Shannon and Weaver, 1949) Thus, *regulation implies capability to prevent occurrence of unfavorable alternatives.* Therefore, it implies *transmission* of these alternatives to the regulator, which in turn must respond (with a command message directed toward preserving the stability of the regulated system).

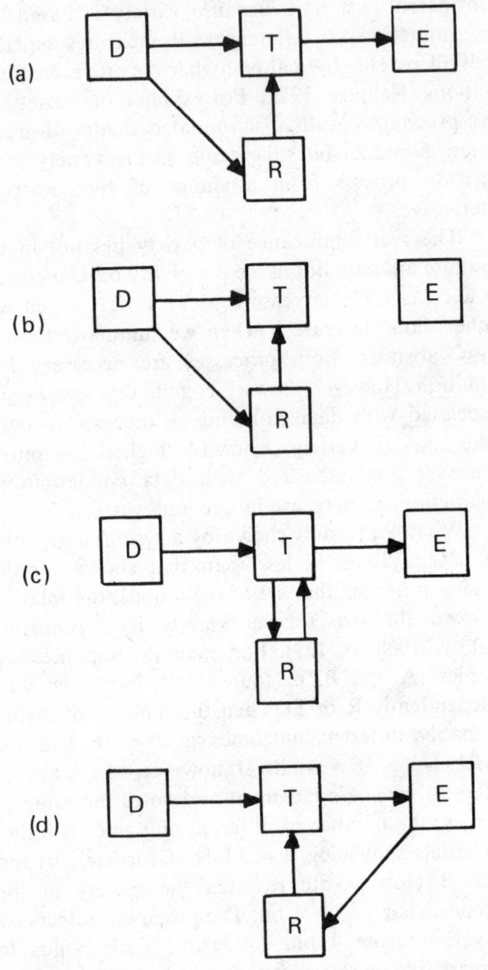


**Fig. 1.** Law of requisite variety. (a) One-step communication channel regulation: D → R. (b) Perfect (one step) regulation: D → R. (c) Two-step regulation: D → T → R. (d) Three-step (error controlled) regulation: D → T → E → R.

Fig. 1 shows the basic elements of a regulatory system. The system whose essential variables (E) are to be kept within certain limits depends on communication of variety (information) between system disturbance (D), the regulator (R), and the environment (T). The most direct regulation is DR, shown in Fig. 1(a). The signal arrives from D in time for R to act on T before T affects E. Figs. 1(c) and 1(d) show paths DTR and DTER, progressively less effective. Perfect regulation [Fig. 1(b)] would leave E isolated from external disturbance—i.e., unaware because of noncommunication that a disturbance had occurred.

A system is said to be well regulated when, through the intervention of the regulator and the environment, a disturbance cannot permanently drive the system from a state in which it is stable (retains its structure and function—"survives"). Lack of regulation occurs when the system is transformed to a state from which it cannot return to a stable state; i.e., cannot survive.

The principal law of cybernetics (credited to Ashby, 1968, p. 206) is the law of requisite variety. This states that if log $V_d$ is the variety in the possible ways in which a disturbance D can affect a system E (to be regulated by a regulator R), and log $V_r$ is the variety in R's alternatives (optional ways of response to D), then the variety in the possible outcomes (log $V_0$) affecting E cannot be forced by R below (log $V_d - \log_r V$), or log $(V_d/V_r) \geq \log V_0$.

This law applies to all forms of regulation, and is independent of field of science or technology or of specific mechanism. Loosely interpreted, it means that—assuming the disturbance, environment, and the system itself are fixed and cannot be altered—the only way to increase E's probability of survival is to increase R's variety (R's versatility, or the number of different modes of response which R can make in order to protect E's stability as affected by D). However, satisfying the law by increasing $V_r$ does not guarantee perfect regulation, i.e., perfect shielding of E. Just as the existence of constraint is necessary but not sufficient for regulation, satisfying the law of requisite variety is necessary but not sufficient for successful regulation (Heilprin, 1973, p. 24).

Space prevents discussion of many prominent cybernetic features such as classification of cybernetic systems by intractability to control (determinate, complex, and "very large"), black-box theory, feedback, isomorphism and homomorphism, and epigenetic theory of regulation. See the references cited and a growing list of periodicals, among which are *Journal of Cybernetics* (American Society of Cybernetics), *Transactions on Systems, Man and Cybernetics* (IEEE), and *Soviet Cybernetic Review.*

REFERENCES

1948. Wiener, N. *Cybernetics or Control and Communication in the Animal and the Machine.* Cambridge, Mass.: M.I.T. Press (New York: Wiley, 1948; 2nd ed., 1965).

1949. Shannon, C. E., and W. Weaver. *The Mathematical Theory of Communication.* Urbana: Univ. of Illinois Press, p. 3.

1968. Ashby, W. R. *An Introduction to Cybernetics.* London: Methuen (University Paperbacks, 1956), chap. 7.

1970. Beer, S. *Decision and Control.* New York: Wiley, chap. 15.

1973. Drozin, V. G., R. Fisher, F. F. Kopstein, G. Pask, and M. Toda. "What is Cybernetics?," *FORUM*, American Society for Cybernetics. Vol V, No. 4 (December), pp. 3–8.

1973. Heilprin, L. B. *Impact of the Cybernetic Law of Requisite Variety on a Theory of Information Science.* College Park, Md.; Univ. of Maryland Computer Science Center, Report No. TR-236, March, ERIC No. ED 073 777, pp. 9–10.

L. B. HEILPRIN

# CYCLE STEALING

For article on related subject *see* MEMORY: Main.

Cycle stealing is a technique for memory sharing whereby a memory may serve two autonomous masters and in effect provide service to each simultaneously. One of the masters is commonly the central processing unit (CPU), and the other is usually an I/O channel or device controller. Fig. 1 illustrates a memory cycle (numbers 3 and 5) being stolen by an I/O channel (from the CPU) between two cycles of memory use by the CPU. This is possible and convenient, at least periodically, because the CPU is self-driven—except possibly between some substeps of a process it is conducting—and has no fixed time demands on memory. Furthermore, there are occasions, particularly in simpler CPU designs, where the instruction being obeyed (e.g., division) is processor-limited and memory access is temporarily suspended.

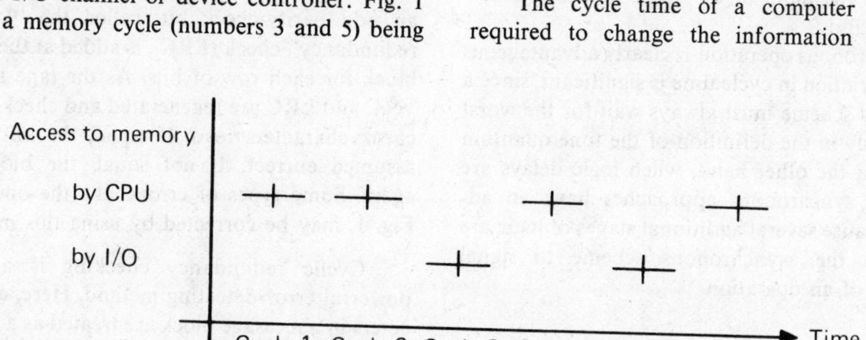


**Fig. 1** Cycle stealing.

The I/O equipment is, on the other hand, quite different. Its use of the memory, though generally less frequent than that by the CPU, is much more time-constrained. For many I/O devices such as disks and tapes, data is produced or required at fixed intervals. The need for data transfer occurs relentlessly at fixed time intervals. In transferring data from a tape to memory, the previous byte or word must have been stored before the next arrives; otherwise data is lost. This problem is somewhat alleviated by the use of single or multiple buffers in the device controller and/or channel, but in any case there are important recurring time demands for memory access. These can be met by the technique of cycle stealing in those CPU designs in which processor activity is suspended for at most a memory cycle while a memory access is made by the I/O system.

K. C. SMITH AND A. SEDRA

# CYCLE TIME

For articles on related subjects *see* LOCAL STORE; and REGISTER.

The cycle time of a computer is the time required to change the information in a set of registers. This is also sometimes called the "state transition" time.

The register cycle time of a processor is sometimes referred to as the "internal cycle time," "clock time," or simply "cycle time"; occasionally, confusion develops between the internal cycle time (referenced to registers) and the main memory cycle time. The memory cycle time is usually several times the internal cycle time.

The internal cycle time may not be of constant value. There are basically three different types of cycle-timing organizations.

1. *Synchronous (fixed)*: In this scheme all operations are composed of one or more cycles, with the fundamental time quantum being fixed by the design. Such systems are also referred to as "clocked," since usually a master oscillator (or clock) is used to distribute and define these cycles.

2. *Synchronous (variable)*: This is a slight variation of the first scheme; certain long operations are allowed to take multiple cycles without causing a register state transition. In such systems there may be several different cycle lengths. For example, a register-to-register transfer of information cycle might take one cycle while a register-to-adder and return-to-register cycle would perhaps be two or three cycles.

The fundamental difference between the fixed and variable synchronous types is that the former stores information into registers at the end of every cycle time, whereas the latter sets information into registers after a number of cycles, depending upon the type of operation being performed.

3. *Asynchronous operation*: In a completely asynchronous machine there is no clock or external mechanism that determines a state transition. Rather, the logic of the system is arranged in stages; when the output value of one stage has been stabilized, the logic signals the input at the stage to admit a new pair of operands.

Asynchronous operation is clearly advantageous when the variation in cycle time is significant, since a synchronous scheme must always wait for the worst possible delay in the definition of the time quantum required. On the other hand, when logic delays are predictable, synchronous approaches have an advantage because several additional stages of logic are required in the asynchronous scheme to signal completion of an operation.

In actual practice, most systems are basically synchronous (either fixed or variable) with some asynchronous operations being used for particular parts of the machine, such as handling access to main memory.

M. J. FLYNN

# CYCLIC REDUNDANCY CHECK

For articles on related subjects *see* CODES; ERROR CORRECTING CODES; and PARITY.

In modern computer systems, data is continuously transferred between the main processor and its peripherals, storage, or terminals. Errors may be introduced during the reading, writing, or actual transmission of this data. Consequently, error control has become an integral part in the design of modern computers and communication systems. The most commonly used methods for error detection involve the addition of one or more bits, called "redundancy" bits, to the information-carrying bits of a character or stream of characters. These redundancy bits do not carry any information; they are merely used to determine the correctness of the bits carrying the information.

Perhaps the most commonly used method for error detection is the simple parity check. Parity may be even or odd, meaning that the sum of the "one" bits of any character, including the parity bit itself, will always be even or odd, depending upon which arrangement is chosen.

Fig. 1 illustrates a form of two-dimensional parity checking used on some magnetic tapes that can detect and even correct some types of errors. The six-bit characters are arranged in columns with a seventh odd parity bit, called the "vertical redundancy check" (VRC), added to make the sum of the "one" bits in each column an odd number. Similarly, an odd parity-check bit, called the "longitudinal redundancy" check (LRC), is added at the end of the block for each row of bits. As the tape is read, the VRC and LRC are regenerated and checked with the check characters read. If equal, the information is assumed correct. If not equal, the block is read again. Some types of errors, like the one shown in Fig. 1, may be corrected by using this method.

Cyclic redundancy checking is a far more powerful error-detecting method. Here, all the characters in a message block are treated as a serial string of bits representing a binary number. This number is then divided modulo 2 by a predetermined binary

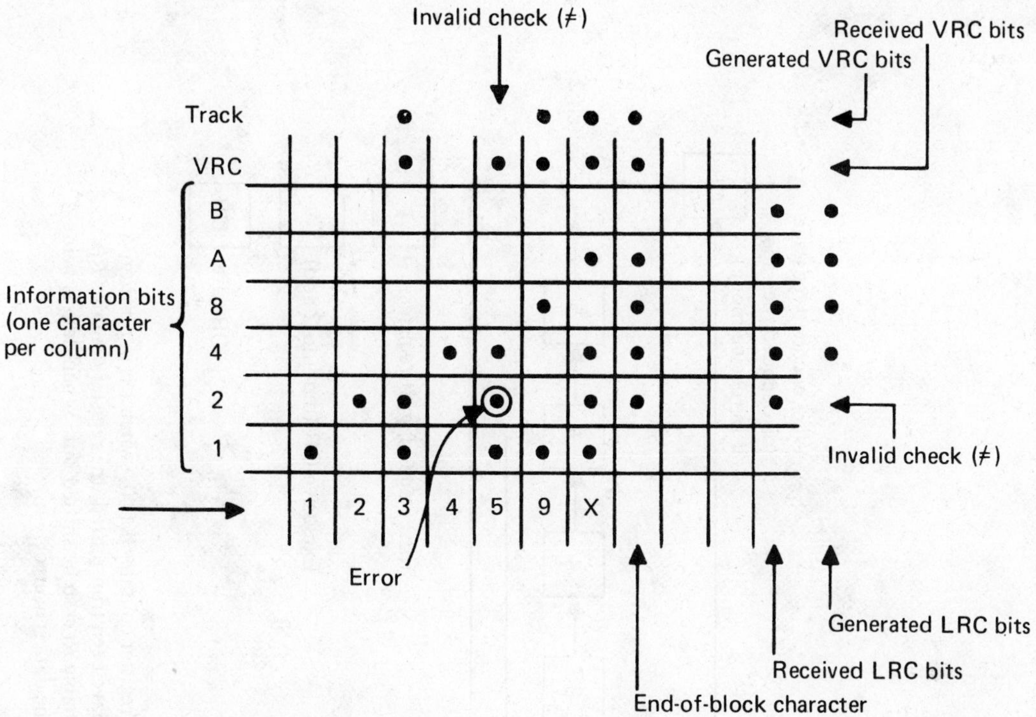


**Fig. 1.** Error detection using LRC and VRC bits. An extra "1" bit has been introduced in the character "5." Assuming no errors in the received check bits, the error must occur at the intersection of the invalid check column and row. The error bit must be reversed. In this case, the "1" must be changed to "0."

number and the remainder of this division is appended to the block of characters as a cyclic redundancy check (CRC) character. The CRC is compared with the check character obtained in similar fashion at the receiving end. If they agree, the message is assumed correct. If they disagree, the receiving terminal will demand a retransmission. This is usually called the ARQ (automatic repeat request) method of error control and is very commonly used in data communication. The CRC character is also called the "cyclic check sum," or simply the "check sum" character.

To show how the CRC is generated, let the message consist of $k$ bits, $a_0 a_1 \cdots a_{k-1}$, $a_i = 0$ or 1. Then we form the $(k - 1)$-degree polynomial:

$$M(x) = a_0 + a_1 x + \cdots + a_{k-1}x^{k-1} = \sum_{i=0}^{k-1} a_i x^i. \quad (1)$$

If we wish to include $r$ CRC bits, $r < k$, $M(x)$ is multiplied by $x^r$ (this is equivalent to shifting the message bits $r$ places to the right). Let $G(x)$ be another polynomial—called the "generator" or "checking" polynomial—of degree $r$, whose coefficients are also 0 or 1. We divide $x^r M(x)$ by $G(x)$, obtaining

$$\frac{x^r M(x)}{G(x)} = Q(x) + \frac{R(x)}{G(x)} \qquad \text{mod } 2 \qquad (2)$$

where the "modulo 2" indicates that all sums and differences of coefficients are taken as 0, if the result is 0 or even, and 1 if it is odd. Thus, from Eq. (2)

$$R(x) = x^r M(x) + Q(x)G(x) \qquad \text{mod } 2 \qquad (3)$$

where $R(x)$ is the remainder and $Q(x)$ is the quotient. The code word $W(x)$ is

$$W(x) = Q(x)G(x) = x^r M(x) + R(x) \text{ mod } 2, \quad (4)$$

and what is transmitted are the coefficients of $W(x)$.

Note that $W(x)$, which is of degree $r + k - 1$, contains the original $k$ message bits (the $x^r M(x)$ term) and $r$ check bits (the $R(x)$ term). Furthermore, $W(x)$ is exactly divisible by $G(x)$. The division by

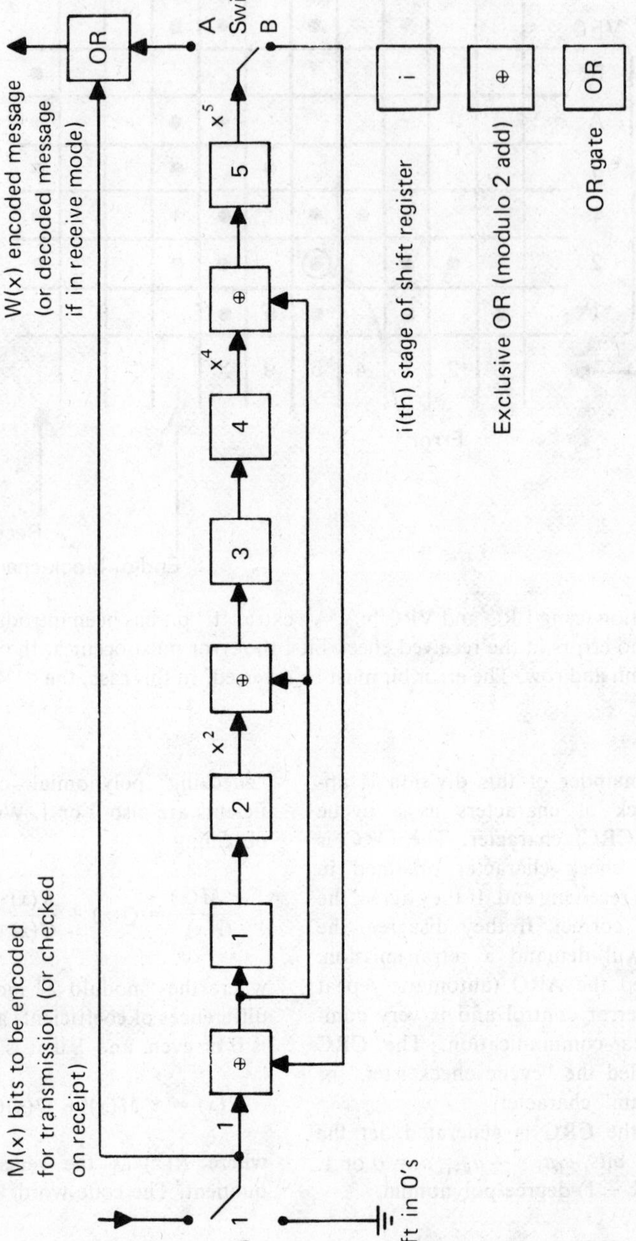


**Fig. 2.** Shift register for $G(x) = 1 + x^2 + x^4 + x^5$. Initially, the register contains 00000, switch 1 is in position A, and switch 2 is in position B. When all message bits have been transmitted, the register contains $R(x)$. Switch 1 now goes to B, and switch 2 goes to A to enable $R(x)$ to be shifted out. When data is being received, the resulting $R(x)$ must be zero; otherwise, the data is in error.

$G(x)$ at the transmitting end is accomplished by an $r$ stage-shift register with feedback paths represented by the coefficients of $G(x)$, as shown in Fig. 2. On the receiving end, $W(x)$ is also divided by $G(x)$, and the remainder in this case must be 0; otherwise, an error has occurred.

Consider the following example related to the shift register shown in Fig. 2. Let the message be 1010010001. Therefore, $M(x) = 1 + x^2 + x^5 + x^9$. With $G(x) = 1 + x^2 + x^4 + x^5$, modulo 2 division of $x^5M(x)$ by $G(x)$ yields

$$Q(x) = 1 + x + x^2 + x^3 + x^7 + x^8 + x^9$$

and $R(x) = 1 + x$. Thus

$$W(x) = 1 + x + x^5 + x^7 + x^{10} + x^{14},$$

and the transmitted message is

| | |
|---|---|
| 11000 | 1010010001 |
| CRC | original |
| bits | message |
| | bits |

The remainder, $R(x)$, is generated by the shift register (which is initially at 00000) as follows:

| *Message Bit* | *Shift Register Contents* Stage 12345 |
|---|---|
| 1 | 10101 |
| 0 | 11111 |
| 0 | 11010 |
| 0 | 01101 |
| 1 | 00110 |
| 0 | 00011 |
| 0 | 10100 |
| 1 | 11111 |
| 0 | 11010 |
| 1 | 11000 |

The final content is $R(x)$. Each successive shift register content represents a successive stage of the division of $x^5M(x)$ by $G(x)$, remembering that only the bits of $x^5M(x)$, which have been already transmitted at each stage, take part in the division. When all message bits have been transmitted, the contents of the shift register are shifted out by five successive right shifts to transmit $R(x)$. Note that during this operation, the zeros are shifted into stage 1 so that after $R(x)$ is transmitted, the contents are 00000; hence, the register is automatically cleared for more transmission.

Codes developed as described above are called "cyclic" codes. Such codes are used for error detection and correction for magnetic tape, disk, and data communication. The generator polynomial $x^{16} + x^{15} + x^2 + 1$, for example, is widely used in synchronous data communication systems. It can detect all odd numbers of error bits, all possible single-error bursts not exceeding 16 bits, 99.9969% of all possible single bursts 17 bits long, and 99.9984% of all possible longer bursts. This is much better than simple parity checking, for instance, which detects only all odd numbers of error bits and no others. Note that parity checking is equivalent to having a generator polynomial $G(x) = x + 1$.

The study of cyclic codes revolves principally upon determining the code characteristics resulting from various generator polynomials. Peterson and Weldon (1972) and Tang and Chien (1969) give some applications and a more thorough mathematical treatment of cyclic and other codes.

### REFERENCES

1969. Tang, D. T., and R. T. Chien. "Coding for Error Control" *IBM Systems Journal*, Vol. 8, No. 1, pp. 48–86.

1972. Peterson, W. W., and E. J. Weldon. *Error-Correcting Codes*, 2d ed. Cambridge, Mass.: M.I.T. Press.

J. S. SOBOLEWSKI

# CYLINDER

For articles on related subjects *see* MEMORY: Auxiliary; and VOLUME.

Many rotating storage devices—drums, disks, data cells, and the like—have fewer read/write heads than recording tracks. Therefore, either the surfaces of these devices must move to position the desired information under a read/write head, or the read/write heads must move to hover above the appropriate recording tracks. The latter strategy is commonly used for large direct-access devices such as disks containing at least 20 million bytes.

For engineering convenience and efficient sequential processing of data, the following design has been adopted by most manufacturers of moving-head disk drives:

1. Tracks are numbered from top to bottom for

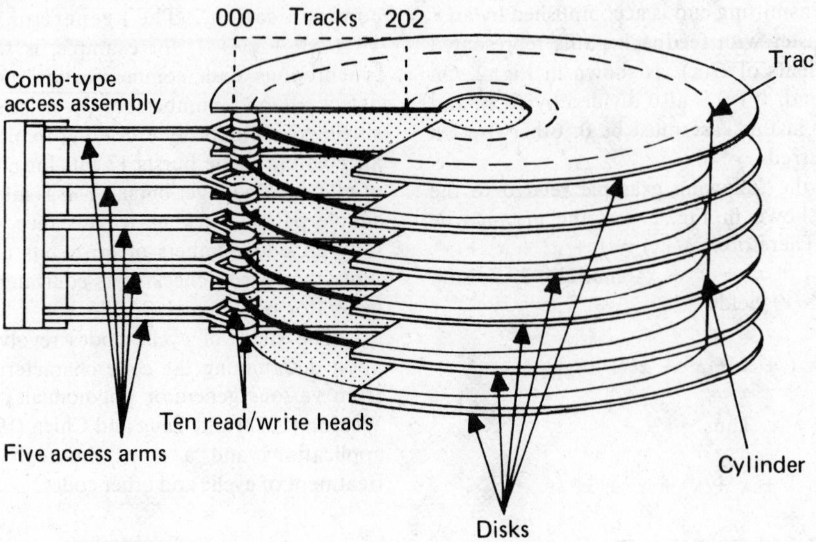


**Fig. 1.** Typical moving-head disk drive and pack.

each horizontal position of the read/write comb, as shown in Fig. 1.

2. During sequential writing operations, as the top track in each vertical plane becomes filled, control circuitry and system software allocate subsequent records to the beginning of the next track. When this is filled, records are started on the third track, etc.

3. Therefore, during sequential reading, a maximum amount of data can be read at one time before the comb must be moved. This is considerably faster than the alternative strategy of writing all tracks concentrically on one surface before advancing to the next surface.

Each vertical set of tracks, one track per recording surface, is called a "cylinder," after the geometrical surface obviously outlined. There are as many cylinders per disk pack as tracks per recording surface (203 cylinders for the illustrated disk pack).

D. N. Freeman

# D

## DPMA. *See* DATA PROCESSING MANAGEMENT ASSOCIATION.

## DANGLING ELSE

For article on related subject *see* PROCEDURE-ORIENTED LANGUAGES.

This picturesque phrase describes a situation in compound conditional statements where it may not be clear to which part of the statement an ELSE belongs. Consider, for example, the following statement in a PL/I-like syntax:

```
IFSEX = FEMALE THEN IF AGE ≥ 30 THEN
        RECONSIDER ELSE PURSUE                    (1)
```

If the ELSE belongs with the second IF-THEN pair, the statement implies pursuit of females under 30. But, if the ELSE belongs with the first IF-THEN pair, the statement implies pursuit of all males, but reconsideration of females 30 and over (and no information on what to do about females under 30; this would have to be taken care of in the next statement in the program, which would be executed if the first condition (SEX = FEMALE) were true and the second (AGE ≥ 30) were false). Because of the ambiguity of which interpretation is correct, the ELSE is said to *dangle*.

One way of avoiding such ambiguities is by the use of compound statements. For example,

```
IF SEX = FEMALE THEN BEGIN IF AGE ≥ 30 THEN
        RECONSIDER ELSE PURSUE END
                                                  (2)
```

makes it clear through the use of BEGIN and END that the first interpretation above is the intended one. (For another solution to the dangling ELSE problem, see Abrahams, 1966.)

In actual practice, of course, statement (1) must be given a specific interpretation by the compiler for the language [in PL/I the interpretation is that given in (2)], but writing statements containing a dangling ELSE is bad programming practice.

### REFERENCE


1966. Abrahams, Paul W. "A Final Solution to the Dangling ELSE of Algol 60 and Related Languages," *Communications of the ACM*, Vol. 9, pp. 679–680.


A. RALSTON

## DATA ACQUISITION COMPUTER

For articles on related subjects *see* DIGITAL-TO-ANALOG CONVERTERS; and SPECIAL-PURPOSE COMPUTERS.

## DATA BANK

Computers have been used for decades to acquire and analyze data generated by instruments such as voltmeters, thermocouples, and electromechanical relays in factories, refineries, missles, or aircraft. Typically data acquisition computers have fast memory-cycle times, so that bursts of signals from real-time physical processes like video scan devices will not be lost. Word sizes for data acquisition computers are short: 16 to 24 bits. Floating-point instructions are generally unnecessary, since data is inherently scaled within ranges determined by the processes being measured.

The main components of a data-acquisition computer are as follows:

1. Analog and digital input cables.
2. Analog to digital converter.
3. Disk or tape cassette for data storage.
4. Central processor.
5. Main memory.
6. Operator console.

For low-volume data acquisition, a paper-tape punch may be substituted for the disk drive or tape cassette.

Programs are loaded from punched paper tape, punched cards, or—in some newer models—from a host computer over a communications link.

Prices of data acquisition computers have decreased considerably since 1965, improving their advantage over manual methods for capturing and transcribing data in many applications. Their inherent reliability—especially central processor, main memory, and disk/tape components—has risen to such levels that they may operate unattended for days at a time.

Many data acquisition computers have been "ruggedized" to function in high-temperature environments such as steel plants or high-acceleration environments such as spacecraft. Data acquisition computers can be built and enclosed in small cabinets, some no larger than a desk or even a briefcase.

For the future, small low-cost data acquisition computers will be installed increasingly close to points at which original data is generated: factory floors, cash registers, continuous-process plants, etc. They will be connected by medium-speed (2,400 bits per second) telephone links to large central computers, which will periodically poll them for data acquired since last polling, status reports on processes being supervised, and hardware-reliability reports on the data acquisition computers themselves.

D. N. Freeman

# DATA BANK

For articles on related subjects *see* COMPUTERS AND SOCIETY; DATA BASE AND DATA BASE MANAGEMENT; and FILES.

A data bank is a file of data derived from a variety of sources and stored in a manner suitable for ready access by a number of users. The term usually denotes a computerized file of personal data about identifiable individuals, which is maintained by an organization that may be able to affect some aspect of personal life and which may be used in making decisions about persons. The term first came into use in the late 1960s for a data system in which a municipal government could combine school, tax, utility, welfare, health, police, and other files. All departments of government could then draw data from this bank in making planning and operational decisions.

Early versions of such municipal management systems encountered strong public protest that the existence of such systems would be a serious threat to personal privacy, since the essence of privacy is that a person should be able to exercise reasonable control over the circulation of information about himself. After investigating the operation of actual data banks in a study for the Computer Science and Engineering Board of the National Academy of Sciences, Westin and Baker reported (1972) that computerized data banks typically contain about the same information as the manually maintained files they replace and are used in much the same ways. Furthermore, they found that computerization of working files had not affected the interchange of information among organizations to any great extent, and had specifically not resulted in the creation of networks of computers through which individual dossiers could be assembled.

Westin and Baker warned, however, that future technical developments might change the situation, and recommended that the federal government set up comprehensive legal protection for the privacy of computerized personal data. However, at the time of their recommendation, Congressional hearings on data banks had already been held, and the Department of Health, Education, and Welfare (under Secretary Elliot L. Richardson) had formed the Secretary's Advisory Committee on Automated Personal Data Systems to prepare the guidelines for protection of the many data banks operated by HEW. The Committee's report recommended that the following principles be made the basis of a code of fair information practice, with statutory penalties to be provided for failure to observe the code in the operation of a data bank:

There must be no personal data record-keeping systems whose very existence is secret.

There must be a way for an individual to find out what information about him is in a record and how it is used.

There must be a way for an individual to prevent information about him, which was obtained for one purpose, from being used or made available for other purposes without his consent.

There must be a way for an individual to correct or amend a record of identifiable information about him.

Any organization creating, maintaining, using, or disseminating records of identifiable personal data must assure the reliability of the data for their intended use and must take precautions to prevent misuse of the data.

The issue of data banks versus privacy has arisen in most of the advanced nations of the world. Nearly all of these nations have taken steps to develop legal structures to allow the evolution of efficient technical methods of dealing with the large masses of personal data required in the running of a modern state while at the same time preserving the fundamental liberties of citizens.

### References

1967. Westin, Alan F. *Privacy and Freedom.* New York: Atheneum.

1971. Westin, Alan F. *Information Technology in a Democracy*. Cambridge: Harvard University Press.

1972. Miller, Arthur R. *The Assault on Privacy: Computers, Data Banks, and Dossiers*. Ann Arbor: University of Michigan Press (New York: Signet Books).

1972. Westin, Alan F., and Michael A. Baker. *Data Banks in a Free Society*. New York: Quadrangle Books.

1973. U.S. Dept. of Health, Education, and Welfare; Secretary's Advisory Committee on Automated Data Systems. "Records, Computers, and the Rights of Citizens." Cambridge, Mass.: M.I.T. Press (Washington, D.C.: U.S. Government Printing Office).

D. H. LUFKIN

## DATA BASE AND DATA BASE MANAGEMENT

For articles on related subjects *see* DATA BANK; DATA SET; FILES; and PROGRAMMING LANGUAGES.

The term "data base" has yet to achieve a widely accepted standard meaning. However, it is to some extent accepted as conveying a more sophisticated concept than the older term "file," which was carried over into data processing terminology from the precomputer era. Unfortunately, it is all too frequently used when all that is implied is a conventional file. The difference between a data base and a file, in terms used prior to the advent of data processing, is perhaps analogous to the difference between a thoroughly cross-referenced set of files in cabinets in a library or in an office and a single file in one cabinet which is not cross-referenced in any way.

The important difference is that the *data base* must be stored in the computer on direct-access storage (such as disks) in order for the computer's central processing unit to be able to utilize the cross-references within a reasonable time. By contrast, a set of cross-referenced *files* could be theoretically stored on magnetic tape. However, the computer would then spend unacceptable amounts of time searching the tapes because it is not possible to access a specific data record on tape without passing over all other data preceding it on the tape. However, despite this disadvantage, magnetic tape is likely to remain the principal storage medium for archival computer files for many years to come, in view of its relatively low cost and high retention qualities.

The term "cross-reference" is not usually used when talking about a data base, the most usual term being "relation." One speaks of a relationship existing between types of records in a data base. A record type is analogous to a color-coded folder in a filing cabinet where different record types are segregated by varied colors. An individual folder may contain a reference to one or more other individual folders elsewhere in a set of cabinets. A referenced folder may have the same or a different color code as the folder that references it. In the data base, such relationships are stored in such a way that searching for records can be done directly without extensive cross-checking. Thus, the user has considerably more flexibility in the way in which he processes the data.

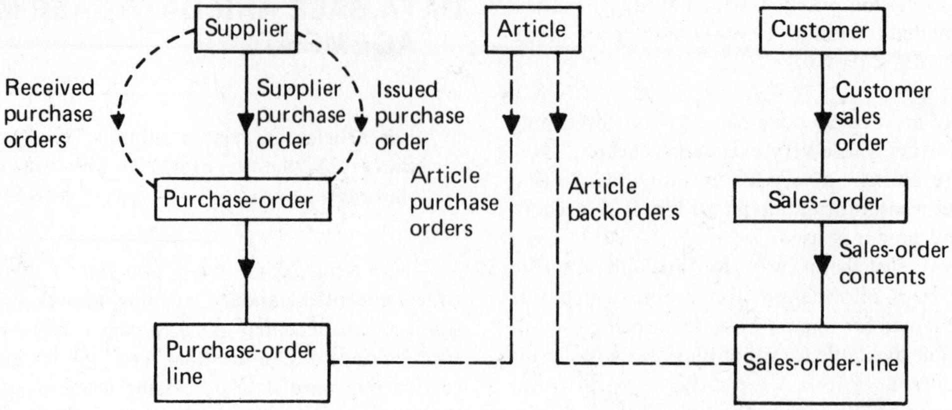


**Fig. 1.** Example: Components of data base in a warehouse system.

**Example of a Data Base.** As an example of a data base, it is interesting to consider the data processing in a warehouse (see Fig. 1). This example is a simplified version of one originally developed by Philips-Electrologica.

The warehouse needs to maintain data about each article to be stored. Articles are ordered in varying quantities by customers. If the stock of a particular article drops below a certain level, then new stocks are purchased from a supplier.

In the data base, it is necessary to have three principal record types: ARTICLE, SUPPLIER, and CUSTOMER. Each time a customer places an order for one or more different kinds of articles, a sales order is built up in the data base. In data processing terms, this means that there is also a SALES-ORDER record type. A single sales order may contain an order for several units of one article. More likely, a customer may order several different classes of articles on the same order. To facilitate the processing of the data base, SALES-ORDER-LINE is then regarded as a different record type, i.e., different from SALES-ORDER, which contains data about the whole sales order, customer identification, date of issue, and so on. The other record type contains data about each line entry in the sales order, such as which article the line refers to and how many units are ordered.

The situation is similar for the purchase order that the warehouse issues to a supplier when the stock of an article is discovered to be low, but there is a slight difference. A sales order and all its lines enter the data base together. A purchase order to a supplier is built up during the course of a day's or a week's processing. At a certain time, a program is run to issue the purchase orders. How many lines there are in a purchase order depends on customer demands for different articles that a supplier provides and also on how many articles the warehouse needs to replenish stock and restore it to its normal inventory level.

In summary, the data base contains seven different *record types*: the three principal record types (article, supplier, customer) and the four respective subsidiary records of sales order, sales-order-line, purchase order, and purchase-order-line.

More important from a data base point of view are the various *relationships* that are defined among these record types. In Fig. 1, eight relationships are illustrated. Four of these eight are denoted by continuous lines, and four by dotted lines. The former are referred to as automatic and the latter as manual relationships. There is an important distinction between these two classes, which is best illustrated by an example.

The relationship between a customer and his sales order is automatic. There is no sense in having a sales order record in the data base if it is not clearly associated with a customer. Furthermore, it is unlikely that a need would arise to move a sales order from one customer to another. Normally, a sales order record would be entered in the data base and immediately associated with a customer record that is already there. In fact, if the sales order contains invalid customer identification, then the sales order should not be allowed in the data base at all. Hence, one can say that each time a sales order record is stored in the data base, it is "automatically" connected in some way to a customer record.

The relationship between a sales-order-line and an article is conceptually quite different. In Fig. 1 this relationship is called "article back orders." It is important to note that the SALES-ORDER-LINE record type is subordinate to two relationships, an automatic one connecting it to SALES-ORDER and a manual one connecting it to ARTICLE. The latter relationship is manual because a sales-order-line is *not* automatically connected to the article being ordered at the time the sales-order-line record is stored in the data base. The name of the relationship, namely, "article back orders," gives the clue to the circumstances under which the connection would be made. At the time the sales-order-line is being processed, it may be discovered that there are insufficient units of the article in stock to meet the order. It is then necessary to hold the sales-order-line in some way so that when new stock enters the warehouse and stock levels are updated in the data base, the back orders that have not been successfully processed can then be easily found in the data base and processed. Hence, when a relationship exists between two record types such that a connection is conditional on circumstances that can be determined only at processing time, the relationship is called "manual."

This entire example illustrates a fairly simple data base structure with seven record types and eight relationships. Of the relationships, four are automatic and four are manual. The fact that three of the record types are subordinate in two or more relationships indicates a structure that is more advanced than that of an ordinary file.

**Data Base Management.** Many techniques have evolved for managing data bases in direct-access storage. Such techniques are used by programmers as they attempt to minimize processing time or storage space required, or sometimes to maximize flexibility. In earlier days, these techniques were used by the customer's application programmer.

During the past decade there has been a significant move by hardware and software manufacturers toward embedding these techniques into a component of systems software. This component is now quite widely referred to as a "data base management system," or DBMS.

DATA BASE MANAGEMENT SYSTEM, DBMS. A DBMS, as mentioned above, is a piece of software. Some vendors regard it as being part of the operating system; others build it in such a way that it is very much an optional extra for which the customer must pay if he decides to use it. It must be emphasized that the reason for identifying DBMS as a piece of software is to avoid any confusion that may arise with what might be called an "integrated management information system," or IMIS. An IMIS *uses* a DBMS. An IMIS comprises human components, appropriate administrative procedures, and application programs, which collectively provide information to management and to others.

Many would argue that an IMIS is not possible without a DBMS. A management information system may be completely manual, but the degree to which one could achieve integration is likely to be modest. The meaning of "integration" in this concept is discussed more completely later in this article under "Integration of Separate Applications."

*Relationship between Data Base and DBMS.* A data base is a set of data stored in some special way in direct-access computer storage. A DBMS is the software that handles the storage and retrieval of the records in this data base. The DBMS cannot exist without a data base. The DBMS is the active partner and the data base is the passive one.

A number of requirements are frequently stipulated for a DBMS in addition to the basic one of handling the data in the data base. Integrity, privacy, and data independence are those most frequently cited.

*Integrity* refers to the ability of the DBMS to protect the data base from hardware and software malfunctions. It should be possible to recognize a problem, report it, reconstruct the damaged part of the data base, and restart the processing. Collectively, these processes are often referred to as a "recovery" system.

*Privacy* identifies a capability to protect the data base against unauthorized access or modification. While the need for this kind of facility varies from one enterprise to another, it always becomes more critical if the data base is to be accessed from on-line terminals.

Finally, *data independence* is a capability that many users regard as of paramount importance. It is defined as the independence of the application programs to structural changes in the data base. In the example of the warehouse, it might be required to add one or two new record types and a new relationship. If the programs that act on the data base do not need to be modified, and possibly not even recompiled after the changes to the data base structure, then it can be said that there is a degree of independence. This capability serves to minimize the reprocessing problem, which has caused major expense when conventional programming methods have been used. Data independence is irrevocably associated with a DBMS. However, astute users have certainly been able to achieve some data independence without using a DBMS.

In summary, a data base management system is a piece of software that is used to manage a data base. A data base is a collection of cross-referenced records stored in a computer's direct-access storage. If the cross-references are not present, then it is safer to say that the data is stored as a file. At the present state-of-the-art in data processing, using files is much more common than using data bases.

Pieces of software are also available for managing files in computer storage. Such a piece of software is called either a "data management system" or, sometimes, a "file management system."

**Data Management System.** Considerable confusion has been caused by mixing the two terms "data management system" (DMS) and "data *base* management system" (DBMS). Some vendors, both hardware and software, refer to their DBMS as a DMS. Others provide both systems and regard them as separate but related items. Some use the term "file management system" to refer to one or the other. In view of the relatively widespread use of the older term, DMS, to identify an operating system's component for handling files of data that are not cross-referenced, it is recommended that this separation and distinction between DBMS and DMS be actively promulgated.

In the more prevalent situation, where the DMS is different and separate from the DBMS, the DMS is always an operating system component that may be little more than a disk input/output controller, namely, a piece of software to transfer blocks of data between disk and central storage. In this case, the DBMS wll always make use of the DMS.

The important element that differentiates the DBMS and the DMS is the ability to define and make use of relationships (i.e., cross-references). If the data is organized into a data base, then a DMS at any one time typically can only process any one file in the data base. There are other differences between a DBMS and a DMS, but these are outside the scope of the present article.

A question that frequently arises concerns how easy it may be for a user to advance from using the DMS to using the DBMS, if and when a DBMS is available. Since using a DMS implies using the operating system facilities for input/output, and is also a fairly conventional approach to application design, a user's decision to use a DMS has no particular significance.

If a vendor does differentiate between his DMS and his DBMS, he may well underplay the problems of migrating from DMS use to DBMS use. Experienced users are justifiably cautious about the problems they predict as a result of any major revolution in the way they do their data processing. They tend to request that any new DBMS they order should make the migration from their present conventional systems as easy as possible.

Vendors are equally aware of the problem of changeover and tend to stress how easy it is to move to the new system. While generalizations on this issue are necessarily vague, apparently it is easier to migrate to a DBMS of modest capabilities than it is to a more powerful one. It may also be possible to migrate from a DMS to a DBMS without actually taking advantage of the added power of the DBMS.

**Classes of DBMS.** In order to clarify the origin of the term DBMS, it is important to note that two basic classes of DBMS have been developed over the years. The two classes are now generally known as "host language DBMS" and "self-contained DBMS." It is the purpose of the following sections to describe and explain the difference between these two classes.

Host Language DBMS. A host language DBMS is simply one that, from a programmer's point of view, represents an extension to an existing programming language. The programming language is often Cobol, but PL/I and Fortran are also used. The extensions are new procedural statements that enable a programmer to access and modify the data records in the data base. This class of languages came into being as the capabilities of computers increased and applications became more sophisticated.

In early days when computers were first used, applications were recognized by users as being "suitable for computerization." What constituted an "application" was in those days rather effectively limited by two factors. One was the early dominance of magnetic tape as a main storage medium for the data. The second was the widespread use of Cobol as a language for programming data processing applications. The design of Cobol in 1959 was itself dominated by the method of processing sequential files stored on magnetic tape. Although some ad hoc modifications were made to the language during the mid-1960s, this basic design philosophy is still prevalent in Cobol today. A process has been under way for some years to update the whole approach.

As some sophisticated users gained experience and insight, and as direct-access storage became more readily available, they developed a somewhat larger view of what constituted an application. They soon realized that this broader scope of application would require better techniques for organizing (or arranging) their application data in the computer direct-access storage. These users felt the need for cross-referencing their data records more thoroughly, using the approach discussed in the opening section of this article. They wanted to take advantage of the extra dimension offered by direct-access storage. More important, they wanted to provide better information to their management at less cost. They felt that this could be done only by "integrating" the data from the files of previously separate application programs into a centralized data base.

The technique of cross-referencing was initially employed by the users' programmers as they built "tailored" (or made to measure) software systems. As the cost of programmer talent increased during the 1960s, largely due to personnel shortage, this tailoring of each individual system became too costly. However, the manufacturers' software designers were fortunately learning how to generalize. In other words, they began to build generalized systems (now called DBMS), which allowed the user to make use of the cross-referencing technique without the expense of tailoring them to each software system.

At this point, the host language DBMS began to come into its own, often as an integral part of the operating system. It provided the more powerful structuring facilities that users needed to take a bigger view of their applications, namely, to integrate them. The DBMS made use of the more readily available direct-access storage in order to do this. Applications programmers then did not have to get involved with the details of physically accessing the data on the direct-access storage.

It must be emphasized that during the period between 1963 and 1969, these application techniques were used relatively infrequently. The concepts were not effectively promoted by those who did understand them, and many users had other, more crucial problems that took precedence over the one that a DBMS of this kind was intended to solve. Such other problems included operating system problems, compiler problems, and the design of the system using conventional techniques.

SELF-CONTAINED DBMS. A self-contained DBMS differs from a host language system in that it is in no way an extension of an existing programming language. On the contrary, it is usually quite independent of any language, although there are examples of self-contained DBMS that can process Cobol files. Recently, self-contained systems have been modified to provide a capability to act on the data structures processed by host language systems. In this context, the self-contained DBMS becomes less self-contained and becomes essentially a supplementary facility in a host language system.

The reasons for developing the self-contained class of DBMS are quite different from those for the host language systems. Throughout the 1960s, and indeed continuing through the 1970s, there has been justifiable concern in many data processing circles about the increasing complexity (and associated cost) of programming, even when using higher-level languages such as Cobol. Consequently, efforts have been made to develop languages that are even easier to use than Cobol, and which therefore can be used by the "nonprogrammer." Another rationale motivating the development was the desire to have quick and easy access to information stored in conventional data files.

The effort to bring nearer to the man the interface between man and machine resulted in a plethora of these languages and associated software packages during the 1960s. Over the years a vast amount of resources has been directed toward this end and is still being expended in many research-oriented organizations.

The terms "retrieval language" and "query language" are often used when referring to "self-contained DBMS" because the major facility in any self-contained DBMS is indeed a query language. Others facilities include update and data definition.

RELATIONSHIP BETWEEN THE TWO CLASSES. It is significant that, historically, there has been no coordination in approach or in thinking between the proponents of the "host language" approach and those advocating "self-contained" systems. On the contrary, the two groups have been in frequent disagreement as to which approach is more meaningful, but since 1971 there has been a growing recognition that the two approaches should be unified. Generally speaking, host language systems have become more important, simply because their very *raison d'être* has been to facilitate integration of smaller applications into a larger coordinated system so that several application programs can access a common or shared data base.

On the other hand, the self-contained system becomes really important to any user after a decision has been taken to utilize a host language system. The techniques embodied in self-contained systems are those that can help meet information needs identified by planning groups and by the higher echelons of management.

The trend of the current state-of-the-art is to make the two classes of systems gradually compatible. It is unreasonable to expect a user organization to store its data in two ways—one for the host language DBMS and the other for the self-contained DBMS, which until 1971 was invariably the case. Since that time, those concerned with software implementation have realized the problems created, and many are developing self-contained systems to operate on the data bases or files primarily created for processing using a host language system.

**Integration of Separate Applications.** Having outlined the concepts of data base, DBMS, and DMS, it is appropriate to examine the task that the DBMS is intended to perform and the problem it is intended to alleviate in any user environment in which it is adopted.

The word "integration" has been used a number of times so far in this article. Experience has shown that, as with many other terms used in data processing terminology, "integration" is open to a number of interpretations. The purpose of the following paragraphs is to identify these and to emphasize the importance of deciding which of these is relevant in any given situation.

For the purpose of discussion, consider two application systems A and B. Whether A and B are major systems or merely components of larger systems is irrelevant to the present discussion. A and B may have some data that is common to both. This means that at least one item of data is updated and used by A, and is also required by B for inclusion in one of its reports or for use in one of its calculations. There are several ways in which system B can get access to system A data.

System A generates reports. Those generated may include some that are specifically designed to meet the requirements of system B; in other words, these reports are requested by the people responsible for system B. If system B indeed requires some of A's data for its own processing, then it may be necessary to copy the data off system A reports onto system B input forms for repunching because system B requires only part of the data generated by system A or because system B requires it in a rather different form. If reprocessing of the data is necessary *for any reason*, then it may be asserted that system A and system B are *not integrated in any sense*; in other words, they are totally uncoordinated.

Suppose, for example, that system B may require system A data, *but in a different form*. This normally means that some item of data that is common (at least in concept) to both systems has two sets of values, one for system A, one (maybe partially overlapping) for system B. On the other hand, the set of values may be the same for each system, but the way they are represented to the computerized system may differ. This introduces the topic of *data representation standards*, which is a problem that must always be addressed if a satisfactory degree of integration is to be achieved. It may happen that system B requires the data in exactly the same form as it is generated and processed in system A. This in itself represents a modicum of integration, by the very necessary standardization of data representation. No meaningful integration of any kind is conceivable unless there is this standardization of data representation.

The designers concerned with systems A and B may agree to pass data from A to B in mechanized form rather than by passing reports from which the system B people can then punch what they need. This level of integration can be thought of as *mechanized interaction*. In this case, system A would arrange to generate files (usually on tape) and system B would include input programs to read these files. This situation represents the first meaningful level of integration. Although magnetic tape files are suggested here, it is possible that the transmittal media could be some other device, such as movable disks. It is implied that system A and system B are separate systems and that they are run at separate times, possibly on separate machines at the same or separate geographic locations.

The most complete degree of integration possible would be achieved if system A and system B were to run concurrently on the same machine. The data they could process would be in one of the following three classes: local to A, local to B, or common. Because the data common to both is the most important consideration, the designers responsible for the two systems must agree on record types to contain the common data. The programs of both systems may be written to access these record types, normally with agreement that only one system—for example, system A—is allowed to update any data in the record, while system B processing is limited to retrieval. It can then be said that systems A and B are *integrated*.

In summary, the following spectrum of potential situations can be identified when two application systems use data conceptually similar:

1. *Totally uncoordinated*: Each system has its own representation and does its own data collection.
2. *Partially interacting*: One system repunches data (and in so doing modifies the form) from reports generated by the other system.
3. *Mechanized interaction*: One system generates files, which can be used as direct input to programs

in the other system. No modification of data representation is necessary.

4. *Integrated*: The two systems have agreed on record types to be used by both systems. Programs of both systems access the records as stored in direct-access storage. There is agreement on which system has authority to update the data contained in records of this type.

**Role of DBMS.** A host language DBMS offers a common and widely used approach toward achieving the maximum integration possible. A self-contained DBMS is of somewhat peripheral interest to this central problem of integrating systems, but nevertheless it has an important role to play in allowing a user to provide for simple ad hoc information requirements that arise in an enterprise.

REFERENCE

Philips-Electrologica BV. "An Application Example of the CODASYL DBTG Proposal," Publication No. 5122 991 24151. Eindhoven, The Netherlands.

T. W. OLLE

# DATA COMMUNICATION NETWORKS

For articles on related subjects *see* ARPA NETWORK; COMPUTER NETWORKS; DATA COMMUNICATIONS; MODEM; MULTIPLEXING; and TELEPROCESSING SYSTEMS.

Data communication may be thought of as the transportation or transmission of data from one location to another location. This requires a data communication network. Such a network consists of a set of nodes connected by a set of links. The nodes may be computers, terminals, or some type of communication control units in various locations, while the links are the communication channels providing a data path between the nodes. These channels are usually private or switched lines leased from a common carrier. Since the transmission over these lines is generally analog, while the data at the nodes is digital, data sets or modems are used to provide the interface between node and link. A simple example of a network is shown in Fig. 1, where the links between modems are the communication lines that may be leased from a common carrier. The communication control unit in city E is used to multiplex or concentrate several lower-speed terminals onto a high-speed line. The single multidrop line also connects several terminals to the host. It is usually routed through several locations, picking up terminals along the way.

Current computer applications of data communication vary widely in function, scope, and requirements. They may be divided into six basic system types: inquiry and response, data collection, data distribution, conversational, remote batch processing, and message-switching systems. The number of such systems is growing very rapidly and will continue to grow. In large systems of this kind, the costs directly related to data transmission are a very significant part of the overall cost; hence the planning and design of data communication networks is very important.

**Network Planning.** Planning and designing a data communication network can be exceedingly complex because of the wide variety of requirements and the large number of possible solutions. The objective is to satisfy all requirements at least cost. Factors to consider in planning include:

1. The type of teleprocessing system used.
2. Volume and distribution of data to be transmitted.
3. Access and response times required.
4. Number and geographical location of nodes.
5. Type of terminal or equipment at each node and its transmission speed.
6. Error rate that may be tolerated.
7. Need for future expansion.
8. Availability, reliability, and maintenance of the network.

**Network Design.** Given the network objectives, the design process includes the choice of terminals, line control procedures, modems, communication control units, common carrier facilities, and network configuration. This can be a very lengthy process, since the number of possible solutions is very large and the various influencing factors are interrelated.

For example, Fig. 2 shows three basic network configurations: the point to point, the multidrop, and distributed connection, as well as a star network, which consists of four point-to-point connections. In the distributed network shown, more than one path exists between nodes. Most present networks are

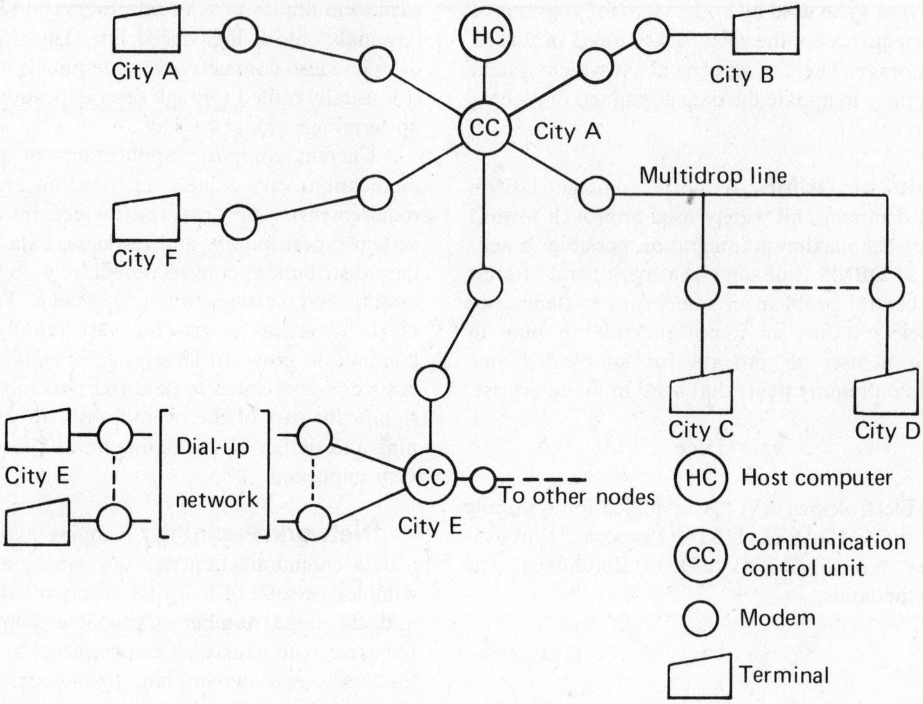


**Fig. 1.** Example of a data communication network.

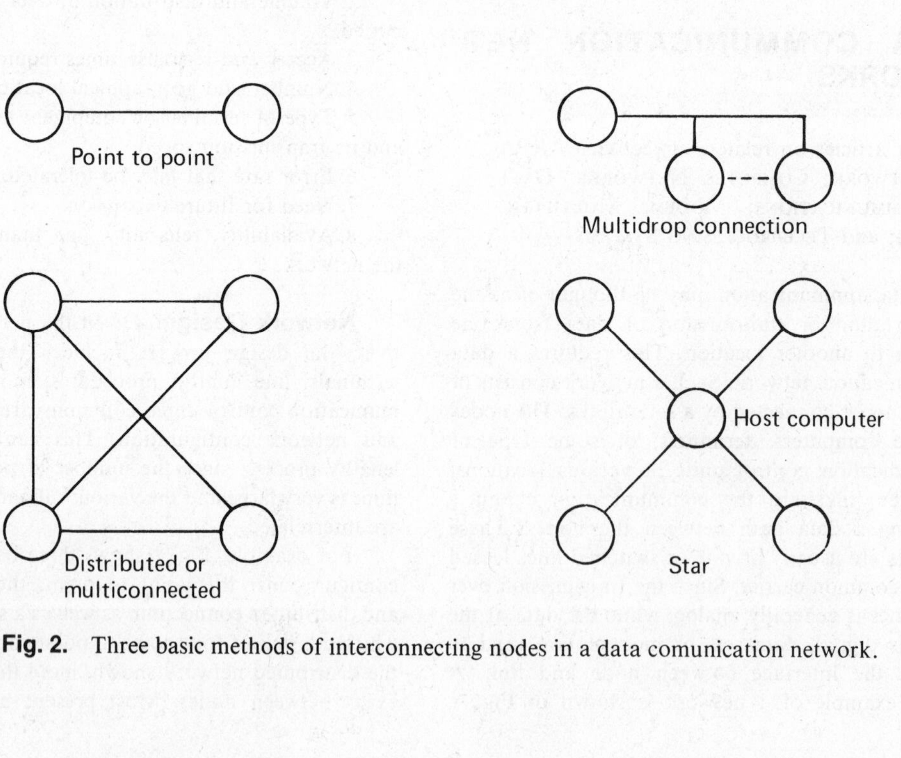


**Fig. 2.** Three basic methods of interconnecting nodes in a data comunication network.

combinations of the three basic configurations.

The cost of the various types of lines or common carrier facilities required are governed by very complex tariffs based upon location, circuit length, and type of line. Both the geometry and types of lines can in turn be greatly influenced by using appropriate communication control units such as multiplexers or concentrators placed at strategic locations within the network. Such units can markedly improve the efficiency of the lines, reducing their number and hence the cost. Furthermore, performance-cost trade-offs are always possible.

Based on the above considerations, a great deal of experience is necessary to design an economical network. The design process is usually iterative in that the designer makes an initial guess at a possible network by deciding on the types of lines that should be used, the auxiliary equipment needed to improve line efficiency, and the network configuration. This initial design is tested to insure that it meets the planned objectives; if it does, it is then evaluated for cost. Special computer programs may then be used to find alternative approaches to minimize the network costs. These programs are usually modular, each module designed to solve a particular segment of the optimization problem, such as finding optimum locations of concentrators, Since computers cannot replace experience and intuition, the programs are interactive in the sense that the designer is in the feedback loop. Should the costs be too high, some of the planned objectives or specifications may be relaxed to lower the cost, and the process is repeated until an acceptable cost-performance network is found.

### Reference

1973. Martin, J. *Systems Analysis for Data Transmission.* Englewood Cliffs, N.J.: Prentice-Hall

J. S. Sobolewski

# DATA COMMUNICATIONS

## GENERAL PRINCIPLES

For articles on related subjects *see* Communications and Computers; Communication Control Unit; Error-Correcting Code; Multiplexing; Teleprocessing Systems; and Terminals.

For articles on related terms *see* Baud; Cyclic Redundancy Check; Packet Switching; and Parity.

From the first time that data had to be passed between one register and another in a computer, the problem of data communications had to be addressed. This article is concerned with the transmission of data from its source to its destination, as shown in Fig. 1. This subject could cover the contents of many volumes. Three general textbooks (Davenport, 1971; Martin, 1969, 1970) are recommended for additional reading. Other references (Bullington et al., 1959; Kretzmer, 1969; Petersen, 1961; Shaw, 1969) deal with more specialized areas.

Normally (see Fig. 1), data is passed in parallel between a computer or peripheral in finite-sized chunks (e.g., 8-bit bytes) to a register, shown as *SO*. This data must be passed via a communication network (*CN*) to a sink (*SI*), where it is passed on in the same or different finite-sized chunks to another computer or peripheral. The communication network usually has the property that the part of it dedicated to the communication between *SO* and *SI* can carry only one bit at a time. Therefore, the data from the *SO* must be serialized in the parallel-series converter (*PS*) and deserialized again in the series-parallel converter (*SP*). The data output of *PS* is usually a bistable binary signal that can be interpreted as one of two states: 0 or 1. To pass through the *CN*, it must usually be used to modulate an analog signal or to emit a short pulse. This is achieved in the modulator (*MOD*), and the digital level is recovered in the demodulator (*DEM*).

If information can flow only from *SO* to *SI* (Fig. 1), the communication is said to be "simplex." If data can flow both from *SO* to *SI* and from *SI* to *SO* simultaneously, the communication is called "duplex." If the data flows in these two directions do not proceed simultaneously, the communication is said to be "half-duplex." In some cases, the communication channels themselves may be full duplex, but either the hardware of *SO* and *SI* or the software associated with them may restrict the communication to half-duplex. Since it is usual for the communication portion of the circuit to be at least half-duplex, it is normal for the functions of modulator and demodulator (Fig. 1) to be combined. The resulting equipment is called a "modem."

Often a character input from a terminal to a computer will be echoed back onto the terminal's printer to show it was received correctly; this mode

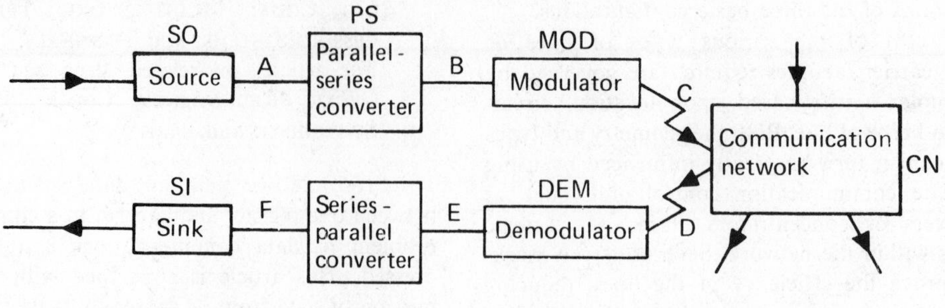


**Fig. 1.** Schematic of communications between source and destination.

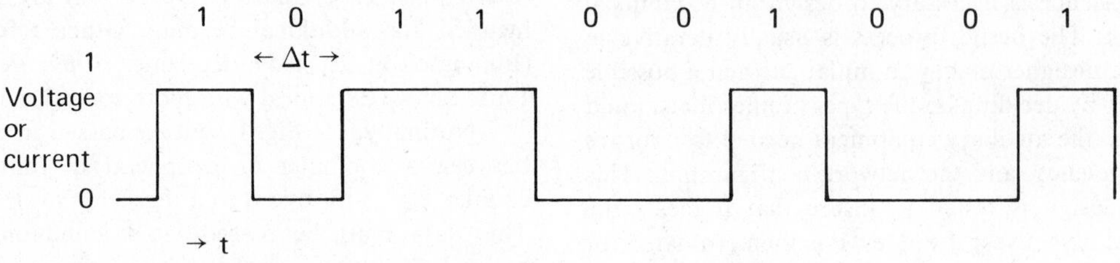


**Fig. 2.** Example of telegraph modulation.

of working is called an "echo-plex." The devices *SP* and *PS*, and the interfaces *A* and *F*, are also often combined, with additional buffers in each to permit duplex working.

It is beyond the scope of this article to say much about techniques of modulation (see Davenport, 1971; Martin, 1969). The simplest way to modulate signals is to use telegraph techniques to insure that the channel has one of two states: with current or without current. An example of this form of signaling is shown in Fig. 2.

The fastest signaling rate of a communication channel is called the "baud rate." In the system shown in Fig. 2, the baud rate is $1/\Delta t$. When only two-level signaling is used, the baud is also equal to the rate of information transfer in bits per second (bps). If multiple-level signaling is used, as shown in Fig. 3 for four-level coding, then the bit rate is higher than the baud rate. To obtain the signals in Fig. 3, each pair of bits in Fig. 2 is taken together, and the four resulting combinations (00,01,10,11) are each coded to one level. Clearly, this approach can be extended to *n* levels, but the circuitry required to discriminate and decode the levels becomes increasingly complex.

The form of signaling described above has problems in long-distance transmission, and it is more usual to use the pulsed signals shown in Fig. 2 or Fig. 3 to modulate the amplitude, frequency, or

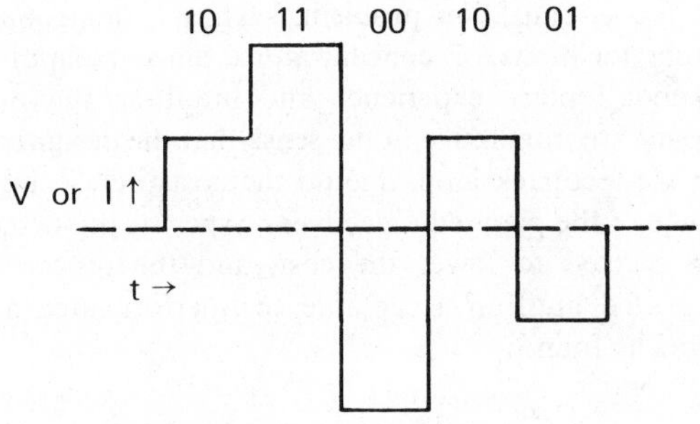


**Fig. 3.** Example of four-level coding.

phase of a carrier sine wave. These forms of transmission are called "analog transmission," and are well suited for use over the conventional telephone system, which is designed for the transfer of analog signals.

Each single communication channel has a certain *bandwidth.* For example, the amplitude response of a standard telephone channel, sketched in Fig. 4, has a bandwith (within a frequency range outside of which the transmitted attentuation rises rapidly) of about 3 kHz (the characteristics are good from about 300 Hz to 3.3 kHz). It has been shown by Nyquist that for all methods of modulation, the maximum signaling rate is about twice the frequency bandwidth. Thus, for a 3 kHz telephone channel, the

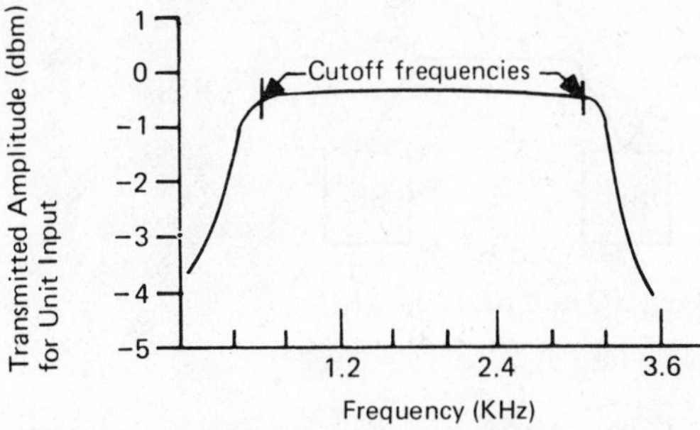


**Fig. 4.** Amplitude response.

maximum signaling, or baud, rate is about 6K baud. The maximum information transfer rate is related to both the baud rate and the number of levels of coding used. Claude Shannon has shown that the maximum information transfer rate, or channel capacity $C$, in a noisy channel is

$$C = BW \log_2(1 + S/N)$$

where $BW$ is the bandwidth and $S/N$ is the ratio of signal strength to random noise level, called the "signal-to-noise ratio." Thus, the more noisy the channel, the less can multiple levels be tolerated. If $S/N$ is 15, the preceding equation shows that the channel capacity is $BW \log_2 16$ (i.e., 4 $BW$) so that four-level coding could be used. With present telephone channels, the maximum signaling rates used are 3.2K baud, with eight-level coding (3 bits) to give 9.6K bps.

It should be noted that, just as two amplitude levels were used in the telegraph modulation of Fig. 2, two frequencies or two phases could be used for frequency or phase modulation of a carrier line wave. For higher-level signaling, more frequencies or phases are used. Thus, for the system of Fig. 3, the pairs of bits, or "dibits," (00), (01), (10), (11) would each be made to refer to a discrete frequency or phase with multilevel frequency or phase modulation. A good discussion of sophisticated multilevel modems is given by Kretzmer (1969).

The mode of modulation may make it possible for the modems to generate timing pulses themselves; such a system is called "synchronous." Both with phase-modulated analog signals and pulse-code modulation, it is possible to synchronize the two modems and produce timing pulses in the modem to indicate when a bit is being sent or received.

A simpler modem is possible when such synchronization is not required. Moreover certain man-oriented peripherals, such as keyboard terminals, need to send data only at irregular intervals. Such systems are termed "asynchronous"; in an asynchronous system, the signaling rate is predetermined, but it is necessary to indicate the start of each piece of information (usually a byte or a character) by sending a start-bit before, and one or more stop-bits (of opposite polarity) after transmission of the data. Thus, a byte 145 (in octal) would be sent as shown in Fig. 5. From the arrival time of the start-bit, the bit timings of the subsequent bits can be deduced. The stop-bit is required to insure for at least a one-bit time that the signal has an appropriate value by which a subsequent start-bit can be recognized.

It is even possible for the data format to be asynchronous (i.e., start- and stop-bits are included) with synchronous modems so that the transmission system is synchronous. Although the start- and stop-bits are redundant in such a system, it is often convenient to include them when the same electronics in $PS$ and $SO$ of of Fig. 1 is to be used with different modems. As described before, an asynchronous system has a fixed length of byte, whereas a synchronous system may have a variable length (see below).

Recently, with the reduction in costs of digital circuitry, it is becoming possible to use pulse-code modulation for transmission. Here, each device is

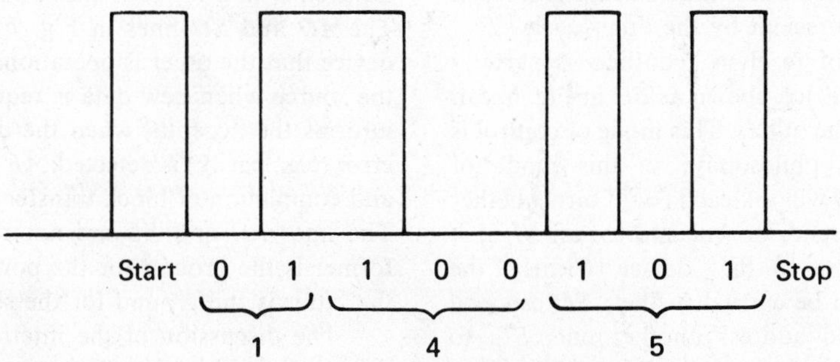


**Fig. 5.** Data sent for 145 in asynchronous system.

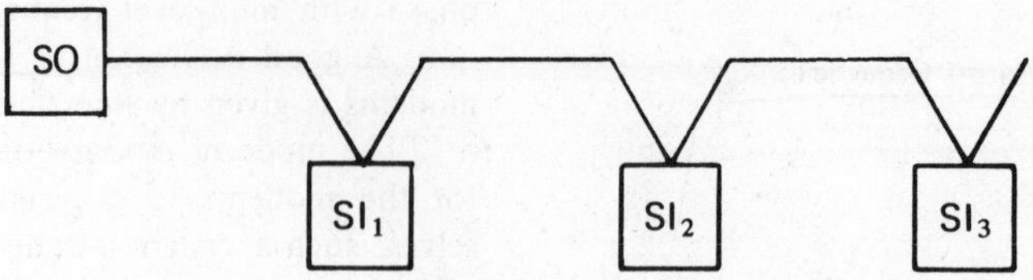


**Fig. 6.** Multipoint connection between *SO* and $SI_1$, $SI_2$, $SI_3$.

given a time slot, and during this period either a pulse is put on the channel or not. This is a modification of the original telegraph techniques, and is the basis of the digital transmission being developed. This form of modulation is really two-level amplitude modulation in a synchronous system.

The communication shown in Fig. 1, in which two parties *SO* and *SI* are connected, is called "point to point." Alternate forms used in some applications are shown in Fig. 6. In the communication circuit depicted by Fig. 6, *SO* can send (or receive) data along the channel connecting it to $SI_1$, $SI_2$, and $SI_3$. By appropriate signaling, it is possible to insure that the data is received at its correct destination, $SI_i$. This type of connection is called "multidrop" or "multipoint." In some cases it is desirable to have the same information received at all stations: $SI_1$, $SI_2$, $SI_3$. This mode of communication is called "broadcast."

If several devices share the same communication channel, as shown in Fig. 6, conflict for use of the channel can occur. One mode of overcoming the conflict is to allow any device to request the channel at will; its efforts to put information onto the channel will then be detected by the others, who will refrain from putting on their information until the message-sending transmitter has ceased. This mode of using a channel is called "contention"; it works well on a point-to-point basis, but reasonably complex strategies must be adopted for successful contention on multipoint channels because of the perceptible delay between information being placed on the channel and its receipt by the other parties.

Another way of resolving conflicts is particularly useful if one device, shown as *SO* in Fig. 6, can be used to control the others. This mode of control is called a "polling" philosophy; in this mode of communication, *SO* will ask each $SI_i$ in turn whether it has anything to send, or will address an $SI_i$ if it wishes to send data to that device. Clearly, the polling strategy can be carried further; *SO* can poll one device $SI_i$ and address another one, $SI_j$, to insure that the data is sent from $SI_i$ to $SI_j$. Alternately, it can poll to see if any device has data to send. The whole question of address control is complex and depends on the nature of the communication channel. A normal telephone channel, for example, is usually point-to-point. A satellite communication channel is fundamentally broadcast, even if it is often used in a point-to-point manner.

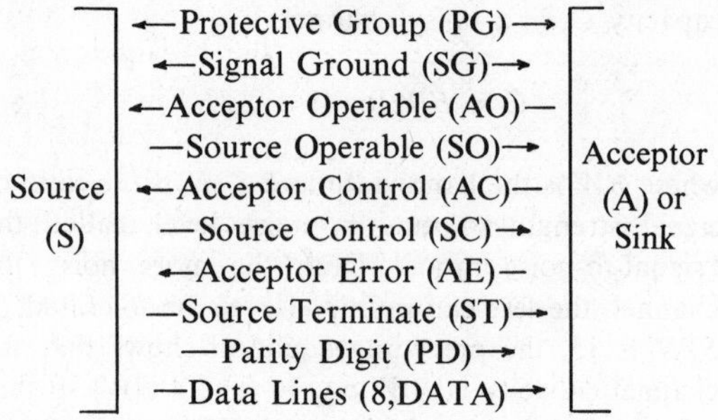


**Fig. 7.** British standard interface (simplified).

To illustrate the problems of the control and synchronization required between *SO* and $SI_j$, we consider the interface inside a single computer system. Here, the data communication path usually has a fairly complex hardware interface with lines for passing data and control. The sort of information passed is indicated in Fig. 7, which is a simplified version of the British standard interface. This interface is for a synchronous autonomous simplex transfer, with 8-bit data lines and a parity line (*PD*). The *AO* and *SO* lines in Fig. 7 are to assure each device that the other is operational. The *AC* informs the source when new data is required, and *SC* then informs the acceptor when the data is ready. If an error (e.g., parity) is detected, *AE* informs the source, and completion of block transfer is indicated by *ST*. The lines *PG* and *SG* are not really relevant. The former is the ground for the power connection and the latter is the ground for the signal lines.

The discussion of the interface of Fig. 7 illustrates one of the key features of data communication. In a local connection, there are a number of control lines to establish synchronization, timing, acknowledgment, error detection, end of transmission, etc. All such control information in the data communication system of Fig. 1 *must be carried with the data.* Moreover, in a local system, errors in transmitting data over the interface of Fig. 7 are usually rare; over long distances, noise and other phenomena will often cause bits to be lost. Since some of these bits may contain control information, care must be taken in the communication environment to insure that the correct action will be taken in all cases at *both sides of the link.* We will discuss below how some of this control information is passed.

In the communication of Fig. 7, the data is carried across the interface in parallel; in that of Fig. 1, it must first be serialized. We discussed previously that in some systems the modems of Fig. 1 established synchronization with each other, the so-called synchronous systems in which the bit timings are developed in the modems. It is merely necessary to establish this synchronization at the beginning of the transmission. Since this takes some time, it is usual to send data in a synchronous system in a block with some header information, followed by the data, and with some control and error detection data at the end. A synchronous system can be used only if the source *SO* of Fig. 6 has a buffer so that it can collect a whole block of information before transmission begins.

We mentioned earlier that the data format could be asynchronous with synchronous data transmission; redundant start- and stop-bits would be transmitted. In the same way even an asynchronous communication system can be used to send block-oriented data, by prefacing it with an appropriate header and ending the block with appropriate end-of-block characters.

It is usual in a data communication system to send some bits additional to the actual useful data to identify the existence of, and possibly to correct, errors. The simplest error detection code is to add to each $n$ bits of data an $(n + 1)$st bit, so chosen that the sum of the $(n + 1)$ bits is of a given parity (even or odd); such an extra bit is called a "parity" bit. In the asynchronous transmission system of Fig. 5, such a parity bit is often sent immediately before the stop-bit.

While this code is simple, it is not adequate if high information integrity is desired. Noise in transmission lines occurs fairly often; $10^{-3}$ is a normal error rate on a switched line. Moreover, the nature of these errors is such that the noise that causes them often lasts more than one-bit time. For this reason, most data transmission systems, other than those involving the simplest keyboard terminals, send their information in blocks and use more sophisticated error-detection codes that act on the whole block. One simple method considers the block as made up of $n$-bit bytes; it then does a parity check on the $i$th bits of each byte, and thus constructs the $i$th bit of a *block parity check* byte. When this block-parity check is combined with a parity check on each byte, only errors that occur in rare combinations would remain undetected. A more sophisticated set of error detection codes is based on *cyclic redundancy checks,* which require rather more logic, but are even safer. The subject of error detection codes is discussed fully by Petersen (1961).

Just as a single byte in Fig. 5 of an asynchronous transmission system was framed by a start-bit (often a parity bit) and a stop-bit, so whole blocks are usually framed by some synchronizing bytes, a start-byte, error-detection bytes, and an end-of-block byte. In some cases the end-of-block byte is replaced by information in the header of the block, stating the number of bytes in the block. For the case of a multipoint or polling situation, the header may also contain polling or addressing information. An international standard on block structure has been developed (Shaw, 1969), but it is not yet in universal use. Most synchronous communication systems are synchronous at the bit level, but are asynchronous at the block level. For this reason, the header and the end-of-block bytes bear the same relation to the block as the start- and stop-bits do to the single byte shown in Fig. 5. Some special synchronizing bytes are sent in the header to obtain the bit synchronization achieved by the start-bit in an asynchronous system.

Just as the interface of Fig. 7 must have an error-return line, so it is usually necessary to acknowledge the correctness of each block sent. In some cases this acknowledgment is made before any new block can be sent. In others, a header contains a block number, which is increased each time a block is sent. It is assumed that each block has been received correctly, unless a *negative acknowledgment* is sent subsequently. If that occurs, either only the faulty block or all subsequent blocks also are retransmitted. The philosophy is particularly important when there are significant delays in the communication network (e.g., when one or more satellite hops are involved) requiring a minimum of 0.5 sec for a round-trip signal.

It is instructive to consider what speeds and modes of data communication are offered currently by the telecommunications authorities over the tel-

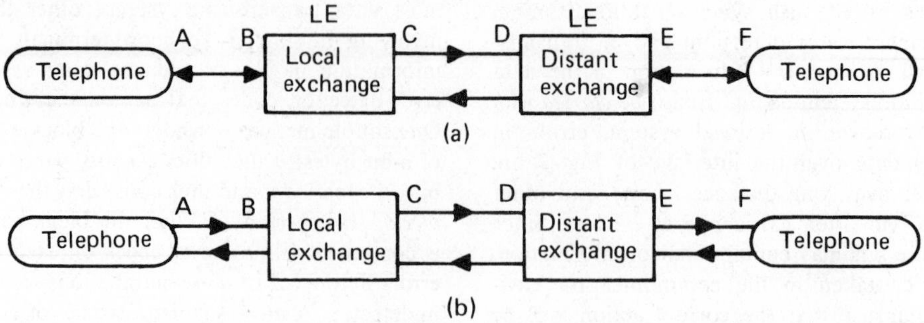


**Fig. 8.** Schematics of telephone networks. (a) Switched telephone line. (b) Four-wire leased telephone line.

ephone networks. They usually offer facilities over both switched and leased lines. In the former, it is possible to dial up any other subscriber on the switched network and to communicate with him; in the latter, connection can be made along only one path (possibly multidrop, as in Fig. 6). On a leased line, because only one path is used, it is possible for the telecommunications authorities to suitably *condition* the line to improve its performance; such conditioning is called *line equalization.* Alternately, both with switched and leased lines, it is possible to arrange for the modems to adjust to line conditions; this is called "equalizing" or "balancing" the modems. On a leased line, this balancing need not be done too often, unless very high performance is required, because the same path is always used. On switched lines, this balancing must be done on each call.

Fig. 8 illustrates the connection between two telephones and their local exchanges. Between the exchanges (*C–D* in Fig. 8), there are separate channels in the two directions, insuring duplex facilities. On a switched line, there is usually only one pair of lines, as shown in Fig. 8(a), between the telephone line and the local exchange; this is called a "two-wire circuit." On a leased line, it is possible to order at comparitively low cost a second pair of lines to the local exchange, as illustrated in Fig. 8(b). In this case, one has a four-wire circuit, and is able to operate at maximum speed simultaneously in both directions. On a single pair, as in *A–B* of Fig. 8(a), it is possible to work at fairly low speeds in both directions simultaneously. It is also possible to work at a much higher speed in one direction with a lower-speed return path. Schematically, this situation is then as shown in Fig. 8(b), but only one pair of physical connections need exist between *A* and *B* or *E* and *F*. This low-speed return path is called a "supervisory return," and varies in speed between 5 and 150 bps. It is used to turn around the line in the half-duplex situation or to signal acknowledgments or enter keyboard data in duplex. Thus, in the true four-wire case of Fig. 8(b), it is possible to have the high-speed data going simultaneously on each line, as shown in the figure, with additional reverse supervisory information. The range of facilities currently offered by the telecommunications authorities are illustrated in Fig. 9.

Finally, a brief discussion of multiplexing techniques is required. A very common situation in data processing involves heavy traffic between one cluster of terminals $T_i$ and a distant computer $C$, as illustrated in Fig. 10. This is similar to the contention mode discussed in relation to Fig. 6. With the present tariff structure and traffic capacity of individual lines, as illustrated in Fig. 9, it is often more economic to use some form of concentrator ($N$), as shown in Fig. 10(b), to concentrate the terminal traffic and pass it over a leased connection to $C$. By adopting such a course, there will often be considerable saving in transmission costs over the solution of Fig. 10(a), which will more than compensate for the cost of the more sophisticated equipment at $N$. One reason for the lower cost is that direct connections to the $T_j$ are often usable only up to 300 bps, whereas $C$–$N$ can run up to 9.6K bps. Thus, by splitting up the channel $C$–$N$ into a number of subchannels, the traffic can be carried more economically.

One method of achieving this subdivision is to allocate to each terminal $T_j$ a frequency set $F_{j1}$, $F_{j2}$, $F_{j3}$, $F_{j4}$ (for both 0 and 1 in the two directions); this is called "frequency division multiplexing" (FDM). A second method is to allocate to each terminal a time slot on the channel; this is called "time division multiplexing" (TDM). These methods extend to the user portion of the system the advantage of cost-saving techniques presently employed by commu-

| Speed Range (K bps) | Switched or Leased | Half- or Full Duplex | Line Equalization Required | Asynchronous or Synchronous | Levels of Coding | Note |
|---|---|---|---|---|---|---|
| Up to 0.2 | S or L | H | No | A | 2 | Uses d-c telegraph techniques |
| Up to 0.3 | S or L | F | No | A | 2 | Uses modems |
| Up to 1.2 | S or L | H | No | A | 2 | May have low speed return |
| 1.2 to 3.6 | S or L | H | No | S | 2–4 | May have low speed return |
| Up to 4.8 | L | F | No | S | 4 | Requires four-wire local connection for full duplex |
| Up to 9.6 | L | F | Yes | S | 4–8 | Requires four-wire local connections for full duplex |
| Up to 72 | L | F | Yes | S | 2–4 | Requires special treatment of the line and possibly repeaters |
| Above 72 | L | F | Yes | S | 2–4 | Required special local lines and transmission facilities |
| 1544 or 2048 | L | F | Yes | S | 2 | Standard pcm digital transmission |

**Fig. 9.** Typical telecommunications facilities available.

nications carriers on their part of the network. The multiplexing techniques can be optimized, however, to the specific capacity, usage patterns, and geography of transmission and switching capacity anticipated by the user.

Still further saving is possible on transmission cost. The terminals $T_j$ are often used only intermittently; a keyboard terminal capable of 30 char/sec is rarely run at an average rate higher than 3 char/sec. For this reason it is possible to store whole messages from or to $T_j$ at the node $N$, and send them in one block over $C$–$N$. This form of line utilization is called "packet" switching. With frequency or time division multiplexing, the frequency or time of the bit identifies the terminal $T_j$; with packet switching, this identification must be carried in a header.

Obviously, packet switching requires more storage and sophistication at $N$ than the other techniques, and is justified only if the transmission costs

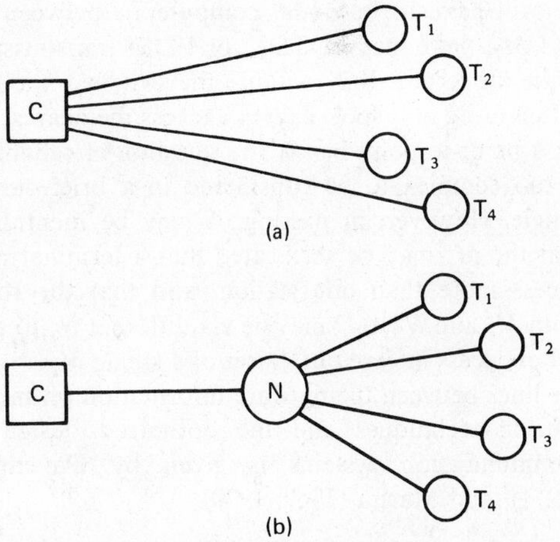


**Fig. 10.** Multiplexing. (a) Direct point-to-point connections. (b) Concentrated terminal usage.

are high. This is exactly analogous to the use of time-assigned speech interpolations (TASI) over transatlantic telephone lines to multiplex $m$ telephone conversations over $n$ communications lines, where $n \leq m$ (Bullington et al., 1959). By this method, messages are interspersed over a smaller number of channels whenever there is a lapse of voice communication on an active channel. When one message is interrupted, another message occupies the vacant time slot, and when the first transmission is resumed, the second message is shifted to the next vacant channel.

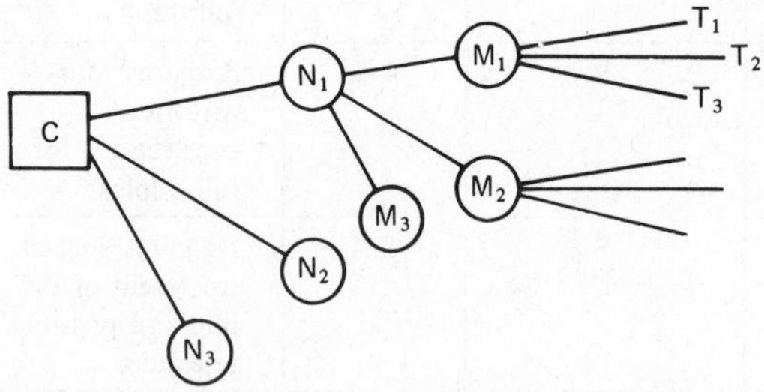


**Fig. 11.** Example of a concentrating hierarchy.

In real systems, a combination of FDM or TDM and packet switching is sometimes used. Over long distances, packet switching is used; over medium distances, FDM or TDM; and over short distances, point-to-point. This situation is illustrated in Fig. 11. Between $C$ and $N_j$, where long distances may be involved, there may be packet switching (the $N_j$ will have to be nodal computers); between $N_j$ and $M_i$, there may be TDM or FDM transmission, while the terminals $T_j$ will use the switched network (often using only local calls) to access the nearest $M_i$ on a point-to-point basis. The question of reliability is too complex to be considered in a brief survey article. However, in passing, it may be mentioned that the $M_i$ may be so located that a terminal may access more than one station, and that the route from $M_i$ and $N_j$ to $C$ may lie via different $N_j$ to give better access in case of failures of a single $M_i$, $N_j$, or the lines between them. More information on multiplexing techniques and the optimized design of communication systems is given by Davenport (1971), and Martin (1969, 1970).

References

1959. Bullington, K., et al. "Engineering Aspects of TASI," BSTJ, Vol. 38, No. 2, pp. 353–364.

1961. Petersen, W. W. *Error Correcting Codes*. Cambridge, Mass.: The M.I.T. Press.

1969. Kretzmer, E. R. "Modem Techniques for Data Communication over Telephone Channels," *IFIP '68 Proceedings*. Amsterdam: North Holland Publishing Co., pp. 716–721.

1969. Martin, J. *Telecommunications and the Computer*. Englewood Cliffs, N.J.: Prentice Hall.

1969. Shaw, R. T. "Basic Control Procedures for Data Transmission," *IFIP '68 Proceedings*. Amsterdam: North Holland Publishing Co., pp. 728–733.

1970. Martin, J. *Teleprocessing Network Organization*. Englewood Cliffs, N.J.: Prentice Hall.

1971. Davenport, W. P. *Modern Data Communication*. London: Pitman Publishing.

P. T. Kirstein

## SOFTWARE

For articles on related subjects *see* Data Communication Networks; Data Communications: General Principles; Error-Correcting Code; and Software.

For articles on related terms *see* Buffer; Interrupt: Real-Time Applications; and Register.

The transmission of messages by electrical means has been a practical reality since the middle of the nineteenth century; the basic concepts in use today do not vary greatly from those used by Samuel Morse in 1838. Morse transmitted his messages a character at a time; each character was encoded as a sequence of "dots" and "dashes." Character encoding and transmission was done by a human operating a key that controlled a buzzer at the receiving point. The reception and decoding was done by the human ear. When the message was received and transcribed on paper, it was either delivered locally or retransmitted to a remote destination. Transmission errors were detected by the human ear.

Some keyboard machines have been developed to both encode and decode the Morse code, but the code does not lend itself to simple mechanization because of the variable lengths of the individual character codes. However, with the introduction of constant character-length codes such as the Baudot code, the mechanization of the character encoding and decoding had become standard in almost all data communication environments by 1950. The next step in data communication mechanization was the introduction of the computer, which made possible the automation of line control, error control, and message-routing procedures.

Data communications software functions that exist in time-sharing networks, military command and control, airline reservation, telegraph, and factory data collection systems are largely application independent. Variations in the content of communications software are caused by the differences in traffic rates, line disciplines, volumes, and gèographical separations rather than by differences in application. In addition to providing the functions of message transmission, message reception, error control, and message routing in a communications environment, the data communications software provides an interface between the communications environment and the EDP environment.

Before discussing the above functions in more detail, we will examine from a software viewpoint the characteristics of the communication lines that connect together the terminals and computer to form a data communications network.

**Communication Line Characteristics.** Communication lines provide a single signal path from transmitter to receiver; information is sent across this path serially, bit by bit. Because there is only one serial path between the transmitter and the receiver, message control information has to be sent along the same path as the message. Over the years, several different message control techniques for distinguishing between the control and message information have developed. Stutzman (1972) gives an excellent review of the techniques used in this area.

The directional characteristics of the line are described by the terms "simplex" (one way only), "half-duplex" (two-way alternate), and "full-duplex" (two-way simultaneous). In a simplex path, information can be transferred only in one direction; e.g., a stock market "ticker tape". Half- and full-duplex lines are capable of transmitting information in both directions. A full-duplex line allows simultaneous transmission of information in both directions; a half-duplex line allows transmission of information in one direction at a time. On a half-duplex line, the line has to be "turned around" before it can be used to transmit information in the opposite direction. Considerable care must be taken with the software for half-duplex lines to avoid *contention* problems, where both ends are transmitting simultaneously, and *lockup* problems, where both are expecting the other to send the next message.

There are two main types of transmission, asynchronous and synchronous. In asynchronous communication the data is sent a character at a time, the character being composed of a fixed number of bits preceded and terminated by control bits. The control bits at the beginning of the character are called the start-bits and those at the end are called the stop-bits (Fig. 1). The time between bits within a character is constant, but the time between characters is variable. Asynchronous communication is most commonly used for communication with slower speed human-operated terminals.

In synchronous communication, the message is sent as a continuous string of fixed-length characters. The message is preceded and terminated by control characters; it may also have control characters embedded within the message [Fig 1(b)]. The message starts with a string of synchonization characters that are used by the receiver to synchronize his clock with that of the sender. Synchronous transmission is used in those instances where a message can be transmitted in one burst, such as is normally done in intercomputer communication. The advantage of synchronous over asynchronous communication is that more useful data bits can be sent in a given time, since synchronous characters do not have any control bits.

The unit used for measuring line speed is the "baud," which is the number of information units transferred in 1 sec. The most commonly used information units are two-level (binary) units in which the value of a unit is either 1 or 0. For binary information units, the baud rate is equal to the number of bits transmitted per second. Baud rates in common use range from 110 to 50,000. This wide variation in speed provides interesting hardware/software trade-offs in the design and configuration of communication computers.

**Message Transmission.** The logic necessary to transmit a message will be described, using a system model in which the communications hardware in the computer is a one-bit transmit buffer that holds the communication line in either the "mark" (one) or "space" (zero) state. The approach of minimal hardware allows the message transmission logic to be described initially in software terms.

The parameters of the message transmission logic are: the directional characteristics (half- or full-duplex), the speed of the line, the transmission type (synchronous or asynchronous), and the message control and code conventions expected by the receiver. These conventions are highly application

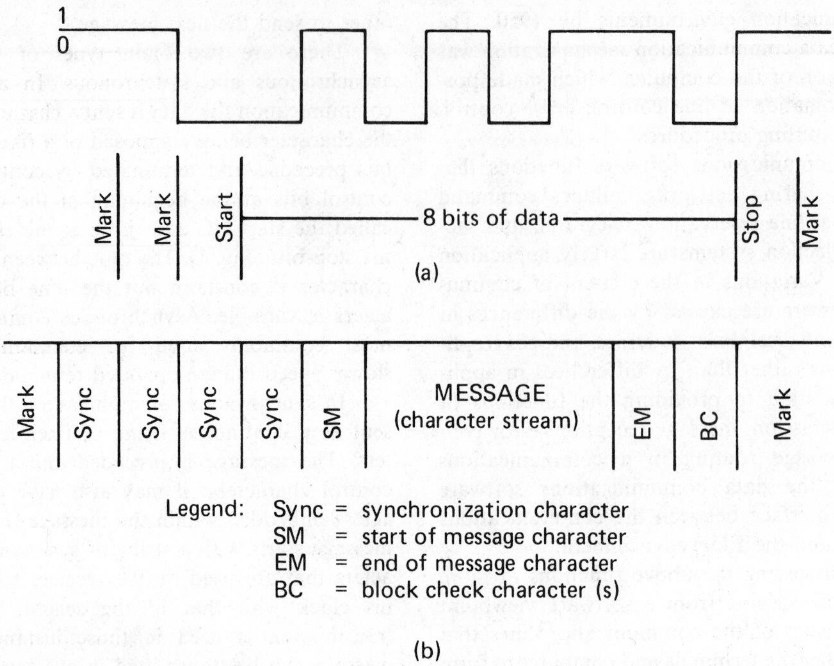


**Fig. 1.** Data transmission. (a) Asynchronous. (b) Synchronous.

and/or manufacturer dependent; because of this, a detailed discussion is beyond the scope of this article. We will restrict our discussion on message transmission to the generic problems associated with asynchronous and synchronous transmission.

With asynchronous transmission, each character in the message is transmitted independently. The character to be transmitted is fetched from store and framed with the required start-stop bits. The first bit (start) of this bit stream is put into the transmit buffer, which changes the line from the "mark" state to the "space" state. At the end of the one-bit time period, the next bit is put into the transmit buffer. The process is repeated until all data and stop bits are sent. If another character is to be sent immediately, then it is fetched and transmitted; otherwise, the transmit buffer is left in its "mark" state. The flowchart in Fig. 2 summarizes this logic.

In the synchronous form of transmission the entire message is sent in a one-bit stream. The message is framed by synchronization and start-of-message characters in front, and by end-of-message and error-detection characters at the rear. Then this new bit string is sent character by character, bit by bit, down the communication line. Normally the control characters are not added to the message buffer but are generated as required (Fig. 3).

**Receive Function.** In this section we consider the logic necessary to detect and to interpret the presence of a serial bit stream arriving on a communication line. Again we will consider minimal hardware; there is a receive buffer that gives the current state of the input line. The receive function is generally more difficult than the transmit function because the receiver has to decode and interpret the bits and characters it receives (which may be in error), whereas the transmitter knows exactly the character sequence it needs to send.

With asynchronous transmission, the character assembly logic must synchronize itself at the start of each character, since there can be a variable time between characters. To do this, the receive logic samples the line at some multiple (say, 16) of the bit rate in order to recognize the transition from the mark to space state at the beginning of the start-bit. Once the transition has been recognized, the logic waits for a half a bit time and samples the middle of the start-bit, which should still be at the space state. The logic then waits one bit time and samples the line to get the first data bit. Each succeeding bit is obtained in a similar manner and is appended to the character being formed. When the character is complete, it is processed and the logic resumes monitoring of the line for the beginning of the next

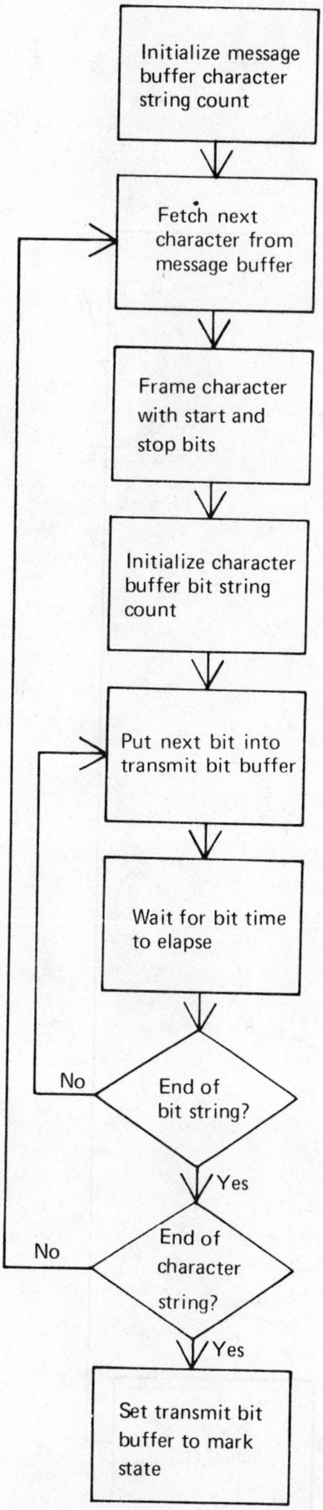


**Fig. 2.** Asynchronous transmit logic.

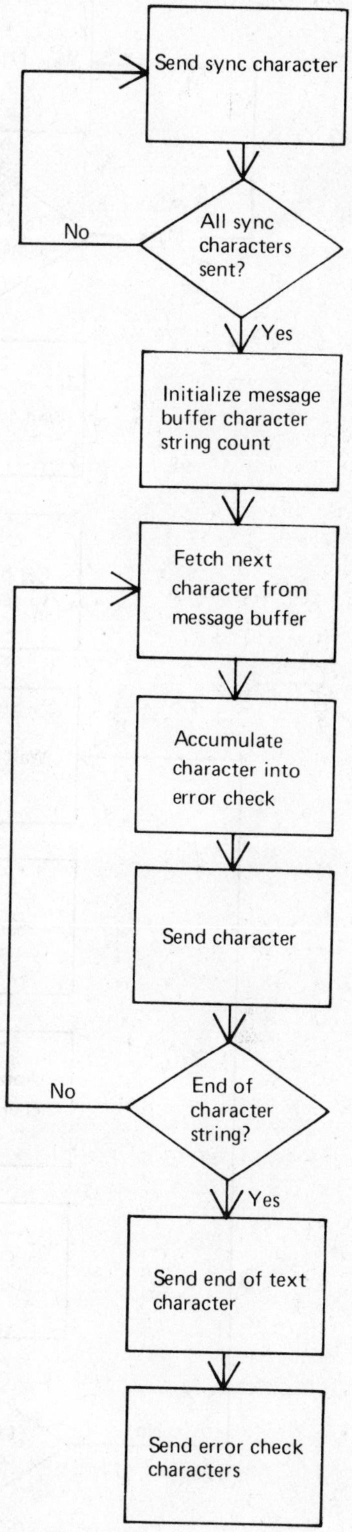


**Fig. 3.** Synchronous transmit logic.

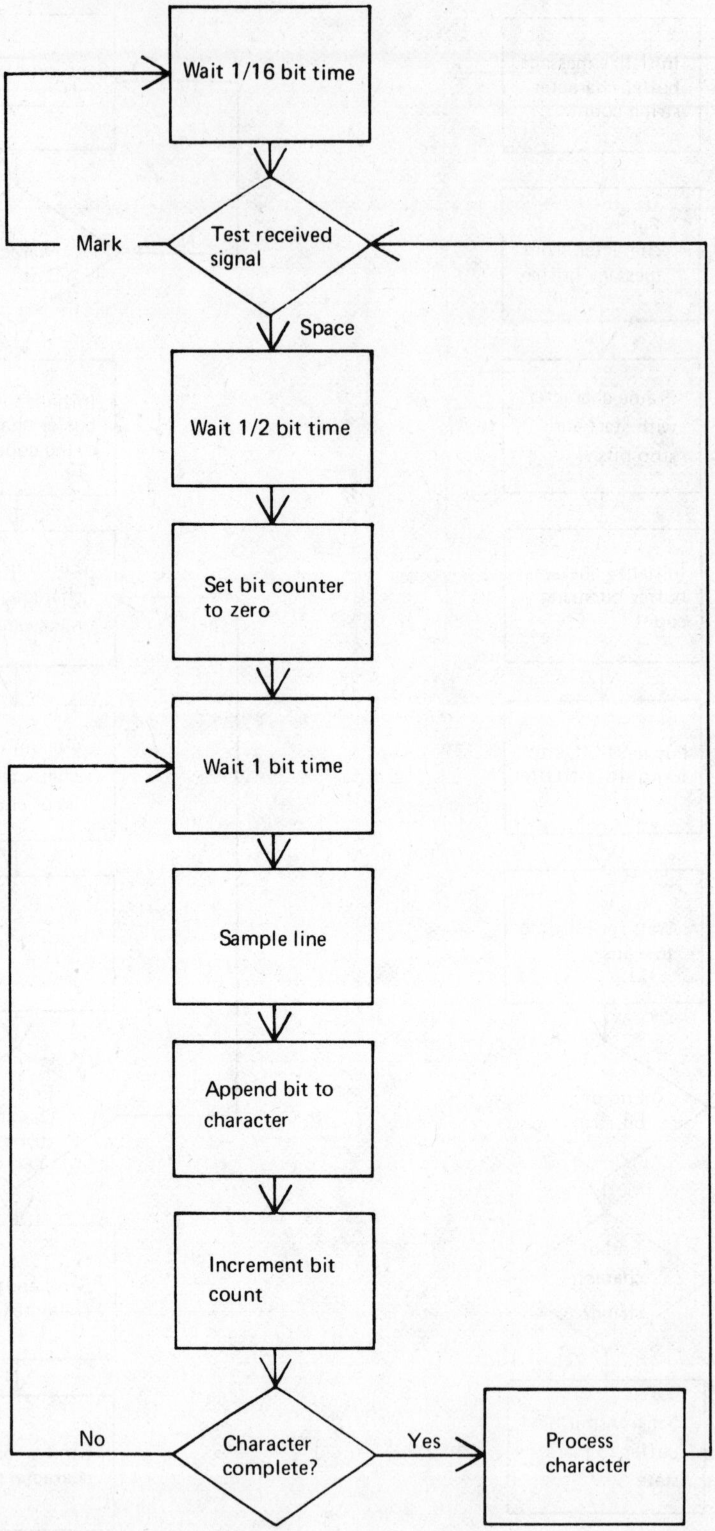


**Fig. 4.** Asynchronous receive function.

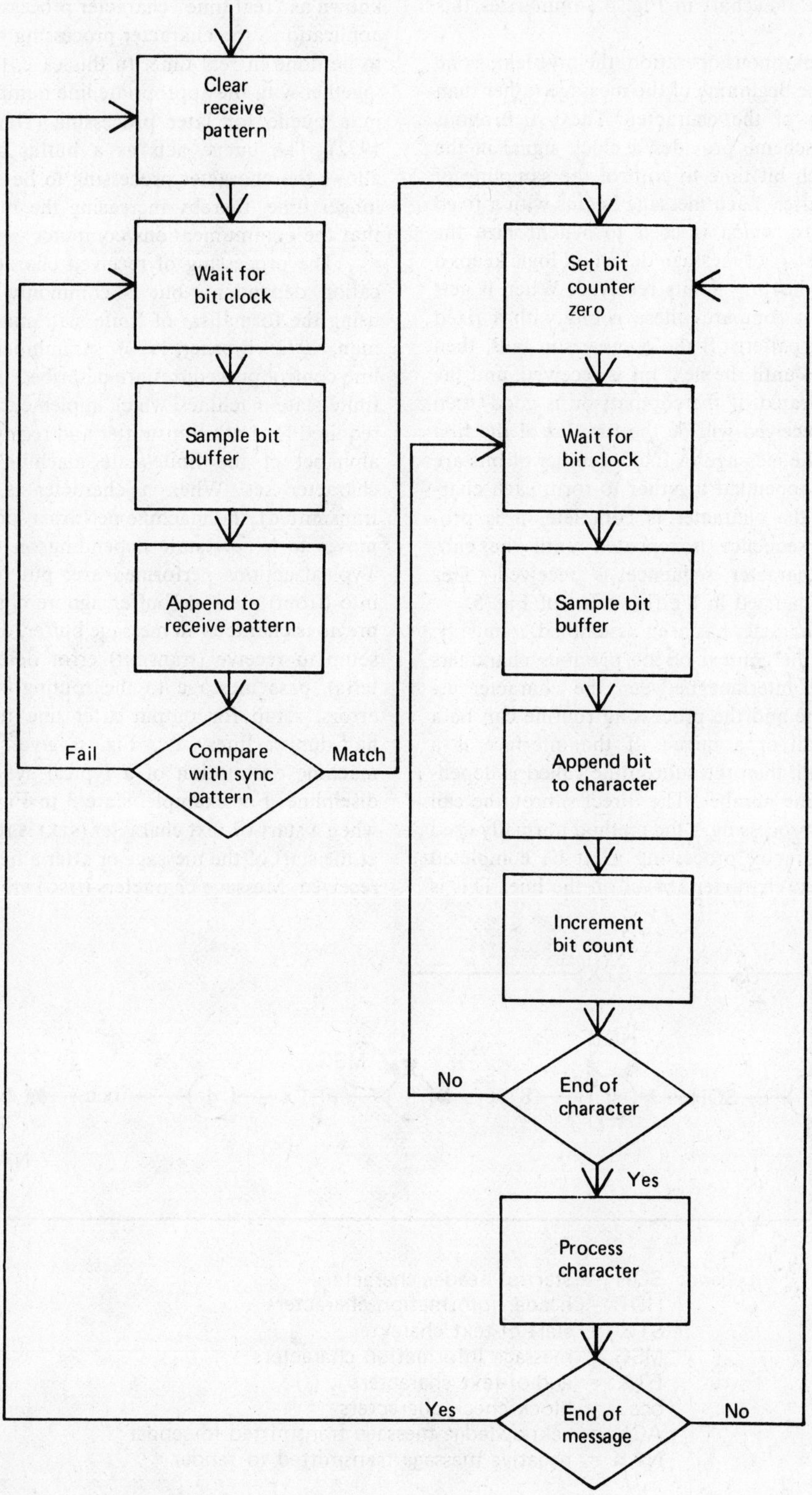


**Fig. 5.** Synchronous character receive.

character. The flowchart in Fig. 4 summarizes this logic.

With synchronous operation, the problem is one of detecting the beginning of the message rather than the beginning of the character. The synchronous transmission scheme provides a clock signal in the middle of each bit time to control the sampling of the receive buffer. Each message begins with a fixed pattern of bits, which is used to synchronize the receiver. The start of message detection logic keeps a record of the last $n - 1$ bits received. When it gets the next bit, it compares these $n$ bits with a fixed synchronizing pattern. If the comparison fails, then the logic waits until the next bit is received, and the process is repeated. If the comparison is good, then the next bit received will be the first bit of the first character of the message. A fixed number of bits are received and appended together to form each character. When the character is complete, it is processed. This sequence is repeated until the end-of-message character sequence is received. This action is summarized in the flowchart of Fig. 5.

After a character has been assembled, it must be processed in the context of the previous characters received. The interface between the character assembly routine and the processing routine can be a subroutine call or a queue. If the interface is a subroutine call, then the subroutine called is dependent on the line number. The direct subroutine call for character processing is the method normally used when the character processing must be completed before the next character arrival on the line. This is known as "real time" character processing. For most applications, the character processing does not have to be done in real time. In this case, the characters together with the appropriate line number are placed in a queue for later processing (Detlefsen et al., 1972). The queue acts as a buffer and therefore allows the character processing to be spread over a longer time, thereby increasing the burst data rate that the communications computer can handle.

The processing of received characters is application dependent, but is commonly implemented using the formalism of finite state machines (Stutzman, 1972; Bjorner, 1970). A number of common line-control procedures are described in terms of the finite-state machines, which implement the discipline required for both transmitter and receiver. The input alphabet of the finite-state machine is the input character set. When a character is received (or transmitted), the machine performs some action and moves to a new state depending on the character. Typical actions performed are: put (get) character into (from) message buffer, ignore character, delete previous character in message buffer, delete message, setup to receive (transmit) error detection character(s), pass message to the routing function if no errors, setup for output after line turnaround on half-duplex lines, etc. Fig. 6 gives a finite-state machine description of a typical synchronous line discipline. For example, state 3 in Fig. 6 is entered when a start-of-text character (STX) is received, either at the start of the message or after a header has been received. Message characters (MSG) are accepted and

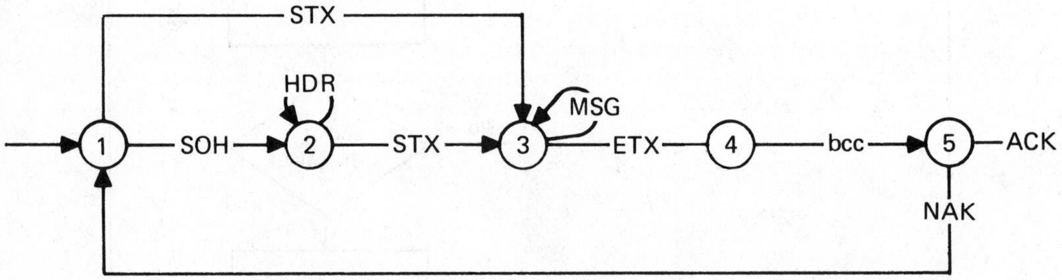


Legend: SOH = start-of-header character
HDR = header information characters
STX = start-of-text character
MSG = message information characters
ETX = end-of-text characters
bcc = block check characters
ACK = acknowledge message transmitted to sender
NAK = negative message transmitted to sender

**Fig. 6.** Typical line control procedure finite-state machine diagram.

put into the message buffer until an end of text (ETX) character is encountered.

**Error Detection and Correction.** The ability to detect and correct errors is determined by the code set and by the transmission disciplines. The details of the error detection and correction techniques tend to be application dependent, although there are some general principles.

The simplest error detection available at the character level is *parity checking*. Parity checking is obtained by including an additional bit (the parity bit) in each character. The parity bit is a function of the data it accompanies. The transmitter generates this parity bit, and the receiver checks incoming characters for correct parity. When it encounters an error, a message may be sent to the transmitter to request retransmission.

For human-operated terminals connected over full-duplex lines, the echo-plex technique is often used. With such a terminal, the keyboard is connected only to the transmitter, and the display device is connected to the receiver. When a key is struck, a character is sent to the receiver at the other end of the line. The receiver retransmits the character back to the terminal, which displays the character typed. The operator can check to see that the character displayed is the same as the character typed.

The second level of error detection and correction applies to the message as a whole. With this scheme, the message is followed by some number of check bits, which are generated at the transmitter as a function of the characters in the message. The receiver applies the same function to the received information to generate a corresponding set of check bits that are compared with those generated by the transmitter. There are several generating functions in use today, but all can be obtained from the theory of cyclic polynomial codes (Peterson, 1961). These polynomial schemes have the capability of correcting as well as detecting errors, but error correction is normally done in practice by software-initiated retransmission. These message-oriented error control schemes are transmission independent, but they are mainly used with synchronous transmission.

**Message Switching.** The message switching logic used in computer-controlled networks is similar to that employed in manual systems; i.e., if the source and destination points are not physically connected by a communication path, then the message is transmitted to an intermediate point (a communication computer) and then retransmitted to another intermediate point or its final destination.

When a message first enters the network, a message header is added to control its flow through the network. The header is removed before the message is delivered to its final network destination, normally a terminal or some EDP program external to the network.

The header contains the network destination, the message priority (which is normally application dependent), and a unique message identification. Message priority is used to determine the order in which messages are switched through the network. The identification is used for retransmission and identification. If the communications logic finds that it does not have an available path either to the final or to an intermediate destination of the message, then the message and its header must be queued within the computer until a path becomes available. In some networks, messages are switched as entities; in others, such as the ARPA network (Detlefsen et al., 1972), messages are broken into "packets" for switching purposes; and in other networks, messages are combined together for switching purposes.

**Hardware/Software Trade-Offs.** In the preceding sections, the transmit and receive logic has been explained in software terms, assuming minimal hardware. Flow diagrams similar to those in Fig. 2 through 5 have been used as the basis of an all software implementation on machines such as the DEC PDP-8. At the other extreme, there are hard-wired communications controllers, such as the IBM 270X with hardware-implemented logic.

The main advantage of an all-software implementation is flexibility in the mix of line speeds, character sets, line disciplines, and terminal types; the disadvantage is in performance loss, particularly at higher data rates. Fig. 7 depicts hardware/software trade-offs by speed.

Hardware can replace software on several levels to improve performance. The first level adds a hardware bit buffer and a software loadable timer register that produces an interrupt when it counts down to zero. With this hardware, the character assembly/disassembly logic is done in the interrupt routine, while the character processing is done by a main program. The significant parameter in such a system is the fraction of time spent in the interrupt routine servicing the bit buffers.

The second level adds hardware shift registers (character buffers) to do the bit-to-character assembly on input and character-to-bit disassembly on output. When combined with a start-bit detector for asynchronous channels or a synchronization pattern

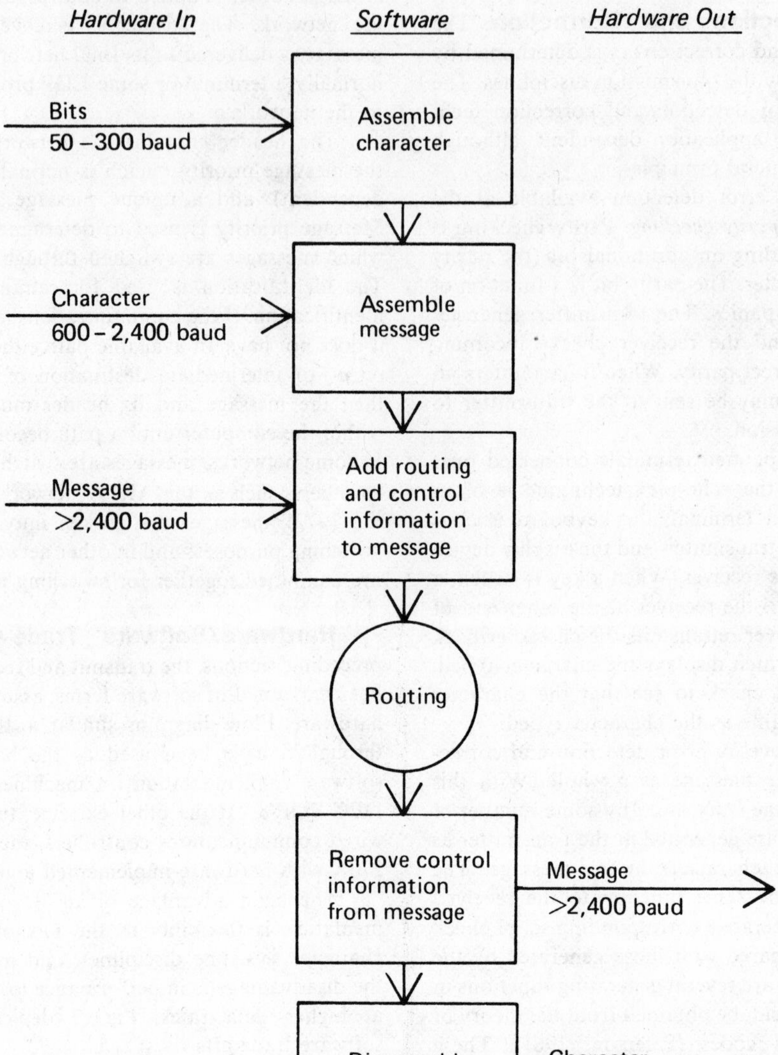


**Fig. 7.** Hardware/Software tradeoffs by speed.

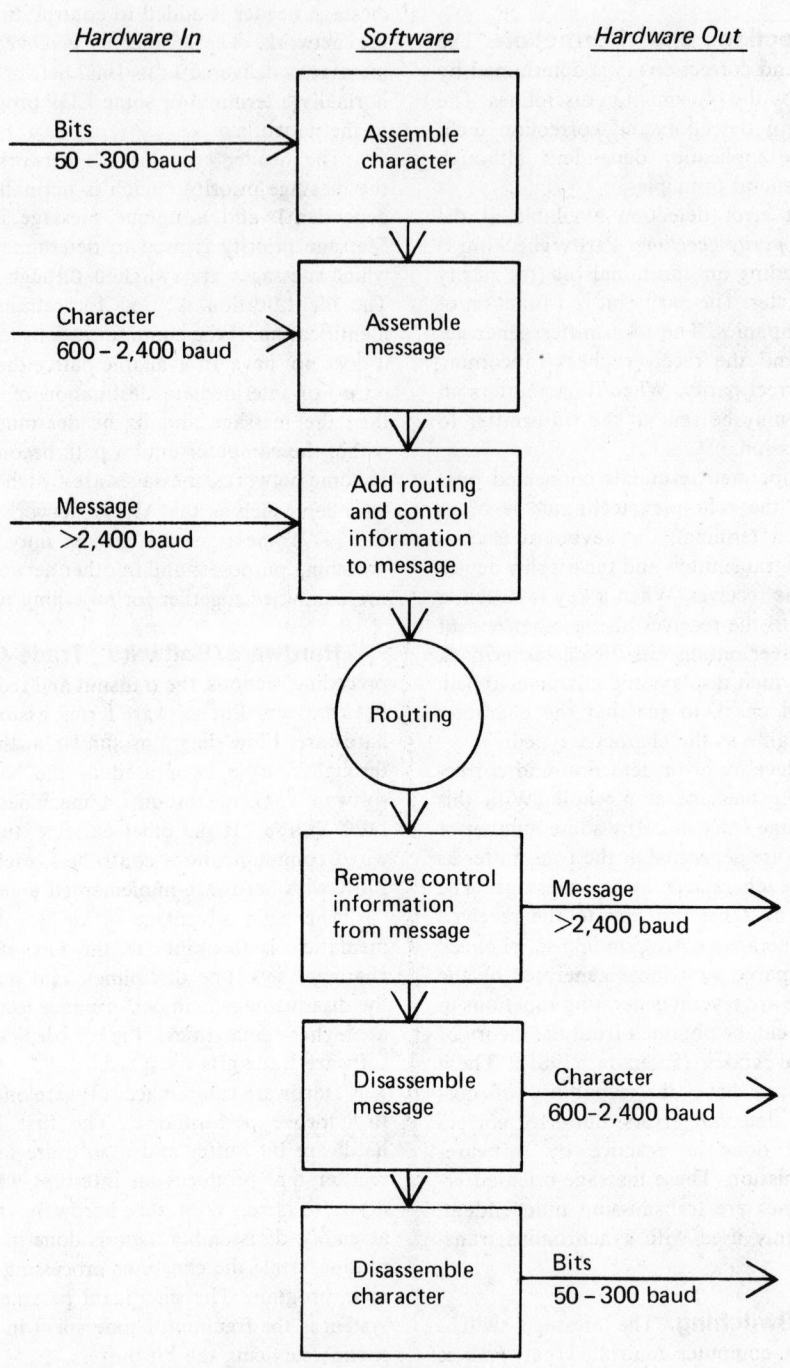

detector for synchronous channels, these character buffers can reduce the interrupt-program processing load by a factor approximately equal to the number of bits per character. Because of their high software processing load, the polynomial error control procedures are also frequently implemented in hardware at the character buffer level. Hardware to implement circular queues in memory has been combined with character buffers in some systems (PDP-11) to reduce the processing load even further.

The third level is direct memory access (hardwired) communication controllers. The hardware in these systems, in addition to transferring the characters to and from memory, must also perform such functions as character parity generation and checking, control character interpretation, and generation of automatic transmission synchronization sequences. The use of hardware to perform these operations reduces the software load considerably, particularly on high-speed (>2,400 baud) channels. Initial implementations (e.g., IBM 270X) of such channels were constrained to operate with the fixed hard-wired message and line discipline. Later implementations (e.g., Honeywell 355) have removed this constraint by allowing the message and line control parameters to be initialized under software control.

Frequently, the three major options of bit buffers, character buffers, and direct memory access controllers are available on the same communication computer and these options provide the user with the ability to configure systems that have widely varying performance and costs.

**Conclusion.** This article describes the major communication software functions. It does not discuss dial-up lines; multipoint lines (Stutzman, 1972); automatic recognition of line speeds; the operating system requirements for communication computers (Detlefsen et al., 1972; Sobolewski, 1972); code conversion; data compression; line monitoring, the data communication requirements on the operating system of EDP computers, or the software content of network traffic analysis and control (Cerf and Naylor, 1972; McKenzie et al., 1972).

REFERENCES

1961. Peterson, W. W. *Error Correcting Codes*. Cambridge, Mass.: The M.I.T. Press.

1970. Bjorner, D. "Finite State Automation-Definition of Data Communication Line Control Procedures," *Proc. FJCC*.

1970. Roberts, L. G., and B. D. Wexler. "Computer Network Development to Achieve Resource Sharing," *Proc. SJCC*.

1972. Cerf, V., and W. Naylor. "Selected ARPA Network Measurement Experiments," *Proc. 6th IEEE Computer Society Conference*.

1972. Detlefsen, G. D., R. H. Kerr, and S. B. Revkin. "Software for Data Communication Networks," *Proc. 5th Australian Computer Conference*.

1972. McKenzie, A. A., B. P. Cosell, J. M. McQuillan, and M. J. Thrope. "The Network Control Center for the ARPA Network," *Proc. First International Conference on Computer Communications*.

1972. Sobolewski, J. S. "Programmable Communication Processes," *Proc. First International Conference on Computer Communication*.

1972. Stutzman, B. W. "Data Communications Control Procedures," *ACM Computing Surveys*, Vol. 4, No. 4.

G. D. DETLEFSEN AND R. H. KERR

## DATA PREPARATION DEVICES

For articles on related subjects *see* AUDIO RESPONSE TERMINAL; CODES; DATA ACQUISITION COMPUTER; DATA COMMUNICATIONS: General Principles; INPUT-OUTPUT DEVICES; OPTICAL CHARACTER READERS; OPTICAL MARK READERS; and TERMINALS.
For article on related term *see* BUFFER.

This article discusses the major data preparation devices including the card punch and paper tape punch through to the magnetic tape encoder, key-to-tape systems, key-to-disk systems, on-line keypunch/verify systems, magnetic character readers, optical character readers, optical mark readers, and direct-entry terminals. Each is briefly described together with its limitations.

The various data preparation devices and their associated data entry techniques can be separated into two main categories:

1. *Transcriptive data entry*: This term covers all data preparation devices where data, prepared on documents at their source or origin, is then transcribed to another medium that is capable of being read and interpreted by a computer. In this category are the following data preparation devices: card punches, paper tape punches, magnetic tape en-

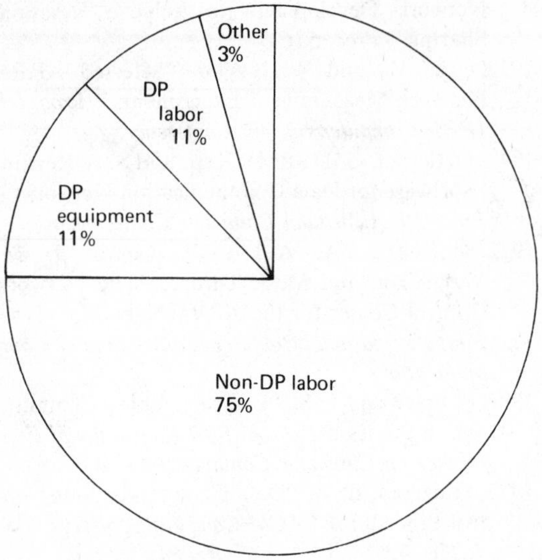


**Fig. 1.** Typical data-entry cost breakdown. Item distribution: DP equipment—computers, peripherals, unit record, DE equipment; DP labor—KP operations, DP operations, DE programming; other—cards, magnetic tape, forms, contracted work, card storage; non-DP labor—initial recording, coding, batching, file reference, document handling.

coders, key-to-tape systems, key-to-disk systems, on-line keypunch/verify systems and magnetic character readers.

2. *Source data entry*: For devices in this category, data is prepared at its source in a machine-readable form such that it can be directly read by a computer without the requirement for a separate intermediate data transcription step. Data entry techniques that fall into this category include optical character reading, optical mark reading, and the direct-entry of information into a computer using terminals at the point of origin of the data.

We will first examine the advantages and shortcomings of these two categories of data entry.

**Transcriptive Data Entry.** Each extra step carried out on data before it finally enters the computer for processing introduces the possibility of the occurrence of errors. Studies have shown that of all of the errors detected in data by the computer, only about 15% of those errors occur in source data content, with the remaining 85% introduced through data transcription.

In order to reduce the number of errors occurring through data transcription, a number of techniques may be used. As data is transcribed into a machine-readable form, the data preparation device may carry out certain checks according to predefined conventions established for that particular data. Some of the editing that can be carried out (Trimble and Penta, 1970) includes:

1. Check digit validation.
2. Field-length check.
3. Check numeric-only fields.
4. Check alphabetic-only fields.
5. Develop batch control totals.

Data that cannot be validated by using check digits or control totals may be verified by keying it a second time, using a verifier unit to check that the second entry of the data agrees with the original entry.

The computer itself may carry out more extensive editing of the validity or reasonableness of information, applying various logical rules to the data, and possibly accessing other information held by the computer on disk or other files for confirmation purposes.

Errors that are detected must be corrected, using the original source document, rekeyed, verified again if necessary, and merged with the original data (Finklestein, 1970). The data is then edited by the computer once more, with errors recycled through the above steps until the data is error-free. Only then is the data ready for computer processing.

In addition to being involved, time consuming, and error prone, transcriptive data-entry techniques require highly trained and highly paid personnel. Indeed, salaries of such personnel can represent as much as 80% of the the total cost of data preparation (Finklestein, 1970). Moreover, these salaries are steadily increasing.

**Source Data Entry.** Studies of the cost of data entry show that while differences occur across companies and industries, approximately 75% of the cost of data entry occurs in nondata-processing personnel labor and delays in availability of data to the computer (see Fig. 1). Of the remaining 25% approximately 11% represents the cost of data processing and data entry equipment, approximately 11% represents the cost of data processing personnel, and approximately 3% represents other costs such as stationery and supplies.

| Data-Entry Work Flow | Card and Paper Tape Punch, Magnetic Tape Encoder, Key-to-Tape System | OCR, OMR, MICR (partially) | Key-to-Disk System, On-Line Keypunch/ Verify System | Direct-Entry Terminal System |
|---|---|---|---|---|
| Initial recording | | X | | X |
| Transport | | | | X |
| File reference | | | X | X |
| Control | | | X | X |
| Transcribe | X | X | X | X |
| Verify | X | X | X | X |
| DP edit | | X | X | X |
| System input | | | X | X |
| Error correction | | | | X |

**Fig. 2.** Impact of data preparation devices on data-entry work flow.

The 75% cost of data entry contributed by nondata-processing personnel and time delays is expended in functions such as:

1. Retyping handwritten information for easier reading and faster operation by data preparation operators.
2. Validation, such as checking the availability of stock to fill an order before that order reaches the data preparation area.
3. Determining the price and discounts applicable for various products ordered in a preinvoicing environment.

These functions take time, with the result that before information reaches the computer, it may be several days old. Thus, the computer can produce results only as accurate and as timely as the input data. The computer in such an environment is being used only as a recording and high-speed printing machine. Its full potential cannot be realized until it is able to accept information as close as possible to the time of origination of that information.

Source data entry removes the need to retype handwritten information for easier reading by data preparation operators. In fact, the need for such data preparation is completely bypassed by entry of the data directly from its source. In addition, the computer itself can check the validity of the information.

In this way, instead of reflecting the status of information that may be several days old, the computer will maintain much more current information. Information, therefore, is available sooner, is more accurate, allows more meaningful decisions to be made, improves customer service, and reduces the amount of time before the organization will be paid for service performed.

The effect of each of the data preparation devices discussed above on the data-entry work flow is summarized in Fig. 2. Each step in the data-entry cycle affected by a particular device is illustrated in Fig. 2 by a cross, with those devices having a similar effect on the work flow grouped together. This figure illustrates the fact that only source data entry, using direct-entry terminals, has an effect on every step in the entry of data into a computer.

We will now examine each of the various data preparation devices in more detail.

## Transcriptive Data Entry Devices

Card Punch and Verifier. Until the 1960s, the capabilities of most card punches were limited. When the punch operator hit a key on the keyboard, the appropriate combination of holes was immediately punched into the card. In many cases, errors made by keypunch operators were detected by them immediately after making the error. However, correction of such an error invariably required that the card be ejected, inserted into the read mechanism, duplicated up to the point of the error, the error corrected, and punching continued. This procedure was time consuming. Examples of these units are the IBM 24, 26, and 29 card punches, and the IBM 56 and 59 card verifiers (see Fig. 3a).

The 1960s saw the development of a buffer on the card punch so that an entire card of information could be keyed, and any error could be corrected by backspacing to the point of the error and rekeying. Only after the punch operator was satisfied with the information keyed was that information released from the buffer for punching.

Other developments provided punches with capabilities of validating check digits and accumulat-

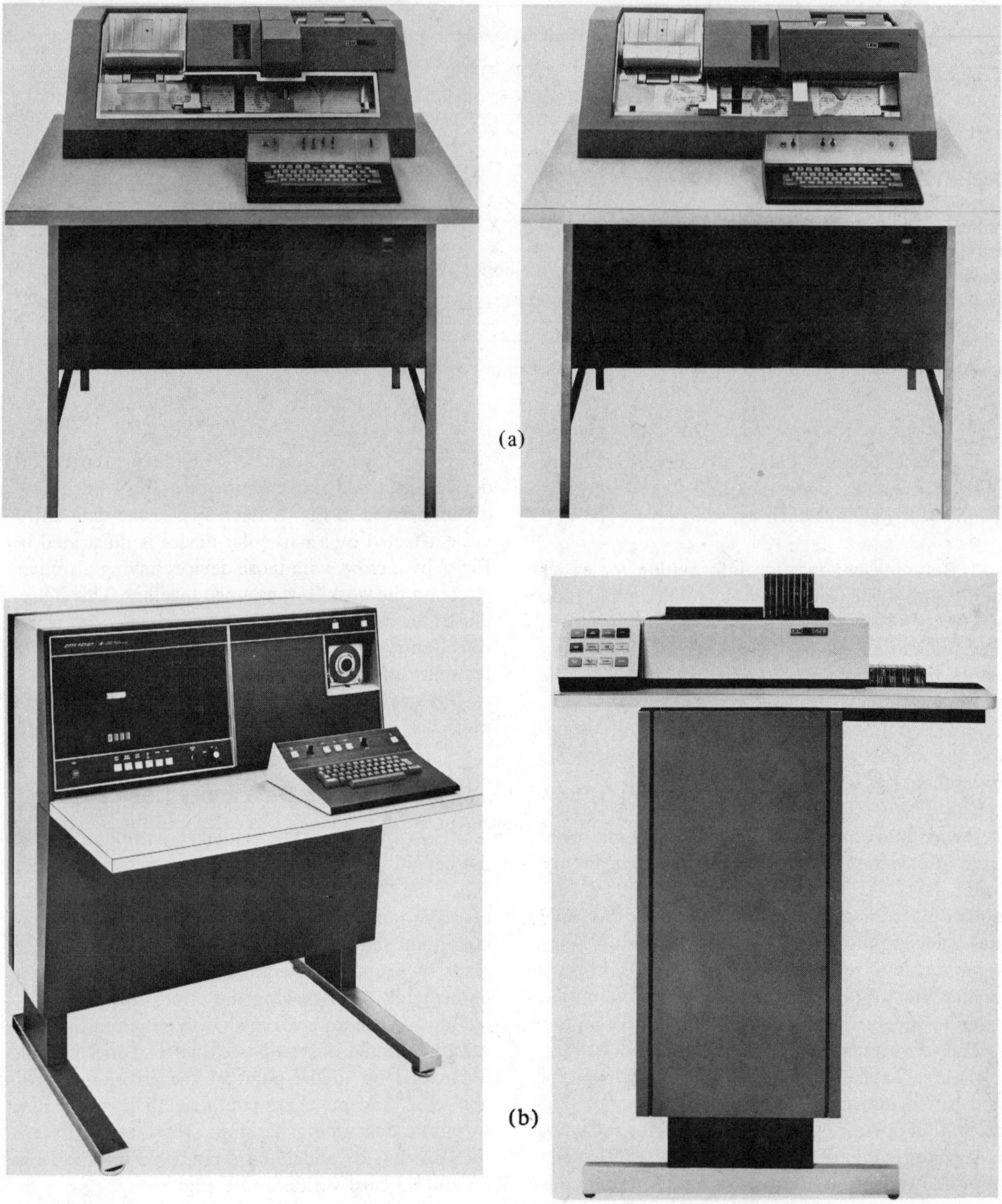


**Fig. 3.** Data preparation devices. (a) IBM card punch and verifier. (b) Data Action 150 magnetic data inscriber and IBM 2495 tape cartridge reader used to transfer data entered on the Data Action 150 into a computer.

ing information for comparison against batch control totals (Trimble and Penta, 1970). The 1960s also saw the emergence of combination devices for both card punching and verifying, thus enabling a keypunch operator to correct a punching error on the same device used for verification. Examples of such units are the Univac 1701 verifying punch, the Univac 1710 verifying interpreting punch, and the IBM 129 card punch.

PAPER TAPE PUNCHES. Paper tape punches permit data to be entered without the restriction of 80 or 96 columns for information on a card. Thus, records of information relating to a particular transaction can contain as much or as little information as necessary, without the physical limitation imposed by the card.

When errors are introduced by the punch operator, the error information on the paper tape is backspaced over, erased by punching a series of delete characters (which are ignored when read by a paper tape reader), and then rekeyed. In many cases, verification of the correction is not used with paper tape; instead, that data is read directly by a computer and edited. In the event of errors being detected, corrections are keyed generally by punching a reversing transaction for the information in error, and then punching the correct information. In addition, information that may have been omitted can be punched on a separate piece of paper tape and then spliced in sequence into the main section of the tape.

Most computer manufacturers like NCR, ICL, Burroughs, CDC, and Univac produce paper tape punches.

MAGNETIC TAPE ENCODERS. The first magnetic tape encoder was announced by Mohawk Data Sciences in 1965, and gained immediate acceptance.

While the magnetic tape encoder can be used for the transcription of data directly to magnetic tape (Finkelstein, 1970; *EDP Analyzer*, Part I, 1971), most magnetic tape encoders such as the Mohawk encoder also have the ability to transmit data from one point to another over telephone lines. Thus, they are well suited for the preparation of data in remote locations, and the transmission of that data to a central point where it may be received by another encoder, recorded directly on magnetic tape, and then used as input into a computer.

As well as recording data directly on half-inch computer magnetic tape, as with the Mohawk encoder, other units have been developed to record data on tape cassettes or cartridges. These cartridges are converted to half-inch computer tape, or read directly into a computer, by a cartridge reader. Examples of these units are the IBM 50 magnetic data inscriber and IBM 2495 tape cartridge reader, the Viatron System 21, and units manufactured by Sycor and by Data Action (Fig. 4).

While magnetic tape encoders remove the need to use cards or paper tape, and feature a buffer for easy correction of keying errors, they still suffer from most of the disadvantages of card and paper tape punches. The data preparation cycle is still involved and time consuming, and errors must be recycled for correction. While most encoders offer features such as check-digit validation and control total accumulation, data cannot be fully validated until it is processed by the computer edit program.

KEY-TO-TAPE SYSTEMS. In 1969, Mohawk announced the 900 Series key-to-tape system, which groups up to 16 key stations around a control unit and pools data from these stations onto magnetic tape. Honeywell produces a similar unit, the Keytape [see Fig. 4a], as does Singer-Friden, who manufactures the 4300 Magnetic Data Recording System.

Key-to-tape systems were developed to overcome the limitations of magnetic tape encoders (*EDP Analyzer*, Part I, 1971). They comprise a number of keyboards, possibly also with television-like cathode-ray tube (CRT) displays, and are connected to a central controlling unit, typically a minicomputer, which collects information from each keyboard. This information is then directed to a magnetic tape.

In addition, the use of a minicomputer allows more sophisticated validation and editing to be carried out at the time of initial entry of the data. Consequently, more errors can be detected earlier than is possible with the devices discussed above, and correction of these errors is simplified.

However, such key-to-tape systems generally do not have the capabilities of accessing other computer files for more complete validation of data. Consequently, errors must still be recycled from the computer edit run for correction. Data preparation is still an involved, time-consuming process.

KEY-TO-DISK SYSTEMS. Key-to-disk systems are effectively equivalent to key-to-tape systems, except that information entered by keyboards is first collected on magnetic disk (*EDP Analyzer*, Part II, 1971). Each keyboard generally uses a separate section of the disk, and is independent of other keyboards. Thus, each keyboard can be working on different types of data at the same time, which results in good operational flexibility in the installation. Data is extracted from the disk when complete, and is copied onto a magnetic tape or another

(a)

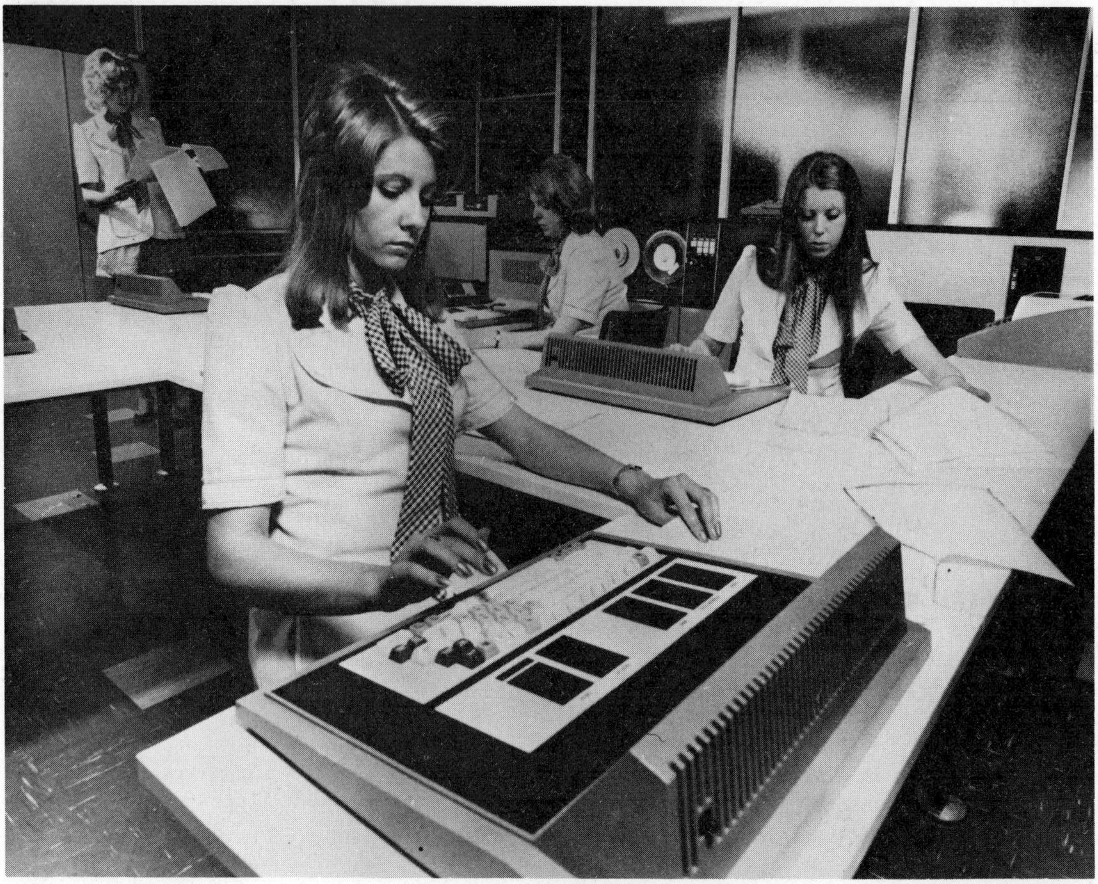

(b)

**Fig. 4.** Data preparation devices. (a) Honeywell KEYPLEX system allows up to 64 operators at KEYTAPE stations to encode data onto magnetic tape. (b) Computer Machinery Corporation (CMC) 18 key-to-disk system can support up to 64 input stations.

disk for further processing on the main computer.

Some key-to-disk systems, such as the IBM 3740 data entry system, are also capable of transmitting data from the disk to a device that copies the data to a magnetic tape for later processing, or transmits it across telephone lines directly to a computer. Examples of key-to-disk systems are the CMC18 Key Processing System, manufactured by Computer Machinery Corporation of Los Angeles [see Fig. 4(b)], the Inforex Key Entry System manufactured by Inforex Inc. of Burlington, Massachusetts, the Honeywell Keyplex System, the Logic Corporation Key Disk System, the IBM 3735 programmable buffered terminal, and the IBM 3740 data entry system.

Most key-to-disk systems generally have limited disk capacity so that they cannot also hold full computer files to allow complete validation and editing. This validation against computer files still must be left until the main computer edit run. Accordingly, errors must still be recycled for correction.

On-Line Keypunch/Verify Systems. On-line keypunch/verify systems, such as IBM's VIDEO/370 program product, provide a software capability similar to that of key-to-disk systems (Finklestein, 1970), but are controlled by a main computer rather than a minicomputer. Consequently, they offer the potential for validation against full computer files, so enabling complete editing of data without requiring a separate computer edit run. In this way, error correction is considerably simplified.

Magnetic Character Readers. Magnetic ink character recognition (MICR) is a transcriptive data entry technique used mainly by banks. Information, such as the amount of a check, is transcribed and printed in magnetic ink when the check is accepted by the particular bank. Examples of magnetic character readers are the IBM 1419 (see Fig. 5), IBM 1259 and IBM 1255 (see Fig. 6), the Burroughs OCR/MICR reader/sorter, and the Honeywell 232 reader/sorter.

Magnetic character readers are designed to be used off-line, away from a computer, for certain editing of information and physical sorting of checks, and also on-line to a computer for direct entry of information from checks. After the computer edit run, errors must still be recycled for correction.

Transcriptive Data Entry Summary. It can be seen from the above discussion that developments in transcriptive data-entry devices have been directed toward increasing the amount of editing that can be carried out when data is initially transcribed

**Fig. 5.** IBM 1419 magnetic character reader.

to a machine-readable form. These developments have also reduced the delays that occur in validating information and correcting errors, and have resulted in up to 30 to 50% increased throughput of key-to-disk systems and on-line keypunch/verify systems over card punching (*EDP Analyzer*, Part II, 1971). However, as was discussed earlier, transcriptive data-entry techniques apply only toward the 25% of the total data-entry cost that is represented by data-entry equipment, data processing personnel labor costs, and supplies (see Fig. 1). Consequently, the net effect of newer devices on the total data-entry cost is an effective increased throughput on the order of 8 to 12%.

## Source Data Entry

Optical Character Readers (OCR). Since typed or numeric hand-printed information capable of being read by OCR's is also readily understood by humans, this is a very useful source data-entry technique. The stylized alphabetic fonts recognized by an optical character reader can be printed by normal electric typewriters at the point of origin, and the need for transcriptive data entry is eliminated (Finklestein, 1970.) This also eliminates the possibility of introduting additional errors, as well as eliminating the high cost of data transcription equipment and personnel.

A large number of OCR's are now available. These include units manufactured by Farrington (3030), Recognition Equipment Inc., Univac, Control Data Corporation (915 and 955 page readers), IBM (1287 and 1288 optical character readers), Optical Scanning Corporation (288 document reader), Honeywell, Scan-Data Corporation, Scan-Optics Inc., and Viatron.

Information printed by the computer can be also used as a turnaround document, with additional

# DATA PREPARATION DEVICES

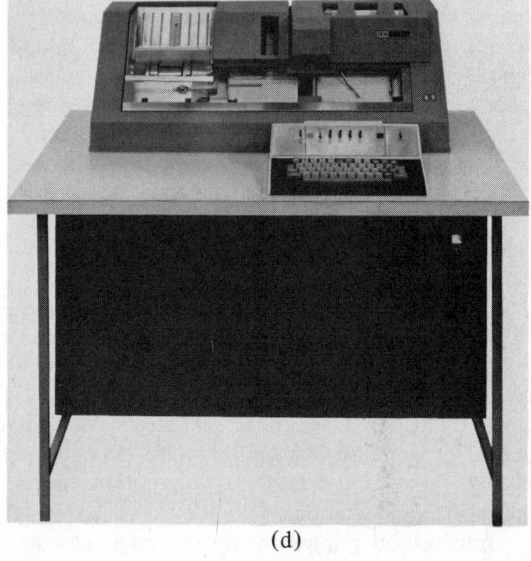

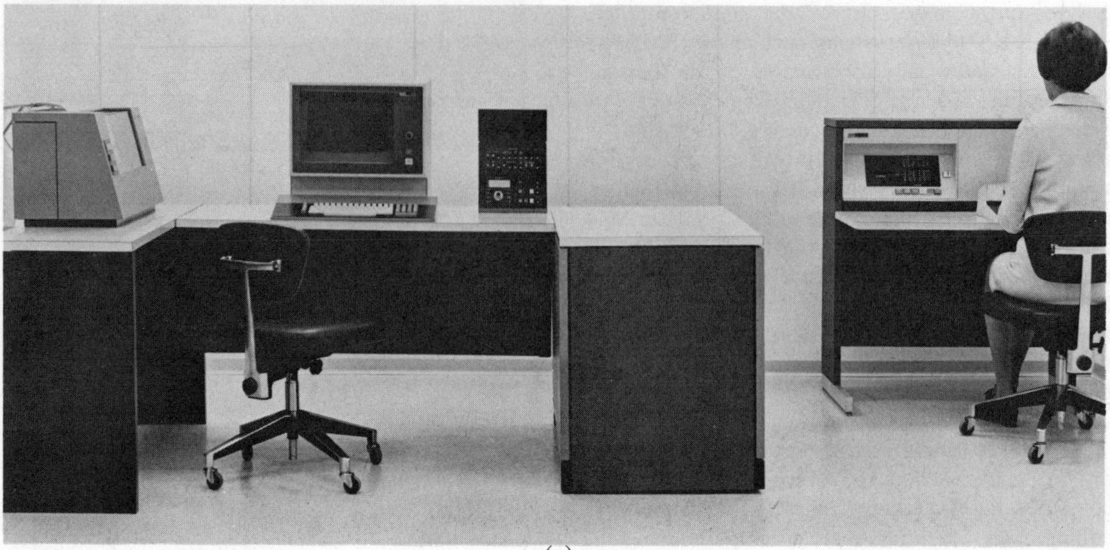

(a)

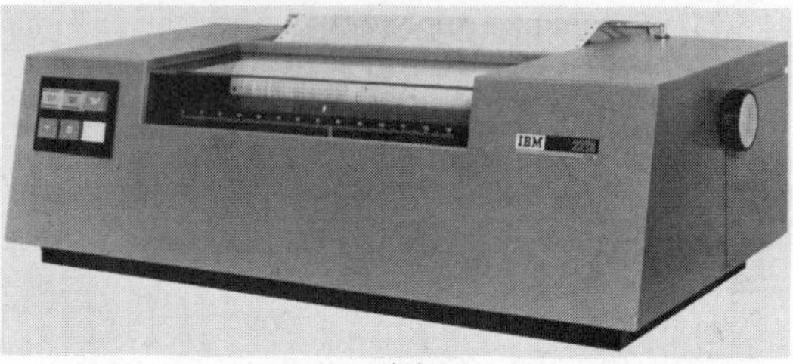


(b)

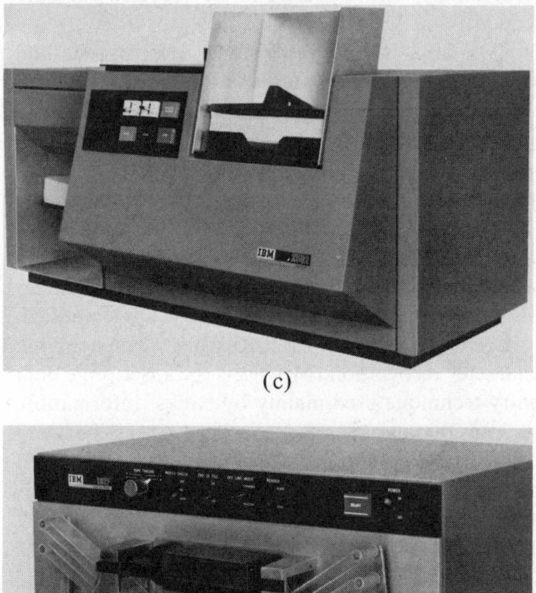


(c)

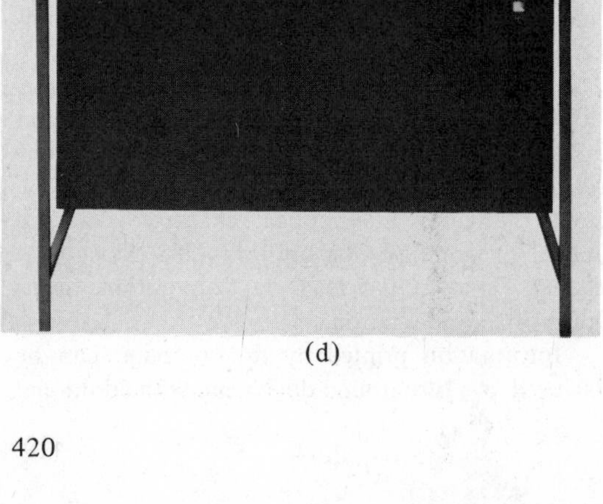

(d)

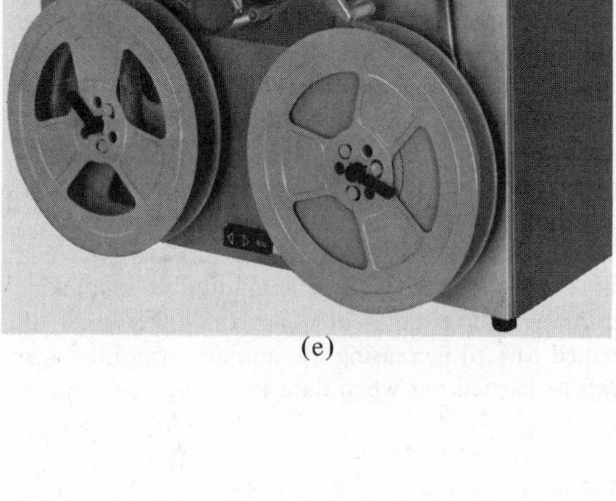


(e)

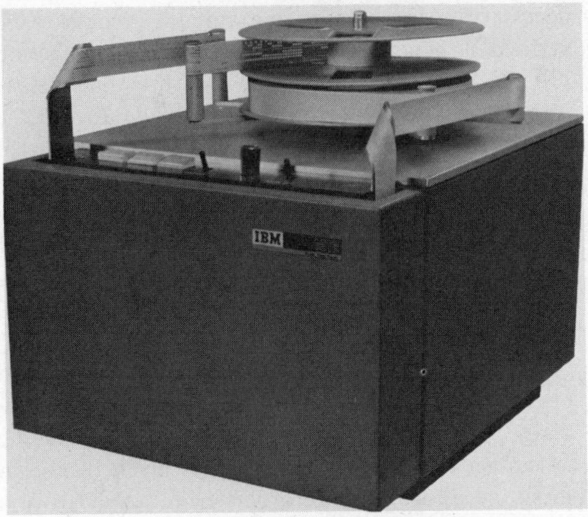

(f)

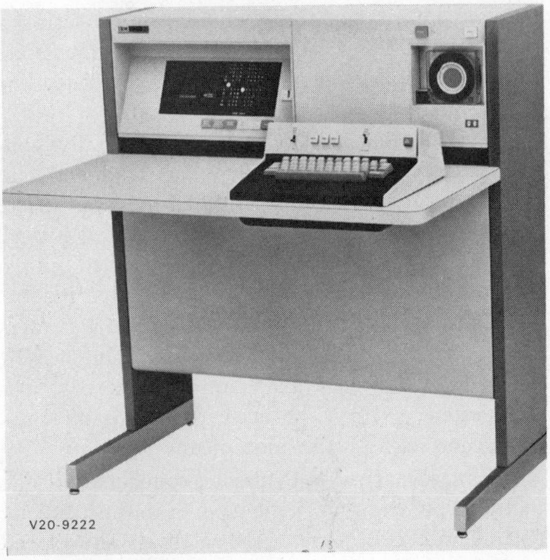


(g)

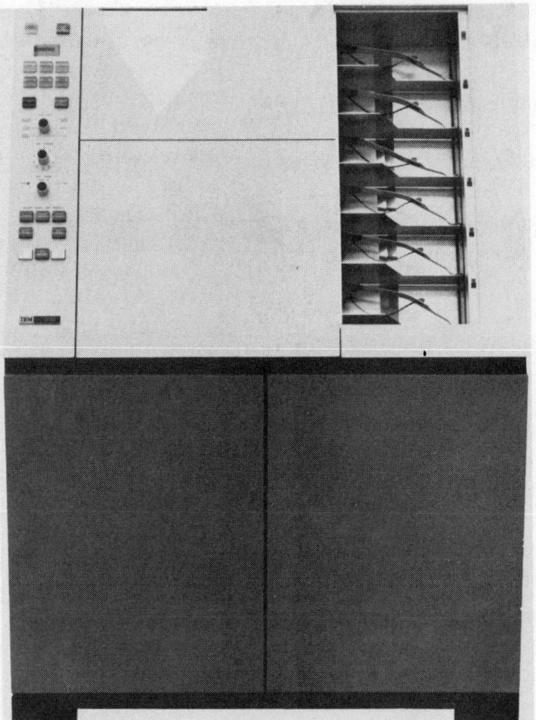

(h)

**Fig. 6.** Components of the IBM 2770 data communications system. (a) 2772 Multi-Purpose Control Unit and Keyboard, 2265-2 Display Station, 2213-2 Printer; (b) 2213-1 Printer; (c) 2502 Card Reader; (d) 545 Output Punch; (e) 1017 Paper Tape Reader; (f) 1018 Paper Tape Punch; (g) 50 Magnetic Data Inscriber; (h) 1255 Magnetic Character Reader.

numeric information being hand printed, using a pencil. Examples of such turnaround documents are insurance policy renewal forms, meter-reading forms, credit authorizations, and so on.

Optical character readers are generally connected directly to a computer, and read and edit documents at high speed. Because of the input speed, computer files generally cannot be accessed for full editing. Any error documents are selected into a separate stacker and must be recycled for correction.

Optical Mark Readers. Optical mark readers (OMR) enable data to be recorded using a soft pencil as a series of marks on a sheet of paper (Finklestein, 1970). Each mark represents information according to its position on the page.

Optical mark readers may be connected off-line to a card punch or magnetic tape, or on-line directly to a computer. Because of the relatively slow speed of such readers, information may be fully edited during data entry, including access to computer files for complete validation. Error sheets can be selected into a separate stacker, corrected by erasure of the error mark, and then recycled.

Examples of optical mark readers include the IBM 1230, 1231, 1232 and 3881, the Optical Scanning Corporation 70 and 100, the Scanak 216, and the Republic Corporation 1500 optical card scanner.

Optical mark readers enable data to be captured very economically directly at its point of origin in a machine-readable form. The only equipment needed is a soft lead pencil and a supply of preprinted optical mark forms. The training necessary to record information accurately for optical mark reading can be carried out in a matter of minutes.

This technique is ideally suited for applications such as surveys, questionnaires, and diagrammatic representation of information, as well as numeric and alphabetic information. Turnaround documents, produced by the computer, can also be used for subsequent input, using optical mark readers.

Direct-Entry Terminals. These terminals enable the computer not only to receive data immediately after it has been entered at its point of origin, but also to edit the data at its time of receipt, allowing computer files to be accessed to validate the information entered, and allowing the terminal operator to be notified immediately of any errors.

Some information (such as dollar values or sales figures) may not be able to be checked against computer files. Such information may instead be verified by rekeying, as for card punches, and the computer can check that the same information was entered each time. While verification may still be necessary in these cases, the amount of data to be verified is generally reduced. Thus, the correction process is greatly simplified, and the time delays associated with the transportation of data from the source as well as the detection and correction of errors are almost eliminated.

A variety of devices can be attached to terminals for communication with a computer. Some of these devices are shown in Fig. 6, which illustrates components that may be attached to the IBM 2770 data communications system.

The power of the computer can also be used to provide information that might not otherwise normally be available at the time. An example of the advantages of source data entry is given by examining the direct entry of orders from terminals in a branch office. An order is entered directly into a terminal at the time it is placed by a customer. Computer customer and product files can be accessed, and the quantity of each product ordered can be checked against the available quantity-on-hand in the product file, and updated. If insufficient stock is available to fill the order, the computer may automatically place the remaining quantity to be supplied on backorder. The price and any relevant discounts of each product ordered can be used to determine the total value of the order, which can then be checked against the customer's credit limit.

When the order has been completely entered, the computer may transmit it directly to a terminal in the warehouse. The products ordered may be sorted by the computer into the same sequence as they are located in the warehouse, to enable a packing slip to be produced on the warehouse terminal. At the same time, a completely calculated invoice may also be produced for inclusion with the order as it is packed, so enabling pre-invoicing to be readily implemented. In addition, a copy of this invoice can be transmitted back to the branch office terminal as confirmation that the order has been accepted. In the same way as stock is received from various suppliers to be placed in the warehouse, these receipts can be entered from the warehouse terminal to update the quantity-on-hand file for each particular product received.

It can be seen from the preceding example that the potential offered by terminals used for source data entry is enormous. The transcription requirement, with its consequent delays and cost, is eliminated, and information is available to the computer at its time of origin rather than several hours or days later. Thus, the computer is able to reflect the actual operation of the company accurately and reliably.

However, the additional cost of data transmission, direct-entry terminal, and computer equipment is a factor that must also be considered.

We will now consider various terminal devices used for source data entry.

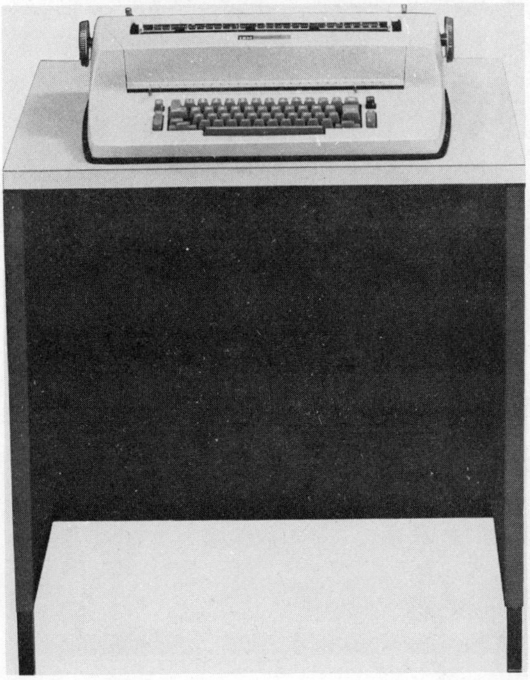

**Fig. 7.** IBM 2741 typewriter communications terminal.

*Typewriter Terminals.* These devices range from the normal office Telex machine used for telegraph communication to terminals that can be used as normal office typewriters when not required as terminals, such as the IBM 2741 (see Fig. 7) and the IBM 2740 communications terminals. Using typewriter terminals, a hard-copy record of information entered via the keyboard and received from the computer via the printer can be recorded on paper for subsequent reference.

In order to share the cost of communication between a number of terminals, typewriter terminals often may all attach to (or be "multidropped" off) the same communication line. In this instance, in order to avoid a tie-up of the line for relatively long periods of time while a terminal operator keys information, such terminals often feature buffers into which the data can be keyed. Once that data has been keyed, it can be input to the computer for transmission at line speed when the line is idle and available for use. The IBM 2740-2 communications terminal is an example of such a buffered terminal.

*Visual Display Terminals.* Visual display terminals, or cathode-ray tube (CRT) terminals as they are sometimes called, generally use a keyboard for entry of information, a television-like screen for the display of that information, and an optional printer for hard copy (see Fig. 8). They are generally characterized by a higher speed of operation than typewriter terminals. Because of the widespread acceptance of such devices, visual display terminals are produced by almost every computer and terminal manufacturer, such as IBM (2260, 2265, and 3270), Univac, NCR, CDC, and Burroughs.

Visual display units (Fig. 9) are well suited as both inquiry and data preparation devices (Finkelstein, 1970). In the event of an error being detected in data entered from the terminal, the computer may display an error message on the screen, and also lock the keyboard and sound an audible alarm to notify the terminal operator (Finkelstein, 1970).

As with typewriter terminals, most visual display terminals may be multidropped off the same communication line. Visual display terminals use a buffer to enable information to be continually regenerated to maintain the image on the screen. This buffer is also useful to enable data to be transmitted at communication-line speeds, thereby sharing that line with other visual display terminals.

*Audio-Response Terminals.* Audio-response terminals feature either a full typewriter keyboard (such as the IBM 2721 portable audio terminal) or only a numeric keyboard, and do not use a printer for output. Instead, the response transmitted from the computer is a spoken response. The computer program can edit the data entered from the keyboard, process that data and construct a reply. This response is directed to an audio-response unit attached to the computer, which converts it to a spoken reply. This spoken response is then transmitted over the telephone line to the audio-terminal speaker. The Touchtone telephone in household use today may be used as an audio data-preparation device. These telephones enable numeric information to be keyed, once the call has been established.

Audio-response terminals may be used for source-data-entry applications (Finkelstein, 1970), such as the order-entry example discussed earlier. In this case, each product number and quantity ordered can be keyed on the audio terminal and the confirmation of acceptance of the order, or any errors can be transmitted back by the computer as a spoken response. The advantage that such audio-

**Fig. 8.** IBM 3270 information display system, showing display screens and printer.

response terminals have over typewriter terminals is their ready availability. Thus, a representative from a company may travel to different customers in his territory, accept orders from the customer on his premises, telephone the computer, and enter those orders directly, using the customer's own telephone.

*Intelligent Terminals.* An intelligent terminal generally has the ability to store data on magnetic tape or disk, and is also able to carry out extensive formatting and editing of information as data is entered and before it is transmitted to the computer. Thus, various edit checks may be carried out as data is entered, and errors may be corrected at that time (Fig. 9). However, it is not possible to carry out full editing by validating information against files until the data is transmitted to the computer at a later time. Therefore, intelligent terminals require the recycling of error corrections, as for transcriptive data preparation devices. However, they offer an effective compromise between the full advantages to be gained through source data entry, and the cost of transmission of large volumes of data across long distances.

Some examples of intelligent terminals are the IBM 3735 programmable buffered terminal, the Burroughs TC500, and minicomputers such as the PDP 8 Series manufactured by Digital Equipment Corporation.

### References

1970. Trimble, Jr., G. R., and A. J. Penta. "Evaluation of Keyed Data Entry Systems," *Datamation* (June), pp. 93–99.

1970. Finkelstein, C. B. "Data Entry Techniques," *Australian Computer Journal* (November), pp. 146–155.

**Fig. 9.** IBM 3270 information display system, being used for payroll inquiries and data entry.

1971. "Improvements in Data Entry," *EDP Analyzer*, Part I, Vol. 9, No. 9 (September); Part II, Vol. 9, No. 10 (October).

C. B. FINKELSTEIN

## DATA PROCESSING

For articles on related subjects *see* ADMINISTRATIVE-BUSINESS APPLICATIONS; INFORMATION AND DATA; INFORMATION PROCESSING; PROCEDURE-ORIENTED LANGUAGES; and SCIENTIFIC APPLICATIONS.

## DATA PROCESSING

For articles on related terms *see* CENTRAL PROCESSING UNIT; DATA COMMUNICATIONS: General Principles; GENERATIONS, COMPUTER; STATISTICAL APPLICATIONS; and TIME SHARING.

Data processing is a widely used term with a variety of meanings and interpretations ranging from one that makes it almost coextensive with all of computing (e.g., IBM's major marketing division is called the "Data Processing" Division) to much narrower connotations in the general area of computer applications to business and administrative problems.

In a broad sense, data processing may be said to be what computers *do*. In this context it should be compared to *information processing*, which some prefer to data processing because "information" does not carry the connotation of "number," as "data" sometimes does. Of course the "data" in data processing is really intended to connote any kind of information in symbolic form. Thus, information may be viewed as "knowledge," while data are the physical symbols used to represent the information.

The term "data processing" is often used with various modifiers, the most common being:

1. Electronic data processing (EDP), a term widely used to describe *all* computing activity—or, at least, the part of computing that focuses on administrative or business applications—and particularly to distinguish computerized applications from manual methods.
2. Automatic data processing (ADP), closely analogous to EDP, since it is intended to distinguish computer data processing from data processing where significant human assistance or intervention is required.
3. Business data processing (BDP) refers specifically to administrative applications (e.g., personnel, payroll, accounting) and to broader business applications (e.g., inventory control, sales forecasting).
4. Scientific data processing, which is still a rather rarely used term and which is meant to imply the increasing recognition that business and scientific applications of computers have much more in common than was once realized or, indeed, than was actually the case in earlier days.

Until the 1960s it was common to divide the world of computer applications into two realms—business data processing and scientific computing—with the latter encompassing all engineering, scientific, or other technical applications of computers where the emphasis was on numerical calculations, usually extensive ones, rather than on the manipulation (sorting, organizing, etc.) of data (together with, at most, very simple arithmetic calculations), which was the province of business data processing.

Another distinct, although related contrast between the two areas was their relative dependence on the central processing unit facilities of the computer on the one hand and on the input-ouput facilities on the other hand. Most scientific calculations seemed to require little input data, produced relatively few numbers as results, but relied heavily on the arithmetic and logical capabilities of the CPU. Indeed, computers that handled mainly large scientific calculations were, and still are, often called "number crunchers." By contrast, business data processing tasks usually involved large amounts of input data (e.g., the entire employee file of a company)—hence the name "data" processing—performed relatively few calculations, and then produced large amounts of output (e.g., all payroll checks for the company).

To a degree, this dichotomy between scientific calculations and business data processing was always misleading. If the paradigm for business data processing—much input and output, little calculation—was, in fact, a rather good generalization, the paradigm for scientific calculation was much less so. Scientific calculations involving large volumes of input data and, more commonly, large quantities of results had been common since the earliest days of computing (e.g., the production of tables of mathematical functions such as the trigonometric or Bessel functions). Still, it has only been in recent years that the dichotomy has been seen to be less and less useful for any purpose.

Increasingly, scientific calculations (e.g., meteorological and high-energy physics applications) process large amounts of input data and produce copious results. Also increasingly, although less so, business applications involve sophisticated mathematical techniques involving large amounts of calculation (e.g., various statistical and related forecasting applications). Thus, while there remain many computer applications that conform to the original business data processing/scientific computing stereotype, it is increasingly common and, this author believes, more reasonable to use the terms "business data processing" and "scientific data processing" to distinguish between applications areas but not between the characteristics of the applications themselves.

The past distinction between business data processing and scientific calculations was reflected in the development of computers ostensibly designed for one application area but not the other. IBM's 700 series of computers of the 1950s illustrates this point. (The 700 series comprised first-generation computers, which utilized vacuum tube technology; with the advent of transistor technology and the second generation of computers, a zero was added, and this became the 7000 series. Thus, the 7040 and 7090 were transistorized and somewhat modified versions of the 704 and 709.) There were two pairs of computers in this series, first the 701 and 702, and later the 704 and 705. (There was also a 709, more powerful but quite similar to the 704.)

Both the 701 and 704 were designed for scientific computing. Their memories were binary and word-oriented and, on the 704, floating-point arithmetic was standard. By contrast, the 702 and 705 were specifically designed for "data processing" applications, meaning business data processing. Their memories were character- and digit-oriented and only fixed-point arithmetic was possible. By the time of the advent of the IBM 360 series of computers in the mid-1960s, the previous sharp distinction between scientific computing and business data processing was becoming blurred so that the existence of separate computers for the two areas was no longer considered necessary. Nevertheless the distinction still was considered important and, for example, one model of the 360 series, the 360-44, was specially designed for scientific computation.

In the 1970s some manufacturers still orient their general-purpose computer line toward particular application areas, most notably Control Data with its 6000, 7000, Cyber 70, and Cyber 170 series of computers intended mainly for scientific applications, but the trend is clearly toward computers for data processing without a distinction between scientific and business applications.

The development of general-purpose higher-level programming languages also parallels the history outlined in the preceding paragraph. The first such language in the mid-1950s, Fortran, was intended (and still is mainly used) for scientific calculations. Even the current version, Fortran IV, lacks the significant character manipulation and good data structure facilities needed for many data processing problems. And its input/output facilities are relatively rudimentary. The second such language in the late 1950s, Cobol, was intended (and still is virtually always used) for business data processing problems. Its arithmetic facilities, lacking as they do a floating-point arithmetic capability, virtually preclude its use for significant numerical calculations.

The development of PL/I in the mid-1960s had, among its motivations, the desire to develop a language that could be used for both scientific and business problems because of increasing cognizance about this time of common properties in these two applications areas. PL/I's failure, up to the mid-1970s at least, to achieve wide popularity cannot be ascribed to any deficiency in this viewpoint. Rather, it is due to the very large inertia among Fortran and Cobol users which prevents them from switching to a new language because of their extensive investment in programs, libraries, and expertise in the older languages.

In the future we may expect the distinctions between the scientific and business applications areas to be further blurred as time sharing, widespread use of data communications, and increasing use of large data bases further pervade all applications areas. The name "data processing," therefore, will remain an inclusive term to describe computer applications of all kinds. It will continue to be one of a few terms (information processing and symbol manipulation are others) that may reasonably be used to denote what a computer does.

REFERENCE

1973. Davis, Gordon B. *Computer Data Processing* (2d ed.). New York: McGraw-Hill.
One of the better books that focuses on business applications.

A. RALSTON

## DATA PROCESSING MANAGEMENT ASSOCIATION (DPMA)

For articles on related subjects *see* AMERICAN FEDERATION OF INFORMATION PROCESSING SOCIETIES; and INSTITUTE FOR CERTIFICATION OF COMPUTER PROFESSIONALS.

**Purpose.** The Data Processing Management Association is one of the largest worldwide organizations serving the information processing and computer management community. It comprises all levels of management personnel and, through its educational and publication activities, seeks to encourage high standards of performance in the field of data processing and to promote a professional attitude among its members. Its specific purposes, as stated in its international bylaws, are as follows:

A. To foster, promote and develop education and scientific inquiry in the field of data processing and data processing management.
B. To inculcate among its members a better understanding of the nature and functions of data processing, and to engage in education and research in the technical methods pertaining thereto with a view to their improvement.
C. To collect through research and to disseminate generally, by all appropriate means, all fundamentally sound data processing principles and methods.
D. To study and develop improvements in equipment related to data processing.
E. To supply to its members current information in the field of data processing management, and to cooperate with them and with educational institutions in the advancement of the science of data processing.
F. To encourage and promote a professional attitude among its members in their approach to an understanding and application of the principles underlying the science of data processing and in their relations to others similarly engaged.
G. To foster among executives, the public generally, and the members of the Association a better understanding of the vital business role of data processing, and the proper relationship of data processing to management.

**How Established.** Founded in Chicago as the National Machine Accountants Association, DPMA was chartered in Illinois on Dec. 26, 1951. At this time the first electronic digital computer had yet to come into commercial use, and the name "machine accountant" was chosen to identify those associated with the operation and supervision of punched card accounting machines. Twenty-seven chapters were organized during the Association's first year. By 1955, the organization had taken on an international character with the admission of Montreal as the first Canadian chapter.

With the rapid advances in information processing techniques brought about by the introduction of computers, the nature of the Association further changed as membership swelled from ranks of computer management. In step with this trend, the Association assumed its present name in 1962. The roster of past presidents includes the following:

| | |
|---|---|
| Robert L. Jenal, 1952 | John K. Swearingen, 1964 |
| Gordon C. Couch, 1953 | Daniel A. Will, 1965 |
| Richard L. Irwin, 1954 | Billy R. Field, 1966 |
| Robert O. Cross, 1955 | Theodore Rich, 1967 |
| Donald L. Gerighty, 1956 | Charles L. Davis, 1968 |
| Willis L. Daniel, 1957 | D. H. Warnke, 1969 |
| Lester E. Hill, 1958 | James D. Parker, Jr., 1970 |
| D. B. Paquin, 1959 | Edward O. Lineback, 1971 |
| L. W. Montgomery, 1960 | Herbert B. Safford, 1972 |
| Alfonso G. Pia, 1961 | James Sutton, 1973 |
| Elmer F. Judge, 1962 | Edward J. Palmer, 1974 |
| Robert S. Gilmore, 1963 | J. Ralph Leatherman, 1975 |

**Organizational Structure.** Individual chapters are organized geographically into 13 regions, each of which holds business meetings, conducts regional conferences and educational seminars, and carries on various types of interchapter educational activities. Governing authority is vested in the International Board of Directors, which consists of one representative from each chapter. An annual meeting of the Board is held in conjunction with the International Data Processing Conference & Business Exposition sponsored by the Association. International directors, appointed by chapters, also represent their chapters at regional meetings.

Implementation of policy established by the Board is carried out by an Executive Council consisting of 21 members: President, Executive Vice-President, Secretary-Treasurer, Immediate Past President, four International Vice-Presidents (with the following areas of responsibility: Planning and Policy, Education, Certification and Testing, and International Affairs and Inter-Association Liaison) and 13 regional Vice-Presidents. Assisting the Executive Council in managing association affairs is a Corporate Operations Committee and a Policy and Planning Committee made up of members chosen from the Executive Council.

The local chapter is the heart of the Association. Every member must belong to a chapter, except those applying for an individual international membership, which is granted to qualified individuals living outside North America upon approval by the International Executive Vice-President. Extensive educational programs are carried on by the local chapters through regular monthly meetings, seminars, and other activities.

Regular membership is granted by the individual chapter Board of Directors to persons engaged as (1) managerial or supervisory personnel in EDP installations; (2) systems and methods analysts, research specialists, and computer programmers employed in executive, administrative, or consulting capacities; (3) staff, managers, educators, and executive personnel with a direct interest in data processing; and (4) holders of the Certificate in Data Processing (CDP). Other types of membership are affiliate, fellow, and honorary.

A computer-equipped international headquarters with modern facilities, located in Park Ridge, Illinois, serves as the administrative nucleus of the Association. It provides a wide range of programs and services to local chapters and contributes to regional educational programs. Major departments are Membership, Research and Professional Services, Conferences and Communications, and Data Processing.

**Programs and Services.** DPMA members attend meetings, seminars, and conferences at the local chapter, and at regional and international levels. A major educational event is the Annual DPMA International Data Processing Conference & Business Exposition, attended by members and nonmembers from all parts of the United States, Canada, and other countries.

The Association was the first to introduce (in 1962) a certification program for computer management personnel. The Certificate in Data Processing (CDP) examination program is dedicated to the advancement of data processing and information management and to this end has established high standards based on a broad educational framework and practical knowledge. In 1970, DPMA also introduced the Registered Business Programmer examination, which seeks to identify those reaching the level of senior business programmers. Both examinations were developed by the DPMA Certification Council and are given annually in test centers at colleges and universities in the United States and in Canada. In 1974 DPMA transferred ownership of these examinations to the Institute for Certification of Computer Professionals (ICCP). Other programs offered to the membership include the Business and Management Principles one-day seminar, the video tape Management Development seminar, and Educator's Night for improving communications with the education community. DPMA encourages and provides assistance to student organizations interested in data processing in colleges and universities. It also offers the Future Data Processors Program for high school students, and provides counseling aid for Boy Scouts seeking the computer merit badge.

Other programs are being constantly developed to keep the membership abreast of changing developments in effective EDP management techniques and in technological advances.

Among DPMA publications are the monthly *Data Management* magazine (included in membership dues); *Guidelines to Data Processing Management; An Executive Briefing on the Control of Computers; Automatic Data Processing—Principles and Procedures*, and several data processing briefings for the student.

Its audiovisual program includes films and slide presentations ranging from introductions to data processing for the layman to general management subjects. In 1969, DPMA originated the Computer-Science-Man-of-the-Year Citation which in that year was presented to Commander Grace Murray Hopper, USNR. Subsequent recipients have been Dr. Frederick Phillips Brooks, Jr., 1970; Robert C. Cheek, 1972; Dr. Carl Hammer, 1973; and Prof. Edward L. Glaser, 1974.

I. L. AUERBACH

# DATA SECURITY

For articles on related subjects *see* COMPUTERS AND SOCIETY; RELIABILITY AND FAULT TOLERANCE; and SECURITY OF COMPUTER INSTALLATIONS, PHYSICAL.
For articles on related terms *see* HARD COPY; and RECORD.

The protection of data against the deliberate or accidental access of unauthorized persons is rapidly becoming a major problem. Ultimately, the security of data depends on some combination of "locks," or access-control measures, for which certain users possess the "keys". No such combination is completely secure. For the intruder, the effectiveness of security measures is really only a matter of the cost of breaking the combination of locks as compared to the value (to him) of obtaining data in this way. Conversely, for someone wishing to maintain the security of data, the cost of devising and implementing a combination of locks on the data must be small relative to the cost of a breach of security.

In the case of, for example, military intelligence data banks, the information contained in them is considered to be of such value that almost no cost is spared to insure data security. Such systems, however, are clearly exceptional. This article deals instead with commercial or public data banks where there are clear limits to the number of high-cost security measures that can be justified.

It is to be noted that in a computer system, the protection of the data itself and of software search and retrieval programs are treated almost entirely in the same manner; thus, the safeguards that apply to program security also apply to data security.

**Classification of Degree of Confidentiality.** In this section the term "user" describes a single person or a group of persons, all of whom have equal rights with respect to accessing a particular body of data and who have a common identity to the system. Three classes of data are defined for an automated system: public, limited-access, and private.

TYPE 1. PUBLIC DATA. Public data is open to all users, and no security measures are necessary as far as reading is concerned. When access is restricted to reading of the data, as it should be where data must remain unchanged, writing should be prevented. If it is not possible to prevent writing, check sums (a simple total of all data items) that should remain constant can be kept with data, and the data can be refreshed from a secure copy whenever a test total of the data does not agree with the check sum. If users are permitted to alter data, a lock must be maintained on the system to insure that while one user is making a change, no other user is permitted access to the data, since normally one user's alterations must be completed before another may begin.

TYPE 2. LIMITED-ACCESS DATA. Only authorized users have access to data of this type. This means that an authorization table must be kept in the system, indicating for each body of data the identity of all users with access rights. When a user requests access: (1) his identity should be authenticated, for example, by personal identification or password; (2) the authorization table should be checked to see that he has appropriate access rights; (3) a record in a log should be made of the event. The purpose of the log is to provide an audit trail or record that can be consulted whenever any trouble is suspected. All unsuccessful attempts to access data should be logged in order to provide an indication of a possible security leak. If the frequency of unsuccessful entry is larger than normal error expectation warrants, an alarm should be generated.

TYPE 3. PRIVATE DATA. This data is open to a single user only. When access to data is requested, the identity of the user should be authenticated to verify the fact that he is the owner of the data. Here again, a record of all unsuccessful attempts at entry should be logged.

**Access Rights to Data.** Data that is not a program is usually organized into discrete files. A *file* is composed of a number of records, or factual statements, each relating to a particular thing; or, in a file containing personal data, each is related to a particular individual. A *record*, in turn, is subdivided into fields. A *field* is a precisely defined location within a record where information may be recorded.

In a file of personal data, certain fields enable the reader of the record to identify the person. Access to a file of personal information is often permitled on the basis of "need to know," and access to a particular record in a file is allowed on the basis of an explicit or implicit consent of the individual to whom the record pertains. It would therefore follow that if a person having access to a record needs to know only the information in certain fields of the record, he should not have access to other fields in the same record. For example, persons who are preparing statistical summaries from files do not need to know the identity of the person to whom each record applies, and therefore should not have access to identifying fields.

Frequently, persons having access to a file have access to *all* fields of *all* records. In a manual file in which records are maintained in a manila folder, it is difficult to arrange to do otherwise. In a computerized system, however, access can be permitted to the entire file, or can be restricted to certain records or to certain fields of the file.

Access rights might be defined as follows: read an item (e.g., file, record, or field); write an item so as to produce a change, either by adding a new item or by changing an existing item; delete an item.

The access rights of a user must be explicitly denoted in any situation where partial rights exist, such as a limited access file, or where reading is permitted but changes and deletions are not. It is possible to have a table or matrix stored with the data (or separately) which lists authorized users of the data and their access rights. Access to this table must be strictly limited to persons authorized to modify the table, usually only the owner of the data. In many cases, access control is assigned to the system itself, since in most computer systems the operations pertaining to the read or write functions are already under system control.

**Physical Storage of Data.** Data in an automated system can exist in many physical forms. Storage media may be classified into five categories: hard copy; display devices; magnetic tape and mountable disks; mounted magnetic tapes, disks, and drums; and magnetic core store.

HARD COPY. This is a term used for recording data that is more or less permanent and that can be stored, read, or written by humans independently of the computer hardware. Included in this category are printed pages, punched paper tape, punched cards, and microfilm. The security of hard copy is similar to the conventional security associated with manual files. The interpretation of the data by an intruder is usually very simple. Also, the destruction of the data requires the destruction of the medium. Machines for shredding hard copy are available.

DISPLAY DEVICES. These are devices on which data may be exhibited to a user but on which it has an evanescent form. As soon as it is no longer required, it will disappear. An example of this form of storage is a cathode-ray tube display. If such devices display sensitive data, they may to have be used in secure rooms where unwanted cameras or persons cannot observe them. When electric circuits are arranged to display images on one cathode-ray tube, stray electromagnetic radiation from these circuits might be amplified to produce a similar display on another such device that has no connection to the first.

Display devices like printers or card readers should also be appropriately shielded to guard against the possibility of electromagnetic eavesdropping. There is the possibility of telephone instruments acting as pickup devices for such radiations even when on the hook.

MAGNETIC TAPE AND MOUNTABLE DISKS. These are media on which data can be recorded as variations in magnetization. They can be erased and used repeatedly, although—as with most erasing processes—small traces of previously recorded information may persist. When the tapes or disks are not mounted on a computer device to read them, they cannot be read, but they can be erased or destroyed, for example, by strong magnets or fire.

A careful banking system in secure rooms under strict control must be maintained to prevent loss or violation of security during off-line storage. When tapes or disks are mounted on read/write devices, they become identical in nature to those integrated in the system (see below) of physical storage; when unmounted, they are similar in nature to hard copy.

MOUNTED MAGNETIC TAPES, DISKS, AND DRUMS. These mounted media are integral parts of the on-line storage system of a computer. They are usually classed as the secondary store, since the time to access information stored on them is long compared with the basic operation rate of the computer. Usually, the time for reading from or writing on them is overlapped by other operations. This means that the individual user does not direct the reading or writing himself, but has to go through the intermediary of the computer operating system. Access control almost always resides in the operating system.

MAGNETIC CORE STORE. This category is the main first-level store of most computers. To operate, a program must be in the core store; to be acted upon, data must be in the core store. Thus, in the final analysis, on-line access to data must first be controlled by controlling access in the core store. Since all users are permitted to use core store, one after another, it is important to erase any residual sensitive data before allowing the next user's program to have control. Some operating systems do this clean-up job automatically; others do not.

**Protection of Data in Core Storage.** Each user in a multiprogrammed computer system is assigned, at a given instant of time, a region of the core store as his own private domain during execution of his program. The right to read from or write into this area of the store is protected by a key (usually through a hardware device). A directory of keys is kept in a table in the core area assigned to the operating system itself. This means that the user cannot alter the directory entry pertaining to his own core area. If he could, it might permit him to access some other user's core area. Each user core area is thus private to an individual user.

Sharing data and programs can be achieved by having an area of core that is common to the users concerned. If only specified users may share the data in this area, an authorization table must be maintained. Often it is sufficient to declare the area as "public" in order to insure that no access control is necessary.

**Protection of Data in Secondary Storage.** In a secure system, all requests to read and write on secondary storage must pass through the input/output control of the operating system. In order to issue a READ or WRITE instruction to a file in secondary storage, it is necessary for a user to alert the operating system that he intends to perform operations on the file by issuing an instruction. At this time, his access rights to the file are examined.

Private files are usually labeled with the name and system identification number of the user, and may even contain in their labels a password that must be matched against one provided by the user at the time of issuing the access request. Only the owner of a limited-access file should be permitted to change the password. When a file has limited access, the access information is frequently stored separately from the data.

**Protection of Data in Transmission.** Wiretapping or electromagnetic eavesdropping is a security threat whenever data travels through the air or over wires that are not in a secure area. Many systems use common carrier facilities, and this presents many problems. Sensitive data that is to be transmitted from one location to another should be transformed (i.e., encrypted) to make it private. Privacy transformations that involve static methods of coding require a certain amount of work to break, but can usually be decoded after some effort.

The best coding techniques involve keys that are as long as the data to be encrypted. The string of characters for the key is generated from a basic starting number, just as a sequence of pseudorandom numbers can be generated. The same starting value yields the same sequence every time. It is nearly impossible to determine the starting value and the generating algorithm from eavesdropping on the transmission. The work required to break the code is very extensive.

**Protection of Data Off-Line.** Stored data in the form of hard copy, or on magnetic tape or removable disks, must be kept in a strictly controlled environment. Protection against accidental or wilful damage or theft must be insured. Access to the data will be basically through a manual system managed by a person charged with its security. There should be a record kept of all deposits and withdrawals from the data bank, after assuring that the person making the transaction has the appropriate access rights.

Frequently, data banks are located near the main computer installation where tapes are requested frequently, but it is common also for systems to have a separate repository of tapes containing data vital to regenerating the system. A remote storage vault in a protected location is essential for basic business or industrial data.

**Integrity of Hardware.** The fashion of having computers prominently displayed to the public is dying out. The need for precise environmental control has always meant that hardware was housed in special rooms, but it is increasingly apparent that protection and control of access to the rooms is also critical to security. Without this isolation, not only could the equipment be destroyed, but data also could be compromised as it is being printed or displayed.

All persons having access to the rooms where hardware is kept should be properly identified and their "need to be present" should be verified. Systems of identification badges are common. Sometimes access is controlled by a security officer; sometimes by locks opened by badges or by combinations. The advantage of locks operated by badges or push-button combinations is that the combination can be more easily changed than can locks operated with ordinary keys. Thus, if there is any suspicion of a compromise of a lock, the combination should be altered. When the key is a badge, the rightful owner may have his picture displayed on it for further identification.

Where a piece of hardware is attached to the main computer hardware through a remote connection, the terminal equipment is often under minimal or no surveillance. As a result, at the present time, highly sensitive data is rarely handled in a computer system with remote terminals. It is important that remote users be properly identified and that the terminals be properly identified, not only at the time of beginning a "conversation," but also from time to time during any extended interaction. This is rarely the case except in military systems. No doubt the security of data in systems with remote terminals will be improved.

**Integrity of Software.** We have indicated that the security of data within the computer depends on the operating system. Many existing systems are complex; to some extent, their complexity protects them from invasion. However, accidental access routes (trapdoors) into the system have been found. When access routes via trapdoors are found, the usual result is that the system becomes inoperative; many of the breakdowns that occur daily in systems are the result of accidental entry into the operating system by an unsuspecting user.

To be secure, operating system structure should be cleanly designed and the documentation openly available. Secrecy should not be a requirement for a secure system. Perhaps only critical parts of operating systems need be under strict security control (e.g., tables of access rights and the programs that validate these rights) to insure data security.

### References

1969. Hoffman, Lance J. "Computers and Privacy: A Survey," *Computing Surveys*, Vol. 1, No. 2 (June).

1970. Friedman, T. D. "The Authorization Problem in Shared Files," *IBM Systems Journal*, Vol. 9, No. 4.

J. N. P. HUME

## DATA SET

For articles on related subjects *see* ACCESS METHODS; and FILES.

This article deals with the software meaning of the term "data set"—a collection of related data items (Clarke, 1966)—and *not* the hardware meaning, which defines "data set" as a device used to couple a computer data link to a telephone line. Examples of data sets within our context are the collection of student records within a university, the collection of inventory items in a warehouse, the set of records describing books in a library, etc. The major objectives of grouping data items into data sets are efficient retrieval, searching, sorting, and recognition.

A data set may be described by a *data set label*, which might contain the name of the data set, its boundaries in physical storage, and certain characteristics of the data items within the set. Within a unit of physical storage (or *volume*), the set of all data set labels may be considered as a "table of contents." Searches, for example, may be expedited by searching the "table of contents" for data set labels exhibiting desired characteristics, and then searching for data items with more specific characteristics among only those data sets whose labels passed the first search.

To enhance the operating characteristics of the storage media used, data sets may be organized in various structures:

1. *Sequential*, as on magnetic tape.
2. *Indexed sequential*, where data items are stored sequentially on a key, but are also accessible via index tables maintained by the system.
3. *Direct*, without index tables; accessing of data items is up to the programmer.
4. *Partitioned*, where sequentially organized data

sets are divided into *members*, and a directory is maintained of members' names and their storage locations.

5. *Telecommunication*, where the data items in the set are messages organized into queues (e.g., for communication between a computer and a remote terminal).

REFERENCE

1966. Clark, W. A. "Data Management," *IBM Systems Journal*, Vol. 5, No. 1.

S. C. BREWER

# DATA STRUCTURES

For articles on related subjects *see* LISTS AND LIST PROCESSING; STACK; STRING; and TREE.
For articles on related terms *see* DATA BASE AND DATA BASE MANAGEMENT; GRAPH THEORY; and QUEUEING THEORY.

The term "structure" is used in many different fields to denote objects that are constructed in a regular and characteristic way from their components. A data structure is a structure whose components are data objects.

EXAMPLE. The arithmetic expression 3 + 4 * 5 is constructed in a systematic way from data components that are integers such as 3, 4, 5, and operators such as + and *. The structure of this expression may be thought of as either a string or a tree structure in which each operator is the root of a subtree whose descendants are operands (Fig. 1).

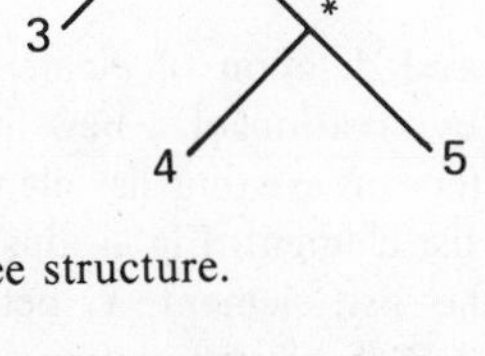

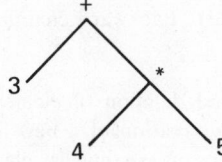

**Fig. 1.** A tree structure.

When this data structure is stored in a computer, it must be stored so that components are readily accessible. This may be done by storing the expression 3 + 4 * 5 as a character string $A$ so that the $i$th character is retrieved by referring to the element $A[i]$ or $A(i)$, with the use of brackets or parentheses depending upon the programming language being used. Alternatively, the string may be stored as a list structure, in which the vertex associated with + has a left son 3 and a right son *, which in turn has left and right sons 4 and 5 (Fig. 2).

Figs. 1 and 2 illustrate the relation between data structures, which specify *logical* relations between data components, and storage structures, which specify how such relations may be realized in a digital computer. The storage structure of Fig. 2 could be represented in a digital computer by five three-component storage cells, where each cell has one component containing an operator and two components respectively containing a pointer to the left and right sons. The three cells that have no successors contain special markers in their pointer fields, here indicated by the word "nil."

In order to define a class of data objects having a common data structure, it is usual to start with a class of primitive data elements called "atoms," or elementary objects, and to specify *construction operators* by means of which *composite objects* may be constructed from the atoms. In the preceding arithmetic-expression example, the atoms are operands (integers) and arithmetic operators. The construction operators specify how expressions are built up from operators and operands. The set of construction rules that specify how operators are built up from operands is sometimes referred to as a "grammar."

In order to access and manipulate composite objects specified by a given set of atoms and construction rules, *selectors* must be defined which allow components of a data object to be accessed, and *creation* and *deletion* operators must be defined which allow components of data structures to be created and deleted. Data structures may be characterized by the nature of their accessing and their creation and deletion operators.

Some of the basic terminology relating to data structures will be mentioned by considering commonly occurring data structures such as arrays, lists, trees, stacks, and queues.

An *array* is a data structure whose elements may be selected by integer selectors called "indexes." If $A$ is a one-dimensional-array data structure, then $A[3]$ or $A(3)$ refers to the third element of $A$. If $B$ is a three-dimensional array, then $B[I,J,K]$ or $B(I,J,K)$ refers to the $I,J,K$ element ($b_{ijk}$) of the array $B$. The set of all elements of an array are generally created and deleted at the same time by means of *decla-*

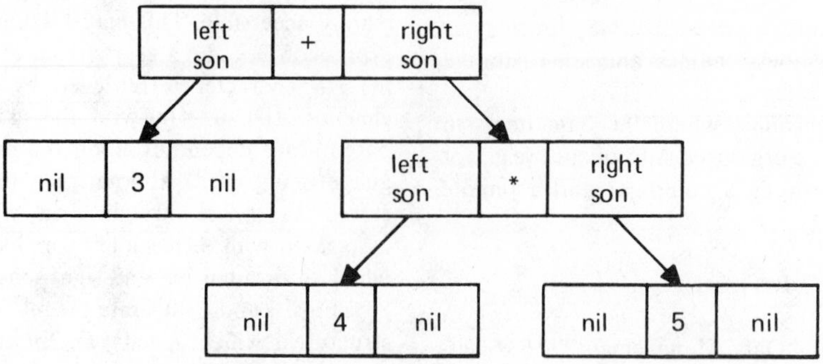


**Fig. 2.** Storage structure for the tree structure of Fig. 1.

*rations*, as illustrated by the following examples:

| | |
|---|---|
| DIMENSION A (1,100) | Fortran array declaration |
| **integer array** A[1:N]; | Algol 60 array declaraion |
| [1:N] **int** A; | Algol 68 array declaration |

In Fortran, the declaration "DIMENSION A(100)" serves to reserve a block of cells for the array $A$ at compile time. In Algol 60 or 68, declarations create an instance of the declared data structure when they are executed. Thus, execution of the declaration "**integer array** $A$[1:N]" causes allocation of a block of $N$ storage cells large enough to hold integers using the current value assigned to the variable $N$, and activates an accessing mechanism so that $A[i]$ will refer to the $i$th allocated cell.

The arrays introduced above are homogeneous because all elements of an array have the same data type, and are rectangular because all vectors in a given dimension have the same size. Programming languages such as Cobol and PL/I permit nonhomogeneous, nonrectangular arrays to be declared. The following is a PL/I declaration of a PAYROLL record with a 50-character name field, fields of the mode FIXED for the number of regular and overtime hours worked, and a field of the mode FLOAT for the rate of pay:

```
DECLARE 1  PAYROLL
           2  NAME CHARACTER(50),
           2  HOURS
              3 REGULAR FIXED,
              3 OVERTIME FIXED,
           2  RATE FLOAT;
```

If it is desired to refer to the number of overtime hours in the record PAYROLL, then this is given by PAYROLL.HOURS.OVERTIME. That is, component names rather than indexes are used to access a given element of the data structure.

List structures, just as array structures, may be characterized by their accessing creation and deletion operators. Elements of a list structure are generally accessed by "walking" along pointer chains, starting at the head of the list. In a linear list, each list element has a unique successor and the last element has an "empty" successor field, usually denoted by the symbol "nil." In general, list elements may have more than one successor, and lists may be circular in the sense that pointer chains may form cycles. Knuth (1968) introduces doubly linked lists that have forward and backward pointer chains passing through each element, and a number of other kinds of lists. Fig. 3 illustrates a doubly linked circular list named $L$ whose head element $H$ is linked both to the next element $A$ and to the last element $B$.

If the forward pointer is referred to by RLINK (for right link) and the backward pointer is referred to by LLINK (left link), then the second list element (labeled A) may be accessed in either of the two following ways:

| | |
|---|---|
| RLINK(L) | Forward chaining |
| LLINK(LLINK(L)) | Backward chaining |

Insertion and deletion of elements in a list is accomplished by creation of a new list cell and by updating pointers of existing list elements and the newly created list element. Fig. 4 illustrates that the insertion of the list element $X$ between the list elements $A$ and $B$ requires updating of the RLINK of $A$, the LLINK of $B$, and initialization of the $R$ and $L$ links of $X$.

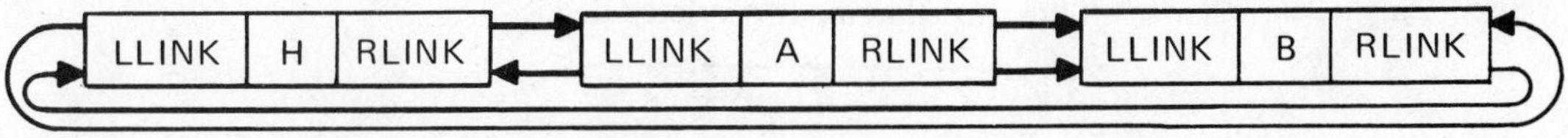


**Fig. 3.** Doubly linked circular list $L$.

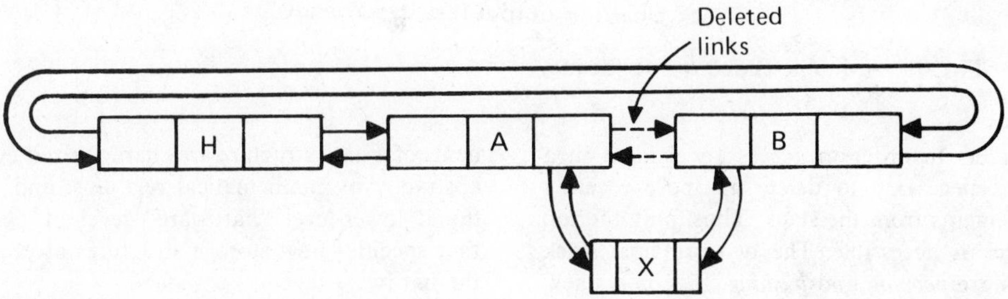


**Fig. 4.** Insertion of $X$ in Fig. 3.

The instructions to perform this insertion might be as follows:

```
create X
RLINK(A) = L(X)   (L(X) - Location of X)
LLINK(B) = L(X)
RLINK(X) = L(B)
LLINK(X) = L(A)
```

The list processing language Lisp, which was developed by John McCarthy in the late 1950s, is probably the most important list processing language. The list format and instruction repertoire of Lisp will be briefly illustrated. For ease of presentation, however, we will use a notation different from that actually used in Lisp.

List elements in Lisp have two components selectable by the selectors *first* and *rest*. If $L$ is a list then $first(L)$ selects the first element of the list, which may be either an atom or a sublist, and $rest(L)$ selects the rest of the list. The list $((A,B),C)$ is represented in Lisp by the list structure of Fig. 5.

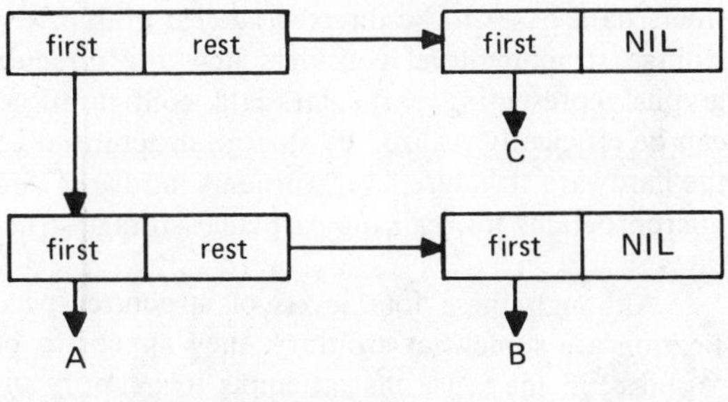


**Fig. 5.** Representation of a list $L$.

For $L = ((A,B),C)$, $first(L) = (A,B)$, $rest(L) = (C)$, $first(first(L)) = A$ and $rest(rest(L)) = NIL$.

Lisp also has a construction operator $cons[X;Y]$ which constructs a list $L$ such that $first(L) = X$ and $rest(L) = Y$, and a predicate $atom(X)$, which is true when $X$ is an atom and false otherwise. In the above example, $atom(first(L)) = false$ since $first(L) = (A,B)$, but $atom(first(first(L))) = true$.

In general, any language for the manipulation of data structures has not only *selectors* for selecting components of a data structure but also *constructors* for constructing data structures from their components, and *predicates* for testing whether a given data object has certain attributes. Lisp illustrates particularly clearly the role of selectors, constructors, and predicates in a programming language.

List structures are a flexible storage structure for objects of variable sizes or tables of fixed-size objects in which insertion and deletion is frequently required. A number of special classes of list structures will now be considered in greater detail.

A *tree* is a list in which there is one element called the "root" with no predecessor and in which every other element has a unique predecessor. That is, a tree is a list that contains no circular lists, and in which no two list elements may have a common sublist as a successor. Elements of a tree which have no successor are called "leaves" of the tree. Tree elements, just as list elements, are generally accessed by walking along a pointer chain. However, the guarantee that there are no cycles or common sublists makes it possible to define orderly procedures for insertion and deletion of subtrees.

A *stack* is a linear list in which elements are accessed, created, and deleted in a last-in–first-out

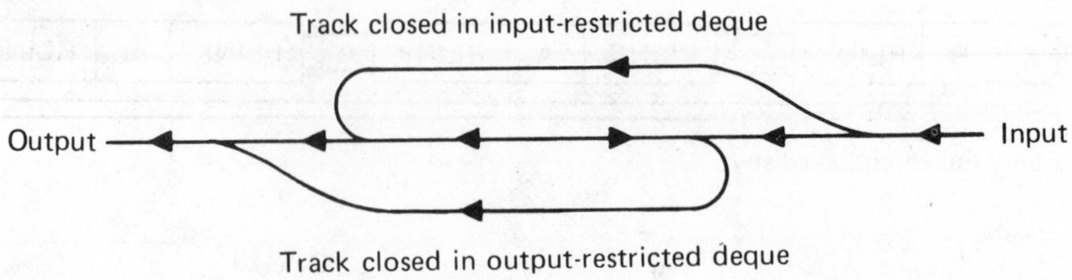


**Fig. 6.** A double-ended queue (deque).

(LIFO) order. In order to access an element in a stack, it is necessary to delete all more recently entered elements from the stack. Thus, only the top of the stack is accessible. The two principal stack operations are *popping* and *pushing*. If $S$ is a stack, then *pop*($S$) causes the top element of the stack to be deleted and *push*($S$,$x$) causes $x$ to be placed on top of the stack.

A *queue* is a linear list in which elements are created and deleted in a first-in–first-out order. A line of people waiting to be served in a cafeteria is a queue, since the person having waited longest is always the first to be served (deleted from the queue). In contrast, employees in a large organization generally form a stack with regard to being fired.

A generalization of queues and stacks in which elements may be added and deleted at both ends of a linear list is called a "deque." A deque is said to be input-restricted if input is possible at only one end, but deletion may occur at both ends. A deque is said to be output-restricted if output may occur at only one end, but input may occur at both ends. Fig. 6 illustrates by means of a railway-switching network the notion of a deque with input and/or output restrictions (see Knuth, 1968, p. 236).

Data structures include numerical structures such as integers that have arithmetic operations applicable to them, and nonnumerical structures such as arrays, list, and trees whose primary purpose is to keep track of relations among data objects rather than to manipulate them.

Computational structures may be studied and analyzed at many different levels of abstraction. We have already remarked on the difference between logical data structures and the storage structures in terms of which they are realized. The characterization of structure by logical relations among components is clearly more abstract than the realization of the logical structure by particular configurations of cells and pointers. It is convenient to introduce an additional higher-level mathematical level of abstraction in which logical relations among components of a data structure are characterized even more abstractly by mathematical relations, and an additional lower-level "hardware" level of abstraction that specifies how storage structures are realized at the hardware level.

1. *Mathematical structure* is defined by specifying a set of objects and a set of operators (functions, relations) for transforming objects into other objects.

2. *Data structure* is defined by labeled-directed graphs that allow characteristic operators on data objects having the given structure to be naturally and simply defined by means of graph transformation rules. A given mathematical structure may, in general, be represented in many different ways by a data structure.

3. *Storage structure* is defined by storage cells with pointers between storage cells. Storage structures, like data structures, are chosen so that operators applicable to computational objects represented by a given storage structure may be simply and efficiently defined. There are, in general, many different storage structures that realize a given data structure.

4. *Hardware structure* specifies how storage structures and transformations of storage structures may be realized at the hardware level.

Example. In modeling data bases, the mathematical level of abstraction models data bases as mathematical relations, the data structure level considers data bases to be directed labeled graphs, the storage structure level considers how the directed graphs representing particular data configurations can be efficiently realized by storage structures, and the hardware structure level considers hardware and microprograms for realizing particular storage structures.

Although these four levels of structure specification are somewhat arbitrary, they appear to be "robust" in the sense that attempts to quantify the notion of abstraction invariably result in something similar to the above characterization. For example, in considering abstraction for program structure, we generally distinguish between mathematical structure, program structure, implementation structure, and hardware realization. These distinctions are very similar to the previously discussed distinctions for the data structure case.

Data structures capture the notion of computational structure at a level that is sufficiently abstract to emphasize logical relations among components of a data object, independently of details of implementation but at the same time sufficiently concrete to preserve some relation between a structure and its computational realization. Data structures thus represent an appropriate and practicable level of abstraction for characterizing computational structure, and it is for this reason that the study of data structures is important in computer science.

REFERENCE

1968. Knuth, D. E. *The Art of Computer Programming*, vol. 1. Reading, Mass.: Addison-Wesley.

P. WEGNER

## DATA STRUCTURES, SET CONCEPTS FOR

For articles on related subjects *see* ACCESS METHODS; DATA BASE AND DATA BASE MANAGEMENT; DATA STRUCTURES; FILES; and STORAGE-MANAGEMENT STRUCTURES.
For articles on related terms *see* LIST-PROCESSING LANGUAGES; RECORD; and SIMULATION.

The data base set concept unifies several programming techniques (table, list, chain, ring, file, and field array) that have been in common usage for most of the history of computers. (This concept is a specialization of the more general mathematical set concept from which the data structure set gets its name and many of its properties.) In this paper the word "set" will always be used in the data structure and not the mathematical sense.

Many software products support the set concept. The list-processing languages, such as IPL-V and Lisp, have used the set concept to support the organization of program structure. Simulation languages, such as Simscript and Simula, have used set concepts to assist in modeling the subject of study. In the data base management area, the Honeywell integrated data store (IDS) system (Bachman and Williams, 1964) pioneered broad usage of the set concept to process complex manufacturing and banking problems. IDS uses the chain form of set implementation. General Motors Research (Dodd, 1966) produced a similar system, Associative Processing Language (APL) for graphic display purposes. After six years of study, the CODASYL Data Base Task Group (ACM, 1971) produced a specification that is being integrated into the Cobol language. The Cobol Data Description and Data Manipulation Language extensions make available the set description and manipulation capabilities of the IDS and APL systems. IBM's Information Management System (IMS II) and Informatic's MARK IV support hierarchical set structures with the multiple-level record array technique. Cobol and PL/I's recognition of the set concept is limited to constructing sets of member records with field arrays.

**Record, Field, and Set Concepts.** The set is one of three complementary concepts (record, field, and set) needed to build and store data structures that closely approximate their natural world counterparts. If the natural world is considered in terms of the entities that exist, the attributes that describe them, and the relationships that associate them, then the equivalent information system concepts are record, field, and set, respectively.

In a simple example taken from a school situation, the entities would be the teachers and the children. Some of the attributes of a teacher are "name," "grade level," and "classroom." Some of the attributes of a child would be "name," "age," and "parent name." A relationship exists between teachers and children. In an information system model of this natural world situation, two classes of records (one for teachers, one for children) would be created. In each teacher record there would be a field to store the teacher's name, another for the grade level, and another for the classroom number. Each child's record would have a field for the child's name, another for his age, and yet another for his parent's name. The information system could tie each child's record to his teacher's record in one of the several ways that have been invented to implement the set concept. This might be done by physically placing all the child records after their teacher's record array in the file. This is called a "table" or "record array."

The data structure set concept thus described is a refinement of the mathematical set concept; i.e., in the data structure set, the set definition is embodied in the instance of the "owner" role. Set membership is embodied in the instance of the "member" role. Records may concurrently have many roles as owner and member of different sets. This property permits the creation and manipulation of complex structures that model the complexity of the real world. In this refinement of the mathematical set concept, one can go reversibly either from owner as definition to members or from any member to owner to reestablish the set definition.

For data structure sets, the set definition is normally based upon the value of some field or fields within the owner record, while the membership in the set is established by the matching value of an equivalent field or fields within a potential member record. Advantage is frequently taken of this phenomenon by removing the fields from the member records that carry the matching data and depending upon the owner record for reconstruction.

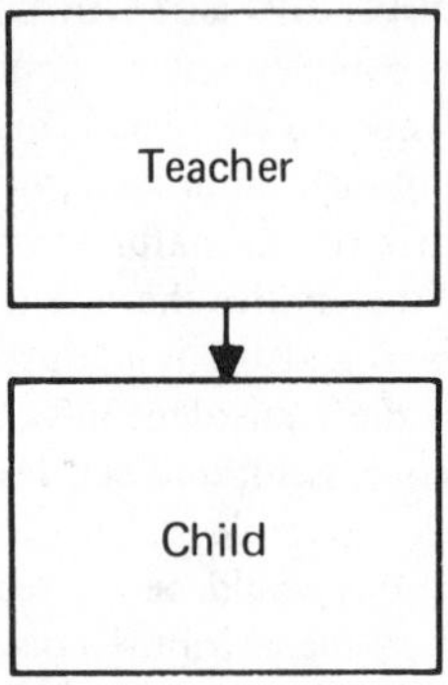


**Fig. 1.** Teacher to child relationship.

A data structure diagram (Bachman, 1969) would illustrate the teacher/child structure as shown in Fig. 1. It uses a box to represent the *entity* class concept and an arrow to represent the *simple relationship* class concept. (A simple relationship is a 1:*n* relationship between entities. Alternately, a complex relationship is an *m*:*n* relationship.) In this case there are two boxes, one for all the teacher entities and one for all the child entities. The arrow symbolizes the relationship that each teacher may have: zero, one, two, or more children. However, each child has only one teacher.

In the school example above, we said that a teacher has the role of "owner" of a teacher/children set. To extend this example, we will recognize that in most schools the relationship between teacher and child is not a simple relationship (1:*n*), but is rather a complex relationship (*m*:*n*), since the children have different teachers for different subjects. This complex relationship of teacher:child may be transformed into a new relationship entity, "pupil," and two simple relationships, teacher:pupil and child: pupil. The teacher has many children as pupils in her classes and, as a pupil, the child has many teachers. This new view is illustrated in Fig. 2. The new "pupil" entity has the attributes "subject" and "hour," which serve to describe and differentiate one relationship entity from another. A child may have the same teacher for several subjects.

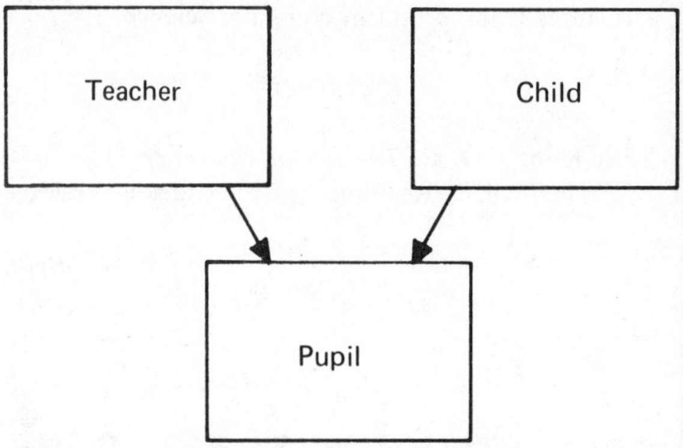


**Fig. 2.** Teacher/pupil/child relationships.

**Set Formalisms.** The data-structure set concept has four basic properties:

1. A set has one, only one, and always one record in the owner role (the teacher in Fig. 1 or Fig. 2).

2. A set has zero, one, or more records in the member role, and the number varies with time (the child in Fig. 1).

3. Any record may be the owner of zero, one, or more sets concurrently.

4. Any record may be a member in zero, one, or more sets concurrently, and thus be simultaneously owned by several owner records (the pupil in Fig. 2). Each record may appear only once as a member of a particular set. The member roles do not interfere with the owner roles.

Fig. 3 expresses the four basic properties of the set concept as a data structure diagram. The numbers used in the list above to enumerate the set properties are shown in order to point out their effect upon the structure. Only slight additions are necessary to complete the data structure concepts that govern data processing.

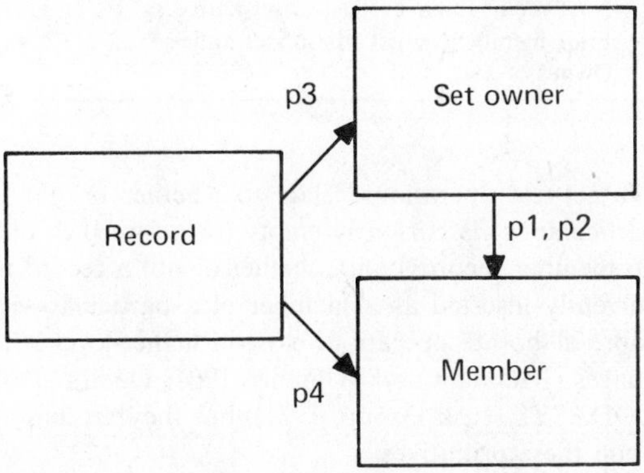


**Fig. 3.** Record/owner/member entity relationships.

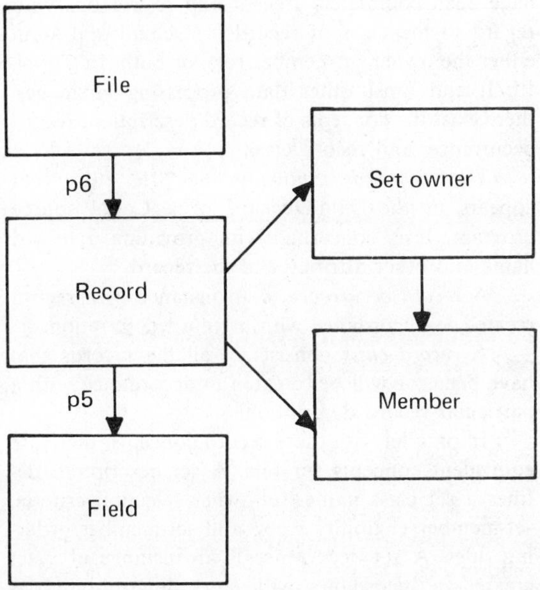


**Fig. 4.** Structure of file/record/field entity relationships

The fields of a record (p5 in Fig. 4) have been previously mentioned as the means of recording the attributes of an entity. All records must be stored in some container for safekeeping and reference. The file (p6) serves this function. Fig. 4 is an extension of Fig. 3, with the field concept and the file concept shown. The arrow from the box marked "file" to the box marked "record" symbolizes the fact that a file may hold zero, one, or more records, but a record may be in only one file. The arrow from "record" to "field" symbolizes the fact that a record may have zero, one, or more fields, but a particular field may appear in only one record.

**Set Ordering.** The notion of "next" and "prior" are important concepts to procedural algorithms that are basic to problem solving in a stored program computer. In addition to the procedural limitation of handling one record at a time, there are important simplifying consequences to an algorithm if the member records within a set can be delivered to it in a predefined data-value ordered sequence or a time-of-insertion ordered sequence (FIFO or LIFO). The notions of "first" and "last" are vital to starting and stopping the iterative execution of these algorithms. Thus, the ordering of members in a set is a prerequisite to rational manipulation of the set.

**Motivation of Set Concept.** The primary motivation of associating records into sets within a file is to model the natural world relationships and to assist in the accessing of selected records within the file that represents some particular relationship. The set access methods fall in between and complement the more traditional access methods. They are listed in Table 1.

**Table 1.** Access methods.

| Method | Use |
|---|---|
| Direct Access | Retrieves one record |
| Data-Key Access | Retrieves one record |
| Set-Owner Access | Retrieves one record |
| Set-Member Access | Used iteratively; retrieves each member of set |
| File-Sequential Access | Used iteratively; retrieves each record in file |

The first four access methods in Table 1 are primarily used in transaction and inquiry processing, where there is a need to determine the recorded status of a particular entity or of a related group of entities, or to update their recorded status. The file-sequential access method is primarily used for periodic batch file updating and report generation. It is possible for the same record to be accessed by any of the five methods, as the occasion may require. Similarly, it is possible to use these access methods in combination to achieve a particular effect.

**Table 2.** Retrieval opportunities.

| Given | Access Method | Determine |
|---|---|---|
| The owner | Set member | First member, or get empty-set notice |
| The owner | Set member | *i*th member, or get out-of-set notice |
| The owner | Set member | Last member, or get empty-set notice |
| Any member | Set member | Next member, or get last-of-set notice |
| Any member | Set member | Prior member, or get first-of-set notice |
| Any member | Set owner | Owner of set |

Taking the example of Fig. 2, a teacher's record might be retrieved by the data-key access method and then her pupils' records could be retrieved by set-member access method. For each pupil record, the child's record may be retrieved with the set-owner access method. Alternately, retrieval might start with data-key access to the child's record and then proceed to access all pupil records of the child, and hence the teacher's records. The basic retrieval opportunities derived from a set are given in Table 2.

**Operations on Sets.** There is a family of primitive operations that apply to sets. These are complementary to the primitive operations on records and fields, which are better known. Table 3 gives the primitive operations on all three for comparison.

**Table 3.** Primitive operations on records, fields, and sets.

| Object | Operation |
|---|---|
| Record | Create |
| | Access |
| | Destroy |
| | Test for record class name |
| Field (content) | Initialize |
| | Reference |
| | Alter |
| | Test for null-value status |
| Set | Insert member |
| | Remove member |
| | Access set owner (record) |
| | Access set member (record) |
| | Test for set emptiness status |
| | Test for member insertion status |

The "insert" and "remove" operations on sets are the means by which a member record is procedurally introduced into a set and extracted. The insertion may be the first or last member, or logically between any two members, depending upon the set-ordering rules established for the set. The two set-access modes were described under "Motivation of Set Concept," and enumerated in Table 2. The two set-test operations relate to whether or not a particular set is currently empty (owner record, but no member records) and whether or not a record is currently inserted as a member of a particular set. More elaborate operations exist in higher-level languages (Bachman and Williams, 1964; Dodd, 1966; CODASYL Task Group, 1971), but they are based upon these primitives.

**Set Descriptions, Set Classes, and Set Occurrences.** The sets described to this point have been completely free of any restrictions with regard to the class of record that could appear in either the owner or member role, or both. In Cobol, PL/I, and most other data processing languages, there exist the concepts of record description, record occurrence, and record class.

The *record description* is the "01" entry that appears in the Data Division of a Cobol source program. It is concerned with providing a record name and other attributes of the record.

A *record occurrence* is an instance of a record created in accordance with a record description.

A *record class* consists of all the records that have been, or will be, created in accordance with a particular record description.

In parallel with these record concepts, there are equivalent concepts for sets. A set description defines a set class name, set-owner selection criteria, set-member eligibility rules, and set-member ordering rules. A set occurrence is an instance of a set created in accordance with a set description. It is owned by a particular record, and it holds specific record occurrences as members. A set class includes all the set occurrences that have been or may be created in accordance with a particular set description.

The main purpose of both the record class and set class concepts is to create a strong organizing force. For example, it changes a data base with a million records from a million special situations into one where 40 or 50 situations exist: one situation for each record class and each set class. It changes the

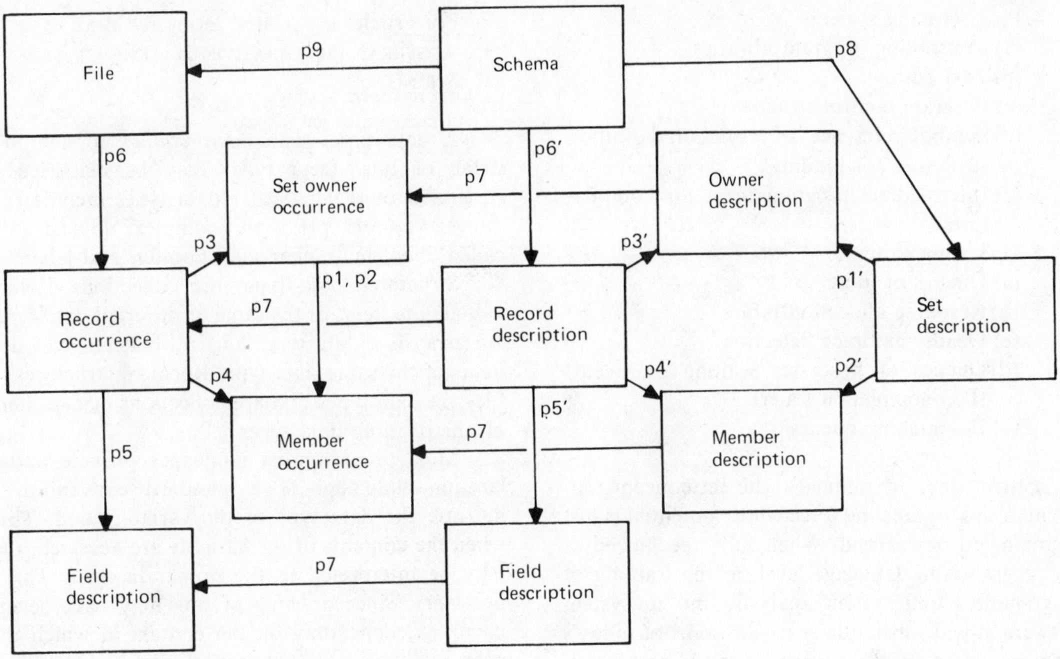


**Fig. 5.** Occurrence/description structures.

problem from something that could be chaos into something that is manageable.

The data structure diagram in Fig. 5 illustrates the integration of the description structure and occurrence structure, for data as illustrated in Fig. 4. There is a corresponding element in the description structure for each occurrence element in the occurrence structure. An arrow points from the descriptive element to its equivalent occurrence element, symbolizing the fact that there may be zero, one, or more occurrence elements for each descriptive element. These occurrence elements are the embodiment of the class property and are all labeled "p7."

The properties p1 through p6, previously described in Figs. 3 and 4, are illustrated on the occurrence structure, and their descriptive counterparts (p1′, p2′, • • • p6′) are mapped onto the description structure. It should be noted that the "set-owner occurrence" block in the occurrence structure is controlled by two description boxes in the description structure. The "owner description" block describes the eligibility of an occurrence of a record class to serve in the owner role, whereas the "set description" block describes the set class as a whole. This separation is necessary because several record classes at the description level may be eligible to serve as set owners while, at the occurrence level, one and only one record is the actual owner of a set occurrence. All the set descriptions in the schema are indicated by the arrow p8. All the files created in accordance with the schema are indicated by the arrow p9.

**Auxiliary Uses of Sets.** Assuming that the major usage of sets is to organize and provide access to records in an application data base, then all other usages within an information system are auxiliary to the primary purpose. The tabulation below lists areas of system software and enumerates for each some usages in its respective area of the set concept. This list is intended to be illustrative of obvious usages and is in no way complete.

1. Data base systems
   (a) Index construction (index sequential and index random).
   (b) Data description structures.
   (c) Shared access control lists.
2. File systems
   (a) Catalog construction.
   (b) Access rights control.
3. Message systems
   (a) Construction of mailbox indexes.
   (b) Queueing messages.
   (c) Accessing multielement messages.

4. Programming systems
   (a) Controlling program libraries.
   (b) Text editing.
   (c) Program control structure.
   (d) Symbol reference and symbol definition structures for binding.
   (e) Intermediate program form for compilation.
5. Operating systems
   (a) Queues of jobs.
   (b) Resource allocation tables.
   (c) Deadly embrace detection.
   (d) Queues of processes waiting on events (I/O completion timer).
   (e) Dispatching queues.

**Summary.** In summary, the set concept represents a new organizing force whose potential is just beginning to be realized. When fully recognized at the programming language level, in the training of programmers and system analysts, and in system software, it will substantially reduce some of today's problems, give clearer direction for file and application design, and improve the tenuous reliability normally associated with the development of new application systems.

REFERENCES

1964. Bachman, C. W., and S. B. Williams. "A General Purpose Programming System for Random Access Memories," Fall Joint Computer Conference.

1966. Dodd, G. G. "APL—A Language for Associative Data Handling in PL/I," Fall Joint Computer Conference.

1969. Bachman, C. W. "Data Structure Diagrams," *Data Base* (Quarterly News Letter of ACM-SIGBDP), Vol. 1, No. 2.

1971. ACM. "CODASYL COBOL Data Base Task Group Report" (April).

C. W. BACHMAN

## DATA TABLET. See RAND TABLET.

## DATA TYPE

For articles on related subjects *see* ARITHMETIC, COMPUTER; DATA STRUCTURES; and PROCEDURE-ORIENTED LANGUAGES.

For articles on related terms *see* BOOLEAN ALGEBRA; DECLARATIVE STATEMENT; and STRING.

A data type is an *interpretation* applied to a string of bits. Data types may be classified as structured or scalar. Scalar data types include real, integer, double precision, complex, logical (also called "boolean"), character, pointer, and label.

Structured data types are collections of individual data items of the same or different data types. An array is a data type that is a collection of data items of the same data type. Records, structures, or files are data types that are collections of data items of one or more data types.

Most programming languages provide a declaration statement or a standard convention to indicate the data type of the variable used. Thus, when the contents of the variable are accessed, they may be interpreted in the proper manner. This is necessary, since a string of bits may have several meanings, depending on the context in which it is used.

The *real* data type, which contains a normalized fraction (mantissa) and an exponent (characteristic), is used to represent floating-point data, usually decimal.

The *integer* data type is used to represent whole numbers, i.e., values without fractional parts.

*Double precision* is a generalization of the real data type, providing greater accuracy and sometimes a greater range of exponents.

*Complex* data contain two real fields representing the real and imaginary components of an imaginary number $a + bi$ ($i$ is the square root of $-1$).

*Logical* data is of the true-false form; i.e., there are only two possible values, true or false.

*Character* data is the internal representation of printable characters. Some coding schemes (BCD) permit 64 characters and use six bits; others (EBCDIC and ASCII) permit up to 256 characters and use 8 bits.

*Label* data refers to locations in the program and *pointer* data refers to locations of other pieces of data.

The commonly used operators for addition (+), subtraction (−), multiplication (*), division (/), and exponentiation (** or ↑) may be applied to real, integer, double precision, or complex data in higher-level language programs, with a few restrictions. The actual operation that takes place depends on the data type of the operands. Although some language processors permit "mixed mode" expressions (i.e., expressions involving operands of differing data types), this is accomplished by converting the operands to a common data type before the operation is performed.

For example, to execute

N = (TEST + 90)/3,

the integer value 90 is converted to a real value, 90.0, so that it may be added to the value of TEST (assumed to be real-valued). Before the resultant real value can be divided, the integer value 3 must be converted to a real value, 3.0. Finally, the real result is truncated and converted to an integer so that it may be stored in the integer location *N*.

The logical operators *and* ( .AND. or AND or &), *or* ( .OR. or OR or |), *not* ( .NOT. or NOT or ¬), *implies*, and *equivalence* may be applied to logical data having true or false values only. Character operations include concatenation and selection of substrings. For all data types, the assignment operator (= or ← or : =) may be used to copy the contents of one location into another, and relational operators may be used to compare values of data items.

Certain programming languages (Snobol or Algol 68) are extendable in the sense that users may define new data types to suit the needs of a particular problem.

REFERENCE

1973. Wirth, Niklaus. *Systematic Programming: An Introduction*. Englewood Cliffs, N.J.: Prentice-Hall.

B. SHNEIDERMAN

# DEADLOCK

For articles on related subjects *see* INTERRUPT; and MULTIPROGRAMMING.
For article on related term *see* TASK.

A task (process) in a multiprogramming system is *deadlocked* if it cannot proceed because it is waiting for an event that will never occur. A system deadlock or a deadlock situation exists if one or more tasks in a system is deadlocked. An example given by Holt (1972) is the following PL/I program, which would cause a deadlock under OS/360:

```
REVENGE:  PROCEDURE OPTIONS (MAIN, TASK);
          WAIT(EVENT);
END REVENGE;
```

The task associated with this program will wait forever unless it is somehow removed by the computer operator, since there is no provision for signaling that EVENT has occurred.

The events waited for by deadlocked tasks are often resource assignments. Suppose tasks PETER and PAUL both require simultaneous use of resources CIRCLE and SQUARE (which might, for example, each be a tape drive) in order to proceed. Assume that PETER has been assigned CIRCLE and PAUL holds SQUARE. Say PETER requests SQUARE, but must wait until it is released by PAUL. However, PAUL will release SQUARE only at task completion time, and in order to proceed to completion it is necessary for PAUL to have CIRCLE, which is held by PETER. The two tasks have requested resources in opposite order and have become involved in a *mutual* deadlock, or *circular wait*. More than two tasks may be involved: A situation may exist in which PETER is waiting for PAUL who is waiting for FRED who is waiting for SAM who is waiting for PETER. Indeed, all tasks in a multiprogramming system may be involved, in which case there is a *total* deadlock. In spooling systems, total deadlock might occur because of competition for spooling space on the disk. This would be the case if no task released disk space until it was completed and no task could complete without additional disk space. (Spooling space is not necessarily continually emptying in this system; it empties only when tasks are complete.)

Another term for deadlock (due to E. W. Dijkstra) is "deadly embrace," and still another is "knot." Some IBM logic manuals call a deadlock an "interlock."

Various ad hoc and systematic methods have been suggested for prevention of deadlocks, or for detection and subsequent recovery. These methods are reviewed in Holt (1972) and Coffman et al. (1971). Included in the ad hoc methods are conventions for requesting resources in specified order, and constraints on the amount of time a task is permitted to wait for an event. That these ad hoc techniques work fairly well is evidenced by the fact that deadlocks are not a serious problem in the operating systems of the mid-1970s. Ad hoc prevention methods are routinely used and deadlocks occur infrequently. Those deadlocks that do occur are resolved mostly by the computer operator, who may abort a deadlocked task, preempt resources from one task in order to allow another task to continue, or restart the system.

It is possible, however, that the deadlock problem may be more pressing in the future as systems are developed with increased resource sharing and stronger concurrency. In this event, the systematic methods would appear more attractive, even through their cost might be relatively high. At present, most systematic methods confine themselves to those deadlocks attributable to contention for resources, as opposed to those caused by faulty synchronization of concurrent tasks, since the latter are more complex and less well understood.

REFERENCES

1971. Coffman, E. G., M. J. Elphick, and A. Shoshani. "System Deadlocks," *Computing Surveys*, Vol. 3, No. 2 (June).

1972. Holt, R. C. "Some Deadlock Properties of Computer Systems," *Computing Surveys*, Vol. 4, No. 3 (September).

A. H. WERKHEISER

# DEBUGGING

For articles on related subjects *see* COMPUTER, USING A; DUMP; ERRORS; FLOWCHART; PATCH; PROCEDURE-ORIENTED LANGUAGES, Programming; PROGRAM; and TRACE.

For article on related term *see* LOOP.

When a program is first ready to be tried out on a computer, the probability is very high that it contains one or more mistakes, introduced at any of several places along the line of preparation. Debugging is the process by which a programmer finds and then corrects the errors in a program. These mistakes may take various forms, such as merely a keypunching mistake; a grammatical error due either to an oversight or to misuse of the syntax of the language; a logical error resulting either in an inability to proceed with the calculation or in proceeding with the wrong calculation; or a choice of method that turns out not to be valid for the particular circumstances. Anticipating this to be the case, the programmer proceeds to establish, with the aid of the computer, the answers to three questions about the program:

1. Is it a *valid* program? Do the statements, individually and together, follow the syntactical rules of the language so that they are capable of being translated into a machine language program?
2. Is it a *working* program? Can the computer execute the program so translated?
3. Is it a *correct* program? Will it accomplish the desired goal? Are the answers produced correct?

**Question 1: Is It a Valid Program?** All compilers determine this. Merely by trying to translate the given program, of necessity they uncover all instances of bad grammar, whether it is a misplaced comma, improper usage, or missing information. Of course, when the programmer makes a mistake resulting in a statement that is syntactically correct but different from what he intended, the compiler can do nothing; but when an error in syntax *is* encountered, it is almost always caught, flagged, and a diagnostic message put out.

Compilers vary greatly in the degree of help they give in such situations. In the early days, when memories were limited, merely an abbreviated error code was often printed, requiring the user to look up in a table or listing to find out the kind of error involved. Now, most compilers print textlike messages, although that does not guarantee their clarity.

For example, omission of an operation symbol is easy to catch, and easy to point out, as in the example:

```
          D = B*B - 4.AC
 *****              $
IMPLIED MULTIPLICATION NOT ALLOWED--USE *
```

However, compiler writers for commercial companies seem rarely to be concerned with the confusion or blankness in the mind of the novice programmer. It is certain that a beginner who forgets to DIMENSION an array (but who has never heard of a statement function) will not find the message

```
          DO 1   I = 1, 3
        1 A(I) = I
   FATAL  ERROR:
   THIS DEFINE PROCEDURE IS DEFINED AFTER AN
          EXECUTABLE STATEMENT
```

very clarifying, and will have to go elsewhere for (human) help. In this respect, the writers of many university-developed compilers, like Watfiv and Forgo, have done far better at anticipating the state of awareness of the programmer, and have tried to give him more helpful information. For the preceding mistake, for example, Forgo says:

```
    DO 1  I = 1, 3
1   A(I) = I
    $
VARIABLE IS NOT DIMENSIONED
```

Sometimes, of course, even the best compiler is reduced to frustration and has to say:

```
UNDECODEABLE STATEMENT
```

Nevertheless, most compilers of today's generation, by and large, do an adequate job (for the experienced programmer, at least) of helping to find mistakes in this first category.

**Question 2: Is It a Working Program?** Assuming that there is a unique interpretation that can be found for every statement, control can be passed over to the resulting object program, and execution can be attempted. If the computer encounters an impasse at execution time—a situation where insufficient information exists, or contradictory instructions are issued—it is usually due to programmer inconsistencies: failing to make sure every quantity is defined (has a value assigned to it) before asking the computer to use it; exceeding the range or the bounds he himself has defined for values, subscripts, or arrays; contradicting himself by supplying the wrong type of data or by calling for a mathematical process that is undefined for the particular values being used, like division by zero.

The response given by different processing systems varies widely here. The error may be one of three types:

A. *Fatal*—execution is terminated.

EXAMPLE 1. A common mistake of beginning programmers (and all too frequently of experienced ones as well) is neglecting to initialize a variable being used iteratively, such as when accumulating a sum. In such a case, the first time the computer is asked to use the quantity, it is told to take the contents of a storage location to which this program has not yet assigned a value. Forgo detects this and stops; a warning message is put out, identifying the situation, the variable, and the location in the source program where the usage occurred.

```
    DIMENSION  A(3)
    DO 1  J = 1, 3
    A(J) = J
1   SUM = SUM + A(J)
    PRINT, SUM
    STOP
    END

$LINKGO

ERROR IN *MAIN*  AT STMT. NO. 00001 + 00
  LINES :
    SUM     UNDEFINED VARIABLE

ABORT
```

EXAMPLE 2. When dealing with arrays, it is all too common for a programmer to fail to keep track of where his subscripts are ranging and, in particular, to let them stray beyond the bounds he himself has declared for them. Again, a good diagnostic processor will catch this and tell the programmer about it.

```
    DIMENSION  N(3)
    DO 1  J = 1, 3
1   N(J) = J
    DO 2  K = 1, 4
2   PRINT, K, N(K)
    STOP
    END

$LINKGO

    1     1
    2     2
    3     3

ERROR IN *MAIN*  AT STMT.  NO. 00002 + 00 LINES :
    N     ERROR IN SUBSCRIPTING

ABORT
```

B. *Nonfatal*—an interpretation is invented, a warning issued, and processing continued.

EXAMPLE 3. The square root of a negative quantity is undefined in real mathematics. What should the processor do when the argument of a SQRT function turns out to be negative? As long as a clear warning is given, almost anything can be used. The important thing is that even a computation with incorrect results may give useful information during debugging; therefore, it is better to do something and continue the computation than just to stop.

```
00102     X = -4.
00103     Y = SQRT(X)
00104     PRINT, X, Y
```

```
****************************************
ERROR DETECTED IN SQRT   ROUTINE
NEGATIVE ARGUMENT  , ARG1 =    -.40000000+01
SQRT   CALLED AT SEQUENCE NUMBER   000103
    OF MAIN PROGRAM
****************************************

     -4.0000      0.0
```

EXAMPLE 4. Sometimes the computer is asked to use the value of an undefined variable only in an output statement. In such a case, some processors will print out a unique and identifiable string (e.g., in Watfiv, a number known as "standardized garbage"; in Forgo a string of □□□□s), and proceed. The justification for this is that such output use of a wrong value may still allow useful calculations that do not involve that value.

```
      DIMENSION N(4)
      DO 1  J = 1, 3
   1  N(J) = J
      DO 2 K = 1, 4
   2  PRINT, K, N(K)
      STOP
      END

      1                  1
      2                  2
      3                  3
      4  □□□□□□□□□□□□
```

C. *Ignored*—an interpretation is invented, *no* warning issued, and processing continued!

EXAMPLE 5. In some Fortran language adaptations, such as Fortran G on the IBM 360, the processor takes whatever value was last stored in the specified location by the preceding program, and goes blithely on.

```
      DIMENSION A(3)
      DO 1  J = 1, 3
      A(J) = J
   1  SUM = SUM + A(J)
      PRINT, SUM
      STOP
      END

      550.9134
```

EXAMPLE 6. In Fortran V on the Univac 1108, the processor at least clears the memory being used to 0's before starting each program, and, if no other value has been defined, zero will be used.

```
      DIMENSION N(4)
      DO 1  J = 1, 3
   1  N(J) = J
      DO 2  K = 1, 4
      L = N(K)
   2  PRINT, K, N(K)
      STOP
      END

      1         1
      2         2
      3         3
      4         0
```

Some programmers may, having learned this, actually count on it and use this feature intentionally. In neither case is the programmer given any warning that the processor has made an assumption and proceeded in spite of incomplete instructions. This, unfortunately, is the case for the great majority of commercially available compilers.

Furthermore, sometimes the invented interpretation will lead to destruction of parts of the program or data, resulting in a later error message that seems to have nothing to do with the original error.

**Question 3: Is It a Correct Program?** If answers are produced by the program and no diagnostic message appears that would invite suspicion, the programmer must now face the question of whether the answers are correct. Here, unfortunately, the computer can do little to help, at least on its own initiative. That is, very little can be built into a processor to operate automatically in this situation. The judgment of the programmer must be used to decide whether the results are acceptable, incorrect, or of uncertain validity. There are, however, several additional techniques and special software features that can be made available to the programmer to assist him in this process of getting the bugs out, or "debugging," as it is commonly called.

If, as often happens, the program does *not* appear to be working as the programmer thinks it should—if it never produces output from a certain section, or appears to be repeating certain sections too many times (called "looping")—a simple procedure is to insert some extra output statements at judicious spots in his program, so that certain intermediate values are printed out for inspection. These may be the results of certain steps, or merely counters or index values. When the troubles are fixed, the extra statements can then be removed, or

```
$LOADGO FORGO

    DIMENSION DATA (10)
 *TRACE
    CALL TRACE (3)
    READ, N, (DATA(I), I=1,N)
    CALL TRACE(0)
    DO 1  I = 1, N
        IF (I .GE. (N - 2))  CALL TRACE (3)
        SUM = 0.
        SUM = SUM + DATA(I)
  1     CONTINUE
    AVE = SUM/N
    PRINT, SUM, N, AVE
    STOP
    END

 $LINKGO
*MAIN* 00000+03         7 1.23 4.56 -7.32 45.32 -9.2 6.89 -2.50
       00000+07 0.0000  SUM     00000+08 -9.2000E+00 SUM     00000+05      6       I
       00000+06 T
       00000+07 0.0000  SUM     00000+08  6.8900E+00 SUM     00000+05      7       I
       00000+06 T
       00000+07 0.0000  SUM     00000+08 -2.5000E+00 SUM     00001+01 -3.5714E-01 AVE

 -2.5000                7     -3.5714E-01
```

**Fig. 1.** Output of a trace program.

merely jumped around.

To simplify this process, many processors offer more or less elaborate capabilities to "trace" a program. Trace programs will produce, usually on the output printer, dynamic information about the progress of the program, such as the flow of control from one part to another, the new value of a variable every time it is changed, index and counter values on each pass through an iteration, and the value of an expression in an IF statement to help see why the program jumped or did not jump. Indiscriminately used, tracing can be extremely expensive, both in the slower execution necessary while producing tracing information, and in the huge volume of output that may be spewed forth. A well-designed general trace package, however, permits the programmer not only to specify at compile time in which parts of the program he would like tracing instructions included, and which variables and arrays he wants traced, but at execution time he can turn the tracing on and off at will.

An example of the output of such a trace program is shown in Fig. 1, produced by the Datacraft version of Forgo developed at the University of Wisconsin. The *TRACE card is a compile-time instruction, and causes trace instructions to be compiled with the rest of the object program. It could have been inserted part way through the program if interest had been centered farther on; CALL TRACE (N) is an execution-time instruction, which turns on the production of trace output, $N$ items per line, if $N > 0$, and turns off the production of output when $N = 0$. For each assignment statement traced, three items of information are printed: (1) the location of the statement, identified in terms of statement numbers and lines counted beyond the last statement number (e.g., 00001 + 01 is the first statement following statement number 1; statement 00000 + 01 is the first executable statement in a program, if unnumbered); (2) the value of the variable named on the left, after execution of the statement; and (3) the name of the variable or array element. If an IF statement is traced, the value of the expression is printed, without a name: a numerical value for an arithmetic IF, a T or F for a logical IF. For each READ statement traced, the location is given, followed by a copy of the data read.

Note that listing of output is suppressed by the

```
$LOADGO FORGO

      DUMP
      DO 1 N = 1, 100
         READ, X, Y
         Z = DIFF(X, Y)
         IF(Z .GT. .05)PRINT, X, Y, Z
    1 CONTINUE
      STOP
      END

      FUNCTION DIFF(R1, R2)
      DUMP
      DIFF = ABS((R1 - R2)/R1)
      RETURN
      END

$LINKGO

4.0000      1.0000      7.5000E-01
6.0000      9.0000      5.0000E-01
7.0000     -3.0000      1.4286
4.0000      0.0000      1.0000

 ERROR IN DIFF   AT STMT. NO. 00000+03 LINES : DIVISION BY ZERO
CALLED IN *MAIN* AT STMT. NO. 00000+04 LINES:

*MAIN*
    X = 0.0000  ,   Y = 5.0000E+00,    N =    5,    Z = 10000E+00

DIFF
    R1 = 0.0000  ,  DIFF = 1.0000E+00,    R2 = 5.0000E+00,
ABORT
```

**Fig. 2.** Output of a Forgo DUMP program.

programmer until the loop is nearing satisfaction, since values near the end are often the critical values. In this case, however, inspection of the trace output quickly reveals (if it had not been apparent before) that the initialization statement has been erroneously included in the loop, and the sum has been reset to zero on each iteration.

Sometimes, even with tracing available, it is difficult to get a clue as to where something is going wrong in a program. It may terminate abruptly with only a cryptic ABEND, or "abnormal termination" message, indicating that "something went wrong somewhere." In such cases the instruction to produce a DUMP, or "post-mortem," showing the status of both program and data at the time the program terminated, may yield valuable information. Systems that produce this information only in terms of core locations or absolute addresses necessitate the use of a "symbol table map" that enables the programmer to determine, at the expense of only a few hours and a finite fraction of his remaining eyesight, what value belonged to what variable, and where the program might have been when it blew up.

Some maps actually give the values in binary or octal code, putting the even more tedious burden of transliteration on the program user. Better designed systems, however, will list selectively the values of only those variables or arrays specified, and will furthermore identify each with its name in source-language terms. Fig. 2 (again taken from Forgo) shows an example of such a DUMP. In this case, the trouble can easily be determined to be an attempt to divide by zero when the fifth set of data is processed. Although in this case it would have been easy to

```
1:          WRITE(6,10)
2:        1 READ, A, B, C
3:          IF(A .NE. 0) GO TO 2
4:          IF(B .EQ. 0) GO TO 7
5:  C
6:  C  EQUATION IS LINEAR
7:  C
8:          ROOT = -C/B
9:          WRITE(6,11) A, B, C, ROOT
10:         GO TO 1
11: C
12: C  ERROR
13: C
14:       7 WRITE(6,16) A, B, C
15:         GO TO 1
16: C
17: C  TEST DISCRIMINANT
18: C
19:       2 D = B*B - 4.*A*C
20:         IF(D .LT. 0.) GO TO 4
21: C
22: C  EQUATION HAS TWO REAL ROOTS
23: C
24:         S = SQRT(D)
25:         ROOT1 = (-B + S)/(2*A)
26:         ROOT2 = (-B - S)/(2*A)
27:         WRITE(6,12) A, B, C
28:         WRITE(6,13) ROOT1, ROOT2
29          GO TO 1
30: C
31: C  EQUATION HAS TWO COMPLEX ROOTS
32: C
33:       4 S = SQRT(-D)
34:         RR = -B/(2*A)
35:         RI = -S/(2*A)
36:         WRITE(6,14) A, B, C
37:         WRITE(6,15) RR, RI
38:         GO TO 1
39:      10 FORMAT(6X,'A',8X,'B',8X,'C'/1X,3(' -------'))
40:      11 FORMAT(3F9.2,' IS A LINEAR EQUATION'/
          *        36X,'ROOT = ',1PE11.4/)
42:      12 FORMAT(3F9.2,' HAS TWO REAL ROOTS')
43:      13 FORMAT(38X,'R1 = ',1PE11.4/38X,'R2 = ',1PE11.4/)
44:      14 FORMAT(3F9.2,' HAS TWO COMPLEX ROOTS')
45:      15 FORMAT(36X,'REAL = ',1PE11.4/
          *        31X,'IMAGINARY = ',1PE11.4/)
47:      16 FORMAT(3F9.2,' NO EQUATION')
48:         END
```

| SYMBOL NAME | REFERENCED AT LINES (MINUS MEANS SYMBOL DEFINED, EXCLUDING SUBPROGRAM CALLS AND EQUIVALENCE |
|---|---|
| SORT | 24 33 |
| S | -24 25 26 -33 35 |
| RR | -34 37 |
| ROOT2 | -26 28 |
| ROOT1 | -25 28 |
| ROOT | -8 9 |
| RI | -35 37 |
| D | -19 20 24 33 |
| C | -2 8 9 14 19 27 36 |
| B | -2 4 8 9 14 19 25 26 27 34 36 |
| A | -2 3 9 14 19 25 26 27 34 35 36 |

| STATEMENT NUMBER | DEFINED AT LINE | REFERENCED AT LINES |
|---|---|---|
| 1 | 2 | 10 15 29 38 |
| 2 | 19 | 3 |
| 4 | 33 | 20 |
| 7 | 14 | 4 |
| 10 | 39 | 1 |
| 11 | 40 | 9 |
| 12 | 42 | 27 |
| 13 | 43 | 28 |
| 14 | 44 | 36 |
| 15 | 45 | 37 |
| 16 | 47 | 14 |

**Fig. 3.** Cross-reference output.

detect by an inspection of the data, in other situations the trouble might have arisen from numbers that were the results of intermediate calculations, and might be much more difficult to track down.

One more type of program aid is sometimes of considerable value in debugging, both after trouble develops, and even more to help keep troubles from getting started. This is a "cross-referencing" program that will produce indexed lists of both the variable names and the statement numbers of a source program, which may be of great value both in tracing the flow through the program and in determining where each variable is used, including which statements have the capability of defining a new value for it. Fig. 3 shows the cross-reference output produced for a simple quadratic equation solving program.

Such a cross-referencing program is of particular value when modifications need to be made to an existing program, either a working program or one still being debugged. It allows a backward trace of the flow path by showing the possible paths that might have been followed to get to a particular point; it tells precisely all the places where a particular variable is used, and which of those are reference usages and which are defining usages. Methodical reference to a cross-referencing program can greatly decrease the incidence of second-order bugs—those *introduced* in the process of trying to fix other bugs.

Besides the use of special processors like tracing and dump programs, programmers often employ all or some of the following techniques, developed out of painful experience, to facilitate debugging their programs:

1. Since most modern compilers will produce a source-language listing of the program as it is being compiled, but not of the data being supplied with it, it is frequently good practice to include an output statement immediately following every input statement, which will print out the values just read. The name "echo checking" or "echo printing" is sometimes applied to this.

2. It is worthwhile for debugging purposes, as well as for the usefulness of the eventual results, to be sure each output value is properly identified by appropriate column headings, captions, or labels, including all independent variable values, count numbers, and other such information. Even though it may be possible to identify an unlabeled output value with a little consideration and comparison, careful anticipation of the appearance of the output page and of the ease and quickness with which meanings can be associated with numbers can greatly speed up comprehension.

3. Liberal use of comment cards in the source program is necessary if anyone else is to make use of the program. It is also extremely helpful to the author himself in the process of debugging when he tries to answer such questions as, "What does this part of the program do?"; "Where is the section that does . . .?"; "What does XYGRAB represent?"; or even, "How did I get here?" Flowcharts carefully correlated with the program in terms of segments, blocks, statement numbers, etc., can also be invaluable in helping to answer such questions.

4. A little extra time spent in careful organization and layout of the source program itself can often save much valuable time in the debugging process. Indentation of subprograms, clear identification of the end of such program segments, and vertical alignment of alternative conditions in branching operations are a few suggestions (see McCracken and Weinberg, 1972).

Such techniques might be summed up in a fifth one:

5. The more care is taken at program construction time, the less hair pigmentation is lost in debugging.

This article has focused on debugging techniques for Fortran programs on some well-known university systems. Although such systems tend to have better than average debugging facilities because they are intended for student use, all higher-level language systems have some debugging facilities of the type described here. Assembler and macro-assembler systems also all have debugging facilities whose details will generally differ from those presented here, but whose spirit—in terms of getting answers to the three questions posed at the beginning of this article—is quite similar to that discussed here.

Some aspects of debugging are beyond the scope of this article. One of these is the increasing use of interactive time-sharing systems for debugging. Although many of the techniques described here are also used in interactive debugging, a number of interactive debugging techniques have been developed to take advantage of the on-line dialog which is possible between the programmer and the computer. Another subject beyond the scope of this article concerns the debugging of large software systems that present problems to the programmer quite different in scope than the debugging of most higher-level language programs (Rustin, 1971).

REFERENCES

1971. Rustin, Randall (Ed.). *Debugging Techniques in Large Systems*. Englewood Cliffs, N.J.: Prentice-Hall.

1972. McCracken, Daniel D., and Gerald Weinberg. "How to Write a Readable Fortran Program," *Datamation*, Vol. 18, No. 10 (October), pp. 73–77.

1973. Hetzel, W. C. (Ed.). *Program Test Methods*. Englewood Cliffs, N.J.: Prentice-Hall.

C. H. DAVIDSON

# DECIDABILITY

For articles on related subjects *see* ALGORITHMS, THEORY OF; and COMPUTABILITY.

For article on related term *see* ALGORITHM.

Decidability is a property of predicates. A *predicate* $P$ with domain $D$ is a property of the elements of $D$, which each particular element of $D$ either has or does not have. If $x$ in $D$ has the property $P$, we say that "$P(x)$ is true"; otherwise, we say that "$P(x)$ is false." The predicate $P$ is said to be *decidable* if there exists an algorithm which, for any given $x$ in $D$, provides us with a definite answer to the question whether or not $P(x)$ is true.

For example, consider the predicate $P$ whose domain $D$ is the set of integers greater than 1, and which is defined as:

$P(i)$ if and only if $i$ is a prime number.

This predicate is decidable. An algorithm is described by Hopcroft and Ullman (1969).

The definition given above is lacking rigor for the following reasons:

1. It is not explained in what form the argument $x$ in $D$ is "given." In particular, this part of the definition makes sense only if elements of $D$ are in some way finitely describable. Thus, the notion of decidability, as described above, makes no sense for a predicate $P$ whose domain is the set of real numbers.
2. The notion of an algorithm is not precise.
3. It is not explained in what sense the algorithm provides us with an answer.

How the notion of decidability of a predicate can be made mathematically rigorous and how the decidability of predicates can be discussed in terms of the computability of functions are explained in the article Algorithms, Theory of

REFERENCE

1969. Hopcroft J. E., and J. D. Ullman. *Formal Languages and Their Relation to Automata*. Reading, Mass.: Addison-Wesley.

G. T. HERMAN

# DECISION TABLES

## PRINCIPLES

For articles on related subjects *see* DECISION TABLES: Languages; and FLOWCHART.

Decision tables are a tabular method of describing or specifying the various actions associated with combinations of conditions. The method is tabular in that it uses a special form of table to present the associations. The actions specified are transformations to be done to data or materials, usually by computers or people. The conditions are data variables that describe the characteristics of the environment and the events that happen in the environment. The relationship among the conditions specified in a decision table is usually the logical AND relationship. The history of the origin and development of decision tables is summarized in Chapin (1967).

EXAMPLE. A simple example of a decision table is given in Fig. 1. This describes a procedure for ordering low-usage products under several conditions. By policy, a target inventory level has been set at 20 units of stock for items covered by this decision table. Consider, as an example of the procedure, the third column from the right in the decision table: If the weekly usage is low (less than 8 units) and the amount on order is not greater than 30 units, then a regular order should be placed if the stock on hand amounts to less than 20 units.

**Terminology.** As indicated in Fig. 2, decision tables are commonly regarded as consisting of four overlapping major parts. Each of these parts is a

| | | | | | | | | |
|---|---|---|---|---|---|---|---|---|
| On hand < 20 | Y | Y | Y | Y | Y | Y | N | ELSE |
| Weekly usage | > 15 | > 15 | 8-15 | 8-15 | 8-15 | < 8 | — | |
| Local vendor available | — | — | N | N | Y | — | — | |
| On order > 30 | N | Y | N | Y | N | N | Y | |
| Rush order | X | | X | | | | | |
| Regular order | | X | | X | X | X | | |
| Cancel order | | | | | | | X | |
| No action | | | | | | | | X |

**Fig. 1.** Example of a decision table.

rectangle within the overall rectangle of the decision table. The proportioning of the four-component rectangles varies from situation to situation.

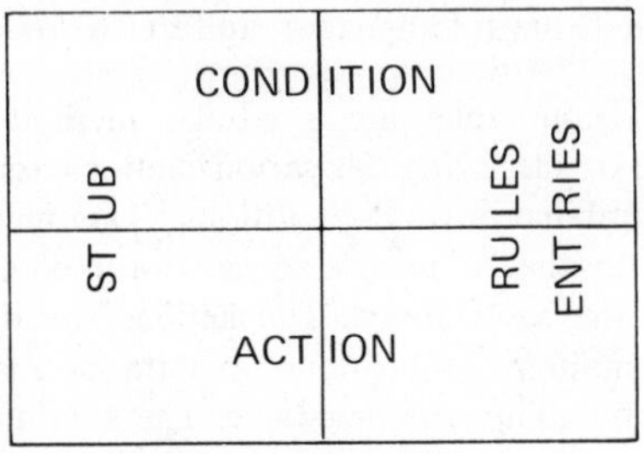


**Fig. 2.** Parts of a decision table.

The upper portion of a decision table is known as the "condition" portion. The lower portion of a decision table is known as the "action" portion. The left-hand portion of a decision table is known as the "stub." The right-hand portion of a decision table is known as the "entry" portion. Each column in it is known as a "decision rule." Because of the overlap, the upper left-hand portion of a decision table is known as the "condition stub." The upper right-hand portion is known as the "condition entries" in the decision rules. The lower left-hand portion is known as the "action stub." The lower right-hand portion of a decision table is known as the "action entries" in the decision rules.

Decision rules are any of the columns in the rules or in the entry portion of the decision table. The rules in decision tables are meant to be read both horizontally and vertically. Thus, read vertically, each decision rule cites some combination of conditions and the associated actions to be taken when that combination of conditions is true (exists or is satisfied). Read horizontally, the rules list the alternative values of of conditions and the presence or absence of the actions to be taken. The stub, read vertically, lists all conditions and actions. Taken together, the decision rules are exhaustive in that they must cover every possible combination of conditions. No such requirement is imposed on the actions, however. Conditions may be of three types: limited entry, extended entry, or mixed entry.

In *limited-entry decision tables*, the condition stub specifies exactly what the condition is, or what the value of the variable is. An example is, "Age is less than 18." Therefore, the condition portion of each decision rule may need only to identify if yes (Y), that condition is met; no (N), that condition is not met; or "don't care" (−), whether or not the condition is met. In the latter case, the rule is insensitive or indifferent to the particular values of that condition.

In *extended-entry decision tables*, the condition stub cites the identification of the condition, but not the particular values. Particular values are entered into the condition portion of the decision rules directly. An example is "Age" in the stub, and "<18," "18," and ">18" in the rules.

In *mixed-entry*, the action portion of the decision rules may be either unsequenced or sequenced. Unsequenced actions, the most common, are identified by any mark (such as *X*) in the rule, with the actions to be performed in the order in which they are listed from top to bottom in the action stub. If needed, actions may be cited more than once in the stub, to get them into the desired sequence for a decision rule. Actions not to be performed are left unmarked in the rule. For sequenced actions, the action entry is a sequence number instead of a mark, and the action stub may list the actions in any sequence.

**Reading and Creating Decision Tables.** The person who creates a decision table must give attention to completeness, accuracy, redundancy, inconsistency, endless loops, and size. For assistance on the first four matters, formal guides and check procedures are available [for examples, see London (1972) and Pollack et al. (1971)]. To avoid all endless loops, the person must require for every decision rule that at least one of the marked actions must change the value of at least one of the conditions cited in the condition stub.

In order to save space in the decision table, and to keep the decision table down to a workable size, rule consolidation is normally practiced as often as possible. This is usually accomplished in two ways. First, when the actions to be taken for different combinations of conditions are identical, and the patterns of conditions can be combined through the use of "don't care" condition entries, then one decision rule can replace two or more decision rules. Second, an "else rule" can be specified for all possible combinations of conditions not explicitly provided for in the other decision rules. Commonly, the else rule is the rightmost rule in a decision table (see, for example, Fig. 1). Large decision tables can be split into a connected group of much smaller decision tables by using decision table parsing techniques.

The user of decision tables commonly reads the decision rules individually from top to bottom, referring to the left to the stub as needed. Except for the "else" rule, the left-to-right sequence of the decision rules in the decision table is of no significance, but is commonly put into a logical order based upon the pattern of changes in the conditions. Having the most commonly used rules at the left is an aid to the user, but having the rules in an orderly progression of condition values is an aid to the creator of the decision table.

To use a decision table, the user first reads the condition stub and, for the situation at hand, notes the input values for each condition. Then he matches these values of the conditions against the condition portion of the decision rules, one rule at a time, from left to right. If the conditions do not match, the user rejects the decision rule and goes to the next decision rule to the right. If the table was correctly created, one and only one decision rule must fit the input values of the conditions, be it only the "else" rule. When the user finds the rule that does match, he accepts the rule and goes to its action portion to find out what actions are to be performed and in which sequence. When these actions are complete, the user applies the decision table afresh with a new set of input values for each condition.

**Use.** Decision tables have enjoyed their widest use in representing logically complex data-handling situations. These are situations where the actions to be taken depend upon the values of a large number of variables, taken in combination. Examples of such situations are commonly encountered in administrative and control applications of computers. Major users include insurance companies and other financial organizations, and manufacturing companies (McDaniel, 1970). Decision tables are rarely used in scientific or research organizations when the situations can be clearly described in mathematical terms. Having or using a computer is not a prerequisite to using decision tables.

Decision tables find use in many phases of computer work, including system analysis, system design, programming, debugging, and documentation. In systems analysis, decision tables help analysts in identifying the significant control variables for the operation being studied. In systems design, decision tables help link the desired action to the control variables. In programming, decision tables can be used as a programming language. In debugging, decision tables can help reduce the time to locate bugs because they force a sharp distinction between control logic in a program and the actual production of the output data. In documentation, decision tables can concisely summarize the system or program in written form.

**Advantages.** Decision tables can serve as a compact means of describing or specifying operations. How compact they are depends on the number of conditions being included, and on the number of possible different actions that need to be taken. In general, the compactness of decision tables decreases about in proportion to the sum of the number of variables included and the number of possible actions.

Because of its compactness, the decision table provides a convenient way of tersely stating logically complex processing. The practical size for a single decision table is approximately what can be put on one page of paper. Larger decision tables can be parsed and linked together.The procedures for creating decision tables provide rules for checking for four types of possible errors: completeness, size, redundancy, and inconsistency (London, 1972; Pollack et al., 1971). These offer valuable aids in systems design and programming, but people must go through the laborious process of doing most of the checking work.

Decision tables can be used to summarize much information in documentation, but in this case are sometimes regarded as being too concise. In programming, their precision and conciseness are major advantages, when supported with additional documentation.

**Disadvantages.** Decision tables have no theoretical size limit, but there are real practical limits imposed by people. Large decision tables become incomprehensible, and can be neither checked nor used well by people. Fortunately, the size can usually be reduced by rule consolidation and by parsing.

Decision tables do not reduce the human labor of thinking or discovery. Human beings still must do the work of defining, specifying, and following to its logical consequences each chain of conditions and actions. Decision tables take away from people none of this arduous work, but they can be used to pinpoint where that work can be best concentrated.

Decision tables ignore the delicate interleaving of logic and action that seems so natural when people think about conditions and actions to be taken. Decision tables force the human user to consider conditions separately from actions.

The advantages of decision tables are drawing an increasing number of supporters, but their disadvantages are sufficiently major to keep this group of users fairly small. Typically, the experience of the first-time user is that he must increase the time and effort he puts in, in order to prepare the decision table. This additional investment may pay off in less debugging and in more efficient operations, as is usually the case for the experienced user of decision tables, but the additional investment by the novice user is difficult to justify.

REFERENCES

1967. Chapin, Ned. "An Introduction to Decision Tables," *DPMA Quarterly*, Vol. 3, No. 3 (April), pp. 2–23.

1970. McDaniel, Herman (Ed.). *Applications of Decision Tables.* Philadelphia: Auerbach Publishers.

1971. Pollack, Solomon L., Harry T. Hicks, and William J. Harrison. *Decision Tables: Theory and Practice.* New York: John Wiley.

1972. London, Keith R. *Decision Tables.* Philadelphia: Auerbach Publishers.

N. CHAPIN

## LANGUAGES

For articles on related subjects *see* DECISION TABLES: Principles; PROCEDURE-ORIENTED LANGUAGES; and PROGRAMMING LANGUAGES.

For articles on related terms *see* DIAGNOSTICS; and SOURCE PROGRAM.

A decision-table language is a higher-level programming language, which in major part has the appearance of, and also serves as, a decision table. A decision-table language is a part of a decision-table programming system, with the decision-table language supported by a translator or processor (or a series of them) to produce executable machine language code.

Decision-table languages differ from other higher-level languages in several respects. First, the syntax, while commonly very close to Cobol or Fortran, goes beyond those languages to allow source language statements, which taken together look like a decision table. This permits the programmer to write a program in decision-table form in part, as illustrated in Fig. 1.

When the analysis and design work have resulted in a decision table, using a decision-table language avoids having the programmer translate the decision table. This greatly speeds up programming and reduces logic bugs. When the analysis and design work have not resulted in a decision table, using a decision-table language for the programming helps provide a check on the completeness and consistency of the design.

Second, the supporting translators or processors often first generate or output Cobol or Fortran source language. In these cases, the decision-table language effectively becomes a preprocessor, an added "front end" to, or alternative way of producing, Cobol or Fortran programs. Third, decision-table languages show great diversity among themselves, enough so that what is acceptable syntax in one is commonly unacceptable in most of the others. Fourth, computer vendors have commonly not provided translators or processors to support decision-table languages. The result has been a profusion of decision-table programming systems from major users and from software houses.

**Background.** Because of the third and fourth points noted above, any brief discussion of this subject must of necessity fail to give a full picture of the convenient and powerful features available in some decision-table languages. The variety is just too much to cover both adequately and briefly. For this reason, a summary discussion such as this one must concentrate on only a selection of features and on the varieties of the decision-table languages likely to be most commonly encountered or likely to be of most significance to most users of higher-level languages. A look at the history of decision-table languages helps clarify this situation..

The first decision-table language was Tabsol, produced in 1961 by the Computer Department of General Electric Company (Chapin, 1967). Its translator went directly to machine language, but by comparison with later developments, the syntax was very limited. In 1962 and 1963, a CODASYL committee proposed a decision-table language extension or addition to Cobol. This effort, Detab, appeared first in an unsupported experimental version Detab-X (CODASYL Systems Group, 1962). This was later (1963–1965) refined to Detab/65 and supported by a decision-table-to-Cobol translator. For some years, the U.S. Navy has distributed an improved version of Detab called DTT, and in 1972 offered a new translator to Cobol, itself written in Cobol.

Concurrently with these developments, a host of other decision-table languages appeared, as well as variations of Detab. Among the later were offerings by IBM, Univac, CDC, Honeywell, and ICL. Among the former, from computer vendors, were offerings by General Electric (Logtab), and IBM (DLT, Decision Logic Translator). From users and software houses came many offerings. Among them were Detap from Information Management Inc., Tabtran from Westinghouse Tele-Computer Systems Corp., and SMP from Trilog Associates Inc., and Tap from Hoskyns Systems Research in Europe. In 1973, the total number of active decision-table languages exceeded two dozen, but only those listed above were popular. A 1969 summary of the major offerings to that year listed 32 decision-table languages (McDaniel, 1970).

**Features.** A comparison of a selection of decision-table languages, based on their major features, helps indicate their variety and range of usefulness. The languages stressed in this comparison are DTT, Detab, SMP, and Tabtran. Where other decision-table languages significantly differ on the points of comparison, note is taken in most cases.

*Source Language.* The programmer writes a decision table on the coding sheet, following some format rules. In some languages, such as DTT, he must provide a header line to describe the size and form of the decision table. In most, he provides no header line, but either must follow a prescribed format (as in SMP, for example) or must follow punctuation rules to enable the translator to identify the parts of the decision table (as in Detab, for example). In all, the programmer must take care in selecting the wording in the stub.

*Target Language.* Nearly all modern translators produce as their output a source language translation of the table input. Most produce Cobol source code, although some, such as Tabtran, may optionally produce Fortran source code. A few languages produce low-level symbolic or assembly language as the target language.

*Output from Translator.* The translator produces a network of comparisons with conditional and unconditional transfers of control to replace the decision rules. The translator usually does not replace the stub at all, but uses the programmer-provided wording directly in the comparisons and as the actions. This means that symbolic names must be fully defined by the programmer or specified in the syntax, be they control entry points, names of items of data, or relations (such as "greater than"). To provide control entry points in the comparison network, the translator usually provides catenated synthetic names. The action-stub names usually become control entry points for exits from the comparison network.

*Entry Form.* All decision-table languages accept limited-entry decision tables, and a few such as Detap accept extended and a mixture of the limited and extended entry forms.

*Number of Rules Permitted in a Table.* The number of decision rules permitted as the maximum has been as follows: DTT, 25; Detab, 50; SMP, 20; and Tabtran, 40.

*Else Rule.* DTT requires the programmer to provide an "else" rule, even though it be only a dummy. For the others, the "else" rule is optional. Detab generates an "else" rule if one is needed but is not provided by the programmer.

*Number of Conditions.* The number of conditions permitted as the maximum has been as follows: DTT, 25; Detab, 50; SMP, more than 1000; and Tabtran, 100.

*Number of Actions.* The number of actions per-

```
00050 000480 PROCEDURE DIVISION.                                                    FIXPOP
00051 000490 000-INITIALIZE-FILES                                                   FIXPOP
00052 000500     OPEN INPUT PCP-FILE CARDS-IN-FILE                                  FIXPOP
00053 000510          OUTPUT CARDS-IN-FILE.                                         FIXPOP
00056 000520     PERFORM 030-READ-A-CARD THRU 030-END-READ-CARD                     FIXPOP
00055 000530     GO TO 040-READ-A-POP-RECORD.                                       FIXPOP
00056 000539 010-DECIDE-DT00   NOTE                      DETAP/IMI V4-0 06/01/70    FIXPOP
00057 000540     DETAP   010-DECIDE                              00001 03 05 05     OP
00058 000550     RL1                                     0  0  0  0  0              OP
00059 000560     RL2                                     1  2  3  4  5  $           OP
00060 000570     CONDITION SECTION                                                  OP
00061 000580     C POP-REC-COLUMN-1 EQUAL TO 'T'         Y  Y  Y  N  N              OP
00062 000590     C POP-REC-COLUMN-3-7                                               OP
00063 000600       CARDS-IN-REC-TEST-NO                  <  =  >  -  -              OP
00064 000610     C WS-SEARCH-OR-PUNCH EQUAL TO           -  -  -  'S' 'P'           OP
00065 000620     ACTION SECTION                                                     OP
00066 000630     A MOVE 'S' TO WS-SEARCH-OR-PUNCH              X                    OP
00067 000640     A MOVE 'P' TO WS-SEARCH-OR-PUNCH           X                       OP
00068 000650     A PERFORM 015-NOT-FOUND                 X                          OP
00069 000660     A PERFORM 020-PUNCH-A-CARD                 X        X              OP
00070 000670     A PERFORM 030-READ-A-CARD THRU                                     OP
00071 000680                030-END-READ-CARD            X  X                       OP
00072 000690     A GO TO 040-READ-A-POP-RECORD              X  X  X  X              OP
00073 000700     A GO TO 010-DECIDE                      X                          OP
00074 000710     TEND.                                                              OP
00075 000712 010-DECIDE SECTION.                                                    FIXPOP
00076 000714 DT00001000.                                                            FIXPOP
00077 000716     IF POP-REC-COLUMN-1 EQUAL TO 'T' GO TO DT00001001.                 FIXPOP
00078 000718     IF WS-SEARCH-OR-PUNCH EQUAL TO 'S' GO TO AT00001004.               FIXPOP
00079 000720     IF WS-SEARCH-OR-PUNCH EQUAL TO 'P' GO TO AT00001005                FIXPOP
00080 000722          ELSE GO TO EL00001001.                                        FIXPOP
00081 000724 DT00001001.                                                            FIXPOP
00082 000726     IF POP-REC-COLUMN-3-7 CARDS-IN-REC-TEST-NO                         FIXPOP
00083 000728          GO TO AT00001001.                                             FIXPOP
00084 000730     IF POP-REC-COLUMN-3-7 CARDS-IN-REC-TEXT-NO                         FIXPOP
00085 000732          GO TO AT00001003 ELSE GO TO AT00001002.                       FIXPOP
00086 000734 AT00001001.                                                            FIXPOP
00087 000736     PERFORM 015-NOT-FOUND.                                             FIXPOP
00088 000738     PERFORM 030-READ-A-CARD THRU 030-END-READ-CARD.                    FIXPOP
00089 000740     GO TO 010-DECIDE.                                                  FIXPOP
00090 000742 AT00001002.                                                            FIXPOP
00091 000744     MOVE 'P' TO WS-SEARCH-OR-PUNCH.                                    FIXPOP
00092 000746     PERFORM 020-PUNCH-A-CARD.                                          FIXPOP
00093 000748     PERFORM 030-READ-A-CARD THRU 030-END-READ-CARD.                    FIXPOP
00094 000750     GO TO 040-READ-A-POP-RECORD.                                       FIXPOP
00095 000752 AT00001003.                                                            FIXPOP
00096 000754     MOVE 'S' TO WS-SEARCH-OR-PUNCH                                     FIXPOP
00097 000756     GO TO 040-READ-A-POP-RECORD.                                       FIXPOP
00098 000758 AT00001004.                                                            FIXPOP
00099 000760     GO TO 040-READ-A-POP-RECORD.                                       FIXPOP
00100 000762 AT00001005.                                                            FIXPOP
00101 000764     PERFORM 020-PUNCH-A-CARD.                                          FIXPOP
00102 000766     GO TO 040-READ-A-POP-RECORD.                                       FIXPOP
00103 000768 EL00001001.                                                            FIXPOP
```

```
00104 000770    DISPLAY 'ELSE RULE NONE SPECIFIED-TBL = 010-DECIDE'.    FIXPOP
00105 000772    STOP RUN.                                               FIXPOP
```

**Fig. 1.** Decision-table in the Detap programming language. This is a replica of a decision table reformatted into Cobol. Note that Paragraph (OP) is now part of the Cobol program and is immediately followed (FIXPOP) by the Cobol source code generaetd by Detap. (Courtesy of Information Management, Inc.)

mitted as the maximum has been as follows: DTT, 25; Detab, 50; SMP, more than 1000; and Tabtran, 150 minus the number of conditions.

*Sequencing of Actions.* Most provide for unsequenced actions. A few, such as SMP, provide only for sequenced actions; and a few, such as Detab, provide for both sequenced and unsequenced actions.

*Diagnostics.* The variety of diagnostics available from the translators is extensive, covering not only syntax matters but also reports on logical errors in the table. Almost all apply tests for rule redundancy and for rule inconsistency. Tests for rule completeness depend in part on the handling of the "else" rule, as do some tests for accuracy. Hence, some languages, such as DTT and Tabtran, provide no diagnostics in these areas, whereas others, such as Detab and SMP, do.

*Size Reduction.* Most of the decision-table translators, as a byproduct of testing for rule redundancy and inconsistency, also attempt to consolidate rules by the use of the "don't care" entry. A minority, including DTT (at least with its prior to 1972 translator), generated equivalent code for rules that could be consolidated. None of the decision-table languages provides for parsing, and all rely on the host language (usually Cobol or Fortran) for the handling of any linkage between tables.

*Other Aids to Users.* Some of the translators are limited to just the handling of the translation, such as DTT. Others, such as Detab, can tie into a larger software package. A few, such as SMP, make the handling of decision tables the keystone to a system of program creation and maintenance, and provide such features as libraries of program versions and cross-references to data names and control entry points.

*Configuration.* To run the translators, the usual practice is to make the minimum computer configuration needed be the same as that required for the host language, usually Cobol or Fortran. Most are available for running under any of the common operating systems that support the host language.

*Optimization.* The effectiveness of the optimization of the object code possible from the translators is moot. In part, it depends on the compiler for the host language. In part, it depends on the algorithms used by the decision-table translator, the effectiveness of which have been questioned. In part, it depends upon the factor chosen for optimization, since the factors are antagonistic (speed of execution versus storage space needed, for example).

*Price and Availability.* Decision-table languages and translators are readily available for immediate delivery, and many have been extensively field tested. Most require a periodic monthly license payment, usually between $200 and $500 per month. Some are available for a period, usually three years, for a one-time license payment of from $1,000 to near $5,000. A few are available only on a purchase basis, at prices from nearly $100,000 to almost free, such as DTT.

### References

1962. CODASYL Systems Group. *DETAB-X*. Santa Monica, Calif: CODASYL Systems Group.

1967. Chapin, Ned. "An Introduction to Decision Tables," *DPMA Quarterly*, Vol. 3, No. 3 (April), pp. 2–23.

1970. McDaniel, Herman. *Decision Table Software*. Philadelphia: Auerbach Publishers.

N. CHAPIN

## DECLARATIVE STATEMENT

For articles on related subjects *see* EXECUTABLE STATEMENT; PROCEDURE-ORIENTED LANGUAGES; PROGRAMMING LANGUAGES; and STATEMENTS.

A declarative statement is one in a higher-level programming language that provides descriptive information (contrasted with an imperative statement that specifies explicit processing operations).

Besides specifying the actual computations, decision rules, and input/output operations involved in the implementation of a particular algorithm, a higher-level language program also must provide the compiler with descriptive information that allows it to perform a variety of organizational tasks directly connected with the production of an executable object program. For example, the description of a variable (its name, together with the type of data to be stored in it) enables the compiler to allocate the proper amount of storage, associate its location with the variable's name, and set up any necessary data conversion mechanisms prior to the assignment of a value to that variable. (This description also defines the set of operations that are applicable to the element.) Similarly, the definition and description of a data file makes it possible for the compiler to establish a relationship between references to that file and a particular collection of data transmitted to or from a specific input/output device.

In most languages, this type of information is supplied through a series of special statements, which often are characterized as being "non-executable" (or more properly, declarative). Once defined, simple variables, arrays, files, and other items can be used throughout the program simply by alluding to their properties by use of their names.

To illustrate the type of information conveyed by declarative statements, consider the following Fortran program, which reads a number $N$ and uses it to compute

$$Y = \sum_{X=1}^{N} X(1 + \sqrt{X}).$$

$N$ and $Y$ are printed with appropriate identification:

```
    INTEGER N
    REAL X,Y
    READ (5,8) N
    Y = 0.0
    DO 6 I = 1,N
    X = I
  6 Y = Y + X*(1.0 + SQRT(X))
    WRITE (6,16) N,Y
  8 FORMAT (I2)
 16 FORMAT (4HN = ,I2,4X,4HY = ,E12.5)
    END
```

The first two declarative statements (underlined) define the three variables and instigate the necessary storage allocation; statement number 8 describes the form in which the input value will be found (a 2-digit integer punched in the first two columns of a card), and statement 16 provides formatting information for the output. Associations with the respective READ and WRITE statements are provided by appropriate statement number references.

Many other languages provide similar declarative facilities which may be interspersed throughout the program. A notable exception is Cobol, in which the declarative facilities are much more formally structured: Each program must consist of four organizational divisions in a fixed order, the first three of which consist entirely of declarative statements.

S. V. POLLACK

# DECREMENT

For article on related subject *see* ADDRESSING.

For article on related term *see* INDEX REGISTER.

The dictionary defines a decrement as a negative increment, but in a computing system, a decrement is a value that is subtracted from the contents of a register.

The term was used in the IBM 704 system and in successor IBM 700 and 7000 systems to denote a field that occurred in instructions to manipulate the index registers. Fig. 1 shows the format of these 36-bit instructions.

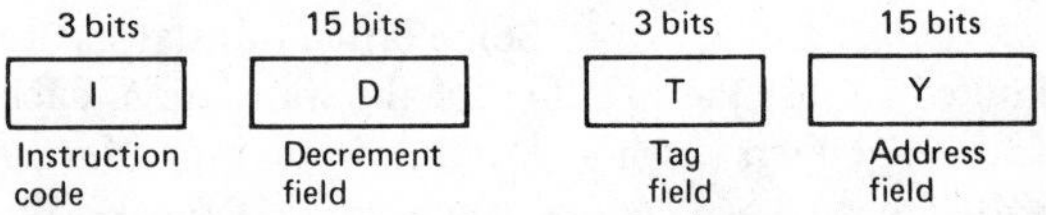


**Fig. 1.** Format of 36-bit instruction with decrement field.

For example, if the first three bits were 010, the instruction was TIX (Transfer on Index). The tag field specified an index register, and this instruction compared the decrement (i.e., the contents of the decrement field) with the contents of the index register. If the decrement $D$ was smaller, the contents of the index register would be decreased (decremented) by the quantity $D$, and a transfer of control would occur to the address $Y$ specified in the address field.

This class of computers, though very widely used, was almost unique in the use of subtracting rather than adding in connection with index registers. It was therefore appropriate to use decrements rather than increments in the index register with the modify-and-test instructions.

S. ROSEN

## DELAY-LINE MEMORY. *See* ULTRASONIC MEMORY.

## DELIMITER

For article on related subject *see* PROCEDURE-ORIENTED LANGUAGES.

A delimiter is an item of lexical information whose form and/or position in a source program denotes the boundary between adjacent syntactic components of that program; this term is also used for a program component whose value controls the number of iterations in a cyclic process.

As is true with natural language, the "meaning" and clarity of statements in higher-level programming languages often depend on the inclusion of explicit indicators that "punctuate" the statement. In the latter context, such signals are termed "delimiters." Since higher-level language statements must be processed by a compiler whose analytical and interpretive facilities must function without the equivalent of human cognition, it is necessary to equip programming languages with a fairly extensive variety of such delimiters, many of them highly specific. The most common of these, of course, is the blank space, whose function as a separator is self-explanatory. As a convenience to programmers, many compilers tolerate superfluous blanks between syntactic components.

Parentheses also represent a commonly used type of delimiter. One of their primary purposes in higher-level languages parallels traditional mathematical usage; i.e., to define the extent of a component in a computational expression. For example, the use of parentheses in the ordinary arithmetic expression

$$A + B(C - 2D) \tag{1}$$

Is clearly paralleled by the equivalent in many higher-level languages. For example,

$$A + B * (C - 2 * D) \tag{2}$$

Many programming languages provide a relatively free physical format where there is no intrinsic association with a specific input medium, such as the punched card or teletypewriter. Consequently, there is no implicit correspondence in such languages between the end of a statement and the physical boundary of the medium, thus necessitating the use of explicit delimiters. The semicolon serves that purpose in PL/I and Algol, for example, so that a statement in those languages may be defined operationally as a string of characters between two semicolons. Similarly, the period delimits certain types of Cobol statements.

In block-oriented languages such as PL/I and Algol, special delimiters are provided to indicate the boundaries of major structural components. For instance, an arbitrarily long sequence of PL/I statements may be identified as a "compound" statement in certain contexts by using the delimiting statements DO and END at the beginning and end of the grouping, respectively. Similarly, a PL/I procedure is bracketed by PROCEDURE and END statements. (The BEGIN and END statements provide the same definition in Algol.)

In a somewhat different context, the term "delimiter" is used to refer to a numerical value (usually expressed as a constant, variable, or arithmetic expression) that controls the number of cycles in an iterative process. A very frequently used technique for implementing such a cycle is exemplified by the following sequence of PL/I statements:

```
Y = 0;
DO I = 1 TO 17;
Y = Y + I;
END;
```

In this construction, a variable $Y$ is set (initialized) to 0, followed by a set of exactly 17 cycles. During each of these, the value accumulated thus far in $Y$ is increased by adding the current value of $I$ to it. As an integral part of this process, the value of $I$ is increased by 1 each time through, so that after the seventeenth cycle has been completed, the final value of $Y$ represents the sum of the first 17 integers. The DO statement contains the information required for the compiler to construct the cycle, and the item following the word TO (17 in this example) is the delimiter of the cycle.

S. V. POLLACK

**DESIGN, LOGICAL.** *See* LOGIC DESIGN.

**DESK CALCULATOR.** *See* CALCULATOR, DESK.

**DETAB.** *See* DECISION TABLES: Languages.

# DIAGNOSTICS

For articles on related subjects *see* DEBUGGING; ERRORS; and MICROPROGRAMMING.

Diagnostics are means of determining whether there are hardware faults in a computer or errors in user programs.

Hardware diagnostics are programs designed to determine whether the components of a computer are operating properly. Circuit components are electronically exercised individually and in groups with the intention of detecting failures. When a failure is detected, the location and identification of the faulty element is printed and the maintenance staff can take action to repair or replace the element.

Hardware diagnostic programs are run as part of a regular schedule of preventive maintenance and in the event of a failure. If a failure has occurred, the hardware diagnostic program may not operate properly, and therefore it may not be of use in determining the source of the difficulty.

Increasingly often hardware diagnostics take the form of microdiagnostics. A microdiagnostic program is a microprogram that tests a specific hardware component such as a bus or store location. Microdiagnostics often provide more accurate location of a fault than hardware diagnostics written in machine language because of the addressability of individual components under microprogramming. Furthermore, these diagnostic programs are so fast that preventive maintenance testing may be interspersed transparently with other processing. Microdiagnostics, consequently, have furthered the development of self-diagnosing and self-repairing computers.

Diagnostic messages in software refer to the error messages produced by compilers, utilities, and system software. These messages are designed to give programmers an indication of where their programs are at fault. Diagnostic messages at compile time may only be warnings to the programmer, or they may indicate invalid syntax, which prohibits execution. In many systems a severity level indicator will be included in the diagnostic message.

Execution-time diagnostic messages are produced by the operating system or an execution-time monitor. These messages indicate attempts to perform illegal operations, such as dividing by zero, taking the square root of a negative number, illegal operation codes, illegal address references, and so on. The diagnostic message may or may not be followed by termination of the program.

Finally, application programs may produce diagnostics when erroneous control cards or data cards are read in. The creator of the application program has complete control over the nature of these diagnostic messages and the action to be taken.

B. SHNEIDERMAN

# DIFFERENTIAL ANALYZER

For articles on related subjects *see* ANALOG COMPUTERS; and DIGITAL COMPUTERS: Early.

In a paper published in the *Journal of the Franklin Institution* in 1931, Vannevar Bush described a machine (Fig. 1) that had been constructed under his direction at M.I.T. for the purpose of solving ordinary differential equations. He christened the machine a *differential analyzer*. This was what would now be called an "analog" computer, and was based on the use of mechanical integrators that could be interconnected in any desired manner. The integrator was in essence a variable-speed gear, and took the form of a rotating horizontal disk on which a small knife-edged wheel rested. The wheel was driven by friction, and the gear ratio was altered by varying the distance of the wheel from the axis of rotation of the disk. The principle is illustrated in Fig. 2.

The use of mechanical integrators for solving differential equations had been suggested by Kelvin, and various special-purpose integrating devices were constructed at various times. Bush's differential analyzer was, however, the first device of sufficiently general application to meet a genuine need, and in

**Fig. 1.** Vannevar Bush shown with the M.I.T. differential analyzer.

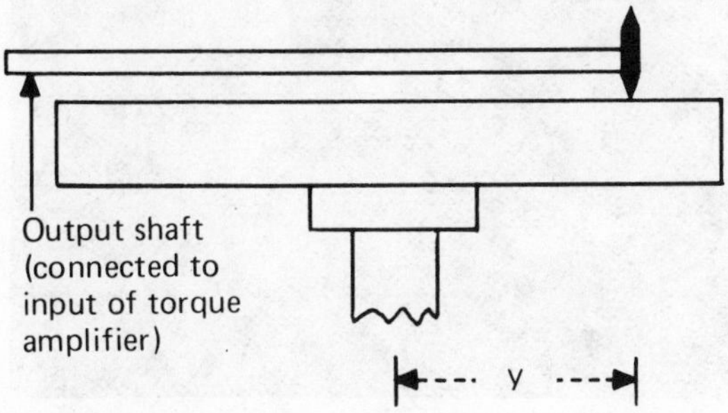


**Fig. 2.** Wheel and disk integrator. If the disk turns through an angle proportional to $x$, the output shaft turns through an angle proportional to $\int y\,dx$.

the period immediately before and during World War II quite a number of these devices were constructed. The one shown in Fig. 1 was installed at the Mathematical Laboratory, in Cambridge, England.

In order to make a practical device, it is necessary to have some means of amplifying the small amount of torque available from the rotating wheel. Bush used a torque amplifier, working on the principle of the ship's capstan, but adapting it for continuous rotation. Fig. 3 is taken from his report (1931) and sufficiently indicates the principle. The friction drums are rotated in opposite directions by a continuously running motor of sufficient power. When the input shaft is turned, one of the cords attached to the input arm begins to tighten on the friction drum round which it is wrapped. Which cord tightens depends on the direction of rotation of the input shaft. A very small tightening, and hence a very small tension in the end of the cord attached to the input arm, is sufficient, in view of the friction of the rotating drum, to produce a large tension in the end attached to the output arm. A small torque applied to the input shaft is thus capable of producing a much larger torque in the output shaft.

The integrators and torque amplifiers can be clearly seen in Fig. 4, together with the system of shafting used for effecting the connections. Changing the problem was a job for someone who did not mind getting his hands covered in oil. The output table on which the results were plotted directly in graphical form can also be seen in Fig. 4, which also shows a number of similar tables that were used for

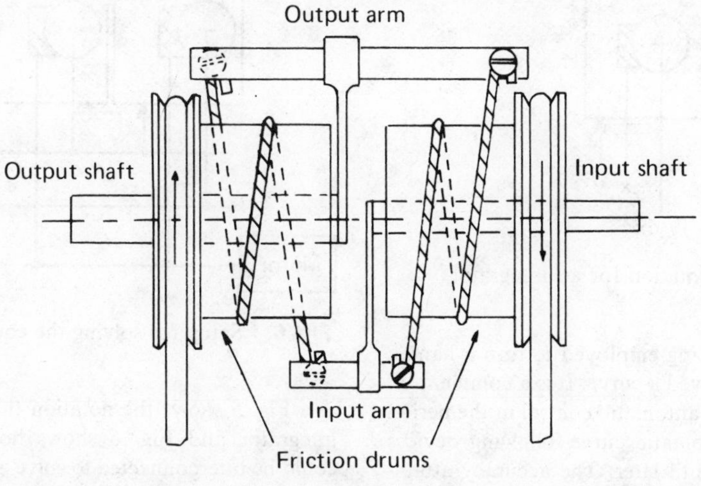


**Fig. 3.** Principle of torque amplifier. (Courtesy of *Journal of the Franklin Institute.*)

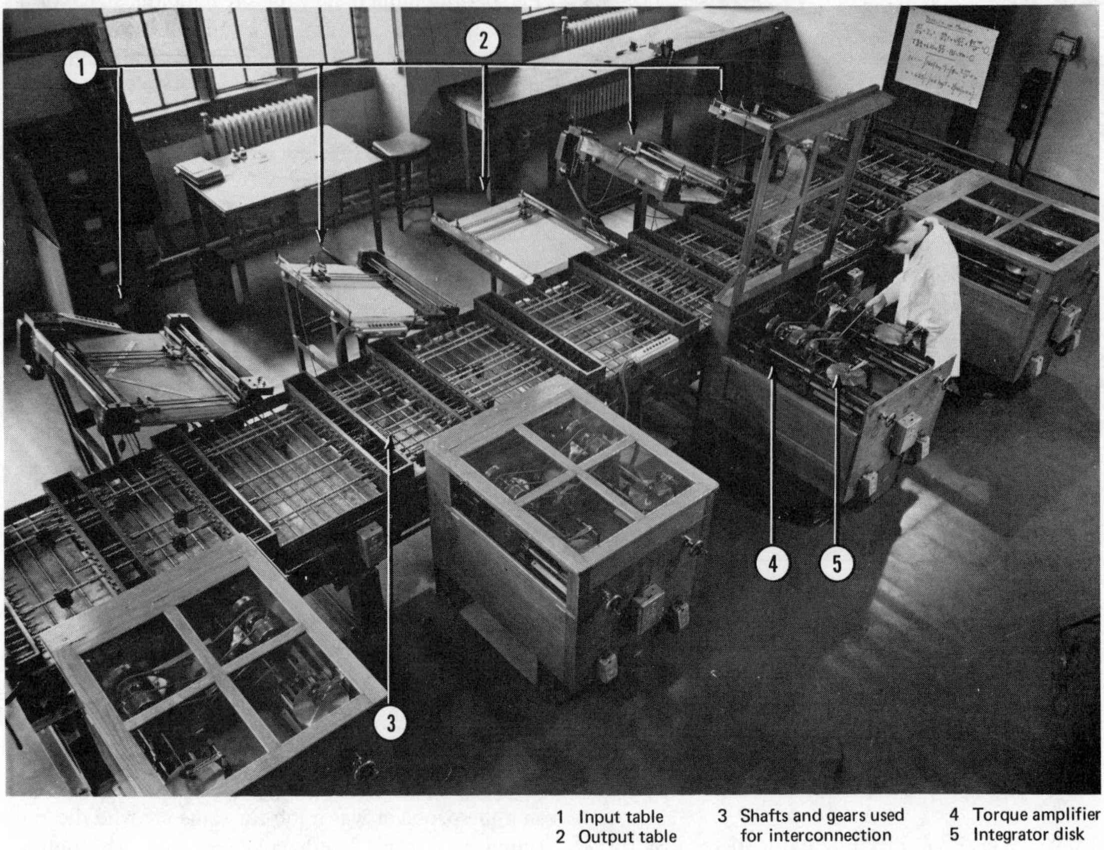


**Fig. 4.** The differential analyzer system, showing integrators, torque amplifiers, and shafting.

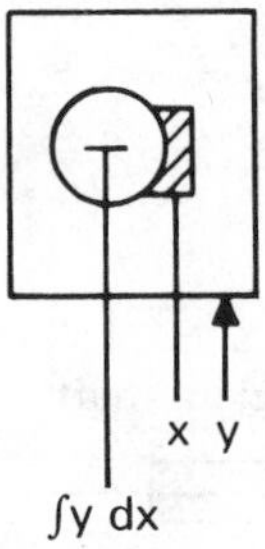


**Fig. 5.** Schematic notation for an integrator.

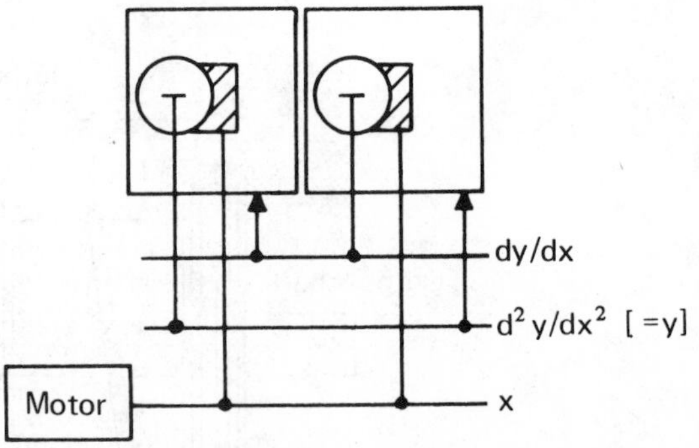


**Fig. 6.** Setup for solving the equation $d^2y/dx^2 = y$.

input, an operator being employed to turn a handle so that a cursor followed a curve. It is a comment on the primitive state of automatic control in the period in question that automatic curve-following devices were not provided until later. The accuracy attainable in a single integrator was about one part in three thousand, but of course a lower accuracy was to be expected in the solution.

Fig. 5 shows the notation that was used for an integrator and Fig. 6 shows how two integrators could be interconnected to solve a simple differential equation. It was not difficult to arrive at a diagram such as Fig. 6, even for a complicated equation, but working out the gear ratios required was a distinctly tedious task calling for some experience, particularly as accuracy required that full use should be made of the available range of integrator motion.

In 1945, Bush and S. H. Caldwell described a new differential analyzer in which interconnection between the integrators was effected electrically instead of mechanically. However, during the decade that followed, competition from electronic analog computers and from digital computers began to build up, and although the new machine ran for a number of years at M.I.T., by 1955 the mechanical differential analyzer was already obsolete.

**Digital Differential Analyzer.** This device is based on the use of a *rate multiplier* as an integrator. In a rate multiplier a constant quantity $y$ is held in a register and, on the receipt of an input pulse, is added to the number standing in an accumulator. If input pulses arrive at a rate $R$, overflow pulses will emerge from the most significant end of the accumulator at a rate proportional to $yR$. If $y$ now varies and if input pulses arrive whenever a certain other variable $x$ increases by $\delta x$, the number of output pulses emerging is proportional to $\Sigma y\ \delta x$ or, approximately, to $\int y\ dx$. Thus, the device serves as an integrator. Normally, $\delta x$ is equal to one unit in the least significant place, and continuously updated values of the variable $x$ can be obtained by feeding the pulses into an accumulator.

The first digital differential analyzer was the MADDIDA developed in 1949 at the Northrop Aircraft Corporation. It had 44 integrators implemented using a magnetic drum for storage, the addition being done serially. There were six tracks in all on the drum, one being used for synchronizing purposes. The problem was specified by writing an appropriate pattern of bits onto one of the tracks. Compared with the digital computers then being built, the MADDIDA was on an impressively small scale. It lost some of its simplicity, however, when adequate input and output devices were added, and in the end competition from general-purpose digital computers proved too much for it. The MADDIDA and its descendants did not, therefore, have the bright future in scientific computation that was predicted for them. However, digital differential analyzers of a simple kind continue to have a place in certain control applications.

REFERENCES

1931. Bush, V. *J. Frank. Inst.*, Vol. 212, p. 447.
1945. Bush, V., and S. H. Caldwell. *J. Frank. Inst.*, Vol. 240, p. 255.
1947. Crank, J. *The Differential Analyser*. London: Longmans, Green and Co.
1962. Huskey, H. D., and G. A. Korn. *Computer Handbook*. New York: McGraw-Hill, pp. 19–14.

M. V. WILKES

# DIGITAL COMPUTERS

## GENERAL PRINCIPLES

For articles on related subjects *see* ANALOG COMPUTERS; ARITHMETIC-LOGIC UNIT; HYBRID COMPUTERS; MEMORY: Auxiliary; MEMORY: Main; and SPECIAL-PURPOSE COMPUTERS.
For articles on related terms *see* CALCULATOR, DESK; CENTRAL PROCESSING UNIT; and FILES.

The digital computer is a machine, a machine which will accept data and information presented to it in its required form; carry out arithmetic, transfer, and logical operations on this raw material; and then supply the required results in an acceptable form. The resulting information (output) produced by these operations is entirely dependent upon the accepted information (input). Thus, the production of correct and complete answers cannot be obtained unless correct and sufficient input data has been provided.

The sequence of the operations required to produce the desired output must be accurately determined and specified by a human—known as a "programmer"—who prepares a set of instructions—known as a "program"—that will automatically process the work from input to output.

**Computer Characteristics.** The main characteristics of the computer are identified as automatic, general purpose, electronic, and digital. Fig. 1 shows a computer installation at Oxford University.

AUTOMATIC. We assume that a machine is automatic if it works by itself without human intervention. But this is not entirely true. Computers are machines: They have no will of their own; they cannot start themselves; they cannot go out and find their own problems and how to solve them. They have to be instructed. They are, however, automatic in that once started on a job, they will carry on until

**Fig. 1.** ICL 1906A computer system at Oxford University.

it is finished, normally without human assistance.

A computer works from a program of *coded* instructions that specify exactly how a particular job is to be done. While the job is in progress, the program is *stored* in the computer, and the parts of the instructions are obeyed. As soon as one instruction is completed, the next is obeyed automatically.

By contrast a desk calculator is semiautomatic; somebody has to set up the numbers on a keyboard and press a button (add, subtract, multiply, or divide) to initiate each individual operation. It should be noted, however, that with one operation, some modern electronic desk calculators are able to perform quite complicated functions.

Because a computer does not need to stop between single operations, it can take full advantage of the high-speed components that enable it to add, subtract, and perform other individual operations in millionths of a second.

General Purpose. Computers (and desk calculators, though they are rarely described as such) are *general-purpose* machines. In other words, a computer can do any job that its programmer can break down into suitable basic operations. Put a payroll program into a computer and you make it, for the time being, a special-purpose payroll machine. Replace the program by one for inverting a matrix, and you make the computer temporarily a special-purpose mathematical machine.

Electronic. The word "electronic" refers, of course, to the components of the machine. It is the nature of the electronic components that make possible the very high speeds of individual operations in modern computers. ("Electronic" is distinct from "electric" in that it suggests not only circuits and currents but also such components as transistors or their equivalent.) The history of electronic digital computers distinguishes three "generations," defined by the nature of the electronic components most prevalent in each. Thus, the first generation made extensive use of vacuum tubes, the second generation used transistors, and the third generation uses integrated circuits.

Most computer users need no special knowledge

of electronics, and the major practical distinctions between the generations—as far as they are concerned—are the reductions in size for a given power and the rapid increases in speed.

DIGITAL. A computer may be either *digital* or *analog*. The two types do have some principles in common, but they employ different types of data representations and are in general suited to different kinds of work. Digital computers are so called because they work with *numbers* in the form of separate digits. More preclsely, they work with information that is in digital or character form, including alphabetic and other symbols as well as numbers.

In a digital machine the data, whether numbers or letters or other symbols, is represented in digital form. An analog computer, on the other hand, may be said to deal with a "model" of the problem, in which the variables are represented by physical quantities such as angular position and voltage. The decimal numbers 136 and 435, for instance, might be represented by by 1.36 volts and 4.35 volts. Using familiar devices, we could say that a slide rule is an analog device because numbers are represented by a linear length. The abacus, on the other hand, is a digital device because movable counters are used for calculating.

Digital computers differ from analog computers much as counting differs in principle from measuring. Both types of machines employ electric currents, or signals, but in the analog system a number is represented by the magnitude (e.g., voltage) of a signal, whereas in a digital computer it is not the magnitude of signals that is important, but rather the number of them, or their presence or absence in particular positions. Analog computers tend to be special-purpose machines designed for some specific scientific or technical application. They are frequently found useful in engineering design for such things as atomic power stations, chemical plants, and aircraft. In commercial and administrative data processing and for mathematical computation, we

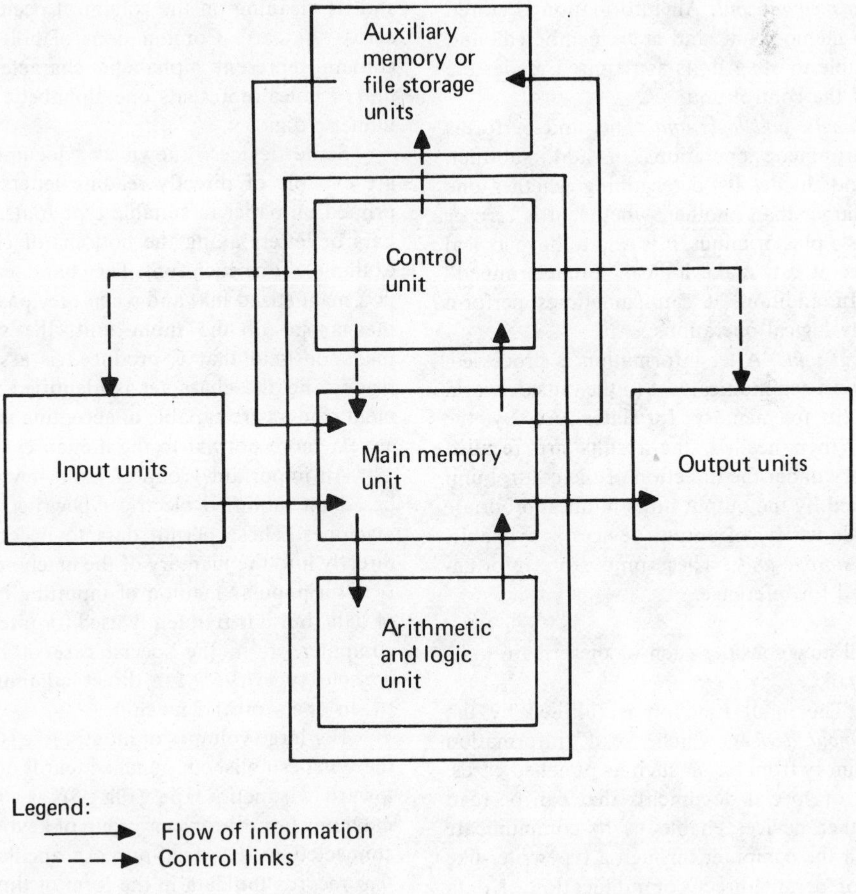


**Fig. 2.** Central processing unit. Grouping of computer components.

are concerned almost exclusively with digital computers.

**Main Units.** Only very rarely indeed does a computer have a unique fixed specification. Normally, it is better described as a computer system, consisting of a selection from a wide variety of units appropriate to meet a defined need. The principal groupings of these units commonly follow the pattern shown in Fig. 2 and are defined as follows:

1. *Input units.* An input unit accepts the data, the raw material that a computer uses, communicated from outside. It is the actual means by which information is converted into electronic pulses, which are then fed into the machine's memory.

2. *Control unit.* The directing force of the computer, the automatic operator, is the control unit. It provides the means of communication within the machine, by moving, advancing, or transferring information. It switches and integrates the various units into a whole system.

3. *Main memory unit.* All information is stored in the main memory unit and is "remembered" and made available to other units as required, under the direction of the control unit.

4. *Arithmetic and logic unit.* This unit performs the four arithmetic operations of add, subtract, multiply, and divide. By determining whether one number is larger than another, whether it is zero or whether it is a plus or minus, it is said to have logical abilities; i.e., it can make logical "predetermined" decisions. In addition, it can sometimes perform other strictly logical operations.

5. *Output units.* After information is processed, an output unit communicates it to the outside world or returns it to memory for later use by the computer. When needed, the results are recalled from memory under the direction of the control unit and presented by the output units in an appropriate form. A wide variety of output devices is available.

6. *File storage units.* These units store information required for reference.

We will now consider each of these main units in some detail.

INPUT. The input function is fulfilled by the individual *input devices*, which "read" information into the memory from *media* such as punched cards, paper tape, or special documents that can be read directly. Other devices enable us to communicate directly with the computer through a typewriter-like keyboard, or permit direct communication of data transmitted from a distance over telephone lines. Only electronic components can give the computer the internal speed of operation that is its great advantage, so its methods of accepting and presenting information are necessarily electronic in nature. But information available outside the machine is perforce initially in the form of written or printed words and figures because these are the only forms interpretable by humans.

The conversion of information from written form to computer form is usually done in two stages (Fig. 3). First, the information is punched into cards or paper tape, where it is represented by patterns of holes punched according to a standard code. At this stage the information may be viewed as being in an intermediate "physical" form. Special electromechanical devices known as card readers and paper tape readers are able to "read" the cards or tape. An input device detects where holes are present and passes corresponding electrical "pulses" into the internal part of the computer, thus completing the two-stage conversion. The value of a hole in a card (Fig. 4) or tape is dependent on the row it appears in and its meaning on the column it occupies, reading across the card. Combinations of holes in a single column represent alphabetic characters. A coded line of holes represents one alphabetic character or numeric digit.

Some devices, known as "document readers," are capable of directly reading letters or numbers printed on paper in suitable type fonts. The vertical bars or letters along the bottoms of checks are an example of one such font. The characters are printed in a magnetized ink, and when they pass the reading mechanism of the input unit, the shape of the magnetic field that is produced is assessed by the reader and the character is identified. Other document readers are capable of accepting type fonts that appear more normal to the human eye.

An important group of input devices are those based on modified electric typewriters or Teletype machines. These permit data to be communicated directly into the memory of the machine. As yet, this is not a popular method of inputting large volumes of data, but it is frequently used for interrogating the computer or, in the special case of the computer console typewriter, for direct communication between operator and machine.

For large volumes of input, there is a trend from the long-established punched card or paper tape toward magnetic tape (Fig. 5) as the recording medium. For example, a group of keyboards may be connected to a special-purpose ancillary computer that records the data in the form of tiny magnetized areas on the tape's surface. The coding is similar to

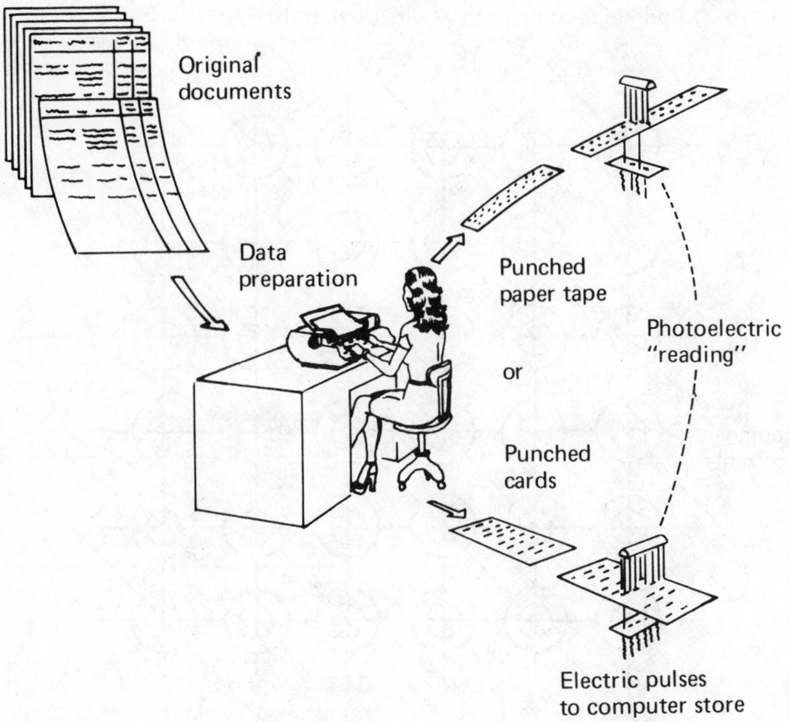


**Fig. 3.** Data preparation and input.

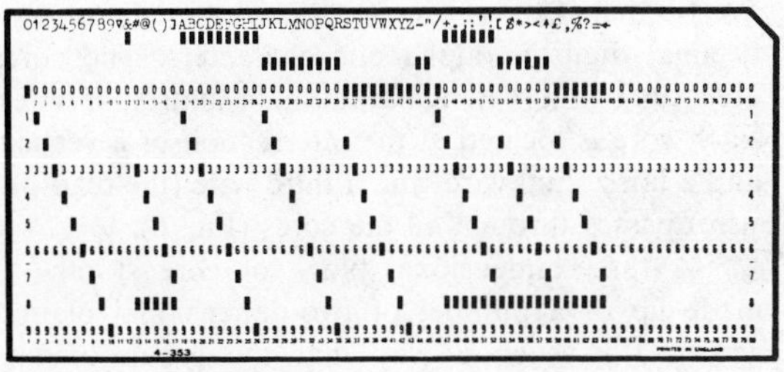

**Fig. 4.** Punched card.

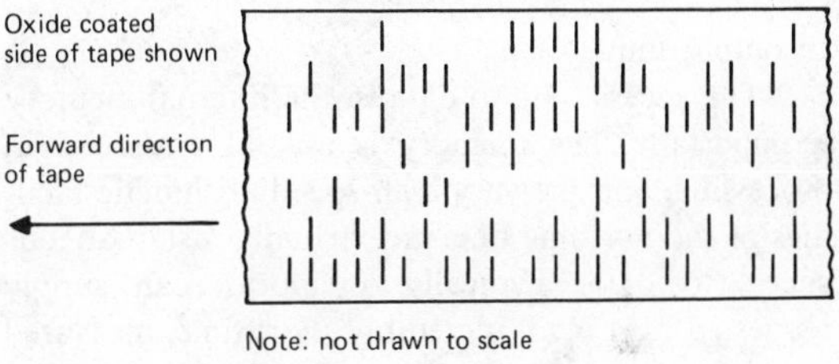


**Fig. 5.** Information recorded on magnetic tape.

that used on paper tape, but the data can be read from the magnetic tape at very much higher speeds than from paper tape or cards. These and other input media are discussed in a later section of this article.

Central Processing Unit. The central processing unit is the focal point of the computer system. It receives data from input units and file storage units, carries out a variety of arithmetic and logical operations on this data, and transmits results to output and file units. It is traditional, and still convenient, to consider the central processor as made up of three principal parts (not necessarily easily identifiable physically): (1) the memory, (2) the arithmetic and logic unit, and (3) the control unit.

1. *The memory*. The memory (or "main memory," as it is sometimes called to distinguish it from file storage or auxiliary memory) is able to hold, for as long as desired, coded representations of numbers and letters in convenient groupings; each group is held in a uniquely addressable part of the memory, from which it can be transferred on demand. The memory may be figuratively described as a large number of pigeonholes, each identifiable by a serial number that in effect is its address.

One purpose of the memory is to hold data. Numbers and letters flow into it from input, are sent for arithmetic processing to the arithmetic unit from which the results return to the memory, and the output information is stored in it before transfer to

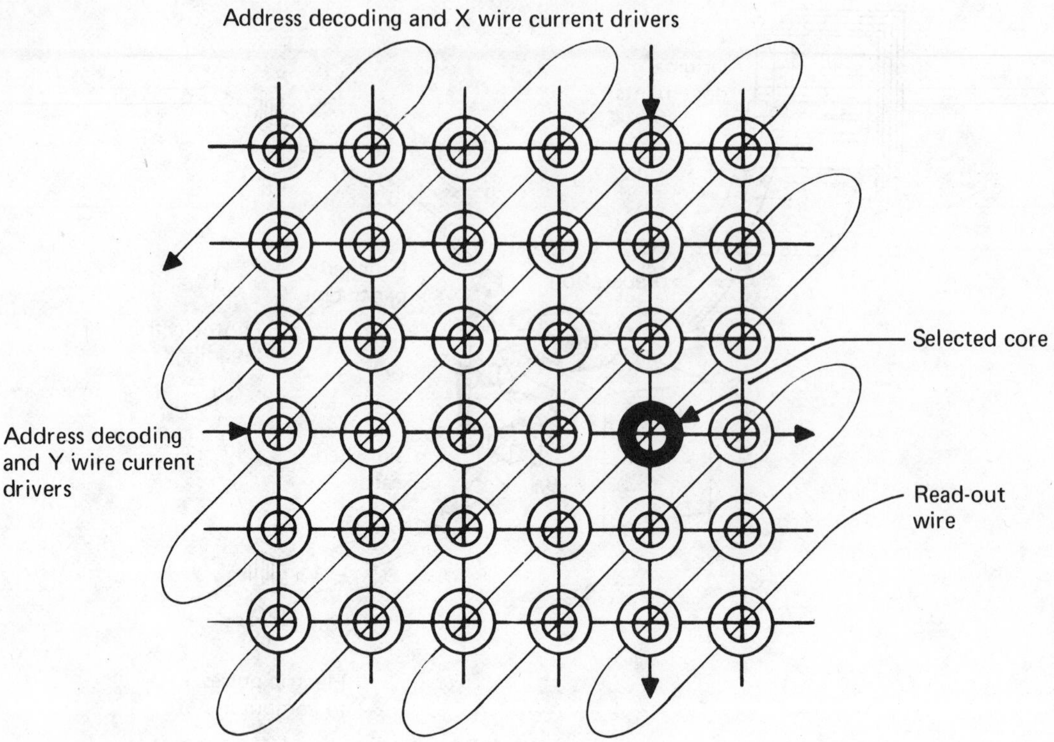


**Fig. 6.** Core storage.

an output unit.

The access time to data in the internal memory is important. The memory is a vital crossroad in processing, and the very high-speed arithmetic facilities of the machine demand virtually instantaneous access to data. Typically, memories can supply requested data in an incredibly short time, measured in microseconds (millionths of a second) or nanoseconds (thousand-millionths of a second); in fact, their speed is usually from 8 $\mu$s down to 200 ns.

The second use of the memory is to hold all the instructions of the program required to carry out a job. These instructions are normally coded in numeric form and can be read into the memory from punched cards, magnetic tape, or any other input medium. They remain in memory indefinitely unless they are deliberately erased.

The most common memory device is the magnetic core. This consists of small ferrite rings that can be magnetized in either of two directions, clockwise or counterclockwise. One state of magnetization denotes 0 and the other denotes 1; hence, each core can represent a binary digit, or "bit." A group of these bits (or cores), using a suitable form of coding (just as in the Morse code), can represent decimal digits or alphabetic characters. The cores are strung on a rectangular mesh, or matrix, of wires. Each core is located at the intersection of a vertical and a horizontal wire, and a third wire (the read-out wire) passes through all the cores (Fig. 6).

A three-dimensional block of core storage is made up of a number of two-dimensional planes, arranged in such a way that the group of bits representing a character can be written magnetically and later read when required.

Core storage works on the principle of permanent electromagnetism. If sufficient current is passed along a wire running through a core, magnetism is induced in a sense (direction) related to the direction of the current (clockwise or counter-clockwise). A core will retain its magnetism indefinitely until a reverse current passes along the wire, when the sense of magnetization will be reversed. By sending a pulse of current along the appropriate wires for a given address, the data or instruction held in that address will be transmitted along the "read" wires for routing to another part of the system.

2. *The arithmetic and logic unit*. This is obviously the part of the machine simplest to understand. It is where actual arithmetic operations are carried out. It

is quite common to find a machine that can add a pair of eight-digit numbers in about ten millionths of a second, and there are models that can do the job in one millionth of a second or even much less!

The term "logic" is used here to describe a nonarithmetic facility of the unit; i.e., its ability to differentiate between positive and negative numbers, and as a result, to take alternative paths in the program. A simple example will easily illustrate its value.

In stock control it is usual to compare a newly calculated stock balance with the preset minimum or danger level, to determine if reordering is necessary. If the "minimum" is subtracted from the "balance," then a positive (excess) result indicates that all is well; a negative result (a shortage) shows a need to reorder. In this latter case only, we can arrange for the machine to jump to a part of the program that prints out reordering information on the printer for management action. If all is well, we need print nothing—one way in which the computer itself can reduce paperwork. This apparently simple facility is of fundamental significance, and a typical program of a few thousand instructions will contain many of the "test and jump to another phase of the program if negative" type of instruction.

The arithmetic and logic unit consists of one or a number of *registers* (each made up of electronic circuits), which may be termed "accumulators." To add a number stored in address 113 of the memory to that stored in address 207, first the contents of address 113 are read into the accumulator and then the contents of address 207 are added into the accumulator. The answer is then read out to another address in memory, thereby leaving the accumulator free for the next operation.

3. *The control unit.* This part of the central processor functions so as to cause the whole machine to operate according to the instructions in the program. Instructions are normally transferred sequentially from the memory to the control unit, where each instruction is interpreted and the appropriate circuits are activated to "execute" the instruction. This strict sequence is broken, for example, when a "test and jump" type of instruction occurs and produces an exceptional result. There is then a "transfer of control" to a program step in a different part of the program, from which the sequential pattern continues until again broken.

The control unit of a computer contains special circuits known as "microprograms." One of these corresponds to each type of elementary operation (and therefore to each type of instruction) in the computer repertoire. It is by the inclusion of a suitable microprogram that a given operation is "built" into the computer.

OUTPUT. The output devices of the computer enable it to communicate results to the outside world. Output form falls into two main categories:

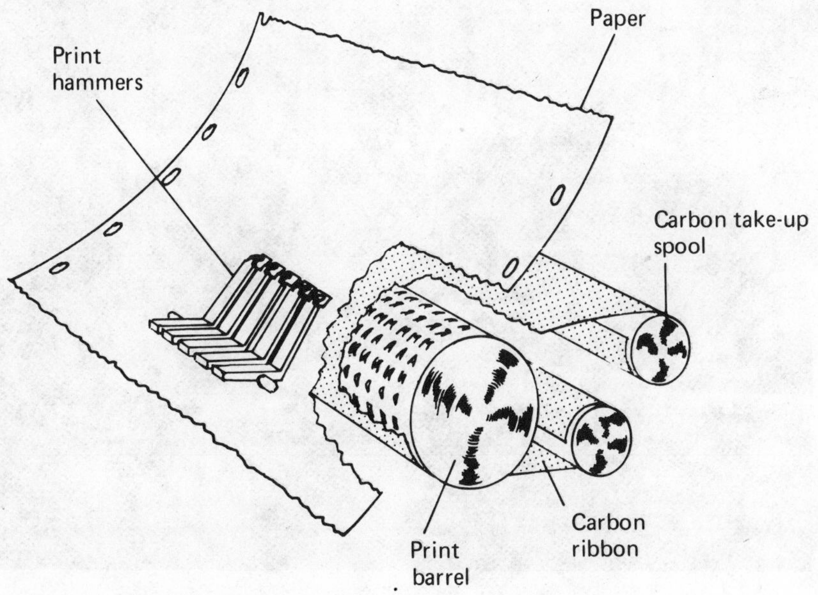


**Fig. 7.** A line printer (barrel type).

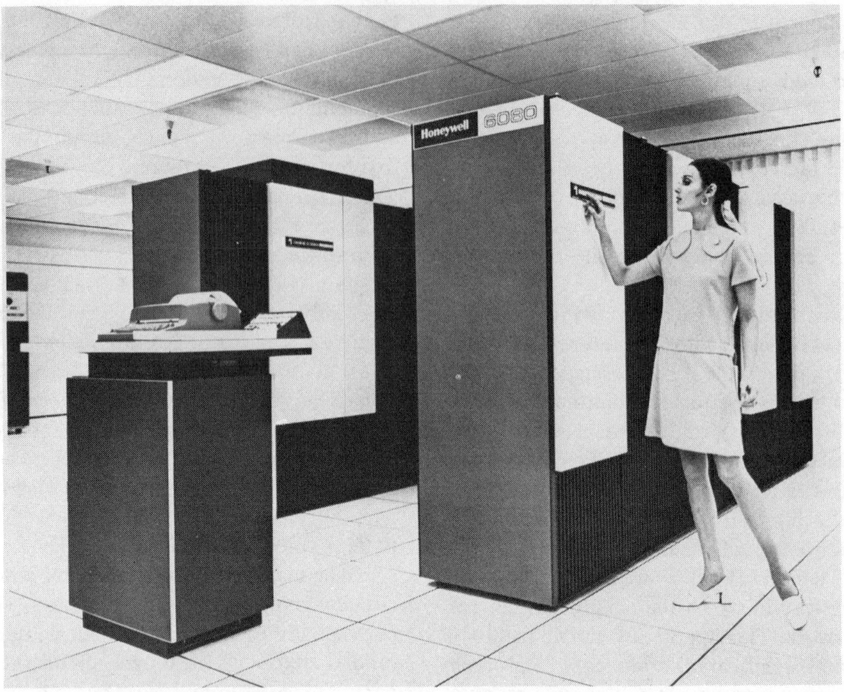


**Fig. 8.** Console typewriter for Honeywell 6080 computer system.

**Fig. 9.** Honeywell 775 cathode-ray tube display terminal.

1. Readily handled and understood by human beings (printers and display units).

2. Intended for further processing by machine (tapes and cards).

The first group contains a number of types of devices. The most obvious of these are printers, designed to produce results in the form of printing on paper.

1. *Printers and display units.* Most printers in current use operate on the same basic principle as the typewriter, in which a character is printed through an impact of a type face on an inked ribbon traversing the paper. There are, however, some printers that generate and print characters electronically.

Where the volume of printing is large, it is usual to use a "line printer," one capable of producing a whole line of print at a time (usually from 120 to 160 characters). Such printers are capable of quite high speeds, typically up to 20 or more lines per second on a continuously fed roll of stationery. It is essential, of course, to have excellent paper-handling facilities to keep pace with such speeds. Such line printers (Fig. 7) are ideal for applications requiring voluminous end-results such as payrolls, or invoices, or inventory listings, but are too often used to print more than necessary. Typewriter-like devices (Fig. 8) are extensively used for such low-volume printed output, and their keyboards permit them to double as input units as well. These devices may be situated close to the computer or at a remote point, receiving the output messages over a telephone line.

A related device, which is becoming increasingly common, is the video-display unit (Fig. 9). This has a keyboard like a typewriter, but the printing mechanism is replaced by a television-like tube on which letters or digits can be projected. Compared with the typewriter, they have the advantage of displaying a large amount of information at once (often several hundred characters), and a fresh display of additional information can be generated very rapidly. On the other hand, they cannot produce "hard copy" or a permanent record. Therefore, they are best used in circumstances where an operator needs to examine a quantity of output information that does not have to be printed.

Video-display units can also be used to display information in graphical form and also diagrams of moderate accuracy. Associated input techniques using a lightpen (a device that effectively draws lines electronically on the face of the tube) manipulate changes or additions to drawings and diagrams. Devices such as the lightpen are increasingly being used for computer-aided design in such fields as car body or electric-circuit design.

Where a permanent record of a graph or drawing is required, or where greater accuracy is needed, a graph-plotter (Fig. 10) can be attached to the computer and can produce intricate drawings on paper.

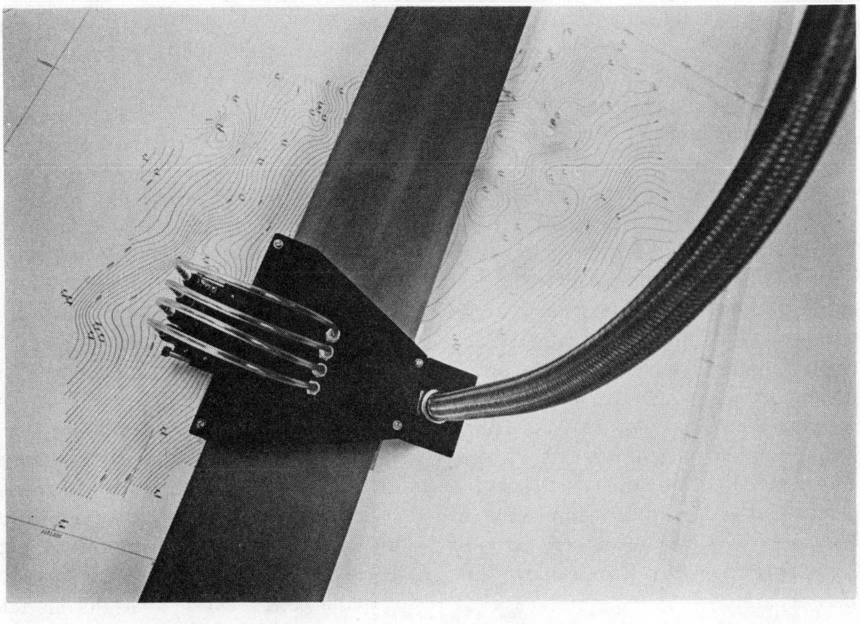

**Fig. 10.** Map being plotted by a flatbed plotter.

2. *Tape and card media.* This second group of output devices produces results in a form for further processing. These include paper tape and card punches. Paper tape can be used for transmission of results over a teleprinter network or as the instructing medium for a numerically controlled machine tool. Punched cards can be interpreted (i.e., the characters represented by the holes can also be printed on the face of the card) and used as documents in their own right; for example, as job tickets or checks. They then provide a means of automatic repetitive input without key punching. This is an example of the "turnaround" document; i.e., a document produced by the computer, readable by a human being, and providing an automatic re-input medium to the machine. With the increasing availability of document readers, output documents printed in an appropriate type face can subsequently be used for input and also serve as "turnaround" documents.

Output data may also be recorded on magnetic tape and used for much the same purposes as paper tape. The principal differences, apart from the method of recording, are that magnetic tape operates at much higher speeds than the paper variety and is also much more expensive. A much more important role of magnetic tape is its role in providing a connecting link for carrying forward the results from one process which are to be the raw material for a subsequent process. Process A, for example, may well produce payroll information that will be subsequently used as input to Process B for a labor cost analysis. A special and vitally important aspect of this type of use is dealt with in the next section, "File Storage."

FILE STORAGE (OR AUXILIARY MEMORY). There are relatively few applications of computers, particularly in the field of business data processing, where the only input is fresh, raw data. For example, in inventory control the new data consists of stock issues and receipts, but data in file storage indicates the number of items left in stock calculated at last inventory and the average value of that stock. These files include more static information about each item, such as its name, dimensions, batch order, quantity, and supplier.

Thus, the computer must also have its "filing cabinets" (albeit electronic ones) if it is to be used in business applications. It is obvious that such file storage units must act as input and output units to the computer, and as they are of special and fundamental importance in these applications, they are treated here separately.

The three most important factors relating to any filing system, whether manual or electronic, are (1) its total capacity, (2) the speed of access to required information—i.e., how long it takes to find what is needed, and (3) the cost per unit of data. The two most commonly used media for holding computer files are magnetic tapes and magnetic disks. Each system has its advantages and disadvantages, and the choice depends on particular circumstances; many installations indeed use both.

### Storage Media

DATA ON TAPES OR DISKS. The different facilities provided by tape and disk give rise to two different philosophies of data processing: "serial access" or "batch" processing using magnetic tape, and "direct access" processing using magnetic disks.

*Magnetic Tape.* Records are held on tape in a serial fashion in a fashion analogous to a tape recorder. Thus, if the records are in no particular sequence, the user is forced to hunt backward and forward along the tape for any desired record. Although tape moves quite quickly on a computer tape unit (up to 12 ft or so per second), a reel of tape is usually 2,400 ft long and contains many thousands of records. (A 1-in. length of tape can accommodate up to 800 or more characters.) Thus, minutes could easily elapse between the location of succeeding required records. It is obvious, therefore, that the records in a magnetic tape file must be held in some predetermined sequence, such as employee-number or customer-number sequence, and that the new data being input in order to bring the file up to date (to "update" the file) must also be in the same sequence.

When used for file storage, magnetic tape units (Fig. 11) are generally operated in pairs: one carrying the brought-forward or current file, which is read by the machine; the other, a new carry-forward or updated file recorded or "written" by the machine, which in turn will become the brought-forward file when the job is next run. (Unaffected items on the brought-forward tape are obviously copied unchanged onto the carried-forward tape.)

Magnetic tape units (or decks, or transports, or stations) differ widely in performance (and price!), with reading and writing speeds varying from about 10,000 characters per second, through a common speed of about 60,000 characters per second, to a maximum speed of over 300,000 characters per second. Obviously, a tape system offers unlimited file capacity at low cost per record, but it is not an acceptable medium when immediate random access is required to every item in the file. A typical magnetic tape deck arrangement is shown in Fig. 12.

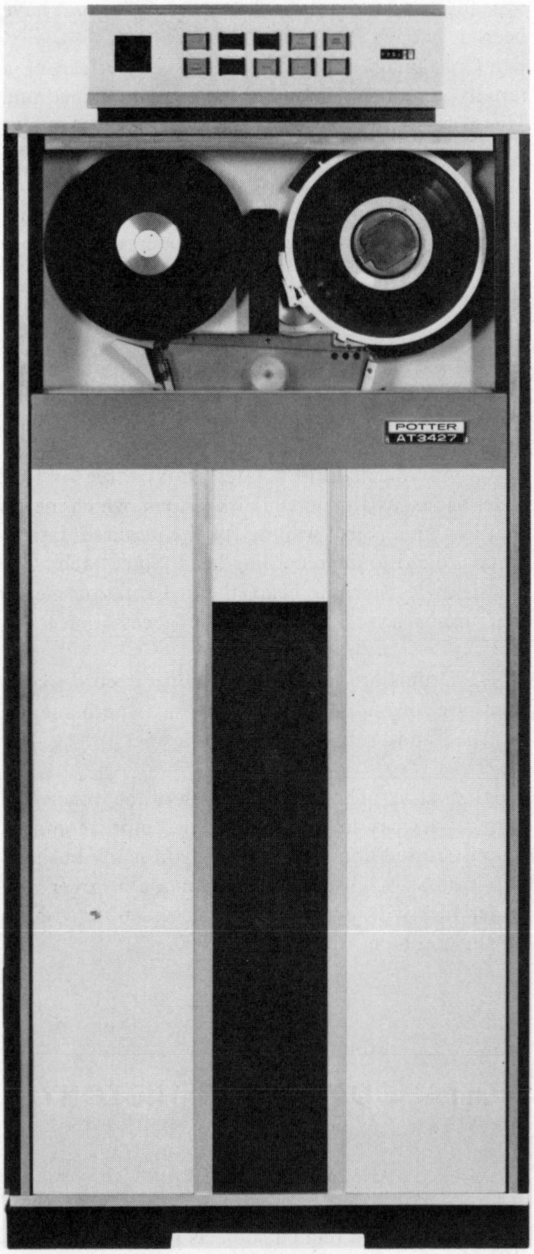


**Fig. 11.** Potter magnetic tape unit.

*Magnetic Disks.* There are two basic forms of the disk unit: In one the disks are usually large (over 3 ft in diameter) and are not removable from the unit; in the other, the "exchangeable disk," or "disk pack," system (Fig. 13) the disks are smaller (about 20 in. in diameter) and are demountable, usually in sets of 6 to 12. This is analogous to putting six phonograph records on a player that is equipped with one pickup for each of the surfaces of the set. (Computers can "play" their disks on both sides without inverting them!)

Unlike the phonograph record, which has one track spiraling from the periphery toward the center, the computer disk has a large number of concentric tracks on its surface, each capable of storing about 4,000 characters. The pickup, or "recording head" can be moved radially across the disk surface to the desired track at very high speed. The total capacity of a set of six exchangeable disks (Fig. 14) is usually between four and eight million characters, and the recording head can move from one track to any other so quickly that direct access to any record at random can be obtained in about one-tenth of a second, or even less in some cases.

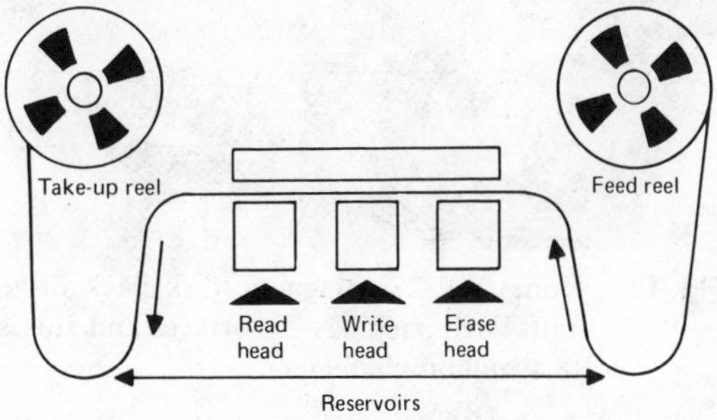


**Fig. 12.** Magnetic tape deck arrangement.

Thus, disks offer the facility of processing data in random sequence without any undue delay in searching for a required item. However, their capacity is much more limited than magnetic tape and their cost is higher. In addition, the fact that essentially random access is possible means that, in contrast to magnetic tapes, data can be corrected or changed and the modified record can be put back on the disk in the same place that it originally occupied. One disadvantage is that the modified data could create an overflow problem, and then a way must be found to correct it.

There are many facets to the problem of choosing between tape and disk for file storage. The simplest basis for choosing one over the other is that tape methods are in general cheaper, whereas disk systems offer greater speed and flexibility in the processing method, especially where the files must be frequently interrogated. Obviously, the choice depends on the application.

Magnetic Drums. Another medium (although less important than tape or disk) used for file storage is the magnetic drum. Historically, it is interesting to

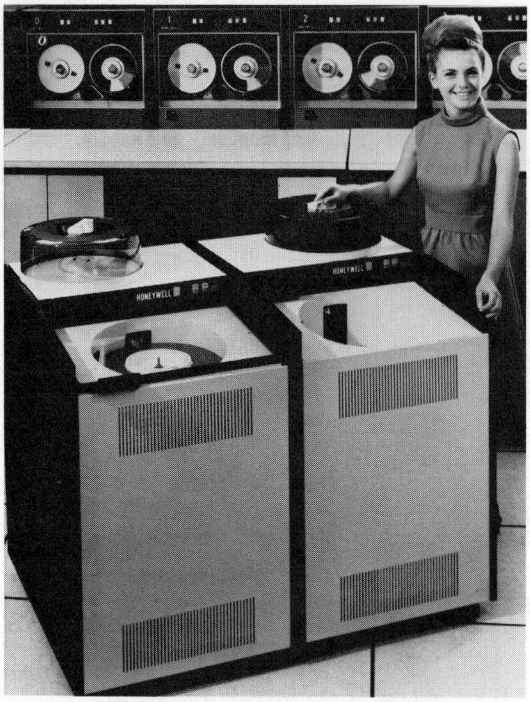


**Fig. 13.** Honeywell 273 magnetic disk pack drive unit. Each pack has 20 surfaces and stores 18.4 million characters.

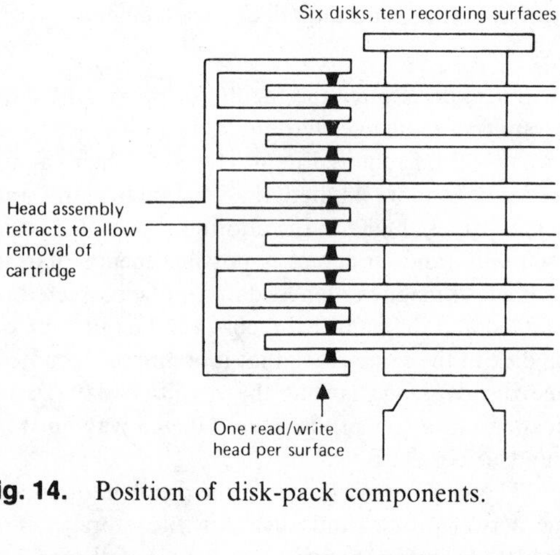


**Fig. 14.** Position of disk-pack components.

note that in early computers a magnetic drum frequently provided the main memory. Its speed of access, however, was such that other processing units were frequently kept waiting for instructions and data, so it was replaced in favor by magnetic core storage.

However, this inherent limitation does not affects its use as a file store, now that drums of large capacity (up to 8 million characters and more) have been developed.

On a magnetic drum the curved surface of a rapidly rotating cylinder is the recording medium. There are a large number of magnetic heads, each of which can read and write data on the drum. Each head is associated with a specific recording track that extends around the circumference of the drum. In many respects the principles of operation and use of the magnetic drum are similar to those for the magnetic disk, but there are the following important differences:

1. Since there is usually a recording head for every track, no time is lost in the physical movement of heads to a required track.
2. A typical drum rotates about three or four times as fast as a magnetic disk system, which means that less time is lost waiting for the required data to come around to the recording head. Since each track has its own recording head, the fast rotation means that drums have a much shorter access time than disks.
3. Drums are more expensive per record stored than are disks. Moreover, they are permanently attached and are not exchangeable.

GENERAL. There are a variety of other file storage devices in addition to the more common ones discussed above. The struggle in many business applications is always to accommodate larger and larger files with an acceptable access time without paying too high a price.

G. J. MORRIS

# DIGITAL COMPUTERS: HISTORY

## ORIGINS

For articles on related subjects *see* DIGITAL COMPUTERS: Contemporary and Future, and Early; MANUFACTURERS, COMPUTER; and STORED PROGRAM CONCEPT.

For articles on related terms and biographical information *see* AIKEN, HOWARD; BABBAGE, CHARLES; ECKERT, J. PRESPER; EDVAC; ENIAC; HOLLERITH, HERMAN; LEIBNIZ, GOTTFRIED WILHELM; MARK I; MAUCHLY, JOHN W.; PASCAL, BLAISE; TURING, ALAN; VON NEUMANN, JOHN; and ZUSE, KONRAD.

Mechanical aids to calculation and mechanical sequence-control devices were perhaps the earliest and most important achievements in the development of computer technology.

The first adding machines date from the early seventeenth century, the most famous of which was invented by the French scientist and philosopher Blaise Pascal, although it is now believed that his work was predated by that of William Schickard. A number of Pascal's machines, which he started to build in 1642, still exist. Even though he had intended them for practical use, their unreliability caused them to be treated mainly as objects of scientific curiosity. During the subsequent two centuries, numerous attempts to develop practical calculating machines were made by Morland, Leibniz, Mahon, Hahn, and Müller, among others. However, it was not until the mid-nineteenth century that a commercially successful machine was produced. This was the "arithmometer" of Thomas de Colmar, the first version of which was invented in 1820, and which used the stepped-wheel mechanism invented by Leibniz.

Mechanical devices for controlling the sequencing of a set of operations, such as the rotating pegged cylinders still seen in music boxes today, date back even earlier. For example, de Caus (1576–1626) used such a mechanism to control both the playing of an organ and the movements of model figures. One of the most famous designers of mechanical automata was Vaucanson. In 1736 he successfully demonstrated an automaton that simulated human lip and finger movements with sufficient accuracy to play a flute. Vaucanson was also involved in the development of what came to be known as the Jacquard loom, in which the woven pattern was specified and controlled by a sequence of perforated cards. The original idea can be traced back to Bouchon in 1725, but such automatic looms did not come into widespread use until early in the nineteenth century after the work by Jacquard.

In 1834 these two lines of development came together in the work of Charles Babbage, who had become dissatisfied with the accuracy of printed mathematical tables. Earlier, in 1822, Babbage had built a small machine, involving several linked adding mechanisms, which would automatically generate successive values of simple algebraic functions, using the method of finite differences. His attempt at making a full-scale model with a printing mechanism was abandoned in 1834, and he then started to design a more versatile machine. In the space of a few years he had developed the concept of a program-controlled, mechanical, digital computer, incorporating a complete arithmetic unit, store, punched-card input and output, and printing mechanism. The machine, which he called an analytical engine, was to have been controlled by programs represented by sets of Jacquard cards, with conditional jumps and iteration loops being provided for by devices that skipped forward or backward over the required number of cards. Internally, the machine was essentially microprogrammed by rotating pegged cylinders that controlled the sequencing of subsidiary mechanisms.

Babbage's work inspired several other people, among whom were Ludgate, who designed an analytical engine in Ireland in 1909; Torres y Quevedo, who, demonstrated the feasibility of an electromechanical analytical engine by successfully producing a typewriter-controlled calculating machine in 1920; and Couffignal, who started to design a binary analytical engine in France during the 1930s. However, Babbage's pioneering efforts were apparently unknown to most of the people who worked on the various computer projects during World War II and who were unaware that the problems they were tackling had been considered and often solved by Babbage more than a hundred years earlier.

The Jacquard loom was perhaps the source of Herman Hollerith's idea of using punched cards to represent logical and numerical data, developed for use in the 1890 U.S. National Census. His system, incorporating hand-operated tabulating machines and sorters, was highly successful and spread rapidly to several other countries. Automatic card-feed mechanisms were soon provided, and the system began to be used for business accounting applications. Following a dispute with Hollerith, the Bureau of the Census developed in time for the 1910 Census a new tabulating system involving mechanical sensing of card perforations, as opposed to Hollerith's system of electrical sensing. James Powers, the engineer in charge of this work, eventually left the Bureau to form his own company, which eventually became part of Remington Rand. Hollerith's company merged with two others to become the Computing-Tabulating-Recording Company, which in 1924 changed its name to the International Business Machines Corporation.

In 1937 Howard Aiken of Harvard University approached IBM with a proposal for a large-scale calculator, to be built from the mechanical and electromechanical devices that were used for punched-card machines. The resulting machine, the Automatic Sequence Controlled Calculator, or Harvard Mark I, was built at the IBM Development Laboratories at Endicott. The machine, which was completed in 1943, was a huge affair with 72 decimal accumulators, capable of multiplying two 23-digit numbers in 6 sec. It was controlled by a sequence of instructions specified by a perforated paper tape; somewhat surprisingly, in view of Aiken's knowledge of and respect for Babbage's efforts, it lacked general conditional jump facilities. After completion of the Mark I, Aiken and IBM pursued separate paths. Several more machines were designed at Harvard, the first being another tape-controlled calculator, built this time from electromagnetic relays. IBM produced various machines, including several plug-board-controlled relay calculators and the partly electronic Selective Sequence Electronic Calculator, which was very much in the tradition of the original Mark I.

Not until well after World War II was it found that in Germany there had been an operational program-controlled calculator built earlier than the Mark I, namely, Konrad Zuse's Z3 machine, which first worked in 1941. This machine, which had been preceded by two earlier but unsuccessful machines, had a mechanical store, but was otherwise built from telephone relays. It could store 64 floating-point binary numbers, and has been described as somewhat faster than the Harvard Mark I. The Z3, like several other machines built by Zuse, did not survive the war; the only one of Zuse's machines to do so was the Z4 computer, which was later used successfully for several years at the Technische Hochschule in Zurich.

Various other electromechanical machines were built during and even after World War II, including an important series of relay calculators at the Bell Telephone Laboratories. The first of these, the Complex Computer, was demonstrated in September 1940 by being operated in its New York City location from a teletypewriter installed in Hanover, New Hampshire, on the occasion of a meeting of the American Mathematical Society. The Complex Computer, or Model 1, was capable of adding, subtracting, multiplying, and dividing two complex numbers, but lacked any sequence-control facilities. Later machines in the series incorporated successively more extensive sequencing facilities, so that the Model 5 relay calculator was a truly general-purpose (tape controlled) computer that achieved very high reliability of operation.

The earliest known electronic digital calculating device was a machine for solving up to 30 simultaneous linear equations, initiated in 1938 at Iowa State College by John Atanasoff and Clifford Berry. Although the arithmetic unit had been successfully tested before the project was abandoned in 1942, the input/output mechanism was still incomplete, so the machine never saw actual use. Other important work on the development of electronic calculating devices was done at IBM, starting in 1942 with the building of experimental versions of various punched-card machines, including a multiplier. This machine was the origin of the electronic multipliers and calculating machines, such as the Type 604 and the Card Programmed Calculator (CPC), which IBM produced in great quantities in the years immediately following World War II and which played an important role until stored program electronic computers became widely available.

The earliest known efforts at applying electronics to a general-purpose, program-controlled computer were those undertaken by Schreyer and Zuse in 1939, but their plans for a 1,500 valve machine were later rejected by the German government. In Britain, a series of large special-purpose electronic computers, intended for code-breaking purposes, was developed by a team at Bletchley Park, with which Alan Turing was associated. The first of these machines, which incorporated about 2000 tubes, was operating in December 1943. It has been described as being, in a very limited fashion, a program-controlled device. Interestingly enough, several postwar British electronic computers were developed by people who had been involved with these secret machines.

However, by far the most influential line of development was that carried out at the Moore School of Electrical Engineering at the University of Pennsylvania by John Mauchly, J. Presper Eckert, and their colleagues, starting in 1943. This work, which derived at least as directly from Vannevar Bush's prewar mechanical differential analyzer as from any digital calculating device, first led to the development of the ENIAC, which was officially inaugurated in February 1946. This machine was intended primarily for ballistics calculations, but by the time it was completed, it was really a general-purpose device, programmed by means of pluggable interconnections. Its internal electronic memory consisted of 20 accumulators, each of 10 decimal digits, and it could perform 5,000 arithmetic operations per second—it was approximately a thousand times faster than the Harvard Mark I. The ENIAC was very much the most complex piece of electronic equipment that had ever been assembled, incorporating 19,000 tubes, and using nearly 200 kW of power. The machine was very successful, despite earlier fears regarding the reliability of electronic components.

However, even before the ENIAC was com-

**Fig. 1.** Family tree of computers to mid-1950s. (Courtesy of the Smithsonian Institution.)

plete, the designers, who had been joined by John von Neumann, started to plan a radically different successor machine, the EDVAC. The EDVAC was a serial binary machine, far more economical on electronic tubes than ENIAC, which was a decimal machine in which each decimal digit was represented by a ring of ten flip-flops. A second major difference was that EDVAC was to have a very much larger internal memory than ENIAC, based on mercury delay lines. For these reasons, the initial design of EDVAC included only one-tenth of the equipment used in ENIAC, yet provided a hundred times the internal memory capacity.

It was apparently the discussions of the various ways in which the capabilities of ENIAC might be extended, together with the knowledge of the possibility of comparatively large internal memories, that led to realization that sequence-control information could be represented by words held in memory along with the numerical quantities entering into the computation, rather than by some external means such as perforated tape or pluggable interconnections. Thus, EDVAC could retain the great speed of operation that had been achieved by ENIAC, but could avoid the very lengthy setup time, often on the order of a day or more, that had made it impractical to use for other than very extensive calculations. The fact that a program could read and modify portions of itself was heavily utilized, since ideas such as index registers and indirect addresses were still in the offing. Of more lasting significance was the practical and attractive proposition of using the computer to assist with the preparation of its own programs.

With EDVAC, therefore, the invention of the modern digital computer was basically complete. The plans for its design were widely published and extremely influential, so that even though it was not the first stored-program electronic digital computer to be put into operation, it undoubtedly was the major initial inspiration that started the vast number of computer projects during the late 1940s.

### References

1961. Morrison, P., and E. Morrison (Eds.). *Charles Babbage and His Calculating Engines: Selected Writings by Charles Babbage and Others*. New York: Dover.

1968. de Beauclair, W. *Rechnen mit Maschinen: Eine Bildgeschichte der Rechentechnik.* Vieweg, Braunschweig.

1969. Rosenberg, J. M. *The Computer Prophets.* New York: Macmillan.
A popular account of the work of many of the computer pioneers.

1972. Goldstine, H. H. *The Computer from Pascal to von Neumann.* Princeton: Princeton University Press.

1973. Randell, B. (Ed.). *The Origins of Digital Computers.* Berlin: Springer.

B. RANDELL

## EARLY

For articles on related subjects *see* DIGITAL COMPUTERS, Contemporary and Future, and Early; MANUFACTURERS, COMPUTER; and STORED PROGRAM CONCEPT.

For articles on related terms *see* AIKEN, HOWARD; ECKERT, J. PRESPER; EDSAC; EDVAC; ENIAC; MARK I; MAUCHLY, JOHN W.; READ-ONLY STORE; REGISTER; TURING, ALAN; ULTRASONIC MEMORY; UNIVAC I; VON NEUMANN, JOHN; WHIRLWIND; and ZUSE, KONRAD.

The digital computer age began when the Automatic Sequence Controlled Calculator (Harvard Mark I) started working in August 1944. This machine was based on the mechanical technology of rotating shafts, electromagnetic clutches, and counter wheels, developed over the years for punched card tabulating machinery. It was constructed by IBM, following the ideas of Howard Aiken, whose original proposals go back at least to 1937. The shaft rotation period, and hence the time required to transfer a number or perform an addition, was 0.3 sec, while multiplication and division took 6 and 11.4 sec, respectively.

No other large machines using rotating shafts were built, but there were a number of successful magnetic relay machines. Bell Telephone Laboratories had been working in this area since 1938. Their first fully automatic computer was the one now referred to as the Bell Model V (Fig. 1), of which two examples were constructed. The first of these began to work at the end of 1946. An addition took 0.3 sec and multiplication and division took up to 1.0 and 2.2 sec, respectively. The last of the series was the Model VI, commissioned in 1949. Harvard Mark II, a relay machine designed by Aiken and following a very different design philosophy, was running in September 1948. A relay computer constructed in Sweden (BARK) was operational early in 1950. Independent work on relay computers had also been done by K. Zuse in Germany, and a Zuse Z4 was running in Zurich in 1950. Relays lend themselves to complex circuit arrangements, and all the machines just mentioned had floating-point arithmetic operation, a feature that did not appear in electronic computers until well after the period now under review here. The Bell machines had elaborate checking arrangements, including a redundant representation for stored numbers. Model VI even had a re-try feature, designed to mitigate the effect of transient relay faults.

The concept of the large-scale electronic computer is due to J. Presper Eckert and John W. Mauchly. They were already building the ENIAC when the Harvard Mark I was commissioned. The ENIAC contained nearly 19,000 vacuum tubes, more than twice as many as any later vacuum-tube computer. Because it was by far the most complex machine constructed up to that time, its construction was a great act of technological courage, both on the part of the designers and of the Moore School of Electrical Engineering in Philadelphia where it was constructed. The ENIAC began to function in the summer of 1945. An addition took 200 $\mu$s and a multiplication took 2.8 ms.

The very early computers were extremely limited in the amount of internal storage that they had. Provision was usually made for tables to be held in read-only storage (banks of switches or punched paper tape) with arrangements for interpolation. It was frequently possible for the programmer to arrange that more than one arithmetic or transfer operation should take place at the same time. The ENIAC was programmed by setting up hundreds of plugs and sockets and switches, an operation that could take several hours. The other computers read their instructions from punched paper tape, endless loops being used for repeated sections of the program.

While the ENIAC was still under construction, Eckert and Mauchly began to realize that, by the application of logical principles, it would be possible to construct a machine not only much more powerful than the ENIAC but also much smaller. They were joined by John von Neumann on a part-time

**Fig. 1.** The second Bell Model V relay calculator installed at Aberdeen Proving Ground. The first was installed at Langley Field, Virginia.

basis, and it was from the group so formed that the ideas of the modern stored-program computer emerged. They were summarized in a document entitled "First draft of a report on the EDVAC," prepared by von Neumann and dated June 30, 1945.

Eckert and Mauchly did not stay at the Moore School to work on the EDVAC, and it was not until January 1952 that a machine bearing that name was commissioned. Instead, they founded the Eckert-Mauchly Corporation, with the object of designing and marketing the UNIVAC. This company was finally absorbed into Remington Rand, but the name UNIVAC has happily survived.

From the beginning the UNIVAC was designed with an eye to business data processing, and the standards set for performance and reliability were very high. In March 1951, the first UNIVAC passed a rigorous acceptance test and was delivered to the U.S. Bureau of Census. It was then a fully engineered machine, with magnetic tape and other peripherals required for large-scale business operations. The Eckert-Mauchly Corporation had demonstrated a smaller machine, the BINAC (Fig. 2), in August 1949, but this was not very successful and they decided to concentrate their efforts on the UNIVAC.

When the Moore School group broke up, von Neumann established at the Institute for Advanced Study, Princeton, a project for the construction of a computer. Von Neumann himself, assisted by H. H. Goldstine, laid down the logical structure of this computer, and the engineering development and design was in the hands of J. H. Bigelow. It was the first parallel computer to be designed, and it introduced techniques that are now commonplace, such as the register economizing device of putting the

**Fig. 2.** The BINAC computer.

**Table 1.** Characteristics of electronic computers (as of early 1951)

| Computer | Serial or Parallel | Decimal or Binary | No. of Addresses | Word length | Clock frequency KH | Memory Type | Memory No. of Words |
|---|---|---|---|---|---|---|---|
| EDVAC[(b)] | S | B | 3 + 1[(d)] | 44 bits | 1,000 | U | 1,024 |
| UNIVAC | S | D | 1 | 12 char. | 2,250 | U | 1,000 |
| IAS[(b)] | P | B | 1 | 40 bits | Asynch. | W | 1,024 |
| EDSAC | S | B | 1 | 35 bits | 500 | U | 512 |
| Ferranti I | S | B | 1 | 40 bits | 100 | W | 256 |
| Pilot ACE | S | B | –[(d)] | 32 bits | 1,000 | U | 360 |
| SEAC | S | B | 3 | 45 bits | 1,000 | U | 512 |
| SWAC | P | B | 4 | 36 bits | 125 | W | 256 |
| Whirlwind I | P | B | 1 | 16 bits | 1,000 | E | 256 |
| Harvard Mark III | S/P | D | 3 | 16 dec. | 28 | D | 4,000[(c)] |
| Burroughs | S | D | 1 or 1 + 1[(d)] | 9 dec. | 125 | D | 800 |
| ERA 1101 | P | B | 1 + 1[(d)] | 24 bits | 400 | D | 16,384 |

Notes: (a) U = ultrasonic delay (mercury tank); W = Williams tube; D = magnetic drum; E = electrostatic (CRT)
(b) Not commissioned until 1952.
(c) Separate 200-word memory for instructions.
(d) Provision for minimum-access coding.

**Fig. 3.** The Ferranti Mark I computer at Manchester University, 1951.

| Max. Memory Access, (time ms) | Operation Time (incl. access) Add, ms | Mult., ms | Divide ms | Input Output | No. of Tubes | No. of Diodes (germanium) | Aux. Memory |
|---|---|---|---|---|---|---|---|
| 0.38 | 0.2–1.5 | 2.2–3.5 | 2.2–3.6 | Paper tape | 3,600 | 10,000 | – |
| 0.40 | 0.5 mean | 2.15 mean | 3.9 mean | Magn. tape | 5,600 | 18,000 | Magn. tape |
| 0.025 | 0.062 | 0.44–1.0 | 1.1 | Cards | 2,300 | 0 | – |
| 1.1 | 1.5 mean | 6 mean | – | Paper tape | 3,800 | 0 | – |
| 0.64 | 1.2 | 3.36 | – | Paper tape | 3,800 | 0 | Drum, 16K |
| 1.0 | – | 2 | – | Cards | 800 | – | – |
| 0.38 | 1.5 max. | 3.6 max. | 3.6 max. | Paper tape | 1,300 | 15,800 | Magn. tape |
| – | 0.064 | 0.38 | – | Paper tape; cards | 2,300 | 3,000 | – |
| 0.016 | 0.049 | 0.061 | 0.1 | Paper tape | 6,800 | 22,000 | – |
| 4.5 | 5 | 13 | 100 | Magn. tape | 5,000 | 1,300 | – |
| 32 | 0.6–17 | 30–50 | – | Paper tape | 3,271 | 6,773 | – |
| 17 | 0.1 min. | 0.35 min. | 0.42 min. | Paper tape | 2,200 | 3,000 | – |

multiplier in the tail of the accumulator and shifting it out as the multiplication proceeds. Although the machine was not working until October 1952, the project had immense influence on the development of the digital computer field. The ultrasonic memory, which had been proposed for the EDVAC, was thought to be too slow for a parallel machine, and it was planned to use instead a memory based on the Selectron proposed by J. A. Rajchman. The Selectron did not fulfill its promise, but fortunately the Williams tube memory came along in time to save the situation.

The experimental computers that came into action first were those that were least ambitious, both in specification and in performance. One of these was the EDSAC, a computer directly inspired by the EDVAC, designed and constructed by myself and W. Renwick in Cambridge, England. This computer did its first calculation on May 6, 1949, and was used for much early work on the development of programming techniques. Activity at Manchester University arose out of work by F. C. Williams on what became known as the Williams tube memory. In order to test this system, Williams and T. Kilburn built a small model computer with a memory of 32 words and with 5 instructions in its instruction set. The only arithmetic instruction was for subtraction. Development work continued, and by the summer of 1949 a computer with a magnetic drum as a backing memory was demonstrated. The Ferranti Mark I computer (Fig. 3), of which the first delivered model was inaugurated at Manchester University in July 1951, was based on this work.

A third center of activity in England was at the National Physical Laboratory, where the inspiration came from Alan Turing. Turing did not stay there long, leaving for Manchester University in 1948, but the Pilot ACE, which was running by December 1950, reflected very strongly his rather personal view of computer design. The Pilot ACE used an ultrasonic memory, and it was necessary for the programmer to know more of the structure of the machine and the timing of pulses within it than was required in the case of other machines.

The first of the American machines to be brought into use was the SEAC, dedicated on June 20, 1950. This was built under the direction of S. N. Alexander at the National Bureau of Standards in Washington and the success of that group is the more remarkable since the SEAC project started after many others. The SEAC was elegant in design and construction, and pioneered the use of small plug-in packages; each package contained a number of germanium diodes and a single vacuum tube. The SEAC used an ultrasonic memory, but a Williams tube memory was later added for evaluation purposes. Meanwhile, H. D. Huskey, who had formerly been a member of the team at the National Physical Laboratory in England and had worked on ENIAC, was completing the SWAC at the NBS Institute for Numerical Analysis at UCLA. This was a parallel machine with a Williams tube memory and was very fast by the standards of the day.

Whirlwind I was a computer with a short word length, aiming at very high speed and power, and intended ultimately for air traffic control and similar applications. It was designed and built under the direction of J. W. Forrester at M.I.T. and was operating in December 1950. From its specification, one would take it to be the first of the minicomputers, but in fact it occupied the largest floor area of all the early computers, including the ENIAC. The memory was of the electrostatic type, but the cathode-ray tubes were of special design and operated on a different principle from that used by Williams.

Table 1 gives brief particulars of the computers mentioned above and also of several additional ones that became operational in the same period.

### References

1951. U.S. Navy, Office of Naval Research. *Digital Computer Newsletter*, vols. 1–3.

1953. U.S. Navy, Office of Naval Research. *A Survey of Automatic Digital Computers.*

1972. Goldstine, H. H. *The Computer from Pascal to von Neumann*. Princeton: Princeton University Press.

M. V. Wilkes

## CONTEMPORARY AND FUTURE

For articles on related subjects *see* Digital Computers: Origins of, and Early; Generations, Computer; Manufacturers, Computer; Microcomputer; and Minicomputers.

For articles on related terms *see* Control Data Corporation 6000 Series; IBM 360-370 Series; Integrated Circuitry; Livermore Automatic Research Computer (LARC); Stretch; and UNIVAC I.

The development of digital computers can be conveniently categorized as successive generations.

**The First Generation.** The modern history of computing starts with the invention of the stored program computer. The first generation of electronic computers is characterized by the use of vacuum tubes as active elements. In the first generation a number of storage media were tried for reasons of economy and reliability and the early computers can be classified according to the nature of their main memory system.

MERCURY DELAY LINE STORAGE. Although mercury delay lines were important in a number of early research computers, UNIVAC I was the only computer delivered commercially that used this type of memory. The first UNIVAC I was delivered on June 14, 1951, several years ahead of the delivery of any competitive system. UNIVAC designers felt at that time that mercury-delay line memory was the only memory available that could provide adequate reliability at reasonably high speed. Average access time to the 1,000-word main memory was on the order of 500 $\mu$s. UNIVAC was a completely serial machine with duplicate arithmetic and control circuitry for detection of errors. The relatively low speed was partially compensated for by the use of minimum access-time coding and other sophisticated software devices. UNIVAC I had a number of features that did not become generally available on other computers until years later. These included a buffered tape system that could read tapes both forward and backward.

ELECTROSTATIC STORAGE. Most of the successful electrostatic storage systems were based on the Williams tube developed at Manchester University in England. Typical memories had from 1,000 to 4,000 words with random access times of from 10 to 50 $\mu$s. There is still some question as to whether these memories ever achieved adequate reliability. IBM's 701 (Fig. 1), of which 18 were delivered between 1953 and 1956, was the most important scientific computer that used this type of memory. Remington Rand offered the only competitive computer in this field, the 1103, which it obtained when it absorbed Engineering Research Associates.

IBM used electrostatic storage on its 702, which it started delivering for commercial data processing in 1955. The 702 was the prototype of many later character-oriented computers, but for a number of reasons, including memory problems, it was soon

**Fig. 1.** An IBM 701 system.

withdrawn from the market.

MAGNETIC DRUM STORAGE. Prototype magnetic drum computers included the Harvard Mark III and the ERA 1101. The magnetic drum provided a large amount of slow memory at relatively low cost. The IBM 700 series and the UNIVAC 1103 series used drums as peripheral storage.

Typical drum-storage systems used a drum that rotated at about 3,600 rpm, providing average random access times of about 17 ms. This seems incredibly slow for a main memory by modern standards, but it was the only way to get moderately priced memory in any quantity in the early 1950s. The development of cheap, reliable magnetic drum systems made it possible for many companies to enter the computer field with a rather modest investment. There were literally dozens of magnetic drum computers of varying capacity that were the small-to-medium sized computers of the first generation. Only a few of those that are historically most important will be mentioned here.

Among the magnetic drum computers delivered as early as 1953 were the CADAC 100 series and the Consolidated Engineering Corporation 200 series. The CADAC was produced by the Computer Research Corporation, which was absorbed by National Cash Register Corporation and became the forerunner of other computers in the NCR line. Consolidated Engineering spun off the ElectroData Corporation, which marketed such computers as the Datatron 203, 204, and 205. ElectroData was absorbed by the Burroughs Corporation and became an important part of Burroughs' computer activity.

IBM's 650 (Fig. 2) was introduced a bit later and soon became the most widely used of all first-generation computers. Many hundreds were delivered between 1955 and 1959. The 650 was somewhat faster than most other magnetic drum computers, but the chief reason for its great success was its well-integrated punched-card input and output and its adaptability to existing punched-card systems.

Remington Rand introduced a perhaps too ambitious UNIVAC file computer, a drum-and-tape based data processing system that was not a commercial success. Toward the end of the first generation, the company introduced the UNIVAC 80 and 90, which were reasonably effective competitors for the IBM 650 systems. The use of solid-state components should perhaps place these computers in the second generation, but the solid-state components in the UNIVAC 80 and 90 were magnetic amplifiers, not transistors. At best, these computers belong in a transitional stage between generations.

MAGNETIC CORE MEMORIES. By 1953, both M.I.T. and RCA had developed working models of coincident-current magnetic core memories. Subsequent litigation awarded patent rights to the group at M.I.T., which made the memory design available to the computer industry. RCA developed the Bizmac,

**Fig. 2.** An IBM 650 system.

**Fig. 3.** Datamatic 1000 computer installed at Michigan Blue Cross–Blue Shield, Detroit.

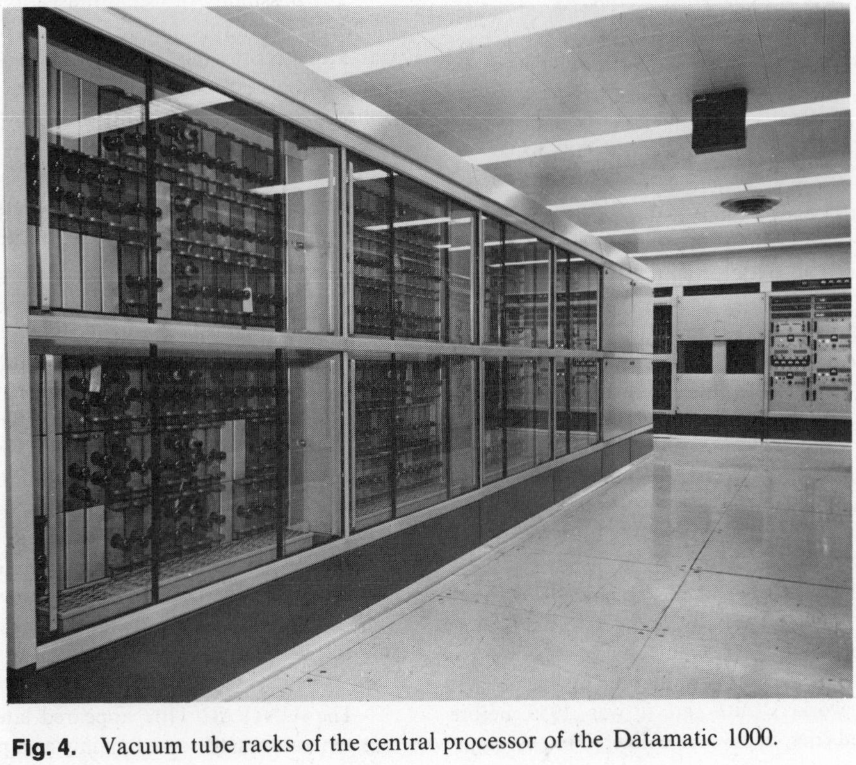

**Fig. 4.** Vacuum tube racks of the central processor of the Datamatic 1000.

a very ambitious commercial data processing system that was unsuccessful for a number of reasons, of which the most obvious was its failure to adequately exploit the capabilities of the magnetic core memory.

IBM moved quickly to adapt the core memory technology to both its scientific and its commercial computer lines, and in 1956 started deliveries on the 704—a very powerful successor to the 701—and the 705, a viable successor to the faltering 702. Core memory was faster and more reliable than the cathode-ray tube memories that were replaced. The hardware floating-point arithmetic and index registers on the 704 and the logical changes that permitted the 705 to work with groups of characters in multiple accumulators, coupled with the development of improved input/output and peripheral devices, made these computers orders of magnitude more powerful than their predecessors.

Remington Rand's UNIVAC divison also quickly absorbed the new magnetic core memory technology and produced the UNIVAC II, which was a compatible extension of UNIVAC I as an upgrade for its data processing customers. The 1103A was the magnetic core upgrade of the Univac Scientific Computer (the 1103), and optional floating-point and interrupt-handling hardware were soon added. The first UNIVAC I had been used to process the voluminous data collected in the 1950 Census. For the 1960 Census, UNIVAC added buffered input/output capacity to its scientific computer, which thus became the UNIVAC 1105. IBM added data channels to provide buffering capabilities to its 704 line, and introduced the 709 just as the first generation was coming to an end.

Other companies were quick to jump on the magnetic core bandwagon. Datamatic Corporation, which later became the computer division of Honeywell, produced a very large computer, the Datamatic 1000 (Figs. 3 and 4), which was used in a very few large data processing applications.

Burroughs produced its 220 system, a medium-size core memory machine that was much more powerful than competitive drum machines, but introduced it too late to have much impact, since its major competition was to come from second-generation machines.

**The Second Generation.** The transistor was invented in 1948, and the advantages of transistors over vacuum tubes for computer applications were recognized almost immediately. There were many technological and production problems that had to be worked out, and it was 1959 before transistorized computers were delivered in any quantity. That year marks the beginning of the second computer generation, in which transistors completely replaced vacuum tubes as the active components of digital computers. All second-generation computers used magnetic core storage systems for main memory. Some of them used magnetic drums and disks in addition to magnetic tapes for auxiliary storage.

LARGE SCIENTIFIC COMPUTERS. Philco Corporation engineers developed the first transistors suitable for really high speed computers. Philco decided to enter the computer field with its own large-scale Transac S-2000 systems, and had moderate success with its Model 211 and later the more powerful 212, but could not generate enough momentum to carry it into the third generation. Philco withdrew from the general-purpose computer field in 1964.

UNIVAC developed one of the first successful, large-scale transistorized computers for military applications, the UNIVAC M460. A group of UNIVAC employees left the company and set up Control Data Corporation, which used the new transistor technology in their 1604 (Fig. 5) computer. The 1604 was followed by a more powerful 3000 series, the 3600 and later the 3800. Control Data established itself as a major supplier of large computers and retained and expanded its position in the third generation.

The possibility of using transistors in very large numbers to produce large and powerful computers was attractive to the Atomic Energy Commission, which sponsored two of the early second-generation projects, Stretch (the IBM 7030) at IBM and Larc at UNIVAC. Both companies tried to market the resulting computers in the early 1960s, but both were unsuccessful because the rapid progress of technology made these early giant computers uneconomical.

IBM produced the 709TX system in 1959 in response to the demand for a transistorized computer for the Ballistic Missile Early Warning System. The 709TX became the 7090, a compatible extension of the first generation 709, designed to run at more than five times the speed of the 709. The 7090, later upgraded to the 7094, dominated the scientific computer market in the period 1960–1964. A similar but slightly less powerful series, the 7040 and 7044 were introduced in 1962–1963. Combinations of the 7040 and 7090 series machines with disk storage formed the direct-coupled systems that were popular from 1964 to 1966 and provided a partial hardware and software prototype of some IBM third-generation systems.

The UNIVAC 1107 appeared late in the second generation and served mainly as a prototype for

**Fig. 5.** CDC 1604-A computer.

**Fig. 6.** NCR 315 system.

the more successful 1108 model in the third generation.

DATA PROCESSING COMPUTERS. Some of the earliest second-generation computers were medium-scale data processing systems. National Cash Register was almost too early with its 304, a joint effort with General Electric. A more successful NCR 315 (Fig. 6) system was introduced in 1962. This system featured an interesting magnetic card cartridge auxiliary memory, CRAM.

The RCA 501 was another of the very early transistorized machines, but had limited performance. It featured one of the very first Cobol compilers. A much more powerful 601 introduced interesting microprogramming features. It was designed primarily for the scientific field, but was not competitive. RCA had most success with its small 301 computer, introduced somewhat later.

IBM introduced its 7070 series in 1960. The 7070 represented a major step up from the first-generation 650 but it did not satisfy the very large number of 705 users. IBM eventually produced the 7080, a large transistorized machine that was compatible with the 705.

Second-generation technology made it possible to build small character-oriented processors at low cost. IBM's 1401, first delivered late in 1960, was the first of a very successful series of such computers. They started out as programmed controllers of input/output devices and developed into full data processing systems, especially when the more powerful 1410 and eventually the 7010 processors were introduced.

Other manufacturers followed with the introduction of small computers in numbers of models too numerous to discuss here.

TRANSITIONAL COMPUTERS. A number of second-generation computers were ahead of their time in introducing features usually associated with the third generation, even though they appeared early in the second generation. The Honeywell 800 introduced an ingenious hardware multiprogramming system along with a very interesting data processing software system, FACT.

The Atlas system, developed jointly by Ferranti and Manchester University in England, introduced the concept of virtual memory implemented through dynamic address translation.

The Burroughs 5000 system introduced a different implementation of virtual memory along with pushdown stacks and other features that help in compilation and in multiprogramming.

**The Third Generation.** Integrated circuits and large-scale integration (LSI) are the most striking technological developments of the current third-generation of computers. However, some very important computers of the third generation make little or no use of integrated circuits. In this discussion, all computers introduced on or after April 7, 1964, will be considered to be third-generation computers, along with several computers introduced earlier whose technology and system design were sufficiently advanced to permit most of their installations to survive into the 1970s.

THE IBM 360 AND 370. April 7, 1964, is the date on which IBM announced its System 360. The 360 was designed to replace all earlier IBM computers, and it represented a very major departure from IBM's second-generation systems. The 360 came in a number of compatible models. The Model 75 at the top of the line used conventional hardware sequencing techniques to implement a large instruction set. The other models (30, 40, 50, 65) used microprogramming in a variety of read-only memory systems to provide the same instruction set on computers with a wide range of memory and circuit speeds. The use of microprogramming in read-only storage also made it possible for these 360 models to run programs written for second-generation IBM computers by emulation, i.e., by hardware-assisted simulation.

Many features of the 360 have become standards in large segments of the computer industry. Among these are the use of eight-bit bytes for the representation of characters and the use of nine-track tapes. Multiple-spindle disk pack systems, first the 2314 and more recently the 3330, were introduced on the 360 and have been adopted, sometimes with variations, on other systems.

The 360 was tremendously successful, and there are many thousands of installations. New models have been introduced at intervals since the initial announcement, including some like the models 20 and 44 that were not quite compatible with the standard 360.

The 360 Model 67 followed shortly after the original 360 announcement, in response to the demand from universities and research laboratories for a large-scale "time-sharing" system. The Model 67 provides dynamic address translation that permits the implementation of "virtual memory" operating systems.

In response to the delivery of the first Control Data 6600 in the fall of 1964, IBM announced a 90 series of a very large and very fast 360. Several of Model 91 and Model 95 were delivered before the series was withdrawn in favor of the Model 85. The

85 introduced the cache, or buffer memory, which provided an automatic multilevel memory system to help match memory speed to the very fast arithmetic speed. The 85 was at the top of the 360 line only very briefly. It was superseded in 1971 by the more powerful 195, which provided a 360 system that was competitive with the CDC 7600 in the scientific computer field.

During 1970, IBM announced its 370 line, which represented a relatively modest step up from the 360. All 360 programs, with a few exceptions, run on the 370. An important feature of the 370 was held back until August 1972, at which time it was revealed that dynamic address translation already existed on the delivered models 135 and 145 and would be standard on new 370 models.

Two new large 370 systems, the 158 and 168, were introduced, whose major difference from the earlier 155 and 165 was the replacement of core memory by faster and much cheaper metal oxide semiconductor (MOS) memories. The MOS large-scale integration technology may very well lead to the rapid obsolescence of magnetic cores in computer memories.

Gene M. Amdahl, one of the designers of IBM's 360 series, left IBM in the fall of 1970 and started a new computer company, Amdahl Corporation. Major financial backing was obtained from Japanese sources. Amdahl's goal was to produce a computer compatible with the IBM 370 series, that would sell at roughly the same price as the Model 168, but would be considerably faster than the 168. The Amdahl computer uses existing IBM 370 software and peripherals. At least one Amdahl 470 V/6 system had been installed by the summer of 1975.

RCA AND UNIVAC. RCA's strategy in the third generation was to accept most features of the IBM 360 as standards for the industry, and to attempt to become an alternate source of supply for users who found that type of equipment attractive. The company introduced the Spectra 70 series whose principal models, the 35 and 45, were designed to fall, respectively, between the IBM 360/30 and 40 models and between the IBM 360/40 and 50. A virtual memory system, the Model 46, was also developed. RCA had only moderate success with the Spectra line, and a series of new virtual memory models introduced in advance of the IBM 370 series met with poor customer response. RCA abruptly departed from the computer business in the fall of 1971, and shortly thereafter Sperry-Rand's UNIVAC Division announced that it would purchase the remnants of RCA's computer division and would provide support for Spectra series installations.

UNIVAC's own entry into the third generation was with the 1108, a compatible extension of its second-generation 1107. The 1108 and its successor in the 1970s, the 1110 (Fig. 7), have made UNIVAC an important factor in the large-scale scientific computer field.

Another important UNIVAC series has been the 400, which has been used in large real-time and control applications.

In the very important small-to-medium scale data processing field, the UNIVAC third-generation 9000 systems followed closely the pattern set by IBM 360 systems. The new models in this line may prove attractive to those of the newly acquired RCA installations that choose to remain with UNIVAC.

CONTROL DATA CORPORATION. The CDC 6000 series easily qualifies as belonging to the third generation, even though the first 6600 was delivered in 1964 and even though the discrete component technology used is more typical of the second generation. For several years after its introduction the 6600 was faster and more powerful than any other computer available, and CDC established a strong position in the large scientific computer field. The speed of the 6600 (estimated by the manufacturer at three million instructions per second) was enhanced by the use of an instruction stack along with multiple arithmetic and logical units. The same system without these features was offered as a lower-priced 6400 system and a multiprocessor 6500 system. All these systems could use a very high speed extended core storage (ECS), a peripheral storage system with transfer rates up to ten million 60-bit words per second.

By 1969, Control Data had delivered its first 7600 system (Fig. 8). The 7000 series provides a good deal of compatibility with the 6000 series at three to seven times the speed of the 6600. Typical Atomic Energy Commission installations use the 6600 as a front-end computer for the faster 7600. Slight upgrades of these machines were marketed in the early 1970s as the CDC Cyber 70 Series. A faster compatible series of computers using integrated circuit technology was introduced as the Cyber 170 Series in 1974.

Another very large computer, the CDC STAR (String Array) 100 was built for Livermore and offered to other customers. The STAR is based on a concept of streaming arrays of data through pipeline arithmetic units at very high rates of speed, and it should prove very effective for some classes of problems. Texas Instruments has developed the Advanced Scientific Computer (ASC), whose size and speed are comparable to the STAR 100 for

**Fig. 7.** Console and CPU of UNIVAC 1110 system.

**Fig. 8.** CDC 7600 system.

(a)

(b)

**Fig. 9.** The Burroughs Corporation B5500(a) and B6700(b) systems.

similar classes of problems.

Control Data has also had reasonable success with the third-generation versions of its 3000 series computers in the small- and medium-size computer field.

Seymour Cray, who was the principal architect of the CDC 6600 and 7600 computers, left Control Data in 1972 to start a new company, Cray Research, Inc. The first product of the company, the Cray-I, is reported to be at least five times as fast as the 7600, with a price roughly the same as the 7600 had when it was first delivered. The first Cray-I was scheduled to be installed at Los Alamos late in 1975.

BURROUGHS. The Burroughs 5000 system was upgraded to the 5500 in 1962. Burroughs introduced a fixed-head disk for system residence and for use in its virtual memory system. Fixed-head disks became an IBM 370 component many years later. During the 1960s Burroughs used the slogan, "Burroughs dares to be different," and its stack organization and use of descriptors for memory addressing were indeed unique in the industry. The 6500 system, announced in 1965, was slow in delivery and in performance, and the very ambitious 8500 never reached completion, but the 6500 was soon replaced by a more capable 6700 and 7700 series. Fig. 9 shows the Burroughs B5500 and B6700 systems.

Meanwhile, Burroughs made great progress with smaller series of computers, the 2500 and 3500, later upgraded to 2700 and 3700. These and the even smaller 1700 series systems have made Burroughs a major factor in the third-generation computer field.

Burroughs also has built the ILLIAC IV, a parallel system based on the use of a large number of synchronized, high-speed arithmetic units. For appropriate problems, the ILLIAC IV is potentially orders of magnitude faster than other computers.

HONEYWELL AND GENERAL ELECTRIC. Honeywell entered the third generation with its 200 computer, which provided upward compatibility with the IBM 1400 series. The 200 grew into a whole series of computers that were very successful in the data processing field.

General Electric's third-generation entry was the 600 series, which provided limited upward compatibility with the IBM 7000 series. GE tried to make a spectacular entry into the large time-sharing computer field with the 645, a computer designed in cooperation with the M.I.T. Multics project, but the IBM 360 Model 67 took away most of that market. GE introduced a 200 and 400 series whose major success was in the time-sharing field. By 1970 it was clear that GE was not making much progress in the computer field, and it sold its computer division to

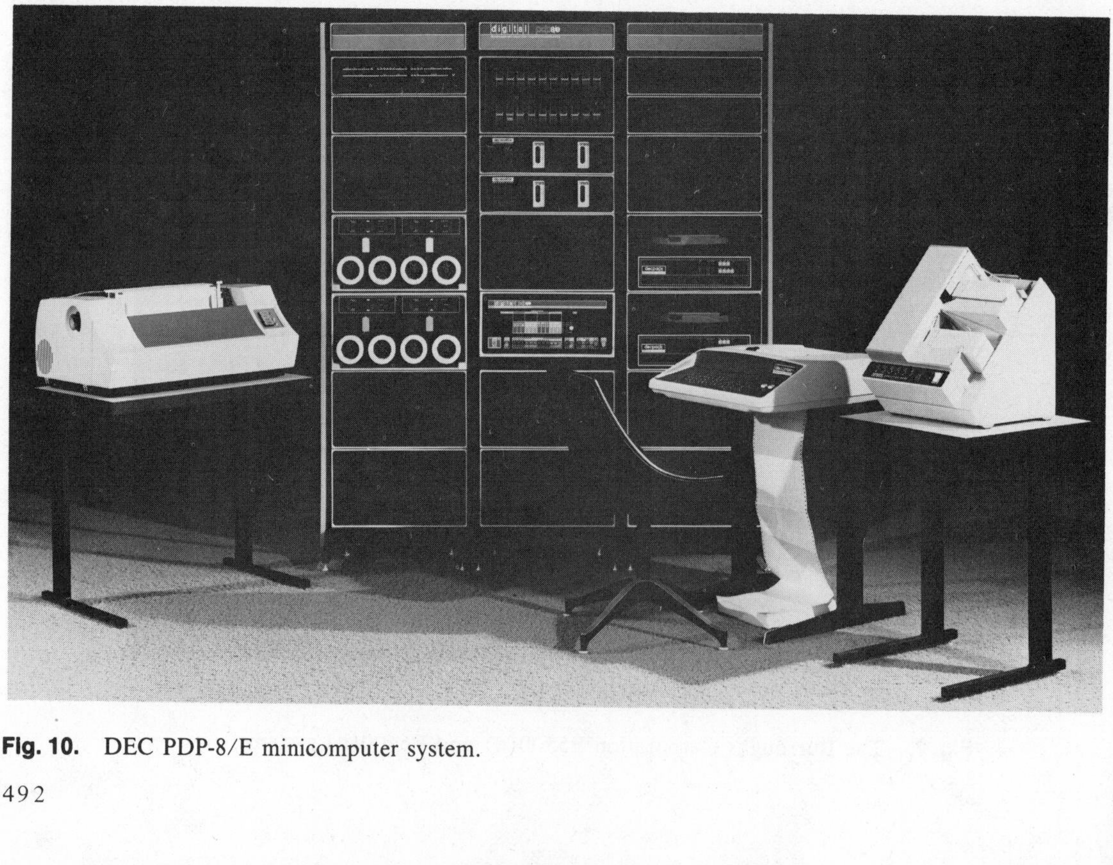


**Fig. 10.** DEC PDP-8/E minicomputer system.

Honeywell. The 600 series was upgraded to a 6000 series of more modern and more powerful computers, and this has helped Honeywell to become a leading contender in the computer industry.

MINICOMPUTERS. The most spectacular growth area in the latter part of the third-generation period has been in the minicomputer field. The largest company in this field is Digital Equipment Corporation, which is famous for its PDP series (Fig. 10). These started in the second generation, but achieved their major success with the third-generation PDP-8, which was first delivered in 1968 and which is installed in thousands of laboratories. The PDP-11 is a newer family of more powerful minicomputers introduced in 1970. These and other minicomputers have impinged on the medium-scale computer field, since large-scale integration technology is being applied to good effect to increase the power and speed of computers that are physically quite small. DEC also has had considerable success with its PDP-10, which is in the medium- to large-scale class. There are many other successful manufacturers of minicomputers, including Data General with their NOVA and Super-NOVA series, Hewlett-Packard, Varian, Interdata, and Microdata. Many minicomputer manufacturers use microprogramming techniques to increase the versatility of their products.

MICROCOMPUTERS. The development of large-scale integration has made it possible to develop quite elaborate computers on just one or two semiconductor chips. Small pocket calculators have been produced by Hewlett-Packard and others that contain the equivalent of tens of thousands of transistors. These calculators are the most conspicuous of the microcomputers that are being used in a very large number of applications.

Just about all areas of automatic control are potential users of microcomputers, whose cost/performance ratio is impressively low. Microcomputers make it possible to build low-cost intelligent terminals. They provide an alternative to many aspects of centralized time-shared computing. It is hard to estimate the full potential of the successors to the "computer on a chip" that first appeared in the early 1970s. Larger microcomputers may very well soon take over most functions of present-day minicomputers.

COMMUNICATIONS AND NETWORKS. An important characteristic of the third-generation computer is its adaptability to data communications. Remote entry of jobs and data has become almost routine. Computer service bureaus offer services of computer networks in national and international hookups. Large corporations link their offices and dealers in elaborate data processing networks. Reservation systems and credit-checking systems have been constructed on a very large scale. Large data bases have been created or are planned with nationwide or even worldwide access by way of communication lines. Much of this type of communications traffic can be handled by standard telephone lines. Special data networks are being developed to provide for special high-speed, high-volume data transmission requirements. Computer network experiments carried on by ARPA and others in the 1960s and 1970s have provided prototypes for the very extensive, high-capacity data networks of the future.

Table 1 summarizes the three generations of computers discussed in this article.

**Future Prospects.** After many years of very rapid development and change in computers, it seems reasonably safe to predict a few years of consolidation, at least in the area of large computing systems, and especially those used in data processing.

There are a number of stabilizing factors in the computer industry. The large computer manufacturers have a very considerable investment in rented equipment. It is in the interest of the manufacturers, when they also function as leasing companies, to avoid too rapid obsolescence of existing equipment. Also, in spite of numerous antitrust suits, IBM's position in the industry continues to grow stronger, and IBM will be increasingly able to control the rate of technological change.

The very elaborate software systems that are now in use, and the increasing complexity of the software systems being developed, also have a stabilizing influence. A new and revolutionary computer, no matter how attractive, will not be considered at most large installations unless it can provide a full range of software products and a guarantee of relatively painless transition from the current system to the new one.

Because of the time lag inherent in the development and marketing of new large systems, it also seems reasonable to predict that the large computers to be used in 1980 will be the ones being marketed in the 1970s. Essentially they will be the same computers that are installed and running today.

There is a strong possibility that these very conservative projections may turn out to be wrong. The chief factor that may bring changes in the computer industry is the very vigorous small computer industry now developing. The major techno-

**Table 1.** Electronic computer generations

| Development | Early First Generation. 1946–1953 | Late First Generation, 1953–1959 | Second Generation, 1959–1964 | Early Third Generation, 1964–1969 | Late Third Generation, 1969— |
|---|---|---|---|---|---|
| *Component technology* | | | | | |
| Vacuum tubes. | — | — | | | |
| Transistors. | | | — | | |
| Hybrid circuits. | | | | — | |
| Monolithic integrated circuits. | | | | — | — |
| Medium- and large-scale integration. | | | | | — |
| *Main memory technology* | | | | | |
| Delay lines. | — | | | | |
| Electrostatic tubes. | — | | | | |
| Magnetic drums. | — | — | | | |
| Magnetic cores. | | — | — | — | — |
| Large-scale integration. | | | | | — |
| *Main memory cycle time* | | | | | |
| 40–40,000 $\mu$s. | — | | | | |
| 10–20 $\mu$s. | | — | | | |
| 2–10 $\mu$s. | | | — | | |
| 0.5–2 $\mu$s. | | | | — | |
| 0.020–1 $\mu$s. | | | | | — |
| *Peripheral storage* | | | | | |
| Magnetic tapes. | — | — | — | — | — |
| Magnetic drums. | — | — | — | — | — |
| Magnetic disks. | | — | — | — | — |
| Laser and magnetic bubbles. | | | | | — |
| *Software systems* | | | | | |
| Subroutine libraries. | — | — | — | — | — |
| Interpreters. | — | — | — | — | — |
| Assemblers. | | — | — | — | — |
| Compilers. | | — | — | — | — |
| Operating systems. | | — | — | — | — |
| Multiprogramming and time-sharing communications systems (networks). | | | — | — | — |
| *Special features* | | | | | |
| Interrupt systems. | | — | — | — | — |
| Virtual memory. | | | — | — | — |
| Microprogramming. | | | — | — | — |
| *Typical examples* | ENIAC,EDVAC<br>SEAC,SWAC<br>Harvard Mark III,IV<br>IAS machine<br>UNIVAC I,1103<br>Whirlwind<br>IBM 701,702 | IBM 650,704, 705,709<br>UNIVAC II, 1103A,SS80<br>Burroughs 205, 220<br>NCR 120,200 series<br>Datamatic 1000<br>RCA Bizmac<br>Many magnetic drum computers | Philco 2000<br>CDC 1604,3600<br>IBM 7000,1400 series<br>Ferranti Atlas<br>RCA 301,501<br>Honeywell 800<br>UNIVAC III, 1107 | Burroughs 5500<br>CDC 6000 series, 3300<br>IBM 360 series<br>UNIVAC 1108<br>Honeywell 200 series<br>RCA Spectra 70<br>NCR Century<br>G.E. 400,600 | IBM 370 series, System 3<br>CDC Cyber 70 series<br>DEC PDP-10,11<br>Honeywell 2000, 6000<br>UNIVAC 1110, 9400<br>Burroughs 6700, 1700<br>Many minicomputers |

logical advance in the past few years has been the development of large-scale integration. For years engineers have been predicting revolutionary changes in the computer industry as a result of LSI, but the actual changes, though important, have been slow in coming. As noted above, it is now possible to produce relatively sophisticated computers on just a few semiconductor chips. Some of today's minicomputers are more powerful than many full-scale second-generation computers.

The manufacturers of the larger computing systems may be in for a shock if the smaller computers begin to compete with the larger ones in speed and capacity, though probably not in price. It is possible that the rapid pace of technological development in the small computer field will force a major upheaval in the whole industry, so that, rather than settling down, the industry will experience an even more rapid rate of change and growth than it has had in the past. A factor that may be significant is the impending entry of the Japanese electronics industry into the small- and medium-scale computer market.

Probably the most far-reaching changes in the computer field will be brought about by breakthroughs in speed, capacity, and price of peripheral storage. Large-scale disk storage systems still cost hundreds of thousands of dollars and provide access times in ten's of milliseconds to less than one billion characters. Recently developed laser technology promises access times in microseconds to larger memories at lower costs. Prototype laser memories are still in the experimental stage and there is little likelihood that they will soon supplant present systems. Regardless, it seems inevitable that the replacement of disks and drums by electronic storage will occur and will usher in a new computer generation.

S. Rosen

# DIGITAL-TO-ANALOG CONVERTERS

For articles on related subjects *see* Analog Computers; Data Communications; Digital Computers; and Hybrid Computers. For article on related term *see* Binary Coded Decimal, Natural.

Whenever it is necessary to communicate between analog and digital systems, analog-to-digital (A-D) and/or digital-to-analog (D-A) converters are required. These converters form basic links between the world of "real" phenomena, where the variables are generally continuous analog quantities, and the "engineer designed" world of digital information processing and data communications, where the variables are discrete quantized quantities.

The number of applications and types of converters available has grown significantly during the past few years. In part, this has resulted from increased recognition of the capabilities of digital, as opposed to analog, signal processing and data transmission. The importance of these capabilities is application dependent; however, in general, the advantages of digital processing and transmission lie in the increased accuracy, noise immunity, processing flexibility, and storage facilities afforded by the digital format. This increasing use of digital processing of analog signals has been aided by the rapid development of sophisticated yet inexpensive minicomputers. At the same time the steady decline in price and increase in the performance of A-D and D-A converters has allowed minicomputers to be effectively coupled to the analog world.

**Some Applications.** Successful and widespread use of digital processing has resulted in numerous examples of A-D and D-A converter use. A simple classification of application areas is given below (also see Hoeschele, 1968).

Digital Control Systems. Fig. 1 is a block diagram illustration of a digital control system. Variables originate within the plant or system. They are sensed by an analog sensor, digitized by an A-D converter, and then transmitted to a digital processor. If the processor merely manipulates and stores this information, then the system is a simple data acquisition system. If, on the basis of the input information, control signals determined by the processor are returned to the plant, then a digital control system is present. A variation on this system, which requires fewer converters, can be designed if the signal frequencies and number of sensors and controllers are not excessive (Fig. 2). Such control systems can be found in a wide variety of situations, from basic industrial processing to aerospace flight systems.

Hybrid Computation Systems. Hybrid computers consist of an analog computer and a digital computer communicating to each other through a fairly sophisticated interface. This interface normally includes several A-D and D-A converters for transforming the signals to the appropriate computer format. While the analog computer is a low-accuracy

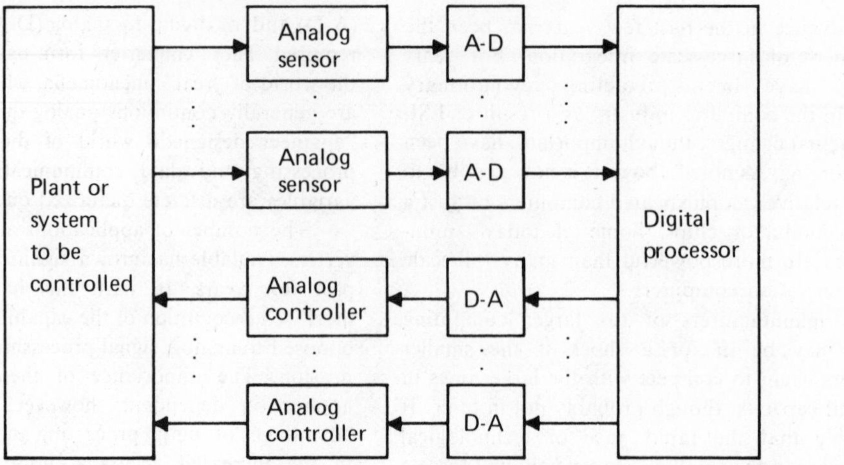


**Fig. 1.** Digital control system.

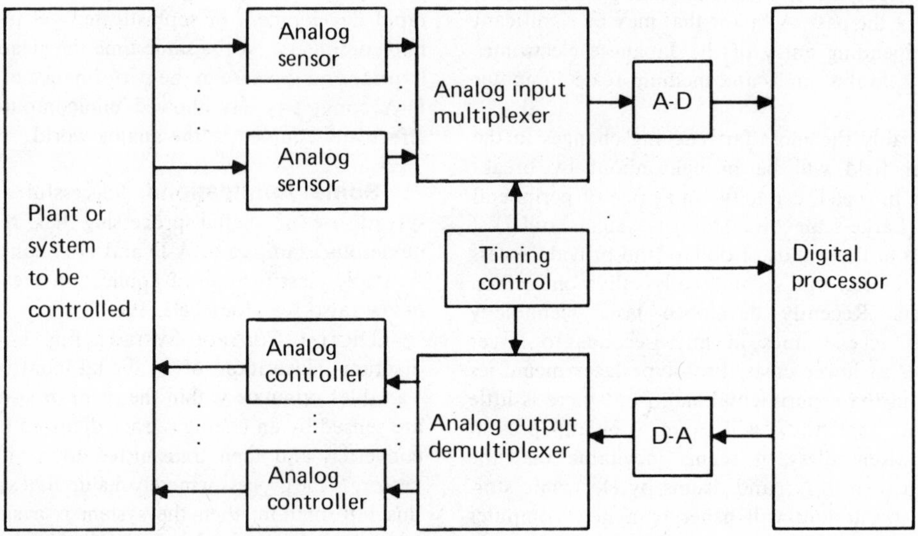


**Fig. 2.** Digital control system with multiplexers.

device, it does permit fast parallel solution of ordinary differential equations. The digital computer, on the other hand, is a high-accuracy serial machine with extensive logic and memory capabilities. Together, communicating through A-D and D-A converters, they permit very efficient solution of certain classes of continuous system optimization and statistical problems. Converters used in this application are often designed with computational capabilities. Thus, a D-A converter may act as a multiplier in addition to a converter.

Communications Systems. The advantages of digital data transmission have resulted in extensive use of converters as parts of telemetering and voice communications systems. In telemetering systems, analog signals originating in remote locations are first converted into digital signals and then transmitted to the control station. Remote weather and defense-related monitoring systems fall in this category of applications.

Voice communications systems are also becoming increasingly oriented toward digital signal processing. Thus, in many situations, analog voice signals are being digitized with A-D converters and subsequently transmitted over time-shared channels, with many conversations being "simultaneously" carried over the same channel. Such systems can be designed to be flexible, and can handle both speech and data at the same time while making "optimum" use of the systems bandwidth capabilities.

TEST, MEASUREMENT, AND MONITORING. In contrast to monitoring systems that require extensive communications capabilities, many applications of A-D converters can be found in test and measurement equipment. Digital voltmeters, for example, have gained widespread acceptance during the past few years. More complex measurement and monitoring applications such as on-line, real-time patient monitoring also have converters as key system elements.

**The Basic Relationship.** Analog variables such as position, temperature, and process rate are typically first converted during measurement into analog voltages and currents. Conversely, to control the analog variables, analog voltages and currents are usually supplied to the inputs of a controlling transducer. Rather than deal with the basic analog variable (e.g., temperature), it is therefore convenient to deal with the voltages or currents available at the output, or produced for the input, of the transducer. The analog variable considered here is thus a pure voltage or current, and questions concerning transducer operation, signal amplification, and signal conditioning are omitted. Material on these important practical matters can be obtained from the references.

Digital information is generally represented by the presence or absence of a fixed voltage or current level. Thus, each unit of information, or "bit," has two states, referred to as the "one" and "zero" states. On a single input line, information can therefore be represented serially by periodically changing the voltage level or state of the line. A set of parallel lines or a grouping of serial bits can be used to represent a digital word where the meaning of this word depends on the number or symbol assigned to each possible combination of bits. This is referred to as the "code."

Different types of codes are used with A-D and D-A converters. However, for simplicity, this article considers only *natural binary* code. Table 1 presents this code for a 3-bit word. In general, each word may have $n$ bits, with the leftmost bit—the most significant bit (MSB)—having a weight of $2^{-1}$, the rightmost bit—the least significant bit (LSB)—having a weight of $2^{-n}$, and the $i$th bit ($1 \leq i \leq n$) having a weight of $2^{-i}$. Signed numbers may be represented by adding an extra bit whose presence or absence indicates whether the number is negative or positive.

**Table 1.** Three-bit natural binary code

| Decimal Value | Binary Value | BIT 1 (MSB) | BIT 2 | BIT 3 (LSB) |
|---|---|---|---|---|
| 0 | .000 | 0 | 0 | 0 |
| 1/8 | .001 | 0 | 0 | 1 |
| 2/8 | .010 | 0 | 1 | 0 |
| 3/8 | .011 | 0 | 1 | 1 |
| 4/8 | .100 | 1 | 0 | 0 |
| 5/8 | .101 | 1 | 0 | 1 |
| 6/8 | .110 | 1 | 1 | 0 |
| 7/8 | .111 | 1 | 1 | 1 |

The basic conversion relationship for a 3-bit binary code is given in Figs. 3(a) and 3(b). Thus, if the input to an A-D converter is properly scaled, then corresponding to any input is a distinct 3-bit code output.

Similarly, any 3-bit digital sequence entering into the D-A converter defined by Fig. 1 results in producing one of eight distinct voltage outputs. The *ideal resolution* of this converter is equal to the value of the LSB, or $2^{-n}$, for an $n$-bit converter. Associated with this resolution is an inherent *quantization error* which reflects an uncertainty in the results of A-D conversion due to quantification of the analog signal. For the system of Fig. 3(a) this uncertainty is 1 LSB; however, if the zero position is offset 1/2 LSB so that transitions occur in the middle of each voltage range, as shown in Fig. 3(b), then the quantization *error* becomes an optimum $\pm 1/2$ LSB. This corresponds to a rounding as opposed to a truncating operation.

In both D-A and A-D converters there is a wide variety of techniques and manufacturers. Davis (1972) provides a list of over 40 firms producing devices in this area. The following two sections discuss several of the more basic techniques used in the conversion process. More elaborate and expensive techniques must be used if very high speed or accuracy is desired.

**D-A Converters.** Fig. 4 shows a block diagram for a D-A converter. Every D-A converter contains switches and a resistor network. The switches are controlled by the digital input code, and establish connections within the network needed to obtain the proper analog voltage.

Fig. 5(a) shows a simple 3-bit plus sign D-A converter. The dashed lines indicate that the switch is controlled by the associated digital bit input. The switches themselves are generally integrated circuits, which ideally would have no resistance when closed and infinite resistance when open. For the 0100

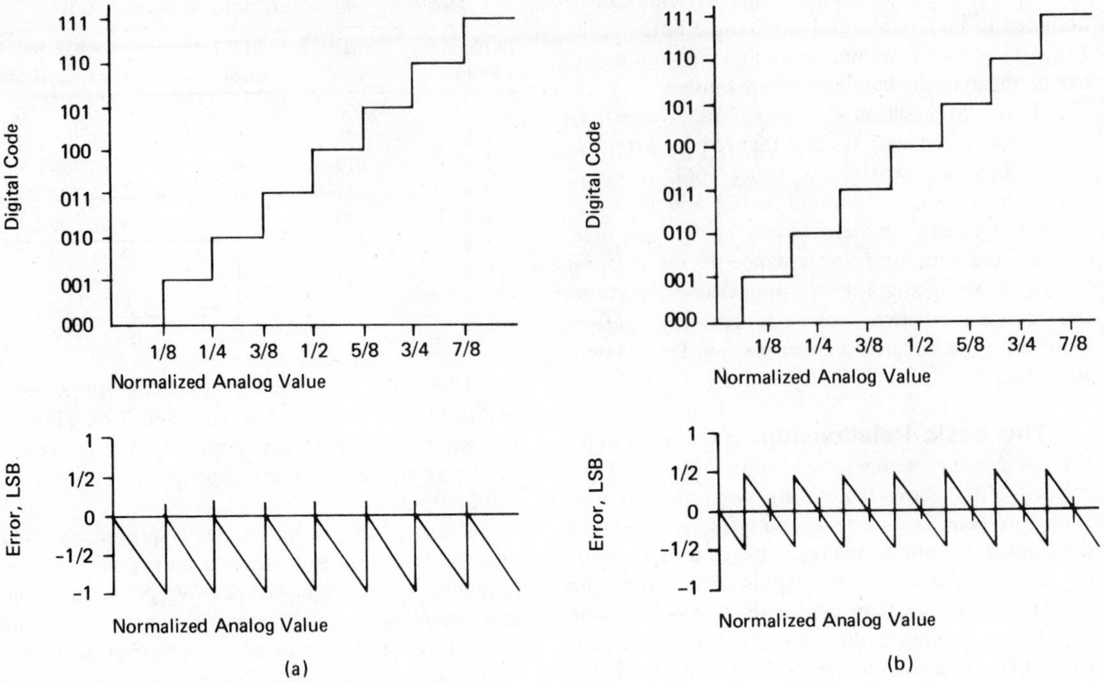


**Fig. 3.** The basic relationship. (a) Maximum quantization error 1 LSB. (b) Maximum quantization error ½ LSB.

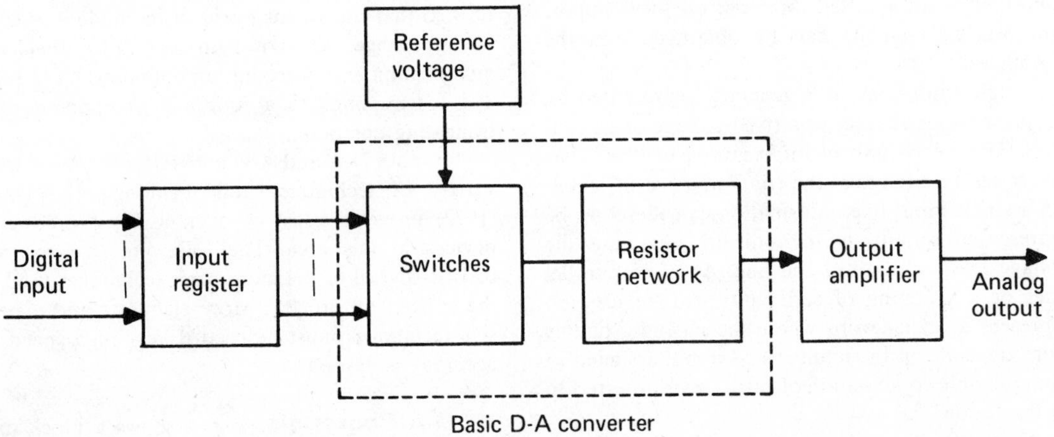


**Fig. 4.** Basic D-A converter and accessories.

input switch configuration shown, the output voltage $V_o$ is easily seen to be $V_R/2$. Similarly the $n$th bit present can be shown to produce an output voltage increment equal to $2^{-n}V_R$; hence, the resulting output voltage is proportional to the binary input. The sign bit controls a voltage reference switch. With certain codes its absence indicates a positive digital input and results in switching in the positive reference voltage $+V_R$. Its presence indicates a negative input and the negative reference voltage $-V_R$ is applied to the network.

Another simple D-A converter based on summing currents is shown in Fig. 5(b). This has the advantage of requiring only one resistor per bit; however, a large range of resistance values is necessary, making it less suitable to monolithic and

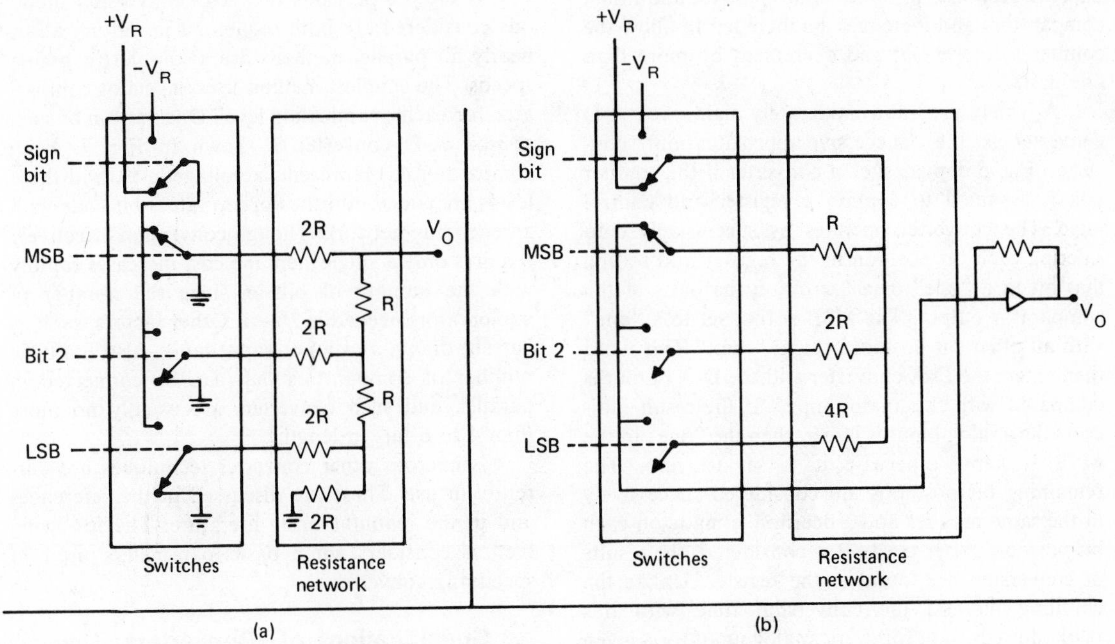


**Fig. 5.** Three-bit plus sign converter. (a) R/2R D-A converter. (b) R/$2^n$R D-A converter.

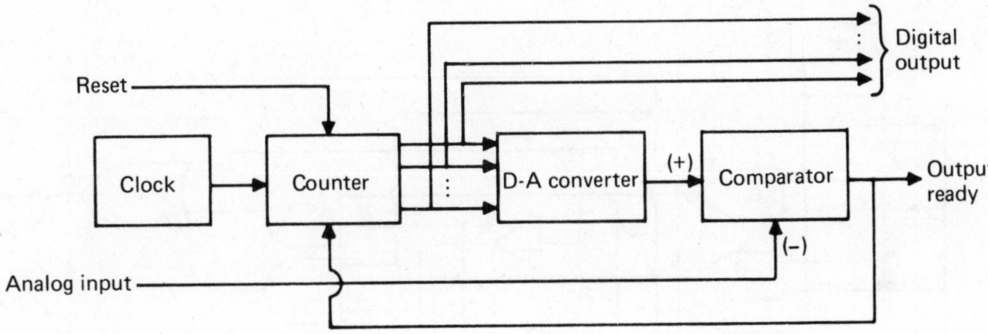


**Fig. 6.** Counter A-D converter.

hybrid circuit manufacturing techniques.

**A-D Converters.** A simple form of A-D converter is shown in Fig. 6. A conversion begins after the reset signal clears the counter. The counter now receives clock pulses and is incremented with each pulse. The counter output is a digital word representing a voltage level. This word, received by the D-A converter, results in an analog signal, which is compared with the incoming analog signal. When the comparator signal becomes positive, then the counter at that point holds the correct digital representation of the analog signal. An "output ready" signal indicates this has occurred.

The method, though simple, requires a relatively long time for a complete A-D conversion, owing to the counting process. This time increases by a factor of 2 for each additional bit and makes the method unsuitable for certain applications. A modification to the above technique, which speeds up the converter, calls for the incrementing counter to be replaced with an "up–down" counter. Here, once a comparison has been made, the counter is designed to increment or decrement on each clock pulse, depending on the output of the comparator. The counter thus follows the analog signal, and the full counting process is not necessary on each conversion if large changes in the analog input do not occur. To improve response to large input changes, additional comparators and logic may be included to allow the counter to increment and decrement by more than one unit.

A widely used and moderately high-speed A-D converter is the "successive-approximation" converter. Fig. 6 depicts such a converter if the counter box is assumed to contain a register and control logic. The converter operates by successively considering each bit position in the register and setting that bit to a "one" or a "zero" on the basis of the comparator output. The MSB is first set to a "one" with all other bit positions set to "zero." This word then enters the D-A converter and the D-A output is compared with the analog input. If the result indicates the analog input is larger, then the "one" in the MSB is kept; otherwise it is set to zero. The remaining bit positions are considered successively in the same manner and a decision is made on each bit position. After the LSB is considered, the results of conversion are found in the register. Unlike the counting method the conversion time with this method is constant for every analog input for a given converter.

While the previous two A-D conversion methods considered are both sequential in nature, all or nearly all parallel methods are available for higher speeds. The simplest method uses an analog comparator for each quantization level. One version of such a 3-bit A-D converter is shown in Fig. 7. Each comparator (C) represents a voltage level, and these levels are coded into the appropriate 3-bit code with an encoding network. Though conversion effectively requires only a single step, the cost increases rapidly with the number of bits $n$, since the number of comparators needed is $2^n - 1$. Other factors, such as current drawn and input capacitance, also limit the number of comparators that can be connected in parallel, and such converters are usually no more than 4 to 6 bits in length.

Numerous other converter techniques are currently in use. These are discussed in the references and in the manufacturing literature. The following section considers some basic parameters used in specifying converters.

**Specification of Converters.** Unfortunately, at this time only limited standardization of

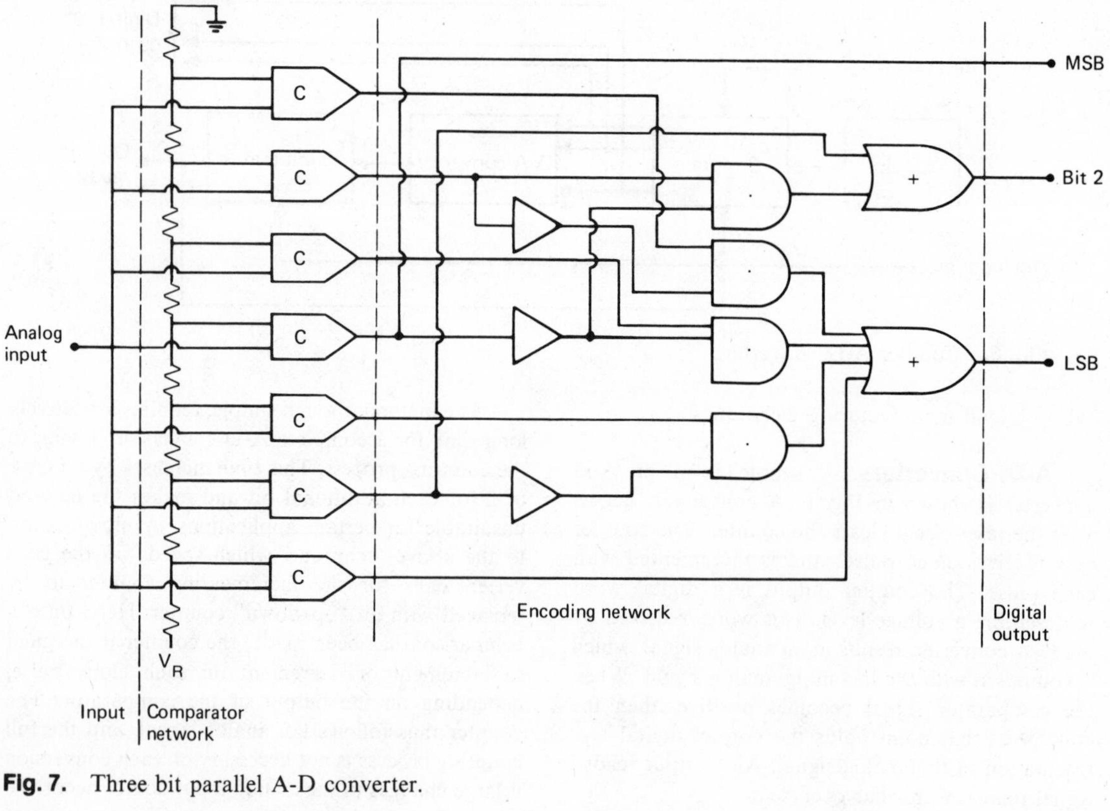


**Fig. 7.** Three bit parallel A-D converter.

converter performance specifications has been achieved. The user should therefore be cautious in evaluating manufacturer specifications and should clearly understand the meaning of the various terms used. Many manufacturers provide literature defining their specification nomenclature.

The application for which the converter is intended should be well understood, since this will determine which of the multitude of converters available offer the best price-performance trade-offs. In addition to accuracy and speed requirements, questions regarding logic levels and codes, scale factors, reference voltages, impedance levels, power levels, temperature stability, and noise levels must be considered. These latter questions are not considered here, and the reader should consult the references for detailed information.

A number of measures are normally used in specifying converter accuracy and speed. These measures in part isolate and indicate the various sources of error. With D-A converters, *accuracy* refers to the deviation of actual analog output from the theoretical output for a given digital input. Though this may vary over the range of the unit, specifications are normally given in terms of a single number representing the maximum error over the range. This may be stated as plus or minus a percentage of full scale or plus or minus a fraction of LSB.

Several common error types which contribute to a loss of accuracy are illustrated in Fig. 8. Fig. 8(a) shows *nonlinearity* in the conversion transfer function. The nonlinearity is, however, *monotonic*, since increasing digital values produce increasing analog values. Fig. 8(b) shows a *nonmonotonic* nonlinearity. Here, two different digital input codes yield the same analog value, a result that could cause oscillations to occur in certain control applications. Figs. 8(c) and 8(d) illustrate *gain* and *offset* errors, which respectively change the slope and zero crossing of the

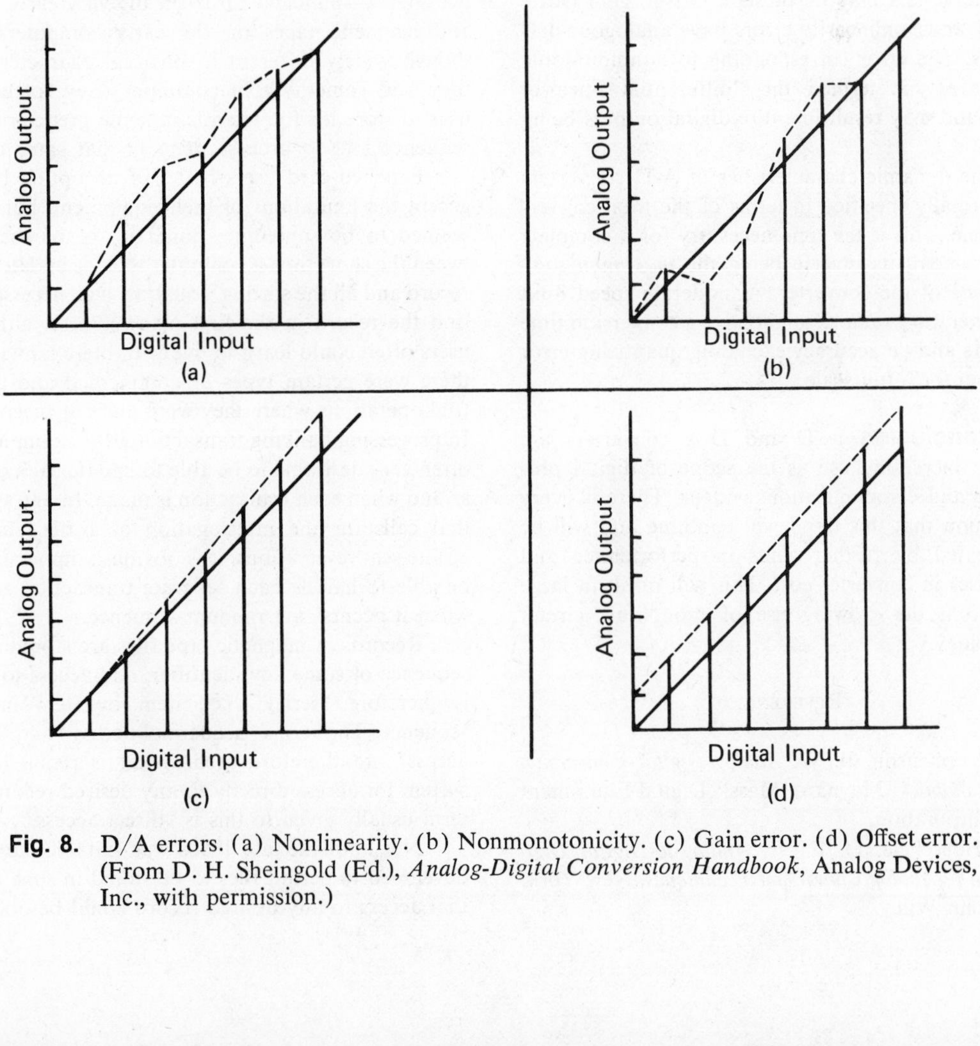


**Fig. 8.** D/A errors. (a) Nonlinearity. (b) Nonmonotonicity. (c) Gain error. (d) Offset error. (From D. H. Sheingold (Ed.), *Analog-Digital Conversion Handbook*, Analog Devices, Inc., with permission.)

transfer function. The difference between the dotted line in the figures and the solid 45-degree angle line is the error associated with each digital input code.

Dynamic characteristics of D-A converters are normally specified in terms of a *settling time*. This is the time between arrival of the digital code and settling of the analog output to within certain specified limits of accuracy. The shorter the settling time, the higher the conversion rate. A typical specification of a moderate speed converter might read 2 $\mu$s to settle within $\pm 1/2$ LSB.

For A-D converters, "accuracy" refers to the deviation of the analog level, represented by the digital output, from the actual analog input. As with D-A converters, this is normally stated as either a percentage of full scale or a fraction of LSB. Errors here may be divided into two parts. The first, *quantization error*, was discussed earlier in this article. This results in an inherent error of $\pm 1/2$ LSB, which can be reduced only by increasing the number of bits. All other errors are equipment errors, and error types directly corresponding to those found in D-A converters may be present. Offset, gain (scale factor), and nonlinearity errors have analogous definitions. The error corresponding to nonmonotonic nonlinearity is termed the "differential linearity error" and may result in entire digital outputs being missed.

The dynamic characteristics of A-D converters are normally specified in terms of the total conversion time. This is the time necessary for a complete measurement, its inverse being the *maximum sampling rate* of the converter. A moderate speed 8-bit converter, for example, might have a conversion time of 40 $\mu$s and an accuracy excluding quantizing error of about 0.2% full scale.

**Conclusion.** A-D and D-A converters are finding increasing use as the scope of digital processing and communications widens. There is every indication that this trend will continue and will be augmented by further gains in performance and decreases in converter cost. This will result in large part from the growing use of monolithic circuit technology.

References

1964. Stephenson, B. W. *Analog-Digital Conversion Handbook*. Maynard, Mass.: Digital Equipment Corporation.

1968. Hoeschele, D. F., Jr. *Analog-to-Digital/Digital-to-Analog Conversion Techniques*. New York: John Wiley.

1970. Schmid, H. *Electronic Analog/Digital Conversions*. New York: Van Nostrand-Reinhold.

1972. Davis, S. "Selection Criteria for A-D and D-A Converters," *Computer Design* (September).

1972. Sheingold, D. H. (Ed.). *Analog-Digital Conversion Handbook*. Norwood, Mass.: Analog Devices, Inc.

M. A. Franklin

## DIRECT ACCESS

For article on related subject *see* Memory: Auxiliary.

For articles on related terms *see* Files; and RAMAC.

Early hardware, developed for the storage of large files in a data processing system, depended on two media—punched cards (in the very early days) and magnetic tapes on the early computers. Although widely different in physical characteristics, they had something in common—they forced the user to store his file records in some predetermined sequence and to process them in that same order.

Punched-card users had had no option but to accept the limitations of their equipment, but there seemed to be something quite out of balance between the short time a computer took to update a file record and all the sorting, collating, etc., necessary to find the record in the first place. Worse, although users often could learn to live with these limitations, there were certain types of commercial and industrial operations where they were quite unacceptable. In processing banking transactions, for example, it is often very desirable to be able to update each record as and when each transaction is made. In any system that calls for the interrogation of a file, such as airline seat reservations, it is obviously imperative to be able to handle each separate transaction as and when it occurs in a random sequence.

Records in magnetic tape files are stored in the sequence of some key identifier, and access to them is therefore "serial", i.e., item by item in that sequence. The terms "sequential access" and "serial access" are therefore used. What is required is a system for access directly to any desired record; the term usually given to this is "direct access."

Not until the late 1950s was suitable hardware developed to permit files to be stored in such a way that access to any desired record could be obtained in the same time as to any other, and in an acceptably short time. The machine that first accomplished this was the IBM 305 RAMAC (Random Access Method for Accounting and Control), and the storage device was the magnetic disk file.

The magnetic tape unit is in many ways like the domestic tape recorder, where we often have to run through many feet of tape to find the recording we want. The magnetic disk file is in many ways like the phonograph, where the recording head can be moved very quickly (given a steady hand) to any desired position on the surface of the disk to select the desired piece of recording. In practice, the computer disk file is usually equipped with a number of disks, with a separate recording head for every disk surface. In this way, the selection of a desired record at random can usually be made in a fraction of a second, and the computer system can therefore respond in an acceptable time scale to the input item, usually in about one-third of a second.

Where higher speeds are required (measured, say, in hundredths of a second), magnetic drums (Fig. 1) are used. These are fast, rotating cylinders with file information stored on tracks along the surface and with a recording head for every track. There is no need, therefore, to move the heads (as with disk files), and the time for access to required information depends only on the speed of rotation of the drum.

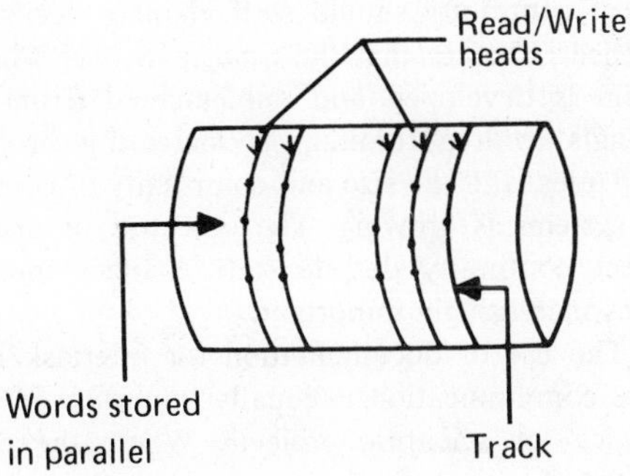


**Fig. 1.** Magnetic drum.

The need for speed in accessing file records is clear. What is even more obvious is the requirement for ultrarapid access to program instructions and data held in the computer's main memory. These are required with an access time measured in millionths of a second or less so that the speed of the arithmetic unit is not wasted.

It is an interesting paradox that one of the fastest devices currently used for random access to files, the magnetic drum, was used in some of the earliest computers for the main memory and was rejected because it was too slow for random access to instructions and data! It was replaced by magnetic core memory units, which still form the majority of main memories in today's computers. These core units are capable of providing required data or instructions in times ranging from a few millionths of a second down to one-fifth of a millionth of a second, speeds compatible with those of arithmetic units. Main memories are therefore also classifiable as "random" or "direct" access.

G. J. MORRIS

# DOCUMENTATION

For articles on related subjects *see* ADMINISTRATIVE-BUSINESS APPLICATIONS; BLOCK DIAGRAM; FLOWCHART; FLOW DIAGRAM; STANDARDS; and SYSTEM CHART.
For article on related term *see* FEASIBILITY STUDY.

Documentation is a vital part of developing and using a computer-based system. In some commercial organizations, 20 to 40% of the total development effort goes into the documentation of the new system, recording how the new system is to work and how it was developed. Documentation of a computer project falls into two broad categories: development documentation and control documentation. Development documentation records how a computer-based system is to operate and gives the background information upon which the design is founded. Control documentation, on the other hand, serves an administrative function: It records the resources used in developing and implementing the system, and includes such documents as project plans, schedules, resource allocation details, and progress reports.

**Functions of Documentation.** Documentation serves four main functions:

1. Intertask/interphase communication.
2. Historical reference.
3. Quality and quantity control.
4. Instructional reference.

The relative importance of each of these depends on many factors. For example, one of the most important is the scope and type of the project; it may be a large-scale commercial system, or a scientific problem-solving program used by one or two technicians on a limited amount of data. Within each category, there are the variations in project size, problem complexity, organization of staff, and the time scale for development and use. Each function of documentation is described below.

INTERTASK/INTERPHASE COMMUNICATION. This operation records what has been done at each stage of the project so that instructions can be issued for the next phase of work, or so that all people involved in the project can agree what has been done before work proceeds to the next step. The amount of time and effort that must be devoted to documentation for this reason is a function of the scope of the system and the number of people involved.

In the development of a major commercial system, which requires procedures such as invoicing, inventory control, payroll, or production control, many people will be involved. In a production control system, for example, the business functions involved could include, among others:

1. Sales forecasting (linking with sales accounts).
2. Parts explosion and production batching/netting (linked with engineering design).
3. Plant resource allocation and scheduling.
4. Materials ordering/tooling and allocation.
5. Monitoring job progress.
6. Scrap and bonus reporting (linking with payroll).
7. Job costing (linking all systems).

Most of these functions are closely related to one another and with other systems in the company. Some 20 or 30 separate job functions or organizational units may be involved with the development, implementation, and running of the computer system. In addition to job functions such as those described above, different levels of user staff will involve senior or executive management, line management, and supervisors and operators. Similarly, a number of job functions will be performed by personnel in the data processing or management services department; for example:

1. Business analysts, internal business consultants who advise management on business methods and who identify areas for improvement.
2. Systems analysts, who investigate, analyze, and specify a new system.
3. Systems designers, who design the new system (computer and manual procedures) in detail.
4. Programmers, who design, code, and test the computer programs for the system.
5. Operators, who are responsible for the day-to-day running of the system.

There may also be general support or service staff within data processing, such as maintenance programmers, software support people, forward planning, and standards analysts. In a small installation, many of the job functions listed above may be performed by one man or a small group of men; in a large installation, each job function may be performed by a specialist group. It can be seen that keeping people informed, passing on information and ideas for approval, and giving instructions involves a complex communications network in which formal documentation plays a vital role.

Fig. 1 is a general schematic of the main lines of communication in developing a commercial computer system. Much information can pass between the various parties to keep people informed of progress, to provide sufficient information for the system design ideas to be approved, and to pass on instructions and specifications for further action.

A failure of communication through poor documentation (or a lack of it) can prove very expensive indeed. The documentation will also help to insure project continuity should staff changes occur. Experience indicates that the time span over which a system is developed and implemented (from first thoughts to live running) is increasing in many companies, and the size and complexity of commercial systems is growing. The objective of insuring project continuity despite staff changes thus becomes increasingly important.

The use of documentation for intertask/interphase communication is equally important in large technical or scientific projects. Where the development of a program or group of programs can be done by only a limited number of technicians, who are quite often both problem proponents and solution programmers, the importance of documentation during the project diminishes. However, the documentation of what has been done and how the programs work will be important for historical or instructional reference, as described below.

*Historical Reference.* The reference function is relevant to both commercial and scientific work. It is the documentation of how the system works that makes it easily changed after it is implemented. All systems are subject to change, with the sole excep-

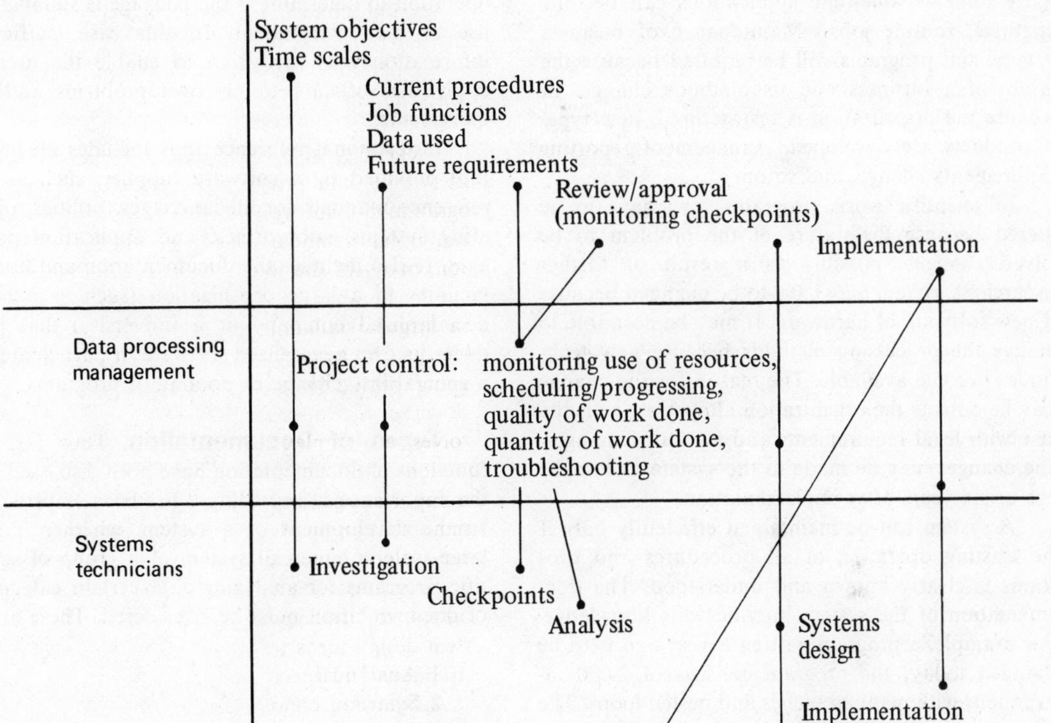

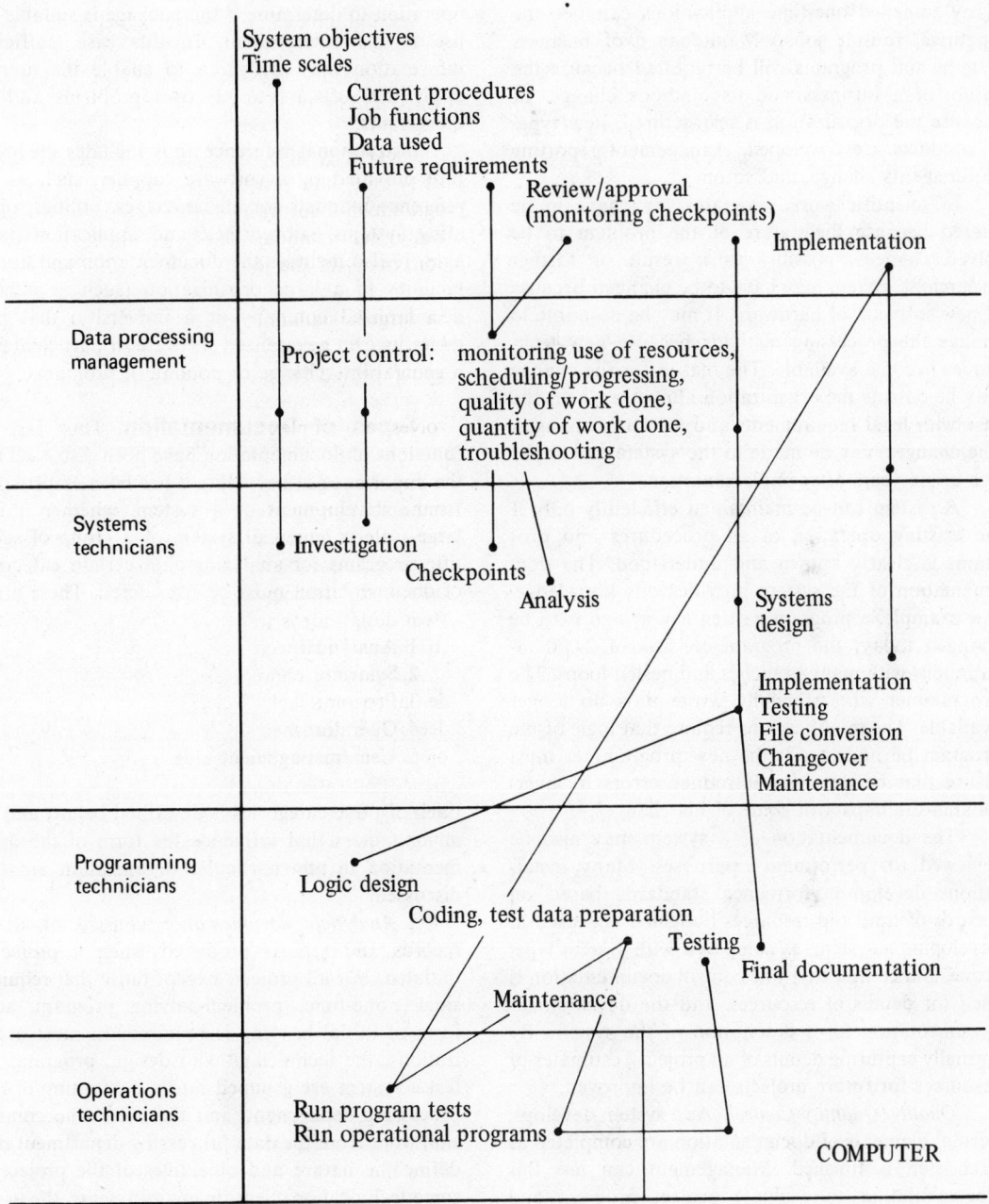


**Fig. 1.** Example of information flow in system development.

tion of one-time problem-solving applications with limited amounts of data; these are usually scientific. (One-time applications should be treated with care. Many so-called one-time applications can become repetitive, routine jobs.) Maintenance of business systems and programs will be required because the nature of a business and its methods change, or because the organization is restructured, new types of products are developed, management reporting requirements change, and so on.

In scientific work, programs may have to be altered because the nature of the problem to be solved changes, possibly as a result of further research. A system may have to be changed because of new software or hardware. It may be desirable to change the processing methods because new techniques become available. The reason for the change may lie outside the organization altogether, as is the case with legal requirements and statutory changes. The changes may be made to the system as long as five or six years after implementation.

A system can be maintained efficiently only if the existing operation of all procedures and programs is clearly known and understood. The documentation of the system provides this knowledge. For example, a program written a year ago is to be changed today; the program consists of 2,000 instructions with many branches and nested loops. The programmer who originally wrote it is no longer available. The modifications require that logic of the program be undestood; the new programmer must insure that he does not introduce errors by overlooking the impact of some of his changes.

The documentation of a system may also be reviewed for performance purposes. Many installations develop performance standards based on records of time and resources budgeted and used in developing a system, as compared with system type, scope, and complexity. The control documentation is used for details of resources, and the development documentation for a description of the system. By formally capturing details of all projects, estimates of resources for future projects can be improved.

*Quality/Quantity Control.* As a system develops, various elements of documentation are completed as each step is finished. Management can use this documentation to evaluate project progress and individual performance.

*Instructional Reference.* The development documentation can be reviewed during and after development for many general purposes. For example, documentation will enable trainees to study a system developed by experienced technicians. This is particularly important for instructional reference to generalized systems or general-purpose software. Another benefit of documentation is that an outside party can evaluate the system and its method of operation to determine if the package is suitable for use in his environment. In this case, sufficient information must be given to enable the user to apply the software to his own problems and requirements.

Instructional reference thus includes all literature provided by a software supplier, such as the reference manuals for all languages, utilities, operating systems, subroutines, and application packages. It also includes the documentation and library facilities in a large organization (such as a large decentralized company or a university) that produces its own generalized software or participates in a general interchange or pooling of programs.

**Types of Documentation.** Thus far, the functions of documentation have been discussed and the importance of providing it has been emphasized. In the development of a system, whether it is a large-scale commercial system or a group of scientific programs for analyzing data, certain categories of documentation must be considered. These are:

1. Analytical.
2. Systems.
3. Program.
4. Operations.
5. User/management aids.

Each of these categories is described below, and the major factors that influence the form of the documentation in any particular organization are then discussed.

1. *Analytical documentation* consists of all the records and reports produced when a project is initiated. For all projects except those that require a single, one-time, problem-solving program, some form of initial briefing is required. In most organizations, the technicians who design, program, and test a system are grouped into a computing or data processing department, and the users who commission work from the data processing department must define the nature and objectives of the project. In some technical or scientific environments, the user is capable of specifying in very exact terms what he requires in the way of processing and outputs. Generally, for any type of project, however (including many business applications), the initial briefing should consist of a *user request*, stating the problem (i.e., what the user wants to achieve); a *feasibility study* that evaluates possible solutions (in

SYSTEMS SPECIFICATION

Title and Administrative Material

1.0 Systems Summary
- 1.1 User Summary
  1. Purpose and Function
  2. Files Maintained and Affected
  3. Input and Input Sources
  4. Output and Output Uses
- 1.2 System Flowchart
  1. Flowchart
  2. Reference Lists
- 1.3 Narrative Description
  1. Definitions
  2. System Flow
  3. General Timing and Size Estimates

2.0 File Specifications
- 2.1 File Identification and Characteristics
  1. General Description
  2. File Abstract
- 2.2 Record Format
- 2.3 Data Element Descriptions
- 2.4 Appendices
  1. Layouts
  2. Edit Lists
  3. Cross-Reference Lists

cont./

3.0 Input Specifications
- 3.1 Identification and Purpose
- 3.2 Transaction Listing (media purpose, programs affected, frequency, volume and source)
- 3.3 Input Layouts and Samples

4.0 Output Specifications
- 4.1 Identification and Purpose
- 4.2 Output Listing (program no., media, frequency, volume, no. of copies, and destination)
- 4.3 Output Description
- 4.4 Output Formats

5.0 Program (Processing) Specifications
- 5.1 Program Specification 1
- 5.2 Program Specification 2
- .
- .
- .
- 5.n Program Specification n

6.0 Systems Test Plan
- 6.1 Identification
- 6.2 Test Organization
- 6.3 Validity Criteria (control, processing, and output)
- 6.4 Test Schedule
- 6.5 Test Cases

7.0 Implementation Plan (timing, resources, responsibilities, and method)

**Fig. 2.** Sample outline of specification documentation. Note that items 2.0, 3.0, and 4.0 are repeated for each file. Data common to a number of programs may be defined in a Data Specification section (not shown). An added section might include a final cost-benefit analysis.

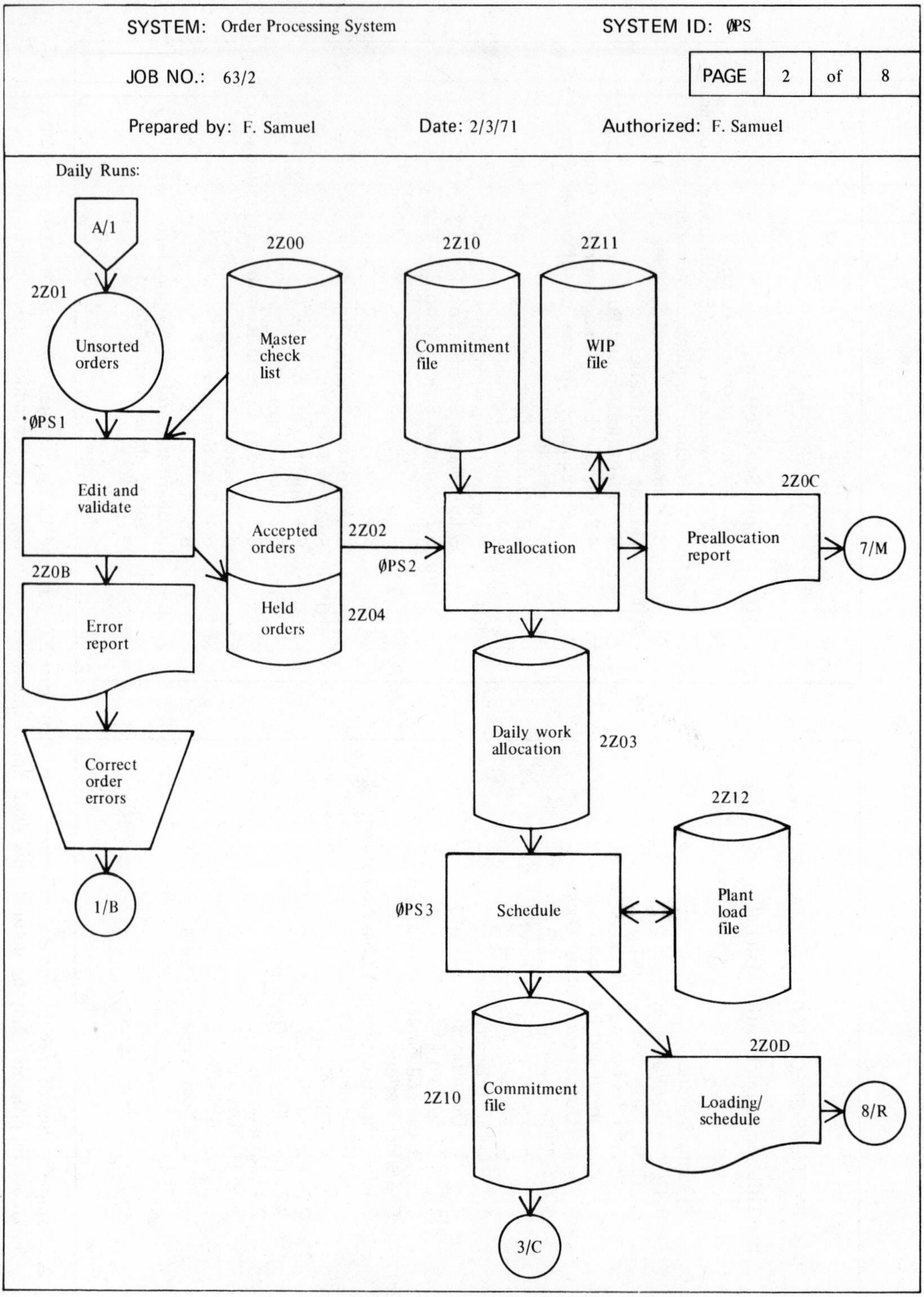


**Fig. 3.** Part of a system flowchart, showing the sequence of manual procedures and computer programs with their inputs and outputs. For each program box a Program Specification will be prepared. Data specifications will be prepared for all inputs, outputs, and files. See also Fig. 6.

outline); and a *project plan* that estimates the time and resources required to develop and implement the system. Failure to produce and agree upon these three statements in the briefing will result in much wasted effort later in the project. They are vital whenever a user commissions work from computer technicians, and must be provided before money is actually committed to the more time-consuming tasks of system design and programming.

2. *Systems documentation* encompasses all information needed to define the proposed computer-based system to a level where it can be programmed, tested, and implemented. The major document is some form of *system specification*, which acts as a permanent record of the structure, its functions and work flow, and the controls on the system. It is the basic means of communication between the systems design, programming, and user functions. In a major project, the system specification comprises a number of documents. A sample outline of specification documentation for a major project is shown in Fig. 2. If the project will result in the development of only one or two programs for restricted use, then only the *program (processing) specification* would be produced. Fig. 3 is an example of part of a system flowchart taken from a system specification (Section 1.2).

3. *Program documentation* comprises the records of the detailed logic and coding of the constituent programs of a system. These records, prepared by the programmer, aid program development and acceptance, troubleshooting, general maintenance, machine/software conversion at a later date, and programmer changeover.

Program documentation covers both specific applications programs and general-purpose or in-house developed software. In addition to documenting *how* a program works (information not always released in the case of general software), instructions for *using* the program must be written for packaged software (this is described in "User/management aids" below).

4. *Operations documentation* specifies those procedures required for running the system by operations personnel. It gives the general sequence of events for performing the job and defines precise procedures for data control and security, data preparation, program running, output dispersal, and ancillary operations.

5. *User/management aids* consist of all the descriptive and instructive material necessary for the user to participate in the running of the operational system, including notes on the interpretation of the output results. Where a software package is produced, this category includes all the material necessary to evaluate the programs and all the instructions for use.

Every installation should establish documentation standards (i.e., rules for the completion of certain documents at certain times) that define the content, format, and distribution of the documents. Many factors influence what documents are to be produced, how, when, and by whom. For example, the extent of *management commitment* is indicated by how much the management of the installation is prepared to allocate time and resources, not only for developing a system, but also for its documentation. Another controlling factor may be *project characteristics*, which consist of the number of projects and their scope, complexity, and duration whether there are to be one or two programs operating on data from limited sources for a limited period of time, or a routine system comprising many programs operating on data from a large number of sources. Crucial to any set of standards is *the organization structure* of both the institution as a whole, and the development and operations departments in particular. This, in turn, is affected by *the technical environment*: the hardware/software techniques used, such as the level of programming language, the quality of documentation produced by the software, and the use of special-purpose documentation programs (flowcharters, etc.).

From this broad picture of the total documentation of a project, we select one type to review in detail: program documentation. We focus on this because the limits of the tasks of programming can be clearly defined, and because this function in programming is similar in many organizations.

**Program Documentation.** Fig. 4 shows the flow of documentation in designing, coding, and testing a program, respectively. The starting point is a program specification. Typically, this is a statement of *what* the program must do; the programmer's task is to determine *how* the program will do it. How much the data formats are predefined and how much is left to the discretion of the programmer depends on installation policy and the project. Other inputs to the programming phase include literature—which describes the software available for the project (either from outside suppliers or from an internal library)—and the programming standards, which give the rules and techniques for programming in that installation.

The outputs include a program manual, which describes the programs in detail (construction, coding, and testing), instructions for use (for a gener-

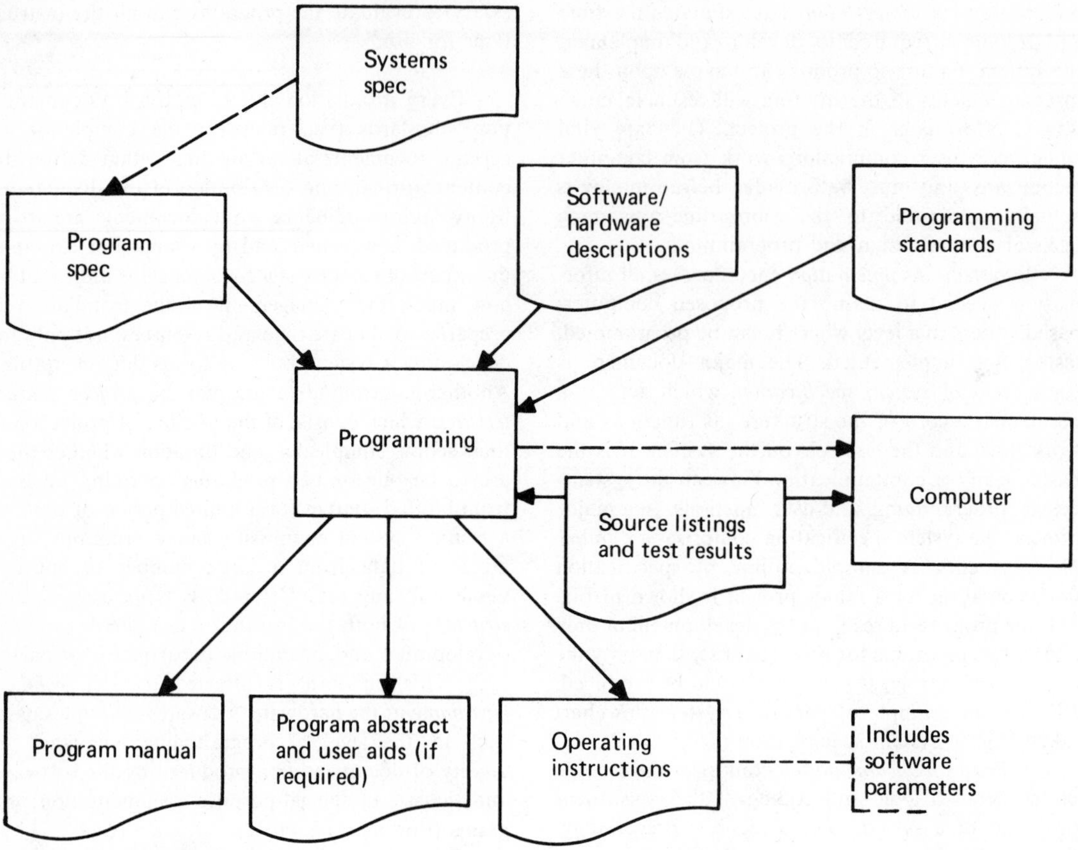


**Fig. 4.** Documentation flow.

alized program), and computer operating instructions for day-to-day running. In many cases the task of documenting a program is one of adding to the initial program specification in order to build up the program manual (see Fig. 5). The various elements of program documentation are discussed below.

PROGRAM SPECIFICATION. This is a statement of the data available for processing, the required outputs, and the details of the necessary processing. The specification can be prepared by the problem proponent, a specialist systems analyst/designer, or the programmer himself. It must be complete, accurate, and unambiguous; changes to the specification after programming begins can be very expensive. The specification usually contains the following information:

1. Input.
2. Output.
3. Major functions performed.
4. The means of communication between this program and previous and following programs.
5. Logical rules and decisions to be followed, including statements of how the input is to be examined, altered, and utilized.
6. Validation and edit criteria.
7. Actions to be taken on error or exception conditions.
8. Special tables, formulas, and algorithms.

(Where a utility program or application package is being used, then some of the data listed will be omitted, and parameters specifically related to the program will be listed instead.) The description of the processing rules (item 5 in the list), can be given in narrative, flowchart, or decision-table form. Figs. 6(a), (b), (c) show the components of a program specification.

PROGRAM MANUAL. From the program specification, the programmer designs, codes, and tests the program. The output of this exercise is the program manual (see Fig. 5). A flowchart from such

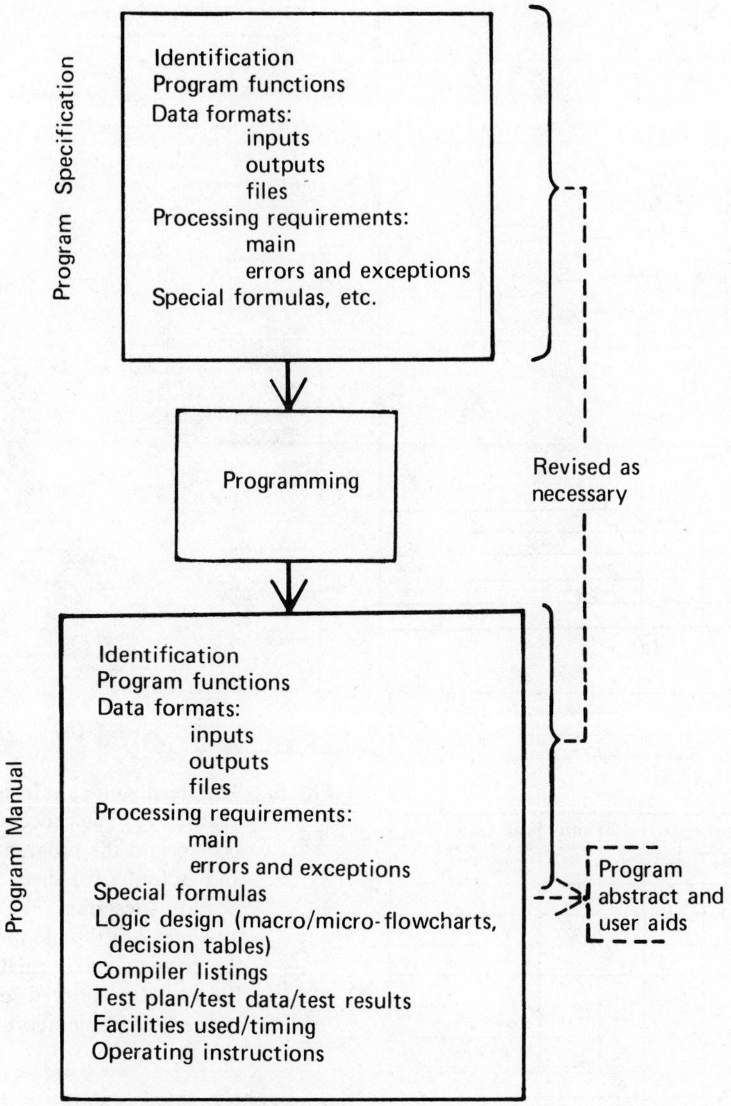


**Fig. 5.** Program specification and program manual.

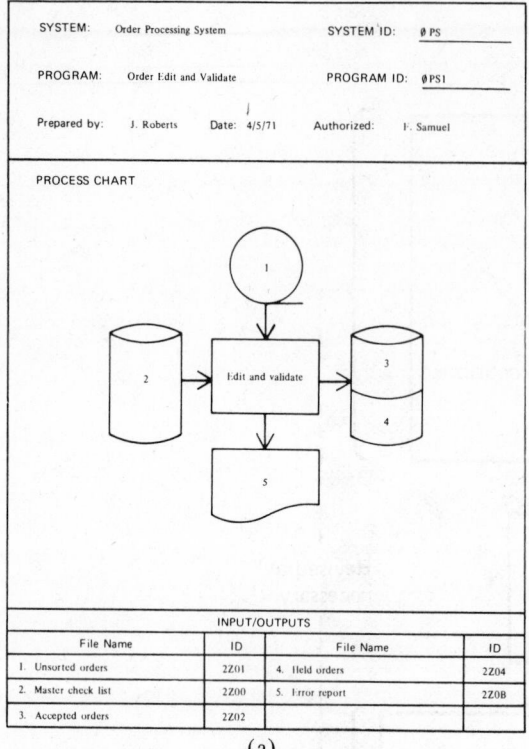

SYSTEM: Order Processing System SYSTEM ID: ØPS

PROGRAM: Order Edit and Validate PROGRAM ID: ØPS1

Prepared by: J. Roberts Date: 4/5/71 Authorized: F. Samuel

PROCESS CHART

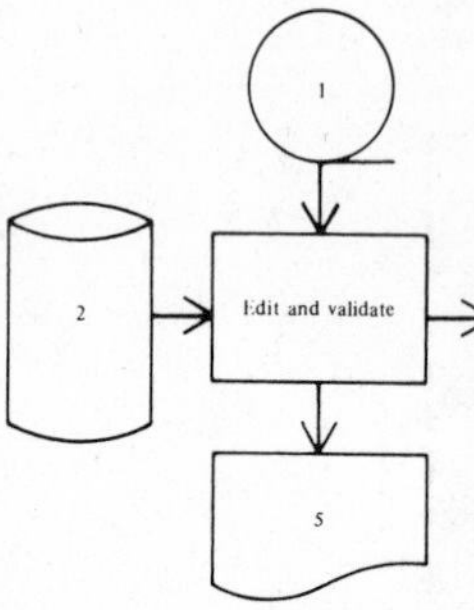


INPUT/OUTPUTS

| File Name | ID | File Name | ID |
|---|---|---|---|
| 1. Unsorted orders | 2Z01 | 4. Held orders | 2Z04 |
| 2. Master check list | 2Z00 | 5. Error report | 2Z0B |
| 3. Accepted orders | 2Z02 | | |

(a)

File Specification FILE ID: 2Z00

File name: Master check list

Prepared by: J. Roberts Date: 4/5/71 Authorized: F. Samuel

Medium: Disk

Contents (record names): Order Identity, Part Request, End Record

Sequence (if any): Key field within record type

Retention and Protection: Master

Used On (program ID's):

File Description:

| Type of record | | Organization | |
|---|---|---|---|
| Blocked | ✓ | Sequential | |
| Unblocked | | Direct Access | |
| Fixed length | ✓ | Index Sequential | ✓ |
| Variable length | | | |
| Undefined length | | | |

| Sizes (bytes) | Average | Maximum | Minimum |
|---|---|---|---|
| Block length: | - | 1232+4 | - |
| Record length: | - | 52+4 | - |
| File length: | 2,300 | 4,000 | 1,400 |

Remarks: Used to validate all input order requests by order identity and part characteristics.

(b)

File Name: Master check list Record Name: Part request

Format codes:
A = characters (alpha/mixed alpha-numeric)
N = zoned decimal
P = packed decimal
B = binary

| Data Description | | | From Byte No. | No. of Bytes or Columns | Range: value (e.g., 1 - 5), blank (b̸), or master reference table |
|---|---|---|---|---|---|
| Field Name | Mnemonic | Format | | | |
| Record type | | N | 1 | 6 | 1 |
| KEY FIELD | | | | | |
| Part number | | A | 7 | 30 | Any character |
| DATA | | | | | |
| Dimension | | A | 37 | 6 | Any character or b̸ |
| Issue code | | A | 43 | 1 | A, C, L, P, or S |
| Status | | A | 44 | 1 | U, N, or b̸ |
| Units | | N | 45 | 5 | 0-99999 |
| Authority | | A | 50 | 3 | Alpha |
| | | | | 52 | |

(c)

**Fig. 6.** Sample documents from a program specification. (a) The process chart identifies the system and the program, and shows inputs and outputs. (b) Sheet 1 of the file specification describes the file as a whole. (c) Sheet 2 of the file specification describes the content and format of a record. Note the use of preprinted forms and the highly stylized, rigid method of completion.

a program manual is shown in Fig. 7. The form of the logic design and the source program listing will depend on the type of application and the software used. For example, if a high-level decision-table preprocessor is used, the tabular program together with the data descriptions and final source listing will be complete enough without the preparation of a flowchart. Similarly, some installations use software for the final documentation; e.g., flowcharters that produce detailed flowcharts, statement by statement from the source program.

One of the advantages of higher-level languages (such as Cobol) is that the source listing itself forms

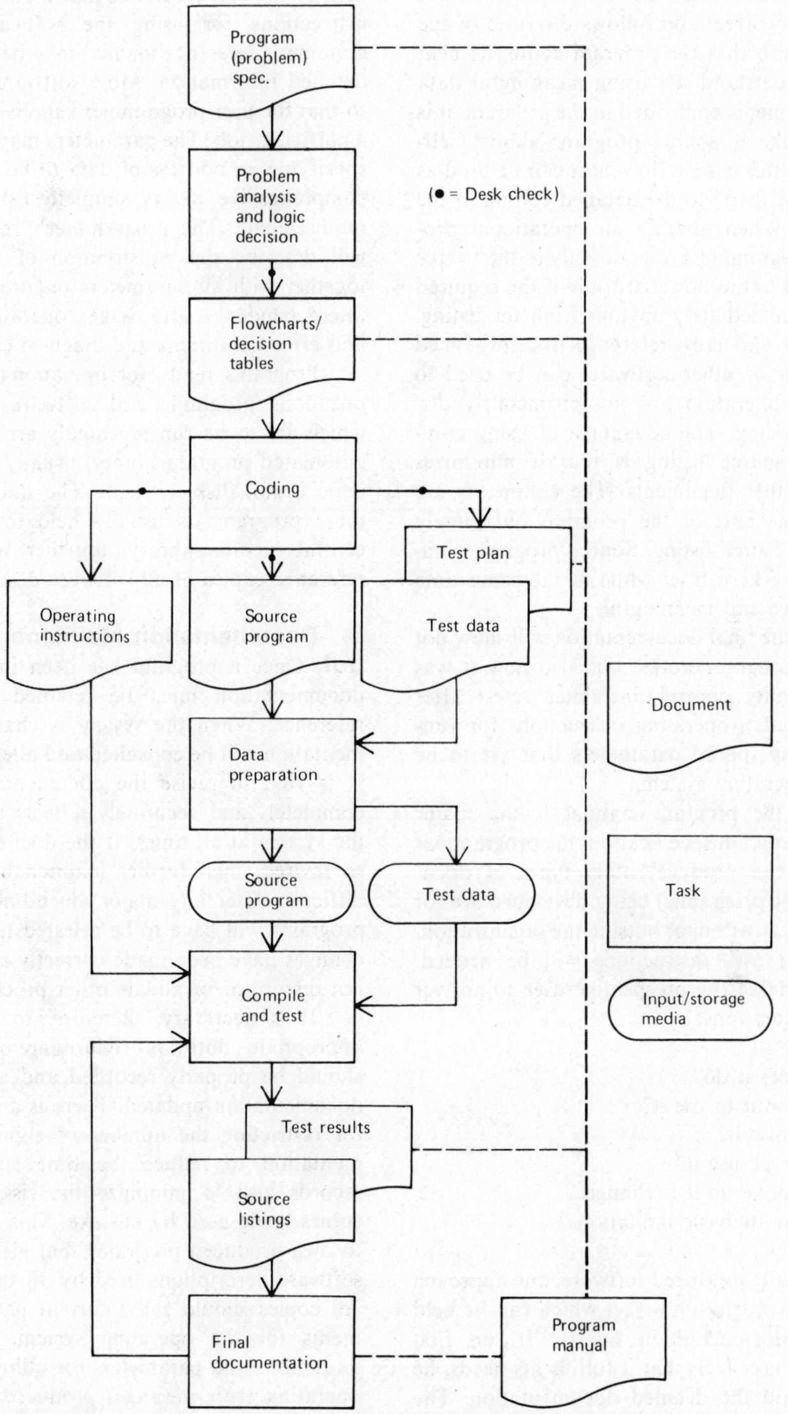


**Fig. 7.** A flowchart from a program manual.

the major part of final documentation. The programmer must insure that the source program not only is logically correct and follows the rules of the language, but also that the program coding is neat and easy to understand. By using meaningful data names and comments embedded in the program, it is possible to make a source program almost self-explanatory. In this case, a flowchart can be used as a general "route map" to the detailed coding in the source listing. When altering an operational program, many programmers refer directly to the source listing and then to the flowchart only if the required change is not immediately obvious from the listing.

Flowcharts and cross-reference lists (produced by the compiler or other software) can be used to check that an alteration has not erroneously disturbed other coding. The advantage of using comments in the source listing is that it minimizes references to other documents. The comments are not compiled as part of the program but merely appear on the source listing. Source program comments should be kept brief while at the same time being descriptive and meaningful.

Note that the final documentation will show not only how the program works, but also how it was tested (for quality control and later retest after changes are made), operating instructions for running it, and any special parameters that are to be given to the operating system.

Although the program manual is the major output of the program specification, the programmer will use (and can produce) other types of documentation. If the program(s) being developed are for general use, either within or outside the organization, then additional user instructions will be needed. They should enable the prospective user to answer the following questions:

1. What does it do?
2. Do we want to use it?
3. Can we use it?
4. How do we use it?
5. What do we do if it changes?
6. What are its basic limitations?

For internally produced software, one approach is to produce a program abstract which can be held in a central documentation library. If, on first inspection, the user feels that it fulfills his needs, he can then consult the detailed documentation. The form of this detailed documentation depends on the scope and complexity of the software. For example, a user's guide may be produced to give a general description of the program(s), the facilities available, the hardware environment required, and example uses of the software. The user's guide may contain instructions for using the software, or a programmer's reference manual may be supplied giving detailed information. Most software is constructed so that the user programmer supplies parameters for a particular job. The parameters may be as simple as specifying an address of data to be processed or as comprehensive as a complete list of processing requirements. The programmer's reference manual will describe the construction of the program(s), together with all parameters required (their format, interdependence, and usage), operating instructions, and error conditions and diagnostics.

Programs ready for operational use (both applications programs and software programs) and which are to be run repeatedly are assigned to the automated program library, usually stored on magnetic drum, disk, or tape. The documentation for these programs is usually held in some form of central records library, together with the master reference copies of all software descriptions.

**Documentation Maintenance and Control.** Once a program has been implemented, the documentation must be retained for subsequent reference. When the system is changed, the documentation will be consulted and altered accordingly. It is vital to revise the documentation so that it completely and accurately reflects the operation of the system at all times. If the documentation is not so revised, then further maintenance will be very difficult. After any major amendment, all affected programs will have to be retested to prove that the changes have been made correctly and that they do not disrupt or invalidate other processing.

It is necessary, therefore, to insure that the appropriate control procedures are used. All changes should be properly recorded and all copies of the documentation updated. There is a strong case here for restricting the number of copies of the documentation to reduce the time spent in revising records and to minimize the risk of out-of-date copies being used by mistake. This applies not only to own-produced programs, but also to generalized software descriptions used by all the programmers. All copies should show current parameter requirements for the operating system, language rules, limitations and parameters for utility programs, and operating error messages produced by all software programs. A large installation will not only create a central records library but also appoint a full-time librarian to cope with amendment distribution control. This is sometimes handled by a "software

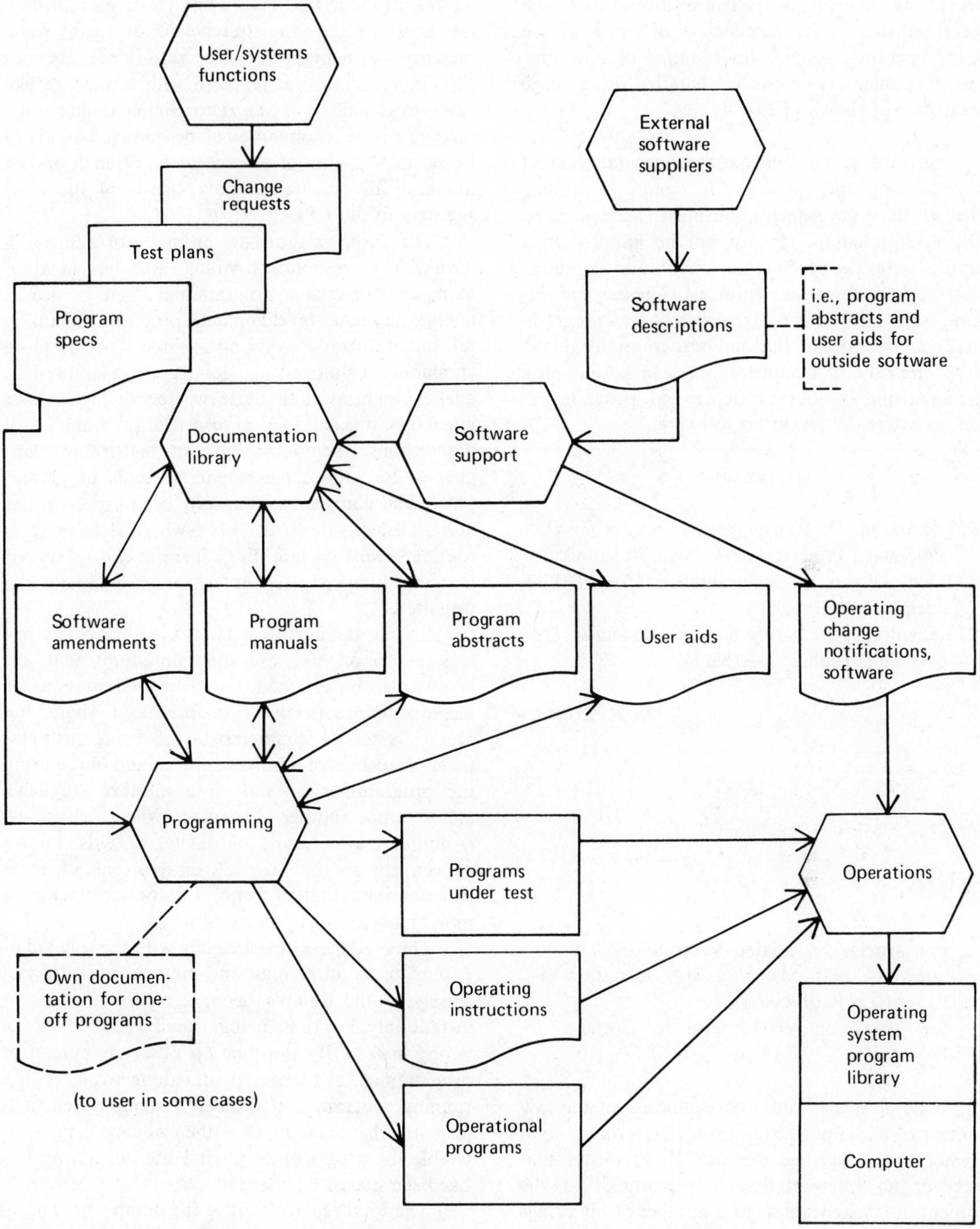


**Fig. 8.** Library and control program documentation. In addition, a documentation library may also accept and control systems documentation.

support" department, which will insure that both programming and operations departments are informed of changes in software availability and operation, such as the introduction of a new release of the operating system. An example of how program documentation will be handled in a large installation is shown in Fig. 8.

**Summary.** Documentation is a vital element in developing and running any computer project, whether in a government, business, academic, or military installation. It must not be handled in a haphazard fashion; formal documentation standards must be laid down and enforced. These standards must cover all areas: users, systems, and programming and operations. In a modern computer installation the flow of documentation can be complex, encompassing in-house systems and programs as well as externally produced software.

REFERENCES

1963. Brandon, D. *Management Standards for Data Processing*. Princeton, N.J.: Van Nostrand.

1972. Van Duyan, J. *Documentation Manual*. Philadelphia: Auerbach.

1973. London, K. *Documentation Standards* (rev. ed.). Philadelphia: Auerbach.

K. R. LONDON

## DUMP

For articles on related subjects *see* DEBUGGING; and MACHINE AND ASSEMBLY LANGUAGE PROGRAMMING.

For article on related term *see* SOURCE PROGRAM.

A dump is a printed representation of the raw content of a computer storage device, usually main memory, at a specified instant. "Raw" means that little or no interpretation is performed on the content; it is taken simply as a number of bit strings and presented to the reader as such.

A few refinements are found in even the simplest dumps that keep them from being mere one-to-one bit maps: The representation is usually in octal or hexadecimal, reducing the dump's bulk by a factor of 3 or 4. The segmentation of memory into words or bytes is reflected in the print format; the address of the leftmost word or byte on each printed line is given; and long stretches of identically filled memory segments (typically, zero-filled) are not printed verbatim, but replaced with a message like LOCATIONS 4000-4177 ALL ZERO. Simple dumps often offer the further amenities of permitting bounds to be set on the area of storage to be printed, and of automatically including the contents of the chief registers in the CPU.

The dump is the most primitive of debugging devices. It corresponds in vintage and sophistication to machine-language programming, and its use in debugging higher-level language programs should be nil, but unfortunately is not. While it is far more commonly employed in debugging assembly-language programs than those written in higher-level languages, it is still the last resort for programs of all descriptions, including those in higher-level languages. Its total replacement by tools of greater power and convenience has long been expected, but accomplished—if at all—only where debugging is routinely done on line. Even there, it can be argued that the dump is often not so much eliminated as disguised.

On-line debugging sessions do not involve extensive dumps, nor are the minidumps that are involved so bit-oriented, but the representations of memory contents that are produced share the dump's essential characteristic of being instantaneous snapshots of a moving object, and of requiring the programmer to shift into another language, almost into another discipline, when debugging. (Another major family of debugging aids, known collectively as the "trace," escapes one of these shortcomings, that of being a static observer of a moving object, but not the other.)

The crudeness of debugging with the sole aid of dumps, program listings, and mother wit is due not merely to the dump's being a record of a single instant only, but to its being, usually, a record of the wrong instant. By the time an observer, human or programmed, has detected something wrong with a running program and ordered a dump taken, it is probable that some or all of the evidence that would enable the programmer to find the underlying bug has been erased or changed.

The total replacement of the dump—or, what is equivalent, the realization of "source-language debugging"—has proved to be more difficult to achieve than had initially been expected, and may still be a long time in coming. It may require the abandonment of the notion of "debugging"—i.e., curative, after-the-fact treatment of faulty programs—in favor of preventive or prophylactic approaches like those suggested in the references given below.

### References

1965. Halpern, M. I. "Computer Programming: The Debugging Epoch Opens," *Computers and Automation* (November).

1971. Worley, W. S. "Toward Automatic Debugging of Low Level Code," IBM Technical Report TR 00.2211.

M. Halpern

# E

## EBCDIC

For articles on related subjects *see* ASCII; CODES; and IBM CARD.

The Extended Binary Coded Decimal Interchange Code (EBCDIC) was developed by IBM for use on the IBM System/360; it is also used exclusively on the IBM System/370. In order to remain compatible with IBM equipment, many other computers also use EBCDIC. The only 8-bit code that is a competitor to EBCDIC for use on computers is ASCII-8.

Fig. 1 shows the 256 ($=2^8$) combinations for EBCDIC, many of which are currently unassigned but may be assigned later as new developments in computer technology occur. The leftmost four bits (or first hexadecimal digit) of the 8-bit code are shown across the top of the Fig. 1 and the rightmost four bits (or second hexadecimal digit) in the second column on the side. Table 1 gives an example.

Also shown in Fig. 1 are the punches on an IBM card corresponding to each of the characters of the code. Zone punches (12, 11, 0, and occasionally 9) for characters above (below) the heavy black lines are shown at the top (bottom). Digit punches (1 to 9) for characters to the left (right) of the heavy black line are shown on the left (right). Table 2 gives an example.

**Table 1**

| | Code | |
|---|---|---|
| Symbol | Binary | Hexadecimal |
| 4 | 11110100 | F4 |
| Y | 11101000 | E8 |
| c | 10000011 | 83 |
| = | 01111110 | 7E |

**Table 2**

| Character | Card Punches |
|---|---|
| 4 | 4 |
| Y | 0-8 |
| c | 12-0-3 |
| = | 8-6 |
| IL | 11-9-7 |

The meanings of the control characters and special graphics, and the card-punch patterns of characters that do not conform to the rules above are shown in Fig. 1.

I. FLORES

# EBCDIC

| Bit Positions 4, 5, 6, 7 | Second Hexadecimal Digit | Digit Punches | | | | | | | | | | | | | | | | | |
|---|---|---|---|---|---|---|---|---|---|---|---|---|---|---|---|---|---|---|---|
| | | | 00 | | | | 01 | | | | 10 | | | | 11 | | | | Bit Positions 0,1 |
| | | | 00 | 01 | 10 | 11 | 00 | 01 | 10 | 11 | 00 | 01 | 10 | 11 | 00 | 01 | 10 | 11 | Bit Positions 2,3 |
| | | | 0 | 1 | 2 | 3 | 4 | 5 | 6 | 7 | 8 | 9 | A | B | C | D | E | F | First Hexadecimal Digit |
| | | | 12 | | | | 12 | 12 | | 12 | 12 | 12 | | 12 | 12 | | | | Zone Punches |
| | | | | 11 | | | | 11 | 11 | 11 | | 11 | 11 | 11 | | 11 | | | Zone Punches |
| | | | | | 0 | | 0 | | 0 | 0 | 0 | | 0 | 0 | | | 0 | | Zone Punches |
| | | | 9 | 9 | 9 | 9 | 9 | 9 | 9 | 9 | | | | | | | | | Digit Punches |
| 0000 | 0 | 8-1 | NUL (1) | DLE (2) | DS (3) | (4) | SP (5) | & (6) | - (7) | (8) | | | | | (9) | (10) | (11) | 0 (12) | 8-1 |
| 0001 | 1 | 1 | SOH | DC1 | SOS | | | | / (13) | | a | j | | | A | J | (14) | 1 | 1 |
| 0010 | 2 | 2 | STX | DC2 | FS | SYN | | | | | b | k | s | | B | K | S | 2 | 2 |
| 0011 | 3 | 3 | ETX | TM | | | | | | | c | l | t | | C | L | T | 3 | 3 |
| 0100 | 4 | 4 | PF | RES | BYP | PN | | | | | d | m | u | | D | M | U | 4 | 4 |
| 0101 | 5 | 5 | HT | NL | LF | RS | | | | | e | n | v | | E | N | V | 5 | 5 |
| 0110 | 6 | 6 | LC | BS | ETB | UC | | | | | f | o | w | | F | O | W | 6 | 6 |
| 0111 | 7 | 7 | DEL | IL | ESC | EOT | | | | | g | p | x | | G | P | X | 7 | 7 |
| 1000 | 8 | 8 | | CAN | | | | | | | h | q | y | | H | Q | Y | 8 | 8 |
| 1001 | 9 | 8-1 | | EM | | | | | | | i | r | z | | I | R | Z | 9 | 9 |
| 1010 | A | 8-2 | SMM | CC | SM | | ¢ | ! | (15) | : | | | | | | | | | 8-2 |
| 1011 | B | 8-3 | VT | CU1 | CU2 | CU3 | | $ | , | # | | | | | | | | | 8-3 |
| 1100 | C | 8-4 | FF | IFS | | DC4 | < | * | % | @ | | | | | | | | | 8-4 |
| 1101 | D | 8-5 | CR | IGS | ENQ | NAK | ( | ) | _ | ' | | | | | | | | | 8-5 |
| 1110 | E | 8-6 | SO | IRS | ACK | | + | ; | > | = | | | | | | | | | 8-6 |
| 1111 | F | 8-7 | SI | IUS | BEL | SUB | \| | ¬ | ? | " | | | | | | | | | 8-7 |
| | | | 12 | | | | 12 | | | | 12 | 12 | | 12 | 12 | 12 | | 12 | Zone Punches |
| | | | | 11 | | | | 11 | | | | 11 | 11 | 11 | | 11 | 11 | 11 | Zone Punches |
| | | | | | 0 | | | | 0 | | 0 | | 0 | 0 | 0 | | 0 | 0 | Zone Punches |
| | | | 9 | 9 | 9 | 9 | | | | | | | | | 9 | 9 | 9 | 9 | Zone Punches |

Card Hole Patterns

| | | | |
|---|---|---|---|
| (1) 12-0-9-8-1 | (5) No Punches | (9) 12-0 | (13) 0-1 |
| (2) 12-11-9-8-1 | (6) 12 | (10) 11-0 | (14) 11-0-9-1 |
| (3) 11-0-9-8-1 | (7) 11 | (11) 0-8-2 | (15) 12-11 |
| (4) 12-11-0-9-8-1 | (8) 12-11-0 | (12) 0 | |

Control Character Representations

| | | | | | |
|---|---|---|---|---|---|
| ACK | Acknowledge | EOT | End of Transmission | PF | Punch Off |
| BEL | Bell | ESC | Escape | PN | Punch On |
| BS | Backspace | ETB | End of Transmission Block | RES | Restore |
| BYP | Bypass | ETX | End of Text | RS | Reader Stop |
| CAN | Cancel | FF | Form Feed | SI | Shift In |
| CC | Cursor Control | FS | Field Separator | SM | Set Mode |
| CR | Carriage Return | HT | Horizontal Tab | SMM | Start of Manual Message |
| CU1 | Customer Use 1 | IFS | Interchange File Separator | SO | Shift Out |
| CU2 | Customer Use 2 | IGS | Interchange Group Separator | SOH | Start of Heading |
| CU3 | Customer Use 3 | IL | Idle | SOS | Start of Significance |
| DC1 | Device Control 1 | IRS | Interchange Record Separator | SP | Space |
| DC2 | Device Control 2 | IUS | Interchange Unit Separator | STX | Start of Text |
| DC4 | Device Control 4 | LC | Lower Case | SUB | Substitute |
| DEL | Delete | LF | Line Feed | SYN | Synchronous Idle |
| DLE | Data Link Escape | NAK | Negative Acknowledge | TM | Tape Mark |
| DS | Digit Select | NL | New Line | UC | Upper Case |
| EM | End of Medium | NUL | Null | VT | Vertical Tab |
| ENQ | Enquiry | | | | |

Special Graphic Characters

| | | | |
|---|---|---|---|
| ¢ | Cent Sign | - | Minus Sign, Hyphen |
| . | Period, Decimal Point | / | Slash |
| < | Less-than Sign | , | Comma |
| ( | Left Parenthesis | % | Percent |
| + | Plus Sign | _ | Underscore |
| \| | Logical OR | > | Greater-than Sign |
| & | Ampersand | ? | Question Mark |
| ! | Exclamation Point | : | Colon |
| $ | Dollar Sign | # | Number Sign |
| * | Asterisk | @ | At Sign |
| ) | Right Parenthesis | ' | Prime, Apostrophe |
| ; | Semicolon | = | Equal Sign |
| ¬ | Logical NOT | " | Quotation Mark |

**Fig. 1.** EBCDIC code combinations.

## ECKERT, J. PRESPER

For articles on related subjects *see* ENIAC; MAUCHLY, JOHN W.; and UNIVAC I.

J. Presper Eckert, co-inventor of ENIAC, was born in 1919 in Philadelphia. He received a Bachelor of Science degree in electrical engineering from the University of Pennsylvania's Moore School of Electrical Engineering in 1941, and his Master's degree under a graduate fellowship from the Moore School in 1943.

**Fig. 1.** J. PRESPER ECKERT.

Dr. Eckert collaborated with Dr. John W. Mauchly, of the Moore School's staff, on developing ENIAC (Electrical Numerical Integrator and Computer) for Army Ordnance between 1943 and 1946. This was the world's first all-electronic digital computer, and could perform 5,000 additions or subtractions per second. Its development launched the computer industry as we know it today.

In 1947, Dr. Eckert and Dr. Mauchly incorporated their venture as the Eckert-Mauchly Computer Corporation. They developed BINAC, the first electronic and fully self-checking computer, in 1949. Their next project, UNIVAC (Universal Automatic Computer), was well under way when Remington Rand acquired the Eckert-Mauchly firm in 1950.

Dr. Eckert became director of engineering for Remington Rand's Eckert-Mauchly Division, which completed UNIVAC I. He became vice-president and director of research in 1955, vice-president and director of commercial engineering in 1957, vice-president and executive assistant to the general manager in 1959, and vice-president and technical advisor to the president of Sperry-Rand, UNIVAC division, in 1963.

Dr. Eckert received an honorary degree of Doctor of Science in Engineering from the University of Pennsylvania in 1964.

In 1969, Dr. Eckert was awarded the National Medal of Science, the nation's highest award for distinguished achievement in science, mathematics, and engineering.

A Fellow of the Institute of Electrical and Electronics Engineers, and a member of the National Academy of Engineering, Dr. Eckert is listed as the inventor or co-inventor on 87 patents.

M. M. MAYNARD

## ECKERT, WALLACE J.

For article on related subject *see* DIGITAL COMPUTERS: Early.

Wallace John Eckert, was born in Pittsburgh, Pa., June 19, 1902 (d. Englewood, N.J., Aug. 24, 1971). Much of the credit for the introduction of machine computation into astronomy belongs to him. The significance of the computer impact on astronomy is comparable to that of the introduction and use of the telescope and photography.

Eckert was raised on a farm in Albion, Pa., the second of four boys born to John and Anna (Heil) Eckert. He received his A.B. degree from Oberlin College in 1925 and his M.A. from Amherst in 1926. In 1931, he was awarded his Ph.D. in astronomy by Yale University. He joined the Columbia University Department of Astronomy as an assistant instructor in 1926.

In 1928, Professor Ben Wood formed the Columbia University Statistical Bureau using punched-card equipment donated by Thomas Watson, Sr., of IBM. It was here that Eckert was first exposed to the possibility of using machines to facilitate computation. From 1929 to 1933 he used the machines in Prof. Wood's laboratory for the interpolation of astronomical data, the reduction of observational data, and the numerical solution of planetary equations. In 1933, with the encouragement of Ben Wood, he convinced Watson to install punched-card equipment and a control unit for astronomical calculations. This led to the formation of the T. J. Watson Astronomical Computing Bureau, jointly operated by Columbia, IBM, and the American Astronomical Society (1937–1945). During this period he published his landmark work (1940), "Punched Card Methods in Scientific Computation."

He was director of the U.S. Nautical Almanac Office in Washington, D.C., from 1940 to 1945. He introduced machine methods to data handling in the Naval Observatory as well as the Almanac Office. During the war he designed the "American Air Almanac," a great navigational influence that is still in use with only minor modifications.

In 1945 he was appointed head of IBM's Pure Science Department and became director of the Watson Scientific Computing Laboratory. The Laboratory not only performed needed computations, but also provided a training ground in machine computation for more than a thousand scientists in crystallography, geology, chemistry, statistics, optics, and solid-state physics, as well as astronomy.

Eckert was instrumental in the construction of IBM's Selective Sequence (Electronic) Calculator (SSEC, 1949) and the Naval Ordnance Research Calculator (NORC, 1954). Using the SSEC, Eckert, Dirk Brouwer of Yale, and G.M. Clemence (1951) of the U.S. Naval Observatory computed the precise positions of Jupiter, Saturn, Uranus, Neptune, and Pluto for the period 1652–2060. This work still serves as the Ephemeris predictions for these planets.

Eckert's most important purely astronomical contributions were in relation to the moon's orbital motion. This and later work in the area of lunar coordinates and orbital parameters (1966) provided the operational basis for NASA's Surveyor, Lunar Orbiter, and Apollo projects.

He retired from IBM in 1967 and as Professor of Celestial Mechanics at Columbia in 1970.

REFERENCES

Anon., "Dr. Wallace J. Eckert" (publications by W. J. Eckert, 38 items), and "Outstanding Contribution Award Report" (n.d.), IBM Archives.

1940. Eckert W. J. *Punched-Card Methods in Scientific Computation*. New York: Columbia University Press.

1951. Eckert, W. J., D. Brouwer, and G. M. Clemence. "Coordinates of the Five Outer Planets, 1653–2060," *Astronomical Papers*, NORC, Vol. 12, U.S. Government Printing Office.

1966. Eckert, W.J. "Transformations of the Lunar Coordinates and Orbital Parameters," *Astronomical Journal* (June).

1971. J. A. "A Great American Astronomer," *Sky and Telescope* (October).

H. S. TROPP

## ECONOMIC APPLICATIONS

For articles on related subjects *see* MODELS; OPERATIONS RESEARCH; and SIMULATION.

Economics is concerned with the interrelated questions of the formation of income, the distribution of income, and the spending of income. Adam Smith's *Wealth of Nations*, 1776, is the first systematic treatment. Alfred Marshall's *Principles of Economics*, 1890, contains the first truly satisfactory explanation of value and the first systematic treatment of price theory.

In 1936, spurred by the depression, J. M. Keynes published his influential *General Theory*. The scope and even the purpose of economics broadened as it became recognized that it belonged to the legitimate domain of governmental responsibility to guide the economy along a full-employment, full-capacity, stable-prices, adequate-growth path, with balance of payments equilibrium and equitable distribution of income as well.

A major step forward toward this goal of controlling the business cycle was Tinbergen's League of Nations study, *Statistical Testing of Business Cycles*, 1939. This was the first systematic attempt to portray the workings of the economy in the form of numerically specified models, i.e., systems of simultaneous equations. Economic theory provides the basis for such relations in *qualitative* terms; statistical time series and econometric estimation techniques (sophisticated versions of regression analysis) provide the *quantitative* specification. The quantitative model will, in general, include variables that the government can influence (taxes, for example) to achieve desired objectives.

Both the estimation procedures and the problem of choosing the appropriate values for the decision variables require vast computations. The most complete model of the United States economy has around 200 equations. One such equation might be that which purports to explain yearly consumption ($C$) as a function of wages ($W$) and nonwage income ($P$) in that year as

$$C_t = \alpha_0 + \alpha_1 P_t + \alpha_2 W_t + u_t \quad (t = 1946, \ldots, 1974).$$

The $\alpha$ coefficients have to be estimated. Even the "best" estimates for the $\alpha$ components will, for most or all years, leave a discrepancy, indicated in the equation by $u_t$. A frequent definition of "best" is that the sum of the squared $u$ values ($\Sigma u_t^2$) is minimized. The parameters of an equation that forms part of a system of equations can be properly estimated only by simultaneous estimation techniques, and require full specification of the rest of the model and extensive computations.

A more or less parallel development began with the publication, in 1944, of Vassily Leontief's *Structure of the American Economy*, introducing the concept of input/output models. Input/output models focus on interindustry deliveries and are designed to determine how a decision in some industry reverberates through the industrial complex: how much steel does a new aircraft carrier require, and how much coal is needed to produce that steel; how many miners to produce that coal, and how many eggs to keep those miners healthy, . . ., and so on. The United States input/output model distinguishes about 80 different industries. As with econometric models, the gathering of data, the statistical estimation and verification, and the manipulation of the model to answer specific questions are voracious consumers of computer time. Without computers, the useful applications of input/output modeling would be impossible.

A more recent development is the widespread use of simulation studies to predict future scenarios for economic systems. The Club of Rome's *Limits to Growth* (Meadows, 1972) is the prototype of this new area. A special Dynamo language has been developed for his purpose. Similar simulation techniques are also widely used in operations research and management science.

### REFERENCES

1965. Theil, H., et al. *Operations Research and Quantitative Economics*. New York: McGraw-Hill.

1972. Maisel, H., and A. Gnugnoli. *Simulation of Discrete Stochastic Systems*, S.R.A., 1972.

1972. Meadows, D. L., et al. *The Limits to Growth*. New York: Universe Books.

J. C. G. BOOT

## EDITOR. *See* LINKAGE EDITOR.

## EDSAC

For articles on related subjects *see* DIGITAL COMPUTERS: Early, and Origins; EDVAC; ENIAC; ULTRASONIC MEMORY; and WILKES, M. V.

For articles on related terms *see* ECKERT, J. PRESPER; MAUCHLY, JOHN W.; and MEMORY: Main.

The EDSAC (Electronic Delay Storage Automatic Calculator) was designed according to the principles expounded by J. Presper Eckert, John W. Mauchly, and others at the summer school held in 1946 at the Moore School of Electrical Engineering in Philadelphia, and which the author of this article was privileged to attend. The objectives in mind from the beginning were (1) to show that a binary stored-program computer could be constructed and operated; (2) to make a start with the development of programming techniques, even then seen to be a subject of more than trivial content; and (3) to apply the techniques developed in a variety of application fields.

In order to accelerate the attainment of the first objective, it was decided to ease the circuit design problems by choosing a conservative pulse repetition frequency (500 kc/s, compared with 1 Mc/s used in most contemporaneous projects) and to bias the logical design in the direction of simplicity rather than speed. This policy was successful, and by May 1949 the project had reached the stage at which the development of programming techniques and the running of practical programs could begin.

The ESDAC (Fig. 1) was a serial binary computer with an ultrasonic memory. The mercury tanks used for the main memory were about 1½ meters long and were built in batteries of 16 tanks. Two batteries were provided. A battery, with the associated circuits, could store 256 numbers of 35 binary digits each, one being a sign digit. An instruction occupied a half-word and it was also possible to use half-words for short numbers. Numbering of the storage locations was in terms of half-words, not full words. The instruction set was of the single-address variety, and there were 17 instructions. Multiplication was included, but not division. Input and output were by means of five-channel punched-paper tape. The input and output orders provided

**Fig. 1.** The EDSAC.

for the transfer of five binary digits from the tape to the memory, and vice versa.

Operation of the machine could not start until a short standard sequence of orders, known as the "initial orders," had been transferred into the ultrasonic memory from a mechanical read-only memory formed from a set of rotary telephone switches. The space that the initial orders occupied in the memory could be re-used when they were no longer required for reading the input tape. The initial orders determined the way in which the instructions were punched on the paper tape, and this was quite an advancement for the period.

One row of holes, interpreted as a letter, indicated the function; this was followed by the address in decimal form, with leading zeros omitted and terminated by a code letter. In the first set of initial orders to be used, this code letter merely determined whether the address referred to a short or a long location; before the end of 1950, however, these initial orders had been replaced by a more elaborate set in which the terminating characters were used to provide relocation facilities for blocks of instructions or data punched on the tape.

The EDSAC did its first calculation on May 6, 1949, and ran until 1958, when it was finally switched off.

### References


1950. Wilkes, M. V. "The EDSAC (Electronic Delay Storage Automatic Calculator)," *MTAC*, Vol. 4, p. 61.

1956. ———. *Automatic Digital Computers*. London: Methuen; New York: John Wiley.


M. V. Wilkes

## EDUCATION, COMPUTERS IN HIGHER.

*See* Higher Education, Computers in.

## EDUCATION IN COMPUTING SCIENCE

For articles on related subjects *see* Computer-Assisted Instruction; Computer-Assisted Learning and Teaching; Computer-Managed Instruction; Computer Science; and Higher Education, Computers in.

For articles on related terms *see* ANALOG COMPUTERS; ARTIFICIAL INTELLIGENCE; COMPUTABILITY; COMPUTER GRAPHICS; DATA STRUCTURES; FORMAL LANGUAGES; HEURISTICS; HYBRID COMPUTERS; INFORMATION RETRIEVAL; INFORMATION SYSTEMS; NUMERICAL ANALYSIS; PROGRAMMING LANGUAGES; SEQUENTIAL MACHINES; STORED-PROGRAM CONCEPT; and SYSTEMS PROGRAMMING.

The forerunners of the modern electronic stored-program computer were first developed at United States universities in the decade of the 1940s, mainly in response to military needs during World War II. However, a lengthy gap then ensued between the conception of computers at universities and their attendant application to the host of educational, research, and administrative processes at these universities. The beginnings of the university computer installation, or the university "computing center" organizational unit, dates only to the mid-1950s; in fact, it was only during the period from 1960 to 1965 that the "computer revolution" really took hold at United States universities. In some cases, the computing center began as a separate organization; more generally, the computing center evolved from a computer initially installed in a department of mathematics or school of engineering for research purposes. Today's computing science curricula often reflect these origins of the computing center by emphasizing the mathematical or engineering content of computing.

**University Programs.** The university academic program in computing began in the mid-1950s under the pressure of early users of computing equipment, or of the computing center staff deluged with questions about the use of these new devices. Initially, the "educational program" might consist only of a short, noncredit course given by the computing center staff; such a course mainly emphasized how to program a problem for computer solution (usually in machine or assembly language). At times, some of the material was absorbed into a regular course in mathematics or engineering, generally in three or four lectures. However, with the rapid growth of university computing installations during the 1960 to 1965 period, it became necessary to establish more formal educational programs in computing.

Usually, these programs started with a collaborative effort between the computing center and the department of mathematics or school of engineering, based again on the organizational origin of the computing center. One of the most influential of these early efforts took place at the University of Michigan, and subsequently at the University of Houston, during the period from 1959 to 1962. These efforts, conducted jointly by the computing center and the college of engineering, were aimed less at establishing computing science as a distinct academic discipline and more at the "Use of Computers in Engineering Education." At approximately the same time, Stanford University, through the joint efforts of its computing center and the department of mathematics, was establishing the discipline of computing science as an optional field of study in the department of mathematics.

These early efforts were capped by the creation of separate departments of computing science. In 1962, Stanford University established a Department of Computer Science in the School of Humanities and Sciences; in the same year, Purdue University created a Department of Computer Science in the Division of Mathematical Sciences. In each case, the bond between the service and academic functions of computing was made evident by the fact that one person was both director of the computing center and chairman of the department; this pattern was followed subsequently by other universities. Another pattern established by Stanford and Purdue was that of initially offering only graduate programs in computing science, at the master's and doctorate levels. This reflected the thinking at the time that there could be no well-defined undergraduate program in computing science, and that specialization in computing should start only at the graduate level. (It also reflected the fact that there were few professors qualified to teach computing at the time.) The arguments for and against a highly concentrated program in computing at the undergraduate level continue even today, and we will return to this point later in this article.

By the mid-1960s, events in computing science education were proceeding at a dynamic pace. Government and quasi-government reports made recommendations that spurred the growth of computing science academic programs. Two of these were of particular importance. The National Academy of Sciences report on "Digital Computer Needs in Universities and Colleges" (1966) recommended among other things that campuses should "increase as rapidly as possible the number of specialists trained annually as computer specialists and the support of pioneering research into computer systems, computer languages, and specialized equipment." The President's Science Advisory Committee report on "Computers in Higher Education" (1967) recommended that "the Federal Government expand its support of both research and education in computer sciences." These reports helped obtain government and university support for the new discipline.

During the same time period, university-sponsored conferences produced reports and books, such as "University Education in Computing Science" (Finerman, 1968), indicating that computing science was truly an emerging academic discipline and not a short-lived curiosity item. Indeed, the "intellectual respectability" of computing science was a controversial issue in the decade of the 1960s. Many educators raised the point that the computer is just a tool, and that a body of study based upon a tool is not a proper academic discipline; others indicated that computing science is not a coherent discipline but rather a collection of bits and pieces from other disciplines; still others felt that computers were not that important and were not proper objects of academic interest. However, by and large, this skepticism was itself short-lived, at times delaying but not preventing the eventual start of academic programs in computing.

Similarly, computing, mathematics, and engineering professional societies sponsored studies of the curricula effects of the new discipline. Reports of the Mathematical Association of America and the Commission on Engineering Education recommended changes in existing academic programs to assure that students in mathematics and engineering received adequate preparation in computing. This preparation was necessitated by the fact that a growing number of mathematics and engineering majors found themselves working in the computing field soon after graduation. The studies of the Association for Computing Machinery (ACM) had the most widespread effect. ACM chartered a Curriculum Committee in Computer Science to recommend necessary academic programs. The subsequent report, "Curriculum 68" (Atchison et al., 1968), for the first time defined the scope and content of a recommended undergraduate program in computing science. Later, ACM also chartered a Curriculum Committee on Computer Education for Management. This committee issued two principal reports, one on undergraduate and the other on graduate programs in information systems. We will return to the recommendations of these committees later in this article.

The effect of all these studies, conferences, and reports was a proliferating and seemingly endless number of computing science academic programs. These now abound at two-year colleges, four-year colleges, universities, and (more recently) have been introduced into secondary schools. Thus, courses in this subject now span the range from high schools through the doctorate. The programs go by different names, such as computing science, information science, data processing, and information systems. (The reader will have noticed that I prefer the phrase "computing science" to the more commonly accepted "computer science." This reflects a personal perspective that "computing" is the more comprehensive term of the two. However, I note that "computer science" departments are much more prevalent than "computing science" departments.) Each name denotes a somewhat different emphasis; for example, computing science indicates a mathematical and scientific flavor, while information systems indicates computing applied to organizational systems. The programs may be housed in a department of computing science, a combined department of electrical engineering and computing science, or given as an option in mathematics, engineering, or business administration. The academic program is now separate from the computing center, and rarely is the same person in immediate charge of both activities.

**Nonuniversity Educational Programs.** We have noted that computing science educational programs originated at universities and spread downward, from graduate to undergraduate to two-year colleges and then to high schools. In the subsequent sections of this article we will deal almost exclusively with the university program, undergraduate and graduate. The university is where an increasing number of students are receiving their education in computing science, where the discipline of computing is being molded, and where the educational programs in computing (while still quite diverse) have their greatest cohesiveness. In this section, we note briefly other educational programs in computing, specifically those offered by high schools, manufacturers of computing equipment, and private technical schools or institutes. We also discuss the educational programs at two-year colleges, in some ways similar to the technical school and in other ways a preparation for four-year undergraduate work.

HIGH SCHOOL PROGRAMS. It is difficult to describe the high school educational program in computing, for as yet there is no such identifiable program. A growing number of high schools are offering courses in computing, and a growing number of high school graduates have received some exposure to computing concepts. Yet, progress has been slow and there is no discipline of computing at the high school level. There are several reasons for this. First, very few high school teachers have taken computing courses, and still fewer understand the subject well enough to teach it. Second, to date, computing equipment has been relatively expensive, and not many high schools are affluent enough to install their own computers, or even terminals to nearby computing centers. Third, there is some doubt as to whether the discipline of computing is fundamental enough—as, for example, are English, mathematics, or physics—to teach at the high school level.

Changes are taking place. A growing number of teachers are being exposed to computing; computing equipment is becoming more affordable; attitudes about computing are being modified as the subject becomes better understood. In general, however, computing programs at the high school level, where they exist at all, consist of a cursory introduction to programming, given either as part of a mathematics course or as a separate course. This situation probably will not change materially in the immediate future.

MANUFACTURERS' PROGRAMS. Manufacturers have been offering courses in computing for years. Indeed, this informal educational activity predates the formal university educational program; probably the greatest number of people entering the computing industry have been exposed only to manufacturer-offered courses. Most such courses are intended only for customers of the manufacturers, and most are concerned only with the equipment offered by those manufacturers. In some cases, courses are as much an exercise in marketing as they are in education; the object is to sell the doubtful customer on the need for bigger and better computers, especially those offered by the manufacturer giving the course. However, some manufacturers have attempted to maintain high standards; some have separated the educational program from the marketing activity. Yet, on the whole, performance has been rather spotty. For years these courses were given free to customers. More recently, manufacturers have begun to offer certain courses for a fee. In these cases, the manufacturer-offered educational program may rival that of the private "computing institute."

TECHNICAL SCHOOL PROGRAMS. Private schools for training technicians have been operating for years. In many fields they serve a worthwhile function by preparing people for jobs as secretaries, dental technicians, draftsmen, and the like. When the computing industry started expanding rapidly, a large number of private industries began offering educational programs in computing. There are many jobs in the industry for which technician training is worthwhile, and the technical school graduate should be qualified to assume such jobs.

Unfortunately, at times, the computing institute may intimate that its training will prepare students for well-paying professional jobs in the computing industry. The technical school graduate often discovers too late that most such positions are filled by college graduates, that the professional career path in computing, as in most other fields, requires a college education. People trained as secretaries are well aware that they will not be hired for, or can advance to, executive positions; draftsmen know that they will seldom become professional engineers —at least not with technical school training only. Perhaps because of the newness of the field and the attendant absence of uniform standards and professional certification, this same fact is not as yet well recognized in computing. Currently, efforts are under way by computing societies to develop certification examinations for computing practitioners, and a number of states have given serious attention to the need for certification. These efforts may, in time, lead to a sharper and more accepted distinction between technicians and professionals.

COMMUNITY COLLEGE PROGRAMS. Two-year community (or junior) colleges have grown phenomenally in recent years, both in quantity and in scope of offerings. Twenty years ago, the community college was rather rare, and usually specialized in such areas as agriculture, forestry, and mining. Today, the community college has become as broadly based and diversified as its university cousin. The community college serves a twofold purpose. One is to train the student for a position as a technician. For these graduates, the two-year Associate degree is proof of better standards than those usually maintained by the technical school; the degree is also proof of a more well-rounded education.

The second purpose of the community college is to serve as a bridge between the high school and the four-year college or university, especially for those students uncertain of their desire or ability to continue with a higher education. For these people, the Associate degree may be an intermediate step on the way towards a bachelor's degree.

Two-year colleges have rapidly expanded their educational programs in computing to fill the same two needs. For those students wishing to terminate at the technician level, the community college education is a more satisfying alternative than the private computing institute. For others, the community college is a valuable stepping stone to the university computing science program. But there are some problems associated with this educational background.

Students terminating after two years and entering industry suffer the same identity problem as the technical school graduate. Indeed, they are more than technicians, but not quite the same as college graduates. More often than not, the career paths open to them are technician-oriented. On the other hand, graduates wishing to continue toward the bachelor's degree sometimes find the transition quite difficult. Community college standards are not always the same as university standards; community college courses are not always identical or even similar to the corresponding courses at the university.

Some of these difficulties are being addressed. Community colleges and universities have been cooperating in facilitating the transition by making courses more compatible, although it still remains a problem. Moreover, the technician versus professional point is far from reconciled. Increasingly, as the "computing profession" evolves and becomes better defined, the broader educational scope of a bachelor's degree becomes a prerequisite for a professional career.

We will not separately detail the usual curricula at two-year colleges. In some cases, these are similar to freshman and sophomore level computing courses at universities. In other cases, the differences are more visible. By and large, university programs are "scientifically" oriented, emphasizing both the scientific underpinnings of computing and the scientific or engineering applications. Two-year college programs tend to emphasize the practical aspects and the business applications (for example, accounting) of computing. The four-year university program allows more time to take unrelated courses outside those in computing, mathematics, and associated technical disciplines. (This is not always so, as we will discuss later.) Community college programs, because of the shorter time span, are more intensely oriented to courses in computing, business mathematics, accounting, and other technical areas.

**Trends in Undergraduate Education.** Let us now consider some general trends in undergraduate education, particularly in the science, technology, and professional fields, and the relation of these trends to academic programs in computing science. At the present time, the general practice in the United States is that technology-oriented students receive an undergraduate education that is highly specialized in their particular fields. For example, engineering students take most of their courses in engineering and related science (mathematics, physics, and chemistry) fields. This practice is followed even more in other countries, where students may take all courses in their particular faculty. In the past few years, various institutions have begun to question whether or not this practice of specialization at the undergraduate level of study denies the student the benefits of a more general education. For example, the Massachusetts Institute of Technology several years ago established a Commission on Undergraduate Education to study the academic program and recommend necessary changes. The Commission identified three basic aspects of undergraduate education and some shortcomings of excessive specialization.

The first aspect concerns integration of knowledge. Modern problems require that students develop the ability to synthesize as well as analyze; these problems point to the need for interdisciplinary curricula. The second deals with facts and values. The most difficult problems we face are those that relate facts and values; these require that intellectual tools from the humanities be included in the programs of engineers and scientists. The third concerns education for citizenship in a democracy. To some people these days, this may sound somewhat old-fashioned, but it has never been more important for students to understand the nature of a democracy and their roles as individuals in it.

This argument of increasing specialization versus a more general education at the undergraduate level is also a controversial issue in computing science education. On the one hand, there are those who believe that the computing science program must be highly specialized, and must emphasize computing, mathematics, and related technical subjects. Otherwise, the computing science major will not be prepared to take a job in industry or continue with his graduate education. On the other hand, there are those who believe that a more liberal undergraduate program is especially necessary in computing. Computing pervades many disciplines, and the computing student should have a background in those disciplines; further, if computing technology is to contribute to the meaningful development of society, the computing scientist must be a well-educated and informed citizen.

There are many more such arguments pro and con, and the controversy continues unabated. At the present time, most university curricula in computing science are highly specialized, following the general trend in undergraduate professional education.

**The Undergraduate Curriculum.** Because computing science is so new, there is as yet no well-established standard curriculum in this discipline. The undergraduate program varies from university to university, depending upon such things as the resources available, the amount of specialization deemed useful, and the interests of the faculty. Even the content of specific courses is, in some cases, quite variable. As we noted earlier in this article, the most scholarly attempt made to date in defining the scope and content of an undergraduate program in computing science has been the work of the ACM Curriculum Committee, "Curriculum 68" (Atchison et al., 1968). Indeed, this report has had a most profound effect on shaping the direction of computing education. Many institutions view its recommendations as the definitive yardstick by which to measure the adequacy of their programs.

Curriculum 68 contains detailed information on four beginning courses (prefixed by the letter B), nine intermediate courses (I), and nine advanced courses (A), a total of 22 undergraduate courses. We list these courses together with a brief description of each, not so much to specify detailed content as to indicate the general range and breadth covered by computing science.

B1. *Introduction to Computing*
The basic knowledge of algorithms, languages, programming, and program structure necessary to use computers effectively.

B2. *Computers and Programming*
The basic structure, language, and internal behavior of computers and the relation among these elements.

B3. *Introduction to Discrete Structures*
Fundamental algebraic, logical, and combinatoric concepts from mathematics and their application to computing science.

B4. *Numerical Calculus*
Fundamental numerical algorithms, in such areas as linear and nonlinear equations, used in scientific work.

I1. *Data Structures*
Elements of data involved in problems, structure of storage media, methods of representing, and techniques for operating on structured data.

I2. *Programming Languages*
Specification of syntax and semantics as applied to algorithms, list processing, string manipulation, and simulation languages.

I3. *Computer Organization*
A continuation of concepts introduced in course B2, the organization, logic design, and components of digital computers.

I4. *Systems Programming*
Software organization and the role of data structures and programming languages in the design and organization of computing systems.

I5. *Compiler Construction*
The organization of compilers, including symbol tables, lexical scan, syntax scan, and object code generation.

I6. *Switching Theory*
Theoretical principles and mathematical techniques involved in the design of digital systems logic.

I7. *Sequential Machines*
Definition and representation of finite state automata and sequential machines, and decision problems of finite automata.

I8. *Numerical Analysis 1*, and

I9. *Numerical Analysis 2*
Mathematically rigorous and computer-oriented methods in the solution of equations, linear systems, and differential equations.

A1. *Formal Languages and Syntactic Analysis*
Theory of context-free grammars and formal languages, and syntactic recognition techniques.

A2. *Advanced Computer Organization*
System design problems and comparison of specific examples of solutions for various computer organizations.

A3. *Analog and Hybrid Computing*
Analog, hybrid, and related digital techniques, operational characteristics of analog components, and conversion methods.

A4. *Systems Simulation*
Simulation and modeling of discrete systems, simulation methodology, and design of simulation experiments.

A5. *Information Organization and Retrieval*
Natural language processing, particularly as applied to the design and operation of automatic information systems.

A6. *Computer Graphics*
Problems and techniques for handling graphic information, such as line drawings, block diagrams, and handwriting.

A7. *Theory of Computability*
Use of abstract machines and models in the study of computability and computa-

tional complexity.

A8. *Large-Scale Information Processing Systems*
The design, organization, and integration of hardware, software, procedures, and techniques.

A9. *Artificial Intelligence and Heuristic Programming*
Application of computing systems to problems that attempt to achieve goals normally considered to require human mental capabilities.

Curriculum 68 recommends that the major in computing science should consist of ten required computing courses (B1 to B4, I1 to I4, and two from I5 to I9), plus perhaps three elective computing courses. In addition, the report lists eight supporting courses in mathematics, covering such areas as calculus, linear algebra, algebraic structures, and probability and statistics. The report notes that an academic program in computing science must be well based in mathematics, since computing science draws so heavily upon mathematical ideas and methods. Consequently, at least six of the mathematical courses listed should be required, and additional electives in mathematics should be encouraged. The program prescribed in Curriculum 68 reflects the viewpoint of those advocating a strong specialization in computing at the undergraduate level; as such, it follows the traditional pattern of most scientific and engineering undergraduate programs. The large component of computing and mathematics courses recommended (between one-half and two-thirds of the total undergraduate course load) plus technical electives in computer-related disciplines, leaves little room for the nontechnical subjects in the humanities and the social sciences.

More liberal undergraduate programs would perhaps limit the recommended number of computing and mathematics courses to one-third of the total course load, and would require that another one-third be taken in the humanities and the social sciences. By allowing flexibility in the remaining one-third, such programs would permit students to take a double major—in computing and in some other discipline such as physics, psychology, or economics.

BUSINESS DATA PROCESSING. While Curriculum 68 emphasized the mathematical and scientific content of computing science education, it paid little attention to the business-oriented computing student. Computers were originally developed for the scientific and engineering applications. Somewhat later, however, the use of computing systems for commercial applications, the "business data processing" aspect, began to exceed the scientific applications. Today, more computers are applied to, and more computing practitioners are engaged in, the data processing end than in the scientific. Yet students interested in this area find few academic programs meeting their needs, except for the host of "data processing" programs at community colleges or sometimes in the undergraduate and graduate programs in schools of business.

But perhaps a more subtle shortcoming of the scientifically oriented computing program is that it does little to prepare students adequately for the more recent applications of computing technology. As users have gained experience and computing capabilities have assumed a more general-purpose nature, the distinction between "scientific" and "business" applications has become increasingly blurred. Many modern applications require the successful integration of the systems analysis approach associated with data processing and the more rigorous mathematical analysis approach associated with scientific processing. Applications in space technology, library information retrieval, airline reservations, and banking are but a few examples of these "large scale" systems.

The large systems bring together many organizational units, technical disciplines, and people-oriented procedures; information flows through and across organizations, and causes problems at the interface; computer programs written by different organizations must be tested, accepted, and integrated into one operational system. Computing science academic programs produce students expert in computing technology but not in management organization, human and organizational behavior, systems analysis and design, economics, and the like. Yet, it is just this type of knowledge as much as the mastery of computing technology that is required to properly implement many large-scale applications.

MANAGEMENT INFORMATION SYSTEMS. As indicated earlier in this article, several years ago the ACM chartered a Curriculum Committee on Computer Education for Management. The approach of this committee has been to design curricula in the field of "information systems," systems in which computing technology is applied to the information needs of the organization. This concept is evident in the two major reports presented by Ashenhurst (1972) and Couger (1973). Couger's report on the undergraduate program recommends a curriculum that gives students knowledge of the organization, its information needs, and its behavior, as well as of computing technology. Students enrolled in this program are required to take certain prerequisite and co-requisite introductory courses in economics, psychology, mathematics, statistics, and computing. (The computing prerequisite may be quite similar to the "Introduction to Computing" course detailed in Curriculum 68.)

Let us examine these courses briefly. They are in four groups: background (prefixed by UB), computing (UC), analysis of organizations (UA), and development of systems (UD).

UB1. *Operational Analysis and Modeling*
Analytical and simulation modeling techniques useful in decision making in the system design environment.

UB2. *Human and Organizational Behavior*
Principles governing human behavior, particularly in organizations, and use of computer-based information systems in organizations.

UC1. *Information Structures*
Structures for representing the logical relationship between elements of information, and techniques for operating on such structures.

UC2. *Computer Systems*
A working view of hardware and software configurations considered as integrated systems.

UC3. *File and Communication Systems*
Basic functions of file and communications systems, current realization of these systems, and analysis of these realizations.

UC4. *Software Designs*
Complex programming tasks; and subdividing such programs for maximum clarity, efficiency, and ease of maintenance and modification.

UA8. *Systems Concepts and Implications*
The basic concepts involved in the systems point of view, the organization as a system, information flows, and information systems.

UD8. *Information Systems Analysis*
Analysis of the design of an information system intended to facilitate decision making and planning and control.

UD9. *System Design and Implementation*
The knowledge and tools necessary to develop a physical design and an operational system from the logical design.

Not all these courses are intended to be required for all students. In particular, students may decide to take an organizational or a technological concentration. For the former, there are two courses, UC8 and UC9, in place of the four courses UC1 to UC4; for the latter, course UB2 may be eliminated. The report also stresses the concept of a double major in information systems and (for example) accounting or engineering. It gives illustrations of sample programs for these two double majors. It is still uncertain whether such programs would be housed in a school of business, a school of engineering, department of computing science, or indeed whether universities would give such programs the priority given in the past to the scientifically oriented programs in computing. It may be that in future years the effects of this report on undergraduate programs in information systems will be as widespread as those of Curriculum 68.

In any event, most departments of computing science or information systems are generally oriented more toward "software" than "hardware." By necessity, and with some exception, students interested in the hardware aspects of computing normally major in departments of electrical engineering. (Indeed, graduates of such programs are referred to as hardware "engineers" rather than computing "scientists," although the distinction is not meaningful.) Courses at the interface (e.g., switching and microprogramming) may be given in computing science or electrical engineering, or both. As noted earlier, computing at some universities is an option in electrical engineering; at others there are combined departments of electrical engineering and computing science.

As a final note on undergraduate programs in computing, many undergraduate courses in computing attract not only the major in computing science (or information systems) but also students majoring in other disciplines. The President's Science Advisory Committee report (Pierce et al., 1967) estimated that about three of every four college undergraduates have need for some educational exposure to computing. The extent of such exposure obviously depends upon the fields in which students are majoring. Those in the liberal arts might benefit only from some introductory knowledge of computing technology. Students majoring in the sciences, engineering, or business administration require a great deal more, in some cases extending to a "minor" or double major in computing. Usually, no special "service" courses in computing are intended mainly for the noncomputing science major. However, the computing science program performs a necessary service function for these students.

**The Graduate Program.** Although graduate programs in computing predate the undergraduate, there are few descriptions in the formal literature of graduate curricula. Curriculum 68 contains a brief desciption of the master's and doctoral program. Finerman's (1968) book is more explicit, since it derived from a conference on graduate academic programs.

A master's program in computing science may be terminal or nonterminal. In the first case, the goal is to develop programming and applied problem-solving capabilities so that the graduate can qualify for a senior position in industry or research organizations. The goal of the nonterminal program is to develop the intellectual capabilities so that the graduate can continue to the doctoral program (although some students go directly from the bachelor's degree to the doctorate). This approach is in the pattern of the traditional master's programs for so-called scientific and professional disciplines. In many sciences, the master's program is viewed as the testing ground for further graduate study. Students who prove they have the necessary capabilities can continue for the doctorate; those who cannot, terminate with the master's degree. However, in professional disciplines, the terminal master's degree is an honorable goal, since most people have no need for the doctorate. In business administration, for example, several excellent universities offer the terminal master's program. Computing science, both a scientific and a professional discipline, increasingly offers the two choices, depending upon the inclination of the student.

The master's program generally has three areas of specialization. The first encompasses information structures and processes. This is quite abstract and theoretical, involving advanced mathematical concepts; it includes such topics as computability, formal languages, and switching and automata theory. The second category covers information processing systems. This deals with practical techniques in such areas as computer organization and design, programming languages, operating systems, and assemblers and compilers. The third category comprises methodologies. This deals with a broad spectrum of techniques appropriate to various computing applications, such as numerical analysis, text processing and graphics, symbol manipulation, simulation, information retrieval, and artificial intelligence.

The master's program in the last two categories —information processing systems and methodologies—might be terminal or not; at many institutions it is assumed that students in these categories will terminate. Students in these areas take one or more courses in the theoretical aspects of computing science, but most courses are in their particular field of specialization, drawn from the intermediate and advanced courses in Curriculum 68 or from graduate versions of these courses. The theoretically inclined student is usually interested in continuing toward the doctorate. Therefore, the first category—information structures and processing—is generally a nonterminal program; again, students in this category are required to take some courses in the other areas. At many institutions, the terminal master's student may elect to perform thesis work, or not; if not, two more courses may be substituted for the thesis or a project may be required. Nonterminal students are expected or required to submit a thesis as further proof of their qualification for the doctorate. Many students enter the master's program with undergraduate degrees that are not in computing science but in the sciences or engineering. Thus they have the essential of a good background in mathematics, especially important for those who expect to continue past the master's degree.

In contrast to this approach to computing science, Ashenhurst (1972) considers the professionally oriented master's program. The philosophy expressed in the undergraduate curriculum carries forward to the graduate level. The program in information systems deals with computing technology as applied to the organization and its systems. As in the undergraduate program, there are four groups of courses. The first involves two background courses: one in operations research and the other in behavior in organizations. The second group, dealing with the environment in which systems function, involves four courses in the organization and systems requirements. The third group contains four courses dealing with computing and information technology. Finally, the fourth group integrates the previous two groups with three additional courses in the analysis and development of systems. The courses are more advanced versions of those at the undergraduate level. Students can enter this program with a background in computing, economics, or other business areas, although the program is equally useful for those with an engineering background. As we discussed previously, computing technology is applied to large engineering or scientific systems as well as to business or commercial systems; in many applications, the "scientific" or "business" distinction is meaningless. The entering student is required to have prerequisite undergraduate courses in mathematics, statistics, computer programming, economics, and psychology.

Most doctoral programs are for students with theoretical or research interests. Courses at this level especially reflect the special interests of the faculty members. In general, however, they are similar to the master's degree programs in the following areas: logical design, switching theory, computer circuits and devices; computer organization, programming languages, compiler and operating systems; computability, formal languages, automata; numerical mathematics, operations research; methodologies such as artificial intelligence, simulation, and modeling. The doctoral thesis, drawn from one or more of these areas, lies at the heart of the doctoral program. It is the means by which the student demonstrates the capability for original contribution to knowledge. This is, of course, the fundamental requirement for the doctorate.

Some universities are reexamining academic programs at the graduate as well as at the undergraduate level. In some cases this examination may lead to broader (and longer) interdisciplinary master's degree programs; in others, predoctoral intermediate degree programs may be established, which do not require original contribution to knowledge but recognize a dimension of excellence in another area. In general, however, the specialized master's degree and the doctorate still are regarded as the accepted graduate programs.

**Summary.** Formal education in computing science is quite new, dating back only to the early 1960s. Educational programs originated at universities, resulting from the increasing use of computers to service the needs of university students, faculty, and administrators. Today, most colleges and universities offer academic programs in computing, mainly as a separate discipline but sometimes as an option in a related discipline. As can be expected in such a new field, the educational program still has fuzzy edges; at times, it overlaps applied mathematics, electrical engineering, business administration, and other disciplines. Yet, in just a few short years, it has become a visible and influential area of study.

Computing science undergraduate programs also provide a service function by making courses available to the major in other disciplines. Usually, these students require some computing courses so that they can better apply computing methods to their fields; often, however, these students become computing practitioners after graduation. Perhaps because of the newness of the field, industrial organizations fill their computing positions with graduates from many disciplines in addition to computing.

Although the discussions in this article apply primarily to computing education in the United States and Canada, experiences in other countries are quite similar. The major difference is that computing science educational programs in other countries were introduced later than those in North America. For example, with some exceptions, western European and Israeli universities initiated such programs around the late 1960s, South American universities around 1970, and African universities during the early 1970s.

One result of these educational programs is a recognition that computing science involves more than the study of a tool. The computer has given entirely new scope to the whole spectrum of computation applications, so much so that people who work with computers have found new approaches to problem solving, even in areas to which the computer as a tool may never be applied. Too often our early educational programs emphasized the study of the computer as a tool; many programs, especially those below the college level, still do. There is now, however, an increasing awareness that the use of the computer stimulates and modifies intellectual processes, and as a result makes it possible for man to expand his intellectual capabilities. This added dimension must be part of any academic program in computing science or information systems.

### References

The early efforts to bring computing methods into engineering education are described in three related volumes:

1960. University of Michigan Study, "Electronic Computers in Engineering Education." Ann Arbor: University of Michigan.

1961. University of Michigan Study. "Use of Computers in Engineering Education, Second Annual Report." Ann Arbor: University of Michigan.

1962. University of Houston Study. "Use of Computers in Engineering Education—A Report of the Advanced Science Seminar." Houston, Texas: University of Houston.

There were two principal government-sponsored studies on computing in universities during the mid-1960s. Both gave background information on the use of computers in universities and recommended government financial support for computing education:

1966. Rosser, J. B., et al. "Digital Computer Needs in Universities and Colleges." Washington, National Academy of Sciences/National Research Council.

1967. Pierce, J., et al. "Computers in Higher Education," The President's Science Advisory Committee, The White House. Washington, D.C.: U.S. Government Printing Office.

There are four principal references for undergraduate and graduate programs in computing. Three have been published in the monthly periodical, *Communications of the Association for Computing Machniery* (CACM), and the fourth is a monograph of the ACM:

1968. Atchison, W., et al. "Curriculum 68," A Report of the ACM Curriculum Committee on Computer Science Education, *CACM*, Vol. 11 (March), pp. 151–197.

1972. Ashenhurst, R. (Ed.). "Curriculum Recommendations for Graduate Professional Programs in Information Systems," A Report of the ACM Curriculum Committee on Computer Education for Management, *CACM*, Vol. 15 (May), pp. 363–398.

1973. Couger, J. D. (Ed.). "Curriculum Recommendations for Undergraduate Programs in Information Systems," A Report of the ACM Curriculum Committee on Computer Education for Management, *CACM*, Vol. 16 (December), pp. 727–749.

1968. Finerman, A. (Ed.). "University Education in Computing Science," ACM Monograph. New York: Academic Press.

A. FINERMAN

# EDVAC

For articles on related subjects *see* DIGITAL COMPUTERS: Early; ENIAC; STORED-PROGRAM CONCEPT; and VON NEUMANN MACHINE.

For articles with related biographical information *see* ECKERT, J. PRESPER; MAUCHLY, JOHN W.; and VON NEUMANN, JOHN.

The EDVAC (Electronic Discrete Variable Automatic Computer) was a direct outgrowth of the work on the ENIAC. During the design and construction of the ENIAC in 1944 and 1945, the need for more storage (only twenty 10-decimal digit numbers in the ENIAC) was realized. The experience with acoustic delay lines for radar range measurement led to the concept of recirculating storage of digital information. The group at the Moore School of Electrical Engineering at the University of Pennsylvania started developmental work on mercury delay lines for such storage, and initiated the design of the EDVAC.

This was the first stored-program computer; the instructions controlling the computational process are stored in the same way that data is stored. The basic logical ideas were described by von Neumann (1945), and computers based on such designs have come to be known as "von Neumann computers." The principles involved in the EDVAC design exerted a strong influence on the computers that followed it.

The EDVAC had about 4,000 tubes and 10,000 crystal diodes. It used a 1,024-word recirculating mercury-delay line memory, consisting of 23 lines, each 384 $\mu$s long. The words were 44 bits long. Instructions were of the four-address type (4-bit operation code and four 10-bit addresses). The arithmetic unit did both fixed and floating-point operations. Input and output were via punched paper tape and IBM cards. Information was all handled as serial pulse trains and the clock frequency was 1 MHz.

Although the conceptual design of the EDVAC was complete in 1946, and it was delivered in 1949 to the Ballistic Research Laboratories at Aberdeen, Maryland, by 1950 the entire calculator had not yet worked as a unit and was still undergoing extensive tests (Stifler, 1950, pp. 200–201). The delay in completion of the EDVAC was primarily due to the efflux of computer people from the Moore School in 1946. Eckert and Mauchly resigned and launched a commercial venture (UNIVAC). Herman Goldstine and Arthur Burks went to Princeton to work with von Neumann, and the author left to work with Turing in England. T. K. Sharpless was put in charge, but he, too, left later to go into business for himself.

The EDVAC finally became operational as a unit in 1951. An Aberdeen Proving Ground report states that during 1952, the EDVAC "began to operate on a production basis." For nine months of 1952 the average available time per week was 47.4 hours (23.3 for code checking and 24.1 for production), and the average "engineering" time was 104.8 hours. Approximately 70.4 hours of this was unscheduled maintenance; 10,000 defective tubes (over twice the complement) and about 3,000 (of 10,000) germanium diodes had been replaced. In a later Aberdeen report, Weik notes that during 1956, the average error-free running period was approximately 8 hours, and that out of a run time of 8,728 hours, 6,752 were good (78%). This gave approximately 130 hours of "good time" per week. The EDVAC was used until December 1962 (Knath, 1970, p. 259).

REFERENCES


1945. von Neumann, John, "First Draft of a Report on the EDVAC," Contract No. W-670-ORD-4926, U.S. Army Ordnance Department. Philadelphia: University of Pennsylvania, Moore School of Electrical Engineering, June 30.

1950. Stifler, W. W., Jr. (Ed.). *High Speed Computing Devices*. New York: McGraw-Hill.

1970. Knuth, Donald E. "Von Neumann's First Computer Program," *Computing Surveys*, Vol. 2, No. 4 (December), pp. 247–260.


H. D. HUSKEY

## ELECTRONIC CALCULATOR. *See* CALCULATOR, ELECTRONIC.

## EMULATION

For articles on related subjects *see* HOST SYSTEM; MICROPROGRAMMING; and SIMULATION.

For article on related terms *see* IBM 360-370 SERIES.

There is little agreement as to which of the many meanings attributed to emulation is valid. Rather than attempt to adjudicate the issue here, a selection of different definitions is presented in chronological sequence followed by a short discussion.

1. "Emulation is the name given to the technique introduced in the IBM System/360 machine series for aiding in the conversion problem [to System/360 from previous IBM computers in the 1400 and 7000 series]. An emulator is a package that includes both special hardware and a complementary set of software ... which runs in the manner of an interpretive routine simulator program but is 5 or even 10 times as fast as a purely software simulator." (S. G. Tucker, 1965)

2. "[An] emulator [is] a complete set of microprograms which, when embedded in a control store, define a machine." (R. F. Rosin, 1969)

3. "Here, emulation is defined as the ability of one system to execute machine language programs written for another system." (S. Husson, p. 15, 1970)

4. "Emulation is defined here as a combined hardware-software approach to simulation. ... An emulator is basically an extension of the host machine's architecture, hardware and software to include the range of the target machine [i.e., the machine being emulated]." (S. Husson, 1970, p. 90)

5. "Emulation (as defined by IBM) means the ability of one [stored-program digital computer] to interpret another's program *at a reasonable performance level*." (Bell and Newell, 1971)

6. "[To emulate is] to imitate one system with another such that the imitating system accepts the same data, executes the same program, and achieves the same results as the imitated system." (Clason, 1971)

Three observations can be made with respect to this list of definitions. First, as can be seen in the preceding definitions, use of the term "emulation" has been subject to the same evolutionary pressures that impact almost all computer science. Indeed, the author of this article is far more in agreement with definitions 3 and 6 than he is with his own outdated interpretation offered in 1969, and included here as definition 2.

Second, the influence of the IBM Corporation, although probably not a result of corporate policy, can be clearly seen in that definitions 1, 4, and 5 are directly or indirectly based on the original use of the term in connection with System/360. Although it might be suggested that alternatives should be found when referring to concepts other than those introduced by IBM, recent publications from that company indicate a strong trend toward a more general interpretation, such as that given in item 6.

Finally, emulation has been strongly associated with microprogramming, as seen in definition 2 and in the title of the source of definitions 3 and 4. However, similar to the trend away from the original, narrow IBM definition, the relationship between microprogramming and emulation is considered quite tenuous in many circles today.

REFERENCES

1965. Tucker, S. G. "Emulation of Large Systems," *Communications of ACM*, Vol. 8, No. 12 (December), pp. 753–761.

1969. Rosin, R. F. "Contemporary Concepts of Microprogramming and Emulation," *Computing Surveys*, Vol. 1, No. 4 (December), pp. 197–212.

1970. Husson, S. *Microprogramming: Practices and Principles*. Englewood Cliffs, N.J.: Prentice-Hall.

1971. Bell, C. G., and A. Newell. *Computer Structures*. New York: McGraw-Hill.

1971. Clason, W. E. *Dictionary of Computers, Automatic Control, and Data Processing*. Amsterdam: Elsevier.

R. F. ROSIN

# ENGINEERING APPLICATIONS

For articles on related subjects *see* COMPUTER-AIDED DESIGN; CONTROL APPLICATIONS; FINITE ELEMENT METHOD; NUMERICAL ANALYSIS; PERT/CPM, PROBLEM-ORIENTED LANGUAGES; and SIMULATION.

Electronic computers have triggered a revolution in the various engineering disciplines. They cover so wide a field that it seems impossible to deal here with their full extent. We will, however, attempt to discuss the following categories:

1. Numerical and process control.
2. Engineering analysis.
3. Simulation.
4. Optimization.
5. Engineering design.

**Numerical Control.** One of the computer applications in production is the numerical control for machining metal parts. These parts are produced by either milling or routing. Essentially, the cutting tool is moved in a predetermined path so that a part is machined from a sheet metal or other heavier metal stock.

If, for example, we wish to cut the two-dimensional contoured shape shown in Fig. 1, the basic operation involved is a movement of the cutting tool in the $x$ and $y$ directions. The cutting tool is advanced in, say, the $x$ direction when the $x$-direction control receives a pulse. These pulses direct the *center* of the cutter, but the cutting is actually performed by the edge of the cutter. Therefore, the offset of the cutter must be determined first.

As far as a production engineer is concerned, cutting a contoured shape involves the following typical steps:

1. Translate the required part on the blueprint into a set of instructions in a user-oriented language, such as APT (Automatically Programmed Tools).
2. Describe the offset path for the cutter.
3. Produce a punched tape by the computer. The tape, containing the information of detailed motions of the cutting tools, is used to control the milling machine.

In the three-dimensional case, the surfaces used to define the end product are of two types. One is the classic type, such as planes, spheres, and cylinders; and the other is commonly known as a "scupltured surface"—complex doubly curved surfaces. The art of machining these complex surfaces has been recently enhanced by extensions to the APT language and its numerical control program.

PROCESS CONTROL. The numerical control described above provides automation of the discrete operations. By contrast, computers may be used to provide automation of continuous operations, known as "process control." A typical example is that of a chemical plant where a definitive sequence of decisions is required to process raw materials. Once all alternative possibilities are predetermined, computers can readily be used to control the entire processing.

The purpose of automatic control of chemical plants is twofold: to achieve optimum production and to obtain the highest possible quality of product. One unique feature of a typical chemical process is the large number of parameters involved, such as flow rate, viscosity, pressure, and temperature. Nonlinear relationships are used as a rule. Typically, information from various measuring stations is transmitted to a computer, which will computerize or make decisions for the control mechanisms so that an optimum operation is maintained.

Computer control is also extensively used in many other fields of engineering. Applications include automatic testing of circuit board assemblies and complex shipboard control systems.

**Engineering Analysis.** Many problems in engineering frequently reduce to one or two standard mathematical problems. Sometimes the explicit

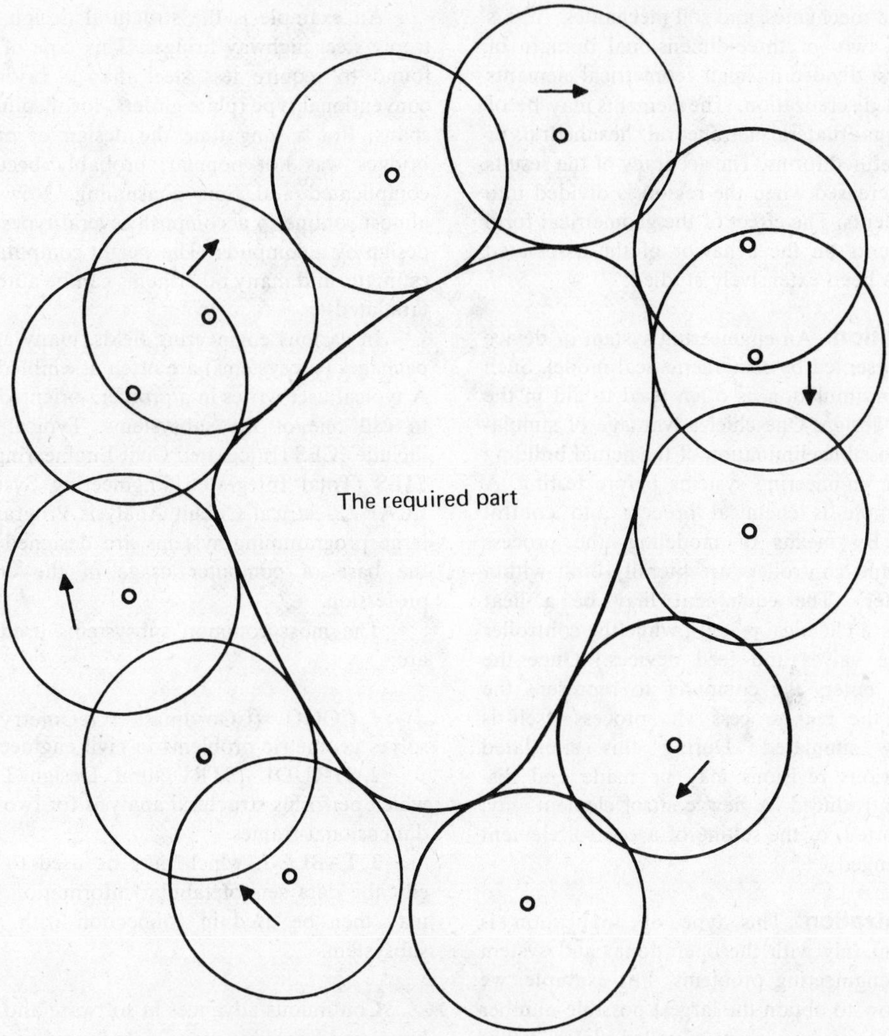


**Fig. 1.** Offset path for the cutter tool in numerical control. The circles indicate some of the successive positions of the cutter. The center of each circle represents the cutter center, which is directed by the control pulses.

solutions may be found, and these are easily programmed for a digital computer. More frequently, they require approximate numerical treatment.

The two most common classes of mathematical problems seem to occur in matrix manipulations and ordinary differential equations. Matrix problems may arise in structural or network analysis, vibrations, and buckling. Usually a continuous system is idealized as a discrete system, a process known as "physical discretization." Matrix problems may also arise from a large class of partial differential equations through the use of finite differences, a process often known as "mathematical discretization." The advent of computer technology has enabled engineers to deal with matrices of very large size. Problems involving matrices on the order 100,000 have been handled successfully.

Ordinary differential equations occur in chemical reaction systems, spring-mass systems, temperature distribution, and many-body systems.

Other standard problems include the solutions of polynomial and transcendental equations, interpolation, curve fitting, and quadrature.

Since the advent of computers, the *finite element method* has gained popularity in various fields of engineering, including structural mechanics, heat transfer, fluid mechanics, and soil mechanics. In this method, the two- or three-dimensional domain of interest is first divided in small geometrical elements —a physical discretization. The elements may be of triangular, quadrilateral, tetrahedral, hexahedral, or other well-defined forms. The accuracy of the results is readily increased when the region is divided into smaller elements. The effect of the geometrical form of the elements on the behavior of the associated matrices has been extensively studied.

**Simulation.** An engineering system or device may be represented by a mathematical model. Such modeling, or simulation, is often used to aid in the engineering design. One chief advantage of simulation is the possible elimination of the actual building of expensive engineering systems before testing. A typical example is chemical process and control simulation. By means of modeling, the process equipment and controllers are literally built within the computer. (The equipment may be a heat exchanger or a chemical reactor, while the controller may include valves and feed devices.) Once the information enters the computer to represent the factors for the real process, the process itself is dynamically simulated. During this simulated process, various revisions may be made and disturbances introduced. A new control element, say, may be inserted, or the setting of a control element may be changed.

**Optimization.** This type of application is concerned mainly with the operational and system aspects of engineering problems. For example, we deal with how to obtain the largest possible number of gusset plates from a sheet of rolled plates, rather than how to design gussets. In a large system, the field data and measurements are usually integrated with some mathematical models and are processed on a large-scale computer. Important techniques include linear and dynamic programming and network analysis. PERT (Program Evaluation and Review Technique) and CPM (Critical Path Method) are also used to assist engineering decision making.

**Engineering Design.** Without computers, for most design problems the engineer would either make a "guestimate" from his experience or, at best, estimate only one or two alternatives in his design. When a digital computer is used, a complete comparative study can be readily obtained to show the effect of numerous parameters. This is a typical situation where a computer is used to perform bulky and repetitive calculations.

An example is the structural design of orthotropic steel highway bridges. This type of bridge is found to require less steel than a bridge of the conventional type (plate girders) for medium or long spans. For a long time the design of orthotropic bridges was not popular, probably because it is complicated and time consuming. Now it seems almost routine to accomplish several types of bridge design by a computer. The weight computation, cost estimate, and many other items can be automatically tabulated.

In various engineering fields, many application packages (subsystems) are often assembled together. A typical user writes in a problem-oriented language to call one of the subsystems. Typical examples include ICES (Integrated Civil Engineering System), TIES (Total Integrated Engineering System), and ECAP (Electrical Circuit Analysis Program). These large programming systems are designed to widen the base of computer usage in the engineering profession.

The most common subsystems used in ICES are:

1. COGO (COordinate GeOmetry), which solves geometric problems in civil engineering.
2. STRUDL (STRUctural Design Language), which performs structural analysis for two- or three-dimensional frames.
3. TABLE-1, which may be used to create or edit the data sets of tabular information. The data may then be used in connection with any other subsystem.

Continuous advances in software and hardware have made possible many new innovations in computer-aided design in engineering and also have permitted a more direct partnership between computers and their human users.

Time sharing, which brings the engineer closer to the computer, is often used in practice. At his own computer terminal, each engineer executes his program in an *interactive* manner.

Another interesting development is in the area of engineering graphics. By using a lightpen on a display scope, as shown in Fig. 2, one can draw two projections of a given object, ask the computer to straighten out lines, or rectify angles, or replace one part of the object with a new one. A sequence of perspective views can be produced by the computer. Similarly, modifications of a surface can be made on a display scope.

Several time-sharing systems have recently been supplemented by virtual memory facilities. Virtual

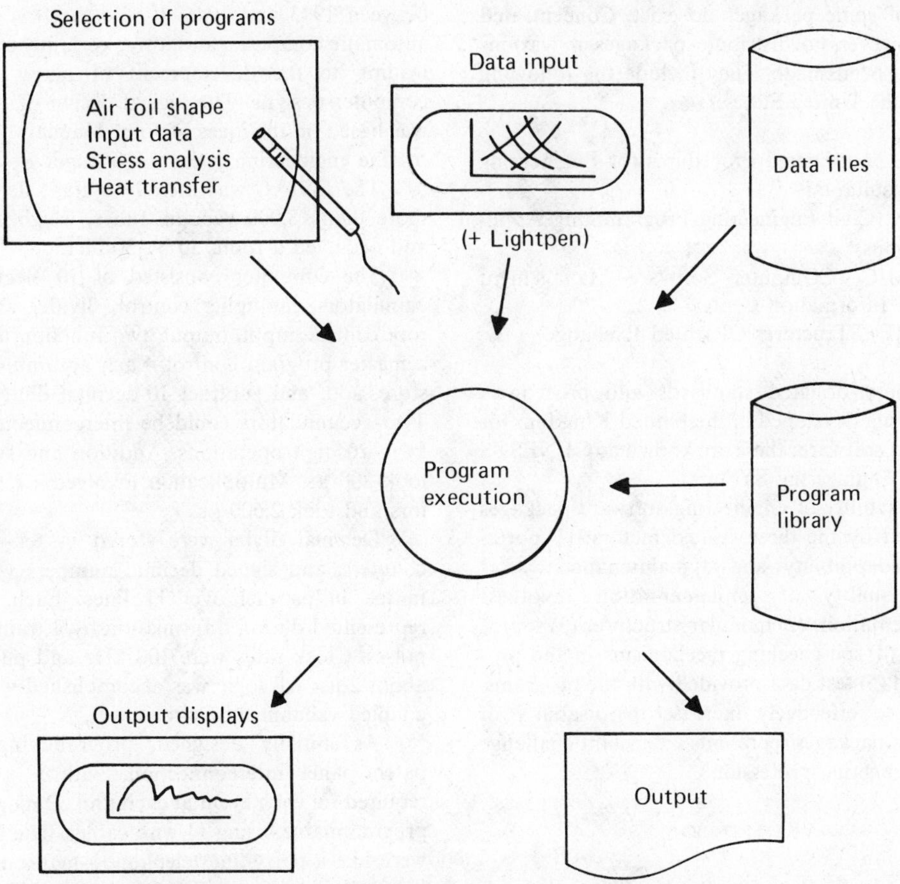


**Fig. 2.** Engineering design using a virtual machine time-sharing system.

memory is a technique that makes a computer appear to have considerably more main storage capacity than it actually has. This makes possible the concurrent processing of programs that in total size would exceed main storage capacity.

The development of a virtual machine time-sharing system with display consoles has been useful in computer-aided design. It allows an engineer to make the computer an integral part of an engineering design sequence through the interactive usage of display consoles. A typical example is the design of jet engine turbine blades. The following steps might be involved:

1. Sitting at a display console, the design engineer calls for a program for airfoil shape. Initial geometric coordinates may be read in through a card reader. The points or lines of the resulting picture on a display scope may then be added, changed, or deleted.

2. The engineer calls for a program such as one to perform static or dynamic stress analysis. The result is graphically shown on the display console. At this point, he may wish to go back to step 1 or go to step 3.

3. The design engineer calls for another program, such as a heat transfer program, and so on.

These steps can be followed in Fig. 2.

**Conclusion.** We conclude our discussion by pointing out some development problems associated with engineering applications.

At the present time, application packages in some engineering disciplines have been developed with relatively little consideration given to language, hardware and software environment, documentation, and maintenance. The growth of these packages is extensive, but it is unmonitored and uncontrolled. As a result, problems of availability and usability of some packages do exist. Concentrated efforts, however, to distribute packages in various fields have been made. They include the following groups in the United States:

APEC (Automated Procedures for Engineering Consultants)
CEPA (Civil Engineering Programming Applications)
COSMIC (COmputer Software Management and Information Center)
STORE (STructures ORiented Exchange).

Computer-oriented standards and procedures are also being developed in the United Kingdom for engineering software; these are known as GENESYS (GENeral Engineering SYStem).

The usability of engineering software packages is measured by the three related factors: (1) portability; (2) adaptability; and (3) maintenance.

The quality of implementation involves: (1) documentation; (2) modular structure; (3) source language; (4) self-checking mechanisms in the programs, and (5) test data provided with the programs.

How to effectively increase the usability of application packages represents a constant challenge to the engineering profession.

### References

1967. Kuo, S. S. *Computer Analysis of Orthotropic Steel Plate Superstructures for Highway Bridges*, (4 vol., PB-173 355 through PB-173 358). Springfield, Va.: U.S. Department of Commerce, National Technical Information Service.

1972. Furman, T. T. (Ed.). *The Use of Computers in Engineering Design*. New York: Van Nostrand-Reinhold.

1972. Kuo, S. S. *Computer Applications of Numerical Methods*. Reading, Mass.: Addison-Wesley.

S. S. Kuo

# ENIAC

For articles on related subjects *see* Digital Computers: Early; Eckert, J. Presper; and Mauchly, John W.

The ENIAC (Electronic Numerical Integrator and Computer) was developed at the Moore School of the University of Pennsylvania in Philadelphia between 1943 and 1946. It was the first electronic automatic computer, and it was certainly a landmark leading to the development of many automatic computer designs. The logical design of the system was based on the ideas of John Mauchly, and credit for the engineering goes to J. Presper Eckert, Jr.

The ENIAC was literally a giant. It contained more than 18,000 vacuum tubes, weighed 30 tons, and occupied a room 30 by 50 feet.

The computer consisted of 20 electronic accumulators, multiplier control, divider and square root control, input, output, two function tables, and a master program control. Each accumulator could store, add, and subtract 10-decimal digit numbers. Two accumulators could be interconnected to perform 20 digit operations. Addition and subtraction took 200 $\mu$s. Multiplication involved six accumulators and took 2,600 $\mu$s.

Decimal digits were stored in ten-stage ring counters, and signed decimal numbers were transmitted in parallel over 11 lines. Each digit was represented during transmission by a train of 0 to 9 pulses. Clock rates were 100 kHz and pulse widths about 2 $\mu$s. All logic was accomplished with direct-coupled vacuum tube circuitry.

As initially designed, programming was by patch panel interconnection, with a wire being required for each event at each unit. Data paths were programmable, using 11 wire cables. The data paths were like a party-line telephone—many units could listen, but only one could transmit. Various units could operate in parallel, being initiated from the same program signal and perhaps using distinct data paths. Interlocks were provided so that independent actions of indeterminate length (e.g., card reading) could complete before follow-on actions were initiated. Signs of results could change the flow of control.

The ENIAC was converted later to a card-programmed computer. In this scheme, certain standard operations were set up in the patch panel wiring, and sequences of these macro operations were initiated from the card reader.

The ENIAC was designed to integrate ballistic equations, and a significant accomplishment at its dedication in February 1946 was the computation of the trajectory of a 16-inch naval shell in less than real time. It was formally accepted a few months after its dedication by the U.S. Army Ordnance Corps, but was still operated at the Moore School until late 1946, when it was dismantled and shipped to Aberdeen Proving Ground in Maryland. It became operational again in 1947, and was operated until Oct. 2, 1955 (Weik, 1961, p. 575).

**Fig. 1.** ENIAC. (Courtesy of Smithsonian Institution.)

The first significant computation on the ENIAC involved atomic energy. Since World War II had ended, there was no longer urgent need for the firing tables that had motivated its design and the support of the Army Ordnance Corps. Among the problems first computed on it, in addition to those involving atomic energy, were random number studies, round-off errors, cosmic ray studies, thermal ignition, wind tunnel design, and weather prediction. It was the major instrument for the computation of all ballistic tables for the U. S. Army and Air Force (Weik, 1961).

Aberdeen Proving Ground reported that during 1952 the "total machine time" for the ENIAC was 7,247 hr., divided as follows: production, 3,491 hr; problem setup and code-checking, 1,061 hr; idle, 195.3 hr; scheduled engineering, 651 hr; and unscheduled "engineering," 1,847.8 hr. The major portion of the scheduled engineering was preventive servicing, the remainder being for improvements and additions; 90% of the unscheduled engineering was devoted to locating and replacing defective tubes. During 1952 approximately 19,000 tubes were replaced (more than 100% of the tube complement).

The ENIAC proved that, with careful engineering, it was possible to build extremely complex logical devices that would perform at electronic speed, without error, for significant periods of time. This was the landmark leading to the development of many automatic computer designs, and paving the way for the "computer revolution." As modestly noted by the Ordnance Corps in *Army Ordnance* (1946), the ENIAC "established the fact that the basic principles of electronic engineering are sound." It was indeed "inevitable that future computing machines of this type would be improved through the knowledge and experience gained on this first one."

Portions of the ENIAC are now in the Smithsonian Institution at Washington, D.C. Other ENIAC materials are in the custody of the Historical Services Division of the Department of the Army in Washington.

### References


1946. U.S. Army Ordnance Corps. "Mathematics by Robot," *Army Ordnance*, Vol. XXX, No. 156 (May–June), pp. 329–331.

1950. Stifler, W. W., Jr. (Ed.). *High Speed Computing Devices*. New York: McGraw-Hill.

1961. Weik, Martin H. "The ENIAC Story," *Army Ordnance*, Vol. XLV, No. 244 (January–February), pp. 571–575.


H. D. Huskey

**EQUATIONS.** *See* PARTIAL DIFFERENTIAL EQUATIONS, NUMERICAL SOLUTION OF; and NUMERICAL ANALYSIS.

# ERROR ANALYSIS

For articles on related subjects *see* ARITHMETIC, COMPUTER; ERRORS; ERRORS, ABSOLUTE AND RELATIVE; INTERVAL ARITHMETIC; MATRIX COMPUTATIONS; NUMERICAL ANALYSIS; ROUNDOFF ERROR; and SIGNIFICANCE ARITHMETIC.

In general the basic arithmetic operations on digital computers are not exact but are subject to rounding or truncation errors. This article is concerned with the cumulative effect of these errors. It will be assumed that the reader has read the article on Matrix Computations since the results will be illustrated by examples from that area.

**Definitions.** There are two main methods of error analysis, known as "forward analysis" and "backward analysis," respectively. They may be illustrated by considering the solution of an $n \times n$ system of linear equations by Gaussian elimination. In this algorithm, the original system is reduced successively to equivalent systems $A^{(r)}x = b^{(r)}$, $r = 1, 2, \ldots, n-1$. In the final system the matrix of coefficients, $A^{(n-1)}$ is upper-triangular, and the solution is found by a back substitution.

In a forward analysis, one adopts the following strategy: Because of rounding errors the computed derived system $\bar{A}^{(r)}x = \bar{b}^{(r)}$ differs from that which would be obtained by exact arithmetic. It seems reasonable to assume that if the algorithm is stable, $\bar{A}^{(r)} - A^{(r)}$ and $\bar{b}^{(r)} - b^{(r)}$ will be small, and with sufficient ingenuity bounds would be found for these "errors." This is perhaps the most natural approach.

Alternatively, one could adopt the following strategy: If the algorithm is stable, presumably the computed solution $\bar{x}$ is the *exact* solution of some system $(A + E)\bar{x} = b + e$, where $E$ and $e$ are relatively small. Of course there will be an infinite number of sets, of which $\bar{x}$ is the exact solution. A successful error analysis will obtain satisfactory bounds for the elements of $E$ and $e$. Such an approach is known as "backward" error analysis, since it seeks to replace all errors made in the course of the solution by an *equivalent* perturbation of the original problem. It has one immediate advantage. It puts the errors made during the computation on the same footing as those arising from the data. Hence, when the initial data is itself inexact, no additional problem is posed.

**Early Error Analysis of Elimination Processes.** In the 1940s the imminent arrival of electronic computers stimulated an interest in error analysis, and one of the first algorithms to be studied was Gaussian elimination. Early analyses were all of the forward type, and typical of the results obtained was that of Hotelling, who showed that errors in solving an $n \times n$ system might build up by a factor $4^{n-1}$. The relevance of this result was widely accepted at the time. Writing in 1946, Bargmann, Montgomery, and von Neumann said of Gaussian elimination: "An error at any stage affects all succeeding results and may become greatly magnified; this explains why instability should be expected." The mood of pessimism was very infectious, and the tendency to become enmeshed in the formal complexity of the algebra of the analysis seems to have precluded a sound assessment of the nature of the problem. Before giving any error analysis we discuss fundamental limitations on the attainable accuracy.

**Norms and Floating-Point Arithmetic.** We will need some way of assessing the "size" of a vector or a matrix. Such a measure is provided by vector and matrix *norms*. A norm of a vector $x$, denoted by $\|x\|$, is a nonnegative quantity satisfying the relations

$$\|x\| \geq 0 \quad \text{and} \quad \|x\| = 0 \quad \text{iff } x = 0,$$
$$\|\alpha x\| = |\alpha| \, \|x\|,$$
$$\|x + y\| \leq \|x\| + \|y\|.$$

We will use only two norms, denoted by $\|x\|_2$ and $\|x\|_\infty$ and defined by

$$\|x\|_2 = (\Sigma |x_i|^2)^{1/2}, \qquad \|x\|_\infty = \max |x_i|.$$

Similarly, a norm of a matrix $A$, denoted by $\|A\|$, is a nonnegative quantity satisfying the relations

$$\|A\| \geq 0 \quad \text{and} \quad \|A\| = 0 \quad \text{iff } A = 0,$$
$$\|\alpha A\| = |\alpha| \, \|A\|,$$
$$\|A + B\| \leq \|A\| + \|B\|,$$
$$\|AB\| \leq \|A\| \, \|B\|.$$

We will use only two norms, denoted by $\|A\|_2$ and $\|A\|_\infty$ and defined by

$$||A||_2 = (\text{max eigenvalue of } AA^H)^{1/2},$$
$$||A||_\infty = \max_i(\Sigma_j |a_{ij}|).$$

It may be verified that

$$||Ax||_2 \leq ||A||_2||x||_2$$
$$||Ax||_\infty \leq ||A||_\infty||x||_\infty.$$

Most of the early error analyses were for fixed-point computation, but since virtually all scientific computation is now done in floating point, we restrict discussion to this case. We use the notation $\text{fl}(x \times y)$ to denote the product of two standard floating-point (fl) numbers as given by the computer under examination, with an analogous notation for the other arithmetic operations. We have the following results for each of the basic operations, using a mantissa of $t$ digits in the base $\beta$:

$$\text{fl}(x \times y) = xy(1 + \epsilon), \quad |\epsilon| \leq m\beta^{-t},$$
$$\text{fl}(x \div y) = (x/y)(1 + \epsilon), \quad |\epsilon| \leq d\beta^{-t},$$
$$\text{fl}(x \pm y) = x(1 + \epsilon_1) \pm y(1 + \epsilon_2), \quad |\epsilon_1|, |\epsilon_2| \leq s\beta^{-t},$$

where $m$, $d$, and $s$ are constants on the order of unity, depending on the details of the rounding or chopping procedure. Described in the language of backward errors analysis, we might say, for example, that the *computed* sum of two numbers $x$ and $y$ is the *exact* sum of two numbers $x(1 + \epsilon_1)$ and $y(1 + \epsilon_2)$, each having a low relative error. On well-designed computers,

$$\text{fl}(x \pm y) = (x \pm y)(1 + \epsilon), \quad |\epsilon| \leq s\beta^{-t}.$$

For convenience from now on we assume that all $\epsilon$ in the above satisfy the bound $|\epsilon| \leq k \cdot \beta^{-t}$, where $k$ is of the order of unity.

By repeated application we have, with an obvious notation,

$$\text{fl}(a_1 + a_2 + \cdots + a_n) = a_1(1 + E_1) + a_2(1 + E_2) + \cdots + a_n(1 + E_n),$$
$$(1 - k\beta^{-t})^{n-1} \leq 1 + E_1 \leq (1 + k\beta^{-t})^{n-1},$$
$$(1 - k\beta^{-t})^{n+1-r} \leq 1 + E_r \leq (1 + k\beta^{-t})^{n+1-r} \quad r = 2, 3, \ldots, n.$$

The bounds on the errors are reasonably realistic and examples can be constructed in which they are almost attained. Naturally, when $n$ is large, the statistical distribution can be expected, in general, to result in some cancellation of errors and, thus, in actual errors substantially less than the bounds.

One of the most important elements in elimination methods is the computation of expressions of the form

$$p = \text{fl}(a - x_1 \times y_1 - \cdots - x_n \times y_n).$$

The computed $r$ and the error bounds are dependent on the order in which operations are performed. If the operations are performed in the order written above, we obtain

$$p = a(1 + E) - x_1y_1(1 + F_1) - \cdots - x_ny_n(1 + F_n),$$

where

$$(1 - k\beta^{-t})^n \leq 1 + E \leq (1 + k\beta^{-t})^n,$$
$$(1 - k\beta^{-t})^{n+2-i} \leq 1 + F_i \leq (1 + k\beta^{-t})^{n+2-i}.$$

If one computes

$$p = \text{fl}(-x_1 \times y_1 - x_2 \times y_2 - \cdots - x_n \times y_n + a),$$

then

$$p = -x_1y_1(1 + E_1) - \cdots - x_ny_n(1 + E_n) + a(1 + F),$$
$$(1 - k\beta^{-t})^{n+3-i} \leq (1 + E_i) \leq (1 + k\beta^{-t})^{n+3-i}, \quad |F| \leq k\beta^{-t}.$$

In describing the last result in terms of backward error analysis, we might say, for example, that it is exact for data $x_i(1 + E_i)$, $y_i$, and $a(1 + F)$, putting all the perturbations in the $x_i$ and $a$. Alternatively, we could say it is exact for data $x_i$, $y_i(1 + E_i)$, and $a(1 + F)$.

Note that although the errors made can be equated with the effect of small relative perturbations in the data, the relative error in the computed $p$ may be arbitrarily high, depending on the degree of cancellation that takes place. Indeed, if the true $p$ is zero, one may have an infinite relative error. One would not think of attributing this to some malignant instability in this simple arithmetic process; it is the natural loss to be expected.

**Inherent Sensitivity of the Solution of a Linear System.** For any computational problem the inherent sensitivity of the solution to changes in the data is of fundamental importance, yet oddly enough the early analyses of Gaussian elimination paid little attention to it. We consider in a very elementary way the effect of perturbations $\delta A$ in the matrix $A$. We have

$$\bar{x} = (A + \delta A)^{-1}b = (A^{-1} - A^{-1}\delta A A^{-1} + \cdots)b$$
$$= x - A^{-1}\delta A x + (A^{-1}\delta A)^2 x - \cdots,$$

giving

$$||\bar{x} - x||/||x|| \leq ||A^{-1}\delta A||/(1 - ||A^{-1}\delta A||),$$

provided $||A^{-1}\delta A|| < 1$. The relative error in $\bar{x}$ will not be low unless $||A^{-1}\delta A||$ is small. Writing,

$$||\delta A|| = \eta ||A||,$$

we see that

$$||\bar{x} - x||/||x||$$
$$\leq \eta ||A||\,||A^{-1}||/(1 - \eta ||A||\,||A^{-1}||).$$

The inherent sensitivity is therefore dependent on $||A||\,||A^{-1}||$, and this is usually known as the "condition number" of $A$ (for the given norm) with respect to inversion or to the solution of linear systems.

We might now ask ourselves what sort of limitation we should expect on the accuracy of Gaussian elimination even if it had no menacing instability. The solution of $Ax = b$ requires $n^3/3$ multiplications and additions, an average of $\frac{1}{3}n$ per element. From the elementary discussion given so far, we might risk the following prophecy: Even if Gaussian elimination is a stable process, then we can scarcely expect to obtain a bound for the resulting error, which is less than that resulting from a perturbation $\delta A$ in $A$ satisfying, say,

$$||\delta A|| \leq \tfrac{1}{3}kn\beta^{-t}||A||.$$

In fact, this bound for the effect is usually reasonably realistic, provided pivoting is used. Indeed, the advantages conferred by the statistical distribution of rounding errors is such that the error is usually less than the maximum error that could be caused by such a perturbation.

**Backward Error Analysis of Gaussian Elimination.** Gaussian elimination provides a very good illustration of the power and simplicity of backward error analysis. The elimination process may be described as the production of a unit lower triangular matrix $L$ and an upper triangular matrix $U$ such that $LU = A$. The solution of the system $Ax = b$ is then carried out in the two steps:

$$Ly = b, \qquad Ux = y.$$

In the backward error analysis one shows that the computed $L$ and $U$ satisfy the relation $LU = A + E$ and obtains bounds for the elements of $E$. One then shows that the computed solution $y$ and $x$ of the triangular systems satisfies the equations

$$(L + \delta L)y = b, \qquad (U + \delta U)x = y$$

and obtains bounds for the elements of $\delta L$ and $\delta U$. The computed $x$ therefore solves *exactly* the system

$$(L + \delta L)(U + \delta U)x = b$$

or

$$(A + E + \delta L U + L\,\delta U + \delta L\,\delta U)x = b.$$

Hence, it is the exact solution of $(A + F)x = b$, where

$$||F|| = ||E + \delta L U + L\,\delta U + \delta L\,\delta U||$$
$$\leq ||E|| + ||L||\,||\delta U||$$
$$+ ||U||\,||\delta L|| + ||\delta L||\,||\delta U||,$$

and from the bounds for $E$, $\delta L$, and $\delta U$, one obtains a bound for $F$.

The simplicity of the technique may be illustrated by presenting the analysis of the solution of the system $Ly = b$. We first make the following observations:

1. The relevant system to be analyzed is that with the computed matrix $L$, *not* the $L$ that would have resulted from exact computation.
2. Since during the course of the analysis we do not attempt a direct comparison between computed and exact values, there is no need to denote computed quantities by bars. It is to be understood that all symbols refer to computed quantities.
3. It is only at the final stage when we have expressed the computed solution as the exact solution of $(A + F)x = b$ and have obtained a bound for $||F||$ that we attempt to compare the computed $x$ with the true $x$, and at this stage we can use the result of the previous section.

At a typical stage in the triangular solution, $y_1, y_2, \ldots, y_{r-1}$ have been computed and $y_r$ is determined from the relation

$$y_r = \mathrm{fl}(-l_{r1}y_1 - l_{r2}y_2 - \cdots - l_{r,r-1}y_{r-1} + b_r),$$

using, of course, the computed values of the $y_i$. Hence

$$y_r = -l_r y_1(1 + E_{r,1}) - l_r{}_2 y_2(1 + E_{r,2}) - \cdots - l_{r,r-1} y_{r-1}(1 + E_{r,r-1}) + b_r(1 + F_r),$$

where the factors $1 + E_{r,i}$ and $1 + F_r$ are of the type discussed in connection with the computation of $p$ above. Hence, the computed $y_i$ satisfy exactly the relation

$$l_r y_1(1 + G_{r,1}) + l_r y_2(1 + G_{r,2}) + \cdots + l_{r,r-1} y_{r-1}(1 + G_{r,r-1}) + y_r(1 + G_{r,r}) = b_r,$$

where

$$(1 + G_{r,i}) = (1 + E_{r,i})/(1 + F_r), \quad i = 1, \cdots, r-1,$$

$$1 + G_{r,r} = 1/(1 + F_r).$$

Notice that by dividing through by $1 + F_r$, we are able to restrict ourselves to perturbations in $L$. The computed $y$ therefore satisfies exactly the relation $(L + \delta L)y = b$, where $\delta L_{ij} = L_{ij} G_{ij}$.

We certainly have

$$(1 - k\beta^{-t})^n \leq (1 + G_{ij}) \leq (1 + k\beta^{-t})^n,$$

most of the factors, of course, satisfying much better bounds. Bounds of the above type are cumbersome to use, and we observe that if $kn\beta^{-t} < 0.1$, as will usually be the case, then, using the binomial theorem,

$$(1 + k\beta^{-t})^n \leq 1 + (1.06)kn\beta^{-t},$$
$$(1 - k\beta^{-t})^n \geq 1 - (1.06)kn\beta^{-t}.$$

Hence, we have

$$|\delta L_{ij}| \leq (1.06)kn\beta^{-t}|L_{ij}|,$$

giving, for example,

$$||\delta L||_\infty \leq (1.06)kn\beta^{-t}||L||_\infty.$$

The analysis is almost trivial, though earlier error analyses of the solution of triangular systems were extremely complicated.

If the computation of $y_r$ had been expressed in the form

$$y_r = \mathrm{fl}(b_r - l_r y_1 - \cdots - l_{r,r-1} y_{r-1}),$$

then we could still obtain a relation of the form $(L + \delta L)y = b$, but in this case the bounds on the elements of $\delta L$ would be appreciably larger.

On many computers it is possible to accumulate either of the expressions for $y_r$ in double precision, rounding to single precision only on completion. If this is done, then we again obtain a relation of the form

$$l_r y_1(1 + G_{r,1}) + l_{r,2} y_2(1 + G_{r,2}) + \cdots + l_{r,r-1} y_{r-1}(1 + G_{r,r-1}) + y_r(1 + G_{r,r}) = b_r,$$

but now the quantities $|G_{r,i}|$ $(i < r)$ have bounds of order $\beta^{-2t}$ and can therefore virtually be neglected, while $|G_{r,r}|$ has the bound $k\beta^{-t}$. We therefore have a result that might well be described as best possible, having regard to the precision of computation. Indeed, the residual vector $b - Ly$ corresponding to the computed $y$ will almost certainly be smaller than that corresponding to the correctly rounded solution!

The analysis of the solution of $Ux = y$ is almost identical to that of $Ly = b$, while the analysis of the factorization process is only marginally more complicated. If the $L$ and $U$ are produced as in classical Gaussian elimination, then one can show that $LU = A + E$, where, denoting the maximum modulus of any element arising during the decomposition by $g$, we certainly have

$$|e_{ij}| \leq (3.02)igk\beta^{-t} \qquad (i \leq j),$$
$$|e_{ij}| \leq (3.02)jgk\beta^{-t} \qquad (i > j).$$

If the factors $L$ and $U$ are determined directly, using the relations

$$l_{ij}u_{jj} = a_{ij} - l_{i1}u_{1j} - \cdots - l_{i,j-1}u_{j-1j} \qquad j = 1, \ldots, i-1$$

and

$$u_{ij} = a_{ij} - l_{i1}u_{1j} - \cdots - l_{i,i-1}u_{i-1j} \qquad j = i, \ldots, n,$$

and the expressions on the right are accumulated in double precision, an even more satisfactory bound may be determined for $E$. Indeed, ignoring quantities of the order of magnitude of $\beta^{-2t}$, we certainly have $|e_{ij}| \leq gk\beta^{-t}$, where $g$ is now the element of maximum modulus in the computed $U$. Again, we have what may be regarded as a "best possible" result.

The reader may be surprised that no reference has been made to pivoting or to the size of the $l_{pq}$. The importance of pivoting is concealed. If any of the multipliers is large, $g$ will usually be much larger than $\max|a_{ij}|$. When pivoting is used $|l_{pq}| \leq 1$, and there will not *usually* be much growth in the size of the elements of the reduced matrices or of $U$ relative to the initial set of $a_{ij}$. When $A$ is positive definite or diagonally dominant, *no* growth can take place, and we have a guaranteed a priori bound for $||E||$ in terms of $A$.

In 1947 von Neumann and Goldstine considered the special case of the inversion of a positive definite matrix with pivoting, and obtained a result for fixed point computation which is only marginally weaker than can be obtained by arguments of the above type, though the analysis was far more complicated. Their analysis is often described as a "forward error analysis," but it is in fact of the backward type, although at no stage are results expressed in a form such as to emphasize this. The final results of an analysis of the above type for the solution of a positive definite system is to guarantee that it is the exact solution of $(A + E)x = b$ and to give a bound for $E$ of the type

$$||E|| \leq f(n)k\beta^{-t}||A||,$$

where $f(n)$ is a modest function of $n$, depending a little on the details of the arithmetic. When backward error analysis is applied to matrix inversion, one cannot show that $X$ is the exact solution of $(A + E)X = I$, with a similar bound for $E$, because it is not true. However, the $r$th column, $x_r$, of $X$ is the exact solution of some $(A + E_r)x_r = e_r$, where $e_r$ is the $r$th column of $I$; the $E_r$ are all different, but have the same satisfactory uniform bound. This result is implicit in that of von Neumann and Goldstine, but it is well concealed!

**Orthogonal Transformations.** Experience with error analyses of matrix processes gradually exposed the fact that control of *growth* in derived matrices is the key to stability. If orthogonal transformations $Q$ are used, then—since $||QA||_2 = |AQ||_2 = ||A||$—no general growth *can* take place. Although the algebra is a little complicated, a fairly general analysis can be given of whole classes of algorithms based on orthogonal transformations, both for the solution of equations and the eigenvalue problem. One can show, for example, that for a sequence of $r$ orthogonal similarity transformations, the final computed transform $A^{(r)}$ satisfies *exactly* a relation of the form

$$A^{(r)} = Q^T(A + E)Q,$$

where $Q$ is *exactly* orthogonal and

$$||E|| \leq rf(n)||A||k\beta^{-t},$$

where $f(n)$ is some quite innocuous function of $n$. Hence, the eigenvalues of $A^{(r)}$ are exactly those of $A + E$, and we are back with perturbation theory.

**A Posteriori Error Bounds.** The bounds discussed so far are of the a priori type. The main function of such an analysis is to show whether or not an algorithm is stable and, if not, to pinpoint the reasons for its instability.

When a solution has been determined, one can usually obtain much sharper backward error bounds. For example, from a computed eigenvalue $\lambda$ and an eigenvector $u$, such that $||u||_2 = 1$, one can compute the residual defined by $r = Au - \lambda u$. This may be written in the form $(A - ru^H)u = \lambda u$, showing that $\lambda$ *and* $u$ are exact for the matrix $A - ru^H$. When $A$ is Hermitian, this implies that $A$ has an eigenvalue in the interval $\lambda - ||r||_2, \lambda + ||r||_2$. Similarly, when solving linear equations one can compute $r = b - Ax$. If $r$ is computed accurately, it can then be used to obtain an improved solution by solving $A\delta = r$. This process is called "iterative refinement."

**Iterative Methods.** It was at one time thought that iterative methods for solving linear equations or the eigenvalue problem would give far greater accuracy than direct methods, since one works with the initial $A$ throughout. In fact this advantage is largely illusory. In Jacobi's method for linear equations, one derives an improved $x_i^{(r+1)}$ from the relation

$$a_{ii}x_i^{(r+1)} = b_i - \Sigma_{j\neq i}a_{ij}x_i^{(r)},$$

but the right-hand side cannot be computed exactly. From the above analysis it is clear that one is really working with a matrix with elements $a_{ij}(1 + e_{ij})$, where the $e_{ij}$ are different in each iteration. When iterative methods are used in practice, iteration is usually terminated before attaining the accuracy given immediately by a direct method, *even without iterative refinement*. Since, as we mentioned earlier, the results obtained with good direct methods are almost "best possible," this is to be expected.

**Interval Arithmetic and Significant Digit Arithmetic.** Attempts have been made to obtain error bounds for computed quantities on the computer itself. In *interval* arithmetic, an ordered pair $[a_l, a_u]$ of floating-point numbers is stored at each stage in the computation, and it is guaranteed that the true number $a$ lies in the interval $a_l \leq a \leq a_u$. Used in a direct manner, the results achieved are very pessimistic; in fact, the computer merely performs numerically the analog of what was done algebraically in the early forward error analysis of the Hotelling type. The intervals become very large. The apparently reasonable assumption that in stable algorithms the computed quantities will be close to those arising in exact computation is frequently quite false. This is particularly true of algorithms for the eigenvalue problem.

In *significant digit* arithmetic, one does not work with normalized floating-point numbers, on the grounds that when cancellation takes place, the zeros introduced are nonsignificant. The possibilities of significant digit arithmetic have been well exploited by Metropolis and Ashenhurst.

The realization that neither interval arithmetic nor significant digit arithmetic provides an automatic answer to error analysis led to an overreaction against them. The provision of the relevant hardware facilities should make them economic, and when combined with a more general appreciation of theoretical error analysis, they have an important role to play.

### References


1963. Wilkinson, J. H. *Rounding Errors in Algebraic Processes*. London: Her Majesty's Stationery Office.

1965. Wilkinson, J. H. *The Algebraic Eigenvalue Problem*. Oxford: Clarendon Press.

1966. Moore, R. E. *Interval Analysis*. Englewood Cliffs, N.J.: Prentice-Hall.

1967. Forsythe, G. E., and C. B. Moler. *Computer Solution of Linear Algebraic Systems*. Englewood Cliffs, N.J.: Prentice-Hall.


J. H. Wilkinson

## ERROR-CORRECTING CODE

For articles on related subjects *see* Codes; and Errors.

For article on related term *see* Parity.

Error-detecting and error-correcting codes arose from the well-known phenomenon that if anything can go wrong, it will. Rather than try to do everything perfectly the first time, error-detecting and error-correcting methods use some form of redundancy to handle the inevitable errors.

*Error detection* has a long history. For example, suppose we have a block of $n$ binary digits and add an $(n + 1)$st digit, chosen so that the whole message has an even (or odd) number of 1s in it. This is called an even (odd) parity check. At the receiving end, the complete block is checked. If there are not the proper number of 1s in the message, then there must be an odd number of errors in the message. If the block is chosen to be reasonably short (with respect to the probability $p$ of an isolated error), so that we may ignore factors of $1 - p$, and if we assume that errors are independent, then to a close approximation there is a probability $(n + 1)p$ of a single error, and a probability $[n(n + 1)/2]p^2$ of two errors.

Upon the detection of an error, the message can be retransmitted, and generally this will produce an error-free message. In some circumstances, especially where it is suspected that the source is slightly defective (say, a magnetic recording), several retrials may be used before giving up. The retrial system is not entirely satisfactory because it takes extra time when errors occur and also requires two-way signaling to call for message repetition. However, if the error is in the original recorded form of the message before encoding, then nothing can be done about the error.

To overcome these difficulties, error-correcting codes are often used. They are based on the use of a high level of redundancy, i.e., repeated parity checks.

There are various ways of explaining how an error-correcting code works. In the algebraic approach, a parity check is assigned to those positions in the code that have a 1 in the rightmost position of their binary representation, a second parity check for those positions that have a 1 in their second to right position, etc. Thus, when a single error does occur, exactly those parity checks will fail for which the binary expansion of the position of the error has 1s. Thus, the pattern of the parity-check failures points directly to the position of the error; in a binary system of signaling, it is easy to change that bit to its opposite value and thus correct the error, with 000 meaning "no error."

As an example, consider the binary encoding of the decimal digits into an error-correcting code. In Table 1, positions 1, 2, and 4 are used for the check positions, leaving positions 3, 5, 6, 7 for the message (where we find the binary coding of the corresponding decimal digit).

**Table 1**

| Decimal | Position 1 | 2 | 3 | 4 | 5 | 6 | 7 |
|---|---|---|---|---|---|---|---|
| 0 | 0 | 0 | 0 | 0 | 0 | 0 | 0 |
| 1 | 1 | 1 | 0 | 1 | 0 | 0 | 1 |
| 2 | 0 | 1 | 0 | 1 | 0 | 1 | 0 |
| 3 | 1 | 0 | 0 | 0 | 0 | 1 | 1 |
| 4 | 1 | 0 | 0 | 1 | 1 | 0 | 0 |
| 5 | 0 | 1 | 0 | 0 | 1 | 0 | 1 |
| 6 | 1 | 1 | 0 | 0 | 1 | 1 | 0 |
| 7 | 0 | 0 | 0 | 1 | 1 | 1 | 1 |
| 8 | 1 | 1 | 1 | 0 | 0 | 0 | 0 |
| 9 | 0 | 0 | 1 | 1 | 0 | 0 | 1 |

The check positions are calculated by even parity checks as follows:

*Parity check column 1*
Columns 1, 3, 5, 7 (columns with a 1 in the rightmost position of their binary representation).
*Parity check column 2*
Columns 2, 3, 6, 7 (1 in second rightmost position).
*Parity check column 4*
Columns 4, 5, 6, 7 (1 in leftmost position).

Let any line be copied and a single error inserted as a simulation of an error in message transmission. When the three parity checks are applied, we will find that if we write a 0 for successful parity check and a 1 for a failure (writing from right to left), the three digits we get will be *exactly* the position of the inserted error.

A second way of looking at the codes is a geometric approach. If an error is to be detected, then the distance between two messages (which we define to be the number of positions for which they differ) must be at least two for every pair of messages. Otherwise, there would be a message that a single error would carry over into another acceptable message, and that error could not be detected. For error correction, the minimum distance must be at least three (as in Table 1); for double error detection, the minimum distance must be at least four; etc.

The encoding process can thus be extended further in protecting against errors. As an example of double-error detection, consider the code in Table 1 with an additional bit added to each message, so chosen that the entire message will have an even number of 1s. If there were a *single* error, the original set of checks would indicate the position, but the last check would fail. If there were a *pair* of errors, the last check would not fail, but some of the original checks would, indicating a double error. The minimum-distance argument can be applied to show that the additional check made each minimal distance one greater, namely, now four.

The preceding examples are the simplest cases. The theory has been highly developed and now makes use of much of abstract algebra, including Galois theory.

REFERENCES


1961. Peterson, W. W. *Error Correcting Codes.* Cambridge, Mass.: The M.I.T. Press.

1968. Berlekamp, E., Jr. *Algebraic Coding Theory.* New York: McGraw-Hill.


R. W. HAMMING

# ERRORS

For articles on related subjects *see* DEBUGGING; DIAGNOSTICS; ERRORS, ABSOLUTE AND RELATIVE; ERROR ANALYSIS; ROUNDOFF ERROR; STRUCTURED PROGRAMMING; and SYNTAX, SEMANTICS, AND PRAGMATICS.
For articles on related terms *see* ALGORITHM; ARITHMETIC-LOGIC UNIT; CENTRAL PROCESSING UNIT; COMPUTER SYSTEMS; GENERATIONS, COMPUTER; MICROPROGRAMMING; SOFTWARE; and VIRTUAL MEMORY.

The indignant customer who receives an incorrect bill from a department store probably does not care what the source of the error was or even that, almost certainly, the fault was not the computer's but its programmer's. Neither is the astronaut descending toward the surface of the moon very concerned about the precise source of the error that caused his on-board computer to fail. But an understanding of the sources of errors in computers is important to anyone who wishes to use or even to comprehend digital computers.

TAXONOMY OF COMPUTER ERRORS. When a computer produces an incorrect result, the error may come from one or more of a number of sources. These sources can be fairly readily grouped under three headings:

*Hardware errors*, which result from a malfunction of some physical component of the computer.

*Software errors*, which result from a coding error in *some* program, but not necessarily in the program that seemed to produce the wrong results (see below).

*Algorithm errors*, which result when the algorithm or method used to solve a problem does not produce correct results, perhaps only under certain conditions and/or for certain input data.

Before proceeding to discuss these three types of errors in some detail, we should stress that, whereas in the early days of computing it was usually rather easy to determine which of the three categories above was the source of an error, it is sometimes very difficult indeed to do this today. To give one example, the increasing use of microprogramming in contemporary computer systems makes it possible for hardware errors to manifest themselves in ways that look like software errors, and vice versa. The difficulty of determining the source of a computer error has heightened the need for good diagnostic techniques, a subject we consider in the last section of this article.

**Hardware Errors.** Considering the staggering complexity of modern computer systems, it is amazing that they work at all. The fact that they are designed to, and often do, operate for hundreds or thousands of hours without failure is even more startling. Modern computers contain literally millions of circuit elements, the failure of any one of which might cause failure of the entire system. This high level of reliability is a tribute to the careful work of circuit designers and the meticulous attention to detail and to testing on the part of the manufacturers. Still, computers are not perfect and the hardware occasionally does fail. The source of a failure may be difficult to determine, since the number of possible faulty components is so large.

A frequent source of errors is in the electromechanical peripheral devices that provide input or output for the central processing unit. The mechanical components of these peripheral devices are likely to wear out as a result of the stresses of frequent use. The staccato motion of movable disk arms, the rapid rotation of disk packs, drums, or tape drives, the stop-and-go movements in card readers and punches, all are possible sources of failures.

The recording medium associated with each of these devices is fragile and consequently a potential source of errors. The delicate magnetic coating of magnetic tapes, disks, or drums can be easily scratched, rendering the information incorrect or inaccessible. A speck of dust or dirt can mar these coatings easily, or tension can stretch a piece of magnetic tape. Punched cards may be folded, spindled, or mutilated, and paper tape reels may easily be torn. The failure of these media may not be fatal to the entire computer, but individual peripheral units may be disabled or data items may be entered incorrectly or lost. Telecommunication devices attached to a computer may also be faulty. Since the quality of the voice-grade telephone lines often used for communication with computers is low, special leased lines are sometimes used to reduce the frequency of errors.

The central processing unit, arithmetic and logical unit, and the high-speed memory are built entirely from electronic components, thereby reducing the chance of failure inherent in mechanical devices. The technology for creating the circuit elements involved in these components is extremely complex. Early computers used vacuum tubes (first generation) as the primary circuit element. These large devices were relatively slow, generated a large amount of heat, required a large amount of power, and wore out easily. The invention of the transistor (second generation) in 1947 made it possible to construct smaller, faster, and much more reliable computers. Combining several transistors and other electronic elements into a single component, called the "integrated circuit" (third generation), enabled designers to create still faster and more reliable computers.

At present, computers are built from a smaller number of large-scale integrated circuits (fourth generation), which extends the notion of combining circuit elements. These highly reliable large-scale integrated circuits contain thousands of discrete circuit elements built into a single replaceable component. These devices are carefully tested during the many stages of a sophisticated fabrication process. Still, they may fail as a result of temperature changes, humidity, shock, or electrical surges. When failure occurs, the faulty circuit component must be located and replaced. This sounds simple enough, but the problem may be hard to locate, since the failure may be intermittent, occurring only when a complex combination of conditions exist. To minimize the deterioration of circuit elements, computer center rooms are air conditioned to keep the temperature and humidity within acceptable ranges. The failure of the air conditioning would lead to overheating of circuit elements and to an increased chance of failure.

Modern computers are designed to monitor their own performance and constantly test themselves to assure that each operation has been performed properly. When a fault occurs, a machine interrupt is issued, and the hardware and software attempt to identify and locate the error. Depending on the severity of the error, the control programs may shut down the entire machine, avoid use of the faulty component, or simply record the fact that an error has occurred.

**Software Errors.** Anyone who has written a computer program knows that debugging can be difficult and tedious. Professionals writing short programs (say, less than 100 lines of code) expect some difficulties and accept the fact that long programs, requiring many man-years of effort, may never be completely debugged. When writing programs in a higher-level language, which require the services of a compiler, utility programs, and an operating system, the number of software modules that come into play is large. Great effort is applied to debug the system software, but it is not currently possible to insure the correctness of such sophisticated programs. If an application program does not operate correctly, the most likely source of the error is in the application program itself. Only after a thorough and careful analysis of the situation can we begin to consider the possibility that the compiler, system utilities, or operating system are at fault. Locating the bug in the system software requires a deep understanding of the code and the expertise of a systems programmer.

Application program errors fall into two basic categories: syntactic and semantic. The syntactic errors include typographic errors, incorrectly spelled keywords and variable names, incorrect punctuation and improper statement formation, all of which result from violations of the programming language syntax. These errors are normally recognized by the language processor, and diagnostic messages are printed to assist the programmer in making corrections. Although some processors will attempt to fix improper syntax, programs with syntactic errors will generally not be permitted to execute.

Assuming all the syntactic errors have been fixed, the program will execute, but there is no guarantee that it will perform as the programmer intended. Semantic errors are a result of an improper understanding of the function of certain operators or mistakes in coding of an algorithm. Typical programming mistakes include exceeding the bounds of an array; failure to initialize variables; overflow or underflow; failure to account for special cases; attempted division by zero; illegal mixing of data types; and incorrect transfers of control. Isolating and locating the error can be a long tedious process and is a skill learned mainly through much experience.

Current research is being directed at reducing the possibility of semantic errors. Improved programming language design and sophisticated compilers are one possible answer. Educating programmers to proper program design techniques such as modularity, top-down structuring, and "go-to-free" programming will hopefully simplify the debugging process. Finally, attempts are being made to prove the correctness of programs through the use of formal mathematical techniques.

**Algorithm Errors.** Computer programs can be viewed as models or representations of real-world situations. Unfortunately, not all aspects of the real-world situation can be accurately represented inside a computer. Decimal quantities such as 1.2 or 6783846.678492104 may have to be approximated when stored in the memory of a binary computer. Since the initial representation is not precise, subsequent operations performed on these values may produce invalid results. The difficulty in locating such faults is that the error will manifest itself only for some sets of data. Thus, the program will produce reasonable results in most cases, but may produce erroneous results erratically.

The heart of this problem is the machine representation of values. While a 60-bit word length may provide a more accurate representation than a 36-bit word or a 32-bit word, a longer word length is not a guarantee of correctness. Since we are limited to the finite length of a computer word, the representation must be rounded off to the closest approximation possible. With each addition or multiplication the result must also be rounded off to fit the representation scheme; hence the name "round-off error."

Another flaw in the representation of the real world occurs when an infinite process must be approximated by a finite series of steps. In summing an infinite series, repeating an iterative process (e.g., the Newton-Raphson or secant methods), or approximating derivatives by differences, the result may become increasingly exact, but is never precisely correct. Since in all these cases an infinite process is cut short and represented by a finite process, this error is called "truncation error."

One of the central concerns of numerical analysis is to estimate the maximum roundoff and truncation errors for various algorithms. This analysis can then be used to select and design the optimum strategy for a given problem.

The goal is to avoid "unstable" algorithms that operate erratically and to identify "ill-conditioned" data sets that are difficult to deal with. The use of double or multiple precision representations and operations may reduce the error, but not eliminate it.

Algorithms that fail sometimes because of roundoff problems are only one type of algorithm failure. Another not uncommon one is the attempted use of an algorithm to solve a problem other than that for which it is intended. An example of this would be the use of an algorithm designed for the solution of a system of linear simultaneous equations with a symmetric coefficient matrix to solve a system with a nonsymmetric coefficient matrix resulting in an inevitably wrong result.

All too common is the development and use of an algorithm that just will not solve the problem at hand for any set of data, due to a design error, for example, or a failure to understand the underlying mathematics. A vital aspect of the avoidance of such errors is the careful debugging of all newly developed programs using data sets for which the results are known.

**Coping with Errors.** Since errors are a fact of life in computing, much has been done to assist programmers in locating errors. Syntactic errors are dealt with by the compiler and are not the source of serious difficulty. Although work remains to be done in the area of improving compile-time diagnostics, most compilers provide a reasonably lucid explanation of what has gone wrong. The programmer must then fix the mistake.

Execution-time errors that result from semantic errors are more difficult to deal with. If the program runs to completion, but does not produce the output that is expected, the programmer must carefully examine the output and attempt to locate the fault. The input data should be checked for validity, and then a careful step-by-step analysis of the program must be performed. If the output does not contain sufficient information to determine what the program was doing, then an additional run with detailed print-outs must be made. Special "trace" packages that print out the execution of the program on an instruction-by-instruction basis can be used. Alternatively, only the transfers of control or subprogram references can be printed. If desired, a particular location can be monitored to indicate when the value was set or referenced. Since the amount of print-out may be voluminous, the programmer must carefully select which features to use. Armed with this material and a thorough understanding of the program, the programmer must perform a careful analysis, which will hopefully lead to the location of the flaw.

If the program does not run to completion but is interrupted as a result of an attempt to perform an illegal instruction, the operating system will (or, at least, should) print a meaningful message. However, since the operating system has no knowledge of what the application program was attempting to do, these messages can be difficult to interpret. Some programming language systems contain an execution-time monitor to produce more meaningful diagnostic messages when an abnormal termination occurs.

If a program successfully executes for a given set of data, there is no guarantee that the program will always perform properly. To verify the correctness of a program, multiple sets of test data should be constructed to exercise the program as much as possible. As many as possible of the reasonable sets of input data should be run to validate the program. Unfortunately, there are many well-documented cases of programs that have run correctly for many years until a particular set of input data was run and resulted in failure. There is no way to guarantee the correctness of large programs, and programmers must accept the possibility of "bugs" in their programs. Large programs such as operating systems are continuously being modified as faults are located. Perfection in programming is illusory.

The diagnosis of hardware errors has become more complex with the advent of sophisticated hardware architecture constructs such as virtual memory and microprogramming. When it is suggested that a particular error may be a result of malfunctioning hardware, a set of hardware diagnostic programs may be run to assist the maintenance engineer in locating the fault. These programs exercise each of the circuit components and print out the location of the faulty element. This technique is not always successful, since the diagnostic program may not run properly because of the fault. Individual components may have to be removed and tested electrically, or components may be replaced until the machine operates properly.

References

1963. Wilkinson, J. H. *Rounding Errors in Algebraic Processes.* Englewood Cliffs, N.J.: Prentice-Hall.

1970. Walker, Terry, and William Cotterman. *An*

*Introduction to Computer Science and Algorithmic Processes*. Boston: Allyn and Bacon.
1972. Chu, Yaohon. *Computer Organization and Microprogramming*, Englewood Cliffs, N.J.: Prentice-Hall.

A. RALSTON AND B. SHNEIDERMAN

# ERRORS, ABSOLUTE AND RELATIVE

For articles on related subjects *see* ERRORS; ERROR ANALYSIS; and NUMERICAL ANALYSIS.

Numerical calculations normally result in an approximation to the true value that is being sought. The *error* in this approximation is a measure of the discrepancy between the true value and the computed result. Estimates of, or bounds on, the error are usually expressed in either *absolute* or *relative* form. Let

$TV$ be the true value of a quantity.
$APP$ be its approximate value.
$E$ be the absolute error.
$RE$ be the relative error.

Then we define

$$E = TV - APP$$
$$RE = (TV - APP)/TV = E/TV$$

For example, if 1/3 is approximated by 0.333, then

$$E = 1/3 - 0.333 = \tfrac{1}{3} \times 10^{-3}$$

and $RE = 10^{-3}$.

More often than not it is $E$ rather than $RE$ that is of interest. For example, if we are calculating the stress on a strut in a bridge, then clearly the absolute error in the calculation is what counts. But in many numerical calculations where the result is very large or very small, relative error is a more meaningful quantity. Thus, if the true value of a quantity is $10^{12}$, an error of $10^4$ is probably not very serious, but this is more meaningfully expressed by noting that $RE = 10^{-8}$.

Much of numerical analysis is concerned with the estimation of $E$ or $RE$, or the calculation of bounds on $E$ or $RE$.

A. RALSTON

# EXCEPTION REPORTING

For article on a related subject *see* ADMINISTRATIVE-BUSINESS APPLICATIONS.

Exception reporting is a technique for screening large amounts of computerized data in order to print reports containing only that information requiring action. It differs from the traditional method of reporting, which entails printing the full contents of files and all activity against those files during some period of time. For example, monthly reports analyzing sales data might show the purchases of all regular customers during the month, for this year to date, during the same month last year, and also the year-to-date sales to this point last year. If an organization has 3,000 customers, the report will have 3,000 lines—one for each customer—plus appropriate totals. The manager who receives such a report must review all entries to determine what situations require action. In many organizations, managers are inundated with reams of computer paper presenting too much data to be assimilated and acted upon. This phenomenon is sometimes called "information overload."

By contrast, exception reports present a user with concise information needed for specific actions. These reports are produced by screening large amounts of information according to predetermined criteria. Exception reports are briefer than conventional reports because they contain only exception data, not all the data in the file. (Fig. 1 illustrates the basic differences between traditional and exception reporting.)

Exception reports generally fall into one of two types, depending on the need they are to meet. Each type is processed according to a different time schedule and uses a different character of screening device. The primary type of exception report is used to isolate exceptions to satisfactory performance. It is produced on a regular, repetitive schedule, and uses a predetermined screening mechanism. Examples of this type of exception reports are monthly inventory reports of all items with balance-on-hand quantities lower than calculated minimums, and monthly and year-to-date sales analyses showing only those customers whose purchases are less than 90% of last year's amounts. (Fig. 1 illustrates this type of report.)

The second type of exception report provides answers to specific inquiries. It is produced only when required, and uses a specially selected screening mechanism. For example, in order to respond to

COMPARATIVE SALES ANALYSIS BY CUSTOMER

PERIOD ENDING 07/31/74 — PAGE 1

| SLMN NO. | CUST NO. | CUSTOMER NAME | THIS PERIOD THIS YEAR | THIS PERIOD LAST YEAR | YEAR-TO-DATE THIS YEAR | YEAR-TO-DATE LAST YEAR | PRCNT CHNG |
|---|---|---|---|---|---|---|---|
| 03 | 4246 | HYDRO CYCLES INC | 3,210.26 | 4,312.06 | 10,010.28 | 9,000.02 | 11 |
| | 7632 | RUPP AQUA CYCLES | 7,800.02 | 2,301.08 | 20,822.60 | 16,020.16 | 29 |
| | 8917 | SEA PORT WEST CO | 90.00 | 421.06 | 900.50 | 593.10 | 51 |
| 10 | 0801 | BOLLINGER ASSOCIATES | 100.96 | 0.00 | 100.06 | 70.00 | 44 |
| | 5641 | MACK HARDWARE CO | 180.60 | 1,420.96 | 8,029.22 | 11,200.00 | 28– |

COMPARATIVE SALES ANALYSIS BY CUSTOMER

PERIOD ENDING 07/31/74 — PAGE (47)

| SLMN NO. | CUST NO. | CUSTOMER NAME | THIS PERIOD THIS YEAR | THIS PERIOD LAST YEAR | YEAR-TO-DATE THIS YEAR | YEAR-TO-DATE LAST YEAR | PRCNT CHNG |
|---|---|---|---|---|---|---|---|
| 86 | 1311 | CHESAPEAKE SUPPLY CO | 2,551.50 | 3,126.57 | 10,914.10 | 16,424.00 | 34– |
| | 3780 | FEDERAL ENGINE CO | 1,421.72 | 1,009.13 | 8,526.44 | 6,290.47 | 36 |
| 98 | 8850 | SOUTH COAST CO | 822.59 | 750.10 | 3,007.06 | 4,285.96 | 30– |

Full Reporting (the traditional method) requires 47 pages of printing

COMPARATIVE SALES ANALYSIS BY CUSTOMER

PERIOD ENDING 07/31/74 — PAGE 1

| SLMN NO. | CUST NO. | CUSTOMER NAME | THIS PERIOD THIS YEAR | THIS PERIOD LAST YEAR | YEAR-TO-DATE THIS YEAR | YEAR-TO-DATE LAST YEAR | PRCNT CHNG |
|---|---|---|---|---|---|---|---|
| 10 | 5641 | MACK HARDWARE CO | 180.60 | 1,420.96 | 8,029.22 | 11,200.00 | 28– |

COMPARATIVE SALES ANALYSIS BY CUSTOMER

PERIOD ENDING 07/31/74 — PAGE (2)

| SLMN NO. | CUST NO. | CUSTOMER NAME | THIS PERIOD THIS YEAR | THIS PERIOD LAST YEAR | YEAR-TO-DATE THIS YEAR | YEAR-TO-DATE LAST YEAR | PRCNT CHNG |
|---|---|---|---|---|---|---|---|
| 86 | 1311 | CHESAPEAKE SUPPLY CO | 2,551.50 | 3,126.57 | 10,914.10 | 16,424.00 | 34– |
| 98 | 8850 | SOUTH COAST CO | 822.59 | 750.10 | 3,007.06 | 4,285.96 | 30– |

Exception Reporting highlights on 2 pages those customers whose purchases this year are significantly less than the previous year

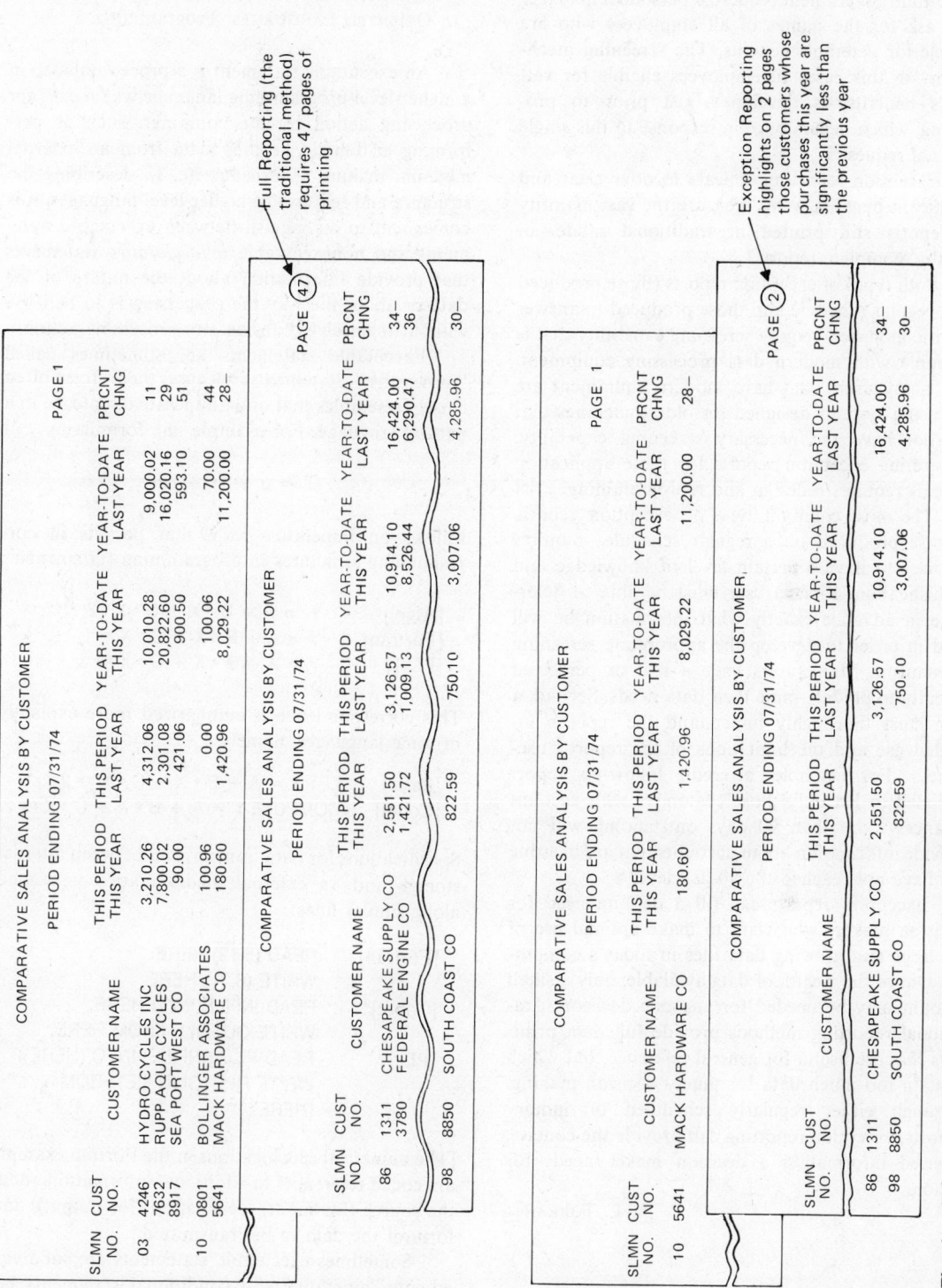

**Fig. 1.** Sales analysis: full versus exception reporting.

a one-time government request, a personnel manager may ask for the names of all employees who are eligible for veteran's benefits. The screening mechanism—in this case, all employees eligible for veteran's benefits—is developed just prior to processing, which occurs once in response to this single external request.

Exception reporting appears to offer clear and significant benefits. Why, then, are the vast majority of reports still printed in traditional mode—in lengthy, complete reports?

Both types of exception reports (those produced on a regular schedule and those produced to answer specific inquiries) require screening capability that is available with modern data processing equipment. Yet, many users who have modern equipment are still using systems designed for older machines that did not have the necessary screening capability. Generating exception reports for these application systems requires redesign and reprogramming.

The most common type of exception reports—those produced on a regular schedule—requires the user to have a certain level of knowledge and sophistication. First, a user must be able to determine in advance exactly what information he will need in order to develop the appropriate screening mechanism. Many users have a real or perceived inability to predetermine their data needs. Second, a user must thoroughly understand the report's intended use and the limitations of the report's usefulness. For example, a credit follow-up report designed to list only those customers with account balances more than 90 days outstanding will not provide information about accounts that are overdue but have not reached the 90-day level.

Exception reports can fill a definite need for decision makers who want to make optimal use of the large and growing data files in today's computers. Out of the wealth of data available, only a small amount may be needed for any one decision. Traditional reporting methods provide full data printouts that are useful for general reference, but which contain too much data for timely decision making. Through either regularly scheduled or inquiry reports, exception reporting can provide the concise, focused information a decision maker needs for action.

A. L. TORRANCE

# EXECUTABLE STATEMENT

For articles on related subjects *see* DECLARATIVE STATEMENT; and PROCEDURE-ORIENTED LANGUAGES: Programming.

An executable statement is a procedural step in a higher-level programming language which calls for processing action by the computer, such as performing arithmetic, reading data from an external medium, making a decision, etc. In describing the structure and features of higher-level languages, it is convenient to distinguish between executable statements and nonexecutable or *declarative* statements that provide information about the nature of the data or about the way the processing is to be done without themselves causing any processing action.

Executable statements are sometimes called "imperative" statements because their form often closely resembles that of an imperative sentence in a natural language. For example, the formula

$$Y = a + bx + cx^2$$

follows an imperative form that persists in corresponding structures in programming statements:

```
[Algol]     Y := A + B * X + C * X ↑ 2;
[Fortran]   Y = A + B * X + C * X ** 2
[PL/I]      Y = A + B * X + C * X ** 2;
```

This correspondence is emphasized more explicitly in some languages, namely,

```
[Basic]     LET Y = A + B * X + C * X ** 2
[Cobol]     COMPUTE Y = A + B * X + C * X ** 2.
```

Specifications for data transmission between internal storage and an external medium are constructed along similar lines:

```
[Fortran]   READ (5,12) HERE
            WRITE (6,21) HERE
[Cobol]     READ INFILE INTO HERE.
            WRITE OUTFILE FROM HERE.
[PL/I]      READ FILE (INFILE) INTO (HERE);
            WRITE FILE (OUTFILE) FROM
            (HERE);
```

[The numerical specifications in the Fortran example are coded references to additional information about the source (for input), destination (for output), and form of the data to be transmitted.]

Sometimes executable statements are subdivided into imperative and conditional statements because the latter, such as the IF statement in Fortran, specify alternate imperative actions linked through a decision mechanism.

A language implementation may have rules about the relative placement of executable and nonexecutable statements. Sometimes it is required that all declarations about data appear before the first executable statement of a program; in other cases it is required only that declarations appear before any information in them is required by an executable statement. One of the distinguishing features of Cobol is its total separation of executable statements (in the "Procedure" division) from nonexecutable statements (in the "Environment and Data" divisions).

The analogy is sometimes made that executable statements are like the verbs in a natural language, which specify actions, and that nonexecutable statements are like nouns and adjectives, which describe entities and their attributes. The analogy is not complete, of course.

D. D. McCracken and S. V. Pollack

## EXTENDED BINARY CODED DECIMAL INTERCHANGE CODE. *See* EBCDIC.

## EXTENSIBLE LANGUAGE

For articles on related subjects *see* Procedure-Oriented Languages; and Programming Languages.

For article on related term *see* Algol 68.

The concept of extensible languages was evolved to permit the user to modify a programming language by adding new features to it or by modifying existing ones. One of the goals was to let the user mold the language to the requirements of his particular area of application, and thus improve his efficiency as a programmer and the clarity of his product.

Extensible languages consist of two basic components:

1. A base language, which provides a complete but minimal set of primitive facilities such as elementary data types, and simple operations and control constructs.

2. Extension mechanisms, which allow the definition of new language features in terms of the base language primitives.

The extension mechanisms can be further subdivided into *semantic extension* facilities and *syntactic extension* facilities.

Semantic extensions introduce new kinds of objects to the languages such as additional data types or operations, whereas syntactic extensions create new notations for existing or user defined mechanisms.

Among others, Algol 68, Basel, EL1 (Extensible Language 1), GPL (General Purpose Language), PPL (Polymorphic Programming Language), and Proteus are languages that are extensible to a higher or lower degree.

As an example of semantic extensibility, consider the mode (i.e., type) and operator definition facilities provided by Algol 68 as demonstrated by the following program segment:

**mode point** = **struct** (**real** x, y);

**Comment:** A new object of the mode **point** is being defined as a structure of two real components. The components are accessed by the selectors *x* and *y*. ¢

**priority** -- = 6;

**Comment:** This is declared to be an infix operator symbol of the priority level 6, i.e., the level of addition. ¢

**op**-- = (**point** p1, p2) **real**:
sqrt ((x **of** p1 − x of p2) ↑ 2 + (y **of** p1 − y **of** p2) ↑ 2);

**Comment:** The symbol --, if applied to operands of the mode *point*, is defined to denote the Euclidean distance of the two points p1 and p2.

The following segment demonstrates how the newly defined objects may be used. ¢

**begin** real a, **point** u, v
u: = (.0,.0), v: = (3.0,4.0); a: = u -- v **end**

**Comment:** *a* is set to 5.0 ¢

It should be noted that all operators so defined are generic, i.e., the same operator symbol may be defined for and used with different operand modes evoking different computations. This is accomplished by checking and matching modes during the compilation.

The above example gives a glimpse at the power of the concept. In a similar fashion, these facilities could be used to define polynomials or logical formulas as objects for programs that manipulate formulas, with operations that, for example, add, multiply, intersect, or unite these objects in a formal rather than a numeric way. In computer graphics applications, pictures could be defined as new objects with operators that overlay, scale, or rotate them, etc.

Both mechanisms demonstrated use only notational patterns that are part of the language Algol 68, namely, the mode declaration and the infix operator notation. Algol 68 does not allow the user to redefine the *syntactic form* of a statement; thus, it does not provide syntactic extensions.

Where syntactic extension mechanisms are available they usually have the general form

*phrase* $\alpha$ *means* $\beta$

where $\alpha$ is a syntactic pattern to be defined and $\beta$ is a program segment consisting of statements of the base language or of extensions previously defined. A GPL program segment will be used for demonstration. In GPL the form

*phrase* $\alpha$ *means* $\beta$

takes on the appearance

**procedure** $\alpha$; $\beta$

As in the Algol 68 program above, the following program defines the distance function for points in a plane. It introduces, however, the novel notation

**dist** a **from** b

for its invocation. The program assumes that the type *point* has been declared previously:

**procedure dist** a **from** b;
**iff point** a, b **take real to be**
sqrt ((x(a) − x(b)) ↑ 2 + (y(a) − y(b)) ↑ 2);

If this operation is now invoked by, for instance,

length: = **dist** x **from** y;

*x* and *y* must be expressions of the type *point*; otherwise, a compile-time error message will be issued.

Among the promising properties of extensible languages, the most important is probably that they should make it possible to implement special-purpose languages with relatively little effort. On the other hand, critics say that present-day extensible languages are not powerful enough to accomplish this goal. Some feel that significant alterations of languages are of an inherent complexity too great to be specified simply. Also, there is a difficult trade-off problem between the flexibility that is provided by the language and the efficiency of both its compiler and the object programs generated.

Nevertheless, some degree of semantic extensibility exists in a number of languages (Algol 68, APL, Lisp, Pascal). Languages of this moderate category are sometimes called "enhanceable." Beyond this, it seems that, particularly for special-purpose language development and implementation, some syntactic flexibility is not only desirable but also necessary.

REFERENCES

1970. Schuman, S. A., and P. Jorrand. "Definition Mechanisms in Extensible Programming Languages," AFIPS Conference Proceedings, Vol. 37, AFIPS Press, pp. 9–20.

1971. "Proceedings of the International Symposium on Extensible Languages" (September 1971 Grenoble, France), SIGPLAN Notices, Vol. 6, No. 12 (December).

J. J. MARTIN

# F

**FFT.** *See* FAST FOURIER TRANSFORM.

## FAST FOURIER TRANSFORM

For article on related subject *see* NUMERICAL ANALYSIS.

The "fast Fourier transform" (FFT) refers to a family of numerical algorithms for computing the discrete Fourier transform (DFT). In complex notation, the DFT is defined by

$$a(n) = \sum_{j=0}^{N-1} x(j)\, W_N^{-nj} \qquad n = 0,1,\ldots, N-1 \tag{1}$$

where $x(j)$, $j = 0,1,\ldots, N-1$ is a given sequence of complex numbers and

$$W_N = \exp(2\pi i/N) \tag{2}$$

is the principal $N$th root of unity. This can be written as a series of sines and cosines by making the substitution

$$W_N^{-nj} = \cos(2\pi nj/N) - i\sin(2\pi nj/N). \tag{3}$$

Most of the important applications of the FFT involve the inversion theorem and the convolution theorem.

The inversion theorem states that Eq. (1) is a solution of the system of equations

$$x(j) = \frac{1}{N} \sum_{n=0}^{N-1} a(n)\, W_N^{nj} \tag{4}$$

This is referred to as the "inverse discrete Fourier transform (IDFT) of $a(n)$."

One important application of a program for computing Eq. (1) is in spectral analysis. Here, one wishes to obtain estimates (with perhaps some smoothing) of the amplitudes and phases given by the $a(n)$ of the sinusoidal components of a signal $x(j)$. Other applications involve the solution of systems of equations by substituting Eq. (4) for the solution and expressing the equations in terms of the $a(n)$. The latter are usually easily solvable and the computation consists mostly of the calculation of the DFT given in Eq. (4).

In some cases, it is expedient to process data by performing operations in the frequency domain, i.e., on the $a(n)$ instead of the $x(j)$. Such applications are usually based upon the convolution theorem, which may be expressed as follows:

Given two periodic sequences $x(j)$, $y(j)$, $j = 0,1,\ldots, N-1$, with DFTs $a(n)$ and $b(n)$, $n = 0,1,\ldots, N-1$, respectively, let the convolution sequence

$$z(j) = \sum_{k=0}^{N-1} x(k)\,y(j-k), \qquad j = 0,1,\ldots, N-1 \tag{5}$$

have the DFT $c(n)$, $n = 0,1,\ldots, N-1$. The convolution theorem states that

$$c(n) = a(n)b(n). \tag{6}$$

Therefore, one may obtain $z(j)$ by computing $a(n)$ and $b(n)$ and then computing the IDFT of their product. While the direct computation of Eq. (5) by accumulating products may take a number of operations (multiplications and additions) proportional to $N^2$, the use of Eq. (6) will require a number of operations proportional to the time required to compute the DFTs, which is proportional to $N \log N$. Since it is fairly typical to process long records of data in slices having a length of approximately $N = 1{,}000$, the computation is reduced by a factor of roughly $N/\log_2 N = 100$.

The FFT algorithms use the fact that if $N$ is composite, i.e.,

$$N = r_1 \cdot r_2 \cdot \ldots \cdot r_m, \tag{7}$$

the series (1) can be expressed as a nested sequence of series of subseries which requires a number of operations proportional to

$$N_{op} = N(r_1 + r_2 + \cdots + r_m). \tag{8}$$

For $N > 4$, this is less than the $N^2$ operations that would be required by a direct accumulation of products for each value of $j$ according to the defining formula (1). The number $N_{op}$ is minimized by using as many factors as possible. If all factors are equal to $r$, then

$$N_{op} = Nr \log_r N = \frac{r}{\log_2 r} N \log_2 N. \tag{9}$$

A frequent choice, for programming efficiency, is to select $N$ to be a power of 2 so that

$$N_{op} = 2 \cdot N \log_2 N. \tag{10}$$

The algorithm is easily derived when $N$ is a product of two factors, $r_1$ and $r_2$. The indices $n$ and $j$ in Eqs. (1) and (4) are, in this case, replaced by index pairs $(n_1, n_2)$ and $(j_1, j_2)$, respectively, defined as

$$\begin{aligned} n &= n_1 + r_1 n_2, \\ j &= j_2 + j_1 r_2, \end{aligned} \tag{11}$$

where

$$\begin{aligned} n_1 &= 0, 1, \ldots, r_1 - 1, \\ n_2 &= 0, 1, \ldots, r_2 - 1, \\ j_1 &= 0, 1, \ldots, r_1 - 1, \\ j_2 &= 0, 1, \ldots, r_2 - 1. \end{aligned} \tag{12}$$

Using Eq. (11), one can perform the factorization

$$W_N^{-nj} = W_N^{-n_2 j_1 r_1 r_2} W_N^{-n_1 j_1 r_2} W_N^{-n_2 j_2 r_1} W_N^{-n_1 j_2}, \tag{13}$$

which is easily simplified by using the relations

$$W_N^{r_1 r_2} = 1, \qquad W_N^{r_1} = W_{r_2}, \qquad W_N^{r_2} = W_{r_1}. \tag{14}$$

The summation may then be taken over $j_1$ and $j_2$ instead of $j$ to give

$$a(n_1 + r_1 n_2) = \sum_{j_2=0}^{r_2-1} \left\{ \sum_{j_1=0}^{r_1-1} x(j_2 + j_1 r_2) W_{r_1}^{-n_1 j_1} \right\} \times W_N^{-n_1 j_2} W_{r_2}^{-n_2 j_2} \tag{15}$$

The inner sum is, for each of the $r_2$ values of $j_2$, a DFT of an $r_1$-point sequence which, for all $r_1$ values of $n_1$, can be computed in $r_1^2$ operations. After multiplication of this result by the phase factor $W_N^{-n_1 j_2}$, or "twiddle factor," the outer sum may be calculated as a DFT of an $r_2$-point sequence, which for each of the $r_1$ values of $n_1$ takes $r_2^2$ operations. If the phase factor $W_N^{-n_1 j_2}$ is absorbed in either of the $W_{r_1}$ or $W_{r_2}$ factors, this will take a total of

$$N_{op} = r_2 r_1^2 + r_1 r_2^2 = N(r_1 + r_2) \tag{16}$$

operations. If $r_2$ can be factored into $r_2' \cdot r_3'$ and the process repeated on the $r_2$-point DFT, it is easily seen that the number of operations will be

$$N_{op} = N(r_1 + r_2' + r_3'). \tag{17}$$

By an inductive argument, one arrives at Eq. (8).

The algorithm described by Eq. (15) may be written so that the data is overwritten by the results, with practically no other storage required except, perhaps, that used for a table of sines.

### References


1976. Cooley, J. W., P. A. W. Lewis, P. D. Welch. *Practical Fourier Analysis, the FFT and Its Applications*. New York: John Wiley.

In process.———. "The Fast Fourier Transform and Its Application to Time Series Analysis," in Enslein, Ralston, and Wilf (Eds.), *Mathematical Methods for Digital Computers*, vol. 3. New York: John Wiley.


J. W. Cooley

# FEASIBILITY STUDY

For article on related subject, *see* DOCUMENTATION.

The feasibility study takes place at the beginning of a systems development project and leads to a *feasibility report*. It is a broad-brush study which seeks to determine two things: the exact nature of the problem to be solved and an outline of one or more solutions to the problem. It seeks to answer three questions: technical—will it work?; economic—will it pay?; operational/political—will it be used? The feasibility report is submitted to the problem proponent (user) who, after review, may authorize the detailed development work on a selected solution, modify the design, or possibly abandon the whole project.

The basis of the feasibility study is that it enables fundamental decisions to be made before time and money are committed to the systems and programming work. Provided the feasibility study is conducted carefully by experienced personnel, the outline solution(s) and cost/timing estimates will be confirmed in the detailed systems work. But, in practice, the findings of the study and the decisions based upon it may be reviewed in the light of the detailed investigation and analysis, and the project modified (or even abandoned) any time up to the beginning of programming. Revisions to the scope of the project or the design approach *after* programming has begun will be very expensive indeed. An example of the contents of a feasibility study report is given in Fig. 1.

As Fig. 1 shows, the study is based on an investigation of the proponent's (user's) problem area. The scope of the investigation and the resources required will depend on the type of project. The feasibility study for the development of a major accounting or production control system in a large company may take several systems analysts a number of months to complete. A study of a small "subsystem" to produce an additional report from an existing system, on the other hand, may take only a few days.

The statement of the user's requirements generally includes the following categories:

1. *Objectives*. States what the user wants the new system to achieve. This should be quantified wherever possible. For example, rather than a general statement of "increase factory throughput," a quantified statement of requirements is preferable, such as "to reduce work in progress by 15% and to increase machine utilization by 5%."

2. *Boundaries and Constraints*. Stipulates what the user does not want changed or sets forth any restriction on the design approach or the facilities used. These may be imposed for various technical and business reasons. Examples: "The job docket currently being used should not be changed." "The system must not be justified on staff displacement." "No more clerks in Grades A and B can be used." "Existing computer facilities must be used."

3. *Time Scale*. Sets the date when the new system is required. There may be many good business reasons for requiring a new system to be operational by a certain date. For example, the new system must be available by the end of the financial year, or before research begins on a new project, or to coincide with next annual stock inventory.

4. *Mandatory Reports*. Lists mandatory output reports, identified by the user, which must be produced in the new system.

This problem definition is the design brief for a systems analyst. His task is to produce and outline one or more solutions that meet the user's needs as described above. A range of solutions is generally preferable because this will give the user an objective choice (rather than "forcing" one solution upon him). For example, if there is an existing system, one alternative solution is "do nothing—do not change method of working"; this will serve as a basis for comparison with new system designs. For each solution there must be sufficient information given to enable the user to answer the following questions:

> "Does the system meet my requirements?"
> "How much will it cost and how long will it take?"
> "Is it worthwhile to proceed?" (a cost benefit analysis of expenditure against savings)

This means that a description of the proposed new system must be given, together with a statement of the objectives that are met by the design. The benefits can be estimated from the latter. Some benefits will be tangible and quantified, others will be intangible and qualified benefits on which no monetary value can be placed. From the outline design, estimates can be made of the resources and time necessary to develop the system; the operational costs of running the system can also be assessed. The cost/benefit analysis, using the appropriate costing methods, can then be drawn up.

K. R. LONDON

**FEASIBILITY STUDY REPORT**

Title
Contents
Administrative Information

1. INTRODUCTION
   1.1 Terms of Reference
   1.2 Method
   1.3 Summary

2. FINDINGS
   2.1 Description of Existing System
   2.2 Identified Problems
   2.3 User Request
       —Objectives
       —Boundaries and Constraints
       —Timescale
       —Mandatory Reports
       —Assumptions and Limitations

3. SYSTEM SOLUTION (repeated for each solution)
   3.1 System Outline
   3.2 Benefits Realized
   3.3 Development Schedule, Resources and Costs
   3.4 Operating Schedule, Resources and Costs
   3.5 Advantages and Disadvantages
       —Cost/Benefit Analysis
       —Impact on Existing Organization/System
       —General Comments and Summary

4. RECOMMENDATIONS AND CONCLUSIONS
   4.1 Conclusions (these may include a comparison of solutions)
   4.2 Recommendations
   4.3 Further Actions

APPENDICES
(Detailed timing and cost figures, document samples, etc.)

**Fig. 1.** Sample feasibility study, table of contents.

# FIFO–LIFO

For articles on related subjects *see* DATA STRUCTURES; and STACK.
For articles on related terms *see* LIST AND LIST PROCESSING; and QUEUEING THEORY.

The terms FIFO and LIFO refer to two techniques for dealing with collection of items to which additions and deletions are to be made. The acronym FIFO stands for first–in–first–out and LIFO represents last–in–first–out. Derived from business accounting and inventory management notions, these techniques have found widespread application in computer science.

The FIFO concept is based on the simple idea of people waiting on line to be serviced at a bank teller's window, a supermarket checkout counter, or a bus stop. The first person to arrive is serviced, and if there is a line of customers the order of entry to the rear of the line is the order of service given at the front of the line. The same concept can be applied to ships waiting to unload at a dock, to jobs waiting to be run in a computer system, or to airplanes waiting to be serviced by a repair shop. The line of people or items waiting to be serviced is called the "queue" (Fig. 1).

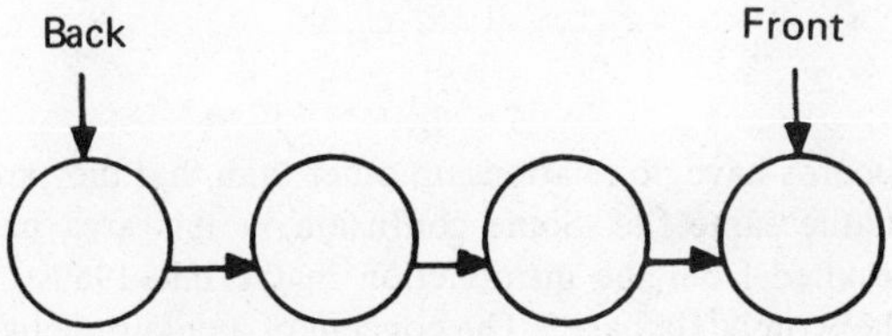


**Fig. 1.** FIFO queue; additions at back; deletions at front.

There are a great number of variations to the basic theme of FIFO arrangement. Multiple-server queues have a single queue, but several facilities that provide service. Some banks and airline ticket counters have adopted this technique by having a single line that feeds to a group of teller windows. Priority queueing permits persons with high priority to move up to the front of the queue. Bounded-length queueing puts an upper limit to the number of persons in the queue.

The LIFO concept is based on the notion that the most recently arrived item is dispatched first. Thus, the freshest vegetables in the grocery are sold first and the inventory items most recently put on the shelf are the first to be sold. This idea is familiar to card players in some games (gin rummy, for example), who may take a card from the top of the pile or place another card face up on the pile. The stack of plates on the spring-loaded dispenser found in cafeterias is another common example of the LIFO principle. The usual definition of this principle includes the specification that only the top element of the collection may be removed and that new items may be placed only on the top of the collection. A collection that has these rules for addition and deletion is called a "stack" or a "pushdown list" (Fig. 2). Automata theorists distinguish between these two terms: In a stack, the interior items may be examined; in a pushdown list, the interior items may not be examined.

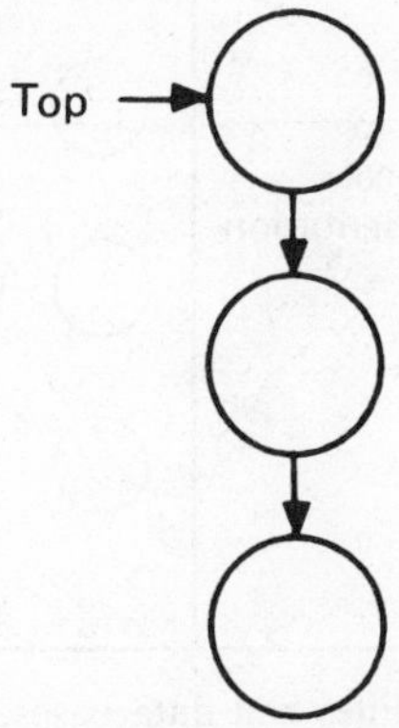


**Fig. 2.** LIFO stack: additions and deletions at top.

The LIFO technique has widespread application in computer science, particularly in the parsing techniques employed by compilers and in the searching of data structures.

B. SHNEIDERMAN

# FILES

For articles on related subjects *see* DATA BASE AND DATA BASE MANAGEMENT; RECORD; and STORAGE MANAGEMENT STRUCTURES.

**Background.** The term "file" must have been one of the first to be used in commercial data processing terminology. Even before the advent of computers a deck of punched cards was often called a "card file," a term also applied to the cabinet in

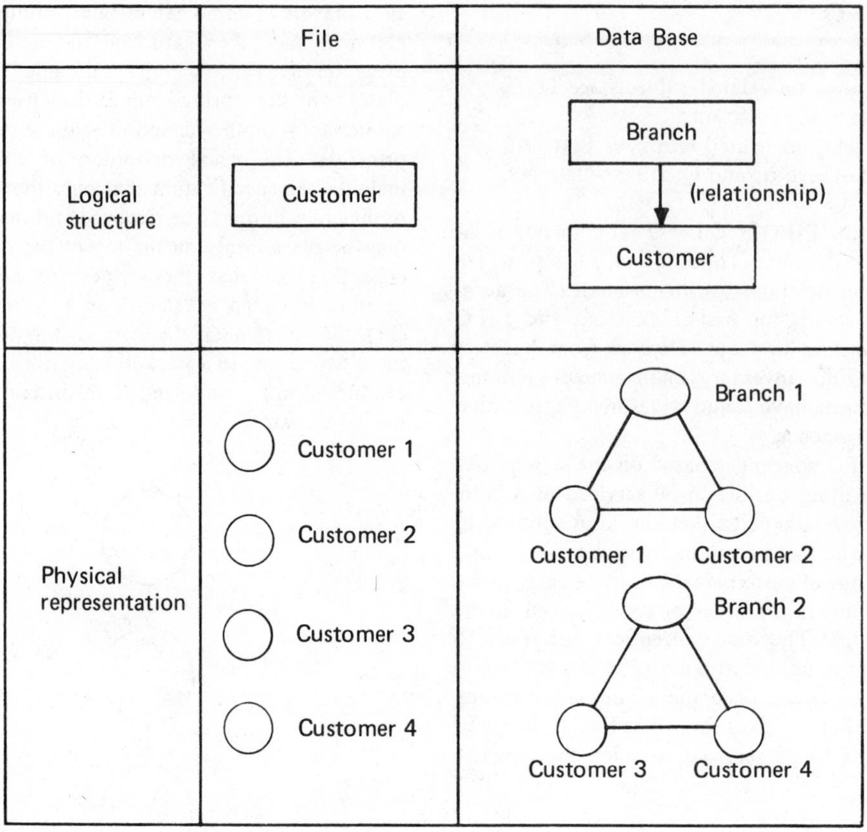


**Fig. 1.** Files and data bases.

which the cards were stored. In the very early days of computers, any collection of data or programs was identified as a file. Magnetic tape was the first storage medium on which data could be stored, detached, and then attached again at a later date. This led to the widespread use of the term "tape file."

When removable disk packs came into use as a storage medium, the concept of a file became slightly more complex. Before the era of data processing, a file was traditionally an ordered collection of similar entities. Magnetic tapes did nothing to disrupt this simple view, but disks and other direct-access devices had an extra dimension. Any record in the file could be accessed without looking first at those preceding it in the order. In this way the concept of an indexed file came into being. Many ways of accessing the records in the file were developed, and each way became known as an "access method."

**Definition.** A file is a collection of data records (possibly of different types) in which the records have no relationship other than that they are in the same file. Some confusion in this area has resulted from the introduction in the mid-1960s of the term "data base." The concept of a data base has become fashionable, and sometimes collections of data which previously had been happily referred to as files received the accolade of "data base." We distinguish these two terms by defining a data base as a collection of data records (of two or more types) in which relationships exist and are represented between record types and between records of the same type.

Fig. 1 illustrates the logical structure and physical representation of a file and a data base.

**Kinds of Files.** The word "file" is used in many ways in data processing. Examples are data file, input file, output file, master file, program file, working file, scratch file, temporary file, transaction file, operating systems file, log file, print file, card file, and job file.

The preceding definition applies essentially to a data file, i.e., a file in which a program may operate during the course of its execution. However, the data may in fact consist of programs, with each program statement as a record in the file.

T. W. OLLE

# FINITE ELEMENT METHOD

For articles on related subjects *see* ENGINEERING APPLICATIONS; MATRIX COMPUTATIONS; NUMERICAL ANALYSIS; and PARTIAL DIFFERENTIAL EQUATIONS, NUMERICAL SOLUTION OF.

The finite element method is a relatively recent and very powerful approximate technique used to solve field problems in various engineering fields. Its development follows closely the increasing usage and availability of large-scale digital computers. Some areas of practical application are:

1. Static and dynamic analysis of complex structures such as airplanes, bridges, buildings, dams, ships, and cars.
2. Fluid flow, diffusion, and consolidation problems.
3. Liquid sloshing in an elastic container.
4. Lubrication problems.
5. Heat conduction and thermal stresses.

In the past decade, through applications of the technique, many engineers, mathematicians, and computer scientists have gained a large amount of direct experience with this new concept. We will briefly discuss this method as seen from the viewpoints of each of these three professional groups.

**The Practicing Engineer.** Practically on the basis of physical intuition alone, this method was initially used for aerospace structural analysis. Essentially, a continuous system is idealized as an assembly of discrete elements (Kuo, 1961). For example, an automobile may be idealized as a set of triangular elements as shown in Fig. 1. The common shape of a discrete element, known as the "shape" function, is the triangle for a two-dimensional structure and the tetrahedron for a three-dimensional one. However, other shape functions have also been used (see Fig. 2). Once this decision is made, the

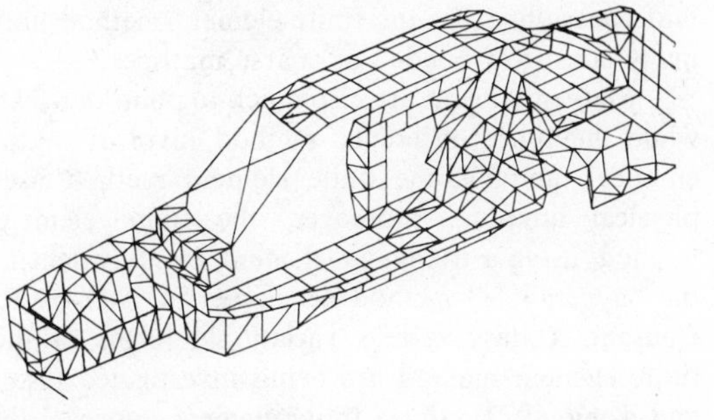

**Fig. 1.** Idealization of a car body using finite elements.

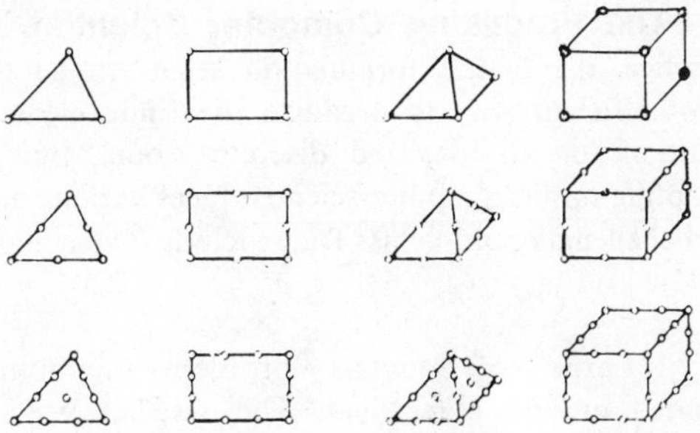

**Fig. 2.** Some common two-dimensional and three-dimensional finite elements.

remaining steps follow a standard procedure. For example, in a structural problem using a stiffness matrix (Desai and Abel, 1972; Zienkiewicz, 1967), they are:

1. Choice of the displacement function for each element, assumed to be a polynomial usually, in terms of displacements at the nodes.
2. Selection of the stress-strain relationship.
3. Development of the stiffness matrix $k$ for an element.
4. Consolidation of internal degrees of freedom.
5. Formation of $k$ for the assemblage.
6. Computation of the displacements, strains, and stresses at various nodal points.

**The Applied Mathematician.** Many applied mathematicians view the finite element method as the approximation of a continuum by elements, each with multiple connecting points. It is similar to the Rayleigh-Ritz method with the following differences: (1) The piecewise continuous field definitions used in the finite element method are used to take care of irregular boundaries; and, (2) the resultant equations from the finite element method normally consist of banded or sparse matrices.

Mathematicians are also quick to point out that, while the finite difference method involves mathematical lumping, the finite element method uses physical lumping. Moreover, the finite element method, using a triangular element, is equivalent to the "hypercircle" method developed in 1943 by R. Courant. Today, various variational forms of the finite element method are being investigated (Pian and Tong, 1972), and a finite element approach to the solution of partial differential equations is being extensively studied (Aziz, 1972).

**The Practicing Computer Scientist.** In practice, the matrix formulation seems to be the most efficient way to organize the finite element solution for an idealized discrete model, but in adopting it, the computer scientist faces various new and challenging problems. They include (Oden et al., 1972):

1. Large-scale matrix problems involving banded or sparse matrices. The associated error bounds and convergence must be studied. Overlay techniques are often used.
2. Automatic mesh generation to avoid the error-prone input of large amounts of data. A typical mesh pattern (automatically generated) is shown in Fig. 3.

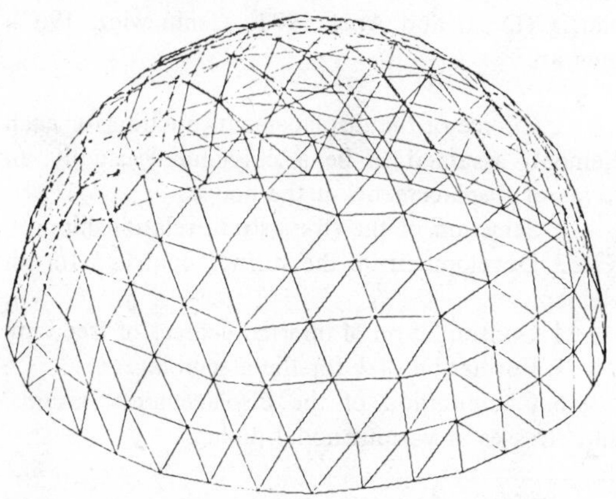

**Fig. 3.** Computer-generated mesh pattern.

3. Computer-oriented interpolation techniques for two-dimensional and three-dimensional problems.
4. Hidden-line computer graphics for output.
5. Design of a general-purpose computer program versus some specially designed programs.

References


1961. Kuo, S. S. "On Jacobi's Method for Real Symmetric Matrices," *Journal of the Aerospace Sciences*, Vol. 28, No. 3, March, p. 255.

1967. Zienkiewicz, O. C. *The Finite Element Method in Structural and Continuum Mechanics*, New York: McGraw-Hill.

1972. Aziz, A. K. *The Mathematical Foundations of the Finite Element Method with Applications to Partial Differential Equations*. New York: Academic Press.

1972. Desai, C. S., and J. F. Abel. *Introduction to the Finite Element Method*. New York: Van Nostrand-Reinhold.

1972. Oden, J. T., R. W. Clough, and Y. Yamamoto (Eds.). "Advances in Computational Methods in Structural Mechanics and Design," Section IV. Huntsville: Program Development, University of Alabama Press.

1972. Pian, T. H. H., and P. Tong. "Finite Element Methods in Continuum Mechanics." In Chia-Shun Yih (Ed.), *Advances in Applied Mechanics*, Vol. 12. New York: Academic Press.


S. S. Kuo

## FIX

For article on related subject *see* Patch.
For article on related term *see* Source Program.

As a verb, the word "fix" means to patch a program in an attempt to correct a bug (an error). More often it is used in computing as a noun. The fix can be made at the machine language level, but commonly, in assembly language or higher-level language coding, the source code is corrected and the entire program is reassembled or recompiled.

F. Gruenberger

## FLOW DIAGRAM

For articles on related subjects *see* Block Diagram; Documentation; Flowchart; and System Chart.

A flow diagram is a variety of flowchart. The flow diagram is distinguished from other varieties of flowchart by its emphasis upon the algorithm. The flow diagram depicts the details of how an algorithm is to transform data when used as a representation for a computer program. Flow diagrams can be distinguished from other varieties of flowchart by the relatively infrequent presentation of input/output operations. An example of a flow diagram is given in Fig. 1.

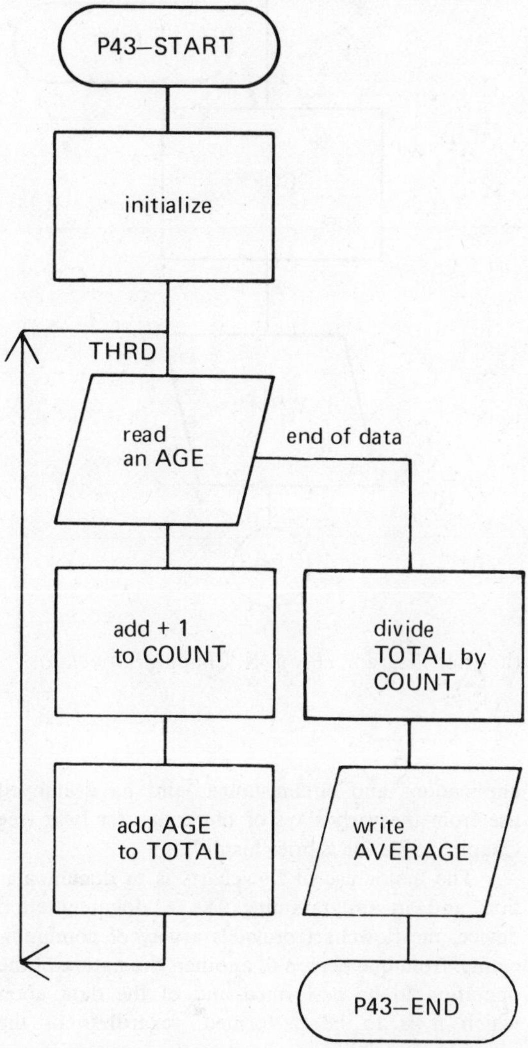


**Fig. 1.** Example of a flow diagram for finding an average. (From Ned Chapin, *Flowcharts*, Petrocelli Books, New York, 1971.)

N. Chapin

# FLOWCHART

For articles on related subjects *see* Algorithm; Block Diagram; Documentation; Flow Diagram; Program; and System Chart.
For article on related term *see* Standards.

**Definition.** Flowcharts are graphic means of describing a sequence of operations done on data. They serve as a means of communication from one person to another about transformations on data. Flowcharts are graphic because they commonly use a two-dimensional pictorial format. The placement of the identifications of the operations in the pictorial format shows the sequence of the operations. The pictorial format typically incorporates wording to identify the data and the operations. The pictorial format is the subject of both an International and an American National Standard (ANSI, 1970).

Flowcharts get their name from their chart (graphic) representation of the flow (orderly passing of control) from one operation to the next in an explicit sequence. Flowcharts go by many other names, including block diagram, flow diagram, logic diagram, system chart, run diagram, process chart, procedure chart, and logic chart (Chapin, 1971). These different names reflect in part a lack of uniformity of nomenclature and in part the particular interests of specialized users. For example, prior to the advent of computers the name "flowchart" was used by systems analysts to designate a means of describing the flow of documents carrying data in an organization.

The two major varieties of flowchart in present-day practice are the system chart and the flow diagram. As indicated in Fig. 1, the flow diagram concentrates on part of what a system chart shows. The unit of data transformation for the two is thus very different. For a flow diagram, the unit of data transformation is usually an operation or short sequence of operations that a computer can perform (such as an instruction or a series of instructions that comprise a subroutine). An example is testing for the presence of leading zeros in a number.

By contrast, in a system chart the unit of data transformation is usually the work done by an entire computer program. Examples are: sorting a file of data, inverting a matrix, or producing a report. Flow diagrams commonly have an algorithmic orientation, stressing how data is transformed, whereas system charts primarily identify inputs and outputs to algorithms, stressing what data is used or pro-

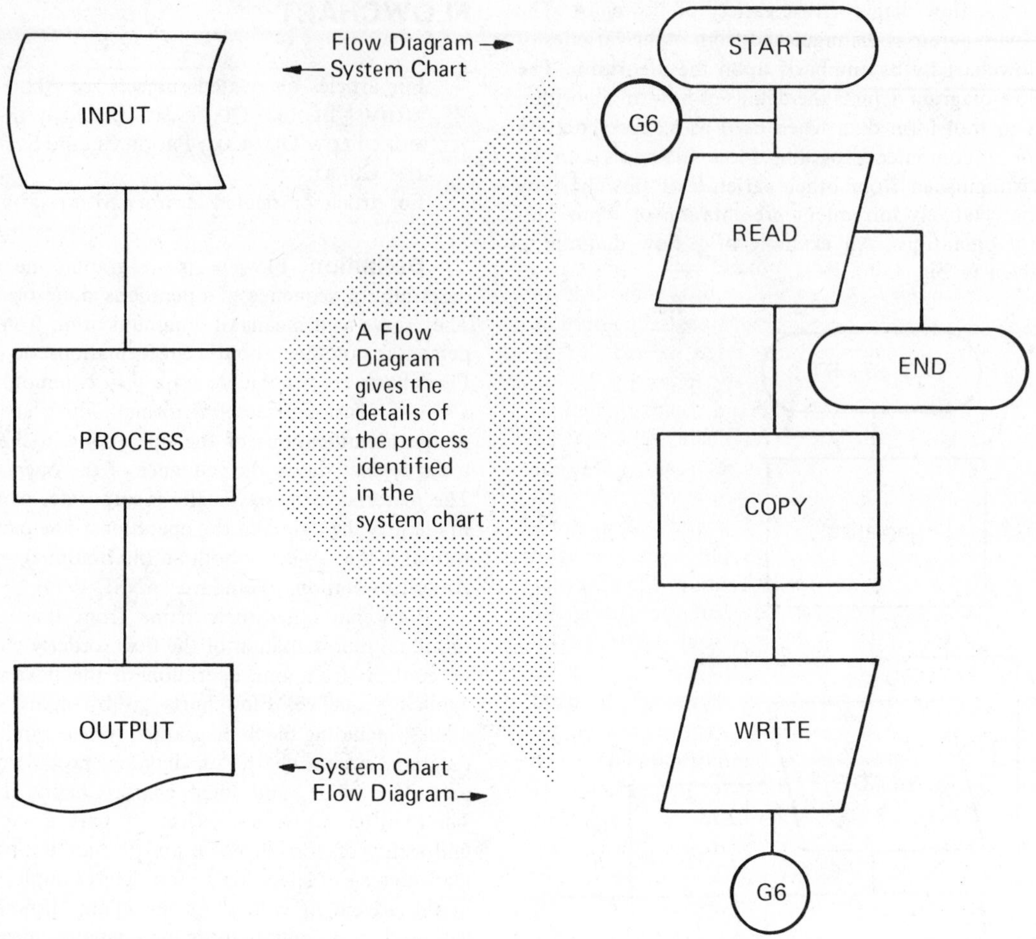


**Fig. 1.** Two types of flowcharts: the system chart and the flow diagram. (From N. Chapin, *Flowcharts,* Petrocelli Books, New York, 1971.)

duced at various points in a sequence of operations. System charts and flow diagrams are described in more detail later in this article.

The major varieties of flowcharts are alike in that they describe operations in sequence on data. They stress "what" and "how." Flowcharts are weak on "when," "why," and "what does the action." The only usual indication of "when" is the relative position in a sequence of operations. Usually, the doer of the action is the computer arithmetic and logic unit for a flow diagram, and the computer itself for a system chart, with exceptions possible.

**Use.** Flowcharts are the most widely used graphic method for describing computer operations. They are adaptable to a wide variety of different applications and circumstances and have enjoyed use from the early days of the computer field (see Chapin, 1971, for a brief history).

The major use of flowcharts is in documentation and in programming. As a documentation device, the flowchart provides a way of communicating, from one person to another, the nature of the operation to be performed and of the data upon which it is to be performed, regardless of the programming language or computer used. Since a flowchart is a graphic means of communication, this feature makes it a good choice for use with the usual programming language and English language descriptions included in most documentation. This alternative means of description can enhance the usefulness of the other means.

As a programming aid, flowcharts are often prepared by systems analysts and designers to describe systems and to specify the work to be accomplished by programs. Programmers use flowcharts as a basis for writing programs and as a means of communicating among each other, particularly when the programming is done as a team effort. Programmers as well as systems analysts also use flowcharts as a source of information for maintenance work on programs and systems.

Flowcharts are more widely used than decision tables, publication languages, or abstract notations (such as the Iverson notation used in APL, or the lambda calculus). This popularity appears to be due to the balance of advantages and disadvantages.

ADVANTAGES. Flowcharts have few features limiting their use. Hence, they are broadly applicable across a wide range of industries, computer applications, and types of work. For example, they are as convenient in administrative file handling as in scientific or engineering computation. This popularity, bred of wide applicability, generates further use as a lingua franca among persons working with computers.

Flowcharts are also largely language independent. Knowledge of a programming language is not normally necessary to be able to use them or to create them. This is always true for the pictorial part of flowcharts, and ideally should be true for the wording or symbols incorporated in a flowchart.

Flowcharts are constraining and precise in ways that are useful to programmers and analysts. They are a limited means of description that force the user to give attention to many significant matters while suppressing attention to a host of less important matters.

Flowcharts are a visual representation, and hence provide a convenient alternative to the usual narrative description for a program or system. This enables a more rapid scan or search of a flowchart than of a narrative description when particular items of information are sought. The graphic format enables a user to comprehend much at a glance.

Flowcharts offer a controllable level of detail. They are usable from the most summary systems level to the most detailed programming level, at the option of the one who prepares the flowchart. This wide range of detail options greatly enhances the communication value of the flowchart. It is generally conceded that the flowchart is most valuable to the user when the level of detail in the flowchart is more summary than that provided in the programming language (for flow diagrams) or in the English language narrative (for system charts). For this reason, the person who creates flowcharts commonly prepares them in a series, arranged from very summary to quite detailed, so that the user may choose the level of detail most convenient for his particular purposes as they change from time to time. In this regard it should be noted that the system chart variety of flowchart inherently provides a more summary view than does the flow-diagram variety of flowchart.

DISADVANTAGES. On the disadvantage side, some programmers and analysts complain that flowcharts are a waste of time, since people do not think in graphic terms. In their view, a flowchart is therefore an unnatural means of communication.

Flowcharts are often cumbersome to use and costly to produce. Because of their graphic format, flowcharts may devote more than a page of space to present what may require from a few lines to less

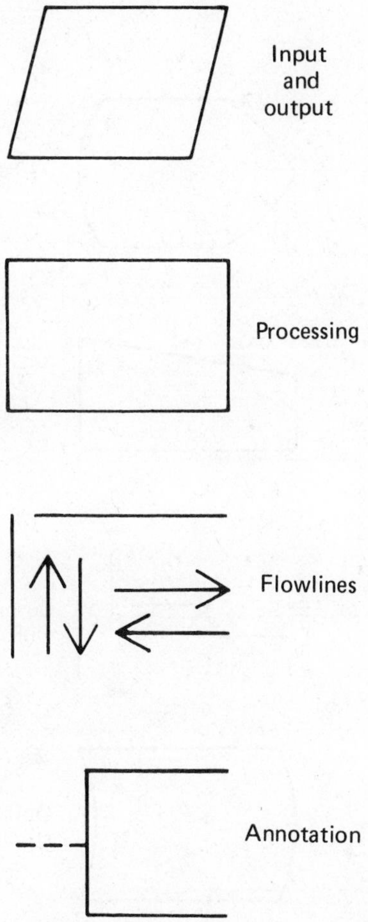


**Fig. 2.** Basic outlines. (From N. Chapin, *Flowcharts*, Petrocelli Books, New York, 1971.)

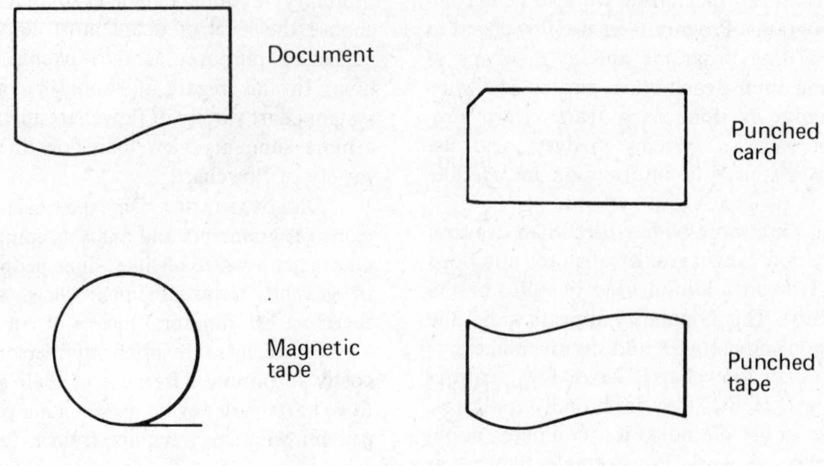
Document
Punched card
Magnetic tape
Punched tape

(a)

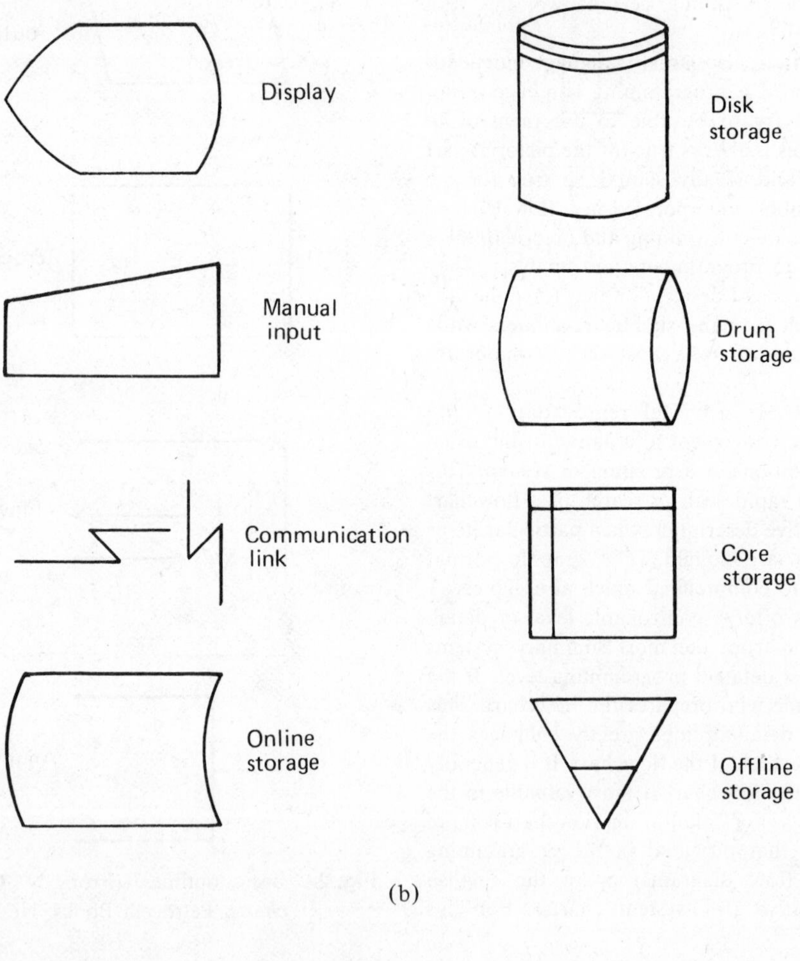
Display
Disk storage
Manual input
Drum storage
Communication link
Core storage
Online storage
Offline storage

(b)

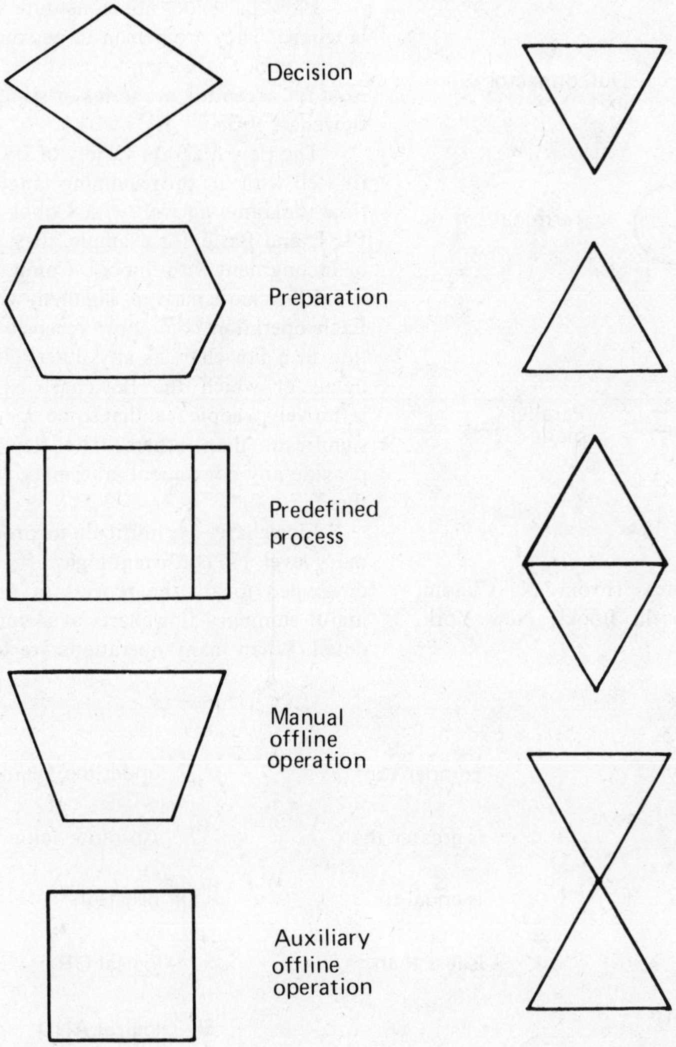


(c)

**Fig. 3.** Specialized outlines. (a) Media. (b) Equipment. (c) Processes. (From N. Chapin, *Flowcharts,* Petrocelli Books, New York, 1971.)

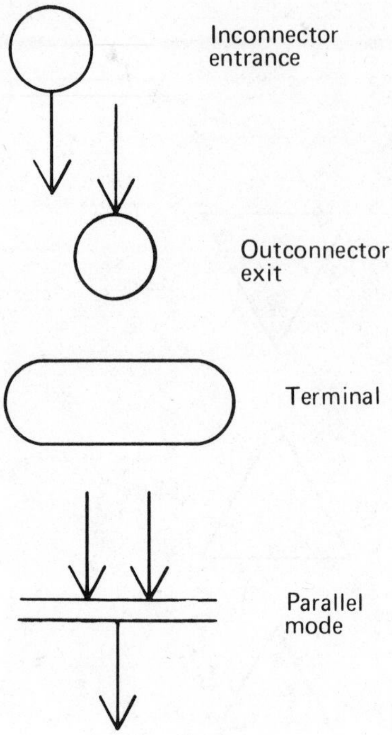


**Fig. 4.** Additional outlines. (From N. Chapin, *Flowcharts*, Petrocelli Books, New York, 1971.)

than a half-page of equally detailed description in some other form. Manual preparation of flowcharts is slow, although detailed flow diagrams can be prepared by computer if the program to be flowcharted exists in source language form.

Flowcharts do not constitute a programming language. They are person-to-person means of communication, not person-to-computer. No translators exist for accepting programs or systems described in flowchart form.

The flow diagram variety of flowchart does not fit well with all programming languages. Although flow diagrams go well with Cobol, Fortran, Algol, PL/I, and Basic, for example, they seem ponderous or incongruent with Snobol, Comit, Lisp, or IPL-V.

Flowcharts may not highlight what is important. Each operation commonly receives as much attention in a flowchart as any other, given the level of detail at which the flowchart is prepared. Yet, intuitively, people feel that some operations are more significant than others. The flowchart does not provide any convenient, automatic way to highlight these.

Flowcharts are difficult to produce at a summary level. No consistent logical rules have yet been developed to aid the process of producing meaningful summary flowcharts at a consistent level of detail. When many operations are to be condensed

| | | | | | |
|---|---|---|---|---|---|
| := ← | is replaced by | : | comparison | — | underline, blank |
| + | plus or addition | > | is greater than | \| \| | Absolute value |
| - | minus or subtraction | = | is equal to | ¬ ~ - | negation |
| * x | multiplication | < | is less than | \| | logical OR |
| ** ↑ | exponentiation | ≯ ¬> | is not greater than | & | logical AND |
| / | division | ≠ ¬= | is not equal to | ' ' | literal (zero level address) |
| EOF | end of file | ≮ ¬< | is not less than | ( ) | grouping, level of address |
| | | | | A ( ) | address constant |

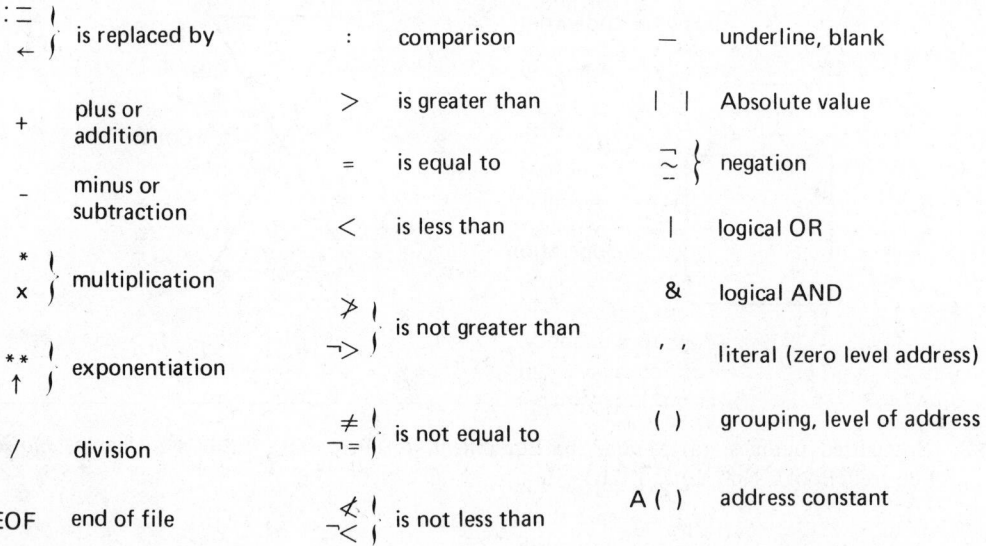

**Fig. 5.** Symbols for use in flow diagrams. (From N. Chapin, *Flowcharts,* Petrocelli Books, New York, 1971.)

and summarized into one operation, serious problems arise. What should be the summary operation? What details are to be suppressed?

**Elements.** Wide agreement exists on the major elements of flowcharts. They are the outlines, flow representation (sequence), and the symbols specifying the operation and identifying the data. Each interacts with and augments the work of the others, to provide the graphic presentation.

The outlines, sometimes called "symbols," but called "boxes" in common speech, are in three groups: the basic, the specialized, and the additional. Complete flowcharts can be drawn using only the basic outlines. These outlines, as shown in Fig. 2, are a parallelogram for input or output, a rectangle for processing, and a line or lines with open arrowheads to represent the direction of flow, as commented upon later. When only the basic outlines are used, the rectangle serves for all operations except input and output. To provide explanatory data, the annotation outline (a partial rectangle attached by a dashed line) can be used, with the comment written within the rectangular part.

Specialized outlines are numerous, as shown in Fig. 3a. These offer a way of visually identifying for the user of the flowchart the media used to carry data; the equipment used for input (Fig. 3b), output, or storage of data; and the general character of a processing operation, such as data transformation (Fig. 3c).

In system charts, the most commonly used of these specialized outlines are usually the document, magnetic tape, on-line storage (for data on magnetic disk, commonly), and punched card outlines. In flow diagrams, the most commonly used are the preparation, the decision, and the predefined process outlines. A predefined process is considered to be a sequence of operations not described in the flowchart but incorporated in the program, as by a call to a subroutine in a library. The manual operation outline is for representing operations done by people, such as "review data for conformance to policy." The auxiliary operation outline is for representing operations done by noncomputer machines, such as "interpret punched cards."

The additional outlines, as shown in Fig. 4, are connectors of three types, and serve to indicate that two or more sequences are to be performed simultaneously (parallel mode). The in-connector and the out-connector are distinguished by the direction of the flowlines leading to and from them. An in-connector, or entrance connector, has a flowline leading from it, and is placed to the left or above the main line of flow or sequence. The out-connector, or exit connector, has a flowline leading into it, and is placed to the right or below the main line of flow or sequence. A terminal connector may also be used in an entrance or exit position as a marker to indicate the beginning or ending of a sequence of operations.

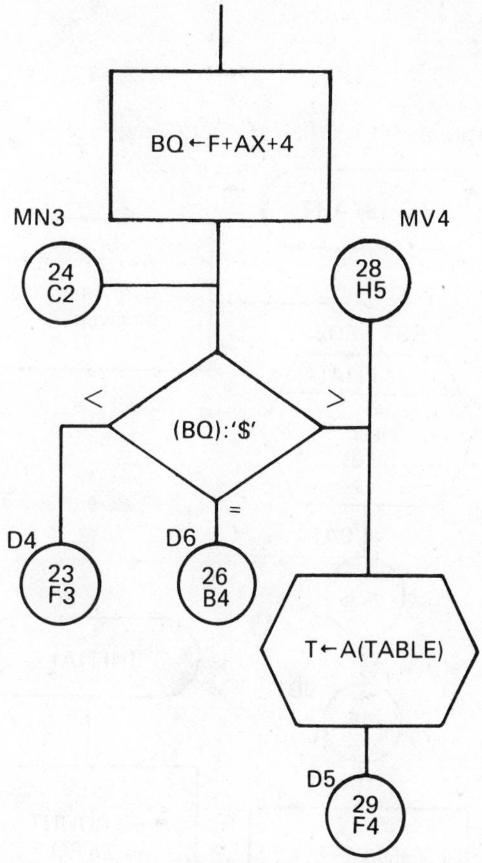


**Fig. 6.** Entry and exit flowlines in a flow diagram. (From N. Chapin, *Flowcharts*, Petrocelli Books, New York, 1971.)

The wording within process outlines identifies the operation and (in flow diagrams) the data involved. The wording within the input or output outlines identifies the data and (in flow diagrams) whether the data is input or output. The wording used within and with the outlines in a flowchart has not been standardized, although the problem has been studied (ANSI, 1965). Common practice depends in major part upon the level of detail to be depicted. In summary flowcharts, English language phrases are the most common. Detailed system charts often include only the names of the inputs, outputs, and programs. Very detailed flow diagrams

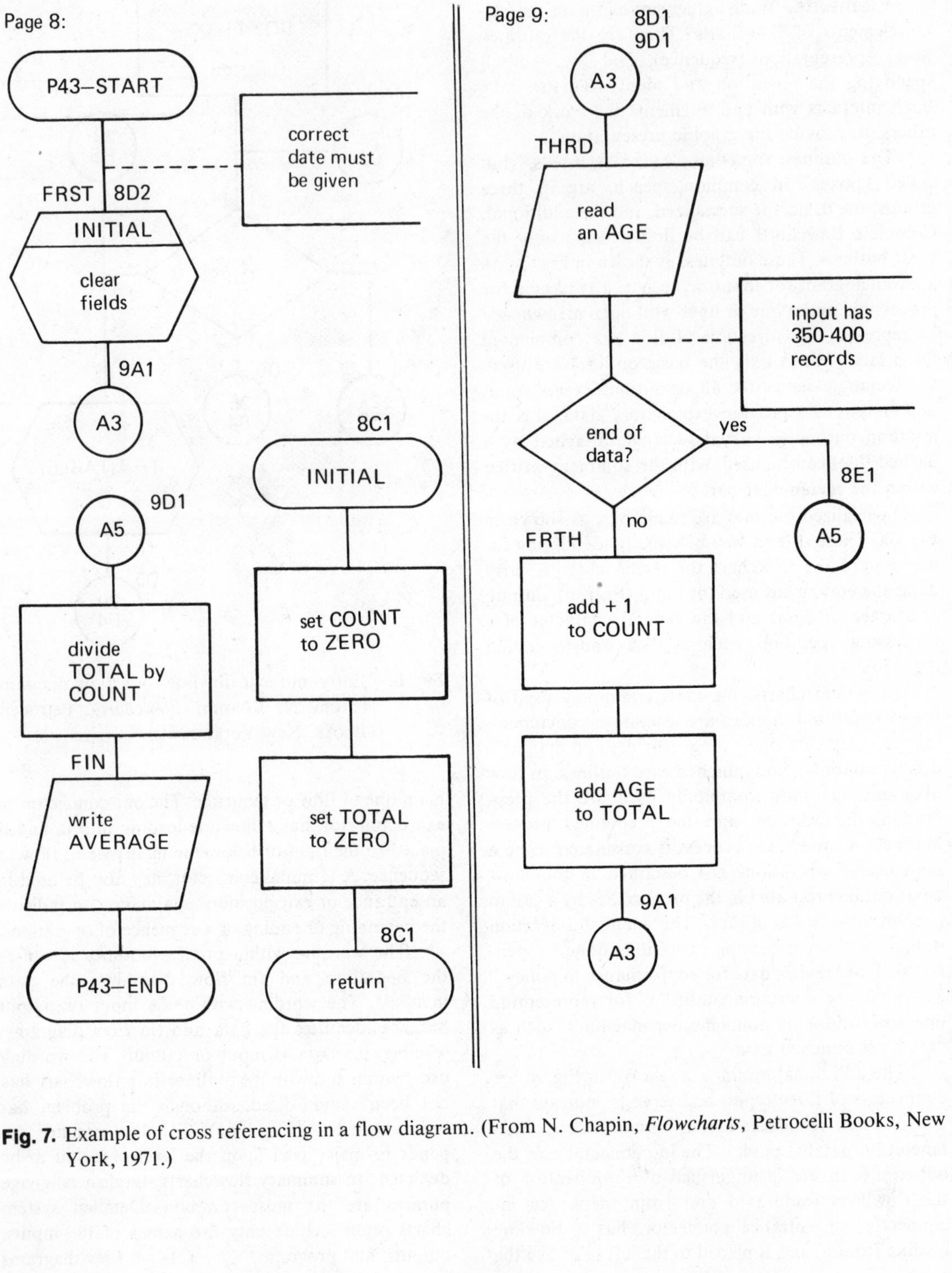


**Fig. 7.** Example of cross referencing in a flow diagram. (From N. Chapin, *Flowcharts*, Petrocelli Books, New York, 1971.)

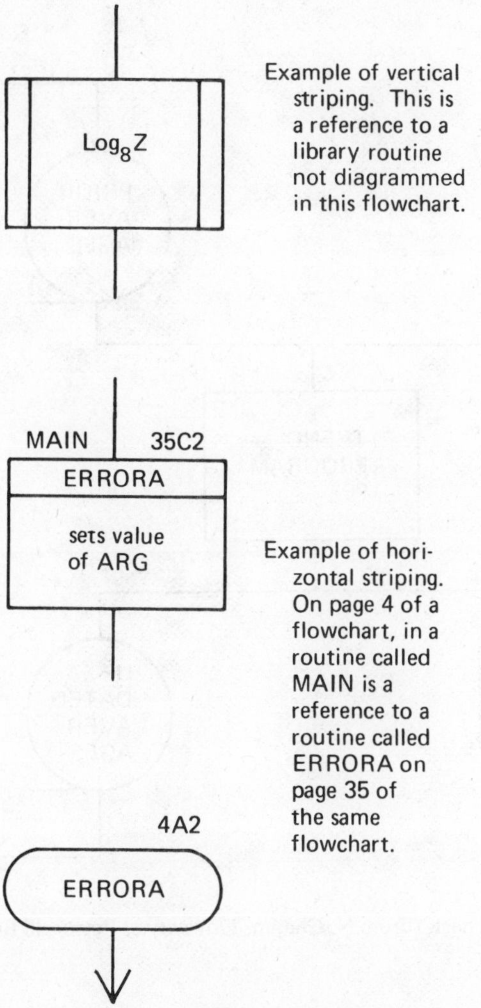
Log8Z
Example of vertical striping. This is a reference to a library routine not diagrammed in this flowchart.
MAIN
35C2
ERRORA
sets value of ARG
Example of horizontal striping. On page 4 of a flowchart, in a routine called MAIN is a reference to a routine called ERRORA on page 35 of the same flowchart.
4A2
ERRORA

**Fig. 8.** Conventions for striping and references. (From N. Chapin, *Flowcharts*, Petrocelli Books, New York, 1971.)

often use programming language instructions within the outlines; less detailed ones use symbols for operations, borrowed largely from logic and mathematics (shown in Fig. 5) or English language words.

**Conventions.** To preserve the graphic format and to improve the usefulness of the flowchart in conjunction with program listings and written system specifications, programmers and analysts use a number of conventions in preparing flowcharts. Some of these conventions apply to ways of depicting convergent and divergent flows, some to the substitution of one outline to represent many, and some to cross-references.

The flow direction (sequence of operations represented) is from top to bottom and left to right. Most deviations from this rule are marked by arrowheads, with the barbs showing the flow direction. Broken flows are marked by connectors in flow diagrams. An exit connector cuts off a flow; an entry connector resumes a flow, as shown in Fig. 6. In system charts, the usual practice is to repeat as input outlines, when resuming a flow, the output outlines that existed when the flow was cut off. Breaks in flows are common at the edges of pages, but may occur anywhere in a flowchart. To facilitate finding the other end of a break in flow, the common practice is to annotate both ends of the break with location cross-references to the other ends, as shown in Fig. 7.

Convergent flows are shown by entrance connectors to create physically joining flowlines, together with location cross-references. Divergent flows are handled differently. In system charts they are represented by just the reverse of the convention used for convergent flows. In flow diagrams, the convention is more complex; divergent flows must come from a decision process. It may be implied, as when an end-of-data condition is encountered in attempting an input operation, but usually it is explicit, based on a comparison process. Each multiple exit flowline from a decision operation must be identified as to the basis for selecting it (see Fig. 6). If a break in flow is also involved, then a location cross-reference is also commonly added, as illustrated in Fig. 7.

At any point in the flowchart, the person who prepares it may add cross-references to other materials, such as system descriptions or program listings. This is usually done by writing in identifying names ("entry points" or "labels") adjacent to a process or connector outline, as shown in Figs. 6 and 7. These names are taken from the corresponding points in the materials referenced. Additional or more extended cross-referencing can be done by using the annotation outline.

To save space in parts of flowcharts in order to provide for a more meaningful presentation of the operations, the horizontal striping convention is an aid. This allows one outline, suitably identified, to represent a sequence of outlines presented elsewhere in the flowchart, as shown in Fig. 8. Most commonly, it applies to process outlines. The person who prepares the flowchart draws a horizontal line through the outline, and identifies by a name the top area thus created in the outline. Then, within ter-

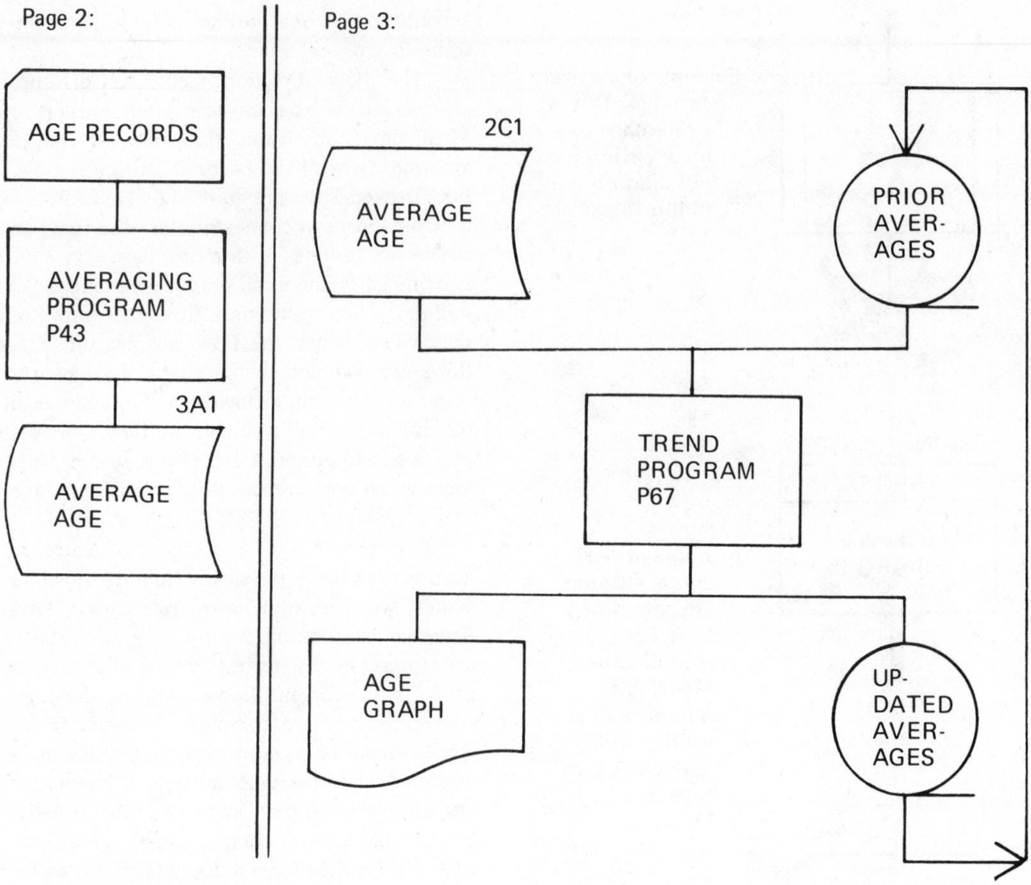


**Fig. 9.** Example of good practice in breaking a system chart. (From N. Chapin, *Flowcharts*, Petrocelli Books, New York, 1971.)

minal connectors in flow diagrams or annotation outlines in system charts, he uses this name to identify the full sequence of operations he cited elsewhere in the flowchart. Adding location cross-references completes the substitution representation.

**System Charts.** The system chart variety of the flowchart identifies major sets or files of input and output data handled by the programs, people, and machines involved in a system. An example of a system chart is shown in Fig. 9. It is commonly prepared from the specialized outlines used to indicate the media or the equipment employed in the system to handle the data. Outlines for data that serve as inputs have flowlines drawn from them to a process outline. Outlines for data that are produced as outputs have flowlines drawn from the process outline to them. An outline that represents output from one process may represent input to another process.

Each process identified in a system chart has at least one input and produces at least one output. Some processes, because of their complexity, require many inputs and produce many outputs. An output that serves as an input later for the same process is usually shown twice (once on each side of the process) with a connecting flowline (see Fig. 9). In general, the structure of a system chart is of alternating layers or process outlines and input/output outlines. An input outline starts the system chart; an output outline ends the system chart.

**Flow Diagrams.** The flow diagram variety of the flowchart describes algorithms, usually as they are implemented in a computer program. Fig. 7 provides an example of a flow diagram for a simple statistical calculation. It is not necessary to identify the media or the equipment used for input or output because, under modern operating conditions, most of the input or output media and equipment typically can be changed from time to time without changing the program, and because computers can operate on data only within their internal storage units. Hence, the specialized media and equipment outlines find little use in flow diagrams. The basic input and output outline is normally the outline of choice.

Conventionally, a flow diagram begins with a terminal outline and ends with a terminal outline. Usually the first part of a flow diagram is concerned with initialization—operations to prepare the storage unit and the arithmetic and logic unit for the main operations.

The main operations and usually the middle part of a flow diagram involve reading in input data, performing some type of transformation action on the data, and producing some output data. Many decision or branching operations with divergent and later convergent flows are common.

The cleanup or final portion of most flow diagrams consists of completing the output data, terminating the use of the input and output equipment, and outputting any summary statistics. This structure is typically more complex than is the structure typical of the system chart, and is far less regular.

The specialized process outlines most used in flow diagrams are the decision, preparation, and predefined process outlines. The decision outline serves as the basis for selecting alternative flow paths, usually based upon comparison or test operations. The preparation outline is reserved for operations upon the program itself, such as setting the starting values of iteration controls, program switches, and the like. The role of the predefined process outline was noted previously.

In a flow diagram, cross-references are especially helpful to the user. This applies both to location cross-references within the flow diagram itself and to cross-references between the flow diagram and other descriptions or materials, such as the program listing.

**Preparing and Using Flowcharts.** Preparing flowcharts is usually a heuristic process of trying to set down a sequence of operations that might get the job done, given the data involved. Commonly, this is done in parts and in stages of increasing precision. Often it is done by elaborating and correcting a former flowchart, and then using it as the basis for a new flowchart. The person preparing a flowchart normally continues this process until he has, given the level of detail he was striving for, completely described the program or system data transformation, step by step.

Most people draw flowcharts initially by hand, typically roughing them out in freehand form. When more neatly prepared flowcharts are desired, plastic templates are available to add a regularity and symmetry to the outlines, as shown in Fig. 10. Flowcharts produced as documentation after a program or system is completely implemented are typically prepared more neatly than are flowcharts produced as working documents for use by programmers and analysts in implementing programs and systems. Detailed flow diagrams can be produced from source-coded programs, whether partial or complete, by the computer.

Using flowcharts is greatly aided by taking full advantage of the graphic character of the flow representation and of the shapes of the outlines. If the user knows what he is looking for, he can use the graphic features to scan even a lengthy flowchart very rapidly. Basic to such a scan, of course, is first identifying the type, either system chart or flow diagram. Sometimes location cross-references and annotation will have to be read to follow a flow. Once he has located the portion of interest, the user can turn his attention to the specific sequence shown, to the operations specified, and to the data acted upon, used in, or produced by the operations. For greater detail or for alternative descriptions, the user can follow the cross-references to related materials. In general, flowcharts are regarded as working documents upon which users freely enter comments, notations of difficulties encountered, changes made, and improvements possible in the program or system.

### References

1965. ANSI. "Graphic Symbols for Problem Definition and Analysis," *Communications of the ACM*, Vol. 8, No. 6, June, pp. 363–365.

1970. ANSI. *American National Standard Flowchart Symbols and Their Usage in Information Processing, X3.5–1970.* New York: American National Standards Institute.

1971. Chapin, Ned. *Flowcarts.* New York: Petrocelli Books.

N. Chapin

**FORMAC.** *See* SYMBOL MANIPULATION.

# FORMAL LANGUAGES

For articles on related subjects *see* AUTOMATA THEORY; DECIDABILITY; LANGUAGE PROCESSORS; LANGUAGE TRANSLATION; and TURING MACHINE.
For article on related term *see* TREE.

**Languages and Grammars.** Formal languages are abstract mathematical objects used to model the syntax of programming languages or (less successfully) of natural languages such as English. For example, consider a simple English sentence, such as

THE MAN ATE THE APPLE.

Let us assume that individual English words are indecomposable objects. Then the study of English syntax attempts to answer the question: When is a string of words a grammatically correct English sentence? And when it is a sentence, how can it be parsed into its grammatical components?

To model this situation, we let $V$ be a finite set of symbols, called a "vocabulary." In the previous example, $V$ contains the four indecomposable words (in this context, called "symbols" or "letters"): APPLE, ATE, MAN, THE. More generally, $V$ might contain all English words and punctuation marks. Let $V^*$ denote all finite-length strings of symbols from $V$. (It is mathematically convenient to include in $V^*$ the *empty string* of length zero.) Then a *formal language* $L$ is simply a set of strings from $V^*$. For example, if $V^*$ is the set of all finite sequences of English words, then $L$ could be the subset of $V^*$ consisting of all grammatically correct sentences. Although $V$ is always finite, in most cases of interest $L$ will be infinite, and we will wish to have a finitely specified way of generating, or recognizing, or parsing the strings in $L$.

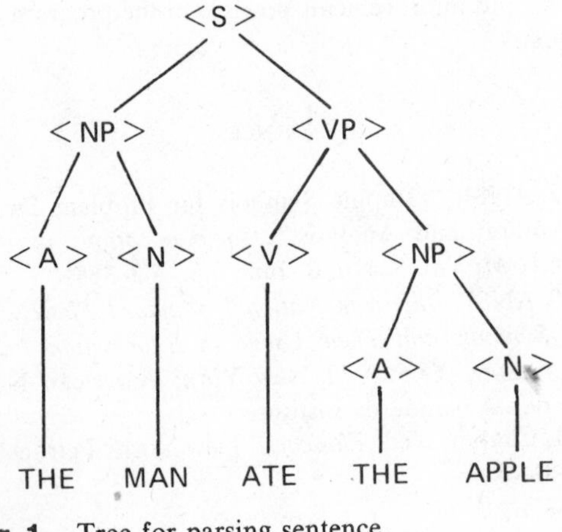


**Fig. 1.** Tree for parsing sentence.

The sample sentence given earlier can be parsed by the treelike diagram in Fig. 1, where $\langle S\rangle$, $\langle NP\rangle$, $\langle VP\rangle$, $\langle A\rangle$, $\langle N\rangle$, and $\langle V\rangle$ are six variables ranging over all *sentences, noun phrases, verb phrases, articles, nouns*, and *verbs*, respectively. Using the "rewriting"

$$\begin{aligned}
\langle S\rangle &\rightarrow \langle NP\rangle\langle VP\rangle \\
\langle NP\rangle &\rightarrow \langle A\rangle\langle N\rangle \\
\langle VP\rangle &\rightarrow \langle V\rangle\langle NP\rangle \\
\langle A\rangle &\rightarrow \text{THE} \\
\langle V\rangle &\rightarrow \text{ATE} \\
\langle N\rangle &\rightarrow \text{MAN} \\
\langle N\rangle &\rightarrow \text{APPLE}
\end{aligned}$$

**Fig. 2.** Rewriting rules.

rules in Fig. 2, it is possible to generate our sample sentence from the variable $\langle S\rangle$. The generation proceeds as follows:

$$\begin{aligned}
\langle S\rangle &\Rightarrow \langle NP\rangle\langle VP\rangle \Rightarrow \langle A\rangle\langle N\rangle\langle VP\rangle \\
&\Rightarrow \langle A\rangle\langle N\rangle\langle V\rangle\langle NP\rangle \Rightarrow \langle A\rangle\langle N\rangle\langle V\rangle\langle A\rangle\langle N\rangle \\
&\Rightarrow \text{THE } \langle N\rangle\langle V\rangle\langle A\rangle\langle N\rangle \\
&\Rightarrow \text{THE MAN } \langle V\rangle\langle A\rangle\langle N\rangle \\
&\Rightarrow \text{THE MAN ATE } \langle A\rangle\langle N\rangle \\
&\Rightarrow \text{THE MAN ATE THE } \langle N\rangle \\
&\Rightarrow \text{THE MAN ATE THE APPLE}
\end{aligned}$$

With these rules we can also generate various improbable but grammatically correct sentences such as THE APPLE ATE THE MAN, and with more rules we could generate more sentences. Rewriting schemes of this sort were introduced by the linguist Noam Chomsky, who called them "context-free grammars." Chomsky observed that these grammars are not good models for the syntax of natural languages, but it was soon discovered that they do closely model the syntax of programming languages, and for this reason they have been studied in great detail.

To see a simple example of context-free rewriting rules that give rise to an infinite language, suppose that the vocabulary consists of two abstract symbols $a$ and $b$, and let $S$ be a variable. Then, using the rules $S \rightarrow aSb$ and $S \rightarrow ab$, we can generate the infinite language

$$L = \{a^n b^n | n \geq 1\} = \{ab, aabb, aaabbb, \ldots\}.$$

Rewriting rules of this type are called "context free" because they permit any occurrence of a variable within a string to be rewritten without regard to the context in which that variable occurs. By contrast, a rewriting rule like $aXab \rightarrow aYZcab$ is not context-free. It is called context "sensitive," since it allows $X$ to be rewritten as $YZc$ only when $X$ occurs in the context $s_1a\_abs_2$, where $s_1$ and $s_2$ are arbitrary strings.

To describe different kinds of grammars more precisely, let us define a *phrase-structure* grammar to be a quadruple $G = (V_N, V_T, P, S)$, where

1. $V_N$ is a finite vocabulary of nonterminal symbols or variables.
2. $V_T$ is a finite vocabulary of terminal symbols.
3. $P$ is a finite set of rewriting rules (also called "productions") of the form $\alpha \rightarrow \beta$, where $\alpha$ is a nonempty string of variables and $\beta$ is an arbitrary string of variables and terminal symbols.
4. $S$ is a particular variable, called the "start" variable.

For all strings $s_1$ and $s_2$, we may write $s_1\alpha s_2 \Rrightarrow s_1\beta s_2$ if $\alpha \rightarrow \beta$ is a production of the grammar $G$. Then the language generated by $G$ is the set of all strings $t$ of *terminal symbols* such that

$$S \Rrightarrow s_1 \Rrightarrow s_2 \Rrightarrow \cdots \Rrightarrow s_n \Rrightarrow t$$

for some choice of intermediate strings $s_1, s_2, \cdots, s_n$. The intermediate strings may consist of both variables and terminal symbols.

Let $\alpha$, $\alpha_1$, and $\alpha_2$ denote arbitrary strings of variables and terminal symbols, and let $A$ and $B$ denote variables. If the productions in $G$ have the specialized form $\alpha_1 A \alpha_2 \rightarrow \alpha_1 \beta \alpha_2$, where $\beta$ represents any nonempty string, then $G$ is a *context-sensitive* grammar. (Frequently, a grammar is called context-sensitive if the productions merely have the form $\alpha \rightarrow \beta$, with $\beta$ at least as long as $\alpha$. These two definitions are in fact equivalent in the sense that the same collection of languages is generated.) If the productions in the grammar $G$ have the form $A \rightarrow \alpha$, then $G$ is context-free. If the productions have the form $A \rightarrow w_1B$ or $A \rightarrow w_2$, where $w_1$ and $w_2$ are strings of terminal symbols, then $G$ is right-linear. A language is called a "phrase-structure" language, or a "context-sensitive," "context-free," or "right-linear" language, if it can be generated by a phrase-structure grammar, or a context-sensitive, context-free, or right-linear grammar, respectively.

To illustrate these ideas, let us examine the language $L = \{a^n b^n c^n | n \geq 1\}$. This language is not context-free because it cannot be generated by context-free productions. For example, suppose we attempt to generate $L$ by imitating the way we used context-free productions to generate $\{a^n b^n | n \geq 1\}$. We might try the productions $S \rightarrow AB$, $A \rightarrow aAB$, $A \rightarrow ab$, $B \rightarrow bBc$, $B \rightarrow bc$.. But these productions generate

$$\{a^m b^m b^n c^n | m \geq 1, n \geq 1\} = \{a^m b^{m+n} c^n | m \geq 1, n \geq 1\},$$

which is not the same as $L$.

The problem here is that the variables $A$ and $B$ interfere with each other. This lack of communication between variables always occurs in the intermediate strings produced by a context-free grammar because the context surrounding a variable has no influence on what that variable can generate. For this reason, no context-free grammar can generate the language $L$. Without some interaction between variables, there is no way to insure that the same number of $a$'s and $b$'s are produced, while simultaneously insuring that the same number of $b$'s and $c$'s are produced. However, the language $L$ *is* context-sensitive because it can be generated by the context-sensitive productions $S \rightarrow ASBC$, $S \rightarrow ABC$, $CB \rightarrow DB$, $DB \rightarrow DC$, $DC \rightarrow BC$, $AB \rightarrow AB'$, $B'B \rightarrow B'B'$, $B'C \rightarrow B'C'$, $C'C \rightarrow C'C'$, $A \rightarrow a$, $B' \rightarrow b$, $C' \rightarrow c$. A typical string in $L$, such as $aabbcc$, could be generated as follows: $S \Rrightarrow ASBC \Rrightarrow AABCBC \Rrightarrow AABDBC \Rrightarrow AABDCC \Rrightarrow AABBCC \Rrightarrow AAB'BCC \Rrightarrow AAB'B'CC \Rrightarrow AAB'B'C'C \Rrightarrow AAB'B'C'C' \Rrightarrow aAB'B'C'C' \Rrightarrow aaB'B'C'C' \Rrightarrow aabB'C'C' \Rrightarrow aabbC'C' \Rrightarrow aabbcC' \Rrightarrow aabbcc$. The diligent reader can verify that terminal strings which do not belong in $L$, like $aabcbc$, cannot be generated by these productions.

The four types of grammars (phrase-structure, context-sensitive, context-free, and right-linear) are also known as type 0, type 1, type 2, and type 3 grammars, respectively. They form a grammatical hierarchy, called the "Chomsky hierarchy." Among the four corresponding families of languages, the smallest family, the right-linear languages, is important because it turns out to consist precisely of those languages that can be recognized by finite-state automata. These languages arise in many different contexts, and they have the advantage of being very easy to parse.

The next family in the hierarchy, the family of context-free languages, is important because context-free languages are good approximations to the syntax of programming languages, even though this syntax is usually a little too complicated to be completely captured by context-free grammars. Context-sensitive languages are powerful enough to encompass any complications in syntax that may have been missed by the context-free model, but they are so general that they are difficult to work with. As a result, they have been studied less than the other models, and various attempts have been made to add to the power of context-free grammars without resorting to the full strength of context-sensitive productions. These efforts have produced various kinds of grammars that are more powerful than context-free grammars, although they are unfortunately more complicated as well: programmed grammars, macro grammars, indexed grammars, and others.

The largest family of languages in the Chomsky hierarchy, the family of phrase-structure languages, is an important family because it represents the largest class with which one is likely to be concerned when modeling natural or artificial languages. This is so because the family of phrase-structure languages is in fact the same as the family of all recursively enumerable languages, i.e., of all languages $L$ such that membership of a string $w$ in $L$ can be verified by some algorithm (or, more precisely, by some Turing machine).

**Languages and Equations.** We have noted that context-free languages are good approximations to the syntax of many programming languages. Consider the following very simple example of syntax specifications in *Backus-Naur form*, or *BNF:*

⟨digit⟩ : : = 0 | 1 | 2 | 3 | 4 | 5 | 6 | 7 | 8 | 9
⟨unsigned integer⟩ : : = ⟨digit⟩ | ⟨unsigned integer⟩ ⟨digit⟩

This means that ⟨digit⟩ and ⟨unsigned integer⟩ are the smallest sets of strings satisfying the following conditions: 0, 1, . . ., 9 are digits (i.e., they are in the set ⟨digit⟩); any digit is an unsigned integer; and any unsigned integer followed by a digit is an unsigned integer. Rewriting these equations in a more algebraic form, we obtain:

$$D = \text{“0”} + \text{“1”} + \cdots + \text{“9”}$$
$$U = D + U \cdot D$$

Consider these as abstract equations. What is their meaning? The unknowns $U$ and $D$ are variables whose values are languages; $X + Y$ denotes the union of the languages $X$ and $Y$; $X \cdot Y$ denotes the product of the languages $X$ and $Y$, obtained by concatenating the strings in $X$ with those in $Y$: $X \cdot Y = \{xy | x \in X, y \in Y\}$; and "0," "1," etc., are constants denoting the languages consisting of just the single symbol 0, 1, etc. In general, the equations corresponding to BNF syntax descriptions can be more complicated than in our example. A typical equation might have the form

$$A = abBAAaAb + BaC + ba.$$

(The letters $a$ and $b$ are terminal symbols; $A$, $B$, and $C$ are variables; and we have omitted the dot in products.) The operations + and • are roughly analogous to addition and multiplication of numbers; only • is not commutative. (If $X$ and $Y$ are languages, $X \cdot Y$ is not generally the same as $Y \cdot X$.) If the product of languages were commutative, then we could write the term $abBAAaAb$ as $aabbA^3B$. This would be similar to a fourth-degree term in a polynomial expression, except that the variables range over languages rather than numbers and the coefficient $aabb$ is a string of symbols instead of a number. Since the product of languages is not commutative, we cannot rearrange terms in this way, but we can still regard these equations as polynomial equations in noncommuting variables. In general, the right-hand side of each equation will be a finite sum of terms, and each term will be a string of variables and terminal symbols. A set of such equations always has a unique smallest solution, so it always makes sense to speak of the "smallest sets of strings" $U$ and $D$ satisfying equations like those in our original example. The languages definable in this way by polynomial equations turn out to be precisely the context-free languages.

As a simple example, the language $\{a^nb^n | n \geq 1\}$ can be specified either as the language generated by the context-free productions $S \rightarrow aSb$ and $S \rightarrow ab$ or as the smallest solution of the equation $S = aSb + ab$. Incidentally, note that this equation is a first-degree or "linear" equation, since each summand contains at most one occurrence of a variable. Languages defined by such equations are called "linear" context-free languages. They can also be characterized as the languages generated by linear context-free grammars; i.e., by context-free grammars having productions of the form $A \rightarrow \alpha$, where the string $\alpha$ contains at most one occurrence of a variable. It should now be clear why right-linear grammars are so named.

In view of the preceding discussion, any programming language whose syntax can be specified in BNF is context-free. Generally, most but not all of the syntax of a programming language can be specified in BNF. So languages such as Algol and Fortran are not quite context-free, but they are close to being so, and context-free languages are useful approximations to their syntax.

**Languages and Automata.** The four families of languages in the Chomsky hierarchy can be obtained from automata as well as from grammars. The phrase-structure languages are just the recursively enumerable languages, i.e., the languages accepted by Turing machines. (A Turing machine is a simple theoretical model of a computer. A Turing machine ($T$) accepts a string $s$ if, when given $s$ as input, $T$ eventually reaches some designated accepting state. The language accepted by $T$ is defined to be the set of all input strings that $T$ accepts.) The context-sensitive languages can be characterized as those languages accepted by linear-bounded automata or *lba*'s; the context-free languages are the languages accepted by pushdown automata; and the right-linear languages are the languages accepted by finite-state automata. For this reason, right-linear languages are sometimes called "finite-state" languages. Usually, however, right-linear languages are known as regular languages or regular sets. This terminology comes from Kleene's theorem, which states that a language is a finite-state language if and only if it can be represented by a *regular* expression. A regular expression is an expression that can be built up from individual strings by using the three operations $+$, $\cdot$, and $*$. The operations $+$ and $\cdot$ are the operations of union and product introduced earlier. (The symbol $\cup$ is sometimes used instead of $+$, and the $\cdot$ may be omitted.) The operation $*$ is called the "Kleene closure" operation. If $L$ is any set of strings, then $L^*$ is defined to be the set of all strings that can be formed by concatenating together sequences of strings from $L$: $L^* = \{s_1s_2 \cdots s_n | n \geq 0$, each $s_i \in L\}$. (By convention, the empty string is always in $L^*$.) For example, $(a + b)^* \cdot aaa \cdot (a + b)^*$ is a regular expression representing the set of all strings of $a$'s and $b$'s containing at least three consecutive $a$'s.

Let us consider the relation between context-free languages and pushdown automata a little more closely. A pushdown automaton is a nondeterministic device having a memory consisting of a finite-state control and a pushdown stack. It receives its input one symbol at a time on request. Every context-free language $L$ is the set of input strings accepted by some pushdown automaton $P$. In fact, we can always find a pushdown automaton $P$ for $L$ that operates in real time; i.e., one that uses up one input letter on every move. This means that $P$ recognizes strings in $L$ very quickly—in fact, in an amount of time proportional to the length of the input string. The catch is that $P$ is a nondeterministic device. It is credited with accepting an input string $w$ if there is *any* sequence of choices of moves (i. e., any sequence of "guesses") it can make while processing $w$ that will lead it to an accepting mode, even though there may be other choices which do not lead to an accepting mode. But if we want to simulate $P$ in the real world, we would systematically have to test every sequence of choices that $P$ could make.

Since $P$ might have several choices available to it on each move, this simulation could take exponentially more time than $P$ does. This might suggest that the task of parsing a context-free language can be prohibitively time consuming, but in fact it is not. General-purpose, context-free, parsing algorithms can be designed to require only time $n^3$, where $n$ is the length of the input. One of the most popular such algorithms is Earley's algorithm. It takes time $n^3$ in the worst case, but for many context-free grammars it takes only a linear amount of time. The $n^3$ bound for an all-purpose, context-free parser can be improved slightly, but it is not yet known how much improvement is possible. In fact, it is conceivable (although very unlikely) that *every* context-free language can be parsed in linear time.

A nondeterministic pushdown automaton is a theoretical construct that is time consuming to simulate in the real world. So, in searching for classes of context-free languages that are easy to parse, it is reasonable to consider *deterministic* context-free languages—those languages that can be recognized by a deterministic pushdown automaton. As one might expect, all deterministic context-free languages can be parsed rapidly; in fact, in a linear amount of time. But not all context-free languages are deterministic. For example, the set of all binary strings (strings of 0's and 1's) which are palindromes is context-free but not deterministic because a pushdown automaton for this language must of necessity operate something like this: Store the first half of the input string on the stack, *guess* when half the input has been read, and use the stack to verify that the second half of the input agrees symbol by symbol, in reverse order, with the first half.

So, nondeterministic pushdown acceptors are more powerful than deterministic ones. Are the corresponding statements true for the other kinds of automata used to characterize the families of languages in the Chomsky hierarchy? For finite-state automata and for Turing machines, the answer is no. It is easy to show that the nondeterministic versions of these devices are no more powerful than the deterministic versions. In other words, the ability to make guesses may enable these devices to do their jobs more quickly, but it will not let them do anything that they could not have done without guessing. But for linear-bounded automata, it is still not known whether the nondeterministic version (which corresponds to the context-sensitive languages) is more powerful than the deterministic version. The answer is thought to be yes. That is, it is widely believed that deterministic *lba*'s are not powerful enough to recognize all context-sensitive languages. But this question, called the "*lba* problem," has remained unresolved for more than a decade.

REFERENCES

1966. Ginsburg, S. *The Mathematical Theory of Context-Free Languages*. New York: McGraw-Hill.
1969. Hopcroft, J. E., and J. D. Ullman. *Formal Languages and Their Relation to Automata*. Reading, Mass.: Addison-Wesley.
1970. Gross, M., and A. Lentin. *Introduction to Formal Grammars*. New York: Springer-Verlag.
1972. Aho, A. V., and J. D. Ullman. *The Theory of Parsing, Translation and Compiling*. Englewood Cliffs, N. J.: Prentice-Hall.
1972. Kain, R. Y. *Automata Theory: Machines and Languages*. New York: McGraw-Hill.
1973. Salomaa, A. *Formal Languages*. New York: Academic Press.

J. GOLDSTINE

**FORTRAN.** *See* PROCEDURE-ORIENTED LANGUAGES: Survey of.

## FRONT-END PROCESSORS

For articles on related subjects *see* CHANNEL; COMMUNICATIONS AND COMPUTERS; COMMUNICATION CONTROL UNIT; HOST SYSTEM; MULTIPLEXING; and PROCESSING MODES.
For articles on related terms *see* INTERRUPT; and MODEM.

A front-end processor is a small, limited capability, digital computer that is programmed to replace the hard-wired input functions of a central computing system (e.g., the control of remote terminals in a time-sharing system). The front-end processor thereby permits the host computer to perform its primary functions with little regard for the slower input/output activities associated with large-scale multiprogrammed or time-shared computing systems.

In addition to receiving and transmitting all data passing through a computing system, front-end processors also support a wide variety of functions, which might include:

1. *Data and/or format conversion*—the conversion of one or more incoming data codes and formats to that of the host system.
2. *Polling*—the determination by a front-end processor of a terminal's readiness to send or receive data.
3. *Assembly of characters and messages*—the assembly and disassembly of all data, input at varying line speeds and in synchronous or asynchronous formats, to insure that the host system receives only complete messages.
4. *Error control and editing*—the detection and possible correction of transmission errors as well as corrections initiated at the terminals, prior to reception by the host system.
5. *Fail-soft functions*—the ability of the front-end processor to keep parts of the system operating (such as terminals) when a major element of the system has failed.
6. *Queueing*—placing incoming messages in transmission order for processing by the host system, or in some cases queueing messages on auxiliary storage devices (spooling).
7. *Message switching*—a function of front-end processors that service more than one central processing unit (Fig. 1).
8. *Direct response*—the front-end processor may have the ability to respond to simple inquiries

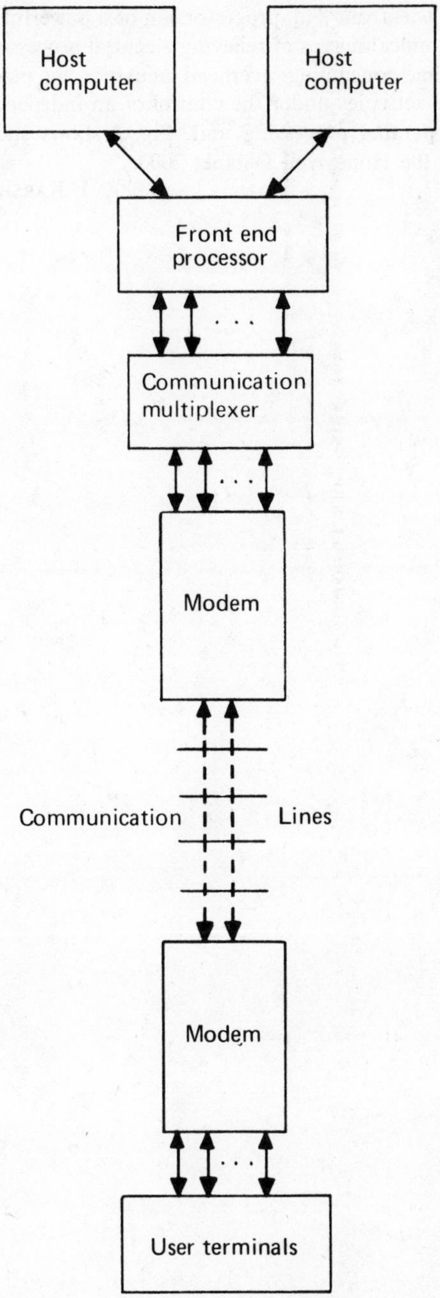


**Fig. 1.** A front-end message switcher.

directly without contact with the host system.

The basic components of a typical front-end processor are:

1. *Processor*—a stored program digital computer that has main memory, which may vary in size from several hundred words to many thousand words, depending on the complexities of the specific application. Two important qualities required of a front-end processor are good facilities for bit manipulation and interrupt handling. The processor may or may not have its own on-line peripheral devices depending on the particular application.

2. *Central processor interface*—the hardware interface that allows the front-end processor to connect directly to the input/output channel of the host system. The host system is then able to communicate with the front-end processor as if it were a standard peripheral device controller.

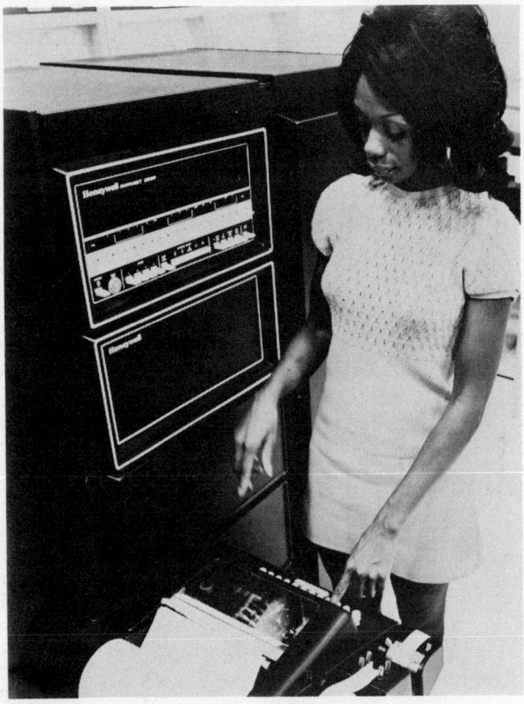

**Fig. 2.** Honeywell Datanet 2000 processor.

3. *Communication multiplexer*—a device with programmable or hard-wired logic which produces logically independent data channels into the front-end processor's main memory from each transmission line serviced. The coordination of the data flow between the multiplexer and processor is handled by the front-end processor's interrupt system.

4. *Line interface units*—the hardware devices that link the communication multiplexer with the modems that terminate each of the communication lines.

5. *Software*—the programs that integrate the functions of the various hardware components of the front-end processor. Included in the software package are such functions as terminal, line and message control, system interface procedures, and whatever other functions are required by a particular installation.

The front-end processor can be a powerful and economical means of relieving a central processor of its time-consuming overhead activities by placing these activities under the control of an independent and parallel processing unit. Fig. 2 shows such a unit, the Honeywell Datanet 2000.

A. I. KARSHMER

# G

## GAMES ON COMPUTERS

For articles on related subjects *see* Artificial Intelligence; Heuristics; and Symbol Manipulation.

When the earliest digital computers were built, scientists immediately became fascinated with the possibility of having them play such games as chess, checkers, and tic-tac-toe. Although this sort of activity proved to be a great deal of fun, the scientists were not just playing around; as it turns out, there are several good reasons to study game playing by computers.

The first reason relates to the popular conception of computers as "giant brains." Even the earliest digital computers could do arithmetic and make decisions at a rate thousands of times faster than humans could. Thus, it was felt that computers could be set up to perform intelligent activities such as to translate French to English, recognize sloppy handwriting, and play chess. At the same time, it was realized that if computers could not perform these tasks, then they could not be considered intelligent by human standards. A new scientific discipline arose from these considerations and became known as "artificial intelligence."

A second reason involves man's understanding of his own intelligence. It is conjectured that computer mechanisms for game playing will bear a resemblance to human thought processes. If this is true, then game-playing computers can help us understand how human minds work.

Another reason for studying games is that they are well-defined activities. Most games use very simple equipment and have a simple set of rules that must be followed. Usually, the ultimate goal (winning) can be very simply defined. Thus, a computer can be easily set up to know the rules of any board game or card game. This allows the computer scientist to devote more effort to the problem of getting the computer to play an intelligent game.

There is also a practical payoff from computer game-playing studies. Specific techniques developed in programming a computer to play games have been applied to other more practical problems. To cite a few, methods of search, which are used to consider alternative moves in chess, have been adapted to find the correct path through a switching network or the correct sequence of steps for an assembly line. Learning methods developed for a checker-playing program have been used to recognize elementary parts of spoken speech. It is felt that the mechanisms of intelligence are general purpose, and therefore the borrowing of techniques from one application to another will continue in the field of artificial intelligence.

**Basic Techniques.** The fundamental reason for the ability of computers to play a variety of games is that computers have the ability to represent arbitrary situations and processes through the use of symbols and logic operations. For example, one can

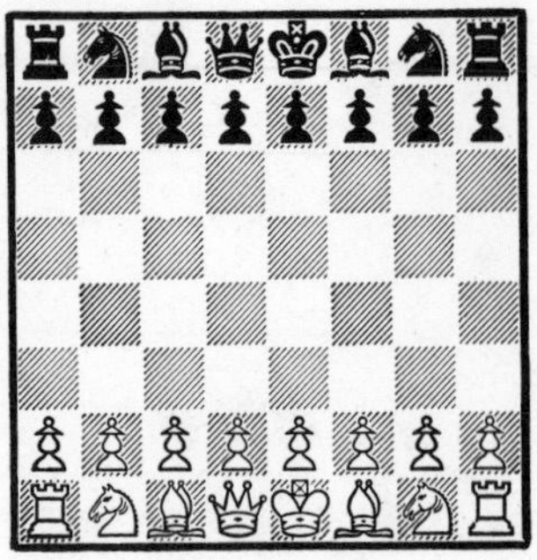

| | | | | | | | |
|---|---|---|---|---|---|---|---|
| -2 | -3 | -4 | -5 | -6 | -4 | -3 | -2 |
| -1 | -1 | -1 | -1 | -1 | -1 | -1 | -1 |
| | | | | | | | |
| | | | | | | | |
| | | | | | | | |
| | | | | | | | |
| 1 | 1 | 1 | 1 | 1 | 1 | 1 | 1 |
| 2 | 3 | 4 | 5 | 6 | 4 | 3 | 2 |

| | | | | | | | |
|---|---|---|---|---|---|---|---|
| -5 | -3 | -3 | -9 | | -3 | -3 | -5 |
| -1 | -1 | -1 | -1 | -1 | -1 | -1 | -1 |
| | | | | | | | |
| | | | | | | | |
| | | | | | | | |
| | | | | | | | |
| 1 | 1 | 1 | 1 | 1 | 1 | 1 | 1 |
| 5 | 3 | 3 | 9 | | 3 | 3 | 5 |

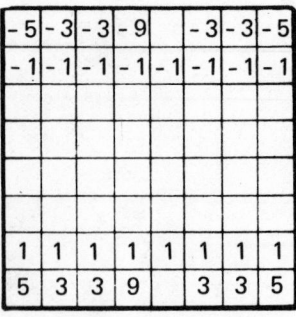

**Fig. 1.** Computer representation of a chess position. In the second array, numbers are used to represent the various pieces. The third array represents the values of the pieces for use by the computer in evaluating trades.

set up a chess position inside a computer by means of an 8 by 8 array of integers, and tentative moves can be made by computer instructions that change the positions of the numbers in the array (Fig. 1). This capability is extremely general. That is, the symbols could represent checker pieces, or with a slight rearrangement, they could be playing cards for poker or bridge.

Fig. 1 also shows the representation of derived information. The values of the pieces are stored in another 8 by 8 array for use by the computer. In effect, they are part of the computer's "knowledge" of the values of chess pieces. (The king may be considered to have an infinitely large value.)

Since symbols can be used to represent the objects of a particular game, computer instructions can be written by a programmer to specify the procedures for playing the game according to the rules and also for playing the game according to a strategy. In order for a set of procedures to be programmable, it is usually sufficient that they be defined in enough detail so that they can be translated into a computer language such as Fortran. For the purposes of this exposition, some game playing algorithms will be stated using English words in place of computer language. The game of tic-tac-toe, for example, can be played perfectly by the following algorithm, in which the word ''row'' refers to a row, column, or diagonal.

ALGORITHM A (THE COMPUTER PLAYS X)

A1. Perform the first applicable step which follows.

A2. Search for two X's in a row. If found, then make three X's in a row.

A3. Search for two 0's in a row. If found, then block them with an X.

A4. Search for two rows that intersect with an empty square, each of which contains one X and no 0's. If found, then place an X on the intersection.

A5. Search for two rows that intersect at an empty square, each of which contains one 0 and no X's. If found, then place an X on the intersection.

A6. Search for a vacant corner square. If found, then place an X on the vacancy.

A7. Search for a vacant square. If found, then place an X on the vacancy.

The algorithm is perfect in the sense that it will find a forced win if it exists and it will never lose. This algorithm may be called a rejection scheme because the first applicable step (following A1) is to be performed and all other steps are rejected or ignored (Fig. 2). A computer can be easily programmed to execute such an algorithm.

For another example, consider the following game, a special case of the game of Nim. It is played

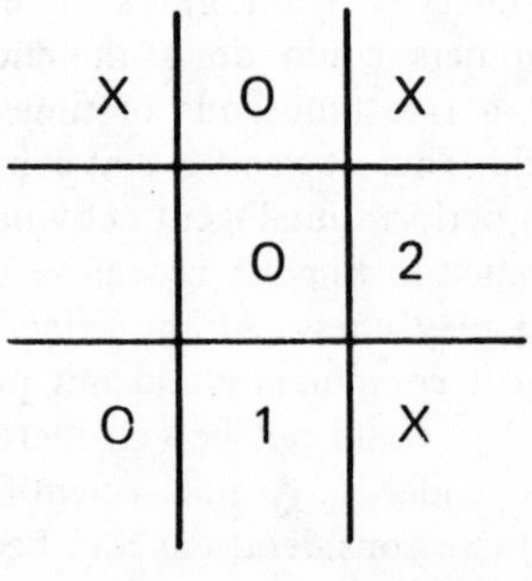


**Fig. 2.** In the position shown here, algorithm A would choose a move at square 2 for a win rather than at square 1, to block the opponent win. This is done because step A2 precedes step A3.

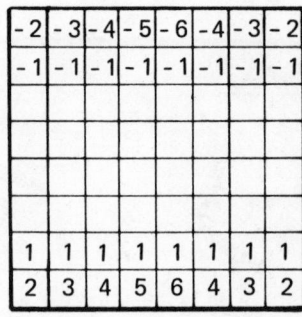

with 13 matches; two players remove matches in turn until one player is forced to take the last match. A player may remove only one to three matches in a single turn, and the player who removes the last match is the loser. This is an algorithm for perfect play.

ALGORITHM B (THE COMPUTER PLAYS SECOND)

B1. Let $n$ be the number of matches taken by the opponent.

B2. Remove $(4 - n)$ matches.

B3. If the game is not over, go to Step B1.

Both tic-tac-toe and Nim are simple examples of a large number of games classed as two-person games of skill. An essential feature of these games is that both players have perfect information about the current state of the game. Chess, checkers, and GO are well-known games of pure skill. It can be shown mathematically that there is an optimal strategy for each player and that its application always gives the same result. In the case of tic-tac-toe, the result is a draw. In the case of the match game, the second player always wins.

In order to show that an optimal strategy exists for two-person games of skill, the principle of *minimax* must be explained. If the state of a game is represented by a circle and the moves from that state are represented by lines (Fig. 3), then a tree can be obtained which represents the set of all possible games. The end nodes of this tree (Fig. 4) can all be labeled with the terms "win," "loss," or "draw" for the first player. Now consider any node that is followed only by labeled nodes. If that node corresponds to the first player's move and it is connected to a node labeled "win," then it may be labeled with the term "win." It may be labeled with a "draw," if it is connected to a draw. Otherwise, it is labeled with a "loss." If it is the second player's move from a position, then a loss is most preferred. This procedure can be repeated to back up the values W, L, and D to the top of the lookahead tree.

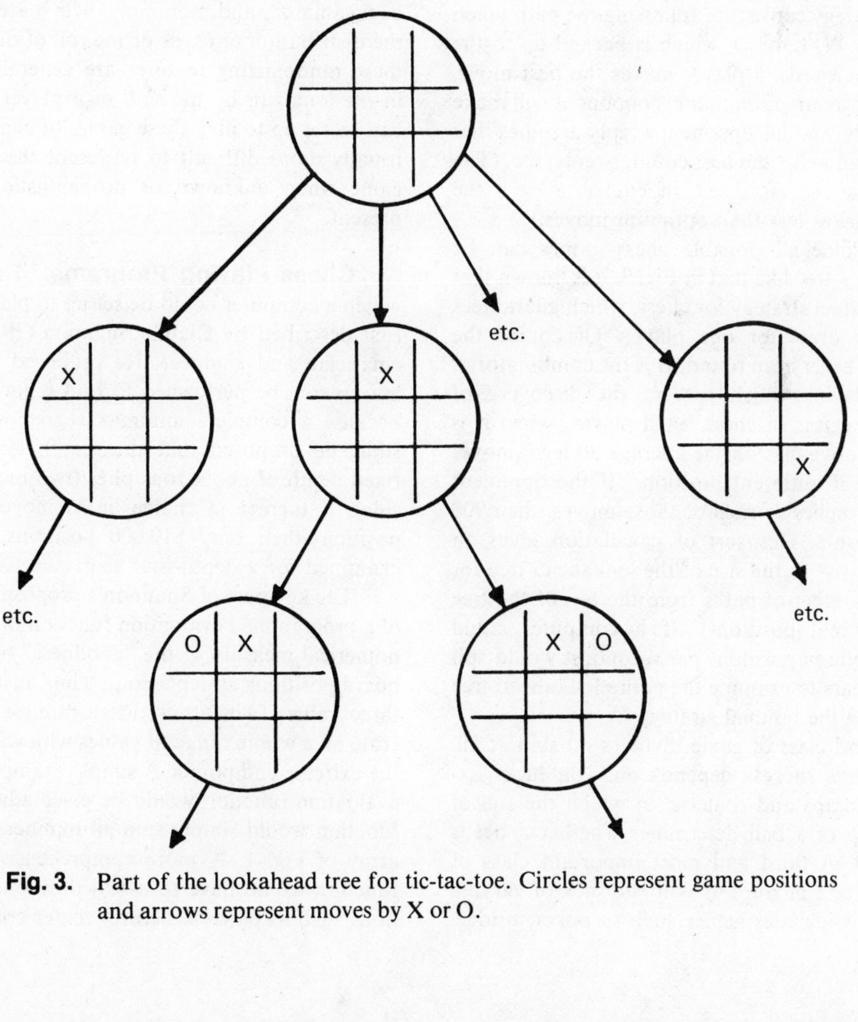


**Fig. 3.** Part of the lookahead tree for tic-tac-toe. Circles represent game positions and arrows represent moves by X or O.

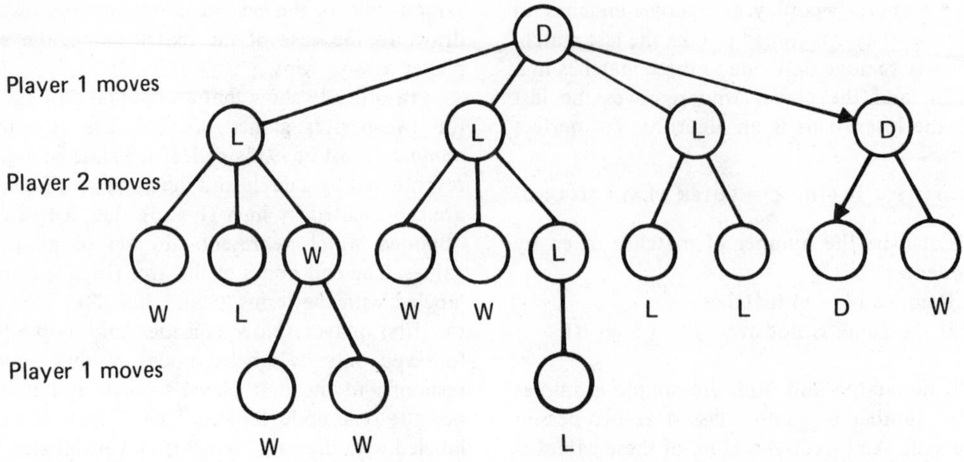


**Fig. 4.** Illustration of the minimax procedure. The values at the bottom are calculated by an evaluation function. The backed-up values shown in circles reflect the result of optimal play. The arrows show the path of optimal play.

Optimal strategy consists of following the path taken by the letter W, L, or D, which is backed up to the top. In other words, a player makes the best move, based on the assumption that his opponent will make the best reply, and his opponent's reply assumes that the player will make the best counter-reply, etc. (The best outcome is guaranteed, of course, even if the opponent makes less than optimum moves.)

Thus, since all possible chess games can be expressed in a tree like that in Fig. 3, it is known that there is a perfect strategy for chess, which guarantees a win or a draw for one player. Of course the strategy has never been found. It is the combinatorics of game playing which prevent the discovery of perfect strategies. In chess, each player, when it is his turn to move, has on the average 30 legal moves resulting in 30 different positions. If the opponent also has 30 replies to each of those moves, then 900 positions result. This sort of calculation gives an estimate of $10^{125}$ as the size of the lookahead tree for chess (the number of paths from the top of the tree to the terminal positions). If a computer could examine a billion positions per second, it would still take $10^{110}$ years to examine the entire lookahead tree to determine the optimal strategy.

A second class of game involves no skill at all, and a player's success depends only on luck. Examples are craps and roulette, in which the roll of dice or drop of a ball determines whether a bet is won or lost. A third and most important class of game involves a mixture of skill and luck of varying degrees. This includes games such as poker, bridge, backgammon, and monopoly, which are affected by the distribution of cards or the roll of dice, although these randomizing features are generally overcome in the long run by the skill of a player. Computers can be set up to play these games of chance, but it is usually more difficult to represent the state of the game when unknown or probabilistic factors are present.

**Chess-Playing Programs.** The means by which a computer could be set up to play chess were first described by Claude Shannon (1950), a mathematician and engineer. He proposed that a minimax search be performed to find a good move, but because a complete minimax search was not possible, he proposed that the search terminate at a fixed depth of about four plies (two moves for each side). If there is a choice of 30 moves from each position, then only 810,000 positions have to be examined for a depth-four search.

The key part of Shannon's proposal was the use of a programmed evaluation function that assigned a numerical measure of the "goodness" of the various board positions at depth four. Thus, instead of using three values (win, draw, loss), minimax would operate on a whole range of values with win and loss as the extreme end points. A simple example of such an evaluation function would be piece advantage. This function would simply sum all numbers in the third array of Fig. 1. A more comprehensive evaluation function would have to assess positional considerations such as pawn structure, center control, mobility, interaction of pieces, etc. Shannon proposed that the evaluation function be a linear sum of the terms expressing the assessment in a quantitative form.

The resulting change to minimax is easy to implement. When the computer has a choice of moves, it always chooses the position with maximum value. The opponent always chooses the position with a minimum value. Thus, the values placed at depth four in the lookahead by the evaluation function can be backed up to level 3 and then to level 2, which determines the best move.

To complete his proposal, Shannon suggested that the computer should not examine as many as 30 moves from a given position. It is usually the case that a majority of moves are ridiculous; if the computer can be given some criteria for selecting or rejecting moves, then the lookahead tree will be "pruned" to a much smaller size. For example, a depth-four lookahead that considers 15 moves from each position has to examine only 50,625 positions.

Unfortunately, the computers of 1950 were too crude for the implementation of Shannon's ideas. In 1953, A. M. Turing tried to simulate the operation of a chess computer by hand. The result was poor play by any standard (and the hand simulation resulted in a logic error as well). The first actual computer program was reported by a group of scientists at Los Alamos (Kister et al.). Their program was set up to play on a 6 by 6 board (omitting bishops) and did not allow castling or *en passant* capture. The program did a minimax search to depth four, but did not prune out bad moves. It was able to beat a human player who had 20 games previous experience.

The first reasonable computer chess player was described by Bernstein and Roberts in 1958. The Bernstein program examined seven moves from each position to a fixed depth of four, resulting in the examination of 2,401 positions in about 2 minutes of computer time. The selection of seven moves for consideration was made according to the following criteria:

C1. If in check, capture the checking piece, interpose a piece, or move the king away.

C2. If exchanges that gain material are possible, make the capturing move to start the exchange.

C3. If castling is possible, castle.

C4. Develop a knight or bishop.

C5. Occupy an open file with a queen or rook.

C6. Move a piece into a pawn chain so that it cannot be attacked by a pawn.

C7. Move a pawn.

C8. Move a piece.

Regardless of the number of possible moves from a given position, these criteria are used to select seven moves for further consideration. The evaluation of board positions at depth four was a sum of four terms: mobility, material, area control, and king defense.

Newell, Shaw, and Simon also described a chess program in 1958 which played a passable amateur game according to the complete rules of chess. Like the Bernstein program, this one selected reasonable moves to limit the size of the lookahead search, but the move selection was made according to "goal generators," which attempted to direct the computer's play toward one or another specific goal.

By 1970, several programs appeared which raised computer chess players to the level of grade C tournament play. The increased proficiency of these programs is due mainly to faster computers and greater programming effort rather than to conceptual breakthroughs in the art of chess programming.

One new idea was described by Zobrist (1973) and Carlson. Apparently, the Shannon-type chess programs are limited by the amount of chess knowledge that can be programmed into a computer, using standard computer languages. Zobrist and Carlson designed a special language for the description of chess knowledge and implemented a program that can interpret that language to play a better game of chess. Figure 5 illustrates the use of their chess language. Their approach is called "advice taking," since it allows a chess player to give advice to the program by means of the chess language.

A computer chess tournament is held each year in conjunction with the ACM annual conference (the Association for Computing Machinery is the main professional organization for computer scientists). Since the participating computers are scattered across the country, moves are communicated via teletype terminals and telephone. This tournament has been held yearly from 1970 through 1975, and has been won every year except 1974 by a series of programs, Chess 3.0 to Chess 4.4, written by David Slate, Larry Atkin, and Keith Gorlen from Northwestern University. The display at the Northwestern computer terminal is shown in Fig. 6. In 1974 the tournament was won by the program TREEFROG, which was written by a group at the University of Waterloo. The first international computer chess tournament, held at the IFIP Congress in Stockholm in the summer of 1974, was won by a Russian program, Kaissa.

```
            COND(7,3,10)         Is the game in the opening stage?

1           MN,MB                Search for a machine knight or bishop.
     (1,A)  RANK(1,1)            Is the knight or bishop on the back rank?
            PREPARE            }
            CODE(1,1)          } Punishment for having a knight or bishop
     (1,F)  WEIGHT(1,-500%)    } on the back rank in the opening.
            CREATE             }
            END
```

**Fig. 5.** An example of chess knowledge as expressed in Zobrist and Carlson's chess language.

**Fig. 6.** Scene from computer chess tournament at 1972 ACM annual meeting.

**Other Games.** The most successful game-playing program of all is Arthur Samuel's (1967) checker player. Though checkers is a fairly difficult game (the game tree for checkers has an estimated $10^{40}$ paths), the checker program plays at a sound master level, having played a world champion to a draw. What is more amazing is that much of the program's skill is due to automatic learning procedures. In one experiment, the program was played against a copy of itself in which the copy was not allowed to "learn." As a result, the program improved itself enough to win consistently over the nonlearning copy. Although the program uses a predetermined set of evaluation criteria, it learns the best means of combining these criteria to arrive at an overall evaluation of a board position.

GO, an extremely difficult game played in the Orient, has been programmed by Zobrist. The main interest here was the difficult problem of representing the derived information that humans use to play the game. GO is played by placing white and black stones on a 19 by 19 grid. The most important feature of play is the emergence of groups or armies of similarly colored stones. Zobrist describes a method that allows the computer to "see" these armies and to represent them internally.

Bridge is an especially interesting case, since there are two distinct phases of play: bidding and trick taking. So far, no one has programmed a computer to play a complete game of bridge, but Wasserman has produced a bridge bidder that achieves an expert level of skill. An unusual feature of his program is that it knows all standard bidding conventions and therefore can be adjusted to be an ideal partner for any player.

The unusual mideastern game Kalah, played using stones and dishes, has been studied extensively. It is only now becoming known in the United States through a game marketed by Kontrell Industries. The game commences (Fig. 7) with an equal number of stones (usually three to six) in each of the side dishes (commonly six in number). The players take turns; in one turn a player takes all stones from one side dish and distributes them, one to a dish, in a counterclockwise fashion, but skipping the opponent's home dish (or Kalah). If the last stone falls in the player's home dish, then he takes a second turn. If the last stone in the first turn falls in an empty dish on the player's side, the stones in the opponent's dish on the opposite side are "captured" and placed in the player's Kalah. The game ends when all dishes on one side are empty, at which point all stones remaining on the other side are placed in that player's Kalah.

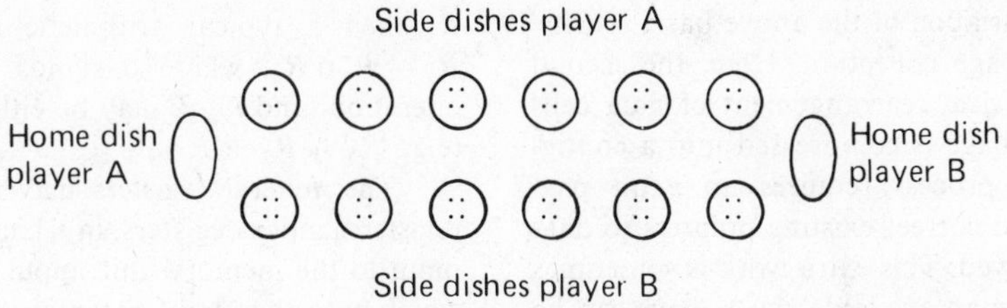


**Fig. 7.** Start of a Kalah game with four stones in each of the side dishes.

REFERENCES

1950. Shannon, C. E. "Automatic Chess Player," *Scientific American*, Vol. 182, No. 2, pp. 48–51.
1953. Turing, A. M. "Digital Computers Applied to Games," in B. V. Bowden (Ed.), *Faster Than Thought*. London: Pitman, pp. 286–310.
1967. Epstein, R. A. *The Theory of Gambling and Statistical Logic*. New York: Academic Press, Chap. 10.
1967. Samuel, A. L. "Some Studies in Machine Learning Using the Game of Checkers, II —Recent Progress," *IBM Journal of Research and Development*, November, pp. 601–617.
1973. Zobrist, A. L. "An Advice-Taking Chess Computer," *Scientific American*, Vol. 205, No. 6, pp. 92–105.

A. L. ZOBRIST

# GARBAGE COLLECTION

For articles on related subjects *see* LISTS AND LIST PROCESSING; and STORAGE ALLOCATION.
For article on related term *see* POINTER.

In most computer programs, fixed regions of memory are allocated for various purposes—such as arrays, constants, temporary storage, etc.—before the computation begins. On the other hand, some systems (including most list-processing systems) permit *dynamic storage allocation*—the assignment and reassignment of memory as determined by requirements during the course of the computation. In such systems, "garbage collection" refers to the automatic process of identifying those memory cells whose contents are no longer useful for the computation in progress and then making them available again for some other use.

Techniques exist that enable dynamic storage allocation to occur without garbage collection. For example, if the programmer has sufficient control of the memory his programs use, he can explicitly reassign storage as necessary and thereby avoid the accumulation of garbage. However, such techniques generally either place an undesirable burden upon the programmer's attention or require excessive use of computer space or time for bookkeeping operations. It has frequently proved more practical to allow programs to use available storage indiscriminately without any careful bookkeeping; then, when all space has apparently been used, the garbage collector is called to generate recycled working space.

Garbage collection generally takes place in two stages: first, identification of the garbage, and then its restructuring into a set of memory cells available for future use. The identification stage can be accomplished by systematically scanning and marking all the nongarbage, i.e., all cells in memory that can be accessed in any way by any current process. In a typical list-processing system, for example, this means starting with a base list of all memory addresses (pointers) that occur in active programs, symbol tables, and the system's temporary storage registers; marking all the cells pointed to; replacing the base list with a list of all pointers found in the cells just marked; and repeating the marking process until no new unmarked cells are reached. (Marking can be done by using a spare bit in each cell, or by using bits in a separate table for this purpose.)

At this point, every unmarked cell in working storage has been identified as garbage. The second stage of collection can then consist of one linear scan through memory to link every unmarked cell into one new long list of available storage (and to unmark every marked cell, in preparation for future garbage collections).

A common variation of the above basic scheme is *compacting* garbage collection. Here, the second stage includes physical rearrangement of data cells so that all the garbage is compressed into a contiguous array. This process requires an extra pass through memory to correct existing pointers to data that have been moved. This extra work is sometimes worthwhile because an available space *array* can be utilized more efficiently than an available space list, especially in paged and swapping memory systems.

B. RAPHAEL

# GENERAL REGISTER

For articles on related subjects *see* ARITHMETIC-LOGIC UNIT; and REGISTER.
For article on related term *see* CHANNEL.

A general register is a storage device that holds the input (operands) and the output (results) of the various functional units of a computing system. It is also used for temporary storage of intermediate results.

The width of the register is directly related to the width of the operational units, as it appears to the programmer, and does not necessarily reflect the width of the main-memory addressable unit. Thus, in the IBM/370, for example, the general registers are 32 bits wide, although the memory is addressed in 8-bit units.

The functional units, referred to in the definition, usually include the arithmetic unit, the memory, the control unit, and various input/output processors.

The registers operate at a speed that is directly connected to the speed of the units they serve. Their speed must be such that they do not slow down in any considerable way the functional units connected to them. In this sense they are the highest-speed storage part in the hierarchy of stores present in a computer.

Among a multitude of hardware reasons for the presence of general registers, one should note in particular their role in reducing the average number of bits needed to specify the operands in a computer program.

As their name implies, the usage of general registers is varied. They may serve as arithemetic registers, in which case they function as dedicated parts of the arithmetic unit. If we denote registers by $R$, then a typical arithmetic instruction will be $R_i \leftarrow R_j \text{ o } R_k$, where o stands for any arithmetic operation, and $i, j, k$ may be either distinct or equal (e.g., $R_2 \leftarrow R_2 + R_3$).

The general registers may also serve as: shift registers; index registers, in which case they serve as input to the memory unit; input/output registers, in which case they hold parameters that specify channels; or channel command registers, etc.

The number of general registers varies widely between 1 to 256 (at the time of this writing). The numbers represent today's architecture and hardware trade-offs, and are not to be taken as magic numbers. There are also computers that possess more than one set of general-purpose registers (and the programmer may switch between them), and computers that possess no general registers at all.

G. FRIEDER

# GENERATIONS, COMPUTER

For articles on related subjects *see* DIGITAL COMPUTERS: Early, and Contemporary and Future; and MANUFACTURERS, COMPUTER.
For articles on related terms *see* CONTROL DATA CORPORATION 6000 SERIES; IBM 360–370 SERIES; IBM 1400 SERIES; and INTEGRATED CIRCUITRY.

In discussions of the history of electronic computers, it is convenient to refer to at least three computer generations.

The first generation is characterized by the use of vacuum tubes as active elements. This generation started with one-of-a-kind computers in university and government research laboratories. Mercury-delay lines and electrostatic storage tubes were the typical memory devices in the early systems.

The development of a reliable magnetic core memory was a major turning point in the first generation. The IBM 704 is an impressive example of the advanced hardware and software technology of that period. The latter part of the first generation also saw the introduction of many computers that used magnetic drums as their main storage.

The second generation is characterized by the use of transistors as active elements. The first important transistorized computers were delivered in 1959, and vacuum tubes rapidly disappeared from computer systems. The second generation was characterized by some powerful computers: Larc, Stretch, IBM 7090, Philco 2000, CDC 3600, etc., and many small systems such as the IBM 1401, RCA 301, CDC 160A, etc.

The distinction between the second and third generation is not nearly as clear-cut as that between the first and second. Computers that use integrated circuit technology are, by definition, third-generation computers, but some of the most powerful computers of the third generation use discrete component technology. It is capability and performance rather than circuitry that makes a large computer a member of the third generation. They are characterized by their ability to support multiprogramming and multiprocessors with a rather elaborate disk-based operating system. A typical third-generation operating system on a large computer handles multiple local and remote job streams and can support a variety of remote on-line terminals.

The third generation is generally considered to have started in 1964. Improvements in technology since that time, especially a trend toward the use of large-scale integration, could be considered the beginning of a fourth computer generation. Most authorities, however, consider the computers introduced since 1969 to be "late third generation" computers. They look for a more significant breakthrough, such as an electronic peripheral storage system to replace disk storage, to characterize a fourth generation.

Many different models of third-generation computers exist at the present time. Some of the better known ones are the IBM 360 and 370 series, UNIVAC 1108 and 1110, Honeywell 6000 series, Control Data 6000, 7000, and Cyber 70 and 170 series, Burroughs 5700 and 6700, Digital Equipment Corporation's PDP-10 and PDP-11, and minicomputers (as well as some larger computers) manufactured by Data General, Hewlett Packard, Varian, Texas Instruments, Microdata, and many others.

S. Rosen

## GIGO

GIGO (garbage in–garbage out) is a popular acronym in computing. A more precise statement of the principle involved is "output is a function of the input and the instructions." The implication is that if the input data is erroneous, or the sequence of instructions is illogical, or both, then it should not be astonishing that the results make little sense. Only if all parts of the computing activity are precisely correct can one expect useful results.

F. Gruenberger

## GLITCH

For article on related subject *see* Bug.

The term "glitch" is a small error of any kind—a bug.

F. Gruenberger

## GLOBAL AND LOCAL VARIABLES

For articles on related subjects *see* Block Structure; and Procedure-Oriented Languages, Programming in.

The quantity (or quantities) referred to by a given variable name in a computer program can generally be accessed (i.e., used or changed) only in certain parts of the program. The domain of the program during which a variable name can be accessed is called the "scope" of the variable.

In a block-structured language, the scope of a variable is the block in which it is declared, but excludes any subblocks that are internal to the defining block *and* in which the same variable name is declared. This is illustrated in Fig. 1, which shows the schematic of an Algol program with an outer block L1 and an inner subblock L2, which in turn contains two further subblocks L3 and L4. Also shown in Fig. 1 is the scope of each variable. Note in particular that a variable like C, defined in the outer block, has a scope L1 minus L4 because C is defined again in L4.

A variable in a block in which it is defined, like G in block L4 in the example, is said to be *local* to that block, and is therefore a local variable. Correspondingly, variable A is *global* to block L4, since it is defined outside this block, although it may be referred to in the block. The variable C defined in the outer block is also global to block L4, but it cannot be referred to in L4 because of the declaration of C in block L4, the latter (but different) C being local to L4.

In a language such as Fortran, where subprograms are separate from the main program, a local variable in a subprogram is one that is defined and used only in the subprogram, while a global variable is one used to communicate with the main program as the name of an input argument from the main program, an output argument to the main program, or both.

```
L1: begin
    real A, C, D; real array B[1:10];
        L2: begin
            real D, E; real array F[-4:6,1:12];
                L3: begin
                    real F, G;
                    .
                    .
                    .
                    end L3;
                L4: begin
                    real B, C, G;
                    .
                    .
                    end L4;
            end L2;
    end L1;
```

| Variable Name | Label of Defining Block | Scope of Name |
|---|---|---|
| A | L1 | L1 |
| B | L1 | L1–L4 |
| C | L1 | L1–L4 |
| D | L1 | L1–L2 |
| D | L2 | L2 |
| E | L2 | L2 |
| F | L2 | L2–L3 |
| F | L3 | L3 |
| G | L3 | L3 |
| B | L4 | L4 |
| C | L4 | L4 |
| G | L4 | L4 |

*Note*: L1–L4, for example, means those parts of the program in block L1 but *not* block L4.

**Fig. 1.** Scope of variable names.

REFERENCE

1971. Ralston, A. *An Introduction to Programming and Computer Science*. New York: McGraw-Hill.

J. A. N. LEE AND A. RALSTON

## GRAMMAR.

*See* GRAMMAR, GENERATIVE; GRAMMAR, REDUCTIVE; and LANGUAGE PROCESSORS.

## GRAMMAR, GENERATIVE

For articles on related subjects *see* GRAMMAR, REDUCTIVE; PARSING; and PROGRAMMING LINGUISTICS.

For article on related term *see* META VARIABLE

A grammar is a set of rules that describes the valid forms of a language on the basis of a set of the "parts of speech" (formally called the set of "metavariables," or "phrase names") and the alphabet or character set of the language. Grammars are most commonly classified into two groups: *context senstive* and *context free*. In the case of context-sensitive grammars, the rules are applicable only when a metavariable occurs in a specified context—for example, the modification of verbs to their plural form in the context of plurality in the rest of the sentence in natural languages. By contrast, in a context-free grammar any occurrence of a metavariable may be replaced by one of its alternatives, irrespective of the other elements in the language. Most programming languages appear to be describable in context-free grammars except where certain declaratives are required, such as the declaration of array dimensions or the specification of a procedure to support a procedure reference. In the discussion that follows, we will restrict ourselves to context-free grammars.

Given a starting phrase name, such as *sentence*, a generative grammar specifies a sequence of replacements that can be applied to that name to form an instance (in this case a *sentence*) in the language. For example, consider the following small grammar:

*sentence* = *noun-phrase verb-phrase*
*noun-phrase* = *article noun*
*verb-phrase* = *verb noun-phrase*

and

*article* = the, a
*noun* = cat, milk
*verb* = drank

where the italicized elements are metavariables

and the nonitalicized elements are from the alphabet of the language. Using these rules, the sentence

The cat drank the milk.

can be generated by the following sequence:

*sentence* → *noun-phrase verb-phrase*.
→ *article noun verb-phrase*.
→ the *noun verb-phrase*.
→ the cat *verb-phrase*.
→ the cat *verb noun-phrase*.
→ the cat drank *noun-phrase*.
→ the cat drank *article noun*.
→ the cat drank the *noun*.
→ the cat drank the milk.

Equally, the sentences "the milk drank the cat" and "the cat drank the cat" can be generated, since they have the required underlying syntactic (grammatical) structure.

Similarly, consider the following grammar for simple forms of arithmetic expressions in higher-level languages (where the vertical bar is to be read "or"):

*add-op* = + | −
*mult-op* = * | /
*exp-op* = **
*primary* = *constant* | *variable*
*factor* = *primary* | *primary exp-op primary*
*term* = *factor* | *factor mult-op factor*
*arithmetic-expression* = *term add-op term*

and where constants and variables then have usual definitions in computer languages. Then the expression

A+B*C**D

could be generated as follows:

*arithmetic-expression* → *term add-op term*
→ *factor add-op term*
→ *primary add-op term*
→ *variable add-op term*
→ A *add-op term*
→ A + *term*
→ A + *factor mult op-factor*
→ A + *primary mult-op factor*
→ A + *variable mult-op factor*
→ A + B *mult-op factor*
→ A + B * *factor*
→ A + B * *primary exp-op primary*
→ A + B * *variable exp-op primary*
→ A + B * C *exp-op primary*
→ A + B * C ** *primary*
→ A + B * C ** *variable*
→ A + B * C ** D

REFERENCES

1963. Chomsky, N. "Formal Properties of Grammars," in *Handbook of Mat. Psych.*, Vol. 2. New York: John Wiley, pp. 323–418.

1969. Hopcroft, J. E., and J. D. Ullman. *Formal Languages and Their Relation to Automata.* Reading, Mass.: Addison-Wesley.

J. A. N. LEE

# GRAMMAR, REDUCTIVE

For articles on related subjects *see* GRAMMAR, GENERATIVE; PARSING; and SYNTAX, SEMANTICS AND PRAGMATICS.
For article on related term *see* META VARIABLE.

A reductive grammar is a set of syntactic rules for the analysis of strings to determine whether the strings exist in a language. As contrasted with a generative grammar, a reductive grammar is designed to permit the reduction of the string to a recognizable metavariable.

In the process of syntactic analysis, a reductive grammar permits the analyzer to commence its operations at the level of the string and to work toward the target of the root symbol in the language. For example, a reductive grammar would take the string

A+B*C**D

and with the reverse series of transformations used with a generative grammar, would achieve the target of *arithmetic-expression*. Such an analysis is known as a "bottom-up" analysis, in contrast to the "top-down" analysis of a generative grammar, which starts from the root symbol (e.g., *arithmetic-expression*) and works down toward the string being analyzed.

In practice, computer language processors normally use a combination of the reductive and generative techniques when doing the syntactic analysis of strings.

J. A. N. LEE

# GRAPH THEORY

For articles on related subjects *see* ALGORITHMS, ANALYSIS OF; COMPUTATIONAL COMPLEXITY; DATA STRUCTURES; and TREE.

For article on related term *see* HEURISTICS.

Informally a graph is a collection of points, any pair of which may or may not be joined by a line. Graph theory is the study of these objects. A graph may be represented by a diagram such as that in Fig. 1.

The uses of graph theory in computer science are diverse, and they include applications such as scheduling in operating systems and elsewhere, resource allocation, flowchart representation, information retrieval, and even sorting. The algorithms developed to solve combinatorial and graph theoretical problems have recently been found to be also of theoretical interest in the area of computational complexity. We attempt here simply to give basic definitions and to summarize the current state-of-the-art in the algorithmic area.

The terminology of graph theory varies from author to author and from application to application; the reader should take care to know what concept is intended when reading articles from diverse fields. We attempt here to use what has become more or less standard vocabulary, and to mention alternative words that are common.

It is frequently pointed out that graph theory had its beginnings with Euler and the Konigsberg bridge problem. The problem is to find a way of taking a walk (in Konigsberg) and to cross each of its seven bridges (Fig. 2) exactly once. Euler showed such a walk to be impossible, by noting that each of the land masses $A,C,D$ has an odd number (three) of bridges. It is noteworthy that Euler's solution to the generalization of this problem (made in 1736), which is known as finding an *Eulerian path* when one exists, remains the basis of the best algorithm known today for the solution to this problem.

A graph $G(V,X)$ is a finite, nonempty collection $V$ of points (nodes, vertices) and a prescribed set $X$ of unordered pairs of distinct points. Such a pair $\{v_1v_2\}$ is called an "edge" (branch, arc, line). The diagram of a graph is sometimes referred to as the graph itself.

A graph is called "labeled" (see the rightmost example in Fig. 1) if its points are distinguished by names. A *directed graph*, or *digraph* (Fig. 3), is a finite nonempty set of points $V$ and a set $X$ of ordered pairs of distinct points for edges. A digraph is said to be *oriented* if both $(v_i,v_j)$ and $(v_j,v_i)$ do not occur in $X$.

Note that the preceding definitions do not allow an infinite set of points, multiple edges, or loops (a line from a point to itself). Some authors allow all or some of these in graphs and reserve some special word (linear graph, for example) to mean the structure we define as simply a graph.

There are two common ways to represent a graph or digraph in a computer: (1) by its *adjacency matrix*, and (2) by its *adjacency structure*. The adjacency matrix for a graph on $n$ vertices is $A = (a_{ij})$, $i,j = 1,2,\ldots n$, where $a_{ij} = 1$ if vertex $v_i$ is *adjacent* to $v_j$ [i.e., if $(v_i,v_j)$ is an edge of the graph], and zero otherwise. The adjacency structure is the listing for each vertex of all other vertices adjacent to it. The adjacency structure has proved to produce faster

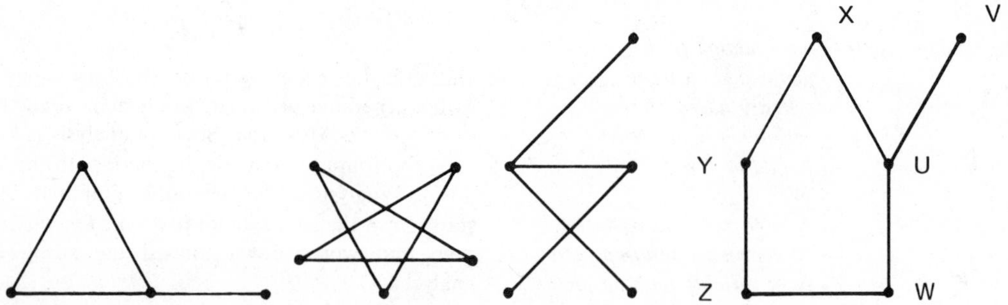


**Fig. 1**

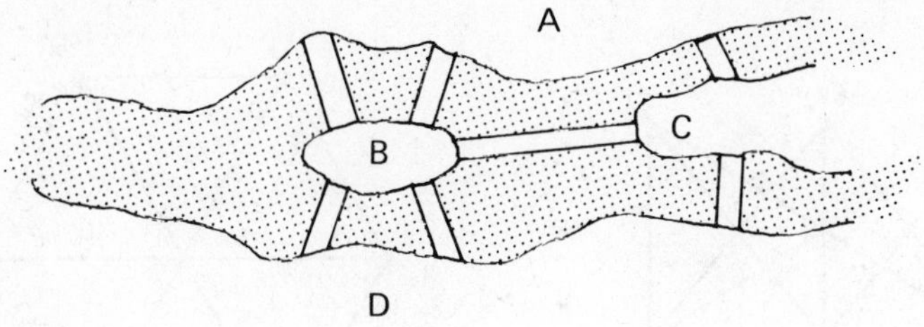


**Fig. 2**

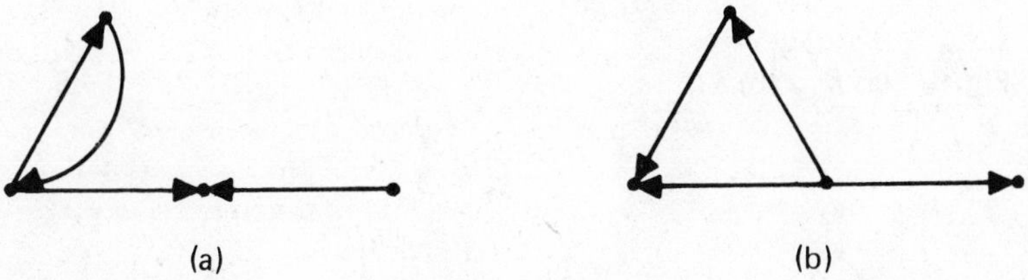


**Fig. 3.** (a) A digraph. (b) An oriented graph.

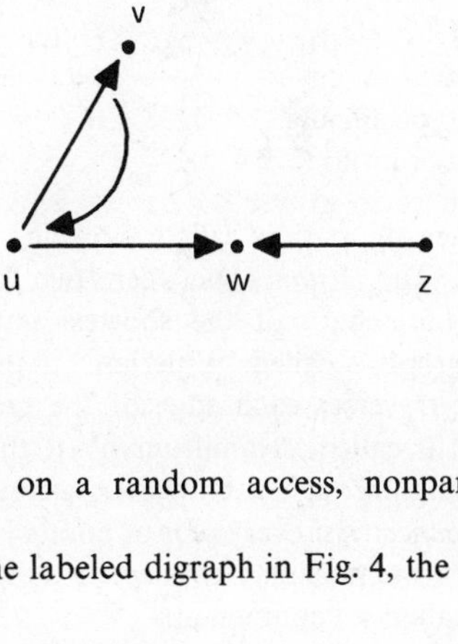


**Fig. 4**

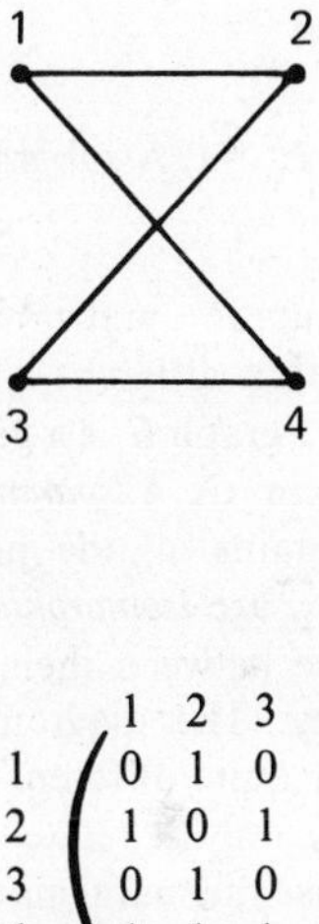


**Fig. 5**

algorithms on a random access, nonparallel machine.

For the labeled digraph in Fig. 4, the adjacency matrix is

$$\begin{array}{c} \\ u \\ v \\ w \\ z \end{array} \begin{array}{c} \begin{matrix} u & v & w & z \end{matrix} \\ \begin{pmatrix} 0 & 1 & 1 & 0 \\ 1 & 0 & 0 & 0 \\ 0 & 0 & 0 & 0 \\ 0 & 0 & 1 & 0 \end{pmatrix} \end{array}$$

and the adjacency structure is

$u$: $v,w$
$v$: $u$
$w$: {empty}
$z$: $w$

Similarly, for the labeled graph in Fig. 5, we have the adjacency matrix:

$$\begin{array}{c} \\ 1 \\ 2 \\ 3 \\ 4 \end{array} \begin{array}{c} \begin{matrix} 1 & 2 & 3 & 4 \end{matrix} \\ \begin{pmatrix} 0 & 1 & 0 & 1 \\ 1 & 0 & 1 & 1 \\ 0 & 1 & 0 & 1 \\ 1 & 1 & 1 & 0 \end{pmatrix} \end{array}$$

and adjacency structure

1: 2,4
2: 1,3
3: 2,4
4: 3,4

The reader will note that if no orientation is given to the edges [i.e., "$(v_i,v_j)$ is an edge" means that $v_i$ is adjacent to $v_j$, and conversely], then the adjacency matrix is symmetric about the diagonal, which is zero when no loops are present. Also, any permutation on the rows and columns ($P^{-1}AP$,

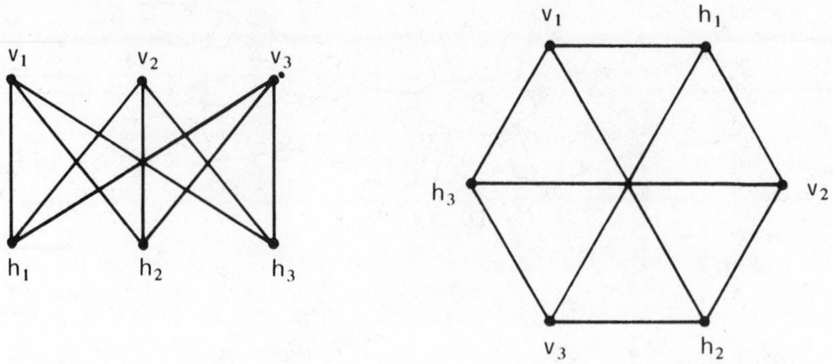


**Fig. 6.** (a) $K_{3,3}$. (b) $K_5$.

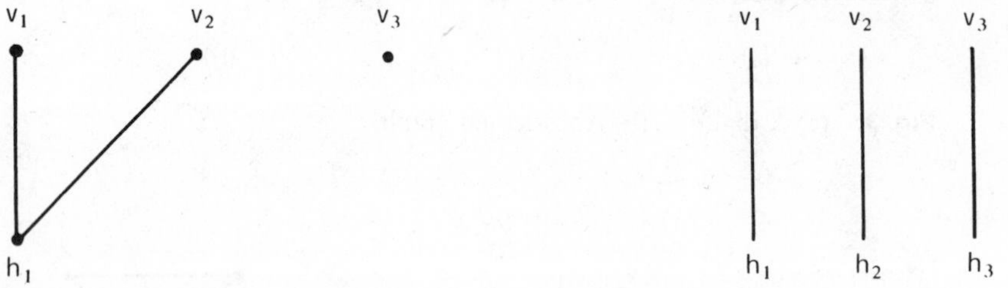


**Fig. 7.** (a) A subgraph of $K_{3,3}$. (b) A spanning subgraph of $K_{3,3}$.

where $P$ is a permutation matrix) simply represents the same graph with a different labeling.

A *subgraph* of a graph $G$ is a graph whose points and edges are all in $G$; a *spanning subgraph* is a subgraph that contains all the points of $G$. Two graphs, $G_1$ and $G_2$, are *isomorphic* if there exists a 1–1 correspondence between their point sets which preserves adjacency. The diagrams of isomorphic graphs may appear quite different (see Fig. 6).

The graph $K_{3,3}$ and the related graph $K_5$ of Fig. 6 are famous because the mathematician Kuratowski showed that a graph is *planar* (roughly can be drawn in the plane without any lines crossing) if and only if it contains no subgraph homeomorphic to $K_{3,3}$ or $K_5$. This theorem has *not* proved useful in computer algorithms to determine whether or not a graph is planar.

For examples of a subgraph, and a spanning subgraph of $K_{3,3}$ see Fig. 7(a) and (b).

A set of vertices $\{v_0, v_1, \ldots, v_n\}$ in a graph $G$ is a *walk* of length $n$ if $\{v_i v_{i+1}\} i = 0,1 \cdots n-1$ is an edge of $G$ and a *path* if all $v_i$ are distinct. Some writers use the word "path" when a given vertex is allowed to appear more than once in the set $\{v_0, v_1, \ldots v_n\}$ and use the term "simple path" to denote what we have called a path. If $n \geq 2$ and $v_0 = v_n$, then the path is called a "cycle" (sometimes "circuit"). The *distance* between two points in a graph is the length of the shortest path between them. A graph is called "Eulerian" if there exists a walk that traverses each edge of the graph exactly once, and is called "Hamiltonian" if there exists a path passing through each vertex exactly once. A graph is *connected* if every pair of points is connected by a path. A maximal connected subgraph of a graph is called a "component."

The *degree* (valence) of a vertex of a graph is the number of lines *incident* to that point. In a digraph, the corresponding idea is expressed by "out degree" and "in degree." Clearly,

$$\Sigma_{v_i \epsilon G} \deg(v_i) = 2q,$$

where $q$ is the number of edges in the graph.

A *complete* graph on $n$ points, denoted by $K_n$, is the $n$-graph containing all possible $\binom{n}{2}$ lines. A *bipartite* (bicolorable) graph, or *bigraph*, is a graph whose point-set can be partitioned into two subsets, $V_1$ and $V_2$, such that any edge of $G$ connects a point of $V_1$ with a point of $V_2$. A graph is bipartite if and only if all its cycles are of even length. A *complete bigraph*, denoted by $K_{m,n}$, contains all possible lines.

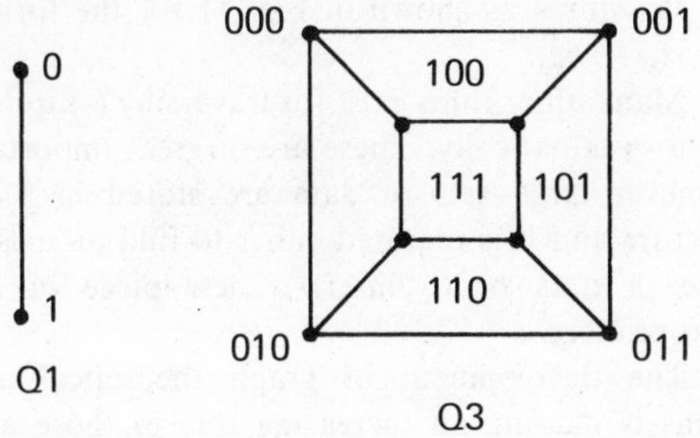


**Fig. 8**

$K_{3,3}$ in Fig. 6 is such a graph, with $V_1 = \{v_1,v_2,v_3\}$ and $V_2 = \{h_1,h_2,h_3\}$.

A graph useful in many applications is the "$n$-cube" $Q_n$; this is a graph on $2^n$ points where each vertex may be denoted by an $n$-bit number. Two points of $Q_n$ (such as $Q_1$ and $Q_3$) are adjacent whenever their binary representation differs in exactly one place, as in Fig. 8.

A *cut-point* (articulation point) of a component of a graph is a point whose removal disconnects that component, and (analogously) a *bridge* (isthmus) is a line whose removal disconnects a component. A graph is *n-connected* if $n$ points must be removed to disconnect the graph. A graph is two-connected or *biconnected* if and only if every pair of points of the graph lies on a cycle.

The graphs called "trees" are used in many computer applications. Knuth (1972) defines a *rooted tree* recursively as a finite set $T$ of *nodes* in which

1. One specially designated node is called the "root" of the tree.
2. The remaining nodes are partitioned into $m \geq 0$ disjoint sets $T_1, T_2, \ldots, T_m$ (or *subtrees*), each of which is a tree.

Fig. 9 illustrates some rooted trees, with the root circled. If there is no point of the tree distinguished as the root, then the tree is called a "free" tree by Knuth, but we will just use the term "tree" here.

It can be proved without too much difficulty that any of the following statements about a graph are equivalent, and hence any one of them may also be used as a definition for a tree. Let $G$ be a graph with $n$ vertices and $k$ edges.

1. G is a tree.
2. G is connected and has no cycles (is *acyclic*).
3. Every two points of $G$ are connected by a unique path.
4. $G$ is connected and has $n - 1$ edges.
5. $G$ is acyclic and has $n - 1$ edges.
6. $G$ is connected, but if any edge of $G$ is removed, then the resulting graph is disconnected.

The word "tree" has lead to much fanciful vocabulary—forest, plantation, leaf, twig, root, palm tree, frond, arborescence, etc., all have technical meanings. In particular, we note that an *end-point*, or *leaf* of a tree is a vertex of degree 1. A *spanning tree* of a graph is a spanning subgraph, which is also a tree. For the application of Kirchoff's laws (which make use of spanning trees) to flowcharts, see Knuth (1972).

If the order of the subtrees formed by deleting the root is important, i.e., if $B$ and $C$ in Fig. 9 are considered distinct, then the rooted tree is called "ordered." Ordered trees are important because computer representations of trees necessarily give rise to rooted ordered trees.

For some reason (possibly in analogy to the "family tree"), rooted trees in computer literature are drawn upside down, with the root at the "top." Computer terminology for tree structures is sexist.

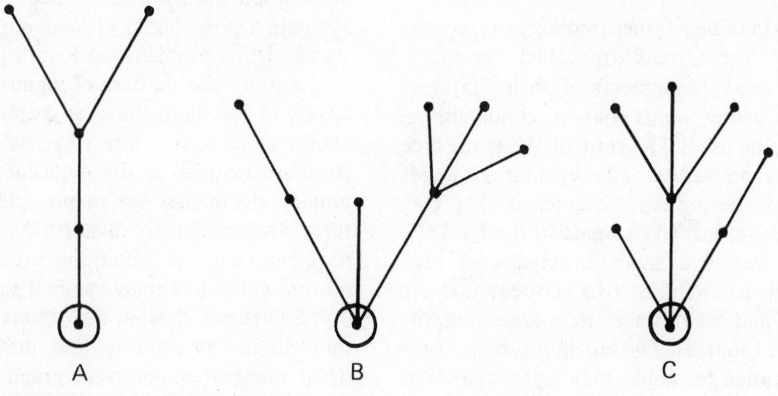


**Fig. 9**

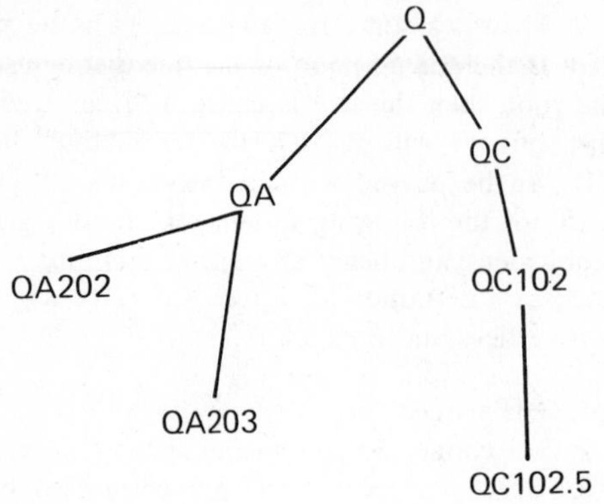


**Fig. 10**

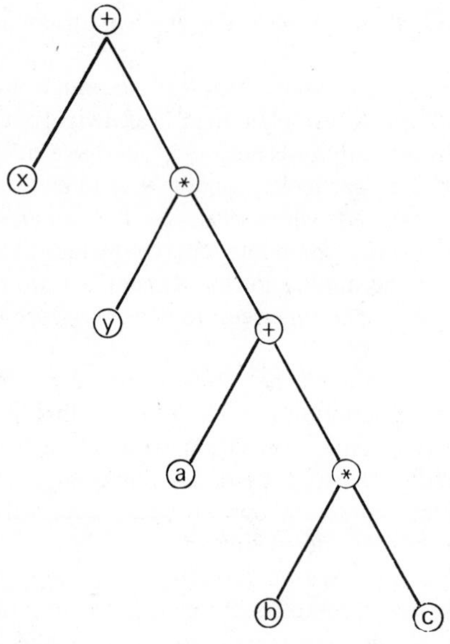


**Fig. 11**

Every root is said to be a father (mother) to the roots of its subtrees. These roots are called "brothers" (sisters) and "sons" (daughters) of their "fathers" (mothers). The neuter words (parent, child, sibling) do not seem to be used. The root of the entire tree (godhead?) has no father. The egalitarian words "ancestor" and "descendant" are terms that may designate nodes several levels apart in the tree.

A *binary* tree is a rooted-ordered tree, each vertex of which has at most two subtrees that are designated left and right. Binary trees arise naturally from a variety of sources. The labeling system of the library classification for books may be thought of as a tree. (See Fig. 10). Algebraic formulas give rise to tree structures as shown in Fig. 11 for the formula $x + y(a + bc)$.

Many algorithms exist for traversing (searching) a tree systematically. These are of great importance whenever large sets of data are stored in a tree structure and it is required either to find an existing piece of data or to insert a new piece of data appropriately.

The development of graph theoretical algorithms is playing an increasing role in those areas that have come to be called "computational complexity," and in the analysis of algorithms. On early computers, lack of main storage prevented the solution of graph problems involving many nodes. Moreover, these computers were not fast enough to handle the very large number of computations that are often required for graph-related computations. Today, large main stores and readily available backing stores have alleviated the storage problem but the time problem still remains, particularly for problems where the obvious algorithm requires $n!$ operations.

For example, the problem of deciding whether or not two graphs are isomorphic is a trivial one for the mathematician, who will simply check all $n!$ mappings of one vertex set onto the other. But the time requirements for a problem of this sort quickly get out of hand. If the solution of this problem would require 6 minutes on a computer when $n = 10$, it would require 9 years for $n = 15$ and 300,000 centuries when $n = 20$. In order to overcome this difficulty, computer scientists have, in recent years, invented new approaches to algorithm design and new algorithms for a number of problems that require much less time than $n!$ algorithms. We should note in this connection the pioneering work of A. M. Ostrowski, who (in 1954)—long before the consideration of such problems was fashionable—posed the question: What is the minimal number of multiplications and/or additions necessary to evaluate a polynomial of degree $n$? For the current status of this problem see Knuth (1969).

Among the matters of significance in the discovery of fast algorithms for graph problems are the choice of data structure (the use of the adjacency structure instead of the adjacency matrix, for example), depth-first search procedures in tree structures, and recursively dividing the problem into two problems, each one-half the previous size but requiring much less than one-half the computation.

Sometimes the new algorithms are heuristic; i.e., they do not attempt to find the optimal solution (least number of colors in graph coloring, for example) but one that is near optimal.

We now briefly summarize problems for which algorithms have been written and give for each problem the currently best-known upper bound for the time of its execution. We assume our graph is an $(n,m)$-graph, i.e., one having $n$ points and $m$ edges.

An algorithm is said to require $0(n^p)$ operations if the number of operations divided by $n^p$ is bounded as $n \rightarrow \infty$. Such an algorithm is said to require polynomial time. Among algorithms that are $0(n)$ are those to determine tree isomorphism and those to determine planarity. It is interesting to note that the bound for planarity algorithms has dropped from $0(n^4)$ to $0(n)$ in the past few years. Most connectivity problems—finding cut-points and/or bridges, determining connectivity, biconnectivity, and three-connectivity—are $0(\max(m,n))$; so is the problem for finding a spanning tree of a graph and that of constructing an Eulerian path if it exists. The best algorithm for subtree isomorphism is $0(n^{2.5})$ and that for finding a minimum spanning tree (the edges are given weights and the spanning tree with minimum total weight is required) is $0(\min(n^2, m \log m))$. An algorithm for the isomorphism problem for planar graphs also exists, which is $0(n \log n)$. The best shortest path (edges are weighted) algorithms are $0(n^3)$, as are the algorithms for more general maximum-flow problems.

Some problems are known to require algorithms that are exponential (i.e., there is no $p$ such that the number of operations is $0(n^k)$). For example, the problems of finding all cliques (a clique is a set of vertices, each of which is connected to all others) in a graph, all isomorphisms between two graphs, and all cycles or all paths in a graph are all known to be exponential.

For a rather large class of problems, the upper bound is unknown. These include: finding the largest clique, general graph isomorphism, vertex coloring, and the traveling salesman problem. However, it is known that if an algorithm requiring polynomial time exists for one of them, then so does one for all of them. If any are shown to be exponential, then they all are.

### References

1962. Berge, C. *The Theory of Graphs and Its Applications*. London: Methuen.

1969. Harary, F. *Graph Theory*. Reading, Mass.: Addison-Wesley.

1972. Knuth, D. E. *The Art of Computer Programming* [vols. 1 (1968), 2 (1969), 3 (1972)]. Reading, Mass.: Addison-Wesley.

P. J. EBERLEIN

## GRAPHICS.

*See* BIOMEDICINE, COMPUTER GRAPHICS IN; and COMPUTER GRAPHICS.

## GROSCH'S LAW

For articles on related subjects *see* PERFORMANCE OF COMPUTERS; and SUPERCOMPUTERS.

In the late 1940s, Herbert R. J. Grosch formulated what has become known as Grosch's law concerning economies of scale in computers. He proposed that computing power increases as the square of the cost of the computer, or

$$P = KC^2,$$

where $P$ = computing power
$K$ = a constant
$C$ = system cost (either lease price or purchase price)

so that, for example, for twice the money one obtains four times the computing power.

While Grosch himself never published his law, it became part of the oral tradition of the computer industry. It was quoted both seriously and humorously, but eventually gained respectability by being cited in several articles.

Grosch's law has received much attention because of its implications, although it is not susceptible to definitive proof. Several studies lend empirical validity to it, but no one has been able to decide whether it reflects the true value in relation to users' cost or if computer manufacturers use its widespread acceptance to price their goods.

It should be kept in mind that there are limits to the extent that economies of scale can be realized; i.e., there is some point at which the state-of-the-art is reached, beyond which it will cost more proportionally to increase computing power. Within this limit, Grosch's law is a rough guide to determining computing power. However, the calculations of Grosch's law are based on a given point in time and are concerned with the new computers released at that point. The existence of a used-computer market, short- and long-term leases, and third-party leases means that Grosch's law cannot normally be applied to the evaluation of computer purchases or leases.

K. E. KNIGHT AND R. P. CERVENY

# GUIDE

For articles on related subjects *see* COMPUTER USER GROUPS; and SHARE.

GUIDE is an international association of users of large-scale IBM computers. It was formed in 1956 as an informal computer users group with members from 44 companies. The name GUIDE originated as an acronym: *G*uidance of *U*sers of *I*ntegrated *D*ata-Processing *E*quipment.

GUIDE was incorporated as a not-for-profit organization in 1970 under the full name of GUIDE International Corporation. As of 1973, GUIDE was made up of 1,300 member installations. The minimum equipment configuration that a member installation has either installed or on order is System 360 Model 40, or larger, or System 370 Model 135, or larger.

GUIDE has three objectives, as follows:

1. *In relation to its members*: To exchange and disseminate information of mutual interest and value, and to promote sound and professional EDP practices.
2. *In relation to the EDP industry*: To communicate to the IBM Corporation user needs in all technical areas of interest; to review, comment, and exchange information on products and services related to IBM large-scale computers; and to influence the development of computer industry standards.
3. *In relation to the public*: An appropriate involvement regarding public opinion as it relates to the data processing industry.

GUIDE holds general sessions semiannually, usually for three days, in the Spring and Fall. Following a prominent keynote speaker, the individual sessions are usually formal presentations that may take the form of tutorials, user experience panels, workshops, or committee reports. The subject matter consists of current topics that deal with all facets of the data processing environment. Normally, over 100 individual sessions are conducted at a GUIDE general session, with an attendance of over 3,000 delegates.

Immediately preceding the general sessions, the Division and Group management and the GUIDE working projects meet to perform the major work of GUIDE. The GUIDE project work has become so valuable to its membership that two more meetings per year have been added. These meetings, called Mini-GUIDE meetings, usually consist of over 80 working projects. The objectives of these projects include sharing of information of mutual interest, suggesting enhancements to existing hardware and software, bringing problems with existing hardware and software to the attention of each other and to IBM, promoting effective usage of existing hardware and software products, and/or suggesting the development of future hardware, software, or management techniques.

The roster of GUIDE presidents includes the following persons:

Ed Law, North American Aviation, 1956–1957
Mel Gross, ESSO, 1957–1959
Carl Byham, Southern Railway, 1959–1960
Les Calkins, U.S. Steel, 1960–1963
Otis Simpson, Boeing, 1963–1965
Ottice Tidwell, A T & T, 1965–1967
Earl Althoff, Eastman Kodak, 1967–1969
Herb Seidensticker, Combustion Engineering, 1969–1971
Garland Cupp, McDonnell-Douglas Automation Co., 1971–1973
Al Burris, Northern Trust Co., 1973–1975

More information can be obtained by writing to GUIDE International Corporation, One Illinois Center, 111 East Wacker Drive, Chicago, Ill. 60601.

B. G. CUPP

# H

## HANDSHAKING

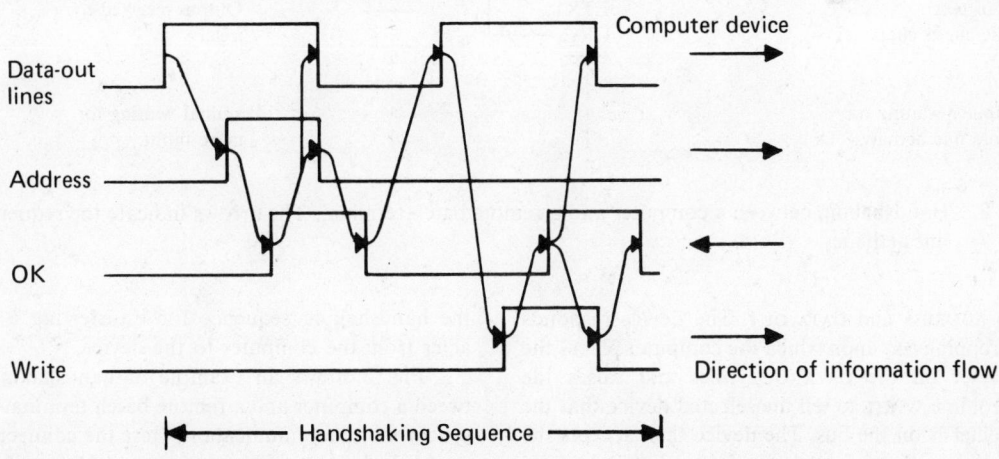

For articles on related subjects *see* DATA COMMUNICATIONS; and TELEPROCESSING SYSTEMS.

The exchange of predetermined sequences of control signals or control characters between two devices or systems to establish a connection, or to break a connection or exchange data and status information, is commonly referred to as "handshaking." This is best illustrated by means of examples.

Consider first Fig. 1, which shows the sequence of signals on the input-output bus of a small computer when writing a character to a device connected to the bus. The computer first places the device address on the DATA OUT lines and raises the ADDRESS control line to tell the device that the data on the DATA OUT lines is an address. The device recognizes its address and raises the control line OK, informing the computer that the device is aware that it has been selected. This causes the computer to

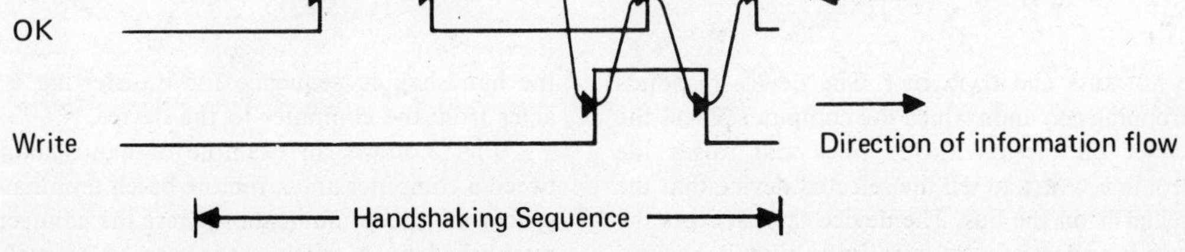


**Fig. 1.** Example of handshaking sequence. The arrows are used to indicate which control signal causes which response during sequence.

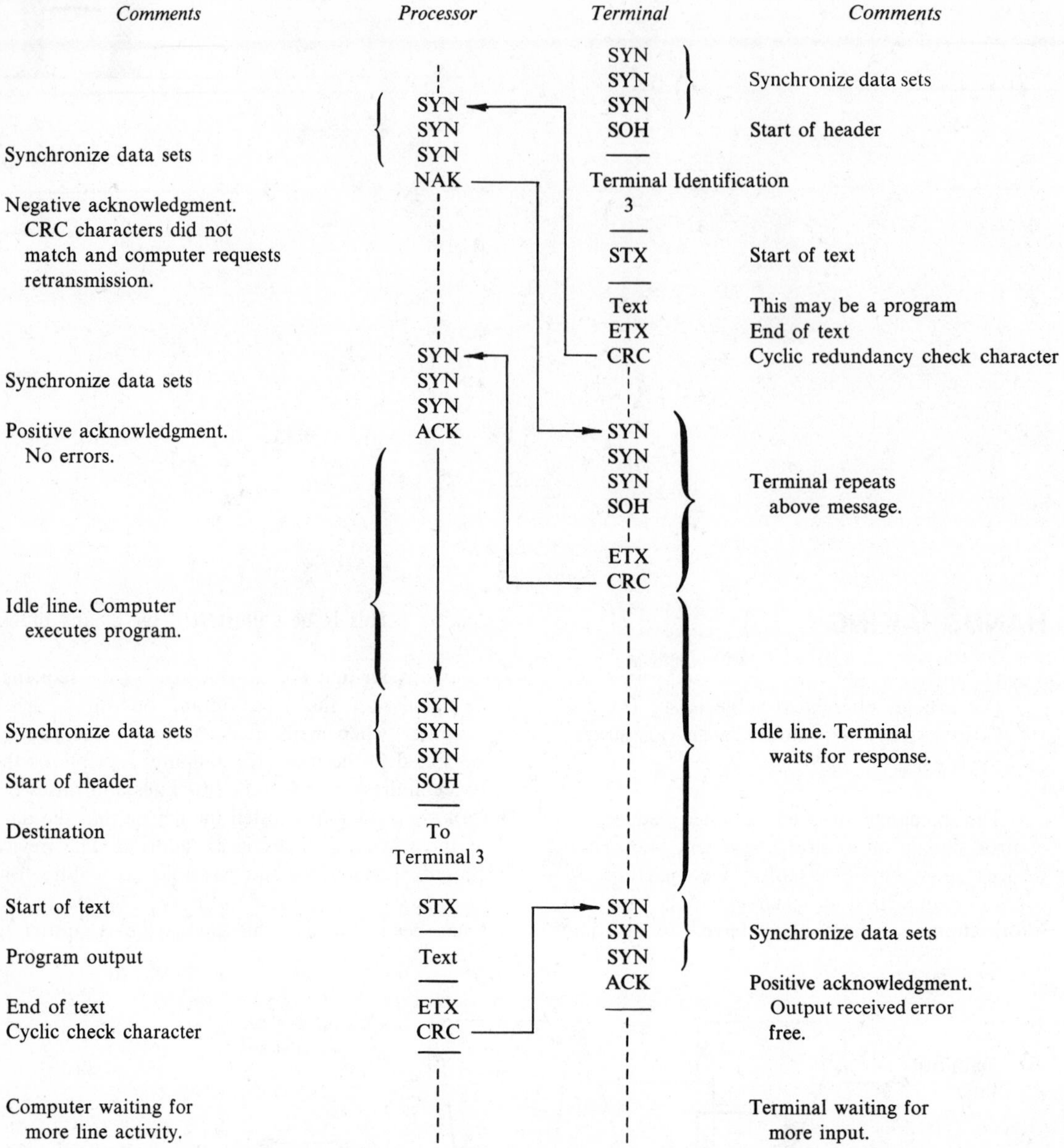


**Fig. 2.** Handshaking between a computer and a remote batch terminal. The arrows indicate the sequence of line activities.

drop ADDRESS and DATA OUT. The device responds by dropping OK, upon which the computer places the character on the DATA OUT lines and raises the control line WRITE to tell the selected device that the character is on the bus. The device then accepts the character and raises OK, signifying that it has accepted it. The computer then drops DATA OUT and WRITE, which causes OK to go down. This completes the handshaking sequence for transferring a character from the computer to the device.

Fig. 2 shows an example of handshaking between a computer and a remote batch terminal using synchronous communication. Here the connection is established by a special sequence of control characters (SYN, SOH, STX, etc.). Such handshaking between remote terminals and a computer is often called "communication protocol," or simply "protocol."

J. S. Sobolewski

## HARD COPY

For articles on related subjects *see* Input-Output Devices; and Machine-Readable Form.
For article on related subject *see* Paper Tape.

Hard copy is used to describe computer output (strictly speaking only at remote terminals) in either printed or graphical form that can be read directly by humans and handled and filed. This is in contrast to information stored in some magnetic form on tape or disk, or temporarily displayed on a screen, or given by voice, or which requires some special device like a microfilm reader to be read. Such hard copy output may be produced simultaneously with other nonreadable output, which happens, for example, when a magnetic tape or disk file is updated and a printed report is also obtained.

The term is also used when a document that can be read by human beings is produced simultaneously with a machine-readable form of the data. This happens, for example, when a typist simultaneously prepares a typewritten document and a punched-paper tape for input to a computer.

J. Necas

## HARDWARE MONITOR

For article on related subject *see* Performance Measurement and Evaluation.
For articles on related terms *see* Central Processing Unit; and Channel.

A hardware monitor is a device for measuring electrical events (e.g., pulses, voltage levels) in a digital computer. It is useful for gathering data for measurement and evaluation of computer systems, particularly when used in conjunction with software monitoring, a technique using programmed steps that lead a computer to examine its own internal operation. Most hardware monitors are external general-purpose devices, but in principle they could be built into a computer if economically justifiable. As an example of use, a hardware monitor might be connected to measure the cumulative time the central processor is idle while all I/O channels are busy. Fig. 1 illustrates the elements of a hardware monitor. The various components are discussed below.

General Probes. A probe consists of a set of signal sensors designed for minimum interference with the host machine and able to drive relatively long cables so that signals can be picked up from various points physically distant from each other and from the central monitor console.

Logic Circuits. The logic circuits accept signals from the general probes and allow logical combinations of the signals (AND, NOR, INVERT, etc.) so that events of interest can be defined.

Counters. A group of counters are used to count the occurrence of various events or to measure the time between events by counting the number of intervening clock pulses.

Comparator Probes. The comparator probes are similar to the general probes. They are used to sense a number of bits that appear in parallel (e.g., as in an address register).

Comparator. This component provides means for comparing the parallel bits with some preset value at an instant defined by a signal on the strobe line.

Data Transfer Register. The transfer register provides means for passing data directly from the host computer to the magnetic tape record. This register could be combined with the counter functions or with the comparator functions.

In addition to refining the basic functions of gathering data, current development in hardware monitors shows a trend toward emphasizing means for processing data during collection and for allowing the host computer and the monitor to alter each other's measurement functions during operation. From the user's viewpoint, the principal differences between hardware and software monitors are:

1. Software monitors can provide more information on cause and effect by relating measured data to the program steps being executed; however, care must be exercised to avoid disruption of time relationships caused by the addition of the measurement programs.

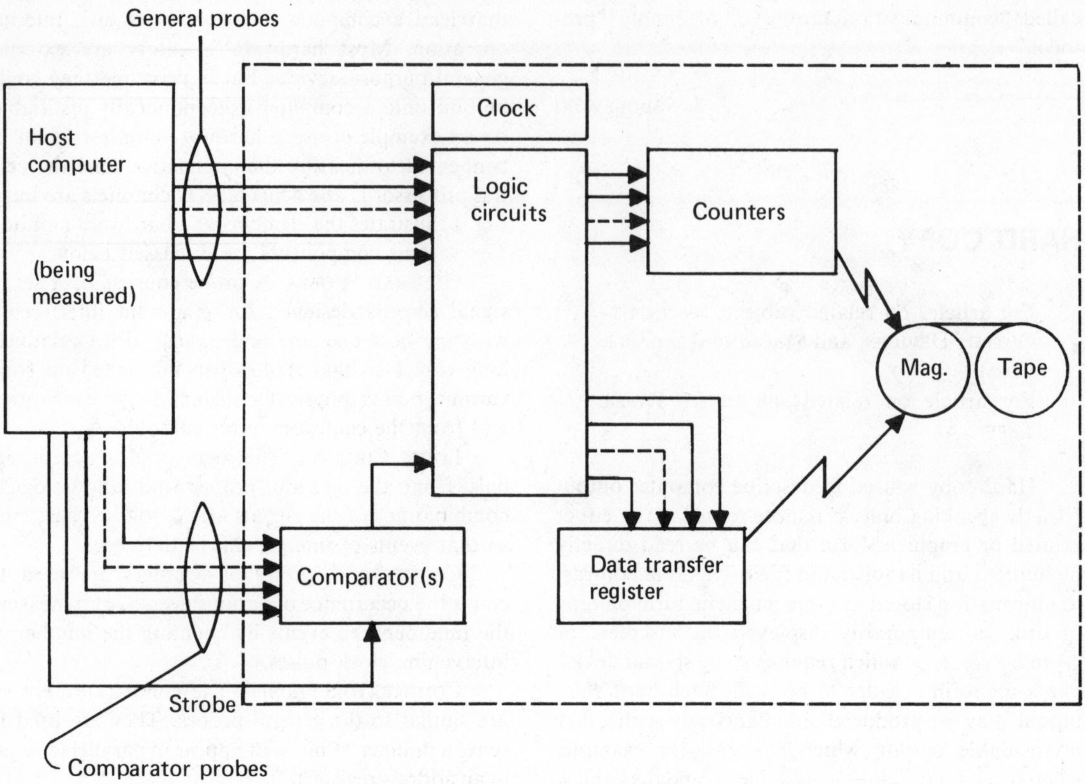


**Fig. 1.** Elements of a hardware monitor.

2. Hardware monitors only measure electrical events at predetermined physical points; hence, it is more difficult to relate measurements to program activity. However, with reasonable care, data may be gathered without interfering with the system being measured.

References

1973. Drummond, M. E. *Evaluation and Measurement Techniques for Digital Computer Systems*. Englewood Cliffs, N.J.: Prentice-Hall, ch. 8, pp. 240–280.

1973. Hughes, J., and D. Cronshaw. "On Using a Hardware Monitor as an Intelligent Peripheral," *ACM Performance Evaluation Review*, Vol. 2, No. 4 (December), pp. 3–19.

1974. Noe, J. D. "Acquiring and Using a Hardware Monitor," *Datamation* (April), pp. 89–95.

J. D. Noe

# HASHING

For articles on related subjects *see* Sorting; and Table Lookup.
For article on related term *see* Key.

Hashing (or hash coding) is a word coined by computer programmers to describe a general class of operations done to transform one or more fields (usually a *key*) into a different (usually more compact) arrangement. Probably "hashing" was first coined because it seemed that "hash" was being made out of integral pieces of data. The rationale for hashing is developed more fully in the article on table lookup, dealing with key transformation. The justification for hashing derives from being able to convert naturally occurring, diverse, ill-structured, scattered key fields into compact, easily manipulated fields—usually some numeric, computer-oriented field such as a word or double word, or a computer memory address to facilitate subsequent references. The transformation from the natural field to the hash address is only a one-way process, however; the natural field cannot be decoded or reconstructed from the hash. Also, the hashed field may not represent only one unique natural field; many natural fields could hash into the same value.

For example, suppose there is a table of automobile part numbers that are ten numeric characters in length, but there may be no more than 10,000 unique part numbers. In order to contain every possible number, the table would have to allow 10 billion ($10^{10}$) positions to handle only $10^4$ possible keys. A scheme can be contrived to transform the original ten-digit key to an integer that will represent the position of that part in a much more compact table.

One simple scheme for hashing is the division-remainder method: Choose a number close to the number of table positions needed. Use that number as a divisor to extract a quotient and a remainder from the dividend (which is the original key). The remainder so obtained is the transformed key. Using 10,000 as the divisor, the transformed key becomes the original key modulo 10,000. Some examples follow.

| Original Key (Part Number) | Transformed Key |
|---|---|
| 00 0000 1000 | 1000 |
| 00 0001 0000 | 0 |
| 00 0001 0001 | 1 |
| 00 0001 0099 | 99 |
| 10 0001 0099 | 99 |
| 22 3333 4444 | 4444 |
| 90 0020 0110 | 110 |
| 99 0020 0112 | 112 |

The examples in this table were constructed to illustrate the occurrence of duplicate transformed keys. In such schemes, prime divisors are normally used in practice.

Ideally, the hashing scheme would convert the original keys to transformed keys with no duplicates. While schemes can be constructed to minimize "collisions" ("hash clash") their possibility cannot be eliminated completely and, because of this, the original key must be stored in the table. Further, some scheme must be used to handle duplicate transformed keys.

The examples and discussion in the article on table lookup will further describe methodology and rationale for hashing. Some other techniques in addition to division-remainder are: (1) folding, (2) radix transformation, and (3) digit rearrangement.

*Folding* consists of splitting the original key into two or more parts, then adding the parts together (or, sometimes, using the exclusive OR operator). This sum, or some part of it, is then used as the transformed key. For example:

Original key = 20 2152 9396
Splitting and adding: 20 + 2152 + 9396 = 11568
Discard high-order digit to obtain four-digit transformed key of 1568.

*Radix transformation* involves changing the radix or base of the original key and either discarding excess high-order digits (i.e., digits in excess of the number desired in the key) or extracting some part of the transformed number. For example, an original key of 12345 (base 10) could be considered a base-16 number, and would be transformed as follows:

$$(1 \times 16^4) + (2 \times 16^3) + (3 \times 16^2) + (4 \times 16^1) + (5 \times 16^0) = 74565.$$

The four-digit key would be 4565 by discarding the high-order excess digit(s).

*Digit rearrangement* consists simply of selecting and shifting digits of the original key. For example, an original key of 1234567 could be transformed to a four-digit key of 6543 by selecting digit positions 3 through 6 and reversing their order.

No one technique is necessarily superior to another in general; however, for specific applications, some may work better than others. The selection of a technique should involve consideration of which technique results in fewest duplicate hash keys.

"Hash" totals are sometimes used for purposes of checking or verification; in this context, hashing has a different purpose than key transformation, inasmuch as the totals may not necessarily be hashed or scrambled. The use of hash totals is for a purpose much like the use of parity bits or self-checking codes for representing characters in digital form on media such as magnetic tapes or punched-paper tapes. When such data is written (or recorded), hash totals are generated and written along with (usually after) the data. Then, when the data is read, the hash totals are recomputed, using the same algorithm, and checked against the ones recorded. If they agree, one can be more certain that the recorded data read is identical to that written and that no bits have been lost or misread.

For example, if a hash total is taken after every

five numbers, that hash total could be recorded (written) after the five numbers, thus:

| | |
|---|---|
| Five data numbers | 12345<br>37654<br>89701<br>00378<br>42270 |
| Total | 182348 |
| Discard excess to obtain "hash" total | 82348 |

Now, upon reading this data and its hash total during some subsequent process, one could recompute the hash total in the same way and thus verify that it matched the one originally recorded.

C. E. PRICE

# HEURISTICS

For article on related subject *see* ARTIFICIAL INTELLIGENCE.
For article on related term *see* ALGORITHM.

The ancient Greek word *heuriskein* means "to find out, to discover." The English adjective "heuristic" and the more recently coined noun "heuristics" came into being via the Latin adjective *heuristicus*. According to the *Random House Dictionary:*

> *heuristic* adj. *1.* serving to indicate or point out, stimulating interest as a means of furthering investigation. *2.* (of a teaching method) encouraging the student to discover for himself. - n. *3.* a heuristic method or argument.

In the general sense, we talk of the "heuristic power" of a technique, the "heuristics in somebody's reasoning," and so on. Pólya (1954) has written several most entertaining books that do not teach, but do make one realize how to approach problems in mathematics and geometry via heuristic ideas. Also, Hadamard's essay on discovery in mathematics yields an interesting insight—a much too rare phenomenon—into how one of the great mathematicians of all time tackles problems.

How does all this concern us in computing? The reason is simple but its application leads to an area that is completely open-ended. Let us consider, for example, a standard task in programming. We wish to find the roots of a higher-order algebraic equation. There are several methods of approximation that yield the solution with estimatable error bounds. We have the formulas to follow, step by step, and eventually we obtain the results. This is the *algorithmic approach.*

Let us now consider a so-called ill-defined problem, and we have millions of them in everyday life. For example, say we want to balance our household budget by following a program. Although our basic needs are reasonably well known (food, shelter, clothing, medical items, transportation, entertainment, etc.), neither the relative weight of the components nor their unit prices are determinable completely. Also, our needs, desires, and tastes change continually. Our interaction with the environment represents a significant modifying factor. Because this problem is terribly ill-defined, no mathematical technique by itself has a chance to solve it. The computerization of the solution requires all those vague, hard-to-quantify ideas that humans in fact make use of in doing this problem. ("Either I go on vacation or buy that new car. ... Let's see, how much longer can I drive my old bomb?") The collection of these rules of thumb, sometimes referred to as insight, intuition, or experience with a particular task, represent what computer scientists call "heuristics" (plural noun).

We resort to heuristic programming whenever an algorithmic solution is prohibitively expensive or impossible to follow, or is unavailable. The role of heuristics is to cut down the time and memory requirements of search. On the average, it should result in appreciable savings when programming our budget to satisfy our basic needs. It must be pointed out that heuristic methods are not foolproof; they can fail a certain proportion of the time. (Algorithms are not supposed to fail. ... However, the fact that a technique is not foolproof does not render it heuristic.)

The larger the range in which a heuristic can be applied, the more powerful it is considered to be. Also, its level of performance is comparable to that of an exhaustive strategy (an algorithm, in fact) or of a random search for a solution.

The following example, originally reported by Simon, should shed some light on the concept under discussion. It is well known that practically any nontrivial game cannot be played by humans *or* by machines algorithmically (because there does not exist an algorithm) or exhaustively (because the memory and time requirements far exceed any available ones). The classical example of intellectual games, chess, has been programmed by several groups of researchers. In all these, heuristic ideas occupy a central role in move selection and position evaluation. In fact, de Groot and other psychologists have shown that the basic difference between excellent and mediocre players is not in their memory capacity or even in their data processing ability *in abstracto*. All players analyze practically the same number of board positions, but not always the same ones. Excellent chess players have developed very powerful heuristics for the *selection* of game continuations to be considered. They may go down to a depth of, say, 20 half-moves along one path and disregard others below a depth of 2 or 3, for reasons of their own.

One of the rather often used heuristics is to leave as little freedom of move selection for the opponent as possible. If all other techniques of comparison assign an equal score to two moves considered, a chess expert usually selects the one that restricts the opponent's mobility to a larger degree. This technique, being a heuristic, works most of the time. There was a famous game, however, between two international masters in which the winner used this heuristic *to his disadvantage*. It has been shown by game analysts that in a particular position, the optimum move (overlooked for the reasons discussed) could have led to an earlier victory. A supplement to this story is that the MATER program by Baylor and Simon (1966), which incorporates the heuristics of fewest-replies, was presented the same particular near-end position and duplicated the mistake made by the international master.

**Outlook.** Except for some introductory efforts (Waterman, 1970; Findler et al., 1971), present heuristics are all preprogrammed in artificial intelligence projects. In other words, it is not the machine that discovers, selects, and optimizes the rules that play an increasingly important role in many problem-solving programs. Therefore, the performance level of these programs is determined by the researcher's experience, insight, and perhaps even luck.

A much more desirable situation would be the one in which the heuristic processes are automated. Learning programs, initially inefficient and possibly even random in their actions, would gradually formulate more and more heuristics on the basis of experience. These heuristics would assume a flexible, or parametric, format so that subsequent optimization processes could raise the overall level of performance.

REFERENCES

1954. Pólya G. *Mathematics and Plausible Reasoning*, vol. I.; *Induction and Analogy in Mathematics*, Vol. II.; *Patterns of Plausible Inference*, Princeton, N.J.; Princeton University Press.

1963. Minsky, M. "Steps toward Artificial Intelligence," *Proc. IRE*, Vol. 49, pp. 8–30. Reprinted in Feigenbaum and Feldman (Eds.), *Computer and Thought*. New York: McGraw-Hill.

1966. Baylor, G. W., and H. A. Simon. "A Chess Mating Combinations Program," *Proc. SJCC*, vol. 28, pp. 431–447.

1970. Waterman, D. A. "Generalization Learning Techniques for Automating the Learning of Heuristics," *Artificial Intelligence*, Vol. 1, pp. 121–170.

1971. Findler, N. V., H. Klein, W. Gould, A. Kowal, and J. Menig. "Studies on Decision Making Using The Game of Poker," *Proc. IFIP Congress* Book TA-7, pp. 50–61. Ljubljana, Yugoslavia.

N. V. FINDLER

# HIGHER EDUCATION, COMPUTERS IN

For articles on related subjects *see* EDUCATION IN COMPUTING SCIENCE; and DIGITAL COMPUTERS.

For articles on related terms *see* ENIAC; MARK I; and SWAC.

**Universities as Computer Builders.** Much of the early research and development of calculators and (later) stored program digital computers was carried out by university personnel. A few examples are the "large systems of linear algebraic equations" solver at Iowa State College (1937–1942); the Mark I or IBM Automatic Sequence Controlled Calculator at Harvard (1939–1944); the ENIAC (Electronic Numerical Integrator and Computer) at the University of Pennsylvania (1942–1946); the EDVAC (Electronic Discrete Variable Computer) at the University of Pennsylvania (1945–1950); the ORDVAC (Ordnance Variable Automatic Computer) and the ILLIAC (Illinois Automatic Computer) at the University of Illinois (1948–1952); the MSUDC (Michigan State University Discrete Computer) at Michigan State; the Whirlwind I at the Massachusetts Institute of Technology (1947–1950); and the SWAC (Standards Western Automatic Computer) at University of California at Los Angeles.

In recent years very few computers have been built by universities. Even the ILLIAC IV developed at the University of Illinois was largely subcontracted to computer manufacturers. However, the University of Illinois continues to be active in computer design with ILLIAC V already under way.

**Universities as Computer Users.** During the early 1950s universities began to acquire computers for general use in their research activities. Many were brought in to handle large-scale statistical and data processing tasks and were usually augmented by large punched-card processing machine installations. Early calculators included IBM's 602A, 604, and CPC (Card Programmed Calculator). The first stored-program digital computer to be utilized by universities in large numbers was the IBM 650, which was made available for several years (approximately 1955–1963) on a 60% educational allowance.

By early 1960 there were approximately 125 colleges and universities in the United States which had one or more stored-program digital computers. Sixty-five of these had the IBM 650, while the remaining 60 were about equally split between smaller machines and those that were larger than the 650 (Keenan, 1959). Table 1 shows that the growth in the numbers of colleges and universities obtaining computers or acquiring access to computers was rapid. By 1975 practically every college and university campus will, indeed *must*, have access to computer facilities for instruction, research, and/or administration.

**Table 1.** Estimated Number of U.S. Institutions of Higher Education with Access to Computer Facilities

| | Total No. of Institutions or Campuses | No. with Access to Computers |
|---|---|---|
| 1960 | 2000 (Est.) | 125 |
| 1965* | 2219 | 707 |
| 1967* | 2477 | 980 |
| 1970* | 2807 | 1681 |
| 1973† | 2850 (Est.) | 2240 |

* John W. Hamblen, 1967.
† John W. Hamblen, 1970.

The use of computers has permeated nearly every discipline. These widespread uses have pushed computer costs upward from 2% to 5% of the institutions' total budgets in most cases. Table 2 shows estimates of the total expenditures and expenditures per student for fiscal year 1970. Approximately three-fourths of computer funds for the 1970 fiscal year came from these institutions' own funds, with the remaining quarter coming from federal government agencies.

**Table 2.** Estimated Expenditures for Computing Total and per Student by Highest Level of Degree Offering 1969–70*

| Highest Degree Offered | Total Expenditure (Millions) | Expended per Pupil ($) |
|---|---|---|
| Associate | 63 | 33 |
| Bachelor's | 26 | 33 |
| Master's | 65 | 36 |
| Doctorate | 318 | 106 |
| Total | 472 | 63 |

* John W. Hamblen, 1967.

By fiscal year 1973 the total expenditures for computing by U.S. institutions of higher education was expected to have reached $600 million and to reach one billion dollars by 1980 (Hamblen, 1967).

DISTRIBUTION OF EXPENDITURES BY FUNCTION. An estimated 30% of the reported expenditures were for on-campus instructional uses of the computing facilities. More than half of these expenditures (18%) were for credit instruction at the institution (see Fig. 1). Approximately 32% was for research and 34% for institutional administration.

In dollar amounts these estimates are roughly $142 million for instruction, $151 million for research, and $161 million for administration. The remaining 4%, or about $19 million, includes services to other educational institutions (estimated to be 3%) and local industry and government agencies (1%).

STUDIES ON COMPUTERS IN HIGHER EDUCATION. The first comprehensive study to be conducted on the status of computers in higher education was conducted by the National Research Council and published in 1966 (Keenan, 1966). This report is commonly known as the Rosser report, after the study committee chairman, Barkley J. Rosser. This was followed by a publication by the

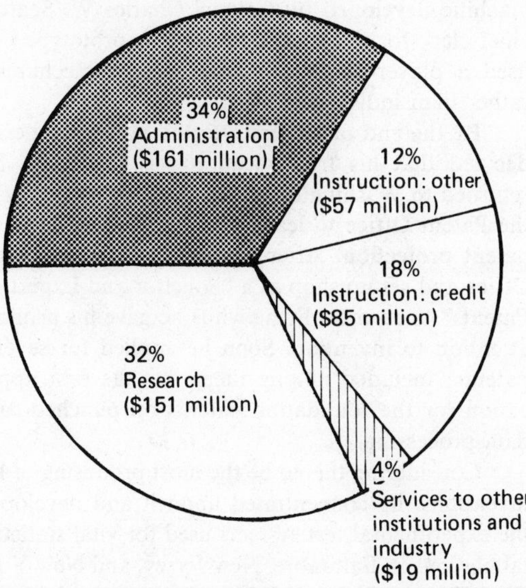


**Fig. 1.** Estimated distribution of expenditures for instruction, research, and administrative uses of computers in U.S. higher education, 1969–1970.

President's Science Advisory Committee (Pierce, 1967), commonly referred to as the Pierce report, and a publication on the first of three national surveys conducted by the Southern Regional Education Board for the National Science Foundation (Hamblen, 1967). Reports have also been published on studies sponsored by the American Council on Education (Caffrey and Mosmann, 1967) EDUCOM (Mosmann, 1973), and the Rand Corporation (Levien, 1971, 1972)

### Associations, Groups, and Societies with Interests in Computers in Higher Education.

ACM/SIGUCC, Special Interest Group on University Computer Centers and ACM/SIGCSE, Special Interest Group on Computer Science Education of the Association for Computing Machinery, 1133 Avenue of the Americas, New York, N.Y. 10036.

AACRAO, American Association of Collegiate Registrars and Admissions Officers, One Dupont Circle, Suite 330, Washington, D.C. 20036.

AEDS, Association for Educational Data Systems, 1201 Sixteenth St. N.W., Washington, D. C. 20036.

CUMREC, College and University Machine Record Conference, 42 Hannah Administration Bldg., Michigan State University, East Lansing, Mich. 48823.

CAUSE, College and University System Exchange, 737 29th St., Boulder, Col. 80302.

EDUCOM, Interuniversity Communications Council, Box 364, Princeton, N. J. 08540.

### References

1959. Keenan, Thomas. "Survey of University Computing Centers," Computing Center, University of Rochester. Rochester, N.Y.

1966. Keenan, Thomas A. (Ed.). *Digital Computer Needs in Universities and Colleges*. Washington D.C.: National Research Council.

1967. Caffrey, John, and Charles Mosmann. *Computers on Campus*. Washington, D.C.: American Council on Education.

1967. Hamblen, John W. *Computers in Higher Education: Expenditures, Sources of Funds and Utilization for Research and Instruction 1964–65 with Projections for 1968–69*. Atlanta, Ga.: Southern Regional Education Board.

1967. Pierce, John R. (Chairman of Study Committee). *Computers in Higher Education*. Washington, D.C.: White House.

1970. Hamblen, John W. *Inventory of Computers in U.S. Higher Education 1966–67: Utilization and Related Degree Programs*. Government Printing Office, Washington, D.C.: Superintendent of Documents, GPO, NS1.2:C75, Catalog No. NS1.2:C73/1969–70.

1971. Levien, R. *Computers in Instruction: Their Future for Higher Education*. Santa Monica, CA.: Rand Corporation.

1972. Goldstine, Herman H. *The Computer: From Pascal to Von Neumann*. Princeton, N.J.: Princeton University Press.

1972. Levien, R., et al. *The Emerging Technology, Instructional Uses of the Computer in Higher Education*. New York: McGraw-Hill.

1973. Hamblen, John W. *Computer Manpower—Supply and Demand—By States*. St. James, Mo.: Information Systems Consultants.

1973. Mosmann, Charles. *Academic Computers in Service*. San Francisco: Jossey-Bass Publishers.

J. W. HAMBLEN

# HOLLERITH, HERMAN

For articles on related subjects *see* DIGITAL COMPUTERS: History; IBM CARD; and NINETY-COLUMN CARD.
For article on related biographical information *see* WATSON, THOMAS, SR.

Herman Hollerith (b. Buffalo, N. Y., 1860; d. Washington, D. C., 1929) was the inventor of punched-card data processing and founder of a firm that evolved to become IBM.

For the quarter-century from 1890 to World War I, he had a virtual monopoly on punched-card data processing. He held the foundation patents on the field (U.S. Patents 395 781–395 783) and nearly 50 other United States and foreign patents on basic techniques and equipment. He developed applications of punched-card data processing to many fields of endeavor, including the Census, medical and public health statistics, railroad and public utility accounting, stock and inventory control, and factory cost accounting.

Many basic decisions he made at, or before, the turn of the 20th century persist today. Punched cards today are the size of dollar bills of that era because Hollerith found it economical to buy cabinets and drawers subdivided in that size. The positional coding used on punched cards (Hollerith code) has evolved directly from decisions he made about card design when designing the first column-by-column keypunch for the 1901 Census of Agriculture. Even the practice of IBM and other firms to lease and maintain their own data processing equipment originated in Hollerith's decisions made prior to 1900.

Upon graduation from Columbia University in 1879, Hollerith took a job with the Census, where he became the protégé of Colonel John Shaw Billings, an Army surgeon who was also serving as director of the division of vital statistics for the Census. Billings suggested to Hollerith that a good machine to do the purely mechanical work of tabulating population and similar statistics was badly needed and that a technique of using cards with the description of each individual punched into them was a good approach to the problem. Intrigued by this suggestion, Hollerith made a study of the problem and determined to his own satisfaction that it was feasible.

In 1882 Hollerith followed General Francis Walker from the Census to M.I.T., where he became an instructor in mechanical engineering. While there he worked hard on his "Census machine" invention, concentrating initially upon a variant of an earlier machine developed by Colonel Charles W. Seaton, chief clerk for the 1870 Census. This prototype had used a player-piano roll type of feed mechanism rather than individual cards.

By the end of his first year at M.I.T., Hollerith decided that his true vocation was invention. He returned to Washington and secured a position with the Patent Office to learn the arts of invention and patent protection. After a year, he left the Patent Office and set up shop as a "Solicitor and Expert on Patents" to earn his living while he gave his primary attention to invention. Soon he applied for several patents; included among them was the first application for the foundation patents on punched-card data processing.

Considering this to be the most promising of his inventions, he concentrated upon it and developed the experimental test systems used for vital statistics tabulations in Baltimore, New Jersey, and New York City. During this period, his system evolved from a simple machine with cards punched by a conductor's ticket punch to a complete system. This system included a pantographlike punch, a tabulating machine with a large number of clocklike counters (each capable of counting up to 10,000 occurrences), and a simple, electrically actuated sorting box for classifying and grouping cards in accordance with the categories punched into them.

In 1889 his system was installed in the Army Surgeon General's office to handle Army medical statistics. A description of this system and his plans for the Census was accepted by Columbia as a doctoral dissertation, and he was awarded a Ph.D. "for achievement" in 1890. Also in 1889, a comparative test made of the Hollerith and two competitive systems caused the Hollerith system to be chosen for use in the 1890 Census. Austria, Canada, Italy, Norway, and Russia were soon investigating and adopting Hollerith equipment for their population censuses. These early systems could only tally, not add or accumulate, totals one at a time.

Shortly after 1900, Hollerith began developing a second generation of his equipment. A new type of card design arranged numeric information in columns and permitted development of a simple, new kind of keypunch, an automatic-feed card sorter, and an automatic-feed tabulator of vastly improved performance. These new systems could accumulate numbers of any size, and thus were obviously applicable to many situations other than census and similar statistical work. Hollerith soon spread their use to an amazing variety of industries. They even went overseas with the American Expeditionary Forces in World War I.

About 1905 the management in the Census Bureau began to object to Hollerith's profits and sponsored alternative developments designed to break his monopoly. These competitive systems were widely adopted, once Hollerith's fundamental patents expired, and often led the data processing industry into new developments. Because this competition resulted in a need for increased capitalization, Hollerith sold his patent and proprietary rights to a holding company in 1912. This relieved him of day-by-day management chores and he became a highly paid consultant. Before long, Thomas J. Watson, Sr., was brought in to head Hollerith's old company, but Watson's commercialism and Hollerith's devotion to purely inventive objectives caused dissension. Watson's interests prevailed, and Hollerith's contributions and achievements were soon absorbed in the greater representative image of IBM.

REFERENCE

Hollerith, Virginia "Biographical Sketch of Herman Hollerith," *ISIS*, Vol. 62, No. 210, pp. 69–78.

W. F. LUEBBERT

## HONEYWELL.

*See* MANUFACTURERS, COMPUTER.

## HOSPITAL INFORMATION SYSTEMS

For articles on related subjects *see* INFORMATION SYSTEMS; MANAGEMENT INFORMATION SYSTEMS; and MEDICAL APPLICATIONS.

The automation of health-care delivery is variously referred to as the development of hospital, health, or medical information systems. These systems have in common a high level of on-line operation and a file structure based on a patient-oriented record.

The physician and nurse are central to a hospital information system (HIS), since most activities in a medical environment are based on a physician's order. Such an order may activate tasks in many areas: the pharmacy, the clinical laboratory, the kitchen, accounting, etc. It is obvious that communication capability is a primary requirement. It has been shown that 20 to 30% of the nursing staff time, and a similar percentage of total hospital costs, are related to information processing. Beyond simple communication services, a HIS system may be used in a pharmacy for the preparation of medication schedules, drug compatibility, and interaction checking. Clinical laboratory tasks such as blood collection schedules, test scheduling and instrument monitoring, result normalization based on standard test samples, and outcome posting, with flags indicating abnormal or out-of-range results may be produced by modules of an HIS. Other tasks can include the generation of patient care plans, diet planning, inventory maintenance, scheduling of staff, etc..

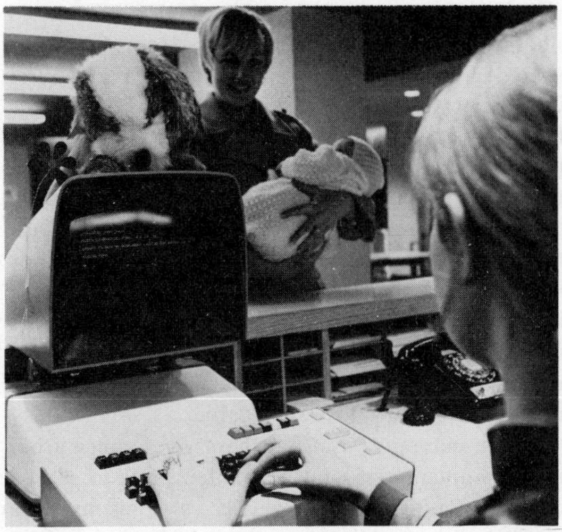

**Fig. 1.** Cathode-ray tube terminal displays clinic scheduling information coming from the Honeywell central computer at Children's Hospital Medical Center, Boston.

For the tasks mentioned above, only a fairly transitory record has to be kept on the patient. In order to impact the medical care to a greater extent, a computerized medical patient record will have to be kept. The entry of physicians' and nurses' observations on the patient, combined with formal categorizations such as problem statements and diagnoses, will allow summarization of a patient's history and progress. Given adequate decision aiding tools, the possibility for useful interaction for the physician emerges. Without such feedback, the utility to the physician of using a computer entry device, no matter how sophisticated, is at best negligible.

Much data entry into actual systems is performed by the nursing staff and ward clerks. A long-term medical record implies extension of the HIS into the outpatient, community pharmacy, and private physician areas. A well-organized medical record may distribute the responsibility for health-care delivery among physicians, nurses, specialists, and medical paraprofessionals, since less will depend on the memory of the physician in attendance. The goal of a complete and integrated medical record is, however, quite elusive, unless supported through forms of comprehensive health insurance.

Systems providing major or minor portions of the tasks outlined above have been provided in a variety of forms. Entry devices may be readers of prepunched cards, large function keyboards, conventional typewriter terminals, as well as CRT terminals. The most successful methods have utilized lightpen or finger-touch selection from CRT-presented choice lists. In a well-structured hierarchy of choices, any specific order may be entered with three to seven screen loads. A major problem has been the poor quality of output presentation. Excessive quantitites of information printed, sometimes noisily, on identical white sheets using lines of uniform uppercase-only characters with unpleasant fonts have made the tasks of searching for relevant information in the record harder instead of easier. A more graphic presentation of the patient's state, as now frequently provided by the nursing staff, may make HIS output more acceptable.

The computer systems themselves range from minicomputers doing fairly isolated tasks to shared computer utilities. Conceptually, systems may be divided into modular systems, which perceive independent development of applications with subsequent linkages, and total systems, which attempt to cover all services within one scheme. Difficulties with modular development have been due to program incompatibilities and lack of intercomputer communication standards, which have prevented the integration of individually successful application modules from many sources into a cohesive network. The total systems have been associated with high initial costs and long delays before they could achieve productive operation. The delays tend to have the effect that the hardware is no longer optimal when the system becomes operational. Total systems have generally employed large central facilities, and here the high demands on file and communication capabilities, which are required to provide CRT terminal interaction with response times on the order of a second, have caused additional problems.

The increasing demands on health-care quantity, quality, distribution, and cost control will have the effect that, even with the problems listed above, continued attempts at HIS implementations will be made. With better understanding of system requirements, a suitable system architecture can be developed. With imaginative human interface engineering, the acceptability of these systems can be increased. With the inclusion of a complete range of services, economic benefits may accrue which will make the concept of an HIS truly viable.

G. WIEDERHOLD

# HOST SYSTEM

For articles on related subjects *see* MICROPROGRAMMING; and MULTIPROGRAMMING.

A host system or a host computer is the physical system that interprets a program. The program is written on a "logical machine", which is usually not the same as the physical machine (host system). These differences arise because the physical system either does not possess or does not allocate all features or resources directly requested by the logical machine (program). The distinction between host system and logical system is especially notable in two areas: multiprogramming systems and microprogrammed (emulated) systems.

In multiprogramming systems the host system is responsible for allocating storage and I/O resources to each of the logical machines (i.e., in effect, active programs), which are usually called "virtual" machines, as they are required. This allows a number of virtual machines to share the physical resources without logical conflict (i.e., without any programmer intervention in the source programs) and at the same time more effectively use the resources of the physical host system.

In microprogrammed systems the notion of host system applies to the physical machine that interprets (emulates) the programs written in other machine languages. The machine being emulated by the host machine is said to be the "image" machine (sometimes the term "virtual" is also used to describe this situation).

M. J. FLYNN

# HUMANITIES APPLICATIONS

For articles on related subjects *see* ARTS APPLICATIONS; INFORMATION RETRIEVAL; and SOCIAL SCIENCE APPLICATIONS.
For articles on related terms *see* COMPUTER GRAPHICS; DATA BANK; HEURISTICS; PATTERN RECOGNITION; and SYNTAX, SEMANTICS AND PRAGMATICS.

The use of the computer in the humanities entails the preparation of information banks, which include data and rules specifying procedures to be used for applications involving either pattern recognition or pattern generation, or both.

**Information Banks in the Humanities.** The preparation of information banks implies preliminary decisions as to formatting and editing. Because many of the traditional categories in the humanities are not rigorously defined, investigators wishing to use such categories often pre-edit the text so as to be able to retrieve information concerning, for example, syntactic or semantic patterns. Thus, at this stage of the use of the computer in the humanities, text formatting and editing sometimes makes use of poorly defined elements and weakly defined or, really, nonexistent models. For example, categories such as image or texture are not sufficiently defined to permit specification by rule for their recognition by the computer; images must be identified in advance by the human being using the computer.

As empirical data gathering, model building, and model testing facilitated by the computer grow, the need for formatting information so as to anticipate the theory upon which the conclusions are based should decline. Rather, it should be possible to "bank" information in its conventional form and then provide rules for sorting the elements in the bank into desired categories. At that point, preparation of information banks will clearly be a step prior to, and separate from, pattern recognition and pattern generation applications in the humanities. At present, although the functional distinction is relatively clear, the methodological distinction is not.

Types of information banks currently used in computer-based applications in the humanities include bibliographies, texts, dictionaries, historical records, and rules for combining discrete elements of whatever artifact is being generated. For the value of bibliographical data for information retrieval, the reader is referred to the article on that subject. The annual Shakespeare bibliography and the U.S. Modern Language Association's annual bibliography are examples of major data banks of this sort for the humanities. General-purpose dictionaries (e.g., Webster's, Random House) that are available in computer-accessible form are used by humanists (Olney and Ramsey, 1970), for example, to search for literary themes; in addition, humanists have prepared special-purpose dictionaries (e.g., The Old English Dictionary) for research related to their special fields of interest (Cameron, Frank, and Leyerle, 1970).

An example of an information bank consisting of historical records is the 11-volume, 8,000-page, 3-million word collection on the London stage, 1660–1800, an

> exhaustive calendar of plays, entertainments, afterpieces, dancing, and singing, together with casts, box receipts, advertising, contemporary comment, and all available information about scenery, theatre construction, costuming, audiences, management, and production, compiled from the playbills, newspapers, and theatrical diaries of the period. (Daland and Schneider, 1971.)

If this material were not available in computer-accessible form, the scholar who

> wished to determine how many times actor X and actress Y performed in the same play together during their careers might find it necessary to scan a period of 15 to 20 years (possibly 800 to 1000 pages) to exhaust all the possibilities of intersection, and yet the list of joint performances might not fill a page. (Daland and Schneider, 1971.)

Historical records of all sorts, ranging from voting records to land use records, are being put into computer-accessible form for scholarly research (see Dollar and Jensen, 1971; *Historical Methods*; Swierenga, 1970).

Information banks of recorded speech are of interest to humanists because research based upon such banks may provide useful analytical categories for the auditory components of language and literature. Speech information banks require formidable quantities of storage (a 2,400-foot magnetic tape will hold 5 to 10 minutes of digitized speech), and techniques for coping with the data are likewise complex.

Information banks comprising rules are currently of importance for pattern generation and will become increasingly significant for pattern recognition as the categories being recognized become ever more amenable to description through a precisely defined procedure. An example of such a bank of rules would be those necessary to enable the computer to approximate the form of a sonnet; e.g., number of lines, number of syllables per line, stress patterns within the line. Some rules (e.g., number of lines) would be obligatory, whereas options would be available as to the selection of some others; e.g., within certain metrical contexts an anapest (∪∪/) might be substituted for an iamb (∪/).

**Pattern Recognition.** Pattern recognition based upon data banks consisting of bibliographies is described in the article on information retrieval. Pattern recognition based upon historical records is analogous to that involved in bibliographies—i.e., searching for either a particular type of record (e.g., cast listings in Daland and Schneider's "London Stage") or a specified word (e.g., the name of a particular actress in the "London Stage").

Pattern recognition for which the data banks are texts in machine-readable form—dictionaries, and indeed sometimes bibliographies and historical records—might be thought of as falling into three divisions: (1) recognition, using categories that derive from standard graphic conventions; (2) recognition, using categories that derive from traditional approaches to language and literature; (3) recognition, using categories that derive from theories or models concerning the description of discrete and continuous events (from the mathematical sciences).

Examples of categories that derive from standard graphic conventions include characters, words, sentences, and strings longer than sentences. Occurrences of single characters or short strings of characters are of interest to humanists concerned with manuscript *stemma* or with various editions of a given text. The derivation of one manuscript from another is of interest for two reasons: One is that the scholar would like to find the manuscript that is either the original or closest to the original manuscript of the text in question; the other is that shifts in spelling provide data for studies in the phonological history of a given language (Mullen, 1971). Comparisons of editions of a given text are undertaken in order to list the variants among them, and thus to arrive at either an edition that seems best to reflect the presumed original or to arrive at an edition that at least exhibits internal consistency (Cabaniss, 1970).

The presence or absence of specific characters in a text may also provide guides to the style of the author. Insofar as linguistics is considered part of the humanities, the character and short strings of characters are important guides to morphology; e.g., the discrimination of roots, affixes, and plural morphs. Such morphological patterns are of obvious importance for the study of foreign languages, traditionally considered humanistic disciplines.

The humanities have used the word as a category most centrally in indexes and concordances. An index is generally taken to be a listing of the word together with locations of its occurrence in the text. A concordance is a listing of the word together with a specific quantity of context for each of its occurrences in the text. For the production of research aids such as these, the computer is now regarded as an indispensable tool by scholars in the humanities. Words are also used to provide stylistic clues, which in turn are sometimes used for author identification (McKinnon and Webster, 1969). For example, the study by Mosteller and Wallace (1964) of the Federalist papers indicated that it is possible to discriminate between those written by Hamilton and those written by Madison on the basis of certain function words (e.g., articles, prepositions, conjunctions) that occur in the known writings of one author at a frequency significantly different from that in the known writings of the other author. Manuscript and text collation also depend heavily upon words, as well as characters, for purposes of comparison (Spencer, 1972).

Sentences and strings longer than sentences, such as paragraphs and chapters, are categories that derive from standard graphic conventions and may provide guides to various components of style. Decisions as to the units by which these strings are measured may well affect their usefulness for a particular problem. For example, although Mosteller and Wallace (1964) could find no significant difference among the sentence lengths of Madison and Hamilton when measured in words, Robert Wachal has suggested in a doctoral dissertation (on Linguistic Evidence, Statistical Inference, and Disputed Authorship) that there may be a significant difference if those sentences are measured in terms of syllables. Whatever the measure, this approach to pattern recognition can be replicated by other scholars as long as the unit is defined according to standard graphic conventions. Perhaps that is the salient point about pattern recognition based upon categories that derive from standard graphic conventions. The conventions can be clearly defined, departures from the conventions can be clearly specified, and experimentation is thus replicable.

It is with the next group of categories, those traditionally used for studies in language and literature, that replicability and reliability become a serious problem. Among the categories that fit into this general class are those drawn from phonology, syntactics, and semantics, as well as terms that refer to readability and terms such as unity and texture which refer to other terms such as structure and content, etc.

Phonology is concerned with the sound of the spoken language, and one might assume that there are categories related to phonology analogous to those, such as characters and words, which relate to the graphic representation of the language. It is indeed possible to produce information banks of digitized speech and subsequently to make statements concerning acoustic properties such as frequency and intensity (amplitude). Unfortunately, the quantity of storage demanded by even short strings of digitized speech has thus far prevented storing literary or linguistic strings in sufficient length to permit the development or discovery of categories arising directly from the acoustic data—categories that would facilitate discussion of metrics, rhythmical patterns, or rhyming patterns. If, given acoustic parameters, the latter categories no longer seem relevant because they lack equivalent precision, then acoustic patterns might be used to distinguish one utterance, or one poem, or one prose work from another.

Current efforts to map the short strings of acoustic signals that are available onto graphic conventions such as characters, combinations of characters, or words are extremely complicated pattern recognition problems. Syllable recognition can now be achieved approximately 80% of the time, but identification of word boundaries is much less successful. (For further discussion of the pattern recognition problem in speech see the article on speech recognition.)

In lieu of direct input and analysis of acoustic signals, phonology has been studied on the basis of human graphic transcriptions of the auditory component of language and literature. Although linguists are extensively trained and become skilled at making such transcriptions, recording variabilities do introduce very serious problems as far as reliable replicability is concerned. Nonetheless, mappings from phonetic transcriptions onto graphic conventions, and vice versa, are of interest to humanists wishing to describe patterns of rhyme, of rhythm, and of auditory phenomena.

Syntactic categories are used for stylistic discrimination applied to author identification or to changes in the style of a given author over time. The syntactic categories used depend upon traditional intuitions concerning parts of speech, plus intuitions concerning the text being examined, or upon a particular linguistic model, e.g., transformational or phrase-structure. (See Burton, 1970; Cluett, 1971; Green, 1971; Koster, 1970; Milic, 1970.) The use of the computer to locate syntactic patterns for which the syntactic units are defined on the basis of traditional intuitions or even on the basis of various models usually implies pre-editing of the text. Because the syntactic categories used in such pre-editing are not sufficiently rigorously defined, efforts to replicate the use of a particular set of categories may not succeed. Insofar as a given scholar is consistent in his use of a set of categories, he may well be able to make statements concerning use of the different categories in the text he is examining. But if another scholar questions his consistency and attempts to replicate his work, difficulties may ensue because the categories themselves are somewhat amorphous (Koster, 1970; Milic, 1970). Computer-based parsers have thus far not been used for extended studies of syntactic patterns in literary or other texts, presumably because such parsers tend to provide so many possible syntactic readings for a given sentence as to make analysis of such readings for extensive quantities of text extremely difficult and time consuming. Probabilistic parsers, which give the single best (most probable) parsing for a given sentence, seem most promising for this application (Stolz et al., 1965).

Semantics, which is just coming into its own in linguistics, has long been of interest to humanists. Categories such as texture, theme, and tone presumably refer to semantic implications of words and to the relations among those words in a text. Computer-based efforts to utilize semantics in literary analysis have depended upon interplay between words in the text and words in standard reference works such as *Roget's International Thesaurus* or portions of the Oxford English Dictionary (Sedelow and Sedelow, 1966, 1967, 1969; Spolsky, 1970). For literary analysis, large stores of semantic information are necessary; hence artificial intelligence efforts to cope with semantics (Quillian, 1969; Winograd, 1972)—efforts that deal with very restricted universes of discourse—are not thus far viable for literary analysis. Rather, computer-based work in the humanities rely on reference works (dictionaries and thesauri) reflecting general use of the language as both validated and modified through time. The difficulty in using such reference works is that their own structures—particularly of thesauri—are not sufficiently characterized so as to ensure that the research scholar knows the biases they introduce into his results. If such references are to be used with assurance, research on modes of characterizing these reference works is necessary; some such research is in progress (Olney and Ramsey, 1970; Revard, 1969; Sedelow and Sedelow, 1969). When semantic networks both external and internal to texts can be more adequately characterized, categories such as texture and tone may either assume new meaning or completely disappear as viable indicators of literary style and structure.

Other traditional categories such as readability and dramatic climax depend either upon categories (e.g., syntactic and semantic) that fall into this general area of categories traditional to language and literature or upon categories such as word length which depend upon standard graphic conventions, or both.

The third major category area important to pattern recognition in the humanities is that derived from the mathematical sciences, particularly statistics and probability, information theory, and analysis (especially relevant to acoustical phenomena). Models in the mathematical sciences can, of course, be rigorously defined and thus tested extensively against data. Because of its quantity, humanistic verbal data is especially appealing to mathematical model builders who in the past have sometimes been dependent upon the restricted number of subjects convenient to social science experiments or to restricted instances of any given case. On the other hand, the application of mathematical and statistical models to natural language data is often hampered by the very quantity of data. Contingency tables, transition matrices, and other structures requisite to mathematical and statistical models quickly become so large that they exceed the capacity of even very large digital computers. Efforts to find models that fit data more adequately (e.g., nonparametric statistical models) as well as to find ways of managing data so as to increase data computability are likely to increase dramatically during the coming years as more data becomes available in computer-accessible form and as more model builders become aware of this large storehouse of data available for model testing.

**Pattern Generation.** In many respects, computer-based pattern generation represents the obverse of pattern recognition. At first blush it might seem to be more difficult because it demands rules specifying the way elements being generated are to be combined. This would seem to be more complicated than, for example, a search through a text for occurrences of specified words. It is probably true that the most elementary generation of poetry is more complicated than elementary searches for words. But as pattern recognition efforts become more comprehensive so as to include, for example, semantic relationships, the pattern recognition task then becomes more complicated than elementary generation tasks. An analog might be the greater ease with which computer-based transformational generative grammars are written than are computer-based transformational parsers. It is easier to generate acceptable sentences than to attempt to parse the infinite variety generated by man.

Pattern generation, like recognition, uses information banks such as dictionaries, thesauri, bibliographical information, and banks of rules based upon models or assumptions appropriate to the artifact being generated. For example, generation of haiku poetry would entail specification of the number of lines, the length of lines, acceptable sequencing of syntactic classes, the vocabulary that falls into the general type of vocabulary appropriate to haiku, and some appropriate semantic relationships among the words. Specification of the latter has been minimal in poetry generated to date. For haiku, a verse form for which semantics is relatively obscure anyway, this specification is not so vital, and in fact, in some contemporary poetry, semantic relationships among words are certainly oblique and often distant. The casual reader may not see a great deal of difference between "a great king packed in an acorn" written by a human and "dance, oh life, like a silent tumbleweed!" written by a machine (Borroff, 1971).

Inasmuch as sophisticated pattern generation of language and literature is extremely complicated, in large measure because of semantics, computer-based pattern generation in the humanities will doubtless be used in the foreseeable future for testing models or parts of models of language and literature. The computer may never write like Shakespeare, but it may be used to identify precisely some aspects of the nature of Shakespeare's writing.

Although computer graphics represents pattern generation in a somewhat different sense, its use in the humanities as a heuristic, or aid to insight, should be mentioned. Graphics can help reveal patterns in the structure of a literary or other text. Thus, graphics can show which themes or ideas tend to cluster together in a text and which never appear together, which metrical patterns tend to dominate and where; in short, graphics can be used to represent those elements of the text that have been specified and identified by the computer. Most often, computer graphics provide visual representations of the results obtained by the application of mathematical and statistical models to data.

**Other Applications.** One of the major areas of the humanities for which the scope of this article does not permit coverage is instruction. Computer-assisted instruction is being used in the teaching of foreign languages, and there is a growing effort to use it in teaching composition. For a detailed presentation of current work in computer-assisted instruction, the reader is referred to the article on that subject.

REFERENCES

1964. Mosteller, Frederick, and David Wallace. *Inferences and Disputed Authorship: The Federalist.* Reading, Mass.: Addison-Wesley.

1965. Stolz, Walter S., Percy H. Tannenbaum, and Frederick V. Carstenson. "A Stochastic Approach to the Grammatical Coding of English," *Communications of the ACM*, Vol. 8, No. 6 (June), pp. 399–405.

1966. Sedelow, Sally, and Walter A. Sedelow, Jr. "A Preface to Computational Stylistics," in Jacob Leed (Ed.), *Computer and Literary Style.* Kent, Ohio: Kent State University Press, pp. 1–13.

1967. Sedelow, Sally, and Walter A. Sedelow, Jr. "Stylistic Analysis," in Harold Borko (Ed.), *Automated Language Processing: The State of the Art.* New York: John Wiley, pp. 181–213.

1969. McKinnon, Alistair, and Roger Webster. "A Method of 'Author' Identification," *Computer Studies in the Humanities and Verbal Behavior*, Vol. 2, No. 1 (March) pp. 19–23.

1969. Quillian, Ross M. "The Teachable Language Comprehender: A Simulation Program and Theory of Language," *Communications of the ACM*, Vol. 12, No. 8, pp. 459–476.

1969. Revard, Carter. "On the Compatability of Certain Monsters in Noah's Ark: Using Computers to Study Webster's New Collegiate Dictionary and the Merriam Webster Pocket Dictionary," *Computer Studies in the Humanities and Verbal Behavior*, Vol. 2, No. 2 (August), pp. 446–461.

1969. Sedelow, Sally, and Walter A. Sedelow, Jr. "Categories and Procedures for Content Analysis in the Humanities," in George Gerbner et al. (Eds.), *The Analysis of Communication Content.* New York: John Wiley, pp. 487–499.

1970. Burton, Dolores M. "Aspects of Word Order and Two Plays of Shakespeare," *Computer Studies in the Humanities and Verbal Behavior.* Vol. 3, No. 1 (January), pp. 34–39.

1970. Cabaniss, Margaret Scanlon. "Using the Computer for Text Collation," *Computer Studies in the Humanities and Verbal Behavior*, Vol. 3, No. 1 (January), pp. 1–33.

1970. Cameron, Angus, Roberta Frank, and John Leyerle, (Eds.). *Computers and Old English Concordances.* Toronto: University of Toronto Press.

1970. Koster, Patricia. "Words and Numbers: A Quantitative Approach to Swift and Some Understrappers," *Computers and the Humanities*, Vol. 4, No. 5 (May), pp. 289–303.

1970. Milic, Louis T. "Comment on Mrs. Koster's Article," *Computers and the Humanities*, Vol. 4, No. 5 (May), pp. 304–306.

1970. Olney, John, and Donald Ramsey. "From Machine-Readable Dictionaries to a Lexicon Tester: Progress, Plans, and an Offer." *Computer Studies in the Humanities and Verbal Behavior*, Vol. 3, No. 4 (November).

1970. Spolsky, Ellen. "Computer-Assisted Semantic Analysis of Poetry," *Computer Studies in the Humanities and Verbal Behavior*, Vol. 3, No. 3 (October), pp. 163–168.

1970. Swierenga, Robert P. *Quantification in American History; Theory and Research.* New York: Atheneum.

1971. Borroff, Marie. "Creativity, Poetic Language and the Computer," *The Yale Review*, Vol. 60, No. 4 (June), pp. 481–513.

1971. Cluett, Robert. "Style, Precept, Personality: A Test Case (Thomas Spratt, 1635–1713)," *Computers and the Humanities*, Vol. 5, No. 5 (May), pp. 257–278.

1971. Daland, Will, and Ben R. Schneider, Jr. "The 'London Stage' Information Bank," *Computers and the Humanities*, Vol. 5, No. 4 (March), pp. 209–214.

1971. Dollar, C., and R. Jensen. *Historian's Guide to Statistics.* New York: Holt, Rinehart and Winston.

1971. Green, Donald C. "Formulas and Syntax in Old English Poetry: A Computer Study," *Computers and the Humanities*, Vol. 6, No. 2 (November), pp. 85–94.

1971. Mullen, Karen A. "Using the Computer to Identify Differences Among Text Variants," *Computers and the Humanities*, Vol. 5, No. 4 (March), pp. 193–202.

1972. Spencer, Christopher. "Shakespeare's *Merchant of Venice* in Sixty-Three Editions," *Studies in Bibliography*, Vol. 25, pp. 89–106.

1972. Winograd, Terry. *Understanding Natural Language*. New York: Academic Press.

1967–present. *Historical Methods Newsletter*. Department of History, University of Pittsburgh, Pittsburgh, Pennsylvania.

S. A. SEDELOW

# HYBRID COMPUTERS

For articles on related subjects *see* ANALOG COMPUTERS; DIGITAL TO ANALOG CONVERTERS; SIMULATION; and SPECIAL PURPOSE COMPUTERS.

For articles on related terms *see* PARALLEL PROCESSING; and PROBLEM-ORIENTED LANGUAGES.

**Overview.** The history of hybrid computers and computation has been brief but remarkably active. The impetus for hybrid computation was provided by the important dynamic system simulation and optimization problems arising from programs of the National Aeronautics and Space Administration (NASA) and Department of Defense (DOD) during the late 1950s to middle 1960s. The speed of analog computers in solving differential equations, coupled with the high precision and programmed control capability of digital computers, proved to be an ideal adjunct to the dynamic system design process.

The hybrid computers of the late 1950s consisted chiefly of ad hoc combinations of standard analog and digital computers connected primarily through high-speed digital-to-analog and analog-to-digital converters. The principal justification for the connection was for the digital computer to compute one or more complicated functions of several variables (e.g., aerodynamic drag as a function of velocity and altitude). In this particular form, the digital computer appeared to the analog computers as one or more computational elements.

As small, inexpensive digital computers became available during the early 1960s, they were integrated into large analog computers to automate the detailed and time-consuming machine diagnostic and problem setup and checkout tasks. These computers, however, were basically analog computers with some digital automation. With the increasing awareness of digital computation techniques and the development of higher-level problem-oriented languages, the middle 1960s saw the development of several commercial product lines of integrated hybrid computers with sophisticated support software. Generally, these integrated hybrid computers provided extensive communication and control paths between the constituent analog and digital computers. The digital computer could simulate one or more functional elements for the analog program and still control the computational sequence, with the analog program appearing as a subroutine to the digital computer program. These computers had real impact on personnel previously oriented solely to the analog computer, and attracted the interest of a number of digital computer enthusiasts as well.

Hybrid computers had significant impact on the success of the NASA Apollo program. Most of the Apollo subsystems were simulated extensively during the design process, and many actual subsystems were evaluated and refined in extensive hybrid computer-based simulations involving both real and simulated hardware. Hybrid simulations were also employed extensively in the training of astronauts and support personnel. During the mid-1960s, hybrid computers were also employed in developing the emerging science of digital process control. Much of the now established success of digital computer control in all process industries (paper, petrochemical, nuclear power, etc.) is due to the testing and refinement of early designs through hybrid simulation.

Most of these successful applications of hybrid computers, however, represented straightforward extensions of analog computer simulation techniques. For a time it appeared as though a new discipline of general-purpose hybrid computation was about to emerge. Significant research effort was directed by universities, NASA- and DOD-sponsored laboratories, and the analog and hybrid computer manufacturers to exploit the potential advantages of hybrid computation. This effort was directed at three basic problem areas: (1) the automation of hybrid computers, (2) the use of hybrid computation in new application areas, and (3) the development of new problem-solving procedures exploiting the advantages of hybrid computation.

With the redirection of the NASA and DOD programs in the late 1960s, much of the impetus for continuing work on these three problem areas was removed. The work on development of new applications and new problem-solving procedures had not progressed to the point where continued work on automation of hybrid computation could be economically justified. With the prospects for continued development of the tool appearing bleak, work on new applications tended to slow down also. The net effect has been a general recognition that, while hybrid computers will continue to serve as valuable special-purpose simulation tools, the prospects for development of a general-purpose hybrid computation field are poor. Hybrid computers are, however, actively manufactured by several domestic and a number of foreign firms, and continue to find application in the aerospace and process industries and in education (Fig. 1).

**Fig. 1.** EAI Mini-AC analog-hybrid computer system for educational and small engineering applications.

Despite this less than promising future for hybrid computation, there are several reasons why hybrid computation merits discussion and attention:

1. Hybrid computation had significant economic and intellectual impact on the development of computers and computational processes during a very active period.
2. Hybrid computers will continue to serve an important function in a number of application areas relating to high-performance dynamic system design and to the educational process.
3. Current predictions of the limited future growth of hybrid computation might well be wrong.

This article presents a brief overview of hybrid computer architecture and a method for classifying hybrid computation. Examples of successful hybrid computer applications are then discussed.

**Hybrid Computers.** As suggested in the preceding section, hybrid computers have involved many combinations of sizes of digital computers, analog computers, and interface systems. The interested reader is referred to Bekey and Karplus (1968) for a complete discussion. For purposes of the present discussion, a hybrid computer is a combination of a high-speed electronic analog computer and a modest size scientific digital computer linked together by a communication interface system. Fig. 2 presents a schematic organization of a typical medium-scale hybrid computer.

The analog computer is a collection of parallel computational elements that is hardware expandable; i.e., problem size capability is increased by adding more elements. Speed capability is increased by increasing the bandwidth of individual computational elements. These elements include summers, coefficient elements, integrators, multipliers, function generators, and logic elements. Once activated, the elements operate continuously and simultaneously in time until deactivated.

Precision is limited because all operations involve continuous signals (e.g., voltage as a function of time) of limited magnitude. Precision decreases with increasing signal frequency, but in modern analog computers it remains fairly high for signal frequencies in the kilohertz range. An analog computer program comprises a collection of elements interconnected to perform the operations necessary to solve algebraic and differential equations. In general, an analog computer is best suited for the solution of ordinary differential equations.

The digital computer is generally a serial computational device that is time-expandable; i.e., problem-size capability is increased by specifying a longer list of sequential instructions, which take a correspondingly longer time to be executed. All computation is performed in a central set of registers on numerical representations of variables. A digital computer program comprises the set of instructions specifying the order in which various arithmetic and logical operations are to be performed. Through proper programming, problem size and accuracy may be made arbitrarily large, but only at the expense of increased solution time.

The communication interface system is composed of three subsystems: control, data, and logic. The control subsystem affords the same degree of control to the digital computer program as enjoyed by a conventional analog computer operator; i.e., operational modes, time scales, coefficient element and relay settings, and state readout of all addressable analog and logic elements. The data subsystem

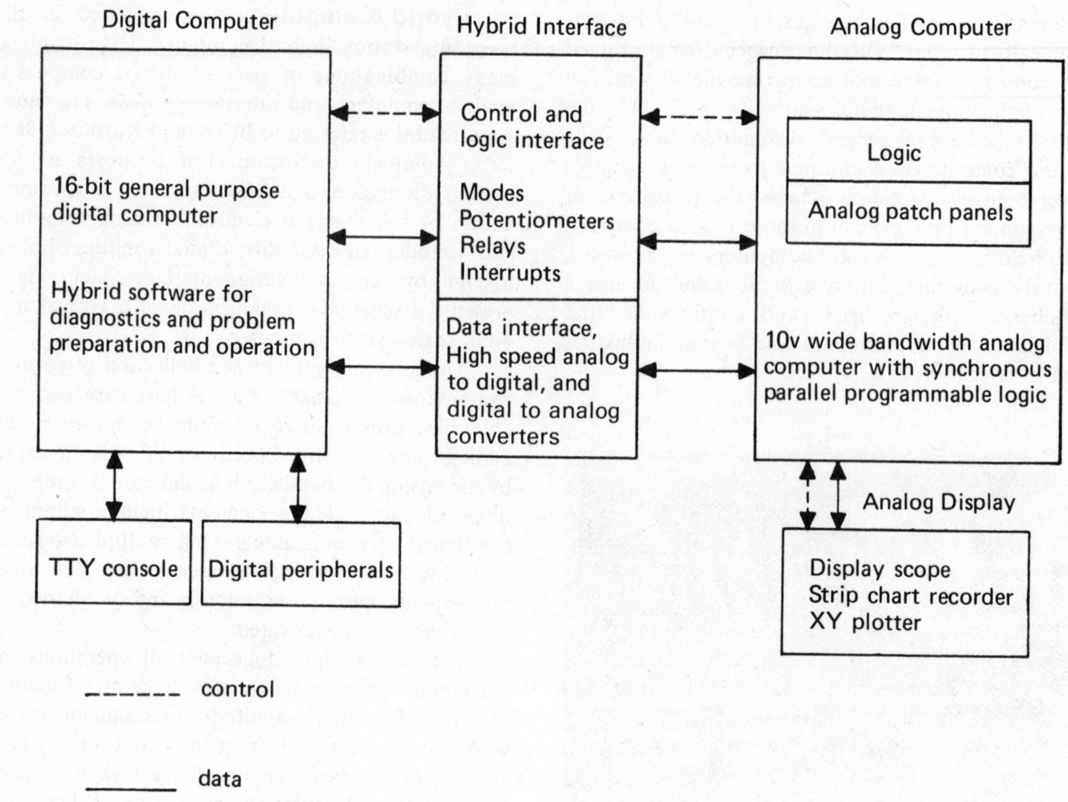


**Fig. 2.** Organization of a medium-scale hybrid computer. (Note: Dashed-line arrows indicate control; solid-line arrows indicate data.)

facilitates the high-speed communication of analog information between the two computers; it includes the high-speed analog-to-digital converter and multiplexer system and a number of digital-to-analog converters and multipliers. The logic subsystem consists of control lines that permit the digital computer program to set and reset logical conditions on the analog, sense lines that permit the digital to read logical conditions on the analog, and a set of interrupt lines that permit conditions on the analog to interrupt the digital program for immediate service.

By making optimal use of the best features of the two types of computers, one can hope to solve certain classes of dynamic system optimization and simulation problems several orders of magnitude faster than is possible with either analog or digital computers alone. The principal problem in hybrid computer programming is the effective utilization of the combined computer complex. The basic idea is to place the high-speed, low-precision, differential equation integrations on the analog computer and the low-speed, high-precision computation and control on the digital computer.

The features of the hybrid computer that distinguish it from the digital and make it particularly well suited for a wide class of dynamic system simulation and optimization problems include:

1. *Speed.* For certain problems, a several hundred thousand dollar hybrid will demonstrate a speed that is orders of magnitude greater than that of a several million dollar digital computer.

2. *Man-Machine Interaction.* The user of a hybrid computer maintains an almost symbiotic relationship with the computer and its high-speed solution of his problem, through the extensive display and control features afforded by the analog computer.

3. *Analog Display.* The analog computer offers intuitively appealing high-speed (display scope and monitor scope) and low-speed hard-copy (stripchart

recorder and X-Y plotter) analog display capabilities.

**Hybrid Computation.** An analysis of different applications from many different fields of engineering and science indicates that the process of hybrid computation is best understood on the basis of control program structure rather than on the origin of the problem to be solved. This classification also contains certain useful information on hybrid computer requirements for satisfactory solution.

CLASSIFICATION OF APPLICATIONS. Hybrid computer progrpams can be classified into four basic levels on the basis of the structural features of the program. Different applications are then easily related to these levels.

*Level 1. Automation of Standard Analog.* Level 1 programs generally involve use of the digital to automate the setup, checkout, and operation of standard analog programs. All communication is through the control interface. A large majority of the work done on hybrid computers in installations with a long history of classical analog computation and many existing application programs fall under this classification.

*Level 2. Digital Control of Analog.* Level 2 programs generally involve use of the digital to control the high-speed operation of the analog computer; structurally, the programs are analog programs, with the digital computer interacting at the beginning and end of each analog solution. Most communication in Level 2 programs is through the high-speed data and logic interfaces, but, in general, it could be handled through the control interface.

Level 2 programs place little emphasis on digital computer speed and no emphasis on time synchronization of the two computers, since the computers alternate operation; i.e., the digital computes new starting conditions on the basis of previous analog runs, initiates a new analog run, waits for completion, etc. In effect, for Level 2 programs, the analog program appears as a high-speed subroutine to the digital program. Many automated design and optimization studies have Level 2 structure.

An example of a Level 2 program would be parameter optimization in a dynamic system where a model of the dynamic system is run on the analog computer and the digital computer program controls a search sequence varying parameters in the analog program, initiating a run, observing the results, modifying the parameters, etc.

*Level 3. Function Storage and Playback.* Level 3 programs generally involve use of the digital computer to store the results of one analog run for playback to successive analog run(s). All run communication in Level 3 programs is through the high-speed data and logic interfaces. As with Level 2, Level 3 programs place little emphasis on the speed of the digital computer and the data interface, but Level 3 does require synchronization of the two computers.

An example of a Level 3 hybrid program would be a solution of a parabolic partial differential equation by a serial continuous space technique: (1) The analog integrates the resulting spatial differential equation at a specific time point, and (2) the digital provides sample information on the function from the preceding time point(s) and samples and stores the results of the analog calculations at the current time point.

*Level 4. Parallel Analog/Digital.* Level 4 programs are the common conception of hybrid programs; i.e., they involve the simultaneous (parallel) interdependent (hybrid) operation of both the analog and digital computers. Level 4 programs place great emphasis on both digital computer and interface speed, as the delay in these components acts as a pure phase shift to that portion of the problem proceeding on the analog. Level 4 programs can be difficult to program and debug because of the exacting synchronization requirements. An example of a Level 4 program would be where the digital program sampled one or more variables from the analog, computed some function of these variables, and sent the new function value to the analog program.

Level 4 programs are characteristically associated with large-scale simulations involving wide dynamic range requirements, extensive nonlinear function generation, and/or extensive simulation of digital subsystem components in a larger dynamic system simulation.

Each of the preceding levels can be further classified on the basis of whether the problem must be solved in "real time." Such a constraint occurs in any simulation involving real system components.

Fig. 3 presents characteristic activity versus time plots for each of the described levels. Also included in Fig. 3 are indications of the flow of information between the active periods of the digital program. This figure should clarify the described level classification of hybrid computation.

**Conclusions.** The future outlook for hybrid computation is not completely favorable. The problems of lack of generality, specialized programming, scaling, poor precision, and poor reproducibility inherent in analog programming tend to be very

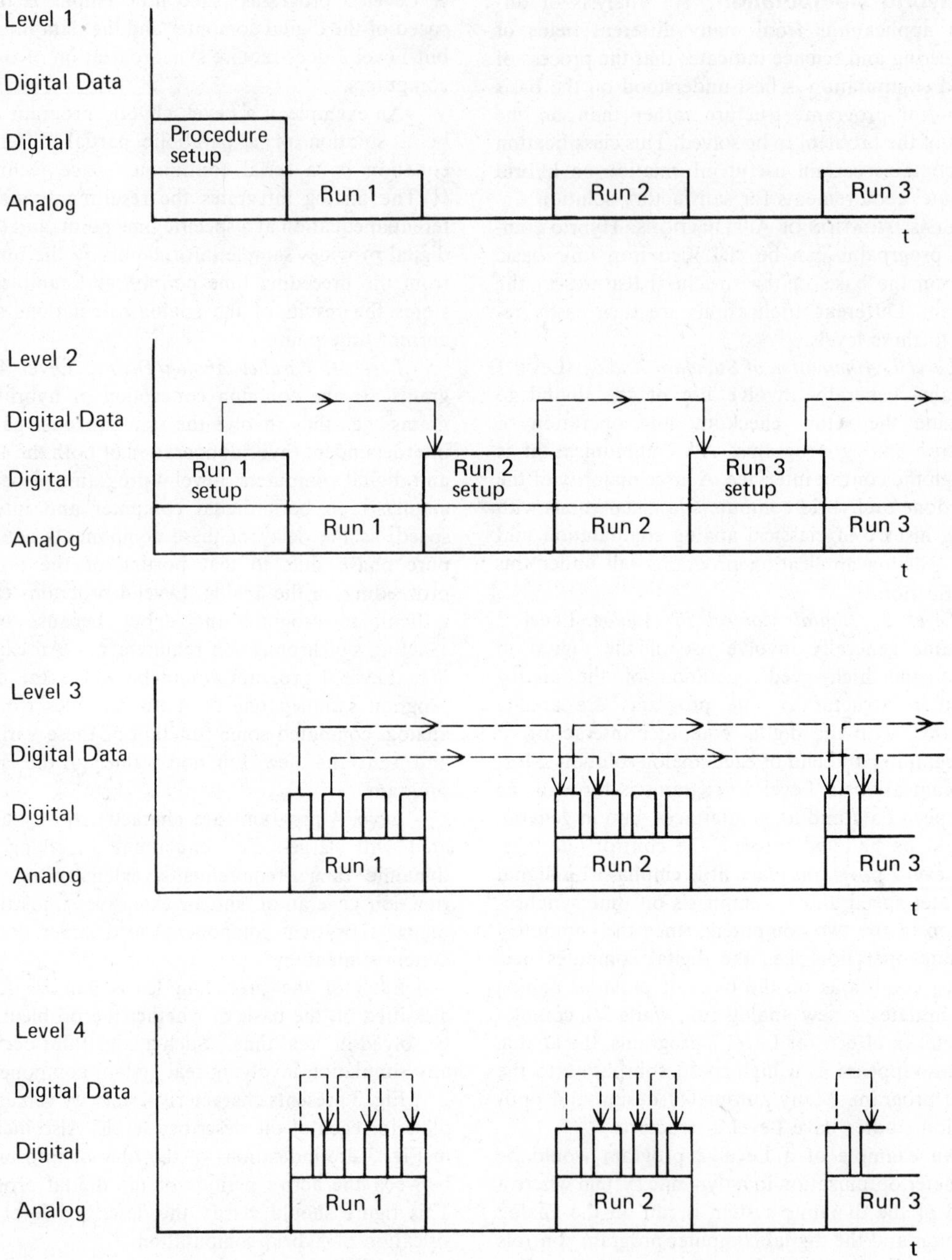


**Fig. 3.** Activity versus time plots for levels of hybrid computation. (Note: Levels 3 and 4 might also have the run setup activity of Level 2.)

difficult to overcome in hybrid programming. The great hope in combining an analog and a digital computer as a hybrid computer is to take advantage of the best features of both; it often turns out that such a combination accentuates the worst features of both in addition to introducing new problems of interconnection.

The best present estimate is that advances in digital simulation languages and techniques, parallel digital computer architecture, and interactive digital graphics will spell the long-term demise of hybrid computation in the form discussed here for all but very special applications. For the present, however, hybrid computers are extremely valuable in a wide range of dynamic system design activities. Current research work on hybrid computation is contributing to a better understanding of the underlying mathematics and is paving the way for future development of computational systems for dynamic system simulation and optimization.

### Reference

1968. Bekey, G. A., and W. J. Karplus. *Hybrid Computation.* New York: John Wiley.

J. C. Strauss

# I

**IBI-ICC.** *See* INTERGOVERNMENTAL BUREAU FOR INFORMATICS.

**IBM.** *See* MANUFACTURERS, COMPUTER.

## IBM 360-370 SERIES

For articles on related subjects *see* GENERATIONS, COMPUTER; MANUFACTURERS, COMPUTER; and OPERATING SYSTEMS: Contemporary.
For articles on related terms *see* CHANNEL; and VIRTUAL MEMORY.

The IBM 360 and 370 systems are so widely used, and many features have been so widely imitated, that it becomes important for everyone in the computer field to be aware of aspects of their hardware and software systems. The literature concerning the 360 and 370 systems would fill a small library. The twentieth edition (IBM document GA 22-6822-19, August 1972) of "IBM System/360 and System/370 Bibliography," which merely "identifies and describes all technical publications and related materials needed by those who plan, program, install and operate the IBM System/360 (model 25 and above) and the System/370," is itself a document that is 283 pages long. The structure of the central computer and its instructions are described in the manual (GA 22-7000) "IBM System/370 Principles of Operation," whose fourth edition, published in January 1973, contains 318 double-column pages. The reader who wishes to gain equivalent insight into the 360 and 370 software systems will not find any single concise manual, but can find a wealth of references in the above mentioned bibliography.

Many features of the 370 are the same as those of the 360, in some cases with minor variations. In the remainder of this article the reader can assume that statements about the 360 apply to the 370 as well. Specific statements about the 370 will not generally apply to the 360, except possibly to some atypical models like the 360 Model 67 and the 360 Model 195.

The basic unit of information in the 360 is the 8-bit byte. Four bytes make up a word. Some of the instructions for the 360s operate on bytes, and others operate on half-words (two bytes), words, double words (eight bytes), and on strings of bytes. An instruction or operand address is always a byte address, the leftmost or most significant byte when a group consisting of more than one byte is being addressed. The 24-bit address field permits the direct addressing of $2^{24} = 16,777,216$ bytes.

The early 360 models were restricted in the size of central memory that could be used. The 360 Model 30 had a maximum of 65,536 bytes of central

**Fig. 1.** The IBM 370 Model 168 multiprocessor system.

memory, and even the top of the line at that time, Model 75, could have only 1,048,576 bytes. The larger models could use auxiliary (though slower) large-core memory of up to 8,388,608 bytes. Large auxiliary, core memory has been eliminated in the 370 series, which permits even the small models to address a virtual memory that spans the full 16-megabyte address space. The amount of real storage permitted is still limited, though growing, on the smaller models. On the larger models, the original announcement limited the amount of real memory to 4 megabytes, but it was clear from the beginning that 370 systems with up to 16 megabytes of real storage would eventually become available. These very large memories are possible because the MOS large-scale integration technology used in the large 370 memories is much more economical than the earlier magnetic core technology.

A special version of the 360 Model 67, which dates back to 1966, provides for the use of full-word (32 bit) addressing, and permits the use of a $2^{32}$ = 4,294,967,296 byte virtual memory. As of this writing it is not known whether this expanded addressing capability will be provided on any models of the 370 series.

The 360 design assumes that the computer will run under control of an interrupt-driven operating system. The system provides for automatic storage in main memory and for automatic loading from a different area of main memory of the contents of essential control registers in response to an interrupt. The contents of these control registers may be considered to form a control word, which is referred to as the "program status word." The program status word contains the address of the next instruction, to permit resumption of a program after an interrupt. It also contains interrupt masks, the storage protection key, and a number of special control fields and control bits. One of these control bits distinguishes between system state and problem state.

The 360 has 16 general-purpose registers that serve as base registers and index registers, and which also serve as fixed-point accumulators and as temporary storage registers. A special instruction provided stores all or a subset of the general registers in memory starting at a specified address. Another instruction can load the general registers (all or a subset) from a specified area of memory. The general registers are 32 bits long, and the most significant 8 bits are ignored in address calculations (except on some of the Model 67 systems mentioned above). The use of the general registers as base and index registers permits the direct addressing of 16,777,216 bytes without requiring that each instruction contain a 24-bit address field. This is illustrated by the RX instruction format, one of several instruction formats used in the 360. Instructions may be one, two, or three half-words long. The RX format uses two half-words as follows:

```
Op Code  R1   X2   B2    D2
-------- ---- ---- ---  ----------
```

The 8-bit op-code specifies the instruction. There are two operands. The first is in the general register, specified by the 4-bit field R1. The second is in memory, at a location determined by adding the 12-bit displacement D2 to the contents of the two general registers specified by B2 and X2.

The 360 has a large and varied instruction set. There are three types of arithmetic: fixed point, floating point, and a special decimal arithmetic that uses strings of 4-bit binary-coded decimal digits as operands. There is a set of privileged instructions that can be executed only in supervisor state. Special instructions are designed to aid in the programming of data-processing applications, of which TRANSLATE AND TEST and EDIT are interesting examples. A special TEST AND SET instruction helps in the handling of interlock problems.

The original 360 system permitted only one multiprocessor model, consisting of two Model 50 central processors. Multiprocessor models of several large 370 central processors have recently become available, with special instructions that permit the processors to signal to each other and to exchange status information.

The central processor has only very rudimentary input/output instructions to start and stop I/O, and to determine the status of an I/O operation that has been started or stopped. Input and output can proceed simultaneously, with computing under control of channels that can directly access main memory and which can execute "channel programs." Selector channels control devices like tapes and disks for fast high-volume data transfers. A multiplexer channel can control large numbers of lower-speed devices.

The most important new peripheral storage device introduced with the 360 series was the 2314, a "direct access" disk storage system consisting of eight disk drives that use removable disk packs. A single controller permits reading or writing from only one disk pack at a time, but a number of seek operations may be proceeding simultaneously. Each pack can hold 28,000,000 bytes of information.

One of the most important new features of the 370 series is the 3330 series of disk systems that replace the 2314s and the block multiplexer channels that control these disk systems. The 3330 stores 100,000,000 bytes per disk pack (200,000,000 bytes in the Model II announced in 1973). The block multiplexer channel and a microprogrammed controller combine to permit much more efficient utilization of disk storage. Fig. 2 is a block diagram of a medium size 370 installation using 3330's for system residence and direct-access storage.

One of the objectives in the introduction of the 370 series was to permit even the small machines in the series to provide large amounts of disk storage, and also to provide communications-handling capabilities that were previously available only on relatively large and expensive models of the 360 series. The very small 370 Model 115, announced early in 1973, is perhaps less powerful as a processor than the 360 Model 30, but it has the full dynamic address translation capability and provides for direct attachment "without need for a separate control unit and selector channel" of up to four 3340 disk units. The 3340, which was introduced at the same time as the 115, has access characteristics similar to those of the 3330, but has a maximum storage capacity of about 70,000,000 bytes per pack.

The central processors of the small 370 models like the 115 and 125 actually consist of several microprogrammed processors in a single compact package. One of these processors executes the central processor instructions. A second handles the disk channel and control functions mentioned above. A third acts as a communications multiplexer, and permits a small number of terminals (up to eight on the 115) to be attached directly to the computer.

The original 360 concept assumed that only one major operating system would be required, which was given the name OS 360 (i.e., Operating System 360). It soon became apparent that many small and intermediate-size 360 systems needed a reasonably sophisticated operating system, but could not afford the high memory space and processor time overhead of OS 360. This led to the early development of an alternative system, DOS (disk operating system), which has been very widely used. Special operating systems were developed for the atypical 360 models such as the 44 and the 67. The time-sharing system, TSS 67, was a very major software effort. IBM also provided an alternative system, CP 67, which achieved greater acceptance than TSS among users of the Model 67. Still another alternative for the Model 67 is MTS (Michigan Terminal System) developed by the University of Michigan.

With the announcement of dynamic address translation as standard for the whole 370 line (except the already obsolescent 155 and 165, and the atypical 195), IBM introduced the VS (Virtual System) operating system. These new operating systems will presumably supersede the earlier OS and DOS systems. The dynamic address translation feature on the 370 series is quite similar to that provided on the 360 Model 67. A number of software systems written for the 360 Model 67 have been converted to

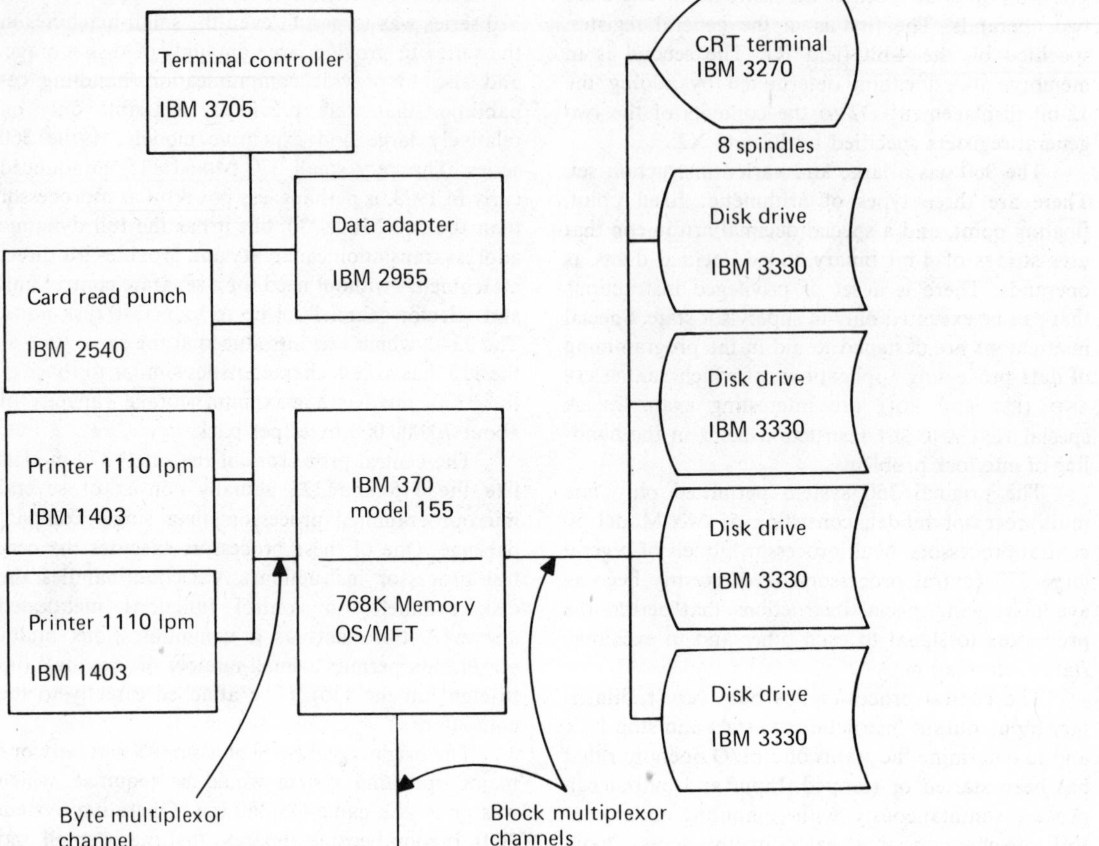

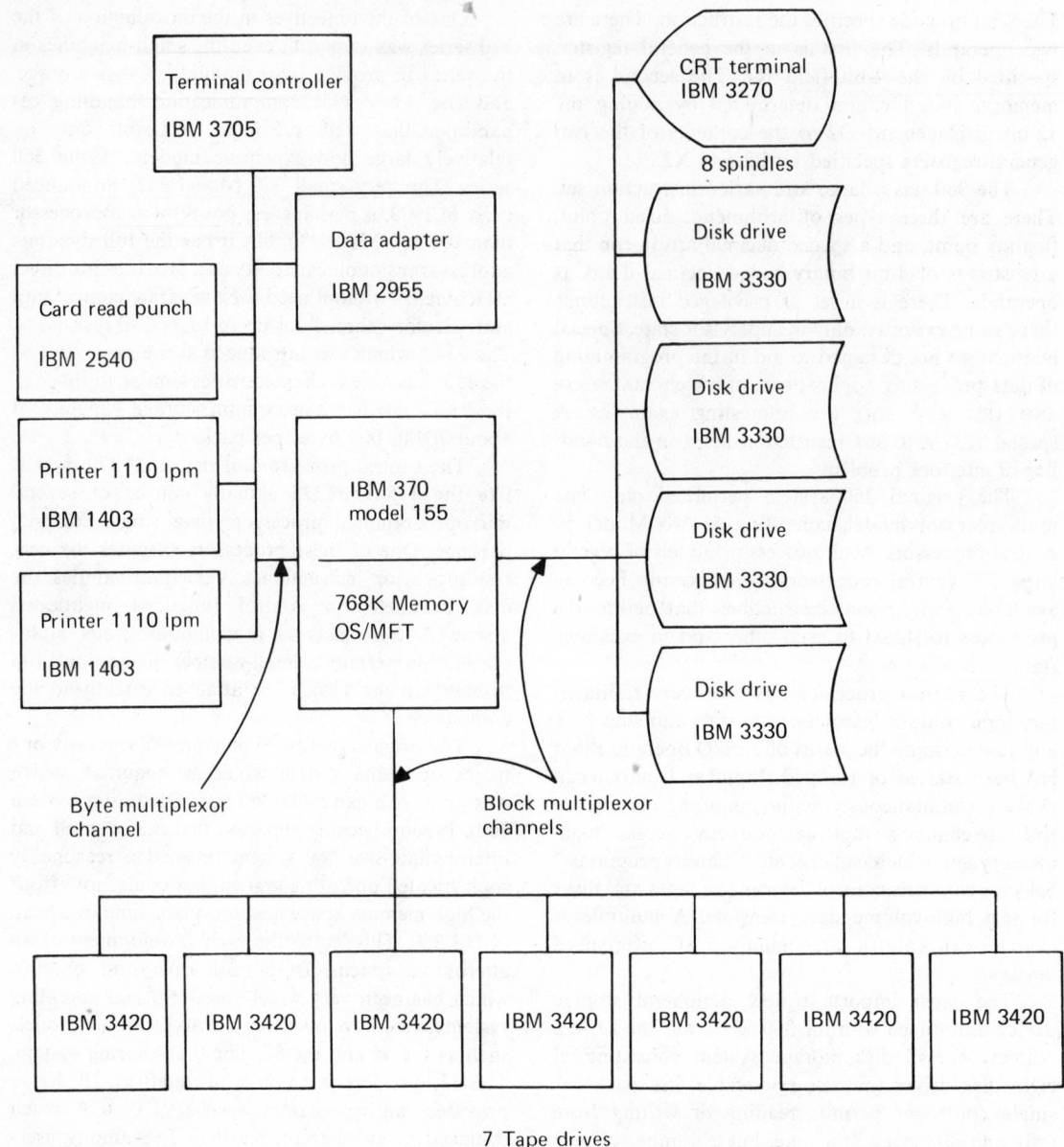

**Fig. 2.** Block diagram of a medium-size IBM 370 installation at Purdue University's administrative data processing center.

run on 370 systems. IBM's virtual machine system VM/370 provides an extended CP67 system for the 370 series. The University of British Columbia has installed MTS on its 370/168. The 370 version of MTS has been used at a number of other universities, including the University of Michigan.

S. Rosen

# IBM 1400 SERIES

For articles on related subjects *see* Digital Computers: Early; Generations, Computer; Manufacturers, Computer; and RAMAC.

The IBM 1400 series data processing systems were introduced to the business world in 1959. This line of equipment had a dramatic impact on the business data processing world at that time. The first of the 1400 series machines, the 1401, rapidly made obsolete the older vacuum tube and electromechanical "unit record" systems. The 1400 system enjoyed widespread use in every type of data processing application from 1959 until "third generation" equipment became available in the mid-1960s.

The 1400 line consisted of five basic computers: 1401, 1440, 1460, 1410, and 7010. The basic main frame, the 1401, was a second-generation, fully-transistorized machine with a magnetic core memory having original capacity options of 1.4K, 2K, and 4K characters, with later announced options of 8K, 12K, and 16K characters.

Internally data was represented in 6-bit BCD code, with additional parity check and "word mark" bits. The memory cycle was 11.5 $\mu$s per character access.

Instruction formats were variable from one to eight characters, and data fields and records could be variable length within the constraints of the peripheral device characteristics and memory size. Instruction and data fields were defined by the presence of a word-mark bit set beneath the leftmost character of the instruction or data field.

The instruction format consisted of a single character op-code, two optional three-character data or instruction addresses, and an optional single character "d-modifier." The instruction set provided for internal data transfer, input/output control, add-to-storage decimal arithmetic, condition testing, and branching operations. A unique (at the time) single instruction provided for versatile printer-field editing. Indirect addressing could be accomplished using any of three standard index registers.

The 1401 (Fig. 1) had an I/O interface that permitted only one I/O operation at a time to take place, regardless of the number of devices on line. I/O operations interlocked the central processor, although some overlap of processing and I/O operation could be gained by the addition of special features.

Although a wide variety of peripheral devices was available for the 1400 series, including MICR and optical readers, paper-tape readers, remote transmission devices, etc., the principal devices in use were:

*1402 Card Reader/Punch.* This unit, somewhat modified, is the presently used 2540. It is capable of reading 800 cards per minute (cpm) and punching 250 cpm.

*1403 Chain Printer.* This device had a maximum rated speed of 1100 alphanumeric lines per minute (lpm), was reliable and comparatively quiet, and had excellent print quality. The speed of this device and its relatively low cost was a significant factor in the widespread acceptance of the 1401.

*729 Magnetic Tape Units.* Seven-track units with speeds ranging from 15,000 to 62,000 characters per second (chps), depending upon the model and the recording density, which could be 200, 556, or 800 characters per inch (chpi).

*7330 Magnetic Tape Units.* These were relatively slow and inexpensive units (7,200 chps at 200 chpi density).

*1405 Disk Storage Units.* These were fixed-disk units with 50,000 or 100,000 directly addressable 200-character records. Records were accessed by a

**Fig. 1.** The IBM 1401 System.

single arm moving laterally and vertically. Average access time was 600 ms.

*1311 Disk Storage Units.* These replaced the 1405-type units with modular disk-pack storage. Each pack stored 2 million characters in the form of 20,000 hundred-character records. The access device was of the "comb" type, requiring only lateral motion. Average access time per record was 250 ms.

Programming for the 1401 was accomplished through the use of several languages. It could be, and often was, programmed in machine language. A basic assembly language SPS (Symbolic Programming System) permitted the use of mnemonic operation codes, symbolic addresses, indirect addressing, data field establishment and definition, and was widely used. A significantly enhanced version of SPS, called "Autocoder"—analogous to basic assembly language for third-generation computers—became the predominantly used language. Autocoder used SPS constructs, but was free form (as opposed to fixed format for SPS statements) and employed macroinstructions for initiating I/O operations. Fortran and Cobol compilers existed, but were not widely used because of either excessive processing time needed for compilation or limitations on the scope of the language due to the limited memory size of the system. Various Report Program Generator (RPG) packages were available, as was a complete set of basic utility packages.

Operating systems were not used with the 1401, 1440, or 1460, although many users developed monitors to permit a rudimentary form of job control by automatic loading of a series of programs as opposed to the conventional method of loading each object program from a card reader before execution.

The 1440 system was initially a disk-oriented 1401 with slower peripherals and lower cost. Internally, the 1440 was, for all practical purposes, identical to the 1401 except that the memory cycle was 11.1 ms as compared to 11.5 for the 1401, and the printer and reader-punch buffers were relocatable in memory.

The 1460 was again basically a 1401 except that it had a 6 $\mu$s memory expandable to a 32K capacity.

The 1410 systems, while having the same basic architecture as the 1401, were significantly more powerful. Memory sizes were 10K, 20K, 40K, 60K, or 80K characters. The internal code was BCD and the use of word-mark bits permitted variable length data and instruction fields. The memory cycle was 4.5 $\mu$s per character. The instruction set was similar to the 1401, but included a table-lookup instruction and 64 different data-move instructions. Fifteen index registers were available. The basic system had a single I/O channel, but a second could be installed. Like the 1401, the processor was interlocked during any I/O operation, though special features were available to provide limited overlap. Autocoder was the predominantly used language, although Cobol and Fortran were widely used. All peripheral equipment was the same as that used in other 1400 series systems except for 1301 and 1302 disk files, which were large fixed-disk units similar to the 350 units used on 305 "RAMAC" machines. The 1401 could be operated in emulated 1410 mode, which provided almost total compatibility with 1401 programs.

The 7010 system was functionally, although not architecturally, an advanced 1410. It used the 1410 instruction set and, unlike the 1410, had a 1410 compatibility feature. The 7010 accessed two characters in parallel on each 2.4 $\mu$s cycle. Four I/O channels could be installed. Memory protection, an interval timer, and a program-level interrupt feature were available. All 1400 compatible I/O devices could be used on the 7010. Comparatively few of these systems were installed, as the system was introduced shortly before the System 360 was announced.

There were approximately 14,000 of the 1401 systems and over 1,000 of the 1410 systems installed. A typical 1401 system rented for $8,000 per month and ranged from $4,000 to $12,000 per month. A typical 1410 system rented for $11,000 per month and ranged from $8,000 to $18,000 per month.

The high-speed card reading and tape and printing ability of the 1401 systems ideally suited them for use as peripheral I/O systems to IBM 7000 series computers.

G. D. Baer

# IBM CARD

For articles on related subjects *see* Manufacturers, Computer; and Ninety Column Card.

For articles on related terms and biographical information *see* ASCII; EBCDIC; Hollerith, Herman; and Watson, Thomas J.

In 1890, Dr. Herman Hollerith was faced with the problem of conducting the U.S. Census and evaluating all resulting information. The data from

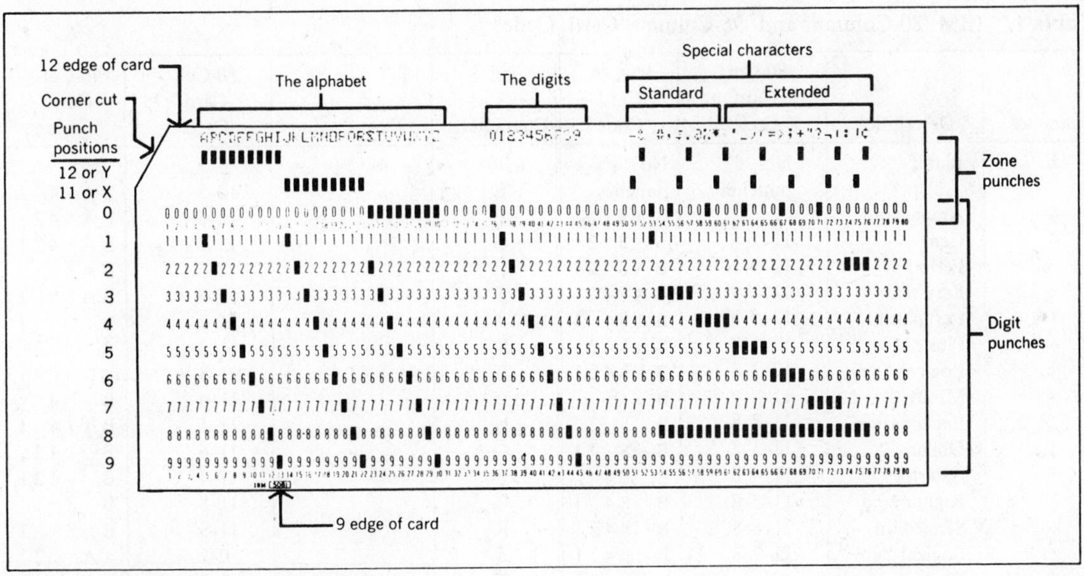


**Fig. 1.** IBM 80-column card format.

the previous census had taken ten years to process manually. To enable this processing to be carried out more efficiently, Dr. Hollerith invented a technique whereby information could be recorded in cards as a series of holes. He also invented a number of machines that were able to read these holes, interpret and accumulate this information, and sort cards into sequence. Using these cards and equipment, he was able to complete the 1890 census by 1892. This card, known almost universally today as the IBM card, is sometimes still called the "Hollerith" card.

Dr. Hollerith patented his ideas and later founded the Tabulating Machine Company. This company became the Computing-Tabulating-Recording Company in 1911. In 1914, Thomas J. Watson, Sr., joined this company, which later became International Business Machines Corporation.

While early cards enabled storage of an amount of information varying from around 30 characters to 90 characters, the card as it is known today has been standardized at a size of 7⅜ in. by 3¼ in., and normally contains 80 characters of information. However, more than 80 characters may be contained in a card if special punching techniques such as binary punching are used.

### The 80-Column Card and Card Codes.

Each card is divided into 80 columns and 12 rows (Fig. 1). Each column is normally used to record one character of information as a series of holes. The top row is called the "12" or "Y" row, and the second row from the top is called the "11" or "X" row. The remaining rows are called the 0, 1, . . ., 9 row, as indicated by the digit printed on the card. Holes punched in the top three rows of the card are called "zone punches."

A decimal digit from 0 to 9 is readily recorded in a column by a punch in the appropriately valued row. In the case of alphabetic information, however, two punches are necessary in a column (see Table 1 for 80-column card codes). The first punch is a zone punch and the second punch is a numeric punch. Thus, the letters A to I are represented by a combination of a 12-zone and the numerics 1 to 9. Special characters (punctuation marks, etc.) are generally represented by a combination of one zone

**Fig. 2.** IBM 5496 data recorder used for punching 96-column cards.

**Table 1.** IBM 80-Column and 96-Column Card Codes

| Character | Description | 80-Col. Card Code | 96-Col. Card Code | Character | Description | 80-Col. Card Code | 96-Col. Card Code |
|---|---|---|---|---|---|---|---|
| b | Blank | No punches | No punches | E | | 12–5 | B A 4 1 |
| & | Ampersand | 12 | A 8 2 | F | | 12–6 | B A 4 2 |
| ¢ | Cent | 12–2–8 | B A 8 2 | G | | 12–7 | B A 4 2 1 |
| . | Period | 12–3–8 | B A 8 2 1 | H | | 12–8 | B A 8 |
| < | Less than | 12–4–8 | B A 8 4 | I | | 12–9 | B A 8 1 |
| ( | Left paren | 12–5–8 | B A 8 4 1 | J | | 11–1 | B 1 |
| + | Plus | 12–6–8 | B A 8 4 2 | K | | 11–2 | B 2 |
| \| | Logical "or" | 12–7–8 | B A 8 4 2 1 | L | | 11–3 | B 2 1 |
| – | Minus | 11 | B | M | | 11–4 | B 4 |
| ! | Exclamation | 11–2–8 | B 8 2 | N | | 11–5 | B 4 1 |
| $ | Dollar | 11–3–8 | B 8 2 1 | O | | 11–6 | B 4 2 |
| * | Asterisk | 11–4–8 | B 8 4 | P | | 11–7 | B 4 2 1 |
| ) | Right paren | 11–5–8 | B 8 4 1 | Q | | 11–8 | B 8 |
| ; | Semicolon | 11–6–8 | B 8 4 2 | R | | 11–9 | B 8 1 |
| ¬ | Logical "not" | 11–7–8 | B 8 4 2 1 | S | | 0–2 | A 2 |
| / | Slash | 0–1 | A 1 | T | | 0–3 | A 2 1 |
| ≠ | Record mark | 0–2–8 | A 8 2 | U | | 0–4 | A 4 |
| , | Comma | 0–3–8 | A 8 2 1 | V | | 0–5 | A 4 1 |
| % | Percent | 0–4–8 | A 8 4 | W | | 0–6 | A 4 2 |
| — | Underscore | 0–5–8 | A 8 4 1 | X | | 0–7 | A 4 2 1 |
| > | Greater than | 0–6–8 | A 8 4 2 | Y | | 0–8 | A 8 |
| ? | Question | 0–7–8 | A 8 4 2 1 | Z | | 0–9 | A 8 1 |
| : | Colon | 2–8 | 8 2 | 0 | | 0 | A |
| # | Number | 3–8 | 8 2 1 | 1 | | 1 | 1 |
| @ | At | 4–8 | 8 4 | 2 | | 2 | 2 |
| ' | Quote | 5–8 | 8 4 1 | 3 | | 3 | 2 1 |
| = | Equals | 6–8 | 8 4 2 | 4 | | 4 | 4 |
| " | Quotation | 7–8 | 8 4 2 1 | 5 | | 5 | 4 1 |
| A | | 12–1 | B A 1 | 6 | | 6 | 4 2 |
| B | | 12–2 | B A 2 | 7 | | 7 | 4 2 1 |
| C | | 12–3 | B A 2 1 | 8 | | 8 | 8 |
| D | | 12–4 | B A 4 | 9 | | 9 | 8 1 |

punch and two numeric punches, as shown in Table 1.

With the advent of computers in the 1950s, it was found necessary to extend the number of different characters that could be recorded on a card. Consequently, various combinations of holes are used to represent up to 256 different values, as in the Extended Binary Coded Decimal Interchange Code (EBCDIC), or up to 128 values, as in the American Standard Code for Information Interchange (ASCII).

**The 96-Column IBM Card and Its Codes.** In 1969, IBM introduced the System/3 computer and the 5496 data recorder (Fig. 2), which use a 96-column card rather than an 80-column card. The 96-column card is physically smaller, measuring only 3 ¼ in. by 2$^{11}/_{16}$ in. and can record 20% more data than the 80-column card (Fig. 3). Information is recorded on the 96-column cards in 32 columns, each column containing three sets of rows (Fig. 4). Each set of rows is called a "tier," and consists of 6 rows instead of the 12 rows found on the 80-column card. From the top down, the first row is the B row; the second, the A row; then the 8 row, the 4 row, the 2 row, and the 1 row. This series of rows is repeated again immediately underneath for the second set of 32 columns, and then again for the third set of 32 columns.

Numeric information is recorded as a combination of punches in the A, 8, 4, 2, and 1 rows, as shown in Fig. 4 and detailed in Table 1 for 96-

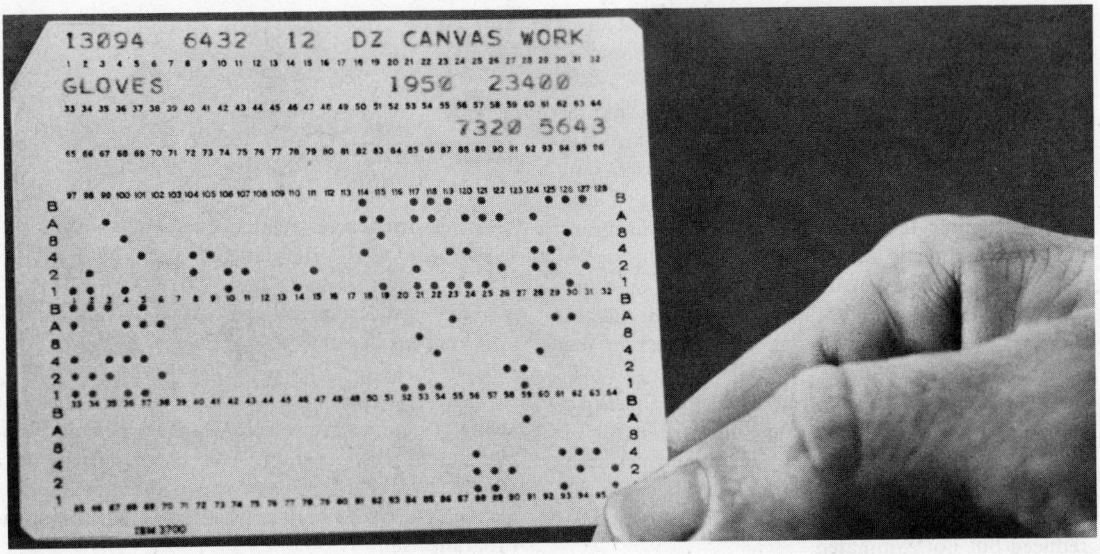


**Fig. 3.** The IBM 96-column card.

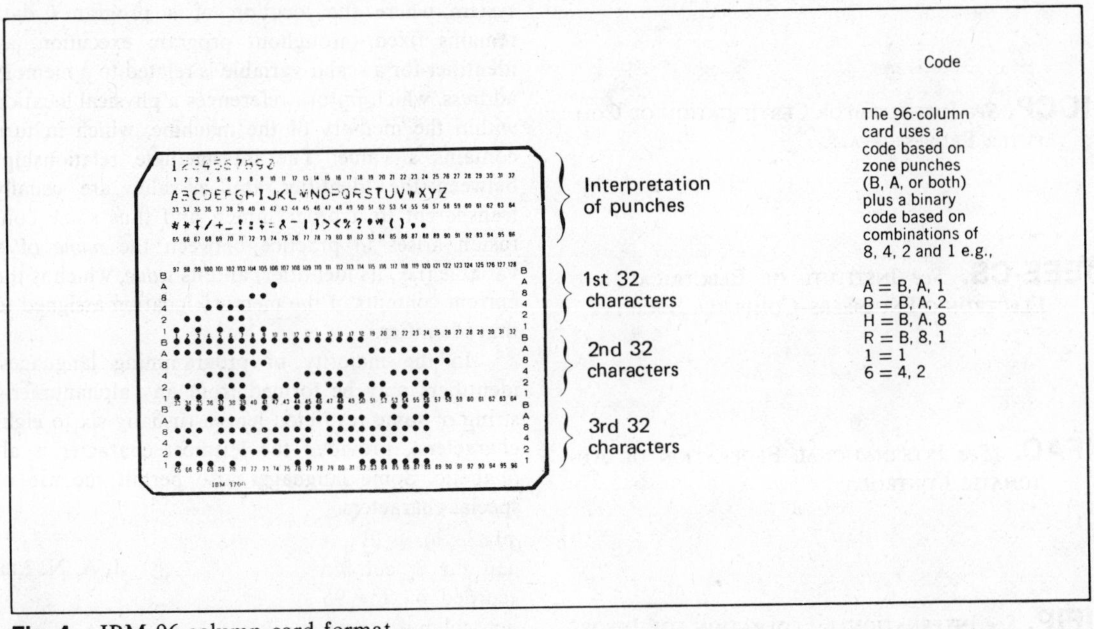


**Fig. 4.** IBM 96-column card format.

column card codes. Note that the B and A rows are used to represent zone punches, with both B and A corresponding to the Y zone punch on the 80-column card, B alone corresponding to the X zone punch, and A alone to the 0 zone punch. Note in Table 1 that the sum of the other punches on the 96-column card is equal to the second punch on the 80-column card for alphabetic characters.

**Justification for the Use of Cards.** The main advantage of a card is that it is a separate unit record of information. Cards are used as a convenient means of recording information relating to transactions used to update master files. Thus, cards are useful for recording separate order transactions to update an orders file, issues and receipts transactions to update a product inventory file, or name and address changes to update a customer master file, for example. Cards are also used for the development of programs, with source program statements being punched into cards for compilation and translation by a computer into actual computer instructions.

The use of computer terminals and time-sharing systems for program development since the late 1960s has resulted in significant improvements in efficiency of program writing and testing. These facilities enable the programmer to enter program instructions directly into the computer, using typewriter terminals, visual display terminals, or other hardware. It is probable, therefore, that the use of the card for programming will be reduced in the future.

The late 1960s introduced devices designed to replace the card as a storage medium for input of transactions into a computer. These devices and advanced techniques will undoubtedly become increasingly dominant, with the use of cards being reduced but not eliminated.

C. B. FINKELSTEIN

**ICCP.** *See* INSTITUTE FOR CERTIFICATION OF COMPUTER PROFESSIONALS.

**IEEE-CS.** *See* INSTITUTE OF ELECTRICAL AND ELECTRONIC ENGINEERS–COMPUTER SOCIETY.

**IFAC.** *See* INTERNATIONAL FEDERATION OF AUTOMATIC CONTROL.

**IFIP.** *See* INTERNATIONAL FEDERATION FOR INFORMATION PROCESSING.

**IMP.** *See* INTERFACE MESSAGE PROCESSOR.

**IOCS.** *See* INPUT-OUTPUT CONTROL SYSTEM.

**IPL-V.** *See* LIST-PROCESSING LANGUAGES.

## IDENTIFIER

For articles on related subjects *see* PROCEDURE-ORIENTED LANGUAGES; and PROGRAMMING LANGUAGES.
For articles on related terms *see* LABEL; and PROCEDURE.

In a programming language, an identifier is a string of characters used to identify (or name) some element of the program. This element may be a statement label, a procedure or function, a data element (such as a scalar variable or an array) or the program itself.

Most commonly, the word "identifier" is used almost synonymously with "variable name." In a system where the location of a program's data remains fixed throughout program execution, an identifier for a scalar variable is related to a memory address, which in turn references a physical location within the memory of the machine, which in turn contains a value. The intermediate relationships between the identifier and a value are usually transparent to a programmer, and thus some confusion arises in practice between the *name* of a variable (i.e., its identifier) and its *value*, which is the current contents of the memory location assigned to that identifier.

In the majority of programming languages, identifiers may be formed from any alphanumeric string of some restricted length (usually six to eight characters), provided the leftmost character is alphabetic. Some languages also permit the use of special characters.

J. A. N. LEE

## IMAGE AND PICTURE PROCESSING

For articles on related subjects *see* ARTIFICIAL INTELLIGENCE; CELLULAR AUTOMATA; CODES; and COMPUTER GRAPHICS.
For articles on related terms *see* AUTOMATA THEORY; GRAMMAR; GRAPH THEORY; and SOFTWARE.

A wide variety of techniques exist for processing pictorial information by computer; these techniques are collectively referred to as *image processing* or *picture processing*. The information to be processed is usually input to the computer by sampling and analog-to-digital conversion of video signals obtained from some type of two-dimensional scanning device (television camera, facsimile scanner, etc.). Thus, at least initially, this information is in the form of a large array (e.g., in the case of ordinary television, about 500 by 500), in which each element is a number representing the brightness (and perhaps color) of a small region in the scanned image. The key distinction between image processing and *computer graphics* is that the latter does not deal with input pictures in array form, though it may construct pictures from input sets of coordinate data.

A digitized image array is sometimes called a "digital picture"; its elements are called "points," "picture elements," "pels," or "pixels." The values of these elements are typically six-bit or eight-bit integers. They usually represent brightness (or *gray level*); color can also be represented, but we will not deal with color here.

**Picture Compression.** A digital picture may contain millions of bits, but most of the classes of pictures encountered in practice are *redundant* (in the sense of information theory), and can be *compressed* without loss of information. One can take advantage of picture redundancy by using efficient encoding techniques in which frequently occurring gray levels, or blocks of gray levels, are represented by short codes and infrequent ones by longer codes. If the pixels are encoded in a fixed succession (e.g., as in a television raster), one can capitalize on the dependency of each gray level on the preceding ones by encoding differences between successive levels rather than the levels themselves. If the dependency is very great, it may even be economical to represent the picture by the positions (or lengths) of runs of constant gray level, or more generally, to specify the positions and shapes of regions of constant gray level.

Except for very simple classes of pictures, only a limited degree of compression can be achieved using efficient encoding. However, for many purposes one need not insist that there be no loss of information; rather, one can approximate the given picture by another picture having lower information content. The digitization process itself, based on spatial sampling and gray-level quantization of a given real

(a) (c)

(b) (d)

**Fig. 1.** Picture approximation. The original was a 256-by-256-point array of 8-bit values. It was divided into 256 16-by-16 point subarrays, and each of these was expanded in a two-dimensional Fourier series. In (a), the picture was reconstructed using only the first 128 coefficients of each series; in (b), using only the first 64 coefficients. In (c), the 128 coefficients of (a) were quantized to 4 bits, and in (d), to 2 bits, before reconstructing the picture. The average number of bits per point in these four approximations is (a)4, (b)2, (c)2, (d)1. (From P. A. Wintz, "Transform Picture Coding," *Proc. IEEE, 60,* July 1972, pp. 809–820.)

image, is a process of approximation. In designing *approximation* schemes (Fig. 1), one can take advantage of the limitations of the human visual system; e.g., quantization can be coarse in the vicinity of abrupt changes in gray level. It is sometimes advantageous to apply approximation techniques to a transform of the given picture rather than the picture itself.

**Image Enhancement.** A picture is not always a satisfactory representation of the original object or scene; e.g., it may have a poorly chosen gray scale (under- or overexposure); it may be geometrically distorted; or it may be blurred or "noisy." Even if the nature of the process that degraded the picture is known, it may not be mathematically possible to invert the process. There are, however, many cases in which one can reduce the difference between a picture and its original by operating on the picture; this is the goal of *image restoration.* More generally, one can operate on a picture to improve its "quality" by making it more "contrasty," less blurred, or less noisy; this is the goal of *image enhancement* (Fig. 2).

One can "sharpen" a picture (increase local contrasts in it, deblur it) by emphasizing its high spatial frequencies. This can be done by multiplying the Fourier transform of the picture by a weighting function whose values increase with distance from the origin, and then taking the inverse Fourier transform to obtain the sharpened picture. Similar effects can be obtained by performing a differencing operation on the picture (e.g., a "Laplacian") and combining the results with the original picture. (Doing just the differencing operation will convert solid regions into outlines). If the picture is not only blurred but also noisy, these methods may make it still noisier. It is often possible to achieve a useful compromise by emphasizing only a selected band of spatial frequencies (or analogously, using a differencing operation based on differences between average gray levels rather than between the gray levels of single pixels).

Similarly, one can "smooth" a picture by deemphasizing its high spatial frequencies or simply by locally averaging it, but this is usually undesirable because it blurs the picture. Here, too, one can compromise by deemphasizing a selected frequency band; this is particularly effective when the noise results from the operation of a sampling process that is periodic (e.g., TV raster lines) or which at least has a characteristic "grain size" (e.g., photographic grain). If the noise is random, and several copies of the picture are available in which the samples of the noise are independent, smoothing without blurring can be achieved by averaging the copies. "Salt and

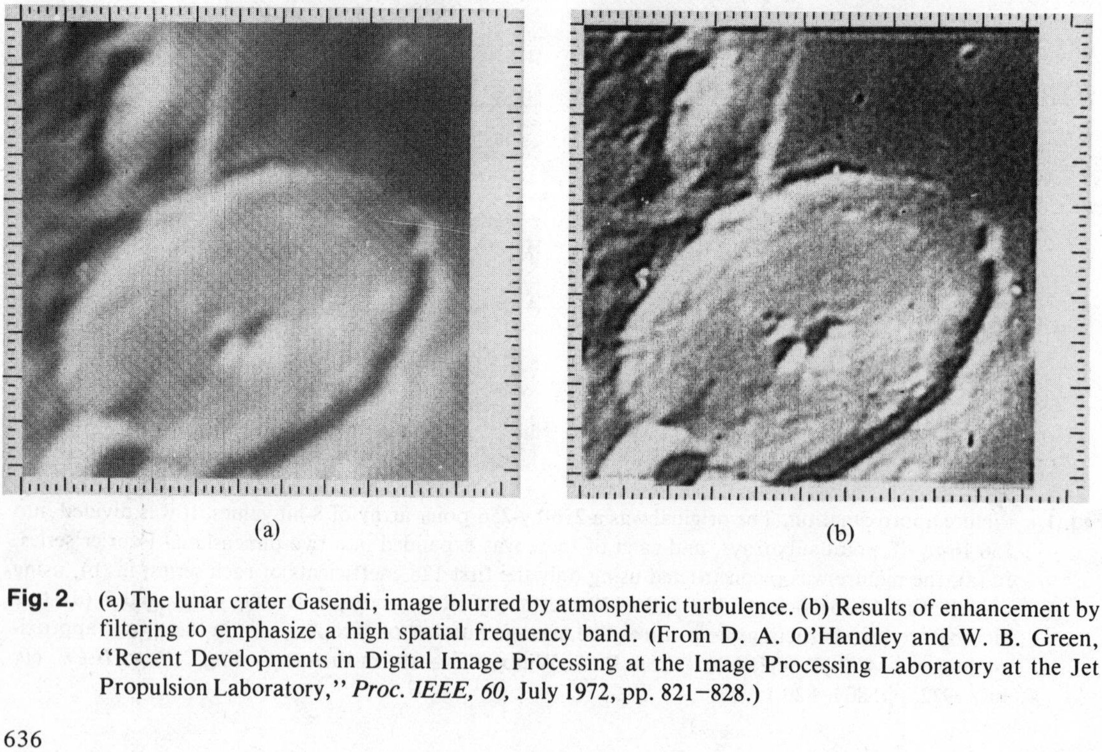

**Fig. 2.** (a) The lunar crater Gasendi, image blurred by atmospheric turbulence. (b) Results of enhancement by filtering to emphasize a high spatial frequency band. (From D. A. O'Handley and W. B. Green, "Recent Developments in Digital Image Processing at the Image Processing Laboratory at the Jet Propulsion Laboratory," *Proc. IEEE, 60,* July 1972, pp. 821–828.)

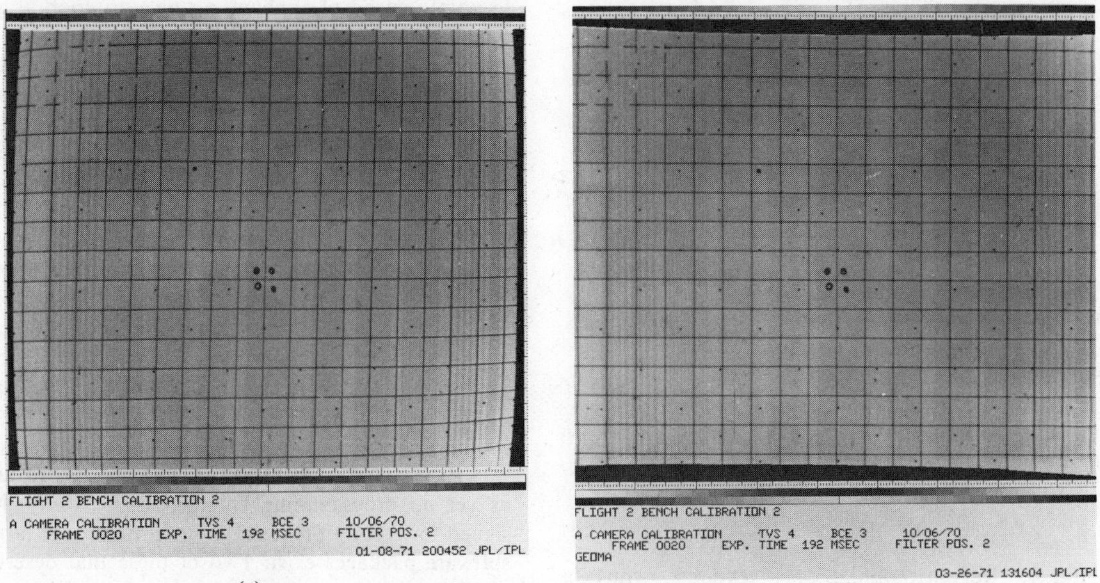


(a) (b)

**Fig. 3.** (a) Mariner 9-grid target, showing geometrical distortion. (b) Results of distortion removal. (From P. A. Wintz, "Transform Picture Coding," *Proc. IEEE, 60,* July 1972.)

pepper" noise (e.g., TV "snow") can be reduced by performing a local averaging operation only at pixels where there are isolated anomalies in gray level.

A known geometrical distortion in a picture can be corrected by resampling it at an irregularly spaced array of positions (as specified by the distortion function) and outputting the samples as a regular array. Gray levels can be assigned to the new samples by interpolation from the levels of the nearby pixels. To correct an unknown relative distortion between two copies of a picture, one can find matches between pairs of distinctive local patterns (Fig. 3), measure the relative displacement of each pair, and construct a geometrical distortion function by interpolation from these displacements. (Local pattern matching is also used to extract relief information from stereopairs of pictures.)

**Pictorial Pattern Classification.** In picture compression and image enhancement, pictures are not only the input but also the output, since the goal is an approximation to, or an improved version of, the input picture. Another major branch of picture processing deals with *picture classification and description*; here the goal is the assignment of the picture to a category or, more generally, the creation of a data structure that contains useful information about the picture.

Pictorial pattern classification systems have been developed for many different applications, including optical character reading, analysis of nuclear bubble chamber pictures, medical diagnosis from micrographs and radiographs, chromosome analysis, recognition of faces or fingerprints, and interpretation of aerial photographs and satellite TV pictures. In such systems, the given picture may first be "preprocessed" to simplify or enhance it; a set of measurements is then made on it ("feature extraction"), and it is then classified on the basis of these measurements.

A wide variety of types of measurements or properties have been used for pictorial pattern classification. Important classes of examples include template properties (degree of match between the picture and a reference pattern, or template) and statistical properties (statistics of the gray levels in the picture (as in Fig. 4) or in a preprocessed version of it; these can be regarded as textural properties of the picture). Local properties, whose values depend only on small parts of the picture, are of particular interest because of their computational simplicity. If the classes of pictures are invariant under certain types of picture transformations (e.g., translation, rotation, change in contrast), one should use properties that are also invariant. One way of insuring this is to "normalize" the picture so that patterns

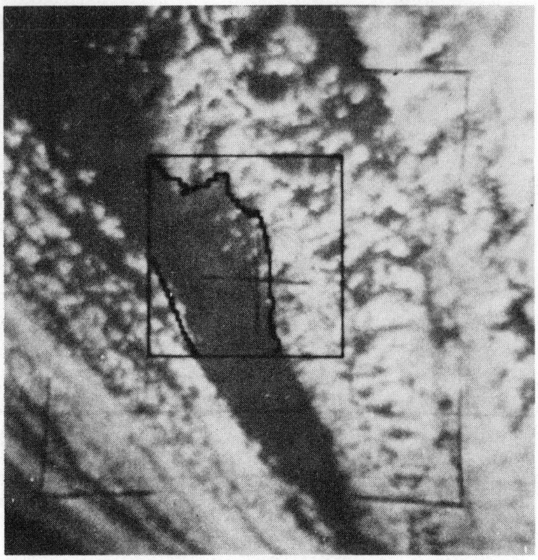

**Fig. 4.** Region outlining on a textured picture (a TIROS VI cloud-cover picture) using differencing of average gray levels. (From J. P. Strong, III, and A. Rosenfeld, "A Region Coloring Technique for Scene Analysis," *Comm. ACM, 16*, 1973.)

differing only by a transformation become identical before measuring the properties.

**Picture Segmentation and Scene Analysis.** Complex pictures, containing many different types of regions or objects, usually cannot be classified or described in a useful way on the basis of measurements made over the entire picture. Such a picture must first be *segmented* into parts (corresponding to regions or objects); once this is done, the picture can be described in terms of the parts, their properties (textures, sizes, shapes, etc.), and their spatial relationships. Picture segmentation and description are the goals of *scene analysis*.

Useful picture segmentations can often be achieved by preprocessing and then thresholding. For example, performing a differencing operation and keeping only the points where the difference value is high will tend to produce outlines of simple regions or objects; differencing of averages, rather than of single-pixel gray levels, can similarly be used to outline textured regions. Thresholding alone can be used to extract regions that are brighter (or darker) than their surrounds. It is usually advantageous to *track* line-like objects, or region outlines, rather than attempt to extract them all at one time; one can then adjust the extraction criteria from point to point instead of applying a single criterion at all points.

Once a picture has been segmented into parts, new segments can be derived by extending, combining, or further splitting the parts. For example, given a picture segment, one can obtain its connected components, its border, its "skeleton"; or one can break it into parts on the basis of shape criteria. One can also measure geometrical properties of the segment (connectivity, area, perimeter, diameter, etc., as well as various shape properties). In addition, one can measure nongeometrical properties (e.g., textural properties) over the segment alone. The properties can then be used to construct descriptions of the picture.

**Picture-Processing Software.** There are as yet no programming languages specifically designed for picture processing, but a number of large software packages exist. Two of these that deserve special mention are Vicar (developed at California Institute of Technology's Jet Propulsion Laboratory) and Pax (developed at the Universities of Illinois and Maryland; originally a simulator for part of the ILLIAC III computer).

Vicar stores pictures as either real or integer arrays; in the latter case, the values of one or more pixels can be stored in a single machine word. This format permits fast execution of arithmetic operations on pictures using hardware instructions; it is thus very appropriate for image compression and enhancement work, which usually involves many such operations. The use of real arrays is important if the processing being done involves Fourier transforms or the like; if one truncates the values in a transform to integers, useful information may be lost.

Pax stores pictures as stacks of "bit planes"; the $i$th bit plane in such a stack is a binary array consisting of the $i$th bits of the pixel gray levels. One advantage of this format is that any number of "overlays," representing segments extracted from a picture, can be stored "in registration" with the picture by adding planes to the stack. Execution of logical operations on the binary planes is fast, since hardware instructions can usually be used to perform such operations on all bits of a machine word—hence, on many pixels—simultaneously. Thus, Pax is an appropriate system for scene analysis work involving many operations on picture segments.

Picture processing can often be greatly facilitated by using special hardware array processors. A variety of analog devices for processing images have also been proposed. In particular, many useful picture-processing operations can be performed optically, but a discussion of nondigital processing techniques is beyond the scope of this article.

**Picture Grammars and Automata.** A variety of formalisms for computations on pictures and for description of picture structure have been studied. Formal grammars can be generalized from strings to arrays, and one can also define automata that have arrays as "tapes." Models for parallel computation on arrays—e.g., by "cellular arrays" of automata—are of special interest. "Perceptrons" (machines that compute linear threshold functions of local properties) have been extensively investigated.

Formalisms for computations on data structures (in particular, on picture descriptions) have also been developed. Grammars can be generalized from strings to graphlike structures, and automata having graph-structured "tapes" can be defined.

One can regard picture segmentation and scene analysis as parsing operations with respect to such formal models. However, a purely "syntactic" approach to scene analysis is unlikely to be adequate except in simple cases. In general, it seems necessary to develop "knowledge-based" scene analysis systems, which make use of "semantic" information about the objects whose images appear in the scene. This approach is being actively pursued in connection with the development of robot vision systems; it constitutes an important area of artificial intelligence research.

REFERENCES

1969. Rosenfeld, A. *Picture Processing by Computer.* New York: Academic Press. (A highly condensed version is in *Computing Surveys, Vol. 1* (September 1969), pp. 147–176.)

1970. Andrews, H. C. (with contributions by W. K. Pratt and K. Caspari). *Computer Techniques in Image Processing.* New York: Academic Press.

1972. *Proceedings of the IEEE.* Special issues on digital image processing and digital pattern recognition (July and October).

A. ROSENFELD

**INCREMENTAL COMPILER.** *See* COMPILER, INCREMENTAL.

# INDEX REGISTER

For articles on related subjects *see* ADDRESS MODIFICATION; ADDRESSING; GENERAL REGISTER; INDIRECT ADDRESS; MACHINE INSTRUCTION SET; and REGISTER.
For article on related term *see* OPERAND.

An index register is a storage device most often used in the determination of an operand address, but which may be used for other purposes, mainly as counters.

In the process of the formation of an address of an operand, one can distinguish three basic parts. Consider, for example, the ADD instruction in a program loop computing the sum of the elements of a vector. The operand address of the ADD instruction is formed from:

1. The address of the base of the vector (its first element) relative to the program module. This address is known when the program is being written.
2. The memory address into which the program module is loaded. This address is known at load time.
3. The offset from the base of the vector, which depends on the element that is currently being added and which is known only at execution time.

Index registers are normally involved with the last of the three parts of the address.

The address computed within the index register is referred to as the *effective address*. The index register accomplishes its role of forming the effective address in one of two ways: Either the address is formed from a constant in the address field of an instruction plus a changing offset in the index register, or the address as a whole is contained in the index register. In the former case, shown in Fig. 1, the index register is used as a counter.

The number of index registers in a machine and the number of index registers used in the formation of the effective address and other attributes of the index registers are highly dependent on the particular architecture. Thus, one finds machines with a single index register, one index register and one dedicated base register, multiple index registers and/or base registers, and machines in which the general-purpose registers may be utilized for indexing and base addressing. The aforementioned possibilities by no means cover all varieties. The number of index registers utilized in forming the effective address is usually one or two; i.e., the address is

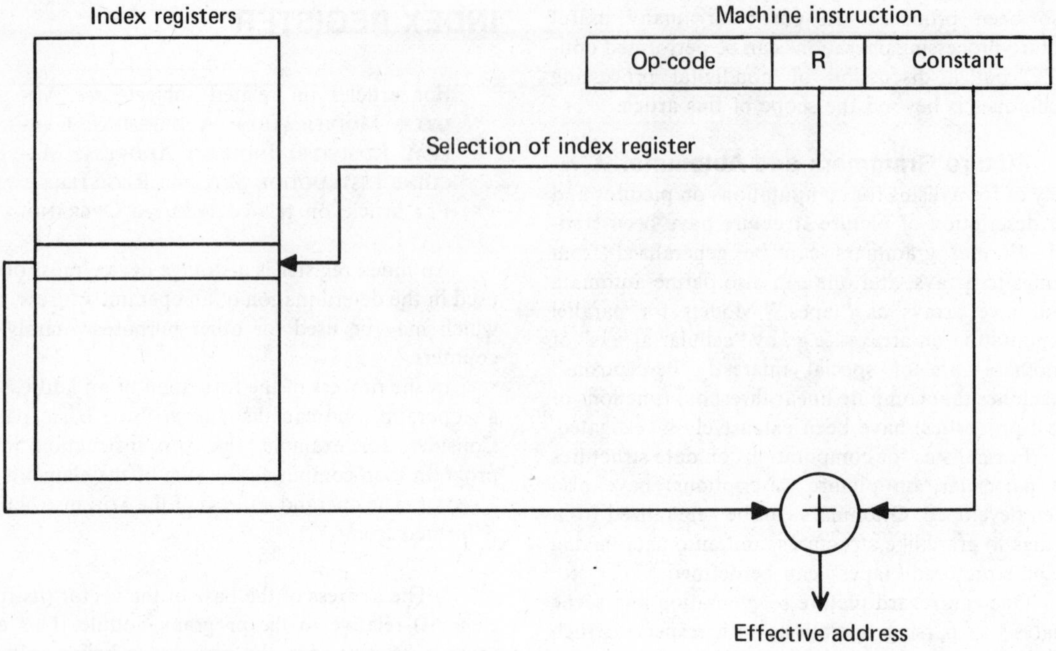


**Fig. 1.** Example of the formation of an effective address.

formed from the constant part of the address field plus the contents of one or two index registers.

As mentioned before, apart from their function in address formation, the index registers can serve as counters. As such, they are used in special instructions that increment or decrement the contents of the index register and check its new contents, thereby exercising control over the program flow.

Special care must be exercised in the use of index registers when the computer possesses an indirect addressing mode. In this case, the index register can be used either to compute the location of the indirect address (pre-indexing) or as an offset to the indirect address itself (post-indexing). When more than one index register is involved in the formation of the effective address, both pre- and post-indexing may be present. Again, the availability of either of the modes varies widely among different machines.

G. FRIEDER

# INDIRECT ADDRESS

For articles on related subjects *see* ADDRESSING; and MACHINE INSTRUCTION SET.

For articles on related terms *see* OPERATION CODE; and VIRTUAL MEMORY.

A simple computer instruction contains an operation code and an address that points to a location in memory. The contents of that location may be the data required by the operation, or may be an address that points to another location in memory. In this latter case, the address in the instruction itself is called an "indirect address," since it references data indirectly by pointing to the address of the data rather than to the data itself.

In some computers, the instruction itself contains a control field (one bit per address is enough) that specifies that the corresponding address is an indirect address. In other computers, tag bits are associated with data words, and these tag bits determine whether the word is to be treated as data or is to be used as an address that points to data.

Many systems support multilevel indirect addressing (see Fig. 1). The address retrieved in the memory word may itself be an indirect address that points to another memory location, which in turn may be an indirect address, etc. Computers that allow multilevel indirect addressing usually have a time-out interrupt facility that causes an interrupt to occur in the case of a nonterminating indirect addressing loop.

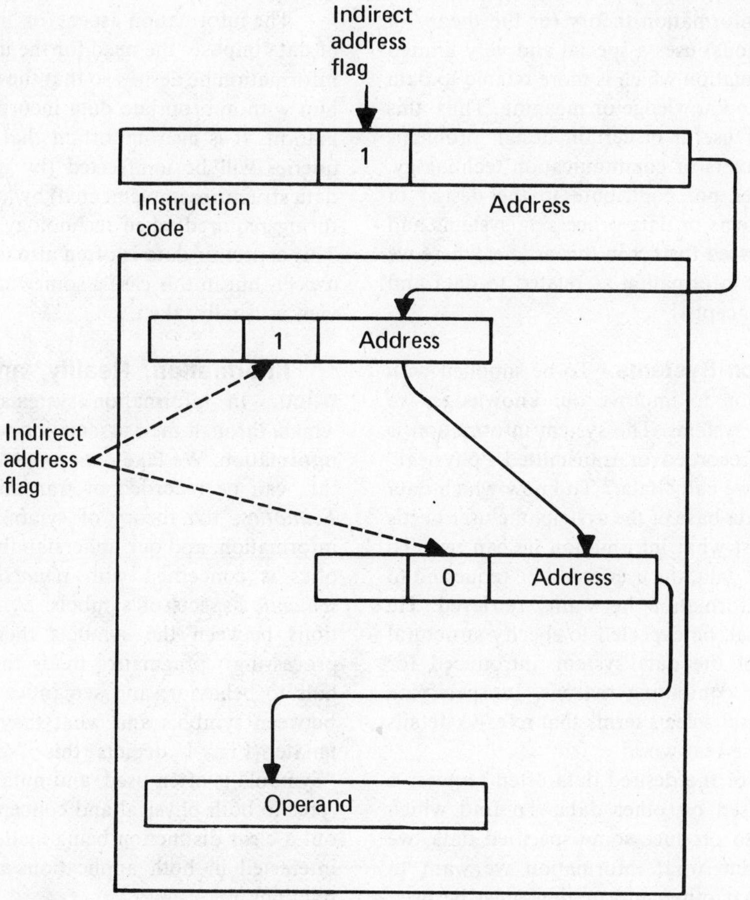


**Fig. 1.** Two-level indirect addressing.

There are many uses for indirect addressing. It has been used most effectively in those systems that require a longer address field than can be conveniently or reasonably provided in each instruction. Many small computers use indirect addressing in this way, but it is also used on many larger ones. Thus, the "descriptors" on large Burroughs systems are indirect addresses in which the address word contains the origin and size of an array that is addressed, to permit an automatic check for out-of-bounds addressing. The Multics system uses two-word indirect addresses to permit the addressing of its very large virtual memory.

S. Rosen

**INFORMATICS.** *See* Information Science.

## INFORMATION AND DATA

For articles on related subjects *see* Data Structures; Data Type; Information Retrieval; and Symbol Manipulation. For article on related subject *see* Syntax, Semantics and Pragmatics.

Data processing is used to produce data that provides people with information to support their decisions or actions.

*Information* may be defined as knowledge, especially as it provides people (or machines) with *new* facts about the real world. *Data* may be defined as physical symbols used to represent information for storage, communication, or processing. To determine what data to use, it is important to decide what information the data is to represent. Ignorance of this fact has caused much trouble in data systems.

## INFORMATION AND DATA

Statistical information theory (or the theory of signal transmissions) uses a special and very limited concept of information which is more related to data or signals than to knowledge or meaning. Thus, this theory has been useful in certain design problems regarding computers or communication technology. However, it does not contribute to the design of information systems or data processing systems and will not be discussed further in this article, where we are interested in information as related to data and to real-world concepts.

**Information Systems.** To be supplied with useful information to improve our knowledge, we use information systems. The system information is represented by recorded or transmitted "physical" symbols, which we call "data." To know which data to have in the data base of the system, the user needs to determine first what information he can use. To retrieve the right data, the user could be requested to specify what information he wants retrieved. He cannot, in general, be expected to specify structural characteristics of the data system, introduced for technological or computing reasons. In specifying information, a user selects terms that refer to details of his view of the real world.

Production of the desired data often requires a computation based on other data. To find which data is needed to produce some specified data, we have to determine what information we want to produce and what other information must be used for the production. We thus need to study *information precedence relations* before we can determine data needs and computation structure.

To determine which information and processing to have in the system, the cost of collecting, storing, and updating must be estimated and balanced against the estimated utility of all its known uses. Some of this must be done informally, but some can be done in a formalized way, using the information precedence relation structure (e.g., analyzing the associated information precedence matrix).

The information aspect (or "infological" aspect) of data imposes the need for the user to specify what information he desires so that the system can provide him with appropriate data incorporating this information. It is also important that his programs and queries will be unaffected (by ignoring the actual data structures implemented) by much of the restructuring required when technology or usage changes. This aspect of data is often also called the *relational aspect,* but in this case a somewhat more formalistic view is usually taken.

**Information, Reality, and Data—Semiotics.** In information systems we use *symbols*, which, through their association with reality, provide information. We take data to mean *physical* symbols that can be recorded or transmitted or processed. *Semiotics,* the theory of symbols, embraces data, information, and our understanding of reality. Semiotics is concerned with *syntactic, pragmatic*, and *semantic* aspects of symbols. Syntactics treats relations between the symbols themselves (including processing); pragmatics treats the relation of symbols to behavior; and semantics treats the relation between symbols and what they stand for or designate. Fig. 1 depicts this "semiotic structure". "Symbol" is often used, and notably in semiotics, to refer to both physical and conceptual symbols without a clear distinction being made. However, we are interested in both applications and in their interrelations.

We use the word "data" to refer to physical symbols and let "data term" (or "data item") stand for the singular form. Then we use "conceptual terms" or "conceptual symbols," which are reference concepts, as our basic concepts of reality, i.e., as the elements of the users' *conceptual model of the real world* and their frame of reference.

For example: "Tom is a boy" is a string of written symbols or data. "T," "o," and "m" are three symbols that form the composite symbol "Tom," which is a data term. The word "boy" is another

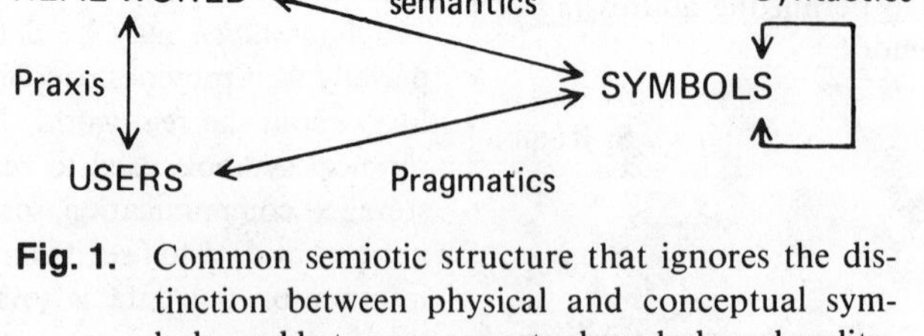


**Fig. 1.** Common semiotic structure that ignores the distinction between physical and conceptual symbols, and between conceptual symbols and reality.

data term, and the string "Tom is a boy" is made up of four data terms.

The data term "boy" is associated by me (as I read it) with the word "boy," which again I associate with the conception of a boy in general (or the idea of all boys). Thus, the word "boy," as perceived by me, acts as a conceptual symbol associated with the concept *boy*.

An important observation, fundamental to all formal treatment of reality, is that the physical symbols, or data, can refer only to our conceptual model of reality, not directly to reality itself. The conceptual terms are the bridge entities between reality and information and between information and data, thus also bridging data and users. The *designata* of data are the conceptual terms of the users. In Fig. 1 we have used the word "praxis" to name the relation between users and the real world. This is to indicate that it is the interaction between the users of the data, information, and the real world (i.e., what occurs in their practical experience) that is of importance. We are now led to a more complex diagram, Fig. 2, where information enters.

**Extended Semiotic Structure.** In Fig. 2, information is introduced into the diagram as the necessary intervening concept to explain how data is able to refer to the real world or is able to influence the users (pragmatics). Note that "users" have to know or determine the information structure (model and conceptual symbols) to be able to specify the data they need, or to understand the data provided to them. Semantics embraces the relation of data to conceptual terms and model. The conceptions are formed in the minds of the users as a result of "praxis," their practical experience.

From the diagram in Fig. 2, we simplify the structure in Fig. 3 and consider the three aspects of the user's requirements: reality, information, and data.

Element of Reality: e-Situation. Information tells what is held to be true—in reality. In a sense, an element of information is a truth statement about an element of reality, and it can reveal, at most, our conception of that element of reality together with a simple property, state, or behavior of it at a certain interval of time. "Simple property" refers to one of all properties prevailing in our conception of that element or object. We may call this an "elementary situation" (an e-situation).

Element of Information: e-Message, e-Fact. An element of information can be seen as a message that informs about an elementary situation. We will refer to such as an "e-message" (elementary message). It is seen that an e-message consists of

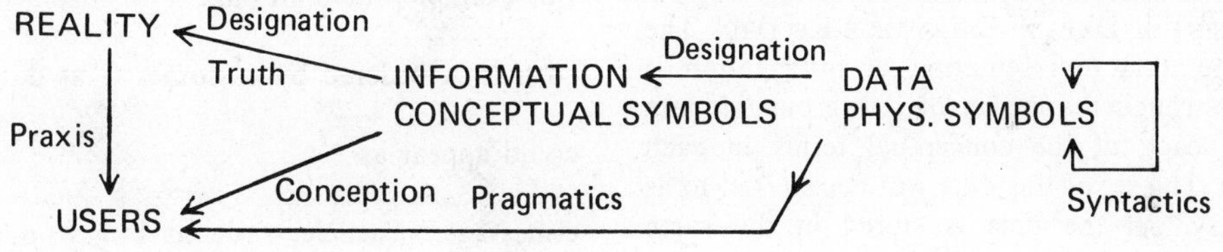


**Fig. 2.** Extended semiotic structure.

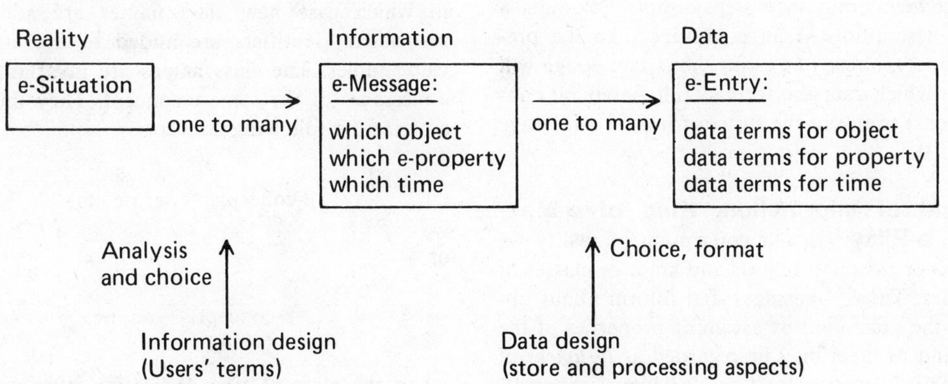


**Fig. 3.** User's requirements: reality, information, and data.

three conceptual terms (conceptual symbols):

$$\text{e-message: } \langle o, A = a, t \rangle$$

where o : object (e.g., Article XY257)
A = a : simple property or behavior (e.g., Manufacturer = COMPANY X)
t : time (e.g., since 1970)

An e-message is a structurally minimal message in the specific sense that if one of its terms is deleted, the rest do not inform of an e-situation.

Formally, an e-message may be regarded as an instance of a *binary relation that is a function of time* (and thus is a ternary relation). The relation has values in the three domains associated with the conceptual terms. While the relational view is formally equivalent, and thus equivalent in data processing with the e-message, the two may be rather distinct from the user's perspective. An e-message is *true* or *false*, depending on whether or not a corresponding e-situation existed at the specified time. A true e-message is an *e-fact*.

In the literature, "associative triple" is often used as almost equivalent to e-message (disregarding the time dimension). The typical "associative triple" has the form, "*attribute* of *object* is *value*" (e.g., "profession of Tom is teacher"). It does not mention at what time interval it is true.

ELEMENT OF DATA: E-ENTRY OR E-RECORD. The link to the data representation of information is obtained through the design of one group of data terms for each of the conceptual terms in each e-message. The set of this data will be referred to as an "e-entry." If the data is stored in the same physical area, it may also be referred to as an "e-record". Thus, there is first a step of information analysis and design before the data design can start (whether we intermix these steps or not). Of course a written description of an e-message (like the preceding one) is already an e-entry, but data design will consider which data and formats (ultimately bit configurations) to use in the system for each e-message (see Fig. 3).

**Kind of Information, Kind of e-Messages, e-Files.** In our conception of reality we use *kinds* or *classes* of objects and kinds or classes of properties. Thus, e-messages that inform about objects of the same kind by assigning properties of the same kind to them may be regarded as *instances* of the same information kind or elementary concepts, or "e-concepts" as we may call them. The kinds of objects and properties conceived are subjective, and sometimes differ strongly among subjects. To achieve a satisfactory intersubjectivity in choosing terms is thus an important part of information design.

The classification of objects, properties, and e-concepts is fundamental to information system design. Without it, we could not organize data for retrieval. Also, algorithms must be designed for the e-concepts in order to hold for all e-messages of the same e-concept. An e-concept is associated with real-world e-situations of the same kind.

As an aid in resolving subjective differences and defining synonyms, *thesaurii* are designed, which define the conceptual terms used. Now we have the form

$$\text{e-message: } \langle oc;\ pc;\ tc \mid oi;\ pi;\ ti \rangle$$

where oc, pc, tc = class names that denote the class of the object, property, and time indication, respectively.
oi, pi, ti = identifiers in the domain of the respective classes and give the *value tuple* of the message.

For example, the e-message

"article A ordered by customer C at date 730328"

could appear as

e-message: ⟨article; ordered by; at date | A; C; 730328⟩

Each class may, of course, be defined hierarchically, in which case new class names are added and associated identifiers are added to the e-message value tuples. The class names are invariant for all e-messages of the same e-concept. They thus characterize the following concept:

$$\text{e-concept: } \langle oc;\ pc;\ tc \rangle$$

or

$$\text{e-concept: } \langle oc,\ pc \rangle$$

when the class of time indication may not be of interest, as in early stages of analysis.

Thus, the e-concept has a simpler description than the e-message. It is therefore the natural thing to specify first in information design.

*Example*

e-concept: ⟨article; ordered by, customer⟩ (Object class: article; Property class: ordered by, customer)

Note that "customer" has the role of a component of the property class specification, although in the general frame of reference it appears as an object class. A collection of e-entries for e-messages of the same e-concept form an *e-file* (elementary file).

TRANSPOSITION (OR PERMUTATION) OF E-CONCEPTS—RELATIONS. In the preceding example, the e-concept was seen as information about articles while also informing about the kind of e-situations. Alternatively, information about this kind of e-situation can be about "customers" or about "ordered by":

e-concept′ ⟨customer; ordered, article⟩
e-concept″ ⟨order; article, customer⟩

We say that we *transpose* an e-concept when we change the roles (as object part or property part of the e-message) of the conceptual terms. Note that transposition implies both a permutation of the terms *and* a change (e.g., a reversion) of the relation involved (e.g., precedence is changed to a succedence). Transposition is not as so simple a change in the system as it may seem. Not only are terms permuted and changed, but the retrieval structure (e.g., sorting order) will probably be changed also. The terms in the e-concept descriptions are the basis for the *primary keys* to be used in the system.

In the same way that an e-message could formally be regarded as an instance of a relation, an e-concept is formally a time-dependent binary relation and thus a ternary relation. (When the conceptual terms are hierarchic groups, the relation appears as *n*-ary, $n > 2$). In such a case, one ignores to some extent the distinction between "object" and "property" (and maybe "time") and regards these as two domains with a relation. The possibility of transposition seems to support such a view. Still, it seems that there are many reasons to retain the distinctions, as in the infological view.

For instance, the binary relation

product group XY, amount sold, 10000$

becomes the ternary relation

product group XY in district D, amount sold, 10000$

where the object is product group XY in district D. It becomes a 4-relation if we add the time:

product group XY in district D, amount sold, 10000$, during 1973.

E-ALGORITHM, E-PROCESS. An elementary algorithm, or e-algorithm, produces e-messages of one e-concept while using other e-concepts as precedents (or input). An execution of an e-algorithm is an e-process that produces an e-message. An e-algorithm is an implementation of the precedence relation between the e-concept produced and its precedent e-concepts. Common algorithms are systems of e-algorithms and e-concepts.

CONSOLIDATION OF E-CONCEPTS AND E-MESSAGES: C-CONCEPTS, N-RELATIONS. Often one is interested in several properties of an object at the same time, calling for several e-messages about the same object, as in Fig. 4(a). One may even be interested in properties of the situation itself, and thus will use e-messages about an e-message. This may be because they are naturally conceived (by some users) as belonging together.

In this case we have a *naturally consolidated* information kind [Fig. 4(b)] or *natural c-concept* (c for consolidated). It may then be a natural *n*-ary relation or *n*-relation (time dependent), *n* being less than or equal to the sum of orders of relations of the e-concepts involved.

Another reason for consolidation is that it will save data transport (e.g., access and transfers) and equipment (e.g., tape handlers). Then it is rather a question of data design and consolidation of e-files into c-files. This is not a natural *n*-relation. Consolidation of e-messages about the same object (and time) will save a number of occurrences of object (and time) references. Consolidation usually is combined with formatted records or entries so that a common record description can be used for a file and each entry is just the tuple of value terms.

*Example.* The message m0:

m0: article # 325; order; quantity 5 pieces; customer # 127; date 720911;

may be seen as a consolidation of two e-messages:

e-m1: article # 325; order; customer # 127; date 720911;
e-m2; e-m1: quantity 5 pieces;

The e-message e-m1 informs about the object "article # 325" and the e-message e-m2 informs about

| | Object | Property | Value | Time |
|---|---|---|---|---|
| e-message 1: | Prodgrp K, article #325, | order, | customer #127, | date 720911; |
| e-message 2: | e-message 1, quantity, | 5 pieces; | | |
| e-message 3: | Prodgrp K, article #17, | order, | customer #127, | date 720911; |
| e-message 4: | e-message 3, quantity, | 11 pounds; | | |
| e-message 5: | Prodgrp M, article #12, | order, | customer #127, | date 720911; |
| e-message 6: | e-message 5, quantity, | 7 gallons; | | |

(a)

| | | | |
|---|---|---|---|
| Order | | | |
| Date | 720911 | | |
| Customer #127 | | | |
| | Product group | Article | Quantity |
| | K | 325 | 5 pieces |
| | | 17 | 11 pounds |
| | M | 12 | 7 gallons |

(b)

**Fig. 4.** (a) Collection of associated e-messages. (b) consolidated message (e-m1 ∪ e-m2 ∪ e-m3 ∪ e-m4 ∪ e-m5 ∪ e-m6).

the object "e-m1"; that is, e-m2 informs that the situation described by e-m1 has the further property "quantity = 5 pieces," so that e-m1 and e-m2 together give the information of m0. Here "order" and "quantity 5 pieces" are regarded as two simple properties.

In a typical, simple query to an information system or a data base, one wants to know the value of a stored instance of a certain term. One cannot, of course, just ask for the term. For instance, one cannot just ask: "What is the quantity?" It is, on the other hand, not possible for a user to specify exactly the location in the system's data structure of the instance desired of the term. The user must be allowed to put his query in terms that are meaningful to him. This is possible because he can specify which e-message it is that contains the term-instance he wants. For example, he may form the *e-query*:

Prodgrp K, article # 325, order, ?, date 720911

by writing the e-message with a question mark replacing the term he wants. The system would reply: "customer # 127" [see Fig 4(a)]. Similarly, if he writes the e-query as "e-message 5, quantity, ?," the reply would be "7 gallons."

The user may know the content of e-message 5, but he may not know that that message has been given the name "e-message 5." He may then replace "e-message 5" by its content, in which case "e-message 5, quantity, ?" is replaced by the equivalent query:

Prodgrp M, article # 12, order, customer # 127, date 720911; quantity, ?;

and the answer would be: "7 gallons" [Fig. 4(a) or, equivalently, Fig. 4(b)].

## References

1961. Carnap, R. *Introduction to Semantics and Formalization of Logic*. Cambridge, Mass.: Harvard University Press.

1964. Bar-Hillel, Y. *Language and Information, Selected Essays*. Reading, Mass.: Addison-Wesley.

1972. Langefors, B. *Theoretical Analysis of Information Systems*. Philadelphia: Auerbach. (Also Lund, Sweden: Studentlitteratur.)

1975. Langefors, B., and B. Sundgren. *Information Systems Architecture*. New York: Petrocelli/Charter.

B. Langefors

# INFORMATION PROCESSING

For articles on related subjects *see* ACCESS METHODS; ARTIFICIAL INTELLIGENCE; INFORMATION AND DATA; INFORMATION RETRIEVAL; and SYMBOL MANIPULATION.

For articles on related terms *see* ADDRESSING; AMERICAN FEDERATION OF INFORMATION PROCESSING SOCIETIES; and INTERNATIONAL FEDERATION FOR INFORMATION PROCESSING.

Information processing might, not inaccurately, be defined as "what computers do." In fact, the broadest professional organizations concerned with computer science are named the American Federation of Information Processing Societies, and the International Federation for Information Processing, respectively.

For information to be processed by a computer or by any other information processing system, it must somehow be represented or symbolized. Hence, information processing is essentially synonymous with symbol manipulation, and the entire discussion in this Encyclopedia of symbol manipulation could be readily retitled "information processing." In this article, we will approach the topic of information processing in a somewhat more philosophical, less technical, vein than in the article Symbol Manipulation.

The phrase "information processing" is often used in preference to "computation" or "data processing," to emphasize the generality of computers —the fact that they are in no way limited to manipulating just symbols that designate numbers, but can operate in any domain, numerical or nonnumerical, where information is represented in symbolic form. The term "information," in turn, carries allusions to the Shannon-Wiener theory of selective information, which emphasizes the role of symbol structures as designating one particular state of affairs out of some larger set of possible states. Thus, if we are dealing with the class of flowers, the symbol "rose" conveys the information that we are concerned with a particular subclass of that class.

Information has other aspects besides the selective aspect emphasized in the Shannon-Wiener theory. However, this selective aspect is closely connected with the way in which information is used by information processing systems such as computers. Information processing systems are capable of executing a *conditional branch* or transfer operation. The conditional branch operation detects which of several different states of affairs prevails (e.g., which of several symbol structures is stored in the working memory of the computer), and sends the subsequent computation along different paths depending on which state of affairs is detected. Thus, as the basis of the selective information available to it, the information processing system behaves in a selective, or informed, fashion.

The use of selective information by conditional branch processes lies at the root of everything complex or clever that a computer can do. In the simplest case, the conditional branch detects when an iteration is done (when the adding of a column of figures has been completed), and transfers control to the next process. (It was with this use in mind that Babbage first invented the conditional branch.) In more complex situations, conditional branching processes enable information processing systems to engage in all kinds of intelligent problem-solving behaviors (whether the intelligence be artificial or natural).

Effective information processing often depends crucially on substituting a high degree of selectivity (that is, a high degree of dependence on selective information) for a large amount of brute-force search through immense spaces of possible alternatives. Popular accounts of the computer often emphasize the impressive speed of its basic arithmetic processes and the vast number of computations it can perform in a short time. In actual fact, apart from "number crunching" applications, the arithmetic speed of the computer is far less important than its capability for selectivity, using information interpreted by the conditional branch processes.

Empirical research on human chess-playing skill, for example, shows that masters do not explore more alternatives than ordinary players—and probably do not even usually look more moves ahead. Instead, their superior performance almost certainly rests on looking at the *right* things—i.e., using information effectively to explore selectively. Similarly, artificial intelligence applications of the computer, whether for chess playing or in other tasks, always require the use of information to behave selectively, rather than rely primarily on the speed of the machine to carry out extensive searches.

We can illustrate this trade-off between selectivity and speed in information processing by two examples: programs for retrieving information from large stores, and programs for solving problems.

**Information Retrieval.** Whenever we have a large store of data—say, a set of customer records

—it becomes expensive to search the entire store sequentially to find a particular piece of data. We would like, instead, to be able to go directly to the point where the data is to be found and to extract it without a lengthy search. A memory that allows us to do this is often called "random access." A better description for it is "addressable, direct access," for there is nothing random about the way in which we approach it. The store is to be *addressable* so that each record in it can be designated, or pointed to, by a symbolized address (name). It is to have *direct access* so that the information processor can be switched to read the desired record directly, once its name is known, without requiring a search.

Now it is well known that to select a particular item from a set of $n$ items requires approximately $\log_2 n$ binary switching operations. Suppose we have a store of 64 records. Since $64 = 2^6$, we can use strings of 6 binary digits each (e.g., 100110) to provide distinct addresses for the 64 records. An appropriate switching device would have to perform six switching operations—one for each digit—to select a desired record. With such a system, the number of switching operations required to select a record increases only with the logarithm of the number of records—6 binary operations, as we have seen, for 64 records; 10 operations for 1,024 records; and 20 operations for more than a million records.

An unindexed book (or a nonalphabetized encyclopedia) frustrates human information processors because it provides no means to find a desired item of information without linear search. Thick books are proportionately more frustrating in this respect than thin books. A good index converts the book into an addressable, direct access store. The cost of retrieving an item can now be expected to increase only with the logarithm of the size of the book.

**Problem Solving.** To illustrate how information permits selectivity in solving problems, we will examine a trivially simple example.

How do we use an information processor to solve this arithmetic equation:

$$5X + 3 = 2X + 7$$

If we depended only on the processor's speed, we might try a simple *generate-and-test* method: Generate various values of $X$ and substitute them in the equation; then test whether the two sides are equal. The futility of this approach is evident as soon as we ask, "Over what class of values shall we generate—integers, rational numbers, real numbers—and in what order?" Of course a very fast computer might solve such problems in a reasonable time, if only problems involving small numbers were presented and possible solutions involving fractions with small numerators and denominators were generated first.

A second approach might be to write the equation as

$$5X + 3 - 2X - 7 = 0.$$

Then we could generate a possible solution and test to find if it gave a positive or negative value to the left side. If the values were positive, this information, communicated to the generator, could cause it to next generate a smaller possible solution; if the values were negative, a larger solution. In this way, the feedback of information could guide the generator to the correct solution by a process of successive approximations. Computational algorithms that employ successive approximations use information in this general way to reduce the amount of search.

Of course a far more effective way to solve the original equation is to observe that the solution is an expression of the form $X = K$, with no constant on the left side, no term in $X$ on the right side, and $X$ having unity as its coefficient. By subtracting 3 from both sides of the original equation, then subtracting $2X$ from both sides, and then dividing the resulting equation through by 3, we obtain the final result, $X = 4/3$, without any search whatsoever. This was accomplished by comparing the given equation with the form of the desired solution, and taking specific actions to bring it into the desired form based on the specific differences noted. Thus, when the constant 3 is found on the left side, where no constant is wanted, it is removed by subtracting 3 from both sides.

At each step, specific information extracted from the problem expression is used to choose a specific action that will alter the expression in the desired way. Since all the required selectivity is provided by the information embedded in the given symbolic expression, no search is required to find the answer. The safe can be opened, so to speak, by reading off the correct combination, rather than by spinning the dials to try different settings. Simple as it is, this example is a prototype for the most sophisticated artificial intelligence system, and contains in rudimentary form the information processes needed for carrying out *means-ends analysis*. (Means-ends analysis involves deleting one or more differences between an actual and a desired situation and then applying operators to reduce one or more of the remaining differences as described in the algebra example above.)

A basic reason, then, why we refer to computers as information processors is that they have to not only provide us with information—by performing a numerical computation, retrieving data from a store, or in some other way—but also to respond to new information, enabling them to substitute a high degree of selectivity for speed in search as a means of solving problems.


REFERENCES

1968. Minsky, Marvin (Ed.). *Semantic Information Processing*. Cambridge, Mass.: M.I.T. Press. Contains examples of how systems use information to guide search in sophisticated ways.

1972. Newell, Allen, and Herbert A. Simon. *Human Problem Solving*. Englewood Cliffs, N.J.: Prentice-Hall, chap. 4. This work discusses selective search, and describes a number of general search methods, including means-ends analysis, and their properties.

1972. Simon, Herbert A., and Laurent Siklóssy (Eds.). *Representation and Meaning*. Englewood Cliffs, N.J.: Prentice-Hall. Further examples of sophisticated search in information processing systems that use information to guide search in sophisticated ways.


H. A. SIMON

# INFORMATION RETRIEVAL

For articles on related subjects *see* CURRENT AWARENESS SYSTEM; DATA SECURITY; DATA STRUCTURES; INFORMATION AND DATA; and INFORMATION SCIENCE.

For articles on related terms *see* COMPUTER NETWORKS; FILES; and INFORMATION SYSTEMS.

Information retrieval (IR) is concerned with the structure, analysis, organization, storage, searching, and dissemination of information. An information retrieval system operates on the one hand with a stored collection of information, and on the other with a user population desiring to obtain access to the stored items. An IR system is thus designed to extract from the files those items that most nearly correspond to existing user needs as reflected in requests submitted by the user population. A library storing books and serving a population of customers is then, among other things, an example of an information retrieval system.

For some years, the information retrieval area has been of concern to the increasing number of people interested in science and technology, in part because of the continued outpouring of potentially useful information—the production of printed materials, for example, is thought to increase yearly at a rate of about 10%—in part because of the ever-mounting costs of information generation, and in part because of the increasing technical difficulties in selectively distributing a large volume of information to a heterogeneous user population.

Conceptually, it is possible to reduce the operations of a typical information retrieval system to the following two main types: *information analysis*, normally consisting of the assignment to each stored item and to each search request of indicators designed to reflect the information content of the given item; and *information organization* and *file search* concerned with the manner in which the stored information is organized in the file and with the corresponding search procedures. Normally, a useful search strategy depends primarily on the organization of the information in storage, on the particular kind of information need expressed by the user, and on the equipment available to carry out the retrieval work.

In recent years, many of the operational retrieval services have implemented on-line operations, using console terminal devices to introduce search queries and to obtain retrieval output. In that case, the information searches may take place *interactively* in such a way that information supplied by the users during the search operation is used to obtain improved search output. Furthermore, *networks* of information centers may be created by supplying suitable connections between individual centers, thereby affording the user population a chance to access the resources of the whole network.

The establishment of information nets, capable of storing large masses of data and of making them available to vast user populations in remote locations, raises complicated legal and social problems, connected in part with the propriety of unlimited duplication and transmission of information that may be subject to legal restrictions (as is the case for patented and copyrighted information), and in part with the preservation of information privacy, where this may be warranted.

Retrieval operations and techniques used in conjunction with library or text processing systems are also of interest in a variety of different information processing systems, including data management systems, selective information dissemination systems, and fact retrieval or question-answering systems.

**Indexing and Content Analysis.** In most operational retrieval situations, information analysis is carried out manually by using subject experts or trained indexers to assign content identifiers to information items and search requests. Such information identifiers are known variously as keywords, index terms, subject indicators, or concepts, and the search operation often consists in matching sets of keywords assigned to stored information items with keywords representing the search requests. The matching is followed by the retrieval of those items whose content indicators exhibit a sufficiently high degree of similarity to the query indicators.

A typical set of words, or word portions, indicative of the notion of "toxicity" is contained in Fig. 1. Such terms might then be assigned for purposes of content identification to documents and queries in the area of toxicity.

| |
|---|
| toxic . . . , poison . . . , lethal dose, LD, side effect, drug allerg . . . , drug reaction, drug sensiti . . . , intoxicat . . . , venom . . . , side action, side reaction, adverse effect, adverse reaction, ill effect, idiosyncra . . . , overdos . . . , overtreat . . . , intoleran . . . , contraindicat . . . , salicylism, goitrogen . . . , nephrotoxic . . . , neurotoxic . . . , hypervitaminosis, untoward, undesirable, deleterious, irritat . . . , irritan . . . , harm . . . , risk . . . , danger . . . , hazard . . . . |

**Fig. 1.** Terms denoting notion of toxicity that may be assigned during document and query analysis.

While the indexing practice is still largely manual, automatic indexing methods are becoming increasingly popular, particularly in a document retrieval environment where references to stored documents are retrieved in response to incoming search requests. The following types of operations are then often used:

1. Expressions are chosen from document or query texts, consisting variously of words, word stems, noun phrases, prepositional phrases, or other content units, which exhibit certain specified properties.

2. Weights may be assigned to each expression on the basis of the frequency of occurrence of the given expression, or the position of the expression in the document, or the type of entity.

3. The expressions originally assigned may be replaced by new ones, or new "associated" expressions may be added to those originally available, based on information contained in stored dictionaries, or on statistical co-occurring characteristics among the terms in a document collection, or on syntactical relations among words.

4. Additional relational indicators between terms may be supplied to express syntactical, or functional, or logical relationships among the entities available for content identification.

The end result of a content analysis procedure is shown in Fig. 2 for two typical queries in the world affairs area. In each case, the resulting query "vectors" are shown, including both term identifications and weights assigned to the terms.

The result of such an automatic indexing process is then similar to that previously outlined in that each stored item is identified by a set of terms representing information content. In operational systems, the automatic indexing practice is still largely restricted to the analysis of document *titles* only—the resulting search products being called "permuted" title indexes or "keyword in context" (KWIC) indexes. However, as larger text portions are made available in machine-readable form, the content analysis will extend to abstracts, summaries, or full texts, with results equivalent to, or exceeding in effectiveness, those now obtainable in manual systems. An example of a KWIC index is given in the article on that subject.

**File Organization and Search Strategies.** Several classes of file organizations are commonly used, the simplest of which is the *serial file.* Here, no subsets of the file are defined, no directories are provided affording access to any subsections of the file, and no particular file order is specified. A search is then performed by a sequential comparison of the query with the identifiers of all stored items. Such a serial file organization is most economical in storage space, since no overhead is incurred for the storage of directories or links between items; furthermore, access is equally con-

```
66          Query number
*FIND   66
AGREEMENT BETWEEN SYRIA AND IRAQ ON FULL ECONOMIC UNITY
AND CLOSER ECONOMIC COOPERATION                                 Query text
                                                                Term number
VECTOR:  162/ 12/, 2302/ 12/, 2535/ 12/,4454/ 24/, 6325/ 12/,7136/ 12/,
         14896/ 12/,16488/ 12/,    0/  0/,                      Term weight
                                   Vector termination
67
*FIND   67
CONTINUING CONFLICT BETWEEN INDIA AND PAKISTAN OVER KASHMIR

VECTOR: 2454/ 12/, 2509/ 12/,6988/ 12/,8022/ 12/,10405/ 12/,   0/  0/,
```

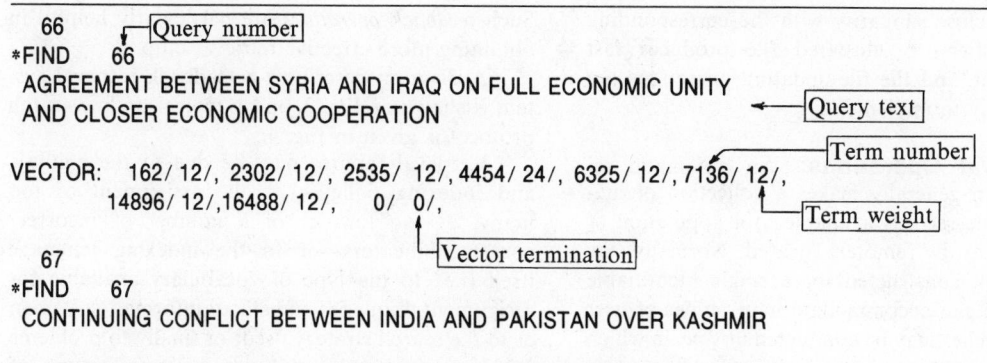

| *English Term* | *Term Number* | | |
|---|---|---|---|
| AGREE | 162 | FULL | 6325 |
| CLOSE | 2302 | IRAQ | 7136 |
| COOPERATE | 2535 | SYRIA | 14896 |
| ECONOMIC | 4454 | UNITY | 16488 |

**Fig. 2.** Typical analysis query vectors.

venient with respect to all keyword classes such as document authors, dates of publication, or content indicators. Unfortunately, a sequential search operation is time consuming and is thus unusable if search output is expected rapidly.

An equally small storage overhead may be incurred in the *computed-access files*, where the stored information is grouped into sets of items mathematically related in some way. In this case, a computation is performed on the set of terms used for accessing, and the "hashed" result of the computation is transformed into one or more storage addresses corresponding to the locations where the requested information may be stored. The search time is very small for computed access files, and no directories may be needed in addition to the main file. However, it is difficult in practice to construct good hashing functions that produce few collisions between distinct items mapping into the same storage address.

*Chained files* are characterized by the fact that all items exhibiting a given common identifier are "chained" together by appropriate links, or pointers; a directory normally provides access to the first item in each chain, and the file is searched by following the pointers within the individual chains. Chained files provide faster access than do serial files, but considerable storage overhead may be incurred to store pointers and directories, and a problem arises when the chain lengths become excessive for certain terms.

The best known and most universally used file organization in information retrieval is the so-called *inverted file*, where a large inverted directory is used to store for each applicable keyword or content identifier the corresponding set of document or item identifications and locations. The file is thus partitioned into sets of items with common keywords, and a search in the document file is replaced by the directory search. Since only small portions of the directory need to be accessed for any given query, acceptable search times are generally obtainable. For this reason, inverted files are currently used with almost all operational on-line retrieval systems.

Inverted file organizations are advantageous in a static environment where the set of terms usable for content identification is not subject to many changes, and where access to the complete term set pertaining to a given stored item is not normally required. In a dynamic situation where changes are made to the content indicators attached to queries and documents, a *clustered file* organization may be preferable. In a clustered file, items that exhibit similar sets of content identifiers are automatically grouped into common classes, or clusters, and a search is performed by looking only at those clusters that exhibit close similarity with the corresponding query identifiers. A clustered file produces fast search output, and the file-updating operations are relatively easy to implement.

**Retrieval Operations.** An automatic retrieval system generally makes a collection of machine-readable records available to a population of users that may be remotely located. Normally, the system is not constructed for a single identifiable purpose, but can accommodate many types of user queries. Searches may be conducted *off line*, in which case a sequential file search may be utilized to obtain responses within several days, or weeks, from the time of query submission; alternatively, an *on-line* search can be carried out directly from a terminal device, using an inverted file organization.

Initially, a user may submit a query statement, which is then transformed—manually or automatically—into a set of terms acceptable to the system; appropriate indicators or connectors may also be defined to express relationships among sets of terms. For example, a request covering "tissue culture studies of human breast cancer," may then be transformed into a statement of the form:

$$\left\{\begin{array}{c}\text{Breast neoplasm}\\ \textit{or}\\ \text{Carcinoma, ductal}\end{array}\right\} \quad \textit{and} \quad \left\{\begin{array}{c}\text{Human}\\ \textit{or not}\\ \text{(any term}\\ \text{indicating}\\ \text{animal or}\\ \text{disease)}\end{array}\right\}$$

$$\textit{and} \quad \left\{\begin{array}{c}\text{Tissue culture}\\ \textit{or}\\ \text{Culture media}\\ \textit{or}\\ \text{Chick embryo}\end{array}\right\} \quad \textit{and} \quad \text{English}$$

If an on-line console search is used, various optional displays may be available to help the user in obtaining acceptable search output. Thus, tutorial sequences may be included to inform the operator about the features of the system; displays of the available term vocabulary may be used during the generation of the query statement; finally, displays of previously retrieved information—i.e., titles or abstracts of items retrieved earlier—may help the user in constructing improved query formulations. Such *feedback operations* are particularly helpful in obtaining more effective retrieval output.

A diagram describing a feedback retrieval system is shown as Fig. 3, and a typical on-line search protocol is given in Fig. 4.

Retrieval failures may be due to the analysis and indexing policy—i.e., the assignment of too many, or too few, or of a number of incorrect content indicators—or to the indexing language itself (i.e., to the type of vocabulary available for assignment to queries and stored information items); or to the search strategy used; or finally to problems arising during user-system interaction. The use of natural language indexing systems may ease some of the restrictions inherent in a controlled indexing language in that it creates many diverse avenues for obtaining access to the stored information; on the other hand, new problems may be introduced by ambiguous or nonstandard uses of the vocabulary. Many of the retrieval problems arising in standard systems from the lack of appropriate user-system interaction are eliminated in modern real-time search systems.

In addition, the *networks of information systems*, which are starting to be created, may relieve the inadequacy of local data banks, provide access to a greater variety of services, and furnish economy and improved use of technical competence. A simplified information network is shown in Fig. 5.

The question of *information privacy*, involving the right of individuals to obtain access to a given piece of information under specified conditions, is most complex, and no solution acceptable to all user classes is likely to emerge soon. On the other hand, it is relatively easy, at least conceptually, to provide *file security* by implementing any given set of privacy decisions. Such security measures may be data independent in the sense that a decision to provide access does not depend on the stored data, but only on the identity of the user and the type of file being manipulated; alternatively, the authority to access may be data dependent. Elaborate systems of user authentication by means of special passwords and of monitoring devices designed to detect unauthorized access are now in use in some installations.

**Retrieval Applications.** The most common type of retrieval situation is exemplified by a *reference retrieval* system performing "on demand" searches submitted by a given user population. Normally, only the bibliographic information is stored for each item, including authors' names, titles, journal or place of publication, dates, and applicable keywords and content identifiers. Often, only the

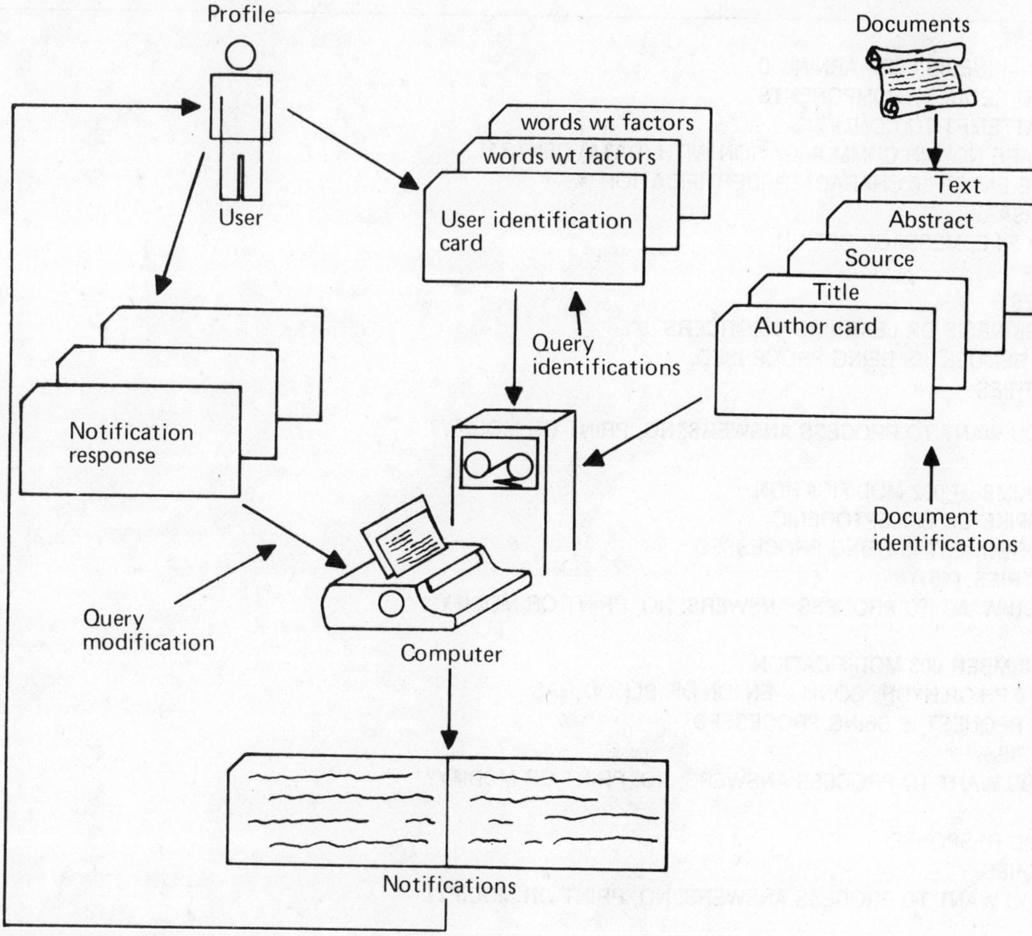


**Fig. 3.** Elements of retrieval system with provision for user feedback.

keywords are usable for search purposes; sometimes the words of the document titles can also be searched; less commonly, more extended text portions such as abstracts, summaries, or even full texts may be stored, in which case a text search (as opposed to a simple keyword search) becomes possible.

In any case, the responses provided by the system consist of references to the bibliographic items that match the user queries. In most conventional situations, the retrieved information is submitted to the users in no particular order of importance; an ordering in decreasing query-document similarity can, however, be obtained in the more advanced systems, which can then be used advantageously for search negotiation and feedback purposes.

A sample search output in decreasing query-document similarity order is shown in Fig. 6.

In a standard reference retrieval system, a search is conducted only when a user actually submits a search request. However, systems also exist which permanently store (and update) user "interest profiles," i.e., dummy queries that express the principal areas of interest for a given user population. Any new information items coming into the system are then periodically matched against the stored interest profiles, and the relevant output is supplied directly to each individual on a dependable, continuous schedule.

Some of the operational systems for such a *selective dissemination of information* (SDI) use response cards, submitted by the user population following receipts of a retrieved document, to update automatically the stored user profiles. Thus, as users become more or less interested in some areas, the positive or negative responses of the recipients are used to add or upgrade (or, correspondingly, to

```
REQUEST
HYPER←KINESIS LER←ARNING D
INVALID REQUEST COMPONENTS
WILL ATTEMPT TO CONTINUE
SSYU ARE NOW IN COMMUNICATION WITH (DATA) CENTRAL.
PLEASE ENTER 10 CHARACTER IDENTIFICATION.
OSEARSAAW.
ENTER FILE, MESSAGE OPTION
EARS,S
REQUEST
HYPERKINESIS OR LEARNING DISORDERS
YOUR REQUEST IS BEING PROCESSED,
16 ENTRIES.

DO YOU WANT TO PROCESS ANSWERS; NO, PRINT OR MODIFY?
M
ADD NUMBER 002 MODIFICATION
AND SPIKE OR EPILEPTOGENIC
YOUR REQUEST IS BEING PROCESSED.
18 ENTRIES. (151)
DO YOU WANT TO PROCESS ANSWERS; NO, PRINT OR MODIFY?
N
ADD NUMBER 003 MODIFICATION
P←AND PH OR HYDROGON← ←EN ION OR BLOOD GAS
YOUR REQUEST IS BEING PROCESSED.
0 ENTRIES.
DO YOU WANT TO PROCESS ANSWERS; NO, PRINT OR MODIFY?
M
INVALID RESPONSE
0 ENTRIES.
DO YOU WANT TO PROCESS ANSWERS; NO, PRINT OR MODIFY?
N
INVALID RESPONSE
0 ENTRIES.
DO YOU WANT TO PROCESS ANSWERS; NO, PRINT OR MODIFY?
PRINT2
ENTER DESIRED OUTPUT, DEVICE.
9,C
DO YOU WANT THE ENTRIES SEQUENCED? YES OR NO.
N
SET PAPER (IF NECESSARY), PRESS SPACE BAR TWICE AND TRANSMIT.
```

**Fig. 4.** On-line search protocol.

delete or downgrade) the respective terms from the profiles.

The rapid development of SDI systems is due in large part to the production and availability of a variety of tape data bases containing titles, references, and sometimes index terms of the published information in various fields.

Data management, or *management information systems*, normally provide general file processing capabilities together with user interface methods to simplify the manipulation and analysis of the stored data. In general, such systems include only simple record-keeping provisions, together with exception reporting, and output-generating capabilities based

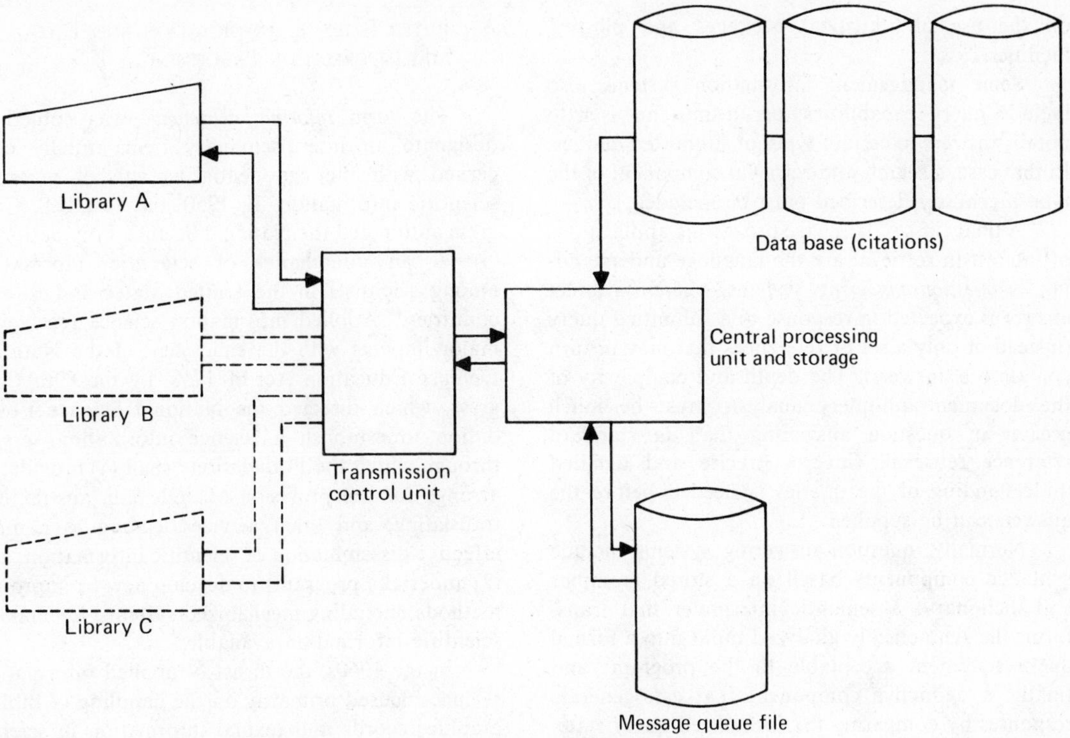


**Fig. 5.** Schematic diagram showing elements of a centralized network.

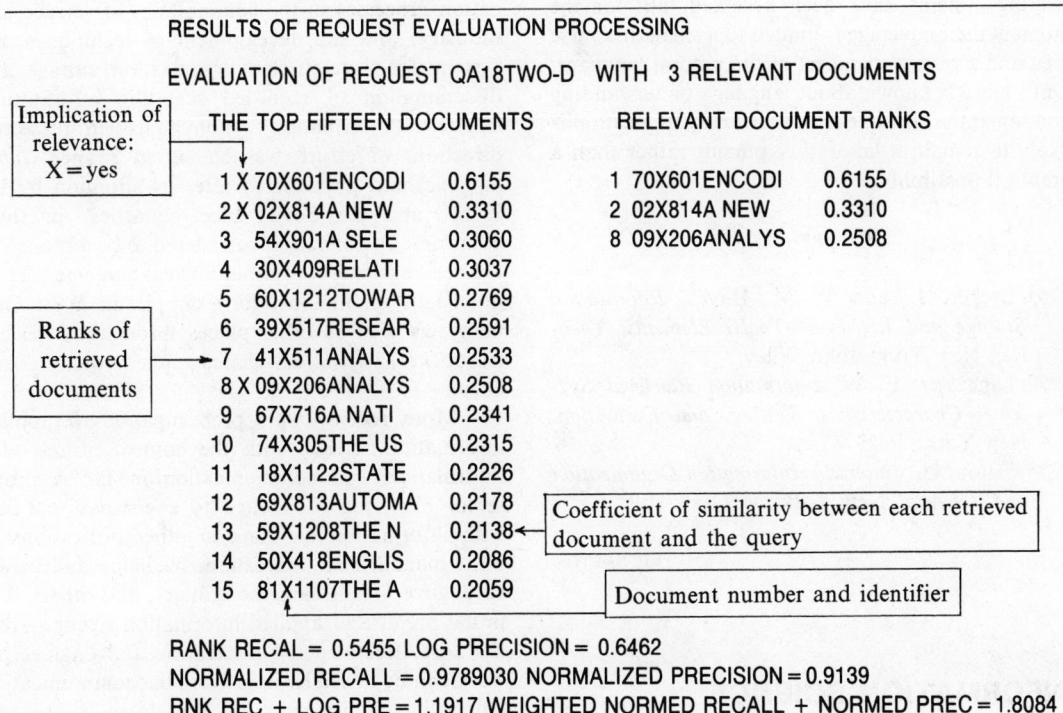

RESULTS OF REQUEST EVALUATION PROCESSING

EVALUATION OF REQUEST QA18TWO-D WITH 3 RELEVANT DOCUMENTS

Implication of relevance: X = yes

Ranks of retrieved documents

THE TOP FIFTEEN DOCUMENTS

| Rank | Relevant | Document | Coefficient |
|---|---|---|---|
| 1 | X | 70X601ENCODI | 0.6155 |
| 2 | X | 02X814A NEW | 0.3310 |
| 3 | | 54X901A SELE | 0.3060 |
| 4 | | 30X409RELATI | 0.3037 |
| 5 | | 60X1212TOWAR | 0.2769 |
| 6 | | 39X517RESEAR | 0.2591 |
| 7 | | 41X511ANALYS | 0.2533 |
| 8 | X | 09X206ANALYS | 0.2508 |
| 9 | | 67X716A NATI | 0.2341 |
| 10 | | 74X305THE US | 0.2315 |
| 11 | | 18X1122STATE | 0.2226 |
| 12 | | 69X813AUTOMA | 0.2178 |
| 13 | | 59X1208THE N | 0.2138 |
| 14 | | 50X418ENGLIS | 0.2086 |
| 15 | | 81X1107THE A | 0.2059 |

RELEVANT DOCUMENT RANKS

| Rank | Document | Coefficient |
|---|---|---|
| 1 | 70X601ENCODI | 0.6155 |
| 2 | 02X814A NEW | 0.3310 |
| 8 | 09X206ANALYS | 0.2508 |

Coefficient of similarity between each retrieved document and the query

Document number and identifier

RANK RECAL = 0.5455 LOG PRECISION = 0.6462
NORMALIZED RECALL = 0.9789030 NORMALIZED PRECISION = 0.9139
RNK REC + LOG PRE = 1.1917 WEIGHTED NORMED RECALL + NORMED PREC = 1.8084

**Fig. 6.** Search output in query-document similarity order.

on the use of statistical packages and plotting facilities.

Some management information systems also include query capabilities, permitting the user to obtain answers to certain types of submitted queries. In that case, a search-and-retrieval component of the type previously described must be included.

A final class of language processing applications of interest in retrieval are the language-understanding, or *question-answering*, systems, wherein a direct answer is expected in response to a submitted query (instead of only a set of references that may in turn contain the answers). The depth and complexity of the document-and-query analysis must be much greater in question answering than in standard reference retrieval, since a precise and detailed understanding of the queries is needed before the answers can be supplied.

Normally, question-answering systems include syntactic components based on a stored grammar and dictionary; a semantic interpreter that transforms the syntactically analyzed input into a formal query statement acceptable to the program; and finally, a deductive component that can generate responses by comparing the formalized query statement with information included in the data base.

Several experimental text-based question-answering systems have been designed, but for the moment their coverage is limited to a small discourse area and a restricted subset of the natural language. Until more is known about language understanding and semantics, the question-answering application is likely to remain a laboratory pursuit rather than a practical possibility.

REFERENCES

1963. Becker, J., and R. M. Hayes. *Information Storage and Retrieval—Tools, Elements, Theories.* New York: John Wiley.

1968. Lancaster, F. W. *Information Retrieval Systems—Characteristics, Testing, and Evaluation.* New York: John Wiley.

1968. Salton, G. *Automatic Information Organization and Retrieval.* New York: McGraw-Hill.

G. SALTON

# INFORMATION SCIENCE

For articles on related subjects *see* COMPUTER SCIENCE; INFORMATION AND DATA; and INFORMATION PROCESSING.

The term *information science* was coined to designate an interdisciplinary field initially concerned with the exponential growth of recorded scientific information. In 1950, the 81st U.S. Congress authorized the National Science Foundation to "foster an interchange of scientific information among scientists in the United States and foreign countries." Applied information science received a major impetus with the enactment of the National Defense Education Act of 1958, by the 89th Congress, which directed the National Science Foundation to establish a science information service through which the Foundation "shall (1) provide, or arrange for the provision of, indexing, abstracting, translating, and other services leading to a more effective dissemination of scientific information, and (2) undertake programs to develop new or improved methods, including mechanized systems, for making scientific information available."

In the 1960s, the thrust of applied information science focused primarily on the handling of bibliographic records and textual information in science and engineering. Two major foci of effort received considerable attention: the study of the communication processes in the communities of science and industry; and the development of techniques and systems for more efficient organization, storage, and dissemination of recorded scientific information. The term "informatics," synonymous with these two directions of effort, was coined in France (*informatique*) and popularized after its adoption by the USSR and the Soviet bloc countries; in these countries, *informatika* is considered to be a branch of the social sciences. (Terminological agreement is by no means unanimous: for example, in West Germany, as well as other places throughout western Europe, *Informatik* designates applied computer science.)

More recently, the preoccupation of applied information science with the control of recorded information and communication in the scientific sector has been broadened to encompass concern with information handling in other professions as well: management, education, medicine and health care, government, law, the military, and others. The initial premise of applied information science—that the cost effectiveness of scientific and engineering work can be raised by improving the communication among its practitioners—has been formulated into a broader assumption: that the cost effectiveness of the human information processes which characterize these professions (e.g., problem solving, decision making, learning, etc.) can be significantly improved through their formalization and gradual delegation to symbol processing machines.

From this assumption, present-day information science and its professions derive their current social mission and long-term objective: the design of information processing systems that augment man's mind and purposeful activities. The significance of the social mission of information science lies in its extending man's historic concern with the efficiency and effectiveness of physical processes into the domain of the symbolic processes of the human mind. So formulated and interpreted, information science subsumes or provides linkages among directions and aspects of other disciplines and professions, including those of applied computer science. Indeed, to the extent that both computer science and information science share these logical aspects of an engineering discipline (an interest in the design and use of information processing engines and systems), they are considered by many to be synonymous.

As reflected in its principal review publication (*Annual Review of Information Science and Technology*) and the programs of its professional societies (in the U.S., the American Society for Information Science), the character of recent information science has been that of a social science and/or an engineering science (technology). Increasingly it is realized, however, that significant progress in the social mission of information science may depend on its ability to develop a natural science branch of the discipline, to be devoted to basic research on the nature and properties of "information" as a fundamental phenomenon, and on primitive information processes. Such a realization motivates a growing number of academic departments in information science, the first of which was established in 1963 at the Georgia Institute of Technology, under the sponsorship of the National Science Foundation. Recently, the term "informatology" was proposed to distinguish the basic science branch of information science from its social and technological orientations.

As a basic science, information science has only begun its search for content and structure. The main direction of this incipient effort in the United States, the USSR, and western Europe is that of semiotics, the study of sign phenomena. (Signs are entities that signify some other thing, called the "object" of the sign, and can be interpreted by a sign interpreter.) This direction includes investigations of the static structure of signs—as represented by fields such as semantics, information theory, and complexity theory—and the study of dynamic sign processes (semiosis) that transfer or transport sign phenomena. In this setting, information science is of metadisciplinary import, due to the semiotic nature of the nonphysical sciences (linguistics, psychology, sociology, history, and others) in which the essential phenomena studied are sign phenomena.

### References

1966. Cuadra, C. C. (Ed.). *Annual Review of Information Science and Technology*. Chicago, Ill.: Encyclopedia Britannica, vol. I.

1973. Debons, A. (Ed.). *Challenges to the Development of a Science of Information: Proceedings of the 1972 NATO Advanced Study Institute in Information Science*. New York: Dekker.

V. Slamecka and C. R. Pearson

# INFORMATION SYSTEMS

For articles on related subjects *see* Computer Systems; Data Base and Data Base Management; Data Processing; Information and Data; Information Processing; Management Information Systems; and Processing Modes.
For articles on related terms *see* Control Applications; Files; Input-Output Devices; Medlars/Medline; Memory: Auxiliary; and String.

An information system can be defined as a collection of people, procedures, and equipment designed, built, operated, and maintained to collect, record, process, store, retrieve, and display information. An information system may utilize various technologies; Sage (1968) describes the historical development of information systems in organizations from Babylonian times. In this article, only systems that contain digital computers as integral parts are considered; sometimes these are called computer-based information systems (CBIS) to distinguish them from earlier (i.e., manual) systems.

Information systems (Fig. 1), as defined above, accept (as inputs), store (in files or a data base), and display (as outputs) strings of symbols that are grouped in various ways (digits, alphabetical characters, special symbols). Users of the information systems attribute some value or meaning to the

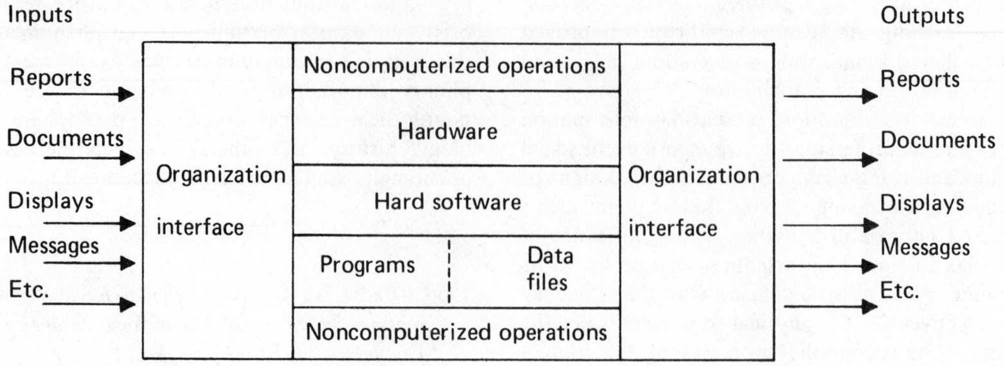


**Fig. 1.** Diagram of an information system.

string of symbols. Sometimes a distinction is made between the mechanistic representation of the symbols, which is called "data," and the meaning attributed to the symbols, which is called "information." A given output datum, under this definition, can result in different information to different users. In this article, the emphasis is on the common characteristics of systems rather than on the meaning attached to the output. The term "Information Processing System" (IPS) is perhaps more appropriate. It will be considered synonymous with "data processing system."

**Structure.** The information system itself consists of the expression, by an appropriate method, of a set of rules by which (1) the contents of the output are determined from the contents of the input and the contents of the data base, and/or (2) the contents of the data base are modified by the contents of the input. Physically, this may be viewed as shown in Fig. 1. First there are machines, or hardware, of which the most important is the CPU (Central Processing Unit) and various input and output devices such as terminals, card readers, printers, etc. Next is a set of software, including operating systems, utility programs, data base management systems, etc. In addition, there are programs specially prepared for the particular system, frequently known as the application software, which is normally prepared in some higher-level programming languages. The data is stored on auxiliary memories, such as disks, tapes, and bulk core.

**Classification of Information Systems.** Information systems may be classified in various ways for various purposes. One method of classification is by the application area, but a more useful classification is by type of service rendered. The following are among the most important classes:

1. *Computing service* systems that provide a general computing service to a number of users. Common examples are university computing centers, computing centers in research institutions, and commercial time-sharing services.
2. *Information storage and retrieval* systems designed to store data (or documents) and retrieve it in response to queries. An example is the medical information retrieval system MEDLARS.
3. *Command and control* systems built to monitor some given situations and provide a signal when predefined conditions occur. An example is the Ballistic Missile Early Warning System (BMEWS).
4. *Transaction processing* systems designed to process predefined transactions and produce predefined outputs as well as maintain the necessary data base. An example is an order-entry billing system.
5. *Message switching* systems that route messages over transmission lines from a point of origin to destination.
6. *Process control* systems designed to control physical processes by monitoring the conditions and signaling appropriate action to the machines. Common examples are systems to control chemical processes and oil refineries.

A summary of the inputs, data base contents, and outputs for these six systems is given in Table 1. Each of these types has certain characteristics that affect the structure of the system, the measures of performance which are appropriate, and the process of designing, building, and operating the system. Many systems in existence today have features from more than one type, and may be considered mixtures of the basic types.

**Table 1.** Typical inputs, data base contents, and outputs by types of system

| Type | Input | Data Base | Outputs |
|---|---|---|---|
| Computing service | Both programs and data supplied by users | Created by individual users for their own purposes. System maintains minimal data base for control and allocating charges. | Specified by users for their own purposes. |
| Information storage and retrieval | Determined by system designers on basis of what is relevant to inquiries to be answered. | Contains all input received. | Produced in answer to user inquiries. |
| Command and control | Obtained from sensors and monitors | Built up from data received by inputs. | Warning and action notices obtained by periodic processing of inputs and data base. |
| Transaction processsing | Predefined transactions. | Contains all data necessary to process transaction and produce outputs. | Specified by system designer to accomplish system objective. |
| Message switching | Messages. | Minimal. Contains data on status of nodes in network. | Messages sent to specified location. |
| Process control | Obtained from sensors and monitors. | Status of all processes under control of systems. | Signals to control operator of physical devices. |

The users of systems may be geographically distant from the physical hardware. Users initiate different types of requests or jobs to be processed. The system has a number of different types of resources, and may have more than one of each type. Any given request or job may need more than one type of resource, possibly given in some order. There are different ways of organizing the resources to accomplish the requests, and systems may be therefore classified by the type of system organization.

Batch or Sequential Processing. Requests are grouped into batches on the basis of common processing requirements, and each batch is processed as a unit, usually at a predetermined time. The individual user therefore gets his results at the conclusion of all operations on the batch in which his request is included.

Store and Forward. Each resource has a queue, consisting of the jobs that require that resource. When a job is finished at that resource, it is sent to the queue at the next resource needed, and the next job in the queue is processed. The user gets his result when all the operations on his job have been performed.

In-Line or Random Processing. Jobs are selected for processing according to some priority scheme; once a job has been started, it is processed completely through to the final result. All the necessary files in the data base are updated.

Interactive. The user communicates with the computing facility via terminals, and his requests are processed as they arrive. He gets quick responses, which he may use to prepare his next input. In order to accomplish this, it is usually necessary to provide some method of time sharing, unless the system is dedicated to a single user.

Real Time, or On Line. When a request is received, it is acted on usually by the in-line processing method so as to provide a response within a given time period. This differs from in-line processing in that feedback is used to control subsequent inputs and in that the demand on response time is stricter.

**Common Features of Information Systems.** The various classifications described above are useful in identifying common features of systems that may appear in more than one type. All six systems have certain features in common, which have important implications:

1. Information systems have to be designed, constructed, operated, and maintained. This is a nontrivial task and has led to the need for methods of system development, operation, and maintenance. An introduction to the topic is given by Benjamin (1971). A survey of current practice appears in the *EDP Analyzer*. Software engineering is a discipline emerging as a partial response to this need.

2. In the development and operation of information systems, both the programs and the data base are important in the benefit/cost performance.

3. Because of the large cost involved in developing information systems, there is an economic need for systems to share hardware, files, and programs.

4. The systems tend to be large and costly to develop, operate, and maintain. This arises because of economies of scale involved in larger hardware and in economies of scale involved in operation and maintenance of systems.

5. The systems involve man-machine communication at various levels, and problems of design and operation include both problems of communication among individuals, of communications with the machine, and of the communication among the various units of the machine. Therefore, documentation is an important aspect.

6. The uses of the systems and the technology on which the systems are developed are continuously changing, as are the organizations using them; consequently, the systems themselves are seldom if ever static.

Information systems are expensive to develop and to operate; consequently, analyses to determine whether they are serving the desired needs of users, and the measurement of their performance, are receiving considerable attention. Performance evaluation must be considered at a number of levels. At the top level, the value of the output of the system to the organization that supports it must be determined. Once these specific outputs have been justified, the performance of the physical system in achieving these outputs must be measured. This performance is a combination of the performance of programs, software, and the hardware equipment itself.

### References

1968. Sage, S. M. "Information Systems: A Brief Look into History," *Datamation* (November), pp. 63–69.

1971. Benjamin, R. I. *Control of the Information System Development Cycle*. New York: John Wiley.

1973. *EDP Analyzer*, Vol. 11, No. 5 (May).

D. Teichroew

## INPUT-OUTPUT CONTROL SYSTEMS

For articles on related subjects *see* Access Methods; Data Base and Data Base Management; Files; Memory: Auxiliary; and Operating Systems.
For articles on related terms *see* Blocks and Blocking; Buffer; Logical and Physical Units; and Supervisor Call.

One of the earliest and most fundamental reasons for the initial development and subsequent growth of operating systems concerns the handling of input/output (I/O) operations. The transfer of responsibility for I/O operations from the programmer to the operating system has been undertaken for several reasons. First of all, the construction of code for handling I/O is one of the more difficult aspects of programming a computer. By not requiring a programmer to know the details of programming I/O operations, computing services have become accessible to a greater number of people. Secondly, as assemblers, compilers, sort packages, and other utilities became available, it was necessary that:

1. Each of these utilities be provided with I/O services.

2. User programs not be permitted to write into areas where these utilities or their work spaces were stored.

A common set of I/O routines could be used by all system facilities (and user programs, too), thus saving duplicated effort. Moreover, a simple, carefully debugged set of routines could provide some measure of protection against destruction of important files of data. The problem of accidental destruction of stored data was further compounded in operating systems that permitted users to construct and maintain private files of programs and/or data. In such systems, the denial of direct I/O capabilities to the user became even more important.

For all of these reasons, the handling of I/O operations has become almost exclusively the province of the operating system. More specifically, it has become the province of the input/output control system (IOCS) portion of a computer operating system.

**Programmer Communication with the IOCS.** Typically, a programmer will communicate with the IOCS by calling various modules as subroutines. The assembly language programmer will generally have available a number of predefined macros, which will be expanded into subroutine calls to IOCS modules, using predefined calling sequences. Similarly, I/O commands in higher-level languages will generally be compiled into subroutine calls to appropriate IOCS modules. In more recent systems, these requests for I/O service have taken the form of supervisor calls.

**The Functions of IOCS.** The global function of an IOCS is, of course, to perform I/O operations for a programmer. This function may be refined to include the following tasks:

1. Interpretation of I/O requests.
2. Execution of I/O requests, once interpreted.
3. Location of the data to be transferred and where it is to be transferred to.
4. Initialization of transfer parameters.

These four topics will be discussed in subsequent sections.

INTERPRETATION OF I/O REQUESTS. Each of the various I/O requests that a user may make (e.g., READ, WRITE, REWIND, OPEN, CLOSE) must be decoded and the parameters checked. This process is accomplished by an I/O request interpreter. The interpreter will check such things as (1) the name of the operation, (2) the name of the logical unit involved, and (3) the parameters specified for the operation. Once checked, the interpreter will enter the parameters into the appropriate table (to be discussed below) and initiate execution of the I/O request.

The I/O request interpreter can, in certain cases, cause a variety of actions based on the I/O request. For example, a request to read a file that has not yet been opened might cause an error condition or simply cause the open request to be generated by the interpreter. Similarly, requests to write on a read-only device, such as a card reader, can be trapped at this level.

EXECUTION OF I/O REQUESTS. Execution of I/O requests involves various kinds of information and routines. Among the tasks that must be handled are:

1. Maintenance of correspondences between logical and physical devices.
2. Generation of physical I/O commands based on requests.
3. Coordination of peripheral activities and maintenance of status information.

Following the distinction between logical units and physical units, it is convenient to divide the portion of the IOCS that is directly concerned with I/O transfers into two parts—logical IOCS and physical IOCS. Logical IOCS will contain routines for managing data on logical units, while physical IOCS will perform analogous functions with respect to physical units. Thus, physical IOCS will contain routines for every physical I/O device attached to the computing system (actually, these routines may be shared among devices that are all of the same type, such as all the tape drives). These routines will handle interrupts from the device and control the execution of I/O transfers without regard for the logical content, format, or organization of the data being transferred. Physical IOCS will also contain routines for handling errors and exceptional conditions received from the device.

The logical IOCS contains routines that perform functions associated with the logical unit, as declared by the programmer (or as predefined by the system). Thus, the logical IOCS will contain routines to handle blocking and deblocking, perform label verification, control error handling and recovery, sense end-of-file and other exceptional conditions, etc., depending on the characteristics associated with a given logical unit. Clearly, logical IOCS will communicate with physical IOCS when transfer of data is necessary. Table 1 illustrates the division between logical and physical IOCS for several I/O requests.

*Tables for Logical IOCS and Physical IOCS.* As mentioned previously, it is common to share the actual routines for performing the various functions mentioned. In order that this may be done, and also provide a capability for users to change certain characteristics, the information that is particular to a given unit is usually organized into a table. The table is then passed to the particular IOCS routine as a parameter. Two types of tables may be distinguished: logical device tables and physical device tables.

Physical Device Tables. Each physical I/O unit

**Table 1.** Division of logical and physical IOCS requests.

| Request | Logical IOCS | Physical IOCS |
|---|---|---|
| Get the next record. | Deblock the next record. If buffer empty, get next block. If end-of-reel condition and file span multiple tapes, mount next reel. | Deliver next block from device. |
| Find a record in a randomly accessed file. | Request index tracks. Search index to find block of record. Request block of record. Find record and deliver to calling program. | Deliver index tracks. Deliver requested track. |
| Store a new record in a randomly accessed file which carries an index. | Add new record to proper block if there is space. Otherwise write new record in a separate area. Update the index to reflect the new data values. | Write updated block. Write a new record. Fetch index blocks and write index blocks. |

(device) will have an associated table containing information such as the following:

1. The device type and an indication of the data paths that may be used to transfer data to or from the device.
2. Status information concerning whether the device is busy, which data path is being used if the device is indeed busy, and whether the device is reserved though perhaps not busy.
3. The I/O operation currently pending on this device.
4. If the device contains storage that can be allocated and freed (e.g., the device is a disk), an indication of which areas are available.
5. The address of the routine that can construct commands for initiation of I/O transfers for this device.
6. The address of the routine that handles interrupts from the device.
7. The address of the routine that processes errors from the device.
8. Pointers to logical device tables associated with this physical device, with an indication of the currently active logical device.
9. Pointers to other physical device tables which share a data path with this physical device.

Fig. 1 gives an annotated version of a portion of a physical device table.

Logical Device Tables. The logical device table is used to keep track of information pertaining to an I/O operation on a logical device. Since several logical devices may share a single physical device (e.g., a disk), there may be several I/O operations outstanding on a given physical device. The current operation on the physical device is, of course, contained in the physical device table, as shown in Fig. 1. The information concerning the various logical device I/O operations will reside in the

Device Status Table (DST) Entry

| Unused | Driver name | Inst. | Entry count | Alternate channel | Primary channel |
|---|---|---|---|---|---|
| Head 1 position | Head 2 position | | Exit count | Inst. | Device busy/ not busy |

Explanation:
Driver name: Name of subroutine that issues physical I/O commands.
Inst: Current physical I/O instruction being executed by the driver.
Entry count: Counts the number of requests on this device.
Primary-Alternate channels: Naming of channels that can be used in conjunction with this device.
Head 1-2 positions: Status information on read/write head positioning.

**Fig. 1.** A portion of a physical device table. (Adapted from *SCOPE 3.1 Manual,* Control Data Corp.)

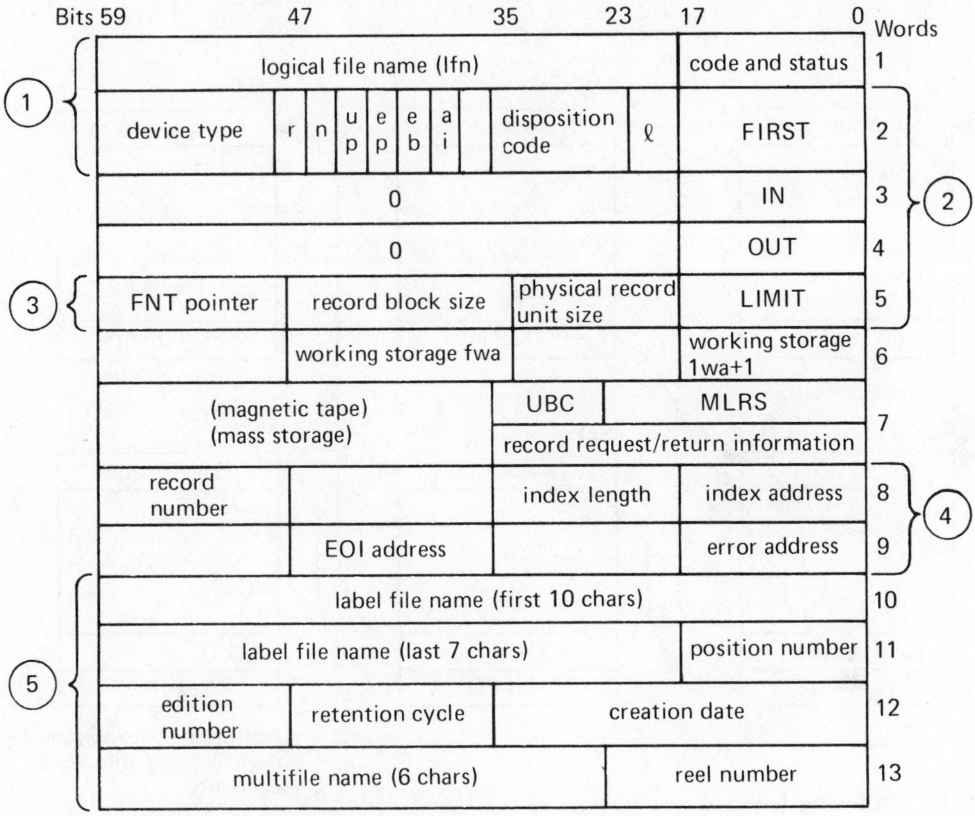

Bits 59
47
35
23
17
0
Words
logical file name (lfn)
code and status
1
device type
r
n
u p
e p
e b
a i
disposition code
ℓ
FIRST
2
0
IN
3
0
OUT
4
FNT pointer
record block size
physical record unit size
LIMIT
5
working storage fwa
working storage 1wa+1
6
(magnetic tape)
(mass storage)
UBC
MLRS
record request/return information
7
record number
index length
index address
8
EOI address
error address
9
label file name (first 10 chars)
10
label file name (last 7 chars)
position number
11
edition number
retention cycle
creation date
12
multifile name (6 chars)
reel number
13
1
2
3
4
5


Explanation:

1. Name of the file and information concerning its corresponding physical device.
2. Buffer pointers for circular buffering.
3. Information concerning blocking factors for blocking/deblocking operations.
4. Indications of index locations for indexed sequential file organization.
5. Label information for verification and future mount requests.

**Fig. 2.** Annotated logical device table (Adapted from *SCOPE 3.0 Manual 60189400,* Rev. I, Control Data Corp.)

logical device table. A logical device table will contain information as follows:

1. The symbolic name of the logical unit.
2. The logical device type and name of the file currently attached to this logical device.
3. The logical I/O request currently pending on this logical device.
4. A pointer to the buffer(s) associated with the logical device, with indications of each buffer's status.
5. The address of the routine used for transferring data to and from buffers.
6. The address of the routine that can process interrupts, errors, and exceptional conditions for this logical device.
7. An indication of which data areas on a shared device belong to this logical device (if appropriate).
8. A pointer to the physical device table for this logical device.
9. Status information concerning the "current" address or position of the logical device, the "current" record number processed, the number of records in a buffer, etc.

Fig. 2 gives an annotated logical device table.

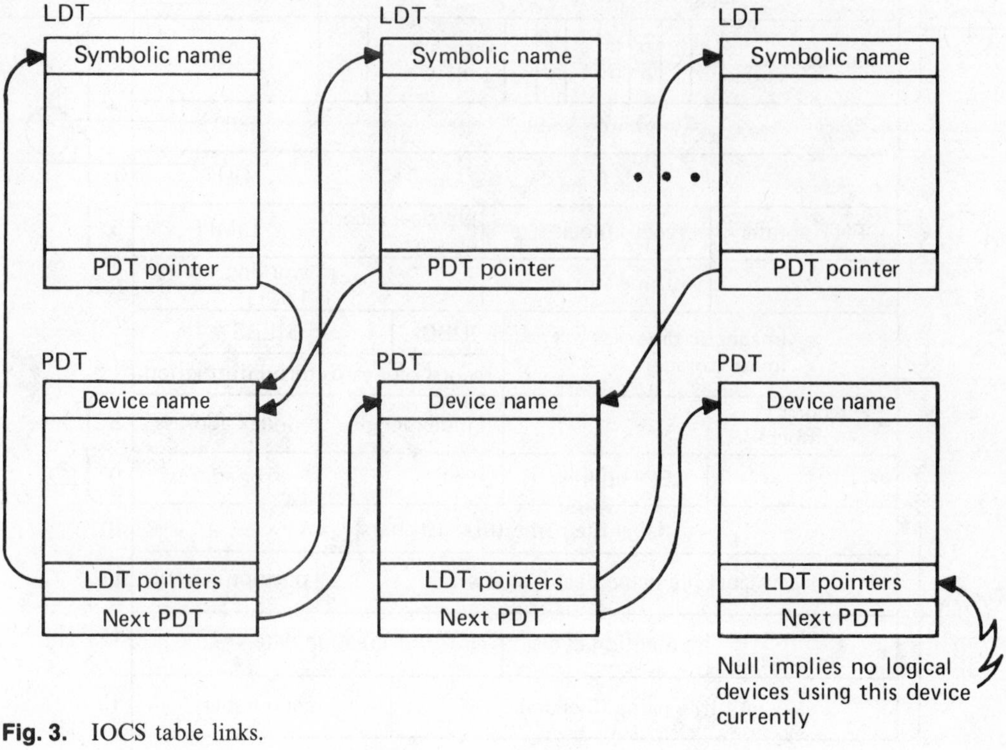


**Fig. 3.** IOCS table links.

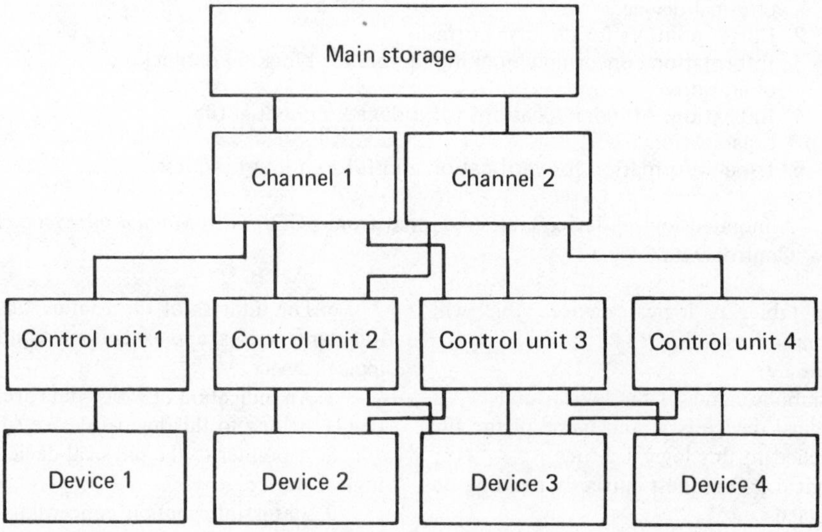


**Fig. 4.** Data paths to I/O devices.

It should be noted that both the logical device tables and the physical device tables contain pointers to routines that perform various functions. A programmer is typically not allowed to provide his own routines to replace those in the physical IOCS. To do so would impinge on the integrity of data stored on the physical device. However, it is common to allow programmers to supply their own routines to perform:

1. Blocking, deblocking, and buffer management.
2. Processing of exceptional conditions such as "end-of-file" or other error conditions on the logical device.
3. Label verification of nonstandard file labels (see below).

In either case, it is clear that substitution of different processing routines in place of the standard ones is simply a matter of changing pointers in the tables (and having the routines available). A programmer effects these changes by declaring that a substitution will be made and by supplying the routine. The IOCS then replaces the pointers in the logical IOCS table with pointers to these user-supplied routines.

Pointers are also used to maintain the correspondences between logical and physical devices. This may be diagrammed as shown in Fig. 3. By using the pointers from logical to physical units, it is possible to discover the physical device associated with a given logical device. Moreover, a change in logical/physical device correspondence is easily accomplished by changing a pointer in the logical device table.

*Coordination of Peripheral Activities and Maintenance of Positioning Information.* The scheduling and coordination of peripheral activities is an especially important IOCS function. In a large computer system, there will often exist a variety of data paths from the central processors through the data channels to the particular devices. Fig. 4 illustrates a typical situation.

Notice in Fig. 4 that a given device may be "attached" to more than one control unit and/or channel in order to form a path that can deliver data to or take data from main storage. This does not imply that data flows to or from the device over two paths simultaneously; only one path to or from a device is used at a given time. The multiple paths exist in order that devices may be kept busy as long as there exists at least one unused path to the device. The multiple paths also allow for continued operation should certain units in a data path break down temporarily. However, the IOCS must keep track of what data paths are currently in use and prevent new requests from using these paths. When a unit signals that a certain component of a path is no longer needed, the IOCS will search the pending requests to see if one can be initiated over the freed path.

In deciding on the next request to be serviced, it is convenient for physical IOCS to have information concerning the current position of read/write heads relative to the position of the data. This is particularly true with disks, which involve movable read/write heads. Requests for data near the current head position can be serviced more quickly than requests that require considerable head movement. Thus, in the scheduling of I/O operations, it is not unusual for physical IOCS to have as part of its status information an indication of current read/write head position. Using this information, it can attempt to optimize requests serviced per unit time (or some similar measure) by scheduling I/O operations based on "nearness" of data to the heads. Note also that the chain of physical device tables in Fig. 3 defines an ordering of physical devices, which can be used for deciding which of a number of devices will be started first when more than one device could be started.

Location of the Data and Initialization of Transfer Parameters. It should be clear that before I/O requests can be interpreted and subsequently executed, the storage area that contains or will contain the data must be located and made accessible to the IOCS. Moreover, various parameters in the logical and physical device tables must be specified. The location and initialization functions are responsible for these tasks.

The location function involves routines for finding the physical devices on which the storage area to be processed resides. This storage area may or may not be directly accessible, depending on the particular computer system involved. If, for example, the programmer has attached a logical device to a tape drive on which a specified tape is to be mounted, then the IOCS must make sure that the tape is indeed mounted. This will typically involve a request to the computer system operator to mount the specified tape. It also usually involves a *label verification* routine. In order to check that the operator has indeed mounted the correct tape, a tape label in a prespecified format will usually exist on the first record of the tape. The label will contain information that identifies the tape, and the label verification routine will match the identification on the tape with the identification information given on the request for tape mount. Lack of a match indicates an error, and an appropriate message will be issued.

If the storage area resides on a disk or other sharable device, a somewhat different kind of location function usually takes place. There will generally exist a catalog of all files that have been created in the system, and a request to attach a logical device to one of these files will trigger a search of this catalog. The catalog will indicate on which disk pack(s) the storage area has been allocated, and a mounting of disk pack(s) onto disk drives may be necessary if the relevant storage areas are not available. Should such a mount be necessary, a verification of the mounted disk pack will take place. However, it should be noted that most interactive systems leave the available disk packs permanently mounted, so this step may not be necessary. Each disk pack will typically have a table of contents, which is essentially a collection of file labels for files on this pack. By searching this table of contents, the file is located.

INITIALIZATION. Once the data have been located, the initialization function can be executed. In order for I/O requests to be executed, various entries in the logical and physical device tables must be filled in. These parameters may be specified on a system control card or by the programmer during execution, but in certain cases they may reside with the data itself, usually as part of the file label. Thus, if it is appropriate, the initialization routines will move a copy of these parameters to the appropriate table entries.

When the file is no longer needed, a final set of IOCS routines will restore the file to a state in which it can be used at a later time. This will involve such things as marking the end of a tape, rewinding it, and informing the operator that it may be dismounted, or updating the table of contents for a file on a disk.

REFERENCES

1966. Clark, W. A. "The Functional Structure of OS/360: Part III—Data Management," *IBM Systems Journal*, Vol. 5, No. 1, pp. 30–51.

1966. Flores, I. *Computer Software—Programming Systems for Digital Computers*. Englewood Cliffs, N.J.: Prentice-Hall, pp. 221–322.

R. W. TAYLOR

# INPUT-OUTPUT DEVICES

For articles on related subjects *see* AUDIO RESPONSE TERMINAL; CARD READING AND PUNCHING TECHNIQUES; COLLATING SEQUENCE; DATA ACQUISITION COMPUTER; DATA PREPARATION DEVICES; KEYBOARD STANDARDS; MEMORY: Auxiliary; OPTICAL CHARACTER READERS; OPTICAL MARK READERS; PAPER TAPE; PRINTING TECHNIQUES; and TERMINALS.

For articles on related terms *see* CURSOR; and LIGHTPEN.

Input is the process of translation of incoming information into electronic patterns suitable for computer processing. Output is the reverse process in which the electronic patterns are translated into a form readable by other machines or understandable by human beings. The translation process is carried out by the input and output devices of the computer system.

The most natural media for communication between a human being and a computer are those which are most natural for communication between people. For input to the computer, this would mean speaking, writing (preferably handwriting) or drawing, and movements of the hands, like pointing, etc. As for computer output, the preferred form by a human being would be hearing (spoken sentences, numbers, and/or sounds like alarm signals, etc.), reading (written messages), or seeing (drawings, graphs, or other types of pictures along with visual sensing of colors). The use of such natural I/O devices is constantly increasing as a result of the recent developments in this field, but these devices will not be discussed further in this article unless they have progressed beyond the research and development stage. However, all those now in general use, as well as some special I/O devices, are described and listed in Table 1, which also shows a few of their characteristics and some typical systems in which they may be used.

In spite of the fact that Table 1 was designed with great care, computer technology (hardware and software) as well as application fields of computer systems change rather quickly. Such changes will surely have impact upon the content of the Table 1, and it should therefore be looked upon as a general guide rather than as correct in every detail. The devices and systems in the table are cross-referenced to sections of this article in the left-hand column,

**Fig. 1.** CDC 3300 console arrangement. (1) Typewriter; (2) typewriter switches; (3) breakpoint switch assembly; (4) console condition switches; (5) access keyboard switches; (6) emergency off-switch; (7) step-rate control; (8) entry switches.

**Table 1.** Uses of Input/Output Devices in Some Typical Systems

*NOTATION. For Characteristics:* * = not so used. – not available or not pertinent. (A), (N), (C), (G) = sometimes, exceptional. $(C)^2$ = R & D stage.

*For Systems:* Y = yes. N = no. (Y) = sometimes, exceptional. (Y)? = unknown. $Y^1$ = operator's console with each processor and at remote stations. $Y^2$ = R & D stage. $Y^3$ = special systems.

| Class | DEVICES Groups and Subgroups | CHARACTERISTICS (1) I, O, or I/O. (2) Type: numerical only (N), alphanumerical (A), graphical (G). (3) Use: terminal (T), conversational mode (C) (1) | (2) | | | (3) | | Off line, conventional computer | On line conventional computer | Terminal, time-sharing system |
|---|---|---|---|---|---|---|---|---|---|---|
| 1 | **NUMERICAL AND ALPHANUMERICAL** | | | | | | | | | |
| | *Operator's control* | | | | | | | | | |
| | Console | I/O | – | A | * | * | * | N | Y | $Y^1$ |
| | *Card readers and punches* | | | | | | | | | |
| | Readers | I | N | A | – | T | – | Y | Y | Y |
| | Punches | O | N | A | – | T | – | Y | Y | Y |
| | Reader/punch | I/O | N | A | – | T | – | Y | Y | Y |
| | *Paper tape readers and punches* | | | | | | | | | |
| | Readers | I | N | A | – | T | – | Y | Y | Y |
| | Punches | O | N | A | – | T | – | Y | Y | Y |
| | *Magnetic-ink and optical-character readers* | | | | | | | | | |
| | MICR document | I | N | A | – | – | – | Y | Y | N |
| | MIMR document | I | N | A | – | – | – | Y | Y | N |
| | OCR page | I | N | A | – | T | – | Y | Y | Y |
| | OCR document | I | N | A | – | T | – | Y | Y | Y |
| | OCR journal tape | I | N | – | – | – | – | Y | Y | N |
| | OMR page | I | N | (A) | – | T | – | Y | Y | Y |
| | OMR document | I | N | (A) | – | T | – | Y | Y | Y |
| | *Printers* | | | | | | | | | |
| | Strip | O | N | A | – | T | – | N | (Y) | (Y) |
| | Digital | O | N | (A) | – | T | – | Y | (Y) | (Y) |
| | Serial | O | N | A | (G) | T | – | Y | Y | Y |
| | Line | O | N | A | (G) | T | – | Y | Y | Y |
| | Simple keyboard | I/O | N | A | – | T | C | (Y) | Y | Y |
| | Complex keyboard | I/O | N | A | – | T | C | (Y) | N | Y |
| | *Direct keying* | | | | | | | | | |
| | Numerical keyboards | I | N | – | – | T | C | N | (Y) | Y |
| | Touchtone phone | I | N | – | – | T | C | N | Y | Y |
| | Alphanumerical keyboards | I | N | A | – | T | C | N | Y | Y |
| | Special keyboards | I | (N) | (A) | – | T | C | N | Y | Y |

| DEVICES USED IN SYSTEMS | | | | | |
|---|---|---|---|---|---|
| | Data Collection Systems | | | | |
| Conversation terminal, time-sharing system | Remote station, single-keyboard system | Remote station, multiple-keyboard with data concentrator | Remote station, multiple-keyboard with message switching | Remote station, multiple-keyboard, direct on line to computer | On line, industrial supervising or process control |
| Y[1] | Y[1] | Y[1] | Y[1] | Y[1] | Y |
| N | N | N | Y | N | N |
| N | N | N | Y | N | N |
| N | N | N | Y | N | N |
| N | N | N | Y | N | (Y) |
| N | N | (Y) | Y | N | (Y) |
| N | N | N | N | N | N |
| N | N | N | N | N | N |
| N | (Y) | (Y) | N | (Y) | N |
| N | (Y) | (Y) | N | (Y) | N |
| N | N | N | N | N | N |
| N | (Y) | (Y) | N | (Y) | N |
| N | (Y) | (Y) | N | (Y) | N |
| (Y) | N | N | N | (Y) | Y |
| (Y) | N | N | N | (Y) | Y |
| (Y) | N | N | (Y) | Y | (Y) |
| (Y) | N | N | (Y) | Y | (Y) |
| Y | Y | Y | Y | Y | Y |
| N | Y | Y | Y | Y | N |
| N | Y | Y | (Y) | Y | Y |
| Y | Y | Y | (Y) | Y | N |
| Y | Y | Y | (Y) | Y | Y |
| Y | Y | Y | (Y) | Y | Y |

*(Table continued to next page)*

| Class | DEVICES Groups and Subgroups | CHARACTERISTICS (1) I, O, or I/O. (2) Type: numerical only (N), alphanumerical (A), graphical (G). (3) Use: terminal (T), conversational mode (C) (1) | (2) | | | (3) | | Off line, conventional computer | On line conventional computer | Terminal, time-sharing system |
|---|---|---|---|---|---|---|---|---|---|---|
| | *Alphanumerical visual display* | | | | | | | | | |
| | Key input checking | I | N | A | – | T | C | N | Y | Y |
| | Alphascope (I/O) | I/O | N | A | (G) | T | C | N | Y | Y |
| | Plasma, and others | O | N | A | – | T | – | N | Y | Y |
| | *Audio* | | | | | | | | | |
| | Input | I | N | A | – | T | (C)[2] | N | N | N |
| | Output | O | N | A | – | T | C | N | Y | (Y) |
| | *I/O in industrial (and similar) processes and systems* | | | | | | | | | |
| | Input (analog/digital) | I | N | – | (G) | T | – | N | N | N |
| | Output (analog/digital) | O | N | – | (G) | T | – | N | N | N |
| | *Special I/O devices* | | | | | | | | | |
| | Ticket vendors | O | – | A | – | T | (C) | N | Y | Y |
| | Cash dispensers | I/O | N | – | – | T | – | N | N | Y |
| 2 | **GRAPHICAL** | | | | | | | | | |
| | *Image input* | | | | | | | | | |
| | Facsimile I/O | I/O | N | A | G | – | – | N | N | N |
| | Manual off-line registration | I | N | (A) | G | – | – | Y | N | N |
| | Manual on-line registration | I | N | A | G | T | C | N | Y | Y |
| | Automatic image input | I | N | A | G | T | C | N | Y | N |
| | *Electromechanical plotters* | | | | | | | | | |
| | Drum-type digital | O | N | – | G | T | – | Y | Y | Y |
| | Flatbed-type digital | O | N | – | G | T | – | Y | Y | Y |
| | *Graphical visual displays* | | | | | | | | | |
| | Graphoscopes, entry | I | – | – | G | T | C | N | Y | Y |
| | Graphoscopes, I/O | I/O | N | A | G | T | C | N | Y | Y |
| | TV display | I/O | N | A | G | T | C | N | Y | Y |
| | *Microflim I/O* | | | | | | | | | |
| | COM graph plotters | O | – | – | G | – | – | Y | Y | N |
| | COM printers | O | N | A | – | – | – | Y | Y | N |
| | COM plotter/printers | O | N | A | G | – | – | Y | Y | N |
| | CIM | I | N | A | G | – | – | N | Y[3] | N |

| DEVICES USED IN SYSTEMS | | | | | | |
|---|---|---|---|---|---|---|
| | | Data Collection Systems | | | | |
| | Conversation terminal, time-sharing system | Remote station, single-keyboard system | Remote station, multiple-key-board with data concentrator | Remote station, multiple-key-board with message switching | Remote station, multiple-key-board, direct on line to computer | On line, industrial supervising or process control |
| | Y | (Y) | Y | (Y) | Y | (Y) |
| | Y | (Y) | Y | (Y) | Y | Y |
| | N | N | N | (Y)? | (Y) | Y |
| | Y[2] | N | N | N | N | N |
| | Y | N | N | N | N | (Y) |
| | N | N | N | N | N | Y |
| | N | N | N | N | N | Y |
| | (Y) | N | N | N | N | N |
| | (Y) | N | N | N | N | N |
| | N | N | N | N | N | N |
| | N | N | N | N | N | N |
| | Y | Y | Y | N | Y | N |
| | Y | N | N | N | N | N |
| | N | N | N | N | N | Y |
| | N | N | N | N | N | Y |
| | Y | (Y) | (Y) | N | (Y) | Y |
| | Y | (Y) | (Y) | N | (Y) | Y |
| | Y | (Y) | (Y) | N | (Y) | Y |
| | N | N | N | N | N | N |
| | N | N | N | N | N | N |
| | N | N | N | N | N | N |
| | N | N | N | N | N | N |

and additional information can be found in other articles in this encyclopedia.

### Alphabetical and Numerical Input and Output Devices

OPERATOR'S CONTROL DEVICES. A *console* is a unit used by the operator for all manual communication with the computer. It also provides a display from the computer, generally in all or some of these forms: visual display, printed message, acoustical signals. The operator communicates with the computer by depression of switches (with specific function assigned to each of them) or by a typewriterlike keyboard. An example of a console arrangement that includes all the components listed is shown in Fig. 1.

The configuration of the console arrangement differs with the computer size and model used. For instance, in some large and fast computer systems, a line printer is used for printing information to speed up the overall performance of the system. Sometimes the console configuration can be extended upon request of the user; e.g., by adding certain features to the unit, such as a pin-feed platen to the typewriter; adding a display unit; a reference typewriter attached to smaller systems using display register and functional switches, etc. Large computer systems usually are equipped with a system console that has two CRTs and one keyboard. However, these devices may be more numerous, with several display consoles being used for controlling independent programs simultaneously.

Remote terminal stations are equipped with data station consoles to control the various I/O devices and to control communication between the data station and the central computer. A data station console generally includes a data set to connect the station to a communications channel, and also has circuits to handle automatic detection and correction of transmission errors.

CARD READERS AND PUNCHES. The punched card has been in use as a data carrier for a long time and is still used as the sole data input medium in many computer and noncomputer systems. The punched card contains data represented in the form of punched holes, which can be sensed by a variety of punched-card machines in order to carry out such functions as sorting, collating, basic arithmetic, and printing. Generally, the card has a standard size of 7.375 by 3.250 in. and a thickness of 0.007 in. It can accommodate 80 to 90 numerical digits and/or alphabetical characters. In the late 1960s, IBM introduced System/3, which uses a small punched card (minicard). This has approximately one-third the area of the standard card, and accommodates up to 96 digits and/or characters and symbols.

With the advent of computers, punched cards continued to be the main data carrier for the source data input in business applications. In addition, they are often used for the transmission of user programs into the computer memory.

The function of the punched card as output from a computer-based information system has greatly diminished, apart from some applications in which the punched card has a dual function, such as a written document and as a data carrier for the machine. It is still used, however, in small punched-card computer systems and sometimes for making error corrections when using the interactive mode, and/or for amendments to programs at the program preparation stage. Also, in some batch-processing systems, short compiled programs are punched on cards.

A computer-based information system needs a wider set of symbols than that used in punched-card machines and often requires different kinds of codes. Card readers and punches, as well as the keyboards of data preparation equipment, can therefore read, recognize, punch, and print (on the surface of the card) a larger set of characters. Some readers and punches can read or punch both binary and decimal cards.

The card transport mechanism of card readers and punches is closely related to the function of the device. The basic functions are reading, punching, selecting, collating (merging, matching), interpreting (which, in the punched card machine terminology, means printing on the face of the card), gang-punching, reproducing, sorting, and computing. Table 2 shows the five basic types of card readers and punches, with their characteristics. Fig. 2 shows a representative card path design for the device in each category. It should be understood, however, that in each category of design, the card path may change to accommodate serial or parallel mode of operation designed for reading and punching, or checking techniques used, or the way errors detected by the checking operations are handled (e.g., selection and separation of cards with errors), or other features peculiar to the system.

*Card Readers.* The speed of operation of card readers is generally between 300 and 1,000 cpm (cards per minute). Also on the market are low-speed readers of 60 cpm, used in applications requiring a small punched card input only, as well as high-speed readers of up to 2,000 cpm. This latter speed seems to be the limit for safe transportation and handling

**Table 2.** Basic Types of Punched-Card Input/Output Devices.

| Characteristics | Basic Types: Reader | Punch | Read-Punch, 1 Hopper | Read-Punch, 2 Hoppers | Multifunction Unit |
|---|---|---|---|---|---|
| Functions | | | | | |
| Reading | Y | N | Y | Y | Y |
| Punching | N | Y | Y | Y | Y |
| Selecting | – | – | – | Y | Y |
| Gang-punching | N | N | Y | Y | Y |
| Collating, merging, matching | N | N | N | – | Y |
| Sorting | N | N | N | N | – |
| Interpreting | N | N | N | N | Y |
| Computing | N | N | N | N | N |
| Features | | | | | |
| Number of hoppers | 1 | 1 | 1 | 2 | 2 or more |
| Number of stackers | 1–2 | 1–2 | 1–2 | 2 or more | 4 or more |
| Speed (for fully punched 80-col. cards), cpm | | | | | |
| Lowest | Appr. 60 | 16 col./sec | Slowest function | Reader plus | Slowest function |
| Average | 300–500 | 100–200 | is decisive | punch performance | is decisive |
| Top | To 2,000 | 500 | | (if independent) | |

Note: Y, yes; N, no; –, possible.

possibilities of the mechanism. The "jams" that occur from time to time in each punched-card machine seriously affect the flow of work, and it is important to be familiar enough with the machine design to remove cards from the machine quickly, determine the number of jammed cards, and determine the damage caused.

*Card Punches*. Card punches perform slower than card readers because of the mechanical action in punching holes in the card. Computer output devices (see Table 2) work at speeds of 100 to 500 cpm when using a parallel punching technique (e.g., row by row) or approximately 16 columns a second when slower serial punching is used.

*Card Reader-Punches*. The speed of operation of the card reader-punch with one hopper is determined by the chosen read or punch function. The speed of operation of the card reader-punch with two hoppers is determined by the type of operation performed. The highest performance is obtained when reading and punching take place independently, with no merging of cards from the two-card paths. Then the performance of the reader is that of a one-hopper reader and the performance of the card punch path is the same as that of a one-hopper card punch. However, if merging of cards from both hopper paths is necessary, the speed of operation is slowed down and may sink as low as the level of the slowest (e.g., punching) path. (See Table 2.)

The last category of card I/O devices in Table 2 is represented by the multifunction card unit. Unlike devices of the four preceding categories, which are used in all computer configurations requiring reading and/or punching of cards, the multifunction card unit is used solely as an input/output device for punched-card computers, (e.g., the IBM 2560 shown in Fig. 3). The operational speed depends upon the actually performed combination of possible types of operations and upon the information content of the cards to be processed (the latter is decisive in determining the collating speed). However, the minimal speed will be equal to the speed of the slowest functional unit used in the device.

PAPER TAPE READERS AND PUNCHES. Functionally, paper tape readers and punches are similar to those of card readers and punches except that the

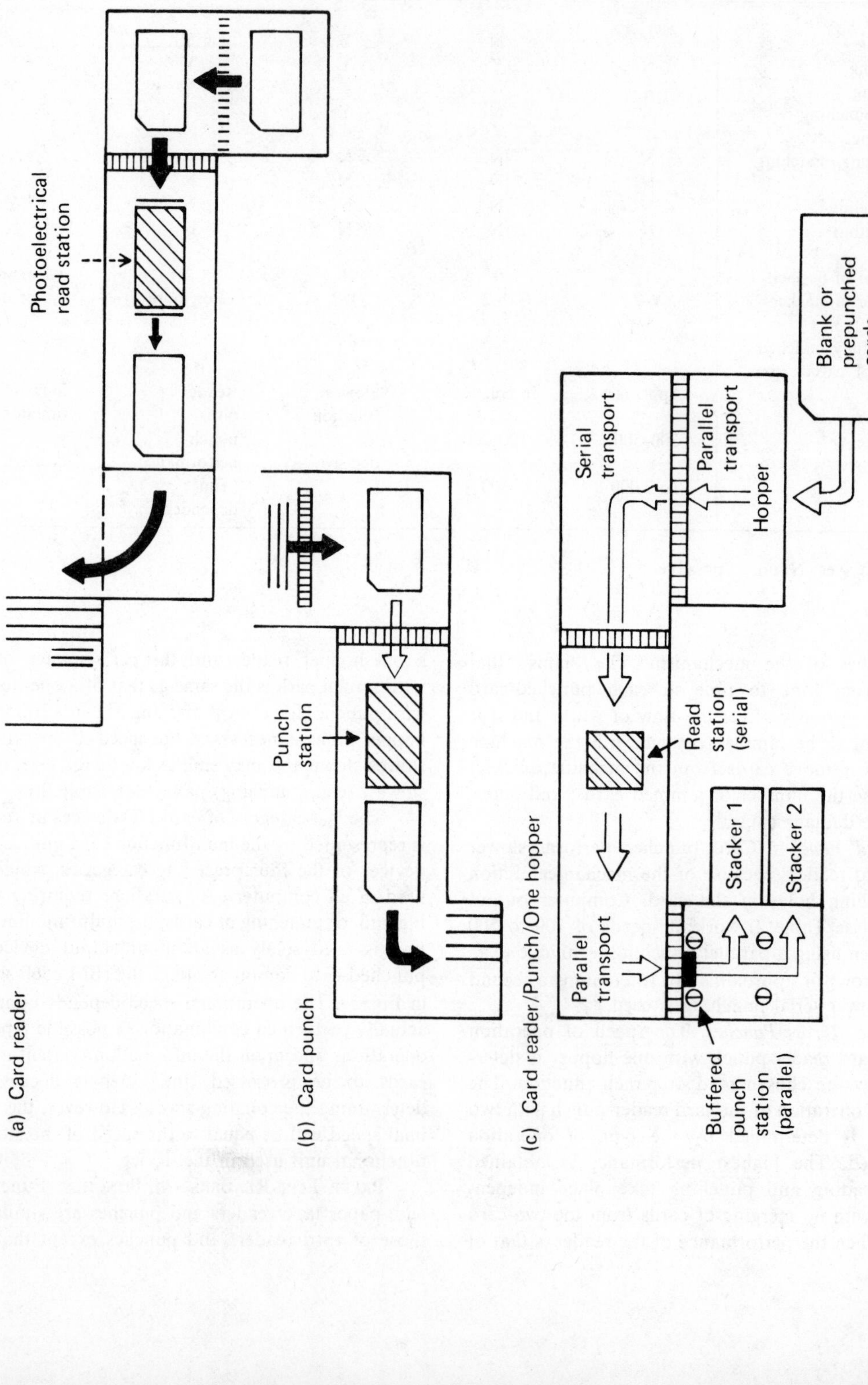
(a) Card reader
Photoelectrical read station
(b) Card punch
Punch station
(c) Card reader/Punch/One hopper
Blank or prepunched cards
Hopper
Parallel transport
Serial transport
Read station (serial)
Stacker 1
Stacker 2
Parallel transport
Buffered punch station (parallel)

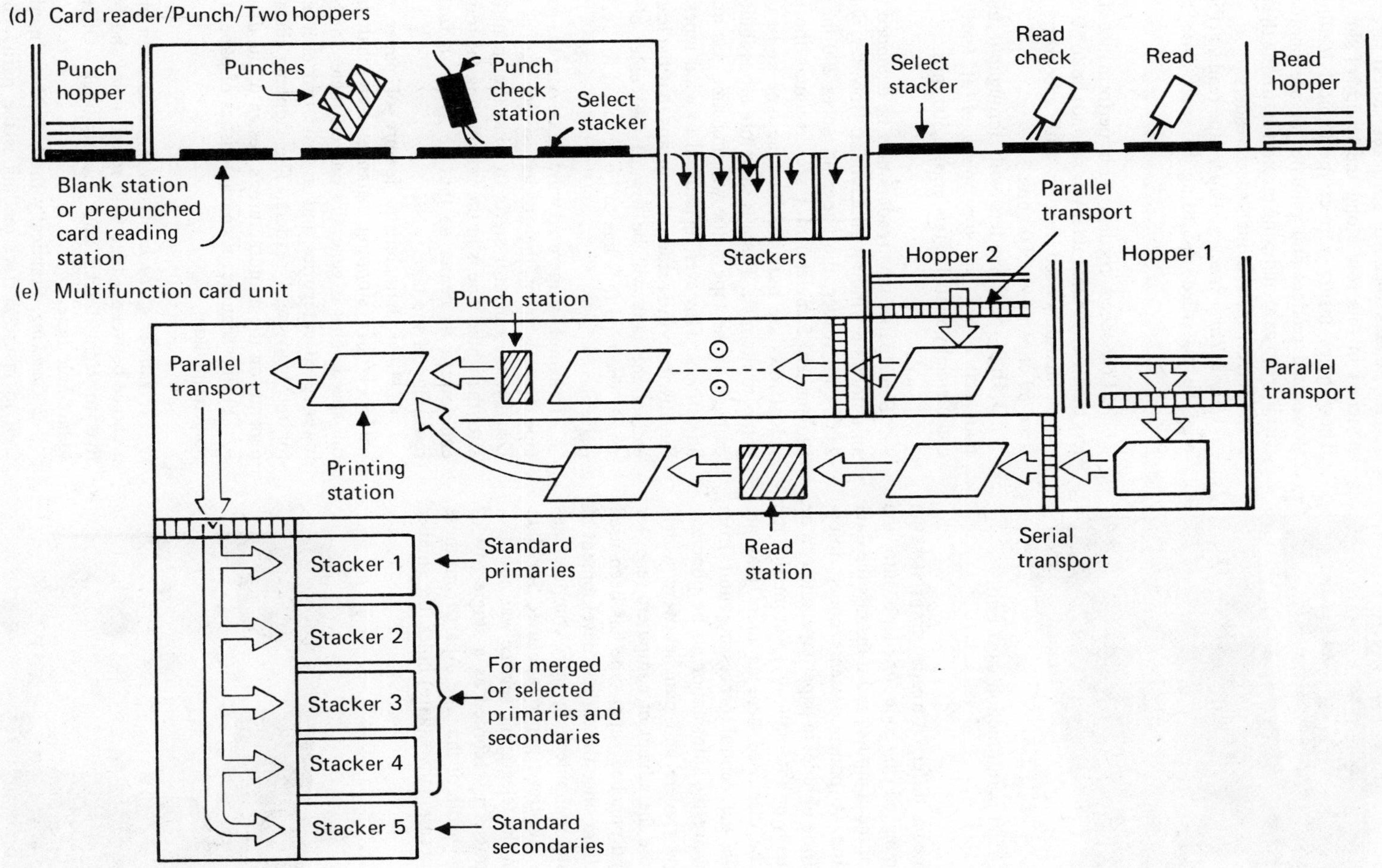


**Fig. 2.** Possible card-path design for each of the five basic punched-card I/O device categories. (a) Card reader; (b) card punch; (c) card reader/punch, one hopper; (d) card reader/punch, two hoppers; (e) multifunction card unit.

**Fig. 3.** IBM 2560 multifunction card unit.

information media differ. A reader translates the information punched in code on tape into the internal code of the computer and transmits the data to the computer. A punch presents coded information in the form of holes in paper tape, and can be operated manually or automatically. Automatic tape punches will be discussed here as units that are connected with the central processing unit from which they receive the information to be punched.

Paper tape readers and punches were widely used long before the advent of computers (e.g., for telegraphy), and punched paper tape has been used as an I/O medium since the earliest development of electronic digital computers. In early computer applications, the five-track paper tape used for data transmission in the telegraphic service was adopted.

Each character is recorded as a single row of holes across the width of the tape. Apart from these larger round (occasionally square) holes, the smaller round holes (so-called sprocket holes) are prepunched in one row along the length of the tape. These holes insure correct mechanical feeding in slow;speed readers and punches or are photoelectrically read as an indexing means for driving the tape at the correct speed in high-speed readers.

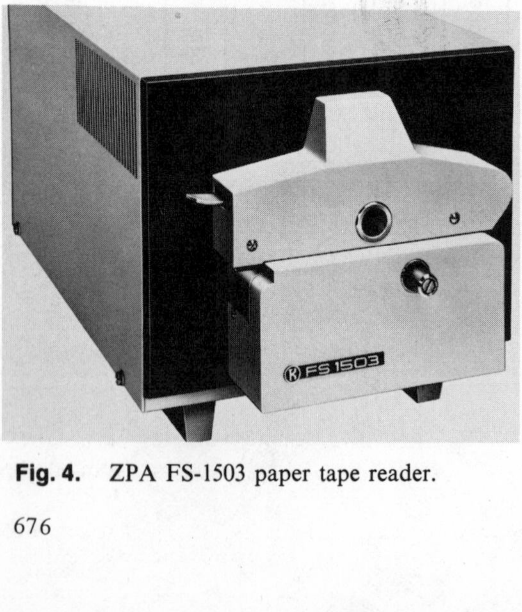


**Fig. 4.** ZPA FS-1503 paper tape reader.

*Paper Tape Readers.* Paper tape readers (Fig. 4) may be classified according to speed into three categories:

1. Low-speed readers with performance from less than 1 chps (character per second) up to 50 chps.
2. Medium-speed readers with speeds ranging from 60 chps up to 500 chps.
3. High-speed readers with throughput higher than 600 chps. The top speed of at least two commercially available readers is 2,500 chps.

Some paper tape readers may be equipped with an automatic winding attachment. However, with a 2,000-chps reader, the paper advances 200 in. (approximately 5 meters) in 1 sec, assuming the individual rows are punched into the tape at 10 characters to the inch. There is therefore a possibility of damage to the tape if the winding unit gets out of adjustment. However, it is usual to wind tapes fed directly from the reader; this means that the leading end of the tape will be toward the center of the spool. The tape thus has to be rewound for further use.

In manually operated winding devices the paper tape coming from the reader is fed into a bin. Usually, the operator starts to wind the spool only after the whole tape is in the bin, putting the trailing end toward its center so that he avoids a further rewinding of the tape.

Another characteristic feature of paper tape readers is their stopping distance after a halt from full speed. This is generally one character for both lower-speed categories and at least two characters for the high-speed readers. The stopping distance depends on the manufacturer's design of the device.

Further significant characteristics of paper tape readers include:

1. *Number of tracks.* Usually the user can make a choice between a tape with round holes and from five to eight tracks and the six-track (Olivetti) square-hole tape.
2. *Checking.* Practically the only check method used to insure correct reading is the parity check (hardware or by a program). However, this method can be applied to seven- or eight-track tapes only. Some devices have no check possibility whatever. To

overcome this disadvantage, check-sum methods are introduced. These require adding a check row or rows on the tape which, when attached to a group of rows, act as a check symbol, allowing a summation (or hash total) check to be made for that item when the tape is used as input to a computer.

3. Possibility for off-line use of the device.

The so-called paper tape reader-punches are two separate devices that are mounted under one cover.

*Paper Tape Punches.* Paper tape punches (Fig. 5) as computer output devices are more complex than a simple keyboard-operated punch; their design demands increased accuracy, maximum speed, and reduced maintenance (mainly the sharpness of the punching die).

**Fig. 5.** Facit 4070 paper tape punch.

As computer output devices, tape punches may be classified by their performance. Low-speed tape punches have speeds ranging from some 15 chps up to less than 100 chps, and high-speed tape punches from 100 up to 300 chps.

Some of the more important features and characteristics associated with tape punches are:

1. Automatic winding attachment; same as for tape readers

2. Immediate visibility of the tape after punching, a very useful feature for the user.

3. Number of tracks on tape; five to eight round holes or six-track square holes.

4. Code translation: automatic, matched, programmed, or by subroutine or plugboard.

5. Check control: echo, verify punch activation, read compare, or none.

MAGNETIC-INK AND OPTICAL CHARACTER READERS. Magnetic-ink and optical-character readers interpret information printed or written on a document. The information may be represented in several forms—by marks, bar codes, numerals, or letters of the Roman alphabet, and by other characters.

Marks are made by hand in preprinted positions on the document, each position having its information significance assigned beforehand to express its meaning. For example, a mark can stand for "Yes" in a questionnaire in a particular position, or it can stand for one chosen digit (or number) in the mark field of several preprinted digits (or numbers), etc. Mark readers have long been used with punched-card machines and so-called test-scoring machines. As computer input devices, they are used for many types of applications, mainly for surveys, census compilations, billing, etc.

Bar codes are printed by machine and usually represent numbers selected in a predetermined manner. Bars look somewhat like Morse code representation, but include some type of check. Bar-code readers are used mainly in point-of-sale and similar terminals for reading price tags, identification cards, etc. They are also sometimes used in optical and magnetic-ink recognition systems for subsequent sorting of documents. Numerical digits and alphabetical characters are either printed or written by machine or by hand in a more or less stylized font. This is a steadily expanding field of computer input form in recent years.

Apart from electromechanical scanning, which seems to be less and less used, there are two distinct groups of scanning techniques, magnetic and optical. Both are used at present with magnetic-ink character recognition, a somewhat older technique. However, the commercial production of optical scanners has made distinct progress in recent years. Both magnetic-ink and optical readers are very similar in performance. However, they differ mainly in four ways;

1. The kind of ink used for printing the information to be read by machine.

2. Types of font, the size and the character set they read.

3. Size of documents and volume of printed information on them to be read by the reader.

4. Scanning technique.

**Table 3.** Characteristics of MICR and OCR readers

| Characteristics | Readers MICR | OCR |
|---|---|---|
| Fonts | | |
| MICR: E-13B | Y | Y |
| CMC-7 | Y | Y |
| OCR: OCR-A (ANSI. I-A or USASCSOCR-A) | N | Y |
| OCR-B (ISO-B) | N | Y |
| Other optical fonts | N | Y |
| Bar codes | N | Y |
| Handwriting | N | Y |
| Ink | | |
| Magnetic | Y | Y |
| Printing (black) | N | Y |
| Typewriter ribbon (black) | N | Y |
| Character Density (pitch) | | |
| 8 characters/inch in a line | Y | – |
| 10 characters/inch in a line | N | Y |
| Printed Forms (derived from applications) | | |
| Page: Typical 14 × 9.0 in. | N | Y |
| Document: 3.75 × 6.0 to 3.67 × 8.75 in. | Y | Y |
| Journal tape: tally roll: 1 ft × 1.3 in. to 350 ft × 4.5 in. | N | Y |
| Readers | | |
| Typical maximum speeds | | |
| Page | N | 400–2,400 chps |
| Document | 1,200–2,400 chps | 200–3,000 chps |
| Journal tape (tally roll) | N | 1,000–3,600 chps |
| Sorting possibility (reader/sorter) | Y | Y |
| Maximum number of lines read per pass | 1 | * |
| Error control: | | |
| Validity check | Y | † |
| Timing check | Y | † |
| Rescan feature | N | Y |

*Notes:* Y, yes; N, no; –, possible; * up to some 15 on documents and 80 on pages depending on device used.

Consequently, their applications are different. Table 3 shows some characteristics of both types of reader. Magnetic-ink mark recognition (MIMR) readers are being rapidly replaced by optical reading devices.

Magnetic-ink character recognition (MICR) readers interpret only information printed in magnetic ink on one line of a document. The font used may be either the E-13B (adopted as a standard by the American Bankers Association) or the CMC-7 (designed by Bull and adopted as standard font by the European banking community). Both fonts are shown in Figs. 6. A picture of an MICR reader-sorter is shown in Fig. 7.

MICR readers are used mainly in check and credit-card applications. Hence, the document has a small size (typically, 2.75 by 6.00 in. up to 3.67 by 8.75 in.) with one line printed in an MICR font and containing the numerals and four special characters used for reading-control purposes. Since checks, postal money orders, and credit cards require handling at different points before their final filing, MICR readers generally have a sorting feature incorporated. Characters to be read magnetically have to be very carefully printed. The reason for using magnetically printed characters on checks is that eventual overprinting by postmarks or smudges will not affect the accuracy of reading. However, some sophisticated OCR methods can also deal with this problem today. Optical readers are described elsewhere in this Encyclopedia.

The preparation of input documents for either magnetic or optical reading should be done with great care. The paper used should be appropriately chosen and print should be clear and well centered. Devices are more or less sensitive to these require-

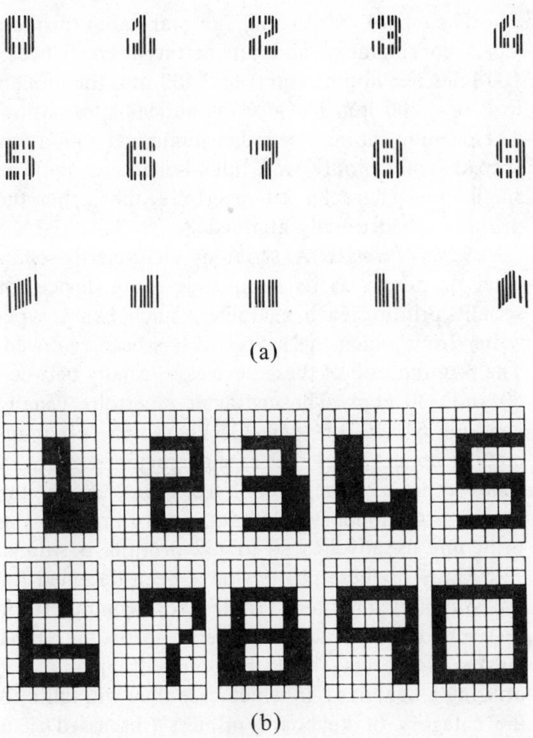


**Fig. 6.** (a) Digits of the CMC-7 MICR font used by the European banking community, and (b) the E-13B font adopted by the American Bankers Association.

**Fig. 7.** The IBM 1419 magnetic character reader/sorter.

ments. Characters not recognized with a high degree of probability are considered as "unknown" and such documents will usually be marked and/or rejected in a special stacker called a "reject pocket." The handling of rejects, if many, may be very troublesome.

Both categories of readers, MICR and OCR, can be used in an on-line or off-line mode to the main processing computer. When used off-line, the possible output information will generally be written on a magnetic tape. However, punched cards or paper tape are sometimes used as well.

Printing Devices. Printers are output devices that convert computed data into printed form. The different printing techniques they use have impact upon several features of these devices; these printing techniques are discussed elsewhere in this Encyclopedia.

From the user's point of view, printing devices can be classified into two main groups, those with and without the capability of data input by means of a keyboard. Printers not having this capability can be further divided (by the paper form of the printed output) into strip printers, digital or journal tape printers, serial (character by character) printers, line printers, and page printers. In this article, only the first four categories are discussed; page printers are used mainly in microfilm I/O devices. However, a few page printers using other than microfilm techniques have been included in the later section entitled "line printers." Note that the term "page" printer is sometimes used to describe the ability of a device to print a page format, as opposed to the "strip" type of printing.

Printers having the keyboard facility have in common (unless directly connected to the computer), besides input and output features, some device to get the connection to the transmission line (e.g., a dial-in telephone). They may be classified into two subgroups, simple and complex devices, depending upon the complexity level of tasks they perform.

Generally, all printers may be used as terminals, but interactive conversational capability is restricted to the keyboard printers.

*Strip Printers.* As the name suggests, a strip printer prints the information along a narrow (usually half-inch wide) paper tape, much like a ticker tape. It is a low-cost device used for special applications in systems where the cost of a multiple-column printer would be prohibitive. Strip printers are used not only as computer peripherals, but also as telegraph or industrial printers.

A typical example of such a device is the strip printer shown in Fig. 8, which has a printing repertoire of 64 characters as follows: capitals A through Z; numerals 0 through 9; and 28 various signs, symbols, and punctuation marks. These characters are arranged on a print barrel in such a way

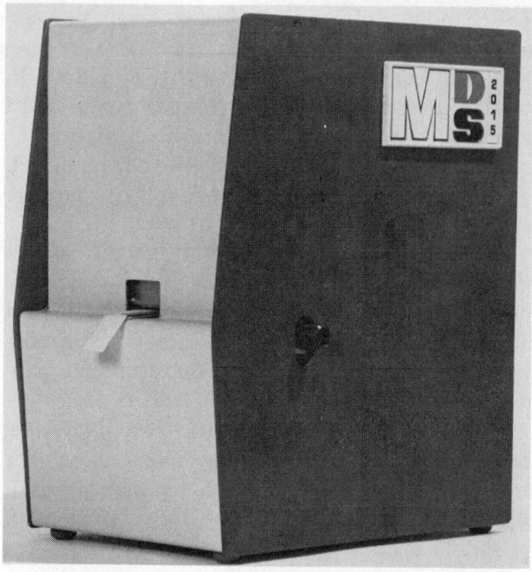


**Fig. 8.** Mohawk Data Sciences Model 2015 strip printer.

that they pass through the print position in the order used in the ASCII code. Average speed is 20 chps; a higher rate is possible for printing numerals only. Characters are printed with their vertical axes perpendicular to the longitudinal axis of the paper strip, 10 characters per inch. The paper stock is a half-inch wide roll approximately 200 ft long.

The usual speed at which strip printers operate is between 10 and 20 characters per second; they can print numerals only, or sometimes also alphabetical characters and special symbols.

*Digital (Journal Tape) Printers.* The primary advantage of a digital printer is its ability to make a permanent, continuous recording of the numerical values indicated by an instrument over a period of time. A similar requirement is sometimes posed for the output of a low-cost scientific computer. However, for this purpose, an electric typewriter is often used because an alphabetical print-out may be also required in some instances.

The name "digital printer" originates in its industrial application, and is used to distinguish this type of print from the analog one. A digital printer used as a computer peripheral is often called a ''line printer.'' However, as the printed line is very short (between 8 to some 32 printing positions) and the stationery does not generally need to have sprocket holes (which are necessary for the paper-advance mechanism in line printers), the printed tape resembles much more closely that of the journal tape printer.

The speed of digital (journal tape) printers varies considerably, and can be anywhere between 100 lines per minute (lpm) to 2,400 lpm for numerical, or 1,200 lpm for alphanumerical information. The printing set may be either numerical with a few special symbols only, or a full 64-character set. The smaller the character set repertoire, the higher the printing speed usually attained.

*Serial Printers.* A serial or character-by-character printer is, as its name suggests, a device for serially printing each character, much like a typewriter from which the keyboard has been removed. The printing rate of these devices is usually between 60 and 330 chps. The character repertoire usually contains 64, 96, or even 128 characters, often including upper- and lower-case characters and sometimes even a larger "boldface" font, as in the Centronics Model 308 impact matrix printer. The print line usually has 80 to 132 printing positions.

Many of these printers have been designed for use with minicomputers, visible record computers, or as terminals; several are offered also on the OEM market. Some may have the optional capability of utilizing a keyboard, in which case they will fall into the category of keyboard printers (discussed in a later section).

*Line Printers.* Line printers are used mainly to print out results of calculations; they can be programmed to print on stationery preprinted as invoices or statements. The individual pages are part of a continuous sheet and are marked out by folds and perforations across the sheet at intervals required by the nature of the document. The stationery is supplied as a pack, and a complete set may consist of several sheets with interleaved carbon paper to produce additional copies.

The continuous-feed paper supply is fed past the print head by a sprocket mechanism engaged through positionable traction clamps. Vertical spacing and skipping of paper is generally controlled by a tape loop in which the positioning of the page is determined by holes in the specific channels (8- or 12-channel tape being most popular today). When this control is not provided, the program within the central processor must control the line spacing of the page.

Fig. 9 shows a vertical-format unit mounted on the left-hand side of the printer. The shaft from the paper-feed clutch extends into the unit to turn a sprocket wheel in correspondence with paper advance. When a format tape is engaged with the sprockets, it is moved between a set of photodiodes and lamps. The tape is prepunched with holes in 12 channels for up to 12 format choices. The holes in

**Fig. 9.** Vertical format unit for line printer.

each channel indicate the line of the form at which the skipping paper-feed cycle is to terminate. As the tape moves over the photodiodes, a pulse is generated by each hole. The output from the selected channel is synchronized with the output of the paper-drive pulse generator to signal the end of the cycle. After being printed, the stationery sets can be split up into single sheets by means of decollators and bursters.

Several manufacturers produce computer form printers that copy the continuous output forms from the computer onto single copies of the same or reduced size. Some of these devices can use masks to eliminate copying of certain parts of the forms, or they can add printed information such as headings or footnotes to the printed image.

Some of the more important line-printer characteristics are as follows:

1. Printing speed differs so much that it is useful to divide line printers into three categories. Low-speed printers have speeds from about 100 lpm to 200 lpm, with 150 lpm as a good average. Medium-speed printers go from more than 200 lpm to less than 1,000 lpm, with an average rate of 600 lpm. High-speed line printers go from 1,000 lpm up to more than 2,000 lpm, with an average performance in this category of 1,100 to 1,200 lpm (Fig. 10). All the rates mentioned are valid for a full alphanumerical character set, usually consisting of about 64 characters. However, if a reduced set is used (e.g., a 48-character set or even a numerical set with only a few special characters), often a much higher rate can be attained, sometimes up to double the rate of the full set. The possibility of using more than one character set for printing depends upon the printing technique used. Printers attaining much higher speeds than those mentioned here are also available.

**Fig. 10.** Potter LP 3403 (1240 lpm) chain printer.

2. The maximum number of printed characters on a line is usually 120, 132, 136, or 160, but any number between 72 and 200 is possible.

3. The print density on a line is usually given in "chpi," the number of characters printed in 1 in. (also called "character pitch"). It is generally 10 chpi; however, MICR font printers use 8 chpi, and other exceptions are also possible.

4. Start-stop or continuous operation is available. Generally, all line printers operate in the start-stop mode. However, printers using certain printing techniques require continuous operation and are used for off-line batch processing.

5. The printing facilities of line printers generally employ the mechanical printing barrel (drum) or the chain (train) techniques.

6. Image printing is not possible with line printers. However, some simple graphs or roughly drawn curved graphs, using the character set available and the overprint or overlay technique, can sometimes be printed (see later section, "Alphanumerical Visual Displays").

7. Checking involves parity, timing, echo, validity, receipt of data, or none.

*Other Printing Facilities.* One field of computer printing application, which is relatively new, is "computer-aided correspondence." The principle of this application is based upon the so-called text-tins, which are short text sentences or articles stored in the computer. Writing of individual letters is done in a batch processing mode of operation (e.g., once a day). Input information for each letter to be written contains identifiers of the "text-tins" to be selected, together with the necessary variables to be inserted into the selected text (such as date, rate, etc.). An optical mark recognition (OMR) reader may be used as an input device for this kind of information. In some applications, as in the banking and security industries, additional information from the computer data base can be added to the text. All this information is then processed on the computer and the required letters are printed.

Computers are used also to prepare magnetic tapes (or paper tapes) to control typesetting machines in the printing industry. The processing generally proceeds like this: The original text is written on a magnetic tape and printed for proofreading. All corrections and amendments resulting from this proofreading are written on a second tape, and both tapes are again processed on the computer. The final output is a magnetic tape containing the corrected text and commands for a typesetting machine. Its operation is subsequently automatically controlled.

In a similar application a computer is used to generate Braille prints. With the aid of translation tables, the computer translates the text to be printed onto some medium suitable for controlling the matrix disk of the Braille dot typesetting device used. Similar systems using Telex and Braillemboss terminals connected with a central computer (used for translation) are under development. Another solution to Braille printing problems has been reported by a manufacturer who supplied a computer system to the Southern College of Business in Orlando, Florida. The system uses an eight-line per inch printer, and a special conversion program changes the alphanumeric print-out into the Braille system of dots. The impressions in the paper are formed by increasing the force of the print hammers, which strike through a specially designed sheet of thin felt, causing the effect of "exploding" the dots.

Line printers are used also as devices in computer graphics (CG) to produce, for example, pictorial data mapping. A software house in Great Britain has developed the LINMAP system, available commercially, which produces statistical maps on a line printer, using ten symbols to simulate the degree of shading density. There is very little restriction on the format of the input data, and up to 400 data items can be handled for each coordinate point. The same firm also offers an additional service, CILMAP, which produces art-printed color maps. This is done by transferring the LINMAP output to magnetic tape and then employing a photoelectronic typesetter.

The Canadian government uses computers to generate a series of alternate land-use maps. The computer output is done in a color-coded system analogous to standard land-use schemata. The scaling technique used makes it possible to select one individual unit of low-density housing and then expand this unit to the size of the entire sheet. Then the program can be used to plan the individual residential unit. Thus, for each individual unit, a series of matrices based on various criteria can be devised to formulate the living patterns of the clients.

A generalized spatial allocation procedure, called "ALOKAT," has been applied to various problems, including individual houses; a neighborhood project; an intensive-care ward of a hospital; a student union in Syracuse; a car manufacturing plant in Algiers; a faculty of law in Marseille; a new university with teaching, research, and laboratory units in Bologna; an office building in Philadelphia; and a simulated town. In all cases except the town (for which a plotter output was used), chain printer output (a special 8 by 10 instead of the standard 6 by 10 chain) was used as the least expensive, most readily available means of producing graphic output. Overprinting of characters was used to give solid borders to the area.

Imperial Chemical Industries, Ltd., England, has developed a set of software packages called "CROSSBOW" for applications in the chemical industry. The set consists of four programs intended for use by universities and research institutes all over the world, since the formulas of chemical compounds are an international language of chemists. One of these programs, for example, is able to answer queries concerning a given compound—such as whether it is original or what other chemical compounds it contains—and directly prints its formula in the conventional way.

Facsimile line printers using dot-printing techniques are used for data and image transmission. However, the number and density of dots is higher than in the conventional line printers, and the spacing between two dots in the line is always the same.

*Simple Keyboard-Printers.* In the subgroup of relatively simple devices, there is always an input keyboard and a printer. The latter can often be used to print both the keyed-in data and the computer output information. In this subgroup are teletypewriters as well as typewriters and typewriterlike devices or printers of some other type with a keyboard added. These devices are often called "keyboard printers."

The input speed of keyboard printers is limited by human ability factor; their output speed is determined by the device and/or transmission capabilities, ranging between 10 and 40 chps for interactive terminals, but up to 180 chps for some terminals. The printing technique used is usually of a serial type, with character-by-character print.

The arrangement of the input keys may be that of a separate keyboard for alphanumerical information—upper and/or lower case—and/or for numerical information entry. Apart from these, some controlling keys are needed; they may be accommodated on the same panel with the others or on a separate keyboard.

The interrogating function is sometimes provided by devices called "interrogating typewriters." A single unit may be connected directly to the processor (generally through an interface channel), or a number of devices may be connected via a communications multiplexer. Besides the interrogating function, the device may be used also for other purposes, such as for program debugging.

This subgroup also includes portable terminals, which incorporate a built-in telephone coupler and typewriterlike input and output features.

*More Complex Keyboard Printers.* This subgroup includes devices of the types mentioned earlier as simple keyboard printers (with the exception of portable terminals), but with some more features added to them, such as reading and/or punching of paper tape. These devices may have some kind of programming feature that allows for a restricted computing facility and printing format, and often for a choice of a few available programs (Fig. 11). These features allow for less complex programming at the computer site and considerably lessen the number of commands transmitted from the computer to the terminal. The programming feature may be external (e.g., plugboard or programming bar) or internal (hardware and/or software type). Devices with more sophisticated (computerlike) facilities are often called "intelligent." Similar "intelligent" terminals are also found in the visual display unit (VDU) group or among graphical devices. There may be systems configurations making use of all these devices.

Direct Keying Devices. Direct keying devices represent a relatively new group of computer input equipment, enabling direct entry of information by

**Fig. 11.** Olivetti TC 300 keyboard-printer terminal with paper tape reader and punch.

means of keyboards (or, exceptionally, dials) operated by humans. Many of these devices are similar to those used in data collection systems that operate in an off-line mode, mainly to keying units in key-to-tape or key-to-disk systems. Direct keying devices, however, are connected with the computer directly, either by cable or transmission lines. Thus, they can also use for validation purposes the files stored in the computer direct access memory. Given proper environmental conditions, they can be used in time-sharing systems that require several types of intermixed data formats to be processed in real-time mode (e.g., updating centralized computer files).

Keyboard devices are used for entry of variable data. However, some of them may have additional features that permit duplication of repetitive data or of personal or other identification, using prepunched or preprinted cards, badges, edge-punched cards, etc.

To allow the operator to correct a typing error detected during the typing operation, the keyboard device is often connected by either some printing means or a simple visual display called "key-input checking VDU." (See the following section, "Alphanumerical Visual Displays.")

As do all devices that use a keyboard, direct keying devices are faced with the problem of the keyboard arrangement, which must be adapted to generation of the character repertoire of the ISO seven-bit ASCII code.

## INPUT-OUTPUT DEVICES

Direct keying devices can be divided in four categories; numerical keyboard devices, Touchtone telephone, alphanumerical keyboard devices, and special keyboard devices. Each of these is discussed in subsequent paragraphs.

*Numerical Keyboard Devices.* These devices resemble those used in key-to-disk off-line systems, but they differ in several respects. The keyboard for a numerical keyboard is arranged in three basic configurations, as follows:

1. Adding machine

```
7 8 9
4 5 6
1 2 3
  0
```

2. Punched-card machine

```
    0
1 2 3
4 5 6
7 8 9
```

3. Telephone

```
1 2 3
4 5 6
7 8 9
  0
```

Differences between these basic types of numerical keyboard arrangements are self-explanatory, as are their uses. A few functional keys are generally added to the ten numerals.

*Touchtone Phone.* The advent of the electronic telephone exchange in the United States made possible the Touchtone phone, which provides a telephone-to-tape data-entry method. The instant response of the new exchange relays eliminates the requirement for a spring-loaded dial as a counter. Instead, the relays respond to unique tones generated by keys that replace the dial on the telephone. Soon after the introduction of Touchtone, it was realized that the instrument provided a new means of entering or preparing data for a computer, particularly where the data has to be collected from a number of remote locations, as in a multi-outlet or branch type of business, or from many different departments situated at some distance from the data processing center.

The Touchtone phone is a special kind of numeric keyboard device. When used in telephone-to-tape communication, it makes use of a translator, an electric device that interprets the unique tones from each phone key, alters them into a computer code, and enters them directly onto tape. The tape and translator are connected to an automatically answered telephone (data set), which allows many phones to input through a single translator onto a single tape. A data set is a device that connects a data processing machine to a telephone or telegraph communication line. A telephone data set is a unit used to connect a data terminal to a telephone circuit; e.g., to transmit data from the terminal to the processing center. Such a data set converts signals from the terminal into a form suitable for transmission over a telephone circuit, and vice versa.

Typical Touchtone telephone users key in about 1.4 digits per second, with a relatively low error rate. Errors of omission are the most serious faults to watch for. Where check-digit verification can be applied, the error rate will be even lower. Further savings may be achieved by the use of a plastic card (originally designed as a self-dialing facility) for entering fixed format information.

The technique of Touchtone data transmission is not limited to batch operations, but can be used on line for any variety of information updates applicable to production, stock, and credit control systems. Increasing use of credit cards opens up a new area of on-line credit validation for all sorts of businesses by keying on line to a central computer. In countries where the electronic exchange is not yet standard, this device can still be used, once a connection has been established through the normal dial telephone. Touchtone pads, linked to any telephone and transmitting through the data set and translator, allow remote data preparation direct to tape.

The Touchtone pad has a single 12-button keyboard and is easy to use. The pad provides the user with the normal ten keys of the Touchtone phone, plus two additional keys (one for "skip," "duplicate," and "data entry" and the other for "error correction"). Data is entered a line at a time; each line can contain as many as 180 characters and can be split into as many fields as required. One key is used to skip from one field to the next; at the end of the line, a final tap on the "skip" key causes the line to be written onto the key tape. If an error is made during the entry of the line, the error-correct key can be used and the line reentered before it is written to tape.

*Alphanumerical Keyboard Devices.* Alphanumerical keyboard devices are similar to the numerical ones previously described, the only difference being the keyboard, which may be one of three

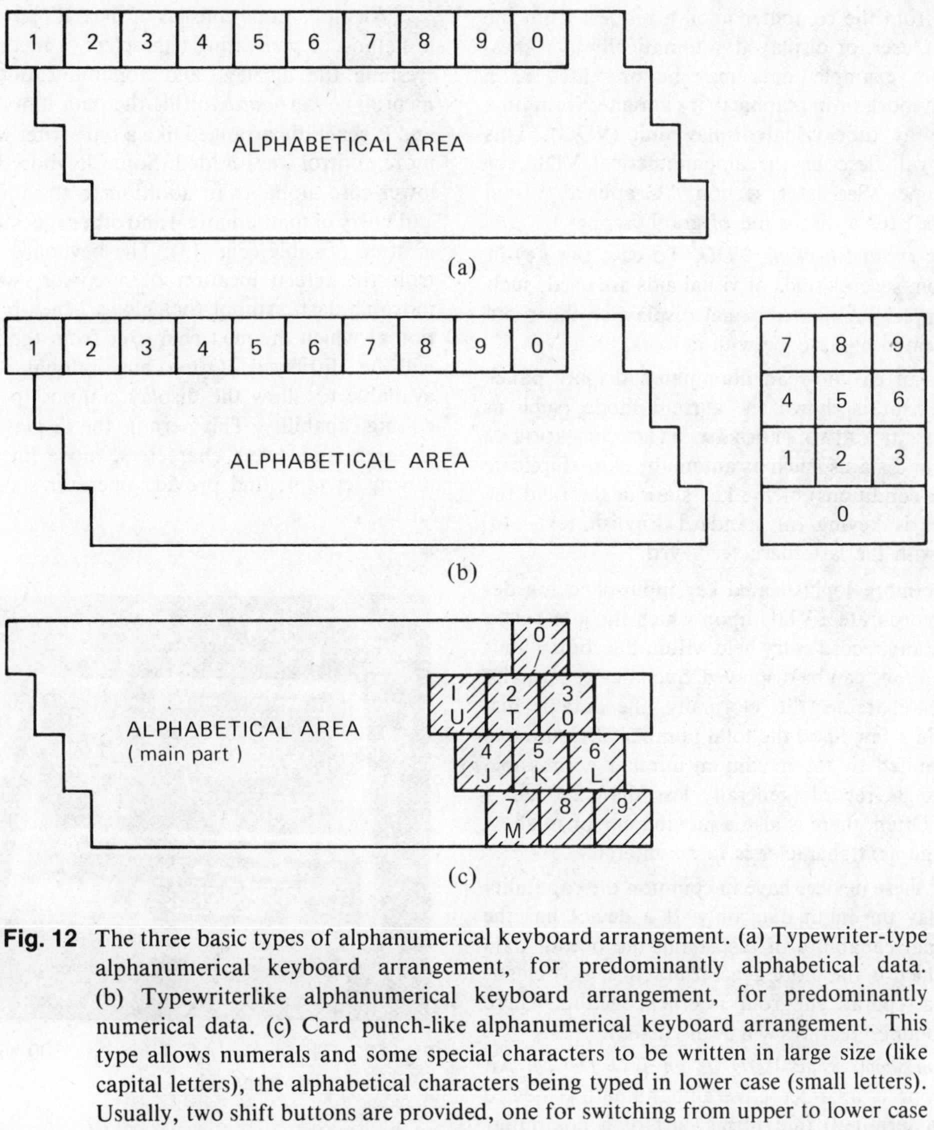


**Fig. 12** The three basic types of alphanumerical keyboard arrangement. (a) Typewriter-type alphanumerical keyboard arrangement, for predominantly alphabetical data. (b) Typewriterlike alphanumerical keyboard arrangement, for predominantly numerical data. (c) Card punch-like alphanumerical keyboard arrangement. This type allows numerals and some special characters to be written in large size (like capital letters), the alphabetical characters being typed in lower case (small letters). Usually, two shift buttons are provided, one for switching from upper to lower case and the other for switching from lower to upper case. If used for printing also, the alphabetical characters would usually be capital letters.

basic types, depending upon the positioning of the numerical characters in the overall layout of the keyboard. A typical layout is shown in Fig. 12.

*Special Keyboard Devices.* Special keyboard devices are of two types. In one, a normal numerical or alphanumerical keyboard is used, but keys are assigned special significance, depending upon the type of work for which the device is being used. The keys may be given special additional labels that identify various types of information when the recording is made. When the recorded data is read into a computer, the computer program is so devised that the significance of the various items of information is recognized.

The second type of special keyboard devices is that especially designed for a given purpose, such as mathematical expressions. This special keyboard device is used mainly in addition to keyboard devices of the numerical or alphanumerical type.

Alphanumerical Visual Displays. A display device allows the operator or user to visually inspect data that is keyed into the computer, and/or retrieved from the computer upon a request from the operator/user, or displayed automatically as a message. For example, data may be presented as a printed report, or in graphical or character form on a cathode-ray tube visual display unit (VDU). This section will describe the alphanumerical VDU, or alphascope. (See later section, "Graphical Visual Displays," for a discussion of graphoscopes.)

*Key Input-Checking VDU.* To ease the key-in operation, several kinds of visual aids are used, such as a simple illuminated panel display or the more sophisticated alphascope with cursors.

On an easy-to-read illuminated display panel, the operator is shown the current mode (such as WRITE, VERIFY, READ, PROGRAM, SELECT, or PROGRAM ENTRY) and status (such as automatic skip/duplicate or error conditions) of the key station, the field the operator is keying (in standard English text), together with the last character keyed.

The more sophisticated key input-checking devices incorporate a VDU upon which the latest data entry or any record entry held within the control unit buffer storage can be displayed. Such devices usually use a 64-character set. Normally, the data is displayed in a few lines, the total number of characters being limited by the maximum number permissible for a single record (generally less than 200 characters). Often, there is also a moving cursor to show where the next character is to be entered.

All these devices have in common the capability to display the input data only. If a device has the additional capability of displaying the output data also, which is the more general practice, it is classified in a separate subgroup (see next section, where some common features will be discussed).

*Alphascope—The VDU as an I/O Device.* An alphascope is an interactive alphanumerical device (often a terminal) that forms part of a computer-based system requiring a short response time for getting answers to queries made by managers, dispatchers, stockkeepers, or clerks. Its purpose is to retrieve these answers from the computer random access memory. The alphascope terminals need only be connected to the computer by an ordinary telephone line. The cost of each terminal unit is about $4,000. Since it is a relatively low-cost unit, it makes possible later extension of the user's facility to true computer graphics, from simple graphs to full vector capability.

The CRT (cathode-ray tube) terminal is not much more complicated than the Teletype, but because it does not depend on a mechanical means of printing, it is considerably more reliable.

An alphascope consists of the CRT, a keyboard, a method of generating characters, a method of refreshing the display, and communications equipment. The *keyboard* fulfills the data input function and is generally arranged like a typewriter with a few more control keys added. Some keyboards have a lower-case alphabet in addition to the upper case, and entry of mathematical and other special symbols is often possible (Fig. 13). The keyboard also controls the screen location of a cursor, which is a movable dash symbol that glows beneath the position at which the next character from the keyboard will be displayed. Often an optional feature is available to allow the display stations to have full editing capability. This permits the display operator to insert and delete characters, move lines up and down, set tabs, and provide operator status to the CPU.

**Fig. 13.** The UNIVAC Uniscope 300 visual display terminal.

*Screens* have generally different diameters, to 20 in. or more, with the display on the whole screen or on part of it. Information is presented from 6 to 20 lines, with up to some 80 positions each, giving a total capacity from 250 to a maximum of some 2,000 characters. The characters are usually displayed in fixed positions on the screen, with the beam moving along each row, character position by character position. More sophisticated systems switch the beam to the next row when no more characters in the row are to be displayed, thus eliminating the need for tracing the path of remaining blank positions in the row. Sometimes a roll feature selects the whole array of characters to be displayed, rolling either in line-by-line or in group-of-lines mode.

Another type of input is a *touchwire* system. Ten or fifteen short pieces of wire are imbedded in a transparent screen over the face of the display tube. The function of each wire is displayed on the screen above it so that it is possible for every character on the keyboard to be displayed by an associated touch, thus eliminating the need for a keyboard. The wire is connected to a balanced electrical bridge and is sensitive to the touch of the operator. By putting his finger on one of the short pieces of wire, the user initiates the start of a computer program.

The user is piloted through the process he controls by labels alongside each touchwire, which are initiated on the display by the computer program. He looks at the displayed diagram (say, an electronic circuit) and points to parts he wishes to alter. Touchwire systems are presently used only to choose the next required display, since a balanced-bridge network is more expensive than a keyboard, and also does not satisfy the sense of touch needed by typists.

For drawing of the required character, a *hardware character generator* is used. Of the many types applied, the most common defines a character by brightening the required dots on a matrix (typically, 7 by 5). Some techniques "paint" lines between points on the matrix (Fig. 14). Very fine characters are produced by a monoscope system, which requires a second tube on which the character set is etched.

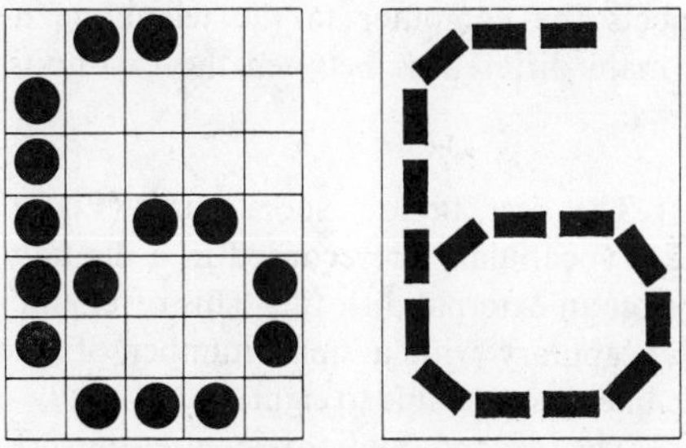

**Fig. 14.** Dot matrix and pointed-line matrix presentation on the IBM 2260 and 2265 VDU, respectively.

For keeping the text displayed, the method of *continuous cyclic refreshment* of the picture (40 to 60 times per second) is generally used. Several problems are connected with storing the picture. The delay lines currently used have the additional problem of temperature control. Use of a core store is almost prohibitive because of its cost. Storage tubes would solve the problem, but they are expensive and cannot be selectively erased (which is a very useful feature required by the user).

The *communications* with the main computer should be much faster than that of a Teletype if the main advantage of the alphascope (the quick presentation of information) is not to be lost. The reading speed should be much higher than that of the human eye. This is essential in many applications because the user scans the displayed text for quick orientation, choosing only the parts required for more detailed study.

Simpler display techniques may be sometimes adequate, depending on functions they have to perform. Fig. 15 shows a display designed to accept input data keyed into a buffer store as well as output retrieved from the internal memory of the computer. However, only numerical data can be displayed on this screen.

**Fig. 15.** Six-character numerical illuminated panel display of Honeywell Bull Gamma 55.

*Plasma and Other Output VDUs.* Other hardware solutions are sometimes considered for visual display output devices, besides CRTs. One of the latest is the plasma display (Fig. 16), consisting of three sheets of glass. The middle sheet is drilled with holes 0.025 in. apart, each containing receptacles filled with illuminant gas (plasma). Both outer glass sheets incorporate strips of transparent conductors, one vertical on the inside sheet and the other horizontal on the outside sheet. The a-c voltage is kept at a level required to make these tiny discharge tubes glow when fired at the user's control station, and any particular spot can be switched on or off. The display provides its own storage, and there is no limit to the size of the screen.

AUDIO DEVICES

*Audio Input Devices.* Audio input devices are still in a research and development stage, although a few systems are commercially available. Automatic recognition of the human voice is extremely difficult,

**Fig. 16.** CDC plasma display at New York Stock Exchange.

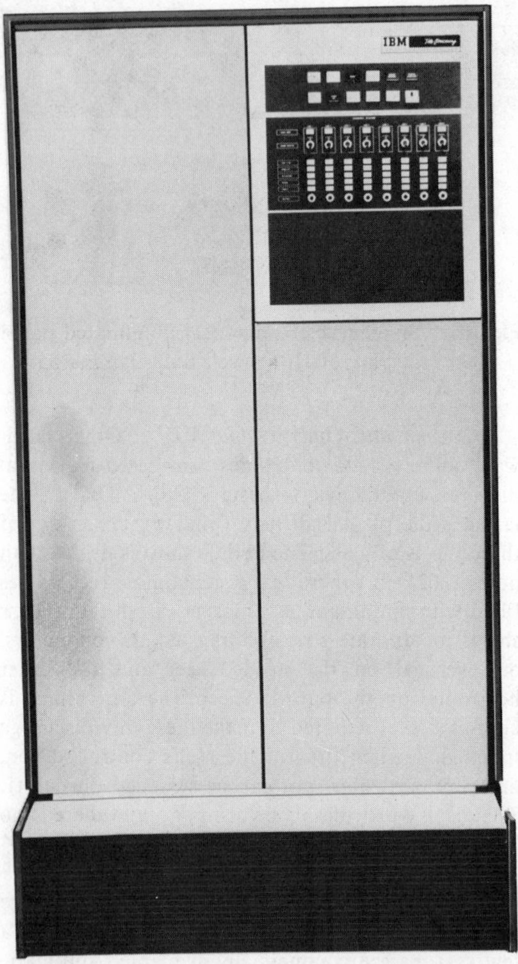

**Fig. 17.** The IBM 7770 audio response unit.

mainly due to the segmentation problem (i.e., the recognition of boundaries between spoken words) and to the extremely wide differences in enunciation among people. However, the recent electronic development of recognizable *voice prints* makes it possible to recognize a person by his mode of speech. At present the use of voice prints is limited, but they may introduce new methods into banking and other money-transfer computer applications, especially in the area of program security. One company, Threshold Technology, has produced some voice recognition systems that can compare a speaker's voice with stored voice patterns. One such system has been attached to a Data General Nova minicomputer to help route baggage and perform other tasks in the United Airlines terminal at O'Hare International Airport in Chicago.

Some computer manufacturers have produced input devices that recognize a few English words (10, 16, etc.) to be used as computer commands, but these devices need much improvement before they can become generally useful.

*Audio Output Devices.* Audio output devices are produced by only a few manufacturers. Figs. 17 and 18 present examples of two different approaches to their design. Both units provide a recorded voice response (optionally, male or female) and sometimes with language options to inquiries made from telephone-type terminals (with dials or Touchtone phone keyboards) and similar computer transmission terminals (with keyboards). They are attached to the computer via the multiplexer channel that connects the computer to the telephone network. The main differences between the two units are as follows:

1. The first audio response unit (Fig. 17) provides a vocabulary prerecorded in a digitally coded voice on an external disk file. This offers an unlimited vocabulary with a small number of lines (two basic lines, expandable to eight).
2. The second audio response unit (Fig. 18) provides a vocabulary prerecorded in analog form on a magnetic drum within the device. This offers a maximum vocabulary of 128 words with many lines (4 basic, expandable to 48).

Devices of the second type are used, for example, to answer calls to out-of-service telephone numbers. An operator asks the caller for the number he wishes to reach and connects it into the system through a simple ten-button keyboard at her station. The computer searches the directory file (stored on a disk) for the new number and then transmits it to the

**Fig. 18.** The IBM 7772 audio response unit.

audio response unit. A voice message is heard by the caller within 10 to 20 sec after placing his call. Devices of the first type are used in more complex systems, but the number of transmission lines is limited.

I/O DEVICES IN CONTROLLED PROCESSES. Processing industries have grown up with analog presentation of data. Digital machines are now coming into this field, some in an indirect capacity—supervising analog controllers—and some observing and optimizing processes. In recent years, with the development of digital computers, digital machines are beginning to take over a very substantial part of process control tasks, often together with some analog elements if necessary, thus forming a new technical field of applications called "DDC" (direct digital control).

There are two main forms of DDC. In one, local control loops take care of subordinate functions and the central processor exercises supervisory control over local loops. In the other form, a large-scale computer sends signals to control devices directly, with virtually all controlling functions being exercised by the computer.

*Input Devices for Processing Industries.* Computer input in process control systems involves the following types of information:

1. Descriptions of type, quality and quantity of the incoming resources to the process (e.g., raw material and energy).
2. Description of the transformation process that takes part in the plant (e.g., process variables such as temperature, pressure of fluids, flow of fluids).
3. Information signaling interrupts of the process and describing their causes (such as equipment breakdown or some other abnormal condition), as well as commands for measures to be taken, which are given automatically by the computer or by the supervising engineer.
4. End-point control information describing type, quality, and quantity of the process output (e.g., finished products, materials and energy not consumed in the process).

With few exceptions, the input information is procured by suitable industrial sensing devices that form the first link in a chain of control equipment. Some of them substitute for human senses:

Feeling: temperature or thickness.
Sight: light, color, smoke density, level of liquids, or granulated solids in open containers, dimensions of solid bodies, etc.
Hearing: human speech recognition.
Taste: acidity, salinity, sweetness, etc.
Smell: presence of odoriferous gases such as ammonia and coal gas.

Some sensing devices have "extrasensory" characteristics beyond direct human perception, such as moisture measurement, chemical analysis, and crack detection.

Before a variable of an industrial process can be controlled, it must first be measured. There are two ways to achieve such measurement. In the first, some physical property of a sensing device can be utilized directly (e.g., a spring, balance, thermometer, barometer, or tachometer). In the second way, comparisons have to be made with a known but adjustable quantity of the same nature, in which the process of measurement involves the accurate assessment of equality between the two qualities (like a scale balance, measuring rule, micrometer, and potentiometer).

The sensing and the measuring functions are usually combined in one instrument. As processes get more complex, both the number and type of variables that need to be controlled increase. Information from a multitude of instruments has to be concentrated and transformed into a standardized digital format that is suitable input information to the computer.

The forms of data presentation from the various sources differ considerably and their frequency can also be widely different. The process variables measured by industrial instruments have to be filtered and amplified, switched, or scanned by multiplexers, which sequentially connect these instruments via analog-to-digital converters to the central computer buffers. Other forms of data presentation may be pulse inputs that enter the buffers via counters, or binary inputs and process interrupts that are connected directly to the buffers.

*Output Devices for Processing Industries.* The computer output has two distinct functions. The first function is the automatic regulation of the process. The output electric signals set up and/or adjust the electric actuators of the regulating devices (valves, etc.), thus forming, together with the automated input, a closed-loop control system. This type of output usually is in the form of electric signals that have to be converted from digital to analog form and then amplified; there may also be a binary or a pulse output that can be used without any intermediate device whatsoever.

As opposed to the machine/machine interface function, the second function of the computer output concerns the man/machine interface. This normally gives up-to-the-minute information to the supervising engineer, usually signaling some abnormal condition or possibly calling for his takeover of control from the computer. It also gives logging information on the process (for further analysis of behavior under varying conditions), using typewriter, Teletype, printer, or plotter.

SPECIAL I/O DEVICES. From time to time input/output devices designed for some special application can be used. Two examples of such devices are discussed here.

*Ticket Vendors.* Early in 1970, two experimental passenger-operated automatic ticket vendors linked to a computer were installed at Chicago's O'Hare International Airport. The ticket vendors accept magnetically encoded credit cards issued by American Express and American Airlines to a selected group of passengers who frequently fly out of Chicago. The system is intended to test whether self-service machines can speed passengers through the airport and how travel agents can benefit from automatic devices.

A passenger with an advance reservation inserts his credit card into the vendor and presses a "Yes" button in reply to whether he has a reservation. He then removes his credit card, and his ticket is delivered within a minute. Without a reservation, a passenger may reserve a first-class flight or coach accommodation on the next available departure to 11 possible destinations.

The automatic ticket vendor consists of a display panel, a credit-card reader, and a ticket issuer. The display panel contains the instruction messages, pushbuttons, and digital display tubes. The display tube assemblies show available flight departure times, controlled by a message from the computer to insure that the correct time appears. The credit card is inserted into the reader while the data recorded on the magnetic track is processed. Data includes the card holder's name, account number, issuer code, and also the qualifier codes used for billing and to check whether the card has been lost or stolen.

Tickets are issued as one or more flight coupons bonded together in a book form with a passenger receipt coupon. Data is written onto the magnetic track across the back of each flight coupon and is then checked. After a ticket has been removed, an auditor's coupon is prepared and stored in the ticket vendor.

The system has developed as a result of problems involved in coping with the expected 300 million air passengers a year in the United States. With the introduction of high-capacity jets, the passenger flow problem at airports is becoming increasingly serious. Similar devices have been designed to form part of computer-controlled issuing systems for betting tickets, and are in operation in France, Australia, and the United States. Figs. 19 and 20 show one such system installed with the Totalizator Agency Board, Melbourne, Australia, and the special telephone display units used at the telephone "betting auditorium."

Some currently offered devices are the

1. Vogue Model 810 airline ticket printer, manufactured by Vogue Instrument Corporation of New York.

2. Di-An Series 8000 from Di-An Controls of Boston.

3. CDC Remote Ticket Issuing Machine (TIM) maunfactured by Control Data Corporation.

These devices are used in various systems: besides airline seat reservation and ticket issuing, they act as totalizators in subway systems and race

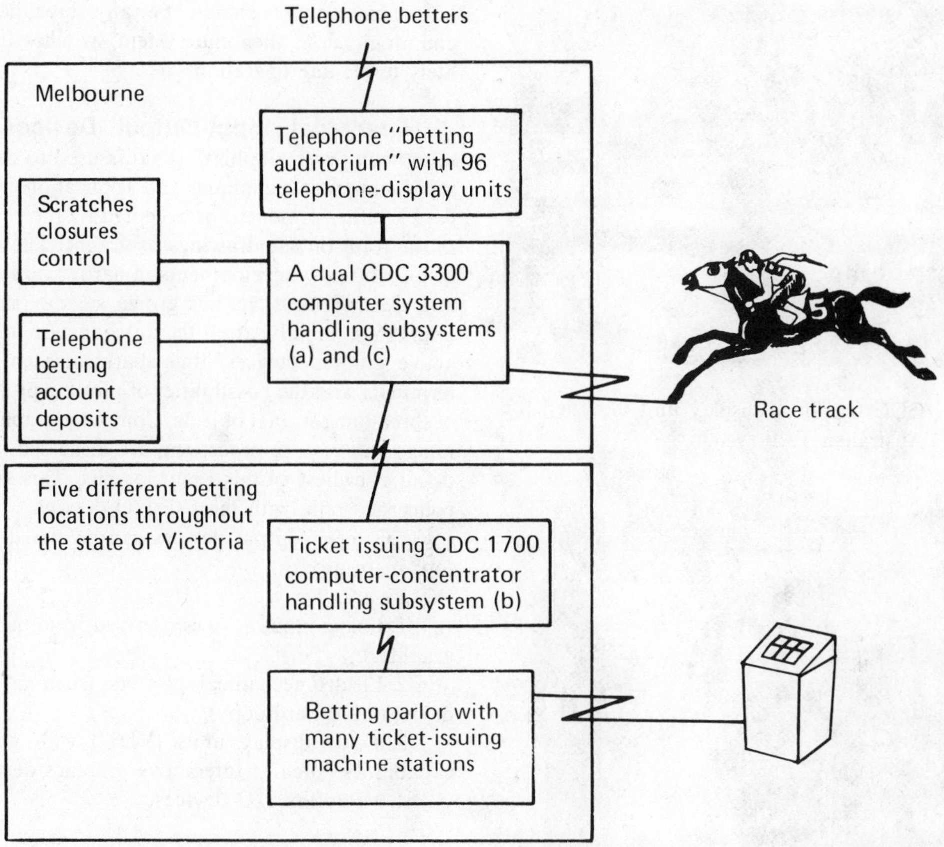


**Fig. 19.** Sketch of the CDC 3300/1700 system used by the Totalizator Agency Board, Melbourne, Australia. Subsystem (a) at the Melbourne Board handles bets placed by telephone only. Subsystem (b) at the betting stations record bets made in person, issues tickets to betters, and pays dividends or winnings. Subsystem (c) at the Melbourne Board finalizes pools, determines dividends, processes miscellaneous business data, and keeps records.

tracks (pari-mutuel), and in sports and theater-seat reservation systems.

*Cash Dispensers.* Cash dispensers, sometimes called "cashpoints" or "self-service banking terminals," (Fig. 21) are computer terminals normally installed in a banking environment or in shopping centers. These terminals allow customers of the bank to withdraw money up to a certain amount. When linked directly to a computer, they extend real-time credit authorization.

Cash dispensers were first introduced in the early 1970s. The main manufacturers were originally Burroughs and IBM. They were equipped with a keyboard and a slot for insertion of a credit card. Depending upon the model used, the transaction took between 10 and 40 sec.

In the Burroughs models, protection against forgery was by means of a secret identification code stored, along with other data, on a three-track magnetic strip on the credit card. In the IBM models, each customer was given a code number, separate from the credit card, which had to be keyed in and which was checked against the same number stored in computer memory. This last method also provided protection against the misuse of lost or stolen cards. The Burroughs system allowed a similar check in which the customer keyed in an account number that was also registered on the magnetic strip. In all systems the keyboard was used for specification of the amount of money required by the customer.

Currently, other manufacturers are also producing cash dispensers, often with additional func-

**Fig. 20.** CDC telephone display unit designed for Australian TAB system.

**Fig. 21.** The IBM 3614 self-service banking terminal, a cash dispenser.

tions such as charging a withdrawal to a credit card account, making deposits, or paying bills. Sometimes, as in the case of Docutel's Total Teller, a receipt is returned to the customer. These more complex systems usually allow customers to perform transactions at any time of the day. They use display panels to guide the user through the specific transaction. Such automatic teller systems are often built around a minicomputer, which may operate off line or on line to the bank's main computer. If, in the latter case, there should be any breakdown in communication, then the system switches immediately to off-line operation.

**Graphical Input-Output Devices.** The term "computer graphics" (CG) is used to denote a set of computer techniques and applications wherein data is either presented or accepted by the computer in the form of line drawings or graphs. The interest in CG and new developments in hardware, software, and their applications has grown steadily since the mid-1960s, mainly after the introduction of interactive graphic devices, time-sharing systems using terminals, and the possibilities of plotting projections of three-dimensional objects. Computer graphics and image and picture processing are discussed in more detail elsewhere in this Encyclopedia. This article is concerned only with the CG I/O devices.

CG input/output devices can be classified into four main groups:

1. Image input devices (derived from hard copy graphics).
2. Electromechanical plotters (such as output devices onto hard copy).
3. Video display units (VDU) with graphical capabilities (such as interactive graphics devices).
4. Microfilm I/O devices.

Nearly all devices of these four types, in addition to their capability to represent graphical images, also allow alphanumerical characters to be represented. These more sophisticated graphical devices are much more expensive than the alphanumerical ones, and the success of their application may be seriously affected by unsuitable or unavailable software.

IMAGE INPUT DEVICES. Many applications require transformation of hard copy images into a proper form for computer processing. Methods used for such computer input are closely connected with those used for facsimile data transmission devices, even when these are not used as computer peripherals. However, some of the scanning methods used and their envisaged incorporation into computer-based systems (like banking, credit card, or message switching systems) make them worth mentioning here.

*Facsimile I/O Devices.* Facsimile data scanners often use some optical raster-scanning method that optically scans all points of an imaginary grid placed over the picture to be transmitted, registering each point as black (part of an image present) or white (part of an image absent). In this technique, even if only a minute portion of the picture is actually filled by an image (e.g., a signature), it is then necessary to transmit details of all the background that carries no useful information. This basic technique can be improved, of course, by application of some methods to eliminate this drawback, improve the shading, introduce colors, etc.

In all facsimile transmission systems the original hard copy picture (or a portion of it) is sent over to the terminal (or terminals) where it is printed or projected onto a screen. The projected image can be microfilmed at the terminal by a camera so that a hard copy representation of the original image can be obtained at some later date. However, in facsimile transmission systems, data is not represented in a digital form.

For graphical processing on computers, the information must be recorded in a digital form, either directly or with the use of a converter, when an analog form is to be translated. In addition to techniques in which the pictures are usually sensed and reproduced line by line, there is another method by which the images are drawn by incremental plotting. Here the information is represented by scales, coordinates, vectors, etc., as well as by identifiers, some descriptive text, and figures, etc. In some parts of the process, where it is necessary to translate the information from one representation to another suitable for computer processing, the computer itself can help substantially, thus reducing the usually great burden connected with manual description of graphical information in the required digital form. Besides the computer itself, the user has a wide variety of devices and means designed to help him in the description task; they can be classified as follows:

1. Devices designed to help the user with the manual description and/or registration of the image data, to be used for subsequent computer processing.
2. Same as the preceding class, but for use in a direct interactive on-line operation mode.
3. Devices used for automatic input of image data to the computer.

Because of the wide variety of devices designed for different applications, only some representative examples of devices in each group will be given here.

*Class 1. Devices designed to help the user with the manual description and/or registration of the image data, to be used for subsequent computer processing.* One of useful devices in this group is the *pencil follower*, which is used for conversion of data presented as graphs, charts, drawings, photographs, and film into digital form for subsequent automatic processing by a computer. It generally consists of two units, the reading table and the electronic console. The pictorial information to be analyzed is placed or projected onto the surface of the reading table. Operation is effected manually by following the trace with the reading pencil or by pointing the pencil at a position. An automatic mechanism beneath the table surface follows the pencil accurately, and position signals are passed to the electronic console where they are visually displayed and converted into suitable form for feeding the output devices (punched cards or tapes, a typewriter, etc.).

Operation of the pencil follower is normally controlled by a foot switch connected to the reading table. Alternatives are a handheld pushbutton; in some cases, a pushbutton is incorporated with the reading pencil.

Usually there are no lines engraved on the reading table for alignment of charts, graphs, or drawings, but such lines may be added by the operator if required. The normal method of reading is to place the graph or chart at any position or angle on the reading table and to take off fiducial points prior to the main analysis, programming the computer to take care of any required correction. Another method requiring special types of pencil followers is the reading of images such as films, high-speed camera films, and other types of photographic work projected on the reading table.

The speed is normally between 18 to 300 symbols a second or between 2 and 30 pairs of coordinates a second, depending upon the ability of the operator and the speed of the output device.

The pencil follower reads out coordinates of points, and no variable origin or scaling facilities are provided. The origin is normally situated at the near left-hand corner of the reading table and a fixed scale of 0.1 mm per digit is used, giving a work area, for example, of 9,999 digits × 4,500 digits. Any corrections for origin and scale would be programmed into the computer. If the chart or image to be analyzed has timing marks or incremental lines along its length, these may be analyzed in several ways:

1. By taking individual readings at the intersection of the trace with the incremental markings.
2. By analyzing the trace fully, using the line mode of output and programming the computer to incorporate the required increments.
3. By using the incremental readout facility, if

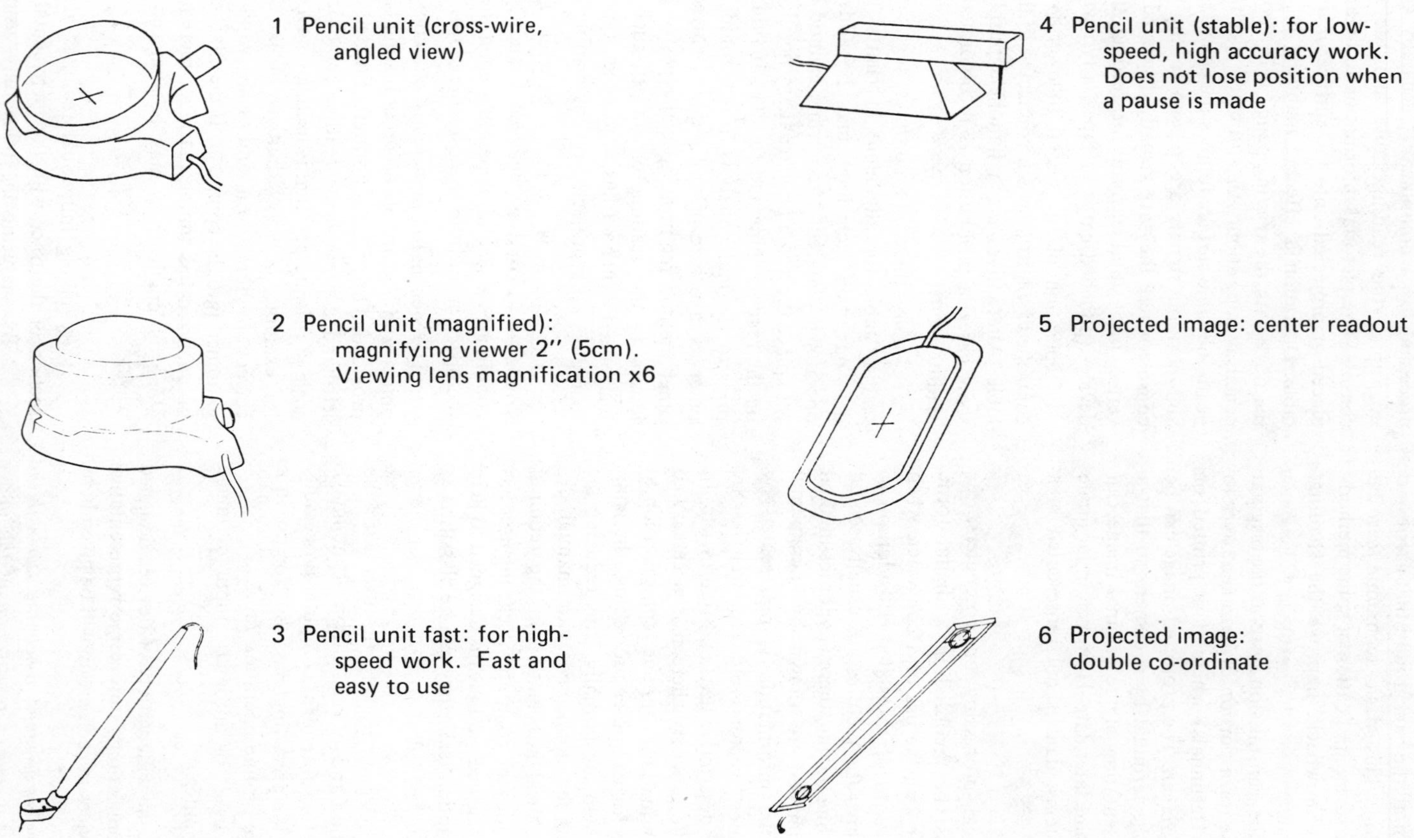


**Fig. 22.** The six types of reading pencil for D-MAC pencil follower (Type PF 10,000, Mark 1B).

the increments are, for example, 1 mm or multiples of it up to 1 cm.

Fig. 22 shows four different types of pencil followers used in the normal method of reading and two types used for reading of projected images.

Another device is *trace analysis equipment that uses two cursors* for tracing the image. The paper trace is placed in the right-hand spool holder and stretched across the length of the illuminated screen. Starting at the left-hand side of the screen, the operator sets the vertical cursor line against the first reference mark on the records and adjusts the quadrant cursor that carries the calibration curve until coincidence is obtained between the vertical line, the calibration curve, and the trace. A foot-switch is then pressed, actuating the attached output equipment—such as typewriter, punch, or plotting table (the latter using a changed scale or calibration corrections to cross-plot one parameter against another)—and the recording is thus completed. The operator moves the cursor to the next reference mark, and the whole operation is repeated.

Trace analysis equipment provides a semiautomatic system for the reduction of analog data recorded on paper or film. Average reading speeds are 1,000 to 2,000 positions per hour. Such trace analysis equipment is used as a computer input device for information that is basically in analog form. The information is converted into digital form by a converter incorporated in the device. This device may also be used if the data should remain in analog form, but the primary information has to be replotted in a different manner; an analog plotter can be attached to the trace analysis equipment.

*Class 2. Devices designed to help the user with the manual description and/or registration of the image data, to be used in a direct interactive operation mode.* Interactive graphic devices used in connection with video display units, like a lightpen, trackball, etc., are described in the later section entitled "Graphical Visual Displays."

As an example of a device working with a hard copy image, the microtrace information processing system will be described. Microtrace enables accurate measurements to be made by moving an electronic "free pencil" around an area or along a line. Measurements are instantly processed by a computer and printed out on an electric typewriter.

The system is simple to use. The operator who is moving the free pencil first records a few control points from the drawings, and is instructed in this procedure by a print-out from the teleprinter, the computer interrogating him with questions designed to discover information about the nature of the task about to be undertaken. The computer is preprogrammed to make its use as simple as possible in offices where there is little existing computer expertise.

Basically, the reading pencil consists of a coil that is coupled inductively to a servodetector system situated beneath the table reading surface. Several types of pencils may be available for trace or for shape analysis and projected image work.

*Class 3. Automatic image scanners as computer on-line or off-line input devices.* There exist special devices designed for specific uses and which have capabilities of automatically scanning charts, often connected with some analytical evaluation method. For example, one such system is an *electronic chart reader*, which scans curves recorded previously by industrial instrument recorders on continuous paper forms and converts them into digital form. This output is then passed to the evaluation unit of the system for analysis. Because the evaluation of the chart in this unit takes place in steps corresponding to previous 15-min registrations (either selected or all of them, on the scanned chart), the system not only permits data registration and conversion, but also a very considerable reduction of the input data. An example of such a recorded chart used for evaluation is shown in Fig. 23.

There is a wide field of application for systems that need some type of automatic pattern recognition device to be used in arriving at image data needed for subsequent processing. An example of such a device is the *pattern recognition system*, which consists essentially of a set of hard-wired digital processor modules that can be combined in many ways to recognize and classify distinct objects of an image, regardless of their orientation.

The choice of source image input devices include *optical-scanning electron microscopes, movie and slide projectors, X-ray systems* and *electron probes*. The image or object is scanned electronically at the rate of one million 720-line frames a second and is converted into 650,000 picture points in a single scan. The digital equivalent of the gray value of the point is processed by the device to determine shapes, sizes, and optical densities, and to classify the objects in the image. This data can be further processed by an on-line, desk-top, or other computer, or it can be output onto computer-compatible paper tape.

An "intelligent" *computer-controlled robot system* has been designed in Japan which can read a technical drawing and, following the information read, can assemble simple machine parts. It is in fact a process-control system consisting of several units,

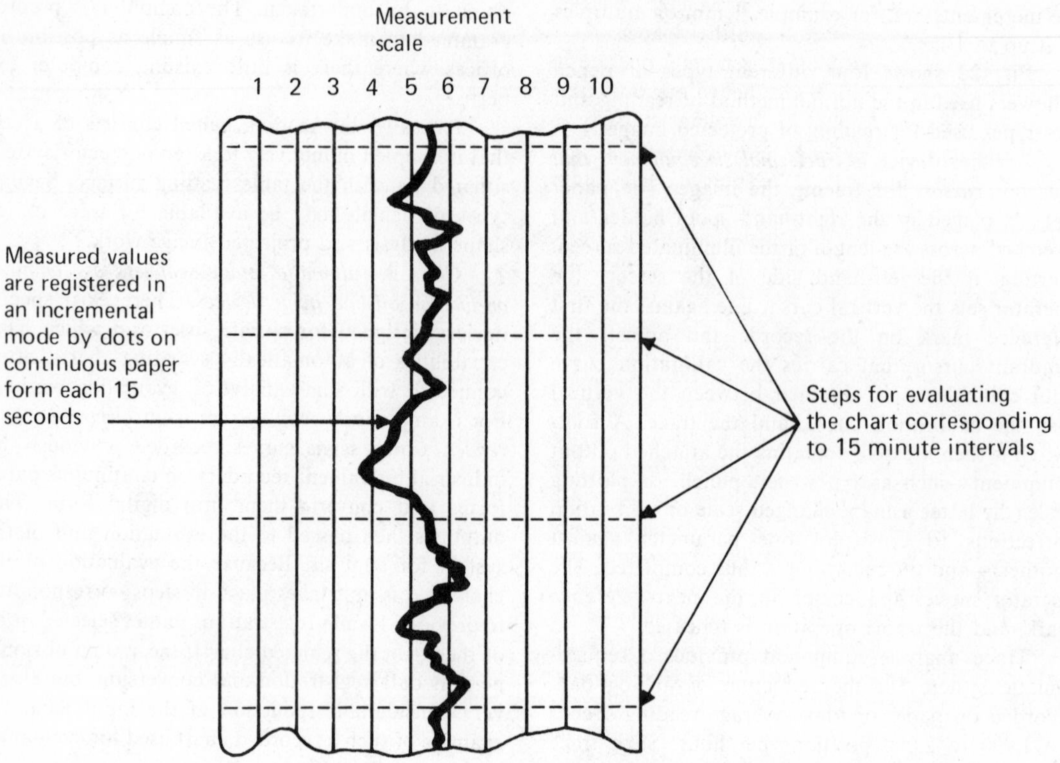


**Fig. 23.** Example of a chart recorded by an industrial instrument to be converted into digital form.

the "eyes" acting as optical pattern recognition devices procuring input data for the "brain," which is represented by a medium-scale computer. The "eyes" are equipped with two television cameras. The first camera surveys and selects parts to be assembled, and the second one reads the drawing (prepared in a conventional way, with special boundary lines drawn between the several different views). Computer output controls the "hands" of the robot system, which are represented by a lever-operated jaw manipulator.

The system operates in such a way that the robot first reads the drawing and then the computer calculates from this data the three-dimensional shapes of the assembly parts and their positioning in the assembly in relation to all other parts. Then the second camera looks for the corresponding part among those prepared on the feeding table by comparing their shapes with that of the computer image; when a match is found, the "hands" catch the selected part and put it to the assigned assembling place, and move it to the proper position.

*Input devices used in microfilm image systems* are described in the last section of this article under the heading "CIM—Computer Input from Microfilm."

Electromechanical Plotters. Automatic plotting devices are used in conjuction with digital computers where graphic or pictorial presentation of computer data on a hard copy are meaningful and easier to use than extensive alphabetic or numeric listings. (A few examples of such simple image listings were discussed earlier under "Line Printers.") They are indispensable when the volume of graphic presentations of output data makes it uneconomical or impossible to perform the task manually.

Electromechanical plotters are impact-plotting devices; hence, they are sometimes called "ink-on-paper" or "pen-on-paper" plotters. They operate generally on the basic digital incremental principle. Decoded input commands from the computer are used to produce increments of movement in either direction along either axis, or at some angle relative to the axes. In the electromechanical ink-on-paper plotters, the plot is produced by movement of a pen relative to the surface of the recording paper.

Electromechanical plotters generally operate in completely digital fashion and hence are drift-free. Accuracy is not dependent upon voltage stability as it is in systems that employ digital-to-analog conversion for positioning of a servomechanism. Since operation is fully incremental, there is no restriction on format. The user has complete freedom of choice in size, type, and orientation of letters, symbols, lines, and axes. Plotters are used for either on-line or off-line operation, often with any standard computer. Some of them may be used as terminals.

The product lines of major digital plotter manufacturers include several model series of electromechanical ink-on-paper digital plotters. Usually, they are all capable of operating in the incremental mode and some of them have added the so-called Zip Mode® capability. In this mode, each input plot command represents a velocity increment, and causes an increase or decrease in speed relative to either or both axes. The Zip Mode allows for high-speed plotting of straight lines and, at the same time, reduces the amount of magnetic tape required for off-line operation.

Two different command structures for the incremental mode are available with electromechanical plotters: an 8-vector structure and sometimes the more precise 16-vector structure. Several increment size options are usually offered with each model, ranging mostly from 0.002 to 0.010 in.; increment size is determined by gears in the plotter. The vector diagrams in Fig. 24 illustrate the direction and incremental values possible with each of the incremental input command formats.

Plotters are of the drum or flat-bed type. The *drum-type plotters* are available in several sizes, usually a 12-in. drum and a 30-in. drum. The plot is produced by rotary motion of the drum ($X$-axis) and lateral motion of the pen carriage ($Y$-axis). Either ballpoint or liquid-ink pens may be used. The drum-type plotter uses special chart paper rolls and can produce continuous plots up to, for example, 120 ft in length. A wide selection of paper is available. An overall view of the equipment is shown in Fig. 25 and its functional diagram is in Fig. 26.

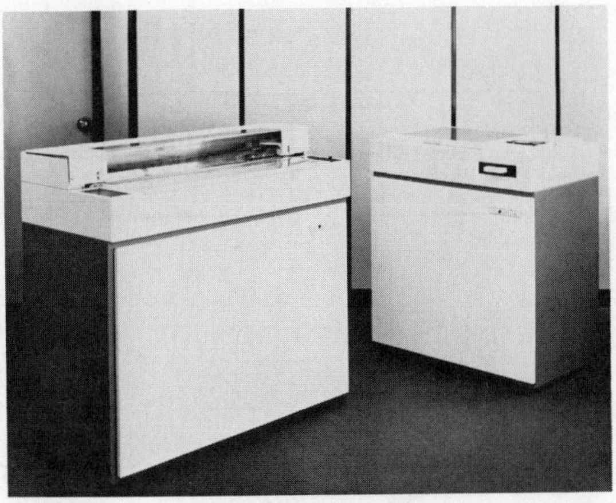

**Fig. 25.** CalComp 1036 drum plotter.

*Flat-bed plotters* are also available in several sizes, such as 31 by 34 in., 54 by 72 in., etc. (plot area). The plot is produced by lateral motion of the beam and vertical motion of the pen carriage. Either ballpoint or liquid-ink pens may be used. The flat-bed plotter provides a continuous display during plotting. It does not require special paper, and can handle a large variety of preprinted forms and special materials. A picture of a flat-bed plotter is shown in Fig. 27.

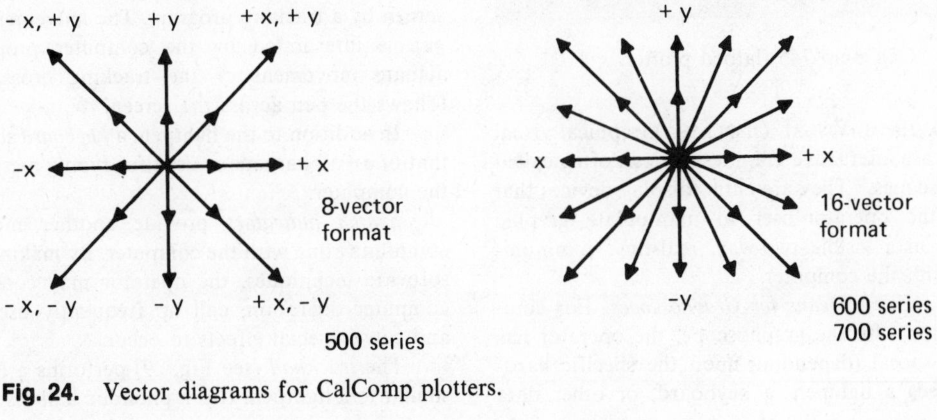


**Fig. 24.** Vector diagrams for CalComp plotters.

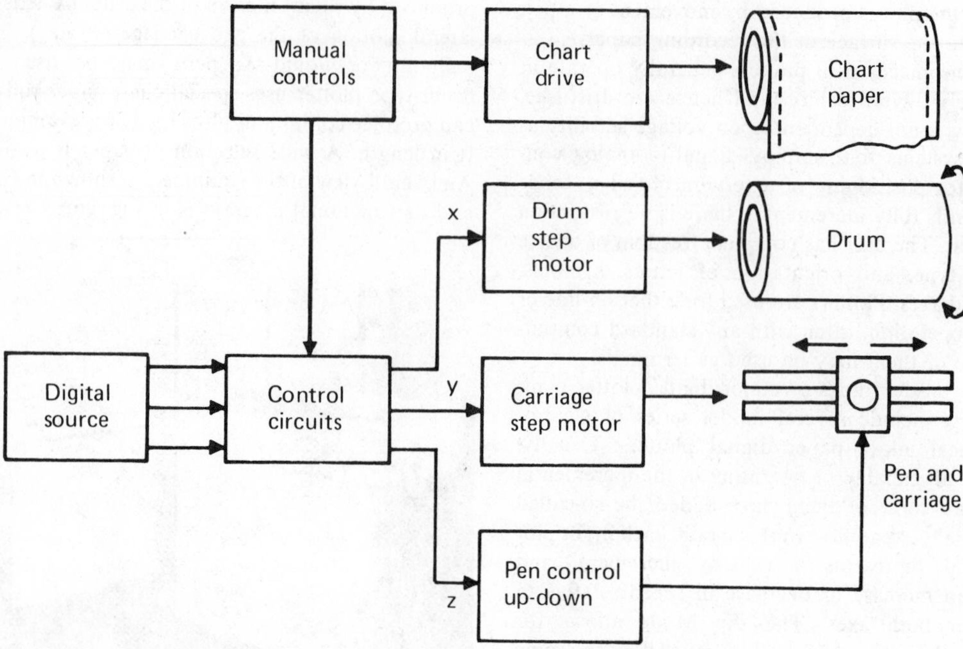


**Fig. 26.** Functional diagram of the CalComp 565 drum plotter.

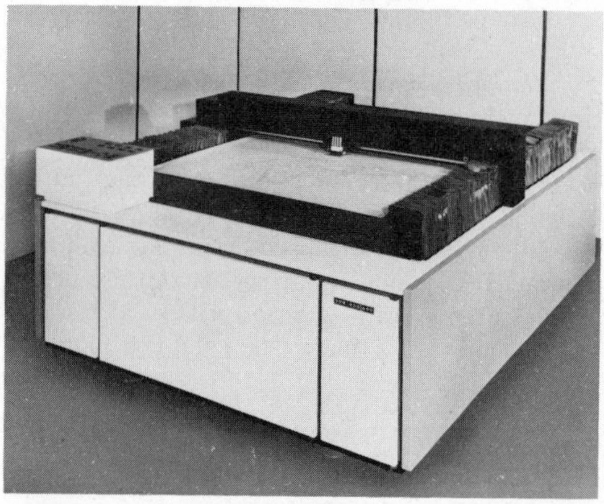

**Fig. 27.** CalComp 745 flatbed plotter.

Graphical Visual Displays. Graphical visual displays are interactive graphics devices, often called "graphoscopes." They are entry/display devices that enable the operator/user to manipulate graphic material in a visible two-way, real-time communication with the computer.

*Data Entry Means for Graphoscopes.* For communication with the graphoscope, the operator has at his disposal (depending upon the specific hardware used) a lightpen, a keyboard, or other data entry means. *A lightpen* is a photosensitive device that generally consists of a small photocell on the end of a rod (Fig. 28), but for better performance (although at higher cost) can use as modem a highly sensitive photomultiplier tube, located inside the cabinet, to which the light is conveyed along a flexible fiber-optic light guide.

The lightpen has two functions: One is to say "there," and the other is to say "do that." Pointing a lightpen at the display indicates that the user wishes to say something about the part of the picture to which he is pointing. When used for drawing, the lightpen is pointed at the center of a small cross, called a "tracking cross," which is displayed on the screen by a tracking program. The movement of the pen is interpreted by the computer program to actuate movement of the tracking cross, which follows the pen across the screen.

In addition to the lightpen, a *keyboard* similar to that of an alphascope is used for typing messages to the computer.

*Switch indicators* provide another means of communicating with the computer. By making use of software techniques, the operator may control the computer operation, call up frequently used data, and cause special effects to occur.

The *trackball* (see Fig. 29) performs a function similar to a lightpen. It is a phonolic ball inset in the

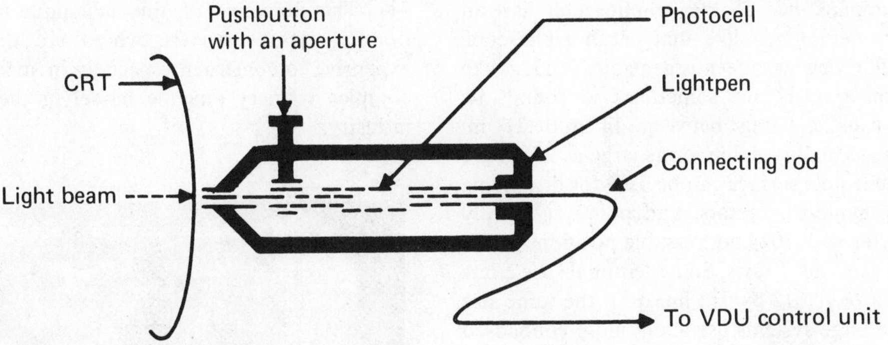


**Fig. 28.** Schematic diagram of a lightpen.

**Fig. 29.** Solid-state magnetic trackball.

display console. When it is invoked by the operator, a cursor appears on the display screen and follows the rotation of the trackball, continuously keeping track of the $X$–$Y$ position. When desired, the operator simply pushes an "interrupt" button to transmit the coordinate data to the computer.

The function of a lightpen is sometimes replaced by a *joystick* or by a *data tablet display*. Compared with the lightpen, these devices have only limited capabilities.

*I/O Functions of Graphoscopes.* Unlike the alphascope, whose prime objective is fast retrieval of the desired information from the computer store, and display it onto a screen, the graphoscope is mainly used for drawing a picture, amending it, and then storing it for further processing or plotting it on a hard copy, as required. However, a graphoscope can also be used for retrieving and displaying stored pictures. Besides its graphical capability, it has to have an alphanumerical feature as well, since the graphs to be displayed have to be presented with adequate headings and notes.

A graphoscope consists of a display unit and some entry device, as discussed previously. Because of its sophisticated nature, its performance has to be monitored by a *controller* interface between the graphoscope and the computer. The controller is equipped with a vector generator, a character and symbol generator, and control logic. Sometimes arc or curve generators are also included, and an addressable buffer store is often added to speed up the overall operation of the system.

**Fig. 30.** User drawing a picture with a lightpen on the IBM 2250 display unit.

The *display unit* of the graphoscope has an appearance very much like that of an alphascope (Fig. 30). The viewing screen is generally oblong, like a television screen, but sometimes is round, its diameter usually being between 14 and 21 in. Diameters as small as 8.5 in. or as large as 25 in. are known. The whole surface can be used for displaying characters, symbols, vectors, and points, generally using a raster with 1024 addressable positions in the *X*- as well as in the *Y*-axis. Some terminals use a less dense raster (e.g., 512 by 512 lines) for the same size area. Some large systems use a still more condensed raster (e.g., the CDC 274 Digigraphic display console, which has a raster of 4096 by 4096 positions over an area of more than 300 sq. in.).

The character set used generally includes approximately 64 different characters and symbols. Several VDUs have, as an option, an extension of the set to 128 characters—to meet requirements for special symbols or different character styles, as well as for displaying characters in more than one size (up to four sizes are often offered).

The number of lines needed to display the alphanumerical text is usually between 16 and 64, depending upon the size of the screen and the size of character set used. Normally, from 32 to 128 characters are displayed on a line.

In underdeveloped countries, special symbols are often used instead of the alphabet for better understanding by illiterate operators.

All functions of the graphoscope have to be done quickly and automatically. The operator should not be bothered with the problem of translating the graphic image and all the manipulating commands into mathematical terms and then into computer language. This is the task of the control unit and the computer, hardware as well as software.

In comparison with the plotter control discussed previously, the software controlling a graphoscope not only must be able to handle a static picture, but also must be very flexible to permit manipulation of the picture (lines and curves in two- or three-dimensional images). Hence, the software considerations are even more important than those of the hardware.

One of many sophisticated techniques developed in recent years is at the Brown University Computing Center in Providence, R.I., where a special program enables the computer at the center to produce a pair of three-dimensional images—differing slightly in perspective—side by side on a graphoscope. When a user looks through a special viewer (stereoscopic), he sees the two images merged into one, with the added dimension of depth (Fig. 31). The objective of this technique is to avoid building actual models, which are difficult and expensive to construct, especially in such cases as a complex refinery pipeline model in the petroleum industry.

**Fig. 31.** Brown University student using stereoscope to get a three-dimensional view of a Möbius strip.

If desired, *devices using microfilm cameras* are used to transfer any displayed picture onto microfilm for a hard copy representation (in one or more copies).

Most present-day interactive computer graphics systems are much more expensive than alphascopes; their average cost is about $100,000. Such a system configuration would include a small general-purpose computer (very likely a microcomputer), a display controller, a display screen, a lightpen, and a keyboard. The system may either work independently or, when a larger computer and/or data-storing facility is required, be connected to an appropriate larger system. Users of these systems are mainly large broad-based companies; they claim, however, that although it is impossible to put a profit or cost-saved figure on graphics, they could not afford to be without computer graphics. Computer-aided design means better design in shorter time, but it is not necessarily cheaper design; computer-aided management seldom means cheaper management.

The economics may change, since recently new types of low-cost graphics terminals have been introduced, but even the most reasonably priced system costs about $8,000 for one unit, which can be used as a remote terminal via telephone lines. Such terminals use either core-refreshed CRTs or storage-

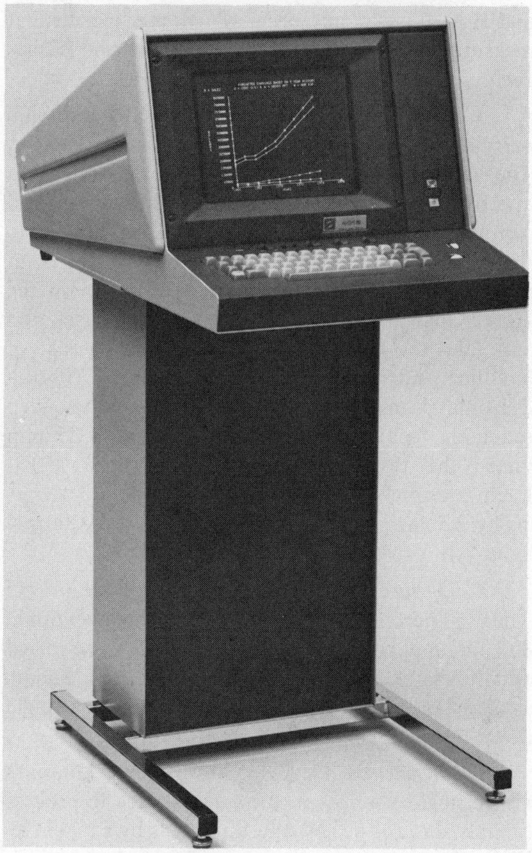

**Fig. 32.** Tektronix 4012 computer terminal with storage tube display.

tube displays (Fig. 32). This type of terminal looks very promising for bridging the gap between alphascopes and interactive graphic systems.

A half-step toward full graphical presentation has been made with the "rear-port" CRT. Permanent information, such as a map or a plant diagram, is back-projected onto the screen of the tube, leaving only the transient alphanumeric data to be handled in the conventional way.

*Television Display Devices.* Television-type displays are sometimes used as a less expensive solution of the image presentation requirement. Color television techniques are also applicable to such displays. A simple two-color presentation needs two separate electron guns to produce different beam energies in the CRT. A special phosphor on the CRT screen responds with red or green light, depending on the energy of the incident electrons.

There are also systems that use color displays as their main components. They may be standard commercial 22-in. TV sets with some minor modifications. In these, the three color points give red, green, or blue color, and other hues can be obtained by mixing these colors. Four different colors can be program-controlled; red, blue, green, and white. The *cursor* and the *trackball* markers have orange color. In alphanumerical mode, the capacity of the screen is 25 lines, with 64 characters each. The individual ASCII characters are built upon a 5 by 7 matrix. In the graphic mode the horizontal and vertical resolution is 384 and 256 points, respectively.

A look into the future projects the use of microcomputers in driving a TV display that could be applied in personal service systems, such as home viewing, where public TV channels are becoming fully utilized. Consider how this range of transmission could be expanded by the application of a chip microcomputer to processing a television picture. According to design standards, each TV channel has a 4.5 MHz bandwidth, with a 540-line raster painted 30 times per second. Assuming 512 lines by 512 elements per line, multiplied by 32 frames per second times four possible signals (off, red, blue, yellow—for halftone reproduction), we come up with $2^{25}$ bits per second. This is close to 32 million bits per second so that a microcomputer with a speed of 10 million instructions per second and 32 bits per word could drive such a display.

Since each frame is $2^9 \times 2^9 \times 2^2$, or $2^{20}$ bits, $2^{16}$ words (64K) in a computer internal store (with 5 bits a word) could hold two frames, or one frame plus instructions. Much more important would be the fact that with a computerized display, we would not need to transmit and retransmit redundant information; that is, those parts of the picture that remain the same from frame to frame could be called from computer storage.

Taking account of the fact that large areas of a picture are of solid colors and that motion from frame to frame is fairly slow and continuous, we can estimate that perhaps only 1 percent of the information would change between successive frames. This means that we could reduce the picture bandwidth by a factor of 100 and that all TV channels presently allotted could be squeezed into the space now reserved for Channel 2. This would have several major effects. The quality of the picture would be higher than the current standard. The range of a transmitter at the reasonably low frequency of Channel 2 would be much greater than at high frequencies and would practically eliminate the present poor reception in fringe areas. Given computer decoding, the cost of receivers would be substantially lower than at present. Most important, this application of computers to TV transmission would free for other uses nearly 400 MHz of the broadcast spectrum, a resource that is in very short supply.

MICROFILM I/O DEVICES. In the past decade, use of microfilm has expanded into a vast range of application areas connected with space-saving archival storage. This has been due not only to the general problems and pressures of information storage and retrieval, but also to the development of a more flexible range of microfilm equipment in parallel with the application of computers.

Some attempts were made earlier to coordinate the two technologies, but without decisive success. Only few years ago, with the introduction of new interfacing equipment, the situation changed rather quickly. Computer people began to look at microfilm as a technique worth considering for inclusion into information systems that need a large data base but not up-to-the-minute response time, with very limited or no need for updating, and with the possibility of storing alphanumeric information as well as graphics in a very condensed manner and for low cost. From all this investigation, new terms emerged: COM (Computer Output on Microfilm), and the not so much used CIM (Computer Input from Microfilm). Before discussing COM and CIM, the different forms of microfilm used in connection with computers will be briefly examined.

Forms of microfilms can be divided into five groups:

1. *Roll microfilm*. This is similar to 16 mm or 35 mm film, but is not perforated. The 16 mm film is used in two different ways, either with one or two tracks of images along the film. With one track, the reduction ratio applied is about 24:1; with two tracks, the ratio is about 43:1. The approximate doubling of the reduction ratio in fact quarters the quantity of film used. Rolls of film are loaded into cassettes, or cartridges, and used in roll-film viewers. There are already a number of double cassettes that overcome the problems of the old single cassette; rewinding is not necessary and the mechanics of the viewer are simplified.

2. *Jackets*. Short strips of microfilm (or individual frames) are inserted into clear plastic covers (acetate sleeves). Related information can be held in one jacket to provide a quick manual retrieval system, since a written reference to the identification codes it contains is put along the top of each jacket like the heading on a index card. Jackets may be updated by inserting new frames or pages of information in the plastic covers. As an example, a Bell and Howell jacket microfilm system uses jackets that measure 5 by 8 in. and hold sixty 16 mm film frames each.

3. *Microfiche*. This is a sheet of 105 mm film carrying an orderly arrangement of micro images. The rectangular transparency of a microfiche is approximately 4 by 6 in. (about a postcard size) and can hold approximately 60 to 70 images, but sometimes holds as many as 224 full-size pages of computer output. (There is at least one printer on the market that automatically arranges the images and annotates the card with headings, allowing ease of handling and retrieval.) NCR, in its PCHI (Photo-CHromatic micro-Image system) uses a two-step reduction technique (the first step being a 35 mm image) that results in a reduction rate up to 250:1. Each microfiche sheet contains more than 3,000 11 in. by 8.5 in. pages, and is generally called "ultrafiche."

4. *Aperture cards*. These were introduced in 1945 when a microimage was inserted in a conventional 80-column punched card, which could then be sorted automatically. Normally, 35 mm film is used. Today, as many as eight images can be inserted into a single card.

5. *Microcards*. Development of new techniques also brought changes in the original idea to process (mainly sort and select) aperture cards by a machine. First, they enabled replacement of the punched code representation of the image identification data in the card by binary coded data printed with higher density, which can be read either optically or magnetically by machine. Thus, more information required for manipulation can be stored on a relatively small area of the card and processed by machine. Second, since the card no longer needs to be processed by the standard punched card equipment, its size can be enlarged. This, together with gains from the data representation change, has made it possible to enlarge the image area. The layout of these microcards (such as Filmorex, Minicard, and Magnavue) is very similar to those of the advanced type of microfiche (and may also contain image identification data).

In all these forms, black-and-white (B and W) microfilm is used, although the use of color microfilm is under study. While B and W can store many levels of information at many places by varying signal densities, from opaque through the gray scale to transparency, color microfilm could store many levels of the same print by varying not only the density but also the color.

Most of the computer microfilm-generating devices have the disadvantage of making positive microfilm, which is commonly known to be not so easily read as negative microfilm on a screen. However, a reversal film especially made for computer print-out has also been produced, at least by one manufacturer.

The arrangement of the pages on the film can usually be varied, depending on the particular unit used, but normally the choice is either the type of arrangement similar to that used in printing comic strips or to that used in movie film, with reduction ratios of around 24:1 and/or 43:1. The choice depends on the sophistication of the equipment.

*COM.* The name "COM" should be related to the overall concept of accessing computer-based information via microfilm. However, more often the term is used to refer to the hardware device that generates the microfilm. Depending upon the technique used, a COM system usually consists of three sections (all of which may be accommodated in one cabinet, or kept as separate units):

1. A *tape drive* in an off-line installation, or a *computer* if the mode of operation is on-line, provide data to be microfilmed.
2. A *control unit*, including a buffer store for speeding up the throughput, a symbol generator for printing alphanumerical and special symbols, a vector generator for drawing graphs, and control logic. The latter coordinates and directs the action of all system elements to achieve the end result of exposed microfilm. It selects the input tape, what is to be recorded, and in what size and position of the "page" it should be located, and when the film is to be advanced to the next frame. It also controls the coding (if any), tape-error conditions, reread, and frame marking to show unreadable characters.
3. The *microfilm recorder* with the microfilm transport and positioning section, and the optical system used for the recording and developing the frame.

In some systems, if hard copy is required, recordings on microfilm can be suppressed and instead the image can be copied in the desired form.

Many COM plotters and/or printers have the ability to superimpose on the printed image one of several program-selectable forms, giving a combined image on microfilm or on hard copy stationery.

The microfilm produced by the COM system can also be used in a conventional way. If hard copy is required, high-speed copying devices using microfilm frames as a copying matrix for producing one or more printed copies are available. Similarly, another device is applied when one or more duplicates of the microfilm are required. The kind of device to be used is determined also by the requirement to ease the selection operation in the information retrieval process. At least two manufacturers produce equipment for automatic microfilm-stored information retrieval.

Generally, all COM systems on the market are offered for off-line operation, but many of them can work on line with the computer. However, there is at least one system that operates in conjunction with the computer in on-line mode only.

Nearly all COM devices translate data from magnetic tape to microfilm via a CRT presented to a microfilm camera, although there are variations of this scheme, such as an electron beam recording directly onto the film or a fiber optics system to present the character image to the camera on line from the computer.

COM hardware on the present-day market is divided into three categories: COM graph plotters, COM printers, and COM plotter/printers: these devices are sometimes known by other names.

*COM graph plotters* use a design technique very similar to that of the pen-on-paper plotters. Drawings are composed by the creation of incremental moves in the $X$- and $Y$-axes by deflection of an electron beam on a CRT. A third move required, equivalent to the raising and lowering of the pen, is achieved by blanking and unblanking the beam. The drawing areas are typically on a raster of 3,000 to 4,000 positions with a standard 15X magnification of the 35 mm microfilm frame, which would give the equivalent of a 0.005 in. increment size resolution on a finished drawing of 11 by 17 in. The plotting speed varies with different models and can be up to 500,000 increments a second. Fig. 33 shows a representative device of this group.

**Fig. 33.** CalComp 1670 microfilm plotting system.

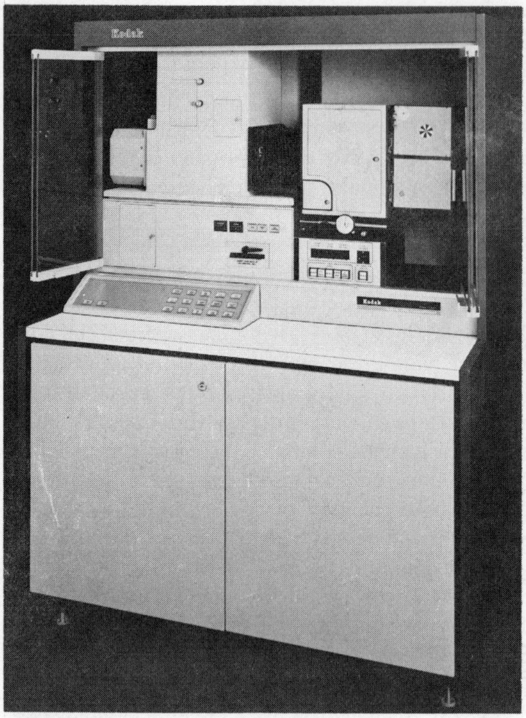


**Fig. 34.** Kodak KOM-90 microfilmer.

**Fig. 35.** CDC 280 recorder and display system.

These plotters can plot graphs as well as alphanumerical characters. They are, however, not suitable for use as high-speed commercial printers.

*COM printers* (Fig. 34) use a symbol generator or other technique to generate characters to be recorded on microfilm and then printed out (all of them, or selectively). Since the microfilm image of the information stored has a form similar to that of a page printed by a high-speed line printer, the COM printers are often called "high-speed page printers." The printing speed varies with the different models

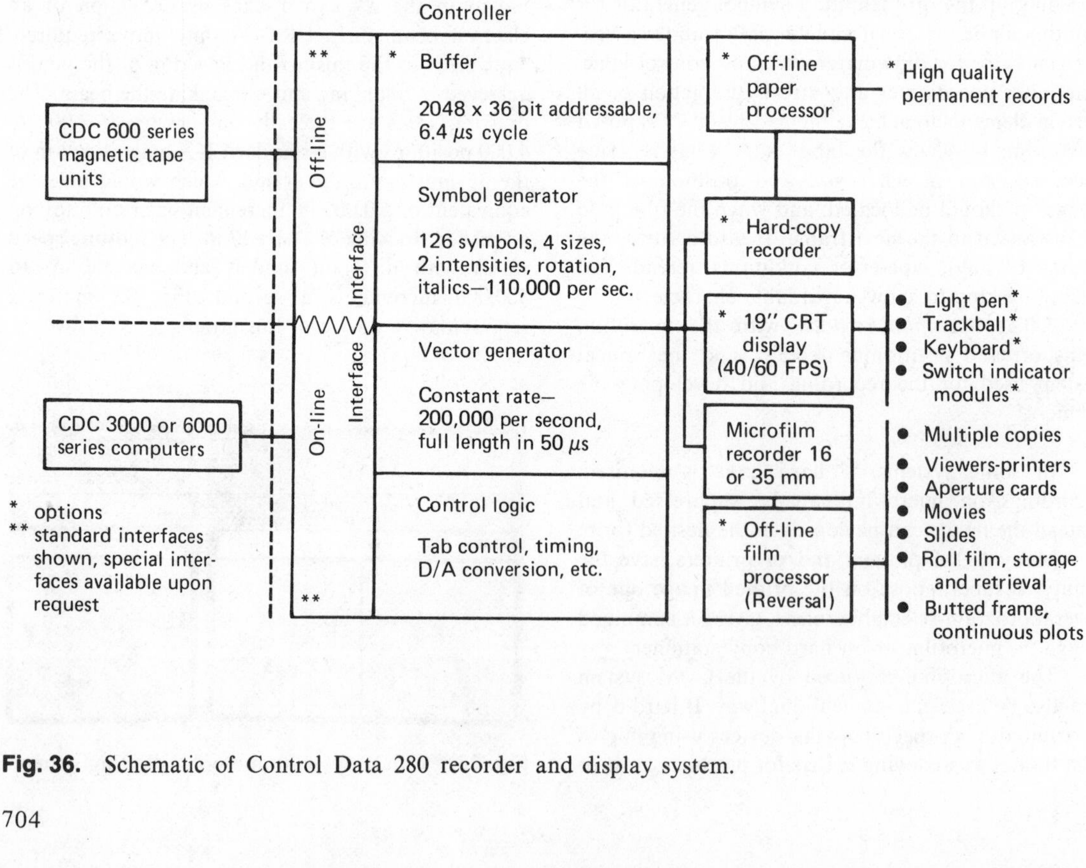


**Fig. 36.** Schematic of Control Data 280 recorder and display system.

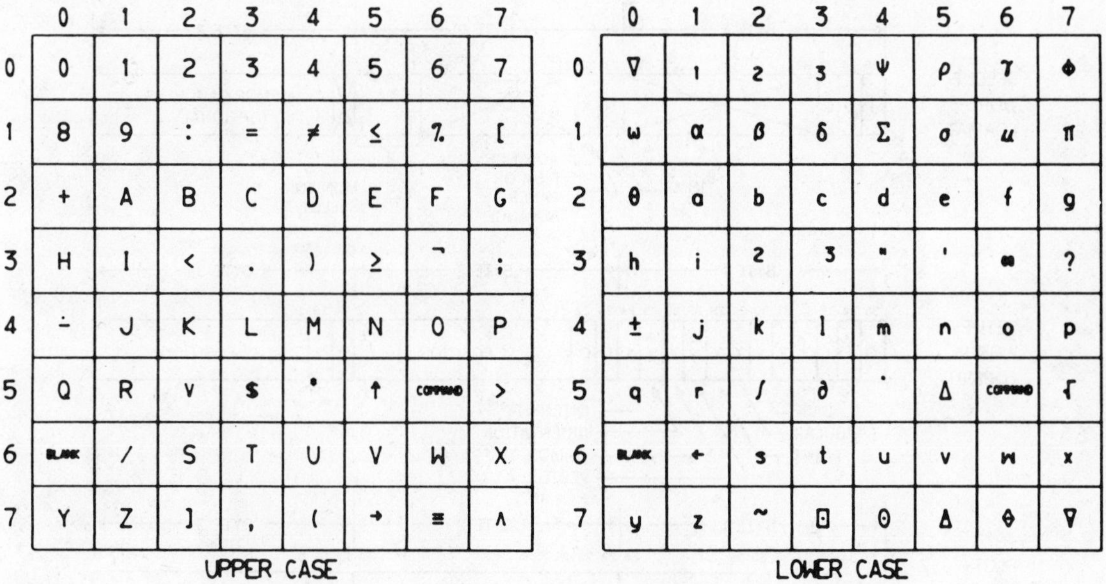

**UPPER CASE**

|   | 0 | 1 | 2 | 3 | 4 | 5 | 6 | 7 |
|---|---|---|---|---|---|---|---|---|
| 0 | 0 | 1 | 2 | 3 | 4 | 5 | 6 | 7 |
| 1 | 8 | 9 | : | = | ≠ | ≤ | 7. | [ |
| 2 | + | A | B | C | D | E | F | G |
| 3 | H | I | < | . | ) | ≥ | ¬ | ; |
| 4 | ÷ | J | K | L | M | N | O | P |
| 5 | Q | R | v | $ | • | ↑ | COMMD | > |
| 6 | BLANK | / | S | T | U | V | W | X |
| 7 | Y | Z | ] | , | ( | → | ≡ | ∧ |

**LOWER CASE**

|   | 0 | 1 | 2 | 3 | 4 | 5 | 6 | 7 |
|---|---|---|---|---|---|---|---|---|
| 0 | ∇ | ι | ζ | ξ | ψ | ρ | γ | φ |
| 1 | ω | α | β | δ | Σ | σ | υ | π |
| 2 | θ | a | b | c | d | e | f | g |
| 3 | h | i | ƶ | ξ | ʺ | ʹ | ϖ | ? |
| 4 | ± | j | k | l | m | n | o | p |
| 5 | q | r | ∫ | ∂ | ˙ | Δ | COMMD | ∫ |
| 6 | BLANK | ← | s | t | u | v | м | x |
| 7 | y | z | ~ | □ | ⊙ | △ | ⊕ | ∇ |

**Fig. 37.** CDC recorder and display system; machine-generated symbols and characters.

used and can be as high as 40,000 lines per minute; there are at least three manufacturers who offer equipment attaining or coming close to this speed. COM printers do not print graphs.

*COM plotter/printers* have features of both the plotters and printers mentioned above. Hence, they can be used in both ways. A representative of this category is shown in Fig. 35. The accompanying diagrams show the possibilities of such systems in a hardware configuration (Fig. 36), in a machine-generated symbol and character set (Fig. 37), and in control word formats (Fig. 38). These plotter/printers which may also use VDU, lightpen, etc., can be considered representative of true *interactive microfilm processing*. Other interactive systems use the computer only for calling up the next required image to be projected onto the screen for viewing by the user, but not for changing the plotted image.

To ease later manipulation with the microfilm, mainly in the selective retrieval operation, the COM system generally prepares, during the COM process, the identification codes for frames, reels, etc., as necessary.

*CIM.* The CIM system may be regarded as the inverse of COM. However, in comparison with COM, CIM is still far more in the research and development stage, with just a handful of systems already installed. The decisive factor that causes difficulties in the design of a CIM device concerns the level of universality of the images to be read, as well as the patterns to be recognized. CIM devices usually can work on line as well as off line. From the few devices available, we will describe three to give the reader some idea of the current range of capability.

*The IBM 2281 film scanner* may be used on line with IBM 360 and 370 systems. Negative images (clear lines on dark background) contained on 35 mm unsprocketed roll film are converted to input data by moving the CRT beam of the IBM 2281 film scanner over the surface of the film in the scanning pattern specified by the program. The complexity of input information that can be handled depends upon the power of the programs written to interpret the data generated by the 2281. Examples of acceptable images are drawings, charts, maps, and graphs.

A frame size up to 1.2 in. square may be scanned before it is necessary to move the film. The film is advanced or backspaced (incrementally, or a full frame at a time) under program control, or manually. Registration of the film image can also be done manually or under program control.

*The Information International Incorporated GRAFIX 1 CIM* configuration is in itself a large computer system containing two processors, the binary image processor (BIP) and a PDP-10 computer with a two billion bit disk store, six tape drives, a number of operator consoles, and a film scanner optical system. The film to be read is positioned frame by frame between a programmable CRT (light source) and a photomultiplier (the image detector).

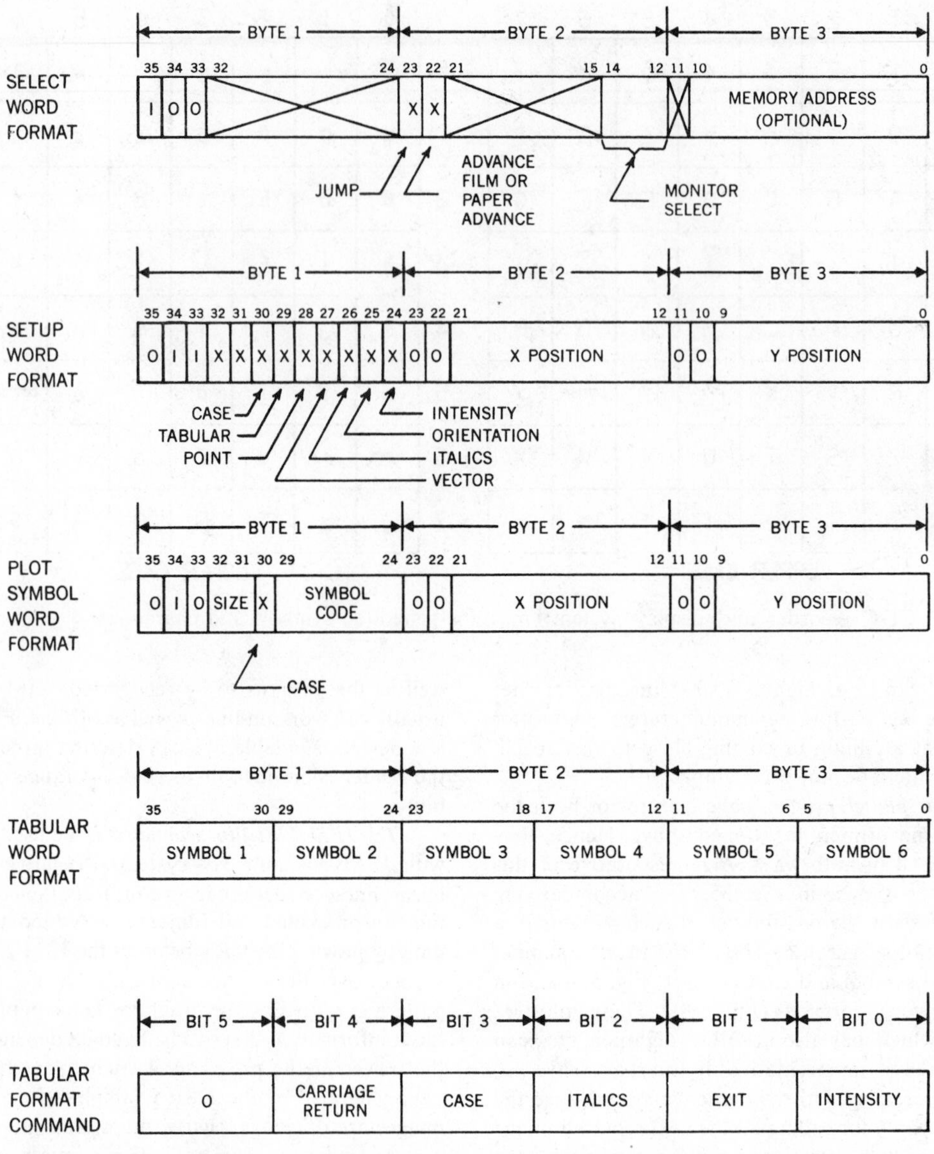


**Fig. 38.** CDC recorder and display system: control word formats.

Under control of the BIP, over a billion points on each frame of the film are examined as potential image constituents. Each character on the film will generate a unique dot pattern within the matrix enclosing it. This pattern is compared with the stored patterns until a match is achieved. Any unrecognizable characters (typically 1:10,000) are displayed on one of the operator consoles for verification. If a previously unknown character represents a member of a new font, the GRAFIX 1 system "remembers" the new style for future reference.

Each font stored in the GRAFIX 1 may consist of up to 92 symbols, and to avoid an average of 46 comparisons in the BIP prior to character identification, the PDP-10 attempts to predict forward characters, using known statistical distributions. The manufacturers claim that this reduces the average number of comparisons in the BIP to 4.6 before a match is achieved. Reading from a known font, the GRAFIX 1 is supposed to input 2,000 chps from microfilm to its backing store.

The GRAFIX 1 is basically a pattern-recognition device and, because of its high degree of resolution, has been used for some interesting experiments, including removing scratches from old Donald Duck cartoons and identifying missile sites from satellite photographs.

*The Oxford Precision Encoding and Pattern Recognition device* (PEPR) was developed for the purpose of identifying and measuring tracks left by the reaction of nuclear particles in hydrogen bubble chambers. Over two million frames of bubble chamber events photographed on 50 mm film have been processed automatically in the first two years of PEPR operation. More recently, PEPR has been used as a converter to read basic rainfall charts recorded by autographic rainfall recording instruments (produced in hundreds of locations throughout the United Kingdom for periods up to 50 years) and to convert them to a complete digital record of rainfall in the U.K. on magnetic tapes for later processing on a computer.

J. NECAS

# INPUT-OUTPUT INSTRUCTIONS

For articles on related subjects *see* CENTRAL PROCESSING UNIT; CHANNEL; INPUT-OUTPUT CONTROL SYSTEMS; INPUT-OUTPUT DEVICES; and MACHINE INSTRUCTION SET.

Input-output (I/O) instructions cause transfer of data between peripheral devices and main memory, and enable the central processing unit to control the peripheral devices connected to it.

Prior to any explanation, a rudimentary model of the logical structure of an I/O setup is necessary. An important point to note is that the model used here is purely logical; i.e., in any actual computer organization, some of the units to be mentioned may be physically nonexistent. Their function, in such a case, will be integrated into the other existing units. This will not change the description of the I/O procedures and operations that will be presented in this article.

The model we use is illustrated in Fig. 1. The central processor and its memory are connected to channels. The number of possible channels is variable. Each one of them has an identifying name (i.e., number). Each channel can accommodate a number of peripheral device controllers. Each controller will control one or more identical, or very similar, devices such as line printers of different speeds, disks, and drums.

In the area of I/O processing, the distinction between hardware and software is extremely vague. In certain cases, vendors of computing equipment include in their hardware manuals a description of I/O instructions, which in reality are parameters to subroutines that incorporate the actual hardware I/O instructions. The questions of the physical existence of channels and controllers must also be carefully dealt with. The reader is advised to keep these gray areas in mind when trying to apply the following discussion to an actual computer.

NOMENCLATURE. Let us now establish some nomenclature. The sequence of I/O operations needed to perform an actual data transfer will be called an "I/O procedure." In an I/O procedure, all devices present in the I/O setup (i.e., the central processor, the channels, and the controllers) take

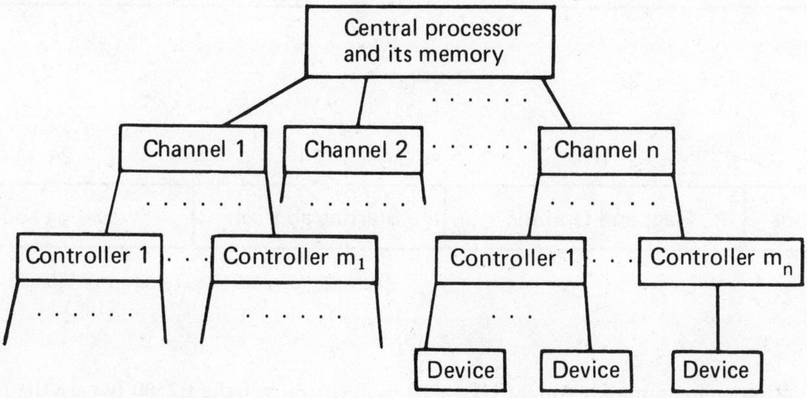


**Fig. 1.** Model of an I/O setup.

part. They operate as independent processors, each performing its own type of operation. We distinguish between I/O *instructions* performed by the central processing units, I/O *commands* performed by the channel, and I/O *orders* performed by the controllers. The degree of independency and concurrency of these operations will be dealt with later.

As usual when introducing nomenclature, it is important to note that different vendors use different words for the same concept. We will follow the more or less established nomenclature, but will introduce synonyms in the proper places.

I/O OPERATIONS. I/O operations are of two classes: control operations and data transfer operations.

Control operations perform the following tasks:

1. Establish the *data path* between the main memory and the peripheral device.
2. Check to verify that the path is legally established and that all devices in the path are operational.
3. Diagnose the success or failure of all data transfer and control operations.

Data transfer operations initiate and terminate the actual data transfer through the preestablished path. These classes cover the whole spectrum of I/O operations.

I/O INSTRUCTIONS. These are regular machine instructions in one of the formats acceptable to the computer. They are decoded and performed by the central processor in the same manner as any other instruction, such as an arithmetic instruction. Examples of such instructions are: START I/O (available on IBM/370 and XDS Sigma, among others), which initiates a channel operation; TEST I/O, which returns status information about the conditions on an I/O path; HALT I/O, etc. The number of basic I/O instructions is usually low, but there are very many variants, which may have different meanings for different devices. These variants are usually included in the address fields of the instruction or deferred to the channel command.

While performing these instructions, the whole central processor is tied up, in the same way that any other type of instruction ties up the CPU.

CHANNEL COMMANDS. Channel commands, sometimes referred to as "channel control words," or I/O descriptors, are bit strings that contain control information for the channel. They are interpreted by the channel, which can therefore be viewed as an independent processor whose instructions are the channel commands, and which is operating in parallel to the central processor. From such a description of the channel, it is clear why the role of the channel can, in certain configurations, be performed by the central processing unit.

The channel commands can be either contained in arbitrary or fixed memory locations (as in most large- and medium-scale computers), or contained in special registers (as in most minicomputers). In each case, the channel operation is initiated by a central processor instruction that passes to the channel the location of the channel commands, or which notifies

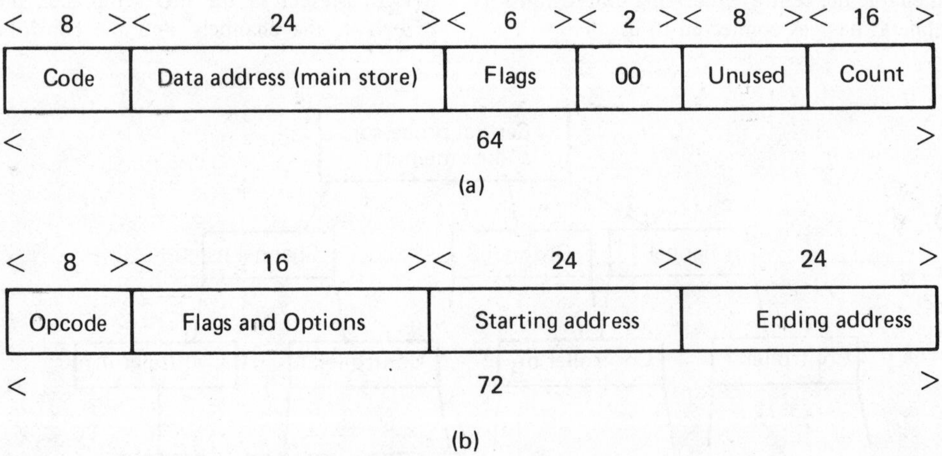


**Fig. 2.** Channel commands for (a) IBM/370, and (b) Burroughs B2500 (where the ending address is not always necessary). Field lengths are given in bits in both (a) and (b).

the channel to start under the assumption that the channel commands are already resident in a predefined, fixed memory location or in predefined registers.

The structure of channel commands is very similar to the structure of regular machine instructions.

In Fig. 2 are two particular examples of channel commands, taken from IBM and Burroughs. The meaning of the various fields is almost self-explanatory. The code (or "opcode") is the actual operation to be performed by the channel: READ, WRITE, READ BACKWARD (in the case of magnetic tape), MOVE (the recording) HEADS (in the case of disks), etc.

The flags and options are usually short fields, sometimes as short as one bit, indicating specific demands and conditions. These may include indications of the course of action to be taken on normal or abnormal completion of the channel command, additional information needed to support some opcodes, enabling or disabling options like command and data chaining (see below), modes of automatic character conversion (if applicable), etc.

The starting address and count, or the starting and ending address, serve to identify the data on which the operation is to be performed. In certain cases, where the amount of information is limited by the nature of the device (i.e., the length of the line in a line printer), it is enough to indicate the beginning of the information.

Once the channel is started, it processes its own commands, which cause the transfer of data to and from the peripheral device controllers. This data, in turn, can be interpreted by the controller, either as an actual data item or as an order to the peripheral device controller. The distinction between data and order can be done in different ways. The transferred item may have identifying information associated with it, or the sequence of arrival of the items will define them to be either orders or actual data.

I/O ORDERS. Orders to controllers may be: START, STOP, TRANSFER status information, GET a data item, MOVE HEADS, REWIND, etc. The orders obviously reflect the nature of the controlled device.

Each step in the sequence instruction-command-order causes, in addition to its normal operation, the creation and storage of status information. This information is usually of two types. One is the setting of the condition codes or status bits of the central processor itself, as expected after each CPU instruction. The other is the creation of a channel status word, sometimes also referred to as "result descriptor." Whereas the condition codes describe the state of the CPU, the channel status words describe the control information that is presented to the channel by the controller (together with data specifying the device itself), and which describes the status of the channel itself.

The structure of the result descriptors varies so widely among manufacturers that examples would be more misleading than beneficial. The reader is advised to consult the manual of the computer in which he is interested.

The various status information items are used to determine the success, or failure, of the I/O process. In the case of failure, the program that initiated that I/O operation can take either corrective or merely diagnostic steps.

A complete I/O procedure will therefore consist of the following steps:

1. Prepare a set of channel commands which will cause the proper set of orders on the device to be activated.
2. Issue instructions that will activate the channel. In this sequence of instructions one should first check to see if the channel is available, i.e., not busy with previous operations or is physically disabled.
3. After completion of the I/O operation, check for success and take necessary steps in case of failure.

Again, the interested reader is strongly advised to follow such a procedure in detail on a particular computer. Procedures of this type are sometimes called "I/O drivers."

We conclude with a number of disconnected remarks and notes. In an actual I/O process, it may be desirable to perform a whole program built from channel commands. The sequencing through the program can be driven by the end of each command, or by the exhaustion of the data to be transferred, without the command being actually finished. These two methods of sequencing channel commands are called "command chaining" and "data chaining," respectively. Not all computers possess this capability. When present, this option is controlled by the flag and option fields of the channel command.

In actual computer systems, the channels are sometimes physically integrated into the CPU. It also happens more and more frequently that the controllers are integrated into the devices themselves. This by no means changes the description of the I/O procedures. The channel commands merely turn into computer instructions. The actual transfer of data, made by the channel, will be done by the central processor hardware. Whether this process will, or will not tie up the computer, is dependent on the sophistication of the hardware.

There exist computer configurations in which not only are the channels not integrated into the CPU, but (as in CDC CYBER 70 series) are turned into full-fledged computers. In this case, one needs a whole interpretive layer of software in these computers to interpret the I/O request posted by the central processor. In other solutions to the question of channels (used, for example, by IBM and Burroughs), the vendors supply factory microprogrammable channels which, on one hand, have the advantage of programmable computers, but on the other hand do not burden the user with software maintenance.

Finally, it is necessary to indicate that no matter which of the former hardware alternatives is present, the I/O process in basically an asynchronous one in which the channels, or their variants, are operating in parallel with the CPU. Thus, one needs a synchronization procedure by which the CPU and channel operations are coordinated. This procedure is indicated by the flag fields and involves either interrupts or polling.

G. FRIEDER

# INSTITUTE FOR CERTIFICATION OF COMPUTER PROFESSIONALS (ICCP)

For articles on related subjects *see* ASSOCIATION FOR COMPUTING MACHINERY; DATA PROCESSING MANAGEMENT ASSOCIATION; and PERSONNEL IN COMPUTERS.

The Institute for Certification of Computer Professionals (ICCP) is an organization of computing societies, established in 1973, for the purpose of sponsoring activity in the areas of testing and certification of knowledge and competence of computing personnel. It is intended to pool the resources and interests of individual societies so that ultimately the full attention of the industry may be focused on the vital tasks of developing and recognizing qualified personnel.

The purposes of the Institute are:

1. To foster, promote, develop, and conduct scientific inquiry and research into any of the several activities related to the development and recognition of knowledge and competence among personnel in the computer and information systems industry.
2. To foster, promote, develop, and conduct scientific inquiry and research into standards of good practice.
3. To formulate and administer testing and evaluation programs designed to determine the aptitude, level of knowledge, and competence of individuals engaging in, or desiring to engage in, disciplines directly related to applied computer and information science.
4. To foster, promote, and develop internationally the purposes of the corporation, including without limitation (i) the establishment of reciprocal standards with, and reciprocal membership for and cooperation with, organizations having similar aims and purposes; (ii) the establishment of international standards of good practice in the worldwide computer and information systems industry; and (iii) the formulation and administration of reciprocal testing and evaluation programs.

**How Established.** ICCP was incorporated as a not-for-profit corporation in the State of Delaware on Aug. 13, 1973. Its establishment was the outgrowth of several years of study by committees of the Data Processing Management Association (DPMA) and the Association for Computing Machinery (ACM) during which the concept of a "computer foundation" to foster testing and certification programs was formulated. An open invitation was extended to other societies to support an organizational period. The organizations that served on the Computer Foundation Organizing Committee and then became charter members of the Institute were:

Association for Computing Machinery
Association of Computer Programmers and Analysts
Association for Educational Data Systems
Automation 1 Association
Canadian Information Processing Society
Data Processing Management Association
IEEE Computer Society
Society of Certified Data Processors
Society of Professional Data Processors

The Organizing Committee was chaired by John K. Swearingen, CDP, of DPMA and Fred H. Harris of ACM, each of whom then became, respectively, the first president and vice-president of the Institute.

On January 1, 1976, Harris succeeded Swearingen as president of ICCP.

**Organizational Structure.** The Institute is governed by a Board of Directors to which each member society designates two directors. Officers of the Institute are elected from the Board at its annual meeting and include a president, vice-president, secretary, and treasurer. The officers constitute an Executive Committee, which may act for the Board between its regularly scheduled quarterly meetings.

Three principal standing committees provide advice to the Board and assist in the management of the Institute: (1) the Program Committee conducts research into the need and feasibility of new projects to be undertaken by the Institute; (2) the Public Information Committee publicizes the programs of the Institute and its concepts; (3) the Budget and Finance Committee prepares the budget for the Board's review and approval, and provides advice on the fiscal affairs of the Institute.

As programs are initiated by the Institute, councils will be established to oversee them and to provide the necessary competence to insure high standards. Councils have policy-making powers, as well as responsibility for quality control, within the appropriate domain of their programs.

Presently, the only council is the Certification Council, which has jurisdiction over the testing and certification programs acquired from DPMA and is responsible for the Certificate in Data Processing (CDP) examination described in the next section.

**Programs of the Institute.** In these first years of its operation, the Institute's highest priority is the improvement of existing certification programs and the establishment of new examinations for various specialties. In 1974 the Institute acquired the testing and certification programs of DPMA, including the Certificate in Data Processing (CDP) examination, which DPMA had begun in 1962 and had administered since then. Since 1962 the CDP examination has been offered annually at designated testing centers, usually colleges and universities.

All candidates for the CDP examination must have at least 60 months of full-time, or equivalent part-time, work experience in a computer-based information systems environment. Candidates may submit college level academic experience for evaluation as partial fulfillment of the current experience qualifications. The amount of credit allowed is determined by the CDP Credentials Committee.

The present CDP examination requires one day to complete, and consists of five sections: Data Processing Equipment, Computer Programming and Software, Principles of Management, Quantitative Methods, and Systems Analysis and Design. Any qualified person may take it, and every candidate must successfully complete all five sections to receive the Certificate.

F. H. Harris

# INSTITUTE OF ELECTRICAL AND ELECTRONICS ENGINEERS—COMPUTER SOCIETY (IEEE-CS)

For an article on a related subject *see* American Federation of Information Processing Societies.

**Purpose.** The IEEE Computer Society was formed to advance the theory and practice of computer and information processing technology. Its objectives are to promote cooperation and exchange of technical information among its members. To achieve this, the Society holds meetings for the presentation and discussion of technical papers, publishes technical journals, and through its chapters and technical committees studies and provides for the professional needs of its members. The scope of the Society encompasses all aspects of design, theory, and practice relating to digital and analog devices, computation, and information processing.

**How Established.** The IEEE Computer Society was so-named in 1972, having originated in October 1951 as The Computer Group of IRE (Institute of Radio Engineers), which on Jan. 1, 1963, merged with the American Institute of Electrical Engineers and became the Institute of Electrical and Electronics Engineers (IEEE). The IEEE represents some 160,000 electrical and electronics engineers throughout the world.

With so many special interests among its members, it was natural for members who wished to concentrate in one area of electronics, or who wanted to exchange knowledge with those of similar interest, to create special-interest groups. The Computer Society with some 21,000 members, is one of these special-interest groups. The IEEE headquarters is located at 345 E. 47th Street, New York, New York 10017.

**Organizational Structure.** The IEEE Computer Society has a Governing Board consisting of a maximum of 23 voting members. The officers include the President, one or more Vice-Presidents, the Junior Past-President, and 20 elected members of the Board. The Board annually elects the President and Vice-Presidents from its membership. The President-elect appoints, from voting members of the Board, a Secretary and a Treasurer for a one-year term coextensive with his term. The President, under direction of the Board, has general supervision of the affairs of the Society.

**Technical Program.** Members of the IEEE Computer Society receive *COMPUTER* magazine, "the voice of the computer systems design profession," which contains tutorial and survey articles, practical applications ideas for the computer professional, a repository of yet unpublished papers, and various other pertinent departments. In addition, they have the choice of receiving the *Transactions on Computers,* which contains papers of archival quality on the theory, design, and practices related to digital and analog computation and information processing, or the *Transactions on Software Engineering,* which contains archival research papers on all aspects of the specification, development, management, test, maintenance, and documentation of computer software, or the *Journal of Solid States Circuits,* which covers devices and systems affecting circuit design.

The IEEE Computer Society sponsors two annual Computer Society Conferences, and cosponsors the annual AFIPS National Computer Conference.

The IEEE Computer Society's technical committees include: Computer Elements, Computer Architecture, Computer Communications, Data Acquisition and Control, Design Automation, Fault-Tolerant Computing, Operating Systems, Packaging, Pattern Recognition, Simulation, and Switching and Automata Theory. Their aim is to promote technical excellence in specific areas by sponsoring seminars, symposia, and sessions at professional conferences.

Other services of the IEEE Computer Society include microfiche and magnetic tapes containing accumulated bibliographic data, data sets to enable researchers with limited resources to obtain access to data bases of other researchers, and the Distinguished Visitors Program, which arranges for leading computer professionals to speak to local chapters of the Society and educational institutions.

Officers of the IEEE-CS since its inception (Oct. 9, 1951) include the following persons:

CHAIRMEN

Jean H. Felker, 1953–1954
H. T. Larson, 1954–1955
Jerre D. Noe, 1955–1957
Werner Buchholz, 1957–1958
Willis H. Ware, 1958–1959
R. O. Endres, 1959–1960
A. A. Cohen, 1960–1962
W. L. Anderson, 1962–1964
K. W. Uncapher, 1964–1965
R. I. Tanaka, 1965–1966
Samuel Levine, 1966–1967
L. C. Hobbs, 1968–1970
E. J. McCluskey, 1970–1971

Name changed to IEEE Computer Society on Jan. 1, 1971.

PRESIDENTS

E. J. McCluskey, 1971
A. S. Hoagland, 1972–1973
S. S. Yau, 1974–1975
D. B. Simmons, 1976–.

I. L. AUERBACH

## INSTRUCTION.

*See* MACHINE INSTRUCTION SET; and PRIVILEGED INSTRUCTION.

## INSTRUCTION COUNTER.

*See* PROGRAM COUNTER.

## INTEGRATED CIRCUITRY

For articles on related subjects *see* COMPUTER CIRCUITRY; and LOGIC DESIGN.

After Bell Telephone Laboratories announced the invention of the transistor in 1948, transistors were manufactured as discrete components in the same way as other electronic components such as diodes and resistors. Logic circuits were built from these discrete components by mounting them on a board with metal-wire connections or on a printed circuit (PC) board. Since transistors consume less power and require less space than vacuum tubes, miniaturization of circuits (which is also referred to as the technique of "microelectronics") has been continuously pursued by circuit engineers. The advantages of microelectronics reach far beyond the apparent reduction of size and weight. They, in fact, improve the reliability of the circuits so much that a drastic increase of system complexity can easily be accommodated.

The earlier semiconductor *integrated circuits* attempted by electronic industry were in the form of the *hybrid integrated circuits* (Warner, 1965). Separated transistors and diodes, resistors and capacitors were mounted on a metallized ceramic substrate. Individual devices were interconnected by a wire-bonding technique. The next important step in the history of semiconductor integrated circuits was the development of the planar transistor. Before the planar technique was developed, junction transistors were fabricated by batch processing in a mesa structure, in which the base layer of a transistor was mounted on top of the collector layer, with the emitter region diffused into the base layer. The surface of mesa transistors is extremely sensitive to ambient conditions, and the product yield of good transistors is usually low.

In the planar approach, the base region is diffused into the collector layer and the emitter region is, in turn, diffused into the base region. The base collector junction of the planar surface is protected from possible contamination of any foreign matter by a layer of silicon dioxide. The metallization (i.e., wiring) patterns, which interconnect various electronic components, can be easily batch-processed by depositing them on top of the silicon dioxide layer. In order to make complete integrated circuits, resistors and capacitors are also fabricated on the same tiny piece of semiconductor material. These tiny pieces of semiconductor are usually referred to as "chips."

When all electronic components like diodes, transistors, resistors, and capacitors are fabricated in a single chip of semiconductor, the name "monolithic integrated circuits," or monolithic circuits, is used to distinguish this circuit from hybrid integrated circuits. As the state-of-the-art progressed, the complexity of monolithic integrated circuits kept increasing. The terms medium-scale integration (MSI) and large-scale integration (LSI) have been introduced. The generally accepted definitions of MSI and LSI are as follows: Medium-scale integration technology refers to the fabrication of integrated circuits with circuit complexity in the 10 to 100 logic-gate range. Large-scale integration technology refers to the fabrication of integrated circuits with circuit complexity of over 100 logic-gate range. A typical logic gate that performs logic functions has approximately half a dozen components (i.e., transistors, diodes, resistors, etc.).

Although a clear-cut dividing point between MSI and LSI in logic-gate counts is provided in the preceding definitions, MSI and LSI technologies actually have no clear-cut boundaries. With some increase in chip size, MSI photolithographic tolerances can be utilized just as well for LSI chips. Both bipolar circuit configurations such as transistor-transistor-logic (TTL), and MOSFET (metal-oxide-semiconductor field-effect transistor) circuit configurations such as the p-channel FET inverter can be used in either MSI or LSI technologies.

Computer logic circuits, in integrated circuit (IC) form, have the advantages of smaller size, lower power dissipation, shorter interconnection delay, and lower cost than those in discrete device form. The IC logic circuits, however, also have some drawbacks (Warner, 1965), which are not present in their discrete device counterparts. These drawbacks include (1) parasitic active devices such as lateral p-n-p transistors, or possible p-n-p-n four-layer diodes among the designed n-p-n transistors; and (2) parasitic capacitances between active and passive devices and the substrate. Extra care is required in IC logic-circuit design and operation in order that the parasitic active elements, if present, will never be turned on to jeopardize the normal operation. The parasitic capacitances, on the other hand, slow down the switching speed or the logic circuits.

Some changes in logic-circuit design have been adapted in IC logic circuits. In discrete device form, transistors cost more than diodes and resistors, while in IC form they cost about the same. Resistor-transistor-logic (RTL), which utilizes resistors to handle its fan-in, is hardly used in IC applications, while transistor-transistor-logic (TTL), which utilizes transistors to handle its fan-in, has gained great popularity. In IC the high switching speed of TTL circuits is obtainable without compromising cost. Based upon the same cost reasoning, it is not uncommon in IC logic-circuit design to utilize bipolar transistors as diodes (Warner, 1965). Either the base-emitter or the base-collector junction of a transistor can be used as a diode. In an integrated field-effect transistor (FET or MOSFET) logic circuit, instead of using a diffused resistor as its loading device, a field-effect transistor that supplies a non-

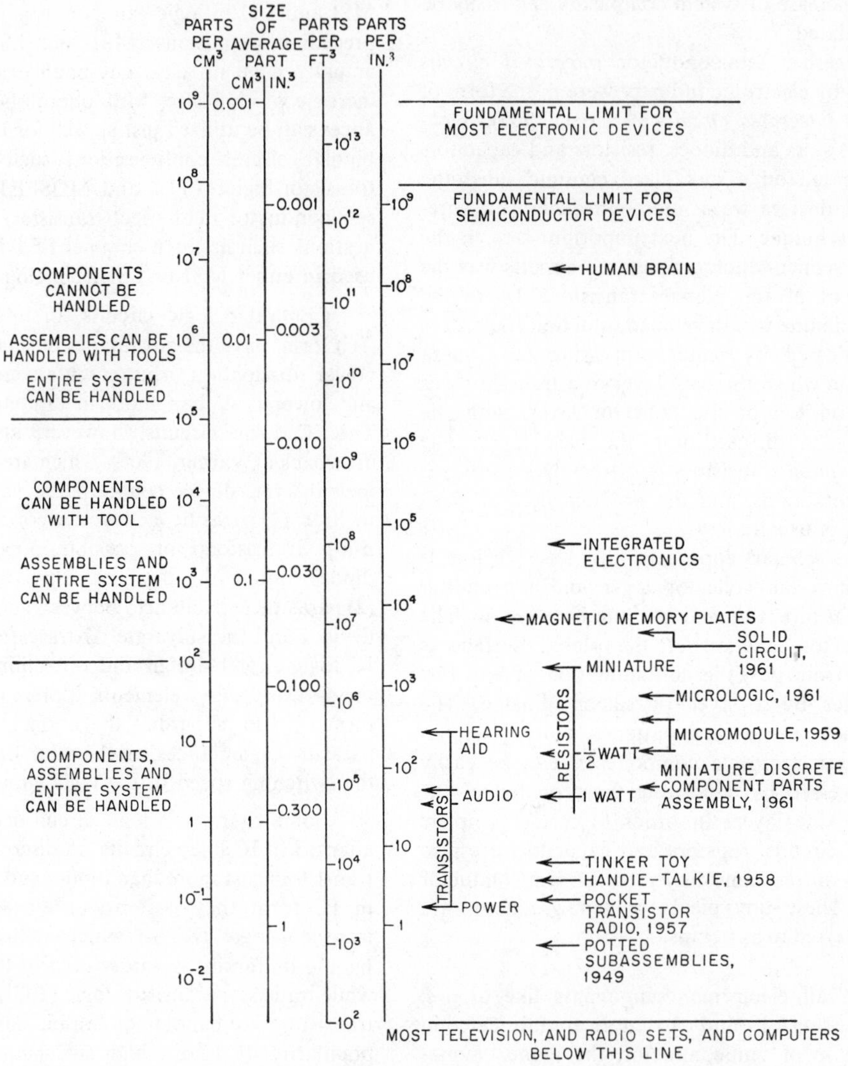


**Fig. 1.** Packing density of electronic devices. (From Keonjian, *Microelectronics,* McGraw-Hill, 1963, p. 6.)

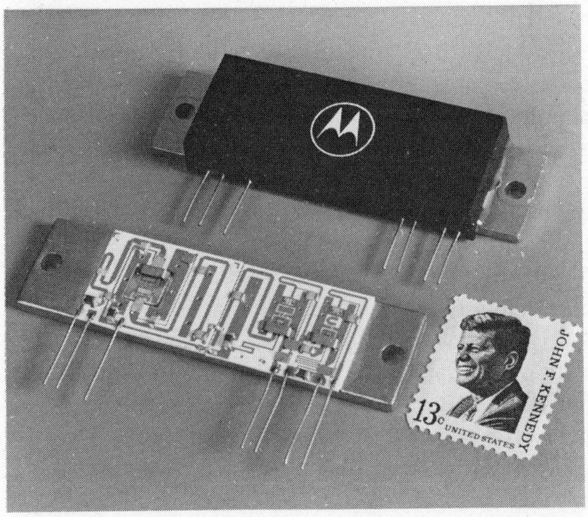

**Fig. 2.** Hybrid integrated circuit. (From Warner, *Integrated Circuits*, McGraw-Hill, 1965, p. 128.)

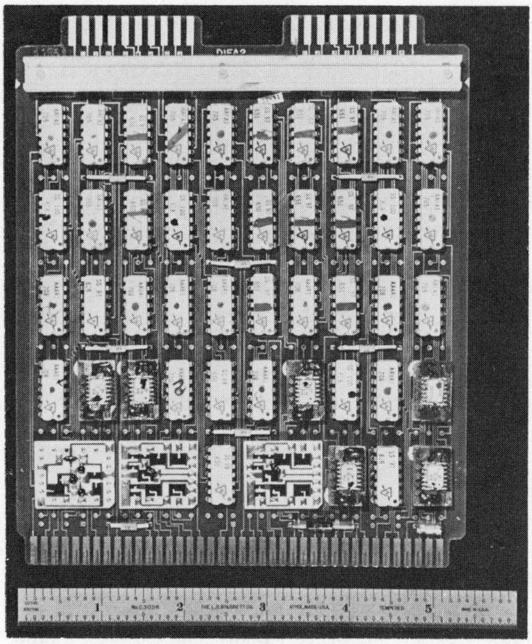

**Fig. 3.** Integrated circuit board used in Honeywell computers.

linear resistance is generally used as the loading device (Carr and Mize, 1972).

Integrated circuits are fabricated in a batch process. Many identical IC chips (typically 150 by 150 mil square) are simultaneously produced on a very thin but large silicon wafer (typically 2½ in. diameter). The process steps in the fabrication commonly include impurity diffusion, epitaxial growth (a technique, by chemical reaction, of growing a thin crystal layer of semiconductor on top of a crystal semiconductor substrate), oxide formation, photo masking, and metallurgy deposition. In each of these processes, many wafers are handled simultaneously. The silicon wafer contained originally either p- or n-type impurity. Diodes, diffused resistors, and field-effect transistors are formed by diffusing one type of impurity (say, p-type) with a chemical compound at an elevated temperature into another type of impurity (say, n-type silicon).

Bipolar transistors are formed, typically, by a double diffusion process. An n-type impurity (emitter) is diffused into a p-type impurity (base), which has itself been diffused into an n-type impurity (collector) previously. In silicon wafers, certain impurity diffusants can be diffused much faster into silicon than into silicon dioxide ($SiO_2$). This particular chemical property is most useful in IC technology in that silicon dioxide can be used as a mask in the diffusion process. Impurity is allowed to get into certain selected areas where $SiO_2$ has been etched away.

In the epitaxial process, a thin film of single crystal silicon with either n- or p-type impurity is grown from a vapor phase on a silicon wafer. To interconnect various active and passive devices on an IC chip, a thin metal film is deposited (typically through vacuum evaporation) on top of a silicon dioxide layer on the processed wafer. The metal film contacts these devices by openings selectively etched through the silicon dioxide layer. The metal film is then etched in a predetermined pattern to form the desired interconnections. After these fabrication processes, certain tests are taken to determine good chips from bad ones. These wafers are then diced into separate chips and each good chip is individually packaged.

The packaging density improvement in electronic systems, due to the introduction of integrated circuit technology, is illustrated in Fig. 1. The reader is cautioned here that the numbers in Fig. 1 are, at best, approximate measures. The packaging density is actually a function of time. As technology advances gradually, IC packaging density improves accordingly. A hybrid integrated circuit is shown in Fig. 2. The actual outside diameter of the package in Fig. 2 is approximately 3/8 in. Fig. 3 shows a circuit board of integrated circuits.

### References

1963. Keonjian, E. (Ed.). *Microelectronics.* New York: McGraw-Hill.

1965. Warner, R. M., Jr. (Ed.). *Integrated Circuits, Design Principles and Fabrication.* New York: McGraw-Hill.

1972. Carr, W. N., and J. P. Mize. *MOS/LSI Design and Application.* New York: McGraw-Hill.

I. T. Ho and S. S. Yau

## INTELLIGENT TERMINAL

For articles on related subjects *see* Data Communications; Data Preparation Devices; Input-Output Devices; Minicomputers; and Terminal.

Computer terminals provide a means of entering data into and receiving a response from a computer that may be located many miles away. When, for some reason, the computer is inoperative and, therefore unable to communicate with its various terminals, there may be serious consequences for the application for which the terminals are being used. To reduce such dependence upon the availability of the computer, intelligent terminals have been developed. Some of the first ones were used in banking, for example, for processing deposit and withdrawal transactions in savings accounts.

In this banking application, the customer presents his passbook to the bank teller. If he is using a terminal connected directly to the computer, the teller may enter the account number, passbook balance, and the amount of the withdrawal or deposit. The computer can validate this information against the customer's account on file, update the passbook balance accordingly, and transmit back to the terminal the information to be printed directly in the passbook.

In the event of a system failure, a bank cannot reasonably refuse to handle deposits or withdrawals. One solution is to do the processing manually by noting the appropriate information on paper and entering that information into the computer at a later stage when it is available once more. A better solution is to use terminals that are capable of editing of information (i.e., checking that the account number is a meaningful number to the bank) and either adding a deposit amount to or subtracting a withdrawal amount from the passbook balance. In addition, the deposit or withdrawal amount is used to update totals of all deposits or withdrawals received by that teller for that day. Provision may sometimes be made to record the deposit or withdrawal transaction on some medium such as paper tape.

The IBM 1060 Data Communications System is typical of the early banking terminals discussed above. This system is called "intelligent" because it has the ability to carry out various processing itself, independent of the main computer.

**Intelligent Terminals.** There are a number of different types of intelligent terminals that use a variety of recording media. One example is the magnetic tape encoder, which has the ability to carry out limited editing, accumulate totals, record information on magnetic tape when not connected to a computer, and subsequently transmit information from magnetic tape to the computer. One example of such an intelligent terminal is the Burroughs TC500.

Often, to increase the flexibility of the terminal, a magnetic disk is used, from which a variety of different programs as well as data, may be obtained. The "intelligent" capability of such terminals has been extended to carry out not only simple arithmetic, but also logical and formatting functions so that sophisticated editing, processing, and formatting of information can take place at the terminal. Examples of disk-oriented intelligent terminals are the IBM 3740 data entry system and the IBM 3735 programmable buffered terminal (see Fig. 1). The 3740 system for example, directly replaces the keypunch, and uses a removable mylar disk for storage

**Fig. 1.** IBM 3735 programmable buffered terminal that uses a magnetic disk and has logical and arithmetic capability.

of programs and data. The unit comprises a keyboard and visual display, and normally operates off line from a computer. It can communicate with a computer, another 3740 station, or a unit that records transmitted data onto half-inch magnetic tape.

**Minicomputers.** The latter half of the 1960s saw the emergence of a large number of minicomputers, in many cases with processing capabilities equivalent to those previously available only in larger computers. The availability of minicomputers has enabled the use of intelligent terminals to be dramatically extended. While many manufacturers now produce minicomputers, the largest supplier is the Digital Equipment Corporation, with its highly successful PDP-8 series.

Minicomputers may be terminals themselves or they may be used to control a number of other terminals, which may be in close proximity to the minicomputer or quite distant. Thus, if the central computer goes down as a result of system failure, the minicomputer can still control its various terminals and accumulate information on disk or tape for transmission to the main computer at a later time. Of course, if the minicomputer goes down, its terminals will not be able to function unless they can communicate with another minicomputer or the main computer.

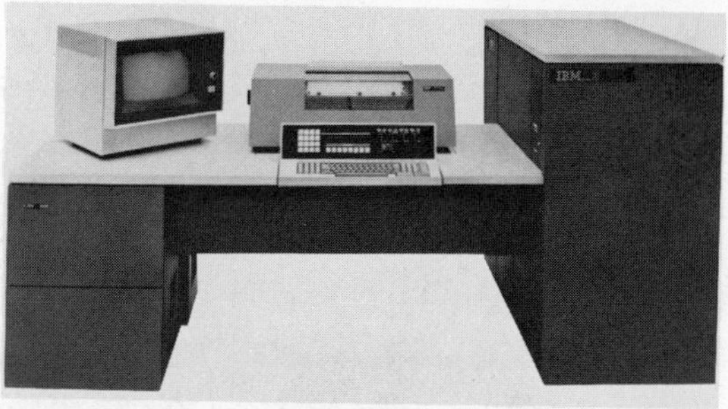

**Fig. 2.** IBM System/3, Model 6, computer, which may be used as an intelligent terminal to another computer.

**Large Computers.** Although minicomputers may communicate with a larger computer, and so appear to that larger computer as an intelligent terminal, large computers can also communicate with each other. In this way, they also act as intelligent terminals, with the ability to carry out considerable processing on their own, without reference to another computer (see Fig. 2). When larger computers are used as intelligent terminals, the system is often said to have *distributed intelligence.*

C. B. Finkelstein

# INTENSIVE CARE, COMPUTERS IN

For article on related subject *see* Medical Applications.
For article on related term *see* Pattern Recognition.

Digital computers have proved themselves able assistants to the medical staff in a hospital's intensive care unit (ICU). The principal reason for the introduction of computers into the ICU is to improve patient care through patient monitoring. Such a computer system can vary in size, configuration, cost, complexity, and function, depending on the degree of sophistication of the monitoring and analysis required and the number of patients to be monitored in a particular ICU. A typical computerized surgical ICU is shown in Fig. 1.

Improved patient care is achieved through computerization for several reasons. First, nurses are able to concentrate on direct patient care when

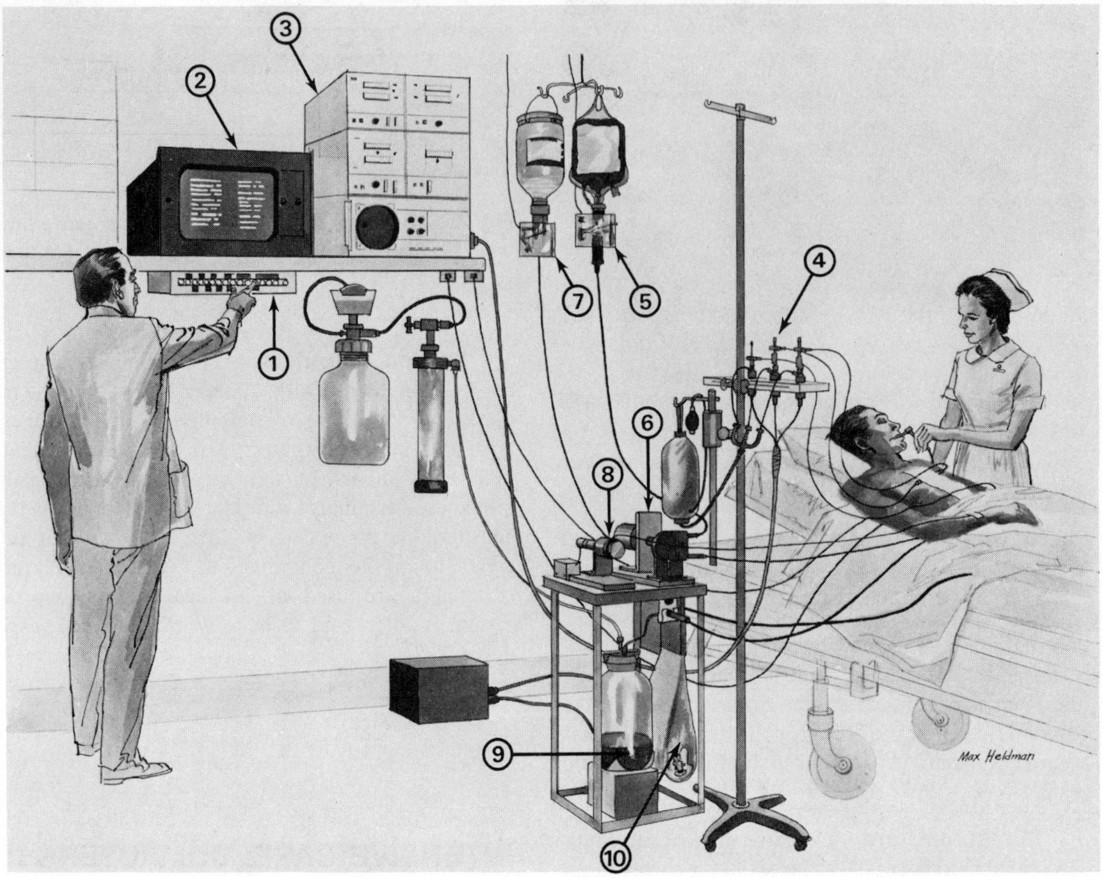


**Fig. 1.** Bedside view at the Cardiac Surgery Post-Operative Intensive Care Unit at the University of Alabama Medical Center, Birmingham, Alabama. Major elements of the automated patient-care system are: (1) numeric keyboard, (2) video display, (3) physiological monitoring devices, (4) blood pressure transducers, (5) blood-drop detector, (6) blood infusion pump, (7) drug and fluid-drop detector, (8) drug and fluid-infusion pump, (9) chest drainage measurement scale and (10) urine output measurement scale. The computer itself, an IBM 1800, is in an adjoining room and continually monitors four such beds on a 24-hr basis. Input to it comes from the numeric keyboard and the monitoring devices. The video display provides the output from the computer. (From "Computer-Controlled Interventions for the Acutely Ill Patient," by L. C. Sheppard et al., in *Computers in Biomedical Research,* Vol. IV, Academic Press, 1974, chap. 6.)

computers take over the repetitive and time-consuming measurement and record-keeping functions. The least sophisticated patient-monitoring systems should fulfill this role by logging the measurements provided by the multitude of commercially available bedside biomedical monitoring devices. These instruments typically provide average values of such parameters as heart rate, blood pressure, respiration rate, and body temperature on front panel meters for visual inspection by the medical staff.

Second, uniformity and reproducibility in data collection from shift to shift and day to day improve the reliability and completeness of the medical record. The more sophisticated systems maintain a data base on each patient, which is reviewable upon request when using bedside display terminals.

Third, a continuous vigil is maintained for out-of-tolerance parameter measures and detectable trends. In advanced systems, trend analyses and multiparameter diagnostic algorithms contribute to a further increase in system capability by providing the physician with an immediate indication of many undesirable and correctable events, such as the presence of abnormal heart rhythms.

Finally, continuous computer adjusment of therapeutic interventions can provide a level of control unattainable by the periodic human supervision of these interventions. For example, the use of sophisticated computer hardware allows the implementation of automated infusion of blood or drugs, under closed-loop control, in response to needs signaled by changes in monitored parameters.

The method by which patient monitoring is physically implemented depends upon the situation in question. In many research environments, or when certain cardiovascular or respiratory monitoring functions are to be performed, it is necessary to analyze physiologic variables on a "heartbeat-by-heartbeat" or "breath-by-breath" basis. The average values produced by standard bedside monitoring devices are not adequate in this application. The digital computer must, in these situations, process the basic time-varying physiologic waveform. The necessary computer programs are generally written by personnel with medical backgrounds or under medical supervision. These pattern recognition programs represent a more complex level of programming than that usually required in other than the beat-to-beat situation.

Regardless of whether preprocessed average values obtained from physiologic waveforms or the waveforms themselves are manipulated within the digital computer, the always necessary analog-to-digital conversion process is a critical area of concern, since data is usually made available to the digital computer as an analog signal, i.e., a voltage that varies as a function of time.

The software utilized in intensive-care monitoring systems can vary as widely as the systems hardware. At one end of the spectrum all monitoring and analysis tasks are performed by a relatively simple program, which sequentially analyzes each of the signals being monitored on a particular patient, permanently records its findings, and then cyclically switches the analog-to-digital converter to the next patient before the program repeats its analysis.

At the other end of the software spectrum are reentrant monitoring and analysis programs which exist in a multiprogramming environment. These programs utilize a hardware priority interrupt system to dynamically respond to the needs of many simultaneously monitored patients. In such a computer installation, data retrieval can be carried out interactively from many independent terminals, utilizing sophisticated graphics and text analysis software. In addition, low priority background processing of nonreal-time tasks is possible to a limited extent.

An open-ended area in the development of patient-monitoring systems is that of diagnostic and statistical analysis programming. The ultimate extent to which computers will contribute to patient care depends upon the growth of techniques utilized in the analysis and extrapolation of all available data. The application of cluster analysis, correlation techniques, nonlinear transformations, and other numeric methods will improve the specificity and accuracy of diagnostic and trend detection functions. The continuing development of diagnostic methods will provide the new criteria to be implemented on ICU computer systems in the future.

Presently, the high cost and the custom-designed nature of ICU computers are the factors that limit the spread of these systems. Advances in computer hardware should, however, continually decrease system cost and increase system capability.

### Reference

1972. Kempner, Kenneth M., William L. Risso, and Daniel Syed. "The Digital Computer as a Tool in an Intensive Care Unit," *Computer*, Vol. 5, (November/December), pp. 39–43.

K. M. Kempner

## INTERFACE MESSAGE PROCESSOR (IMP)

For articles on related subjects *see* ARPA NETWORK; COMPUTER NETWORKS; DATA COMMUNICATIONS; and TELEPROCESSING SYSTEMS.

The term "Interface Message Processor," or IMP (Heart et al., 1970), is generally associated with the ARPA network, which provides a capability for geographically separate computers, called "hosts," to communicate with each other via lines leased from a common carrier. Each host is connected into the network through a small local computer called an IMP. Each IMP (Fig. 1), in turn, is connected to one or more other IMPs in the network via wideband leased lines.

In normal operation, a host wishing to communicate with another will pass a message, including the destination address, to its local IMP. This message will then be passed from IMP to IMP until it reaches its destination. The choice of the path that the message will traverse is determined dynamically. Each IMP forwards each message on the path it determines to be best to assure prompt delivery, taking account of network loading or failures. Alternate routings do exist, since the network is multiconnected to insure reliability. Since a message generally must traverse several nodes in going from source to destination, a copy of the message is stored at each node until it is received correctly at the following node. The IMP is therefore a type of *store and forward* message switcher.

**Fig. 1.** Interface message processor used in the ARPA network.

The hardware consists of a 16-bit word length general-purpose computer with a 12K word memory

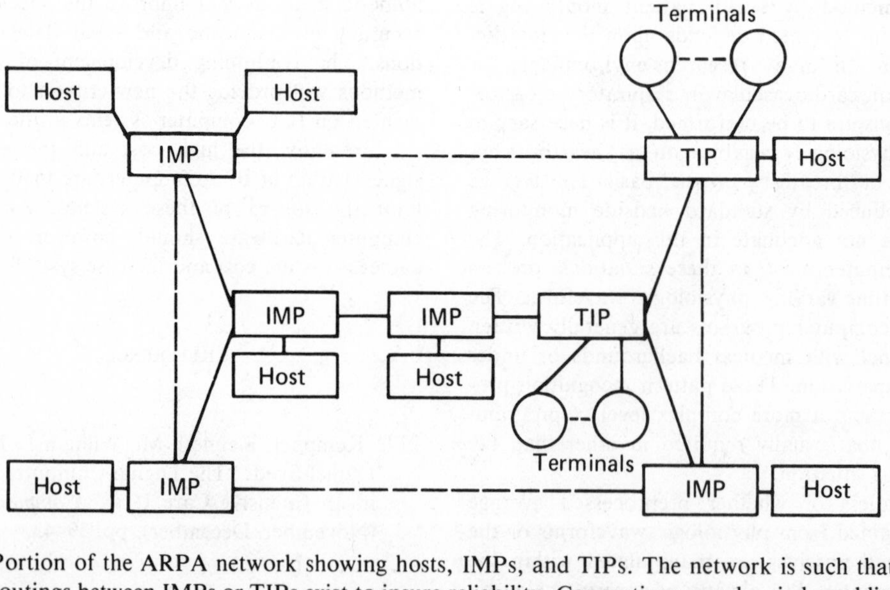


**Fig. 2.** Portion of the ARPA network showing hosts, IMPs, and TIPs. The network is such that alternate routings between IMPs or TIPs exist to insure reliability. Connections may be via leased lines at 9.6K to 230.4K bits per second, but most are at 50K bits per second.

and suitable interfaces to the host and the network. The software includes routines for handling, buffering, and routing messages. Particular attention has been paid to hardware and software features, insuring reliability and fast system recovery.

The IMP enables only host computers to be connected to the network. At any location where terminals only or terminals and host require access to the network, a terminal IMP or TIP (Ornstein et al., 1972) must be used as shown in Fig. 2. The essential hardware difference between the IMP and TIP is that the latter has a multiline controller (MLC), which allows connection of up to 63 terminals to the TIP, directly or via modems. The terminals may be synchronous or asynchronous, and work at bit rates up to 19.2K bits per second. The TIP also has an additional 8K words of memory for the extra programs required for the terminal handling.

The IMPs or TIPs may be connected to as many as four local hosts and five remote IMPs or TIPs via lines from 9.6K to 230.4K bits per second. Further work is being done to extend this to over one million bits per second and to include satellite links to overseas nodes.


### References

1970. Heart, F. E., R. E. Kahn, S. M. Ornstein, W. R. Crowther, and D. C. Walden, "The Interface Message Processor for the ARPA Computer Network," Proceedings of the AFIPS 1970 Spring Joint Computer Conference, Vol. 36, pp. 551–567.

1972. Ornstein, S. M., F. E. Heart, W. R. Crowther, H. K. Rising, and S. B. Russell, "The Terminal IMP for the ARPA Computer Network," Proceedings of the AFIPS 1972 Spring Joint Computer Conference, Vol. 40, pp. 243–254.


J. S. Sobolewski

## INTERGOVERNMENTAL BUREAU FOR INFORMATICS (IBI)

For articles on related subjects *see* International Federation of Automatic Control; and International Federation for Information Processing.

**Purpose.** The Intergovernmental Bureau for Informatics (IBI) is an organization of states that are members of the United Nations or of the United Nations Educational, Scientific and Cultural Organization (UNESCO) or of one of the other specialized agencies of the United Nations. All became parties to the Convention establishing the IBI by depositing an instrument of acceptance with the Director General of UNESCO. The member states are

| | |
|---|---|
| Algeria | Argentina |
| Brazil | Cameroons |
| Chile | Cuba |
| Ecuador | France |
| Ghana | Iraq |
| Israel | Italy |
| Madagascar | Mexico |
| Nigeria | Spain |

The objective of IBI is to promote scientific research, computer education and training, and the exchange of knowledge between developed and developing countries, carrying out activities mainly oriented toward the promotion of informatics particularly in developing countries.

**How Established.** IBI was created by the initiative of the Economic and Social Council (ECOSOC) under the auspices of UNESCO (by Resolution 2.24 adopted at the sixth session of its General Conference). It was established by an International Convention, and went into operation as an autonomous organization in November 1961, as the International Computation Centre (ICC). In 1969 the designation Intergovernmental Bureau for Informatics was added to the original name. This new name signified a change in operating policy, particularly with regard to the promotion of informatics in developing countries. In 1975 this was further reflected by dropping the International Computation Centre from the name.

**Organizational Structure.** The General Assembly, which consists of a representative of each member state of IBI and a representative of UNESCO, is the supreme body of government and meets every two years. The Executive Council, which is composed of six persons elected by the General Assembly and a UNESCO representative, meets twice a year, and is responsible for the program of IBI and administrative and financial matters.

The Director, who is appointed by the General Assembly, conducts the work of the organization in accordance with General Assembly Directives and at the direction of the Executive Council. The current and previous directors of the organization are:

| | |
|---|---|
| Prof. F. A. Bernasconi | 1969– |
| L. A. Lombardi | 1967–68 |
| Claude Berge | 1964–67 |
| Stig Comet | 1962–63 |

IBI headquarters is at 23 Viale Civilta del Lavoro 00144 Roma - EUR, Italy.

**Technical Program.** The activities of IBI center on the following technical programs:

1. Organization of conferences and seminars at an international level.
2. Promotion and organization of regional training courses on the use of informatics at governmental level.
3. Promotion of the use of informatics in the field of management through training courses on the technology and the management of information systems at national and regional levels.
4. Assistance in the creation of regional centers to conduct training, education, and research in informatics.
5. Cooperation with universities and education centers in formulating programs on informatics and in carrying them out by means of direct technical assistance.
6. Action on important research and development projects that cannot be implemented otherwise than on an intergovernmental and interdisciplinary basis.
7. A research grant program designed to grant subventions to research and educational institutes operating in developing countries in the field of informatics, or to institutes operating in industrialized countries for projects to be utilized in developing countries.
8. A fellowship program designed to permit professionals from member countries to participate in courses, conferences, and seminars.

In addition to its own program an IBI/UNESCO Joint Program is being developed. The IBI also administers a Special Fund of Informatics for Development (SFIDE), which is included in the general program. SFIDE resources are made up by contributions from computer manufacturers, institutions, and organizations interested in the promotion of informatics as a tool for development. It is used basically for organization of conferences and courses, for fellowships, scholarships, and technical assistance to developing countries.

I. L. AUERBACH

# INTERLEAVING

For article on related subject *see* MEMORY: Main.

In large systems with more than one autonomous memory module, considerable advantage in system speed may be acquired by arranging that sequential memory addresses occur in different modules. By this means the total time taken to access a sequence of memory locations can be much reduced, since several memory accesses may be overlapped by a high-speed CPU. Two-way and four-way interleaving are commonly encountered.

Assume, for example, a memory with 0.6 $\mu$s access time (i.e., the time to get a word from memory to the processor) and a 1.2 $\mu$s cycle (i.e., the time after the initiation of an access before the memory can be accessed again), and a processor requiring 0.2 $\mu$s to prepare a memory request and a further 0.2 $\mu$s to handle the result. Also assume processor and memory overlap.

Under these conditions, as illustrated in Fig. 1, a sequence of four memory accesses would take 4.6 $\mu$s with no interleaving, 2.4 $\mu$s with two-way interleaving, and 1.6 $\mu$s with four-way interleaving. Notice in this example that four-way interleaving provides a smaller incremental advantage than does the two-way. This is a result of the particular choice made of CPU and memory timing, which happens to be fairly well suited for two-way interleaving. Notice further that four-way interleaving leaves the CPU fully occupied (at least as far as the example goes). The result is that more than four-way interleaving will provide no increase in speed. The system speed for four-way (or more) interleaving has become CPU-limited rather than memory-limited, as is the case shown in Fig. 1(a).

K. C. SMITH AND A. S. SEDRA

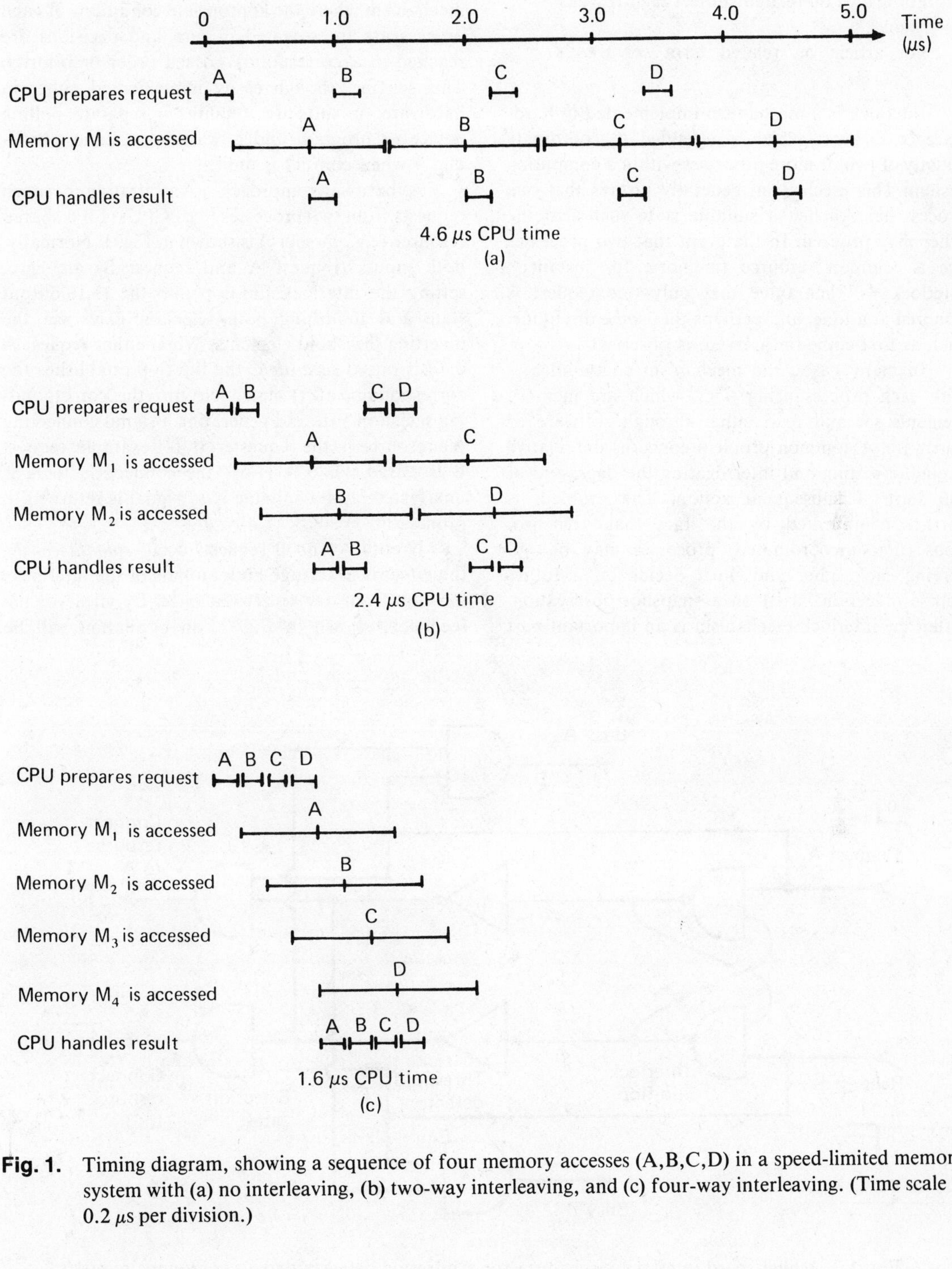


**Fig. 1.** Timing diagram, showing a sequence of four memory accesses (A,B,C,D) in a speed-limited memory system with (a) no interleaving, (b) two-way interleaving, and (c) four-way interleaving. (Time scale is 0.2 μs per division.)

# INTERLOCK

For article on related subject *see* MEMORY: Main.
For article on related term *see* STACK.

Interlock is a mechanism implemented in hardware or software which is intended to coordinate activity of two or more processes within a computing system. This mechanism generally insures that one process has reached a suitable state such that the other may proceed. In the event that two processes use a common resource (memory, for instance), interlock will guarantee that only one request is honored at a time, and perhaps that some discipline, such as first-come-first-served, is observed.

In many cases, the mechanism communicates with each process using *flags*, which are memory elements set and read either through software or hardware. A common problem concerns the relative timing of setting and interrogating the flags, and of the start of subsequent action. The problem is further complicated by the fact that asynchronous (time-uncoordinated) processes may be observing each other and must decide on a future course of action based on a snapshot observation. Often the interlock mechanism is an important part of the timing of each process; hence, it should be very fast.

One solution to interlock incorporates a polling mechanism where the appropriate conditions of each process are interrogated in turn and decisions are reached in a corresponding fixed order or priority. This scheme, though easily implemented either in hardware or software, requires a separate polling device or program and is wasteful of time, particularly when conflict is unlikely.

A hardware approach to arbitrating between requests from two processes (e.g., CPUs) for a shared resource (e.g., memory) is shown in Fig. 1. Normally, both inputs (request A and request B) are zero, setting the interlock flip-flop into the (1,1) output state and inhibiting both selection gates via the inverting threshold elements. When either request A or B is raised *separately*, the flip-flop establishes the corresponding (0,1) state, selecting the corresponding selection gate and generating a signal connecting the resource to the requester. If, for example, request B is raised while A is up, the connection to A is unaffected, and a suitable busy signal is returned to process B.

If both A and B requests occur *simultaneously*, the effect is to change both outputs of the interlocks flip-flop from one to zero at once. By virtue of the feedback, shown in Fig. 1, an oscillation will be

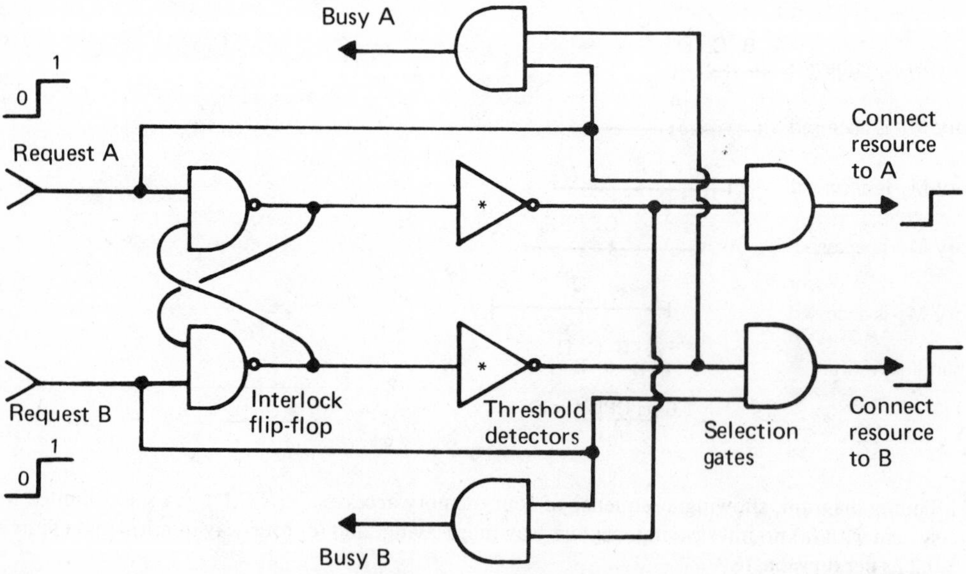


**Fig. 1.** A high-speed interlock mechanism for arbitrating between two asynchronous requests for a single resource.

produced in which each output changes in phase at a very high frequency. The amplitude of the oscillation is so small that the threshold of the detectors following can be set to ignore it.

Eventually, due to minute timing differences in the inputs, random electrical noise, circuit asymmetry, etc., the circuit will establish a stable state in which one and only one of the requests is honored. In practice, this oscillatory decision process occurs very rarely. In one study conducted using 10 ns logic, oscillation of any significance was observed only when input signals were within 100 ps of simultaneity. For signals within 10 ps of simultaneity, oscillation was maintained for about 1 $\mu$s before a decision was reached.

A. S. SEDRA AND K. C. SMITH

## INTERNATIONAL ASSOCIATION FOR ANALOG COMPUTATION

For article on related subject *see* ANALOG COMPUTERS.
For articles on related terms *see* INTERNATIONAL FEDERATION OF AUTOMATIC CONTROL; and INTERNATIONAL FEDERATION FOR INFORMATION PROCESSING.

The object of the International Association for Analog Computation (AICA) is to facilitate the exchange of scientific information among specialists, builders, or users interested in analog and hybrid computation methods by periodically organizing international meetings, displays of equipment and works, by issuing scientific publications and establishing frequent contacts with scientific associations in the whole world for the study of arithmetical methods of computation.

**How Established.** The Association was established in response to a proposal of the presidents of the sessions of the first International Meeting for Analog Computation, Sept. 26 to Oct. 2, 1955. Professor J. Hoffmann, chairman and organizer of the meeting, was elected as a provisional chairman of the Managing Committee of the new Association.

The Association has a constitution approved by a Belgian royal decree dated Feb. 20, 1956. During the second International Congress of Analog Computation in Strasbourg during 1958, Professor Hoffmann was confirmed, and since then he has been reelected by each of the general assemblies up to the present day.

**Organizational Structure.** According to the statutes, the Managing Committee is composed of a minimum of 6 and a maximum of 15 members, selected internationally from among specialists in experimental mathematics. At least one member, a chairman or a vice-chairman, must be of Belgian nationality. There may not be four members of the same nationality belonging to the committee.

The Association is composed of individuals and associated members (industrial firms and public administrations, institutes for research and training), of delegates appointed by the associated members, and, finally, of some honorary members.

The seat of the Association is established in Brussels, and at present is at 50, Avenue Franklin D. Roosevelt, 1050 Brussels. A few individual members have agreed to be official delegates of the Association in their respective countries.

**Technical Program.** According to its rules, the Association organizes an international congress every three years, followed by a general assembly, which elects one-third of the members of the Managing Committee. Between such congresses, the Association organizes small international meetings on more specialized subjects. The Association also supports some national meetings. Since the time of the third congress, which was held at Opatija (Yugoslavia), the program of the congresses has included methods of computation and hybrid simulation.

The Association publishes the official acts of its congresses and of its other international meetings. A scientific publication on more specialized subjects is published quarterly under the title of "Annales de l'Association Internationale pour le Calcul analogique" (Proceedings of the International Association for Analog Computation), with a subtitle: "Revue internationale des methodes de Calcul et de Simulation Hybrids" (Hybrid Computer Simulation). All publications are written in the language of their authors. The official languages of the Association are French, English, and German.

Congresses of the Association were held as follows:

Brussels, Sept. 26 to Oct. 2, 1955
Strasbourg, France, Sept. 1–6, 1958
Opatija, Yugoslavia, Sept. 5–8, 1961
Brighton, Great Britain, Sept. 14–18, 1964

Lausanne, Switzerland, Aug. 28 to Sept. 2, 1967
Munich, West Germany, Aug. 31 to Sept. 4, 1970
Prague, Czechoslovakia, Aug. 26–31, 1973

The eighth international congress is to be held in Delft, Netherlands, in 1976.

The Association has also organized the following small meetings (colloques) and seminars:

Brussels, April 21–23, 1960: Seminar on analog methods in nuclear energy problems.
Brussels, Nov. 21–23, 1960: Seminar on analog computation applied to the study of chemical processes.
Paris, May 28–30, 1962: Colloquium on modern techniques of industrial computation and automation.
Liege, Sept. 9–12, 1963: Symposium on analog and digital techniques applied to automation.
Versailles, Sept. 16–18, 1968: Symposium on analog and hybrid computation applied to nuclear energy.
Tokyo, Sept. 3–7, 1971: Symposium on the simulation of complex systems.

**Foreign Relations.** The International Association for Analog Computation has joined the "Five International Associations Coordinating Committee" (FIACC), established in Paris during a meeting of the delegates of the five contracting associations, which was held on June 2–3, 1970, under the presidency of Professor Victor Broida, chairman of the IFAC. The five members of the international federation include:

AICA, International Association for Analog Computation
IFAC, International Federation of Automatic Control
IFIP, International Federation for Information Processing
IFORS, International Federation of Operational Research Societies
IMEKO, International Measurement Confederation

I. L. AUERBACH

## INTERNATIONAL FEDERATION OF AUTOMATIC CONTROL (IFAC)

For article on related subject *see* INTERNATIONAL FEDERATION FOR INFORMATION PROCESSING.

The International Federation of Automatic Control (IFAC) is a multinational federation of national member organizations, each one of which represents the engineering and scientific societies that are concerned with automatic control in their respective countries. At present, 38 countries (see Table 1) have formed appropriate national member organizations and joined IFAC.

IFAC is concerned with advancing the science and technology of control—which in the broad sense includes engineering, physical, biological, social, and economic systems—and in promoting the dissemination of information about such systems throughout the world. The primary means for accomplishing these aims are:

1. International congresses, held every three years.
2. Between congresses, IFAC sponsors many symposia covering particular aspects of control systems, with topics ranging from "Automatic Control in Space," to "Systems Approaches to Developing Countries."
3. The IFAC Journal *Automatica*, which publishes both selected papers from symposia in expanded form, and original material of particular interest.

IFAC is also concerned with the impact of this advancing technology on society. The technical committee on the Social Effects of Automation acts as the focal point for the collection and dissemination of information in this field.

IFAC takes an active role in public affairs, making its broad technical expertise available to the United Nations family and other international and regional organizations. The IFAC Committee on Public Affairs maintains technical liaison with agencies such as the Office of Science and Technology of the United Nations, and nominates representatives to serve as advisors and consultants on a task basis.

**How Established.** IFAC came into existence because scientists and engineers working in the field of automatic control realized their need to become more closely associated to exchange information regarding their activities. In 1956, at an International Symposium on Automatic Control at Heidelberg, V. Broida (France), O. Grebe (FGR), A. M. Letov (USSR), P. J. Nowacki (Poland), R.

# INTERNATIONAL FEDERATION OF AUTOMATIC CONTROL

**Table 1.** IFAC National Member Organizations

| | |
|---|---|
| Dem. People's Rep. of Algeria | Commissariat National a l'Informatique (C.N.I.) |
| Argentina | Secretaria de SADECA |
| Australia | The Institution of Engineers Australia |
| Austria | Osterreichisches Produktivitats-Zentrum, Arbeitsgemeinschaft fur Automatisierung |
| Belgium | Federation IBRA/BIRA |
| Bulgaria | The National Centre of Cybernetics and Computer Technique to the Committee for Science, Technical Progress & Higher Education |
| Canada | Associate Committee on Automatic Control, National Research Council |
| People's Rep. of China | Chinese Association of Automation |
| Republic of Cuba | Centro de Automatizacion Industrial |
| Czechoslovakia CSSR | Ceskoslovensky narodny komitet IFAC |
| Denmark | Danish Automation Society |
| Fed. Rep. of Germany | VDI/VDE-Gesellschaft fur Mess- und Regelungstechnik |
| Finland | The Finnish Society of Automatic Control |
| France | Association Francaise pour la Cybernetique Economique et Technique (AFCET) |
| German Dem. Rep. | Deutsche Gesellschaft für Messtechnik u. Automatisierung (DGMA) in der Kammer der Technik (KDT) |
| Greece | Technical Chamber of Greece |
| Hungary | Computer and Automation Institute, Hungarian Academy of Sciences |
| India | The Institution of Engineers (India) |
| Iran | Iranian Association of Automation and Control |
| Israel | Israel Committee for Automatic Control |
| Italy | Commissione Italiana per l'Automazione |
| Japan | National Committee of Automatic Control, Science Council of Japan |
| Dem. People's Rep. of Korea | Central Committee for Automation Association |
| Mexico | Mexican Association for Automatic Control (Asociacion Mexicana de Control Automatico-AMCA) |
| Netherlands | Koninklijk Institut van Ingenieurs |
| Norway | Norsk Forening for Automatisering |

**Table 1.** IFAC National Member Organizations (cont'd)

| | |
|---|---|
| Poland | Polski Komitet Pomiarow i Automatyki, Naczelna Organizacja Techniczna w Polsce |
| Socialist Rep. of Rumania | Comisia de Automatizare |
| Republic of South Africa | South African Council for Automation and Computation |
| Spain | Comite Espanol de la IFAC |
| Sweden | Svenska Kommitten for IFAC |
| Switzerland | Schweizerische Gesellschaft für Automatik |
| Turkey | Turk Otomatik Kontrol Kurumu |
| United Arab Republic (UAR) | The General Organization for Industrialization |
| United Kingdom (U.K.) | United Kingdom Automation Council |
| United States of America (U.S.A.) | American Automatic Control Council |
| Union of Soviet Socialist Republics (USSR) | USSR National Committee on Automatic Control |
| Yugoslavia | Yugoslav Committee for Electronics and Automation |

Oldenburger (U.S.A.), and J. Welbourn (U.K.) formed the Organizing Committee of IFAC, with Dr. Broida as president and Dr. G. Ruppel as secretary. A general assembly was convened in Paris, France, and on Sept. 12, 1957, IFAC became a reality with 19 member organizations. The constitution and bylaws were adopted in London on June 21, 1966.

The presidents of IFAC have been:

Dr. Harold Chestnut (U.S.A.), 1957–1959
Prof. Dr. A. M. Letov (USSR), 1959–1961
Prof. E. Gerecke (Switzerland), 1961–1963
Prof. J. F. Coales (U.K.), 1963–1966
Dr. P. J. Nowacki (Poland), 1966–1969
Dr. V. Broida (France), 1969–1972
Mr. J. C. Lozier (U.S.A.), 1972–1975

**Organizational Structure.** IFAC is governed by a general assembly, consisting of delegates from each national member organization, which meets during the triennial congresses. Between congresses, the federation is run by an Executive Council, headed by the president, and elected for three years. The day-to-day work of IFAC is administered by the secretariat, whose address is IFAC, Postfach 1139, Dusseldorf 1, Germany. The legal seat of IFAC is in Geneva, Switzerland.

**Technical Program.** The technical activities of IFAC are carried on primarily by technical committees, which play a major role in the generation of the technical program for the triennial congresses. The initiative for generating symposia in appropriate topics in their respective fields also lies with the technical committees. The list of technical committees is as follows:

Theory.
Applications.
Components and Instruments.
Education.
Terminology and Standards.
Space (started 1964).
Systems Engineering (started 1966).
Social Effects of Automation (started 1971).
Economic and Management Systems (started 1972).
Computers (started 1972).

**Conferences and Symposia.** IFAC has had six congresses: in Moscow, 1960; Basel, 1963; London, 1966; Warsaw, 1969; Paris, 1972; and Cambridge, Mass., 1975.

Full proceedings of the congresses and most of the symposium papers are published.

I. L. AUERBACH

For articles on related subjects *see* AMERICAN FEDERATION OF INFORMATION PROCESSING SOCIETIES; and INTERNATIONAL FEDERATION OF AUTOMATIC CONTROL.

## INTERNATIONAL FEDERATION FOR INFORMATION PROCESSING (IFIP)

The International Federation for Information Processing is a multinational federation of professional-technical societies (or groups of such societies) concerned with information processing. In any country, only one such society or group—which must be representative of the national activities in the information processing field—can be admitted as a full member. As of Jan. 1, 1975, 34 national societies were members of the federation, as follows;

| Country | Society |
|---|---|
| Algeria | Commissariat National a l'Informatique |
| Australia | Australian Computer Society |
| Austria | Austrian Productivity Centre (APC) |
| Belgium | Societe Belge pour l'Application des Methodes Scientifiques de Gestion |
| Brazil | Sociedate dos Usuários de Computadores e Equipamentos Subsidiários |
| Bulgaria | Bulgarian Academy of Sciences |
| Canada | Canadian Information Processing Society |
| Chile | Chilean Computer and Information Processing Association |
| Cuba | Academia de Ciencias de Cuba |
| Czechoslovakia | Czechoslovak National Committee |
| Denmark | Danish Federation for Information Processing |
| Finland | Finnish Association for Data Processing |
| France | Association Francaise pour la Cybernetique Economique et Technique (AFCET) |
| German Democratic Republic | Academy of the German Democratic Republic |
| Germany, Federal Republic of | Deutsche Arbeitsgemeinschaft für Rechenanlagen (DARA) |
| Ghana | Information Processing Association of Ghana |
| Hungary | John von Neumann Society |
| India | Computer Society of India |
| Ireland | Irish Computer Society |
| Israel | Information Processing Association of Israel (IPA) |

| | |
|---|---|
| Italy | Associazione Italiana per il Calcolo Automatico (AICA) |
| Japan | Information Processing Society of Japan |
| Netherlands | Nederlands Rekenmachine Genootschap |
| New Zealand | The New Zealand Computer Society |
| Norway | Joint Committee for Data Processing Societies |
| Poland | Polish Academy of Sciences |
| South Africa | Computer Society of South Africa |
| Spain | Consejo Superior de Investigaciones Cientificas |
| Sweden | Swedish Society for Information Processing |
| Switzerland | Swiss Federation for Automatic Control |
| United Kingdom | British Computer Society |
| U.S.A. | American Federation of Information Processing Societies (AFIPS) |
| USSR | The Computing Centre of the USSR Academy of Sciences |
| Yugoslavia | Yugoslav Committee for Electronics and Automation (ETAN) |

The aims of IFIP are:

1. To promote information science and technology.
2. To advance international cooperation in the field of information processing.
3. To stimulate research, development, and application of information processing in science and in human activity.
4. To further the dissemination and exchange of information on information processing.
5. To encourage education in information processing.

IFIP is both a catalyst and a focal point for conceptual and technological developments that advance the state of the information processing art, thereby accelerating technical and scientific progress. It also performs a vital function in working toward the maximum dissemination of significant information about the digital computer and its applications.

**How Established.** The genesis of IFIP took place in June 1959 at the UNESCO-sponsored First International Conference on Information Processing in Paris. As conference chairman, Professor Howard H. Aiken stated at the conference in his closing speech, "The suggestion to hold this meeting was originated by Mr. Isaac L. Auerbach on behalf of the (U.S.) Joint Computer Committee in the form of a letter to Professor Pierre Auger, UNESCO. The importance of the subject and of the proposal made was such that UNESCO acted immediately and this conference was called."

Even before the success of this conference was confirmed, it was apparent in the planning sessions that future international meetings and other activities were essential to the worldwide development of information sciences. A committee was organized under the leadership of Isaac L. Auerbach (U.S.A.), to draft appropriate statutes and lay the foundation for future activities. The members of this committee were: J. Carteron, France; S. Comet, Sweden; A. Panov, USSR; J. G. Santesmases, Spain; A. Walther, Germany; A. van Wijngaarden, Netherlands; M. V. Wilkes, U.K.; H. Yamashita, Japan.

During the First International Conference on Information Processing, Paris, in June 1959, representatives of 18 national computer societies met to formulate the preliminary structure of IFIP. Statutes for the federation were reviewed and, in the months that followed, were ratified by 13 national societies —6 more than the minimum required. IFIP came into official existence on Jan. 1, 1960.

The presidents of IFIP have been

Isaac L. Auerbach (U.S.A.), 1960–1965
Ambros P. Speiser (Switzerland), 1965–1968
A. A. Dorodnicyn (USSR), 1968–1971
Heinz Zemanek (Austria), 1971–1974
Richard I. Tanaka (U.S.A.), 1974–

**Organizational Structure.** The supreme authority of IFIP is the General Assembly, which meets annually to take action on all matters of policy, program activities, admissions, elections, and budget. It is made up of one representative from each of the member societies and Isaac L. Auerbach U.S., Honorary Life Member; R. J. McQuaker, Chairman of the IFIP International Applications Group (IAG), Associate Member.

The executive body of IFIP is composed of the officers: president, three vice-presidents, secretary, and treasurer, who are elected by the General Assembly. The day-to-day work of IFIP is administered by a Secretariat, whose address is 3, rue du Marche, Geneva, Switzerland.

The Council, consisting of the executive body and up to six elected trustees, meets twice a year and makes decisions as required between General Assembly meetings.

**Technical Program.** In a continuing program devoted to a common basis for the world-wide development of the information sciences, IFIP has established a number of technical committees, working groups, and special-interest groups whose influence is strongly felt at the international as well as the national levels.

The technical committees (TC) and Working Groups (WG) established within IFIP are listed in the accompanying table.

| TC/WG | Area of Work | Established |
|---|---|---|
| TC-1 | TERMINOLOGY | 1962 |
| WG1.1 | Terminology | 1967 |
| | (Both dissolved in 1974) | |
| TC-2 | PROGRAMMING | 1962 |
| WG 2.1 | Algol | 1962 |
| WG 2.2 | Programming Language Description | 1965 |
| WG 2.3 | Programming Methodology | 1969 |
| WG 2.4 | Machine Oriented Higher Level Languages | 1973 |
| WG 2.5 | Numerical Software | 1975 |
| WG 2.6 | Data Bases | 1975 |
| TC-3 | EDUCATION | 1963 |
| WG 3.1 | Secondary School Education | 1968 |
| WG 3.2 | Organization of Educational Seminars | 1968 |
| WG 3.3 | Instructional Uses of Computers | 1971 |
| WG 3.4 | Post-Secondary Education and Vocational Training | 1972 |
| TC-4 | MEDICINE | 1967 |
| WG 4.1 | Education of Medical and Paramedical Personnel | 1968 |
| WG 4.2 | Requirements for Interfaces for Input and Output Procedures in Medical Computers Applications | 1971 |
| WG 4.3 | Guidelines for Testing and Validating ECG-Analysis Programs | 1974 |
| TC-5 | COMPUTER APPLICATIONS IN TECHNOLOGY | 1970 |
| WG 5.1 | Transportation Systems | 1972 |
| WG 5.2 | Computer-Aided Design | 1972 |
| WG 5.3 | Discrete Manufacturing | 1972 |
| WG 5.4 | Common and/or Standardized Hardware and Software Techniques | 1972 |
| WG 5.5 | Continuous Process Manufacturing | 1974 |
| WG 5.6 | Maritime Industries | 1974 |
| TC-6 | DATA COMMUNICATIONS | 1971 |
| WG 6.1 | International Packet Switching | 1973 |
| WG 6.2 | International Information Networks | 1974 |
| TC-7 | OPTIMIZATION | 1972 |
| WG 7.1 | Modeling and Simulation | 1972 |
| WG 7.2 | Computational Techniques in Distributed Systems | 1974 |
| WG 7.3 | Computer System Modeling | 1974 |
| TC-8 | INFORMATION SYSTEMS | 1975 |
| WG 8.1 | Analysis of Organizations' Needs for Information | 1975 |
| WG 8.2 | Utilization of Information Within Organizations | 1975 |
| TC-9 | RELATIONSHIP BETWEEN COMPUTERS AND SOCIETY | 1975 |

The IFIP International Applications Group (IAG), which emphasizes administrative data processing, was established in 1967 as a special-interest group to serve the needs of the administrative data processing community to promote research, education, and the exchange of experience in the field of information processing as applied to problems in public and business administration. IAG conducts an extensive educational program. Its headquarters is located at 6, Stadhouderskade, Amsterdam, The Netherlands.

Each of the technical committees, working groups, and special-interest groups convenes conferences as appropriate to the fulfillment of its objectives. In addition, the main event in the IFIP program of activities is the triennial congress. These have been held in Munich, Germany, August 1962; New York City, U.S.A., May 1965; Edinburgh, Scotland, August 1968; Ljubljana, Yugoslavia, August 1971; and Stockholm, Sweden, August 1974. The next one will be in Toronto, Canada, in August 1977.

From most of these meetings and the work of the technical committees, proceedings and publications are prepared for broad dissemination of current developments in the information sciences.

REFERENCE

IFIP Secretariat. *IFIP Information Bulletin.* (3 rue de Marche, 1204 Geneva, Switzerland.)

I. L. AUERBACH

# INTERPRETER

For articles on related subjects *see* LANGUAGE PROCESSORS; MACROLANGUAGES; and MICROPROGRAMMING.
For articles on related terms *see* COMPILER; OBJECT PROGRAM; and SOURCE PROGRAM.

There are two primary methods by which statements in a source program in a higher-level language are translated in order to have the specified computations or manipulations carried out. One is the compiler method and the other, which will be discussed here, is the less well known interpreter method.

In both methods, it is necessary to take the original source-language program and to analyze and decipher it statement by statement in order to convert it into the machine language object code with which the computer actually operates. With the compiler method, the entire source-language program is first converted, by a program called a "compiler," into run-time computer object code to give the object program. At any later time, when use of the program is desired, the object program is loaded into the computer and set into action to operate upon data to produce the desired results.

With the interpreter method, a quite different approach is used. The interpreter program consists of two parts. The first part analyzes and recognizes the various kinds of statements found in the higher-level source program. The second part consists of a set of subroutines, where each subroutine is a package of compiled object code capable of executing one of the kinds of statements used in the programming language of the source program. The operation of the interpreter involves, therefore, analysis of each statement in the source program, followed by activation of the appropriate subroutine that executes the statement using the actual data of the problem.

The use of interpreters has a number of real or potential advantages:

1. Because they deal with the translation of one statement at a time, whereas compilers must translate the entire object program at once, interpreters are more easily written than are compilers.
2. The subroutines that execute each kind of statement give interpreters flexibility and power, particularly by allowing elegant tracing and other diagnostic techniques used in debugging to be incorporated much more easily than with compilers.
3. Extensions and modifications of the source language (e.g., new statements, new data structures) are relatively easy to incorporate by writing new subroutines or modifying existing ones.

Because of these advantages, high hopes were held out for interpreters in the early years of computers (1948–1952), but interpreters were found to have one basic disadvantage. Consider the Fortran statements:

```
    DO 10 J = 1, 50
10  A(J) = B(J)*C(J)
```

Using a compiler, these are translated once and then the object program equivalent to statement 10 is executed 50 times. But if an interpreter is used, statement 10 must be *translated* 50 times, which creates a time penalty that is often overwhelming. Thus, by 1955–1960, the use of interpreters was rather rare, despite their theoretical advantages.

Various developments are now beginning to bring interpreters back into favor. The first is the emergence of higher-level languages in which the execution time of individual statements may be quite long compared with the translation time. For example, in a string processing language, a single command may initiate a lengthy string search.

A second development is the increasing use of time-sharing systems for the development and debugging of programs. Because of the advantages of interpreters in this area, some systems use interpretation for the translation process for an incomplete or undebugged program and then use a compiler for actual production of results, using the complete, debugged program.

Another motivation for the use of interpreters is the emergence of fast microprogrammed control memories. These make it practical to think of such things as "Fortran machines"—i.e., machines with microprogrammed interpreters for operating directly on higher-level source-language programs—without any need for an intervening translation step.

C. N. MOOERS

# INTERRUPT

For articles on related subjects *see* CHANNEL; OPERATING SYSTEMS; PRIVILEGED INSTRUCTION; and SUPERVISOR CALL.

For articles on related terms *see* CENTRAL PROCESSING UNIT; INTERVAL TIMER; PROGRAM STATUS WORD AND STATE VECTOR; and TRACE.

Program interrupt, an important feature of most modern computer systems, permits them to respond quickly to events that occur at unpredictable times. Some events of this type are: signals generated by instruments, or sensors monitoring some laboratory or industrial process, or a user at a Teletype terminal signaling that he has finished typing a message that requires computer analysis and response. Since the event times are unpredictable, they usually occur while the computer is executing some program that is logically unrelated to the event. To respond to the interrupt signal, the current program must be gracefully stopped, i.e., *interrupted*, and the computer then switched to the program designed to service the interrupt request.

An interrupt facility is very common in most operating systems and real-time applications. It not only enables a computer to communicate with a rich variety of external devices, but is also helpful to the system in managing its own device and program resources. Although basically implemented by hardware, the logical power of interrupts is also provided in a convenient form to users of some modern programming languages, as by the ON type of statement in PL/I.

Each possible event that can cause an interrupt will be called an "interrupt-request-line," and this may be visualized (and even implemented) as a single physical line, which by its 1 or 0 state signifies that the event (i.e., an interrupt request) has or has not occurred. Two examples of interrupt requests were mentioned above. Others include: overflow of arithmetic registers; operation-completion of an I/O device such as end-of-data transmission from a card reader, disk, or tape; a signal from the machine's *interval timer*, signifying the end of a preset time interval. Machine malfunctions, as detected by various internal checking circuits, also typically activate interrupt request lines.

The basic function of interrupt handling is to accept and store interrupt requests and respond to the requests by calling appropriate programs.

To simplify the following discussion, we assume a "classical" system consisting of only one programmed central processing unit (CPU), but containing also several programmed device controllers (IBM and some other manufacturers call these "channels"). Although this structure is relatively simple compared to some multiprocessor configurations reported in the literature, it still accounts for most of the presently installed data processing capacity. Furthermore, most of the principles illustrated for the case of a single CPU system also apply to multiple CPU systems.

**A Simple Example.** To get some idea of what interrupts are and what machine facilities handle them, consider the hardware logic for the simple example interrupt system shown in Fig. 1. Circled numbers indicate relative times of events. At the top of the figure we see the interrupt request lines, which, for reasons of economy, are partitioned into *groups*, each group represented by a single line. The group lines are combined with *mask* signals supplied from the mask field of the program status word (PSW) register. The interrupt mask can be set by the program (or by interrupt events, as will be seen below). The purpose of the mask is to give program control (especially to a program for handling interrupts) over the order in which interrupt requests will actually be permitted to cause an interrupt. This is done by permitting an interrupt to take place only when an interrupt request is present (= 1) *and* the corresponding mask bit is 1.

Thus, for example, if the program controlling interrupts desires at some point to inhibit all interrupts, it simply stores all zeros (0) in the interrupt mask field. Conversely, an interrupt mask field of all ones (1) will cause *any* interrupt request to cause an interrupt. As suggested in Fig. 1, whenever there is a conjunction of a 1 bit of a group request line and the corresponding mask line, the master interrupt line is

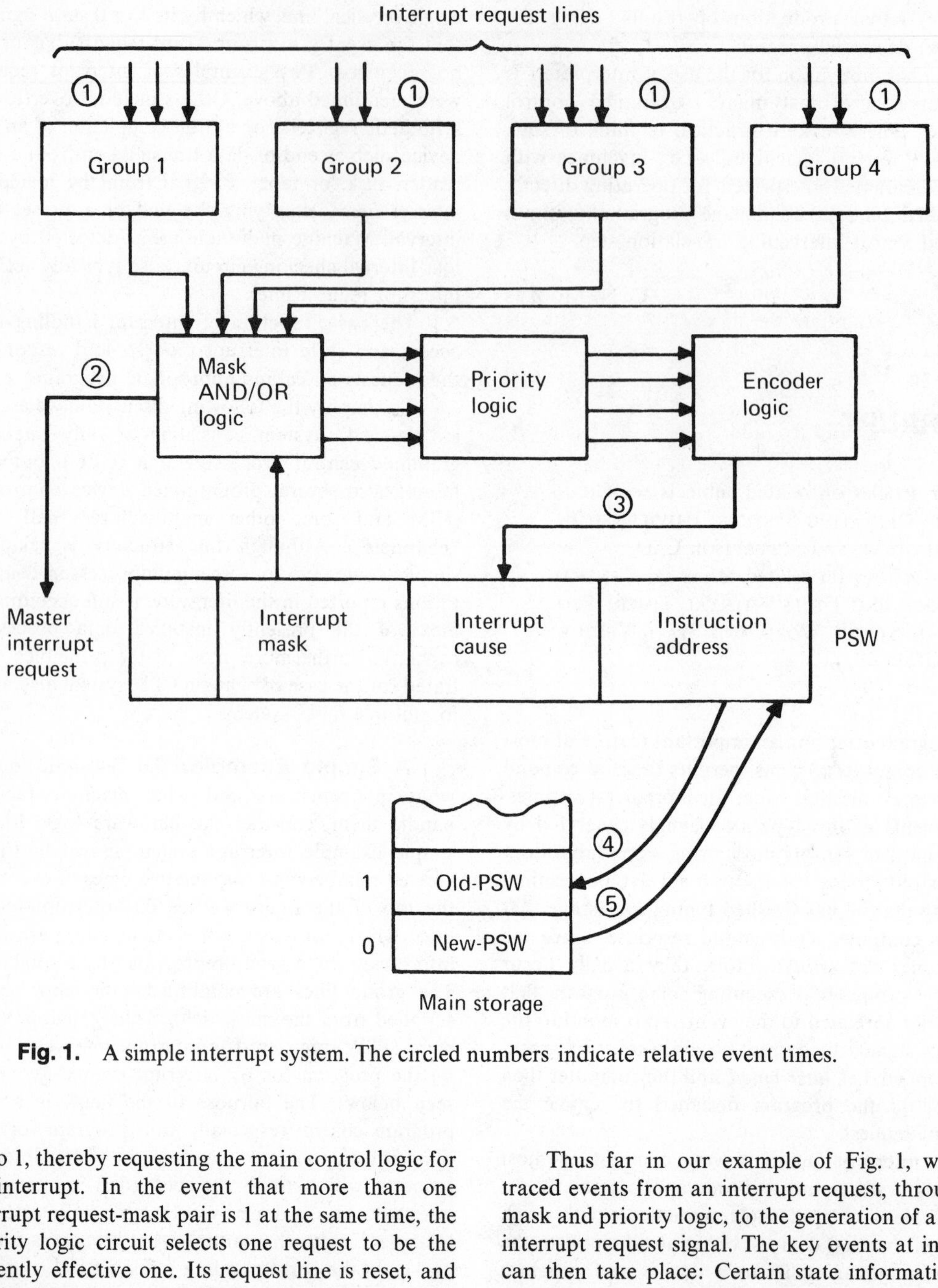


**Fig. 1.** A simple interrupt system. The circled numbers indicate relative event times.

set to 1, thereby requesting the main control logic for an interrupt. In the event that more than one interrupt request-mask pair is 1 at the same time, the priority logic circuit selects one request to be the currently effective one. Its request line is reset, and its identifier is recorded in the PSW register as the interrupt cause.

Normally, detailed timing is arranged so that the interrupt will not actually occur until after completion of the current CPU instruction. In some systems, however, to guarantee very fast interrupt response times, interruption of the execution of certain lengthy instructions is permitted.

Thus far in our example of Fig. 1, we have traced events from an interrupt request, through the mask and priority logic, to the generation of a master interrupt request signal. The key events at interrupt can then take place: Certain state information will next be saved in main storage; then a branch to a new program will be forced. The state information has two main components. First is the identification of the exact cause of the interrupt, since the program for responding to the interrupt must know this in order to respond properly. A second component of the state is the instruction address of the interrupted program, which is the location in storage of the instruction next to be executed in that program, and hence the point where this program is to be resumed later.

The rationale for the PSW register can now be seen: It is simply a "packaging" into one register of essential state and associated information. Thus, a main interrupt event is to store the PSW register into some standard main-storage location (address 1 in Fig. 1). This address is sometimes called the "Old-PSW." Having saved the state of the interrupted program and identification of the request cause, the next step is to initiate the new program, which, of course, requires a new value for the instruction address and hence for the PSW register. This is done by reloading the PSW register from some standard address in main storage (address 0 in our example). Note that this "New PSW" also respecifies a new set of interrupt mask bits.

Control over masking and the selection of the program entered by interrupt is done in part by specifying the New-PSW at word location 0. Usually, in a system like Fig. 1, this New-PSW would contain all zeros in its mask field, to (temporarily) inhibit all interrupts, and the instruction address field would point to a SAVE program that stores CPU registers, moves the Old-PSW to a stacking area of main storage, and then branches to the start of a cause-decode program that eventually uses the interrupt-cause to determine the appropriate response program. At this point, the PSW mask bits may be set to all 1s to permit interrupt requests to be effective again.

The preceding description suggests that, in many ways, response to an interrupt is similar to linking to a subroutine, and an interrupt-handling system may be designed to resemble a subroutine structuring system.

In the example here, some of the principles of interrupts have been illustrated. However, it must be emphasized that the great diversity in the logic and implementation of interrupt schemes precludes coverage of all variations in any single example.

**General Functional Features.** The example in the preceding section illustrates the following six general classes of functions found in most interrupt systems.

1. Storage of interrupt requests.
2. Interrupt masking and enabling.
3. Priority selection from among concurrent requests.
4. Request decoding to the address of the response program.
5. Storage of processor state.
6. Initiation of a new processor state.

A combination of hardware (logic circuitry) and programs is used to implement these functions. In general, the more of the implementation done in hardware, the greater can be the speed of response, but the higher the hardware cost and less flexible the system will be to changes in interrupt logic. Systems differ greatly in the choice of functions for hardware implementation (see the subsequent section, "Implementations").

**Interrupt Types.** Most of the interrupt types fall into the following classes:

1. Processor operations.
2. Privileged operations.
3. Machine malfunctions.
4. Input/output.
5. Timer.
6. Supervisor CALL instruction.
7. External device.

Class 1 includes register overflows, divide checks, addresses that are out of bounds, illegal operation codes. Class 2 refers to a class of exceptional conditions that may arise because many modern computers reserve certain functions for a *privileged* mode of the machine, so that certain key-resource scheduling and storage-protection instructions can be executed *only* by the system supervisor program. A class 2 interrupt occurs if any of these privileged instructions is attempted when the machine is not in the privileged mode. Classes 3 and 4 are rather obvious in principle and will not be discussed further. Class 5 refers to an interval timer that can be set to any reasonable, positive value by program instruction. The value is counted down automatically, and when it reaches zero, generates an interrupt request. Class 6 refers to the ability to initiate an interrupt by a special instruction designed for this purpose. In effect, this instruction is usually a request for some program that is part of the operating system. Class 7 refers to interrupt requests that may be typically generated by sensor devices, or instruments, or relay closures.

**Implementations.** Thus far we have discussed an interrupt system primarily from the viewpoint of its hardware features, and then only for one example configuration. In most cases, as indicated in the section on functional features, interrupt handling is done by a combination of hardware and software.

The software is usually a part of the operating system program that manages the assignment of all hardware/software resources to workload demands. In fact, most operating systems are *interrupt-driven*; i.e., the interrupt system is the mechanism for reporting all changes in resource states; and such changes are the events that induce new assignments. Incidentally, this fact makes interrupt handling an excellent place for monitoring resource-use for performance analysis and billing. Many performance monitors called "traces" do their jobs by intercepting each interrupt and recording the cause and time of occurrence as a trace record. A stream of such records is a comprehensive log of system activity.

Because of the very close relationship between interrupts and the operating system that handles them, and the very great diversity in operating system logic, it is difficult to discuss the software aspects of interrupt implementation in any generality. For this reason, most of the following discussion is confined to options that appear in hardware implementations in some systems.

The number of request lines is clearly a logic-design decision. Some systems offer a small number as standard; the customer may add more at a modest cost.

The grouping structure is subject to hardware/software/speed trade-offs. We will call each source of a New-PSW an interrupt level. Thus, for example, the case of Fig. 1 represents a one-level system. Since each level, which points to the start of an interrupt service program, constitutes a partial decoding of the interrupt cause, fast response requires a large number of levels. On the other hand, as long as the cause is recorded, only one level is logically essential, since the interrupt-handling program can use the cause-field of the Old-PSW to determine the response routine.

Another implementation issue is the amount of information to be stored automatically (by hardware) at each interrupt. The result of an interrupt is the initiation of a new program that will require the same kind of CPU facilities as the interrupted program. The PSW represents the near-minimum of such facilities; a scheme that stores only the PSW automatically will have to store other components of the state of the CPU by program instructions during the interrupt response. This has two deleterious effects on response time. First is the actual time to store the registers and to reload them for the new program. Second is the fact that during this time the system cannot be interrupted, and it is therefore possible that interrupts might be lost. Maximum speed is attainable by supplying multiple sets of important CPU registers, and this is done in some systems. Sometimes the sets are made available in increments at incremental costs. The optimum number of register sets will, of course, depend on the interrupt speed specifications.

Finally, we should maintain a hardware/software feature that is most desirable but is often lacking in an interrupt system. This is the ability to set any interrupt request line by a program instruction, although, of course, normally such requests are generated by natural events. Such program control over requests is a most desirable feature for system testing and debugging.

### REFERENCES

1962. Buchholz, W. (Ed.). *Planning a Computer System.* New York: McGraw-Hill, pp. 136–147.

1973. Hellerman, H. *Digital Computer System Principles* (2d ed.). New York: McGraw-Hill, pp. 379–382, 418–424.

H. HELLERMAN

## INTERVAL ARITHMETIC

For articles on related subjects *see* ARITHMETIC, COMPUTER; NUMERICAL ANALYSIS; and ROUNDOFF ERROR.

For article on related term *see* ALGORITHM.

For as long as numeric computation has been done, there has been a need to assess the accuracy of computed results. The traditional concepts of significant-digit calculation have evolved to meet this need, and are usually applicable in short computations when the quantities involved are largely independent. The starting premise of significant-digit computation is that the accuracy of approximating numbers is inferred from the way in which they are represented; e.g., "correct to within half a unit in the last place quoted." When an arithmetic operation with such numbers has developed a value, a representation must be chosen which implies the accuracy of the computed result. The stringency with which the choice is made depends on whether rigorous or probable (in some sense) error estimates are desired.

Applied pessimistically, significant-digit rules can result in loss of information; applied optimistically, they can lead to unacceptably large errors. For example, if "$x = 1.63$" means that $x$ has some value between 1.625 and 1.635, then $x^2$ will have some value between 2.640625 and 2.673225. We could choose to represent $x^2$ as 2.66, 2.7, or 3, but none of these choices is entirely satisfactory. Thus, Paul Dwyer proposed in 1951 that "range arithmetic," a modification of significant-digit arithmetic providing finer resolution, be employed to prevent loss of information while retaining an indication of accuracy. This kind of computation is now called "interval arithmetic."

Rather than deal with approximations to variables, in interval arithmetic we suppose that lower and upper bounds are known; i.e., each datum is contained somewhere within a closed interval on the real line. Then each arithmetic operation can compute an interval result containing all values that could have resulted from operating on any numbers selected from the interval operands.

Suppose, given variables $x$ and $y$, we wish to compute $z = x + y$. If exact values of $x$ and $y$ are not available, but we know instead that $a \leq x \leq b$ and $c \leq y \leq d$, then the rules of arithmetic inequalities tell us that $a + c \leq x + y \leq b + d$. If we now designate by $X$, $Y$, and $Z$ the intervals in which $x$, $y$, and $z$ are known to be contained, we could write $X = [a, b]$, $Y = [c, d]$, and $Z = X + Y = [a + c, b + d]$. Thus, we have defined addition on intervals consistent with the computational goal stated above. Further, this interval sum is the narrowest possible interval that can guarantee *rigorous* upper and lower bounds for the computed results.

However, error may be introduced into the computation of $a + c$ and $b + d$, since these will not necessarily be representable floating-point values even if $a$, $b$, $c$, and $d$ are. To insure that error bounds remain valid at each computational step, it is necessary to modify the rounding rules when computing interval end-points so that the computed value of $a + c$ will be rounded to an algebraically lower value and the computed value of $b + d$ will be rounded to an algebraically higher value, *but only when they must be rounded at all.*

In theory, interval analysis is concerned with problems of the following type: If bounds on the input data are known, how can we compute results on which rigorous bounds are of realistic width? This question is easily answered in the case of the elementary arithmetic operations. The rules of interval arithmetic are

$$
\begin{aligned}
[a, b] + [c, d] &= [a + c, b + d],\\
[a, b] - [c, d] &= [a - d, b - c],\\
[a, b] * [c, d] &= [\min(ac, ad, bc, bd),\\
&\qquad \max(ac, ad, bc, bd)],\\
[a, b] / [c, d] &= [\min(a/c, a/d, b/c, b/d),\\
&\qquad \max(a/c, a/d, b/c, b/d)],\\
&\qquad (\text{provided } cd > 0).
\end{aligned}
$$

For example, we have the following correspondences:

$$
\begin{aligned}
-1 \leq x \leq 2 &\qquad X = [-1, 2],\\
1 \leq y \leq 3 &\qquad Y = [1, 3].\\
0 \leq (x + y) \leq 5 &\qquad X + Y = [0, 5],\\
-4 \leq (x - y) \leq 1 &\qquad X - Y = [-4, 1],\\
-3 \leq (x * y) \leq 6 &\qquad X * Y = [-3, 6],\\
-1 \leq (x/y) \leq 2 &\qquad X/Y = [-1, 2].
\end{aligned}
$$

Each inequality is sharp, so each corresponding interval end-point can be attained, provided $x$ and $y$ are independent. If they are not, the inequalities will certainly still be valid, but may not be sharp. If, for example,

$$-1 \leq x \leq 2 \quad \text{and} \quad y = 1 + |x|,$$

then, although, as above $1 \leq y \leq 3$, in place of the inequalities, we have instead:

$$
\begin{aligned}
1 &\leq (x + y) \leq 5,\\
-3 &\leq (x - y) \leq -1,\\
-2 &\leq (x * y) \leq 6,\\
-1/2 &\leq (x/y) \leq 2/3.
\end{aligned}
$$

Naturally, it is important to keep the error bounds as narrow as possible. Since the outcome of each elementary arithmetic operation does not depend on past or future computational context, mathematical relationships that would hold for exact operands are not necessarily honored by interval arithmetic. For example, the evaluation of the expressions $A * (B + C)$ and $(A * B) + (A * C)$ in interval arithmetic will not always produce the same result, since the equivalence of the two occurrences of $A$ is not taken into account. In practice, interval analysis is concerned with finding computational sequences to minimize the excess interval width that this phenomenon induces.

Interval arithmetic monitors error dynamically and is directly applicable in cases in which conventional forward error analysis gives realistic bounds. However, it is not a panacea for rounding error problems. Computations that are inherently ill conditioned in floating-point arithmetic, and algorithms that induce instability, will behave similarly in interval arithmetic in that the computed interval results will be so wide as to contain only the negative information that something is wrong someplace. Because this often happens when interval arithmetic is applied naively, it is often supposed that it is hopeless to do nontrivial calculations in interval arithmetic. Nonetheless, good interval algorithms have been found for the solution of linear and nonlinear systems of equations, the algebraic eigenvalue problem, and the solution of ordinary differential equations. However, very few people are willing to work on interval problems because there is practically no higher-level language support for the expression of interval algorithms, nor is there hardware support to do correctly rounded interval arithmetic.

The chief current utility of interval arithmetic is as a diagnostic tool. As such, it can save much human effort, which might otherwise be spent doing (or taking the consequences of not doing) error analysis. It is also useful in laboratory and engineering environments in which physical measurements subject to error are used to compute other quantities. If the variation of the output as a function of the input is critical, interval arithmetic is a natural tool.

The alternatives to interval arithmetic are the various significance arithmetics, including unnormalized arithmetic. Sensitivity of results to input variation is also sometimes evaluated by repeated computation with perturbed data. Such methods offer some confidence, but none offers complete reliability, so results obtained from these styles of computing are difficult or impossible to interpret. By contrast, interval results are very easily understood. When a computation produces narrow intervals, the drudgery of an error analysis is not required to know what accuracy has been attained.

References

1951. Dwyer, P. S. *Linear Computations.* New York: John Wiley.

Chapter 2 of this book explains the motivations for the use of interval arithmetic and provides a good introduction to the issues raised in approximate computation.

1966. Moore, R. E. *Interval Analysis.* Englewood Cliffs, N.J.: Prentice-Hall.

This is the standard reference, the only book devoted to the basic elements of interval analysis.

1969. Hansen, E. R. (Ed.) *Topics in Interval Analysis.* New York: Oxford.

This is a collection of papers presented at a conference in 1968. Much of the material has been superseded, but it conveys the flavor of work in interval analysis.

F. N. Ris

## INTERVAL TIMER

For articles on related subjects *see* Computer Accounting and Resource Control; Multiprogramming; and Operating Systems.

An interval timer (sometimes called a "real time clock") is a mechanism whereby the time of day can be monitored by a computer system. In most systems, a word in memory is set aside to be used as the interval timer. This mechanism, usually at the low end of memory, cannot be used for anything else, since the computer is wired to increment it automatically by one interval every millisecond (or other fixed period). Although some timers are incremented as infrequently as 60 times per second, most are incremented much more frequently than that.

For timing purposes it is useful to have a timer capable of monitoring the execution of a few thousands, or tens of thousands, of instructions. Hence, in a computer with some instructions requiring only 1 $\mu$s, a millisecond timer will be incremented once for every thousand of those instructions, which is about as low a rate as can be tolerated. If the system stores the time of day (say, at start-up time) in another word, then any program needing to report the current time of day need only read the start time and add to it the number of milliseconds in the timer to obtain the current time of day.

The timer is useful for reporting the date and time of execution of various parts of a job. Equally important is its use in checking the timing for segments of a routine. To figure the average time required to compute a square root, for example, a program could call up the interval timer, save the contents, calculate 10,000 square roots, read the timer again, and obtain the difference.

In multiprogrammed systems, care must be taken to maintain an interval timer with each job. The time of day will be global to all jobs, of course, but for timing purposes the programmer is usually interested in time elapsed only while the CPU is assigned to his job (as opposed to running other jobs or performing input/output operations for his or other jobs). While a stopwatch might be adequate for timing large components of routines in a nonmultiprogrammed system, an interval timer is essential for timing components of multiprogrammed systems, since time may be allocated to jobs in increments of only a few hundreds (or even tens) of milliseconds.

C. L. MEEK

# ITERATION

For articles on related subjects *see* NUMERICAL ANALYSIS; PROCEDURE-ORIENTED LANGUAGES; and RECURSION.

To *iterate* means to do repeatedly. In computer programming, *iteration* is the repeated execution of lines of code or statements until some condition is satisfied.

For example, ten numbers A(1), A(2), A(3), . . ., A(10) can be summed using the following Fortran program:

```
      L = 10
      I = 1
      SUM = 0.
15    SUM = SUM + A(I)                         (1)
      I = I + 1
      IF (I .LE. L) GO TO 15
      . . .
```

The statement 15 and the two following it are executed repeatedly until I becomes 11.

In contrast, the sum could be computed by

```
SUM = A(1) + A(2) + A(3) + A(4) + A(5) + A(6)
                                                (2)
          + A(7) + A(8) + A(9) + A(10),
```

which does not involve iteration. This last statement is more efficient in the example given, since the sum is obtained with fewer program steps. However, if more elements are to be summed, then statement (2) must be changed by adding more terms to it. In the first program, however, to sum more elements, only the value of L (which could be an input quantity) need be changed. Therefore, when the number of elements to be summed increases, a point is eventually reached where the effort needed to write the program in form (2) becomes greater than for form (1). This illustrates the use of iteration to reduce the effort of the programmer at the price of using more computer time. At some point, of course, (2) will require more time to compile than (1).

All worthwhile computer programs are iterative in some way. For example, in the time that one can write program (2) above, one could perform the actual summation by hand. Thus, solving a problem by computer is worthwhile only if: (1) the programming effort is small compared with the amount of computing (which means that some of the program is executed repetitively), or (2) the program is applied to a succession of input data values. Although this last process is less often called "iteration," the program is repeatedly executed.

Another advantage of the iterative approach is the greater ease of generalization. For example, the first program could be part of a subroutine, and the control of the iteration could be done by means of a parameter.

```
      SUBROUTINE ABC (L)
      . . .
      I = 1
      SUM = 0.
15    SUM = SUM + A(I)
      I = I + 1
      IF (I .LE. L) GO TO 15
      . . .
```

Calling the subroutine with

```
CALL ABC (10)
```

would compute the sum of ten elements.

**Control of Iteration.** DO, FOR, and WHILE statements may be used to control an iteration. For example, the Fortran program

```
      SUM = 0.
      DO 5 I = 1, 10                           (3)
5     SUM = SUM + A(I)
```

accomplishes the same effect as program (1).

In PL/1, the program (3) can be written as

```
SUM = 0;
DO I = 1 TO 10;
SUM = SUM + A(I);                              (4)
END;
```

In Algol, this same program (3) would be

```
SUM := 0;
for I := 1 step 1 until 10 do                  (5)
    SUM := SUM + A(I);
```

Note that in the language APL the same summation can be written as

```
+/A                                                    (6)
```

Here, at the language level, no iteration is involved. However, at the level of the interpretive program that evaluates the APL statement, iteration may occur.

The iteration may be repeated a number of times depending upon the values involved. For example, the summation (1) may be terminated if an A(I) = 0:

```
     SUM = 0.
     DO 5 I = 1, 10
     IF (A(I) .EQ. 0.) GO TO 6
  5  SUM = SUM + A(I)                                  (7)
  6  CONTINUE
     ...
```

In Algol, this program would be

```
SUM := 0;
I := 1;
while A(I) ¬= 0 do
  begin                                                (8)
    SUM := SUM + A(I);
    I := I + 1;
  end
```

Another type of example is illustrated by a SQUARE ROOT subroutine:

```
      SUBROUTINE SQRT (X,Y,E)
      IF (X .LT. 0.) GO TO 50
      Y = 1.
30    IF (ABS(Y*Y-X) .LT. E) GO TO 70
40    Y = (X/Y + Y)*.5                                 (9)
      GO TO 30
50    ...error code...
70    RETURN
      END
```

Line 40 of program (9) computes an improved value of the square root. If X = 1.0, it is not executed at all (assuming E is of appropriate size relative to the arithmetic precision of the computer on which the problem is run). Otherwise, the number of iterations depends both on the value of X and on the value of E.

**Iteration in Numerical Methods.** Many numerical problems can be solved by iterative techniques. Here, a succession of values for one or more variables are computed. It is hoped that the successive values approach the true values. The iterative process is terminated when some error criterion is satisfied. The square root program (9) above is an example of an iterative numerical procedure. Although the successive partial sums of the first example (1) do approach the final sum, this procedure is not usually called an iterative numerical procedure. Thus, numerical iteration is usually characterized by the use of successive approximations and termination depending upon error bounds.

**Hardware Iteration.** The distinction between hardware and software activity is less and less clear as more complex processors are designed. This is particularly true in using microprogramming techniques and read-only memories.

In a simple example, a number in a register (Register 2 of Fig. 1) may need to be shifted a number of binary positions determined by a number stored in a second register (Register 1). The shift circuits of Register 2 are repeatedly pulsed until the contents of Register 1 are counted down to zero. Although the activity of the shift circuits are iterative in character, very few logical designers would use the term.

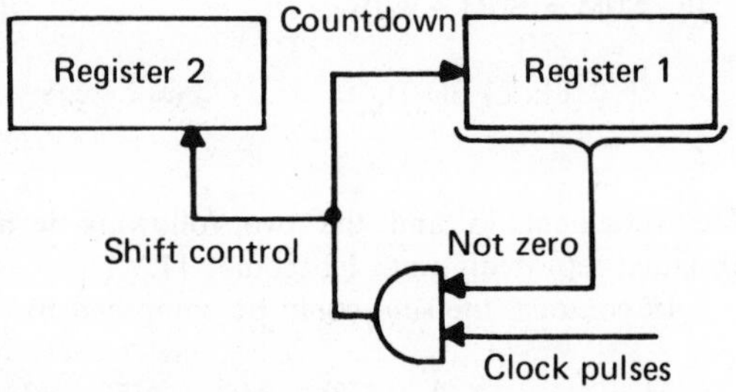


**Fig. 1.** Simple example of hardware iteration.

In more complex processors the term may be more appropriate. For example, the summation of the elements of a vector (as discussed above) may be done entirely by hardware. This involves a complex sequence of events including: incrementing an address register to access successive components; performing a floating-point addition which itself involves comparing exponents; shifting mantissas; and perhaps normalizing results. Thus, the same pattern of activities are iteratively performed until all components of the vector are accounted for.

**Iteration versus Recursion.** A program is recursive if the defining statements refer to the program itself. For example, in Algol, one may write

```
procedure ABC(X);
    ...
    ...
ABC(Y);                                   (10)
    ...
    ...
end;
```

This requires a so-called STACK mechanism to keep track of parameters, and RETURN locations for each level of call. Needless to say, other statements in the program must in some way limit the levels of calling. A frequently used example is the *factorial* (Arden, 1963, p. 300; or Bauman et al., 1964, p. 83):

```
procedure FACTORIAL (X);
if X = 1 then FACTORIAL = 1
   else FACTORIAL = X * FACTORIAL(X - 1);   (11)
end;
```

Although portions of this code (11) are executed repetitively, the control is by reference to the named procedure. Therefore, this example is said to be *recursive*, and not iterative.

The factorial of N can be computed iteratively.

```
       J = 1;
       FACT = 1;
TEST:  if J = N then go to NEXT;
       J = J + 1;
       FACT = FACT * J;
       go to TEST;
NEXT:  ...
```

For most examples, *recursion* requires more memory space and involves the execution of more instructions than *iteration*. For instance, in the factorial example, each call involves the establishment of a parameter X. This must occur many times for an X of reasonable size, so both more memory space and execution time are required.

### REFERENCES


1963. Arden, B. W. *An Introduction to Digital Computing*. Reading, Mass.: Addison-Wesley.

1964. Baumann, R., M. Feliciano, F. L. Bauer, and K. Samelson. *Introduction to Algol*. Englewood Cliffs, N.J.: Prentice-Hall.

1970. Acton, F. S. *Numerical Methods That Work*. New York: Harper & Row.


H. D. HUSKEY

# J

## JCL. *See* COMMAND AND JOB CONTROL LANGUAGES.

## JOB

For articles on related subjects *see* MULTIPROGRAMMING; OPERATING SYSTEMS: Principles and Theory; PROCESSING MODES; and TASK.
For article on related term *see* FILES.

A job is a task or group of tasks to be performed by a computer. The number of tasks (or steps) per job is usually a preference of the programmer, but is also subject to the conventions of the operating system. For example, many empty temporary files supplied by the operating system are automatically closed and released at the end of a job. If a programmer wishes to use one of these temporary files to store some intermediate information between two steps, then the two steps must be contained within the same job. On the other hand, if the programmer uses a permanent file, then he may have a step that creates the file in one job and a step that reads it in another job. In a batch-processing environment, where jobs are run one at a time, the programmer needs only to insure that the job which reads the file is *submitted* to be run after the job that creates it. But in a multiprogrammed environment, where several jobs are run concurrently, there is need to insure that the jobs are *executed* in sequence. To accomplish this automatically, many multiprogramming operating systems allow job sequencing, which allows the programmer to specify that a job cannot be selected for execution until its predecessor has been completed.

A job is also the smallest accounting unit on most machines. That is, computer resources are normally charged against one account number per job.

C. L. MEEK

## JOB CONTROL LANGUAGES. *See* COMMAND AND JOB CONTROL LANGUAGES.

## JOINT USERS GROUP (JUG)

For an article on a related subject *see* ASSOCIATION FOR COMPUTING MACHINERY.

The Joint Users Group (JUG) is an organization of digital computer user groups. The membership as of early 1976 is given in Table 1.

**Table 1.** JUG Membership

| *Name* | *Membership* |
|---|---|
| 1. DECUS | *D*igital *E*quipment *C*omputer *U*sers *S*ociety represents users of all DEC systems. |
| 2. EMR | EMR Computer Users Group represents users of Electric Machinery Corporation computers. |
| 3. FNU | *F*ederation of *N*CR *U*sers represents all NCR computer users belonging to member groups of the Federation. |
| 4. FOCUS | *Fo*rum of *C*ontrol Data *Us*ers represents users of the various CDC computers. |
| 5. GUIDE | Represents users of large-business IBM computers. |
| 6. HUG | *H*oneywell *U*ser *G*roup represents users of H-200/2000 systems. |
| 7. SEL | *S*ystem *E*ngineering *L*abs represents users of SEL computers. |
| 8. SWAP | *S*ociety for *W*ang *A*pplications and *P*rograms represents users of Wang Laboratories minicomputers. |
| 9. TI-MIX | *T*exas *I*nstruments *M*inicomputer *I*nformation Exchange represents users of Texas Instruments minicomputers. |
| 10. USE | *U*nivac *S*cientific *E*xchange represents Univac large-scale scientific users. |
| 11. UUA | *U*nivac *U*sers *A*ssociation represents business users of Univac computers. |
| 12. VIM | Represents scientifc users of Control Data systems. |

The group had its inception in the late 1950s, and was formally accepted as an activity of the Association for Computing Machinery (ACM) in 1961.

The purpose of the group is stated in the bylaws as follows: "The objective of the Joint Users Group is the establishment of communications among digital computer user groups to promote study, exchange of information and cooperative effort in areas of common interest."

The activities of the group include establishment of a program documentation exchange service among member groups, the compilation of a directory of computer programs submitted to user groups, and holding workshops on user group administration and on various topics of common interest.

The activities of the group also include the formulation of user group comments and positions on computing standards, and communication of these comments to applicable standards bodies. The group has a vote, as a representative of the computing user community, in the X3 Committee of the American National Standards Institute (ANSI).

B. R. Faden and R. H. VanDenburg, Jr.

# JOYSTICK

For articles on related subjects *see* Computer Graphics; Lightpen; and Rand Tablet.

The joystick is a manual input device for graphics display consoles which allows the user to specify simultaneously the two or three coordinates of a point in two- or three-dimensional space. Typically, the current coordinate values specified by the joystick are indicated on the screen with a point or cursor, which is "coupled" to the joystick by hardware or software. By driving the cursor around the screen and having the program sample the successive positions, the user can input freehand drawings. By providing a comparator circuit, the joystick can also be used to provide a lightpen type *picking* function.

Physically, the device consists of a stubby lever that rotates with two or three degrees of freedom, similar to a pitch/yaw control joystick in a small airplane. Angular displacements of the internal shaft encoders are transduced to electric voltages, which are analog-to-digital converted to *x-y* values and stored in computer-accessible registers for subsequent processing. The third degree of freedom (*z* value) can be provided by having the knob of the joystick rotate about the axis of the stick.

A. van Dam

**JUG.** *See* Joint Users Group.

# JUSTIFICATION

For article on related subject *see* Text Editing Systems.

In the context of programming, *justification* refers to the left or right alignment of a piece of data, typically a bit or character string, in a field that is assumed to be larger (i.e., greater in length) than the data. Thus, "right justifying" a bit string of length 2 in an 8-bit byte means that the rightmost of the two data bits is placed in the rightmost position of the byte. Remaining positions in the field are usually occupied by as many copies as needed of a specified or assumed "fill character." These nondata characters or bits "pad" the data on the left if the data is right-justified, or on the right if the data is left-justified.

In the context of text processing, the term "justification" pertains to left- and/or right-margin alignment. Conventionally, typeset text such as that found in books and magazines appears with straight (justified) left and right margins. By contrast, typewritten letters usually have a left-justified ("flush left") margin but a "ragged right" margin. On some output devices such as computer line printers, where each character in the print line has a uniform size (monospace), computer-based typesetting algorithms can force alignment by inserting additional blanks between words or after punctuation.

A. van Dam

**Fig. 1.** A joystick on table below screen.

# K

## KEY

For articles on related subjects *see* COLLATING SEQUENCE; and TABLE LOOK-UP.

A key in the computer programming sense is a particular field or combination of fields in a data record upon which some "lookup" or ordering process is performed. Other fields in the record would be considered ancillary to the key during such a process. Usually, a group of records (a file) will be ordered and controlled (i.e., added, revised, or deleted), based on some key field. For example, in a file containing personnel records, the person's social security number could be used as a record key. Computer processing of the key will usually involve comparisons of one key field with another or use of the key as an index. Thus, the programmer must be familiar with the characteristics of such keys: how characters making up the key are represented, how fields are justified, and how padding is handled if necessary.

In a computer hardware sense, the term "key" may be used to describe a computer memory area used for certain purposes. In an associative or content-addressable memory, an associative key field is used to reference items. The key, which may be specified as part of an instruction, provides a value that is compared against corresponding fields in each memory cell. The contents of that cell(s) for which there is a key match are retrieved. In some hardware, a protection key is used to define and control resource privileges. In the hardware, a key field is put in correspondence with blocks of memory and used to enable or disable access to such blocks by an executing process. Both central processing unit (CPU) and channel references may be controlled in this way. In more general protection systems, the protection key is associated with a process and defines the privileges owned by the process (e.g., use of files or transfer of control to other processes).

C. E. PRICE

## KEYBOARD STANDARDS

For articles on related subjects *see* ASCII; and STANDARDS.

Although there is significant need for international standards for keyboards on devices for the preparation and collection of input data for computers or for direct input into computers, there is still a lack of standardization with respect to

1. The arrangement of the keys for special symbols and functions.
2. The number of printing keys (usually 42 to 46 on the alphabetic keyboard).
3. Even the arrangement of the alphabetic and numeric keys themselves.

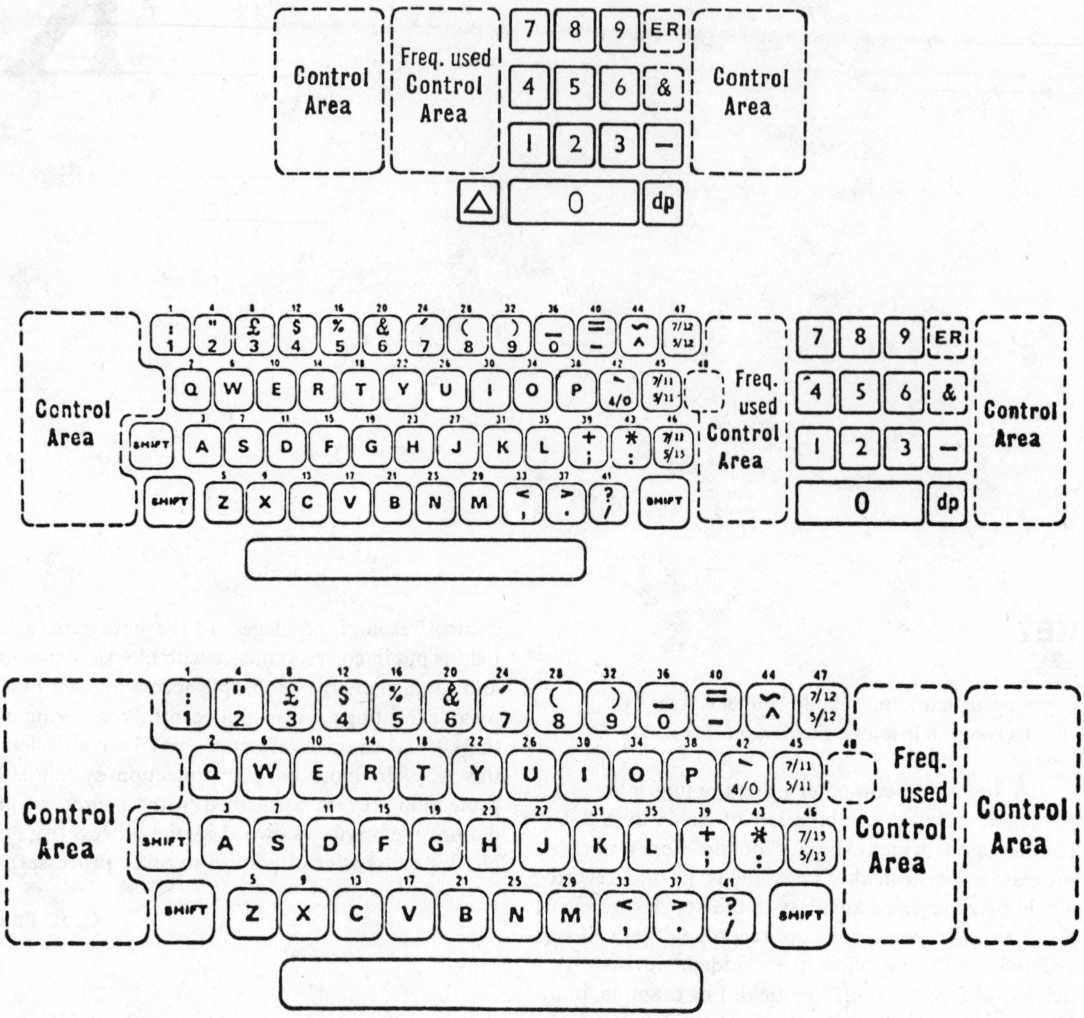


**Fig. 1.** Three types of keyboard depicted in ECMA Standard 23 for keyboards generating the code combinations of characters in the ECMA seven-bit coded character set (promulgated June 1969). (a) Numerical keyboard for exclusively numeric data (dp = decimal point representation; Δ = space; ER = error key). (b) Alphanumerical keyboard for predominantly numeric data. (c) Alphanumerical keyboard for predominantly alphabetic data.

A number of factors have led to this situation, among them changing requirements and new applications for computer input and data collection equipment, the need for special symbols for individual national alphabets, and lack of coordination among national and international standards bodies.

Keyboard standards are needed for a number of reasons: to save manufacturing costs by making both the keyboards and the interfaces with other equipment standard; to save operator training costs and to achieve higher operator efficiency; to make it possible to use several national alphabets in the same information system as the use of international networks grows. Despite the problems posed by the large investment in current keyboard equipment, progress toward keyboard standardization is being made steadily. The present International Standards Organization (ISO) recommendations for international keyboard standards do not include the relation of individual keys to coded character sets, as opposed to the ECMA (European Computer Manufacturers Association) standard. As an example of current keyboard standards, Fig. 1 shows the three keyboards of the ECMA Standard 23 for generating the code combinations of the characters of the ECMA 7-bit coded character set.

J. NECAS

## KEYWORD-IN-CONTEXT (KWIC) INDEX

For article on related subject *see* INFORMATION RETRIEVAL.

One of the oldest, automatically produced information search tools is the keyword-in-context (KWIC) index. Typically, the index is a list produced by filtering titles, text, or text portions extracted from documents, using a preconstructed "stop list" to eliminate words that are not indicative of content (such as "and," "of," and "or") and including in the index an entry for each of the remaining text words. Each line of text may thus appear many times in the list.

An entry in a KWIC index normally consists of one line of text printed in such a way that the particular keyword characterizing the entry appears in alphabetical order in the middle of the line, with both left and right contexts and with the corresponding document reference number. Thus, a phrase such as "diseases of the liver in mice" is entered three times in the index: once under D for diseases, once under L (liver), and once under M (mice). An excerpt from a KWIC index is shown in Fig. 1.

The advantages of the KWIC approach are its simple mechanized production—consisting principally of text reading, filtering, and automatic sorting routines—and the simplicity of utilization of the uncontrolled, natural-language vocabulary. The disadvantages include the chopped-up appearance (restricted to one line) of many entries, and the fact that the size of the resulting multientry index makes it necessary to use only very small text excerpts. In practice, only the titles of the documents are usually used for indexing purposes, the index then becoming a "permuted title index." Since titles are sometimes not indicative of content, a KWIC index can never become a perfect search tool.

Some related automatic indexing products are author lists, keyword lists, and so-called KWOC (keyword-out-of-context) listings in which a full title

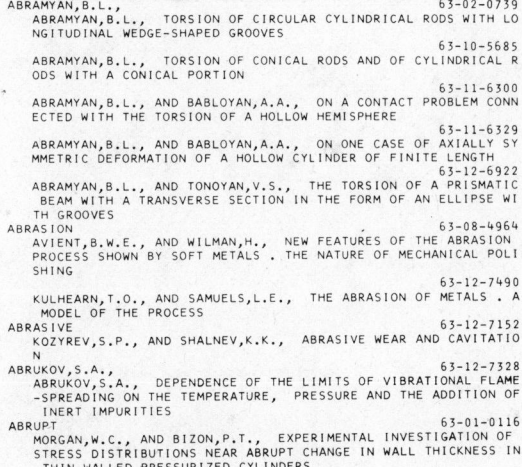

```
ABRAMYAN,B.L.,                                           63-02-0739
   ABRAMYAN,B.L.,  TORSION OF CIRCULAR CYLINDRICAL RODS WITH LO
   NGITUDINAL WEDGE-SHAPED GROOVES
                                                         63-10-5685
   ABRAMYAN,B.L.,  TORSION OF CONICAL RODS AND OF CYLINDRICAL R
   ODS WITH A CONICAL PORTION
                                                         63-11-6300
   ABRAMYAN,B.L., AND BABLOYAN,A.A.,  ON A CONTACT PROBLEM CONN
   ECTED WITH THE TORSION OF A HOLLOW HEMISPHERE
                                                         63-11-6329
   ABRAMYAN,B.L., AND BABLOYAN,A.A.,  ON ONE CASE OF AXIALLY SY
   MMETRIC DEFORMATION OF A HOLLOW CYLINDER OF FINITE LENGTH
                                                         63-12-6922
   ABRAMYAN,B.L., AND TONOYAN,V.S.,  THE TORSION OF A PRISMATIC
    BEAM WITH A TRANSVERSE SECTION IN THE FORM OF AN ELLIPSE WI
   TH GROOVES
ABRASION                                                 63-08-4964
   AVIENT,B.W.E., AND WILMAN,H.,  NEW FEATURES OF THE ABRASION
   PROCESS SHOWN BY SOFT METALS . THE NATURE OF MECHANICAL POLI
   SHING
                                                         63-12-7490
   KULHEARN,T.O., AND SAMUELS,L.E.,  THE ABRASION OF METALS . A
    MODEL OF THE PROCESS
ABRASIVE                                                 63-12-7152
   KOZYREV,S.P., AND SHALNEV,K.K.,  ABRASIVE WEAR AND CAVITATIO
   N
ABRUKOV,S.A.,                                            63-12-7328
   ABRUKOV,S.A.,  DEPENDENCE OF THE LIMITS OF VIBRATIONAL FLAME
   -SPREADING ON THE TEMPERATURE,  PRESSURE AND THE ADDITION OF
    INERT IMPURITIES
ABRUPT                                                   63-01-0116
   MORGAN,W.C., AND BIZON,P.T.,  EXPERIMENTAL INVESTIGATION OF
   STRESS DISTRIBUTIONS NEAR ABRUPT CHANGE IN WALL THICKNESS IN
    THIN-WALLED PRESSURIZED CYLINDERS
```

**Fig. 2.** Excerpt from word-and-author index.

```
                                      Terms in                                Corresponding
                                      context                                 document
                                                                              numbers
ETERMINATION OF VERTICAL WIND DISTURBANCES                                    --------
T OSCILLATIONS CAUSED BY WIND GUSTS                                           --------
                         WIND LOAD ON TOWERS                                  --------
                 FORM OF WIND PROFILE IN NEAR-GROUND LAYER O                  --------
                       A WINDTUNNEL INVESTIGATION INTO THE P                  --------
ON A 45 DEGREE SWEPTBACK WING AT TRANSONIC SPEEDS                             --------
                         WING PLAN FORMS FOR TRANSONIC SPEED                  --------
ISTRIBUTION ON SYMMETRIC WING PROFILES IN THE CASE OF HIGH-S                  --------
SIS OF AN ASPECT-RATIO-1 WING WITH FAN AT 0.354 CHORD                         --------
ESSURE DISTRIBUTION ON A WINGSURFACE IN A NON-UNIFORM SUPERS                  --------
```

**Fig. 1.** Excerpt from KWIC index.

may be entered, together with the particular keyword listed separately (i.e., out of context). When author names also function as main index entries, a "keyword and author" index results, as shown in Fig. 2.

G. SALTON

## KLUDGE

The word "kludge" is a term coined by Jackson Granholm in an article "How to Design a Kludge," in *Datamation* (February 1962). The definition is given as "an ill-sorted collection of poorly matching parts, forming a distressing whole." The design of every computer contains some anomalies that prove to be annoying to the users and which the designer wishes he had done differently. If there are enough of these, the machine is called a "kludge."

By extension, the term has now come to be applied to programs, documentation, and even computer centers, so that the definition is now "an ill-conceived and hence unreliable system that has accumulated through patchwork, expediency, and poor planning."

The first kludge article triggered five others ("How to Maintain a Kludge," etc.) in subsequent issues of *Datamation*. Four of the articles may be found in the book, *Faith, Hope and Parity,* edited by Jack Moshman, Thompson Book Company, 1966.

F. GRUENBERGER

## KWIC. 

*See* KEYWORD-IN-CONTEXT INDEX

# L

**LSI.** *See* Integrated Circuitry.

## LABEL

For articles on related subjects *see* Machine and Assembly Language Programming; and Procedure-Oriented Languages.

A label is an identifier that may be appended to a statement (possibly a compound statement) in a program, which enables the statement to be referenced by other statements in the program. Label identifiers may be either alphanumeric or numeric, depending on the language.

In most symbolic assembly languages, statement labels are formed as strings of alphanumeric characters. Such labels are the identifiers of the storage locations in which the assembled statement is located. Where the statement is an instruction, the label permits references to the assembled instruction for the purpose (among others) of using it as the destination of a branching instruction or for the use of the instruction in some self-modifying code. Where the label is attached to a declaration of a data element or data area, instructions in the program may utilize the symbolic label as the name of the element. For example (Gruenberger, 1969):

| LOC'N | OP | ADDR | |
|---|---|---|---|
| BEGIN | LDA | JIM | Reference to data (LDA-LOAD ADDRESS) |
| | . | | |
| | . | | |
| | . | | |
| | STA | OHIO | Modifying an instruction (STA-STORE ADDRESS) |
| OHIO | LDA | 0000 | |
| | . | | |
| | . | | |
| | . | | |
| | LDA | OHIO | Using an instruction as data |
| | . | | |
| | . | | |
| | . | | |
| | BZE | OUT3 | Branch reference (BZE-BRANCH ON ZERO) |
| | . | | |
| | . | | |
| | . | | |
| | BRA | BEGIN + 4 | Relative reference (BRA-BRANCH) |
| OUT3 | HAL | | |
| JIM | DEC | 0 | |
| | . | | |
| | . | | |
| | . | | |

In languages of a higher level than symbolic assembly languages, such as Fortran and Algol, labels are used in connection with either executable statements or formatting specifications. Since the storage allocation of variables is transparent to the programmer, there is no provision made in these languages for the user to specify relationships between names and storage. In the majority of higher-level languages, little provision is made for providing a means by which the user can be assured of the relative position of variable locations; one notable exception is the COMMON statement in Fortran. Without these requirements, the use of a label as the identifier of a storage location is not necessary in these languages.

Thus, the usage of labels is confined to references to executable statements as the destination of a branching instruction (such as a **goto** in Algol), as specifying the limit of a block of code (such as in the DO range of a Fortran program), or the identification of a formatting specification for an input/output instruction (as in Fortran). For example (Hare, 1970):

```
5   DO 70 I = 1,10 ← Reference to a range
    DO 60 J = 1, 250
      .
      .
      .
    GO TO 60 ← Specification of destination
      .
      .
      .
60  CONTINUE
      .
      .
      .     ↙ Format reference
70  WRITE(6,80) NGAMES,SIMU,ACTU,ERROR
      .
80  FORMAT(/,1X,115,3F15.6)
```

In certain languages designed for use in conversational systems (such as Basic and APL), labels may be required with each statement so as to exactly specify the physical ordering of the statements. In these cases the labels are used by a sorting routine to order the statements prior to compilation of the program, since it is not required that the user enter the program in exactly the correct order. Thus, the statement labels are also used as line numbers and are required to be in ascending numerical order. For example, in Basic,

```
100 READ A,B,C,D,E
110 IF A < 7500 THEN 800
120 IF D > A/52 THEN 800
130 IF B <= 3 THEN 900
140 IF C >= 3 THEN 900
800 PRINT "CASE NO." E "CREDIT REJECTED"
805 GO TO 100
900 PRINT "CASE NO." E "CREDIT APPROVED"
905 GO TO 100
```

### REFERENCES

1969. Gruenberger, F. *Computing: An Introduction.* New York: Harcourt, Brace & World.

1970. Hare, V. C. *Introduction to Programming, A BASIC Approach.* New York: Harcourt, Brace, and World.

A. RALSTON AND J. A. N. LEE

## LAMBDA CALCULUS

For articles on related subjects *see* LIST PROCESSING LANGUAGES; and PROGRAMMING LINGUISTICS.

For article on related term *see* SYNTAX, SEMANTICS AND PRAGMATICS.

The λ-calculus is a mathematical formalism developed by the logician Alonzo Church (1951) in the 1930s to model the mathematical notion of substitution of values for bound variables. Consider the definition $f(x) = x + 1$, which defines $f$ to be the successor function. The variable $x$ in this definition is a *bound variable* in the sense that replacement of all instances of $x$ by some other variable (say, $y$) yields a definition $f(y) = y + 1$, which is semantically equivalent. In the λ-calculus, the successor function $f$ may be defined by the λ-expression $\lambda x(x + 1)$. The subexpression $(x + 1)$ is referred to as the "body" of the λ-expression. The subexpression $\lambda x$ is referred to as the "bound variable part" and specifies that $x$ is to be regarded as a bound variable in the body with which $\lambda x$ is associated.

The application of $\lambda x(x + 1)$ to the integer argument 3 may be specified by the λ-expression $f(3) = \lambda x(x + 1)(3)$. The subexpression $\lambda x(x + 1)$ is referred to as the "operator part" of this lambda expression; the subexpression 3 is referred to as the "operand part" of this lambda expression. The substitution rules (reduction rules) of the lambda calculus specify that the operator part $\lambda x(x + 1)$ may be applied to the operand part 3 to yield the value $(3 + 1) = 4$.

Consider next the lambda expression $\lambda h(h(3) + h(4))(\lambda x(x + 1))$. The substitution rules of the λ-calculus specify that $\lambda x(x + 1)$, which is the operand part of this expression, is to be substituted for all instances of $h$ in the body of the operator part, yielding the λ-expression $(\lambda x(x + 1)(3) + \lambda x(x + 1)(4))$, which on further substitution yields $((3 + 1) + (4 + 1)) = 9$.

The binding of $h$ to $\lambda x(x + 1)$ in $h(3) + h(4)$ may be expressed in one of the following ways:

1. Let $h = \lambda x(x + 1)$ in $h(3) + h(4)$.
2. $h(3) + h(4)$ where $h = \lambda x(x + 1)$.

The notations (1) and (2) are said to be syntactically "sugared" versions of the original λ-expression in the sense that they are semantically equivalent to the original λ-expression but are easier to read. The above syntactically sugared specifications illustrate that certain notational conventions of real programming languages may very easily be converted into semantically equivalent lambda notations.

The following example illustrates even more clearly that the bound variable $h$ of the λ-expression given above represents a procedure that is initialized to the successor function $\lambda x(x + 1)$ at the time of binding, and is then called with the arguments 3 and 4:

**procedure** $h(x)$; **result** $\leftarrow x + 1$;
**value** $\leftarrow h(3) + h(4)$;

This example also illustrates that, in order to realize the functions determined by lambda expressions in a conventional programming language, it is necessary to introduce the assignment operator and to realize binding and substitution in terms of assignment.

In the preceding examples, λ-expressions were allowed to contain extraneous symbols, such as +, which allow arithmetic operations to be embedded in the substitutive mechanism of the λ-calculus. The pure λ-calculus does not contain such extraneous operators, and requires all transformations to be substitutions of values for bound variables. In the remainder of this article we will be concerned with the pure λ-calculus.

The pure λ-calculus may be thought of as a programming language with a very simple syntax and semantics. The syntax of λ-expressions may be defined by a BNF grammar whose terminal symbols are λ, (, ), and a class V of variable names, and whose productions are $E \rightarrow V \mid \lambda VE \mid (EE)$, where $E$ denotes the class of λ-expressions. An expression of the form $\lambda VE$ (say, $\lambda xM$) denotes a one-parameter function and has a bound variable part $\lambda x$ and a body part $M$. An expression of the form $(EE)$ [say, $(M_1\ M_2)$], is referred to as an operator-operand combination, and has an operator part $M_1$ and an operand part $M_2$. An occurrence of a variable $x$ in a λ-expression $M$ is said to be bound in $M$ if it occurs within a subexpression of the form $\lambda xM_1$ within $M$, and is said to be free otherwise.

*Note:* The above syntactic definition requires application of an operator $f$ to an operand $x$ to be specified as $(fx)$ rather than as $f(x)$.

The "computational semantics" of the λ-calculus may be defined by transformation rules that specify how λ-expressions may be converted into "semantically equivalent" λ-expressions. The principal computation rule is the *reduction rule* (sometimes called the "β-rule"):

REDUCTION RULE. An operator-operand combination of the form $(\lambda xMA)$ may be transformed into the expression $S_A^x M$, obtained by substituting the λ-expression $A$ for all instances of $x$ in $M$, provided there are no conflicts of variable names. The condition that there be no conflicts of variable names may be explicitly specified as follows:

1. $M$ contains no bound occurrences of $x$.
2. $M$ contains no bound variables that occur free in $A$.

A second transformation rule called the "renaming rule" (α rule) allows conflicts of variables to be eliminated.

RENAMING RULE. A bound variable $x$ in a λ-expression $M$ may be uniformly replaced by some other bound variable $y$, provided $y$ does not occur in $M$.

Any λ-expression of the form $(\lambda xMA)$ may be converted into a λ-expression of the form $(\lambda xM'A)$ satisfying conditions (1) and (2) above by renaming of the bound variables of $M$, using the renaming rule, and may then be reduced to $S_A^x M'$ using the reduction rule.

*Example.*
$$(\lambda x(x\lambda xx)(pq)) \underset{\alpha}{\rightarrow} (\lambda x(x\lambda tt)(pq)) \underset{\beta}{\rightarrow} ((pq)\lambda tt).$$

A λ-expression $P$ that has no subexpressions of the form $(\lambda xMA)$ is said to be in *reduced form.* A λ-expression that cannot be converted to a reduced form by a sequence of renaming and reduction rules is said to be *irreducible.*

*Example.* $P = (\lambda x(xx)\lambda x(xx))$ is irreducible, since it is of the form $(\lambda xMA)$ with $M = (xx)$ and $A = \lambda x(xx)$, and application of the reduction rule produces $(\lambda x(xx)\lambda x(xx))$.

The question of whether an arbitrary λ-expression $P$ has a reduced form is undecidable; i.e., there is no algorithm which, given an arbitrary λ-expression $E$, can determine in a finite number of steps whether or not $E$ has a reduced form.

The notion of a reduced form corresponds to the intuitive notion of a value in arithmetic computation. For example, the arithmetic computation $(3 + (4 * 5)) \rightarrow (3 + 20) \rightarrow 23$ is accomplished by two applications of operators to their operands, corresponding to reductions in the λ-calculus. The result, 23, corresponds to a reduced expression because it contains no more instances of operators that can be applied to their operands.

If a λ-expression contains more than one subexpression of the form $(\lambda xMA)$, then there is more than one "next step" in the computation, and the evaluation process becomes nondeterministic. The following important theorem states that for any λ-expression, all sequences of computation which yield a value will yield the same value.

CHURCH-ROSSER THEOREM. If a given λ-expression is reduced by two different reduction sequences, and if both reduction sequences yield a reduced form, then the reduced forms are equivalent up to renaming of bound variables.

However, there are λ-expressions that give rise to both terminating and nonterminating sequences.

*Example.* The λ-expression

$$(\lambda x\lambda yy(\lambda x(xx)\lambda x(xx)))$$

has the form $(\lambda xMA)$, where $M = \lambda yy$ and $A = (\lambda x(xx)\lambda x(xx))$. If $A$ is substituted for occurrences of $x$ in $M$ before $A$ is evaluated, then the value of $\lambda yy$ is obtained, while if an attempt is made to evaluate $A$ before substituting it in $M$, then an infinite reduction sequence is obtained.

The choice among different orders of evaluation in the λ-calculus has its counterpart in function evaluation for real programming languages. For example, in evaluating $f(g(x))$, we can choose to evaluate $g(x)$ and use the resulting value in the evaluation of $f$, or we can pass the unevaluated function $g(x)$ to $f$ and evaluate $g(x)$ whenever it is needed in $f$. The first alternative is referred to as "inside-out" evaluation and corresponds to "call-by-value" in Algol 60 (Naur et al., 1963), while the second alternative is referred to as "outside-in" evaluation and corresponds to "call-by-name" in Algol 60. Call-by-value is more efficient than call-by-name when the value of $g(x)$ is used more than once during the evaluation of $f$, but it is less efficient if $g(x)$ is never used during the evaluation of $f$. In particular, if $g(x)$ results in an infinite computation sequence but is never used in $f$, then the call-by-value strategy results in disaster, whereas the call-by-name strategy is always adequate.

The λ-expression

$$(\lambda xMA) = (\lambda x\lambda yy(\lambda x(xx)\lambda x(xx)))$$

is of the form $f(g(x))$, where $f = \lambda x\lambda yy$ has a function body with no occurrences of the parameter $x$, and $g(x) = (\lambda x(xx)\lambda x(xx))$ results in an infinite computation. The call-by-name evaluation strategy for λ-expressions corresponds to always reducing the instance of $(\lambda xMA)$ whose component $\lambda x$ occurs farthest to the left. This strategy is called the "leftmost" evaluation strategy. The universal adequacy of the call-by-name strategy is captured by the following theorem.

THEOREM. If for a lambda expression $E$ there is a terminating reduction sequence yielding a reduced form $E$, then the leftmost reduction sequence will yield a reduced form that is equivalent to $E$ up to renaming.

The λ-calculus is equivalent in computational power to the class of Turing machines in the sense that any computable function may be represented as a λ-expression. However, the notation and computation mechanism of the λ-calculus is closer to that of programming languages than in the case of Turing machines. This has led to attempts to model programming languages such as Algol 60 in terms of the λ-calculus (Landin, 1965). Such models capture certain concepts such as nested block structure, binding of variables, and the order of evaluation, but have difficulty in capturing other concepts such as assignment, sharing of values by references, side effects, and unconditional branching. Thus, although the λ-calculus is useful for gaining insights into certain computational mechanisms arising in real programming languages, it appears to be unnatural as a framework for modeling complete programming languages. In order to model complete programming languages in a natural way, it is appropriate to introduce (as a primitive notion) cells whose values may be updated and which may be referred to by references.

The λ-calculus is of computational interest because it allows us to factor out certain aspects of computational structure and study these features independently of the complexity of real programming languages. It is of mathematical interest because it provides a framework for characterizing the substitution of values for bound variables and for studying the notion of function application. The λ-calculus thus provides a bridge between mathematics and the theory of computation. However, since the λ-calculus is a natural model for only a very restricted class of computational mechanisms, it is likely to remain of limited value as a tool in the analysis of computing systems.

REFERENCES

1951. Church, A. "The Calculi of Lambda Conversion," *Ann. Math. Studies*, No. 6. Princeton, N.J.: Princeton University Press.

1963. Naur, P., et al. "Revised Report on the Algorithmic Language ALGOL 60," *CACM*, January.

1965. Landin, P.J. "A Correspondence Between Algol 60 and Church's Lambda Notation," *CACM*, February and March.

P. WEGNER

## LANGUAGES.

*See* ALGEBRAIC MANIPULATION LANGUAGES; ALGOL 68; ASSOCIATIVE LANGUAGES; AUTHORING LANGUAGES AND SYSTEMS; COMMAND AND JOB CONTROL LANGUAGES; DECISION TABLES: Languages; FORMAL LANGUAGES; LIST PROCESSING LANGUAGES; MACHINE AND ASSEMBLY LANGUAGE PROGRAMMING; MACROLANGUAGES; METALANGUAGE; NONPROCEDURAL LANGUAGES; PASCAL; PROBLEM-ORIENTED LANGUAGES; PROCEDURE-ORIENTED LANGUAGES; PROGRAMMING LANGUAGES; SIMULATION: Languages; and STRING PROCESSING LANGUAGES.

## LANGUAGES, PROGRAMMING.

*See* PROGRAMMING LANGUAGES.

## LANGUAGE PROCESSORS

For articles on related subjects *see* ASSEMBLERS; INTERPRETER; PARSING; PROGRAMMING LANGUAGES; and PROGRAMMING LINGUISTICS.

For articles on related terms *see* BINDING TIME; DELIMITER; MACHINE AND ASSEMBLY LANGUAGE PROGRAMMING; OBJECT PROGRAM; and SOURCE PROGRAM.

**The General Translatory Process.** Given the fundamental language of communication with a computer—namely, *machine language*—there exists an almost intolerable barrier between the person who desires to solve some problem using the computer and the description of the solution in terms of the machine language. Although the ability of some programmers to communicate in terms of machine languages is exceptional, the minute attention to detail required to develop a program is generally beyond the scope of most computer users. Thus, early in the history of computer development, there was a drive to moderate this communications gap.

The primary efforts toward simplification led to a symbolic form of machine language in which code sequences were represented by mnemonic character sequences (such as ADD for the operation of addition, or JMP for the instruction to break normal sequential processing and "jump" to some other designated instruction), and where references to data elements were in terms of symbolic names instead of through the memory address of the data element. This language development lead to the requirement for a processor (program) that would convert programs represented by a symbolic code into their equivalent machine language representation. This process was (and still is) known as "*assembly*," and the processor was known as an "*assembler*." It is important to note that the assembler performs no task other than the generation of an equivalent machine language program based on a symbolic language program and, in particular, takes no part in the actual execution of the generated program.

The development of symbolic languages and assemblers was followed closely by the development of *autocoders*, in which the programmer's language was more closely related to mathematical notation than to the machine operations. Most of the first autocoders were primitive by the standards of the 1970s, permitting only simple one-operator expressions and restricted naming of data elements. However, the autocoder required the development of more sophisticated conversion processors, thus leading to a study of the general translatory processes.

The methods of program conversion and subsequent execution of a user's program can be classified into two basic techniques: compilation and execution, or interpretation. Both systems utilize a translatory system in which the original program (the *source program*) is converted into some other language (*target* language). In the case of the compilation process (performed by a *compiler*), the target language is either machine language or its corresponding symbolic language. In the latter case, the compiler must be supplemented by an assembler in order to complete the conversion process. Once the compiler has generated the equivalent program in machine language, the program may then be executed independently. In the case of interpretation (performed by an *interpreter*) the two steps of conversion and execution are continuously interleaved so that the generated code corresponding to a portion of the source program is executed as it produced. In this manner the interpreter maintains control over both conversion and execution.

In the preceding exposition, the term "conversion" has been used in place of the term "translation," since we wish to reserve the latter for a very specific purpose. The American National Standard Vocabulary for Information Processing (ANSVIP; 1970) provides a strict definition of this term:

> **translate**
> To *transform statements* from one *language* to another without significantly changing the meaning.

In this sense, a programmer must insist that a compiler or the conversion process within an interpreter should be a translator, since the meaning associated with a source program *must* be carried over to the target language program. The ANSVIP also provides definitions associated with the process of compilation and interpretation:

> **compile**
> To prepare a *machine language* program from a *computer program* written in another *programming language* by making use of the overall logic structure of the program, or generating more than one *machine [language] instruction* for each symbolic *statement*, or both, as well as performing the function of an *assembler*.
>
> **interpreter**
> (1) A *computer program* that *translates* and executes each *source language* statement before translating and executing the next one.

In practice, there rarely exists a compiler or an interpreter which adheres precisely to these definitions; most languages possess certain features that cannot be compiled, and most interpreters initially preprocess the source program into some intermediate form, from which the original program can be reconstructed, and operate over that code rather than the original form.

The steps that compose the process of translation of the statements of a higher-level computer programming language into machine language are shown in Fig. 1.

In Fig. 1, the processor portions of the translation system are shown in rectangular blocks and the data groups over which they operate and which they develop are in ovals. This diagram is extremely formalized, the individual processors not being readily recognizable in most translatory systems. Nor is it necessary, as may be inferred from this diagram, that each phase of translation is completed before the next is entered.

The lexical analyzer used in the lexical scan performs the task of preparing the source text (the user's program in machine-readable form) for the syntactic analyzer phase. At the same time it attempts to condense the text so as to improve the efficiency of later examinations of the text. For example, in Fortran, the inclusion of blanks in the statements is tolerated by the language so as to provide a more readable text for the programmer. In fact, except in Hollerith constants (i.e., literal strings), blanks may be inserted randomly.

However, such niceties can considerably slow down the statement scanning routines, which must examine each and every character of the statement. Hence, one of the assigned tasks of a Fortran lexical scan will be to eliminate nonsignificant blanks and condense the statements to their "raw" symbolic content. Further, to assist the syntactic analyzer, the delineation of the statements into words or phrases can be accomplished for some languages. For example, in Basic, the design of the language (to ease implementation) is such that the first three characters following the line number are a unique characterization of the type of statement that follows. Thus, if the lexical analyzer separates these characters into (say) one word, the recognition of the type of statement by the syntactic analyzer can be facilitated.

Further, considering Basic as a simple language for compilation, it is possible to recognize variables and language constants by simple lexical rules (as opposed to syntactic rules). Any string that starts with (has as the leftmost character) an alphabetic character is a candidate for recognition as a variable. The right delimiter of such a string is any nonalphanumeric character, except in the case of FOR statements, where special character sequences (TO and STEP) are of importance. However, it is possible

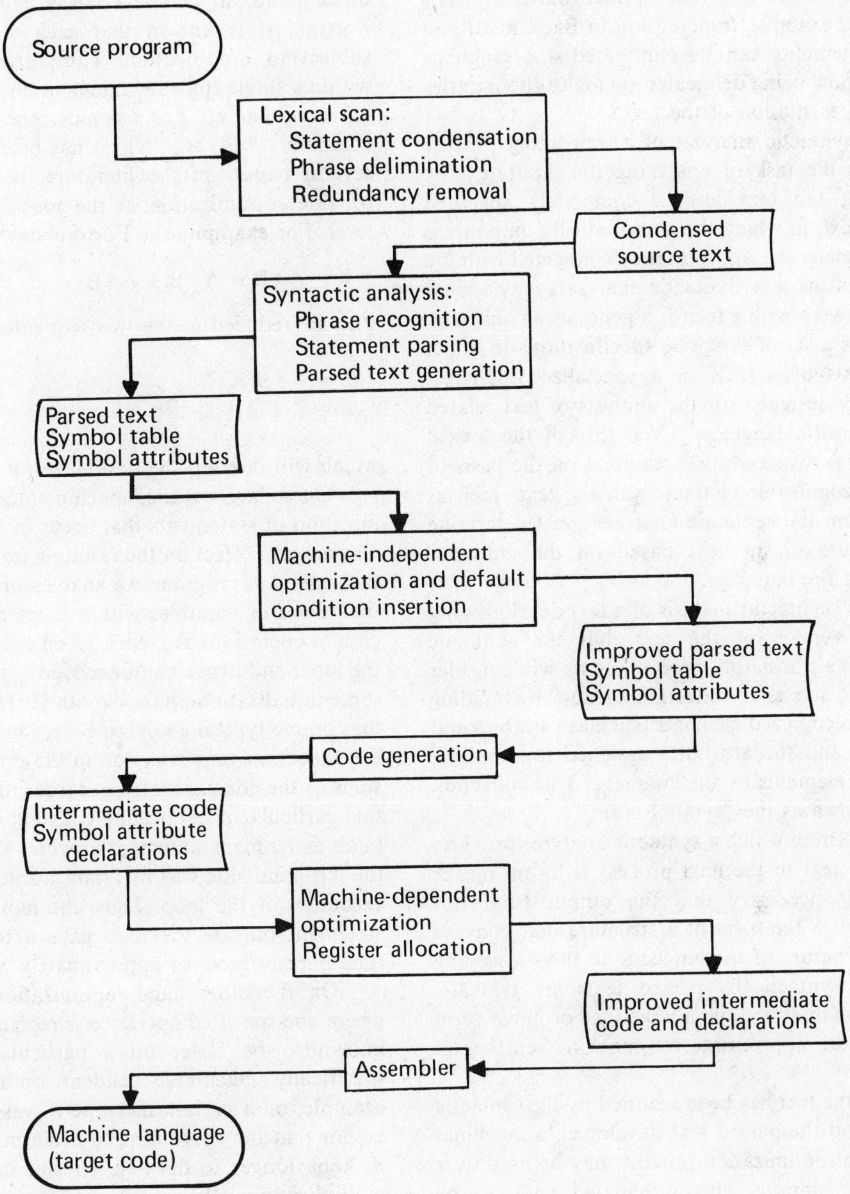


**Fig. 1.** The detailed process of language translation from a higher-level programming language to a machine language.

in a lexical scan to recognize about 90% of all instances of variables and constants and to collect the characters that compose those language elements into words or other well-defined units. By this means, for example, punctuation in Basic READ and PRINT statements can be eliminated, the language elements now being delineated by logical boundaries in the representation of the text.

The syntactic analyzer of a translatory process completes the task of analyzing the input text by converting the text into a completely specified (parsed) text, in which the grammatical components of the language are appropriately connected with the elements of the text. Syntactic analyzers may appear in one of two possible forms: a generalized analyzer, which uses a set of syntactic specifications to direct the analysis of a text; or a specialized analyzer, specifically designed for the analysis of text related to one specific language. Even though the lexical analyzer has "worked over" the text on the basis of readily recognizable characters in the text, such as punctuation, the syntactic analyzer must determine the structure of the text based on the grammar (syntax) of the language.

"Pure" syntactic analysis of a text develops only a parsed version of the text, but the syntactic analyzer in a translatory process (as we will consider it here) also acts as a "collection agency" by building a table of recognized elements (such as variables and constants) and the attributes assigned (or implied) over those elements by the language. This collection will be known as the "symbol table."

The form in which a syntactic analyzer provides the parsed text to the next process is by no means fixed. It is necessary that the output from this analyzer be in the form of a structure that conveys the nested nature of the language to the succeeding processes. Syntactically parsed texts are typically displayed as trees, though a linked list or linear form may be more appropriate for machine representation.

Once the text has been scanned by the syntactic analyzer and the parsed text developed, a machine-independent optimization process may be used over the text to improve the anticipated code to be generated in a later phase. Machine-independent optimization can be distinguished from the later stage of machine-dependent optimization, not only by the fact that the domains of the two optimization processes are different but also by mechanisms of optimization. In the case of machine-dependent optimization, it is the general intent to eliminate instructions that are either repetitious or redundant.

In this latter type of optimization over self-modifying code, it is not always possible to reorganize instruction sequences and be assured that the optimizing changes will not affect the result. On the other hand, at the level of a language such as Fortran, it is known that each statement is not subject to modification. Thus, any change made within a single Fortran statement does not affect any other statement. For example, the recognition of common subphrases, which has been the subject of several papers in the literature, is a process that provides optimization at the machine-independent level. For example, the Fortran statement

```
X = A * B + A * B + A * B
```

may be reduced to the two sequential statements

```
Z = A * B
X = Z + Z + Z
```

which will develop the desired result in X.

On a larger scale, machine-independent optimization of statements that occur in loops can have a significant effect on the resulting execution time of the generated program. An analysis of the changes in the values of variables within loops can reveal that certain operations are repeated on each pass through the loop, and hence can be moved out of the loop to some initialization phase. Knuth (1971) has reported that in one typical analyzed program, almost 18% of the execution time was due to the repeated conversions of the constant 0 from integer to real mode. In this particular program, the constant was contained in an assignment statement in which the variable on the left-hand side was invariant during the repeated execution of the loop. Thus, the movement of this statement outside the loop gave a total execution time improvement of approximately 30%.

On the other hand, optimization of the type where one specified operation is replaced by another known to be faster on a particular machine is specifically machine-dependent optimization. For example, on a certain machine it was found by the author that the subroutine to perform the operation $A^I$ took longer to develop a result than successive multiplications when $I$ was an integer less than 15. Thus, a compiler written for that machine took this knowledge into account and transformed the Fortran phrase A**I into A*A*A* · · · *A in those circumstances. On the other hand, optimization of an expression to eliminate sign reversals, and thus minimize the number of operators in the expression, is not machine-dependent.

Prior to the machine-independent optimization of the statements of a language, the implied elements of the language must be inserted. For example, in the FOR statement of Basic, the absence of a STEP clause implies that the step size (or more accurately, the value) is one. Thus, at this stage the FOR statements in the parsed text would be examined and this default condition applied where necessary. Further, still in Basic, arrays whose size was not declared in a DIM statement would be presumed to have a dimension of 10 elements (or 10 × 10 if a table), and an appropriate entry would be made in the symbol table. Further, since the attributes of the elements of the text had been collected into the symbol table, the declaratives of the program would be eliminated from the text. Code generation is the process of generating from the parsed, economized, optimized text, a code relative to the target language of the machine on which the program is to be run. This code may also be optimized later and then assembled into absolute machine language (ACM, 1970).

**Binding Time.** Given a program in (almost) any language and the derivation therefrom of the set of identifiers, constants, references, and other language elements, there must occur at some time a mapping from this user's set of elements onto the available memory locations of the computer that is to execute or which is executing the generated program. The majority of higher-level computer languages do not provide the programmer with the ability to describe explicitly the organization of memory at object time (except in the case of Fortran COMMON), and rarely (with the exception of Fortran EQUIVALENCE) do they allow the user to specify relationships between identifiers and other language elements. Thus, the implementer is free to devise some mapping algorithm between the language elements and their assigned storage locations (at object time), provided a certain criterion is met. This criterion is that the values assigned to some identifier (variable, array element, statement identifier, etc.) should be retrievable at some later (possibly restricted) time.

The instant at which all the information is available, which is necessary to permit the allocation of object time memory to some language element, is one of the bounds on the *binding time* of that element. That is, there must exist two bounds (which in certain instances may be identical) on the time during which memory may be assigned to a language element. The latest time (bound) available to assign a memory location to a language element is obviously the instant prior to its first usage in the program.

Conversely, if all the attributes of a language element are not only known but are also known to be fixed (i.e., static) at the instant that the element is first encountered in the translatory process, then it is possible to assign (allocate) memory at this earliest time. This period may be further subdivided by considering the type of memory referencing to be performed. For instance, if the earliest binding time is taken as that instant when an absolute address can be assigned to a language element, then binding time might be defined as load time (i.e., the time at which the program is loaded into memory).

Binding time may be a language feature or it may be implementation-defined. For example, in APL, the left-arrow (assignment operator ←) operation has the side effect (actually, an initial effect) of assigning the attributes of the expression to its right to the operand on its left. Thus, the instant at which all the information is available to enable the assignment of storage to the operand on the left is the instant of executing the assignment operation. Hence, APL has dynamic attribute specifications, and binding time (earliest and latest) is execution time. Lacking explicit (and static) declarations of attributes, the APL interpreter itself determines attributes at execution time. Conversely, Basic, in the case of missing (omitted) array-size declarations, inserts the missing attributes so as to permit compile-time binding of variables.

In choosing a binding time within the established bounds, the implementer is free to choose any particular instant. However, the later that binding takes place, the greater the difficulty in generating effective code and the more time it will take to both store and retrieve the values of language elements. For instance, if an absolute address had been assigned to a variable, then all references to that variable in the generated code may be made directly. However, if the binding time is delayed until (say) the last moment, then each reference to that variable will require the system to look up the assigned location. Thus, the work of the symbol table is delayed until execution time and may be performed repeatedly rather than just once as would be the case for compile time binding of variables. In any case, it should be a general principle that the earliest binding time should be used always.

**Compilation vs. Interpretation.** Many factors must be considered by a language implementer before the decision is made to compile or interpret, to develop optimized code or not, to develop a load-and-go system, or to completely separate the translation and execution phases. The environment within which the system is to operate may help to determine the type of system to be developed. For example, if it is expected that the system will be used primarily for education, then an interpretive system may be advantageous, provided error reports are related to the source code directly. Or in a mixed education and research environment where many programs will run but few will ever become production programs and be run repeatedly, a load-and-go system may suit the needs best. That is, the code developed by a compiler is stored directly in the memory of the computer instead of being output on some intermediate storage system, control is transferred to the first executable statement in the compiled program after compilation is complete, with the developed code not being saved for subsequent executions. In the same type of situation, where the number of compiles is high, an extremely efficient (or fast) compiler is necessary, and thus the optimization phases may be omitted on the basis that the overall cost of compilation does not justify the cost of execution. Conversely, in a shop where compiled programs are to be developed into production systems and one compile may result in many thousands of runs, then a methodical compiler that develops highly optimized machine code is of importance.

The answer to the question of whether to compile or to interpret—all other economic questions being equal and assuming that the source code is susceptible to either interpretation or compilation —may depend on other factors that are less easy to express in quantitative terms. With regard to storage, it can be realized that the amount of storage required by a compiler is not substantially different from that required to perform the same tasks within the interpreter; in fact the interpreter will contain additional features to perform the execution phase of the problem solution. On the other hand, while it is obvious that there need be no significant differences between user data-storage requirements of an interpretive system over that of a compiler system, nor differences between the storage requirements for the symbol tables of the two systems, a judicious design of the interpretive symbol table can substantially reduce the combined storage requirements of the symbol table and the user data storage.

Conversely, the interpreter must be self-sufficient and, except in comparatively large computer systems with fast access ancillary storage facilities, the interpreter should also have, readily available in memory, all anticipated library routines. On the other hand, the compiler can take advantage of the hiatus between compilation and execution to load into memory only those which are needed by this particular program.

It has been shown empirically many times that the amount of storage required by the compiled code of a source text is not substantially different (but is almost always less) than that for the source text itself.

Based on these premises we may deduce two interesting relationships. *For the same program* (source text):

$$
\begin{aligned}
IM_{\text{interpreter}} &> CM_{\text{compiler}} \\
IM_{\text{user data}} &= EM_{\text{user data}} \\
IM_{\text{symbol table}} &= CM_{\text{symbol table}} \\
IM_{\text{source text}} &= EM_{\text{target code}} \\
IM_{\text{library}} &>> EM_{\text{library}}
\end{aligned}
$$

where IM stands for interpretative memory, CM stands for compile-time memory, and EM stands for execute-time memory. If $\Sigma IM$ is the sum of all necessary parts of the memory for the interpreter, $\Sigma CM$ is the sum of used memory at compile time, and $\Sigma EM$ is the memory used at execute time, then it is obvious that $\Sigma IM > \Sigma CM$ and $\Sigma IM >> \Sigma EM$.

Other features relevant to the problem of whether to interpret or to compile are listed in Table 1.

The question of whether a program written in a certain language can be compiled or can be interpreted is not directly related to the question of whether to interpret or to compile except as related to available storage. Obviously, if the average-size program (determined by some undefined means) cannot be interpreted because of a lack of available storage, there is a possibility that it may be compiled, and thus the question of to compile or to interpret is answered. However, it may be that some languages are not susceptible to compilation but which must be interpreted, although it would seem that any language that can be compiled can also be interpreted (storage requirements aside). There are some languages which contain elements that cannot be compiled but which must be interpreted, thus raising the possibility of "hybrid" translator systems. In fact, Fortran is in the latter category: Due to the inclusion in the language of variable FORMAT, which is specified by the user at execution time, a portion of the compiler is left in the generated program to interpret the corresponding READ or WRITE statement. Similarly, those languages (such as PL/I or APL) that permit dynamic storage allocation must be interpreted to some extent.

**TABLE 1.**

| *INTERPRETERS* | *COMPILERS* |
|---|---|
| 1. Available storage should contain at the same time the interpreter, the source text, the symbol table, *all* library routines, and the data. Hence, the size of program (as measured by the numbers of statements in the program and the number of data elements defined) is restricted compared to that available for use with a compiler system. | The available storage at compile time must contain the compiler, the symbol table, and *one* statement from the source text. At execute time, the available storage must contain the compiled code, the required library routines, and the data. |
| 2. There is always a direct relationship between the source text and the code being executed; hence there is a good relationship between detected errors and the source text, which promotes easy debugging. | The relationship between the source text and the code being executed is remote. Hence the burden of error/source relations is placed on the programmer and his knowledge of the machine and its compiler. |
| 3. Syntactic errors detected by the interpreter can be corrected during a run (at the request of the interpreter) and do not require the whole run to be restarted. Execution errors may be reported to the programmer and source text changes can be made under the same controls. | Syntactic errors can be corrected at the instant of recognition, but the loss of the source text at execution time requires that corrections be made in the source text and recompilation of the whole text be performed. |
| 4. Because of 2 and 3 above, and recognizing that condition 1 may not be too restrictive in this mode, an interpreter may be well suited to a conversational time-sharing mode of programming. | Compared to the interpreter, a compiler system is better suited to batch environments. |
| 5. Due to the successive recompilations of the statements in the source text and the need to reference all data through the symbol table, an interpretive system is expensive to use. | A compiler system makes best use of the available resources of the computer system. |

**The Symbol Table.** In the organization of any translatory system in which several subprocesses of translation take place (such as lexical analysis, syntactic analysis, and code generation), the vehicle for the transference of extracted or deduced information regarding the text is the symbol table. The symbol table provides a base for the coalescence of data relating to the various elements of the source text and provides a possibility for describing certain relationships between the text and the target machine, such as the assigned (possibly relative) addresses of variables. In a static environment the symbol table will serve the purpose of providing (say) assigned addresses to the compiler's code generator for substitution into instruction masks (see the last section of this article), while the symbol table in a dynamic environment may exist also at run time to provide a key to currently allocated memory space. Between the time of ending compilation and beginning the execution of the generated program (assuming that the generated code is not resident), the symbol table will provide necessary data to the loader for the acquisition of library-provided subprograms and will, in turn during run time, act as a transfer vector for the linkage of the generated code and those subprograms.

The compile-time symbol table of an algebraic language processor will contain entries pertinent to the various data elements that may occur within the source text. In general these may include variables (both simple and *n*-dimensional), statement identifiers, subprogram (or block) names, and constants. Among this data will appear not only the deduced (or defined) attributes of the language element but also data pertinent to the compilation of the statements in which they either appeared or are expected to appear.

In some language systems the symbol table may play an extremely important part of the run-time characteristics of the system. For example, in any system that includes the ability to allocate and free storage, or in a system that is implemented so that storage is dynamically controlled, the symbol table is the key between the executable code and the data set.

During the various phases of compilation or interpretation, in any procedural or block-structured language there may exist several differing symbol tables, each relating to a particular block or procedure. While the *raison d'être* and the means of establishment of each symbol table may be distinct, the means by which symbol tables in general are organized is common to all.

The purpose of a symbol table is to provide a common data source to the various components of a translatory system relating to the elements of the source text and, in particular, to provide a source of data pertinent to the specified or deduced attributes of those elements. The symbol table is thus being accessed by many routines during the process of translation and therefore must be amenable to rapid access and data retrieval. The routine that organizes the symbol table directs a number of tasks, among them the following:

1. Post an item and its associated data.
2. Retrieve the data associated with any item.
3. Delete an item and its associated data.

All these activities involve the searching of the table to locate the item or to recognize the absence of that item, and hence the efficiency of this search affects the efficiency of the whole compiler.

McClure (1972) states that the majority of productive working compilers use some variant of the *hash link* method of symbol table organization. This technique combines hash addressing based on the symbol table entry representation (i.e., the character string that comprises the language element representation) to locate an initial entry in a fixed-size table, with a linked list emanating from the initial entry.

**Expression Analysis and Code Generation.** The action of a compiler is best exemplified by the analysis of a simple arithmetic expression and the subsequent generation of machine language (or corresponding symbolic code) as the equivalent program to evaluate that expression. Within arithmetic expressions (i.e., expressions involving the operations of addition(+), subtraction(−), multiplication(*), and division(/)), each operator can be assigned a hierarchical level that determines its place in the sequence of operations which will evaluate the expression. Together with a rule to specify that the leftmost operation of two (or more) with the same hierarchical level is the first to be evaluated, a simple algorithm for evaluating simple arithmetic expressions can be evolved:

1. Scan the expression and associate with each operator a hierarchical-level number.
2. Scan the expression and locate the leftmost operator with the highest valued hierarchical-level number.
3. Evaluate the term in which that operator is included and replace the term in the original expression by the resulting value. The term associated with an operator is *always* the operator and its immediately adjacent operands. (In the case of $n$-ary operators [$n \neq 2$], special care must be taken to select the correct operands.)
4. If no other operators remain in the expression, there must exist only one operand that is the value of the expression.

A suitable hierarchical assignment of levels for the operators is as follows:

| | |
|---|---|
| +, − | level 1 |
| *,/ | level 2 |

Using the preceding algorithm over expressions that contain only constant-valued operands, we find that the following example typifies the actions:

```
expression:        3 + 5 * 2/5 - 4
operator levels:     1   2 2   1
```

In this expression the leftmost highest-level operator is the operator of multiplication, which is associated with the operands 5 and 2 in the term 5 * 2. Evaluating this term, the expression is reduced to

```
expression:        3 + 10/5 - 4
operator levels:     1    2   1
```

Repeating the algorithm over this new expression until no operators remain, the expression is finally reduced to

```
expression:    1
```

which is the value of the expression.

The presence of parentheses in an expression creates no new problem other than specifying an embedded subexpression, which must be evaluated prior to the evaluation of the enclosing expression. While the algorithm could be modified to scan the expression for parenthesized expressions, a simpler modification is possible. It is merely necessary to assure that the operators contained within parentheses are assigned a hierarchical value that forces their early participation in an evaluation procedure. This may be accomplished by modifying step 1 in the algorithm:

1(a) Set the base value of the hierarchical table to zero.

1(b) Scanning the expression from *left to right*, assign hierarchical-level numbers to operators as the addition of the base value plus the level from the table above.

1(c) If a left parenthesis is encountered, increase the base value of the hierarchical table by (say) 10. When a right parenthesis is encountered, reduce the base value by the same amount. (Note that if the base value has not returned to zero when the complete expression has been scanned, then there exist unmatched parentheses in the expression.)

Using this modified algorithm, the expression below can be evaluated:

| | |
|---|---|
| expression: | 3 + 5 * (2/5) − 4 |
| operator levels: | 1 2 12 1 |

As may be seen directly, the operator contained within the parentheses in this expression will be processed first as a result of this modification.

Using the same algorithm, algebraic expressions may be prepared for evaluation by identifying the terms in the expression. That is, if the *evaluated term* in step 4 of the algorithm is taken to mean the name given to the result of the evaluation, then a sequence of evaluation steps can be determined which describes the method of evaluating the expression.

Consider the algebraic expression

$$a + b * (c/d) - e$$

in which the operators obviously have the same hierarchical levels as in the expression

$$3 + 5 * (2/5) - 4$$

If we represent the names of intermediate results of the evaluation process by $t_i$ we can easily see that the sequence of steps for evaluating the preceding expression is

$$t_1 = c/d$$
$$t_2 = b * t_1$$
$$t_3 = a + t_2$$
$$t_4 = t_3 - e$$

where $t_4$ is the name associated with the value of the expression. This set of *triplets* (operands and operator) can be directly related to sequences of machine instructions in a computer. For example, let us consider a hypothetical computer with the following instructions:

| | | |
|---|---|---|
| LDA | c | load the accumulator with the contents of memory address c. |
| ADD | c | add to the current contents of the accumulator the contents of memory address c. |
| SUB | c | subtract from the current contents of the accumulator the contents of memory address c. |
| MUL | c | multiply the current contents of the accumulator by the contents of memory address c. |
| DIV | c | divide the current contents of the accumulator by the contents of memory address c. |
| STO | c | store the current contents of the accumulator into memory address c. |

Based on these machine instructions (specified in their symbolic form), the generation of code from statements of the form

$$x = y \# z$$

is a direct mapping into an instruction mask (or template)

```
LDA  y
(#)  z
STO  x
```

where (#) is the transformation of the operator into its corresponding machine operation code; i.e.,

+ → ADD,  − → SUB,  * → MUL,  / → DIV

The processes of expression analysis given here provides a basis for more sophisticated expression analyzers that cover a far greater range of operators and *n*-ary functions, including subscripted array elements and whole arrays. Simple optimization techniques can be added to eliminate back-to-back store and load operations over the same memory location, and tabular methods of analysis speed up the processing time considerably.

REFERENCES


1960. Samelson, K., and P. I. Bauer. "Sequential Formula Translation," *CACM*, Vol. 3 (February), pp. 76–83.

1964. Randell, B., and D. J. Russell. *Algol 60 Implementation*. London: Academic Press.

1966. Ingerman, P. Z. *A Syntax Oriented Translator*. New York: Academic Press.

1967. Lee, J. A. N. *The Anatomy of a Compiler*. New York: Van Nostrand-Reinhold.

1968. Wegner, P. *Programming Languages, Information Structures, and Machine Organization*. New York: McGraw-Hill.

1969. Hopgood, F. R. A. *Compiling Techniques*. New York: American Elsevier.

1970. American National Standards Institute. *Vocabulary for Information Processing*, Doc. No. X3.12–1970. New York: ANSI.

1970. Association for Computing Machinery. "Proceedings of a Symposium on Compiler Optimization," *SIGPLAN Notices*, Vol. 5, No. 7 (July).

1970. Cocke, J., and J. T. Schwartz. "Programming Languages and Their Compilers—Preliminary Notes," *Courant Inst. of Math. Sciences*, New York University.

1971. Knuth, D. E. "An Empirical Study of FORTRAN Programs," *Software—Practice and Experience*, Vol. 1, pp. 105–133.

1972. Gries, D. *Compiler Construction for Digital Computers*. New York: Wiley.

1972. McClure, R. M. "An Appraisal of Compiler Technology," *Proc. S.J.C.C.*, Vol. 40. AFIPS Press, Montvale, N.J.


J. A. N. LEE

## LANGUAGE TRANSLATION

For articles on related subjects *see* ARTIFICIAL INTELLIGENCE; PROGRAMMING LINGUISTICS; and STRING-PROCESSING LANGUAGES.

The idea of using a computer as an aid for language translation seems to have originated in 1946 in a discussion between Warren Weaver and A. D. Booth. The computers of those days were so limited in storage and availability that until the mid-1950s it was hardly practical to use them for experimentation. Nevertheless, interest grew in the subject and was accelerated in the United States by the circulation of a memorandum by Warren Weaver and by important techniques such as pre- and post-editing of text, and stem-ending decomposition Locke and Booth (1965), microglossaries, and binary dictionary search (Booth, 1953) which originated in this period. Probably the best account of early machine translation is that given by Locke and Booth.

In the 1950s and early 1960s a number of projects came into being particularly in the United States, encouraged by generous research funding and increasingly available computer time. Among the notable ideas emerging were those of predictive analysis—linguistic depth—which is concerned with the extent to which human beings can comprehend sentences (like the present one) in which clauses are embedded within other clauses, and proposals for the efficient mechanization of dictionaries (Oettinger, 1960). The end of the decade was notable for the development of Comit, the first higher-level language dedicated to text processing, and for Chomsky's work on transformational grammars.

In England a translation program from French into English, using a microglossary, was tested; the powerful computer of the National Physical Laboratory was utilized for a Russian-English translation experiment; and the idea of a thesaurus as an aid to the problem of multiple meaning was investigated.

On the European continent, projects emerged in Italy, France, and Germany, but only in Russia was support available on anything like the scale of that in the United States. Booth (1967) and Josselson (1971) are perhaps the best general references for this phase of machine translation (MT).

The majority of these projects concentrated, for political reasons, on the language pair Russian-English, and when Canada entered the field in the mid-1960s, politics also prompted supporting by the National Research Council of two projects directed toward English to French translation. Outstanding techniques emerging from this work are modified forms of transformational grammars, allowing the insertion of parameters and conditions and a rapid method of parsing, using statistical data.

In late 1966 a report by the National Academy of Sciences (NAS) in the United States presented a gloomy view of the future of MT and suggested that funds should be diverted to computational linguistics. This, combined with the general reduction in research finances, has led to a change in emphasis or to the elimination of many projects in the United States.

The NAS report, which is open to criticism on technical grounds, was undoubtedly partly inspired by the unrealistic claims made by some groups, chiefly industrial, of the imminent availability of fully automatic, high-quality translation from computers. Such claims were, of course, unjustified and led to a reaction against MT. It is unfortunate to note a recrudescence of them in recent literature.

**Linguistic Problems of MT.** At the lowest level of machine-aided translation, the computer is used merely as a mechanical dictionary, rendering translations of words or phrases as requested. As has been demonstrated at the German Armed Forces Translation Centre at Mannheim, this can be a very useful service to human translators. All research projects, however, have aimed at more ambitious targets, ranging from the provision of technical translation good enough to be comprehensible directly or (after post-editing) by an expert in the field to the unattained goal of perfect machine output without human intervention.

As soon as even the simplest of these goals is attempted, the problem of syntax arises. That is, in order to produce translation at any level (as distinct from transliteration), some analysis must be made of the function of words in a sentence and their relation to one another in the source language. Moreover, since languages often differ in structure, transformations may be necessary before the target language sentence can be produced. Thus the sentence "He was given a difficult book by the teacher" becomes "Le maître lui a donné un livre difficile" in French (literally; the teacher to him has given a book difficult). In order to make the translation, it was necessary first to recognize that, "he," "book," and "teacher" are respectively the subject, direct object, and agent in the English sentence, and that "book" is therefore a noun rather than an adjective or verb. Second, a transformation must be made to remove the passive construction, which would not be grammatical in French, and finally the order of adjective and noun must be reversed in French.

More subtle (and mostly unsolved) difficulties are that the teacher might in fact be feminine, requiring the translation of *La maîtresse*, and that the sense of the surrounding text might require a completely different translation, such as *instituteur* or *professeur*. This illustrates the limitation of attempting translation by using only the local context of a single sentence. Most machine translation schemes do just this, and are thereby restricted in scope. In fact, to produce a perfect translation, the global context of a paragraph—or, indeed, of the complete text—may sometimes have to be considered.

The process of translation is thus seen to involve at least four stages;

1. Lookup of each word in a source language dictionary to determine properties and possible functions.
2. Analysis to determine the function of words and groups of words in the sentence.
3. Rearrangement and transformation of the results of (2) to conform with the syntax of the target language.
4. Substitution of target language equivalents.

As well as these four stages, any realistic translation scheme must include an idiom-processing routine, usually incorporated in stage 1. This is necessary because of the numerous phrases that are so peculiar to a language that they cannot be rendered on a word-to-word basis into another language (e.g., French *boîte de nuit* = English "night club").

The four stages defined above may in fact overlap and entwine each other in practice, but the important conclusion which is implied is that a precisely defined form of the syntax of source and target language must be provided to act as a basis for the program. This, together with the provision of adequately fast methods for applying this information, has been the crucial problem in MT.

It cannot be said that the problem has yet been solved in the sense that any one of the many schemes proposed and tested is greatly superior to any other in quality of resulting output, speed of operation, and extent of application. Some characteristic approaches are outlined briefly below. For a more extensive survey see Booth (1967) and Josselson (1971).

TRANSFORMATIONAL GRAMMARS. Many of the proposed methods of machine translation utilize transformational grammars of the type discussed by Chomsky. A very simple example of such a grammar might be:

⟨sentence⟩ ⟶ ⟨subject phrase⟩ ⟨verb⟩
⟨subject phrase⟩ ⟶ the ⟨noun⟩
⟨verb⟩ ⟶ has | sees
⟨noun⟩ ⟶ cat | dog

The elements enclosed by ⟨⟩ are the syntactic elements, or nonterminal symbols, of the language and the words "the," "has," "cat," etc. are called "terminal symbols." The "rules" are known as transformations or productions, and should define all possible legal sentences in the language under consideration. The vertical stroke | means "or".

Although attractive from the theoretical point of view, both because the precise style of formulation lends itself to computer interpretation and because (in theory) new "rules" can be added without altering the interpreting program, methods based on this idea suffer two disadvantages. When applied to "real life" languages, the number of rules required tends to be very large, and the ambiguous nature of many of the terminal symbols (words) of a language means that many permutations may have to be tested before the correct parsing is found.

As an example, consider the following very simple grammar in which the abbreviations used are: Noun = N, Verb = V, Adjective = A, Subordinator (while, when, etc.) = S, Determiner (a, the, etc.) = D, Connector (and) = C, Adverb = B.

Verb Phrase (VP) → ⟨V⟩ | ⟨V⟩ ⟨B⟩
Noun Phrase (NP) → ⟨N⟩ | ⟨D⟩ ⟨N⟩ |
⟨D⟩ ⟨A⟩ ⟨N⟩
Subordinate Clause (SC) → ⟨S⟩ ⟨A⟩
Main Clause (MC)→⟨NP⟩ ⟨VP⟩
Sentence →⟨MC⟩ ⟨•⟩ | ⟨SC⟩ ⟨,⟩ ⟨MC⟩ ⟨•⟩ |
⟨MC⟩ ⟨,⟩ ⟨MC⟩ ⟨C⟩ ⟨MC⟩ ⟨•⟩

Suppose we try to parse the sentence:

While contented, the man works well.

The individual words of this sentence can take the following possible parts of speech:

| | |
|---|---|
| contented | V or A |
| man | N or V or A |
| the | D |
| well | N or V or A or B |
| while | N or S |
| works | N or V |

On a first try, "while" and "the man works" might be identified as noun phrases, and "contented" and "well" as verb phrases. These then group to give two main clauses, but an attempt to form the construct ⟨MC⟩ ⟨,⟩ ⟨MC⟩ ⟨C⟩ ⟨MC⟩ would fail. We might next try "while contented" parsed as a subordinate clause, and the final parse as a sentence is then obtained from ⟨SC⟩ ⟨,⟩ ⟨MC⟩ ⟨•⟩. This, of course, is incorrect semantically, but correct as far as our grammar is concerned. Further investigation would then show that the alternative, and correct, parse "the man" = NP, "works well" = VP would also give a valid sentence.

As well as showing that "backtracking" and the investigation of alternative parses may be necessary, this example illustrates that a parsing method must produce *all* possible analyses for a given sentence.

TRANSITION NETWORK GRAMMARS. This method of parsing is best described by an example. Suppose that the syntactic element *Noun Phrase* is defined as a noun possibly preceded by a determiner, or an adjective, or both, and possibly followed by a connector and a second noun. Thus,

[Determiner] [Adjective] {Noun} ([Connector] [Noun])

where the braces {} indicate that the element must be present, the brackets [] indicate optional elements, and parentheses ( ) indicate that the enclosed elements must be present together if at all. The process of parsing such a phrase can be represented by a *transition network*, which has an entrance node Ⓘ with at least one path leading from it, and an exit node Ⓧ with at least one path leading to it and no paths emerging from it. These are connected by a series of nodes indicating the elements that must be recognized if the particular syntactic element is to be identified. Thus the transition network for *Noun Phrase* will be as shown in Fig. 1. Every syntactic element in the language will have such an associated network.

SEMANTIC MODELS. As remarked earlier, the fundamental problem behind any attempt at translation is that of analyzing the "meaning" in the source language and conveying it into the target language. The use of semantic models, or templates, is one approach suggested as an aid in this process.

A number of such models are defined, each designed to express a particular "message," and these are matched against the source sentence. For example, one model might be

Actor-Act-Object

which would match the sentence

Men eat apples

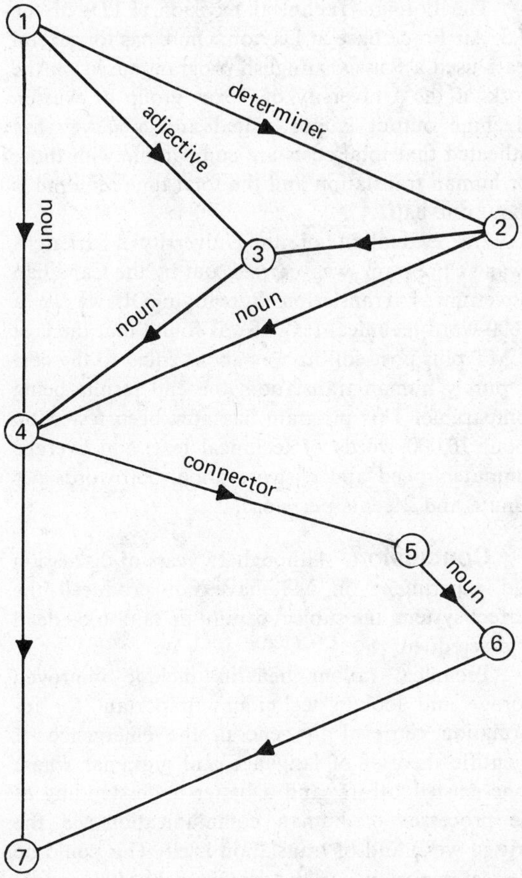


**Fig. 1.** Transition network for Noun Phrase.

because the dictionary would contain the information that *Men* is in the semantic class "actor," *eat* in the class "act," etc.

It is not yet clear how far such a system can cope with a more convoluted sentence structure, or how many models will be needed.

DEPENDENCY THEORY (HAYS, 1967). Developed by the MT group in Georgetown University and by workers in the Rand Corporation, this method seeks to analyze sentences in terms of governor and dependent units. Analysis proceeds to higher and higher levels of grammar until, in general, a single ungoverned symbol is obtained. Most words and units have multiple functions and may be either governors or dependents.

Q AND W SYSTEMS. The MT group at the University of Montreal has developed two grammars based on transformational grammars, but with the modifications that parameters can be introduced and the application of the rules can be governed by certain conditions. These grammars are called Q and W systems (after A. Querido and A. van Wijngaarden); in application to MT, the source language is first transformed to a "normalized" form. This leads to a normalized form of the target language, which is finally transformed to the actual target language.

FORMATIONAL THEORY. Developed at the University of Texas, this method is closely related to a transformational grammar, and assumes that the formation of symbol strings can be defined mathematically. A meta language is used as an intermediate stage between the source and object language.

WAYNE STATE UNIVERSITY MT PROGRAM. An initial analysis of a sentence identifies elements or "blocks"; these are used in subsequent analysis to identify the main sentence units such as subject, predicate, and object. Although the blocking process will generally not be unambiguous, the resulting reduction in the number of elements that must be handled in the final phase simplifies the latter.

PREDICTIVE ANALYSIS (OETTINGER, 1960). The MT group at Harvard University has utilized the method of predictive analysis, first suggested by Rhodes. Analysis of a sentence is performed in a left-to-right scan, and predictions are recorded at each stage of the possible outcome. When a prediction is either fulfilled or shown to be untenable, it is erased. A practical difficulty, which was later removed to some extent by Plath, lay in the number of predictions that had to be followed through in some cases.

STATISTICAL ANALYSIS. At the University of Saskatchewan—and subsequently at Lakehead University, Thunder Bay, Ontario—a completely different approach has been tested, in which a preliminary parsing classifies the words of a sentence into 16 categories, using statistical data. Subsequent scans identify larger units, such as noun and verb phrases, and syntactic elements such as subject and object. From this analysis the application of a set of rules enables the target language sentence to be produced. This method has been tested extensively on "scientific" text and has the advantage that it appears to be much faster than most methods that employ a transformational type of scheme. Because of the inevitable errors (about 3.5%) when a statistical method is used, post-editing is considered necessary.

This survey does not pretend to be exhaustive, but is enough to give an idea of the scope of methods that have been proposed for MT. The references list further reading in depth.

**Computational Problems of MT.** The representation of textual as distinct from numeric data in a computer presents no problem—at any rate, in theory. Letters and punctuation are coded numerically and are thereafter manipulated within the computer. The perfect computer, from the point of view of anyone wishing to process text, would undoubtedly be able to accept as input and print out the full range of lower and upper-case letters together with accents and other diacritics peculiar to the language under consideration. However, no such computer exists, and recourse has to be made to further coding, which is serviceable, though sometimes clumsy.

Programming has been assisted by the development of such higher-level languages as Comit and Snobol, although translation programs have been produced in such unlikely languages as Algol-60 and Cobol, and many are written at least partly in machine language for the sake of speed.

The great problem in the early days of experimentation was restriction in storage space, but this is now a thing of the past. One technique developed to overcome this, and which is still in use to a certain extent, is that of stem-ending decomposition (Locke and Booth, 1965). This considerably reduces the number of dictionary entries required in languages such as Russian or French, which are heavily inflected, but puts an added burden on the lookup program.

**MT in Practice.** A very desirable feature of any MT program is that it should have been extensively tested on "real" text and not merely used on such artificial and unrealistic examples as the famous sentence, "They are flying planes." It is often difficult to determine how far this has been done. Some authenticated tests and realistic estimates of time and cost, etc., however, do exist and are worth mentioning.

At Oak Ridge National Laboratory, Tennessee, a program based on the work of the Georgetown University group has been in operation for some years, producing Russian-English translation of technical text. No post-editing is done, and the total time required is said to be one-quarter of that needed for human translation, while the cost is competitive.

The Foreign Technical Division (FTD) of the U.S. Air Force Base at Dayton, Ohio, has for several years used a Russian-English program based on the work of the University of Texas group at Austin. Machine output is post-edited and a survey has indicated that total costs are comparable with those for human translation and the total time required is about one-half.

An evaluation of the University of Saskatchewan's program was carried out by the Canadian Government Translation Bureau in Ottawa on a 2,600-word technical text. It was found that the cost of MT plus post-editing was about equal to the cost of purely human translation, the end results being comparable. This program has now been tested on about 10,000 words of technical text, and average computer speed and cost are about 350 words per minute and 2 cents per word.

**Conclusion.** Although 25 years of discussion and experiment on MT have not produced the perfect system, the subject cannot be said to be dead or discredited.

Technical fallout benefits include improved storage and lookup techniques, important for information retrieval in general, the emergence of scientific theories of language and grammar where none existed before, and a better understanding of the processes of human communication via the written word and of translation itself. This could be of great importance in the development of languages for information retrieval systems seeking to provide a "natural" query form.

Work is still in progress and improvements are being made in existing MT programs. The price of computer time versus cost of human translators will surely decrease, rendering MT more attractive financially. Thus, although those who predicted or expected "perfect" MT have been disappointed, the more realistic majority of investigators, who envisioned machines as merely aiding and abetting human translators rather than replacing them, have been encouraged by the continuing progress.

### References

1953. Booth, A. D. "Mechanical Translation," *Computers and Automation*, Vol. 2, No. 4.

1960. Oettinger, A. G. *Automatic Language Translation.* Cambridge, Mass.: Harvard Univ. Press.

1965. Locke, W. N., and A. D. Booth (Eds.). *Machine Translation of Language*. Cambridge, Mass.: M.I.T. Press, 3d printing.
1967. Booth, A. D. (Ed.). *Machine Translation*. Amsterdam: North-Holland Publishing.
1967. Hays, D. G. *Introduction to Computational Linguistics*. New York: American-Elsevier.
1971. Josselson, H. H. "Automatic Translation of Language Since 1960: A Linguist's View," *Advances in Computers*.

K. H. V. BOOTH AND A. D. BOOTH

**LARC.** *See* LIVERMORE AUTOMATIC RESEARCH COMPUTER.

## LATENCY

For article on related subject *see* ACCESS TIME; DIRECT ACCESS; and MEMORY: AUXILIARY.

Latency is the rotational delay in reading/writing a record to a direct-access auxiliary memory, e.g. disk, drum, or data cell (see Fig. 1). *Maximum* latency is the time for an entire revolution of the recording surface. A program suffers maximum latency—generally undesirable from an efficiency standpoint—if it requests a record whose starting point has just passed under the read/write heads. *Minimum* latency is zero delay, by definition. *Average* latency is half the maximum.

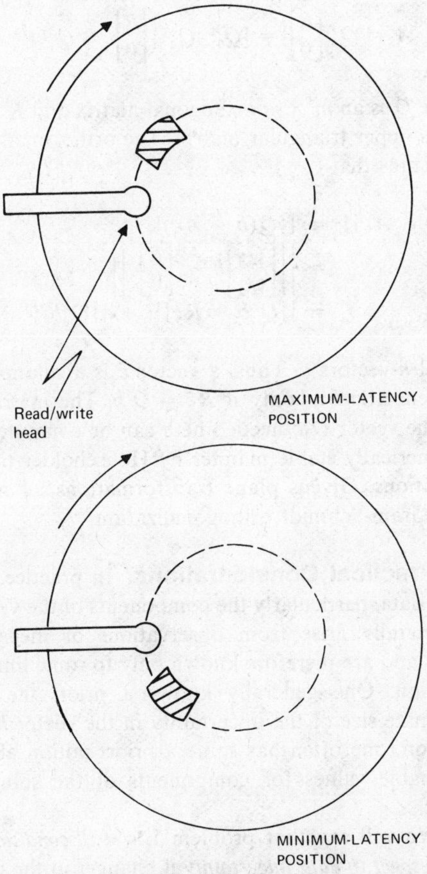


**Fig. 1.** Maximum and minimum latencies for various head-record orientations. Time: just after channel commences search for indicated record.

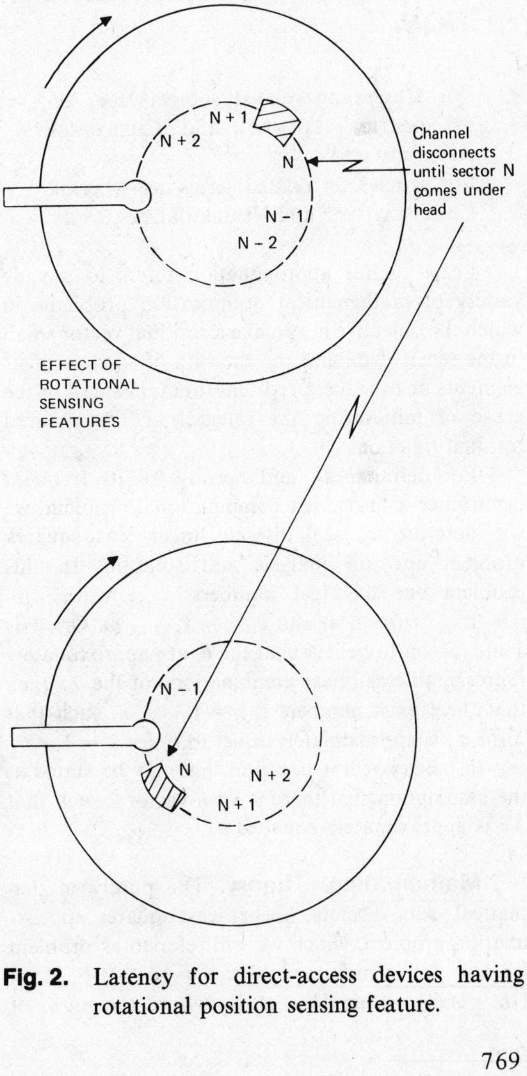


**Fig. 2.** Latency for direct-access devices having rotational position sensing feature.

Newer direct-access devices often have a rotational position sensing (RPS) feature; they do not attempt to access a record until it is almost under their heads, as shown in Fig. 2. By dividing each track into $N$ equal-sized *sectors* ($N$ typically is 128), disk drives having the RPS feature reduce channel latency, but not drive latency. Channel latency blocks activity on all drives attached to the channel; while the channel awaits correct positioning of the record on one drive, no other drives can be active. The RPS feature permits a channel to service other drives while the requested sector is rotating toward the read/write head, as shown in Fig. 2.

D. N. FREEMAN

## LEAST-SQUARES APPROXIMATION

For articles on related subjects *see* APPROXIMATION THEORY; and CHEBYSHEV APPROXIMATION.

For articles on related terms *see* MATRIX COMPUTATIONS; and NUMERICAL ANALYSIS.

Least-squares approximation refers to a wide variety of mathematical optimization problems in which the objective is to make a residual vector small in the sense of minimizing the sum of squares of its elements or to make a residual function small in the sense of minimizing the integral of the squared residual function.

For definiteness, and because of its frequent occurrence as a real-life computational problem, we will describe the real discrete linear least-squares problem and its analysis and solution. In this problem one has real numbers $a_{ij}, i = 1,\ldots, m$, $j = 1,\ldots, n\,(m > n)$ and $b_i$, $i = 1,\ldots, m$. One has some reason to believe that the $b_i$ are approximately representable as linear combinations of the $a_{ij}$ (i.e., that there exist numbers $\tilde{c}_j\, j = 1,\ldots, n$, such that $\sum_{j=1}^{n}\tilde{c}_j a_{ij}$ is approximately equal to $b_i$ for $i = 1,\ldots, m$). In matrix-vector notation this may be stated as the assumption that there is an $n$-vector $\tilde{c}$ such that $A\tilde{c}$ is approximately equal to $b$.

**Mathematical Theory.** The purely mathematical, real, discrete, linear, least-squares approximation problem, which we will refer to as problem LS, is to find an $n$-vector $\tilde{c}$ such that $\|b - A\tilde{c}\| = \min\|b - Ac\|$, where the *norm* of a vector $v$, $\|v\|$, is defined as the square root of the sum of the squares of the components of $v$. A solution for this problem always exists. It is unique if and only if the rank of $A$ is $n$.

A vector $\tilde{c}$ is a solution vector for problem LS if and only if the associated residual vector, $\tilde{r} = b - A\tilde{c}$, is orthogonal to all column vectors of $A$. This orthogonality condition may be written as $A^T(b - A\tilde{c}) = A^Tb - A^TA\tilde{c} = 0$. From this latter expression one obtains the system of equations, $A^TAc = A^Tb$, called the "normal equations" for problem LS. Forming the normal equations and solving them by the Cholesky algorithm is a common method of computing a solution for problem LS.

Other solution methods providing superior numerical reliability at a cost of about twice as many arithmetic operations are based on the *QR decomposition* of $A$. Thus, $A$ can be written as

$$A = Q^T\begin{bmatrix}R\\0\end{bmatrix} = [Q_1{}^T\!:\!Q_2{}^T]\begin{bmatrix}R\\0\end{bmatrix} = Q_1{}^TR$$

where $Q$ is an $m \times m$ orthogonal matrix and $R$ is an $n \times n$ upper triangular matrix. The orthogonality of $Q$ assures that

$$\begin{aligned}\|b - Ac\|^2 &= \|Q(b - Ac)\|^2\\ &= \left\|\begin{bmatrix}Q_1\\Q_2\end{bmatrix}b - \begin{bmatrix}R\\0\end{bmatrix}c\right\|^2\\ &= \|Q_1b - Rc\|^2 + \|Q_2b\|^2\end{aligned}$$

for all $n$-vectors $c$. Thus, a vector $\tilde{c}$ is a solution of problem LS if and only if $R\tilde{c} = Q_1b$. The matrix $R$ and the vector $Q_1b$ needed here can be computed in a numerically stable manner by Householder transformations, Givens plane transformations, or modified Gram-Schmidt orthogonalization.

**Practical Considerations.** In practice, the given data, particularly the components of the vector $b$, generally arise from observations or measurements and are therefore known only to some limited precision. One generally knows a priori the approximate size of the uncertainty in the vector $b$. In addition, one often has some a priori notion about reasonable values for components of the solution vector.

We will say that problem LS is *ill-conditioned with respect to data uncertainty* if changes in the data matrix $[A\!:\!b]$ of the order of magnitude of the uncertainty in this data can cause changes in the solution vector which are regarded as significant by the problem originator. In such a case, even though the rank of $A$ may be $n$, there will commonly be a set of significantly different $n$-vectors that are almost as good as the unique best-solution vector if "goodness" is measured only by the criterion of reducing the residual norm.

In practice, it is desirable to have a systematic way of recognizing the occurrence of an ill-conditioned problem, of identifying the data dependencies that cause the ill-conditioning, of quantitatively characterizing a set of candidate solutions, and of selecting from the candidate solutions one that is suitable for the application at hand. Singular-value analysis and Levenberg-Marquardt analysis provide practical means for obtaining this information.

Singular-value analysis makes use of a matrix decomposition of the form $A = USV^T$, where $U$ and $V$ are orthogonal matrices and $S$ is a diagonal matrix. The Levenberg-Marquardt analysis studies solutions of the augmented least-squares problem

$$\begin{bmatrix} A \\ \lambda I \end{bmatrix} c \cong \begin{bmatrix} b \\ 0 \end{bmatrix}$$

as a function of the parameter $\lambda$.

As an example of an ill-conditioned least-squares problem, consider the problem $Ac \cong b$ with

$$A = \begin{bmatrix} 0.780 & 0.563 \\ 0.913 & 0.659 \\ 0.133 & 0.096 \end{bmatrix}, \quad b = \begin{bmatrix} 0.481 \\ 0.560 \\ 0.082 \end{bmatrix}$$

The exact mathematical solution for this problem is

$$\tilde{c} = [477, -660]^T$$

with a residual vector $\tilde{r} = b - A\tilde{c} = [0.0010, -0.0010, 0.0010]^T$ and residual norm $||r|| \doteq 0.0017$.

By either singular-value analysis or Levenberg-Marquardt analysis one can find that there are other candidate solution vectors that are much smaller in norm than $\tilde{c}$ and which have residual norms only slightly greater than the minimal norm $||\tilde{r}||$. For instance, the vector $\hat{c} = [0.404, 0.292]^T$ gives a residual vector

$$\hat{r} \doteq [0.0015, -0.0013, 0.0002]^T$$

whose norm is $||\hat{r}|| \doteq 0.0020$.

In most practical situations, particularly where there is uncertainty in some of the data defining $A$ and $b$, the vector $\hat{c}$ would be preferred in place of the vector $\tilde{c}$, whose components are larger by three orders of magnitude. The reason for preferring smaller solution vector components will be different in different contexts, but often this is related to the preference for a simpler, more economical explanation of the real-world phenomenon being modeled.

For a more complete discussion of the concepts mentioned above, see Lawson and Hanson (1974).

### Reference

1974. Lawson, C. L., and R. J. Hanson. *Solving Least Squares Problems*. Englewood Cliffs, N.J.: Prentice-Hall.

C. L. Lawson

## LEGAL PROTECTION OF SOFTWARE

For articles on related subjects *see* Copyrights and Patents, Computer Aspects of; Programming Languages; and Software.

In order to buy, sell, and otherwise trade computer software in commerce, as with other goods and services, an adequate system of property right protection in software items must be developed, understood, and used. Otherwise, after the creation of a valuable software property—which involves the expenditure of much effort and funds for development and debugging, as well as advertising to gain widespread public interest—it would be possible for an interloper to pirate the product and to reap the merchandising benefits, with no effective recourse available to the developer.

The term "software" applies to all sorts of computer programs, supporting documentation, flowcharts, tapes, records, systems, compilers, and even definitions of computer languages. The importance of adequate protection of computer software becomes apparent when it is realized that investment in software development, services, and purchases now exceeds the cost of development and purchase of hardware. This being so, it is perhaps indicative of the immaturity of the computer profession that relatively very little attention has been directed to property rights in software and to the legal and other aspects of its protection. Our purpose here is to consider some of the possibilities and pitfalls of legal and other methods of protection for this valuable property.

**Forms of Protection Available.** A variety of forms of "protection" are available to owners of computer software. Some offer little or no protection at all, while other forms that are surprisingly inexpensive are very effective. Because of the relatively recent arisal of the problem, none of the current patent or copyright laws or other case law specifically relate to computer software, and few of them can be interpreted as applicable. However, a great deal of case law from other fields is relevant to this problem of protection, and certain management techniques can provide some degree of security. The legal and other methods to be discussed in this article are:

1. Simple secrecy.
2. Obfuscation.
3. Contract.
4. Trade secret.
5. Remedies for unfair trade practices.
6. Patent.
7. Trademark and service mark.
8. Copyright.

SIMPLE SECRECY. The method of "simple secrecy" is a very inexpensive and effective method, when it applies. It means that you protect a software development by telling no one about it. No one, at all! This method suffers from the obvious disadvantage that such a software development cannot be marketed without giving up the secrecy, and thus the protection it brings.

Simple secrecy is useful during the period when a software product is under development. If there are several people working on the development, every employee having knowledge of it should be under a nondisclosure contract with the employer. In case of loss of the secret, action would lie in a suit for breach of confidentiality by the person who, without authorization, disclosed the secret to outsiders. This kind of secrecy merges into the area of "trade secret," which is discussed below.

The merits of simple secrecy are its effectiveness, minimal expense, and lack of legal complexity when only one or a few trusted people are involved. This method is widely used.

OBFUSCATION. Another method of protection is "obfuscation." This widespread, nonlegal method is consciously used by a select few, and unconsciously by many others. Software protection by this method depends upon the fact that some kinds of software are, or can be made, so confused, so opaque, and so difficult to unravel that there is no point in stealing them.

When the obfuscation method of protection is used, the software package cannot be transported easily to a new situation unless the purloiner has gained a great deal of additional support by having full access to "inside" system documentation.

Obfuscation has a very definite use where object code is to be put into libraries, into time-shared systems, into operating systems, and the like, and where the system support is contained in a users' manual that provides only the directions for use of the command language. In such cases, flowcharts, source programs, and other resources are not made available outside the vendor's organization. Of course, if someone is willing to dump out a core listing and put in the required effort to "crack the code," without acquiring other documentation, the obfuscation method provides no legal recourse to the owner.

CONTRACT. The method of "contract" is employed by some in an attempt to secure a degree of protection of computer software or its documentation. For example, in a two-party contract agreement between the buyer and the seller, the buyer may promise not to do certain things—such as not to "disclose" the code of a program or the method of a program, not to make copies of program tapes, not to give such copies to others, or not to do other things that compromise ownership.

However, such protection is limited because a contract cannot bind third parties, and it cannot claim reservations in the nature of patent rights, copyright rights, etc., when these proprietary grants do not exist. Attempts to control disclosure or piracy in this manner merge into the "trade secret" method, discussed in the next section.

It appears that the use of contracts for the protection of legal rights in computer programs and software should merely complement other legal methods of protection that have a statutory legal basis such as patent, trademark, or copyright. For example, a contract between the vendor and the buyer may spell out how the vendor wishes his legal copyright or other interests to be protected, with the contract stipulating what the buyer can and cannot do.

TRADE SECRET. The method of "trade secret" for protection of software seems to have been extended far beyond its safe security limitations. Judicial opinions are very narrow concerning the circumstances in which a true "trade secret" situation is considered to exist. The "secret" must indeed be a secret, and be identified as a secret. It must be known only to a few, and only to those within the company that uses and benefits from the trade secret. The secret cannot be general or widespread knowledge. Moreover, the secret must convey substantial competitive advantages to the single company that possesses and actually uses it. (Consider Coca-Cola.) If a trade secret, or any articles that *embody and disclose* the secret, are put on the market generally, to be used by a number of buyers or licensees, by definition it is no longer a trade secret, irrespective of the words in any auxiliary contract.

Thus, for example, if a computer time-shared service bureau has come up with an improved operating system, it *may* be a trade secret. However, it stops being a trade secret when others have access to it and can examine it, or when the operating system is generally marketed to other service bureaus or companies, or if an employee gives out its secret details. In the latter case, the only recourse of the owner is to sue the errant employee for breach of confidence, and try to get an injunction to stop its use by those who gained the secret. Because of its many limitations, the trade secret method should be treated with caution.

Unfair Trade Practices. Reliance upon remedies for "unfair trade practices" or "unfair competition" is another means which must be considered with regard to misappropriation of computer software, documentation, or information, or for other acts that are commercially damaging. Involved here are all kinds of fraud, misrepresentation, deception, and other methods of unfair or unethical practices by a competitor which are damaging to the owner of the computer software, to his relationship with his customers or potential customers, or to his title to rights in his software. Some of these problems touch upon trademark rights, discussed below.

Unfortunately, protection through remedies for "unfair trade practices" are, for the most part, applicable only after the trouble has developed. Then, the sooner the remedies can be applied, the better. Because of the great complexity of this subject, not much more can be said about it here. However, this avenue of remedy should not be overlooked when such troubles occur.

Patent. The "patent" method for the protection of computer software may also have received an undue amount of emphasis and attention. Only a very small proportion of new programs contain the kind of completely new, brilliant, "inventive step" that is required by law for patentability.

Most computer programs represent merely competent, well-worked-out applications of widely known methods. Much of their value resides in the fact that the program has been completely checked out and is free of any bugs. Developments of this kind (quite apart from the fact that the development is a computer program) are simply not patentable.

A very few computer programs that do represent a new process or method are being granted patents by the United States Patent Office. The cost of obtaining a patent is on the order of several thousand dollars, and usually takes at least two years to issue.

If a valid patent is obtained, it gives the owner exclusive right to "make, use, or vend" the article or method protected. However, patent rights have traditionally been very difficult and costly to monitor and enforce. Patents on program methodology would be harder, not easier, to enforce than hardware patents.

The Patent Office has been very much opposed to granting patents on methods that it likes to characterize as "computer programs." This is partly because of the expected increased work load that program patents might impose on the Patent Office. It is also because the Office holds that a computer program is in fact merely a "mathematical theory," or a "computation," or a "series of mental steps," and that these are not patentable branches of technology under the law.

Accordingly, in 1972, the Patent Office, through the Justice Department, brought to review by the Supreme Court a test case on what they characterized as a "program patent." In its decision, the Supreme Court denied issuance of the patent, as the Patent Office had requested. On the other hand, the Court stated that its decision should not be viewed as precluding patent protection for any program servicing a computer.

Trademark. The method of "trademark" and "service mark" is inexpensive and quick. It provides legal protection for the chosen name for your software, systems, or services. If others use the trademarked name for describing their similar or competing goods or services, they can be promptly stopped by an injunction and sued for recovery of damages resulting from their actions.

A trademark is created by actual use of the chosen mark in commerce with your products or services. The mark may appear in sales, advertising, or even in a descriptive technical paper. It may be a word or phrase, such as *ZILCH*. At the earliest time that the mark is used, and always thereafter, there should be an indication of the "trademark status" of the mark. This is signified by means of a tiny little "TM" placed alongside the mark: ZILCH™. Legal assistance should be obtained to verify the uniqueness of the chosen mark before using it. Many kinds of words (place names, personal names, descriptive names, etc.) are not acceptable for trademark.

The mark should always be used as an adjective, not as a noun. If the mark "ZILCH" is for a new program, always use the mark in expressions like "Do it with the ZILCH program" and not in expressions like "Do it with ZILCH."

The legal rights in a trademark are, for the most part, secured by the simple use of the mark in commerce. A trademark or service mark can be registered in the U. S. Patent Office. A registered trademark or service mark gives the owner the additional right to bring suit in a federal court, and enjoys a few other useful increments in legal rights over the unregistered mark.

COPYRIGHT. The method of "copyright" is in many instances the best method for protection of computer software. For the strongest protection, copyright should be used together with trademark and various kinds of auxiliary contracts. Like trademark, copyright is inexpensive and quick.

Computer programs have many manifestations: tapes, cards, printed listings, etc. The manifestation on which copyright is focused is the printed program on paper, i.e., the source program, in whatever programming language. Copyright protection on the printed program then extends to any other version derived from it.

The legal protection of copyright (U.S. and internationally) is achieved by inserting a simple notice such as:

Copyright © 1972 Calvin N. Mooers

on the first or title page of any documentation or listing. Legal copyright exists from the instant that a copy with such a notice is "published," providing that the copyright is promptly registered. "Publication" consists of offering it for sale, or lease, or otherwise distributing it publicly.

*Beware:* If publication occurs without the notice, all rights in copyright are lost forever! Therefore, many people consider it prudent to apply the legal copyright notice to all valuable new documentation (on every page, and on all drawings, diagrams, and figures) and thus avoid the chance that some Xerox copy of it might inadvertently be "published" at an unplanned time.

Copyright is directed to the original "writing" that constitutes the copyrighted document—irrespective of what the writing is "about." It is immaterial whether the writing is a computer program, a poem, a nonsense song, or whatever. Neither does it matter what manner of printing or reproduction is used, or how many copies are made. Copyright gives immediate, enforceable legal protection against the making by others, without authorization, of any copies, translations, or any other version derived from the copyrighted writing.

With software, as with all other kinds of writings, the legal protection of copyright applies to any writings or versions whatsoever which are in whole or in part derived from the protected copyrighted writing. When the copyright is applied to a computer source-language program, then translations of the program into other computer languages, compilations, assemblies, adaptations, tape copies, and all other transformations are protected by the language of the law. Copyright on a defining document for a computer language system thus provides protection against the unauthorized writing and selling of compilers for the language, since the latter are also "writings" derived from the former. Opinion is divided on whether running a copyrighted program constitutes an infringement, but caution recommends that it should not be done.

It is desirable that the legal copyright notice be applied to each of the derived forms that is put on sale or is distributed. The advice and guidance of a copyright lawyer should always be sought in order to comply with the many legal requirements and to avoid future grief.

**Conclusion.** Of the various methods for protection of computer software, this author recommends use of ordinary discretion or secrecy for developmental work, the use of trademark or service mark for the name of the product, and use of copyright on the written software when the product is to be marketed. Certainly, the minimal cost, and the instant creation of strong legal rights, by both the trademark and copyright approaches strongly commend them.

Serious consideration should be given to adopting a company policy that systematically and *always* registers claims for trademark and copyright to *all* software products and literature from the very beginning of public exposure and the marketing cycle. It costs very little, and much may be gained. The protection is then systematically created at the only time it can be created. If it is decided at some later time that the protection is not needed, the rights in trademarks and copyright can be simply abandoned.

Conversely, any initial publication without copyright notice legally and irrevocably dedicates the rights to the public. Similarly, if an initial notice of a trademark claim is not made to a mark, then trademark rights in the mark can be developed later only with substantial hazard.

The other legal methods of protection—namely, patent, remedies for unfair trade practices, and trade secret—have application only to special situations, and are very expensive. This author believes that reliance on them could be hazardous.

REFERENCES

1969. Computers-in-Law Institute. "The Law of Software, 1969 Proceeding". National Law Center, George Washington University, Washington, D.C.

1972. Goldberg, David. "Legal Protection of EDP Software," *Datamation* Vol. 18, No. 5 (May), pp. 66–70.

C. N. MOOERS

## LEIBNIZ, GOTTFRIED WILHELM VON

For articles on related subjects *see* DIGITAL COMPUTERS: History; and PASCAL, BLAISE.

Gottfried von Leibniz (b. Leipzig, 1646; d. Hanover, 1716) had obtained an excellent education in his father's library before entering the University of Leipzig at fifteen years of age and receiving a bachelor's degree at seventeen. At twenty he received a doctorate in jurisprudence from Altdorf, and for six years thereafter pursued a career of law and diplomacy, working to create an effective defense for the German states against Louis XIV. These diplomatic intrigues took him to Paris (1672), where he spent the four most fecund years of his mathematical career. Under the tutelage of Huygens, Leibniz systematically studied mathematics, especially the work of Descartes and Pascal.

Pascal's calculating machine stimulated Leibniz's interest. By adding a movable carriage operating on wheels utilizing an active-and-inactive pin principle and a delayed carry mechanism, Leibniz modified Pascal's machine so that it would multiply and divide directly (i.e., without the operator's using an algorithm). However, in the only extant Leibniz machine (Hanover Museum), a later model, Pascal's ratchet-carry mechanism is replaced by a primitive

**Fig. 1.** Gottfried Wilhelm von Leibniz, from a painting by A. Scheits. (Photograph by courtesy of the Herzog Anton Ulrich-Museum.)

Geneva gear system that accomplishes the discontinuous carry of digits by a series of five-point star gears. Eliminating the ratchet mechanisms made subtraction and division possible by simply reversing the rotation of the addition and multiplication mechanisms.

In 1673, Leibniz made discoveries in differential calculus and observed (in 1675) that the summation process of integration was equivalent to reversing the operation of differentiation, the fundamental theorem of calculus. Newton had also made this observation in the 1660s, but Leibniz was apparently unaware of it.

In 1676 Leibniz left Paris for Hanover, where for the next forty years he was a historian and librarian actively pursuing philosophy, theology, diplomatic missions, and scientific correspondences, and intermittently worked on his calculating machines. In 1700 he organized the Berlin Academy of Science (an idea he first articulated in 1668) and at his death was carrying on the now-famous correspondence with Clarke about the theological implications of Newton's *Principia* and *Opticks*.

C. V. JONES

## LIBRARY, PROGRAM. *See* PROGRAM LIBRARIES.

## LIFO. *See* FIFO-LIFO.

## LIGHTPEN

For articles on related subjects *see* COMPUTER GRAPHICS; and INPUT-OUTPUT DEVICES.

The lightpen is one of the most common manual input devices on graphic displays (and even on some alphanumeric ones), for use in identifying ("picking") information displayed on the screen for subsequent computer processing. For example, in text editing, pointing at a certain character on a certain line with the lightpen might indicate to the program that a string of characters about to be typed by the user should be inserted after the identified character. Pointing the lightpen at a particular resistor in an electronic schematic on the screen might mean that the user wants that particular resistor moved, scaled up, deleted, or manipulated in some other specified way.

Physically, the lightpen (Fig. 1) is a photosensitive transducer that converts light emanating from the screen to an electric signal, which is typically used to interrupt the processor servicing the display. Associated with the interrupt is some sense data, usually either the $x - y$ coordinates of the lightpenned display element (point, line, or character) on the screen, and the address in the display buffer of the display command which caused display of the element that the lightpen detected.

In either case, the program has the problem of relating such coordinate or address sense data to the particular text character or logical picture entity which the user selected for processing by the program. This process is known as *correlation* of the physical sense data to the logical subpicture item that the user wanted to indicate, and usually involves

**Fig. 1.** A lightpen pointing to a picture on a display screen.

some amount of table searching.

Some lightpens aid the user in accurate positioning by projecting "finder beams" of light on the spot on the screen where the lightpen photodetector is focused. Nevertheless, most lightpens are not easily used for fast, accurate picking, and have the additional disadvantage that they are not natural for freehand input. A data tablet with its stylus allows such input without special programming aids, while a lightpen must be provided with special "tracking" algorithms. In such an algorithm, the program displays a tracking cursor, or cross, and makes it follow the lightpen.

A. VAN DAM

## LINEAR PROGRAMMING. *See* MATHEMATICAL PROGRAMMING; and SIMPLEX METHOD.

## LINGUISTICS. *See* PROGRAMMING LINGUISTICS.

## LINKAGE EDITOR

For articles on related subjects *see* ASSEMBLERS; LOADERS; and PROGRAM LIBRARIES. For article on related term *see* GLOBAL AND LOCAL VARIABLES.

The function of the linkage editor (sometimes called the "consolidator" or "composer") is to combine into a single module a number of program segments that have been independently compiled. Some of the segments may be held in a library (on disk or tape), and the linkage editor will normally provide facilities for the automatic incorporation of any library segments that have been referenced. The output of the linkage editor is usually a relocatable binary program suitable for loading by a relocating loader.

If a section of program has been independently compiled, there will be three kinds of items in the compiler output:

1. Constants (absolute items whose value does not depend on the ultimate position of the segment in memory).
2. Items (usually addresses or address constants), whose value is known relative to the value of a specified location counter at the start of the segment.
3. External references, whose value cannot be determined until all segments are present.

The complete output of the compiler will therefore typically consist of

1. A "code" block consisting of binary words tagged to show their absolute, relative, or external character, and, in the case of relative items, the appropriate location counter.
2. A table of external references, containing for each reference the (relative) address in the code section at which it occurs and its symbolic form.
3. A table of external (global) symbol definitions, containing the name and (relative) value of each symbol globally defined in the segment.

The linkage editor operates in a number of passes. The first pass determines which segments are missing, by comparing the external reference tables with the global definition tables. If there are "missing" segments, the directories of specified library files are scanned. If the relevant names are found, the corresponding segments are added to the program. Pass 2 scans the segment headers and computes the sizes of the blocks corresponding to the various location counters. This information is placed in a header block for the use of the loader. Pass 3 performs relocation of all subsequent segments relative to the first segment so as to produce a relocatable program based on a single set of origins.

The process is simple: The location counters are all set to zero at the start of the first segment. Their values at the start of segment $n$, together with the information in that segment's header block, determine their values at the start of segment $n + 1$. During this pass, the entries in the global symbol definition tables and in the external reference tables are relocated relative to the origin of the first segment, and the entries from the tables associated with each segment are merged to give a single global symbol table and a single table of external references. Finally, these two tables are used to fill in all the unresolved external references, and the end result is a single module of relocatable binary.

The operation of linkage editing is commonly done as a disk-to-disk operation, using temporary work files as necessary. It is evident that it is a trivial extra complication to perform the final relocation at the same time, thus producing an executable binary module. Such a system is called a "linking loader."

REFERENCES

1972. Barron, D. W. *Assemblers and Loaders*, 2d ed. New York: American Elsevier.

1972. Presser L., and J. R. White. "Linkers and Loaders," *Computing Surveys*, Vol. 4, pp. 149–168.

D. W. BARRON

## LISP. 

*See* LIST PROCESSING LANGUAGES.

## LIST PROCESSING. 

*See* LISTS AND LIST PROCESSING.

## LIST PROCESSING LANGUAGES

For articles on related subjects *see* ARTIFICIAL INTELLIGENCE; DATA STRUCTURES; GARBAGE COLLECTION; LAMBDA CALCU-

LUS; LANGUAGE TRANSLATION; LISTS AND LIST PROCESSING; POINTER; PROGRAMMING LANGUAGES; and RECURSION.
For articles on related terms *see* DECREMENT; and INTERPRETER.

List processing languages are computer languages that facilitate the processing of data organized in the form of lists. Lisp, Comit, Sail, and Pop-2 are typical list-processing languages.

**External List Representation.** We begin with some simple examples to show what kinds of problems are solved by list processing and also how the lists look as they are used for input and output.

| *Traditional Notation* | *List Notation* |
|---|---|
| French to English translation: | |
| Où est le Métro ? | (OU EST LE METRO ?) |
| Symbolic integration: | |
| $\int xe^{x^2}dx$ | (INT X *(E ** (X**2))) |
| Logic: | |
| $(\forall x)(Q(x) \vee \sim P(x))$ | (ALL X(QX)OR(NOT(PX))) |
| Automatic question answering: | |
| Who is on first ? | (WHO IS ON FIRST ?) |

A list is simply a sequence of elements of any kind. The elements can be words, numbers, code groups, mathematical symbols, punctuation marks, or even lists. The list is a convenient way of representing nonnumerical data such as English sentences, mathematical formulas, a position in a game, logic theorems, or computer programs. The structure of a list is a natural way to represent the structure of data for the computer. By nesting sublists, sub-sublists, etc., one can create list structures of arbitrary complexity. List-processing techniques are especially useful for data that has variable structure, such as languages.

Some of the terms used in connection with list processing do not have precise definitions. They are used in slightly different ways by different writers. Nevertheless, some rough definitions can be given:

An *atom* is the basic list element. It is not a list. An atom corresponds to a word in English. In the examples above, EST, INT, **, X, and WHO are some of the atoms.

An *element* is one item on a list. It may be an atom or another list. Synonyms sometimes used for element are *node, item, record, entity*, and *bead*.

A *string* is an ordered sequence of elements (usually characters). A string lacks the complex structure that a list may have.

A list structure is a list whose elements may be atoms or lists or list structures.

A list is represented externally to the computer in terms of characters, and internally in terms of memory cells. The external representation (shown in the tabulated examples above) is designed for the convenience of the user and is used by the computer for input and output operations. The exact rules for writing a list vary from one language to another. In the above examples we have used the notation of Lisp. Parentheses indicate the beginning and end of a list, and blanks separate atoms.

**Internal List Representation.** The internal representation of a list is the way in which the computer stores the list in its memory cells. This varies from one language to another, and also may be different in different implementations of the same language (interpreters or compilers written by different programmers or for different machines).

An important part of list processing concerns the way lists are stored in memory. In order to clarify this point, a comparison will be made between the way lists might be stored in a conventional language such as Fortran and the way lists are usually stored in a list-processing language such as Lisp.

Fig. 1 is a simple list—(SEE (THE BIG) DOG)—as it might be stored in a Fortran array and also as it might be stored in the memory of a Lisp system. Each rectangle represents one memory cell or word. In the Fortran array, the list is stored in the conventional form of coded characters, one atom to a memory word. We assume here that the words are filled with blanks and right-justified. Markers are needed to indicate the beginning and ending of sublists, and we normally use parentheses for that purpose.

The same list is represented in a Lisp system in the form of *pointers*. A pointer is the address of a memory word. Other terms sometimes used for pointer are "link" and "reference." In this example, each memory word is divided into a front half and a rear half. Each half contains the address of another memory word. Each such address is represented in the diagram as an arrow pointing to the word to which it refers. The characters of the atoms are located in a special part of the memory reserved for characters. The arrow pointing to SEE represents the address of a special memory word that represents the

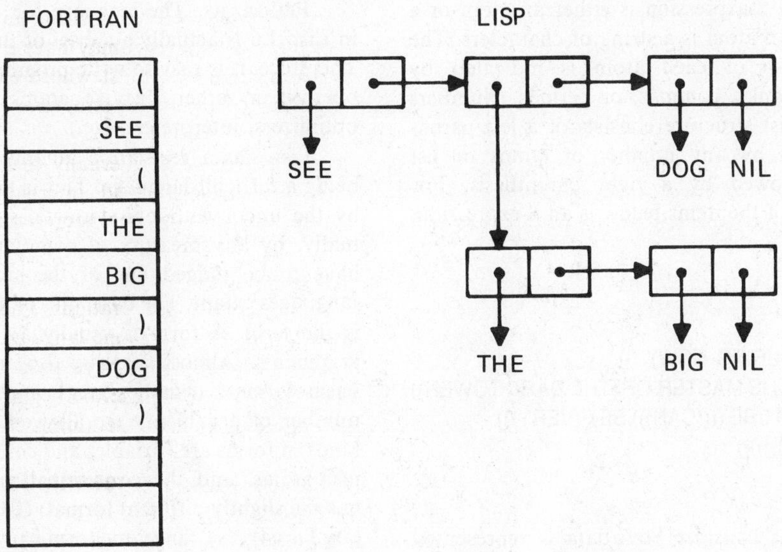


**Fig. 1.**

atom SEE. The other arrows pointing to atoms have a similar meaning. The special atom NIL is used to mark the end of a list.

This type of representation makes it easy to see several advantages of the pointer system of memory organization:

1. When adding or deleting items in the Fortran array representation, it is necessary to move down or move up all elements below the point at which the addition or deletion is made, whereas in the pointer type of organization one can add or delete an element by changing only two pointers. If a list contains hundreds of elements, this is an important saving of time.

2. Sublists are represented in the Fortran array by storing in the array every character in the sublist. In Lisp, one uses a pointer to the sublist. Thus, if a single sublist appears in many main lists, it can be represented by one pointer in each main list instead of repeating the entire sublist many times. This can be a considerable saving in memory space.

3. In Lisp, a sublist of any size can be added to or deleted from a main list by changing just two pointers. Thus, the processing of large sublists is more efficient.

4. In the Fortran array, adjacent elements of the list are physically adjacent in the memory. In Lisp, adjacent elements are linked by pointers, so the memory cells need not be adjacent. This means that any available memory word can be used in any list. This allows more efficient use of memory space.

5. The Fortran programmer must estimate the maximum size of each list and then reserve that number of words for each array. In Lisp the computer decides where to store lists while the problem is being run. This is called "dynamic storage allocation" and saves programmer effort.

6. Another advantage of the Lisp representation is that, when searching a main list, one can easily skip over the sublists if this is desirable, but in the Fortran representation one must search through each sublist in detail.

## The Lisp Language

DATA. Perhaps the best way to gain a good understanding of list processing is to describe a typical list-processing language in considerable detail. Lisp (short for LISt Processing) is one of the most popular of such languages. Lisp was developed by John McCarthy and his associates at M.I.T. during the late 1950s and early 1960s. Here we discuss Lisp 1.6, which is a version of the Lisp language developed at the Stanford Artificial Intelligence Project. In the interest of brevity, some of the finer details will be skipped over.

First we will define the data language that is used in Lisp: An "S-expression" (short for symbolic expression) is the general name for legal input data in Lisp 1.6. An S-expression is either an atom or a list structure. An atom is a string of characters. The start and finish of each atom is indicated by parentheses, blanks, commas, or periods. Numbers are atoms. A list structure consists of a left parenthesis followed by any number of atoms or list structures, followed by a right parenthesis. For example, each of the items below is an S-expression.

```
DOG
1984
(WHERE IS TURING NOW)
((MCCARTHY) IS MASTER OF (THE DARK TOWER))
(LIST STRUCTURE ((((CAN))) BE (((VERY)))
   ((((((DEEP))))))))
```

Now let us consider how data is represented internally in the computer memory. The memory is divided into two parts: free storage and full-word space. The free storage contains the list structure in pointer form, as described earlier. The full-word space contains the characters in the atoms.

An atom is represented internally as a special list in free storage space. In order that the computer may distinguish between an atom and ordinary list structure, a special marker is placed in the first half of the first word of a list representing an atom. The second half of the first word of an atom is a pointer to the property list of the atom. This property list contains information about that particular atom. Some typical properties are *print name* (a pointer to the characters of the atom name in full word space), *value* (if the atom is a variable), and *function definition* (if the atom is a function name). Also, the programmer can add additional properties to any atom at will. For example, an atom that is an English word might be given ADJECTIVE or NOUN as a property.

The Lisp reading routine checks each newly read atom against a list of all atoms known to the system. If the atom is already known, then a pointer to the existing atom is used. Otherwise, a new atom is created. Thus, if one uses the word DOG several times, each occurrence will be represented internally by a pointer to one unique atom.

Numbers may also be used in Lisp 1.6. They may be integers, fixed-point, or floating-point numbers. All Lisp functions that operate on numbers automatically test the number type and perform needed conversions. The word NIL is a special atom in Lisp 1.6 and is used to mark the end of a list. By itself, NIL just means the "empty list"( ).

PROGRAMS. The language for writing programs in Lisp 1.6 is actually a subset of the data language. Therefore, it is easy to write programs in Lisp which operate on other Lisp programs (e.g., compilers, optimizers, interpreters, etc.).

Lisp has a reputation among programmers as being a difficult language. This is an illusion caused by the unconventional syntactic style of Lisp. Actually, by any measure of complexity, Lisp would have to be judged one of the simplest computer languages extant. The basic unit of a program in Lisp is the *form*. A form is usually a function with its arguments. Almost all Lisp 1.6 forms follow the basic format: (function arg1 arg2 arg3 . . .). Any number of arguments are allowed. The only other kinds of forms are variables and constants, which are just atoms, and the conditional expression, which has the slightly different format: (COND (arg1 arg2) (arg3 arg4) . . .). Since one form can be the argument for another, large programs can be built up by nesting.

Lisp has very few special rules, exceptions, etc. It was designed by a group of mathematicians and therefore has the virtues of mathematical elegance and simplicity.

The semantics of Lisp are also straightforward. The Lisp 1.6 system contains a program called "interpreter." The interpreter reads a Lisp form and then prints the value of that form. To understand a Lisp program (a form), one must know what value the interpreter will produce when evaluating that form.

The simplest form is a variable. A variable is any atom to which a value has been assigned. The value is a pointer to some S-expression. For example, a variable X may have as value a list of three elements (A B C). Values may be assigned to variables by a LAMBDA form, described below. Given a variable, the interpreter returns its value. If the variable is part of a larger form, this value will be used in evaluating that form.

The other atomic Lisp form is the constant. A constant is simply a variable that has been assigned itself as a value. Typical constants are numbers, T, and NIL. The constant T means "true," and NIL means "false" and also "end of list."

The QUOTE form is written (QUOTE a), where "a" can be any S-expression. The value of (QUOTE a) is "a." The argument is not evaluated. This is how data is put into a program.

The next type of Lisp form is the SUBR form (short for subroutine); CAR is a SUBR function that returns the first element of a list. If X has the value (A B C), then (CAR X) has the value A. A companion to CAR is CDR, which returns the rest of the list. The value of (CDR X) is (B C). One can use nested sequences of CARs and CDRs to isolate any desired fragment of an S-expression. The names CAR and CDR are historical fossils. They are assembly language instructions on the IBM 704 computer, the first machine on which Lisp was implemented. The term CAR is short for "Contents of the Address part of Register," and CDR is short for "Contents of the Decrement part of Register."

The SUBR function CONS (short for construct) is used to build up S-expressions; CONS takes two arguments. The second is an existing list and the first is a new element for that list. If Y has the value A, then (CONS Y X) has the value (A A B C).

Lisp also contains predicates: ATOM is a predicate of one argument. A predicate is either true or false: (ATOM X) has the value T for truth if X is an atom; otherwise NIL for false.

Predicates are particularly useful in conditional forms, the Lisp equivalent of a branch instruction. The following is a typical conditional form:

```
(COND ((ATOM X) X) (T (CAR X)))
```

The arguments of a conditional form come in pairs. In each pair, the first is the predicate part and the second is the value part. The interpreter evaluates conditional pairs from left to right. If the predicate has a value T, the interpreter then evaluates the second portion of the conditional pair and returns this as the value of the entire conditional form. If the predicate is NIL then the interpreter starts to work on the next pair. If X is (A B C), then the value of the sample conditional form above is A, since (ATOM X) is NIL and (CAR X) is A.

The LAMBDA form is a way of assigning local or temporary values to variables. The LAMBDA form consists of a LAMBDA function followed by some arguments. A LAMBDA function is a list of three elements; for example,

```
(LAMBDA (X Y) (CONS Y X))
```

The second element is a list of lambda variables, the third is a form that uses those variables. Arguments may be added to a LAMBDA function to make a complete form according to the usual syntactic rule: (function arg1 arg2 . . .).

The result looks more complex than other forms, since the LAMBDA function is a list of three elements instead of just one atom like the other functions. An example of a complete LAMBDA form is:

```
((LAMBDA (X Y) (CONS Y X)) (QUOTE (A B C))
(QUOTE A))
```

The interpreter first evaluates the arguments. These values are then assigned to the corresponding variables on the lambda variables list. The form in which the lambda variables appear (the internal form) is then evaluated, and this value is then the value of the entire LAMBDA form. If the lambda variables had other values at the start, these values would be saved during evaluation of the internal form and then restored afterward.

In the example above, X will have the value (A B C) and Y will have the value A. Thus, the internal form, (CONS Y X), will have the value (A A B C), and this will be the value of the entire LAMBDA form.

The EXPR function is a function written by the Lisp programmer. The programmer can make any atom into a function by assigning to that atom a suitable Lisp expression (usually a LAMBDA function). This is usually done with the DE function (short for "define"). Below is an example of a simple EXPR function being defined and then used. In this example, TIMES means multiply.

```
(DE SQUARE (X) (TIMES X X))
(SQUARE 9)
```

The DE form above will assign to the atom SQUARE, an EXPR property with the value (LAMBDA (X) (TIMES X X)). When evaluating (SQUARE 9), the Lisp interpreter will first look up the definition of the EXPR function, as given on the property list of the atom, and then evaluate the function according to that definition. Thus, the value of (SQUARE 9) is 81.

RECURSIVE FUNCTIONS. A very useful property of Lisp is the ability to evaluate a recursively defined function, i.e., a function that uses its own name as part of its definition. For example,

```
(DE LAST (X) (COND
         ((ATOM (CDR X)) (CAR X))
         (T (LAST (CDR X)))     ))
```

where LAST searches a list of any length and returns the last element of that list. (ATOM (CDR.X)) is true only if X is a list of just one element. If X is a list of two or more elements, LAST calls itself and shortens the list by removing the first element. Eventually, the list is shortened to just one element.

Then (CAR K) is returned, which is the last element of a one-element list.

How can a recursively defined function be evaluated? When the Lisp interpreter is evaluating an EXPR function and it encounters another call of the same function, it simply obtains a pointer to the definition from the property list of the atom. The interpreter saves its place in the old definition by putting a pointer on an internal structure known as the "pushdown stack." The evaluation procedure is exactly the same, whether the function happens to be the same as the one currently being evaluated or a different one. During evaluation the Lisp interpreter only reads the expression representing a function, but does not modify it in any way. Therefore, exactly the same list structure can be used by the Lisp interpreter at different levels of its evaluation procedure. This just means that the pushdown stack will contain several different pointers to the same expression. In the preceding example of the function LAST, the recursion depth will be equal to the number of elements in the list being searched.

A Lisp function may also call itself at several different places in its definition (possibly with different arguments). A Lisp function may also call itself implicitly; i.e., function FNA may call FNB, which then calls FNA again. One must take care that a recursive function is not given a circular definition.

THE RECLAIMER. The "reclaimer," or "garbage collector," performs dynamic storage alocation in Lisp. It periodically searches memory to locate list structures that are no longer needed. The memory cells in this "garbage" are then added to the "list of available space" to be used in making new list structures. Reclaimers are also used in most other list-processing languages.

**A Practical Lisp Program.** As a practical example to illustrate the use of Lisp, we will now write a program to differentiate algebraic expressions. First, let us choose the notation to be used for the algebraic expressions. Polish prefix notation is quite convenient. Variables may be indicated by letters of the alphabet such as X, Y, and Z. Constants may be indicated by other letters or by numbers. These may be added or multiplied by the special symbols PLUS and TIMES as used in Polish prefix notation:

```
(PLUS X A)   = X + A
(TIMES 3 X)  = 3X
```

Larger expressions may be built up by nesting these symbols:

(PLUS 3 (TIMES X X)) = 3 + $X^2$

The program will carry out four mathematical rules of differentiation:

1. $dX/dX = 1$.
2. $dA/dX = 0$.
3. $d$(PLUS $Y$ $Z$)$/dX$ = (PLUS $(dY/dX)$ $(dZ/dX)$).
4. $d$(TIMES $Y$ $Z$)$/dX$ = (PLUS (TIMES $dY/dX$ $Z$) (TIMES $dZ/dX$ $Y$)).

The program to carry out these rules is quite straightforward. The top-level function, called DIF, takes two variables—E the expression to be differentiated and X the variable of differentiation. Also, DIF uses a conditional form to decide which of the four rules should be applied. The fifth alternative is an error message, in case none of the four rules applies.

Each of the four subfunctions, DIF1, DIF2, DIF3, and DIF4, applies one of the four rules of differentiation as given above: DIF1 and DIF2 have no arguments, but DIF3 and DIF4 each take three arguments, E2, E3, and X; E2 and E3 are the second and third elements of the expression E, which was given to DIF. One may see in DIF the form (CAR (CDR E)), which obtains the second element of E, and also the form (CAR (CDR (CDR E))), which obtains the third element of E.

The last subfunction, DIF5 is called by DIF4 to handle the innermost part of the TIMES differentiation rule.

Note that DIF3 and DIF5 call DIF, the top-level function. Thus, DIF is a recursive function. This recursive design allows DIF to differentiate expressions that are nested to any depth. Thus, this simple program can handle algebraic expressions of arbitrary complexity. Here is the program listing.

```
(DE DIF (E X) (COND
  ((EQ E X) (DIF1))
  ((ATOM E) (DIF2))
  ((EQ (CAR E) (QUOTE PLUS))
     (DIF3 (CAR(CDR E)) (CAR(CDR(CDR E))) X))
  ((EQ (CAR E) (QUOTE TIMES))
     (DIF4 (CAR(CDR E)) (CAR(CDR(CDR E))) X))
  (T(CONS (QUOTE ERROR) E)) ))

(DE DIF1 () 1)
```

```
(DE DIF2 () 0)

(DE DIF3 (E2 E3 X) (CONS (QUOTE PLUS)
   (CONS (DIF E2 X)
   (CONS (DIF E3 X) NIL))) )

(DE DIF4 (E2 E3 X) (CONS (QUOTE PLUS)
   (CONS (DIF5 E2 E3 X)
   (CONS (DIF5 E3 E2 X) NIL ))) )

(DE DIF5 (E2 E3 X) (CONS (QUOTE TIMES)
   (CONS E2
   (CONS (DIF E3 X) NIL ))) )
```

Below is a use of DIF and the value that is returned by the computer. The problem is to differentiate $3X^2$:

```
(DIF (QUOTE (TIMES 3(TIMES X X))) (QUOTE X))
```

to get the result 6X

```
(PLUS(TIMES 3(PLUS(TIMES X 1) (TIMES X 1)))
(TIMES(TIMES X X)0))
```

It is obvious that this program could use a subroutine to simplify the answers.

## Other List Processing Languages.

IPL-V is the grandfather of all list-processing languages. It was developed by Allen Newell and his associates at the RAND Corporation and later at Carnegie-Mellon University. IPL is an acronym for Information Processing Language, a choice that reflects the lack of competition when the name was selected. IPL-V is the fifth member of the IPL family. It is also the most highly developed and the best known (IPL-V was designed but never implemented).

IPL-V was the first language to use lists made of memory cells linked with pointers, but garbage collection is the programmer's responsibility. IPL-V programs resemble assembly language in format.

Below is an IPL-V program to test if two symbols are equal, and to return one symbol if they are equal or the second symbol if they are not equal. This could be expressed in Lisp as a conditional form:

```
(COND ( (EQ X0 X1) X1) (T X0) )
```

Here is the IPL-V version:

| Name | PQ | Symbol | Link | Comments |
|---|---|---|---|---|
| E0 | | J2 | | Test if H0(0) = H0(1) |
| | 70 | 9-1 | | Branch if not equal |
| | 30 | H0 | | Pop H0 (= H0(0)–the communication cell) |
| 9-1 | | J0 | | Dummy instruction |

According to the conventions of IPL-V, there is a special memory cell called H0 (the communication cell), which is used to transmit arguments to subroutines. The H0 cell is actually the head cell of a pushdown list, so that any number of arguments may be stored there. The notation H0(0) is the top symbol on the H0 pushdown list, and H0(1),H0(2), ... refer to the deeper elements. Thus, if a subroutine such as the example above takes two arguments, they will be placed in H0(0) and H0(1) by the calling program, and the answer of the subroutine will be placed in H0(0).

Now let us consider the example above, where E0 is the name of the subroutine. After being defined, it can be called by this name. The call J2 is to an existing subroutine, called a "primitive," which tests the equality of the first two arguments. H0(0) and H0(1). If they are equal, the test cell H5 is set plus; otherwise, H5 is set minus. In the next instruction there is no name, but the P part which is 7 means "conditional branch." The Q part, 0, means direct rather than indirect addressing. This instruction calls for a branch to 9-1 if the test cell is minus or to the contents of the LINK field if the test cell is plus. If the LINK field is empty, the next instruction is assumed. Thus, the third instruction will be executed only if the arguments are equal.

The P part of the third instruction is 3, which means pop the pushdown list named by the symbol part. The Q part, 0, again means "direct addressing." Thus, the effect of this instruction is to pop H0. This means that all arguments in the list are moved up one place; H0(1) becomes H0(0), H0(2) becomes H0(1), etc. The symbol that was at the top of the list is lost. The last instruction, 9-1, is a dummy to provide a place to branch to, like the CONTINUE statement in Fortran.

This brief example will give the flavor of IPL-V. The programmer must follow certain conventions to save arguments, reclaim free storage cells, etc.

The programming language Comit was originally designed for research on the mechanical translation of Russian into English. It was based on the notations used by some linguists working on this problem. However, Comit has now been generalized into a general-purpose language sufficiently powerful to perform any data processing task. In addition to the usual list-processing advantages of automatic storage allocation and efficient manipulation of strings, Comit also has a pattern-matching capability.

Basic Comit notation is a production rule or rewrite rule. An example is:

```
THE + DOG = 1 + BIG + 2
```

This means that the computer must search a certain list called the workspace, until two adjacent atoms, THE and DOG, are found. These two atoms are then replaced by what is defined by the right half of the production rule. The numbers refer to elements of the left-hand side; i.e., 1 + BIG + 2 evaluates to THE BIG DOG.

The left half of a rewrite rule defines a pattern that is to be found. The right half tells how to rearrange the elements of the pattern after it is found.

The left half can include various pattern variables in addition to specific atoms; for example, $1 means one atom of any type and $3 means three atoms. The right half may contain special symbols that specify complex operations in addition to rearrangements. A Comit program consists of a series of such rewrite rules.

The language Slip differs from other list-processing languages in two main ways: It is embedded in Fortran and it uses symmetric lists. Embedding in Fortran means that, except for a small number of assembly language subprograms, all Slip primitive functions are written in the form of Fortran subprograms. Slip programs are written as a series of Fortran subroutine calls. This makes it easy to use standard Fortran subroutines with a Slip program.

Data is represented in memory by Slip cells. A Slip cell is two or three memory words (depending on the implementation) that are physically adjacent. The cell represents one element of a list. It contains a pointer to the next cell on the list, a pointer to the preceding cell on the list, and some alphanumeric data. The data may be an atom or the name of another list.

Since Slip cells contain pointers in both directions, it is as easy to search a Slip list backward as forward. This is why Slip lists are called "symmetric." Many Slip functions come in pairs, one forward and one backward. This property is extremely convenient for certain types of list processing. In most other list-processing languages the programmer must save a pointer to the start of a list and start from there if any backtracking is necessary.

Below is a sample Slip program. This program searches a list structure of English sentences, called TEXT, and counts the number of times the word CARL appears.

```
    DATA CARL/4HCARL/
    K=LRDROV(TEXT)
    J=-1
100 J=J+1
200 X=ADVSER(K,F)
    IF(F) 500,300,500
300 IF(EQUAL(CARL,X)) 200,100,200
500 CONTINUE
```

The syntax of the program is, of course, the same as Fortran. The instruction ADVSER is a Slip subroutine, which contains an advancing mechanism that searches a list structure. Every time it is called, it advances one cell and returns the data part of that cell. The instruction LRDROV initializes the advancing mechanism on a particular list structure.

The language Pop-2 is a descendant of Lisp and Algol. It was developed by R. J. Popplestone in the Department of Machine Intelligence and Perception at the University of Edinburgh. Programs written in Pop-2 look very much like Algol. Pop-2 is a very general language with many ingenious features. It might be described as a combination of Algol and Lisp plus every other feature known to man. The pushdown stack is accessible to the programmer. The compiler is a subroutine that can be called by a program. An automatic reclaimer is available. Pop-2 is also extensible in terms of data structures. The programmer can invent new data structures, and the programs to handle them, with little difficulty. Pop-2 has been described as a "kitchen sink" language. This powerful language has been used for many years by research workers at Edinburgh.

**Recent Progress.** The trend in the 1970s is toward the development of list-processing languages with capabilities in four main areas:

1. *Data types*: The programmer is allowed to define new data types in a convenient way. Examples are *n*-tuples, unordered sets, statements in a mathematical language, statements in a computer language.

2. *Control structures*: Multiarchies are now replacing hierarchies. In a hierarchy the main program calls subroutines, each subroutine calls sub-subroutines, etc. The program control structure is like that of a tree. Multiarchies allow greater freedom. In some languages, any subroutine may call any other. Two subroutines may be executed simultaneously (simulated). Conditional interrupts, known as "demons" are sometimes used.

3. *Deduction*: Built-in deductive mechanisms allow the programmer to specify what result is desired without telling the computer exactly how to do it. Planner, Conniver, Micro-Planner, and Popler are four languages with powerful deductive capabilities.

4. *Pattern matching*: The style of matching found in Comit has been extended in other languages. Patterns for matching are known as "skeletons," or "templates." They can be specified by the programmer in a very natural way. They can then be used for automatic search of large data bases.

REFERENCES

1961. Newell, A. (Ed.). *Information Processing Language-V Manual.* Englewood Cliffs, N.J.: Prentice-Hall.

1964. Information International Inc. *The Programming Language LISP: Its Operation and Applications.* Cambridge, Mass.: The M.I.T. Press.

1967. Rosen, Saul (Ed.). *Programming Systems and Languages.* New York: McGraw-Hill.

1967. Weissman, C. *LISP 1.5 Primer.* Belmont Calif.: Dickerson Pub. Co.

1968. Quam, L. H. *Stanford LISP 1.6 Manual.* (Stanford U. Artificial Intelligence Program.) Stanford, Calif.: Stanford University Press.

1969. Knuth, Donald E. *The Art of Computer Programming,* vol 1. Reading, Mass.: Addison-Wesley.

1971. Burstall, R. M., J. S. Collins, and R. J. Popplestone. *Programming in POP-2.* Edinburgh University Press.

1971. Findler, N. V., J. L. Pfaltz, and H. J. Bernstein. *Four High Level Extensions of Fortran IV: SLIP, AMPPL-II, TREETRAN and SYMBOLANG.* New York: Spartan Books.

1972. Feldman, J. A., et al. "Recent Developments in Sail—An Algol Based Language for Artificial Intelligence," Proceedings of the Fall Joint Computer Conference.

1973. Bobrow, Daniel G., and Bertram Raphael. "New Programming Languages for AI Research," Xerox Research Center, Palo Alto, Calif., Report CSL-73-2, August.

J. R. SLAGLE, J. K. DIXON, AND T. L. JONES

# LISTS AND LIST PROCESSING

For articles on related subjects *see* ARTIFICIAL INTELLIGENCE; LIST PROCESSING LANGUAGES; and STORAGE ALLOCATION.
For articles on related terms *see* DATA TYPE; GARBAGE COLLECTION; POINTER; and SYMBOL MANIPULATION.

Anyone who uses a digital computer to solve a problem must go through three major phases:

1. *Representation*: the creation of formal objects that are understandable by an existing computer system and adequately represent interesting aspects of the real problem.

2. *Computation*: actual operation of the computer to manipulate the data and produce results.

3. *Interpretation*: translation of the computer-produced results into meaningful information about the real problem situation.

Most discussions of the use of computers focus upon the second phase, computation, which concerns the operation of the computer itself. However, representation and its inverse, interpretation, play a crucial role in making the calculation meaningful.

**The Representation Problem.** Some obvious or "natural" representations exist for most problems. For example, in the most common computer applications—business tasks such as payroll preparation and scientific tasks such as matrix calculations—the natural representation for much of the significant data is numeric; numbers appear on paychecks and as parameters in scientific equations. Since these same numbers can be stored and manipulated in computer registers, the numbers merely stand for themselves, so that the representation and interpretation phases are trivial and may be ignored.

In nonarithmetic problems, on the other hand, representation is frequently the most crucial phase. Fig. 1 gives some examples of primarily nonarithmetic tasks for which computers have been used. Note that there is no obvious way of uniquely

| Task | Natural Representation | Example | List Representation |
|---|---|---|---|
| Symbolic mathematics | Mathematical notation | $\int_0^{\infty} \frac{e^{-x}}{x^2+1}\,dx$ | (INTEGRAL 0 INF DX (DIV(EXP E(MINUS X)) (PLUS(EXP X 2)1))) |
| Information retrieval | Bibliographic data in standard citation form | Duda, R.O., and Hart, P.E., *Scene Analysis and Image Processing,* John Wiley & Sons (1973) | (AUTHOR((DUDA R O)(HART P E)) TITLE(SCENE ANALYSIS AND IMAGE PROCESSING) PUBLISHER WILEY DATE 1973) |
| Picture processing | Photographs |  | (FACE(EYES SHIFTY) (EARS POINTED) (BEARD BUSHY) (SHAPE ROUND) (NOSE WIDE) (GLASSES RIMMED) (HAIR THICK DARK PARTED |
| Chess playing | Chess publication notation |  | ((WHITE(KING Q7) (KNIGHT Q4 KN4) (BISHOP K8 KR4)) (BLACK(KING KN2) (PAWN KR2))) |

**Fig. 1.** Representations.

representing by numbers the data from the examples in the third column of Fig. 1. Of course numeric codes can be invented—e.g., all possible chess positions could be enumerated in some systematic way so that the last example in Fig. 1 might be identified as position number 3,275,117—but such arbitrary encodings tend to obscure significant aspects of the problem situation, and thus complicate the tasks of programming and debugging.

For most research purposes, it is preferable to program directly in terms of nonnumeric data. Such data would have to be able to represent significant aspects of many different problem domains in a natural, intuitive manner, and at the same time would have to have sufficient uniform formal structure to permit manipulation within a single general-purpose programming system. Several data types, such as strings, trees, and graphs, have been proposed for such purposes and are available in various programming languages. However, the most familiar and widely used standard nonnumeric data type is the *list*.

Lists provide a convenient way for keeping track of things in our everyday life: shopping lists, laundry lists, lists of things to be done, and so on. Similarly, lists provide a convenient way for representing arbitrary nonnumeric information in a computer. The last column of Fig. 1 shows how the knowledge in the natural representations of the examples might be encoded into lists.

The remainder of this article will deal with the list as a formal data type, and will explain how it is represented and manipulated in a computer.

## Lists

BASIC CONCEPTS. In everyday informal use, the simplest written list is usually a sequence of items, one written below another. For example:

Milk
Eggs
Butter
Jam
Bread

For computer use, a simple list is also defined as a sequence of items. However, the meanings of the terms "item" and "sequence" must be more precise. The most elementary items, sometimes called "atomic symbols," usually are strings of upper-case alphanumeric symbols that do not contain certain special punctuation characters, such as spaces. The sequence of items is enclosed in parentheses as delimiters for readability by both the computer and the programmer. Items within the list may be separated by placement on separate lines, or they may appear on the same line to save space if they are separated by spaces or commas. Thus, the preceding informal grocery list could be represented by the computer list

(MILK EGGS BUTTER
JAM BREAD)

Note that the appearance of this machine-readable data structure is extremely close to the "natural" data representation.

Thus far we have been concerned with the appearance of lists on paper, i.e., external to the computer. When a list is read into computer memory, all the information in the list—namely, the list items *and their sequence*—must be captured by the internal computer representation. A key property of internal list representation is that *the sequencing information is stored explicitly with each list item* and does not depend upon the implicit sequencing of computer memory addresses. These explicit sequencing data are crucial for efficient list processing, because they play a key role in the operations of inserting and deleting items on lists. (See the later section entitled "List Processing.")

Each word in that portion of computer memory used for lists is divided into two parts called "fields": One contains a list item, and one contains a sequence pointer to the word containing the next item on the list. Such a memory word may be denoted by a rectangle, where the arrow indicates that the

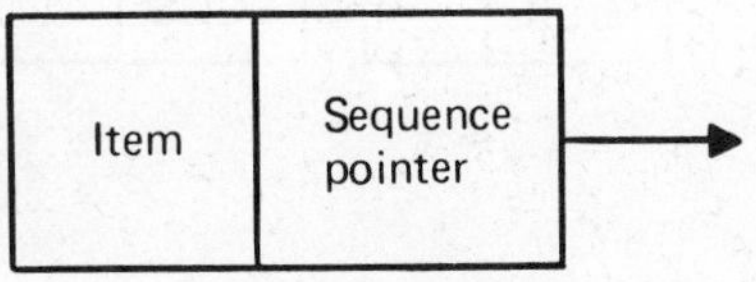


pointer field contains the address of another memory word. In this notation our grocery list looks like the illustration on the top of p. 788 where

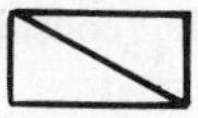

represents a special symbol used to mark the ends of lists. (We assume that atomic symbols always fit into item fields. Actually, these fields generally contain pointers to a part of memory where only atomic symbols are stored.)

## LISTS AND LIST PROCESSING

KINDS OF LISTS. The basic kind of list described above consisted simply of atomic symbols and forward pointers. We now define some more complex kinds of lists that have been found useful, either because of their ability to represent conveniently more complex data or because of the efficiency with which they may be manipulated.

*List Structures*. Suppose the grocery list is modified to read

Milk
Eggs
Butter
Strawberry Jam
Bread

An obvious formal representation,

(MILK EGGS BUTTER STRAWBERRY JAM BREAD)

might result in a shopping basket containing, among other things, a jar of cherry jam and a single strawberry! To resolve this ambiguity, the fourth item on the list can itself be made into a list:

(MILK EGGS BUTTER (STRAWBERRY JAM) BREAD)

or, in internal notation,

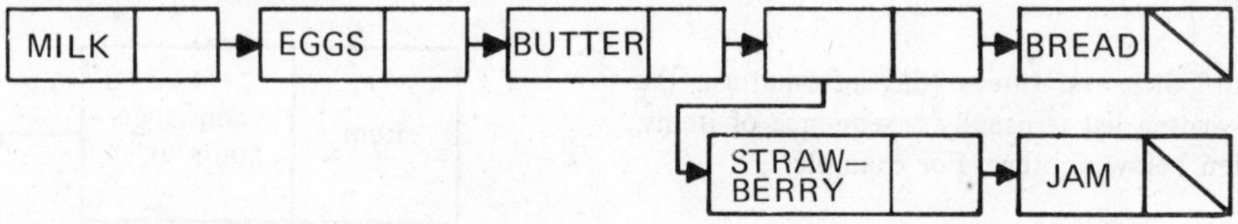


Thus, a *list structure* may be defined (recursively) as *a list, each item of which is either an atomic symbol or a list structure.*

List structures may be nested to any finite depth. For example, consider a more complete version of our grocery list:

2 qts milk
6 eggs
$^1/_4$ lb butter
1 jar strawberry jam
1 rye bread

The representation phase now consists of setting up some conventions:

1. The grocery list will contain a sublist for each food.
2. Each sublist will contain two items: a food and its quantity.
3. Each food will be represented either by its name or by a list of the name followed by modifiers.
4. Each quantity will be represented either by a number or by a list on which the number is followed by its units.

The resulting list structure, in external and internal notations, is shown in Fig. 2.

External Representation

```
((MILK (2 QUARTS))
 (EGGS 6)
 (BUTTER (.25 POUNDS))
 ((JAM STRAWBERRY)(1 JAR))
 ((BREAD RYE) 1))
```

Internal Representation

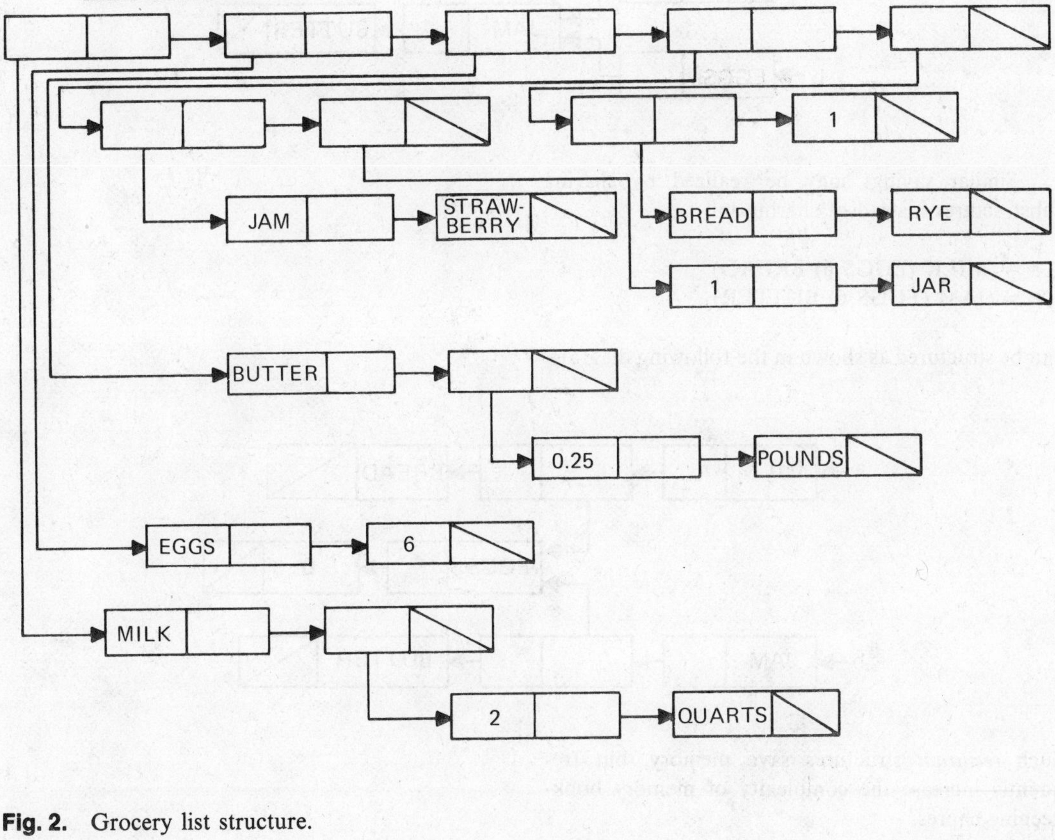


**Fig. 2.** Grocery list structure.

*Reentrant Lists.* Suppose we wish to consider simultaneously two alternative shopping lists:

a = (MILK JAM BUTTER)

and

b = (EGGS JAM BUTTER)

Instead of needing the six memory words in the following diagram, all the information can be cap-

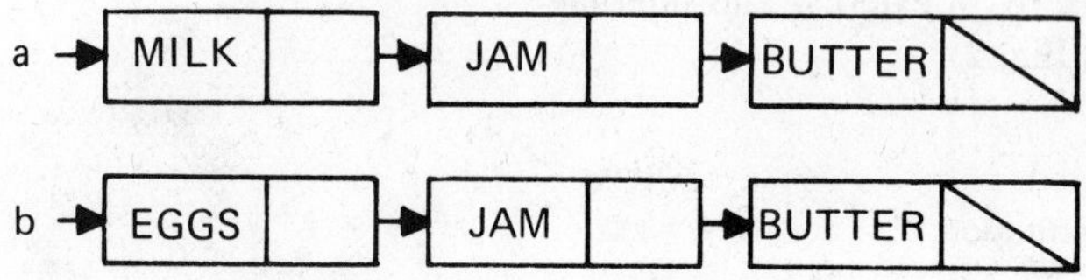


tured with four words by sharing the "tails" of the two lists:

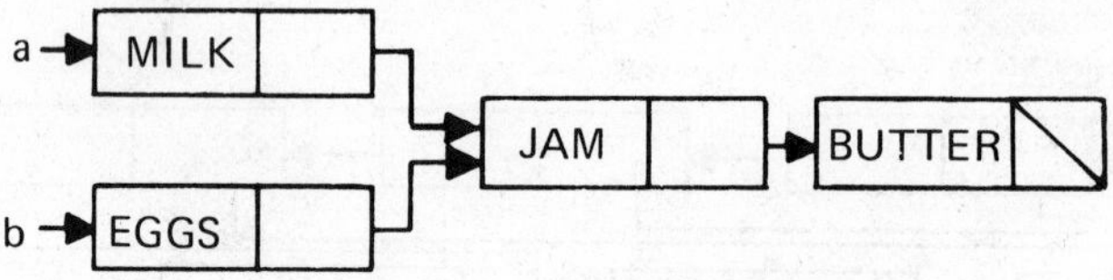


Similar savings may be realized by sharing substructures instead of sharing tails; e.g.,

a = (MILK (EGGS 6) BREAD)
b = (JAM (EGGS 6) BUTTER)

can be structured as shown in the following diagram.

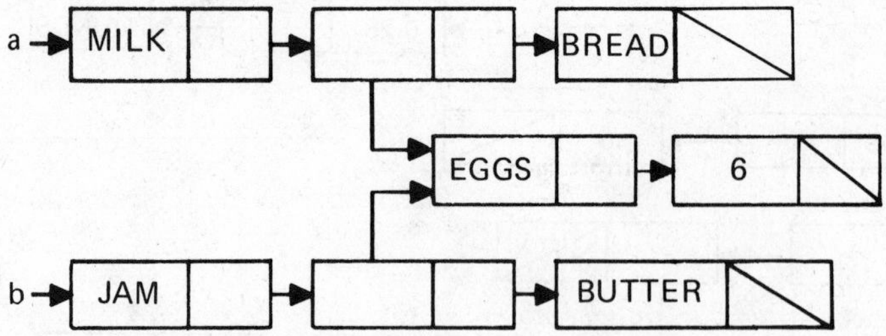


Such *reentrant* structures save memory, but frequently increase the complexity of memory bookkeeping chores.

*Circular Lists.* Circular lists look like the next structures. Unless the first, or *header,* cell in such

and

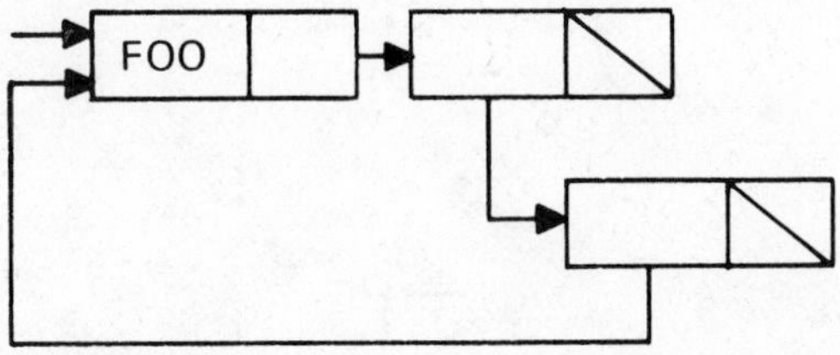


lists is specifically denoted, circular lists cannot be described by the usual external notation. They are, therefore, rarely used in normal list-processing operations because any attempt to copy, search through, or print out such structures could create endless looping.

*Symmetric Lists.* The lists discussed thus far contain only forward sequencing information. Occasionally it is useful to go from the location of one list item to the preceding item. At such times, *symmetric* lists—*lists with sequencing pointers to previous as well as subsequent items*—may be useful. A common implementation uses a pair of memory words for each symmetric list cell; one word of the pair contains the list item, and the other contains both forward and backward sequencing pointers. For example, the symmetric list

(EGGS MILK BUTTER)

would look internally like

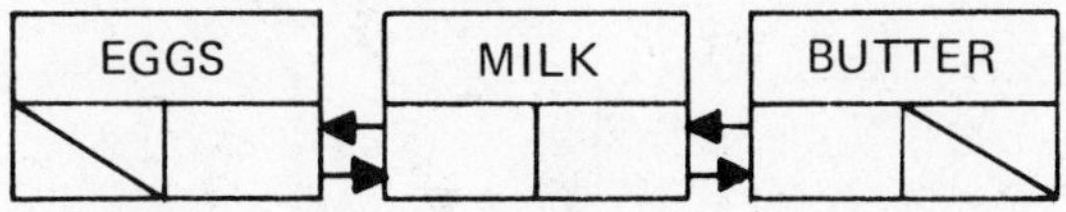


*Multiple Association Lists.* The multiple association list is a generalization of the symmetric list concept. Why restrict the number of pointers per cell to one or two? Why require the pointers to identify only the (forward or backward) adjacent item? In at least one widely used language (called "$L^6$" or "L-sixth," which was developed at the Bell Laboratories) the user may specify during the problem representation phase the number, arrangement, and use of sequencing pointers, with considerable generality. Of course such flexibility carries with it a responsibility for considerable detailed bookkeeping, since many automated features of simple list-processing systems depend upon more rigid, predefined pointer conventions.

*Property Lists.* The term "property list" refers to a list in which the data items are organized in a particular way, rather than a list that has some special internal pointer structure. Each property list is considered to describe some object or concept. The first, third, fifth, and every odd-numbered item on the list names a *property* or *attribute* of a relevant class of objects, and the item following the property name is the particular *value* of that property for the described object. For example, the following property list might be associated with a baseball:

(SHAPE SPHERE SIZE (4 INCHES)
COLOR WHITE MATERIAL HORSEHIDE)

Property lists provide a convenient way to represent an arbitrary amount of information about objects. The order of the attribute-value pairs on a list is generally ignored; one simply scans the list for a desired attribute, and returns the next item on the list as the corresponding value.

*Pushdown List.* The term "pushdown list" refers to the way a list is used, rather than to either its information organization or pointer structure. Pushdown lists are only accessed from the front, i.e., only the first element is ever read, inserted, or deleted. This restricted use permits pushdown lists to be implemented in a different, more efficient manner than other lists. Therefore, their use is beyond the scope of this article.

**List Processing.** The term "list processing" refers to the collection of operations that must be performed on list-structured data in the course of solving a problem. These operations are usually specified by statements in some programming formalism, called a "list-processing language." Here we consider the basic data-manipulation operations themselves, and see how they can be carried out by altering the contents of fields in the memory of a computer.

INSERT. A fundamental advantage of list structures over other data forms is the ease with which items may be inserted into lists. To add an item to the middle of an array, one must copy and move half the elements of the array, whereas to add an item to the middle of a list, one must merely change the contents of two memory cells.

For example, suppose we wish to insert EGGS after BUTTER on the list (MILK BUTTER JAM BREAD). In internal notation (with small letters

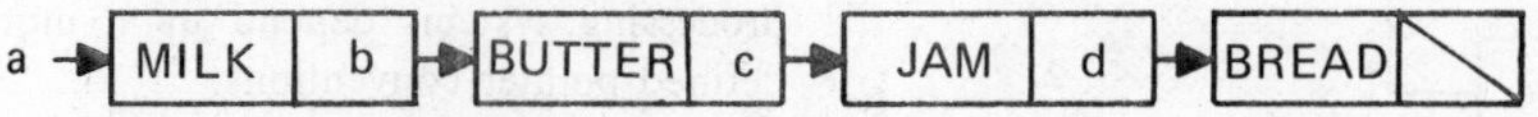


(1)

naming the individual computer words), we have, initially, the arrangement in (1). The insertion operations requires us to obtain some unused cell (say, "e") and place the new item, EGGS, in its item field.

Now the insertion may be completed by changing the pointer field of the cell containing BUTTER from "c" to "e," and placing "c" in the pointer field of "e" to link back into the rest of the list, as in

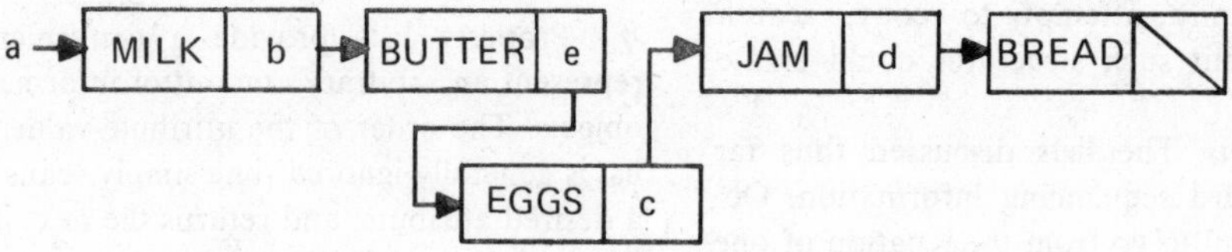


(2)

arrangement (2). This resulting structure represents the desired list:

(MILK BUTTER EGGS JAM BREAD)

List *structures* may be built up almost as easily as simple lists. Suppose instead of merely adding eggs to the list (1), we wanted to specify a half-dozen eggs. First we would have to build up a sublist describing the new item; say, in cells x, y, z, and w.

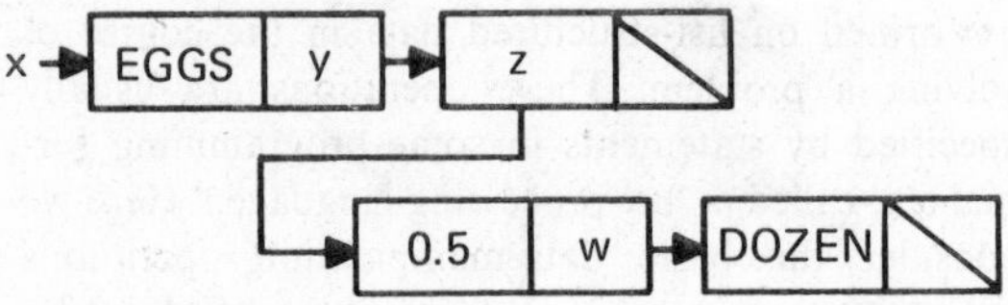


One additional cell, "f," is needed to contain the name of the sublist, "x," in its item field:

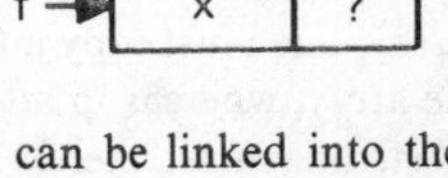

Now "f" can be linked into the original list in the same way that "e" was in the previous example:

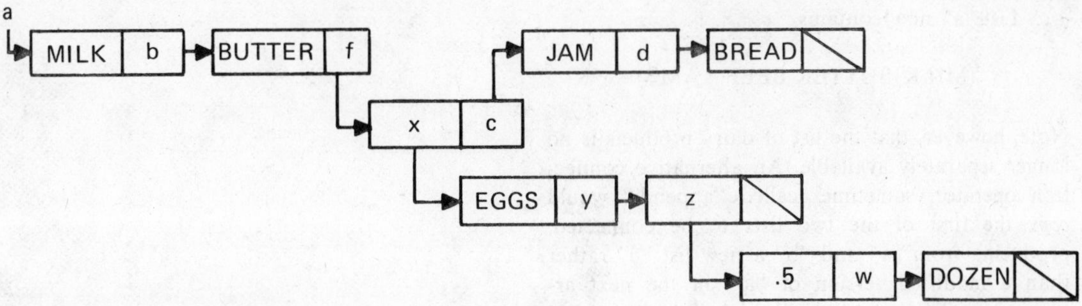


The external representation is

(MILK BUTTER (EGGS (0.5 DOZEN)) JAM BREAD)

as desired.

DELETE. Deletion of list items is even easier than insertion. Because no new cells need be obtained, only some pointers need be changed. For example, to delete BUTTER from structure (2), we have only to replace pointer "b" by "e" in cell "a", as shown in the diagram. Cell "b" is now no longer needed, and it is therefore available for other uses. The fact that it currently points into the active data at "e" is immaterial because it will not be noticed when we follow the pointer structure beginning at "a."

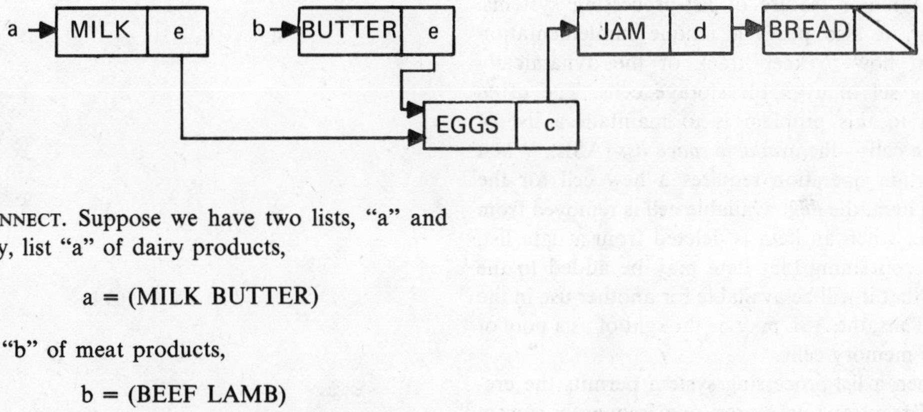


CONNECT. Suppose we have two lists, "a" and "b"; say, list "a" of dairy products,

a = (MILK BUTTER)

and list "b" of meat products,

b = (BEEF LAMB)

and we wish to combine them into a single shopping list. One way would be to find the end of list "a" and link it into "b," changing

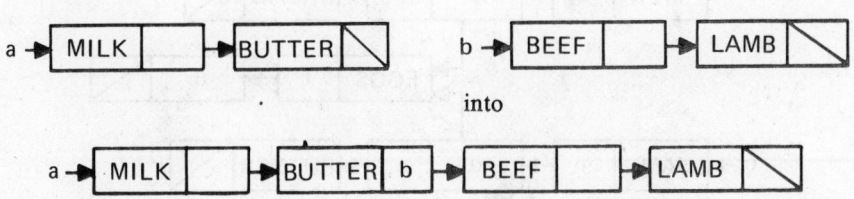


into

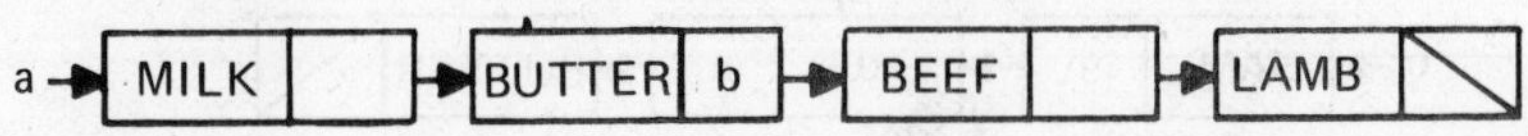

List "a" now contains

(MILK BUTTER BEEF LAMB)

Note, however, that the list of dairy products is no longer separately available. An alternative connection operator, sometimes called "append," would *copy* the first of the two lists to be connected, producing from "a" and "b" a new list "c" rather than a modified version of "a," in the next arrangement. This approach allows "a," "b," and "c"

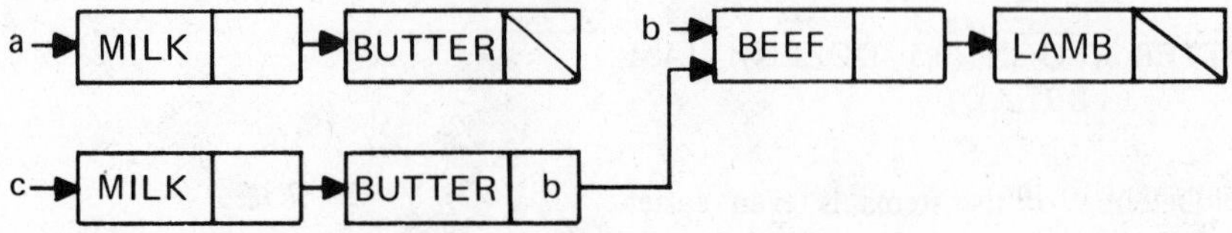


to be referenced independently. Of course subsequent changes to the structure of "b" must be undertaken with care, since such changes would also affect "c."

**Storage Management.** As we have seen in the preceding examples, memory cells may be added to or deleted from list structures in the course of a calculation. This ability for *dynamic storage allocation* is a major feature of list-processing systems. However, it also poses a unique implementation problem: how to keep track of the dynamically changing set of available storage cells. The usual solution to this problem is to maintain a list of available cells—the *available space list* (ASL). When an insertion operation requires a new cell for the inserted item, the next available cell is removed from the ASL; when an item is deleted from a data list, the cell containing that item may be added to the ASL so that it will be available for another use in the future. Thus, the ASL may be thought of as a pool of inactive memory cells.

When a list-processing system permits the creation of reentrant structures, one frequently cannot tell whether or not deleted cells should be returned to the ASL. Let us reconsider an earlier example:

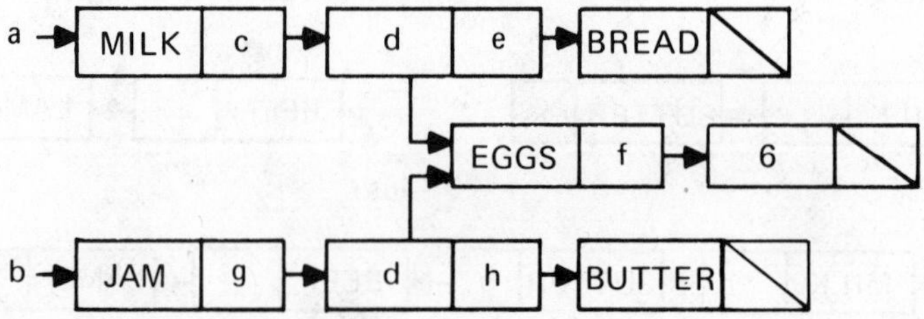

Suppose we wish to delete the eggs from list "a," leaving just (MILK BREAD), as shown in the diagram below. Clearly, cell "c" is no longer needed

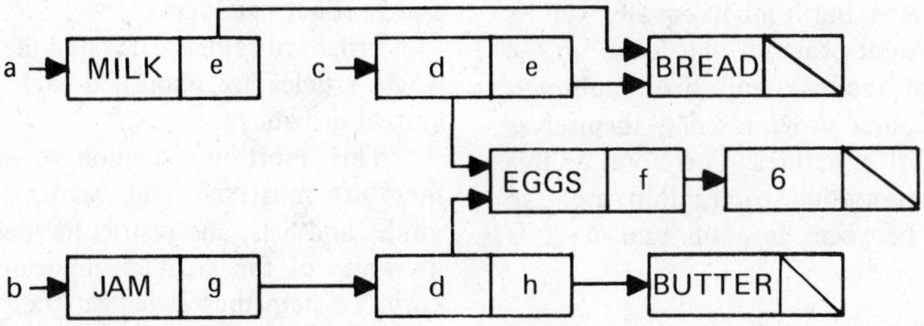


and may be returned to the ASL. But what about cells "d" and "f"? They had better not be disturbed because they are still part of list structure "b."

Subsequently, we may decide to delete the eggs from list "b" also, reducing it to (JAM BUTTER), and of course returning cell "g" to the ASL, thus:

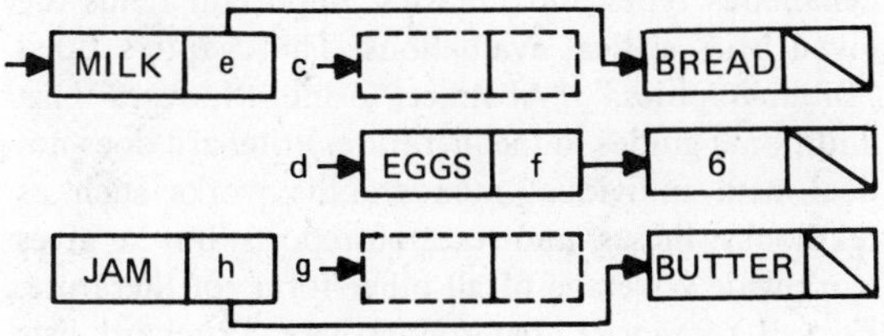


But now what about cells "d" and "f"? Unless they are returned to the ASL, they will be lost forever to the system. This kind of bug in some early list-processing programs caused memory to seem to shrink away and disappear during a computation.

This problem, called the "responsibility problem"—how to assign responsibility for returning cells to the ASL—has been solved in various ways. A trivial solution is simply to forbid reentrant structures, and automatically to return all detached cells to the ASL whenever anything is deleted. Another approach has been to give complete responsibility (and control) to the programmer, requiring him explicitly to erase abandoned cells to prevent their loss.

The *reference count method* is a novel approach in which each shared substructure contains a number indicating how many structures access it. This additional bookkeeping provides enough information for the system to decide when cells on a sublist may be returned to the ASL.

A well-known solution to the responsibility problem is based upon a technique called "garbage collection." In this approach, abandoned cells—the garbage—such as cells "d" and "f" in the preceding example, are simply ignored until they are needed, i.e., until the ASL is completely exhausted. At that point, a special program—the garbage collector—is invoked to find all the garbage and assemble it into a new ASL.

**New Directions.** List-processing techniques have been in wide use since about 1960 and have provided the basis for much of the research in such fields as artificial intelligence and computational logic. Recent advances in computer science suggest some modifications and extensions of the techniques that are currently evolving. We conclude this article by mentioning some of these new influences.

PAGING. A large list-structured memory is extremely inefficient when used in a paged memory such as that common in current time-sharing environments. This problem has been partially overcome by having separate ASLs for each hardware page, thereby requiring more complex bookkeeping procedures.

INTERACTIVE SYSTEMS. Time-shared use of list-processing techniques makes powerful new debugging methods possible. It also substantially increases the complexity of the operating system.

NEW DATA TYPES. Programmers are beginning to move beyond lists to new symbolic data types such as sets. Methods for representing such types and techniques for implementing the basic operations one wishes to perform with them are currently being studied.

PROCEDURAL REPRESENTATION. Many researchers now believe that the best way to represent certain real concepts in a computer is not by static data items such as numbers or lists, but rather directly by *procedures* or programs in some appropriate language. For example, the volume of a box might be represented by a number telling how many cubic inches the box contains, but it might equally well be represented by an Algol program that looks up the three dimensions of the box and then multiplies them together. Of course programs may themselves be represented by list structures. Therefore, as this new mode of representation comes into use, the classic distinction between program and data is beginning to blur.

REFERENCES

1968. Bobrow, D. G. (Ed.). *Symbol Manipulation Languages and Techniques*, North Holland.

B. RAPHAEL

# LITERATURE IN COMPUTING

For article on related subject *see* COPYRIGHTS AND PATENTS, COMPUTER ASPECTS OF.

Prior to the late 1940s the only computer literature concerned analog computers (then called "analyzers"), punched-card machines, and calculations made with pencil and paper or desk calculators. No periodicals were devoted to the subject. The literature was scattered in the publications of mathematics, statistics, physics, electrical engineering, education, and the earth sciences, especially astronomy. At that time a few books—for instance, Whittaker and Robinson (*Calculus of Observations*), Scarborough (*Numerical Mathematical Analysis*), and Eckert (*Punched Card Methods in Scientific Computation*)—could be said to deal exclusively with computing. Even the literature of science fiction contained no foreshadowing of the stored program digital computer.

Between 1945 and 1964 the situation changed dramatically with the appearance of more than 300 computer periodicals and about as many books. By 1972 the total number of periodicals had passed 600 worldwide, more than half in the United States, and books in print on computers exceeded 1,000. (Periodicals seem to be doubling in number every four to six years, as compared with the doubling period of 10 to 14 years for science and technology generally.) In addition, there is a wide variety of other literature such as research reports, trade publications, theses, patents, proceedings of conferences, abstracts and indexes, glossaries, handbooks, data compilations, and product catalogs.

Pritchard (1) has estimated that 40,000 to 50,000 single articles are published each year, with a 10% annual growth rate.

This short introduction to such an array of literature must refer the reader to comprehensive guides and lists, and restrict its specific comments to literature of the greatest importance in each category. To help the reader get the publications mentioned, a list of addresses follows the references at the end of the article.

## Bibliographic and Basic Literature

GUIDES AND LISTS. Pritchard (1) is the best and most comprehensive guide. Each of 26 chapters in this book deals with a different form of computer literature, ranging from those that report original work through abstracts and bibliographies to miscellaneous types and libraries. Important items are given brief critical evaluations. The chapters titled "Bibliographies," "Abstracts," and "Indexes" list additional guides to the literature. Pritchard does not deal with individual monographic works such as textbooks, theses, and research reports, but he gives worldwide coverage of all other forms of literature. For all categories that follow here, Pritchard lists more specific titles than the few examples listed in this article.

Second only to Pritchard is Carter (2), a master reference to information sources in the computer sciences. It is an annotated "finding" tool essential to reference librarians, indispensable to professional information seekers, and highly useful to generalists. Some 900 basic information sources have been given a critical evaluation based on the author's extensive knowledge and understanding of the field. The sources are listed in ten categories. The first two are human: Professional Organizations, and Research and Information Centers. The remaining eight are literature: Bibliographies and Bibliographic Aids; Conference Literature; Encyclopedias, Anthologies, and Surveys; Vocabulary; Directories and Catalogs; Handbooks and Manuals; Computer Industry; and Journals and Other Periodicals.

Couger (3) annually lists all the books in print that are useful in teaching business applications of the computer. He classifies the books as to purpose; e.g., introductions, programming, and systems analysis. The principal classes omitted are those having to do with mathematics and the design of computers.

The largest bibliography covering computer books, pamphlets, and reports is the *International Computer Bibliography* (4). More than 7,000 items are listed, with author and subject indexes. Annotations are in English, German, or French. Coverage of European work, both East and West, is particularly good.

The first 20 years of periodical literature, conference proceedings, and books with chapters by individual authors are covered selectively by W. W. Youden (5,6). Articles are listed by publication, by author, and by title permuted into a Kwic index, but are not annotated or abstracted.

The most useful bibliographies are those that list the publications relating to a specific field or that critically annotate each entry. The abstract journals listed in the following section of this article publish bibliographies at irregular intervals. The articles in *Computing Surveys* or annual reviews will often have reference lists that amount to comprehensive bibliographies. The ACM Special Interest Group newsletters will sometimes publish bibliographies.

All regularly produced serials in the field of computers and their applications are listed in *A World List of Computer Periodicals* (7). This includes periodicals, newsletters, looseleaf data books (which are regularly updated), regularly produced directories, and book series that appear under a common title (e.g., *Advances in Computers*). The first edition covers 1916 to 1970. A second edition is in preparation.

Periodical lists giving publisher's addresses are printed annually in *Computing Reviews, Data Processing Digest, Computer Abstracts*, and in each issue of *New Literature on Automation*.

There is no comprehensive listing of miscellaneous literature, although Pritchard (1) gives some suggestions and hints for searching. Publications catalogs of the principal computer societies list their available conference and symposia proceedings, and reports of their technical and special interest divisions.

ABSTRACTS. As with all technical and scientific publications, more computer literature is published than anyone can read. Furthermore, although most of the significant material appears in a few "core" journals, there is much relevant material in journals of other disciplines, this being particularly true because the extensive use of computing by all scientific and engineering activities results in much computer literature being interdisciplinary. Current abstract services ameliorate this problem of volume and scatter of computer literature.

The seven principal abstract services are listed below. They all overlap in their coverage of periodicals, conference proceedings, research reports, patents, books, movies, and academic theses, but no one service attempts to cover everything. All are issued monthly, have indexes, and regularly publish cumulative indexes.

*Computer Abstracts* (8). United Kingdom and international orientation. Strong in applications.

*Computing Reviews* (9). United States orientation. Strong in programming, software, mathematics. Unique in that reviews are critical and signed.

*New Literature on Automation* (10). International orientation. Strong in business data processing. Abstracts may be in the language of the article. All titles given in English, German, French, and Spanish.

*Computer and Control Abstracts* (11). United States and United Kingdom orientation. Strong in computer hardware, control technology, and subjects related to electrical engineering.

*Data Processing Digest* (12). United States orientation. Strong in business systems and practices. Occasionally includes extended essays.

*Referativnyi Zhurnal Avtomatika Telemekhanika Vychislitel'naya Tekhnika* (13). Russian, East European, and Asian orientation. Strong in hardware and programming.

*Cybernetics Abstracts* (14). Translation of some of the abstracts from *Referativnyi Zhurnal Kibernetika*. Russian, East European, and Asian orientation. Strong in theory, mathematics, and applications.

GLOSSARIES AND DICTIONARIES. There are three authoritative glossaries: *American National Standard Vocabulary for Information Processing* (ANSI 1970): *Glossary of Terms Used in Automatic Data Processing* (British Standards Institution 1962); and *IFIP-ICC Vocabulary of Information Processing* (North Holland 1966). These overlap, but although the definitions are seldom identical, the conflicts are usually not substantive. The International Standards Organization is preparing a glossary based on these three, which may dissolve the differences.

*IFIP Guide to Concepts and Terms in Data Processing* (North Holland 1971) is an updated version of the earlier IFIP glossary.

## LITERATURE IN COMPUTING

The *IEEE Standard Dictionary of Electrical and Electronics Terms* (Wiley 1972) is an expanded glossary that includes computer-related terms.

Correspondence between terms in several natural languages will be found in the second volume of the *IFIP Guide* as well as in *Elsevier's Dictionary of Computers, Automatic Control and Data Processing* (Elsevier 1971), which gives English, Dutch, French, German, Italian, and Spanish, and *Four-Language Technical Dictionary of Data Processing, Computers, and Office Machinery* (Pergamon 1970), which gives English, German, French, and Russian.

ANNUAL REVIEWS. A few commercial firms specialize in the publication of annual reviews. "Annual" refers to the frequency of publication and not to the period reviewed. The contents are a collection of usually well-written articles, intermediate in length and comprehensiveness between journal articles and books, summarizing segments of the subject field. The selection as to what is to be covered in each volume seems to be random and chiefly dependent on the current interests of the editors and the availability of authors. The chief entries are *Advances in Computers* (Academic Press), *Annual Review in Automatic Programming* (Pergamon Press), *Advances in Information Systems Science* (Plenum Press), *Methods in Computational Physics* (Academic Press), and *Advances in Control Systems* (Academic Press). Since the articles are usually replete with references, they are good entry points for literature searches. In most cases each volume lists the contents of its predecessors.

INTRODUCTORY BOOKS. In 1974 Couger (3) listed 98 titles intended as introductory books to the field of computer science. The best for the intelligent and concerned person seeking a general understanding of computing are those by Crowley (*Understanding Computers*, McGraw-Hill, 1967), Gruenberger (*Computing: An Introduction*, Harcourt, Brace & World, 1969), and Rothman and Mosmann (*Computers and Society*, Science Research Associates, 1972). The best for a businessman or student of business seeking to understand how computers may be used are those by Awad (*Business Data Processing*, Prentice-Hall, 1968), Chapin (*Computers, A Systems Approach*, Van Nostrand, 1971), Davis (*Computer Data Processing*, McGraw-Hill, 1969), and Sanders (*Computers in Business, An Introduction*, McGraw-Hill, 1972). The mathematician, scientist, or engineer seeking broad understanding should start with Crowley, Hamming (*Computers and Society*, McGraw-Hill, 1972), Forsythe et al. (*Computer Science, A First Course*, Wiley, 1970), Ralston (*Introduction to Programming and Computer Science*, McGraw-Hill, 1971), or Rice and Rice (*Introduction to Computer Science*, Holt, Rinehart & Winston, 1969).

HANDBOOKS. There are only three important general handbooks on computing. Volume 2 of Grabbe (*Handbook of Automation, Computation, and Control*, Wiley, 1961) is sound on fundamentals, dated in some detail, and of course void on recent developments. Huskey & Korn (*Computer Handbook*, McGraw-Hill, 1962) covers components, theory, and applications. Klerer & Korn (*Digital Computer Users Handbook*, McGraw-Hill, 1967) covers programming, numerical techniques, statistical methods, and applications. All three have good bibliographies appropriate to their dates.

TEXTBOOKS. Textbooks on computing reflect the instructional demand and the efforts of almost 200 publishers to satisfy it. About a quarter of the computer-related textbooks in print deal with programming, the subject of Fortran being the most popular. Books on specific subjects are referred to in other articles in this work.

### Original Contributions

PERIODICALS. Three major types of periodicals may be distinguished on the basis of their character, objectives, and audience. Academic periodicals report original results, are refereed, and are published for the benefit of the authors' peers. Other commercial periodicals interpret original results for practitioners, are professionally edited for clarity and interest and occasionally for originality and precision. News publications are a form of commercial publication in which currency is the most significant criterion applied in content selection.

The leading English language academic periodicals are those of the principal societies: the *Journal* and *Communications* of the ACM; the *Computer Journal* of the BCS: *Transactions on Computers* of the IEEE Computer Society: *Mathematics of Computation* of the AMS; the SIAM journals on *Computing, Applied Mathematics*, and *Numerical Analysis*; and *Management Informatics* (formerly the *IAG Journal*). The two principal Russian academic periodicals are available in translation: (*Avtomatika i Telemekhanika (Automation and Remote Control*, Plenum Press), and *Zhurnal Vychislitel'noi Matematiki i Matematicheskoi Fiziki (USSR Computational Mathematics and Mathematical Physics*, Pergamon). Some academic periodicals are published commercially, notably by Academic Press, Elsevier, and Pergamon. The best of the commercially published academic periodicals, because of rigid reviewing, outstanding editing, and intra-corporate rewards to authors are the *IBM Journal of Research and Development*, the *IBM Systems Journal*, the *Bell System Technical Journal*, and the *Journal of Computer and Systems Sciences* (Academic Press), all equal in content quality to the best of the society journals.

The commercial periodical with the largest circulation, a reflection of the satisfaction of readers and advertisers, is *Datamation*. Others of less appeal and circulation in the United States are *Infosystems* (formerly *Business Automation*), *EDP Analyzer, Computer Design, Computer Decisions*, and *Computers and Automation*; and in the United Kingdom, *Data Processing* and *Data Systems*. On the basis that the technical content is not limited to original results, the *Computer Bulletin* of the BCS, *Data Management* of DPMA, the *Journal of Systems Management* of the AMS, *Computer* of the IEEE Computer Society, and *Computing Surveys* of the ACM must be categorized with commercial periodicals although in each case refereeing procedures are applied to the technical content.

Several of the commercial periodicals undertake to provide news coverage, but *Computerworld* (U.S.), *Computing* (U.K.), and *Computer Weekly* (U.K.), make news their principal reason for existence. This is also true of a family of overlapping news journals issued by EDP News Service, Inc.

House journals published by computer firms range down from the best, mentioned above, through mediocrity to pure puffery.

CONFERENCE PROCEEDINGS. Publication of papers in proceedings of professional conferences in the U.S. often takes the place of publication in academic periodicals. Pritchard (1) cites a 1958 study indicating that about half of the papers presented at conferences are never published except in their proceedings. Although the refereeing of conference papers is often not so strict as that applied by the leading academic journals, the material is often significant. The major regular conference is that sponsored each year by the American Federation of Information Processing Societies (AFIPS), the National Computer Conference, which in 1973 replaced the twice-yearly Joint Computer Conferences. The other important regular conferences are the annual meetings of the principal computer societies, the ACM, largely concerned with programming and the mathematics of computing; the IEEE Computer Society, more concerned with hardware than software; and the DPMA, concerned with applications of a business nature. Proceedings of other computer conferences are also published by other technical and scientific societies with central and peripheral relationships to the discipline. The proceedings of the conferences and symposia of the special interest groups of the ACM, both periodic and aperiodic, are particularly important to specialists. Those available are listed in each issue of the *Communications of the ACM*.

The International Federation for Information Processing (IFIP) publishes proceedings of its triennial congresses and of the irregular international conferences held by IAG (International Applications Group), the IFIP Administrative Data Processing Group.

The only regular conferences in the United Kingdom are the biennial Datafair of the BCS and the more frequent Infotech state-of-the-art seminars.

While conferences held at regular intervals develop a reasonable standard of quality of content or die, the occasional or one-time-only conference cannot depend for its quality on any tradition but even so may be outstanding when time, place, participants, and subject, by design or by luck come together in just the right way.

## Collections of Data

HARDWARE AND SOFTWARE INFORMATION SERVICES. Auerbach Information, Inc. publishes authoritative and comprehensive reference material on hardware and software. The major work is the 11-volume *Standard EDP Reports*, which gives detailed coverage of the characteristics, price, and performance of United States hardware. The presentation is uniform, the data is reliable, and the arrangement makes the material easy to use. Parts of this basic work are summarized in *Minicomputer Reports, Computer Notebook International*, and *Computer Characteristics Digest*. Other Auerbach reports in specialized areas are *Data Communications Reports, Communications Terminal Digest, Data Handling Reports, Graphic Processing Reports*, and *Time Sharing Reports*.

Datapro Research Corporation publishes an equally authoritative and reliable reference service covering hardware and software, titled *Datapro 70*, with supplements on minicomputers and banking automation.

GML Corporation publishes *Computer Characteristics Review*, a pocket-size summary tabulation of price and characteristics of United States, European, and Japanese hardware.

*Computers in Europe*, published by Computer Consultants, Ltd., covers European computers, but not with the depth or authority of the Auerbach reports on United States hardware.

*Auerbach Software Reports* give the details on applications packages. *Auerbach Software Notebook*, extracted from the *Standard EDP Reports*, covers operating systems, compilers, and the like.

The *ICP Quarterly* lists abstracts of commercially available software of all kinds, including systems software and application programs. NASA's *Computer Program Abstracts* lists government-sponsored computer programs that are available to the private sector, including those distributed by COSMIC at the University of Georgia. *Computer Programs Directory* of the CCM Information Corporation gives the abstracts of programs available from the principal computer users' groups. *CALGO (Collected Algorithms from the Communications of the ACM)* is an updated loose-leaf collection of all the algorithms and supporting material published in the *Communications,* and, starting in 1975, in the ACM *Transactions on Mathematical Software.*

Program listings are available for almost all the specialist fields of computing, including the disciplines that computing serves. The lists do not seem to be much used.

DIRECTORIES. There is no general printed directory of all United States computer installations or of vendors of computers and computer services. Extensive, although certainly incomplete, lists are issued annually as commercial publications; for example, the *Official Directory of Data Processing* (25,000 users and 5,000 vendors), *Computer Yearbook and Directory*, and *Computer Industry Annual.* Commercial periodicals often issue directories; for example, *Computers and Automation*'s (annual) *Computer Directory and Buyer's Guide.*

In the United Kingdom the two main directories are *Computer Directory* and *Computer User's Yearbook. Facts and Figures about Computers in Europe* lists European installations. There are individual installation lists for some European countries, Canada, and Japan. Also, there are several international directories; for example, the *International Directory of Computer and Information System Services, Who Is Related to Whom in the Computer Industry*, and the *World Directory of Computer Companies.*

STATISTICAL INFORMATION. In almost all computer industry statistics, the definition problem regularly causes difficulties and discrepancies. For example, in counting computer installations or machines, should punched card machines, minicomputers, or process control computers be included or excluded? What is a computer installation? In short, there are no agreed upon and universally accepted standard definitions that apply to the collection of statistical data. Since the basis for the statistical reports that are privately published are usually mail surveys of uninterested respondents, and the collection process is unaudited and untested, the results should always be considered in the light of the publisher's self-interest and never accepted as more than gross indicators.

While there is a standard industrial classification covering computer hardware, there is none for software or computing services. There is no computer industry association of sufficient scope and strength to collect and publish comprehensive and reliable statistical data.

The basic source for statistical information on installed computers is International Data Corporation, which publishes *EDP Industry Report* and *EDP Europa Report*, containing censuses and market analyses drawn from a file on more than 50,000 United States and 30,000 other installations. *Computers and Automation, Datamation*, and *ADP Newsletter* also publish statistical reports.

## Miscellaneous Literature

STANDARDS. The most significant standards relating to computing are produced by the American National Standards Institute (ANSI)—formerly the American Standards Association and the U.S.A. Standards Institute—and the National Bureau of Standards (Federal Information Processing Standards) in the United States, and the British Standards Institution and the National Computing Centre in the United Kingdom. International standards, usually derivative from those of the U.S. and U.K. bodies, are published by the International Standards Organization (ISO). Two other international standards organizations, the International Electrotechnical Commission and the European Computer Manufacturers Association (ECMA), cooperate closely with ISO.

The National Bureau of Standards annually publishes *Federal Information Processing Standards Index*, which summarizes standards publications at all levels: federal, national, and international.

TRADE LITERATURE. Vast quantities of descriptive or publicity material are distributed free to potential and actual customers by hardware and software vendors. The purely factual descriptive and instructional manuals are valuable and important, and are often the only reference material available for a new computer or software system. The remaining trade literature is a form of commercial advertising, and is usually worth what the vendor charges for it. There is no general listing or abstracting of such literature, each vendor maintaining his own listing, usually in a rather uncoordinated fashion. IBM has the only really comprehensive list of its own literature.

PATENTS. Although, in principle, patents (publically available at a nominal fee from the U.S. Patent Office) should provide complete and comprehensible descriptions of the devices, methods, processes, or programs patented, their titles are deliberately vague and uninformative, and the disclosures themselves are written in an arcane, wordy, and laborious jargon that makes them generally useless as informative literature.

TRANSLATIONS. Only about 5% of the computer literature in English has been translated from another language, almost all of that is from Russian. Pritchard (1) gives a list of translated periodicals.

BIOGRAPHICAL INFORMATION. The only regular biographical publication is *Who's Who in Computers and Data Processing,* published by *Computers and People* (formerly *Computers and Automation*) and giving brief, subject-prepared, summary entries for 15,000 people.

Book-length biographical treatment has been given only to Alan M. Turing (*Alan M. Turing*, by Sara Turing, Cambridge, 1959, a mother's biography), and Thomas J. Watson, Sr. (*The Lengthening Shadow*, by Thomas and Marva Belden, Little, Brown & Co., 1962, the authorized life story; and *THINK*, by William Rodgers, Stein and Day, 1969, the unauthorized biography).

CRITICAL LITERATURE. *Computing Reviews* is the only regular critique of the current literature, although commercial periodicals run occasional book reviews, which tend to be more critical than informative. A few well-conceived and thought-provoking books have been published which are works of scientific criticism addressed to computing. Worth mentioning are *Computers and Common Sense* by Mortimer Taube (Columbia University press, 1961), *What Computers Can't Do* by Hubert L. Dreyfus (Harper & Row, 1972), and *Run, Computer, Run* by Selma Marks and Anthony G. Oettinger (Harvard University Press, 1969). As with most critical literature, the vigor of the controversy they arouse is a measure of their effectiveness.

FICTION AND HUMOR. Literary works dealing with computers are limited to a great deal of average-quality science fiction, and some initial attempts by essayists and social science writers to grapple with the philsophical and humanistic implications of computers and computing. Anthologies by Taviss (*The Computer Impact*, Prentice-Hall, 1970) and Pylyshyn (*Perspectives on the Computer Revolution*, Prentice-Hall, 1970) are typical. Snow's "two cultures" gap remains unbridged.

Computer-related humor is generally represented by cartoons in the technical and popular press, and short items in *Datamation*. Some of this material has been collected into hard covers in the now out-of-print *faith, hope and parity* (Jack Moshman, Ed., Thompson Book Company, 1966).

REFERENCES


1. Pritchard, Alan. *A Guide to Computer Literature*, 2d ed., 1972. Shoe String Press, 995 Sherman Av., Hamden, Ct. 06514.
2. Carter, Ciel. *Guide to Reference Sources in the Computer Sciences*, 1974, Macmillan Information, 886 Third Avenue, New York, N.Y. 10022.
3. Couger, J. Daniel (Ed.). *Computing Newsletter for Instructors of Data Processing, Annual Bibliography of Computer Books*. 2611 Northridge Drive, Box 7345, Colorado Springs, Col. 80933.
4. *International Computer Bibliography*, 1968, Studiecentrum voor Informatica, Stadhouderskade 6, Amsterdam 13, The Netherlands.
5. Youden, W. W. *Computer Literature Bibliography, 1946–1963*. National Bureau of Standards, Misc. Pub. 266, 1964 (out-of-print).
6. Youden, W. W. *Computer Literature Bibliography, Vol. 2, 1964–1967*. National Bureau of Standards, Spec. Pub. 309, 1968. Superintendent of Documents, U.S. Government Printing Office, Washington, D.C. 20402.
7. *National Computing Centre Ltd. A World List of Computer Periodicals*, 1970. Quay House, Quay Street, Manchester M3 3HU, England.
8. *Computer Abstracts*. Technical Information Company, Martins Bank Chambers, P.O. Box 59, St. Helier, Jersey, British Channel Islands.
9. *Computing Reviews*. Association for Computing Machinery, 1133 Avenue of the Americas, New York, N.Y. 10036.
10. *New Literature on Automation*. Stichting Het Nederlands Studiecentrum voor Informatica, Stadhouderskade 6, Amsterdam 13, The Netherlands.
11. *Computer & Control Abstracts*. IEEE, 345 East 47th Street, New York, N.Y. 10017.
12. *Data Processing Digest*. 6820 La Tijera Blvd., Los Angeles, Cal. 90045.
13. *Referativnyi Zhurnal Avtomatika Telemekhanika Vychislitel'naya Tekhnika*. Moscow.
14. *Cybernetics Abstracts*. Scientific Information Consultants, Ltd., 661 Finchley Road, London NW2, England.

ADDITIONAL LITERATURE ADDRESSES

*Associations*

American Federation of Information Processing Societies (AFIPS), 210 Summit Ave., Montvale, N.J. 07645.
American National Standards Institute (ANSI), 1430 Broadway, New York, N.Y. 10018.
Association for Computing Machinery (ACM), 1133 Avenue of the Americas, New York, N.Y. 10036.
British Computer Society (BCS), 29 Portland Place, London W1N4AP, England.
IEEE Computer Society, 5855 Naples Plaza, Suite 301, Long Beach, Cal. 90803.
Institute of Electrical and Electronics Engineers (IEEE), 345 East 47th Street, New York, N.Y. 10017.
Society for Industrial and Applied Mathematics (SIAM), 33 South 17th Street, Philadelphia, Pa, 19103.

*Commercial Publishers*

Academic Press, 111 Fifth Avenue, New York, N.Y. 10003.
Datamation, 1801 S. La Cienega Blvd., Los Angeles, Cal. 90035.
McGraw-Hill Book Company, 1221 Avenue of the Americas, New York, N.Y. 10020.
Pergamon Press, Ltd., Headington Hill Hall, Oxford OX3 OBW, England.
Petrocelli/Charter, 641 Lexington Ave., New York, N.Y. 10022.
Plenum Publishing Corp, 114 Fifth Avenue, New York, N.Y. 10011.
Prentice-Hall, Inc., Englewood Cliffs, N.J. 07632.
John Wiley & Sons, 605 Third Avenue, New York, N.Y. 10016.

*Data Collections*

Auerbach Information, Inc. 121 N. Broad Street, Philadelphia, Pa. 19107.
Computers and People, 815 Washington Street, Newtonville, Mass. 02160.
Datapro Research Corp., Delran, N.J. 08075.
GML Corporation, 594 Marrett Road, Lexington, Mass. 02173.
ICP Quarterly, International Computer Programs, Inc., 2506 Willowbrook Pkway., Indianapolis, Ind. 46205.
International Data Corporation, 60 Austin St., Newtonville, Mass. 02160.
Official Directory of Data Processing, 3435 Wilshire Blvd., Lower Plaza, Los Angeles, Cal. 90010.

E. A. WEISS

# LIVERMORE AUTOMATIC RESEARCH COMPUTER (LARC)

For article on related subject *see* STRETCH.

The LARC (Livermore Automatic Research Computer) was one of the first of the high-performance giant computers. It was developed at the Sperry UNIVAC engineering facilities in Philadelphia during the 1959–1960 period. LARC represented a manyfold increase in speed over any existing computer of that period.

Two LARC computers were manufactured. One was supplied to the Lawrence Radiation Laboratory in Livermore, California; the other was delivered to the former David Taylor Model Basin (now the Naval Ships Research & Development Center) located near Washington, D. C. Both computers were phased out of service in the period 1968–1969. The consensus was that LARC was a technical success, but the high costs of manufacture did not justify further sales effort.

The basic LARC system was composed of two units. One was an input/output processor designed primarily to provide flexible, parallel, and coordinated control of the input/output equipment. The second was a computing unit designed to perform the arithmetic functions of the system. If increased computing capacity was required, the basic system could be expanded to include an additional computing unit. The computing unit was a parallel computer capable of both fixed and floating-point arithmetic operation. The number system was binary-coded decimal. Except for certain intercommunication facilities, the computing units and the input/output processor operated independently. Additions were performed in 4 $\mu$s, multiplication in 8 $\mu$s.

LARC had a high-speed magnetic core memory shared by the processor and computing units. The memory was divided into units, each of which was capable of storing 2,500 computer words of 11 decimal digits plus a sign digit. Each unit of the memory contained all the necessary switches, read-write regenerate circuits, and intermediate storage to operate independently and in parallel with other units. The high-speed memory could be expanded to

**Fig. 1.** The LARC computer.

a maximum of 39 units, equivalent to 97,500 words. Eight units were used in the basic system on a high-speed bus to provide an effective rate of one word every ½ μs.

The high-speed memory was backed up by a magnetic drum-file memory. Up to 24 magnetic drums could be included in the system. Each drum was capable of storing 250,000 computer words of 12 decimal digits. The magnetic drums featured an air-floated read/write head assembly, which achieved high reliability with high pulse densities because of the absence of mechanical contact between the head and the drum surface. A continuous data-transfer rate of 2,500 words every 83 ms was achieved between the drums and the computing unit by interlacing the sequential operation of the two drums.

M. M. MAYNARD

# LOAD-AND-GO COMPILER

For articles on related subjects *see* COMPILER; LANGUAGE PROCESSORS; and OBJECT PROGRAM.

For article on related term *see* DEBUGGING.

The process of running a computer program is generally a two-step sequence: the process of translating the program (compilation) from its humanlike language into executable machine code, and then the execution of that code. Where the program is expected to be used many times without modification, such as in an accounting or payroll situation, the cost of repeated compilation can be avoided by separating the two processing steps: (1) a single compilation stage (which provides an object program that is stored on some auxiliary storage medium such as disk), and (2) (at later times) the repeated execution of the resultant code. In this situation the compiler should be as efficient as possible in generating the minimal code for the program. Therefore, additional computer time is justified at the compilation stage in order to save considerably more time during the succeeding execution runs.

On the other hand, in a "debugging" or "educational" environment where the expectation of repeated runs of the same compiled program is minimal, the cost of highly efficient compilation and its consequent time consumption must be weighed against the time used in executing the generated code. In general, in this type of environment, the time used in generating efficient code far outweighs the time saved by that code, and thus a fast compilation is more desirable than a quick execution.

Further, since the compilation is expected to be followed immediately by the execution of the generated code, the two phases can be permanently linked together. Where possible, the generated code is retained in the working memory (as contrasted with the process of generating an intermediate output onto a scratch tape and then requiring the reentry of the code prior to the execution phase) so that, as soon as the compilation is complete, control can be transferred to the generated code without delay. This process is known as "load and go" and is the basis for many university systems, such as the WATFOR (University of Waterloo Fortran) and PUFFT (Purdue University Fast Fortran Translator).

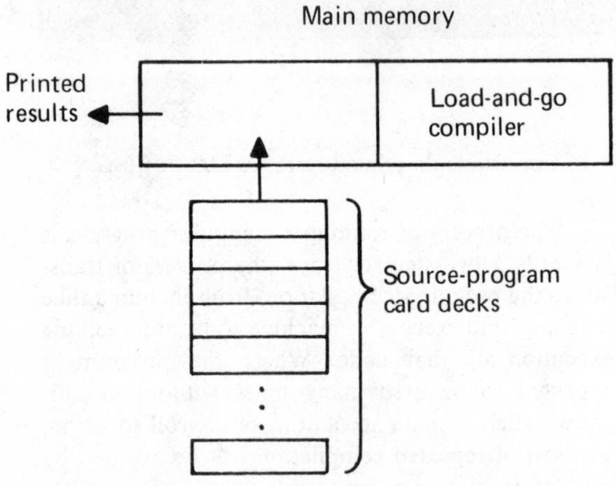


**Fig. 1.** Operation of load-and-go systems.

When used in university environments, load-and-go systems generally operate as shown in Fig. 1. A batch of source program decks are read into main memory (or first onto auxiliary storage and then into main memory) one at a time. The load-and-go compiler compiles and executes these programs one at a time. In contrast to nonload-and-go systems, where the compiler is read into memory again each time a new source program is compiled, the load-and-go compiler remains resident in memory until the whole batch of source programs has been compiled and executed.

REFERENCES

1967. Shantz, P. W., et al. "WATFOR—The University of Waterloo Fortran IV Compiler," *Communications of the ACM*, Vol. 10, No. 1 (January), pp. 41–44.

1965. Rosen, S., et al. "PUFFT—The Purdue University Fast Fortran Translator," *Communications of the ACM*, Vol. 8, No. 11 (November), pp. 661–666. (Also contained in—1967, S. Rosen (Ed.), *Programming Systems and Languages*, McGraw-Hill, New York.)

J. A. N. LEE

# LOADER

For articles on related subjects *see* ASSEMBLERS; and LINKAGE EDITOR.
For article on related term *see* BOOTSTRAP.

The function of a loader is to transfer a program held on some external storage medium (e.g., paper tape, magnetic tape, disk) into the main memory of the machine in a form suitable for execution. There are three main types of loaders: binary, relocating, and linking. An important variant of the binary loader is the bootstrap loader, which is used for the initial loading of program into an empty machine.

**Binary Loaders.** For a binary loader, the external form of the program to be loaded is an exact image of the binary pattern to be established in main memory. Thus, the loading process consists of one or more read transfers, and such complication as there is resides mainly in the sum checks or longitudinal parity checks used to verify the correctness of the transfers. If the external medium is paper tape, there is a trap for the unwary if certain binary combinations are treated by the hardware as control characters (e.g., to halt the reader). Special shift conventions have to be employed in this case.

A further difficulty is that there must be room in memory for both the loader and the program being loaded. The loader may be kept in a reserved area, or it may be placed in a position where it is known that no program will be loaded (e.g., the blank COMMON area for a Fortran program). A more sophisticated solution is to include in a header block not only the address at which loading is to commence but also the size of the program to be loaded. The loader, which is itself written in relocatable form, reads these items and then copies itself into a place in memory outside the area to be loaded.

**Relocating Loaders.** A relocating loader differs from a binary loader in that some of the addresses in the program to be loaded are expressed relative to the start of the program rather than in absolute form. These addresses have to be adjusted by the loader by adding a suitable constant to put the program into an executable form. This type of source material, commonly called "relocatable binary," is typically produced as output by a linkage editor.

If the machine in question uses a base-and-displacement addressing system (as, for example, the IBM System/370), only address constants will need relocating. If the architecture is such that instructions include absolute addresses (strictly speaking, absolute in the virtual address space), then all memory reference instructions will require relocation. The relocation information may be concentrated in one place in a relocation map that contains in coded form the positions of all the addresses requiring relocation, or each individual word may be tagged to show whether or not it is to be relocated.

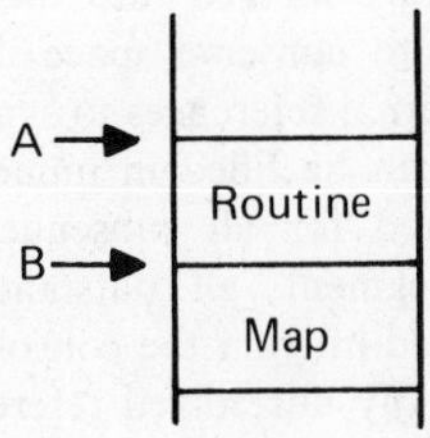


**Fig. 1.** Initial action of loader.

In the first case, the loader first reads the routine and its map into store, as shown in Fig. 1. (The routine is preceded by a header block giving its length, thus allowing address B to be computed.) The map is then scanned and the specified words in the routine are relocated by having the address A added to them. If individual words are tagged, the loader examines the flag associated with each incoming word to decide whether or not to add the relocation constant (i.e., the address of the start of the routine). When the routine is completed, the relocation constant is updated (i.e., set to B) and the process continued by reading the next routine and its map into core, starting at B.

A more elaborate form of relocating the loader will deal with multiple location counters. [For example, an assembler output (Fig. 2) may contain code and literal constants: At run time, the literal constants for the entire program must be in a contiguous block, so they are conveniently described as being relative to a different location counter (Fig. 3). Similarly, COMMON areas in Fortran can conveniently be dealt with using additional location counters.]

In this case each instruction is tagged to show to which location counter (if any) the address in that item is relative. The loader now becomes a two-pass process: The first pass computes the sizes of the blocks for each location counter and determines the displacement of their origins, and hence the appropriate relocation constants. The second pass loads and relocates, using the origins determined in the first pass. This process is illustrated in Figs. 2, 3, and 4. Observe in Fig. 4 that the loader is now performing a storage-allocation function.

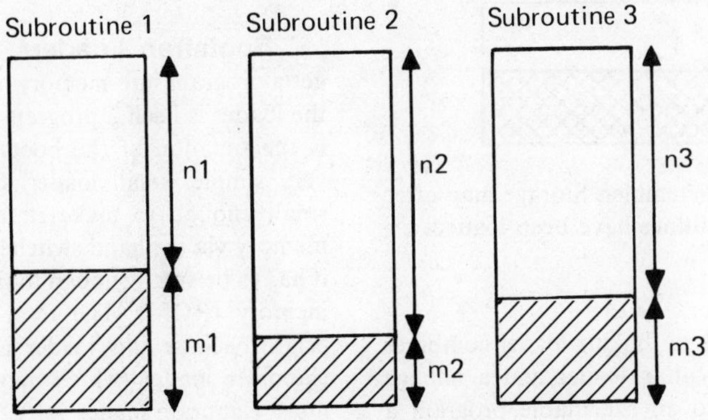


**Fig. 2.** Output of the assembler. Shaded areas denote items stored relative to location counter 2.

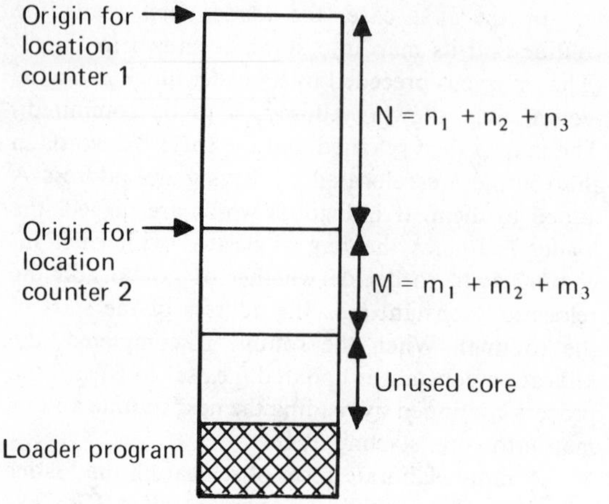


**Fig. 3.** Output of the assembler. Storage allocation after first pass.

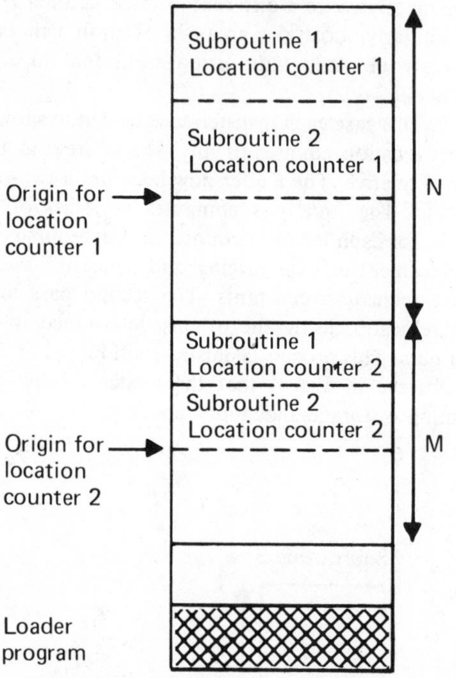


**Fig. 4.** Output of the assembler. Storage map after first two subroutines have been loaded.

**Linking Loaders.** A linking loader combines the functions of a relocating loader and a linkage editor. It combines into an executable program a number of program segments that have been independently compiled; thus, in addition to relocation, it must resolve the cross-references between the segments.

An independently compiled segment contains three kinds of information: absolute information, which is independent of the final position in memory (e.g., operation codes); relative addresses, which are expressed as displacements from the start of the segment; and external references. The output of the compiler will typically consist of a number of binary words, a relocation map as before, a table of external references, and a table of global symbol definitions. The external reference table contains the (relative) address of each external reference together with the symbolic form of the reference, and the table of global definitions contains the symbolic form and value (as a relative address) of each defined symbol.

The linking loader reads the first segment and its tables, noting the origin of the segment. This origin is used to adjust all relative addresses in the segment (via the relocation map), and in the external reference and definition tables. The entries from these two tables are copied to form the start of consolidated external reference and definition tables in some safe place (e.g., the top of the memory). The relocation origin is then reset to the end of the segment, and the next segment is read in, overwriting the tables of the preceding segment. The process of relocation is repeated and the external reference and definition tables are merged into the consolidated tables. (In order to conserve space in the consolidated tables, external references to symbols that are already defined can be filled in immediately.) The process is repeated for all subsequent segments: After the last segment, all outstanding external references are filled in from the consolidated global definition table. Any unresolved references may be treated as errors or may be used to trigger the automatic scanning of a library of precompiled segments. The process is illustrated in Fig. 5.

**Bootstrap Loaders.** It is apparent that to get a program into memory, we require a loader. But the loader is itself a program: How is it loaded? This is the function of the bootstrap loader, which is a very simple, small loader. Originally it had to be small enough to make it feasible to enter it into memory via the hand switches on the console. Today it has to be small enough to fit into a small read-only memory (ROM). The term "bootstrap" is appropriate because this loader is used to load a more elaborate loader (which may in turn load an even more elaborate loader . . . ).

A typical system might consist of an 8-word program held in a read-only memory that is capable

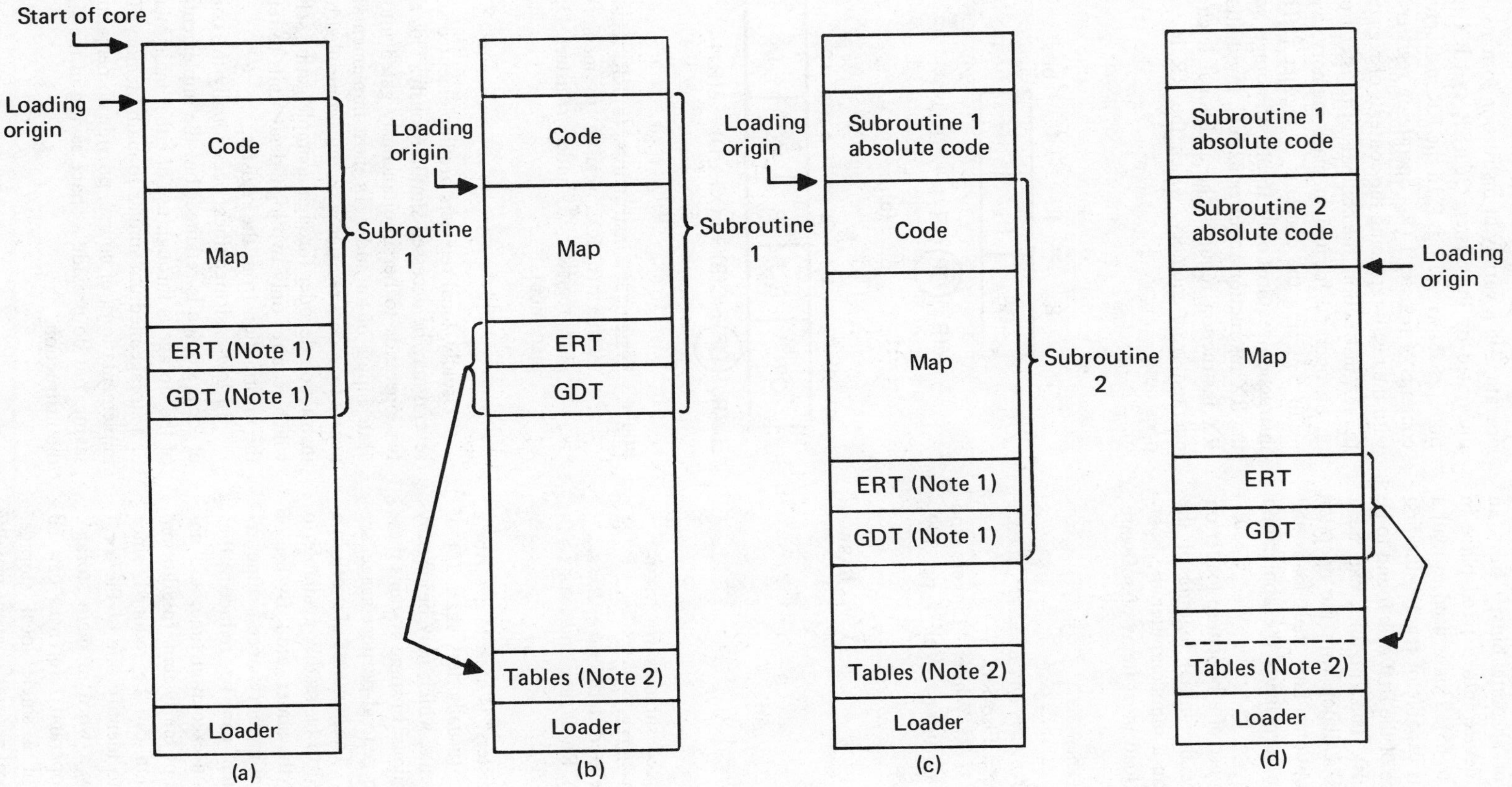


Notes:
(1) External reference table (ERT) and global definition table(GDT) entries have values relative to start of subroutine.
(2) Table entries now have values relative to start of core.

**Fig. 5.** Stages in link loading: (a) after first subroutine read-in, (b) immediately prior to reading of second subroutine, (c) immediately after reading second subroutine, (d) immediately prior to reading third subroutine.

of reading 64 words of absolute binary from an unalterable peripheral device into a fixed place in memory (e.g., words 0 to 63). This is used to load a 64-word program that is capable of reading the first track on the first surface of the first disk found to be on line (say, 256 words). This, in turn, can be a program that conducts a dialog with the operator concerning available options, and then loads the "real" loader, which in turn loads the application program.

The most common use of a bootstrap loader on a large machine is for the initial loading of the operating system, but on a minicomputer the bootstrap loader is used to load most items of software.

References

1972. Barron, D. W. *Assemblers and Loaders* (2d ed.). New York: American Elsevier.

1972. Presser, L., and J. R. White. "Linkers and Loaders," *Computing Surveys*, Vol. 4, pp. 149–168.

D. W. Barron

# LOCAL STORE

For articles on related subjects *see* Memory: Main: and Register.

For articles on related terms *see* Base Register; General Register; and Index Register.

The term "local registers" is used to describe a relatively small number (usually less than 32) of high-speed storage elements, which may be directly referred to by the instructions. In some systems these registers, because of their general-purpose usage, are called "general registers." The contents of a cell in a local register is presumed to be readily available to the execution resources (the adder, etc.). By use of local registers, the main memory access time required for operand fetch can be reduced, thus minimizing the instruction execution time, and improving the performance of the system. In addition, the size of the instruction can be reduced, since fewer bits are required to identify one of the local registers than to identify a word in main storage.

Of course, not all operand references can be conveniently arranged in a single local storage. Machines that use the local register concept usually operate with a variety of instruction formats. This is illustrated by the System/360 RR and RX instructions, as shown in Fig. 1. In the RR instruction, the contents of register 1 ($R_1$) operate on register 2 ($R_2$), with the result replacing the contents of register 2. In the RX instruction, the contents of register 1 operate on an operand located in main memory, with the result replacing the contents of register 1. The RR instruction requires only 16 bits of storage, whereas the RX instruction requires 32 bits. In addition, the RX instruction requires the additional fetch of an operand from memory, which the RR instruction does not.

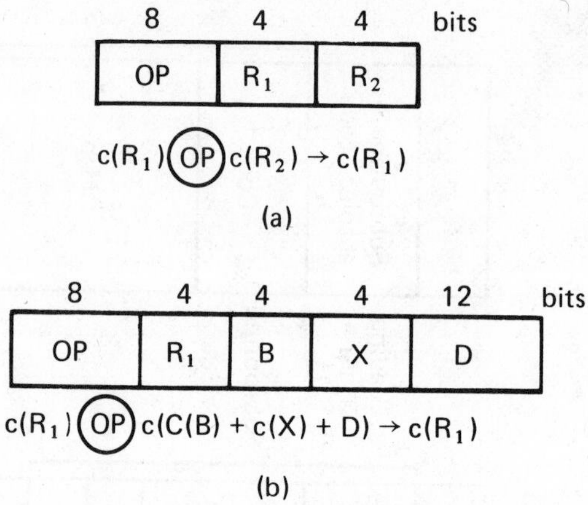


**Fig. 1.** System/360 instructions. (a) RR, register to register. (b) RX, register to memory: B, base register; X, index register; D, displacement.

Usually, local registers are implemented so that several may be accessed simultaneously. This allows two operands to be simultaneously gated into separate inputs of an adder. In most implementations, access to a local register is directly controlled by the instruction decoder through a simple gating scheme, which requires only two logic delay units to retrieve the information from the register.

In low-cost machines, occasionally the concept of local storage is retained, but the implementation of the storage is through use of either main memory or a storage medium similar to main memory. These implementations, of course, provide no performance saving, but do provide a space saving in the size of the instruction.

M. J. Flynn

# LOCKOUT

For articles on related subjects *see* CONTENTION; MULTIPROCESSING; and SEMAPHORE.

When several processes are executing simultaneously, it may happen that two (or more) of these processes want to access the same data. For example, in a system with multiple CPUs, two processors can be idle and request a new task at the same time. If no precaution is taken, both will access the table where the list of waiting tasks is stored, and both may initiate the same task. In a multiprogramming system a READ process and a WRITE process might share the same buffer area, so that the writer has to be protected from having its data garbled by the reader before the output is completed. To circumvent this problem, means must be provided to protect the shared data from unorderly changes. Such means are usually called "lockout," or "mutual exclusion." The portion of code in a process that accesses a shared area is called a "critical section" of that process.

At the hardware level, one can use instructions such as TEST AND WAIT and SET, or the equivalent pair, LOCK/UNLOCK. Similar schemes have been proposed for higher-level languages. In order to allow programs to be more independent, Dijkstra (1968) has defined a new type of variable, called a "semaphore," which can take only nonnegative integer values. Dijkstra's elegant solution is based on two primitive and indivisible operations on semaphores, namely:

$V(S)$ defined as $S \leftarrow S + 1$.

$P(S)$ defined as $L$: **if** $S = 0$ **then go to** $L$ **else** $S \leftarrow S - 1$.

Basically, the philosophy behind the use of semaphores is as follows: For purposes of clarity we restrict the semaphore $S$ protecting a shared data base to take only the values 0 and 1. Initially, the semaphore is set to 1. Before entering a critical section, the process performs a $P$ operation. If $S$ is 1, the process decrements $S$ and enters its critical section. Since $S$ is now 0, no other process may enter its critical section. If $S$ were 0, then the process would be blocked and would remain so as long as another process was executing in a critical section. When a process terminates its critical section, it performs a $V$ operation, setting $S$ to 1 and thus allowing another process to enter its critical section.

The semaphore concept is now widely recognized as an efficient means of protection between cooperating processes, and has been implemented in various forms in several operating systems.

REFERENCE

1968. Dijkstra, E. W. "Cooperating Sequential Processes", in F. Genuys (Ed.), *Programming Languages*. New York: Academic Press.

J. L. BAER

# LOGIC DESIGN

For articles on related subjects *see* BOOLEAN ALGEBRA; COMPUTER CIRCUITRY; and INTEGRATED CIRCUITRY.
For article on related term *see* BINARY CODED DECIMAL, NATURAL.

The term "logic design" refers to the process of specifying an interconnection of logic elements in digital computer hardware so that a desired function is performed. Examples of this process might be the design of a circuit that would accept data representing numbers in a gray code and convert this data into a binary-coded decimal representation, or the specification of the gates and interconnections required to implement the arithmetic unit of a computer. Both formal and ad hoc techniques are used to achieve the desired design.

All digital logic networks in current use operate on signals that are restricted to two possible values only, and are thus called "binary values." While it is theoretically possible to design logic networks in which a larger number of discrete values are allowed for the signals (so-called multiple-valued logic networks), the discussion here will be restricted to binary logic networks, since these are the only type of networks in current use. For some binary networks it is possible to specify the desired performance by means of tables of combinations as shown in Table 1, which lists each possible combination of binary signals on the inputs to the network and the

**Table 1.** Combinations for Elementary Gates

(a) Inverter

| Input f | Output f′ |
|---|---|
| 0 | 1 |
| 1 | 0 |

(b) AND gate

| Inputs A B | Output f |
|---|---|
| 0 0 | 0 |
| 0 1 | 0 |
| 1 0 | 0 |
| 1 1 | 1 |

(c) OR gate

| Inputs A B | Output f |
|---|---|
| 0 0 | 0 |
| 0 1 | 1 |
| 1 0 | 1 |
| 1 1 | 1 |

(d) XOR (exclusive OR) gate

| Inputs A B | Output f |
|---|---|
| 0 0 | 0 |
| 0 1 | 1 |
| 1 0 | 1 |
| 1 1 | 0 |

(e) NAND (not AND) gate

| Inputs A B | Output f |
|---|---|
| 0 0 | 1 |
| 0 1 | 1 |
| 1 0 | 1 |
| 1 1 | 0 |

(f) NOR (not OR) gate

| Inputs A B | Output f |
|---|---|
| 0 0 | 1 |
| 0 1 | 0 |
| 1 0 | 0 |
| 1 1 | 0 |

*Note:* See Fig: 1.

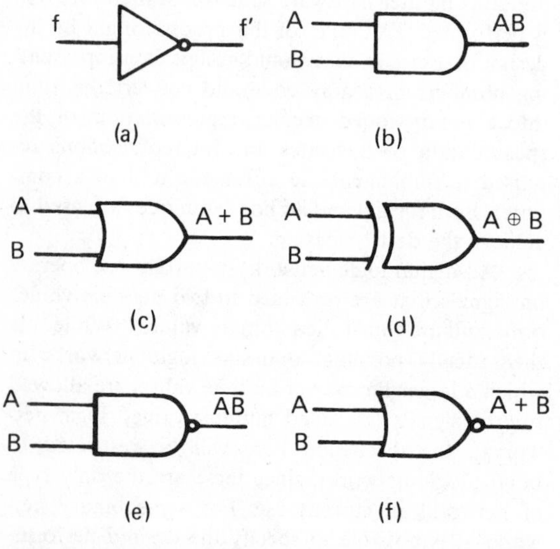


**Fig. 1.** Elementary gate symbols: (a) inverter; (b) AND gate; (c) OR gate; (d) XOR gate; (e) NAND gate; (f) NOR gate.

corresponding combination of desired output signals.

In Table 1, (a) shows the combinations for a network having one input and one output. The output of this network will have a signal representing the zero value on it whenever the input signal represents a 1, and will have an output signal representing a 1 value whenever the input signal has a zero. Such a network is called an "inverter," and the symbol used to represent it is shown in Fig. 1(a).

Actually, a network having such a simple performance as that of an inverter is usually realized as a single logic element and is not constructed out of more elementary subnetworks. An inverter is thus one of the basic building blocks from which more complex logic networks are constructed. Other basic building blocks, or *elementary gates*, are shown in Table 1 as (b), (c), (d), (e), and (f), with the corresponding logic symbols shown in Figs. 1(b), 1(c), 1(d), 1(e) and 1(f).

The combinations for a more complex logic network are shown in Table 2. This network has four input signals and four output signals. If the four binary signals appearing on the network inputs represent one decimal digit encoded in the 8-4-2-1 code (i.e., binary-coded decimal, or BCD), then the four output signals will represent the encoding of the 9s complement of the input digit. Notice that in addition to having entries of 1 or 0, there are also entries in this table that are represented by a "d."

**Table 2.** Combinations for Generating the Complement of a BCD (8421) Digit

| | Inputs | | | | Outputs | | | |
|---|---|---|---|---|---|---|---|---|
| | $b_8$ | $b_4$ | $b_2$ | $b_1$ | $c_8$ | $c_4$ | $c_2$ | $c_1$ |
| (0) | 0 | 0 | 0 | 0 | 1 | 0 | 0 | 1 |
| (1) | 0 | 0 | 0 | 1 | 1 | 0 | 0 | 0 |
| (2) | 0 | 0 | 1 | 0 | 0 | 1 | 1 | 1 |
| (3) | 0 | 0 | 1 | 1 | 0 | 1 | 1 | 0 |
| (4) | 0 | 1 | 0 | 0 | 0 | 1 | 0 | 1 |
| (5) | 0 | 1 | 0 | 1 | 0 | 1 | 0 | 0 |
| (6) | 0 | 1 | 1 | 0 | 0 | 0 | 1 | 1 |
| (7) | 0 | 1 | 1 | 1 | 0 | 0 | 1 | 0 |
| (8) | 1 | 0 | 0 | 0 | 0 | 0 | 0 | 1 |
| (9) | 1 | 0 | 0 | 1 | 0 | 0 | 0 | 0 |
| | 1 | 0 | 1 | 0 | d | d | d | d |
| | 1 | 0 | 1 | 1 | d | d | d | d |
| | 1 | 1 | 0 | 0 | d | d | d | d |
| | 1 | 1 | 0 | 1 | d | d | d | d |
| | 1 | 1 | 1 | 0 | d | d | d | d |
| | 1 | 1 | 1 | 1 | d | d | d | d |

*Note:* See Fig. 2.

This notation is used to indicate the fact that certain input combinations would not be expected to appear at the input of the network. Such entries are called "don't cares." A table of combinations that contains "don't care" entries is an *incompletely specified table of combinations.*

An incompletely specified table of combinations is actually a representation for a whole family of completely specified tables of combinations that would satisfy the given design requirements. Techniques exist that effectively choose a completely specified table of combinations that leads to the most efficient network design. An efficient network to realize the specifications of Table 2 is shown in Fig. 2. Using Table 2, the reader may verify that the equations given in Fig. 2 are correct.

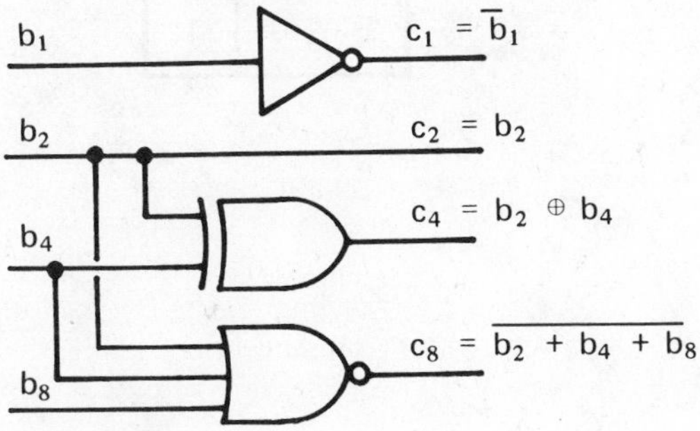


**Fig. 2.** Network for Table 2.

The types of networks described thus far all have the property that the output values at any given instant of time are dependent solely upon the input values present at the same time. Such networks are called "combinational logic networks." The other type of logic network is called a "sequential logic network" or a *sequential circuit.* These networks have the property that their outputs are dependent not only on their present inputs but also on the inputs that may have been present previously.

An example of a sequential circuit is a network whose input is a series of pulses on a single lead and whose outputs display the count modulo *n* of the number of input pulses. Such a circuit is called a "counter" (Gschwind and McCluskey, 1975). Since the output of a sequential circuit at any particular time may depend on previous inputs, there must be contained in the circuit some mechanism for recording some information about these previous inputs. This function is achieved by providing feedback loops in the circuit, which are capable of storing information in them. The most commonly used type of feedback loop consists of two gate elements interconnected, as shown in Fig. 3.

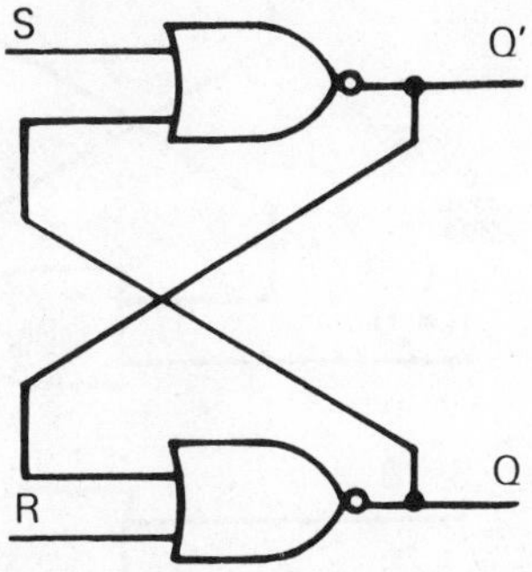


**Fig. 3.** Interconnected NOR gates forming a flip-flop.

In order to understand how this circuit works, consider the situation shown in Fig. 4. In Fig. 4(a), the input $S = 1$, $R = 0$ is applied to the circuit. Table 1(f) shows that when at least one input of a NOR gate is equal to 1, then the gate output must be equal to 0. Thus, the output of gate A in Fig. 4(a) must be equal to 0. It follows from this that both inputs to gate B are equal to 0 and, again from Table 1(f), the output of gate B must be equal to 1. Suppose now that the $S$ input is changed from 1 to 0. Then the situation in Fig. 4(b) will occur. Here, $S = R = 0$ and $Q = 1$. If $R$ is then made equal to 1, the situation in Fig. 4(c) will occur, with $Q$ changing to become equal to 0, since setting $R$ equal to 1 forces gate B output to change to 0. Fig. 4(d) shows the situation if the $R$ input is next returned to 0. The output $Q$ remains unchanged (at 0). The inputs to the circuit are the same in Fig. 4(b) and 4(d) ($S = R = 0$), but the outputs are different ($Q = 1$ or $Q = 0$). Thus, the output of this circuit when $S = R = 0$ depends not only on the signals on the inputs, but also on the previous input signals. This circuit can thus be used to "store" information.

There is a whole class of memory elements in which information is stored in two interconnected gates. Such elements are known as "flip-flops." Just as a table of combinations is a formal representation for the performance of a combinational circuit, *flow tables* or *state diagrams* or *regular expressions* are used as formal specifications for the action of a sequential circuit (see McCluskey, 1965).

Formal techniques exist for determining logic networks that correspond to specifications given in the form of a table of combinations or a flow table.

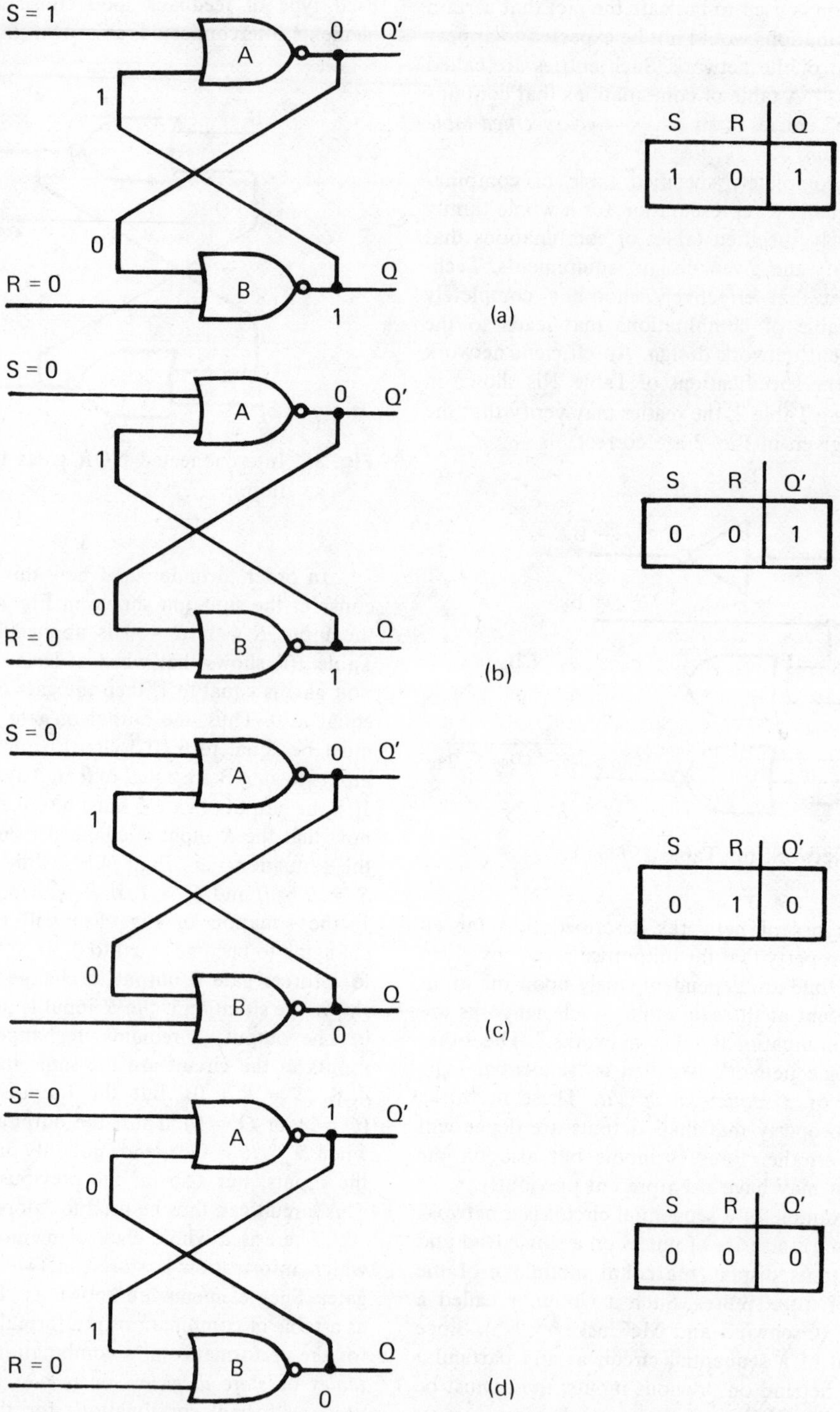


**Fig. 4.** Sequence of situations in a simple flip-flop of two NOR gates. (a) Situation with $S = 1$, $R = 0$; (b) situation occurring after (a) if $S$ is changed to 0; (c) situation with $S = 0$, $R = 1$; (d) situation occurring after (c) if $R$ is changed to 0.

These formal techniques are the subject of the discipline known as "switching theory" (McCluskey, 1965). Classical switching theory is concerned mainly with the problem of designing optimum networks that correspond to given formal specifications. Algorithms have been developed for designing networks that contain a minimum number of gates under certain constraints; e.g., the condition that there be no more than two gates connected in series between any input and any output. While a great deal of attention has been devoted to the *minimization problem*—that of obtaining minimum element networks—this problem has been solved only for networks having very specific constraints, such as those mentioned above. General design algorithms with flexible constraints have proved to be very difficult to discover.

Formal techniques for the design of logic networks have an inherent limitation in that the size of the table of combinations, or flow table, tends to be proportional to $2^n$, where $n$ is the number of network inputs. A logic network with ten inputs is not a particularly large one, but a formal specification for such a network would require over 1,000 entries. The approach taken to overcome this difficulty is to partition logic networks into subnetworks of a convenient size. The overall network is then structured by interconnections of the subnetworks, the interconnections being determined by ad hoc rather than formal techniques.

Other motivations besides design convenience also lead to the use of building blocks more complex than elementary gates. With present-day integrated circuit technology used to realize the logic elements, much of the cost of an element is in its packaging and interconnections, and thus it pays to minimize the number of such packages and external connections. The way in which this can be done is by incorporating in an individual package a circuit more complex than an elementary gate. Two general approaches have been taken to determine the nature of the complex building blocks to be used. One approach is to attempt to identify the more common types of subnetworks that occur, and to manufacture individual integrated circuit packages incorporating the functions performed by these subnetworks. This approach is commonly called "medium scale integration" (MSI). Some typical MSI elements are:

1. Full adder.
2. Arithmetic logic unit.
3. Parallel binary multiplier.
4. Magnitude comparator.
5. Odd/Even parity generator.
6. Shift register.
7. Register file (8 words of 2 bits, 4 words of 4 bits).
8. Data selector/multiplexer.
9. Decoder/demultiplexer.
10. Counter.
11. Priority encoder.

Each of the major manufacturers of integrated-circuit logic elements publishes its own manual on techniques for interconnecting the MSI elements, perhaps making use of some elementary gates (called "SSI," small scale integration), in connection with the MSI elements (Barna and Porat, 1973).

Another approach is to manufacture generalized networks in one package, which can be specialized in some fashion to provide the desired function. The most successful technique along this line has been one that incorporates a memory in a single package. This package can be used as a specialized logic network by, in effect, storing the table of combinations, or flow table, in the element itself.

In summary: For small specialized switching networks the logic design can be accomplished by using the formal techniques of switching theory. For larger, more complex networks, the logic design is usually accomplished by using ad hoc rather than formal techniques to specify interconnections of more complex networks.

### References

1965. McCluskey, E. J. *Introduction to the Theory of Switching Circuits*. New York: McGraw-Hill.
1973. Barna, A., and D. I. Porat. *Integrated Circuits in Digital Electronics*. New York: John Wiley.
1975. Gschwind, H., and E. J. McCluskey. *Design of Digital Computers*. New York: Springer-Verlag.

E. J. McCluskey

# LOGICAL AND PHYSICAL UNITS

For articles on related subjects *see* Input-Output Devices; and Memory: Auxiliary.

A *physical* (input/output) *unit* is an input/output device and its associated recording medium. Thus, tape units, disks, drums, card readers, and printers are all examples of physical units. A *logical unit* is a convenient abstraction of a physical unit; it is an extra level of naming of input/output devices, which gives both the programmer and the system added flexibility in operations.

The usage of a two-level naming scheme may be compared to the usage of call numbers in a library card catalog. The call number of a book is sufficient to identify the book, but it bears no permanent relationship to the location of the book on the shelves. Rather, to locate a book physically, knowing only its call number, it is necessary to consult a directory that tells (for example) on which floor a particular collection of call numbers is located. The library staff is then free to change the physical location of the books, provided the directory is updated accordingly.

A similar two-level naming scheme is used for input/output operations on a computer. Each physical input/output unit in a computer has associated with it a physical unit name (number) in order that communication with the central processor can be established. When data is being transferred, these physical unit names are ultimately used. However, a programmer frequently finds it convenient to use logical unit names in place of these physical unit names, and to provide a correspondence (i.e., directory) between logical and physical units. Thus, for example, in the familiar Fortran statement

```
READ (5,100) X,Y,Z
```

the number 5 is a logical unit name, which indicates where the data (X, Y, and Z in the format given in the statement numbered 100) is to be found. Elsewhere, the programmer (or the operating system, by default) will provide the correspondence that logical unit 5 is currently associated with physical unit 007, which might be a card reader, for example. Data will then be transferred from Card Reader 007.

This two-level naming provides a number of advantages, both to the programmer and to the operating system. First of all, it is possible to reassign the physical unit associated with a given logical unit without recompilation of the program, since the program is written in terms of logical units only, and the correspondence is made during program execution by looking in the directory. Thus, for example, the card reader used for processing jobs may vary from time to time, with the programs still executing properly, provided the correspondence between logical and physical devices is properly maintained.

Similarly, a programmer processing tapes may have them mounted on whatever drives the system operator finds convenient (it is not necessary for a tape to be mounted on the same physical unit each time). This is especially important in a multiprogrammed system where there is no way to predict in advance which physical units will be in use.

A programmer can also gain *device independence* by using logical units. A program is said to be device independent if the successful execution of the program (without recompilation) does not depend on the type of physical unit associated with a given logical unit. Thus, a device-independent program can "attach" logical device 5 to a card reader on one run and to a tape unit on another. This is, once again, accomplished by changing the logical unit/physical unit correspondences.

The advent of sharable physical units such as disks further emphasizes the importance of logical units. A disk will typically contain files of data belonging to several users, or several files belonging to the same user, or both. In such cases, a programmer will associate a logical device with a particular file of data on the physical unit rather than with the physical unit itself. It is thus possible to have several logical units associated with (usually) different files on the same physical unit.

The correspondence between logical and physical units is very often declared in control statements that precede the program using the particular correspondence. Particularly with tapes, the declaration of logical unit is often part of the request to mount the tape onto a tape drive. It is also sometimes possible to associate a logical unit and a file during execution of a program. This is most often true in time-sharing systems, which usually offer the user a capability to maintain permanent files.

Many operating systems reserve a set of logical unit numbers for internal use. It is also common practice to establish default assignments for certain commonly used logical/physical units. Typical logical/physical default assignments will involve the system-input card reader, the system-output printer, the system card punch, the user's console keyboard, and the user's console teleprinter.

R. W. TAYLOR

# LOOP

For articles on related subjects *see* ADDRESS MODIFICATION; INDEX REGISTER; ITERATION; and PROCEDURE-ORIENTED LANGUAGES.

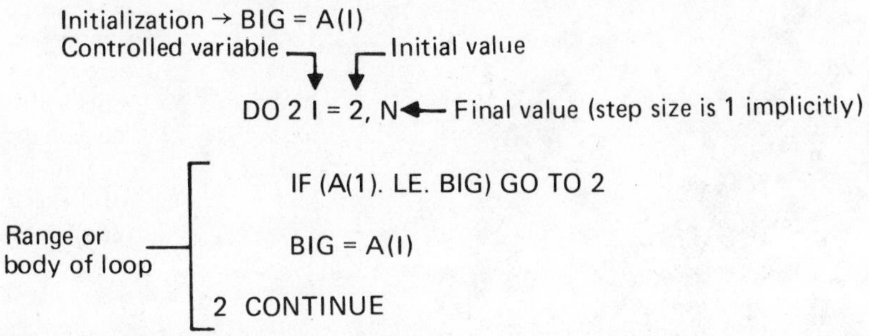
Initialization → BIG = A(I)
Controlled variable
Initial value
DO 2 I = 2, N
Final value (step size is 1 implicitly)
IF (A(1). LE. BIG) GO TO 2
Range or body of loop
BIG = A(I)
2 CONTINUE

**Fig. 1.** Largest number loop in Fortran.

A *loop* is a program fragment designed to be executed repeatedly during each run of the program. This ability to re-use the same instructions, normally with fresh operands at each iteration, is the great advantage offered by the stored-program computer, and is the basis of practically all programs of interest and value.

The creation of a loop, whether accomplished explicitly by an assembly language programmer, or implicitly by a compiler language programmer, involves three steps beyond those required by non-iterative routines: *initialization* (putting various registers and storage locations in the proper state for starting execution of a loop); *address modification* (to select the operands to be manipulated at each successive iteration); and *index modification and testing* (to record the number of times the loop has been traversed since its most recent initialization, and to exit from it when it has been traversed the required number of times).

The assembly language programmer has to write code to accomplish each of these tasks, usually using the index registers provided in the machine for the purpose. Loop initialization requires loading an index register with a value that is a function of the number of desired iterations, and another index register with the quantity by which operand addresses are to be modified at each iteration. Address modification is accomplished by referencing the index register in each loop instruction for which a new operand is to be selected; the machine modifies an address so tagged at each execution of such an instruction. Index modification and testing, finally, are accomplished by instructions that test the index register —to see if it has reached its terminal value—and cause either an exit from the loop or another iteration with modified index register value, depending on whether or not that value has been reached.

The compiler language programmer is relieved of much of this detail. The language he uses almost invariably contains at least one statement, which —given the range of statements that are to form the body of a loop, and the name, initial value, terminal value, and step size of the index or controlled variable—will generate all the necessary code. Fig. 1 illustrates the form and parts of a loop in Fortran to compute the largest of an array of numbers $A(1), \ldots, A(N)$. Other compiler language control statements giving the same effect direct that while (or until) a given logical or arithmetic condition obtains, a specified routine is to be performed. (In case of such "while" and "until" statements, the programmer assumes responsibility for modifying some variable forming part of the conditional expression and thus insuring that the loop terminates.)

Loops can be nested—i.e., contain other loops —to a depth usually limited only by storage capacity, with the number of times an inner loop is iterated being the product of its own iteration count and those of all the loops it nests within. This gives code within a deeply nested loop enormous leverage for good or bad; it may be executed millions of times in a single run of the program, and if any of it is redundant, the consequent waste of time is proportionately great. The desire to avoid such extreme penalties for small lapses has been a principal motivation for the inclusion of optimization phases in compilers, whose most fruitful efforts are perhaps those devoted to moving instructions out of an inner loop and into the less frequently executed loop (or ordinary straight-line code) in which it is embedded. Since it is common for a sizable program to be itself one big loop containing many multilevel nests of loops, the question of creating and optimizing loops is, taken broadly, practically identical to that of good program design itself.

M. Halpern

# M

**MIS.** *See* MANAGEMENT INFORMATION SYSTEMS.

**MACHINE.** *See* SEQUENTIAL MACHINES; TURING MACHINE; and VON NEUMANN MACHINE.

## MACHINE AND ASSEMBLY LANGUAGE PROGRAMMING

For articles on related subjects *see* ADDRESSING; ASSEMBLERS; BINDING TIME; COMPUTERS, MULTIPLE ADDRESS; DEBUGGING; DUMP; LINKAGE EDITOR; LOADER; MACROINSTRUCTION; NUMBERS AND NUMBER SYSTEMS; PROGRAMMING LANGUAGES; STORAGE ORGANIZATION; SUBPROGRAMS, CALLING; and SUBROUTINE.
For articles on related terms *see* INDIRECT ADDRESS; REGISTER; and TRAP.

Throughout this article, ML stands for machine language, and AL for "[symbolic] assembly [program] language." For the sake of clarity, the coding examples offered throughout are for a now obsolescent machine family (the IBM 704-709-7090-7094 series), which lends itself to piecemeal elementary presentation better than its successors. This can be done without loss of generality, as the mathematicians say, because newer machines—although faster, bigger and more complicated—embody no new principles.

**Definition of ML.** Machine language has traditionally meant that particular representation of instructions and data immediately interpretable by the hardware of the machine concerned. But, as the variety of implemented machines grows to fill the available conceptual space, a simple and precise definition of ML becomes as hard to give as one of "democracy." It no longer suffices to call it the language of the hardware now that microprogramming is coming into wider use, nor to call it machine—rather than application-oriented—now that machines (Fairchild's SYMBOL, for example) are appearing with compilerlike languages wired in.

All that can or need be done here is to indicate, by listing essential characteristics, what is meant in this article by that term. ML, then, is that programming language that is immediately executable by the machine concerned, and whose typical statement consists of a single operator-operand pair. The operand part of the statement, or instruction, is typically an address; i.e., a binary integer designating one of the storage segments usually called either "words" or "bytes." ("Byte" is the usual term where the machines's addressable storage segment is designed to hold one alphanumeric character, and is hence six, seven, or eight bits long; "word" is more often reserved for the addressable segments of machines whose special strength is in handling numbers rather than characters, and may be anything from 8 to 60 bits in length, with 32 or 36 being perhaps both mean and mode.)

The operator part of an ML statement will typically call for the performance of a dyadic arithmetic or logical operation upon the contents of (1) the addressed segment of storage and (2) any of several special registers where those operations can occur; or it will move contents between one of the special registers and a storage segment; or between either of these and one of the machine's input/output devices. The bit pattern in an addressed word will, if the operator is an arithmetic one, be treated as the representation of a scalar quantity in base 2 or an integral power of 2, such as hexadecimal.

(The foregoing describes a typical ML instruction only; for an idea of the range of possible variants, note that some machines, chiefly older ones, offer multiple-address instructions; i.e., instructions that include the addresses of two or more operands, such as the augend and addend of an addition operation. Again, many machines offer some instructions whose operand parts are immediate, i.e., they are interpreted not as the addresses of data, but as being themselves the data. Finally, all machines include instructions, variously called "jumps," "transfers," or "branches," whose function is to change the standard sequence in which instructions are executed.)

One further note on the usage of the term ML: Because genuine ML is rarely used, its name has come sometimes to be used loosely as a synonym for assembly language. This regrettable practice has sometimes forced those to whom the distinction is important to use "binary," "absolute ML," or just "absolute" to insure being understood when they mean ML. In this article, the terms "machine language" and "assembly language" will be kept quite distinct, with ML standing solely for that language (characterized above) which requires no software to translate it, and makes no concession whatever to human readability or convenience.

*Example.* In the computer from which we will draw our illustrations, as in most computers, arithmetic is usually done in a special register called an accumulator; the instruction that causes the quantity in a word—word number 100, say—to be brought to the accumulator is, in its full binary glory,

000101000000000000000000000001100100 (1)

The leftmost 12 bits of instruction (1) comprise the operation code, which in this case specifies that a quantity in memory is to be brought to the accumulator; the rightmost 15 (the "address field") specify that the particular word to be fetched is number 100 (note that 1100100 in binary is 100 in decimal). The other available bits in this instruction type are not used in the present example.

The instruction that adds the quantity in word 101 to the quantity we have just put in the accumulator is

000100000000000000000000000001100101 (2)

and the instruction that stores the quantity in the accumulator into word 102 is

000110000001000000000000000001100110 (3)

These three instructions constitute a tiny program. If they were loaded into the computer in the order just given, at locations $n$, $n + 1$, and $n + 2$, and the computer were directed to execute instructions starting at location $n$, then the sum of the quantities that happened to be in locations 100 and 101 would be formed in the accumulator and stored in location 102.

**Uses of ML.** Many programmers have to be able to recognize and interpret ML when they see it in memory dumps and assembly listings, but very few have had occasion to use it as a programming tool since alternative languages were first offered. The occasions that still arise for its use are virtually limited to the patching of a program already in ML (physically, in the form of a card deck produced by an assembler) and to the implementation of the first assembler for a new machine (but see below).

Patching is an expedient that may be attractive to a programmer who has found a bug in a sizable program, or for whom turnaround time is a critical consideration. Wanting to avoid a complete reassembly, he may decide to play the role of assembly program himself for the few instructions that need to be added to correct the object deck. This involves punching the ML instructions and data required into cards in the correct format, and computing whatever relocation information, card-loading addresses, and check sums are demanded by the loader that will read the deck into the computer. This exercise calls for a degree of patience and exactitude uncommon even among programmers, but when the alternative is the reassembly of a big program at a heavy cost in computer time, turnaround time, or both, it may be justified.

It must be borne in mind, too, that while ML patching demands the greatest accuracy of mind, hand, and eye, it yields no documentation, so that the continued usefulness of the assembly listing from which the programmer has been working depends upon its manual updating to correspond to the revised state of the object program. He will also want to make the identical change in the assembly-language version of the program against the day of reassembly that will inevitably come if the program continues to be used.

ML is a necessary tool to programmers developing the first assembler for a computer. (An alternative, at least in principle, is the development of an assembler for machine A by means of a meta assembler running on machine B; this approach, for a variety of reasons both technical and psychological, has not yet established itself in practice.) The usual approach is to write the assembler in its own language, as if it already existed, and then assemble it by hand in the manner just described for ML patching. Hand translating from an assembly-language original carries the advantage of working from a complete specification rather than, for example, a comparatively abstract flowchart; in addition, it can serve as a check on the assembly algorithm as well.

If the programmer "plays computer," strictly following the logic of his assembler in the process of translating its assembly-language representation into ML, he will, as a bonus, discover many of the bugs in it. Often it will be sufficient to hand-assemble only a certain essential core of the new assembler, after which the rest of it can be written in a perhaps restricted assembly language and translated by the part already running. A curious result of this approach is that the first ML version of a new assembler, the hand-translated one, usually has its own assembly-language image for its first source program, and usually finds itself discarded after translating that one source program, since the version it has assembled on the computer is probably both richer in facilities and freer from bugs than the hand-assembled prototype.

A third and even more marginal application of ML may be found in the use of the unofficial instructions that enterprising programmers have sometimes discovered among a machine's capabilities, although not advertised by or perhaps even known to the developers of the machine's assembly language. While it has happened several times that bit configurations not recognized in an assembly-language manual have turned out to be interpretable by the hardware as instructions, the discovery is seldom more than a curiosity. Almost without exception, these windfall instructions cause effects for which it is difficult to think of practical uses; if programmers manage to use them at all, it is generally by twisting the design of programs so as to make a place for them. Whatever the wisdom of using such instructions, it is clear that, if used at all, they are used in ML form. (They will generally be represented in the assembly-language source program as octal or hexadecimal constants, if that feature is available, but since they must first have been conceived as bit configurations, their appearance in any form may be regarded as ML usage.)

None of the ML applications just described, especially the last two, is part of the common experience of programmers today, and apart from these applications, ML may be said to be a dead language.

**Features of AL.** The earliest assemblers were little more than routines for translating some more convenient representation of ML instructions into ML, with none of the additional features now expected as a matter of course. The primitive assembler offered the programmer only a symbolic representation of operators—ADD instead of 000101000000 for example, with decimal or octal representation of operand addresses; or octal representation of the entire instruction, 050000003770—instead of 36 binary digits.

It is instructive to note how much extra programming capability is achieved with even so rudimentary an assembly language as this last mentioned octal representation, though it amounts to just the octal-constant feature that is today considered a very minor adjunct to assembly language (AL). The 3:1 compression ratio, together with the use of eight of the familiar decimal digits, makes errors of transcription and keypunching both harder to commit and easier to spot. In addition, when represented by octal digits, at least the more common instructions become recognizable on sight.

What AL means today, though, is "symbolic" AL—a language in which all operators and all operands are normally represented by names chosen for their explanatory and mnemonic power. Some of these names, those for the operators particularly, will have been chosen by the AL designers (although many modern assemblers allow users to rename operators); operands are left for the user to name within each source program.

*Example.* The three instructions given in ML form in (1), (2), (3) would appear in AL as

```
CLA  100
ADD  101        (4)
STO  102
```

or, if the programmer cared to assign names by

means explained below to the locations involved, they could be

```
CLA  AUGEND
ADD  ADDEND          (5)
STO  SUM
```

This more convenient form for the writing of instructions is, however, only one part, and perhaps the least important part, of the advantage offered by AL. In introducing a software intermediary between programmer and computer, AL provided a framework within which all kinds of new conveniences and features could fit. The new notational features, which gave programmers more convenient access to powers already in ML, were valuable; the new substantive features—powers having no direct counterparts in ML, and made possible only by the existence of the assembler—made programming really practical. (It is essential in evaluating software to bear in mind that an accumulation of minor conveniences, none of them indispensable or even particularly impressive considered by itself, can in the aggregate amount to a breakthrough, an arrival at a new plateau of capability in programming.)

Among these substantive new features offered by the assembler are those allowing data to be defined in octal, decimal, character string, or other "natural" form; the reserving of execution-time storage space; the production of a printed, cross-indexed listing of the program, with programmer-written comments and assembler-generated warnings of known or suspected errors, all being features that let the programmer do explicitly and directly things otherwise so difficult to do that in effect they would be impossible.

*Example.* The way in which the operand names used in (5) would be assigned, for example, would be through the use of one or another of these new, assembler-born features—the pseudo-operations, as they are frequently called, since they look like machine operation codes or instructions, but are not; they are addressed to the assembler for its use in assembling the real machine instructions that form the bulk of the program. (The distinction between operations and pseudo-operations is analogous to that between a manuscript to be typed and the author's marginal notes to the typist; the latter are not to be typed, but give the typist instructions as to how to type the manuscript.) The names AUGEND, ADDEND, and SUM, for example, would have been assigned through use of pseudo-ops such as these:

```
AUGEND  PZE  0
ADDEND  PZE  0        (6)
SUM     PZE  0
```

or

```
AUGEND  PZE  0
ADDEND  DEC  1        (7)
SUM     PZE  0
```

where PZE stands for "Plus ZEro," meaning that the word in question is to contain the internal representation of $+0$, which is all zeros; DEC is for "DECimal," meaning that the number so introduced is to be interpreted as decimal rather than octal or binary. The example in (6) simply reserves the next three available words of storage (the next available word being that whose address is one greater than the last used, unless the programmer specifies otherwise) and assigns them the names given in the left-hand column, setting their contents to zero; nonzero values would presumably be stored in locations AUGEND and ADDEND before the first execution of the program given in (5), or the result would be simply to add zero to zero, and store the resulting zero in a word whose contents were already zero. The variant form (7) does what (6) does, but adds one more feature: It gives ADDEND the initial value of 1. The pseudo-op DEC instructs the assembler to interpret the number that follows as a decimal number, and to put its binary representation in the word reserved.

Each of the names so assigned to storage locations is entered into a symbol table or dictionary maintained by the assembler as it does its job, along with the actual address of the location to which it has been assigned. In this way the programmer is free to use the name alone to refer to the quantity stored in the word, leaving it to the assembler to replace this mnemonic symbol (which is meaningful only to the programmer) with the binary address that is meaningful to the machine. It must be emphasized that a programmer-chosen mnemonic symbol is simply an arbitrary string of characters to the assembler and the computer, and it is up to the programmer to see to it that the value of a location actually mirrors its name. There is nothing to prevent him, for example, from calling a location ONE, but storing a value of two or two thousand in it.

Probably the most important of the unexpected advantages of programming in symbols rather than bit patterns is the control it gives the programmer over what has come to be called "binding," the assignment of directly machine-computable values to the quantities the program is to manipulate. Since the computer cannot execute a program until it is in ML form, a narrow concept of efficiency would seem to dictate that it be reduced to that form as quickly as possible. The forced deferral of final translation that is entailed by the use of AL turns out, though, to carry advantages more important even than those originally aimed at in AL.

Programming in a symbolic language both enables the programmer to see the potential generality of a program he is currently working on, and encourages him to realize it. In doing so he may spend a little more time writing (and documenting) today's program; his reward will be that he will not have to rewrite that program tomorrow to deal with slightly changed circumstances. If the program computes a payroll, for example, the fact that AL will encourage the programmer to represent a tax rate throughout the program as TAXRATE rather than as 17.25%, defining it numerically just once, will not only make writing the program more convenient, but will also allow it to survive a change in the tax rate with unimpaired usefulness at no greater cost than reassembly with a newly defined TAXRATE. Not only that, but by forcing the programmer's mind to the slightly elevated abstraction of the symbolic level, AL tends to make him consider treating as variables other quantities he would almost certainly have treated as constants if he were programming in ML: the total number of paycheck deductions to be provided for, the number of governmental levels for which tax is to be withheld, and so on. If the possibility of changes in these quantities has occurred to the programmer before he finishes the program, it is easy for him to provide for it in any of several ways:

1. He can, as already suggested, provide a new value for a variable by substituting a new definition of it in the source program, and reassembling.
2. He can design the program to accept a possible new value from the data given it at run time.
3. He can even, under some operating systems, have the computer operator set one or more program-testable switches, thereby selecting one from among several alternate values built into the program.

But the possibility of achieving this flexibility at acceptable cost hinges on the programmer's seeing the need for it while the program is being written, at the latest. What is still very easy to do at that stage is often so hard to do after the program is written as to be practically impossible. And this is where a symbolic assembly language rewards its user by putting a certain distance between him and his immediate problem, forcing him to consider it somewhat more generally and detachedly, and thus investing it with a degree of adaptability that may save him or a colleague from having to write essentially the same thing over again.

Because the final assignment of a computable value to a program variable (e.g., 17.25% to TAXRATE) is called "binding," and its moment of occurrence "binding time," the AL property just discussed may be called "binding-time control." The degree of such control offered by a modern, multipass assembler working in conjunction with a sophisticated linking loader and an indulgent operating system is very great. Symbols can be defined in terms of other symbols to form an indefinitely deep regression, with the definition of those at the most primitive layer of the hierarchy deferred until the end of the source program or even—to push matters to the limit—until program load time.

The loaders that are prepared to handle so-called object programs in which so much binding remains to be done are misnamed, in fact, since their loading function is by this point incidental. They are actually the last (and sometimes the longest) pass of the assemblers they work with, and their use amounts to a return to the old "load-and-go" concept in which final assembly is followed immediately by loading and execution, rather than simply the production of an object program that is to be executed only when the programmer so orders. The object program (whether in the form of a card deck, tape file, or disk file) produced by the assembler part of such an assembler-loader partnership is not in ML, but in some nameless intermediate language dictated by the needs of the loader. (Here, as in the attempt to define ML, the proliferation of variants and extreme cases makes it possible to maintain a stable terminology only at the cost of a measure of arbitrariness: despite the observations just made, we will continue to refer to these translators that fail to produce ML as assemblers, and to the processors that carry these incomplete assemblies all the way to completion as loaders.)

Perhaps most important of all the possibilities opened up by binding-time flexibility is that of having variables in one program defined by values assigned to them in another. This makes it possible for a number of independently written programs —provided they observe the conventions governing the use of such "external" symbols—to join forces and become in effect one large program, and in so doing greatly extend the usefulness of the constituent programs.

Important as it is, though, binding-time control is only one aspect of a broader and more fundamental principle that was introduced into programming along with AL: decoupling. This is the technological version of the military principle, "divide and conquer"; as applied to programming, one of the things it means is the separation of potential problems and their isolation from one another so that they can be separately dealt with, and so that errors cannot propagate from one to another. Binding-time control permits decoupling the writing of an expression that relates many variables in elaborate ways from the task of giving those variables specific numeric or other computable values.

But AL programming promotes other exploitations of decoupling. The symbols used in such a program, for example, will probably be defined by the programmer in a group at the end of the source program; if there are a substantial number of them, he will probably divide them further into subgroups of constants, storage reservations, and so on, creating something very like Cobol's Data Division. In doing so, the AL programmer is led naturally to apply the decoupling principle, not merely on the level of the individual expression and its component variables, but also on that of the entire program algorithm and the data it operates on. The strikingly superior managability of programs so organized —their relative transparency to those who have to study and maintain them, their amenability to revision, and their resistance to obsolescence as circumstances change—collectively amount to an enormous advantage over ML programming, one probably far more important than the convenience an assembly language offers in simply getting a program running.

### Subroutines and Macroinstructions.

Decoupling can be seen again in the practice of subroutinizing, in which routines that have been written once are preserved so that they need not be written again—the decoupling is between work done and work yet to do. The occasion for creating a subroutine arises when a programmer notices that he has been writing essentially the same routine (e.g., one that converts external-representation numerals to internal, computable form) over and over, possibly with minor variations. Creating a subroutine for the function in question will save him from ever having to do it again, and this promise gives him the incentive to invest great care in generalizing it, debugging it, making it as compact or as fast as possible, documenting and otherwise perfecting it.

Subroutinizing, it should be noted, is not the same thing as modularizing, with which it is often confused. Both subroutines and modules are chunks of code that have been deliberately isolated, but for quite different, even opposed, reasons. The ignorance of context that is a corollary of their isolation is, for the subroutine, a fault—probably its major fault; in the module, this trait is the very reason for its existence. The success of a subroutine is often dependent on the degree to which it can be made sensitive to its environment at each call; it will be expected to approximate the efficiency of the tailor-made code it has replaced.

A module, on the other hand, like a member of a cloistered religious order, is supposed to remain ignorant of the world it lives in for the sake of higher things. The module is intended to limit the area of concern of any one programming-team member, and to minimize the impact of later changes. It does this by isolating and formalizing the channels of communication, or interfaces, between itself and other program components. A common application is the funneling of all a program's input/output requests through one module, which alone makes I/O requests on the operating system or the hardware. If the I/O facilities of the system later change in ways that affect a program that has been so modularized, only its I/O module need be revised. The module, then, can accomplish its objective only if its relations with the rest of the system are sharply restricted. A subroutine, on the other hand, will often succeed to the extent that it can adapt to the state of the calling program at each call; it should be as worldly as the module should be sequestered.

Once created, a subroutine need only be assembled along with an assembly-language program (or loaded with its ML representation) to be available as often as needed throughout that program. At whatever points in the program the function performed by the subroutine is required, a "call" to the subroutine can be written by the programmer, and a transfer to it will be made. After it has been executed, a return transfer from the subroutine to a point some fixed number of locations from the call just honored is automatically made, and the program continues. The subroutine need never be written again, nor need it ever appear more than once in a program, however often its services may be required. (What is being discussed here is, strictly speaking, the "closed" subroutine; there is also an "open" variety that is physically copied as a whole into the calling program at each point of call. This type is of little interest; it was never widely used, and has been replaced for all practical purposes by the macroinstruction, discussed below.)

Subroutinizing is useful even when practiced by a solitary programmer within one large program, but its advantages grow enormously if subroutines can be freely traded back and forth within the entire community of programmers working with one kind of computer. The possibility of doing this depends on the observance by all concerned of a number of conventions for creating and using subroutines, and these are usually set forth in the AL manual of a computer as if they were built into the hardware or the assembler. These conventions, while absolutely necessary to the interchangeability of subroutines, are responsible also for many of the unsatisfactory features of subroutine usage (discussed below), and account at least in part for the rise of an alternative form of subroutinization, the macroinstruction. Like the subroutine, the macro (as it is usually called) is a way of packaging routines for future use, but the conventions governing both its creation and its use differ greatly from those of the subroutine. The root of the difference is that the macro facility is made possible by a special processor that can be embedded within an assembler or exist as a separate piece of software; if separate, it will be given as input a source program consisting of macros and AL statements, expand the macros into the language, and pass the resulting program to a simple assembler. The consequent differences between programming with macros and with subroutines may be summarized in four categories: point of creation, appearance of call, trapping ability, and code-generating economy.

POINT OF CREATION. The new macro can be created, or defined, at any point in a program. Since the macro processor, whether embedded in an assembler or not, is put in a special macro-defining mode by the appearance of a definition, the creation of a macro does not generate any instructions in the program; only an explicit call does that.

Until called, the instructions constituting a macro definition are stored in an area under the control of the macro processor, and do not appear in the object program being assembled. By contrast, the defining of a subroutine, since it is indistinguishable from ordinary programming as far as the assembler is concerned, actually inserts the instructions of which it is composed in the host program at the point of definition. If the programmer wants the subroutine to be stored at the end of the object program when it is loaded, as he usually does, he must make its definition appear at the end of the source program.

*Example.* A subroutinized version of the miniature program created in (5) would take a form like this:

```
TRISUM CLA* 1,4
       ADD* 2,4
       STO* 3,4                    (8)
       TRA  4,4
```

In this little routine, which we have given the name TRISUM, some new programming features are used. The addresses of the four instructions refer, respectively, to the first, second, third, and fourth locations following the instruction that has just called TRISUM (the 4 following the comma is the designation of a special register, an index register, one of whose uses is to record the location of the instruction in the main program from which a subroutine (in this case, TRISUM) has been called. Its action is such that an address in the subroutine of the form "n,4" will refer to the *n*th location following that call). Another notation new to this example is the "*" following three of the instructions, denoting "indirect" use of the address that follows. Indirect addressing means that the address, modified as necessary by any index register used, is to be taken not as the location of the data, but as the location of the *address* of the data. The interpretation in this context of CLA* 1,4 is: "Bring to the accumulator the quantity whose address is one word below that in which the call to this subroutine was found, as shown in (10) below.

An equivalent macro would take this form:

```
TRISUM MACRO A,B,C
       CLA   A
       ADD   B                     (9)
       STO   C
       END   TRISUM
```

The first line of this macro definition declares that TRISUM is its name, and that this name, when used to call upon the macro, will normally be accompanied by three values (parameters) that are to replace A, B, and C, respectively, wherever these symbols occur in the definition. The ways in which the TRISUM subroutine and the TRISUM macro are called upon are explained in the next section.

APPEARANCE OF CALL. The macro is called by what is in appearance and placement just another AL operator (but one invented by the macro definer or user). The values that are to be passed down into the defining instructions when they are inserted into the program text in answer to this particular call

—the "parameters," as they are frequently called —will usually follow the macro name on the same line in a format that closely parallels that of the operands supplied with a standard AL operator.

The subroutine is traditionally called by a stereotyped series of AL instructions [see (10) below] known as a "calling sequence." This consists of transferring to the subroutine, via a special transfer instruction that records its own location before doing so; followed by a fixed number of locations reserved for the parameters that are to be passed to the subroutine with each call; and one or more for the subroutine to transfer back to when its execution is done, depending on the number of exit conditions for which it is wished to provide separate paths. In the more advanced macro processors the difference in appearance may be greater yet; they may permit the programmer to give the parameters accompanying each call on a macro in an order convenient to him on that particular occasion. The more "natural" appearance of macro calls, besides making for a more readable source program, offers a most important advantage in the trapping capability described in the next section, "Trapping Ability."

*Example.* To call upon the subroutine TRISUM defined in (9) above, we would insert into the main program at the point where it was wanted the following "calling sequence":

```
TSX  TRISUM,4
PZE  LOCA
PZE  LOCB                                   (10)
PZE  LOCC
```

The first of these instructions, TSX, is the special transfer instruction, referred to earlier, that transfers to TRISUM while marking its own location in an index register (4 in this case). This location-marking is needed so that instructions in the subroutine can reach back for the parameters being held (or, as in this example, whose addresses are being held) in the calling sequence, and so that a return transfer can be made to the proper location when the subroutine has been executed.

The three PZE pseudo-ops that follow are simply dummies whose function is to hold, in their address parts, the addresses at which parameters A, B, and C can be found by the subroutine. Each call upon the subroutine, then, would cost the execution time of the TSX and the return transfer at the end of the subroutine, plus the storage space for these two instructions and the three PZEs.

To call upon the macro TRISUM we would write, at the point where it was wanted:

```
TRISUM ALPHA, BETA, GAMMA                   (11)
```

where ALPHA, BETA, and GAMMA are the values we want to be substituted for A, B, and C on this occasion. The macro would generate into the program, at the point of call, the wanted instructions, and only them:

```
CLA  ALPHA
ADD  BETA                                   (11)
STO  GAMMA
```

The overwhelming economic superiority of the macro form over the subroutine in this example is due to our employment of an unrealistically brief piece of code as the core of each. In particular, the illustration is unfair to the subroutine in making it so trivial that it is actually shorter than the calling sequence that connects it to the main program; a more realistic impression is gotten by postulating that TRISUM is a routine of 50 or more instructions. On the other hand, the macro, too, can do better than this example would suggest; see the section, "Code-Generating Economy," and the example in the next section.

TRAPPING ABILITY. A unique property of the macroinstruction, and one having no subroutine counterpart, is its trapping ability. This enables the macro user to define any standard AL operator as a macro, and thereby trap it for special treatment. This valuable capability rests on two seemingly trivial points: first, the fact that macro calls are (or can be) identical in format to ordinary AL operators; second, the fact that macro processing precedes (or can be made to precede) ordinary assembly. By virtue of these two facts, any symbol defined both as an ordinary operator and macro name is effectively a macro name only, and will cause the generation into the object program of whatever instructions the macro author has specified. This feature would, for example, allow the programmer (1) to trap every transfer instruction in his program (or a selected portion of it) and generate instead, or in addition, instructions that would compute at execution time the actual addresses to which control is being ordered transferred; (2) compare these with limits set by the programmer; and (3) allow the transfer to be executed only if within those limits.

Preventing the execution of wild transfers would, in turn, much facilitate debugging, whose difficulty is greatly aggravated when a program is allowed to run on after a bug shows up, and particularly so when control is thereby transferred into unknown territory. When this occurs, the program is very likely to wipe out the evidence a bug hunter will need to correct it, or at least so confuse matters as to make the run useless for debugging. A similar redefinition of operations that write information into storage will accomplish, to give another example, equally useful feats in the precise protection of storage.

*Example.* A macro that would trap and test an ordinary transfer instruction (mnemonic op-code TRA) is in Fig. 1. (The new instructions introduced in this example are not explained in the same way as those introduced in earlier ones, but in pictures showing the effect they have on the accumulator or the storage location addressed.) The following shorthand notation is employed:

AC means accumulator
IR means index register
C(n) means contents of n (e.g., C(AC) means contents of the accumulator)
Y stands for the apparent address of the TRA (see explanation following example 6.1)
X stands for the index-register designation (0,1,2 or 4) in the TRA

First, this macro defines the mnemonic op-code TRA to be a macro instruction instead, so that it will be caught at the macro processing stage and expanded into the instructions shown, rather than simply passed unchanged to the assembler and there translated into its ML equivalent. The body of the macro computes the effective address of the TRA instruction evoking it (i.e., the address as written by the programmer, minus the quantity in any index register modifying it) and compares that effective address to a permissible range defined by the programmer-supplied bounds LOWLIM and HILIM.

If the address lies outside that range, the TRA instruction is not executed and control is transferred instead to one of the two error routines, TOOLOW and TOOHI. If its address falls within the permissible range, the TRA instruction is executed and the program being debugged proceeds. (The macro as given contains some simplifying assumptions, among them that the symbol ZERO has elsewhere been given the value zero; that SAV is a location having a TRA in its instruction part and zeros elsewhere; that LOCMAC is where the TRA instruction currently under test is stored, and so on.)

CODE-GENERATING ECONOMY. The macroinstruction and the subroutine differ most obviously in that each call of a macro causes a fresh copy of its defining instructions to be inserted into the text of the program being translated, while a subroutine appears in the program using it just once, no matter how often called. This distinction should not, however, be taken to mean, as it frequently is, that macro usage entails a wasteful repetitive generation of coding that could be avoided by the use of subroutines instead.

The economics of programming are such that the advantage sometimes lies with generating the substantive code as many times as it is to be executed, sometimes with generating only multiple calling sequences to a single copy of that code. The decision will hinge on such considerations as the length of the calling sequence versus that of the routine to be executed, and the relative importance of storage space and time during execution. While a decision to save time clearly points to the macro as the instrument of choice, a space-saving strategy

```
                                                                    AC            SAV
TRA MACRO  ZERO               (Define TRA to be a macro)
    CLA    LOCMAC             Fetch to AC the TRA to test     |TRA|X|Y|     |TRA|0|0|
    TIX    NOTAG, ZERO,0      Skip computation of
                              effective address if X= 0 or C(X)=0
                                                                            |TRA|0|C(X)|
    SXA    SAV,ZERO           Store C((X) into SAV
    SUB    SAV                Form Y–C(X);i.e., effective address  |0|?|Y-C(X)|
NOTAG PAX  0,1                Put effective address into IR 1
    TXL    TOOLOW,1,LOWLIM    Address too low—trap to TOOLOW
    TXH    TOOHI,1,HILIM      Address too high—trap to TOOHI
    XEC    LOCMAC             Address legal—execute original TRA
    END                       (End of definition of TRA macro)
```

**Fig. 1.**

does not point to the subroutine; it merely suggests that the macros to be employed should generate not the entire routine, but only a calling sequence to a subroutinized version of it.

In short, there is no hard choice to be made. A macro facility incorporates the ability to use subroutines as well, and to call them by means of macros, with the superior writability and readability of that form. In at least one macroinstruction processor based on assembly language, the programmer is allowed to include within a macro definition both a subroutine and its calling sequence; at the first use of the macro, the processor copies both the calling sequence and the subroutine into the object program, the former at the point where the macro was used and the latter back with the data. Subsequent uses of the macro cause only the calling sequence to be copied, the processor recalling that it has already incorporated the subroutine into the program.

*Example.* Schematically, the kind of macro subroutine combination referred to would look like this:

*Macro definition*:

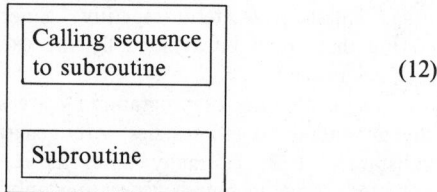

| Calling sequence to subroutine |
| Subroutine |

(12)

Calls upon such a macro would generate code as follows:

First call in a program:

| Calling sequence to subroutine |
| Subroutine ← Probably placed at end of program |

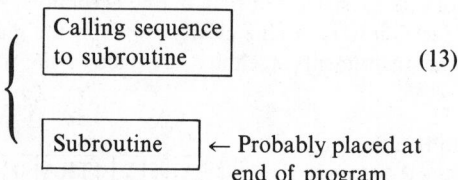

(13)

Second and all succeeding calls:

| Calling sequence to subroutine |

(14)

**Roles and Applications of AL.** It has long been expected, and from time to time announced, that compiler languages would supplant AL as thoroughly as it in turn had supplanted ML. This replacement has not occurred; AL survives and even flourishes. The fundamental reason is clear: AL is a general language, standing to the compiler languages as English stands to the jargons of various trades and professions. AL allows the programmer to do with the computer anything it can do at all, while compiler languages trade this versatility for superior applicability to a limited range of problems. If compiler languages existed for every conceivable application, no role might be left to AL, but such complete coverage is unlikely in the foreseeable future. For one thing, new applications continue to arise with no end in sight. For another, the cost of developing and maintaining a compiler language and all its supporting sub- and superstructure is such that a very large community of users is needed to justify it economically, and it may well be that the science-engineering and business markets served chiefly by Fortran and Cobol, respectively, are the only ones large enough to support such efforts.

Beyond these general grounds for the continued importance of AL lie several specific roles for which it seems uniquely well suited—ecological niches into which it fits so well as to insure its survival against any competitor now visible. Among these at least five are worthy of being named and examined: fine tuning, early responsiveness, machine accessibility, pioneering, and craftsmanship.

FINE TUNING. Because only the AL programmer directly and consciously determines the machine-language instructions that are to be executed, and the detailed internal representation of the data upon which they are to operate, he alone can guarantee that a program will fit within a given area of storage or execute within a given period of time. He is also the programmer who can most plausibly claim (no guarantee is possible here) that a program has been so written as to take either the least possible space or the least possible time to execute.

Programs, or program segments, may be arbitrarily restricted in execution time because they are real-time applications, i.e., directly linked to other equipment or processes operating fast enough so that even a computer is pressed to keep up with their demands. Examples of such equipment and processes include the evaluation of radar signals to produce target-tracking displays, and antenna-steering commands, which typically involve computer linkage to equipment based on the same technology that supports the computer itself, and hence have comparable speed in input demand and output generation. With a permissible slight stretching of terminology, it may be said that in such applications the computer is rushed because it is trying to satisfy another computer.

Programs may be arbitrarily restricted in the storage space (particularly in highest-speed, or CPU, storage) available to them because they are to be executed by a multiprogramming system in which each task is allotted a partition of predetermined size within which it must reside. This is becoming an increasingly common strategy of computer resource allocation as attempts are made to keep all components of a computing system productively busy by having them deal concurrently with several distinct programs. Such space constraints may be due, however, to nothing more than the absolute size of the machine involved.

Where the computer has to operate within a missile, aircraft, or other highly weight- and space-limited environment, its storage size may be such as to make the program hard to fit in, even though the machine may be dedicated to one task alone.

Whatever the circumstances, a requirement that a program be executable within critical time or space constraints generally implies that it should be written in AL. (It is possible to write such a program in a compiler language, if one is available, and then, if the program so compiled should exceed the given limits, to rewrite parts of it in AL so as to make it fit. This approach requires a very detailed knowledge of the way in which the compiler generates its object code if the hand-written code being introduced is to work smoothly with its host. The difficulty of deciding what part to rewrite, and the uncongeniality to programmers to revise others' coding rather than write their own, make this a seldom-chosen alternative.)

*Example.* A problem that occurred in the development of the original Fortran compiler for the IBM 704 offers a vivid example of a situation in which AL alone will do. It was found at a late stage in the development of that compiler that a quantity had been put into the wrong index register, and that if the omission were to be rectified without extensive modification to the compiler, it would have to be done under drastic constraints. These constraints dictated that space for only two instructions was available to load the index register with the requisite value, and that this two-instruction sequence had to be absolutely autonomous. It could not affect storage or arithmetic registers, nor could it assume the existence of any particular value in any location other than that of the desired value in another index register. The following two instructions did accomplish this seemingly impossible task (the source and target index registers are here arbitrarily taken to be 1 and 2, respectively):

```
LXD  *+1,2                                    (15)
TXI  *+1,3,0
```

The first of these instructions loads the target index register (number 2) with the quantity (0) in the so-called decrement portion of the next instruction ("next" symbolized by *+1). The second location contains an instruction whose exact identity was unimportant (any of several would have done). Its only functions were (1) to contain a value of zero in its decrement part so that the LXD would know where to find one (recall that this patch could not take for granted the contents of any location outside itself) and (2) to address the nonexistent index register 3.

The 704 had but three index registers (1, 2, and 4); if the numbers 3, 5, 6, or 7 were used where an index-register number was expected, the index registers affected would be those whose numerical designations summed to form the number given. The effect on the actual index registers so designated was to form the logical OR of their contents and store the value so formed into each of them. It should be apparent how the storing of a zero in the target index register (number 2), followed by the execution of an instruction that involved a reference to the mythical index register 3, could achieve the desired movement of the value in index register 1 to index register 2. A compiler language (such as Fortran itself) would not have permitted the programmer to specify the index register into which a quantity was to be loaded, let alone a nonexistent index register. Solving this problem was possible only through a combination of intimate knowledge of the machine and the availability of AL to exploit that knowledge.

Another common fine-tuning application of AL is the writing of segments of code that are to be executed so often as to make their time or space-optimization economically worthwhile, if not strictly necessary. These include practically anything that has been found worth turning into a subroutine, practically all general-purpose software (to be discussed separately), and the critical parts of big, long-lived, compiler-language application programs. This last category is worth emphasizing because its hazards are seldom appreciated until they present a serious problem.

The compiler-language application programs that are candidates for this treatment are those whose execution consumes a substantial part of the total machine time available at their installation, and hence offer real savings if they can be speeded up. If such a program has been written in a compiler language, a clever programmer, familiar with the code the compiler has generated and also with the characteristics of the program at hand, is very likely to be able to improve it significantly by rewriting in AL some small but critical section. It would not be very remarkable for such a programmer to be able to speed up such a program tenfold by rewriting a few hundred lines of code. This can often be accomplished, in fact, by essentially negative actions involving no substantive new coding at all. Just the deletion of stretches of code that (representing the compiler writer's desire to serve a wide range of needs) offer options or safeguards not relevant to the program at hand, or the removal of a few instructions from the innermost loop of a deep nest, or the mere reordering of a number of file searches to reflect the programmer's knowledge of the probable contents of those files may be sufficient to show dramatic improvements in execution time.

With such rewards awaiting him, an installation manager is strongly tempted to relax the edict that only Fortran (or Cobol, or whatever) is to be used in his shop, but if he succumbs to this enticement, all his big compiler-language programs will tend inexorably to become hand-written AL programs that use a thin shell of compiler-generated code just to interface with the operating system they must run under. The danger of this practice is sometimes unrecognized until the installation that has permitted it decides to replace its computers. Thinking that all his principal programs are, for example, Fortran-language programs, the installation manager supposes that only their recompilation through the new machine's Fortran compiler will be needed to get them running on it. The discovery that many of these programs are substantially handwritten on the old machine in AL, usually by programmers who are no longer available and who did not much care for documenting their work, can be a painful one.

If an installation adopts the policy of allowing compiler-generated programs to be improved by the implanting of handwritten AL—and there may be excellent reasons for doing so—it should adopt it formally, with explicit recognition of the attendant dangers and careful provision against them. Essential among the safeguards will be putting all such optimization work under the direction of someone who believes wholeheartedly in the importance of full and lucid documentation.

EARLY RESPONSIVENESS. To insure that their development will be carried on in an orderly and thoughtful way, and above all in a way that will not jeopardize their machine independence, the standard compiler languages have been entrusted to various national and international standards organizations (in the United States chiefly to the American National Standards Institute, known as ANSI). These organizations, which attempt to include or at least consult representatives of all concerned parties, issue formal definitions of the languages entrusted to their care, and entertain proposals for their enrichment and revision. Part of the price that must be paid for this elaborate and necessarily slow-moving apparatus of consultation and deliberation is that additions to the compiler languages, even if approved at every stage of review, are a very long time in coming. Usually, years pass between the first proposal that a new feature be incorporated and the actual appearance of that feature in manufacturer-supplied software. This gap between programmer requirement and compiler response leaves another opening for AL, which, under the sole control of the manufacturer concerned, can be used at the one-for-one level to get the job done immediately or, if time permits, to enrich the system with subroutines or macros, either by the manufacturer or by users.

MACHINE ACCESSIBILITY. As "early responsiveness" reflects the immediate answer of AL to the requirements generated by application programmers, so "machine accessibility," refers to its unique responsiveness in making available all the capabilities built into the machine by its manufacturer. Providing such access is generally impossible for the compiler languages, which—again because of their need to remain machine independent—cannot refer to any machine facility not common to all on which those languages are to be offered. If some, but not all, of the machines on which a compiler is to run include, say, a program-testable real-time clock, then the compiler language cannot be augmented with statements that let users refer to that clock without restricting the transferability of source programs that do so, or without forcing the compiler to generate coding that simulates such a clock on those machines not having it in the hardware.

Since neither of these penalties is acceptable (the second is not always even physically possible), the outcome is that such nonuniversal features are simply ignored in the standard compiler languages. For most purposes, this partial disabling of the machine is tolerable; for a few, and most particularly for systems programming, it is not. Whatever distinctive features a machine offers must be usable by its software, or they may as well not exist. Since software itself is a major consumer of machine time, time so spent is felt to be nonproductive overhead by application-minded programmers and budget-minded installation managers, so it is doubly important that a system be as fast as possible. This requirement means that software has to be written in a language that allows access to all machine features, and thus normally rules out the standard compiler languages.

Computer manufacturers and other regular software producers have long sought to develop for their own in-house use a special language that would combine most of the advantages of compiler languages with the fine machine control offered by AL. They would thus acquire for their internal task a tool as good as those they provide for their customers. Many such projects have been mounted, and many interesting languages have come out of them, but none has yet proved completely satisfactory. Therefore AL remains, so far, the standard language for the writing of software.

PIONEERING. Because of those attributes listed above, particularly under "Machine Accessibility," AL is almost the invariable choice when a wholly new computer application is being pioneered, even though the necessity for its use may not be clear at the outset. When it is uncertain what the demands of the new species of program are going to be, the safest course is to use the language that imposes no constraints. After a number of AL programs have been written in the new application area, it may turn out that one of the existing compiler languages (almost always with some modifications) is adequate, or it may be found that the new application is sufficiently different (and economically important) to warrant the development of a language tailored to its needs. AL programming experience forms, among many other things, the breeding ground for specialized language development.

CRAFTSMANSHIP. One reason for the continued use of AL, which has caused some clashes between programmers and their managers, is that its programming is widely felt to be the most professional and demanding kind, and many career programmers will seek to use it even when none of the reasons discussed above applies. To a considerable extent, the programmer's private wish to use AL can coincide with the best interests of his installation. No matter how adamant management may be about running a pure Fortran or Cobol shop, there must always be a few programmers behind the scenes who can read dumps, help the application programmers with special debugging problems, understand the operating system, and deal as equals with the computer manufacturer's systems engineers.

Furthermore, a knowledge of AL often helps the programmer to use compiler languages more efficiently, clarifying the relation between what he writes and what the compiler produces, and warning him about the hidden points in compiler-language usage where the price of execution may suddenly rise tenfold because the code compiled has exceeded some critical machine dimension. And if AL specialists in what is nominally a pure compiler-language shop are to keep their skills sharp, they must be allowed to practice them. Even in such a shop, then, some AL programming will take place, with the connivance if not the wholehearted approval of installation management.

Beyond these reasons for tolerating AL usage in a compiler-language shop—reasons that make sense from management's viewpoint—there is the good programmer's personal desire to learn more about the machines and systems his programs depend upon, to be able to understand dumps and other operating system messages, and in general to upgrade his skills and deepen his understanding, even when there is little or no foreseeable benefit to his present employer in his doing so. This instinct to practice one's craft at the highest possible level of capability is a perennial one that will, independent of economic considerations, continue to turn many programmers toward AL.

Neither the roles discussed above nor the qualifications of AL to fill them would seem to be in any immediate danger of vanishing. By means of such devices as the macroinstruction, the subroutine, and the externally defined symbol, this language potentially affords its user the chief powers of the higher-level languages, embedded in a general programming language that is oriented to no one application, but which gives access to all the powers of the computer to a programmer who knows how to use them. This combination of power and generality suggests that, contrary to innumerable predictions of its imminent extinction, AL has a long and vigorous future before it.

**Source Literature.** ML programming seems to have generated no literature, and AL has had little of any consequence written about it. On most topics that the reader may want to pursue further, relevant articles in this Encyclopedia will probably be the best resource. On the loading of programs that have been translated into ML, and the linking together of such separately translated programs when they refer to each other symbolically, see Presser and White (1972). For the internal workings of assemblers, see Barron's (1972) lucid explanation.

REFERENCES

1972. Barron, D. W. *Assemblers and Loaders*, 2d ed. New York: American Elsevier.

1972. Presser, L., and J. White. "Linkers and Loaders," *Computing Surveys*, Vol. 4, No. 3 (September), pp. 149–167.

M. HALPERN

# MACHINE INSTRUCTION SET

For articles on related subjects *see* ADDRESSING; INPUT-OUTPUT INSTRUCTIONS; MACHINE AND ASSEMBLY LANGUAGE PROGRAMMING; OPERAND; OPERATION CODE; PRIVILEGED INSTRUCTION; and SHIFTING. For articles on related terms *see* BOOLEAN ALGEBRA; and MICROPROGRAMMING.

A machine instruction is a string of numbers in the base in which the machine operates. When interpreted by the hardware, the instruction causes a unique and well-defined change in the state of the computer.

This rather rigorous definition calls for a more loosely worded explanation. Most computers today are based on the binary system. Therefore, for most cases, the "string of numbers" will be a string of bits, each having the value 0 or 1. In what follows, we will refer to instructions with bits only, although for convenience we will express those bits using hexadecimal notation.

In the definition given above, the words "interpreted by the hardware" really mean "used by the hardware." The change in state of the machine is, in fact, a change in the contents of various registers or memory locations. The changed registers may be those explicitly, or implicitly, referred to by the instruction, or they may be some internal registers not directly known to the user. For example: The 16-bit string 1010000100100001 (hexadecimal A121), when interpreted by the hardware of one of the IBM System 370 computers, causes the contents of register 1 to be added to register 2, the result replacing the previous contents of register 1. In this case, the change of state is apparent to the user of the machine. On the other hand, on the same machine, the bit string 0000011111110001 (hexadecimal 07F1) causes an inaccessible internal register, the program counter, to set its value to that of register 1, thus causing the next instruction that has to be interpreted by the hardware to be taken from the location whose address is the contents of register 1.

It is important to realize that each computer possesses its unique instruction set. The same bit string may mean completely different things on two different computers, even if the number of bits needed for expressing an instruction is the same on the two machines. Thus, the bit string A121 (hexadecimal), which we used as an example on the IBM/370 and which caused addition of two registers, when interpreted by a Data General Corporation NOVA computer will decrement by one the contents of the memory location whose address is in location 18 and skip the next instruction if the result is zero. This different interpretation for the same bit string makes it clear that bit strings are not a good basis for classification of machine instructions. We will therefore introduce several categories in order to be able to find some patterns in the multitude of instructions available on various computers.

**Classification of Machine Instructions.** We have already hinted that machine instructions differ in length, i.e., in the number of bits needed to express an instruction. There is usually a simple relation between the length of the computer word or addressable unit and the instruction length. Thus, we find up to four instructions per word in the B5500 and CDC 6000 series, but one instruction per word in most minicomputers.

The length of the instruction need not be fixed. For example, in the IBM/370 we find instructions whose length is 16, 32, or 48 bits. In most minicomputers we have single-length (i.e., one word) instructions and double-length instructions.

The bit string representing a machine instruction is generally divided into two major fields: the operations (or "op") field and the operand(s) field, usually referred to as the address field. Note that this is completely analogous to the way a mathematician denotes a function; i.e., $g(x,y,z)$ means the function (operation) $g$ on the variables (operands) $x,y,z$. The number of operands available in each instruction is generally different, not only between different machines but also in the same machine between different operation types, as we will see later. However, neither the question of number of operands nor the question of the way they are addressed will be discussed here. The interested reader is referred to the coverage of "addressing" elsewhere in this Encyclopedia. This article concentrates on the operation field only.

The types of operations available on contemporary machines are roughly divided into arithmetic, logical, data move, and control operations.

ARITHMETIC OPERATIONS. Arithmetic operations are usually confined to the four basic ones (plus, minus, multiply, and divide) and to the "compare" operation, which serves to record status information about the relative magnitude of the operands. These arithmetic operations may operate on different types of operands, such as integers and floating-point numbers, with different precision (half-, single-, or double-word length numbers). The operands may assume various bases. Binary is the usual one, but decimal is also common, especially on business-oriented machines. In specialized machines, one may find arithmetic operations of a more sophisticated nature, such as exponentiation or square root, but this is rare.

An example of an arithmetic operation is: Add an integer number in register 2 to an integer in register 1, replacing the previous contents of register 1 by the sum. Instructions of this type are found on various computers. In an IBM 370 computer, this instruction will be coded a A121 (hexadecimal). This is the instruction used at the beginning of this article. Fig. 1 gives the structure of an IBM 370 instruction, and from it we can gain some preliminary insight into the actual structure of a machine instruction. Thus, the first eight bits (i.e., hexadecimal A1) are the actual operation code, the last eight bits (i.e., hexadecimal 21) being the address field. In this particular instruction, the address field specifies register 2 with the first four bits and register 1 in the last four bits. On a Data General Corporation NOVA computer, the same instruction has the hexadecimal code CE10. Not only is the code different, but the breakdown of the instruction into fields is also completely different.

LOGICAL OPERATIONS. The logical operations usually contain boolean operations on the bit values of the operands. Although there are 16 possible boolean operations between two operands, usually only a subset of these (typically AND, OR, and NOT) is available. This subset is sufficient to reproduce all other boolean operations. In this category, one usually includes also the various possible shift instructions, although in some classifications these form a category of their own.

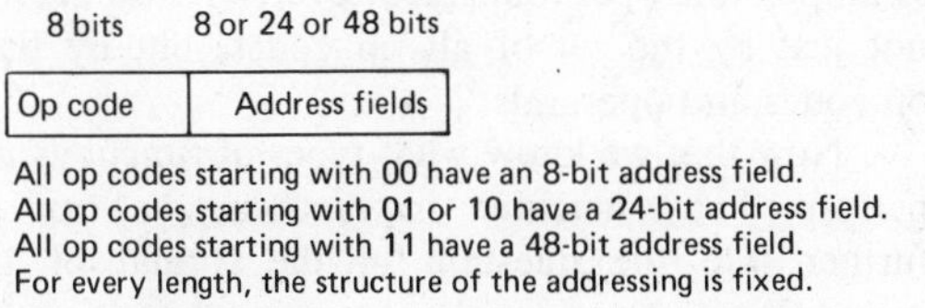
8 bits
8 or 24 or 48 bits
Op code
Address fields
All op codes starting with 00 have an 8-bit address field.
All op codes starting with 01 or 10 have a 24-bit address field.
All op codes starting with 11 have a 48-bit address field.
For every length, the structure of the addressing is fixed.

**Fig. 1.** Typical structure of a vertical instruction set (IBM 370 series).

Boolean operations are most easily represented by truth tables. A truth table describes all the possible outcomes of a boolean operation on a pair of bits, in a way similar to that in which a multiplication table describes the possible outcome of the multiplication of two numbers. For example, the boolean operation AND has the following truth table, which should be read as follows: 0 AND 0 yields the result 0; 0 AND 1 yields 0; etc.

| A | B | AND (A,B) |
|---|---|---|
| 0 | 0 | 0 |
| 0 | 1 | 0 |
| 1 | 0 | 0 |
| 1 | 1 | 1 |

Boolean operations are used for the manipulation of parts of words, for decision processes, and for nonnumerical processing. As an example, consider the following problem: Given a data item in a register, isolate the last six bits of it. By inspecting the AND operation truth table, one finds that the result of an AND with 0 is always zero, whereas the result of an AND with 1 reproduces the operand. Thus, an AND operation between the given data item and an operand that has 0 in all places except in the last six bits (all of which are one) will isolate the last six bits of the given data item. Thus:

| | |
|---|---|
| Given data item: | Arbitrary bit string |
| Second operand: | 0 . . . 0 111111 |
| Result of AND: | 0 . . . 0 6 last bits of given data item. |

Operations like this are called "masking" operations. Note that the bit string representing the instruction is completely independent of the actual data. On an IBM/370, assuming that the first operand is in register 3 and the second in register 4, the instruction will be hexadecimal 1434.

Other common boolean operations are the OR operation with the following truth table and the NOT operation, which changes 0 to 1 and 1 to 0. Note that the AND and OR operations have two operands, whereas NOT has only one.

| A | B | OR (A,B) |
|---|---|---|
| 0 | 0 | 0 |
| 0 | 1 | 1 |
| 1 | 0 | 1 |
| 1 | 1 | 1 |

Shifting operations, as their name implies, shift the bits in a word to the left or right. The differences between types of shifts affects what happens to the bits being shifted out of a word and what bits are shifted in. For example, in logical shifts, the bits shifted out are lost and the bits shifted in are zeros. In an instruction that will shift two places to the left logically, the leftmost two bits of a data item are lost, and the last vacated two positions are filled with zeros. A discussion of "shift operation" appears elsewhere in this Encyclopedia.

DATA MOVE OPERATIONS. The data move instructions include moves of data between memory locations and registers, and the input/output instructions necessary for communication between the central processor and peripheral devices. Examples of the former operations are instructions to load and store a register and to move data from one location in memory to another. The input/output operations are of such a complexity that no useful example can be given without an extensive explanation.

CONTROL OPERATIONS. The control instructions include those operations that are necessary for the proper sequencing of the instructions so that the programmed task can be performed correctly. These include conditional and unconditional branches, test instructions, and status-changing instructions.

As an example of this category of instructions, there may be instructions like BRANCH to a given sequence of instructions when the result of the last operation is negative, or if there was an arithmetic overflow. There are also instructions that swap the contents of the user accessible registers with internal registers, thus causing a change in the state of the computer; in particular, this may cause execution of a completely different sequence of instructions. The reader is reminded here that program flow can be affected not only by explicit control instructions issued by the programmer, but also by special conditions known as "interrupts," which are covered elsewhere.

This rough division of instructions into types is not necessarily exclusive. Referring to the previous example of a NOVA (compared with IBM 370 in Fig. 1), the bit string represented by the hexadecimal number A121 will perform both an arithmetic operation (decrease; i.e., subtract 1) *and* a control operation (skip the next instruction if the result is zero).

An important remark has to be made at this point. Since addressing is not discussed here, it is not evident that the different instruction types usually possess different numbers of operands. Whereas arithmetic operations usually refer to three operands (two for the data locations and one for the result location), either explicitly or implicitly, certain control instructions may have one or no operands at all. For example, an unconditional BRANCH has one operand, but a HALT instruction has none. In addition to the operands involved in the instruction execution, there are also condition codes involved. Generally speaking, condition codes are indicators, usually one-bit long, which describe the properties of the results and the validity of the operation performed.

Examples of condition codes are explicit indications of (1) the sign of the result, (2) whether or not an overflow has occurred, (3) what the relative magnitudes of the operands are, (4) whether there is a parity in reading or writing to memory. Similar to the instruction repertoire, the variety of condition codes differs between computers. There is also a difference in the way that condition codes are used. In some computers they are incorporated directly in the instructions, especially conditional branches (like BRANCH on overflow), and in others they can be transferred into registers and then manipulated as data.

**Machine Language and Instruction Formats.** The previous examples indicated that what a computer does can generally be expressed in terms of what operations take place in the registers of the machine. In such a computer the operation code fully defines the operation to be done. The *machine language* is defined to be the set of all possible operations, and in a computer of the type discussed previously, this boils down to the set of all possible operation codes (op codes).

There are, however, other types of computers such as the tagged architecture machines in which the operation code *does not* fully describe the operation to be done. In such a computer, part of the operation performed is defined by the type of the operand. For example, there is only *one* ADD operation, and this is done in floating-point or integer mode, depending on the type of the operand. The machine language of such a computer is still the set of all possible operations. However, it is now defined not just by the set of all op codes, but by both op codes and operands.

Now that we know what types of functions are performed by machine instructions, we can go further into the question of the format of the instruction, but again without treating the addressing in any detail. As we have mentioned, a machine instruction can be written, using mathematical notation, as $g(x_1, x_2, \ldots, x_n) = g(x)$, where $g$ is the operation performed on the $n$ operands:

$$x_1, \ldots, x_n = x.$$

The natural question to ask is: Can we have multiple operation instructions in the form

$$g_1(x_1)g_2(x_2)g_3(x_3) \cdots g_n(x_n) \quad (1)$$

where the operations $g_i$ are performed on the operands $x_i$ and the operand sets are either identical, partially overlapping, or distinct from each other? The answer is that machines with such instruction sets do, in fact, exist. Quite roughly, we can divide instruction sets into vertical and horizontal. Vertical instructions are those of the type *g(x),* where a single operation or a time-ordered series of a *fixed* number and *type* of operation is performed on a single set of operands. Vertical instructions are usually highly coded (see below).

Horizontal instructions are those of the form (1). Here the functions $g_i$ are *independent* and are performed on the respective operands in parallel or in a well-defined time sequence.

The instruction set of an IBM/370 series computer is an example of a vertical instruction set (see Fig. 1). That of the Digital Scientific Corporation META-4 computer is an example of a horizontal instruction (see Fig. 2). This second example requires some explanation. In the META-4 computer, there are four types of instructions, each having a different field structure (i.e., in each type the interpretation of the various bits is different). We have chosen one of the possible instruction formats. It has six operations done in parallel, two of them control the arithmetic/boolean devices and one controls the program flow. The functions $g_i$ shown in form (1) are thus two arithmetic, two shift, and two control. In Fig. 2 they are denoted by $A$, $A$, $S$, $S$, $X$, and $F$, respectively.

Vertical instructions are found in most machines today. Horizontal instructions are mainly found in microprogrammed machines and in certain minicomputers.

The structure of the operation code itself, i.e., the structure of the contents of the operation field, is also of interest. In principle, if one wants a certain number of instructions, it seems sufficient to associate a function with each number expressible in the operation field. The operation then is determined by *all* the digits (in the binary case, the bits) in the field. By inspecting a part of that field, we generally have no meaningful information about the operation. We call such an arrangement a "highly coded" one. In the highly coded arrangement, the number of possible instructions is equal to the total information contents of the field. In a field of $n$ bits, this means a total of $2^n$ possible instructions.

On the other hand, one can envision a completely different situation in which each part of the instruction code conveys some information about the type of the operation. For instance, the first bit in the field may determine if the instruction is arithmetical or nonarithmetical. The second bit may determine the length of the operands; the third, the arithmetic mode (real or integer), etc. In this case we speak about a "low level of coding." The number of instructions expressible in this case is smaller than the total information content of the op code field, since some of the combinations may be unused. For example, if the instruction is logical, the arithmetic mode may be irrelevant. The low decoding level needed for this type of instruction, and the strict interpretation of the various bits, enable a high degree of parallelism in the decision process that the hardware has to go through in order to decide which instruction has to be performed.

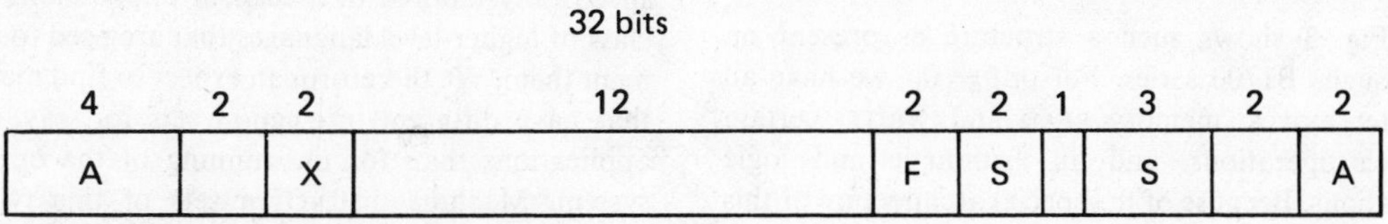


A, A – Arithmetic/Boolean Controls (functions)
X – External Control
S, S – Shifter Control
F – Program Flow Control

**Fig. 2.** Typical structure of a 32-bit horizontal instruction (DSC META-4). Nonmarked fields are used for addressing. A,A = arithmetic/boolean controls (functions); C = external control; S,S = shifter control; F = program flow control.

Up to this point we have assumed that the operation field is of fixed length, and in the case of a low decoding level, the bits have fixed meaning. Neither of these assumptions is either necessary or actually used in all machines.

The basis of coding theory teaches us that it may be advisable to have codes of different lengths, utilizing short ones for the more frequently used combinations and long ones for the least used. Indeed, one finds computers that possess what can be called a "tree-structured" instruction code, i.e., the operation field is divided into parts and each part is interpreted in sequence, with the meaning attached to it dependent on the results of interpretation of the preceding part. This not only solves the problem of meaningless bit settings that we encountered in the low decoding level combinations, but it also enables us to terminate the op code interpretation at a different point for different instructions.

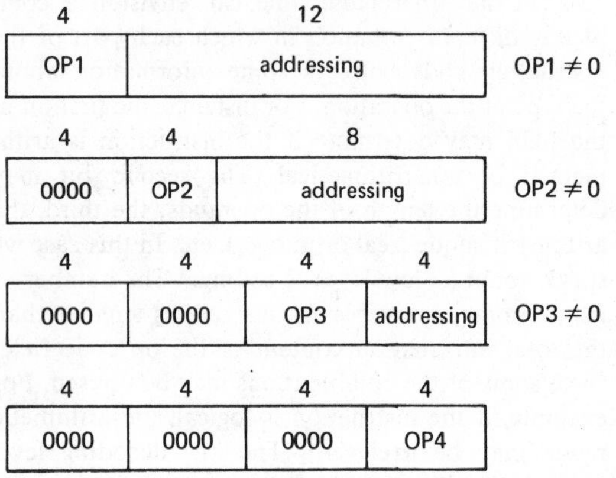


**Fig. 3.** Typical structure of a 16-bit variable length instruction code (Burroughs 1700). Note that the addressing structure is different for each type of instruction.

Fig. 3 shows such a structure as present on Burroughs B1700 series. For op1 $\neq 0$, we have all register moves, memory READ and WRITE, certain branch operations, and all arithmetic and logic operations. Because of the special architecture of this machine, part of the operation is defined by the structure of the address field, a feature that enables a large number of operations even though there are only 15 bit patterns for op1 $\neq$ 0. For op1 = 0, op2 $\neq$ 0, we find memory/register swap operations, register clear, shifts, and register increments and decrements. The instructions with op1 = op2 = 0, op3 $\neq$ 0, and those with op1 = op2 = op3 = 0, op4 $\neq$ 0, are used far less frequently. Computers that possess this feature need smaller numbers of bits to express a sequence of instructions than do other types of computers (possibly excluding machines that rely heavily on stacks).

**General Remarks.** This article has described single machine instructions according to their length, operation type, the degree of parallelism in the specification of the operation, the number of operations specified, and, finally, the degree of coding. We conclude with some general remarks on the capabilities of machine instruction sets.

It goes without saying that instructions are built into a machine in order to be utilized. This is, however, easier said than done. One has to realize that, at this time, higher-level languages are the main means of program implementation. Thus, instructions that are present in the machine, but which are difficult to include in the code produced by a higher-level language compiler, may have limited use. If those instructions have been included to support types of applications that are usually coded in higher-level languages, they are useless.

Generally speaking, a machine instruction set is a grouping of instructions according to their intended application. As always in statements of this kind, the grouping is extremely vague. For example, it is well accepted that floating-point operations are to be considered as part of a scientific instruction set. These instructions, however, may prove quite useful in many other complicated data processing computations. String manipulation and sophisticated data moves, for example, are of value both in business data processing and in compiling. Thus, in this classification, we rely more on instinct or on the choice made by a vendor than on a strict set of rules.

With the advent of microprogramming, it is possible to implement instruction sets that will be specifically tailored to a class of applications and a class of higher-level languages that are used to implement them. We therefore can expect to find machines that have different instruction sets for, say, Cobol applications than for the running of the operating system. Machine instruction sets of this type are usually referred to as language-oriented instruction sets. At the time of writing this article, such sets have been proposed for APL, Fortran, Cobol, and operating system and compiler writing. Examples of complete instruction sets are available in most computer manufacturers' manuals.

G. FRIEDER

## MACHINE-READABLE FORM

For articles on related subjects *see* INPUT-OUTPUT DEVICES; OPTICAL CHARACTER READERS; and OPTICAL MARK READERS.

Machine-readable form refers to the form in which information is encoded for direct, automatic input into a computer. Punched cards contain information in machine-readable form, for example, because machines are able to "read" the information by sensing where the holes are. Information handwritten in script is typically not machine-readable, because devices are not yet available which can handle the wide variations in style. One exception to this is carefully hand-printed characters on certain forms (e.g., social security numbers or driver's license renewals), which are read directly by optical scanning devices.

**Fig. 1.** Honeywell Type 236 MICR-document reader/sorter, which can handle up to 1,625 documents per minute.

In general, punched cards, punched paper tape, magnetic tape, disks, drums, data cells, etc. carry information in machine-readable form for the express purpose of being read exclusively by computers. Some printer and typewriter output on paper can be machine-read by optical scanners, and is also directly readable by humans, unlike the magnetic coding on tape or disk. Magnetic-ink characters, used principally for coding bank-accounting information on checks, are readable by humans (optically) and by machines (magnetically). Such magnetic-ink character recognition is often referred to by its abbreviation MICR. A typical MICR reader is shown in Fig. 1.

C. L. MEEK

## MACHINE TRANSLATION. *See* LANGUAGE TRANSLATION.

## MACRO LANGUAGES

For articles on related subjects *see* MACROINSTRUCTION; PROGRAMMING LANGUAGES; and STRING PROCESSING LANGUAGES.
For articles on related terms *see* ASSEMBLERS; COMPILER; STRING; and SYMBOL MANIPULATION.

A macro language is a string-manipulation language that makes use of macros. A "macro" is a stored string in which particular sites of the string are marked so that other strings can be inserted in the sites when the stored string is brought forth from storage. A fully developed macro language is capable of conditional branching, arithmetic, control at run-time of string input and output, and dissection of strings into single characters and chunks. It is also able to make use of files, and has diagnostic and tracing facilities.

An unusual feature of a macro language is that all commands in the language, such as string storage, string retrieval, and arithmetic, are considered to be valid data objects. Thus, sequences of such commands may be stored as strings or macros like any other strings. When the stored string with commands is brought forth, the commands in the string or macro are executed. A macro language is run interpretively, i.e., a program in a macro language is not compiled. The result is a very powerful though unusual kind of computer language.

A macro language system should be contrasted with the "macro processors" and "macro generators" that are often found embedded, in a subsidiary role, in certain assemblers and compilers. Such macro processors used in programming systems are constrained by the requirements of the particular programming system in use. This is especially true of their command format and in their lack of control of input and output at run time. For this reason, such macro processors are not able to exploit fully the general string-manipulation capabilities inherent in the macro concept.

Macro languages were developed as derivatives or as descendents of the macro techniques used in macro assemblers. Around 1960, Eastwood and McIlroy observed that when the output of a macro assembler was taken to be in assembly language, the macro assembler was actually putting out a sequence of alphanumerical symbol strings. They were able to show (as a tour de force) that their macro assembler could, with great contortions, be made to perform symbolic differentiation. The macro assembler that they developed, BE-FAP, powerfully influenced later macro assemblers. While widely used in program development, it was not used extensively for general symbol manipulation.

The two actual "macro languages" that have appeared (as contrasted to program-development macro processors) are GPM and TRAC® (a registered service mark of Rockford Research, Inc.). GPM, for "general-purpose macrogenerator," was developed by Christopher Strachey (1965). The TRAC language was developed by Mooers (1966). These two macro languages have a remarkable similarity in principle, though they were developed completely independently.

GPM was developed with the intent of providing a very general tool to assist in assembly-language computer programming. It is classed here as a macro language because it was not specialized to program development. It was used to some extent in Cambridge, England, for program development, but has not apparently been given continued support.

The TRAC language is a more elaborately developed macro language than GPM. In the following discussion of macro languages, the notation and elements of the TRAC language will be used for the sake of definiteness.

The operation of the TRAC macro processor takes place on strings in a "workspace." The strings are scanned character by character until a fully formed executable statement is formed, and this statement is then executed. Execution may produce another string or a side-effect action, or sometimes both. If an executable statement produces a "value string," this value string replaces the executable statement in the workspace. Typically, the scanning action resumes in the workspace at the head end of the new value string. In other words, the new string is again scanned.

For example, #(RS) is an executable statement in TRAC language. This statement may be immersed in a surrounding string in the workspace:

```
ABC#(RS)XYZ
```

When the scanning action has fully marked out the statement #(RS), execution takes place. Suppose that it produces the value string

```
THIS IS TEXT
```

The new value string replaces the executed statement, giving in the workspace the string

```
ABCTHIS IS TEXTXYZ
   @
```

The scanning action resumes at the location of the character @.

TRAC language executable statements are prefixed by either #( or ##( . They are terminated by ) . Executable statements may be concatenated or nested inside others to any degree. They may have several argument strings, such as

```
#(DS,A1,THE FAT OLD CAT)
```

The commas separate the several arguments in the expression. The action of this expression is to store the string THE FAT OLD CAT with the name A1. The kind of action to be taken is specified by the first argument, DS. The abbreviation DS stands for "define string" or "define and store."

The simplest form of an executable statement, i.e., one that has no other nested executable statements, is called a "primitive." TRAC language has 34 kinds of primitive executable statements. Each kind is given a two-letter designation, which is used in the first argument of the primitive expression.

The expression #(RS) is actually an expression controlling input of strings from an on-line typewriter. The abbreviation RS stands for "read string." When #(RS) is executed, the processor receives characters as they are typed at the connected reactive typewriter. Finally, when the TRAC meta character ' is typed, the input action stops and the string that has been received is inserted into the workspace, replacing the # (RS) expression.

Output of strings in TRAC language is controlled by the "print string" primitive, illustrated by #(PS,CAT). When this primitive is executed, the string CAT is printed out on the reactive typewriter. The expression has a null string (no characters) as its value string. This null string replaces the expression after its execution; in other words, the expression disappears and nothing is put in its place. The define-string primitive DS also has a null-string value.

A stored string may be copied (nondestructively) into the workspace by means of the "call" primitive with abbreviation CL. Thus, the stored string named A1 may be brought back into the workspace with the call #(CL,A1), whose value string after execution is

THE FAT OLD CAT

Expressions may be nested to produce compound effects. Thus, the string named A1 can be brought into the workspace and then typed out with the expression

#(PS,#(CL,A1))

Execution begins with the innermost expression, so at an intermediate stage there is

#(PS,THE FAT OLD CAT)

Finally, the string is typed out at the typewriter.

Executable expressions can also be stored, to be executed at some later time. For example, the expression

```
#(DS,A23,(#(PS,#(CL,A1))))
         *                *
```

will cause the storage of the executable expression #(PS,#(CL,A1)) under the name A23. The two asterisks * are inserted here merely to mark the pair of parentheses that serve to protect the contained expression from going into execution before the storage action takes place. These parentheses are removed in the scanning operation, and the enclosed string goes into storage.

Execution of the stored expression is initiated by the call #(CL,A23). This call places the stored expression into the workspace, where it is scanned, and execution takes place. The final result is that the string THE FAT OLD CAT is typed out at the typewriter.

Such a stored expression can also be copied into the workspace without causing execution by the call ##(CL,A23). The effect of the prefix ##( is to cause the scanning to resume following the tail end of the value string resulting from the call.

Branching in the TRAC language is the result of two primitives: (1) for testing for string equality, and (2) for testing whether one number is greater than another. They are illustrated by

#(EQ,AB,BB,YES,NO)

which produces the string value NO, since the strings AB and BB are different. If they had been the same, the string value would have been YES. Numerical comparison is illustrated by

#(GR,13,5,ABCD,XXX)

which produces the string value ABCD, since 13 is greater than 5. In both these primitives, any argument string may be used in the different argument positions. In particular, the last two arguments may contain calls to different executable expressions, thus causing branching of control. TRAC language does not have a GO TO.

Formal variables can be inserted into the stored strings, such as the string named A1, by means of the SS primitive expression. For example, the result of

#(SS,A1,CAT,FAT)

is to cause the stored string with name A1 to be modified so that it becomes

THE 2 OLD 1

When called, such a modified string can have new strings inserted into these formal variable positions. For example,

#(CL,A1,DOG,HAPPY)

has the string value THE HAPPY OLD DOG, which replaces the call expression in the workspace.

Portions of stored strings may be brought forth by means of several special primitives. Thus the "call character" primitive #(CC,A1) produces the single letter T the first time it is used. The next time it is used, it produces H, then E, and so on, ignoring the markers for the formal variables.

In comparison with TRAC language, GPM might be said to have only two primitives, the define string and the call. It has no explicit input/output control as first defined. Various actions on strings are synthesized by clever combinations of the available tools. Instead of the SS primitive, GPM requires the explicit writing of the formal variable markers at the time the string is stored. Because of its very limited repertoire of primitives, GPM requires a very high level of ingenuity in order to get it to do relatively simple things, such as addition. Accordingly, it has been used relatively little as a macro language outside of program development. On the other hand, because of its very minimal amount of "apparatus," it deserves study by the serious student from the theoretical or logical standpoint.

REFERENCES

1965. Strachey, C. "A General Purpose Macrogenerator," *Computer Journal*, Vol. 8, No. 3.

1966. Mooers, Calvin N. "TRAC, A Procedure-Describing Language for the Reactive Typewriter," *Comm. ACM*, Vol. 9, No. 3 (March).
1969. Brown, P. J. "A Survey of Macro Processors," Vol. 6, Part 2. *Annual Review in Automatic Programming*, pp. 37–88.

C. N. MOOERS

# MACROINSTRUCTION

For articles on related subjects *see* ARGUMENT; ASSEMBLERS; MACHINE AND ASSEMBLY LANGUAGE PROGRAMMING; MACRO LANGUAGES; PROGRAMMING LANGUAGES; SUBPROGRAMS, CALLING; and SUBROUTINE.

In its simplest form, a macroinstruction (which is usually called, simply, a "macro") is a single computer instruction that stands for a given sequence of instructions. This can be illustrated by taking an analogy from the English language. Originally, people working with computers spoke of a "binary digit," but since this is a frequently used term, people got tired of saying it and coined the more concise word "bit" to use instead. The word "bit" is therefore a macro that stands for "binary digit."

To implement macros, it is necessary to have a piece of software called a "macro processor." Macro processors are available on almost all computers, but there has been no standardization in their design. Hence, each computer tends to have a different kind of macro processor implemented for it, though fundamentally all macro processors are much the same. The job of a macro processor is simple. The programmer supplies some macro definitions, which define the macros and what is to replace them, and the macro processor then replaces any occurrence of the macro accordingly.

This is best illustrated by an example, which will be taken from the assembly language of a hypothetical computer. Assume, for instance, that at several points in his program a programmer needs to increase a variable, whose name is COUNT, by 1. Assume further that this takes three assembly-language instructions:

```
LOAD  COUNT
ADD   1
STORE COUNT
```

It would be wasteful of a programmer's time to keep writing out these three instructions in full. It would be much better for him to choose a single name (BUMPCOUNT, say) to stand for these instructions, and then to write the name every time he wished to specify the three instructions. He would then process his program according to Fig. 1.

The macro definitions define BUMPCOUNT and instructions that are to replace it. In practice, there would probably be several other macro definitions as well. The macro processor then scans the program, replacing each occurrence of BUMPCOUNT by its expanded form. It would similarly process any other macros that had been defined. As a result of this, the program is then in pure assembly language and can be passed on to the assembler, which processes it in the normal way.

The reader may wonder why the assembler itself cannot be adapted to deal with BUMPCOUNT, thus obviating the need for the two-part process illustrated above. The answer is that assembly languages, as are almost all other computer languages, are inflexible, and the ordinary programmer is not allowed to change them. To return to the earlier analogy, the assembler is akin to a person who has been taught about "binary digits," and he is not going to understand anyone who calls them "bits." Hence, if anyone does speak of bits, he needs an interpreter—the analogy of the macro processor—to convert to the assembler's style of language. In summary, therefore, computer languages are intrinsically inflexible, but with a macro processor to act

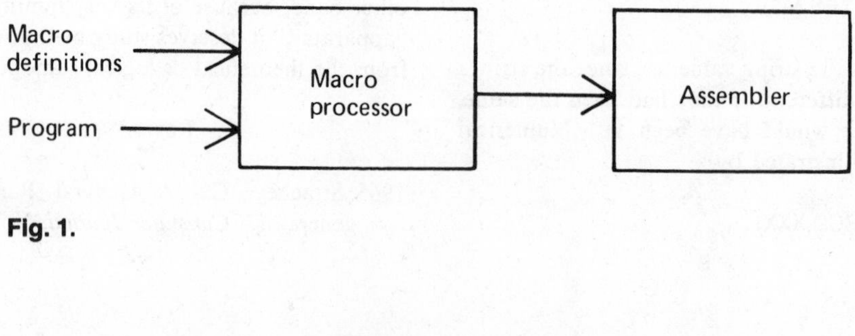


**Fig. 1.**

as interpreter, this need not inconvenience the programmer.

Thus far our picture of macros has been an oversimplified one in that the most important and powerful aspect has not been mentioned. This concerns macros with variable elements.

To return to the example of the BUMPCOUNT macro, the defect of this macro as it stands is that it works only for one variable, COUNT. In practice, it would be much more useful to have a general macro (called, say, BUMP) that could be used to increment any variable by 1. This can, in fact, be done. The name of the variable to be incremented is written immediately after BUMP, and is called the "argument" of the macro. The macro processor can be told to insert the argument at various points in the replacement of the macro. Thus,

```
BUMP     (name)
```

would be replaced by

```
LOAD     (name)
ADD      1
STORE    (name)
```

where any name of a variable could occur as *name*.

It is possible to have more than one argument to a macro. For example, it would be possible to specify a macro of form

```
PRODUCT     X,Y,Z
```

which for any *X, Y*, and *Z* would compute *X* to be the product of *Y* and *Z*.

Beginners at programming often find it hard to distinguish between the concept of a macro and that of a subroutine. The difference is, in fact, clear-cut. A macro is actually replaced by its expanded form. Hence, if a program contains *n* occurrences of a macro, then *n* copies of the instructions it stands for are inserted into the program. (Note, however, that if the macro possesses arguments, the instructions need not be identical in all the cases.) A subroutine, on the other hand, involves a break in the flow of a program. If a sequence of instructions occurs frequently in a program, then these can be written as a subroutine, and each occurrence in the program is replaced by an instruction to jump to this subroutine, execute it, and then return. There is then only one copy of the sequence of instructions. (Viewed at a more fundamental level, a subroutine is a run-time replacement and a macro a replacement at the time of translation.)

Macros are most often used to represent relatively short sequences of instructions or sequences that involve a relatively large number of insertions of arguments. But sometimes macros are quite long sequences of instructions, in which case the macroassembler will normally generate a calling sequence to a subroutinized version of the macro. Often a set of macros is combined into a library; a very common example of this is a library of macros to aid communication with an operating system.

Looked at from another viewpoint, a macro is a way of extending a language. Thus, once the BUMP macro has been defined, a programmer can treat BUMP as an extra assembly language instruction. It is common practice to build an extensive group of macros, and it often happens that a program is built entirely of macros and devoid of true assembly-language instructions. In this case the macros can be thought of as forming a new language in their own right. Macros are therefore a useful tool for building up programming languages, though they are not normally powerful enough to build up from assembly languages to such higher-level languages as Fortran.

Needless to say, such relatively sophisticated uses of macros require more facilities than have been described here. In particular, it is necessary for macro processors to contain a decision-making facility so that the instructions to replace the macro can depend on the form of a macro argument and the context in which it occurs.

The examples considered so far have shown macros for assembly language, as this is the most popular use of macros. Indeed, a macro processor is often combined with an assembler to make it appear to the programmer as if the two are a single unit, called a "macro assembler." However, macros can be used with any programming language and, perhaps most interestingly of all, as an end in themselves.

As an example of the latter, assume that a computer is being used to print invitations. Each invitation is identical except for the name of the person to be invited. One way to do this would be to define a macro called, say, INVITE, which generates the invitation, inserting the argument at the necessary places. This macro could then be used by writing

```
INVITE     STAN       JONES
INVITE     MONICA     SMITH
. . . etc.
```

In more general applications, macros can be used to provide a replacement facility in any written text. At the simplest level, macros may be used to replace one word by another throughout a document, and can therefore be used to correct systematic errors or make systematic changes. To deal with applications such as this, there exist so-called *general-purpose* macro processors.

REFERENCES

1960. McIlroy, M. D. "Macro Instruction Extensions of Compiler Languages," *Comm. ACM*, Vol. 3, No. 4 (April), pp. 214–220.
This is a classic early paper on macros and gives a good insight into their potential power.

1969. Kent, W. "Assembler Language Macroprogramming," *Computing Surveys*, Vol. 1, No. 4 (December), pp. 183–196.
A tutorial paper on macro assemblers, particularly the macro assembler for IBM System/360.

1971. Macleod, J. A. "MP/I—A FORTRAN Macroprocessor," *Computer Journal*, Vol. 14, No. 3 (August), pp. 229–231.
One example of a macro facility designed for a higher-level language.

1974. Brown, P. J. *Macro Processors and Techniques for Portable Software*. New York: John Wiley.

P. J. BROWN

# MAIN FRAME

For articles on related subjects *see* CENTRAL PROCESSING UNIT; and MEMORY: Main.

For article on related term *see* MULTIPROCESSING.

The main frame of a computer system is the cabinet that houses the central processor and main memory. It is therefore separate from the peripheral devices (card readers, printers, tape drives, etc.) and device controllers. Typically, it is the largest component in size and cost, but modern electronics have allowed great reductions in both in recent years. The main frame usually has many indicator lights (sometimes as part of the operator's console) to show fault conditions, memory contents, etc. The central processor and main memory are housed together as an aid in increasing processing speeds (cable lengths will be short) and improving reliability (e.g., both will be at similar temperatures and humidities). The term "main frame" comes from the use of "frame" as a device to hold electronics (rack is also frequently used); and the frame holding the electronics that do the computing might reasonably be the main frame.

In modern systems with very large main memory, some memory modules are housed in cabinets separate from the main frame. Frequently, they are attached and thus become part of the main frame cabinet. Multiprocessor systems with more than one central processor (CPU) are referred to as two- or three-main frame systems, in which case the main frame refers only to the CPU and not to the main memory.

C. L. MEEK

# MAIN MEMORY. *See* MEMORY: Main.

# MAINTENANCE OF COMPUTERS

For articles on related subjects *see* PERFORMANCE OF COMPUTERS; REDUNDANCY; and RELIABILITY AND FAULT TOLERANCE.

Like all sophisticated equipment, computers undergo the cycle of repair, check-out, operational readiness, failure, and back to repair. When the cost of a machine's not being in service is high, methods must be applied to reduce these out-of-service, or downtime, periods. The cost of downtime is not simply the lost revenue when the computer is not used, but also the cost of having to rerun programs that were interrupted by the ailing system, perhaps loss of real-time data, loss of control of external processes, opportunity costs, and costs related to user inconvenience, dissatisfaction, and reduced confidence in the system. Other costs are related directly to the diagnosis and corrective repair actions, and associated logistics and bookkeeping.

Due to the complexity of the equipment, as well as managerial judgment, many users, even some sophisticated computer-knowledgeable users, often decide not to maintain the system (processors, memory, system software, peripherals) themselves, but rather to have a maintenance contract with the system manufacturer. The cost of a maintenance contract over the useful life of the equipment in relation to its capital cost is quite high. It is also a good indicator of the expected unreliability. High costs due to unreliability and maintenance needs are a strong argument for designing dependability, maintainability, and serviceability into the equipment.

Decisions such as whether to have one's own maintenance personnel, what spare parts to stock and in what quantities, what test instruments are required, etc., have to be faced. Mathematical tools offered by operations research, such as dynamic programming and others, are often used to model the system in an attempt to arrive at optimal solutions to this complex problem.

**Preventive Maintenance.** One means of reducing the direct cost associated with an unexpected system failure is to provide scheduled downtimes for the purpose of preventive maintenance. Obviously, a deliberate scheduled shutdown is less disruptive than that due to an unexpected system failure. During the downtime the general idea is to tune up the system so that things that are in marginal working condition will be identified and remedied. Diagnosis should be made by exercising all aspects of the system to catch latent failures and those that may have already occurred but have been lying undetected. Failed portions of the system are likely to be undetected if they have never been called into service, and therefore their operational readiness would not have been verified.

Typically, most computer centers use a few hours every week, (say, Saturday mornings) for scheduled preventive maintenance. Especially prepared diagnostic programs may be run to exercise the hardware, benchmark programs may be run to verify timing and accuracy considerations, peripherals may be serviced by oiling, removing dust, and paper chad, replacing ribbons, etc. The typical cyclical behavior of a maintained system is shown in Fig. 1. The number of tasks and the sequence of possibilities between the detection of a malfunction and the resumption of operating time are shown in the flowchart of Fig. 2. The complexity of time relationships is codified in Fig. 3.

**Maintainability.** For the purposes of better understanding and for controlling maintenance requirements, we will attempt to quantify the foregoing considerations by defining quantitatively the applicable terms, such as maintainability and availability,

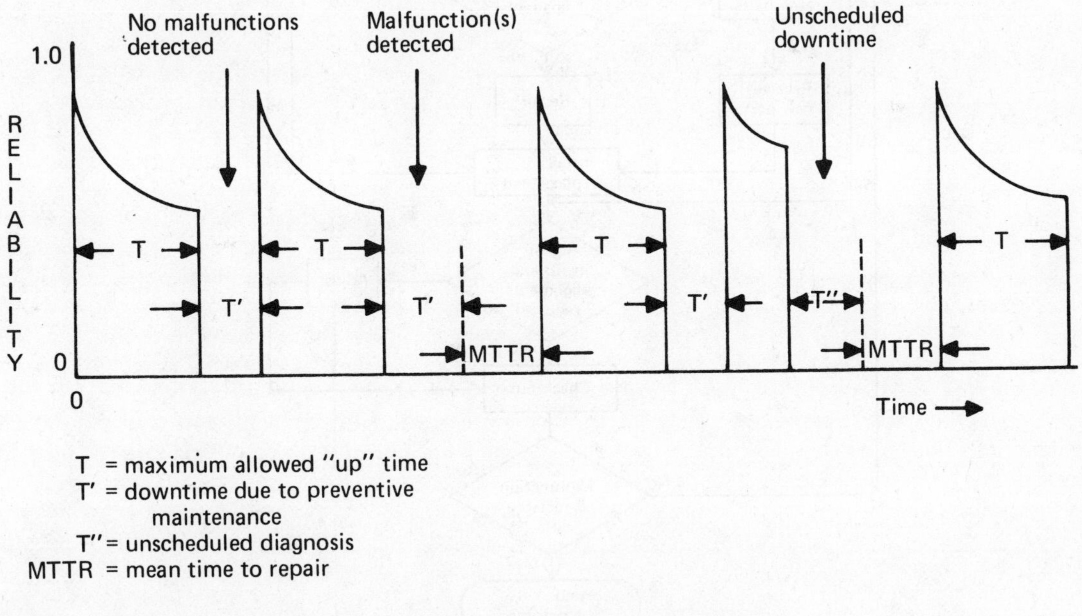


**Fig. 1.** Cyclical behavior of a maintained system. T = maximum allowed "up" time; T′ = downtime due to preventive maintenance; T′′ = unscheduled diagnosis; MTTR = mean time to repair.

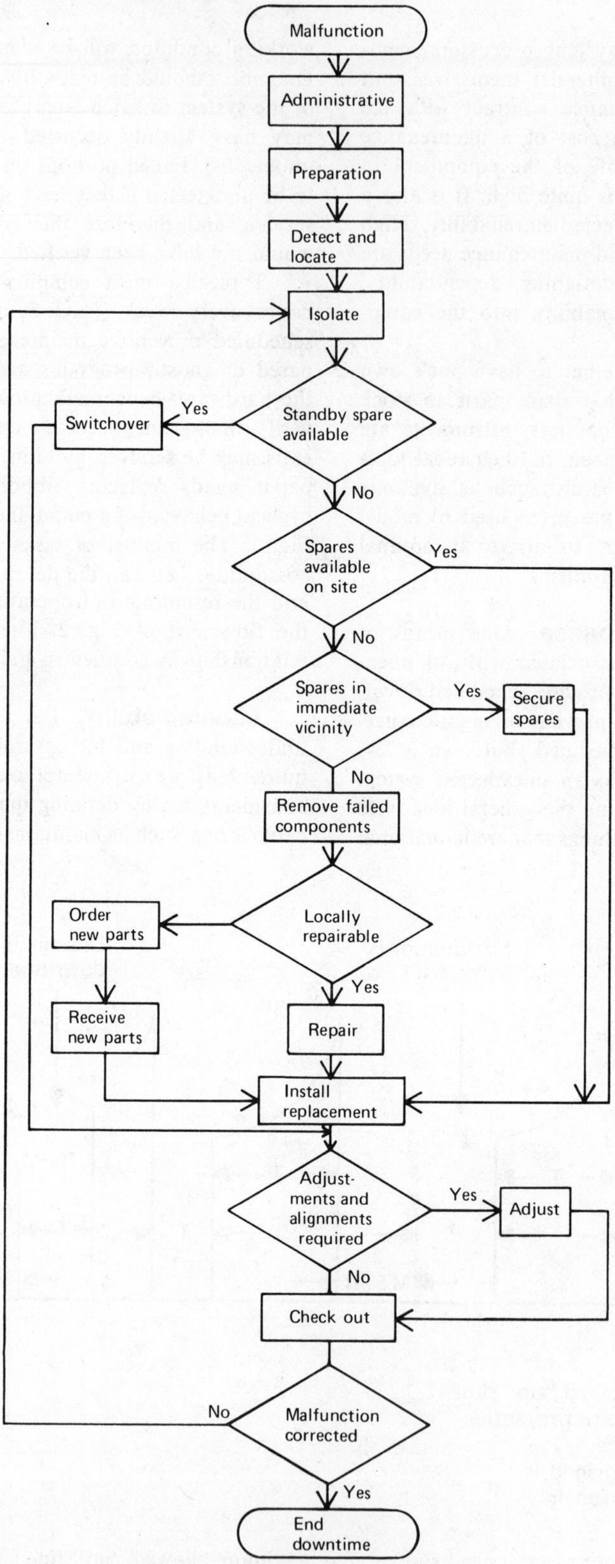


**Fig. 2.** Flowchart for maintenance operations.

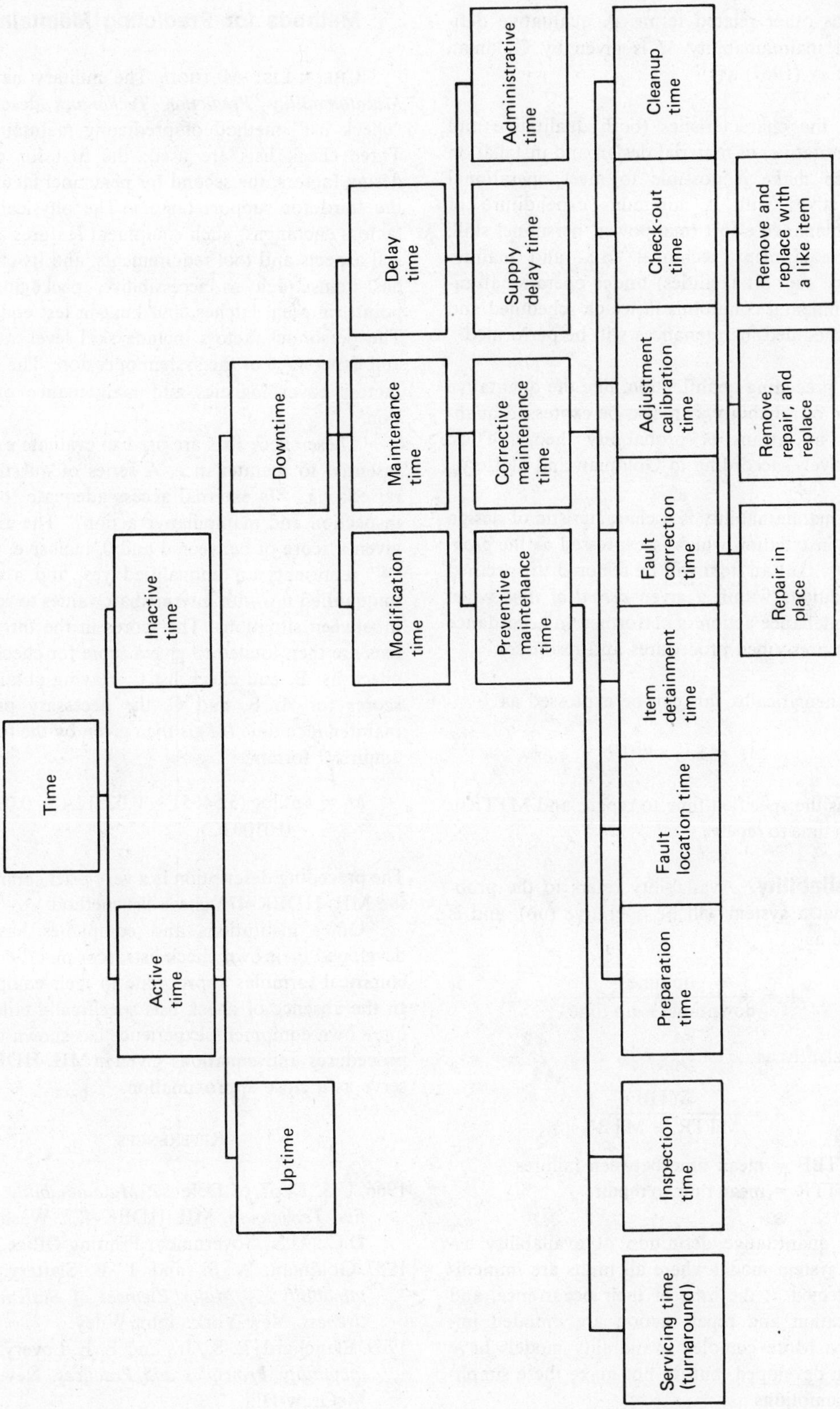


**Fig. 3.** Time relationship. (Adapted from O.A. Meykar, "Maintenance Terminology Supports the Effectiveness Concept," *IEEE Trans. on Reliability*, Vol. R-16, No. 1, May 1967.)

as well as other related terms. A qualitative definition of maintainability $M$ is given by Goldman and Slattery (1967) as

> ... the characteristics (both qualitative and quantitative) of material design and installation which make it possible to meet operational objectives with a minimum expenditure of maintenance effort (manpower, personnel skill, test equipment, technical data, and maintenance support facilities) under operational environmental conditions in which scheduled and unscheduled maintenances will be performed.

The preceding qualification, like the qualitative definition of reliability, can also be expressed quantitatively by means of probability theory. Thus, quantitatively, according to Goldman and Slattery,

> ... maintainability is a characteristic of design and installation which is expressed as the *probability* that an item will be restored to specified conditions within a given *period of time* when maintenance action is performed in accordance with prescribed procedures and resources.

Mathematically, this can be expressed as

$$M = 1 - e^{-t/\mathrm{MTTR}}$$

where $t$ is the specified time to repair, and MTTR is the mean time to repair.

**Availability.** Availability refers to the probability that a system will be operative (up), and is expressed as

$$A = \frac{\text{up time}}{\text{downtime} + \text{up time}}$$

or equivalently as

$$A = \frac{\mathrm{MTBF}}{\mathrm{MTTR} + \mathrm{MTBF}}$$

where MTBF = mean time between failures
MTTR = mean time to repair

The quantitative definition of availability assumes a system model where all faults are immediately detected at the time of their occurrence, and fault location and repair action are initiated immediately. More complex availability models have also been developed, but do not make these simplifying assumptions.

## Methods for Predicting Maintainability

CHECK-LIST METHOD. The military handbook *Maintainability Prediction Techniques* describes a "check list" method of predicting maintainability. Three check lists are used: the first for physical design factors, the second for personnel factors, and the third for support factors. The physical design factors encompass such equipment features as physical aspects and tool requirements, and its check list has items such as accessibility, packaging, test-points, internal latches, and built-in test equipment. The personnel factors include skill level, attitudes, and experience of the system operators. The support factors cover logistics and maintenance organization.

These check lists are used to evaluate each step essential to maintenance. A series of questions are raised: e.g., "Is external access adequate for visual inspection and manipulative action?" The answer is given a score of between 4 and 0, inclusive, where a "4" represents an unqualified yes, and a zero an unqualified no, with intermediate values to represent inbetween situations. The scores in the three check lists are then totaled to give a score for check list A, check list B, and check list C. Having obtained the scores for A, B, and C, the necessary predicted maintenance time ($M$) is then given by the following empirical formula:

$$M = \text{antilog}\,(3.54651 - 0.02512\mathrm{A} - 0.03055\mathrm{B} - 0.01093\mathrm{C}).$$

The preceding description is a very brief summary of the MIL-HDBK-472 check list method.

Other institutions and companies have also developed their own check lists, scoring criteria, and empirical formulas appropriate to their equipments. In the absence of check lists specifically tailored to one's own equipment, experience has shown that the procedures and equations given in MIL-HDBK-472 serve as a close approximation.

### REFERENCES

1966. U.S. Dept. of Defense. *Maintainability Prediction Techniques*, MIL-HDBK-472. Washington, D.C.: U.S. Government Printing Office.

1967. Goldman, A. S., and T. B. Slattery. *Maintainability: A Major Element of System Effectiveness*. New York: John Wiley.

1969. Blanchard, B. S., Jr., and E. E. Lovery. *Maintainability Principles and Practices*. New York: McGraw-Hill.

1972. Cunningham, C. E., and W. Cox. *Applied Maintainability Engineering*. New York: Wiley-Interscience.

F. P. MATHUR

# MANAGEMENT INFORMATION SYSTEMS

For articles on related subjects *see* COMPUTER SYSTEMS; DATA BASE AND DATA BASE MANAGEMENT; INFORMATION SYSTEMS; MODELS; PLANNING APPLICATIONS; and SIMULATION: Principles.

Management information systems are devised to aid management in organizational planning, operation, and development. Beyond such a general characterization there is no accepted definition of the term. The two most prominent characteristics of a management information system (MIS) are the emphasis on managers as the users of the system and the orientation of the design of the system around a "corporate data base." Both characteristics have developed historically as a result of the evolution of computer use in business and manufacturing organizations.

## EVOLUTION OF ORGANIZATIONAL INFORMATION SYSTEMS

The initial use of computers in organizations was directed toward replacement of existing clerical operations by an automated (computerized) system. This was the result of the need to demonstrate the economic benefits of the computer to the organization through reduction of clerical costs. This type of application was identified as business data processing (BDP), electronic data processing (EDP), or automatic data processing (ADP), and usually consisted of regularly scheduled processing of large numbers of similar transactions such as time cards and commodity orders. Each application was organized around one or more master files, usually stored on magnetic tape.

As the individual applications were mechanized, it became evident that the results of one application were frequently input to another system, but had to be manually transcribed or at least reformatted by the computer. During this period, the more powerful late-second and early-third generation systems became available. The second generation of BDP systems placed more emphasis on outputs to help management control the organization and aid decision making at the operations level by producing summary reports similar to those received earlier, but which were compiled more rapidly and contained more data. With the increasing capability of computers to store larger amounts of information, and the fact that many of the applications which can be economically computerized have already been computerized, a wider range of computer use has evolved. Attention now focuses on systems that are designed to aid management in planning and decision making, and the term MIS emphasizes this change. The interrelationship of operations, control, and planning applications is shown in Fig. 1. Many of these applications, such as planning, models, and simulation, are discussed elsewhere in this Encyclopedia.

**Organization of the Data Base.** One other characteristic of MIS concerns the orientation in the design of the system. In the routine data processing applications, the system tends to be organized around sequential files and the operations performed on the files. This was necessary previously for the type of application for which computers were effective because sequential magnetic tape files were the only large file storage then available. However, the problems of management are continuously changing, and it is difficult to forecast the exact data that will be needed. Therefore, the emphasis has shifted to the design of an integrated data base, which contains the information that is "basic" to the organization.

Now MIS can be considered an information storage and retrieval system with the capability to answer the queries raised by management, based on all relevant data. Data base management software provides the capability to use the data base, interactively if possible.

**Performance Evaluation.** In order for a system to have the capability to answer inquiries, the necessary data must be available. Much of the data needed for management information systems comes from the routine data processing system of the organization. However, additional information has to be obtained from external sources, since management is concerned to a large extent with interaction with the outside environment. The cost of maintaining the data base can be expensive, and it is frequently difficult to determine the benefits precisely. Hence, the benefit/cost analysis of manage-

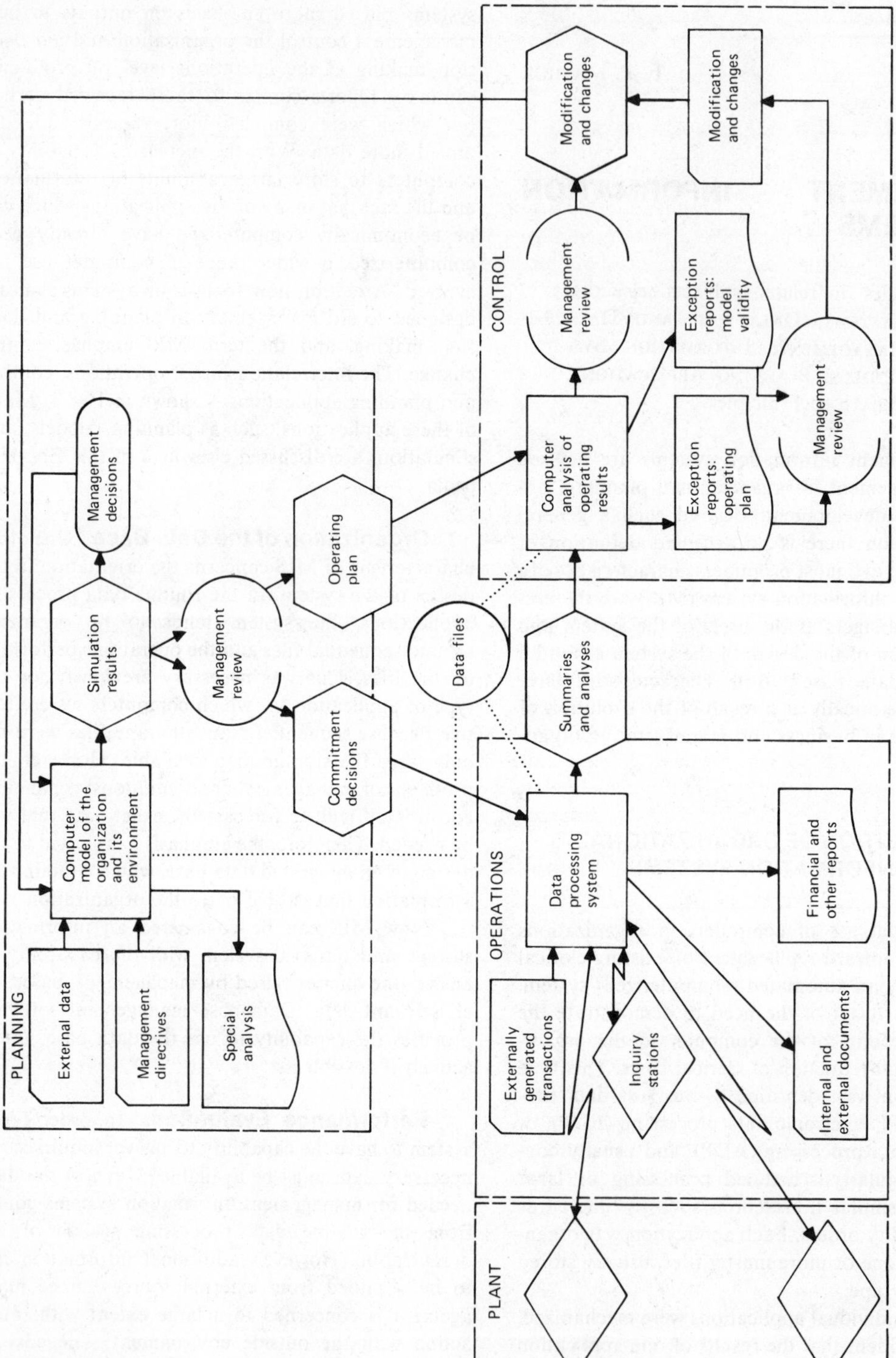


**Fig. 1.** An integrated operations, control, and planning system. (From D. Teichroew, "Data Display in Business Information Systems," *Stanford Graduate School of Business Bulletin*, Vol. 32, No. 3, 1963.)

ment information systems tends to be much more difficult than is the case for routine data processing systems where benefit is more easily identifiable in terms of cost reduction.

**Design of MIS.** The general principles for the design of management information systems are essentially those for the design of any information system. There is, however, a considerable literature devoted to design of management information systems, especially with regard to the type of information needed for management decision making and the characteristics of the display devices. These system designs are oriented toward the managers *as users* of the system.

**Experience with MIS.** Many systems labeled as MIS have been announced and have raised great expectations. However, many have not lived up to their promises. Their problems frequently have more to do with organization than with technology. While most organizations now have extensive computer-based information systems that accomplish routine processing, provide data for decision making at the operational level, and provide some data for management decision making and planning, there is considerable debate about the impact that such systems have had on management. Precise, controlled experiments are difficult in this situation, and therefore the literature consists mostly of case studies and personal opinion.

However, several reasons lead us to believe that the impact of MIS will be greater in the future. In particular, the cost of hardware is decreasing and the capability in terms of larger memories, faster processing, and better display is increasing. (The latter is particularly important because developments in MIS also emphasize the use of quick response and display of information by terminals, graphical formats for reports, etc.) Consequently, larger and better systems can be built at reasonable cost. Also, considerable research has been devoted to the development of software systems that will make it easier for management to interact with the computer to get the necessary information. Considerable experience has been gained in the use of these systems.

Management itself is learning to use the systems. It is common experience that once any computer-based system is developed, its users want more from it, once they learn to use what they are getting. It is likely that management will find MIS more useful and valuable as managers become more familiar with them and/or the MIS get better.

**Sources of Information on MIS.** The literature on MIS is voluminous and continuously growing. Among the academic articles casting doubt on the MIS approach are those by Dearden (1972) and Ackoff (1967). A view of MIS by an executive is contained in two papers by Hanold (1968, 1972).

The Society for Management Information Systems (SMIS), 221 North LaSalle, Chicago, Illinois 60601, is the major society devoted specifically to MIS. The proceedings of the SMIS 1971 Conference in Denver describe the experience of two large corporations (Westinghouse and Weyerhaeuser) and MIS. The proceedings of the SMIS 1972 Conference in Montreal give examples of systems at each of the levels: operational control, tactical planning and control, and strategic planning and control.

Publications on the general management aspects of MIS appear in references in publications such as the *Index to Business Periodicals.* For example, a paper by Kennedy (1970) reports on a survey of what companies are doing about MIS. Another source of information is the *EDP Analyzer*, published by Canning Publications, 928 Anza Avenue, Vista, California 92083. Information about specific management information systems for particular industries or types of organizations is usually covered in the publications for those industries or organizations. Information regarding the computer-related aspects of MIS appear in the publications of computer societies such as ACM; *Computer Reviews*, for example, has a section entitled "Management Applications."

References

1967. Ackoff, Russell L. "Management Misinformation Systems," *Management Science*, Vol. 14, No. 4 (December), pp. B147–B156.

1968. Hanold, Terrance. "A President's View of MIS," *Datamation* (November), pp. 59–62.

1970. Kennedy, David W. "What a President Needs to Know About MIS," *Financial Executive* (December), pp. 52–56.

1972. Dearden, John. "MIS Is a Mirage," *Harvard Business Review* (January-February), pp. 90–99.

1972. Hanold, Terrance. "An Executive View of MIS," *Datamation* (November), pp. 65–71.

D. Teichroew

# MANUFACTURERS, COMPUTER

For articles on related subjects *see* CONTROL DATA CORPORATION 6000 SERIES; DIGITAL COMPUTERS: Early; IBM 360-370 SERIES; IBM 1400 SERIES; RAMAC; and WATSON, THOMAS, SR.

For articles on related terms *see* DATA PROCESSING; ECKERT, J. PRESPER; EDSAC; ENIAC; MAUCHLY, JOHN W.; MINICOMPUTERS; SEAC; SWAC; and WHIRLWIND.

The earliest computers, both in the United States and abroad, were developed at universities, and the concept of computer manufacturer must be extended to embrace the ENIAC (Univ. of Pennsylvania), the EDSAC (Cambridge Univ., England), and various other early computers built by universities or scientific establishments, e.g., SEAC and SWAC (the National Bureau of Standards). These were generally one of a kind, for either use of the university, or to order for a specific user.

**United States: Early Developments.** The first commercial company specifically organized to manufacture electronic computers was the Electronic Control Company (1946), which later became the Eckert-Mauchly Corporation in 1947. Remington Rand (later Sperry-Rand), by purchasing Eckert-Mauchly, was in the computer manufacturing business before 1950. So also were Raytheon, Engineering Research Associates, and, more conservatively, IBM, which moved from its Mark I, an electromechanical computer, to the SSEC (Selective Sequential Electronic Calculator) utilizing both vacuum tubes and electronic relays in 1948, and later to the 604, which used punched cards but computed at electronic speeds. Burroughs had computers under development in the late 1940s, and RCA was working on computer memory systems.

By 1950 extensive mergers and realignments had taken place among the spate of computer manufacturers, and the diversity of (mostly acronymic) names for computers (ENIAC, EDVAC, EDSAC, MANIAC, Whirlwind) had begun to be replaced by manufacturer and model number (Remington Rand 1101 and 1102; IBM 701). The loss of color, however regrettable from a literary point of view, appropriately signified the much broader universe of computer users.

By the early 1950s, data processing by industrial and business organizations had unexpectedly but unmistakably become at least as important a market for computer manufacturers as the numerical/mathematical calculations of scientific and technical establishments. The demands of this opulent market accelerated the production of new designs, new auxiliaries, new capacities—from improved input and output devices to a shift from punched cards to magnetic tape, and rapid advances in storage concepts and devices (cathode-ray tubes, magnetic cores). Processing speeds, of course, improved with every revision, and an epochal change resulted from the application of transistors to replace vacuum tubes in computer technology. Later, there was the impetus of many refinements: thin film memories, printed circuits, and a constant flood of breakthroughs in theory and realizations.

Various manufacturers took different approaches that gave each of them some technical advantage for a time before the concept entered the common stock of computer knowledge. UNIVAC introduced, for example, recording to magnetic tape from a typewriter keyboard; RCA was the first to utilize coincident-current magnetic core memory in a commercially produced computer; IBM (in its 650) had the first high-speed magnetic drum (12,500 rpm); and the Electro-Data Corporation (in its Datatron) offered a hardware index register and introduced floating-point hardware.

Computer manufacturers proliferated in the early 1950s. The market was apparently insatiable; the basic principles of design were generally known, creative and enthusiastic technical staff was available, and entrepreneurs were eager to back new undertakings in the incredibly promising open-horizon industry. The United States spawned new companies from coast to coast. In the east, the Electronic Computer Corporation (later part of the Underwood Corp.) produced the ELECOM; Computer Research Corporation, the CADAC and the 102A; Consolidated Engineering, the CEC201; Honeywell (then called Minneapolis-Honeywell) combined with Raytheon to form Datamatic and produce the 1000 at Newton, Mass.; and later, having bought out Raytheon's interest, the 800. NCR specialized early in the nonscientific sector of the computer market, with one of the earliest transistorized computers, the 304 (designed by NCR but built by GE). Philco's TRANSAC, S-2000, built to order for government agencies, was a transistorized computer that, improved and marketed as the 2000, echoed features of the IAS machine (originally designed by John von Neumann at the Institute for Advanced Study, Princeton).

DEVELOPMENTS IN LATER YEARS. Interplay with the eager consumer was an unusually important factor in the development by manufacturers of new models of computers. Higher speeds, greater storage capacity, facilitated interaction between operator and computer, all these were advances that often came about because users, often government users, contracted with manufacturers beforehand for models incorporating these superiorities. Occasionally, a company was formed to manufacture a computer because a contract with a large government agency had been obtained. This had been an early tradition: The first UNIVAC was built to order for the Bureau of the Census; later, NORC was built by IBM for the Naval Weapons Laboratory, and then Stretch (the commercial version became known as the 7030) was built by IBM for the AEC, which also commissioned the LARC from UNIVAC, and the CDC 6600. Control Data Corporation is a classical (but by no means a unique) example of the creation of a new company in this burgeoning computer field. Digital Equipment (in the east) and SDS (in the west) also exemplify this workable concept. Individuals from various going concerns, moved by entrepreneurial ambitions, combined their engineering knowledge, managerial skills, and market contacts to secure contracts for large-scale computers not yet even designed, and thence to find funding for the long-range undertaking.

An odd feature of market competition in computer manufacturing was the recurring practice of having one organization pick up sectors of the market abandoned (or neglected) by another. The huge investments by individual users in programs (software) linked to a specific computer model provided the occasion for such salvaging endeavors. Thus, Honeywell addressed itself to those who had developed programs for the IBM 1401 and, when IBM dropped that series, marketed an improved version of its own 200, which, in offering compatibility with the 1401, obviated the user's need to rewrite his programs.

By the late 1950s, the computer industry was clearly becoming oligopolistic; a few giants increasingly dominated the market for complete computers; the manufacture of peripherals that were compatible for use with the various models of the major computer manufacturers became a booming industry. The products ranged from devices that would clean and rehabilitate much-used tapes, to off-line equipment that offered economic alternatives to wasteful use of the high-cost central processing unit.

In the oligopolistic stage, certainly from 1960 on, when IBM's share of the market was about 70%, some smaller manufacturers realistically maximized their prospective market by offering computers that were compatible with the various IBM series. And IBM itself generally stressed the compatibility with earlier series when introducing a radically new model. The concept of compatibility on the equipment side was matched by the concept of generality or portability on the program side, but manufacturers who offered software support to users of their computers seldom concerned themselves with the portability of such software support.

**Foreign Developments.** Great Britain (appropriately for the land of Charles Babbage and Alan Turing) may in some measure lay claim to having achieved the first working electronic computer, since Cambridge University's EDSAC was developed by Maurice Wilkes, who had been an early "student" of Eckert and Mauchly at the Moore School. The EDSAC was quickly followed by the ACE at the National Physical Laboratory (Teddington) and by the Manchester University variation on the Mark I, MADM. The earliest major British manufacturers in the field were Ferranti, Elliot Bros., International Computers & Tabulators, Lyons Electronic Office (a subsidiary of the Lyons Tea Company), the English Electric Co. (which developed the DEUCE based on the ACE), and Associated Electrical Industries (AEI). Mergers and consolidations occurred rapidly in Great Britain. By 1968 these mergers and acquisitions culminated in the formation of International Computers, Ltd., the giant of the industry, with special status that often required British users to give ICL preference when purchasing computers. There were British-based affiliates of American and European manufacturers (notably IBM, and Siemens), but by 1973 the significant British companies represented a short list: ICL, Business Computers, Ltd., Computer Technology, GEC-AEI, and Plessey.

In Germany, Konrad Zuse had been working on program-controlled relay computers during World War II. As in America and Great Britain, technical institutions took the lead in producing computers: Gottingen achieved the G-1 and later, with the Max Planck Institute, the G-3. The DERA at Darmstadt and the PERM at Munich were essentially based on American developments. Commercial manufacture was slow to enter the field, Siemens being among the earliest, and remaining the most prominent, manufacturer that was not an affiliate of an American company. The Zeiss Company (East Germany) marketed the OPREMA in 1954; Standard Electric Lorenz, the ER 56; and Telefunken, the TR 4 in 1956.

In France, Bull (the GAMMA, in operation in

1952) was the outstanding name for many years (later purchased by the General Electric Co.). Compagnie Internationale pour Informatique (CII) effectively met the international competition for major computers, and is now the chief France-based manufacturer, with a position analogous essentially to that of ICL in Great Britain. Telemecanique should also be cited.

The information on hardware in the Communist countries is limited; as state ventures these systems are perhaps not comparable to those of commercial manufacturers in the western bloc. The Soviet Union with its URAL and BESM computers in their various models is of major importance, supplying the satellites and, at one time, even China. In May 1973, an unprecedented glimpse at the state-of-the-art for the Soviet computer manufacturing industry was provided by the RIAD exhibition in Moscow. The emphasis was on complete systems, CPUs through peripherals. The RIAD (an acronym of the Russian words for Unified System of Electronic Computing Machines) series displayed comprised six CPUs ranging from the smallest R-10 through the largest R-50, with related peripherals. The literature available indicated general compatibility with variant models in East Germany, Hungary, and Czechoslovakia. Projected production quantities and delivery schedules (with some sales abroad indicated) seem relatively better for the smaller systems.

Italy, apart from affiliates with foreign companies, has its Laben and Olivetti. Israel early produced the WEIZAC (at the Weizmann Institute); the chief commercial company is Elbit.

Japan's first computer was a relay machine, the ELT, developed by the Electrotechnical Laboratory

**Fig. 1.** Assembly and test area at IBM plant in Poughkeepsie, New York.

of the Ministry of International Trade. By 1973, the Japanese computer industry was flourishing; the major companies include (alphabetically) Hitachi, Mitsubishi, Nippon Electric, Panasonic, and Toshiba. The affiliates of foreign companies have their share of the market (e.g., Nippon Univac Sogo Kenkyusho, organized in 1969).

Sweden early organized a mathematics machinery project group and produced its earliest computers, the BARK in 1950 and the BESK in 1954, both with state support. The chief commercial manufacturer, who entered the field much later, is Datasaab.

Switzerland completed the production of Konrad Zuse's Z4, and in 1955 produced the R4S computer at the Eidgenossische Technische Hochschule.

The Scandinavian countries also have the Danish Regnecentralen, the Norwegian Norsk-Data Elektronikk, as well as the Swedish Datasaab; Holland, the Philips Electrologica.

The Latin American market is only now developing some independence from the American giants. Canada has been in constant interplay with the United States, its scientists and engineers contributing to the American development of computers: hardware, software, and theories. Canada has, in parallel, also drawn on its relation to Great Britain for computer manufacturing. Two companies may be cited: Automatic Electronic Systems and Canadian Westinghouse.

**Special-Purpose Peripherals and Minicomputers.** The manufacturers of main-frame computers, from the very beginning, have turned to other companies ready to supply a wide variety of electronic, electrical, and mechanical products. Quite early, some suppliers began to concentrate on aspects of the computer that were not the prime manufacturer's real concern. Inevitably, the specialists (e.g., in cathode-ray tubes) improved their products with a vivid sense of the new market implicit in the expanding use of computers. But from intimate knowledge of the actual situation in the computer room, from the anomaly of urgent orders for equipment that did not yet exist, a diversity of new auxiliaries were invented, developed, and modified. Salient examples involve the input/output ends of the computer. In the mid-1960s, Mohawk Data Corporation marketed a technique for going directly from keyboard to magnetic tape (bypassing the punched-card stage) with such significant economies of time and effort that the company's expansion was spectacular—the price of its stock increased 400% in less than a year. Stromberg-Carlson devoted itself to facilitating photographic processing and recording of computer output for many uses not satisfied by a line printer; its 4020 series produced various film and microform records of computer output.

Baird Electronics, Rabinow, Recognition Inc., and others developed scanners that permitted a computer to read different typefaces, thus bypassing the keypunching operation and achieving input directly from printed or typed documents. Various point-of-sale, special-purpose, input devices proliferated; NCR, for example, provided a machine-readable recording-accounting-billing flow, starting with the sales-slip/cash-register operation. California Computer Products (Calcomp) specialized in meeting the needs of those whose problems required graphic manipulations and visualizations rather than numeric calculations and printouts. Other companies developed faster card and tape readers, new principle data-storage devices, or significantly improved memory functions of familiar devices. The ramifications of special-purpose computers—tiny enough to fit in the nose cones of projectiles, activate an adding machine by voice, or provide a calculator that could be held in the hand—were paralleled by developments of satellite computers and then by minicomputers. Noteworthy examples of these special-function computers are those for numerical control of machine tools and the composition of text for books, magazines, and newspapers.

The value of the minicomputer is that, as a component in a system, it minimizes hardware costs by restricting equipment to the function necessary for the specific usage. It sacrifices the configurations of the general-purpose computer and by adroit modular planning adapts the central processing unit, memory capacity, etc., as appropriate and sufficient for the performance required. Since minicomputers can be produced with much smaller investment than that required for general-purpose computers, various companies have entered this field and compete with manufacturers who produce them for special markets. Early entrants were Digital Equipment Corporation (with its PDP series) and Systems Equipment Laboratories (SEL 840 and 890). By 1973, Bunker-Ramo, Computer Automation, Data General, Micro Systems, and Varian Data were among the manufacturers of minicomputers.

**Recent United States Advances.** The computer industry suffered its first recession in 1969. Abruptly, markets became smaller and tighter; there was actually unemployment on the production lines —and even for programmers! Although the market began to recover in the 1970s, the glorious era of endless vistas of expansion had apparently ended. Even in the oligopolistic states, there were now significant realignments and defections. RCA had entered the field in the mid-1950s (first with the Bizmac, and then with a transistorized machine, the 501), and in the mid-1960s had committed itself to the Spectra 70 series, which was highly compatible with IBM's 360 series and often nearly filled gaps between the different levels of the 360 series. But in 1971 RCA announced it was going out of the computer business. Rather untypically for a major manufacturer of an established product, this was not a case of selling a model and line to another manufacturer, but an outright abandonment of the field—production facilities, equipment know-how, and all. In a later arrangement, Sperry-Rand UNIVAC absorbed RCA's computer line.

**Fig. 2.** Manufacturing area at IBM's Kingston, New York, facility, where IBM System/370 is built. Shows various elements of the computers as they are brought together. The wires suspended from the ceiling power each assembly and test area.

In 1969, Honeywell acquired the computing division of GE, an operation now named GE-Honeywell. As of late 1973, the tally of major computer manufacturers is appreciably smaller than it was in the late 1960s, much smaller than at the highpoint of the industry's golden period of development in the early 1960s. Check lists of manufacturers are inappropriate here but, summarizing empirically (by their having models in the categories of very large, large, and medium systems), as of late 1973, the major computer manufacturers were (alphabetically) Burroughs, Control Data, Digital Equipment, Hewlett Packard, Honeywell, IBM, Memorex, NCR, Singer, UNIVAC (Sperry-Rand), and Xerox. The latter became in 1975 the most recent major manufacturer to go out of the main-frame business. For the tally of manufacturers of smaller equipment, special-purpose computers, peripherals, and the like, comprehensive lists with descriptions are found in *Computer Characteristics Review* (frequently updated) and similar publications.

In as active an industry as computing, all statistics rapidly become outdated, but at the end of 1973, approximately 82,000 computers were in use. The industry as a whole is reported to have passed the $11 billion level of sales in 1973. According to the *Fortune* 500 list for 1973, it appears that fewer than ten computer manufacturers (all main-frame companies) are on the list, and leading them is of course IBM, which still commands nearly 70% of the market.

**Sources of Information.** Various "computer trees" have been devised to trace graphically the development and interrelation of different "computer lines and families." One of the earliest, and best, trees (mainly the work of W.W.Youden) was produced at the National Bureau of Standards, Washington, D.C. It has been updated to the late 1960s. Others are available from the files of the Computer History Project, Smithsonian Institution, Washington, D.C. Announcements of new major products from the first were reported in the issues of *Computers and Automation* and, for the later years, in the news columns of *Communications of the ACM* and in *Datamation*. Frequently, particularly in the 1950s and 1960s, announcements and descriptions were presented at the semiannual Joint Computer Conferences (later the National Computer Conferences) and may be found in their "Proceedings."

A prime source of much of the material presented in this article is Rosen's (1969) survey, which, in addition to its richly detailed account of who, where, and when offers an excellent bibliography. Also, *Computer Characteristics Review*, GML Corporation, Lexington, Massachusetts, is an invaluable quarterly for detailed information on computer and peripheral manufacturers and their products, compactly presented in tabular form.

REFERENCES

1958. Alt, Franz L. *Electronic Digital Computers*. New York: Academic Press.

1953. Bowden, B. V. *Faster Than Thought*. London: Pitman.

1953. U.S. Dept. of Defense, Office of Naval Research. *A Survey of Automatic Digital Computers*. Washington. D.C.: U.S. Government Printing Office.

1969. Rosen, Saul. "Electronic Computers—A Historical Survey," Computing Surveys, Vol. 1, No. 1 (March), pp. 7–36.

1972. Goldstone, H. H. *The Computer from Pascal to Von Neumann*. Princeton, N.J.: Princeton University Press.

L. REVENS

## MARK I

For articles on related subjects *see* AIKEN, HOWARD; and DIGITAL COMPUTERS: Early.

The Harvard Mark I, also called the IBM Automatic Sequence Controlled Calculator, was the first large-scale, automatic, digital computer. The gift of the International Business Machines Corporation to Harvard University in August 1944, Mark I marked the beginning of the era of the modern computer.

The Mark I was the brainchild of Howard Hathaway Aiken, who conceived the idea for a general-purpose computing machine for scientific calculations while working on his Ph.D. at Harvard. In 1937 he approached IBM with this idea. Thomas J. Watson, Sr., supported the plan to adapt the components and techniques of IBM statistical machines to an automatic scientific calculator.

The machine was designed in collaboration with IBM engineers Clair D. Lake, Francis E. Hamilton, and Benjamin M. Durfee (U.S. Patent 2,616,626) at the IBM Research Laboratory at Endicott, New York. Final construction of the machine was delayed by United States entrance into World War II. When placed in operation at Harvard in 1944, the Mark I was operated round-the-clock for the Navy's Bureau of Ships, under the supervision of Professor Aiken, then Commander, USNR.

The Mark I was a parallel, synchronous calculator with a word length of 23 decimal digits, plus the algebraic sign. It was 51 ft long (see Fig. 1), stood 8 ft high, and weighed approximately 5 tons. It used many standard components from IBM equipment,

**Fig. 1.** The Mark I, or Automatic Sequence Controlled Calculator.

including relays, counters, cam contacts, typewriters, card feeds, and punches. The sequence mechanism, the primary innovation of the Mark I, governed the automatic operation of the machine from instructions encoded on punched paper tape; by much the same method, Babbage envisioned the control of his analytical engine by Jacquard cards. The fundamental time cycle of the Mark I was 300 ms, the time necessary to advance the sequence tape. One cycle was sufficient for addition; multiplication, division, and functional computations required from 10 to 200 cycles.

The machine consisted of 60 constant registers set by dial switches, 72 storage counters used for arithmetic operations and temporary storage, a multiplying/dividing unit, functional counters for computing logarithmic and trigonometric functions, three interpolators capable of interpolation from tables of previously computed values punched on paper tape, and the sequence mechanism. Input was by interpolator tape, punched cards, and constant registers; output, by punched cards or IBM Electromatic typewriters. A 4 hp, 25 kw motor provided the mechanical drive for the counters and functional units through electromagnetic clutches controlled by relays.

The flexibility of the automatic computer was demonstrated by the Mark I solution of various defense problems, including logistics, firing tables, and a highly secret, mathematical simulation of the first atomic bomb. The base load of the Mark I for many years was the computation of Bessel functions. Later electronic machines outrivaled the Mark I in speed, but its suitability for the computation of tables insured its continued operation until 1959. Results of this work are used by almost every computing laboratory. After more than 15 years of service in the Harvard Computation Laboratory, the Mark I was retired and dismantled. Pieces of the machine may still be seen at Harvard, IBM headquarters in New York, and the Smithsonian.

For many pioneers, their early training on the Harvard Mark I set the stage for later important contributions to the development of the computer. Though this electromechanical machine was soon surpassed by the electronic computer, the Mark I—as the first completed, operational, automatic, general-purpose, digital calculator, the fulfillment of Babbage's dream—is assured a permanent place in history.

REFERENCE

1946. Computation Laboratory, Harvard University. "Manual of Operation for the Automatic Sequence Controlled Calculator," *Annals of the Computation Laboratory*, Vol. 1. Cambridge, Mass.: Harvard University Press.

E. L. STOLL

# MARKOV ALGORITHMS

For articles on related subjects *see* ALGORITHM; COMPUTABILITY; and TURING MACHINE.

Markov algorithms have been proposed for the purpose of making the concept of an algorithm precise. They are due to the Russian mathematician A. A. Markov (1903– ). A concise description of Markov algorithms can be found in Hermes (1965), who refers to them as *normal algorithms*.

A normal algorithm operates on strings of symbols (words) over an alphabet, $A$. Its way of operation is described by a finite sequence of *substitution formulas*:

$$\begin{array}{c} W_1 \rightarrow (.)W'_1 \\ W_2 \rightarrow (.)W'_2 \\ \vdots \\ W_m \rightarrow (.)W'_m \end{array}$$

$W_i$ and $W'_i$ are themselves words over $A$ and the parentheses around the dots mean that there may or may not be a dot in the substitution formula. (An example is given below.)

For every word $U$ over $A$, the normal algorithm defines a possibly terminating sequence of words $U = U_0, U_1, U_2, \ldots$ $U_k$ is a terminal word, if it has been obtained by the use of a substitution rule with a dot in it, or if it does not contain any of the $W'_i$ as a subword. Otherwise, $U_{k+1}$ is defined by replacing in $U_k$ the first occurrence of the subword $W_i$ by $W'_i$, where $i$ is chosen as the smallest integer such that $W_i$ is a subword of $U_k$.

Let $f$ be a function whose domain and range are subsets of the set of nonnegative integers. Let us say that $f$ is *Markov computable* if and only if there exists a normal algorithm that contains 0,1, and \$ in its alphabet $A$, and which is such that, for any non-negative integer $n$, if $U_0$ is the binary representation of $n$ followed by \$, then:

1. If $n$ is in the domain of $f$, then the sequence $U_0, U_1, \ldots$ terminates in some $U_k$, and $U_k$ is the binary representation of $f(n)$,
2. If $n$ is not in the domain of $f$, the sequence $U_0, U_1, \ldots$ does not terminate.

For example, let $A = \{0,1,\$\}$, and let the substitution formulas be

$0\$ \rightarrow \cdot 1$
$1\$ \rightarrow \$0$
$\$ \rightarrow \cdot 1$

This normal algorithm computes the successor function $s(n) = n + 1$. Two typical computations are

101\$, 10\$0, 110
111\$, 11\$0, 1\$00, \$000, 1000

A similar definition can be given to define when the function $f$ is *Turing computable*, using a Turing machine instead of a normal algorithm. It can be then proved that a function $f$ is Markov-computable if and only if it is Turing-computable. The equivalence of such precise replacements of the intuitive notion of a computable function is one of the strongest arguments in favor of Church's thesis, discussed in the article ALGORITHMS, THEORY OF.

REFERENCE

1962. Markov, A. A. *The Theory of Algorithms*. U.S. Dept. of Commerce. (English trans.)
1965. Hermes, H. *Enumerability, Decidability, Computability*. Berlin: Springer-Verlag.

G. T. HERMAN

# MASKING

For articles on related subjects *see* MACHINE INSTRUCTION SET; and SHIFTING.
For articles on related terms *see* IBM 360–370 SERIES; and INTERRUPTS.

The information items required by a computer program may be of lengths that are not matched to the usually fixed length of the storage unit in the computer memory. Therefore, either an item may require several storage units or several items may be packed into one unit. In the latter case, a mechanism is necessary in order to get to the information item that is needed, without interference from other items that are stored in the same memory unit. Masking is the procedure that enables one to "open a window" on the desired information while suppressing or masking out the undesired one.

The basis of the masking operation is the boolean operation AND. The AND operation between two variables $D$ and $M$ is defined as follows:

| $D$ | $M$ | $D$ and $M$ |
|---|---|---|
| 0 | 1 | 0 |
| 1 | 1 | 1 |
| 0 | 0 | 0 |
| 1 | 0 | 0 |

This truth table may be rewritten as

$D$ AND $1 = D$
$D$ AND $0 = 0$

The variable $M$, therefore, functions as a mask. Whenever its value is 1, the result of the AND operation is to duplicate the value of $D$, whereas if $M = 0$, the value of $D$ is "masked out."

As an example, let us assume that in an eight-bit byte we would like to gain access to the middle four bits. The necessary mask is 00111100. The AND operation of this mask with the data byte produces a result in which the first two and last two bits are masked out. This result can then be aligned to the byte boundary (or any other boundary) with the aid of shift operations.

There are other masking operations concerned with control information. Various control items can be grouped; those that are required can then be chosen by masking all nonrequired items with a zero mask. For example, a user of an IBM/370 system may choose one of four possible condition codes by structuring a mask of four bits, with values of one and zero corresponding to the selection or masking of the appropriate condition. The same type of masking is used in order to mask out undesired interrupt conditions, control bits, etc. One has to note that in these cases, as opposed to data masking, one cannot use shift operations because the information to be masked is not data in the usual sense.

G. FRIEDER

# MATHEMATICAL PROGRAMMING

For articles on related subjects *see* NUMERICAL ANALYSIS; OPERATIONS RESEARCH; and SIMPLEX METHOD.

This article provides an overview of mathematical programming—its scope, its methods, and the associated computer feasibility and efficacy of the methods. Mathematical programming as discussed here has nothing inherently to do with computer programming. Although mathematical programming is usually done by computer, this term refers to mathematical *optimization*, with or without constraints. A mathematical programming problem can be written without loss of generality as

$$\begin{array}{lll} \text{Maximize} & c(x_1, \ldots, x_n), & (1) \\ \text{Subject to} & a_i(x_1, \ldots, x_n) \leq 0. & (i = 1, \ldots, m) \end{array}$$

In the formulation (1), $x_1, \ldots, x_n$ are real decision variables for which values are desired which will maximize the objective function $c(x_1, \ldots, x_n)$, subject to the $m$ constraints $a_i(x_1, \ldots, x_n) \leq 0$. There may be further restrictions requiring that the values of $x_j (j = 1, \ldots, n)$ are a proper subset of those values that satisfy the constraints. For example, all or some of the variables may be required to be integers.

With some imagination one can see that almost any well-defined deterministic optimization problem (a problem in which all numbers in the functions of expression (1) are known constants) can be formulated as a mathematical programming problem. Many nondeterministic problems (those in which some numbers in the functions of expression (1) are probabilistic, i.e., are random) can be formulated in this manner as well. Solving mathematical programming problems in general is quite another matter. Although certain classes of problems are relatively inexpensive to solve computationally, others are very expensive.

Methods of mathematical programming may be divided into three groups: linear programming, integer linear programming, and nonlinear programming. Linear programming methods solve the problem for which the functions $c(x_1, \ldots, x_n)$ and $a_i(x_1, \ldots, x_n)$ are linear and the $x_j$ may take on any values that satisfy the constraints. Linear programming problems are relatively easy to solve, and computers have great capability for solving such problems. Integer linear programming problems are those in which some or all variables must be integers. Nonlinear programming is literally everything else in mathematical programming. As might be expected, because of the availability of computer programs to solve large linear programming problems efficiently, there has been a great incentive to find nonlinear programming problems that are in some manner similar or reducible to linear programming problems so that linear programming methods can be used to solve (or approximately solve) them. In addition, special methods have been developed to solve certain nonlinear programming problems not similar to linear programming problems.

This article discusses linear and nonlinear programming problems and methods for their solution. Also discussed are some useful necessary conditions for an optimal solution to a nonlinear programming problem which are also sufficient under restrictive circumstances. Finally, integer programming problems and methods are discussed, and some comments on computational feasibility are presented.

**Linear Programming Problems.** Linear programming is used to solve problems of resource allocation in which the employment of a resource in different activities has proportionately constant returns. This means that, for example, if four units of a resource can be employed to produce one unit of a product, then eight units of the resource can be used to produce two units of the product. Similarly, each unit of a product produced contributes the same amount to cover profits and overhead.

The general linear programming problem may be written as follows (minimization problems may be solved by maximizing the negative of a function, and variables unrestricted in sign may also be incorporated):

$$\begin{array}{ll} \text{Maximize} & c_1x_1 + \cdots + c_nx_n, \\ \text{Subject to} & a_{i1}x_1 + \cdots + a_{in}x_n + x_{n+i} = b_i \\ & \qquad i = 1, \cdots, m \\ & x_1, \cdots, x_{n+m} \geq 0. \end{array} \qquad (2)$$

The $a_{ij}$, $c_j$, and $b_i$ are constants. By reference to the set of constraints, it can be seen that the solution set is underdefined. Choosing any $n$ variables (subject to consistency limitations) to be set to some particular values, the remaining $m$ variables are uniquely determined. Further, considering that the objective function is concave and the constraint set is convex (see the next section on nonlinear programming), it can be shown that some *basic solution* (obtained by setting $n$ variables to zero so that the remaining set of equations has a unique solution) is optimal. A naive way to solve linear programming problems would be to enumerate all basic solutions and choose the one that is optimal and *feasible* (all $x_j \geq 0$).

A more practical way to solve linear programming problems is to begin with a basic solution that is feasible and then proceed to find a sequence of basic feasible solutions in which each member of the sequence has one variable of a nonzero value different (and therefore one different variable with a zero value) from its predecessor solution. By further assuring that the value of the objective function is monotonically increasing, and therefore that no basic solution can be repeated, an optimal solution is attained. This is the essence of the methods currently used to solve linear programming problems.

APPLICATIONS. Linear programming has been used for a number of years by business, government, and industry to solve certain resource allocation problems. Some examples of applications include the following:

1. *Blending problems* in which a lowest-cost blend is desired to satisfy certain requirements subject to material availability, etc. The blending of animal feeds, peanut butter, gasoline, and specification of foods in hospital diets are examples of blending problems that have been solved using linear programming.

2. *Product-mix problems* in which the maximal-profit mix of products is desired consistent with facility and material limitations, sales commitments to customers, and sales potential of products. Product-mix problems in the aluminum, manufacturing, oil, and steel industries (among others) have been solved by linear programming.

3. *Distribution problems* in which least-cost procedures are desired for distributing products from plants or warehouses to customers.

4. *Dynamic production planning* over a time projection.

Linear programming has also been used to help make advertising and investment decisions, and it has been used in numerous other ways such as in education planning. For a comprehensive, reasonably up-to-date bibliography of linear programming applications, see Gass (1969).

EXAMPLE OF A LINEAR PROGRAMMING PROBLEM. We will now develop an example of a linear programming problem that will also illustrate related concepts.

A small shop has two machines used to make two products. Both machines are each operated 12 hours each day. Product 1 requires 2 hr on machine A and 1 hr on machine B, and produces a net profit (above the costs of materials) of \$15. Product 2 requires 0.25 hr on machine A and 0.5 hr on machine B, and produces a profit of \$10. The proprietor of the shop wants to maximize his total profits. Assume that raw materials are abundantly available, and that all production will be saleable. To formulate the problem, let $x_1$ and $x_2$ be the number of units of product 1 and product 2 produced on a given day, respectively. The number of hours of machine A time required for production of product 1 is

$$\frac{2 \text{ hr}}{\text{unit}}(x_1 \text{ units}) = 2x_1 \text{ hr}$$

and the number of hours of machine A time required for production of product 2 is

$$\frac{0.25 \text{ hr}}{\text{unit}}(x_2 \text{ units}) = 0.25x_2 \text{ hr.}$$

The total amount of machine A time required for $x_1$ units of product 1 and $x_2$ units of product 2 is, then,

$$2x_1 + 0.25x_2.$$

Incorporating the 12-hr limitation per day on machine A, we then have

$$2x_1 + 0.25x_2 \leq 12, \tag{3}$$

where $\leq$ means "is less than or equal to," or "must not exceed."

Similarly, we have that $x_1 + 0.5x_2$ hr of machine B time are required to produce $x_1$ units of product 1 and $x_2$ units of product 2. Incorporating the 12-hr daily availability of machine B, we then have

$$x_1 + 0.5x_2 \leq 12. \tag{4}$$

Since the number of units of a product to be

produced must be nonnegative, we have further that

$$x_1, x_2 \geq 0 \tag{5}$$

Total net profits (or, more properly, contributions to overhead and profits) may be expressed as $15x_1 + 10x_2$, whose value we wish to maximize. Writing the objective function and constraints together, we have

$$\begin{aligned} \text{Maximize} \quad & 15x_1 + 10x_2 \\ \text{Subject to} \quad & 2x_1 + 0.25x_2 \leq 12 \\ & x_1 + \phantom{0}0.5x_2 \leq 12 \\ & x_1, x_2 \geq 0. \end{aligned} \tag{6}$$

The problem may be solved graphically by plotting $x_1$ and $x_2$ as coordinates and graphing the constraints. A graph for the example is given in Fig. 1, in which the shaded area represents the set of feasible solutions to the problem. The dashed lines of the form $15x_1 + 10x_2 = K$, are lines of constant profit $K$. We desire the line having the greatest value of $K$ which intersects the area enclosed by the solid line. As can be seen, $K = 240$ is the maximum value of profits for which the associated line of constant profit intersects the solution set. Accordingly, that is the optimal value of profits obtainable, and the solution is the intersection of the line with the constraint set. That intersection is usually, but not always, a unique point. For this example, it is a unique solution: $x_1 = 0$, $x_2 = 24$.

Problems having more than two variables cannot be solved graphically. A method for solving such problems (which was roughly outlined above) in general is called the "simplex method." [For more information on the simplex method and its variants see, e.g., Gass (1969) or Zionts (1973).] This method is quite efficient, and computer programs capable of solving problems having thousands of constraints, with virtually no limit on the number of variables,

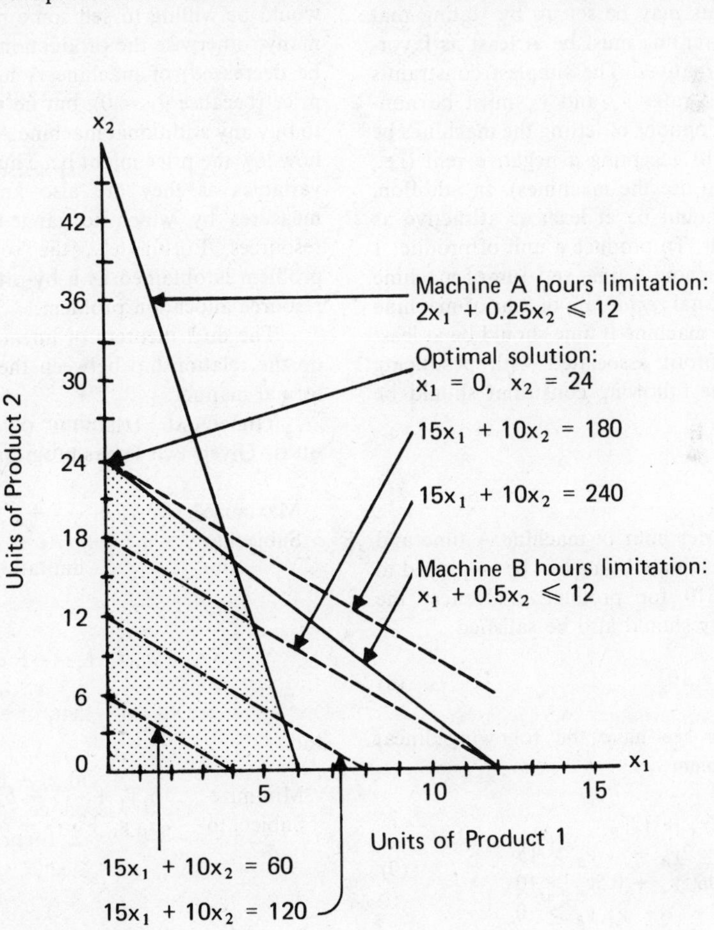


**Fig. 1.** Graphical representation of example.

are available for many computer systems.

DUALITY. Closely associated with the preceding problem is another linear programming problem called the "dual" problem. This is a pricing problem, as opposed to a resource allocation problem, and has both practical and theoretical importance.

*Example of a Dual Problem.* Suppose the owner of a shop has been approached by an individual who would like to rent the facilities of the shop for one day. The assets of the shop consist of hours on machine A and hours on machine B. Designating the rental rate for each kind of hour as $y_A$ and $y_B$, respectively, the owner will receive a daily rental of $12y_A + 12y_B$. The *lowest* value of this rental must be computed so that the owner will know what minimum offer will be economically acceptable to him. (The linear programming problem of determining the minimum acceptable price is distinct from the *bargaining* or *gaming* approach by the owner for achieving the *highest* rental price that he can obtain.)

The constraints may be set up by stating that the alternative of renting must be at least as favorable as other alternatives. The simplest constraints are that the rental rates $y_A$ and $y_B$ must be nonnegative, since the options of letting the machines be idle is preferable to accepting a negative rent (i.e., paying someone to use the machines). In addition, the rental rates should be at least as attractive as producing products. To produce a unit of product 1 requires 2 hr of machine A time and 1 hr of machine B time. Thus, the total *rental* rate of 2 hr of machine A time and 1 hr of machine B time should be at least as great as the profit associated with producing product 1; i.e., the following constraint should be satisfied:

$$2y_A + y_B \geq 15 \tag{7}$$

Similarly, one-quarter hour of machine A time and one-half hour of machine B time can be employed to earn profits of \$10 for product 2. Hence, the following inequality should also be satisfied:

$$0.25y_A + 0.5y_B \geq 10 \tag{8}$$

Thus, all together we have the following linear programming problem:

$$\begin{array}{ll} \text{Minimize} & 12y_A + 12y_B \\ \text{Subject to:} & 2y_A + y_B \geq 15 \\ & 0.25y_A + 0.5y_B \geq 10 \\ & y_A, y_B \geq 0 \end{array} \tag{9}$$

The solution to (9), which may be found graphically, is $y_A = 0$, $y_B = 20$, with a total rental of \$240. It should not be surprising that the minimum acceptable rental is the same as the maximum level of profits that can be achieved. The owner should accept any offers of more than \$240 rental per day, and reject any offers of less than \$240 per day. He should be indifferent to an offer of \$240. (The reader may wonder why someone would be willing to pay a rental of more than \$240 per day. Possibly such a person may have other options that the owner does not have available.)

Individual rental rates are of interest also. They give the marginal values of each resource. Thus, if there were a market for renting hours on each machine, the owner of the shop would be willing to purchase some number of hours on machine B if the rental price were less than $y_B$ = \$20/hr. Similarly, if the market rental price were greater than $y_B$ = \$20/hr, the owner would be willing to sell some number of machine B hours. The owner of the shop would be willing to sell some number (but not too many; otherwise the production of product 2 would be decreased) of machine A hours at any positive price (because $y_A = 0$), but he would not be willing to buy any additional machine A hours, regardless of how low the price might be. Thus, the prices, or dual variables as they are also known, give valuable measures by which to gauge the cost of limited resources. Fortunately, the solution of the dual problem is obtained as a by-product of solving the resource allocation problem.

The dual theorem of linear programming sums up the relationship between the two problems in a formal manner.

THE DUAL THEOREM OF LINEAR PROGRAMMING. Given two linear programming problems:

$$\begin{array}{ll} \text{Maximize} & c_1x_1 + \cdots + c_nx_n \\ \text{Subject to} & a_{11}x_1 + \cdots + a_{1n}x_n \leq b_1 \\ & \vdots \\ & a_{m1}x_1 + \cdots + a_{mn}x_n \leq b_m \\ & x_1, \ldots, x_n \geq 0 \end{array}$$

and

$$\begin{array}{ll} \text{Minimize} & b_1y_1 + \cdots + b_my_m \\ \text{Subject to} & a_{11}y_1 + \cdots + a_{m1}y_m \geq c_1 \\ & \vdots \\ & a_{1n}y_1 + \cdots + a_{mn}y_my_m \geq c_n \\ & y_1, \ldots, y_m \geq 0 \end{array}$$

1. If one problem has an optimal feasible solution, then so does the other, and the objective function values of the solutions to the two problems are identical.

2. If one problem has an infinite optimal solution (i.e., the constraint set is not bounded and the optimal solution is infinite), then the other problem does not have any feasible solutions.

As a corollary to the dual theorem, there are the complementary slackness conditions, which we now state informally and give examples of from our problem: (The word "resource" is used in a general sense; every constraint is assumed to limit a resource. Similarly, the word "product" is used in a general sense; every variable is assumed to be a product.)

1. If the value of a resource is positive, it should all be used up. ($y_B = 20$ implies that machine B has no idle hours: $x_1 + 0.5x_2 = 12$)

2. If a resource is not all used up, its value is zero. (That machine A is not fully utilized or that $2x_1 + 0.25x_2 < 12$ in the optimal solution implies that $y_A = 0$.)

3. If the value of resources required to produce a unit of product exceeds the profit of producing that product, the product will not be produced. (For product 1, $2y_A + y_B > 15$ implies that $x_1 = 0$.)

4. If a product is produced, the value of the resources used to produce the product exactly equals the profit associated with producing the product. (That product 2 is produced, or $x_2 > 0$, implies that $0.25y_A + 0.5y_B = 10$.)

References for linear programming include Gass (1969) and Zionts (1973), and many others.

**Nonlinear Programming Problems.** In this section we consider nonlinear programming problems and methods, but we do not consider nonlinear integer programming problems. There are some methods for solving nonlinear integer programming problems; further information may be found in Garfinkel and Nemhauser (1972), for example. Nonlinear programming methods have been used in solving many problems: e.g., engineering design, inventory and production planning, and portfolio investment.

We now present some necessary conditions for an optimal solution. These conditions are referred to as the "Kuhn-Tucker conditions," after the individuals who developed them. The Kuhn-Tucker theorem states the following:

Given the general mathematical programming problem (1), then if $c(x_1, \ldots, x_n)$ and $a_i(x_1, \ldots, x_n)$ are continuous and their first derivatives are continuous, and certain constraint qualifications hold (intuitively that there exist no needlelike cusps pointing out from the constraint set), then necessary conditions for an optimal solution are:

1. The solution satisfies the constraints of (1).
2. There exist multipliers $y_i \geq 0$ such that $\partial c/\partial x_j = \Sigma_{i=1}^{m} (\partial a_i/\partial x_j) y_i$ for $j = 1, \ldots, n$.
3. The solution is such that $y_i a_i = 0$ for all $i$.

An intuitive interpretation of these conditions is that the gradient (vector of partial derivatives) of the objective function $c$ can be expressed as a nonnegative linear combination of the gradients of the constraints $a_i$ on the solution. Further, the $y_i$ are analogous to the variables of the dual problem in linear programming. An even more intuitive interpretation is that the tangent to a contour of constant objective function value at an optimal solution either is tangent to the constraint set at the optimal solution or intersects the constraint set only at the optimal solution. Two examples are shown in Fig. 2.

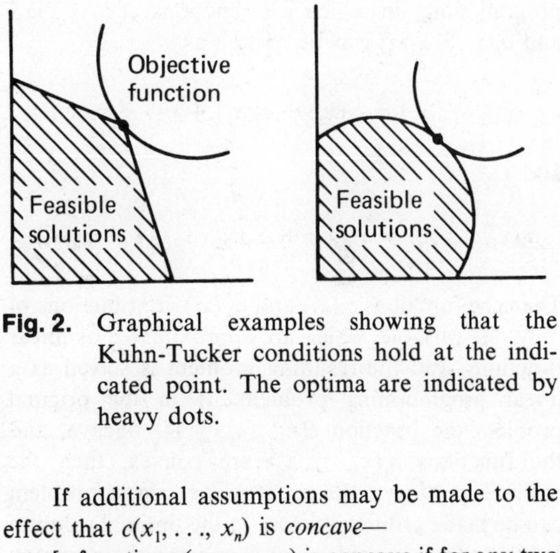


**Fig. 2.** Graphical examples showing that the Kuhn-Tucker conditions hold at the indicated point. The optima are indicated by heavy dots.

If additional assumptions may be made to the effect that $c(x_1, \ldots, x_n)$ is *concave*—

[a function $c(x_1, \ldots, x_n)$ is concave if for any two points $v_1, \ldots, v_n$ and $w_1, \ldots, w_n$, and for all $\alpha$, $0 \leq \alpha \leq 1$, $\alpha c(v_1, \ldots, v_n) + (1 - \alpha)c(w_1, \ldots, w_n) \leq c(\alpha v_1 + (1 - \alpha)w_1, \ldots, \alpha v_n + (1 - \alpha)w_n)$]

and all $a_i(x_1, \ldots, x_n)$ are *convex*—

[a function $a_i(x_1, \ldots, x_n)$ is convex if the function $-a_i(x_1, \ldots, x_n)$ is concave],

then the Kuhn-Tucker necessary conditions are also sufficient to assure an optimum. (Examples of convex and concave functions are given in Fig. 3.)

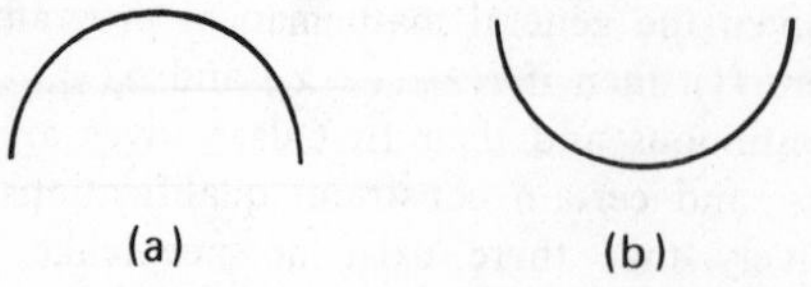


**Fig. 3.** Concave (a) and convex (b) functions.

Although the Kuhn-Tucker conditions provide a useful way of testing for an optimal solution, they do not directly give a method for solving nonlinear programming problems. The conditions have been used to develop methods for solving quadratic programming problems in which the objective function is quadratic (concave if the quadratic form of $c$ is negative semidefinite) and the constraints are linear. For the quadratic programming problem, the Kuhn-Tucker conditions are sets of linear inequalities except for the nonlinear side conditions given as condition 3 in the preceding list. As a result, methods based on the simplex method have been found to be quite efficient in solving quadratic programming problems. For further information, see Wagner (1969), for example.

Other methods for solving nonlinear programming problems are quite similar to the simplex method in certain respects. These include separable programming, in which all functions $c(x_1, \ldots, x_n)$ and $a_i(x_1, \ldots, x_n)$ can be written as

$$c(x_1, \ldots, x_n) = c_1(x_1) + c_2(x_2) + \cdots + c_n(x_n),$$

and

$$a_i(x_1, \ldots, x_n) = a_{i1}(x_1) + a_{i2}(x_2) + \cdots + a_{in}(x_n).$$

Then the functions $c_j(x_j)$ and $a_{ij}(x_j)$ are functions of only one variable, which are approximated as linear functions, and the resulting problem is solved as a linear programming problem. If in the original problem the function $c(x_1, \ldots, x_n)$ is concave, and the functions $a_i(x_1, \ldots, x_n)$ are convex, then the optimal solution to the linear programming problem can be made arbitrarily close to the optimal solution for the original problem by increasing the accuracy of the approximation. If the function $c(x_1, \ldots, x_n)$ is not concave or some $a_i(x_1, \ldots, x_n)$ are not convex, or both, then either some side conditions in the linear programming problem solution must be employed, or integer programming methods must be used to solve the problem to assure that a global optimum is achieved. Many large-scale linear programming computer systems have built-in capabilities for handling separable programming problems.

There are numerous other methods of nonlinear programming beyond the scope of this article. We will, however, briefly mention the penalty methods by which a constrained optimization problem may be converted into a sequence of unconstrained optimization problems. The idea is to begin with a feasible solution to the problem and then solve a sequence of unconstrained optimization problems, using search techniques (or, more precisely, gradient techniques). We illustrate these by an example.

Suppose that we wish to maximize $x_1x_2^2$ subject to $x_1^2 + x_2^2 \leq 25$, $x_1, x_2 \geq 0$, and that we have a starting solution $x_1 = x_2 = 0.5$. We might then solve a sequence of unconstrained problems of the form

$$\text{Maximize} \qquad x_1x_2^2 - r/(25 - x_1^2 - x_2^2) \qquad (10)$$

The effect of the second term of (10), or the penalty term, is to provide an incentive to "keep away" from the boundary of the set. Begin with a reasonable value of $r$ and find a solution that is approximately optimal for (10). Then reduce $r$ to a smaller value and find a solution that is approximately optimal to (10), using the most recent solution as a starting point. Repeat until the change found in the solution to (10) as $r$ decreases becomes sufficiently small. Only one type of penalty function has been indicated here, but there are others. Fiacco and McCormick (1968), who have contributed significantly to the development of penalty methods, call this method the "sequential unconstrained minimization technique" (SUMT) and have had considerable success in the computer implementation of it.

**Integer Linear Programming.** Solving linear programming problems with the stipulation that some or all variables be integer-valued might seem to be a rather useless activity, particularly if we are concerned with determining the optimal number of Chevrolet Impala four-door sedans General Motors should produce next year. It would appear that rounding a solution value such as 102,376.35 to a nearby integer value would make a negligible difference in the objective function value. On the other hand, if a variable represented the number of new bridges to be built across the Niagara River between the United States and Canada, and the optimal linear program solution value were 0.53, rounding to 0 or 1 would indeed make a great deal of difference in the objective function value.

We may infer from the above that, generally, large integer variables may be rounded arbitrarily, whereas small integer variables may not; this seems most reasonable. In addition, the use of integer variables may be made to assure that certain logical conditions are fulfilled [e.g., of two alternatives ($x_1$ and $x_2$) exactly one must be selected: $x_1 + x_2 = 1$, where $x_1, x_2 \geq 0$ and integer], or that certain peculiar nonlinear functions are involved which do not correspond to maximizing a concave function over a convex set. (The solution set of an arbitrary constraint set of a mathematical programming problem (1) is convex when all $a_i(x_1, \ldots, x_n)$ are convex; e.g., linear constraint sets are convex). See Garfinkel and Nemhauser (1972) or Zionts (1973) for further information.

Thus, there are many applications for integer variables in addition to the obvious one that the number of units to be produced are to be integer. Integer programming methods have been successfully utilized to solve problems of airline-crew scheduling, capital budgeting, and bank-check clearing for large companies, as well as other problems.

We briefly describe integer programming methods and indicate which methods tend to be successful in practice. For our discussion we categorize the methods into four types:

1. Cut methods.
2. Group theoretic methods.
3. Branch-and-bound methods.
4. Implicit enumeration methods.

Further, we will refer to the problem as an all-integer problem if all variables are required to be integer, and as mixed integer if not all variables are required to be integer.

Cut Methods. Cut methods, which were among the first methods developed, employ cut constraints derived from the original problem. Cut constraints have the desirable property that they exclude or cut off parts of the feasible solution space without cutting off any integer solution points. Some cut methods first require the solution of the linear programming problem before cut constraints are added; others do not. If the linear programming optimal solution should happen to have the required variables integer, it is optimal. Otherwise, a cut constraint is added and a new optimal solution to the augmented problem is found. The procedure is continued until an integer solution is obtained. Other cut methods do not first solve the linear programming problem; instead they generate and utilize a cut constraint at every step of the solution process. There are cut methods for both all-integer and mixed-integer problems.

Currently, cut methods are not used much in practice; some experimentation on using cut methods in conjunction with other methods has been undertaken.

Group Theoretic Methods. Group theoretic methods can be used only for problems in which all variables are required to be integers. The method begins by solving the linear programming problem. Assuming that the solution is not integer, the method then systematically constructs an integer solution to the problem by increasing to positive integer values certain variables that were set equal to zero in the optimal linear programming solution. Quite often, the constructed solution will be the optimal solution to the integer programming problem; where it is not, additional construction is required to generate the integer optimum. The method is based on mathematical group theory and works reasonably well on some problems. Although there is little available data on the efficiency of the methods, commercial computer codes using the technique are in use.

Branch-and-Bound Methods. Branch-and-bound methods are generally the most successful for solving integer programming problems—both for all integer and mixed integer. We outline one of a number of variations of the branch-and-bound procedure.

First solve the linear programming problem. If the solution does not satisfy the integer requirements, choose a variable in the solution which should be integer, but which is not. Supposing that the variable chosen has a solution value of 3.4, two new linear programs are solved, one stating that the variable must not exceed 3, and the other stating that the variable must be at least 4. Then the two problems and their solutions are stored in a list. The following procedure is then used.

Pick the best solution from the list; if it is integer, it is optimal. Otherwise, as above, choose a variable in that solution which is not integer, but should be, and solve two linear programming problems, storing the resulting solutions in the list. Then the best solution on the list is chosen, a variable is branched upon, and so on. The method is particularly successful because feasible integer solutions are usually found early in the solution process. Once such a solution has been found, the solution can be terminated at any time, as is often done in practice. A bound on how far the solution can be from optimal is known; it is the difference between the objective function value of the best-known integer solution and the objective function value of the best noninteger solution on the list. In addition, the cost of altering and resolving the problem is usually quite low.

IMPLICIT ENUMERATION METHODS. Implicit enumeration methods are methods for solving all-integer problems. Most of the successfully implemented variations also require that all integer variables be zero or one, but more general methods have been developed. The idea of the method is straightforward: if there are $n$ variables there are $2^n$ possible solutions to enumerate; explicit enumeration would require explicit consideration of each of them. By using tests that follow conceptually from using implied upper and lower bounds on variables, generally only a tiny fraction of all possibilities need to be considered with the implicit treatment of all possibilities. Some auxiliary techniques used to accelerate implicit enumeration have been derived from linear programming.

*Example.* To briefly illustrate the methods consider the following problem.

$$\begin{aligned} \text{Maximize} \quad & z = 1.1x_1 + x_2 \\ \text{Subject to} \quad & 2x_1 + 3x_2 \le 14 \\ & 3x_1 + 2x_2 \le 14 \\ & x_1, x_2 \ge 0 \quad \text{and integer.} \end{aligned}$$

The optimal solution, ignoring the requirement that $x_1$ and $x_2$ be integer, is $x_1 = x_2 = 14/5$, $z = 5.88$. (Note that rounding in this case yields a solution that violates both constraints.) Using one of the cut methods, a cut constraint $3x_1 + 3x_2 \le 16$ is added to the original problem and the problem is resolved, yielding the solution

$$x_1 = \frac{10}{3}, x_2 = 2, z = 5\frac{2}{3}.$$

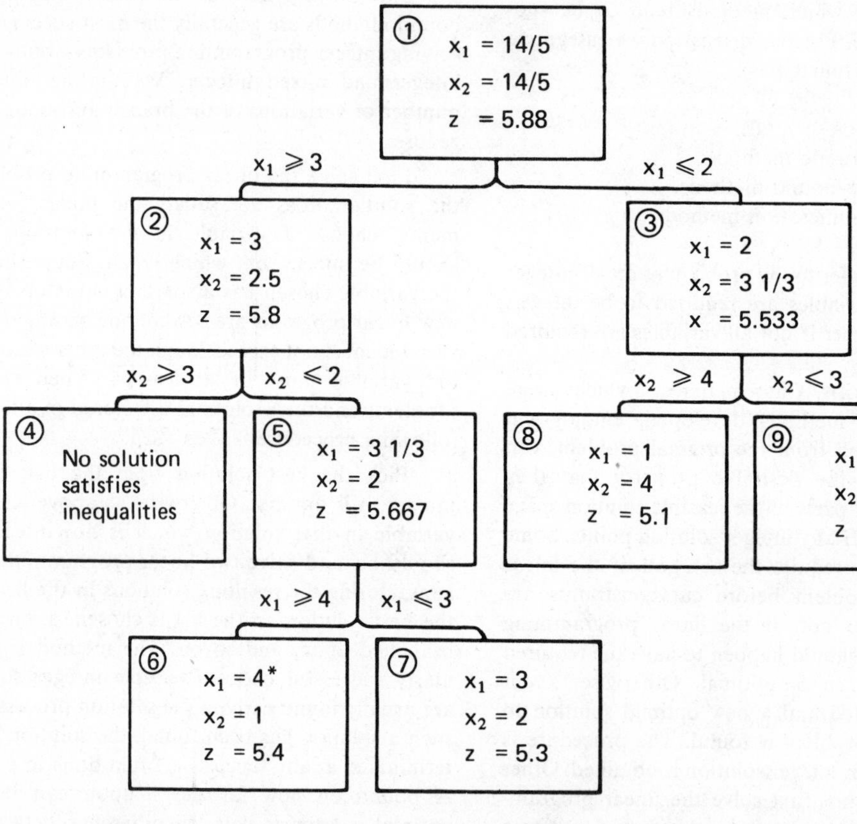


**Fig. 4.** Sequence of solutions to the example problem, using branch-and-bound augmentation of the original problem. Notes: An asterisk (*) indicates optimal solution; circled numbers in the blocks indicate the position in sequence in which the respective problem was solved; all constraints along the path from a problem to the first problem have been added to the original problem in solving that problem. For problem 6, these are $x_1 \geqq 4$, $x_2 \leqq 2$.

Because this solution is not integer, a new cut constraint $x_1 + x_2 \leq 5$ is added, yielding the optimal integer solution $x_1 = 4$, $x_2 = 1$, $z = 5.4$.

Using branch-and-bound, the linear programming problem is solved, and then variations of the problem are solved. The sequence of solution for the example is given in Fig. 4.

Implicit enumeration requires that all variables be zero or one. Such a transformation can be accomplished by substituting $x_1 = w_1 + 2w_2 + 4w_3$ and $x_2 = v_1 + 2v_2 + 4v_3$, where each $w_j$ and $v_j$ is either zero or one. For this problem there are 64 possible solutions; only five need be examined to determine and confirm the optimal solution.

**Putting the Computational Considerations into Perspective.** We conclude this article with a few comments about the current state of computational efficiency in mathematical programming. Very large linear programming problems (having thousands of constraints) may be solved, and have been solved, inexpensively, although it is certainly possible to dream up problems that are too large for solution. Fairly large nonlinear programming problems (including quadratic programming and separable programming) that employ methods based on linear programming methods may be solved at reasonable cost. Beyond that, linear constraints are much easier to handle than nonlinear constraints, and the size capabilities of the remaining methods are somewhat smaller. In integer programming, although some fairly large problems have been and are being solved on a routine basis, there are still many relatively small problems that are computationally difficult to solve.

In perspective, mathematical programming gives a potentially very powerful means for formulating and solving optimization problems. Numerous methods have been developed and implemented in many computer systems, and are becoming a viable means of solving all kinds of optimization problems.

REFERENCES

1968. Fiacco, A. V., and G. P. McCormick. *Nonlinear Programming*. New York: John Wiley.
1969. Gass, S. I. *Linear Programming*, 3d ed. New York: McGraw-Hill.
1969. Wagner, H. M. *Principles of Operations Research*. Englewood Cliffs, N.J.: Prentice-Hall.
1972. Garfinkel, R., and G. L. Nemhauser. *Integer Programming*. New York: John Wiley.
1973. Zionts, S. *Linear and Integer Programming*. Englewood Cliffs, N.J.: Prentice-Hall.

S. ZIONTS

## MATHEMATICAL SOFTWARE

For articles on related subjects *see* ALGORITHM; ALGEBRAIC MANIPULATION LANGUAGES; APPROXIMATION THEORY; MATRIX COMPUTATIONS; NUMERICAL ANALYSIS; and SYMBOL MANIPULATION.
For articles on related terms *see* BABBAGE, CHARLES; and EDSAC.

Mathematical software is the set of *algorithms* in the area of mathematics. The exact scope of the term is slightly vague, but it is generally accepted to include algorithms whose primary interest or motivation is mathematical and not merely the application of mathematics. Thus, a computer program to solve a system of first-order differential equations is considered to be mathematical software. A program to solve a chemical reaction problem is not mathematical software, even though the essence of the program might be an algorithm for solving differential equations. The scope of the term is much broader than a pure mathematician's view of mathematics; it includes some aspects of programming languages and computer systems. The scope is also much broader than traditional *numerical analysis*, for it includes such areas as statistics, symbolic mathematical analysis, and linear programming, which are clearly mathematical in nature.

The historical origins of mathematical software go back to ancient developments of algorithms for arithmetic operations. Indeed, the word "algorithm" is derived from the name of a ninth-century Arab mathematician, *Al-Khuwarizmi*, who worked in this area. The modern connotation of computer programs perhaps originates with Lady Lovelace, who wrote "programs" for Babbage's analytical machine in the 1840s. However, the real origins of mathematical software came with the advent of modern computers. A Mark 1 routine for sin(x) was published in 1944 and the first operational electronic computer (*EDSAC*) had a well thought-out subroutine library before 1950. Activity and interest in the area grew steadily, and by 1970 mathematical software began to be recognized as a separate subdiscipline of the mathematics-computer science area.

## MATHEMATICAL SOFTWARE

Mathematical software can be classified from several points of view, and one of the most natural is according to complexity or mathematical level. At the bottom are algorithms for arithmetic, i.e., addition, multiplication, division, and subtraction. In many instances these algorithms are more appropriately called "mathematical hardware," since they are carried out by the hardware of central processing units. The wide variety of algorithms here stems from the different representations and types of numbers used. Not only are there different radices (base 2, 10, and 16 are common, and then there is biquinary), but there are also different lengths (6 to 15 decimal digits are common) plus multiple-precision, fixed- and floating-point (or integers and reals), and complex numbers. More specialized arithmetics of interest include interval and significance arithmetic. Each combination of these representations and types requires algorithms for the basic arithmetic operations.

The next higher mathematical level includes the evaluation of the functions of algebra, trigonometry, and analysis (e.g., roots and powers, sines and cosines, exponentials, logarithms and a selection of "higher" functions). These are the *elementary functions* that are commonly included as the built-in mathematical routines of higher-level languages (e.g., Algol, Fortran, and PL/I). These built-in routines allow one to state:

```
X = SIN(3.2) + ALOG(4.7)/5.1    (Fortran)
X:= SIN(3.2) + LN(4.7)/5.1      (Algol)
X = SIN(3.2) + LOG(4.7)/5.1     (PL/I)
```

Without computers, one must use tables or, for low accuracy, a slide rule to evaluate functions like sine and logarithm. With computers, however, it is much more efficient to evaluate these functions by means of algorithms (i.e., computer programs). This is a simple example of mathematical software, and as an illustration the following approach is typical of that used to evaluate the sine function SIN(x):

Set $Y = X \bmod (2\pi)$
If $Y > \pi$ then set $Y = Y - \pi$, SIGN = − 1
else set SIGN = 1.

If $Y > \frac{\pi}{2}$ then set $Y = \pi - Y$

Set $Z = Y/3$
Compute SIN(Z) = cubic polynomial accurate to 10 decimal places.
Set SIN(X) = SIGN * SIN(Z) * (3 − 4 SIN² (Z))

One may obtain 20-decimal-digit accuracy by replacing the cubic polynomial by an appropriate sixth-degree polynomial. The state-of-the-art for this software is such that high-quality programs are tailored to exploit the specific characteristics of each computer's arithmetic unit.

The next level of mathematical software includes the algorithms of linear algebra (e.g., solving linear systems of equations) and the operations of calculus and advanced calculus (e.g., integration, differentiation, and solving nonlinear equations). These mathematical problems are of an order of magnitude more difficult than those discussed above. A thorough discussion of the theory and techniques for any of these mathematical procedures requires a thick book. This software is distinguished from the previous level by two other characteristics. First, it is well known that it is impossible to solve most of the underlying mathematical problems in generality. Thus, given any algorithm for integrating functions, one can construct a function where the algorithm fails. This is true whether the integration algorithm is symbolic or numerical or a combination. Second, it would not be surprising to discover new algorithms that are much superior to currently known ones. Indeed, one should expect superior algorithms to appear for many of these procedures.

The highest level of mathematical software is the integrated system for mathematics. A wide variety of experimental systems have been developed, but none of them has become widely available. There are two primary goals of these systems. The first is to have a language that is closely related to standard mathematics and which allows a natural expression of a variety of mathematical procedures. Thus, such a language includes statements similar to

$$A = \int_0^{1.5} \cos(x^2 + 1)\sqrt{x+2}\,dx$$

$$\text{SOLVE } B*X^2 - 3.1e^{-X} = \text{HBAR FOR X, GUESS } X = 2.0$$

$$F(T) = A'(T) + \int_0^{T+1} \sin(x)/(A(x) + 1)dx$$

The second goal is to incorporate high-quality algorithms to carry out the mathematical procedures allowed in the language. These algorithms are integrated with one another and the overall system so that results of one are automatically compatible with any algorithms to be applied later to these results. The development of such systems involves a broad range of mathematics and computer science (e.g., symbolic manipulation, numerical analysis, languages, compilers, and operating systems).

Mathematical software can also be divided into two classes according to whether the program is "static" or "deterministic," or whether it is "dynamic" or "heuristic." This division is not precise (and the terminology is not standardized) and, indeed, every algorithm and computer program is deterministic (provided the hardware and systems software operate correctly). Nevertheless, this division serves a useful intuitive purpose. An algorithm is said to be *static* if its operation is known in advance. Examples of static algorithms are those of arithmetic, symbolic differentiation, Simpson's rule for quadrature, and the evaluation of $\sin(x)$. The ambiguity of this classification arises from the word "know," and the division depends on how much one knows. An algorithm is *dynamic* or *heuristic* if its operation is somewhat unpredictable in advance.

Unpredictability normally comes from logical decisions that are made on the basis of quantities that are computed during the operation of the algorithm. An example of such software is a *polyalgorithm*, which is a set of static algorithms plus a strategy for choosing and switching among them. Polyalgorithms were first introduced in attempts to automate numerical analysis. Other dynamic algorithms have been used for symbolic integration and numerical integration (adaptive quadrature). Only a small portion of current mathematical software is dynamic, but this is an area with great potential significance and growth.

Another common division of mathematical software is between *symbolic* and *numerical algorithms*. This division is easily seen in simple cases. Integer addition and symbolic differentiation of polynomials are symbolic; the exact results are obtained after a finite number of symbolic operations. Newton's method for polynomial zeros and Simpson's rule for integration are numerical; approximate results are obtained, but they can be made as accurate as one pleases with sufficient effort and precision in the arithmetic. The algorithms of arithmetic are symbolic, but—unfortunately and unavoidably—they are incorrect due to the fixed precision of arithmetic. This incorrectness introduces ambiguity in the distinction between symbolic and numerical algorithms.

For example, many of the algorithms of linear algebra are symbolic (e.g., Gauss elimination for solving linear equations), but are considered to be part of numerical analysis. This is perhaps because one of the most important questions is the effect that incorrect arithmetic has upon these algorithms. On the other hand, symbolic polynomial manipulation is considered to be symbolic, and yet programs for this typically take $(2X + 3) + 1/2*(3X - 4)$ to be $3.5X + 1$, and thus are also subject to incorrectness due to the arithmetic. The depth and difficulty of understanding this distinction is much greater than one might conjecture. For example, there is a well-known formula to express the roots $X_0$ and $X_1$ of $ax^2 + bx + c = 0$ in terms of $a$, $b$, and $c$. However, given that $a$, $b$, $c$, $X_0$, and $X_1$ are representable in a particular computer, as yet there is no known program to produce $X_0$ and $X_1$ from $a$, $b$, and $c$, which will be always correct (for this computer).

Mathematical software is still an emerging subdiscipline, and it contains a number of significant problem areas. Most of these are, of course, related to specific mathematical procedures, but there are three general problems and areas of great importance. One of these is the *dissemination of software*, and while it may be a somewhat mundane problem, it is also a very difficult one. The objective is simple: Make the best and most effective software available to *everyone* in a natural, efficient, and automatic manner. Materials that fall into this area include *computer center libraries, textbooks, published algorithms, user group libraries*, and *computer manufacturers' libraries*. All these materials are prone to weaknesses in documentation, effectiveness, efficiency, ease-of-use, and ease-of-access.

A second problem area of great theoretical and practical interest is the evaluation and proof of algorithms. The problems here range from the foundations of mathematics to experimental investigations. Symbolic algorithms have been studied from the point of view of pure mathematics, and a variety of proof techniques of a very rigorous nature have been used. Complex and/or numerical algorithms are much less tractable for rigorous and mathematical proofs, and new techniques (both mathematical and experimental) of proof and evaluation are needed.

Most mathematical software algorithms attempt to solve a certain class of problems, and one productive approach to evaluation is to attempt to precisely define the domain of problems that the algorithms solve. This is particularly appropriate where it is known that no algorithm can solve all the problems and where almost any algorithm manages to solve some of the problems. The experimental approach is deceptively simple: One picks a set of test problems and evaluates an algorithm's performance on this set. The delicate yet crucial point is an appropriate choice of test problems and of criteria to measure the performance. There seem to be no general guidelines for these choices and each algorithm and problem area requires special consideration. On a more mathematical level, one would describe a problem domain in terms of some attributes (e.g., the integration of functions defined between 0 and 1, consisting of at most five convex pieces and with values between $-1$ and $+1$); then one could prove that the algorithm produces an estimate of the integral, which is accurate to $\pm 0.001$. A major difficulty here is the lack of suitable terms to describe relevant *problem domains*, especially for dynamic algorithms.

Finally, we come to the *resource allocation* aspect of mathematical software. A simple example of this is the trade-off between computation time and memory used. There are frequent instances where significantly faster execution results by using significantly larger amounts of memory. The advent of sophisticated multiprogramming systems and hierarchies of memories has introduced another dimension to the creation and evaluation of mathematical software.


REFERENCES

1968. Klerer, M., and J. Reinfelds. *Interactive Systems for Experimental Applied Mathematics*. New York: Academic Press.

1972. Association of Computing Machinery. *Comm. ACM* (July).
This publication contains several articles on mathematical software.

1971. Rice, J. *Mathematical Software*. New York: Academic Press.


J. R. RICE

## MATHLAB. 

*See* SYMBOL MANIPULATION.

# MATRIX COMPUTATIONS

For articles on related subjects *see* ERROR ANALYSIS; NUMERICAL ANALYSIS; and SCIENTIFIC APPLICATIONS.
For article on related term *see* ITERATION.

A large proportion of the scientific calculations performed on computers involves matrices. Partly, this is because of the ubiquity of matrices in the mathematics of scientific problems, but it is also partly due to the fact that the use of matrices is ideally suited to the iterative type of calculation in which computers realize their full power.

**Notation and Definitions.** From the point of view of this article, a matrix is defined to be a rectangular array of elements, each of which will generally be a real or complex number. An $m \times n$ matrix will be denoted by a capital Roman letter, and the elements of such a matrix $A$ will be denoted by $a_{ij}$, $i = 1, \ldots, m$, $j = 1, \ldots, n$. If $n = 1$, the matrix is called a "column vector" and a lower case Roman letter will be used. The elements of a vector $x$ of order $m$ are denoted by $x_i$ ($i = 1, \ldots, m$). The *transpose* $B$ of an $m \times n$ matrix $A$ is an $n \times m$ matrix defined by $b_{ij} = a_{ji}$. It is commonly denoted by $A^T$ or $A'$. Similarly, the $1 \times m$ transpose of a column vector is denoted by $x^T$, and is called a "row vector." The *Hermitian transpose* $B$ of an $m \times n$ matrix $A$ is defined by $b_{ij} = \bar{a}_{ji}$, where the bar over $\bar{a}$ denotes the complex conjugate, and is commonly denoted by $A^H$ or $A^*$; $x^H$ is defined similarly.

If $A$ and $B$ are of the same dimension, their sum $C$ is defined by $c_{ij} = a_{ij} + b_{ij}$. The product $C$ of an $m \times k$ matrix $A$ and $k \times n$ matrix $B$ is defined by

$$c_{ij} = \sum_{s=1}^{k} a_{is} b_{sj}.$$

The definition applies immediately to the product $y$ of an $m \times n$ matrix $A$ and an $n \times 1$ column vector $x$; we have

$$y_i = \sum_{s=1}^{n} a_{is} x_s$$

Finally, the product $C$ of a matrix $A$ by a scalar $\alpha$ is defined by

$$c_{ij} = \alpha a_{ij}.$$

A matrix or vector is said to be *null* if all its components are zero. Either "null" or "zero" will be denoted by the same symbol used for the zero scalar, the context providing adequate identification.

The classes of square matrices defined below are of special interest in matrix computations:

*Symmetric:* $A = A^T$ (i.e., $a_{ij} = a_{ji}$).
*Positive definite:* $A$ *real, symmetric* and $x^T A x > 0$ for all real $x \neq 0$.
*Hermitian:* $A = A^H$ (i.e., $a_{ij} = \bar{a}_{ji}$).
*Orthogonal:* $A$ real and $AA^T = A^T A = I$.

*Upper (lower) triangular:* $a_{ij} = 0, \quad i > j \ (i < j)$.
*Tridiagonal:* $a_{ij} = 0, \quad |i - j| > 1$.
*Upper-Hessenberg:* $a_{ij} = 0, \quad i > j + 1$.

The *identity matrix* of order $n$ is denoted by $I_n$, or by $I$ if the order is obvious, and is defined by

$$i_{kk} = 1, \qquad i_{kl} = 0 \qquad (k \neq l).$$

The elements are usually denoted by $\delta_{kl}$ rather than by $i_{kl}$. From the definitions, $IA = A = IA$ whenever the dimensions are such that they exist.

It will be assumed that the reader is familiar with the concept of the scalar function of a square matrix $A$, known as its "determinant" and denoted by $\det(A)$. A square matrix $A$ is said to be *singular* if $\det(A) = 0$; otherwise it is *nonsingular*. The matrix formed by the elements at the intersection of any collection of rows and columns is called a "submatrix." The determinant of a square submatrix is called a "minor"; if the submatrix is formed from the intersection of the first $r$ rows and columns, its determinant is called a "leading principal minor." The *cofactor* $A_{ij}$ of the element $a_{ij}$ of an $n \times n$ square matrix $A$ is defined by

$$A_{ij} = (-1)^{i+j} \det(\text{matrix formed by omitting row } i \text{ and column } j).$$

The $n \times n$ matrix $X$ with $x_{ij} = A_{ji}$ is called the "adjoint" of $A$, and it follows from the elementary properties of determinants that

$$AX = \det(A)I = XA.$$

Hence, if $A$ is nonsingular, the matrix $Y$ defined by $Y = X/\det(A)$ satisfies the relation $AY = YA = I$; $Y$ is called the "inverse" of $A$ and is denoted by $A^{-1}$.

The *rank* $r$ of an $m \times n$ matrix $A$ is defined to be the highest order of nonzero minor. Clearly, $r \leq m,n$.

A set of matrices $A^{(1)}, \ldots, A^{(k)}$ is said to be *linearly dependent* if there exists a set of scalars $\alpha_i$, not all zero, such that

$$\sum_{i=1}^{k} \alpha_i A^{(i)} = 0;$$

otherwise they are said to be *linearly independent*. The concept is of particular interest when the $A^{(i)}$ are row or column vectors. If $A$ is of rank $r$, then it has $r$ independent rows and $r$ independent columns; any $k$ rows (or columns) with $k > r$ are linearly dependent.

**The Solution of Simultaneous Linear Algebraic Equations.** Perhaps the most fundamental of all computations is the solution of a system of $m$ simultaneous linear equations in $n$ unknowns:

$$\sum_{j=1}^{n} a_{ij} x_j = b_i \qquad (i = 1, \ldots, m) \quad \text{or} \quad Ax = b,$$

where $A$ is the $m \times n$ matrix $(a_{ij})$, and $x$ and $b$ are column vectors of orders $n$ and $m$, respectively. The mathematical theory is well known, the following being a brief summary.

Solutions exist if and only if rank $(A,b)$ = rank $(A)$. The general solution is based on the ability to solve any $r \times r$ system $Cy = d$, where $C$ is nonsingular. Such a system has the unique solution

$$y = C^{-1}d,$$

the inverse $C^{-1}$ existing since $C$ is assumed to be nonsingular.

If rank $(A,b) >$ rank $(A)$, then there is no solution. If rank $(A,b)$ = rank $(A) = r$ (say), then the solutions are determined as follows: Since $A$ is of rank $r$, there is a nonsingular $r \times r$ submatrix of $A$; arrange the order of the equations and the order of the variables so that the leading principal $r \times r$ matrix is nonsingular. Then any solution of the first $r$ equations is automatically a solution of the remainder. The first $r$ equations may be written in the form

$$\begin{aligned} a_{i1}x_1 + \cdots + a_{ir}x_r &\\ = b_i - a_{i,r+1}x_{r+1} - \cdots - a_{in}x_n &\\ = d_i \text{ (say)} \quad (i = 1, \ldots, r), & \end{aligned}$$

or

$$Cx^{(r)} = d^{(r)},$$

where $C$ is a nonsingular $r \times r$ matrix and $x^{(r)} = (x_1, \ldots, x_r)^T$. Hence, $x_{r+1}, \ldots, x_n$ may be chosen arbitrarily, and for each such choice $x_1, \ldots, x_r$ are given uniquely as the solution of $Cx^{(r)} = d^{(r)}$. If $r < n$, there is an $(n - r)$fold infinity of solutions. If $r = n$, the solution is unique.

Of particular importance is the case $b = 0$; the system is then called "homogeneous." For such systems, rank $(A,b)$ certainly equals rank $(A)$, and hence they are necessarily compatible, but if $r = n$, the only solution is $x = 0$, the *null* solution. If $r < n$, there is an $(n - r)$fold infinity of nonnull solutions.

**The Practical Solution of a Nonsingular $n \times n$ System.** The difficulties involved in solving a system of equations are almost entirely of a practical nature. It is essential that a method should be stable with respect to rounding errors and be as economical as possible. Since the fundamental problem is the solution of a system with a square nonsingular matrix of coefficients, we now concentrate on this case. There are two main classes of methods. In *direct* methods the solution is obtained in a finite number of operations; without the intervention of rounding errors, it would be exact. In *iterative* methods a sequence $x^{(k)}$ of solutions is obtained such that $x^{(k)} \to x$, the true solution, as $k \to \infty$. In practice, iteration is terminated after a finite number of steps.

DIRECT METHODS. The best-known direct method is *Gaussian elimination*, which is merely a systematic version of the high-school method of successive elimination of variables. We denote the original set of equations by

$$a_{i1}x_1 + a_{i2}x_2 + \cdots + a_{in}x_n = b_i \quad (i = 1 \cdots n).$$

The variable $x_1$ is eliminated in each of equations $i = 2, \ldots, n$ by subtracting a multiple $m_{i1} = a_{i1}/a_{11}$ of the first equation from it. This gives the first derived set:

$$\begin{aligned} a_{11}x_1 + a_{12}x_2 + \cdots + a_{1n}x_n &= b_1 \\ a_{22}^{(1)}x_2 + \cdots + a_{2n}^{(1)}x_n &= b_2^{(1)} \\ \cdots \quad \cdots \quad \cdots \quad & \cdots \\ a_{n2}^{(1)}x_2 + \cdots + a_{nn}^{(1)}x_n &= b_n^{(1)} \end{aligned}$$

The variable $x_2$ is now eliminated from each of equations $i = 3, \ldots, n$ by subtracting a multiple $m_{i2} = a_{i2}^{(1)}/a_{22}^{(1)}$ of the second row from it. After $n - 1$ such steps, we obtain an *equivalent* derived system of the following form:

$$\begin{aligned} a_{11}x_1 + a_{12}x_2 + a_{13}x_3 + \cdots + a_{1n}x_n &= b_1 \\ a_{22}^{(1)}x_2 + a_{23}^{(1)}x_3 + \cdots + a_{2n}^{(1)}x_n &= b_2^{(1)} \\ a_{33}^{(2)}x_3 + \cdots + a_{3n}^{(2)}x_n &= b_3^{(2)} \\ \cdots \quad \cdots \quad \cdots \quad & \cdots \\ a_{nn}^{(n-1)}x_n &= b_n^{(n-1)} \end{aligned}$$

or, in matrix form, $Ux = b^{(n-1)}$, where $U$ is *upper triangular*. This triangular set may now be solved by *back substitution*, computing $x_n$ from the $n$th equation, $x_{n-1}$ from the $(n - 1)$st equation, ..., $x_1$ from the first.

The process breaks down if at any stage $a^{(r)}_{r+1,r+1} = 0$. This may be avoided by a simple modification. In the $r$th derived system, the last $n - r$ equations involve only the last $n - r$ variables. Any of these equations may be used to eliminate $x_{r+1}$ from the remaining $n - r - 1$. We may choose that equation which has the largest coefficient of $x_{r+1}$. It is convenient to think in terms of interchanging this equation with equation $r + 1$. This modified process is known as Gaussian elimination with *partial pivoting*. Breakdown cannot now occur unless $A$ is singular. (More accurately, unless $A$, modified by the rounding errors, is singular.) With this modification $|m_{ij}| \leq 1$. A more sophisticated form of pivoting is sometimes used. In the $r$th reduced set, the largest element $|a_{ij}^{(r)}|$ $(i, j \geq r + 1)$ is determined. If this is $a_{st}^{(r)}$, then equation $s$ is used to eliminate $x_t$ from the remaining $n - r - 1$ equations. This is best thought of in terms of interchanging the appropriate rows and columns. This process is *complete pivoting*. In general, Gaussian elimination with pivoting is remarkably stable with respect to rounding errors, but without pivoting it may be arbitrarily unstable.

If a matrix $L$ is constructed from the multipliers $m_{ij}$ by taking $l_{ij} = m_{ij}$ $(i > j)$, $l_{ii} = 1$, $l_{ij} = 0$ $(j > i)$, then the resulting unit lower triangular matrix (i.e., lower triangular with diagonal 1s) is such that $LU = A$. (In the case where partial pivoting has been used, the relation is $LU = \tilde{A}$, where $\tilde{A}$ is $A$ with its rows suitably permuted; with complete pivoting, $LU = \tilde{A}$, where $\tilde{A}$ is $A$ with both its rows and columns suitably permuted.) The factorization $A = LU$ may be derived directly without producing the intermediate matrices $A^{(k)}$, and it is not difficult to combine this direct factorization with the equivalent of partial pivoting. The solution of $Ax = b$ is then achieved by solving $Ly = b$, $Ux = y$. There is an analogous factorization in which $U$ is unit upper triangular.

An important class of direct methods is based on the factorization of $A$ into the product of an orthogonal matrix $Q$ and an upper triangular matrix $R$. (The notation $R$ is used rather than $U$, for historical reasons). If $A = QR$, then $Q^T A = R$, where $Q^T$ is of course also orthogonal, and the factorization is commonly achieved in this way. $Q^T$ is not derived directly, but as the product of a number of simple orthogonal matrices. Such factorizations are associated with the names of Givens and Householder. The $QR$ factorizations have slightly more reliable numerical stability than the $LU$ factorization with pivoting, but since they involve more work, the $LU$ factorization is more commonly used for solving linear equations. However, the $QR$ factorizations are of fundamental importance in connection with the eigenvalue problem and the least squares problem.

ITERATIVE METHODS. Basically, the simplest iterative methods for solving linear systems are those of Jacobi and Gauss-Seidel. The relations are most simply expressed if we write $A \equiv D - E - F$, where $D$ is the set of diagonal elements, $-E$ the set of subdiagonal elements, and $-F$ the set of superdiagonal elements. Jacobi's method may then be expressed in the form

$$Dx^{(k+1)} = b + Ex^{(k)} + Fx^{(k)}.$$

Clearly, the method can be applied only if the diagonal elements are nonzero. Writing $D^{-1}E = L$, $D^{-1}F = U$, this becomes

$$x^{(k+1)} = D^{-1}b + (L + U)x^{(k)}.$$

If $x$ is the true solution, then

$$x = D^{-1}b + (L + U)x,$$

and writing $e^{(k)} = x - x^{(k)}$, we have

$$e^{(k+1)} = (L + U)e^{(k)} = Pe^{(k)},$$

giving $e^{(k+1)}) = P^k e^{(1)}$.

The process is therefore convergent if $P^k \to 0$ as $k \to \infty$, which is true if all the eigenvalues of $P$ are less than unity in modulus (see later sections of this article). In the Gauss-Seidel method the most up-to-date value of each component is used at each stage, the relevant relations being

$$Dx^{(k+1)} = b + Ex^{(k+1)} + Fx^{(k)},$$

giving

$$(I - L)x^{(k+1)} = D^{-1}b + Ux^{(k)}.$$

The error matrix now satisfies the relations

$$(I - L)e^{(k+1)} = Ue^{(k)}$$

or

$$e^{(k+1)} = (I - L)^{-1}Ue^{(k)} = Qx^{(k)},$$

and the process is convergent if $Q^k \to 0$. When both methods are convergent, one might expect the Gauss-Seidel to converge faster, since it always uses the most recent information; this is true generally, but not always.

Research on iterative methods has mainly been concerned with *sufficient* conditions for convergence and methods for *accelerating* the rate of convergence. If $A$ is real and symmetric with a positive diagonal, then a *necessary* and *sufficient* condition for Gauss-Seidel to converge is that it be positive definite. If $L$ and $U$ are nonnegative, then Gauss-Seidel and Jacobi are either both convergent or both divergent. In the former case, Gauss-Seidel converges the more rapidly.

A class of matrices that arises frequently in the study of partial differential equations is that for which the equations and variables can be reordered so that $L + U$ is of the form

$$\begin{bmatrix} 0 & P \\ Q & 0 \end{bmatrix}$$

where the null submatrices are square. These are said to have *Young's property A*. For matrices of this kind, when Gauss-Seidel converges, it does so twice as fast as Jacobi.

Acceleration of convergence of Gauss-Seidel can be achieved by making a change in each component which is $\omega$ times as great as that determined by Gauss-Seidel itself. The relevant relation is therefore

$$x^{(k+1)} - x^{(k)} = \omega[D^{-1}b + Lx^{(k+1)} + Ux^{(k)} - x^{(k)}],$$
$$(I - \omega L)x^{(k+1)} = x^{(k)} + \omega[D^{-1}b - (I - U)x^{(k)}],$$

giving

$$e^{(k+1)} = (I - \omega L)^{-1}[(1 - \omega)I + \omega U]e^{(k)}.$$

If $\omega > 1$ ($<1$), the method is known as *successive over-relaxation* (*under-relaxation*). The effectiveness of the method depends on a judicious choice of $\omega$. Young has investigated fully the case when $A$ has property $A$, and has shown that the optimum choice of $\omega$ is $2/(1 + (1 - \theta^2)^{1/2})$, where $\theta$ is the largest eigenvalue of $L + U$.

In iterative methods one works throughout with the original matrix $A$, and for this reason it was at one time thought that such methods would be much more stable with respect to rounding errors than would direct methods. This advantage has proved to be less important than was thought. Much more important is the fact that if $A$ has a high percentage of zero elements, then it is easy to take advantage of this and thereby reduce the storage requirements and the number of arithmetic operations. In direct methods such as Gaussian elimination, the zero elements in the original matrix do not persist in the successive derived matrices.

**The Algebraic Eigenvalue Problem.** The practical importance of the algebraic eigenvalue problem springs mainly from its relation to the problem of solving a system of $n$ simultaneous linear differential equations of first order with constant coefficients. In standard form such a system may be written as

$$\frac{dx}{dt} = Ax,$$

where $A$ is an $n \times n$ matrix and $x$ a vector. By substitution, $x = ue^{\lambda t}$ is a solution if $\lambda u = Au$. Conversely, if $\lambda$ and $u \neq 0$ satisfy $\lambda u = Au$, then $x = ue^{\lambda t}$ is a solution. The *algebraic eigenvalue problem* is the determination of such $\lambda$ and $u$. From the theory of linear algebraic equations, nonnull solutions exist if and only if $\det(\lambda I - A) = 0$. This is a polynomial equation of degree $n$, the coefficient of $\lambda^n$ being unity. It is known as the "characteristic equation" of $A$. The roots of this equation are called the "eigenvalues," "latent roots," or "characteristic values" of $A$. Taking into account multiplicities, there are always precisely $n$ eigenvalues. Corresponding to each eigenvalue there is at least one nonnull solution $u$, and this is known as a corresponding *eigenvector*. The number of independent eigenvectors corresponding to a given eigenvalue $\lambda$ may be less than its multiplicity; it is equal to $n - k$, where $k$ is the rank of $A - \lambda I$.

Since the calculation of the eigenvalues is equivalent to finding the roots of the characteristic equation (an *apparently* simpler problem), early methods were based on the explicit determination of this equation. All such methods are inherently unstable, since very small errors in the coefficients of the equation may correspond to large changes in its roots even when the eigenvalues are not unduly sensitive to changes in the elements of $A$.

If the transformation $x = Py$ is made in the system of differential equations, it becomes $dy/dt = (P^{-1}AP)y$, assuming that $P$ is nonsingular. The matrix $P^{-1}AP$ is said to be *similar* to $A$. Since $\det(P^{-1}AP - \lambda I) = \det(A - \lambda I)$, the eigenvalues of $A$ are the same as those of any similar matrix. This is intuitively obvious from consideration of the differential equations. Many of the most effective methods for finding eigenvalues are based on determining a similarity transformation such that eigenvalues of $P^{-1}AP$ are readily available. The eigenvalues of a triangular matrix are its diagonal elements, and hence reduction to this form gives the eigenvalues immediately.

The theory of similarity transformations shows that for any $A$, there exists a nonsingular $P$ such that $P^{-1}AP$ is upper-triangular. In fact such a transformation is always possible even if $P$ is restricted to the class of *unitary* matrices, i.e., matrices such that $PP^H = P^HP = I$. A real unitary matrix satisfies $PP^T = P^TP = I$ and is therefore orthogonal. Unitary similarity transformations are numerically very stable, and several of the best algorithms are based on their use. For such matrices, $P^{-1}AP = P^HAP$.

When $A$ has distinct eigenvalues, there is always a $P$ such that $P^{-1}AP = \mathrm{diag}(\lambda_i)$, the diagonal matrix with $\lambda_i$ on the diagonal. If $A$ has any multiple eigenvalues, reduction to diagonal form is not generally possible, and hence *general* algorithms are not usually based on such a reduction.

Real Symmetric Matrices. When $A$ is symmetric, there is an advantage in taking $P$ to be orthogonal, since $P^TAP$ is still symmetric. It is known that a real symmetric matrix is always reducible to diagonal form via an orthogonal $P$; Jacobi's method, one of the most effective algorithms, is based on such a reduction. $P$ is not determined directly, but as a product of a sequence of elementary orthogonal matrices of the form $R_{pq}$, where

$$\begin{aligned} r_{pp} &= r_{qq} = \cos\theta, \\ r_{pq} &= -r_{qp} = \sin\theta; \\ r_{ij} &= \delta_{ij} \quad \text{(otherwise)} \end{aligned}$$

This is known as a rotation in the $p,q$ plane. Denoting the successive derived matrices by $A^{(k)}$, if $a^{(k)}_{p_k,q_k}$ is the off-diagonal element of largest modulus, then the next transformation is given by

$$A^{(k+1)} = R^T_{p_k,q_k} A^{(k)} R_{p_k,q_k},$$

with the angle $\theta$ being chosen so that

$$a^{(k+1)}_{p_k,q_k} = 0.$$

In general, an infinite number of transformations are needed to give the diagonal form, and iteration is terminated when the off-diagonal elements are all negligible. To reach this point approximately $12n^3$ multiplications and additions are required.

A real symmetric matrix can be reduced to symmetric tridiagonal form by $\frac{1}{2}n(n-1)$ elementary orthogonal similarities of the above type, involving less than 10% of the computation in Jacobi's method. This algorithm is due to Givens; an alternative reduction involving orthogonal similarities and requiring half as much work is due to Householder.

The calculation of the eigenvalues of a symmetric tridiagonal matrix is a very economical process. Two methods are widely used. The first is due to Givens and is based on the fact that if $T$ is tridiagonal, the leading principal minors $p_r (r = 0, \ldots, n)$ of $(T - \lambda I)$ can be computed from the relations

$$p_0(\lambda) = 1,$$
$$p_1(\lambda) = t_{11} - \lambda,$$
$$p_r(\lambda) = (t_{r,r} - \lambda)p_{r-1}(\lambda) - (t_{r,r-1})^2 p_{r-2}(\lambda).$$

For any given value of $\lambda$ the number of agreements in sign between consecutive members of the sequence $p_0, p_1, \ldots, p_n$ equals the number of eigenvalues greater than $\lambda$. Any individual eigenvalue may be found by repeated bisection using this property, given only an initial upper and lower bound. The second method is described in the next section.

EIGENVALUES OF GENERAL MATRICES. The most efficient method for general matrices is based on the unitary similarity reduction to upper-triangular form. For real matrices, an analogous *real* reduction may be achieved, using only orthogonal similarities to give a triangular matrix apart from $2 \times 2$ diagonal blocks corresponding to complex conjugate pairs of eigenvalues. This reduction is much more economical if the original matrix is first reduced to upper-Hessenberg form, which can be done by $\frac{1}{2}n(n-1)$ elementary orthogonal similarities, as in Givens' reduction of a symmetric matrix to tridiagonal form. Again, Householder has given an alternative requiring only half as much computation.

The Hessenberg matrix is then reduced to the quasi-triangular form by the Francis $QR$ algorithm. In the basic $QR$ algorithm, a sequence of similar matrices $A_s$ is produced via the relations

$$A_s - k_s I = Q_s R_s, \qquad R_s Q_s + k_s I = A_{s+1},$$

where $Q_s$ is orthogonal, $R_s$ is upper-triangular, and the $k_s$ are chosen so as to accelerate convergence. The matrix $A_s$ tends to the quasi-triangular form, the speed of convergence being extraordinarily satisfactory. Upper-Hessenberg form is preserved by this algorithm and this greatly reduces the volume of computation.

The $QR$ method is also extremely effective for finding the eigenvalues of a real symmetric tridiagonal matrix. The symmetric tridiagonal form is preserved, giving great economy in the volume of work. For finding all the eigenvalues, it is the most efficient of known methods.

**The Main Areas of Research.** In the solution of linear systems, the main area of research is devoted to the economical solution (by direct methods) of large sparse systems, i.e., systems for which the matrix of coefficients has a low percentage of nonzero elements. The main problem is that of taking advantage of sparseness without sacrificing numerical stability.

In the eigenvalue field, the main areas are sparse matrix techniques and the generalized eigenvalue problem. The latter is related to the solution of the differential equation of system

$$A_r \frac{d^r x}{dt^r} + A_{r-1} \frac{d^{r-1}x}{dt^{r-1}} + \cdots + A_1 \frac{dx}{dt} + A_0 x = 0,$$

which gives rise to the solution of the algebraic problem

$$(A_r \lambda^r + A_{r-1}\lambda^{r-1} + \cdots + A_1 \lambda + A_0)u = 0.$$

REFERENCES

1962. Varga, R. S. *Matrix Iterative Analysis*. Englewood Cliffs, N.J.: Prentice-Hall.

1964. Householder, A. S. *The Theory of Matrices in Numerical Analysis*. New York: Blaisdell.

1965. Wilkinson, J. H. *The Algebraic Eigenvalue Problem*. Oxford: Clarendon Press.

1971. Wilkinson, J. H., and C. Reinsch. *Handbook for Automatic Computation: Linear Algebra*, vol. 2. Berlin: Springer-Verlag.

1971. Young, D. M. *Iterative Solution of Large Linear Systems*. New York: Academic Press.

1972. Rose, D. J., and R. A. Willoughby. *Sparse Matrices and Their Applications*. New York: Plenum Press.

J. H. WILKINSON

# MAUCHLY, JOHN WILLIAM

For articles on related subjects *see* DIGITAL COMPUTERS: Early; ECKERT, J. PRESPER; ENIAC; and UNIVAC I.

John Mauchly (b. Cincinnati, Ohio, Aug. 30, 1907) is one of the major visionaries and pioneers of our current electronic digital computer era. The dedication of his brainchild, ENIAC, in 1946 totally changed the scientific and commercial information processing environment.

In 1925 Mauchly received a scholarship to attend the engineering school of The Johns Hopkins University. After two years, however, he decided that he didn't care for engineering and switched to physics. His Ph.D. was awarded in 1932 with a thesis on an analysis of the carbon monoxide molecule. He remained at Johns Hopkins the following year as a research assistant to Professor Joseph Eachus, where his work included calculating the energy levels of the formaldehyde spectrum. This research project, as well as his thesis work, involved a great deal of calculation, and Mauchly began to be interested in devising special techniques to cut down on the work involved.

**Fig. 1.** John William Mauchly

He taught physics at Ursinus College from 1933 to 1941. During this period he developed an interest in the problem of weather prediction, and built an analog computer to do harmonic analysis of weather data. This work led to a paper (1940) on the quasi-periodicity of precipitation. He spent the summer of 1940 with H. Helm Clayton, who was interested in long-range weather forecasting, and he also presented a paper during this period to the Geophysical Union, using a statistical approach to the causes of sunspots.

In the summer of 1941, with the impending war, he attended a defense training course in electronics at the Moore School of Electrical Engineering (University of Pennsylvania). He was subsequently invited to join the faculty of the Moore School as an instructor. The Moore School had long had a contract with Army Ordnance to calculate ballistics tables, and Mauchly was assigned to this work in addition to his regular teaching duties. All of his work of the past decade seemed to come together in these ballistics calculations, and in 1942 he wrote a memorandum proposing that an electronic calculator be constructed to perform these vital computations. This original proposal was rejected, but it was revived a year later by Herman Goldstine, who had been assigned to Aberdeen Proving Ground to expedite the production of the firing data. Thirty months later, ENIAC, conceived by Mauchly and engineered by J. Presper Eckert, was publicly demonstrated (February 1946). From the standpoint of speed of computation, it was a quantum jump, increasing that ability by a factor of 1,000.

ENIAC, now retired to the Smithsonian Institution, operated successfully at Aberdeen Proving Ground for ten years. It well deserves its description as the first truly electronic, general-purpose computer and the precursor of all that was to come.

Mauchly and Eckert left the Moore School in 1946 to found the Electronic Control Co., which became the Eckert-Mauchly Corporation in 1947. The company's first contracts were to design a small binary computer for the Northrop Aircraft Corporation (BINAC) and a computer for the Bureau of the Census (UNIVAC I). In 1951 the Eckert-Mauchly Corporation became a division of the Remington-Rand Corporation, and Mauchly remained with it in various capacities until 1959, when he formed Mauchly Associates. He is a member of many learned societies, including the American Physical Society and the Franklin Institute. He has received numerous awards, including the Howard Potts Medal of the Franklin Institute (1949), the John Scott Award (1961), and most recently (jointly with J. P. Eckert), the Philadelphia Man of the Year Award (1973).

## References

1946. Kennedy, T. R., Jr. "Electronic Computer

Flashes Answers, May Speed Engineering," *N.Y. Times* (Feb. 15), pp. 1,16.

1971. Rosen, Saul. "Electronic Computers: A Historical Survey," *Computing Reviews*, Vol. 1, No. 1 (March). Reprinted in "A Quarter Century View," *ACM*, pp. 9–36.

H. S. Tropp

# MEDICAL APPLICATIONS

For articles on related subjects *see* Biomedicine, Computer Graphics in; Hospital Information Systems; Intensive Care, Computers in; and Medlars-Medline.

Applications of computers are found throughout the spectrum of tasks that are part of the world of medicine. This article will cite examples ranging from medical research via clinical applications to health care administration.

**Organizational Support.** A large fraction of the reported work is government-supported. In the United States, the National Institutes of Health (and more recently the National Center for Health Services Research and Development) have promoted the use of computers in medicine. The Biotechnology Resources branch of the NIH has funded shared computer facilities, complementing the specific mission-oriented grants of other institutes and departments. In Europe, much activity has been sponsored through the national health maintenance schemes, and hospital computer systems have had specific governmental encouragement in Scandinavia, France, and Germany. Medical documentation has been encouraged in the Netherlands; and Switzerland, Italy, and Japan have supported pharmacological data analysis. Studies of biological systems based on the application of cybernetic concepts have been produced in eastern European countries as well as in France and Germany. Computerized medical instrumentation is being produced in Europe and Japan, and also in the United States. Due to the need for multidisciplinary capabilities, many of the efforts are associated with major medical centers. Interest in medical application of computers can be found throughout the world. This summary merely illustrates the geographical breadth of computer applications in the field of medicine.

Societies. Some of the organizations that provide a focal point for medical computing are:

The Society for Computer Medicine
Roger Shannon, M.D.
S. 2325 Garfield,
Spokane, Washington 99203

Special Interest Group on Biomedical Computing (SIGBIO)
Association for Computing Machinery
1133 Avenue of the Americas
New York, N. Y. 10036

Society for Advanced Medical Systems
c/o Dr. Morris Collen
The Permanente Medical Group
Medical Methods Research
Oakland, Calif. 94611

Hospital Information Systems Sharing Group
c/o W. E. VanDerHaak
Presbyterian Hospital
622 West 168th Street
New York, N. Y. 10032

Biomedical Engineering Group
Institute of Electrical and Electronics Engineers
345 East 47th Street
New York, N. Y. 10017

A number of journals dedicated to medical computation are listed in the references. Many relevant articles are found in the literature of the specific medical application areas.

Annual conferences at which recent developments can be presented are sponsored by the Society for Computer Medicine, by SIGBIO in conjunction with the annual ACM Conferences, by the Texas Medical Center, Inc., in Houston under the title "Symposia on Biomathematics and Computer Science in the Life Sciences," by the IEEE and UCSD among others as the "San Diego Biomedical Symposia," by IBM as "Medical Symposia" in Poughkeepsie, N.Y., by the French government research organization IRIA in Toulouse as "Journées d'Informatique Médicale," and by the HISSG organization.

**Research.** Medical research has stressed computer technology in several areas, and a number of developments that are significant outside the medical area proper can be reported.

Medical Statistics. The need to make statistical tabulation and analytical procedures available as a tool to health-care personnel provided the impetus to Drs. Dixon and Massey of UCLA to publish statistical algorithms, which became the basis for the BioMeDical Statistical Program Library. This BMD series of programs is still being expanded and refined by the Health Sciences Computing Facility at UCLA. A feature of the programs is a common input specification, which allows multiple procedures to operate on a collection of data without requiring additional data transformation and selection programs. Statistical procedures are essential in medicine to test potential causal relationships in biological systems. Applications include the evaluation of new and old drugs, of medical procedures, of environmental and hereditary causes of disease, as well as studies on normal population groups.

SIMULATION. In order to develop a better understanding of biological processes, computer-based models of portions of the human metabolism system have been built. Some of these models use analog computers, but digital computation predominates now. The programs may be written in languages such as CSMP (Continous System Modeling Program), which allow models to be constructed of elements familiar to model builders, such as integrators, delays, attenuators, and threshold functions. A specialized medical simulation language has been implemented and used by Garfinkel at the University of Pennsylvania. An extension to CSMP, which provides interactive graphics for the medical researcher, has been developed at RAND Corporation under the name BIOMOD.

Other models have been written in algebraic languages such as Fortran in order to utilize commonly available facilities. A formal separation of the constructive specification of the model and the parameters describing its current state has been advocated and used by Yamamoto and Raub in order to provide a basis for scientific evaluation and development of models. Significant models have been constructed in the areas of respiratory behavior, the cardiac cycle, responses to a number of drugs, and adrenaline production in reaction to stress. Models of cell life cycles promise to give some guidance to sequential radiation treatments in cancer therapy.

GRAPHICS. Frequently, graphic representation of computer-produced results is required, so that CRT technology has received a significant impetus from the biomedical area, beginning from the first graphic-oriented minicomputers, the LINC machines, by Cox, and others at MIT; and, later, at Washington University in St. Louis. Today, graphics applications in medicine include the use of Evans-Sutherland systems for the study of organic molecules. (Fig. 1) Graphic languages have been developed at UCLA-HSCF (GRAF and IMGRAF) by Yeaton and Ryden as well as at RAND by Lincoln. A system to serve pharmacological research, PROPHET, has been developed by Bolt, Beranek, and Newman of Cambridge, Mass., and provides not only graphic output, but also graphic input by means of an electronically scanned input tablet.

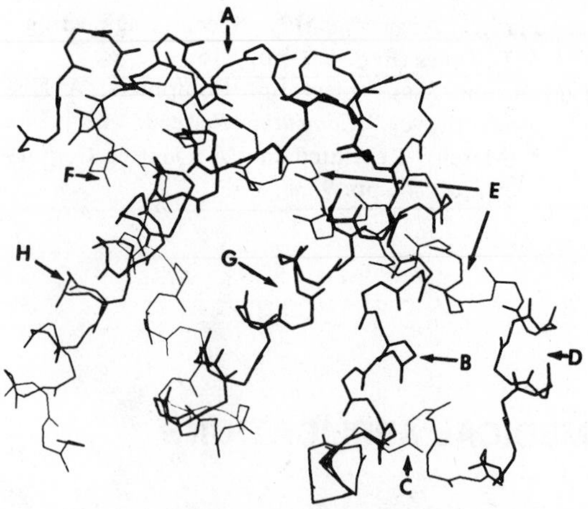


**Fig. 1.** This computer graphic presentation of complex molecules shows a model of the polypeptide backbone of myoglobin. Each helix is lettered (A-H), starting with the nitrogen terminal of this amino acid. (Courtesy of Prof. Andrew Tometsko, School of Medicine, University of Rochester.)

DATA ACQUISITION. A large number of medical research projects use data that can be acquired directly from instruments. (See Fig. 2.) Typical sources are electroencephalogram and electrocardiogram recorders, which measure surface electric potentials due to neural and muscular activity in the brain and in the heart, and blood-pressure measurements via catheters. More conventional instrumentation includes strain gauges for the measurement of motion, thermistors, and Geiger counters. Also important are instruments that operate on biological material removed from the patient. These include highly automated blood and urine analysis systems. Most of these instruments are relatively slow and operate in tune with human metabolic rates. Data acquisition speeds per channel rarely exceed 1,000 samples per second and are frequently considerably lower. Higher data rates are generated by mass spectral analysis of biological samples as well as by data that is received in image form by optical, X-ray, gamma-ray, or ultrasonic cameras. On-line and

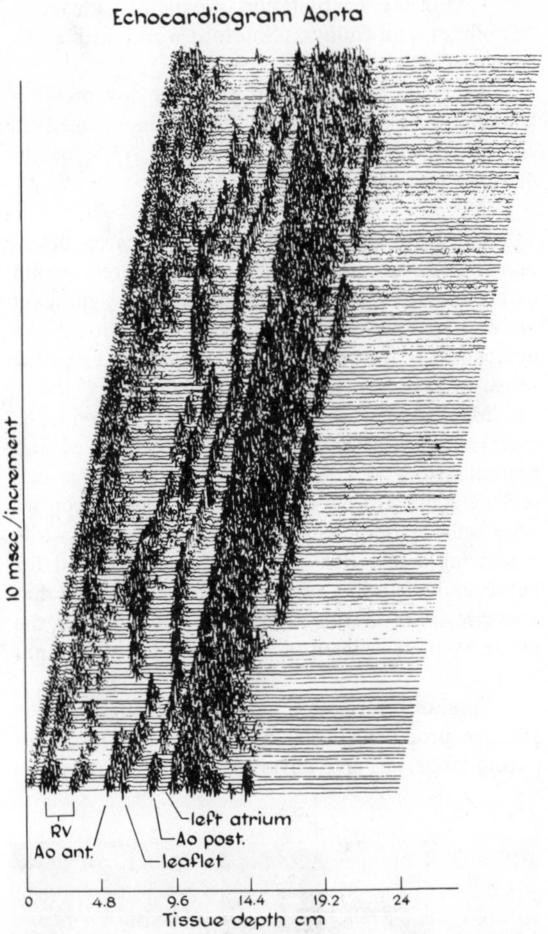


**Fig. 2.** A time/motion presentation of heart-structure motion over a few heart beats, using a Picker ultrasound transducer. Data were recorded on analog tape and anayzed at 1/32 real time on a PDP-12 computer for presentation on a Houston plotter. (Courtesy of Dr. Eugene Dong, Stanford University.)

real-time data acquisition is very demanding on computer operation. Such computers are frequently dedicated to one research problem. Kirklin in Birmingham, Ala., operates a closed-loop system that controls the intravenous administration of fluids to patients.

In some centers (e.g., the Brain Research Institute at UCLA under Adey, and the Cardiology Laboratory at the Latter-day Saints Hospital in Salt Lake City under Warner), fairly large machines are operated with a professional staff in order to support a number of projects concentrated in one specific research area. At Stanford, ACME, a time-shared system designed by Wiederhold, attempts to let researchers from a variety of disciplines share the resources and convenience attainable with a larger computer and interactive operation, while providing data acquisition capabilities. In studies using laboratory animals (Fig. 3), electric probes are sometimes implanted in the brain or near the heart. A closed-loop experiment has been carried out by Dong at Stanford, in which the computer stimulates the vagal nerve, which has been shown to control the heartbeat rate through a phase-dependent mechanism. Signals may be transmitted by telemetering from implanted monitors. Implantable devices for bloodflow measurement, using Doppler effects in the ultrasonic frequency range, have been constructed by Meindl at the Stanford Electronics Laboratory.

In order to handle the higher data rates adequately, dedicated computers or computing modules will have to execute data selection and reduction

**Fig. 3.** Animal surgery laboratory showing catheter and EKG inputs and pen-recorder outputs to the ACME system. (Courtesy of Dr. Mesel, Stanford University.)

algorithms. There is a need to develop better and more routine procedures in the area of biological data preprocessing so that this facet of automation becomes as accessible to medical researchers as statistical tools have become through the BMD programs. The availability of the Fast Fourier Transform and work by Gersch at the University of Hawaii on automatic spectrum analysis promise further breakthroughs in this area.

The use of mass spectral analysis on urine samples, now still too costly for routine care, has been shown by Jellum of the University of Oslo in Norway to be an extremely powerful tool in the diagnosis of metabolic diseases. There is also a need to enhance languages in order to describe two- and three-dimensional images adequately, without which work in physiology and anatomy is severely hampered. It may be generally observed that medical computing problems demand more memory relative to processing capability than do applications in other areas of science. Development of flexible as well as economical systems remains important; fortunately many systems can give adequate performance, even if written in higher-level languages, due to the the high speed of modern computers.

**Education.** Programs to train scientists in biomedical computing have been instituted by Saunders in Winnipeg, by Gremy in Paris, by Blois and Starkweather at the University of California in San Francisco, and by others. These programs are oriented to close the gap that is frequently felt when computer scientists attempt to solve biomedical problems without adequate awareness of the medical environment or when medically oriented personnel invest in efforts that do not benefit from the state-of-the-art in computer science. Many projects have suffered greatly through this mutual lack of understanding. The traditional organization of medicine, as well as the social aspects of health-care problems, has inhibited or impeded many computer scientists who have been interested in biomedicine.

Even without specific programs in medical information science, educational opportunities exist at many major medical centers where current research is being done. Specifically worth mentioning are Harvard, with its associated Massachusetts General Hospital: the University of California in Los Angeles: Stanford University: the University of Alabama in Birmingham: and the University of North Carolina at Chapel Hill.

Use of computer-assisted instruction has received encouragement at various schools in Canada and the United States. Augsburger in Heidelberg uses CAI in the rehabilitation of patients with severe disabilities, and Colby at Stanford works with autistic children.

The National Library of Medicine now provides terminal access to its index files at many medical centers, in addition to the MEDLARS batch-oriented bibliographic services.

**Clinical Use.** A number of research developments are moving into the area of direct health care. Many of these projects still carry a significant research component and are supported through the dedication of individuals who expect that routine usage will occur in due time.

MONITORING. A prime area of application is the monitoring of patients, as exemplified by Weil and Shubin's work at USC (Fig. 4). Such a system can replace some aspects of the tedious task of continuous bedside monitoring by nursing personnel, while preserving a historical record that can be used for better understanding of the onset of conditions that give rise to an alarm. A limiting factor here is the difficulty of instrumenting a potentially mobile patient.

Monitoring of vital signs during anesthesia is another promising area. Monitoring of the fetus during labor can give advance warning of potential

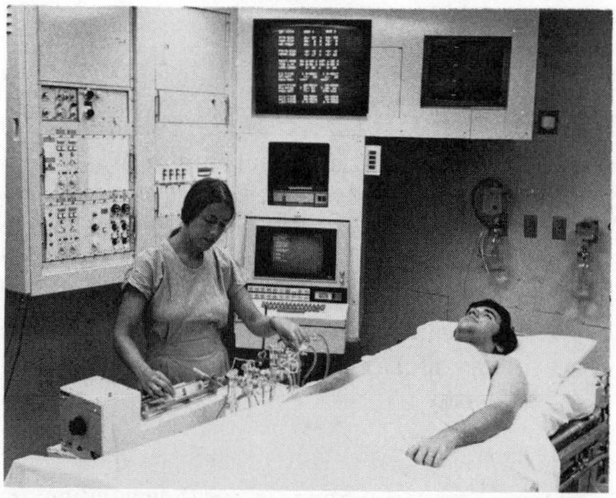

**Fig. 4.** Bedside arrangement in the Shock Research Unit, Center for Critically Ill, Hollywood Presbyterian Hospital. The oscilloscope (upper right) displays electrocardiographic and pressure waveforms. The TV monitor (left) provides status display. The CRT and the video terminal present trend plots, summaries of patient data, and records data into the system. (Courtesy of Dr. Herbert Shubin and Dr. Max Weil.)

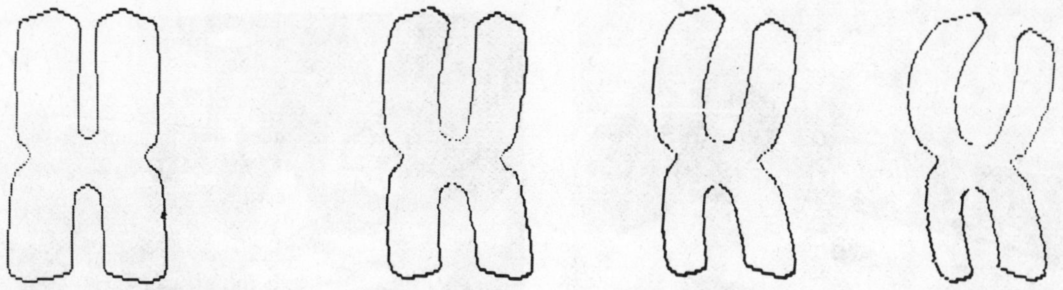

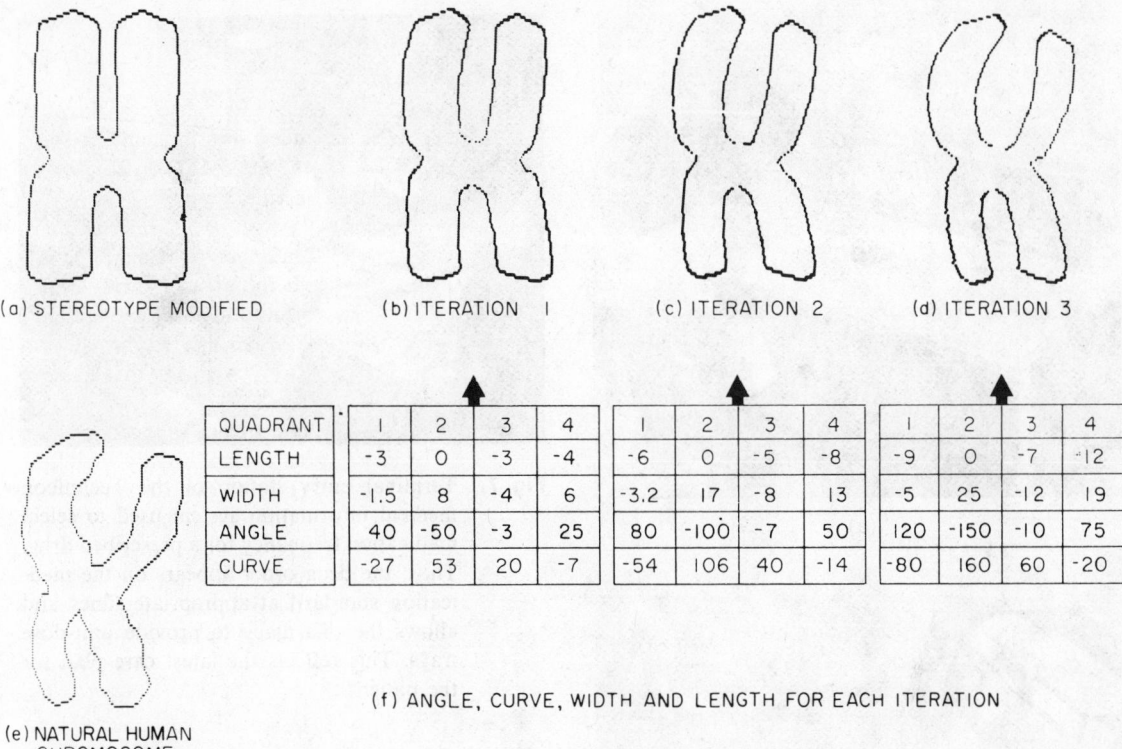

(a) STEREOTYPE MODIFIED (b) ITERATION 1 (c) ITERATION 2 (d) ITERATION 3

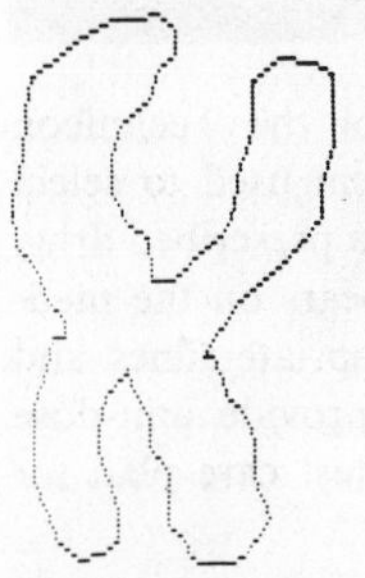

(e) NATURAL HUMAN CHROMOSOME TO BE FITTED

| QUADRANT | 1 | 2 | 3 | 4 | 1 | 2 | 3 | 4 | 1 | 2 | 3 | 4 |
|---|---|---|---|---|---|---|---|---|---|---|---|---|
| LENGTH | -3 | 0 | -3 | -4 | -6 | 0 | -5 | -8 | -9 | 0 | -7 | -12 |
| WIDTH | -1.5 | 8 | -4 | 6 | -3.2 | 17 | -8 | 13 | -5 | 25 | -12 | 19 |
| ANGLE | 40 | -50 | -3 | 25 | 80 | -100 | -7 | 50 | 120 | -150 | -10 | 75 |
| CURVE | -27 | 53 | 20 | -7 | -54 | 106 | 40 | -14 | -80 | 160 | 60 | -20 |

(f) ANGLE, CURVE, WIDTH AND LENGTH FOR EACH ITERATION

**Fig. 5.** Pattern matching of individual chromosomes. A standard stereotype matches the image of a natural chromosome. Length parameters are critical for chromosome classification. (Courtesy of Prof. B. Widrow and Robert Melen, Information Systems Laboratory, Stanford University.)

problems. (See Fig. 5) The monitoring and analysis of data during catheterization can shorten the procedure and at the same time increase the reliability of the obtained data. Analysis of sequences of images of the heart is used to estimate heart-stroke volume. Video disks are used here for fast playback and analysis of an image frozen at a particular instant of time. The analysis, or at least the selection of abnormal intervals of electrocardiograms, developed initially by Caceras (now at George Washington University) has attained routine use.

Requirements of reliability and availability have caused most of those clinical systems to be based on minicomputer technology. The computer is frequently not explicitly visible to the physician, but is part of the complex of medical instrumentation.

Clinical Services. Less demanding, but still with high availability requirements, are applications that are one step removed from the patient himself. Important uses of computers can be found in radiation treatment planning, for which specialized systems have been developed by Cox. These provide the contours of radiation intensity in the body for a sequence of treatments so that the effects may be concentrated on tumors and minimized in other areas. (See Fig. 6.) The checking for potential interaction between a combination of drugs (Cohen at Stanford) and the data reduction, test scheduling, and quality control in clinical laboratories (Berkeley Scientific and Meditech) are among areas of application where computers are now becoming routine.

Medical Records. The collection of some of the data for the medical record has been automated. One aspect of this area is the collection of medical history data from a patient by a programmed structured and branching interview sequence, which was initiated by Slack at the University of Wisconsin. Another is the administration of a routine battery of tests as part of a regular checkup procedure, multiphasic screening, as initiated by Collen

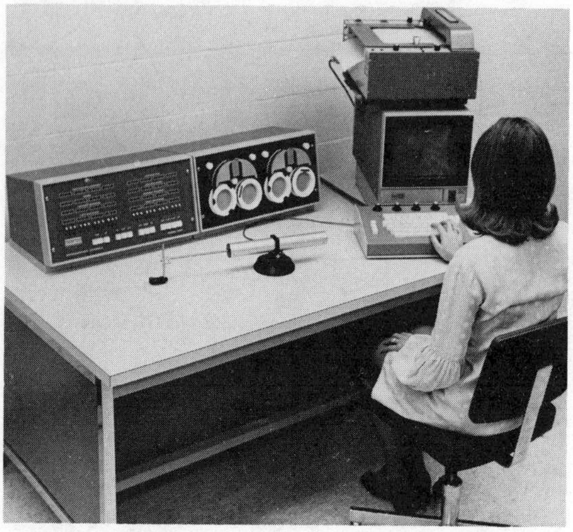

(a)

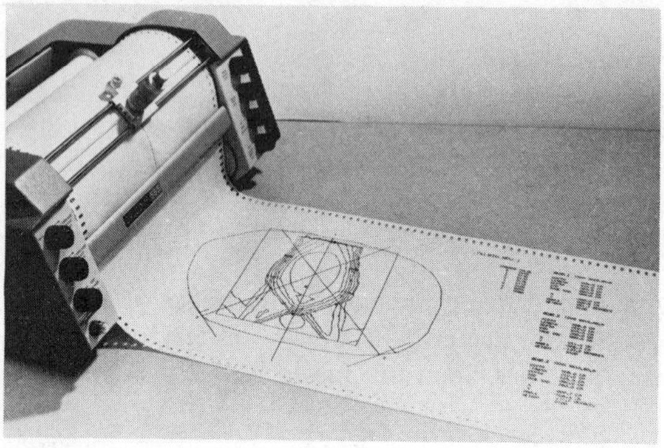

(b)

**Fig. 6.** Programmed console for radiation treatment planning. Data concerning the patient are entered from radiographic information by tracing with stylus, and the drawings are displayed on the storage scope. Descriptions of ionizing radiation beams are stored on digital tape units. Final results are reproduced on an incremental plotter.

**Fig. 7.** Terminal entry station of the Technicon medical information system used to select medication frequency for a prescribed drug. Thus, the drug order appears on the medication standard at appropriate times and allows the pharmacy to provide unit-dose trays. This reflects the latest care plan for the patient.

at Kaiser Foundation in Oakland. Data banks of test information are being developed which may eventually be used to determine more individual limits of normalcy and abnormalcy of test results. The decision process that leads to an optimal sequence of tests in order to arrive at a specific diagnosis is also a candidate for computerization.

A capability to follow patients over long periods of time is needed to make studies on patient medical data useful. This capability does not exist in general in the United States, outside of health maintenance organizations such as the Kaiser plan. The Kaiser Foundation is one of the few organizations that attempts to maintain long-range medical records in an on-line accessible form. In Europe, such potential exists, and many countries assign health-care identification numbers, which are used in every aspect of health-care delivery. Some population studies by American researchers are in fact done on foreign population groups so that adequate follow-up can be maintained. The data processing problems become quite complex in such instances.

Many specialized clinics maintain detailed computerized records on their chronic population, but do not use them to replace the conventional paper record. Weed at the University of Vermont advocates and has implemented a computerized version of a more systematic approach to medical record keeping where the data acquired is not only associated with a patient, but also with a particular problem of the patient. Such a record organization will not only aid in the delivery of care, but also make the processing problem more tractable and enable the medical record to be used for the prediction of the effectiveness of medical procedures on specific patient groups. Developmental work in this area is being done by Feistein at Yale and Fries at Stanford.

The development of automatic clinical decision-making (Lusted at the University of Oregon in Portland) or advice-giving procedures demands both a basis of normal data as well as collections of detailed disease specific records.

Off-line processing of narrative pathology and radiology reports, resulting in automatic classification of problems found, can provide another formal input to the medical record, as shown by Pratt (NIH), Lamson (UCLA), and Robinson (Bowman-Gray, N.C.).

**Hospital Management.** Most hospitals use their own or service bureau computers to do their daily account processing. The data processing cycle is typically based on a midnight census against which all daily transactions are posted. The processed results are generally available by the following morning. Considerable difficuties are encountered because of the varying requirements of the third-party organizations that pay for a large fraction of the hospital expense. Cost justification may include disease diagnosis and severity information, which is generally not available in convenient form and has to be coded by specialized personnel.

Many commercial computer system manufacturers produce census, charging, and billing packages, which may be modified to specific requirements. A more complete automation of hospitals has been provided by a number of cooperative efforts of hospitals and computer system designers. Here, appropriate terminals are installed in the nursing areas of the hospital, as well as in the pharmacy (Fig. 7), the laboratories, and other service areas. Such a computer system functions mainly as a communication device, transmitting physicians orders, laboratory results, etc., to their proper location. An extraction of appropriate data can provide the inputs to the hospital administrative processing.

The methodology of such systems varies from large shared processors (Technicon in Sunnyvale) to proposed networks of minicomputers (Blois and Henley at UCSF). Many modules of such systems have been developed, using the interpretive system MUMPS. This system, which includes a tree-structured mapping of data onto disk—replacing the conventional concept of data files—was developed at Massachusetts General Hospital by Barnett. The economical and operational justification of all these systems is still being debated.

Some nationwide services, specifically PAS (Professional Activity Study) run by the Commission on Professional and Hospital Activities, Ann Arbor, Michigan, collect and summarize abstracted data from many hospitals in order to provide performance feedback to their subscribers.

Modeling of hospital processes has been another tool to aid management in the allocation and scheduling of resources. Valbona at the Texas Institute for Research and Rehabilitation uses computers directly to schedule services to patients.

It is clear that medical computing will remain an area of much activity in the coming decade. Computers will also play a role in the measurement of their own effects on health care as well as in the evaluation of other changes in the delivery of care.

**Source Information.** One of the principal sources of current material is the journal. *Computers in Biomedical Research*, published since 1967 by Academic Press, New York. Another current source is the *Revue de l'Informatique Médicale*, published since 1970 by L'Expansion Scientifique, Paris CEDEX 06. Proceedings of annual meetings, specifically the IBM and San Diego symposia, provide further reference material. Material from the IRIA meetings as well as from other sources has been published since 1970 in the *International Journal of Biomedical Computing*, by American Elsevier Publishing Company. Stacy and Waxman have edited a three-volume series reviewing medical computing, *Computers in Biomedical Research*, published by Academic Press in 1965 (vols. 1 and 2) and 1969 (vol. 3). The National Center (Rockville, Md.) has produced a series of monographs on health-care delivery systems. In Great Britain, the Nuffield Provincial Hospitals Trust has documented *Computers in the Service of Medicine* through a series under that name published by the Oxford University Press.

Real-time data problems have been discussed in a six-volume series, *Data Acquisition and Processing in Biology and Medicine* by Pergamon Press, which report on conferences held in Rochester from 1961 to 1966.

Other periodicals in the area include *Methods of Information in Medicine*, published by the Schattauer Verlag, Stuttgart 1 since 1962; *Computing in Biology and Medicine*, by Pergamon Press; and *Computer Programs in Biomedicine*, by North Holland in Amsterdam, the last two published since 1970. In addition to application reports in the medical and health-care management literature, a number of relevant articles can be found in the *IEEE Transactions on Biomedical Engineering* and in the Annals of the N.Y. Academy of Sciences.

G. WIEDERHOLD

# MEDLARS/MEDLINE

For articles on related subjects *see* INFORMATION RETRIEVAL; MEDICAL APPLICATIONS; and TIME SHARING.

The National Library of Medicine initiated a program for access to the biomedical literature nearly 100 years ago under the guidance of Dr. John Shaw Billings. *Index Medicus*, a guide to the medical literature, was first published in 1879. In 1962, the library began to develop a computerized system for the production of *Index Medicus*; the system went into operation in January 1964. This computer system, called MEDLARS (Medical Literature Analysis and Retrieval System), incorporated the first operational photocomposition system. As a by-product, the system could provide partially individualized bibliographies ("demand searches") for a requesting health professional. The demand for such services grew with time and with the size of the computer file, reaching a peak in 1970 with a total of 24,000 searches in the United States and participating foreign centers. The search service was provided, at times, from 10 computers in the United States and 11 computers in foreign countries. Foreign MEDLARS centers were established in Australia, Canada, France, Germany, Japan, Sweden, the United Kingdom, and at the World Health Organization in Geneva.

To obtain a search, a qualified health professional submitted a written request describing the details of the information needed. This request was then "formulated" by a trained analyst, coded into the vocabulary of MEDLARS for input to one of the computers, and processed on the computer. The output was reviewed by the same search analyst who had formulated the query; finally, in three to four weeks, the requester received his bibliography. The entire MEDLARS file now contains 1.8 million citations, but at that time only about 800,000 were maintained in a current file that was available for routine searching. A limited number of searches were processed against the total file. The data base was searched with the same controlled vocabulary used in indexing the documents, containing about 8,900 hierarchically arranged subject terms.

On Oct. 29, 1971, NLM initiated a nationwide, on-line, bibliographic retrieval system as a general service for the biomedical community. This service, called MEDLINE, now allows almost instantaneous, interactive searching of over 450,000 citations from the world's biomedical serial literature. This service has superseded the MEDLARS-batch demand search service. The service now supports an average

```
.
.
.
.
USER:                          (Indicates user is to type command)
xyy                            (Command to search for term xyy)
PROG:
PSTG(1)                        (Program has found one posting of this term in current month's file)
USER:
"print"                        (Command to print citation)
PROG:
AU-NIELSEN J              |
AU-CHRISTENSEN AL         |    4 authors (AU) of article
AU-SCHULTZ-LARSEN J       |
AU-YDE H                  |
TI-A PSYCHIATRIC-PSYCHOLOGICAL STUDY                    } Title(TI)
   OF PATIENT SMW WITH THE XYY SYNDROME ...             } Source (SO) Journal
SO-ACTA PSYCHIATR SCAND 49 159-168 1973
```

(By using further MEDLINE facilities, the user could the search in the retrieval file for past data to look for other related documents on the XYY syndrome.)

**Fig. 1.** Excerpt from a MEDLINE search. Lower-case in the left column represents typing by the user; capital letters are entries by the terminal.

of 25 simultaneous users, 43 hour per week. In July 1973, 16,124 searches were processed, a rate of nearly 200,000 searches per year. Service is provided through a data communications network that allows access through a local Dataphone call in any of 50 major metropolitan areas across the nation. Over 180 institutions with over 250 terminals are using the service. The communications network also has a node in Paris and is being used regularly by the French MEDLARS center for a trial period. Ten Canadian centers are a regular part of the network. The MEDLINE data base is also operated from a computer in Sweden, and access is provided by remote terminals in eight locations in Sweden through regular telephone lines, with one each in Denmark, Finland, and Norway.

Access to the MEDLINE retrieval service is provided by a simple language at a typewriterlike device (although the indexing vocabulary is rather complex) connected through a telephone line to the computer at the NLM. When a word or words are entered at the terminal, the computer assumes (unless told otherwise) that it should attempt to search on them. A word or words in quotation marks are commands to the computer to do something other than search, for example, to print a set of retrieved citations. Fig. 1 is an excerpt from a MEDLINE search.

The base of bibliographic citations in MEDLINE consists of all references published in *Index Medicus* from January 1970 to the present for approximately 1,200 journls. Since the entire printed *Index Medicus* covers about 2,200 journals, MEDLINE thus includes about 60% of the material in *Index Medicus*.

REFERENCES

1967. Austin, Charles J. *MEDLARS 1963–1967*. Bethesda, Md.: National Library of Medicine (Public Health Service Publication No. 1823), 76 pp., bibliography.

1973. McCarn, Davis B., and Joseph Leiter. "On-line Services in Medicine and Beyond," *Science*, No. 181 (July 27), pp. 318–324.

D. B. McCarn

# MEMORY

The information in this article is organized in two major sections: *Main* and *Auxiliary*.

For articles on related subjects *see* Associative Memory; Cache Memory; Ultrasonic Memory; and Virtual Memory.

## MAIN

For articles on related subjects *see* Addressing; Associative Memory; Cache Memory; Computer Circuitry; Cycle Stealing; Direct Access; Interleave; Interlock; Memory: Auxiliary; Read-Only Store; and Storage Hierarchy.

For articles on related terms *see* Access Time; Cycle Time; and Integrated Circuitry.

Different levels of storage (or memory) are usually employed in a computer system. This article concerns itself with the computer main memory, which is usually the most rapidly accessible memory and the one from which most, often all, instructions in programs are executed. However, due to the rapid change of computer technology and its impact on the design philosophies of computers, some items traditionally unrelated to main memory techniques will be briefly treated.

In this article, each of the key terms related to main memory will be defined and illustrated. A concise description of the different organizations, technologies, and system techniques associated with memory design are then given.

Memory performance and cost are the twin keys to computer technology. It is fair to say that without the faster and cheaper memories that have been developed in recent years, the innovations in electronic device technology, processor organizations, and software systems would not have had their enormous impact on computer technology.

**Definitions and Terminology.** From a hardware point of view the computer main memory is formed by a large number of basic units referred to as "memory cells." Each memory cell is a device or an electronic circuit that has two or more stable states. In current practice, only two state devices are commonly available; each is capable of storing a binary digit, or bit. The physical grouping of these cells or bits into chunks such as bytes, or words, and the rationale behind each grouping scheme is discussed in detail in the section "Dimensional Quantization." At this stage it is sufficient to note that all the digits in a quantum (referred to as a word for the present) in a main memory are simultaneously accessed for a READ or WRITE operation. Two important characteristics of main memory are: (1) The main memory is a *read/write* memory (RW or R/W) permitting data to be stored or retrieved at comparable intervals. This should be contrasted to *read only* memories (ROM) and *read mostly* memories (RMM), which permit reading at the same high speeds of RW memories, but for which the writing operation is restricted. ROM's may be written only once and cannot be changed thereafter. RMM's may be erased and written again, but the erase and write operations are usually much slower than the read operation. (2) The main memory is a *random access* memory (RAM); i.e., the time to access each stored word is constant, independent of the sequence in which words were stored. This should be contrasted with *serial memories* such as disks, drums, tapes, and shift registers in which data is available only in the same sequence as originally stored.

Viewed from the system standpoint, a main memory can be considered as $W$ words, each of $B$ bits for a total storage capacity of $W \times B$ bits. Storage capacity may be stated in bytes, each of which consists usually of eight or nine bits. As mentioned before, the $B$ bits of one word are available in parallel for reading or writing, as schematically indicated in Fig. 1.

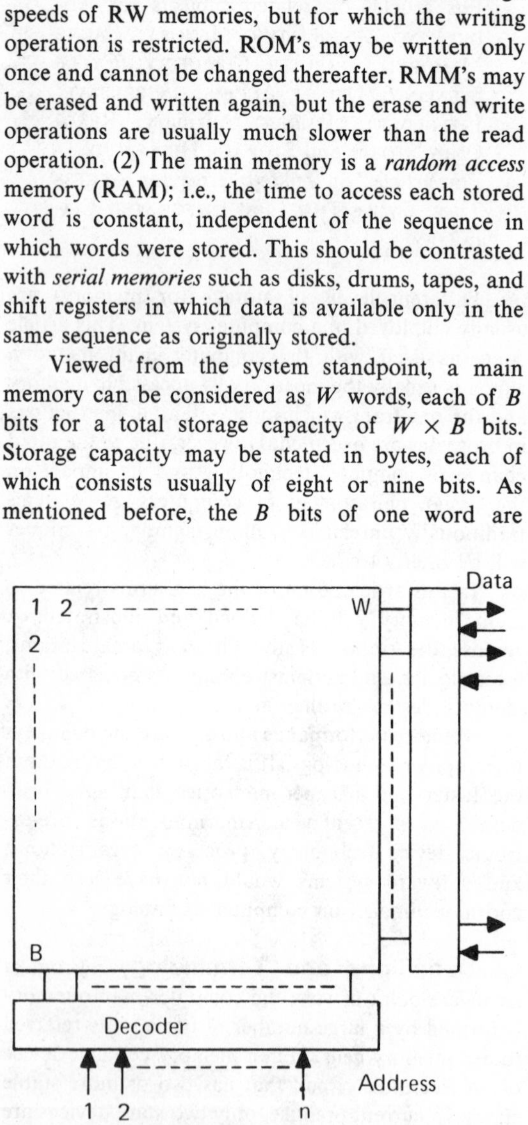


**Fig. 1.** Memory consisting of $W$ words of $B$ bits, each requiring an address of $n$ bits ($n = \log_2 W$).

With respect to memory timing, we speak of *access time* and *cycle time*. Access time is the time required to read out any randomly selected word from memory. Cycle time is the minimum time interval required between the initiation of two successive, independent memory operations. In some memory technologies, such as bipolar semiconductor, the read cycle and write cycle times are almost equal. On the other hand, for magnetic cores, the reading operation is destructive. Thus, a core has to be rewritten after each reading, resulting in a cycle time equal to the time required to read and rewrite.

From the definitions above we distinguish between memory technologies that necessitate a *destructive readout* (DRO), such as magnetic cores, and those for which the readout is *nondestructive* (NDRO), such as semiconductors. The rapid growth of semiconductor technology introduced, in addition to other terminology, the terms "static" and "dynamic" memories. A static memory is one whose cells retain their states indefinitely as long as the system power is applied. Such memories do not fundamentally need a clock for their operation. Clocks may be used but are required only to synchronize memory operation with the other elements in a computer system. Magnetic cores provide static memories. Static semiconductor memories employ a bistable flip-flop for each memory cell. On the other hand, dynamic memories usually store a binary digit as charge on a capacitor. Since capacitors will discharge with time, a dynamic memory cell needs periodic refreshing. This is accomplished by reading the cell content and rewriting it periodically under clock control. The details of the refresh operation, as well as its implication on the memory system design, will be considered later.

We should also distinguish between *volatile* and *nonvolatile* memories. A nonvolatile memory is one that retains its contents even if the power supply is removed. This property, considered important by many computer system designers, is present in ferrite core memories. On the other hand, semiconductor memories are volatile. Since main memory is not used for long-term storage of instructions or data, volatility is not a major concern. Nonvolatility, however, is an essential attribute of mass storage systems.

**Memory Technologies: An Overview.** The oldest, and still predominant, memory technology is that of ferrite cores. (See Riley, 1971; Hodges, 1972; Renwick, 1964.) In spite of the challenge posed by the newer technologies such as plated wires, thin film, and (more recently) semiconductors, magnetic-core memories continue to exist. Part of the reason is perhaps psychological, since system designers have become accustomed to thinking in terms of cores. More important are the large investments by manufacturers in core fabrication equipment, and hence their reluctance to adopt a new technology.

In the section "Ferrite-Core Memories," we consider their characteristics in detail. We wish at this point, however, to make some general observations concerning them. The trend in ferrite-core memories over the years has been to reduce the cost per bit and simultaneously increase the operating speed. Cores have the obvious advantages of zero standby power, reasonable cost and speed for general-purpose applications (especially in large systems), and nonvolatility. Most important, though, is that the technology of magnetic cores is mature and proven.

Ferrite-core memories do, however, present a number of disadvantages, such as large currents needed for writing and small signals obtained in readout; both imply sophisticated read and write circuitry. The cost of such circuitry is an overhead on the system, which results in uneconomic magnetic memories for small systems. In addition to being bulky, magnetic-core memories are a foreign technology in relation to the rest of the computer system components. Stated in other terms, both the mechanical and electrical interfaces and power supplies present added problems.

Meanwhile, advances have been made in other magnetic memory technologies such as thin films and plated wires. Plated wires, pioneered by UNIVAC, appeared in 1967 and became competitive in the main-frame market. In 1970, the output of plated wire memories was about 2.5% of the estimated total for all types of random access memory, and most of this production was for the UNIVAC 1100 and 9000 series computers.

We note, however, that for normal speeds, plated wires do not offer distinct advantages over magnetic cores. Although simpler in wiring than cores, plated wires have the disadvantage of low bit density. They are, however, capable of much higher speeds of operation. The readout obtained with plated wires is nondestructive, reducing the complexity and cost of the associated electronics, but the readout signals are very small. Accordingly, considerable cost is still incurred in the electronics part of the memory system and in interfacing this magnetic technology with the integrated circuit technology dominant throughout the rest of the computer. Similar problems exist with thin films.

This brief overview of magnetic memories suggests that the development and growth of semiconductor memories is a logical step toward faster and cheaper computer systems. Indicative of this trend is the data in Table 1, which shows that semiconductors have already overtaken cores in the area of main frame memory.

**Table 1.** Add-on* Main Memory Systems Shipped by United States Manufacturers (in $ millions)

| Memory Type | 1973 | 1974 | 1978 (Estimated) |
|---|---|---|---|
| Cores | 175 | 165 | 115 |
| Semiconductors | 150 | 250 | 690 |

*"Add-on Memory" refers to memory purchased to augment a basic computer system.

The data in Table 1 is even more startling when it is realized that the price per bit of semiconductor memory systems has been traditionally higher than that of cores. Although core prices are reasonably stable, those for semiconductor memories continue to decline. In fact, for small systems at present, semiconductor memories are cheaper than cores. With this competition, plated wire and thin-film technologies are no longer in contention for the main memory market.

Semiconductor memory is known by various names: monolithic memory, integrated circuit memory, large-scale integrated (LSI) memory, active memory, and transistor memory. All these names refer to binary digital memories that employ an electronic circuit for each memory cell.

Traditionally, semiconductor memories have been used in computer systems for applications requiring high operating speed such as scratch-pad memories. These were low-density, high-cost units employing bipolar junction transistors as flip-flops for the memory cells. Note in the following that we refer to semiconductor memories employing integrated circuit bipolar junction transistors as "bipolar memories." This will be contrasted with MOS memories, which employ metal-oxide-semiconductor field-effect transistor technology.

Recently, semiconductor memories have made their way to the computer main memory area. Examples of this trend include the IBM System 370/145 and the ILLIAC IV process-element memory. The bulk of these memory systems are bipolar chips containing 256 bits of storage.

In the remainder of this article we consider in some detail magnetic-core memories and semiconductor memories. The former are considered because they are still predominant, and the latter are considered because of their very rapid growth and their potential for eventual complete replacement of magnetic technology in main-frame applications.

**Dimensional Quantization.** Digital memory is dimensionally quantized as to both the number of words and the bits per word. The quantization naturally depends on the application for which the memory is intended, but also on some constraints produced by technology.

For "small" computers, the number of words required is often available in one "module," and the complete memory consists entirely of a single module. For magnetic-core memories, the natural physical unit (or module) is called a "stack." Depending on the speed of technology and other factors, a stack may be 1,024 (called 1K), 2K, 4K, or 8K words. Thus, for small machines, a single core memory stack may suffice.

However, for "large" applications, the number of words required may easily exceed the number in a single stack. Thus, a number of modules may be required, in which case a new opportunity for functional quantization arises. If the total number of words required by a system is at least twice that naturally available in one module, it is possible to apply the technique of address interleaving (or simply "interleaving") in the system. In an interleaved memory consisting of $M$ independent modules, consecutive addresses occur in physically separate modules. This arrangement in large systems makes possible the very high speed access of a sequence of contiguously addressed words, since all modules operate nearly simultaneously to obtain $M$ words. In the event that sequentially accessed words are not in contiguous addresses, the reduction in total access time will not be so great, but will be still meaningful.

Though the digit or bit dimension (i.e., the number of bits per word) of a main-frame memory appears constrained by the system in which it is embedded, internally the memory may operate in a way that is technologically constrained. For example, though a memory may appear to the user to have addressing at a bit level, this appearance would normally be implemented by a combination of word addressing, and then subsequent bit-from-word selection.

The number of bits available from each quantum selection is constrained by the simultaneous need for speed and economy. For a speed of data access fixed by the technology chosen, it is obvious that the peak memory data rate in bits per second increases as more and more bits are retrieved by a single word access. Thus, there is a tendency to increase the number of bits per word to improve system speed. Another reason for increasing the number of bits per accessed quantum is that, for a given memory capacity, this reduces the total number of words and thus the total cost of the word-access mechanism. But bit sensing and standardization circuitry are costly. Furthermore, the cost of a system in effectively using a large number of simultaneously accessed bits is high. In addition to bit-group (or word) selection circuitry costs, also to be considered is the cost of underutilization of many bits available, but seldom used.

Whether a memory is most economically accessed by bit, byte, fraction of a word, half-word, word, double word, or multiple word will depend on the relative costs of the word-and-bit access mechanisms. Often the solution chosen balances in some sense the word and digit dimensions to produce a "square" design. In a "square" design there is a rough equality among the speed, cost, or space (or some combination) of mechanisms for selection in the word direction and for bit recovery in the digit direction.

**Memory Selection—The Numbers Game.** Even modest memories require prodigious numbers of individual binary storage cells. For example, a memory of 4,096 words of 16 bits each, suitable only for very modest minicomputer configuration, contains $2^{16}$ (=65,536) memory elements. Clearly, even this small size results in an enormous technological problem in the selection of the desired bits. This has been solved in practical main memory technology by the concept of multidimensional access. One dimension, the digit dimension, is implicitly identified in the original memory specification. For each word selected, $2^4$ (or 16) bits are accessed. However, there remains the need to select from one of $2^{12}$ (or 4,096) words. The notion of coordinate selection suggests itself.

If each memory cell typically containing one bit of information is conceived to be at the crossing points of a two-dimensional $X \times Y$ unit grid, or 2D array, then the number of grid points is $XY$. Clearly, for a memory of $2^N$ cells: $XY = 2^N$. By this means, an important advantage has accrued—namely, that the number of selection lines has been reduced from one per cell, $2^N$, to $X + Y$, where $XY = 2^N$. The reduction is greatest when the array is nearly square; i.e., when $X$ is as close to $Y$ as possible. For $N$ even, the best choice is $X = Y = 2^{N/2}$, in which case the required number of wires is $2 \times 2^{N/2}$ for a $2^N$ cell array.

Now that we have identified $2^N$ nodes in a conceptual *array*, it is necessary to implement some physical node-selection mechanism. What is needed in practice is a *nonlinear* element with a threshold. A fundamental example of such an element is a semiconductor diode that conducts current in only one direction with a few tenths of a volt drop while accepting large voltages in the reverse direction but allowing no current to flow. An example of a suitable array is shown in Fig. 2. One can see that current will flow in diode $D_{11}$ only if the voltage $V_{Y1}$ on $Y_1$ is positive, and if the voltage $V_{X1}$ on $X_1$ is negative. Further, one can see that if all other $Y$ wires are held negative and all other $X$ wires positive, current will not flow in any other diode.

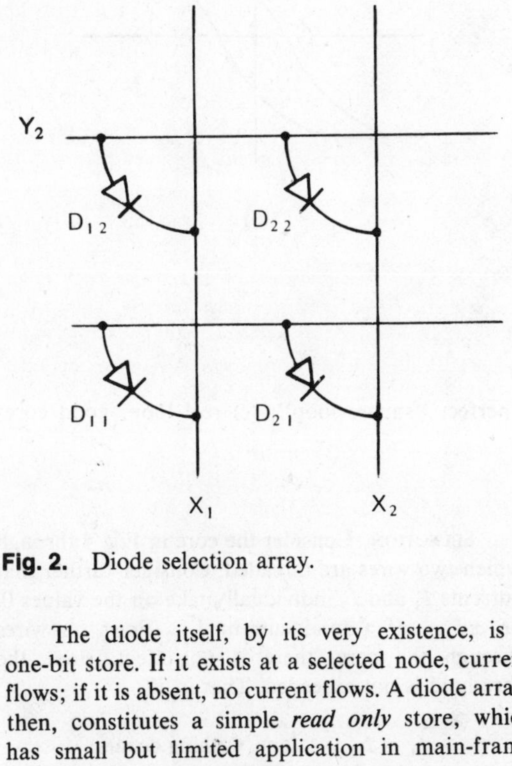


**Fig. 2.** Diode selection array.

The diode itself, by its very existence, is a one-bit store. If it exists at a selected node, current flows; if it is absent, no current flows. A diode array, then, constitutes a simple *read only* store, which has small but limited application in main-frame technology as a permanent subroutine or as a constant storage mechanism with fast access.

More generally, if the diode current accesses a digital storage mechanism, one has succeeded in selecting one of $2^N$ storage locations by energizing two of $2 \times 2^{N/2}$ wires. In this role the diode nonlinearity is performing a logical AND function. If both $X_1$ and $Y_1$ are simultaneously energized, then current flows in $D_{11}$, selecting cell $C_{11}$. Logically, $C_{11} = X_1 \cdot Y_1$. This is a necessary property of all coordinate selection systems. Each selected entity is driven by an ANDed coincidence of selection variables. For two-dimension (2D) select, there are two selecting variables; for three-dimension (3D) select, there are three selecting variables. Because we have introduced no constraint on the order of energizing the $X$ or $Y$, the array so obtained is said to be "random access."

**Ferrite-Core Memories.** A realization of the possibility of using magnetic square-loop toroids in a digital memory organization came to Jay Forrester at M.I.T. in 1950. Though his invention incorporated Permalloy tape-wound cores at first, the concept was quickly extended to the more easily mass-produced ferrite material.

Two critical properties of an ideal memory element happen to coexist in a single square-loop magnetic device: The first of these is memory, or *remanence*, permitting the fundamental storage of information. The second is threshold, or nonlinearity, facilitating noncritical *selection*.

Figure 3(a) shows a toroid of appropriate (ferrite) magnetic material through which a wire is run. In actuality, this toroid, or magnetic core, or core can be very small. Typical paired values of outer and inner diameters expressed in units of $10^{-3}$ in. includes 80/50, 50/30, 30/18, 18/12, 12/7, 7/4. The incentive to use smaller and smaller cores, besides the obvious one of miniaturization, is that less and less energy is needed to operate the device, and, with available switches, speed improves if smaller currents are required.

In actual use, as we will see, more than one wire threads each core. Thus, depending on the particular memory design parameters, including number of wires per core and number of cores on each selecting wire, some particular small core becomes a standard at any time corresponding to the current state of fabrication technology.

An ideal core such as that shown in Fig. 3(a) might have an ideal relationship between its controlling parameter, wire current $I$, and its controlled internal magnetization $M$, such as shown in Fig. 3(b) as a *perfect square* (meaning rectangular) *loop*. Real cores are, however, less than perfect, as shown in Figs. 3(c) and 3(d). Assuming that the core is initially in the remanent state $M_B$, application of a current $I_A$ moves the state of the core into the fourth quadrant until, when $I_A$ exceeds $I_{\text{threshold}}$, the core *switches*. If

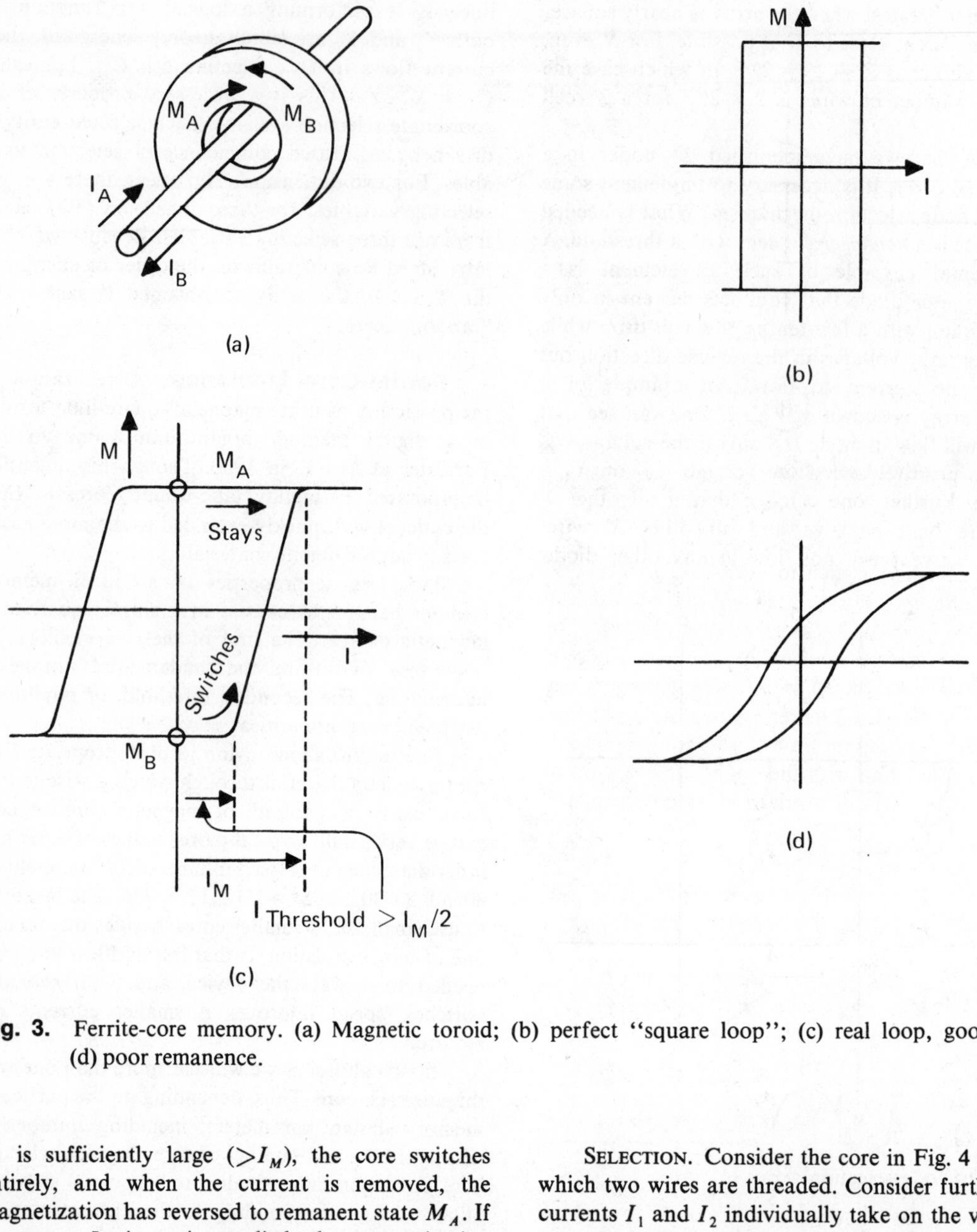


**Fig. 3.** Ferrite-core memory. (a) Magnetic toroid; (b) perfect "square loop"; (c) real loop, good core; (d) poor remanence.

$I_A$ is sufficiently large ($>I_M$), the core switches entirely, and when the current is removed, the magnetization has reversed to remanent state $M_A$. If a current $I_A$ is again applied, the magnetization remains essentially constant. If, however, the current $I$ is reversed to $I_B > I_M$, the state of magnetization will permanently change back to $M_B$.

Remanence per se does not depend strongly on the shape of the *MI* curve, and in fact the core in Fig. 3(d) has distinct remanent states. However, for purposes of selection, the shape of the "square loop" is very critical. It is very important, as we will see, that for a core to be safely selected [Fig.3(c)] $I_{\text{threshold}}$ must exceed $I_{M/2}$.

SELECTION. Consider the core in Fig. 4 through which two wires are threaded. Consider further that currents $I_1$ and $I_2$ individually take on the values 0, or $\pm I_{M/2}$. If a total current $I_{M/2}$ flows on wires through the core, there is no effect, since the threshold is not exceeded. That is, if

$$I_1 = I_{M/2} \quad \text{alone, nothing occurs,}$$

or if

$$I_2 = I_{M/2} \quad \text{alone, nothing occurs}$$

but if $I_1 = I_2 = I_{M/2}$, the core threshold is overcome

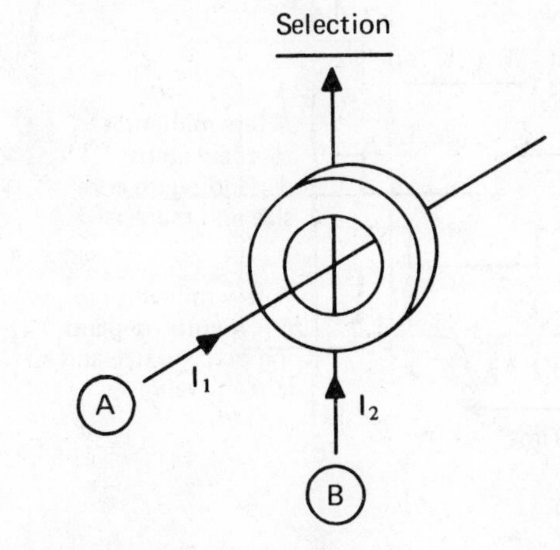


**Fig. 4.** Threshold selection.

and the core may switch to state A. To reverse the state of the core (state B), it will be necessary to apply $I_1 = I_2 = -I_{M/2}$, or alternatively, a current of $-I_M$ on one wire.

OUTPUT. A voltage is induced on every wire coupling of the core if its remanent state is changed. Fig. 5 shows an output on a third wire coupling the core in conjunction with the application of currents $I_{M/2}$ on two others in overlapped time sequence.

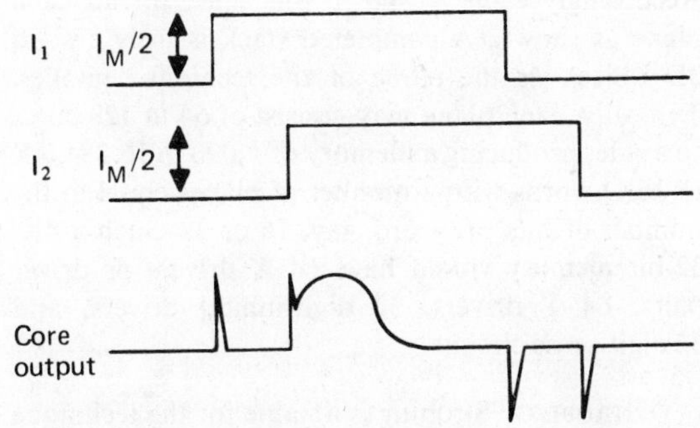


**Fig. 5.** Output voltage on third wire coupling the core of Fig. 4 due to application of select currents $I_{M/2}$.

Application or removal of just one of the select currents causes the core to traverse the relatively flat upper and lower branches of the *MI* curve. For each such traversal occurring at the leading and trailing edges of the select pulses, a small, short output signal is produced. The effect is similar to coupling in a linear magnetic transformer, and reverses with the polarity of the current change. Because the change is not permanent and not related to the remanent property of the core, it is said to be "reversible." These reversible changes occur as noise on the bit-signal line. Each of the two signals to be interpreted as binary stored information is preceded by one of these reversible outputs appearing as an initial spike before the longer-term output, caused by permanent reversal of the magnetic domains within the core. In the case that the core is remanent at the state to which it is being sent, essentially only the reversible part appears.

Noise due to reversible core coupling and other magnetic and capacitive coupling between wires is a serious system problem in memories. As a result, it is common practice (and technologically more natural) not to provide perfect pulses as shown, but rather ones that have controlled rise and fall times. Rise times must, of course, be less than the *fundamental ferrite switching time*. Fig. 6 shows a typical sequence of operations in the selection of one core in a memory array. The figure is realistic with the exception of the implied perfection of the current pulses. Their rise time is normally somewhat increased, and pulse shape is not necessarily perfect. The currents applied to the core on wire 1 and wire 2 are intentionally shown noncoincident so as to represent the propagation delay of currents along each dimension of a real two-dimensional core array. One can see that as a result of this delay, select pulses must be longer, to ensure an adequate overlap that allows time to permit complete core switching.

As can be seen, only a small noise output results from a half-selected core where only one selection pulse is supplied. It is very important, of course, that this half-select output be small, since on a line of $N$ cores, only one is selected while $N - 1$ are half-selected. The total accumulation of $(N - 1)$ half-selects is often a limiting factor in core-memory array dimensions.

If the core is selected and reverses state, a relatively large and long output is produced. This is shown in Fig. 6 arbitrarily as "Read with a one output." Since there is an output, the core was in a "one" state, but is now in a "zero" state. A subsequent read of the same polarity labeled "Read with zero output" produces no output. The rewrite of a "one" is shown to require reversal of both select currents to drive the core into its former remanent state. Though an output is produced at this time, it is rarely used. Thus, we see that reading is a destructive process, and therefore each read operation is normally followed by a restoring rewrite cycle.

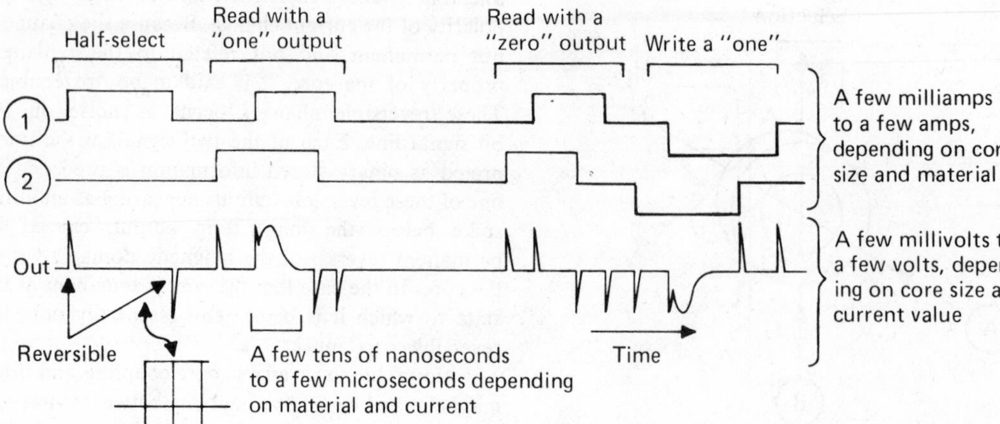


**Fig. 6.** A sequence of operations in the selection of one core in a memory array, illustrating the destructive nature of the read operation. In normal operation each read cycle is usually followed by a restoring write cycle.

WIRING ORGANIZATIONS

*3D or Bit Organized.* Fig. 7(a) shows a memory plane organization, traditionally called "bit organized," or 3D. The complete memory system shown in Fig. 7(c) is composed of edge-connected planes wired as in Fig. 7(a) where a short diagonal line represents each core. The particular wiring shown within the plane is called "3D–4 wire, simplified."

Each core in a given core plane is threaded with four wires. The role of the wires in Fig. 7(b), labeled *X* and *Y* is similar to that described previously. However, for simplicity of electronic control, the current waveforms on each are invariant, consisting of a bipolar pulse doublet as shown in Fig. 7(b), independent of the data to be read or written. In order to write zeros and ones, an additional single line called "bit inhibit" threads every core in the same sense as the *X* line. A simple monopolar pulse applied to it, when present, cancels one half-select at the selected core, preventing the rewrite of the "one" state and leaving a zero. A fourth wire called "bit sense" threads every core. As a result of the simplicity of its diagonal path, the pulse naturally traverses alternate cores in a reverse sense from its previous path. Hence, the polarity of the signal available between its ends varies from core to core. In operation, accordingly, the signal available has three states, either a positive or negative pulse called a "one," or nothing but noise for a zero. Since the contribution from each threaded core alternates, the noise accumulation from half-selects is reduced considerably.

In use, each plane is assigned to one bit of all words in the *collection of planes*, called the "stack." Accordingly each X and Y line must thread each plane as shown. A completed stack is truly a solid 3D object, as the name of the technique implies. Typically, each plane may consist of 64 to 128 cores to a side, producing a memory of 4,096 to 16,384 (4K to 16K) words with a number of planes equal to the number of bits per word, say, 16 or 32. Such a 4K, 32-bit memory would have 64 *X* drivers or driver pairs, 64 *Y* drivers, 32 digit-inhibit drivers, and 32 digit-sense circuits.

STROBING. Strobing is a name for the technique required to time-synchronize data appearing as pulses at the output of a memory. It is implemented by a gate within each sense amplifier (connected to each digit line), which is opened at a predetermined optimum time at which the correct digit readout is expected. It is intended to solve two problems: The first is the fact that a core plane is a noisy environment, and the selection of a legitimate logic 1 signal from the accumulation of half-selects, reversible signals, and driven line induction requires some precision. Luckily, the timing of the noise, particularly of the reversible and induced signals,

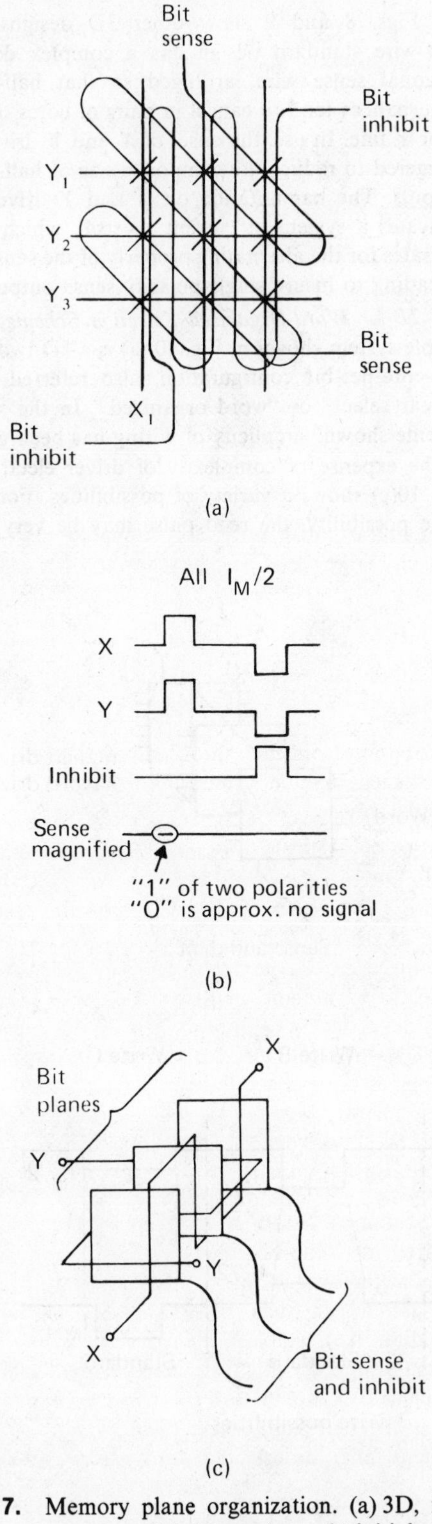


**Fig. 7.** Memory plane organization. (a) 3D, four-wire, simplified core plane; (b) initial pulses on $X$ and $Y$; (c) 3D core stack.

and including the half-selects, is earlier than the true signal.

The second problem that strobing must solve complicates the solution to the first selection. This problem concerns the time delay of transmission within each plane and within the stack. Clearly, the bit lines indicated in Fig. 7 are very long and consist of a wire having a distributed load of magnetic cores. The result is a transmission line having considerable delay per bit. It is apparent that a signal originating at a core deep within a plane will appear at the bit-sense terminals somewhat later than the one originating near the ends of the sense line. This is a difficult problem to solve with strobe timing, and often limits the size of the core plane that can be used. In some designs it is possible to vary the strobe, and hence the bit-sensing time, with the *address* of the bit selected, thus allowing somewhat longer bit lines.

In designing the digit strobe circuitry, account must also be taken of the delay along the $X$ and $Y$ select lines. In a bit-organized 3D memory, this is particularly easy, since the $X$ and $Y$ lines are relatively short, being $d/\sqrt{2n}$ times the length of the bit lines for $d$ ($n \times n$) bit planes* ($n^2$ words of $d$ bits each). Furthermore, it is easy to adjust the strobe for each bit to cancel $X$ and $Y$ delay if necessary.

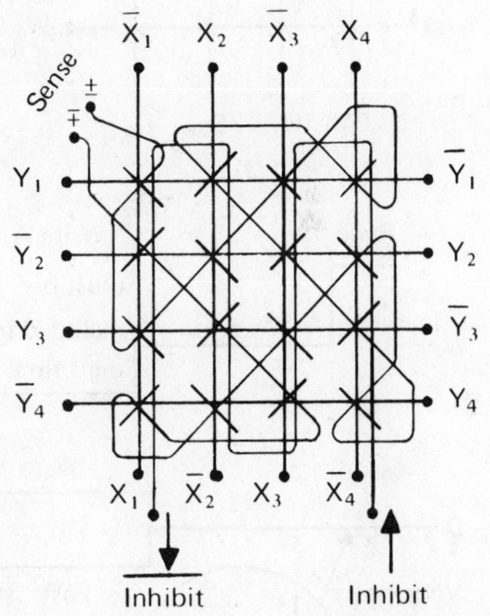


**Fig. 8.** Another 3D, four-wire, standard core plane.

* This may be seen by observing that the digit line of each digit plane consists of $2n$ diagonal bit lines of variable length equivalent to $n$ lines of length $\sqrt{2}$ times the plane side length.

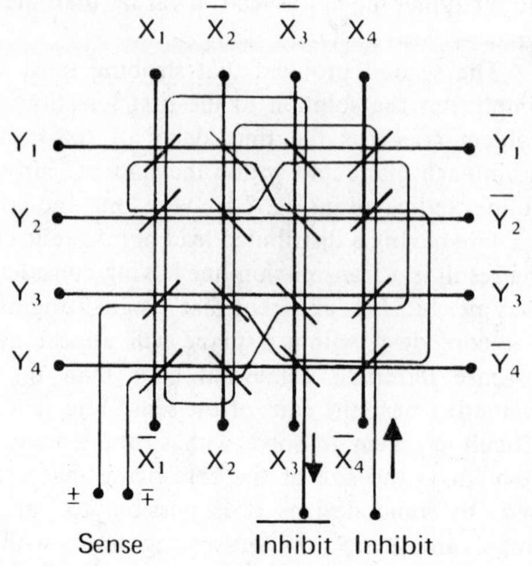


**Fig. 9.** A 3D, four-wire, rectangular core plane.

Figs. 8 and 9 show other 3D designs. The four-wire standard design has a complex double-diagonal sense wire, arranged so that half-select disturbances tend to cancel in pairs of cores on any $X$ or $Y$ line. In use, the onset of $X$ and $Y$ drives are staggered to reduce the composite size of half-select outputs. The bar notation on $X$ and $Y$ drive lines indicates a system of current reversal, which compensates for the alternating property of the sense line threading to insure single-polarity sense outputs.

*2D or Word-Organized Selection Schemes.* The simple system shown in Fig. 10 (a) is a 2D two-wire, one-core-per-bit configuration, also referred to as "linear select" or "word organized." In the simple scheme shown, simplicity of wiring has been gained at the expense of complexity of driver electronics. Fig. 10(c) shows a variety of possibilities. For each write possibility, the read pulse may be very large

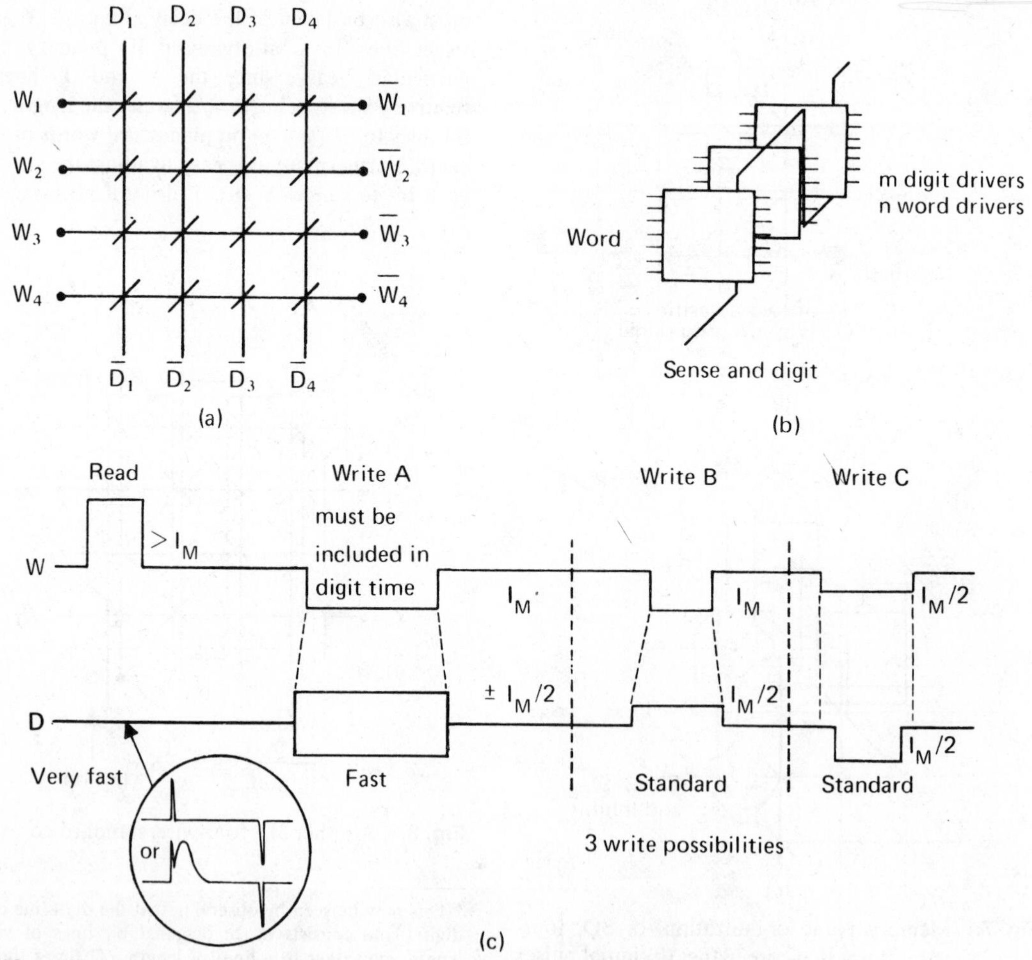


**Fig. 10** A linear-select system. (a) 2D, two-wire, one-core per bit plane; (b) 2D core stack; (c) read/write waveforms.

($>I_M$), since no selection function is required. The excess current available very quickly switches to zero each core of the word storing a "one," rapidly producing a relatively large output voltage.

Three rewrite schemes are possible. One, using a word line current of $I_M$ and a digit current of $\pm I_M/2$ is very fast, since the switching current applied is $3/2(I_M)$. The other two schemes result in a net core drive of $I_M$ and accordingly are standard in speed. In the event that switching or sensing electronics must be simplified for speed or otherwise, it is very easy to parallel wires in the array. Thus, a single wire and bipolar drive (for example) may be replaced by two wires and monopolar drivers.

The one greatest difficulty with this system is the variable load presented to the word line by a collection of bits that may be either all ones or all zeros. Under these extreme conditions, either all or no cores switch, making driver design difficult.

Another 2D two-wire scheme uses two cores per bit, as shown in Fig. 11. This offers the advantage of a constant word-line load, since one of the two cores per bit always switches. It has the additional advantage that for short word lines, the reversible components of the output signal from the two cores cancel. This, together with the fact that the output signal on the digit line provides a one and zero of opposite polarity, makes fast low-noise operation possible. The immediate cost is the second core per bit, but this is often compensated by simpler driver design.

*2½D, Two-Wire Systems.* The polarity-pair selection shown in Fig. 12 is a combination of 2D or word-select and 3D or bit-select schemes. It resembles the two-core-per-bit scheme, but uses alternating polarity pulses on the digit line to access each of the two cores. It conveniently doubles the number of digits per word available from a two-core-per-bit

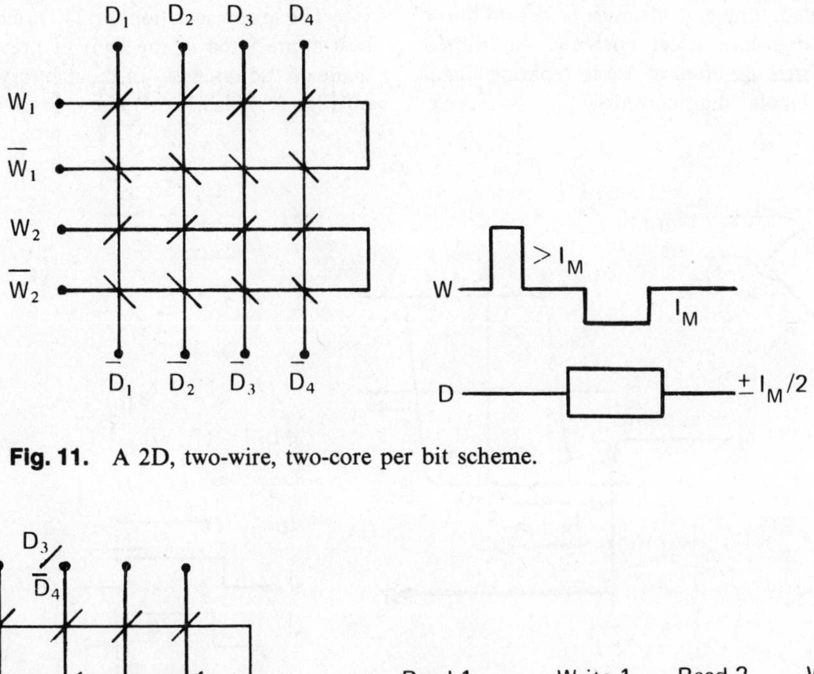


**Fig. 11.** A 2D, two-wire, two-core per bit scheme.

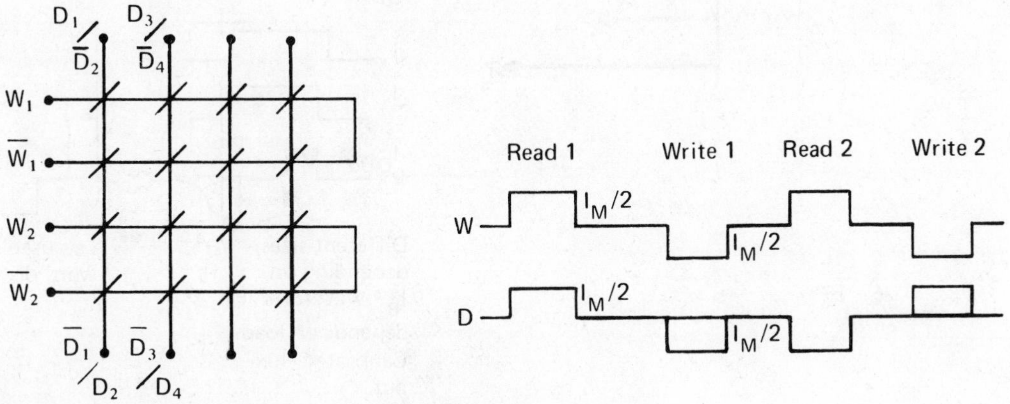


**Fig. 12.** A 2½D, two-wire, polarity-pair selection.

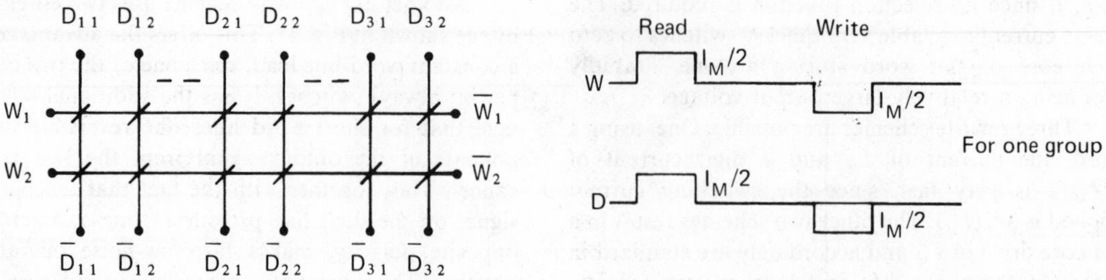


**Fig. 13.** A 2½D, two-wire, group selection.

frame at the expense of more complex driver protocol and bit sensing, and a reduction in speed. The latter results from the use of *half-select currents* to distinguish bits and not because of the unconstrained currents usable in two-core-per-bit systems. Like the two-core-per-bit system, reversible digit signals and disturbances produced by the word current are canceled, though digits must be sensed in the presence of digit-line select currents. Additional parallel digit lines are often of use to separate signal sensing from bipolar digit currents.

Another approach to 2½D, called "group selection," is shown in Fig. 13. Here, again, both a word line and a group of digit lines are activated simultaneously. Though the word may be very long, only a fraction of its bits will switch; however, disturbances and reversible components from all bits accumulate as word line load.

The group selection, or 2½D, technique may be best appreciated in the light of previous comments made on "squareness" of the memory (see discussion of Fig. 3). Clearly, if the cost of word select is

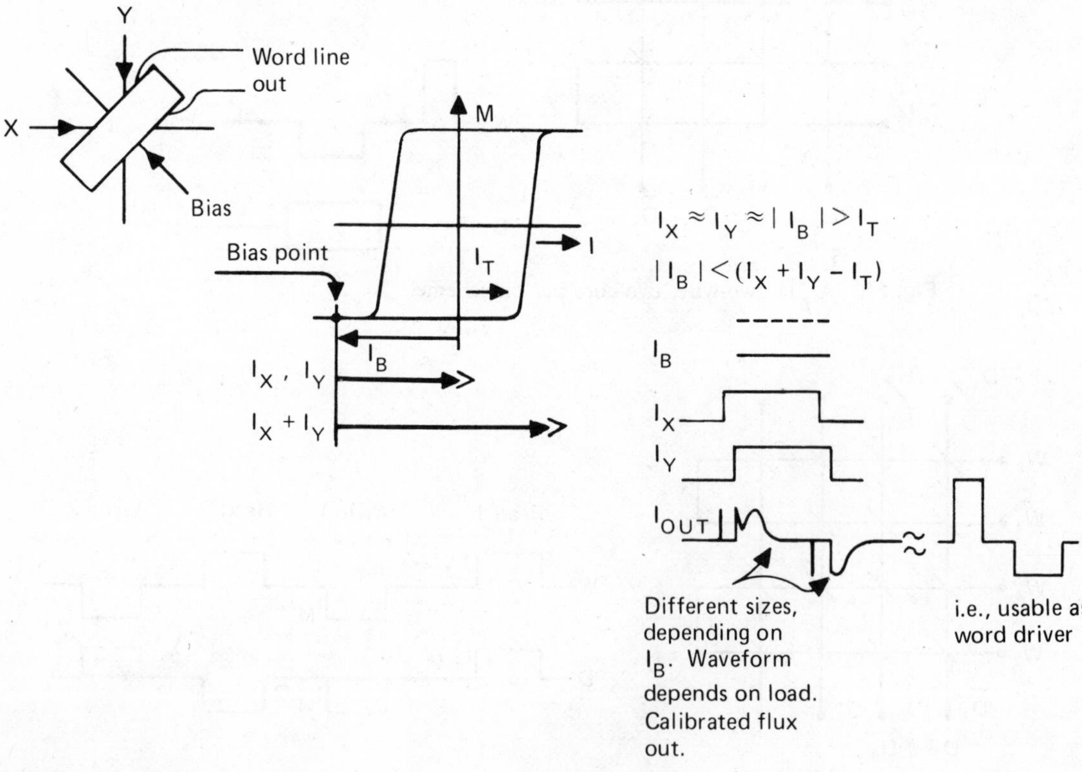


**Fig. 14.** Switch-core word selection.

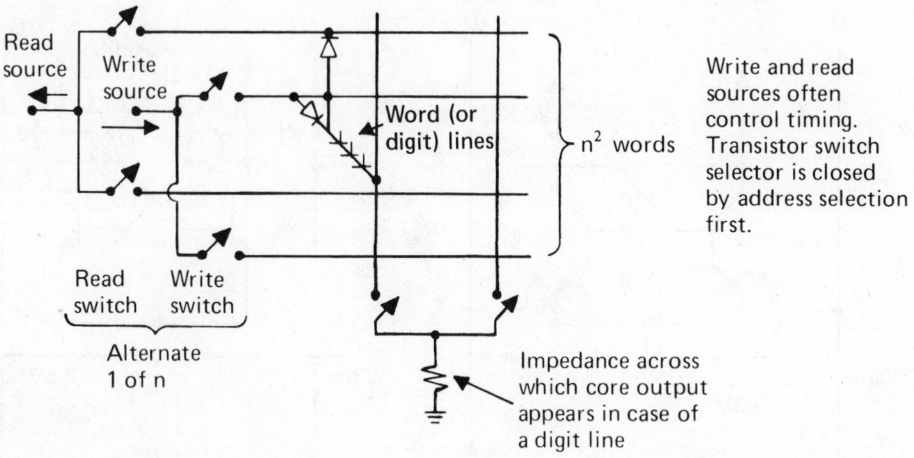


**Fig. 15.** Diode word selection.

relatively great per word in 2D designs, it may be recovered somewhat if words are made longer. However, what does one do in a system (particularly a small one) with the extra bits available, particularly if they cost money? The answer is found in this group selection scheme, in which only some of the bits in a long word are accessed and the bit-accessing digit drivers and sense circuits are shared between several groups of bits in a word.

WORD SELECTION. Though the linear or word-select schemes are potentially fast, they are limited by the requirement for one word driver per word. Various schemes for external coordinate word selection have been used, incorporating "switch cores" or diodes, for example.

The switch-core scheme uses relatively large cores arranged in a biased rectangular array having $X/Y$ selection, as indicated in Fig. 14, and an output from each, providing word drive. The word drive so produced is bipolar, and accordingly is appropriate for many of the linear-select schemes. For an $n$-bit word, the switch core, being larger, can be arranged to supply $n$ units of flux upon reversal, thus calibrating a drive in current rather than flux units. This is particularly appropriate for two-core-per-bit designs where the word-line load is constant.

Diode selection schemes that may be used resemble those introduced previously in Fig. 2, where each diode has a word line in series with it. Since word-line currents required are bidirectional, two such diode select matrices are often necessary. Such an arrangement is shown in Fig. 15. The switches shown are typically implemented with integrated circuits—as may be the entire selection scheme, including in effect the diodes.

## Semiconductor Memories

BIPOLAR MEMORIES. As mentioned in the preceding section, there are basically two types of semiconductor memories, bipolar memories and MOS memories. Fig. 16 shows the two commonly used bipolar transistor memory cells. The multi-emitter cell is the earliest one, and is the one used in the Fairchild 256-bit package to be described shortly. The diode-coupled cell, using Schottky diodes for coupling the cell to the digit lines $D$ and $\overline{D}$, consumes less standby power without sacrificing speed (Hodges, 1972).

Each memory cell is coupled to a word line $W$ and two digit lines $D$ and $\overline{D}$. The memory cells on a single silicon chip are usually physically organized in a square matrix. The logical organization, however, of an $n$-cell chip is that of $n$ words by 1 bit. As an example, consider the Fairchild 93410, with a 256-bit fully decoded memory chip. The chip is housed in a 16-pin dual-in-line package. Fig. 17 shows the package outline and terminals. The chip is organized as 256 words by 1 bit. Selection is achieved by means of an 8-bit address applied to terminals $A_0$ to $A_7$. The three chip-select inputs are provided to permit some logic flexibility in the application of this package to large memory systems. The read and write operations are controlled by the state of the *write enable* ($\overline{W}_E$) line. With $\overline{W}_E$ held low and the chip selected, the data at $D_{IN}$ is written into the addressed location.

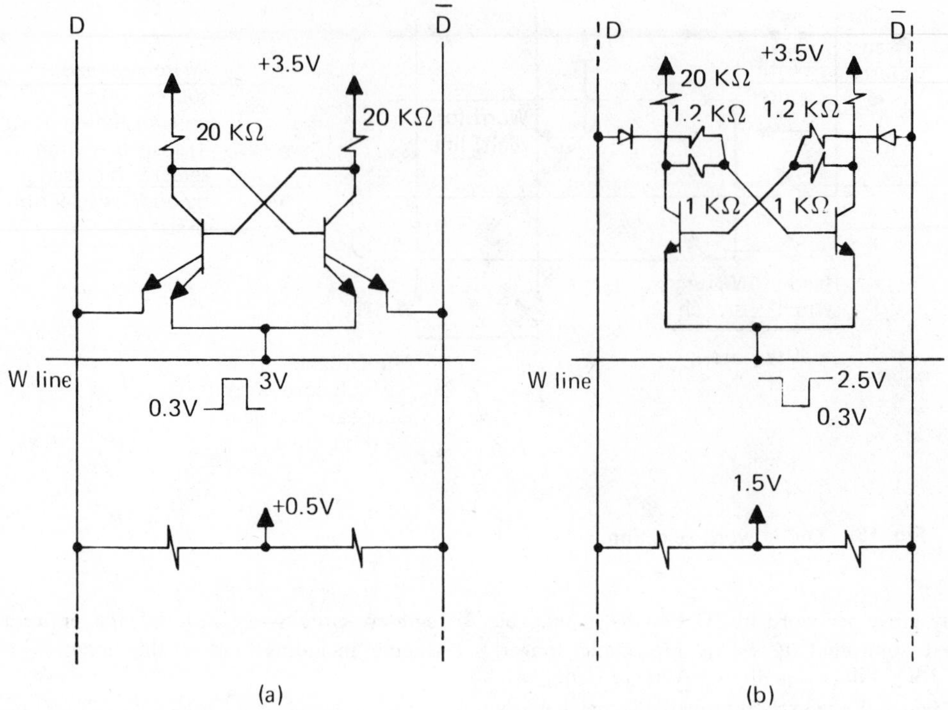


**Fig. 16.** Two commonly used bipolar memory cells. (a) Emitter coupled; (b) Schottky diode coupled.

To read, $\bar{W}_E$ is held high and the chip is selected. Data in the location specified is presented at $D_{OUT}$.

As contrasted to magnetic memories, semiconductor memories provide their outputs as direct-current (dc) levels that will stay as long as the particular cell is accessed, thereby considerably simplifying the readout electronics. The interface problems are almost nonexistent, since both input and output levels are compatible with integrated circuit logic technology.

The particular package of Fig. 17 is specified to have a maximum read-access time of 50 ns, with 1.8 mW per bit power dissipation. In general, it is fair to say that bipolar memories commercially available in the 1970s obtain high operating speeds at the expense of high standby power and increased cost. They are therefore useful only for the parts of the memory system that require this high speed. It should be mentioned that this technology is continuously developing, and more recently reported designs (Luecke et al., 1973; Tsang, 1974) might lead to further gains for bipolar memory technology.

An understanding of bipolar memories is perhaps enhanced by reviewing the operation of a typical basic cell. Consider the multi-emitter cell shown in Fig. 16(a). The two transistors form a flip-flop that stores a binary digit 0 or 1, according to which of the two devices is on or off. Normally, the word line is at the low level (0.3 volt) and the current is conducted over one of the inner emitters. When the word is selected, the $W$ line is raised to the high level (+3 volts). Since the digit lines $D$ and $\bar{D}$ are normally at about +0.5 volt, the flip-flop current is transferred to one of the outer emitters and the inner emitter junctions are both reverse-biased. Depending on which transistor is on, one of the two digit lines will carry a current of about 0.25 mA. The sense amplifier is simply a differential amplifier connected across the $D$ and $\bar{D}$ lines. To write into the cell, the $W$ line is first raised in potential, and current is applied to either the $D$ or $\bar{D}$ (to write a 1 or a 0) to force the flip-flop to the desired state. Note that for the component values shown, this cell dissipates about 900 $\mu$W in standby.

MOS MEMORIES. MOS memories are the most popular type of semiconductor memory at the present time. Chips containing 4K bits are available at moderate prices. Indeed the only serious challenge to

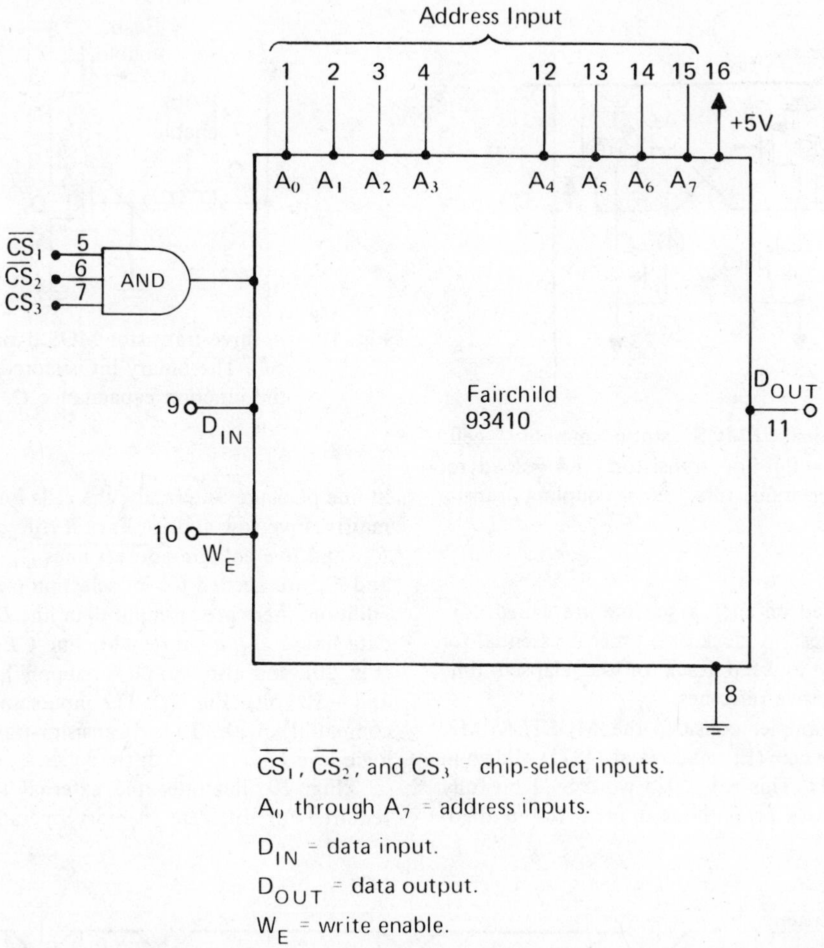


**Fig. 17.** Package outline of the Fairchild 93410 fully decoded 256-bit bipolar memory chip.

the magnetic-core technology is perhaps the MOS memory technology.

First consider static MOS memories. As mentioned before, a static MOS memory employs a flip-flop per memory cell, such as the one shown in Fig. 18. All the transistors are *p*-channel-enhancement MOS devices (PMOS). Transistors 1 and 2 are the flip-flop transistors, and transistors 3 and 4 provide the load resistors. The flip-flop is coupled to the digit lines $D$ and $\bar{D}$ through two transistors, 5 and 6. The latter are controlled by the word line and are normally off. Energizing the $W$ line turns on the coupling transistors, enabling the cell content to be impressed on the digit lines for reading, or enabling a change in the flip-flop state in response to voltage applied to the appropriate digit line for writing.

A matrix of such cells results in a static PMOS memory chip, with each cell requiring six transistors. Although the resulting memory dissipates less power and is easier to manufacture than bipolar memories, speed is sacrificed, and the power and area saving is not substantial. This is the motivation to consider dynamic memory cells.

Fig. 19 shows one possible three-transistor dynamic memory cell. The binary digit is stored as a charge on the gate-to-substrate (ground) capacitance of $Q_1$, while $Q_2$ and $Q_3$ serve as gating switches for reading and writing, respectively. Since the capacitance-stored charge decays with time, the memory needs periodic refreshing. By "refreshing" we mean reading the cell content and rewriting it. This has to occur at a certain specified minimum frequency.

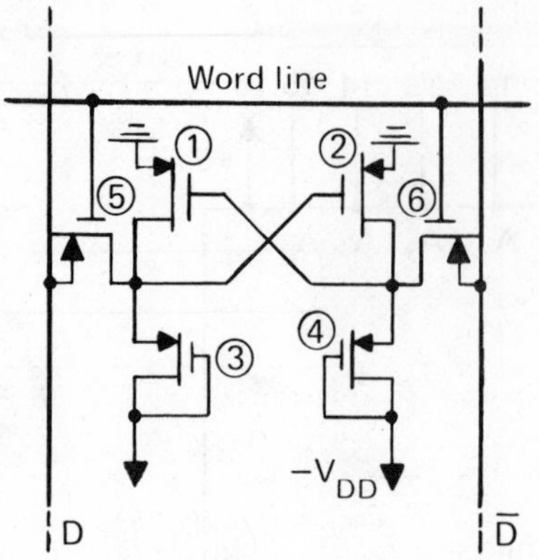


**Fig. 18.** Typical PMOS static memory cell: 1,2 = flip-flop transistors; 3,4 = load resistor transistors; 5,6 = coupling transistors.

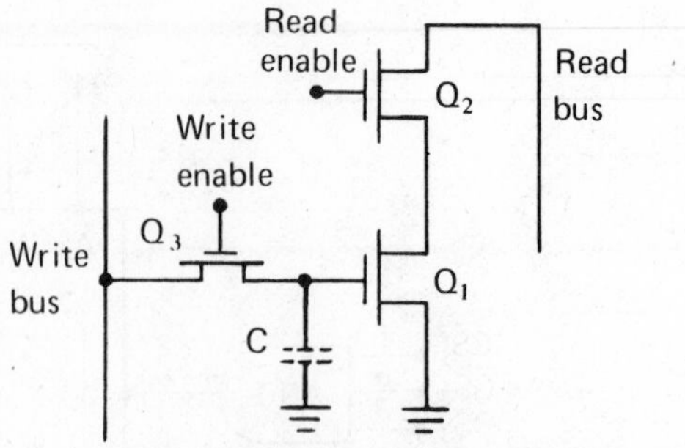


**Fig. 19.** A three-transistor MOS dynamic memory cell. The binary bit is stored as charge on the junction capacitance $C$.

Memories based on such a scheme are called "dynamic memories." A clock or a timer is essential for the operation, to keep track of the elapsed time between successive refreshes.

As an example, consider the MOSTEK MK 4006P memory chip (Erdmann et al., 1971), shown in Figs. 20 and 21. This is a 1,024 word by 1 bit fully decoded memory array housed in a 16-pin dual-in-line package. Internally, the cells form a 32 by 32 matrix. Five-row address lines $R_A$, $R_B$, $R_C$, $R_D$, and $R_E$, and five column-address lines $C_A$, $C_B$, $C_C$, $C_D$, and $C_E$ are needed for bit selection (see Fig. 21). In addition, there are an input data line $D_{IN}$, an output data line $D_{OUT}$, a chip-enable line $CE$, a $R/W$ line (Fig. 20); and also two power-supply lines, +5 volts and −12 volts (Fig. 21). The inputs and outputs are compatible with TTL (transistor-transistor logic) logic levels.

Fig. 20 illustrates the external timing signals required for different memory operations. A write

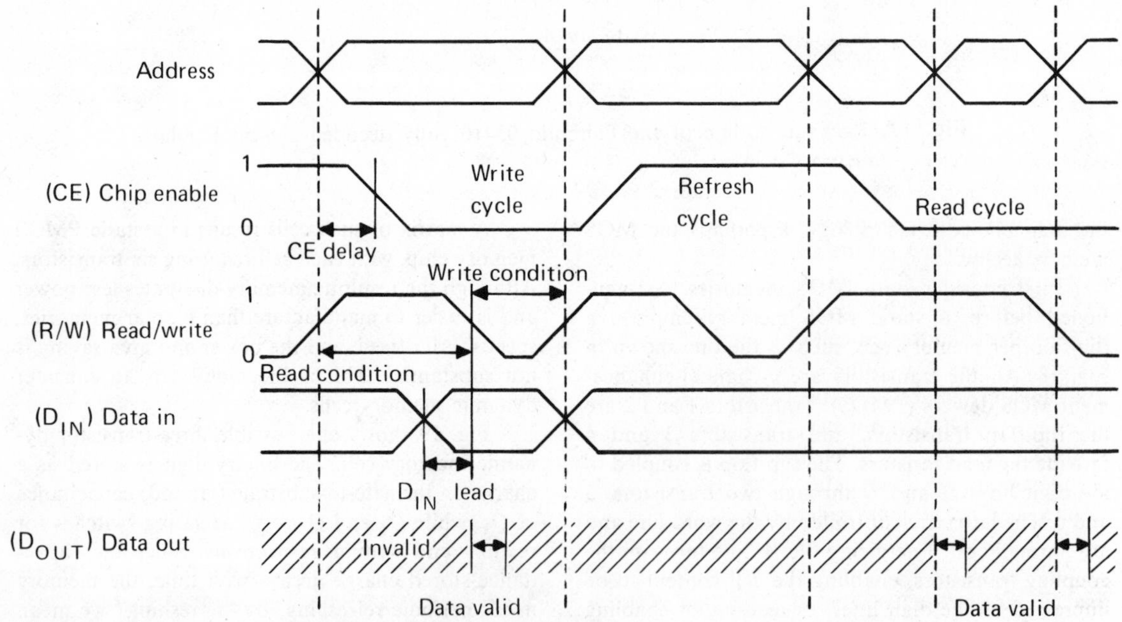


**Fig. 20.** Timing for the MK4006P memory chip. (Courtesy of Erdmann et al. and IEEE; redrawn from a paper presented at the Third Annual IEEE Seminar.)

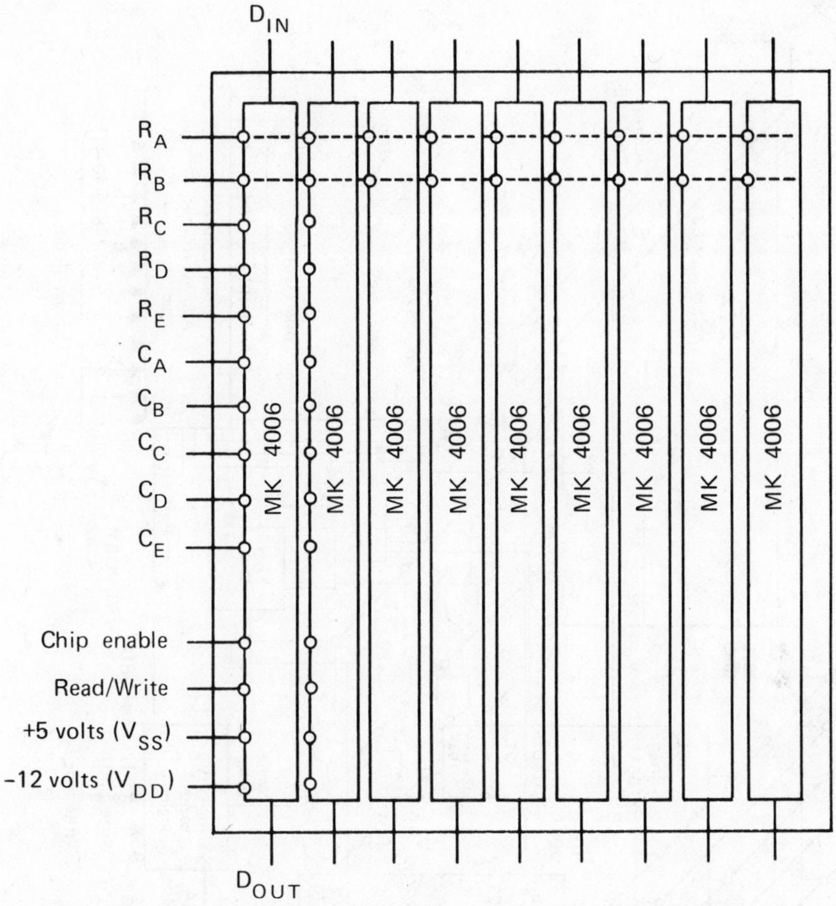


**Fig. 21.** A 1,024-word by 9-bit memory plane. (Courtesy of Erdmann et al. and IEEE; redrawn from a paper presented at the Third Annual IEEE Seminar.)

cycle followed by a refresh cycle and two read cycles are shown. For a read operation, the address code is applied to the address lines and the chip is selected by lowering the level on the *CE* line. The *R/W* line is first raised to logic "1" level. This puts the chip in a "read" mode. After a delay of about 400 ns, the content of the addressed cell ("0" or "1") becomes available at the $D_{OUT}$ line. Although not obvious from the above description, the contents of the other 31 cells in the selected row become available at some internal nodes.

Assuming that the data to be written in the selected cell in the chip is already available at the $D_{IN}$ line, the *R/W* line is lowered, placing the chip in the "write" mode (Fig. 20). Subsequently, the selected cell will be written in. Also, the other 31 cells in the selected row will be rewritten with their original data; i.e., refreshed. The writing time requires about 250 ns. The complete write cycle, therefore, occupies a total of 650 ns.

For the refresh cycle, the CE line (Fig. 20) is raised to the logic "1" level, thus disabling the chip and isolating it from the $D_{IN}$ line. A particular address code is applied to select one of the 32 rows, and the memory chip is placed in a read mode. After the 400 ns required for reading, the contents of the 32 cells in the selected row become available at internal nodes. Subsequent placing of the memory in the write node rewrites this data in the original 32 locations. In this way a complete row has been refreshed. A refresh cycle therefore takes about 650 ns. Thus, to refresh the complete memory chip, we need 32 refresh cycles (i.e., 20 $\mu$s). Since each cell has to be refreshed at least once every 2 ms, only 1% of the time will be spent in refreshing. Finally, we note that a read cycle requires placing the memory in the

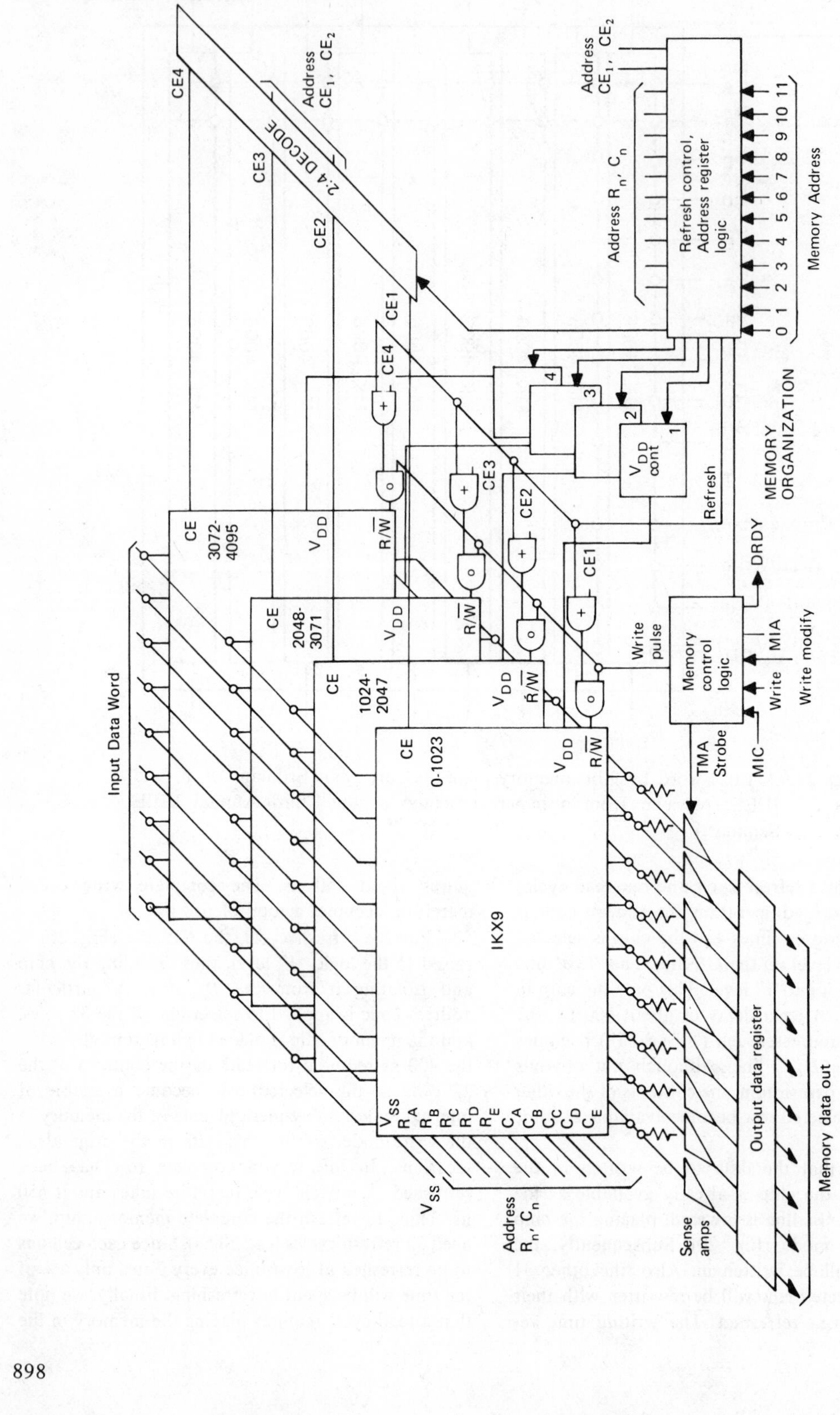


**Fig. 22.** The complete 4,096-word by 9-bit memory system. (Courtesy of Erdmann et al. and IEEE; redrawn from a paper presented at the Third Annual IEEE Seminar.)

**Table 2.** Comparison of Memory Systems

| | Technology | Access/Cycle Time (ns) | System Pwr. (mW/bit) | Density (bits/cm³) | Bits/Chip |
|---|---|---|---|---|---|
| IBM 360-85 | Bipolar | 40/80 | 5.5 | 5 | 64 |
| IBM 370-145 | Bipolar | 125/150 | 0.6 | 54 | 128 |
| COGAR 15C06 | Bipolar | 125/150 | 2.7 | 14 | 128 |
| Fairchild-Illiac | Bipolar | 188/200 | 3.8 | 5 | 256 |
| Semi RAM 300 | Bipolar | 300/400 | 0.7 | 31 | 128 |
| COGAR 30C06 | MOS | 250/400 | 0.4 | 70 | 1024 |
| STD Logic-1103 | MOS | 450/550 | 0.5 | 32 | 1024 |
| EM & M 3000 | Core | 300/650 | 0.5 | 50 | — |

*Source:* David A. Hodges, *Semiconductor Memories*, IEEE Press, 1972.

read condition and waiting 400 ns for the data on the $D_{OUT}$ line to be valid.

To illustrate the application of the memory chip described above, consider the design of a memory system of 4,096 words of nine bits each. Fig. 22 shows the connection of nine packages to form a 1,024-word by 9-bit memory plane. All the address lines, the *CE* lines, the *R/W* lines, and the power-supply lines of the nine chips are connected in parallel. The lines at the top are those of the nine-bit input word, while the lines at the bottom are those of the nine-bit output word.

The connection of four such memory planes together with some control logic form the entire memory system. The detailed description of the operation of this system is beyond the scope of this article. The interested reader is referred to Erdmann et al. (1971). However, it is worth noting that, to conserve power, the full power supply is applied only to the memory plane in which an operation (read or write) is to be performed. The three other planes are operated in the "power down" mode; i.e., at a reduced voltage and reduced standby power. In this mode the memory cells still hold their contents.

Another feature worth noting is that the refreshing is done by hardware and does not require software attention. The refresh control circuitry (not shown) is very simple and consists fundamentally of a timer set to 62.5 $\mu$s (2 ms/32). Whenever the interval elapses, the memory (if not busy) is placed in a refresh cycle. In each refresh cycle, one row of every chip in the memory (a total of $32 \times 9 \times 4$ cells) is simultaneously refreshed. Note that this adds more memory planes, but does not change the time spent on refreshing. During a refresh cycle the memory does not respond to requests from the CPU. This refresh scheme is referred to as "memory-controlled priority request." There are, of course, other schemes employing software control for performing the refresh operation. The memory system described has a read cycle time of 475 ns and write cycle time of 725 ns.

In concluding this article, we present Table 2, which shows a comparison of some of the memory systems employing bipolars, MOS, and magnetic cores.

## References


1964. Renwick, W. *Digital Storage Systems*. London: SPON.

1971. Erdmann et al. "A 1024 Bit Dynamic RAM Using Ion Implant Techniques and Its Applications," paper presented (April 1971) at the Third Annual IEEE Seminar, Paris, France.

1971. Riley, W. B. (Ed.). *Electronic Computer Memory Technology*. New York: McGraw-Hill.

1972. Hodges, David A. (Ed.). *Semiconductor Memories*. New York: IEEE Press.

1973. Luecke, G., J. Mize, and W. Carr. *Semiconductor Memory Design and Applications*. New York: McGraw-Hill.

1974. Tsang, F. "A 1024-Bit Bipolar RAM," 1974 International Solid State Circuits Conference, *Digest*, p. 200.


K. C. Smith and A. S. Sedra

## AUXILIARY

For articles on related subjects *see* Access Time; Block and Blocking; Data Acquisition Computer; Direct Access; Latency; Memory: Main; Scratch File; and Storage Hierarchy.

For articles on related terms *see* ARITHMETIC-LOGIC UNIT; and OPEN AND CLOSE A FILE.

Auxiliary memory (AM) is distinguished from main memory (MM) by the fact that only from the latter are instructions taken for execution. In most computers, the arithmetic logic unit (ALU) and MM comprise a carefully designed pair of machine components, matched for speed and data-path width. AM comprises all other memories whose contents (instructions and data) must be fetched into the MM before processing by the ALU.

An exception to the foregoing statement is large-core storage (LCS), an AM out of which instructions can be directly executed by some ALU's. In such cases, LCS behaves like an MM, but slows ALU speed by a factor of 3 to 10.

AM is rewritable; i.e., it can be written, read, rewritten, etc., many times without deterioration. Thus, punched cards, paper tape, and printer paper are not classified as AM's, although the first two store instructions and data in re-readable form. AM generally uses electromagnetic digital technology for storing data.

There are some eight different types of AM's in use today, and the variety and number continue to grow rapidly:

| | |
|---|---|
| Magnetic tapes | Moving-head disks |
| Cassette tapes | Data cells |
| Drums | Photocopy storages |
| Fixed-head disks | Large core storages |

**Magnetic Tape.** Magnetic tapes are long, narrow ribbons (typically 2,400 ft long and 0.5 in.

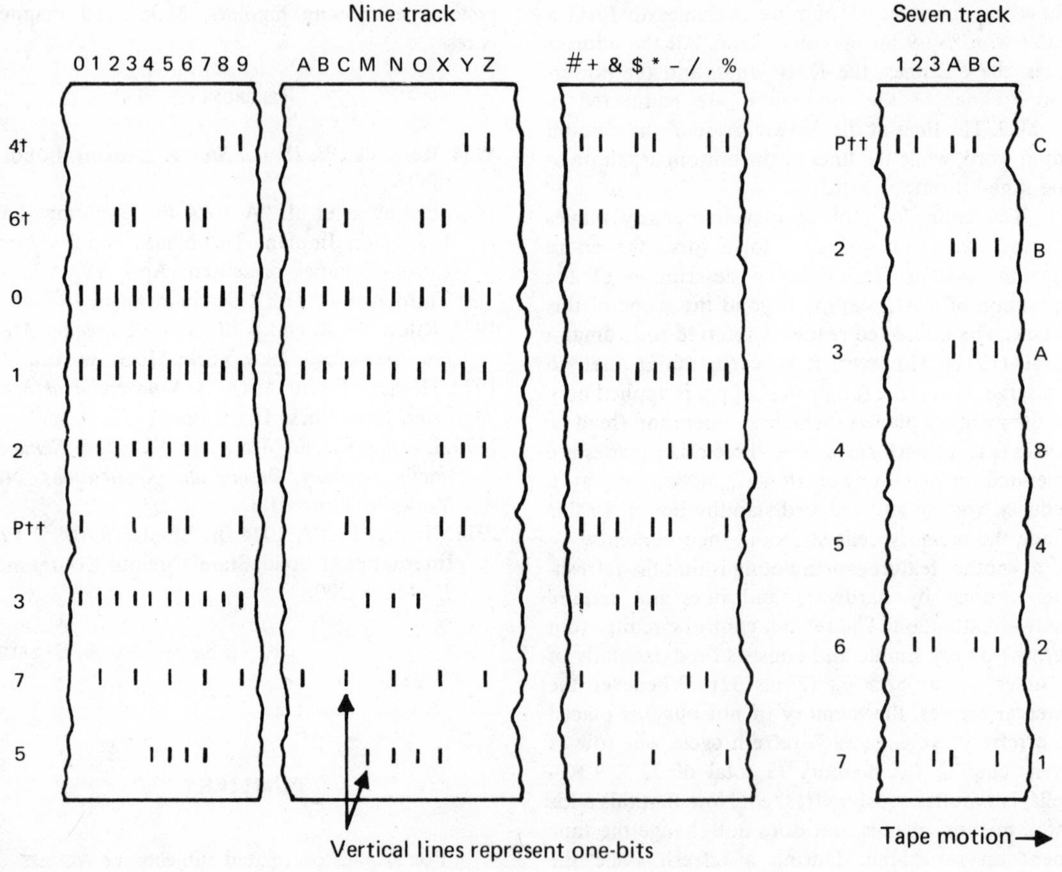


**Fig. 1.** Nine- and seven-track tape data format. *Notes:* † Track numbering shows order in which bits are accumulated into bytes (characters); bit 0 is leftmost character and bit 1 is next, etc. Therefore, the character 0 has the bit representation 11110000 on a nine-track tape. †† The parity bit.

wide) of plastic film coated with iron oxide, wound on hard-plastic reels approximately 1 ft in diameter. Information is stored transversely on tape, usually seven or nine bits per *frame* (character or byte of data recorded on tape; see Fig. 1). Longitudinally, data is stored at one of the following densities: 200, 556, 800, or 1,600 frames per inch. (Advanced tape drives store over 6,200 frames per inch.) Thus, a fully-written reel of tape, recorded at 1,600 frames per inch (also called "bits per inch," bpi), contains over 40 million bytes: (2,400 ft × 12 in./foot × 1,600 bytes/inch) = 46,080,000 bytes.

**Fig. 2.** Magnetic tape units on Honeywell Model 8200 computer.

Data is read from a magnetic-tape AM into MM via a tape drive (also called "tape station," or "tape controller"), depicted in the photo in Fig. 2 and the schematic in Fig. 3. Referring to Fig. 3, the tape is pulled from the supply reel to the takeup reel by motors driving the two hubs. These motors operate independently, so that the length of tape between the two reels varies from instant to instant. This permits the takeup reel to accelerate quickly at the start of each read/write (R/W) operation without requiring synchronized acceleration of the supply reel. The interhub strand of tape droops into two vacuum columns in many widely used tape drives, where it is held lightly taut by air-pressure differences (Fig. 4). As the loop drops below a vacuum-sensing hole in the takeup column, an electric signal engages the takeup motor with the corresponding reel. The motor disengages as soon as the loop is pulled above a second vacuum-sensing hold (Fig. 5). Analogous controls keep a varying-length loop suspended in the supply column.

The foregoing describes *forward* R/W operations; *backward* R/W operations are commonly

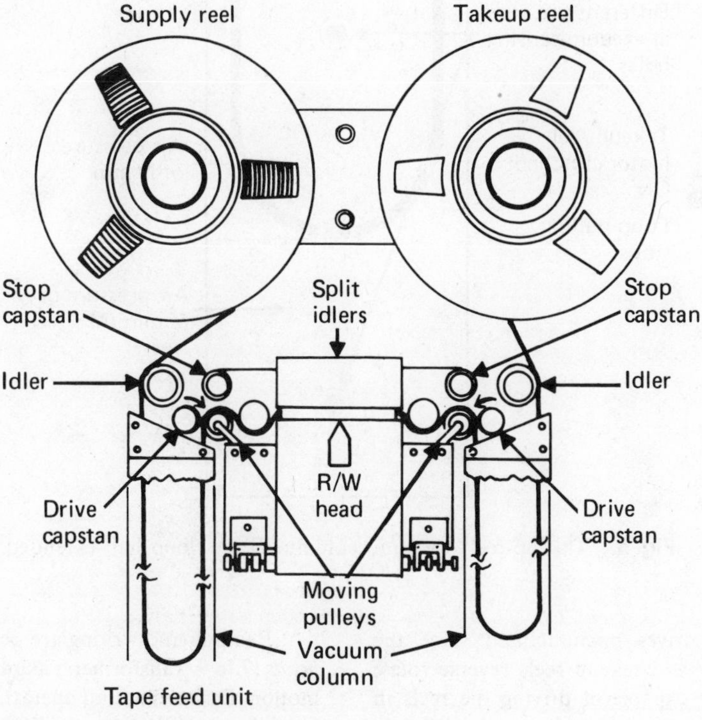


**Fig. 3.** Tape-drive schematic.

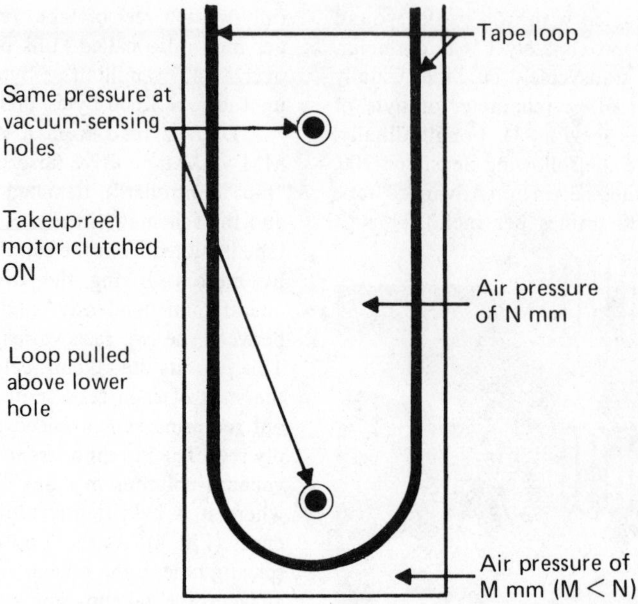


**Fig. 4.** Takeup-reel vacuum column. Tape loop fully extended.

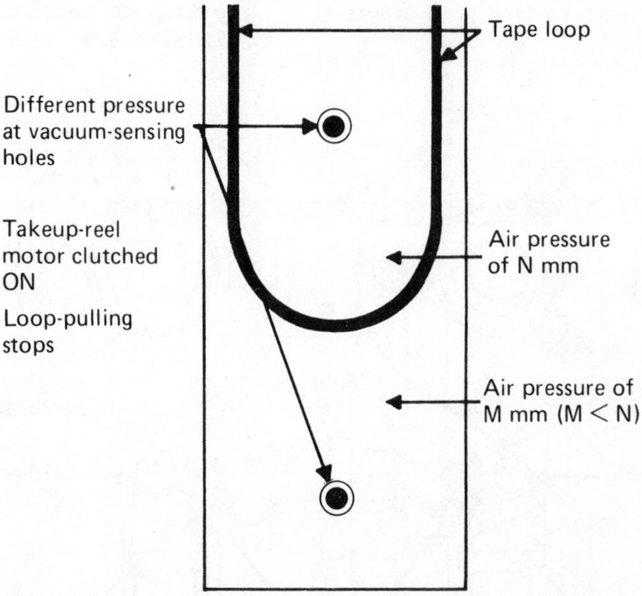


**Fig. 5.** Takeup-reel vacuum column. Tape loop half-extended.

available on tape drives manufactured since the early 1960s. Supply and takeup reels reverse roles; the two motors are capable of driving the reels in either direction.

Reading and writing are performed by a pair of *heads* (7 to 9 transformers) aligned transverse to tape motion. During reading operations (Fig. 6), the *write head* is inactive; the *read head* senses the flux

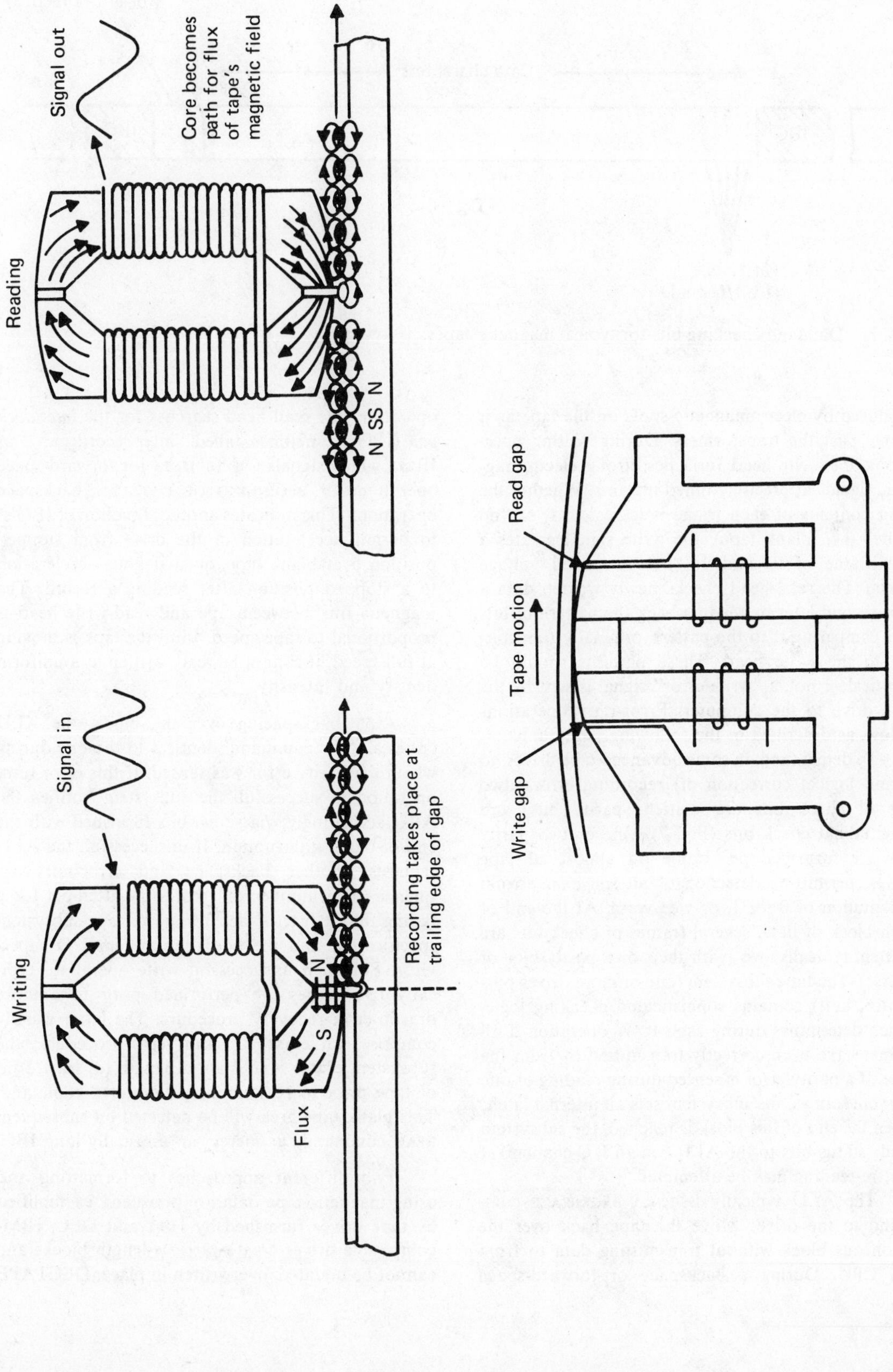


**Fig. 6.** Two-gap read/write head.

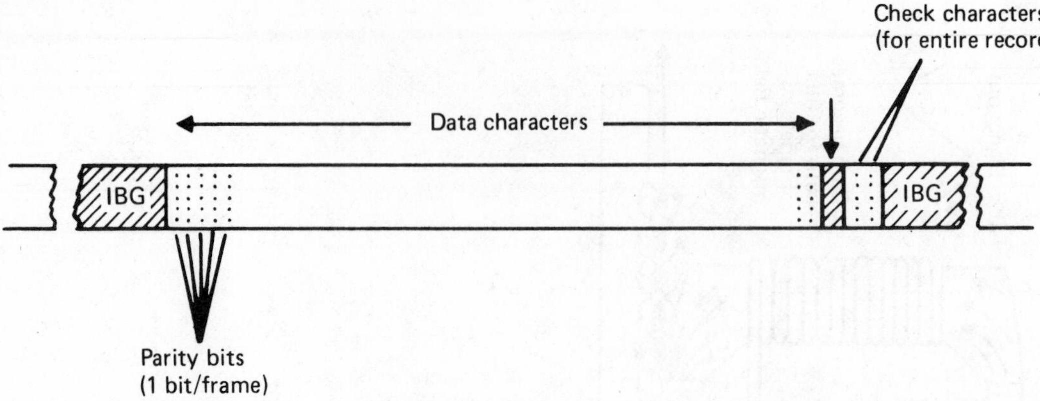


**Fig. 7.** Data and checking bits for typical magnetic tapes.

produced by electromagnetic spots on the tape as it moves past the transformers. During writing operations, the write head furnishes strong electromagnetic signals at precisely timed instants. Whether the prior contents of each frame is logical 0, 1, or "no value" (i.e., blank tape), the write signal creates a new frame of 0s and 1s (predetermined voltage levels). The read head checks newly written data a split second later by reading back the pattern of bits and comparing it to the pattern originally transmitted to the write head. These patterns should be identical; if not, a "write error" signal is sent by the tape drive to the computer. Error-retry operations follow, as described in the following paragraphs.

To detect (and, in some advanced tape drives, to permit logical correction of) recording errors, two sets of check bits are written: parity bits, and longitudinal check bits (Fig. 7). One or two parity bits are furnished per frame on almost all tape drives, permitting detection of all *single-bit* errors: substitution of 0 for 1, or vice versa. At the end of each block of data, several frames of check bits are written, typically two (with their own parity bits, of course). The tape subsystem (one or more drives plus control unit) contains sophisticated checking logic, which determines during each R/W operation if all frames have been correctly transmitted to/from the tape. If a parity error is sensed during reading of one or more frames, the subsystem sets an internal latch; when the end of this block is reached, the subsystem sends status bits to the ALU (via an I/O channel) so that re-reading may be attempted.

The ALU typically issues a BACKSPACE command to the drive: Move the tape back over the erroneous block without transmitting data to/from the CPU. During a backspace or forward-space operation, the read head searches for the *interblock gap* (IBG; sometimes called "inter-record gap," or IRG), which signals END OF DATA for forward-space operations or BEGINNING OF DATA for backspace operations. This indicates another function of IBG's: to permit acceleration of the drive from stopped position over blank tape, or analogous deceleration to a stopped position after reading a record. The magnetic flux between tape and read-write head is proportional to tape speed; until the tape is moving at full speed, it cannot be read/written at a uniform density and intensity.

After backspacing over the block, the ALU issues a R/W command identical to the one during which the parity error was sensed. If this error-retry operation is successful, the subsystem notifies the ALU accordingly, via status bits furnished with the end-of-block interruption. If unsuccessful, the ALU requests another backspace and error-retry sequence. The number of error-retry attempts for a failing block varies according to tape-subsystem specification and the operating system I/O supervisor. For each unsuccessful write operation, typically five retries are performed prior to a more drastic error-recovery procedure. The latter usually comprises an erase gap and retry procedure; the subsystem erases a substantial length (at least 2 in) of tape prior to reattempting the WRITE command. This blank-tape area will be detected on subsequent READ commands as merely an unusually long IBG.

Two different approaches to formatting and using magnetic-tape data are prevalent, exemplified by tape drives furnished by IBM and DEC. IBM-compatible drives create variable-length blocks and cannot be updated/overwritten in place, DECTAPE

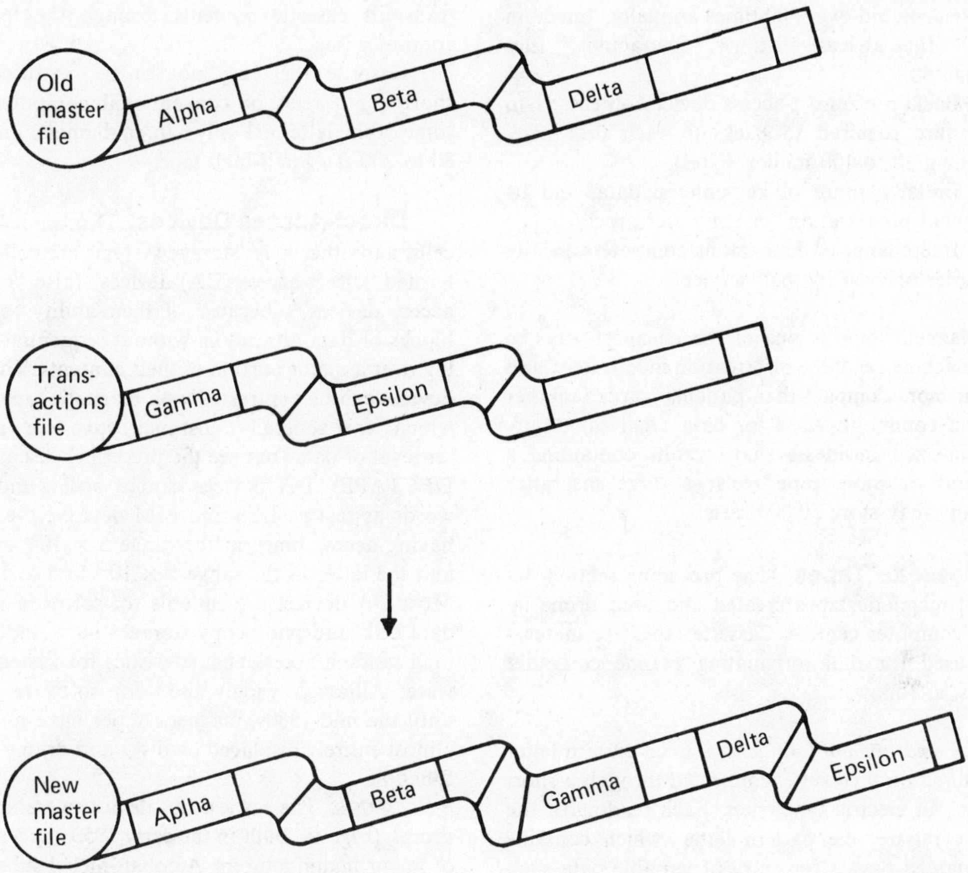


**Fig. 8.** Tape file maintenance.

drives create fixed-length blocks that can be updated/overwritten with new information. To update a tape file using an IBM-compatible subsystem, the old master file must be completely copied onto a new master file, with transaction data merged in as appropriate (Fig. 8). With DECTAPE drives, the master file need only be spaced forward to blocks requiring updating. In this respect, DECTAPE drives can be used like direct-access devices (see next section). However, it is often desirable in commercial data processing and certain scientific applications) to continually create backup copies of tape master files. In such environments, recopying required by IBM-compatible drives is consistent with local data-security practices. The old master file is called the "father," the new master file the "son"; when the next updating is performed, a new generation of this file is created; the "father" file becomes the "grandfather," the "son" becomes the "father," etc. Often, 30 or more generations are kept for vital corporate master files; e.g., daily updatings for a month.

TYPICAL USAGE. Until the early 1960s, magnetic tape was the prevalent AM for scientific and commercial data processing; direct-access devices were used only for executable programs and data (e.g., drums on the IBM 650 and Burroughs 205 computers), or for on-line, real-time applications such as inventory control and satellite monitoring. From 1963 to 1968, many sequentially stored files were transferred from magnetic tape to direct-access devices. *Scratch files* (intermediate storage required by compilers, sort and utility programs, and application programs), allocated to tape drives on second-generation computers, were typically allocated to disk and/or drum devices on third-generation computers.

Nonetheless, magnetic tape drives are found on most third-generation systems (and their successors), where they fulfill the following roles:

1. Retention of low and medium-activity master files. Common terminology is that "high activity"

files are accessed over 300 times annually, "medium activity" files at least 50 times, "low activity" files less than 50.

2. Backup of direct-access-device contents (1 to 3 reels are required to back up each disk pack containing 20 to 100 million bytes).

3. Initial capture of key-entered data, and its subsequent presentation for computer processing.

4. Interchange of data among computers, locally by courier or even by mail service.

Magnetic tape is one of the cheapest ways to store machine-readable information indefinitely, and it is far more compact than punched cards (another medium commonly used for data archives). Many medium-sized businesses have vaults containing a thousand or more tape reels; a large insurance company may store 50,000 reels.

**Cassette Tapes.** The preceding section described magnetic tapes created and used primarily *within* computer centers. Cassette tapes are increasingly used for data originating *outside* computer centers, as follows:

1. *Preparation of form letters.* Each pattern letter is captured on a cassette, connected through a short cable to an electric typewriter. Each reading of the cassette retypes the pattern letter, which contains programmed pauses for entry of variable data such as addressee and salutation.

2. *Acquisition of data from laboratory instruments.* Analog voltages are digitized and written onto a cassette. Paper-tape punches have performed these data acquisition functions for decades; cassette and cartridge-disk devices are beginning to displace paper tape.

3. *Cash register, gasoline credit card, and other retailing applications.* Some cassette-oriented devices are small and light enough to be handheld.

Typically, cassette tapes are ¼-in. wide and store $10^5$ characters, in contrast to full-sized tapes, which are ½-in. wide and store $10^6$ to $10^7$ characters.

Many minicomputers and some full-sized third-generation computers have cassette drives as I/O devices. For minicomputers used in data-acquisition environments, cassette tapes are often the principal AM, used both to load programs into MM and to capture data. On other computers, cassette readers serve primarily for original input of data. Cassette drives are often installed on terminals, serving as a local data-capture AM. After all data is on the cassette, the user dials up a computer and transmits cassette contents through the terminal-computer link.

Cassette reels are not to be confused with short-length reels of conventional computer tape; some of the latter are only 5 in. in diameter and wind 50 to 200 ft of half-inch tape.

**Direct-Access Devices.** Drums, disks, data cells, and other mass storage systems are collectively termed "direct-access (DA) devices" (also "random-access devices"), because of their ability to access blocks of data at random without sequentially passing over a major portion of their contents. Thus, DA devices can be contrasted with magnetic tape drives, which are generally cost-ineffective for random retrieval of data (but see the preceding discussion of DECTAPE). DA devices cannot access individual words as fast as LCS and MM devices, the former having access times in the range $5 \times 10^{-3}$ to 5 sec, and the latter in the range $5 \times 10^{-8}$ to 5 to $10^{-6}$ sec. Most DA devices are suitable for software storage; data cells and photocopy storages have undesirably long random-access characteristics for systems software. Although widely used for software storage until the mid-1960s, magnetic tapes have now been almost entirely displaced by disks and drums for this function.

DRUMS. The earliest DA devices were magnetic drums (Fig. 9), built in the early 1950s by a number of major manufacturers. A cobalt-nickel substrate is coated with iron oxide, which is magnetized and sensed much as in magnetic-tape operations. Drums are typically 8 to 20 in. in diameter, 2 to 4 ft in length, and revolve at 1,500 to 4,000 rpm. Each character is stored on one or more tracks circumferentially, blocks of characters being separated by IRG's of several thousandths of an inch. (IRG's mark the beginning and end of each record, to be sensed by the read/write heads.) Bit densities of 4,000 per inch are commonplace, yielding R/W rates of 1 to 3 million characters per second.

As with magnetic tape, two types of formatting are possible: fixed-length blocks (often called "sectors") and variable-length blocks. With either format—and in contrast to tape—it is possible to update blocks in place, i.e., without copying their contents to another part of the device. This facility is vital to the updating activities commonly performed during random retrievals from master files. In fact, all AM's, except certain magnetic tapes and the photocopy/laser-holography devices, permit updating in place.

Drums hold considerably less data than do disks, data cells, magnetic tapes, etc. (Although

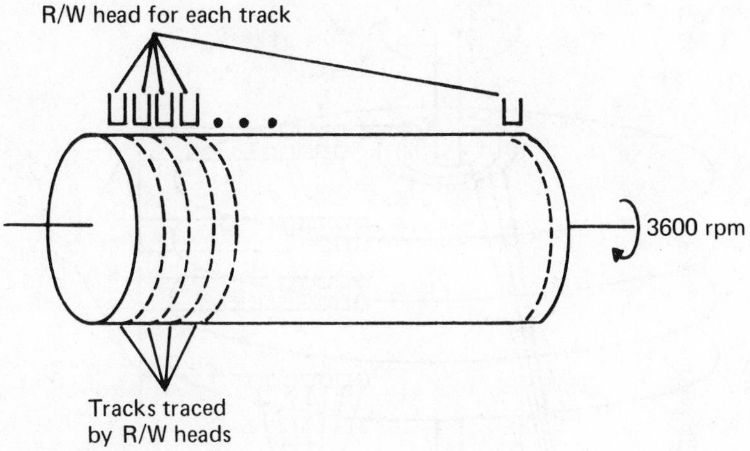


**Fig. 9.** Magnetic drum.

Sperry-Rand UNIVAC built hundred-megabyte drums in the 1950s and early 1960s, these are now disappearing in favor of large-capacity disk drives.) However, they can access blocks of data at random more quickly than most other DA devices, 5 to 8 ms on the average. (Since a drum is a narrow cylinder, its typical rotational speed of 3,600 rpm is considerably higher than that of disk drives, typically 2,400 rpm. A speed of 3,600 rpm means an average rotational time of 16.7 ms. This is compared to 12 to 100 ms for disk drives, the next fastest devices during the 1955–1970 time frame. Therefore, drums have typically been used for the following functions:

1. Prior to the development of magnetic-core memories in the mid-1950s, drums were used as MM's (e.g., on the IBM 650 and Burroughs 205 computers).

2. Thereafter, frequently needed software (inter-job monitors, portions of the I/O-error and program-error supervisors, compilers and sort programs, etc.) has been stored permanently on drums. Since drum storage is nonvolatile because electric power can be turned off and on without disturbing contents, it is well suited for permanent storage of continually used software.

3. High-activity scratch files for the operating system, compilers, and other software are often allocated to drums.

4. Backing storage for virtual-memory (VM) machines has been a major role for drums since the Ferranti Atlas systems of the late 1950s. Thousand-word blocks of MM contents are shuttled to/from drums by the VM control program.

5. In many airborne computers (and similar high-stress environments), drums are used for MM's or AM's because of their high reliability, insensitivity to sudden force changes, and relatively light weight and small bulk.

DISKS. Two major varieties of disk drives are widely used:

1. *Fixed-Head, Multiple-Platter* (Fig. 10). Although their geometry is considerably different from that of drums, fixed-head (FH) disks (Fig. 11) have comparable access times and transfer rates. They have approximately the same capacity as commonly used drums: disks in the range $3 \times 10^6$ to $10 \times 10^6$ bytes, and drums approximately $4 \times 10^6$ bytes.

Over the past 20 years, computer manufacturers have vacillated between stressing drums or fixed-head disks in their newer configurations. Functional repertoires are essentially identical, as are their reliability and cost per character. It seems safe to predict several years' persistence of both in computer configurations, even though they are functionally equivalent.

Each FH drive contains from five to ten steel platters coated with iron oxide, aligned vertically on a common spindle. R/W heads extend between the platters, facing up and down from the *comb* suspending the heads and containing signal cables. Since there is a head for each track, the only delays in accessing a random data block are due to *rotational latency* (i.e., 0 to 15 ms required for the block to revolve beneath the corresponding R/W head). (Although track *lengths* vary linearly with distance from the spindle, R/W heads are calibrated in such a way

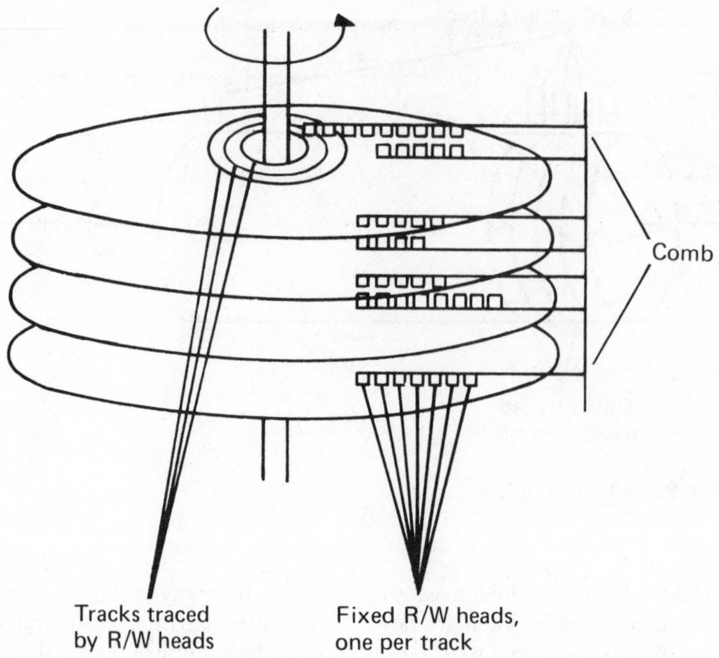


**Fig. 10.** Fixed-head disk drive.

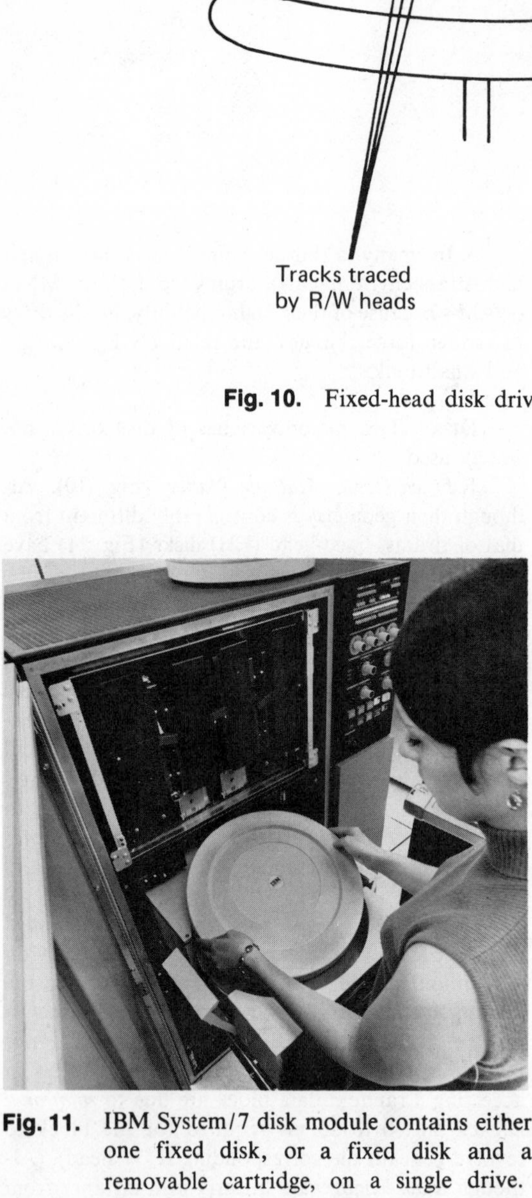

**Fig. 11.** IBM System/7 disk module contains either one fixed disk, or a fixed disk and a removable cartridge, on a single drive. Capacity: up to 2.46 million 16-bit words.

that track capacities are all identical. Therefore, there is a universal transfer rate for data, whether read from inner or outer tracks.) The average delay for reading a random block is half the maximum rotational latency, although recent hardward/software developments in rotational positions sensing (RPS) considerably reduce inefficiencies caused by I/O, as follows:

The I/O supervisor keeps the queue of disk requests (i.e., R/W operations pending for one or more programs) ordered by angular displacement from *index point*, a universal logical origin for the tracks. Index points for all platters are vertically aligned (Fig. 12). As each R/W operation terminates, the I/O supervisor searches its queue for the nearest request in terms of angular position. This request may reference any track in the FH file, not necessarily that from which the preceding block was read. If $N$ requests are enqueued with uniformly distributed angular displacements—a reasonable assumption for most computer environments—the average *interoperation latency* is only $(1/N + 1) \times$ (max latency).

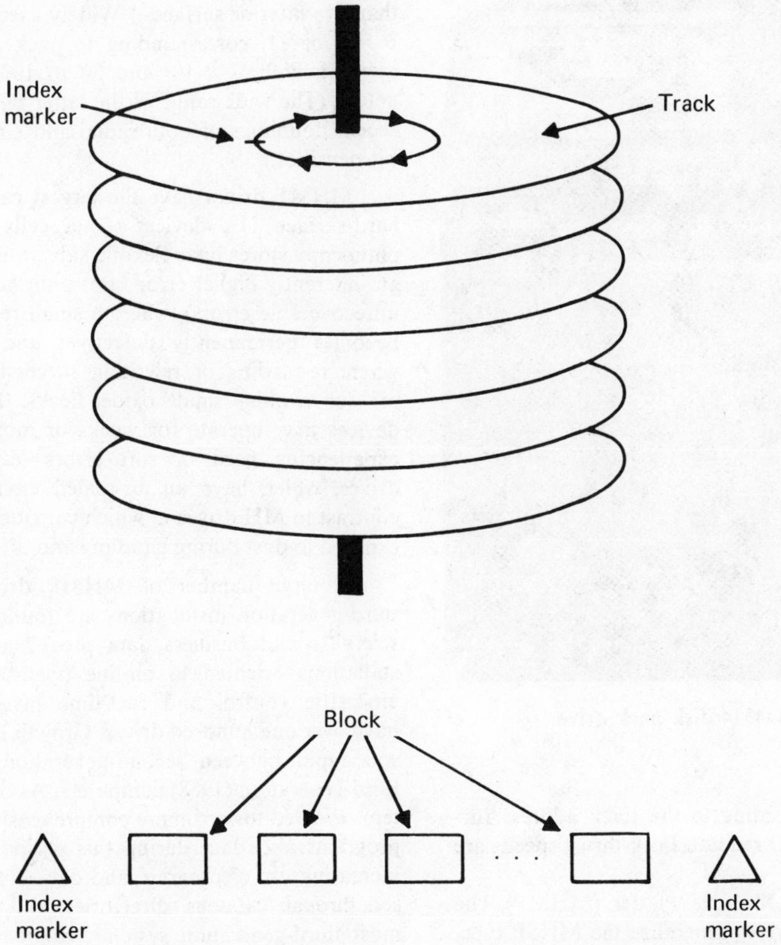


**Fig. 12.** Track format for disk storage.

*Moving Head.* Since only two heads and associated electronics are required per platter, moving-head (MH) drives are considerably cheaper to build than FH drives, although the former require sophisticated servomechanisms to move their read-write heads over the platters. Per-character cost for MH storage is typically 15 to 25% of the cost for FH storage. Furthermore, MH drives generally permit removal of their disk-and-spindle socket assemblies: *disk cartridge* in the case of a single platter, *disk pack* (Fig. 13) in the case of multiple platters. An installation can store an indefinite number of cartridges/packs off line, mounted as required by various application programs.

Most batch-processing installations with MH drives designate one subset as *resident* (also called "permanently mounted," although this is a logical designation rather than a physical attribute), containing the operating system, scratch storage, and frequently referenced data files. Another subset of drives is designated "mountable," where cartridges/packs are set up as required.

Most on-line installations (i.e., devoted to real-time and telecommunications applications) keep cartridges/packs resident, since data requests originate unpredictably and generally require response within a few seconds (or milliseconds), too short for a computer operator to retrieve and mount a shelf-stored cartridge/pack.

Moving head drives may be either single platter of multiple platter:

Moving Head Single Platter (MHSP). This type is shown in Fig. 14. Typically the *fork* (two-tined comb) contains two R/W heads; it is inserted/with-

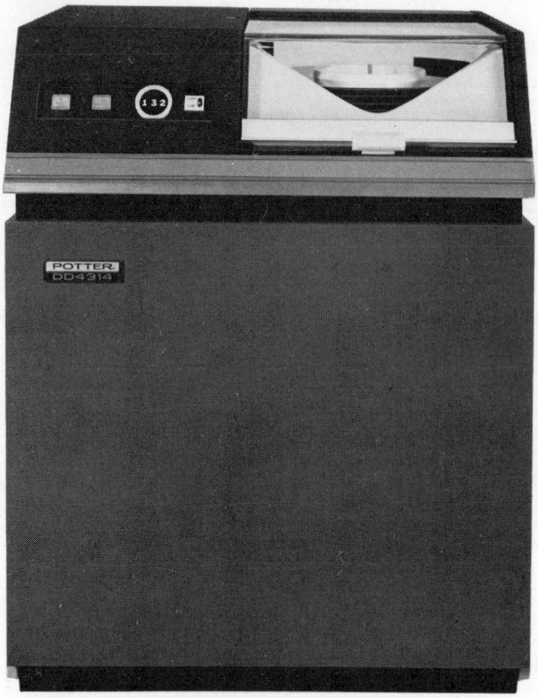


**Fig. 13.** Potter DD4314 disk pack drive.

drawn radially according to the track address furnished with each I/O request. Fork-thrust speeds are given in Table 1.

Moving Head Multiple Platter (MHMP). The MHMP (Fig. 15) drives generalize the MHSP type, with combs containing 2P-2 heads, $P$ being the number of platters. (The top surface of the top platter and bottom surface of the bottom platter are not used on MHMP packs, since they are much more exposed to scratches and dust contamination than are interior surfaces.) Widely used drives have $P = 6$ or 11, corresponding to pack capacities of approximately $7 \times 10^6$ and 30 to $100 \times 10^6$ characters. (The wide range of the latter figure is due to recent doublings of both radial and circumferential bit densities.)

MHMP drives have the largest capacity of all hard-surface DA devices. Data cells, tapes, and photocopy stores have flexible substrates, and hence an inherently higher error rate: both *hard errors* (or unrecoverable errors), where a small recording area becomes permanently defective; and *soft errors*, where re-reading or rewriting successfully brushes off (or avoids) small oxide flecks. Hard-surface devices may operate for weeks or months without experiencing hard or soft errors—especially FH drives, which have an air-sealed environment, in contrast to MH drives in which cartridges/packs are exposed to dust during handling and off-line storage.

A large number of MHMP drives in most third-generation installations are found performing scientific and business data processing. Large installations oriented to on-line operations such as air-traffic control and real-time inventory, often have over one hundred drives. Growth in their usage was rapid between second-generation (1962) and third-generation (1968) computers. As operating systems evolved toward more comprehensive control of programs and data during this period, they made increasing use of program and data libraries, accessed through catalogs, directories, and indices. For most third-generation systems, catalogs and directories were stored exclusively on DA devices, generally disks and drums; increasingly, libraries themselves are being stored on disk drives to take advantage of their superior transfer rates, random access, and reliability versus soft-surface AM's.

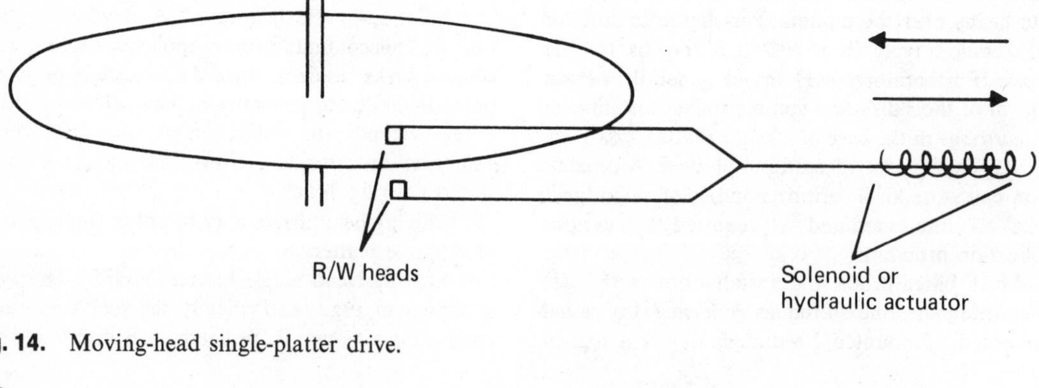


**Fig. 14.** Moving-head single-platter drive.

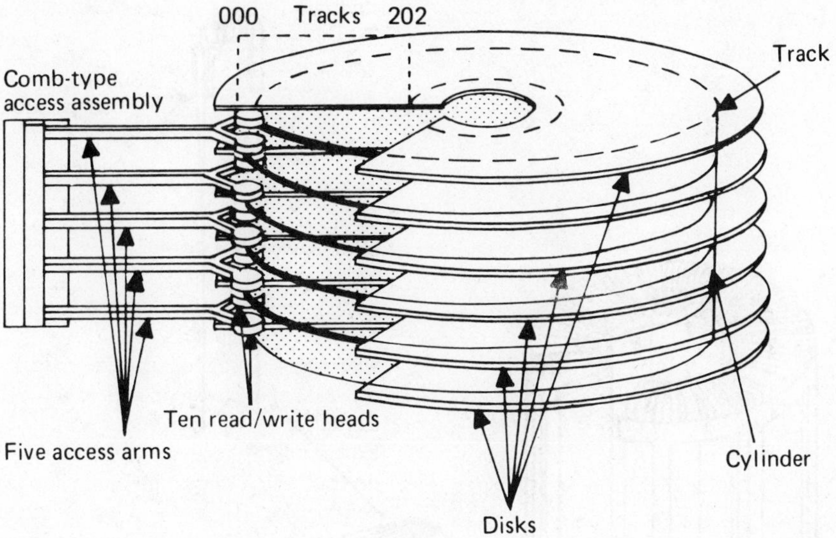


**Fig. 15.** Moving-head multiple-platter drive.

Soft-Surface DA Devices. Data cells, CRAM files (Card Random Access Memory, trademark of NCR Corporation), and similar devices are rapidly being displaced by MH disk drives, except for a few enormous data-base applications, typically requiring $10^{11}$ to $10^{12}$ bits of on-line DA storage, which are experimenting with photocopy and laser-holography storages. Soft-surface DA devices have the following design elements in common:

1. Iron-oxide coats a plastic substrate: magnetic-tape strips (considerably wider than reel-wound tape) for data cells (Fig. 16), and coated flexible cards for CRAM files.
2. A complex electromechanical "picker" selects one strip/card out of a magazine, extracts it with tweezerlike fingers, and wraps it around a R/W drum. Typically, vacuum holes on the drum hold the strip/card in place (Fig. 17).
3. R/W heads move parallel to the drum spindle, thus passing over the recording area to the requested track.
4. When one strip/card is no longer required for a sequence of R/W operations, it is automatically peeled off the drum and returned to the magazine. This is necessary prior to retrieval of another strip/card onto this drum.
5. Random access requiring retrieval of a new strip/card takes 0.5 to 2 sec.

Data cells, CRAM files, etc., have been used for large on-line data bases in which individual master records are relatively infrequently accessed, typically no more than once weekly. These devices have no functional advantages over MH disk drives, and their aggregate reliability is considerably poorer. In particular, if the picker or R/W drum malfunctions, the entire data base becomes inaccessible (unless individual magazines are moved to a standby device). In the mid-1960s, data cells and CRAM files had a considerable per-character cost advantage over MH disk drives; this has been significantly diminished by recent advances in disk-recording densities. Furthermore, random-access times and transfer rates for soft-surface DA devices are approximately 10 to 15 times slower than for hard-surface DA devices.

Photocopy and Laser-Holography Storages. A few manufacturers offer nonmagnetic DA devices with enormous capacities. Precision Instrument's UNICON device uses a laser beam to burn microscopic spots in a holographic substrate. This is therefore a *write-once medium*: Data can be re-read indefinitely by sensing a lower-energy laser beam through previously "burned" holes, but the latter cannot be overwritten by the laser. IBM's photocopy storage records bits of data on high-resolution film; after developing, this information can be read by shining a sharply focused light beam through the

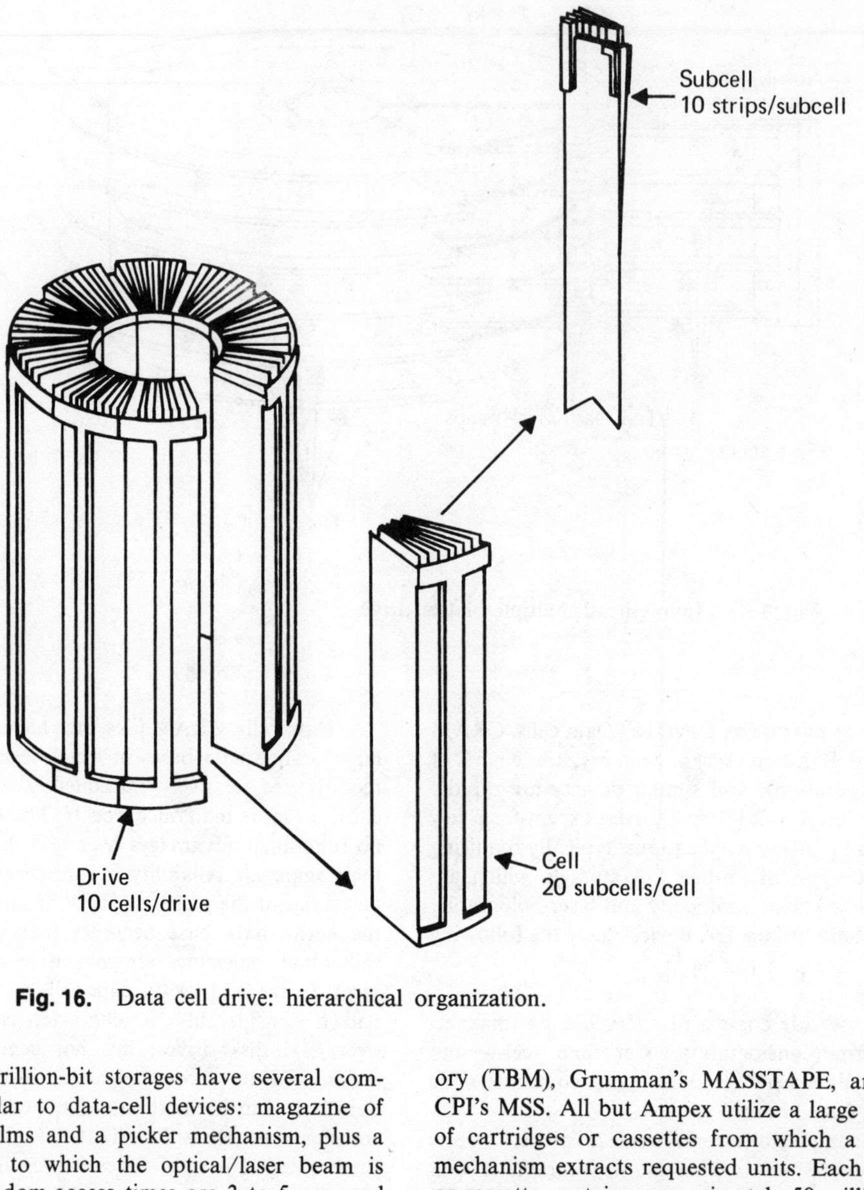


**Fig. 16.** Data cell drive: hierarchical organization.

film. These trillion-bit storages have several components similar to data-cell devices: magazine of holographs/films and a picker mechanism, plus a reading area to which the optical/laser beam is directed. Random-access times are 3 to 5 sec, and transfer rates are comparable to disk drives.

**Other Mass Storage Systems (MSS).** During the early 1970s, several manufacturers developed trillion-bit storage devices based on reels, cartridges, or cassettes of videotape. In late 1974, marketing of these MSS devices to commercial users commenced with the IBM 3850 Mass Storage System, whose online capacity is 50–500 billion bytes ($0.4 - 4 \times 10^{12}$ bits). Other manufacturers and corresponding products include Ampex's Terabit Memory (TBM), Grumman's MASSTAPE, and CDC-CPI's MSS. All but Ampex utilize a large magazine of cartridges or cassettes from which a transport mechanism extracts requested units. Each cartridge or cassette contains approximately 50 million bytes, comparable to a fully-packed reel of conventional digitally recorded magnetic tape. A full MSS of this type contains 500–5000 cartridges or cassettes, together with transports and read/write stations. Often the transports and R/W stations are duplexed or triplexed to assure continuity of operation should one of these complex electromechanical devices malfunction.

The Ampex TBM utilizes reels of two-inch video tape rather than cassettes or cartridges. Each reel can hold 11 billion bytes ($9 \times 10^{10}$ bits). A full TMB system contains 31 tape read/write stations.

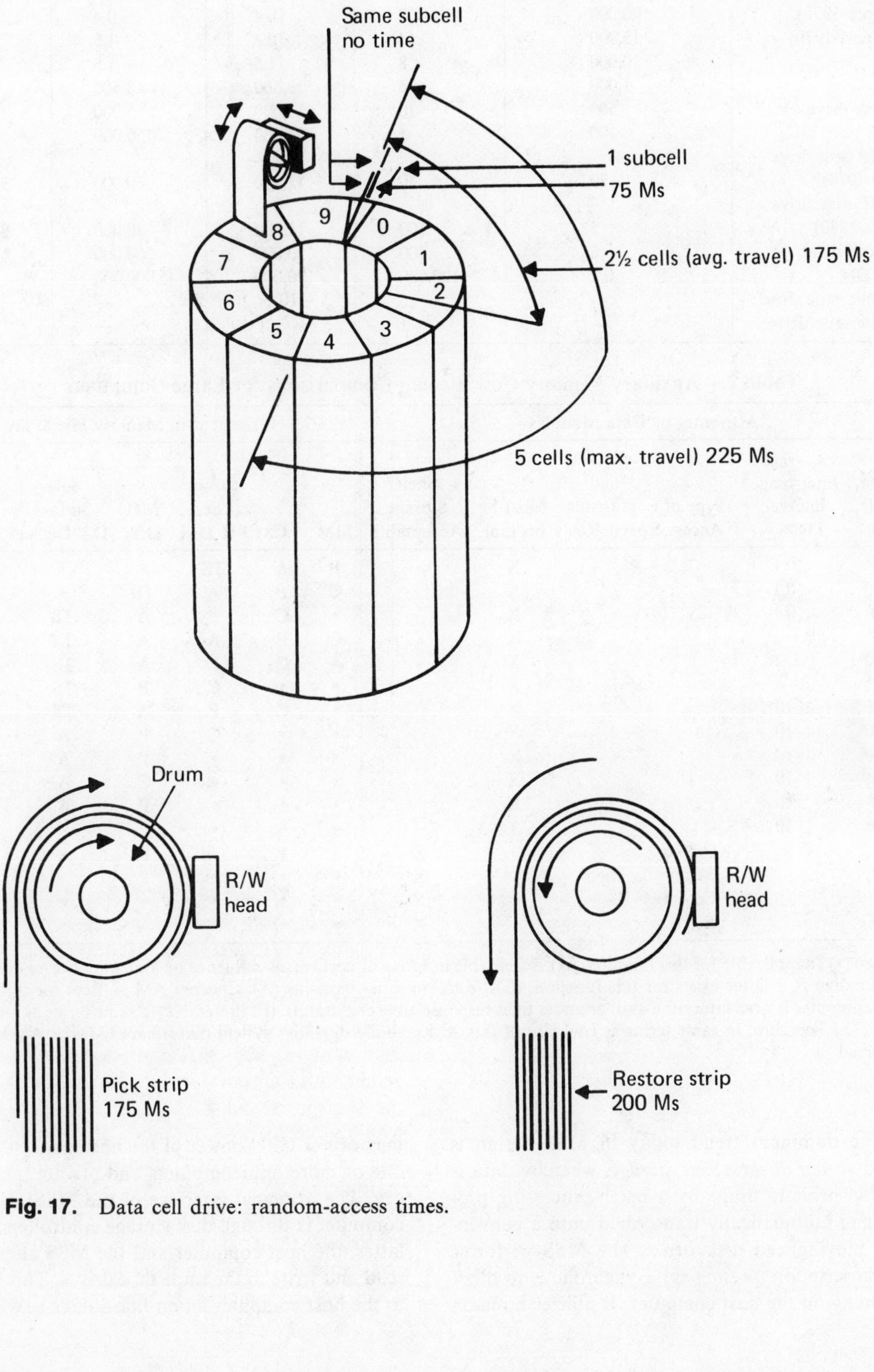


**Fig. 17.** Data cell drive: random-access times.

**Table 1.** Capacity, Speed, and Cost of Memories

| Memory | Typical Rental Cost, \$, per $10^6$ char/month | On-line Capacity ($\times 10^6$ char.) | Sequential Access Time, $\mu s$ | Random-Access Time, $\mu s$ | Transfer Rate, char./sec |
|---|---|---|---|---|---|
| MM (pre-1970) | 40,000 | <2 | 0.4 | 0.4 | $10^7$ |
| MM (post-1970) | 15,000 | <4 | 0.3 | 1.5 | $10^7$ |
| LCS | 10,000 | <8 | 1.5 | 1.5 | $10^6$ |
| Drum | 1,000 | 4 | 8,500 | 8,500 | $10^6$ |
| FH disk drive | 500 | 10 | 5,000 | 5,000 | $10^6$ |
| MHSP | 300 | 1 | 25,000 | 150,000 | $10^5$ |
| MHMP disk drive (pre-1970) | 20 | 30 | 12,500 | 60,000 | $3 \times 10^5$ |
| MHMP disk drive (post-1970) | 5 | 100 | 12,500 | 30,000 | $8 \times 10^5$ |
| Data cell drive | 6 | 400 | 30,000 | 500,000 | $6 \times 10^4$ |
| UNICON | 0.2 | 100,000 | 20,000 | 5,000,000 | $10^6$ |
| Magnetic tape drive | --- | 25 | $3-10 \times 10^3$ | --- | $60-300 \times 10^3$ |
| Cassette tape drive | --- | 1 | $3-10 \times 10^3$ | --- | $10^3$ |

**Table 2.** Auxiliary Memory Cost/Benefit Comparisons for Large Computers

| Attributes of Data Modules | | | | | | Placement in Memory Hierarchy | | | | | |
|---|---|---|---|---|---|---|---|---|---|---|---|
| Size of Module, chars. | Average Inter-usage Interval, secs. | Type of Access | Reliability and Transfer Speed Req's. | Must be on Line | Shelf Storage Acceptable | MM | LCS | Drum or FH Disk | MH Disk | Soft-Surface DA Device | Magnetic Tape |
| $<10^4$ | <0.1 | | | X | | P | A | TS | * | * | * |
| $10^4$–$10^5$ | <0.1 | | | X | | C | P | A | TS | * | * |
| $>10^5$ | <0.1 | | | X | | * | C | P | A | TS | * |
| $<10^4$ | 0.1–1 | | | X | | C | P | A | A | TS | * |
| $10^4$–$10^6$ | 0.1–1 | | | X | | * | C | P | A | TS | * |
| $>10^6$ | 0.1–1 | | | X | | * | * | C | P | TS | * |
| $<10^5$ | 1–10 | | | X | | * | C | P | A | TS | * |
| $10^5$–$10^6$ | 1–10 | | | X | | * | * | C | P | A | * |
| $10^6$–$10^8$ | 1–10 | | | X | | * | * | * | P | A | * |
| $>10^8$ | 1–10 | | | X | | * | * | * | C | A | * |
| $<10^8$ | >10 | | | X | | * | * | * | P | A | * |
| $>10^8$ | >10 | | | X | | * | * | * | C | P | * |
| | | Random | | | X | * | * | * | P | * | * |
| $<10^7$ | | Seq. | High | | X | * | * | * | P | * | A |
| $<10^7$ | | Seq. | Low | | X | * | * | * | * | * | P |
| $>10^7$ | | Seq. | | | X | * | * | * | A | * | P |

*Notes:* (*) Inapplicable for this function. (A) Acceptable in terms of cost versus influence on system performance; inferior to alternative *P* if latter exists for this function. (C) *Costly*, in same terms as (A). Cheaper AM suffices for this function unless computer is near saturation and/or under tight response-time constraints. (P) Preferable, in same terms as (A) to other AM's. (TS) Too slow, in same terms as (A). Use of this AM severely degrades system performance; faster AM should be considered.

The dominant trend today in MSS design is toward *virtual direct access storage*, whereby data is retrieved prior to usage by a batch-processing program and automatically transcribed onto a conventional movinghead disk drive. The MSS performs this transcription (*prestaging*) asynchronous to other computing on the host computer. It utilizes no main memory or CPU power of the host, since it contains one or more minicomputers and private main memory. The principal interface of the MSS to the host computer is through disk storage controllers. Via the latter, the host computer and the MSS alternatively read and write to the same disk drives. This provides to the host computer an on-line data base whose unit

**Table 3.** Auxiliary Memory Cost Benefit Comparisons for Small Computers

| Attributes of Data Modules | | | | | | Placement in Memory Hierarchy | | | | | |
|---|---|---|---|---|---|---|---|---|---|---|---|
| Size of Module, chars. | Average Inter-usage Frequency, secs. | Type of Access | Reliability and Transfer Speed Req's. | Must Be on Line | Shelf Storage Acceptable | MM | Drum or FH Disk | MHSP Disk | MHMP Disk | Magnetic Tape | Cassette Tape |
| $<10^4$ | $<0.1$ | | | X | | P | A | TS | * | * | * |
| $>10^4$ | $<0.1$ | | | X | | C | P | TS | * | * | * |
| $<10^4$ | 0.1–1 | | | X | | C | A | P | A | * | * |
| $10^4$–$10^6$ | 0.1–1 | | | X | | * | P | A | A | * | * |
| $>10^6$ | 0.1–1 | | | X | | * | C | C | A | * | * |
| $<10^6$ | $>1$ | | | X | | * | C | P | A | * | A |
| $>10^6$ | $>1$ | | | X | | * | * | C | P | A | * |
| $<10^6$ | | Random | | | X | * | * | P | A | * | A |
| $>10^6$ | | Random | | | X | * | * | * | P | A | * |
| $<10^6$ | | Seq. | High | | X | * | * | P | * | A | A |
| $<10^6$ | | Seq. | Low | | X | * | * | A | * | A | P |
| $>10^6$ | | Seq. | High | | X | * | * | * | P | A | * |
| $>10^6$ | | Seq. | Low | | X | * | * | * | A | P | * |

*Notes:* (*) Inapplicable for this function. (A) Acceptable in terms of cost versus influence on system performance; inferior to alternative *P* if latter exists for this function. (C) *Costly*, in same terms as (A). Cheaper AM suffices for this function unless computer is near saturation and/or under tight response-time constraints. (P) Preferable, in same terms as (A) to other AM's. (TS) Too slow, in same terms as (A). Use of this AM severely degrades system performance; faster AM should be considered.

storage cost is comparable to conventional magnetic tape with accessibility—after transcription to disk—approximately the same as for a 100-megabyte disk drive (8.4 milliseconds average sequential access time, transfer rate exceeding 800KB).

Average random access time to MSS units is 10-20 seconds. However, this time is essentially invisible to the host computer, since MSS devices are not generally used for servicing on-line transactions submitted to the host.

**Large-Core Storage.** Large-core storage (LCS), also called "extended-core storage/memory (ECS/ECM)," has been offered by large-system manufacturers since the mid-1960s on a small variety of computers, primarily for the following functions:

1. Temporary storage of large matrices whose individual elements have low activity.
2. Resident, low-activity elements of the operating system, such as trace tables, OPEN/CLOSE logic, etc.
3. Interchange medium between two ALU's, each of which has a private MM as well.
4. Swapping/paging target for VM programs (or conventional overlay or message-processing programs) in a time-critical environment (e.g., spacecraft missions) in which drums or fixed-head disks have inadequate random-access speeds.

LCS is fabricated and attached to the ALU and other machine components much like the MM magnetic-core. It typically operates 5 to 10 times slower than MM. It is used for software components that have an inherently large size, random reference patterns, high reference frequency (vis-a-vis other software), and low ALU content (i.e., relatively few instruction/operand references per usage of this software component). It is, for example, inefficient to execute out of LCS an instruction loop with 1000 iterations. It is better to move the loop to MM and execute it there, due to the ALU speed degradation of at least 3:1 cited above. For some LCS memories (e.g., Control Data ECS for the 6600 computer), direct executions are not permitted; a special MOVE instruction transmits large blocks of data between ECS and MM. For other LCS memories (e.g., IBM System/360), the ALU and I/O channels can operate directly into LCS.

LCS memories are less important to the current generation of computers than during the 1960s, when large MM's were difficult and costly to build. LCS memories are invariably "two wire" or "three wire" (number of wires passing through each ferrite core), whereas high-speed (0.6 to 1 $\mu$s) MM's usually require four wires per core. Although these MM's were rather cost-ineffective in terms of 1960 technology, their speed was essential to computer performance, since the rate of instruction/operand references by a typical ALU was already so high.

In the 1970s, new memory-hierarchy and non-core technologies have overcome the MM price/performance problems of the 1960s. MM's of over two million characters are increasingly common, at prices comparable to LCS. This has tended to reduce considerably the cost-attractiveness of LCS memories, although they are still widely used on *purchased* third-generation computers.

Tables 1, 2, and 3 provide comparative data for the various memory types, and also gives cost/benefit comparisons of large and small computer applications.

D. N. Freeman

**MEMORY ADDRESSING.** *See* Addressing.

**MEMORY ALLOCATION.** *See* Storage Allocation.

**MEMORY ORGANIZATION.** *See* Storage Organization.

## MEMORY PROTECTION

For articles on related subjects *see* Addressing; and Base Register.

For articles on related terms *see* IBM 360-370 Series; Multiprogramming; and Operating Systems.

Memory protection, as used in this article, is a hardware mechanism that limits or prevents access to specified areas in the central memory of a computer.

Memory protection first became important when systems became capable of permitting or requiring more than one program to be resident in memory at the same time. The possibility then existed that, while one of the programs was running, it might inadvertently (e.g., because of a bug) write in the area occupied by the other program and thus invalidate that program.

In uniprogramming operating systems—and most first-generation systems were uniprogramming systems—there were typically two programs resident in memory, an executive program and a user program. The earliest memory protection mechanism provided a switch register that could be set to a memory address which marked the upper limit of a protected area. The lower limit was zero. No program running outside the protected area could write into any location inside the protected area. The executive routine, presumably debugged, would reside *in* the protected area. The user program would run on the outside, and if it did anything improper it could hurt only itself. The execution of a user program instruction that would result in a write into the protected area would abort the user program, and then, either automatically or through operator intervention, control would be returned to the executive, which could proceed to the next user program.

With the development of multiprogramming systems, more elaborate memory protection mechanisms were needed. In such systems, supervisory programs and a number of user programs may reside in memory simultaneously. While a user program is running, it is important to be able to designate the areas that belong to that program and to limit its access to other areas. The supervisory programs must be able to designate and change the areas under protection, and the user programs must be denied this capability. Although some systems limited themselves to *write protection* (i.e., a program could *read* from any area in memory, but could not *write* outside its own area), it was recognized quite early that a more general access protection was desirable.

The first effective memory protection mechanism for a multiprogramming system used a base register (also called a "relocation register") and a limit register. A program must reside in a contiguous area of memory; when that program is to run, the executive places the program's origin (i.e., its lowest address) in the base register and its length in the limit register. Any attempt by a program to access a memory location outside its own area causes control to go to the executive routine.

It is, however, often desirable for a program and its associated data to reside in disjoint areas of memory. In such cases, it is nevertheless necessary to protect the program and data as a unit. In the IBM

360/370 series, for example, each block of 2,048 consecutive bytes has an associated protection code register that holds a four-bit protection key set by an executive routine operating in "supervisor" state. A running program runs under its protection key, and an interrupt results from any attempt to access a block whose protection key is different from that of the running program. Protection code 0000 is reserved for executive routines and has special significance in that a program with protection code 0000 has access to all memory.

Memory protection is an important feature of multiprogramming systems, but it does create problems in systems in which routines and data are to be shared among programs simultaneously present in memory. Some virtual memory systems have been designed to permit and encourage such sharing. The problems of protection in such systems can be very complicated and are beyond the scope of this article.

Memory protection can be important within a single program. One of the most usual of program bugs occurs when a program calculates a subscript that causes a value to be stored outside the array that is being referenced. Automatic checking of array boundaries (as provided, for example, on many Burroughs' computers) can be an extremely useful memory protection feature.

S. ROSEN

## MERCURY DELAY-LINE MEMORY.

*See* ULTRASONIC MEMORY.

## META CHARACTER

For articles on related subjects *see* LANGUAGE TRANSLATION; and MACRO LANGUAGES.

For article on related term *see* DELIMITER.

Meta characters in computer programming language systems are characters that have some controlling role with respect to other characters with which they may be associated. The terminology comes from the Greek stem *meta* (meaning "after," "along with," "beyond," or "behind"). In an interactive macro language, an input string from the interactive typewriter is terminated by a meta character. The meta character is a signal to the connected processor that the preceding input string is complete and is ready to be acted upon. In this case, the meta character is discarded, and is not considered to be a part of the input string.

In a similar view, the delimiter characters such as + and = might also be considered meta characters of arithmetic expressions. This is because of their lexically controlling role with reference to the alphanumerical characters with which their operands are constructed.

C. N. MOOERS

## META LANGUAGE

For articles on related subjects *see* BACKUS-NAUR FORM; PROGRAMMING LANGUAGES; and PROGRAMMING LINGUISTICS.

A meta language is a set of symbols and words used to describe another language (in which these symbols do not appear). The most common application is in the definition of programming languages. The first and best known example was the definition of Algol-60, and a small section of this follows as an example.

The meta language used in this case consists of the symbols <, >, |, : : =, together with a number of meta-linguistic variables that are used to define the elements of Algol. The brackets < > are used as delimiters for the meta-linguistic variables, the vertical stroke | has the meaning "or," and the symbol : : = means "is defined as." The following extract from the report on Algol-60 gives the definition of an integer and illustrates the use of the symbols:

```
⟨digit⟩ : : = 0 | 1 | 2 | 3 | 4 | 5 | 6 | 7 | 8 | 9
⟨unsigned integer⟩ : : = ⟨digit⟩
                 | ⟨unsigned integer⟩ ⟨digit⟩
⟨integer⟩ : : = ⟨unsigned integer⟩
                 | + ⟨unsigned integer⟩
                 | −⟨unsigned integer⟩
```

The complete definition of Algol in this form, together with some semantic interpretation, takes about 26 pages.

It will be observed that in order to define the symbols of the meta language, we had to make use of another language, namely, English. This causes no confusion in the present case, but might do so if we were to try to define English itself by a meta language.

In the example above we made use of three meta-linguistic variables: digit, unsigned integer, and integer. In defining the complete language, there will normally be one meta-linguistic variable that is never used in the definition of any other variable; this is known as the "starting type." In programming languages this would normally be ⟨program⟩, and in natural languages it might be ⟨sentence⟩.

The digits 0, 1 • • • 9 and the signs + and − are *terminal symbols* of the language; i.e., they will appear in statements written in the language. For this reason they are often printed in heavy type to distinguish them from the *nonterminal symbols* (digit, integer etc.), sometimes called "defined types."

REFERENCES

1967. Rosen, S. *Programming Systems and Languages*. New York: McGraw-Hill.

1969. Sammet, J. E. *Programming Languages*. Englewood Cliffs, N.J.: Prentice-Hall.

K. H. V. BOOTH

## META VARIABLE

For articles on related subjects *see* BACKUS-NAUR FORM; and GRAMMAR, GENERATIVE.

In the description of languages by syntactic rules, it is necessary to identify elements of the language, such as phrases, by names. In natural languages these are termed "parts of speech" and are identified by such terms as *noun, verb*, etc.

The formal description of computer languages ascribes the names "meta variable," "phrase name," or "component name" (among others) to these language elements. For example, in the simple grammar for an arithmetic expression given in the article on generative grammar, the meta variables are *constant, variable, add op, mult op, exp op, primary, factor, term*, and *arithmetic expression*. In describing a language in printed form, the meta variable must be distinguished from the actual strings of the language by some technique, such as the italics used here.

J. A. N. LEE

## MICROCOMPUTER

For articles on a related subject *see* INTEGRATED CIRCUITRY; and MINICOMPUTER.

The term "microcomputer," which was first used to denote a subclass of minicomputers dedicated to a single task and which was seldom if ever reprogrammed, has now become a category in its own right and refers to a concept of a complete computer central processor. Microcomputers are sometimes called "single chip LSI processors," "component processors," or "pico-computers," no one term having become generally accepted. One definition of a microcomputer describes it as a parallel arithmetic and logic processing unit, implemented by using large-scale integration (LSI), and providing a general-purpose data bus for communication with external devices. Elsewhere, it has been defined as a single-chip computer, although there are implementations using up to three chips. (An LSI chip is the name given to a slice of silicon, about 3/4 in. long, on which a large number of circuits are fabricated). There is no reason to suppose that the present trend toward reducing the size of chips and augmenting the number of elements a chip can accommodate will not continue. It seems safe to predict that before 1980, a microcomputer requiring only one chip will be selling for $1.00 to $10.00.

A typical microcomputer will have 16,000 words of memory of 32 bits each, a modest but carefully chosen instruction set, a handful of general-purpose registers, and I/O connections into and out of at least one of these registers. The 32 bits of the word length will provide for 8 bits for the operation code, 8 for a modifier field, and 16 for selection of one of the 65K bytes of local store. This local store will hold both program and data. No autonomous I/O processor will be provided.

Among the present and potential applications of microcomputers are:

1. Various control applications for which minicomputers, somewhat larger than current microcomputers, are presently used.
2. Adding capabilities to more or less standard computing installations (i.e., as part of a terminal device that connects the user with a central computer). With an intelligent terminal that incorporates a microprocessor as a peripheral controller, much of the operating system normally associated with a complex peripheral can be brought directly into the microcomputer itself, thus simplifying both the com-

**Fig. 1.** A typical microprocessor which is capable of performing control functions previously handled by minicomputers.

puter software and the peripheral interface, and reducing overhead in the main processor. For example, a visual display unit (VDU) with an internal microcomputer would be an easy-to-use, if limited, computational tool. The cost of such a system may soon be no more than $100. In addition, other devices such as a cassette unit, a disk, a printer, a communication modem, or a minicomputer could be deployed directly from the VDU via its microcomputer.

3. To provide enhanced logical functions for noncomputer products such as an automated wristwatch with some form of a digital display, or as a device to drive a specialized television display.

J. NECAS

## MICROPROCESSOR. *See* MICROCOMPUTER.

## MICROPROGRAMMING

For articles on related subjects *see* COMPUTER ARCHITECTURE; CONTROL POINT; CYCLE TIME; DIGITAL COMPUTERS; EMULATION; HOST SYSTEM; LOGIC DESIGN; MACHINE INSTRUCTION SET; and READ-ONLY STORE.

For articles on related terms *see* ADDER; INDEX REGISTER; PROGRAM COUNTER; and WILKES, M. V.

Microprogramming is a technique used by designers to implement the control functions of a computer. As with the case of a number of other terms relating to computer systems, microprogramming has gradually evolved and broadened its meaning—as, in fact, the understanding of the term "control" has also broadened. Microprogramming, as originally conceived by M. V. Wilkes in 1951, was a specific technique "to provide a systematic approach and an orderly approach to designing the control section of any computing system." In Wilkes' context, the term "control" is taken to mean the interpretation and execution of a machine instruction. The timing for this is shown in Fig. 1.

The interpretation and execution of the instruction involves four phases:

1. Fetching the instruction into the instruction register (IR).
2. Decoding the instruction and generation of the data address.
3. Fetching the data.
4. Final execution of the instruction.

Each of these phases is broken into a number of steps. The steps are defined by the notion of a "cycle": One cycle is the smallest time quantum in the control process. Generally, it is the time required to reconfigure (i.e., change the contents of) the data registers of the system. Thus, the notion of step or cycle is roughly equivalent to the notion of a register-state transition or register-state transformation. Many cycles are required to execute one machine instruction, usually between 3 and 5 cycles are required per phase or between 12 and 20 cycles per instruction execution for even a simple instruction.

The machine, exclusive of control, consists largely of register and combinatorial execution resources (adders, shifters, etc.). Each register position in the system can be gated or directed to one of a number of other registers during one cycle. The register interconnections, together with the registers and resources, are referred to as the "data paths" of the system. The output of each register drives a series of AND gates, which are directed to each of the desti-

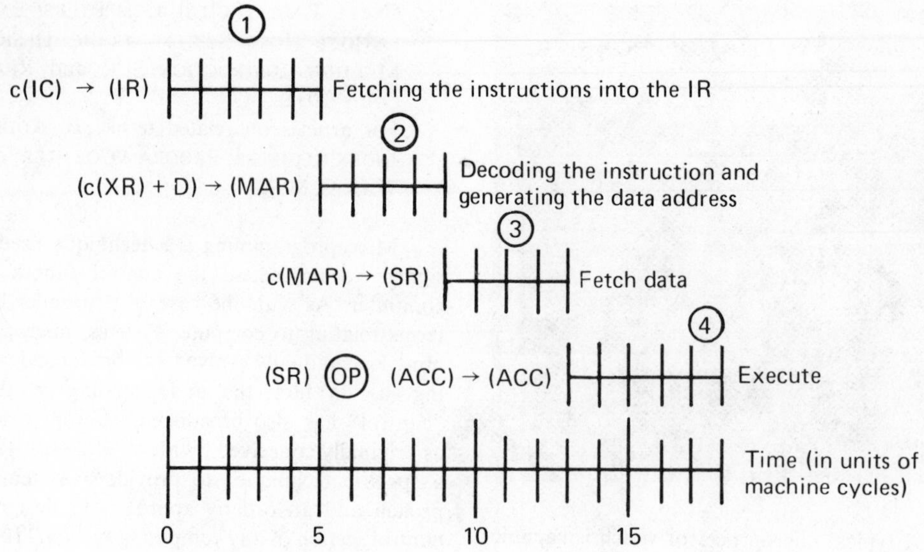


**Fig. 1.** Sequencing through a simple instruction. Instruction in the form c(c(XR) + D) OP (ACC)→(ACC), where c() = contents of; SR = storage register; MAR = memory address register; IR = instruction register; XR = index register; OP = operation specified by the instruction; D = address displacement; ACC = accumulator; IC = instruction (program) counter.

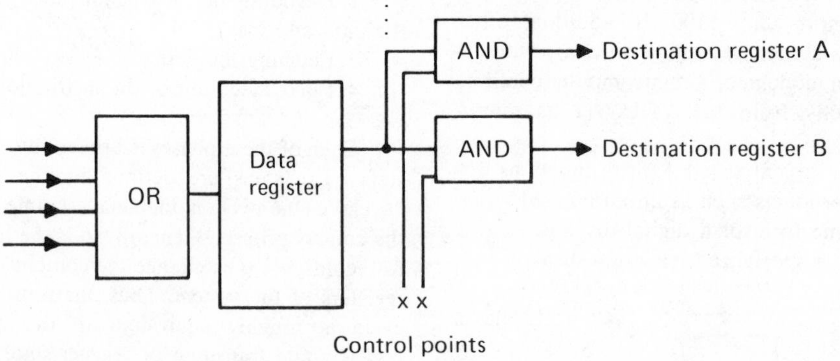


**Fig. 2.** Gating logic.

nations that may be reached from the source register in one cycle. See Fig. 2.

There are two types of data movements:

1. Those paths that connect the source register to a destination (perhaps itself) directly, i.e., without any intervening transformational logic.

2. Those paths that are connected from a source register into an execution resource and then directed to a destination register.

These two types are illustrated in Fig. 3. Shown in Fig. 3. is the *i*th bit of a storage register-adder-accumulator. In this example, the accumulator register must be added to a word in memory that has been placed in the storage register, and the sum must be returned to the accumulator. This occurs during the execute phase (step 4) in Fig. 1.

A simple ADD instruction may have a three-cycle execution. One cycle will be used for inspection of the signs of each of the operands before the

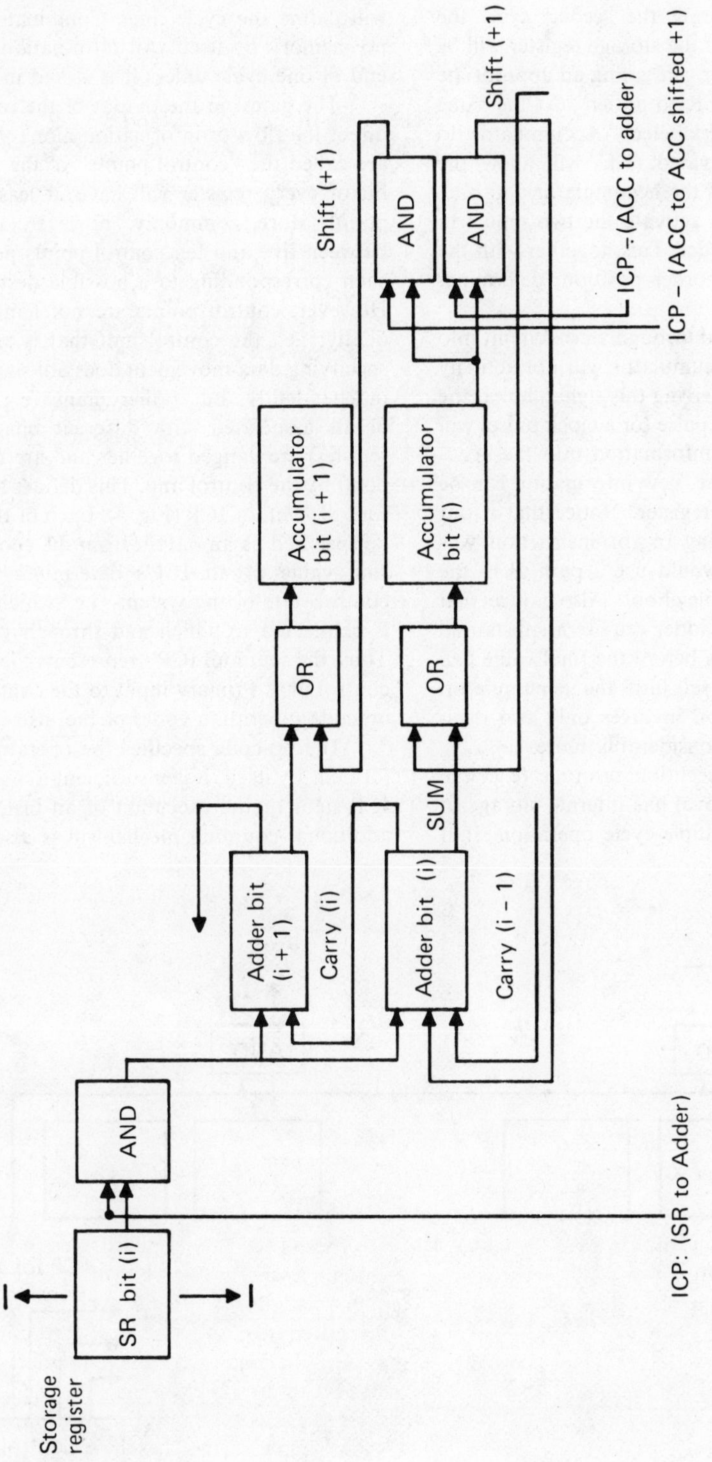


**Fig. 3.** The *i*th bit of storage register-adder-accumulator.

addition; the second cycle will represent the absolute addition; and the third cycle is used for sign and overflow inspection. During the second cycle the information in the bit $i$ of the storage register will be gated to bit $i$ of the adder, activating an appropriate control signal, labeled "SR to adder". At the same time the control signal labeled "Accumulator to adder" will also be activated. This will allow the information from bit $i$ of the accumulator and bit $i$ of the storage register to activate the two inputs to the $i$th position of the adder. This, together with the "carry" from the lower order position, determines the sum.

The sum will be gated through an OR circuit into the accumulator. The accumulator will not actually change its value upon receiving this signal, but at the end of the cycle a sample pulse (or a clock pulse) will be used to set this new information into the accumulator. At the same time, new information can be entered into the storage register. Notice that if our instruction, instead of being an ADD instruction, was a SHIFT instruction, we would use a path from the accumulator to its next neighbor. Also notice that operations involving the adder require a substantial number of logic decisions before the final value can be determined and be set into the accumulator. While the SHIFT operation involves only two decisions, the ADD requires considerably more.

In general, if the execution resource (e.g., the adder in the example above) has internal storage, it may be treated as a multiple-cycle operation. If it does not, then the time to direct information from a register through the resource and back to a register will define the cycle time. Combinatorial logic has no memory by itself. All information is lost at the end of one cycle unless it is stored in a register.

The gates on the output of the registers, which direct the flow of information along the data paths, are called the "control points" of the system. Every bit of every register will have at least one control point. More commonly, however, there will be between five and ten control points per register bit, each corresponding to a possible destination point. However, control points are not handled independently; i.e., the control unit that is responsible for specifying data movement does not signal each point independently, but rather many (e.g., the control points associated with different bits of the same register) are ganged together and are treated as one point by the control unit. This defines an *independent control point*, or ICP (Fig. 4). Each of the ICP's must be specified as an output from the control unit. The sum value of all ICP's determines the complete control state of the system—i.e., which data register is connected to which and through what resource. Thus, the set of all ICP's represents the output of the control unit. Primary input to the control unit is the op-code (operation code) of the instruction.

The op-code specifies the operation to be performed; by itself, it is insufficient to specify multiple ICP steps or the execution of an instruction. Some additional counting mechanism is also required. If

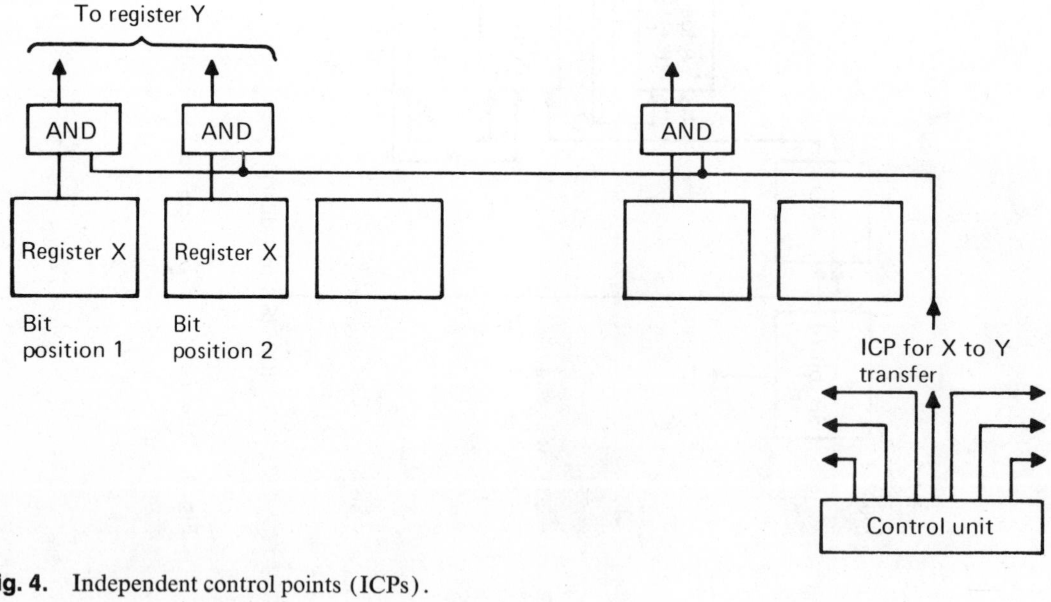


**Fig. 4.** Independent control points (ICPs).

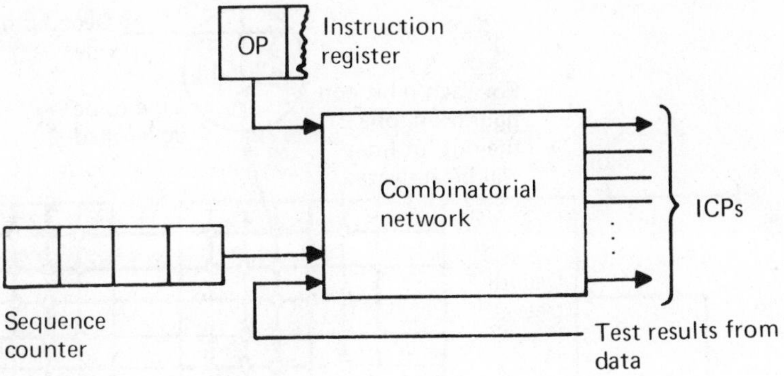


**Fig. 5.** Hardwire control.

the control implementation is to be done with the "hardwire" implementation, using a combinatorial network (Fig. 5), then the counting mechanism will be in the form of a sequence counter. This counter identifies the particular step of the instruction which is executed at any moment. The combination of the sequence count and the operation is the input to the network, which then describes the exact state of each ICP on each cycle of every instruction.

The microprogramming technique to implement the control function substitutes storage for the boolean combinatorial network and sequence counter. This serves as both a sequence and a combinatorial translator. The op code specifies the first microinstruction. The next microinstruction in the sequence, which interprets the instruction, may lie "in line" (i.e., following the address of the first microinstruction) or, alternately, the successor microinstruction may have its address contained in one of the fields of the first microinstruction. A MICRO-ONE microprocessor is shown in Fig. 6.

**Fig. 6.** Micro-One microprocessor. (Courtesy Microdata Corporation.)

**The Evolution of Microprogramming.** Microprogramming has evolved through three distinct phases. Phase 1 involved the use of microprogramming for engineering convenience. The storage contained simple descriptions of the gating patterns of each of the ICP's for each cycle. Ease of engineering change and design were important considerations. For these early microprogram implementations, diode matrix technology was well suited. Microprogrammed implementations of control during this era are best illustrated perhaps by Wilkes' ideas (Fig. 7). Wilkes viewed the microprogrammed control store as consisting of two diode matrices. The first matrix would determine the control information for the data paths, while the second matrix would determine, at least in part, the next microinstruction selected to continue the interpretation of the given instruction. The next microinstruction could be influenced by some selected datum (e.g., the sign bit of an accumulator). If the sign were negative, one microinstruction would be called; if the sign bit were positive, another might be invoked.

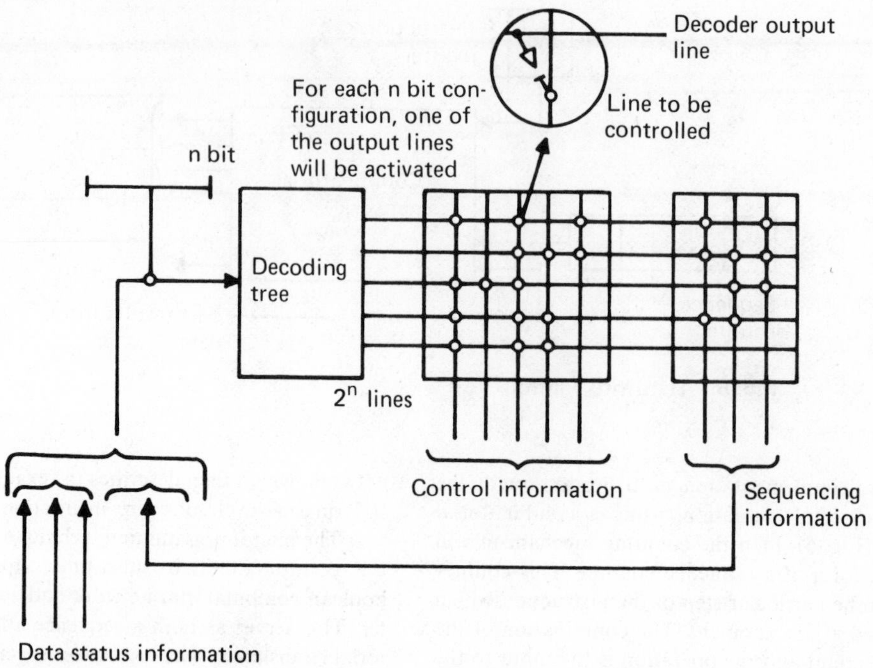


**Fig. 7.** Wilkes' microprogrammed control storage.

This was required so that proper complementation rules could be used for addition and substraction.

The decoding tree shown in Fig. 6 has the function of transforming a pattern of $n$ bits into a unique selection of 1 out of $2^n$ possible outputs. Thus, for example, a four-bit binary input into a decoder tree would have four input variables. These would define 16 possible configurations, from 0000 to 1111. The output of the tree would be 16 lines or possible events. Each output line would correspond to one and only one of the input configurations. When an output line is activated, it will also activate all lines out of the matrix that are connected to it (via diodes). The diode action essentially allows current to pass from the drive or input line into the output line. Of course, if no diode connects an input line to an output line, no current will be transmitted, and that line will remain in a "down state." These diode arrays give a simple and regular implementation to the control function. However, speed could be a problem.

In early implementations, no speed problems developed because main memory was quite slow, on the order of 10 $\mu$s cycle time, and the diode matrix had an access time of under 1/2 $\mu$s. The ratio of control access to the main memory access time was an important one; namely, as long as there was a large number of internal cycles in each memory cycle, the microprogramming task was relatively simple and straightforward. One register to register transformation was performed per internal cycle, and performance was essentially limited by the main memory cycle. As the main memory access time decreased, however, microprogramming techniques became correspondingly more sophisticated. If only one or two internal machine cycles are available for each main memory cycle, it is necessary to have multiple data transfers in each machine cycle. That is, the microinstruction has to simultaneously control a number of resources internal to the system. This gave rise to a type of internal parallelism within the processor.

The second generation of microprogrammed systems was distinguished by its small number of internal machine cycles per main memory cycle. By the early 1960s, main memory speed had dropped below 1 $\mu$s; yet the technology for control store had not noticeably improved, and the best access for read-only store varied between 200 and 400 ns. In addition, the read-only storage technologies tended to be exotic: The technology was not common with any other part of the machine and not always reliable. However, by this time the arguments for using microprogramming went well beyond the reasons cited by Wilkes. In the beginning of 1964, with the announcement of the IBM System 360, an important application for microprogramming was added—*emulation* of multiple machines on a single host system. This was intended to make the customer's transition from an old to a new system much more palatable, in that the customer could, with one system, support his old software as well as develop new applications with new programming languages and facilities (Husson, 1970).

The third generation of microprogramming dates from about 1970 with the advent of fast read-write control store (Flynn and Rosin, 1971). The development of bipolar monolithic technology created a storage medium with the same access time as combinatorial decisions, since essentially they are made out of the same material. The writable capability of control store represents an important transition, since now the control store becomes a true member of the memory hierarchy. It is unnecessary for control store to contain dynamically all interpretations for each and every instruction for each and every machine that must be emulated. Rather, emulated routines may be overlaid, as required, into a common microstorage. Similarly, the same storage may be used to hold parameters and buffer data values. Where the flexibility of high-performance operation over a variety of machine languages is not required, the data buffering function can be split off into a separate memory, again with the same technology. Here, references to main memory are anticipated by transferring blocks of data into the buffer. This gives rise to the "cache" type systems. Later, in the more general context of machine organizations, we will examine the impact of third-generation microprogramming on computer architecture. Fig. 8 shows a medium-scale computer system, which features microprogrammable processors.

**Fig. 8.** The Burroughs B1728 (B1700 series) medium-scale computer that features microprogrammable processors.

**Microinstructions.** The microinstruction is, by definition, the control mechanism that causes a single data-register state transition; i.e., it actuates an internal cycle. One can view this as the action of two separate machines—(1) a control machine whose output activates the data, or (2) an operational machine. The flexibility of these activations gives rise to a variety of possible microinstructions; terms such as horizontal, vertical, nanoinstruction, and packed or unpacked microinstructions have been used to describe the diversity of activations. These terms arise, sometimes ambiguously, to describe certain differences (Fig. 9):

1. If, within the control of a single resource, the microinstruction contains a separate description of each independent control point in the resource (i.e., the true description of the control gating), that activation is said to be an *unpacked* or *exploded form* of the microinstruction. Clearly, this form is most expensive in terms of space, but it provides the ultimate flexibility in that any combination of ICP values may be specified at any time in the future. As an alternate to this unpacked form, a specific number of combinations of ICPs may be choosen. These combinations, then, may be coded into a smaller number of code points, and through the use of a decoder can be regenerated when the microinstruction is executed. Thus, only the packed form of the microinstruction is stored, in effect saving space at the expense of flexibility. Occasionally the distinction between packed and unpacked forms of microinstructions are referred to as "vertical" and "horizontal" microinstructions, respectively.

2. As previously mentioned, the resources of the system may be partitioned into a number of independent units which can be simultaneously activated. If this partitioning is done, then the microinstruction that activates each of these resources simultaneously contains a separate information field for each of these resources. Thus, in Fig. 9(c), a resource might be an adder, a shifter, a unit for loading and/or storing information into a register or a test and branch unit. Notice that each of these could be operated at the same time, as long as they did not make conflicting use of a data operand.

The distinction between the control of the single resource through the use of ICPs [whether packed or unpacked—Figs. 9(a), (b)] and the multiple resource control situation [Fig. 9(c)] should be noted. Of course

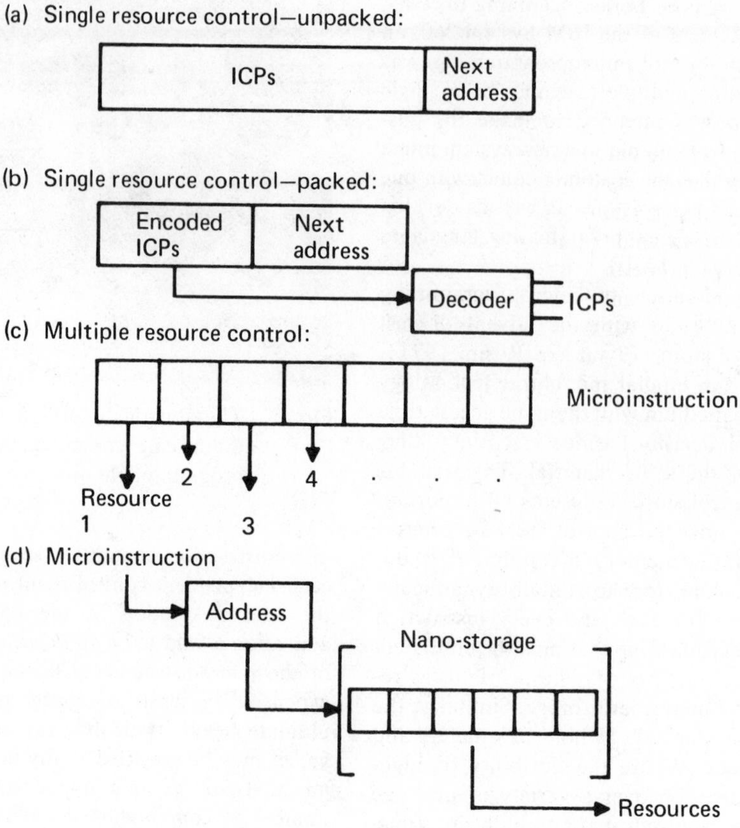


**Fig. 9.** Some concepts used in microinstruction formats.

the control for an adder still requires a set of ICPs, whether or not a microinstruction is specifying only the adder action or multiple units. This simultaneous use of resources gives rise to a type of internal parallelism that is explicit (visible to the microprogrammer), yet within the single instruction stream. This is unlike the type of internal parallelism of certain highly overlapped machines such as the CDC 6600 and IBM 360 Model 91, whose parallelism is transparent to the programmer. In any event, this use of the microinstruction for identification of possible simultaneous use of resources in conjunction with a partitioned set of resources has also been referred to as a "horizontal" microinstruction. The alternative is to use a universal single resource (unpartitioned); its corresponding control mechanism is sometimes referred to as a "vertical" microinstruction.

These two notions are independent; i.e., one can have an unpacked single resource microinstruction or a packed parallel-control-type microinstruction. In any event, a "vertical" microinstruction is a short form of a microinstruction, usually using a coded (packed) specification of an operation and also usually referring to only one type of operation. The "horizontal" microinstruction usually has either an unpacked specification of an operation and/or specification of multiple simultaneous operations.

3. There is an allied notion relating to the structure of a microinstruction, associated with the concept of residual control, called "a nanoinstruction." In this mode, a packed instruction (the microinstruction), with usually only one or two fields, is used as the basic control mechanism. However, instead of driving the resources directly, it indirectly refers to the resources through another storage level, the nanoinstruction. The nanoinstruction is the "horizontal" instruction that contains the exploded form of the control description. This technique is used on machines such as the Nanodata Corporation's QM1.

Fig. 9(d) illustrates this concept in which the nanoinstructions are a sequence of addresses in which each address points to a microinstruction. A microinstruction may be horizontal and may have multiple resource specifications. The purpose of this technique is to reduce the size of the storage needed to represent the program.

**Emulation.** An emulator (Rosin, 1969; Husson, 1970) is the collection of routines and programs that interprets a language. Languages that are efficiently interpreted are said to have the directly executable language property. "Efficiency" in this sense is a relative measure, and includes factors such as the amount of storage required to represent the statement in a language, as well as the amount of time required to interpret that statement (Fig. 10).

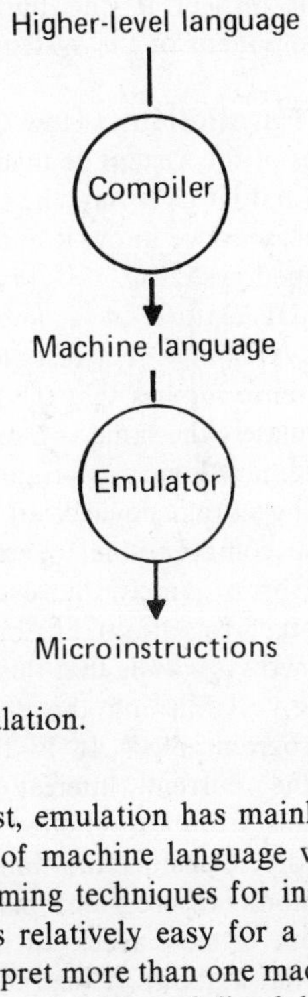


**Fig. 10.** Emulation.

In the past, emulation has mainly involved the interpretation of machine language with the use of microprogramming techniques for instruction interpretation. It is relatively easy for a single physical system to interpret more than one machine language. The physical machine, as defined by its microinstructions and their actions, is called a "host machine." Machine languages that are emulated by sets of microprogrammed routines are called "image machines." It is, of course, possible to write an emulator for one image machine in terms of another image machine language; thus, one can conceive of layers of emulators. However, more common usage of the term "emulator" implies that the interpretive set of programs is written in the microlanguage of the host processor.

Probably the most widely known use of emulation is that of IBM System 360. Most of the models of System 360 and System 370 are microprogrammed (with the notable exception of the Models 91 and 195). Each model of the System/360 and System/370 is quite a distinct machine, with widely differing performance characteristics, data path size, etc. However, each has the common machine language of System/360. In all the microprogrammed models of the System/360, the interpretation of the assembly language is done by an emulator that resides in microstorage. This emulator consists of a series of routines; each routine represents a particular System/360 instruction.

The emulation of a non-360 machine on a 360 machine is not so straightforward. Consider a Model 65 that emulates a 7090 (Table 1). The "emulation" of a 7090 on a Model 65 is more accurately described as a simulation of the 7090, using a combination of techniques, which includes 360 instructions, special instructions, and 7090 type instructions. The hybrid approach to emulation reduces the size of microstorage needed to provide emulation for both the 360 and the 7090. In the Model 65, each 7090 instruction is interpreted by an emulation subroutine that is contained in main memory (Fig. 11). This subroutine uses special instructions as well as conventional System 360 instructions. One of the most notable of the special instructions is the DIL (Do Interpretive Loop), which is a microprogrammed routine that does a

**Table 1.** Emulation of 7090 Instructions

| 7090 instruction | 360 Emulation routine | |
|---|---|---|
| AXT address to index true | EAXT | Microroutine that does AXT |
| | DIL | Microroutine that does fetch and interpretation of next instruction |
| AXC address to index complemented | LCR | 360 instruction that complements the address |
| | EAXT | Microroutine (see above) |
| | DIL | Microroutine (see above) |
| TMI transfer if minus | ESTO | Microroutine that puts the value into a work area of the 360 (the simulated accumulator) |
| | TM | 360 instruction, test under mask (to get the sign bit) |
| | EBC | Microroutine that does a 7090 branch if the test is satisfied |

fetch and interpretation of the next 7090 instruction. In addition to the DIL routine, a number of other subroutines are added to the microstorage to assist in emulating specific 7090 instructions. The configuration of main storage during emulation, as well as the emulation of three 7090 instructions, are shown in Fig. 11.

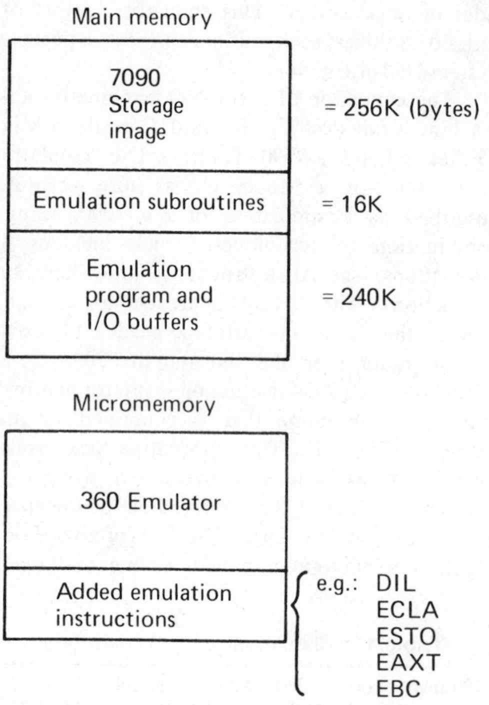


**Fig. 11.** Configuration of main memory and micromemory in a 360 Model 65 that is emulating a 7090.

**Microprogramming and Computer Architecture.** The availability of read-write storage can be expected to play an important role in the evolution of machine organizations (Flynn and Rosin, 1971). Traditional second- and third-generation machines have been organized about two artifacts:

1. The importance of the machine language as a ready interface with the human.
2. The access time to main memory for data and instructions is quite long compared with the time required to move data from a register.

The machine language programmer of today does not program in assembly code for convenience. He codes almost exclusively for reasons of efficiency; i.e., in order to control the physical resources of the system in an optimal way. Ease of use is not so important a consideration in the development of a machine language as efficiency. This, coupled with technological improvements, especially in the area of memory, portend the first significant change in computer organizations—the increase in use of parallel or "concurrent" operation of the resources of the systems. Since the hardware is inexpensive, units are made independent in the hope that their concurrent operation will produce more efficient program performances. "Efficient" in this sense is used with respect to the user program and its performance, not with respect to the busyness of some internal subcomponent of the system.

**Explicit Parallelism.** How can the control of the resources of the system be made visible to the programmer? First let us review the evolution of the machine language as we know it and compare it to microprogrammed systems.

An essential feature of a microprogrammed system is the availability of a fast storage medium. "Fast" in this sense implies that the memory access time is approximately the same as a sequence of such as "and/or" ordinary logical operations. That is, the access time of the storage device is of the same order as the primitive combinational operations that the system can perform, namely, the cycle time of the processor. Another important attribute of modern microprogrammed systems is that this "fast" storage is also writable, establishing the concept of "dynamic microprogramming." It is the latter that distinguishes the current interest in microprogrammed systems from earlier attempts that used read-only memory. Consider the timing chart for a conventional (nonmicroprogram) machine instruction (Fig. 1). Due to slow access of instruction and data, a substantial amount of instruction execution time is spent in these overhead operations. Contrast this with the situation shown in Fig. 12, illustrating the microprogram's instruction. In Fig. 12 there is an implicit assumption of homogeneity of memory; i.e., data and operands are all located in the same fast storage as the instructions. The latter assumption is valid when the control storage is writable.

The preceding statement implies another significant difference in conventional machines and microprogrammed machines, i.e., the power of the operation to be performed by the instruction. In the conventional machine, given the substantial accessing overhead, it is very important to orient the

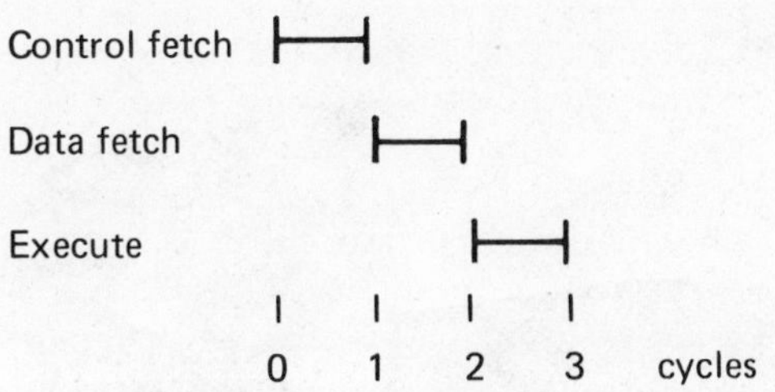


**Fig. 12.** Microinstruction execution.

operation so that it will be as significant as possible in computing a result. To do otherwise would necessarily involve a number of accessing overheads; thus, we have the evolution of the rich and powerful instruction sets of the second- and third-generation machines. With dynamically microprogrammed systems (Fig. 12), the powerful operation will do no more than a sequence of steps. Indeed, the rich instruction operation may (if its richness is done at the expense of flexibility) cause an overall degradation in system performance.

In the traditional system, since the overhead penalties are so significant, there is little real advantage in keeping the combinational resources of the system simultaneously busy or active. This would mean perhaps that instead of 20 cycles, 17 or 18 would be required to perform an instruction—hardly worth the effort. A much different situation arises with the advent of dynamic microprogramming. Consider a system partitioned into resources (e.g., adder, storage resources, addressing resources) If the microinstruction can be designed in such a fashion that during a single execution one can control the flow of data internal to each one of these resources, as well as communicate between them, significant performance advantages can be derived. Of course these advantages come at the expense of a wider microinstruction.

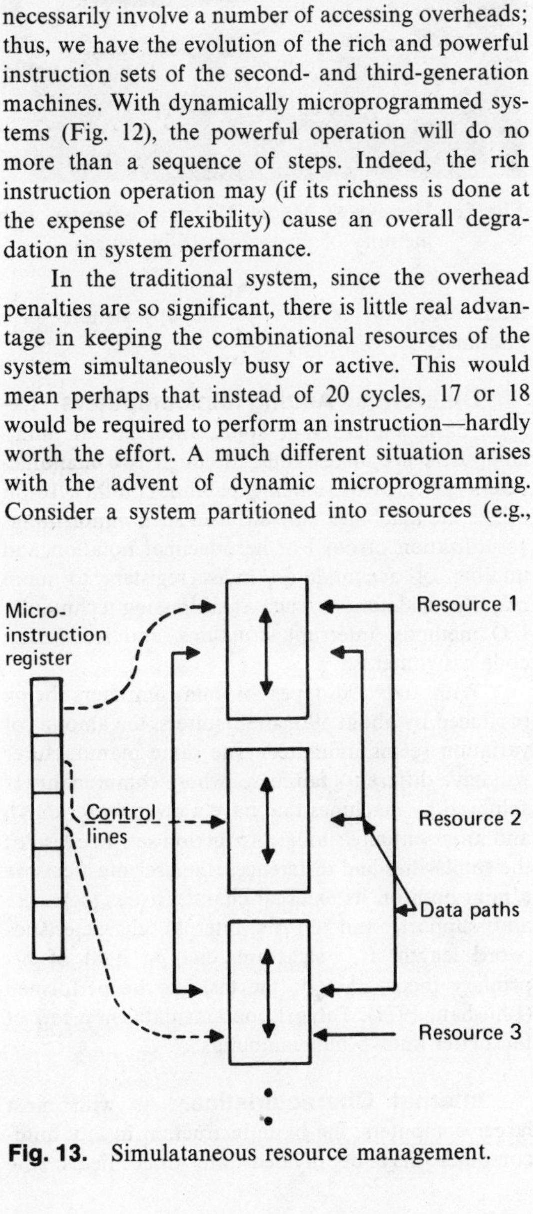


**Fig. 13.** Simulataneous resource management.

In any event, computer architecture cannot help but be influenced strongly by the availability of fast memory and the use of primitive (one cycle) operations, and explicit parallelism to simultaneously control the resources of the system (Fig. 13). The third-generation microprogrammed systems can achieve a performance speed-up in direct proportion to the reduced access time of microstorage memory over main memory. Thus, an order of magnitude performance improvement is a potentially available factor.

References

1969. Rosin, R. F. "Contemporary Concepts in Microprogramming and Emulation," *Computing Surveys,* Vol. 1 (December), pp. 197–212.

1970. Husson, S. S. *Microprogramming: Principles and Practices*. Englewood Cliffs, N.J.: Prentice-Hall.

1971. Flynn, M. J., and R. Rosin. "Microprogramming: An Introduction and a Viewpoint," *IEEE Transactions on Computers*, Vol. C-20, No. 7 (July), pp. 727–731.

M. J. Flynn

# MINICOMPUTERS

For articles on related subjects *see* Addressing; Computer Systems; Digital Computers: Contemporary and Future; Machine Instruction Set; Microcomputer; and Microprogramming.

For articles on related terms *see* Coroutine; Interrupt; Read-Only Store; and Subroutine.

Today's minicomputer can be broadly classified as an 8, 12, 16, 18, 24, or 32 bit word length machine with a memory size ranging from 4K to 256K provided in modules of 4K or 8K. Nearly all minicomputers employ a parallel internal processor structure with a high-speed bus and a clock rate of 1 to 10 MHz. The basic configuration cost ranges from $4,000 to $20,000, with the cost of peripheral devices usually far outstripping the cost of the machine. The use of low-cost MSI and LSI logic has removed many of the initial design constraints, such as:

1. Limited addressing capability.
2. Lack of general-purpose registers and accumulators.
3. Elementary I/O processing and devices.
4. Limited interrupt schemes.

Indeed, the minicomputer is a product of our technology which can provide us with machines that exhibit significant architectural designs at very modest prices.

Minicomputer usage differs from that of a large-scale machine primarily in the following ways:

1. The shorter world length limits the precision of various data types to be used (or requires multiple-precision software).
2. Although higher-level languages are usually available, the use of assembly language for writing user programs is much more common.
3. The machine is normally run in an open-shop environment, with the user acting as operator, programmer, and application analyst. A typical installation is shown in Fig. 1.
4. The system operates in a dedicated environment for which the system has been specifically configured.
5. The user must, in general, be more sophisticated and ingenious, since large and complex operating systems do not exist, thus requiring the user to program what is more routinely provided by the large-scale computing system.

The trend of the minicomputer market has shifted from an OEM to an end-user market, and as a result, more sophisticated software (requiring additional hardware) is being developed so as to allow the user to buy a turnkey minicomputer system that has a complete operating system capable of supporting one or many users simultaneously.

The languages available on these machines include Fortran, Basic, and Algol, besides other proprietary dialects of these standards. As we go through new generations of minicomputer systems, it seems clear that the day may soon arrive when the mini and the large computer appear as one, at least from the point of view of the applications programmer.

**Fig. 1.** Honeywell Model 316 minicomputer with memory of up to 32K 16-bit words.

**Differences Among Minicomputers.** Despite basic similarity of appearance, not all minicomputers are alike. Thus, although two manufacturers may provide similar capabilities on their 16-bit minis, the machines may differ in such minor things as utilization of octal or hexadecimal notation and number of accumulators/index registers to more major considerations, such as addressing techniques, I/O methods, interrupt structures, and instruction code assignments.

With over 90 types of minicomputers being produced by about 50 manufacturers, the amount of variation seems unlimited. The same manufacturer will have different "families," whose commonality is achieved by machines that have a given word length and an essentially similar instruction set. Because of the similarities and differences, the user must choose a mini both on its external characteristics (software and support) and on its internal characteristics (word length, I/O structure, etc.) in light of his primary focus, namely, the tasks to be performed (Bhushan, 1971). Table 1 contains data on a few of the better known minicomputers.

**Internal Characteristics.** As with most larger computers, the basic instruction in any minicomputer may be divided into three fields: the

**Table 1.** Some Characterisitcs of Some Well-Known Minicomputers

| Company/ Model | Word Length/ Instruction Length | Add Time, μs | Memory Sizes, K = 1,024 words | Number of Basic Instructions | Addressing Modes | Number of Register Accumulators | Extensive Software | Basic Cost, $ |
|---|---|---|---|---|---|---|---|---|
| Cincinnati Milacron CIP/2100 | 8/8,16,24, or 32 | 6.4 | 4K–32K | 89 | 8 | 6 | No | 5,875 |
| Data General Supernova | 16/16 | 0.8 | 4K–32K | 11 | 4 | 4 (16 memory) | Yes | 11,700 |
| Digital Equipment PDP-8/E | 12/12 or 24 | 2.6 | 4K–32K | 8 | N/A | 1 | Yes | 4,500 |
| PDP-11/20 | 16/16,32, or 48 | 2.3 | 4K–32K | 56 | 8 | 8 | Yes | 10,800 |
| Hewlett-Packard 2100A | 16/16 | 2.0 | 4K–32K | 80 | N/A | 2 | Yes | 7,250 |
| Interdata Model 70 | 16 or 32/8, 16 or 32 | 1.0 | 4K–32K | 113 | N/A | 16 | Yes | 7,000 |
| Microdata Micro 800 | 8/16 | 0.22 | 0K–32K | 15 | N/A | 16 | No | 5,000 |
| Texas Instr. 960A | 16/32 | 3.2 | 4K–64K | 76 | N/A | 16 | Yes | 2,900 |
| Varian 620/f | 16/16 or 32 | 1.5 | 4K–32K | 159 | 8 | 4 | Yes | 10,500 |

**Fig. 2.** Instruction format.

operation to be performed, the address mode to be used, and the address field (see Fig. 2). The size of each field is very important in that it determines much of the internal machine characteristics (e.g., how many registers, how much memory may be referenced directly, how many distinct opcodes will exist.).

OPERATION CODES. Since the size of the op code field of an instruction is greatly limited by the short word length, the number of distinct op codes is increased by a simple trick. Instructions that do not reference memory do not have address fields. Instead, these instructions are lumped together under one basic op code and the address field is used as an extension of the basic op code so as to specify a particular operation within the group.

For example, the "operate" instruction for the PDP-8 computer is shown in Fig. 3. This instruction (octal operation code = 7) allows the programmer to test and/or manipulate data that is held in an accumulator and associated "link" bit. Bits 4 to 11 of the instruction specify whether the accumulator is cleared (the CLA bit), the link bit is cleared (CLL), the accumulator is complemented (CMA), the link bit is complemented (CML), the accumulator and link bit are rotated right (RAR), rotated left (RAL), and if the contents of the accumulator are to be incremented by 1 (IAC). When taken in combination, the operate bits allow the programmer to perform such operations as: (1) two's complement the accumulator (CMA IAC), (2) set the link to a one (CLL CML), and (3) set the accumulator to two (CLA IAC RAL).

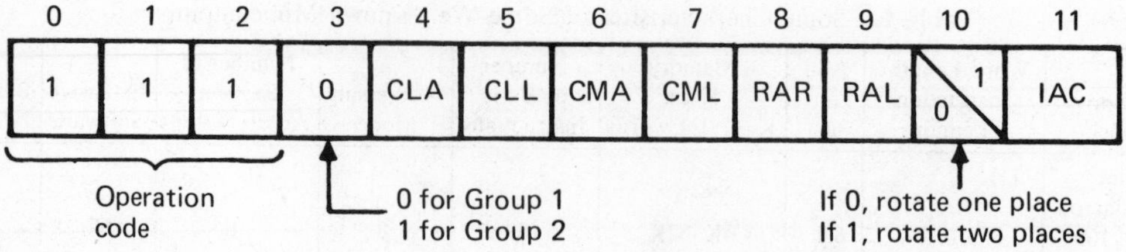


**Fig. 3.** Operate instruction. The instructions are separated into two groups. Group 1 contains manipulation instructions and Group 2 contains testing operations.

On some machines, the extension field is likened to horizontal microprogramming, where the individual bits can be used independently to perform such functions as clearing the accumulator, skipping if a register is zero (or positive or negative), and shifting the contents of a specified register/accumulator. As a result of these instruction extenders, most minicomputers have large instruction sets when all the various legal combinations are considered.

ADDRESSING CHARACTERISTICS. As mentioned earlier, part of the basic instruction word is the address mode field. Possible addressing options include absolute/relative addressing, direct/indirect addressing, and indexed/no-indexed addressing. These different modes allow the programmer to expand the range of possible addresses that his program can generate. Since the number of bits available for specifying the address is small, it is absolutely essential that various addressing options be part of the addressing structure.

Although some minis may address all of memory directly and absolutely, such is not the normal case. Instead, it is more common to be able to address only 256 (8-bits) or 4,096 (12-bits) memory locations. As a result, the address field of the instruction is used to relatively address small portions of memory by combining its value with the current program counter value, resulting in a floating page of fixed size, or with a page-register value, such as the high-order bits of the program-counter value, resulting in a fixed page of fixed size.

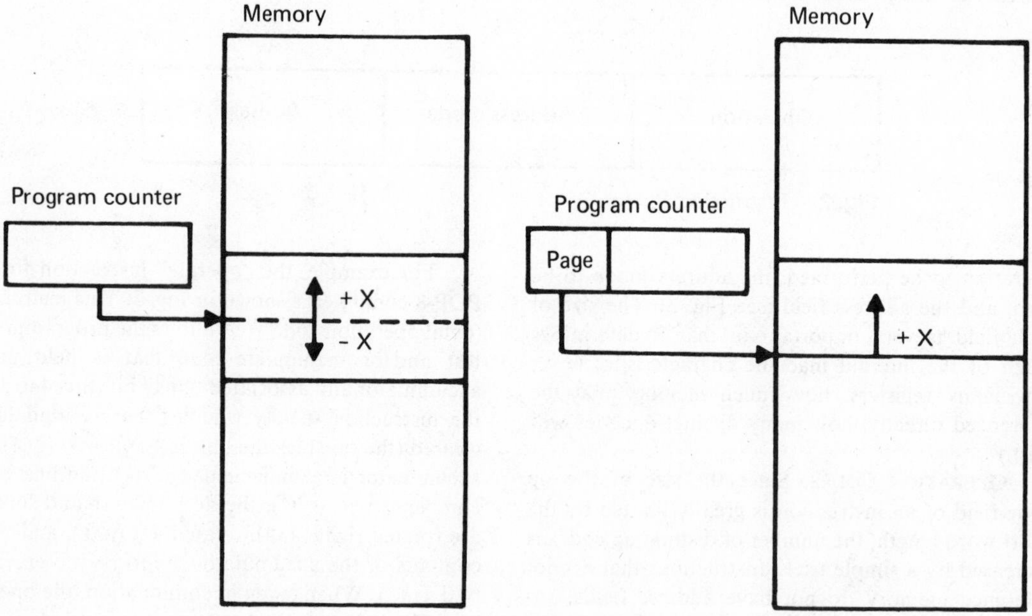


**Fig. 4.** Fixed and floating pages. (a) Floating page: effective address = PC±X. (b) Fixed page: effective address = Page + X.

Fig. 4 depicts both the floating and fixed page addressing schemes. In Fig. 4(a), the program-generated address X is added algebraically to the program-counter value, generating the effective memory address. In Fig. 4(b), only the page bits of the program counter are used with X to generate the effective address. In this second case, the value of X is always assumed to be positive, so that the page is fixed in both size and position.

One advantage of relative addressing is the position independence of the generated code. Since only the relative distance between instructions and data are preserved as part of the instruction word, the word can be easily moved around in memory without requiring the services of a relocatable assembler and loader.

When indirect addressing is utilized, the entire word pointed to as the address field can be utilized, thus expanding significantly the addressing space of the instruction. The level of indirectness may be single or multilevel, of course, depending on whether the indirect bit is associated with the instruction or the address field.

Current technology has produced minicomputers with truly general-purpose registers that may be used as index registers, accumulators, program counters, and stack registers. When used as index registers (and when implemented in active logic rather than as special-purpose memory locations), general-purpose registers allow large blocks of memory to be referenced without requiring additional instruction execution time. Additionally, these registers (whether part of memory or separate hardware locations) may be used in an auto-indexing fashion such that when utilized indirectly, their contents are automatically incremented (or decremented). Auto-indexing is useful for loops, for stepping through arrays, and for subroutine parameter passing.

When it is possible to utilize all the addressing modes described, the order of execution for calculating the effective address becomes quite important. Depending on the size of the address field, post- or pre-indexing is performed after "derelativizing" the address field. For small address field machines, post-indexing is preferred, since the indirect address field can address a larger portion of memory, which is then indexed. On the other hand, for a large address field where more of memory can be addressed, it is particularly convenient to perform indexing before indirect addressing for such things as subroutine parameter passing, where the parameters may be addresses that have to be indirectly referenced.

Finally, there is another type of addressing scheme, which is associated with the variable-length instruction minicomputer. These machines use an extra memory word for the address field (when necessary) and specify that the instruction is more than one word long by setting the appropriate bits in the address-mode field. These machines require extra memory cycles for fetching the extra words, but clearly the time is no more than the time required to perform indirect addressing.

**Input/Output.** The range of peripheral devices that may be connected to a minicomputer is quite large and includes teletypewriters, paper tape, card readers and punches, line/page printers, disks, drums, cassette/cartridges, magnetic tapes, CRT's, plotters, and telecommunication equipment. Because of the simplicity of the I/O interface, it is easy to attach almost any kind of peripheral device to the minicomputer I/O bus.

Data and control information is transferred to the I/O device either through the mini's accumulator or through special device registers. Once initiated (by making a request to the device controller), the I/O device is capable of operating concurrently with the CPU. Indeed, it is often possible to have several devices running simultaneously with the CPU, stealing memory cycles as needed.

Many minicomputers include a direct memory access (DMA) feature as part of the computer's structure. A DMA port allows an I/O device to communicate directly with memory without tying up the I/O bus or the CPU. Typical devices for which a DMA port would be useful are high-speed mass-storage devices and special-purpose interfaces to time-critical processes, such as graphical displays.

One of the key features found on most minicomputers is the interrupt structure. Depending on the application, the sophistication of the interrupt system may be more important than machine speed or instruction repertoire. The interrupt structures commonly found on minis range from single-level without priority to multilevel with priority.

A direct consequence of the multilevel interrupt structure is the automatic stacking of the processor state words. By means of a stack register, any level of interrupt nesting is possible. In addition, by utilizing the stack register for the automatic stacking of state words during subroutine activation, recursive programming and coroutine structures are more easily facilitated. Further, by introducing trap instructions into the instruction set, it is possible to link together easily independently written software systems and/or emulate/simulate hardware features, e.g., multiply/divide, floating point) not part of the basic instruction set.

**Software.** The range of software packages available for most minicomputers is quite large. At the very minimal level, most systems will include an absolute assembler, an absolute loader, an editor, an I/O programming system, a debugging tool, and a mathematical utilities package. Each of these programs can be executed on the basic or minimal hardware configuration.

As the size of memory is increased, more sophisticated software becomes available to the user. This software includes higher-level and special-purpose languages, and mini time-sharing systems capable of supporting from 4 to 32 simultaneous users.

By adding a mass-storage device, such as a disk to his system, the minicomputer user gains the flexibility of a single-user disk operating system or a batch operating system if a card reader is attached. In addition, by adding memory hardware for protection and relocation, background/foreground programming becomes possible, sometimes with manufacturer-supplied software.

As a result of the recent trend to provide more sophisticated software, it is becoming more common to find minicomputers serving as general-purpose computing machines. On the other hand, the number of potential applications is almost limitless, and minicomputers can be found in a wide range of environments.

**Applications.** By and large, the greatest use of minicomputers has been in areas other than general-purpose computing. These areas include:

1. Industrial applications such as control of power generation, petrochemical systems, data acquisition, and testing of equipment and devices.
2. Biomedical control for experiment monitoring.
3. In larger computer systems for communication and peripheral control, such as data concentrators, satellite peripherals, and intelligent terminals.
4. Intelligent graphic terminals and interactive graphic systems that may be part of general-purpose, graphic-oriented computing.
5. Microprogrammable minicomputer systems that are capable of being tailored to specific applications and/or environments.

The systems shown in Figs. 5 and 6 are typical of models used in these applications.

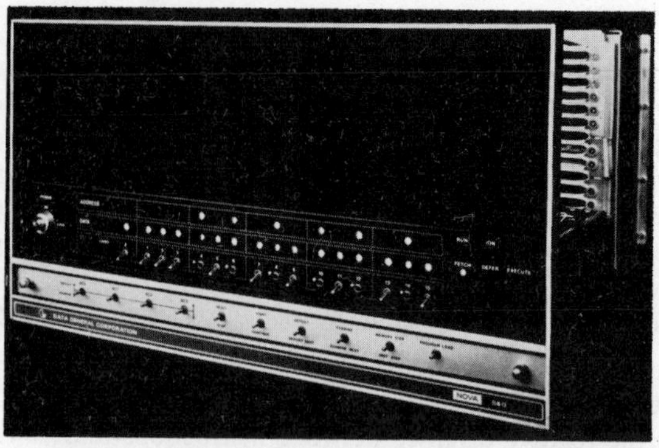

**Fig. 5.** Data General Nova 840 minicomputer.

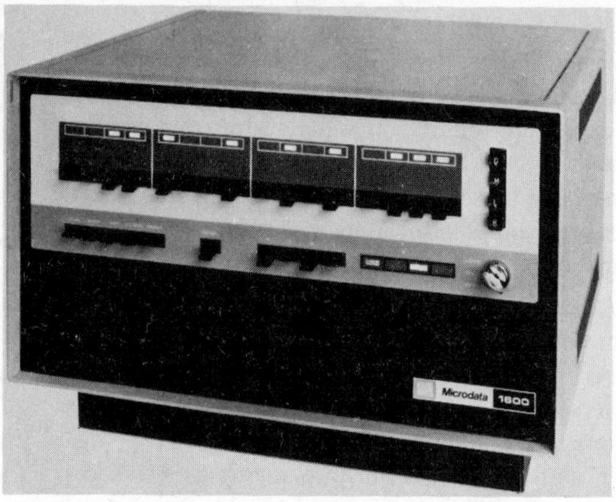


**Fig. 6.** Microdata 1600 minicomputer.

It is important to distinguish between microprogrammable computers and the simple operation-code extension mentioned earlier. The value of the microprogrammable machine can be found in its compatibility with other different machines by emulation of the same instruction set; in its ability to allow the user to tailor his machine at the most primitive level to accommodate his particular requirements; or in its ability to allow the user the flexibility of experimenting with new ideas and designs.

Another distinction occurs between microprogrammable minis and minis with read-only memories (ROM). Although ROM's are often used to hold microprograms, they may also be used to store programs for minicomputer applications that do not change and where the instructions may be locked into memory, providing decreased memory cycle time and greater integrity against accidental destruction.

**Future Developments.** As the cost of the hardware goes down with new technological advances, the cost/performance ratio of minicomputer hardware will continue to improve more dramatically than for large computer systems, where cost has remained fairly constant and performance has changed only slightly. As a result, there will be an increasing use of minicomputers in new applications areas (e.g., hospital record keeping, retail inventory management, and specialized commercial applications areas). Indeed, as the sophistication of the software improves, it will become increasingly difficult to distinguish minicomputer systems from larger computer systems.

REFERENCES

1970. Carter, W. C. "Getting to Know Your Mini," *Computer Decisions* (November), pp. 17–21.

1971. Bhushan, A. K. "Guidelines for Minicomputer Selection," *Computer Design* (April), pp. 43–57.

1971. Theis, D. J., and L. C. Hobbs. "The Minicomputer Revisted," *Datamation* (May 15), pp. 24–34.

R. H. ECKHOUSE, JR.

# MODELS

For articles on related subjects *see* OPERATIONS RESEARCH; and SIMULATION.
For articles on related terms *see* MATHEMATICAL PROGRAMMING; and QUEUEING THEORY.

Large, complex systems—including scientific, engineering, business, and social systems—are difficult to exercise and properly evaluate. System exercise is costly, usually very difficult, and often impossible, especially during design and implementation phases. Yet, the necessity for analysis and evaluation is always present and critical. So, in the past, various research and analysis techniques have been applied to obtain answers to questions dealing with various system aspects, such as systems reaction and effectiveness, and in the future we can anticipate even wider and more exotic applications. At present perhaps the most effective research and analysis technique is the representation of a system, concept, or operation, by a logical-mathematical model. Typically, then, computer simulation is used to analyze and study the model.

The development of computer simulation has opened a new technique for analyzing problems in our institutions and technologies. Simulation is a useful tool for analysts, scientists, engineers, designers, managers, researchers, social scientists, and students to test existing or conceptual systems and operations, as well as ideas created in men's minds. We can apply simulation to: (1) determine parameter sensitivity, (2) optimize or evaluate system design, (3) test and experiment system design concepts, (4) evaluate overall system effectiveness or utility, (5) generate relevant information, and (6) examine a system under any conceivable situation. Actually, a computer simulation is not restricted by real-world constraints, so we are at liberty to exercise the simulation in any manner whatever.

Unquestionably, computer simulation is one of the most important applications of the computer to a vast array of problems whose methods of solution are amenable to mathematical modeling.

**History.** The development of computer simulation techniques has paralleled the development of the electronic digital computer, and the technique has evolved within the constraints of computer hardware and software. This is an apparent fact, since any technique dependent on a technology cannot exceed the capabilities of that technology. In other words, computer simulation technique cannot exceed the capabilities of computer technology in relation to storage space, command structure, and available software.

It was in the late 1940s that computers were first manufactured and sold commercially. And it was in the 1950s when pioneer work was started on computer simulation. Simulation had been applied before, but it was physical analog simulation, such as wind tunnels used to simulate an operational environment for aircraft models.

During the decade beginning in 1950, researchers gradually converted certain physical analog and manual models to digital computer simulation. This took place primarily in military defense projects conducted at several laboratories, such as the Applied Physics Laboratory at Johns Hopkins University, and in various military installations. However, some work went on in nondefense disciplines as well, such as the business games developed at Northwestern University, Carnegie Institute of Technology, and the University of California at Los Angeles.

Early computer simulations were very simple, and because available digital computers at that time had limited memory space of usually a few hundred words, many of the model manipulations had to be carried out manually by the analyst while working closely with the computer. Computer programs requiring more memory than was available had to be segmented, and each part had to be loaded and run on the computer separately.

With the increased use of computers in the 1950s came an awareness of computer simulation as a powerful technique, frequently far more efficient than other simulation techniques such as physical analog simulation. The development of programming languages (notably Fortran) and subsequent simulation languages (e.g., GPSS, Simscript, and Simula) gave further impetus to the technique of simulation.

By the 1960s the technique was firmly established as an important and useful tool to apply to a broad range of problems. Its potential was recognized by many researchers, the technique was gradually applied over a wide spectrum of problems and disciplines. Simulation models were built to: (1) evaluate the performance of conceptual systems described by parameters only, (2) simulate hypothetical systems and optimize system design, (3) determine effects of natural and induced environments on system performance, and (4) evaluate in advance the performance and effectiveness of conceptual systems.

Applications in business and economics, traffic and transportation, military systems, engineering systems, natural science, social science, human science, and education proliferated. These are all significant areas of application; however, the technique is now being applied in other subject areas as well, but those listed above are representative of hundreds of computer simulations designed and developed in the decade between 1960 and 1970.

In the 1970s and beyond, an extension and expansion of the technique can be expected.

**Advantages.** There are many advantages in using computer simulation. The following are a few of the more significant ones:

1. With computer simulation there are no real-world constraints on model manipulation and application. The only constraints are those limitations inherent in the computer hardware and software, as well as the limitations of manpower resources allocated to the problem solution.

2. Extreme flexibility is found in the simulated time and spatial domains in the control of simulated environment, and in system configuration and operation. Almost any conceivable situation or condition, actual or hypothetical, can be simulated.

3. Results can be generated quickly and reliably, and results can be realized as fast as the simulation designer can implement the model and the computer can produce a meaningful output.

4. Problems that often could not be solved by any other scientific technique are subject to attack.

5. Computer simulation can be used advantageously in various applications in order to: (a) evaluate ideas, (b) test system concepts before building the system, (c) aid in the design phase of a system, (d) test operational systems, (e) aid in growth processes carried through various system generations, (f) aid as training and learning devices in the classroom or laboratory, and (g) aid in managerial decisions.

6. Simulation is always under complete human control. No real-world difficulties, such as a hostile environment, are encountered.

7. The model designer and user can do anything with computer simulation within the capabilities of the computer, its peripherals and software, and resources available.

**Philosophy and Rationale.** Consider the difficulties encountered in trying to manipulate real-world parameters while conducting an experiment.

First are problems in the *time* domain. We cannot turn the clock backward or forward to conduct an experiment. We cannot stop time, slow it down, or speed it up. This places very severe constraints upon any research that requires long spans of time; e.g., the slow growth processes of plant life.

Second are the problems in the *spatial* domain. In the real world we cannot move people and objects easily and quickly from one geographic location to another. Many problems are created in the attempt to conduct experiments that require moving long distances or communicating with several different locations.

Third are the problems in controlling the *environment*. Some parts of the environment cannot be controlled at all; e.g., climate or topography. This also includes problems in measuring environmental parameters in order to determine their effects on the experiment.

Fourth are the problems in *system* exercise and control. Depending upon the systems being manipulated, there are serious problems in controlling the system and in rearranging system elements to give the necessary data. We cannot easily change system characteristics in order to examine different features.

Despite the enormous difficulties encountered in solving problems in the real-world context, researchers continue to solve many problems in this manner. Sometimes from necessity, and sometimes as an expediency, a researcher still uses real-world elements to solve many social, political, and economic problems without first trying other techniques. For example, new products are often introduced in the marketplace without sufficient marketing analysis to determine needs and utility, and many engineering systems are still built by trial-and-error methods, often at great costs to society.

Time, space, environment, and the system cause basic problems when an attempt is made to manipulate real-world elements. On the other hand, the "principles of simulation" rather than manipulation of real-world elements can be applied. We can solve certain problems by (1) structuring the problem elements in a simulated world; (2) exercising and manipulating this simulated world; and (3) determining, transferring, and applying effective solutions to the real-world situation. These are the underlying principles that give validity and integrity to computer simulation techniques, and transform pseudoscience into a workable scientific method of problem solution. This tremendous advantage provides a wide range of simulation applications in solving problems that can be represented in quantitative terms.

Consider the flexibilities of computer simulation. We can select a simulated time interval as large or as small as is necessary. We can turn the simulated clock backward, forward, stop it, slow it down, or speed it up without any restrictions whatsoever. We can move simulated objects in simulated space in any direction at any speed or to any location as fast as is required. We can change or increment the simulated environment in any manner we wish. We can manipulate the configuration of the simulated system in any manner in order to solve the problem. We can do all these things without disturbing the simulation or the real world.

**The Elements of Simulation.** Since digital computers operate only on discrete quantities, we must transform all simulations to a set of procedures that involve discrete calculations and logic. These procedures may include all mathematical processes, from the simplest arithmetic operations to the most complex, deterministic as well as nondeterministic features, and a logic whose basic elements are reducible to yes-or-no decisions. Thus, within the constraints of the computer, the simulated world provides a convenience of flexibility for problem solution that is often impractical or impossible in the real world.

From these principles of simulation, a rational foundation for computer simulation techniques can be developed.

We start with a "problem." Assume that the problem exists and can be solved by computer simulation; i.e., the problem can be modeled by discrete calculations and logic. Also assume that the existence of the problem is recognized, there is a desire to attack the problem, and sufficient resources are available.

Now look at the real world in relation to the problem, and be sure to include all aspects of the real world which bear upon the problem. The real world, in the present or future time frame, contains systems and subsystems that are relevant to the problem. These systems may be actual and presently in existence, or they may be planned or conceptual systems that might be developed in the future.

The system to be investigated operates in a natural environment and may also operate in an induced environment, such as urban location. This environment may contain friendly elements that are benevolent to system operation, as well as hostile elements that are detrimental and act as impediments to proper system function. For example, fog may be a benevolent element for a military unit trying to evade the enemy, or fog is a hostile element in landing planes safely at an airport. Thus, benevolence or hostility of the environment is determined by the context of the problem.

Manned systems, such as transportation systems, involve people who interact with those who are applying the system to perform some function or functions. Unmanned systems, such as the solar system, may not directly involve people; however, there may be some direct or indirect effect on people. Thus, in every system, some interaction between human beings and the system is found. Normally, there is always some interaction between the system and the environment, and between humans and the environment.

Thus, we have a complex that consists of system elements, human beings, and an environment. In some cases, only two elements interact and in others there are interactions among all three. This complex can be modeled by application of appropriate logical-mathematical techniques.

The mathematical model of the system is an analog, or approximation, of the system to be simulated, which transforms the elements of the system into a symbolic representation expressed in a set of processes. Thus, on one hand, we have the real-world system, and on the other hand we have a symbolic interpretation (the model) of the system.

Mathematical models can be either continuous or discrete. Continuous-change models are used to represent systems that consist of a continuous flow of information or material, counted in the aggregate rather than as individual items (e.g., flow of gas in a pipeline). Continuous models are usually represented by differential or difference equations that describe rate of change of the variables over time. Discrete-change models represent systems in which changes in the state of the systems are conceptualized as discrete rather than continuous (e.g., messages arriving at a switchboard). Discrete models are usually represented by queueing theory and stochastic processes.

Certain basic problem forms are associated with certain mathematical models. Several of the basic forms are classified as follows:

1. *Allocation*. This form comprises specified resources required to meet desired objectives, and is concerned with the activity-analysis problem of allocating resources to maximize gains, the production scheduling problem to vary production to meet demands, and the transportation problem. Mathematical programming techniques (such as linear programming) are used to solve allocation problems.

2. *Inventory*. This is concerned with the maintenance of resources in an idle state to provide response to future demands; e.g., maintenance of spare parts.

3. *Queueing*. Queueing relates to the rate of servicing at a facility (e.g., shoppers arriving at a check-out stand).

4. *Sequencing*. This is concerned with the order in which units requiring service are serviced for example (e.g., first-come-first-served policy at a ticket-sales counter).

5. *Routing*. Choosing the preferred path for progressing from A to B (e.g., the traveling salesman seeks the best route for his sales journey) is a routing problem.

6. *Replacement*. This is concerned with items, such as electronic components, that must be replaced due to obsolescence or repeated failure.

7. *Search*. The continuing problem of management of resources is the detection of risk objects or conditions (e.g., police patrols to detect crime).

8. *Game Theory*. This involves situations of conflict or competition in which decisions of one decision maker are affected by decisions of other decision makers (e.g., business and management games to test marketing strategies).

When we are sufficiently convinced that we have a valid model within acceptable confidence limits, we can then transform the model into a computer model or computer program, for which programming techniques are available to effect the transformation. Once this task has been accomplished satisfactorily, the computer model is ready for manipulation on the computer or in an operator/computer mode.

The computer simulation is exercised by using a set of inputs that initiate model manipulation by the computer. Simulation inputs consist of system inputs and environmental inputs, which are frequently referred to as "endogenous" and "exogenous" inputs, respectively. These inputs may be based upon real-world data when they are available, or the inputs may consist of hypothetical values. In exercising the simulation, there are none of the constraints that must be considered when exercising a part of the real world.

In the exercise of the computer model, whatever data is germane to the problem and its solution is observed and recorded. The selection of which data to record is made on the basis of the results desired from the simulation.

Finally, simulation outputs are analyzed and evaluated, and the results are applied to effect a solution to the problem. Frequently, and this is not uncommon, many of the procedures have to be iterated before arriving at a feasible solution.

**Methodology.** An initial approach in the use of the computer simulation technique is to look at what others have done in similar situations. In the 1960s, much work was done in simulation by various industries, government agencies, universities, and other research organizations throughout the world. Most of the work has been documented and is available from various sources.

Even though every problem is unique, certain procedures are generally applicable to all problems that are amenable to solution by computer simulation. To espouse universal commonality on one hand, or to deny any commonality among problems on the other hand, would be oversimplification. Every problem cannot be forced to fit a single mold, but we can benefit from the commonalities that exist among all simulation problems.

As techniques and technologies change and are improved, the emphasis on specific procedures may also change, and breakthroughs may result in more efficient implementation of given procedures. However, certain general phases of simulation will not change basically, regardless of the technology. These phases—conceptualization, implementation, and results—are discussed below.

*Conceptualization.* In this phase the problem is defined, its scope determined, and appropriate resources are allocated to achieve a meaningful solution. The parameters, variables, and measures of effectiveness are determined, and the appropriate mathematical approximations to simulate the system are selected. The conceptual model is defined, the inputs and outputs are described, methods of experimentation are chosen, and the model is validated in order to determine the degree of confidence with which the model measures or describes what it is supposed to measure. This phase of model construction can be carried out with or without the aid of a digital computer.

*Implementation.* The conceptual model is transformed into a tangible computer simulation that is ready to generate simulation outputs. The manner of effecting this transformation is highly dependent upon, and affected by, the technology, both computer hardware and software. Thus, the specific procedures followed in model implementation depend upon the sophistication of computers, peripheral equipment, and programming or simulation languages applied. For example, the uses made of interactive or batch processing, plotting, visual displays, and the GPSS or Simscript simulation languages are all affected by the specific implementation procedures. Thus, model implementation is closely dependent on and related to state-of-the-art computer technology and software.

*Results.* Interpretation and evaluation of simulation outcomes and their subsequent application to problem solution can also be carried out with or without the aid of the digital computer.

This versatility of the simulation technique has made it a valuable tool in science, business, and other disciplines where problem solving has been often impossible in the past. Real-world models have brought into reality the seemingly fantastic imagery expressed in fictional projections of space travel, communication satellites, and hundreds of similar achievements in medicine, chemistry, and physics. The future of modeling and computer simulation using these models promises almost unlimited horizons.

### Reference

1968. Martin, F. F. *Computer Modeling and Simulation.* New York: John Wiley.

F. F. Martin

## MODEMS

For articles on related subjects *see* Acoustic Coupler; Data Communications; and Teleprocessing Systems.

Most existing common-carrier communication facilities have been designed for voice communication. To transmit digital signals over these channels, which pass frequencies between 300 and 3,000 Hz, the digital signal must be modulated at the transmitting end before it can be transmitted over the communication line. At the receiving end, it must be demodulated to convert it back to the original digital signal. Since communication must, in general, be in both directions, each end must include a *mod*ulator-*dem*odulator pair, or *modem*, as shown in Fig. 1. In addition to connecting computers or terminal equipment with communication circuits by performing the basic translation function between the digital signals of the terminals and the modulated voice frequency signals of the communication line, a modem also performs a number of control functions that coordinate data flow between the various terminals.

**Modem Types.** Modems, often referred to as "data sets," "data phones," "line adapters" or "subsets" (rare) can be classified according to their performance type:

1. Synchronous or asynchronous transmission.
2. Dedicated (leased) line or dial-up line.
3. Half- or full-duplex operation.
4. Long haul or short haul.

Some modems handle characters serially, while others handle an entire character in one bit time by receiving or transmitting the individual bits in parallel on several voice channels. Also, some modems, called "acoustic couplers," can be acoustically coup-

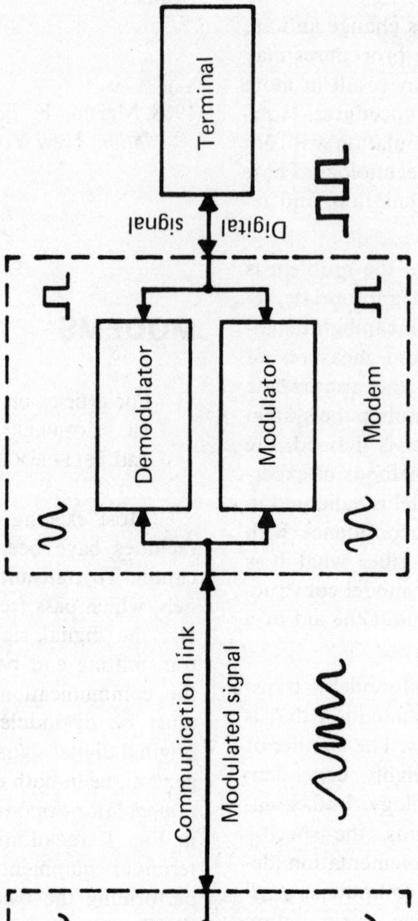

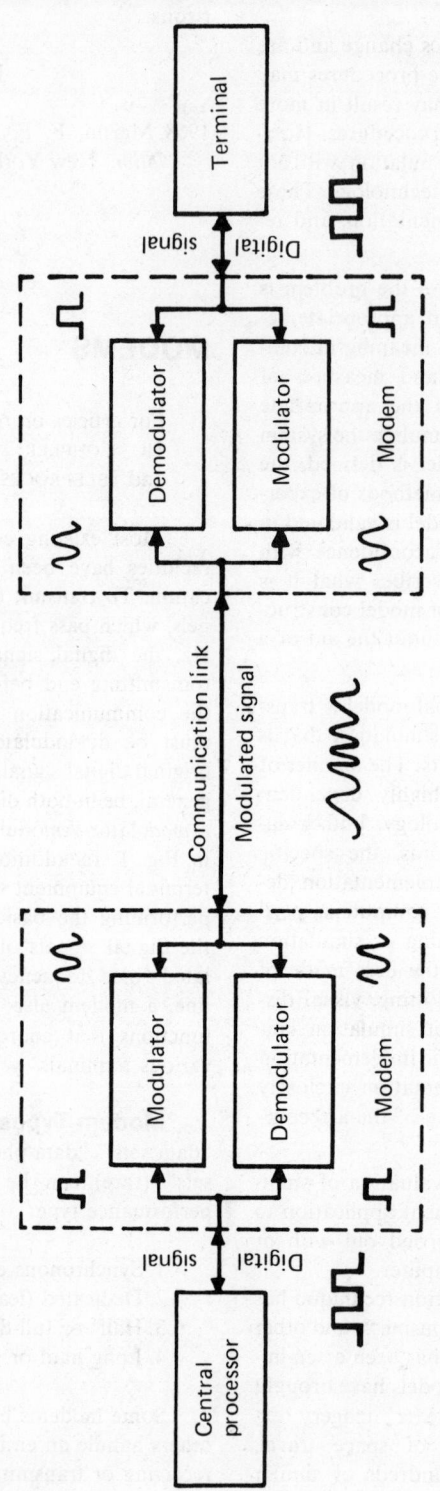


**Fig. 1.** A communication link using modems.

led to the telephone handset. However, since parallel modems and acoustic couplers are not so common, further comments will be limited to the modems that transmit and receive characters serially by bit and do not use acoustic coupling.

Synchronous transmission, in which the characters are transmitted at a fixed rate, with the transmitter and receiver synchronized, is usually used for high-speed transmission (above 2,000 bits/sec) between buffered terminals. Synchronization is achieved by using several special characters (SYNCH characters) at the beginning of each message. In asynchronous transmission, in which the time interval between characters can vary arbitrarily, synchronization is accomplished by adding start-and-stop bits to each character. For this reason it is mainly used for lower-speed (usually less than 2,400 bits/sec), unbuffered terminals such as keyboard devices. Synchronous transmission is more difficult to implement, but is more efficient because start-and-stop bits are not needed for each character. On the other hand, software to handle many asynchronous terminals is generally easier to implement than that for a similar number of synchronous terminals.

Modems designed to work on the switched network must usually have an auxiliary set (dialing unit) to allow dialing from the remote terminal, as shown in Fig. 2. Dial-up modems may be provided by the telephone companies or independent vendors, the latter usually providing equipment with a better cost/performance ratio and greater flexibility. However, in the latter case, it may be necessary to interface a data-access arrangement (DAA) between the modem and the switched network to provide protection to the switched network by limiting the modem's output signal level. Modems on leased lines do not usually require a DAA and have no dialing units. They are usually preferred because of the greater reliability and potentially higher transmission rates. In practice, the choice between leased lines and dial-up lines is usually determined by the amount of data to be transmitted and the relative costs of the two services.

Channels, and therefore modems, are also classified on the basis of simultaneity, the three basic types being simplex, half-duplex, and full duplex. Simplex refers strictly to unidirectional transmission, and consequently is rarely used. Full duplex refers to *simultaneous* transmission in both directions, while in half-duplex systems information may flow in both directions, but *not simultaneously*. Most modems built today are designed to work satisfactorily in any of the three modes, the choice being determined by the communication line and the terminal device.

Initially, most modems were long haul; i.e., they would function satisfactorily over unlimited distances, using the telephone company switched- or

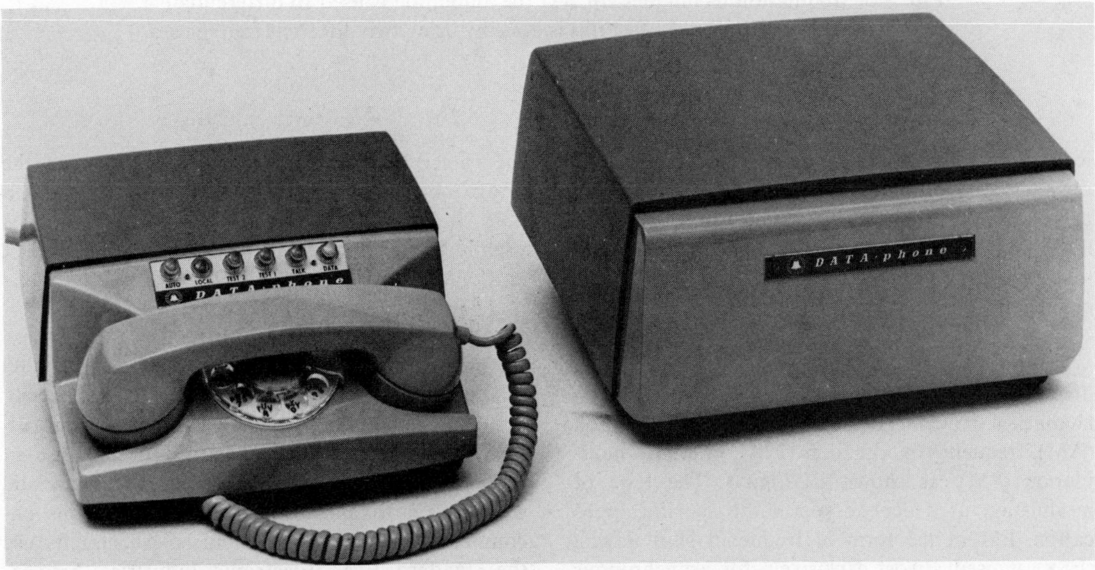


**Fig. 2.** A modem (data set) with auxiliary set for use on dial-up lines. Auxiliary sets are not required for use on private or leased lines. (reproduced with permission from American Telephone and Telegraph Company.)

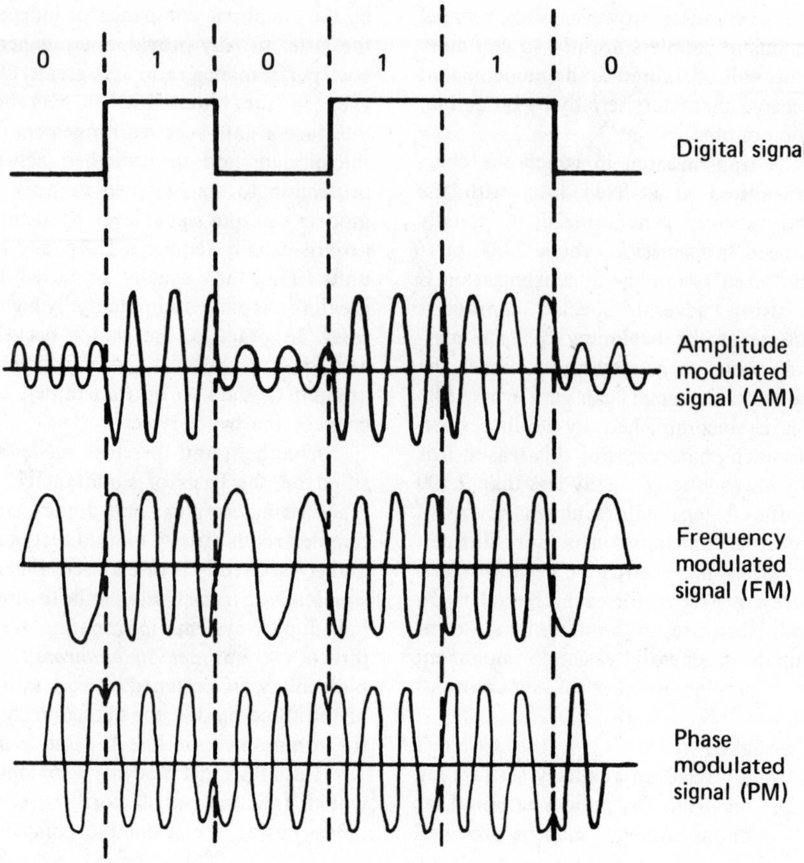


**Fig. 3.** Modulation techniques. In AM the amplitude is used to differentiate a "0" from a "1." In FM this is done by using two different frequencies, while PM uses a change in phase.

leased-line network. Today, one may obtain limited-distance or short-haul modems. These are specifically designed to work on short point-to-point leased lines, and offer substantial cost savings over their long-haul counterparts with similar performance characteristics.

**Modulation Techniques.** To modulate a digital signal for transmission over a communication channel, a modem may use amplitude modulation (AM), frequency modulation (FM), or phase modulation (PM), as shown in Fig. 3. The type of modulation used depends upon the specific application. FM in the form of frequency-shift keying (FSK) is used almost exclusively for asynchronous communication up to 1800 bits/sec. A form of PM is used for synchronous communication at 2,000 and 2,400 bits/sec. For the 4,800 to 9,600 bit/sec range, the choice is much wider, and depends upon the design objectives and the quality of channels available. In these cases the modulation technique is usually more complex, being some combination of AM, FM, and PM.

**Modern Modem Design.** On dial-up lines the current limits of reliable transmission are 4,800 bits/sec. On leased lines, the limit is 9,600 bits/sec, although special circuits for higher rates are available. Above 4,800 bits/sec, the modem must use an elaborate modulation technique and have automatic equalization to allow for the wide variations encountered in voice-band channels. All circuits use the standard EIA (Electronic Industries Association) Standard RS-232 specifications for the interface between the modem and terminal equipment. The higher the operating speed, the more self-testing arrangements are provided to aid in isolating causes of faulty operation.

With the rapid improvement in integrated circuit technology, modems will become smaller and cheaper. Reliability will be greatly increased and some will even have integrated error detection and correction capabilities.

REFERENCES

1970. O'Hare, R. A. "Modems and Multiplexers," *Modern Data*, Vol. 3, No. 12 (December), pp. 58–79.

1972. Davey, J. R. "Modems," *Proc. IEEE*, Vol. 60, No. 11 (November), pp. 1284–1292.

J. S. SOBOLEWSKI

# MODULAR PROGRAMMING

For article on related subject *see* STRUCTURED PROGRAMMING.
For article on related term *see* SUBROUTINE.

A program module can be defined as a logically self-contained and discrete part of a larger program. A complete program can thus be considered to be a collection of modules. A properly constructed module accepts input that is well defined as to content and structure, carries out a well-defined set of processing actions, and produces output that is well defined as to content and structure. A properly constructed module, as the term is normally used, has only one entry point and only one exit point. If it is a subroutine, it always returns only to the statement following the one that called it into play.

In many languages a subroutine is functionally equivalent to a module, although most languages permit violations of the guidelines just stated, such as allowing multiple entry and exit points.

The purpose of modular programming is to break a complex task into smaller and simpler subtasks, which, among other things, facilitates writing correct programs. A program consisting of modules of properly designed scope (typically a page or two of coding at most) is much simpler to design, write, and test than is the same program when it is not so modularized. Further, the interactions between parts of a program can be rigidly restricted to the interactions between modules, which greatly simplifies the understanding of how a program works.

All this, in turn, makes it much more likely that the program can be made to be correct in a reasonable time. Finally, realizing that all programs that are used over a period of time have to be maintained and modified, good modularization also aids in doing these chores more quickly and accurately.

Good program design starts with the most general definition of the function of the program, and proceeds through a sequence of increasingly detailed specifications. This technique, called "top-down," is an aspect of structured programming, and is greatly enhanced by modular programming.

D. D. MCCRACKEN

# MONTE CARLO METHOD

For articles on related subjects *see* RANDOM NUMBER GENERATION; and SIMULATION.

In applied mathematics, the name "Monte Carlo" is given to the method of solving problems by means of experiments with random numbers. This name (after the casino at Monaco) was first applied around 1944 to the method of solving deterministic problems by reformulating them in terms of a problem with random elements, which could then be solved by large-scale sampling. But, by extension, the term has come to mean any simulation problem that uses random numbers.

A classical example of what we would now call the Monte Carlo method is that of Buffon, who in 1733 pointed out that $\pi$ could be found experimentally by repeatedly throwing a needle onto a ruled surface, and counting the number of times the needle crossed a line (see Fig. 1). The idea is more remarkable for its sophistication in geometric probability than for its practicality—a more accurate Monte Carlo evaluation of $\pi$ could be done with a piece of string, a ruler, and the plates and saucers in your kitchen. But the idea of Monte Carlo had been conceived, although the difficulty of using physical devices for sampling and the lack of suitable statistical theory made it little more than a curiosity until the advent of large-scale computers.

The development and proliferation of computers was accompanied by widespread use of Monte

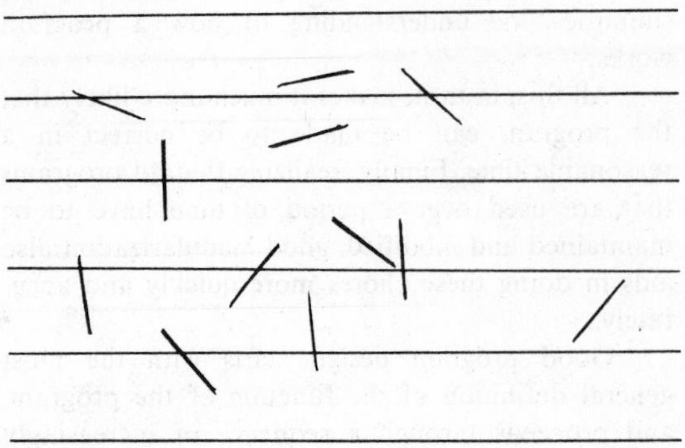

**Fig. 1.** Buffon's needle problem. If a needle of length $L - 1$ is dropped on a ruled surface that has parallel lines spaced one unit apart, the probability that the needle will cross a line is $2/(\pi L)$. If the needle is dropped $N$ times, the number of line crossings (say, $X$) should be about $2N/(\pi L)$, and hence $\pi = (2N)/(LX)$.

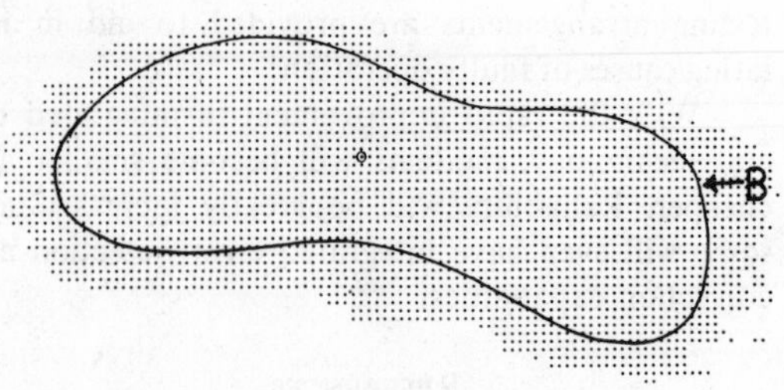


**Fig. 2.** Monte Carlo solution to a boundary problem. To find the value $u(x_0,y_0)$ of a function $u(x,y)$ which satisfies $\partial^2u/\partial x^2 + \partial^2u/\partial y^2 = 0$ for $(x,y)$ in the region enclosed by boundary $B$, and for which $u(x,y) = f(x,y)$ for points $(x,y)$ on the boundary $B$, start 1,000 random walks at $x_0y_0$ (center circle) so as to get 1,000 border crossing points. The average of $f(x,y)$ over the border crossing points is then approximately $u(x_0,y_0)$. The random walk moves from each point on the lattice to the four neighbors, with probability 1/4.

Carlo methods in virtually all branches of science, ranging from nuclear physics (where computer-aided Monte Carlo was first applied) to astrophysics, biology, engineering, medicine, and operations research. Note that the use of ther term has become so extensive that it now serves as an adjective (as in a Monte Carlo problem) as a noun (as in the previous sentence), and even as a verb (as in "Let's Monte Carlo it") meaning to get an idea of the answer to a complicated problem with random elements by having a computer run through the problem as many as thousands of times, using random numbers to assign values to the random or unpredictable parts of the problem.

The examples and nearly 500 references listed by Hammersley (1964) and Shreider (1966) give an idea of the variety of applications that have been reported. Since the time of those publications, the method has become even more widespread. Today the Monte Carlo method of solving complicated problems by using random numbers in a computer —either by direct simulation of physical or statistical problems or by reformulating deterministic problems in terms of ones involving random processes (e.g., partial differential equations or integral equations in terms of diffusion processes or random walks, multidimensional integrals as expected values of certain random events) has become one of the important tools of applied mathematics. An example of a Monte Carlo solution to a boundary value problem is in Fig. 2.

References

1964. Hammersley, J. M. and D. C. Handscomb. *Monte Carlo Methods*. London: Methuen.
1966. Shreider, Yu. A. (Ed.). *The Monte Carlo Method, The Method of Statistical Trials*. New York: Pergamon Press. (Translated from the Russian.)

G. Marsaglia

## MULTIPLEXING

For articles on related subjects *see* Communication Control Unit; Communications and Computers; Computer Networks; Data Communications: General Principles; Data Communication Networks; Modem; Packet Switching; and Time Sharing.

For articles on related terms *see* Bandwidth; and Terminals.

In general terms, the word "multiplexing" refers to the use of a single facility to handle simultaneously several similar but separate operations. Most computers, for example, have high-speed multiplexing input/output channels to handle many peripheral devices such as line printers or card readers, all of which may operate simultaneously. The main use of multiplexing, however, is in the field of data communication, where it is used for the transmission of several lower-speed data streams over a single higher-speed line. The primary motivation behind multiplexing is the reduction of costs, although in many cases an increase in reliability is an additional benefit.

Basically, there are two methods of multiplexing: frequency-division multiplexing (FDM) and time-division multiplexing (TDM). Before describing these further, it is appropriate to mention that the words "multiplexing" and "concentration" are sometimes used synonymously. *Concentration*, however, is a TDM method that uses a sharing technique in which statistics and queueing play an important role. This usually involves a small computer, and the word "concentrator" is therefore usually reserved for a small computer, programmed to perform the functions of a multiplexer.

**Frequency Division Multiplexing.** In FDM, a high bandwidth line is divided into several lower-frequency bands, with each band capable of carrying a channel of data. As an example, Fig. 1

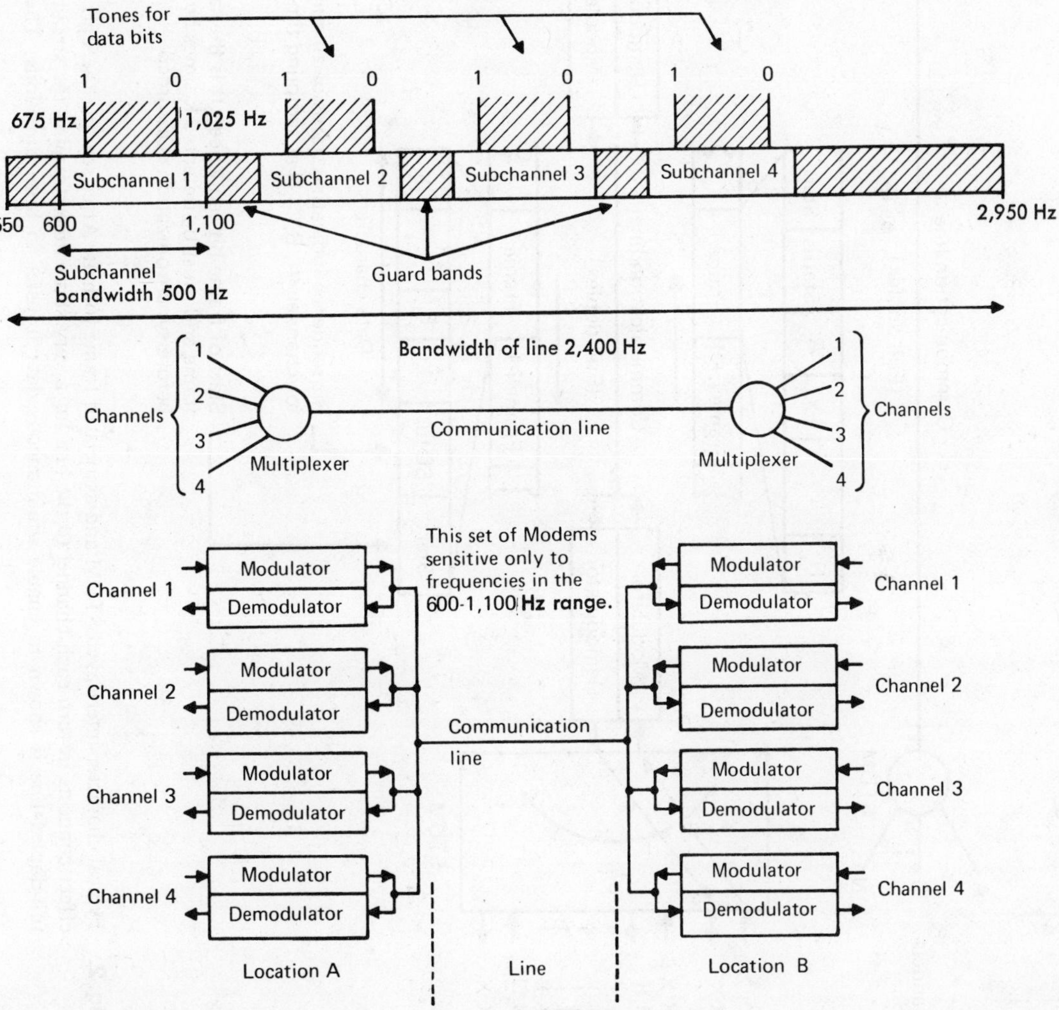


**Fig. 1.** Signaling-frequency assignments in a simple FDM system for digital data. The modulator-demodulator sets are sensitive only to the range of frequencies within a particular channel, and hence provide signal separation.

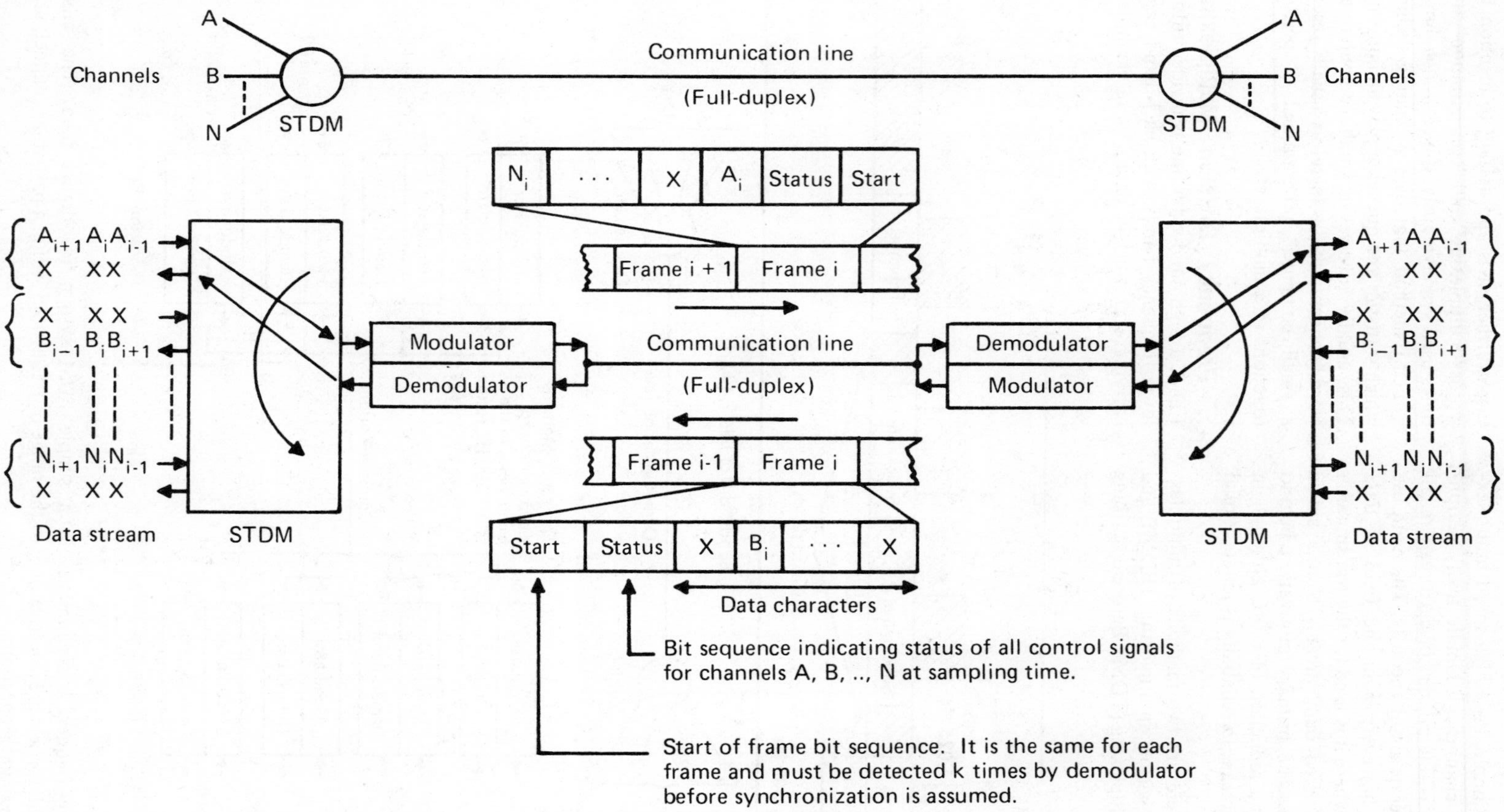


**Fig. 2.** Typical character-interleaved STDM and associated frame format. After sending the start and status bit sequences, the STDM in effect connects in turn each channel to the line for a very short time, forming the stream of data characters for each frame. A full-duplex line is shown to enable simultaneous data transfer in both directions. The X's represent an idle-line condition.

shows a voice-grade line with a bandwidth of 2,400 Hz split up into four sub channel bands of 500 Hz each. Each 500-Hz band is capable of carrying bidirectional data, using frequency shift keying. Thus, on the 600 to 1,100 Hz channel, "0" data bits may be transmitted at 675 Hz, and "1" data bits may be transmitted at 1,025 Hz. Other channels are split up in similar fashion, the matched pairs of modulators and demodulators with appropriate filters insuring channel separation. The guard bands, as illustrated, enhance the channel separation still further.

Fig. 1 illustrates how several low-speed terminals may send data concurrently on a single voice-grade line. This sharing reduces the connection costs per terminal. In similar fashion, several voice-grade lines could be multiplexed together to share a still higher bandwidth line, reducing the effective costs of each voice-grade line.

A familiar example of FDM is television broadcasting. Stations broadcast programs continuously at different frequencies, the atmosphere being the transmission medium. The tuning circuits in the television tuner select and separate one channel from all others.

**Time-Division Multiplexing.** In TDM, the time is divided up into small slots, and each time slot is used to perform a segment of the desired operation. In data communication, this operation may be the transmission of a portion of the signal. Perhaps a more familiar example of TDM is a time-sharing computer. Here, a large number of users access the computer simultaneously, and the operating system schedules the computer resources to each user for very short periods of time on a demand basis. This occurs so rapidly that users think that they have the computer to themselves.

The time slots may be allotted on a fixed, predetermined (a priori) basis or on a demand basis. The allotted time slices may be fixed in length or

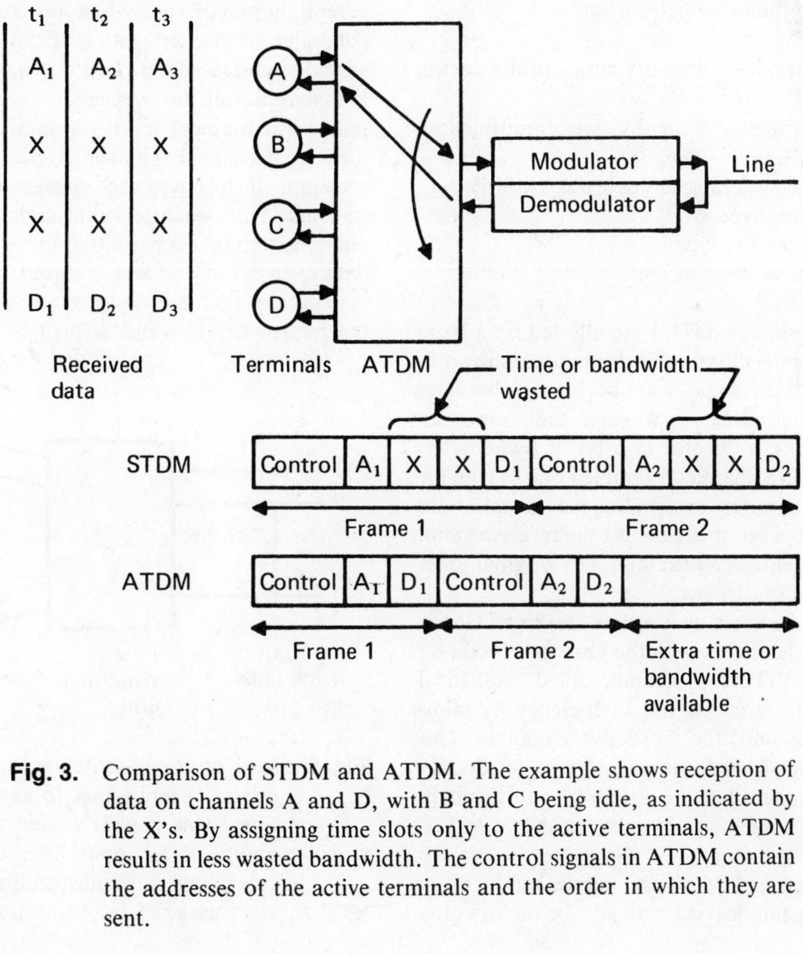


**Fig. 3.** Comparison of STDM and ATDM. The example shows reception of data on channels A and D, with B and C being idle, as indicated by the X's. By assigning time slots only to the active terminals, ATDM results in less wasted bandwidth. The control signals in ATDM contain the addresses of the active terminals and the order in which they are sent.

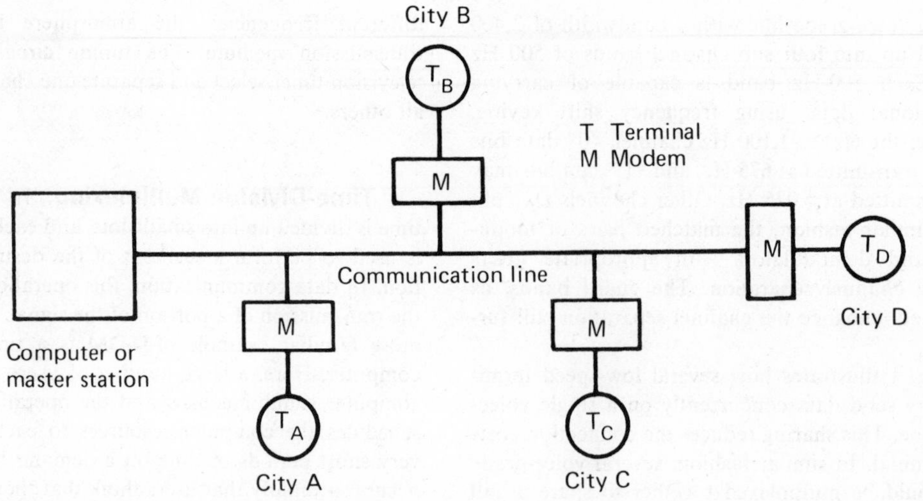


**Fig. 4.** Multiplexing by polling or by contention.

may be variable. TDM is therefore usually subdivided into the following categories:

1. Synchronous time-division multiplexing (STDM).
2. Asynchronous time-division multiplexing (ATDM).
3. Message-switching multiplexing (MSM):
   (a) Polling type.
   (b) Contention type.
   (c) Remote concentrator.

The time slots in STDM are allotted on a fixed basis, usually in a round-robin fashion, as shown in Fig. 2. The data stream may be bit or character interleaved, depending on whether each time slot within the frame is devoted to a bit or a character, respectively. Each channel is sampled one by one for one bit or character time, and the samples are assembled into a serial stream. At the receiving end, the stream is disassembled and the original data channels are reconstructed.

It should be noted that a time slot in STDM is allotted for a channel even in the absence of data on that channel. ATDM (sometimes called "statistical multiplexing") overcomes this inefficiency by allotting time slots only for the active channels. This requires a special header in each frame to identify the active channels, but the efficiency and throughput may be increased significantly, as shown in Fig. 3.

STDM and ATDM may be interleaved by bit or character. The interleaving may also be on an entire message basis. Fig. 4 shows one line connecting several terminals, party-line fashion, to a central computer or master station. Each terminal is assigned a unique address and the master station does the multiplexing by *polling* or by *contention.* In a polled environment, each terminal is addressed in turn to determine whether it has information to transmit. If it does, the master authorizes it to transmit. Thus, each terminal is polled in turn and only one terminal is permitted to transmit or receive data over the line at any one time. In a contention system, any terminal desiring to communicate with the master station waits until there is no traffic on

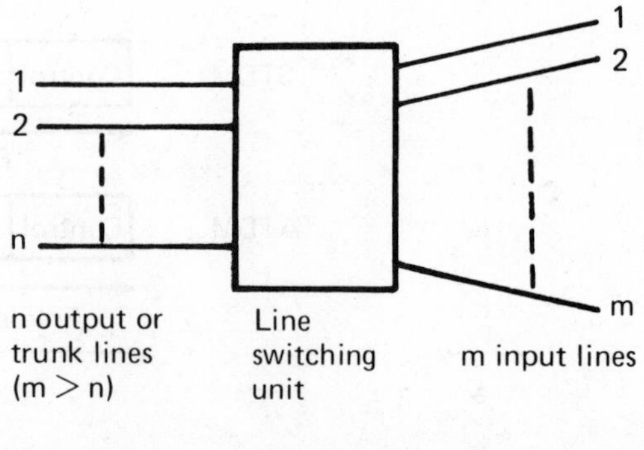


**Fig. 5.** Line or circuit-switching unit connects any one of *m* input lines to any one of *n* trunk lines. This is widely used where the probability of all input lines being used at a given time is small, resulting in more efficient usage of the trunk lines.

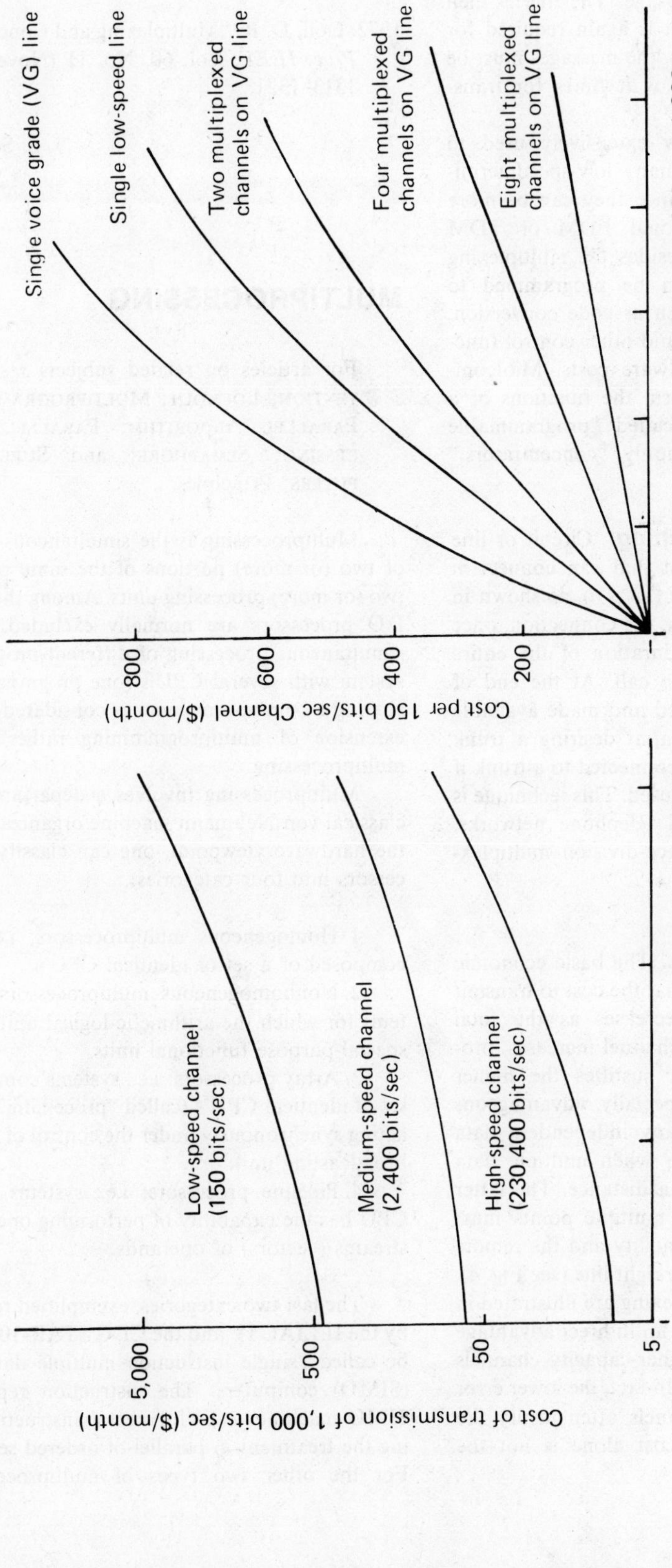


**Fig. 6.** Comparative costs showing economics of multiplexing (a) Cost of transmitting 1,000 bits/sec using low-, medium-, and high-speed channels. Note how costs decrease on higher-speed channels. (b) Reduction in costs for low-speed channels.

the line and then seizes the line for the length of time required to transmit the message. The line is then released until such time as it is again required for transmission. In such systems, the messages must be short, to avoid unduly long wait times for transmission by other terminals.

Minicomputers are now extensively used to multiplex or "concentrate" many low-speed terminals onto high-speed lines, since they can be more efficient than the conventional FDM or TDM techniques just described. Besides the multiplexing function, minicomputers can be programmed to perform additional tasks, such as code conversion, error detection, line polling, and other control functions, at no additional hardware costs. Minicomputers programmed to perform the functions of a multiplexer are sometimes called "programmable multiplexers" or, more commonly, "concentrators."

**Line or Circuit Switching.** Circuit or line switching refers to equipment that can connect $m$ inputs to $n$ output trunk lines ($m > n$), as shown in Fig. 5. In a typical application, the connection, once established, is held for the duration of the entire transmission of data or voice call. At the end of transmission, the trunk is freed and made available for assignment to the next input desiring a trunk connection. An input can be connected to a trunk if at least one trunk is not being used. This technique is mainly used in conventional telephone networks, and is sometimes called "space-division multiplexing."

**Uses of Multiplexing.** The basic economic advantage of multiplexing is that the cost to transmit a fixed amount of data decreases as the total capacity of the transmission channel increases, provided the amount of traffic justifies the higher capacity. Multiplexing is especially advantageous when there is a need for many independent data paths between two points, or when multiple data paths parallel each other for a distance. The latter includes the situation where multiple points must communicate with a central facility and the remote points are more or less on a straight line (see Fig. 4).

The economics of multiplexing are illustrated in Fig. 6. It should be noted that an indirect advantage of using multiplexing and higher-capacity channels is the reduction of error rates. In fact, the lower error rates on higher-capacity channels often justify the use of such facilities when cost alone is not the overriding factor.

References

1972. Doll, D. R. "Multiplexing and Concentration," *Proc. IEEE*, Vol. 60, No. 11 (November), pp. 1313–1321.

J. S. Sobolewski

## MULTIPROCESSING

For articles on related subjects *see* Contention; Lockout; Multiprogramming; Parallel Algorithm; Parallel Processing; Semaphore; and Supercomputers: Principles.

Multiprocessing is the simultaneous processing of two (or more) portions of the same program by two (or more) processing units. Among the latter, the I/O processors are normally excluded. Also, the simultaneous processing of different programs on a system with several CPU's (one program per CPU) sharing a common memory is considered here as an extension of multiprogramming rather than true multiprocessing.

Multiprocessing involves a departure from the classical von Neumann machine organization. From the hardware viewpoint, one can classify multiprocessors into four categories:

1. Homogeneous multiprocessors; i.e., systems composed of a set of identical CPU's.
2. Nonhomogeneous multiprocessors; i.e., systems for which the arithmetic-logical unit is a set of special-purpose functional units.
3. Array processors; i.e., systems composed of a set of identical CPU's (called "processing elements") acting synchronously under the control of a common broadcasting unit.
4. Pipeline processors; i.e., systems where the CPU has the capability of performing operations on streams (vectors) of operands.

The last two categories, exemplified respectively by the ILLIAC IV and the CDC STAR-100, can also be called "single instruction multiple data stream" (SIMD) computers. The instruction repertoire of SIMD machines calls for vector instructions allowing the treatment in parallel of ordered sets of data. For the other two types of multiprocessors, the

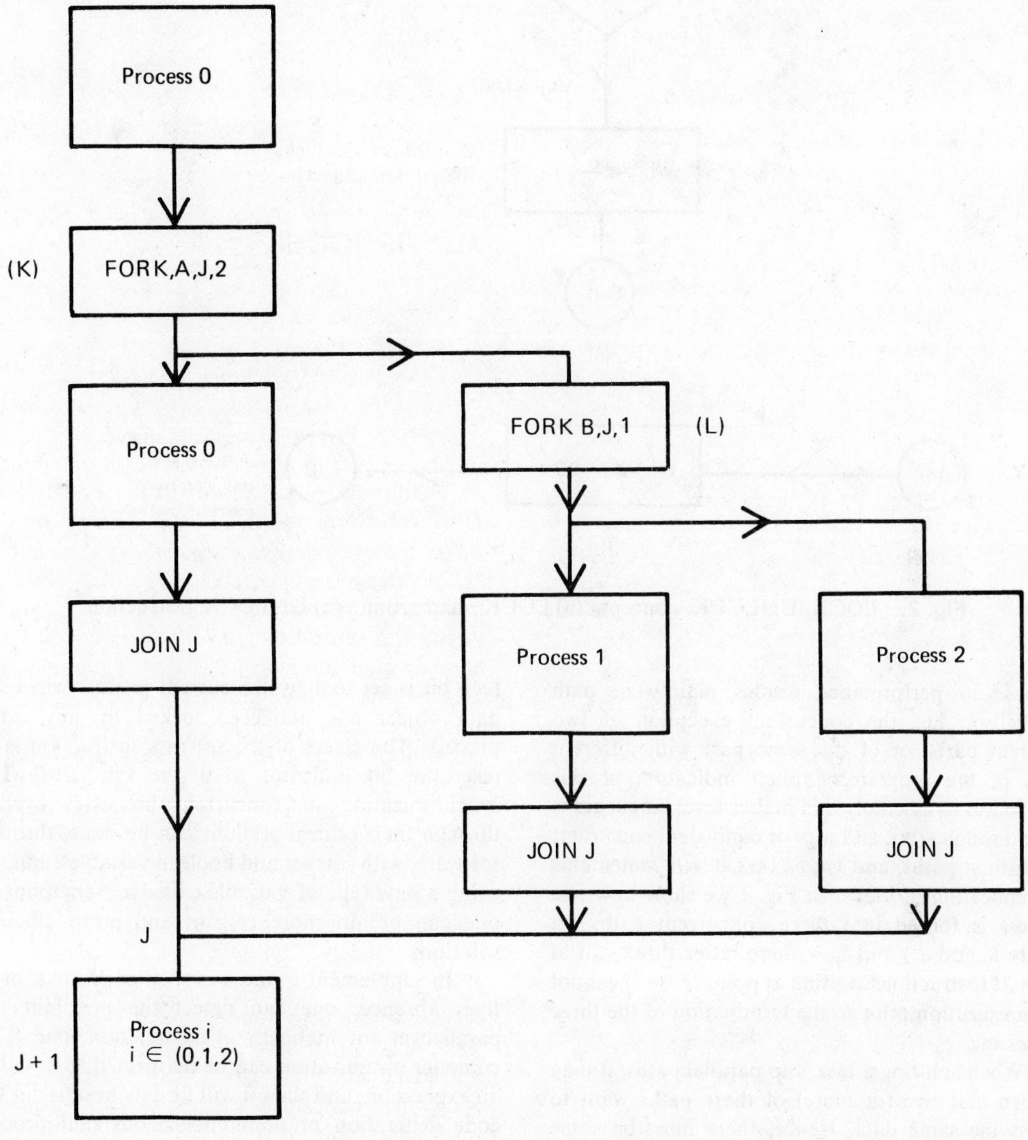


**Fig. 1.** FORK-JOIN concept. FORK A,J,N: (1) Initiate process at address A; (2) continue current process at next instruction; (3) increment counter at address J by N. JOIN J: (1) Decrement counter at address J; if zero, initiate processing at address J + 1, else (2) release the processor executing the JOIN.

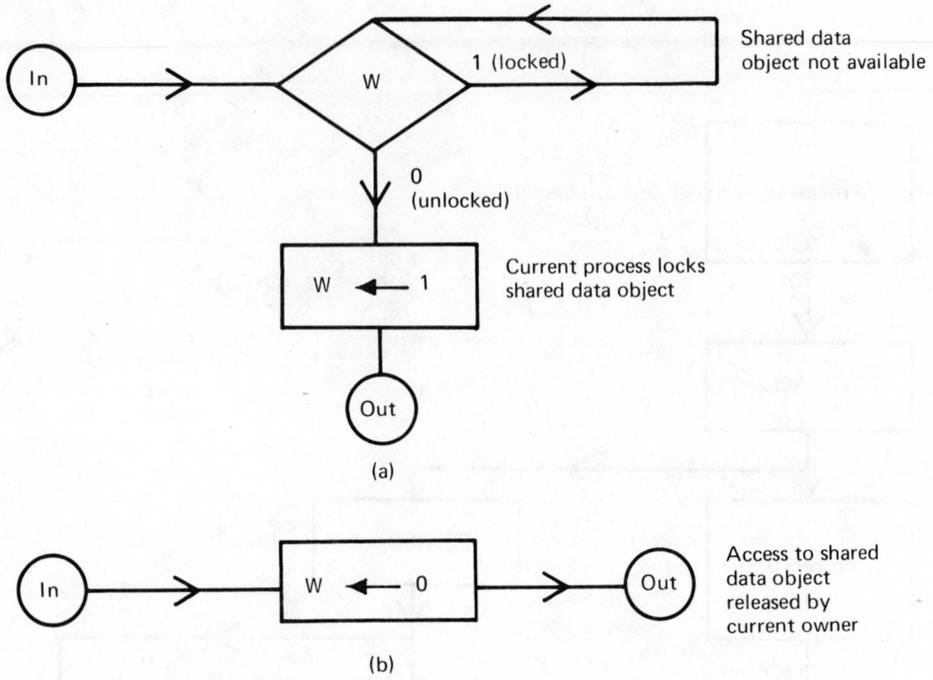


**Fig. 2.** LOCK/UNLOCK concept. (a) LOCK instruction; (b) UNLOCK instruction.

increase in performance resides mainly in path parallelism; i.e., the concurrent execution of two different parts, or of the same part with different data, of the program. Explicit indication of this parallelism in assembly and higher-level languages is done through FORK and JOIN or equivalent constructs for distinct paths, and via PARALLEL FOR statements for replication of loops. In Fig. 1 we show how one process is forked into three concurrent paths (at points $K$ and $L$) and how these latter three join at point $J$. Instructions starting at point $(J + 1)$ cannot begin execution prior to the termination of the three processes.

When splitting a task into parallel paths, it may happen that two (or more) of these paths want to access the same data. Hence, there must be some means of preventing unorderly changes in the shared data base. This has been referred to as the "lockout," or "mutual exclusion," problem. The portion of code (in a path) that accesses the shared data is called the "critical section" of that path.

One way to provide the necessary protection is by having instructions of the form TEST AND WAIT and SET or the equivalent pair LOCK/UNLOCK. A possible realization is to associate a one-bit lock indicator $w$ with each shared data object. The effect of the LOCK instruction is shown in Fig. 2(a). The lock bit is set to 1 by the current process when the data object has not been locked by any other process. The effect of the UNLOCK instruction is to reset the bit indicator to 0 [see Fig. 2(b)]. The synchronization of concurrent processes cycling through their critical sections can be done, through software, with integer and boolean variables; but, by using a new type of variable called a "semaphore," one can obtain more elegant and more efficient solutions.

In supplement to these explicit constructs, or in their absence, one can detect the possibility of parallelism automatically at compilation time. This compiler optimization can be performed first within an expression, and then it will find its best use in the code generation of nonhomogeneous multiprocessors such as the CDC 6600. Second, one can detect the independence of statements or blocks of code, as well as the possible replication of loops. In this case, the optimization is mainly directed toward programs running on homogeneous multiprocessors.

The presence of several CPU's adds a new dimension to the scheduling problem. In almost all cases, optimal schedules cannot be attained even with an a priori knowledge of the exact time requirements of each task. Models have been devised, analytical solutions have been investigated, and a number of heuristic methods have been proposed to assess the projected performance of multiprocessing systems.

REFERENCE

1973. Baer. J.-L. "A Survey of Some Theoretical Aspects of Multiprocessing," *Computing Surveys*, Vol. 5, No. 1 (March), pp. 31–80.

J.-L. BAER

## MULTIPROGRAMMING

For articles on related subjects *see* COMPUTER UTILITY; DATA SECURITY; INPUT-OUTPUT CONTROL SYSTEM; OPERATING SYSTEMS; PARALLEL PROCESSING; PROCESSING MODES; SCHEDULING ALGORITHM; and TIME SHARING.
For articles on related terms *see* CONTENTION; DEADLOCK; JOB; OVERHEAD; PRIVILEGED INSTRUCTION; and TASK.

Most modern computer systems can provide more resources than one typical program requires. By *multiprogramming*—i.e., overlapping and interleaving the executions of more than one program—an attempt is made to put all the resources of a modern computer system to work.

Early computer systems executed only one program (or *job*) at a time. It was quickly observed that certain jobs were *input/output* (I/O) *bound*; i.e., their rate of progress was limited by the speed of input/output units such as tape drives or card readers. Other jobs rarely used these I/O devices after they began calculating; these *central processing unit* (CPU) *bound* jobs performed mostly numerical calculations, with little input/output. Neither of these types of jobs fully utilized the power of the computer system. But it was found that if we can multiprogram, and thereby concurrently execute more than one job, better utilization of the available equipment could be realized.

In modern computing systems, many resources can be active simultaneously. For example, once a card reader has begun to read a card, the processor can execute instructions while data is being transferred into an area of memory that is being used as a *buffer*. If we have a single CPU, then it can perform work for many different jobs by switching from one to another while being devoted at any one moment to a particular *task*. Each program requires memory space to hold the data and instructions to be executed, and this memory cannot be simultaneously occupied by two different jobs. If sufficient memory and other resources exist, and can be allocated to many programs in a manner such that each makes effective progress, then we can consider using a multiprogrammed computer system.

Fig. 1 is an example of how two programs can be interleaved and overlapped by multiprogramming. The first program (shown in Fig. 1(a)) is heavily input/output-bound, and uses the CPU only 10% of the time. The second program, shown in Fig. 1(c), has the opposite nature, and would like to use the CPU 90% of the time. If these programs were executing alone, each would behave as shown in Figs. 1(a) and 1(c), respectively, but Fig. 1(b) shows how often the demands of the first program and those of the second conflict because each wants to use the same resource. Notice that this happens about 20% of the time. We could have calculated this number by realizing that the program in Fig. 1(a) would like to use the CPU 10% of the time, but that the program in Fig. 1(c) probably wants to do the same. Conversely, the program in Fig. 1(c) wants to do some input/output about 10% of the time, when it is very likely that the program in Fig. 1(a) does also. Thus, we estimate that for 20% of the time there is a conflict for resources, while for 80% of the time the programs might be able to overlap by using different resources [Fig. 1(d)].

Fig. 1(d) shows one way in which we can multiprogram these two programs. The following rules are used to determine which program will be active and which resource it can use: Whenever both programs request the use of the same resource, the CPU-bound program is allowed to proceed, and the I/O-bound program must wait, subject to the restriction that once an input/output operation is begun, it cannot be stopped and must be finished. (These decision rules are shown only as an example and are not necessarily the "best" rules to use for the types of jobs shown.) We see that, in the 50 units of time displayed, either the CPU or an I/O device is in use for 71 units. Since together we have resources for 100 units of work (50 from the CPU and 50 of I/O), we are achieving 71% *utilization* of the system. Separately, the program in Fig. 1(a) or Fig. 1(c) would use only 50% of the available resources, so we have improved utilization of the system by about 40%. We could not expect utilization to go much beyond 90% (excepting some unusually favorable

## MULTIPROGRAMMING

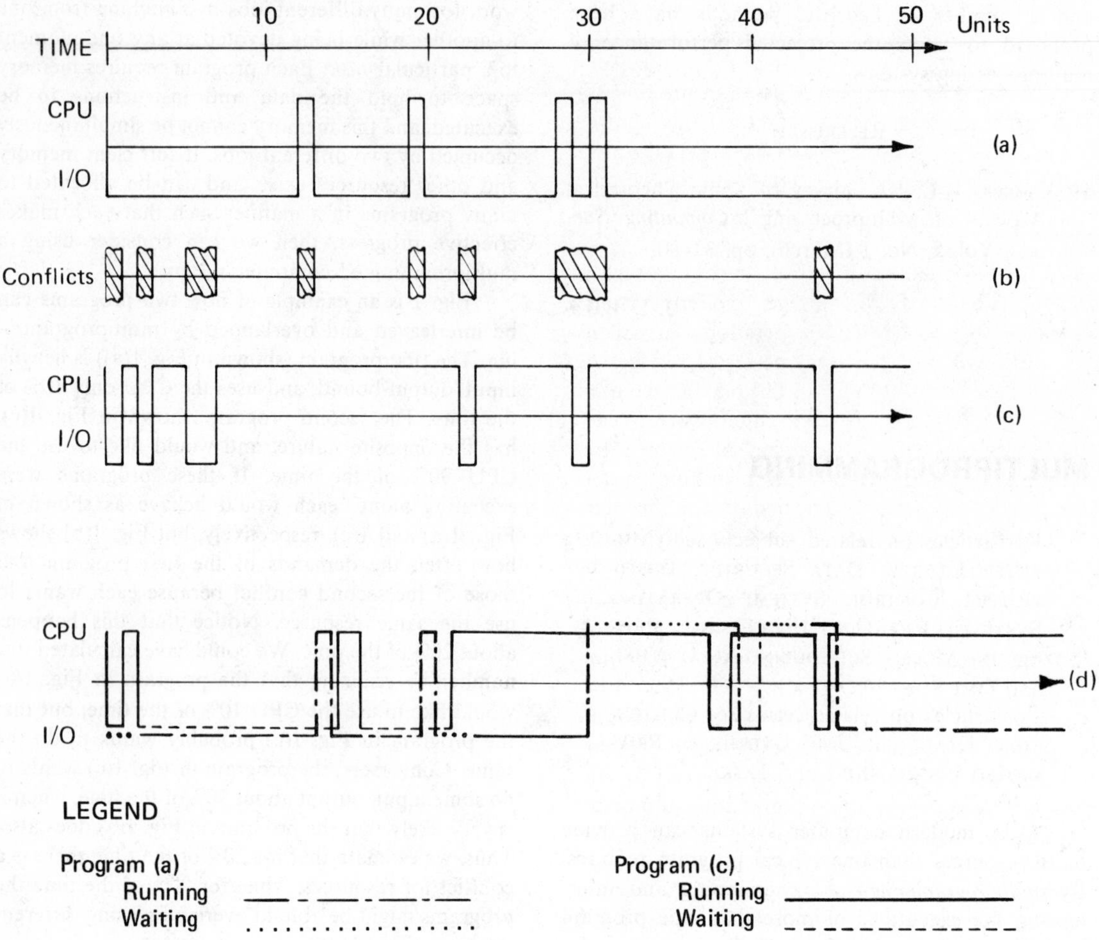


**Fig. 1.** An example of the advantages of multiprogramming. The area of overlap between the I/O-bound program (a) and CPU-bound program (c) is shown in (b). In (d) one way of multiprogramming these two programs is shown.

circumstances), since we calculated that for 80% of the time both resources could be in use, and that for 20% of the time only one resource is busy while one program waits for the other.

Multiprogramming does not require a large operating system in order to coordinate the demands of each program. On a small computer, such as is used for process control, it is common to provide a *background/foreground* system that permits two programs to execute. The foreground, or real-time program, may consist of a job to periodically monitor a number of instruments and perform some corrective adjustment. In between each measurement, the system may have sufficient resources to permit a background program to execute, doing compilations or calculations. These two programs might cooperate by mutual understanding; i.e., the programmers could insure that each would not interfere with the use of the system by the other.

While in very simple situations it may be feasible to multiprogram cooperatively, often we must be sure that, if one program somehow violates the rules of the system, it does not corrupt the whole environment. Thus, most multiprogramming systems require a *monitor* (also called an "executive" or "supervisor").

It is the responsibility of the monitor to maintain the integrity of the system. In the case of the background/foreground system used as an example previously, we would like the monitor to guarantee that the foreground real-time program will be able to take its measurements, even if the background program goes into a loop and never voluntarily relinquishes control. Thus, our computer system must have the capability to preempt a resource (such as the CPU) from a program and to insure that the foreground program or the monitor gains control. The monitor must be *protected* from accidental or malicious destruction by a program (which we refer to as a *user* program, in contrast to the supervisor itself).

In order to control effectively resources such as space for data or file storage, modern systems centralize all input/output operations in an *input/output control system* that performs services on behalf of the user programs. In this manner the users of the multiprogrammed system cannot corrupt each other's data or invade the privacy of secure information. The multiprogrammed operating system may provide accounting information for the management of the computer system, and this information should not be destroyed by a user program.

To permit the construction of a monitor with these capabilities, computer systems generally possess a *privileged* class of instruction that user programs cannot execute. For example, all input/output instructions, or those instructions associated with the protection of one area of memory from a program executing in a different area, are reserved for the monitor. When the computer is executing in monitor (or *master*) mode, these functions are permitted. The monitor has the responsibility of insuring that when control is given to a user program, the system is switched to user (or *slave*) mode. In slave mode, any attempt to execute privileged instructions will give control back to the monitor without permitting any violations of resource control.

In addition to the monitoring function, the executive of a multiprogrammed operating system must perform a *scheduling* function. If too many jobs are begun, they can interfere with each other and waste resources. In fact, it is even possible to cause a *deadlock* to occur when a number of programs have begun but cannot continue until additional resources are available, and yet those resources are tied up by other jobs. The algorithm used for scheduling must have enough information to avoid such situations, or should possess the means to "untangle" them if they occur.

Scheduling in a multiprogrammed environment is often complex. The concept of multiprogramming entails the *global* optimization of the resources of the entire system. However, each user generally is concerned with his own task, and attempts to optimize *locally*; i.e., he tries to make his program perform better or faster, without regard to the total environment.

Consequently, it is common to find the ultimate scheduling performed external to the system itself, either by administrative decisions concerning the categories (or *classes*) of jobs that are permitted at certain times of day, or by the operator of the system. The operator may be able to start or suspend programs from an operator's console based on the performance of the system. Meanwhile, the scheduler program of the multiprogrammed operating system performs the microscopic decisions such as initiating input/output operations or deciding which program is to be given the resources of the central processor.

One common form of scheduling is provided by a *priority* assigned to each job or task within the system. The actual value of the priority may be based on external factors such as the fact that the results are needed quickly (or the converse), or it may be based on the overall resource requirements of the job when submitted to the computer system. This priority may change dynamically as the program evolves, or it may increase as time progresses if the job is not making effective progress. It may also be changed by an operator from a console. The detailed nature of scheduling depends heavily on the nature of the service the system is expected to provide.

Multiprogramming of modern computer systems can be done in a variety of fashions. Some systems, such as the IBM System/360 Operating System Multiprogramming a Fixed Number of Tasks (OS/MFT) allocate certain resources in a static fashion. Memory is divided into *partitions* of fixed sizes, and each job submitted to the system must specify which partition is to be used. Other systems, such as OS/MVT (the IBM System/360 Operating System with a Variable number of Tasks), distribute the memory space according to the request of the user. This additional flexibility requires extra complexity and possibly extra *overhead*, but may be critical in the effective use of a system where many users submit programs of widely differing sizes.

Fig. 2 is a highly schematic representation of the partitioning of memory in a simple multiprogrammed system, and illustrates some of the information that the monitor uses in controlling and scheduling jobs. In this example, memory has been split into five major areas [Fig.2(a)]. The partitions P1, P2, and P3 are for the execution of user-written programs or system-provided programs such as language translators. The monitor program itself occupies another area, and provides job supervision,

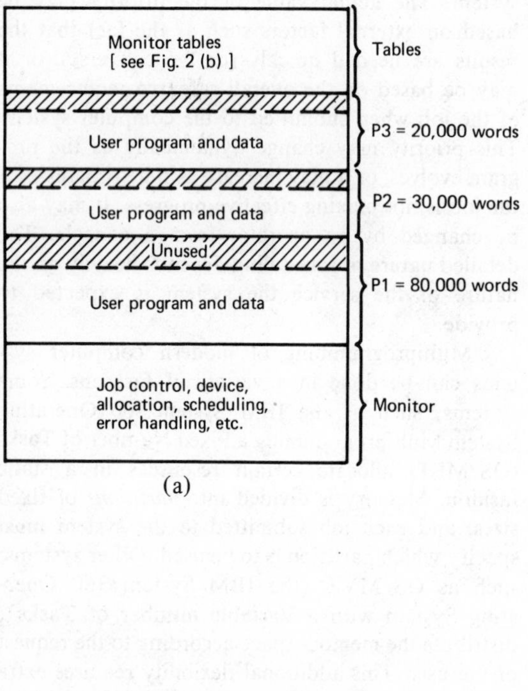


(a)

①

| Input Queue | | | | |
|---|---|---|---|---|
| Job number | 201 | 203 | 205 | 206 |
| Job name | LOUIS | ANNE | DAVID | FRAN |
| Priority | 10 | 8 | 10 | 15 |
| Memory request | 12,000 | 70,000 | 15,000 | 3,000 |
| Device needs | 2 tapes, printer | 3 tapes | Card-reader, 1 tape | Console |

| Waiting Jobs (by partition) | |
|---|---|
| *Partition Number* | *Input Queue Number* |
| 1 | 201,205,206 |
| 2 | none |
| 3 | 203 |

| Device Requests of Waiting Jobs | | |
|---|---|---|
| *Device Type* | *Input Queue No.* | *Quantity* |
| Reader | 205 | 1 |
| Punch | none | |
| Printer | 201 | 1 |
| Tape | 201 | 2 |
| | 203 | 3 |
| | 205 | 1 |
| Console | 206 | 1 |

②

| Jobs in Progress | | | |
|---|---|---|---|
| Partition no. | 1 | 2 | 3 |
| Job number: | 200 | 202 | 204 |
| Job name: | FRED | JOHN | MARY |
| Priority: | 6 | 8 | 15 |
| Memory req' std | 60,000 | 25,000 | 18,000 |
| Devices assigned | Tape 1, tape 3 | Card-reader, printer | Console 1 |
| Status | Executing | Awaiting card input | Awaiting console input |

| Device Assignment Table | | |
|---|---|---|
| *Name* | *To Whom* | *Status* |
| Cardreader | JOHN | Input in progress |
| Cardpunch | Free | |
| Printer | JOHN | Free |
| Tape 1 | FRED | Rewinding |
| Tape 2 | Free | |
| Tape 3 | FRED | Reading |
| Console 1 | MARY | Input in progress |
| Console 2 | Free | |
| Console 3 | Free | |

(b)

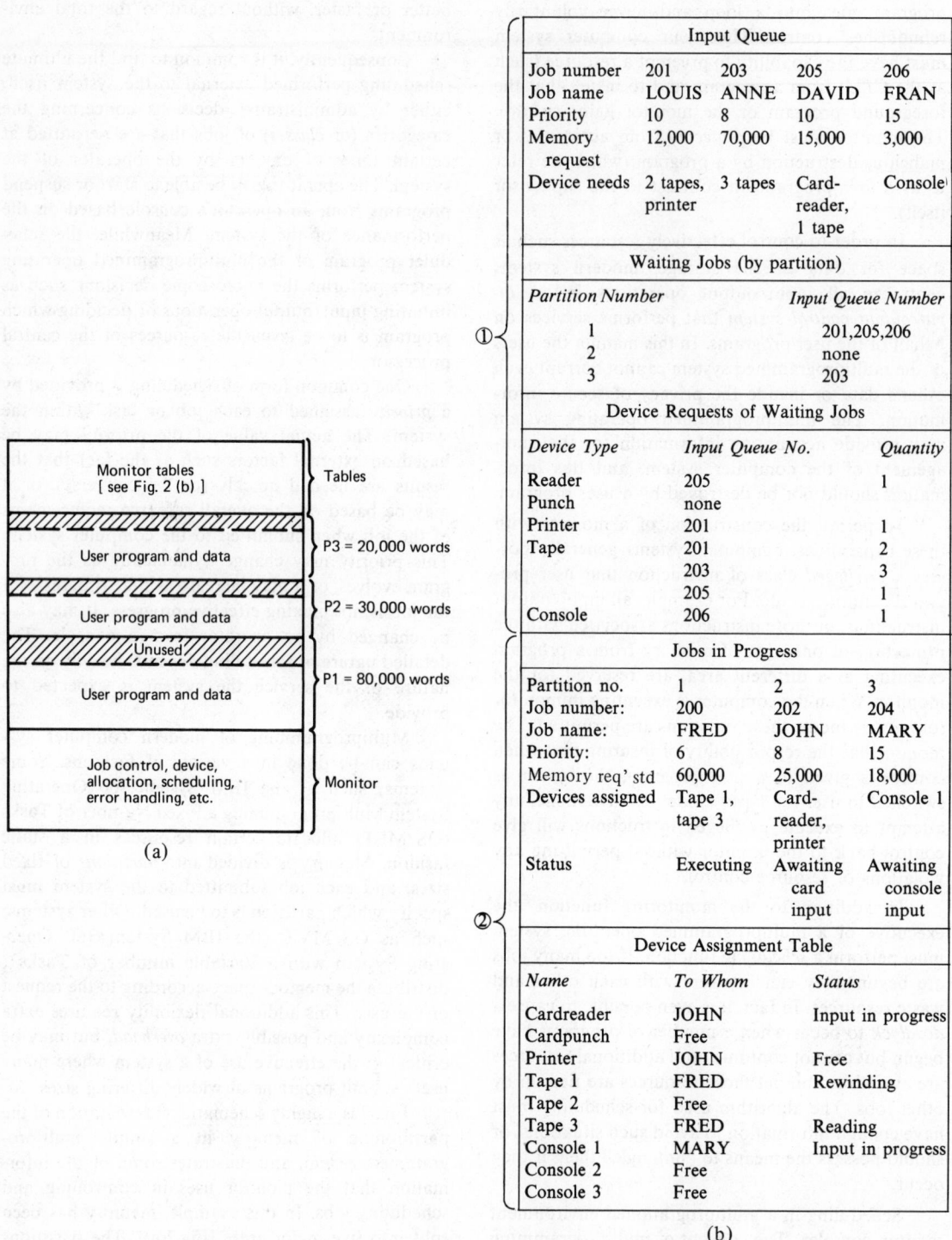

**Fig. 2.** Schematic representation of the partitioning of memory in a multiprogrammed system. (a) Memory layout. (b) Samples of monitor tables: Group 1 represents the information concerning future jobs; Group 2 represents the information concerning present jobs.

resource scheduling, allocation of memory and input/output devices, and other services for user programs. Finally, space is reserved for a large variety of tables used by the monitor in carrying out its tasks. Within these tables are all the critical data regarding the status of the system and of additional requests that will have to be handled. Fig. 2b shows only a small fraction of the actual information that a real multiprogrammed monitor would use to make its decisions.

The tables fall into two classes, those containing information about the present jobs being executed, and tables relating to jobs that have been submitted for execution, but are not yet being multiprogrammed. We can locate information about each partition (such as the job name), or we can determine the status of an input/output device (such as to whom it has been assigned). In order to determine which job should be entered into the multiprogrammed *mix* next, we can see which jobs are awaiting a particular partition or are waiting for some input/output device to be available. Notice that many pieces of information are repeated in different tables in order to locate rapidly the relevant jobs whenever any significant change takes place.

Multiprogramming may also take place within a single job. For example, the system may be able to overlap the computational needs of a single program with its input/output needs. In IBM's OS/MVT, a program may spawn (or create) additional tasks that are to be multiprogrammed as if they were jobs, but which possess a filial relationship to the mother task. Each of these tasks may have differing requirements for resources, and may cause concurrent utilization of system facilties.

Multiprogramming is accepted as the standard means of utilizing all but the smallest of today's computer systems. A computer utility that provides service to many users who may be sitting at remote consoles, communicating with an executing program in an interactive fashion, can serve many individuals while others are thinking or responding.

A *time-sharing* system attempts to provide rapid response to the interactive requests of users at consoles; a *multiprogrammed* system may be required in order to provide time-sharing facilities, but multiprogramming connotes, in itself a concern with resource utilization and not with rapid response time. The advantages offered by multiprogramming are now filtering down to even very small systems, and may be found on a large number of computers that until recently were used in a dedicated, one-user environment.

### References

1972. Lorin, H. *Parallelism in Hardware and Software: Real and Apparent Concurrency.* Englewood Cliffs, N.J.: Prentice-Hall.

1973. Katzan, H., Jr. *Operating Systems: A Pragmatic Approach.* New York: Van Nostrand-Reinhold.

H. J. Saal

# N

## NETWORKS. *See* ARPA NETWORK; and COMPUTER NETWORKS.

## NETWORKS FOR INSTRUCTION

For articles on related subjects *see* COMPUTER ASSISTED INSTRUCTION (CAI); COMPUTER ASSISTED LEARNING AND TEACHING; and COMPUTER NETWORKS.

The future for instructional use of computers depends to a large extent on the distribution of effective learning materials through networks. For example, a "star" network (central computer serving widely distributed users) extends the audience for programs and materials developed by the instructional computing staff at a central location. A "distributed" network (different kinds of computers connected so that the special capabilities of all are available to a user of any one) maximizes utilization of those computing resources that are available to education. A nationwide communication network will encourage the application of quality standards to computer-related materials.

Obstructions to expanded use of computers in the instructional process have been encountered, such as high cost and the lack of a definite theory of instruction in computer-assisted learning and teaching. One means of working around these obstructions is through networks that deliver material directly from the originating site to a large number of users.

Economic and academic incentives for development and validation of computer-based learning materials will be derived when a large number of users find access convenient. Authors whose programmed material has passed a critical review procedure should receive credit, as they do for traditional publications. Furthermore, authors or sponsoring organizations should receive some return on financial investments, probably in proportion to the amount of material made available through the network. The distribution may be via digital cassette tape or other portable medium that can be read by the computers at many user sites. Long-distance communications may be used to connect a user anywhere in the country with the most current version of a program at the originating site or a central library.

The PLATO project at the University of Illinois in Urbana has established a centralized system, distributing some training and author assistance as well as finished programs through the communications network. Materials developed at one location in the country are stored centrally and are immediately available (with permission of the author) to any other location. Groups of users of the PLATO system exchange information among themselves, using the system for communication and storage.

CONDUIT is a consortium of regional computing services. Each regional center has agreed to give special attention to sharing instruction-related computer programs and associated materials with other regional services in the group. A variety of means have been explored for transporting materials successfully from the site of the originator to the site of the user, such as personal visits, workshops, video tapes of the originator, and detailed user guides. The North Carolina Educational Computing Service makes good use of circuit riders, who maintain communication not only in the sense of a "star" network from central site to users and back, but also in the important connections among users throughout the state.

EDUCOM (the Inter-university Communications Council with headquarters in Princeton, N.J.) has been giving careful attention to networks in higher education for some time. Helpful publications include the report of a summer conference in 1966, selected reports of the fall and spring meetings, and the report of three symposia on a national science network.

The idea of a collection of networks serving as an information utility is very attractive at a time when demands on institutions are increasing and financial resources are held steady or decreasing.

### Reference

1974. Greenberger, Martin, Julius Aronofsky, James L. McKinney, and William F. Massey (Eds.). *Networks for Research and Education.* Cambridge, Mass: M.I.T. Press.

K. L. Zinn

## NINETY-COLUMN CARD

For articles on related subjects *see* Hollerith, Herman; IBM Card; and Manufacturers, Computer.

Today the familiar rectangular-hole, 80-column "IBM card" has no serious competition as the international standard for data processing punched cards. Until about 1960, however, the IBM card had significant competition from cards of the same size, which were punched with round holes and contained 90 columns of information, known as the Powers or "RemRand" cards (Fig. 1).

This is the background. Until about 1909, Herman Hollerith (whose firm evolved to become IBM) enjoyed a monopoly on punched cards as a result of his patents. He charged the Census Bureau for processing on a per-card basis (65¢ per 1,000 cards tabulated). Although he gradually introduced technological improvements, such as automatic card feed, which reduced the processing costs, he did not correspondingly lower his prices. Because the Census Bureau objected to what it viewed as monopolistic overpricing, it sponsored the development of a competitive system. John Powers, an imaginative and competent mechanical engineer, became head of this effort. He managed to get patent rights on the inventions involved in a new system which successfully skirted Hollerith's patents by using sophisticated mechanical linkages to substitute for many of Hollerith's electrical techniques. After the new system was well started, Powers left the bureau to manufacture and sell these systems. In 1927 the Powers Accounting Machine Company, the Remington Typewriter Company, and Rand Cardex merged to form Remington Rand, a well-capitalized and serious competitor to IBM.

The Powers/RemRand system offered many technological innovations. It provided positive "die set" punching with the possibility of visual verification of the entire card entry before all holes were punched simultaneously (initially by depressing a foot treadle; later by an electrically driven punch). It was the first system to offer card punches with automatic card feed, the first to offer a printing tabulator, the first to offer a multiplying punch, the first to link a typewriter and a card punch, and the first with many other important innovations in punched card processing.

There is a direct line of evolution from the punched cards used by Hollerith in the 1890 census to the modern IBM card. In the early 1900s, Hollerith cards used round holes in a 45-column card of the same size as the modern card. There were 12 punch positions in each column. The Powers/RemRand cards initially used this standard.

The two systems diverged in the late 1920s and early 1930s. In 1924–1925, the Powers system introduced its first alphanumeric punch and tabulator along with a technique for doubling the amount of information in each card. The 12 rows were split into two 6-row banks, in effect giving two 45-column half-cards stacked one above the other (a 90-column card). A six-bit code requiring multiple punches per column was introduced, since there were only six punching positions to represent a digit or number. In 1929–1931, when IBM moved to meet the competition, it adopted an entirely different approach and standard. It adopted a 12-row code, the Hollerith code, which always used a single punch in a column

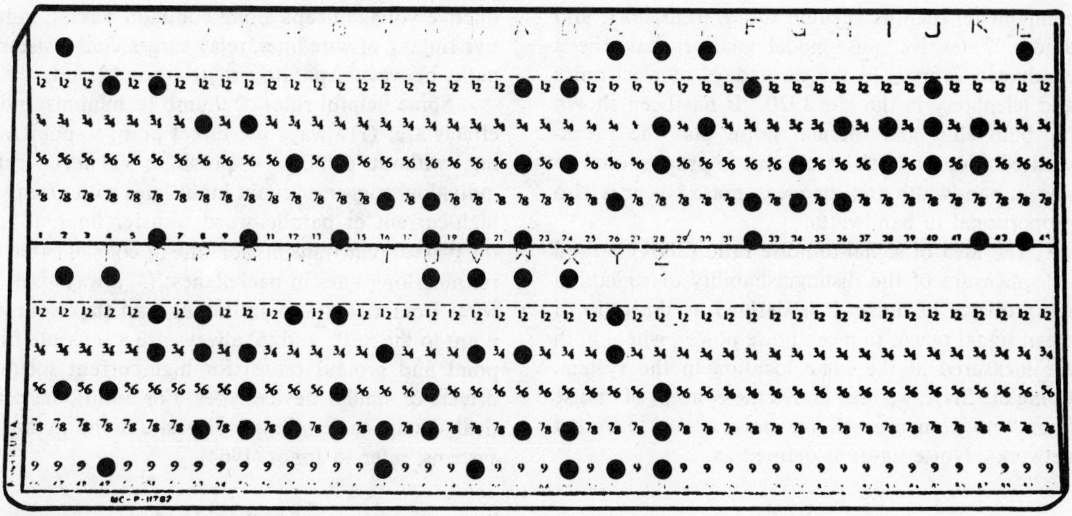

**Fig. 1.** The 90-column punched card.

to represent a number, and two punches to represent a letter. It got more columns onto the card by a very different technique. It changed from round holes to narrow, rectangular holes, which permitted 80 columns to be squeezed into a card of the same size.

Twice the Powers/RemRand system had major opportunities to take over as the predominant system. In the 1930s it might have become the *de facto* U.S. Government standard if its equipment had won the competition for mechanization of the social security system. Again, in the 1950s, it had a unique opportunity when its parent firm, Remington Rand, seemed to have an almost insurmountable lead in the evolving technology of computers. Though IBM was then preeminent in punched cards, it seemed possible that the RemRand UNIVAC computers would be able to drag the RemRand corporate standard (90-column) punched card along with them into data processing predominance. However, in both cases, RemRand failed to grasp its opportunity, and today the 90-column, round-hole punched card has all but disappeared.

### References

1933. Comrie, L. J. *The Hollerith and Powers Tabulating Machines*. Printed for private circulation, London. (Available at Library of Congress)

1965. Truesdell, Leon E. *The Development of Punch Card Tabulation in the Bureau of the Census, 1890–1940*. U.S. Dept of Commerce (U.S. Government Printing Office).

W. F. Luebbert

## NOISE

For articles on related subjects *see* Data Communications; and Reliability and Fault Tolerance.

One fundamental limitation of information transmission in communication systems is the presence of noise. By "noise" is meant any spurious or undesired disturbance that tends to obscure or mask the signal to be transmitted.

One can distinguish between different types of noise produced by fundamentally different means: man-made, erratic disturbances, and spontaneous fluctuations. The primary difference between the erratic and spontaneous types is that the former is not continuously present whereas the latter is.

Two basic types of spontaneous fluctuations are present in electric circuits. One is the so-called shot effect due to the random emission of electrons; the other type of spontaneous fluctuation is that due to thermal interaction between the free electrons and vibrating ions in a conduction medium.

If the noise spectrum is flat at all frequencies, noise possessing such a flat spectrum is called "white noise." This term is derived from optics, since white includes all colors or frequencies. Unlike shot noise, thermal noise is an illustration of white noise, since it has been shown that the thermal noise spectrum is uniform up to extremely high frequencies on the order of $10^{13}$ Hz.

Equivalent noise circuits have been modeled for the thermal and shot noise effects for various components such as vacuum tubes, transistors, and diodes. Extensive noise-model analyses have been conducted ever since the early days of electronics and telephony in the late 1920s. It has been shown for both shot and thermal noise that the mean-squared noise voltage or current is proportional to system bandwidth and the mean noise power is also proportional to bandwidth.

The idea of signal-to-noise ratio (SNR) is used as a measure of the distinguishability of signals in the presence of noise. It is defined as the ratio of mean signal power to mean noise power, where both are measured at the same location in the system. Using the SNR, we may derive the concept of "noise figure" to compare relative noisiness of different networks. Noise figure is defined as

$$F = \frac{S_s/N_s}{S_0/N_0}$$

where $S_s/N_s$ is the SNR at the system input (source) and $S_0/N_0$ is the SNR at the system output. An ideal network will have $F = 1$, since this corresponds to the case where the system itself contributes no additional noise.

With reference to digital system design, the term "noise" can be considered as any unwanted signal that produces an unwanted result. In practical design terms, there are three sources of noise: (1) high-frequency effects within the circuitry and associated wiring, (2) extraneous pulses that may be caused by circuit interaction or "time races" within the logical system, and (3) sources outside the system.

Digital systems deal with pulse waveforms that are square (ideally). It may be shown by Fourier analysis that square pulses are equivalent to the summation of an infinite series of successively higher frequency components. Such high-frequency components of the primary pulse waveform are much faster than the pulse repetition rate of the clocked pulses. These high-frequency components of the pulse get differentiated by the distributive wire-to-wire capacitances of the circuit or by backplane wiring and thus become the major source of "noise spikes." Another source of susceptibility to noise is due to self-resonance of circuitry and wiring that tend to pick up pulse components from adjacent lines.

Various other causes of noise in digital systems are electrostatic interference in backplane wiring, effects due to capacitive coupling, effects due to inductive coupling (since the lines act as primary and secondary windings of air-core transformers), inductive voltage drops along common busses, inductive ringing of wire lines, relay surges, and resistance paths between separate circuit ground points.

Some helpful rules of thumb to minimize noise effects are: (1) always use direct point-to-point wiring, without cabling, if possible; (2) never cable individual trigger or count input lines with groups of high-current or parallel-word transfer lines; (3) use the twisted pair transmission line or coaxial cable for running long lines in backplanes; (4) always fan out wires from a central point rather than step from one point to the next; and (5) always use a separate filter point and ground return for high-current solenoid drivers or similar device types. For additional practical details in handling noisy situations in digital systems, refer to Jones (1964).

### References

1959. Schwartz, M. *Information Transmission, Modulation, and Noise*. New York: McGraw-Hill.

1964. Jones, J. Paul. *Causes and Cures of Noise in Digital Systems*. W. Concord, Mass.: Computer Design Publishing Corporation.

F. P. Mathur

# NONPROCEDURAL LANGUAGES

For articles on related subjects *see* Administrative-Business Applications; Problem-Oriented Languages; Procedure-Oriented Languages; Programming Languages; and Simulation: Languages. For articles on related terms *see* Data Processing; and IBM 360-370 Series.

This article defines nonprocedural languages, describes their purpose and historical development, and compares them to procedural languages. An explanation of the most widely used nonprocedural commercial language, Report Program Generator (RPG), is then given.

**Definition.** A nonprocedural language is one in which the program does not follow the actual steps a computer follows in executing a program. For a normal data processing application, these steps and their general sequence are:

1. Housekeeping: clear memory, initialize counters and work areas, etc.

2. Open files and check labels.

3. Read input records.

4. Perform arithmetic and logic functions on the input records.

5. Produce output records.

6. Repeat steps 3 through 5 until all records are processed.

7. Print any final output records; close files.

8. End program or return control to supervisor or monitor.

These steps are typically followed when preparing programs for procedural languages because the source program with procedural languages tends to be translated in a more direct manner into the object (machine language) program.

For nonprocedural languages, there is very little relationship necessary between the *sequence* of the source language statements and the sequence of the resulting machine language instructions. Thus, the source program language is freed from the eight-step process listed above, and can be more closely related to the following aspects of the program: (1) a description of the files and records to be read or output; and (2) the arithmetic and logic operations to be performed on the input data.

**Purpose.** Nonprocedural languages tend to be more problem-oriented than do procedural languages. This is particularly true for the programming of commercial (business) applications. The major purpose (and value) of nonprocedural languages is to permit the programming activity to focus more strongly on the problem being solved, rather than on the computer resources (hardware, software) being used. Nonprocedural languages have numerous benefits and some limitations when compared to procedural languages. Exhibit 1 compares the functions and uses of these two types of languages for commercial programming purposes.

The key advantage of nonprocedural languages is the lower amount of programming effort required to produce a working program, when compared to most procedural languages. The reason for this is that much of the internal logic of the object program is provided by the "generator program," which translates the source program into the object program. The basic disadvantage of nonprocedural languages is their lack of flexibility; for example, the loss of programmer control over the input/output functions of the computer and the inability to minimize the use of memory or of execution time through more direct control of hardware operations. These latter functions are better performed with a procedural language having a close relationship between the source language and the machine language so that control over the machine functions is increased.

**Historical Development.** Nonprocedural languages made their first significant appearance in commercial computer installations in the mid-1950s with the introduction of the Report Program Generator (RPG) language for the IBM 1401 data processing system, commonly referred to as 1401 RPG. The purpose of this language was to permit easy preparation of business reports from a description of the records and basic processing involved. This language was followed by other report generator languages during the 1950s and early 1960s, developed by IBM and other computer manufacturers and software firms.

In June 1964, IBM announced the System/360 line of computers. The programming languages for these computers included a greatly expanded version of RPG, with some similarities to the earlier RPG but with significant improvements permitting it to be used in a much wider variety of situations.

The System/360 RPG language became extensively used in the late 1960s at installations of smaller IBM computers (such as the System/360 Model 20) and was shortly adopted by the UNIVAC 9000 Series of the UNIVAC Division of Sperry Rand, by RCA in its Spectra/70 Series, by Honeywell in its H-200 Series, and by Burroughs in the 1700 Series. Its use was primarily concentrated in smaller commercial computer installations having monthly rentals below $5,000. The use of RPG and other commercial report-generating languages has continued to expand in the 1970s, and an RPG-type language is offered with most minicomputers now marketed for commercial applications. Further enhancements continue to be added to these languages because of the rising programming costs that have increased the demand for efficient nonprocedural languages.

Other nonprocedural languages in use today include decision-table processing languages, simulation languages, and special-purpose languages. Several of these special-purpose languages are discussed below.

APT (AUTOMATICALLY PROGRAMMED TOOLS). For use in instructing numerically controlled machine tools by describing the operations to be performed in English-like terms. Developed in 1957 by member companies of the Aerospace Industries Association with the assistance of Massachusetts Institute of Technology (M.I.T.).

| *NONPROCEDURAL* | *PROCEDURAL* |
|---|---|
| *Advantages* | *Disadvantages* |
| Less attention to utilization of hardware resources | Use of hardware resources involved in planning program |
| Little attention to housekeeping of files or areas of memory | Considerable attention to opening and closing files, label checking and establishment of constants and counters in memory |
| Little need to concentrate on mechanical relationships of I/O and processing | Must carefully think through the program sequence in the order the computer will perform it |
| Focuses programmer's attention on the problem (input, processing, output) itself, and not on the requirements of the computer | Programmer's time divided between understanding the problem and understanding the computer |
| Mostly self-documenting | Requires additional effort to properly document |
| Relatively simple to learn | Moderate to difficult to learn |
| Easier to produce working programs due to more extensive diagnostics and automatic inclusion of internal structure of object program | Requires more time to debug programs |
| *Disadvantages* | *Advantages* |
| Does not provide complete control over I/O functions, particularly with multiple input files | Relatively complete control over all I/O functions |
| Requires considerable knowledge of the internal logic provided in order to use the language most effectively | Little knowledge of special internal logic needed, as programmer provides this |
| Capability to handle various forms of I/O generally limited to standard forms | Generally all forms of I/O are supported |
| Less efficient use of memory | Programs can be written to minimize memory usage |
| Programs require somewhat more time to be executed | Programs can be written to minimize execution time by taking into account specific hardware characteristics |

**Exhibit 1.** Features and use of nonprocedural and procedural languages for business data processing.

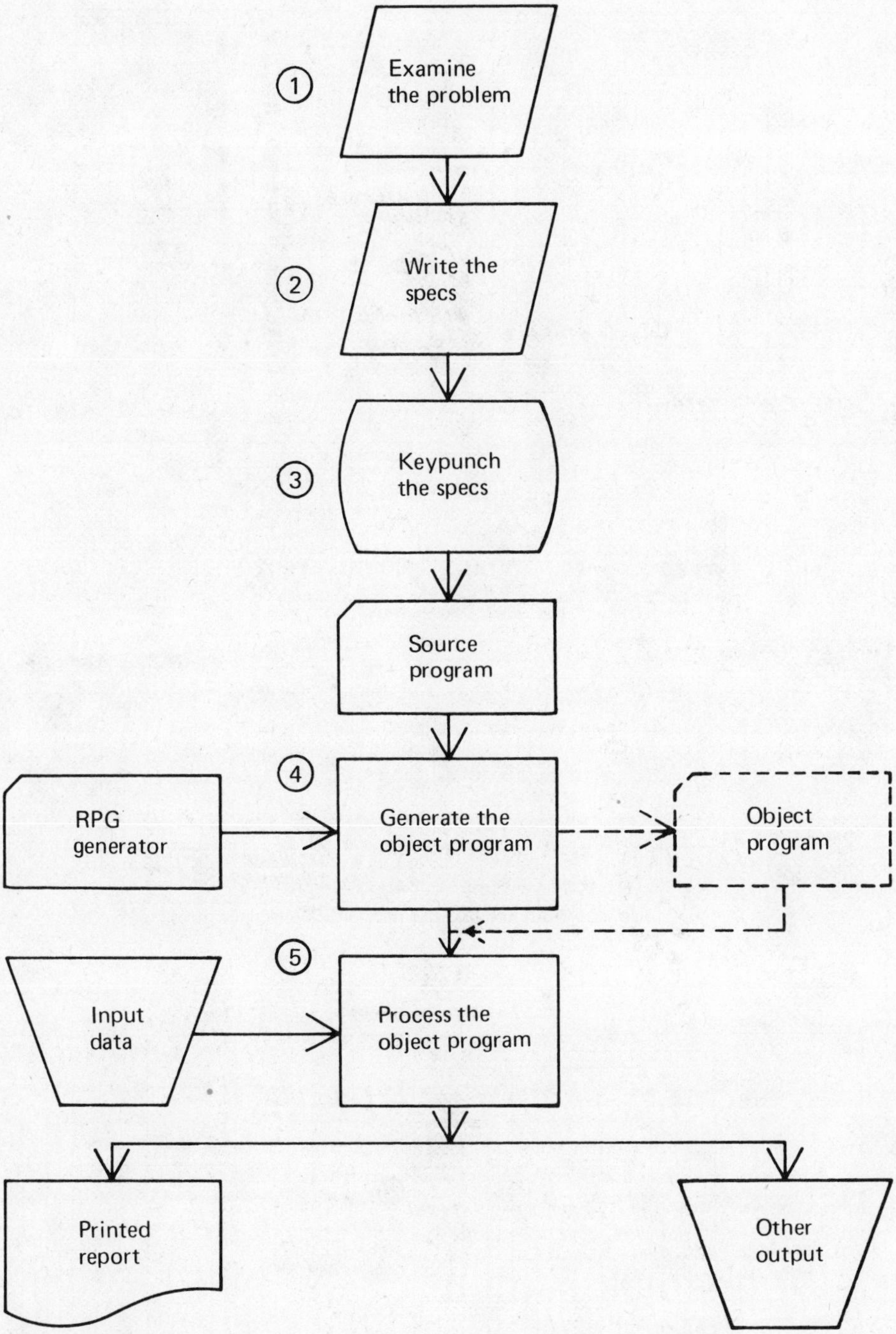


**Exhibit 2.** Steps in processing an RPG program.

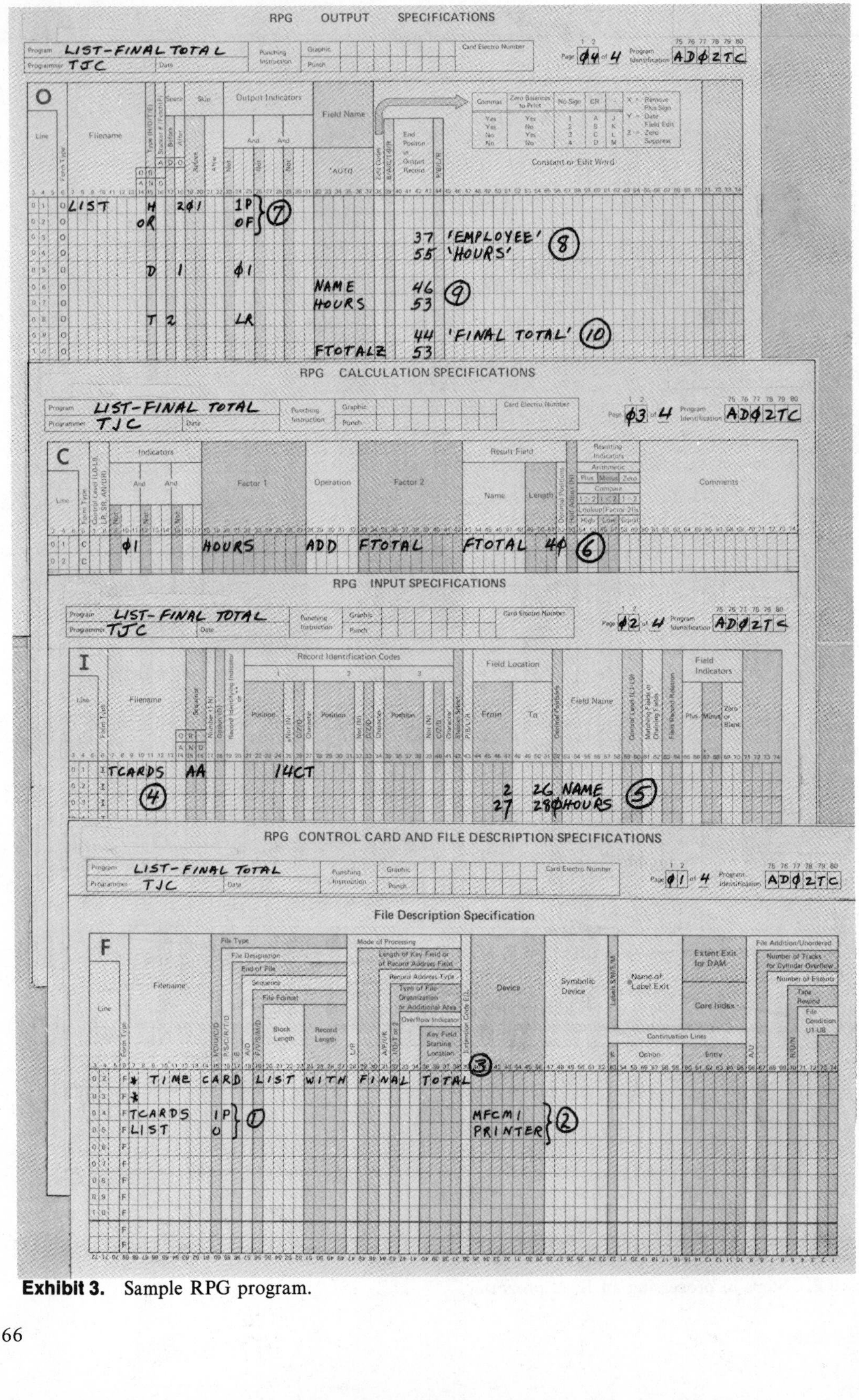
RPG OUTPUT SPECIFICATIONS
Program LIST-FINAL TOTAL
Programmer TJC
Page ϕ4 of 4
Program Identification ADϕ2TC
LIST H 2ϕ1 1P
OR OF
37 'EMPLOYEE'
55 'HOURS'
D 1 ϕ1
NAME 46
HOURS 53
T 2 LR
44 'FINAL TOTAL'
FTOTALZ 53
RPG CALCULATION SPECIFICATIONS
Program LIST-FINAL TOTAL
Programmer TJC
Page ϕ3 of 4
Program Identification ADϕ2TC
ϕ1 HOURS ADD FTOTAL FTOTAL 4ϕ
RPG INPUT SPECIFICATIONS
Program LIST-FINAL TOTAL
Programmer TJC
Page ϕ2 of 4
Program Identification ADϕ2TC
TCARDS AA 14CT
2 26 NAME
27 28ϕHOURS
RPG CONTROL CARD AND FILE DESCRIPTION SPECIFICATIONS
Program LIST-FINAL TOTAL
Programmer TJC
Page ϕ1 of 4
Program Identification ADϕ2TC
File Description Specification
* TIME CARD LIST WITH FINAL TOTAL
*
TCARDS IP MFCM1
LIST O PRINTER
1
2
3
4
5
6
7
8
9
10

**Exhibit 3.** Sample RPG program.

| Entry | Comment |
|---|---|
| 1 | Assigns the name TCARDS to the card file and LIST to the output print file. |
| 2 | Specific names that the programmer uses to tell the generator program what type of hardware I/O devices are used. |
| 3 | A comment line for documentation purposes; ignored by the generator program. |
| 4 | Assigns the indicator "01" to be turned on when a card in the TCARDS file is read with the character T in column 01. |
| 5 | Defines two data fields in the card described in the line above; with the data in columns 2 through 26 placed in a field called NAME, and the data in columns 27 and 28 placed in a field called HOURS. |
| 6 | This line describes a calculation that is to take place when the "01" indicator is on (a card described above in entry 4 has been read). The data in the HOURS field from the card is added to a counter defined as FTOTAL with four positions. |
| 7 | These two lines are similar to entry 4 in that they identify a record, in this case an output record that is to be output to the LIST file (printer) on the first page (1P condition) or when the page overflows (OF condition). The printer carriage is told to skip to channel 1 on the carriage control tape before printing and to double space after printing. |
| 8 | The data for the record described in entry 7 is indicated as two constants, EMPLOYEE and HOURS, to print with their rightmost characters in print positions 37 and 55, respectively. |
| 9 | Lines 05 through 07 on the coding sheet cause a detail line to be printed when the "01" indicator is on, printing the contents of the data fields NAME and HOURS in rightmost positions 46 and 53, respectively. |
| 10 | Lines 08 through 10 cause a line to be printed at the end of the job, with the constant FINAL TOTAL printed next to the data in the field FTOTAL. |

**Exhibit 3.** (continued)

COGO (COORDINATE GEOMETRY). For use in solving plane geometry problems required in surveying. Developed by the Civil Engineering Department of M.I.T. in 1960.

SIMSCRIPT. A simulation language developed by the Rand Corporation in the early 1960s for developing discrete simulations. The language permits description of a system in terms of *sets* of *entities* and the *attributes* associated with the entities.

STRESS (STRUCTURAL ENGINEERING SYSTEMS SOLVER). A language for civil engineers; solves structural problems associated with framed structures. It was developed by M.I.T. in the early 1960s.

**Description of RPG.** The RPG language used by IBM, UNIVAC, RCA (whose computers are now marketed by UNIVAC), Honeywell, Burroughs, and many of the makers of minicomputers is the most widely used nonprocedural commercial language.

The preparation of a report or other desired output with RPG consists of the following steps, which are diagrammed in Exhibit 2:

1. The programmer analyzes the report requirements to determine the output format for records and reports, the input records required and calculations (arithmetic and logic) to be performed on the input, and the types of controls to be maintained.

2. The description of the files, input record formats, calculations, and output record formats are entered on specialized RPG specifications forms (see Exhibit 3).

3. Cards are keypunched from the RPG specifications forms to obtain the source program deck.

4. The source program deck is processed, using the RPG generator program (on disk, tape, or cards) to produce the object program (on disk, tape, or cards). A listing of the source program is produced, which contains diagnostic messages for errors in the source program.

| EMPLOYEE | HOURS |
|---|---|
| ACKERMAN, JAMES A. | 40 |
| ANDREWS, WALTER J. | 20 |
| BROWNE, TIMOTHY R. | 40 |
| COMPTON, JOE Q. | 40 |
| EVANS, ANTHONY B. | 33 |
| FARMER, FRANCES K. | 31 |
| HALO, HANNAH F. | 27 |
| INGRAM, JEROME E. | 40 |
| JACKSON, THOMAS R. | 40 |
| FINAL TOTAL | 311 |

**Exhibit 4.** Output for sample RPG program.

5. The actual input data is processed, using the object program to produce the desired output. A portion of the sample program in Exhibit 3 is shown as output in Exhibit 4.

A significant variation of the above procedure in the use of nonprocedural languages is the "load and go" facility. Here, the object program is generated in memory and immediately used to process the input data, in which case the object program cannot also be stored for later use.

### References


1967. Fletcher, Dennis A., and Thomas J. Cashman. *IBM System/360 RPG Programming: Volume I—Introduction* and *Volume II—Advanced Concepts*. Fullerton, Calif.: Anaheim.

1970. Brightman, Richard W., and John R. Clark. *RPG I and RPG II Programming: System/3 and System/360.* New York: The Macmillan Company.

1972. Murach, Mike. *System/360 RPG*. Palo Alto, Calif.: Science Research Associates.


D. A. Fletcher

# NUCLEUS

For articles on related subjects *see* Input-Output Control System; Operating Systems: Principles and Theory; Scheduling Algorithm; Swapping; and Task. For articles on related terms *see* Interrupt; Interval Timer; and Virtual Memory.

The term "nucleus" (and sometimes "kernel") is used for that set of programs in an operating system which implements the most primitive of that system's functions. The precise interpretation of nucleus programs, of course, depends on the system; however, typical nuclei contain programs for three types of functions:

1. *Task management*: routines for switching the processor among tasks; for scheduling; for sending messages or timing signals among tasks; for creating and removing tasks.
2. *Memory management*: routines for placing, fetching, and removing pages or segments in or from main memory.
3. *Basic I/O control*: routines for allocating and releasing buffers; for starting I/O requests on particular channels or devices; for checking the integrity of individual data transmissions.

In some systems the nucleus is larger and provides for more than these three functions; in others, it is smaller. Each of the three classes of nucleus programs contains interrupt handling routines for interrupts pertaining to the class function; for example, clock interrupts are handled in class 1, page faults and drum completion interrupts in class 2, and channel completion interrupts in class 3. Some systems order the classes hierarchically (e.g., in order 1,2,3) so that programs in a given class can invoke services of programs preceding them in the ordering; for example, memory management (in class 2) can be implemented by a collection of properly coordinated system tasks, the coordination of which is managed by task management routines (in class 1).

The reader should not confuse the system nucleus with that portion of the operating system which is continuously *resident* in main memory. Two criteria determine whether a particular system module (either routine or table) should be resident: (1) its frequency of use, and (2) whether the system can operate at all without it. Examples of the latter include portions of the nucleus, but may include virtual memory mapping tables and other critical information describing activated tasks.

### Reference


1973. Hansen, Per Brinch. *Operating Systems Principles*. New York: Prentice-Hall, Ch. 8.


P. J. Denning and D. E. Denning

# NUMBERS AND NUMBER SYSTEMS

For articles on related subjects *see* ARITHMETIC, COMPUTER; INTERVAL ARITHMETIC; NUMERICAL ANALYSIS; PRECISION; and SIGNIFICANCE ARITHMETIC.

Since almost everyone uses numbers every day, it is at first glance surprising that so many laymen have difficulty understanding the rather simple variations on the decimal system theme that are widely used in computing. The crux of the problem seems to be that, while the layman may use and manipulate (e.g., do arithmetic with) numbers with some facility, there is all too often little understanding of what is being done. What needs to be understood, however, is simply that the representation in which we normally write numbers, for example

$$276.1069, \tag{1}$$

is nothing more than shorthand symbolic representation for the precise mathematical equivalent

$$2 \times 100 + 7 \times 10 + 6 \times 1 + 1 \times 0.1 + 0 \times 0.01 + 6 \times 0.001 + 9 \times 0.0001 \tag{2}$$

or

$$2 \times 10^2 + 7 \times 10^1 + 6 \times 10^0 + 1 \times 10^{-1} + 0 \times 10^{-2} + 6 \times 10^{-3} + 9 \times 10^{-4} \tag{3}$$

The representations (2) and (3) express clearly that the decimal system we use has a "base," or "radix," 10. By analogy, therefore, the "binary," or "base 2," system so commonly used with computers can become immediately understandable, as presented below. The notation (1)—often called "positional notation" because the position of a digit specifies the power of 10 in (3), which is associated with it—may effectively hide for many the real mathematical content of a number.

**Radix Representation.** The notation in (2) or (3) above is called the "radix representation" of a number. The general form of any decimal number may be written

$$\Sigma_{i=-m}^{n} d_i \cdot 10^i \qquad 0 \leq d_i \leq 9 \quad (d_i \text{ an integer}),$$

which in the case of (3) specializes to

$$\begin{aligned} m &= -4, & n &= 2 \\ d_{-4} &= 9, & d_{-3} &= 6 \\ d_{-2} &= 0, & d_{-1} &= 1 \\ d_0 &= 6, & d_1 &= 7, & d_2 &= 2 \end{aligned}$$

The three other number systems most important in computers are the binary, the octal, and the hexadecimal.

1. The "binary," or base 2, system, in which numbers are represented by

$$\Sigma_{i=-m}^{n} b_i \cdot 2^i \qquad b_i = 0 \text{ or } 1. \tag{4}$$

2. The "octal" (formerly called "octonal"), or base 8, system representation

$$\Sigma_{i=-m}^{n} o_i \cdot 8^i \qquad 0 \leq o_i \leq 7 \quad (o_i \text{ an integer}).$$

3. The "hexadecimal," or base 16, system, represented by

$$\Sigma_{i=-m}^{n} h_i \cdot 16^i \qquad 0 \leq h_i \leq 15 \quad (h_i \text{ an integer}).$$

We will now consider the characteristics of each of these systems briefly.

BINARY. The rule for generating successive numbers in any number system is given in Fig. 1. If $R = 10$, this algorithm will generate successfully the familiar sequence of decimal numbers. But, if $R = 2$, we get the sequence of binary numbers, the first few of which are

| | | | | | |
|---|---|---|---|---|---|
| 0 | 11 | 110 | 1001 | 1100 | 1111 |
| 1 | 100 | 111 | 1010 | 1101 | 10000 |
| 10 | 101 | 1000 | 1011 | 1110 | 10001 |

The addition and multiplication tables for binary numbers are particularly simple (Table 1) and, once learned, so is binary arithmetic using these tables. Fig. 2 gives examples of all four arithmetic operations in binary, with the corresponding decimal arithmetic also given. Finding the equivalent decimal integer to a given binary integer is very simple using expression (4). Thus, for example,

$$\begin{aligned} 1011010 &= 1 \times 2^6 + 0 \times 2^5 + 1 \times 2^4 + 1 \times 2^3 \\ &\quad + 0 \times 2^2 + 1 \times 2^1 + 0 \times 2^0 \\ &= 64 + 16 + 8 + 2 \\ &= 90 \end{aligned}$$

Later on in this article we will consider the general

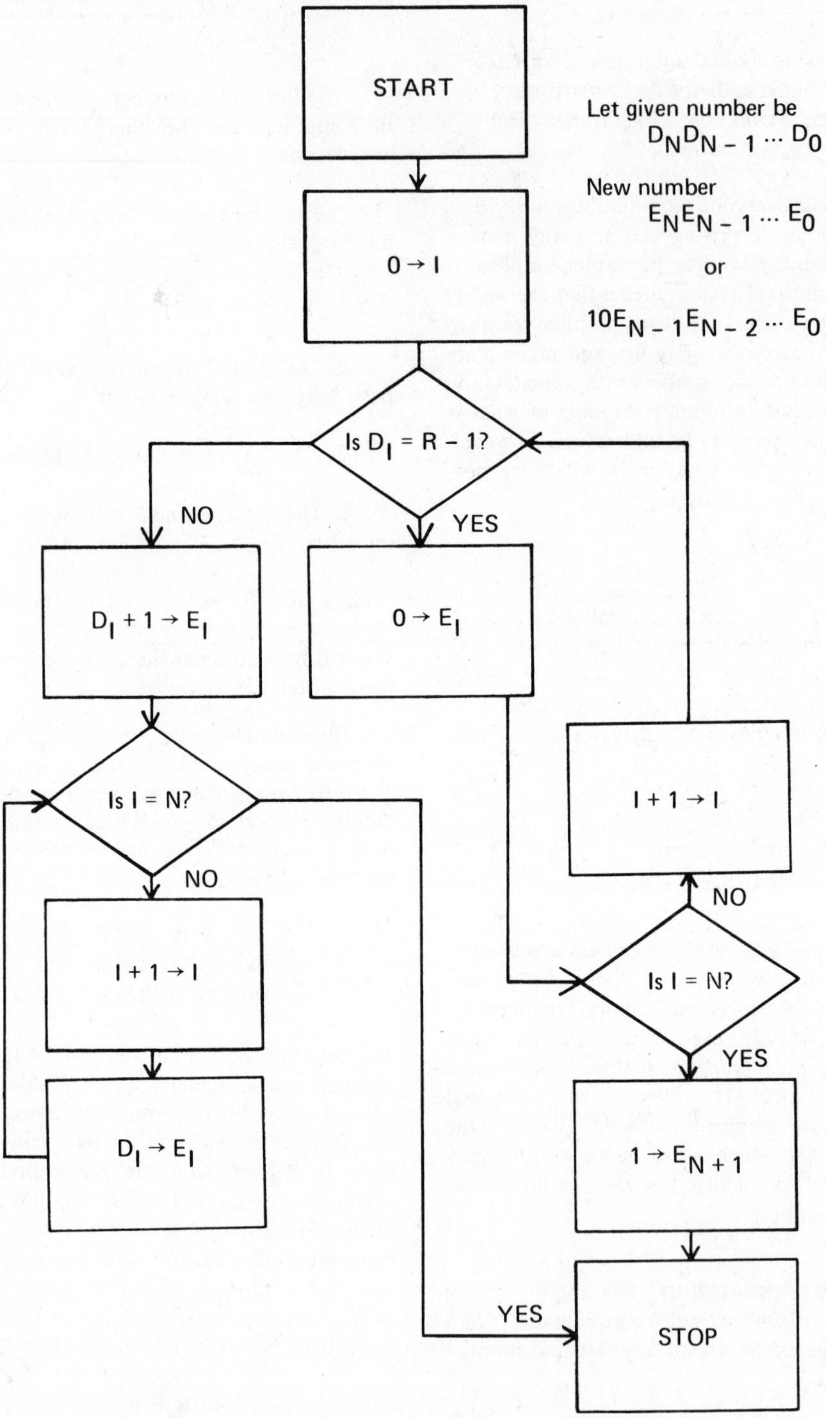


**Fig. 1.** Flowchart for generating next number in a number system with radix *R*.

```
Addition                          Subtraction

Carries   10011                   Borrowing   10     1     1
                                        0     ø     1ó    1ó    10
          11001      25                 ⁄1    ⁄1    0     0     0      24
         +10011     +19                -0     1     1     0     1     -13
         ------     ---            -----------------------------     ---
         101100      44                       1     0     1     1      11


Multiplication                    Division

      1101           13                       11                 3 1/9
     x1110          x14           1001 | 11100                9 | 28
     -----          ---                  1001
     11010           52                  ----
    1101            13                   1010
   1101            ---                   1001
  --------         182                   ----
  10110110                                  1
```

**Fig. 2.** Binary arithmetic.

**Table 1.** Binary addition and multiplication tables

| + | 0 | 1 |
|---|---|---|
| 0 | 0 | 1 |
| 1 | 0 | 10 |

| × | 0 | 1 |
|---|---|---|
| 0 | 0 | 0 |
| 1 | 0 | 1 |

**Table 2.** Octal addition and multiplication tables.

| + | 0 | 1 | 2 | 3 | 4 | 5 | 6 | 7 | × | 0 | 1 | 2 | 3 | 4 | 5 | 6 | 7 |
|---|---|---|---|---|---|---|---|---|---|---|---|---|---|---|---|---|---|
| 0 | 0 | 1 | 2 | 3 | 4 | 5 | 6 | 7 | 0 | 0 | 0 | 0 | 0 | 0 | 0 | 0 | 0 |
| 1 | 1 | 2 | 3 | 4 | 5 | 6 | 7 | 10 | 1 | 0 | 1 | 2 | 3 | 4 | 5 | 6 | 7 |
| 2 | 2 | 3 | 4 | 5 | 6 | 7 | 10 | 11 | 2 | 0 | 2 | 4 | 6 | 10 | 12 | 14 | 16 |
| 3 | 3 | 4 | 5 | 6 | 7 | 10 | 11 | 12 | 3 | 0 | 3 | 6 | 11 | 14 | 17 | 22 | 25 |
| 4 | 4 | 5 | 6 | 7 | 10 | 11 | 12 | 13 | 4 | 0 | 4 | 10 | 14 | 20 | 24 | 30 | 34 |
| 5 | 5 | 6 | 7 | 10 | 11 | 12 | 13 | 14 | 5 | 0 | 5 | 12 | 17 | 24 | 31 | 36 | 43 |
| 6 | 6 | 7 | 10 | 11 | 12 | 13 | 14 | 15 | 6 | 0 | 6 | 14 | 22 | 30 | 36 | 44 | 52 |
| 7 | 7 | 10 | 11 | 12 | 13 | 14 | 15 | 16 | 7 | 0 | 7 | 16 | 25 | 34 | 43 | 52 | 61 |

problem of conversion from a number in one system to another.

OCTAL. The octal system is used widely in computing only because of its simple relation to binary. To convert a binary number to octal, it is only necessary (since $8 = 2^3$) to group the binary digits in sets of three and convert each set to its binary equivalent. (Note that three binary digits—hereafter we will use the common contraction "bits" for binary digits—can represent the digits from 0 to 7 or one octal digit.) Thus, the binary equivalent of one million in decimal is

11 | 110 | 100 | 001 | 001 | 000 | 000

↓ ↓ ↓ ↓ ↓ ↓ ↓

3 6 4 1 1 0 0

and the octal equivalent is 3641100. Correspondingly, to go from octal to binary, each octal digit is converted into its binary equivalent. Thus,

647.0534

↓

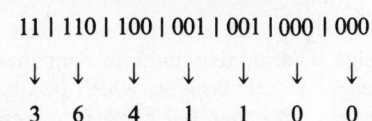

110100111.000101011100

The advantage of octal over binary is shown clearly by the preceding two examples. For all large numbers or numbers with a significant number of decimal places, the octal representation is much more compact, and therefore is easier to write and manipulate than its binary equivalent. Table 2 gives the octal addition and multiplication tables.

HEXADECIMAL. This system became important with the advent of the IBM 360 and 370 systems, which, while binary internally, from the user's point of view are hexadecimal machines. Because hexadecimal requires 16 distinct characters, 6 characters in addition to 0, 1, . . ., 9 are needed to represent "10", "11", . . ., "15". These are usually taken to be $A,B,C,D,E,F$.

Just as octal is related to binary using three-bit groups, hexadecimal is related to binary using four-bit groups. Thus,

$$111 \mid 1010 \mid 0001 \mid 0010 \mid 0001$$

becomes

$$7 \quad A \quad 1 \quad 2 \quad 1$$

in hexadecimal.

## Other Number Systems

BALANCED DIGIT SYSTEMS. In a balanced digit system the allowable digits in each position are from a value $-s$ to $+s$, with negative numbers usually denoted by an overbar. Thus, a balanced binary system might have digits $-1$, 0, 1 with $-1$ written as $\bar{1}$. In this system,

$$10\bar{1}\bar{1} = 2^3 - 2^1 - 2^0 = 5$$

and

$$\bar{1}101 = -2^3 + 2^2 + 2^0 = -3.$$

One property of such a system, sometimes useful in the design of arithmetic units in computers, is the *redundancy* of such systems, which occurs when a number has more than one possible representation. For example, in the system described above, 5 may, as in the usual binary system, also be represented by

$$101$$

In any balanced digit system where $s$ is less than the base, the leftmost digit gives the sign of the number so that no explicit sign is needed. In addition, given any number $A$, its negative may be found by changing all digits to their negatives (i.e., removing all overbars and inserting overbars where there were none). Thus, for example,

$$10\bar{1}10 = 2^4 - 2^2 + 2^1 = +14$$

and

$$\bar{1}01\bar{1}0 = -2^4 + 2^2 - 2^1 = -14.$$

A particularly interesting balanced digit system, which does not yet appear to have been applied in computers, is *balanced ternary* (Knuth, 1969), which has radix 3 and where, as above, the digits, called "trits," are 1, 0, and $\bar{1}$. This system is nonredundant and, in addition to the properties mentioned above, has the additional useful property that a number may be rounded to the nearest integer merely by deleting its fractional part. Thus,

$$10\bar{1}.\bar{1}\bar{1} = 3^2 - 3^0 - 3^{-1} - 3^{-2} = 7\tfrac{5}{9}$$

and

$$10\bar{1} = 8.$$

RESIDUE SYSTEMS. A residue system is one in which (1) each digit position corresponds to a different radix; (2) all pairs of radices are relatively prime; i.e., the only common divisor of any two radices is 1; (3) the value of the digit $d_i$ for integer $A$ in position $i$ corresponding to radix $r_i$ is given by $d_i = A$ modulo $r_i$, i.e., the remainder when $A$ is divided by $r_i$.

For example, if $r_2 = 5$, $r_1 = 3$, $r_0 = 2$, then 13 is represented by

$$311$$

and 25 is represented by

$$011.$$

Because of property 2, the range of value that can be expressed is from 0 to 1 less than the product of the radices used.

**Radix Conversion.** We now consider how to take a number in one system to base $p$ and convert it to a number in base $q$. To do this, we consider the integer and fractional parts of the number separately. Let $(I)_p$ and $(F)_p$, respectively, be the integer and fractional parts of the number in base $p$,

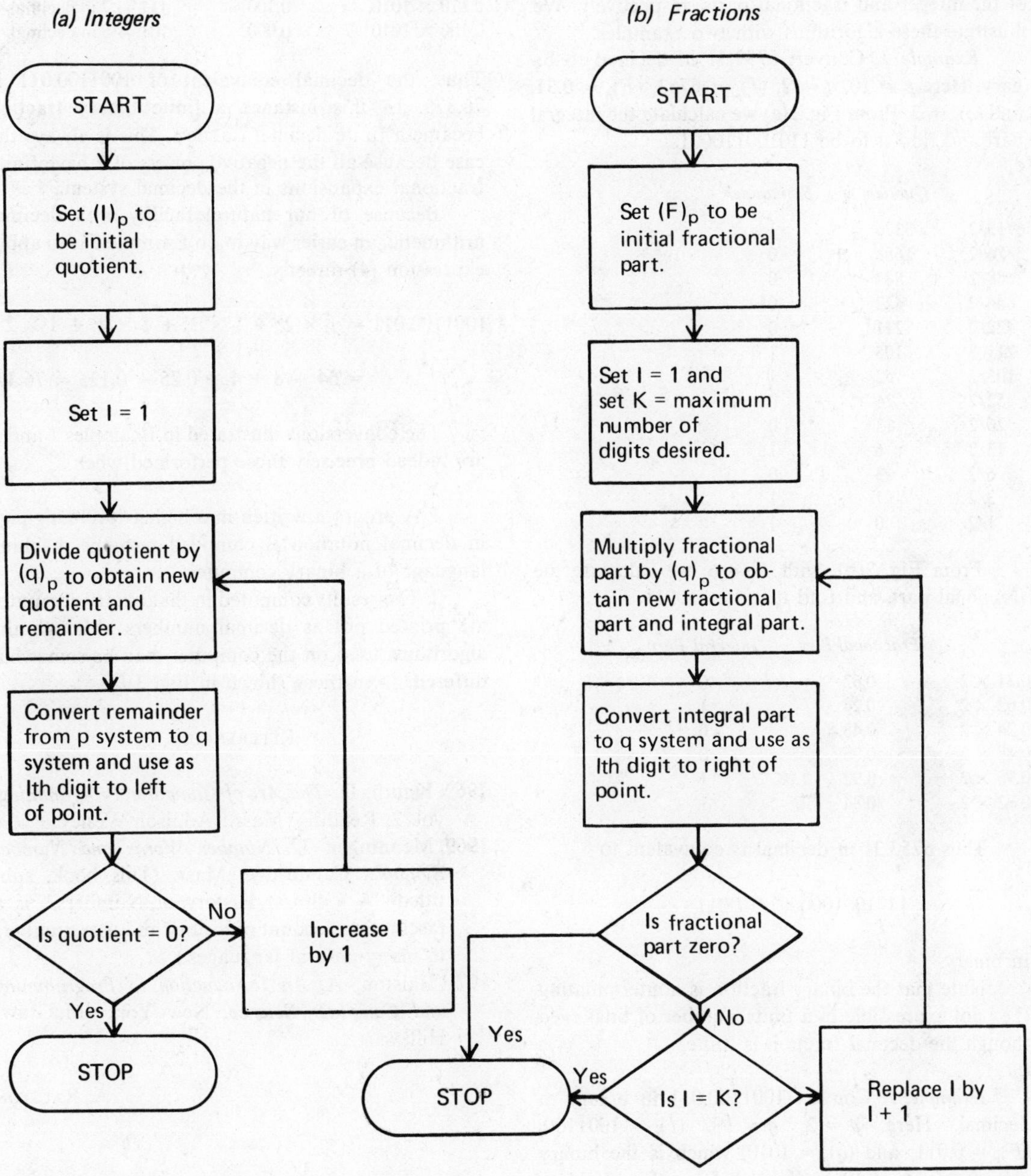


**Fig. 3.** Radix conversion.

which we wish to convert to base $q$; let $(q)_p$ be the expression of $q$ in the $p$ system (e.g., to convert from binary to decimal $(q)_p = (10)_2 = 1010$). Figures 3(a) and 3(b) are flowcharts to perform the conversions of the integer and fractional parts, respectively. We illustrate these algorithms with two examples.

*Example 1.* Convert 6753.31 in decimal to binary. Here $p = 10$, $q = 2$, $(I)_p = 6753$, $(F)_p = 0.31$, and $(q)_p = 2$. From Fig. 3(a) we calculate the integral part and find it to be 110100110001.

| | *Quotient* | *Remainder* |
|---|---|---|
| 6753/2 | 3376 | 1 |
| 3376/2 | 1688 | 0 |
| 1688/2 | 844 | 0 |
| 844/2 | 422 | 0 |
| 422/2 | 211 | 0 |
| 211/2 | 105 | 1 |
| 105/2 | 52 | 1 |
| 52/2 | 26 | 0 |
| 26/2 | 13 | 0 |
| 13/2 | 6 | 1 |
| 6/2 | 3 | 0 |
| 3/2 | 1 | 1 |
| 1/2 | 0 | 1 |

From Fig. 3(b), with $K = 6$, we calculate the fractional part, and find it to be 010011.

| | *Fractional Part* | *Integral Part* |
|---|---|---|
| 0.31 × 2 | 0.62 | 0 |
| 0.62 × 2 | 0.24 | 1 |
| 0.24 × 2 | 0.48 | 0 |
| 0.48 × 2 | 0.96 | 0 |
| 0.96 × 2 | 0.92 | 1 |
| 0.92 × 2 | 0.84 | 1 |

Thus 6753.31 in decimal is equivalent to

1101001000001.010011 · · ·

in binary.

Note that the binary fraction is nonterminating (i.e., not expressible in a finite number of bits) even though the decimal fraction is finite.

*Example 2.* Convert 1001100.011 in binary to decimal. Here, $p = 2$, $q = 10$, $(I)_p = 1001100$, $(F)_p = 0.011$, and $(q)_p = 1010$, which is the binary representation of 10 in decimal. From Fig. 3(a),

| | *Quotient* | *Remainder* |
|---|---|---|
| 1001100/1010 | 111 | 110 → 6 in decimal |
| 111/1010 | 0 | 111 → 7 in decimal |

Thus, the integral part of the decimal number is 76. From Figure 3(b).

| | *Fractional Part* | *Integral Part* |
|---|---|---|
| 0.011 × 1010 | 0.110 | 11 → 3 in decimal |
| 0.110 × 1010 | 0.100 | 111 → 7 in decimal |
| 0.100 × 1010 | 0.000 | 101 → 5 in decimal |

Thus, the decimal equivalent of 1001100.011 is 76.375. In this instance a finite binary fraction became a finite decimal fraction. This is always the case because all the negative powers of 2 have finite fractional expansions in the decimal system.

Because of our natural facility with decimal arithmetic, an easier way to do Example 2 is to apply expression (4) directly:

$$1001100.011 = 1 \times 2^6 + 1 \times 2^3 + 1 \times 2^2 + 1 \times 2^{-2} + 1 \times 2^{-3}$$
$$= 64 + 8 + 4 + 0.25 + 0.125 = 76.375$$

The conversions illustrated in Examples 1 and 2 are indeed precisely those performed when

1. A program written in a higher-level language in decimal notation is compiled into the machine language of a binary computer.
2. The results computed in that binary computer are printed out as decimal numbers although the algorithms used on the computer may be somewhat different from those shown in Fig. 3.

REFERENCES

1969. Knuth, D. *The Art of Computer Programming.* vol. 2. Reading, Mass.: Addison-Wesley.

1969. Menninger, K. *Number Words and Number Symbols.* Cambridge, Mass. (This book, subtitled "A Cultural History of Numbers," is a fascinating account of history and uses numbers in many natural languages.)

1971. Ralston, A. *An Introduction to Programming and Computer Science.* New York: McGraw-Hill.

A. RALSTON

# NUMERICAL ANALYSIS

For articles on related subjects *see* ALGORITHM; APPROXIMATION THEORY; ERROR ANALYSIS; ERRORS, ABSOLUTE AND RELA-

TIVE; MATHEMATICAL PROGRAMMING; MATHEMATICAL SOFTWARE; MATRIX COMPUTATIONS; and PARTIAL DIFFERENTIAL EQUATIONS, NUMERICAL SOLUTION OF.

Numerical analysis is concerned with the development, analysis, and use of algorithms that simulate physical and social processes. It is a practical science, involving as it does the production of numbers that approximate the solution of mathematical models of physical and social systems. It is a very old science. Many famous mathematicians from the eighteenth and nineteenth centuries—including Gauss, Newton, and Fourier, to mention a few—developed algorithms for solving problems, which are still widely used. The advent of computers provided a tremendous impetus to the study and development of numerical analysis, and indeed led to so many new advances that it is now common to refer to the period from 1950 to the present as the era of "modern numerical analysis." High-speed computers have made it possible for us to solve ever more complex problems and, as a result, to gain much better insight into complex processes. It is quite accurate to say that modern technological achievements in such areas as space and atomic energy would have been impossible without high-speed computers and advances in numerical analysis.

Computers have affected the direction of numerical analysis in several important ways. They have forced numerical analysis to search for algorithms that are computationally fast and efficient, and to search for a better understanding of error analysis. Algorithms that produce speed-up factors on the order of 100 or more have been discovered in such areas as harmonic analysis, the solution of large linear systems by iterative methods, and matrix eigenvalue problems, to mention a few. Computers have also generated new problems for numerical analysts. For example, because computers work with finite word lengths and because of the inexactness of conversion from one number base to another, round-off errors are inevitably introduced. These errors in turn propagate in very complicated ways. Numerical analysts are concerned about the effect of the totality of such errors on the accuracy of the results. Statistical methods of error analysis yield some promise in this area, but the most effective approach to date is that of backward-error analysis, due to Wilkinson (1960).

In backward error analysis one shows that the *computed* results are the exact solutions of a perturbed problem and that the bounds for the perturbations can be obtained numerically. By comparing the perturbed problem and the given problem, one can then decide on how much confidence one can place in the computed results.

Another problem introduced by computers is that of numerical instability. Errors introduced into a computation, from whatever source, propagate in different ways. In some algorithmic processes these errors tend to grow exponentially, with disastrous computational results. An algorithm that exhibits such exponential error growth is said to be "numerically unstable." Numerical analysts therefore seek algorithms that are not only fast and efficient, but also stable at the same time.

The complexity of error analysis has also led to the development of automatic error analysis procedures. In such automatic error procedures an attempt is made to have the computer monitor the error at each stage of the computation and to adjust parameters automatically so as to reduce the error in subsequent computations. The adaptive integration schemes for quadrature, which will be described in a later section, provide one example of such automatic error-monitoring algorithms. Traditional numerical analysis usually deals with the following topics:

1. Root-finding methods for a single equation or for systems of equations.
2. Interpolation.
3. Approximation.
4. Numerical differentiation.
5. Numerical quadrature.
6. Solution of linear systems.
7. Matrix eigenvalue problems.
8. Solution of ordinary differential equations.
9. Solution of partial differential equations.

In an article of this length, one can hope to provide only a brief glimpse of the algorithms available in each of these areas. In this section are brief discussions of algorithms for root finding, interpolation, numerical differentiation, numerical quadrature, and ordinary differential equations. Ralston (1965), Conte (1972), and Hamming (1973) give a more detailed treatment of each of these areas. Topics 3, 6, 7, and 9 above are discussed in separate articles in this encyclopedia.

**Roots of Equations.** We consider first the problem of finding the roots of equations of one variable. Some examples of equations that arise in physics and engineering are:

1. $x^3 - x - 1 = 0.$

2. $e^x - \cos x = 0$.
3. $2x - \tan x = 0$.

It is only rarely possible to find roots of such equations explicitly, and we must therefore rely on numerical methods that produce approximate solutions.

The simplest of all methods for finding a simple real zero of a continuous function $f(x)$ is the "bisection method." The process begins by finding an interval $(a_0,b_0)$ which contains the desired zero $\alpha$. If the zero is simple, then $f(a_0)$ and $f(b_0)$ must be opposite in sign, the usual test for this being based on the inequality

$$f(a_0)f(b_0) < 0.$$

The next step is to bisect the interval $(a_0,b_0)$; i.e., compute $m = \frac{1}{2}(a_0 + b_0)$. We then evaluate $f(m)$ and form the product $f(x_1)f(m)$. If this product is negative, then we know that the zero lies in the interval $(a_0,m)$; otherwise, it must be in the interval $(m,b_0)$. Of course, if $f(x_1)f(x_m) = 0$, then $m$ is the desired zero. We now bisect the smaller interval, which is known to contain the zero $\alpha$, and the entire process is repeated until the zero is obtained to the accuracy desired. The procedure is summarized in algorithmic form below.

THE BISECTION ALGORITHM. Given a function $f(x)$ continuous on the interval $(a_0,b_0)$ and such that $f(a_0)f(b_0) \leq 0$.
For $n = 0,1,2,\ldots$, until satisfied, do:
Set $m = (a_n + b_n)/2$.
If $f(a_n)f(m) \leq 0$, set $a_{n+1} = a_n$, $b_{n+1} = m$.
Otherwise, set $a_{n+1} = m$, $b_{n+1} = b_n$.
Then $f(x)$ has a root in the interval $(a_{n+1}, b_{n+1})$.

The phrase "until satisfied" used in this algorithm must be made precise in a program and is usually based on one of the following criteria:

(i) $|f(m)| < \epsilon$;
(ii) $|b_{n+1} - a_{n+1}| < \delta$.

where $\epsilon$, $\delta$ are selected to achieve the desired accuracy.

As a simple example, consider the function $f(x) = x^3 - x - 1$. It is easy to verify that

$$f(1) = -1 < 0 < 5 = f(2).$$

Hence, there must be at least one zero of $f(x)$ on the interval (1,2). In fact, there is exactly one zero on (1,2). We call this zero $\alpha$. The midpoint of the interval (1,2) is 1.5, and we know that $\alpha \approx 1.5$ with an absolute error of at most 0.5. Now $f(1.5) = 0.875$ and $f(1)f(1.5) < 0$; hence, the zero lies in the interval (1,1.5). Therefore, $\alpha \approx 1.25$, with absolute error less than 0.25. After 20 steps of this algorithm we find that

$$1.3247175 = a_{20} \leq \alpha \leq b_{20} = 1.3247184,$$
$$f(a_{20}) = (-1.857\cdots)\,10^{-6},$$
$$f(b_{20}) = (2.209\cdots)\,10^{-6}.$$

At this point we have six significant digits of accuracy. As this example shows, the bisection method always brackets the zero and provides an automatic bound on the approximation. Its simplicity makes it ideal for computer solution. On the other hand, it usually converges very slowly. If the function is complicated, this method is not very efficient and we are led to a search for methods that converge faster.

One such method is due to Newton. The algorithm for Newton's method is also quite simple.

NEWTON'S ALGORITHM. Given $f(x)$ continuously differentiable and a starting approximation $x_0$. For $n = 0,1,2,\ldots$, until satisfied, do:

Calculate

$$x_{n+1} = x_n - \frac{f(x_n)}{f'(x_n)}. \tag{1}$$

Geometrically, Newton's method takes as a next approximation the intersection of the tangent to the curve $f(x)$ at the point $x_0$ with the $x$-axis (see Fig. 1). We note that Newton's algorithm requires that the derivative $f'(x)$ be available.

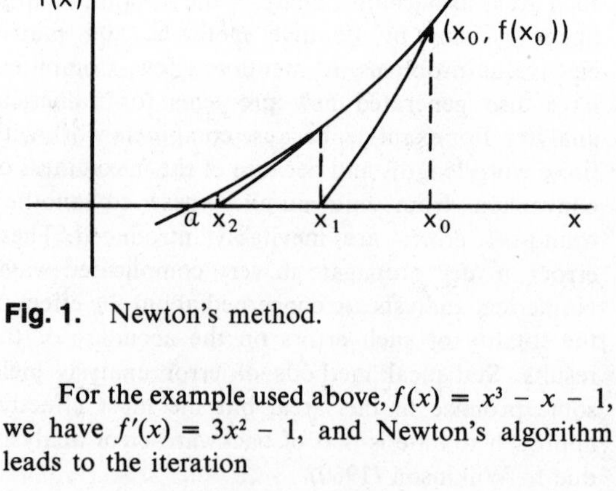


**Fig. 1.** Newton's method.

For the example used above, $f(x) = x^3 - x - 1$, we have $f'(x) = 3x^2 - 1$, and Newton's algorithm leads to the iteration

$$x_{n+1} = x_n - \frac{x_n^3 - x_n - 1}{3x_n^2 - 1}.$$

Starting with $x_0 = 1$, we obtain the values in Table 1.

**Table 1.** Newton's method applied to $f(x) = x^3 - x - 1$.

| $n$ | $x_n$ |
|---|---|
| 0 | 1.0 |
| 1 | 1.5 |
| 2 | 1.3478261 |
| 3 | 1.3252004 |
| 4 | 1.3247182 |
| 5 | 1.3247180 |

Since the iterates $x_4$, $x_5$ agree to seven significant digits, we take $x_5$ as an approximation to $\alpha$, which is correct to at least that many digits.

The rapidity of convergence in this problem, even considering the fact that we do more work per step, shows that Newton's method is much more efficient than the bisection method. The tabular results also illustrate another important feature of this method. The number of correct digits, those underlined in Table 1, appears to double with each iteration. This observation is made more precise by the following theorem.

*Theorem: Newton's Method.* Let $f(x)$, $f'(x)$, $f''(x)$ be continuous and bounded on an interval containing the zero $\alpha$. If $x_0$ is picked sufficiently close to $\alpha$, then the iteration of Eq. (1) converges; moreover, for $n$ large enough,

$$(x_{n+1} - \alpha) \approx K(x_n - \alpha)^2, \tag{2}$$

where $K$ is a constant that depends on the derivatives of $f(x)$ at the point $\alpha$.

The last inequality shows that the error of the $(n + 1)$st iterate is proportional to the square of the error at the $n$th iterate, and demonstrates the eventual quadratic convergence of Newton's method. For this reason it is a very popular method. The most important disadvantage of Newton's method is that it will sometimes diverge or that it will converge to some zero other than the one desired. While the theorem guarantees convergence if $x_0$ is sufficiently close to $\alpha$, it is difficult in practice to know what "sufficiently close" implies. A second disadvantage of Newton's method is that it requires that $f'(x)$ be computable. In many cases we may know $f(x)$ but not $f'(x)$.

A method that retains most of the advantages of Newton's method, but which does not require knowledge of $f'(x)$, is the secant method. It can be derived directly from Eq. (1) by replacing $f'(x_n)$ by a difference quotient:

$$f'(x_n) \approx \frac{f(x_n) - f(x_{n-1})}{x_n - x_{n-1}}. \tag{3}$$

We know from calculus that this difference quotient is a reasonable approximation to $f'(x_n)$, provided $x_{n-1}$ is sufficiently close to $x_n$. Substituting expression (3) into Eq. (1), we obtain the secant iteration:

$$x_{n+1} = x_n - f(x_n)\frac{x_n - x_{n-1}}{f(x_n) - f(x_{n-1})}.$$

Stated in algorithmic form, we have

THE SECANT ALGORITHM. Given a function $f(x)$ and two points $x_{-1}$, $x_0$. For $n = 0, 1, 2, \ldots$ until satisfied, do:

Calculate

$$x_{n+1} = x_n - f(x_n)\frac{x_n - x_{n-1}}{f(x_n) - f(x_{n-1})}. \tag{4}$$

Geometrically, as shown in Fig. 2, the secant method takes $x_{n+1}$ as the intersection with the $x$-axis of the secant passing through the points $(x_n, f_n)$ and $(x_{n-1}, f_{n-1})$.

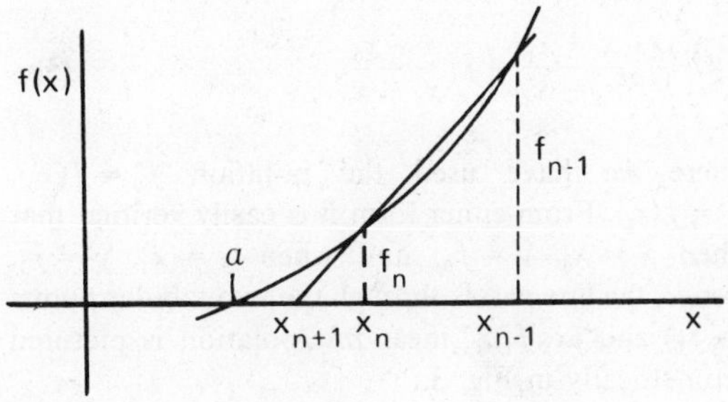


**Fig. 2.** Secant method.

This method converges much more rapidly than the bisection method, but less rapidly than Newton's method. Its primary advantage is that it requires no knowledge of $f'(x)$.

There are many other methods that could be considered, including fixed-point iteration, the modified regula falsi, Steffensen iteration, etc. Those mentioned above are, however, used most commonly in practice. Moreover, each of these methods can be generalized to apply to systems of nonlinear equations. As applied to systems, however, these methods frequently fail to converge, and in fact a great deal of research remains to be done to produce an effective computational method for finding zeros of nonlinear systems.

**Interpolation.** We now describe briefly the process of interpolation. In its simplest form we are given the values of a function $f(x)$ at a selected set of points $\{x_i\}(i = 0, 1, \ldots, n)$. The function $f(x)$ is usually not known explicitly, but its values at the selected points can be obtained either from a table of values or experimentally. The problem is to estimate the value of $f(x)$ at some nontabular point $\bar{x}$. In Table, 2, for example, we are given the values of an unspecified function $f(x)$ at the indicated points. We may now be required to estimate the value of $f(x)$ at, say, $\bar{x} = 2.1$, or at any nontabular point. To do so, it is customary to select a simple class of functions, most commonly polynomials, which agree with the function $f(x)$ at the tabular points. We can then evaluate this polynomial at the point $x = \bar{x}$ to obtain the desired estimate. The simplest case is that of linear interpolation. Here we are given two points $\{x_0, x_1\}$ and the corresponding values $\{f(x_0), f(x_1)\}$. The equation of the linear polynomial (a straight line) which passes through the points $(x_0, f(x_0))$ and $(x_1, f(x_1))$ may be written in the following equivalent forms:

$$y = f_0 + \frac{f_1 - f_0}{x_1 - x_0}(x - x_0), \tag{5a}$$

$$y = f_0 \frac{x - x_1}{x_0 - x_1} + f_1 \frac{x - x_0}{x_1 - x_0}, \tag{5b}$$

where we have used the notation $f_0 = f(x_0)$, $f_1 = f(x_1)$. From either form it is easily verified that when $x = x_0$, $y = f_0$; and when $x = x_1$, $y = f_1$. Hence, the line passes through the two tabular points $(x_0, f_0)$ and $(x_1, f_1)$. Linear interpolation is pictured geometrically in Fig. 3.

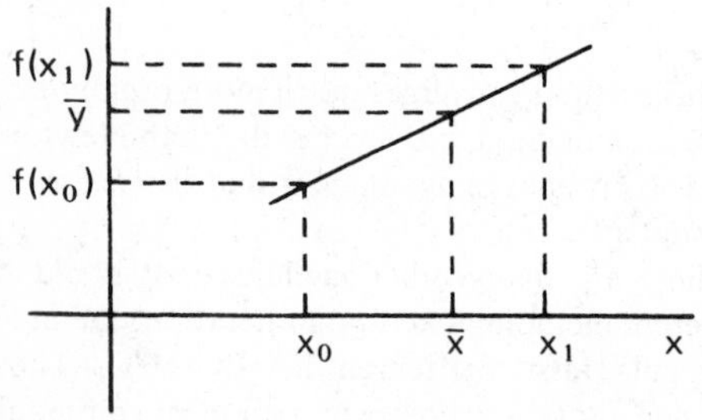


**Fig. 3.** Linear interpolation.

**Table 2**

| | | | | |
|---|---|---|---|---|
| $x$ | 2.0 | 2.2 | 2.4 | 2.6 |
| $f(x)$ | 0.30103 | 0.34242 | 0.38021 | 0.41497 |

To estimate $f(2.1)$ for the data in Table 2, using linear interpolation, substitute $x = 2.1$ into Eq. (5a) to obtain

$$y = 0.30103 + \frac{0.34242 - 0.30103}{2.2 - 2.0}(2.1 - 2.0)$$

$$= 0.30103 + 0.020695 = 0.321725.$$

This result "appears" to be reasonable, but we cannot say much about its accuracy. If the function varies greatly over the interval $[x_0, x_1]$, linear interpolation will generally give poor accuracy. It is reasonable to expect that if the actual function $f(x)$ is smooth, interpolation based on a higher degree polynomial will give better results than that based on lower-degree polynomials.

If we are given $n + 1$ values of $x$ and $f(x)$, say $\{x_i, f_i\}(i = 0, 1, \ldots, n)$, then we can pass a polynomial of degree $n$ through these points. It can be proved that if the points $x_i$ are distinct, the interpolating polynomial of degree less than or equal to $n$ is unique. However, it can be expressed in many different forms. Two such forms are

$$p_n(x) = a_0 + a_1 x + a_2 x^2 + \cdots + a_n x^n. \tag{6a}$$

$$p_n(x) = a_0 + a_1(x - x_0) + a_2(x - x_0)(x - x_1) + \cdots + a_n(x - x_0)(x - x_1)\cdots(x - x_{n-1}). \tag{6b}$$

Of these, the most convenient one to derive and use in practice is Eq. (6b). It is known as the "Newton divided difference form" of the "interpolating polynomial." The coefficients in this form depend on the given data points. If, for simplicity, we assume that the $x_i$ are equally spaced with spacing $h$ so that $x_i = x + ih (i = 0, \ldots, n)$, then the coefficients in Eq. (6b) turn out to be

$$a_k = \frac{\Delta^k f_0}{k!h^k},$$

where $\Delta^k f_0$ is the $k$th forward difference of $f(x)$ at $x = x_0$. If we define $\Delta f(x) = f(x + h) - f(x)$, then the forward difference operator $\Delta^k f_0$ of order $k$ is defined as

$$\Delta f_0 = f_1 - f_0;$$
$$\Delta^2 f_0 = \Delta f_1 - \Delta f_0;$$
$$\cdots\cdots\cdots\cdots\cdots$$
$$\Delta^k f_0 = \Delta^{k-1} f_1 - \Delta^{k-1} f_0.$$

These differences are conveniently obtained from

forward difference Table 3.

**Table 3.** Forward difference table.

| | | | | | |
|---|---|---|---|---|---|
| $x_0$ | $f_0$ | | | | |
| | | $\Delta f_0$ | | | |
| $x_1$ | $f_1$ | | $\Delta^2 f_0$ | | |
| | | $\Delta f_1$ | | $\Delta^3 f_0$ | |
| $x_2$ | $f_2$ | | $\Delta^2 f_1$ | | $\Delta^4 f_0$ |
| | | $\Delta f_2$ | | $\Delta^3 f_1$ | |
| $x_3$ | $f_3$ | | $\Delta^2 f_2$ | | |
| | | $\Delta f_3$ | | | |
| $x_4$ | $f_4$ | | | | |

The Newton formula (6b) expressed in terms of the differences $\Delta^k f_0$, which appear along the upper diagonal in Table 3, then becomes

$$p_n(x) = f_0 + \frac{\Delta f_0}{h}(x - x_0) + \frac{\Delta^2 f_0}{2 \cdot h^2}(x - x_0)(x - x_1) + \cdots + \frac{\Delta^n f_0}{n!h^n}(x - x_0)(x - x_1)\cdots(x - x_{n-1}).$$

To apply this formula to the data of Table 2, we note that there are four tabular points; hence, $n = 3$, and with $x_0 = 2.0$, $h = 0.2$, we obtain Table 4. Substituting into Eq. (7), we obtain

$$p_3(x) = 0.30103 + \frac{0.04139}{0.2}(x - 2) - \frac{0.00360}{2(0.04)}(x - 2)(x - 2.2) + \frac{0.00057}{6(0.008)}(x - 2)(x - 2.2)(x - 2.4).$$

Now, to find an estimate for $f(2.1)$, we set $\bar{x} = 2.1$ to obtain

$$f(2.1) \approx p_3(2.1) = 0.30103 + 0.020695 + 0.00045 + 0.0000356 = 0.3222106. \quad (8)$$

**Table 4**

| $x$ | $f(x)$ | $\Delta f$ | $\Delta^2 f$ | $\Delta^3 f$ |
|---|---|---|---|---|
| 2.0 | 0.30103 | | | |
| | | 0.04139 | | |
| 2.2. | 0.34242 | | −0.00360 | |
| | | 0.03779 | | 0.00057 |
| 2.4 | 0.38021 | | −0.00303 | |
| | | 0.03476 | | |
| 2.6 | 0.41497 | | | |

This example illustrates two important features of Newton polynomial interpolation. First, we can increase the degree of the interpolating polynomial by simply adding on additional terms. No recalculation of coefficients once obtained is necessary. Second, the error of the interpolating polynomial of a given degree can be estimated by examining the next term. Thus, in Eq. (8) the error in linear interpolation is approximately 0.00045, while the error in second-degree interpolation is 0.0000356. Notice that each term decreases in magnitude. A thorough study of the error in the interpolating polynomial is beyond the scope of this article. While it is true that for most smooth functions the error decreases as the degree of the interpolating polynomial increases, this does not always hold. In practice, it is usually better to use a low-degree polynomial over a smaller range of the points of tabulation than to use a high-degree polynomial over a larger range. This method of interpolation is called "piecewise polynomial interpolation." Interpolation is discussed in Wilkinson (1960) and Ralston (1965).

**Numerical Differentiation.** We turn next to a consideration of numerical differentiation. In the calculus differentiation is a well-defined process if the function to be differentiated is given explicitly. Thus, if $f(x) =$ sin $x$, $f'(x) =$ cos $x$ and if $f(x) = x$ sin $x$, then $f'(x) =$ sin $x + x$ cos $x$. If, however, the function is not known explicitly, $f(x)$ may, for example, only be known at a set of tabular points. How do we then obtain an estimate of the derivative at a point? One answer is to rely on finite difference approximations to the derivative. The simplest of these approximations is the "forward difference formula," given by

$$f'(x_0) \approx \frac{f(x_0 + h) - f(x_0)}{h} = \frac{\Delta f_0}{h}. \quad (9)$$

Since the limit on the right as $h \to 0$ is the definition of $f'(x_0)$, if it exists, then we can expect that for $h$ small enough, the difference quotient will be close to $f'(x_0)$. Geometrically, as shown in Fig. 4, the dif-

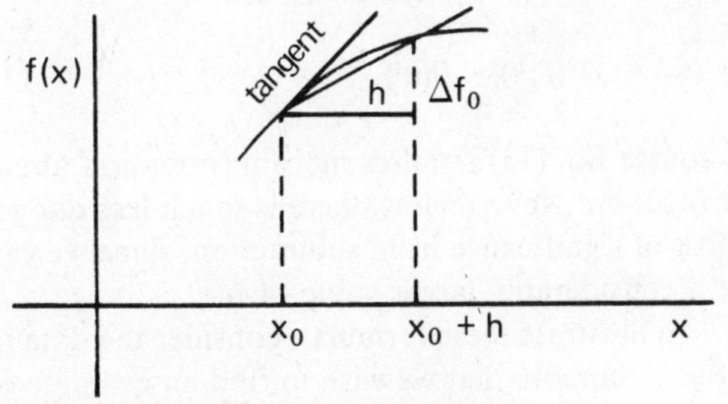


**Fig. 4.** Numerical approximation to $f'(x_0)$.

ference quotient is the slope of the chord joining the points $(x_0, f(x_0))$ and $(x_0 + h, f(x_0 + h))$.

It can be shown that the error in the forward difference formula is proportional to $h$. Hence, the approximation (9) is generally quite poor unless $h$ is very small. If, however, $h$ is taken very small, then there is a possibility of serious loss of accuracy due to the fact that we will be subtracting two quantities, $f(x_0 + h)$ and $f(x_0)$, which are nearly equal in magnitude. This type of error arises because computers have fixed word lengths. It is usually referred to as a "loss of significant digits due to subtraction." For example, if $f(x_0) = 0.76482122$ and $f(x_0 + h) = 0.76482333$, then $f(x_0 + h) - f(x_0) = 0.00000211$, which in floating-point arithmetic will be written as $0.211 \cdot 10^{-5}$. Even if $f(x_0)$ and $f(x_0 + h)$ were correct to eight significant digits, the difference will be correct to only three significant digits. How, then, do we avoid this loss of significance? One way is to use a formula that has a smaller error term and hence will not require so small a value of $h$ for a desired accuracy. One such formula is the "central difference formula":

$$D(f,h) = \frac{f(x_0 + h) - f(x_0 - h)}{2h} . \qquad (10)$$

The error term for this formula is of the order $h^2$ ($0(h^2)$); i.e.,

$$f'(x_0) - D(f,h) = ch^2 \qquad (11)$$

for some constant $c$, while the error for the forward difference formula is only $0(h)$. An even more accurate formula is

$$D^2(f,h) = -\frac{1}{12h}\{f(x_0 + 2h) - 8f(x_0 + h) + 8f(x_0 - h) - f(x_0 - 2h)\} \qquad (12)$$

The error of this formula is given by

$$f'(x_0) - D^2(f,h) = 0(h^4). \qquad (13)$$

Of course Eq. (13) requires more information about the function. Nevertheless, there is much less danger of loss of significance from subtraction, since we can use a considerably larger value of $h$.

To illustrate these formulas, consider the data in Table 5. Suppose that we wish to find an estimate of $f'(1)$, using this data. The function tabulated in Table 5 is $f(x) = e^x$, and since $f'(x) = e^x$, $f'(1) = e = 2.7183$. Using the forward difference formula (9) with $h = 0.1$, we get

$$f'(1) \approx \frac{f(1.1) - f(1.0)}{0.1} = \frac{3.0042 - 2.7183}{0.1} = 2.8590,$$

while for $h = 0.01$, we get

$$f'(1) \approx \frac{f(1.01) - f(1.0)}{0.01} = \frac{2.7456 - 2.7183}{0.01} = 2.7300.$$

Neither result here is very good.

**Table 5**

| $x$ | $f(x)$ |
|---|---|
| 0.80 | 2.2255 |
| 0.90 | 2.4596 |
| 0.96 | 2.6117 |
| 0.98 | 2.6645 |
| 0.99 | 2.6912 |
| 1.00 | 2.7183 |
| 1.01 | 2.7456 |
| 1.02 | 2.7732 |
| 1.04 | 2.8292 |
| 1.10 | 3.0042 |
| 1.20 | 3.3201 |

If we now use the central difference formula (10) with $h = 0.1$, we obtain

$$f'(x_0) \approx \frac{f(1.1) - f(0.9)}{0.2} = \frac{3.0042 - 2.4596}{0.2} = 2.7230,$$

while for $h = 0.04$ we obtain

$$f'(x_0) \approx \frac{f(1.04) - f(0.96)}{0.08} = 2.7188.$$

Finally, for $h = 0.01$ we find that

$$f'(x_0) \approx \frac{f(1.01) - f(0.99)}{0.02} = 2.7200.$$

These results are clearly better than those for the forward difference formula, but notice that the results for $h = 0.01$ are worse than those for $h = 0.04$. This is again due to loss of significance. If we now use formula (12) with $h = 0.1$, we obtain

$$f'(x_0) \approx \frac{1}{-12h}\{f(1.2) - 8f(1.1) + 8f(0.9) - f(0.8)\} = 2.7185,$$

a greatly improved result even with a rather coarse step $h$.

As this example shows, numerical differentiation is an unstable process. Even under the best of circumstances it is usually difficult to obtain good accuracy. By contrast, numerical integration, which we discuss next, is a very stable process.

**Numerical Integration.** We turn now to a consideration of numerical integration. The problem here in its simplest form is to compute an approximation to the definite integral

$$I = \int_a^b f(x)\,dx. \tag{14}$$

Geometrically, we can interpret this problem as that of finding the area between the curve for $f(x)$ and the $x$-axis on the interval $(a, b)$ (see Fig. 5).

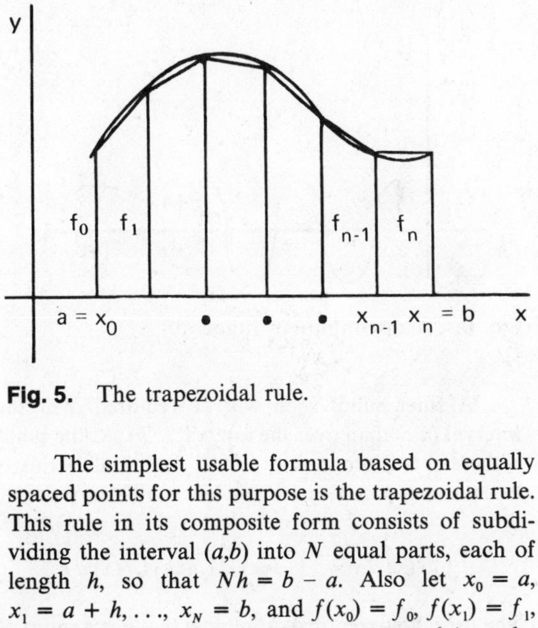


**Fig. 5.** The trapezoidal rule.

The simplest usable formula based on equally spaced points for this purpose is the trapezoidal rule. This rule in its composite form consists of subdividing the interval $(a,b)$ into $N$ equal parts, each of length $h$, so that $Nh = b - a$. Also let $x_0 = a$, $x_1 = a + h, \ldots, x_N = b$, and $f(x_0) = f_0$, $f(x_1) = f_1$, etc. The area of a trapezoid over one panel (say, the first) is

$$T = \frac{h}{2}(f_0 + f_1).$$

Adding the areas over each panel leads to the composite trapezoidal formula

$$T_N = \frac{h}{2}(f_0 + 2f_1 + 2f_2 + \cdots + 2f_{N-1} + f_N).$$

How good is $T_N$ as an approximation to the integral $I$? It is impossible to answer this question for all integrable functions $f(x)$. Sometimes the results are remarkably accurate, in some cases even exact. If we assume that the class of function we are considering is sufficiently smooth, then we might try to answer the question by examining the error in the approximation $T_N$. It can be shown that the error is given by

$$E = I - T_N = \frac{h^2(b-a)}{12} f''(\eta), \qquad a < \eta < b$$

The error here is called the "discretization error." In general we will not know $f''(\eta)$, but we see that the error in $T_N$ is proportional to $h^2$, where $h = (b - a)/N$. We can achieve any desired accuracy, at least mathematically, by taking $h$ sufficiently small. As we decrease $h$, however, the required number of function evaluations will increase and the danger of round-off error accumulation will also increase.

We have thus encountered a situation that arises frequently in numerical computations. The total error comes from two sources: a discretization error caused by using an approximate expression for the true mathematical operator, and a round-off error. To achieve good accuracy in the mathematical sense, i.e., to reduce the discretization error, we need to take smaller divisions of $h$. Round-off error, however, is inversely proportional to $h$. Hence, decreasing $h$ increases roundoff error. The numerical analyst must therefore seek algorithms that in some sense minimize the totality of errors, those due to the sum of the absolute values of the discretization and round-off errors.

Table 6 presents the results of applying the trapezoidal rule for various values of $N$ to the integral

$$I = \int_0^1 e^{-x^2}\,dx$$

calculated using both single precision (SP) and double precision (DP) arithmetic.

**Table 6.** Trapezoidal rule results for $I = \int_0^1 e^{-x^2}\,dx$

| $N$ | $T_N$(SP) | $T_N$(DP) |
|---|---|---|
| 50 | 0.74679947 | 0.74679961 |
| 100 | 0.74681776 | 0.74681800 |
| 200 | 0.74682212 | 0.74682260 |
| 400 | 0.74682275 | 0.74682375 |
| 800 | 0.74682207 | 0.74682404 |

The correct value of $I$ to eight significant figures is 0.74682413. As $N$ increases from 50 to 400, $T_N$(SP) approaches the correct result. However, for $N = 800$, the results are worse. The difference between the single precision result and the double precision result shows that the poorer results are due entirely to round-off error. Thus, for this example, the optimum single precision result would be obtained for a value of $N$ considerably less than $N = 800$. Even $N = 400$ requires considerable computational effort. This effort can be reduced by using a formula with a smaller discretization error.

One such formula is known as "Simpson's rule." It begins by subdividing the interval $(a, b)$ into $2N$ equally spaced panels, each of length $h$. Hence, $2Nh = b - a$. Again the subdivision points are labeled $x_i$ $(i = 0,1,\ldots, 2N)$ and the functional values $f(x_i) = f_i$ $(i = 0,1,\ldots, 2N)$. Over each panel of width $2h$ one now assumes that the function $f(x)$ can be approximated by a polynomial of degree 2 passing through the points $(x_{2j}, f_{2j})$, $(x_{2j+1}, f_{2j+1})$, $(x_{2j+2}, f_{2j+2})$ $(j = 0,1,\ldots,N-1)$. Integrating the polynomial over this panel then yields an approximation to the integral $f(x)$ over this panel. Adding these approximations over all subpanels of width $2h$ leads to Simpson's quadrature formula $S_{2N}$:

$$S_2N = \frac{h}{3}(f_0 + 4f_1 + 2f_2 + 4f_3 + \cdots + 4f_{2N-1} + f_{2N}). \qquad (15)$$

The error of this formula is given by

$$I - S_{2N} = \frac{-h^4(b-a)}{180} f^{iv}(\xi), \qquad a < \xi < b.$$

Again we do not in general know $f^{iv}(\xi)$, but the error is proportional to $h^4$. Thus, for functions that are sufficiently smooth, Simpson's formula should require fewer subdivisions, at least theoretically, to obtain a required accuracy compared with the trapezoidal rule. In fact, for the example considered above, Simpson's rule with $N = 50$ yields the result 0.74682400 in single precision and the result 0.74682413 (which is correct to eight significant figures) in double precision. Obviously, Simpson's rule is computationally much more efficient than the trapezoidal rule in this case, and this remains true in general for most functions $f(x)$.

Having selected a method and a step $h$ in either Simpson's formula or the trapezoidal rule, we are faced with the question: "How good are the results produced?" The error term normally provides little help, since we usually cannot evaluate the derivatives involved. One way to build some confidence in the results is to solve the same problem several times with different values of $h$ and then to compare the results. Thus, if one uses Simpson's rule with a step $h$ and then with a step $h/2$, one will have two approximations to the integral. If these two approximations agree to $s$ significant figures, the assumption is then made that the results are correct to $s$ significant figures. This method, while not conclusive mathematically, does provide some basis for confidence in the results. Each halving of the step size doubles the amount of work, however, and if the function $f(x)$ is not "smooth," the halving process may have to be repeated many times. We will not precisely define "smoothness" of a function here. However, a function that wiggles a great deal on part of an interval will be harder to integrate than one that does not, and some functions may even have singularities within the interval. In Fig. 6 we exhibit a function of this type.

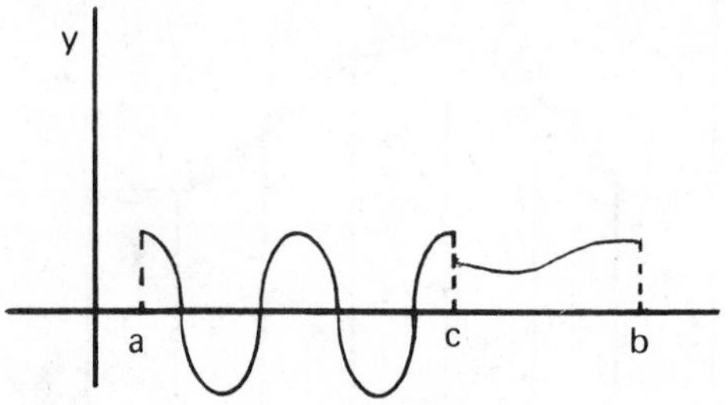


**Fig. 6.** A discontinuous function.

A finer subdivision will be required over the interval $(a,c)$ than over the interval $(c,b)$. At the point $c$ there is a discontinuity in the function. If this is known to the user, then it is reasonable to write

$$\int_a^b f(x)\,dx = \int_a^c f(x)\,dx + \int_c^b f(x)\,dx.$$

The user, however, may not know that $c$ is a point of discontinuity. An automatic approach, which has been used to handle such a situation in an efficient manner, is known as "adaptive integration." It can be based on any basic integration formula, but we choose Simpson's rule for illustrative purposes. We are given an interval $(a,b)$, the function $f(x)$, and an error $\epsilon$, and a starting step size $h$.

The procedure for adaptive integration is as follows:

1. Divide the interval $(a,b)$ into two equal parts. Call these $I_1, I_2$.

2. Using the subdivision $h$, integrate over each part separately to obtain $S_h(I_1), S_h(I_2)$.

3. Replace $h$ by $h/2$; apply Simpson's rule again to obtain $S_{h/2}(I_1), S_{h/2}(I_2)$.

4. If $| S_h(I_1) - S_{h/2}(I_1) | \leq (\frac{1}{2})\epsilon$, accept $S_{h/2}(I_1)$ and store. If $| S_h(I_2) - S_{h/2}(I_2) | \leq (\frac{1}{2})\epsilon$, accept $S_{h/2}(I_2)$ and store.

5. If both or either of these are not satisfied, divide the interval or intervals into two parts. For definiteness, assume the test is not passed on $I_2$. Divide $I_2$ into two parts $I_3$ and $I_4$. Compute $S_{h/2}$ and $S_{h/4}$ on each part and test again, this time using a test like $| S_{h/2}(I_3) - S_{h/4}(I_3) | \leq (\frac{1}{4})\epsilon$, where the coefficient of $\epsilon$ is the ratio of the subinterval to the interval $b - a$.

6. Continue the process until the test is passed on each portion. The sum of the integrals over all portions then yields the desired approximation.

The advantage of adaptive schemes is that they do only as much work as necessary on each subinterval. Even discontinuities can be handled reasonably well by this approach.

Among other formulas based on equally spaced formulas, one should mention the Newton-Cotes formulas and Romberg integration. These quadrature formulas are capable of producing higher order error terms and thus hold the promise of further reduction in computational error.

Somewhat different in nature are integration formulas of the Gaussian type. All the formulas considered above are based on equally spaced points. In Gaussian formulas one attempts to select the integration points as well as the weights so as to produce a "best" integration formula. Such formulas have the form

$$I = \int_a^b f(x)\,dx \approx \sum_{i=0}^{n} w_i f(x_i),$$

where the points $x_i$ as well as the weights $w_i$ are to be determined. Such formulas, for a given number $n$ of points, are capable of much higher accuracy. Gaussian methods can also be used to treat integrals with singularities. They are not, however, popularly used, primarily because the weights $w_i$ and the points $x_i$ turn out to be irrational numbers.

A more complete discussion of integration formulas can be found in Davis and Rabinowitz (1975).

**Differential Equations.** Now we consider methods for solving ordinary differential equations. We restrict ourselves to a first-order initial value problem; i.e., we are given an equation involving a function $y(x)$ and its derivative

$$y' = f(x,y) \tag{16a}$$

and an initial value such as

$$y'(x_0) = y_0. \tag{16b}$$

We seek a continuous function $y(x)$ which satisfies Eq. (16a) subject to the initial value (16b). The theory of differential equations tells us that Eqs. (16a) and (16b) have a unique solution, provided certain conditions on $f(x,y)$ are satisfied. Closed-form solutions are sometimes, but not very often, possible. For example, the differential system

$$y' = y, \qquad y(x_0) = y_0$$

has the solution $y(x) = y_0(\exp(x - x_0))$. More often we must rely on numerical methods to obtain an approximation to the solution over a given interval.

Let a solution be required over an interval $(x_0,b)$. We first subdivide the interval $(x_0,b)$ into $N$ equal parts of length $h$ so that $Nh = b - x_0$, and we label the subdivision points $x_n = x_0 + nh$ $(n = 0, 1, \ldots, N)$ with $x_N = b$. We will consider several methods that yield approximations $y_n$ to the true solution $y(x_n)$ at the subdivision points. The simplest of all methods is that of Euler, depicted in Fig. 7.

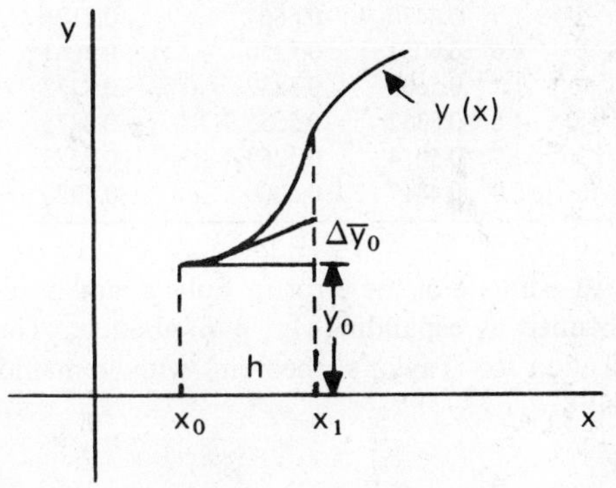


**Fig. 7.** Euler's method.

Geometrically, we find an approximate value of $y$ at $x_1$ by extending the tangent to $y(x)$ at $x_0$ to the line $x = x_1$ and then adding to $y_0$ the increment $\Delta y_0 = hf(x_0,y_0)$. We thus obtain

$$y(x_1) \approx y_1 = y_0 + hf(x_0,y_0).$$

Note in Fig. 7 that the slope to the curve $y(x)$ is

available immediately from the given equation $y' = f(x,y)$. Now that we have an estimate $y_1$ at $x = x_1$, we can calculate $y' = f(x_1,y_1)$, and thus we can step ahead to obtain

$$y(x_2) \approx y_2 = y_1 + hf(x_1,y_1).$$

The general formula, which yields $y_{n+1}$ when we know $x_n,y_n$, is

$$y_{n+1} = y_n + hf(x_n,y_n), \qquad n = 0,1,\ldots, N-1. \tag{17}$$

As an example, consider the equation

$$y' = -y^2 \quad y(1) = 1 \tag{18}$$

We choose $h = 0.1$ and apply formula (17) over the interval (1,2). The results are given in Table 7. The exact solution of Eq. (17) is $y = 1/x$. The results of Euler's method was a step $h = 0.1$ produces about one-digit accuracy.

**Table 7**

| $n$ | $x_n$ | $y_n$ | $y(x_n) = 1/x_n$ | $f(x_n,y_n) = -y_n^2$ |
|---|---|---|---|---|
| 0 | 1. | 1. | 1. | -1. |
| 1 | 1.1 | 0.0 | 0.9090 | -0.81 |
| 2 | 1.2 | 0.819 | 0.8333 | -0.6708 |
| 3 | 1.3 | 0.7519 | 0.7692 | -0.5654 |
| 4 | 1.4 | 0.6954 | 0.7143 | -0.4836 |
| 5 | 1.5 | 0.6470 | 0.6667 | -0.4186 |
| 6 | 1.6 | 0.6051 | 0.6250 | -0.3661 |
| 7 | 1.7 | 0.5685 | 0.5882 | -0.3232 |
| 8 | 1.8 | 0.5362 | 0.5555 | -0.2875 |
| 9 | 1.9 | 0.5074 | 0.5263 | -0.2575 |
| 10 | 2.0 | 0.4817 | 0.5000 | -0.2320 |

An estimate of the error in Euler's method can be obtained by expanding $y(x_n + h)$ about $x_n$. Thus, application of Taylor's theorem with remainder yields

$$y(x_n + h) = y(x_n) + hy'(x_n) + \frac{h^2}{2}y''(\xi_n), \quad x_n < \xi < x_n + h.$$

Hence, the error in one step of Euler's method is

$$y(x_n + h) - \{y(x_n) + hf(x_n,y_n)\} = \frac{h^2}{2}y''(\xi_n).$$

This is called the "local error" since it is based on the assumption that $x_n$, $y(x_n)$ are known exactly. Errors committed at each step will themselves propagate, and the global or total error at the end of $N$ steps will be considerably larger. In fact the global error of Euler's method can be shown to be of order $h$ instead of $h^2$. To achieve any kind of accuracy for the problem presented above will clearly require a much smaller value of $h$. As we decrease $h$, however, the amount of work increases because we must evaluate $f(x,y)$ once for each step and, in addition, our round-off error problems will increase. In practice, therefore, it is advisable to use formulas that are of higher order; i.e., we seek formulas for which the error is $0(h^p)$ with $p$ greater than 1.

A direct use of Taylor's theorem carried to more terms would yield a formula of the form

$$y(x_n + h) = y(x_n) + hy'(x_n) + \frac{h^2}{2}y''(x_n) + \cdots + \frac{h^k}{k!}y^{(k)}(x_n) + \frac{h^{k+1}}{(k+1)!}y^{(k+1)}(\xi_n) \tag{19}$$

If we use the first $k + 1$ terms of this formula to predict $y(x_{n+1})$, then the error would be of order $h^{k+1}$. Taylor's theorem in this form is difficult to use because the higher derivatives of $y(x)$ are generally not easily computable. Runge first discovered formulas that achieve agreement with the Taylor expansion for different values of $k$, but which depend only upon the evaluation of $f(x,y)$. One such formula is

$$y_{n+1} = y_n + \frac{h}{6}(k_1 + 2k_2 + 2k_3 + k_4), \tag{20}$$

where:

$$k_1 = hf(x_n,y_n),$$

$$k_2 = hf\left(x_n + \frac{h}{2}, y_n + \frac{k_1}{2}\right),$$

$$k_3 = hf\left(x_n + \frac{h}{2}, y_n + \frac{k_2}{2}\right),$$

$$k_4 = hf(x_n + h, y_n + k_3).$$

The local error of this method is $0(h^5)$ and the global error is $0(h^4)$. It is called a "Runge-Kutta fourth-order" method; no derivatives of $y$ other than $y' = f(x,y)$ are required. We note, however, that we must evaluate $f(x,y)$ at four different points for each step of the integration. By comparison with Euler's method, this Runge-Kutta method is far more efficient and, in addition, round-off error is considerably less for the same accuracy. For the example presented in Eq. (18), again using $h = 0.1$, at $x = 1.1$ we obtain $y_1 = 0.090909$, which agrees with the exact result 1/1.1 to all digits shown, indeed a remarkable improvement over the Euler result. The Runge-Kutta method and variations of it are very popular. It provides good accuracy, it is simple to program, it requires minimum storage, and it is stable. Its principal disadvantage, compared to methods based on finite differences, is that it requires four function evaluations per integration step.

Next we discuss the so-called multistep methods which make it possible to achieve comparable accuracy with about half the amount of work. Runge-Kutta methods are called "one-step" methods because they use information at a single point to estimate $y$ at the next point. Let us suppose that we have already estimated $y(x)$ at several successive subdivision points. For definiteness, assume that we know

$$(x_n, y_n, f_n), \qquad (x_{n-1}, y_{n-1}, f_{n-1}),$$
$$(x_{n-2}, y_{n-2}, f_{n-2}), \qquad (x_{n-3}, y_{n-3}, f_{n-3}),$$

where $f_n$ represents $f(x_n, y_n)$, etc. How can this information be used to extrapolate a value for $y$ at $x_{n+1}$? The theory of interpolation suggests one possible approach. If we integrate the equation $y' = f(x,y)$ from $x_n$ to $x_{n+1}$, we obtain

$$y(x_{n+1}) - y(x_n) = \int_{x_n}^{x_{n+1}} f(x, y(x))\, dx.$$

Since we know the value of $f$ at the four successive points $x_n$, $x_{n-1}$, $x_{n-2}$, $x_{n-3}$ we can pass a polynomial of degree 3 through these points. Integrating the resulting polynomial and evaluating it between the limits $x_n$ to $x_{n+1}$ will then yield an approximate formula for $y(x_{n+1})$. One such formula is that of Adams, which after simplification, takes the form

$$y_{n+1} = y_n + \frac{h}{24}(55f_n - 59f_{n-1} + 37f_{n-2} - 9f_{n-3}). \tag{21}$$

The local error of this formula is $0(h^5)$ and the global error $0(h^4)$, just as for the Runge-Kutta method of order 4, discussed earlier. Notice that only one new function evaluation is required to compute $y_{n+1}$. It would thus appear that a formula of this type should be computationally more efficient than the Runge-Kutta method. It turns out that the accuracy of Adams formula (21) is not quite so good as that of the Runge-Kutta method, even though both are of the same order, because the coefficient in the error term is somewhat larger. It is customary to consider the result of applying Eq. (21) as a predicted value and to correct it by using the formula

$$y^c_{n+1} = y_n + \frac{h}{24}\{9f(x_{n+1}, y^p_{n+1}) + 19f_n - 5f_{n-1} + f_{n-2}\}, \tag{22}$$

where $y^p_{n+1}$ is the value obtained from Eq. (21). The global error of Eq. (22) is also $0(h^4)$. The pair of formulas (21) and (22) is called a "predictor-corrector" pair. It yields results comparable in accuracy to the Runge-Kutta method, with about half as much work. Multistep formulas like (21) and (22) have the disadvantage of requiring special techniques for starting, since initially we have information at one point only. Some multistep methods also suffer from numerical instability, a phenomenon that can lead to disastrous results, and hence they should not be used indiscriminately. Other predictor-corrector formulas are described in Ralston (1965).

As with all numerical methods, we must ask: "How accurate are the results?" The fact that a method achieves good accuracy on one problem is no assurance that it will give comparable accuracy on another. One commonly used technique, analogous to the quadrature case, is to integrate the given differential equation twice, once with a step $h$ and again with a step $h/2$. If the two solutions at the common subdivision points agree to $s$ significant figures, we can then have some confidence in them. Indeed, if we are using the Runge-Kutta method and we let $y_{n+1}(h)$ represent the computed solution at $x_{n+1}$, then the discretization error can be represented roughly as

$$y(x_{n+1}) - y_{n+1}(h) = ch^4. \tag{23}$$

If we now replace $h$ by $h/2$, the error is

$$y(x_{n+1}) - y_{n+1}\left(\frac{h}{2}\right) = c\left(\frac{h^4}{16}\right) \tag{24}$$

In these equations we assume that $c$ is a constant that does not depend on $h$. Of course this assumption is not usually valid, but in many practical problems $c$ will change only slowly, and in such cases the following analysis is valid. Even though we do not know the exact solution $y(x_{n+1})$, we can solve (23) and (24) for $ch^4$ and substitute in (24) to obtain

$$y(x_{n+1}) - y_{n+1}\left(\frac{h}{2}\right) = \frac{y_{n+1}(h/2) - y_{n+1}(h)}{15}. \qquad (25)$$

This equation states that the error in $y_{n+1}(h/2)$ is given by the right side of Eq. (25), and this quantity is computable. Notice, however, that to obtain this error estimate we pay a severe price in computational effort, in fact more than twice the effort for a single solution.

On the other hand, if we run a multistep predictor-corrector formula such as either Eq. (21) or (22), a similar error estimate can be obtained with almost no additional effort. This can be seen from the equations

$$y(x_{n+1}) - y^p_{n+1} = c_1h^4,$$
$$y(x_{n+1}) - y^c_{n+1} = c_2h^4,$$

where $c_1, c_2$ are known constants. Eliminating $h^4$ as in Eq. (25), we obtain the error estimate

$$y(x_{n+1}) - y^c_{n+1} = \frac{c_2}{c_1 - c_2}(y^c_{n+1} - y^p_{n+1}).$$

The right-hand side, which is easily computable, is the error in going from one point $x_n$ to the next point $x_{n+1}$. It can therefore be used as a basis for deciding whether the step size $h$ is too small, too large, or about right. This is perhaps the most important advantage of multistep methods. It provides a basis for automatic monitoring of the error at little additional cost.

**Conclusion.** In a short article on numerical analysis, one can hope to present to the reader only a synopsis of the work of the numerical analyst. We have discussed only a small number of algorithms. These algorithms work well on some classes of functions, but no algorithm is uniformly best for all classes of functions. The numerical analyst must be constantly alert to indications that an algorithm is not functioning properly. We have tried to stress those qualities of good algorithms which are important for computational purposes. These qualities are speed, efficiency, and automatic error analysis and control. There are many good books on numerical analysis at various levels for the reader interested in pursuing this subject, among which are Ralston (1965), Conte (1972), and Hamming (1973).

REFERENCES

1960. Wilkinson, J. H. "Error Analysis of Floating Point Computations," *Num. Math.*, No. 2, 319–340.

1965. Ralston, A. *A First Course in Numerical Analysis.* New York: McGraw-Hill.

1972. Conte, S. D., and Carl J. deBoor. *Elementary Numerical Analysis: An Algorithmic Approach.* New York: McGraw-Hill.

1973. Hamming, R. W. *Numerical Methods for Scientists and Engineers*, 2nd ed. New York: McGraw-Hill.

1975. Davis, P., and P. Rabinowitz. *Methods in Numerical Integration.* New York: Academic Press.

S. D. CONTE

# O

**OCR.** *See* Optical Character Readers.

**OEM.** *See* Original Equipment Manufacturer.

## OBJECT PROGRAM

For articles on related subjects *see* Computer, Using a; Procedure-Oriented Languages; and Source Program.

An object program is the output of a translating program, such as an assembler or a compiler, which has converted a "source program" written in one language into another language, such as machine language, capable of being executed on a given computer.

This output may be in one of several forms: It may be in an intermediate language, needing further translating; it may be "relocatable," in which data and program references are still expressed relative to a base address; or it may be "absolute," in which all linkages between program elements have been made, and absolute address assignments established, so that the program is ready to be loaded and executed. Usage varies as to which of these may be called the "object program." Properly, any output of a translating program is the object of that step, and hence is an object program.

C. H. Davidson

## OPEN AND CLOSE A FILE

For articles on related subjects *see* Blocks and Blocking; Files; Input-Output Control System; and Logical and Physical Units.
For articles on related terms *see* Buffer; Job; Tape Label; and Update.

A file is considered *open* when it may be accessed for reading, writing, or possibly both. It is considered *closed* when it cannot be so accessed. The open routines change the state of a file from closed to open; the close routines do the opposite.

The open and close routines are the primary mechanisms by which various parameters in the logical device tables and physical device tables are initialized, or stored, and the associations between logical and physical device tables are maintained. The open and close routines also handle the initialization and update of tape and file labels. After the open routines have been executed, all data needed for further processing is available in the appropriate table. When a file has been closed, the file is in a state suitable for subsequent reopening.

When a programmer opens a data file, he often declares a number of attributes that the file will have. It is the responsibility of the open routines to initialize the proper table entries to reflect the declared attributes. For example, a file of data typically may be opened for reading only, writing only, or in some cases for both reading and writing (update). As another example, most systems allow a programmer to create a file for temporary storage of data. In such cases, the temporary file will be destroyed at the end of the job.

Upon receipt of a request to open an existing permanent file, the open routines must first find the file, which usually involves the accessing of the system catalogs and/or, if the file is one of several on the same tape reel, the positioning of the tape at the appropriate point. With indexed sequential files where the index is to be kept in main storage, the open routines will locate the index and read it into an internal buffer. If the file has been declared as temporary, then the open routines will interact with the secondary storage allocation routines to reserve space for the data that will be saved.

The next task is one of label verification and initialization of logical and physical device tables with parameters that are carried in the label. Assuming the file resides on a tape and that the operator has mounted the correct reel, the open routines will locate such file parameters as the blocking factor, the density at which information is recorded, and the description of allocated storage areas and storage formats. These parameters will be copied to the proper fields in the logical and physical device tables.

The open routines will also set the read/write/update status so that subsequent requests can be checked for validity. If the file is to be written, then a fresh label must be created, giving the date written, the edition number (multiple copies of files with the same name are updated by editions, much like newspapers), and all other pertinent data that resides in the tape label.

If the file resides on a disk or similar shared device, control information similar to that in a tape label will be accessed by the open routines in order to initialize tables. Like a tape label, this file-control information is stored with the file and gives information concerning blocking factors, storage allocation, and storage organization. The storage organization information will often be more complex than with a file on tape. For example, the strategy to be used when storing new records that might not fit in a given storage area (overflow policies) would be part of the file control information for some files stored on a disk.

Unlabeled files are also allowed in most systems. They are the normal case for data residing on punched cards. In such situations, the open routines will ignore the label verification phase. Needed control information such as physical record size must be provided by other means—e.g., as an argument to the open routines—so that table entries can still be initialized.

The routines to close a file have a number of tasks to perform before the file is ready for subsequent reopening. First, some of the data that has been logically "written" may still reside in a buffer because the buffer was not full and no physical "write" had been generated. The close routines will cause that data to be transferred to the recording medium. An end-of-file marker and perhaps also an end-of-file label will then be written if the file resides on tape. Alternately, if the file is on a direct-access device, the routines to close a file will restore indices and file-control information to their allotted storage locations, updating them to reflect any changes in the status of the file. Closing a temporary file usually results in the release of the allotted file space.

When the file is on tape, the closing routines may or may not rewind the file; often the programmer specifies which option is desired. If the file is rewound, then subsequent reopening causes the first record of the previously closed file to be processed. If not, then the next file on the tape will be processed on the subsequent opening.

Closing a file also results in the logical device table for the appropriate logical device being restored to a state that indicates that there is no file currently attached to this device. This allows subsequent requests on the logical device to be invalidated.

R. W. TAYLOR

# OPEN AND CLOSED SHOP

For articles on related subjects *see* COMPUTING CENTER; and SECURITY OF COMPUTER INSTALLATIONS, PHYSICAL.
For articles on related terms *see* MINICOMPUTERS; and MULTIPROGRAMMING.

The terms open shop and closed shop refer to operating policies and procedures of a computer center. An *open shop* permits users to enter their programs into the computer and to operate consoles and peripheral equipment without assistance from a professional staff. A *closed shop* requires users to submit their source programs to an operator (I/O handler, control clerk, etc.), who enters them into the computer.

Most minicomputer installations operate as open shops, since (1) equipment and software are simple to operate, (2) the cost of the installation is relatively small, and hence (3) inefficiencies incurred by letting users operate the equipment are less costly than maintaining a staff of computer operators. Also, (4) minicomputer users tend to be more knowledgeable about machine operations than are users of a large, closed-shop facility.

Most large, multiprogrammed computers are operated as closed shop, since the second-by-second cost of the facility is too high to permit waste of time by amateur operators. Also, the complexity and physical security aspects of large installations require a full-time operations staff to police the machine room for hazards, unauthorized visitors, etc., as well as to continually service the consoles and peripheral equipment of the computer.

D. N. FREEMAN

## OPERAND

For articles on related subjects *see* ADDRESSING; and OPERATION CODE.

An operand is the entity on which operations are performed. In a typical computer, an instruction will specify one or more operations such as FETCH, ADD, MOVE, MULTIPLY, EDIT, etc. It will also usually specify one or more operands (see Fig. 1). The operands are the data items that will be fetched, added, moved, multiplied, edited, etc.

In some special cases the operand itself may be contained in the instruction, in which case it is usually called "immediate." Usually, the instruction contains a memory address, or a number of fields from which a memory address can be calculated. That memory address is then a pointer that points to the operand and which permits the operand to be retrieved.

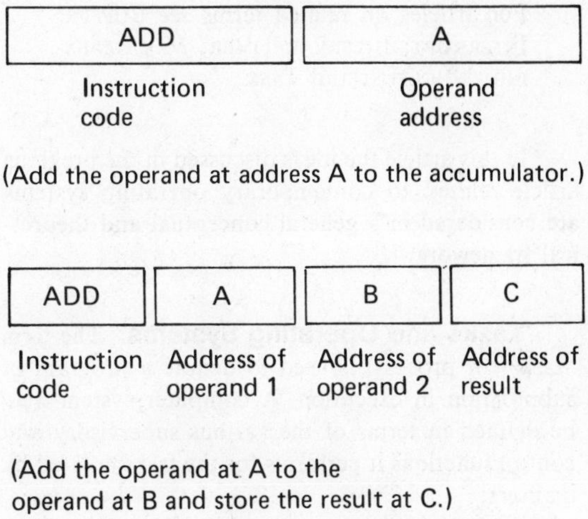


**Fig. 1.** Typical single operand and multiple operand computer instructions.

Many computers provide single-precision arithmetic operations in which the operands are numbers stored in single computer words. Some provide double-precision or multiple-precision operations in which operands may occupy two, three, or more words each.

In many nonarithmetic operations (and even in some arithmetic ones), the operands are strings of characters (or bytes). The operand address points to the beginning of the string. The extent of the string may be specified in the instruction, but in many cases it is determined by a count field or by a termination code in the operand itself.

S. ROSEN

## OPERATING SYSTEMS

### PRINCIPLES AND THEORY

For articles on related subjects *see* COMMAND AND JOB CONTROL LANGUAGES; COMPUTER ACCOUNTING AND RESOURCE CONTROL; FILES; MULTIPROCESSING; MULTIPROGRAMMING; PARALLEL PROCESSING; PROCESSING MODES; and TIME SHARING.

## OPERATING SYSTEMS

For articles on related terms *see* BUFFER; INTERRUPT; INTERVAL TIMER; MULTIPLEXING; NUCLEUS; and TASK.

In this article the ideas discussed in the previous article related to contemporary operating systems are considered in a general conceptual and theoretical framework.

**Tasks and Operating Systems.** The term "task" (or process) is used to denote a program or subprogram in execution. A computer system may be defined in terms of the various supervisory and control functions it performs for the tasks created by its users:

1. Creating and removing tasks.
2. Controlling the progress of tasks—i.e., insuring that each logically enabled task progresses at a positive rate and that no task can indefinitely block the progress of others.
3. Acting on exceptional conditions arising during the operation of a task—e.g., arithmetic or machine errors, interrupts, addressing snags, attempted execution of illegal or privileged instructions, protection violations.
4. Allocating hardware resources among tasks.
5. Providing access to software resources—e.g., file editors, compilers, assemblers, subroutine libraries, utility programs.
6. Providing protection, access control, and security for information.

**Table 1.** A Summary of the Characteristics of the Generations of Computers

| | Generations | | | |
|---|---|---|---|---|
| Characteristics | First | Second | Third | Late Third |
| Electronics | | | | |
| Components | Vacuum tubes | Transistors | Integrated circuits | Same as third |
| Time/operation | 0.1–1.0 ms | 1–10 $\mu$s | 0.1–1.0 $\mu$s | Same as third |
| Main memory | | | | |
| Components | Electrostatic tubes and delay lines | Magnetic drum and magnetic core | Magnetic core and other magnetic media | Semiconductor registers (cache) |
| Time/access | 1 ms | 1–10 $\mu$s | 0.1–1.0 $\mu$s | 0.1 $\mu$s |
| Auxiliary memory | Paper tape, cards, delay lines | Magnetic tape, disk, drum, paper cards | Same as second, plus extended core and mass core | Same as third |
| Programming languages and capabilities | Binary code and symbolic code | Higher-level languages, subroutines, recursion | Same as second, plus data structures | Same as third, plus extensible languages and concurrent programming |
| Ability of user to participate in debugging and running his program | Yes (hands on) | No | Yes (interactive and conversational programs) | Same as third |
| Hardware services and primitives | Arithmetic units | Floating-point arithmetic, interrupt facilities, microprogramming, special-purpose I/O equipment | Same as second, plus microprogramming and read-only storage, paging and relocation hardware, generalized interrupt systems, increased use of parallelism, instruction look-ahead and pipelining, datatype control | |
| Software and other services | Assemblers, compilers, limited-batch monitor, subroutine library features | Subroutine libraries, batch monitors, special-purpose I/O equipment | Same as second, plus multiaccessing and multiprogramming, time sharing and remote access, central file systems, automatic resource allocation, relocation and linking, one-level store and virtual memory, segmentation and paging, context editors, programming systems, sharing and protection of information | |

*Source:* P. J. Denning, "Third-Generation Computing Systems," *Computing Surveys*, Vol. 3, No. 4 (December 1971), pp. 175–216. (© Association for Computing Machinery, Inc.)

7. Providing a means of communicating messages or signals among tasks.

These functions must be provided by the system, since they cannot be handled adequately by the tasks themselves. The computer system software that assists the hardware to implement these functions is known as the "operating system." Table 1 shows the principal characteristics of computer and operating systems as they have evolved over the years.

Users seldom (if ever) perform a computation without assistance from the operating system. Thus, they often come to regard the entire hardware/software system, rather than the hardware alone, as "the machine." Moreover, many systems permit users to redefine or add to all but a small *nucleus* of operating-system programs; an operating system is therefore not immutable, and each user can be presented with a different "machine." The combination of the hardware plus the operating-system software, which defines the environment within which a given user may perform his tasks, is often called the "virtual machine" seen by that user.

**Types of Systems.** The range of computing systems available today is enormous. It includes general-purpose programming systems, real-time control systems, time-sharing systems, information service and teleprocessing systems, and computer network systems. All systems provide one or the other (and sometimes both) of *batch-processing* and *interactive* service.

Under batch-processing service, the user submits the program and data of his task together with control information describing what the system is to do with his task. All this is typically submitted in the form of cards, either to a single entry station in the computing center or to a remote entry station connected by a communication link to the computing center. The cards describing what the system is to do with the task cards are called the "control cards." They describe such information as processing time, memory space, and other resource requirements of the task. They also show the names of files to be used as input to, or output from, the task; the names of library procedures to be included as part of the task; the name of the language translator to be used to compile the task; and whether the task is to be loaded and executed after compilation. The system reads the cards, stores their content in a file, and places the file in a queue for processing. The details of this are presented in a later section of this article, on Job Control. After a suitable delay, the processing of the task is completed, and the original cards plus output are returned to the user.

In contrast, a system providing interactive service does not usually require the user to specify his task as a deck of cards. The function of the control cards is replaced by a set of *commands* interpreted by a *command system*, which receives control information directly from the user at a console. Each command issued by the user causes a task to be executed for him, the output of which is usually transmitted directly to him at his console. It is possible in some systems for the user to interact with the task, modifying it or its behavior as he sees fit. Interactive systems fall into four main categories:

1. Dedicated *transaction* systems, such as airline and other ticket reservation systems, in which the user may initiate tasks that perform transactions on a data base, the set of allowable transactions being fixed and small.

2. Dedicated *interactive* systems, such as Joss (Johnniac Open Shop System), Quiktran, or Basic, in which users may program tasks in a single simple language.

3. General-purpose *interactive* systems, as are offered by many time-sharing service bureaus, in which users may write and execute tasks in any one of a collection of languages supported by the system.

4. *Extensible* systems, such as M.I.T.'s CTSS (Compatible Time-Sharing System) or Multics (Multiplexed Information and Computing Service), in which users (usually by the medium of a file system that permits long-term storage and sharing of files) may extend the basic system by implementing their own languages and subsystems and making them available for others to use.

Almost all systems require that each user make prior arrangements with the computing center management before he can use the system at all. Each user will negotiate with the computing center for an account number and will pay for services rendered. Often the arrangements involve limitations on the amount of resources he can use, and new arrangements will have to be made when he has consumed his ration. (Exceptions to this most often include dedicated transaction systems and dedicated interactive systems where a user, by virtue of gaining access to a dedicated terminal, gains access to the system.) Thus, the first control card of a job submitted to a batch-processing system, or the first command issued to an interactive system, will serve to identify the user to the system; he will be permitted access only if he has an account with the system and can properly identify himself.

Because of the high degree of task/user communication in interactive systems, there is typically more overhead involved in switching resources (especially the processor and main memory) among tasks, and the execution of tasks is correspondingly less efficient than in a batch-processing system. To balance this, an interactive system provides a highly efficient environment for program development: editing, debugging, and testing. Thus, batch-processing systems are most often found in computing centers where program development is considered to be a minor part of the overall activity, and efficient production runs are considered to be the major part. Interactive systems are often found in centers where program development is considered the primary activity, and in centers where interaction is dictated, of course, by the nature of the problems being solved (e.g., ticket reservation systems, real-time control systems).

**Common Properties of Systems.** The views taken by programmers and designers of systems are almost as varied as the systems themselves. Some are viewed as large and powerful batch-processing facilities, offering a wide variety of languages, programming systems, and services (e.g., most of the IBM 360 and 370 series, most of the CDC 6000 series). Some are viewed as highly efficient environments for specific purposes (e.g., Algol on the Burroughs B5700/B6700 machines, Cobol on the Burroughs B1700). Some are viewed as extensions of some language or machine (e.g., M.I.T. Multics, IBM CP-67 virtual machine system). Others are viewed as information management systems (e.g., the SABRE airline reservations system). Still others are viewed as information utilities or extensible machines (e.g., M.I.T. Multics, the BBN TENEX system for the PDP-10, A/S Regnecentralen RC4000 system, IBM TSS/360).

Despite the diversity of system types and views about them, most operating systems have a great deal in common, arising from three basic and common design objectives: an efficient environment for program development, debugging, and execution; a wide range of problem-solving facilities; and low-cost computing through the sharing of resources and information. The characteristics in common are listed below. Not all need be found in any single system.

CONCURRENCY. This property is associated with two or more activities that are in progress simultaneously; e.g., the central processing unit can be executing instructions from some task at the same time a peripheral processor is carrying out an input/output operation. The notion of "parallel processes" or "parallel tasks," is a form of concurrency, though at a logical rather than physical level; it means that at any given time, more than one task may be observed between its initiation and termination.

ASYNCHRONISM. This refers to the potential unpredictability of the order in which events occur. Asynchronism is a consequence of concurrency and sharing. Because of dependence on total load, inaccuracies in prior information supplied by programmers with regard to the demands of their programs, and the speed differentials among the various hardware units of the system, the order in which resources are assigned, released, or accessed by tasks is unpredictable. The mechanisms for handling concurrency and sharing must be designed to allow for this. When it is desired to impose a logical ordering on certain events, synchronization mechanisms must be part of a system's design, and their use must appear explicitly in the programming of the tasks. These mechanisms cause one task to be stopped at a given point until a signal or message has been received from another task.

AUTOMATIC RESOURCE ALLOCATION. A centralized resource-allocation mechanism appears in many systems in order to monitor resource usage to satisfy objectives of good service and efficiency, especially since there is the possibility that otherwise independent tasks can interfere with one another by competing for the same resources. System control of resource allocation is a consequence of the goal of removing as much as possible of the burden of resource allocation from the programmer, in order that he may concentrate his energies fully on the logical properties of his algorithms. Moreover, the unpredictable nature of demands in systems supporting concurrent activity places the programmer at a severe disadvantage in making efficient resource allocation decisions on his own.

SHARING. This term has two related uses. First, it refers to the fact that resource *types* can be shared, irrespective of whether individual *units* of those types are sharable. Examples of resource types include hardware types such as processor and memory, and software types such as files and messages. Examples of corresponding units are, respectively, a single processor, a page of memory, a file, or a message. A unit of physical resource type is typically subject to exclusive control by the task to which it is assigned (since the task may manipulate the internal "state" of the resource unit), and some form of *multiplexing* (see below) must be used to implement the sharing. Second, the term refers to sharing of information.

Information sharing is motivated in part by the desire to be able to use, in one's own programs, subprograms or modules constructed by others; in part by the existence of problems involving the use of a central data base; and in part by a desire to avoid multiple, redundant copies of a procedure that is to be used by more than one task.

LONG-TERM STORAGE. Second-generation systems provided long-term storage only under severe limitations (e.g., it was restricted to subroutine libraries accessible only via compilers or loaders), which considerably simplified the problem of managing and protecting this information. However, many third-generation systems endeavor to provide a mechanism by which users can store files for indefinite periods, giving rise to three nontrivial implementation problems:

1. A file system must be designed to manage information entrusted to it, using symbolic file names provided by users.
2. There must be guarantees that the information will survive system failures, and even users' own mistakes.
3. A protection mechanism is required to permit access to files only as authorized.

MULTIPLEXING. This is a technique under which time is divided into disjoint intervals, and a unit of resource is assigned to at most one task during each interval. The time interval during which a task is granted exclusive control of a unit of resource may be defined naturally by the task's alternating between periods of demand and nondemand for a unit of that type, or it may be defined artificially by "time slicing" and preemption. The latter method is used primarily in time-sharing systems and other systems in which response-time deadlines must be satisfied.

The prefix *multi-* is frequently added to a term to denote some form of sharing or multiplexing:

1. *Multitasking* refers to the capability of a system to support two or more active tasks simultaneously.
2. *Multiprogramming* refers to the capability of a system to have programs or program segments of two or more tasks in main memory simultaneously. Multiprogramming implies multitasking, but not conversely; a system that has many active tasks, but loads only one at a time into main memory, is an example. The purpose of multiprogramming is to permit the concurrent operation of the devices in the system by maintaining a supply of tasks to which the central processor can be switched should the one it was processing stop to use an input/output device.
3. *Multiaccessing* refers to the capability of a system to be accessible through two or more terminal stations. It does not imply, nor is it implied by, either multitasking or multiprogramming.
4. *Multiprocessing* is used to refer to the capability of a system to provide two or more processors for the execution of tasks. (Actually, the word "multiprocessoring" should be used because "multiprocessing," taken at face value in English, means the same as "multitasking.") To be practical, multiprocessing implies multiprogramming, and therefore multitasking.

*Time sharing* is a technique used in certain multiaccess, multitask systems to permit different users simultaneously to receive the services of the system by multiplexing processor and main memory rapidly among the active tasks.

**A Model of Multitask Systems.** At the heart of most modern operating systems is the mechanism for implementing multitasking. An understanding of this mechanism is a prerequisite to an understanding of the operation of most other parts of an operating system. Accordingly, a simple model for a multitask mechanism in a single processor system is presented here.

TASK DESCRIPTORS. Each task in the system will be identified by a unique index $i$, which is a positive integer. A task in the system is described at any time by its *task descriptor*:

$$D = (ep, ip, pc, mc)$$

in which $ep$ is an environment pointer (designating, for example, the base of a region of main memory containing the program and data of the task, or the base of a page table describing the virtual address space of the task); $ip$ is the instruction pointer, designating the next instruction to be executed by the task; $pc$ is a protection code indicating the protection state or domain of the task (e.g., user or supervisor state); and $mc$ is the machine conditions (processor stateword—contents of programmable processor registers) of the task. The descriptor D of a task is given a new value at the end of each instruction execution. Observe that, to start or resume a task, all one must do is load its descriptor into a processor and start the processor. To preempt a processor from a task, one needs only to signal the processor to pause at the end of the current instruction-execution, whereupon the value of D is saved.

Since a task completely describes the sequence of its descriptor values, the preceding definitions guarantee that we can interrupt any task and preempt processor and memory resources from it without interfering with its logical progress.

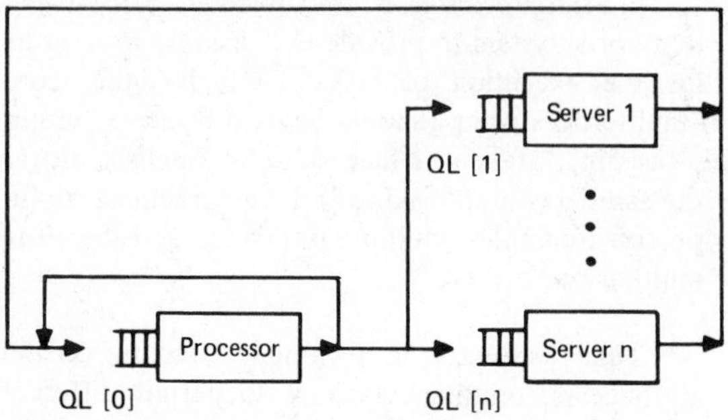


**Fig. 1.** Network diagram of system.

STRUCTURE. The system is assumed here to be equivalent to a network of queues and servers, as shown in Fig. 1. There are $n + 1$ servers, server 0 being the (single) processor and servers $1, \ldots, n$ being other types of service that tasks may request (e.g., supervisor functions like file handling or input/output operations). Associated with each server is a queue of tasks waiting for that type of service. (We assume here that the queues are FIFO [first-in first-out]; the FIFO assumption is merely a matter of convenience, for the system is straightforwardly modified to include priority and other types of queues.) A data structure called the "queue list" (QL[0:*n*]) will implement these queues. In particular, QL[*j*] will designate a FIFO queue containing the indices of tasks waiting for service of type *j*. QL[0] will be called the "ready list." Associated with server *j*, for $1 \leq j \leq n$, is a special task, the *overseer task* (O-task for short), whose duty it is to render service of type *j* to the tasks whose indices are listed in the QL[*j*]. (The scheduling of the O-tasks is discussed later.)

The *interrupt handler tasks* (tasks invoked by interrupts, faults, or exceptions, such as arithmetic errors, machine errors, protection violations, addressing snags, device completion signals) are *not* considered as O-tasks in the model described here. However, various supervisor functions are regarded as "servers" (e.g., file systems, intertask message transmission facilities, input or output operations, compilers, loaders, job initiators, and terminators). The distinction between overseer tasks and interrupt handler tasks is not essential, being made here partly as a matter of convenience and partly because most systems make such a distinction: The interrupt handler tasks are considered to be on a level of abstraction below the overseer tasks, and may therefore be used to invoke or schedule the overseer tasks.

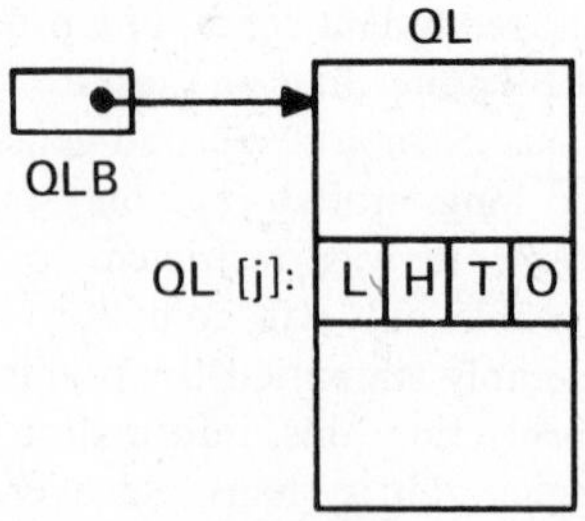


**Fig. 2.** Queue list structure.

As noted above, the queue list QL[0:*n*] designates a list of FIFO queues for the various servers. As will be shown shortly, the FIFO queues themselves are stored in another structure, the task list. As indicated in Fig. 2, the structure of a typical entry in the queue list is

QL: (QL.L, QL.H, QL.T, QL.O)

where QL.L is an integer giving the length of the queue, QL.H is the index of the task at the head of the queue, QL.T is the index of the task at the tail of the queue, and QL.O is the index of the O-task of the queue. A cell QLB (which we assume for convenience to be a processor register) contains the base address of the queue list.

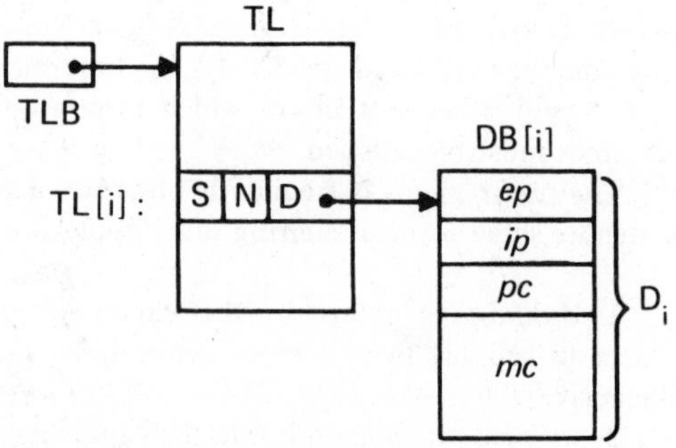


**Fig. 3.** Task list structure.

There is an additional structure, the *task list* TL[0:*m*], containing one entry for each task in the system, where *m* is the maximum number of tasks that can exist simultaneously in the system. Task 0 is an "idle task," which is executed whenever no other task is available for execution. As shown in Fig. 3, the structure of a typical entry in the task list is

TL: (TL.S, TL.N, TL.D)

where TL.S is the status of the task (i.e., the index of the queue in which the task is waiting or being served), TL.N is the index of the next task after this task in the queue whose index is in TL.S, and TL.D is a pointer to the descriptor block of the task. The *descriptor block* of task $i$, denoted by DB[$i$], is simply a contiguous set of main memory locations used for storing the descriptor of task $i$, the base address of DB[$i$] being stored in TL.D[$i$]. A cell TLB (which we assume for convenience to be a processor register) contains the base address of the task list. Fig. 4 shows the configuration of TL and QL when tasks $i_1, i_2, \ldots, i_k$ are waiting for service of type $j$.

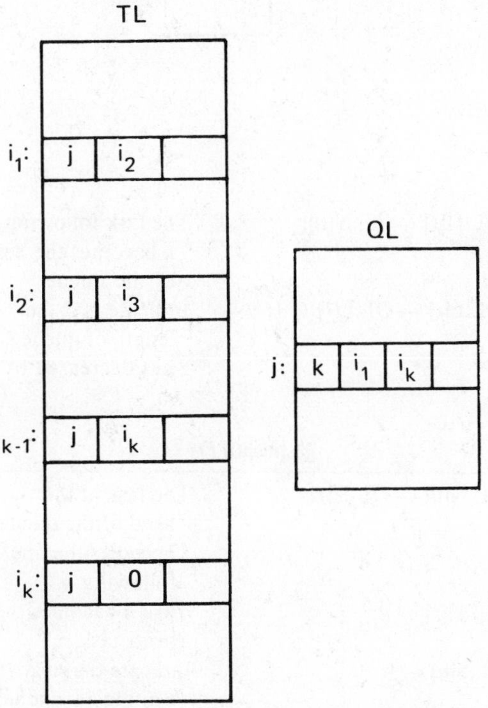


**Fig. 4.** Configuration of queue list and task list.

HARDWARE ASSUMPTIONS. The processor is assumed to contain the usual registers for holding a descriptor D of a task; the register QLB pointing to the base of the queue list; the register TLB pointing to the base of the task list; and a register T holding the index of the task currently assigned to the processor. Registers QLB and TLB are set when the system is initialized. Register T is set whenever a new task is assigned to the processor. The following special instructions are provided:

SAVE — Causes the descriptor of task $i$, where $i$ is the contents of the T register, to be saved in DB[$i$]; the base address of DB[$i$] is found in TL.D[$i$].

RESUME — Causes the descriptor of task $i$, where $i$ is the contents of the T register, to be loaded from DB[$i$], after which the processor begins executing instructions.

LOAD-T,x — Load the T register from location $x$.

STORE-T,x — Store the T register into location $x$.

SC, j (service call of type $j$) — Causes the index of the currently running task to be appended to the queue of QL[$j$] and the next task waiting for the processor (at the head of QL[0]) to be resumed (see below).

DISABLE — Turn off the interrupts (see below).

ENABLE — Turn on the interrupts (see below).

To switch the processor to another task whose index is stored in location $x$, a task needs to execute the sequence

SAVE; LOAD-T,x; RESUME;

The ability of a task to execute the above instructions may depend on the protection code (*pc*) part of its descriptor, as may its ability to alter the *ep*, *ip*, and *pc* parts of its descriptor. An attempt to execute any of the instructions when not authorized by the *pc* in the descriptor will cause an interrupt, which will invoke the interrupt handler task that acts on protection violations.

Fig. 5 summarizes the relations among the above structures. As shown, task $i$ is running on the processor, so that the *ep* register points to the address space $A_i$ of task $i$ and the *ip* register points to the next instruction task $i$ is to execute. Another task $j$, which is not running, has its descriptor stored in DB[$j$] so that the next time it is resumed, it can continue from the point designated by the value of its descriptor.

OPERATIONS. Three operations on the lists QL and TL are defined: **enqueue**($u$,$j$) causes task index $u$ to be added to the end of the queue QL[$j$]; **dequeue**($u$,$j$) causes the first entry in QL[$j$] to be removed and assigned to $u$; and **push**($u$,$j$) causes $u$ to become the first element of QL[$j$], the remaining elements of QL[$j$] being as before but starting at the

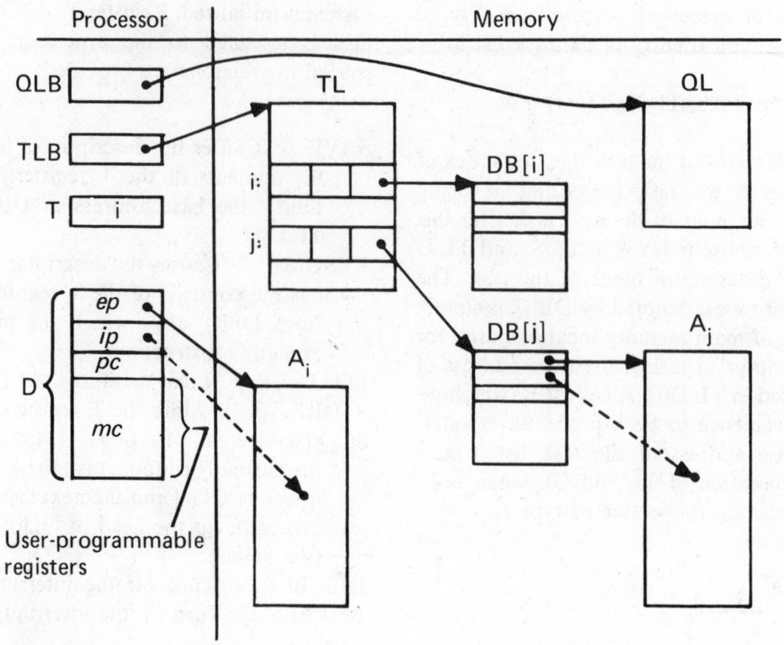


**Fig. 5.** Structure of system.

second position of the queue. For FIFO queues, these operations are defined as follows:

**enqueue**$(u,j)$

| | |
|---|---|
| **if** QL.H[$j$] = 0 **then** QL.H[$j$] ← $u$ **else** TL.N[QL.T[$j$]] ← $u$; | If the queue is empty, put $u$ at its head; otherwise, let $i$ be the task at the tail and $u$ be the task following $i$. |
| TL.N[$u$] ← 0; | Indicate that no task follows $u$ in the queue. |
| TL.S[$u$] ← $j$; | Indicate that $u$ is waiting in queue $j$. |
| QL.T[$j$] ← $u$; | Indicate that $u$ is at the tail of queue $j$. |
| QL.L[$j$] ← QL.L[$j$] + 1; | Indicate that the length of queue $j$ has increased by 1. |

**dequeue** $(u,j)$

| | |
|---|---|
| $u$ ← QL.H[$j$]; | Let $u$ be the task at the head of the queue. |
| QL.H[$j$] ← TL.N[$u$]; | The task following $u$ becomes the head of the queue. |
| QL.L[$j$] ← QL.L[$j$] − 1; | Indicate that the length of queue $j$ has decreased by 1. |

**push**$(u,j)$

| | |
|---|---|
| TL.N[$u$] ← QL.H[$j$]; | The task at the head of the queue becomes the one following $u$. |
| QL.H[$j$] ← $u$; | Task $u$ becomes the head task. |
| TL.S[$u$] ← $j$; | Indicate that $u$ is waiting in queue $j$. |
| QL.L[$j$] ← QL.L[$j$] + 1; | Indicate that the length of queue $j$ has increased by 1. |

Since the queue manipulation operations are critical sections of code, they must be executed with the processor in uninterruptible mode (see below). Often we write **enqueue**$(T,j)$, **push**$(T,j)$, and **dequeue**$(T,j)$, which of course implies the use of the LOAD-T and STORE-T instructions.

The hardware is assumed to contain a set of 1-bit *condition cells* $X[1{:}c]$ such that the event $X[k]$: $0 \rightarrow 1$ signifies the occurrence of the $k$th *exceptional condition* where $1 \leq k \leq c$. (Condition cells corresponding to channel completion signals are sometimes called "channel indicators.") Define the signal $X$ to be 1 whenever $X[k] = 1$ for some $k$, and 0 otherwise. We assume that the hardware also contains a 1-bit *mask cell* $M$ such that $M = 1$ indicates that conditions are to be recognized and acted on (interrupts are "enabled") and $M = 0$ indicates that action on condition-occurrences is to be deferred (interrupts are "disabled" or "masked off").

As noted earlier, two instructions are provided for setting the mask cell: DISABLE causes the action $M \leftarrow 0$; and ENABLE causes the action $M \leftarrow 1$, but this action is deferred until *after* the completion of the next instruction so that a new task can be resumed if necessary before another interrupt is recognized (see below). The signal $Y = MX$ is 1 if and only if both $M$ and $X$ are 1. At specified points in the execution of instructions—usually at the end of the instruction cycle or on references to memory—the processor will execute an action equivalent to

**if** Y = 1 **then** {$M \leftarrow 0$; DISPATCH;}

where

| DISPATCH | |
|---|---|
| **push**(T,0) | Save the index of the running task at the head of the ready list. |
| SAVE; | Save the descriptor of the running task. |
| LOAD-T, H[k]; | Load the index of the interrupt handler task corresponding to the index $k$ of the condition being recognized. |
| RESUME; | Load the descriptor of the interrupt handler task and begin execution. |

Here, $k$ is a signal generated by the hardware, having as value the index of the interrupt condition to be acted on—usually $k$ will designate the interrupt of highest priority (e.g., $k = \min\{i \mid X[i] = 1\}$—and H[1:$c$] is an array whose position is known to DISPATCH such that H[$k$] contains the index of the handler task for condition $k$. (The array H is sometimes called an "interrupt vector" and is sometimes implemented as registers in the processor.) Since RESUME (in DISPATCH) does not cause the action $M \leftarrow 1$, the condition handler task will operate with the interrupts off. When it completes its action, the handler executes the sequence

**dequeue**(T,0); ENABLE; RESUME;

which resumes the task at the head of the ready list. Since the effect of ENABLE is deferred until after the next instruction-execution, the RESUME operation will be completed before the interrupts come back on.

Let us consider the schema of an O-task. It was mentioned that the instruction SC,$j$ is available for a user-task to signal the need for service of type $j$; this instruction is supposed to place the task executing it at the end of QL[$j$]. Since the number of possible types of service may be variable (e.g., some functions are implemented in software) and the operation of SC is relatively complex, most systems are designed so that the SC instruction uses the interrupt mechanism

SC,j: {J $\leftarrow$ j; X[$k_{SC}$] $\leftarrow$ 1;}

where J is a special register and $k_{SC}$ is the index of the exceptional condition caused by an SC instruction. Another reason for using the interrupt mechanism for invoking O-tasks is protection: it guarantees that control is transferred only to the entry point of the O-task (i.e., it implements "protected entry point"). The handler task operates as follows:

| task H[$k_{SC}$] | |
|---|---|
| X[$k_{SC}$] $\leftarrow$ 0; | Turn off the condition cell. |
| **dequeue**(u,0); | Save the index of the task at the head of the ready list in the variable *u* (so that *u* is the task interrupted by the SC interrupt). |
| **enqueue**(u,J); | Place *u* on the queue for service requested (the index of the service requested being in the J register). |
| **if** TL.S[QL.O[J]] $\neq$ 0 **then enqueue**(QL.O[J],0); | The index of the O-task for queue J is in QL.O[J]; if this task is not in the ready list, it is placed there. |
| **dequeue**(T,0); ENABLE; RESUME; | Resume the next ready task. |

The fourth step above schedules the O-task for the service requested if that O-task is not already on the ready list. (Recall that TL.S[*i*] for any task *i* indicates the index of the queue in which task *i* is waiting.) Although the fourth step above shows the O-task being placed at the end of the ready list, a more realistic system would give it priority in the ready list. The operation of the O-task is

O-task j

| | |
|---|---|
| Perform service j for task QL.H[j]; | Perform the requested service for the task at the head of queue *j*. |
| DISABLE; | Turn off the interrupts, as subsequent actions will manipulate the queue list and task list. |
| **dequeue**(u, j); | Let *u* be the index of the task at the head of queue *j* (which task has now had service completed for it). |
| **enqueue**(u,0); | Place *u* at the end of the ready list. |
| reinitialize DB[O-task j]; | Since O-task *j* could have been interrupted before the DISABLE, the descriptor block needs to be reinitialized so that future resumptions of this task start at the beginning. |
| **if** QL.L[j] > 0 **then enqueue**(T,0) **else** TL.S[O-task j] ← j; | If there is more work for O-task *j*, place its index on the ready list. Otherwise, indicate that this task is not ready and is in fact waiting for work to appear in queue *j*. |
| **dequeue**(T,0); ENABLE; RESUME; | Resume the next ready task. |

In the case of a channel-driving task, the action "perform service j" will check to see if the channel is busy and if so take no further action; otherwise, it will specify work for the channel (in the form of a channel program) and start the channel. The channel completion interrupt will invoke an interrupt handler task that will initiate the channel for the next task (see below).

Note that the queue-manipulation portion of O-task *j* operates with the interrupts off; some O-tasks may be designed to operate entirely in uninterruptible mode, in which case DISABLE would become the first step. Some O-tasks may be intended to complete all work in QL[*j*] before relinquishing the processor, in which case the task could follow the design:

O-task j

| | |
|---|---|
| DISABLE; | Turn off the interrupts while manipulating queue. |
| L1: **if** QL.L[j] = 0 **then goto** L2; | If queue *j* is empty, there is no more work to do. |
| ENABLE; | Turn on interrupts while performing service *j* for task at head of queue. |
| Perform service j for task QL.H[j]; | Perform service for task at head of queue. |
| DISABLE; | Turn off the interrupts. |
| **dequeue**(u,j); **enqueue**(u,0); | Move task for which service now is complete back to the ready list. |
| **goto** L1; | Repeat for next task in queue *j*. |
| L2: TL.S[O-task j] ← j; | Indicate O-task *j* not in ready list. |
| reinitialize DB[O-task j]; | Reinitialize its descriptor block. |
| **dequeue**(T,0); ENABLE; RESUME; | Resume the next ready task. |

Next we need to consider the operation of the exceptional condition handler tasks (we mentioned one, task H[$k_{SC}$], above), since these tasks are the only tasks other than the O-tasks with authority to manipulate the queues. Suppose $k_{ERR}$ is the index of some error condition caused by the running task; the action to be performed is one of three:

A. Rectify the error and resume the task.
B. Stop the task and report to a superior of the erroneous task.
C. Stop the task and report the error to the task's user.

If action A is intended, the handler task schema is

task H[$k_{ERR}$]

| | |
|---|---|
| X[$k_{ERR}$] ← 0; | Turn off the condition cell. |
| Perform action A; | Take intended action. |
| **dequeue**(T,0); ENABLE; RESUME; | Resume next ready task. |

If actions B or C are intended:

task H[$k_{ERR}$]

| | |
|---|---|
| X[$k_{ERR}$] ← 0; | Turn off condition cell. |
| **dequeue**(u,0); | Get index of interrupted task from head of ready list. |
| Perform action B or C on task u; | Perform intended action. |
| **dequeue**(T,0); ENABLE; RESUME; | Resume next ready task. |

Note that task H[$k_{ERR}$] does not save its own descriptor on completion—DB[H[$k_{ERR}$]] is thus never altered, so that later resumptions of this task will always start it with the initial value of its descriptor.

Next consider the form of a handler task for a condition *not* caused by the interrupted task. One important such condition is the completion signal from a device or channel started previously by some O-task. Suppose $k_j$ is the index of the condition corresponding to a completion signal from channel $j$, and the tasks waiting for service on channel $j$ are queued in QL[j]:

task H[$k_j$]

| | |
|---|---|
| X[$k_j$] ← 0; | Turn off condition cell. |
| **dequeue**(u, j); **enqueue**(u,0); | Move completed task to ready list. |
| **if** QL.L[j] > 0 **then**{specify work for the device or channel, to be performed on task QL.H[j]; start the device or channel;} | If tasks are waiting, specify work and start the channel on the next task. |
| **dequeue**(T,0); ENABLE; RESUME; | Resume next ready task. |

Another important such case is the *clock interrupt*, which is used to force the preemption of the running task after some time limit, if that task has failed to relinquish the processor for some other reason. In systems having a clock interrupt, a hardware clock is initialized with some value $v$; after $v$ time units, the clock generates an exception signal. The clock handler task is

task H[$k_{CLK}$]

| | |
|---|---|
| X[$k_{CLK}$] ← 0; | Turn off condition cell. |
| **dequeue**(u,0); **enqueue**(u,0) | Move interrupted task to tail of the ready list. |
| LOAD-CLOCK, v; | Load the value of a time limit (quantum) into the clock. |
| **dequeue**(T,0); ENABLE; RESUME; | Resume next ready task. |

**Message Sending.** It is frequently necessary to be able to transmit messages among tasks in the system, these messages being useful to request service and to receive replies from service tasks. A simple extension of the previous system will handle this. With each task is associated a private *message queue*, consisting of a linked list of *message buffers*. Each buffer contains a single message, and all buffers reside in a system buffer area (outside the address spaces of tasks). For the purposes of this discussion, it is convenient to assume that all message buffers are of the same size (say, $b$ words). The first word of a buffer is a *link field*, and is used to point to the next buffer on the chain. The second word of a buffer is an *identification field*, and is used to contain the *index of the task which sent the message*. (See Figs. 6 and 7.) The structure of each task-list entry is extended to include pointers to the head (TL.MH) and tail (TL.MT) of the chain of message buffers.

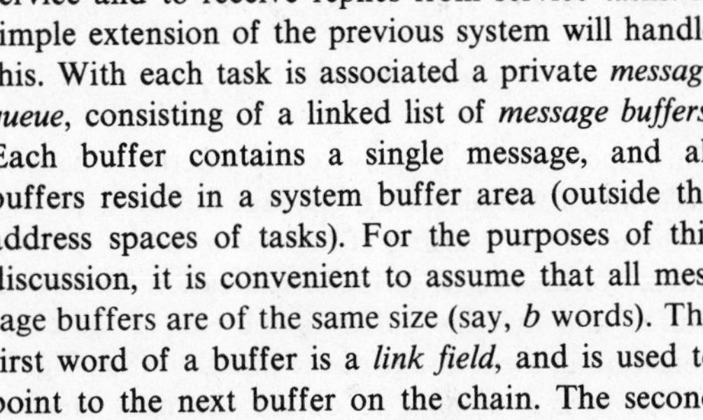

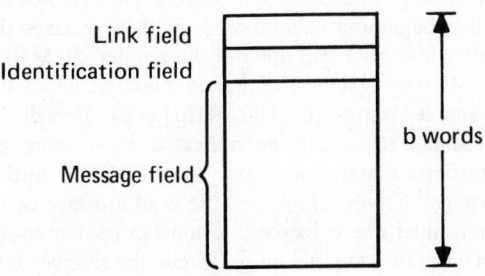


**Fig. 6.** A message buffer.

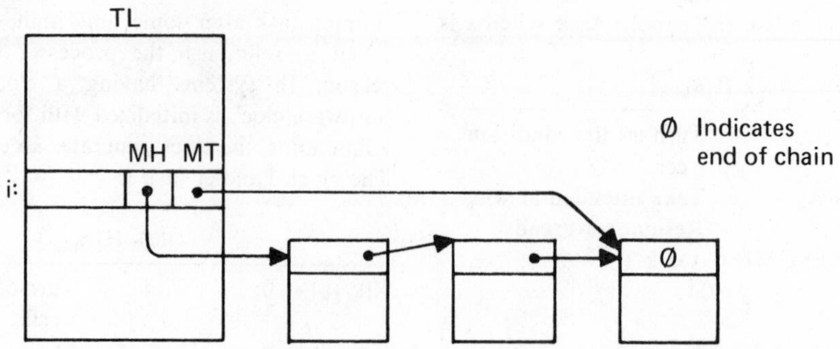


**Fig. 7.** A chain of messages in TL[$i$].

The identification field serves two purposes: First, it allows a task to send a *return message* to another task. Second, it is very useful for implementing *protected entry points*, since a receiver always knows the identification of the sender and there is no way for a sender to "enter" the receiver except at the point where the receiver examines its message buffer.

A task $i$ wishing to send a message to task $j$, places the message in a region with base address $a$ of its address space ($A_i$); it then executes the operation

**send message** (a, j).

This operation will activate an interrupt handler task, which will allocate a message buffer, copy into it the message (starting at address $a$ in $A_i$), put the index $i$ of the sender in the identification field of the buffer, and link the buffer to the end of the chain constituting the message queue in task $j$. (See Fig. 7.)

A task $i$ wishing to obtain the next message from its message queue executes the operation

**get message** (a).

This operation will activate an interrupt handler task, which will copy the message (including the identification field) from the buffer at the head of the message queue into the address space ($A_i$) of the caller, beginning at address $a$; it then releases the buffer to a pool and updates the pointer TL.MH[$i$].

If task $i$ should request a message when the queue is empty (i.e., TL.MH[$i$] = 0), it will be suspended (this can be indicated by placing an appropriate status indicator into TL.S[$i$]) unitl a message arrives. Therefore, the **send message** operation must check to see if when the next message becomes the only one in the queue the receiver task is waiting for a message; if so, the **get message** operation previously initiated by that task is completed. Instead of forcing a task to wait when it attempts to get a message from an empty queue, it is possible to implement an operation that tests whether a message is present; if there is no message present, the testing task could presumably perform other work and retest for a message later on. This is usually considered undesirable: it is easy for a task waiting for a message to enter a *busy loop* testing for the presence of a message, and thereby wasting processor time.

**File Storage.** Many systems provide each task with access to files on secondary storage for use during execution. In the majority of cases, a system will provide a capability only for a task to use temporary files during its execution, such files being deleted when the task terminates. A few systems provide long-term storage facilities, according to which a user can store a collection of files of his own choosing for indefinite periods; in particular, his files continue their existence even at times when there is no active task authorized to use them.

A basic file capability is easily added to the multitask system model. Associated with each user account is a *file directory*, containing pointers to all the user's permanent files. (If he has no permanent files, the directory will, of course, be empty when the user is not using the system.) When the user successfully gains access to the system, his task will be provided with a pointer to his file directory; this pointer is stored in an extension (TL.F) to a task list entry. Fig. 8 shows task $i$ having access to an input and an output file. Whenever a task calls for service from a file-manipulation task, it is an easy matter for the latter to locate the file directory (and therefore the files) of the former.

**Job Control.** The basic multitask system of the previous sections now has the capabilities to

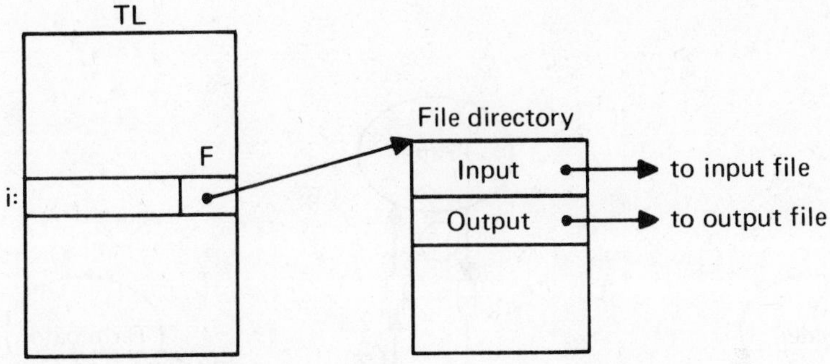


**Fig. 8.** Files belonging to a task.

support the execution of a job submitted by the user. To avoid unnecessary detail, a simple example of a typical batch job will be given. It will suffice to show the principles of operation in this case. A typical job submitted in the form of cards will be equivalent to the following:

```
Job Step    Cards
            //JOB BEGIN, IDENTIFICATION
   1        //COMPILE IN LANGUAGE L
   2        //LOAD
   3        //EXECUTE
   4        //PRINT OUTPUT
            //PROGRAM BEGIN
                .
                . (program cards)
                .
            //PROGRAM END
            //DATA BEGIN
                .
                . (data cards)
                .
            //DATA END
            //JOB END
```

The submitted cards are of two types: *control cards,* which begin with a special marking ("//" in the example), and *program or data cards*. The former specify how the job is to run; the latter specify the job itself. As indicated above, the example job has four main *job steps* indicated on the control cards. The following system tasks will be involved in carrying out the job steps:

Reader: Read the cards. Authenticate user identification information.
Create a file directory pointing to three files:
*commands*: images of the control cards
*program*: images of the program cards
*input*: images of the data cards
Send to the control card interpreter a message containing a pointer to this file directory.

Control Card Interpreter: Get the next message (using the **get message** operation). Using the file directory pointer in the message, access the *commands* file, and obtain the next unexecuted control card. If the control cards are exhausted, delete the file directory and all files. Otherwise, send to the task that implements the command on the control card a message containing the pointer to the file directory.

Compiler (of language L): Get the next message (using the **get message** operation). Using the file directory pointer in it, access the *program* file, and compile it, producing a new file *compiled program*. Place a pointer to this file in the directory. Send to the control card interpreter a return message containing the pointer to the file directory.

Loader: Get the next message (using the **get message** operation). Using the file directory pointer in it, access the file *compiled program* and load it, together with any routines required from the system library, into a file *address space*. A pointer to this file is placed in the directory. Send to the control card interpreter a reply message containing the pointer to the file directory.

Initiator: Get the next message (using the **get message** operation). Using the file directory pointer in it, obtain the pointer to the file *address space*. Find an unused task index, $i$, and create a task list entry for it, with a pointer to *address space* and an initial descriptor in DB[$i$], and the pointer to the file directory in TL.F[$i$]. Add a pointer for the file *output* to the file directory. Add the new task to the ready list.

Terminator: Gains control (by the SC instruction) when a task terminates. Create a message con-

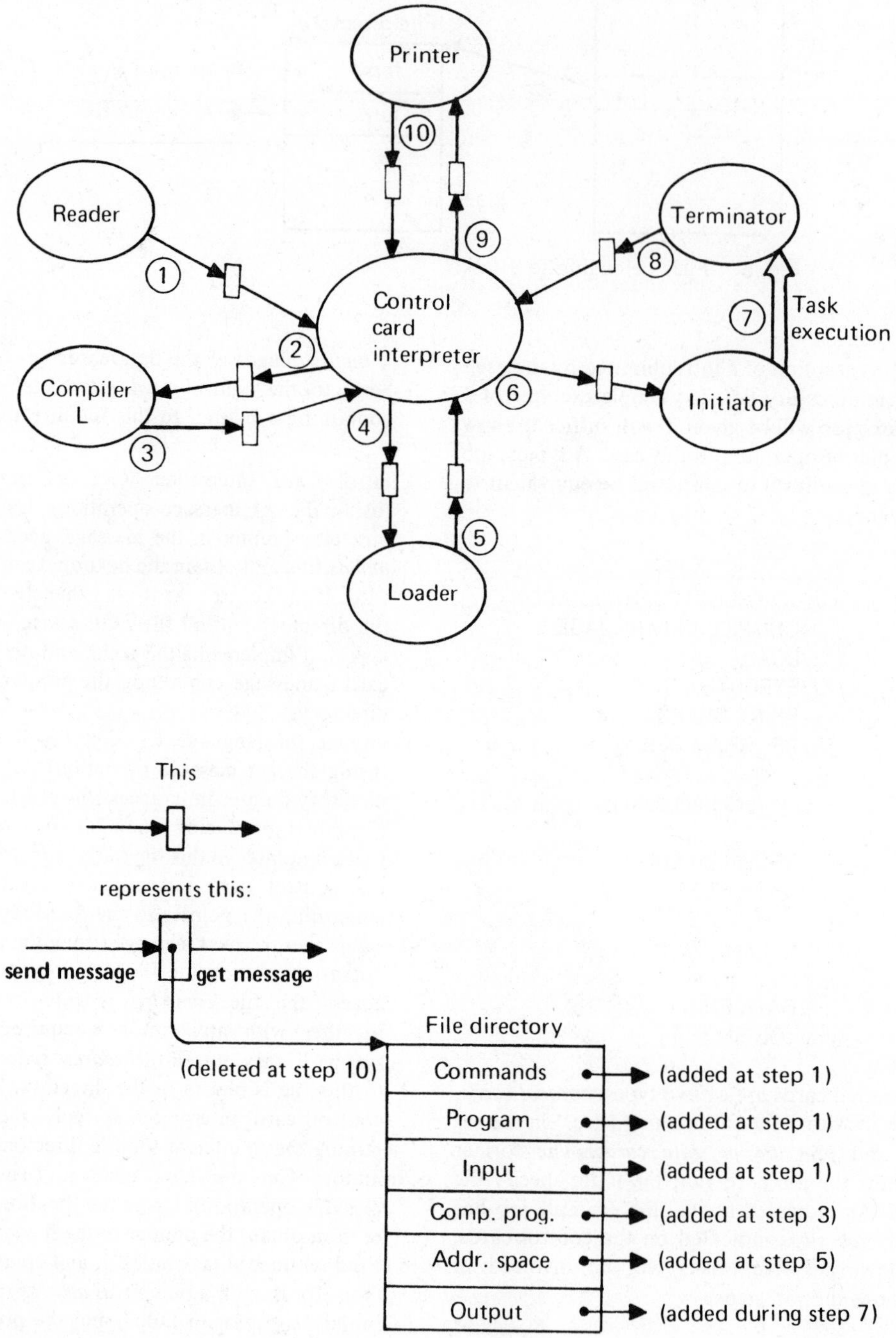


**Fig. 9.** Flow of job steps.

taining the pointer to the file directory of the terminated task. De-allocate the task list entry TL[*i*]. Send the message to the control card interpreter.

Printer: Get the next message (using the **get message** operation). Using the file directory pointer in it, access the *output* file and print it. Send to the control card interpreter a return message containing a pointer to the file directory.

When the task created by the initiator comes into existence, it executes the program in its address space. Any input/output operations (which are invoked by the SC instruction) refer to the *input* and *output* files listed in the task's file directory.

Fig. 9 shows the flow of messages among the tasks mentioned above as they cooperate in carrying out the steps of a job. There are ten message transmissions in the example given. Note that each message contains a pointer to the file directory containing the file to be processed by the task receiving the message.

In the example, the control card interpreter deletes the file directory and the files when the job is completed. In a more general implementation, each file would be designated "temporary" or "permanent," and only the temporary files would be deleted. In a time-sharing system, the basic operations above are the same except that there is usually a unique *command interpreter* task, associated with each active terminal, to process the commands (and other input and output) from that terminal.

### References

1971. Denning, P. J. "Third Generation Computer Systems," *Computing Surveys*, Vol. 3, No. 4 (December), pp. 175–216.

1972. Organick, E. I. *The MULTICS System: An Examination of Its Structure*. Cambridge, Mass.: M.I.T. Press.

1972. Wilkes, M. V. *Time Sharing Computer Systems* (2d Ed.). New York: American Elsevier.

1973. Coffman, E. G., Jr., and P. J. Denning. *Operating Systems Theory*. Englewood Cliffs, N.J.: Prentice-Hall, Inc.

1973. Katzan, H. *Operating Systems: A Pragmatic Approach*. New York: Van Nostrand-Reinhold.

1973. Organick, E. I. *Computer System Organization: The B5700/B6700 Series*. New York: Academic Press.

1974. Shaw, A. *The Logical Design of Operating Systems*. Englewood Cliffs, N.J.: Prentice-Hall.

1975. Graham, R. M. *Principles of Systems Programming*. Reading, Mass.: Addison-Wesley.

P. J. Denning

## CONTEMPORARY FEATURES

For articles on related subjects *see* Addressing; Buffer; Command and Job Control Languages; Computer Systems; Data Base and Data Base Management; Data Security; Input-Output Devices; Memory: Main; Memory: Auxiliary; Memory Protection; Multiprocessing; Multiprogramming; Processing Modes; Program Libraries; Software; Spooling; and Time Sharing.

For articles on related terms *see* Data Processing; Data Set; Files; IBM 360–370 Series; Job; Overlay; Swapping; Throughput; and Turnaround Time.

This article briefly surveys the features provided by computer operating systems. Basically, an operating system is the software (programs and data) that initiates the interaction of the electronic and electromechanical components of a computer so that they constitute a useful system for carrying out calculations. The operating system is responsible for sharing the computer equipment among users and is therefore sometimes identified by functional names such as *control programs, supervisors, executives*, or *monitors*, although these names have gradually fallen out of use.

From the viewpoint of a *user* of a computer system, the purpose of an operating system is to provide a convenient and economical means of processing his programs, but from the viewpoint of the person who manages a computer system, the purpose of an operating system is to share the computer equipment among several users in such a way as to maximize the system's throughput. That is, the objective of a system manager is to maximize the amount of useful work performed by the system. This difference in objective is analogous to that between a purchaser and seller of retail goods. The buyer wants the best buy he can get for the money he spends, and the merchandiser wants the best price for the quality of goods and services he sells. In a computer system, the operating system is supposed to effect a satisfactory match between user and manager objectives.

**Equipment Needed to Satisfy User Requirements.** This article gives examples of computer services required by users, and then discusses the actual computer equipment and the technological constraints (speed and size) which this equipment imposes upon the system.

Economy and Convenience for the User. A user of a computer system typically submits a *job* to the computer center. This job consists of a program to be run by the computer (as well as data to be processed by the program). There is a tremendous variation in the characteristics of jobs that are submitted to different computer systems by different users. We give four examples.

1. *A Typical Small, One-Time Job.* Most commonly, these are submitted by students at a high school or university and may consist, for example, of 60 punched cards. The student's job description might print out a table of values of the sine function. Student jobs such as this one require little calculation; the reading of the student's cards and the printing of his answers may take longer than does the calculation. The student wants good *turnaround time*; i.e., he wants to see his results soon after he submits his job.

2. *A Typical Scientific Calculation.* A physicist may need to calculate the focusing properties of a proposed set of lenses for a telescope. He writes a computer program to determine these properties for various lens configurations. He punches his program onto cards (say, 1,500 cards) and submits the cards as a job to the computer center. Scientific jobs such as this one require a lot of calculation. Although the scientist wants good turnaround time, he is also concerned that his job will not *cost* too much to run. In many systems, the manager bills each user, such as the physicist, for the time required to process the user's jobs.

3. *A Typical Business Data Processing Job.* Let us suppose that the electric utility company in a small town keeps the accounts for its customers on punched cards. Each month a billing card is keypunched for each customer to record the amount of electricity used. At billing time, a job is submitted to the computer system in order to read account cards and billing cards, and to print bills to be sent to customers. The job will perform simple calculations such as multiplying the electricity usage of a customer times the cost per kilowatt-hour of electricity. Data processing jobs, such as this one, often require a lot of printing and reading of *files*, such as the reading of the file of account cards. On the other hand, these jobs typically require little computation. The electric utility company does not require a short turnaround time (after all, bills are printed only once a month). However, the company is very concerned about *reliability*, for its own sake as well as the customer's.

4. *A Typical Interactive Programming Session.* Some computer systems support interactive consoles (typewriterlike devices). These consoles allow the user to interact with the computer on a line-by-line basis. By contrast, in the first three examples, an entire job was submitted as a unit. Consider a civil engineer who wishes to evaluate a complicated formula for the thickness of concrete pillars required to support a given bridge. He could type the formula into the computer, using his console, and then receive back the required thickness. But the engineer also wants good *response time*; i.e., he wants the computer to evaluate his formula in at most a few seconds.

These four examples are not intended to illustrate *all* uses of computer systems, but to demonstrate the *diversity of needs* of computer users. We now turn to the equipment needed to satisfy these requirements.

Equipment in a Computer System. If cost could be ignored, we could dedicate a computer system to every user. Unfortunately, computer systems remain quite expensive, and many users are able to run their jobs only because the cost of the system is supported by many users. We can regard the operating system as a necessary evil, which must be tolerated in order to share the equipment and to distribute its operational cost among individual users.

By seeing that the equipment is used efficiently, the operating system can increase throughput and thus decrease cost to users. The designer of an operating system will need to have an intimate understanding of the equipment, in order to see that equipment can be used efficiently. We now list the items of equipment comprising a computer system.

1. *Central Processing Unit (CPU).* This part of the system actually performs the calculations required by users. Calculations are broken into basic operations (e.g., addition); each operation may take a microsecond (0.000001 sec) or less to perform its work. That is, modern CPU's can perform a million or more operations per second.

2. *High-Speed Memory, or Memory.* The memory holds programs and data; the programs are sequences of operations to be performed by the CPU. Memory is typically divided into *bytes*, each of

which can hold one character of information. Memory sizes for different computer systems range from a few thousand bytes to several million bytes.

3. *Magnetic Disks, or Disks.* Disks provide storage for programs and data; this storage is cheaper (per byte) and larger than high-speed memory. Programs and data stored on a disk cannot be directly accessed by the CPU. Before being used, information must be transferred from the disk into high-speed memory. The transfer of a block of information (say, 1,000 bytes) from the disk to memory may require 10 ms (0.01 sec). Although 10 ms seems like a very short time to a person, it is not so short to a CPU; a CPU can perform around ten thousand operations in 10 ms. A typical disk can hold about 10 million bytes of information. In computer systems, it is common for the information capacity of the disks to be 10 to 1,000 times that of the high-speed memory. The purpose of disks is to hold programs and data that are not currently active in the high-speed memory.

4. *Card Readers.* These devices read punched cards and transfer their contents into memory. A typical card reader can read 300 cards a minute (i.e., 5 cards per second). Note that a CPU with a microsecond ($\mu$s) instruction time can perform 200,000 operations in the time taken to read one card.

5. *Printers.* These devices take lines of text from memory and print them on paper. A typical printer can produce 300 to 2,000 lines per minute.

6. *Consoles.* These are typewriterlike devices. A person can type information into the computer and the computer can type information back to the user. A typical console can print about a line a second. Hence, the CPU can perform about a million operations in the time taken to print a line. Most computer systems have an *operator's console*; the person who is the *operator* for the computer system can give commands to the system via this console.

For brevity's sake, we have limited this discussion to the six classes of devices listed above. Actual computer systems often have other pieces of equipment, such as magnetic drums, magnetic tape drives, card punches, paper-tape readers and punches, etc.

We have given the speeds and capacities of the above six types of devices in order to illustrate their diversity. It is a great challenge to the operating system to transform these seemingly mismatched speed ratios (varying by as much as a million to one) into a convenient and efficient system.

Traditionally, the CPU and the high-speed memory have been the most expensive components of a computer system. The operating system must see that the CPU does not remain idle while work is to be done, and that memory is occupied by active programs and data. We now present features of operating systems that are designed to accomplish these aims.

**Features of Operating Systems.** In some *very small* computer systems, there is little need for an operating system. In those systems, the sharing of the equipment can be handled on a *manual* basis. For example, a user may sign up to use the system between 10:00 and 11:00 A.M. It is the user's responsibility to provide all software to run the system. At the end of his allocated time, the user relinquishes the machine to the next user.

AUTOMATIC JOB SEQUENCING. The problem with manual scheduling is that the equipment may be idle for relatively long periods between the time when one user finishes his work and the next user sets up the machine for his job. For larger and more expensive computer systems, it is advantageous to provide software that automatically begins running the next job as soon as the current job finishes. This software is called a "sequential batch operating system."

Introducing a sequential batch operating system can more than double the throughput of the system simply by eliminating idle time between jobs. The obvious disadvantages of such a system over manual scheduling are (1) the expense of writing the software that does the sequencing, and (2) providing memory and disk space to store the operating system.

COMMON INPUT/OUTPUT ROUTINES. When a number of users share a computer system, it becomes convenient to write a common set of routines to control the input/output devices (printers, readers, etc). These routines schedule these devices and are absorbed into the software comprising the operating system.

OFF-LINING OF INPUT/OUTPUT. Once the idle time between jobs has been minimized, the mismatch between the speed of the CPU and the input/output devices emerges as an important source of inefficiency. For a typical job, the CPU time used may approximately equal the time the input/output devices spend in reading and writing. If the CPU remains idle while the input/output devices are running, and vice versa, then the CPU and input/output devices will each be idle about 50% of the time.

One solution to this problem is to move the card reader and printer to a cheaper off-line system and replace them on the main system with high-speed magnetic tape drives. In the off-line system, a sequence (batch) of user jobs is loaded onto a magnetic tape. The tape is then manually transferred to the main system, which runs the jobs on the tape and places the output from those jobs on another magnetic tape. Finally, this output tape is carried to the off-line system, which prints the results. This process of separating card reading and printing from the actual running of jobs is called "off-lining."

The primary advantage of off-lining is that the CPU of the main system does not need to wait for relatively slow devices, such as card readers and printers, and therefore can spend much more of its time in processing jobs.

The obvious disadvantages of off-lining are the cost of the tape drives, of the off-line system, and of the operator who must move the tapes. There is another disadvantage. The user must now wait for his job to be loaded onto a tape with a batch of other users' jobs; he will not be able to see the results of his job until the whole batch has been processed by the main system. Even though the user has a very small job (he may be a student with a small test program), he will be forced to wait for the completion of large jobs, such as data processing jobs, which are in the same batch.

BUFFERING OF INPUT/OUTPUT. There is another technique that solves the problem of having the CPU wait while input/output devices are working. This allows the CPU and the input/output devices to operate *concurrently* (i.e., simultaneously). The computer equipment is augumented by simple or special-purpose processors, often called *channels* ("peripheral processors" and "input-output controllers" are terms also in use), which keep the input/output devices running at the same time the CPU is working. Cards are read before they are actually needed by the user's job. Some high-speed memory, called a "buffer," is set aside to hold the information from cards until it is required by the running user's job. Similarly, a buffer is set aside in high-speed memory to hold print lines that have been produced by a user's job, but which have not yet been printed. This technique is called "buffering." By allowing the CPU to continue working while input/output is in progress, the buffering technique can more than double the throughput of a computer system.

Once the CPU and the input/output devices run concurrently, a new type of problem arises for the operating system designer. He must now produce software that can cope with the *asynchronous* activity of equipment. His software (the operating system) must *synchronize* the user job's input request with the continuing operation of the card reader. The difficulty is that the operating system must simultaneously keep track of (1) the running user's job and (2) the running input/output devices. Fortunately for the efficiency of computer systems, and unfortunately for the complexity of operating systems, asynchronous activity is a fact of life in modern computer systems.

COMMON LIBRARY ROUTINES. Users of computer systems have found that they can save time and money by using computer programs that other users (or the computer manufacturer) have previously developed. For example, once programs have been developed to evaluate trigonometric functions, they can be used again and again. One way to provide users with common routines is to store such software on a magnetic disk. When a user wishes to use one of the routines, he includes a card in his job which asks the operating system to fetch the desired routine from the disk and attach it to his job.

USER FILES. A user of a computer system may find it convenient to store his private programs and data on a magnetic disk (or, for that matter, on a magnetic tape). For example, the electric utility company described in a previous example may wish to store its customers' accounting records on a disk. We call a collection of information, such as this type of accounting record, a "file" or a "data set." Most operating systems provide their users with a means of "long term" storage of files on disks or tapes, where "long term" means days, months, or years.

The primary purpose of some computer systems is to maintain a large set of files which can be queried or updated. A large set of files is called a "data base," and a computer system that handles queries to and updates the files is called a "data-base management system."

A user will be willing to place information in the long-term storage of a computer system only if he is confident that the information will not be scrambled or destroyed. He would not like to be told that "the janitor unplugged the disk by mistake and so your accounting records are lost." Hence, the operating system must be carefully designed to maintain the *integrity* of files, i.e., to see that files are not lost.

If several users of a computer system are using long-term storage, then a situation may arise in which one user does not wish to allow another user to inspect his files. For example, two competing department stores might keep their lists of active sales items in separate files in the same computer system. Each department store wants to be guaranteed that its files are secure against accidental or purposeful access by the other company. In such an arrangement the operating system must be carefully designed to maintain the *security* of its users' files, i.e., to see that access to files is limited to authorized users.

LOGGING OF SYSTEM ACTIVITY. Operating systems commonly keep a *log* of the activity of the computer system. In small systems, the log is usually made by printing on the operator's console. The log may record the time each job is started and finished, as well as the resources (CPU time, input/output time, etc.) consumed by the job. This information can be used to bill users for the jobs they run. The log may also record the usage of the various pieces of equipment in the computer system. This information helps the computer system manager to adjust the system and improve its efficiency. The log may also be used to record failures in the computer equipment or software. These entries can be used for maintenance of the equipment and for improving the system's reliability.

COMMAND OR JOB CONTROL LANGUAGE. Some computer systems provide their users with a variety of services, such as several computer language translators, file-managing programs, and application programs. The user of a computer system can specify which service his job requires by using *control cards*. For example, an engineer who wishes to run a Fortran program adds to his card deck a control card requesting use of the Fortran translator. The operating system reads control cards and sees that the requested services are provided. The control cards accepted by a particular computer system are called a "job control language" (JCL) or a "command language."

MULTIPLE PROGRAMS IN MEMORY (MULTIPROGRAMMING). In computer systems where there is a lot of concurrent input/output activity, especially on a large number of devices, it may be advantageous to load more than one user's program into memory at a given time. This technique is called "multiprogramming."

Consider a large business data processing job that uses little CPU time, but which uses a lot of disk time in updating a file of customers' accounts. Such a job will leave most of the system's resources idle, the exception being the disk. This is not only wasteful of equipment, but also means that users with small jobs must wait a long time while the large data processing job ties up the system. Multiprogramming can be used to solve these problems. In a multiprogramming operating system, more than one job is active at a time. This means that when one job leaves the CPU idle because it is waiting for an input/output operation to finish, the operating system can start the CPU working on another job. Similarly, if one job is not using part of the system's equipment (e.g., the magnetic-tape drives), then another program which requires the idle equipment can be activated.

Multiprogramming can also solve the problem of poor turnaround time for small jobs by allowing small jobs to be started and completed while a large job is in progress.

In computer systems that support interactive consoles, many users' programs are active at one time. The operating system automatically switches CPU attention from one user to another. This technique is called "time sharing" because it shares CPU time among many active users. Since the CPU is very fast and consoles (and users) are relatively slow, time sharing gives each user the impression that he has the CPU all to himself.

With the introduction of multiprogramming, a number of technical problems must be solved. We now briefly discuss some of them: memory protection, program relocation, and CPU scheduling.

*Memory Protection and Program Relocation.* Since multiprogramming allows more than one program in memory at one time, the operating system must see that misbehavior on the part of one program does not ruin another program. This problem is solved by adding *memory protection hardware* to the CPU, which guarantees that a program accesses only memory to which it is authorized.

Another problem with multiprogramming is that there is no longer a unique position in memory where a program can expect to be loaded. To solve this problem, the CPU is augmented by *relocation hardware*, which allows a program to be run in any available place in memory. This hardware allows the operating system to load a user's program into any currently unused part of the memory.

Protection hardware and relocation hardware require in turn a mode of CPU operation called "supervisor state." When the CPU is running in supervisor state, it is possible to set the memory access rights and the relocation properties of user's programs. Supervisor state is used by the operating system in assigning memory to user jobs. (Users' programs are not allowed to use supervisor state.)

*CPU Scheduling.* Since more than one program is simultaneously active in a multiprogramming system, the operating system must *schedule* the CPU for use by the various programs; this is sometimes called "dispatching" the CPU. If the operating system consistently assigns the CPU to an inopportune program, the result can be poor equipment utilization, poor response time for interactive users, and poor turnaround time. The operating system must use a relatively sophisticated strategy for assigning the CPU to jobs in order to keep the CPU, memory, and input/output devices productive while simultaneously providing good service to users.

USING MULTIPROGRAMMING TO IMPLEMENT SPOOLING. Once multiprogramming is available in a system it can be used by the operating system to simulate off-lining (described above). The operating system can use special programs that are active concurrently with user programs. One special program can read cards from the card reader onto magnetic disk or tape. The cards representing a user's job will be stored until the system is ready to process the job. Similarly, when a user job produces lines to be printed, these lines are temporarily stored on a disk or tape. Later, a special program reads the stored lines and sends them to the printer. This arrangement is called "spooling"; it is similar to off-lining, as described previously, but has an advantage in that it is not necessary to transport the input and output tapes between the main system and the off-line system.

When user jobs are stored on a disk rather than on tape, this arrangement provides a scheduling advantage. In particular, if there are several jobs on the disk waiting to be run, the operating system can choose to run first those jobs that require fast turnaround.

We have covered various aspects of the use of multiprogramming, and will now summarize its advantages and disadvantages. Multiprogramming can (1) improve CPU and input/output equipment utilization, (2) improve turnaround time for small jobs and (3) provide good response for interactive consoles. The disadvantages of multiprogramming are that it requires expensive hardware and a sophisticated operating system. Unfortunately, a sophisticated operating system is expensive to produce, consumes valuable system resources such as CPU time and memory space, and requires costly programmer time for adjustments to accommodate new equipment and changes in users' applications.

AUTOMATIC SHARING OF MEMORY. The obvious method of running a user's program is to place the entire user's program in memory and leave it there until the program has finished running. This method has the advantage of simplicity, and it is commonly used. However, it has several drawbacks. First, a long-running program can prevent short jobs from receiving good turnaround time. Second, during the running of a program, only parts of the program are active at a given time. In fact, it often happens that some parts of a program never become active in a given job. This means that memory space reserved for a job is not effectively used. Finally, some programs are just too large to fit into high-speed memory; some means must be provided for dividing such programs into smaller pieces, each of which fits into memory.

Complicated techniques have been developed with the aim of solving these problems and increasing the utilization of memory. We now present two such techniques, called "swapping" and "paging."

*Memory Swapping.* The simplest scheme for automatically sharing memory involves temporarily suspending the progress of the running program and moving the program onto a magnetic drum or disk. The high-speed memory occupied by the suspended job is then reassigned to another more pressing job. When the memory once again becomes free, the suspended job can be restored to memory from the drum or disk and allowed to continue running. This scheme is called memory "swapping," or "roll-out/roll-in" (the suspended job is "rolled out" to the drum or disk and later "rolled" back into memory). One of the prime advantages of swapping is that it allows short jobs to overtake longer ones. This technique can also be used to share the computing power of the system among a number of interactive consoles.

*Paging.* A more sophisticated scheme, called "paging," divides the high-speed memory into equal-sized parts called "pages." Typically, a page may hold 4,000 bytes of information. The operating system assigns to a job only the number of pages required for the active parts of the job program (and data). Extra hardware is added to the CPU so that it is not necessary to assign contiguous pages of memory to a given program. The user writes his program as if it were to be all in memory at the same time; it is then the responsibility of the operating system to see that pages are made available to the program as they are required.

The result is that each user job is provided *virtual memory*, i.e., the apparent (but not real) dedication of enough high-speed memory to hold the user's entire program.

One of the advantages of paging is that it decreases the memory requirements for running a given job. A second advantage of paging is that the user is provided with a convenient method of running programs that exceed the size of the high-speed memory. The paging technique does not require the entire program to be in memory at one time. This allows the operating system to implement for the user a virtual memory larger than the actual memory. In the absence of a large virtual memory provided by paging, a user with a large program may be forced to invent his own scheme for successively *overlaying* real memory with different parts of his program.

Some computer systems, such as the Burroughs 5500, use a technique similar to paging, the difference being that the high-speed memory is divided into parts of *variable* size. These variable-size parts of memory are called "segments." Some computer systems, such as the Honeywell Multics system, provide variable-length segments, which are in turn subdivided into fixed-length pages.

MULTIPLE CPU SYSTEMS. Large computer systems, such as the CDC 6600, sometimes include more than one CPU. When more than one CPU is present, the system becomes a *multiprocessing* system.

**Features of Commercially Available Systems.** The foregoing description of operating systems has introduced increasingly complex and sophisticated features. In general, smaller and older computer systems have simpler operating system features, and larger and newer computer systems have more complex features.

Small computers (minicomputers) such as the Digital Equipment PDP-8, the Hewlett Packard 2100, and the IBM 1130 are commonly run using no operating system or using a sequential batch-operating system.

The larger and older IBM 7090 normally ran with a sequential batch system supported by spooling.

Medium-scale systems, such as the IBM 360/65, the CDC 3600, and the Titan, are typically run under multiprogramming operating systems.

Paging and/or segmenting has been available for years on some machines, such as the Atlas and the Burroughs 5500. IBM has recently provided these facilities on its 370 series of computers.

TWO EXAMPLES OF OPERATING SYSTEMS. There is a tremendous variation among contemporary computer systems and their operating systems. Some computer systems cost millions of dollars and occupy several rooms. Other systems cost a few thousand dollars and occupy no more space than a writing desk. Some systems provide their users with a nearly infinite variety of services. Other systems provide only a single service. Some models of computers, with their respective operating systems, have been installed in thousands of businesses, industries, and universities. Others are one-of-a-kind systems.

To illustrate this variation in computers and their operating systems, we present two examples. The first is the small, specialized T.H.E. multiprogramming system, and second is the large, general-purpose OS/360 system.

T.H.E. MULTIPROGRAMMING SYSTEM. In the early 1960s, a team of six computer scientists at the Technical University of Eindhoven in the Netherlands constructed a small special-purpose multiprogramming system. Since the name of their university, in Dutch, is Technische Hochschule Eindhoven, the system is called the T.H.E. multiprogramming system.

The system was designed for one purpose: to run users' Algol programs. The system provides its users with the following services and advantages:

1. Users can run Algol programs that are punched on paper tape. (The system does not accept punched cards). Users can edit (modify) their paper tapes by running a special editing program.

2. Good turnaround is provided to small jobs; these jobs can overtake larger jobs which have already started running. Since small jobs occupy only a fraction of the system resources (e.g., memory), and since other jobs can concurrently be using the other resources, it is not costly to run small jobs.

3. Users can run jobs with larger memory requirements than provided by the system's actual high-speed memory. The system provides a large virtual memory, and hence programmers need not worry about the memory requirements of their programs (within reasonable limits).

The common library of the T.H.E. system provides its users with an Algol translator and support routines (e.g., trigonometric functions) for Algol programs. There are no other translators available and there is no assembler. The system provides no facility for maintaining user files. Any user files must be kept by the users on paper tape.

The system uses an Electrologica X8 computer; this is a Dutch machine of which few were manufactured. The system's equipment includes the following items:

CPU: instruction time of about 2.5 $\mu$s.
Memory: capacity of about 150K bytes.
Magnetic drum: capacity of about 1,500K bytes.
Operator's console.
One printer.
Three paper-tape readers.
Three paper-tape punches.
One plotter.

The user's programs and data are read by the paper-tape readers. The user's programs can produce output on the printer, the plotter, and the paper-tape punches.

The operating system provides multiprogramming: up to five user jobs can be running on the system at the same time. It also gives higher priority to small jobs, and thus provides them with good turnaround. Larger slow jobs, such as those producing pictures using the plotter, can remain in the system for long periods of time without disturbing turnaround time for small jobs.

The operating system supports paging: the active parts of running user jobs are kept in high-speed memory, while the inactive parts are stored on the magnetic drum. Hence, high-speed memory is not wasted by holding inactive parts of programs. The total size of a user's program is thus limited by the size of the drum (which is relatively large) instead of by the size of the high-speed memory (which is about one-tenth the size of the drum).

Since the system provides its users with only one language translator (for Algol), its designers took advantage of this fact by integrating the translator into the operating system. They solved the problem of protecting user programs from each other by having the translator provide checks to keep each user within his authorized memory. They also used the translator to help them implement paging. (It is more common in the design of systems to separate the operating system and the language translators.)

The T.H.E. multiprogramming system is interesting to study because it has a simple, well-described structure, and because it is highly reliable and reasonably efficient. However, its narrow range of service is of value only to a limited number of applications. We now describe an operating system that provides a very broad range of the services.

THE OPERATING SYSTEM FOR THE IBM 360 SERIES. In the IBM System/360 series of computers, each has the same instructions for its CPU and the same input/output channel arrangement. However, the speeds, the memory capacities, and the attached input/output devices on these systems vary dramatically. The Model 30 of the 360 series is a relatively small machine, having typically 128K bytes of memory; it is comparable to the Electrologica X8 of the T.H.E. system. The Model 91 of the 360 series is a very large computer with 4,000K bytes of memory. There is a range of 360 models between the Model 30 and the Model 91.

IBM supplies the OS/360 operating system, designed to support the 360 series of computers. Not only does it support many different computer models, but it also provides its users with a vast variety of services. OS/360 is really a whole series of operating systems rather than a single one, which offer a large complement of programs that support user applications. Therefore, it is not surprising that OS/360 is a big system; it is one of the most expensive software developments ever undertaken. The programs that comprise OS/360 utilize over 200K lines of code, and required thousands of man-years to produce.

Services provided by OS/360 include:

1. Higher-level languages; most commonly used are Cobol, Fortran, and PL/I.
2. Assembly language.
3. A very sophisticated job-control language.
4. A filing system, together with a set of "utility programs" for maintaining user files.

There are many other services available in using OS/360, such as interactive programming, special subsystems to run student jobs, special subsystems to manage large business data bases, etc.

As OS/360 is actually a family of operating systems, we limit our attention to one of its most common variants, called "OS/MVT," in which MVT stands for "*m*ultiprogramming with a *v*ariable number of *t*asks," which means that OS/MVT can concurrently run a number of user jobs, the number depending upon the memory requirements of the jobs.

OS/MVT is sometimes augmented by a spooling subsystem (such as the Houston automatic spooling program (HASP) subsystem), which controls the system's card readers and printers. This subsystem minimizes the time jobs spend waiting for readers and printers, and as a result decreases the time during which jobs occupy memory.

The OS/MVT operating system does not support paging. Instead, memory is assigned to a user's program when the program begins running; the assigned memory remains dedicated to the program until the program terminates.

Since OS/360 supports a series of machines together with diverse applications, it is necessary to tailor an operating system to a particular computer installation. This is accomplished by a process called "system generation," which selects from among the available operating system features, attempting to fabricate an operating system that is well suited to the particular installation.

OS/360 is one of the most widely used operating systems. The reason for this is that there are more 360 series computers in use than any other type of computer. Because of its generality, OS/360 has proved useful in a great range of applications. However, as a result of this generality, OS/360 is not

**Table 1.** Operating Systems for Some Widely Used Large-Scale Computers

| Operating System | Computers Supported | Comments |
|---|---|---|
| EXEC-8 | Univac 1107 and 1108 | Commonly used in scientific and teaching applications. The most commonly used language is Fortran. |
| MCP | Burroughs 5000 series and 6000 series | MCP (master control program) is used by the Burroughs Corporation as the name of its various operating systems. Generally, these systems have been oriented toward the Algol language and have been written in that language. |
| MULTICS | GE-645 and Honeywell 6045 | Originally developed at M.I.T. for the GE-645 computer. The Honeywell Corporation has now taken over the effort and uses the software on its 6045 computer. MULTICS provides its users with powerful means of managing and sharing files. |
| OS/360 | IBM 360/370 series | Widely used in business data processing, teaching, and research. The most commonly used languages on this system are Cobol, Fortran, PL/I, and 360 Assembler. |
| SCOPE | CDC 6000 series | Commonly used in scientific and teaching applications. The most commonly used language is Fortran. It provides a simple job-control language for batch processing. |
| TENEX | DEC (Digital Equipment Corporation) PDP-10 | Developed by BBN (Bolt, Beranek, and Newman Corporation) for use on the PDP-10 computer. It is oriented toward scientific interactive computing. |

an easy system to understand, and can be difficult and expensive to use. Table 1 lists operating systems used on some commonly available large-scale computer systems.

**General Remarks about Operating Systems.** In this survey of operating systems we have tried to emphasize their great diversity in terms of (1) services provided to users, (2) types of equipment managed by the system, and (3) methods of managing the equipment. Across this diversity, the main purpose of an operating system is to provide convenient and economical computer services by efficiently sharing the computer equipment among users. Complex methods of managing input/output devices and assigning high-speed memory to users' jobs can improve equipment utilization and thus decrease the cost to the users. In general, the simpler of these techniques (such as automatic job sequencing) are used on smaller computer systems, and more complicated techniques (such as paging) are used on larger computer systems.

REFERENCES

1972. Hoare, C. A. R., and R. H. Perrot. *Operating Systems Techniques*. New York: Academic Press.

1973. Hansen, P. Brinch. *Operating System Principles*. Englewood Cliffs, N.J.: Prentice-Hall.

1974. Tsichritzis, D. C., and P. A. Bernstein. *Operating Systems*. New York: Academic Press.

R. C. HOLT

# OPERATION CODE

For articles on related subjects *see* ADDRESSING; MACHINE INSTRUCTION SET; MICROPROGRAMMING; and OPERAND.

The operation code (abbreviated as op code) is the part of a computer instruction which specifies what operation has to be performed on the operands.

The selection of the operands is done by other parts of the computer instruction or by defaults. Operation codes are either of fixed or variable length. They may be either highly encoded or possess a low degree of encoding (see below).

Fixed-length op codes are utilized in most computers. They reflect a design decision not to take advantage of the relative frequency of usage of the various instructions, and thus they do not use any minimal coding. The fixed-length op code is easy to handle, both in hardware and in software.

Variable-length op codes take into account both the frequency of the operation and the length of the address field of the instruction. This data is used in order to produce minimal coding for the op code, so that the memory utilization for a typical program is as low as possible.

A highly encoded op code is one in which the function of the instruction can be induced only by observing a high number of code elements (i.e., bits in the op code). High encoding enables a high number of possibilities in a relatively short field, as all possible code combinations can be utilized. Thus, in $n$ bits, up to $2^n$ instructions can be specified.

An op code is considered to be of low encoding if there is a direct correspondence between partial fields of the op code and specific subunits of the computer. No encoding at all is present when every single bit of the op code has a predefined function, controlling one aspect of one unit, completely independently from all other bits.

In practice, most op codes are somewhere between the two extremes of high and low encoding. Recently there has been inclination to associate low encoding with microprogramming. Additional elaboration and details are given elsewhere in this Encyclopedia.

G. FRIEDER

# OPERATIONS RESEARCH

For articles on related subjects *see* MATHEMATICAL PROGRAMMING; MODELS; QUEUEING THEORY; and SIMULATION.
For article on related term *see* STOCHASTIC PROCESS.

Operations research (operational research in the United Kingdom) is the quantitative study, both experimental and theoretical, of operations in action. An operation is defined as the cooperative action of man and machine to accomplish some repetitive task, to which some measureable goal has usually been assigned, either explicitly or implicitly. An active production line, an operating inventory system or sales campaign, a bombing mission, or a network of police patrols in action, all these are operations. Their details can be analyzed and observed, stochastic theories can be devised to simulate their dynamic behavior and the results can then be used to predict changes in output resulting from possible changes in equipment or rules of operation. Understanding the dynamics of an operation is of importance to management, for with this understanding they can choose the rules of operation and the equipment so as to produce the desired result as efficiently as possible. In addition, studying operations and devising of mathematical models to simulate their actions is of interest in the abstract; it is one of the areas of social science that can be quantified.

The boundaries between operations research and systems analysis on the one side and management science on the other have never been, and may never be, clearly defined. In general, systems analysis deals more with the complex of equipment that might be used in some operation; it tends to be more concerned with the design of not-yet-operating systems; it uses the findings of operations research to assist in the design. On the other hand, management science is more interested in the application of operations research to the particular ongoing system being managed; it tends to concentrate more on the human aspects. Operations research lies midway between these, and is sometimes considered to encompass them both.

Since its beginnings during World War II, work in operations research has induced the development of many theoretical models of elements of, and interconnections between, various operations. Many of the theoretical aspects and applications of computers discussed in this Encyclopedia have had their inception in the study of some operations research problem. Computer systems designers also use the theoretical tools of operations research. For example, queueing theory, Markov process theory (mentioned later in this article), and, to some extent, linear programming are theoretical tools, developed for use in operations research, which have been found useful in the systems engineering problems encountered in designing a complete computing system, particularly of the time-sharing variety.

Workers in operations research naturally have used computers from the start to carry out the data processing and calculating required in analyzing and solving their complex problems. In fact, the Operations Research Group of the U.S. Navy was the first to routinely use Hollerith cards, sorters, and tabulators to process naval operational data and to compute weapons effectiveness during World War II, even before the advent of internally programmed computers. The whole subject of mathematical programming, with its subdivisions of linear programming and dynamic programming, was developed to solve problems of allocation, scheduling, and routing, which arise in many operations research studies. Today the related applications programs, usually written by the operations research worker, have become standard items of computer software. This is also true of various simulation programs (e.g., Simula) that have been written to provide a surrogate to some complex operational system such as automobile traffic or warfare or urban development, which can be experimented with as the original system cannot. The usefulness as well as the dangers of such surrogate experimentation are obvious.

In view of the ubiquity of the relationship between operations research and the use of computers, all that can be done in this article is to describe a few of the mathematical and/or computational models that have been found most useful in operations research. For more complete treatment, see Morse and Kimball (1950), Ackoff and Sasieni (1968), or van der Veen (1967).

Since human variability and the vagaries of boundary conditions (such as supply and demand) on the operations influence strongly the outcome of an individual operation, the theory of probability, and in particular the theory of stochastic processes, provides the basis of many of the mathematical models (see Thomasian, 1969; Parzen, 1960; Drake, 1967).

When the system is such that its condition at any time is expressible in terms of a denumerable set of states, and if one is interested only in the state of the system at the end of one or another of a discrete sequence of time periods, then the dynamics of the operation can be simulated by a Markov process (see Bharucha-Reid, 1960; Feller, 1957).

The probability $p_n(t+1)$ that the system is in state $n$ at the end of the $(t+1)$st period is related to the probability $p_m(t)$ that the system is in state $m$ at the end of the $t$th period by the equation

$$p_n(t+1) = \Sigma_m p_m(t) T_{mn}(t,t+1) \qquad (1)$$

in a Markov process. Quantity $T_{mn}(t,t+1)$ is called the "transition probability" from state $m$ to state $n$ in the single period from $t$ to $t+1$. In many cases of practical interest, $T_{mn}(t,t+1)$ is independent of $t$ over a sufficient number of periods, so that it is feasible (as well as convenient) to concentrate on finding solutions of Eq. (1) when $T_{mn}(t,t+1)$ is independent of $t$. In this case, the process described is called a "Markov chain," and the transition probability may be written $T^{(1)}_{mn}$. This matrix element is a conditional probability; if the system is in state $m$ at the end of a period, the probability that it is in state $n$ at the end of the next period is $T^{(1)}_{mn}$. Thus, the matrix is a *stochastic matrix*, i.e., $\Sigma_n T_{mn} = 1$, the sum of each row of the matrix is unity, and all elements of the matrix are nonnegative.

From these single-period transition probabilities one can derive the matrix elements covering multiple periods. Successive applications of Eq. (1) show that

$$T^{(r+s)}_{mn} = \Sigma_p T^{(r)}_{mp} T^{(s)}_{pr}. \qquad (2)$$

This is known as the *Chapman-Kolmogorov equation.* $T^{(r)}_{mp}$ is the probability that the system is in state $m$ at the end of a period and in state $p$ at the end of $r$ subsequent periods. With a number of exceptions, rarely encountered in practice but which are discussed in Bharucha-Reid (1960) and Feller (1957), the sequence of transition matrices $T^{(r)}_{mn}$ as $r$ goes to infinity usually approaches an asymptotic form that is independent of the initial state $m$:

$$T^{(r)}_{mn} \to P_n \qquad (\text{as } r \to \infty). \qquad (3)$$

One can show that $P_n$ is the *steady-state probability* that the system is eventually in state $n$, according to the equation

$$P_n = \Sigma_m P_m T^{(1)}_{mn}. \qquad (4)$$

If these equations are viewed as the stochastic analogs of the equations of motion of a dynamic system, then the $t$-dependent probabilities are equivalent to the transient behavior of the system and the probabilities $P_n$ correspond to its steady state after the system "has forgotten how it started." It is not that the stochastic system has stopped changing from state to state. It is just that the occupancy frequency $P_n$ has ceased to depend on the initial state.

Of course the transient solutions of Eq. (1) may be obtained by iteration of the matrix multiplication, but a formal solution will provide greater insight into the nature of the process. The characteristic values of the matrix $T_{mn}$, the roots of the secular equations

$$D(\mathcal{T} - \mu\mathcal{I}) \equiv \begin{vmatrix} T_{11}-\mu & T_{12} & T_{13} & - & - \\ T_{21} & T_{22}-\mu & T_{23} & - & - \\ - & - & - & - & - \\ - & - & - & - & - \end{vmatrix} = 0 \qquad (5)$$

never have magnitudes greater than unity because matrix $\mathcal{T}$ is stochastic. At least one root (which we will label $\mu_1$) is unity. The others ($\mu_\sigma$, $\sigma > 1$) usually have magnitudes less than unity. The corresponding characteristic vectors, with normalized components $e_j(\sigma)$ and $e_i^{-1}(\sigma)$, are solutions of

$$\begin{aligned} &\Sigma_i T^{(1)}_{ij} e_j(\sigma) = \mu_\sigma e_i(\sigma); \\ &\Sigma_i e_i^{-1}(\sigma) T^{(1)}_{ij} = \mu_\sigma e_j^{-1}(\sigma); \\ &\Sigma_\sigma e_i(\sigma) e_j^{-1}(\sigma) = \delta_{ij}; \\ &\Sigma_i e_i(\sigma) e_i^{-1}(\tau) = \delta_{\sigma\tau}. \end{aligned} \qquad (6)$$

For the unity root $\mu_1 = 1$, it can be shown that

$$e_j(1) = 1 \qquad \text{and} \qquad e_i^{-1}(1) = P_i. \qquad (7)$$

Finally, it can be shown that the matrices defined in terms of the characteristic components,

$$M_{ij}(\sigma) = e_i(\sigma)e_j^{-1}(\sigma)$$

can be used to express the higher-order transition probabilities,

$$T_{mn}^{(r)} = \Sigma_\sigma(\mu_\sigma)^r M_{mn}(\sigma);$$

also (8)

$$T_{mn}^{(0)} = \delta_{mn};\ T_{mn}^{(1)} = \Sigma_\sigma \mu_\sigma M_{mn}(\sigma).$$

Since, with the exceptions mentioned earlier and discussed in the references, all the roots except $\mu_1 = 1$ have magnitudes less than unity, as $r \to \infty$, the transition matrix $T_{mn}^{(r)}$ approaches asymptotically the form

$$T_{mn}^{(r)} \to e_m(1)e_n^{-1}(1) = P_n \qquad (\text{as } r \to \infty),$$

which is the same as Eq. (3).

If one must consider time as a continuous variable, these equations can be subjected to a limiting process, for determining the rate of change with time of the state probability $p_n(t)$. This results in the fundamental equation

$$\frac{d}{dt}p_n(t) = \Sigma_m p_m(t) R_{mn}, \tag{9}$$

where we have assumed, as we did for Eq. (4), that $R_{mn}$ is independent of time. The matrix element $R_{mn}$ is the probabilistic *rate of transition* from state $m$ to state $n$. If $p_n(t)$ is to be a true probability distribution ($p_n \geq 0$, $\Sigma p_n = 1$), then all nondiagonal elements of the matrix must be nonnegative and the sum of all elements in each row must be zero:

$$\Sigma_n R_{mn} = 0;\ R_{mn} \geq 0 \qquad \text{for } n \neq m,$$

i.e., (10)

$$R_{mm} = -\sum_{n \neq m} R_{mn}$$

Solutions of Eq. (9), for the initial conditions $p_m(0)$, follow closely those for the discrete-time case. The roots $\rho_\sigma$ of the secular equation

$$D(\mathscr{R} - \rho_\sigma \mathscr{I}) = 0$$

have nonpositive real parts and (with the usual exceptions), only one, $\rho_1$, is zero. As before, the characteristic vectors,

$$\begin{aligned} &\Sigma_j R_{ij} e_j(\sigma) = \rho_\sigma e_i(\sigma);\\ &\Sigma_i e_i^{-1}(\sigma) R_{ij} = \rho_\sigma e_j^{-1}(\sigma);\\ &\Sigma_\sigma e_j(\sigma) e_j^{-1}(\sigma) = \delta_{ij};\\ &\Sigma_i e_i(\sigma) e_i^{-1}(\tau) = \delta_{\sigma\tau}; \end{aligned} \tag{11}$$

and the solution of Eq. (9) is

$$p_n(t) = \Sigma_m p_m(0) T_{mn}(t),$$

where (12)

$$\begin{aligned} T_{mn}(t) &= \Sigma_\sigma \exp(\rho_\sigma t) e_m(\sigma) e_n^{-1}(\sigma)\\ &\to e_m(1) e_n^{-1}(1) \qquad (\text{as } t \to \infty), \end{aligned}$$

since all roots but the first, $\rho_1 = 0$, have negative real parts. As before, we have $e_m(1) = 1$ and $e_n^{-1}(1) = p_n$, the steady-state probability that the system is in state $n$, a solution of the set of the equations for conditions $p_m(0)$ after time variation has ceased:

$$\Sigma_m P_m R_{mn} = 0 \tag{13}$$

In many cases only the steady-state distribution is of interest, so only the set of the equations for Eq. (13) need be solved.

Eqs. (9) to (13) provide the model for a large number of processes in ecology and in operations research. Such processes are often called "birth-and-death" processes because of their obvious biological connotations (see Harris, 1963). When the matrix elements $R_{mn}$ are nearly all zero, except for a few diagonals adjoining the main diagonal, the equations are representative of some of the *queueing processes* often encountered in operations research (see Morse, 1958; Saaty, 1961; Cooper, 1963).

In such processes, arriving units (with some distribution of arrival times) appear at a *service facility*, where the unit is serviced within a service time that may vary from unit to unit. After one unit is serviced, another is taken on if one should be waiting. The number of units waiting to be serviced is called the "queue." A queue may consist of various kinds of units: persons waiting in front of a check-out counter at a supermarket; airplanes stacked above an airfield, waiting to land; telephone subscribers waiting for a nonbusy, long-distance line; or pieces of equipment, the "arrival" of which is some breakdown in their operation and for which the "service" process is their repair. Sometimes the service facility has several channels operating in parallel (several check-out counters, several landing strips, etc.); sometimes several service operations must act in series on each unit, with possible queues forming in front of each (as in a production line).

In most cases the steady-state solution is the most useful. Usually the quantities of practical interest are the *mean number* of units in the queue; the average time interval between a unit's arrival and its entry into service (*mean time in queue*), or its discharge from service (*mean time in the system*); and, occasionally, the distribution in time of discharge of units from service (*exit distribution*). The characteristics of the queueing system which must be specified if solutions are to be obtained, include such items as:

1. *The mean rate of arrival*, $\lambda$, of the units and the *distribution* of *arrivals* in time. In many cases the arrival distribution is Poisson, or nearly so, which simplifies considerably the equations describing the process and the procedures for solution.

2. *The queue discipline.* The freedom or lack of freedom of the arriving units to leave the queue before being serviced is a factor that profoundly affects the characteristic behavior of the process. The solution also is adversely affected if some units have priority for admission to the service facility. Also, the order in which the units in the queue are taken into service (which may be first-come-first-served or random) influences some properties of the operation.

3. *The mean rate of service* $\mu$ and the *distribution of service times.* In a surprising number of cases this distribution turns out to be close to exponential (corresponding to Poisson arrivals), in which case the solution is further simplified. In fact, Eq. (13), with $P_m$ representing the steady-state probability that there are $m$ units in the system, is a valid model only in the case of Poisson arrivals and exponential service times; but this turns out to be a good approximation to reality in a surprising number of cases. Other, more complicated methods of analysis have to be used when this is not the case (e.g., see Takács, 1962).

In all cases where units are captive and none is allowed to leave without being serviced, the system can become saturated if arrival rate $\lambda$ exceeds service rate $\mu$, in which case there is no steady-state solution, and the queue increases without limit. In fact, in nearly all cases of this kind, the mean length of queue and the mean time in queue have a factor $(\mu - \lambda)^{-1}$ appearing in their steady-state formulas for $\mu > \lambda$. This illustrates a common problem with elements of a larger operation; if one tries to *increase* service efficiency by reducing the fraction of time $(\mu - \lambda)/\lambda$, the service facility is idle; then both the waiting time and length of queue increase, which usually *decreases* the efficiency of other parts of the operation.

When, in addition to the time variable, the state variable is continuous, with $m$, $n$ changing to $x$, $y$, further modification of the equation of motion must be made. In this case, the behavior of the limiting form of the transition probability

$$T_{mn}(t,t + dt) \rightarrow \Phi(x,y;t)$$

for regions of $x$ and $y$ closest to the main diagonal $(x = y)$ is important. It usually turns out that only the first two of the "cross-diagonal" moments of $\Phi$ are of first order in $dt$ and thus are of importance in the limit,

$$\begin{aligned} \int \mu^2\Phi(x,x + \mu;t)\, d\mu &= \gamma(x)\, dt; \\ \int \mu\Phi(x,x + \mu;t)\, d\mu &= \beta(x)\, dt, \end{aligned} \tag{14}$$

and, of course, $\int \Phi(x,x + \mu;t)d\mu = 1$.

The Chapman-Kolmogorov equation, in the limit,

$$T(x,y;t_0,t + dt) = \int T(x,u;t_0,t)\, \Phi(u,y;t)\, du,$$

goes over into a partial differential equation for the transition probability $T(x,y;t_0,t)$ from state $x$ to state $y$ in the time interval from $t_0$ to $t$:

$$\begin{aligned} \frac{\partial}{\partial t} T(x,y;t_0,t) = &- \frac{\partial}{\partial y}[\beta(y)T(x,y;t_0,t)] \\ &+ \frac{1}{2}\frac{\partial^2}{\partial y^2}[\gamma(y)T(x,y;t_0,t)] \end{aligned} \tag{15}$$

Quantities $\gamma$ and $\beta$ measure the behavior of the stochastic force tending to change coordinate $x$ in the elementary interval $dt$, $\gamma$ measuring its variance about zero, and $\beta$ its preference for one direction over the other. Eq. (15) is the well-known *Fokker-Planck equation*, used extensively in theories of Brownian motion and related problems of plasmas (see Reif, 1965; Wax, 1954).

Another mathematical model, useful in a variety of operational problems, is the *theory of search*, which was developed during World War II to aid in solving problems related to the search for submarines (see Koopman, 1956; Morse and Kimball, 1950, pp. 87–89, 105–109). It has more recently been found useful in the analysis of the *search for information* (see Morse, 1970).

The searching unit has a measurable *rate of search* $\rho$ for finding the desired item, defined by the equation

$$P(\rho t) = 1 - e^{-\rho t} \qquad (16)$$

where $P$ is the probability of finding the item after searching for a time $t$. This simple function, which assumes a certain amount of randomness in the search, and which turns out to correspond reasonably well to the realities of most search, exhibits the well-known characteristics of diminishing return: Doubling the time of search does not double the probability of success.

This property of diminishing return requires that the efficient allocation of search effort must be quite nonlinear when the search takes place in a region of variable probability of presence of the searched-for item. For example, it requires that search be often entirely omitted in regions where the item is least likely to be. The case is discussed in some detail in Koopman (1956) and associated references mentioned above.

Another mathematical model, *game theory*, is particularly useful for operations involving competition, such as warfare, some police activity, and some marketing operations. The literature on this theory is quite voluminous (e.g., see von Neumann and Morgenstern, 1953; Dresher, 1961).

For large-scale systems, where variability is less important than sheer number of variables, and where one wishes to determine the values of the variables that will optimize the output of the operation, *mathematical programming* has been developed (e.g., see Dantzig, 1963; Bellman, 1957; Howard, 1960).

Where values of some of the parameters cannot at a specific time be measured or calculated, but must be determined from a consensus of experienced operators, *decision theory* has become useful (see Pratt, Raiffa, and Schlaifer, 1965; Schlaifer, 1969). This theory is useful also in the study of public systems, where opinions, as well as physical limitations, are controlling.

Other special models have been devised for special cases. For example, both fluid dynamics and probabilistic analysis have been used to represent the flow of automobiles (see Herman, 1961), and other models have been used for library operations (see Morse, 1968; Swanson and Bookstein, 1972; Morse, 1972).

Finally, when the system becomes too complex to be expressed in terms of an analytic model, it may be *simulated* on a computer. Applications of this method are legion, from Monte Carlo simulations of nuclear reactor operation to representations of automobile traffic flow and even of the development of whole cities. The general methods, together with a review of the numerous pitfalls encountered, are outlined in Machol (1965).

**Sources of General Information.** Applications of operations research make up a large literature by now. One should refer to the journal literature, such as *Operations Research*, the journal of the Operations Research Society of America, and *International Abstracts in Operations Research*, published by the International Federation of Operational Research Societies. For a general review, see Ackoff and Sasieni (1968), and for the important and rapidly growing field of applications in the public sector, see Drake, Keeney, and Morse, (1972), both of which are listed in the references below.

### References

1950. Morse, P. M., and G. E. Kimball. *Methods of Operations Research*. Cambridge, Mass.: M.I.T. Press.

1953. von Neumann, J., and O. Morganstern. *Theory of Games and Economic Behavior*. Princeton, N.J.: Princeton University Press.

1954. Wax, N. (Ed.). *Noise and Stochastic Processes*. New York: Dover.

1956. Koopman, B. O. "The Theory of Search," *Operations Research*, Vol. 4, pp. 324, 503.

1957. Bellman, R. *Dynamic Programming*. Princeton, N.J.: Princeton University Press.

1957. Feller, W. *An Introduction to Probability Theory and Its Applications,* 2nd ed. New York: John Wiley (chaps. 14–17).

1958. Morse, P. M. *Queues, Inventories and Maintenance*. New York: John Wiley.

1960. Bharucha-Reid, A. T. *Markov Processes and Their Application*. New York: McGraw-Hill.

1960. Howard, R. A. *Dynamic Programming and Markov Processes*. Cambridge, Mass.: M.I.T. Press.

1960. Parzen, E. *Modern Probability Theory and Its Applications*. New York: John Wiley.

1961. Dresher, M. *Games of Strategy—Theory and Applications*. Englewood Cliffs, N.J.: Prentice-Hall.

1961. Herman R. (Ed.). *Theory of Traffic Flow*. New York: American Elsevier.

1961. Saaty, T. *Elements of Queueing Theory*. New York: McGraw-Hill.
1962. Takács, L. *Introduction to the Theory of Queues*. New York: Oxford.
1963. Cooper, R. B. *Introduction to Queueing Theory*. New York: Macmillan.
1963. Dantzig, G. B. *Linear Programming and Extensions*. Princeton, N.J.: Princeton University Press.
1963. Harris, T. E. *The Theory of Branching Processes*. Berlin: Springer.
1965. Machol, R. E. (Ed.). *Systems Engineering Handbook*. New York: McGraw-Hill, chap. 33.
1965. Pratt, J. W., H. Raiffa, and R. Schlaifer. *Introduction to Statistical Decision Theory*. New York: McGraw-Hill.
1965. Reif, F. *Fundamentals of Statistical and Thermal Physics*. New York: McGraw-Hill, pp. 577–581.
1967. Drake, A. W. *Fundamentals of Applied Probability Theory*. New York: McGraw-Hill.
1967. van der Veen, B. *Introduction to the Theory of Operations Research*. Berlin: Springer.
1968. Ackoff, R. L., and M. W. Sasieni. *Fundamentals of Operations Research*. New York: John Wiley.
1968. Morse, P. M. *Library Effectiveness*. Cambridge, Mass.: M.I.T. Press.
1969. Schlaifer, R. *Analysis of Decision under Uncertainty*. New York: McGraw-Hill.
1969. Thomasian, A. J. *The Structure of Probability Theory with Applications*. New York: McGraw-Hill.
1970. Morse, P. M. "Search Theory and Browsing," *Library Quarterly*, Vol. 40, p. 391.
1972. Drake, A. W., R. L. Keeney, and P. M. Morse (Eds.). *Analysis of Public Systems*. Cambridge, Mass.: M.I.T. Press.
1972. Morse, P. M. "Optimal Linear Ordering of Information Items," *Operations Research*, Vol. 20, p. 741.
1972. Swanson, D. R., and A. Bookstein (Eds.). *Operations Research: Implications for Libraries*. Chicago: University of Chicago Press.

P. M. Morse

# OPTICAL CHARACTER READERS

For articles on related subjects *see* Data Preparation Devices; Input-Output Devices; Machine-Readable Form; Optical Mark Readers; and Pattern Recognition.

Optical character recognition (OCR) can be defined as a high-speed process of recognizing and translating machine-printed or hand-printed words, letters, symbols, and numbers into computer-processable information. The data is directly machine readable while still being readable by people.

Optical character recognition was developed by using the techniques of optical mark reading. Whereas optical mark readers generally use a single photocell to detect the presence or absence of an optical mark in a given marking position, early optical character readers used a matrix of photocells onto which the character to be recognized was projected. If the character is from a defined stylized font, the image can be decoded into a particular character. The advent of "flying spot" electronic and laser scanners saw an increase in reliability of recognition to the point where OCR has become an acceptable and viable means of inputting data.

**Scanning Methods.** Before a character can be converted into a machine representation, it must pass through two systems: an optical scanning system and a recognition system (the analysis and decoding of optical output). The optical system not only governs the speed and flexibility of the scanner, but also determines the range of inks and paper-surface qualities needed. The scanning process determines the presence or absence of a mark or stroke by the amount of light reflected from the area being scanned. The main scanning techniques are as follows:

1. Mechanical disk: The document to be scanned is flooded with ordinary light. Between the document and a single photocell is a spinning disk (a "nipkow" disk containing special holes or slots). This effectively breaks down the character into very thin slices. Thus, a rapid series of character bits of varying intensity are presented to the photocell, which provides usable input to the recognition circuits.

2. Flying spot: The beam from a cathode-ray tube is moved across the character position in a given scanning pattern. This scanning pattern may vary with the type of font being read. The most common pattern is a "raster" scan, in which the beam oscillates up and down over the character in a very close sawtoothed pattern. The light reflected is

received, converted from an analog to a digital signal, and its pattern is analyzed. For stylized characters, this is more reliable than the mechanical technique in which a single stroke may be crossed several times. This type of scanner also allows curve tracing, wherein the beam is used to follow the shape of the character. This permits a great deal of flexibility, since the character leads the beam, and the size and shape do not have to be programmed or designed into the system. Feature analysis provides recognition. The scanner can adapt itself easily to varying sized characters and characters out of alignment. Machines that read handwriting may use this approach.

3. Video sensing: The document is flooded with light from an ordinary light source. The image of the character is reflected onto the face of a reviewing cathode-ray tube and scanned by an electron beam. The resulting video signals are converted to digital information for recognition.

4. Matrix of photocells: The character to be analyzed is projected onto a matrix of photocells. For a given photocell to register the presence of a mark, the cell must be at least 50% covered. Each photocell is sampled in a given order and the pattern of zeros or ones representing the absence or presence of a mark is decoded to represent a character. It follows that the presence of extraneous ink marks or the presence of large voids in a stroke can give a bit pattern that is not valid. This results in rejection of the character. Because this technique resembles the way the human eye sees, it is sometimes called a "retinal array."

5. Light-emitting diode (LED): The light source is a special diode (junction of two dissimilar metals) that emits light when a current is passed through it. This light is reflected off the document onto an adjoining photodetector. To generate a raster scan, the bank or column of diodes is turned on and off sequentially. The resulting signal is passed on to the recognition system. The analysis and decoding of the output from the optical scanning system can be performed by either hardware or (because storage is becoming less expensive) by standard software routines, or by microprograms such as for the IBM 3888 optical character reader.

**Optical Fonts.** The problems of reading printed characters by a machine increase drastically with a significant increase in the number of characters in the set. Obviously, the least expensive readers are those designed to read only a single stylized upper-case type such as ISO-A (see below). Stylizing a type font reduces the number of similarities between characters, making their identification easier for the machine. Adding a lower-case font increases the recognition problem. The major standard fonts, defined by specification R1073 of the International Standards Organization, are:

1. ISO-A (see Fig. 1): This was formerly called USASCSOCR, or OCR-A. The "A" designation indicates that it is the first character set to be designated as a standard by ISO, the organization for international standards.

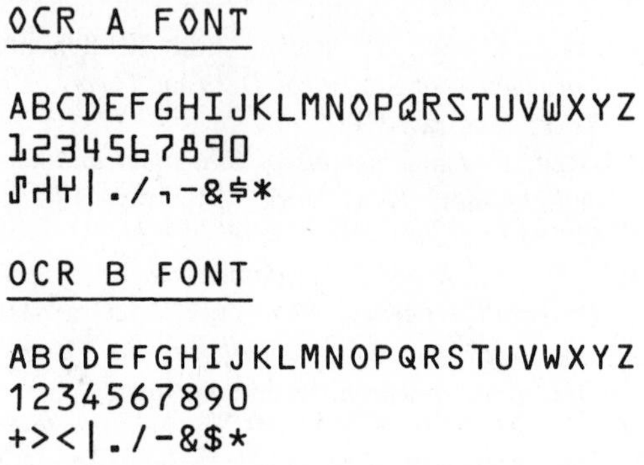


**Fig. 1.** Optical character recognition fonts ISO-A and ISO-B.

2. ISO-B (see Fig. 1): This OCR is strongly promoted by ECMA, the European Computer Manufacturers Association, and is less stylized than ISO-A. It is also designated OCR-B.

Some other optical fonts (but nonstandard) in use are:

1. IBM 1428 font: This is a numeric subset with several alphabetic special characters that became largely incorporated into the OCR-A character set.

2. NOF: The National optical font (NCR Corporation) was developed to enable the reading of printed output on journal rolls produced by cash registers or adding machines. It is a numeric subset with six special function characters.

3. 7B: The 7B font is a development of the Farrington Manufacturing Company. Its main use is in special printing, such as on credit cards.

4. IBM 1403: Although not a standard OCR font, several OCR readers are equipped to read the standard output from an IBM 1403 printer.

5. 3/16 in. Gothic: This, also, is not a standard OCR font. Serial numbering of OCR documents in this font has proved a reliable system control.

As yet, no standard has been developed for numerics that are hand-printed. However, guidelines for shapes must be followed closely to enable reliable recognition. A specification for a standard is at present being considered.

**OCR Readers.** Not all readers require electric typewriters to produce the input. Many can read alphanumeric information from high-speed computer printout. Some optical readers can also read hand-written numerical information (Fig. 2). Some scanners can read pencil marks placed in certain positions. Others read information prepared on cash registers, adding machines, and accounting machines. However, typewritten input is—and will continue to be—the major source material for optical readers.

Optical character readers are classified by reader and paper-handling capabilities.

1. Reading capability:

(a) Single font readers recognize only one type style, usually highly stylized (e.g., CDC 915).

(b) Multifont readers have a wide range of optical fonts (e.g., Scan Data 300, REI Retina, IBM 3886).

(c) Mark sense readers recognize marks entered by pencil. These are not true optical readers as they do not interpret a character into machine language, but merely signal the presence or absence of a mark in a given position.

2. Paper-handling capability:

(a) Journal tape readers read cash register tapes, adding machine tapes, or other continuous strips (e.g., IBM 1285, IBM 1287).

(b) Document readers (Fig. 3) are capable of reading lines or fields on a coupon, stub card, or document (e.g., Farrington 3010, IBM 1287).

(c) Page readers read multiple lines of type in normal page format. This is sometimes known as "unformatted" reading. Examples of these are IBM 1288, REI Retina, Scan Data 300, CDC 915, Farrington 3030, IBM 3886.

All OCR readers fall into one or more of the two classifications. The market for OCR readers has divided naturally, along lines of price and performance, between two families: single, stylized-font readers in the $4,000–6,000 per month price range, and multifont readers in the $10,000–20,000 per month range. For example, the IBM 1287 can read the following fonts: IBM 1428, IBM 1428E, ANSI/A Size 1, ANSI/A Size IV, ISOOCR/A Size I, and (with special features) numeric hand printing, NOF, 3/16 in. Gothic and 7B fonts.

**OCR Application Areas.** OCR has developed as an alternative solution to the data input bottleneck problem. OCR enables the source documents themselves to pass information directly to the computer. The time frequently lost between source documents and computer-processed information is reduced or eliminated. The exact savings depends on the method of document creation and the system that OCR can replace. For example, using handwritten source documents can eliminate a transcription and keying operation. Typewriting significantly increases keying rates over those of other keyboard devices. In most cases the source document itself can be redesigned and adapted as an OCR input document.

Two basic areas suit OCR input:

1. Regular data entry: Used, for example, in retailing—cash register journal tapes, stocktaking, order entry, sales checks. Transport—shipping lists, cargo manifests, invoices. Banking—stock transfers, savings and loan accounts. Education—test records, registrations. Finance—Loan applications, mortgage payments. Manufacturing—inventory control, payroll, time-and-output recording.

2. Computer-generated turnaround, i.e., reentry documents (see Fig. 4): Information from a master file is printed by a high-speed printer on an OCR document. This information can be modified or added to by numeric hand printing and reentered into the computer system (e.g., utility meter billing, commercial credit accounts, auto renewal registrations, and stocktaking, where key numbers and descriptions are printed for easy recognition by coding personnel, and reentered to update master files).

While OCR can be applied to a large range of data entry applications, there are conditions under which this technique may not be the optimal method. Generally, this is the case when the input cannot be controlled and maintained at an acceptable level of quality. These conditions occur when OCR documents are subject to extensive handling, multilation, or crumpling, or when the documents cannot be kept clean (e.g., in a machine shop) or are not prepared in a controlled environment.

**OCR Quality.** Good print quality is the key to reading performance and subsequent overall OCR

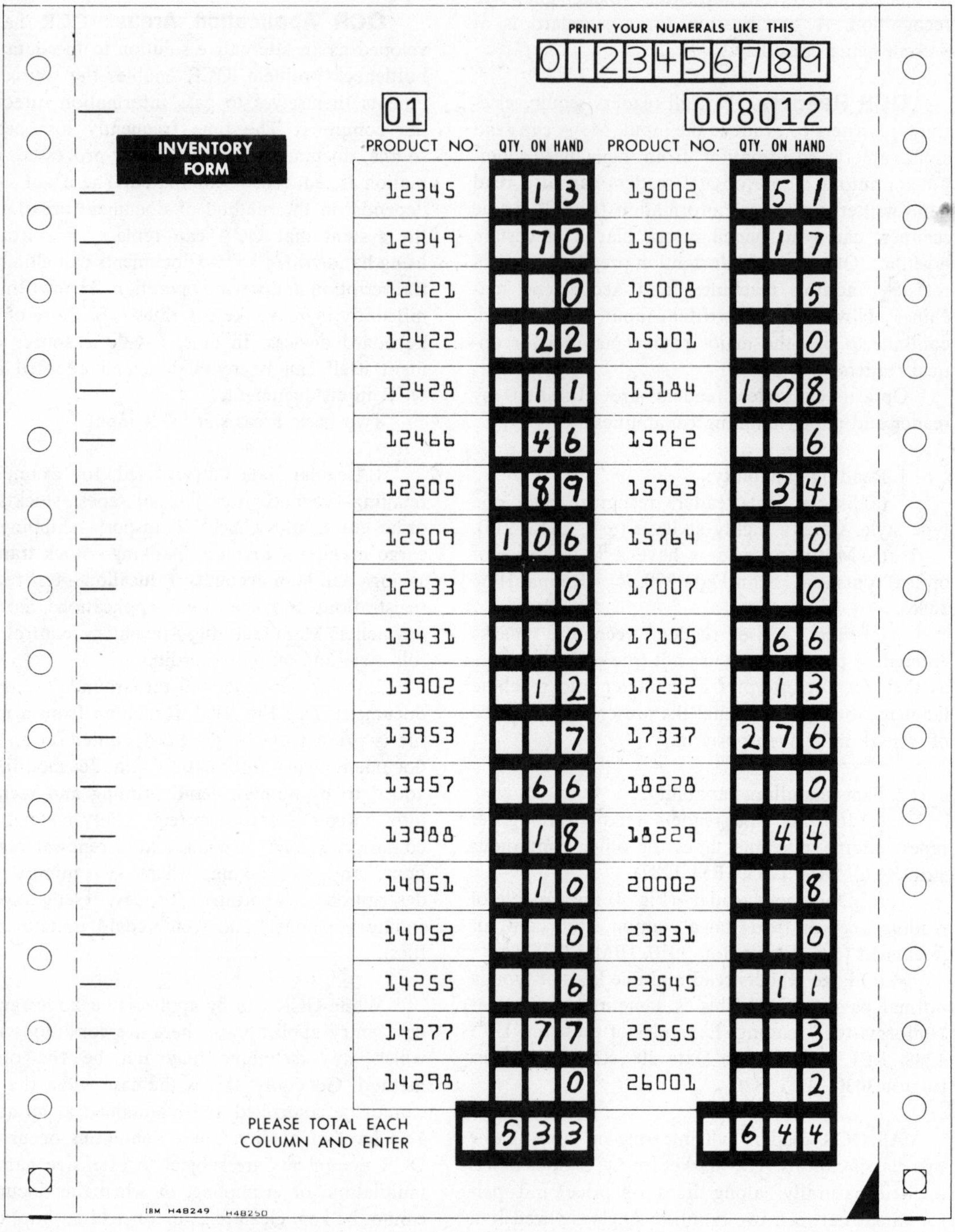

INVENTORY FORM

PRINT YOUR NUMERALS LIKE THIS

0 1 2 3 4 5 6 7 8 9

01 | 008012

| PRODUCT NO. | QTY. ON HAND | PRODUCT NO. | QTY. ON HAND |
|---|---|---|---|
| 12345 | 13 | 15002 | 51 |
| 12349 | 70 | 15006 | 17 |
| 12421 | 0 | 15008 | 5 |
| 12422 | 22 | 15101 | 0 |
| 12428 | 11 | 15184 | 108 |
| 12466 | 46 | 15762 | 6 |
| 12505 | 89 | 15763 | 34 |
| 12509 | 106 | 15764 | 0 |
| 12633 | 0 | 17007 | 0 |
| 13431 | 0 | 17105 | 66 |
| 13902 | 12 | 17232 | 13 |
| 13953 | 7 | 17337 | 276 |
| 13957 | 66 | 18228 | 0 |
| 13988 | 18 | 18229 | 44 |
| 14051 | 10 | 20002 | 8 |
| 14052 | 0 | 23331 | 0 |
| 14255 | 6 | 23545 | 11 |
| 14277 | 77 | 25555 | 3 |
| 14298 | 0 | 26001 | 2 |
| PLEASE TOTAL EACH COLUMN AND ENTER | 533 | | 644 |

IBM H48249 H48250

**Fig. 2.** Document used for hand-printing OCR input to inventory system.

**Fig. 3.** The Recognition Equipment, Inc. OCR/S 2000 system reads OCR ISO-B and IBM 1403 fonts plus special symbols. Also reads documents at up to 2,400 characters per minute and can be directly connected to a computer. It can also be used for microfilming and sorting.

system performance. The quality of the printing will affect both total process time and error recovery effort on line and/or off line. Also, the sensitive physics of light impose specifications of paper quality, background inks, and print quality on OCR forms no less rigid than those of the scanning machines themselves.

In a very real sense, the forms manufacturer has great responsibility for the success of the optical scanning operation, since he determines the type of paper used and the inks used for any preprinting on the form. Each new advance in machine sophistication has been met with equal sophistication in forms technology. Background papers must be completely free of extraneous marks and dirt. Cleanliness requirements are so stringent that there must never be more than 150 "marks" per thousand square inches of raw stock. In this context, a "mark" is considered to be any visible imperfection larger than four millionths of a square inch.

Also, characteristics of strength, weight, thickness, paper smoothness, and optical density are evaluated against strict criteria. The background inks must satisfy constant and rigid quality requirements. The slightest variations in ink color shades can affect the scanner operations. The reflective characteristics of ink batches must be measured and tested against the specifications of the particular scanner with which the ink will be used.

Since machine-readable data is being created by a human being, human factors must be considered if quality output is to be produced at all times. An OCR application can succeed only if optimum quality output is given at all times. To achieve this, the person must feel motivated to produce optimum output. A person must receive training and education to a depth and intensity appropriate to the level of personnel involved. Perhaps the most important factor, however, is individual feedback of quality attainments. Individual feedback or group feedback is necessary so that future performance will be as good as, or better than, past performance as measured against an acceptable set of criteria.

**Cost Advantages.** With continually decreasing prices of OCR machines, more and more applications have become feasible because they show distinct cost advantages. The recent advent of

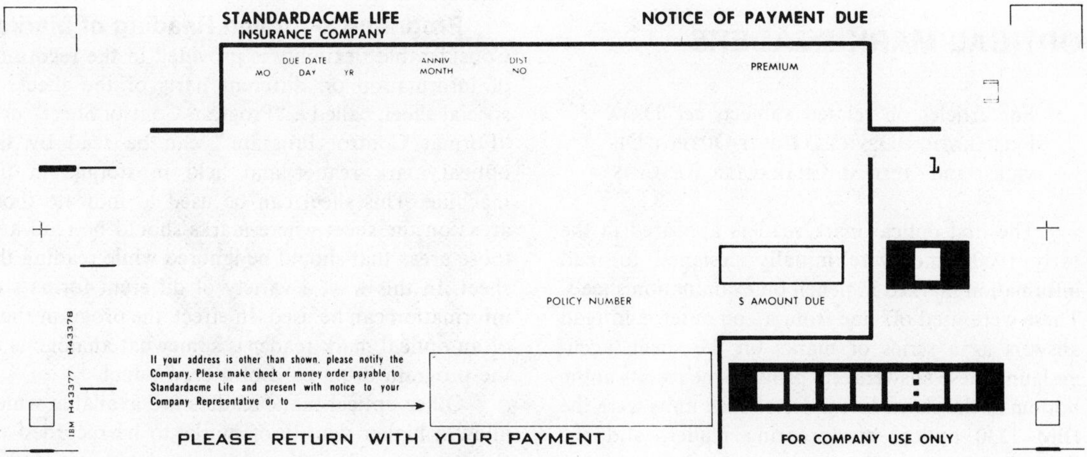


**Fig. 4.** Turnaround billing document for OCR input.

OCR service centers makes possible the improvements in economics of data preparation by allowing a low-volume customer to use a small portion of the processing capabilities of a highly sophisticated machine.

The greatest cost advantages are obtained if the OCR document is created at the source of information. A person currently fulfilling a hand-printing or typewriting function can create original input data. This eliminates completely the need for keypunches, verifiers, or other keyboard devices. Other tangible areas of savings are reduction in card or paper-tape costs, reduction in capital equipment costs, (e.g., keypunches, verifiers, and other card handling equipment), reduction in supervision or reconciliation costs, and reduction in floor-space costs. Other possible advantages are reduction in data preparation time and subsequent total data processing cycle time, and elimination of transcription errors.

Factors such as fast turnaround, changes in training procedures, office space, and cost of errors contribute significantly to the cost effectiveness of OCR. On direct capital and associated overhead savings alone, however, an OCR reader costing \$25,000–\$50,000 represents the equivalent of about 8 to 12 keypunch operators. But, compared with cost, the volume of data that can be processed represents the output of approximately 50 punches and verifiers. The capacity for expansion and greater cost savings is obvious.

M. J. F. POULSEN

# OPTICAL MARK READERS

For articles on related subjects *see* DATA PREPARATION DEVICES; INPUT-OUTPUT DEVICES; and OPTICAL CHARACTER READERS.

The first optical mark readers appeared in the early 1960s and were initially designed to read information marked in pencil on examination sheets. These were used off line from a computer, and read answers as a series of marks on the sheet, accumulating these answers and printing the results at the bottom of the sheet. Examples of such units were the IBM 1230 optical mark-scoring reader, and the Optical Scanning Corporation's Model 100 test-scoring reader.

As the uses of optical mark reading expanded to other applications, the availability of other optical mark readers increased in the early and mid-1960s. These later models were designed to attach either directly to a computer or to off-line card punches or magnetic tape.

**Reading Optical Marks.** In optical mark reading, information is read as a series of marks on a sheet of paper, which is generally 8 1/2 by 11 in. in size (see Fig. 1). The sheet is divided into a number of separate mark-response positions, up to 1,000 positions in the case of the IBM Models 1231 and 1232 optical mark page readers (see Fig. 2), and 2,500 positions for the Optical Scanning Corporation Model 70 optical mark page reader. Ten response positions are used to make up one word of information (or, with the IBM 1231 and 1232, to represent the digits zero to nine). Two words can appear side by side on the page, comprising one row, with 50 rows of 100 words (or 1,000 positions) on the sheet.

The pencil marks are read optically. Lamps direct beams of light onto the paper, which are reflected back from the paper; the amount of light reflected is measured by a photocell. When a pencil mark is present, the amount of light reflected is much less than when the mark is absent. In many readers, separate lamps and photocells are used to read each column of mark response positions on the sheet.

In order to control the reading of information from row to row down the sheet, timing marks are used (see right side of Fig. 1). These are normally preprinted on the sheet away from the marking area and are read by a separate lamp and cell.

**Program-Controlled Reading of Marks.** Considerable flexibility is provided in the recording of information on different parts of the sheet. A special sheet, called a "Program Control Sheet" or a "Format Control Program," can be read by the optical mark reader and held in storage in the machine. This sheet can be used to indicate those areas on the sheet where marks should be read and those areas that should be ignored while reading the sheet. In this way, a variety of different formats of information can be used. In effect, the program sheet of an optical mark reader is somewhat analogous to the program drum card of a card punch.

Other optical mark readers are available which allow a higher density of marks to be recorded on the page, as well as allow different sized sheets (other than 8 ½ by 11 in.) to be read. An example of these is

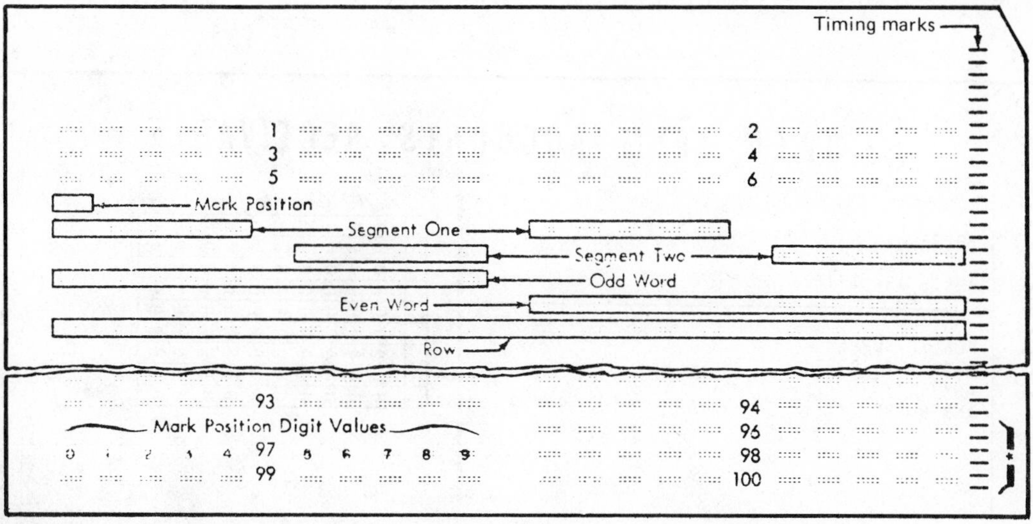


*These six control timing marks are used for counter read out controls in the IBM 1230.

5065

**Fig. 1.** Typical mark reader data sheet format.

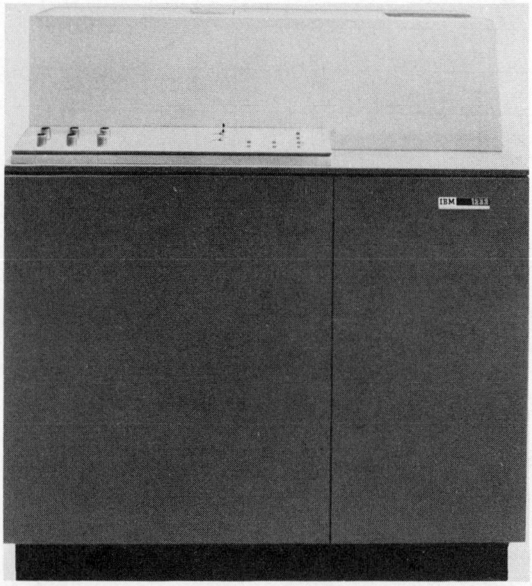

**Fig. 2.** IBM 1232 optical mark page reader.

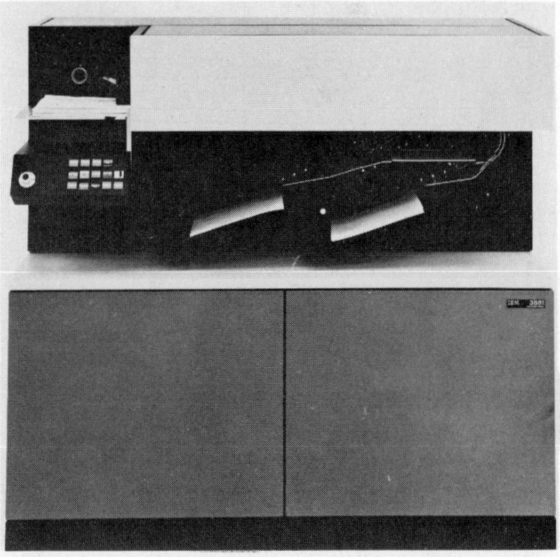

**Fig. 3.** IBM 3881 optical mark reader, which handles documents ranging from small cards to page-size forms.

the National Computer Systems mark reader, which can read pages up to 11 by 42 in. In some optical mark readers (Control Data Corporation), the appropriate digit can be drawn in its relevant position on the page. While the mark, or digit, is given a particular value only according to its relative position on the sheet, this technique can be very useful in allowing information recorded on the sheet to be understood more readily by humans.

Optical mark readers are relatively low-speed input devices, compared with other computer input equipment. The speed is generally on the order of a few thousand documents per hour.

Recently, the development of optical mark readers has been directed toward increasing the amount of information that can be recorded on a page, and toward increasing the speed of input. Examples of these advanced readers are the IBM

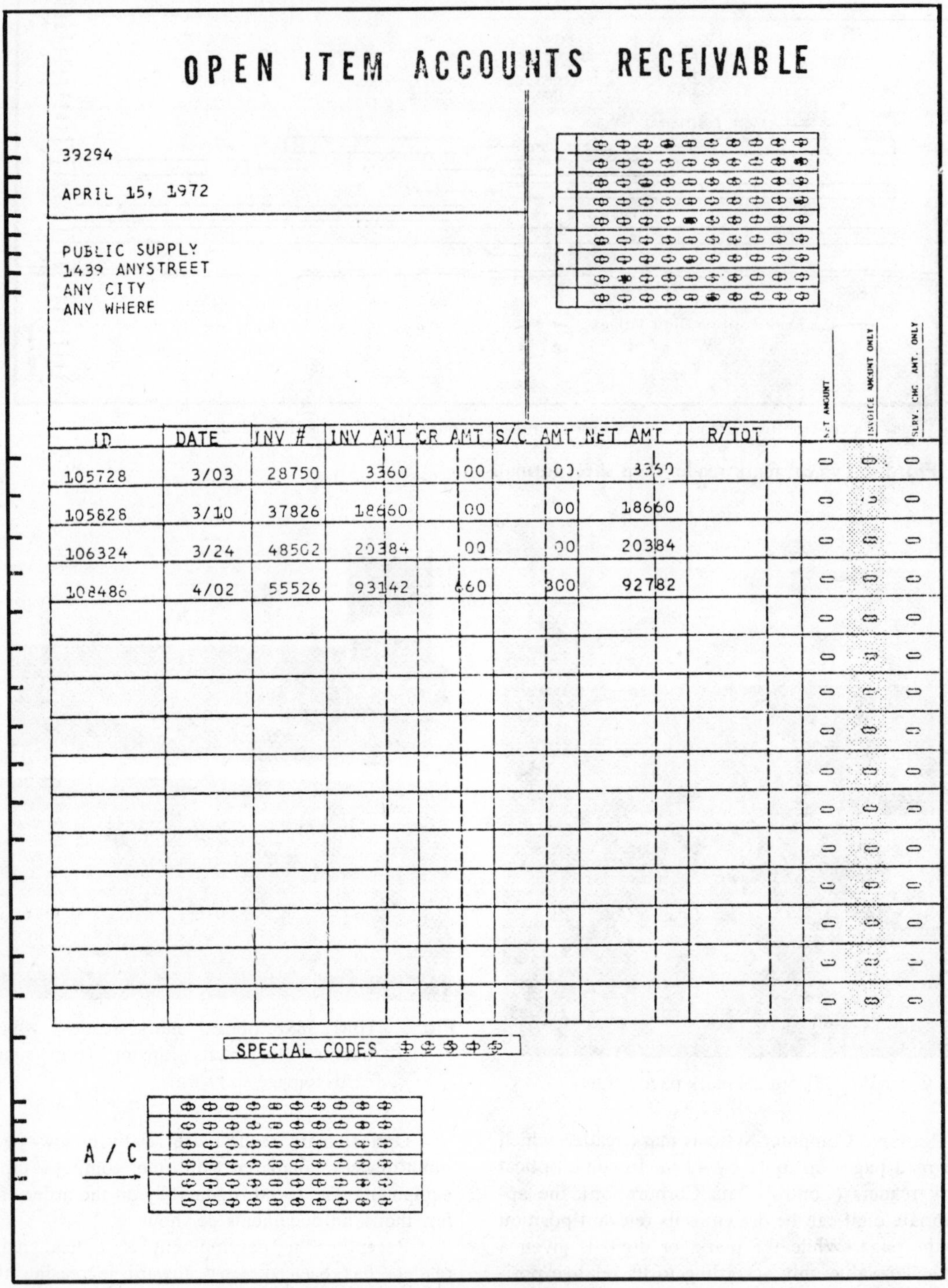

OPEN ITEM ACCOUNTS RECEIVABLE

39294

APRIL 15, 1972

PUBLIC SUPPLY
1439 ANYSTREET
ANY CITY
ANY WHERE

| ID | DATE | INV # | INV AMT | CR AMT | S/C AMT | NET AMT | R/TOT | NET AMOUNT | INVOICE AMOUNT ONLY | SLPV. CHG. AMT. ONLY |
|---|---|---|---|---|---|---|---|---|---|---|
| 105728 | 3/03 | 28750 | 3360 | 00 | 00 | 3360 | | | | |
| 105828 | 3/10 | 37826 | 18660 | 00 | 00 | 18660 | | | | |
| 106324 | 3/24 | 48502 | 20384 | 00 | 00 | 20384 | | | | |
| 108486 | 4/02 | 55526 | 93142 | 660 | 300 | 92782 | | | | |

SPECIAL CODES

A / C

**Fig. 4.** Typical accounts receivable optical mark format.

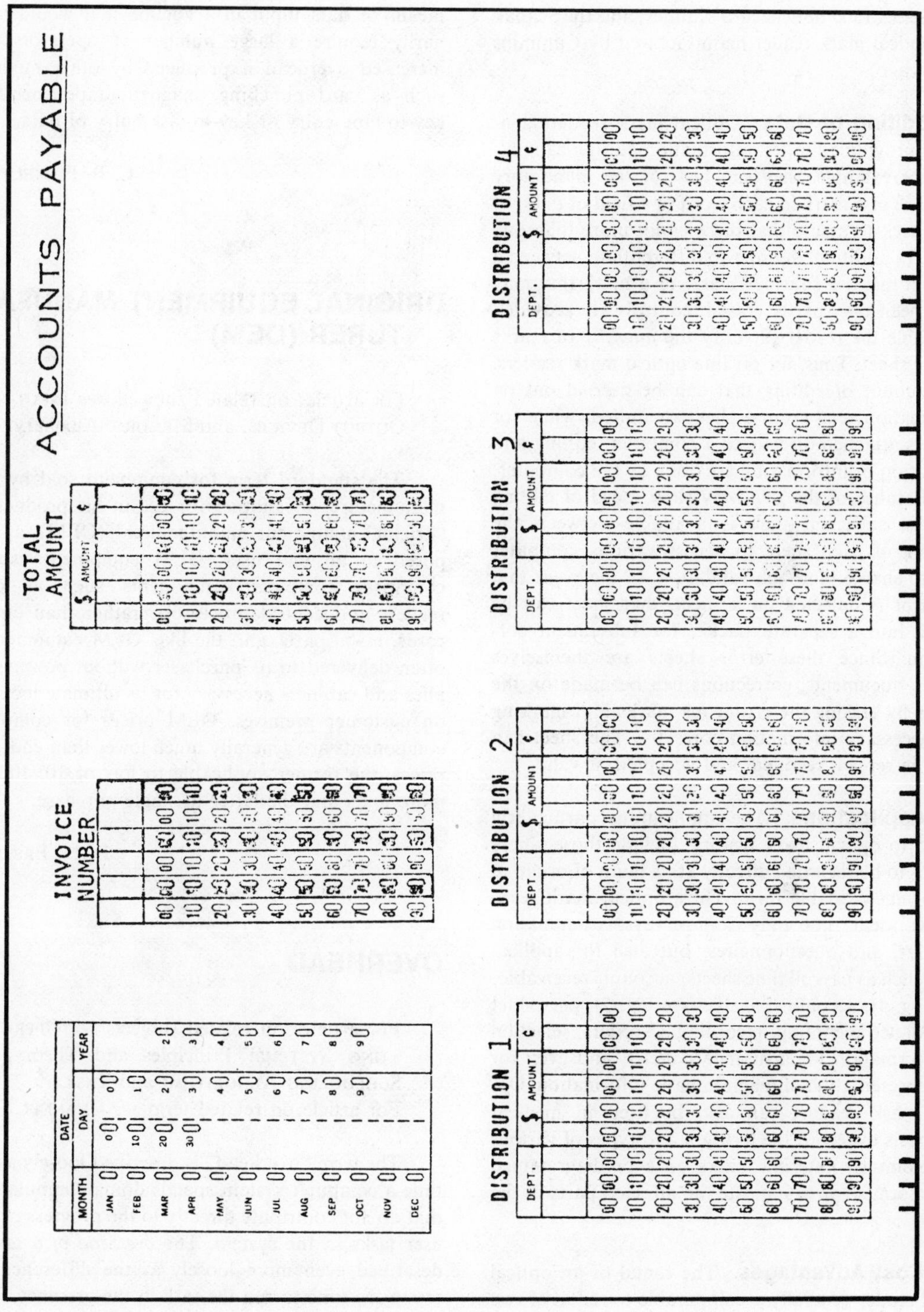


**Fig. 5.** Typical accounts payable optical mark form.

3881 optical mark reader, the National Computer Systems mark reader (Fig. 3), the Republic Corporation Series 1500 optical card scanner, and the Scanak 216 optical mark reader manufactured by Cummins in Chicago.

**Editing of Data.** Optical mark readers generally provide a limited information-editing capability. For example, they can test for the mandatory presence of a mark in each word in a field of data, or can check to assure that there is not more than one mark. In addition, in order to differentiate between a distinct mark, a spurious mark, or a mark that may have been only partly erased, controls are provided to enable the reader to verify the *intensity* of marks on the sheet. Thus, for off-line optical mark readers, the amount of editing that can be carried out on information read from a sheet is limited, while for readers attached directly to a computer, editing and validation of information are done by the computer.

Because of the relatively slow speed of editing devices, sufficient time is available between the reading of each sheet to access various computer files to enable thorough validation. In the event that an error is detected on a sheet, that sheet can be sorted into a separate stacker for subsequent correction. Since these error sheets are themselves source documents, corrections can be made on the sheets by erasing the erroneous marks and marking the necessary information correctly. The sheet can then be reread, reedited, and accepted, if valid.

**Applications.** The applications particularly suited to optical mark reading include those where data is to be recorded directly at its point of origin in a machine-readable form. Thus, optical mark reading is ideal, not only for surveys, examination answers, and questionnaires, but also for applications such as payroll time sheets, accounts receivable, (see Fig. 4), accounts payable (see Fig. 5), personnel attendance recording, recording of orders, selection of information for insurance policies, and even for the representation of diagrammatic information. Optical mark reading can also be used in medical diagnosis to record the location and types of various symptoms by entering marks on a prediagrammed body form so as to indicate the affected parts of the body.

**Cost Advantages.** The rental of an optical mark reader generally is comparable to rental of two to four card punches and the cost of associated operator's salaries, but typically the reader has the capability of reading the same volume of data as would be produced by 20 to 40 card punches. Thus, optical mark reading provides a very economical means of data input in a volume that would ordinarily require a large number of operators and increased overhead if produced by other methods such as card punching, magnetic tape encoding, key-to-tape entry or key-to-disk entry of data.

C. B. FINKELSTEIN

## ORIGINAL EQUIPMENT MANUFACTURER (OEM)

For articles on related subjects *see* INPUT-OUTPUT DEVICES; and MEMORY: Auxiliary.

The standard term for equipment sold by one manufacturer to another for use in his products is "original equipment manufacturer" (OEM), as opposed to an end user. OEM equipment usually comprises complete components such as card readers and central processors, rather than circuit cards, metal parts, and the like. OEM equipment is often delivered to its purchaser without power supplies and cabinets necessary for its ultimate location on customer premises. OEM prices for computer components are generally much lower than end-user prices, the former applicable to lots of 10, 100, or more units and the latter to single purchase.

D. N. FREEMAN

## OVERHEAD

For articles on related subjects *see* OPERATING SYSTEMS: Principles and Theory; SCHEDULING ALGORITHM; and TASK.
For article on related term *see* CHANNEL.

The term "overhead" is described loosely as the time a computer system spends doing computations that do not contribute directly to the progress of any user tasks in the system. The *overhead of a task* is described even more loosely as the difference between the time to run the task in the presence of all other tasks in a system and the time to run the task if it had the entire system to itself. A precise definition of overhead is difficult to obtain, and a measurement of overhead in a given system must be interpreted carefully.

Offhand, it might seem that whenever an operating system program is executing, no user task is making progress and the time so spent should be attributed directly to overhead. Overhead, according to this definition, is easily measured as the time the central processor spends in the "supervisor state." The imprecision of this definition becomes clear when one considers that (1) many systems have peripheral processors and channels dedicated to the execution of systems programs, whereupon the central processor has little occasion to execute systems programs; and (2) many important functions and services employed by user tasks are implemented as part of the operating system (e.g., input and output programs, file system programs, and error handling programs) so that one cannot always say that no progress on any task is being made whenever the processor is observed to be executing a systems program. The point is, overhead cannot be measured simply as the time the central processor spends in supervisor state; it must be measured in terms of the total system resources expended on system functions.

Thus, for example, an observation that an IBM System 370 spends 80% of its time in the supervisor state cannot be interpreted to mean that the system spends only 20% of its time doing useful work: We need to know what portion of the 80% is spent on running systems programs specifically requested by some user task. Or, an observation that a CDC 6600 processor spends 90% of the time running user tasks cannot be interpreted to mean that overhead is low, as there are eight or more peripheral processors concurrently carrying out systems functions.

There are at least four sources of overhead in most systems: allocation of resources, responding to exceptional conditions, providing protection and reliability, and accounting. Each will consume some system resources to provide, for example, time on central and peripheral processors to execute systems programs, or space in various memory devices to store information about the running tasks and the system state.

With respect to *resource allocation*, a portion of system capacity will be devoted to functions such as scheduling the use of resources, initiating and terminating tasks, switching processors among tasks, allocating space in primary and secondary memory, and managing information transfers among levels of memory. With respect to *exceptional conditions*, a portion of the system's capacity will be devoted to handling such errors as arithmetic contingencies, data transmission failures, addressing snags, and illegal actions by tasks. With respect to *protection and reliability*, a portion of the system's capacity will be devoted to monitoring accesses to various resources for authenticity, to periodic testing of equipment, and to periodic dumping and copying of information off line. With respect to *accounting*, a portion of the system's capacity will be devoted to collecting information on each task's usage of resources, figuring costs and billings for users of the system, and generating statistics on resource usage and performance.

The costs of the overhead functions mentioned above are usually borne by the users of the system. Where possible, these costs are allocated to the tasks that caused the overhead function to be performed (e.g., initiating a task, switching a processor to a task, moving information of a task among the levels of memory). Otherwise, these costs are distributed among all users according to some pro rata formula.

It is important to recognize that overhead detracts from system performance only to the extent that the overhead functions interfere with the processing of user tasks. As noted earlier, many services are provided by the system to relieve programmers from having to provide these functions themselves. As long as the system can provide these functions more efficiently than the users, the resulting increases in overhead may well be offset by better service, improved performance, and lower overall costs to the users.

P. J. Denning and D. E. Denning

# OVERLAY

For an article on a related subject *see* Procedure-Oriented Languages: Programming in.

When a section of computer code is loaded into a central memory area that was previously allocated to another section of the same executing program, the process is called "overlaying," and the loaded section of code is called an "overlay." An overlay may contain instructions or data, or a combination of instructions and data.

The technique of overlaying is used to permit jobs to run on a computer even if their total memory requirement is larger than the amount of memory available to them. The amount of memory available may be all of central memory in a simple uniprogramming environment. It may be only a fraction of the total memory in a multiprogramming environment.

In a program using overlays, an initial part of the program is loaded into main memory; the remainder is held in peripheral storage. During the running of the program, instructions are executed to cause all or part of the core-resident program to be overlayed by specified program sections in peripheral storage.

A very simple overlaying system called "chaining" was used in a number of early Fortran systems. The chained overlays were relatively independent and self-contained. A link of the chain would be loaded into memory and would execute until it terminated by loading another link (i.e., overlay) over itself. The next link would then execute and terminate in the same way by loading an overlay over itself and giving control to the new overlay. A common non-overlayed data area in memory, declared by the Fortran COMMON statement, provided the only communication between the links of the chained program.

More recent and more sophisticated systems permit the programmer quite a bit of flexibility in handling overlays. In a typical system the programmer can specify an overlay tree, as in Fig. 1. The programmer specifies a *root segment R*, which remains in memory throughout the running of the program. The memory area just beyond the end of the root segment may be occupied by one of the first level overlays *A*, *B*, or *C*. If it is occupied by *A*, then the area just past the end of *A* may be occupied by *D* or *E*. If it is *D*, then either *K* or *L*; if *E*, then *M* or *N* may occupy the next area of storage. However, *K* or *L* cannot be in memory unless *D* and *A*, and of course the root segment, are present.

If *R*, *A*, *D*, and *K* are in memory, a reference in *D* to a location in *L* will cause the loader to bring in *L* and overlay *K*. A reference in *A* to a location in *E* will cause *E* to be loaded over *D*, extending over part of *K* or *L* if necessary. A reference in the root segment to a location in *C* will load *C* over *A*, effectively removing *A* and all of its lower levels from central memory. A reference to *F* in the root segment will cause both *B* and *F* to be loaded. At any given time, one path through the overlay tree is current, and any segment can be loaded through references from any point above it in the tree.

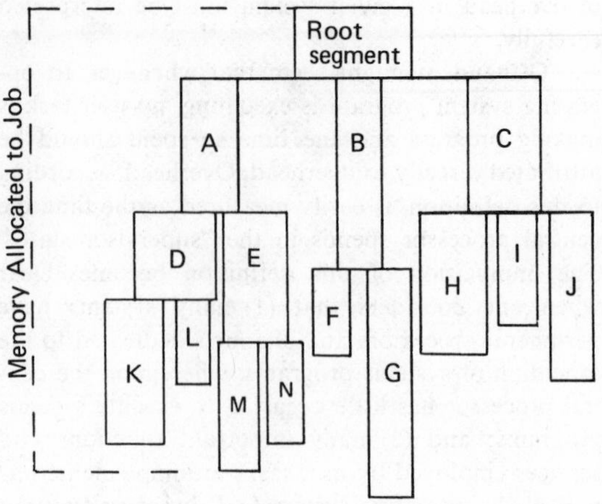


**Fig. 1.** An overlay tree structure.

The programmer must specify the beginning and end of each segment and its position in the tree structure. The language processing system organizes the object code modules along with necessary control information into a structure that resides in peripheral storage during program execution and from which the appropriate overlays are loaded.

The development of an appropriate and efficient overlay structure for a long and complicated program can be very difficult. One of the aims in the development of virtual memory systems has been to make the handling of overlays completely automatic.

S. ROSEN

# P

**PL/I.** *See* PROCEDURE-ORIENTED LANGUAGES; and PROCEDURE-ORIENTED LANGUAGES, PROGRAMMING IN.

## PMS NOTATION

For article on related subject *see* COMPUTER SYSTEMS.
For article on related term *see* BLOCK DIAGRAM.

PMS (*p*rocessor-*m*emory-*s*witch) notation was developed by Bell and Newell (1971) to provide a clearer, more concise description of the physical structure of computer systems than is provided by the equivocal "block diagrams" of computers. There are only a few primitive components in the PMS notation:

- *M* A *memory* component is capable of storing information. An *M* only retains information for subsequent use by other components; it cannot alter the information it is given to store.
- *L* A *link* transmits information between other PMS components. Like an *M*, an *L* is not capable of altering information.
- *S* A *switch* constructs links between other components. It has an associated set of *L*'s that it enables or disables to make the required connections.
- *D* A component performs the *data operations* of creating and altering information. *D*'s are the only PMS components that modify the meanings of the information in the computer system. (An arithmetic unit is a classic *D* component.)
- *K* A *control* unit evokes the other PMS components into operation. All other components are intrinsically passive and require a *K* to evoke an action from them.
- *T* A *transducer* couples a computer structure to the physical world. In other words, it translates between the logic levels of digital circuits and the holes in a punched card, images on a TV screen, keystrokes at a terminal, etc.

With no more than these six PMS components, we are able to describe the basic structure (Fig. 1) of a conventional computer. The symbol *X* is used to denote the external environment of the computer. The PMS components are interconnected with solid and broken lines to specify the various information paths. The solid lines indicate the flow of data and the broken lines indicate the transfer of control information. We usually indicate links as broken or solid lines and reserve the more explicit *L* notation for instances when we want to draw attention to some attribute of the link. There is a solid and broken line between *M* and *K* in Fig. 1 to indicate

## PMS NOTATION

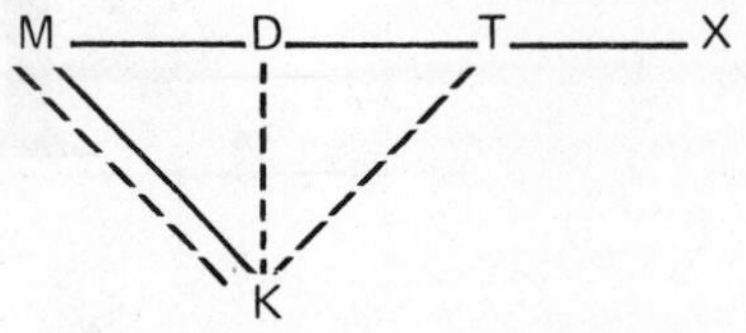


**Fig. 1.** PMS components of a conventional computer.

the flow of instructions from *M* to *K* (a data transfer) and the control of *M* via control signals from *K*. Although boxes convey no additional information, PMS components are sometimes enclosed in them to give a more familiar "block diagram" appearance.

The *D* and *K* pair in Fig. 1 are commonly referred to as the "central processor," and in general it is useful to define a *processor* as a nonprimitive PMS component.

*P* is a component that is able to interpret a sequence of instructions and execute a corresponding sequence of actions.

Our PMS description of a simple computer now reduces to

$$M — P — T —$$

Note that we have also suppressed the control lines from the *K* to the *M* and *T*. Control lines are often omitted when there is little chance of confusion. This structure of a conventional computer is so common that it is often helpful to define the *computer*, *C*, as another nonprimitive PMS component. Many large computer systems will include smaller *C*'s as components.

In order for the PMS notation to describe the rich variation in each of the components, the following form is provided to allow a more detailed

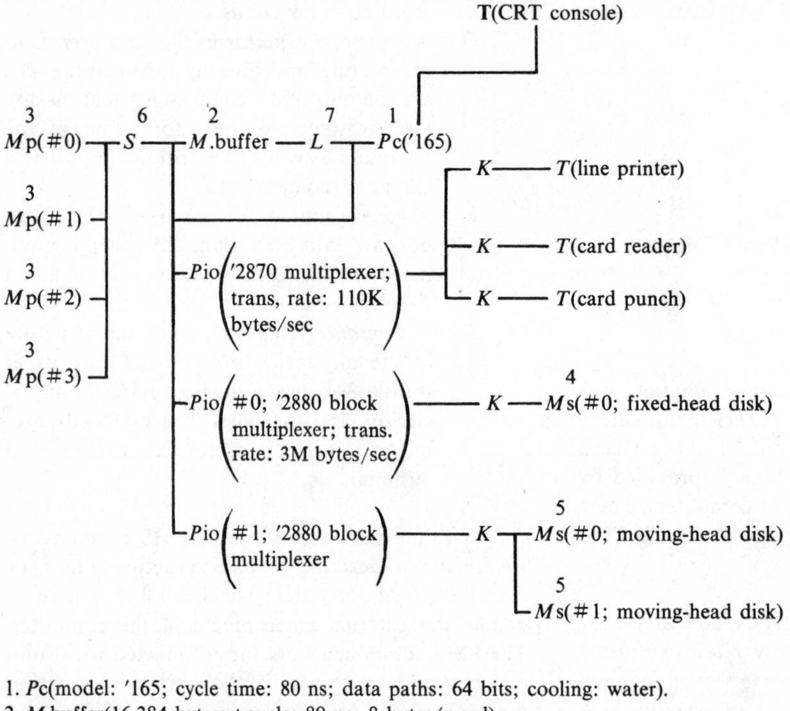


1. *P*c(model: '165; cycle time: 80 ns; data paths: 64 bits; cooling: water).
2. *M*.buffer(16,384 bytes; t.cycle: 80 ns; 8 bytes/word)
3. *M*p(262,144 bytes; t.cycle: 2 μs)
4. *M*s('2305 Model 2 fixed-head disk unit; capacity: 11M bytes; rotation: 0.01 sec; transfer rate: 1.5M bytes/sec)
5. *M*s('3330 moving-head disk unit: capacity: 2 disk packs and 100M bytes/pack; transfer rate: 806K bytes/sec)
6. *S*(bandwidth: 16M bytes/sec; data path: 8 bytes)
7. *L*(bandwidth: 50M bytes/sec; data path: 8 bytes)

**Fig. 2.** PMS diagram of an IBM 370/165.

description of an arbitrary PMS unit $U$:

$$U(a_1{:}v_1;\ a_2{:}v_2;\ \cdots),$$

where the $a_i$ are attributes and the $v_i$ are their corresponding values. For example,

*P*(function: control; name: 'UNIVAC I; addition time: 525 μs; word length: 12 characters; t.operation: March 1951; technology: vacuum tubes)
*M*(t.cycle: 1.0 μs; capacity: 16,384 words; word length: 36 bits)

Some attributes are so common that a series of progressively abbreviated descriptions have been included in the notation. The following example illustrates the derivation of *P*c, the PMS equivalent of CPU:

*P*(function: control)
*P*(control)
*P*.control
*P*.c
*P*c

Fig. 2 is a PMS diagram of an IBM 370/165 computer installation that includes one million bytes of main memory, three I/O channels, a fixed-head disk, eight disk packs, and an assortment of unit record devices. This diagram is considerably more detailed than the earlier PMS diagrams of a computer, and in general the PMS notation is capable of describing computer structures to varying degrees of detail.

### Reference

1971. Bell, C. G., and A. Newell. *Computer Structures: Readings and Examples.* New York: McGraw-Hill.

S. H. Fuller

**PSW.** *See* Program Status Words and State Vectors.

## PACKET SWITCHING

For articles on related subjects *see* ARPA Network; Communications and Computers; Data Processing; and Data Communication Networks.

Packet switching is a term used to describe the internal operation of a particular type of data communication network that has a fixed internal topology and uses software to dynamically route messages through the network from source to destination. A packet-switched data communication network is usually composed of a number of geographically separate nodes connected by dedicated high-speed data links. The nodes are (usually) stored program computers that have internal data link connections to the other nodes and external data links connected (usually) to local terminals and computers. Fig. 1 illustrates an example of a packet-switched data communication network with four nodes.

A terminal wishing to communicate with another terminal sends to its node a message composed of a start-of-header (SOH) signal, a header that specifies the destination as node address and terminal address, a start-of-text (STX) signal, the message text, and an end-of-text (ETX) signal, possibly followed by some error check information.

Fig. 2(a) illustrates a typical message entering the network from the computer on terminal 1 of node A destined for the Teletype on terminal 1 of node D. The node processor stores the header information for subsequent use in routing packets of data through the network to their destination. The node processor divides the message text into fixed-length packets (around 1,000 bits is common), which are prefixed by a fixed-length header containing routing and network control information. The packet header usually contains the source and destination addresses, a message number, and the packet number within the message. Fig. 2(b) shows the example message divided into four packets.

The packets are then routed through the network to the destination node, and may pass through a number of intermediate nodes before they reach their destination node. Sequential packets may take different routes through the network, depending on the load and availability of the internal data links, and may arrive at the destination node out of order. Fig. 3 gives a sample packet-routing sequence in the event of failure of an internode link.

The destination node assembles the packets of the message into their correct order and sends the message to the destination terminal, preceded by a header containing the address of the source and followed by an end-of-message signal. When the

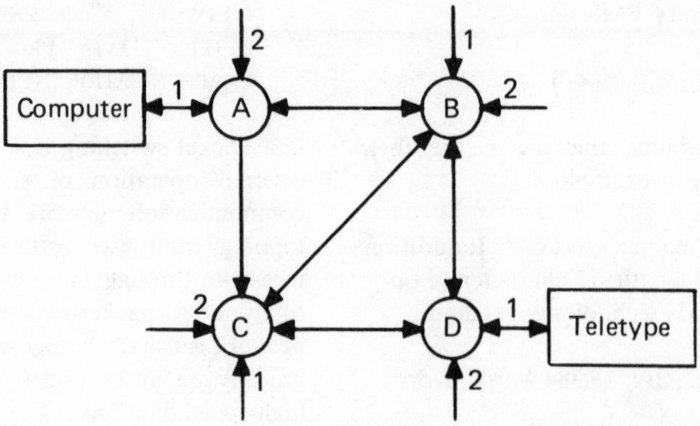


**Fig. 1.** Example of a packet-switched data network.

SOH D 1 STX ··· 256 characters ··· ETX

(a)

| | | | | | |
|---|---|---|---|---|---|
| SOH | A 1 | D 1 | 1 | 1 | STX ··· 1st 64 characters ETX |
| SOH | A 1 | D 1 | 1 | 2 | STX ··· 2nd 64 characters ETX |
| SOH | A 1 | D 1 | 1 | 3 | STX ··· 3rd 64 characters ETX |
| SOH | A 1 | D 1 | 1 | 4 | STX ··· 4th 64 characters ETX |
| | SA | DA | MN | PN | |

(b)

**Fig. 2.** Typical message entering network. (a) Sample message. (b) Resulting packets. SA = source address; DA = destination address; MN = message number; PN = packet number.

| Packet | Route | | | | | |
|---|---|---|---|---|---|---|
| 1 | A | B | D* | B | C | D |
| 2 | A | C | D | | | |
| 3 | | A | B | C | D | |
| 4 | | A | C | D | | |
| | 1 | 2 | 3 | 4 | 5 | 6 |
| | time | | | | | |

**Fig. 3.** Sample packet-routing sequence. Asterisk denotes that internode link BD fails in time period 2–3, causing packets 1, 3 to be rerouted via C. Order of arrival at node D = 2,4,3,1.

message has been received by the destination terminal and acknowledged, an acknowledgment packet is constructed and sent back through the network to the source node. The source node then sends an acknowledgment signal to the source terminal.

When the messages sent into the network from a source terminal are short and go to a varying set of destinations, the packet-switched network has a much shorter network setup time than a circuit-switched network, which must first construct a digital path from source to destination before transmission of data can begin. The packet-switched network can make more efficient use of the channel capacity of the internode data links because it can take advantage of gaps in the terminal-to-terminal conversation by multiplexing packets from several sources on a single internode data link. The choice of fixed-length packets allows one error detection scheme to be used for all transmissions and simplifies the internal network scheduling.

The best-known examples of an operational packet-switched data network are the ARPA network (Carr et al., 1970; Heart et al., 1970) and the General Electric time-sharing service network (Feeney, 1972).

### References

1970. Carr, C. S., S. D. Crocker, and V. G. Cerf. "HOST-HOST Communication Protocol in the ARPA Network," *Proc. SJCC,* pp. 589-597.

1970. Heart, F. E., R. E. Kahn, S. M. Ornstein, W. R. Crowther, and D. C. Walden. "The Interface Message Processor for the ARPA Computer Network," *Proc. SJCC,* pp. 551-567.

1972. Feeney, G. J. "The Future of Computer Utilities," *Proc. First International Conf. on Computer Communications,* Washington, D.C.

R. H. Kerr

# PAPER TAPE

## GENERAL

For articles on related subjects *see* CODES; DATA PREPARATION DEVICES; and INPUT-OUTPUT DEVICES.

For articles on related terms *see* ASCII; and EBCDIC.

Punched paper tape is a storage medium used for the preparation, storage, and transmission of data in various applications. Slow-speed paper tape may be used as a control device for numerically controlled machine tool operations. At higher speeds, paper tape may be used for typesetting, telegraphic and data transmission, and automated typewriting, as well as for storing computer programs and data, and also for other data processing functions (e.g., to control the carriage movement in line printers).

The use of punched paper tape for data preparation, storage, and transmission is not a new technique. It was introduced by Sir Charles Wheatstone in 1857 for telegraphic purposes, just 21 years after the first practical demonstration of the electric telegraph. One year later, in 1858, a Morse tape reader-transmitter operated at 100 words per minute. Five-track tape keyboard punches were in common use in 1908. In 1925, five-track readers were commonly operating at four letters, or 20 bits per second. When multiplexed for transmission use, the line speed was 80 bits per second. Adoption of this technique for data processing has seen a vast increase in applications of punched paper tape.

Speed requirements and therefore performance have increased manyfold, and the available number of tracks has increased from five to eight to accommodate the various alphabets required. Small sprocket holes appear along the length of the tape and are used to feed the tape mechanically as they engage toothed wheels in slow-speed readers; in high-speed machines, these sprocket holes (or feed holes) act as a clock pulse when a tape is read by a photoelectric head (see Fig. 1). Data is recorded in the tape by punching holes in a row across the width. Each row represents one character, and the pattern of the holes punched indicates the particular character.

In the narrowest tape (with five tracks, and which is 11/16 in. wide), since a hole can be punched in any track, the number of unique hole combinations possible is $2^5$, or 32. Thus, 32 characters can be represented by a five-hole code. More than 32 separate items can be identified if each code group is made to represent two or more characters, and a special character (e.g., letter or figure shift) precedes the punched data to indicate which interpretation is to be used (see Fig. 2). In certain circumstances this arrangement can be cumbersome; hence, it has resulted in the development of tape with more information tracks so that a larger number of characters can be identified uniquely. Nevertheless, economic considerations caused many first-generation computer manufacturers (especially in the U.K.) to opt for five-track paper tape input, and many of them designed their own five-track paper tape code.

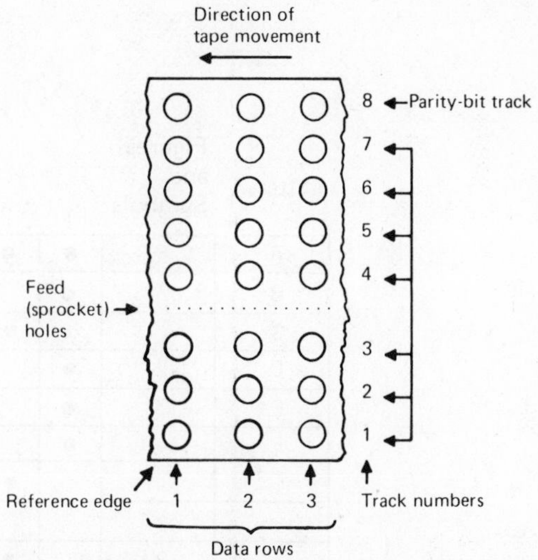


**Fig. 1.** Punched paper-tape terminology. Note: Each data row represents one seven-bit character.

With the advent of the second generation of computers, the limitations of the five-track tape led to introduction of a sixth track, giving the possibility of 64 code combinations. To this was also added a parity track, resulting in seven-track paper tape whose width was about 7/8 in. IBM's paper tape code, however, used seven data tracks and had a single character ("new line") in the eighth track. This resulted in a tape width of 1 in., and the maximum number of code combinations was increased to 65. IBM's eight-track paper tape has been widely adopted by office machine manufacturers because it provides enough codes for various miscellaneous commands.

The demand for further paper-tape code combinations was brought about by the larger character sets of third-generation computers. These computers had discrete codes for upper- and lower-case characters, a larger number of special symbols for both control and graphical characters, and transmission

| Letters | Figures and Symbols | Code 1 | 2 | 3 | 4 | 5 ← Track numbers |
|---|---|---|---|---|---|---|
| A | – | ● | ● | | | |
| B | ? | ● | | | ● | ● |
| C | : | | ● | ● | ● | |
| D | Who are you? | ● | | | ● | |
| E | 3 | ● | | | | |
| F | | ● | | ● | ● | |
| G | | | ● | | ● | ● |
| H | | | | ● | | ● |
| I | 8 | | ● | ● | | |
| J | Bell | ● | ● | | ● | |
| K | ( | ● | ● | ● | ● | |
| L | ) | | ● | | | ● |
| M | . | | | ● | ● | ● |
| N | , | | | ● | ● | |
| O | 9 | | | | ● | ● |
| P | 0 | | ● | ● | | ● |
| Q | 1 | ● | ● | ● | | ● |
| R | 4 | | ● | | ● | |
| S | , | ● | | ● | | |
| T | 5 | | | | | ● |
| U | 7 | ● | ● | ● | | |
| V | = | | ● | ● | ● | ● |
| W | 2 | ● | ● | | | ● |
| X | / | ● | | ● | ● | ● |
| Y | 6 | ● | | ● | | ● |
| Z | + | ● | | | | ● |
| Blank | | | | | | |
| Letters shift | | ● | ● | ● | ● | ● |
| Figures shift | | ● | ● | | ● | ● |
| Space | | | | ● | | |
| Carriage return | | | | | ● | |
| Line feed | | | ● | | | |

**Fig. 2.** Reproduction of the five-track code standardized by the International Communications Union, known as Alphabet CCITT No. 2.

control codes. Seven-bit codes for information interchange were set up and internationally adopted as ISO Standard No. 646 (revised 1973). Many national standards have been based upon it, such as ASCII Eight-track paper tape was then used so that the first seven tracks accommodated the seven-bit code and the eighth track was used for parity. Despite the adoption of the ISO standard, many other codes are still in use (e.g., the six-bit BCD code and the seven-bit EBCDIC).

Paper tape for computers is normally supplied in an 11/16 in. width (which satisfies the teleprinter tape standard now established at 11/16 in. wide by 1,000 ft long in coil form), or 7/8 in. or 1 in. widths to suit the requirements of 5-, 6-, 7-, or 8-track information. Tapes for most applications are supplied in coils with a nominal length of 1,000 ft and an outer diameter of 8 in. The center supporting cores are available in plain and serrated plastic.

Several kinds of substances are available for paper tape manufacture, depending upon the application and the machines in which the tape is to be used. For computer applications, the most suitable substance is a low-filler paper tape, either with or without the inclusion of oil. There are also more durable tapes of the paper variety suited for long-life cyclic uses, and long-life polyester plastic tapes are used for continuous cyclic work that needs tapes of exceptional durability.

The advantages in using paper tape for data processing are:

- Simplicity in handling and transport.
- Permanency of record.
- Possibility of fixed- as well as variable-length records, with practically no upper limits imposed.
- Preparation as a by-product by some other machine operation; e.g., from a cash register, adding machine, electric typewriter, ticket-issuing machine, accounting and invoicing machine, visible-record computer, desk-top computer, etc. (in some of which paper tape is also accepted as an input medium).
- Reading at 1,500 characters per second without difficulty.
- Comparative inexpensiveness.

There are some disadvantages also:

- Information punched in a tape is very difficult for people to read.
- Records punched on tape cannot be sorted (as can punched cards).
- Recordings on tape are not erasable.
- Correcting an error on a tape may mean that the tape must be repunched (but, provided individual tapes are generated for batches of transactions with suitable batch control totals, this problem does not represent a severe constraint).
- Relative slowness as a computer input medium.

In machines producing paper tape as a by-product, the present trend seems to be toward cassette recorders. As a keypunch medium, paper tape is being superseded by magnetic tape in key-to-tape devices. The overall prospects for paper tape as an input medium do not seem very bright.

J. Necas

## READING AND PUNCHING TECHNIQUES

For article on related subject *see* Input-Output Devices.

**Tape Reading.** Electromechanical techniques are used for reading low-speed paper tape on devices that operate at approximately 50 characters per second (chps). On higher-speed readers, photoelectric reading is generally the normal practice.

Photoelectric reading of paper tape is similar to the technique used in high-speed punched-card reading, in which a pencil-beam of light is projected through holes in each track so that it strikes a photoelectric cell (or photocell).

Fig. 1 shows the design of a high-speed paper tape reader. The feed mechanism consists of an electromagnetic brake (A) at the start of the tape, and an electromagnetic clutch (B) at the winding end of the tape. The clutch consists of a divided, rotating drum (C) with a permanently magnetized, internal, fixed excitation winding, superposed by a roller (D). When the winding is energized, the roller presses against the drum and the paper tape moves between them as a result of friction.

The brake at the input of the tape consists of a U-shaped electromagnet and a flat armature. The clutch and brake are energized in such a way that electric current can be switched to either one, thus permitting transport of the tape and a start/stop operation of the device.

The photoelectric reader part of the device consists of a light bulb (E) and an optical system (F)

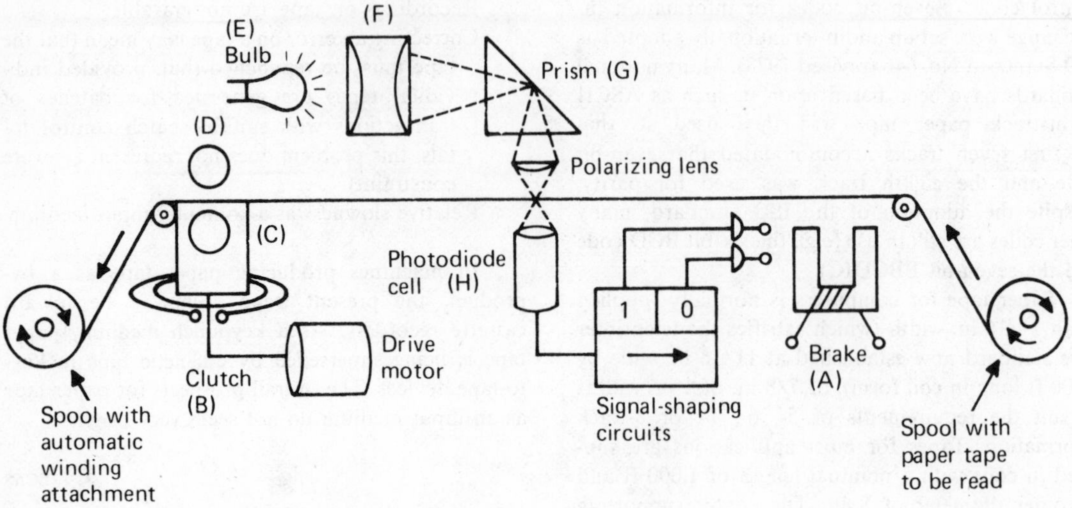


**Fig. 1.** Simplified diagram of paper tape path in a high-speed reader.

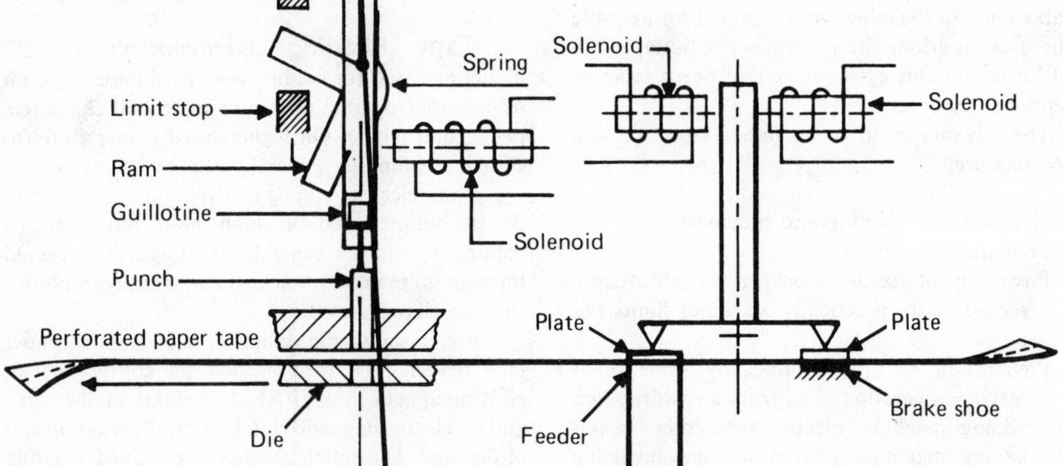


**Fig. 2.** Solenoid-controlled punch mechanism of the FACIT PE-1500 punch.

that concentrates light through a prism (G) into a narrow rectangular beam that is perpendicularly oriented at the punched paper-tape centerline and which passes through the punched holes in the tape. Below the tape the polarized light falls on a photocell (H), which converts the light rays into electric current that feeds into the signal-shaping circuit inputs. The signal-shaping circuits vary their outputs in proportion to the amount of illumination entering the photocell. The rectangular outputs of these circuits are then adapted by means of matching circuits.

**Tape Punching.** Tape is punched by five- to eight-track rows of dies striking against a steel matrix with a corresponding number of holes while the paper tape passes between the dies and matrix. The dies are activated by a mechanism under the control of computer output signals. Mechanisms used for the punching operation differ mainly in the movement of the dies and/or the steel matrix. Although patents have been granted for punches that have no moving parts because they are activated by compression (air pressure waves) and operate at a speed of 1,000 chps, no such devices are known to be in production.

The design of paper tape punches is complicated by the need to examine the tape immediately after punching. This means that the tape has to be punched in a horizontal plane, with the chads, or chips, from the punching being ejected upward. Fig. 2 shows a solenoid-activated punch mechanism used for paper tape punching.

J. NECAS

# PARALLEL ALGORITHMS

For articles on related subjects *see* MULTIPROCESSING; NUMERICAL ANALYSIS; and PARALLEL PROCESSING.
For articles on related terms *see* GRAPH THEORY; and SIMULATION.

With the advent of multiprocessors, parallel algorithms and models for parallel computation have received a great deal of attention. It must be noted that some computations which should be thought of as parallel (e.g., addition of two vectors) have been transformed today into a series of sequential steps because of the restrictions imposed by the architecture of the majority of the current machines. The same holds true for a number of algorithms, applicable mostly to scientific problems, such as the Jacobi method of solving a system of linear equations. Thus, one has to differentiate algorithms that are conceptually in parallel form and those that have to be transformed into a parallel representation.

In numerical analysis, several processes intended to be run on single processors, by design or by force, have been recast in parallel form. Frequent examples can be found in the fields of optimization theory, root finding, solution of differential equations, and resolution of systems of linear equations. The improvements in the completion times range from log $N$ to $N$, where $N$ is the number of parallel machines.

Concurrent with this development, as well as that of the hardware, numerous models (e.g., directed graphs, networks, program schema) have been proposed to investigate properties of parallel systems. Depending on the investigators' approach and background (engineers, logicians, mathematicians), investigative goals have been somewhat different. Among such objectives are:

- Design of modular parallel systems and their interconnection.
- Control techniques that allow sharing of procedures and data among processors.
- Relations between sequential programs and their transformed representation for parallel processing.
- Prediction of increased performance and cost when using a multiprocessor instead of a conventional single processor.

These models are generally represented in graphical form. A convenient frame of reference to describe them is to consider a triple $P = (W, U, C)$ where

$W = \{w_1, w_2, \ldots, w_n\}$ = set of operators (of computations),
$U = \{u_1, u_2, \ldots, u_m\}$ = set of variables,
$C$ = control link,

where C links (e.g., by a directed graph representation) members of $W$ to members of $U$, and vice versa.

For example, consider the representation of the computation of the root of $y = f(x)$ by the Newton-Raphson method, i.e.,

$$x^{(i)} = x^{(i-1)} - \frac{f(x^{(i-1)})}{f'(x^{(i-1)})},$$

with an error less than $\epsilon$. The graph of Fig. 1 shows how $f(x)$ and $f'(x)$ can be computed in parallel. Nodes of the graph represent computational tasks ($w_1$ is the start; $w_2$, the iteration node; $w_3$, the computation of $f(x)$; $w_4$, the computation of $f'(x)$; $w_5$, the computation of $x^{(i)}$ and the test for convergence; and $w_6$, the end node). Arcs represent flow of control and/or holdings of variables ($a_1$ holds $x^{(0)}$ and $\epsilon$; $a_2$ and $a_3$ hold $x^{(i-1)}$ and $\epsilon$; $a_4$ and $a_5$ also hold $x^{(i-1)}$ and $\epsilon$, and $f(x^{(i-1)})$ and $f'(x^{(i-1)})$, respectively; $a_6$ holds $x^{(i)}$; and $a_7$, the solution $y$). The control of the parallelism is indicated by the sign *, which at the output of a node indicates a FORK (i.e., possible parallel initiation) and at the input indicates a JOIN (i.e., all predecessors of this node must terminate before it can initiate). The usual branching and looping is indicated by +.

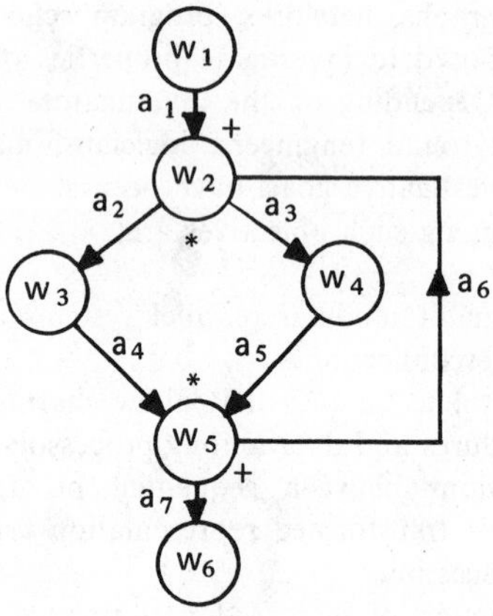


**Fig. 1.** Graph model for parallel computation.

With each operator is associated an input set $I_i = \{u_{i1}, \ldots, u_{ik}\}$ and an output set $O_i = \{u_{o1}, \ldots, u_{op}\}$. In our example, let $u_1 = x^{(i)}$, $u_2 = \epsilon$, $u_3 = f(x^{(i)})$, and $u_4 = f'(x^{(i)})$. Then $I_1 = O_1 = \{u_1,u_2\}, \ldots, I_4 = \{u_1,u_2\}$, $O_4 = \{u_1,u_2,u_4\}, \ldots, I_6 = \{u_1\}$, $O_6 = \Phi$.

A simulation on the model is defined by

For each variable $u_i$, a domain $D_i$ of values which the variable may assume.

For each operator $w_i$, a mapping $O_i = f(I_i)$. This mapping can be both computational (i.e., values associated with members of $O_i$ are defined in terms of values associated with members $I_i$) and logical (i.e., control conditions can be dictated by operators).

A set of initial values for members of $U$.

A variable history $h_i$ is the sequence of values associated with $u_i$ during a simulation on $P$. A program history is the $m$-tuple $\{h_1, \ldots, h_m\}$ consisting of the variable histories of the elements of $U$.

An important property of a parallel program model is its determinacy. A program is said to be determinate if and only if each simulation results in a unique program history. Often, less stringent conditions, such as proper termination, are considered. Two models, $P$ and $P'$, are equivalent if they have the same set of variables and if their program histories are the same.

The objectives of the model dictate the amount of interpretation given to the mapping $O_i = f(I_i)$. If the main goal is to describe specific algorithms or systems, then a total interpretation will be most convenient. In our example this would mean the description of the computation of a specific $f(x)$, and a fortiori of $f'(x)$. A model of this type can be regarded as a programming language. On the other hand, if the derivation of general formal properties and the characterization of parallel algorithms are of prime interest, then an interpretation is necessary and schema have to be introduced. In the case here, this would mean simply looking at Fig. 1 without being interested in the computations associated with the nodes of the graph. Generally, models will be partially interpreted in order to retain some descriptive power without losing formal properties. This is what has been done in the preceding example by giving some indication of the purpose of each node and arc.

The importance of these models for the design of multiprocessors, the synchronization of parallel processes, and the evaluation of performance of parallel systems is becoming more and more evident. The most prominent modeling realizations study structures at levels of detail ranging from asynchronous circuits to the computer-aided design of full machines and the evaluation of operating systems. Simultaneously, new methods, or modifications of existing ones, for taking advantage of the parallelism of future machines are constantly being investigated.

REFERENCE

1973. Baer, J-L. "A Survey of Some Theoretical Aspects of Multiprocessing," *Computing Surveys*, Vol. 5, No. 1 (March), pp. 31–80.

J-L. BAER

# PARALLEL PROCESSING

For articles on related subjects *see* CHANNEL; COMPUTER ARCHITECTURE; MULTIPROGRAMMING; MULTIPROCESSING; OPERATING SYSTEMS; PARALLEL ALGORITHM; SUPERCOMPUTERS; and TIME SHARING.
For articles on related terms *see* LOCKOUT; MULTIPLEXING; and TASK.

Processing of more than one task on a computer system may be *truly* simultaneous or *apparently* simultaneous. True simultaneity can be achieved only with duplicate hardware. It involves the proliferation of equipment, the isolation of functions, and the (at least partial) decentralization of control.

**Forms of Parallelism.** For a system to write on a tape at the same time it performs a floating divide (true simultaneity) there must be a

1. Unit for performing a divide.
2. Unit for performing a tape write.
3. Capacity for units to independently control their own functions.

*Apparent* concurrency or simultaneity may be achieved with either hardware or software. The effect is achieved by multiplexing, and depends upon differences in operational speeds between units. Hardware multiplexing involves a family of units to be serviced and a servicing unit. The servicing unit interleaves its attention in such a way that the serviced units appear to be receiving constant attention. A number of card readers may be supported by a single multiplex channel. If the rate at which characters are presented to the channel is enough smaller than the rate at which the channel can transfer characters into storage, then during the time taken to read a card, the multiplex channel can accept characters from many card readers. The actual transmission by the channel is serial, but each card reader gives the appearance of having an independent, separate, duplicate "parallel" path to storage.

Software multiplexing is used in the support of time-sharing and multiprogrammed systems. In both types of systems a software algorithm is used to multiplex the attention of a CPU between programs waiting for CPU service. The rate of CPU multiplex as opposed to the rate of terminal operation sustains the time-sharing illusion that programs are actually being performed "in parallel," as if there were a processor for each program. Actually, service is entirely serial, with cyclic intervals of partial service granted to each program. The concepts of true and apparent concurrency are illustrated in Fig. 1.

One of the design decisions of hardware/software architects is the degree to which hardware replication or multiplexing should be used in order to balance or enhance the operation of a system.

**A. TRUE SIMULTANEITY**
**Events happen at the same time. For example, *read* tape while computing actually occurs at the same time.**

| Event | Time Units | | | | | | | | | | | |
|---|---|---|---|---|---|---|---|---|---|---|---|---|
| | 1 | 2 | 3 | 4 | 5 | 6 | 7 | 8 | 9 | 10 | 11 | 12 |
| CPU DIV inst. | X | X | X | X | X | | | | | | | |
| CHAN. READ tape | | X | X | X | X | X | X | X | X | X | | |
| CPU STORE inst. | | | | | | X | X | X | | | | |
| CPU ADD inst. | | | | | | | | | X | X | X | X |
| CPU summary: (DIVIDE, STORE, ADD) | X | X | X | X | X | X | X | X | X | X | X | X |

*SUMMARY:* Overall time period = 12 units. CPU operating time = 12 units, consisting of: DIV (1–5) = 5; STORE (6–8) = 3; ADD (9–12) = 4. Tape operating time (2–10) = 9. CPU-only (1, 11–12) = 3. Channel-only operating time = 0. Overlapped units of time (2–10) = 9.

**B. APPARENT SIMULTANEITY**
**Events appear to happen at the same time. For example, time-sharing terminals.**

| Event | Time Units | | | | | | | | | | | | | | |
|---|---|---|---|---|---|---|---|---|---|---|---|---|---|---|---|
| | 1 | 2 | 3 | 4 | 5 | 6 | 7 | 8 | 9 | 10 | 11 | 12 | 13 | 14 | 15 |
| User 1 req. | X | | | | | | | | | | | | | | |
| User 2 req. | | X | | | | | | | | | | | | | |
| User 3 req. | | | X | | | | | | | | | | | | |
| CPU serv | | | | 1 | 2 | 3 | 1 | 2 | 3 | 1 | 2 | 3 | | | |
| User 1 resp. | | | | | | | | | | | | | X | | |
| User 2 resp. | | | | | | | | | | | | | | X | |
| User 3 resp. | | | | | | | | | | | | | | | X |
| User time ref. | ←— A —→ | | | | | ←— B —→ | | | | | ←— C —→ | | | | |

*Note:* Users perceive time in five-unit groups so that terminals appear active at the same time in A and C, and appear to be receiving simultaneous CPU service in time reference B.

**Fig. 1.** Comparison of true and apparent simultaneity

**Levels of Parallelism.** Whether parallelism is real or apparent depends upon the "level" of function to be performed. There are numerous operational levels at which parallel operation may occur:

1. Basic data flow.
2. Between stages of an instruction.
3. Between instructions.
4. Between "regions" of a program.
5. Between formal tasks of a structured program.
6. Between independent programs.

BASIC DATA FLOW. This level defines the "width" of the paths that move data from one place to another in the system. An early meaning of "parallelism" was the concurrent transfer of multiple bits. Machines were at one time characterized as "serial by character, serial by bit," or "serial by character, parallel by bit," etc. Contemporary high-performance machines generally move more characters at a time than do small or medium machines. The IBM 360/195, for example, transfers 64 bytes into a processor on one reference to memory. This parallel transfer capacity decreases the time a processor must wait for data from memory. Parallel data flow is always a part of hardware design.

BETWEEN STAGES OF INSTRUCTION. Parallelism between stages of an instruction, called "lookahead" (Fig. 2), is a hardware-defined capability that depends upon the definition of at least two instruction stages. The two traditional stages are the I (instruction) stage (when the instruction is being fetched and prepared for execution) and the E (execution) stage (when the instruction is performed). If no I and E stage circuitry is shared, a processor may be preparing one instruction while executing a predecessor. The effect of this is to overlap execution as shown in Fig. 2. The potential of lookahead may as much as double the rate of execution. This is rarely achieved because of contention for memory access, of conditional transfer instructions that delay fetch of a next instruction until the direction of transfer is known, and of variable execution times that allow "long instructions" (e.g., divide) to occupy execution units for extended periods and consequently delay the release of successor instructions.

BETWEEN INSTRUCTIONS. Parallelism between instructions is a hardware-defined capability that depends upon the proliferation of hardware units. It is an extension of lookahead in which multiple instructions may be in the same stage at the same time. The parallelism may be constrained to concurrent execution stages. The CDC 7600, for example, has a family of specialized execution units that operate independently of each other. The instruction-preparation unit distributes an instruction to an appropriate specialized execution unit. At any single time, instructions for floating multiply, a transfer to memory, a fixed add, etc., may be proceeding concurrently.

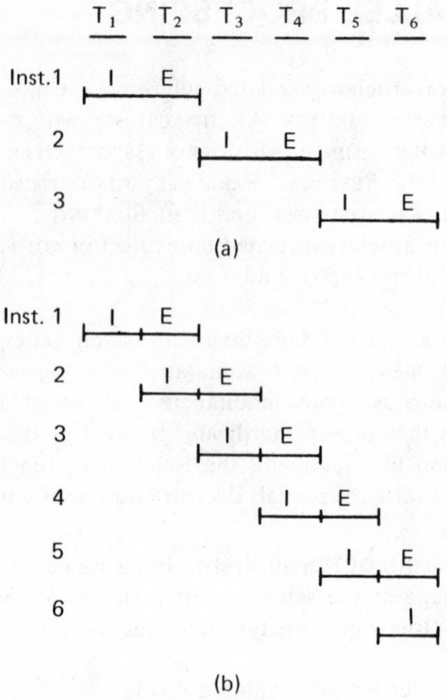


**Fig. 2.** Basic lookahead. (a) No lookahead. (b) Lookahead.

The IBM 360/195 achieves a similar capability by providing a "pipelining" capability. "Pipelining" is a considerable extension of lookahead. Instructions are broken into numerous small stages and a small queue is provided at each stage. At any time in the system a population of instructions are in various stages. With both the CDC 7600 and the IBM 360/195 systems it is necessary to apply explicit instruction sequencing techniques that recognize the dependency of one instruction upon a predecessor. The overlap of I/O and CPU instructions is merely a special case of multiple execution units. The contrast between "parallelism" and "pipelining" is shown in Fig. 3.

When the capability for concurrent processing of I-stage functions exists in a machine, it is called a "multiple I-stream machine." The added capability allows instructions from different programs to join

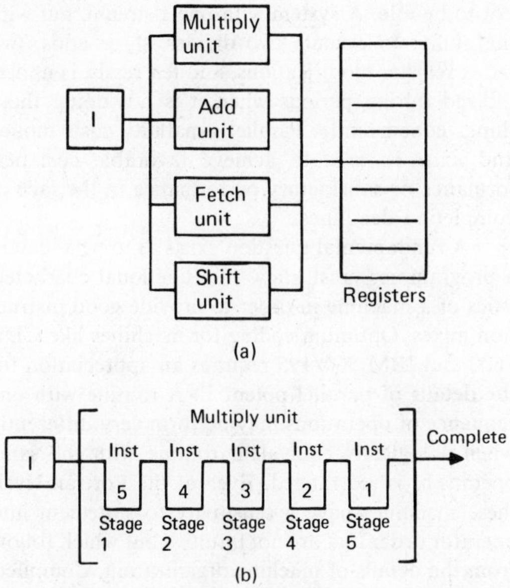


**Fig. 3.** Parallel and pipeline operation. (a) In parallel operation I issues instructions to specialized execution units, each of which operates independently and concurrently. (b) In pipeline operation, MULTIPLY takes five stages, each of one cycle. The effective rate of MULTIPLY, however, is one cycle, since a MULTIPLY is completed every cycle. At cycle 5, instruction 1 completes; at cycle 6, instruction 2 completes; etc. Stages 1 through 5 are executed in parallel on a series of instructions.

the mix of instructions using the pool of execution capability. "Multiprocessors" are a form of the multiple I-stream machine in which parallel capability is most often achieved by providing duplicate I and E stage hardware, but in which the system is so packaged that I-E sets are isolated from each other. In a UNIVAC 1108-II multiprocessor, for example, there are multiple instruction preparation units and multiple execution units, but each I-E set is an 1108. An instruction fetched by one instruction preparation unit must be executed by the execution units associated with the I unit. A variant form of instruction parallelism is found in machines that provide for a number of processing elements to execute synchronously the same instruction on private data. ILLIAC IV is such a machine. The term "parallel" processor is often loosely used to designate machines like ILLIAC IV or multiple I-stream machines.

BETWEEN REGIONS. Parallelism between "regions" of a program is achieved by hardware/software combinations of various kinds. If there is to be true concurrency, then some multiple instruction-preparation capability must exist in the system. The system must be "a multiple I-stream machine." Apparent concurrency between "regions" of a program can be achieved by multiprogramming software. The definition of a region is not especially precise. A program may contain a number of computational steps that are independent, but which are represented serially in code because of the serial nature of programming languages. A region is an area of coding that begins at a transfer point and continues until a point is reached where another transfer is made or where there is an entry. For example, instructions for, say, three regions might be as follows:

Region 1

```
ALABEL:    A = B + C;
           D = A * W - 5;
           Z = R + D ** 2;
           GO TO NEXT;
```

Region 2

```
BLABEL:    E = B - C;
           F = E * W - 10;
           H = R + D ** 3;
```

Region 3

```
CLABEL:    I = Z - X;
           T = Y * D - W;
           GO TO NEXT;
```

Each of these regions of a program could be executed at the same time because they are independent of each other; they do not pass values to each other, nor do they depend upon each other's prior completion. The software/hardware technique necessary for either true or apparent concurrency between region 1 and region 2 involves: (1) a means for recognizing their independence; (2) a means for starting the "parallel" execution; (3) a means for establishing the conditions for execution of the region beginning at NEXT.

BETWEEN FORMAL TASKS. Parallelism between formal tasks of a structured program is currently supported by an operating system responding to programmer directives. OS/360 has a service macro called "ATTACH," which enables a program to request the execution of a subprogram. In multiprogramming systems the ATTACH function causes the attached task to be placed on a dispatching queue where it and its "mother" (the task that executed ATTACH) are serviced according to system dispatching algorithms. In contemporary multiprocessing systems (such as the UNIVAC 1108-II and the IBM System 360/65 multiprocessor), processors share the dispatching queue, and it is possible for a mother and daughter (task named in ATTACH) to be executing at the same time. In either the multiprogramming or multiprocessing environments, synchronizing functions in addition to ATTACH are required to report subtask completion in order to coordinate access to shared resources. Some of these are WAIT, which causes a process to suspend processing pending a system event; LOCK, which guarantees exclusive use of a system resource; ENQUE, which requests a system resource.

The fundamental difference between regional and task parallelism is the size of the unit to be performed and the use of the operating system. Regions of programs, iterations of loops, or subexpressions in assignment statements cannot afford the overhead of software services if they are to run effectively in parallel. A major issue of multiprocessor design is the lowest effective level at which program elements may be profitably run in parallel. A program with a collection of 50 $\mu$s regions cannot run usefully in parallel if the start-up mechanism requires 100 $\mu$s of execution time. The efficiency of the start-up mechanism and other service functions defines the level of program parallelism appropriate for a system. The efficiency of a multiprocessor is affected by the level of parallelism. The higher the level of the profitably parallel program unit, the smaller will be the population of independent tasks that are available to utilize individual CPUs. The cost/effectiveness of multiprocessing at any installation depends upon the availability of things to be done in parallel.

BETWEEN INDEPENDENT PROGRAMS. The ultimate parallel capability is the ability to run entirely independent job streams. This is achieved in multiprogramming systems that do not allow subtasking (i.e., DOS for IBM 360). In multiprocessing systems it is supported by very loose associations of processors. Little or no coordination between independent streams is required, beyond normal operating system queueing for shared physical channels and devices. Each stream is dedicated to a processor so that load-balancing capabilities are limited to proper initial selection of streams.

**Problems.** The critical problem for a system with any level of parallel capability lies in finding sufficient work of the proper "shape" to utilize parallel potential. A system with five processors must have five processes ready to go if processors are not to be idle. A system with one I-stream, but with the ability to execute two divides, three adds, two index register modifications, and ten reads, is underutilized during periods when it is not doing those things concurrently. Parallel capability costs money and *must be used* to achieve favorable cost/performance or satisfactory performance in the face of completion deadlines.

A fundamental question exists as to what extent a programmer must know the functional characteristics of a machine in order to provide good instruction mixes. Optimum coding for machines like CDC 7600 and IBM 360/195 requires an appreciation for the details of parallel potential. A routine with one sequence of operations may perform very differently when a logically equivalent routine with the same operations is rearranged. Even at the Fortran level, these machines have a sensitivity to statement and operator order that are not intuitive but which follow from the details of machine organization. Compilers may undertake program rearrangement to facilitate parallel operation, but may still be unable to achieve the results of careful programming.

For multiple I-stream machines the problem of availability of work is extended to problem definition. To what extent should an analyst know the potential capability for parallel execution at the regional or the task level? To what extent should the programmer be asked to direct explicitly the concurrent execution processes? To what extent should assembly languages and higher-level languages contain directions like FORK (to request a processor), JOIN (to release a processor), and other synchronizing functions.

A further aspect of programming parallel processes concerns the relations between the operating system and programs. A set of problems in resource allocation and operating system interface must be resolved. For example, should the operating system be involved in starting and coordinating parallel processes, or should a program be permitted to perform such coordination privately? To what extent should the acquisition and release of processors be dynamic? To what extent must the system guarantee $N$ processors; to what extent should code be written to be independent of the number of processors, etc.?

Software may attempt to ameliorate the problem of expressing parallelism by building compilers that optimize for parallel machines. Fortran statements and groups of statements are rearranged to make better use of the parallel organization of a machine. Work has been undertaken to analyze DO loops for the possibility of executing iterations in parallel. Parallelism at a higher level is still largely the responsibility of the programmer or the operating system. Work has been done on the global analysis of programs for parallel potential, and it is reasonable to expect that analytic tools may be developed to help programmers recognize what can be done in parallel.

The hardware side of the problem of matching resources against usage is reflected in decisions about machine balance, configurability (the ability to define or redefine the active components of a system), and processor intercommunication. The machine architect must design overlap with an appreciation for programming habits. The proper definition of instruction stages, the ratio of execution times between various instructions, the size and location of local buffers, and the degree of replication of function are decisions that must be based on an appreciation for expected instruction mixes and sequences. To some extent, instruction execution can be hardware rearranged, but a machine built to maximize the parallel execution of floating-point instructions will not justify its cost for programs that make sparse use of floating-point operations.

Multiple I-stream machines have additional problems of balance. In order to execute separate processes, there must be space enough for them in memory and sufficient I/O capability to keep them supplied with data. There are problems of contention between processes. Processors may interfere with each other by making references to the same memory banks, by enqueueing on the same channels, by referring to system serially reusable resources. To the extent that processors delay each other, they reduce the effectiveness of parallel components.

A very high degree of system configurability helps the problem of balance. The ability to decide how many CPUs, channels, or memory banks there should be active in the system or associated with a process at any time allows matching hardware to requirements at the time of installation. Beyond this, the idea of ordering so many adders, so many multipliers, etc., has appeared in the literature from time to time. Associated with configurability is the degree to which resources are shared and transferable throughout the system. Multiprocessing systems commonly share primary storage, but the level of use of I/O as a common sharable pool differs widely from system to system. In the IBM System 360/67 Duplex, any processor may reach any I/O device as easily as another, whereas in the multiprocessor System 360/65 there are "private" and preferred devices or paths associated with each processor. Potentially multiprocessor systems could be designed to have multiple I-units that share execution power (E-units). The degree to which an installation finds it profitable (in terms of cost performance) to grow into a multiprocessor version of a given system, rather than to a faster system, depends upon the proportion of incremental expense to incremental performance. Systems having defined components so that additional processors or I/O elements can be added at relatively small cost can grow smoothly from uniprocessor systems to multiprocessor systems.

The degree of hardware support given to processor intercommunication will determine how "parallel" a system can be. In those systems where acquisition and release of processors, process coordination, and communication are supported by hardware, more effective parallelism can be obtained. Because the overhead for controlling concurrent activities is low, very small processes or only partially parallel processes may be profitably run together. When processor intercommunication is provided only by software routines, the overhead is high and concurrency will be profitable only for larger, truly independent tasks.

Characteristically, the goal of reducing an execution time of $T$ to $T/N$ by providing $N$ processors is not realized because

1. Problems are not easily segmented into executable fragments of equal size.
2. The segments of a problem often cannot be allocated to available resources without causing some resource contention and consequent delay.
3. The overhead of controlling parallel processes adds nontrivial execution time.

**Final Remarks.** The realization of optimally effective parallel processing is difficult and complex to effect by hardware and software design. Despite this, increasing the potential parallelism of a system is, in general, an excellent and effective way to increase system speed and effective utilization. Some applications (weather forecasting) can be realized only in reasonable time frames by the application of parallel processing. Whether the best form of parallelism is multiprogramming a very large and highly pipelined uniprocessor or multiprocessor depends very much upon the "shape" of work at the installation—the size of processes and the relations between them, and the details of system realization.

REFERENCES

1966. Flynn, M. "Very High Speed Computing Systems," *Proc. IEEE* (December).

1969. Gonzalez, M. J., and C. V. Ramamoorthy. "A Survey of Techniques for Recognizing Parallel Processable Streams," *AFIPS*, Vol. 35, pp. 1–15, Fall Joint Computer Conference.

1972. Lorin, H. *Parallelism in Hardware and Software*. Englewood Cliffs, N.J.: Prentice-Hall.

H. LORIN

# PARITY

For articles on related subjects *see* CODES; and ERROR CORRECTING CODE.

Parity is a synonym for equality. Parity checking is an extensively used error-checking facility provided to insure correct recording of data, its input into a computer system, and its transfer within the system, transmission included. A parity check consists of adding up the bits in a unit of data, calculating the parity bit required, and checking the calculated parity bit with that transferred with the data item. This form of check will normally be performed by hardware.

A parity bit is a check bit whose binary value (0 or 1) depends upon whether the sum of bits with value 1 in the unit of data being checked is odd or even. If the total number of bits with value 1, including the parity bit (or bits), is even, the unit of data is said to have even parity; if it is odd, it has odd parity. Checking methods use either even or odd parity. Each information system must use the same parity principle, even or odd throughout. An error caused by incorrect parity detected as a result of a parity check is called a "parity error."

The unit of data to which a parity check is applied may be a character, a byte, a word, etc., the character parity check being the one mostly used. The smaller the unit of data to which the check is applied, the higher the probability that compensating errors will not occur.

J. NECAS

# PARSING

For articles on related subjects *see* GRAMMAR, GENERATIVE; GRAMMAR, REDUCTIVE; and SYNTAX, SEMANTICS AND PRAGMATICS.
For articles on related terms *see* SOURCE PROGRAM; STRING; and TREE.

Parsing is the process by which the phrases in a string of characters in a language are associated with the component names of the grammar that generated the string. The structural description of the string that results from parsing is called the "parse." A parse is often shown as a *tree*, as in the following example of the parse of the English sentence, "The cat drank the milk" (see Fig. 1).

An equivalent parse of this sentence is

$$({}_S({}_{NP}({}_A\,\textit{the})_A({}_N\,\text{cat})_N)_{NP}$$
$$({}_{VP}({}_V\,\text{drank})_V({}_{NP}({}_A\,\text{the})_A({}_N\,\text{milk})_N)_{NP})_{VP})_S$$

which has the advantage of being linear (i.e., one-

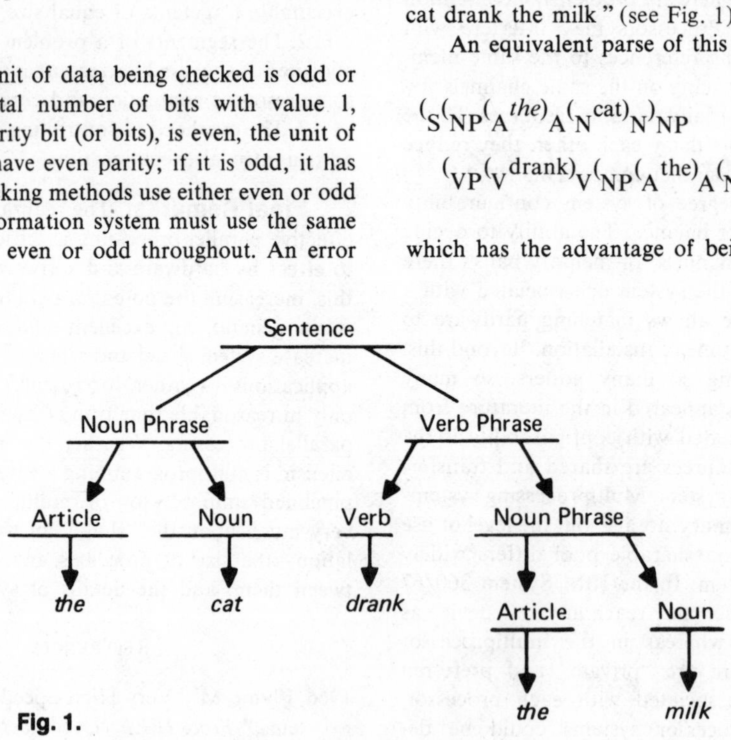


**Fig. 1.**

dimensional), but may have the disadvantage of being harder to visualize.

Parsing is the heart of the process of compilation of source programs in a higher-level language into machine language. The compiler must take the string of characters written by the programmer and associate appropriate substrings of characters with the syntactic components of the higher-level language in order to determine the structure of the given program so that it can be translated into machine code. For example, the arithmetic assignment statement

$$A = B + C * D$$

might be parsed as in Fig. 2. Hidden in this example are many subtleties, such as: How can the compiler know that $B + C * D$ should be interpreted as $B + (C * D)$ rather than $(B + C) * D$?

There are two extremes in the manner in which compilers determine the syntactic structure of a program. One is the *top-down* strategy whereby (in the example above) the starting point would be "Arithmetic Assignment Statement" and from this the tree would "grow" downward until it matched the given string. In the other extreme, or *bottom-up* strategy, the starting point is the given input string and the tree would "grow" upward until all branches joined at a single root. In practice, most language processors employ a combination of these strategies.

### Reference

1972. Presser, L., in A. F. Cardenas, L. Presser, and M. A. Marin (Eds.). *The Translation of Programming Languages in Computer Science.* New York: Wiley-Interscience.

J. A. N. LEE AND A. RALSTON

## PARTIAL DIFFERENTIAL EQUATIONS

For articles on related subjects *see* FINITE ELEMENT METHOD; MATRIX COMPUTATIONS; and NUMERICAL ANALYSIS.

A major scientific application of large-scale digital computers is the numerical solution of prob-

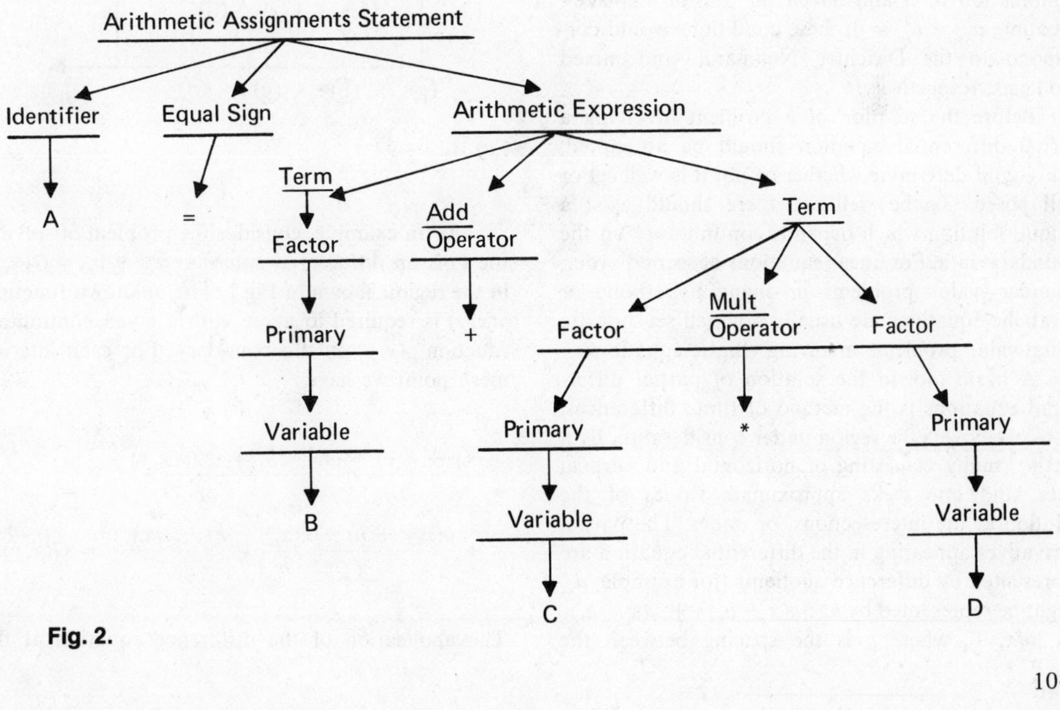


Fig. 2.

lems involving partial differential equations. These problems have application in such areas as weather forecasting, nuclear diffusion studies for reactor design, fluid flow, supersonic flow, and elasticity. An important class of partial differential equations is the class of *linear equations of second order* in two independent variables. The most general such equation is

$$L[u] = Au_{xx} + 2Bu_{xy} + Cu_{yy} + Du_x + Eu_y + Fu = g,$$

where $A$, $B$, $C$, $D$, $E$, $F$, and $G$ depend on $x$ and $y$. The equation is elliptic, hyperbolic, or parabolic at a point $(x, y)$ according as the discriminant $B^2 - AC$ is negative, positive, or zero. Simple examples are Laplace's equation $u_{xx} + u_{yy} = 0$ (elliptic); the wave equation $u_{xx} - u_{yy} = 0$ (hyperbolic); and the heat or diffusion equation $u_{xx} - u_y = 0$ (parabolic).

Two important classes of problems involving partial differential equations are *initial-value problems* and *boundary-value problems*. For an initial-value problem in two variables the desired function $u(x,y)$ is to satisfy the differential equation in an unbounded region $R$ and to satisfy auxiliary conditions on the boundary $S$. Such conditions might involve prescribing the values of $u(x,y)$ on $S$ or (as for the Cauchy problem) $u$, and the normal derivative $\partial u/\partial n$ might be prescribed on $S$. For a boundary-value problem the region $R$ is bounded, and one prescribes either $u$, $\partial u/\partial n$, or a linear combination of $u$ and $\partial u/\partial n$ on $S$. For Laplace's equation, $u_{xx} + u_{yy} = 0$; these conditions would correspond to the Dirichlet, Neumann, and mixed problems, respectively.

Before the solution of a problem involving a partial differential equation should be attempted, one should determine whether or not it is well set or well posed. To be well set, there should exist a unique solution which depends continuously on the boundary data. For linear equations of second order, boundary-value problems involving hyperbolic or parabolic equations are usually not well set, nor are initial-value problems involving elliptic equations.

A basic tool in the solution of partial differential equations is the method of finite differences. Here one covers the region under consideration by a mesh, usually consisting of horizontal and vertical lines, and one seeks approximate values of the solution at the interesections, or nodes. The partial derivatives appearing in the differential equation are represented by difference quotients (for example, $u_{xx}$ might be represented by $h^{-2}[u(x + h, y) + u(x - h, y) - 2u(x, y)]$, where $h$ is the spacing between the adjacent lines in the mesh. Substituting the difference quotient in the differential equation leads to a difference equation. For a boundary-value problem, one then obtains a system of linear algebraic equations, with the number of equations equal to the number of interior mesh points. It can usually be shown without difficulty that the linear system has a unique solution. However, if the number of mesh points is large (as must frequently be the case in order that an accurate solution can be obtained), the practical solution of the linear system may present a formidable computational problem. Frequently, iterative methods are used to solve the linear system. Commonly used methods include the *successive overrelaxation* and the *alternating direction implicit method*. An extensive theory has been developed concerning the rapidity of convergence of these and other iterative methods.

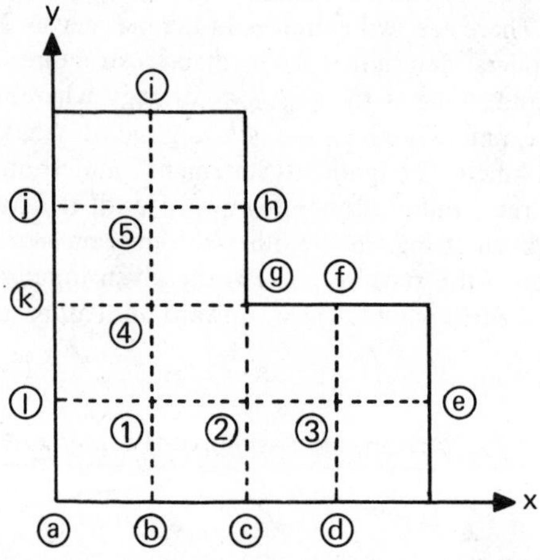


**Fig. 1.**

As an example, consider the problem of solving the Poisson differential equation $u_{xx} + u_{yy} = G(x,y)$ in the region shown in Fig.1. The unknown function $u(x,y)$ is required to agree with a given continuous function $g(x,y)$ on the boundary. For each interior mesh point we have

$$\frac{u(x + h, y) + u(x - h, y) - 2u(x, y)}{h^2} + \frac{u(x, y + h) + u(x, y - h) - 2u(x, y)}{h^2} = G(x, y).$$

The application of the difference equation at the

point labeled 1 leads (after multiplying by $-h^2$) to the linear equation

$$4u_1 - u_2 - u_4 - u_l - u_b = -h^2G(x_1,y_1).$$

where the subscripts refer to the points with those labels. Similar equations correspond to the other interior points ②, ③., ④, and ⑤. The values $u_a$, $u_b$, . . . , are equal to the known values $g_a$, $g_b$, . . ..

Another alternative procedure for solving boundary-value problems is the *finite element method*. Here, again, one eventually obtains a linear system. However, instead of using finite differences, one considers a variational formulation of the problem (for example, the Dirichlet problem is equivalent to minimizing $Q[u] = \int\int (u_x^2 + u_y^2)\,dx\,dy$ over a suitable class $C$ of functions with the required boundary values). One constructs a subclass $C'$ of functions which have certain properties relative to a set of "elements" covering the region, and one seeks a function in $C'$ which minimizes $Q[u]$.

One class of initial-value problems involves the differential equation $u_t = L[u]$, where $L[u]$ is an elliptic operator in one or two "space" variables. Frequently, one is given $u(\vec{x},0)$ for all $\vec{x}$ in the region and $u(\vec{x},t)$ for $\vec{x}$ on the boundary and for all $t > 0$. In the method of finite differences, one constructs a mesh in the space variables, as in the case of a boundary-value problem. In the *forward difference method* one replaces $u_t$ by $[u(\vec{x},t + \Delta t) - u(\vec{x},t)]/(\Delta t)$ and sets it equal to $L_h[u](\vec{x},t)$, where $L_h[u](\vec{x},t)$ is a finite difference representation of $L[u](\vec{x},t)$. The determination of $u(\vec{x},\Delta t)$, $u(\vec{x},2\Delta t)$, etc., can be carried out explicitly. However, numerical stability considerations require that $\Delta t/h^2$, where $h = \Delta x = \Delta y$, be bounded as $h \to 0$. The work required because of the excessively small value of $\Delta t$ is usually prohibitive.

A more popular method, which greatly relaxes the restriction on $\Delta t$, is the *Crank-Nicolson method*, where one replaces $L_h[u](\vec{x},t)$ by $\frac{1}{2}[L_h[u](\vec{x},t) + L_h[u](\vec{x},t + \Delta t)]$. An implicit rather than an explicit procedure is thus developed. However, with one space dimension, the implicit calculation involves solving a linear system with a tridiagonal matrix. (This is relatively easy.) With two space dimensions, one must solve a boundary-value problem on each time step. However, certain iterative methods can be shown to converge much more rapidly than in the case of a pure boundary-value problem.

As an example, consider the diffusion equation $u_t = u_{xx}$ for $0 < x < 1$, $t > 0$, subject to the boundary conditions $u(0,t) = g_1(t)$, $u(1,t) = g_2(t)$, for $t > 0$, and the initial condition $u(x,0) = f(x)$. Here, $g_1(t)$, $g_2(t)$, and $f(x)$ are given. The forward difference method is given by

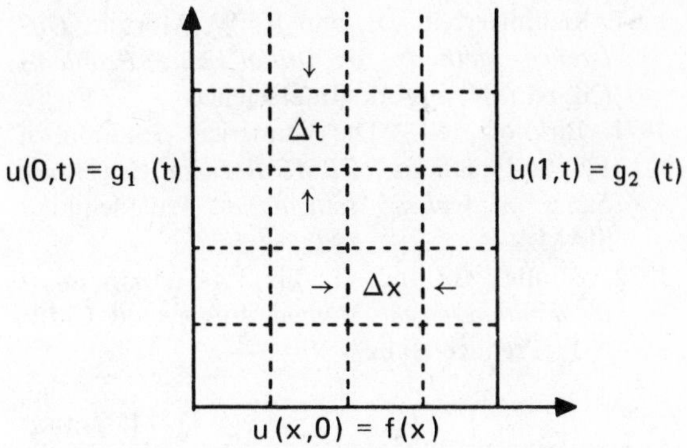


**Fig. 2.**

$$\frac{u(x,t + \Delta t) + u(x,t)}{\Delta t} = \frac{u(x + h,t) + u(x - h,t) - 2u(x,t)}{h^2}.$$

From this, the values of $u(x,t + \Delta t)$ can be calculated explicitly in terms of values of $u(x,t)$. For the Crank-Nicolson method, the right-hand side is replaced by

$$\frac{1}{2}\left\{\frac{u(x + h,t) + u(x - h,t) - 2u(x,t)}{h^2} + \frac{u(x + h,t + \Delta t) + u(x - h,t + \Delta t) - 2u(x,t + \Delta t)}{h^2}\right\}$$

Hyperbolic equations of the form $u_{tt} = L[u]$ can often be treated in a manner similar to that described above. Other hyperbolic equations, or systems of equations, are treated by the *method of characteristics*.

The book by Forsythe and Wasow (1960) treats hyperbolic, parabolic, and elliptic equations. Initial-value problems are treated in depth by Richtmyer and Morton (1967). For a modern treatment of elliptic equations, the monograph by Birkhoff (1971) is recommended. For finite element methods, the book by Strang and Fix (1972) is recommended.

REFERENCES

1960. Forsythe, G. E., and W. R. Wasow. *Finite Difference Methods for Partial Differential Equations.* New York: John Wiley.

1967. Richtmyer, R. D., and K. W. Morton. *Difference Methods for Initial-Value Problems* (2d. ed.). New York: Interscience.
1971. Birkhoff, G. "The Numerical Solution of Elliptic Equations," *CBMS Regional Conference Series in Applied Mathematics*. Philadelphia.: SIAM.
1972. Strang, G. and G. Fix. *An Analysis of the Finite Element Method.* Englewood Cliffs, N.J.: Prentice-Hall.

D. M. YOUNG

## PASCAL, BLAISE

For articles on related subjects *see* DIGITAL COMPUTERS: Origins; and LEIBNIZ, G. W.

Pascal (b. Clermont, France, 1623; d. Paris, 1662) was educated by his father Etienne, and after discovering a proof to Euclid's Proposition 32 at age 12, he became a participant in Mersenne's Circle. Four years later he presented to them his well-known theorem in projective geometry.

In 1640, he started developing a calculating machine to help in his father's tax work in Rouen.

**Fig. 1.** Death Mask of Blaise Pascal. (Courtesy N.Y. Public Library.)

He completed the first operating model in 1642 and built 50 more during the next ten years. The machine was a small box with eight dials (resembling telephone dials), each geared to a drum that displayed the digits in a register window. Pascal's fundamental innovation was a ratchet linkage (*sautier*) between the rotating drums, which transferred rotating motion from one drum to the next higher-position drum only during carryover. This kept the digit of each drum aligned with its display window. The machine added and subtracted directly, and multiplied and divided by using repeated additions and subtractions, analogous to present-day pencil-and-paper algorithms. The machine was presented publicly in 1645.

In 1646 Pascal learned of Torricelli's experiment with the vacuum and successfully repeated it. Because of illness, he moved back to Paris in 1647, where he associated with Roberval, met Descartes, published treatises on the vacuum and on conics, and prepared the Puy-de-Dômes (barometer) experiment. Around 1651, he met the Duc de Roannez and the Chevalier de Mere, became reinvolved in research; in 1654 he produced two papers establishing the foundations of the integral calculus and of probability theory. In 1658, using the pseudonym Amos Dettonville, he challenged mathematicians to a mathematical contest and created a controversy by awarding himself the prize. No further significant research followed.

Pascal had been converted to Jansenism in 1645, and in 1654 he had an ecstatic religious experience which drew him into the Port-Royal Jansenists' machinations with the Jesuits, resulting in his writing the *Provincial Letters*, the beginning of French classical literature. His general health, which had been poor, degenerated and he became more mystical in his interests. During his last months in 1662, he created the first public transportation system—an omnibus service in Paris.

C. V. JONES

## PASCAL

For articles on related subjects *see* PROCEDURE-ORIENTED LANGUAGES; and STRUCTURED PROGRAMMING.

Pascal is an Algol-related language that was developed by Wirth (1971) in the early 1970s following some earlier work by Wirth and Hoare (1966). Its existence is due to its originators' dissatisfaction with the features and constructs of the (then) existing procedure-oriented languages. Pascal was designed to serve as a language for teaching computer programming as a systematic discipline, while at the same time proving that a reliable (error free) and efficient (in size and speed) implementation of a large procedure-oriented language could be created on presently available computers.

Pascal is one of the few programming languages specifically designed to help the programmer find coding errors quickly. Extensive error checking is performed during compilation and (optionally) during execution. It is not unusual for Pascal programs, once syntactically correct, to execute error free almost immediately. This phenomenon can be attributed to (1) the requirement for declaring how each programmer-defined symbol is to be used (there are virtually no defaults in the language), and (2) the existence of a rich set of data types plus a variety of programming structures permitting programs to be closely related to their intended meaning. The latter is the essence of structured programming, i.e., writing programs that are easy to read and understand, are less prone to programming errors, and are easy to maintain (i.e., update and debug).

The Pascal statements that make it an excellent host language for structured programming are: *repeat-until, case,* plus the Algol-like constructs of *if-then-else, while-do,* and *for-do.* The statement *goto* is also permitted in Pascal; however, its use—strongly criticized by structured programming advocates (Habermann, 1973)—can almost always be avoided by a suitable choice of program organization.

Pascal can be generally characterized as including Algol 60 as a subset. In all but a few cases, conversion of an Algol 60 program to Pascal is a negligible effort of transcription (Wirth, 1971). The principal differences between the two languages lie in the area of data-structuring facilities (data types), which determine the kinds of values that user-defined variables may assume. For example, in addition to the integer, real, array of integer, and array of real that Algol permits, Pascal provides (among others) scalar, set, record, file, pointer, and character types plus arrays to accommodate each. Pascal also provides a primitive input/output (I/O) facility, which is easy to understand and apply in

```
const n = 25; { number of primes to compute }
type index = 1..n; { scalar data type is subrange of integer }
var x: integer;
   i,k,limit: index; { variables i,k,limit are of type index }
   prime: Boolean; { prime is either true or false }
   p: array[index] of integer; { p[i] is ith prime }
begin p[1] := 2; { first prime }
      write(2,eol); { output prime and end of line terminator }
      x := 1; limit := 1; { initialize method }
      for i := 2 to n do { compute next n-1 prime numbers }
      begin
         repeat
            x := x+2; { only odd numbers need be considered }
            if sqr(p[limit])<x then limit := limit+1; { to determine greatest prime needed as a divisor }
            k := 2; prime := true;
            while prime ∧ (k<limit) do
               begin
                  prime := (x div p[k])*p[k]≠x;
                     { div results in integer part of quotient }
                  k := k+1
               end
         until prime; { if prime true no prime divisor of x exists }
         p[i] := x; { save prime found in array p }
         write(x,eol) { output the prime }
      end { of for loop }
end. { of prime number generator }
```

**Fig. 1.** A sample Pascal program. (Adapted from Wirth, 1973.)

most cases but is somewhat difficult to use in programs with complex I/O requirements.

The sample Pascal program shown in Fig. 1 is adapted from Wirth (1973).

### REFERENCES

1966. Wirth, N. and C. A. R. Hoare. "A Contribution to the Development of Algol." *Communications of the ACM,* Vol. 9, No. 6, pp. 413–431.

1968. Dijkstra, E. W. "GOTO Statement Considered Harmful," *Communications of the ACM,* Vol. 11, No. 3, pp. 147–148.

1971. Wirth, N. "The Programming Language PASCAL," *Acta Informatica,* Vol. 1, pp. 35–63.

1972. Dahl, O. J., E. W. Dijkstra, and C. A. R. Hoare. *Structured Programming.* New York: Academic Press.

1973. Habermann, A. N. "Critical Comments on the Programming Language PASCAL," Dept. of Computer Science. Pittsburgh: Carnegie-Mellon University.

1973. Wirth N. *Systematic Programming: An Introduction.* Englewood Cliffs, N.J.: Prentice-Hall.

1974. Lecarme, O., and P. Desjardins. "Reply to a Paper by A. N. Habermann on the Programming Language PASCAL," *SIGPLAN Notices,* Vol. 9, No. 10, pp. 21–27.

1975. Jensen, K., and N. Wirth. *PASCAL User Manual and Report,* 2nd ed. New York: Springer Verlag.

M. KESSLER

# PATCH

For articles on related subjects *see* DEBUGGING; and MACHINE AND ASSEMBLY LANGUAGE PROGRAMMING.

A patch is a piece of code that (1) represents a programmer's afterthought, (2) is generated by more primitive means than was the program it is to be applied to, and (3) is usually overwritten on code or data in the program to be patched. As a verb, therefore, to "patch" is to modify a program in a rough or expedient way.

A typical example of patching would begin with the discovery of a bug in a sizable compiler-language program, and the realization that it would be very costly or inconvenient to fix it by recompilation. An alternative procedure is to patch—i.e., to generate the required new code either by writing it in assembly language and assembling it, or even by writing it directly in machine language—and loading it after the program to be modified. If the patch is no greater in size than the code to be replaced (if any), it can simply be overlaid on that code, possibly with a terminal transfer over some remaining undesired old code. If it is larger than the code to be replaced, it will be necessary to find "patch space" in which to load it, and to insert transfer instructions to and from the patch so as to link it in at the appropriate point. Depending on the loader that will be inserting the patch, it may be necessary for the programmer to concern himself with check sums, load addresses, and relocation quantities or bits.

The advantages of a patch (over reassembly or recompilation) are that it does not incur the cost, in time or money, involved in submitting the entire program in source form to the appropriate processor. The disadvantages include a much greater liability to error and a loss of correspondence between the latest program listing and the program. Since one of the greatest advantages of the patch is its saving of turnaround time, the coming of on-line programming has deprived the patch of one of its chief reasons for being.

M. HALPERN

**PATENTS.** *See* COPYRIGHTS AND PATENTS, COMPUTER ASPECTS OF; and LEGAL PROTECTION OF SOFTWARE.

# PATTERN RECOGNITION

For articles on related subjects *see* ARTIFICIAL INTELLIGENCE; IMAGE AND PICTURE PROCESSING; MEDICAL APPLICATIONS; and OPTICAL CHARACTER READERS.

Since recognizing patterns is intrinsic to all intelligent activity, an early motivation for work on automatic pattern recognition was the modeling of human intelligence. On the other hand, the emergence of computer-related technology and needs led to, and made feasible, serious attempts to automate the reading of printed alphanumeric characters; the analysis and classification of military aerial photographs, weather-satellite photographs, bubble chamber, blood cell, and chromosome pictures; speech sounds, and sonar; electrocardiogram, and electroencephalogram waveforms; and analysis, clustering, and classification of data obtained in diverse fields, from anthropology to zoology.

Through an abuse of the language, words such as "recognition" and "learning," which refer to fairly complex capabilities of humans and animals, have been applied to machine systems that implement classification and estimation algorithms. Unfortunately, this abuse of the language is here to stay, and so we also will speak of "machine recognition." Basing his arguments on the linguistic school of philosophy, Kenneth Sayre (1969) points out that "classification of a group of objects is a matter either of sorting them according to a given set of categories or of devising a set of categories by which they can be sorted. Either procedure is a process and not itself an attainment," whereas, according to his analysis, recognition is an attainment. He goes on to say, "Even though I could not recognize a strange flower found among the flowers in my backyard, I could easily identify it—i.e., point it out for my neighbor when he arrives to inspect it." Further, "If I recognize an object it is something I could not have done more effectively, more thoroughly or more satisfactorily."

The understanding that pattern recognition is an attainment, a goal—rather than a process, method, or technique—explains why machines embodying some classification algorithms can lead to "recognition" of certain patterns without necessarily having anything in common with the methods used by humans or animals to recognize those same patterns. This also suggests that alternative models and methods exist for recognition problems. Some of the models and methods proposed for machine recognition are outlined here.

**Models for Automatic Pattern Recognition.** In the current literature on pattern recognition, one discerns two proposed models for automatic pattern recognition. These are the feature extraction-classification, and linguistic, or syntactic, models. While much is made of the difference between these two approaches, the syntactic model may be viewed as a particular case of the first model.

FEATURE EXTRACTION-CLASSIFICATION MODEL. The feature extraction-classification model is shown in Fig. 1. In this model, recognition is achieved by making measurements on the patterns to be recognized, and then deriving features from these measurements. These features form the input to a classification procedure that gives a class, group, or category assignment for each pattern. The available information from the pattern environment is thereby reduced (in stages) ultimately to a small number of categories. Thus, the process is one of information reduction, or data compression.

In waveform classification, an approach may be to expand the waveform in a suitable set of orthogonal functions and use the coefficients of the expansion as the features. In optical character recognition (OCR), such features may not be relevant, whereas length and position of certain strokes may contain sufficient information for classification.

A commonly used version of the feature extraction-classification model is one in which the features are treated as components of a vector $x = (x_1 \cdots x_n)$. Each pattern is then considered to be a point in the resulting $n$-dimensional feature space. Classification becomes a problem of dividing this $n$-dimensional space into exclusive regions $R_j$, $j = 1, 2 \cdots K$, such that when a feature vector falls into $R_j$, the pattern is assigned to class $j$ (Fig. 2). This division might be effected on the basis of statistical or nonstatistical considerations.

Note that any type of feature may be used in this model. As an example, let us consider the recognition of a character as in Fig. 1(b). The measurement process here consists of scanning a region of the paper where the character is written. This region is divided into small (usually rectangular) subregions, and the average gray level for each subregion is measured. In this scanned form the information about the character consists of a two-dimensional array of gray-level values. The gray levels in each of these regions may be used as a feature. Of course, if suitable preprocessors are available, one might define other features, such as a binary-valued feature to indicate the existence of a certain stroke.

In the simplest case where there is no variability within pattern classes, classification reduces to the procedure called "template matching," in which an observed pattern is matched against a prototype (template). For example, since the variability in machine-printed characters of a single type style (font) is introduced mainly by the printing process, template-matching approaches have been very useful in designing optical character readers (Fig. 3). A special OCR font, which is well suited to a template-matching approach, has been designed and accepted as standard for character readers (Fig. 4).

When the variability is limited, it may be possible to extend this idea to the feature space and

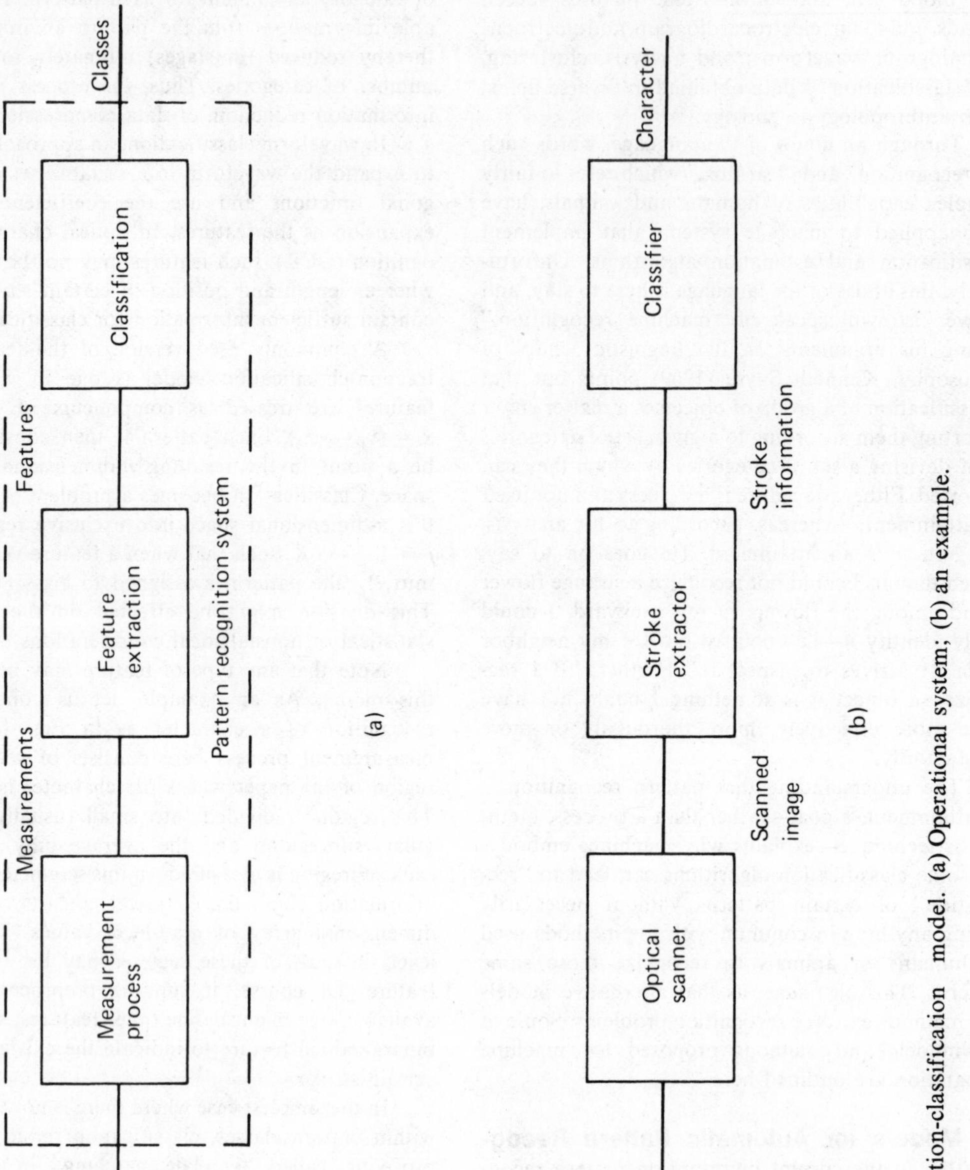

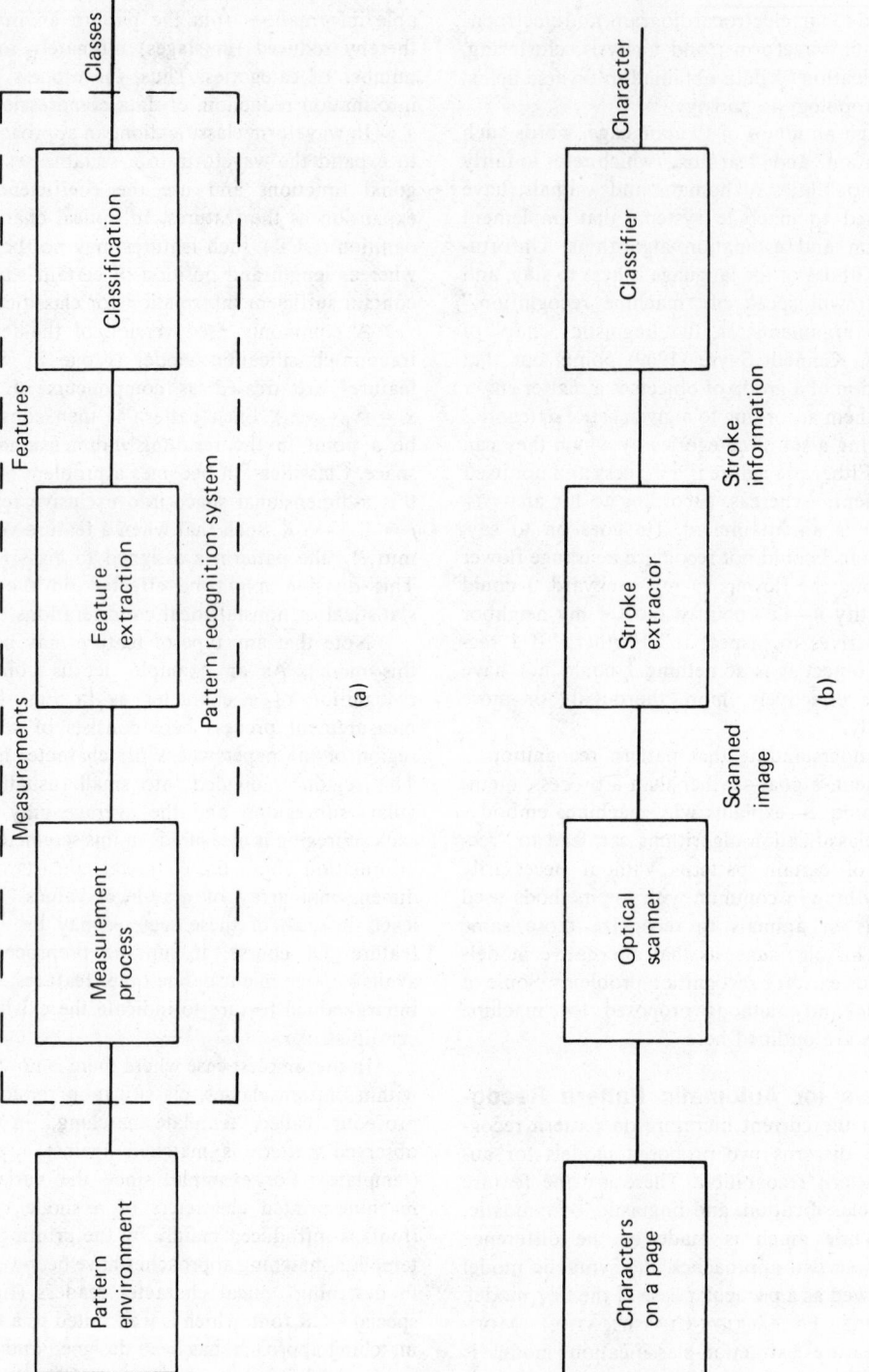

**Fig. 1.** Feature extraction-classification model. (a) Operational system; (b) an example.

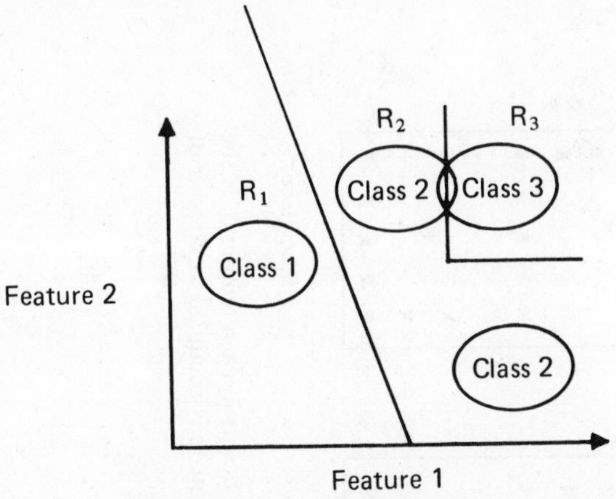


**Fig. 2.** Separation of classes in feature space (regions $R_1$, $R_2$, $R_3$). Sample is assigned to class $i$ if corresponding feature vector lies in region $R_i$. Here, classes 1 and 2 are separable; class 2 is bimodal; classes 2 and 3 overlap. Because classes 2 and 3 are inseparable, a classification procedure defined by these two regions will result in errors.

classify patterns according to their distance from the nearest prototype. In most real-life problems, neither of these procedures leads to adequate classification performance; instead, one needs to employ more sophisticated methods of multivariate statistical classification for defining the regions $R_j$.

LINGUISTIC (SYNTACTIC) MODEL. The commonly used version of the feature-extraction classification model has been criticized for focusing primarily on statistical relationships among the features while ignoring the structural properties that seem to characterize the patterns. In the structural, or "linguistic" approach, one defines a class of patterns as satisfying a certain set of relations among suitably defined "primitives." The relations might be boolean expressions in a relatively simple case, or might be specifiable by a generative grammar in a more complex case. Again, in the case of an alphabetic character, the set of primitives might be a "vertical stroke" a "horizontal stroke," etc., and the structural relationship specifies how the strokes are to be juxtaposed to qualify as a certain character. For example, the "2" in Fig. 3 consists of three horizontal strokes and two half-vertical strokes. The top and middle horizontal strokes are connected by a top-right half-vertical stroke. For a character to be recognized as a "2," using this approach, various strokes have to be detected first, and then the stroke positions have to conform to the "known" structural relationship for "2". The recognition of primitives is another pattern recognition problem, albeit of a lower complexity. The term "linguistic" is especially preferred when generative grammars are used, in obvious analogy to language analysis.

The stress on the distinction between the feature-extraction classification model and the linguistic or syntactic model misses the obvious points that, even in the syntactic model, the primitives are nothing more than features that have to be extracted from measurements, and that associating a pattern with a generative model is essentially the same as classifying the pattern into categories represented by the generative models. Clearly, the generative models need not be restricted to formal grammars and could include such familiar models as a differential equation model, a functional equation model, or a stochastic model such as a finite state Markov chain model.

A recent theoretical development is the introduction of fuzzy sets in the classification process. Unlike classical set theory in which the characteristic function of a set is binary valued (i.e., 0 or 1), fuzzy sets are defined to have a membership function that can take any real value between 0 and 1. For example, the degree of membership of a female in the class of "beautiful women" is very much a function of the beholder. Simultaneously, she could be considered fairly beautiful by some and not so beautiful by others. This produces a nonexclusive assignment of a pattern to a class. The concept is different from a probabilistic assignment of patterns to classes. In the latter case, a pattern may be probabilistically assigned to one class or the other, but it does not simultaneously belong to both classes, as is the case in the fuzzy-set model.

**Development of a Pattern Recognition System.** An operational pattern recognition system looks deceptively simple. Arriving at the final design requires a highly iterative trial-and-error process, with the designer bringing to bear all knowledge he can garner about the problem (Fig. 5). In problem-oriented, pattern-recognition investigations, the starting point is usually some samples of patterns. The question then asked is whether or not the recognition of patterns such as these can be automated, and if it can, how complex a machine is needed.

To go from these initial vague questions to an actual pattern recognition system involves a series of refinements and formalizations concerning the deterministic, probabilistic, or mixed structure: what can

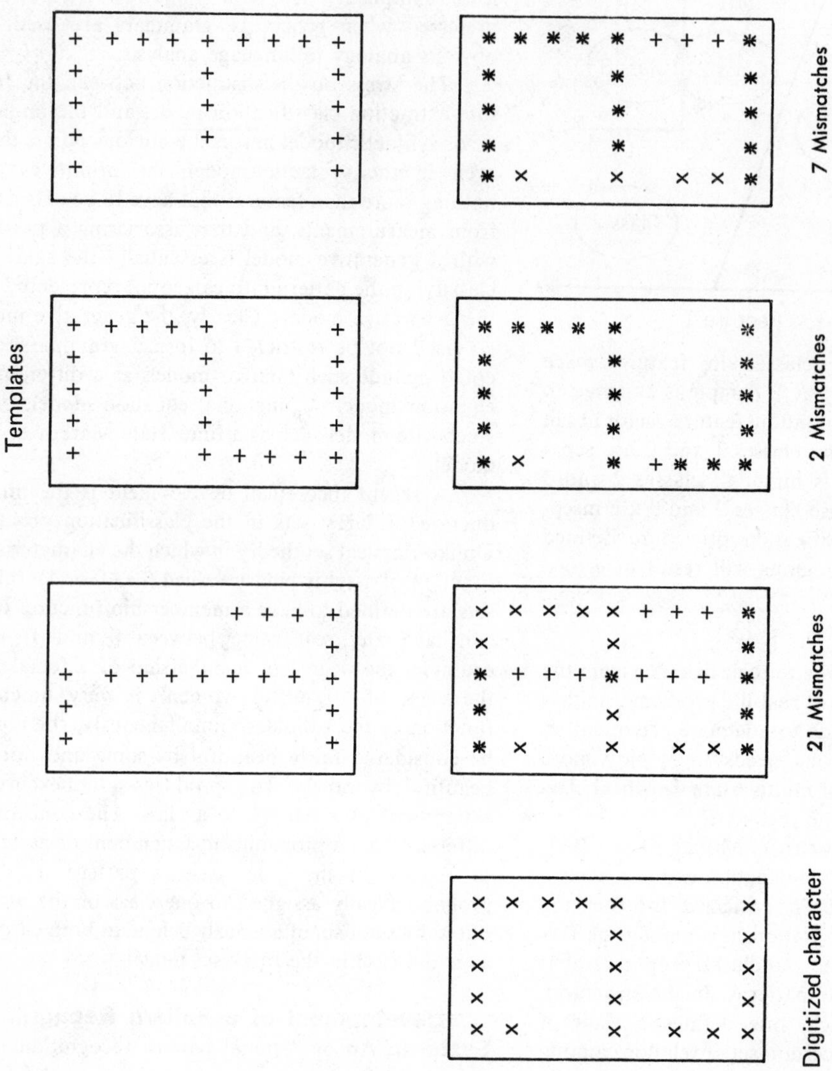


**Fig. 3.** Template matching. All points of the digitized character are compared with corresponding points in each template. If the two are not the same (i.e., both 0 or both 1), a mismatch is counted. Here, the second template is occupied as a result of minimum mismatch.

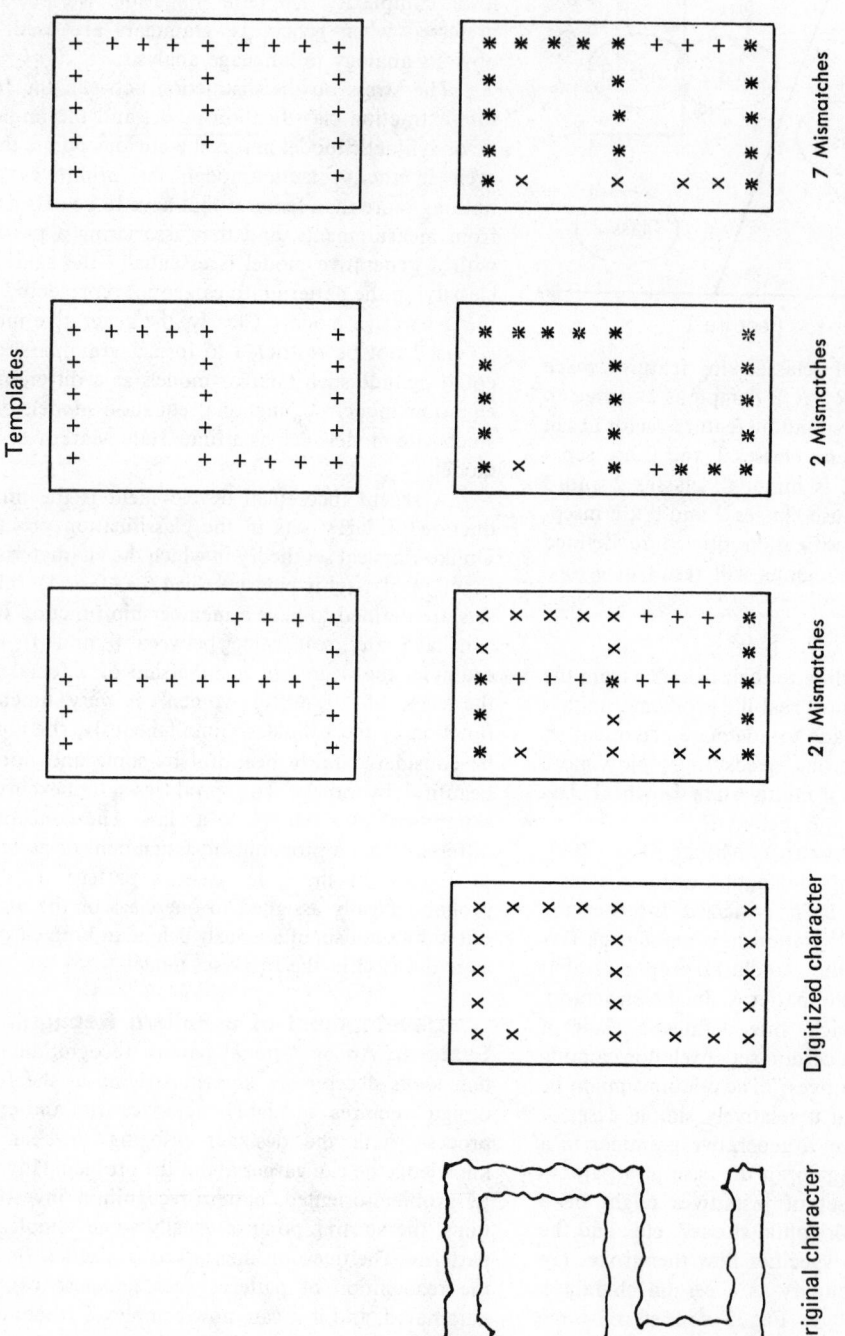

*ANSI OCR Size A Type Font (lowercase omitted)*

**Fig. 4.** Standard OCR character set.

be inferred about the patterns; what level of performance is desirable; what competing design approaches are worth considering; and what manner of implementation is relevant.

When deterministic descriptions are the basis for the decision logic, a large amount of information has been transmitted to the classifier. To infer the same type and amount of information using statistical methodology would take an inordinately large number of samples. But the within-group variability of patterns in most nontrivial real problems is such that—following a purely deterministic approach without severe constraints on the input—the performance of practical pattern recognition systems is marginal or unacceptable. In most real-life pattern recognition problems, we are thus faced with the necessity of inferring both deterministic and probabilistic structures governing the patterns and pattern classes in order to achieve good classification performance. Furthermore, in order to understand the variability in relatively unconstrained data and to come up with solutions, we need to study the detailed peculiarities of a large data base. Thus, pattern analysis is the first step in designing a pattern recognition system.

**Pattern Analysis.** Pattern analysis consists of using whatever is known about the problem at hand to guide the gathering of data about the patterns and pattern classes, and then applying techniques of data analysis to help uncover the structure present in the data. Data analysis techniques derived from clustering and statistical discriminant analysis have been found useful, and the process of uncovering structure is often facilitated by special graphical presentations of the data. Fig. 6 shows a graphical display of handprinted 9s and 7s on a two-dimensional linear projection that is designed to bring out the separation between the classes.

Clustering algorithms attempt to detect and locate the presence of groups of vectors, in a high dimensional-multivariate space, which share some property of similarity. A widely used measure of similarity is the mean distance of each sample from the closest cluster center. Based on such similarity measures, clustering algorithms iteratively assign samples to clusters while employing merging and splitting rules on each iteration to define the clusters.

In addition to detecting cluster structure in the data, clustering routines can be used for data com-

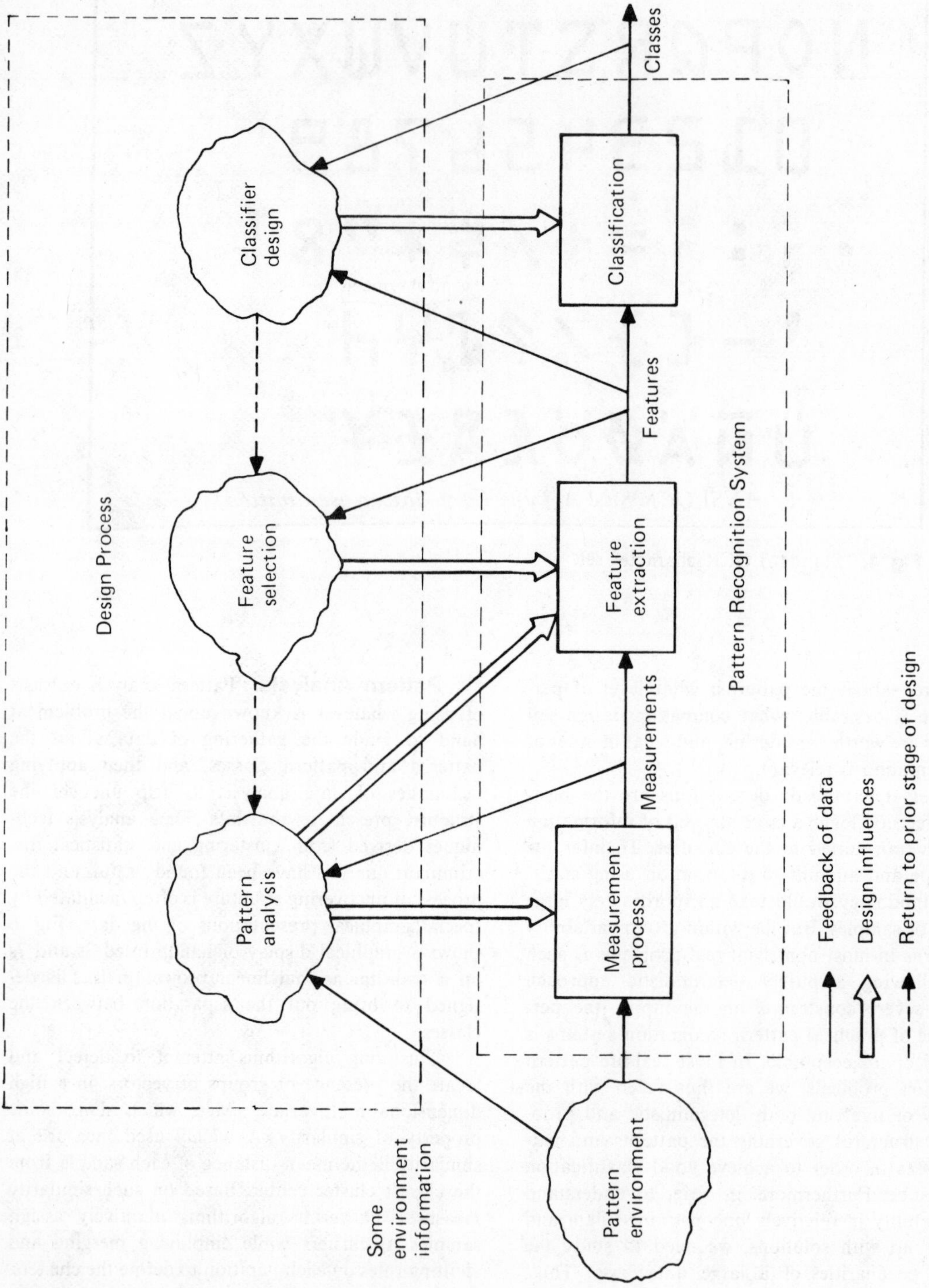


**Fig. 5.** Development of pattern recognition systems: lightweight arrow = feedback of data; heavy arrow = design influences; dotted arrow = return to prior stage of design.

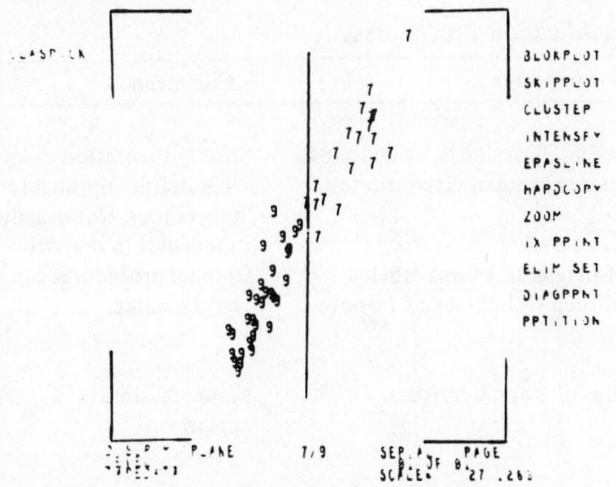

**Fig. 6.** Projection of handwritten numerals on an Optical Discriminant Plane in which the horizontal axis is the Fisher direction and the second axis is derived under the additional constraint of being orthogonal to the first direction.

pression. The large amount of data gathered for analysis can sometimes be handled by representing all vectors in a cluster by a prototype vector. An additional insight into the structure may be gained by examining in detail the points that do not belong to any cluster. The study of outliers, i.e., points that lie outside a cluster and between clusters, is often revealing.

A number of other linear and nonlinear mapping techniques have also been found useful, especially when the analysis is carried out in an interactive environment using a graphics terminal.

**Feature Selection.** The quality of decisions we make depends on the quality of questions we ask. The ultimate test of a set of features is their utility for classification as measured by the classification error. Unfortunately, in most situations, the analytical relationship between the classification error and the features used is not available. Hence, various measures of information, distance, and separation have been proposed to measure the effectiveness of a given set of features for classification. The relationship of such measures to classification error is a subject of current research. Feature extraction or feature formation is problem specific, but methods of selecting features from a given set apply across problems.

**Classification.** Pattern information is presented to the classifier in the form of an $n$-dimensional feature vector $x = (x_1, x_2 \cdots x_n)$. The task of the classifier is to assign $x$ to one of $k$ categories. This is achieved by examining the regions $R_j$, $j = 1, \ldots k$ of the $n$-dimensional feature space and finding the region $R_i$ in which $x$ lies. The pattern is then assigned to category $i$. The necessary information about the region $R_j$ is usually stored in one of two forms:

1. Each region may be described by storing its boundaries, which may be linear or nonlinear and may or may not be simply connected. The classifier examines the class participation of the pattern by examining sequentially or in parallel where it lies with respect to the boundaries. These boundaries are often called "discriminant functions."

2. A typical location for each region (e.g., the mean vector) may be stored. The classifier computes the location of the feature vector relative to various classes, and makes an assignment. This procedure tends to specify the region boundaries implicitly, and does not require storing the details of the boundaries.

Minimization of storage and computation required to implement a classifier is a usual goal often achieved by restricting the form of the classifier to a linear or piecewise linear function of the features. It should be noted that nonlinear functions (e.g., powers) of features may be treated as linear functions in a higher-order feature space, but the apparent theoretical increase in discriminating ability is usually not realizable in practice because of problems involved in estimating the fine structure represented by the higher-order relationships among the features.

In problems where the system may observe a number of samples not belonging to the classes it knows about, a reject option is often provided. This is effectively achieved by assigning closed regions for known classes and labeling all others of the feature space as the reject region.

The techniques for designing a classifier depend on the information available about the feature space and classes. The applicable techniques for various situations are summarized in Table 1.

The performance of classifiers designed on a training set strongly depends on the size and structure (representativeness) of the training set. A number of open problems in this area relate to the dimensionality of the feature space and the sample size, and their relationship to the probability of error achievable by a classifier.

**Table 1.** Statistical Classification Procedures

| Assumptions | Techniques Applicable | Comments |
|---|---|---|
| Parametric Assumptions | | |
| 1. Structural form of all probability density functions along with the parameter values are given. | Hypothesis testing, Bayesian decision techniques, sequential probability ratio test. | Strictly theoretical case that defines optimality procedures. Not usually applicable in practice. |
| 2. Structural form of all probability density functions and a set of labeled samples given. The values of a few parameters not given. | Estimation of parameters using labeled samples and then techniques of 1 above. | Optimal procedures can be generated. |
| 3. Structural form of all probability density functions and a set of unclassified samples given. The values of a few parameters not given. | Uses techniques of 2 and heuristics. | Rarely feasible in practice. |
| Nonparametric Assumptions | | |
| 1. A set of classified learning samples. | (a) Minimization of appropriate criterion. (b) Stochastic approximation. Minimization of criterion involving probability distribution functions. | Evaluation of performance difficult; rough estimate obtainable from independent test samples. |
| 2. A set of unclassified learning samples. | Clustering<br>Bootstrap techniques along with 1(b). | |

**Table 2.** Some Applications of Pattern Recognition

| Problem | Input to Pattern Recognition System | Output of Pattern Recognition System |
|---|---|---|
| Military Applications | | |
| Interpretation of aerial reconnaissance imagery | Visual, infrared radar, multispectral imagery | Tanks, personnel carriers, weapons, missile launchers, airfields, campsites |
| Detection of enemy navy vessels | Passive/active sonar waveforms | Surface vessels, submarines, whales, fish |
| Detection of underground nuclear explosions | Seismic waveforms | Nuclear explosions, conventional explosions, earthquakes |
| Medical Applications | | |
| Identification and counting of cells | Slides of blood samples, microsections of tissue | Types of cells |
| Detection/diagnosis of disease | Electrocardiogram waveforms<br>Electroencephalogram waveforms<br>Slides of blood samples | Types of cardiac conditions<br>Classes of brain conditions<br>Various types and proportions of normal and abnormal cells |
| Prosthetic control devices | Myopotentials | Categories of (muscle) movements of limbs |
| X-ray diagnosis | X-ray photograph | Presence or absence of specific conditions |
| Commercial/Government Applications | | |
| Automatic detection of flaws: impurities in sheet glass, bottles, paper, textiles, printed-circuit boards, integrated circuit masks | Scanned image (visible or infrared, etc.) | Acceptable vs. unacceptable, markings, bubbles, flaws, radiation patterns, etc. |

**Table 2.** (Continued)

| | | |
|---|---|---|
| Classification/identification of fingerprints | Scanned image | Fingerprint descriptions based on Henry system of classification |
| Traffic pattern studies | Aerial photographs of highways, intersections, bridges<br>Road sensors | Automobiles, trucks, motorcycles, etc., to determine the characteristics of traffic flow |
| Natural resource identification | Multispectral imagery | Terrain forms, agricultural land, bodies of water, forests |
| Identification of crop diseases | Multispectral imagery | Normal and diseased crops |
| Economic predictions | Time series of economic indicators | Economic conditions |
| Speech Recognition<br>Remote manipulation of processes<br>Parcel post sorting<br>Management information systems<br>Voice input to computers | Speech waveform | Spoken words, phonemes |
| Weather forecasting | Weather data from various land-based, airborne, ocean and satellite sensors | Categories of weather |
| Object recognition<br>Parts handling<br>Inspection of parts<br>Assembly | Scanned image | Object types |
| Character Recognition | | |
| Bank checks | Magnetic response waveform<br>Optical scanned image | Numeric characters, special symbols |
| Automatic processing of documents<br>Utility bills<br>Credit card charges<br>Sale/inventory documents | Optical scanned image | Alphanumeric characters, special symbols |
| Journal tape reading | Optical scanned image | Numeric characters, special symbols |
| Page readers<br>Automatic typesetting<br>Input to computers<br>Reading for the blind | Optical scanned image | Alphanumeric characters, special symbols |
| Label readers | Optical scanned image | Alphanumeric characters, special symbols |
| Address readers | Optical scanned image | Letters/numerals combined into zip codes, city/state names and street addresses |
| Other readers<br>License-plate readers<br>Telephone traffic counter readers | Optical scanned image | Alphanumeric characters, special symbols |

**Evaluation Criterion.** To be acceptable, a pattern recognition system should make very few errors in assigning classes to the observed patterns. The probability of misclassification is the most important evaluation criterion. However, it is very difficult to estimate this probability from a small number of samples. Because of the inherent optimistic bias in the error estimates obtained from a training set, an available finite set of samples needs to be partitioned into independent test and training sets. The classical statistical method of dividing a sample into equal proportions for training and test does not lead to an unbiased error estimate except for a very large sample size. Error estimation from $N$ runs, in each of which one observation is kept for testing and the remaining $N - 1$ samples are used for training, is preferable. Also preferable are related techniques of sample rotation and cross validation, which use different partitions of the total observations into training and testing sets, and interchange the role of training and testing samples before deriving an error estimate.

| True class \ Assigned class | 1 | 2 | 3 | 4 | 5 |
|---|---|---|---|---|---|
| 1 | 48 | 0 | 1 | 0 | 1 |
| 2 | 0 | 43 | 2 | 3 | 2 |
| 3 | 2 | 0 | 45 | 2 | 1 |
| 4 | 1 | 3 | 2 | 40 | 4 |
| 5 | 0 | 0 | 0 | 0 | 50 |

**Fig. 7.** Confusion matrix.

A useful way of representing errors is in the form of a confusion matrix, in which the *ij*th element represents the number of samples from class *i* which were classified as class *j*. Fig. 7 shows an example of a confusion matrix. As there are a number of ways in which a classifier makes errors, the evaluation criteria are often constructed on the basis of such errors. Some of the commonly used criteria are:

1. The probability of error averaged for all classes.

2. A cost function that is a weighted sum taking into account the cost of making each kind of error. This criterion is meaningful when certain types of errors are less critical than other types. Note that if the cost for all misclassifications is considered equal, this criterion becomes the same as criterion 1.

In some applications a machine is allowed to reject samples on which it cannot reach a decision. As these samples may be examined separately, one may be willing to accept a higher reject rate if the error rate can be kept low. This type of performance is very typical of character readers that are designed to flag rejected samples and allow the operator to classify such samples. A trade-off between errors and rejects can be achieved by appropriately adjusting the parameters of the classifier. Achieving very low error rates may, however, require very high reject rates. A relationship between these error and reject rates can be exploited to estimate the error rate from the reject rate.

**Applications and Concluding Remarks.** The methodology being developed in the area of pattern recognition, which has been only briefly outlined in this article, is applicable to problems in a variety of fields. A sample of such problems is displayed in Table 2. Some of these applications (e.g., OCR, blood-cell analysis, and ECG analysis) have reached a commercial stage, and many others are subjects of active research and development.

We can summarize the present state of affairs as follows: Whatever successes have been achieved in machine recognition of patterns have been the result of an effective transformation of a perception-recognition problem into a classification problem. Transforming a recognition problem into a classification problem involves the generation and selection of features that form the inputs to the decision device in pattern recognition systems. The difficult problems in the field are those in which the generation of suitable, complete sets of features has been formidable.

We do not have a general theory for anything except certain classification aspects of machine recognition problems. If we assume that an adequate set of features is at hand, we have quite an arsenal of solutions for classification problems under various conditions. But the boundaries between feature selection and classification are not sharp. We need feedback between feature selection, and design and testing of the classifier, and we need many iterations of the feedback process. This is naturally an interactive operation.

The problem-dependent nature of the front end of a pattern recognition system and the many possible techniques that may be applicable make it necessary for the designer to interact with the problem data and selectively explore solutions, rather than rely completely on automatic procedures. Interactive graphics-oriented technology currently being developed is expected to play a major role in providing viable solutions for pattern recognition applications.

**Source Material.** The annual volume of published papers and books in this field is very large. Journals regularly carrying papers in pattern recognition include:

*IEEE Transactions on Information Theory*
*IEEE Transactions on Computers*
*IEEE Transactions on Systems, Man and Cybernetics*
*Pattern Recognition*
*Information Sciences*

REFERENCES

1968. Kanal, L. N. (Ed.). *Pattern Recognition.* Silver Spring, Md.: Thompson (L.N.K. Inc.).
1969. Sayre, K. M. *Consciousness: A Philosophical Study of Minds and Machines.* New York: Random House.
1969. Watanabe, S. (Ed.). *Methodologies of Pattern Recognition.* New York: Academic Press.
1972. Fukunaga, K. *Introduction to Statistical Pattern Recognition.* New York: Academic Press.
1972. Watanabe, S. (Ed.). *Frontiers of Pattern Recognition.* New York: Academic Press.
1973. Chen, C. H. *Statistical Pattern Recognition.* New York: Hayden (Spartan Books).
1973. Duda, R. O., and P. E. Hart. *Pattern Classification and Scene Analysis.* New York: John Wiley.

L. N. KANAL AND A. K. AGRAWALA

# PERCEPTRON

For articles on related subjects *see* ARTIFICIAL INTELLIGENCE; and PATTERN RECOGNITION.

In 1958 the psychologist Frank Rosenblatt proposed the network structure of Fig. 1 as a cognitive machine embodying aspects of the brain and the visual system of animals. This was called a "perceptron," or specifically, the Mark I Perceptron (Rosenblatt, 1962).

A basic building block of a perceptron is an element that accepts a number of inputs $x_i$, $i = 1 \cdots I$, and computes a weighted sum of these inputs, where the weights $\omega_i$ can be only $+1$ or $-1$ for each input. The sum is then compared with a threshold and an output, $y$ equal to 1 or 0 is produced, depending on whether or not the sum exceeds the threshold. In other words,

$$y = \begin{cases} 1 & \text{if } (\Sigma_{i=1}^{I} \omega_i x_i) \geq \theta \\ 0 & \text{if } (\Sigma_{i=1}^{I} \omega_i x_i) < \theta \end{cases}$$

The receptor of the perceptron is analogous to the retina of the eye, and is made of a rectangular array of light-sensing elements or photocells. Depending on whether or not a photocell is excited, it produces a binary output. A randomly selected set of retinal cells is connected to the next level of the network, called "A units," or associative elements. Each A unit behaves like the basic building block discussed above. The $+1$, $-1$ weights for the inputs to each A unit are randomly assigned. The threshold for all A units is the same.

The binary output of the $k$th A unit ($k = 1,m$) is multiplied by a weight $a_k$, and a sum of all $m$ weighted outputs is formed in a summation unit that is the same as the basic building blocks with all weights equal to $+1$. Each weight $a_k$ is allowed to be positive, zero, or negative, and may change independently of other weights. The output of this block is again binary, depending on a threshold that is normally set at zero. The binary values of the output are used to distinguish or classify two classes of patterns which may be presented to the retina of a perceptron. The design of a perceptron to distinguish between two given sets of patterns involves adjusting the weights $a_k$, $k = 1, m$, and the threshold $\theta$.

Rosenblatt (1962) proposed a number of variations of the following procedure for "training" perceptrons. The set of given patterns of known classification are presented sequentially to the retina, with the complete set being repeated as often as needed. The output of the perceptron is monitored to examine if a pattern is correctly classified. If not, the weights are adjusted according to the following "error correction" procedure: If the $n$th pattern was misclassified, the new value $a_k(n + 1)$ for the $k$th weight is calculated as

$$a_k(n + 1) = a_k(n) - y_k(n) * \delta(n),$$

where $\delta(n)$ is 1 if the $n$th pattern is from class 1 and $\delta(n)$ is $-1$ if the $n$th pattern is from class 2. No adjustment to the weight is made if a pattern is correctly classified.

If there exists a set of weights such that all patterns can be correctly classified, the pattern classes are said to be *linearly separable.* It was conjectured by Rosenblatt that, when the pattern classes are linearly separable, the error correction "learning" procedure will converge to a set of weights which correctly classifies all the patterns. Many proofs of this perceptron convergence theorem were subsequently derived, culminating in a short proof by A. J. Novikoff.

Rosenblatt's brilliant conjectures and the colorful names for his "self-organizing" machines attracted wide attention. He had high hopes for his "artificial intelligences." They were to be replace-

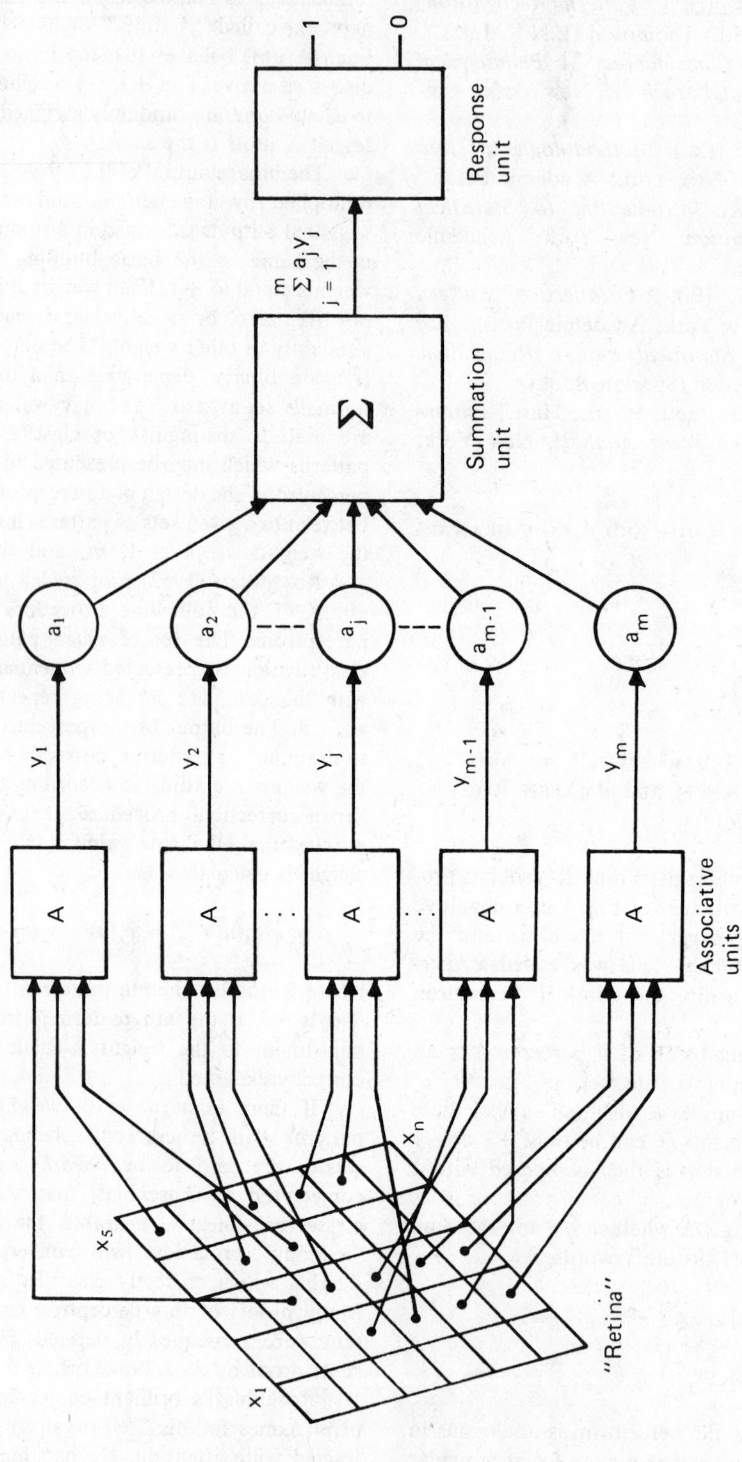


**Fig. 1.** Mark-1 Perceptron structure.

ments for human perceivers, recognizers, and problem solvers. Over the next few years after his proposal there followed a flock of other "adaptive" and "learning" machines. As was to become evident, the true contribution of the brilliant conjectures, catchy names, and audacious claims for these machines was not in providing a general approach to pattern recognition, but rather in creating an air of excitement about automatic pattern recognition and learning machines. Today, perceptrons are properly viewed as a class of machines with interesting but restricted properties; in particular, Minsky and Papert (1969) prove many theorems about a class of perceptrons, some of which indicate their limited pattern-recognition capabilities.

### References

1962. Rosenblatt, F. *Principles of Neurodynamics*. New York: Spartan Books.

1969. Minsky, M., and S. Papert. *Perceptrons*. Cambridge, Mass.: M.I.T. Press.

A. K. Agrawala and L. N. Kanal

## PERFORMANCE EVALUATION AND REVIEW TECHNIQUE.

*See* PERT/CPM.

## PERFORMANCE MEASUREMENT AND EVALUATION

For articles on related subjects *see* Computing Economics: Acquisition and Operation; Hardware Monitor; Operating Systems; Performance of Computers; System Generation; Time Sharing; and Throughput.

For articles on related terms *see* Benchmark; Models; and Simulation.

There are as yet no techniques for characterizing the overall performance of a computing system in the abstract. The trouble is that we do not have any adequate and accepted method of quantifying the "information work" that a given job entails. For a given system, in a given environment, such measures as *job throughput* or *terminal response time* may be regarded as adequate characterizations of how well the system is performing. However, it is very difficult to compare the performance of two systems that provide rather different sets of facilities and interfaces to the external world, or even of two identical systems in environments that provide radically different workloads.

One approach to performance measurement is therefore to rely on "benchmark" work loads, which, when used for purposes of comparison, usually exercise only the "lowest common denominator" of the facilities provided by each of the systems under comparison. Benchmarking has other problems: it is time consuming, and the task of producing a benchmark work load that adequately models the real work load is often very difficult. However, it is presently the standard method of making a comparative evaluation of rival systems for purposes of computer selection.

Although the problem of assessing the overall performance of a computing system is still somewhat intractable, much can be gained from efforts at measuring and evaluating various aspects of the internal activities of a computing system, such as the average lengths of the more important queues for operating system services, or the levels of utilization of major hardware components. Such efforts can be used to assist the development of a system by providing a valuable form of feedback to the designers, or can be used to learn more about the behavior of an existing system—usually in the hope of finding ways in which the system can be improved.

Performance evaluation does not necessarily have to involve monitoring, i.e., the measurement of the actual system, either while in normal use or while running benchmark work loads made up of selected jobs or specially constructed programs. Instead, evaluation can be based on models, either analytic or simulated, although it is then necessary to demonstrate that the model is indeed a sufficiently accurate representation of the particular aspects of the computer system which are of interest. Analytical models, which are usually based on queueing theory, have to be comparatively simple if they are to be mathematically tractable; typical examples are models of time-sharing schedulers, or of system components such as drums and disks. Simulation models can be considerably more complex, although there is a danger of achieving apparent realism at the expense of actual validity.

Detailed simulation models have been made of particular operating systems, and have been used for such purposes as investigating the probable effects of changes to the hardware configuration or the operating system strategies. Indeed, there are simulation models that are claimed by their designers to be capable of providing accurate comparative evaluations of a whole range of computer systems. As a final example, simulation models have been used extensively to assess the design of a new processor and memory intended as an addition to a series of computers with compatible architecture; such models have the advantage that they can take actual programs as their input data. Thus, simulation models may range from being quite abstract representations of a complete system to faithful and detailed models of system components.

Performance monitoring is coming into increasing use by computing center personnel as an aid to improving the effectiveness of a system. Present large-scale computing systems, particularly those involving remote terminals and telecommunications devices, are so complex that even the problem of maintaining an awareness of whether the system is continuing to function normally can be nontrivial. However, performance monitoring really comes into its own as a means of obtaining information about the inner workings of a system.

The operating systems that computer manufacturers provide can often be described as generic systems, in the sense that they are designed to be used in a large (some might say an "excessively large") variety of versions, each catering to a different hardware configuration and different type of work load. In any given environment it is necessary to create a particularized version of the generic system. This involves selecting the desired system components from the total set of components that comprise the generic system, and choosing settings of the many and varied parameters that govern the actions of the system. These decisions can be very difficult; performance monitoring can provide data on which to base the decisions and can be used afterward to determine how well founded they were. It can also play a similar role in decisions about hardware configuration changes, about the layout of data in a disk store, etc.

Performance monitoring involves the counting, and perhaps timing, of selected events, either continuously or on a sampling basis. This can be done with the aid of special hardware or solely by software. The earliest hardware monitors were simply electrical probes connected to recording counters through a modest amount of combinatorial circuitry. Later hardware monitors were more sophisticated, even in some cases to the extent of being themselves program-controlled computers. The advantage of such hardware monitors is that they are capable of very high resolution, and need not interfere with the operation of the system being monitored. They are particularly convenient for monitoring low-level hardware-related events such as concurrent channel and processor activity, and frequency of accesses to particular store modules. However, it may be very difficult to find hardware events that can be interpreted in terms of high-level events such as use of a particular operating system facility or a resource utilization on behalf of a particular user. In such cases, software monitoring is usually much more convenient, although the addition of the necessary extra instructions into the code of the system being monitored can have the effect of disturbing the behavior of the system. (The addition of such data collection facilities to an existing operating system may be a very awkward business. The tendency now is to try to foresee what events will need to be monitored, and to build the necessary facilities into the system from the outset.)

With either type of monitoring, the tabulation and analysis of the recorded events can be very time consuming. However, the major difficulties are deciding what events to monitor in order to obtain the required data, and then interpreting the results. As a result, various companies now offer a monitoring and evaluation service to users of the more widespread generic operating systems. Particularly in the case of a computing system that has a fairly stable work load, it is not uncommon for considerable savings to result from quite simple modifications arising out of the data collected during a day or so of monitoring. This, of course, says much about the state of the original system and about the inability of many installations to cope with the complexity that is characteristic of present large-scale operating systems.

After changes have been made to a system in order to improve its performance, the obvious way to evaluate their effects again involves monitoring techniques. This is not too difficult if the work load is a stable, repetitive one. Otherwise, one has to choose between monitoring an artificial benchmark work load, and attempting to disentangle the effects of the changes from all other variables that may be affecting the situation (e.g., by regression analysis techniques).

In summary, despite the problems of finding a satisfactory and widely applicable definition of system performance, even somewhat ad hoc efforts at performance measurement and evaluation can be of very great value. However, despite any impression to the contrary that may be gained from much of the literature, the problems of monitoring and measurement are comparatively simple. They consist merely of deciding what to monitor and how to evaluate the results (which is difficult), both of which demand high skills and detailed knowledge of the structure of the system under consideration.

### REFERENCES


1969. Naur, P., and B. Randell (Eds.). *Software Engineering: Report on a Conference Sponsored by the NATO Science Committee, Garmisch, Germany, 7–11 Oct. 1968*. Scientific Affairs Division, NATO, Brussels (January).
Contains extensive discussions on system measurement and evaluation, and an article by Pinkerton on performance monitoring.

1971. Bard, Y. "Performance Criteria and Measurement for a Time-Sharing System," *IBM Systems J.*, Vol. 10, No. 3, pp.193–216.
An example of monitoring a system in ordinary use so as to evaluate the effects of changes.

1971. Lucas, H. C. "Performance Evaluation and Monitoring," *Computing Surveys*, Vol. 3, No. 3, pp. 79–91.
An introductory article on the topic.


B. RANDELL

# PERFORMANCE OF COMPUTERS

For articles on related subjects *see* BENCHMARK; GROSCH'S LAW; PERFORMANCE MEASUREMENT AND EVALUATION; and SUPERCOMPUTERS.

For articles on related terms *see* BUFFER; CENTRAL PROCESSING UNIT; GENERATIONS, COMPUTER; INDEX REGISTER; LEAST SQUARES APPROXIMATION; and REGRESSION ANALYSIS.

While the idea that present-day computers are faster and more efficient than their predecessors is universally accepted, ideas about how they arrived at this level are not. One school of thought holds that computer performance has progressed by major breakthroughs, which are discreet and quantifiable, and are evidenced by "generations." Another maintains that progress has been fairly steady over the years and, rather than the result of major breakthroughs, is the sum of many improvements.

Over the past few years, several methods of comparing computer power have been developed. The technique used here is one that lends itself readily to comparing computer technology levels by year (see Knight, 1968; 1972). It consists of developing a value for computer power, which is then compared with its cost to yield a technology level for a given year. The results of this comparison show that computer technology has advanced each year without major jumps in the rate of advancement.

**Calculation of Computing Power and Cost.** The variables used in comparing computer power $P$ (measured in operations per second) with seconds of operations-per-unit cost $C$ are expressed in the following formula:

$$P = \frac{10^{12}[((L - 7)(T)(WF))/(32{,}000)(36 - 7))]^{i}}{t_{\mathrm{CPU}} + t_{\mathrm{I/O}}}$$

where

$$t_{\mathrm{CPU}} = 10^{4}[C_1A_{F1} + C_2A_{F2} + C_3M + C_4D + C_5\mu]$$

$$\begin{aligned} t_{\mathrm{I/O}} &= p \times OL_1 \\ &\quad \times 10^{6}[(W_{I1} \times B \times (1/\mathrm{K}_{I1})) \\ &\quad + (W_{O1} \times B(1/\mathrm{K}_{O1}))]R_1 \\ &\quad + (1 - p)OL_2 \times 10^{6}[(W_{I2} \times (1/\mathrm{K}_{I2})) \\ &\quad + (W_{O2} \times B \times (1/\mathrm{K}_{O1}))]R_2. \end{aligned}$$

Symbols used in these equations are defined in Table 1 for the variable attributes of each computing

**Table 1.** Definitions of Symbols in the P Formula: Variables—Attributes of Each Computing System

| | |
|---|---|
| $L$ = | word length (in bits) |
| $T$ = | total number of words in memory |
| $t_{\mathrm{CPU}}$ = | time for the CPU (central processing unit) to perform one million operations |
| $t_{\mathrm{I/O}}$ = | time the CPU stands idle waiting for I/O to take place while one million operations are performed |
| $A_{F1}$ = | time for the CPU to perform one fixed-point addition |
| $A_{F2}$ = | time for the CPU to perform one floating-point addition |
| $M$ = | time for the CPU to perform one multiply |
| $D$ = | time for the CPU to perform one divide |
| $\mu$ = | time for the CPU to perform one logic operation |
| $B$ = | number of characters in each word |
| $K_{I1}$ = | input transfer rate (chps) of primary I/O system |
| $K_{O1}$ = | output transfer rate (chps) of primary I/O system |
| $K_{I2}$ = | input transfer rate (chps) of secondary I/O system |
| $K_{O2}$ = | output transfer rate (chps) of secondary I/O system |
| $R_1$ = | 1 plus fraction of useful primary I/O time required for nonoverlap rewind time |
| $R_2$ = | same as $R_1$ for secondary I/O system |

**Table 2.** Definitions of Symbols in the *P* Formula: Semiconstant Factors

| Symbol | Description | Scientific Computation | Commercial Computation |
|---|---|---|---|
| $WF$ | Word factor: | | |
| | (a) fixed-word-length memory | 1 | 1 |
| | (b) variable-word-length memory | 2 | 2 |
| $C_1$ | Weighting factor representing percentage of fixed add operations: | | |
| | (a) computers without index registers or indirect addressing | 10 | 25 |
| | (b) computers with index registers or indirect addressing | 25 | 45 |
| $C_2$ | Weighting factor indicating percentage of floating additions | 10 | 0 |
| $C_3$ | Weighting factor indicating percentage of multiply operations | 6 | 1 |
| $C_4$ | Weighting factor indicating percentage of divide operations | 2 | 0 |
| $C_5$ | Weighting factor indicating percentage of logic operations | 72 | 74 |
| $P$ | Percentage of I/O using primary I/O system: | | |
| | (a) systems with only a primary I/O system | 1.0 | 1.0 |
| | (b) systems with primary and secondary I/O systems | Variable | Variable |
| $W_{I1}$ | Number of input words per million internal operations using primary I/O system: | | |
| | (a) magnetic tape I/O system | 20,000 | 100,000 |
| | (b) other I/O systems | 2,000 | 10,000 |
| $W_{O1}$ | Number of output words per million internal operations using primary I/O system | Same as for $W_{I1}$ | Same as for $W_{I1}$ |
| $W_{I2}/W_{O2}$ | Number of I/O words per million internal operations using secondary I/O systems | | |
| $OL_1$ | Overlap factor 1: fraction of primary I/O system time not overlapped with compute: | | |
| | (a) no overlap, no buffer | 1. | 1. |
| | (b) read or write with compute, single buffer | 0.85 | 0.85 |
| | (c) read, write, and compute; single buffer | 0.7 | 0.7 |
| | (d) multiple read, write, and compute; several buffers | 0.6 | 0.6 |
| | (e) multiple read, write, and compute with program interrupt; several buffers | 0.55 | 0.55 |
| $OL_2$ | Overlap factor 2: fraction of secondary I/O system time not overlapped with compute: | Same as for for $OL_1$ (a-e) | Same as for $OL_1$ (a-e) |
| $i$ | Exponential memory weighting factor | 0.5 | 0.333 |

system and in Table 2 for semiconstant factors. The factor 32,000 (36 − 7) in the numerator reflects the need to evaluate P relative to a standard memory size, chosen here to be 32,000 36 bit words with the − 7 reflecting a penalty for short word lengths.

As indicated in Table 2, *P* can be computed for both commercial and scientific applications. The results for the commercial calculation are very similar to those for the scientific calculation and therefore are omitted in Table 3. The calculation of *P* also omits all software considerations, thus allowing comparisons to be made on hardware developments alone.

The value of *C* is arrived at by taking the cost of the computer in terms of its lease price per month and dividing that into the number of useful seconds in a month. Table 3 contains the values of computing power, cost, and date of introduction for a representative sample of computers introduced over the period 1963–1971.

The values of *P* and *C* shown in Table 3 are average numbers for one configuration of each machine listed. They should not be taken as "measures" for any machine, as there are thousands of combinations possible. The major use of these figures is not to compare computers but to observe changes in the level of technology and economies of scale. The relative values of $P$ and $C$ for any two computers should not be taken to mean that one is "better" than another.

**Computer Performance Over the Years.** A regression technique can be used to determine cost as a function of power for any year. The graph of the regression equation (Fig. 1) depicts the technology available in any given year per unit of cost.

The regression equation has the form

$$\ln(C) = \alpha_0 + \alpha_1 \ln(P) + \beta_1 Z_{63} + \beta_2 Z_{64} + \beta_3 Z_{65} + \beta_4 Z_{66} + \beta_5 Z_{67} + \beta_6 Z_{68} + \beta_7 Z_{69} + \beta_8 Z_{70} + \beta_9 Z_{71}$$

In this equation the $\alpha$'s and $\beta$'s represent the regression coefficients to be determined by the least squares analysis, and the $Z$'s are dummy variables (or shift parameters) for the different years considered (1963–1971). Natural logarithms are used for $P$ and $C$ because of the range of values for both variables.

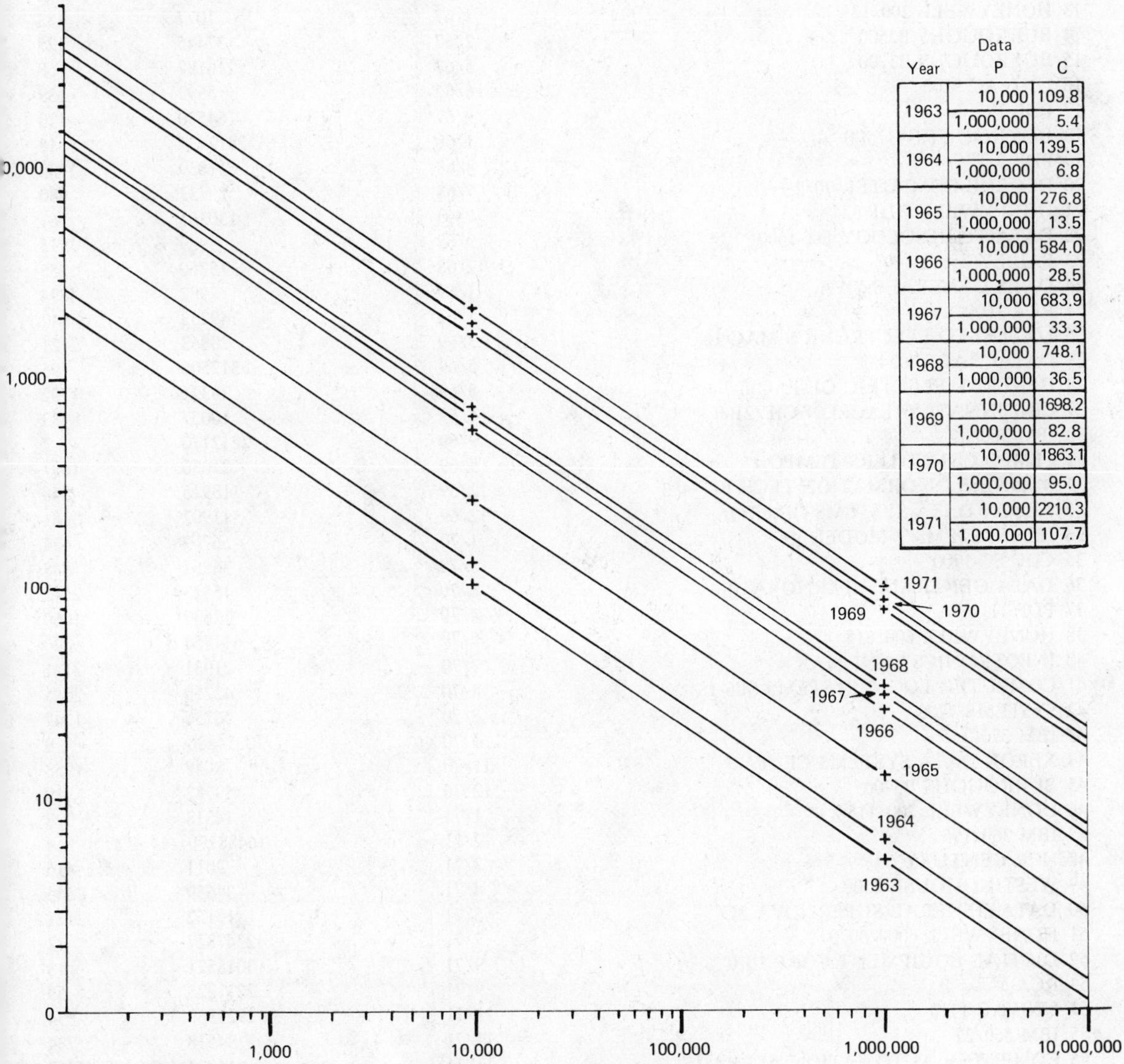


Data

| Year | P | C |
|---|---|---|
| 1963 | 10,000 | 109.8 |
| | 1,000,000 | 5.4 |
| 1964 | 10,000 | 139.5 |
| | 1,000,000 | 6.8 |
| 1965 | 10,000 | 276.8 |
| | 1,000,000 | 13.5 |
| 1966 | 10,000 | 584.0 |
| | 1,000,000 | 28.5 |
| 1967 | 10,000 | 683.9 |
| | 1,000,000 | 33.3 |
| 1968 | 10,000 | 748.1 |
| | 1,000,000 | 36.5 |
| 1969 | 10,000 | 1698.2 |
| | 1,000,000 | 82.8 |
| 1970 | 10,000 | 1863.1 |
| | 1,000,000 | 95.0 |
| 1971 | 10,000 | 2210.3 |
| | 1,000,000 | 107.7 |

**Fig. 1.** Graph of regression calculations for scientific computation.

**Table 3.** Values of *P* and *C* for Representative Computing Systems

| Number and Name | Date Introduced | Scientific *P* (ops/sec) | *C* (sec/$) |
|---|---|---|---|
| 1 IBM 7040 | 4/63 | 32912 | 45 |
| 2 PDP 5 | 9/63 | 18787 | 312 |
| 3 BURROUGHS 273 | 1/64 | 999 | 88 |
| 4 CDC 3200 | 5/64 | 275634 | 52 |
| 5 NCR 315-100 | 11/64 | 8700 | 156 |
| 6 IBM 360/20 | 1/65 | 8020 | 1039 |
| 7 NCR 315 RMC | 7/65 | 182545 | 62 |
| 8 IBM 1800 | 2/66 | 67472 | 480 |
| 9 UNIVAC 494 | 3/66 | 608537 | 21 |
| 10 HONEYWELL 110/G-115 | 4/66 | 1019 | 260 |
| 11 PDP 9 | 12/66 | 225598 | 1247 |
| 12 SDS SIGMA 7 | 12/66 | 787899 | 42 |
| 13 HONEYWELL 200/125 | 1/67 | 1077 | 183 |
| 14 BURROUGHS B2500 | 2/67 | 37445 | 125 |
| 15 BURROUGHS B3200 | 5/67 | 216187 | 68 |
| 16 UNIVAC 9200 | 6/67 | 5592 | 139 |
| 17 PDP 10 | 9/67 | 164530 | 170 |
| 18 BURROUGHS B7500 | 1/68 | 2812447 | 18 |
| 19 PDF 8/I | 4/68 | 11859 | 1732 |
| 20 DECADE COMPUTER 70/2 | 7/68 | 19437 | 480 |
| 21 HONEYWELL DDP-324 | 7/68 | 130361 | 61 |
| 22 DATA TECHNOLOGY DT-1600 | 9/68 | 989 | 3915 |
| 23 BAILEY 855/25 | 12/68 | 15260 | 255 |
| 24 DATA GENERAL NOVA | 1/69 | 7982 | 4894 |
| 25 RCA 1600 | 1/69 | 149233 | 312 |
| 26 LOCKHEED ELECTRONICS MAC-16 | 3/69 | 20863 | 2121 |
| 27 DATACRAFT 6024/3 | 5/69 | 312506 | 795 |
| 28 GENERAL ELECTRIC GE-PAC30-2 | 5/69 | 38321 | 1792 |
| 29 CINCINNATI MILACRON CIP/2100 | 6/69 | 10057 | 8483 |
| 30 IBM 360/85 | 9/69 | 2212170 | 7 |
| 31 TEMPO COMPUTERS TEMPO I | 9/69 | 21056 | 1697 |
| 32 BUSINESS INFORMATION TECH BIT-483 | 12/69 | 118915 | 848 |
| 33 XEROX DATA SYSTEMS OF CF 16 | 12/69 | 11902 | 3181 |
| 34 IBM SYSTEMS/3 MODEL 10 | 1/70 | 6769 | 624 |
| 35 CDC SC-1700 | 3/70 | 36567 | 848 |
| 36 DATA GENERAL SUPERNOVA | 4/70 | 15513 | 2545 |
| 37 PDP 11 | 4/70 | 12697 | 1060 |
| 38 HONEYWELL 600/615 | 6/70 | 411354 | 20 |
| 40 INFOTRONICS MINI/MAX | 7/70 | 21931 | 2121 |
| 41 COMPUTER LOGIC SYSTEMS SLS-18 | 8/70 | 42250 | 2545 |
| 42 SYSTEMS 7200 | 8/70 | 56236 | 1247 |
| 43 IBM 370/165 | 8/70 | 20054886 | 9 |
| 44 XEROX DATA SYSTEMS CF-16A | 11/70 | 8648 | 1958 |
| 45 BURROUGHS B5700 | 12/70 | 159782 | 19 |
| 46 HONEYWELL 200/115-2 | 1/71 | 14318 | 328 |
| 47 IBM 360/195 | 2/71 | 16488290 | 4 |
| 48 NCR CENTURY 50 | 3/71 | 2011 | 416 |
| 49 WESTINGHOUSE 2500 | 4/71 | 34659 | 2545 |
| 50 DATA GENERAL SUPERNOVA SC | 5/71 | 16152 | 2121 |
| 51 HONEYWELL 6000/6070 | 7/71 | 2347827 | 12 |
| 52 DIGITAL EQUIPMENT CORP 1070 | 9/71 | 3018521 | 18 |
| 53 RCA 6 | 9/71 | 2231223 | 59 |
| 54 UNIVAC 1110 | 11/71 | 2921860 | 14 |
| 55 IBM 360/22 | 11/71 | 34518 | 734 |
| 56 COMPUTER AUTOMATION ALPHA-16 | 11/71 | 14224 | 6362 |
| 57 CDC CYBER 70 MODEL 76 | 12/71 | 6913355 | 3 |

Data

| Year | %Change |
| --- | --- |
| 63-64 | 27.0 |
| 64-65 | 98.8 |
| 65-66 | 111.0 |
| 66-67 | 17.1 |
| 67-68 | 8.6 |
| 68-69 | 127.0 |
| 69-70 | 9.7 |
| 70-71 | 18.6 |

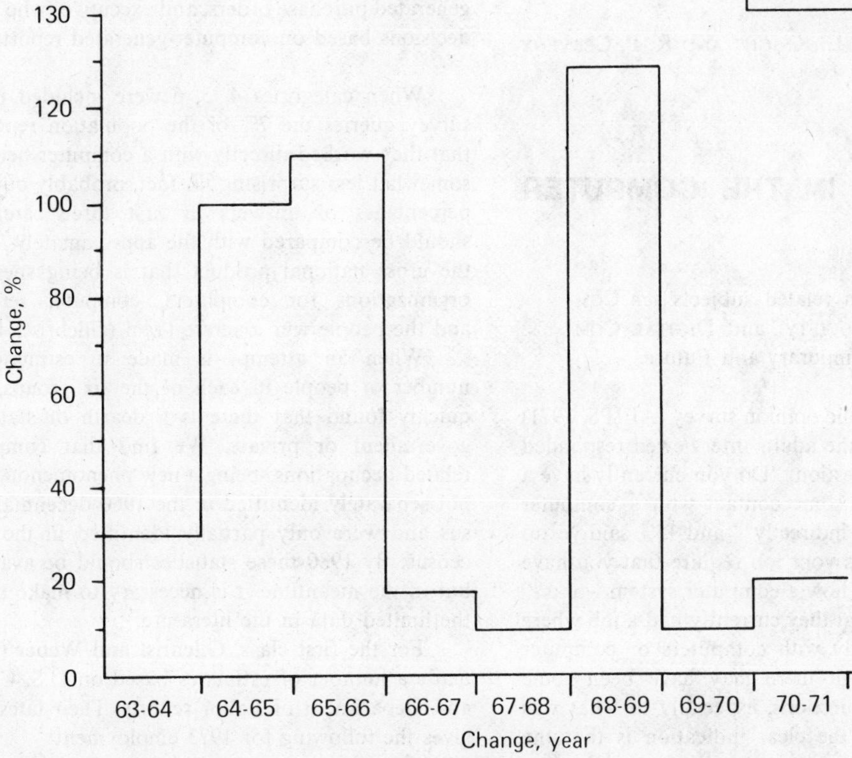


**Fig. 2.** Average yearly shift of the technology curve: power $P$ change for constant cost $C$.

Using the data of Table 3 and other data not shown, the coefficients in the preceding equation can be calculated. The results are shown in Fig. 1 and lead to two observations: (1) Computer technology, in terms of how much computing power one may buy per dollar cost, has been improving on a yearly basis since 1963 (Fig. 2 illustrates the yearly change); (2) economies of scale, as predicted by Grosch's law, are still obtainable.

The regression equation given above may be used to test Grosch's law for the years 1963 through 1971. Rewriting the equation,

$$C = K \cdot P^{\alpha_1} \quad \text{or} \quad \text{Cost} = \frac{1}{C} = \left(\frac{1}{K}\right) P^{-\alpha_1}$$

where $K$ is a constant that represents a combination of $\alpha_0$ and the yearly shift parameters. Grosch's law predicts that computing power increases as a function of cost squared, so that for twice the cost, one should have four times as much computing power.

The actual $\alpha_1$ used in Fig. 1 is $\alpha_1 = -0.656$. Grosch's law predicts $-\alpha_1 = 0.5$, so the agreement is quite good.

REFERENCES

1968. Knight, K. E. "Evolving Computer Performance 1963–1967," *Datamation*, Vol. 14, No. 1 (January), pp. 31–35.

1972. Knight, K. E. "Application of Technological Forecasting to the Computer Industry," in J. R. Bright and M. F. Schoeman (Eds.), *A Guide to Practical Technological Forecasting*. Englewood Cliffs, N.J.: Prentice-Hall, pp. 377–403.

K. E. KNIGHT AND R. P. CERVENY

# PERSONNEL IN THE COMPUTER FIELD

For articles on related subjects *see* COMPUTERS AND SOCIETY; and DIGITAL COMPUTERS: Contemporary and Future.

A national public opinion survey (AFIPS, 1971) found that 30% of the adults interviewed responded positively to the question, "Do you currently have a job which requires some contact with a computer—either directly or indirectly?" and 15% said yes to the question: "Does your job require that you have some knowledge of how a computer system works?" Another 7% said that they currently had a job where they worked directly with computers or computer equipment. Although there may have been some ambiguity in the questions, especially in what was meant by *directly*, the clear indication is that the computer is being used by, or in some way affecting, a significant percentage of the American labor force.

Those in the labor force who are affected by computers or who have jobs created by the computer may be divided into the following broad classes:

1. Those directly concerned with the operation of computers and associated equipment (e.g., programmers, systems analysts, computer operators, and key punch operators).
2. Those involved directly with providing management and administrative support to computer facilities (e.g., managers, tape librarians, receptionists, and clerical employees).
3. Those involved in the manufacture, sales, and servicing of computers.
4. Those who use computers as an integral part of their jobs in other disciplines (e.g., engineers, accountants, and scientists).
5. Those who rely on computers in order to perform their job, but who only use them in particular limited ways (e.g., stock brokers using a quotation system, airline reservation clerks, and retail clerks using point-of-sale terminals connected to a computer).
6. Those who use the output of computers (e.g., accountants who are given computer-produced financial statements, buyers who receive computer-generated purchase orders, and executives who make decisions based on computer-generated reports).

When categories 4, 5, 6 were included in the survey queries the 7% of the population reporting that they worked directly with a computer becomes somewhat less surprising. In fact, probably only the percentages of answers in first three categories should be compared with the approximately 2% of the gross national product that is being spent by organizations for computers, computer services, and the people who operate them (Gilchrist, 1973).

When an attempt is made to estimate the number of people in each of the six groups, it is quickly found that there is a dearth of statistics, government or private. We find that computer-related occupations, being a new phenomenon, were not separately identified in the 1960 decennial census and were only partially identified in the 1970 census. By 1980 these statistics should be available but in the meantime it is necessary to make use of the limited data in the literature.

For the first class, Gilchrist and Weber (1974) made a number of estimates based on U.S. Census and Department of Labor reports. Their latest one gives the following for 1973 employment:

| | |
|---|---|
| Keypunch Operator | 395,000 |
| Computer Operator | 165,000 |
| Programmer | 100,000 |
| Systems Analyst | 140,000 |

These estimates are lower than earlier ones and considerably less than projections made in the mid-1960s. Several factors may contribute to this, such as the greater emphasis on cost control by computer users, the expanded use of proprietary software, and the more automated operation of the larger computer systems. In addition, it should be remembered that employees involved on a part-time basis in any of the four occupations were probably not counted.

Estimating the number of individuals in the second class is difficult because of the wide variety of job definitions used in computer installations and in many cases the problem of deciding whether a support position is attributable solely to the computer facility or should be divided between it and other areas. A rough idea of the size of the group can, however, be seen from a 1972 salary survey conducted by *Infosystems Magazine*, which found that for the average computer installation, the total of all employees engaged in EDP was 4.4 times the number of programmers and systems analysts. Using this result in conjunction with the numbers estimated for the first class gives a rough estimate of 500,000 people providing direct management and administrative support to computer facilities.

Although IBM and a few other large companies are best known to the public for the manufacture, sales, and servicing of computers, there are actually many hundreds of companies in the industry. The U.S. Department of Labor collects data on employment by industry, and for the last few years has been reporting just under 200,000 employees in SIC code 3573 (Electronic Computing Equipment). However, inspection of the annual reports of major companies indicates that the number of domestic employees in data processing manufacture, sales, and servicing is more probably in the range of 300,000 to 400,000. (It should be noted that this does not include employees of the companies' overseas operations, nor does it include those employed in non-data processing product lines.)

The employment estimate for the first three classes is about 1.5 million people directly involved with computers. This total represents 2% of all United States employment, which approximately corresponds to the portion of the gross national product being spent on the purchase and use of computers.

No estimates are available for the number of individuals in the remaining three classes, but probably they outnumber considerably those in the first three. They may even approach the 30% figure found by the survey quoted earlier. Considering the importance of knowledge in our post-industrial society, this high percentage should not be surprising. In fact, employment will probably continue to increase as the computer becomes an even more ubiquitous tool.

REFERENCES

1971. AFIPS. "A National Survey of the Public's Attitudes Toward Computers." Joint Project of the American Federation of Information Processing Societies and *Time Magazine*. Montvale, N.J.: AFIPS Press.

1973. Gilchrist, B., and R. E. Weber (Eds.). *The State of the Computer Industry in the United States*. Montvale, N.J.: AFIPS Press.

1974. Weber, R. E., and B. Gilchrist. *Numerical Bias in the 1970 U.S. Census Data on Computer Occupations.* Montvale, N.J.: AFIPS Press.

B. GILCHRIST

## PERT/CPM

For article on related subject *see* PLANNING, COMPUTER APPLICATIONS IN.

The development of project management techniques using network methods, of which PERT (project evaluation and review technique) and CPM (critical path method) are the most widely known, was undertaken in the late 1950s by several independent groups working on different types of projects. The most widely publicized of these efforts was the use of PERT in conjunction with the design of the Polaris submarine system. It was credited with saving substantial time and cost on Polaris, which caused its use to be made mandatory on all significant development projects undertaken for and by the U.S. Department of Defense. Knowledge of this and other successful applications soon became widespread, and many variants, additional features, and computerized aids were developed and publicized. As a result, project management techniques have become the most extensively used of the quantitative tools for management, with the possible exception of linear programming.

Most uses of these techniques are in the defense and construction industries, although they are suitable for any situation where:

The *project* consists of a collection of *activities* or tasks.

The activities can be started and stopped independently of each other (in contrast to a sequential flow of processing), even if the resources employed on the various activities are not independent.

Precedence relationships exist which preclude

the start of certain activities until others are complete (e.g., surfacing a road must be preceded by the laying of the road bed).

Specific and general examples of successful use include:

Apollo mission development and countdown procedures.
Construction projects such as a building.
Procedures for closing accounts in a bank or firm (e.g., payroll).
Ship or aircraft repair projects.
Implementation of a computer system, from ordering and site preparation through installation and checkout.

The techniques can be used in both planning and control of projects. *Planning* in this context consists of the overall layout of the project, with rough estimation of the time and resources required, and the detailed scheduling of the timing and order of activities. In short, it concerns the set of decisions made before the start of the project. By contrast, *control* takes place during the project. As actual resource use and completion times are obtained, project management techniques can be used to reallocate resources according to the revised criticality ratings of activities.

**Computation of a Critical Path.** All variants of the project management technique compute what is called a "critical path." Since a project consists of an ordered set of independent activities, it can be represented as a network (Fig. 1), where activities are shown as branches connected at nodes to immediately preceding and immediately following activities. (Other conventions are possible, but the idea of a network remains.)

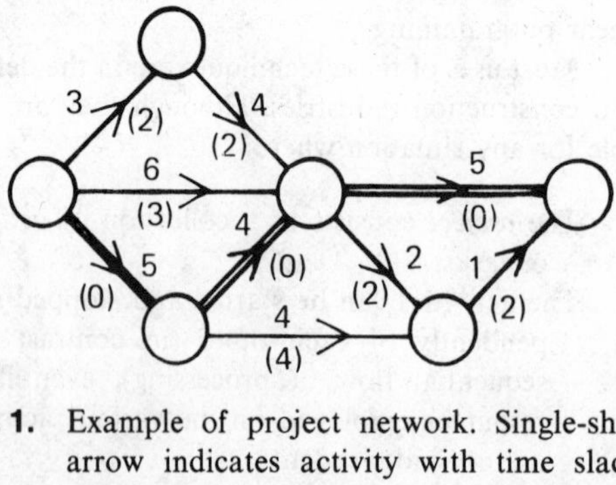


**Fig. 1.** Example of project network. Single-shaft arrow indicates activity with time slack; double-shaft arrow represents critical path.

A *path* through the network is any set of successive activities which goes from the beginning to the end of the project. Associated with each activity in the network is a single number that best estimates the time which that activity will consume; differences in the way this number is obtained distinguish the major variants of the technique. A *critical path*, then, is one whose sum of activity times is longer than that for any other path through the network (multiple critical paths with equal total times are, of course, possible). This path is important because, if everything goes according to schedule, its length gives the shortest possible completion time of the overall project.

In addition, a *slack time* can be associated with each activity in the project. This is the difference between the latest possible completion time of each activity which will not delay the completion of the overall project, and the earliest possible completion time, based on all predecessor activities. Activities on a critical path have zero slack time, and conversely, activities with zero slack time are on a critical path.

The critical path and associated slack times for a project are found by simply working forward through the network, computing the earliest possible completion time for each activity, until the earliest possible completion time for the total project is found. Then, by working backward through the network, the latest completion time for each activity is found, the slack time computed, and the critical path identified.

This procedure is so straightforward that it is clearly easily programmable for a computer. For example, the complete data input, computation, and output of results can be done in less than 40 Fortran statements. Not surprisingly, there is a wide proliferation of programs that perform this computation, many with special features tailored to a specific industry or type of problem. Nearly every commercial time-sharing system or service bureau has such software available for use by its customers.

**PERT Assumptions.** The variant of the technique described above, which carries the name PERT, was first used in conjunction with the Polaris systems development cited earlier. Because of imperfect knowledge of the times of individual development activities, it is felt necessary to have a means to incorporate uncertainty in the estimation of such times. To do this, a three-point estimate of optimistic, pessimistic, and most likely completion times is obtained for each activity. These are used to estimate the mean and standard deviation of each activity time. The means are in turn used to find the critical path and slack times, as described in the preceding section, implying that a given activity is or is not critical. Then continuing on the assumption that activities are independent, the estimates of individual activity standard deviation are used to estimate the standard deviation of completion time for the whole project.

It seems clear that only a few additional program statements are required to convert a basic critical-path program into one that computes the results based on the foregoing assumptions. To relax the assumptions about criticality and independence requires a much more sophisticated code. To date, most practical success has been obtained by using Monte Carlo simulation to obtain the mean and variance of total project time as well as a "probability of criticality" for each activity. Research continues into the development of computational methods for relaxing these assumptions without resorting to expensive simulation.

**CPM Assumptions.** The variant known as CPM was developed for the construction industry, where the times for each activity are assumed to be perfectly known, but controllable within limits depending on the amount of additional effort to be expended. Computation typically proceeds by first assuming a nominal time for each activity, and then using this to find a critical path in the normal manner. Activities on the critical path become candidates for "crashing," i.e., for a reduction in their times by payment of a premium for early completion. By successively relaxing activities on the critical path, a curve showing total project cost versus time to completion can be obtained. These computations can be done using a simple embellishment of the basic critical-path program. If, in addition, the value of the project as a function of its completion time is known, the mix of crash and normal activity times which best balances the crash-cost premiums against the overall value of the project can be found.

### Other Major Variants

Costing Methods (e.g., PERT/COST). The structure provided by the network representation of the project is used as a framework for collecting and allocating project cost, replacing standard functional allocation schemes. This provides a more appropriate means for aggregating the individual costs of project activities. Software that performs this costing in conjunction with a project network is available, but is more limited than the critical-path computations themselves. Such methods are used in surprisingly few projects, probably because of a reluctance to abandon standard cost-accounting methods, however inappropriate.

Resource Allocation. The assumption of unlimited resources available when necessary is replaced by an assumption of limited resources of various sorts (e.g., computer time, carpenters, bulldozers). The problem then becomes one not only of scheduling activities to avoid delaying the overall project, but also of insuring that the scarce resources are available when necessary. This becomes particularly interesting in the so-called *multiship, multishop* problem, where several projects compete simultaneously for the same resources. Some computer codes available for this purpose are usually based on heuristic methods of optimization.

Reference

1969. Wiest, J. D, and F. K. Levy. *A Management Guide to PERT/CPM*. Englewood Cliffs, N. J.: Prentice-Hall.

E. G. Hurst, Jr.

## PHYSICAL UNIT. *See* Logical and Physical Units.

## PICTURE PROCESSING. *See* Image and Picture Processing.

## PICTURES, BASIC STRUCTURE

For articles on related subjects *see* Computer Graphics; Image and Picture Processing; and Pattern Recognition.

The basic structure of any photograph or reproduced picture consists of small areas, known as picture elements, of light, shade, and possibly color. The amount of detail in the picture depends on the size and number of elements making up the picture. For fine detail, the picture elements should be small and numerous, as in an ordinary photograph, and should not be individually visible except on very close inspection. However, if the picture elements are few and large, they will show quite plainly, as they do in photographs reproduced in newspapers. The number and size of picture elements required for satisfactory visual representation depend upon two factors: the amount of detail desired and the distance at which the picture is to be viewed.

All images to be processed by a computer may be divided into two categories: those made up solely of lines and curves, such as engineering drawings (so-called line drawings); and those, such as photographs, that include areas of tone (often called halftone or gray scale pictures). Images of the first category, in which there is no shading of the lines and curves, can be read by devices such as curve followers and can be subsequently reproduced by any standard plotting device. Images of the second category, including line drawings in which lines can be drawn with varying intensity, can only be recognized or reproduced by devices that not only distinguish between white and black, but also recognize *shades* of black and white. Therefore, general purpose computer image-input devices must have the ability to distinguish multiple levels of gray and to convert ("digitize") them into digital representations; similarly, computer image-output devices must be able to distinguish these levels of gray, for example, by representing picture elements by dots of different size or by dots of varying darkness (or color).

It is obviously more convenient to have a computer use an input device to "read" a picture directly and then to analyze it instead of first having the picture digitized off-line and then using the computer only for analysis. To accomplish such computer-controlled input, such devices must incorporate some kind of sophisticated scanning (and possibly even recognition) technique for the digital representation and analysis of the picture. A common technique is to employ a light-sensitive receiver like a photo-multiplier tube or photo diode to make an enumerative raster scan for conversion of the picture into its digital representation. The term *raster* can be defined as two mutually perpendicular sets of parallel lines, with all lines in each set drawn at the same distance from one another. Each rectangular area of the raster represents one picture element. A raster of reasonable size often contains as many as several hundred thousand picture points (for example, 512×512). The density of the raster cross lines is usually called its *resolution*. The optical beam of the raster scan proceeds sequentially from one picture element to another, normally horizontally across the picture and then from top to bottom as in a TV raster deflection. The scan produces a large matrix of digitized gray values. For a single picture such a matrix may require as many as one million bits of storage. To proceed from the scan to recognition of the picture then requires analysis of these gray values. Examples of devices that use a raster scan are fingerprint readers and automatic signature verification terminals, both of which, however, are still in the research and development stage.

Raster scan techniques are also widely used by computer output devices such as electrostatic printer/plotter systems, which print one or more raster lines at a time and advance the paper, and some COM (computer output on microfilm) systems. Some systems can plot points at arbitrary places in the raster, not just contiguous ones, and thus do not use a raster scan; they move the electron beam from one point in the raster to another and can draw the vector between the two points under program control ("random" positioning.) These can be used to "print" solid areas by adjoining many vectors to achieve a cross-hatched effect.

In color graphic display systems, raster or random positioning techniques are also used. Each picture element is represented not just by a single value but by an array of values for the different colors.

J. NECAS

# PINGPONG

For article on related subject *see* MEMORY: Auxiliary.
For article on related term *see* FILES.

The term "pingpong" means to alternate two or more storage devices (e.g., magnetic tape drives) so that processing may take place on a virtually endless set of files. For example, a program may operate on a file of a dozen reels of tape, but the program, when executed, requires a computer with only two tape drives. Reel 1 is mounted on drive A, and reel 2 on drive B. The end-of-file signal on drive A causes the program to switch to drive B, at which time the console operator can demount reel 1 and mount reel 3 on drive A. This procedure continues, "pingponging" the two drives, until all 12 reels have been processed.

F. GRUENBERGER

# PLANNING, COMPUTER APPLICATIONS IN

For articles on related subjects *see* Administrative-Business Applications; PERT/CPM; Planning Systems, Characteristics of; and Statistical Applications.

The variety of descriptive and normative works published on the topic of planning in the past 50 years offer a selection of definitions for this activity (see Sackman and Citrenbaum, 1972). A set of decisions common to all these definitions provides for the decision maker a procedural base for tentatively allocating overall resources to his possible alternative activities in the future. These definitions range over a variety of organization types in which the decision-making takes place at different levels. For this reason, planning is a difficult procedure to characterize by a single example.

However, the use of computers in planning has enhanced the ability to make more complex decisions rapidly. In order to describe this application of data processing, as well as to indicate the diversity of levels at which planning takes place, this article presents several examples of popular uses of the computer in planning.

Production and Operations Planning. These types of planning generally tend to be focused on one narrow function or operation in the enterprise, whether it is a manufacturing or service firm, an educational institution, or a government organization. The most common example is the planning and scheduling of the production line in a factory, where data consists of the number of jobs to be done, their completion due dates, available resources of equipment and workers, and other production factors, all of which are combined to plan a proposed factory schedule. On the other hand, the scheduling of classes in a school, the scheduling of the tasks in a health-care facility, and even the choice of a call schedule for salesmen can be regarded strictly as operations planning. Planning of this sort is characterized by the relatively low level in the organization at which it takes place, and by the fact that it is relatively frequently performed. For these reasons, operations planning has adapted somewhat sooner to computerization than have the examples given later.

Still, in spite of the potential benefits made possible by the frequency of performance, operations planning includes a large number of individual choices that must be made and which are of relatively low financial importance, and which compete with satisfactory performance in decision making by humans without computers. These characteristics mean that computer methods, particularly those that seek exact optimal solutions, are not yet economical in all applications. In spite of this, a number of computer software manufacturers and service bureaus offer packages that attempt to solve such problems either approximately or exactly. Some of these have proved quite successful. Many of the early business applications of the first-generation scientific computers were in this area.

Project Planning. This form of planning is oriented toward a specific project rather than a continuing operation. Formal project planning first gained prominence during the development of the Polaris submarine system, in which it was necessary to take into account the interrelationships among new engineering and scientific developments, each having uncertain costs and times to completion. A scheme was developed for deciding what jobs were critical and how long the total project would take. Because of its well-publicized success in saving both time and money, the technique soon became adopted for development projects in the U.S. Department of Defense.

Among the methods for dealing with project scheduling problems are the CPM (critical path method) and PERT (program evaluation and review technique). While these techniques are used only once for planning every project (although they are often used as a control measure throughout the project), and while every project has unique features, there are enough characteristics in common in specifying structure, processing times, and costs for a given project so that standardized computer packages can be used to good advantage. Many such packages are now available, from simple programs handling small problems on time-sharing systems through very sophisticated systems containing a variety of options which can solve mammoth problems.

Financial Planning. A growing area of planning made popular largely by the advent of computer systems is the area of financial planning. Although financial planning itself is not new, the ability to examine quickly the probable financial consequences of a number of alternatives has become possible because of the availability of specially designed computer systems. As an example, consider the preparation of the projected cash-flow statements of a firm. Forecasts of sales and costs are combined with the likely values of delays and other internal factors to produce probable cash-flow summaries under various sets of assumptions. A number of firms have custom-built systems for their internal financial planning needs. There also exist several general-purpose programs or sets of programs, developed for the most part by large commercial banks, which are available on time-sharing systems. These programs tend to have built in the structure of the standard financial reports, and require only that detailed projections and historical data specific to the individual firm be input.

STRATEGIC PLANNING. Strategic planning is the term commonly given to consideration of high-level, one-of-a-kind, long-term, complex decisions about different alternate courses of action which face the entire enterprise. Because of its characteristics, it is not nearly so amenable to computerized analysis as are lower-level forms of planning. In the past, the cost of programming a model structure unique to the strategic decision has in most cases far exceeded the benefits derived. However, with the rise in the economic consequences of the strategic decisions being made, and the enhanced ease of programming and analysis of such decisions brought about by the development of specially designed planning systems, the computer is becoming increasingly useful and used in the strategic planning area.

**Common Features of Planning Applications.** A variety of different tools used for planning, in addition to those named above, emphasize application areas rather than methods (see References). Although widely varying in both level and context of application, planning decisions have several features in common which distinguish them from other types of decisions:

1. The need to take an overall view of whatever entity is under consideration.
2. A large number of interrelated decisions.
3. A relatively long period of time during which the decisions are effective.
4. A context in which changing behavior over time is often important.
5. Less frequent processing of the set of decisions.

These five characteristics of planning decisions have tended to prevent computers supplanting humans, especially for operating decisions made in the same environment. They also tend to make use of computers relatively more difficult.

**Advantages of Computers in Planning.** Despite the handicaps introduced by the preceding five factors, computers have also brought certain advantages to planning applications. Many of these are similar to the advantages brought by computerization of decision processes in general, although some are unique to planning. The most important advantages include:

1. *The speed at which results can be obtained.* Reports can be obtained in seconds or minutes rather than in days.

2. *The increased number of iterations for a given planning cycle.* Multiple passes through a plan can be made, a greater selection of parameter values can be explored, and various facets of the plan can be highlighted during different phases of planning.

3. *Representation of greater complexity and therefore realism.* This enhanced realism can take two forms:
   (a) Problems of a larger size can be handled.
   (b) More complex, and therefore realistic, formulas for representing relationships in the system can be manipulated.

4. *The use of more sophisticated analysis techniques* such as optimization, risk analysis, multivariate sensitivity analysis, and others to examine the plan.

5. *The use of the computer for tedious tasks.* This can free the user for other nonrepetitive tasks which he performs better than the computer. It may permit him to explore nonquantitative facets of the plan for which he would not have had the time before.

6. *The discipline enforced.* Having to model the structure of the entity being planned, and having to gather data complete enough to be analyzed by the system can force an organized look at the problem which may help to drive out fuzzy thinking.

**Directions for Future Applications.** All the elements mentioned in the following areas of probable growth are available to a limited extent today, but each should assume even more importance as improved planning systems are developed.

1. Planning systems will be increasingly capable of solving higher level unstructured planning problems. This means that:
   (a) Larger and more complex problem structures will be representable.
   (b) The larger volume of data necessary for predicting outcomes will be accessible.
   (c) The two foregoing steps will become economical.

2. The user of the plan will be increasingly able to deal directly with the planning system rather than through an intermediary. This is happening because:

(a) The capability for writing sophisticated models and manipulating them in natural languages will give the user the ability to model his own problem, rather than being bound by a ready-made model whose structure does not represent the entity being planned.

(b) The increasing availability of interactive computer systems will permit the user of plans to interact directly with the planning system at his normal thinking speed, rather than at a speed set by the system.

3. The plan will be immediately usable for control of the plan, with no additional modeling effort. The quicker availability of real data directly accessible by the planning system itself will mean that the plans can be monitored by the system and the user signaled when there appears to be a problem. This sort of control is already readily available for chemical processes and other production operations, and will be used increasingly for higher planning levels and contexts.

REFERENCES

1971. Benton, William K. *The Use of the Computer in Planning*. Reading, Mass.: Addison-Wesley.

1972. Sackman, Harold, and Ronald L. Citrenbaum (Eds.). *Online Planning*. Englewood Cliffs, N.J.: Prentice-Hall.

E. G. HURST, JR.

## PLANNING SYSTEMS, CHARACTERISTICS OF

For articles on related subjects *see* PLANNING, COMPUTER APPLICATIONS IN; and REAL TIME APPLICATIONS.
For article on related term *see* MONTE CARLO METHOD.

A planning system is a special-purpose, problem-oriented software system intended for the easy representation and manipulation of models and data appropriate to strategic planning decisions. These systems are characterized by three mandatory features and two optional ones.

### Mandatory Features

SPECIAL MODEL BUILDING LANGUAGE. This implies the ability to tailor-make the model for the user's own problem, rather than being forced to use a fixed and perhaps inappropriate model structure. Often, the modeling language is itself one of the procedural formula-translation languages, such as Fortran or Basic, although a trend toward more natural and declarative modeling languages is evident.

ANALYSIS CAPABILITIES. These consist of a set of analysis tools that can be used to manipulate the data and model. The contents of the set varies considerably from system to system. Among the most common types are:

(a) *Data analysis*. The ability to input historical data and manipulate it into a forecast suitable for direct input into the model.

(b) *Case analysis*. The ability to evaluate outcomes for a given set of input values.

(c) *Parametric (what if . . . ) analysis*. The ability to vary a set of input values systematically and observe the effect on the outcomes.

(d) *Sensitivity analysis*. The ability to determine the relative effect on the outcomes of changes in the values of the input variables.

(e) *Break-even (how get . . . ) analysis*. The ability to find the value of an input variable that yields a desired outcome (the opposite of parametric analysis).

(f) *Risk analysis*. The ability to determine the effect on the potential outcomes of randomness in the input variables, usually by Monte Carlo simulation.

(g) *Optimization*. The ability to seek the values of the controllable input variables which yield a "best" value of one of the outcomes.

(h) *Comparison*. The ability to compare the results of two or more runs with different assumptions, or to compare predicted with actual results.

(i) *Command sequences*. The ability to write, execute, and save for later use a regularly executed series of analysis and report commands.

REPORT GENERATION AND CHANGE. To accompany his tailor-made model, the user should be able to custom-design his reports. This ability may range from controlling only the variables that appear in a standard report format all the way to a complete design of report content, line spacing, column spac-

**Table 1.** Summary of Some Planning Systems.

| IDENTIFICATION | | MODELING CHARACTERISTICS | | | |
|---|---|---|---|---|---|
| Name | Supplier[1] | Mode[3] | Model Language | Automatic Multiperiod? | Financial Function[3] |
| BPL (business planning language) | International Time Sharing Jonathan Industrex Chaska, Minn. 55318 | T | Special report-oriented | Y | P,D,A |
| BUDPLAN (budgets and plans generator) | IBM (Various locations) | B,R | Special, interface with PL/1 | Y | P,D,A,C,O |
| DYLAN (dynamic language) | University of Toronto Computer Systems Research Group Toronto 5, Canada | T | PL/1 | Y | P,A |
| EA1000 | Ebeling Associates, Inc. 2063 Coolidge Place Schenectady, N.Y. 12309 | T | Basic | N | N |
| FAL (financial analysis language) | G.E. Information Services (various locations) | T | Fortran with Basic-like variables | Y | P,D,A,C |
| Foresight | Foresight Systems, Inc. 270 Madison Avenue New York, N.Y. 10016 | T,B | Report-oriented | Y | P,D,A,C,O |
| FP/70 (financial planning for the 1970s) | Bonner and Moore (various locations) | B,R | Card/form oriented, Fortran linkable | Y | P,D,A,C,O |
| GPOS (general-purpose operating system) | On-Line Decisions, Inc. 20 N. Wacker Dr. Chicago, Ill. 60606 | T,B,R | Fortran with extensive subroutines | Y | P,F,D,A,C,O |
| IPSY (interactive planning system) | Interactive Planning Systems, Inc. 18 W. 44th Street New York, N.Y. 10036 | T,B | Special highly declarative | Y | D,A,C,O |
| Oracle | Time-Sharing, Ltd. 179-193 Portland St. London WIN STB England | T,B,R | Special Fortran-like | Y | P,D,A,C |
| PA300 | GE Information Services (various locations) | T | Basic | N | N |

| ANALYSIS OPTIONS[4] | | | | | | | | REPORT OPTIONS | | | |
|---|---|---|---|---|---|---|---|---|---|---|---|
| Data[5,6] | Parametric[7] | Sensitivity | Breakeven | Risk | Optimization | Comparison | Command Sequences | Std. default rept.? | Rept.[8] Languages | Graphic[6,9] Capabilities | Other Features |
| N | N | I | I | N | I | N | Y | Y | Y | O | Model editor; interface with Fortran + Basic |
| W;R | Y | Y | N | N | N | N | Y | Y | M | W;V,T | Easy file storage and maintenance |
| N | Y | N | Y | Y | Y | N | Y | Y | N | N | |
| W;R | 4 | Y | N | Y | 10 | N | Y | Y | N | W;P | Process flow diagrams; extensive data diagnostics; convenient probability specifications |
| N | N | N | N | N | N | N | N | N | M | N | |
| W;R,E | N | N | N | N | N | N | Y | N | M | N | |
| W;R | Y | Y | N | N | N | N | Y | N | Y | N | Extensive model diagnostics |
| W;R,E | 1 | Y | Y | N | I | N | Y | N | Y | W;V,T | Extensive consulting service available |
| W;R,A | N | Y | Y | N | N | Y | Y | Y | Y | W;V,T | Dimensional checking in model; extensive tracing; simple type ahead |
| O;R,E, B | 1 | Y | Y | N | N | N | Y | Y | Y | O;V,T | Scrambling for security; easy results transfer between models |
| N | Y | N | N | Y | Y | N | N | Y | S | W;P | Convenient probability specifications |

**Table 1.** (Continued)

| IDENTIFICATION | | | MODELING CHARACTERISTICS | | |
|---|---|---|---|---|---|
| Name | Supplier[1] | Mode[3] | Model Language | Automatic Multiperiod? | Financial Function[3] |
| Plato (planning tools) | IBM (various locations) | B | PL/I | Y | F,A,C,O |
| Prophit II | SBC<br>600 Mamaroneck Ave.<br>Harrison, N.Y. 10528 | T | Report-oriented | Y | C |
| Prosper | ICL, Putney<br>London, SW1, England | R | Parametric input | Y | P,F,D,A,C |
| PSG II (planning systems generator) | IBM (various locations) | B | Fortran IV | Y | P,F,A,C,O |
| Sigma | GMD, D-5205<br>St. Augustin 1, Germany | B | Special | N | P,A |
| Stratplan | IBM (various locations) | T | Fortran-like, less procedural | Y | P,D,A,C,O |
| Supreme (système universel de prevision et de modelisation) | SIA<br>35 Boulevard Brune<br>Paris 14 France | T | Report-oriented, terse statements | Y | P,D,A,C,O |

*Explanatory Notes:*

1. Specific computers on which the system is available are not indicated, since this is both rapidly changeable as well as largely transparent to the user of a proprietary system. Likewise, cost figures are omitted because of their changeability and lack of comparability.
2. Modes of operation: T, time sharing; R, remote batch; B, batch.
3. Financial functions available in the modeling language: P, present value; F, compounded future value; D, discounted rate of return; A, accumulation over time; C, consolidation of results from several submodels; O, others (e.g., depreciation, ROI and other ratios, amortization and repayment schedules, cost allocation, loss carry-forward).
4. A response of "Y" indicates that the feature is available as one of the analysis system commands, and can be used on any appropriate variables after the model is built. "I" means that the feature is available as a special function within the modeling language, so that its use must be anticipated at model building time; use on a set of variables different from those originally anticipated requires modification of the model. "N" means that any use of such analysis must be built into the model in the modeling language itself. A numerical response in any column indicates the number of variables which can be simultaneously used in the analysis indicated.

| ANALYSIS OPTIONS[4] | | | | | | | | REPORT OPTIONS | | | |
|---|---|---|---|---|---|---|---|---|---|---|---|
| Data[5,6] | Parametric[7] | Sensitivity | Breakeven | Risk | Optimization | Comparison | Command Sequences | Std. default rept.? | Rept.[8] Languages | Graphic[6,9] Capabilities | Other Features |
| W;R | N | N | N | N | N | N | Y | Y | Y | N | Complex data structures: multidimensional |
| W;R | N | N | N | N | N | N | Y | N | M | W;T | Easy ratio analysis |
| N | 26 | Y | N | Y | N | N | Y | N | M | W;V,T,P | Variable time structures; text editing |
| W;R | Y | Y | N | N | N | N | Y | N | Y | W;T | |
| N | Y | Y | N | N | N | N | Y | N | Y | W;P | |
| O;R,E, A | N | I | I | I | I | Y | N | Y | M | W;V,T | Result statistics; input time shifts; alter model during run; built-in report hierarchy |
| W;R | 1 | Y | Y | N | N | Y | Y | Y | M | N | Hierarchical report structure with automatic consolidation; prompting for model building |

5. Available data analysis functions: R, regression analysis; E, exponential smoothing and extensions (e.g., seasonal analysis); B, Box-Jenkins time series analysis; A, analysis of variance.

6. Location of capability: O, outside the planning system in a separate system using compatible files; W, within the command structure of the planning system itself.

7. All systems can do a simple "what if . . . " analysis, using temporarily changed values of a subset of the input variables. Parametric analysis here is taken to mean an ability to vary one or more input variables systematically (as in a loop) and observe the results.

8. Available report language options: N, nothing but standard report formats available; S, no special report language available in system, but special reports possible, using capabilities outside the planning system; M, modeling language used to generate reports, either within the main model itself or using a second model file; Y, full report language separate from the model language.

9. Available graphical options: V, plots variables against each other (e.g., scattergram); T, plots variables against time; P, plots histograms or other pictoral representation of probabilistic results.

ing, etc. (Graphical displays are also commonly available report options.)

**Optional Features.** Other features of a planning system which are desirable and common, but not mandatory, include:

1. *Real-time interaction with the user.* Although interaction is available on time-sharing services that permit questions and answers back and forth between the user and the system, some planning systems are available only on batch computers. Whatever its mode of operation, the system should react quickly enough to give a timely evaluation of the alternatives being generated by the planner.

2. *Special modeling features,* notably:
(a) Automatic advancement of time, where a model given for one period can be repeated with different data for several periods.
(b) Functions peculiar to financial analysis, such as discounting of results, accumulation of results over time, and allocation of costs or returns across profit centers.

**Summary.** A planning system is a combination of most of the features of a report-generation language, many of the features of a simulation language, some of the features of an inquiry or data management language, along with extra modeling and analysis facilities necessary for representing and solving unique planning problems.

Table 1 summarizes features of a sample of the planning systems available at the time this article was prepared. New systems continue to appear and new features are added to existing systems, so the table should be taken only as a sample of planning system characteristics rather than an exhaustive list of available systems. Interested readers should consult the individual suppliers for up-to-date and more detailed information.

E. J. Hurst, Jr., and T. Thilemann

# POINT-OF-SALE TERMINAL

For articles on related subjects *see* Administrative-Business Applications; and Terminals.

A point-of-sale terminal is a device connected to a computer which takes the place of a manual cash register or similar device. Point-of-sale (PoS) systems offer notable advantages over conventional cash registers in inventory control, credit authorization (if required), and recording sales, while at the same time reducing the time, manpower, and paperwork needed for such operations.

Many attempts have been made in the past to find an acceptable solution to the problem of gathering and recording data in machine-readable form when a sale is made. For example, cash registers have been equipped with paper tape punches or have produced tally rolls printed in a machine-readable optical font. Some of these techniques, however, required a conversion to translate the information created at the counter and transfer it onto a medium suitable for computer input, but all these techniques required that the data be processed only in the batch mode. Recent extensive use of time-sharing computer systems, together with the drop in price of small computers and terminals, has led to development of a solution without these drawbacks, namely, the point-of-sale terminals and systems.

*A single-keyboard PoS system* is based upon electronic cash registers as stand-alone units equipped with a few registers and some programming capability that enables up to 100 different totals to be accumulated and several types of transactions to be handled. The hardware usually comprises, among other things, a numeric keyboard, some functional keys, an operator guide-display panel, and a sales data display panel. Such a machine can guide a check-out clerk through the different types of retail transactions, clearly indicating on a display panel every step and any mistake made; then, if necessary, it can automatically print out a bill or invoice with all items, subtotals, and totals detailed. Often, all transactions are simultaneously recorded on a magnetic tape cassette for later processing.

*In a multiple-keyboard PoS system* a group of such electronic machines (without programming capability, however) is placed at all check points and linked either to one central data collector with a magnetic tape or to a minicomputer with disk, and perhaps also magnetic tape, storage. Such configurations enable the transmission at any time of all current transaction data to a remote computer for immediate processing. In this way, management is provided with continuous, almost up-to-the-minute details of sales by product and department. This is usually considered to be the most significant benefit to be derived from the use of electronic cash registers. Moreover, the minicomputer configuration

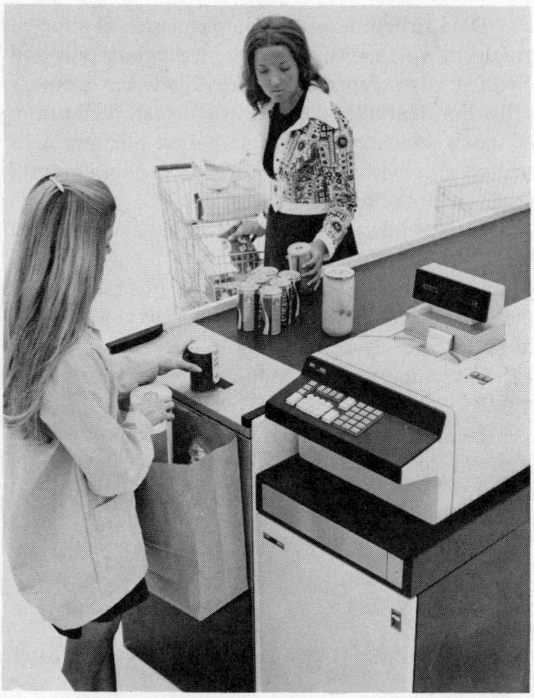

**Fig. 1.** IBM 3660 point-of-sale terminal at supermarket check-out counter.

**Fig. 2.** Optical scanner reads Universal Product Code at a check-out counter.

allows the possibility of on-line access to prices of all items and on-line credit authorization.

An important recent development in PoS systems is the ability to read automatically the labels attached to goods. This is achieved by an electronic data-capture terminal, which is usually a pen-shaped wand, hand-held by a checking clerk, which optically or magnetically scans (see Fig. 1) specially printed bar-coded labels attached to the selected goods over which it is passed. Or, in case of supermarkets, it is a fixed-head (usually laser beam) scanner mounted on a conveyor at the check point, which reads the bar-coded label attached to goods, either automatically while they are passing the reading station or when it is moved along the reading slit by the checking clerk. Several manufacturers are currently delivering such devices, which differ one from another mainly in the design of the bar code.

Generally, some method of binary coding of the data is used so that the bar code will represent a numerical or alphanumerical subset of the full 128 ASCII characters. The lack of uniformity of these devices creates a labeling problem. The ideal system would be a standard product number that would uniquely identify each item of merchandise handled in any shop, but the practical implementation of such a system is difficult. The most highly developed system is the one known as the Universal Product Code (see Fig. 2) adopted in 1972 in the United States.

Leading manufacturers of PoS systems are Singer Data Systems and the National Cash Register Company, closely followed by the Sweda division of Litton Industries. There are some two dozen other manufacturers of PoS equipment, many of them just entering the field (for example, IBM and Univac). Retail terminal PoS systems are being installed in rapidly increasing numbers in department stores in the United States and in Europe. By the end of 1973, some 200,000 terminals had been installed or were on order, and the future is very promising.

J. Necas

# POINTER

For articles on related subjects *see* Addressing; Data Structures; Storage Organization.

For article on related term *see* Tree.

A digital computer memory contains *cells*, which may be referred to by *addresses*. The address of a memory cell is sometimes referred to as a "pointer," since it may be thought of as pointing to the memory cell to which it refers.

Pointers may occur at the level of machine language both as direct addresses and as indirect addresses.

| | |
|---|---|
| LOAD 100 | This assembly-language instruction specifies that the content of memory cell 100 is to be loaded into the accumulator. The address 100 is a pointer to the memory cell whose address is 100. |
| LOAD*100 | This indirect-addressing assembly-language instruction specifies that location 100 contains the address of the quantity to be loaded into the accumulator. The address 100 is a pointer to a pointer. |

In general, a pointer $p_1$ may point to a cell containing a pointer $p_2$, and the pointer $p_2$ may in turn contain a pointer to a cell containing a pointer $p_3$. A sequence of pointers $p_1 p_2 p_3, \ldots$ such that $p_i$ points to a cell containing $p_{i+1}$ for $i = 1,2, \ldots$ is called a "pointer chain."

Pointers may also occur in higher-level languages such as PL/I:

| | |
|---|---|
| P = ADDR(A); | This PL/I statement assigns to the variable P the address of the variable A. The value stored in P is a pointer to the variable A, and P is said to be a pointer-valued variable. |

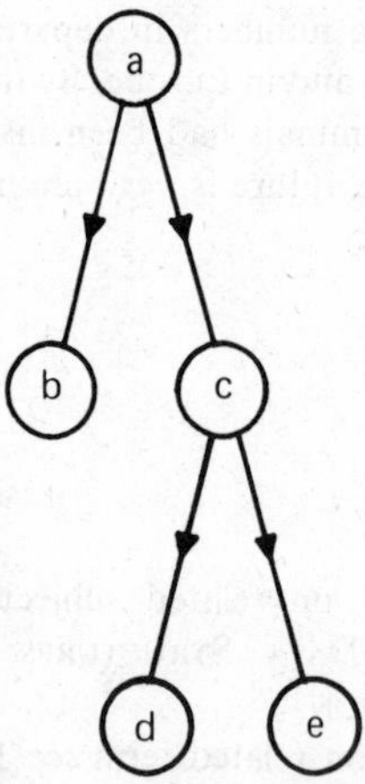


Data structures may be implemented as directed graphs in which vertices represent memory cells and directed edges represent pointers between memory cells. For example, the tree structure at the bottom of the previous column contains five memory cells *a, b, c, d, e,* with a pointer from *a* to *b* and pointer chains from *a* through *c* to *d* and *e*.

In general, pointers may be used to connect individual memory cells and also to point from one composite data structure to another. For example, in the diagram the pointer from *a* to *c* may be thought of not merely as a pointer from *a* to the cell *c*, but also as a pointer from *a* to the subtree having *c* as its root.

Pointers are essential in any composite data structure for linking components of the data structure.

P. WEGNER

# POLISH NOTATION

For articles on related subjects *see* BOOLEAN ALGEBRA; LANGUAGE PROCESSORS; and PROCEDURE-ORIENTED LANGUAGES.

In 1951, the Polish logician Jan Lukasiewicz devised a *parenthesis-free* notation for logic. This notation, extended for use in algebra and other operator-operand systems, has become known as "*Polish notation.*" Basically, by consistently placing operators before or after their operands, the need for parentheses is eliminated, provided each operator has a fixed number of operands. The *prefix* form, in which the operators precede the operands, is used in APL, while the *postfix* (or *suffix*) form, in which the operators follow the operands, is used as an intermediate expression form by many compilers.

Parenthesis elimination is made possible by the fixed number of operands for each operator. Thus if "+" denotes ordinary addition, we expect two operands. Hence, "+ab" (prefix) and "ab+" (postfix) are as clearly understood as "a+b". Similarly, if "~" denotes logical negation, exactly one operand is expected. The minus sign causes a problem, since it may be associated with one operand (negative numbers) or two (subtraction). Agreement to limit its use to defining negative numbers solves this problem at the expense of writing subtraction as "a+(−b)" rather than "a−b". Table 1 gives several examples of Polish notation.

**Table 1.** Polish notation.

| Expression | Prefix | Postfix |
|---|---|---|
| a+(−b) | +a−b | ab−+ |
| (−a)+b | +−ab | a−b+ |
| a*(b+c) | *a+bc | abc+* |
| (p⊃q)≡(∼p∨q) | ≡⊃pq∨∼pq | pq⊃p∼q∨≡ |

If a prefix expression is evaluated from right to left, then whenever an operator is encountered, its operands are those that have most recently been evaluated. Hence, the operator can be immediately processed. The same is true of a postfix expression evaluated from left to right. For example, the evaluation sequence for *a+bc is c, b, +bc, a, *a+bc. Similarly, the expression +*abc (i.e., (a*b)+c) is evaluated in the order c, b, a, *ab, +*abc. These two properties—ease of evaluation and unique representation of an expression without use of parentheses or other punctuation—justify Polish notation for use with computer language and in language processors.

R. R. KORFHAGE

# PORTABILITY

For articles on related subjects *see* COMPATIBILITY; SOFTWARE; and SOFTWARE FLEXIBILITY.
For articles on related terms *see* ASSEMBLERS; MACROINSTRUCTION; and OPERATING SYSTEMS.

It often happens that a program that runs on one computer is required on a second computer that is of a type different from the first. If the program has been written in a sufficiently flexible way for such a transfer to be made relatively easily, the program is said to be "portable." A program written in an assembly language is tied to a particular computer and therefore is not portable. On the other hand, a program encoded in a machine-independent, higher-level language may be portable.

When talking of portability, one cannot ignore the question of efficiency. If a program is transferred from one computer to another, but runs unnecessarily slowly or occupies excessive storage on the second computer, then it is not truly portable. For example, a program might be written in such a way that it manipulates character strings on a character-by-character basis. If this program is transferred, without any logical changes, to a computer that possesses instructions that can manipulate entire strings of characters, then this computer could not be properly exploited and the program might run several times slower than it needed to. Similar considerations apply even more strongly to the use of auxiliary storage.

To date, it has been impossible to find a method whereby all programs can be encoded in a form that will run efficiently on all computers; for some time to come, huge sums of money will therefore continue to be spent in moving programs between computers. However, there have been some successful partial solutions to the portability problem. For numerical programs the use of a higher-level language such as Fortran provides a solution, and the Cobol language covers data processing programs. For nonnumerical programs, such as system software, that need to be implemented efficiently, the DLIMP technique (*d*escriptive *l*anguage *i*mplemented by *m*acro *p*rocessor) has proved effective. In this technique the program is encoded in a "descriptive language" made up of a sequence of machine-independent macro calls, the macros being specially tailored to describe the program in hand. The macros represent an ideal *abstract machine* for running the program. When it is desired to implement the program on a given computer, the macros are written to map into the assembly language of that computer, and the program is then fed to a macro processor that performs the required translation.

Some computer manufacturers have eased portability problems between their machines by producing a range of compatible computers sharing a common machine code. Even when programs are transferred between computers of a similar type, however, problems may arise when the computers have incompatible operating systems, which impose different constraints on the programs that they control.

REFERENCES

1971. Richards, M. "The Portability of the BCPL Compiler," *Software—Practice and Experience*, Vol. 1, pp. 135–146.

This describes how a compiler can be made portable.

1972. Newey, M. C., P. C. Poole, and W. M. Waite. "Abstract Machine Modelling to Produce Portable Software—A Review and Evaluation," *Software—Practice and Experience*, Vol. 2, pp. 107–136.
An evaluation of three separate DLIMPs.

P. J. BROWN

## PORTS, MEMORY

For article on related subject *see* MEMORY: Main.

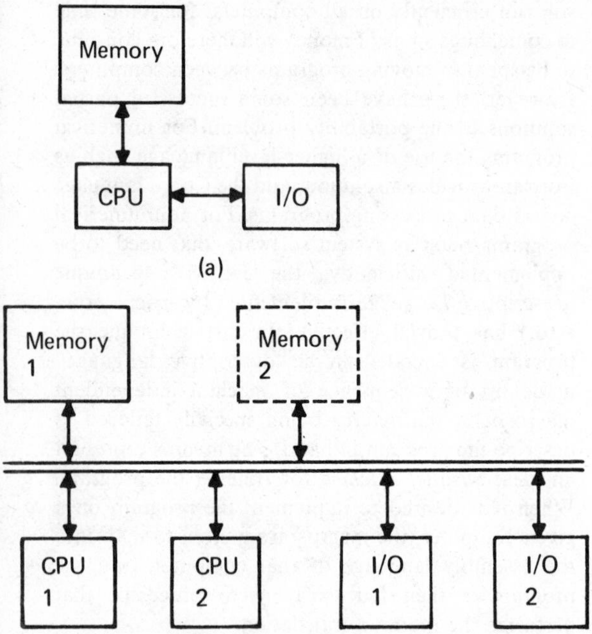

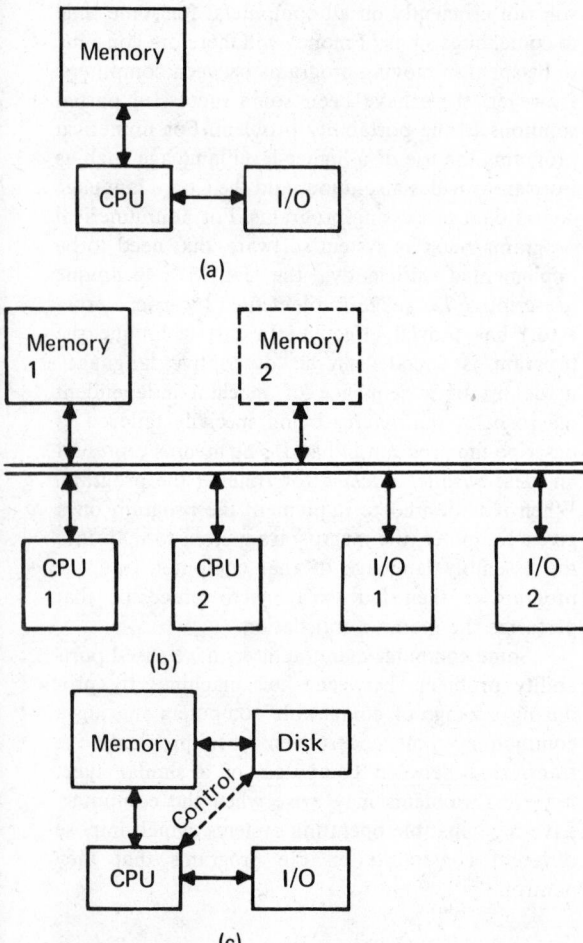


**Fig. 1.** Memory port connections: (a) single port, simply connected; (b) single-port, bus-connected; (c) double-port, servicing disk and CPU on separate ports.

In simple systems the main memory has a single port or logical connection through which data is transferred under CPU control. In more elegant systems (e.g., PDP-11), a single memory port is connected to a *bus* via which several CPU's and I/O equipment have memory access. On still larger systems, bus traffic can become sufficiently intense that speed of some important high-speed activity may be sacrificed. Because the CPU to memory path is normally high speed, a second port for the CPU may be added to the memory. Since data rates are high and overrun is possible, another port for backup store or bulk store may be provided. For example, a DEC PDP-10 may have several ports connected typically to CPU, disk, or special high-speed I/O. In some cases (e.g., the Sigma 500), multiport memory is used to interface between autonomous busses in multiprocessor, multimemory systems; this allows, for example, the I/O and internal busses to communicate as needed through memory but to proceed normally without interference from each other's traffic.

Within a multiport memory there must, of course, be some form of interlock mechanism to arbitrate conflict between port requests. Often a cyclic polling scheme guarantees access to memory by each of the ports on some priority basis with a guarantee of minimum service.

K. C. SMITH AND A. S. SEDRA

**PRAGMATICS.** *See* SYNTAX, SEMANTICS, AND PRAGMATICS.

## PRECEDENCE

For articles on related subjects *see* GRAMMAR; and PROGRAMMING LINGUISTICS.

The subject of *precedence grammars* is discussed elsewhere in this Encyclopedia along with *operator precedence grammars*. In this article we consider the narrower topic of operators in higher-level languages and the types of precedence relations, or *hierarchy*, that exist among them.

As an example of the need for such relationships, consider the expression

$$A+B*C$$

Is this to be interpreted as A+(B∗C) or (A+B)∗C? One way to solve this problem would be to enforce a strict left-to-right or (as in APL) a right-to-left order of evaluation. In APL, therefore, the expression is interpreted as A+(B∗C), but (also in APL) C∗B+A would be interpreted as C∗(B+A). To minimize the effect on interpretation of the order in which an expression is written, precedence relations among operators exist in most languages. A major purpose of such relations is to assure that as many expressions as possible have their "natural" interpretation (e.g., most people would regard A + (B*C) as the natural interpretation of A+B∗C).

The operator hierarchy includes not only arithmetic operators but also relational operators (<, >, ≤, etc.) and logical operators, as well as (in PL/I) the concatenation operator (||). Table 1 gives the operator hierarchy in Fortran, Algol, and PL/I. It is to be interpreted as follows: In an expression containing more than one operator, the operator to be applied first is the one that is highest in the hierarchy. Thus,

| | *Expression* | *Interpretation* |
|---|---|---|
| Fortran: | A+B/C−D | A+(B/C)−D |
| | −A∗B | (−A)∗B |
| Algol | −A↑B | −(A↑B) |
| | A∧B∨C | (A∧B)∨C |

**Table 1.** Operator Hierarchy

| | Fortran | Algol | PL/I |
|---|---|---|---|
| High | ** | ↑ | ¬** − (unary) |
| | /* | /*÷ | /* |
| | + − | + − (binary and unary) | + − |
| | (binary and unary) | | \|\| |
| | Relational operators | Relational operators | Relational operators |
| | .NOT. | ¬ | & |
| | .AND. | ∧ | \| |
| | .OR. | ∨ | |
| | | ⊃ | |
| Low | | ≡ | |

+ Addition
− Subtraction
∗ Multiplication
/ Division
÷ Integer Division
Exponentiation: **, ↑
Negation: .NOT., ¬
Conjunction (logical product): .AND., ∧, &
Disjunction (logical sum): .OR., ∨, |
Implication: ⊃
Equivalence: ≡
Concatenation: ||

Note that the position of the relational (=, <, ⩽, >, ⩾, ≠) and logical operators relative to the arithmetic operators is forced if expressions containing a combination of these operators are to be meaningful. Thus, the Fortran expression (.NE. means ≠)

A+B .NE. C .OR. D

makes sense only if interpreted as

((A+B) .NE. C) .OR. D

When an expression contains two operators of equal precedence, the usual rule is to evaluate them from left to right (although in PL/I the highest precedence class is evaluated right to left). Thus, A/B∗C is to be interpreted as (A/B)∗C. Finally, in all languages, parentheses may always be used to override the precedence rules. Put another way, the precedence rules (or left-to-right rule) are never applied across parentheses.

Reference

1971. Ralston, A. *An Introduction to Programming and Computer Science.* New York: McGraw-Hill.

A. Ralston

# PRECISION

For articles on related subjects *see* Arithmetic, Computer; Numbers and Number Systems; Significance Arithmetic; and Significant Digit.

For a numeric representation system that employs strings of symbols from a finite alphabet to represent numbers, the *precision attribute* of a symbol string denotes the length of the string, and possibly also positional information for determining a base point of the string. Those numbers representable by finite length symbol strings are termed the "finite precision numbers" of that numeric representation system.

For the fixed-point radix representation $d_m d_{m-1} \cdots d_1 d_0 \cdot d_{-1} d_{-2} \cdots d_l$, $d_m \neq 0$, the precision attribute is the triple $(m - l + 1, -l, m + 1)$; e.g., 310.25 has precision (5, 2, 3) and 0.0024 has precision (2, 4, −2). If $l \leqq 0 \leqq m$, then $-l$ and $m + 1$ may be interpreted as the number of digits in the fractional and integer parts, respectively, of the $m - l + 1$ digit number. The precision triple $(m - l + 1,\ -l,\ m + 1)$ thus provides both the number of digits and base-point normalization information.

For a radix number system where computed radix representations are truncated to exhibit only significant digits, the precision attribute identifies the significant digits. In this restricted environment, precision is a measure of accuracy. For integer radix-number systems such as the "8-digit decimal integers" or the "6-digit hexadecimal integers," the precision attribute provides simply a measure of the magnitude of the representable integers.

The precision attribute is utilized for numeric formats in input, output, and internal storage allocation in higher-level programming languages. In PL/I, for example, precision rules are employed to compute the precision attribute of program variables at compile time to help optimize storage utilization.

D. W. MATULA

# PRINTING TECHNIQUES

For article on related subject *see* INPUT-OUTPUT DEVICES.

Present-day printers used either for on-line or off-line computer output fall into two main classes, impact and nonimpact printers, depending upon whether or not there is impact of the printing element on the paper. In this article the main principles of the most commonly used techniques are considered.

**Impact Printing Techniques.** A printed character can be represented either by a complete image formed by uninterrupted strokes or by dots in close proximity so that they give the reader the impression of having been printed by uninterrupted strokes. Hence, impact printers are classified as face-character or dot-character (or simply dot) printers. Both categories include serial (character-by-character) as well as parallel (line, or line-at-a-time) printers. All impact printer design is based on electromechanical principles, sometimes with supplemental electronic improvements.

FACE-CHARACTER IMPACT PRINTING TECHNIQUES. These can be classified in four categories:

1. Type-bar and type-wheel printing.
2. Drum (or barrel) printing.
3. Chain and train printing.
4. Alloy belt printing.

In parallel *type bar printing* there are as many type bars (and hammers) as there are print positions (or columns) on the line, thus avoiding the horizontal shifting of the carriage. Each bar contains all the characters that can be printed and is elevated to a print point determined by the character being printed. Here it rests while being struck by the hammer (plunger), and then it returns to its home position. In the printing position the character to be printed faces the printing cylinder; the ribbon and the paper move between them. This technique is used, for example, in some punched card accounting machines. Alphanumerical printers of this type operate at 100 lines per minute (lpm), and numerical ones at 150, 200, or 300 lpm.

For serial type bar printing a slightly different technique is applied resembling that of a conventional typewriter. Here the number of type bars generally equals the number of different characters to be printed, each bar having a different character. The printing of a character is effected by actuating the type bar with the appropriate character to be printed. After the type bar returns to its home position, the carriage moves horizontally into the next print position on the line. Serial printers of this type operate at up to some 10 characters per second (chps).

On some typewriters and serial printers the conventional type bars and moving carriages have been replaced by a single type head of a "golf-ball" shape (Figs. 1 and 2). This type head skims across the printed line while the typewriter or printer carriage does not move. As this head is removable, it may be changed for another type head with other than Roman script or with a different size of Roman font such as the elite or pica, or OCR-A, OCR-B, etc. These printers are used by many computer manufacturers as console typewriters, interrogating typewriters, or as printers for small scientific or business computers (Fig. 3). The speed of these printers when used as computer output devices is up to 16 chps, which may be doubled by using two separate type heads to print in parallel on each half of the print line.

Sometimes *vertically rotating* type wheels are used as printing heads. On such a type wheel more

**Fig. 1.** "Golf-ball" printing element for IBM Selectric II typewriter.

**Fig. 2.** IBM typewriter with "golf ball" installed.

**Fig. 3.** IBM Selectric with rotating type head in use as a console unit.

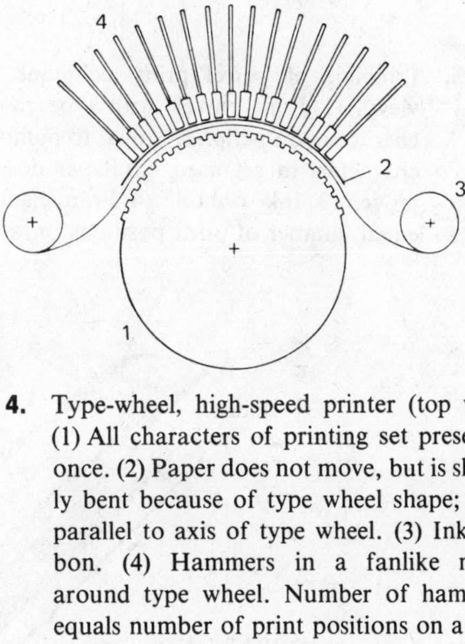


**Fig. 4.** Type-wheel, high-speed printer (top view) (1) All characters of printing set presented once. (2) Paper does not move, but is slightly bent because of type wheel shape; runs parallel to axis of type wheel. (3) Ink ribbon. (4) Hammers in a fanlike mode around type wheel. Number of hammers equals number of print positions on a line.

characters can be accommodated than on a type bar; moreover, the printing speed is higher. Type wheels are used for serial as well as for parallel printing. This principle of printing is used in the printer shown in Fig. 4, with a printing speed of approximately 600 lpm. A similar technique, except that it uses a type tape instead of a type wheel, is used in a Japanese printer that prints at a rate of approximately 300 lpm.

UNIVAC has developed a printer that uses *a horizontally rotating* type wheel. The type characters are located around a single wheel on a carrier. When the chosen character appears on the rotating wheel, a hammer pushes the paper against the character. Horizontal movement is achieved by a rotating, threaded shaft. The carriage runs on a pinion, which is attached to the carriage. The resultant mechanism is very simple and rugged, with a minimum of reciprocating parts.

In the *print barrel (drum)* method, all characters in the character set are engraved on the surface of a rapidly rotating, solid barrel (drum). The printing is effected by hammers that strike the paper at the moment when the appropriate character on the barrel is in the correct position relative to the paper.

This method is similar to one that uses multiple wheels locked together to form a print drum. Fig. 5 illustrates this principle.

Another similar printing device is the *chain* or *train* of print slugs. The only difference between the two is that in a chain the characters for printing are linked together, which is not the case in the train of print slugs. One advantage of the train is that it can be moved at a higher speed than a chain. A typical example using both variations is shown in Fig. 6.

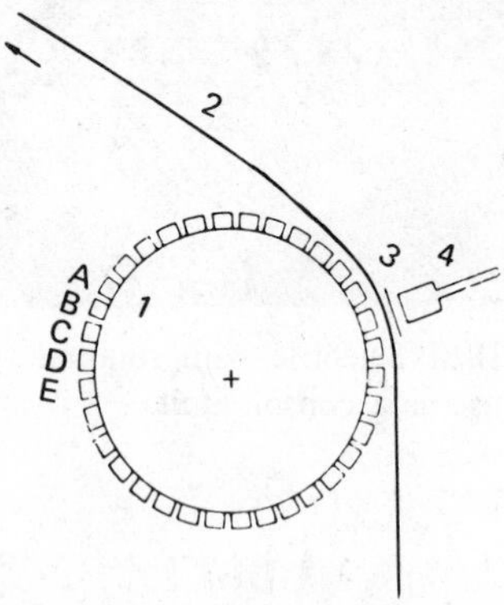


**Fig. 5.** Principle of barrel print technique (side view). (1) Print barrel, with type rows of characters on periphery equal to number of characters in set used. (2) Paper does not move. (3) Ink ribbon. (4) Print hammers equal number of print positions on a line.

Some models of the IBM 1403 printer use a chain and have a maximal speed of 600 lpm; others use a train with a maximum speed of 1,100 lpm. Special-print character configurations may be used to allow upper- and lower-case alphabets (Fig. 7), other than Roman script, national additions to the Roman alphabet, or (for special purposes) fragmental print (Fig. 8), among others. Fragmental print is not a standard typeface and is used for printing large sized letters and numerals, called "bill" (poster or placard) font. On a line printer, each character of this font is composed of fragments printed in several adjacent horizontal positions and lines on the paper; hence, the name "fragmental printing."

Recently developed printers of the train type attain a speed of 2,000 lpm when using a standard 48-character set, repeated nine times on the train. A speed of 2,500 lpm is possible with a 36-character set. Spacing and skipping are controlled by a program-loaded buffer in the control unit. A metal *alloy belt* of print slugs is sometimes used because chain and drum printers are rather heavy and expensive to manufacture. A thin metal alloy belt is lighter, and easier and less costly to produce.

The Data Products Model 2550 line printer uses a print drive system, known as Charaband, which is designed to overcome the wear problems of the train printer while retaining its flexibility and interchangeability. The Charaband is reversible, with one character set on each side of the band. The design of the type cap makes it easy for the operator to replace

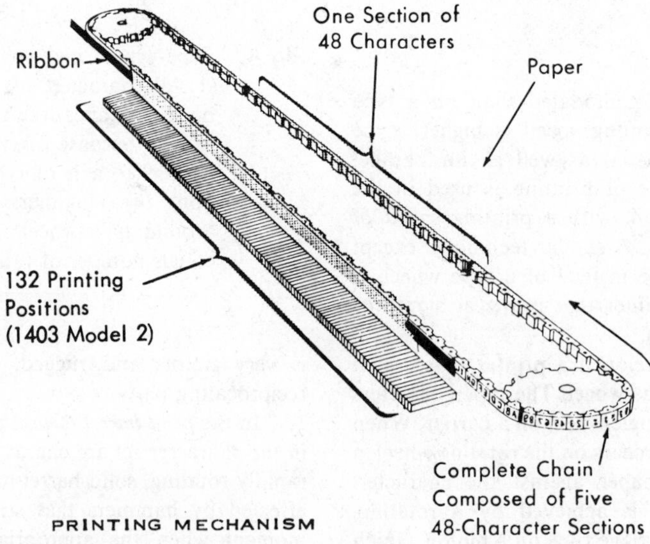


**Fig. 6.** The IBM 1403 printer chain.

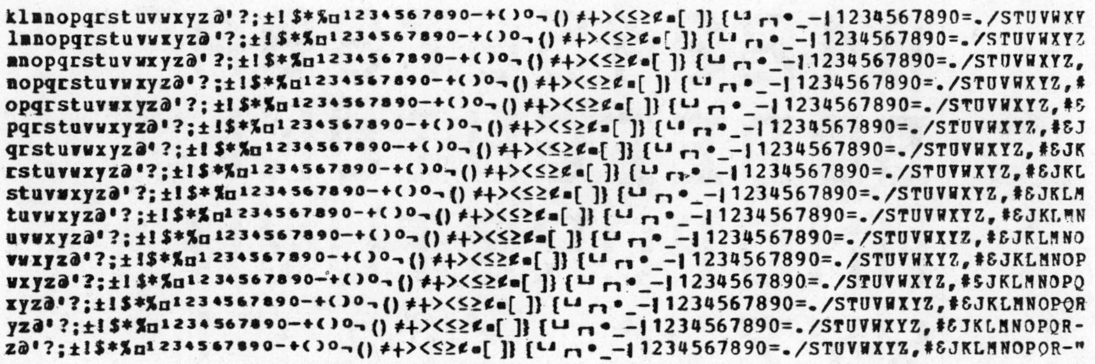

**Fig. 7.** Print test on IBM 1403 printer with standard character set; possible speed is up to 1,400 lpm for numerical and 1,250 lpm for alphabetical printing.

**Fig. 8.** Fragmental print on an IBM 1403 printer. (Designer: R. Haardt, Alfred Hagelstein Maschinfabrik, Lübeck-Travemünde, Germany.)

worn characters or mount special characters in a few minutes. The characters are mounted in pairs on metal caps, which are mounted on a plastic carrier slug. The slug is attached to a broad polyurethane band strengthened by a thinner steel band, and rides on roller bearings.

Dot-Character Impact Printing Techniques. Matrix or array dot-printing techniques are sometimes referred to as "mosaic print." In these techniques, characters are formed by a number of pins appropriately selected from an array or matrix (usually 5 columns by 7 rows) that strikes the paper. The pins are generally electromagnetically or hydraulically actuated, can be moved quickly, and attain printing speeds of up to 200 lpm or more. One of the advantages of these techniques is that the number of characters in a set generally does not affect the printing speed. Matrix printing techniques are used for both serial and parallel printing.

*Serial* dot-character impact printing is applied, for example, in the Centronics Model 306 impact matrix printer, which employs a movable print head that is driven back and forth across the page by a single-speed clutch. Mounted in this print head are seven solenoids together with their associated print wires, the ends of which come together in a vertical plane in front of an inked ribbon. As the head moves from left to right, it detects its lateral position by photoelectrically scanning an optical strip and fires the print wires up to a maximum of seven times for any given character. The nylon ribbon is thus pressed against the paper and each character is constructed from a matrix of small ink dots. This device can print at 100 chps or 60 lpm (with 80 characters per line). Several Centronics printers using the same technique are available with speeds ranging from 100 to 330 chps, 60 to 200 lpm, and 80 or 132 characters per line.

Serial dot-character impact printing may be applied to any kind of printing device. Its application for a printing card punch is shown in Fig. 9.

*Parallel dot-character* impact printing is performed similarly to serial printing except that a whole line of dots is printed in parallel at a time. For example, in the Tally Series 2000 line printers, the heart of the print mechanism is a lightweight, single-piece, 132-hammer print comb. The impact face of each of the hammers consists of a small dot-sized steel ball. A dot is formed when the hammer is struck against a fixed platen that is mounted behind the paper and inked ribbon. The print comb is positioned in front of the ribbon and paper, with one hammer for each character, across

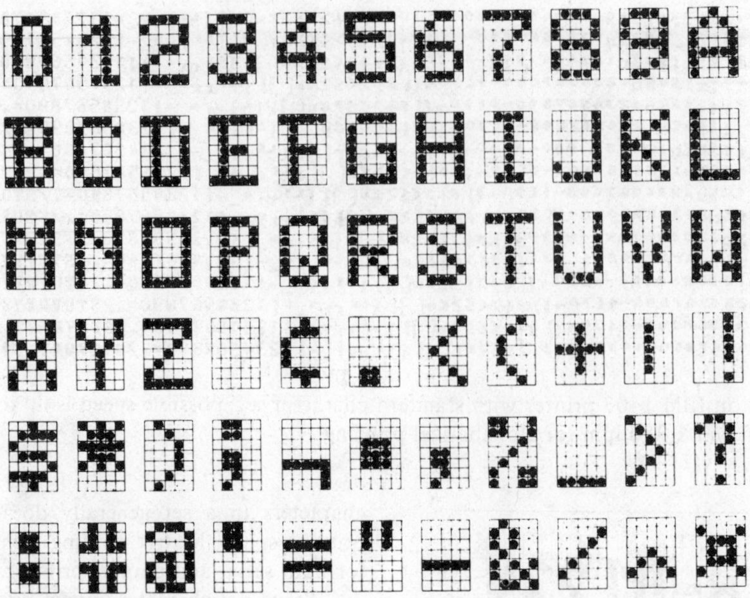

**Fig. 9.** Mosaic print character set of the ARITMA 130 printer card punch.

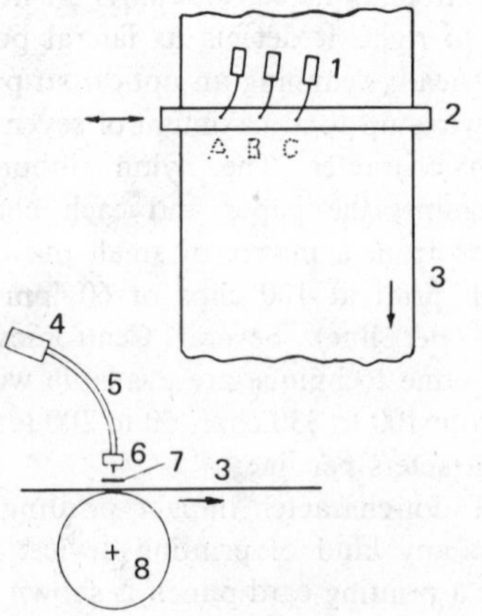


**Fig. 10.** Electromechanical mosaic printing by ITC Samastronic line printer. (1) Pin print heads. Number of heads on bearer corresponds with number of printing positions on line. (2) Bed bearer and guide bar, which moves during each printing cycle along the printed line across stationery (see arrows). (3) Paper moves in direction of arrow. (4) Magnets actuate dot print head. (5) Bowden. (6) Print head with print pin. (7) Ink ribbon. (8) Print base.

the width of the 132-character line. Each hammer in a position that is to be printed is simultaneously pulled back by its own fixed electromagnet and then released to fly forward and create a dot. The comb then moves horizontally to the next adjacent dot position, and the process is repeated until one row of dots is complete. The paper is then advanced vertically one dot row and the horizontal printing cycles are repeated. After the complete line matrix has been scanned, the paper advances in preparation for the next line of print. Clear and consistent quality of print is achieved on up to six copies.

Parallel impact printers are often used as minicomputer peripherals and remote batch-printing terminals. An example of a parallel dot-character impact printer is shown in Fig. 10. It uses a 5 by 7 dot matrix and prints all characters of a line in five horizontal and seven vertical steps corresponding to the number of dots forming the width and the height of the character.

**Nonimpact Printing Techniques.** In contrast to impact printers, nonimpact printers work without contact of the printing element with the paper. Nonimpact printers may also be divided into the face-character and dot-character categories. Commercially available nonimpact printers are

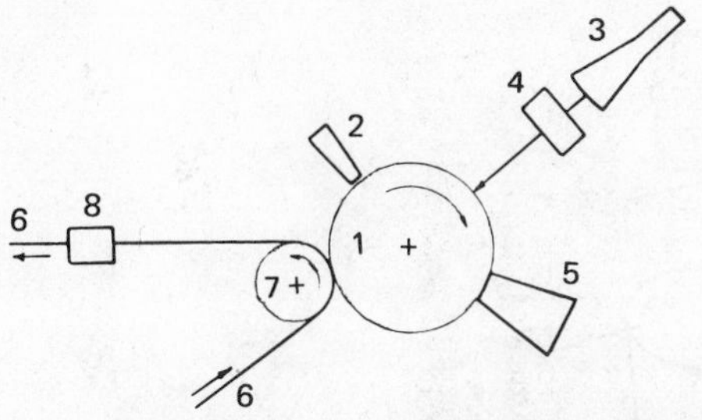


**Fig. 11.** Xerographic printer (side view). (1) Secondary cylinder with selenide coating. (2) Device for automatic charging of cylinder surface. (3) CRT. (4) Optical system. (5) Powdered-ink input surface. (6) Stationery. (7) Pressure cylinder. (8) Heating device.

**Fig. 12.** NCR 260 thermal printer for use as a terminal.

based, more or less, upon electrostatic principles, which implies that the printing image is generally formed on a paper medium through the use of electric charges. However, techniques based upon this principle differ in the way in which the character is transferred (via a CRT or a special process such as xerography) and by the way the image is fixed on the paper (by use of heat or by other means). See Fig. 11. These techniques are interesting because of the speeds they achieve and because they offer the possibility of printing graphics. However, they also have some drawbacks: They can produce only one copy at a time; the quality of print is often not very good, and therefore not suitable for many uses; and special, more expensive paper stock must often be used (Zaphiropoulos, 1973).

FACE-CHARACTER NONIMPACT PRINTING TECHNIQUES. At the present time the only techniques in this category are those using a *xerographic process* based on static electricity and photoconductivity, such as currently used in xerographic copying and reproducing machines. The problem of this technique in printing computer output directly is that it can be used only after the image of a character, line, column, or whole page has been created (on a CRT, drum, etc.).

Xerographic line printers were developed in the United States in the late 1950s. However, because of the problems mentioned above only a relatively small number of these devices is in use. In Europe, one of the first xerographic printers was installed in the Lyons bakery in London in 1965.

In late 1973, a computer printer (the Xerox 1200) employing xerographic techniques was test marketed in the United States by Xerox Corporation. The 1200 prints standard 132-character length lines in a 66 line-per-page format, which is almost an industry standard, but the printing is done on 8½ by 11 in. paper instead of the 11 by 14⅞ in. stock that is normally used on line printers. Drawing heavily upon the technology of the Xerox 3600 copier system, the 1200 prints at approximately one page per second, or 4,000 lpm, using a 95-character ASCII set that includes both upper- and lower-case characters. The 1200 has several advantages over conventional line printers, including unlimited multiple copies (which are printed one after the other) and the ability to print forms and data at the same time. Two versions are available, an off-line model with a Xerox magnetic tape drive, and an on-line model for use as a peripheral with Xerox computers. Approximately at the same time as the Model 1200 machine was announced, Upster announced a nonimpact printer that uses a similar technique, and also prints reduced-size pages at a speed of 4,340 lpm.

DOT-CHARACTER NONIMPACT PRINTING TECHNIQUES. There are several printing techniques commonly used in this category, among which are:

1. A linear array or matrix of scanning styli.
2. Ink-jet printing.
3. Thermal printing.
4. Electrostatic printing.

The *linear array* technique uses a linear array or matrix of scanning styli, placed either in a horizontal or vertical position relative to the paper. The hori-

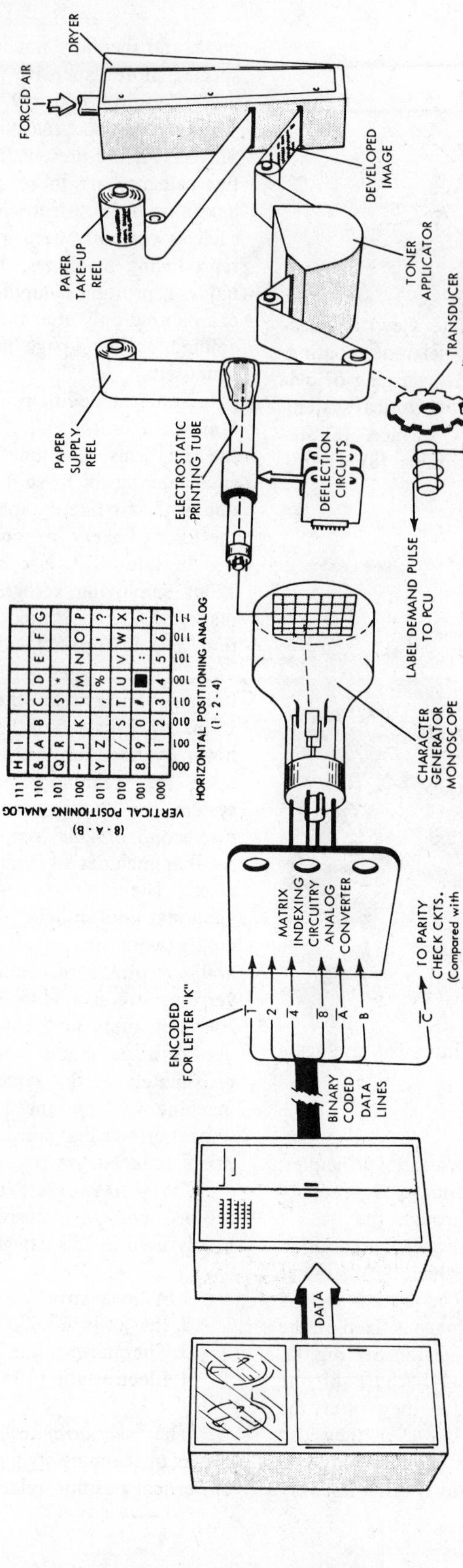


**Fig. 13.** A.B. Dick electrostatic VIDEOGRAPH 915 address printer.

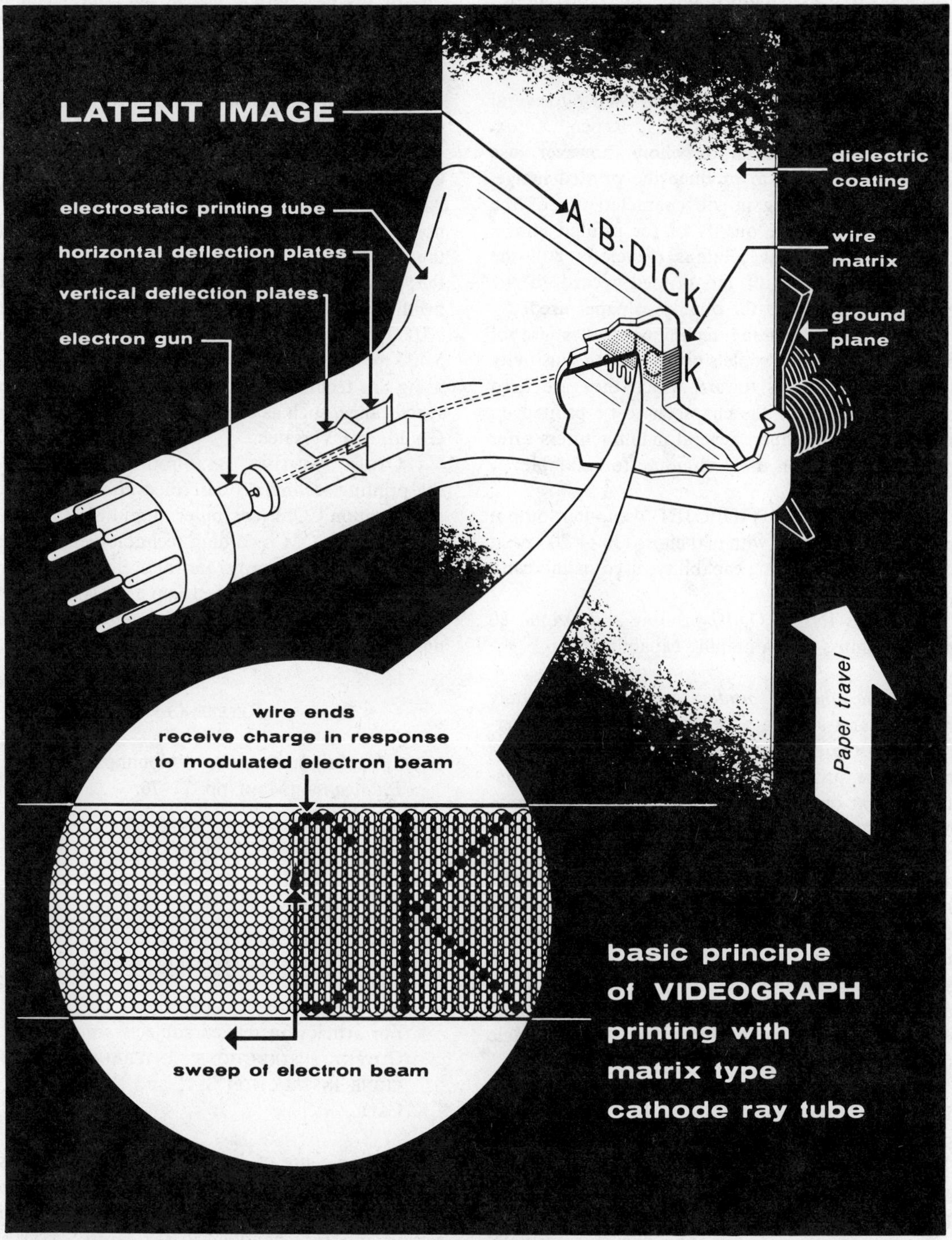


**Fig. 14.** Basic principle of electrostatic printing with matrix type CRT.

zontal method has been used in a Radiation line printer in which a high-voltage discharge burns selectively under each protruding stylus (corresponding to each of the print columns) on the surface of a special-quality moving paper. The printing speed is 30,000 lpm, 120 columns per line.

The vertical method has been used by several manufacturers such as Motorola, Repco, Xerox, Data Interface, etc., all of whom, however, use different techniques to produce the printed image, the differences being in the characteristics of the printing element, the quality of the printed image, the number of print columns (generally 80), the immediate visibility of the printed record to the operator or user, and the quality of paper used.

The *ink-jet* printing technique makes use of electrically charged droplets of ink, whose sensitivity to the electric fields toward which they are fired causes the image of the character to be printed on standard quality paper. Several manufacturers offer printers based upon this technique; for example:

1. A. B. Dick's VIDEOJET computer output printer, Model 9600, with 600 chps, 136 or 200 print columns, and a graphic capability; used mainly with minicomputers.
2. ITT's INKTRONIC printing at 120 lpm, 80 print columns, with a graphic capability.

In the *thermal printing* technique, the only moving parts are the paper advancement and perhaps also the print head; the printing operation is silent. The process itself involves generating controlled heat on each stylus in contact with thermochronic paper, the chemical compounds in the paper changing color with the heat applied. Input can be accepted from a variety of sources, and is usually received in an ASCII serial digital-code format. It is then converted into a parallel form and applied to the heating matrix in the printing head (which, in a serial printer, moves across the paper) to form alphanumeric characters and graphics. Only special-quality paper can be used, and only a single copy at a time can be printed.

Several manufacturers offer thermal printers, including Texas Instruments with a 20 lpm, 132 column printer, using 3M papers; and Anderson Jacobson, using NCR papers, and NCR with its 260 printer terminal. A few manufacturers produce portable thermal-printing terminals (NCR 260, Fig. 12), making remote computing available virtually at any place that has a telephone. The visibility of these portable terminals is generally good, and they weigh under 30 lb. One of these devices is a terminal made by Computer Devices for users of Honeywell's MULTICS system.

In the *electrostatic matrix dot-print* technique, electrostatic charges are selectively transferred as small dots directly onto a conductive paper substrate coated with an insulating layer, and the printed image is then placed in contact with a toner. This technique was used for a line printer as long ago as 1960. In 1968, such a printer, called VIDEOGRAPH, produced by A. B. Dick was installed in Amsterdam at Time-Life International. It can print up to 135,000 address slips an hour. Fig. 13 shows the configuration of the system and Fig. 14 outlines the printing principle. By comparison with other printing techniques, the maximum speed attained is 20,000 chps, which corresponds to approximately 5,400 lpm, 132 columns per line. However, printers using this technique usually fall into 500 to 600 lpm speed range, such as those manufactured by Varian, Gould, and Versatec.

OTHER PRINTING TECHNIQUES. In addition to the printing techniques described above, we should also mention COM (computer output on microfilm). Three basic COM recording technologies are in use today: CRT, electron beam, and fiber optics with light-emitting diodes. Speeds up to 40,000 lpm are attainable. COM is being used extensively by business as a replacement for printers.

### REFERENCE

1973. Zaphiropoulos, R. "Nonimpact Printers" *Datamation* (May), pp. 71–76.

J. NECAS

# PRIVILEGED INSTRUCTION

For articles on related subjects *see* INPUT-OUTPUT INSTRUCTIONS; INTERRUPT; MACHINE INSTRUCTION SET; and SUPERVISOR CALL.

Improper use of certain instructions can easily affect system integrity in a multiuser environment. These instructions usually include storage protection setting, interrupt handling, timer control, I/O, and special processor status-setting instructions.

In order to prevent accidental or intentional misuse of these instructions, many computers have a special privileged mode in which instructions of the aforementioned type, called "privileged instructions," can be executed. In a processor that possesses such a mode, the instructions are divided into sets; each set can be executed in its own mode. The privileged mode includes *all* instructions, whereas all other modes include some of them. The number of modes may be one (which means essentially the absence of a privileged mode) or two (one user mode and one privileged mode) or more. In the case of the PDP 11/45, for example, the computer has three modes: user, supervisor, and kernel.

Which instructions are to be made privileged varies widely, reflecting different approaches to the solution of the problem of the protection of system integrity. In the IBM/370, for example, all instructions that may be harmful to the system are included in the privileged set and are not accessible to the user. In other computers, the protection is provided by other means (e.g., via the addressing mechanism). Thus, the PDP 11/45 has only three privileged instructions, but has different addressing registers for the different modes.

The treatment of privileged instructions in a nonprivileged state also varies. One procedure is an illegal instruction trap, causing an interrupt. Another is to ignore it completely, which is equivalent to the former if the interrupt is disabled.

Another possible approach to the division of instructions into privileged and user subsets is to structure the computing system into two or more independent processors, each dedicated to one subset. Such division was made, for example, in the CDC 6000 series of computers. In those machines, the central processor had no instructions that caused any system functions unless explicitly directed to do so by another processor. (This was later changed by adding one additional instruction to the central processor so that later machines did not have this property).

G. FRIEDER

# PROBABILISTIC AUTOMATA

For articles on related subjects *see* AUTOMATA THEORY; FORMAL LANGUAGES; and SEQUENTIAL MACHINES.
For article on related term *see* STOCHASTIC PROCESS.

A probabilistic or stochastic automaton [sequential machine]—in what follows all bracketed comments refer to probabilistic sequential machines—is a device with a finite number of internal states, capable of scanning input words over a finite alphabet and responding by successively changing its internal state in a probabilistic way [and printing output words probabilistically, over a finite output alphabet].

With each probabilistic automaton [probabilistic sequential machine], one can associate a function from the set of all input words [input-output pairs of words] into the 0–1 interval as follows: Let $\rho$ be a vector with entries $\rho_i$ representing the probability that the automaton [machine] was in its $i$th state to begin with; let $A(x)$ [$A(y|x)$] be a matrix with entries $a_{ij}(x)$ [$a_{ij}(y|x)$] representing the probability that the automaton moved to state $j$ from state $i$ upon scanning the symbol $x$ [the machine printed the symbol $y$ and moved to state $j$ from state $i$ upon scanning the input symbol $x$]. Let $\eta$ be a column vector with some entries equal to one, the other entries being equal to zero [with all entries equal to one]. Then,

$$p(x_1 \cdots x_k) = \rho A(x_1) \cdots A(x_k)\eta$$
$$[p(y_1 \cdots y_k | x_1 \cdots x_k) = \rho A(y_1|x_1) \cdots A(y_k|x_k)\eta]$$

is a function representing the probability that the automaton entered a designated final state [the machine printed the output word $y_1 \cdots y_k$] after scanning the input word $x_1 \cdots x_k$. The function $P$ associated with a probabilistic automaton can be used as a sorting criterion to define the probabilistic language consisting of all input words $x_1 \cdots x_k$ with $p(x_1 \cdots x_k) > \lambda$, $\lambda$ being a preassigned given threshold.

The study of probabilistic automata is concerned mainly with the study of probabilisitic languages, their closure properties and relation to other types of formal languages. The study of probabilistic machines is concerned with the input/output relations induced by the machines, minimization of states of given machines, and other engineering-oriented problems connected with input/output information systems with random characteristics.

*Example.* Consider a physical system (or animal) assumed to be in one of two possible internal states (healthy or ill), with probabilities 0.2 and 0.8 correspondingly (the states may or may not be observable). If a sequence of stimuli (medicines) is applied to the system (animal), it undergoes probabilistically successive changes of its internal states.

Assume that the transition characteristics of the first stimulus are

$$\begin{pmatrix} 0.7 & 0.3 \\ 0.9 & 0.1 \end{pmatrix}$$

meaning that with probabilities 0.7 and 0.3, the system will stay in its first state, or will go to the second state, respectively, if the stimulus has been applied while the system was in its first state, etc. The probabilities of being in one of the two states after the application of the first stimulus (after swallowing the medicine) will then be

$$(0.2 \quad 0.8)\begin{pmatrix} 0.7 & 0.3 \\ 0.9 & 0.1 \end{pmatrix} = (0.86 \quad 0.14)$$

and the process will continue in the same way. The transition characteristics of the first stimulus are depicted in Fig. 1.

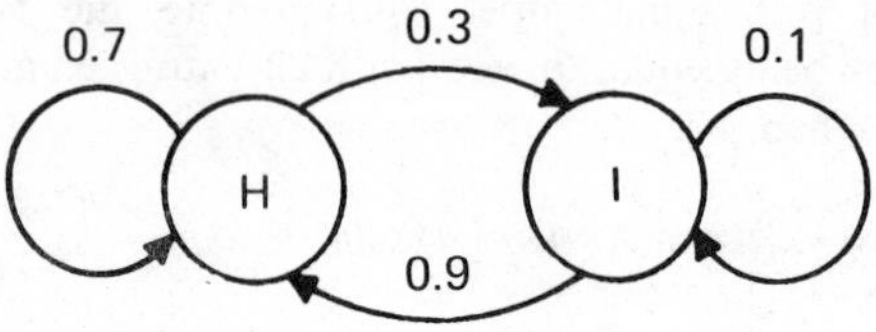


**Fig. 1.** Transition characteristics.

REFERENCES

1969. Carlyle, J. W. "Stochastic Finite-State System Theory," in L. A. Zadeh and E. Polak (Eds.), *System Theory*. New York: McGraw-Hill, Chap. 10.

1971. Paz, A. *Introduction to Probabilistic Automata*. New York: Academic Press.

A. PAZ

# PROBLEM-ORIENTED LANGUAGES

For articles on related subjects *see* COMMAND AND JOB CONTROL LANGUAGES; ENGINEERING APPLICATIONS; PROCEDURE-ORIENTED LANGUAGES; and PROGRAMMING LANGUAGES.

For articles on related terms *see* DATA STRUCTURES; and SIMULATION: Languages.

The term "problem-oriented" languages, if taken literally, is too general to be useful in the taxonomy of programming languages. In its most general meaning, one would have to include any programming language that helps solve problems. Thus, Fortran is a problem-oriented language when one solves scientific or numeric problems. Cobol (COmmon Business-Oriented Language) is problem oriented, even in its title, for business problems. However, accepted usage in computer science literature has imposed a narrower context for problem-oriented languages than one that could encompass Fortran and Cobol. From this more restricted point of view, synonyms for "problem oriented" are "applications oriented" or "special purpose."

This article discusses a number of applications-oriented and special-purpose programming languages. Some languages have been designed for very special applications such as numerical control programming or electronic circuit analysis. Others are applications oriented, but at the same time are more general purpose. Examples of these would include simulation languages, statistical packages, and information retrieval systems. Discussion of the more general-purpose, problem-oriented languages is found in other sections of this Encyclopedia.

Numerous problem-oriented languages have been developed. It is obvious that this article can only touch upon a small part of the vast work that has been done in this field. Many of these languages have been described by Sammet (1969), and the reader is directed to her work for additional details. The best source of technical information about a language is generally the reference manuals provided by the developers or suppliers of the software.

Before looking at specific problem-oriented languages in current usage, we present an example of one of the earliest such languages and then review the characteristics of the more commonly used languages in numerical control, civil engineering, and electrical engineering. Finally, we will have a few things to say about trends in the future use and development of problem-oriented languages.

**An Early Problem-Oriented Language—DYANA.** Shortly after the successful introduction of Fortran as a programming language for scientific and engineering calculations, the General Motors Research Laboratories developed a specialized language for describing vibrational and other dynamic systems. DYANA (dynamic analyzer) was developed originally for the IBM 704 in 1958 and was an extension of Fortran. See Theodoroff (1958).

DYANA provided for the definition of variables to specify the elements, excitation, and dependent and independent variables in a dynamic system. These variables have meaning in both Fortran and non-Fortran statements. The variables are constructed in such a way as to define the topology of the mechanical system. Fig. 1 illustrates a simple mechanical system. The topology of the system is contained in the variables themselves, using the letters *E* for element, *K* for spring, *M* for mass, *F* for force, etc. For example, E03K02 stands for the spring element, which is contained between the two elements 03 and 02. E03K02 is also used as the coefficient of damping for that spring element when the variable appears in Fortran arithmetic or input/output statements.

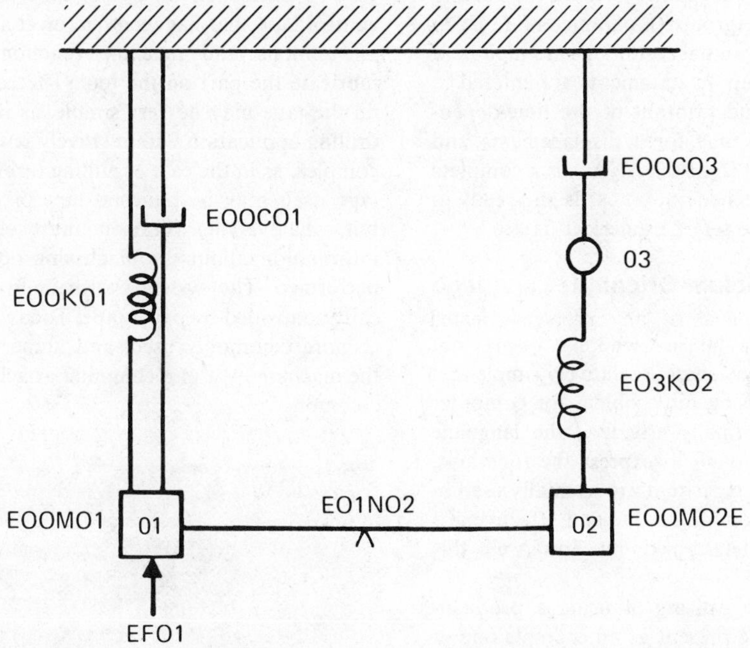


INPUT WITH DIAGNOSTIC COMMENTS FLAGGED BY AN X

```
X     SYSTEM DESCRIPTION                                        CARD  1
      EOOMO1,EOOMO2,EOOKO1,EOOCO1,EOOCO3                        CARD  2
      EO3KO2,EO1NO2,EFO1                                        CARD  3
X     PRE-COMPUTATION                                           CARD  4
      EO3KO2 = 2.4 + 0.6 * EOOKO1                               CARD  5
X     DAMPING RATE, EOOCO3(XO3)                                 CARD  6
      EOOCO3 = A * XO3 + B                                      CARD  7
X     FORCE, EFO1                                               CARD  8
      EFO1 = F *SINF(W *TIME)                                   CARD  9
X     INPUT VARIABLES                                           CARD 10
      A,B,F,W                                                   CARD 11
X     PRINT PRECOMPUTATION ANSWERS                              CARD 12
      EOOMO1,EOOMO2,EOOKO1,EOOCO1,EO3KO2,EO1NO2,A,B,F,W         CARD 13
X     PRINT TIME DEPENDENT ANSWERS                              CARD 14
      TIME,EFO1,XO1,XO2, XO3,DXO1,DXO2                          CARD 15
X     TRANSLATIONAL                                             CARD 16
X     TRANSIENT                                                 CARD 17
X     END                                                       CARD 18
```

**Fig. 1.** Sample DYANA program. (From J. E. Sammet, *Programming Languages: History and Fundamentals,* Prentice-Hall, 1969.)

In Fig. 1, the DYANA language is first used to define the system description (group 1). This is done by listing all system elements, with each element name showing its relationship to each other element, and defining its type (mass, spring, force, etc.)

Next (group 2), a series of Fortran arithmetic statements specify the functional relationship of the coefficients of damping of the two spring elements, the damping rate of element E00C03 as a function of the displacement of the point 03, and the forcing function EF01. Next (group 3), parameters *A*, *B*, *F*, and *W*, and the other initial conditions are input and printed. Finally (group 4), statements are entered to begin the analysis and printout of the time-dependent answers, such as time, force, displacements, and velocities. The output from DYANA was a complete Fortran program punched out on cards and ready to run with the requisite set of numerical data.

### Using a Problem-Oriented Language

**APT.** The essential goal of any problem-oriented language is to provide the user, who may or may not be a computer specialist, with a relatively simple and direct way of expressing his problem for computer solution. To be maximally effective, the language must be complete enough to express the functions, algorithms, and data types that are normally used in the specific application. The value and effectiveness of a language is determined by how well this criterion is met.

To illustrate the process of using a problem-oriented language, we present as an example one of the most successful problem-oriented languages ever devised, namely, APT (ITT, 1967).

APT stands for "automatically programmed tools." It was first developed at M.I.T. in the early 1950s to assist in the production of punched tapes for numerically controlled machine tools. The early versions of APT were restricted to two-dimensional objects, using only straight lines and circles. Later developments, which were sponsored by the Aerospace Industries Association, resulted in a system called APT II. APT II utilized a specialized language to describe geometric surfaces. In the 1960s the APT Long-Range Program, sponsored by numerous industries and conducted by the Illinois Institute of Technology Research Institute, developed APT III, which eventually became the de facto standard for numerical control applications. Most of the currently used languages for numerical control programming are extensions, variations, or subsets of APT.

THE APT SYSTEM. The utilization of numerical control for machine tools is one of the most significant modern developments in manufacturing. It has made possible the machining of components of great complexity, with tolerance conditions and repeatability never attained by conventional machining methods. It has provided great flexibility and economy in the production of both simple and complex parts. Numerical control (N/C) has been applied to milling machines, drilling and boring machines, lathes, machining centers, automatic wiring machines, welding and flame-cutting machines, etc.

To utilize an N/C tool, one must prepare a control tape that has recorded on it a description of all motions and machine functions required to fabricate the part on the tool. The control program on the tape may be very simple, as in the case of a drilling application with relatively few holes, or very complex, as in the case of milling turbine blades. The tape itself may be punched tape or magnetic tape, but, whatever its form, it must contain all the information about the machining operations to be performed. The system shown in Fig. 2 is numerically controlled by paper tape. Today, magnetic tape is more commonly used, and numerical control of the machine by a minicomputer attached to it is also common.

**Fig. 2.** Large milling machine numerically controlled by paper tape units (behind glass in center). Units at left record information on paper tape received from remote computer, which is then transferred to unit at center. (Courtesy of Illinois Institute of Technology Research Institute.)

In all but the simplest applications, a certain number of computations must be performed before the control tape can be produced. In the case of continuous path-control systems, literally thousands of computations must be performed to prepare a

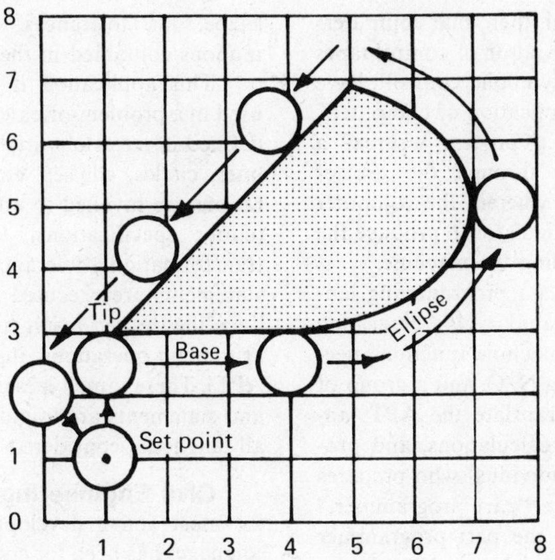


| Part Program | Explanation |
|---|---|
| CUTTER/1 | Use a 1 in. diameter cutter. |
| TOLER/.005 | Tolerance of cut is 0.005 in. |
| FEDRAT/80 | Move tool at feed rate of 80 in./min. |
| HEAD/1 | Use head #1. |
| SPINDL/2400 | Turn on spindle. Set at 2,400 rpm. |
| COOLNT/FLOOD | Turn on coolant. Use flood setting. |
| PT1 = POINT/4,5 | Define point PT1, as point with coordinates (4,5), used later to define ellipse. |
| FROM/(SETPT = POINT/1,1) | Start tool from point called SETPT, defined as point with coordinates (1,1). |
| INDIRP/(TIP = POINT/1,3) | Aim tool in direction of point called TIP, defined as point with coordinates (1,3). |
| BASE = LINE/TIP, AT ANGL, 0 | Define line called BASE as line through point TIP, which makes angle of 0 deg. with horizontal. |
| GO/TO, BASE | Go to the line BASE. |
| TL RGT, GO RGT/BASE | With tool on right of part with respect to direction of motion, go right along line BASE until tangency with next surface, the ellipse, is reached. |
| GO FWD/(ELLIPS/CENTER,PT1, 3,2,0) | Go forward along ellipse with center at PT1, semi-major axis = 3, semi-minor axis = 2, and major axis making angle of 0 deg with horizontal. |
| GO LFT/(LINE/2,4,1,3,), PAST, BASE | Go left along line joining points (2,4) and (1,3) past line BASE. |
| GOTO/SETPT | Go to point SETPT in a straight line. |
| COOLNT/OFF | Turn off coolant flow. |
| SPINDL/OFF | Turn off spindle. |
| END | This is end of machine control unit operation, |
| FINI | and the finish of part program. |

**Fig. 3.** An APT program for the two-dimensional cam shown at top. (From J. E. Sammet, *Programming Languages: History and Fundamentals*, Prentice-Hall, 1969.)

control tape. It is only natural, then, that computers have been applied to the preparation of control tapes for N/C tools. The words "symbolic control" have been used to describe this application of computers. Symbolic control describes a process wherein a human controls a machine through the use of language (i.e., symbols), and wherein the computer serves as his translator and calculator to produce the numerical signals for controlling the machine.

The APT system includes a programming language, which provides a vocabulary for describing the geometry, motions, and machine functions necessary to produce a part using N/C, and a group of computer programs, which translate the APT language, perform the required calculations, and produce the control tape. The individual who prepares the APT program is called a "part programmer." The APT language provides the part programmer with a vocabulary to describe a large variety of two- and three-dimensional part geometry, to define tool shape, to specify tolerance, to command cutter motion, to indicate machining functions, to perform in-line computations, and to execute program logic and specify geometric transformations. These features, when used individually and in combination, offer the part programmer the possibility of producing simple or complex parts efficiently and economically.

THE APT LANGUAGE. We will illustrate the APT language by describing the process of writing a part program for a two-dimensional cam (Fig. 3). The APT language is used to:

1. Give names or symbols to the different geometrical elements of the part.
2. Describe the dimension and shape of the tool with which the part is to be cut.
3. Specify the computational tolerance. This tolerance is used by the computer to calculate the offset of the tool from the surfaces of the part and to determine successive cutter locations. By changing tolerances from run to run, machining can be varied from rough cuts to finer cuts.
4. Define the geometry of the part.
5. Describe the motion of the tool. Here, the part programmer acts as if he were sitting on the tool and driving it, like a car, around the part.
6. Specify auxiliary functions of the controller-machine tool combination.

With these elements, one obtains the part program shown in Fig. 3. The APT computer system calculates successive cutter positions to fabricate the part specified, taking into account the defined tool shape, the tolerances, part geometry, and tool motions contained in the part program.

This application is typical of the procedures used in a problem-oriented language. The problem is defined in terms of variables and data types (points, lines, circles, ellipses, etc., in APT), certain declarations are invoked to establish proper environment (cutter specifications, tool positions, coordinate transformations, tolerance, etc., in APT), and then statements are executed in a specific order to produce the desired result (tool motion, program logic, arithmetic operations, input/output control, etc., in APT). These same types of expressions, declarations, and statements are found in one form or another in all languages considered here.

**Civil Engineering Applications.** Some of the most active development of problem-oriented languages has been for civil engineering applications. The computer was recognized very early as an invaluable tool to the civil engineer in performing the numerous calculations in his work and in handling the complex data that are involved in the design and construction of bridges, building highways, harbors, etc.

The solution of civil engineering problems involves many disciplines. For example, in the design of a highway interchange, the engineer utilizes surveying, highway engineering, soil mechanics, structural engineering, hydraulic engineering, transportation engineering, etc. Computer aids to each of these fields have been developed over the past 20 years. Recent work has been done in combining these separate applications into an integrated package of programs known as ICES (Integrated Civil Engineering System). This section discusses some of the work that led up to the design and implementation of ICES, and then discusses ICES as an example of a unified system approach to problem-oriented languages.

COGO. Cogo (coordinate geometry) is a programming language used to perform the geometric calculations required in surveying. It was developed originally by Professor C. Miller of the M.I.T. Civil Engineering Department around 1960. It is now available on most computers and has been also implemented under several time-sharing systems.

Cogo provides the civil engineer with a large number of commands and associated programs to perform plane geometry computations. Some examples of Cogo commands are given below:

| | |
|---|---|
| DIVIDE/LINE | To divide a line into a specified number of segments. |

| | |
|---|---|
| LOCATE/AZIMUTH | To define a point, given the distance and azimuth from a specified point. |
| AREA | To calculate the area of a triangle, given the three vertices. |

STRESS. Structural Engineering Systems Solver (Stress) was developed (Fenves, 1964) with the objective of facilitating the use of computers in analyzing structures. The principal objective of Stress was to provide a wide variety of structural analyses with a minimum of programming effort. It can be used to analyze two- and three-dimensional structures, with either pinned or rigid joints, with prismatic or nonprismatic members, and subjected to concentrated or distributed loads, support motions, or temperature effects.

Stress was developed in the early 1960s under the direction of Professor S. J. Fenves at M.I.T. Numerous computer implementations of this language have been accomplished since this early work. The following statements are examples of types found in Stress.

*Header Statement.* The word STRUCTURE followed by any identifying information serves to start a new problem.

*Size Descriptors.* Several statements are needed to define the size of the problem to be handled. These include:

NUMBER OF JOINTS
NUMBER OF SUPPORTS
NUMBER OF MEMBERS
NUMBER OF LOADINGS

*Structural Data Descriptors.* To describe completely a framed structure, it is necessary to provide information about its geometry, topology (interconnection of members and joints), mechanical properties (load-deflection relationships of the members), and the presence of local releases (such as hinges or rollers). Six types of statements are provided:

1. Geometry is specified in terms of joint coordinates by the statement

JOINT COORDINATES

followed by the $X$, $Y$, $Z$ coordinates of each joint (or $X$, $Y$ for plane structures). These statements are also used to describe the status (i.e., free or support) of the joints.

2. The presence of hinges or rollers at support joints is given as

JOINT RELEASES

followed by the joint numbers and the designation and orientation of the released (zero) force components.

3. The interconnection of the members is specified by the statement

MEMBER INCIDENCES

followed by a list giving the starting and ending joint of each member. The meaning of this statement is best illustrated by the descriptive input form, which for a typical member may be MEMBER 17 GOES FROM JOINT 10 TO JOINT 7.

4. The load-deflection properties of the members are specified as

MEMBER PROPERTIES

followed by a statement for each member, giving the type of member, and the labels and numerical values of the properties.

5. The presence of hinges in the members is given as

MEMBER RELEASES

followed by the member numbers, and the position and orientation of the released force components.

6. Constants associated with the members are specified by the

CONSTANTS

statement.

*Loading Data Descriptors.* The loading applied to the structure is specified in terms of loading condition descriptors, descriptors of individual loads, and descriptors of groups of loads, as follows:

1. The word

LOADING

followed by any identifying information, delineates groups of loads (together comprising a loading condition) and serves as a loading condition header.

2. Individual loads are specified by statements such as

JOINT LOADS

followed by the joint numbers and the components of applied load,

JOINT DISPLACEMENTS
MEMBER DISTORTIONS
MEMBER LOADS

followed by a statement for each load, giving the member number, the orientation, magnitude, and type of the load.

3. Certain loading specifications involve general information such as

COMBINE

followed by a list of loading conditions to be combined.

*Modification Descriptors.* To permit rapid evaluation of alternate designs, the following statements can be used after an initial problem has been defined:

| | |
|---|---|
| MODIFICATION | (with information for output identification) |
| ADDITIONS<br>CHANGES<br>DELETIONS | (interspersed with pertinent statements of all the above types describing the modification) |

*Termination Statements.* These statements terminate the input of portions of or all statements of a problem:

SOLVE
SOLVE THIS PART
FINISH

ICES. The problem-oriented languages discussed to this point have provided the user with language capability to solve very special problems, such as producing tapes for numerically controlled machine tools, solving problems in plane geometry, and performing structural analysis. The integrated civil engineering system (ICES), on the other hand, was designed to function as a series of subsystems, each subsystem corresponding to an engineering discipline (Roos, 1967). Each subsystem in ICES utilizes its own data structure; nevertheless, it provides for common files of problem data. ICES also provides an engineering programming language, command-definition language, and data-definition language to create subsystems. Thus, ICES is a framework within which engineering programs can be embedded.

The engineering programming language is Icetran, which is an extension of Fortran designed to handle civil engineering programming. With Icetran, a programmer can develop problem-oriented subsystems that become part of the ICES package.

To provide for a common method of defining the language elements, the subsystem designer makes use of a command-definition language (CDL) to specify the commands needed for the necessary problem-solving capabilities, as well as the external data requirements and the internal data processing required for each command. This information is transmitted to the computer in the command-definition language. The command-definition language requests are processed by the command-definition system program (an ICES subsystem), which produces a command dictionary, a COMMON map, and command data blocks for the subsystem. The dictionary and the command data blocks are used by ICEX, the ICES executive program, which processes the engineer's problem-oriented language commands.

There are two types of commands in ICES: system commands and subsystem commands. System commands are used by an engineer to specify the name of the ICES subsystem he wishes to use. Examples of system commands are Cogo, Strudl (structural design language), Sepol (settlement problem oriented language), etc. Subsystem commands refer to the engineering commands in each subsystem. The engineer specifies the appropriate system command, followed by the relevant subsystem commands. Assume, for example, that a structural engineer is working on a bridge-design problem. He will first give the BRIDGE system command, followed by BRIDGE subsystem commands. When he wishes to design the bridge geometry, he will issue the Cogo system command, followed by the Cogo subsystem commands. After the bridge geometry has been calculated, he will issue the BRIDGE system command, which returns him to the bridge subsystem.

Thus, the essence of ICES is the generation of appropriate subsystems for specific engineering applications, which are then used to solve a given class of problems. Once a new subsystem is generated, it becomes a part of the ICES package. The generation of a subsystem requires that a programmer:

1. Write a description of each subsystem command in CDL.
2. Write programs in Icetran to carry out the computations.
3. Design the load module structure.
4. Design the subsystem COMMON area.

*Example Subsystem.* As an example, let us consider the generation of a subsystem to analyze simple beams. The specifications for this subsystem will permit the engineer to input the length of the beam and a set of uniform and/or concentrated loads acting on it, and to obtain as output the reactions at the left and right ends resulting from this loading. After examining the reactions, the engineer could add new loads to the beam and recompute the reactions. Loadings may be deleted by applying negative loads to the beam. Only one beam will be maintained by the system at a time.

Summarized below is the information which the subsystem designer must specify to the ICES system.

Internal Structure. The data necessary for this subsystem are (1) the length of the beam, and (2) the position and magnitude of each load. Since only one beam is considered at a time, the beam length is stored as a scalar in COMMON. The information relating to each load is stored in dynamic arrays. The size of each dynamic subarray is determined by the type of loading (specification of a concentrated load requires less information than does specification of a uniform load).

The algorithms for solving the problem can be described quite simply. When a new beam is introduced, information (one array in this case) will be initialized, and the length of the beam will be stored in COMMON. An Icetran subroutine called FJSTRT will be used for this task. For each load applied to the beam, data subarrays will be defined, and information about the magnitude and position of the forces will be stored in them. A subroutine called FJLOAD will perform this task.

Finally, when the reactions are requested, a subroutine called FJREAC will be called to carry out bookkeeping functions on the stored loads. Then FJREAC calls FJRCAP for concentrated loads and FJRCAU for uniform loads. Subroutine FJRCAP handles concentrated loads by distributing the load between the two ends according to the ratio of the distances from the ends to the load. For example, a load that is three-quarters of the way across the beam will send three-quarters of its value to the support at the right end (closest support) and only one-quarter of its value to the left support. Subroutine FJRCAU handles uniform loads by finding the equivalent concentrated load and then calling FJRCAP.

Structure of the Commands. The convention of *underlining* that part of each command or identifier which is required is followed below. Data or identifiers in parentheses may be omitted. The name of the subsystem is FJSBEAM. Thus, the prefix of all programs will be FJ. When the engineer desires to use the system, he will give the name of the subsystem, followed by the length of the simple beam he wishes to analyze:

FJSBEAM length

where "length" will be the length in feet, a real number. Note that the entire word "FJSBEAM" must be used. If no value for "length" is given, 10 ft will be assumed. The use of the command implies that all information related to previously defined beams is to be deleted.

To add loads onto the beam, the engineer will have available the following command:

```
      { UNIFORM w        (POSITION) l1 (FROM) LEFT/RIGHT (TO) l2 (FROM) LEFT/RIGHT }
FORCE {                                                                       }
      { CONCENTRATED p   (POSITION) l3 (FROM) LEFT/RIGHT                        }
```

Here "w" is the load in pounds/foot, "p" the load in pounds, and "$l_1$", "$l_2$", and "$l_3$" are positions in feet on the beam. One of the choices of type of load *must* be made, and the magnitude of the specified load must be supplied. All optional words, if present, must be spelled out in full. If positional information is omitted, the following is assumed: For concentrated loads, the left end ($l_3$ = 0.0 FROM LEFT) is assumed; if a distance but not a support is given, the support is assumed to be left. On uniform loads, $l_1$ = 0.0 FROM LEFT, $l_2$ = 0.0 FROM RIGHT are assumed if not specified. Therefore, if no other information than the magnitude of the uniform load is given, that magnitude will be assumed to act on the entire beam.

Finally, when the reactions are desired, the engineer requests

REACTIONS

Note that any word starting with REAC is permitted. The routines needed for each command are shown in Fig. 4.

| Command | Icetran Programs Executed |
|---|---|
| FJSBEAM | FJSTRT |
| FORCE | FJLOAD |
| REACTIONS | FJREAC ↗ FJRCAP<br>FJREAC ↘ FJRCAU → FJRCAP |

**Fig. 4.** Relation between commands and Icetran programs (FJSBEAM).

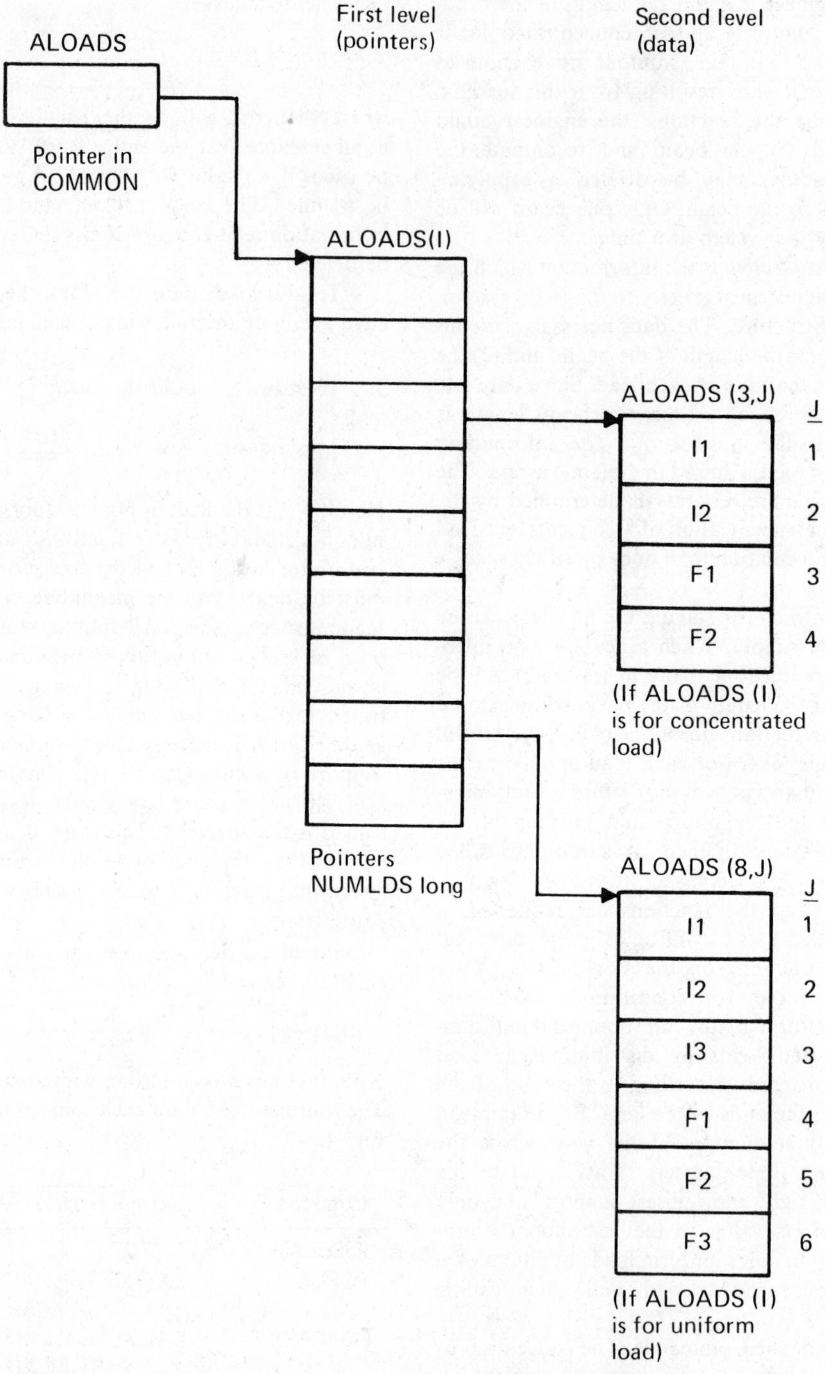


**Fig. 5.** The FJSBEAM data structure.

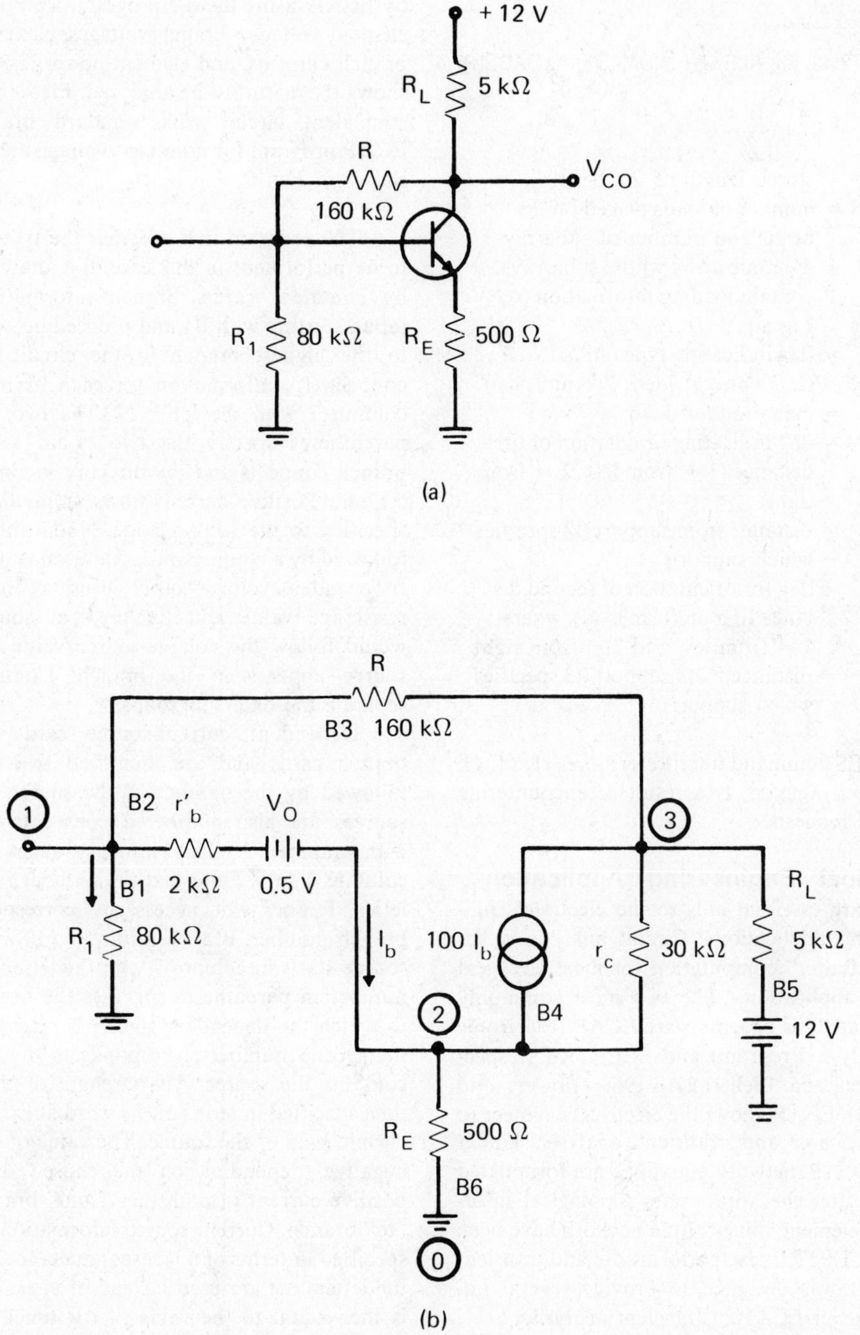


**Fig. 6.** Circuits on which ECAP program analyzes quiescent voltage. (a) Transistor amplifier; (b) equivalent circuit showing standard branches. ECAP program at bottom. (Copyright © 1971 by International Textbook Company. Reprinted from *Computer Analysis of Circuits* by David J. Comer by permission of Intext Educational Publishers, New York.)

Data Structure. Storage in COMMON is structured as follows:

I1, F1, I2, F2, I3, F3, ALENGT, NUMLDS, ALOADS(P)

where:

| | | |
|---|---|---|
| ALENGT | = | stored length of the beam |
| NUMLDS | = | number of loads placed on the beam and number of subarrays |
| ALOADS | = | dynamic array whose subarrays contain loading information (see Fig. 5) |
| I1 | = | flag indicating type of load (1 = concentrated; 2 = uniform) |
| F1 | = | magnitude of load |
| I2 | = | flag indicating orientation of first distance (1 = from left; 2 = from right) |
| F2 | = | distance from support (I2 specifies which support) |
| I3 | = | flag for orientation of second distance (if a uniform load), where 1 = from left and 2 = from right |
| F3 | = | distance from support (I3 specifies which support) |

The ICES command interpreter stores I1, F1, I2, F2, I3, F3, and ALENGT as a result of encountering data storage requests.

**Electrical Engineering Applications.** Computers are essential aids to the electrical engineer in many applications. Circuit analysis is the "bread and butter" computation for most electrical engineering applications. The two most commonly used circuit analysis programs are ECAP (Electronic Circuit Analysis Program) and SCEPTRE (respectively: Jensen and Lieberman, 1968; Bowers and Sedore, 1971). ECAP allows the electrical engineer to perform d-c, a-c, and transient analysis. Under control of ECAP, network equations are formulated and solved after the appropriate topological information and element values of the network have been provided. SCEPTRE also performs d-c and transient analysis, but was designed to provide several improvements over ECAP in transient analysis.

To illustrate the use of ECAP, a d-c analysis is performed (Comer, 1971). A transistor amplifier has been reduced to an equivalent circuit using the standard branches allowed in ECAP. The only branches permitted in ECAP in the d-c analysis program are independent d-c sources, dependent d-c current sources, and resistance or capacitance. Among the output quantities that can be calculated by ECAP, using the d-c program, are node voltages, element voltages, branch voltages, element currents, branch currents, and element power losses. Fig. 6(a) shows the circuit to be analyzed. Fig. 6(b) shows the equivalent circuit with standard branches. The ECAP program for quiescent voltage analysis is also shown in Fig. 6.

The program first specifies the type of analysis to be performed; in this case, d-c analysis followed by comment cards. Branch information is then input, starting with B1 and proceeding consecutively to the highest branch in the circuit. The nodal connectivity information for each branch starts in column 7 with the letter N. The two numbers in parentheses specify the two nodes to which the branch connects and the direction defining positive current. Positive current flows from the first node specified to the second node. Nodal information is followed by a comma and a finite value of resistance. Independent voltage-source information follows the resistance value and independent source current would follow the voltage-source value if a current source appears in the branch. Commas always separate the data subgroups.

Dependent current-source cards follow the branch cards and are identified by the letter T, followed by the number of the source. Dependent sources are also numbered consecutively, starting with number 1. This information is located in columns 1 to 5. Note that the number following the letter T does not necessarily correspond to the branch number. Branch information for the current source starts in column 7 with the letter B. The first number in parentheses specifies the branch current to which the dependent source is proportional, and the second number corresponds to the branch that contains the source. The strength of the source is then specified in terms of the word BETA, which is the current gain of the source. The value of BETA can be negative, depending on the chosen directions of positive current in both the "from" branch and the "to" branch. Current-source information can also be specified in terms of a transconductance. In this case the letters GM are used instead of BETA. The current is then equal to the value of GM times the voltage appearing across the resistance of the "from" branch.

There are only four circuit elements recognized by the ECAP d-c analysis program; resistors (or conductances), independent voltage sources, independent current sources, and dependent current sources. All these elements except independent cur-

**Table 1.** Representative Problem-Oriented Languages

| Application Area | Program Name |
|---|---|
| Statistics | SPSS: Statistical package for the social sciences |
| | Omnitab. |
| Computer-assisted instruction | PLATO: Programmed logic for automatic teaching operations |
| | Coursewriter. |
| Simulation | GPSS: General-purpose systems simulator |
| | Simscript. |
| | CSSL: Continuous system simulation language |
| Data-base management | IMS: Information management system |
| | GIS: Generalized information system |
| | TDMS: Time-shared data management system |
| Software engineering | AED: Automated engineering design |
| | Bliss: Basic language for implementing system software |

rent sources are used in the preceding program. After the topology of the network is described by B-cards (branches) and T-cards (dependent sources), an output specification card determines the output block of data to be printed.

**Other Problem-Oriented Languages.** Literally hundreds of problem-oriented languages have been developed over the past 20 years. We have looked in detail at the areas of numerical control, civil engineering, and electrical engineering. Table 1 summarizes some other representative languages, showing their areas of application. These, of course, are only a small percentage of the numerous languages in use today.

**Future Developments in Problem-Oriented Languages.** As the computer continues to enter new fields, the need for problem-oriented languages will increase. Computer science research in programming languages will impact future developments in special-purpose languages. One new area of research is the development of techniques to permit users to define their own language requirements and have an automatic procedure for generation of the translator for that language. The growth of interactive systems will permit a man-machine dialog for the definition, refinement, and generation of the user-developed language. The system would then produce the necessary language documentation, tutorial material, and compiler or interpreter to translate and execute programs in the new language.

As pointed out by Sammet (1969), the controversy over language structure will continue into the future. Some people advocate the use of English as a programming language. Others insist that many applications require a precision of expression which would be aided by a more formal and structured language than would be available when using natural language. Since this controversy is unlikely to subside in the near future, it seems reasonable to press for user-defined languages. In this way, the personal preference of the specific user could be satisfied. However, research in this field is only now beginning in earnest.

Another development in computer science, which is impacting problem-oriented languages, and will continue to do so, is the growth of time-sharing systems and interactive graphics. Many of the languages discussed in this article have been modified to include interactive processing. Numerical control, civil engineering, and electrical engineering are only some of the disciplines that are becoming heavily involved in the application of interactive graphics to problem solving. The design of future problem-oriented languages will be influenced by the availability of inexpensive graphics terminals as part of every time-sharing service.

Finally, new theoretical and practical work in compiler design, in extensible languages, in program complexity, in artificial intelligence, and in many other areas of computer science will influence the design, utility, accessibility, and application of new problem-oriented languages. The use of problem-oriented languages will continue to expand because specialists in every discipline will want to communicate with the computer in languages that are comfortable for them to use and which provide them with the greatest degree of expressiveness possible.

REFERENCES

1958. Theodoroff, T. J. "DYANA: Dynamics Analyzer-Programmer, Part I, Description and Application," *Proc. Eastern Joint Computer Conference,* pp. 144–147.

1964. Fenves, S. J., et al. *STRESS: A User's Manual.* Cambridge, Mass.: M.I.T. Press

1967. IIT Research Institute. *APT Part Programming.* New York: McGraw-Hill.

1967. Roos, D. *ICES Systems Design.* Cambridge, Mass.: M.I.T. Press.

1968. Jensen, R. W., and M. D. Lieberman. *IBM Electronic Circuit Analysis Program—Techniques and Applications.* Englewood Cliffs, N.J.: Prentice-Hall.

1969. Sammet, Jean E. *Programming Languages: History and Fundamentals.* Englewood Cliffs, N.J.: Prentice-Hall.

1971. Bowers, J. C., and S. R. Sedore. *SCEPTRE: A Computer Program for Circuit and Systems Analysis.* Englewood Cliffs, N.J.: Prentice-Hall.

1971. Comer, D. J. *Computer Analysis of Circuits.* Scranton, Pa.: International Textbook.

B. MITTMAN

# PROCEDURE

For articles on related subjects *see* ARGUMENT; BLOCK STRUCTURE; PROCEDURE-ORIENTED LANGUAGES; SUBPROGRAMS, CALLING; and SUBROUTINE.
For article on related term *see* STRING.

A procedure is a portion of a higher-level language program which performs a specific task necessary for that program. This term is normally used interchangeably with the terms "subprogram" and "subroutine" when referring to higher-level languages, although the term "subroutine" has a wider meaning outside higher-level languages. The use of procedures is so central to programming in general-purpose, higher-level languages such as Fortran, Algol, and PL/I that these languages are often known as "procedure-oriented" languages.

Early in the development of programming languages, it was recognized that programs would be written in which the same process was to be executed at several different locations within the program. One example of such a process is the evaluation of mathematical functions such as logarithms and exponentials, or trigonometric functions such as sine or cosine. To accomplish this conveniently, a facility was needed to permit the programmer to code such a procedure once and then to call that process whenever it was needed.

**Table 1.** Fortran Functions

| Name of function | Mathematical Definition | Fortran Name |
|---|---|---|
| Sine | sin x | SIN |
| Cosine | cos x | COS |
| Exponential | $e^x$ | EXP |
| Natural logarithm | ln x | ALOG† |
| Absolute value | $\|x\|$ | ABS |
| Maximum | Value of maximum of $x_1, x_2, \ldots, x_n$ | AMAXI† |

†The A in front of these names is required because Fortran names beginning with L or M automatically have integer values.

Procedures in higher-level languages are of two types: intrinsic (or built-in) and programmer written. Intrinsic procedures are those provided with the language so that the programmer need only call them in his program and have them automatically *invoked.* This invocation requires only that the programmer give the *name* of the procedure and its *arguments.* Fortran, for example, has numerous built-in functions, a short list of which is given in Table 1. If a program contains a variable X and the programmer wishes to compute the cosine of the current value assigned to that variable, he has only to write

```
COS(X)
```

If he wishes to assign to variable A the absolute value of the sum of the cosine and sine of the argument, he may write

```
A = ABS(COS(X) + SIN(X))
```

If he wished B to be the maximum of the sine and exponential of the arguments, he writes

```
B = AMAXI(SIN(X),EXP(X))
```

Other higher-level languages have different sets of intrinsic procedures. Algol has a much smaller number of intrinsic procedures than Fortran and PL/I has a much larger number. For example, PL/I has a built-in function that allows the programmer to extract a *substring* from a named string of characters which is an argument of the function. Intrinsic procedures are often called "functions" because they involve common mathematical functions and because they are used in arithmetic expressions in higher-level languages just like mathematical functions.

The availability of intrinsic functions clearly suggests the need for a parallel facility to permit the programmer to define his own procedures at the same time that he writes the referencing or *main* program. Thus, the programmer could write "subprograms" in the language and then reference these in the same manner as intrinsic procedures. All general-purpose, higher-level languages have such a facility, although the details of how it can be used and how it is implemented vary considerably.

In Fortran, programmer-written procedures are called subprograms and distinguished in two types: FUNCTION subprograms and SUBROUTINE subprograms. The former are directly analogous to intrinsic functions in that FUNCTIONs are invoked or *called* just like intrinsic functions. Fig. 1 is an example of a programmer-written FUNCTION to calculate the sum of the products of the corresponding elements of two 100-element arrays together with two main program statements calling this function. Note in particular that the *value* of the function is the value assigned to its name (PROD in Fig. 1).

```
     Main program
       —
       —
       —
  A=C+(D*E)/PROD(F,G)
       —
  Q1=Q2*PROD(Q3,Q4)

  FUNCTION PROD (X,Y)
  REAL X(100),Y(100)
  PROD = 0.
  DO 2 I=1,100
2   PROD = PROD + X(I)*Y(I)
  RETURN
  END
```

**Fig. 1.** A FUNCTION in Fortran.

```
      Main Program
        —
        —
        —
        —
    CALL TRANS (B,100,100)
        —
        —
    CALL TRANS (C,50,50)
        —
        —
        —

    SUBROUTINE TRANS (A,M,N)
    REAL A (M,N)
    DO 2 I=1, M
    I1=I+1
    DO 2 J=I1, N
C   NOTE NEED TO SAVE A (I,J)
C   BEFORE REPLACING IT BY A (J,I)
      TEMP=A(I,J)
      A(I,J)=A(J,I)
2     A(J,I)=TEMP
    RETURN
    END
```

**Fig. 2.** A Fortran SUBROUTINE.

```
begin
  real B[1:100,1:100],C[1:50,1:50];
  real procedure TRANS (A,M,N);
    real array A; real TEMP; integer M,N,I,J;
      for I=1 step 1 until M do
        for J=I+1 step 1 until N do
          begin
            TEMP:=A[I,J];
            A[I,J]:=A[J,I];
            A[J,I]:=TEMP;
          end
      —
      —
      —
      —
        TRANS(B,100,100);
      —
      —
      —
      —
        TRANS(C,50,50);
  —
  —
  —
  —
end
```

**Fig. 3.** An Algol procedure.

In Fortran, SUBROUTINE subprograms differ from FUNCTION subprograms in the method by which they are called and in the lack of any requirement that a specific result as such be produced. Fig. 2 is an example of a SUBROUTINE subprogram to transpose the elements of a two-dimensional array [i.e., interchange the (I,J) and (J,I) elements]. Note that the only "result" of the subprogram is the input matrix with its elements interchanged, and that the subprogram is not called in an assignment statement but by a CALL statement.

Also in Fortran, as shown in Figs. 1 and 2, procedures are physically separate from the main program, but in block-structured languages they are an integral part of the main program. Fig. 3 shows an example from Algol corresponding to that in Fig. 2 for Fortran. Here the procedure is a *declaration* at the start of the *block* which is the Algol program, although a procedure may be declared in any subblock of the program also. The procedure is called by giving just its name followed by its arguments.

Algol also has a procedure facility analogous to Fortran functions. PL/I is also a block-structured language and has procedure facilities very similar to those in Algol. By contrast with block-structured languages and Fortran, Cobol has a quite rudimentary procedure facility that integrates subprograms into the main program in a much more restrictive context than with languages like Algol or PL/I.

The contrast between the physically separate procedures of Fortran and those integrated into the main program, as in block-structured languages, needs to be noted and understood. The former allows separate compilation of the main program and subprograms, which may be convenient during debugging. Block-structured languages require recompilation of the procedure every time the program is recompiled, but the integration of procedures into the main program is an aid of great value to programming and to thinking about programming.

J. A. N. LEE AND A. RALSTON

# PROCEDURE, PURE

For article on related subject *see* REENTRANT PROGRAM.

A pure procedure is one that never modifies any part of itself during execution. Thus, any data subject to modification during execution of the pure procedure must be stored in memory associated with the calling program. A reentrant program is, therefore, generally a pure procedure.

A. RALSTON

# PROCEDURE-ORIENTED LANGUAGES

## SURVEY

For articles on related subjects *see* ALGOL 68; ITERATION; LANGUAGE PROCESSORS; LIST PROCESSING LANGUAGES; MACHINE AND ASSEMBLY LANGUAGE PROGRAMMING; PASCAL; PROGRAM-ORIENTED LANGUAGES; PROGRAMMING LANGUAGES; STRING PROCESSING LANGUAGES; STANDARDS; and SUBPROGRAMS, CALLING.
For articles on related terms *see* BACKUS-NAUR FORM; and META LANGUAGE.

A procedure-oriented language (POL) is a way of expressing commands to a computer in a form somewhat similar to such natural languages as English and mathematics. It is distinguished from machine language and assembly language—in which we are constrained to express ourselves in a form much closer to the language of the machine itself—and problem-oriented languages, in which we state our problem and leave the system to choose a procedure for solving it. It is also distinguished from list-processing and string-processing languages, which do in fact express procedures and not problems, but which are different in that the information processed is almost entirely symbolic. All of these and other forms of programming languages are treated elsewhere in this Encyclopedia.

In one sense a computer can understand only its own machine language. From this point of view a procedure expressed in any other language must be translated into machine language before it can be executed. The translation is done by another program of machine instructions, called a "translator," "processor," or (most commonly) a "compiler." The process is usually called "compilation." The input to the compilation, the program written in a POL, is the source program, and the output is a machine-language program called the object program. It is the object program that is actually executed to process data.

**Advantages and Disadvantages.** When the early POLs were introduced in the 1950s, they were seen primarily in relation to assembly language, compared with which they promised several advantages and some disadvantages. Most of these considerations still apply, although today the choice is seldom solely between assembly language and POLs.

POLs offer savings in programming time. Since the programmer can concentrate on the procedure and worry less about how the machine will carry out the details, his productivity is usually higher. There is a further speed factor because a line of coding in a POL generally produces—after compilation—many machine instructions.

Since the procedure is written in a form closer to human means of communication, documentation and program understandability are enhanced. If the programmer takes a little additional care in writing the program, using meaningful data names, for example, the program may become—at least to some extent—its own documentation.

All programs that are used over an extended period of time have to be maintained because requirements and procedures change. When programs are written in assembly language, rather simple-appearing changes in such things as data formats can mean extensive reprogramming, which is time consuming, expensive, and error prone. In a POL it is generally a simple matter to make the necessary changes and recompile the entire program.

A program written in a POL can be used on any computer for which an appropriate compiler exists. For the more widely used POLs, such as Fortran and Cobol, compilers are available for all medium- and large-sized computers and for many minicomputers. With hopefully only a few changes having to do with minor language and machine differences, a POL program that has been running on one machine can be transferred to another one with only a simple recompilation required.

Finally, a POL is usually rather easier to learn than an assembly language. This assertion can be challenged in terms of the full reach of the most powerful POL's, but relatively few people need to know *everything* about the language they are using, especially the more powerful ones. Ease of learning obviously eases the programmer training problem. Furthermore, this training is transferable just as programs are: A person who knows Cobol can write programs for any computer that has a Cobol compiler (which is most), with only modest retraining to become familiar with minor language differences and what little needs to be known about machine differences.

The advantages of POLs outweigh their disadvantages, in most peoples' minds, but there are disadvantages. The compilers are expensive to write, are often delivered late, and routinely have many errors in them at first. The direct expense is usually borne by the manufacturer, but naturally the customer pays in the end. They take more computer storage space than an assembler, and if the user does not otherwise need the extra storage, this cost must be considered.

The claims for transferability or portability of programs and programmer training are sometimes exaggerated, since the languages implemented by different manufacturers are not really identical. A few differences can be explained by machine differences, but beyond that there is a great temptation for every implementor to add extra features that he considers desirable. These features, regardless of how valuable they may be, detract from the ability to move a program or a programmer to another installation that uses a different system.

The early POLs had compilers that were quite slow, and produced programs that executed much more slowly than corresponding assembly language programs written by an accomplished programmer. The charge against POLs, accordingly, was that they were expensive in machine time and that this was an unavoidable price that had to be paid for such advantages as speed of programming. This argument has nearly died out as compilers have been steadily improved over the years, and as it has become obvious that there will never be enough accomplished assembly language programmers to write all the programs that are needed.

On balance, it is clear that the advantages dramatically outweigh the disadvantages, and that POLs are here to stay. Improvements and modifications will be made, presumably indefinitely, but the basic concept will be with us for the foreseeable future.

**Fortran.** The first POL to be widely used was Fortran (see McCracken, 1963), an acronym that was coined from the words "FORmula TRANslation." Work on Fortran began in the mid-1950s by a committee composed of people from IBM and some of its customers. The name of John W. Backus of IBM is most closely associated with the effort.

Fortran was designed initially for use on problems of a mathematical nature, and it is still most commonly used for solving problems in mathematics, engineering, and science. Nothing in the language actually forces this specialization, however, and Fortran is widely employed as a vehicle for teaching computer applications and programming to students without extensive mathematical backgrounds because it is fairly easy to learn.

For problems of a technical nature, Fortran is by far the most widely used computer language. Since there are more business than technical applications of computers, however, Cobol is more widely used on an industry-wide basis.

An illustrative program, shown in Fig. 1, demonstrates some of the features of the language. The program is designed to find the roots of the quadratic equation $ax^2 + bx + c = 0$, which are given by the formula

$$x = \frac{-b \pm \sqrt{b^2 - 4ac}}{2a}.$$

The program is to read values of $a$, $b$, and $c$ from a card, compute and print the roots, and then go back to read another card. Each time a card is read, a check is made to determine whether $a = 0$, which will be used to signal that the end of the deck of data cards has been read. We will assume that the equation does have real roots, which means that the discriminant (the quantity under the square root sign) will always be positive.

```
  5  READ (5, 100) A, B, C
100  FORMAT (3F10.0)
     IF (A .EQ. 0.0) STOP
     DISC = B**2 - 4.0*A*C
     X1 = (-B + SQRT(DISC))/(2.0*A)
     X2 = (-B - SQRT(DISC))/(2.0*A)
     WRITE (6, 200) A, B, C, X1, X2
200  FORMAT (1X, 5F12.5)
     GO TO 5
     END
```

**Fig. 1.** A Fortran program.

Looking at the program in Fig. 1, we see that it begins with a READ statement, which is a command to read an input record (a card, usually) and assign three values from it to the variables named A, B, and C. The 5 in parentheses identifies a card reader, and the 100 is the statement number of the FORMAT statement that follows. Within parentheses in the FORMAT, we describe the numbers as they will be punched on a card: The 3 means three numbers, the F means "fixed format," the 10 means that each number will occupy ten columns, and the zero means that if we do not punch a decimal point, the numbers will be taken as having zero places after the decimal point (i. e., as being integers). Since we will in fact punch decimal points in the numbers, the zero has no effect.

The IF statement is an example of a conditional: If the logical expression in parentheses is true (i.e., if A is equal to (.EQ.) zero), program execution is to stop.

The calculation of the discriminant is done with an arithmetic assignment statement in which we see how arithmetic operations are designated by various symbols. The minus sign for subtraction and the asterisk for multiplication are fairly obvious; two asterisks together call for raising to a power (exponentiation). We see in the following statement the plus sign for addition and the slash (/) for division. An arithmetic assignment statement is a command to evaluate the expression on the right of the equal sign, using values for the variables that have been previously read or computed, and assign that value to the variable named on the left. In the following two assignment statements we have examples of the use of parentheses to indicate groupings of quantities, and of a function to compute the square root. When the compiler encounters the function name SQRT it calls upon a library of previously programmed subroutines and makes provision to incorporate the square-root routine in the program that will later be executed.

The WRITE statement calls for the printing of the data values and the roots. The FORMAT statement that is referenced this time specifies single spacing with the 1X, and with the 5F12.5 calls for each of the five numbers to be printed in 12 character positions with 5 digits after the decimal point.

The GO TO statement causes a transfer of control back to the statement labeled with the number 5, to repeat execution of the program. The END is a notice to the Fortran compiler that the end of the program has been reached and that compilation can be completed.

In Fig. 2 we have a sample of the output that could be produced after this program has been compiled and is being executed. We see in the first line, for instance, that the roots of the equation $x^2 - 1.5x - 4.5 = 0$ are 3.0 and $-1.5$.

The program shown in Fig. 3 exhibits some additional Fortran features, especially the handling of an array of data as distinguished from a single value. Here the name Z stands for 100 separate data

| | | | | |
|---|---|---|---|---|
| 1.00000 | -1.50000 | -4.50000 | 3.00000 | -1.50000 |
| 1.00000 | -2.00000 | 1.00000 | 1.00000 | 1.00000 |
| 100.00000 | -200.00000 | 100.00000 | 1.00000 | 1.00000 |
| 1.00000 | -10.00000 | 25.00000 | 5.00000 | 5.00000 |
| 1.00000 | -3.00000 | 2.00000 | 2.00000 | 1.00000 |
| 2.00000 | -6.00000 | 4.00000 | 2.00000 | 1.00000 |
| 1.00000 | 1.00000 | -2550.00000 | 50.00000 | -51.00000 |
| 1.43200 | 9.87600 | -4.56700 | 0.43500 | -7.33164 |
| 8.81300 | -1.31000 | 0.0 | 0.14864 | 0.0 |
| 2.30030 | 1.99170 | 0.0 | 0.0 | -0.86584 |

**Fig. 2.** Output of program of Fig. 1.

```
      DIMENSION Z(100)
      READ (5, 50) N
 50   FORMAT (I3)
C CHECK FOR N OUT OF RANGE
      IF ( N .LT. 1 .OR. N .GT. 100 )STOP
C READ DATA VALUES
      DO 60 K = 1, N
 60   READ (5, 70) Z(K)
 70   FORMAT (F10.0)
C CLEAR SUMMING LOCATION TO ZERO
      SUMSQ = 0.0
C GET SUM OF SQUARES
      DO 80 K = 1, N
 80   SUMSQ = SUMSQ + Z(K)**2
      WRITE (6, 90) N, SUMSQ
 90   FORMAT (1X, I5, 1PG15.6)
      STOP
      END
```

**Fig. 3.** Fortran program showing additional features.

elements, which fact is specified by the DIMENSION statement. We wish to read some number of data items, probably fewer than 100, and form the sum of their squares. The program reads the value of N from a card, then reads N additional cards, assigning the data values from them to the successive elements of the array named Z. The DO statement says to carry out the READ statement N times, with the index variable named K running from 1 to N. This index is used as the subscript that identifies a particular element of Z. The formation of the sum of squares is handled by another DO loop, as it is called, in which a variable named SUMSQ accumulates the squares after having been started at zero. We note the use of comments (lines beginning with a C) to make the meaning of the program clearer.

An important feature of most POLs is the ability to write subroutines that can be compiled separately, if desired, and then combined with a main program and run. This permits more effective division of effort on large projects, improves documentation, facilitates program checkout, and saves effort when previously programmed routines can be used. In Fortran this capability is provided by the FUNCTION and SUBROUTINE features, of which we illustrate the latter.

Suppose that a subroutine is desired which will accept the coefficients of a quadratic equation and return the roots. The program of Fig. 4 begins with a notice to the compiler that this is a SUBROUTINE, and gives its name and the names of the three input and two output arguments. The assignment statements are as before, after which we have a RETURN. The scheme is that during the execution of some other program, we would encounter a statement calling for the execution of this subroutine, at the end of which control would be transferred back to the calling program. In calling the subroutine, we specify actual arguments. If we want the roots of the equation $x^2 - 4x + 3 = 0$, assigning them to the variables named $R$ and $S$, we would write

```
CALL QUAD(1.0, -4.0, 3.0, R, S)
```

If the three coefficients were Y, Z(13), and F+12.3,

```
SUBROUTINE QUAD(A, B, C, X1, X2)
DISC = B**2 - 4.0*A*C
X1 = (-B + SQRT(DISC))/(2.0*A)
X2 = (-B - SQRT(DISC))/(2.0*A)
RETURN
END
```

**Fig. 4.** A Fortran subroutine.

with the roots being array elements T(1) and T(2), we would write

```
CALL QUAD(Y, Z(13), F+12.3, T(1), T(2))
```

To find the roots of different equations the subroutine could thus be called many times from the same calling program.

A subroutine can be designed to carry out alternative calculations, and then convey information about its execution back to the calling program. In our quadratic equation illustration, we might wish to have the subroutine tell the calling program whether the roots are real or complex, calculating them in either case. To do this, we would need to have two parameters for the real and imaginary parts of the roots if they are complex, and an additional parameter to carry the real or complex information. This latter parameter might be set to zero for real and to one for complex, for example, or any other convention that might seem convenient. The calling program could test this parameter to determine how to process the roots, or perhaps to choose appropriate printing formats for the two cases.

Some of the more important features of Fortran, which it is not possible to illustrate here, include the details of handling input and output, complex and double precision operations, and the control of storage allocation with the COMMON and EQUIVALENCE statements.

Standards on Fortran were adopted by the American National Standards Institute, ANSI, in 1966, with provision for occasional revision. Most Fortran implementations differ from the standard (and from each other), most commonly in the way they add features not covered in the standard. Some of these features offer considerable convenience and power to the programmer, but at the expense of a partial loss of such POL advantages as program and programmer transferability and ease of learning.

One variation of Fortran deserves mention because of its importance and wide use. Watfor and its successor Watfiv were developed at the University of Waterloo, Canada, originally for student use. They offer simplified input and output operations, very fast compilation, and extensive error diagnostics. They are ideal for beginning students, but they also have value to the experienced programmer in the early stages of program checkout because of the error diagnostics. Since the source language is little different from other Fortrans, it is a simple matter to check out a program using Watfiv and then make a final compilation on some other compiler that may produce a faster-running object program.

**Cobol.** Cobol is intended for use in the solution of problems in business data processing; the acronym stands for COmmon Business Oriented Language. It was developed in the late 1950s by a group of computer manufacturers and users, especially the U.S. government. The work built on several other POL's, which had been developed earlier. The name of Grace Murray Hopper of the Sperry-Rand Corporation and the U.S. Navy is most closely associated with the effort.

Cobol is probably used by a majority of those business computer installations for which a Cobol compiler is available. It is by a good margin the most widely used POL. Cobol, like Fortran, has been standardized by the American National Standards Institute; but, also like Fortran, many implementations differ from the standard (McCracken and Gerbassi, 1970).

Major goals of the early Cobol efforts were easy readability of computer programs and as much machine independence as possible. This latter means that it was to be possible to run a Cobol program on any computer for which a compiler existed with only minor modifications. This would simplify programmer training, too, it was hoped, and there were hints at one stage that persons without training in programming might be able to write their own programs. This has not turned out to be the case, but other advantages have been realized.

A Cobol program is composed of four divisions, each with a distinct function and with varying degrees of machine independence. We will consider some of the features of the divisions in conjunction with a very simple but complete Cobol program. The function of the program is to read records containing the number of hours a man worked in a week and his hourly pay rate, and compute his gross pay, with time-and-a-half for any hours over 40. For each record read, a line is to be printed giving the input data and the gross pay, with appropriate decimal points and a dollar sign included. The program is shown in Fig. 5.

The IDENTIFICATION DIVISION in this case consists of just one line giving a name to the program, and has no other effect on the compilation.

The ENVIRONMENT DIVISION functions to link the DATA DIVISION (which is mostly machine independent) and the PROCEDURE DIVISION (which is almost entirely machine independent) with the actual equipment that will be used. Using the SELECT verb, we designate the devices that will hold the input and output files. We have used symbolic names (CARD and PRINTER) so that the final decision on what the devices will be can be postponed to the latest

```
IDENTIFICATION DIVISION.
PROGRAM-ID. PAYROLL.

ENVIRONMENT DIVISION.
INPUT-OUTPUT SECTION.
FILE-CONTROL.
    SELECT IN-FILE ASSIGN TO UT-S-CARDS.
    SELECT OUT-FILE ASSIGN TO UT-S-PRINTER.

DATA DIVISION.
FILE SECTION.
FD  IN-FILE
    LABEL RECORDS ARE OMITTED.
01  IN-RECORD.
    02  HOURS-WORKED                PICTURE 99V9.
    02  PAYRATE                     PICTURE 9V999.
    02  FILLER                      PICTURE X(73).
FD  OUT-FILE
    LABEL RECORDS ARE OMITTED.
01  OUT-RECORD.
    02  HOURS-WORKED-EDITED         PICTURE ZZ99.9.
    02  PAYRATE-EDITED              PICTURE ZZ9.999.
    02  GROSS-PAY-EDITED            PICTURE $$$$$$$9.99.
    02  FILLER                      PICTURE X(56).
WORKING-STORAGE SECTION.
01  EXTRA                           PICTURE 99V99.
01  GROSS-PAY                       PICTURE 999V99.

PROCEDURE DIVISION.
INITIALIZATION.
    OPEN INPUT IN-FILE, OUTPUT OUT-FILE.
PROCESSING-ROUTINE.
    READ IN-FILE RECORD
        AT END GO TO WRAPUP.
    MULTIPLY HOURS-WORKED BY PAYRATE GIVING GROSS-PAY ROUNDED.
    IF HOURS-WORKED GREATER THAN 40
      COMPUTE EXTRA ROUNDED = 0.5 * (HOURS-WORKED - 40) * PAYRATE
      ADD EXTRA TO GROSS-PAY.
    MOVE SPACES TO OUT-RECORD.
    MOVE HOURS-WORKED TO HOURS-WORKED-EDITED.
    MOVE PAYRATE TO PAYRATE-EDITED.
    MOVE GROSS-PAY TO GROSS-PAY-EDITED.
    WRITE OUT-RECORD.
    GO TO PROCESSING-ROUTINE.
WRAPUP.
    CLOSE IN-FILE, OUT-FILE.
    STOP RUN.
```

**Fig. 5.** A Cobol program.

possible time, when the object program is actually run, to gain further flexibility.

In the preceding paragraph we called the word SELECT a *verb*. This is an important concept in POLs, and is perhaps the most important of several borrowings from the terminology of English grammar. A verb, as the term is used here, is an imperative, a command to carry out some action. In Cobol, the verb is always the first word of the sentence, which greatly simplifies the work of the compiler in determining the meaning of the sentence. Moreover, the verbs (as well as other Cobol words) are *reserved words* and therefore cannot be used also as data names. If the verb calls for action on data, the data names can be thought of as nouns. If two or more data items have the same name, and therefore have to be qualified as to which record or other data group they are in, the qualifiers can be thought of as adjectives, although the terminology is not used as such. Finally, for our purposes here, the term "declaration" is used to denote POL language elements that do not call for any processing actions, but rather describe such matters as data formats, the grouping of data items into arrays, and record layouts. Everything in the Cobol DATA DIVISION, described next, consists of declarations.

The DATA DIVISION is used to describe all files that will be used by the program, together with the arrangement of information into records within the files. In our case we have two files, named IN-FILE and OUT-FILE. The record description for IN-RECORD begins with 01, which is called the "first level." The second level consists of the data items within the record, which is the lowest level in this simple program. We could have such things as a date at one level broken into month and day, and year at the next level. Within the PROCEDURE DIVISION it would be possible to refer either to the entire date or to any of its components. This kind of data structure is widely used in business data processing, and is an important feature of Cobol.

Each of the items at the lowest level must be described as to format: the number of characters, whether digits or letters, where the assumed decimal point is, any initial value, etc. This is handled here with the PICTURE clause, with which we essentially provide an illustration of what the item looks like. Other ways are provided for conveying the same information, but are less commonly used. In the PICTURE clauses for the output record OUT-RECORD, we see that for printing the output the PICTURE can be used to control format. The z's call for the suppression of leading zeros, embedded decimal points call for insertion of decimal points into the output (the v's in IN-RECORD indicate the position of the decimal point on input), and the dollar signs call for a "floating dollar sign," i.e., one dollar sign immediately to the left of the first significant digit. The FILLER is used to describe unused space.

The working storage section in this case provides temporary storage for quantities between the time they are computed and the time they are converted to a form suitable for printing.

The PROCEDURE DIVISION specifies the processing to be done. Since Cobol verbs are all ordinary English words, a person without extensive training can understand this division more readily than with most POLs. We note that computation can be specified either by words (MULTIPLY HOURS-WORKED BY PAYRATE. . .) or by using a formula style much like Fortran except that it is introduced by the verb COMPUTE.

```
40.0 3.000  $120.00
42.0 3.000  $129.00
37.5 3.888  $145.80
40.0 3.888  $155.52
41.0 3.888  $161.35
50.0 3.888  $213.84
44.0 2.200  $101.20
44.0 9.876  $454.30
22.0 2.876   $63.27
```

**Fig. 6.** Output of program of Fig. 5.

Fig. 6 shows the output produced when the program was compiled and run with representative data.

We see in this program that data names can be much longer than in Fortran, up to 30 characters, and that they may be hyphenated. If a Cobol program is written with an eye to easy readability, using meaningful data names, it can indeed be quite readable.

One of the important innovations in Cobol was the rigid separation of the data and procedure divisions, a separation that is left partly implicit in many POLs, as in Fortran. When processing or data specifications change, as they frequently do in most applications, appropriate changes can be made in just the items affected and the programs can be recompiled. Something as simple as the expansion of a data item from two digits to three can result in changes in almost all parts of the object program. Without some way of keeping the data descriptions from being embedded in the procedure description, programs become extremely inflexible and difficult to change.

Important Cobol features that we are not able to cover here include details of input and output processing, the handling of conditionals and subscripts, and the facilities for controlling loops.

**Algol.** Algol (ALGOrithmic Language) was developed by an international committee that began work in the late 1950s (McCracken, 1962). The goal, as the name suggests, was to devise a language for expressing algorithms, whether intended for later execution on a computer or not. The language as defined was very machine independent, although particular implementations of necessity develop some dependence on the machine used.

Compared with Fortran, which Algol followed by a few years, Algol introduced a number of important concepts. Some of the new features offered easier and more powerful ways of doing common information processing operations. The means for controlling loop execution are much more flexible and comprehensive than in Fortran; it is possible to specify what is to be done on both branches of a conditional statement instead of only on the "true" path; there are facilities for grouping a set of statements into one compound statement that can be treated as a whole by other program elements. Algol distinguishes between global variables, which are known in all parts of a program, and local variables, which are known only in the program block where they are declared. (Some variation of this distinction appears in most POLs.) This concept of block structure, whereby we are able to divide a program into precisely defined and named segments, with explicit control over the blocks in which variables are "known," is one of the most significant contributions by the designers of Algol to the development of POLs.

We will illustrate a few of these features, this time without showing a complete program.

The Algol **for** statement is used to control loop execution; it is a much more powerful version of the Fortran DO. To find the sum of the squares of the N elements of the array named Z we could write:

```
sumsq := 0.0; for k := 1 step 1 until N do
sumsq := sumsq + Z[k] ↑ 2;
```

We see that statements are followed by semicolons as delimiters; that the combination := is used to specify the replacement of a variable value by the value of an expression; and that the exponentiation operator is denoted by an upward-pointing arrow instead of the double asterisk that we have seen in Fortran and Cobol. In the language as defined, variable names may be of any length and may use both upper and lower-case letters; actual implementations may place restrictions on this freedom.

An interesting example of the **for** statement, suggested by Donald E. Knuth, shows how much can be done with one statement in Algol. The Newton-Raphson iteration method for finding the square root of a positive number A requires repeated evaluation of the formula

$$x = ((A/prevx) + prevx)/2$$

where $x$ at one stage becomes *prevx* at the next stage, until $x$ and *prevx* are the same to within some tolerance. The variable *prevx* has to be given a starting value, which can be 1:

```
prevx := 1;
for x := (A/prevx + prevx)/2
while abs(x - prevx)>tolerance do prevx := x;
```

This **for** statement calls for repeated application of the formula and replacement of *prevx* by $x$, as long as the absolute value of the difference between $x$ and *prevx* is greater than the tolerance.

Algol was defined in a report in 1960 that was itself an innovation in that the Algol language was described in another language (therefore called a meta language) ascribed to John Backus and to Peter Naur of Denmark. This Backus-Naur Form (BNF) provides a clear and unambiguous way to express the syntax of a POL (i.e., the rules for forming correct programs).

The language itself was the first major POL to use recursion, which describes a procedure that is able to call itself. The usual illustration is the factorial function, which can be evaluated with the following Algol procedure (subroutine):

```
real procedure factorial (n);
if n = 1 then factorial := 1 else
factorial := n×factorial (n - 1);
```

We see that the entire procedure body consists of one **if** statement. It asks whether $n$ is equal to 1 and sets the factorial equal to 1 if so. Otherwise, it multiplies $n$ by the value of the same procedure evaluated for $n - 1$. In other words, the procedure calls itself repeatedly until the argument is reduced to 1, and then multiplies out the integers.

This is not an effective way to compute factorials in actual practice. The example is widely used to show what recursion is about, since practical applications are usually much more complex.

Algol provides for arrays (subscripted variables) in a form that is more flexible than Fortran, but it does not provide the data structures of Cobol, since it was not intended for extensive use in business data processing.

The Algol language provides for a degree of dynamic storage allocation, which means that assignment of storage to variables can be delayed until program execution reaches the block where the variable is used, and the storage released when the work of the block is finished. This can be important in problems involving large amounts of storage.

Algol is more widely used in Europe than in the United States. A number of implementations are available in the United States, but comparatively few installations have adopted it as the primary programming language. It is, nevertheless, a landmark in the development of programming languages, and has had an influence on almost everything done later.

All living languages change, and Algol is no exception. Various individuals and groups have suggested revisions, leading to a new but related language called Algol 68 to distinguish it from the earlier Algol 60 that has been the basis for our description.

One way of characterizing Algol 68 is to say that it generalizes many of the concepts underlying Algol 60. For example, there are any number of modes of values rather than the three types of real, integer, and boolean in Algol 60. Array elements may be structures, containing values of possibly differing modes. Control of storage allocation is more flexible. Some facilities for parallel execution of programs are introduced. The Algol 60 concept of subscripting is replaced by the concept of indexing, which allows the selection not only of a single element of an array but also of subarrays with the same or smaller dimensionality. (This facility is also available in PL/I and APL.)

One of the most interesting features of Algol 68 is the provision for extensibility. That is, it is possible to construct new modes of data from existing ones, and to define new operators. It is possible that future POLs will ordinarily include such features.

A number of implementations of Algol 68 are expected.

**PL/I.** PL/I (Programming Language One) was developed for the IBM System/360 in the mid-1960s by a committee composed of representatives of IBM and two organizations of users of its large computers, GUIDE and SHARE (Weinberg, 1966). The committee drew upon the work that had been done on Fortran, Cobol, and Algol, so that PL/I has characteristics of each. It was presumably the hope of IBM that PL/I would replace both Fortran and Cobol, thus reducing the cost of maintaining compilers. This has not occurred, but PL/I probably is the third most commonly used POL on large IBM computers. An increasing number of universities are

```
QUAD:    PROCEDURE OPTIONS (MAIN);

         /* A PL/I PROGRAM TO FIND ROOTS OF QUADRATIC EQUATIONS*/

         DECLARE (A, B, C, DISC, X1, X2) FLOAT ;

         GET LIST (A, B, C) ;
REPEAT:  DO WHILE (A ¬= 0.0);
              DISC = B**2 - 4.0 * A * C;
              X1 = (-B + SQRT(DISC)) / (2.0*A);
              X2 = (-B - SQRT(DISC)) / (2.0*A);
              PUT LIST (A, B, C, X1, X2) ;
              GET LIST (A, B, C) ;
         END REPEAT ;

         END QUAD ;
```

**Fig. 7.** The PL/I version of program of Fig. 1.

using it for instruction. There is slow movement toward PL/I by other manufacturers.

PL/I is by a wide margin the "richest" POL now available; i.e., it provides the programmer with the most features for handling a variety of applications in a variety of ways. One of the distinguishing features of the language is that it can be used effectively for both scientific and business data processing applications (to the extent that a clear distinction can always be made between the two). This can be a benefit in terms of reducing the number of compilers required in an installation.

It would be quite simple to fill this entire article with examples of programs that use PL/I features, without important duplication. We will have to be content with the briefest indication of what PL/I programs look like, followed by a description of other aspects of the language.

Fig. 7 is a PL/I version of the Fortran program shown in Fig. 1. Since it appears as the label of the PROCEDURE statement, QUAD becomes the name of the program. Following that we see a comment, so recognized because it appears between the delimiters /* and */. A comment may appear anywhere a blank is permitted. We see that statements end with a semicolon. A PL/I program is to be thought of as a linear string of characters, quite independent of its assignment to lines. As with Algol and Cobol, a statement may continue over more than one line, with no indication of the fact required; more than one statement may appear on one line. Blank lines may be used to improve understandability, which, surprisingly, is not permitted in all languages.

The DECLARE statement is one example of the features furnished to provide the information of the Cobol DATA DIVISION about variables, data layouts, etc. The GET statement calls for input of values for A, B, and C from a list of numeric values separated by spaces or commas. Numerous other input forms are permitted. Most of the rest of the program is not greatly different from the Fortran version except for the method of stopping program execution. Here, we first read one card, then go into a loop that is repeated indefinitely as long as (WHILE) the value of A is not equal to zero. Thus, the program does not involve any GO TO statements; it is therefore easier to understand and more likely to be correct when first written.

Fig. 8 is a PL/I version of the Fortran program of Fig. 3 for finding the sum of squares of an array. New features here include the use of the underline (called the "break" character) in place of hyphenation in data names, provision of an initial value in a declaration, and the vertical bar for the OR function.

```
SQUARE: PROCEDURE OPTIONS (MAIN);
        /* A PROGRAM TO FIND THE SUM OF SQUARES OF THE
              ELEMENTS OF AN ARRAY */

        DECLARE Z(100) FLOAT,
                 SUM_SQUARES FLOAT INITIAL (0),
                 (K, N) FIXED;

        GET LIST(N);

        IF N<1 | N>100 THEN GO TO WRAPUP;

READ_LOOP:    DO K = 1 TO N;
                    GET LIST(Z(K));
              END READ_LOOP;

SQUARE_LOOP: DO K = 1 TO N;
                    SUM_SQUARES = SUM_SQUARES + Z(K)**2;
              END SQUARE_LOOP;

       PUT LIST (N, SUM_SQUARES);

WRAPUP: END SQUARE;
```

**Fig. 8.** The PL/I version of program of Fig. 3.

```
PAYROLL:    PROCEDURE OPTIONS (MAIN);

            DCL HOURS_WORKED FIXED (3,1),
                PAYRATE      FIXED (4,3),
                EXTRA        FIXED (3,1),
                GROSS_PAY    FIXED (5,2);

            ON ENDFILE (SYSIN) GO TO WRAPUP;

START:      OPEN FILE (SYSIN) INPUT;
            OPEN FILE (SYSPRINT) OUTPUT;

PROCESSING_ROUTINE:
            GET EDIT (HOURS_WORKED, PAYRATE) (COLUMN(1), F(3,1), F(4,3));
            GROSS_PAY = PAYRATE * HOURS_WORKED;
            IF HOURS_WORKED > 40 THEN BEGIN;
              EXTRA = 0.5 * (HOURS_WORKED - 40) * PAYRATE;
              GROSS_PAY = GROSS_PAY + EXTRA;
            END;
            PUT SKIP EDIT (HOURS_WORKED, PAYRATE, GROSS_PAY)
                 (F(5,1), F(8,3), P'$$$$$$$9V.99');
            GO TO PROCESSING_ROUTINE;

WRAPUP:     CLOSE FILE (SYSIN);
            CLOSE FILE (SYSPRINT);

            END PAYROLL;
```

**Fig. 9.** The PL/I version of program of Fig. 5.

Fig. 9 shows the Cobol program of Fig. 5 rewritten in PL/I. We note the use of the abbreviation DCL for DECLARE; a variety of abbreviations are available. (Incidentally, there are no reserved words in PL/I as there are in Cobol; any word may be used as an identifier if it will be clear to the compiler from the context that it has no special meaning in PL/I. This is quite different from Cobol.) The OPEN statements carry out various necessary actions in getting started on input and output operations; previously, we let the system do these actions on its own initiative when first encountering GET and PUT statements. Implicit opening of files is the only way in Fortran; it is not provided in Cobol, and is (characteristically) optional in PL/I.

The GET used in this program is the EDIT version, which means that we provide information about the arrangement of input, in a way not too different from Fortran although with considerably more flexibility. The format information associated with the PUT includes a picture specification similar to a Cobol feature. We see the explicit file closing.

We now turn to a brief sketch of some of the characteristic features of PL/I. PL/I provides for fixed, floating, binary, and character data, with length and radix-point location specifiable. These and various other attributes may be specified in DECLARE statements; if not so specified, there are prescribed defaults. Array features are much like Algol, and various data structures are reminiscent of Cobol; the elements of an array may themselves be structures.

If not specified otherwise, storage is allocated to variables upon entry into the procedure in which the variables are defined. But variations are possible, such as fixing storage allocation at the time the procedure is loaded into storage, or leaving allocation to the programmer through explicit statements. Facilities are available for making the name of a variable known outside the procedure block in which it is declared.

A multiple assignment statement gives a value to more than one variable, using a form such as

```
A, X = B + C;
```

An assignment statement may use arrays and structures in whole or in part, rather than elements or elementary items. For example, if R, S, and T are all arrays of the same size, we can write

```
R = S + T;
```

which means to perform an element-by-element addition of the two arrays. When a variable name appears as part of more than one structure, data name qualification can be used to specify which is meant, or sometimes the compiler can be left to deduce the correspondences. It is possible to call for actions on some subset of the elements of any array (i.e., a specified row or column of a two-dimensional array). This is called a "cross section" of the array.

The loop control facilities match the generality of Algol and are similar. Some kinds of loops can be replaced by functions that have been provided to accomplish tasks that arise frequently. For example, the sum of all the elements of an array is given by the function SUM, and the function INDEX returns the position of the first occurrence of one string in another string.

It is possible to specify that various conditions should be tested for, during the execution of a program, together with the action that should be taken if they arise. Examples include END-OF-FILE on input, the existence of a subscript that is out of specified range, and arithmetic overflow. It is also possible to describe the desired handling of asynchronous interrupts, which means that two or more processes can be executed concurrently within the same program.

Input and output divides most basically between the stream and record types. All of the examples above were of stream I/O, where the characters are transmitted as a continuous flow. The PL/I verbs used in this case are GET and PUT. Record I/O deals with data grouped into records, with the records usually being further grouped into blocks to achieve speed and space efficiencies. The verbs in this case are READ and WRITE.

In summary, PL/I offers many powerful features and a high degree of generality. Well-written PL/I programs can be more compact, and more likely to be initially correct, than programs in most other languages. On the other hand, the great flexibility and generality leads to very large compilers and to long training periods. Acceptance of PL/I increased when compilers of the Watfiv type (very fast compilations, good diagnostics) became available.

**Basic.** Basic (Beginner's All-Purpose Symbolic Instruction Code) was developed in the mid-1960s at Dartmouth College under the direction of John Kemeny and Thomas Kurtz (Kemeny and Kurtz, 1967). It was intended to be very simple to learn and inexpensive to implement and use, so that large numbers of users could take advantage of it for learning purposes. It was designed as an interactive language, i.e., one in which the programmer gets immediate response to what he types at a terminal connected to the computer. A few batch-mode compilers do exist, however.

Basic was developed for use by beginning students, who would be expected to convert to other languages as their skills and needs developed. It has since turned out to be useful for others than beginners in some circumstances, and has found acceptance in business and industrial applications.

Many of the characteristics of Basic can be seen in the example in Fig. 10. This is a program to generate drill in subtraction for the writer's seven-year-old daughter. We see that every statement must have a line number, which serves as the statement label, and the line numbers are in ascending sequence. The first thing after the line number is a word that establishes the nature of the statement. We first have a remark introduced by REM. Next are three assignment statements, which always begin with LET. We see here string variables, one of the data types permitted in Basic, which have as their second character a dollar sign. Variable names in Basic consist of a single letter or of a letter followed by a digit. Subscripted variables do not require a dimension statement unless they have more than ten elements. One- and two-dimensional arrays are allowed.

A random number function (RND), which generates random numbers in the range 0 to 1, is used to help produce the numbers for the drill: minuends between 1 and 9, inclusive, and subtrahends between zero and the minuend. The integer (INT) function discards the fractional part of its argument. The rest of the program controls the drill logic, in which the student is given the correct answer after the second and succeeding errors, and is forced to enter the correct answer before being given another exercise. We note the rather simple conditional statement, in which the action is implied: GO TO the statement named. The PRINT with no arguments at 210 is to produce a blank line. Fig. 11 shows a few sample interactions.

Other features of Basic include programmer-defined functions, simple subroutines, and matrix operations.

```
0 REM A PROGRAM TO PROVIDE DRILL IN SUBTRACTION
10 LET L$(1) = 'TRY AGAIN'
20 LET L$(2) = 'THE CORRECT ANSWER IS:'
30 LET L$(3) = L$(2)
40 REM THE NEXT TWO STATEMENTS USE THE RANDOM NUMBER
50 REM     FUNCTION TO GENERATE THE TWO NUMBERS
60 LET A = INT (9 * RND(0) + 1)
70 LET B = INT (A * RND(0))
80 LET C = A - B
90 REM T COUNTS THE NUMBER OF TRIES
100 LET T = 1
110 PRINT A; ' -'; B; ' ='; 
120 INPUT D
130 IF C = D THEN 200
140 PRINT L$(T);
150 LET T = T + 1
160 IF T = 2 THEN 120
170 PRINT C
180 LET T = 3
190 GO TO 110
200 PRINT 'GOOD'
210 PRINT
220 GO TO 60
230 END
```

**Fig. 10.** A Basic program.

```
6  -    1 = ?5
GOOD

3  -    1 = ?1
TRY AGAIN  ?2
GOOD

2  -    0 = ?2
GOOD

9  -    1 = ?7
TRY AGAIN  ?6
THE CORRECT ANSWER IS:  8
9  -    1 = ?8
GOOD

8  -    5 = ?3
GOOD

4  -    2 = ?2
GOOD

2  -    1 = ?1
GOOD
```

**Fig. 11.** Typical user-computer dialogue for program of Fig. 10.

Basic is the second most widely used POL for a first programming course in universities in the United States, after Fortran. Basic and APL are the two most widely used interactive programming languages.

**APL.** APL (A Programming Language) was defined in a 1962 book by Kenneth E. Iverson, now of IBM, describing a language he developed while teaching at Harvard (Iverson, 1962; Pakin, 1972). It is a procedure-oriented language, like the others treated in this article, in that it is used to express procedures for solving problems. Since it is used almost exclusively in the interactive mode, however, a "procedure" can be in the most rudimentary form: If we type 2 + 2 at an APL terminal and press the return key, the system responds at once with a 4. The plus sign alone serves as a sufficient command for the system to take action. It is also possible to write procedures of the more common type, where a group of operations is defined in advance and then applied to data.

The word "rudimentary" used above should not mislead the reader into the notion that APL is limited or that APL programs are always trivial to understand. APL is a very powerful language indeed, having operators that carry out actions requiring possibly dozens of statements in other languages. The language thus has the attractive characteristic that the beginner can get started doing meaningful work very quickly—within minutes, in fact—and still have available language features of great power and range.

The power of APL is built upon the use of arrays as the basic data elements and a set of operators of remarkable scope for manipulating arrays. All operators that operate on scalars, such as the arithmetic and logical operations, exist in both monadic and dyadic form. For example, the operator that produces the maximum of two values, if applied to a single value, returns the smallest integer that is greater than or equal to the argument. There is an operator that produces the factorial of a single argument or the binomial coefficient of two. One operator is a random number generator. All these operators apply without change to arrays, as long as dimensions are compatible.

One of the unusual features of APL is that there is no hierarchy of operators as in the other POLs discussed here: In the absence of parentheses, expressions are evaluated from right to left; thus $2 \times 3 + 4$ is 14, not 10, because the addition is done first, followed by the multiplication.

An operation called "reduction," denoted by a slash, applies a stated operator to all the elements of a vector. If A is a vector, for example, the expression +/A forms the sum of all the elements of A.

The subscript of an array can itself be an array. Since there is an operator that produces a vector giving the order in which the elements of another vector would have to be taken to be in ascending sequence, sorting a vector is a matter of writing a simple subscript expression. Thus an action that would require at least a dozen statements in most other POLs is done as one part—perhaps a small part—of a single APL statement. This is not an isolated example. There are operators that transpose matrices, rotate the rows or columns of an array, reshape a vector into any type of array, perform number base conversion or a substitution cipher in a single operation, or generate all the integers from 1 up to the argument. Assignment of new values to variables is done with an assignment operator that may be embedded within a statement that does many other things. Most of the operators generalize in logical ways to arrays of any dimensionality. Matrix multiplication, for example, is designated by just three symbols besides the names of the two matrices.

APL has been used as a convenient notation for describing complex information processing succinctly, without involving a computer at all. Considered as a POL for running on a computer, however, APL is an interactive language. In fact, there is ordinarily no compilation into a separate object program at all: The statements are interpreted as they are carried out. There is a provision for the use of functions, but they cannot be compiled separately. There are provisions, however, for making use of preprogrammed routines that may be available in the system. Functions may be recursive.

Since the language was intended for use at an interactive terminal with modest amounts of storage, the input and output facilities are very limited. The business concerns that provide APL time-sharing service, however, have developed file systems that have much more storage capability, combined with appropriate input and output facilities.

Two examples of APL functions will have to suffice to give a hint of the flavor of the language. These are taken from *APL 360 User's Manual*, by A. D. Falkoff and K. E. Iverson, published by IBM.

The first is a simple routine to give drill in multiplication, as shown in Fig. 12. The first line is called the "function header"; it gives the name of the function, the name of the argument (N), and establishes Y and X as local variables that will be used only in this function and have no relation to any other variable of the same name elsewhere. The scheme is this: When we want drill in multiplication, we will type MULTDRILL followed by two integers that give the maximum sizes of factors that we want to use. Thus, N becomes a vector of two elements; the fact that it is a vector instead of a scalar will be established by usage—no declaration is necessary.

```
    ∇MULTDRILL N;Y;X
[1]  Y←?N
[2]  Y
[3]  X←⎕
[4]  →0×⍳X='S'
[5]  →⍳X=×/Y
[6]  'WRONG, TRY AGAIN'
[7]  →3∇
```

**Fig. 12.** An APL program.

Statement 1 generates two random numbers, using the ? operator, and assigns them to the vector Y. Statement 2, since it does not say to do anything else with the variable named, will print these two values. Statement 3 calls for a number to be read from the terminal; this would be the student's answer to the implied question as to the product of the two elements of Y that have been printed. Thus, X is a scalar. Statement 4 determines whether the student typed the letter S (for Stop) instead of a number, and must be read from right to left: If X is equal to the letter S the comparison produces a 1, and the iota operator (ɩ) of this is also 1. One times zero is zero, and we transfer (the right-pointing arrow) to statement zero, which means to leave the function. If X is not equal to S, the comparison produces a zero: The iota function of zero is null (which is different from zero!), which multiplied by zero is still null, and the transfer is not taken.

Statement 5 establishes whether the answer is correct by asking whether the product of the two elements of Y is equal to X and transferring back to statement 1 for another exercise if so. If the answer is wrong, we print a comment to that effect and transfer back to ask for another try at the answer.

Fig. 13 shows a complete APL program for finding the inverse of a square matrix. It would not serve our purposes to explain its operation, which would take many pages, but perhaps the reader can still gather the extreme power of the APL operators when it is realized that this procedure would take dozens of statements in most other POLs.

An APL program, as this example shows, can be extremely condensed. This can sometimes make it difficult to explain and understand, which in turn becomes a potential handicap to producing correct programs. It is not always in the programmer's best interest to take full advantage of APL to produce absolutely the shortest possible program.

APL has attracted many staunch supporters. Implementations exist for machines of most manufacturers, some of the implementations having been produced in university environments for educational use. Whether APL will continue to gain popularity at the expense of the more conventional POLs remains to be seen.

**The Future of POLs.** The future of programming languages is not entirely clear. On the one hand, there are strong economic and psychological forces tending toward a relatively gradual evolution along lines already well mapped out. On the other hand, there is the observation that, if the use of computers is to grow as rapidly as it has in the past, programming languages will be forced to change, unless the entire adult population is to consist of programmers. Some researchers are convinced that the answer to this problem is the development of programming languages that are closely akin to the natural languages of the various applications areas, whether that be ordinary English, a notation suitable for expressing kinship relations in anthropology, the reactions of subatomic particles, or whatever. Others question whether any natural language has sufficient precision for expressing procedures as rigidly as computers seem to require. The question is still open.

The reader interested in programming may reasonably expect Fortran and Cobol and all the others languages to be in use for many years yet—with evolutionary modifications, to be sure—but revolutionary new developments are a distinct possibility.

### REFERENCES

1962. McCracken, D. D. *A Guide to Algol Programming.* New York: John Wiley.

1962. Iverson, K. E. *A Programming Language.* New York: John Wiley.

1966. Weinberg, G. M. *PL/I Programming Primer.* New York: McGraw-Hill.

1967. Kemeny, J. G., and T. E. Kurtz. *Basic Programming.* New York: John Wiley.

1967. Rosen, S. (Ed.) *Programming Systems and Languages.* New York: McGraw-Hill.

1969. Sammet, J. E. *Programming Languages: History and Fundamentals.* Englewood Cliffs, N.J.: Prentice-Hall.

1970. McCracken, D. D., and U. Gerbassi. *A Guide to Cobol Programming* (2d ed.). New York: John Wiley.

1972. McCracken, D. D. (Ed.). *A Guide to Fortran IV Programming* (2d ed.). New York: John Wiley.

```
    ∇Z←INV M;I;J
[1]   M←⌽(1 0 +⍴M)⍴(,⌽M),~J←1<⍳I←1↑⍴M
[2]   M←1⌽(J,1)⌽[1]M − (J×M[;1])∘.× M[1;]←M[1;]÷M[1;1]
[3]   →2×⍳0≠I←I−1
[4]   Z←M[;⍳1↑⍴M]
    ∇
```

**Fig. 13.** An APL routine for finding the inverse of a square matrix.

1972. Pakin, S. *APL/360 Reference Manual* (2d ed.). Chicago: Science Research Associates.

D. D. McCRACKEN

## PROGRAMMING

For articles on related subjects *see* DATA STRUCTURES; DEBUGGING; DIAGNOSTICS; INPUT-OUTPUT DEVICES; LANGUAGE PROCESSORS; LOOP; MODULAR PROGRAMMING PASCAL; PROCEDURE; PROGRAMMING LANGUAGES; STRUCTURED PROGRAMMING; SUBROUTINE; and TRACE.

For articles on related terms *see* COMPILER; OBJECT PROGRAM; and SOURCE PROGRAM.

In contrast with tremendous advances in machine speed, miniaturization, and versatility, the basic level at which most machine languages operate has changed relatively little over the past two decades. Instructions can be executed only if they are submitted to the processor's control unit as sequences of numerical codes. Moreover, with a small number of specific exceptions, the typical machine language instruction represents an activity that is trivial by human standards, offering no direct correspondence with our idea of a "step" in an overall problem solution.

Consequently, there continues to be a gap between what the programmer wants to say and what the processor is designed to recognize. The predominant vehicle for bridging that gap is provided by the higher-level programming language, supported by its translator. It is in this context that one may examine the major conveniences provided by such languages, together with their effects on programming techniques.

There are hundreds of higher-level programming languages currently in use, each designed with a particular set of objectives in mind. Some are intended for use over a wide range of applications; others address themselves to a more limited spectrum of problem types that are characteristic of a specific discipline. Regardless of basic orientation, there is a common property that is reflected in any higher-level program: The elemental vehicle for expressing the programmer's intention (i.e., the individual language statement) is constructed to convey a level of complexity consistent with the nature of the procedure being represented. This means that the activity which can be described in a single "instruction" or "command" bears no direct resemblance to a single machine operation. Instead, there has been substantial effort to provide some similarity between a higher-level language statement and its counterpart in the notation appropriate to the area of application. For example, the following statement in the Fortran language,

```
H = 0.023*(C/D)*((D*V*R/U)**0.8)*((U*P/C)**0.4)
```
(1)

is easily related to the same formula in conventional algebraic form:

$$H = 0.023\frac{C}{D}\left(\frac{DVR}{U}\right)^{0.8}\left(\frac{UP}{C}\right)^{0.4}. \quad (2)$$

This equation would ultimately require a considerable number of machine operations to produce the specified result (i.e., a value for $H$) on most computers. Accordingly, the parallelism between the Fortran statement and the equivalent sequence of machine language instructions produced by the language-translating program (the compiler) is much less obvious.

The ability to establish such extensive insulation between machine and programmer has had a profound effect on the growth of the population of computer users and the range of successful applications. Most programs are written in a higher-level language, and most of the people who write programs are not computer specialists. Moreover, these languages have engendered basic changes in the techniques used to construct and implement programs. We will examine a number of these important techniques within the perspective of this reorientation in which the programmer's mode of expression is moved away from that required by the machine and comes closer to that desired by the human.

Toward this end, a number of fundamental programming facilities will be examined briefly. Once their basic functions have been defined, they will be used in combination to synthesize programs and program segments. The discussions will be built around several widely used languages whose properties typify the general power and convenience embodied in such programming vehicles; many of the facilities will be illustrated using Fortran, Algol, and PL/I, all of which implement syntactically similar instruments for computations and decision mechanisms. Where appropriate, they will be contrasted with Cobol, which is directed away from a formulaic expression and more toward narrative description. Occasional examples will be shown in the Snobol language to illustrate the types of programming techniques engendered by its highly implicit approach.

Because an essentially different set of programming techniques is required to exploit their specific advantages, interactive programming languages will not be discussed here. However, two such languages will be mentioned briefly with regard to some of the programming conveniences they offer. Certain illustrations will be expressed in Basic to show the minimal approach that reflects its emphasis on ease of learning. By way of contrast, the discussion will include some program segments in APL to illustrate its highly compact syntax, the complexity of specifiable operations, and its general orientation away from the vernacular.

**Descriptions and Specifications.** Regardless of the language in which a program is written originally, the final result must be an operationally equivalent sequence of machine instructions. For almost all computing systems, this consists of a numerical string in which each operation is designated by its respective code, defined for it as part of the machine's design. References to operands (data items on which specified operations are to be performed) cannot be expressed in terms of names or symbols. Instead, reference to a variable is expressed in terms of its address, i.e., the storage location associated with that variable.

For example, if a step in some procedure calls for the addition of variables $X$ and $Y$, the eventual implementation of that step in machine language is devoid of any knowledge of an $X$ or a $Y$. Having previously established association between those variables and particular storage locations, the instructions that actually will be executed when the program runs will be in terms of the contents of those locations. Thus, instead of saying "add Y to X," the implied activity is to "add the contents of the location associated with Y to the contents of the location associated with variable X."

Similarly, when an algorithm includes a decision mechanism requiring a choice of processing sequences, the programmer sets up appropriate branches to different parts of the procedure, associating each destination with a particular activity. However, when this structure is represented in its final machine language form, these references are stripped of any procedural association. The destination of a branch is given as a storage location containing the instruction to be executed next.

If the final machine language form of a program is being prepared manually, then it is the programmer who must define and guarantee the associations between locations in storage and their contents vis-a-vis their significance with respect to the procedure. The necessity of keeping track of these myriad relationships accounted for much of the tedium and effort required to turn out a reliable machine language program, and helped motivate the development of higher-level languages.

Consequently, every higher-level language includes features that relieve the programmer of most of these bookkeeping tasks, shifting them to the underlying software. The extent of this transfer depends primarily on the sophistication of the language and the general class of procedures or problems toward which it is oriented. In all cases, however, the programmer is no longer responsible for defining the direct relationships among the variables and the actual storage locations in which they will reside. It is still necessary for the programmer to make sure that ample storage is allocated to the various data items, but the allocation process is greatly simplified (from the programmer's viewpoint). The programmer treats each variable in conventional terms, giving it a meaningful name that will apply throughout the program.

Within this general framework, the mechanism for expressing such specifications varies from one language to another. For many languages, the first stated activity involving a variable (such as the initial assignment of a value or input of data) is sufficient to trigger a mechanism that automatically reserves storage and establishes the necessary association. For example, if we consider the Fortran statement shown in (1) as part of a program and if the reference to the variable H in that statement constitutes its initial appearance in that program, the compiler will recognize that, automatically allocating storage under that name for the result of the specified computations. Subsequent references to H will be processed routinely. Some languages include facilities for the explicit reservation of storage. For instance, each of the three following statements,

```
REAL X,Y,Z          (Fortran)
real X,Y,Z;         (Algol)        (3)
DECLARE X,Y,Z;      (PL/I)
```

reserves storage for three variables X, Y, and Z. Each of these is to accommodate a numerical value to be placed there at some subsequent point in the program. Since no further information is specified, internally implemented language rules (called defaults) will determine the amount of storage to be reserved and the form in which the numerical values ultimately will be expressed. Various means are available to the programmer for overriding these defaults. In languages such as Fortran and PL/I, where such explicit specifications are optional, they serve as a convenience to the programmer, providing a record of variable names and allocations.

Cobol, because of its predominant concern with data records and files, requires a hierarchical description of the items for which storage is to be allocated. That is, unless specifically defined otherwise, each variable is considered to be a component of a more comprehensive data structure. Moreover, the amount of storage associated with each variable must be specified in terms of the type of information to be accommodated. For example, the following specification,

```
01  RENEW-INFO.
    02  R-DATE.
        03  R-MONTH PICTURE 99.
        03  R-DAY PICTURE 99.                (4)
        03  R-YR PICTURE 99.
    02  RENEW-RATE PICTURE 999V99.
```

reserves storage for a group of variables known collectively as RENEW-INFO. This structure consists of two basic components, R-DATE and RENEW-RATE. The first of these is a collection of three variables (R-MONTH, R-DAY, and R-YR), each of which is a two-digit integer. The second component is a single variable whose value will be expressed as a five-digit number having two decimal places.

The basic facility for naming variables extends to the identification of statements within a program. It is possible to attach unique labels as prefixes to statements in a higher-level language program, thereby providing an unambiguous way of alluding to a desired point in the processing. In most languages, statements may be associated with symbolic names such as those used for variables. In Fortran and Basic, the syntactic rules require the exclusive use of numbers for statement labels. The equivalent assignment statements shown below illustrate the labeling conventions for several languages:

```
CALC2:  C: = A + Y*B;        (Algol)     (5a)
    17  LET C = A + Y*B      (Basic)     (5b)
    24  C = A + Y*B          (Fortran)   (5c)
CALC2:  C = A + Y*B;         (PL/I)      (5d)
CALC2   C = A + Y*B          (Snobol)    (5e)
CALC2.                       (Cobol)     (5f)
  COMPUTE C = A + Y * B
```

**Specification of Complex Activities in Simple Terms.** The illustrative program statement given in (1) exemplifies the primary convenience that a higher-level language brings to its users—the ability to specify arbitrarily intricate procedural steps with little loss in correspondence between the conventional description of a step and its representation in a program. Syntactically, this intent is reflected in the structural characteristics of a language's elemental "sentence" or statement. In general, the limitation on the length and complexity of a single statement in such a language is designed to be sufficiently large so that it never (or hardly ever) places a restriction on the programmer's ability to maintain the integrity of a procedural step. Thus, in a higher-level language, it is usually the programmer, and not the computing system or the language, that determines the amount of activity to be specified in a single program "step," without serious regard to the number of actual machine steps these actions eventually will entail.

TERMS, OPERATORS, AND EXPRESSIONS. The effect of this shift in limitations away from the computer and more toward the user is seen perhaps most dramatically in terms of statements denoting internal manipulative operations (i.e., "computing"). In many higher-level languages, the type of statement most commonly associated with such operations is the assignment statement. When specifying mathematical computations, the assignment statement bears a close resemblance to an equation, as exemplified in (5a) through (5f). The resemblance, though not exactly complete, is quite close. For many languages, particularly those emphasizing mathematical capabilities, the assignment statement is some variant of the general structure

$$\textit{variable} \leftarrow \textit{expression} \tag{6}$$

The ← in this construction symbolizes the operation of *replacement*, so that the general sense of the assignment may be represented as follows: "Evaluate the expression on the right-hand side of the ← by performing the indicated operations; then, let the result be the new value for *variable*, replacing its current value." In many widely used higher-level languages, replacement is denoted (expectedly) by the symbol =; Algol uses :=, and APL has the actual symbol ←. Because of this basic characterization, *variable*, the item to the left of ←, is structurally restricted to a single variable. Thus, a formulation such as

$$\frac{A + B}{C^2} = \frac{32.96(D + C)}{D} \tag{7}$$

would have to be rewritten with the desired variable (say, $B$) isolated on the left; i.e.,

$$B = \frac{32.96C^2(D + C)}{D} - A \tag{8}$$

before the formula could be represented as a program statement.

An expression consists of a combination of *terms* and *operators* in which the rules of construction constitute a somewhat restricted version of those applying to ordinary algebra. The three basic restrictions given below are imposed to accommodate certain of the computer's functional limitations and to avoid grave logical problems in the construction and implementation of compilers:

1. Each individual arithmetic operation in an expression must be indicated explicitly; it may never be implied. (For example, the expression $A(B + C)$, quite understandable in algebra, must be written as A*(B + C) in a program statement.)

2. Expressions must be in linear form. For example, the expression (A + B)/(C − D) is a slightly more awkward, but unavoidable, substitute for the conventional algebraic equivalent

$$\frac{A + B}{C - D}$$

This restriction reflects a physical limitation imposed by input/output media rather than any linguistic constraint.

3. Each compiler uses certain internal rules to evaluate expressions. Unless the user is familiar with these rules for a particular compiler, there may be constructions that appear ambiguous to him. For example, the expression A + B/C*D may be thought to represent

$$A + \frac{B}{CD}, \quad A + \frac{BD}{C}, \quad \text{or even} \frac{A + B}{CD}.$$

Higher-level languages allow the programmer to avoid such ambiguity by using parentheses to indicate the exact intent. Thus, the linear expressions A + B/(C*D), A + (B/C)*D and (A + B)/(C*D) are the respective equivalents of the three algebraic expressions.

Additional limitations are those imposed by the necessity of insuring that there is a value associated with each variable appearing in an expression. This must be guaranteed by the programmer, since compilers generally are designed to proceed on that assumption. Thus, once the programmer makes sure that the variables have been defined (i.e., storage specifically has been made available for them and values have been provided), the language presents no further obstacles with regard to the length or complexity of an expression.

To illustrate, we refer again to equation (1), which uses the Fortran language. Assuming that current values are available for each of the variables D, V, R, U, and C, the programmer has the prerogative of computing a value for H via a single statement, as in (2), or using several statements to produce partial results that are stored in separate variables and used subsequently:

```
V1 = D*V*R/U
V2 = U*P/C                                  (9)
 H = 0.023*(C/D)*(V1**0.8)*(V2**0.4)
```

Depending on the particular case, the attendant penalties in additional storage and machine time may be accepted willingly in the light of the improved legibility that such fragmentation may provide.

For an increasing variety of applications, the category of "internal manipulations," or "computation," extends to include operations on strings of letters and other nonnumeric symbols. While most higher-level languages accommodate such information, their facilities generally are limited to the simple movement and display of strings, treating them as labels or headings. However, capabilities for substantive processing of character strings are included in a number of languages that allow the use of nonnumeric data as constants and variables, and implement the manipulations through the general-assignment statement mechanism. A fundamental operation is concatenation, the synthesis of strings from smaller ones. This process is exemplified below for three such languages to show the parallelism with arithmetic assignments. In each instance, we form a string consisting of the letters IDENTICAL and assign it to the variable W3:

PL/I:

```
DECLARE W1 CHARACTER (4),
        W2 CHARACTER (3),
        W3 CHARACTER (9);                   (10a)
W1 = 'DENT'; W2 = 'CAL';
W3 = 'I'||W1||'I'||W2;
```

APL:

```
W1←'DENT'
W2←'CAL'                                    (10b)
W3←'I',W1,'I',W2
```

Snobol:

```
W1 = 'DENT'
W2 = 'CAL'                (10c)
W3 = 'I' W1 'I' W2
```

BUILT-IN FUNCTIONS. To enhance the analogy between a procedural step and a program statement, higher-level languages include features that expand considerably the range of processes expressible in a statement. The general objective of these capabilities is to allow the programmer to specify as "single" operations a variety of activities, each of which actually embodies a number of steps, even by human standards. Prototypical is the extraction of the square root, a process viewed as a single mathematical operation and represented that way in conventional notation. To preserve this integrity within the structure of a programming language, a procedure designed to produce the square root is embedded in the language and made available to the programmer via a simple reference name (SQRT in most languages). Thus, the structure of a formulation such as

$$C = \sqrt{A^2 + B^2} \tag{11}$$

still can be preserved in a language statement:

```
C = SQRT(A**2 + B**2)        (Fortran)   (12a)
C = SQRT(A**2 + B**2);       (PL/I)      (12b)
LET C = SQR(A**2 + B**2)     (Basic)     (12c)
C:= SQRT(A↑2 + B↑2);         (Algol)     (12d)
```

This type of facility is known as a "built-in function." Most higher-level languages provide a repertoire of such functions, with their exact nature being determined by the orientation of the particular language. Accordingly, languages such as Fortran and Basic reflect their emphasis on arithmetic computations in terms of substantial mathematical function libraries (e.g., logarithms, trigonometric functions), while the functions provided by Snobol and other languages directed away from predominantly mathematical procedures offer a different spectrum of operations.

The presence of a standard collection of built-in functions represents part of a more general facility that allows the programmer in effect to augment the language with additional functions of his own design. Inclusion of such functions is a relatively straightforward process, which varies with the particular language but is independent of the complexity of the function or its intended permanency.

DECISIONS AND DECISION STRUCTURES. Building on a modest assortment of simple comparison operations available at the machine level, a higher-level language characteristically provides the programmer with a vehicle for expressing arbitrarily complicated tests and decision rules. As is the case with arithmetic and other internal operations, the language structure makes it possible for the programmer to construct the decision mechanisms on his own terms, consistent with the requirements of the algorithm being implemented.

The structural element that forms the basis for decision statements in many higher-level languages can be represented graphically by the flowchart component in Fig. 1. The nucleus of the decision mechanism is the test condition, formulated as a comparison with two possible outcomes (true or false). Accordingly, when the condition is tested, its outcome will dictate which of the two alternative actions will ensue. The power of this construction can be summarized in terms of three basic properties:

1. The formulation of the decision statement usually is simple and "natural," reflecting the flowchart given above: "Test the specified condition. If it exists (true) perform the alternative action *A*, ignoring *B*. If it is false, perform *B*, ignoring *A*. Upon completion of the appropriate action, continue with that part of the processing that is independent of the test condition."
2. The test condition may be arbitrarily complex.
3. Both or either of the alternative actions may be arbitrarily complex, ranging from a very long sequence of program statements to no action at all.

The testing facilities in the Basic programming language, though rudimentary, typify the form underlying the more extensive mechanisms available in other languages. In general terms, the condition to be tested (in Basic) consists of a pair of arithmetic expressions connected by an operator that defines the nature of the comparison. Thus, the construction

```
X*Y <= Z                     (13)
```

specifies a comparison to determine whether the product XY is less than or equal to Z (in which case the outcome would be "true") or not. Only one type of action is specifiable—a branch to some other place in the program, at which point the appropriate processing presumably continues; the alternative merely is to ignore the branch. Accordingly, the test

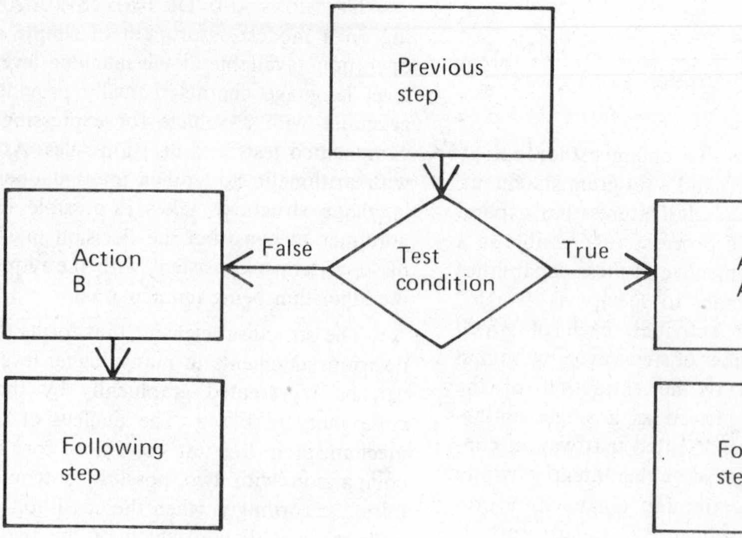


**Fig. 1.** Flowchart for basic higher-level language decision structure.

and branch are combined to form a complete statement:

IF X*Y <= Z THEN 70 (14)

as shown in Fig. 2. The "70" refers to the statement number attached to the branch's destination.

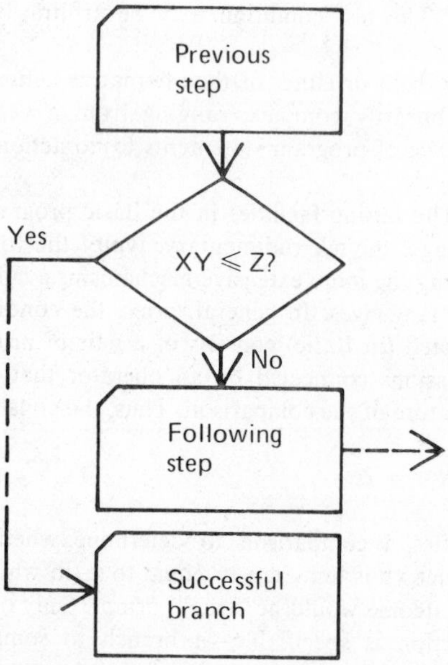


**Fig. 2.** Example of testing and branching in the Basic language.

Numerous procedural occasions require the type of test whose outcome is based on several comparisons. To preserve the integrity of such tests, logical operators are provided for connecting individual comparisons to form compound-decision rules. For example, assume that a particular action is to be performed only when XY is less than or equal to Z and at the same time some variable W exceeds 29.6. The entire decision rule can be implemented in Fortran with one compound statement:

```
IF((X*Y).LE. Z .AND. W .GT. 29.6) GO TO 140
```
(15)

The same rule could be expressed in Basic, which does not accept compound comparisons:

```
50  IF X*Y <= Z THEN 70
60  GO TO 80
70  IF W > 29.6 THEN 140
80  Further processing
```
(16)

Note, however, that the feeling of a single procedural test is lost. Moreover, the programmer is forced into the awkward construction shown above in order to avoid the performance of the second test, once the first one fails. Alternatively, the additional GO TO statement could be removed; but in so doing, the programmer would have to reverse the first decision rule, thereby departing again from the sense of the test:

```
50  IF X*Y > Z THEN 70
60  IF W > 29.6 THEN 140                              (17)
70  Further processing
```

Additional flexibility is provided by including actions other than branching within the overall structure of the decision statement. For example, the programmer writing in Fortran may specify an assignment statement as the action prompted by an outcome of "true". Thus, decision rule "A", "If the product $XY$ is less than or equal to $Z$, add 7.8 to the current value in $X$; otherwise do not. In either case, compute $XYZ$ $(2.5Y + W)$ and assign it to $T$," can be expressed simply by saying

```
IF(X*Y .LE. Z) X = X + 7.8
T = X*Y*Z * (2.5 * Y + W)                             (18)
```

This is very convenient as long as the situation is such that one of the alternatives is to do nothing. As soon as that restriction is inapplicable, this facility is ineffectual. To illustrate, the decision rule "A" will be expanded: "If the product $XY$ is less than or equal to $Z$, add 7.8 to the current value in $X$; otherwise subtract 1.6 from the current value. Then, in either case, compute $T$ as $XYZ$ $(2.5Y + W)$." Accordingly, the Fortran and Basic implementations do not differ:

Basic:

```
30  IF X*Y < = Z THEN 60
40  LET X = X - 1.6
50  GO TO 70                                          (19a)
60  LET X = X + 7.8
70  LET T = X*Y*Z*(2.5*Y+W)
```

Fortran:

```
    IF(X*Y .LE. Z) GO TO 14
    X = X - 1.6
    GO TO 20                                          (19b)
14  X = X + 7.8
20  T = X*Y*Z*(2.5*Y+W)
```

Languages like Algol and PL/I provide less awkward vehicles by allowing the explicit specification of alternative actions, thereby mirroring directly the graphic representation in Fig. 1. This is seen in the following implementations of the decision rule "A".

Algol:

```
if X*Y = Z then X:= X + 7.8
            else X:= X - 1.6;                         (19c)
T:= X*Y*Z * (2.5 * Y + W);
```

PL/I:

```
IF X*Y <= Z THEN X = X + 7.8;
             ELSE X = X - 1.6;                        (19d)
T = X*Y*Z * (2.5 * Y + W);
```

The same facility is present in Cobol in a more narrative form:

```
IF X * Y <= Z ADD 7.8 TO X
  ELSE SUBTRACT 1.6 FROM X.                           (19e)
COMPUTE T = X * Y * Z * (2.5*Y+W).
```

The structural simplicity made possible by the THEN ··· ELSE coupling is not very useful without a corresponding enlargement in the range of activities which may be attached to a decision rule. This is recognized in languages like Cobol, PL/I, and Algol, which include syntactic components wherein sequences of statements are handled as a single (conceptual) activity. As an example, the decision rule "A" will be complicated further: "If $XY$ is less than or equal to $Z$ and, at the same time, $Z$ is greater than $2.9W$, do the following: Add 7.8 to $X$, double $Y$, and subtract 2.2 from $Z$; otherwise, subtract 1.6 from $X$, make $Y = 0.85$ times its current value, and leave $Z$ alone. In either case, compute $XYZ$ $(2.5Y + W)$ and store the result in $T$." The construction of appropriate program segments is as follows:

Algol:

```
if X*Y < = Z and T = Z > 2.9*W
        then begin X: = X + 7.8;
                   Y: = 2*Y;
                   Z: = Z - 2.2;                      (20a)
             end
        else begin X: = X - 1.6;
                   Y: = 0.85*Y; end
T: = X*Y*Z*(2.5*Y + W);
```

PL/I:

```
IF X*Y <= Z & Z > 2.9*W
  THEN DO;
       X = X + 7.8; Y = 2*Y; Z = Z - 2.2;
       END;                                           (20b)
  ELSE DO;
       X = X - 1.6; Y = 0.85*Y;
       END;
T = X*Y*Z* (2.5*Y + W);
```

Compound statements also may appear in Cobol, with a more casual syntax:

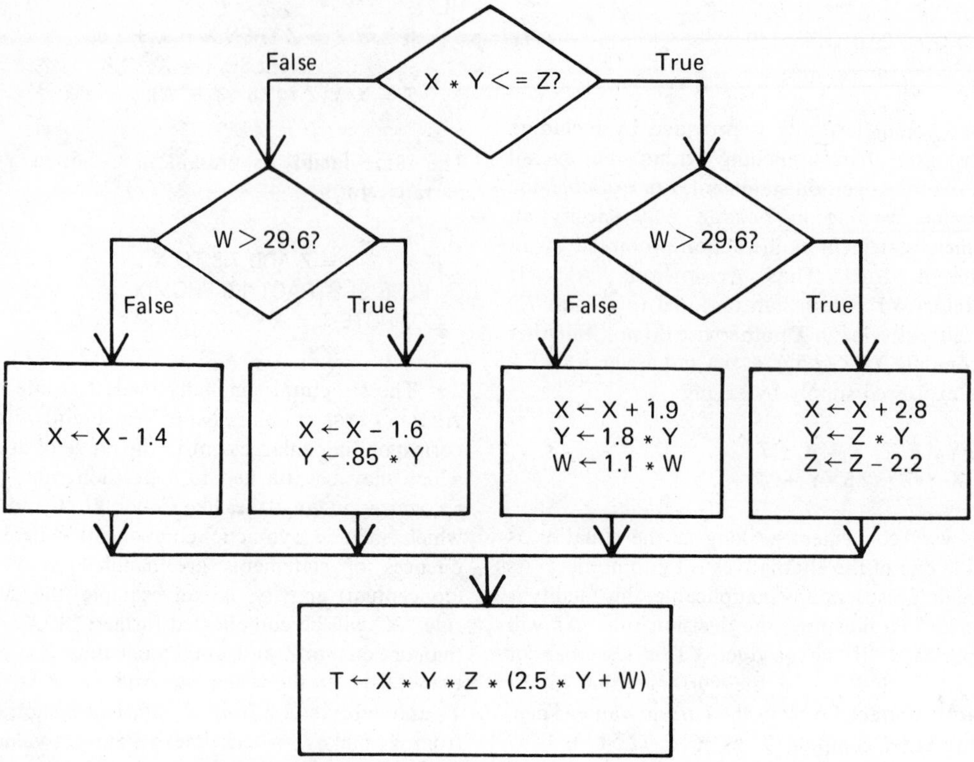


**Fig. 3.** Flowchart of sequential decision structure.

```
IF X * Y IS <= Z AND Z IS > 2.9 * W ADD 7.8 TO X
  MULTIPLY 2 BY Y SUBTRACT 2.2 FROM Z ELSE
  SUBTRACT 1.6 FROM X MULTIPLY 0.85 BY Y.
COMPUTE T = X * Y * Z * (2.5 * Y + W).            (20c)
```

Some languages are designed with the expectation that their users will frequently seek to implement decision networks in which a number of conditions are to be evaluated sequentially, with various consequent actions at each step. A simple structure of this type is shown in Fig. 3.

The intent of these decision rules is conveyed rather directly in languages such as PL/I or Algol by accepting constructions such as IF···THEN···IF···etc. Expression of the sequential tests then becomes straightforward. For example, in PL/I:

```
IF X*Y <= Z THEN IF W > 29.6 THEN DO;
                          X=X+2.8;
                          Y=2*Y;
                          Z=Z-2.2;
                          END;
                       ELSE DO;        (21a)
                          X=X+1.9;
                          Y=1.8*Y;
                          W=1.1*W;
          ELSE IF W > 29.6 THEN DO;
                          X=X-1.6;
                          Y=0.85*Y;
                          END;
                       ELSE X=X-1.4;
T = X*Y*Z*(2.5*Y+W);
```

The Algol programming is similar. This organization must yield to a more cumbersome one when sequential tests are not accommodated. Thus, the same decision rules in Fortran could be represented as follows:

```
      IF (X*Y.LE.Z) GO TO 110
        IF (W.GT.29.6) GO TO 220
          X = X-1.4
          GO TO 300
220       X = X-1.6
          Y = 0.85*Y
          GO TO 300
```

```
110  IF (W.GT.29.6) GO TO 120                    (21b)
          X = X+1.9
          Y = 1.8*Y
          W = 1.1*W
          GO TO 300
120       X = X+2.8
          Y = 2.0*Y
          Z = Z-2.2
300  T = X*Y*Z*(2.5*Y+W)
```

PROGRAMMING LOOPS. The use of loops pervades all aspects of programming. Consequently, every higher level language offers some kind of vehicle to facilitate the description and control of sequences of steps that are to be repeated several times in succession.

The fundamental capability for constructing loops enables the programmer to identify the beginning and end of the loop, specify the number of times the loop is to be repeated, and define a specific indicator (termed an index) that will keep track of the number of cycles through the loop.

These mechanisms can be examined conveniently by setting up another example involving arrays. This time, an array Al will have its 14 elements set respectively to values of 1, 2, . . ., 14. A second array A2, also consisting of 14 elements, will receive respective values of 3,5,7,9, . . ., 29. The sequences in Basic, Fortran, Algol, and PL/I are quite similar.

Basic:

```
10  DIM AI (14), A2(14)
15  FOR I = 1 TO 14
20     LET A1(I)=I                              (22a)
25     LET A2(I)=2*I+1
30  NEXT I
```

Fortran:

```
    DIMENSION A1(14), A2(14)
    DO 30 I = 1, 14
       A1(I) = 1                                (22b)
       A2(I)=2*I+1
30  CONTINUE
```

Algol:

```
integer array A1,A2[1:14];
for I: =1 step 1 until 14 do
begin                                           (22c)
    A1[I]: =I; A2[I]: =2*I+1;
end
```

PL/I:

```
DECLARE A1(14), A2(14);
    DO I=1 TO 14;                               (22d)
    A1(I)=I; A2(I)=2*I+1;
    END;
```

The mode of expression in Cobol is characteristically less formulaic:

```
01  ARRAYS.
    02 A1 OCCURS 14 TIMES PICTURE 999V99.
    02 A2 OCCURS 14 TIMES PICTURE 999V99.
                  .
                  .
                  .
77 I PICTURE 99.                                (22e)
                  .
                  .
                  .
PERFORM BUILDUP VARYING I FROM 1 BY 1 UNTIL
    I GREATER THAN 14.
BUILDUP.
    COMPUTE A1 (I) = I.
    COMPUTE A2 (I) = 2 * I + 1.
```

In Snobol the construction uses a test mechanism as part of a compound statement. Thus, the condition LE (I,14) shown in (22f) determines whether I is less than or equal to 14. If it is, the test is *successful*, and the statement operates as if the test were not there. That is, I is increased by 1. Furthermore, the :S(BUILD) stipulates that the action precipitated by a successful test should culminate in a branch to the statement identified as BUILD. Failure prevents processing of both the assignment and the branch:

```
         A1 = ARRAY(14)
         A2 = ARRAY(14)
         I = 1
BUILD    A1<I> = I                              (22f)
         A2<I> = 2*I+1
         I = LE(I,14)I+1      :S(BUILD)
```
*Further processing*

APL, because of its strong emphasis on arrays, treats such operations as being much more fundamental. Accordingly, much of the processing is implied, and the necessary programming reduces to

```
A1←ι14
A2←1+2×ι14                                      (22g)
```

where ι is an operation that creates an array named by the identifier to the left of ←; the number of elements is specified by the item to the right of ι, and respective values are assigned in accordance with the function (between ← and ι) that operates on successive positive integers beginning with 1. Using this construction as a point of departure, these languages include supplemental facilities that enable the programmer to implement loops in which the number of cycles and the method of cycling may vary with each use.

For some languages, the ability to specify the number of cycles through a loop is complemented by another method for specifying such control. Instead of specifying a particular number of cycles, this augmented capability enables the programmer to construct a loop in which some arbitrarily defined criterion automatically terminates the repetitions, irrespective of the number of cycles. To see how this works, we consider the following example: *X* is an array of 100 numbers, values for which were made available earlier in the program. Starting with the first element, the program is to accumulate the sum of successive elements until that sum reaches or exceeds a value *Y* (said value also having been made available to the program earlier). To simplify matters, it will be assumed that *Y* will be equaled or exceeded before all of *X* elements are used. Thus, the problem is to construct some type of automatically controlled loop, with the number of cycles being a consequence of some other activity.

Some languages include a specific mechanism to deal with such situations conveniently. For instance, a solution to the problem described above can be represented quite conveniently in PL/I:

```
TOTAL = 0;
DO I = 1 TO 100 WHILE (TOTAL < Y);
TOTAL = TOTAL + X(I);                    (23a)
END;
Further processing
```

In the absence of this automating feature, the programmer is obliged to set up the decision mechanism manually. Accordingly, an equivalent sequence in Fortran would be expressed as follows:

```
      TOTAL = 0.0
      DO 25 I=1,100
      IF (TOTAL .GE. Y) GO TO 30
      TOTAL = TOTAL + X(I)               (23b)
   25 CONTINUE
   30 Further processing
```

Despite the difference in appearance, both sequences embody the same mechanism—a test to determine whether the program will make another cycle through the loop or branch out of it to subsequent processing. The fact that this mechanism need not be explicitly stated in languages such as PL/I is much more than a convenience. Rather, it carries some important implications with regard to the structure of higher-level language programs. Although the example shown above is sufficiently simple so that there is no conspicuous difference in legibility between the two versions, use of numerous branches in more complex loops and other decision structures may lead to overly intricate, logical mazes that are extremely difficult to analyze. In such contexts, the branch may represent an operational intrusion that detracts from the resemblance between a procedural component and its implementation in a program.

As knowledge about the properties of programming languages and the design of programs becomes more systematized, there is a corresponding expansion of language features that facilitate the representation of increasingly complex logical situations without the use of explicit branch statements. This approach, known as "structured programming," or "GO-TO-less" programming, has prompted a reexamination of higher-level languages currently in use and has motivated the formulation of new languages and compilers.

INPUT-OUTPUT OPERATIONS. One of the most conspicuous aspects that continues to characterize development in computer hardware is the ability to equip a processor with a widening assortment of input/output devices. To accommodate this capability, it is necessary to use more and more complicated interfacing structures between these peripherals and the central processing unit. As a result, the growth in versatility has been accompanied by a corresponding increase in the complexity of input/output operations. In some configurations this has become sufficiently severe so that programmers working in even the lowest-level languages find it impractical to specify relatively straightforward data transmission operations without the use of multiple layers of software. Even with this intervening software, the resulting programming vehicle still tends to be rather cumbersome.

This situation makes it all the more difficult for higher-level languages to provide the same type of insulation that users enjoy with respect to other types of programming operations. Ideally, the language must seek to reconcile two often conflicting requirements: While offering a simple mode of expression for specifying input/output operations, it must preserve the versatility of the computing system and make it available to the programmer.

Many languages handle input/output operations in one of two ways. The first of these is to provide a unified form for specifying all data transmission. Specific circumstances pertaining to a particular input/output operation then are defined within the general structure of the statement. In Fortran, for example, all input and output operations are represented respectively by the general statement

READ (*n,m*) *v1, v2, etc.*
WRITE (*n,m*) *v1, v2, etc.* (24)

Access to the various peripheral devices is provided by *n*. Each device in a particular computing constellation is given a unique number, and a table of these designations is made available to Fortran within the supervisory software system under which it operates. (These assignments are fairly standard, but they may easily be redefined at each individual installation.) Accordingly, the programmer specifies the device number involved in a particular data transmission, and the appropriate association is established. The second indicator in parentheses, *m*, gives the number of a statement in that program in which the data format is described. For input (i.e., in a READ statement), statement *m* gives an item-by-item description of the appearance of the data (number of digits, location of the decimal point, number of spaces between consecutive values, etc.). Each description corresponds to a variable named in the input list *v1, v2,* etc. To illustrate, assume that values for three variables *X*, *Y*, and *Z* are keypunched on a card as shown in Fig. 4. Using 5 to represent the card reader, the appropriate Fortran statement would be

```
   REAL X,Y,Z
   READ (5,12) X,Y,Z                    (25)
12 FORMAT(F4.1,1X,F6.2,2X,F4.1)
```

In the WRITE statement, the information in statement number *m* describes the listed data items as they are to appear on the output medium.

PL/I facilities for handling input/output operations are embodied in two pairs of statement types: GET and PUT for transmission of individual data items, and READ and WRITE for transmission of multiple data items organized into records. Input with the GET statement is roughly analogous to the process triggered by the READ statement in Fortran. This can be seen in the general construction

GET FILE *filename* EDIT (*v1,v2*,etc.) (*format description*); (26)

The list of items to be read is specified as in Fortran, and the item-by-item descriptions of the input are similar except that they appear as part of the same statement, thereby obviating the reference to a separate format statement. Designation of the data source is through *filename*, the name of a collection of data from which these items are taken. The connection between this name and the appropriate physical input device is established outside the program.

Since the card reader is a very common source of input, it is possible to define that device (or some other device, for that matter) as a standard input unit, in which case its designation may be implied, resulting in a simplified form of the GET statement:

GET EDIT (*v1,v2*, etc.) (*format description*); (27)

**Fig. 4.** Values of variables X,Y,Z keypunched for statement (25).

Accordingly, a sequence of PL/I statements to read the card shown in (25) would appear as follows:

```
DECLARE X,Y,Z;
GET EDIT (X,Y,Z) (F(4,1),X(1),F(6,2),X(2),F(4,1));        (28)
```

Further simplification is possible when dealing with input in which the data items are separated by blanks. The *X* in both Fortran and PL/I causes the program to skip the indicated number of spaces, irrespective of their contents. Thus, there could have been anything at all between the data items in (25) without affecting the result. When input items are separated specifically by blanks, it is possible to exploit a special scanning mechanism within PL/I, thereby simplifying the GET statement even further. For example, the card used above can be read with the statement

```
GET LIST (X,Y,Z);        (29)
```

Another variation within the general structure of the GET statement allows the programmer to submit input values in the form of miniature assignment statements, accompanied by variable names. Using the previous values as an example, there are contexts in which it may be convenient to prepare them in the form shown in Fig. 5, in which case they may be read by the statement

```
GET DATA (X,Y,Z);        (30)
```

Corresponding output facilities are implemented by means of the PUT statement, whose structure parallels that of the GET statement completely. In addition, the various simplifications discussed above may be used, in which case the programmer relinquishes control of the appearance of the output and accepts a standard format built into the language.

Complementing PL/I GET and PUT facilities are those oriented around the transmission of entire records. The data items in such a record are organized hierarchically in much the same way used by the Cobol language and illustrated in (4). Input is handled via the general construction

READ FILE (*filename*) INTO (*place*); (31)

where *filename* has its previous meaning and *place* refers to an area in storage reserved for the input record. Once the record has been read in as an entity, access may be made to individual data items for further processing. Transmission of output follows the same general mechanism:

WRITE FILE (*filename*) FROM (*place*); (32)

Individual data items are assembled in *place* to form the record, after which it is written as a structural whole.

As an alternative approach to implementing input/output handling facilities, some languages provide separate vehicles for transmitting data to and from standard peripheral devices (usually the card reader and line printer), keeping these constructions simple. Data transmissions involving other

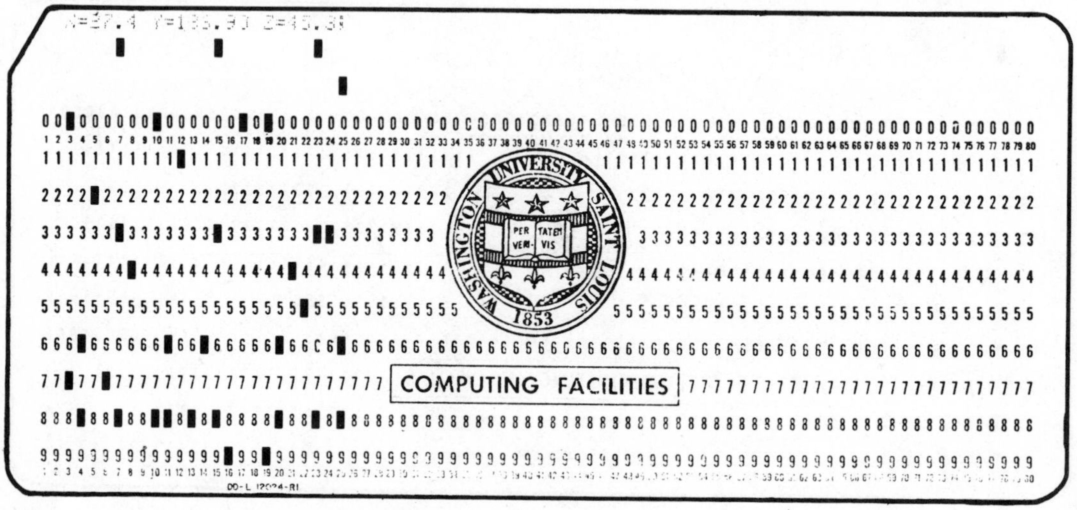


**Fig. 5** Values of variables keypunched for statement (30).

devices are specified with different types of statements designed to express whatever complications those processes may entail. Along these lines, the general facilities in Cobol are expressible through READ and WRITE statements that resemble (and are ancestral to) their namesakes in PL/I. However, if the programmer simply wants to read data from a card, he may do so with the statement

ACCEPT *place*. (33)

where *place* refers to an area in storage that is to serve as the destination for the 80 characters of data read in. Subsequent extraction of desired items from *place* is handled on the basis of its hierarchical description given earlier in the program. Similarly, the DISPLAY statement produces a line of output on the printer from a designated area in storage in which that line is constructed.

Standardized input/output is made even more convenient in Snobol, where the language word INPUT implies the reading of a card and OUTPUT implies the printing of a line. For example, the statement

DEST = INPUT (34)

reserves enough storage under the name DEST to accommodate a cardful of data, reads the next available card from the card reader, and stores its contents in DEST. Similarly, the statement

OUTPUT = DEST (35)

takes the information currently stored in DEST, pads it with blanks to fill a print line (normally 132 characters long), and prints it. In fact, the combined processes of reading a card and printing it can be specified in the single statement

OUTPUT = INPUT (36)

The input/output handling facilities currently incorporated in most Algol systems are relatively complex, reflecting the language's primary concern with internal manipulations and logical organization. APL and Basic, being languages designed for interactive use, assume the availability of a single external device that serves the dual purpose of transmitting input and receiving output. Consequently, the data transmission statements are very limited in scope and correspondingly simple in form.

**Organization of Programs.** Efforts by designers to increase the parallels between statements in a language and steps in an algorithm have helped shape the techniques surrounding the preparation of programs. In contrast to early approaches in which sequences of statements were put together to produce something that "worked," increasing emphasis is being placed on facilitating the programming process through systematic exploitation of higher-level language features. Some of the underlying motivations are worth nothing.

On innumerable occasions, the cost involved in designing and debugging a program outstrip that of using the finished product. Moreover, many programs tend to be unstable in that a combination of accumulated experience and external events precipitates procedural changes, which ultimately must be accommodated in terms of corresponding modifications to the program. When the program's construction is somewhat haphazard to begin with, any but the most trivial changes are awkward to incorporate. In many cases, such modification is aggravated by the programmers' inability to follow the tortuous path of events in their own programs after being away from them even for a short time. Under these conditions it is understandable that a small number of such episodes often result in a decision to scrap a program and start over.

An important factor in reducing this type of chaos has been the advocacy of modular programming, an approach in which an explicit effort is made to construct a program from a series of components, each representing an identifiable procedural activity. That is, instead of viewing a program as a sequence of individual statements, it is treated as a combination of modules. Although this orientation has been applied to some limited extent in machine-language program design, its major impetus stems from the introduction of higher-level languages whose features encourage and facilitate modularity.

To illustrate some aspects of this approach, a number of the features discussed in previous sections will be integrated to construct complete programs representing solutions to the following problem:

> An array of input values X consists of 32 numbers, each in the form YY.Y. The array is to be divided into two component arrays X1 and X2 such that each member of X1 has a value smaller than that specified by an additional input variable named CUTOFF, with the remaining elements being assigned to X2. The program is to print three lines of output: the first of these is to repeat the input value for CUTOFF; the

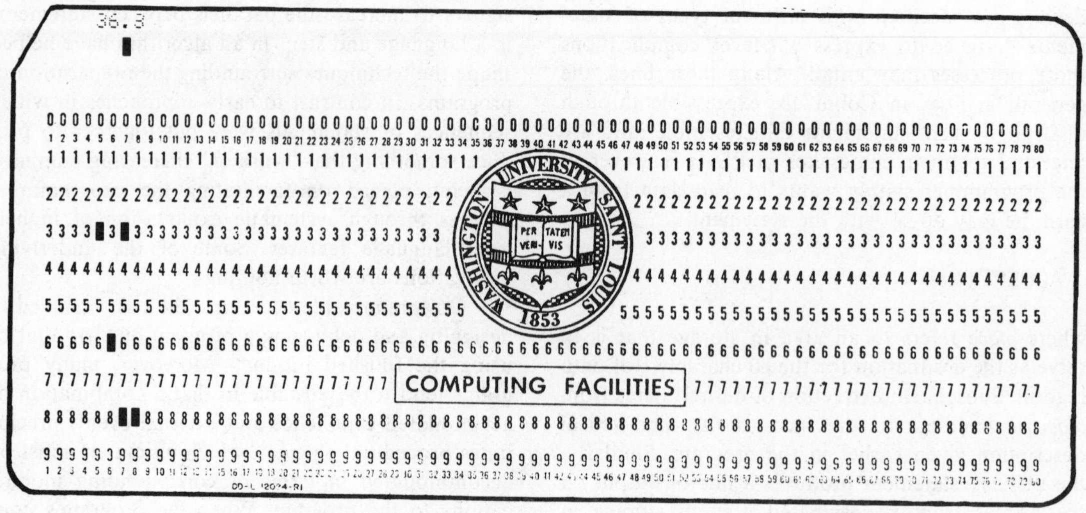


(a)

CUTOFF = 36.8
SUM1 = 263.8 N1 = 13 SMALL1 = 1.4 BIG1 = 34.7
SUM2 = 1227.6 N2 = 19 SMALL2 = 36.8 BIG2 = 99.7

(b)

**Fig. 6.** Representative data and results for programs in Figs. 7–10. (a) Sample input; (b) sample output.

```
0001          REAL X(32),SUM1,SUM2,SMALL1,SMALL2,BIG1,BIG2,CUTOFF,X1(32),X2(32)
0002          INTEGER N1,N2
        C
        C  A 'REAL' VARIABLE IN FORTRAN IS STORED AS A FLOATING POINT NUMBER.
        C  THIS IS EQUIVALENT TO A DEFAULT DECLARATION IN PL/I, E.G.,
        C  DECLARE SUM1, SUM2; WITHOUT FURTHER QUALIFICATION.
        C  EACH READ STATEMENT HANDLES AT LEAST ONE CARD, TAKING ONLY THE
        C  INFORMATION INDICATED BY THE VARIABLE NAME(S) IN ACCORDANCE WITH
        C  THE FORMAT SPECIFICATIONS.
        C
0003          READ(5,10)CUTOFF
        C
        C  SINCE X IS DEFINED AS CONSISTING OF 32 ELEMENTS, THE DESIGNATION
        C  IN THE FOLLOWING READ STATEMENT IS SUFFICIENT TO INSTIGATE THE REA-
        C  DING OF 32 ITEMS. STATEMENT 11 DESCRIBES THE ARRANGEMENT OF AN
        C  INDIVIDUAL CARD CONTAINING 16 VALUES. CONSEQUENTLY, WHEN THAT CARD
        C  IS EXHAUSTED, THE NEXT CARD WILL BE READ AUTOMATICALLY, USING THE
        C  SAME SPECIFICATIONS AGAIN.
        C
0004          READ(5,11) X
0005       10 FORMAT(4X,F4.1)
```

**Fig. 7.** Listing of Fortran program for producing the output of Fig. 6.

```
   11 FORMAT(16 (F4.1,1X))
C
C  SMALL1 AND SMALL2 ARE INITIALIZED TO 99.9, THEREBY FORCING THE FIRST
C  ASSIGNMENTS FROM THEIR RESPECTIVE ARRAYS, AFTER WHICH THE LOOP WILL
C  PROCEED ROUTINELY. THE SAME REASONING PUTS THE LOWEST POSSIBLE
C  VALUES (IF WE ASSUME NO NEGATIVES) IN THE TWO MAXIMA.
C
      SMALL1 = 99.9
      SMALL2 = 99.9
      BIG1 = 0.0
      BIG2 = 0.0
      N1 = 0
      N2 = 0
      SUM1 = 0.0
      SUM2 = 0.0
C
C  SINCE THERE IS A CERTAIN AMOUNT OF BOOKKEEPING BEHIND A DO LOOP,
C  IT CAN BE SOMEWHAT MORE EFFICIENT TO KEEP THE NUMBER OF LOOPS DOWN.
C  THUS, WE ARE SEARCHING FOR THE SMALLS AND THE BIGS WITHIN THE SAME
C  LOOP, RATHER THAN DOING IT IN SEPARATE LOOPS AFTER THE ARRAYS X1
C  AND X2 HAVE BEEN SEGREGATED. THIS IS A MATTER OF JUDGEMENT, BECAUSE
C  OVERZEALOUS USE OF THIS PRACTICE COULD IMPAIR THE PROGRAM'S CLARITY.
C
      DO 20 I = 1,32
      IF (X(I) .LT. CUTOFF) GO TO 16
         N2 = N2 + 1
         X2(N2) = X(I)
         SUM2 = SUM2 + X(I)
         IF (X(I) .LT. SMALL2) SMALL2 = X(I)
         IF (X(I) .GT. BIG2) BIG2 = X(I)
         GO TO 20
   16 N1 = N1 + 1
      X1(N1) = X(I)
      SUM1 = SUM1 + X(I)
      IF (X(I) .LT. SMALL1) SMALL1 = X(I)
      IF (X(I) .GT. BIG1) BIG1  =  X(I)
   20 CONTINUE
C
C  EACH WRITE STATEMENT AUTOMATICALLY STARTS ON A NEW LINE. THE FOR-
C  MAT DESCRIPTION MUST ACCOUNT FOR EVERY SPACE ON THE LINE, SO THAT
C  THE BLANKS, AS WELL AS THE IDENTIFIERS, ARE INCLUDED IN STATEMENTS
C  30, 31 AND 32.
C
      WRITE(6,30)CUTOFF
      WRITE(6,31)SUM1,N1,SMALL1,BIG1
      WRITE(6,32)SUM2,N2,SMALL2,BIG2
   30 FORMAT(5X,9HCUTOFF = ,F5.1)
   31 FORMAT(5X,7HSUM1 = ,F7.1,3X,5HN1 = ,I2,3X,9HSMALL1 = ,F5.1,3X,
     *       7HBIG1 = ,F5.1)
   32 FORMAT(5X,7HSUM2 = ,F7.1,3X,5HN2 = ,I2,3X,9HSMALL2 = ,F5.1,3X,
     *       7HBIG2 = ,F5.1)
      END
```

**Fig. 7.** (continued)

```
STMT LEVEL NEST
  1                     PG1: PROCEDURE OPTIONS (MAIN);
                          /*****************************************************************/
                          /** ALL PL/I PROGRAMS ARE EXPRESSED AS PROCEDURES, BE-          **/
                          /** GINNING WITH A PROCEDURE STATEMENT AND CONCLUDING           **/
                          /** WITH AN END STATEMENT.                                       **/
                          /** THE DESIGNATION FIXED(3,1) DESCRIBES NUMBERS OF THE         **/
                          /** FORM XX.X; FIXED(5,1) SPECIFIES THE NUMERICAL FORM          **/
                          /** XXXX.X.                                                      **/
                          /*****************************************************************/

  2    1                DECLARE (X(32),X1(32),X2(32),SMALL1,SMALL2,BIG1,BIG2,CUTOFF)
                               FIXED(3,1), (SUM1,SUM2) FIXED(5,1), (N1,N2) FIXED(2);

  3    1                GET LIST(CUTOFF,X);
                          /*****************************************************************/
                          /** BIG1 AND BIG2 ARE SET TO ZERO SO THAT THE FIRST COM-         **/
                          /** PARISON WITH AN ARRAY ELEMENT INEVITABLY WILL FORCE         **/
                          /** A REPLACEMENT. THE SAME REASONING MOTIVATES THE INI-         **/
                          /** TIALIZATION OF SMALL1 AND SMALL2 TO 99.9, THE LAR-           **/
                          /** GEST POSSIBLE VALUE THAT CAN BE ACCOMMODATED THERE.          **/
                          /*****************************************************************/

  4    1                X1 = 0; X2 = 0;
  6    1                N1,N2,SUM1,SUM2,BIG1,BIG2 = 0;
  7    1                SMALL1,SMALL2 = 99.9;

  8    1                DO I = 1 TO 32;
  9    1    1           IF X(I) < CUTOFF THEN DO;
 11    1    2                      SUM1 = SUM1 + X(I); N1 = N1 + 1; X1(N1) = X(I);
 14    1    2                      IF X(I) < SMALL1 THEN SMALL1 = X(I);
 16    1    2                      IF X(I) > BIG1 THEN BIG1 = X(I);
 18    1    2                          END;
 19    1    1                      ELSE DO;
 20    1    2                      SUM2 = SUM2 + X(I); N2 = N2 + 1; X2(N2) = X(I);
 23    1    2                      IF X(I) < SMALL2 THEN SMALL2 = X(I);
 25    1    2                      IF X(I) > BIG2 THEN BIG2 = X(I);
 27    1    2                          END;
 28    1    1           END;
                                                                 /****************************/
 29    1                PUT SKIP DATA(CUTOFF);                   /* THE WORD SKIP FORCES     */
 30    1                PUT SKIP DATA(SUM1,N1,SMALL1,BIG1);      /* THE START OF A NEW       */
 31    1                PUT SKIP DATA(SUM2,N2,SMALL2,BIG2);      /* LINE OF PRINT.           */
                                                                 /****************************/

 32    1           END PG1;
```

**Fig. 8.** PL/I program for producing output in Fig. 6.

second line is to display the sum of all the values assigned to array X1 (SUM1), the number of elements assigned to X1 (N1), the smallest element in X1 (SMALL1), and the largest value assigned to X1 (BIG1). The final line of output is to show similar values for array X2 (SUM2, N2, SMALL2, and BIG2, respectively). Note that the arrays X1 and X2 are not needed to obtain the required results. Their inclusion presumes that they would be processed further in a more extensive procedure.

Several versions of solution programs are shown to compare structural possibilities in various languages. Additional explanatory material is embedded in each program by exploiting the ability of the language to accept and display incidental information that is not part of the actual program. As a point of reference, sample input and output are shown in Fig.6.

The Fortran program shown in Fig. 7 embodies no particular attempt at modularity. Although most of the sequences are straightforward, the awkwardness of Fortran structural limitations regarding decision mechanisms already is apparent, even in the simple process of assigning elements to X1 or X2. It is not difficult to extrapolate this type of situation to realistically complex networks whose convolutions would be most difficult to follow.

The ability to specify compound statements in languages such as PL/I affords some organizational simplification. Use of these statements in constructing the program's basic decision mechanism (Fig. 8) establishes an immediate parallel to the basic flowchart representation as depicted in Fig. 1.

An additional convenience is seen in the substitution of the PL/I simplified GET LIST and PUT DATA facilities to read the input and print the results, both in the same form shown in Fig. 6.

The basic formal step toward program modularity pivots around a reorganization in which major activities are expressed as *subprograms*. These are brought together and logically connected through the main program, which carries the sense of the overall procedure and makes reference to a subprogram as its activity is needed.

A salient feature of many higher-level languages is the ability to define and integrate subprograms easily and to make them very general. This has revolutionized program techniques at numerous computer installations, motivating an overall approach in which frequently used procedural activities are constructed as subprograms and maintained in an extensive library. Then, a new set of procedural requirements are fulfilled by selecting appropriate library routines and combining them by means of a relatively small main program, adding those special sequences not otherwise covered. In using this construction, each activity can be treated as a "black box" whose input requirements are known and whose results are defined, thereby enhancing the program's legibility. Furthermore, there may be a considerable reduction in the effort required to produce a working program, since each of these prepackaged activities is known to work and need not be redeveloped. When a new program must be constructed from the ground up because available subprograms are inappropriate, careful modularization may allow several people to work on components of the program concurrently.

This approach is seen in the reorganized PL/I program in Fig. 9 (an equivalent Fortran program is fairly similar). Assignment of an element from array *X* to another array is handled by a separate procedure, which is called each time through the loop. Once all *X* elements have been processed, a second subprogram is called twice, once for each of the arrays *X1* and *X2*, to find the respective extreme values.

There are additional language features that allow further organizational improvements, such as the ability to vary the sizes of arrays *X*, *X1*, and *X2* independently to suit each set of requirements as they become known. This reflects direction toward a straightforward approach, which tends to reduce preparation time and cost so that accompanying penalties in the program's ultimate efficiency usually are justified.

A strikingly different construction is required by Cobol, consistent with its narrative orientation. The program in Fig. 10, operationally equivalent to the previous ones, shows the four required formal divisions. Variables are described in the DATA DIVISION, providing a completely detailed record of all names and storage allocations. The implied intent —that the program serve as its own documentation —carries over into the PROCEDURE DIVISION, where the actual processing steps are specified.

In addition to other language features that permit more concise expression, Cobol also includes provisions for subprograms. However, the descriptive aspect still is preserved. See Fig. 10.

**Aids in the Debugging Process.** In the process of freeing the programmer from the minutiae of the machine, higher-level languages also have removed him from his vantage point, so that he is no longer in a position to know what is going on inside.

```
                PG3: PROCEDURE OPTIONS (MAIN);

STMT LEVEL NEST
  1                     PG3: PROCEDURE OPTIONS (MAIN);
  2     1                    DECLARE (X(32),X1(32),X2(32),SMALL1,SMALL2,BIG1, BIG2,CUTOFF)
                                   FIXED(3,1),(SUM1,SUM2) FIXED(5,1),(N1,N2) FIXED(2);

  3     1                    GET LIST(CUTOFF,X);

  4     1                    SUM1,SUM2,N1,N2 = 0;
  5     1                    X1 = 0; X2 = 99.9;
  7     1                    SMALL1,SMALL2 = 99.9; BIG1,BIG2 = 0;

                  /******************************************************************/
                  /** THE LOOP IS STRUCTURALLY THE SAME AS BEFORE, EXCEPT          **/
                  /** THAT THE ASSIGNMENT OF EACH OF X'S ELEMENTS TO THE           **/
                  /** APPROPRIATE ARRAY IS HANDLED BY THE SUBPROGRAM FIND.         **/
                  /** THE SUBPROGRAM NEED NOT BE IN THE IMMEDIATE PROXI-           **/
                  /** MITY; THE CALL STATEMENT IMPLIES A BRANCH TO THE             **/
                  /** START OF THE SUBPROGRAM AND A RETURN TO THE REGULAR          **/
                  /** SEQUENCE, AS IF ONE STATEMENT HAD BEEN EXECUTED.             **/
                  /******************************************************************/

  9     1             DO I = 1 TO 32;
 10     1     1       IF X(I) < CUTOFF THEN CALL FIND(X1,SUM1,N1);
 12     1                                  ELSE CALL FIND(X2,SUM2,N2);
 13     1     1       END;

                  /******************************************************************/
                  /** THE PROGRAM ARRIVES AT THIS POINT ONLY AFTER THE             **/
                  /** LOOP HAS BEEN CYCLED 32 TIMES, I.E., ALL ELEMENTS            **/
                  /** HAVE BEEN PROPERLY ASSIGNED. NOW ANOTHER SUBPROGRAM           **/
                  /** (NAMED RANGE) IS CALLED TO FIND THE EXTREME VALUES           **/
                  /** FOR EACH OF THE ARRAYS X1 AND X2.                            **/
                  /******************************************************************/

 14     1             CALL RANGE(X1,N1,SMALL1,BIG1);
 15     1             CALL RANGE(X2,N2,SMALL2,BIG2);

 16     1             PUT SKIP DATA(CUTOFF);
 17     1             PUT SKIP DATA(SUM1,N1,SMALL1,BIG1);
 18     1             PUT SKIP DATA(SUM2,N2,SMALL2,BIG2);
```

**Fig. 9.** Reorganized PL/I program employing subprograms.

```
                  /*****************************************************************/
                  /** HERE ARE THE TWO SUBPROGRAMS USED BY THE MAIN PRO-          **/
                  /** GRAM. THEIR PLACEMENT HERE IS CONVENIENT RATHER THAN        **/
                  /** OBLIGATORY. SINCE EACH IS BRACKETED BY A SET OF             **/
                  /** PROCEDURE AND END STATEMENTS, THEY WILL BE BYPASSED         **/
                  /** IN NORMAL SEQUENTIAL PROCESSING, BEING ACCESSIBLE           **/
                  /** ONLY BY MEANS OF A CALL STATEMENT.                          **/
                  /*****************************************************************/

19    1         FIND: PROCEDURE (Y,TOTAL,M);
                      /*****************************************************************/
                      /** THIS PROCEDURE IS GIVEN THE NAME OF AN ARRAY,               **/
                      /** THE NUMBER OF ELEMENTS OCCUPIED THUS FAR, AND              **/
                      /** THE SUM OF THOSE ELEMENTS. EACH TIME IT IS                 **/
                      /** CALLED, IT FILLS THE NEXT AVAILABLE POSITION               **/
                      /** WITH THE VALUE OF THE INPUT ARRAY ELEMENT CUR-             **/
                      /** RENTLY BEING EXAMINED AND UPDATES THE TOTAL.               **/
                      /*****************************************************************/
20    2               DECLARE Y(32) FIXED(3,1), TOTAL FIXED(5,1), M FIXED(2);
21    2               M = M + 1; Y(M) = X(I); TOTAL = TOTAL + X(I);
24    2               RETURN;
25    2               END FIND;

26    1         RANGE: PROCEDURE (Z,L,S,B);
                        /*****************************************************************/
                        /** THIS SUBPROGRAM LOOKS THROUGH THE INDICATED                **/
                        /** NUMBER OF OCCUPIED ELEMENTS IN AN ARRAY AND               **/
                        /** FINDS THE LARGEST AND SMALLEST VALUES.                     **/
                        /*****************************************************************/
27    2                 DECLARE (Z(32),S,B) FIXED(3,1), L FIXED(2);
28    2                    DO J = 1 TO L;
29    2    1               IF Z(J) < S THEN S = Z(J);
31    2    1                       ELSE IF Z(J) > B THEN B = Z(J);
33    2    1               END;
34    2                 RETURN;
35    2                 END RANGE;

36    1         END PG3;
```

Fig. 9. (continued)

```
       IDENTIFICATION DIVISION.
       PROGRAM-ID. 'PG4'
       REMARKS. THE FIRST TWO DIVISIONS, SHOWN IN MINIMAL FORM HERE,
                REFLECT AN INTENT TO HAVE THE COBOL SOURCE PROGRAM
                SERVE AS ITS OWN DOCUMENTATION.
       ENVIRONMENT DIVISION.
       CONFIGURATION SECTION.
       SOURCE-COMPUTER. IBM-360.
       OBJECT-COMPUTER. IBM-360.
       DATA DIVISION.
      *
      *           THE VARIABLES S1,S2,SM1,SM2,B1,B2 ARE USED TO
      *    STORE THE COMPUTER RESULTS. WHEN COMPUTATION IS COMPLETE,
      *    THEY WILL BE REPRODUCED, RESPECTIVELY, IN SUM1,SUM2,SMALL1,
      *    SMALL2,BIG1 AND BIG2, FROM WHENCE THEY WILL BE PRINTED.
      *
       WORKING-STORAGE SECTION.
       77  I PICTURE 99.
       77  SM1 PICTURE 99V9 VALUE IS 99.9.
       77  SM2 PICTURE 99V9 VALUE IS 99.9.
       77  B1 PICTURE 99V9 VALUE IS ZERO.
       77  B2 PICTURE 99V9 VALUE IS ZERO.
       77  S1 PICTURE 9999V9 VALUE IS ZEROS.
       77  S2 PICTURE 9999V9 VALUE IS ZEROS.
       77  C PICTURE 99V9.
      *
      *           THERE IS NO CONVENIENT WAY TO READ KEYPUNCHED DATA
      *    WITH EMBEDDED DECIMAL POINTS. CONSEQUENTLY, THE INTEGER
      *    AND FRACTIONAL PORTIONS VT AND VU ARE DEFINED AS SEPARATE
      *    VARIABLES THAT WILL BE COMBINED, ONCE THEY ARE READ, TO
      *    FORM C. THE SAME IS DONE WITH EACH OF THE ELEMENTS IN THE
      *    INPUT ARRAY, PARTITIONING THE VALUES INTO TX AND UX.
      *
       01  FIRST-CARD.
           02  FILLER PICTURE X(4).
           02  VT PICTURE 99.
           02  VP PICTURE X.
           02  VU PICTURE 9.
           02  FILLER PICTURE X(72).
       01  IN-ARRAY.
           02  INHERE OCCURS 32 TIMES.
               03  TX PICTURE 99.
               03  TP PICTURE X.
               03  UX PICTURE 9.
               03  FILLER PICTURE X.
       01  WORKING-ARRAYS.
           02  X1 PICTURE 99V9 OCCURS 32 TIMES.
           02  X2 PICTURE 99V9 OCCURS 32 TIMES.
           02  X PICTURE 99V9 OCCURS 32 TIMES.
      *
      *           EACH OF THE THREE LINES OF PRINT IS SET UP EXACTLY
      *    AS IT WILL APPEAR, WITH THE LABELING PREDEFINED AND THE
```

**Fig. 10.** Cobol program listing.

```
 *    SPACES RESERVED FOR THE NUMERICAL RESULTS.
 *
  01  LINE-1.
      02  FILLER PICTURE X(4).
      02  L11 PICTURE X(9) VALUE IS 'CUTOFF = '.
      02  CUTOFF PICTURE 99.9.
      02  FILLER PICTURE X(115).
  01  LINE-2
      02  FILLER PICTURE X(4).
      02  L21 PICTURE X(7) VALUE IS 'SUM1 = '.
      02  SUM1 PICTURE 9999.9.
      02  L22 PICTURE X(8) VALUE IS '  N1 = '.
      02  N1 PICTURE 99 VALUE IS ZEROES.
      02  L23 PICTURE X(12) VALUE IS '   SMALL1 = '.
      02  SMALL1 PICTURE 99.9.
      02  L24 PICTURE X(10) VALUE IS '   BIG1 = '.
      02  BIG1 PICTURE 99.9.
      02  FILLER PICTURE X(75).
  01  LINE-3.
      02  FILLER PICTURE X(4).
      02  L31 PICTURE X(7) VALUE IS 'SUM2 = '.
      02  SUM2 PICTURE 9999.9.
      02  L32 PICTURE X(8) VALUE IS '  N2 = '.
      02  N2 PICTURE 99 VALUE IS ZEROS.
      02  L33 PICTURE X(12) VALUE IS '   SMALL2 = '.
      02  SMALL2 PICTURE 99.9.
      02  L34 PICTURE X(10) VALUE IS '   BIG2 = '.
      02  BIG2 PICTURE 99.9,
      02  FILLER PICTURE X(75).
 *
 *            THE FINAL (PROCEDURE) DIVISION CONTAINS THE ACTUAL
 *    PROCESSING STEPS. THE PERFORM STATEMENT IS MUCH LIKE A CALL
 *    TO A SUBROUTINE. IN THIS CASE THE SINGLE STATEMENT WITH THE
 *    LABEL 'BUILD' WILL BE USED AS THE NUCLEUS OF A LOOP. ON THE
 *    OTHER HAND, 'FIND' REFERS TO AN ENTIRE SECTION, COVERING
 *    ALL OF THE PROCESSING FROM 'FIND-1' THROUGH 'AWAY'.
 *
  PROCEDURE DIVISION.
      ACCEPT FIRST-CARD.
      COMPUTE C = VT + VU / 10.
      ACCEPT IN-ARRAY.
      PERFORM BUILD VARYING I FROM 1 BY 1 UNTIL
      I IS GREATER THAN 32.
      PERFORM FIND VARYING I FROM 1 BY 1 UNTIL
      I IS GREATER THAN 32.
  COMMENTS-1.
      NOTE THE PLACEMENT OF C'S VALUE IN CUTOFF INCLUDES THE
      INSERTION OF THE ACTUAL DECIMAL POINT, DESIGNATED BY
      CUTOFF'S DESCRIPTION IN THE DATA DIVISION. THE SAME HOLDS
      TRUE FOR THE OTHER OUTPUT VALUES.
  OUTPUT-PREP.
      MOVE C TO CUTOFF.
```

**Fig. 10.** (continued)

```
            DISPLAY LINE-1.
            MOVE S1 TO SUM1.
            MOVE B1 TO BIG1.
            MOVE SM1 TO SMALL1.
            DISPLAY LINE-2.
            MOVE S2 TO SUM2.
            MOVE B2 TO BIG2.
            MOVE SM2 TO SMALL2.
            DISPLAY LINE-3.
            GO TO ENDALL.
        BUILD.
            COMPUTE X (I) = TX (I) + UX (I) / 10.
        FIND SECTION.
        FIND-1.
            IF X (I) IS LESS THAN CUTOFF GO TO ADD-ON-X1 OTHERWISE
            GO TO ADD-ON-X2.
        ADD-ON-X1.
            ADD 1 TO N1.
            COMPUTE S1 = S1 + X (I).
            MOVE X (I) TO X1 (N1).
            IF X (I) IS LESS THAN SM1 MOVE X (I) TO SM1.
            IF X (I) IS GREATER THAN B1 MOVE X (I) TO B1.
            GO TO AWAY.
        ADD-ON-X2.
            ADD 1 TO N2.
            COMPUTE S2 = S2 + X (I).
            MOVE X (I) TO X2 (N2).
            IF X (I) IS LESS THAN SM2 MOVE X (I) TO SM2.
            IF X (I) IS GREATER THAN B2 MOVE X (I) TO B2.
        AWAY.
            EXIT.
        ENDALL.
            STOP RUN.
```

**Fig. 10.** (continued)

This becomes a crucial problem when something is wrong in the program or the processing, since it may be impossible to relate an event concerning an individual machine instruction to the corresponding point in the procedure as the programmer perceives it.

To reestablish some measure of control, the software structure within which a higher-level language operates is equipped with diagnostic mechanisms to provide the programmer with appropriate clues that will facilitate the process of locating, identifying, and repairing difficulties. Since any software structure inherently contains a set of rules whose violation prevents the system from operating properly, the general approach is to supplement these rules by a corresponding repertoire of messages. Then, if a rule is broken, the appropriate message is displayed as part of the system's response to the transgression. The rest of the response often is to curtail the processing at that point, but not before the programmer has been given some information.

There is continuing controversy over what is "appropriate." Many users would like their higher-level language implementation equipped with extensive arrays of messages that delineate the type of difficulty as well as its source. Designers, more directly concerned with the size and operating overhead of a software system, favor a minimal set of aids in which the location of the difficulty is identified but no attempt is made to specify its nature. This general philosophy derives from the idea that once the user is directed to a trouble spot, then presumably he will determine what is wrong and correct it. The direction of the inevitable compromise varies widely from one language to another and from implementation to implementation in a given language.

A number of diagnostic facilities will be examined within two basic contexts: The first of these deals with the compilation process during which a higher-level language *source program* is analyzed to produce an equivalent machine language *object program*; the second general situation is concerned with events preventing a successfully compiled program from operating.

AIDS DURING THE COMPILATION PROCESS. Every programming language has its syntactic rules, which permit the unambiguous and reproducible analysis of a source language program by an appropriately designed compiler. As part of the same process, then, the compiler can detect and classify violations of those rules, calling the programmer's attention to them.

To become acquainted with the general nature of these responses, the illustrative procedure shown in Figs. 7–10 has been contaminated with the following syntactic errors:

1. The closing parenthesis on the storage allocation for array X has been omitted. (This type of oversight is fairly common).
2. Storage for array X2 has not been reserved.
3. The variables SUM1 and SUM2 have not been initialized.

The Fortran version of this procedure was processed by a particular compiler, producing the listing shown in Fig. 11. For this version, an additional error was introduced by relieving statement number 16 of its label, leaving the branch on card number 14 with an unknown destination. (Note also that the comments have been deleted for brevity).

As seen from Fig. 11, this compiler display mechanism is constructed to intersperse the source program listing with error messages immediately following the statement in which syntactic violations have been detected. (A $ is placed by the compiler at the possible trouble spot.) It is seen that the general approach is to indicate that something is wrong, without providing extensive details. (The accompanying codes, e.g., IEY008I, refer to entries in a separate manual containing more information.) Thus, the message following card number 0001 alerts the programmer to the fact that there is something wrong with the allocation of X. This type of error is particularly catastrophic because so many subsequent activities in the program make use of and depend on array X. Consequently, other statements, which are syntactically correct in themselves, elicit protests from the compiler as a result of the inconsistency precipitated by the absence of X. Accordingly, each of the numerous references to elements in array X carries an error message.

Failure to allocate storage for array X2 produces an appropriate error message following card 0016. Absence of a labeled destination for the branch in card 0014 is not noted directly. However, a more subtle mechanism calls attention to the deficiency. Although the unlabeled statement on card 0021 seems structurally legitimate, the fact that it is preceded immediately by a GO TO statement means that it will not be reached in the normal sequence of processing. Rather, it is itself the destination of some other transfer, and therefore ought to be labeled.

Note that the compiler finds nothing "wrong" with the uninitialized variables SUM1 and SUM2. All the statements involving these two variables have proper construction and are processed routinely by the compiler.

A somewhat different display is produced when the same program is processed by another Fortran compiler (Fig. 12), this one designed primarily for educational use. The basic format is the same as before in that the error messages are included in the source listing. However, their volubility displays a clear attempt to be self-sufficient and to provide specific information about the possible difficulty. (In the case of card 1, much of this effort is misdirected, since the missing parenthesis forces the compiler to treat the ensuing names as additional pieces of information relating to X.) Thus, the unavailability of X as a 32-element array is felt throughout the rest of the program, as was seen with the other compiler.

The equivalent PL/I program was processed by a compiler for a compatible subset of the language. A single error message appears in the listing (Fig. 13), correctly pointing out the missing right parenthesis; most of the diagnostic information (Fig. 14), which follows the listing, implies a more aggressive design philosophy, resulting in a compiler that attempts to take some corrective action as part of its response to errors. The basic objective is to allow the compiler to complete its job and produce a program that is likely to run, even though it could differ drastically from the intended product. Despite its apparent futility, it may give the programmer an opportunity to scrutinize the results of the compiler's operation on his entire program, thereby finding and correcting errors that otherwise would have to be handled in several stages, each requiring a separate compilation run. Accordingly, each message is accompanied by a description of the compiler's action and the "corrected" statement produced thereby.

```
   card no.
   0001               REAL X(32 ,SUM1,SUM2,SMALL1,SMALL2,BIG1,BIG2,CUTOFF,X1(32)
                                $
**********01)   IEY008I ALLOCATION**********************************************
   0002               INTEGER N1,N2
   0003               READ(5,10)CUTOFF
   0004               READ(5,11) X
   0005            10 FORMAT(4X,F4.1)
   0006            11 FORMAT(16 (F4.1,1X))
   0007               SMALL1 = 99.9
   0008               SMALL2 = 99.9
   0009               BIG1 = 0.0
   0010               BIG2 = 0.0
   0011               N1 = 0
   0012               N2 = 0
   0013               DO 20 I = 1,32
   0014               IF (X(I) .LT. CUTOFF) GO TO 16
                          $
**********01)   IEY013I SYNTAX**************************************************
   0015                  N2 = N2 + 1
   0016                  X2(N2) = X(I)
                          $
**********01)   IEY011I UNDIMENSIONED*******************************************
   0017                  SUM2 = SUM2 + X(I)
                                    $
**********01)   IEY013I SYNTAX**************************************************
   0018                  IF (X(I) .LT. SMALL2) SMALL2 = X(I)
                            $
**********01)   IEY013I SYNTAX**************************************************
   0019                  IF (X(I) .GT. BIG2) BIG2 = X(I)
                            $
**********01)   IEY013I SYNTAX**************************************************
   0020                  GO TO 20
   0021               N1 = N1 + 1
             $
**********01)   IEY002I LABEL***************************************************
   0022               X1(N1) = X(I)
                        $
**********01)   IEY011I UNDIMENSIONED*******************************************
   0023               SUM1 = SUM1 + X(I)
                                 $
**********01)   IEY013I SYNTAX**************************************************
   0024               IF (X(I) .LT. SMALL1) SMALL1 = X(I)
                          $
**********01)   IEY013I SYNTAX**************************************************
   0025               IF (X(I) .GT. BIG1) BIG1  =  X(I)
                          $
**********01)   IEY013I SYNTAX**************************************************
   0026            20 CONTINUE
   0027               WRITE(6,30)CUTOFF
   0028               WRITE(6,31)SUM1,N1,SMALL1,BIG1
```

**Fig. 11.** Listing of Fortran program with diagnostic messages. (continued)

```
0029          WRITE(6,32)SUM2,N2,SMALL2,BIG2
0030       30 FORMAT(5X,9HCUTOFF = ,F5.1)
0031       31 FORMAT(5X,7HSUM1 = ,F7.1,3X,5HN1 = ,I2,3X,9HSMALL1 = ,F5.1,3X,
             *      7HBIG1 = ,F5.1)
0032       32 FORMAT(5X,7HSUM2 = ,F7.1,3X,5HN2 = ,I2,3X,9HSMALL2 = ,F5.1,3X,
             *      7HBIG2 = ,F5.1)
0033          END
```

**Fig. 11.** (continued)

```
   1          REAL X(32 ,SUM1,SUM2,SMALL1,SMALL2,BIG1,BIG2,CUTOFF,X1(32)
**ERROR***  UNMATCHED PARENTHESIS
**ERROR***  VARIABLE X       ,USED WITH VARIABLE DIMENSIONS,IS NOT A SUBPROGRAM PARAMETER
**ERROR***  VARIABLE DIMENSION SUM1    IS NOT ONE OF SIMPLE INTEGER VARIABLE,SUBPROGRAM PARAMETER
**ERROR***  VARIABLE DIMENSION SUM2    IS NOT ONE OF SIMPLE INTEGER VARIABLE,SUBPROGRAM PARAMETER
**ERROR***  VARIABLE DIMENSION SMALL1  IS NOT ONE OF SIMPLE INTEGER VARIABLE,SUBPROGRAM PARAMETER
**ERROR***  VARIABLE DIMENSION SMALL2  IS NOT ONE OF SIMPLE INTEGER VARIABLE,SUBPROGRAM PARAMETER
**ERROR***  VARIABLE DIMENSION BIG1    IS NOT ONE OF SIMPLE INTEGER VARIABLE,SUBPROGRAM PARAMETER
**ERROR***  VARIABLE DIMENSION BIG2    IS NOT ONE OF SIMPLE INTEGER VARIABLE,SUBPROGRAM PARAMETER
**ERROR***  MORE THAN 7 DIMENSIONS NOT ALLOWED. CUTOFF  IS INVALID
**ERROR***  VARIABLE DIMENSION CUTOFF  IS NOT ONE OF SIMPLE INTEGER VARIABLE,SUBPROGRAM PARAMETER
**ERROR***  MORE THAN 7 DIMENSIONS NOT ALLOWED. X1  IS INVALID
**ERROR***  VARIABLE DIMENSION X1      IS NOT ONE OF SIMPLE INTEGER VARIABLE,SUBPROGRAM PARAMETER
**ERROR***  EXPECTING OPERATOR BUT ( BEFORE          32 WAS FOUND
**ERROR***  MISSING OPERATOR,UNEXPECTED          32
   2          INTEGER N1,N2
   3          READ(5,10)CUTOFF
   4          READ(5,11) X
   5       10 FORMAT(4X,F4.1)
   6       11 FORMAT(16 (F4.11X))
   7          SMALL1 = 99.9
   8          SMALL2 = 99.9
   9          BIG1 = 0.0
  10          BIG2 = 0.0
  11          N1 = 0
  12          N2 = 0
  13          DO 20 I = 1,32
  14          IF (X(I) .LT. CUTOFF) GO TO 16
**ERROR***  WRONG NUMBER OF SUBSCRIPTS SPECIFIED FOR VARIABLE X
**ERROR***  ARITHMETIC OR INVALID EXPRESSION IN LOGICAL IF
  15                 N2 = N2 + 1
  16                 X2(N2) = X(I)
*WARNING**  A STATEMENT FUNCTION DEFINITION APPEARS AFTER THE FIRST EXECUTABLE STATEMENT
**ERROR***  WRONG NUMBER OF SUBSCRIPTS SPECIFIED FOR VARIABLE X
  17                 SUM2 = SUM2 + X(I)
**ERROR***  WRONG NUMBER OF SUBSCRIPTS SPECIFIED FOR VARIABLE X
  18                 IF (X(I) .LT. SMALL2) SMALL2 = X(I)
**ERROR***  WRONG NUMBER OF SUBSCRIPTS SPECIFIED FOR VARIABLE X
**ERROR***  ARITHMETIC OR INVALID EXPRESSION IN LOGICAL IF
**ERROR***  WRONG NUMBER OF SUBSCRIPTS SPECIFIED FOR VARIABLE X
  19                 IF (X(I) .GT. BIG2) BIG2 = X(I)
**ERROR***  WRONG NUMBER OF SUBSCRIPTS SPECIFIED FOR VARIABLE X
**ERROR***  ARITHMETIC OR INVALID EXPRESSION IN LOGICAL IF
**ERROR***  WRONG NUMBER OF SUBSCRIPTS SPECIFIED FOR VARIABLE X
  20                 GO TO 20
  21          N1 = N1 + 1
```

**Fig. 12.** Diagnostic messages produced by an educationally oriented Fortran compiler. (continued)

```
*WARNING**     UNNUMBERED EXECUTABLE STATEMENT FOLLOWS A TRANSFER
   22            X1(N1)=X(I)
*WARNING**     A STATEMENT FUNCTION DEFINITION APPEARS AFTER THE FIRST EXECUTABLE STATEMENT
**ERROR***     WRONG NUMBER OF SUBSCRIPTS SPECIFIED FOR VARIABLE X
   23            SUM1 = SUM1 + X(I)
**ERROR***     WRONG NUMBER OF SUBSCRIPTS SPECIFIED FOR VARIABLE X
   24            IF (X(I) .LT. SMALL1) SMALL1 = X(I)
**ERROR***     WRONG NUMBER OF SUBSCRIPTS SPECIFIED FOR VARIABLE X
**ERROR***     ARITHMETIC OR INVALID EXPRESSION IN LOGICAL IF
**ERROR***     WRONG NUMBER OF SUBSCRIPTS SPECIFIED FOR VARIABLE X
   25            IF (X(I) .GT. BIG1) BIG1  =  X(I)
**ERROR***     WRONG NUMBER OF SUBSCRIPTS SPECIFIED FOR VARIABLE X
**ERROR***     ARITHMETIC OR INVALID EXPRESSION IN LOGICAL IF
**ERROR***     WRONG NUMBER OF SUBSCRIPTS SPECIFIED FOR VARIABLE X
   26         20 CONTINUE
   27            WRITE(6,30)CUTOFF
   28            WRITE(6,31)SUM1,N1,SMALL1,BIG1
   29            WRITE(6,32)SUM2,N2,SMALL2,BIG2
   30         30 FORMAT(5X,9HCUTOFF  =  ,F5.1)
   31         31 FORMAT(5X,7HSUM1  =  ,F7.1,3X,5HN1  =  ,I2,3X,9HSMALL1  =  ,F5.1,3X,
                *         7HBIG1  =  ,F5.1)
   32         32 FORMAT(5X,7HSUM2  =  ,F7.1,3X,5HN2  =  ,I2,3X,9HSMALL2  =  ,F5.1,3X,
                *         7HBIG2  =  ,F5.1)
   33            END
*WARNING**     END STATEMENT NOT PRECEDED BY A TRANSFER
**ERROR***     MISSING STATEMENT NUMBER      16 USED IN LINE      14
```

**Fig. 12.** (continued)

The uninitialized SUM1 and SUM2 go unnoticed as before.

The types of diagnostic services exemplified above represent but one layer of such facilities, available by default (i.e., without requiring explicit requests). Many compilers include more elaborate diagnostic structures that may be activated at the programmer's option.

DIAGNOSTIC AIDS DURING PROGRAM EXECUTION. Successful compilation in no way guarantees subsequent execution of the resulting machine language program. An endless variety of anomalies and inconsistencies can appear during processing, and hardware/software systems contain features for detecting and dealing with some of these difficulties. Of course it is impossible for the system to anticipate each particular situation. Instead, the diagnostic mechanisms are sensitive to certain types of events whose occurrence can be expected to cause trouble. Typical categories include attempts to divide by zero, a reference to a nonexistent storage address, or the involvement of a nonnumeric data item in an arithmetic operation. Once such a situation is encountered, the resulting diagnostic message usually gives the general category, together with some indication of the place in the program at which the difficulty occurred.

To illustrate: The errors in the Fortran example (Fig. 11) have been corrected, except for the failure to initialize SUM1 and SUM2. (Some compilers ignore this type of problem altogether.) Compilation will be successful, but when the program executes, its attempt to add to an indeterminate quantity will not fare well. The diagnostic system used for Fig. 11 indicates this by showing asterisks where SUM1 and SUM2 would have appeared (Fig. 15). A more direct message (Fig. 16) is produced by the other system used.

The PL/I system used for Fig. 8 incorporates a less direct mode of diagnostic expression. For example, execution of the PL/I program with SUM1 and SUM2 uninitialized is terminated at some point and produces a message (Fig. 17) requiring two supplementary sources of information to make it useful: the error type refers to information cataloged under that code in a manual; the point at which execution stopped is expressed as a storage address whose relation to a particular source-language statement is defined in a separate reference table produced by the software.

```
        PG1: PROCEDURE OPTIONS (MAIN);

   STMT LEVEL NEST BLOCK        SOURCE STATEMENT

     1                          PG1: PROCEDURE OPTIONS (MAIN);
     2    1          1                    DECLARE (X(32 ,X1(32),      SMALL1,SMALL2,BIG1,BIG2,CUTOFF)
                                             FIXED(3,1), (SUM1,SUM2) FIXED (5,1), (N1,N2) FIXED(2);
IN   2               ERROR       SY04 MISSING )
PL/C USES                       DECLARE(X (32,X1 (32),SMALL1,SMALL2,BIG1,BIG2,CUTOFF) FIXED (3,1),(SUM1
                                ,SUM2) FIXED (5,1),(N1,N2) FIXED (2));

     3    1          1                    GET LIST(CUTOFF,X);
     4    1          1                    N1,N2,BIG1,BIG2 = 0;
     5    1          1                    SMALL1,SMALL2 = 99.9;
     6    1          1                    DO I = 1 TO 32;
     7    1     1    1                    IF X(I) < CUTOFF        THEN DO;
     9    1     2    1                                            SUM1 = SUM1 + X(I); N1 = N1 + 1; X1(N1) = X(I);
    12    1     2    1                                            IF X(I) < SMALL1 THEN SMALL1 = X(I);
    14    1     2    1                                            IF X(I) > BIG1 THEN BIG1 = X(I);
    16    1     2    1                                               END;
    17    1     1    1                                            ELSE DO;
    18    1     2    1                                            SUM2 = SUM2 + X(I); N2 = N2 + 1; X2(N2) = X(I);
    21    1     2    1                                            IF X(I) < SMALL2 THEN SMALL2 = X(I);
    23    1     2    1                                            IF X(I) > BIG2 THEN BIG2 = X(I);
    25    1     2    1                    END;

    26    1     1    1                    PUT SKIP DATA(CUTOFF);
    27    1     1    1                    PUT SKIP DATA(SUM1,N1,SMALL1,BIG1);
    28    1     1    1                    PUT SKIP DATA(SUM2,N2,SMALL2,BIG2);

    29    1     1    1                END PG1;
```

**Fig. 13.** Listing of program processed by PL/C compiler.

```
IN STMT      2  ERROR  SM4E X1 HAS TOO MANY SUBSCRIPTS.  SUBSCRIPT LIST DELETED
PL/C USES                      DECLARE (X (32,X1,SMALL1,SMALL2,BIG1,BIG2,CUTOFF) FIXED (3,1),(SUM1,SUM
DECLARED IN BLOCK                        1    1     1     1   1   1     1           1
                                    ) FIXED (5,1),(N1,N2) FIXED (2));
DECLARED IN BLOCK                             1  1

IN STMT      7  ERROR  SM4F X HAS TOO FEW SUBSCRIPTS.  SUBSCRIPT LIST DELETED
IN STMT      7  ERROR  SM42 WRONG STRUCTURE OR DIMENSIONALITY FOR EXPRESSION
PL/C USES                           IF '1'B

IN STMT      9  ERROR  SM4F X HAS TOO FEW SUBSCRIPTS.  SUBSCRIPT LIST DELETED
IN STMT      9  ERROR  SM5E ASSIGNMENT SOURCE INCOMPATIBLE WITH TARGET
PL/C USES                           SUM1 = 1;
DECLARED IN BLOCK                       1

IN STMT     11  ERROR  SM4E X1 HAS TOO MANY SUBSCRIPTS.  SUBSCRIPT LIST DELETED
IN STMT     11  ERROR  SM4F X HAS TOO FEW SUBSCRIPTS.  SUBSCRIPT LIST DELETED
IN STMT     11  ERROR  SM5E ASSIGNMENT SOURCE INCOMPATIBLE WITH TARGET
PL/C USES                           X1 = 1;
DECLARED IN BLOCK                     1
                                                 .
                                                 .
                                                 .
```

**Fig. 14.** Diagnostic messages for the program in Fig. 13.

```
CUTOFF =  36.8
SUM1 = *******    N1 = 13    SMALL1 =  1.4    BIG1 = 34.7
SUM2 = *******    N2 = 19    SMALL2 = 36.8    BIG2 = 99.7
```

**Fig.15.** Output of Fortran program with uninitialized SUM1 and SUM2 (standard system).

```
***ERROR***    VALUE OF SUM1    IS UNDEFINED
```

**Fig. 16.** Output of Fortran program with uninitialized SUM1 and SUM2 (Watfiv system).

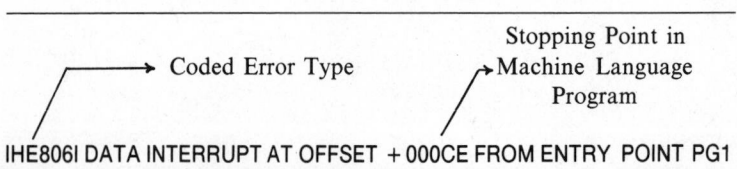

```
                                             Stopping Point in
      ------> Coded Error Type              ->Machine Language
     /                                     /      Program
    /                                     /
IHE806I DATA INTERRUPT AT OFFSET +000CE FROM ENTRY POINT PG1
```

**Fig. 17.** Diagnostic message produced by PL/I system after attempt to run with SUM1 and SUM2 uninitialized.

```
****** IN STMT     9  ERROR  EXB7 SUM1 HAS NOT BEEN INITIALIZED. IT IS SET TO 0.

CUTOFF =     36.8;
SUM1 =       32.9        N1 =   1          SMALL1 =  32.9        BIG1 =    0.0;
SUM2 = //////            N2 =   0          SMALL2 =  99.9        BIG2 =    0.0;
****** IN STMT    18  ERROR  EXB7 SUM2 HAS NOT BEEN INITIALIZED. IT IS SET TO 0.

CUTOFF =     36.8;
SUM1 =       32.9        N1 =   1          SMALL1 =  32.9        BIG1 =    0.0;
SUM2 =       44.4        N2 =   1          SMALL2 =  44.4        BIG2 =    0.0;
CUTOFF =     36.8;
SUM1 =       32.9        N1 =   1          SMALL1 =  32.9        BIG1 =    0.0;
SUM2 =      105.4        N2 =   2          SMALL2 =  44.4        BIG2 =   61.0;
CUTOFF =     36.8;
SUM1 =       32.9        N1 =   1          SMALL1 =  32.9        BIG1 =    0.0;
SUM2 =      180.9        N2 =   3          SMALL2 =  44.4        BIG2 =   75.5;

                                 .
                                 .
                                 .
                                 .
                                 .

CUTOFF =     36.8;
SUM1 =      263.8        N1 =  13          SMALL1 =   1.4        BIG1 =   34.7;
SUM2 =     1112.0        N2 =  17          SMALL2 =  36.8        BIG2 =   99.7;
CUTOFF =     36.8;
SUM1 =      263.8        N1 =  13          SMALL1 =   1.4        BIG1 =   34.7;
SUM2 =     1154.9        N2 =  18          SMALL2 =  36.8        BIG2 =   99.7;
CUTOFF =     36.8;
SUM1 =      263.8        N1 =  13          SMALL1 =   1.4        BIG1 =   34.7;
SUM2 =     1227.6        N2 =  19          SMALL2 =  36.8        BIG2 =   99.7;
```

**Fig. 18.** PL/C diagnostic output for program with uninitialized SUM1 and SUM2.

Increased emphasis on debugging capabilities is seen in the PL/C system (a teaching subset of PL/I system developed at Cornell University) approach to the same situation (Fig. 18). Direct designation of the type of error is supplemented by the results of automatically triggered action based on the assumption that initialization to zero is reasonable. (In this case, it is.) Subsequent results are printed each time through the loop (only a few cycles are shown). Thus, even if the assumed initialization were improper, the programmer could see the consequences.

While there is a loose parallelism between the processes of producing a successful compilation and a successful run, the techniques associated with the latter activity are conspicuously different. Despite the extensive diagnostic aids that are available by default or by request during a program's execution, it often is impossible for the user to exploit them passively. Since these facilities necessarily must be general, the information they provide may be useless unless it is accompanied by more specific qualifications actively supplied by the programmer. To do this, the programmer uses a simple but effective technique: The source program is equipped with supplementary statements designed specifically to provide helpful information for debugging purposes. A common practice, for instance, is to print the input "as is" as soon as it is read (this is often referred to as an echo), thereby providing a very convenient reference point. Displays of intermediate results also may be very revealing.

A frequently occurring situation is one in which execution is terminated and the regular diagnostic services report that there was an attempt to divide by zero somewhere in the program corresponding to a particular statement in the original higher-level language sequence. However, there are complications because that statement turns out to be part of a loop and there is no indication of the number of cycles that had been completed before the tragedy occurred. Insertion of a statement that prints the value of the index (and, perhaps, other crucial variables) each time through the loop may be all that is required to identify the problem. Once the difficulty is found and appropriate safeguards are installed (e.g., testing potential divisors for a value of zero and specifying evasive action should this be true), the now extraneous output statement may be removed for the program's final version.

This technique is especially helpful in dealing with the more insidious types of situations in which a program runs to completion but is procedurally wrong: Input was read properly and the program printed when it should have printed, but the output values make no sense. Correction is strictly up to the programmer, who must decide which items of information will be most revealing and at which time their display will be of greatest use.

Diagnostic facilities of many systems include features that facilitate this type of scrutiny. Rather than require the programmer to insert explicit statements at strategic points, he may request a *trace* during which designated variables are monitored automatically. In this mode of operation, the value of a variable is printed every time it undergoes a change, together with information regarding the point in the program at which that change occurred. Another type of trace documents the sequence of events during execution. This is very useful in procedures containing numerous modules and/or complex decision networks that provide a wide choice of possible actions and sequences.

**Future Directions.** Despite the abundance of syntactic and operational restrictions, there still is sufficient latitude to make higher-level language programming a surprisingly subjective endeavor. There is no "ultimate" language (nor is its eventual definition assured), and there are no rigorous "laws" characterizing programs or the techniques pertinent to their construction. Consequently, the development of higher-level language programming can be described perhaps as a dynamic, spiraling process in which a continuous accumulation of experience and insight identifies linguistic deficiencies remedied by new languages or extensions to existing ones. (Similar impetus is provided concurrently by newly emerging hardware, software, and applications.) These more powerful instruments of expression engender new programming techniques and higher levels of algorithms that stimulate further linguistic developments, and so it goes. The overall result is a turbulent and challenging arena to all people involved with computers and computing.

REFERENCES


1968. Maurer, W. D. *Programming: An Introduction to Computer Languages and Techniques*. San Francisco: Holden-Day.

1973. Andree, R. V., J. P. Andree, and D. D. Andree. *Computer Programming: Techniques, Analysis and Mathematics*. Englewood Cliffs, N.J.: Prentice-Hall.

1973. Elson, M. *Programming Techniques*. Chicago: Science Research Associates.

1974. Pollack, S. V., and T. D. Sterling. *Essentials of PL/I*. New York: Holt, Rinehart and Winston.


S. V. POLLACK AND T. D. STERLING

## PROCESS. *See* TASK.

## PROCESSING MODES

For articles on related subjects *see* COMPUTING CENTER; REAL TIME APPLICATIONS; TIME SHARING; and TURNAROUND TIME.

For articles on related terms *see* DATA ACQUISITION COMPUTER; MEMORY: Main; and MEMORY: Auxiliary.

Six distinct categories of computing activity can be distinguished at modern computing installations:

1. Card-oriented batch processing.
2. Keyboard-oriented batch processing.
3. Interactive computing (also called "time sharing").
4. On-line inquiry.
5. Message switching.
6. Data acquisition and control ("DAX").

Of these processing modes, the last four are on line and in real time; response to input stimuli (or input transactions) is almost instantaneous. The batch-processing modes differ in that substantial queues of unprocessed transactions ("jobs") are held in the computer throughout normal operation. Likewise, substantial queues of output reports are printed/punched continuously for card-oriented batch processing. (These queues are presented on request during keyboard-oriented batch processing.) Time lines for input, computer processing, and output responses for the six modes are shown in Figs. 1 through 3.

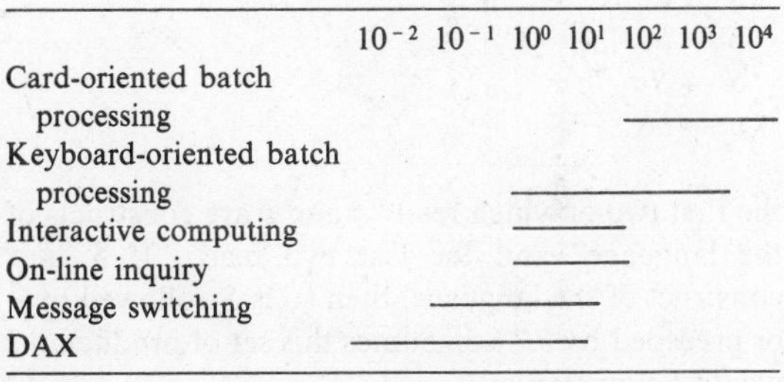


**Fig. 1.** Response times to input stimuli, in seconds.

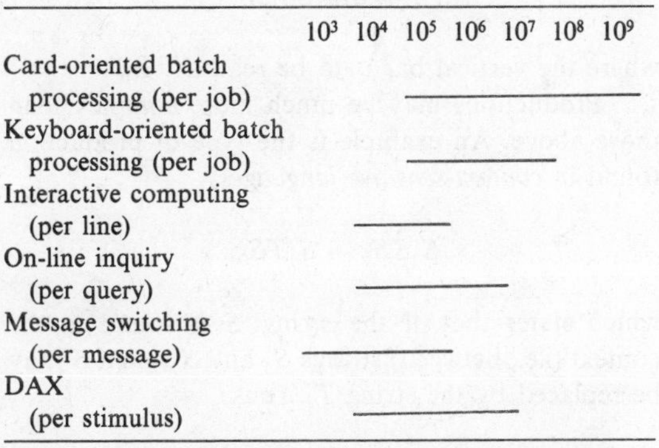


**Fig. 2.** Instructions executed per input stimulus.

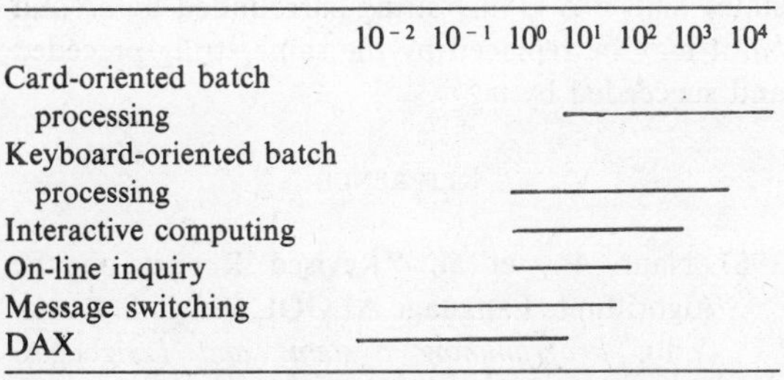


**Fig. 3.** Duration of output stimuli (transactions), in seconds.

*Batch processing* utilizes programs and data stored at all levels of a memory hierarchy:

1. Main memory
2. Auxiliary memory
3. Card decks, paper tapes, cassettes, etc.

Each batch installation maintains a library of systems and applications programs on fast auxiliary memory: magnetic tapes, drums, or disks. Users of card-oriented batch processing prepare input data on keypunches, Teletype, or other off-line devices not connected to a computer. Input data (and specialized programs associated with the data) is submitted to a computer all at once in a high-speed stream, typically through a local/remote card reader. Little validation of data is performed during this input phase. Checks are performed for correct parity and punched-card patterns (local card readers), or for error-free transmission (remote card readers).

Users of *keyboard-oriented batch processing* prepare input data and programs much the same as for card-oriented processing. However, certain validation and syntax checking are performed as statements are typed directly into the computer. When accepted, these statements are stored temporarily/permanently on disk storage. Typically, a broad repertoire of commands is available for inserting, updating, and other editing of partially developed programs.

After all input records have been read into the computer, the *job* (processing task defined by these records) is enqueued for execution. If it is a small, short, urgent job, it may be selected for execution a few seconds later. If it is a large, low-priority job, it may remain enqueued for hours, even days.

When the control program selects the job for execution, its control statements are scanned for consistency and completeness. If valid, source data and programs are processed on a nonstop, minimal-intervention basis. Output records are generated at this time, typically accumulated on tape or disk rather than flowing directly to a line printer, card punch, or display device.

*Interactive computing* supports programmers who wish to develop programs in *real time*, correcting errors as soon as the latter are detected by the computer. (This contrasts with debugging in the batch-processing mode, where most errors cause immediate termination of jobs, accompanied by diagnostic printouts.) Also, programs and data may be validated as entered: syntax checked, consistency with prior program statements established, and range tests on variable values performed.

Of the six processing activities, the two batch-processing modes and interactive computing are appropriate for creating and checking new programs, and for general scientific and business calculations.

*On-line inquiry* uses the computer as a communications channel to an instant-access repository of data. Processing time per query is typically trivial (see Fig. 2) compared with times required to enter and display information. On-line inquiry has been made feasible by development and widespread usage of large disk drives, whose capacities range from 7 to 200 million characters per drive. Complete and up-to-date master files can be accessed by authorized clerks, management personnel, etc., using typewriter terminals or CRT (cathode-ray tube) displays.

*Message switching* resembles on-line inquiry in that processing per input stimulus (message, query) is trivial. Whereas the inquiry mode permits retrieval and display of disk-stored records, the message-switching mode receives streams of characters (*messages*) from one site and routes them to other sites automatically according to *destination headers* describing (for each block) where it is to be sent. Message switching is almost invariably used in conjunction with the public telephone network; large commercial, manufacturing, and governmental enterprises use message switching for high-speed communications among offices and for efficient usage of their telephone networks.

*Data acquisition and control* has many operational similarities to message switching: modest requirements for computational power and main memory, fast processing of incoming cassette tape or punched paper tape. As data is received from such instruments as voltmeters, gas chromatographs, and thermocouples, it is scaled and tested to see that it lies within normal operating ranges for these instruments (and associated physical processes). When the computer detects an out-of-range condition, it notifies appropriate personnel such as a plant guard, fireman, or operating engineer. Typically, the DAX-oriented computer types out a warning message, rings an alarm bell, or flashes an alarm light continuously until the out-of-range condition is corrected.

D. N. FREEMAN

# PRODUCTION

For articles on related subjects *see* FORMAL LANGUAGES; GRAMMAR; PARSING; PROGRAMMING LINGUISTICS; and WELL-FORMED FORMULA.

A production is a rule, often called a "rule of inference," in a grammar that describes how parts of a string (or word, or phrase, or construct) can be replaced by other strings. The set of productions of a grammar describe all the rules by which strings of the language can be generated by the grammar.

As an example, consider the grammar whose alphabet consists of the characters *a* and *b* and which is to generate any string consisting of any number (including zero) of *b*'s followed by any number (including zero) of *a*'s. A set of productions which generate this language is

$$S \rightarrow a$$
$$S \rightarrow b$$
$$S \rightarrow Sa$$
$$S \rightarrow bS$$

the first two of which read "*a* and *b* are constructs of the language" and the last two read, "If $S$ is a construct of the language, then so is $S$ followed by *a* or preceded by *b*." Sometimes this set of productions would be written as

$$S \rightarrow a|b|Sa|bS$$

where the vertical bar is to be read as "or".

Productions may be much more complex than those above. An example is the type of production found in *context-sensitive languages*,

$$S_1SS_2 \rightarrow S_1TS_2,$$

which states that, if the string $S$ is found in the context (i.e., between) strings $S_1$ and $S_2$, then $S$ may be replaced by the string $T$. Thus,

$$abSba \rightarrow abaSaba$$

states that, if $S$ is any string surrounded by *ab* and *ba*, it may be replaced by the same string preceded and succeeded by *a*.

REFERENCE

1967. Naur, P., et al. "Revised Report on the Algorithmic Language ALGOL 60," in S. Rosen (Ed.), *Programming Systems and Languages*. New York: McGraw-Hill.

J. A. N. LEE AND A. RALSTON

# PROGRAM

For articles on related subjects *see* ALGORITHM; ASSEMBLERS; COMPILER; MACHINE

AND ASSEMBLY LANGUAGE PROGRAMMING; MODULAR PROGRAMMING; PROBLEM-ORIENTED LANGUAGES; PROCEDURE; PROCEDURE-ORIENTED LANGUAGES; PROGRAMMING LANGUAGES; STORED PROGRAM CONCEPT; and STRUCTURED PROGRAMMING.
For article on related term *see* TASK.

In order to solve a computational problem, its solution must be specified in terms of a sequence of computational steps, each of which may be effectively performed by a human agent or by a digital computer. Systematic notations for the specification of such sequences of computational steps are referred to as programming languages. A specification of the sequence of computational steps in a particular programming language is referred to as a program. The task of developing programs for the solution of computational problems is referred to as programming. A person engaging in the activity of programming is referred to as a programmer.

Programming is sometimes contrasted with *coding*. Coding generally refers to the writing and debugging of programs for given program specifications, while programming includes the task of preparing the program specification as well as that of writing the program. The text of a program is sometimes referred to as *code*, and lines of program text are referred to as lines of code, especially in the case of machine-language programs. The term "coder" is used, sometimes pejoratively, to describe a person engaged exclusively in implementing program specifications prepared by others.

The programs for the earliest digital computers were written in a *machine language*. Pure machine-language programming required the programmer to write out the sequences of binary or decimal digits by which each instruction was represented in the computer memory. By the mid-1950s it was realized that programmers could specify instruction codes and memory locations by symbolic mnemonics, which could be translated into the internal machine language by a translation program called an *assembler*.

In the late 1950s and in the 1960s, *problem-oriented languages* were developed to allow programmers to specify algorithms in a notation natural to the problem being solved. Programs specified in a problem-oriented language were translated into the internal language of a particular computer by a translation program called a "compiler." The commonly used programming languages in the 1960s and 1970s include Fortran, Algol 60, Cobol, PL/I, and APL. The reader is referred to Sammet (1969) for brief descriptions of over a hundred programming languages developed in the 1950s and 1960s.

The flavor of programs in problem-oriented languages is illustrated by following the Algol 60 procedure for finding the maximum of a set of numbers in Fig. 1.

A problem specification is generally given in terms of a desired relation between inputs and outputs which specifies *what* is to be computed. An algorithm or program for a given problem specifies *how* the given relation between inputs and outputs is to be achieved. It is the task of the programmer to convert "static" input/output specifications of what is to be computed into dynamic specifications that specify how the computation is to be performed.

A given input/output relation may be realized by a wide variety of different algorithms, and each algorithm may in turn be realized in a variety of different programming languages. There is thus considerable freedom in developing a program for the solution of any given problem. This freedom of choice in developing programs leads to the notion that programming is an art rather than a science.

Although the set of all programs for realizing a given problem specification is in general infinite, there are a number of criteria other than correctness which may be used to restrict the class of acceptable programs that realize a given problem specification.

```
procedure MAX(X,N);
  integer N; array X;
      begin integer I; real T;        {Declares data types of
      T:=X[1];                        {procedure parameters (X,N)
                                      {and local variables (I,T)

      for I:=2 step 1 until N do      {Tests each component of X
        if X[I]>T then T:=X[I];       {in sequence against largest
                                      {found thus far (T)

      MAX:=T;                         {Sets name of procedure (MAX)
  end                                 {to largest of set (T)
```

**Fig. 1.**

A good program should economize both on computation time and on the storage space required to represent the program and data structures. It should have a modular structure in the sense that each well-defined subtask should be specified by a well-defined subprogram. Modular design of a program is important because it makes the program easier to understand, facilitates debugging, and allows modifications to be made more easily. It is usually worth paying a price in computation time and memory space in order to achieve greater modularity. Modular construction is especially important in large programs, since the human mind is severely restricted in the complexity it can handle, and systematic modularity reduces the number of factors the human mind must handle at any given moment, thereby allowing the understanding of a larger system than would otherwise be possible.

Programming was regarded as an art rather than a science in the 1950s and 1960s because it was felt that the choices among different styles of implementing a given problem were creative choices based on intangible criteria of style, just as in the case of literature. However, as more experience was gained in writing large programs, the freedom of the programmer to develop his own style became increasingly restricted by programming conventions designed to mechanize programming style. For example, it has become accepted that *goto* statements should be avoided whenever possible, and that operators that preserve modularity, such as *while* statements, should be more heavily used. Wirth (1973) gives a good introduction to the basic notions of *structured programming*.

REFERENCES

1968. Knuth, D. E. *The Art of Computer Programming*. Reading, Mass.: Addison-Wesley.

1969. Sammet, J. *Programming Languages—History and Fundamentals*. Englewood Cliffs, N.J.: Prentice-Hall.

1973. Wirth, N. *Systematic Programming*. Englewood Cliffs, N.J.: Prentice-Hall.

P. WEGNER

# PROGRAM CORRECTNESS, PROOF OF

For articles on related subjects *see* ALGORITHMS, THEORY OF; DEBUGGING; PARALLEL ALGORITHMS; and PROGRAMMING LANGUAGE MODELS.

For articles on related terms *see* INTERVAL ARITHMETIC; LAMBDA CALCULUS; RECURSION; STRUCTURED PROGRAMMING; and SUBROUTINE.

Verifying that a computer program is correct is clearly a most important activity, and may be performed with varying degrees of rigor. It is an activity in which all programmers are engaged, and throughout the years good and bad techniques have been established. *Debugging* normally consists of testing a program or parts of a program on a specially selected set of test data; more often than not, this proves to be inadequate, and errors show up later when situations arise not covered by the test data. However, for many programs, or parts of programs, it is possible to state their desired properties precisely, usually in the form of relations between output values and input values. Moreover, since a program is a well-defined mathematical structure, it should be possible to give a proof of its correctness in all situations. Even if the complete program specification is not easily formalized, certain properties of the program may well be formalizable; for example, it should not go into a loop if certain restrictions on the data are met or it should not alter the value of certain variables. These properties should be provable.

It is not possible to give a rigorous proof concerning a program unless one has a theory as to how meaning is to be attached to it. Some languages have been given a formal semantics and some (such as Lisp) have had their formal semantics defined at the same time as the language definition, but, for the most part, workers in the area of proofs of programs have exhibited proof techniques without explicitly defining semantics. Thus, their techniques in effect become a way of formally defining the semantics of a programming language, and this has indeed equally motivated some of the work. It should also be noted that we cannot expect to find completely general techniques for proving most of the interesting properties of programs because they are usually undecidable. Nevertheless, the underlying reasons why programs are correct are very rarely other than a large collection of basically simple ideas; general proving techniques aided by mechanical symbolic manipulations should be feasible.

One technique that has been widely investigated for producing rigorous proofs is that of attaching *assertions* to programs. This technique was suggested independently by R. W. Floyd and P. Naur in 1966. Naur calls the assertions "general snapshots," although the idea occurs in an earlier paper by Goldstine and von Neumann. Assume the program is written in a simple language and consists only of assignment statements and conditional jumps. Attach an assertion to certain program statements (i.e., a relation between the values of the variables) which should be true whenever the statement is about to be executed. These assertions will often also involve the initial values of the variables. The assertion attached to the exit of the program will express a relation between final values and initial values, and is the property of the program we are trying to prove correct. Other assertions must be assigned so that there is at least one in every loop of the program.

Now a set of consistency relations may be derived—for example, if $P(x,y)$ is an assertion immediately before the assignment statement $y := f(x,y)$, and $Q(x,y)$ is an assertion immediately after it, then the consistency relation is: $P(x,y)$ implies $Q(x,f(x,y))$. Assuming that all the consistency relations can be proved valid, then it will indeed be true that the final assertion is correct, unless the program becomes stuck in a loop.

As a simple example, consider the flowchart in Fig. 1, whose purpose is to test whether any of $A_1$, $A_2, \ldots A_N$ is zero. Control is to reach point A if all are nonzero; point B if one or more are zero. Let *NZA(I)* mean that *I* is between 1 and *N* inclusive, and that all of $A_1$, $A_2, \ldots A_I$ are nonzero, an assertion of what should be true at Q. Let *ZA(I)* mean that *I* is greater than zero and that at least one of $A_1, A_2, \ldots A_I$ is zero.

Attach the shown assertions at A and B as being the desired properties of the program. By attaching assertions at the other points, as shown, it is readily seen that the various consistency relations are valid; for example, from P to Q it must be shown that

$$[[I = 1 \;\; or \;\; \{NZA(I-1) \;\; and \;\; I \neq N+1\}] \;\; and \;\; A_I \neq 0] \;\; implies \;\; NZA(I).$$

This assertion must therefore be proved from some suitable definition of NZA, or perhaps merely listed along with the program as being a condition on which the correctness of the program depends.

The assertions are normally made in a logical system known as the *first-order predicate calculus,* which provides a language specially designed

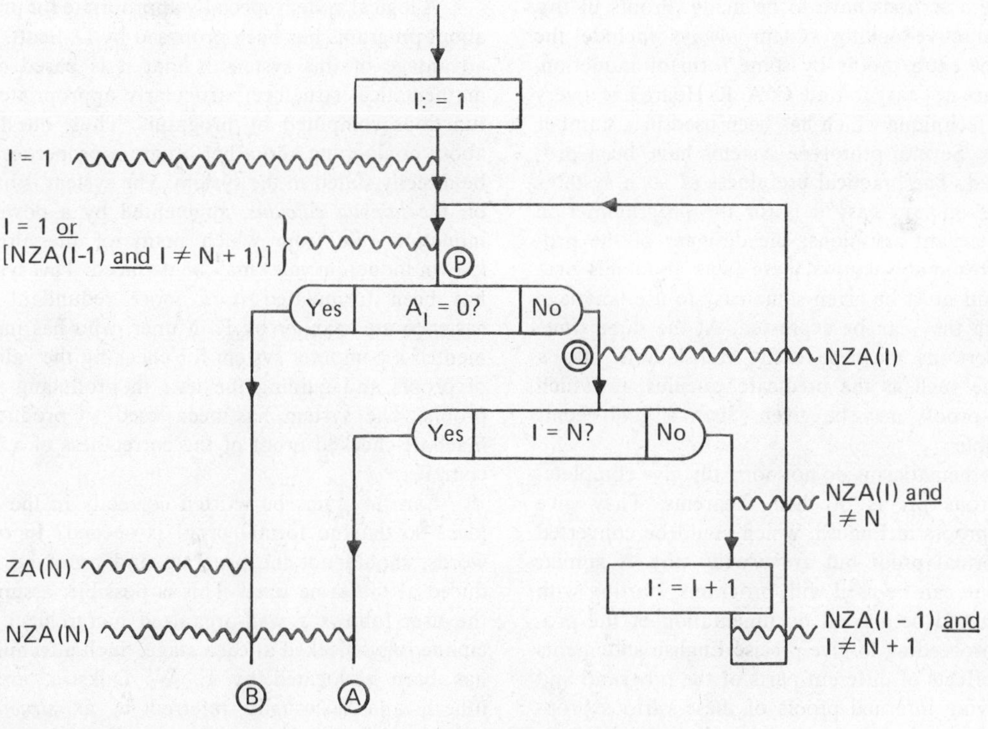


**Fig. 1.** Flowchart for testing whether any element of A is 0.

for the specification of theorems and the statement of rigorous proofs. Various techniques have been suggested for proving such theorems by computer; hence, it is possible to envisage a complete system that, given the assertions, will derive the consistency relations and attempt to prove them valid. The task of mechanical proof is made more difficult by the fact that knowledge (usually in the form of axioms) is needed of the specific area, such as numbers or lists. Moreover, complete mechanical verification is almost certainly beyond the capabilities of existing theorem provers and probably always will be. However, it is reasonable to expect mechanical aids to prove the simpler theorems that emerge from a system—experience indicates that very large numbers of these are generated—thus leaving what one hopes is a small set of possible theorems on whose validity the correctness of the program depends.

The assertion method has been extended so that it applies to programs that include facilities such as recursive definitions, arrays, parallel programs, and subroutines. An analogous system in which relations are attached to program sections, rather than as assertions to program points, has been developed. Extensions have also been made so that proof of nonlooping can be included and so that no intermediate assertions have to be made. Proofs in this last attractive-looking system always include the need for extra proofs by some form of induction, which are not easy to find. C. A. R. Hoare has a very similar technique which has been used in a number of cases. Several prototype systems have been programmed. The practical usefulness of such systems depends on how easy it is for the programmer to make relevant assertions; the designer of the program presumably knows these facts about his program and must be given some easy-to-use language in which they can be expressed. At the same time, the assertions must be easily translatable into a language such as the predicate calculus, in which formal proofs may be given. Such a goal seems achievable.

Mathematicians do not normally give completely rigorous proofs of their theorems. They give sketch proofs in English, which could be converted to a formal proof but are usually not. A similar technique can be used with programs, starting with what should be a good documentation of the program, proceeding to give precise English statements of the effects of different parts of the program, and then giving informal proofs of these various properties. This technique has been used, primarily by R. London (1972), on a variety of quite complex programs such as a bridge-bidding program, programs for interval arithmetic, and a Lisp compiler. These proofs are useful in pointing out proof methods that can be formalized, and in methods for integrating complete proofs of whole programs from proofs of the correctness of small sections. The proofs always involve an induction argument of some kind, and often make considerable use of proof by case analysis. This involves dividing the values of some variables, or of the data, into different sets and proving the desired result separately for each set. Since some form of induction argument is a part of most proofs, investigations into appropriate variants of mathematical induction have been made.

One of the first techniques for proving program correctness, due to J. McCarthy, was a form of induction known as "recursion induction," which is specially applicable to programs in a recursive language such as Lisp. This is essentially an induction argument based on the structure of the program. Different data structures also generate appropriate versions of induction; thus, for a tree, if one can prove that some property $P$ is true of the "empty" tree and also, assuming $P$ is true of the left subtree and the right subtree, if one can prove that $P$ is true of the composite tree, then $P$ must be true for all trees.

A logical system specially appropriate for proofs about programs has been proposed by D. Scott. The advantage of this system is that it is based on a mathematical structure particularly appropriate for functions computed by programs. Thus, questions about nonlooping and other program properties can be directly stated in the system. The system is based on the *lambda calculus*, augmented by a powerful induction rule from which many of the already known induction rules may be deduced. This system has been formulated in a more redundant but easier-to-use manner by R. Milner, who has implemented a computer system for checking the validity of proofs and guiding the user in producing such proofs. The system has been used to produce a machine-checked proof of the correctness of a Lisp compiler.

Can programs be written correctly in the first place so that no formal proof is needed? In other words, should not the program and proof be produced at the same time? This is possible, assuming the user follows a well-organized hierarchical discipline fully checked at each stage. Such a technique has been advocated by E. W. Dijkstra, among others, and is usually referred to as *structured programming*. An alternative approach is to produce a *program-writing system*, i.e., a system which, given desired properties, mechanically produces a program satisfying these properties. Such a system has been designed by R. Waldinger and others; it essentially works by proving a theorem that a program exists with the required property, and then extracting the program from the proof. The system has been useful in preparing plans for robots (these are essentially simple programs), but it is unlikely that a sufficiently powerful theorem prover will be created to produce more complex programs. The system does, however, shed light on the relation between programs and mathematical logic.

An ultimate goal for this type of work is the production of some general language for communicating with computers, a language in which we can construct parts of programs, state properties of the programs, and give proofs of these properties either at an informal or a formal level. Every programmer would then be expected to provide with his program a formal definition of its properties, together with a sketch proof. When challenged, this informal proof must be made formal (perhaps with the aid of a computer) and can then be mechanically checked. Hopefully, only one integrated language would be needed, rather than the present (for the most part) dual systems of one programming language and one logical language.

REFERENCES

1972. ACM. *Proceedings of ACM Conference on Proving Assertions about Programs*. Las Cruces, New Mexico, Jan. 6–7.

1972. London, R. L. "The Current State of Proving Programs Correct," *Proceedings of 1972 ACM Annual Conference*.

1972. Elspas, B., K. M. Levitt, R. J. Waldinger, and A. Waksman. "An Assessment of Techniques for Proving Program Correctness," *Computing Surveys*, Vol. 4, No. 2 (June).

D. C. COOPER

## PROGRAM COUNTER

For an article on a related subject *see* MACHINE INSTRUCTION SET.

For an article on a related term *see* REGISTER.

Typically, a computer instruction is the specification of an operation to be performed, the address of two operands on which the operation will be performed, the address for the location of the results, and a specification (an address) of the next instruction in the sequence. These specifications or addresses may be explicitly placed in the instruction or implicitly defined. By "implicit" is meant that the machine will assume that an operand will be in a certain place (e.g., the accumulator) rather than have it specified in each instruction. In the case of the specification of the next instruction location, it is common for the machine to assume that the instructions lie in sequence. That is, the next instruction is contained in the address following the location of the current instruction. The location of the current instruction is kept in a register called the "program counter." During the execution of an instruction, the program counter is advanced by one address unit.

If the instruction lengths are not uniform (i.e., there are several different sizes), then the implementation of the program counter must take this into account. For example, in IBM System/360, instructions are of three different sizes: 2 bytes, 4 bytes, or 6 bytes. Since addresses always refer to bytes, the program counter must be incremented by either 2, 4, or 6, depending upon the type of instruction currently being executed.

In all systems that use program counters, there must be an additional mechanism for initializing the value and for changing values at certain points in the program. This mechanism is a special instruction, usually called "branch." There are two basic kinds of branch instructions: unconditional branch and conditional branch. The unconditional branch causes a new value to be placed in the program counter and hence defines the start of the location of a new sequence of instructions. The conditional branch has a similar action except that it is dependent upon the state of certain data items. Thus, whether the next instruction will be simply the next instruction in the current sequence or the beginning of a new sequence will depend upon the result (e.g., positive or negative) of a preceding instruction.

M. J. FLYNN

## PROGRAM LIBRARIES

For articles on related subjects *see* COMPUTING CENTER; DOCUMENTATION; and SOFTWARE PACKAGES.

## PROGRAM LIBRARIES

For articles on related terms *see* DATA PROCESSING; MANAGEMENT INFORMATION SYSTEMS; RANDOM NUMBER GENERATION; SUBROUTINE; and TIME SHARING.

A program library is a collection of computer programs made available to computer users to reduce the work of programming.

Libraries are often associated with a computer installation, a manufacturer, the government, or user groups. A library for an installation will usually have programs written for the computers being used at the installation. A manufacturer maintains libraries for all its computers and systems that are sold to users. The government has provided centers where programs developed by government agencies are distributed. User groups have also established libraries where the users have control over development and distribution of programs.

Program libraries originated in order to avoid costly duplication of effort in programming. The early programs in libraries were collected on punched cards and reproduced for distribution. With increasing volume and complexity, programs were more commonly stored and distributed on magnetic tape and disk.

More recently, with the development of interactive time sharing, libraries have been provided in a form accessible to users at terminals, which may be remote from the computer installation. Programs in the library of the central computer can be obtained by the user for use at his terminal, perhaps to be modified and then stored in his own files.

The contents of program libraries may be classified into several categories, such as data processing, utility, and computation. For data processing, there might be programs for accounting, inventory, payroll, and data retrieval. Utility programs might include programs for code conversion, such as BCD to internal binary, programs for listing and copying tapes, or punching and listing cards. Programs for computation would include categories like engineering, mathematics, and statistics.

Programs in libraries may range from subroutines for specific functions to complete subsystems. Subroutines for specific functions would include programs for such things as the square root, trigonometric functions, random-number generation, code conversion, and other general data processing procedures. Subsystems may involve language processors (e.g., Snobol, GPSS), management information and data retrieval systems, and complicated data handling and analysis systems such as SPSS (statistical package for social science).

Libraries have catalogs or directories to keep track of the programs and enable users to find the programs available for particular types of computing.

Programs in libraries must be documented so that the user of a program will know what it does and how to use it. Generally, the documentation consists of a written description of the program, flowcharts, tables of variables, record layouts, operating instructions, a program listing, sample input and output, and (for computational programs) references to published reports and certification of

---

```
FETCH*5 REGRES
OK. DATE FILED:  05/12/71.

RUN
 8K

DO YOU WANT INSTRUCTIONS (-YES- OR -NO-)
?YES

REGRESSION ANALYSIS - LEAST SQUARES

AT CERTAIN TIMES THE FOLLOWING QUESTION WILL BE TYPED
OPTION
?

WHEN THIS OCCURS, THE FOLLOWING OPTIONS ARE AVAILABLE
```

**Fig. 1.** Example of a self-documented program.

```
ENTRY       RESULT
----------  ----------------------------------------------

-DATA-      PROGRAM READY TO ACCEPT DATA TABLE
-DLET-      PROGRAM READY TO ACCEPT TABLE DELETIONS
-LIST-      PROGRAM LISTS CURRENT DATA
-PLOT-      PROGRAM PLOTS CURRENT DATA
-CALC-      PROGRAM CALCULATES AND PRINTS RESULTS
-STOP-      RUN IS TERMINATED

OTHER QUESTIONS MAY BE ANSWERED BY -YES- OR -NO-

WHAT IS THE TABLE LENGTH ( MAX. = 100 )
?4
INPUT        4 ALTERNATING VALUES OF X AND Y
?1.0  2.5
?2.0  4.4
?3.0  6.6
?4.0  8.3

OPTION
?CALC

*****************************************************

Y = A + BX
              B                      A                      R
       .196000E+01           .550000E+00           .998908E+00
*****************************************************

DO YOU WANT TO SEE THE EVALUATION RESULTS
?

YES

NO.        X               Y               PRED. Y          RESIDUAL          RESIDUAL**2
-----  ---------------  ---------------  ---------------  -----------------  -------------------

 1     .1000E+01        .2500E+01        .2510E+01        -.1000E-01         .1000E-03
 2     .2000E+01        .4400E+01        .4470E+01        -.7000E-01         .4900E-02
 3     .3000E+01        .6600E+01        .6430E+01         .1700E+00         .2890E-01
 4     .4000E+01        .8300E+01        .8390E+01        -.9000E-01         .8100E-02

SUM OF RESIDUAL**2 ( DELETIONS, IF ANY, EXCLUDED ) =   .420000E-01

OPTION
?STP_OP
 00200,STOP

TIME:    1.901 SEC.
```

**Fig. 1** (continued)

accuracy. Program documentation guidelines are usually compiled as follows:

A. Identification
   1. Title.
   2. Programmer.
   3. Programming language.
   4. Date.
B. Purpose
   1. Description of what program accomplishes.
C. Environment description
   1. Elements of hardware used.
   2. Software routines and functions used.
   3. Limitations pertaining to number of variables, etc.
D. Internal description
   1. A list of flags, constants, tables, arrays, and a description of their use, meaning, and format.
   2. Format and description of input and output areas.
   3. Explanation of program control cards.
   4. Explanation of error messages, if any.
   5. Cautions to user.
E. Computational procedure
   1. Method of computation.
   2. Special algorithms or procedures.
   3. References to literature or origin of program.
F. Functional flowchart of detailed logic descriptions
   The content of the flow chart should be sufficiently descriptive so that a nonexpert in the field can grasp the intent.
G. Well-annotated listing of the program
H. Tests performed on program
I. Sample listing of input and computed results
J. Source and object decks, sample data deck

Programs in interactive time-sharing systems, in addition to the above type of documentation, may be self-documenting in that the documentation is part of the program as stored in the library and the user may request as much of this documentation as he needs while using the program. Fig. 1 is an example of this type of program library.

Some libraries contain programs where the documentation falls short of that specified above. Such programs may be in the form of control cards and source code, and nothing else, leaving the user on his own to make the program run. Many "free" programs fall in this category.

*Source Material.* A number of publications available on a more or less periodic basis are helpful in pursuing this subject. Among them are:

*Computer Program Abstracts*, Superintendent of Documents, Government Printing Office, Washington, D.C. 20402

*Collected Algorithms*, Association for Computing Machinery, 1133 Avenue of the Americas, New York, New York 10036

*JUG Computer Programs Directory*, CCM Information Corporation, 909 Third Avenue, New York, New York 10022

REFERENCES

1969. Walsh, D. *A Guide for Software Documentation.* New York: Advanced Computer Techniques Corporation.

1972. University of Georgia. *SHARE Program Library Catalog* (January). Information Services, University of Georgia, Athens, Georgia 30601.

1973. Harper, W. L. *Data Processing Documentation: Standards, Procedures, and Applications.* Englewood Cliffs, N.J.: Prentice-Hall.

ROBERT H. GONTER

## PROGRAM STATUS WORDS AND STATE VECTORS

For articles on related subjects *see* INTERRUPT; MASKING; MEMORY PROTECTION; MULTIPROGRAMMING; SCHEDULING ALGORITHM; and TASK.

For articles on related terms *see* KEY; and REGISTER.

In multitask computer systems the processor or processors must be switched among the tasks or processes of the system. The mechanism for accomplishing task switching must guarantee the integrity of the tasks: By saving all vital information about a task, switching should not interfere or affect in any way the computation performed. For protection purposes, it may be also desirable that no information about a previous task should remain behind in a processor after the switching operation is done. To interrupt the processor from one task and assign it to another, it is necessary to save the state of the processor at the time of interruption; later, the processor state can be restored to this value and the task resumed at the point of interruption. The state information about the task to be saved is called the "task state descriptor," or "state vector," of the task. In some systems, notably IBM, a portion of the state descriptor is called the "program status word;" this term is, however, misleading, not only because the state concept applies to the dynamic behavior of a task and not to the static program that generates it, but also because a state descriptor often requires several words of storage to represent, whereas a program status word normally requires only one.

A task's state description can be represented as a vector of four components:

$$D = (ep, ip, mc, pc).$$

The component *ep* is called the "environment pointer;" it is usually contained in a set of one or more base registers, and designates where the instructions and data code for the task are located. In the case of a CDC 6000 series system, *ep* is the content of a base/limit register, defining a contiguous main memory region containing the task. In the case of IBM OS/360 system, *ep* is implicit in the *storage key* (which is part of the program status word) and designates a unique region of memory whose *lock register* contains the same value as the storage key. In the case of virtual storage systems, *ep* is the content of a register pointing to the mapping tables, defining the address space of the task; and in the case of the Burroughs B6700, *ep* is the content of the *display*, which is a stack of base registers pointing to activation records of the task. The component *ip* is called the "instruction pointer"; it is simply the address of the next instruction to be executed by the task from its address space as designated by *ep*.

The component *mc* is called the "machine conditions" of the task; it comprises the contents of all programmable registers in the processor, such as arithmetic and index registers. The component *pc* is called the "protection code" of the task; it specifies the protection domain of the task, i.e., the authorizations it has to perform certain actions. The simplest form of protection code is the value of the supervisor/user mode flip-flop, the setting of which to the "user" state indicates that certain instructions (e.g., those that load base registers) may not legally be executed by a user task.

In IBM systems, a state descriptor is of the form $D = (ip, mc, psw)$, where *psw* is the program status word. The environment pointer *ep* is embedded in *psw* as the "storage key" mentioned above, and the supervisor/user protection code *pc* is embedded in *psw*. Also contained in *psw* are:

1. A *condition code*, indicating the outcome of the most recently executed arithmetic or boolean operation.
2. A collection of interrupt *masks*, indicating which exceptional conditions (e.g., overflow, underflow, zero-divide) are enabled for the task.
3. *Channel masks* indicating which channels may interrupt the task by their completion signals.

There is some question whether the channel masks ought to be part of a task state descriptor, since the channels operate independently of user tasks. Many systems have all interrupt masks, except for interrupts that can be enabled from a programming language (e.g., ON conditions in PL/I), implemented separately and independently of task state descriptors.

P. J. DENNING AND D. E. DENNING

## PROGRAMMING.

*See* APPLICATIONS PROGRAMMING; MICROPROGRAMMING; MODULAR PROGRAMMING; STRUCTURED PROGRAMMING; and SYSTEMS PROGRAMMING.

## PROGRAMMING, MATHEMATICAL.

*See* MATHEMATICAL PROGRAMMING.

## PROGRAMMING LANGUAGE MODELS

For articles on related subjects *see* MARKOV ALGORITHM; PROGRAM CORRECTNESS, PROOF OF; and TURING MACHINE.
For articles on related terms *see* INTERPRETER; LAMBDA CALCULUS; STACK; and VIENNA DEFINITION LANGUAGE.

There are three sides to the definition of a programming language: the syntax (what sets of strings are grammatically correct?), the semantics (what do grammatically correct strings mean?), and pragmatics (what is practically useful?). This article is concerned with ways to define the semantics of a programming language. Meaning has to be attached to programs in any language. Normally, this is done informally in a programming manual. However, there has been quite a lot of research on formal techniques for defining semantics. There are two main reasons for providing a formal definition of a language. First, there is compatibility; we need to specify precisely the meaning of, say, Fortran so that users and compiler implementers agree on their interpretations of programs. Second, we need such a formal theory if we are to make rigorous arguments that particular programs satisfy certain properties, such as two programs being equivalent or the results of a program being related to the input data in a certain way. The formal semantics should also reveal the underlying structure of programs in a clearer way than is done by the sequence of characters representing the program.

One very simple way to give a formal definition is to define a particular compiler on a particular computer as being correct. The only advantage this method has is its lack of need for any mathematical techniques; anyone can understand it. The technique is rather poor for compatibility (How can I be convinced a compiler written for a different computer defines the same language?), and the technique is useless for proving results about programs and also reveals very little of the basic structure of the language.

Certain structures in a language can often be easily and clearly described in terms of other structures. Thus, the Algol 60 report, which gives a formal definition of the syntax of Algol 60 and informal descriptions of the semantics, defined the semantics of a *for* statement by showing how to construct an equivalent sequence with a conditional statement. Thus, this rule can be used to eliminate all *for* statements, and we need only specify the semantics of a simpler language. This process can be carried a long way; we can eliminate such concepts as block structure, multidimensional arrays, function definitions, and even *goto* statements (as long as we have procedures). Reversing the process, we can start with some very simple language for which we have a semantic definition and then build up a more complex, but useful, language by successively defining new structures in terms of existing structures, ending up with a language like Algol 60 or Fortran. For a starting language, one can use a language for defining a *Turing machine*, or perhaps it is better to start with *Markov algorithms*, which operate directly on strings of characters. An alternative approach is to start with the *lambda calculus*. One method can easily be combined with others, using an alternative semantics definition technique on some intermediate language.

At the same time as J. McCarthy developed the list-processing language Lisp, he provided a rigorous definition of its semantics. This was done by defining a Lisp function APPLY(P,D) in Lisp itself, which, given a program *P* and some particular data *D* represented as lists, computed the result of applying program *P* to data *D*. Such a function is known as an "interpreter." The Lisp interpreter is defined in Lisp itself, a circular definition but none the less a useful one since APPLY was an easy-to-follow short function; understanding this one function enables one to give meaning to any Lisp program.

McCarthy further developed a semantics theory applicable to languages with more structure than Lisp. Two main ideas introduced were *abstract syntax* and *state vector*. In the abstract syntax of a language we specify the syntactical form of the different components of the language without specifying in detail the form as sets of strings of characters. Thus, in some formal language, we specify a term as being one of a number of different forms, one of which is a sum and (if it is a sum) has two components that are terms. This is similar to BNF, but we do not commit ourselves to a particular string, say, "*a+b*" or "*+ab,*" or "PLUS(*a,b*)." The state vector is to be thought of as the set of current values of all variables of the program. These "variables" are to include everything on which execution might depend, such as the values in a stack or in modifiers, accumulators, etc., depending on the language being defined. A set of basic operations on the state vector can be defined to select and update its components. The meaning of a program in the language is defined by specifying the abstract syntax and giving the meaning of the individual components in terms of the operations on the state vector, such as "alter the value of the component corresponding to a certain variable." In one application of this method, a simplified Algol-like language has been defined, an assembly codelike language defined, a compiler defined, and the correctness of this compiler proved in the system.

A group in Vienna has extended McCarthy's ideas by providing a more appropriate data structure in terms of which both the abstract syntax and the states can be defined, and by specifying how these structures change as the program is executed. In this system (Vienna Definition Language), the whole of the semantics of the language PL/I has been defined, a very considerable task. Some proofs of equivalence of different techniques for implementing parts of compilers, identifier-accessing, for example, have also been made in the system.

C. A. R. Hoare has suggested an axiomatic approach to the semantics of a programming language. This is closely related to the method of *assertions*; indeed, it was pointed out by R. W. Floyd in his paper suggesting this method that a technique for proving program correctness must in itself involve a theory of the semantics of the language. Hoare introduces a notation $P \{S\} Q$, where $P$ and $Q$ are predicates (i.e., expressions that can be true or false) and $S$ is part of a program, perhaps an assignment statement or a sequence of statements. The notation is an assertion that, assuming $P$ is true, if the statement $S$ is obeyed, then $Q$ will become true. For example y=a {x:=y} x=a is a true assertion in Hoare's notation, assuming x:=y is an Algol assignment statement. The semantics of a language can be defined as a set of axioms in this notation, and, by using these axioms, deductions may be made about the properties of particular programs.

Many deductions about programs may be made which do not depend on the specific meaning of the basic operations; for example, conditions under which statements may be interchanged or under which statements inside a loop may be taken outside the loop. This idea has motivated work into *program schemes*; these have the form of programs, but no particular meaning is to be attached to operations such as $x+y$ or $f(x,y)$. Thus, two schemes are to be thought of as equivalent if they produce identical answers, no matter what interpretation is placed on these function symbols and no matter what the data is. Theoretical properties of schemes have been investigated—such as, for what kind of schemes can we have an algorithm to decide if two schemes are equivalent, and what is the relation between different schemes such as those allowing recursion and those that do not.

Finally, the work of Scott and Strachey (1971) must be mentioned, in which the semantics problem is looked at from the point of view of finding the kinds of mathematical structures which are relevant for description of higher-level languages. An important beginning has been made here; the interested reader should refer to Scott's papers.

REFERENCES

1966. Steel, T. B. (Ed). *Formal Language Description Languages for Computer Programming*. Amsterdam: North-Holland.

1971. "Symposium on Semantics of Algorithmic Languages," in *Lecture Notes in Mathematics,* vol. 188. Berlin: Springer-Verlag.

1971. Scott, D., and C. Strachey. "Toward a Mathematical Semantics for Computer Languages," Proc. of the Symposia on Computers and Automata, in *Microwave Research Institute Symposia Series,* vol. 21. Polytechnic Institute of Brooklyn.

1972. Wegner, P. "The Vienna Definition Language," *Computing Surveys,* Vol. 4, No. 1, pp. 5–63.

D. C. COOPER

# PROGRAMMING LANGUAGES

For articles on related subjects *see* ASSEMBLERS; COMPILER, SYNTAX-DIRECTED; COMPILER, INCREMENTAL; LANGUAGE PROCESSORS; LANGUAGES; MACHINE AND ASSEMBLY LANGUAGE PROGRAMMING; PROCEDURE-ORIENTED LANGUAGES; and PROGRAMMING LINGUISTICS.

For articles on related terms *see* APPLICATIONS PROGRAMMING; OBJECT PROGRAM; SOURCE PROGRAM; and SYSTEMS PROGRAMMING.

The definition of the term "programming languages" is a controversial subject and by no means agreed to by all experts in the field. In order to lead up to the one proposed by this writer, we must consider various levels of languages used for dealing with the computer.

At the lowest level is pure binary. This is so impractical to use that humans almost never use this even though it is actually the only language the machine "understands." A step above this is what is generally referred to as "machine code" or "symbolic machine code." In this case the user generally writes his instructions in some type of alphabetic symbols (e.g. SUB for subtract, TRA for transfer control, etc). Machine addresses are written in normal decimal form (e.g., 1723). At the next higher level is the "symbolic assembly language" in which the names of variables are written in symbols (e.g., ALPHA, TEMP, X, Y, Z) so that the location can be referred to symbolically rather than numerically. Thus a user might write

```
CLA Z          (CLA = clear accumulator and add)
ADD ALPHA
STO TEMP               (STO = store)
```

meaning: "Add the variables stored in locations named Z and ALPHA and store the result in a location named TEMP." A program called an "assembler" assigns absolute storage locations to the variables and fills in the numeric values for machine addresses in the instructions. The term "assembly language" is sometimes used for what was called above (symbolic) "machine code," and is sometimes used for what was called "symbolic assembly language."

The next level of complexity involves a macro-assembler in which the user may define new "instructions" and use them in his program, with their definitions being given elsewhere in the program; for example, INCR ALPHA might represent the use of the macro INCRement which automatically adds 1 to the variable ALPHA. This would be shown elsewhere in the program as

```
MACRO   INCR   VAR
        CLA    VAR
        ADD    CON
        STO    VAR
        CON    1
        END
```

The previous levels bring us to what is frequently called "higher-level language." This author uses that term interchangeably with the term "programming language," although some others include the concept of assembly language in the term "programming language." The term "source program" means a program written in a higher-level language. It is generally translated to an "object program," which is in a form directly understandable by the computer. The translation is usually done by a program called a "compiler."

### Definition of Programming Language.*

A programming language is a set of characters and rules for combining them, which has the following four characteristics:

1. It requires no knowledge of machine code on the part of the user. In other words, the user need only learn the particular programming language, and can use this quite independently of his (perhaps nonexistent) knowledge of any particular machine code. This does not mean that the user can completely ignore the actual computer. For example, he may need to know how floating-point numbers are represented, or he may wish to take advantage of certain machine resources that are known to him and which provide more efficient programs. In particular he obviously cannot use input/output equipment that does not exist on a particular computer configuration. However, the fundamental point is that he does not need to know the basic machine code for the given computer.

2. A programming language must have some significant amount of machine independence. This means that there must be some high potential of having a source program run on two computers with different machine codes without completely rewriting the source program. (In the early development of programming languages this characteristic was often stated or implied as "complete machine independence." The state-of-the-art in 1976 does not provide such a capability, so the objective is to minimize the changes required to go from one computer to another.)

3. When a source program is translated into machine language, there is normally more than one machine instruction per executable unit created. For example, an executable unit in a programming language might be something of the form "A = B + C * D" or "OPEN FILE ALPHA." Normally, each of these executable units would be translated into more than one machine instruction.

4. A programming language normally employs a notation that is somewhat closer to that of the specific problem being solved than is normal machine code. Thus, for example, the example "A = B + C * D" might be translated into a sequence of machine instructions such as

```
CLA   C
MPY   D
ADD   B
STO   A
```

which is clearly less understandable than the programming language form.

### Advantages of Programming Languages.

As always, one cannot obtain something for nothing, and therefore there are both advantages and disadvantages to programming languages, where the alternative is some type of assembly language. Let us consider the advantages first.

The primary advantage of a programming language is that it is easier to learn than a machine language. It must be emphasized that there is a relative aspect involved in this advantage. An ex-

* This section and the succeeding three sections are rewritten versions of material taken from Jean E. Sammet, *Programming Languages: History and Fundamentals*, © 1969, Prentice-Hall, Inc., Englewood Cliffs, N.J., pp. 9–22.

tremely powerful programming language might be harder to learn in its entirety than an assembly language on a computer which has only a dozen instructions. However, given programming and assembly languages of approximately the same complexity in their relative classes, the programming language will be easier to learn. This actually has two facets to it. The programming language may itself be extremely complex, but its ease of learning often comes because the notation is somewhat more related to the problem usage than is the machine code; furthermore, more attention can be paid to the language itself rather than to the idiosyncrasies of the physical hardware, which is necessary when one deals in machine code.

A problem written in a programming language is generally easier to debug for two major reasons. First, the program is usually shorter than its assembly language equivalent because of the expansion factor indicated as the third characteristic of a programming language. Since the number of errors is roughly proportional to the length of the program, there will normally be fewer errors. A second reason for the program's being easier to debug is that the notation itself is somewhat more natural, and therefore more attention can be paid to the logic of the program with less attention paid to details of the machine code.

A program coded in a programming language is generally easier to understand and to transfer to someone other than the originator because of the notational advantages and relative conciseness already mentioned.

Fourth, the notation of a programming language automatically provides a part of the necessary documentation because the notation is easier to understand and the logic is easier to follow.

Finally, the above advantages tend to accumulate into two general advantages, which are that the total calendar time and the total cost required for the problem solution are generally reduced significantly.

**Disadvantages of Programming Languages.** There are disadvantages to programming languages which have varying importance in specific instances. First, the additional process of compilation obviously requires machine time, which may exceed the time saved by easier debugging.

Second, the compiler might produce very inefficient object code. This would significantly affect production runs (i.e., programs that are run repeatedly) because the machine-time requirements might be increased significantly by any inefficiencies. (The counter argument to this, of course, is the fact that compilers today generally produce code that is at least as good as the average programmer can produce, and there are only a few really expert programmers who can write the most efficient machine code.)

Finally, the program may be much harder to debug than an assembly language program if the user does not know machine code and if the compiler does not provide the proper type of diagnostics and debugging tools. A user who must look at a memory dump in octal, which he does not understand, is going to have more trouble than debugging an assembly language program in which he understands what is happening.

In the opinion of this author, and generally supported by common practice, the advantages of programming languages in the 1970s far outweigh the disadvantages. The normal mode for writing (at least) application programs is to use a higher-level language, and the burden of justification for not doing this falls on the proponent of assembly language.

**Classifications of Programming Languages.** As indicated earlier, it is very difficult to define a programming language. However, it is a little easier to propose definitions for classes of programming languages, although these definitions are themselves controversial and not agreed on by everyone. The terms to be defined are the following: procedure-oriented and nonprocedural; problem-oriented, special-application and special-purpose; problem-defining, problem-describing, and problem-solving; hardware, publication, and reference. Note that some of these are overlapping and that a particular language may fall into more than one of these categories.

A *procedure-oriented* language is one in which the user specifies a set of executable operations that are to be performed in sequence and which specify a procedure. The key factor here is that these are definitely executable operations, and the sequencing is already specified by the user. Fortran, Cobol, and PL/I are examples. (The relation of these to domains of application is discussed later.)

The term *nonprocedural language* has been used for years without any attempt to define it. A definition is not really possible because nonprocedural is actually a relative term, meaning that decreasing numbers of specific sequential steps need be provided by the user as the state-of-the-art improves. The closer the user can come to stating his problem without specifying the steps for solving it, the more nonprocedural is the language. Furthermore, there can be an ordered sequence of steps, each of which is "somewhat nonprocedural," or a set of executable operations whose sequence is not specified by the user. Both cases contribute to more "nonproceduralness." Thus, before the existence of such languages as Fortran, the statement

Y = A + B * C - D/E

could be considered nonprocedural because it could not be written as one executable unit and translated by any system. In the mid-1970s the sentences CALCULATE THE SQUARE ROOT OF THE PRIME NUMBERS FROM 7 TO 91 AND PRINT IN THREE COLUMNS and PRINT ALL THE SALARY CHECKS are nonprocedural because there is no compiler available that can accept these statements and translate them; the user must supply the specific steps required. As compilers are developed to cope with increasingly complex sentences, the nature of the term changes. Thus, what is considered nonprocedural today may well be procedural tomorrow. The best examples of currently available nonprocedural systems (not really languages) are report generators (RPG) and sort generators in which the individual specifies the input and the desired output without any description of the procedures needed to obtain the output.

The term *problem-oriented* has been used in many ways by different people, but it seems that the most effective use of this term is to encompass any language that is easier for writing solutions to a particular problem than assembly language would be. Any current programming language illustrates this; thus, in this author's opinion, the term "problem-oriented" is a general catchall phrase. However, it is worth noting that many other people use the term to refer to languages for very specialized application areas.

It is a frequent misunderstanding that there is a separate category of languages called *application-oriented.* In reality, *all* languages are application-oriented, but some are for larger or smaller application areas than others. For example, Fortran is primarily useful for numerical scientific problems, whereas Cobol is best suited for business data processing. On the other hand, PL/I is useful in both those application areas, and therefore has a wider area of application. The term "general purpose" is sometimes used for PL/I (and even for Fortran), although in this author's opinion there is *no* truly general-purpose programming language; if there were, we would not need the others. In this writer's view, the following application areas are sufficiently wide and important to justify particular consideration: numerical and nonnumerical (i.e., formal algebraic) scientific applications, business data processing, string and list processing. Subjects other than these (or combinations of them) seem to be more specialized (e.g., graphics, simulation, machine-tool control, equipment checkout). Languages for application areas other than those defined as fairly general should be called "special-application-oriented."

A *special-purpose* language is one designed to satisfy a single objective. The objective might involve the application area, the ease of use for a particular application, or pertain to efficiency of the compiler or the object code.

A *problem-defining*, or *specification*, language is one that literally defines the problem and may specifically define the desired input and output, but it *does not* define the method of transformation. There is a significant difference among a problem (and its definition), the method (or procedure) used to solve it, and the language in which this method is stated.

A much more general type of language classification is that referred to as *problem-describing*, in which the objective is described only in very general terms (e.g., CALCULATE PAYROLL). All this does is cite, in the most general way, the problem to be solved, but it gives no indication of its detailed characteristics, let alone how to solve it.

Finally, a *problem-solving* language is one that can be used to specify a complete solution to a problem. Like the term "nonprocedural," this is a relative term, which changes as the state-of-the-art changes. All procedure-oriented languages are problem-solving languages.

A *reference* language is the definitive character set and form of a language. It usually has a unique character for each concept or character in the language, is one-dimensional, and need not be suitable as computer input. In some cases, the reference language contains English words considered as single characters; in other cases, a fixed set of symbols is provided. The concept of having a reference language, as distinguished from a publication or hardware representation language (discussed below), was introduced by the Algol committee in its first report. The reference language need not be particularly easy to read.

A *publication* language is some well-defined variation of the reference language that is suitable for publication. It is designed to be suitable for printing and/or writing; therefore, it will have reasonable rules and characters for such things as subscripts, exponents, spaces, and Greek letters. The publication language would normally be the means of communication between people (using printed media). There can be many publication languages and they can contain different characters, but there must be a well-defined mapping between the publication and reference languages. An illustration of this is the use of an "up" arrow ↑ to denote exponentiation in the Algol reference language, but the use of a raised symbol in the publication language e.g., A ↑ 2 becomes $A^2$.

A *hardware* language, sometimes called a "hardware representation," is a mapping of the reference language into a form suitable for direct input to a computer. The number and types of characters used must be those accepted by the computer involved, and is often determined by those available on input devices such as keypunches. A hardware language must have a well-defined mapping between itself and the reference language; for example, ** might be a hardware representation of the ↑ in the reference language, and **begin** might be represented by 'BEGIN'.

**History and Statistics.** A large number of higher-level languages have been developed since the first ones in the early 1950s. By 1973 there were more than 200 implemented (Fig. 1) and in use just in the United States, and over 40 more have lived and died in the interim. Of these, roughly half were languages for specialized application areas (e.g., graphics, simulation, computer-assisted instruction, machine-tool control, equipment checkout, systems programming). The remainder are divided among the application areas cited earlier as being important and general. However, of this large number of languages developed in a 20-year time span, only a handful have been truly significant, and even fewer have been widely used.

In approximate chronological order, the languages of major significance, and the approximate dates of their earliest public documentation and/or general availability, are shown below.* In some instances, notably IPL-V and Algol 60, earlier versions of the language contributed significantly to the ones listed here.

APT (*A*utomatically *P*rogrammed *T*ools); 1956. The first language for a specialized application area.

**Fig. 1.** The Tower of Babel, representing the large number of programming languages, is a concept that first appeared in the *Communications of ACM*. The form shown above was used as the jacket design for *Programming Languages: History and Fundamentals* by J. E. Sammet, © 1969, Prentice-Hall, Inc., Englewood Cliffs, N.J.

Fortran (*FOR*mula *TRAN*slation); 1956. The first higher-level language to be widely used. It opened the door to practical usage of computers by large numbers of scientific and engineering personnel.

Flowmatic; 1956. The first language suitable for business data processing and the first to have heavy emphasis on an "English-like" syntax.

IPL-V (*I*nformation *P*rocessing *L*anguage *V*); 1958. The first—and also a major—language for doing list processing.

Comit; 1957. The first realistic string-handling and pattern-matching language; most of its features appear (although with different syntax) in any other language attempting to do any string manipulation.

Cobol (*CO*mmon *B*usiness-*O*riented *L*anguage); 1960. One of the most widely used languages on an absolute basis, and the most widely used for business applications. Technical attributes include real attempts at an English-like syntax and at machine independence.

* This list and subsequent text are based on material excerpted from "Programming Languages: History and Future," by Jean E. Sammet, in *Communications of the ACM*, Vol. 15, No. 7 (July 1972). By permission. pp. 603–604.

Algol 60 (*ALGO*rithmic *L*anguage); 1960. Developed for specifying algorithms-primarily numerical. Introduced many specific features in an elegant fashion and, combined with its formal syntactic definition, inspired most of the theoretical work in programming languages and much of the work on implementation techniques. More widely used in Europe than in the United States.

Lisp (*LIS*t *P*rocessing); 1960. Introduced concepts of functional programming combined with facility for doing list processing. Used by many of the people working in the field of artificial intelligence.

Jovial (*J*ules *O*wn *V*ersion of *IAL*); 1960. The first language to include adequate capability for handling scientific computations, input/output, logical manipulation of information, and data storage and handling. Most Jovial compilers were written in Jovial.

GPSS (*G*eneral-*P*urpose *S*ystems *S*imulator); 1961. The first language to make simulation a practical tool for people.

Joss (*J*OHNNIAC *O*pen-*S*hop *S*ystem); 1964. The first interactive language; it spawned a number of dialects, which collectively helped to make time sharing practical for computational problems.

Formac (*FOR*mula *MA*nipulation *C*ompiler); 1964. The first language to be used fairly widely on a practical basis for mathematical problems needing formal algebraic manipulation.

APL\360 (*A* *P*rogramming *L*anguage); 1967. Provided many higher-level operators, which permitted extremely short algorithms and caused new ways of looking at some problems.

Some other languages are now more widely used or more comprehensive than those on the list, specifically Basic, PL/I, Simscript, and Snobol. In many cases, they have almost completely replaced some of the languages on the list (e.g., Basic for Joss and its derivatives, Snobol for Comit). The four "obvious candidates" cited above are omitted from the list of languages of major significance for the following reasons: Basic, although simple and economical, added no new concepts, was not the first on-line language, and was not the first to be of major practical importance. PL/I has capabilities derived from Fortran, Cobol, and Algol, but has not (yet?) succeeded in one of its implicit objectives, which was to replace these languages. It was preceded by Jovial in the attempt to combine capabilities for several application areas. Simscript built on the previous discrete simulation languages. Snobol was a good but fairly obvious improvement to the concepts introduced in Comit.

REFERENCES

1967. Higman, B. *A Comparative Study of Programming Languages.* New York: American Elsevier.

1969. Sammet, J. E. *Programming Languages: History and Fundamentals.* Englewood Cliffs, N.J.: Prentice-Hall.

J. E. SAMMET

# PROGRAMMING LINGUISTICS

For articles on related subjects *see* AUTOMATA THEORY; FORMAL LANGUAGES; LANGUAGE PROCESSORS; PROGRAMMING LANGUAGES; and STRING PROCESSING LANGUAGES.

For articles on related terms *see* BACKUS-NAUR FORM; CHARACTER SET; CONCATENATION; META LANGUAGE; PARSING; PRODUCTION; PROGRAM; RECURSION; SYNTAX, SEMANTICS AND PRAGMATICS; and VIENNA DEFINITION LANGUAGE.

Languages for communication between any two systems, be they human or mechanical, can be described by three intertwining concepts: syntax, semantics, and pragmatics. Together these form the area of study known as semiotics.

**Semiotics.** In natural languages, the *syntax* of a language is known as its grammar, and it defines the valid relationships between the elements of the language. While syntax (or grammar) implies nothing about the meaning of the valid sentences (or phrases), *semantics* is the definition of meaning that is prescribed for the sentence by the originator of the sentence; i.e., by the speaker or writer. *Pragmatics*, on the other hand, is the meaning received by a listener or reader.

In computer languages, the set of symbols available for the composition of sentences (or, in languages like Fortran or Algol, statements) is highly restricted, and therefore syntactic specifications can be predicated on individual symbols rather than on words, prefixes, and suffixes. Further, since computer languages are artificial languages, it can be prescribed that there exists no difference between the semantics and the pragmatics of a language. Thus, in this article we omit any consideration of the pragmatics of computer languages, and confine our attention to those aspects of linguistics that are in use in relation to computer languages.

**Context-Free and Context-Sensitive Grammars.** A grammar of a language is a formal system of description of the relationships among the symbols that comprise the language, over the operations of symbol substitution and concatenation. A grammar is composed of four parts:

1. Alphabet of the language (character set or symbol set).
2. Set of parts of speech (known as the "component" names).
3. Basic language element, such as "sentence" or "speech".
4. Set of rules which directs the formation of instances of the language (called *productions*).

In the case of a language that may be described syntactically by rules of direct unconditional substitution and concatenation, such that the substitution of a phrase for a component name is independent of the context of that component name, the language (and its grammar) is said to be *context free*. On the other hand, where such a substitution depends directly on the symbols or component names surrounding the component being replaced by substitution, the language is said to be *context sensitive*.

**Language Descriptors.** The terminology in which a language may be defined is a *meta language,* and must be uniquely distinguishable from the language being described. Thus, attempts to define a language in terms of itself can lead to paradoxes due to the indistinguishability of the meta language and the language. For example, we may say in the meta language of English that a sentence has certain qualities, such as; *it is grammatically correct* or *that sentence is true*. Consider, then, the sentence: *This statement is false*. If one is not given the information as to whether this sentence is written in the language or a meta language, one assumes that the word *this* refers to the statement itself; then the sentence is paradoxical. However, the same utterance on the part of a scholar pointing to some other statement is clearly valid. Thus, the meta language for Algol, for instance, must be clearly distinguishable from Algol. By these requirements, the symbolism of a meta language must not include the symbols used in Algol. Hence, there is a necessity to provide a distinct meta language that has applicability to the class of languages known as programming languages.

Mathematically, a grammar can be considered to be the definition of sets in terms of elements of other sets. For example, a member of the alphabet of Basic is a member of the set named (say) *character*; i.e.,

$$character = \{A,B,C,D,E, \ldots X,Y,Z,0,1, \ldots 8,9,+,*,/,-, \ldots\},$$

and, further, the class of objects named *variable* is composed of objects that are instances of the roman alphabet ($roman = \{A,B,C, \ldots X,Y,Z\}$) or the set of single instances of roman letters concatenated with single instances of the set of digits; i.e.,

$$variable = roman \cup (roman \times digit)$$

where $digit = \{0,1,2, \ldots 8,9\}$ and the operation $\times$ signifies the cross-product of the two sets.

The most commonly used form of syntactic specification is the Backus-Naur form (BNF), which was originally developed for the specification of the syntax of Algol 60 (Naur, 1960). This method of specification has since been widely used in the literature of computer science and has become widely accepted as a result of its ease of use and its readability.

This notation is applicable to an alphabet which is composed of the union of the alphabet of the language being described and the set of component names (names of the "parts of speech") of the language. To distinguish between the character set (alphabet) of the language and the component names, the BNF system encloses component names in angle brackets, or corner braces (⟨ and ⟩), whereas the actual alphabet symbols are free of any enclosing marks.

The rules for generation of sentences in the language is composed of a set of productions in which each rule has the form

$$\alpha ::= \beta_1\beta_2\beta_3 \ldots \beta_n \qquad (n \geq 1),$$

where $\alpha$ is a member of the set of component names and $\beta_i$ is a member of the union of the set of component names and the alphabet of the language being defined. The string (or phrase) $\beta_1\beta_2\beta_3 \ldots \beta_n$ represents the concatenation of the individual ele-

**Table 1.** BNF Notation vs. Set Notation

| Symbol | BNF Meaning | Set Meaning, or Equivalent |
|---|---|---|
| ⟨*X*⟩ | Component named *X* | An instance class of objects named *X* |
| *x* | Actual symbol *x* | the actual object *x* |
| : : = | . . . is to be replaced by . . . | . . . is a member of the set of strings . . . |
| \| | "or" (the exclusive "or") | (When the separator between two class names) set union U; (when the separator between two elements of the alphabet) the set punctuation ',', |
| ⁀ | Operation of concatenation* | Product of the two sets |
| $\{z\}_i^j$ | If $z^k$ represents *k* concatenated occurrences of *z*, then: $\{z\}_i^j = z^i \mid z^{i+1} \mid \ldots \mid z^j$ | $\{z^i, z^{i+1}, \ldots, z^j\}$ |

* Represented on the printed page by juxtaposition.

ments $\beta_i$. The construct itself is taken to mean that the occurrence of $\alpha$ in any string may be replaced by the string $\beta_1\beta_2\beta_3 \ldots \beta_n$.

Table 1 defines the symbolism of BNF and compares the notation with set notation.

Where there exists more than one possible substitution for any given component name $\alpha$, two methods of description are possible: Either there exist several production rules in which $\alpha$ occurs on the left-hand side, or the list of alternatives is specified on the right-hand side of a single production rule, separated by the alternation symbol |. Thus, the definition of a language composed of the set of binary digits (0 and 1) may take either of two forms:

⟨*binary digit*⟩ : : = 0
⟨*binary digit*⟩ : : = 1

or

⟨*binary digit*⟩ : : = 0|1

The set of production rules that comprises a grammar is constrained so that its combinations cover the requirements for the completeness of the grammar. While there exists no algorithm to determine the completeness of a grammar, the following rules are generally adequate:

1. There shall exist only a single language component that is not derivable from other language elements. This component is known as the "root component", or root symbol, and generally is given the name of the object that the grammar describes, such as *program* or *sentence.*

2. All other components shall appear on the left-hand side of at least one construct rule, thereby assuring that there are no "dead ends" in the grammar.

3. For every component in the grammar, there must exist at least one sequence of substitutions using the production rules that will lead to a string composed totally of the characters in the alphabet of the language.

4. Starting at the root symbol, there must exist for each component in the language a sequence of substitutions based on the production rules which will result in a string in which the component occurs; i.e., there are no "useless" components.

5. For every string of characters in the language, there shall exist at the most one sequence of substitutions which permits the generation of that string; i.e., the language must be unambiguous.

As an example of a syntactic definition, consider the simple programming language (SPL) developed by Neuhold (1971) as the vehicle for the description of the Vienna Definition Language. This language has two basic components, named *numbers* and *variables:*

⟨*number*⟩ : : = ⟨*digit*⟩ | ⟨*digit*⟩ ⟨*number*⟩
⟨*digit*⟩ : : = 0|1|2|3|4|5|6|7|8|9
⟨*variable*⟩ : : = ⟨*letter*⟩ | ⟨*variable*⟩ ⟨*letter*⟩
⟨*letter*⟩ : : = A|B|C| . . . |X|Y|Z

In these two definitions, a recursive description system has been used, which basically consists of two parts: a starter and an expander. That is, each definition contains an alternative, which does not depend on the component type being formed, and an alternative, which creates another instance of the component named on the left-hand side, given an instance of that component. Such recursive definitions permit the unbounded generation of strings of characters. Where an implementation restricts the length of a string (i.e., the number of characters that comprise the string), two alternate methods of description are available; either the set of permitted strings can be described individually, or a bounded repetition notation can be employed. The equivalence of these two descriptive methods is obvious. For example, let us assume that a particular implementation has restricted strings that represent *numbers* to three characters in length. Then the two representations could be

⟨*number*⟩ : : = ⟨*digit*⟩ | ⟨*digit*⟩ ⟨*digit*⟩
| ⟨*digit*⟩ ⟨*digit*⟩ ⟨*digit*⟩

or

$$\langle number \rangle ::= \{\langle digit \rangle\}_1^3$$

where the $\{\ \}_j^i$ notation represents repeated concatenation of the object within the braces with itself, and the indices specify the upper and lower bounds of the number of repetitions.

The SPL uses these elements to form programs that comprise statements that may be labeled optionally:

⟨*label*⟩ : : = ⟨*letter*⟩ | ⟨*letter*⟩ ⟨*label*⟩
⟨*statement*⟩ : : = $\{\langle label \rangle\}_0^1$⟨*statement body*⟩
⟨*program*⟩ : : = ⟨*statement*⟩ | ⟨*program*⟩;⟨*statement*⟩

An SPL statement may take one of two forms: an arithmetic assignment statement (set statement) or a conditional branching statement (goto statement).

⟨*statement body*⟩ : : = ⟨*set statement*⟩ | ⟨*goto statement*⟩

⟨*set statement*⟩ : : = SET ⟨*variable*⟩ TO ⟨*expression*⟩
⟨*goto statement*⟩ : : = GO TO ⟨*label*⟩ IF ⟨*expression*⟩

In the latter two descriptions (productions), the upper-case characters are elements of the language being described, and therefore are without the angle brackets. Finally, the description of an *expression* is required:

⟨*expression*⟩ : : = ⟨*simple expression*⟩ | ⟨*simple expression*⟩ ⟨*operator*⟩ ⟨*expression*⟩
⟨*simple expression*⟩ : : = ⟨*number*⟩ | ⟨*variable*⟩
| (⟨*expression*⟩)
⟨*operator*⟩ : : = + | −

This set of constructs completes the description of the syntax of the language and conforms to the five formation rules set forth previously.

The Backus-Naur form of syntactic description suffers from one deficiency: an inability to specify context-sensitive restriction rules. In most programming languages, there exist rules for the formation of programs that are totally independent of meaning (i.e., semantic meaning) and yet which are not adequately described in BNF. These are rules of the form, "if there exists in the program an element *x*, then there must also occur a declaration statement describing the attributes of the element *x*," or "there may only occur one element named *y*." Such a statement occurs in the verbal description of SPL: "(in describing the action of a GOTO statement) . . . To identify a target statement, the same label (mentioned in the GOTO statement) must appear exactly once as the prefix to some statement in the SPL program." While some completely formal descriptions of languages that include descriptions of both syntax and semantics include tests for multi-defined program elements as part of the semantic definition portion, work is currently underway to extend syntactic descriptive techniques to include such provisions independently of the semantic description.

Several other forms of syntactic definition exist, including forms in which the distinctions between component names and the alphabetic characters are maintained in terms of different type settings. Of particular importance is the two-dimensional syntactic description system utilized for the description of Standard Cobol (ANSI, 1968). This descriptive system uses lower-case strings to denote language components (called *generic terms* in the Cobol Standard) and upper-case string to symbolize actual

Cobol language characters. Further, upper-case strings that are underlined occur as key words in the language and must appear exactly as printed. On the other hand, upper-case characters that are not underlined are optional, and may or may not be present in the program. There are two sets of parentheses: brackets, [ ], which denote users' options and which may or may not appear in the program; and braces, { }, which denote alternatives, one of which must occur in the program. In this notation, the elements of the brackets or braces are listed vertically. There also exists a notation that means "and so on" which is represented by the symbolism ( ... ). According to the Cobol Standard (Chapter 5, Section 2.1.5), the meaning of this becomes apparent in context.

Using this method of syntactic specification, the simple programming language (SPL) described earlier in BNF can be described as follows:

program: statement [; statement] ...

$$\text{statement: [label]} \left\{ \begin{array}{l} \underline{\text{SET}} \text{ variable } \underline{\text{TO}} \text{ expression} \\ \underline{\text{GOTO}} \text{ label } \underline{\text{IF}} \text{ expression} \end{array} \right\}$$

label: letter [. . .]
variable: letter [. . .]
number: digit [. . .]

$$\text{expression:} \left\{ \begin{array}{l} \text{number} \\ \text{variable} \\ \underline{(}\text{ expression }\underline{)} \end{array} \right\} \left[ \left\{ \begin{array}{c} \pm \\ = \end{array} \right\} \text{expression} \right]$$

$$\text{letter:} \left\{ \begin{array}{c} \underline{\text{A}} \\ \underline{\text{B}} \\ \underline{\text{C}} \\ \ldots \end{array} \right\}$$

$$\text{digit} \left\{ \begin{array}{c} \underline{0} \\ \underline{1} \\ \underline{2} \\ \ldots \end{array} \right\}$$

**Syntactic Ambiguity.** As described in the preceding section, a grammar is considered to be ambiguous when there exists more than one sequence of substitutions that permit the generation of a single string of characters. In the English language, examples of syntactic ambiguities are common and appear most frequently in signs or titles. For example, consider the various ways in which the following three phrases can be interpreted (or formally "parsed"):

a half baked chicken
hot tiled showers
home made bake shop

Typically, an ambiguous grammar is one that contains a production rule, which on its right-hand side references the same meta variable more than once, and does it in such a manner that it is impossible to discover the method of production of string from its form. There is no known algorithmic technique to test for the existence of ambiguities in a grammar. However, examples of ambiguous grammars may help to indicate common sources of ambiguity. For example, consider the grammar

⟨*integer*⟩ : : = ⟨*digit*⟩ | ⟨*integer*⟩ ⟨*integer*⟩
⟨*digit*⟩ : : = 0|1|2|3|4|5|6|7|8|9

Using this syntax, there are at least two possible generation sequences to generate any string composed of three or more digits. For example, consider the string 123:

Generation sequence (1)
⟨*integer*⟩→⟨*integer*⟩⟨*integer*⟩→⟨*integer*⟩⟨*digit*⟩
→⟨*integer*⟩3→⟨*integer*⟩⟨*integer*⟩3
→⟨*integer*⟩⟨*digit*⟩3→⟨*integer*⟩23→⟨*digit*⟩23→12
Generation sequence (2)
⟨*integer*⟩→⟨*integer*⟩⟨*integer*⟩→⟨*digit*⟩⟨*integer*⟩
→1⟨*integer*⟩→1⟨*integer*⟩⟨*integer*⟩
→ ⟨*digit*⟩⟨*integer*⟩→12⟨*integer*⟩→12⟨*digit*⟩→123

The differences between these two generation sequences can best be seen by examination of the generation trees (syntactic trees) corresponding to these sequences. In these trees, the replacement of a component by the use of a production rule is represented by a single-level tree structure, with the component being replaced at the top and its replacement(s) below, and branch lines connecting the component and its replacement(s). Thus, sequence (1) is represented by the tree shown in Fig. 1, and sequence (2) is shown in Fig. 2. Obviously, these two trees are not equivalent, and thus we may state that this grammar appears to be ambiguous.

However, apparent ambiguity can result from a failure to be consistent in the order in which components in the partially expanded string are replaced. In fact, any rule that contains in its right-hand part more than one component is a potential source of apparent ambiguity. Thus, we insist that the order of replacement of components in a string be strictly left-to-right or right-to-left. That is, the leftmost (rightmost) component in a string is

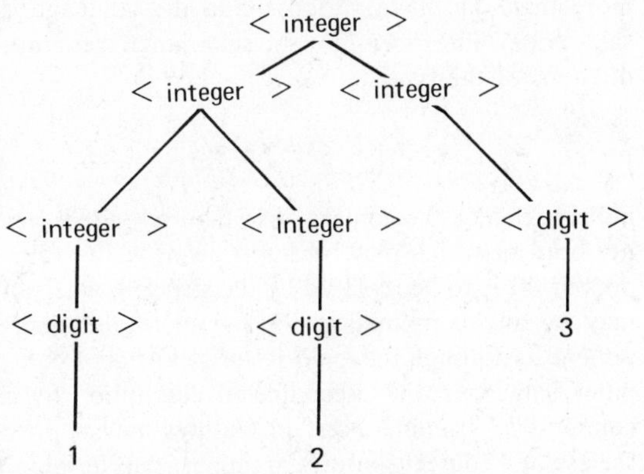


**Fig. 1.** Generation sequence (1).

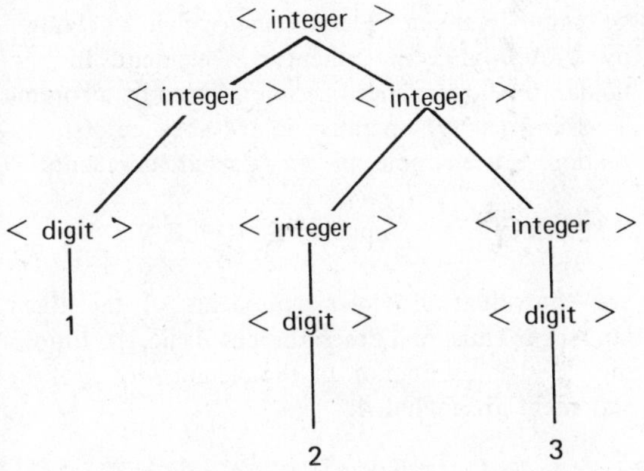


**Fig. 2.** Generation sequence (2).

the candidate for replacement at each generation stage. Such a strict sequence of generation is known as "canonic" generation.

Returning to the definition of a digit string given above, it may be seen that a canonic generation would not alleviate the ambiguousness of the grammar. However, a simple change in the grammar would solve this problem:

$$\langle integer\rangle ::= \langle digit\rangle \mid \langle integer\rangle \langle digit\rangle$$
$$\langle digit\rangle ::= 0|1|2|3|4|5|6|7|8|9$$

From this grammar, it would appear that there are at least two distinct manners of generating the string 123, depending on the order of application of the production rules, i.e., left or right canonic generation:

Left canonic generation sequence (3):

$$\langle integer\rangle \rightarrow \langle integer\rangle\langle digit\rangle \rightarrow \langle integer\rangle\langle digit\rangle\langle digit\rangle \rightarrow \langle digit\rangle\langle digit\rangle\langle digit\rangle \rightarrow 1\langle digit\rangle\langle digit\rangle \rightarrow 12\langle digit\rangle \rightarrow 123$$

Right canonic generation sequence (4):

$$\langle integer\rangle \rightarrow \langle integer\rangle\langle digit\rangle \rightarrow \langle integer\rangle 3 \rightarrow \langle integer\rangle\langle digit\rangle 3 \rightarrow \langle integer\rangle 23 \rightarrow \langle digit\rangle 23 \rightarrow 123$$

While it would appear that these two generation sequences are distinct, their generation trees are in fact identical, as is shown in Fig. 3.

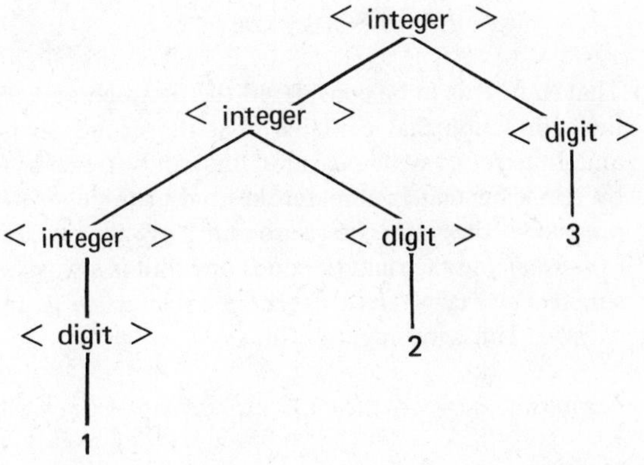


**Fig. 3.** Canonic generation tree for sequences (3) and (4).

In general, an ambiguous grammar will be formed when two grammars are combined to define languages that have at least one element in common. For example, consider the grammar

$$\langle this\rangle ::= \{A\}_1^3$$

which corresponds to the language with the sentences A, AA and AAA. Then, if this were to be combined with the grammar

$$\langle that\rangle ::= AA$$

there would be two canonic generation sequences to develop the string AA. Thus, the grammar

$$\langle this\text{-}or\text{-}that\rangle ::= \langle this\rangle \mid \langle that\rangle$$

is ambiguous.

Similarly, in connection with programming languages, it is important that languages be defined so that the desired meaning of a statement is unambiguous. As an example, it should be clear in defining an arithmetic expression that the implied meaning of an expression is unambiguous. Consider the simple expression

$$A - B - C$$

The interpretation (or parsing) of this string should be equivalent to the string

$$(A - B) - C$$

and not

$$A - (B - C)$$

That is, A–B is to be considered the first operand of the subtraction that contains C as its second operand. In terms of syntactic rules, this can be described by requiring that in unparenthesized arithmetic expressions, the left (first) operand is always an *expression* and the right (second) operand is always a simple *element*, where a degenerate *expression* is an *element*. Thus, we might define

$$\langle \textit{expression} \rangle ::= \langle \textit{element} \rangle \mid \langle \textit{expression} \rangle - \langle \textit{element} \rangle$$

If we now add a semantic interpretation scheme over the syntactic form, which specifies that only *expressions* can be evaluated and *elements* are number representations, we may see that

$$9 - 7 - 2$$

can be generated only by a sequence of productions such that 9 − 7 is an *expression* (and hence can be evaluated) that is part of the larger *expression* $\overline{9-7}-2$, where the overscore identifies the left-hand operand, which must have a value (i.e., be evaluated) in order to evaluate the second subtraction term.

**Context Sensitivity.** In the use of syntax productions, the progression from the root symbol to the actual string of characters may be visualized as the progressive substitution of components until all components have been replaced by elements of the character set of the language. This may be further visualized as the progression through certain branches of a tree structure wherein each branch is independent of all other branches. However, this treelike structure with no interdependence of branches exists only for *context free* languages. If the left-hand side of a production contains more than one meta variable, then the production of the right-hand side is dependent on the occurrence of more than one meta variable, and the language is said to be *context-sensitive*. In such languages, productions of the type

$$\langle a \rangle \langle b \rangle \langle c \rangle ::= \langle a \rangle \pi \langle c \rangle$$

indicate that in the context of ⟨a⟩ and ⟨c⟩ (either but not both of which may be empty strings), the component ⟨b⟩ is to be replaced by the string $\pi$, where $\pi$ may be any combination of characters and components. Although the majority of elements of computer languages are susceptible to description by a context-free grammar, certain features may require the use of a context-sensitive grammar, thus developing a totally context-sensitive grammar for that language. For example, one feature of the Basic language is susceptibility to context-sensitive definition. In Basic, the punctuation of a PRINT statement may be omitted between a literal string (which is delimited by quotes) and any other print element. In particular, the format specification inferred by a comma is assumed to be operative in the absence of punctuation. For example, the two partial statements

"EXAMPLE",X      and      "EXAMPLE"X

are equivalent in PRINT statements of the Basic language. Thus, in a description of Basic, the following rules of production of the elements of a PRINT statement are included:

$$\begin{array}{l}
\langle \textit{print st} \rangle ::= \text{PRINT}\langle \textit{print string} \rangle \{\langle \textit{punct} \rangle\}_0^1 \\
\langle \textit{punct} \rangle ::= ,\mid ; \\
\langle \textit{message} \rangle ::= {''}\{\langle \textit{char} \rangle\}_1^n{''} \\
\langle \textit{char} \rangle ::= \langle \textit{letter} \rangle \mid \langle \textit{digit} \rangle \mid \langle \textit{special char} \rangle \\
\langle \textit{print string} \rangle ::= \langle \textit{message} \rangle \mid \langle \textit{expression} \rangle \\
\qquad \mid \{\langle \textit{print string} \rangle\}_1^n
\end{array}$$

The following four context-sensitive productions specify the permitted forms of punctuation in a print string:

$$\begin{array}{l}
\langle \textit{null} \rangle \langle \textit{message} \rangle \langle \textit{expression} \rangle \\
\qquad ::= \langle \textit{null} \rangle \langle \textit{message} \rangle \{\langle \textit{punct} \rangle\}_0^1 \langle \textit{expression} \rangle \\
\langle \textit{null} \rangle \langle \textit{expression} \rangle \langle \textit{message} \rangle \\
\qquad ::= \langle \textit{null} \rangle \langle \textit{expression} \rangle \{\langle \textit{punct} \rangle\}_0^1 \langle \textit{message} \rangle \\
\langle \textit{null} \rangle \langle \textit{message} \rangle \langle \textit{message} \rangle \\
\qquad ::= \langle \textit{null} \rangle \langle \textit{message} \rangle \{\langle \textit{punct} \rangle\}_0^1 \langle \textit{message} \rangle \\
\langle \textit{null} \rangle \langle \textit{expression} \rangle \langle \textit{expression} \rangle \\
\qquad ::= \langle \textit{null} \rangle \langle \textit{expression} \rangle \langle \textit{punct} \rangle \langle \textit{expression} \rangle
\end{array}$$

In these context-sensitive productions, the component ⟨*null*⟩ has been included for clarity; in fact, every pair of elements in a string is separated by the null string, and thus ⟨*null*⟩ matches the element in the string immediately to the left of either message or expression in the above productions. Similarly, ⟨*null*⟩ on the right-hand side has no effect on the result; this element is specifically indicated here in order to match the left-hand side elements with the three-element general form specified previously; i.e.,

$$\langle a\rangle\langle b\rangle\langle c\rangle ::= \langle a\rangle\,\pi\,\langle c\rangle$$

For a discussion and formal definition of context-sensitive languages, see Ginsburg (1966).

**Syntactic Analysis.** The problem of associating a given string of symbols through a grammar to a language, such that an answer to the question "does this string belong to the language?" may be determined, is known as "syntactic analysis." It is intended that in determining the existence of the string in the language, the syntactic tree for that string can be created. In fact, in terms of syntactic trees, the process of analysis can be thought of as the determination of the syntactic tree that was used to generate the string.

Cheatham (1967) has likened the problem of tree generation to the game of dominoes, wherein the dominoes contain the left-hand side and the right-hand side of each syntactic production. The problem, then, is to fit the dominoes together in such a manner that there exists a complete tree between the

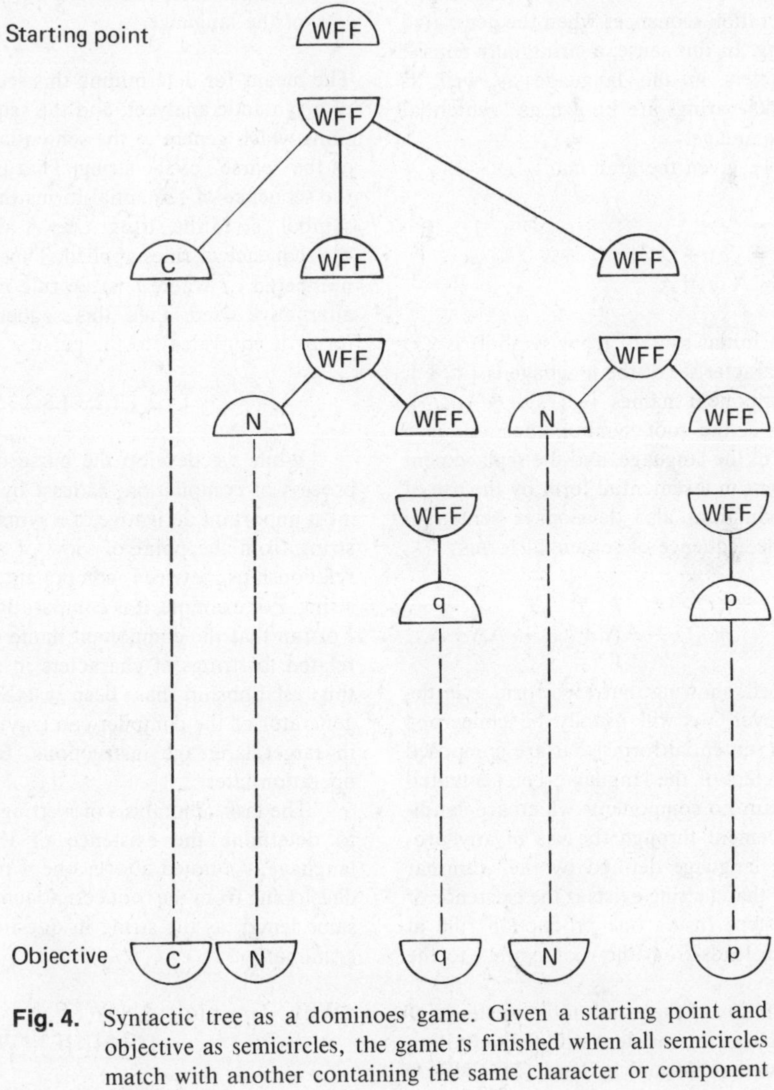


**Fig. 4.** Syntactic tree as a dominoes game. Given a starting point and objective as semicircles, the game is finished when all semicircles match with another containing the same character or component name.

root symbol and the string in question. Such a structure is shown in Fig. 4 and is discussed later in this section.

Another means for validating the existence of a string in a language is to generate all possible strings of that language and then to investigate the existence of the string in question in the generated set. Obviously, in some languages this is impossible, since the language is infinite. However, given a string of a prescribed length (i.e., number of distinct characters in the string), it is possible to generate all sequences of that length, provided the null element is rejected from the grammar. That is, if each and every production in a given grammar either maintains or increases the length of the generated string upon application, then it is possible to discard many alternative generation sequences when the generated string is too long. In this sense, a string may consist of both characters in the language as well as components. Such strings are known as "sentential forms" of the language.

For example, given the grammar

(1) $\langle s \rangle ::= \langle e \rangle$
(2) $\langle e \rangle ::= \langle e \rangle + \langle t \rangle \mid \langle t \rangle$
(3) $\langle t \rangle ::= \mathrm{A} \langle t \rangle \mid \mathrm{A}$

we see that the initial symbol (root symbol) is $\langle s \rangle$ and that the character set of the language is $\{\mathrm{A}, +\}$. The set of component names is $\{\langle s \rangle, \langle e \rangle, \langle t \rangle\}$. Given that $\langle s \rangle$ is the root symbol, then $\langle s \rangle$ is a sentential form of the language, and the replacement of any component in a sentential form by the use of one of the productions also develops a sentential form. Hence, the sequence of sentential forms

$$\langle s \rangle \to \langle e \rangle \to \langle e \rangle + \langle t \rangle \to \langle t \rangle + \langle t \rangle \to \mathrm{A}\langle t \rangle + \langle t \rangle \to \mathrm{AA} + \langle t \rangle \to \mathrm{AA+A}$$

may be developed, showing that each form is *in* the language. However, we will usually be concerned with only those sentential forms that are composed totally of characters of the language; i.e., sentential forms that contain no components which are candidates for replacement through the use of any production. In the language defined by the grammar above, the *proof* that a string exists is the existence of a sequence of steps (using one production rule at each step) which leads from the root symbol to the desired string.

Such a definition of the proof of the existence of a string in a language is consistent with the definition of *proof* as related to formal systems (Mendelson, 1966):

> A proof . . . is a sequence $A_1, A_2, \ldots A_n$ of well formed formulas such that, for each $i$, either $A_i$ is an axiom (of the system) or $A_i$ is a direct consequence of some preceding well formed formula by virtue of one of the rules of inference.

In terms of syntactic forms, the existence proof may be defined as follows:

> An existence proof over a string of characters $\emptyset_n$ in the language is a sequence $\emptyset_1, \emptyset_2, \ldots, \emptyset_n$ of sentential forms of the language such that, for each i, $\emptyset_i$ is a sentential form which is the result of applying one of the production rules of the grammar to $\emptyset_{i-1}$ and where $\emptyset_1$ is the root symbol of the language.

The means for determining this sequence is the task of a syntactic analyzer, and the sequence of productions which generates the sentential forms is known as the "parse" of the string. That is, for example, in the sequence of sentential forms that relate the root symbol $\langle s \rangle$ to the string AA+A above, the parse is the sequence of rules applied. Thus, if the rules were numbered $i.j$ where $i$ is the rule number and $j$ the alternative used, then this sequence of sentential forms is equivalent to the parse

1.1,2.1,2.2,3.1,3.2,3.2

While we develop the parse of a string in the process of compilation, at least by implication, the most important derivative of a syntactic analysis of a string from the point of view of a compiler is the relationships between component names and the string. For example, it is comparatively easy to see in Fortran that the component name ⟨*variable*⟩ can be related to strings of characters in statements. Once this relationship has been established, then the generator of the compiler can (say) create addresses in target language instructions. But more of this operation later.

The task of analysis of a string must be initially to determine the existence of the string in the language. As noted above, one way to do this is by developing from the root component all strings of the same length as the string in question. Consider the grammar

$$\langle \mathrm{WFF} \rangle ::= \mathrm{p|q|r|s|N}\langle \mathrm{WFF} \rangle \mid \{\mathrm{C|A|K|E}\}_1^1 \langle \mathrm{WFF} \rangle \langle \mathrm{WFF} \rangle$$

This simple grammar (Allen, 1970) permits the

production of well-formed formulas (WFF); the upper-case characters (N,C,A,K,E) represent the operators, and the lower-case characters (p,q,r,s) represent the simple operands. Fig. 5 shows Cheatham's domino game form of the generation tree of the string CNqNp. Now, obviously, since the definition of this language includes a recursive production, the language is an infinite language, and hence it will not be feasible to generate all possible strings in the language to test against any string that is believed to exist in the language. However, it is possible to generate all strings of a certain length and then to check the existence of some string in this generated set. For example, consider again the string CNqNp. This string is composed of five characters (symbols in the language); and, by an examination of the possible substitutions that can be made, it can be seen that there are approximately 2,500 five-character strings that may be generated from this grammar! Thus, even for strings with comparatively few (5 even) characters, the number of alternatives in the algorithm for analysis is extremely large. Therefore, we must search for an alternate approach.

Syntactic analyzers can broadly be classified into two methods: (1) the predictive methods, which, starting from the root symbol, attempt to predict the means by which the string was generated; and (2) the reductive methods, which attempt to reduce the string to the root symbol. These methods are loosely termed the *top-down* and *bottom-up* methods, respectively. The direction implied by these terms is related to the syntactic trees that may be generated wherein the root symbol is at the top of the page and the string at the bottom. It may then be seen that a predictive (top-down) method starts at the top of the (yet unconstructed) tree and builds down toward the string, whereas the bottom-up (reductive) method starts at the string and attempts to develop a tree that converges onto the root symbol.
It can be seen, using Cheatham's domino game, that starting from the basic game board containing only the root symbol (at the top) and the string to be analyzed (at the bottom), the two stages of analysis are well exemplified by the order in which the players fit the pieces into the puzzle.

A further class of syntactic analyzers is based on a particular form of grammar known as "precedence grammar." Precedence grammars may be described by the use of Backus-Naur form or the two-dimensional Cobol form, provided the resulting rules conform to a set of relational properties over the elements of the language. Precedence relationships exist between two symbols (components or characters) in the language when the following relationships hold:

1. The relationship $A \doteq B$ is said to exist between the symbols of the vocabulary A and B when there exists in the syntax a rule of the form

$$C \rightarrow \alpha AB\beta$$

where $\alpha$ and $\beta$ are symbol strings of which either or both may be the empty string.

2. The relationship $A \lessdot B$ is said to exist between two symbols of the vocabulary if there exists in the grammar a construct rule of the form

$$C \rightarrow \alpha A\rho\beta$$

and where by some substitution sequence $\rho$ is developed into the string $B\lambda$, where $\alpha$, $\beta$, and $\lambda$ are (possibly empty) symbol strings.

3. The relationship $A \gtrdot B$ is said to exist between two symbols of the vocabulary of the language when either of two situations exist in the grammar:

(a) There exists a construct rule of the form

$$C \rightarrow \alpha\rho B\beta$$

and, for some substitution sequence, $\rho$ is developed into the string $\lambda A$; or

(b) There exists a construct rule of the form

$$C \rightarrow \alpha\rho\sigma\beta$$

and for some substitution sequences, $\rho$ is developed into the string $\lambda A$ and $\sigma$ is developed into the string $\varnothing B$, where $\alpha$, $\beta$, $\varnothing$, and $\lambda$ are (possibly empty) symbol strings.

4. Where two symbols of the vocabulary of the language never occur in sentential forms in any of the above relationships, they are said to have a *null* relationship.

The preceding relationships are not reflexive, and hence $A \doteq B$ does not imply $B \doteq A$, since there is a distinct ordering of the symbols in any sentential form in the language. A grammar in which there exists a unique relationship between every pairing of symbols (both language components and characters of the alphabet), including the null relationship, is a precedence grammar.

Where a language can be described by a precedence grammar, there exists a very simple and straightforward method of analyzing strings in that language. Examining a syntactic tree for strings in a language that is described by a precedence grammar, one may see that the relationships $\doteq$, $\langle\cdot$, and $\cdot\rangle$ are also relationships of tree level. In performing a bottom-up analysis, symbols of the vocabulary at a lower level must be reduced to higher-level components before reductions can occur at a higher level. In fact, if the relational symbols are inserted between the symbols in a string that is being analyzed, matching $\langle\cdot$ and $\cdot\rangle$ relational symbols denote a subtree that can be reduced to a single component. The relational symbol $\underline{\blacktriangle}$ denotes a continuation of a level. Where two symbols have no relationship in a precedence grammar, they can never validly occur in juxtaposition. This provides an automatic error-detection scheme built into the grammar. For an example of a language that is defined by a precedence grammar see Wirth and Webber (1966).

A modified class of precedence grammars is that termed "operator precedence" grammars. In these grammars, relationships are expressed only between characters of the language and where pairings occur in strings, possibly separated by components. Where relationships are expressed between the operators of expressions (such as arithmetic or logical expressions), it can clearly be seen how the concept of analysis can be extended to a special class of languages. The conditions of relationship for operator precedence grammars are as follows:

1. The relationship $\doteq$ holds between two characters of the alphabet $a$ and $b$ if there exists in the grammar the construct rules of form

$$C \rightarrow \alpha ab\beta \qquad \text{or} \qquad C \rightarrow \alpha a A b\beta$$

where A is a component of the language and $\alpha$ and $\beta$ are (possibly empty) strings of language symbols.

2. The relationship $\langle\cdot$ exists between two characters of the alphabet $a$ and $b$ if there exists in the grammar a construct rule of form

$$C \rightarrow \alpha a A\beta$$

where, by some substitution sequence, A is developed into either the string $b\lambda$ or the string $\mathrm{D}b\lambda$, where A and D are components of the language and $\alpha$, $\beta$, and $\lambda$ are (possibly empty) strings of symbols.

3. The relationship $\cdot\rangle$ exists between two characters of the alphabet $a$ and $b$ if there exists in the grammar a construct rule of the form

$$C \rightarrow \alpha A b\beta$$

where, for some substitution sequence, A is developed into either of the strings $\lambda a$ or $\lambda a\mathrm{D}$, where A and D are components of the language and where $\alpha$, $\beta$, and $\lambda$ are (possibly empty) symbol strings.

Using the same technique as with strings that were produced from precedence grammars, strings in languages which are the subject of operator grammars can be analyzed.

**Semantic Descriptions.** The formal description of the semantics of programming languages is currently in a state of active development, with several competing techniques, each emphasizing some aspect of definitional technology. There exist methods of semantic definition which are based on automata theory; these methods model processes and languages by modeling techniques. Other systems have developed abstract machines that closely resemble actual machines and which have a language of instruction that is used to describe a process or language. Although tremendous strides have been made in the methods of definition, including several examples of defining the semantics of actual languages and using those descriptions to guide the development of compilers and interpreters for those languages, there has been little practical work done in the area of formally validating those definitions. Conversely, there is a growing body of knowledge related to the proof of assertions about simple programs, which can be expected to develop to more meaningful proof techniques and systems in the future.

REFERENCES

1960. Naur, P. "Documentation Problems: ALGOL 60," *Communications of the ACM*, Vol. 3, No. 5 (May), pp. 299–314.

1963. Floyd, R. W. "Syntactic Analysis and Operator Precedence," *Journal of the ACM*, Vol. 10, (July), p. 316.

1966. Ginsburg, S. *The Mathematical Theory of Context Free Languages*. New York: McGraw-Hill.

1966. Mendelson, E. *Introduction to Mathematical Logic*. New York: Van Nostrand.

1966. Wirth, N., and H. Webber. "Euler: A Generalization of ALGOL, and Its Formal Definition," *Communications of the ACM*, Vol. 9 (January-February), pp. 13, 89.

1967. Cheatham, T. E. *The Theory and Construction of Compilers*, 2d ed. Wakefield, Mass.: Computer Associates.

1968. ANSI. *American National Standard COBOL, X3.23-1968.* New York: American National Standards Institute.

1969. Lucas, P., and K. Walk. "On the Formal Description of PL/I," *Annual Review in Automatic Programming*, Part 3. Oxford, U.K.: Pergamon Press.

1970. Allen, L. E. *Wff'n Proof.* New Haven, Conn.: Antotelic Instructional Materials, Publ.

1971. Branquart, P., et al. "The Composition of Semantics in ALGOL 68," *Communications of the ACM*, Vol. 14, No. 11, (November), p. 697.

1971. Neuhold, E. J. "The Formal Description of Programming Languages," *IBM Systems Journal*, Vol. 10, No. 2, pp. 86–112.

1972. *Proceedings of a Symposium on Proving Assertions about Programs, SIGPLAN Notices*, Vol. 7, No. 7, (January). New York: Association for Computing Machinery.

J. A. N. LEE

## PROOF OF PROGRAM CORRECTNESS. *See* PROGRAM CORRECTNESS, PROOF OF.

## PROPRIETARY PROGRAM

For articles on related subjects *see* COPYRIGHTS AND PATENTS, COMPUTER ASPECTS OF; and LEGAL PROTECTION OF SOFTWARE.

Strictly speaking, a "proprietary" program is one *owned* by someone, and therefore has a "proprietor." It is distinguished from a program that is in the public domain and which is open and available for use by everyone without charge or restriction. The term is more commonly used, however, to identify only the first of three subsets of nonpublic domain ("owned") programs. This subset consists of programs being exploited commercially as separate products.

The second of the other two subsets of owned programs consists of those used primarily by their proprietors for internal processing in their own businesses and not generally made available separately to third parties for profit. An example of this type is the payroll program used by a service center in its processing of payrolls for customers. These are sometimes called "production" programs. The third subset consists of programs marketed commercially as an integral part of a much larger group of products, of which their value represents a relatively small fraction. An example is the software marketed by a hardware manufacturer in a package including the computer main frame itself. These are frequently called "bundled" programs.

The three subsets of owned programs are not mutually exclusive, and the same program may fall within two and sometimes even all three categories. The term "proprietary program" is the most significant commercially, however, and if the program is being publicly marketed as a separate product to any significant extent, it will usually be called a "proprietary program," irrespective of what other terms also apply.

Commercial exploitation of a proprietary program is dependent upon the proprietor's exclusive rights to the program under three branches of law: patent law, copyright law, and trade-secret law. None of these represents either certain or complete protection, and the U.S. Congress and a number of organizations and persons concerned with program protection are giving thought to new and different ways of balancing the many important and conflicting social and economic issues involved.

Patent protection is the most legally powerful form of protection. It gives the patentee the right to exclude all others from use of the patented subject matter for the life of the patent. However, it is limited to only those novel programs that would not be obvious to one skilled in the art of programming. Despite the relative ease of obtaining patents from the Patent Office, the courts in recent years have been more and more restrictive in upholding all kinds of patents. In its first decision relating to a patent on a program as such, the U.S. Supreme Court in 1972 unanimously (although with only six of the nine justices participating) ruled against patentability. The impact of that decision is still unclear, however, and the Patent Office and the Court of Customs and Patent Appeals continue to validate some kinds of patents that relate to programs. It may be a decade or more before there is certainty in this area as the result of further judicial decisions or action by Congress. Finally, issued patents are published and available to all, and patentees sometimes have great difficulty discovering whether the patented subject matter is being used by others without permission.

Copyright protection is probably the most certain of the three forms of protection, but it is usually also the least valuable. Although no court has yet ruled on the issue, the Copyright Office has been granting copyrights for programs since the mid-1960s, and the majority view in legal circles is that one who actually copies a copyrighted program will be held liable to the owner for damages. However, copyright protection protects only against "copying," so that (unlike patent protection) one who admires the output of another's specially programmed computer is free to develop his own program if he does so independently without copying, even if it turns out to be an exact duplicate of the copyrighted program.

Damages for copyright infringement are limited. Furthermore, the extent of program copyright protection is not yet clear. It has not been decided, for example, that one who uses a copyrighted program in his computer is an infringer any more than one who reads a copyrighted book in a library violates the copyright. Determination of this issue will probably depend on whether in legal consequence the computer is technically "copying" or simply "reading" each time it runs the program. Registered copyrights must be published in the same fashion as issued patents and therefore they are subject to the same problem of policing.

Trade-secret protection is the form most commonly in use. It protects the program only against improper access by a third party, and is therefore dependent upon a series of security operating precautions, contractual secrecy provisions with licensees and franchisees, restrictive employment agreements, and other security and legal measures designed to assure the proprietor that unauthorized persons will not be able to copy the program without doing something wrong. Although, for this reason, trade-secret protection is the most difficult of the three forms to obtain, it is at the same time usually also the most effective in the practical sense because, by the very nature of the form of protection, the program will not be available publicly for others to examine in the Library of Congress, the Patent Office, or elsewhere. However, in recent years decisions of the U.S. Supreme Court have limited the scope of trade-secret protection. Although its general availability seems clear, it may be several years before the precise limits of trade-secret protection are all fully spelled out by the judiciary or Congress.

REFERENCES

1965. Wessel, M. "Legal Protection of Computers," *Harvard Business Review*, Vol. 43, No. 97.
On the subject of trade-secret protection.

1973. Cambridge Research Institute. "Omnibus Copyright Revision." American Federation of Information Processing Societies (Am. Soc. of Information Science).
On the subject of copyright protection.

1973. Soltysinski. "Computer Programs and Patent Law: A Comparative Study," *Rutgers Journal of Computers and the Law*, Vol. 3, No. 1.
On the subject of patent protection.

M. WESSEL

**PROTECTION, MEMORY.** *See* MEMORY PROTECTION.

**PUNCHED CARD.** *See* IBM CARD; and NINETY COLUMN CARD.

**PURE PROCEDURE.** *See* PROCEDURE, PURE.

# Q

## QUEUEING THEORY

For articles on related subjects *see* COMMUNICATIONS AND COMPUTERS; OPERATIONS RESEARCH; SIMULATION; STATISTICAL APPLICATIONS; and STOCHASTIC PROCESS.

Waiting lines have become an accepted and often frustrating fact of modern life. Whenever congestion occurs in production, transportation, communication, computers, or other kinds of systems, waiting lines are built up, resulting in a blocking of resources and resulting in losses of time, money, patience, and goodwill. Efforts to control congestion are thus of vital importance, and have led to a rapid growth of research activity in "queueing theory," which is the study of waiting-line processes through the use of mathematical and/or simulation models.

**Queueing Models.** The basic queueing context can be described as follows: Units from some source arrive at a service facility, wait if necessary in a queue or system of queues, receive service at a time or times determined by some service policy or queue discipline, and depart after having their demands serviced. Thus, the study of a queueing process requires the specification of each of the following elements:

1. Source. The source, finite or infinite, is a population or a group of populations from which the units demanding service emanate. These units may be people; paperwork, such as orders, invoices, letters, or computer program decks; malfunctioning machines; or electronic signals as in telecommunications systems.

2. Input Process. The statistical pattern by which units arrive at the service facility is called the "arrival-time distribution," which is most often taken to be the negative exponential distribution (also called "random arrivals" or "Poisson arrivals").

3. Queue Structure. The waiting line of a system may consist of a queue or a system of queues. Each queue may have a finite maximum length or be unlimited in length. The waiting line may be conceptual rather than physical, as in the case of remote terminals waiting to be polled by a computer.

4. Service Facility. The service facility may consist of one or more service channels in parallel; each channel may have one or more servers in series. A queueing model must specify the arrangement of the service facilities. The "server" need not be a person but may be a machine (e.g., a computer).

5. Service Process. The time required to completely service a unit at any server is referred to as that server's "service (or holding) time." A queueing model must specify the probability distribution of service times for each server (possibly for each type of unit entering the system). The types commonly used are the negative exponential and the constant service time distributions.

6. Service Discipline. The rules by which units are selected and serviced constitute the service

discipline. Service may be first-come-first-served (or FIFO, first-in—first-out), random, or according to some priority procedure. In the latter case, the priorities may be externally or internally determined, and service may be on a preemptive basis in which service on a "low" priority unit is interrupted in order to service a "high" priority unit. Whatever service discipline is to be used must be specified.

**Problem Areas.** The problems associated with queueing theory may be classified as (1) analytical or theoretical, and (2) operational or applications problems.

ANALYTICAL PROBLEMS. After the mathematical model of a queueing situation has been formulated by specifying all its assumptions, the model may be studied analytically in order to better understand the behavior of the system. The characteristics of usual interest are the queue length (number of units waiting at time $t$), the waiting time (the time a new arrival will have to wait until his service begins), and the length of the busy period (the length of time the server is continuously busy).

Under certain conditions, a queueing system that has been in operation for a sufficiently long time settles down to a behavior independent of time. The system is then said to be in an equilibrium (or steady state) condition. Because the steady-state condition is less difficult to study analytically than the initial transient condition, the majority of queueing results concern steady-state behavior.

A great deal of insight into the steady-state behavior of queues can be gained through the results for the simplest models; consequently, a few single-demand models are summarized in Table 1, which

**Table 1.** Some sample steady-state queueing results

| Model Description | $p_n$ | $p_0$ | $L$ | $Q$ |
|---|---|---|---|---|
| 1. Birth-death process<br>Arrival rate = $\lambda_n$<br>Service rate = $\mu_n$ | $\left(\dfrac{\Pi_{i=1}^{n-1} \lambda_i}{\Pi_{i=1}^{n} \mu_i}\right) p_0 = R_n p_0$ | $\dfrac{1}{1 + \Sigma_{n=1}^{\infty} R_n}$ | $\Sigma_{n=0}^{\infty} np_n$ | $\Sigma_{n=c}^{\infty} (n - c)p_n$ |
| 2. Poisson input, exponential service times.<br>Arrival rate $\lambda_n = \lambda$ for all $n$.<br>Service rate $\mu_n = \mu$ for all $n > 0$. | $\left(\dfrac{\lambda}{\mu}\right)^n p_0 = \rho^n p_0$ | $1 - \rho$ | $\dfrac{\lambda}{\mu - \lambda}$ | $\dfrac{\lambda^2}{\mu(\mu - \lambda)}$ |
| 3. Poisson input, arbitrary service times<br>Arrival rate $\lambda_n = \lambda$.<br>Service time has mean $1/\mu$ and variance $\sigma^2$. | | $1 - \rho$ | $\rho + Q$ | $\dfrac{\rho^2 + \lambda^2\sigma^2}{2(1 - \rho)}$ |
| 4. Poisson input, constant service time.<br>Arrival rate $\lambda_n = \lambda$ for all $n$.<br>Service time = constant = $1/\mu$. | | $1 - \rho$ | $\rho + Q$ | $\dfrac{\rho^2}{2(1 - \rho)}$ |
| 5. Poisson input, exponential service time, finite max. queue length $M$.<br>Arrival rate $\lambda_n = \lambda$ for $n \leq M$.<br>Service rate $\mu_n = \mu$ for $n > 0$. | $\rho^n p_0$ | $\dfrac{1 - \rho}{1 - \rho^{M+1}}$ | $\dfrac{\rho}{1 - \rho} - \dfrac{(M + 1)\rho^{M+1}}{1 - \rho^{M+1}}$ | $L - (1 - p_0)$ |
| 6. Finite source population (size $N$) exponential service<br>$\lambda_n = \begin{cases} (N - n)\lambda & \text{if } n = 0,1,\ldots,N \\ 0 & \text{if } n \geq N \end{cases}$<br>$\mu_n = \mu$ for all $n > 0$ | $\dfrac{N!}{(N - n)!} \rho^n p_0 =$ $C_n \rho^n p_0$ | $\dfrac{1}{1 + \Sigma_{n=0}^{N} C_n \rho^n}$ | $N - \dfrac{\mu}{\lambda}(1 - p_0)$ | $N - \dfrac{\lambda + \mu}{\lambda}(1 - p_0)$ |

uses the following notation:

$p_n$ = probability that the number of units in the queueing system (line length) is $n$.
$p_o$ = probability that system is idle.
$L$ = average line length.
$Q$ = average queue length, where queue length is the line length minus the number of units being serviced.
$W$ = average waiting time in the system (includes service time).
$W_q$ = average waiting time in the queue (excludes service time).
$\lambda_n$ = mean arrival rate (expected number of arrivals per unit time) of units when the line length is $n$.
$\mu_n$ = mean service rate (expected number of units being serviced per unit time) when the line length is $n$.

The first line of Table 1 gives the general results for such processes (often called "birth-death" processes). Subsequent lines of Table 1 give results for a number of special cases.

As the table indicates, most queueing-system results depend upon the specific assumptions made; however, the following results hold under quite general conditions. Assume that $\lambda_n = \lambda$ for all $n$. Then $L = \lambda W$ and $Q = \lambda W_q$. Further, if $\mu_n = \mu$ for all $n$, then $W = W_q + 1/\mu$. These relationships enable us to determine all four quantities ($L$, $Q$, $W$, and $W_q$), if any one of them can be found analytically. Also, $\rho = \lambda/\mu$ is the utilization factor for the service facility; i.e., the expected fraction of time the server is busy.

Operational Problems. The study of real queueing systems is motivated by the objectives of improving their design, their control, and/or their effectiveness. The decisions that can be made usually involve: the number of servers, the service rate(s) of the servers, the number of service facilities and their placement, and the service discipline.

All these decisions involve the general question of the appropriate level of service to provide and the appropriate trade-off to make between the costs incurred by providing the service and the costs incurred by waiting for service.

In attempting to use theoretical models for practical applications a number of statistical problems arise, mainly involving verification of the basic assumptions of the model in order to avoid misusing mathematically derived results. In many applications, the queueing problem cannot be described in a mathematically amenable manner. Computer simulation may be used to obtain results in these cases. Several higher-level computer programming languages such as GPSS (General Purpose Systems Simulator) and Simscript II have been designed with the simulation of queueing processes in mind.

One important service discipline that should be discussed in a time-shared computer context is the "round-robin" discipline, which is useful when the processing times of arriving units are unknown. This discipline may be used to automatically give priority to those units that have the smaller service-time requirements. In this method, a unit entering service is processed for a time period called a "quantum." If during this quantum the unit completes service, that unit departs and service begins on the next; otherwise, the uncompleted unit rejoins the queue to await further service. The concept appears to have arisen from the desire to provide faster responses and minimize delay times for users with short requests in time-sharing computer systems.

Though the earliest works in queueing (the classical studies by Erlang, a Danish mathematician) were concerned with the highly practical problem of designing telephone exchanges, relatively little attention has been given to the practical application of queueing theory to optimal decision making. If waiting lines are not to be the bane of existence in the future, great strides must be made in this area of queueing theory.

References

1961. Saaty, T. L. *Elements of Queueing Theory with Applications*. New York: McGraw-Hill.
1969. McKinney, J. M. "A Survey of Analytical Time-Sharing Models," *Computing Surveys*, No. 1, pp. 105–116.
1972. Cooper, Robert. *Introduction to Queueing Theory*. New York: Macmillan.
1973. Fishburn, G. S. *Concepts and Methods in Discrete Event Digital Simulation*. New York: John Wiley.

J. M. McKinney

# R

## ROS. *See* Read-Only Store.

## RPG. *See* Nonprocedural Languages.

## RAMAC

For articles on related subjects *see* Digital Computers: Early; and Manufacturers, Computer.

The IBM 305 RAMAC (random access method of accounting and control) was among the first—if not the first—data processing systems to employ a magnetic disk file permitting direct random accessing of data records. It was essentially a unit record system enhanced by a stored program capability and the direct access capability provided by its disk file.

The basic 305 consisted of a processing unit, a disk file, an operator console, a printer, card reader, and card punch. The processing unit permitted the storage of only a hundred instructions, which were loaded to and serially accessed from a magnetic drum. The drum provided four 100-character areas for working storage. The instruction set was, by today's standards, extraordinarily limited. The set provided for data transfer, decimal arithmetic, disk

**Fig. 1.** The IBM 305 RAMAC.

I/O operations, and switch setting. All I/O operations, including formatting, print editing, and all branching operations, were accomplished by wired plugboards located in the I/O and processing units. The execution of each job required that a stored program be loaded and the appropriate control panels be mounted in each unit. Programming was done in machine language only. Program overlays from disk to drum were commonly used.

The disk file consisted of 50 magnetic disks with 100 recording tracks on each surface. Each track stored 10 to 100 character records. The total disk capacity of a 305 could be expanded to 20 million characters, and a single file could be shared by two systems. The access mechanism consisted of one or two arms, which moved vertically past the disks and laterally between them. Records were directly addressed by a sequential record address. The cylinder concept of file management was programmatically implemented by users, but the hardware did nothing to facilitate the concept. Access time was less than 1 sec.

The printer was a very slow serial-stick printer and could be replaced with a 407 unit record accounting machine, operating at a maximum speed of 150 lpm. Multiple printers could be attached to a single 305.

The 305 was employed for most common in-line applications such as inventory control and distribution accounting. The first management operating system, integrating many business applications, was developed by IBM and implemented on the 305 as a user package. Experience gained with this system led to the development of file management techniques, such as address randomization and chained file structures, which were employed on subsequently developed disk systems. However, the 305 was quickly made obsolete by the introduction of the IBM 1400 series and similar second-generation computers.

G. D. BAER

## RAND TABLET

For article on related subject *see* COMPUTER GRAPHICS.

The Rand (or data) tablet is a manual input device for graphics display consoles. It consists of a flat writing surface (the tablet itself) and a stylus, typically the size of a ballpoint pen, which the user moves over the tablet as if writing on a normal note pad. Some tablets also have a *z*-axis input, which is the height of the stylus above the tablet, and which allows the stylus tip to be moved through some predefined three dimensional volume. As with the joystick, successive stylus tip positions can be sensed, digitized, and left in a register pair (or triple) for subsequent processing. The data tablet is an excellent vehicle for digitizing already existing drawings or for freehand input.

With the addition of suitable "comparator" circuitry, a tablet can also be used to generate an interrupt when the stylus cursor, which tracks the stylus position on the screen, moves within a preset distance of some graphic element already on the screen. The tablet with comparator can therefore be used as a functional equivalent to the lightpen, but is found by most users to be superior to it from an ergonomic point of view.

Physically, tablets use either analog or digital techniques for locating the stylus. Analog tablets use electromagnetic or sonic pickups (detectors) to relate the strength of a received signal to the distance between the stylus tip and the boundaries of the tablet. Sonic, or spark tablets, for example, transmit an ultrasonic pulse train that is detected by receivers at the corners for triangulation on the stylus position. Digital tablets (for example, the earliest and best-known Rand Corporation tablet) usually have transmission lines inscribed in the tablet along which pulse trains are transmitted. The stylus receives the pulse trains characteristic of the wires it is near, and these trains can be decoded by digital logic to determine the position of the stylus.

A. VAN DAM

## RANDOM ACCESS. *See* DIRECT ACCESS.

## RANDOM NUMBER GENERATION

For articles on related subjects *see* MONTE CARLO METHOD; SIMULATION; and STOCHASTIC PROCESS.
For article on related term *see* SHIFTING.

A *random-number generator* is basically a set of computer instructions which scrambles the digits of an integer to produce a new integer. Here, "scramble" means to mix and combine by means of simple computer operations. The idea is to produce a sequence of integers which, in spite of being produced by a fixed procedure, will serve as random variables in computer simulations such as Monte Carlo, which is used to describe any simulation problem that uses random numbers. For reasons of speed, simplicity, and repeatability, virtually all Monte Carlo programs in computers use a set of random numbers that is produced by a fixed procedure, chosen in such a way that the results pass extensive tests for randomness. The following examples (using decimal digits, although most generators scramble binary digits) are representative:

1. *Mid-Square Generator*. Given an 8-digit decimal integer, square to get 16 digits; keep the middle 8 digits:

current $I$ = 45086273,
$I^2$ = 2032772013030529,
new $I$ = 77201303.

2. *Congruential Generator*. Given an 8-digit integer, multiply by a constant, say, 7654321; then keep the last 8 digits:

current $I$ = 45086273,
$I \times 7654321$ = 345104806235633,
new $I$ = 06235633.

3. *Shift-Register Generator*. Given an 8-digit integer, shift right 3, do a no-carry add, shift left 4, then another no-carry add:

| | | |
|---|---|---|
| current $I$ = | 45086273 | |
| | 00045086 | shift right 3 |
| | 45021259 | no-carry add |
| | 12590000 | shift left 4 |
| new $I$ = | 57511259 | no-carry add |

Each of these examples produces a sequence of integers that seem to jump around haphazardly within the allowable range (word size) of the computer. No doubt the reader could make up a few procedures that would appear to do as well. There are two basic problems: (1) to make sure that the generator does not begin to repeat itself too soon, and (2) to somehow test the output for randomness.

Problem 1 is usually resolved, sometimes after some difficult mathematics. If there is no satisfactory solution, as in the case of the mid-square generator, the method is abandoned. The question of the suitability of a generator for Monte Carlo problems can never be completely resolved. All we can do is try the generator for more and more problems for which we know an exact or approximate answer, or, as in the case of congruential generators, use some theoretical arguments to suggest Monte Carlo problems for which results will not be satisfactory.

The examples above are from the three types of random-number generators that have dominated both practical use and theoretical discussion in the literature. The *mid-square* generator is now considered obsolete. Used in early computers, it produced important results in Monte Carlo studies of neutron diffusion, particularly in the development of atomic bombs, reactors, and shielding. *Congruential* generators, by far the most commonly used method for the past 25 years, have been the subject of scores of papers. Recent discoveries have shown, however, that congruential generators are not so satisfactory as they were thought to be. *Shift-register* generators,

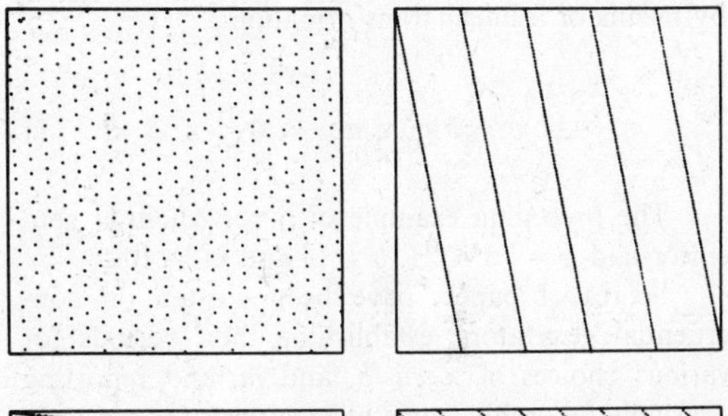

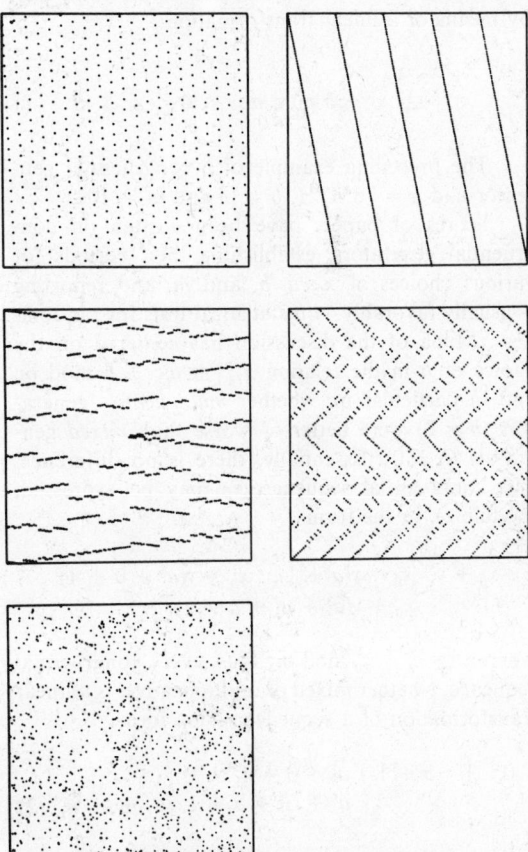

**Fig. 1.** Regularities in congruent and shift register generators with pairs of random numbers shown as points in the plane. Top: Patterns produced by two congruent generators. Middle: Two shift registers. Bottom: A satisfactory pattern produced by combining two congruential generators (algorithm M). Regularities are a consequence of the linear nature of the generators and cannot be removed by choice of parameters.

used for many years in communication theory, coding theory, and cryptography, have been recently heralded as the best alternative to congruential generators. However, shift-register generators have regularities that appear to be more serious, though not so easy to establish as those of the congruential generators. Regularities in congruential and shift-register generators are illustrated in Fig. 1 and discussed below.

**Congruential Generators.** These are more properly called "linear" congruential generators because they produce a sequence of residues of a large modulus $m$ (usually the word size of the computer) by means of a linear transformation:

$$x_0, x_1, x_2, x_3, \ldots \quad x_{i+1} \equiv ax_i + b \bmod m, \qquad 0 \leq x_i < m. \tag{1}$$

The preceding example of a congruential generator had $a = 7654321$, $b = 0$, and $m = 10^8$.

Scores of papers have been written on congruential generators, establishing their periods for various choices of $x_0$, $a$, $b$, and $m$, and reporting —usually favorably—on statistical tests for randomness. Much of the discussion has centered on the choice of $b$ in the relation $x_{i+1} \equiv ax_i + b \bmod m$, and in particular on whether *multiplicative* generators ($b = 0$) were better or worse than *mixed* generators ($b \neq 0$). Essentially, there is no difference. The congruential sequence (1) may be expressed, modulo $m$, in the form

$$x_0,\ x_0 + v,\ x_0 + v(a + 1),\ x_0 + v(a^2 + a + 1),\ x_0 + v(a^3 + a^2 + a + 1),\ \ldots$$

where $v \equiv x_1 - x_0 \bmod m$; thus, every congruential sequence, whether mixed or multiplicative, is a linear transformation of a sequence of the form

$$0,\ 1,\ a + 1,\ a^2 + a + 1,\ a^3 + a^2 + a + 1, \ldots \bmod m. \tag{2}$$

Thus, the choice of $x_0$ and $b$ are of no importance, except that a poor choice may shorten the period. But as long as $v = x_0(a - 1) + b = x_1 - x_0$ has no factors in common with the modulus $m$, then the period and the "randomness" of sequences (1) and (2) are the same.

Marsaglia (1972) gives a complete development of the theory of linear congruential sequences. The particular case $m = 2^\beta$, the one most commonly encountered with modern computers, is summarized here.

**Congruential Generators for Modulus $2^\beta$.** To find the period of the sequence:

$$x_0, x_1, x_2, x_3, \ldots \qquad x_{i+1} \equiv ax_i + b \bmod 2^\beta, \tag{3}$$

write $a = 1 + k \cdot 2^\alpha$ or $a = -1 + k \cdot 2^\alpha$ according to whether $a \equiv 1 \bmod 4$ or $a \equiv -1 \bmod 4$, with $k$ odd and $2 < \alpha < \beta$. (The case $\alpha = \beta$ is of no interest.) When $b$ is odd, sequence (3) has period $2^\beta$ for $a = 1 + k \cdot 2^\alpha$, and period $2^{\beta-\alpha+1}$ for $a = -1 + k \cdot 2^\alpha$. However, in either case, sequence (3) has *effective period* $2^{\beta-\alpha}$ in that it is made up of a block $\{B\}$ of $2^{\beta-\alpha}$ residues, followed by translates of that block:

$$\{B\}, \{B + c\}, \{B + 2c\}, \{B + 3c\}, \ldots \bmod 2^\beta.$$

When $b = 0$, the sequence becomes

$$x_0,\quad ax_0,\quad a^2x_0,\quad a^3x_0, \ldots \bmod 2^\beta,$$

and the period is $2^{\beta-\alpha}$ in either case, provided $x_0$ is odd. If $x_0$ is multiplied by a power of 2, the period is divided by that power of 2.

*Example*: $a = 2^7 + 1$, $b = 1$, $m = 2^{35}$. The generator

$$x_{i+1} = (2^7 + 1)x_i + 1 \bmod 2^{35}$$

was suggested in 1960 because one can quickly multiply by $2^7 + 1$ with a shift and an add. Since $a = 1 + 2^7$, the period is $2^{35}$, but the effective period is $2^{28}$; the full sequence is made up of 128 translates of a block of $2^{28}$ residues.

REGULARITIES IN CONGRUENTIAL GENERATORS. For most uses, the integers produced by a random-number generator are divided by the modulus (usually $2^k$ for $k$-bit computers) to get random numbers between zero and one. If we use $n$-tuples of these numbers to represent points in the unit cube in $n$-space, we find that the points, rather than appearing to be randomly spread throughout the $n$-cube, may form patterns that suggest the random-number generator will give poor results for certain types of Monte Carlo problems. Both congruential and shift-register generators show regularities of this type, illustrated for 2-space in Fig. 1.

In the case of congruential generators, the pattern is very regular; points in $n$-space fall on a lattice with relatively large spacing compared to the lattice of points with integer coordinates that is the theoretical limit of resolution of a computer with a fixed word size. The particular shape of the lattice associated with a congruential generator depends on the multiplier used in the generator.

If we characterize a lattice in $n$-dimensions by the smallest number of hyperplanes that contain all points produced by the generator, we find that all points, for a congruential generator with modulus $m$, must lie in fewer than $(n!m)^{1/n}$ parallel hyperplanes. For example, in a binary computer with 32-bit words, $m = 2^{32}$, and no matter what the multiplier or starting value of the congruential sequence, fewer than 2,953 hyperplanes will contain all 3-tuples, fewer than 566 hyperplanes will contain all 4-tuples, and fewer than 41 hyperplanes will contain all 10-tuples.

In Fig. 1 the lattices are for modulus $2^{10}$, so that $(n!m)^{1/n} = (2\times 2^{10})^{1/2} \cong 45$ In fact, all points are contained in 21 lines for the first lattice and 5 lines for the second.

**Shift-Register Generators.** The theory can be described by means of a linear transformation over a binary vector space. We start with a vector of zeros and ones; say, $\beta = (1,0,1,1,0,1)$. Then, if $T$ is a $6 \times 6$ matrix with elements in the field with two elements (0 and 1, with arithmetic modulo 2), we form a sequence of vectors by repeated multiplication by the matrix $T$:

$$\beta,\ \beta T,\ \beta T^2,\ \beta T^3, \ldots.$$

If $T$ is nonsingular, this sequence will repeat with the smallest integer $k$, such that $\beta = \beta T^k$; i.e., $\beta$ is a characteristic vector belonging to the characteristic root 1 of $T^k$. Details depend on factors of the characteristic polynomial of $T$. Excellent accounts are in the books by Berlekamp (1968) and by Golomb (1967).

In practice, we seek matrices $T$ and a starting vector $\beta$ so that the period is long and so that multiplication by $T$ can be carried out with a few computer instructions. For example, for $1 \times 6$ binary vectors, we might choose $T = (I + R^2)(I + L^3)$, where $R$ and $L$ are matrices that produce right and left shifts:

$$R = \begin{pmatrix} 0 & 1 & 0 & 0 & 0 & 0 \\ 0 & 0 & 1 & 0 & 0 & 0 \\ 0 & 0 & 0 & 1 & 0 & 0 \\ 0 & 0 & 0 & 0 & 1 & 0 \\ 0 & 0 & 0 & 0 & 0 & 1 \\ 0 & 0 & 0 & 0 & 0 & 0 \end{pmatrix}$$

$$L = \begin{pmatrix} 0 & 0 & 0 & 0 & 0 & 0 \\ 1 & 0 & 0 & 0 & 0 & 0 \\ 0 & 1 & 0 & 0 & 0 & 0 \\ 0 & 0 & 1 & 0 & 0 & 0 \\ 0 & 0 & 0 & 1 & 0 & 0 \\ 0 & 0 & 0 & 0 & 1 & 0 \end{pmatrix}$$

Then $R^s$ and $L^s$ will produce right or left shifts of $s$ positions, and the multiplication of $\beta$ by, say, $T = (I + R^2)(I + L^3)$ can be carried out by shifting and adding (exclusive "or") as follows:

$$\begin{aligned} (1\ 0\ 1\ 1\ 0\ 1) &= \beta \\ (0\ 0\ 1\ 0\ 1\ 1) &= \beta R^2 \\ (1\ 0\ 0\ 1\ 1\ 0) &= \beta(I + R^2) \\ (1\ 1\ 0\ 0\ 0\ 0) &= \beta(I + R^2)L^3 \\ (0\ 1\ 0\ 1\ 1\ 0) &= \beta(I + R^2)(I + L^3). \end{aligned}$$

Many of the shift-register generators for large computers are of this type. For $1 \times 31$ binary vectors, any of these three choices of $T$,

$$\begin{aligned} T &= (I + R^3)(I + L^{28}), \\ T &= (I + R^6)(I + L^{25}), \\ T &= (I + R^{13})(I + L^{18}), \end{aligned}$$

(or their transposes) will generate all possible nonnull vectors; i.e., the period is $2^{31} - 1$ and any nonnull starting vector may be used.

For $1 \times 32$ binary vectors (the full word for IBM 360 machines), there is no matrix of the above form that has full period; however, $T = (I + R^{15})(I + L^{17})$ or its transpose has period 99.95% of the possible maximum of $2^{32} - 1$.

A *simple* shift-register generator is one for which the matrix $T$ is a particularly simple matrix, called a "companion matrix," of the form (say, for $n = 6$)

$$C = \begin{pmatrix} 0 & 1 & 0 & 0 & 0 & 0 \\ 0 & 0 & 1 & 0 & 0 & 0 \\ 0 & 0 & 0 & 1 & 0 & 0 \\ 0 & 0 & 0 & 0 & 1 & 0 \\ 0 & 0 & 0 & 0 & 0 & 1 \\ c_0 & c_1 & c_2 & c_3 & c_4 & c_5 \end{pmatrix}$$

If $R$ is the right-shift-one matrix and $\gamma$ is the constant binary vector $(c_0, c_1, \ldots, c_5)$, then $\beta C$ is either $\beta R$ or $\beta R + \gamma$, depending on whether the last element of the vector $\beta$ is 0 or 1. Simple shift-register sequences are very easy to generate in a computer, but they are obviously unsuitable for general Monte Carlo use, since half of the time a new point will be produced by shifting coordinates of the previous point one position. Thus, half of the points $(x, y)$ will be on the line $2y = x$. This is a flaw common to all shift-register generators: If $\beta, \beta T, \beta T^2, \ldots$ is any shift-register sequence, there is a nonsingular matrix $Q$ such that half of the points produced by successive pairs of elements in the sequence $\beta Q, \beta TQ, \beta T^2Q, \ldots$ will lie on the line $2y = x$.

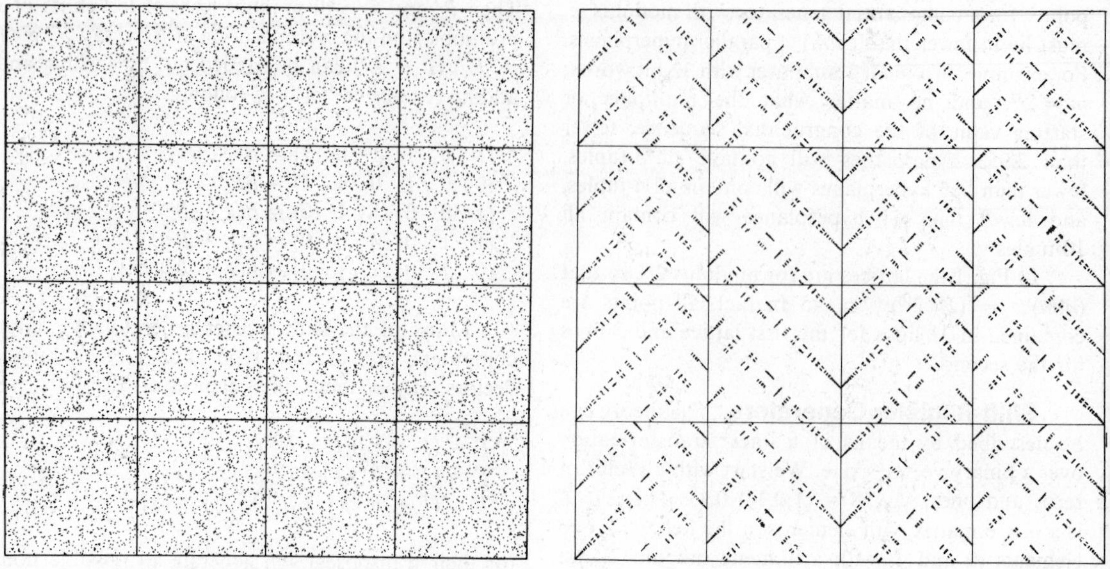

**Fig. 2.** The parking-lot test where each sector has a capacity of 1,000 cars (random points). Left: Bird's-eye view of a lot filled with a good generator (algorithm M). Right: The lot filled with the 31-bit shift-register generator discussed in text.

REGULARITIES IN SHIFT-REGISTER GENERATORS. Since the theory of shift-register generators is similar to that of congruential generators, in the sense that we have a linear transformation on binary vectors rather than on the residues of some modulus *m*, we should expect to find some sort of linear patterns in the output. We do, except that when the binary vectors are viewed as the representation of an integer to the base 2, the linear patterns get folded over and distorted, much as the original linear sedimentary patterns in the earth are distorted and folded over to produce the patterns we observe millions of years later. Two examples of this type of regularity are in Fig. 1.

Regularity in shift-register generators is not so easy to characterize as that of congruential generators, but it is there all the same, and should be taken into account in considering the kind of Monte Carlo problems for which the generator is used.

The examples in Fig. 1 are for a 12-bit word, to illustrate the situation. Ordinarily, for 32-bit words or larger, regularities in 2-space are not evident for congruential generators, and only in higher dimensions do they become a problem. However, shift-register regularities may cause trouble in the plane, even with a large computer such as the IBM 360. For example, Fig. 2 shows the results of the "parking lot" test applied to a shift-register generator and to a good generator. In this test, "cars" are parked in a large car park until each of its 16 sections with capacity of 1,000 cars is filled. The left picture is a bird's-eye view of the lot filled by a good random-number generator, and the right picture shows the result of filling the lot with the very shift-register generator (31 bits, right shift 3, left shift 28) that was proposed as the successor to congruential generators for the IBM 360, after regularities in congruential generators were discovered.

**Combining Generators.** Congruential and shift-register generators have regularities that make them individually unsuitable for general Monte Carlo use, but combining the generators in various ways appears to produce satisfactory sequences. For example, in a 32-bit machine, the congruential sequence $x_{i+1} \equiv 69069 x_i \mod 2^{32}$ and the shift register sequence $\beta \rightarrow \beta(I + R^{15})(I + L^{17})$ may be combined by adding (either by an *arithmetic* or an *exclusive "or"* addition). The result appears to be a quite random sequence with period about $5 \times 10^{18}$.

Another method, known as algorithm M, combines two sequences of uniform variates $U_1$, $U_2$, $U_3$, . . . and $V_1$, $V_2$, $V_3$, . . ., with magnitude between 0 and 1, produced by two simple methods (e.g., a congruential and a shift-register generator). Suppose, say, that memory locations $C(1)$, $C(2)$, . . ., $C(100)$ are filled with $U$. Then one generates a new $V$, uses it to get an index $J$ from 1 to 100 by taking the greatest integer in $1 + 100 * V$, uses $C(J)$ as the next random number, and then fills location $C(J)$ with a newly generated $U$.

Both methods for combining generators have passed extensive tests for randomness and have also resisted attempts to display regularities of the type shown in Fig. 1 for congruential or shift-register generators used alone. Thus, at the time of this writing, it appears that by perhaps doubling or tripling the time required for the simplest generators (combining them in various ways), satisfactory sequences can be produced for general Monte Carlo use. There is no assurance that a new level of sophistication for simulation problems will not find these methods unsatisfactory, but the situation looks promising, since regularities in the latest methods appear to be of the magnitude of limitations imposed by the fixed word size of the computer.

### References


1964. Hammersley, J. M., and D. C. Handscomb. *Monte Carlo Methods*. London: Methuen.

1967. Golomb, S. W. *Shift Register Sequences*. New York: Holden Day.

1968. Berlekamp, E. R. *Algebraic Coding Theory*. New York: McGraw-Hill.

1969. Knuth, Donald E. *The Art of Computer Programming*, vol. 2 (*Seminumerical Algorithms*). Reading, Mass.: Addison Wesley.

1972. Marsaglia, G. "The Structure of Linear Congruential Sequences," in S. K. Zaremba (Ed.), *Applications of Number Theory to Numerical Analysis*. New York: Academic Press.


G. Marsaglia

## READ-ONLY STORE

For articles on related subjects *see* Cycle Time; Memory: Main; Microprogramming; and Storage Hierarchies.

For articles on related terms *see* Access Time; and Bootstrap.

Read-only storage is based on a wide spectrum of storage technologies, many of which should be more accurately referred to as "slow write" storages. The basic idea behind the read-only store is that, for a number of applications, the contents of the storage are relatively fixed for a long period of time. In fact, for some applications, the contents of storage are not altered during the life of the machine. For example, tables that translate coded representations of numbers from one type to another can be easily implemented by read-only storage.

**Fig. 1.** A 24,000-bit read-only store chip, using field-effect transistor technology packaged in a 1-in. square metallized ceramic substrate.

The memory cycle of read-only storage is shortened because it does not have to be regenerated, since its contents are fixed. In addition, since a store operation cannot be performed by the system, the accessing mechanism usually can be designed to operate faster than otherwise. Also, in most situations, the read-only memory system will be less expensive than a read-write memory with corresponding performance.

Many technologies have been used and applied to read-only store. These include the diode matrix, the card-capacitor approach, and magnetic or transformer type read-only storage.

Read-only storage has been used quite extensively for microprogrammed implementations of the control function—controlling the action of an instruction execution. For this function, the read-only storage has to be as fast as the basic cycle time of the machine.

Another use of read-only storage is the area of the bootstrap loader, which is a program that is permanently stored as part of the main memory of the system. Control is transferred to this program on machine startup so that other programs can be called in an orderly way and control can be transferred to them.

REFERENCE

1970. Husson, S. S. *Microprogramming: Principles and Practices*. Englewood Cliffs, N.J.: Prentice-Hall.

M. J. FLYNN

## REAL-TIME APPLICATIONS

For articles on related subjects *see* ADMINISTRATIVE-BUSINESS APPLICATIONS; COMMUNICATIONS AND COMPUTERS; DATA BASE AND DATA BASE MANAGEMENT; MULTIPROGRAMMING; REENTRANT PROGRAM; and TERMINALS.
For articles on related terms *see* APPLICATIONS PROGRAMMING; CENTRAL PROCESSING UNIT; FRONT END; OPERATING SYSTEMS; and SOFTWARE.

Real-time applications have been well established in the field of computer systems for at least the past decade, and in certain areas of computer usage have become virtually the exclusive mode of data processing. This approach to computer applications can perhaps be best described by contrasting it with "batch" processing, the prevailing form of computer utilization before the advent of the more sophisticated systems concepts that underlie real-time processing.

**What Are Real-Time Applications?** In batch processing, transactions against a file of data are accumulated until a sufficient number are present to warrant mass updating of a master file. This type of processing is particularly suitable for accounting applications such as payroll accounting or accounts receivable, in which master files are updated with new transactions periodically and in which output is produced according to a predetermined processing cycle. The processing cycle for this type of system is ordinarily defined by the frequency with which the master file must be updated.

Fig. 1 provides a simplified illustration of a batch data processing system for billing. During each processing cycle, receipts and new charges are batched for entry, as are status changes (open account, close account, change address, etc.). After keypunching, both classes of input go into an edit/convert run where they are validated as to correctness of account number and completeness of information. After editing, each item is written out to magnetic tape for subsequent processing. The next processing step is to sort these transactions into the same sequence as the master file. The master file may then be updated during what is by far the most complicated and time-consuming run in the system. Outputs from this run include the updated master (which will become input to this same run during the next processing cycle) and other tapes, which go into output-edit runs to produce new bills and management reports.

What is a real-time system, and how does it compare with the batch-processing type of system just described? Real-time systems can best be differentiated by their quality of *responsiveness*. Conventional systems "respond" to their business environment by producing the requisite journals, reports, and other outputs according to their carefully prescheduled batch-processing cycles. Real-time systems, in contrast, can respond immediately at the *time* a transaction occurs. Thus, a bank teller using a terminal can obtain immediate information about a customer's current balance while the customer waits at the window for completion of the transaction.

The question of how responsive a system must be before it merits designation as real-time is, of course, a relative one. In some situations, usually those in which the customer is awaiting a decision based upon the computer's response, the reply will be required within a few seconds; in other circumstances, a longer response time can be tolerated. Real-time systems in which there is rapid and frequent interaction between human and machine are sometimes said to operate in a "conversational" mode.

Most real-time applications require hardware and software that provide fast responses to the terminal operator. From a human factors standpoint, a system response time of 3 to 5 sec on the

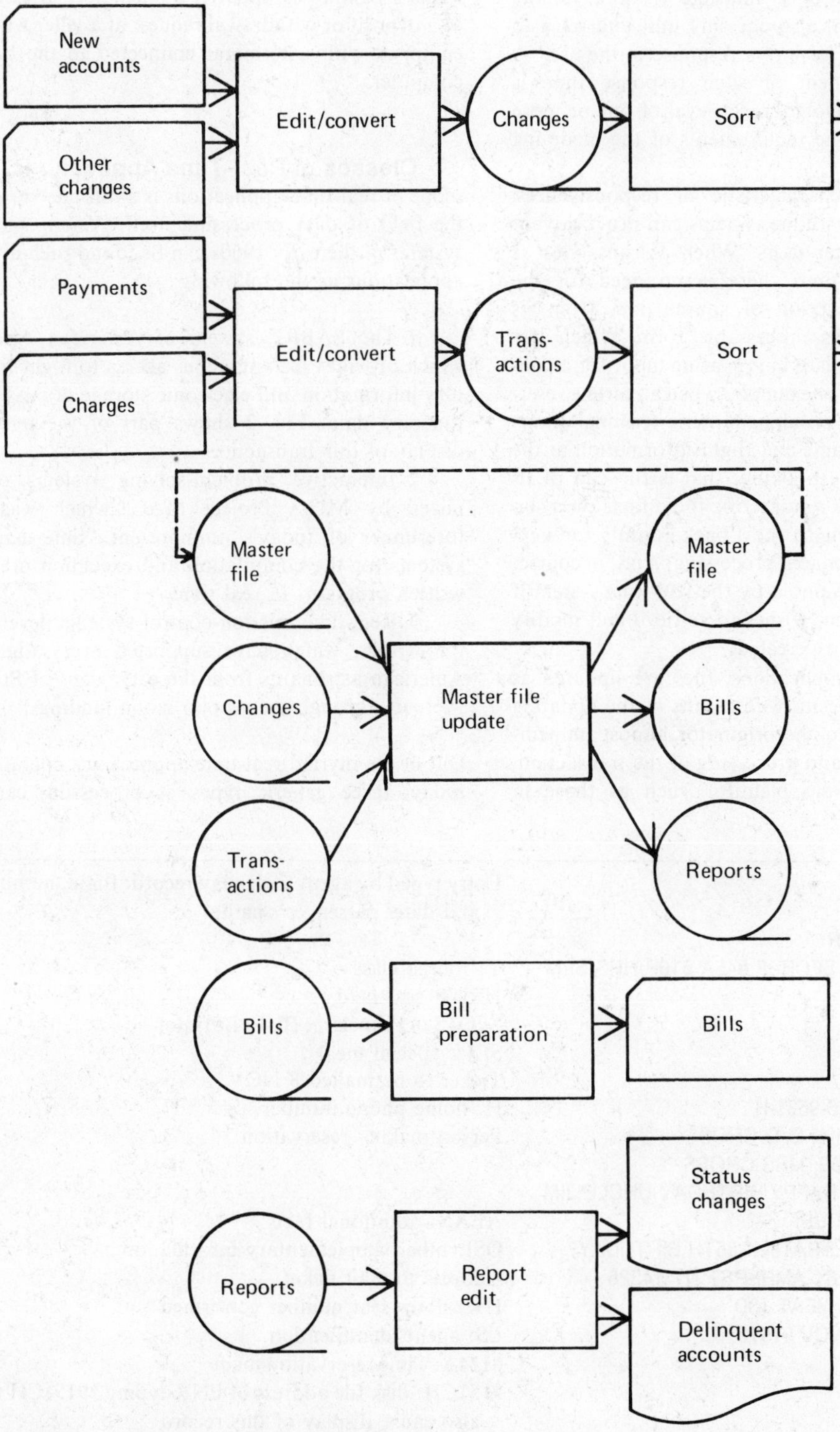


**Fig. 1.** Batch-processing application.

average is desirable. This covers the elapsed time from the dispatch of a message from a remote terminal into a central processing unit and back to the terminal in the form of a response to the user. A significant component of such response time is usually the time devoted to retrieval of one or more records to satisfy the requirements of the incoming transactions.

Besides this characteristic of responsiveness, other features of real-time systems can prove advantageous to computer users. When a transaction is processed in real-time, there is no need for the laborious retranscription of source data from its original form to its processable form, which frequently must take place in preparing input for a conventional system. For example, when an airline reservation agent using an alphanumeric terminal enters each passenger's name and flight information at the time she makes the booking, that is the end of it. There is no need to retranscribe these facts on a slip of paper to be sent to the "back room" for keypunching and subsequent processing. And, of course, there is no delay imposed by the real-time system if the reservation agent wishes to retrieve and modify the record she has just created.

In real-time applications, files are updated as new transactions occur, with results of the updating transmitted back to the originator almost immediately upon receipt and processing of the transaction. Examples of this are plentiful, such as those in savings bank accounting systems in which the customer's balance is updated immediately after entry of a deposit or withdrawal request at a teller window equipped with a terminal connected to the bank's computer.

**Classes of Real-Time Applications.** The scope of real-time applications is almost as varied as the field of data processing itself. Among pioneer systems of the early 1960s can be found such diverse applications as the following:

1. The SABRE system of American Airlines, which provides instantaneous access to flight inventory information and electronic storage of passenger itinerary data. Fig. 2 shows part of the terminal display of this transaction.
2. Interactive problem-solving systems epitomized by MIT's Project MAC, which was the forerunner of today's omnipresent "time-sharing" systems for the compilation and execution of user-written programs in real time.
3. Real-time mission-control systems developed for NASA, which have supported every flight of American astronauts from the early days of Project Mercury through the Apollo moon landings.

Out of the myriad real-time applications operational today, three generic types of processing can be

| | |
|---|---|
| *92/10 NOV-HART | Entry typed by agent to display record: flight, number and date, passenger's name |
| HART/JAMES MR | |
| 1. 92Y10NOV HS1 SFOBUF 845A 516P HRS SPM | Y: tourist class<br>HS1: 1 seat held<br>SFO: San Francisco; BUF: Buffalo;<br>SPM: special meal |
| TKTG TAM0 8NOV/ | Ticket to be mailed 8 NOV. |
| FONE NYC-212 AA6-9531-H | H: home phone number |
| NYC-212 TW9-6431-H C/O CROSS | Person making reservation |
| RCVD-PSGRS NIECE, MRS CROSS | |
| AFAX CAKE WITH HAPPY BIRTHDAY UNCLE JIM SFO SKY CHEF | AFAX: additional facts |
| OSI PSGR IS CELEBRATING 85TH BIRTHDAY | OSI: other supplementary information |
| TAM 475 FOREST ST AMHERST NY 14226 | Address to mail ticket |
| JFK 17Y10NOV HK SEAT 18D | HK: notes seat number confirmed |
| NYC-LS 0124A/04NOV 9151CH | LS: agent identification<br>0124A: Time reservation made<br>9151CH: disk file address of PNR-typing *9151CH will also cause display of this record |

**Fig. 2.** Annotated sample of terminal display of passenger name record (PNR) on the SABRE system.

identified which correspond to these landmark efforts.

There is, first, transaction-oriented processing in which clerical personnel interact with a computer for the entry and recording of business transactions such as airline reservations. One characteristic of such transaction processing is that the terminal operator is carefully guided through a set of input/output operations by the computer, which responds with an error message should an erroneous or unacceptable entry be submitted. For example, an airline reservation agent would be notified if she tried to book a passenger on a nonexistent flight or on a flight already sold out. Similarly, a bank teller would be reminded if she entered an inactive account number or a withdrawal request that caused a deposit balance to become negative.

A second class of real-time processing involves interactive problem solving in a manner less highly structured than transaction processing. Here, terminal users are provided with generalized software packages such as those for information retrieval, which allow them to enter the parameters of a retrieval request and trigger a search of system files. For example, a data base of personnel information might be interrogated to find out how many employees fit a pattern of more than ten years of service with salary level greater than $10,000 or who have a college degree. Another category of interactive processing permits on-line program development, whereby program instructions are input at a terminal with a request that the program be immediately compiled and executed.

A third class of real-time system is found in industrial applications in the field of continuous process control, where a computer is utilized to adjust the performance of other equipment in a continuous process such as petroleum production. Such process-control systems may be of the "open loop" variety in which the computer prints out, on an exception basis, messages requiring remedial action by an operator to adjust system flows, or they may be "closed loop" in which the computer itself is able, through links to sensors and control equipment, to adjust the production process without human intervention. In either case, there must be feedback from the process control equipment to the computer in real time, and resultant messages must be output from the computer within the same immediate time frame.

**Equipment Requirements for Real-Time Applications.** Real-time applications of the kinds described are operational on a wide range of equipment, from minicomputers with limited storage capacity serving only a few terminals, up to the largest systems available today which embody multiple processing units and memory modules, billions of characters of immediate access storage, and hundreds of terminals. But regardless of size, the equipment employed in real-time systems has a number of common characteristics. Although not all real-time applications require all these features, the vast majority will be found to employ them at least to some degree. Fig. 3 provides a schematic of the major equipment elements usually present in a real-time processing environment. Descriptions of these elements follow.

TERMINALS. Terminals for real-time applications are almost as varied as the applications themselves. In some instances, the terminal may be a simple numeric input device, such as a Touchtone telephone keyboard, with responses provided by computer-generated voice answer. At the other end of the complexity scale, one can find "intelligent" terminals, which in actuality may be minicomputers with enough storage capacity and logic to perform extensive preliminary processing before accepting a transaction for transmission to the central processing unit.

Terminals for real-time applications can also be differentiated as special-purpose or general-purpose types. Special-purpose terminals are employed in such applications as stock quotation, airline reservations, and on-line banking. Such terminals may be equipped with special-purpose function keys, specialized print symbols, and templates or masks for specialized displays. However, many real-time applications, in particular those for handling relatively unstructured retrieval requests or interactive problem solving, require only a standard low-speed Teletype device or an input keyboard combined with a data display screen.

COMMUNICATIONS FRONT END. A communications front end is necessary to interface the lines connecting remote terminals to the central processing unit. It performs such functions as assembling incoming messages, detecting transmission errors, and routing responses back to the terminal operators. In large systems, this front-end equipment may be a minicomputer and may have associated with it magnetic tapes or disks for message queueing. In smaller systems, front-end functions may be integral to the central processing unit rather than assigned to a separate processor.

CENTRAL PROCESSING UNITS. Two central processing units are shown in Fig. 3 to reflect a characteristic of many real-time configurations that

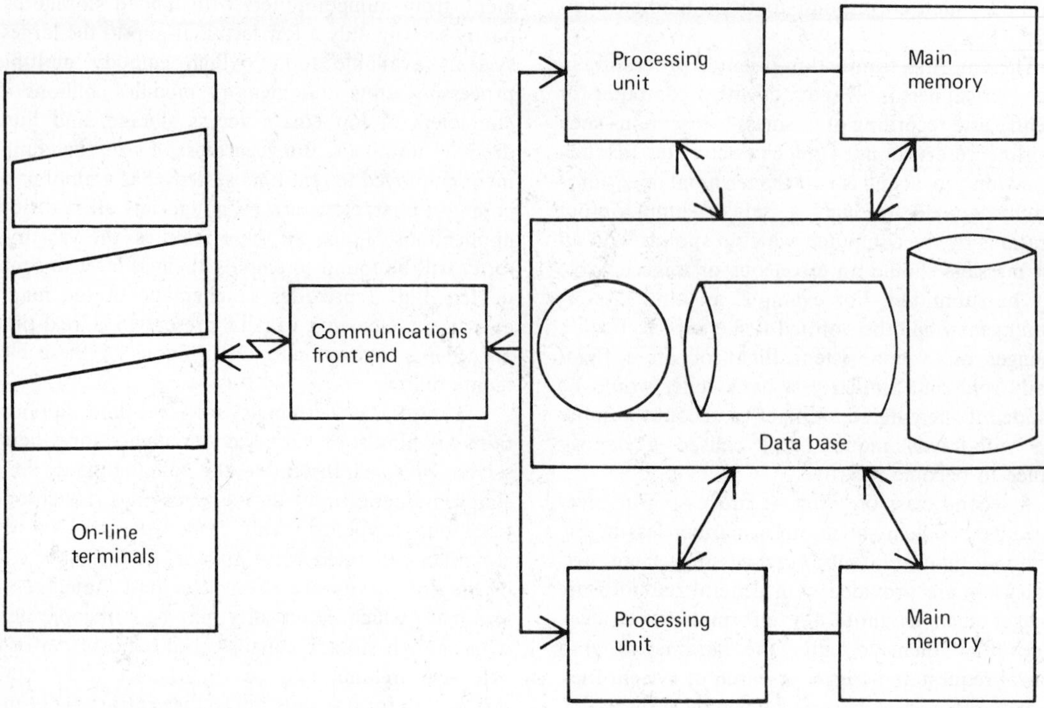


**Fig. 3.** Real-time equipment configuration.

contain dual processing units for greater reliability. In such systems, one processing unit may perform high-priority transaction processing while the other performs lower priority work, perhaps batch processing, with the capability of the second processing unit assuming the on-line processing work load if there is a malfunction in the first.

MAIN MEMORY MODULES. As in the case of the central processing unit, two or more main memory modules may be configured for work-load sharing and enhanced reliability.

IMMEDIATE ACCESS STORAGE. Immediate access storage is found in virtually all real-time applications, and sometimes ranges into the billions of characters for storage of large data bases that must be immediately accessible. In many systems, there is a hierarchy of such storage, ranging from fixed-head drums or disks with access times of a few milliseconds up to large-capacity disk files with access times averaging 100 ms or more. Removable disk storage is also present in many configurations so that files can be conveniently removed and stored, once processing against them is completed. In multiprocessing configurations, each processing unit may have a channel to all the immediate access storage.

OTHER DEVICES. Magnetic tape drives continue to be utilized in real-time applications for such purposes as logging incoming transactions, maintaining duplicate copies of files and transactions for recovery purposes, and performing sorting and other batch processing for low-priority batch applications. More exotic types of storage devices are now beginning to appear as substitutes for, or augmentations of, conventional disk storage units, such as laser memory systems that provide access to billions of characters of storage within a few seconds.

**Software Requirements for Real-Time Applications.** The operation of real-time systems dictates the need for certain kinds of software that might not otherwise be required. Fig. 4 illustrates the major software components typically present in real-time applications. These packages may, in some cases, be housed in a single computer; in more complex systems, they may be distributed among multiple computers (e.g., communications front ends and central processors).

THE OPERATING SYSTEM. All the software functions illustrated in Fig. 4 are under control of an operating system. The operating system maintains

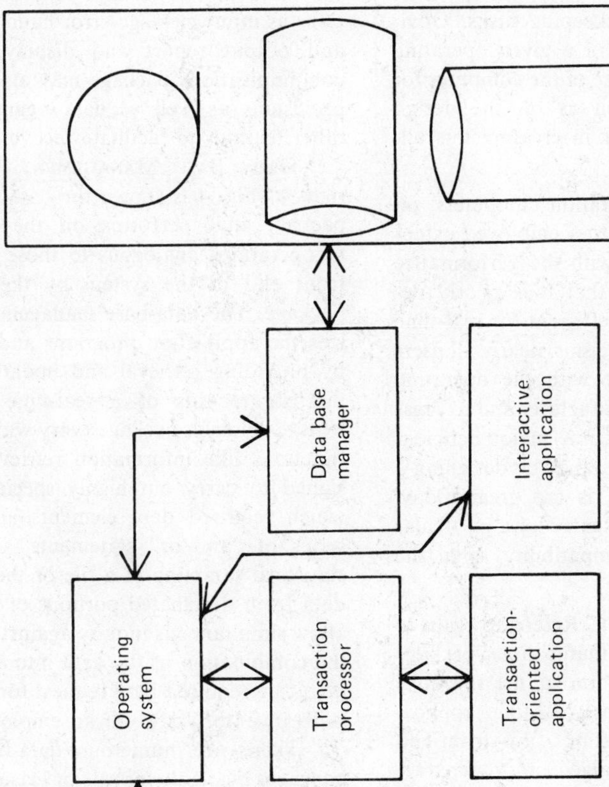

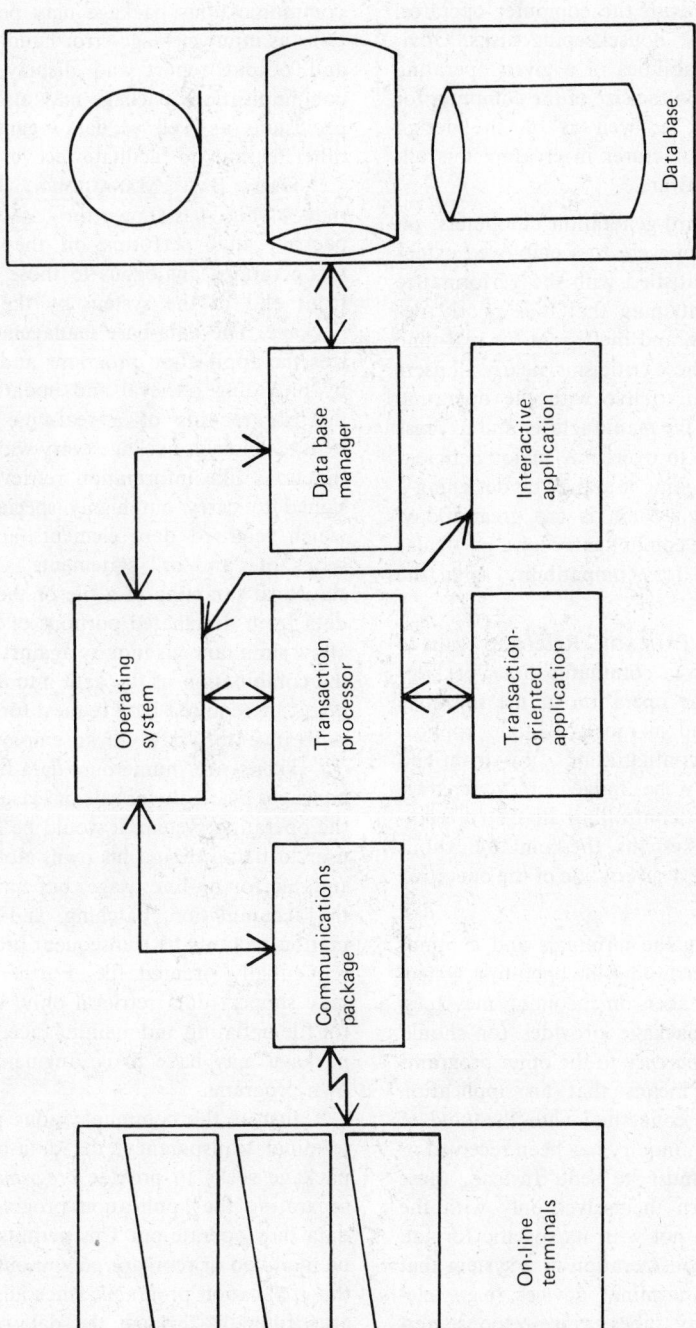


**Fig. 4.** Real-time software packages.

overall control of system operations by scheduling the execution of all other programs, allocating main memory, establishing job priorities, servicing interrupts, communicating with the computer operator, and performing similar housekeeping tasks. Obviously, the precise capabilities of a given operating system are dependent on the size of the computer for which it was written, as well as on the design objectives of the manufacturer in creating this all-important piece of software.

Many users of third-generation computers, on which operating systems were first employed extensively, have been dissatisfied with the performance of this software, maintaining that it is poorly designed, overly complex, and inefficient for real-time applications. Despite these criticisms, nearly all users have made a decision to live with the operating system as delivered by the manufacturer and to press for improved versions to overcome major deficiencies. The penalty for "going it alone" by designing a nonstandard operating system is too great today, since all other software componentry for a particular machine is designed for compatibility with the operating system.

Communications Package. Referring again to Fig. 4, we can identify a communications package required to control the operation of the multiple, remote terminals found in most real-time applications. In some large configurations, this front-end software may actually be lodged in a separate computer dedicated to controlling all system communications. In small systems, the communications package may simply be a subroutine of the operating system.

Besides controlling the terminals and communication lines, and interrupting the operating system when action must be taken on incoming messages, the communications package provides (or should provide) *terminal transparency* to the other programs in the system. This means that an application program need not be concerned with the *kind* of terminal from which an inquiry has been received or to which a message must be sent. Instead, these programs need concern themselves only with the substance of the data, not with its specific format. This is an important consideration in a system that employs a variety of terminal devices (e.g., teletypewriters, cathode-ray tubes, voice-response terminals, or graphics terminals). It is often necessary to change terminal types or upgrade terminal capability as new information needs are identified or as new hardware becomes available. With terminal transparency, flexibility can be achieved by making changes only in the communications front end, *not* in the application programs themselves.

Besides communications network control, a communications package may perform such functions as input message-error handling, input editing, and output report and display formatting. The communications package may also contain security provisions as well as data-logging capability and other features to facilitate recovery.

Data Base Management Package. At the right of Fig. 4 is shown the data-base management package that performs on the data base a set of operations analogous to those performed at the front end of the system by the communications package. The data-base management package services the application programs and the system users by providing retrieval and updating capability for the file records of a real-time system. Specific features of such packages vary widely, especially for functions like information retrieval. Some are designed to carry out highly specialized searches in which required data elements are qualified by a series of "and/or" statements. Others permit the statistical sampling of a file or the accumulation of data from designated portions of a file. Still others allow simultaneous inquiry against multiple files and the combination of file data into a single output, as might be required by a request for both payroll and skills inventory data for an employee.

There are numerous data-base management packages available for sale or lease. As in the case of the operating system, it would be imprudent for the user to try to design his own. Not all packages are suitable for on-line usage, but may instead require the accumulation, batching, and sorting of information requests for subsequent processing against a sequentially ordered file. Further, some packages may support data retrieval only, with no provision for file updating and maintenance, in which case the package may have to be augmented by the user's own programs.

Just as the communications package aims for terminal transparency, the data-base management package seeks to provide *program independence* by separating the application programs from the file data they operate on. This permits the data base to be modified or reorganized without unduly affecting the application programs, since all requests for data are "filtered" through the data-base management package. This is in marked contrast to earlier practice, in which the application programmer was free to design his own files and records, and embed references to these records within his program wherever he, unconstrained by outside standards, found it convenient. Such practice is intolerable in a system in which files frequently must be expanded or reorganized, based on their degree of usage, with data shifted from one physical storage medium to another. The objective of program independence is to permit these changes to the data base without requiring inordinate changes in the application programs that reference the data base.

TRANSACTION PROCESSING PACKAGE. This is the newest category of software package utilized in real-time applications. In earlier real-time systems, transaction-processing functions were performed by specially tailored software; today, many of these functions have been sufficiently well defined that they can be generalized and packaged.

The purpose of the transaction processor is to handle large volumes of specifically defined transactions in a highly efficient manner. Examples of such transactions can be found in booking airline passenger reservations or in recording deposits to savings bank accounts. Transaction processing should be contrasted with interactive problem solving in which the nature of the processing to be performed is determined by the user as he proceeds with his interactive session. In transaction processing, the features and options available to the terminal operator are carefully structured in advance and are performed by specialized application programs under control of the transaction-processing software. Any deviation from the predetermined processing scenario by the operator, such as the entry of an invalid date, results in discontinuation of processing and transmission of an error response.

In a transaction-oriented real-time system, the transaction processing package is activated by the operating system upon receipt of an incoming transaction. It performs initial validation of data, establishes what application program action is required, and reacts to error and other special conditions.

The transaction processor is responsible for maintaining control over real-time application program scheduling. Following the scheduling of an application program as the result of the arrival of a transaction, the transaction processor delivers the input transaction to the application program.

The transaction processor may initiate recovery procedures following abnormal termination of an application program. Such recovery procedures could include scheduling a special routine to repair any files damaged by the malfunctioning program; shutting the program down; releasing any facilities, such as main memory, assigned to the program; and apprising the operator of the problem. The transaction processor may also maintain statistics on such data as transaction volumes processed by type.

**Real-Time Application Processing.** As previously suggested, real-time applications imply a high degree of simultaneity of processing in order to provide fast responses to large numbers of system users. One approach to achieving a high level of throughput in real-time applications lies, of course, in multiprocessing. Here, more than one processing unit is available to handle transactions, as suggested in Fig. 3. But there is a practical limit, especially in business applications, to the amount of simultaneity that can be achieved through the addition of multiple hardware components and the distribution of incoming transactions among them.

Software techniques are commonly employed in transaction-oriented systems to enhance throughput capability. Two of the most common are multiprogramming and reentrancy.

MULTIPROGRAMMING. What is multiprogramming and why does it have such an important role in real-time systems? Like so many other terms in current usage among computer specialists, it has taken on a variety of shades of meaning. In this discussion a multiprogrammed system is defined as one in which several transactions may be in process at the same time inside the central processing unit. This is in contrast to a sequentially programmed system, which disposes of transactions one by one, not permitting a new action to enter the processing cycle until the current one has been completely processed.

Fig. 5 illustrates how a multiprogrammed system operates on inputs received from several remote terminals. An entry is received from terminal 1 and is immediately subjected to analysis by the transaction processor to determine the type of action required. This processing is interrupted by receipt of an entry from terminal 2. After the same preliminary action-code analysis of this second entry, the transaction processor completes its scrutiny of the first entry and activates Application Program A. Application Program A is interrupted by receipt of an entry from terminal 3, which must be given the same preliminary transaction code analysis as were the two preceding entries. On completion of this analysis, the transaction processor reactivates the program that has been interrupted, namely, Application Program A.

Application Program A has by now been twice interrupted, each time because of an external event: receipt of entries from terminals 2 and 3. Now that Application Program A has regained control, it

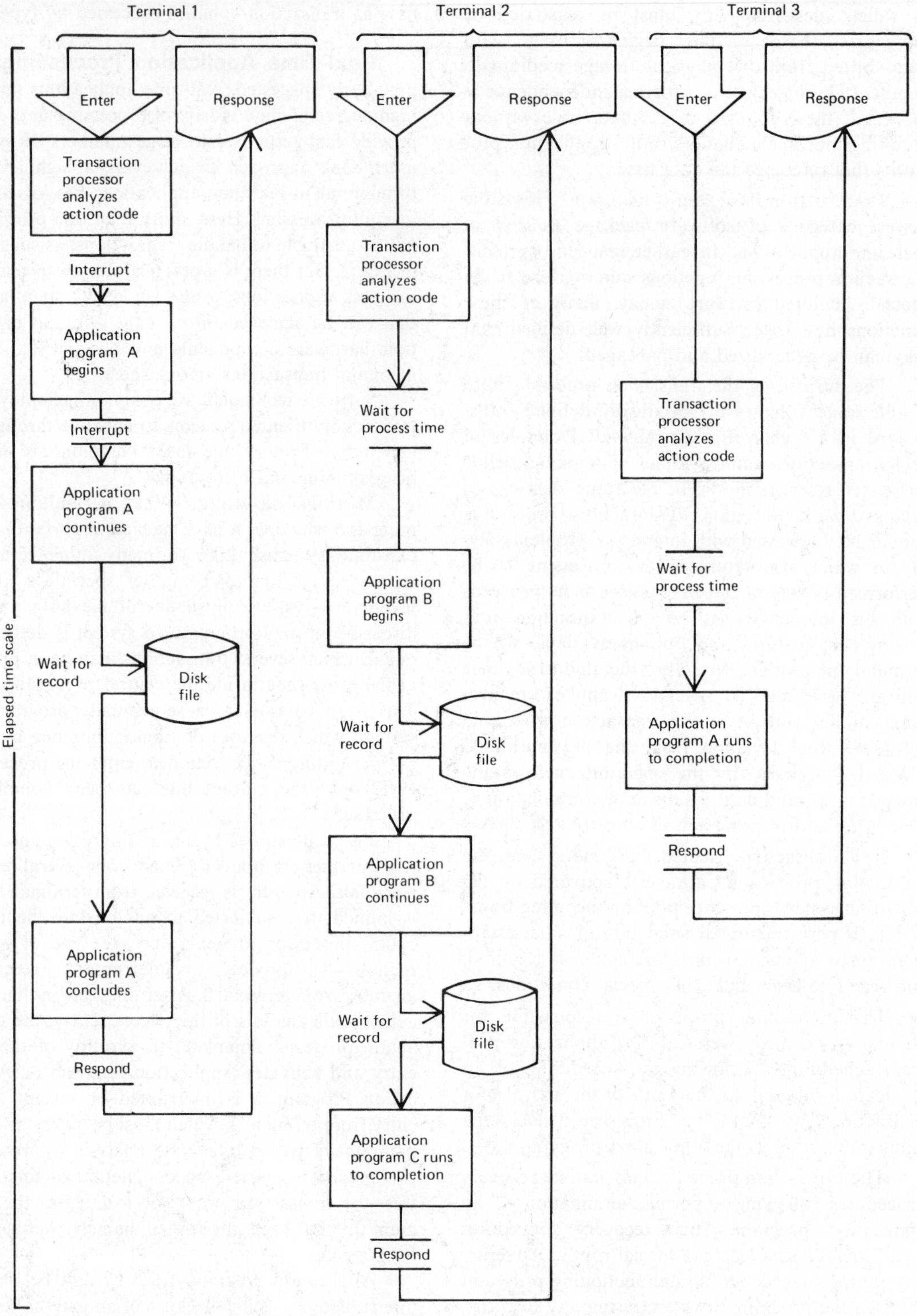


**Fig. 5.** Multiprogrammed system operating on inputs received from remote terminals.

proceeds to a point where it must pause to request a record from the file. At this point, Application Program A requests the transaction processor to obtain the needed file record, and relinquishes control until the record is available. The transaction processor initiates the request and then asks, "Is any other work to be done during this waiting period?" The answer is "Yes," since entries from terminals 2 and 3 are both in queues awaiting processing. The transaction processor selects the entry received from terminal 2 and activates Application Program B, which begins processing and continues until it requires a file record. This wait permits the transaction processor to initiate the processing of the entry from terminal 3.

The entry from terminal 3 is interesting in two respects. First it runs through to completion with no waits for file records and generates a response to the terminal ahead of the other two entries, even though it entered the system after them. It also makes use of the same program (Application Program A) as did the first entry, but because of a difference in the input data, a different processing path through Application Program A is selected. Both entry 1 and entry 3 might, for example, be airline reservations, but 3 might contain an erroneous date, which obviates the need to consult any file records.

After entry 3 is disposed of, the transaction processor discovers that the file record requested by Program B is now ready, and so control returns to this program, which almost immediately relinquishes control with a request for a second file record. This is a rather typical occurrence, in which the first record requested might be an index containing the file address of a second, or master, record. At any rate, during this second wait, Program A can be reactivated, as the file record requested by it is now ready. The availability of this record permits Program A to process entry 1 through to completion.

All that now remains is to dispose of entry 2. This can be done as soon as the second record requested by Program B is available. Note, however, that there is a transfer of control from Program B to Program C, which contains the logic for operating on the newly obtained record and for preparing the response to terminal 2.

Several revealing inferences can be drawn from the preceding example:

1. The usage of relatively slow disk storage with the resultant waits for records to be fetched into main memory constitutes one of the principal reasons for multiprogramming. Essentially, the idea is to let some other program make use of the central processing unit while the access mechanism is seeking file records.

2. There are two sources of interruption of an application program: receipt of input from the outside world and receipt of input from the file on completion of a seek.

3. The processing sequence and the time required to process a given input are dependent upon what other inputs also happen to be undergoing processing. If, in the example, entry 3 had *not* come into the system, entries 1 and 2 would not have been interrupted so frequently. And, if the entries from the three terminals had been received in a slightly different sequence (say 2-3-1), we would have to redraw the schematic entirely to gain a picture of the processing operations.

4. A transaction processing package is essential to determine what must be done next by the system.

The schematic is, of course, greatly simplified. There may be tens or hundreds of terminals associated with a system, each capable of generating any one of two or three dozen different kinds of entries. And the reference files in the system may be on several modules of disk storage, on drums or tapes, or on all these in combination. Multiprogramming can make a real-time system efficient, but at the same time dangerously complex in its operation. And the planning, programming, and system testing required to produce this efficient but complex system are technically formidable and costly.

REENTRANCY. In addition to the multiprocessing and multiprogramming approaches, further simultaneity of operations and hence greater throughput and responsiveness can be achieved in real-time systems by means of program reentrancy. By employing this programming technique, one resident copy of an application program can be used to process multiple transactions of the same type in a highly efficient manner. Suppose, for example, that a banking system simultaneously receives several requests to debit customer account records from various terminals. It would be desirable if the transaction processor were able to initiate the processing of a second transaction and perhaps a third or fourth before the first transaction had been completely processed by the application program involved.

As we have seen, an application program frequently interrupts its processing of a transaction at some intermediate point prior to completion of processing; at that point, processing could begin on another transaction of the same type. But this is possible *only* if the application program is reentrant, i.e., written in such a manner that it is capable of starting to process the new transaction without switches, variables, or working storage locations still set to handle the suspended processing of the first transaction.

Simultaneity in processing several identical transactions could, of course, also be achieved by having multiple copies of the same application program resident in main memory and assigning a single transaction to each, but the preferred method is to write these programs in such a manner that simultaneity is achieved through the ability to re-enter one resident copy of an application program with a new transaction at any time.

**System Reliability.** No discussion of real-time processing is complete without emphasis on the heightened requirements for reliability in these kinds of systems. Special provision must be made to compensate for equipment malfunctions or program errors in such a way that these can be isolated and corrected or bypassed without causing the entire system to "crash" and without destroying or damaging file data. This implies software capability, in conjunction with hardware features, to accomplish "graceful degradation" that could, for example, permit one processor to assume the entire work load in the event of malfunction in a multiprocessing configuration. It also implies programs and procedures for recovering from errors and restoring the system and its associated files to its users in such a manner that work can proceed with minimum need for manual reentry of transactions or file data.

As real-time systems evolved from their tentative beginnings more than ten years ago, there has been a steady increase in the numbers of applications and the size of the systems devoted to such processing. Today, real-time processing is the normative mode for numerous applications in stock brokerage, transportation, banking, and retail merchandising as well as countless nonbusiness applications. Today's equipment and software packages are, because of the importance of such processing, becoming increasingly oriented to providing the high level of performance and reliability that are mandatory for real-time applications.

REFERENCES

1967. Martin, J. *Design of Real-Time Computer Systems*. Englewood Cliffs, N.J.: Prentice-Hall.

1967. Yourdon, E. (Ed.). *Real-Time Systems Design*. Cambridge, Mass.: Information and Systems Institute.

1969. Blumenthal, S. C. *Management Information Systems: A Framework for Planning and Development*. Englewood Cliffs, N.J.: Prentice-Hall.

1972. Head, R. V. *Manager's Guide to Management Information Systems*. Englewood Cliffs, N.J.: Prentice-Hall.

R. V. HEAD

## REAL-TIME CLOCK. *See* INTERVAL TIMER.

## RECORD

For articles on related subjects *see* BLOCK AND BLOCKING; DATA SET; and FILES.

A record is an aggregate of data transcribed, or in a form suitable for transcription, between a computer and an external medium. Each record comprises data that have an underlying relationship to one another. For example, a personnel record usually contains data such as Social Security number, first name, middle initial, last name, date of birth, next of kin, and home address. All these data are *attributes* (descriptors, locators, identifiers, etc.) peculiar to this individual.

Data elements in a record may be of similar or dissimilar types: bits, numbers, character strings, etc. The contents of punched cards and printer lines are often called "unit records," since these document lengths are predefined by associated electromechanical devices. Magnetic tape and disk drives usually accommodate *variable-length records* in which the amount of data per record varies according to activity, age, etc., of the individual. Records of the same type are usually grouped into larger aggregates, called "files" or "data sets." When written sequentially into a file, records are collected into intermediate aggregates called "blocks," whose lengths are efficient for transcription to tape or disk devices. In theory, a file could comprise a single block containing all its records. In practice, a large file may contain hundreds or thousands of blocks, each containing one or more records.

D. N. FREEMAN

# RECURSION

For articles on related subjects *see* ITERATION; LOOP; and STACK.
For articles on related terms *see* BACKUS-NAUR FORM; SYMBOL MANIPULATION; and TURING MACHINE.

Recursion refers to several related concepts in computer science and mathematics. One or more functions of an integer variable are defined by giving initial values and by giving the value for larger integers in terms of smaller ones. No single definition is generally accepted, so we will give examples of increasing complexity.

## Recursive Relations

1. The Fibonacci sequence is given by the equations

$$f_0 = 1,$$
$$f_1 = 1,$$
$$f_{n+1} = f_n + f_{n-1}.$$

2. When differential equations are to be solved numerically, recursion relations such as

$$f(x_0 + nh) = F(f(x_0 + (n - 1)h), f(x_0 + (n - 2)h), \ldots, f(x_0 + (n - k)h))$$

arise where $f$ is, in general, a vector of real numbers.

3. When linear differential equations are solved by series, recursion relations for the coefficients of the powers of the independent variables arise.

**Recursive Functions.** The systematic study of recursion began in the 1920s when mathematical logic began to treat questions of definability, computability, and decidability. An important role is played by *primitive recursive functions*.

Primitive recursive functions are integer functions of integers built up from addition and multiplication of integers, and previously defined primitive recursive functions by the primitive recursion scheme:

$$f(0, x_2, \ldots, x_k) = g(x_2, \ldots, x_k),$$
$$f(x_1 + 1, x_2, \ldots, x_k) = h(f(x_1, \ldots, x_k), x_1, \ldots, x_k).$$

Here, $g$ and $h$ are primitive recursive functions of $k - 1$ and $k + 1$ arguments, respectively. As an example, we define $n!$ by $n! = f(n)$ (where $f(0) = 1$ and $n$ is a positive integer) and $f(n + 1) = (n + 1) \cdot f(n)$. So, in this case, $g$ is a function of 0 arguments, namely, the constant 1, and $h(u,v) = (v + 1)u$.

All the common functions of number theory are primitive recursive. Moreover, many important functions on countable domains other than the integers correspond to primitive recursive functions when we choose a specific enumeration for the domain.

Primitive recursive functions are included in general recursive functions. The definition of general recursive functions is like that given above for primitive recursive functions, except that the relations are replaced by an arbitrary finite collection of equations relating the values of $f$ for different arguments, and the function is considered defined if and only if a unique value of $f(x_1, \ldots, x_k)$ can be deduced from the equations for each $k$-tuplet $(x_1, \ldots, x_k)$. Naturally, if someone gives you an arbitrary collection of such relations, you may not be able to determine whether $f(x_1, \ldots, x_k)$ is uniquely determined, so you may not know whether you have a general recursive function. This difficulty is unavoidable. There is no way to give a definition scheme that is always guaranteed to give a function but which will give all computable functions. This fact is itself expressed in the terminology of recursive function theory by the statement that the set of computable functions is recursively enumerable but not recursive. The famous example of a general recursive function that is not primitive recursive is the Ackermann function, defined by the equations

$$A(0,n,p) = n + p, \quad A(1,0,p) = 0$$
$$A(m + 2,0,p) = 1$$

and

$$A(m + 1,n + 1,p) = A(m,A(m + 1,n,p),p).$$

An important result for computer science is that the general recursive functions coincide with the functions defined by a Turing machine, which is a simple form of computer. They also coincide with the functions of integers defined by Algol or Fortran programs, assuming that the program can cope with whatever size integers arise.

Both programs and general recursion schemata, in general, give partial functions because the computation may terminate for some values of the arguments and not for others.

The study of computable functions is the domain of recursive function theory, an active branch of mathematics. The connection between current research in recursive function theory and computing practice, or even current research in computer science, is rather tenuous. This situation might change because of developments in either field.

**Recursive Procedures.** In programming, it is frequently convenient to have a procedure use itself as a subprocedure. If the procedure does this, it is called "recursive." Recursive procedures are particularly natural in dealing with symbolic expressions because the structure of the programs often matches the structure of the data. As far as programming languages are concerned, recursive procedures are quite natural; it requires a special statement in the definition of the language to forbid them. However, implementing them requires that a special kind of object code be compiled, and early programming languages like Fortran do not allow them. The problem is that variables in the program correspond to locations in the machine, and when the program is called by itself, it will use these same locations, overwriting their previous contents. Therefore, recursive programs use an array, called the "stack,"to store the contents of registers that must be saved. This storage can be done by the calling routine before it enters the subroutine, or it can be done by the subroutine before it uses the registers, the latter being more common.

After the registers have been saved on the stack, the index into the stack is increased by the number of registers stored, so that subsequent saving on the stack will use fresh registers. When the subroutine exits, the contents of the saved registers are restored from the stack to their previous values, and the stack pointer is reduced by the amount it was previously increased. This is done by the caller or by the subroutine, according to whether the caller or subroutine did the original storing. An alternative technique is to use the stack for all temporary registers. In this case, it is unnecessary to move data around, and it is only necessary to change the stack pointer when subroutines are entered and left. However, this technique uses up the indexing capabilities of some machines that may be wanted for other purposes. Recursive programs can be written in any programming language by explicitly programming the saving and restoring.

The first languages to use recursive subroutines on a regular basis were the IPL languages of Newell, Shaw, and Simon. Lists were used for the stack and the saving and restoring was done explicitly by the programmer. The first language to provide an automatic mechanism for recursion was Lisp. Algol 60 and its successors also allow recursion.

Many computers have special instruction for handling stacks (e.g. the PUSH and POP instructions of the Digital Equipment PDP-10). Other machines, such as the Burroughs 5000 and its successors, have instructions that use a hardware stack directly. These special facilities give a modest increase in the efficiency of recursive programming.

**Recursive Conditional Expressions.** The recursive use of conditional expressions provides an economical and elegant way of specifying the functions that are computable in terms of a collection of base functions. This technique is the basis of the Lisp programming language and also of the theoretical system of D. Scott for studying the properties of computer programs. A conditional expression has the form, in Algol notation, of

$$\textbf{if } p \textbf{ then } a \textbf{ else } b.$$

It is evaluated by first evaluating the propositional expression $p$. If $p$ is TRUE, the value of the conditional expression is that of $a$, and if the value of $p$ is FALSE, the value of the conditional expression is that of $b$. It is important to note that only one of $a$ or $b$ is actually evaluated.

A simple example of the use of conditional expressions is to define the absolute value of a number by

$$|x| = \textbf{if } x < 0 \textbf{ then } -x \textbf{ else } x.$$

Conditional expressions are used to define functions recursively by writing the definition in the form

$$f(x, \ldots, z) \leftarrow \boldsymbol{E}\{x, \ldots, z, f, g, \ldots, h\},$$

where $\boldsymbol{E}$ is an expression involving the variables $x, \ldots, z$, the function $f$ being defined, and known or previously defined functions $g, \ldots, h$. An example of such a definition is

$$n! \leftarrow \textbf{if } n = 0 \textbf{ then } 1 \textbf{ else } n(n-1)!. \quad (1)$$

The general method for evaluating recursive conditional expressions is illustrated by using the above definition to evaluate 3!. Namely, we have

$$\begin{aligned} 3! &= \textbf{if } 3 = 0 \textbf{ then } 1 \textbf{ else } 3\cdot(3-1)! \\ &= 3\cdot 2! = 3\cdot(\textbf{if } 2 = 0 \textbf{ then } 1 \textbf{ else } 2\cdot(2-1)!) \\ &= 3\cdot 2\cdot(\textbf{if } 1 = 0 \textbf{ then } 1 \textbf{ else } 1\cdot(1-1)!) \\ &= 3\cdot 2\cdot 1\cdot(\textbf{if } 0 = 0 \textbf{ then } 1 \textbf{ else } 0\cdot(0-1)!) \\ &= 3\cdot 2\cdot 1\cdot 1 = 6. \end{aligned}$$

Note that the rule for evaluating conditional expressions ensures that the computer never attempts to evaluate $(-1)!$. This is necessary since its evaluation would not terminate.

As a second example, the Ackermann function mentioned above is written as a recursive conditional expression as follows:

$$A(m,n,p) \leftarrow \\ \quad \textbf{if } m = 0 \textbf{ then } n + p \\ \quad \textbf{else if } n = 0 \textbf{ then } (\textbf{if } m = 1 \textbf{ then } 0 \textbf{ else } 1) \\ \quad \textbf{else } A(m-1, A(m, n-1, p), p).$$

Several remarks are worth making:

First, in a programming language that uses recursive conditional expressions, 3! would not be evaluated by the above symbolic manipulation. Either (1) would be compiled into a recursive subroutine (i.e., a subroutine of the type explained above that calls itself and uses a stack to save intermediate results and return addresses), or a recursive interpreter would interpret a list structure version of (1).

Second, (1) can easily be replaced by another expression for the factorial that can be compiled into a nonrecursive program. Namely, we write

$$n! \leftarrow \text{fact}(n, 0, 1) \tag{2}$$

where

$$\text{fact}(n, m, p) \leftarrow \textbf{if } m = n \textbf{ then } p \\ \quad \textbf{else } \text{fact}(n, m+1, (m+1)p).$$

Now (2) can be translated into a nonrecursive program because the only occurrence of "fact" on the right-hand side of the definition appears at the outer level; i.e., fact $(n, m+1, (m+1)p)$ gives the value of fact $(n, m, p)$, in contrast to the the situation in (1) where $(n-1)!$ must be multiplied by $n$ to give $n!$. This allows the object program to contain an ordinary jump to itself rather than a subroutine call. When this is possible, the function definition is called "iterative." Thus, "fact" is iterative, while the definition (2) is not. Recursive definitions cannot in general be replaced by iterative definitions except by encoding the stack as a variable in the program, and if this has to be done, there is no advantage in the replacement.

Third, there may be several occurrences of the function being defined on the right-hand side of the recursive definition, and whether the evaluation terminates may depend on which occurrence is evaluated first. The following example due to Morris shows this:

$$f(x,y) \leftarrow \textbf{if } x = 0 \textbf{ then } 0 \textbf{ else } f(x-1, f(y-2, x)).$$

The reader should evaluate $f(2,1)$ to convince himself.

It is also possible to use recursive conditional expressions to define functions that take functions as arguments or give functions as results. However, there remain unsolved problems in getting compiling algorithms that give efficient object code and give the "right" answers in all cases.

The term *"recursive"* is sometimes also applied to the the Backus-Naur form used to define classes of strings of symbols.

**Source Material.** There is no good reference to the use of recursion in programming. McCarthy et al. (1962) has some discussion of its implementation in Lisp, and Randell and Russell (1964) discuss the implementation of recursion in Algol. Peter (1967) has a thorough treatment of subclasses of general recursive functions. The standard reference on recursive functions. The standard reference on recursive function theory was written by Kleene (1952), who gave a more elementary treatment in a later book (1967).

Two aspects of recursion are current research topics in computer science. First, the notion of recursive program is being extended in various ways, and methods of implementing these extensions by compilers and interpreters are being studied (Bobrow and Raphael, 1973). Second, the formal properties of recursive programs are being studied as part of the mathematical theory of computation, which has as its major object the ability to prove assertions about programs and check these assertions on a computer (Manna, 1974).

REFERENCES


1952. Kleene, S. C. *Introduction to Metamathematics.* Princeton, N.J.: Van Nostrand.

1962. McCarthy, J. et al. *LISP 1.5 Programmer's Manual.* Cambridge, Mass.: M.I.T. Press.

1964. Randell, B. and L. J. Russell. *Algol 60 Implementation: Translation and Use of Algol 60 Programs by Computers.* New York: Academic Press.

1967. Kleene, S. C. *Mathematical Logic.* New York: John Wiley.

1967. Peter, R. *Recursive Functions.* New York: Academic Press.

1973. Bobrow, D. and B. Raphael. *New Programming Languages for AI Research.* Palo Alto: Xerox Research Center.
1974. Manna, Z. *Introduction to Mathematical Theory of Computation.* New York: McGraw-Hill.

J. McCarthy

# REDUNDANCY

For articles on related subjects *see* Errors; Error Correcting Codes; and Reliability and Fault Tolerance.
For article on related term *see* Integrated Circuitry.

A system is said to be *nonredundant* or is said to have a *simplex structure* if it is designed in such a manner that only the absolute minimum amount of hardware is utilized to implement its function. If, even after utilizing the finest components available, the desired system reliability is not achieved, or if failure tolerance is desired as a system capability, then *redundancy* as a design procedure is resorted to; i.e., more system elements are used than are absolutely necessary to realize all the system's functions. The additional system elements, referred to as the redundant elements, need not all necessarily be hardware elements, but may also be additional software (software redundancy), additional time (time redundancy—performing a computation more than once and comparing the results), and additional information (information redundancy—e.g., the application of error-detection and correction codes).

Naturally, redundancies are often interrelated. Additional software requires additional memory storage, and additional time is used to execute the added software. The term "protective redundancy" is often used to characterize that redundancy which has an overall beneficial effect on the system attributes, since redundancy alone without proper application may well become a liability. Protective redundancy is utilized to realize *fault-tolerant digital systems and self-repairing systems* by such means as triple or $N$-tuple modular redundancy (TMR, NMR), quadded redundancy, standby-replacement redundancy, hybrid redundancy, software redundancy, and the application of error-detection and correction codes.

Redundancy as a procedure for designing more reliable systems than allowed by the intrinsic reliability of the constituting components is as old as the discipline of engineering itself. An example of the use of redundancy in ancient times is provided in structures where more than the absolute minimum required number of struts were provided to uphold a structure. Thus, early uses of redundancy were used as insurance against (1) the lack of accurate knowledge of underlying phenomena, and (2) the lack of confidence in the available data on the materials used. Redundancy as a procedure is even more basic. This is evidenced by the testimony of evolutionary processes of life, which make abundant use of it (e.g., in the human body there are two kidneys, two lungs, two cerebral hemispheres, etc.). Also, in societal systems, protective redundancy is advocated by the truism "two heads are better than one," and conversely, the improper use of redundancy by "too many cooks spoil the broth." Among other societal systems exhibiting the principles of redundancy is the typical committee, which is constituted by an odd number of members so that a tie in balloting may never occur. This is analogous to the majority voting redundancy used in some computer systems. Other examples will readily occur to the reader.

For the computer age, redundancy has been used at all levels of technology, from that of medium-scale-integrated (MSI) devices, circuitry logic, subsystem computers, and even to entire networks of digital systems.

F. P. Mathur

# REENTRANT PROGRAM

For articles on related subjects *see* Multiprogramming; Procedure, Pure; and Time Sharing.

In a time-sharing or multiprogramming environment a number of user programs may be sharing a common pool of subprograms or processors. Therefore, it is necessary that the shared programs be written in such a form that each can be applied to, say, user program 1 without running to completion, then be interrupted and applied to some other user program (perhaps, or perhaps not, running to completion), and then later be *reentered* at the point of interruption of user program 1 without loss of information.

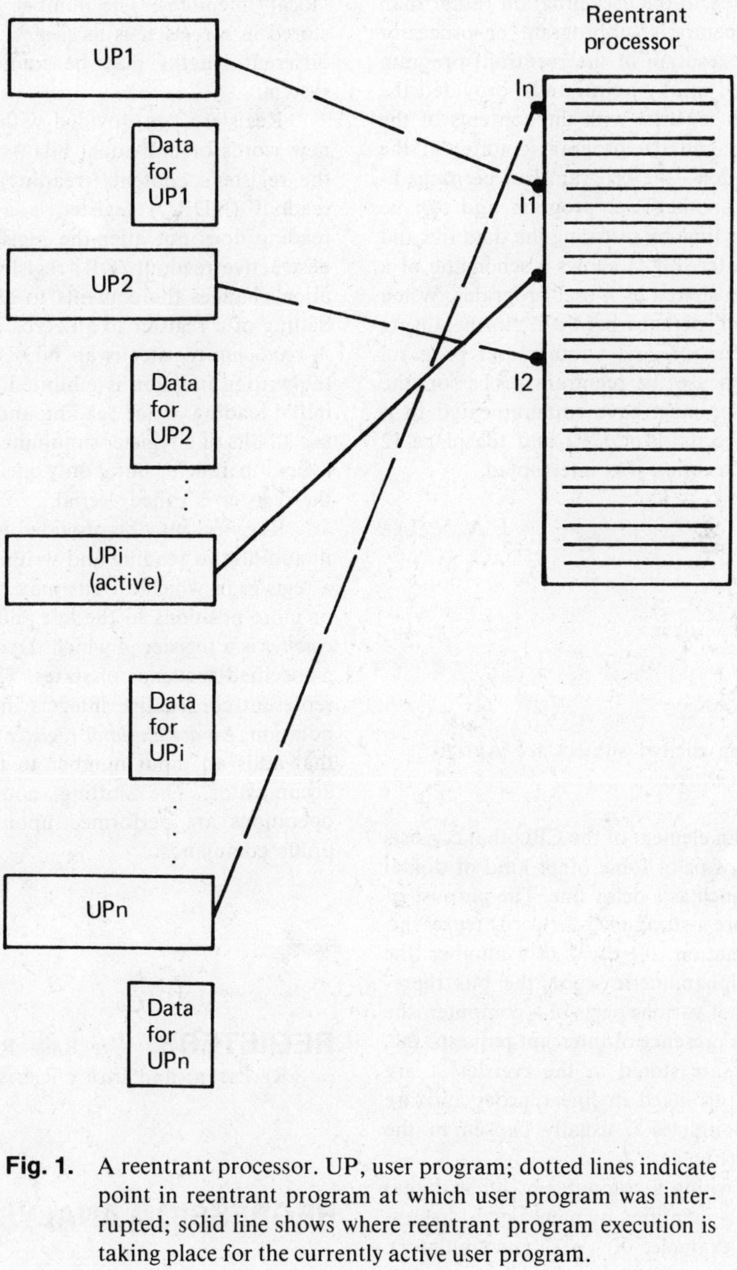


**Fig. 1.** A reentrant processor. UP, user program; dotted lines indicate point in reentrant program at which user program was interrupted; solid line shows where reentrant program execution is taking place for the currently active user program.

In order to allow this reentrance ability, the programs must be written so that they contain no self-modifying features and so that all data required by the reentrant program can be maintained in a separate file related to the user program rather than as part of the reentrant subprogram or processor itself. Then the execution of the reentrant program can be interrupted at any point, and—provided the data file is stored together with the contents of the machine registers and the program counter at the point of interruption—the program can be immediately applied to another user program and can be resumed at a later time by restoring the data file and the program counter. Fig. 1 shows a schematic of a reentrant program shared by *n* user programs. When UPi is interrupted, perhaps before it finishes using the reentrant processor, and another user program (say, UP2) gets to use the reentrant processor, the reentrant processor must have communicated to it the location of the data for UP2 and the place I2 where previous execution was interrupted.

J. A. N. LEE

## REGISTER

For article on related subject *see* ARITHMETIC-LOGIC UNIT.

A register is an element of the CPU that consists of several flip-flops or of some other kind of digital storage element, such as a delay line. The purpose of a register is to store a string of bits (word) representing related information: the digits of a number, the symbols of an alphanumeric word, the bits representing the status of various parts of a computer, the bits indicating the presence of interrupt requests, etc. The bits $X_i$ that are stored in the register $X$ are considered to be arranged in linear order and are identified by the indices $i$, usually chosen in the range $0 \leq i \leq n$ (Fig. 1).

All registers within a computer or other digital device are uniquely identified by names or addresses. The names—for example: X, ACC (accumulator), MSW (machine status word), index register—often indicate the function of a register. The addresses are a set of consecutive integers $A$ $(0 \leq A \leq N)$ which identify registers within a storage array (often called "local" memory). The number of bits that can be stored in a register is its *length*. Registers of several different lengths may be found within the same system.

| | | | | | | | |
|---|---|---|---|---|---|---|---|
| $X_7$ | $X_6$ | $X_5$ | $X_4$ | $X_3$ | $X_2$ | $X_1$ | $X_0$ |

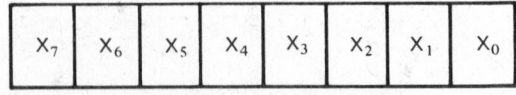

**Fig. 1.** An eight-bit register X.

Registers are provided with the means to *load* new words or individual bits (writing) and to *sense* the register's contents (reading). A nondestructive readout (NDRO) register is a register in which reading does not alter the register's contents. In a destructive readout (DR) register the reading operation changes the contents to all zeros or all ones. Setting of a register to all zeros is called "clearing." A *read-only* register is an NDRO register in which the writing function is inhibited or deleted after the initial loading. If the reading and writing operations use all bits of a register simultaneously, the register is called "parallel," but if only one bit at a time is used, the register is called "serial."

Registers may be provided with other functions in addition to reading and writing. A *shift register* is a register in which all bits may be displaced by one or more positions to the left and/or to the right. A *counter* is a register in which the contents go through a specified sequence of states. The states frequently represent consecutive integers in binary or decimal notation. An *accumulator register* has a built-in adder that adds an input number to the contents of the accumulator. The shifting, counting, and adding operations are performed upon receipt of appropriate commands.

A. AVIŽIENIS

**REGISTERS.** *See* BASE REGISTER; GENERAL REGISTER; and INDEX REGISTER.

## REGRESSION ANALYSIS

For article on related subject *see* STATISTICAL APPLICATIONS.

Regression analysis is used for many different purposes. The most important is to build models explaining a dependent variable in terms of a set of independent variables. The hope is that extrapolation into new population sets other than those observed can be performed by choosing values of the independent variables for new cases and thereby predicting the most likely value of the dependent variable. For example, one might wish to predict age at death (the dependent variable) on the basis of life habits, genetic characteristics, and physiology (the independent variables).

The basic bivariate linear regression equation is

$$Y = a + b\,(X - \bar{X}),$$

where $Y$ is the dependent variable, $a$ is a constant, $b$ is the regression coefficient of $X$ on $Y$, the $X$ are independent observations, and $\bar{X}$ their mean. To follow Fisher (1958), $Y$ might be height, $b$ the coefficient with which height changes with age, and $X$ the age. The equation is easily extended to multiple independent variables, in which case $b$ would be a row vector, and $X$ and $\bar{X}$ column vectors. Nonlinear regression is also possible. Many forms exist, including polynomial, quadratic, and higher order. An example of a polynomial regression equation of order 3 (cubic) would be

$$Y = a + b_1(X - \bar{X}) + b_2(X^2 - \bar{X}^2) + b_3\,(X^3 - \bar{X}^3).$$

The reader is again referred to Fisher for further details of these aspects. Regression analysis is thus used to build models and, as an extension, to allow extrapolation from the model to predict future values of the dependent variable.

The effect of high-speed, large central memory computers on the use of regression analysis has been very considerable. While the calculations are basically simple, the presence of numerous variables and observations, particularly if the independent variables are interrelated (nonorthogonal), can cause the total amount of calculation to be very large. The major use of regression analysis on computers has paralleled the development of the *stepwise regression* method. Perhaps the most widely used stepwise regression program has been BMD02R (lately replaced by BMDP02R), which was written as part of the UCLA Library of computer programs (Dixon, 1973). The method is basically that of M.A. Efroymson (1964), later elaborated upon and further refined by R. Jennrich (1976). These programs were the first to address themselves to the problem of selecting variable subsets that reduced the residual sum of squares (i.e., increased the multiple correlation coefficient) the most. After entering into the equation that variable with the largest partial correlation coefficient with the dependent variable, its effect is removed from the correlation matrix and then the most important variable is entered. This process continues until some criterion for terminating the process is reached. Mantel (1971) has pointed out that the step-up method of selecting variables leaves much to be desired because it is possible to miss the more important variables. He suggested instead (but was not the first to use) stepdown procedures wherein all variables are initially used and those that explain the smallest amount of variance are removed, one by one.

A method which has come into use in recent years is ridge (or damped) regression, first formally described by A. E. Hoerl and R. W. Kennard (1970). In this method, damping factors are added to the diagonal of the correlation matrix prior to inversion. This tends to orthogonalize interrelated variables, and by the study of the robustness of the regression coefficients with changes in the damping factors (ridge trace), one determines sets of variables that should be removed. This method also permits one to deal with the overdetermined case, i.e., one in which there are more variables than observations.

Still another method not infrequently used is optimum regression, due to Lamotte and Hocking [see Hocking (1976)] in which all possible two-variable, three-variable, etc., subsets are evaluated under various constraints. The user is then free to chose whatever combination of variables is of most interest to him, on the basis of the multiple correlation coefficient and the variables contributing to that coefficient.

In regression analysis, particular attention must be paid to outliers, i.e., values that do not "fit" the scheme of the majority of the observations. Outliers may swing regression coefficients in a way that makes them lack robustness. The importance of an analysis of the residuals from the regression calculation cannot be overemphasized. The lack of this analysis is frequently the cause for the failure of regression equations to be imbued with sufficient confidence.

Present restrictions on regression analysis are mostly due to computational power. The stepwise and ridge methods can be used with up to approximately 400 variables and an essentially unlimited number of observations. The optimum regression method is presently limited by computer time to approximately 50 variables.

### References

1958. Fisher, R. A. *Statistical Methods for Research Workers.* New York: Hafner, (13th ed.), pp. 129ff.

1964. Efroymson, M. A. "Multiple Regression Analysis." In A. Ralston and H. S. Wilf (Eds.), *Mathematical Methods for Digital Computers*, vol. 1. New York: John Wiley.

1970. Hoerl, A. E., and R. W. Kennard. "Ridge Regression: Biased Estimation for Nonorthogonal Problems," *Technometrics*, vol. 12, pp. 55–67.

1971. Mantel, N. "Why Stepdown Procedures vs. Variables Selection." *Technometrics*, vol. 12, pp. 621–625, and vol. 13, pp. 455–457.

1973. Dixon, W. J. (Ed.). *BMD Biomedical Computer Programs*. Berkeley: University of California Press.

1976. Hocking, R. R. "Selection of the Best Subset of Regression Variables," in K. Enslein, A. Ralston, and H. S. Wilf (Eds.), *Statistical Methods for Digital Computers* [vol. 3 of *Mathematical Methods for Digital Computers (Series)*]. New York: John Wiley.

1976. Jennrich, R. I. "Stepwise Discriminant Analysis," in K. Enslein, A. Ralston, and H. S. Wilf (Eds.), *Statistical Methods for Digital Computers* [vol. 3 of *Mathematical Methods for Digital Computers (Series)*]. New York: John Wiley.

K. ENSLEIN

# REGULAR EXPRESSION

For article on related subject *see* AUTOMATA THEORY.
For article on related term *see* CONCATENATION.

The formal description for a language acceptable by a finite automaton or for the behavior of a sequential switching circuit is known as a "regular expression." It tells how a language is built up from atomic languages, using regular operations. The atomic languages are the empty language $\phi$ and the singleton sets $\{a\}$, where $a$ is a letter of some previously specified alphabet. The regular operations are *union, catenation*, and *catenation closure*. Union is the ordinary set theoretical union; the catenation $XY$ of two languages $X$ and $Y$ consists of all words $xy$ with $x \in X$ and $y \in Y$; and the catenation closure $X*$ of a language $X$ consists of the empty word and of all words of the form $x_1 \cdots x_n$, where $n \geqslant 1$ and each $x_i \in X$. For example, $(ab \cup b)*$ is a regular expression for the language $X$, obtained by catenating $ab$ and $b$ in an arbitrary fashion; i.e., $X$ consists of the empty word and of all words over the alphabet $\{a,b\}$ ending with $b$ and having no subwords $aa$.

A formal definition of regular expressions is now given. Assume that $V$ and $V_1 = \{\phi, \cup, *, (, )\}$ are disjoint alphabets. A word $\alpha$ over the alphabet $V \cup V_1$ is a regular expression over $V$ if and only if (1) $\alpha$ is a letter of $V$ or the letter $\phi$, or (2) $\alpha$ is of one of the forms $(\beta \cup \gamma)$, $(\beta\gamma)$, or $\beta*$, where $\beta$ and $\gamma$ are regular expressions over $V$. Each regular expression $\alpha$ over $V$ denotes a language $|\alpha|$ over $V$ according to the following conventions:

1. The language denoted by $\phi$ is the empty language.
2. The language denoted by $a \in V$ consists of the word $a$.
3. For regular expressions $\alpha$ and $\beta$ over V,

$$|(\alpha \cup \beta)| = |\alpha| \cup |\beta|, \quad |(\alpha\beta)| = |\alpha|\,|\beta|, \quad |\alpha*| = |\alpha|*.$$

Very different looking regular expressions may denote the same language; e.g., each of the regular expressions

$$(a \cup ab \cup ba)*, \quad (ba \cup a*ab)*a*, \quad a*(ab \cup ba*a)*$$

denotes the same language.

The behavior of a finite automaton or a sequential switching circuit is very often better understood after a simplification of the corresponding regular expression. Especially helpful is the reduction of the star height, i.e., the maximum number of nested stars in the regular expression. A finitary axiomatization can be given to all equations among regular expressions, although rules of inference stronger than substitution are necessarily needed. Various algorithms are known for the transition from a regular expression to a finite automaton, and vice versa.

REFERENCES

1968. Ginzburg, A. *Algebraic Theory of Automata*. New York: Academic Press.

1969. Salomaa, A. *Theory of Automata*. New York: Pergamon.

A. SALOMAA

## RELIABILITY AND FAULT TOLERANCE

For article on related subject *see* DATA SECURITY.

The domain of reliability engineering involves considerations of all aspects of design, development, and fabrication so as to minimize the chance of equipment breakdown. Neglect of reliability considerations can prove to be very costly, from the loss of consumer acceptance of the product to the possibility of endangering human life. Success of complex missions such as rocket launching of spacecraft depends heavily on reliability engineering. Failure of a single component could result in the total loss of the system.

Reliability in a qualitative sense can mean a host of different things relating to the confidence in the goodness of the equipment, and is closely connected but often confused with the concepts of maintainability, availability, safety, and even security of the system. Quantitatively, reliability can be formulated mathematically as the probability that the system will perform its intended function over the stated duration of time in the specified environment for its usage.

As equipment becomes more complex, the chance of system unreliability becomes greater, since the reliability of any equipment depends on the reliability of its components. The relationship between parts reliability and the system reliability can be formulated mathematically to varying degrees of precision, depending on the scale of the modeling effort. The mathematics of reliability is based on parts-failure rate statistics and probability theoretic relationships. The mathematical theory of reliability is used to model, simulate, and predict proneness of the equipment to failure under expected operating conditions.

There have been two distinct and viable approaches taken to enhance system reliability. One is based on component technology; i.e., manufacturing capability of producing the component with the highest possible reliability, followed by parts screening, quality control, pretesting to remove early failures (infant mortality effects), etc. The second approach is based on the organization of the system itself (e.g., fault-tolerant architectures that make use of protective redundancy to mask or remove the effects of failure, and thereby provide greater overall system reliability than would be possible by the use of the same components in a simplex or nonredundant configuration).

Fault tolerance is the capability of the system to perform its functions in accordance with design specifications, even in the presence of hardware failures. If, in the event of faults, the system functions can be performed, but do not meet the design specifications with respect to the time required to complete the job or the storage capacity required for the job, then the system is said to be *partially* or *quasi fault-tolerant*. Since the number of possible hardware failures can be very large, in practice it is necessary to restrict fault tolerance to prespecified classes of faults from which the system is designed to recover.

Faults may be classified as *transient* or *permanent, deterministic* or *indeterminate, local* or *catastrophic*. The first category refers to the duration of the fault, the second to its effect on the values of the system design parameters, and the third to the propagation of the fault to its neighboring elements.

Fault tolerance is provided by the application of protective redundancy, or the use of more resources so as to upgrade system reliability. These resources may consist of more hardware, software, or time, or a combinations of all three. Extra time is required to retransmit messages or to reexecute programs, extra software is required to perform diagnosis on the hardware, and extra hardware is required to provide replication of units.

Hardware redundancy may be of the fault-masking or self-repair types, or a hybrid of these two. In fault masking, redundancy is of a static nature; faults are masked instantly and the operations of fault detection, location, and correction are indistinguishable. In self-repair, redundancy is used dynamically; faults are selectively masked and are detected, located, and subsequently corrected by the replacement of the failed unit by an unfailed replica. Examples of the former are triple modular redundancy (TMR) and quadding (see below), and (of the latter) standby-replacement (SR) systems and reconfigurable systems. Schemes using a combination of these two basic approaches are called "hybrid" or adaptive redundancy.

**Some Fundamental Principles.** A fundamental principle of reliability is that it must be not only inherent but also a function of how the component is used. Another important principle is that, to achieve reliability by means of protective redundancy, the redundancy must be applied to the lowest level of component complexity in the system in order to maximize gain in reliability. This is the idealized state; in practice, tradeoffs due to overhead are required in utilizing redundancy techniques (e.g., providing voters in TMR systems and detection-switching requirements in standby systems). The application of the mathematical theory of reliability in modeling such systems provides quantitative design guidelines that make such tradeoffs and optimizations possible and practicable.

In addition to the foregoing first and second principles of fault tolerance, a third principle is that a system may be made arbitrarily reliable, provided the degree of redundancy is made high (i.e., a sufficiently large number of replicas are provided). Again, this principle holds only in an idealized situation; in practice, since the probability of detecting a failure and correctly switching over to a spare is less than unity, this parameter, called "coverage," limits the advantages postulated by the third principle.

A fourth principle concerns the problem of requiring the checking elements (those elements that are used for the diagnosis of the rest of the system and the subsequent reconfiguration of the system units) also to be checkable. This is the problem of "checking the checker." Thus, the fourth principle states that any system utilizing protective redundancy will have major and minor "hard cores" (i.e., unprotected system elements), and that these cannot be totally eliminated from the system design; however, they may be made arbitrarily small by judicious use of a mixture of different, protective redundancy techniques.

**Mathematical Theory of Reliability.** Some relationships among reliability parameters and the underlying probability theoretic relationships are as follows: If a fixed large number $N_0$ of identical items is being tested, of which $N_s$ is the number of items surviving after time $t$ and $N_f$ is the number of items that failed during time $t$, then $N_0 = N_s + N_f$ for all $t$. Now, for a sufficiently large $N_0$, the reliability $R(t)$ of an item is $N_s/N_0$. The failure rate $\lambda(t)$, which is defined to be the rate at which the population changes at time $t$, can be shown to be given by

$$\lambda(t) = -\frac{1}{R(t)}\frac{dR(t)}{dt}, \qquad (1)$$

so that

$$R(t) = \exp\left(-\int_0^t \lambda(\tau)\, d\tau\right) \qquad (2)$$

The reliability function $R(t)$ is often called the "survival probability function," since it measures the probability that failure of an item does not occur during the time interval $[0,t]$.

**Failure Rate.** Statistical data on equipment failure yields a characteristic "bathtub" curve, as shown in Fig. 1. When the equipment is first put into service, inherently weak components fail early; this stage is also called "infant mortality." Subsequently, the failure rate stabilizes quickly to a relatively constant value; this period is called the "useful life period." After much usage, failure rate begins to increase rapidly as a result of deterioration and wear.

**Exponential Failure Law.** In general, the failure law of a component is the probability distribution effective from the moment at which a component enters service up to the moment of its failure. In practice the most commonly used failure law is the exponential law, which applies when a component is subject only to failures that occur at random intervals and the average number of failures is the same for equal time periods. These constraints are valid for a component that is no longer subject to infant mortality failures and whose failure rate is a constant within the "useful life" span. Thus, for

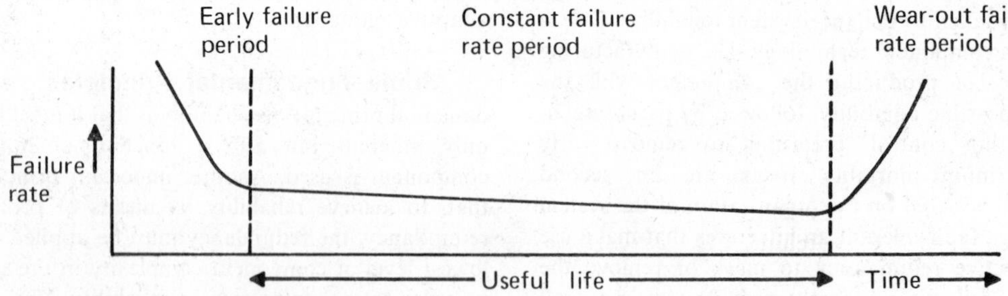


**Fig. 1.** Bathtub curve of failure rate.

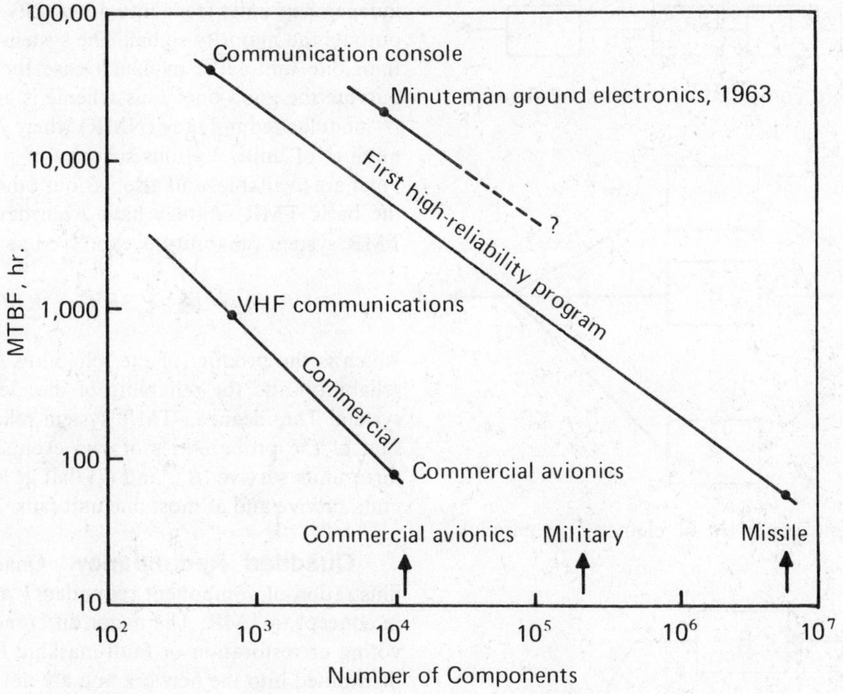


**Fig. 2.** Comparison of mean time between failures for commercial equipment and high-reliability military equipment. (From E. J. Nalos and R. B. Schultz, "Reliability and Cost of Avionics," *IEEE Trans. Reliability,* October 1965. By permission.)

operating periods within the useful life, the component reliability over a period of time $t$ can be expressed as $R(t) = e^{-\lambda t}$, where $\lambda$ (usually expressed in failures per hour or per million hours) is the constant failure rate of the device. A characteristic of the exponential failure law is that the reliability of the device within the useful life period is the same for operating times of equal duration.

From the definition of $R(t)$ it follows that the mean time between failures (MTBF) or the mean time to first failure (MTTF), usually expressed in hours (Fig. 2), are given by $\int_0^\infty R(t)\,dt$; i.e., it is the area underneath the reliability curve $R(t)$ plotted versus $t$. This result is true for any failure distribution. For the specific case of the exponential failure law, the MTBF, $m$, is equal to $1/\lambda$. Further, when the product $\lambda t$ is small, the equation for $R(t)$ may be approximated by $R(t) \approx 1 - \lambda t$. Thus, if $\lambda t = 0.01$, $R(t) = e^{-0.01} = 0.99.$, or 99.0%. The product $\lambda t$ is often referred to as the "normalized" time, since $\lambda t = t/m$; i.e., the mission time $t$ is normalized with respect to the MTBF.

**Series Reliability.** If a system is composed of elements in such a way that the failure of any one element causes a failure of the system, then these elements are considered to be functionally in series. For the system to survive, each element must survive. The probability of survival for the system cannot be better than the element with the lowest probability of survival; e.g., a chain is no better than its weakest link. When these series elements are independent of each other, then, by the probability multiplication law, the system survival probability is the product of the individual survival probabilities of the elements. This is known as the product rule:

$$R_{\text{system}} = \Pi_{i=1}^{n} R_i,$$

where $R_i$ is the reliability of the $i$th element of an $n$-element system (Fig. 3).

**Parallel Reliability.** Parallel reliability is an illustration of protective redundancy. The system is composed of functionally parallel elements in such a way that if one of the elements fails the parallel unit will continue to do the system function. See Fig. 4. The system reliability, under the assumption of

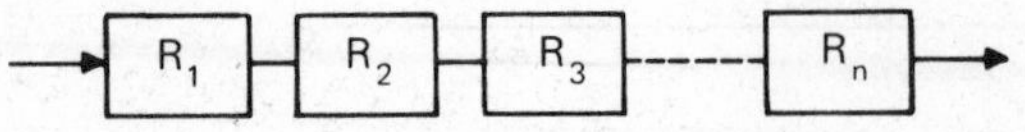


**Fig. 3.** System composed of a series of elements.

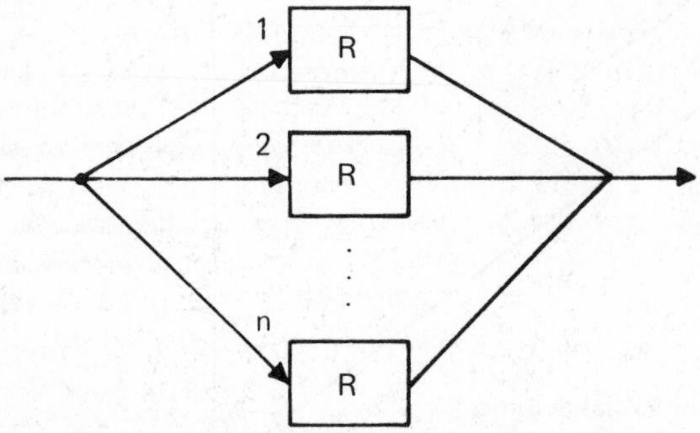


**Fig. 4.** System composed of elements in parallel.

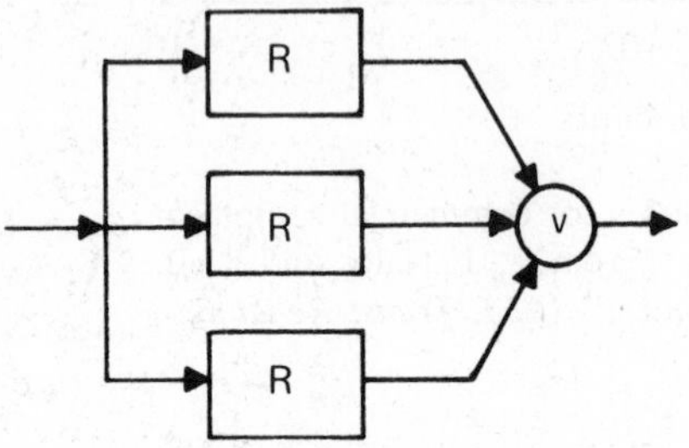


**Fig. 5.** Triple modular redundancy.

independence of failure of the elements, is expressed by

$$R_{\text{system}} = 1 - (1 - R)^n,$$

which is the probability that not all $n$ elements have failed. The term $(1 - R)$, known as the unreliability of a unit, is the probability that a unit will fail. The term $(1 - R)^n$ by the product rule is the probability that all $n$ units will fail and one minus that is the probability that not all units will have failed. An example of parallel reliability is given by electronic diodes in parallel; if one diode open-circuits, the other will still provide the function.

**Triple Modular Redundancy (TMR).** TMR is also known as the "multiple-line voting" system. One of the earliest and most influential schemes was developed by J. von Neumann. The simplex unit is triplicated and each of the three independent units feeds into a majority voter, which outputs the majority signal. The system fails if more than one unit fails, in which case the failed units outvote the good one. This scheme is generalized to $N$-modular redundancy (NMR) where $N$ is any odd number of units. Various schemes of protecting the voter are available, and also various other variants of the basic TMR strategy have been developed. The TMR system reliability is expressed as

$$R_{\text{system}} = [R^3 + 3R^2(1 - R)]R_v,$$

which is the product of the reliability $R_v$ (the voter reliability) and the reliability of the idealized TMR system. The idealized TMR system reliability is the sum of the probabilities of two events: (1) that all three units survive, $R^3$; and (2) that at least any two units survive and at most one unit fails, $3R^2(1 - R)$.

**Quadded Redundancy.** Quadding is an illustration of component redundancy and is similar in concept to TMR. The major difference is that the voting or restoration or fault-masking functions are distributed into the network and are not separable as in TMR. An example of quadding is shown in Fig. 6 where the nonredundant logic circuit in Fig. 6(a) is shown "quadded" in Fig. 6(b). The process of how an error downstream is subsequently corrected upstream is illustrated.

In general, the quadding procedure requires that each logic gate be quadruplicated and that each of the gates in a quad stage will have twice as many inputs as the nonredundant gate replaced. The outputs of a stage are interconnected to the inputs of the succeeding stage by a connection pattern in such a way that the effects of errors in earlier stages get subsequently "restored" in the latter stages; i.e., the originally intended "good" signal is restored.

**Standby Replacement Redundancy.** In standby replacement redundancy (Fig. 7), only one unit is operational at a time, unlike TMR. When the active unit fails, this event is detected by additional circuitry, and a spare unit from a reserve of spares is switched in as a replacement of the failed unit, thereby restoring the system to its operational state. The reliability of this system is expressed as

$$R_{\text{system}} = 1 - (1 - R)^{S+1},$$

which is the probability that not all units have failed.

**Hybrid Redundancy.** Hybrid redundancy is a synthesis of TMR and standby replacement re-

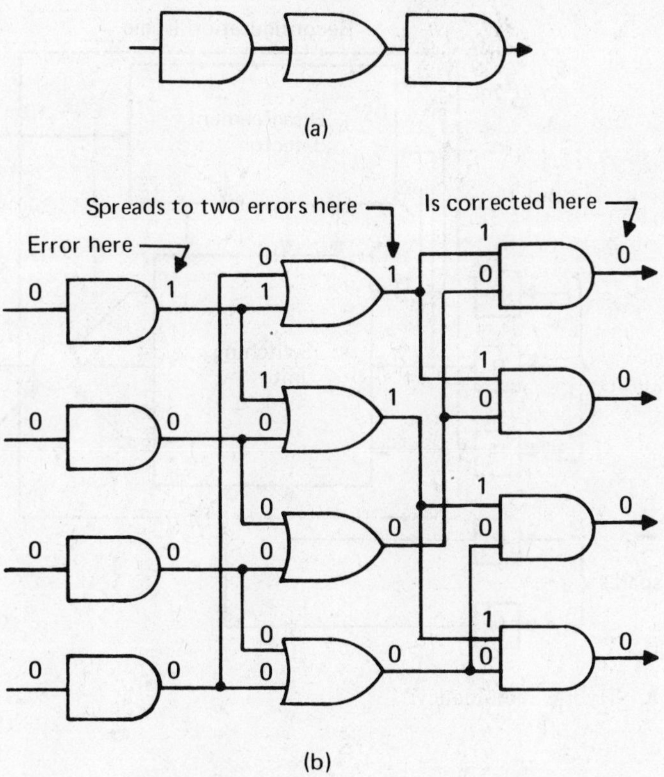


**Fig. 6.** An example of quadding: (a) nonredundant circuit; (b) circuit in (a) protected by quadding.

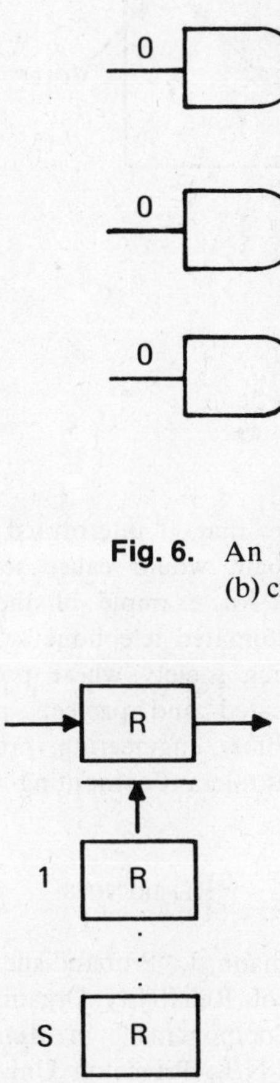


**Fig. 7.** Standby replacement redundancy.

dundancy (see Fig. 8). It consists of a TMR system (or, in general, an NMR system) with a bank of spares so that when one of the TMR units fail, it is replaced by a spare unit. Failure detection is achieved by means of the disagreement detectors, which compare the individual outputs of each of the triple modular redundancy units with the system output. If there is a difference, the disagreement detector signals the switching network to replace the failed unit by a spare unit. When all spares are utilized, the hybrid redundancy system reduces to a TMR system. Variations of the hybrid or adaptive redundancy schemes are available. The system reliability in its simplest terms may be expressed as

$$R_{\text{system}} = 1 - [(1 - R^{S+3} + (S + 3)(1 - R)^{S+2} \cdot R],$$

which is the probability that not all $S + 3$ units fail and that not any $S + 2$ units fail with one not failing.

**Summary.** Redundancy as a procedure for designing more reliable systems than allowed by the intrinsic reliability of the constituent components is as old as the discipline of engineering itself. In fact, even in the evolutionary processes of life, Nature makes abundant use of it (e.g., in the human body there are two kidneys, two lungs, etc.).

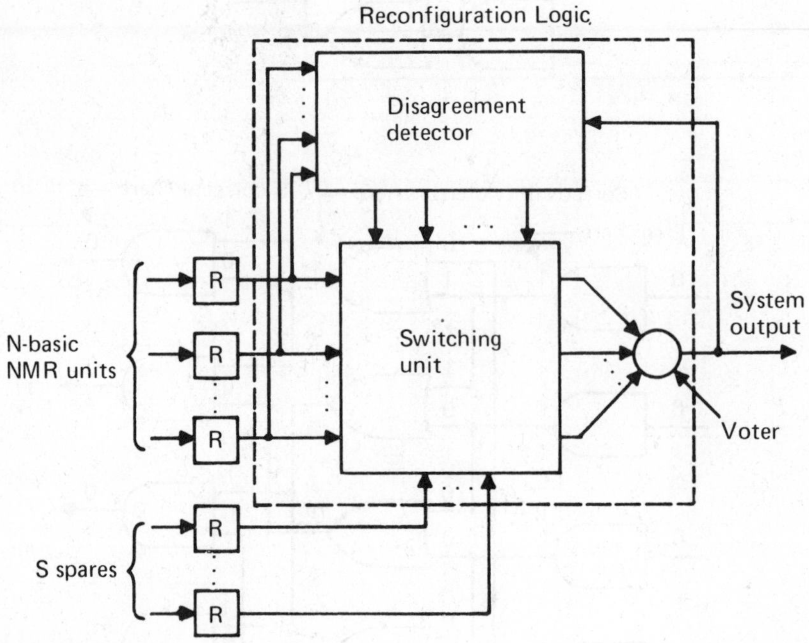


**Fig. 8.** Hybrid redundancy.

Examples of the use of redundancy in ancient times are provided in the construction of temples and bridges, where more than the absolutely required number of pillars is provided to uphold a structure; thus, should one pillar sustain damage, the remaining pillars would still be able to successfully share the load.

In the computer age, all the basic techniques described here have been applied, to various degrees of sophistication, to the design of ultrareliable computing systems. TMR has been successfully applied in designing the guidance and control computer of the SATURN V launch vehicle. Quadding is utilized to a great extent in the design of the spacecraft computer of the Orbiting Astronomic Observatory (OAO). Standby replacement redundancy was extensively used in the Raytheon RAYDAC computer and in the Jet Propulsion Laboratory's self-test and repair (STAR) computer. The latter also utilized hybrid redundancy to protect the monitor subsystem of the self-repairing computer.

In addition, these techniques are also finding application in protecting the automated computerized controls of modern high-speed transit systems and in other applications where cost of using redundancy is justifiable because it minimizes danger to human life, or increases the continuous availability of services that, if interrupted by failure and subsequent repair, would cause severe consumer dissatisfaction. An example of the latter is the present-day automated telephone switching system. In an expanding society where products become more sophisticated and projects proliferate, the scope of reliability engineering, protective redundancy and fault-tolerant computing will continue to grow.

## References

1956. von Neumann, J. "Probabilistic Logics and the Synthesis of Reliability Organisms from Unreliable Components," in *Automata Studies*. Princeton, N.J.: Princeton University, pp. 43–98.

1961. Bazovsky, I. *Reliability Theory and Practice*. Englewood Cliffs, N.J.: Prentice-Hall.

1962. Lloyd, D. K., and M. Lipow. *Reliability, Management Methods, and Mathematics*. Englewood Cliffs, N.J.: Prentice-Hall.

1971. IEEE. *Transactions on Computers: Special Issue on Fault-Tolerant Computing*, Vol. C-20, No. 11 (November).

F. P. Mathur

# REMOTE JOB ENTRY

For articles on related subjects *see* COMMUNICATIONS AND COMPUTERS; DATA COMMUNICATIONS; INPUT-OUTPUT DEVICES; PROCESSING MODES; and TELEPROCESSING SYSTEMS.
For article on related term *see* JOB.

Remote job entry (RJE) refers to the submission of jobs to a central computer from a location at least several hundred feet, and sometimes many miles, distant from the computer. Job entry becomes "remote" when the length limits of cable connections between input/output devices are exceeded, in which case the telephone or another common-carrier communications link must be used to bridge the gap, as shown in Fig. 1.

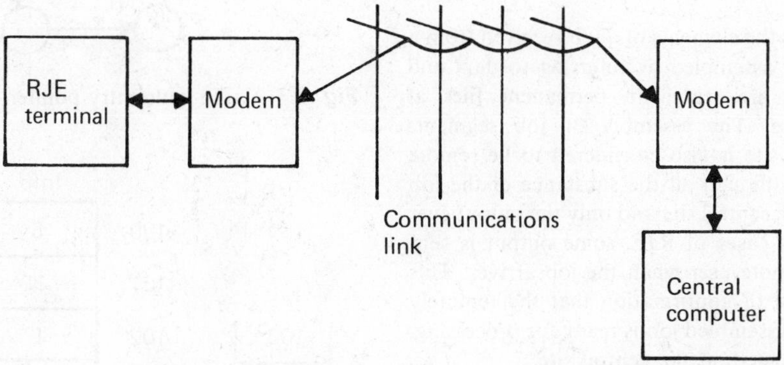


**Fig. 1.** Connections for remote job entry to a computer through a communications link.

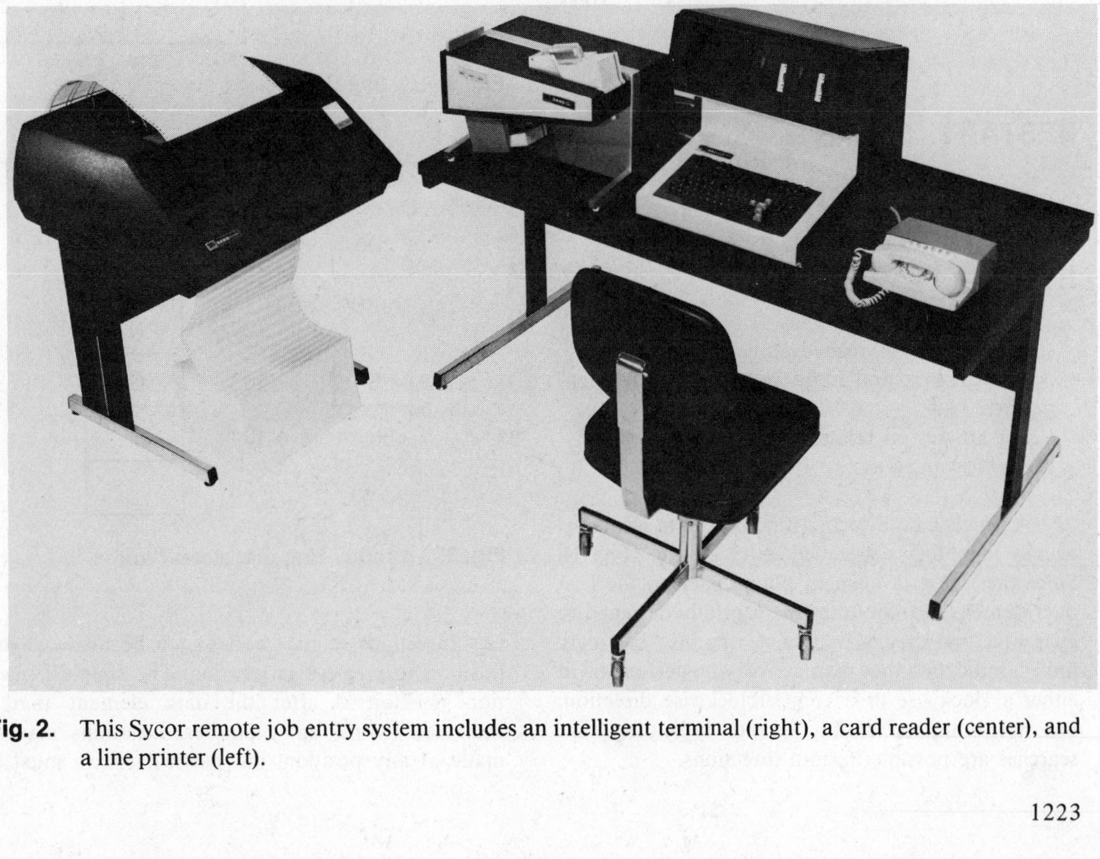

**Fig. 2.** This Sycor remote job entry system includes an intelligent terminal (right), a card reader (center), and a line printer (left).

Remote job entry is usually combined with so-called "remote job receipt," since a remote terminal can enter the job on the computer and can also receive output results returned by the computer. Often the output device speed at the remote terminal is quite slow, so that only jobs with very small amounts of output (a few lines in the case of typewriter-speed devices) can or should be received remotely. In such cases, larger amounts of output must or should be printed at the central computer site, and then sent to the remote user via mail or courier.

Sometimes the elements of a job received from a remote site are assembled by referring to data and programs that are stored in permanent files at the central site. The assembly of job segments from a remote site is also considered to be remote job entry, even though all the substance of the job originates at the central site and only the output ever leaves it. In all cases of RJE, some output is sent back to the remote user when the job arrives. This consists at least of confirmation that the remotely submitted and assembled job is ready for processing, or is being executed, at the central site.

A typical remote job entry system is shown in Fig. 2.

C. L. MEEK

## RESTART. *See* CHECKPOINT AND RESTART.

## RING

For articles on related subjects *see* DATA STRUCTURES; and LISTS AND LIST PROCESSING.

For articles on related terms *see* POINTER; STRING; and TREE.

A ring is a cyclic arrangement of data elements, usually including a specified entry pointer (Fig. 1). Since the last data element points back to the first data element, searches must be carefully designed to guarantee that they terminate. A ring may be singly linked, indicating that searches may be performed in either a clockwise or a counterclockwise direction, but not both; or doubly linked, indicating that searches are possible in both directions.

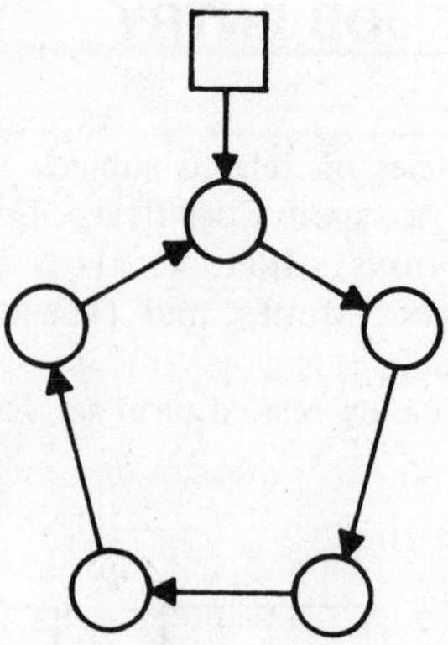

**Fig. 1.** A ring with entry pointer.

Entry: 103

| | Info | Link |
|---|---|---|
| 100 | S | 103 |
| 101 | N | 105 |
| 102 | I | 101 |
| 103 | R | 102 |
| 104 | | |
| 105 | G | 100 |

**Fig. 2.** A ring that stores "RINGS."

Entry: 100

Length: 5

| | Info |
|---|---|
| 100 | R |
| 101 | I |
| 102 | N |
| 103 | G |
| 104 | S |
| 105 | |

**Fig. 3.** Another ring that stores "RINGS."

Insertions of new nodes may be made at any position to create a larger ring. The simplest insertion position is after the data element that is indicated by the entry pointer. Deletions may be made at any position, but particular care must be taken if the data element referenced by the entry pointer is deleted. Doubly linked rings may simplify the insertion and deletion operations, but there is substantial overhead cost for the use of space to store the second set of pointers.

The ring structure is a logical view of data access paths, for which there can be several physical implementations. A ring may be implemented in the processor storage by the use of pointer fields that contain the address of the next data element (Fig. 2). Another implementation in the processor storage might involve sequential allocation of storage locations (Fig. 3). An index may be incremented or decremented to reach the next node, with a special test included to determine when the first or last location has been reached. In this implementation, it would be difficult to insert or delete a node, since a potentially large portion of the data elements would have to be shifted. Finally, the ring structure could be implemented on a direct-access device, with pointers to region numbers containing the next data element.

The greatest use of rings is in connection with other data structures. Ring structures appear in the implementation of lists, strings, and trees. Certain data base management systems utilize a ring structure for the fields of a record and use indices to enter the ring at any position for the start of a search. Another application example might be that of putting into a ring all records of the employees in each corporate division. Then, if any employee's record were to be accessed, it would be a simple matter to retrieve all co-workers by traversing the ring once.

REFERENCE

1968. Knuth, Donald. *The Art of Computer Programming*, vol. I, *Fundamental Algorithms*. Reading, Mass.: Addison-Wesley.

B. SHNEIDERMAN

# ROUNDOFF ERROR

For articles on related subjects *see* ERRORS; and NUMERICAL ANALYSIS.

Computers typically deal with numbers of fixed length (i.e., with a fixed number of digits or bits) when performing arithmetic (although there are exceptions to this). For example, when multiplying two numbers, each of which has $n$ bits, the resulting $2n$ bit product is *rounded* (or, on some few computers, truncated) to $n$ bits. The error that results from this is called "roundoff error", or sometimes "rounding error." With pencil and paper calculations, such roundoff is seldom significant, but with the thousands or even millions of arithmetic operations performed in computer calculations, the effects of roundoff can be considerable and sometimes disastrous. In addition, even a single roundoff error can be disastrous in large problems solved on a computer (see below for an example of this).

Roundoff also occurs when the data for a calculation, which may be known exactly, must be rounded to $n$ bits when read into and stored in the computer.

As examples of the magnitude of a single roundoff error, we consider two cases, both assuming the use of fixed-point arithmetic on a computer using 32-bit numbers with binary point at the left end as shown in Fig. 1.

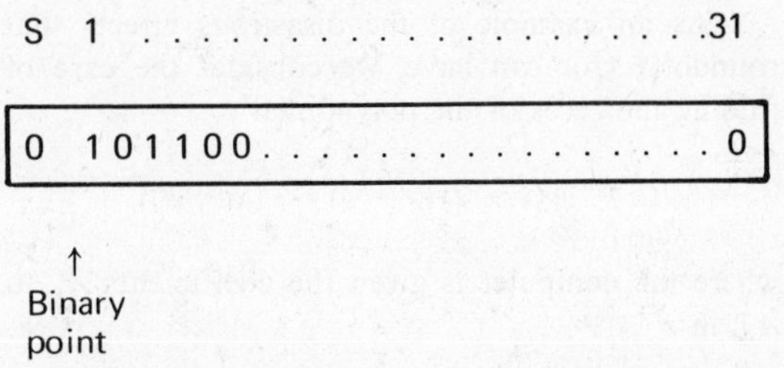


**Fig. 1.** The 31-bit number shown with positive sign (0) has the value .1011 = 11/16.

CASE 1. *Multiplication of two 31-bit numbers rounded to a 31-bit product*. Rounding to a 31-bit product means that the thirty-second bit of the product is examined. If it is 0 (i.e., bits 32–62 represent less than $\frac{1}{2} \times 2^{-31}$), then nothing is done; if it is 1 (i.e., bits 32–62 represent greater than or equal to $\frac{1}{2} \times 2^{31}$), then 1 is added into bit position 31 of the product. The magnitude of the error in the product is therefore no greater than

$$\tfrac{1}{2} \times 2^{-31} = 2^{-32}.$$

CASE 2. An exact datum is read into the computer and rounded to 31 bits. If the rounding is done as above, by looking at the thirty-second bit, then again the magnitude of the error is no greater than $2^{-32}$.

The analysis of roundoff error in a long calculation is usually very difficult. Sometimes, by considering the worst possible error magnitude in each roundoff, a bound on the worst error in the result can be obtained, but this bound may be very conservative (i.e., much larger than the actual error). For example, suppose each of $N$ numbers read into the computer, as in Case 2 above, are added. The quantity $N \cdot 2^{-32}$ is then a bound on the error in the sum, but this bound will occur only if all numbers have the maximum possible roundoff error *with the same sign.* Generally, individual roundoff errors will be less than the maximum possible and will have both positive and negative values so that there will be some cancellation of errors when they are added. Probabilistic analysis shows that for this addition example, the *probable error*, defined as the value exceeded by the actual roundoff error one-half of the time, is given approximately by $0.2 \times \sqrt{N} \times 2^{-32}$. The *square root rule* (i.e., replacing the number of operations $N$ by $\sqrt{N}$) is often used as a rule of thumb in making probable error estimates from maximum error bounds.

As an example of the disastrous effects that roundoff error can have, we consider the case of finding the zeros of the polynomial

$$(x - 1)(x - 2)(x - 3) \cdots (x - 20),$$

where the computer is given the coefficients $A_0$ to $A_{19}$ in

$$x^{20} + A_{19}x^{19} + A_{18}x^{18} + \cdots + A_2x^2 + A_1x + A_0.$$

It is easily calculated that $A_{19} = -210$. Now suppose that the coefficients $A_0, A_1, \ldots A_{18}$ are all stored exactly in the computer, but that, because of a roundoff error, $A_{19}$ is stored as $-210 - 2^{-23}$, noting that $2^{-23}$ is approximately one ten-millionth. This one error changes the polynomial so that—even if the computer then calculated the zeros exactly (i.e., with no further roundoff errors)—instead of 1,2, . . ., 20, it would obtain (correct to three decimal places)

| | | |
|---|---|---|
| 1.000 | 6.000 | $10.095 \pm 0.644i$ |
| 2.000 | 7.000 | $11.794 \pm 1.652i$ |
| 3.000 | 8.007 | $13.992 \pm 2.519i$ |
| 4.000 | 8.917 | $16.731 \pm 2.813i$ |
| 5.000 | 20.847 | $19.502 \pm 1.940i$ |

Not only have the larger zeros become quite inaccurate, but ten of them have also changed from real to complex conjugate pairs, all because of one error in the seventh decimal place. Problems in which a single, small roundoff error in the data or in subsequent calculation results in much larger errors in the answers, are called "ill-conditioned." Recognition of ill-condition may be difficult, although some classes of problems—such as the calculation of the zeros of higher-degree polynomials—are known to be generally ill-conditioned. Unless an ill-conditioned problem can be somehow transformed to well-conditioned form, it is usually true that the only way to overcome ill-condition is by using multiple precision arithmetic in which the individual roundoff errors will be much smaller.

### Reference

1963. Wilkinson, J. H. *Rounding Errors in Algebraic Processes.* Englewood Cliffs, N.J.: Prentice-Hall.

A. Ralston

**RUN TIME.** *See* Compile and Run Time.

# S

**SCS.** *See* Society for Computer Simulation.

**SDI.** *See* Current Awareness System.

## SCHEDULING ALGORITHM

For articles on related subjects *see* Interrupt; Multiprogramming; Operating Systems; Processing Modes; Swapping; Time Sharing; and Time Slice.

For articles on related terms *see* Algorithm; and Real-Time Applications.

Operating systems, particularly for medium- and large-scale computers, use many algorithms to schedule the work in the computer. Whenever there is a choice of things to do, a scheduling algorithm decides which is to be done first. There are identifiable bodies of code in most time-sharing and multiprogrammed operating systems that accomplish the following:

1. Selection of the next job to be initiated for execution.

2. Selection of the next of several "currently running" programs to be executed on the CPU.

3. Selection of the next of several already posted I/O operations to be started (in order to minimize disk arm movement and/or rotational latency).

4. Selection of the next program or program fragments to be swapped between primary and secondary storage.

5. Selection of the next program output to be transferred to printer, punch, plotter, or other symbiont (spooled) output device.

6. Decisions controlling the use of physical resources (particularly tapes and private disk packs, but also bodies of code and access to public files of data).

Scheduling algorithms have enjoyed a wide popular and theoretic appeal. As a prestige work assignment for system programmers, they have been the subject of many mathematical analyses, simulation studies, and doctoral dissertations. The objective of most of these studies, especially the early ones, was to find algorithms that optimized hardware performance. Recently, more attention has been paid to the optimization of the entire use of the machine (including human factors), which requires high-speed response and good job turnaround time in addition to good hardware utilization for a system that may, for example, simultaneously service 10 to 100 on-line users together with 2 to 10 batch job partitions.

The earliest and most durable interest has been in execution-time scheduling. The earliest algorithm, called "round-robin" scheduling, simply cycled from user program to user program, giving each program the opportunity to use the CPU for a period of time equal to the established "time slice." Of course it never was just that simple. After all, the primary purpose of the whole time-sharing system was the need to provide fast response to commands just issued by users at their terminals. Thus, such users were more important than others—say, for example, those whose programs had already been running for several minutes.

Early systems classified each concurrently running program into one of several states, depending on its most recent activity. Most important of these states were (1) waiting for the completion of terminal input, (2) waiting for the completion of terminal output, (3) ready-to-run (input or output having arrived), and (4) running without requiring terminal I/O for at least the last time slice. Thus, the execution scheduling could be relatively straightforward: Those programs waiting for input from a terminal or completion of output to a terminal need not be considered for execution: those ready to run should be serviced quickly in order to achieve timely response; and finally, those in the fourth state could be round-robined at the time-slice frequency until there was another program ready to run and which required immediate attention.

It was quickly determined that this simple algorithm was inadequate because it did not provide sufficient bias in favor of short, small programs; both too much CPU time and too much overhead (due to swapping) were given over to long, large jobs. Since in many installations the greater number of user programs were short and small, the best response could be achieved by biasing the scheduling algorithm in their favor. In early systems, this problem was solved through the observation that the longer a program had already been running, the longer it was likely to run before entering one of the waiting states. Thus, one or more lower-priority running queues were created to which both long-running and large programs were demoted. These queues were serviced less frequently (which provided better service to the short program), but were also given longer execution time slices, which decreased overhead and thus increased system efficiency.

This problem was of critical importance in early systems, which had only a single program in core memory at a time, and therefore there was nothing to do during the time one program was being swapped for another. Following the introduction of memory paging or program relocation hardware, more than one program could occupy core at a time; thus, the CPU could be working on one program while another was being swapped.

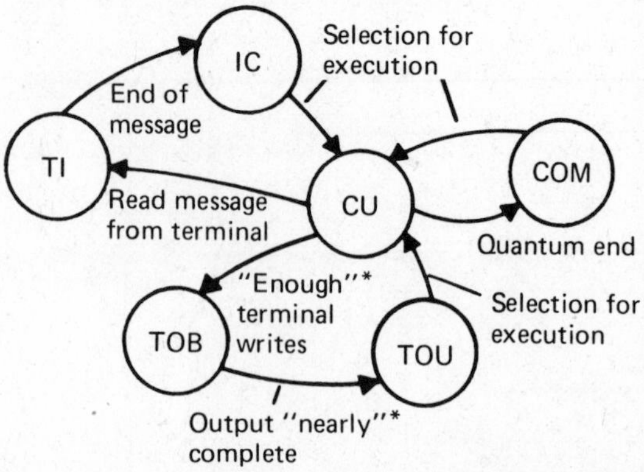


**Fig. 1** State diagram of a scheduling algorithm. Priority lists: *Execution and Swap*—IC, TOU, CU, COM; *Outswap*—TI, TOB, COM. CU = current CPU user, TI = terminal inputting, IC = terminal input message complete, TOB = terminal output blocked, TOU = terminal output unblocked, COM = compute bound. *Proper setting of parameters "enough" and "nearly" depends on terminal speed. "Enough" writes limits amount of buffering required for characters destined for terminal. Blocked program restarts when number of characters remaining is "nearly" enough to cover scheduling and swapping time, thereby providing continuous output at terminal.

The state diagram in Fig. 1 illustrates a simplified version of the operation of a scheduling algorithm similar to that used by several time-sharing systems. Each node represents one of the states in which a user's program may be. Events generated by the program, the system, the user's terminal, and the clock cause transitions of the program from one state to another. The system maintains a FIFO list of users in each state and schedules from priority lists. One list contains all programs in states ready for execution or inswap and then execution. The other contains all programs in states that make them candidates for outswap. The scheduler makes its selections after each event (e.g., end of time quantum for CU program; completion of input message for program) occurs. First a swap is determined by finding the highest-priority out-of-core user on the inswap list and a corresponding in-core user from the outswap list, if any. Second, a user is selected for execution by finding the highest-priority user on the execution list. Responsiveness to terminal requests is achieved by giving high priority for both swap and execution when a complete input message arrives for the user's program. When only compute-bound users are active, then simple round-robining among them at the established time slice quantum occurs.

Following the introduction of these multiprogrammed systems, scheduling algorithms took into account more of the states of user programs, and based scheduling on more events than those driving the simple scheduling algorithms described above. Xerox's CP-V system on Sigma 6 and Sigma 9 machines, for example, expands the number of scheduling states to 30, and uses them to form the scheduling priority lists not only for execution scheduling but also for scheduling of nonresident programs to be swapped into core as well as resident programs to be swapped out. (The objective, of course, is to try to trade waiting programs in core for runnable programs out of core.)

The most important of the new states are those recording the initiation, progress, and completion of file I/O operations. It appears that the best throughput is achieved by giving higher CPU priority to programs that have just completed an I/O operation, since they have an established history of short CPU use and rather longer I/O operations. Such an algorithm admits the possibility that several I/O-bound programs will fill core memory and thereby lock out a CPU-bound program for some period of time, though practically this does not seem to be a serious problem.

The same hardware that permitted the interrupt-driven systems and asynchronous I/O described above also produced real-time systems used in process control. These systems are scheduled by hardware priorities established for each of the possible interrupt events. Instead of time-slicing of programs at the same interrupt level, these systems provided a priority hierarchy of execution levels, with the highest levels running to completion (or until I/O initiation) before execution of a lower priority program. In the 1970s, systems were introduced that combined batch-program execution, time sharing, and real-time programming in a single multi-use system. Digital Equipment's DEC System 10 and Xerox's CP-V are examples of such multipurpose systems.

Some numerical algorithms have been used in various systems to control the priority scheduling of jobs. These, as do all scheduling algorithms, reflect the policies of machine use established by the installation management. It is typical in time-sharing systems to establish a policy that favors short computational tasks interleaved with terminal interaction, and to demote long computational tasks. Terminal response time is to be minimized for small, short, interactive tasks. An example of such an algorithm is that due to Corbató in the CTSS system, and since extended to MULTICS. Each user is assigned a queue level based on his size according to

$$l = \left[ \log_2 \left( \frac{Wp}{Wq} \right) + 1 \right],$$

where $Wp$ is the number of words in the program and $Wq$ is the number of words transferable to and from secondary storage in one quantum. A user on level 1 is allowed to execute for $2^l$ time quanta before being demoted one queue level. The quantum is reset upon terminal interaction. Since queues are served from lowest $l$ to highest $l$, those programs that are small and interact rapidly, using small amounts of CPU time, get the best service, which is the desired policy.

### References

1966. Bryan, G. E. *JOSS: Introduction to the System Implementation.* The Rand Corporation, P-3486 (November); also published by the Digital Equipment Computer Users Society, DECUS Proceedings.

1972. Wilkes, M. V. *Timesharing Computer Systems* (2d ed.). New York: American Elsevier.

G. E. Bryan

# SCIENTIFIC APPLICATIONS

For articles on related subjects *see* Information Retrieval; Numerical Analysis; Pattern Recognition; Simulation: Principles; and Statistical Applications.

Computation has always played a central role in the closed cycle known as the "scientific method." A new theory gains acceptance or falls by the wayside in direct proportion to its success in explaining known phenomena and predicting new ones, not just qualitatively but also quantitatively. Einstein's theory of relativity predicted not just that light should be deflected in passing by a massive object such as the sun, but also the precise amount by which it should be deflected. No computer is needed for such a prediction (indeed, the first such calculation antedated electronic computers by almost a half-century), but a certain minimum amount of arithmetic computation is nonetheless required. This is typical of any new scientific discovery, since the truly fundamental physical phenomena are governed by equations that describe what happens to small particles or energy bundles as they move through space and time.

It is often of scientific interest to calculate the behavior of not just one particle, but also aggregates of such particles over large regions of space or within long time intervals. Scientists facing such a task usually have a choice of two basically different approaches. One can calculate the flight of an individual particle until it is scattered by a second particle, absorbed, or leaves the region of observation (Fig. 1). The exact history of each particle depends on a sequence of random numbers chosen and used in such a way as to constrain the particle to experience one event or another in accord with its correct probability. Tracking and accumulating statistics on thousands of such particles then enable calculation of quantities of physical interest. Such a technique is called the Monte Carlo method, for obvious reasons, and finds application in such diverse situations as the behavior of neutrons in a reactor, the light quanta or "photons" in stellar atmospheres, and automobiles in heavy traffic. Monte Carlo calculations are inherently time consuming, even on very fast electronic computers, because of the necessity to follow a sufficiently large number of particles to obtain results that are accurate within statistically acceptable limits of error.

The second principal line of computational attack occurs more often, namely, when (1) the behavior of the quantity of interest is known to obey a linear or nonlinear algebraic equation, a differential equation, an integral equation, or an integro-differential equation over some region of space/time of given shape, and when (2) the desired quantity obeys specified boundary conditions in space (and initial conditions in time in time-dependent problems). Taking differential equations as an example, the simplest situations occur when the desired quantity (the dependent variable) is a function of only one independent variable, perhaps time or one-space dimension. Such differential equations are called "ordinary." In such cases, either an analytic solution is obtainable or use of a simple difference equation approximation will allow production of desired answers in a few seconds of computer time.

When the dependent variable is a function of two or more independent variables, the appropriate differential equation is called a "partial differential equation" because it involves partial derivatives that indicate the change in the dependent variable as one or another of the independent variables change while holding all other independent variables fixed. Except under special circumstances, the solution of such equations is computationally formidable. As an example, consider an electromagnetic wave imping-

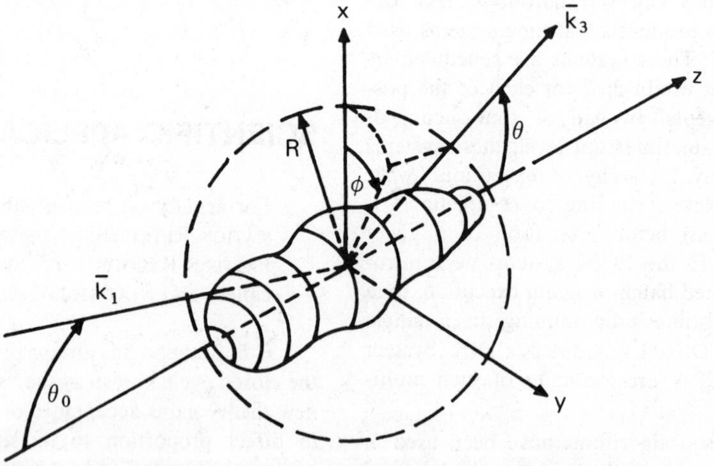


**Fig. 1.** Geometry for scattering from an arbitrarily shaped body of revolution. (From E. D. Reilly, Jr., in *Journal of Computational Physics,* April 1973, Academic Press, New York.)

ing on a target of given shape and internal composition. In principle, Maxwell's system of differential equations and attendant boundary conditions completely specify the behavior of the radiation scattered from the target. When the target is either a metallic (perfectly reflecting) sphere or a penetrable sphere of homogeneous and isotropic internal electrical properties, Maxwell's partial differential equations reduce to three ordinary differential equations, one each specifying the behavior of the scattered wave with the $r$, $\theta$, and $\phi$ directions in spherical coordinates. This has been known at least as far back as 1908, and so-called Mie calculations (after their originator), while tedious, can be programmed and normally take only a few seconds of computer time.

Imagine the target, while still spherical, to have internal electrical properties that are a function of radial position. Perhaps the core is dense and surrounded by a diffuse fringe, for example. Then Maxwell's equations still separate into three ordinary differential equations, but the radial equation, which in the homogeneous case was known to have solutions familiar to scientists (Bessel functions), must now be solved from point to point by difference methods. A digital computer is now a virtual necessity.

Now envision a progression of relaxations of symmetry conditions; each will greatly extend computer running time: Nonspherical, but still axially symmetric, targets will require several minutes to an hour of computer time and anisotropic targets will need a few minutes to an hour or more (depending on spatial symmetry), and so on up to completely nonsymmetric anisotropic targets, which would take several hours, even on the fastest computers presently available.

The situation described above is typical of a number of physical situations. A scientist will often know that the subject of his study is governed by equations whose full complexity places exact solutions beyond the capability of the computer available to him. A sufficient number of approximations is then made to bring a typical calculation down to an acceptable bound, usually an hour or less, on the available computer. When the installation serving him increases its capability by, say, a factor of 4, he will not necessarily be content to run four times as many cases in unit time, but will often remove a restriction or approximation, which will bring total running time back to an hour or so.

In reactor design, for example, it is known that neutron behavior is governed by a complex integro-differential equation known as Boltzmann's equation. This equation takes into account that, at any given spatial point, the rate of neutron flow depends on their speed and direction, and to a certain extent on their past history. The solution of such an equation everywhere throughout reactor volume for all possible neutron velocities is a task beyond presently available computers. However, what can be, and usually is, done is to make approximations that replace the Boltzmann equation with a series of coupled partial differential equations, each of which calculates neutron flux at a particular energy (speed) at a given space point. Each such equation, a so-called diffusion equation, is then calculated in either one-, two-, or three-space dimensions, whichever the symmetry of the reactor (or expediency) demands. Any horizontal plane through a reactor core is obviously best modeled in cartesian $(x,y)$ coordinates, but other geometric arrangements often dictate use of polar $(r,\theta)$ or cylindrical $(r,z)$ coordinates. Any of these geometries reduces to this simple situation: Given that $p$, $a$, $c$, $d$, and $e$ are known functions of position (precalculated and stored in computer memory prior to the time-consuming calculation of neutron flux), we would like to know what values of neutron flux $\phi_P$, $\phi_A$, $\phi_C$, $\phi_D$, $\phi_E$ balance the equation

$$p\phi_P - a\phi_A - c\phi_C - d\phi_D - e\phi_E = 0$$

at every mesh-point $P$, where left, right, bottom, and top neighboring points are designated $A$, $C$, $D$, and $E$, respectively. All questions of geometry, material composition, and boundary condition are buried in the calculation of the coefficients. Any one such equation has five unknowns, and hence cannot be solved uniquely, but since a similar equation must hold at every mesh point, a 10,000-point model (say) represents 10,000 equations in 10,000 unknowns. In principle, this can be solved by inverting a $10{,}000 \times 10{,}000$ matrix. Such an attempt would be not only foolish but unnecessary. Since most elements of such a matrix would be zero (the result of using only a nearest-neighbor numerical approximation to derivatives in the diffusion equation), the desired fluxes are best obtained iteratively. There is a variety of methods for doing this, but most process a line of points at a time, sweeping all lines a sufficient number of times to obtain the desired convergence. Here, "sweeping" means the consistent solution of just the 100 (say) points on a line by a systematic forward-elimination/backward-substitution method applicable to so-called three-term linear systems (matrices whose only nonzero elements are on the diagonal or next to the diagonal).

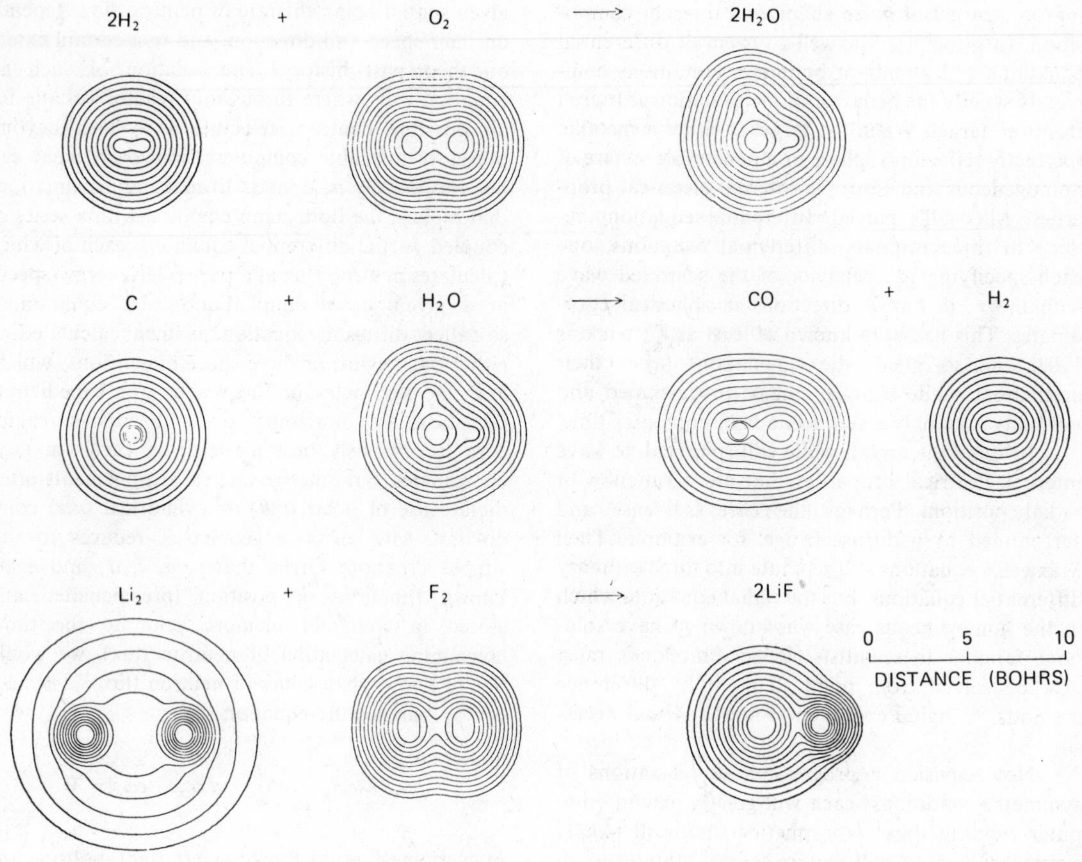


**Fig. 2.** Three chemical reactions portrayed in terms of changes in computer-produced electron-density diagrams. Top shows two hydrogen molecules combining with an oxygen molecule to form two water molecules. Middle shows a carbon atom and a water molecule combining to form a carbon monoxide molecule and a hydrogen molecule. Bottom shows a lithium molecule and a fluorine molecule combining to form two lithium fluoride molecules. Although these are simple reactions, it appears reasonable to expect that this general approach can be extended to much more complicated reactions. (From Arnold C. Wahl in *Scientific American,* April 1970, fig. 5.)

Although the preceding discussion assumed use of a two-dimensional slice taken from a full three-dimensional reactor, the technique can be extended (at great expense in computer time) to all three space dimensions, and can be used to calculate quantities of interest other than neutron flux.

In some fields, the increasing speed and memory capacity of successive generations of digital computers have transformed the image that the computer conveys to the scientist from that of a tool—albeit a powerful one—to that of a new experimental device in its own right. Chemistry is a good example. The basic equation that governs the behavior of molecules, atoms, and (low velocity) electrons has been known for almost 50 years—the Schrödinger equation. Without a computer, only simple systems consisting of two or three particles can be studied in any detail (see Fig. 2). With the latest computers, however, ions of much larger atomic number can be followed kinetically as they interact with other ions to form molecules. If the chemist is able to watch the progression of such a reaction on a TV-like display device attached to the computer, it is just as good or better (and less messy) than mixing the reagents in the laboratory. ("Better" because he has only limited means of varying the speed of an actual reaction, but could cause the simulated reaction to proceed at "instant replay" slow motion on the display device through appropriate variation of program parameters.)

**Inverse Calculations.** All of the examples cited thus far are examples of "direct" calculational situations. We know the characteristics of a target and want to calculate its scattering properties. We know the reactor configuration and desire its lifetime behavior. We know the reagents and want to know their reactivity. As time-consuming as such calculations can be, they are routine in their demand for computer time compared to indirect or "inverse" calculations, where we have access to experimental data but no access at all to the source of the phenomena generating the data.

An example is the problem of interstellar dust particles. Astrophysicists and cosmologists would like to know the quantity, shape, and composition of these particles, since this knowledge has a bearing on theories of the origin and evolution of the universe. We cannot yet send space ships to retrieve such matter, but we can observe quantities such as the polarization and absorption of light of various wavelengths passing through it. What kinds of particles produce scattered light: spherical? elongated? metallic? anisotropic ferrite needles? dirty ice? The question is far from settled, and the astrophysicist will need to experiment with many different models to achieve success without being at all sure that the answer is unique.

Crystallographic calculations are another example of inverse computations. It would be straightforward to calculate the pattern of x-rays diffracted from a known spatial distribution of known atoms, but we cannot get inside crystals or molecules the way Asimov's fictional scientists traveled through the circulatory system in "Fantastic Voyage." We can observe the pattern of diffracted x-rays or neutrons impinging on a crystal of unknown structure, but in doing so, certain basic information (phase relations between atoms) is lost. Using what information is available, however, such as intensity data, suspected symmetries, and chemical formulas learned through destructive testing of portions of the same material, crystallographers are now able to use an organized trial-and-error method to deduce the structure of quite large molecules of up to 100 atoms or so, and the frontier is pushed ahead with each advance in computer technology.

As complex as they are, the structures of several proteins as well as the vitamin $B_{12}$ have been determined by computer techniques. Some programs are so sophisticated that they produce as a final result a stereo pair (Fig. 3) of similar views of the predicted molecular structure; viewing them through an appropriate optical device brings out the spatial arrangement and vibrational characteristics of crystal constituent atoms in stunning detail.

Just as the astrophysicist and the crystallographer are barred from entering the domain of the

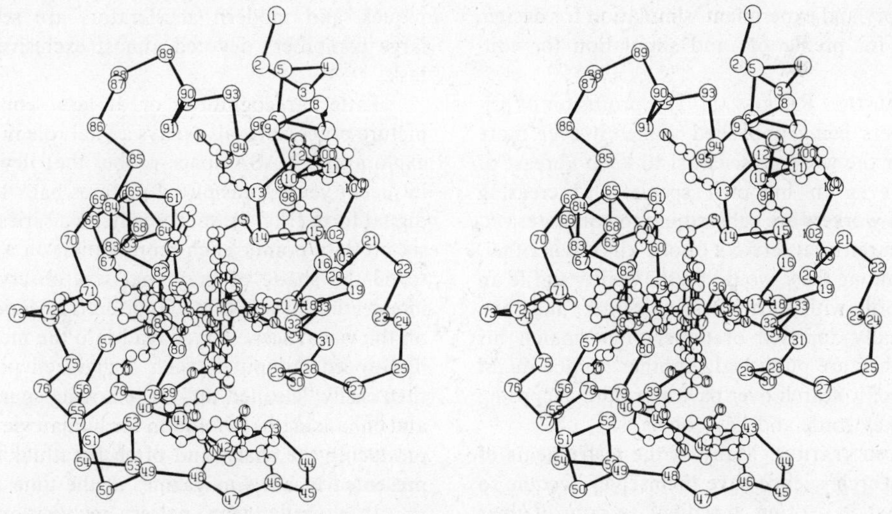

**Fig. 3.** Stereoscopic pair of front view of reduced cytochrome *c* molecule from a tuna. (Source: R. E. Dickerson, California Institute of Technology.)

objects of their interest, so is the geophysicist unable to examine more than an infinitesimal fraction of the interior of the earth. There is data, however, that gives extremely pointed clues as to the internal composition of the earth, namely, that provided through seismological records taken during periods of earthquake, volcanic eruption, and atomic testing. The earth, like any (approximate) sphere of given internal composition, has certain characteristic modes of vibration, and allows elastic waves to propagate at certain speeds from point to point on its surface. By using digital computers to vary appropriate parameters in the equations that govern such phenomena, geophysicists have derived a profile of the earth's interior with reasonable certitude, a confidence founded on agreement between the predicted characteristics of their model and observed properties. Based on such methods, they already predict a molten liquid core, and their detailed predictions of its shape and composition are being sharpened as they make increasingly detailed comparisons with experimental data of the effects the liquid core might have on the earth's rotational and magnetic properties. Similar methods are allowing geologists to map strain energies in the earth in an attempt to understand earthquake phenomena.

**Ancillary Roles.** In addition to their obvious value for direct and inverse calculation, digital computers play a role in automating many other aspects of the scientist's personal work load. These will be discussed under the headings information retrieval, instrumentation, data reduction, comparison of theory and experiment, simulation for design, simulation for prediction, and simulation for education.

INFORMATION RETRIEVAL. The profusion of scientific papers being published makes it ever more difficult for the working scientist to keep abreast of his field, even in his own specialty. Increasing numbers of workers are subscribing to computerized information retrieval services of one kind or another. Principal among these would be the ability to file an interest profile with such a service center, and then be continually apprised of papers that match his profile as they are published; another service might make a specific search over past literature according to certain keywords and key concepts.

INSTRUMENTATION. Many of the instruments of modern research science have themselves become so complex that it is often expedient to control their operation automatically with a small computer directly connected to the instrument. Nuclear reactors and particle accelerators are often controlled or at least monitored in this way, as are a wide range of other devices such as radio and optical telescopes, nuclear magnetic resonance equipment, crystallographic apparatus, electron microscopes, and satellites forced to obey telemetered signals emanating from computers on the ground below.

DATA REDUCTION, PRESENTATION, AND PATTERN RECOGNITION. The data produced by an experimental instrument is seldom directly usable. It usually needs some kind of scaling, noise filtering, time integration, or other treatment that is ideally suited to computer processing. As a by-product of this data reduction, a properly equipped computer can also display the reduced data either in hard-copy form on a graph plotter or in a transient visual form on a cathode-ray tube display device. Thus, a scientist may monitor an experiment in progress and perhaps even input feedback information that alters the later course of his work.

Some of the more interesting applications of data reduction occur in a pattern-recognition context. The classic example is the widespread use of devices called "bubble chambers" in high-energy physics. Particles passing through such devices leave visible tracks composed of tiny bubbles, which can be photographed and scanned for the occurrence of interesting branchlike structures that indicate the presence of a collision or reaction between particles. Although humans can do this quite well, a bubble chamber can snap a new picture every few seconds and easily reach an annual production of over a million frames. Such prodigious output can be coped with only by computerized pattern-recognition techniques, and modern accelerators are serviced by large computers devoted almost exclusively to this task.

Pattern recognition, or at least computerized picture processing, also plays a vital role in planetary exploration. NASA space probes that flew by Mars in recent years transmitted pictures back to earth in digital form (Fig. 4), specifically, as a series of 40,000 six-bit data points, each representing on a scale of 0 to 63 the shade of gray that was observed at the intersection of a $200 \times 200$ grid array superimposed on the visual scene. Once read into the memory of a high-speed computer, such a digitized picture was then easily "cleaned up" by removing spurious noise and enhancing its resolution for human viewing, thus producing the sharp and often breathtaking photos presented in news magazines at the time.

In a similar vein, pattern recognition by computer has been used by scientists in other fields. Biologists have successfully identified mutant chromosomes among normal ones through such tech-

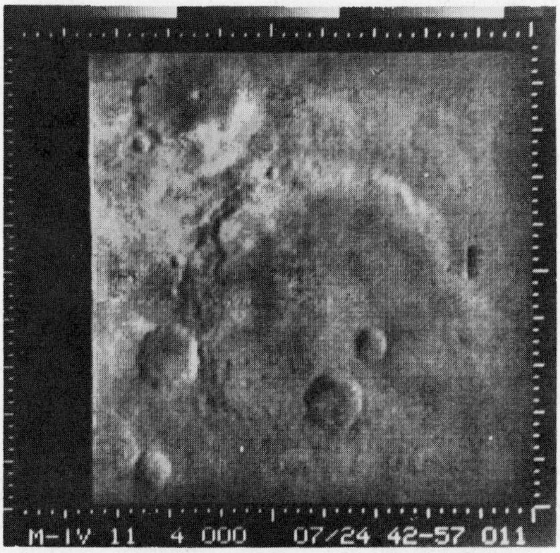


**Fig. 4.** A computer enhanced photograph of a portion of the surface of Mars. (Source: Jet Propulsion Laboratory.)

niques. Atmospheric scientists are experimenting with attempts to identify cyclonelike disturbances in cloud-cover satellite photos. Archeologists have successfully reconstructed murals from Egyptian temples by fitting together photographs of stone fragments as if they were pieces in a gigantic jigsaw puzzle solved by computer matching of similar patterns. In a similar application, but with far fewer pieces to worry about, earth scientists have tested theories of continental drift by doing a computerized comparison of how well the east coast of North and South America fits the west coast of Europe and Africa, and found the answer to be very plausible indeed.

COMPARISON OF THEORY AND EXPERIMENT. Some physical situations are insufficiently well understood to be described according to fundamental principles and therefore must be treated phenomenologically. This implies that an equation devised to cover the phenomena contains a number of adjustable parameters whose values are not known in advance, or known only within certain bounds. An example is the scattering of nuclear particles such as protons and electrons from atomic nuclei. In principle, the scattering properties are known (through solution of Schrödinger's equation) when the strength and shape of the force field or "potential" causing the scattering (i.e., the target nucleus) is known, but such characteristics of nuclei are extremely difficult to calculate quantitatively from first principles.

The solution is to characterize the potential as having a certain functional form containing several adjustable parameters such as potential depth, nuclear radius, degree of surface diffuseness, etc., up to as many as eight or nine such parameters. It then becomes a task worthy of a modern computer to vary these parameters to achieve that degree of agreement between theory and experiment that gives the best fit, in the least squares sense. This is not a trivial task; it is something like trying to achieve the sharpest possible picture on a color TV set that has nine adjustable knobs and where adjusting one may make it necessary to readjust knobs already set by earlier trial and error. To achieve a reasonable fit, the computer must effectively search through an $n$-dimensional parameter space, recalculating the scattering at reasonably small steps in the parameters along the way. It is not unusual to consume hours of computer time in the process, but the scientist who does this considers the additional insights gained into nuclear structure well worth the effort.

SIMULATION FOR DESIGN. The calculational problems associated with the behavior of neutrons in a reactor have been discussed previously, but the rationale for studying these problems was not considered. Initially, through the late 1940s and early 1950s, research data was reasonably fundamental, since the properties of neutron propagation in various materials under a variety of operating conditions were imperfectly understood. As in other fields, however, the widespread use of digital computers accelerated the natural progression of a given type of activity, from research to applied science to engineering. The point has now been reached where most reactor calculations are part of a design engineering process whose aim is to simulate performance of tentative reactor designs in lieu of constructing an experimental prototype. By this technique, many hundreds of design variations can be tested in theory and only the most promising results need be tested in practice.

The preceding example is typical of many applications of simulation to design practice. In the same vein, other large scientific instruments can be engineered to desired specifications through preliminary simulation of a large number of alternative designs. It would now be extremely difficult for humans using precomputer methods to design the large accelerators used in high-energy physics research or the large radio telescopes used in astronomy.

SIMULATION FOR PREDICTION. Another reason for simulating a complex physical system is to

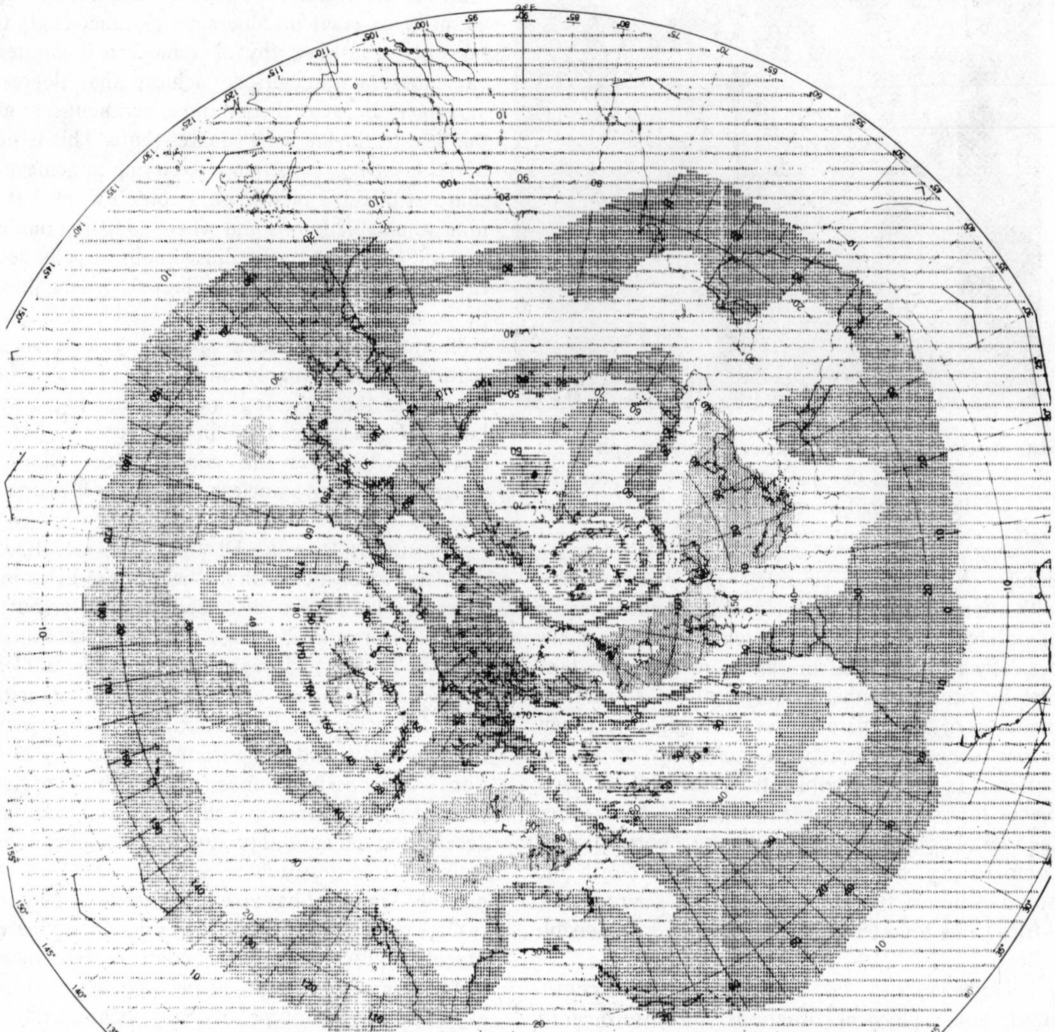


**Fig. 5.** Computer-produced weather map of the Northern Hemisphere with geographical outlines superimposed. The four-digit numbers are observed geopotential heights of the 1,000 mbar surface. The shaded swaths represent lines of constant geopotential intervals and are a rough measure of wind direction, with narrower channels indicating stronger winds.

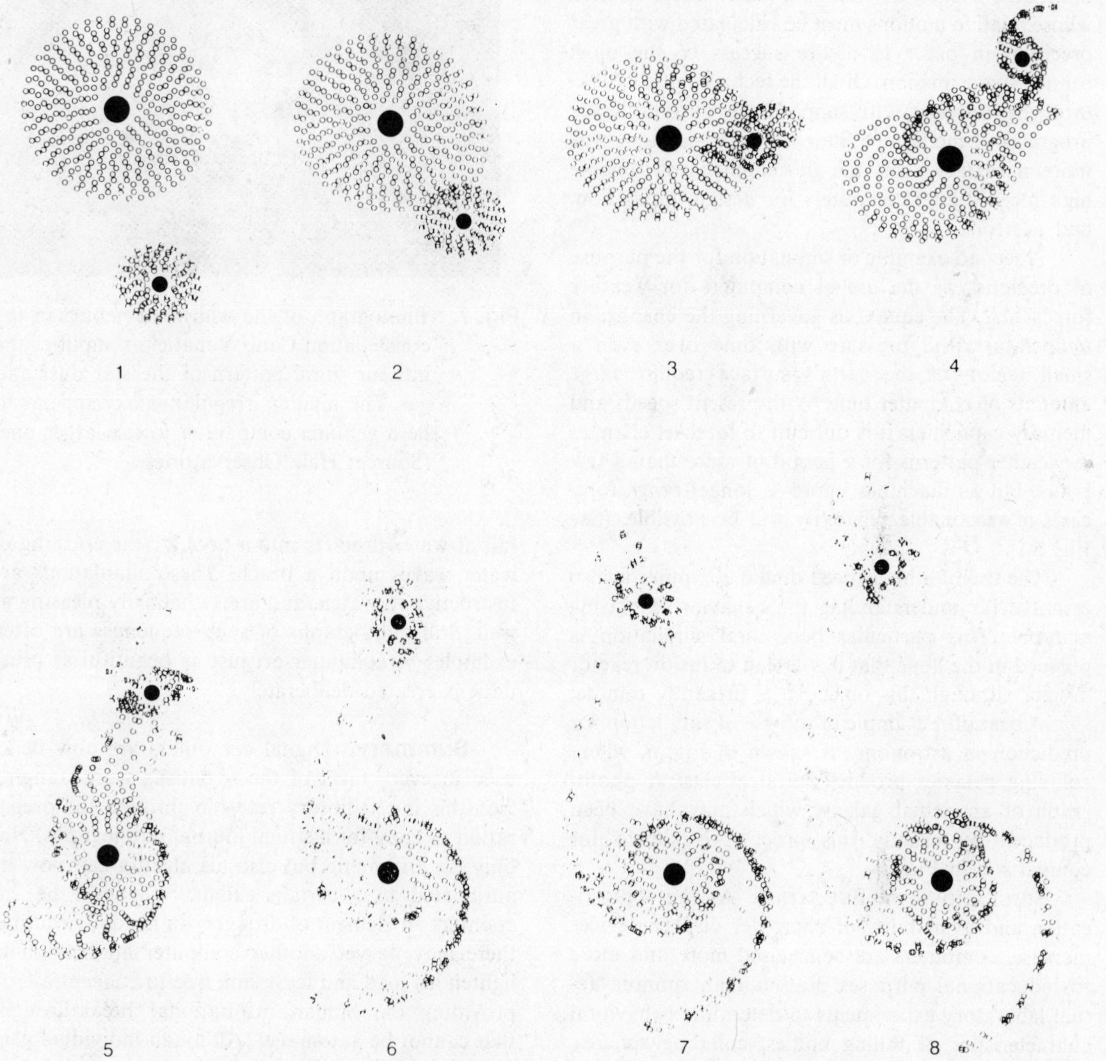


**Fig. 6.** Computer simulation of flyby of small galaxy past a larger one. In time frames *1* and *2*, the barely distorted small galaxy is still rising toward the viewer. At its closest approach to the larger galaxy (*3*) it passes as much in front of it as to the right of it. The tidal effects in both disks (*4*) are distinctly two-sided. As the smaller galaxy recedes (*5-7*), the tide it raised on the side of the larger disk closer to it evolves into a narrow bridge connecting the two galaxies. The similar bulge that it caused on the far side wraps into a fine counterarm that will become sparse and eventually disappear. (From Alar and Juri Toomre, "Violent Tides between Galaxies," © December 1973 by *Scientific American, Inc*. All rights reserved. With permission.)

predict its behavior. The physical laws governing the motion of planetary bodies are intrinsically simple for two-body systems, but they are intractable analytically for the complex systems of earth, moon, multistage rockets of changing mass, satellites, etc., whose relative motions must be calculated with great precision in order to assure success of the most routine space mission. Of all the technological breakthroughs necessary to support the current space programs of the United States and Russia, none was more necessary than the development of reliable high-speed digital computers for design, prediction, and control.

A second example of simulation for the purpose of prediction is the use of computers for weather forecasting. The equations governing the changes in temperature and pressure with time over even a small region of the earth's surface require large amounts of computer time. With present speeds and memory capacities, it is difficult to forecast changes in weather patterns for a period of more than a few hours, but as machines improve, longer-range forecasts of reasonable reliability will be possible. (See Fig. 5.)

The use of a high-speed digital computer is also essential for understanding the behavior of plasma material. This particular behavioral simulation is pursued in the hope that it will lead to fusion reactor design, although this objective is presently remote.

A beautiful example of the use of simulation for prediction in astronomy is shown in Fig. 6, where colliding galaxies produce spiral effects. A photograph of an actual galaxy, which may have been produced by exactly this process, is shown for comparison in Fig. 7.

**Fig. 7.** Photograph of the whirlpool nebula in the constellation Canis Venatici exemplifies the interior spiral pattern of the star dust and gas. The smaller, irregular galaxy appears to be a genuine companion to the larger one. (Source: Hale Observatories.)

SIMULATION FOR EDUCATION. As the sophistication and availability of computer display devices increase, computers are being used more and more for educational purposes. Rather than running actual laboratory experiments to determine behavioral characteristics of falling bodies, colliding spheres, pendulums, projectiles, etc., the event to be studied can be simulated at any desired rate on a cathode-ray tube display device. The student can then interact with the computer to study the effect of changing parameters, such as the mass of a pendulum bob, the angle of elevation of the initial launch of a rocket, or any one or more of other factors that affect the experiment at hand.

Using such numerical simulation and display techniques one can even examine phenomena that are closed to easy observation in the laboratory; for example, the tunneling of a quantum mechanical particle through a potential barrier, the slow-motion fall of water droplets into a pool, or the crashing of water waves upon a beach. These simulations are instructive to watch, and are esthetically pleasing as well. Still photographs of such sequences are often examples of computer art just as beautiful as other designs created deliberately.

**Summary.** Digital computers are now being used in every facet of the scientist's work, ranging from his initial library research through the preparation of copy for his final journal publications. Not only his arithmetic but also his algebra can now be automated to a certain extent. Whenever he encounters an element of drudgery in his daily routine, there may be yet another computer application to lighten his load and leave him free to concentrate on providing the human inspirational breakthroughs that cannot be automated. Although individual genius will create new systems in the future, as it has in the historic past, the average working scientist today cannot be competitive unless he has access to a digital computer and is reasonably proficient in its use.

REFERENCES

*Note:* The weekly magazine *Science*, a publication of the American Association for the Advancement of Science in Washington, D.C., contains frequent articles on the application of computers to science.

1970. Fernbach, S., and A. Taub (Eds.). *Computers and Their Role in the Physical Sciences.* New York: Gordon and Breach Science Publishers.

1971. Oettinger, A. "The Use of Computers in Science," *Scientific American* (September 1966). Reprinted in R. Fenichel and J. Weizenbaum (Eds.), *Computers and Computation—Readings from Scientific American.* San Francisco: W. H. Freeman.

E. D. REILLY, JR.

## SCRATCH FILES

For articles on related subjects *see* FILES; and MEMORY: Auxiliary.

During the processing of substantial files of data, it often becomes necessary to create temporary files for later use by copying all or part of a data set to an auxiliary-memory device—tape, disk, or drum. Such a temporary file (or the associated storage device) is called a "scratch file." Sometimes, scratch-file data is unchanged from what was originally read into the computer, e.g., during sorting. In other applications (compilations, data editing, etc.), scratch-file data is partially processed.

In most installations, scratch-file devices are the fastest available: drums or fixed-head disk drives; other disk drives; or high-speed magnetic tapes. In large installations, several disk drives (or tape drives, or both) are often allocated permanently for general-user scratch-file storage. In a multiprogramming environment, several users can simultaneously allocate modest amounts of scratch-file storage from this pool. This tends to economize the number of disk drives required at an installation, compared to the alternative strategy of having each user furnish private packs for his scratch files.

D. N. FREEMAN

## SEAC

For articles on related subjects *see* DIGITAL COMPUTERS: Early; EDVAC; and SWAC.

In 1947, with the encouragement of the U.S. Navy, the National Bureau of Standards (NBS) established the National Applied Mathematical Laboratories under the leadership of John Curtiss. The purpose was to create a centralized national computation facility equipped with high-speed automatic computers, which would provide a computing service for other governmental agencies and play an active part in the further development of computing machinery.

The Census Bureau, the U.S. Air Force, and the U.S. Navy all supported the Laboratories, and negotiations for the acquisition of computers from Eckert and Mauchly (later acquired by Sperry Rand), from Engineering Research Associates (a supplier to the security agencies), and from Raytheon Corporation (RAYDAC), were under way in 1948. Impatient with the slow development of computers, and feeling the need for more "hands-on" expertise, the NBS decided at a meeting in May 1948 to build its own computer; later in the same year the decision was made to build a second computer at the Institute for Numerical Analysis, an NBS field station located at the University of California at Los Angeles. These two bureau computers became known as the SEAC and SWAC (Standards Eastern and Standards Western Automatic Computers).

The SEAC, built under the direction of Samuel Alexander, used mercury-delay lines for storage. Its design was based on the EDVAC work at the University of Pennsylvania. The original memory used the same type of mercury-delay lines, consisting of 64 eight-word lines operating at a clock rate of 1 mH. Initial input and output was by punched paper tape. Later, magnetic wire and magnetic tape replaced the paper tape, and a Williams' tube memory was added to the system.

Addition time (including storage access) ranged from 192 to 1,540 ms, and multiply time from 2,300 to 3,600 ms. The SEAC was the first stored-program computer to run in the United States. It was dedicated in May 1950 and was in operation until October 1964.

REFERENCES

1951. Alexander, S. N. "The National Bureau of Standards Eastern Automatic Computer (SEAC)," *IRE Eastern Joint Computer Conference, 1951*, pp. 84–89.

1953. Shupe, P. D., Jr., and R. A. Kirsch. "SEAC—A Review of Three Years of Operation," *IRE Eastern Joint Computer Conference, 1953*, pp. 83–90.

H. D. HUSKEY

## SECURITY. *See* DATA SECURITY.

## SECURITY OF COMPUTER INSTALLATIONS, PHYSICAL

For article on related subject *see* DATA SECURITY.

This article deals with protection of hardware and software against physical threats. Each subsection describes a physical threat and useful countermeasures that have been successfully applied in a number of installations. Physical security measures are intended to reduce or prevent disruptions to operations or loss of assets. Because in most organizations there is a growing dependence on the computer, its disruption can have a devastating effect upon the organization's performance as well as cause a large loss of assets. Before selecting specific security measures, management should review assets and operations and possible threats against them to select the optimum security program, bearing in mind its cost and effect on productivity as well as its protective features.

When developing physical security plans, examination should be made of the possibility of insuring the computer installation. Most large organizations have on their staff an insurance specialist who might be called a "risk" manager. This individual should be contacted and asked to determine if insurance should be purchased for the computer center. If the organization does not have this type of expertise available from within, the insurance broker or agency with whom it normally deals should be asked to make recommendations concerning purchase of insurance for the computer installation. A benefit of this study will be that the insurance company will make a survey of the computer installation to determine its level of protection before any policy will be issued.

The measures discussed below, if fully implemented, will give an extremely secure environment. All installations will, of course, not need all these measures. For example, a university research computing center that handles no sensitive or classified data or information will probably not be concerned about access control. However, it may develop an extremely effective fire safety program, since destruction of the center may have a fairly major impact on carrying out the research program of the university if there is no way of obtaining backup computer services within a reasonable period of time. Another example is the average industrial computing center, which probably would not develop a backup power source to assure continuing power during blackouts or brownouts, whereas a medical center, which has life monitoring systems connected to its computer, would probably want to do everything possible to assure a continuing power supply.

**Fire.** Fire damage of the computer room may be caused by a fire outside the building in which the computer is located, inside the building, or interior to the room itself. Consequently, one should consider all these possibilities. If possible, one should avoid high hazards in or near the building; e.g., chemical or petroleum operations, warehouses, lumber yards. Internal fires may originate in trash, electric wiring, inside the computer hardware or in forms storage, data encoding, or in programming areas. Smoke, heat, and corrosive gases from fires may enter the area through doors, windows, elevator shafts, or air conditioning ducts. Tapes and disk packs can be destroyed by temperatures as low as 150°F.

A good fire safety program for computer hardware and software has five parts: (1) building design, construction, and location; (2) building operation; (3) fire detection; (4) fire fighting; and (5) loss control.

BUILDING DESIGN. The preferred building is of fire-resistive construction, well separated from hazardous materials and operations (e.g., chemicals, plastics, paint, packing materials, etc.) stored or used in it. The computer facility should be located on an upper floor where it will be less exposed to water damage, intrusion, and vandalism. In the case of a large installation, a special building embodying maximum fire and safety features can sometimes be set aside for the computer complex.

BUILDING OPERATIONS. Rigorous measures should be taken to minimize the risk of fire, including prompt trash removal; unobstructed fire doors; careful maintenance of fire detector and extinguisher equipment, and of heating, ventilating, and cooling equipment; protection of fuel lines and other potential fire sites. Regular inspections are required to assure compliance.

FIRE DETECTION. The fire detection system should provide *prompt, positive* detection. The preferred system uses (1) products-of-combustion detectors in the computer area located above hung ceilings, at ceilings, under raised floors, in air conditioning ducts entering the computer area, electrical equipment closets, and other key areas; (2) less expensive rate-of-temperature-rise detectors in adjacent areas, and preferably throughout the building; and (3) flow alarm switches in sprinkler systems and hose lines. The control panel design should include enough indicators to make it easy to locate a fire. If possible, the detection system should be connected by telephone line to the fire department. Alarm bells should be located to assure a response at *all* times.

FIRE FIGHTING. Prompt effective response to all alarms, of course, increases considerably the likelihood of quick extinguishment and minimum damage. A fire brigade should be appointed and trained for first-aid fire fighting, not as a substitute for professional fire fighters, but as a deterrent force to extinguish minor blazes before they become major. This is obviously not to be done at the expense of life endangerment of the employees. Local fire departments often will be happy to assist in training fire fighters. Provide ample Class A and Class C portable extinguishers, some of which should be light enough for women to carry easily. An automatic sprinkler will provide highly reliable protection against catastrophic loss; the preaction/recycle type minimizes water damage. HALON-1301 extinguishing systems (see NFPA Standard No. 13-A) are preferable for tape vaults, underfloor areas, and other locations where the contents must be protected against damage or where conventional extinguishment is difficult to apply; however, their cost is significantly higher than sprinklers, and of course protection is lost after discharge until HALON containers are recharged.

LOSS CONTROL. Loss and disruption can be minimized, and recovery can be accelerated if steps are taken to control smoke and water damage. Individuals should be designated, trained, and equipped to take steps like the following: conduct an orderly shutdown of hardware; dismount and protect tapes and disk packs; cover hardware with plastic sheeting; protect documentation and source documents. Fire-rated vaults for tapes and disk packs can be kept nearby for emergency use.

**Water Damage.** Water damage may come from natural flooding, broken pipes, or water from fire fighting. Hardware is surprisingly resistant to water damage, and tapes and disk packs inside canisters are usually safe unless subjected to immersion. However, wiring, air conditioning equipment, paper, furnishings, and the like can be seriously damaged or destroyed, and actual flooding in the computer room will halt operations.

No computer should be located where it is subject to natural flooding, nor should it be in a basement where water may collect or drains may back up. Exterior windows should have burglar-resistant glass that protects against water as well. Overhead water, steam, fuel, and drain pipes should be avoided if possible, or inspected regularly. All openings in the floor above should be sealed with cement, and positive drainage should be provided for the computer area.

**Earthquake.** If the computer facility is located in an earthquake-prone area, backup facilities should be outside the area. One must assume that little or no support, including personnel, will be available locally for backup operation in the event of an earthquake. The building containing the computer complex should be constructed to the highest standards. Particular attention should be paid to eliminating internal and adjacent fire hazards, and to providing on-site energy and other utilities.

**Air Conditioning.** The air conditioning system should be of adequate capacity, with good controls, adequate air filtering, and properly located outside air-intake louvers. Louvers should not be located at ground level where they are subject to sabotage attacks, nor should they be near sources of harmful gases.

Reliability depends on proper design and effective preventive maintenance. Each element of the system—air handling unit (AHU), chiller, cooling tower unit, circulating pump, etc.—should be redundant. Each of these should be sized and interconnected in such a way that the failure of any single unit will not cause interruption or shutdown of computer operations. If the AHUs in the computer room are supplied by a central system, it may be possible to eliminate comfort air conditioning elsewhere in the building during an emergency. Except when the outside air is above 80°F, increased outside air can be used in an emergency, but humidity controls may not work. The computer operations staff should be familiar with the air conditioning system operation and alarm panel and should oversee arrangements for preventive maintenance and emergency repairs. An individual should be designated to inspect temperature and humidity recorder charts on a regular basis and to resolve any out-of-limits operation.

**Electric Power.** There are three possible sources of electric power trouble: (1) transients or "spikes," which may propagate into logic hardware and cause erratic operation and scrambled data; (2) subnormal line voltage or "brownouts" (or possibly overvoltages), which may prevent computer (and, in extreme cases, air conditioning) hardware from functioning properly; and (3) power failures, which immediately halt operations. Transients may be caused by high-current devices in the building, switching transients (which often occur between 7:00 and 8:00 A.M.), or lightning strikes on the transmission or distribution system within a few miles of the building. Brownouts usually are imposed deliberately when power demand overloads the available generating capacity. Power failures may result from an electrical fault or fire in the building, destruction of a utility pole, an accident at the supplying substation, or in very rare cases a system-wide disturbance.

A review of recent reliability and quality of the power source and an estimate of the cost of reruns and delayed processing will indicate the amount (if any) appropriate to spend for countermeasures. An electric power monitor connected to all three phases with a strip-chart recorder will help to pinpoint problems caused by electric power fluctuations, particularly transients. These records will help correlate occurrence of systems problems with power fluctuations.

There are a number of countermeasures. Voltage-regulating transformers will compensate for brownouts. Diesel- or turbine-driven generators can generate power locally if protection against long-term power failures is needed. Uninterruptible power systems (UPS) filter out transients and protect against brief power failures, by storing energy internally. Rotary UPSs use a motor-generator with a flywheel for energy storage; they are relatively inexpensive, but are noisy, require regular maintenance, and can support the load for only 10 to 15 sec when power fails. Electronic UPS use a solid-state rectifier-inverter set with a battery, which can carry the load for 15 to 45 min. The ultimate system, using an electronic UPS, a diesel or turbine generator set, and transfer switches, will assure high-quality power and can survive an indefinitely long power failure. A solid-state bypass switch will transfer the computer load to the incoming electric power source in a few milliseconds if a UPS fails.

The emergency power system must have enough capacity to support the computer hardware, communications and data encoding equipment, air conditioning, a minimum of lighting and (possibly) elevators, dumbwaiters, and security hardware. Only uninterruptible or transient sensitive loads need be connected to the UPS. Proper design of the UPS, emergency generator, transfer and bypass switches, and their integration into the building's electrical service must be done by qualified engineers for best results.

**Deliberate Destruction.** The possibility of sabotage, vandalism, arson, or bombing must be considered. Depending on public "image"—the local crime rate, character of the neighborhood, and similar factors—the computer facility may be exposed to damage from vandals, extremists, extortionists, striking workers, a rioting mob, or a disgruntled customer or employee. Countermeasures include: building location and construction; controls over access to and from the building and computer area; computer operations rules; personnel selection, training, and supervision.

If possible, high-crime areas and proximity to production plants (potential picket lines) should be avoided. The exterior of the building should be designed and built to make covert or forced entry difficult and to provide resistance to riot damage or sabotage. For example, all first-story windows should be protected as well as doors. Electric power and communications lines, cooling towers, etc., should be hidden or protected. Entrances and parking lots should be safe for employees, particularly at night. Exterior signs designating the building as a computer facility, or building directories that give the room number of the computer room, should be omitted.

Access control simply means that only authorized persons—employees, service personnel, proper visitors, and vendor representatives—enter the building, and that all materials which enter or leave the building are properly screened to deter both theft and sabotage. It may be adequate to depend on personal recognition if there are no more than 50 employees, *but* all employees must be trained to challenge strangers, and supervisors must be alert to compliance with property-pass procedures and the like. In larger facilities, it may be necessary to adopt more formal procedures, including visible badges and access control zones; i.e., individual access to sensitive areas limited to only those assigned or authorized.

Enforcement of access controls may require the use of a security force, guards and receptionists, in large facilities. Undue dependence should not be placed on door locks, as even exotic card-key systems are vulnerable. Perimeter fences, intrusion detectors, closed-circuit television, and similar security devices can help to secure and control a building, *but only if used by alert people with respon-*

*sibility for security*. All employees should be briefed on their responsibilities for secure operation. Issuance and recovery of keys, ID cards, and badges should be closely controlled. For example, all locks and badges should be periodically changed. A designated staff member should regularly verify proper functioning of security devices and compliance with security and access control procedures.

**Personnel Screening.** Ideally, *all* personnel who enter sensitive areas should be prescreened as trustworthy or should be under direct supervision. Supervisors should be sensitive to the attitudes and deportment of their staff in order to discover disgruntlement before it causes problems and to take corrective action. For reasons of both personal safety and security, individuals should never work alone. Through their own strict compliance with control and security procedures, supervisors at all levels should set a good example for their subordinates.


REFERENCES

1968. Healy, R. J. *Design for Security*. New York: John Wiley.

1971. Brown, W. F., M. B. Greenlee, and R. V. Jacobson. *AMR's Guide to Computer and Software Security*. AMR International.

1974. Jacobson, R. V., W. F. Brown, and P. S. Browne, *Guidelines for Automatic Data Processing Physical Security and Risk Management*. Washington, D.C.: National Bureau of Standards, 1974, FIPS Pub. 31.


W. F. BROWN AND R. V. JACOBSON

## SEGMENT. *See* OVERLAY.

## SELECTIVE DISSEMINATION OF INFORMATION. *See* CURRENT AWARENESS SYSTEM.

## SEMANTICS. *See* SYNTAX, SEMANTICS, AND PRAGMATICS.

## SEMAPHORE

For articles on related subjects *see* LOCKOUT; PARALLEL PROCESSING; and THRASHING.
For article on related term *see* PROCESS.

Where two parallel processes rely on each other for their continued operation (including perhaps the activation of other processes), some form of elementary communication is needed between them to signal when significant events have taken place. This can be accomplished by the use of a shared memory cell, which is used to indicate (by its contents) when such events have occurred; such a cell is known as a "semaphore."

For example, if a process A cannot proceed past a point $\alpha$ in its execution without a datum that will be provided by another process B, process A will initially set the semaphore associated with this datum to the negative value $-1$, meaning that execution of A cannot proceed past $\alpha$. When process B computes the required data, it will add 1 to this semaphore, making its value 0 and allowing process A to proceed.

This idea is clearly extendible to more than two processes and to the need to satisfy multiple requirements before a process can proceed.


REFERENCE

1968. Dijkstra, E. W. "The Structure of the 'THE' Multiprogramming System," *Communications of the ACM*, pp. 341–346.


J. A. N. LEE

## SEQUENTIAL MACHINES

For articles on related subjects *see* AUTOMATA THEORY; FORMAL LANGUAGES; and REGULAR EXPRESSION.
For articles on related terms *see* BOOLEAN ALGEBRA; GRAPH THEORY; SHIFTING; and STOCHASTIC PROCESS.

**Basic Concepts.** A sequential machine is a mathematical model of a certain type of sequential switching circuit. It has an input $\sigma$ which can take on any value from a finite set $\Sigma$, called the "input

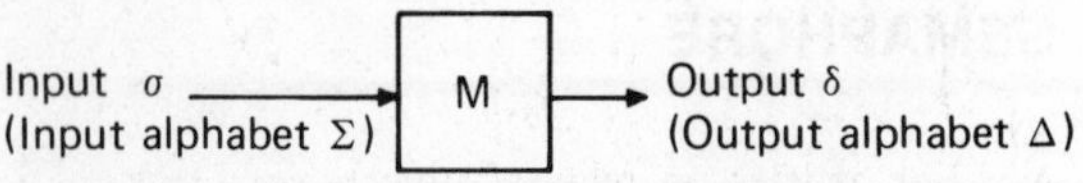


**Fig. 1.** Sequential machine symbol.

alphabet," and an output $\delta$, from a finite "output alphabet" $\Delta$, as shown in Fig. 1. The input and output values are of interest only at certain instants of time; these instants are usually referred to as instants 1,2,3, . . .. At any time $t$, the output $\delta(t)$ depends not only on the present input $\sigma(t)$, but also on the past input sequence . . . $\sigma(t - k),\sigma(t - k + 1), \ldots, \sigma(t - 2),\sigma(t - 1)$; hence, the name "sequential machine."

The dependence of the output on past inputs implies that a sequential machine has memory. Usually, this memory is finite and corresponds to a finite set $Q$, called the set of "internal states." At time $t$, the machine $M$ is in some (present) state $q(t)$. It receives an input value $\sigma(t)$, and this present input and the present internal state determine the next internal state $q(t + 1)$.

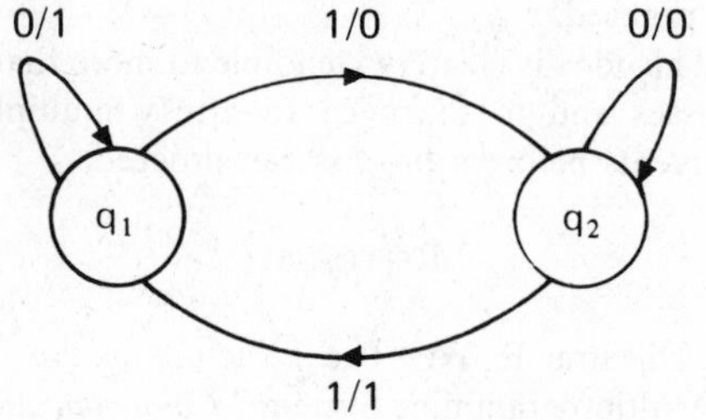


**Fig. 2.** Machine $M_1$.

An example of a sequential machine is shown in Fig. 2. The machine is represented by a directed graph, a *state graph*, where the nodes correspond to internal states and the labeled edges to transitions among internal states. The labels are of the form $\sigma/\delta$, where $\sigma$ is the input value causing the transition and $\delta$ is the corresponding output value. For example, if $M_1$ of Fig. 2 is in state $q_1$ at time $t$, and if $\sigma(t) = 1$, then the transition labeled 1/0 is relevant, $\delta(t) = 0$, and at time $t + 1$ the state of $M_1$ will be $q_2$. If we are given an initial state $q(1)$—i.e., the value of $q$ at $t = 1$—and an input sequence $\sigma(1),\sigma(2), \ldots ,\sigma(t)$, we can determine from the state graph the resulting state sequence $q(2), \ldots, q(t + 1)$ and the corresponding output sequence $\delta(1),\delta(2), \ldots, \delta(t)$. A typical computation is shown in Fig. 3, where it is assumed that $q(1) = q_1$. The reader will verify that if $M_1$ is started in state $q_1$, it will produce an output of 1 at time $t$ if and only if the number of 1's in the sequence $\sigma(1),\sigma(2), \ldots, \sigma(t)$ is even.

With each sequential machine we associate two functions: the *transition function f*, which determines the next state from the present state and the present input, and an *output function g*. In the machine $M_1$, the present output depends on both the present state and the present input. The model in which the output depends on both the state and the input—i.e., where $\delta(t) = g(q(t),\sigma(t))$—is the *Mealy model*. In another useful model, the *Moore model*, the present output is uniquely determined by the present state, i.e., $\delta(t) = g(q(t))$.

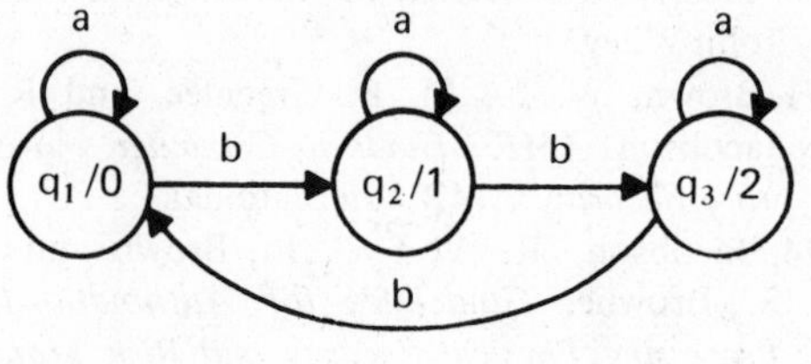


**Fig. 4.** Machine $M_2$.

An example of a Moore machine is shown in Fig. 4. The input and output alphabets are $\Sigma = \{a,b\}$ and $\Delta = \{0,1,2\}$, respectively. Given an initial state and an input sequence, we can determine the state sequence, as in the Mealy model. Since the output is determined solely by the state, we associate it with the nodes of the state graph rather than with the edges. A typical computation for $M_2$ is shown in Fig. 5, assuming $q(1) = q_1$. The behavior of $M_2$ can

| | | | | | | | | | |
|---|---|---|---|---|---|---|---|---|---|
| Time instants: | 1 | 2 | 3 | 4 | 5 | 6 | 7 | 8 | 9 |
| Input sequence: | 0 | 1 | 0 | 0 | 1 | 1 | 0 | 1 | |
| State sequence: | $q_1$ | $q_1$ | $q_2$ | $q_2$ | $q_2$ | $q_1$ | $q_2$ | $q_2$ | $q_1$ |
| Output sequence: | 1 | 0 | 0 | 0 | 1 | 0 | 0 | 1 | |

**Fig. 3.** Sequences for $M_1$.

| Time instants: | 1 | 2 | 3 | 4 | 5 | 6 | 7 | 8 | 9 | 10 |
|---|---|---|---|---|---|---|---|---|---|---|
| Input sequence: | b | a | b | a | b | b | b | a | b | |
| State sequence: | $q_1$ | $q_2$ | $q_2$ | $q_3$ | $q_3$ | $q_1$ | $q_2$ | $q_3$ | $q_3$ | $q_1$ |
| Output sequence: | 0 | 1 | 1 | 2 | 2 | 0 | 1 | 2 | 2 | 0 |

**Fig. 5.** Sequences for $M_2$.

be described as follows: The input value $a$ is "ignored" by $M_2$ in the sense that no change of state results when $\sigma(t) = a$. The input $b$ advances the state of $M_2$ cyclically. If the machine is started in $q_1$, the output $\delta(t + 1)$ is congruent modulo 3 to the number of $b$'s in the input sequence $\sigma(1), \sigma(2), \ldots, \sigma(t)$.

The differences between the Moore and Mealy models are only technical. From a general point of view, these models are equivalent as far as computational power is concerned. Another model equivalent to these in the general sense is the *finite automaton* model. This is a special case of the Moore model, where $\Delta = \{0,1\}$. If the output corresponding to an internal state is 1, that state is called "accepting," or *final*; if the output is 0, the state is called a "rejecting" state. A single *initial state* $q_0$ is usually specified in the finite automaton model. A finite automaton $A$ can be viewed as an *acceptor* of input sequences. For the input sequence $\sigma(1), \ldots, \sigma(t)$, let $q(t + 1)$ be the state reached by $A$, when started in $q_0$. If $q(t + 1)$ is a final state, the sequence is accepted; otherwise, it is rejected. An alternate point of view considers a sequential machine as a *sequence transducer*—a machine that transforms an input sequence into an output sequence, as in Figs. 3 and 5.

### Realization of Sequential Machines.

The behavior of a sequential machine can be realized by a sequential switching circuit. We now describe an idealized model of such circuits, which we call a "sequential network." The sequential network reflects the logical properties of the switching circuit, but not its electronic properties. Thus, it has the advantage of being independent of actual technological implementation while retaining many of the basic structural properties.

A block diagram of a switching network is shown in Fig. 6. As is usually the case, we assume that all signals in a sequential network are binary, with 0 and 1 as the two possible values. The network has a finite number of binary inputs $x_1, \ldots, x_n$ and binary outputs $z_1, \ldots, z_m$. If the output values $z_i(t)$ are uniquely determined by the input values $x_j(t)$,

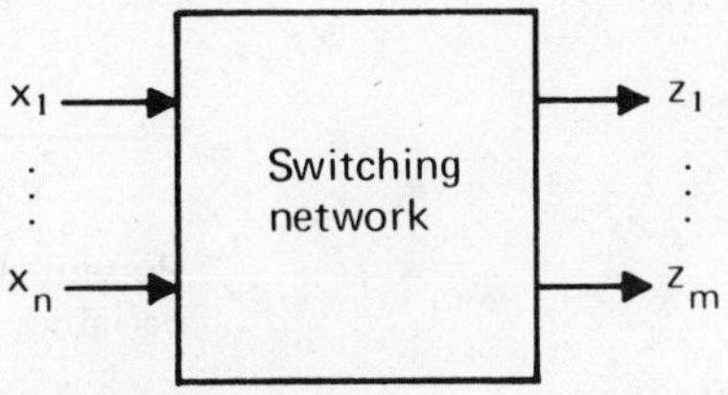


**Fig. 6.** Switching network.

then it has no memory. In that case, it is called a "combinational" network, and its behavior can be described by $m$ boolean functions, one for each output $z_i$. A combinational network can be implemented by a network of gates *without* any feedback loops.

A switching network with memory is called "sequential." The function of memory can be performed by gate networks *with* feedback. In general, such networks have no special timing signals and are called "asynchronous." If a special periodic input, called "clock," is provided to control the action of the network, the network is "synchronous." In that case, the response of the network is of interest only at certain times, once during each clock period. These times correspond to the instants 1,2,3, . . . mentioned earlier.

A synchronous sequential network can be divided into a combinational part and a memory part. The units corresponding to memory are rather complex asynchronous gate networks called "flip-flops." For theoretical considerations, the simplest memory module is the *unit delay*, whose output $y$ is equal to the input $x$ delayed by one unit of time; i.e., $y(t) = x(t - 1)$. The general form of a synchronous sequential network with unit delays as memory elements is shown in Fig. 7. The network can be described by two sets of equations.

1. Next-state equations:

$$Y_i(t) = y_i(t + 1) = f_i(x_1(t), \ldots, x_n(t), y_1(t), \ldots, y_s(t)), \quad i = 1, \ldots, s.$$

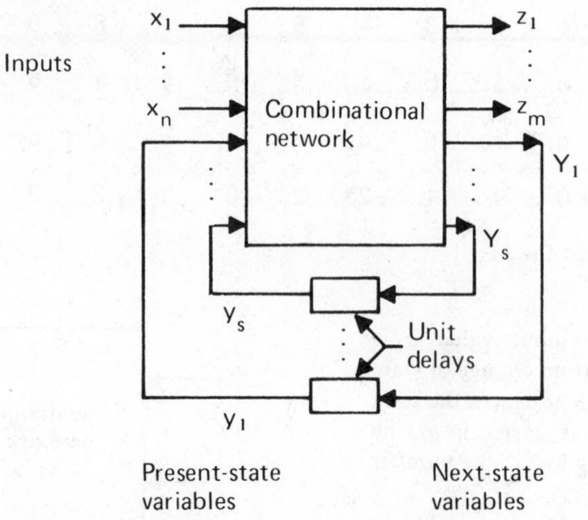


**Fig. 7.** Sequential network with unit delays.

2. Output equations:

$$z_j(t) = g_j(x_1(t), \ldots, x_n(t), y_1(t), \ldots, y_s(t)),$$
$$j = 1, \ldots, m,$$

In (1) the $f_i$ and in (2) the $g_j$ are boolean functions.

The reader will easily verify that the sequential network model of Fig. 7 is a special case of the Mealy model, where $\Sigma$ is the set of all binary $n$-tuples (binary words of length $n$) and $\Delta$ is the set of all binary $m$-tuples.

Any abstract sequential machine can be realized by a sequential network of the type shown in Fig. 7. This can be done by representing each element of $\Sigma$ by a suitable $n$-tuple $x_1, \ldots, x_n$, and $\Delta$ and $Q$ must be coded similarly.

The unit delay is sometimes called the "D flip-flop." Other types of flip-flops are the "T" (toggle or trigger) type, the "SR" (set-reset) type, and the "JK" type. Each type of flip-flop can be used to realize any sequential machine. In Fig. 8 we define the four types of flip-flops by *state tables,* which constitute a common way (equivalent to the state-graph representation) of representing sequential networks. The rows of the state table correspond to the internal states, and the columns to input combinations. The entries represent the next state. The most general type of flip-flop is the JK. The condition $J = 0$, $K = 0$ is the *remember* condition, where no change takes place. $J = 0$, $K = 1$ corresponds to *reset* condition (the flip-flop is reset to 0); $J = 1$, $K = 0$ is the *set* condition; and $J = 1$, $K = 1$ is the *toggle* condition (the state changes, or "toggles").

**Behavioral Properties.** Two states $q$ and $q'$ of a sequential machine $M$ are *indistinguishable* if the input/output behavior of $M$ started in $q$ cannot be distinguished by any external experiment from that of $M$ started in $q'$. In other words, a given input sequence applied to $M$, started in $q$, produces the same output sequence as in the case when $M$ is started in $q'$. Otherwise, $q$ and $q'$ are *distinguishable.* A sequential machine in which every pair of states is distinguishable is called "reduced."

Two sequential machines $M$ and $M'$ are indistinguishable if for every state $q$ of $M$ there exists a state $q'$ of $M'$ such that the input/output behavior of $M$ started in $q$ is the same as that of $M'$ started in $q'$, and vice versa. For every sequential machine $M$ there exists a unique (up to isomorphism) reduced sequential machine $M_0$ indistinguishable from $M$. The machine $M_0$ is the minimal-state version of $M$.

A set of sequences over a finite alphabet is called a "language." It is natural to associate certain languages with sequential machines. For example, in the case of a finite automaton $A$, we define the *language,* $L(A)$, *accepted by* $A$ to be the set of all accepted sequences. Similarly, the set $L_{ij}$ of all sequences taking a sequential machine from state $q_i$ to state $q_j$, or the set $L_\delta$, of all sequences resulting in a particular output value $\delta$, represent useful languages. All such languages of the form $L(A)$, $L_{ij}$, or $L_\delta$ are *regular languages.* It can be shown that any language defined by a sequential machine in the above sense is regular and, conversely, for every regular language there exists a sequential machine "recognizing" that language.

| q(t) \ D(t) | 0 | 1 |
|---|---|---|
| 0 | 0 | 1 |
| 1 | 0 | 1 |

q(t + 1)

(a)

| q(t) \ T(t) | 0 | 1 |
|---|---|---|
| 0 | 0 | 1 |
| 1 | 1 | 0 |

q(t + 1)

(b)

| q(t) \ S(t) R(t) | 00 | 01 | 10 |
|---|---|---|---|
| 0 | 0 | 0 | 1 |
| 1 | 1 | 0 | 1 |

q(t + 1)

(c)

| q(t) \ J(t) K(t) | 00 | 01 | 11 | 10 |
|---|---|---|---|---|
| 0 | 0 | 0 | 1 | 1 |
| 1 | 1 | 0 | 0 | 1 |

q(t + 1)

(d)

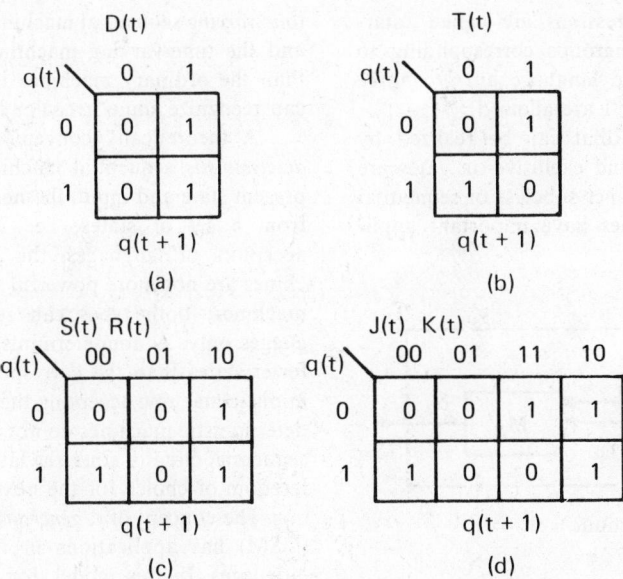

**Fig. 8.** State tables. (a) D flip-flop, (b) T flip-flop. (c) SR Flip-flop; note that S = R = 1 is not used. (d) JK flip-flop.

An important application of sequential machines is in counting. When the number of states is finite, a sequential machine can only count modulo an integer.

Another unique characterization of sequential machines is provided by the *syntactic semigroup* of the machine, defined as follows: For each input $\sigma$, the set $Q$ of states of a reduced machine is transformed according to the transition function. The set of all transformations of states performed by all input sequences constitutes the syntactic semigroup. This representation is useful for certain structural properties.

**Structural Properties.** In a general network, as shown in Fig. 7, there may be feedback loops. For example, $Y_1$ may be a function of $y_2$, and $Y_2$ may be a function of $y_1$. In the special case where no such loops exist, the network is called "definite." An example of a simple definite network is shown in Fig. 9.

The languages recognized by definite networks are particularly simple, since the behavior of the machine depends only on the last $k$ symbols of the input sequence, for some $k$. In general, feedback is required in order to realize the behavior of an arbitrary sequential machine. It can be shown, however, that every sequential machine can be realized by a sequential network having a single feedback loop.

When SR flip-flops (instead of unit delays) are used as memory elements, the class of machines realizable without feedback is considerably larger than the class of definite machines. The languages recognized by machines in this class are the so-called *noncounting* regular languages. Such machines can only "count to a threshold," in the following sense: If the threshold is the integer $k \geq 0$, then the machine may be able to determine whether a certain sequence of symbols occurs in the input sequence $0, 1, \ldots$, or $k - 1$ times. After this, it cannot distinguish $k$ occurrences from $k + 1$ occurrences, but can only conclude that the number of occurrences is at least $k$. Therefore, such machines cannot count modulo any integer greater than 1, and are called "counter-free." The languages corresponding to counter-free machines constitute a natural subclass of regular languages. They can be defined by regular expressions that use only boolean operations and

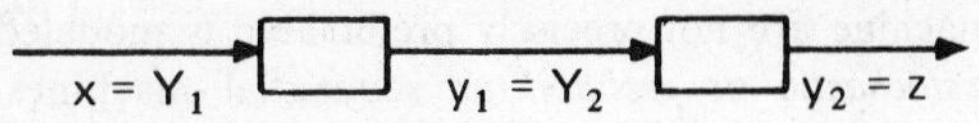


**Fig. 9.** A definite network.

concatenation. Such expressions are called "star-free." The syntactic semigroups corresponding to this class of machine and language are *group-free* (i.e., only groups of order 1 are allowed).

Sequential machines that can be realized by networks of unit delays and exclusive-OR gates are *linear* and constitute a proper subclass of sequential machines. Linear machines have important applications in coding theory.

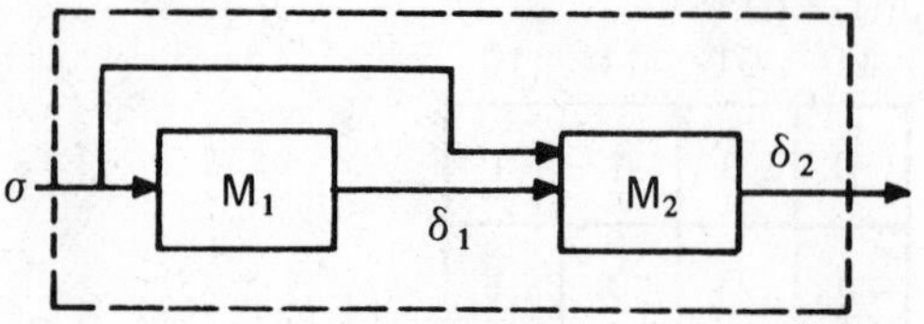


**Fig. 10.** Cascade connection.

The problem of decomposing a sequential machine into a *cascade connection* of smaller sequential machines has received much attention. The cascade connection of two machines is shown in Fig. 10. This connection is also known as the *series connection*. The *parallel connection* of two machines is a special case of the cascade connection, where neither machine influences the other. We have already mentioned that definite machines correspond to cascade connections of unit delays, and counter-free machines correspond to cascade connections of SR flip-flops. The Krohn-Rhodes theory shows that, in general, arbitrary sequential machines correspond to cascade connections of (1) machines whose syntactic semigroups are simple groups, and (2) SR flip-flops.

Such results are of theoretical interest. For practical applications, an often-used cascade connection is a *shift register*, which is a very simple cascade connection of flip-flops. Shift registers and counters constitute basic modules in the design of sequential networks.

**Related Models.** In practical applications, certain state-input combinations of a sequential machine may never occur. In this case, the next state and output may be irrelevant and need not be specified. The *incompletely specified* sequential machine model handles such cases.

The situation where the next state and output of a machine are not precisely predictable is modeled by *stochastic* or *probabilistic* sequential machines. The case where the transition function and the output function vary with time is modeled by *time-varying* sequential machines. Both the stochastic and the time-varying machines are more powerful than the ordinary machines in the sense that they can recognize some irregular languages.

A theoretically convenient model is the *nondeterministic* sequential machine. Here, for a given present state and input, the next state can be chosen from a set of states; i.e., it is not unique. As acceptors of languages, the nondeterministic machines are not more powerful than the deterministic machines; both types can recognize regular languages only. A nondeterministic machine can have fewer states than the corresponding reduced deterministic machine accepting the same language. Nondeterministic machines do not correspond directly to sequential circuits, since the latter do not possess any freedom of choice for the next state.

The concept of a *generalized sequential machine* (GSM) has applications in the theory of formal languages. In this model, for a given present state and input symbol, the machine can produce a sequence of output symbols, whereas the standard model permits only one output symbol. The GSM is also a more powerful model than the standard one.

In the discussion above, we have tacitly assumed that the term "sequential machine" implies that the number of states is finite. *Infinite-state* sequential machines have also been studied. They are obviously much more powerful than the finite-state machines, and most of the results discussed above do not apply directly to the infinite-state case. Infinite-state linear sequential machines provide an example where a number of results from the finite-state case have their generalized counterparts in the infinite case.

REFERENCES

1964. Moore, E. F. (Ed.). *Sequential Machines: Selected Papers*. Reading, Mass.: Addison-Wesley.

1967. Brzozowski, J. A. "Synthesis of Sequential Machines," in J. F. Hart and S. Takasu (Eds.), *Systems and Computer Science*. Toronto, Ont.: University of Toronto Press.

1968. Ginzburg, A. *Algebraic Theory of Automata*. New York: Academic Press.

1970. Kohavi, Z. *Switching and Finite Automata Theory*. New York: McGraw-Hill.

1971. McNaughton, R., and S. Papert. *Counter-Free Automata*. Cambridge, Mass.: The M.I.T. Press.

J. A. BRZOZOWSKI

# SERVICE BUREAUS, DATA PROCESSING

For articles on related subjects *see* ADMINISTRATIVE-BUSINESS APPLICATIONS; COMPUTING CENTER; PROCESSING MODES; and SOFTWARE MANAGEMENT.

For articles on related terms *see* DATA BASE AND DATA BASE MANAGEMENT; and HOSPITAL INFORMATION SYSTEMS.

Although the data processing services industry has achieved significance in only the past decade, the first data processing service company dates back to approximately 1910. By 1935 a number of small firms were offering "tabulating services," for the most part in the "statistical" area of commercial data processing. By 1970 a wide range of services in both the scientific and commercial fields was available from some 1,700 firms. Therefore, to say "computer service industry" today is much like saying "transportation industry" as all-inclusive terms for identifying the nature of their activities.

Some pertinent statistical data, supplied by the Association of Data Processing Service Organizations (ADAPSO), 210 Summit Avenue, Montvale, N.J. 07645, for the year 1972 is as follows:

> Total revenues: $2.73 billion. The average service center employs 39 people, serves 113 clients, and has annual revenue of some $550,000. ... The average revenue per client in 1972 was $5,092. ... Computer service centers provided services to the full spectrum of industries; however, the wholesale/retail and manufacturing industries were by far the largest users, accounting for 41% and 26% of revenues, respectively. ... All indices indicate a substantial growth over the past five years, and projections are for continued substantial growth through 1975.

**Definition of the Industry.** A definition of the industry is best achieved by considering two major elements of the industry together: (1) The end product or service, and (2) the means employed in achieving the end product or service. Each of these two criteria apply to the three major categories of applications: commercial, scientific/engineering, and business sciences.

The first category accounts for the bulk of computer services provided today. The second category, while considerably smaller in terms of dollar revenue, is at present the major category utilizing advanced communications and time-sharing technologies. The third category, which includes applied computer techniques such as operations research, economic models, and management sciences, is a relatively small user of computer services today; however, it is the most promising area for development in the 1980s.

**Services.** Historically, clients have utilized the computer service center in either of two broad categories:

1. Repetitive, recurring service, usually applications oriented to and consisting of general accounting and reporting systems.
2. Overflow, nonrecurring service, usually time-oriented and consisting of peak-load or conversion efforts.

Whereas service centers in the 1950s tended to be generalistic in nature, the trend since that time has been increasingly toward specialization. In some cases this has been industry-oriented. For instance, a given center might specialize to a major extent in "hospital data processing." In this case, the center would offer hospital administrators a unique blend of specific knowledge with respect to that particular enterprise, together with data processing systems and operating expertise.

In other cases, specialization was concentrated in a single area, such as payroll processing. In this case, a computer center developed a particular expertise in the processing of payrolls and offered to process payrolls for a broad range of industries.

In each of the three broad application categories listed in the preceding section, the end product or service may be categorized as utilizing

1. A common data base with variable programs.
2. A common program with variable data.
3. Variable programs and variable data.

In the commercial area, an example of the first would be a credit-data file, which would be accessed for different information in various formats by a variety of users. An example of the second would be any one of the various "packages," such as a "payroll package" that employs the same programs for a number of users, each of whom introduces his own data. The third category is typical of the "custom" service wherein both the program and the data are unique to the individual user.

A further categorization may be made using the technology employed:

1. Batch processing.
2. Remote batch processing.
3. Interactive batch processing.
4. Real-time transaction processing.

Until recently there has been little in the fourth category, other than dedicated systems such as airline reservations, and on-line savings and loan passbook updating. However, recent introductions such as point-of-sale cash registers, which are in fact remote terminals and can be on-line to a computer, hold significant promise for this particular technology in the next five to ten years.

There is essential difference between the scientific/engineering field and the commercial field with respect to data processing requirements. The former is characterized by a small volume of input, very extensive computations, and a small volume of output. Commercial requirements tend to be just the opposite, involving a large volume of input, minimal computations, and a large volume of output. For this reason, time-sharing and economy-of-scale in hardware have been major factors in the growth of scientific services. These factors have been less important in the commercial services market, where the availability of expert personnel and of applied computer techniques have been the principal attraction to the user.

For the past 20 years or so, the commercial data processing service firms have served to bridge the gap which has existed between the executive management of most companies—with their complete knowledge of their business operations (the "businessman")—and the computer technologist whose hardware expertise was often handicapped by unfamiliarity with business functions in the real world. This "bridge" was built as those computer technicians who went into business (the service center) soon became "businessmen" in their own right so as to survive in a very competitive market. This, together with the fact that, in serving a variety of business clients, technologists gained a broad spectrum of experience with a wide variety of problems in many industries, made the service center attractive to many business managers.

Another advantage enjoyed by the computer service center has been the honing and sharpening effect on the center management of constant pressure in a competitive marketplace. The "in-house" data processing department is in effect a "protected monopoly." As such, it is subject to "empire building" and to all the inefficient performance characteristics sooner or later endemic to most monopolies. The service center manager knows that operating inefficiency, poor expense control, lax procedures, and so forth, will put him out of business or, at least, cost him direct out-of-pocket dollars. The cost/effectiveness of a properly managed service center cannot be matched by any single-user data processing facility engaged in general-purpose computer operations; i.e., multiple applications of an accounting nature.

Services offered by computer service centers cover the entire range of data processing:

1. One-time or overload processing.
2. Continuing processing of a single application.
3. Continuing processing of the full range of applications required by a given client.
4. Sale of only computer time, in which the client himself uses the center's facility for one of the three preceding functions,

In addition, many service centers will also:

1. Manage all data processing operations at the clients' facility.
2. Prepare input only, referred to as "data conversion," subsequently to be processed by the client.
3. Initially set up and convert systems for a client who will ultimately take up the processing in house.
4. Perform systems design and programming of a specialized nature for an existing in-house operation.
5. Monitor existing hardware on the client's premises to effect maximum utilization.

**Charges and Fees.** Application services in a service bureau, such as payroll, job-cost analysis, sales analysis, and so forth, may be purchased in either "customized" or "packaged" forms. That is, the particular system may be designed and programmed to unique specifications provided by the client, or the client may choose an application that has been designed and programmed for sale to a wide range of users.

The "custom" application involves systems design and programming, for which the center will charge a programming fee as a one-time cost. In the packaged application, "setup" charges will normally consist only of those costs involved in converting the client to the system, such as keypunching balance-forward items, special forms, and so forth. The setup cost is obviously much less in packaged applications than in custom systems, which can be very substantial, depending upon the complexity and extensiveness of the required system. The tradeoff is the degree to which the client obtains a system addressed specifically to his own personal requirements.

Once a client is using a system, the center will charge a fee for processing the data involved and issuing the required reports. In general, the fee will be based upon the number of transactions processed in the given report cycle. In charging for computer time, those centers utilizing larger-scale systems will generally have various rates, depending upon how much of the total hardware configuration is used, so that a system consisting of eight tape drives, eight disk drives, and two printers would cost more per hour than another utilizing only four tape drives.

Charges for time-sharing systems are still in the evolutionary stages, particularly in the commercial area. In general, the system resources involved are the number of ports (entry points) available, the processing power itself, and (in some cases) certain proprietary software or programs. Charges, then, are based upon the extent to which these resources are used: "connect time," or use of a port; "cycle time," or use of computer power; and a surcharge of some amount for use of a proprietary program. In some cases there is also a charge for the amount of memory used.

**Facilities Management.** More than anything else, the commercial service center industry has served thus far as a pool of skilled technologists combining computer expertise with an understanding of business functions. Hardware economy of scale has been most elusive and, to date, not a significant factor. The centers have also served, although unwittingly, as the first phase of a user's move into automated systems; i.e., a client would use a center until he had sufficient applications so that the fees paid to the center were high enough for him to install his own machinery. In this way the service center industry has been midwife to thousands of in-house installations.

Some centers and/or individuals followed their former clients to provide management services to the client's own computer. Thereby began what has come to be known today as "facilities management." This type of service has become quite broad and comprehensive, in many cases involving total direction of all data processing services, often including the maintenance of all personnel involved on the facility manager's payroll.

**The Future.** Almost every major industry has three identifiable levels: production (or manufacturing), distribution (wholesale) and end user (retail). The computer industry today has only two tiers, manufacturing and end use. There is, at least in the commercial area, no distributor tier insofar as computer power is concerned, although this does exist to some extent in the scientific area via time-sharing services.

A number of factors make this "distributor of computer power" role not only possible but also inevitable as the primary function of the computer service center. Within the next 10 to 15 years, the data processing industry will consist of:

1. *Manufacturers*, enjoined by antitrust regulations from services and/or distribution in the same way movie producers have had to divest theater chains and airframe manufacturers have had to divest passenger service lines.
2. *Service centers* (wholesale), consisting in the main of large-scale installations providing raw computer power to users via telephone or microwave transmission to high-speed line-printing terminals.
3. *End users*, both today's in-house installation and those data processing service centers providing a specialized service.

L. J. Palmer

# SHARE

For article on related subject *see* Computer User Groups.
For article on related term *see* GUIDE.

SHARE is an organization of users of medium- and large-scale IBM data processing systems (essentially 360/50 and larger and including system 370) whose objective is the exchange and dissemination of ideas and information pertinent to the use of such systems. SHARE membership is open to all organizations that can demonstrate competence and a legitimate interest in SHARE activities.

The organization conducts semiannual general meetings, for which *Proceedings* are published, as well as other smaller meetings for specialized purposes. Additionally, SHARE sponsors—either wholly or jointly with other organizations—workshops and symposia open to all qualified data processing practitioners. A monthly newsletter, *SHARE Sec-*

*retary's Distribution*, together with a variety of irregular publications supplements the face-to-face information exchange derived from meetings.

SHARE, the first *computer user group*, was established in August 1955. The founding fathers were Lee Amaya of Lockheed Aircraft, Paul Armer of RAND, and Jack Strong and Frank Wagner of North American Aviation. Invitations were sent to all known prospective IBM 704 installations, and the response was virtually total. The first SHARE meeting was held in Santa Monica, California, and 46 persons representing 17 installations participated.

Since the IBM 704 was designed for *scientific computation*, the composition of SHARE remained oriented to this domain for some time. *Business data processing* became an area of major concern only after the announcement of IBM's System 360 in April 1964. Well before this time, the users of IBM equipment concerned with business data processing had established a sibling organization, GUIDE, to serve their needs. Much of the energy of both organizations in the late 1960s was devoted to developing a modus operandi for cooperation, resulting in a merger proposal that was rejected by the memberships. At present, approximately 20% of the membership of SHARE (currently about 1,000 installations) also belong to GUIDE as well.

The early thrust in SHARE was toward development of conventions, standards, and procedures necessary to permit and promote exchange of programs. While this objective remains explicit in SHARE activities today, the current emphasis is directed to critique vendor-supplied products for the purpose of providing a consensus on functional need to the vendors.

Central to SHARE's interests are *programming languages, operating systems*, and (more recently) *data base systems*. Software associated with specific application areas has always been of secondary interest in SHARE. A complete listing of SHARE activities is beyond the scope of this article, but it is fair to say that almost all data processing subjects not directly concerned with the design of hardware have been given scrutiny by some subgroups of the organization.

SHARE has responded to growth and change in the computer industry in various ways. An administrative office with full-time personnel has been established, legal counsel has been retained, the by-laws have been redrawn to remove explicit organizational structure, and the original SHARE organization was dissolved by the transfer of its assets and good will to a newly created not-for-profit corporation, SHARE, Inc., in January 1969. Funding is provided solely by the registration fees paid by meeting participants and by receipts from sale of publications. As a consequence, SHARE is not obligated to IBM or any other vendor, and is now taking steps to broaden its interests beyond its original area of concern.

The roster of presidents and the dates of their service follows.

Jack Strong, 1955–1956
Frank Engel, 1956–1957
Frank Wagner, 1957–1958
Ben Ferber, 1958–July 24, 1959 (resigned)
Ed Jacks, 1959 (appointed by Executive Board, 7/24/59)
Frank Verzuh, 1959–1960
Harry Cantrell, 1960–1961
Aaron Finerman, 1961 (resigned 10/16/61)
John Jordan, 1961–1962 (promoted from vice-president, 10/16/61)
George Ryckman, 1962–1963
Jim Rowe, 1963–1964
Jim Babcock, 1964–1965
Roy Dickson, 1965–1966
Jim Tupac, 1966–1967
Phil Cramer, 1967–1968
John Noerr, 1968–1969
Philip Dorn, 1969–1970
E. David Callender, 1970–1971
David M. Smith, 1971–1972
George E. Gautney, Jr., 1972–1974
Shirley Prutch, 1974–1975
Edward J. Farrell, 1975–1976

T. B. Steel

# SHIFTING

For articles on related subjects *see* ARITHMETIC-LOGIC UNIT; and MACHINE INSTRUCTION SET.

Shifting is the process of moving data that is stored in a storage device relative to the boundaries of the device (as opposed to moving it in and out of the device). The device in which the shift is performed is called a "shift register."

In order to discuss the various modes of the shift operation, we assume that the register in which the shift is to be performed is $n$ bits wide, and number the bits from left to right, $1 \cdots n$.

A *left shift* is the operation in which the $i$th bit is replaced by the $(i + 1)$st one. This operation can be

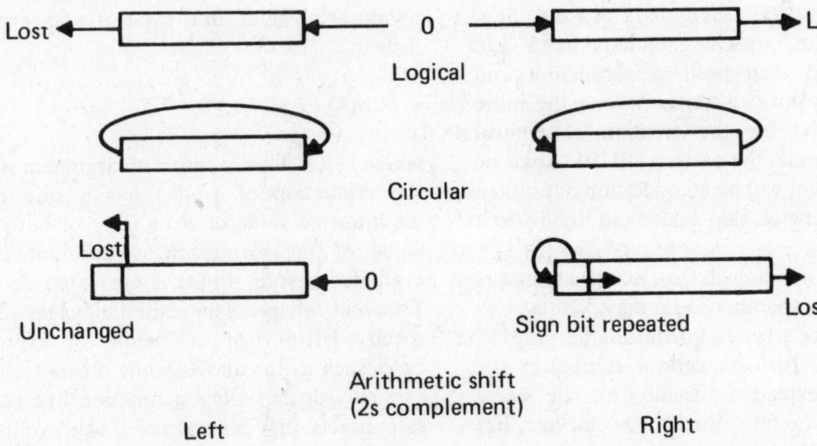


**Fig. 1.** The various shift operations.

repeated an arbitrary number of times so that one can shift left by any number of positions. The question of what replaces the *n*th (last) bit will be dealt with later, as will the question of what happens to bit 1.

A *right shift* is the operation in which the *i*th bit is replaced by the $(i - 1)$st bit. Again, this is easily generalized to a right shift by any number of positions.

There are three types of shifts: logical, circular, and arithmetic (see Fig. 1). They differ in the treatment of the first and last bits, both in the left and right shift.

*In logical shifts*, the bit shifted out is lost, and the bit shifted in is zero. Note in the left shift that the bit shifted out is bit 1, and the bit shifted in occupies position *n*, whereas in the right shift, the bit shifted out is the *n*th one and the bit shifted in occupies position 1.

*In circular shifts* the bit shifted out of one end is shifted into the other end. There is, therefore, no loss of information in the circular shift.

*The arithmetic shift* is designed to take orderly advantage of the fact that shifting a bit string left multiplies the binary number represented by it by 2, whereas shifting it right divides it by 2. Multiplication and division of positive numbers by 2 can therefore be accomplished by logical shifts. However, when negative numbers are present, special care must be exercised in dealing with the sign bit.

In the sign-magnitude representation of negative numbers, the sign bit should be left intact. In the 2s complement representation, it should be kept intact on left shift and should be repeated on right shift; i.e., in the right shift, bit 2 should be replaced by bit 1 (the sign bit) and bit 1 should be left in its previous value. In the 1s complement representation, the equivalent operation is done by circular shifts. In either of these, there are cases in which overflow or incorrect results can be generated.

The precise definition of an arithmetic shift depends, therefore, on the way negative numbers are represented in the computer. For 2s complement representation (Fig. 1), the definition is as follows:

> In a right arithmetic shift, the *n*th bit is shifted out and the first bit is repeated. In a left arithmetic shift, the sign bit is left intact, the *n*th bit is filled with zero, and the second bit is lost. Most computers will set condition codes to indicate possible overflow or other incorrect results in arithmetic shifts.

Some examples of the effect of the various shift operations on various five-bit strings are presented in Table 1.

**Table 1.** Examples of Shift Operations

| Bit String | Operation | Result | Comments |
|---|---|---|---|
| 01011 | Left logical | 10110 | |
| 01011 | Right logical | 00101 | Last bit lost |
| 01011 | Right circular | 10101 | |
| 01011 | Left circular | 10110 | |
| 01011 | Right arithmetic | 00101 | |
| 01011 | Left arithmetic | 00110 | Result incorrect (overflow) |
| 11001 | Left arithmetic | 10010 | |
| 11001 | Right arithmetic | 11100 | |
| 11001 | Left logical | 10010 | |
| 11001 | Left logical 2 | 00100 | |

Shift operations are usually used in field alignments, packing and unpacking of data items into storage units, and high-speed multiplication and division, especially by constants. Among the more exotic uses is that for the creation of control patterns. For example, the pattern 10110111 can be used for a switch that will do an operation once, then skip (0), then do it twice, skip again, and finally do it three times.

It should be mentioned that many computers allow double-shift operations. In these shifts, two $n$-bit storage devices are used for shifting purposes as one $2n$-bit device. Also, in certain computers the shift register is extended, usually by the carry indicator, so that the bit shifted out is not lost, but rather is shifted into the extra bit storage.

G. FRIEDER

**SIAM.** *See* SOCIETY FOR INDUSTRIAL AND APPLIED MATHEMATICS.

## SIDE EFFECT

For articles on related subjects *see* ARGUMENT; PROCEDURE; and PROCEDURE-ORIENTED LANGUAGES: Programming In.

A side effect is a consistent result of a procedure that is in addition to or peripheral to the basic result. It is often evidenced as a change in values of variables that are not local to the procedure. Although a side effect may be of no consequence or undesired, in many cases it is just what is desired from the procedure—as, for example, when one of the procedure arguments is an output argument. But side effects can result in nasty problems in the evaluation of arithmetic expressions. To understand this consider the expression

```
A+B*C
```

It is most convenient to evaluate this expression by multiplying $B$ times $C$ and then adding $A$, for otherwise we must first add $A$, store it away temporarily, multiply $B*C$, and then add back the temporary value. But what if the expression is instead

```
FCN(A)+B*C
```

where FCN is a procedure with argument $A$? Suppose the evaluation of FCN(A) has a side effect that modifies the value of $B$ or $C$ or of both. Then the value of the expression is different if $B*C$ is evaluated before FCN(A) is evaluated or afterward. To avoid this problem some languages (e.g., Algol) specify left-to-right evaluation of expressions in cases such as the above, while others (e.g., Fortran) explicitly do not allow a function like FCN to have side effects that may affect other variables in the expression.

1968. Wegner, P. *Programming Languages, Information Structures and Machine Organization.* New York: McGraw-Hill.

A. RALSTON

## SIGNIFICANCE ARITHMETIC

For articles on related subjects *see* ARITHMETIC, COMPUTER; NUMBERS AND NUMBER SYSTEMS; PRECISION; and SIGNIFICANT DIGIT.

The significant digits of a radix approximation (from some finite precision radix-number system) to a true number implicitly convey information on the accuracy of the numerical approximation. Significance arithmetic is a quick and dirty accuracy-monitoring technique providing rules for estimating the number and positions of the significant digits of the radix approximation that results when an arithmetic operation is applied to operands in radix approximation form.

Suppose the positional digit sequence $d_m d_{m-1} \cdots d_l \cdots$ is the standard base $\beta \geq 2$ radix representation of the real number $x$ with most significant digit $d_m \neq 0$. The absolute error in approximating $x$ by the $m - l + 1$ digit real number $\tilde{x} = d_m d_{m-1} \cdots d_l$ with least significant digit $d_l$ less than $\beta^l$. A bound on the relative error $|(x - \tilde{x})/x|$ is given uniformly for any $x$ by $1/\beta^{m-l}$. As a function of $x$, a sharper bound on the relative error is found by

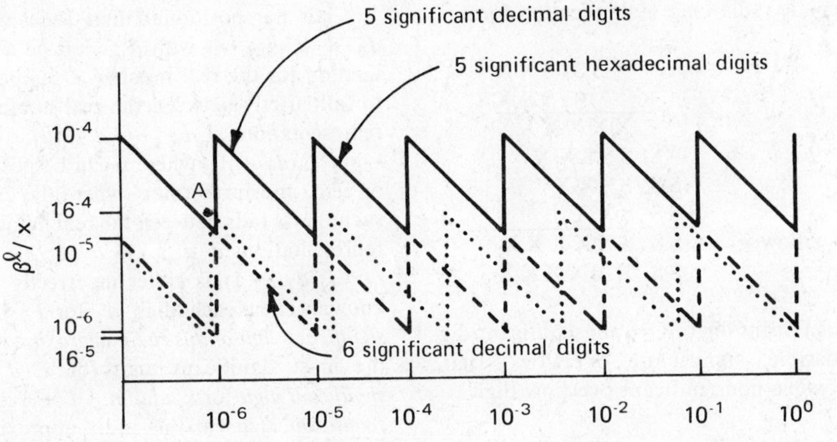


**Fig. 1.** Three cases of the gap function.

plotting the gap function $\beta^l/x$. This function may be interpreted as the absolute error bound divided by the true value $x$. The gap function then yields a bound on the relative error, which varies with $x$ in a log periodic manner, and is best illustrated on a log-log plot (Matula, 1970).

The solid line in Fig. 1 shows the gap function for radix approximations truncated to $n = m - l + 1 = 5$ significant decimal digits; the dashed line corresponds to six significant decimal digits; and the dotted line to five significant hexadecimal digits. The decimal gap functions in Fig. 1 illustrate the rule that an additional significant digit in the base $\beta$ radix approximation provides a uniformly tighter error bound on the relative error by a factor of $1/\beta$. It is also evident that an $n$ significant digit base $\beta$ radix approximation with a leading digit of unity will provide only a slightly better relative error bound than an $n - 1$ significant digit radix approximation with a leading digit of value $\beta - 1$. For example, 1.065 as a four-digit approximation to 1.065 ··· has only a slightly smaller relative error bound than that of 0.978 as a three-digit approximation to 0.978 ··· (this explains why four digits are as easily obtained on the left-hand side of a slide rule as are three digits on the right-hand side).

The significance arithmetic rule for radix conversion (Matula, 1970) is that an $n$ significant digit base $\beta$ radix approximation will, upon conversion to base $\gamma$, yield approximately ($n \log \beta / \log \gamma$) significant digits in the base $\gamma$ radix approximation. This estimate is inherently crude, since Fig. 1 implies that five significant digit hexadecimal radix approximations can in some regions yield more accuracy than seven significant digit decimal approximations, whereas in other regions they will yield less accuracy than five significant digit decimal radix approximations (see point A in Fig. 1).

The significance arithmetic rule for addition/subtraction of radix approximations is that (if no overflow to a higher indexed most significant digit occurs) the position of the least significant digit is the higher index of the least significant digit positions of the operands, and (if overflow occurs) the least significant digit position is taken as one unit higher. The most significant digit of the result is the highest indexed nonzero digit of the result, providing this position is at least as great as the least significant digit position. Note that subtractive cancellation can result in a severe decrease in the number of significant digits, with a possibility of leaving no resulting significant digits. In schematic radix addition form:

| | |
|---|---|
| | SSSS.SSXX |
| | SSS.SXX |
| With no overflow: | SSSS.SXXX |
| With overflow: | SSSSS.XXXX |
| Cancellation example: | 000S.SXXX |

where S = significant digit and X = nonsignificant digit.

The significance arithmetic rule for multiplication/division is simply that the number of significant digits in the result is the minimum of the number of significant digits in the operands.

In schematic radix long multiplication form,

```
                          SS.SXX
                      ×    S.SSX
                       .ⓍXXXXX
                     Ⓢ.SSSXX
                    ⓈS.SSXX
                   ⓈSS.SXX
With no overflow:     SS.SXXXXX
With overflow:       SSS.XXXXXX
```

where S = significant digit, X = nonsignificant digit, Ⓢ = possible significant overflow digit, and Ⓧ = possible nonsignificant overflow digit.

In summary, significance arithmetic provides rules for estimating the significant digits of an arithmetically computed radix approximation, which in turn provides an estimate of the error of this approximation. The overall error estimate is crude but easy to compute.

### Reference

1970. Matula, D. W. "A Formalization of Floating-Point Numeric Case Conversion," *IEEE Trans. Comp. C-19*, pp. 681–692.

D. W. MATULA

# SIGNIFICANT DIGIT

For articles on related subjects *see* ARITHMETIC, COMPUTER; NUMBERS AND NUMBER SYSTEMS; PRECISION; and SIGNIFICANCE ARITHMETIC.

Let the positional digit sequence $d_m d_{m-1} \cdots d_0 \cdot d_{-1} d_{-2} d_{-3} \cdots$ with $d_m \neq 0$ be an exact radix representation for the real number $x$. Each digit $d_i$ for $i \leq m$ is termed a *significant digit of the exact representation* for $x$, and the leading nonzero digit $d_m$ is the *most significant digit* for $x$. For example, with $x = 0.030200\ldots$, $d_{-2} = 3$ is the most significant digit for $x$. Note that the leading zero digits $d_0 = 0$ and $d_{-1} = 0$ are not considered significant digits for $x$, even though the representation utilizes $d_{-1} = 0$ to properly position the significant digits; $d_{-3}$ is significant because it falls after the most significant digit.

Let the positional digit sequence $d_m d_{m-1} \cdots d_0 \cdot d_{-1} d_{-2} d_{-3} \cdots$ with $d_m \neq 0$ be a radix approximation for the real number $x$. Suppose $x$ is known to fall strictly between the real numbers with radix representations $d_m d_{m-1} \cdots d_{l+1}(d_l - 1)$ and $d_m d_{m-1} \cdots d_{l+1}(d_l + 1)$, where $l$ can be positive, negative, or zero, and furthermore where the digit value $d_{l-1}$, such that $x$ falls between the real numbers with radix representations $d_m d_{m-1} \cdots d_l(d_{l-1} - 1)$ and $d_m d_{m-1} \cdots d_l(d_{l-1} + 1)$, is either incorrectly chosen *or* unknown. Then each digit $d_i$ for $l \leq i \leq m$ is a *significant digit of this radix approximation* for $x$, $d_m$ is the most significant digit for $x$, $d_l$ is the least *significant digit* for $x$, and $m - l + 1$ is *the number of significant digits* in this radix approximation for $x$. For example, the decimal approximations 03.0, $\underline{3.142}50$, $\underline{3.1415}80$, $\underline{3.1416}03$, and the binary approximation $0\underline{11.001}11$ for $\pi = 3.1415926 \cdots$ have the significant digits underlined. In these cases the digit following the least significant digit is incorrect in each case. The statement that a measured value, (say, 23.185) has three significant digits merely indicates that the digit value $d_{-2}$ is not known with certitude, although $d_{-2} = 8$ might be possible (and perhaps represents a "best guess").

D. W. MATULA

# SIMPLEX METHOD

For articles on related subjects *see* MATHEMATICAL PROGRAMMING; and MATRIX COMPUTATIONS.

We consider the linear programming problem $P$: Minimize

$$Z = c'x$$

subject to the constraints

$$Ax = b, \qquad x \geq 0,$$

where $A$ is an $(m,n)$-matrix $(m \leq n)$ of full rank, $c$ and $x$ are $n$-vectors, $b$ is an $m$-vector, $Z$ is a scalar referred to as the "objective function," and the prime denotes the transpose. The rank assumption on $A$ is not an unreasonable one even though most linear programs encountered in practice do not satisfy it. A full rank is always achieved by including in $A$ up to $m$ unit vectors corresponding to "artificial" variables, which eventually are set to zero at the optimal solution (see discussion on Step 0 below). Similarly, any inequality constraints are assumed to have been converted to equalities by the addition of "slack" variables.

For convenience, we let $J$ represent the set of all column indices of $A$. Any set $\underline{J}$ (*basic set*) of $m$ linearly independent columns of $A$ forms a *basic matrix* $\underline{A}$, with the remaining set of column indices forming $\bar{J}$ (the *nonbasic set*), $J = \underline{J} \cup \bar{J}$. Similarly, $c' = (\underline{c}', \bar{c}')$, $A = (\underline{A}, \bar{A})$, $x' = (\underline{x}', \bar{x}')$.

A *basic solution* (*bs*) to $P$ is defined as: $\underline{x} = \underline{A}^{-1}b$ and $\bar{x} = 0$. A *basic feasible solution* (*bfs*) to $P$ is a *bs* with $\underline{x} \geq 0$. A *degenerate bfs* is a *bfs* with $\underline{x}_i = 0$ for at least one $i \in \underline{J}$. A *basic dual feasible solution* (*bdfs*) is a *bs* for which $(u'a_j - c_j) \leq 0$ for all $j \in J$, where $u' = \underline{c}' \underline{A}^{-1}$ and where equality holds for all $j \in \underline{J}$. A *degenerate bdfs* is a *bdfs* for which $(u'a_j - c_j) = 0$ for at least one $j \in \bar{J}$.

The (primal) "simplex method," first proposed by G. B. Dantzig in 1947, is an iterative procedure that generates a monotone sequence of *bfs*'s to $P$ with nonincreasing objective function values. With some appropriate precautions to avoid degeneracy, the algorithm is shown to be finite. Computational experience shows that the number of iterations required to solve most problems $P$ is of the order of $m$. In 1953, C. E. Lemke discovered an analogous method, the "dual simplex method," which generates a monotone sequence of *bdfs*'s with nondecreasing values of the dual objective function $U = b'u$. At any feasible solution, $Z \geq U$, and at the optimal solution $Z = U$. Both methods are used widely today. A third approach, the "primal-dual simplex method," was proposed by G. B. Dantzig, L. R. Ford, and D. R. Fulkerson in 1956. The latter has found wide applicability for specially structured linear programs such as network flow problems. Table 1 outlines the "revised" forms of the primal and dual simplex methods.

Step 0 of the algorithms requires clarification: In RPSM a *bfs* is obtained by solving a "Phase I" problem, which is the same as $P$ except that $p(\leq m)$ unit vectors have been included in $A$ corresponding to "artificial variables." The vector $c$ is temporarily ignored and replaced by $c' = (0, s')$, where $s$ is a $p$-vector of all 1s corresponding to the artificial variables. The RPSM is then applied until $c'x = 0$. If Phase I terminates with a *bs* $\underline{x}^*$ such that $\underline{c}'\underline{x}^* > 0$, $P$ has no feasible solution. Otherwise (i.e., $\underline{c}'\underline{x}^* = 0$), the *bfs* $\underline{x} = \underline{x}^*$ is used to start Phase II by restoring the original $c$ and by applying the RPSM once again with the following restrictions: (1) Nonbasic artificial variables are discarded, and (2) basic artificial

**Table 1.** Primal and Dual Simplex Methods

| "Revised Primal Simplex Method" (RPSM) | "Revised Dual Simplex Method" (RDSM) |
|---|---|
| *Step 0.* Obtain a *bfs*: $\underline{x} = \underline{A}^{-1}b \geq 0$, the corresponding basis $\underline{A}$ and the sets $\underline{J}, \bar{J}$. Let $u' = \underline{c}'\underline{A}^{-1}$ and $W = \underline{c}'\underline{x}$, where $W$ denotes $Z$. | *Step 0.* Obtain a *bdfs*: $\underline{x} = \underline{A}^{-1}b$, the corresponding basis $\underline{A}$ and the sets $\underline{J}, \bar{J}$. Let $u' = \underline{c}'\underline{A}^{-1}$ and $W = u'b$, where $W$ denotes $U$. |
| *Step 1.* Choose a column $a_k$ to *enter* the basis by $(z_k - c_k) = \text{"op"}\{(z_j - c_j) \mid (z_j - c_j) > 0; j \in \bar{J}\}$ where "op" is usually "max" and where $z_j = u'a_j$. If $z_j - c_j \leq 0$ for all $j \in \bar{J}$, then $\underline{x}$ solves $P$, stop. Else, compute $y_k = \underline{A}^{-1}a_k$. | *Step 1.* Choose a column $a_l$ to *leave* the basis by $\underline{x}_l = \text{"op"}\{\underline{x}_i \mid \underline{x}_i < 0; i \in \underline{J}\}$ where "op" is usually "min". If $\underline{x} \geq 0$, then $\underline{x}$ solves $P$, stop. Else, let $v' = e_k'\underline{A}^{-1}$, where $e_l$ is the $l$th unit vector. |
| *Step 2.* Choose the column $a_l$ to *leave* the basis by $\underline{x}_l / y_{lk} = \min\{\underline{x}_i / y_{ik} \mid y_{ik} > 0; i \in \underline{J}\}$ If $y_k \leq 0$, $P$ has an infinite solution, stop. Else, go to step 3. | *Step 2.* Choose the column $a_k$ to *enter* the basis by $(z_k - c_k) = \min\{(z_j - c_j)/y_{lj} \mid y_{lj} < 0; j \in \bar{J}\}$ where $z_j = u'a_j$ and $y_{lj} = v'a_j$. If $y_{lj} \geq 0$ for all $j \in \bar{J}$, $P$ has no feasible solution, stop. Else, go to step 3. |

*Step 3.* Implement the pivot step identified in steps 1 and 2 by: $\underline{A}^{-1} \leftarrow E_l \underline{A}^{-1}$; $\underline{x} \leftarrow E_l \underline{x}$; $W \leftarrow W - (z_k - c_k)\underline{x}_l / y_{lk}$; $\underline{J} \leftarrow \underline{J} + \{k\} - \{l\}$; $\bar{J} \leftarrow \bar{J} + \{l\} - \{k\}$; $u' \leftarrow \underline{c}'\underline{A}^{-1}$, where $E_l$ is an "elementary matrix" consisting of a unit matrix with its $l$th column replaced by the vector: $\eta_i = (1/y_{lk})(-y_{1k}, \ldots, -y_{l-1.k}, 1, -y_{l+1,k}, \ldots, -y_{mk})$.
Go to step 1 (of the method being executed).

variables, which necessarily have a zero value at the conclusion of Phase I, are kept at zero value.

In RDSM, Phase I is somewhat different: First, some basic $\underline{A}$ is chosen from $A$, i.e., some $\underline{J} \subseteq J$. Second, the "artifical constraint" row $\bar{s}'\bar{x} + x_+ = K$ is appended to problem $P$, where $\bar{s}$ is an $(n-m)$ vector of all 1s, $K$ is a large positive scalar, and $x_+$ is a "slack variable." Third, the *bs* $\underline{x}$ is computed for this new system as defined above, with the sole exception that the pivot in this artificial row is chosen at the $k$th position, where $k$ is defined by $(z_k - c_k) = \max(z_j - c_j; j \in J)$. The resulting $\underline{x}$ is a *bdfs*. Then, RDSM is applied. The condition $x_+ = 0$ at the solution implies that $P$ has an infinite solution.

Step 1, as stated in Table 1 (and the subsequent application of Step 2), is a simplification in the interest of expediency of the computationally much more expensive step:

RPSM:

$$\frac{(z_k - c_k)\underline{x}_l}{y_{lk}} = \max\left\{(z_j - c_j)\left(\min\left\{\frac{\underline{x}_i}{y_{ij}}\middle| y_{ij} > 0; i \in \underline{J}\right\}\right)\middle| (z_j - c_j) > 0; j \in \bar{J}\right\}$$

RDSM:

$$\frac{(z_k - c_k)\underline{x}_l}{y_{lk}} = \max\left\{\underline{x}_i\left(\min\left\{\frac{(z_j - c_j)}{y_{ij}}\middle| y_{ij} < 0; j \in \bar{J}\right\}\right)\middle| \underline{x}_i < 0; i \in \underline{J}\right\}$$

This choice of the pivot element would produce the maximum change in $Z$ per iteration, and thus RPSM (or RDSM) would qualify as a "steepest descent (or ascent)" method. The simplified choice employed in Step 1 with "op" = "max" (or "op" = "min") results in convergence rates comparable to those under the more complicated choices above. For some problems, improved convergence rates may be obtained by specifying as "op" various "pricing strategies." This capability exists in most large scale LP codes.

If during the RPSM iteration, $\underline{x}_l = 0$, then $Z$ remains unchanged. Similarly, $U$ remains unchanged if during an RDSM iteration $z_k - c_k = 0$. This condition arises when the initial *bfs* (or *bdfs*) is degenerate, and/or when the minimum in Step 2 is not unique. These iterations, referred to as "degenerate" or "unproductive," *may* cause a particular $\underline{J}$ to be repeated after a number of such iterations (cycling), thus rendering the sequence infinite. Almost invariably, degenerate iterations are encountered in practice, but seldom cause cycling. For this reason, most LP codes do not employ existing methods to avoid degeneracy beyond simple tie-breaking rules for selecting an index among the alternate minima in Step 2.

The matrix $A$ is normally stored on a slower storage device and reviewed sequentially by columns, for each iteration. Nevertheless, it is clear that in order to have any semblance of efficiency, one must use main storage for $\underline{A}^{-1}$, $\underline{x}$, $y_k$, $a_j$, and $u$ for RPSM and an additional vector $v$ for RDSM, requiring $(m^2 + 4m)$ and $(m^2 + 5m)$ locations, respectively. This arrangement, in particular the high density of nonzero elements in the explicit form of $\underline{A}^{-1}$, prevents the solution of large problems with thousands of rows and tens of thousands of columns, even though such problems possess extremely sparse matrices $A$. In most commercially available LP codes, this difficulty is remedied by using the "product form of the inverse" (PFI) for the RPSM or RDSM. The PFI consists of keeping $\underline{A}^{-1}$ in the product form of the elementary matrices $E_t$; i.e., $\underline{A}^{-1} = E_tE_{t-1} \cdots E_1$ (actually only the index $t$ and the nonzero elements of the vector $\eta_t$ are stored). Each iteration $t$ creates one such $\eta_t$, which may be stored sequentially on a slower device (e.g., disk). Since $\underline{A}^{-1}$ is only used to premultiply or postmultiply a vector, the sequence $\{\eta_t\}$ is reviewed in the "forward" or the "backward" order of its creation. Currently, most large-scale LP codes use the PFI and achieve a sparsity for the $\eta$ vectors comparable to that of the original matrix $A$.

Step 3 and the PFI are implementations of the Gauss-Jordan elimination method. The corresponding implementations of the Gauss elimination method lead to the "elimination form of the inverse" (EFI), whose application in large-scale LP is the subject of current research and appears extremely promising.

For more detailed information on the simplex methods, and its various extensions and applications, the reader is referred to the References.

## References

1962. Hadley, G. *Linear Programming*. Reading, Mass.: Addison-Wesley.

1963. Dantzig, G. B. *Linear Programming and Extensions*. Princeton, N.J.: Princeton Univ. Press.

1964. Gass, S. I. *Linear Programming Methods and Applications,* 2d ed. New York: McGraw-Hill.
1966. Simonnard, M. *Linear Programming.* Englewood Cliffs, N.J.: Prentice-Hall. (Transl. by W. S. Jewell.)
1968. Orchard-Hays, W. *Advanced Linear Programming Computing Techniques.* New York: McGraw-Hill.
1973. White, W. W. "A Status Report on Computing Algorithms for Mathematical Programming," *Computing Surveys*, Vol. 5, No. 3 (September).

M. D. Grigoriadis

## SIMSCRIPT. *See* Simulation: Languages.

## SIMULATION

For articles on related subjects *see* Models; Operations Research; Performance Measurement and Evaluation; Programming Languages; and Queueing Theory.
For article on related term *see* Block Diagram.

Simulation is the representation of certain features of the behavior of a physical or abstract system by the behavior of another system. In computing, therefore, simulation refers to the employment of the computation process to implement a model of some dynamic system or phenomenon. The purpose of simulation is usually to make experimental measurements or predict behavior, although simulation is also used for teaching purposes. Simulation has been one of the most consistently useful and productive applications of computer science. Simulations, both large and small, have been used by industry, academia, and government for as long as the modern digital computer has been employed. Indeed, the concept of simulation preceded the advent of digital computation through the use of analog systems, and even preceded the use of analog computers through the use of physical models in, for example, wind tunnels and towing tanks.

This treatment of digital simulation is divided into two categories: the process and applications of simulation; and the techniques, or languages, of simulation.

### PRINCIPLES

Historically, the concept of modern digital simulation was early proposed by John von Neumann, who visualized the application of computation enabling the automation of gathering repetitive, statistical data on modeled phenomena. This was termed the "Monte Carlo" process because it imposed randomly generated parametric changes on the model (Naylor et al., 1966). Among the earliest published applications of digital simulation were the solutions of problems related to job shops, the allocation and distribution of resources to production scheduling. Among the latest applications of digital simulation is, curiously, the prediction of the performance of computers themselves. Both examples are illustrative of one of the prime justifications for employing simulation, namely, that the economics or logistics of experimenting with the actual system are prohibitive. Since simulation is an expensive (both labor-intensive and computation-intensive) tool to use, economic justification for its application is of great importance.

Other situations where simulation has been economically feasible are those in which a model or substitute system must be used to attain predictive data: system-design concept evaluation (the system is not physically available); system-destruction or safety experiments (too dangerous); system-reliability or failure testing (economically unfeasible). Simulation has also been employed to replace elements of systems or entire systems too large or cumbersome to test, e.g., spacecraft docking and maneuvering; world weather dynamics; large man/machine systems; weapon effects. It is employed in lieu of a closed-form, mathematical means of predicting behavior. The term "prediction" is an important concept. Simulation enables the mapping of the analyst's concept of the real world. Because mapping is an approximation, the results are approximate rather than precise.

In the modern sense, digital simulation began about 1959 with the reporting of several job-shop simulators developed by large industrial corporations. In 1962 came the documentation of the first general-purpose simulation languages, Simscript and GPSS. The technology has burgeoned in the intervening years. Practitioners of simulation hold three yearly national conferences on general subjects, and there are a number of symposia devoted to special applications (e.g., simulation of computers). Several major technical societies have simulation-oriented component organizations. There is at least one technical organization devoted exclusively to simulation. Many academic institutions, responding to the rapidly increasing demand for this useful technology, give courses in simulation which are sponsored mainly in the multidisciplinary curricula: computer science, operations research, or industrial management. This is appropriate because simulation is, in essence, a multidisciplinary technology, comprising elements of mathematics, engineering, and management science.

## The Process of Simulation

DEFINITIONS. Simulation is a process that employs a computerized model of certain significant features of some physical or logical system. The object of the process of simulation is to provide an experimental model for the accumulation of data on the target system. The process of simulation comprises the steps of experiment definition, modeling, computer implementation, validation, and data gathering.

Simulators are programs developed to apply the process of simulation. The term "simulator" usually implies the incorporation of some model elements (job-shop simulator; computer simulator) even though the tool may be quite flexible and thus useful for many modeling adaptations.

Simulators are distinguished from "simulation languages," which are general purpose and contain no model bias.

Simulaters (often called simulators) are persons who perform simulation.

EXPERIMENT DEFINITION. The problem to be solved by simulation can be considered as the identification of the behavior of some dynamic system. "Dynamic" and "simulation" are interrelated terms. Systems that are dynamic—i.e., whose states change with time—are those which are customarily defined to be simulatable.

What the problem solver must determine at the outset of the process is the extent and detail of the model required, and correspondingly the scope of input and output data required.

"Extent" and "detail" are also interrelated. The extent of a system is the broadness of system function encompassed by the simulation model. The number of functions modeled is the detail or level of structure incorporated in the model. Because the computer size and speed presents a finite boundary on any application, the numerical product of extent and detail may be considered to be essentially a constant. Thus, the broader the scope of the system considered, the less detail is likely to be included. For example, the synthesis of a model of airport service might include planes landing, alighting, taxiing, and loading-unloading. Corresponding detail might be the actual runway routing and the unloading ramp services. Broader specification might include descent, ascent, flight routing, and holding. Finer structure might involve fueling, inspection, crewing. In the broad extent, the incorporation of finer levels of detail would usually be irrelevant, and vice versa.

The desired output data and available input data are important ingredients in defining the simulation process. The data detail should be at a level comparable to that of the complexity of the model definition. Input data is frequently considered a simulation problem area. Hypothesized or poor-quality input data may degrade the validity of output data, but it may not diminish the viability or utility of the simulation process if the validity problem is taken into account (see later section, "Validation.")

MODELING. The target system, thus defined, is modeled. Many types of simulation models exist. They are classified by the nature of the systems they represent. The most frequent classification criterion is the dynamic-change property of the system variables: continuous or discrete.

*Continuous-variable* models usually represent those systems that are describable by mathematical expressions which depict the continuous change of variables with time. Physical systems represented by differential equations, where time is the independent variable, are of this nature. What continuous-variable simulation implements is the behavior of the system during transient responses to perturbations. Continuous-variable simulation is often carried out on analog or digital computers but will not be considered further here.

Systems to be considered here are those where the dynamic state changes in discrete steps. In this case, no smooth, mathematical function can be solved to obtain system behavior. The changes are abrupt, steplike. Interstate transients are not considered. Such system behavior usually results from the disruption of system status caused by the allocation and deallocation of resources within the system. Queueing is an important consideration in systems describable by discrete-event models.

COMPUTER IMPLEMENTATION. By *implementation* we mean the process of computerization of the discrete-event model. Simulation programming may be accomplished by using various programming tools, such as higher-level languages and languages specifically designed to implement simulation. It should be noted that most discrete-event simulation models could be exercised by manual computation, although this would be tedious. However, it is sometimes a useful method for checking the operation of the computerized model.

Computerization of the simulation model affords the benefit of automated data gathering and storage. Automation of these functions, using modern digital computers, enables representation of complex dynamic processes and (optionally) the performance of Monte Carlo experiments on target systems. Monte Carlo experiments involve the perturbation of the system with randomly varying quantities, and the accumulation of large and statistically sufficient output data samples.

Another benefit accruing from computerization is the reduction of the experimental data to produce summary reports on important system variables. Thus, the experimenter may receive deterministic or statistical output data that depicts system status and performance during and at the end of specified time intervals in individual experiments or (in Monte Carlo models) at the conclusion of the desired statistical sample.

*Discrete-event* models are frequently implemented using such general-purpose, higher-level languages as Fortran. Occasionally they are programmed in machine assembly language. Most commonly, languages especially designed to enhance this implementation process are used. These are called "discrete-event" simulation languages. They can be described by various properties: event orientation (transaction versus process); modeling purpose (general versus specific purpose); or coding level (statement versus data base). Some, such as Simscript and GPSS, are available on a wide range of host machines; others designed for special machines and purposes have limited availability. Specific languages are discussed in a later section.

VALIDATION. Validation is the most perplexing aspect of the simulation process. In the simulation community there is a wide range of opinion as to the meaning, necessity, and techniques of validation. Validation, in general, refers to estimating the degree of validity of the simulation results and is a property somewhat comparative to accuracy.

However, while accuracy has an "absolute" connotation, validity has a "relative" connotation. Validity, therefore, assumes the nature of *relative* accuracy (Morris and Roth, 1975). To state the validity of a result, one must impute to it an accuracy related to an understood criterion. This is important because simulation itself is an approximate process, frequently employing hypothetical or statistically varying data, constructs, and parameters. In this context, simulation results with a specified accuracy may be valid for one purpose but invalid for another. For instance, accuracies in simulated performance of a computer system of, say, 70% may be quite valid for configuration analysis for use in marketing, but the same results would be entirely invalid for some other purpose, such as final source selection. The process requires the use of an understood *criterion of validity*.

Simulation is itself a substitute for real experimentation, and usually is conducted in the absence of a complete set of "real" data. Even when a real data comparison about some system point is accomplished, absolute accuracy of extrapolated system states is impractical, for the modeling process itself imparts assumptions, linearities, and qualified detail to the target system model. In any case, establishing the final accuracy (hence, validity of the model) involves an iterative process whereby successive runs and adjustments converge and lead to some accepted criterion.

Other means of partially validating the results of a simulation are *comparison* (for a limited range) with a hand-computed solution, and an *estimation* of relative validity. This refers to an order-of-magnitude/polarity comparison of simulated and predicted behavior when subjecting the system to selected stresses.

DATA GATHERING. Data obtainable from discrete-event simulations fall into three primary classifications: timing, resource utilization and queueing, and historical.

*Timing data* includes the statistics of system or event timing: time to complete a job or process, or time allocation to a system user, or number of users per-unit-time. These are useful for gauging the dynamic performance of various systems entities, i.e., customers processed through facilities, speed of service, etc.

*Resource utilization and queueing data* includes the number of calls, time utilized, waiting time, length of queue, etc., for the system resources. This is useful for determining system-flow bottlenecks and balance of resources.

*Historical data* usually is represented by a chronological event-by-event trace for entire or partial simulations. This is useful for debugging models and programs, and for examining transient conditions in the simulated system.

DISCRETE-EVENT MODELS. Discrete-event models, while possibly differing in "world view" (organization of model logic and structure) may be considered to have a common, basic purpose and therefore a common basic set of elements. Discrete-event models basically are focused on system users, who consume system resources and expend time. Where resources are unavailable, queueing and queue-serving may occur. Models may differ in the generation of events and in method of accumulation of time and queueing statistics. However, all discrete-event models possess the basic element set: users, resources, queues, and demand. Elements may be described as entities having referenced attributes, which enable classification and accumulation.

*Users* are the consumers of resources. They may be, for example, supermarket customers, computer applications, or factory orders. User entities may have defining attributes. Supermarket customers may be differentiated by sex, number of selections, point of origin (i.e., parking location). Computer applications may be differentiated by data set, number of segments processed, type of origin (i.e., remote terminal, batch load, etc.). Factory orders may be differentiated by type of product ordered, number of production operations required, shipping destination. A commonly employed attribute is *priority*. This is usually invoked to influence the competition for resources. Priority may be of a ranking nature or may be preemptive.

*Resources* may be described as single entities, pools or sets of entities, and storage entities. Resource entities may also have classifying attributes. A single entity is one that has uniqueness. Resources having common attributes and considered as interchangeable may be grouped in sets. Resources having multiplicity of storage capacity may be considered as multiserver facilities.

The manager of a supermarket is a resource likely to have unique attributes because there is only one in each unit of the supermarket system. However, the carts of a supermarket may be considered as having common, indistinguishable attributes, and therefore comprise a set of interchangeable units. A facility may be illustrated by the storage area of some store or shop, where a number of elements of occupancy exist. This is figuratively the inverse of an element set. The set becomes empty during use; the facility becomes filled.

An interesting attribute is spatial location. Entities may be transferred during use from one location to another—for example; locomotives on a rail system; program segments in memory; supermarket carts from store to parking lot. Most simulators can enable assignment of resources by location attribute, with some difficulty.

*Demand* is the schedule of events, users, or customers to be processed through the target system. Demand specification may be expressed in deterministic or probabilistic fashion: Transactions may be scheduled at predetermined times or as the result of random selection from some statistical ensemble. A supermarket demand example is the specification of the arrival of shoppers of various types during, say, a peak hour.

*Queues* are entities that hold and order the users waiting for resource service. A stated service discipline controls the ordering, usually by user priority and time of request. Queues having length may be usually associated with specific resources, such as the supermarket check-out waiting line, the computer application scheduling stack, the job-shop subassembly storage bin. The waiting line may be infinite or be limited by floor space; the stack is necessarily limited by memory size; the storage bin, while holding a queue, is itself a facility occupied, and may, in turn, be queued.

## The Tools of Computer Simulation

DISCRETE-EVENT SIMULATION PROGRAM OPERATION. Discrete-event simulation programming languages are, at the execution level, quite similar. They differ mainly in the method available to the programmer for communicating the model programmatically. Basically, programs in all simulation languages manipulate files, or sets, which contain elements describing simulated time, event resource-and-time requirements, resource status, etc.

The main operation of a typical simulation program consists of the updating of a "next event" file. Other main operations are the maintenance of a "queue" file, a resource status file, and data collection files (Fig. 1).

The queue file maintains a "time stamped" record of all events awaiting resource servicing and which have previously been denied resources.

The heart of the typical simulation program is the "next event" file, which has the function of maintaining a list of all events to be processed and also serves as the "clock," allowing simulated time to be updated. An entry in the next-event file is made whenever the initiation time for a future event is established. Types of events handled by this file are:

1. Simulation events: the starting time of some process or string of events, the starting time of individual events, the termination time of events or processes.
2. Reporting events: start of interim or final simulation output reports.
3. End of the simulation.

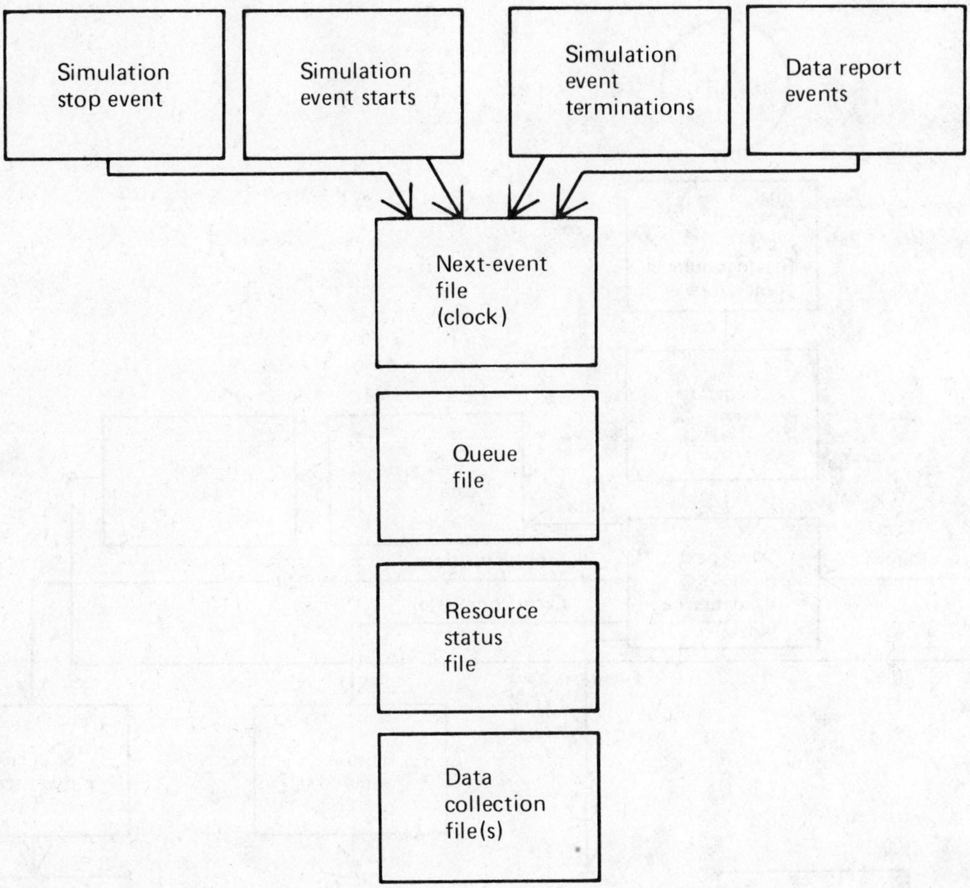


**Fig. 1.** Typical main simulation files.

At the beginning of a simulation, the starting times for all predetermined events may be loaded into the next-event file. For simulation events, these may consist of occurrence times generated from random ensembles or by deterministic specification. The times for reports and for the end of the simulation may also be input.

Processing of the next-event file, and hence the clock, then becomes a continous updating of the start and finish of various events. Obviously, all event terminations and many event starts cannot be predetermined because of blockage or delays induced by resource contention and random selection of timing and decision.

Initially, the next-event routine (Fig. 2) scans the next-event file to find the next event. In the case of a scheduled-event start, it advances the file time-status NOW (or clock) to the time of this start, and then exits to a resource allocation routine, which either assigns resources or initiates queueing. If resources are successfully assigned, the event-service time is added to NOW, and this time is entered into the next-event file as a future completion event, and the scanning for other events occurring at NOW is resumed. If resources are unavailable, an entry is made into the queue file naming this event, requesting appropriate resources, and indicating NOW as the time of request. Control is then returned to the next-event routine to continue scanning for the next event in the file.

In the case of an event completion (meaning that the clock has advanced so that NOW equals the event completion time), the next-event routine exits to a routine that restores the resources used by the event to their unbusy states and appropriate files. At this point, the event-scan routine will likely pass control to a queue-servicing routine, which determines if the required resources are now available for a queued event. The queue-servicing routine then scans the queue file for events which, at this point,

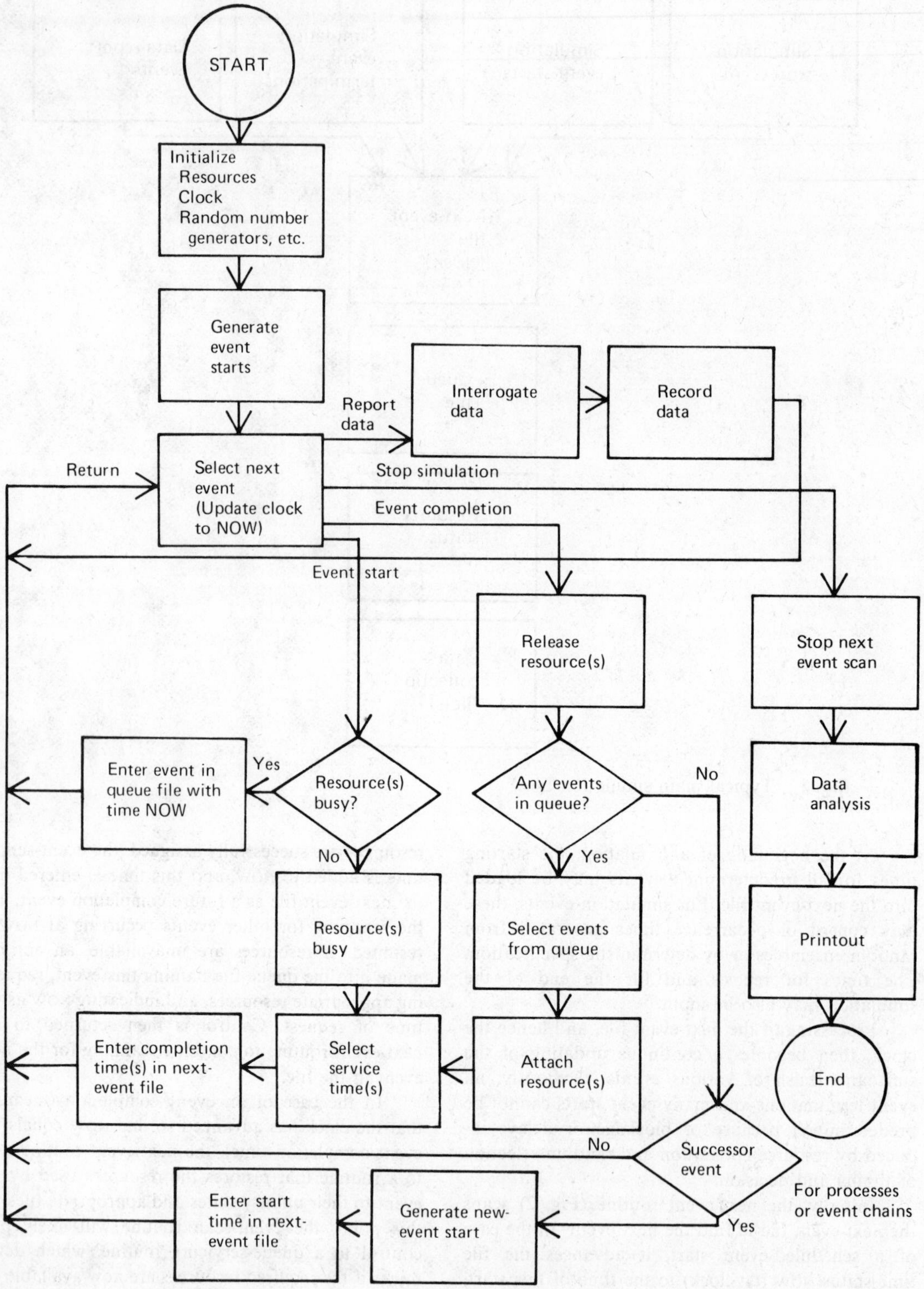


**Fig. 2.** Typical next-event routine for discrete- event simulation.

can be assigned resources. If any events can be so assigned, they are effectively "reactivated," i.e., removed from the queue file by having their completion times entered in the next-event file. Control is then given back to the next-event routine, which enters the scan mode and proceeds to look for other events at NOW. If current (NOW) events are exhausted, the "clock" scanning continues until the next event is found. This constitutes in effect a two-modal scan: the "clock" scan, looking for events chronologically, and the "event" scan, looking for events during the current value of NOW.

Note that, at the current time, many things may happen simultaneously. Events may start and finish; reporting may occur. The ordering of these occurrences during this "time freeze" is influenced by the order of insertion of events into the next-event file, which may be the result of various random processes.

It should also be noted that the clock is usually updated in asynchronous, random-time quanta, not in synchronous time steps. Periodic reporting occurs when the next-event routine senses a reporting notice in the next-event file. Control is then given to the report-generation section of the program.

Final programmatic stopping of the simulation occurs usually in one of two ways: The next-event routine may determine that no more simulation events are scheduled, or it may sense a STOP notice at some value of NOW. Usually, either stop condition will automatically generate a final data report.

## LANGUAGES

OVERVIEW. The preceding section described the operation of a typical simulation program so as to illustrate its purely list-processing and nonmathematical nature. Reference to specific programs was intentionally omitted in order to convey this nature in an abstract sense. This operation is at the inner, execution level. In the context of simulation implementation, however, the most important language concepts are not those of execution, but rather of language communication of simulation models to the computer so that execution may occur.

Simulation languages, as distinguished from general-purpose languages, are problem-oriented. Such languages are usually written in a largely computer-independent notation for a particular problem area, and contain statements or constructs appropriate for formulating solutions to specific types of problems. Of course general-purpose compiler-type languages such as Fortran are also widely used in discrete event simulation. A recent estimate indicates that 75% of all discrete event simulation is performed using Fortran. Of the remaining 25%, GPSS and Simscript are the most popularly favored, with the former more highly favored.

These use patterns probably reflect the already established familiarity with such tools as Fortran rather than an objective preference based on features. Also, such factors as training time and cost may weigh to some extent. However, an important decision factor in the choice of a simulation language is the complexity and freedom of model representation accommodated. This choice is frequently a trade-off between factors such as complexity of expression accommodated, language bias, cost of running, ease of programming, availability of program, and method of documentation of results.

The complexity accommodated refers to the programmatic features of the language. The language bias refers to the modeling conventions imposed by the language. Obviously, a language such as Fortran has the widest range of expression and imposes the least bias upon the model to be programmed. This is at one end of the language spectrum. The remainder of the spectrum consists of various discrete-event simulation languages with varying degrees of expression and/or bias.

Simulation languages contain, to varying extents, constructs or structures that facilitate communication of a model to the computer. Control features such as data aggregation, event-timing routines, entity generation and destruction, data collection and presentation, and random variable generation are contained as subroutines or procedural operations in simulation languages. General-purpose programming languages require that these operations be programmed ad hoc.

One class of simulation languages, examples of which are Simscript and Simula, provide a basic, precompiled set of simulation support and control routines, but require the modeler to communicate the model by using formal program language statements: Simscript uses Fortran-like statements; Simula uses Algol-like statements. Another type of simulation language, such as GPSS, incorporates not only control routines but also general-purpose model structures, which are precompiled. This enables the communication of the model through specification of "blocks," which represent specific model routines. Programming this type of model consists of ordering block operations and specifying parameters through the use of rigid, formatted, data input files. This, of course, constrains the model basically to the "world view" of the simulation language developer.

**Table 1.** General Information about Digital-Discrete Simulation Languages

| Language Name | Type | Developing Organization | Authors | Computer Implementation | Documentation or Reference |
|---|---|---|---|---|---|
| Boss | Process | Burroughs | Meyerhoff, Roth, Shafer | B5000, B6000 series | Boss Mark II Reference Manual, Report 66099A; Burroughs Corp., Paoli, Pa. 1972 |
| Flow Simulator | Process | RCA CSD | Unknown | RCA 3301 Spectra 70 series | Flow Simulator Reference Manual 70-00-617, April 1969 |
| Gasp | Event | U.S. Steel, Arizona State | Kiviat & Pritsker | With appropriate modification, any computer with Fortran IV compiler | *Simulation with GASP II*, Kiviat & Pritsker, Prentice-Hall, 1969; *The GASP IV Simulation Language*, Pritsker, Wiley, 1974 |
| Gesim | Process | GE | Unknown | HIS Sys. 600 & 6000 series | GESIM User's Manual GES-1022 |
| GPDS | Process | Xerox | Unknown | Sigma 5-9 | Xerox General Purpose Discrete Simulator, Sigma 5-9 Computers, Xerox Data Systems, April 1971 |
| GPSS | Process | IBM | Gordon et al. | IBM 7090, 7094, 7040, 7044, System 360/370; UNIVAC 1107/1108/1110; CDC 6000 series; Honeywell 600, 6000 series | General Purpose Simulation System/360 CS Version 2 Users Manual, SH20-0694-0, IBM Corp. |
| GPSS/360 Norden | Process | Norden Div., United Aircraft | Katzke & Reitman | IBM System 360 w/2250 display unit | Norden Report 4269R0003, Users Guide to Conversational GPSS, December 1969 |
| Quiksim | Process | National Cash Register | Weamer | NCR 315 RMC | Proc. Third Conference on the Applications of Simulation, December 1969 |
| Simon | Process | Bristol College of Science & Technology and ICL | Unknown | Elliott 503, 803; ICL 1900 series | ICL Reference Manual 4138, Simulation Language SIMON, January 1969 |
| Simscript | Event | RAND | Markowitz, Hausner, & Karr | IBM 7090, 7094, 7040, 7044, 360/370; CDC 3600, 3800, 6400, 6600, 7600; UNIVAC 494, 1107, 1108, 1110; RCA Spectra 70 series; NCR 200 series; PHILCO 2000 series; HIS 615, 625, 635, 655, 6030, 6040, 6060, 6080; STANDARD IC-6000 | *SIMSCRIPT, A Simulation Programming Language*, Markowitz, Hausner, & Karr, Prentice-Hall, 1963 |

| | | | | | |
|---|---|---|---|---|---|
| Simscript II | Event | RAND | Kiviat, Markowitz, Hausner, & Villaneueva | IBM System 360/370; RCA Spectra 70 | *SIMSCRIPT II—A Programming Language*, Kiviat, Villaneueva, & Markowitz, Prentice-Hall, 1969 |
| Simpl/1 | Event | IBM | Unknown | IBM 360/370 | SIMPL/1 General Information Manual (GH19-5053), IBM, 1972 |
| Simula | Process | Norwegian Computer Center | Dahl & Nygaard | UNIVAC 1107; 1108, 1110; CDC 6400, 6600, 6700, 7600; Burroughs B5000, B6000, B7000 series | Simula—A language for programming and description of discrete event system; Users Manual, Dahl & Nygaard, Norwegian Computer Center, 1965 |
| Sol | Process | Burroughs, Case Inst. of Tech. | Knuth & McNeley | Burroughs B5000/B5500; UNIVAC 1107/1108 | Sol—A symbolic language for general-purpose systems simulation, Knuth and McNeley 1963 |

*Source:* From I. M. Kay, "Digital Discrete Simulation Languages. Discussion and Inventory," in Ira M. Kay and John McLeod (Eds.), *Progress in Simulation*, vol. 2, Gordon and Breach Science Publishers, New York, 1972.

The statement-like languages discussed previously impart less "world view," and hence more modeling flexibility.

Simulation languages can be discriminated from another standpoint: their method of processing modeled events. The major distinction is between the "process-oriented" and "event-oriented" languages. The process-oriented language views the world as a set of fixed objects or facilities, which are employed to service the active transactions (users) that are created and which traverse the system. A supermarket can be modeled as a set of fixed resources (carts) assigned to the users (customers) who enter the store. In event orientation, the event occurs at some scheduled time and searches for a facility to process it. An example of event orientation is a repairman looking for a failed piece of equipment to service.

It is interesting to note that statement simulation languages comprise primarily both process (Simula) and event (Simscript) orientation. Block languages such as GPSS tend to be process-oriented. However, most are sufficiently flexible to be used as desired by the inventive simulater.

Various human and economic factors must be considered in language selection. The block-diagram approach greatly eases the process of access to the computer. The precompiled nature of the block language requires only new data inputs to change the model structure and parameters, since compilation is eliminated from the simulation process. By contrast, a statement simulation language requires statement preparation, subsequent compilation, and debugging for each model respecification. Conversely, the statement language offers a potentially greater efficiency in running than does the block diagram language, and therefore lowers the computer cost. However, again, this may be offset by the potentially lower cost of programming a block-oriented simulation where it is applicable.

Another consideration is the level of expertise required to implement either approach. A statement language requires programming and syntax rigor; a block language requires only the ability to manipulate a data base to map the model; hence, the modeler or problem solver is presented with a shorthand method of communicating with the computer.

**Description of Languages.** The following material describes three event-type (Simscript, Simscript II, Gasp II) and three process-type (GPSS, Simula, Boss) languages and is followed by a detailed listing of major discrete-event languages. This material and Table 1 have been abstracted from an exhaustive compilation by Kay (1972).

*Simscript*. Developed by H. Markowitz, G. Hausner, and H. Karr at the RAND Corporation, Simscript is available on a wide range of computers. It was one of the original discrete-event simulation languages. Since its statements equip the user with a Fortran-like instrumentation set, Simscript requires scientific programming ability. Simscript permits broad specification of an event-oriented model, but it does not provide any automatic statistical analysis or output. However, a Report Generator provides code for specifying output without the use of input-output statements per se. Subsequent to the RAND version, new compilers appeared for various machines under a copyrighted name, Simscript I.5.

*Simscript II.* This is a scientific programming language, which enables discrete-event simulation. A descendant of, but not compatible with, the original Simscript, it was designed by Markowitz and Karr, with additional work done by P. Kiviat and R. Villaneueva at RAND. Simscript II contains five "levels," which provide a wide range of capability for use as a scientific and/or data processing language, as well as providing event-oriented simulation capability. It is also available in copyrighted versions: Simscript II Plus and Simscript II.5.

*Gasp II (General Activity Simulation Program).* This is a simulation language that essentially augments Fortran with a set of event-oriented simulation structures such as event timing, set manipulation, and statistical data collection and reporting. The Gasp user must be familiar with Fortran. Gasp II was developed by Kiviat and A. Pritsker. Lately, Pritsker and associates have developed a PL/I version, Gaspl-I, and a new scientific language version of Gasp, Gasp IV.

*GPSS (General-Purpose Systems Simulator).* GPSS, developed originally by G. Gordon at IBM, is the most popular discrete-event simulation language. GPSS is process-oriented, containing a repertoire of flowchart-like blocks (Gordon, 1969). It also provides a large variety of autonomously generated measurements about the simulated model. Since its original version, it has appeared in subsequent, more powerful versions: GPSS-II, -III, -IV, -V, and -360. Current versions provide limited capability for using Fortran and assembly language subroutines. GPSS-360 Norden is a proprietary version developed by Reitman and associates, which through a CRT display unit, provides conversational features, user-interactive input, and control.

*Simula.* Simula, an extension of Algol developed at the Norwegian Computing Center by O.-J. Dahl and K. Nygaard, is process-oriented: A process (user) continues until it is prevented from execution. An operative process is considered "active"; a queued or suspended process is considered "passive." Simula contains recursiveness, list-processing capability, and allows complete user access to Algol. An advanced version, also called Simula, is a general-purpose scientific language containing simulation capability.

*Boss (Burroughs Operational System Simulator).* This language was developed at the Burroughs Corporation by A. J. Meyerhoff, P. F. Roth, P. Shafer, and J. P. Troy. While not following GPSS block format, Boss is similar in that it allows the use of its own flowchart-like blocks for coding processes. Boss blocks, however, contain multiple functions; for instance, it has implicitly invoked queueing when a process task cannot obtain a resource. This imparts to Boss an extremely compact notation that is sufficiently powerful for most modeling applications.

**Comparative Example.** To illustrate simulation languages and their differences, the coding of a simple, single-server queueing model is illustrated, using a block-diagramming language and a statement language.

Fig. 3 represents the logical flow of events for a discrete-event mapping of a rather general single-server situation. In this case, it is assumed that one server constitutes the fixed resource of the system, and the user activity is represented by the flow model. Discrete events occur as the service user is created or generated; i.e., it arrives at the system for service; tests the status of the server (currently busy or unbusy) and branches accordingly; is queued awaiting service (if busy) and then dequeued; obtains possession of the server (busies it) for a time; releases the resource; and exits the system. Time parameters (left unspecified here for generality) that must be imparted to the system are the arrival time and the service time; these may be generated in Monte Carlo fashion or otherwise specified. The time in the queue is conditional upon the availability of the server; thus, it may have a value from zero to any number, based on the demand on the server.

A simulation comparison is shown by discussing the coding of such a model in GPSS, the major block-diagram language, and Simscript II, one version of the most popular statement language. These coding examples are abstracted from a detailed treatment given by Fishman (1973). Only code specifically related to model implementation is discussed here, although complete programs are illustrated (Figs. 4 and 6).

*GPSS—Single-Server Example.* The GPSS coding for the single-server model is shown in Fig. 4. The coding for the specific events of the single-server process are given in lines 9 through 17 of the code, and is represented symbolically by the GPSS block diagram in Fig. 5. Each block in the diagram represents a verb in GPSS code, with its appropriate parameters. Each verb, in turn, assembles GPSS code for execution. A complete set of verb/blocks may be found in the literature.

In the code example, lines 1–8 consist of initializing statements, with lines 3–8 specifying a two-valued table, which stores the coordinates of an

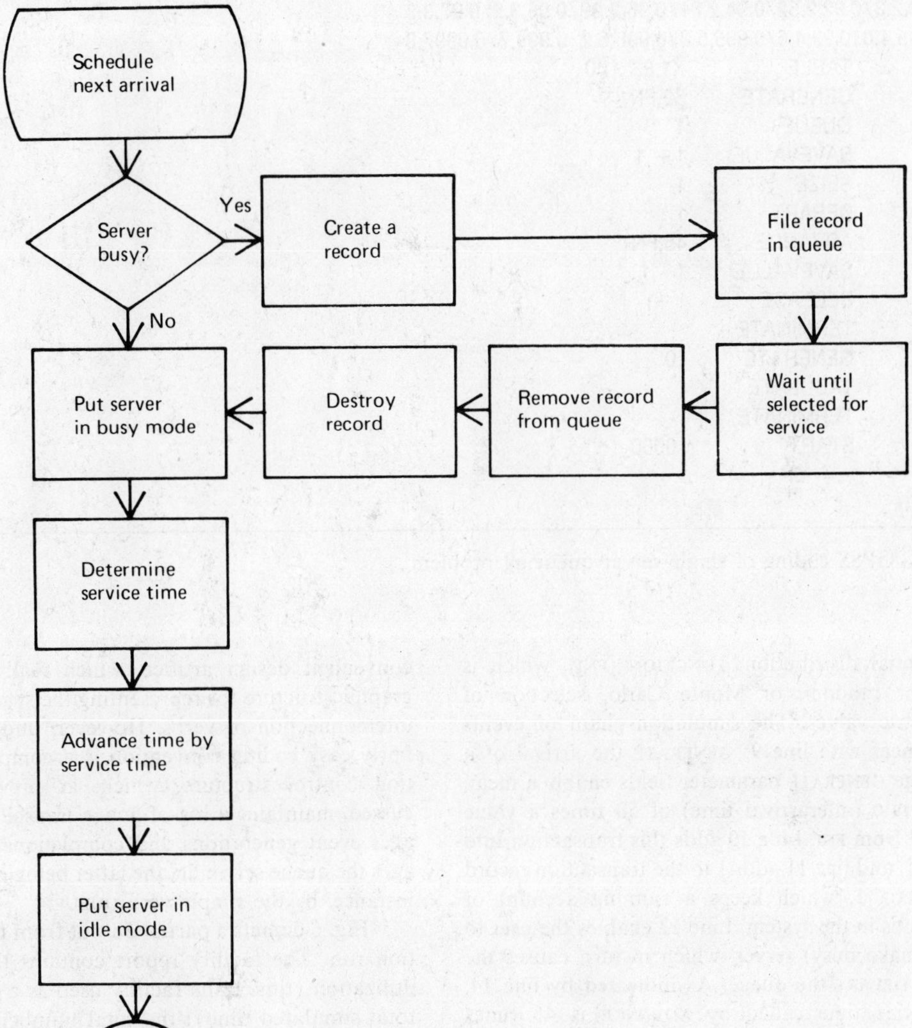


**Fig. 3.** Single-server queueing model.

```
Line
1           SIMULATE
2           SINGLE SERVER QUEUEING PROBLEM
3   1       FUNCTION      RN1,C24
4   0.0,0.0/0.1,0.104/0.2,0.222/0.3,0.355/0.4,0.509/0.5,0.69
5   0.6,0.915/0.7,1.2/0.75,1.38/0.8,1.6/0.84,1.83/0.88,2.12
6   0.9,2.3/0.92,2.52/0.94,2.81/0.95,2.99/0.96,3.2/0.97,3.5
7   0.98,4.0/0.99,4.6/0.995,5.3/0.998,6.2/0.999,7/0.9997,8
8   1       TABLE         X1,0,1,100
9           GENERATE      50,FN1
10          QUEUE         1
11          SAVEVALUE     1+,1
12          SEIZE         1
13          DEPART        1
14          ADVANCE       45,FN1
15          SAVEVALUE     1-,1
16          RELEASE       1
17          TERMINATE
18          GENERATE      10
19          TABULATE      1
20          TERMINATE     1
21          START         10000
22  *
23  END
```

**Fig. 4.** GPSS coding of single-server queueing problem.

exponential distribution, FUNCTION (FNI), which is used for random, or Monte Carlo, selection of parametric values. The simulation chain of events commences with line 9: GENERATE the arrival of a user. The GENERATE parameter fields enable a mean arrival rate (interarrival time) of 50 times a value selected from FNI. Line 10 adds this transaction into QUEUE 1, and line 11 adds 1 to the transaction record SAVEVALUE 1, which keeps a running account of active jobs in the system. Line 12 enables the user to SEIZE (make busy) server, which in turn causes the user to DEPART the queue. As indicated by line 14, the service time called by ADVANCE is 45 times another value selected from FNI at random. This time is effectively inserted into the next-event file of the simulation control program, and causes this user flow to suspend until the selected time elapses, at which time reactivation of the flow occurs. At this reactivation, lines 15 and 16 RELEASE the server (make it unbusy) and decrement the transaction record (SAVEVALUE 1). This records the departure of the user from the system, which is effected by the TERMINATE instruction in line 17.

It should be fairly obvious that this GPSS type of coding from a block diagram is merely a very convenient design artifice, which really creates a graphic structure for representing the succession and interconnection of verbs. However, underlying this fairly easy coding convention is a complex simulation control structure, which, as previously discussed, maintains a log of active transactions, manages event generations and completions, and manages the queue servicing, the latter being invoked, for instance, by the simple verb QUEUE.

Fig. 6 depicts a partial output from this simulation run. The facility report contains the average utilization (time units facility used as a fraction of total simulated time); the total number of entries (times the facility was used); and the average time-per-use for a transaction.

The queue report contains the maximum and average contents (i.e. length) of the queue; the total number of entries (transactions requesting service); the number and per cent of zero entries (transactions requiring no queueing); and the average transaction times (time an entry remains in the queue).

*Simscript II Single-Server Example.* The Simscript II coding (Fig. 7) for the same sort of single-server situation is basically distinguished from the GPSS code in that it is a closer approximation of a "program" because formal statements are written

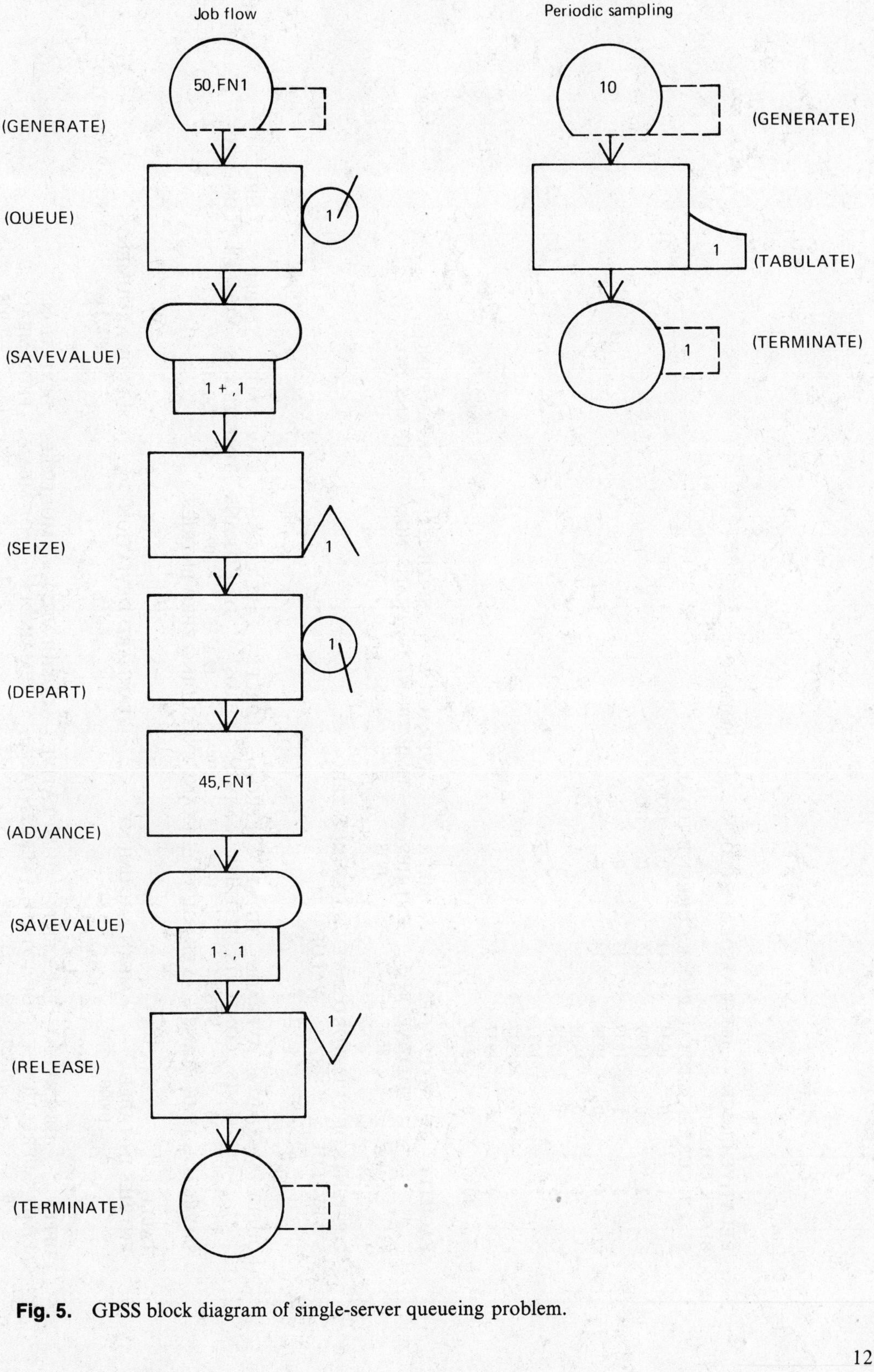


**Fig. 5.** GPSS block diagram of single-server queueing problem.

RELATIVE CLOCK 100000 ABSOLUTE CLOCK 100000

BLOCK COUNTS

| BLOCK | CURRENT | TOTAL | BLOCK | CURRENT | TOTAL |
|---|---|---|---|---|---|
| 1 | 0 | 1934 | 11 | 0 | 10000 |
| 2 | 0 | 1939 | 12 | 0 | 10000 |
| 3 | 1 | 1939 | 13 | 0 | 5 |
| 4 | 0 | 1938 | 14 | 0 | 5 |
| 5 | 0 | 1938 | | | |
| 6 | 1 | 1938 | | | |
| 7 | 0 | 1937 | | | |
| 8 | 0 | 1937 | | | |
| 9 | 0 | 1937 | | | |
| 10 | 0 | 10000 | | | |

| FACILITY | AVERAGE UTILIZATION | NUMBER ENTRIES | AVERAGE TIME/TRAN | SEIZING TRANS. NO. | PREEMPTING TRANS. NO. |
|---|---|---|---|---|---|
| 1 | .865 | 1938 | 44.682 | 27 | |

CONTENTS OF FULLWORD SAVEVALUES (NON-ZERO)

| SAVEVALUE | NR. | VALUE |
|---|---|---|
| | 1 | 2 |

| QUEUE | MAXIMUM CONTENTS | AVERAGE CONTENTS | TOTAL ENTRIES | ZERO ENTRIES | PERCENT ZEROS | AVERAGE TIME/TRANS | $ AVERAGE TIME/TRANS | TABLE NUMBER | CURRENT CONTENTS |
|---|---|---|---|---|---|---|---|---|---|
| 1 | 36 | 5960 | 1939 | 239 | 12.3 | 307.397 | 350.614 | | 1 |

$ AVERAGE TIME TRANS = AVERAGE TIME TRANS EXCLUDING ZERO ENTRIES

TABLE 1

| ENTRIES IN TABLE | MEAN ARGUMENT | STANDARD DEVIATION | SUM OF ARGUMENTS | |
|---|---|---|---|---|
| 10000 | 6.825 | 6.769 | 68251.000 | NON-WEIGHTED |

| UPPER LIMIT | OBSERVED FREQUENCY | PER CENT OF TOTAL | CUMULATIVE PERCENTAGE | CUMULATIVE REMAINDER | MULTIPLE OF MEAN | DEVIATION FROM MEAN |
|---|---|---|---|---|---|---|
| 0 | 1327 | 13.26 | 13.2 | 86.7 | - .000 | —1.008 |
| 1 | 1019 | 10.18 | 23.4 | 76.5 | .146 | —.860 |

| | | | | | | |
|---|---|---|---|---|---|---|
| 2 | 889 | 8.88 | 32.3 | 67.6 | .293 | —.712 |
| 3 | 776 | 7.75 | 40.1 | 59.8 | .439 | —.565 |
| 4 | 738 | 7.37 | 47.4 | 52.5 | .586 | —.417 |
| 5 | 646 | 6.45 | 53.9 | 46.0 | .732 | —.269 |
| 6 | 674 | 6.73 | 60.6 | 39.3 | .879 | —.121 |
| 7 | 574 | 5.73 | 66.4 | 33.5 | 1.025 | .025 |
| 8 | 420 | 4.19 | 70.6 | 29.3 | 1.172 | .173 |
| 9 | 377 | 3.76 | 74.3 | 25.6 | 1.318 | .321 |
| 10 | 276 | 2.75 | 77.1 | 22.8 | 1.465 | .468 |
| 11 | 258 | 2.57 | 79.7 | 20.2 | 1.611 | .616 |
| 12 | 192 | 1.91 | 81.6 | 18.3 | 1.758 | .764 |
| 13 | 207 | 2.06 | 83.7 | 16.2 | 1.904 | .912 |
| 14 | 203 | 2.02 | 85.7 | 14.2 | 2.051 | 1.059 |
| 15 | 218 | 2.17 | 87.9 | 12.0 | 2.197 | 1.207 |
| 16 | 144 | 1.43 | 89.3 | 10.6 | 2.344 | 1.355 |
| 17 | 204 | 2.03 | 91.4 | 8.5 | 2.490 | 1.503 |
| 18 | 157 | 1.56 | 92.9 | 7.0 | 2.637 | 1.650 |
| 19 | 111 | 1.10 | 94.0 | 5.9 | 2.783 | 1.798 |
| 20 | 89 | .88 | 94.9 | 5.0 | 2.930 | 1.946 |
| 21 | 66 | .65 | 95.6 | 4.3 | 3.076 | 2.093 |
| 22 | 55 | .54 | 96.1 | 3.8 | 3.223 | 2.241 |
| 23 | 63 | .62 | 96.8 | 3.1 | 3.369 | 2.389 |
| 24 | 50 | .49 | 97.3 | 2.6 | 3.516 | 2.537 |
| 25 | 34 | .33 | 97.6 | 2.3 | 3.662 | 2.684 |
| 26 | 39 | .38 | 98.0 | 1.9 | 3.809 | 2.832 |
| 27 | 45 | .44 | 98.5 | 1.4 | 3.955 | 2.980 |
| 28 | 24 | .23 | 98.7 | 1.2 | 4.102 | 3.127 |
| 29 | 43 | .42 | 99.1 | .8 | 4.249 | 3.275 |
| 30 | 8 | .17 | 99.3 | .6 | 4.395 | 3.423 |
| 31 | 9 | .08 | 99.4 | .5 | 4.542 | 3.571 |
| 32 | 10 | .09 | 99.5 | .4 | 4.688 | 3.718 |
| 33 | 12 | .11 | 99.6 | .3 | 4.835 | 3.866 |
| 34 | 14 | .13 | 99.8 | .1 | 4.981 | 4.014 |
| 35 | 7 | .06 | 99.8 | .1 | 5.128 | 4.162 |
| 36 | 6 | .05 | 99.9 | .0 | 5.274 | 4.309 |
| 37 | 6 | .05 | 100.0 | .0 | 5.421 | 4.457 |

**Fig. 6.** Partial output from this simulation run. Shown are the printout for facility utilization ("FACILITY") and queuing activity ("QUEUE"). These are gathered and reported autonomously by GPSS. "TABLE 1" is a histogram presenting statistics about queue length, this report having been specifically user-programmed using GPSS coding. The table also lists the frequency distribution for each occurring queue length. The mean queue length ("Mean argument") as well as the maximum length (37) differ from the one in "QUEUE". Because the user-commanded counting operation (SAVEVALUE) considers queue length to include the number of jobs in the facility, the built-in QUEUE report only considers jobs "waiting".

*Declarations*

```
PREAMBLE
THE SYSTEM OWNS A QUEUE AND HAS A SERVER
.
.
.
DEFINE IDLE TO MEAN 0
DEFINE BUSY TO MEAN 1
DEFINE S AS A REAL, 1-DIMENSIONAL ARRAY
.
.
.
END
```

*Initialization*

```
MAIN
READ MEAN.INTERARRIVAL, MEAN.SERVICE, INITIAL.Q, N
.
.
.
IF INITIAL.Q>0,
    LET SERVER = BUSY
    SCHEDULE A DEPARTURE IN
    EXPONENTIAL.F(MEAN.SERVICE,2)MINUTES
        FOR I = 1 TO INITIAL.Q-1, DO
            CREATE A TASK
            FILE THIS TASK IN THE QUEUE
        LOOP
ELSE
SCHEDULE A COLLECTION IN 1 MINUTE
SCHEDULE AN END.OF.SIMULATION IN N MINUTES
SCHEDULE AN ARRIVAL NOW
```

*Arrival Event*

```
EVENT ARRIVAL SAVING THE EVENT NOTICE
RESCHEDULE THIS ARRIVAL IN EXPONENTIAL.F(MEAN.INTERARRIVAL,1) MINUTES
    LET T = TIME.V*1440
    ADD T-T.1 TO S(N.QUEUE+SERVER+1)
    LET T.L = T
    LET MAX.Q = MAX.F(MAX.Q,N.QUEUE+SERVER+1)
IF SERVER = BUSY
    CREATE A TASK
    FILE THIS TASK IN QUEUE
    RETURN
ELSE
LET SERVER = BUSY
SCHEDULE A DEPARTURE IN
EXPONENTIAL.F(MEAN.SERVICE,2) MINUTES
RETURN
END
```

**Fig. 7.** Simscript II coding of single-server queueing problem.

*Departure Event*

```
EVENT DEPARTURE SAVING THE EVENT NOTICE
LET T = TIME.V*1440
ADD T-T.1 TO S(N.QUEUE+SERVER+1)
LET T.1 = T
IF QUEUE IS EMPTY,
     LET SERVER = IDLE
     RETURN
ELSE
REMOVE THE FIRST TASK FROM THE QUEUE
DESTROY THIS TASK
SCHEDULE THIS DEPARTURE IN
EXPONENTIAL.F(MEAN.SERVICE, 2) MINUTES
RETURN
END
```

*Collection Event*

```
EVENT COLLECTION SAVING THE EVENT NOTICE
RESCHEDULE THIS COLLECTION IN 1 MINUTE
LET T = TIME.V*1440
LET X(T) = N.QUEUE + SERVER
RETURN
END
```

*End of Simulation Event*

```
EVENT END.OF.SIMULATION
FOR I = 1 TO MAX.Q+1, DO
     LET S(I) = S(I)/T.1
     COMPUTE QBAR AS THE SUM OF (I-1)*S(I)
LOOP
FOR I = 1 TO MAX.Q + 1, COMPUTE QVAR AS THE SUM OF
S(I)*(I - 1 - QBAR)*(I - 1 - QBAR)
NOW REPORT
CALL ANALYSIS (N)
FOR I = 1 TO EVENTS.V,
     FOR EACH ITEM IN EV.S(I), DO
          REMOVE THE ITEM FROM EV.S(I)
          DESTROY THIS ARRIVAL CALLED ITEM
     LOOP
RETURN
END
```

*Output Report*

```
ROUTINE REPORT
DEFINE N.PRIME AS A REAL VARIABLE
START NEW PAGE
```

(continued)

```
 70  PRINT 1 LINE THUS
 71  SIMULATION RESULTS
 72  SKIP 3 LINES
  .
  .
  .
 88  PRINT 2 LINES WITH QBAR AND SQRT.F(QVAR) THUS
 89  AVERAGE QUEUE LENGTH IS ****.** TASKS
 90  STD.DEV. IS ****.**
 91  SKIP 3 LINES
 92  BEGIN REPORT
 93  BEGIN HEADING
 94  PRINT 2 LINES THUS
 95  QUEUE LENGTH HISTOGRAM
 96  NO.     FREQ.
 97  END
 98  FOR I = 1 TO MAX.Q + 1, PRINT 1 LINE WITH I-1 AND
     S(I) AS FOLLOWS
 99  ***     *.***
100  END
101  SKIP 3 LINES
102  PRINT 2 LINES THUS
103  ANALYSIS OF SERVER
104  IDLE     BUSY
105  PRINT 1 LINE WITH S(1) AND1 - S(1)
106  *.***     *.***
107  RETURN
108  END
```

**Fig. 7.** (continued)

and simulation control and model instructions are intermixed and explicit. However, certain primitive simulation-control macroinstructions, or "shorthand," are incorporated.

The declarations and initialization sections of the program set up the simulation control, the data structures, and the random-number generation. The MAIN routine initializes the program, starts the simulation, and terminates program execution.

The START SIMULATION command (line 18) transfers control to the arrival event segment, which immediately executes the arrival scheduled on line 17. Execution of the service event, conducted in the arrival event and departure event segments, essentially divides the system flow into two parts. Following EVENT ARRIVAL (line 18), the next arrival time is scheduled (line 19), and lines 20–22 update the system clock. Lines 24–27 test for "busy server" to CREATE A TASK TO FILE . . . IN QUEUE for servicing. Line 29 busies an unbusy server and line 30 SCHEDULE(s) A DEPARTURE event, i.e., causes a notice that the service will end after some randomly selected time. The RETURN statements in lines 27 and 31 cause the simulation to return to the next-event control (MAIN) routine. Therefore, the final outcome of the arrival event segment is either a notice in the next-event file to end this service (DEPARTURE) or a notice in the queue file requesting service of the server.

The departure event segment has two main functions: to terminate an event and to service queued events. Lines 33–36 reactivate the departure event and update the clock. Lines 37 through 39 test for tasks awaiting service in the queue. If none, the SERVER is made IDLE; otherwise, the FIRST TASK FROM THE QUEUE is selected and destroyed. As in an arrival event, a departure time is selected with a notice placed in the events list. The "task," which is destroyed, is a temporary entity created by Simscript II to record the queueing event. The RETURN statements (lines 39 and 44) allow the program to return to next-event control, with the outcome of this segment execution being the release (or "unbusying") of the server, thus ending a service event or

```
SIMULATION RESULTS

STREAM 1 STARTING RANDOM NUMBER =    2116429302
     STREAM 1 LAST RANDOM NUMBER =    215867681
STREAM 2 STARTING RANDOM NUMBER =    683743814
     STREAM 2 LAST RANDOM NUMBER =    181518447

INITIAL QUEUE LENGTH =  0
MEAN INTERARRIVAL TIME =  5.00 MEAN SERVICE TIME =  4.50
AVERAGE QUEUE LENGTH IS  7.34 TASKS
STD.DEV. IS      6.12

QUEUE LENGTH HISTOGRAM
NO.        FREQ.
  0         .090
  1         .080
  2         .072
  3         .070
  4         .069
  5         .070
  6         .067
  7         .070
  8         .062
  9         .058
 10         .060
 11         .039
 12         .026
 13         .024
 14         .018
 15         .015
 16         .013
 17         .015
 18         .011
 19         .014
 20         .011
 21         .011
 22         .010
 23         .004
 24         .002
 25         .003
 26         .004
 27         .005
 28         .002
 29         .002
 30         .002
 31         .001
 32         .000

ANALYSIS OF SERVER
IDLE        BUSY
 .090        .910
```

**Fig. 8.** Single-server queueing problem: Simscript II report routine statistics.

entering a notice in the next-event file to end the service commenced in the queue-servicing routine, i.e., a DEPARTURE.

The collection routine effectively emulates the SAVEVALUE operation of GPSS, enabling the counting of system users.

The end of simulation event segment computes summary statistics for presentation in the output report segment, which executes an explicitly programmed, free-format report (Fig. 8).

One of the distinct trade-offs between the Simscript and GPSS language approaches is clearly illustrated by the versatility of the Simscript coding and reporting structures versus (of course) the shorthand approach to model implementation gained through the GPSS block repertoire.

### References

1966. Naylor, T. H., J. L. Balintfy, D. S. Burdick, and K. Chu. *Computer Simulation Techniques.* New York: John Wiley.

1969. Gordon, G. *System Simulation.* Englewood Cliffs, N.J.: Prentice-Hall.

1972. Kay, I. M. "Digital Discrete Simulation Languages. Discussion and Inventory," in Ira M. Kay and John McLeod (Eds.), *Progress in Simulation*, vol. 2. New York: Gordon and Breach.

1973. Fishman, G. S. *Concepts and Methods in Discrete Event Simulation.* New York: John Wiley.

1976. Morris, M. F., and P. F. Roth. *Computer Performance Evaluation.* New York: Mason Charter (Petrocelli Books).

P. F. Roth

**SNOBOL.** *See* String Processing Languages.

# SOCIAL SCIENCES APPLICATIONS

For articles on related subjects *see* Computers and Society; Data Bank; Regression Analysis; Simulation: Principles; and Statistical Applications.

For article on related term *see* Data Set.

The analysis of large bodies of data is the principal use of the computer made by social scientists. The data processing power of the computer has considerably enriched social analysis, but the debt is not all one way. Social studies have in turn contributed to data processing technology: the punched card was itself developed by Hollerith for the analysis of the U.S. Census of 1890. Using manual methods of analysis, research is limited to thousands of items of data (tens of observations on hundreds of subjects). The use of the punched card technology without computers (sorters, tabulators, etc.) increases the range by some two orders of magnitude (hundreds of observations on thousands of subjects). A computer effectively removes all restrictions and enables the social scientist to work close to the intrinsic limits of his problem. But apart from scale, social science data is likely to have features that mark it off from that occurring in other computer applications.

**Data of Social Analysis.** Records in social studies may take on very complex structures. A record describing a family, for example, might include a master section with data on family circumstances, a subrecord for each member of the family, and possibly sub-subrecords for each school attended by each child and each job for the adults. In a simpler case, it is common for a questionnaire, particularly in market surveys, to include branches so that the respondent answers one set of questions or another, depending on his answer to a previous question.

Complicated structures are also generated where subjects are retested over time. This is typical in medical surveys. The respondent may miss an examination, or take part in special tests. These types of records are difficult to accommodate within a normal computer file system. Their analysis has therefore anticipated many data base techniques and will in turn benefit when this technology becomes cheap and simple.

Most branches of statistical analysis are bedeviled by the problem of missing observations. This is often overcome by discarding units of the sample which are incompletely described. With human subjects, however, the frequency of missing observations and the expense of data collection make it both statistically and economically difficult to jettison a subject. This problem alone has often made the use of general statistics programs unsuitable for social science research.

Although nonnumeric data can occur in any study, in social studies they are normal. Variables such as sex and voting preference are not always easy to handle with standard methods because even when they can be coded and manipulated as numbers, their values still do not lie along a true numeric scale. Moreover, certain topics such as purchasing habits or readership typically give rise to analysis variables that may take on multiple values. For example, when asked which newspapers he read last week, a respondent may name two, three, or more journals, all of which must be considered in the analysis. Even an apparently orthodox integer value, such as age in years, may in practice be treated with values grouped in classes of unequal size, with a special value to indicate missing data.

**Analysis of Surveys.** Most social data is therefore unsuitable for the classical types of statistical analysis, so that cross-tabulation, which allows the underlying significance of data to be grasped with a minimum of calculation, has traditionally been the main analytical tool in this field. More recently, its power has been enhanced by the wider availability of methods for establishing objectively the significance of a cross-tabulation. Textbooks such as those by Davis (1971) and Rosenberg (1968) have influenced a larger public in acquiring a far more sophisticated attitude toward the assessment of social science data.

Methods of carrying out cross-tabulation on precomputer punched card equipment have reached a high level of sophistication. The capabilities of the tabulator and specialized statistical sorters (e.g., the IBM 101) were pushed to their limits in producing cross-tabulations of large files with minimal handling of the data. The early attempts to use a computer for survey analysis often retained the precomputer conceptual basis and used the computer to emulate a counter-sorter. The larger group of statistical analysts, however, had never found punched cards very useful and so approached computers with less preconception.

The publication in 1961 of the manual for the collection of biomedical computer programs (then known as BIMD and later as BMD) was a landmark in the provision of flexible and reliable statistical programs on a large scale. The name of the system indicates its orientation, but it has been widely used in the social sciences. The 1973 edition describes 53 programs covering the following areas:

Description and tabulation
Multivariate analysis
Regression analysis
Time-series analysis
Variance analysis

To illustrate the range of programs in a particular section, here are those in regression analysis:

Simple linear regression
Stepwise regression
Multiple regression with case combination
Periodic regression and harmonic analysis
Polynomial regression
Asymptotic regression
Nonlinear least squares

BMD is now written entirely in IBM 360 Fortran IV. It consists of a library of main programs, which carry out the required analysis, and a set of common subroutines. It has been developed at the School of Medicine at UCLA under the direction of Professor Wilfred Dixon. The need by social scientists for just such a set of statistical routines is indicated by the wide use of BMD. However, the existence of an early offshoot, called XTAB, illustrated that BMD could not properly cope with the special needs of large-scale data analysis. (The name XTAB, derived from the word "cross-tabulation," emphasizes the system's bias.)

XTAB was originally developed by Professor Frank Massey of UCLA, who was also involved in BMD. Technically, its main difference from BMD is small but significant. BMD expects to hold all the data in main store throughout the analysis. It forms a matrix with one row for each subject and one column for each variable. XTAB, however, reads the data case by case from secondary store or the primary input medium (usually cards), and adds into the current tables being formed. Thus, the data uses less of the main store, and the limits that BMD places upon the number of cases (as low as 2,000) are relaxed.

The late 1960s saw an enormous proliferation of programs and packages for the analysis of data for social surveys. Problems of classification make an exact count impossible, but the total must be over a thousand. Two important examples may be cited.

1. The "multiple variate counter" (MVC) was developed by Dr. Andrew Colin while at the University of London. Technically, its main feature is that it is a full compiler that translates the user's specification (written in an Algol-like language) into an executable program. It gives the user facilities to input, recheck, and manipulate variables arising from surveys. These variables may then be formed

into tables. Here is an example of the specification of a table in MVC:

*title* 'Table 2'
*tabulate* by class
*count* education, marital status, leisure
*sum* income tax, days ill
*mean* income tax, days ill
*chisquare* education, marital status, leisure
*finish*

2. The "statistical package for the social sciences" (SPSS) was developed under Professor Norman Nie of the National Opinion Research Center, University of Chicago. Like BMD, it has become very widely used indeed, and the user manual can be purchased in bookshops. By June 1970 it was already in use at over 60 universities and research centers and its use has spread continuously since then. SPSS gives the user powerful facilities for filing data and reaccessing it. It also permits the user to carry out the following statistical tests in addition to cross-tabulation, histograms, and descriptive statistics:

Pearson and rank-order correlation
partial correlation
multiple regression
Guttman scale
factor analysis

**Data Banks.** With the rapid increase in the amount of official data kept on members of the public, the use of existing files rather than samples becomes more feasible. The central problem here is that the information relating to any one person is scattered throughout several different data banks. Variants and mistakes in basic items of identifying data such as name, address, data of birth, and even sex can render it quite difficult to tie these scattered records together. Pioneering work by the Oxford Record Linkage Study in the United Kingdom, among others, has shown already how valuable this work can be in the health field, but has shown up even more clearly the inherent difficulties. Without computers, this sort of project could hardly be contemplated, particularly as the basic data itself is increasingly held on computer media.

The use of data banks has required many social scientists and other computer users to face unexpected ethical problems. The strong social value of medical and law-enforcement projects has been offset by a generalized fear of an overdocumented society. In the social sciences these problems have not been so critical, as surveys are generally based on samples, and the national censuses, the largest surveys in this field, are generally surrounded by careful rules controlling access.

**Simulation.** Social data is expensive to collect and difficult to control. Experimentation is usually impossible, for ethical and practical reasons. An attractive solution to this problem is to set up dynamic models of a social situation, allowing the researcher to set whatever values he may wish to the parameters of his model. The intrinsic complexity of social interaction gives the computer as large a role in this sort of simulation as it does in the analysis of real data.

Simulation techniques have been used, for example, in the analysis of personal belief systems and of patients in a drug trial. Business games and models of national economies use other facets of the same techniques. Professor Leslie Stone and his colleagues at Cambridge attempted computer simulation of the British economy in the early 1960s (Klein et al., 1967).

Large-scale simulation of the patterns of urban communication and behavior probably hold out the strongest hope of a basic understanding of these phenomena. Recently, for example, the population control program in Costa Rica has been modeled on a computer. Experiments with the model show what change in fertility is due to the control program itself and what is due to outside factors such as the changing age structure. They also show that the model can be used as a training device for the administration involved in the project.

**Anthropology.** Although the impact of the computer has inevitably been biggest in the study of large-scale industrial societies, anthropologists have not neglected its aid (Burton, 1970). Field surveys can generate bodies of data large enough to warrant automatic analysis. Even in the 1950s punched cards were being used by E.P.Murdoch for cross-cultural studies, and the use of computers enlarges the possibility of extending this investigation. For example, Eleanor R. Heider (1972) used a computer in analyzing the possibility of correctly structuring the color system of a language community in the case of the Dani of Papua.

Simulation techniques can be as useful here as in urban studies; more specialized uses include the storing and analysis of genealogies, the simulation of small group dynamics, and the study of linguistic and mythological texts. Analysis of material culture records has been a valuable use of computers for archaeologists and anthropologists alike.

**Applied Social Sciences.** In the more directly applied social sciences, the use of computers has recently been described both in political studies (as in an analysis of concept frequencies described in political texts) and in political campaigning. For example, James Lee and Allan Kornberg (1973) used a computer to simulate the recruitment of candidates to parliamentary office in Canada.

In social administration we have the intersection of the research use of computers and of organizational data processing. Although this area of activity can be classified as an applied social science, it is better viewed in the wider context of management and business data processing.

REFERENCES

1961. Klein, L. R., et al. *An Econometric Model of the United Kingdom*. Oxford: Oxford University Press.

1968. Rosenberg, M. *The Logic of Survey Analysis*. New York: Basic Books.

1970. Burton, M. I. "Computer Applications in Cultural Anthropology," *Computers and the Humanities*, Vol. 5, No. 1.

1971. Davis, J. A. *Elementary Survey Analysis*. Englewood Cliffs, N.J.: Prentice-Hall.

1972. Greenblat, C. S. "Gaming and Simulation in the Social Sciences: A Guide to the Literature," *Simulation and Games*, Vol. 3, No. 4.

1972. Heider, E. R. "Probabilities, Sampling, and Ethnographic Method: The Case of Dani Colour Names," *Man*, Vol. 7, No. 3 (September).

1973. Lee, J., and A. Kornberg. "A Computer Simulation Model of Multiparty Parliamentary Recruitment," *Simulation and Games*, Vol. 4, No. 1.

B. C. ROWE

# SOCIETY FOR COMPUTER SIMULATION (SCS)

For article on related subject *see* AMERICAN FEDERATION OF INFORMATION PROCESSING SOCIETIES.

For article on related term *see* SIMULATION.

**Purpose.** The Society for Computer Simulation promotes the advancement of simulation and allied computer arts by sponsoring meetings and informal discussions, by publishing reports of these meetings and papers, and by cooperating with other technical societies and with educational and other organizations in activities that contribute to the advancement of simulation and allied arts.

**How Established.** The Society began on the initiative of John McLeod, who called a meeting in Oxnard, California, on Nov. 7, 1952, of people (mostly from Southern California) who were using simulation in their work. Thirty-nine people from 13 organizations attended this meeting and created "The Simulation Council," carefully excluding any reference to the type of equipment used for modeling and simulation.

McLeod was elected chairman at the organization meeting, and he and his wife Suzette immediately began putting out at their own expense a mimeographed monthly *Simulation Council Newsletter*, which quickly developed national circulation and spread the Simulation Council idea across the country. In 1956, regional simulation councils elected two directors each to serve on the Board of Directors of Simulation Councils, an unincorporated association created to provide coordination and better communication among the regional councils and to advance the art of simulation.

On June 3, 1957, Dov Abramis, Dr. George Bekey, and Norman L. Irvine formed a California nonprofit membership corporation called Simulation Councils, Inc. (SCI), which is the legal name, though the Board in adopted 1972 and uses the name "The Society for Computer Simulation" as one that better describes the organization's activities. Eligibility for membership requires professional training and experience, and professional engagement in simulation or allied sciences. There were approximately 1,500 members as of January 1973.

The following people have served as chairmen of the Board of Directors, an office that was retermed "President" in 1962.

Dr. Robert M. Howe, 1956–1957
B. Dov Abramis, 1958–1959
Stanley Rogers, 1959–1960
J. E. Sherman, 1960–1962
Maughan S. Mason, 1962–1964
P. J. Hermann, 1964–1966
James E. Wolle, 1966–1968
David R. Miller, 1968–1969
Francis C. Rieman, 1969–1971
Jon N. Mangnall, 1971–1972
Dr. George A. Rahe, 1972–1973

Robert D. Brennan, 1973–1975
Paul A. Berthiaume, 1975–1976

The Society is a member of the American Federation of Information Processing Societies (AFIPS) and of the Association Internationale pour le Calcul Analogigue.

**Technical Program.** The Society participates in the AFIPS National Computer Conferences and cosponsors Summer and Winter Computer Simulation Conferences and the annual San Diego Biomedical Symposium. Annually, the Society holds a National Invitation Seminar on Advanced Simulation at a secluded location, to stimulate thinking about problems related to simulation and about contributions the Society may be able to make. Professional development seminars are a part of the Society's program.

The Society publishes the following periodicals:

*Simulation*, a monthly technical journal containing technical articles and information on the state-of-the-art and organization activities.

*Simulation Councils Proceedings*, a semiannual series of hard-bound books, each dealing with a topic in the field of simulation and each edited by an expert in that field.

*Simulation Today*, an annual collection of four-page tutorial papers on the technology of simulation and its application, all originally published in *Simulation*.

The EAI Senior Scientific Simulation Award consisting of $500 and a plaque in recognition of outstanding contributions to the art of simulation is financed by Electronic Associates, Inc., of West Long Branch, New Jersey. Winners of this award are:

1965 John McLeod, Consultant, Editor of *Simulation*
1966 John R. Ragazzini, Columbia University
Robert H. Randall, City College of New York
Frederick A. Russell, Newark College of Engineering
1968 Granino A. Korn, University of Arizona
1969 Robert M. Howe, University of Michigan
1970 A. Ben Clymer, Consultant
1971 Stanley Rogers, Consultant
1972 Walter J. Karplus, University of California at Los Angeles
1973 Jack E. Sherman, Lockheed Missile and Spare Co.

The EAI Student Papers Competition consists of a certificate and $50 in cash or reference books, and up to six awards may be made each year.

The Mary Emerson Memorial Award of $500 and a plaque, funded by Comcor, a division of Denelcor, Inc., Denver, Colorado, is awarded for effective methods of using simulation as a classroom teaching aid in a recognized institution of higher learning. This award has been won by:

Dr. Ladis Kovach
Dr. Avrum Soudack
Dr. Donald C. Martin

I. L. AUERBACH

## SOCIETY FOR INDUSTRIAL AND APPLIED MATHEMATICS (SIAM)

For article on related subject *see* AMERICAN FEDERATION OF INFORMATION PROCESSING SOCIETIES.

The Society for Industrial and Applied Mathematics (SIAM) is a professional membership association of the United States established in 1952 to:

Further the application of mathematics to industry and science.
Promote basic research in mathematics leading to new methods and techniques useful to industry and science.
Provide media for the exchange of information and ideas between mathematicians and other technical and scientific personnel.

To support these objectives, SIAM publishes numerous periodicals and monographs containing research and expository papers; conducts national meetings, research conferences, and section activities; and sponsors the SIAM Institute for Mathematics and Society to promote the application of mathematics to the social sciences.

The presidents of SIAM since its founding are as follows:

William E. Bradley, 1952
Donald B. Houghton, 1952–1954

Harold W. Kuhn, 1954–1955
John W. Mauchly, 1955–1956
Thomas E. Southard, 1956–1958
Donald L. Thomsen, Jr., 1958–1959
Brockway McMillan, 1959–1960
F. J. Weyl, 1960–1961
Robert F. Rinehart, 1961–1962
Joseph P. LaSalle, 1962–1963
Alston S. Householder, 1963–1964
J. Barkley Rosser, 1964–1966
Garrett Birkhoff, 1966–1968
J. Wallace Givens, Jr., 1968–1970
Burton H. Colvin, 1970–1972
C. C. Lin, 1972–1974
Herbert B. Keller, 1974–

SIAM publishes six research journals, of which two are of particular interest to computer scientists:

*SIAM Journal on Computing*. Contains research articles in mathematics that apply to the problems of computer science and the nonnumerical aspects of computing. Four issues per year; first issue, March 1972.

*SIAM Journal on Numerical Analysis*. Contains research articles on the development and analysis of numerical methods. Six issues per year; first issue, 1964.

I. L. Auerbach

## SOFTWARE

For articles on related subjects *see* Operating Systems; Program Libraries; Programming Languages; and Software Packages.
For articles on related terms *see* Data Processing: Input-output Control System; Multiprogramming; Software Engineering; and Structured Programming.

Very early in the development of computers, people referred to the actual physical components —the tubes and relays, the resistors and wires, and chassis—as computer *hardware*. It soon became popular within the computer industry to use the word "software" to describe the nonhardware components of the computer, in particular the programs that were needed to make the computers perform their intended tasks. The word "software" caught on rapidly, and was in quite general use by 1960. One speaks of software people, software shops (i.e., organizations that produce software), software maintenance, and more recently, software engineering. Actually, software is a very general term that includes many areas discussed elsewhere in this Encyclopedia. The most significant are operating systems, programming, and programming languages.

Although the word "software" can be used in connection with all kinds of programs, it is usually used to denote programs whose use is not limited to one particular job or application. Thus, one speaks of systems software, of software systems, of mathematical software, of software for business applications, etc.

The following is a quotation, which remains accurate, from an unpublished document that I wrote in 1960.

> There exists a class of computer programs which are not designed to solve specific computational or data processing problems. These are the programs which are used to aid in the production, debugging, maintenance, and orderly running of other programs. They are collectively known as computer software. As computers have grown larger, more powerful, and more complex, computer software has become as important as and, in some cases, more important than computer hardware in determining the productivity of computer installations. The programs that make up the "software package" are usually supplied and maintained by the computer manufacturer. For large-scale computers such programs represent an investment of many millions of dollars, an investment that would be prohibitive except for the fact that it is spread over many computers of the same model. A good deal of computer software is produced by users ... who often have very special requirements along these lines.

Early computers could run with relatively simple software systems. A loader and a library of subroutines was considered sufficient for most first-generation computers. There were some very significant and sophisticated software developments associated with UNIVAC I. Grace Hopper and her colleagues designed the first, very general sorting systems, and developed the first higher-level languages for business applications. Anatol Holt and William Turanski introduced many software system concepts in their GP (Generalized Programming) system, such as the "extended machine," which refers to the *combination* of hardware and software that the user sees as the machine for which he writes his programs.

Still in the first generation, John Backus and his colleagues from IBM and from several IBM user installations developed the Fortran compiler for the IBM 704, perhaps the most significant piece of software ever written. Fortran became the language of discourse for scientific programmers throughout the world and throughout the computer industry, and once and for all established the importance and usefulness of higher-level languages.

The separation of hardware and software, the idea that software was superimposed on hardware in order to enhance its capabilities, persisted throughout the first- and most of the second-generation computers. Even though this was already true in some earlier computers, especially those built by UNIVAC, it is perhaps the distinguishing characteristic of third-generation systems that the hardware system is designed to operate under control of a rather sophisticated software system, and will perform very poorly or not at all in the absence of such a system. Especially in a multiprogramming and/or multiprocessor system, it is essential that there be an operating system (almost always software) that maintains control of the allocation of system resources and that avoids problems of conflict, blocking, interference among simultaneous users of the system. In particular, the input/output functions and the management of central and peripheral storage are software system functions that must be centralized and carefully controlled if chaos is to be avoided. These topics are discussed in detail in the article on operating systems.

The operating system provides a set of interfaces and conventions for using them which are reflected in all other major software products. A complete software system will contain, in addition to the operating system, a set of compilers for various languages, one or more system loaders, one or more filing systems, sets of utility routines, special- and general-purpose debugging systems, and generalized subsystems for applications such as sorting and merging, mathematical programming, engineering design, report generation, simulation, graphics, etc. All of these must interface with the operating system and its input/output system, and in this sense they all form part of a single software system. In general, the individual components cannot be moved from one operating system to another without considerable modification in areas in which they interface with other system routines.

Software systems for general-purpose computers are usually supplied by the manufacturers of the hardware systems. Up until about 1969 it was generally assumed that the purchase or rental of a computer hardware system entitled the customer to all general-purpose software produced by the manufacturer for that computer at no extra cost. The independent software industry, to the extent that it existed, was limited mostly to work on special-purpose systems and to applications programming. Software companies could attempt to produce software systems for sale that were better in some significant ways than those produced by the hardware manufacturers, but this could rarely be done on a profitable basis. The software companies argued that the manufacturers were actually selling software to their customers and including its cost in the price of the hardware. The hardware customer had to buy a bundle consisting of the hardware plus all available software. They urged the "unbundling" of software. This would presumably benefit the buyer, who would only have to pay for as much software as he needed. It would also permit competitive marketing of software products.

In June of 1969, IBM announced that it was introducing a new policy to implement the unbundling of computer software. With the exception of essential operating system software, all new software products would henceforth be priced separately.

The decision to unbundle software was made under pressure as a response to charges of unfair competition, but it was probably not made reluctantly. It must have been clear to IBM that software rental could become a major source of revenue to computer manufacturers. Almost all other hardware manufacturers followed the lead of IBM and unbundled their software products.

**Scientific and Mathematical Software.** The first software systems were libraries of mathematical subroutines. In view of their very long history, it is rather surprising that major efforts in this area have continued and will continue on into the future. In fact, it was only in the early 1970s that some attempt was made to consolidate these efforts. A program supported by National Science Foundation, was initiated with the aim of taking whatever steps are necessary to make sure that high-quality scientific software is available to the whole community of scientific users of computers. Most earlier efforts in this area underestimated the magnitude of the problems, and attacked them with insufficient resources.

A number of mathematical software packages have achieved very wide distribution and very general use on computers of very diverse characteristics produced by a number of different manufacturers. One of the best known is the Bi-Med (BMD) series of statistical programs produced at UCLA. Another is the EISPAK eigenvalue package produced at the Argonne National Laboratory.

**Software Engineering.** Techniques of software development developed on an ad hoc basis along with the earliest computers. Application of these techniques to the production of really large software systems (e.g., the SAGE system) resulted in unexpectedly large expenditures for the relatively inefficient programs that were produced.

There has been a great deal of thought devoted to the technology of software production. In the current third-generation of computers the cost of producing software seems to be excessive, and the methods used often show little or no advance over those used on some of the earliest systems.

Attempts have been made, with varying amounts of success, to apply to the problems of software production the engineering principles that have been reasonably successful in other disciplines. The most usual proposal is to develop sets of modules that can be used as "off the shelf" components in the development of software products. One of the factors that has limited the success of such ventures has been the continuing high rate of technological development of computer hardware. Thus, the increased use of large-scale integration and the projected development of large-scale, low-cost, fast bulk memory may produce very radical changes in software requirements and in software technology.

A more theoretical approach to the problems of program development has developed from the work of Perlis, McCarthy, Dijkstra, Wirth, Naur, Floyd, and others. This approach is based on "structured programming" and on the use of mathematical verification and proof techniques in connection with the production of programs. The aim is to produce programs that have been proved to be correct before they are tested on a computer, and thereby to eliminate much of the program-testing activity. Proponents of this methodology claim a tremendous increase in programmer productivity at little if any cost in program-running efficiency.

REFERENCES

*Note*: There are many books and journals devoted to the software field. Among the most important software journals are the *Communications of the ACM* and the recently launched IEEE *Transactions on Software Engineering.*

1967. Rosen, S. (Ed.). *Programming Systems and Languages*. New York: McGraw-Hill.
A survey of software up to the mid-1960s.

S. ROSEN

## SOFTWARE, LEGAL PROTECTION OF.

*See* COPYRIGHTS AND PATENTS, COMPUTER ASPECTS OF; and LEGAL PROTECTION OF SOFTWARE.

## SOFTWARE, MATHEMATICAL.

*See* MATHEMATICAL SOFTWARE.

## SOFTWARE ENGINEERING

For articles on related subjects *see* SOFTWARE; SOFTWARE MANAGEMENT; SOFTWARE PACKAGES; and STRUCTURED PROGRAMMING.
For article on related term *see* HOST SYSTEM.

From the very beginning, until recent years, the design of computers was dominated by *hardware* development. *Software*, the term coined in ironical contrast to hardware, was underestimated in its economic importance as well as in its key role for future development. Thus, software has been built to accommodate hardware. In the near future, software may turn out to be the more expensive part of a computer system, and hardware may have to be built according to the requirements of software.

**Software and Hardware.** Software and hardware show typical differences:

1. Hardware has substance and therefore is subjected to an aging process; software is not.

2. Within some limits, software can be continuously improved, i.e., completed and then further developed; hardware depends on technology and its stepwise development. The arrival of a new technology tends to make all existing computers obsolete.

3. While manufacturing costs for hardware show a falling tendency, mainly in view of mass production, manufacturing costs for software show an increasing tendency as the result of increasing demand for individualistic service.

**The Paradox of Nonhardware Engineering.** A paradox is inherent in the combination of the words "engineering" and "software." Engineers usually deal with material subjects, with hardware in the most literal sense. One may object to this, since electricity is not a tangible material. Although electrical engineers seem to be somewhat more abstract in their approach than other engineers, the common bond is that all deal to some extent with physical objects. And here lies the difference: Software is *not a physical object*; it is nonmaterial. Software needs physical objects only as carriers, and is totally nonspecific about the physical nature of the carrier.

Since the material needed is cheap (a paper carrier is sufficient) and the tools are at hand (usually mental processes), producing some software is a beginner's introduction to the computer field.

The products of structural engineering can generally be measured, tested, and judged by measuring instruments. This is not generally possible with software.

IS SOFTWARE PATENTABLE? According to the German patent law, software consisting of "instructions to the human mind" is not patentable, despite the fact that it usually needs "ingenuity" and that its production may be relevant to various aspects of the national economy. The situation is similar in France, Switzerland, The Netherlands, and the United Kingdom. Efforts have been made in the United States to make software patentable. These efforts are supported by the software companies but are opposed by hardware manufacturers. Legal actions have not yet decided the issue. Practical solutions to protect software against piracy are necessary, but even these have met obstacles.

**The Software Crisis.** In the mid-1960s the first signs appeared that for further development in "big science," programming efforts were becoming a bottleneck. Similar problems exist in principle in a number of other application areas. The situation is aggravated by the difficulty of interchangeability among products of different manufacturers, which thus inhibits desirable competition in the software field. In this situation, a definition of software engineering assumes negative implications, which are expressed as follows:

1. Existing software production is frequently done by amateurs (regardless of whether at universities, software houses, or manufacturers).
2. Existing software development is frequently done by tinkering (at the universities) or by the human-wave ("million monkey") approach in manufacturing departments.
3. Existing software is frequently unreliable and needs permanent "maintenance." Here, the word "maintenance" is misused to denote correction of errors that are expected to be present at the very beginning by the producer.
4. Existing software frequently is messy, lacks transparency, and prevents improvement or extension (or at least requires too high a price to be paid for this).
5. Existing software comes too late and at higher costs than expected, and does not fulfill the promises made for it.

**The Positive Approach to Software Engineering.** The aim of software engineering is to meet the needs of users for economical software that is reliable and efficient on real machines. To accomplish this objective, software engineers have developed various requirements and techniques.

RELIABILITY. The demands on the reliability of software are becoming crucial, and existing programs are expected to deliver good and correct results to many users on different computers for a long period.

FLEXIBILITY: PORTABILITY AND ADAPTABILITY. The characteristic of flexibility applies to both the *machine end* and *user's end*, which has been regarded in the past as a fixed requirement. For the user's end, it means that a changing user environment enforces changes, adaptations to new situations both foreseen and unforeseen. This flexibility in software is interpreted as *adaptability*. In machines, flexibility means changing machine characteristics, foreseen or unforeseen (usually the case with a new machine). Software adaptability has also been called "portability." In this context the word "foreseen" contributes nothing, since a foreseen problem can be corrected at the beginning. Nor is the word "availability," which has been used sometimes in this connection, a proper term.

On the other hand, portable and adaptable software imply that something has to be altered, because of an *unforeseen* change. The objective is to keep change to a minimum, and the method to achieve it seems to be suitable structuring.

**Software as an Industrial Product.** The idea of software as an industrial product, to be purchased at regular prices in an open market, is not fully accepted today. Software design and production is an industrial engineering field, and therefore certain principles and procedures must be observed.

1. Large projects should be split up into partial projects in which the great importance of planned and directed communication is recognized.
2. Division into manageable parts is urgently required. With software projects, it is difficult to design the interfaces in such a way that the number and structure of the interfaces remain comprehensible.
3. The route from the design to the usable product is a long one, much less clearly prescribed than normal engineering tasks, and therefore requires careful delineation.
4. The computer helps to settle the difficult tasks by computerized surveillance: The whole design, production, and maintenance process should be subjected to computerized surveillance. The points to be looked at in particular are:

(a) Automatic updating and quality control of working documentation.

(b) Selective dissemination of information to all project staff.

(c) Surveillance of deadline plans.

(d) Collection of data for final quality control.

(e) Automatic production of manuals and maintenance material.

**Structured Programming—A Hierarchy of Conceptual Layers.** The essential procedure for construction of good software is to organize the software project in conceptual layers. This technique is known under different names. It is essentially what Dijkstra calls "structured programming" (Dahl et al., 1972).

Stepwise abstraction is advocated; the writing of a program should start with the most abstract form. But, in doing this, one must choose a sequence of languages, the highest being the user's language (usually problem-oriented) and the lowest usually being the machine language. In this form, the technique has been used rather widely since first described (to our knowledge) in the 1958 UNCOL report, where three levels of languages were advocated, the intermediate level being the "Universal Computer Oriented Language." The essence of such a hierarchical structuring, however, was given by Zurcher and Randell (1968), who proposed (as did Dijkstra) designing "from the outside inwards," using different "levels of abstraction" and achieving "successively greater detail." The direction is here "top-down," and is the same approach as in modern top-down teaching of programming. There is, however, also the choice of adopting a bottom-up approach to design, illustrated by Poole and Waite (1969), who start from the machine level (defined by a real machine), and then introduce a sequence of *abstract machines*, each one being defined in terms of one or some of its predecessors. For the final structure, neither the direction matters nor is there any fundamental difference between abstract machines and *intermediate languages*.

The structure is represented by the *hierarchy* of *linguistic levels* defined by successive layers of software. Each level of this hierarchy is a computer system characterized by the data types and primitive operations of its language. Each level is (or, is potentially) the *host system* for the definition of linguistic levels through the addition of further software systems. The meaning of *host system* is illustrated by an example.

For an operating system, the host system may be the processing units and main memory hardware. The operating system is then a software system, having many software modules and appropriate mass storage devices to hold files. This computer system may then serve as the host system for a software system that implements the Basic language. This software system consists of an editor, an interpreter, and a command processor. If the host system does not include a communications-like controller, the implementer of Basic would find it necessary to add one to the host as part of the new computer system.

Hierarchy is a tool of software engineering. If properly used, it permits the components of several levels to be designed and developed separately. Of course this separate development of system levels is possible only if the languages corresponding to the boundaries between layers of software have been precisely specified and agreed to. For success, the implementers of a software system should not find it necessary to alter any component of the host system. Such need would expose incompleteness or inefficiency of the host language—the inability to realize the objectives of the software system. This principle is often violated in practice; for example, when an inner layer of an operating system must be modified so that an accounting procedure can be implemented within an outer software layer.

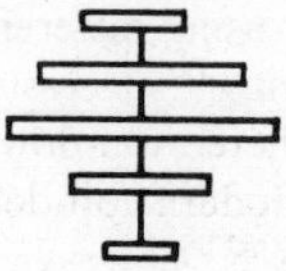

**Fig. 1**

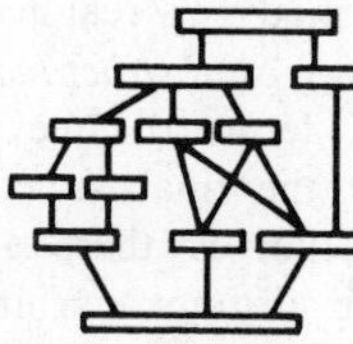

**Fig. 2**

**Fig. 3**

In the simplest case, we have a linear ordering (Fig. 1) of layers, each representing an increased level of detail over the layer preceding it. More generally, there will be a partial ordering only, in which the levels as such disappear and we speak of layers only, in which pairs of layers that are not directly related may exist (Fig. 2). Since more than one man and/or one machine (i.e., a multiprocessor) is also possible, the most general situation is that of Fig. 3. Further details are given in Bauer (1973).

References

1968. Zurcher, F. W., and B. Randell. "Iterative Multi-level Modelling." *IFIP Congress Proceedings,* pp. D138-D142. Amsterdam: North Holland.

1969. Poole, P. C., and W. M. Waite, "Machine Independent Software," *Proc. ACM Second Symposium on Operating Systems.* Princeton, N.J.: Brandon/Systems Press.

1972. Dahl. O. J., E. W. Dijkstra, and C. A. R. Hoare. *Structured Programming.* New York: Academic Press.

1973. Bauer, F. L. (Ed.). "Advanced Course on Software Engineering," in *Lecture Notes in Economics and Mathematical Systems Series 1.* Berlin: Springer-Verlag.

F. L. Bauer

## SOFTWARE FLEXIBILITY

For articles on related subjects *see* Compatibility; and Portability.
For article on related term *see* System Generation.

Flexibility is a property of software which enables it to change easily in response to different user and system requirements. The necessary changes can be classified roughly according to their purpose:

1. To alter the user image,
2. To adapt to different machine organizations.
3. To meet different system constraints.

These categories are not truly independent. For example, we might meet certain system constraints by changing the user image to remove expensive features. Nevertheless, the classification is a useful one because changes in different categories are normally achieved by somewhat different means.

The user image of a program is usually altered by making textual changes, principally excision of source code and selection of one of several alternatives. This implies that the body of text representing the source program incorporates the implementation of all possible user images, and is so structured that relevant changes can be made easily. Thus, some care must be taken during the implementation to modularize "by feature," avoiding if possible the use of a single procedure to provide several distinct facets of the user image. Also, wherever possible, the variations of the user image should provide a hierarchy of facilities. Changes then consist simply of removing all routines that deal with facilities above a certain level.

To solve a particular problem on a particular computer, one must model the operations and data types required for the solution in terms of the operations and data types provided by the computer. Part of this modeling is carried out by the programmer when he writes a program to solve the problem, and part is carried out when his program is translated to machine code. Adaptability for different machine organizations is enhanced when the program is written in terms of operations and data types that are more closely related to the problem than to a particular computer. Changes then involve redefinition of these operators and data types in terms appropriate to the target computer. An important point to note is that the definition of an operator or data type is independent of its use, so that the number of such definitions does not grow with the size of the program. Hence, a redefinition involves far less effort than would be required to recode the program.

System constraints include such items as peripheral complement, memory size, word length, and arithmetic (precision, rounding). Careful organization of the algorithm is necessary to provide flexibility in meeting these constraints, with the key point being the preservation of suitable fall-back positions. For example, the program should (if possible) be structured so that sections could be overlaid to meet a memory constraint. This consideration has implications for the procedure linkage and the segmentation of data; it may affect the algorithm chosen to solve the problem.

Some form of parameterization is generally used to achieve all aspects of flexibility: Symbols are used to denote key constants such as table sizes, and conditional operations are executed during translation to select different parts of the code according to the desired user image. Assembly languages and general-purpose macroprocessors provide the most powerful facilities for parameterization; most higher-level languages are deficient in this respect. The best examples of software that can be adapted through parameterization are found in the nucleus of an operating system. "System generation" is the process of adapting the body of text supplied by the manufacturer to the user image desired by the installation management and to the constraints of their hardware configuration.

Flexibility is important because it increases the useful life of a piece of software and extends its range of application. This permits the development cost to be recovered over a wider market, and hence reduces the price to the user.

### Reference

1973. Poole, P. C. and W. M. Waite. "Portability and Adaptability," in F. L. Bauer (Ed.), *Advanced Course in Software Engineering*. Berlin: Springer-Verlag.

W. M. Waite

## SOFTWARE MAINTENANCE

For articles on related subjects *see* Compatibility; Debugging; Errors; Program Libraries; Software; and Software Packages.

For article on related term *see* Structured Programming.

Because of the complexity of large software systems, there are almost always errors (bugs) and inadequacies in running them. Software maintenance is the activity that addresses itself to the correction of software errors and to remedying the inadequacies that may exist.

Computer manufacturers and other producers of software products have large software maintenance groups whose tasks vary from simple correction of typographical errors to major changes and extensions to existing software programs. These groups usually provide a formal mechanism whereby users can submit evidence of errors or of inadequate performance. Corrections are then usually distributed to all users.

After a number of changes have been made, it is inconvenient to make additional changes, especially if new changes change the results of earlier changes. Also, in some cases, very extensive changes require major changes in the documentation of the software product. In such cases it is usual to release a new version of the software product, which contains all changes to data and which serves as a new base for future changes. For example, IBM's Release 20 of OS 360, which went into use in 1972, is quite different from Release 16, which was current in 1968, and is radically different from some of the earlier releases.

In order to ease the impact on the users, the manufacturer usually continues to maintain several earlier software releases for some time after a new version is released. Ultimately, however, the older versions are declared to be obsolete and are taken off maintenance. When this happens, even reluctant users usually convert to the newer versions.

New versions of software products often have subtle effects on a user's applications systems, and large users usually require their own software maintenance personnel, not only for maintenance of the application systems, but also to install new versions of supplied software and make modifications that may be necessary to move their application programs from one version to another.

As software development and software maintenance have grown into major activities involving very large numbers of people and very large amounts of money, there has been considerable effort devoted to improving the efficiency and productivity of the whole software process.

Some software projects have claimed spectacular results through the use of a programming discipline that has come to be known as "structured proramming" (Dahl et al., 1972). "Top-down" programming and the use of a "chief programmer team" are related concepts (Baker, 1972).

The use of structured programming often is associated with the development of methods for proving the correctness of programs. The aim is to produce error-free programs whose correctness can be guaranteed. Proponents of the structured programming approach argue that the universal adoption of their methods will do away with the need for software maintenance. Even if this cannot be achieved, the systematic study of programming methodology, as exemplified in areas like structured programming, will probably have significant influence on the ways in which software will be produced and maintained in the future.

REFERENCES

1972. Baker, F. T. "Chief Programmer Team Management of Production Planning," *IBM Systems Journal*, Vol. 11, No. 1.

1972. Dahl, O. J., E. W. Dijkstra, and C. A. R. Hoare. *Structured Programming*. New York: Academic Press.

S. ROSEN

# SOFTWARE MANAGEMENT

For articles on related subjects *see* COMPUTING CENTER; DOCUMENTATION; SOFTWARE ENGINEERING; and STRUCTURED PROGRAMMING.

For articles on related terms *see* DATA SECURITY; MULTIPROGRAMMING; OPERATING SYSTEMS; and TIME SHARING.

An increasing portion of the cost associated with data processing installations is allocated to the development of programs for both existing and new applications. This trend is due to the increasing complexity of applications and the decreasing cost of hardware. This has directed increasing attention to the management of software development.

One of the reasons for increasing complexity is the trend toward large collections of data subject to analysis by many independent users. For example, census data on population and income provides local government with the basis for taxation and zoning, and for transportation, school, fire, police and water district boundaries. Another reason for complexity is the ability of modern computer systems to permit several programs to run concurrently and share system resources. Such multiprogrammed and time-shared use of computers requires considerable understanding of the operating system and the specific system configuration in order to achieve reliable and efficient operation.

Thus, the problem of managing software development is a function of the complexity of the application and operating system. Another factor that influences software development is the degree to which the problem requires new and untried approaches. There is considerable experience in managing the development of general commercial applications, which account for the majority of today's data processing installations. Such experience is well documented (Shaw and Atkins, 1970) and should be a valuable guide to less experienced managers. On the other hand, the development of new and very complex programming systems that require advances in the state-of-the-art continues to present very difficult problems. The related management issues are receiving increasing attention (Weinwurm, 1970; Kay, 1969), but as yet there are no generally accepted guidelines for coping with these problems. Some of these issues will be considered after presenting an outline of current management practice in the development of the more common applications.

## Current Management Practice

ORGANIZATION. It is generally recognized that the position and role of the data processing department within an organization is crucial to its effectiveness. Where the organizational objectives include or aim to provide an integrated management information system, the department often reports to a vice-president for information systems or, along with the controller and treasurer, to the vice-president for finance and administration. Not only the costs of the data processing function, but also its potential influence upon the responsiveness of the entire organization have led to this key role. Thus, along with a steering committee made up of executives from the other departments of the organization, the director or vice-president for information systems assumes responsibility for determining what computer system projects should be undertaken and which organizational objectives are to be served. This places heavy emphasis on the analysis of system requirements and the specification of those requirements, planning of an implementation, projection of cost and schedules, testing and evaluation, and a maintenance plan. With increasing complexity, coding and debugging of programs will more and more give way to system analysis as the major task of programming development.

PROJECT MANAGEMENT. The ability to manage software development on a project basis stems from an established, recognized discipline with structured patterns and methods, which in turn provide a basis for control (Shaw and Atkins, 1970). Project planning, scheduling, and control are documented and reviewed during the entire course of the project, to provide management with the opportunity to assess increasing commitments periodically. Such periodic review permits progressive reduction of risk as increasing organizational commitment is required. Experience has demonstrated the value of early involvement of the operational groups that must ultimately assume responsibility for the utilization of the programming system. Their understanding of the rationale and familiarity with the implementation is necessary for the initial acceptance and ultimate success of the project.

**The Management of Advanced and Complex Software Development.** Modern operating systems and large real-time applications, such as airline reservation systems, are examples of large systems that invariably require innovation in order to meet the many demands of sheer size, speed, efficiency, reliability, and flexibility. Probably the most difficult problem is the assessment of the degree of innovation required. Only the most experienced practitioners can hope to qualify this aspect of the development task. Extensive simulation at various levels of detail often is carried on throughout the development cycle to test new concepts.

When such projects require large numbers of people (i.e., too many to allow close proximity and continuous personal contact for all) and involve several levels of management, communication and awareness of current status become hard to manage. What is more, new and advanced requirements are often difficult to define and specify. For example, concepts such as data security and reliability are not easily spelled out, let alone evaluated when they are applied to a complex system as yet not fully specified.

While certain management techniques are accepted in principle, their application remains controversial. There are divergent views of the organization of the project team and the manner in which control can be exercised to maintain consistent documentation and test standards. General agreement on the desirability of modularity in a programming system has not helped to define how a given function can be assigned to a particular module to minimize the complexity of the interfaces between modules.

Documentation of software has come to be recognized as one of the most effective management tools because it provides the only visible evidence of progress during the development process. While documentation in itself does not guarantee the success of the final product, good documentation of any program, large or small, is essential to the ultimate users. The effort associated with documentation can be a major part of the software development, another reason for its importance to the management of software.

Only recently has there been evidence of an emerging programming methodology, defined with some degree of rigor. The chief programmer team and top-down and structured programming are examples of concepts that have been tested in practice (Baker, 1972). The variation in individual programmer performance, and the difficulty of establishing quantitative criteria for programmer productivity and program quality, contribute further to the difficulties of managing large software development efforts. These difficulties can assume major proportions, since the difference in productivity from the average to the best programmers can be more than an order of magnitude. Growing effectiveness will come with the emergence of competent software engineers who have developed relevant experience and insight to provide effective management. Relevant insight will increasingly relate to the objectives of the organization and people to be served as software engineering gets on firmer ground.

REFERENCES

1969 Kay, R. H. "The Management and Organization of Large Scale Software Development Projects," *AFIPS Conference Proceedings*, Vol. 34. Montvale, N.J.: AFIPS Press, pp. 425–433.

1970. Shaw, J. C., and W. Atkins. *Managing Computer System Projects*. New York: McGraw-Hill.

1970. Weinwurm, C. F. (Ed.). *On the Management of Computer Programming*. Philadelphia: Auerbach.

1972. Baker, F. T. "Chief Programmer Team Management of Production Programming," *IBM Systems Journal,* Vol. 11 (Spring) pp. 56–73.

1974. Stevens, W. P., G. J. Myers, and L. L. Constantine. "Structured Design," *IBM Systems Journal*, Vol. 13, pp. 115–139.

R. H. KAY

# SOFTWARE PACKAGES

For articles on related subjects *see* ADMINISTRATIVE-BUSINESS APPLICATIONS; APPLICATIONS PROGRAMMING; DOCUMENTATION; ENGINEERING APPLICATIONS; MATHEMATICAL PROGRAMMING; and PORTABILITY.
For article on related term *see* FLOWCHART.

A software package is a program for performing some specific function or calculation, which is useful to more than one computer user and which is sufficiently well documented to be used without modification on a defined configuration of some computer system. Such a package may include options that are available only on certain hardware configurations, or which may be of use only to a limited number of potential users. It may also be constructed so as to admit easy adaptation or amendment, and thereby be *portable*, to other machines or to other configurations of the same machine.

Packages sold or rented are rather evenly split between systems software and applications programs. Revenues in the United States amounted to $375 million in 1973, but this must be compared to an estimated $8.5 billion spent on system design and programming "in-house" (i.e., inside the organization with the computer). This balance is, however, changing in favor of software packages as more reliable and acceptable packages reach the market.

**Example of Software Packages.** There have been many attempts to produce successful packages, and several thousand have been offered for sale, but few have succeeded in achieving general distribution. Two of the most successful have been Autoflow and Mark IV. Both are essentially aids to the programmer to carry out his task. Mark IV is a complete and somewhat complex system developed by Informatics Inc. It gives the user a simpler way to manipulate files and the data in them in conjunction with the facilities provided by the manufacturer, which would not be possible without the system. It has achieved wide distribution because manufacturers, in providing a common operating system for a range of machines, have to make compromises that reduce the efficiency of their system on any particular member of that range. To a considerable extent, Mark IV enables the user to improve the efficiency of his particular configuration in the range, particularly if it is a comparatively large one. Moreover, the package contains diagnostic facilities superior to those available through the manufacturers, thus cutting down on debugging time.

The Autoflow package enables the programmer to compare a number of important features of his own program with those which it was planned for it to have. Before writing a program in computer language, it is often convenient to draw up the logic being used in the form of a *flowchart*. When the program is actually written, not only will the logic of the flowchart become obscure, but mistakes may creep in and sections can become omitted. Some of the mistakes and omissions will be detected by the *compiler* used, but mistakes and omissions in logical sections (if the program relating to them is actually executable) will not be detected. Autoflow constructs the logic actually being followed by the program (with respect to data fed to it) in the form of a flowchart, thus enabling a comparison to be made with the original logic. This saves time in debugging and also leads to substantial savings in machine time, since the cost of running Autoflow is usually less than the cost of the debugging runs it saves.

Autoflow is a particularly simple package to use, since the information needed to construct the flowchart is not much greater than that contained in the program itself; i.e., the parameters of Autoflow are primarily the program statements themselves. However, some additional information may be needed if special techniques have been used in programming.

Other areas in which application packages have been produced are payroll, production control, frame stressing, machine tool control, pipe design and layout, registration of shares of stocks, various mathematical and statistical calculations, market survey processing and resource-distribution techniques such as networking and mathematical programming. Of these, none has achieved universal acceptance, and only a small number can be considered successful.

Payroll, invoicing, and production-control packages usually require extensive adaptation to be useful in a particular context. To some extent, each expresses a relationship among the employer, the employed, and the customer. Because this varies widely between firms in the same industry as well as between one industry and another, it is generally in a somewhat unsettled state. Thus, it is not altogether surprising that no one package has proved to be acceptable to more than a limited set of customers or to be adaptable to more than a further limited set.

A more limited application, such as stock-share registration, is more likely to be successful, but the market for such an application may well be too small to allow success. On the other hand, APT (Automatically Programmed Tools), which was developed by a consortium of aircraft firms, has achieved a measure of acceptance and success. Substantial mathematical calculations are likely to provide a good basis for a general package, but even here different methods play a part; for instance, every statistician has his own preferred technique of regression analysis. However, in the statistical field, the BIMED (biomedical computer program) package developed at UCLA (see Source Information, par. 2) has proved generally valuable and has been widely used.

Where substantial calculations are associated with engineering applications, it has often been difficult to distinguish the line between computer and manual methods. Thus, early packages tended to include only the calculations and did not take into account the very real data processing problems that arose in applying them. Therefore these packages did not greatly diminish the work of the users. As this has become better understood, packages have become more comprehensive—and thus more expensive to develop. This comprehensiveness has sometimes led to incorporation of operating approaches that are peculiar to the originator of the packages, which has inhibited general acceptance. For example, a succession of packages for pipe-stressing calculations has exhibited this tendency. A package may begin with the calculations associated with free pipes, introduce more and more anchors, heating coefficients, and so on, until it has advanced to a complete pipe system design. However, all this may apply only to the standards of the originator (either a consulting firm or a chemical group), which are not necessarily widely accepted.

Similar problems have played a part in stress analysis, although there has been less tendency to go into the final selective stage. At present there are at least two widely used packages in finite element analysis (see Source Information, par. 3). Some packages, such as ICES at M.I.T., however, have become so complicated and so difficult to maintain that clearly they cannot be regarded as "portable" in anything but name.

Undoubtedly the most widely accepted and "profitable" packages so far devised have been those associated with linear programming. Starting from some early and interesting work by such pioneers as Dantzig, the first really useful package, SCROLL, was built by Orchard-Hays for the IBM 704. Successor packages include LP 90, LP 90/94, CAPLINE, UMPIRE, and MPS 360, almost all of which were based on the work begun with SCROLL. Successive developments involved substantial technical enhancements in capability, but in many ways, and more importantly, they provided better ways to manipulate data and to present results. LP 90 was especially interesting because it contained a compiler/compiler system for updating purposes and was one of the first packages to facilitate ready maintenance on a widely distributed network of sites.

**Documentation.** The importance of documentation in dealing with packages is obvious. Good documentation of programs is always needed, of course, but since packages are (or should be) designed for widespread distribution, it is particularly important that this documentation rule be observed. Moreover, it may well be that the user's complete understanding of the process is undesirable (see below). Hence, it is important to keep user documentation and programmer documentation rigidly separate.

At least three manuals are needed, one for the user (who needs to know how to communicate his wishes to the package), one for the operator (who needs to know what tape or disk to put where, how to prepare and put in the data, how to control runs, and especially how to detect and deal with failures, restarts, errors, etc.), and one for the programmers (who may become involved in amending or adding to the package). To expect any one of these three persons to be knowledgable of all three aspects is probably impossible. Therefore, each manual must be comprehensible to a "layman," or at least to a programmer coming to the system for the first time.

**Development and Marketing.** By means of the examples given above, some problems of developing a successful package have been discussed, and some common mistakes that have been made have been mentioned. Clearly, a potential market must not be too small, but this should not imply that a software package should attempt to cover every requirement, since such requirements may be incompatible. It is preferable to choose an area in which use of the package is likely to be considerable, even though packages may cost more to develop than expected, and may require considerable maintenance and adaptation in the field.

Assuming that a suitable potential market has been chosen, development of the package ought to be planned as carefully as that of any other commercial product. Unfortunately, this obviously sensible approach has seldom been followed. For the most part, packages have tended to grow out of work done under contract for a specific application, and their development has not been carried out systematically and on a market-oriented basis. This has been especially true of packages developed by software companies, few of which have ever been in a financial position to finance adequate development work. Usually, market-oriented and adequately funded development has been sponsored by the manufacturers. However, this has often been aimed primarily at selling machines to a particular group of prospects, who have stipulated the existence of a particular package before buying, but who have as a group rarely, if ever, insisted on an adequate assessment of its quality, taking into account the complete system (beyond the computer) which will be involved in its use. Too often, therefore (though perhaps less since unbundling), the manufacturer's package has been directed primarily at increasing hardware sales rather than at solving the problems of the customer.

Marketing a package, even when it has been satisfactorily developed, is not easy. Because little or no legal protection exists (despite recent decisions on patent and copyright cover), secrecy is mandatory and the salesman must sell his product without divulging sufficient details to illustrate its superiority until after the contract is signed. Even then, there may be problems with enforcement of the contract, and it is wise to retain control over the "secrets" as long as possible.

One way to maintain control over the product while making money on it is to market it only as a bureau facility, charging "royalty" for the machine time used. However, this may be objectionable to clients because they do not have the same control over running priorities as they would on their own equipment. Nevertheless, particularly for packages requiring the support of specialist manpower, such as model builders or engineers, this is frequently used as a way of marketing LP, or finite element, packages.

In order not to disclose details of the package, the user may be given only the user and operator documentation, and be supplied with a machine-readable "object deck" or "binary tape," which (even if printed out) is practically uninterpretable without the programmer's documentation. This is done, for example, with Mark IV.

It is fair to say that unless such methods are used, the package developer cannot expect to enjoy more than two years without competition from new packages. These competitors use "derived" techniques, with or without the connivance of the originator's customers, and notwithstanding any contractual obligations he may have imposed. This unfortunate circumstance is due in part to the relative mobility of staff and the "open" atmosphere in the subject engendered by close connection with the university world—from which, of course, the package developer as well as his competitors benefit.

## Source Information

The most current literature relating to software packages is obtainable from various developers. A number of related articles also appear in this Encyclopedia. A selected list of these sources follows:

1. Mark IV manuals are obtainable from Informatics Inc., Los Angeles, California. Autoflow manuals (for the IBM 360) are obtainable from Applied Data Research Inc., Princeton, New Jersey, or CAP, Ltd., Europe. For other machines, several similar packages exist, notably BLOCKCHARTER developed by J. Harwell Data Processing for the ICL 1900 and System 4 Series. Packages measuring the frequency of occurrence of statements in programs include COTUNE for the 360, and LANDMARKER for the 1900.
2. The BIMED package was developed at the Health Sciences Computing Facility of the University of California in Los Angeles, from whom details are available.
3. See also the article in this Encyclopedia on the Finite Element Method. Packages available in-

clude (a) ASAS for Static and Dynamic Stress Analysis, available through W. S. Atkins Research and Development Division, Epson, Surrey, U.K.; (b) ASKA, developed at the Institute für Statik und Dynamik, University of Stuttgart, Germany, by C. Argyris and others; (c) NASTRAN, developed by McNeil, Schendler, Inc., for NASA; (d) SESAM, developed and marketed by Computas AS, Oslo, Norway; and (e) a package developed by Nordisk ADB of Stockholm and marketed by Leasco Systems and Research, Ltd., and Reliance Systems and Research, Inc. of Washington, D.C.

4. See also articles in this Encyclopedia on Mathematical Programming and the Simplex Method. Up-to-date packages include (a) MPS 360, available through IBM; (b) XDLA available from ICL; (c) Ilona available from Univac; (d) FMPS available from University Computing Corporation (developed by Bonner and Moore); (e) UMPIRE, available from Scientific Control Systems, Ltd. (formerly CEIR, Ltd.); (f) APEX I and II, available from Control Data Corporation; (g) LP/6000 available from Honeywell. Other manufacturers also have packages for their machines, and several commercial companies (notably Bonner and Moore and Haverlee Systems) offer packages for use on specific machines.

A. S. DOUGLAS

# SORT/MERGE PACKAGES

For articles on related subjects *see* SOFTWARE PACKAGES; SORTING; and UTILITY PROGRAM.
For article on related term *see* OPERATING SYSTEMS.

A sort/merge package is a set of programs capable of sorting and merging data files. The package is usually a part of the operating system and may be used either externally as a set of independent programs activated by control cards, or internally as a set of subroutines or macros callable from a user program.

**Capabilities.** Four types of application are possible:

1. *Sort.* A data file is sorted to create a new file, using a sequence of internal sorts and merges.

2. *Merge.* A merge operation is done on a number of presorted files.

3. *Combination Sort and Merge.* First a data file is sorted and then the output file is merged with other presorted files.

4. *Sequence Check.* A special case of a merge application in which only one input file is specified. This checks whether the file is in the proper sequence.

**Organization.** A typical sort/merge package comprises a monitor and four phases: edit, internal sort, external sort, and final merge phases.

The monitor communicates with the operating system and maintains the interphase communication between the various phases. At the start of the run, the monitor transfers control to the edit phase. When the edit phase completes its functions, the monitor in turn calls other phases according to the particular application.

The edit phase reads the parameters supplied by the user, checks them, issues appropriate error messages if necessary, determines (from the parameters) information relevant to the particular application, and stores it in tables common to all other phases.

The internal sort phase reads data records into core storage and sorts them into ordered strings (sometimes called "runs," "sequences," or "sections"). These are written in turn on intermediate storage devices and are merged later. For efficiency, most internal sort phases use either quicksort or one of its modifications.

The external sort phase merges the strings previously produced by the internal sort phase. It performs a number of passes, each of which increases the average length of a string and reduces the number of strings, and it continues up to the point where the final merge phase can combine the strings into a single file in one pass. If the initial number of strings is small enough, the external sort phase may be bypassed by the monitor and control can be transferred directly to the final merge phase.

The final merge phase is used as the last merge pass of the run. It produces a single, sorted output file according to mode and blocking specifications supplied by the user. For a merge application, this phase is called by the monitor immediately after the edit phase (i.e., the internal and external sort phase are bypassed).

Today, almost every operating system includes a sort/merge package. Those of the IBM 360, OS and DOS, and the CDC 6000 series, are widely used and similar in many respects. Both offer disk and tape variants and permit the user to add modification routines at some points in the sorting process. Both use the replacement-selection technique for internal sorting, and either the balanced, the polyphase, or the oscillating techniques for external sorting. They are good examples of efficient, general programs which are useful in many applications and yet are used mainly by experienced programmers because of the many details involved in using them. Manufacturers' manuals for these three packages give more extensive details. For additional information, consult:

1. IBM System/360 OS Sort/Merge Form GC28-6543.
2. IBM System/360 DOS, Tape and Disk Sort/Merge, Form GC28-6676.
3. CDC 6000 Computer Series: SORT/MERGE Ref. Manual, Pub. 60343900.

D. SALOMON

# SORTING

For articles on related subjects *see* BINARY SEARCH; COLLATING SEQUENCE; FILES; KEY; RECORD; and SORT-MERGE PACKAGES.
For article on related term *see* DIRECT ACCESS.

Sorting is the process by which a list of items or *records*, normally disordered, is put into order according to some criterion based on the content of each record. Why is it important to have ordered lists rather than disordered ones? A simple example will suffice to illustrate this. Consider a list of a thousand records. Suppose we wish to find a particular record. Whether the list is ordered or not, we must look at 500 records on the average to find the record we want, if our search is conducted serially from beginning to end. Indeed, for an unordered list, there is no better procedure than a serial search. And if the list does not contain our record, we must examine *all* the records in the list to find this out. But if the list is ordered, certain techniques will greatly reduce the searching effort, whether or not the record is present. For example, using binary search, the search for a record and determination of its presence in or absence from an ordered list of 1,000 records takes only ten passes on the average. In addition, if a number of records are sought and these records are arranged in order according to their keys, then serial search requires only one complete examination of the ordered list to obtain all records. To summarize, the ordered list provides the following three advantages:

1. Faster search for a single record, using various sophisticated search techniques.
2. Faster determination if a sought record is present or absent.
3. More rapid retrieval of several records sought at once.

Before discussing various methods of sorting, we must first present some definitions and notation concerning records and files.

**Definitions and Notation.** Data is rather useless unless it corresponds to something real. The correspondents are *entries* or *individuals*, which might be, for example, people for a payroll application, accounts for bookkeeping applications, or items for an inventory application. In all cases we have a collection of these individuals which comprises a *universe*. Corresponding to each individual, there is a record. The set of records is called a "file." Hence, there is one record in the file for each individual in the universe.

The record comprises a partial description of the entity, which may have many attributes, but of which only some are of interest in our data processing application. Each attribute has a name. If the attribute interests us, there is a corresponding *field* in our record. Each attribute must have two or more values. For example, sex can be described (currently) in one of two ways. On the other hand, a description of a person's wealth may require many digits.

The field in the record carries the *field value*, which is a reflection of the attribute value. The field value may represent the attribute value itself. For instance, the *weight* field in a personnel record may contain a value corresponding to the individual's weight in pounds at the time of measurement. To represent the state where an individual lives, the field value could be alphabetic (e.g., CONNECTICUT) or an abbreviation (e.g., CONN), or a *coded* value (e.g., 07 to represent that Connecticut is the seventh state in the alphabetical listing of states).

To use our file effectively, and in particular to enable us to order it, we must uniquely identify each record. The field in the record which so identifies it is often referred to as the *record key*, or simply as the "key."

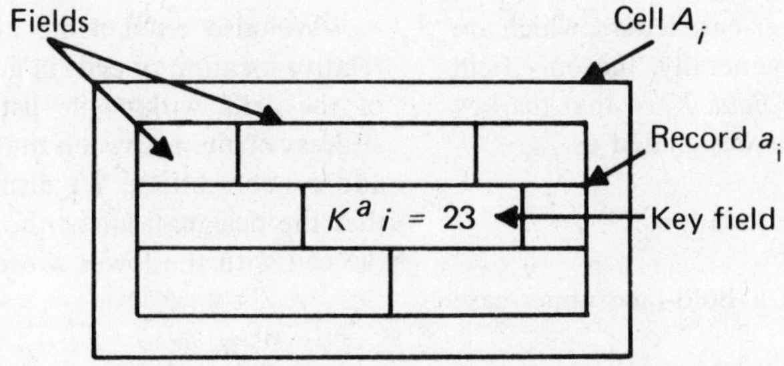


**Fig. 1.** A cell containing a record with a key field.

Thus far, our definitions are unrelated to the use of a computer for sorting. In a computer, all or some portion of the file must be stored in a tangible, nameable location. We define:

A *cell* to be the location or locations in memory or on an auxiliary medium where a record is stored.
A *list* to be the location where a file is stored.

Fig. 1 shows a cell with a record in it. The record key is also displayed; note that it need not be in any special position in the record.

A list, then, is a collection of cells. Records of a file are stored in cells of the list. However, it is not necessary that every cell of a list contain some record of the file. When all the cells of the list have records of the file, the list is called "dense." Should there be cells in the list which do not contain records (are empty), as in Fig. 2, the list is said to be *loose*, or *thin*. These empty cells must have some recognizable unique feature so that the sorting program will identify them as empty.

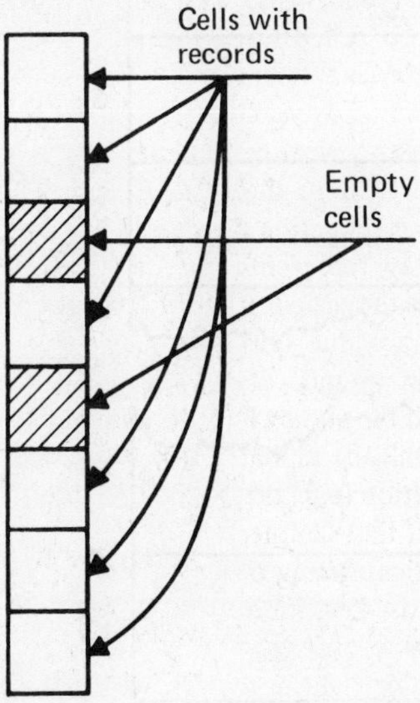


**Fig. 2.** A loose list.

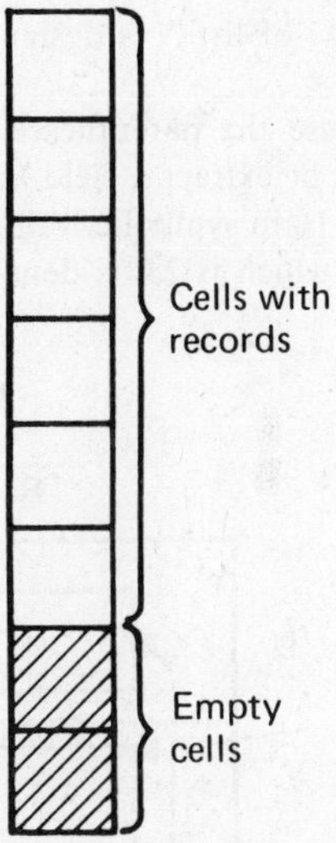


**Fig. 3.** A semidense list.

It is often useful for a contiguous portion of the list to hold the file compactly, as shown in Fig. 3, where the top six cells contain the six records that constitute the file. However, there are two more cells in the list, which are empty. Intuitively we feel that the list is both dense and loose; the top part is dense; all the cells are not occupied, so the list is loose; such a list is called "semi-dense."

We use the following notation to describe the various *quantities* involved in sorting:

The *file* is designated by boldface lower-case letters, e.g., **a**.
*Records* are designated by subscripted lower-case italic letters, e.g., $a_i$.

*Fields in records* use lower-case letters, which are doubly subscripted; generally, the only field referred to is the *key field, K*, so that the key in record $i$ of file **a** is designated as ${}_Ka_i$.

Upper-case letters designate locations:

A *list* is designated by a bold-face upper-case letter, e.g., **A**.
A *cell* is designated by a subscripted upper-case italic letter, e.g., $A_i$.
The *field location* within a cell uses the double-subscript notation, so that the location of the key in cell $i$ of list **A** is designated ${}_KA_i$.

Finally, we use the parentheses to extract the contents of a cell or extract a field from a cell. For instance (see Fig. 1), in symbolic form, the key in the $i$th cell of list **A**, which is 23, is denoted by

$$({}_KA_i) = {}_Ka_i = 23. \tag{1}$$

We also need some notation to indicate the relative location of cells in a list. In a list **R** the order of the cells within the list is determined by the address of the cell, such that the cell with the lower address comes first. We display this fact by insuring that the designation for the lower address contains the cell with the lower subscript. In symbolic terms

$$i < j \supset R_i < R_j, \tag{2}$$

which should be read, "if $i$ is less than $j$, then the cell labeled $R_i$ precedes the cell labeled $R_j$." The symbol $\supset$ represents "implies."

Now let us suppose we have a dense list. Each record contains a key. For a *sorted list*, the order in which we encounter records in the cells of the list should correspond to the size of the key assigned to each record. This is stated symbolically as

$$R_i < R_j \supset ({}_KR_i) < ({}_KR_j), \tag{3}$$

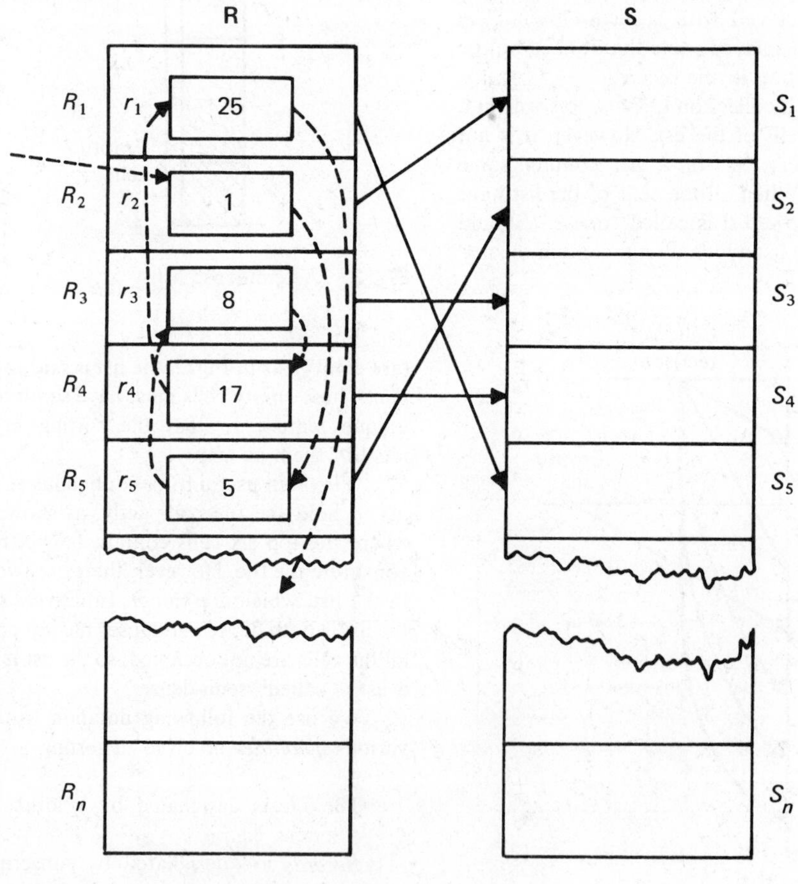


**Fig. 4.** Action required for sorting.

and in words, "if cell $R_i$ precedes cell $R_j$, then the key of the record contained in $R_i$ is smaller than the key of the record contained in $R_j$." It should be obvious that we have imposed order upon the list **R** by the position of the records contained in that list with respect to the key contained in those records.

This is not the only order we might impose on the list **R**. For example, we can place a list into either ascending or descending order. The relation (3) describes a list in *ascending sequence*. To make a similar statement for an ordered list in *descending sequence*, we write

$$R_i < R_j \supset ({}_K R_i) > ({}_K R_j). \tag{4}$$

This says that as we proceed through the list to cells of larger numerical address, we encounter records with smaller keys. In what follows we consider only the case of ordered lists in ascending order.

To recapitulate the foregoing, we refer to Fig. 4, which illustrates a disordered list **R** and its ordered counterpart **S**. The incoming dotted arrow points to $r_2$, indicating that it is the smallest record found in **R**. The dotted arrow from $r_2$ to $r_5$ in **R** shows that it is the next smallest; $r_5$ points to $r_3$ which should come next, etc. On the right of Fig. 4 we see the sorted list **S**. The first cell, $S_1$, contains $r_2$, which has been moved from its position in list **R**. $S_2$ contains $r_5$; $S_3$ contains $r_3$, etc. In a general sense it is easy to see how the sorted list **S** can be created from the unsorted list **R**. However, there are many ways the comparisons and the move operations can be performed. Much work has gone into finding good ways to do this. In what follows, we examine some of these methods.

**Computer Sorting.** Generally, the lists to be sorted on a computer are large. The lists are supplied using intermediate or external media such as punched cards or magnetic tape, disk, or drum. As far as the user is concerned, he supplies a list on such a medium and the computer returns a similar list, but in ordered form. What happens in between?

INTERNAL SORTING. When the entire list can be brought into the main computer memory and sorted in memory, this process is called "internal sorting." Internal sorting can be done at least in two ways. Both are illustrated in Fig. 5.

For the *double-list sort*, the unordered file **t** is placed in a list area of memory, designated in Fig. 5(a) as **R**, using the buffer to load it from an external or auxiliary medium. The internal sort action then takes place, creating the sorted list **S**, generally in another area of memory. This becomes the output file **u**.

*Entry sorting* [Fig. 5(b)] takes place as records are brought into the buffer from **t**. The sorting program sets up a buffer area where one record or a block of a few records is placed as it is brought in from the external medium. Entry sorting takes records from the buffer and places them in the sorted list **S**. This action takes place a bufferful at a time until the input file is exhausted.

EXTERNAL SORTING. When the input file grows large, the size of the computer memory becomes a limiting factor in the case of internal sorting. The technique provided in most sorting programs is to produce a string of sorted records by an internal sort. Thus, in Fig. 6 we see the input file **t**, which is brought into memory a piece at a time (to **R**) and sorted internally in **S**. As each sorted sublist is produced, it is placed on an auxiliary storage medium, shown in Fig. 6 as the list **U**. When this action is completed, **U** consists of ordered sublists. These are subsequently acted upon by the computer to form a single-ordered list; the action thus performed

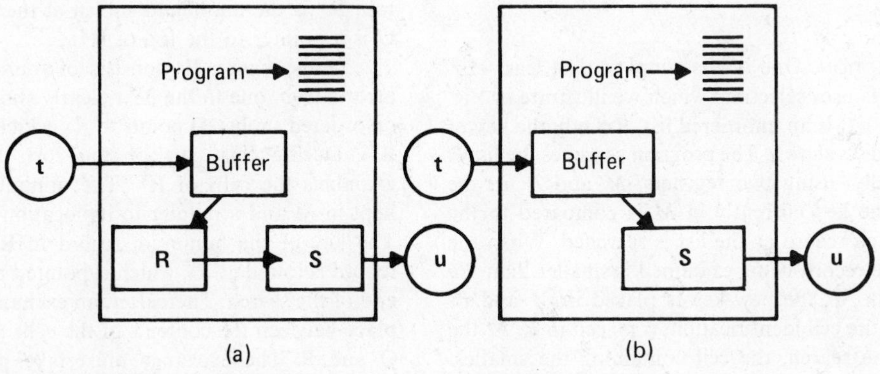


**Fig. 5.** Internal sorting. (a) Double-list sort. (b) Entry sort.

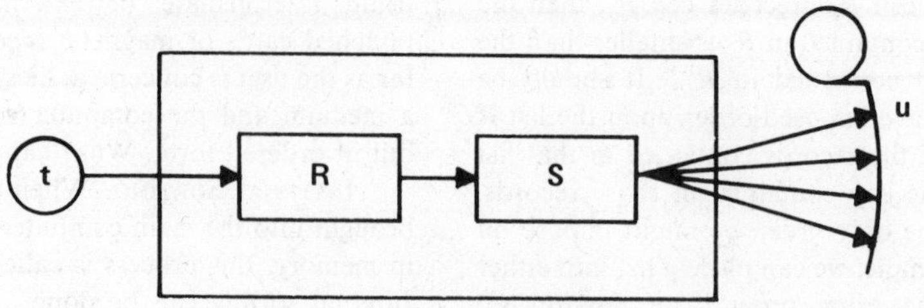


**Fig. 6.** An internal sort of a long list produces a list of ordered sublists.

is called an *external sort* and uses *merging*, which will be described shortly.

**Internal Sorting Techniques.** In this section we examine a number of the simpler types of internal sorts. The more complicated sorts have much space devoted to them in the literature (Flores, 1969; Knuth, 1973; Lorin, 1971).

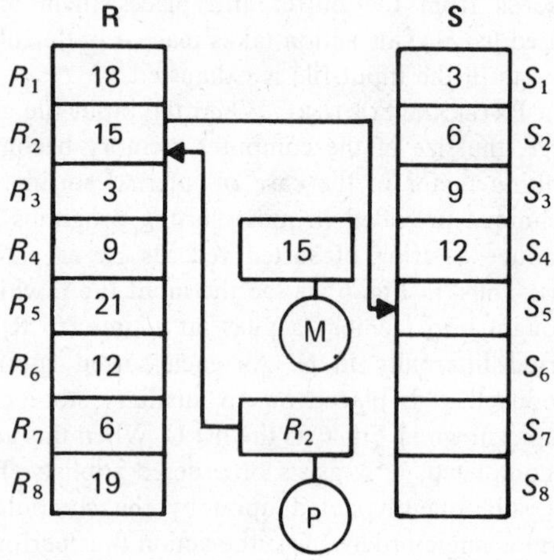


**Fig. 7.** Sort by selection.

SELECTION. One of the simplest (but least efficient) sorts uses selection, which we illustrate in Fig. 7. On the left is an unordered list, **R**. Only the key of the records is shown. The program searches the list **R** sequentially, using two registers, $M$ and $P$, in the figure. The key currently in $M$ is compared to the key of each record as the list is searched. When the key of the record being examined is smaller than the number in $M$, the new key is placed in $M$ and its location, the cell identification, is placed in $P$. At the end of the search, the cell containing the smallest record is pointed to by $P$. This record is transferred to $S_i$, the proper location in **S**.

A problem arises for the next selection. If nothing is done with the list **R**, the search will come up with the same least record. Hence, after a record has been transferred from its location in **R**, a *flag* must be inserted in **R** to indicate to the program to skip this call. One way to do this is to change the key in the cell from which a record has been transferred to the highest possible key; that way it can never be least.

In Fig. 7, the four smallest records of **R** have already been placed in cells of **S**. The next least record to come from **R** for **S** is now in $R_2$. It should be clear from the description how this record is found and moved.

SELECTION AND EXCHANGE. Several improvements can be made on the selection sort. One such, called "selection and exchange," is a sort performed *within* the list area—a separate area **S** is not required. We describe it briefly. First, the list **R** is scanned for the smallest record. This record is moved to the top cell and the record in the top cell is moved down to the position of the list record—thus the reason for "exchange" in its name. One advantage obtained from selection and exchange is that, as it proceeds, fewer and fewer cells need be examined. Another is that it uses less memory. In Fig. 8, **R** is divided into two sublists, where $\mathbf{R}^o$ is the ordered sublist at the top; $\mathbf{R}^X$ is the unordered sublist at the bottom; and Q is a pointer to the top of $\mathbf{R}^X$.

In the figure, $\mathbf{R}^o$ consists of four records; the arrows from one to the next clearly show that this is an ordered sublist. Q points to $R_5$, which is the top of $\mathbf{R}^X$. During this part of the sort, the program examines the cells of $\mathbf{R}^X$. The minimum record is kept in M and a pointer to its location is kept in P. The key of the minimum record in $\mathbf{R}^X$ is 15; this record is found at $R_7$, which is pointed to by P at the end of the search. Thereafter, an exchange must take place between the contents of the cells pointed to by Q and P. The exchange must take place so that neither record is altered. If the entire record is in M, $R_5$ can go at once to $R_7$, and M to $R_5$.

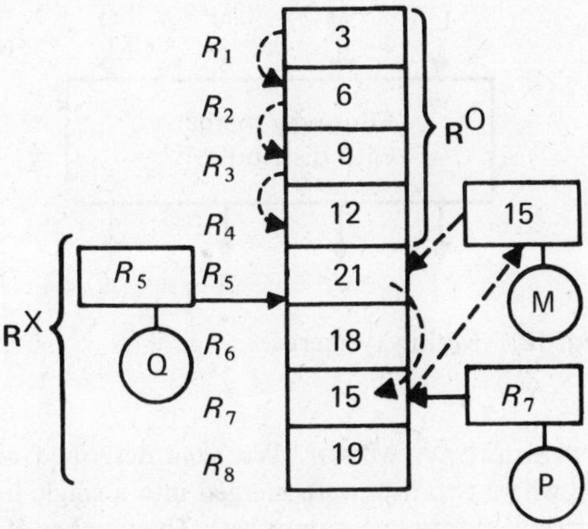


**Fig. 8.** Sort by selection and exchange.

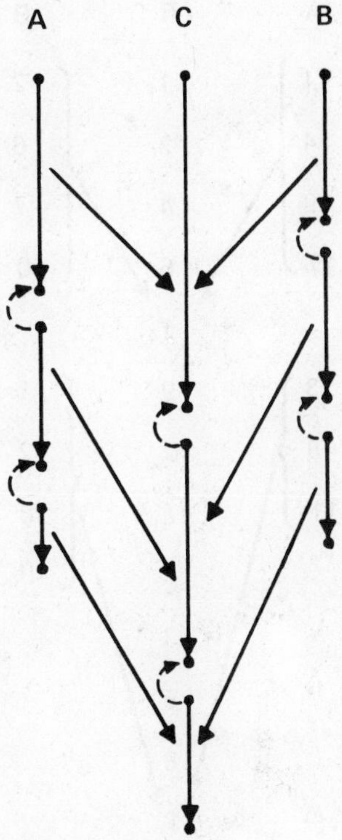


**Fig. 9.** A merge.

The sort described above is sometimes known as a *bubble sort*. Consider the record with the smallest key to be the lightest. During each phase of the sort, the lightest record bubbles up to the top of the unordered sublist. In actuality, the bubble sort described in the literature is more complicated and less efficient than selection and exchange because the comparisons and transfers are not done in exactly the order described.

**Merging.** In its simplest form, *merging* consists of taking two ordered lists and creating a single ordered list out of them. This can be extended so that the input lists can consist of ordered sublists, as shown in Fig. 9. Lists **A** and **B** each consist of several sublists. The end of one sublist can be distinguished from the beginning of the next because the first cell of the next sublist has arrows that point both forward and backward to preceding and succeeding cells, respectively. Merging then consists of producing a single ordered sublist for corresponding ordered sublists in the two input lists. The action is better seen when numbers are actually used to represent the keys of records in the sublists as they are being merged, as shown by Fig. 10. The algorithm for performing the merge is introduced below and described in detail in Flores (1967).

Sorting by Merging. Merging is conveniently combined with internal sorting for large lists that cannot be stored conveniently in memory. Consider one of the internal sorts that take records from an input list and create an ordered sublist of them. The output of repeated internal sorts would be a *single list* of ordered sublists, which would not be suitable for later merging. To produce two lists of ordered sublists, a distribution action is necessary during the internal sort. As ordered sublists are created by the internal sort, they are distributed alternately to two lists on an intermediate medium such as tape or disk. After this *internal phase* of the sort, we have two *volumes*, each containing two lists and each mounted on separated devices.

Fig. 11 shows two lists, **L** and **M**, consisting of ordered sublists. These are submitted to the computer, which contains a *merge* program. An ordered sublist is produced from each two ordered sublists, one each from **L** and **M**, which have been merged together. If no further action is taken during this merge, the output would be a single list of ordered sublists and would be unfit for further merging. To remedy this, *distribution* occurs during each merge: Merged ordered sublists are presented alternately to each of two output media. Now these new lists, **P** and **Q** in Fig. 11, are candidates for further merging. The second merge produces two new lists, **U** and **V**. These new output lists become input for the next merge activity. This continues until the production of the merge is a single list that is entirely ordered.

Suppose **L** and **M** consist of four sublists each; **P** and **Q** would each contain two ordered sublists; **U** and **V** would contain one sublist each. **W**, the result of merging **U** and **V**, is the required ordered list.

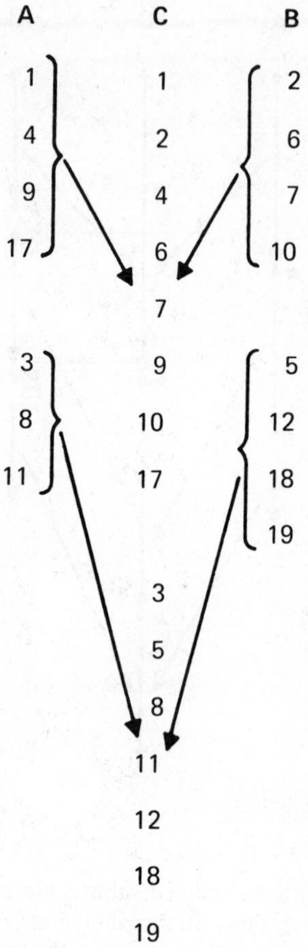


**Fig. 10.** Merge details.

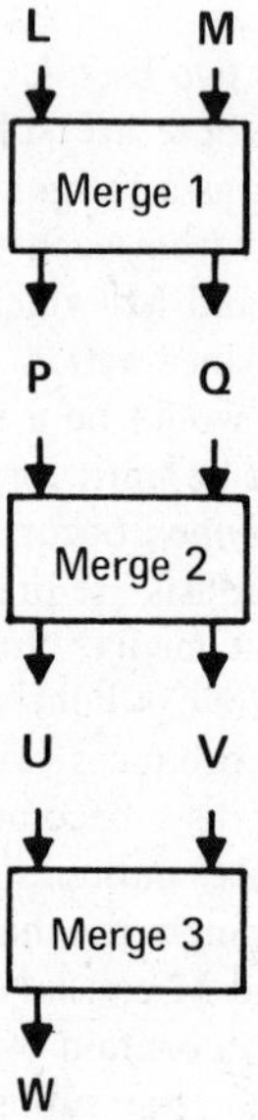


**Fig. 11.** Sorting by merging ordered sublists.

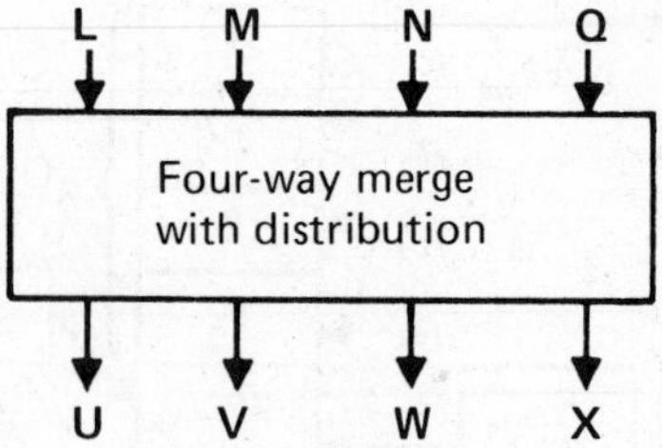


**Fig. 12.** Multiway merge.

MULTIWAY MERGE. We have described merging where two lists were merged into a single list or distributed into two output lists. The number of lists that can be merged at one time is limited only by the complexity of the merge program and by the amount of main memory available in the machine. Fig. 12 shows a four-way merge, where **L**, **M**, **N**, and **Q** are input lists of ordered sublists and distribution takes place to **U**, **V**, **W**, and **X**. One sublist each from **L**, **M**, **N**, and **Q** is merged into a single sublist and distributed to the proper output list. This method is described in detail in Flores (1969, p. 109).

The advantage of the multiway merge is that it gets the job done much more quickly. The disadvantage is that it uses many I/O devices—the four-way merge uses eight devices, although this is not a serious objection if disks rather than tapes are used.

CASCADE MERGE. To reduce the number of devices holding input or output media, more complicated merge sorts have been devised. The *cascade merge* was one of the first of these and possibly the easiest to explain. In the example of Fig. 13 we begin with four lists labeled **U**, **V**, **W**, and **X**. **U** is a list comprising 14 sublists. Each of these sublists was created during an internal sort. To indicate the length of each sublist, a subscript is used. A unit sublist is one the length of which is the same as the sublist produced during the internal sort. **V** contains 11 such sublists, and **W** contains six. During the first phase, sublists of unit length from each list are merged by a three-way merge producing six sublists, each of which is three units long. These are placed on **X**. During the second phase, a two-way merge produces five sublists, each of length 2 on **W**.

It might seem that we are ready to do another merge. However, this sort was designed for magnetic tape. Although the tapes can be read backward, control becomes more complicated when we try to do a merge reading **U** forward, and **W** and **V** backward. Hence, **U** is copied onto **V** in phase 3. Now it is possible in phase 4 to read **V**, **W**, and **X**, all

The polyphase sort requires a distribution procedure that is performed during the internal sort and which is quite uneven; it is based on a complicated algorithm. The origin and principle of the algorithm is explained in Flores (1969, p. 145).

Using the notation we developed for the cascade sort, let us examine Fig. 14, which shows how the polyphase sort works. The sort displayed uses four magnetic tape units. The internal sort has produced 13 sublists of unit length on the left-hand tape unit, 11 of these on the next one, and 7 on the third unit. The fourth unit contains a working tape. Actually, this can be on the input tape unit from which the original tape was removed and a working tape mounted to secure the integrity of the original file during the sort.

During the first phase, a three-way merge produces seven sublists, each of unit length three. These go to the fourth tape unit. As the last sublist from the third unit is merged, we find that no more sublists remain on that unit. The program senses this and makes an alteration in the I/O device assignment.

During the second phase, another three-way merge occurs. The output of this merge goes on to the third tape unit. Notice during this merge that the first and second tape units continue to read forward. However, the fourth tape unit had just been written backward, merging sublists of each into sublists of length 6.

The reader can now follow how the rest of the merge is done using three- and two-way merges and copies (see Flores, 1969, p. 136).

Polyphase Sort-Merge. The polyphase sort-merge provides a more advanced merge facility. It is used in most manufacturer-supplied tape sorts. It enables the user with $N$ tape units to have $N - 1$ of these in use for merging most of the time. To take advantage of the sort, the tape units should be capable of reading backward and forward, and the program must be able to energize the tape units in different directions during any given phase of the sort.

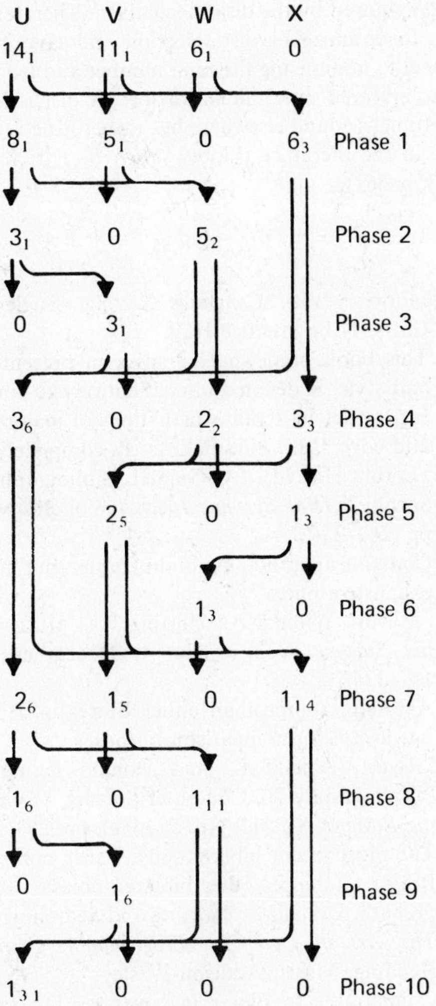


**Fig. 13.** Cascade merge.

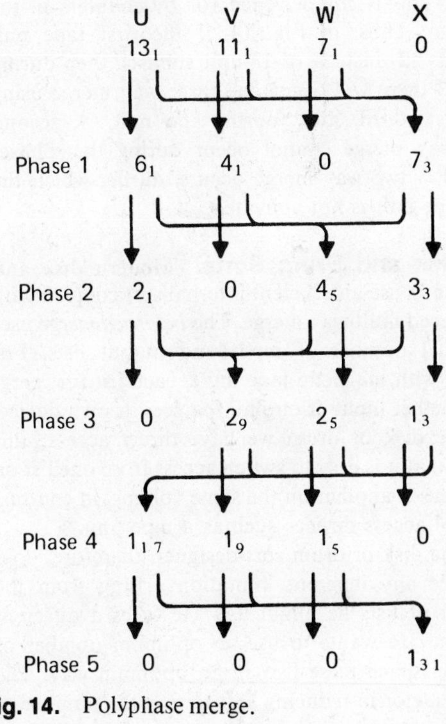


**Fig. 14.** Polyphase merge.

upon; to save rewinding time, it is read backward. This may cause complications as sublist lengths get large. If the allocated buffer in main memory cannot hold the whole sublist, trouble arises, since we cannot merge the end of one sublist with the beginning of another sublist. For this reason, some polyphase sorts are designed so as to rewind the destination unit after it has accepted the proper number of sublists.

At the end of phase 2, the first tape unit has two unit sublists left and is still reading forward; the second tape unit is empty; the third tape unit has just received four sublists of length 5 and is ready to read backward; the fourth tape unit has three sublists of length 3 and continues to be read backward.

From the figure it should be clear how the five phases required for this particular sort are performed. During the distribution phase, the allocation of sublists to each tape unit is very sensitive. An algorithm creates the assignment numbers, which are known as perfect numbers (not to be confused with perfect numbers in mathematics). The perfect numbers corresponding to 31 sublists are 13, 11, and 7 when four tape units are involved.

If we have only 30 sublists, we find that no perfect numbers can be generated. Several alternatives are available. The simplest of these to understand is the creation of a null sublist so that the program thinks there are 31 sublists when there really aren't. This is compensated for by counters in the program. Thus, in Fig. 14, if the first tape unit contains 12- instead of 13-unit sublists, then during phase 3 there will occur one three-way merge using the first, third, and fourth tape unit. A second three-way merge cannot occur during this phase; instead, a two-way merge occurs, during which the first tape unit is not activated.

**Disk and Drum Sorts.** Modern disk and drum sorts use an efficient internal sort coupled with a balanced multiway merge. The *balanced merge* uses an equal number of input and output lists. For sorting with magnetic tape units, each list for merging, whether input or output, requires its own device. For the disk or drum we have direct access; this means that it is easy to switch access from one list on a volume to another on the same volume, in contrast to serial access devices such as a tape unit.

The disk or drum sort designer, therefore, does not face any inherent limitation arising from the number of lists he might use. He faces a different problem. He wants to use an optimum number of lists and space these lists in an optimum way. The crucial factor in reducing sort time is the number of seeks required by the disk mechanism. Therefore, he tries to optimize his list selection and layout with respect to minimizing the total number and length of seeks involved over the entire sort. A discussion of this topic is found elsewhere but rather little is available in the literature (Flores, 1969, p. 172; Knuth, 1973, p. 361).

### References

1969. Flores, Ivan. *Computer Sorting*. Englewood Cliffs, N.J.: Prentice-Hall.
This book, somewhat complex in presentation and style, is devoted almost entirely to sorting. It provides in-depth explanations of major sorts and covers the wide field fairly completely.

1971. Lorin, Harold. "A Guided Bibliography to Sorting," *IBM Systems Journal*, Vol. 10, No. 3, pp. 244–254.
Contains an annotated bibliography, but not an exhaustive one.

1971. Martin, William A. "Sorting," *ACM Computing Surveys*, Vol. 3, No. 4 (December), pp. 147–174.
A briefer source than either Flores or Knuth, but useful for comparison purposes.

1972. Rivest, Ronald L., and Donald E. Knuth. "Bibliography 26, Computer Sorting," *Computing Reviews*, Vol. 13, No. 6 (June), pp. 283–289.
The most recent bibliography. Fairly complete. It also references other bibliographies.

1973. Knuth, Donald E. "Sorting and Searching," in *The Art of Computer Programming*, Vol. 3. Reading, Mass.: Addison-Wesley.
Comparable to Flores in coverage, but rather difficult to assimilate.

I. Flores

## SOURCE PROGRAM

For articles on related subjects *see* Computer, Using a; Object Program; and Procedure-Oriented Languages.
For article on related term *see* Machine and Assembly Language Programming.

A source program is a computer program written in a language one or more steps removed from the "machine language" of a given computer. Machine language consists of the very explicit set of instructions and operation codes capable of direct execution by the hardware of the computer. It is, however, extremely tedious and error producing to use, for it requires that instructions be spelled out in almost microscopic detail, specifying all data and program references in terms of actual addresses within the computer memory. Accordingly, other languages have been developed to make it easier for a programmer to express his desires. A program written in such a language is called a "source program," and must be translated by one means or another into the language of the machine before it can be executed. Fortunately, other programs can carry out this translation on the computer itself.

If the source program is in assembly (i.e., symbolic) language, the process of translating it is called "assembling," and the result is an "object program" in machine language, ready to be executed. If the source program is in a higher-level language like Fortran or Cobol, the translating process is called "compiling," and may involve one or more stages (e.g., a Fortran program may be first compiled into assembly language, and then that program assembled into machine language).

Source programs in higher-level languages have great advantages in portability, for with only minor changes they can often be compiled to run on various machines.

C. H. DAVIDSON

# SPECIAL-PURPOSE COMPUTERS

For articles on related subjects *see* ANALOG COMPUTERS; DATA ACQUISITION COMPUTER; DIGITAL COMPUTERS; and HYBRID COMPUTERS.
For articles on related terms *see* FAST FOURIER TRANSFORM; MICROPROGRAMMING; MINICOMPUTERS; and MULTIPLEXING.

It is difficult to define a rigid boundary to distinguish special-purpose (SP) from general-purpose (GP) computers. The rationale expressed in this article is that a computer is special purpose if it displays a dedication in its architecture or in its implementation which reflects the application or environment for which it was designed and which makes its use elsewhere impractical. In this article we are concerned with stored program, electronic, and digital machines, and with systems that incorporate such machines. We exclude analog computers, mechanical and electromechanical computers, and devices that do not normally have an internally stored program, such as calculating machines.

This survey will discuss four application areas where special-purpose computers are of considerable interest. A summary section will draw general conclusions about trends in architecture, implementation, and system configuration.

**Industrial Automation.** Possibly the simplest machine that warrants our interest is the programmable logic controller (PLC). This is a stored-program device intended to replace relay logic used in sequencing, timing, and counting of discrete events. Instead of physically wiring relays, pushbuttons, limit switches, etc., a PLC is programmed to test the state of input lines, to set output lines in accordance with the input state, or to branch to another set of tests. The instruction sets of these machines generally exclude all arithmetic and boolean operators, but do include vital decision instructions such as skip, transfer unconditional, transfer conditional, and even transfer and link. (See Fig. 1.)

Another step up the ladder in complexity is the direct digital controller (DDC). This special-purpose machine replaces an analog set-point controller, such as a flow-rate or temperature controller. (See Fig. 2.) Such controllers compare a measured value to a set value and compute a correction signal. A typical equation is

$$S = K_1E + K_2 \int E \, dt + K_3 \frac{dE}{dt}$$

where $S$ is the output signal and $E$ is the error value.

The desirability of a digital implementation is indicated by the need for accuracy, for a means to change set points dynamically, and for the ability to modify the algorithm easily. Since the cost of even a special-purpose digital machine would be greater than that of the analog device, all designs for DDCs have been based on the capability of one processor to handle at least 16, and as many as a thousand, control loops.

During the mid-1960s, numerous DDC machines were designed. Generally, the digitized inputs were scanned at a constant rate. The algorithmic constants and required historical data for each point were kept on a small magnetic drum (or, later, a core memory). A special-purpose arithmetic unit, often a digital differential analyzer, was used to solve the

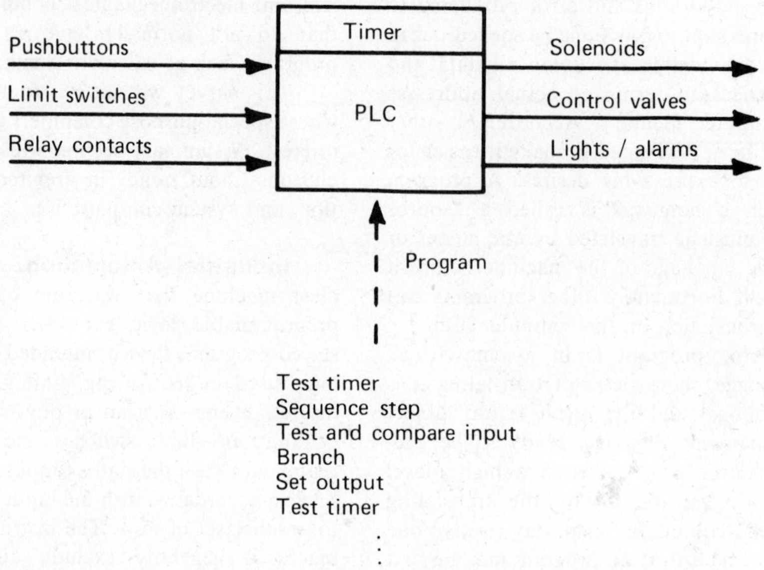


**Fig. 1.** Descriptive schematic of programmable logic controller (PLC).

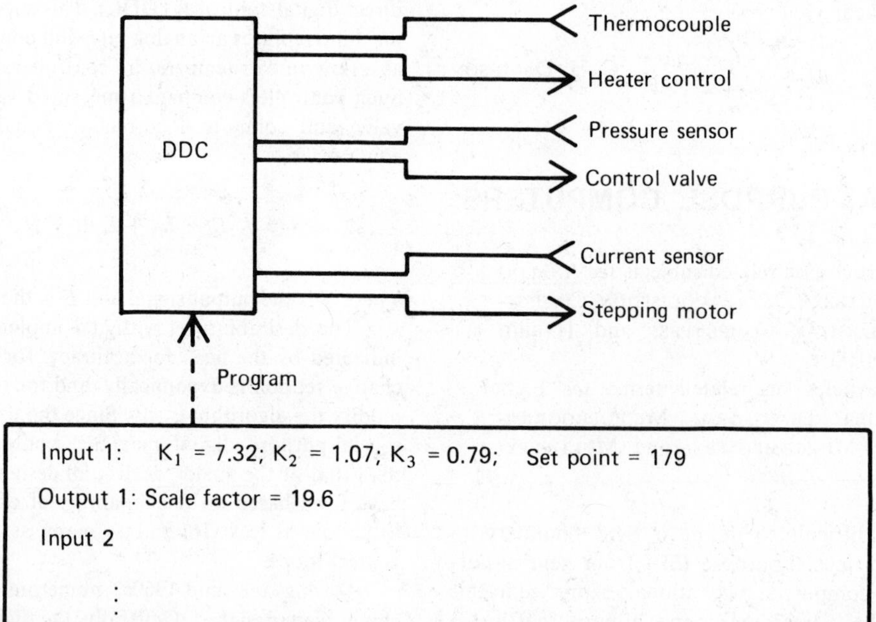


**Fig. 2.** Descriptive schematic of direct digital controller (DDC).

equation repetitively. Few special-purpose DDCs were ever installed because GP computers could be programmed to do the DDC actions and could also perform valuable other functions in the process-control cycle.

Before discussing such functions, it is desirable to digress briefly and describe one of the most complex and crucial aspects of process-control system design, the input and output of analog signals. The level, linearity, or frequency content of such signals are not well standardized. In addition to analog-to-digital conversion of sensor inputs and the digital-to-analog conversion of output signals, the input signals must usually be scaled into a usable range, and often they must be adjusted for nonlinearities of the sensors. Output signals may require similar treatment.

The major problems in the I/O section are concerned with the inherent accuracy of the sensors or actuators, the control of electrical noise and spurious signals, the high cost of long wiring runs, the multiplexing of signals to the signal amplifiers, and the design of these rather crucial amplifiers. These problems remain invariant whether the digital section is SP or GP. The I/O interfaces are often the most expensive and the most limiting aspect of an on-line control system.

Progress from the PLC to the DDC to the data acquisition system (DAS) is another step in a continuing spectrum of sophistication. The DAS scans digital and analog inputs in an order and at a rate controlled by a program. The input signals are first scaled and corrected. The resulting values may be compared against stored limits. Out-of-limit values can result in attention alarms, or they may be logged (printed out). (See Fig. 3.)

In an SP implementation, the conversion, print-control, and limit-testing functions are wired in. Programming is then limited to simple selection techniques, often provided by patch cords or a fixed program on paper tape. In more sophisticated applications, measured values are used in computation of process performance parameters. In such a case, the need for a GP machine, which can clearly also perform the rote functions, is indicated. The DAS with GP computation provides an industrial control capability that can be used in process optimization and in control of very complex industrial systems.

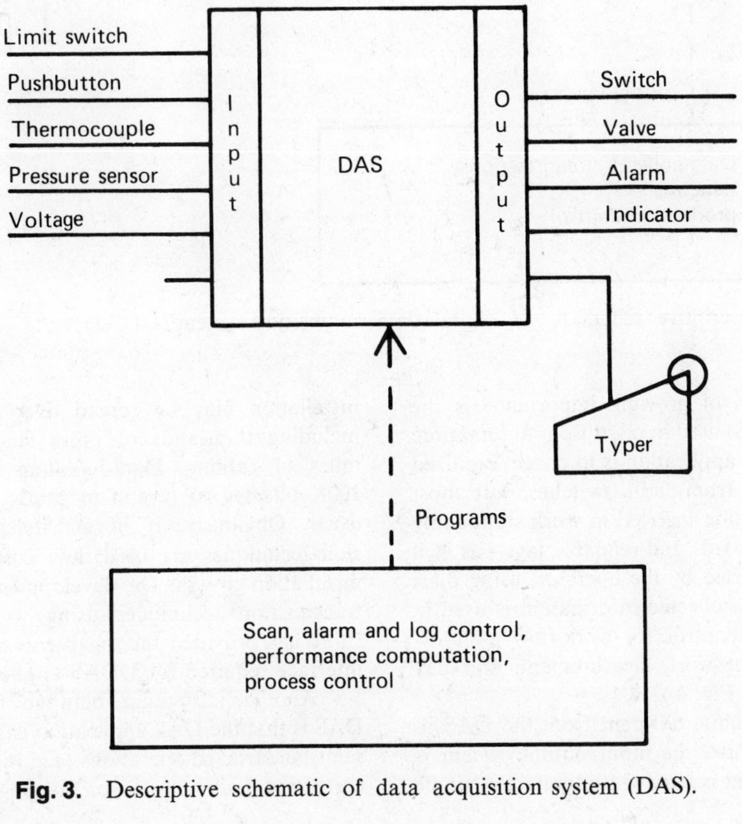


**Fig. 3.** Descriptive schematic of data acquisition system (DAS).

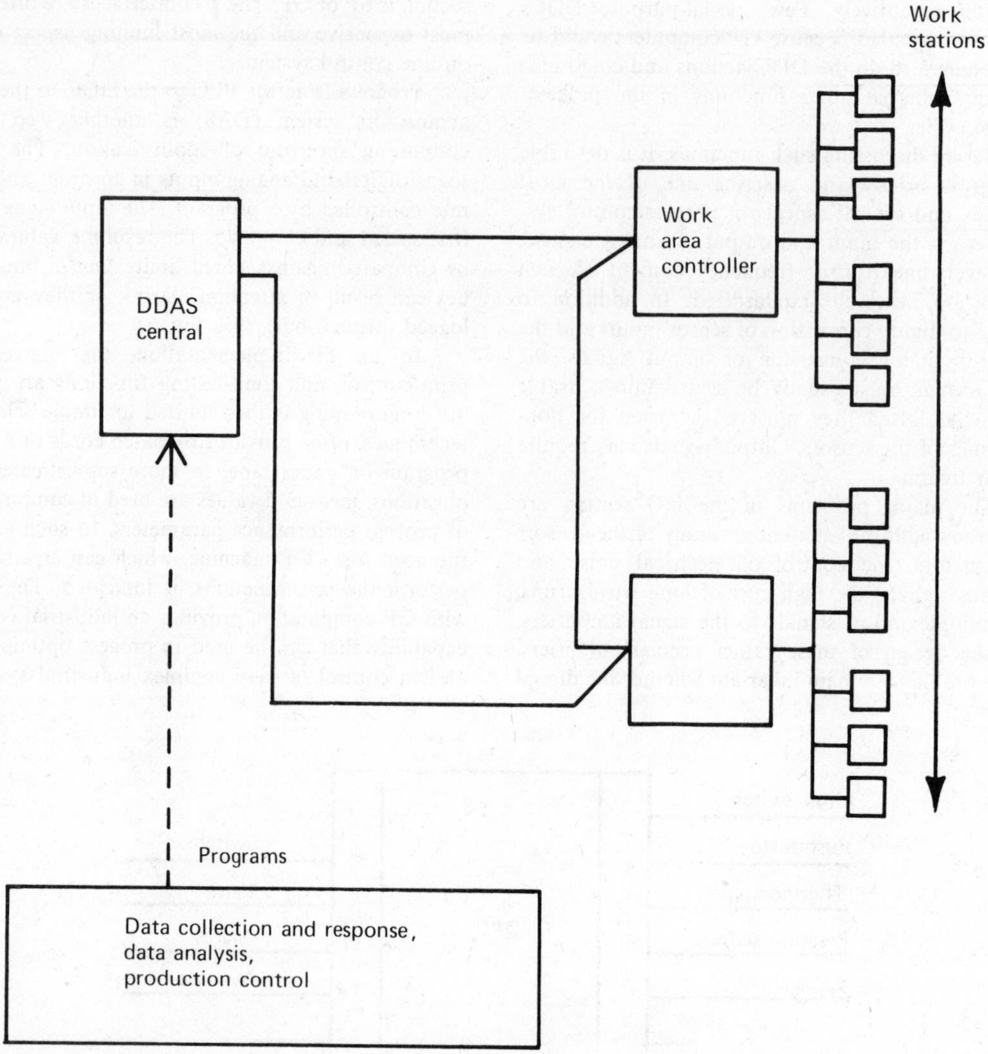


**Fig. 4.** Descriptive schematic of digital data acquisition system (DDAS).

An application of growing importance is the digital DAS (DDAS) used in plant floor automation. The purpose of this application is to collect digitized data—occasionally from limit switches, but most often from information inserted in work stations by means of punched cards and readable tags—as well as information inserted by the operator, using dials or a keyboard. The collected information is used in dynamic inventory control, for work-flow monitoring and control, for work measurement, and pay determination. (See Fig. 4.)

The DDAS is quite different from the DAS in two major ways. First, the input/output system is not noise-limited, but is bandwidth limited. A single installation may be spread over many buildings, including thousands of input stations and many miles of cabling. Data-handling requirements of 100K bits/sec to several megabits/sec are not unusual. Obviously, if normal telephone transmission techniques are used, line costs severely limit installation growth. The development of time-shared transmission techniques using wide-band coaxial cable has provided the inexpensive communication interface required for DDAS applications.

Another difference between the DDAS and DAS is that the DAS application is based on a set of semistandardized operations (e.g., signal scaling and correction, limit comparison, logging and recording).

In the DDAS applications the type of data collected and the uses to which it is put are less well defined, thus demanding complete freedom in programming. As a result, while the local work stations are very simple SP digital devices, a GP central computer is clearly needed.

So far, in industrial automation applications, we have described the PLC, DDC, DAS, DAS with computation, and DDAS. It is clear that, excepting input/output, the functions of any of these applications could be performed by a general-purpose machine. Historically, this has not been the case. For example, in the early 1960s when DAS came into widespread use in process control, the implementations were nearly all special-purpose arithmetic units. In some early implementations, input selection, correction and conversion constants, and logging control signals were prerecorded on a paper tape loop or were programmed on plugboards. The inflexibility of such designs led to the use of small magnetic drums for storage of constants and programs. The instruction sets remained limited, and the typical DAS did not have the capability to store or recall the data on which it operated.

The desire to obtain on-line performance analysis, combined with the advent of cheaper and more reliable transistorized circuitry, led to a variety of experiments in the mid-1960s. In some of these, the special-purpose DAS was retained as a "front end," but selected data was passed to a general-purpose computer for analysis.

The logical problems of communicating with a batch-oriented GP machine, the physical communication problems, and the poor availablity (up time) of the large GP machine quickly led to design of small GP machines that reflected the needs of real-time in the form of priority interrupt systems and fast computation via small core memory backed by larger drums. Such a machine could be economically justified if it performed both the computational and the DAS functions.

Early SP implementation, with later replacement by a GP machine, is a distinct characteristic of industrial application: Technological changes reduce the cost and increase the reliability of GP computers. This, combined with the desire for more function, quickly leads to the disappearance of the historically important special-pupose machine.

Early process-control computers were somewhat special in implementation as well as architecture. The many soldered joints, connectors, and (even within the memory of some readers) vacuum tubes led to the need for environmental protections against vibration, shock, acoustic noise, and corrosive atmophere. Many early machines were constructed with sealed drawers, built-in air conditioning, and extensive vibration mounts. The resulting service difficulties quickly led to other solutions, such as containing the computer in a separate room. Newer technologies are more reliable and require less space. Today, not even implementation distinguishes most industrial computers from other GP machines.

**Numerical Machine Control.** Control of lathes, milling machines, and other metal-cutting tools represented an early and continuously changing interplay between special- and general-purpose techniques. The idea is simple: Given that a cutter is at a position $X1, Y1$, it is desired to move it to $X2, Y2$ at a known velocity. In order to maintain great precision of the path, many thousands of control signals must be given the drives for each inch of total motion. With high cutting rates, the data transmission rates are significant. The computation technique is to sense the $X$ and $Y$ positions, and then calculate and transmit the proper increments for the desired path. Linear, circular, and parabolic paths are most common. With modern high-speed machines, output data rates of 1.0 to 1.5M bits/sec are not unusual.

The earliest machines used a paper tape input, which provided the constants needed to define the terminal positions and velocity vector between positions. Digital differential analyzers (DDA) were commonly used to provide the required calculation, or more correctly, interpolation. The DDA is well suited for this application in that incremental corrective calculations of great accuracy can be provided by a simple computer.

The numerical machine controller generally also provided means of controlling discrete operations such as starting and stopping motors, coolant and lubricant feeds, selecting the proper tool from a rotating tool holder, etc. In addition, some interpolators were designed to operate in three dimensions, thus providing full contouring capability. An obvious constraint is that the paper tape program is inflexible. Such tapes are usually prepared on a general-purpose computer. Any change in the desired path, feed rate, or in the setup characteristics of the holding jigs or cutting tools requires generation of a new program.

In the late 1960s, several manufacturers announced centralized systems, using GP computers that could handle a multiplicity of machines. (See Fig. 5.) In these, the operator could insert new information via a data link, and the central computer could modify or generate the needed program.

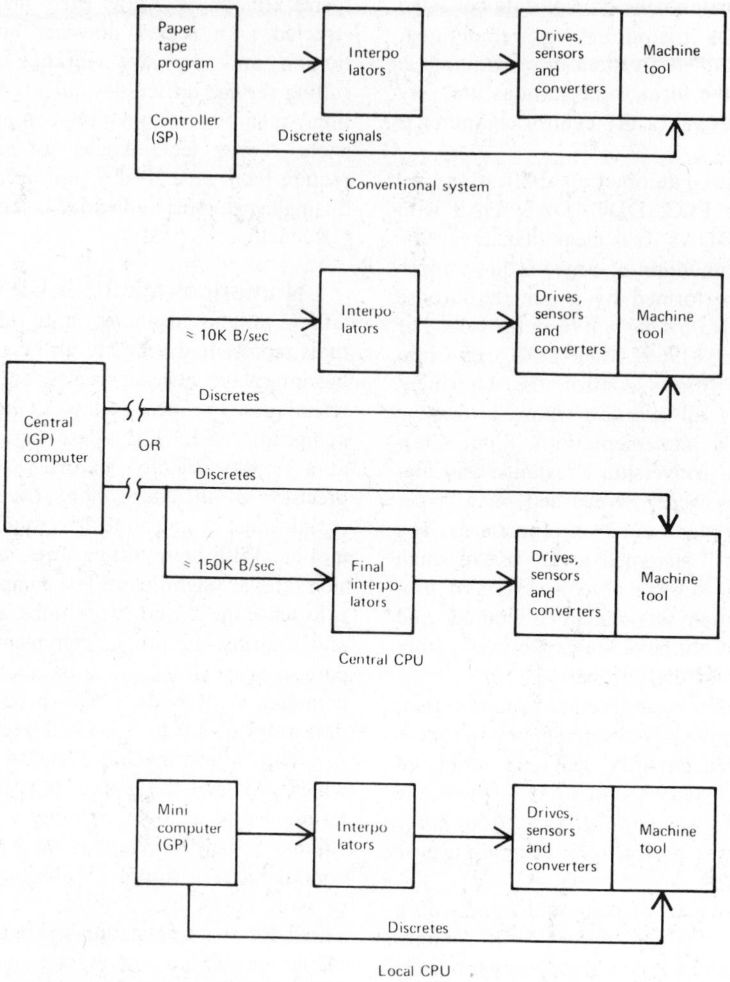


**Fig. 5.** Numerical control systems.

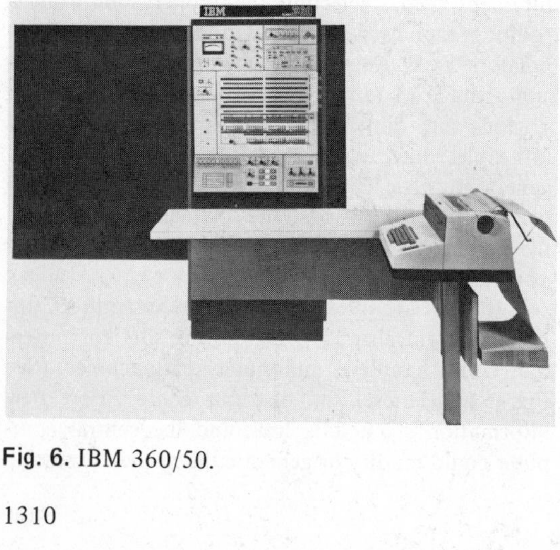


**Fig. 6.** IBM 360/50.

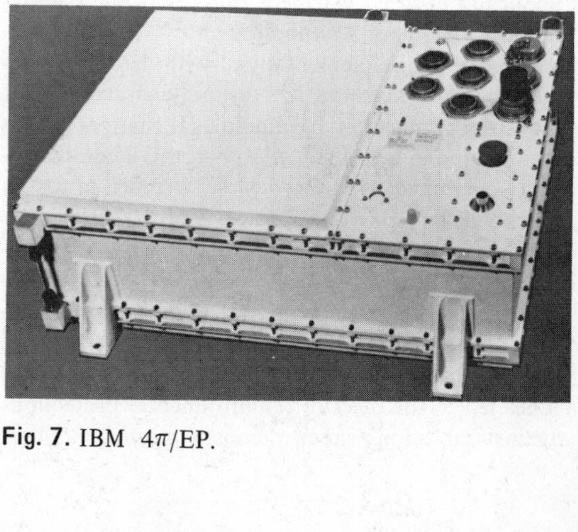

**Fig. 7.** IBM $4\pi$/EP.

One great difficulty was the data rate; none of the systems attempted direct attachment to the position drives. Some offered a modified interpolator, which reduced rates by a factor of 10, while others retained the full interpolator, which reduced rates by a factor of 100. Obviously, the latter system represents a greater cost/machine controlled; the computer provides flexibility, but, except for the paper tape reader, the remainder of the equipment at the machine tool had to be retained.

Rather suddenly, in the early 1970s, the minicomputer inspired a new system design. The functions of the central GP could be provided with a single minicomputer at each machine tool (or group) site. The interpolator can be retained or replaced by the minicomputer. In some installations, the minicomputer may be able to call on a central computer to access the data base and to report on work accomplished.

Numerical machine control is instructive in that special-purpose computers and general-purpose systems are often intermingled. There is a tendency to combine specialized front ends with local and/or central GP computers. In such configurations, the GP portion will absorb all appropriate work, but excessive data rates and highly repetitive fast computation may demand special-purpose facilities; in fact, these front ends are often the key to application feasibility.

**Scientific Applications.** The father of modern computers, ENIAC, built by Eckert and Mauchly in 1946, was a special-purpose machine designed for calculating ballistic trajectories. For each program, the machine had to be rewired by means of strategically located patch cords. There was no logical branching facility, although ENIAC did possess all common arithmetic functions, including very fast multiply and square root features. The IBM 603, the first production electronic calculator (also 1946), was limited to multiplying one 6-digit field by another and punching out a 12-digit result (Rosen, 1969).

By the mid-1950s, machines were fundamentally GP, but even then they exhibited at least partial dedication, especially a scientific versus commercial dichotomy. The scientific machines generally were I/O limited and had fast arithmetic and multiply units. Floating-point binary representations rapidly came into use. Commercial machines tended toward a much greater I/O versatility and less emphasis on arithmetic capability and utilized decimal representations.

The use of highly specialized processors *in conjunction with* general-purpose machines first occurred in a primitive form in 1948 when an IBM 603 was coupled to an IBM Type 405 accounting machine by Northrop Aviation, Inc. The RCA BIZMAC made use of a special-purpose sorter to perform its tape sorts at much higher speed than could be done otherwise. Selection of the tapes to be directed to the sorter could be controlled over a telephonelike dial-up switched network.

In 1959, Prof. G. Estrin of UCLA described a prewired special-purpose machine to be attached to an IBM 7090. Projected speed gains ranged from 2.5 to over 1,000 (for a quadratic sieve). The projected system configuration consisted of the GP computer, a means of transferring arguments to the prewired SP computer, and supervisory control, which coordinated the operations of the two machines.

Other special-purpose computers intended for use with a general-purpose machine include fast Fourier transform (FFT) machines and array processors. The FFT algorithm can, of course, be programmed on a GP machine. In certain signal reduction and analysis applications (e.g., radar data reduction), a substantial portion of the entire computational capability is used in preparing a Fourier transformation on the incoming data. Thus, the use of a specialized "front end" can substantially reduce the total GP requirement. In general, this "front end" activity requires little storage and may operate more or less concurrently with the other GP workload (Bergland, 1969).

The array processor represents a somewhat different problem. As used in data reduction, the array processor is not a front end, but is rather a specialized high-speed executor for special operations. The array processor can be attached to the GP machine so that the arguments are transferred to the array-processor local storage. Unless the operations on the arguments are quite extensive, or the local store is very large, the memory interference generated by the data transfers can seriously slow both the parent and the attached processor.

The array processor generally has a limited instruction set, which can operate on one or a few data types. The local store and the built-in indexing techniques are very fast so that a repetitive series of instructions can proceed much faster than on a GP machine. As an example of attainable results, a commercially available array processor can provide approximately a 50% improvement over a large-scale commercial machine in performance of matrix multiplication (Ruggiero and Coryell, 1969).

Two other aspects of special-purpose scientific computation are noteworthy. The first, the array of processors (single instruction stream, multiple data stream) such as the SOLOMON and ILLIAC familiy. The second is the use of microprogramming to achieve a specialized order set.

In a given machine, a special microprogram can achieve greater speed than a series of "machine instructions," to the extent that the microprogram can reduce memory accesses or reduce computation cycles. Usually, because the capacity of the working registers addressed by the microcode is rather small, memory accesses become the controlling factor in limiting performance gain. Since many contemporary machines already use techniques to overlap and conceal next instruction fetches, gains due to microprogramming are limited to instances where a few operands require an extensive and complex manipulation. In the author's experience, the instances of real gain from specialized microprograms have been very rare, and then more often related to more efficient machine control functions than to more efficient application functions.

**Aerospace Applications.** Aerospace applications (see Buchman, 1968) encompass such a diversity of performance levels and uses that generalizations could be misleading. One statement that can certainly be made is that while most computer applications are sensitive to performance and cost, aerospace computer applications are also particularly sensitive to reliability and physical characteristics such as power, weight, and volume. Table 1 relates several typical aerospace applications to the desired characteristics of the computer.

The earliest aerospace computers were special purpose in architecture as well as implementation. Ballistic missiles were guided by a computer that calculated present position, using DDAs to integrate and rotate the acceleration vectors in accordance with a reference plane established by an inertial reference. The present position was compared to a precalculated trajectory, and steering correction signals were generated.

A more sophisticated approach used the on-board computer to calculate the desired trajectory. This gave considerable freedom in target selection, allowed for optimization of the path, and permitted alternate paths or alternate destinations to be generated. Such machines generally used magnetic drums. Because the DDA function is so easily implemented on a rotating drum, its use for calculating "present position" persisted for many years.

It is apparent that the architectural similarity to machine tool applications is remarkably close, including the use of DDAs and of combined GP and SP machines. As in machine tool control, missile control requires sensing and issuing of discrete commands to control timing and sequencing. In some cases, the computer may also be used to monitor on-board facilities, and even to direct the vehicle in responding to on-board failures that require overt compensation or choice of alternate paths.

The architecture of such computers is now rarely of a special-purpose nature. There may be directly implemented or microprogrammed trigonometric functions to speed up vector rotation, and the input/output section may be quite special in order to accommodate sensor or actuator signals. Such features alone do not warrant a SP classification. The contemporary ballistic missile or launch vehicle computer has special purpose characteristics because of its implementation with stringent emphasis on weight, volume, and reliability.

**Table 1.** Mission Requirements

| Application | Performance* | Reliability† | Physical Characteristics‡ | | |
|---|---|---|---|---|---|
| | | | Power | Weight | Volume |
| Ballistic missiles | 2 | $1 \times 10^4$ | 1 | 2 | 2 |
| Launch vehicles | 4 | $1 \times 10^5$ | 1 | 1 | 1 |
| Unmanned short duration | 10 | $1 \times 10^4$ | 2 | 2 | 2 |
| Manned orbital** | 20 | $1 \times 10^5$ | 2 | 2 | 2 |
| Unmanned long duration | 1 | $1 \times 10^8$ | 3 | 3 | 2 |
| Integrated avionics system | 10 | $1 \times 10^4$ | 1 | 2 | 2 |
| Airborne command and control** | 40 | $1 \times 10^3$ | 1 | 1 | 1 |

* Relative scale: 10 approximates computational capability of IBM 7090.
† Mean time between failure (hours) for system performance of critical functions.
‡ 1 = requirements reasonable; 2 = requirements quite demanding; 3 = requirements crucial and difficult to meet.
** Independent high-reliability guidance system also available.

Before discussing implementations, let us briefly note that computers used in unmanned space flight are often merely sequencing, counting, and timing units that perform functions similar to the PLC described under Industrial Automation. Such machines are clearly special purpose in architecture, and in fact these "programmers" are usually designed specifically for a mission or even for a particular flight. At the other extreme, airborne command and control systems are supplements to, or substitutes for, similar ground-based systems, which demand extensive telecommunication, display, and data base facilities. Thus, the airborne command post is actually only a version of a GP ground-base system. As we shall see, implementation is the distinguishing factor.

Aerospace applications have been a primary testing ground for transistors, integrated circuits, thin-film memories, nondestructive read and read-only memories, high-frequency power conversion, multilayer connection boards, etc. Such techniques received early attention in aerospace applications because most of them led to reduced power consumption, reduced weight, smaller size, and greater reliability. Many of these technologies, after initial development and proof testing in aerospace applications, were adopted for ground-based applications.

**Table 2.** Comparison of Computer Specifications

| | IBM 360/50 | IBM 4Pi/EP |
|---|---|---|
| Weight, lb | 5,200 | 75 |
| Volume, $ft^3$ | 200 | 1.88 |
| Power, kVA | 7 | 0.365 |

*Common characteristics* of both computers. 96K bytes, multiplex channel, standard instruction set.

To emphasize the impact of these technologies, let us compare specifications for two late-1960 machines almost identical in architecture and performance (see Table 2). The IBM 360/50 was intended for ground application and the IBM 4Pi/EP was designed specifically for an aerospace command and control mission. These gains in physical characteristic do not come without a price. First, there is the high development and design cost of the basic technologies. Because of the difficulty of making changes after the parts are assembled, the design must be thoroughly evaluated before construction begins. Most important, minor changes in customer specifications, such as added instructions, additional channels, and modifications to the testing interface can often result in the need for major redesign or retesting. Thus, the user of an aerospace processor must submit his requirements early and be prepared to live with the consequences (see Figs. 6 and 7).

The desire for enhanced reliability sometimes outstrips the technological capabilities currently available. In several cases, special internal designs or special system configurations have been used to enhance processor reliability. For example, the IBM computer used to control the SATURN launch vehicle utilized a "majority voting" scheme. Much of the logic was triplicated; voting circuits inspected outputs, and if a disagreement was indicated, passed on the signal agreed on by two of the inputs. In this processor, the core memory was also duplicated in part to protect vital data.

Since the machine had 3.5 to 4 times as many components as a more conventional organization, the part-failure rate was 3.5 to 4 times higher than a simpler version. Obviously, extremely careful partitioning of the logic and placement of the voters was required to assure usable reliability gains. The result is interesting: For short intervals (hundreds of hours) the probability of success is considerably greater than for a simplex machine. For longer intervals—i.e., when the probability of two failures into a voting node becomes significant—the machine had a lower probability of success than a simplex version.

In addition to such hardware redundancy, much recent work in using encoding techniques to enhance reliability has been done by A. Avižienis and others.

**Trends.** In 1961, an authoritative text on control systems, in justifying the need for special-purpose techniques to control machine tools, stated:

> Furthermore, the furnishing of 15,000 new pieces of data per second would strain the capacities of even the fastest presently available computing instruments, to say nothing of the high cost of such machines (upwards of one million dollars). (Rosenberg, 1961.)

Today, a richer function than the author intended is easily provided by a minicomputer costing less than $10,000. This anecdote clearly illustrates the principle underlying the trend in special-purpose computers; when the economics of an application mitigate against a GP architecture, designers will exert ingenuity to devise a specialized digital technique that can perform the limited function indicated. As technologies improve, the performance/cost and reliability of GP machines increase, and soon the functional limitations of the special-purpose architecture are no longer acceptable: The SP machine is replaced by a GP machine.

Occasionally, GP machines adopt architectural features such as priority interrupt features, fast task switching via multiple register sets, and special machine instructions, all of which further enhance the capability of absorbing time-dependent or specialized functions. Current technologies are sufficiently reliable so that the implementation used for GP and SP machines is similar except in aerospace computers. The advent of large-scale integration may narrow the gap to the point that only exotic machines, such as space-borne computers, are distinguished by implementation as having a special-purpose character.

Counter to the trend of architectural and implementation conformity is a trend toward joining a number of separate machines onto a system configuration wherein the function performed by each individual machine is dedicated to a specific purpose. The advent of low-cost logic and the prospect of CPU-on-a-chip design invite the agglomeration of several machines in a single set to serve specialized functions. This leads to GP computers that contain somewhat specialized quasi-independent internal processors that are asynchronously coupled. These "second level" processors perform functions such as sequence control, floating-point instruction execution, or handling of I/O operations.

Combinations of cooperative machines are often framed into explicit networks where some of the independent processors are specialized in function, such as the "front end" FFT processor or telecommunication handler. The independent processors may act to distribute the intelligence of the network, especially to reduce communication costs by transferring part of the system intelligence to remote sites. Examples are display generator-controllers and terminals with built-in computation capability. Such networks may have secondary nodes between the terminals and the central computer. These nodes are often communication controllers, which can route, edit, multiplex, and even store-and-forward messages. Many of these cooperating machines are special, at least in their balance of I/O versus computational capability.

The trend toward tightly coupled systems of processors to achieve new levels of performance or reliability will motivate continuing development of highly specialized second-level machines. The trend toward distributed intelligence networks will assure the continuing development of digital machines that are balanced in performance and functional characteristics toward a specific purpose.

Nonetheless, stand-alone SP computers are becoming rare except where the functions are very limited. Although GP computers may show some dedication to a particular application, the architectural and implementation differences among them are no longer strong. That is, the distinction is not DDA versus GP, but "mini" versus commercial, or floating-point performance versus I/O performance.

### References

*Note: Control Engineering*, published monthly by Dun-Donnelley Publishing Company, has been a continuing source of information in the industrial automation application area.

1961. Rosenberg, J. "Numerical Control of Machines," in Grabbe, Ramo, and Woolridge (Eds.), *Handbook of Automation, Computation and Control*. New York: John Wiley.

1968. Buchman, A. S. "Aerospace Computers," in *Advances in Computers*, vol. 9. New York: Academic Press.

1969. Bergland, G. D. "A Guided Tour of the FFT," *IEEE Spectrum* (July).

1969. Rosen, Saul. "Electronic Computers: A Historical Survey," *Computing Surveys*, Vol. 1, No. 1 (March).

1969. Ruggiero, J. T., and D. A. Coryell. "An Auxiliary Processing System for Array Calculations," *IBM Systems Journal*, Vol. 8, No. 2.

A. S. Buchman

# SPEECH RECOGNITION

For articles on related subjects *see* Artificial Intelligence; and Pattern Recognition.

For article on related term *see* Bandwidth.

It is clear that if a computer could be programmed to recognize human speech, this would provide a means of great power and flexibility for human/computer communication. In order to grasp the magnitude of this problem, it is necessary first to understand some of the characteristics of human speech.

The energy in speech covers a wide range of audible frequencies, although those components above 3 kHz are not important for human communication.

A particularly meaningful representation of the speech signal is produced by the sound spectrograph. This records the short-term power spectrum as a function of the two dimensions: frequency (vertical axis) and time (horizontal axis). The local power density is represented by the blackness of the trace. This record is called a "spectrogram" (Fig. 1).

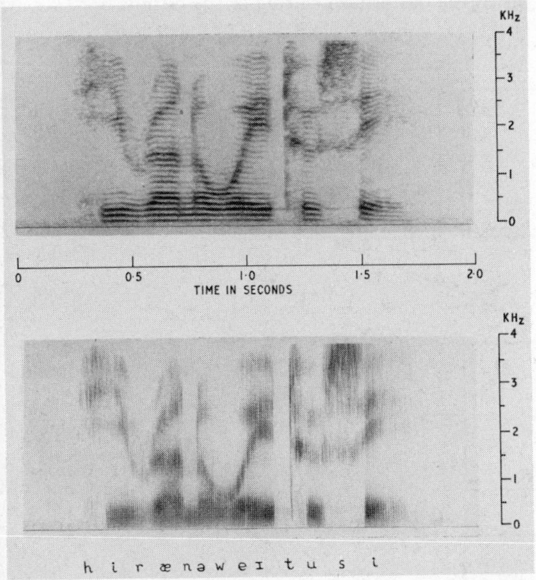


**Fig. 1.** Spectrogram of the sentence "He ran away to sea." The upper record is a narrow-band analysis made with a 30-Hz bandwidth filter. The fine horizontal lines are due to individual harmonics in the buzzing sound produced at the larynx. The lower record is a wide-band analysis made with a 240-Hz bandwidth filter. The fine vertical lines are due to the sound of individual pulses of air emitted by the larynx. The dark bands, or formants, are due to resonance peaks in the acoustic response of the vocal tract. Below the bottom figure the spoken phrase is written in phonetic symbols of the International Phonetic Association. Each "letter" represents a single sound.

The dark bands seen in the spectrogram are called "formants." They are caused by the lowest frequency modes of resonance in the vocal tract (the mouth, nose, and throat cavities), and they are particularly significant in human speech perception.

There are two distinctly different sources of sound in speech. One occurs during "voiced" speech sounds such as the vowels (e.g., "EE," "AH," "AW") and vowel-like consonants (e.g., "W," "L," "M"). Vibrations of the vocal folds (or vocal cords) breaks up the flow of air from the lungs into sharp pulses. These occur typically at a repetition rate of 70 to 250 Hz, and the sound is very rich in harmonics. The other source of sound is a hiss caused by air turbulence in the mouth. This is heard in the "unvoiced" consonants such as "S," "SH," "F."

Source spectrum components that coincide with vocal tract resonances are enhanced, giving rise to the formant patterns. The formants move about in frequency as the tongue, lips, jaw, etc., move during speech.

A more detailed discussion of speech production and speech signal analysis can be found in Flanagan (1972).

An automatic recognizer can normally be considered as a two-stage device (Fig. 2). The first stage performs signal analysis and data reduction, resulting in a simplified pattern or a set of extracted characteristic features. The second stage performs pattern classification, ending in a decision about which word or words were spoken. There are two general classes of recognizer, which will be referred to here as the *pattern-matching* type and the *feature-detecting* type.

The pattern-matching word recognizer (Fig. 3) stores a quantized representation of the frequency-amplitude-time pattern for a representative utterance of each word in the recognition vocabulary. The stored patterns are called "standards" or "templates."

A word of unknown identity is then classified by comparing its pattern with each template pattern to see which one it most nearly resembles. The comparison is often determined in the form of a score obtained by summing the squared differences between the signal levels in corresponding cells on the quantized frequency-time plane. The process can be thought of as finding the distance between multidimensional vectors representing the word patterns. Since the words can be spoken at different rates, it is common to normalize the pattern time durations before making the comparisons.

The pattern-matching recognizer has several advantages when the input words are spoken in isolation. It does not require any linguistic or other knowledge; the recognition vocabulary can be changed simply by replacing the stored examples;

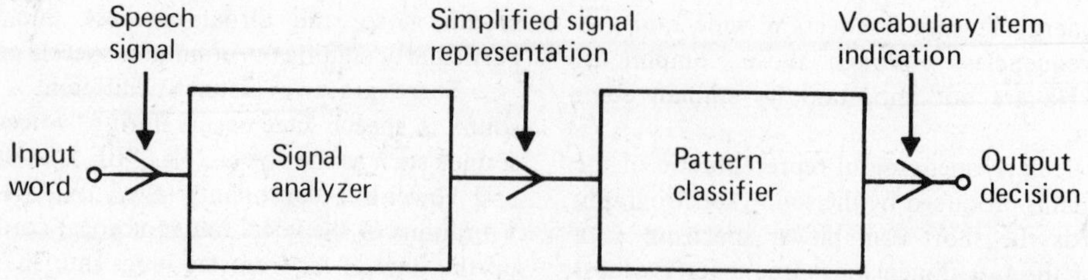


**Fig. 2.** Highly simplified view of an automatic speech recognizer. The signal analyzer transforms the very complex speech waveform into a simpler representation, hopefully without losing any information needed for word identification. The pattern classifier decides which item of the machine's recognition vocabulary was intended by the speaker, on the basis of the pattern appearing at the output of the signal analyzer.

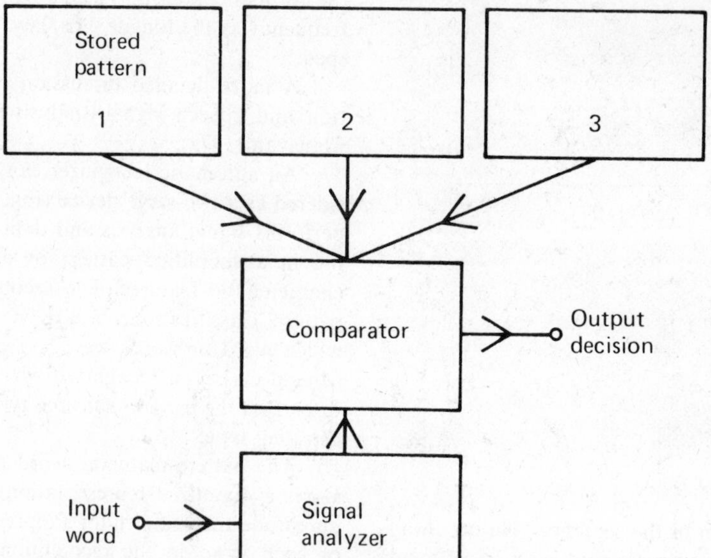


**Fig. 3.** Pattern-matching word recognizer. The pattern produced by signal analysis is compared with a set of stored patterns derived from words of known identity. The input word is assumed to be the same as the word whose stored pattern is most similar.

and the processing is closely related to optical pattern recognition, for which a large body of knowledge and experience exists. Disadvantages include the fact that complete word patterns must be stored, and it is usually found that more than one example of each word is required to cover the normal range of pronunciation.

A different philosophy is employed in the feature-detecting word recognizer (Fig. 4). This attempts to identify the various spectral and temporal characteristics that distinguish the sound segments of which words are composed. The spoken word is then classified on the basis of the sequence of sound segments indicated by the detected feature ensembles.

The sound segments are usually thought of as the equivalent of letters in the written language. The phonetician would refer to elementary sound units of this type as *phonemes*; and *speech recognizers*, which identify sound segments, are often referred to as *phoneme recognizers*, although the term "phone recognizer" would be more correct.

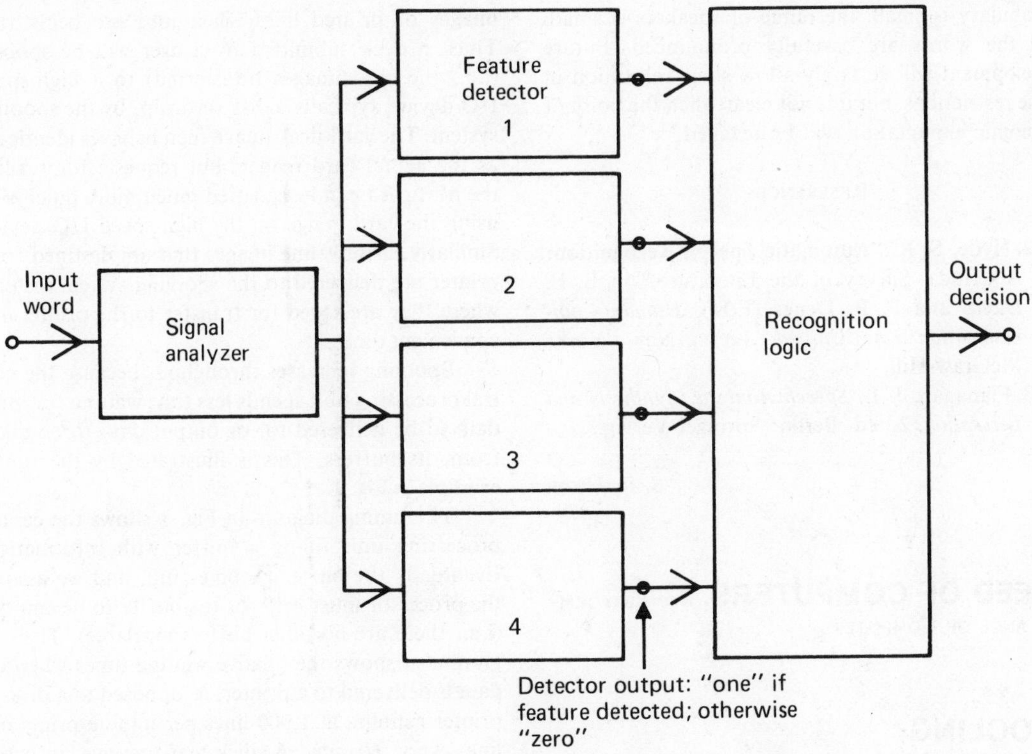


**Fig. 4.** Feature-detecting word recognizer. Each detector is designed to detect the occurrence of one characteristic feature in the word pattern. The recognition logic decides on the identity of the input word, on the basis of the ensemble of detected features. This decision may rely on lookup tables of feature sets, probabilities, etc., and many incorporate error-correcting procedures.

When the recognition vocabulary is large, the feature-detecting recognizer should require less information storage than the pattern-matching recognizer, and it is more appropriate for the recognition of connected speech. But there are serious difficulties in the isolation and identification of the characteristic features, and present knowledge of these features is inadequate for proper exploitation of these advantages.

The literature up to 1970 (Hyde, 1972) describes more than 60 different recognition schemes which have been studied. The first successful recognizer was demonstrated at Bell Telephone Laboratories in 1952. It could recognize ten digits with a high degree of accuracy when these were carefully spoken, one at a time, by the one speaker for which it was adjusted.

In the 1950s, recognizers were built entirely in special-purpose hardware. With the advent of powerful, fast computers, it became possible to implement complete recognition systems; but for speed and simplicity it has been quite common to use a hardware signal analyzer, based on well-established principles, followed by a software pattern classifier.

The amount of success in the field of automatic speech recognition has not been very great. Research over the past 20 years has not brought us far from first-generation techniques, and many recent studies have simply repeated earlier ones, using new analysis tools. There is considerable doubt whether an economic automatic recognizer can be designed for use with real conversational speech, considering the knowledge available at present.

Speech is designed for communication between sophisticated and intelligent beings under noisy environmental conditions. The information is highly redundant, and is encoded on a range of processing levels: acoustic, phonetic, linguistic, semantic, etc. On any one level, it may appear highly ambiguous.

Even under favorable conditions, normal conversation involves processing at the highest levels of human intellect. To match human ability in this respect will require an (literally) intelligent machine. Present techniques can be made to work well for simple tasks such as machine control, provided the vocabulary is small, the range of speakers is small, and the words are carefully pronounced. Future development will certainly allow some relaxation in these restrictions, but it is not clear when the point of economic exploitation will be reached.

REFERENCES

1972. Hyde, S. R. "Automatic Speech Recognition: A Critical Survey of the Literature," in E. E. David and P. B. Denes (Eds.), *Human Communication: A Unified View*. New York: McGraw-Hill.

1973. Flanagan, J. L. *Speech Analysis, Synthesis and Perception*, 2d ed. Berlin: Springer-Verlag.

S. R. HYDE

## SPEED OF COMPUTERS. *See* PERFORMANCE OF COMPUTERS.

## SPOOLING

For articles on related subjects *see* INPUT-OUTPUT CONTROL SYSTEM; INPUT-OUTPUT DEVICES; and MEMORY: Auxiliary.

For articles on related terms *see* BUFFER; JOB; MULTIPROGRAMMING; and TASK.

Spooling (simultaneous peripheral operations on line) is a method of handling low-speed input/output devices commonly implemented in operating systems to increase throughput. This increase is accomplished by using only high-speed I/O devices to supply images of decks of punched cards or to receive images of printed lines when jobs are being run. Thus, a deck submitted by a user will be spooled (i.e., the card images transferred) to a high-speed I/O device, typically a disk or drum, by the spooling system. The card-deck image then behaves identically as the actual card reader, but requests for reading the next card can be satisfied much more quickly by using the card image on the high-speed I/O device. Similarly, a job's line images that are destined for a printer are delivered to the spooling system instead, where they are saved for transfer to the printer at a convenient time.

Spooling increases throughput because the central processing unit spends less time waiting for input data to be delivered to, or output data to be taken from, its buffers. This is illustrated by the simple example in Fig. 1.

The timing diagram in Fig. 1 shows the central processing unit filling a buffer with information. Eventually the buffer becomes full, and we assume the processor must wait for the buffer to be emptied (i.e., there are no other buffers available). The diagram also shows the relative waiting times when the data is delivered to a printer, as opposed to a disk. A printer running at 1,000 lines per minute prints one line every 60 ms. A disk can receive information about four times as fast, i.e., one line in 15 ms. Thus, the disk unit empties the buffer more quickly and less time (potential main-processor working time) is spent waiting. Of course the images will have to be transferred to the printer eventually, but not at the expense of main processor waiting time.

The idea of transferring card images to a higher speed I/O device (say, tape) before actual job processing—and similarly for line images destined for the printer—existed in early operating systems. In those systems, the "card to tape" and "tape to printer" functions were carried out on a separate

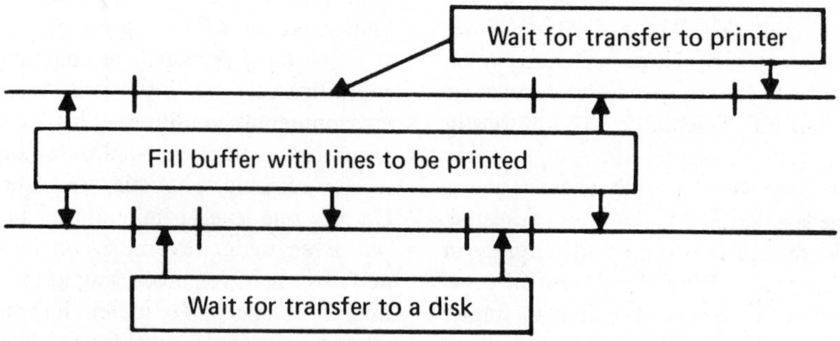


**Fig. 1.** Relative waiting times of output data delivered to a printer and to a disk.

computer, which either operated independently of the main processor or communicated with it. In both cases, there were at least two computers present. This is not the case with a spooling system. Rather, on a single system that is capable of supporting multiprogramming, the tasks "card to disk" and "disk to printer" are incorporated as members of the set of tasks to be supported. Thus, the I/O devices used by the spooling system are truly on line with respect to the main computer. System throughput is increased because these two tasks take relatively little processor time, and at the same time reduce the time that user tasks (the ultimate producers or consumers of data) wait for I/O.

Normally, spooling packages perform many other services in addition to the transfer of data from low- to high-speed I/O devices, and vice versa. For example, assuming that some jobs occupy the main computer for a long enough time so that several other new jobs can be spooled to a disk, it is not necessary to initiate the new jobs in the same order that they were spooled. Particularly time, storage, I/O device, or other estimates can be used to initiate jobs in a manner that will increase throughput. Similarly, actual numbers of lines generated for printing can be used to schedule the flow of work through the printers.

Other desirable benefits that accrue from a spooling system are the ability to simulate the operation of several independent card readers, using only a single one (thus creating the effect of multiple-batch streams); and the ability to print multiple copies of a job's output. Both advantages are due to the ability to locate directly and/or re-read the card or line images on the direct-access storage device.

R. W. TAYLOR

# STACK

For articles on related subjects *see* DATA STRUCTURES; LISTS AND LIST PROCESSING; POLISH NOTATION; RECURSION; and SUBPROGRAMS, CALLING.
For articles on related terms *see* FIFO-LIFO; and TREE.

A *stack* is a linear list for which all insertions and deletions, and usually all accesses, are made at one end of the list. The properties of a simple stack may be illustrated by a railroad switching network having a track into which railroad cars may be inserted and removed from only one end, as in Fig. 1. At any given time, only the most recently entered railroad car may be removed from the track. Railroad cars are said to enter and leave the track in a *last-in-first-out* (LIFO) order.

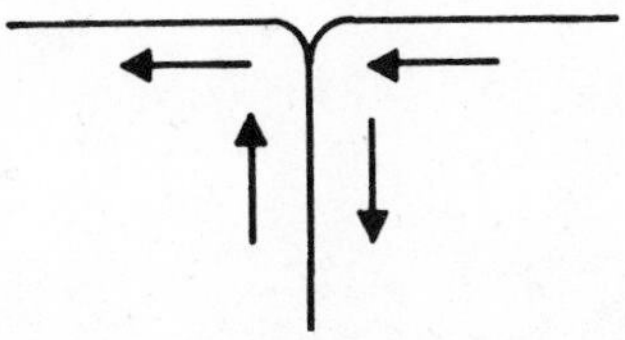

**Fig. 1**

A stack may alternatively be defined as a linear list whose elements may be created and deleted only in a last-in-first-out order. Stacks arise in computational processes dealing with structures whose components are nested, as in the following example.

*Example from Arithmetic Expression Evaluation.* The expression (3+(4*5)) has a subexpression (4*5), which is nested within the complete expression and is conveniently evaluated by first converting it to the parentheses-free postfix notation 345*+ (in which the operator * immediately follows its operands 4, 5, and the operator + immediately follows its operands 3 and 45*), and then using an operand stack for evaluation. The evaluation of the expression 345*+, using a stack, is illustrated in Fig. 2, and is defined in detail below.

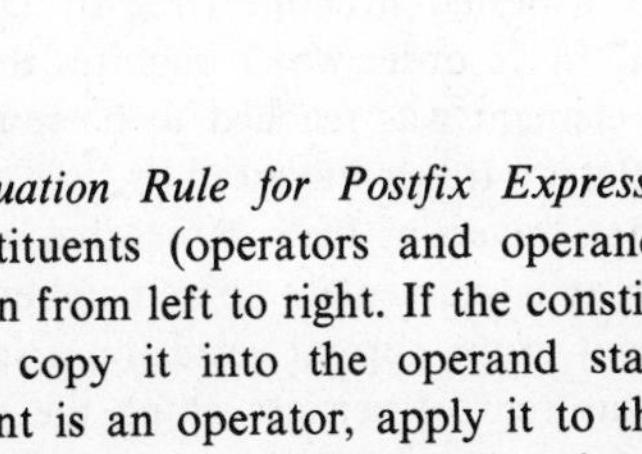


**Fig. 2**

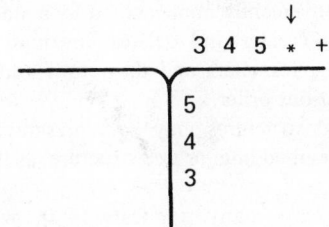

*Evaluation Rule for Postfix Expressions.* Scan the constituents (operators and operands) of the expression from left to right. If the constituent is an operand, copy it into the operand stack. If the constituent is an operator, apply it to the two top elements of the operand stack and replace these two elements by the result of applying the operator to its operands.

A(B,C(D,E))

1 A
2 B
2 C
3 D
3 E

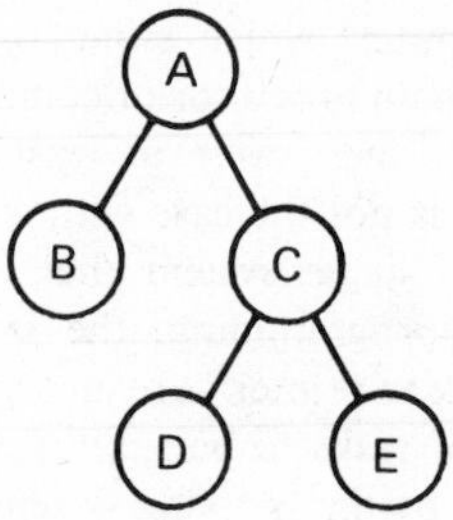


Fig. 3

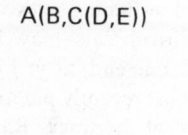

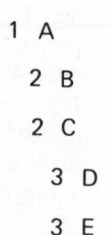

The elements 3,4,5 in Fig. 2 have been placed in the operand stack and the operator "*" is about to be scanned. According to the evaluation rules, * is applied to the two top elements (5 and 4) of the operand stack, which causes the elements 5 and 4 to be replaced by the value 20. The operator + is now applied to the two top elements (20 and 3) of the operand stack, which causes these elements to be replaced by the value 23.

Arithmetic expression evaluation is conveniently implemented by stacks because expressions may contain subexpressions nested inside them to an arbitrary level. A further example of nested program structure arises in the case of subroutines (procedures).

Subroutine calls have the property that a called subroutine must be completely executed before return to the higher-level subroutine that called it. Thus, subroutines are executed in a last-in–first-out order (relative to the order in which they are called), and are conveniently implemented by a stack mechanism that creates and deletes information about subroutine parameters and the return address in a last-in–first-out order.

Nested structures may be represented by parentheses, embedding, or tree structure, as illustrated in Fig. 3.

There are many applications in which the elements of a nested structure (tree structure) must be "visited" in an order which requires the path by which the element was reached to be remembered. For example, if a tree is traversed by first visiting the root and then traversing the subtrees in a left-to-right order, then it is convenient to remember the path from the root to the current vertex on a stack, since successor subtrees of vertices along the path from the root to the current vertex must be examined in a last-in–first-out order if they are to complete the traversal of all vertices of the tree.

REFERENCE

1968. Knuth, D. E. *The Art of Computer Programming*, vol. 1. Reading, Mass.: Addison-Wesley.

P. WEGNER

# STANDARDS

For articles on related subjects *see* ASSOCIATION FOR COMPUTING MACHINERY; CONFERENCE ON DATA SYSTEMS LANGUAGES; DATA PROCESSING MANAGEMENT ASSOCIATION; and JOINT USERS GROUP.

The availability of standards within any industry provides both the manufacturer and the consumer with a basis for the efficient operation of their respective tasks while at the same time promoting and encouraging fair trade. To the manufacturer, standardization provides monetary savings through the use of mass production techniques over a range of closely related products, by the production of uniform quality items, and through the decrease in developmental costs by the use of standard designs and equipment. To the user, standards improve his ability to evaluate adequately the products of competitive vendors and, by the use of interface standards, to develop systems which better suit his needs and requirements by the utilization of mixed manufacturer configurations.

**Computer Industry Standards.** Although the benefits of standardization of the elements of the computer industry are obvious, the timing of the publication and acceptance of standards is highly critical. Throughout the brief history of the development of standards related to the computer industry, the process of development has been continually greeted by the opinions of "too early" or "too late." On one hand, the premature standardization of computer elements can lead to a stagnation of the development of the product by being overly restrictive and therefore stifling further research in that area. In addition, standards adopted at an early stage of the development of a product can associate it so closely with the (then) current technology that no advantages can be taken of later technological developments.

The major benefit to be attained by early standardization is that the standard might recognize and codify the fundamental features of the element under consideration, and provide a uniform and logical means for the further development of the element.

On the other hand, the development of standards after the fact of product development can lead to confusion and rejection (by either misuse or misinterpretation) of the proposed standard. Where a product has been in the marketplace for some considerable period, and where there exists more than one manufacturer for the product, with a not inconsiderable body of consumers or users, the "Johnny-come-lately" approach to standardization is predestined to effective failure. Although standards would be beneficial in such situations, it is obvious that few manufacturers can afford to rewrite their software or to retool an assembly line; further, consumers will not have interest in modifications as long as their current requirements are met. Only when software is to be rewritten or an assembly is to be retooled in any case, is it advantageous to the manufacturer to contemplate conformance with the standard, and only when considering upgrading or replacing software or equipment is it worthwhile for the consumer or user to refer to the standard. On the national scale, such situations must occur daily, but on the individual scale, the standard that is "too late" has little direct influence.

Rarely, if ever, has the process of standardization of elements of the computer industry reached the middle ground between the two extremes of "too early" and "too late." Without any means for enforcement of standards in the United States, industry is paying dearly for its lack of attention to standardization efforts. It has been estimated that one-quarter of the total available computer power in the United States is being used to provide conversion systems between dissimilar, nonstandardized (or nonstandard) elements of computer systems. One need only look at the complexity of input/output conversion (software) packages to realize that a standard, common representation system would be highly beneficial. Even in other countries where government control and enforcement of standards is stricter, the predominance of United States companies in the computer industry effectively controls the production of national standards.

**Standards Organizations.** Within the United States, standards are developed and published on a voluntary basis, since there exists no governmental agency with direct control over the use of standards within the computer (or any other) industry. Further, there exist no congressional authorizations or appropriations that directly support or fund the development of standards for use within the United States. However, the National Bureau of Standards (a division of the Department of Commerce) has direct responsibility for the development of standards for use within the federal government and for compliance with those standards by vendors of equipment to the federal government. Since the majority of computer equipment manufacturers are vendors not only to the U.S. Government, but also to all consumers and users (nationally and internationally), federally enforced standards can be expected to be de facto industry standards, merely to save the cost of producing two separate lines of equipment. While the National Bureau of Standards has the authority to develop independent federal standards, the recognition of what would be the overall costs of purchasing special custom-designed equipment for the Government requires the Bureau to actively participate in and promote the voluntary standards efforts of the computer industry.

The American National Standards Institute (ANSI) is the national clearinghouse and coordinating agency for voluntary standards in the United States. It is a nonprofit (membership) organization incorporated under the laws of the State of New York and is located at 1430 Broadway in New York City. It is a federation of approximately 140 trade associations and professional societies, together with 750 companies that are dues-paying members.

ANSI was originally organized as the American Engineering Standards Committee (AESC) in 1918 by five engineering societies: American Institute of Electrical Engineers, American Society of Mechanical Engineers, American Society of Civil Engineers, American Society of Mining and Metallurgical Engineers, and American Society for Testing Materials. The AESC's initial purpose was to provide means for coordinating the standards issued by its founders, eliminating confusion and duplication among those standards. Its first act was to invite three federal government departments to join and work with the founding societies; the War Department, the Navy Department, and the Department of Commerce accepted the invitation. Enlarged in 1920 by the addition of trade associations, as well as more technical and professional societies, the AESC in 1928 was reorganized as the American Standards Association (ASA) to provide a more workable structure. The principles and procedures that were developed by the founders basically applied to the work of the American Standards Association through 1966, when ASA became the United States of America Standards Institute (USASI). In 1969, the present name, American National Standards Institute, was adopted.

As the national clearinghouse for standards, ANSI provides the machinery for developing and approving standards that are supported by a national consensus. Its constitution states: "In standardization practice a consensus is achieved when substantial agreement is reached by concerned interests according to the judgment of a duly appointed authority. Consensus implies much more than the concept of a simple majority, but not necessarily unanimity."

Since its inception, ANSI has published over 2,800 American National Standards, of which about 35 are directly related to the computer industry.

ANSI is the United States member body of the International Standards Organization (ISO). The United States' viewpoints to be presented in the technical work of the ISO may be developed through the interested ANSI sectional committee, through a competent committee of another standards organization, or through a committee specifically organized as an Advisory Committee to an ISO Technical Committee. The work of the technical committees eventually results in ISO Draft International Standards (DIS), which may be embodied in the national standards of the ISO member bodies. Conversely, national standards of the member bodies may be embodied in DIS, and through this mechanism develop into other national standards.

To provide direct supervision of the hundreds of ANSI technical activities, there exists within ANSI a number of boards, each responsible for several efforts in a particular area of standardization. One such board is the Information Systems Technical Advisory Board (ISTAB). American National Standards Committee X3 (ANSC-X3) for Computers and Information Processing, along with the standards committees for Office Machines (ANSC-X4), Terminology for Automatic Control (ANSC-85), and Library Sciences and Documentation (ANSC-X39) are advised by the ISTAB. The ISTAB is responsible for all aspects of standardization of systems that transmit, store, or process analog, symbolic, or encoded representations of information, including satellite or control systems, peripheral equipment, and auxiliary devices that significantly influence the effective utilization of composite information processing systems.

The American National Standards Committee for Computers and Information Processing (ANSC-X3) was established in 1960 and was given the task of standardization related to systems, computers, equipments, devices, and media for information processing systems. The Committee is sponsored by the Computer and Business Equipment Manufacturers Association (CBEMA), 1828 L Street, N.W., Washington, D.C. 20036. As the sponsor, CBEMA acts as the secretariat providing essential administrative support and, through its standards committee, is responsible to ANSI for the general administration of ANSC-X3. CBEMA has the authority to appoint the chairman of ANSC-X3, and through its administrative services is responsible for the processing of proposed standards to be forwarded to ISTAB and for publication as an American National Standard.

The membership of the ANSC-X3 is approved by CBEMA and represents associations, professional societies, manufacturers (both of hardware and software), government agencies, and other bodies with an express interest in standards related to computers and information processing. These member bodies are categorized into three groups (consumer, general interest, and producer), the members of which are so chosen that no group has a majority. The major responsibilities of the ANSC-X3 include the development and approval of standards related to the computer industry and the development of national positions for presentation to the corresponding ISO committee (ISO/TC 97). ANSC-X3 accomplishes these tasks through two major committees: SPARC (Standards Planning and Requirements Committee) and SSC (Standards Steering Committee).

The first committee (SPARC) is the research and study arm of ANSC-X3, responsible to and responsive to the ANSC-X3 committee for the identification of the needs and requirements of the industry for standards. The process of determining the need, the justification, and the availability of resources and technical ability for the development of a standard is performed by a subcommittee. Having identified the need, justified the work, con-

**Table 1.** Listing of ANSC-X3 Organizations

| | |
|---|---|
| X3 | Computers and Information Processing |
| ISTAB | Information Systems Technical Advisory Board |
| X3/IAC | International Advisory Committee |
| X3/SPARC | Standards Planning and Requirements Committee |
| X3/SPARC/DISP | Display Parameters |
| X3/SPARC/DOCN | Documentation |
| X3/SPARC/FDII | Format Description for Information Interchange |
| X3/SPARC/JOVL | JOVIAL |
| X3/SPARC/OSCL | Operating System Control Languages |
| X3/SPARC/PERF | Performance Evaluation |
| X3/SPARC/TEXT | Codes for Textual Data |
| X3/SSC | Standards Steering Committee |
| X3A1 | Optical Character Recognition (OCR) |
| X3A1A | Font Design |
| X3A11 | Handwritten Characters for OCR |
| X3A12 | Print Quality Specifications |
| X3A13 | Applications and Evaluations |
| X3A7 | Magnetic Ink Character Recognition |
| X3B1 | Magnetic Tape |
| X3B2 | Perforated Tape |
| X3B3 | Punched Cards (Physical) |
| X3B4 | Edge Punched Cards |
| X3B7 | Interchangeable Magnetic Disk Media |
| X3B71 | Mechanical Characteristics of Magnetic Disks |
| X3B72 | Magnetic Characteristics of Magnetic Disks |
| X3B73 | Magnetic Disk Control Formats |
| X3J1 | Composite Language Development |
| X3J3 | Fortran |
| X3J4 | Cobol Standards |
| X3J41 | Surveys |
| X3J42 | Compiler Feature Availability |
| X3J43 | Cobol Information Bulletin |
| X3J44 | Cobol Standard Maintenance |
| X3J7 | APT |
| X3J8 | Algol |
| X3K1 | Project Documentation |
| X3K2 | Flowcharts |
| X3K3 | Alphanumeric Presentation |
| X3K5 | Terminology and Glossary |
| X3K51 | Dictionary Maintenance |
| X3K52 | International Vocabulary |
| X3K53 | General Dictionary |
| X3K6 | Network-Oriented Project Management |
| X3L2 | Character Codes |
| X3L21 | Transition to ASCII |
| X3L5 | Data Formats, Related Sets and Applications |
| X3L8 | Representations of Data Elements |
| X3L81 | Data Standardization Criteria |
| X3L82 | Time Designations |
| X3L83 | Individual and Business Identifications |
| X3L84 | Geographic Units |
| X3L86 | Quantitative Expressions |
| X3S3 | Data Transmission |
| X3S33 | Data Communications Formats |
| X3S34 | Data Communications Control Procedures |
| X3S35 | System Performance |
| X3S36 | Digital Data Transmission Speeds |
| X3T9 | I/O Interface Standards |

firmed the availability of resources, and determined that the work is within the limits of current technology, SPARC recommends to ANSC-X3 the establishment of a technical committee under the supervision of SSC for the actual standard development. Once approved by ANSC-X3, the Standards Steering Committee establishes the technical committee and oversees the work of the committee.

It is important to note that at the technical committee level (including SPARC, its subcommittees, and SSC), all membership is based on technical qualifications rather than organizational membership. Thus, while the membership of ANSC-X3 represents specific organizations, the membership of the other committees consists of individuals. In the early 1970s, the committees of ANSC-X3 (listed in Table 1) were working on approximately 120 separate projects, including the tasks of maintaining and updating existing standards. The list of approved American National Standards developed by ANSC-X3 is given in Table 2.

Although ANSI is responsible for the coordination of national voluntary standards in the United States, the Institute has never established itself as the sole organization for the development of standards-related information. In fact, over one-third of the standards published by ANSI originated from outside the ANSI organization. The only requirement placed on these externally originating standards is that they be submitted by competent organizations, developed through their own procedures, and be supported by a consensus of the interested organ-

**Table 2.** List of ANSC-X3 Standards (as of 1974) on Computers and Information Processing.

| | |
|---|---|
| X3.1-1969 | Synchronous Signaling Rates for Data Transmission |
| X3.2-1970 | Print Specifications for Magnetic Ink Character Recognition |
| X3.3-1970 | Bank Check Specifications for Magnetic Ink Character Recognition |
| X3.4-1968 | Code for Information Interchange |
| X3.5-1970 | Flowchart Symbols and Their Usage in Information Processing |
| X3.6-1965 | Perforated Tape Code for Information Interchange |
| X3.9-1966 | Fortran |
| X3.10-1966 | Basic Fortran |
| X3.11-1969 | Specifications for General Purpose Paper Cards for Information Processing |
| X3.12-1970 | Vocabulary for Information Processing |
| X3.14-1972 | Recorded Magnetic Tape for Information Exchange |
| X3.15-1966 | Code for Information Interchange in Serial-by-Bit Data Transmission |
| X3.16-1966 | Character Structure and Character Parity Sense for Serial-by-Bit Data Communication in the American National Standard Code for Information Interchange |
| X3.17-1966 | Character Set for Optical Character Recognition |
| X3.18-1967 | One-Inch Perforated Paper Tape for Information Interchange |
| X3.19-1967 | Eleven-Sixteenths Inch Perforated Paper Tape for Information Interchange |
| X3.20-1967 | Take-Up Reels for One-Inch Perforated Tape for Information Interchange |
| X3.21-1967 | Rectangular Holes in Twelve-Row Punched Cards |
| X3.22-1973 | Recorded Magnetic Tape for Information Interchange (800 CPI, NRZI) |
| X3.23-1968 | Cobol |
| X3.24-1968 | Signal Quality at Interface Between Data Processing Terminal Equipment and Synchronous Data Communication Equipment for Serial Data Transmission |
| X3.25-1968 | Character Structure and Character Parity Sense for Parallel-by-Bit Communication in the American National Standard Code for Information Interchange |
| X3.26-1970 | Hollerith Punched Card Code |
| X3.27-1969 | Magnetic Tape Labels for Information Interchange |
| X3.28-1971 | Procedures for the Use of the Communication Control Characters of American National Standard Code for Information Interchange in Specified Data Communication Links |
| X3.29-1971 | Specification for Properties of Unpunched Paper Perforator Tape |
| X3.30-1971 | Representation for Calendar Date and Ordinal Date for Information Interchange |
| X3.31-1973 | Structure for the Identification of the Counties of the United States for Information Exchange |
| X3.32-1973 | Graphic Representation of Control Characters of ASCII |
| X3.34-1972 | Interchange Rolls of Perforated Tape for Information Interchange |
| X3.38-1972 | Identification of States of the United States (including the District of Columbia) for Information Interchange |
| X3.39-1973 | Recorded Magnetic Tape for Information Exchange |
| X3.40-1973 | Unrecorded Magnetic Tape for Information Interchange |
| X2.3.4-1959 | (To be redesignated as an X3 standard) Method of Charting Paperwork Procedures |

izations in the field of application. In the particular area of Data Systems Languages, ANSC-X3 is supported by developmental work by the Conference on Data Systems Languages (CODASYL).

CODASYL is not a standards-setting body, but instead an informal and voluntary organization specifically established to design and develop techniques and languages to assist in data systems analysis and implementation. Specifically, CODASYL operates four committees: the Data Definition Language Committee, the Programming Language Committee, the Planning Committee, and the Systems Committee. The overall organization is supervised by the Executive Committee, the membership of which is by individual nomination and election.

The most widely known products of CODASYL are the Cobol language, which was subsequently accepted as the basis for the American National Standard Cobol X3.23, and the Data Base Reports. The Programming Languages Committee also publishes, on an as-needed basis, a Cobol Information Bulletin (CIB) which reports on the proposals for the development of Cobol, and gives interpretations and clarifications of existing specifications.

The international aspects of standardization are important to United States manufacturers of both hardware and software, since they provide over 30% of the equipment to the free world outside the United States. Of particular importance to the information-processing community is the work of the International Standards Organization (ISO) and its technical committee TC 97 (Computers and Information Processing).

ISO was established in 1947 to promote the development of standards in order to facilitate international exchange of goods and services, and to develop mutual cooperation in areas of intellectual, scientific, technological, and economic activity. Its objectives, as specified in its constitution, are: "... to facilitate the coordination and unification of the standards of Member Bodies.'' In connection with this goal, ISO may "organize the exchange of information regarding the work carried out by each Member Body ... , set forth principles for the guidance of Member Bodies in their work ... , cooperate with other international organizations dealing with related questions ... , set up international standards provided [that] in each case no Member Body dissents."

Present membership in ISO includes 54 member bodies. A member body is an organization of an individual nation which best represents the standardization activities of its nation. Only one such body for each country can be an ISO Member Body. The ISO Member Body that represents the United States is the American National Standards Institute (ANSI).

The standardization work of ISO is accomplished by technical committees. Any ISO Member Body or any organization outside ISO may request the study of a technical subject. If the study is approved by a majority, and at least five member bodies are willing to take an active part, a technical committee is established by the Council.

For each committee, the Council designates one member body to act impartially as a secretariat. This member body also has its own delegation in the technical committee, with the same status as other participating member bodies. The secretariat is responsible for the satisfactory conduct of the technical committee's work and annually reports to the Council.

Currently, over 130 technical committees have been established. Members who take an active part in the work of a technical committee are known as "(P) Members" (participating) and have the right to vote. Members who wish only to be kept informed of a committee's work are called "(O) Members" (observers) and may not vote.

Members participating at the committee, subcommittee, and working group levels of ISO/TC 97 include the following countries:

(P) Members

| | | |
|---|---|---|
| Australia | Germany | Rumania |
| Brazil | Italy | Sweden |
| Canada | Japan | Switzerland |
| Czechoslovakia | Netherlands | United Kingdom |
| Denmark | Poland | United States |
| France | Spain | USSR |

(O) Members

| | | |
|---|---|---|
| Austria | India | Pakistan |
| Belgium | Iran | Portugal |
| Chile | Ireland | South Africa |
| Colombia | Israel | Turkey |
| Greece | New Zealand | Yugoslavia |
| Hungary | Norway | |

One other standards organization has considerable impact on the computer industry of the United States. That is the European Computer Manufacturer's Association (ECMA). This body parallels CBEMA of the United States organizationally, but restricts membership in the standards development and approval processes to manufacturers only. Since the majority of United States computer manufacturers also have a market in Europe, they also have a voice in the development of standards within ECMA. Although ECMA is not a member of ISO, it is regarded as being a competent standards development body, and its proposals are accepted as a basis for ISO Draft International Standards. In the early 1970s ECMA was responsible for the development of a proposed standard for the PL/I language.

**Installation Standards.** Contrasted with industry standards, installation standards exist not specifically for the efficient interchange of information between organizations or companies, but rather to provide guidelines for the efficient operation of an individual installation. While such standards do not prohibit or nullify such interchanges, their primary purpose is to provide for clear, concise documentation of programs and systems for use in a single installation.

There exists no organization either in the United States or internationally which has undertaken such standardization, although the individual professional organizations have attempted to provide guidelines for their own members. These include the following organizations.

Association for Computing Machinery (ACM);
ACM Special Interest Group on Computer Systems Installation Management (SIGCOSIM);
Joint User's Group (JUG);
Data Processing Management Association (DPMA).

J. A. N. LEE

## STATE VECTOR. *See* PROGRAM STATUS WORDS AND STATE VECTORS.

## STATEMENTS

For articles on related subjects *see* DECLARATIVE STATEMENT; EXECUTABLE STATEMENT; PROCEDURE-ORIENTED LANGUAGES; PROGRAMMING LANGUAGES; and STRING PROCESSING LANGUAGES.

In much the same way that a sentence is the structural unit of expression in a stream of natural language discourse, the statement may be viewed as the elemental organizational component of a higher-level language program. As such, it embodies a unit of activity in terms of the algorithm being implemented. This is quite different from, and bears no direct correspondence with, processor activity. Although many types of statements are "executable" in that they instigate the higher-level language compiler to produce operationally equivalent sequences of machine language instructions, this relationship is arbitrary: A given type of statement may be expanded or contracted to designate a wide range of activities, all within the syntax of that statement. For example, the following two statements,

```
A = 7.82
B = (22.4 + (X/Y)**3) * (X * Y - Z)        (1)
```

are both syntactically legitimate assignment statements in the Fortran language, but there is clearly a considerable difference in the amount of computation each one specifies. This is completely consistent with the underlying idea that the user, rather than the processor, be the determining factor with regard to the amount of processing expressed in a higher-level language statement.

Not all higher-level language statements can be related to instructions in the machine language program ultimately produced. Many languages include statement types whose primary purpose is not to convey the intent of an algorithm, but rather to provide supportive information for compilation and other processes auxiliary to the actual execution of the program. These statements, which pertain to matters such as the allocation of storage and description of variables, correspond to a range of activities that do not generally show up as equivalent sequences of machine instructions. Accordingly, they are *nonexecutable*, and usually are treated as a distinct syntactic set.

It is not always possible to provide the programmer with unlimited scope for expression in a single statement. Yet such capability is needed if the linkage between the statement and a meaningful activity is to be preserved. There are innumerable occasions in which a sequence of associated events, while clearly identifiable as a single procedural activity, contains arbitrarily diverse machine processes whose specification in a single statement would be linguistically impractical. Most higher-level languages accommodate this necessity by allowing some type of compound construction. In some cases the construction is formed as a single statement with multiple clauses; in others, the idea of the "compound" statement is implemented as a group of single statements enclosed in special organizational statements or special words that serve as delimiters.

**Executable Statements.** Since these statement types are characterized by their ultimate relationship to explicit processing action in the object program, their general form tends to resemble the imperative sentence in many natural languages. Accordingly, it often is true that the language elements used for specifying activities are verbs. For example, an input activity in Fortran is expressed in the form

READ(*i*, *j*)*list* (2)

where *i*, *j*, and *list* specify the source, form, and destination of the input, respectively. The same construction prevails when data is to be transmitted from the central processor to the outside, with the verb WRITE indicating the direction. In less predominantly formulaic languages, the resemblance to imperative syntax is more pronounced. Thus, one of PL/I's constructions for data transmission has the form

READ FILE (*source*) INTO (*destination*); (3)

and

WRITE FILE (*destination*) FROM (*source*);

for input and output, respectively. When similarity to natural language is a primary design objective, the correspondence may be complete, as in the following Cobol statement:

ADD *a* TO *b* GIVING *c*. (4)

The narrative construction persists in an alternative, more formulaic form:

COMPUTE $c = a + b$. (5)

The Basic language designates the same operations in a similar manner:

LET $c = a + b$. (6)

The words COMPUTE and LET are included in the fixed vocabularies of their respective languages specifically to enhance the parallels with "real" sentences; the language translators clearly can operate properly without them (at some slight inconvenience), as they do in such languages as Fortran, Algol, and PL/I. It should be noted, however, that the absence of such verbs does not change the inherently imperative syntax; though now more implicit, it still remains. Thus, the PL/I statement equivalent to the previous examples, namely,

$c = a + b$; (7)

can be read as a highly implicit form of the sentence "the value in *c* is to be replaced by the result of the indicated operation on *a* and *b*".

The same construction generally carries over to compound statements. Though higher-level languages vary in the type and extent of compounding their syntaxes allow, there is one category of compound activity sufficiently basic to all computing work to compel its representation across the entire spectrum of higher-level languages. This is the fundamental decision mechanism, in which a comparison is specified in conjunction with a procedural step based on the outcome of that comparison. A "natural" way to articulate such combinations would be with some form of conditional sentence: "If a particular condition exists, take the action specified here; if it does not exist, ignore the specification." This construction is followed closely in many languages.

To illustrate: Consider a situation in which two variables *X* and *Y* are to be compared. If *X* is less than *Y*, the *X* value is to be doubled; otherwise, *X* is to be unchanged. In either case, a variable *Z* is to be computed as the product *XY*. The appropriate compound statements for several languages appear below:

```
(Algol)     if X < Y then X: = 2 * X;
            Z: = X * Y
(Cobol)     IF X IS LESS THAN Y MULTIPLY 2 BY
            X. COMPUTE Z = X * Y.
(Fortran)   IF (X.LT.Y) X = 2.0 * Y                  (8)
            Z = X * Y
(PL/I)      IF X < Y THEN X = 2 * X;
            Z = X * Y;
```

Additional extension may be allowed to accommodate decision structures in which mutually exclusive alternative actions are to be specified. Referring to the preceding example, we augment the decision rule

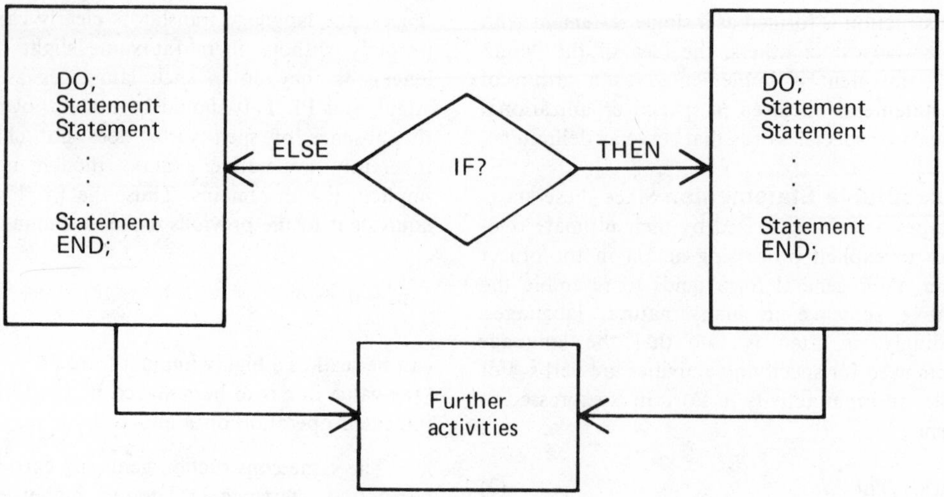


**Fig. 1.** Implementation of alternative activity groups in PL/I.

so that $X$ is to be decreased by 8.2 if it is found not to be less than $Y$:

```
(Algol)   if X < Y then X: = 2 * X;
                    else X: = X - 8.2;
          Z: = X * Y;
(Cobol)   IF X IS LESS THAN Y MULTIPLY 2 BY X
                    ELSE SUBTRACT 8.2 FROM X.
          COMPUTE Z = X * Y.                      (9)
(PL/I)    IF X < Y THEN X = 2 * X;
                    ELSE X = X - 8.2;
          Z = X * Y;
```

(This additional facility is not present in Fortran and must be implemented in other, more awkward ways.)

Aside from a limited number of specific cases, most languages cannot accept further extensions without additional organizational programming. One such extension is possible in PL/I, for example, which allows either or both alternative actions at the ends of an IF statement to be IF statements themselves.

The language Snobol has a syntactic construction which emphasizes compound statements. Moreover, the language is characterized by a fundamental shift away from the sentence-like appearance of its statements; many of the crucial operations are either highly symbolic or completely implied. Both properties are illustrated in the statement

```
HERE  VSTR 'BC' = 'W'     :S(HERE)     (10)
      next statement.
```

which may be paraphrased roughly as follows: Search the string VSTR for an occurrence of a B followed by a C, replacing that pair of characters with a single W; if the search was successful (that is what the S after the colon stands for), execute the statement again (i.e., return to the statement labeled HERE). When the search fails, continue with the next statement. Thus, a single compound statement embodies a request to find and process any or all occurrences of a particular set of characters in another, larger character string.

The ability to treat arbitrarily long sequences as single procedural activities receives formal emphasis in languages like Algol and PL/I, whose vocabularies include special organizational statements to indicate the bounds of such sequences. This type of facility is intended to encourage a modular approach to program design wherein the implementation of an algorithm is treated as a synthesis of related but logically (and structurally) distinct activities. Languages so oriented are often termed "block structure" languages. In PL/I, for example, decision alternatives may be extended arbitrarily by bracketing them with the DO and END statements, as depicted in Fig. 1

The group of statements in each of the processing boxes in Fig. 1 is considered as a "unit" of activity, irrespective of its extent. The delimiters **begin** and **end** serve the same purpose in Algol. On a somewhat larger scale, this method is used to enclose subprograms and other major program components (e.g., PROCEDURE and END statements in PL/I and

SUBROUTINE and END statements in Fortran). Examples of these statements and their use are found in the article on Procedures.

**Nonexecutable Statements.** Completion of a higher-level language program usually requires the inclusion of statements that do not correspond directly to steps in the algorithm being implemented. Rather, they provide the compiler with essential information from which it may determine the allocation of storage and other organizational characteristics of the final program. The command structure in these nonexecutable statements bears a less consistent resemblance to the imperative sentence than is found in other statement types.

A primary type of information transmitted by such statements concerns the definition and description of variables to be used in a program. For example, each of the following statements,

```
(Algol)     real X,Y, integer Z;
(Fortran)   REAL X,Y
            INTEGER Z                            (11)
(PL/I)      DECLARE (X,Y) FLOAT BINARY,
              Z FIXED BINARY;
```

associates the names X and Y with certain amounts of storage, indicating further that the contents of these locations are to be treated as numerical values in floating-point form. In addition, the name Z is associated with storage whose contents represent an integer value. Note that the expandability inherent in other statement types is present here, too, since it is possible to combine an arbitrary number of different declarations in a single statement.

Definition of entire arrays is no more complicated, since the same basic descriptive structure is used, augmented by information about the array's extent. For instance, the following declarations

```
(Algol)     real X,Y, integer array Z(1:18);
(Fortran)   REAL X,Y
            INTEGER Z(18)                        (12)
(PL/I)      DECLARE (X,Y) FLOAT BINARY,
              Z(18) FIXED BINARY;
```

define variables X, Y, and Z as they did in (11), except that Z now is an array of 18 elements, each of whose contents represents an integer value.

This descriptive process is much more formalized in Cobol, where the definitions and descriptions of variables are a required major organizational component of every program.


REFERENCES

1967. Higman, B. *A Comparative Study of Programming Languages.* New York: American Elsevier.

1969. Sammet, J. *Programming Languages—History and Fundamentals.* Englewood Cliffs, N.J.: Prentice-Hall.


S. V. POLLACK AND T. D. STERLING

# STATISTICAL APPLICATIONS

For articles on related subjects *see* ECONOMIC APPLICATIONS; MEDICAL APPLICATIONS; PATTERN RECOGNITION; REGRESSION ANALYSIS; SCIENTIFIC APPLICATIONS; and SOCIAL SCIENCE APPLICATIONS.

The advent of high-speed, large, central memory computers has greatly expanded the application of statistics. However, for other than elementary applications such as quality control, simple means and standard deviations, and the like, the actual practical application of computers to statistics has severely lagged behind methodological development. There are in fact relatively few practitioners of computer applications of statistics, particularly of multivariate statistics.

The literature of statistical computing methodology is considerable. A reasonable sampling of this literature can be found in Enslein et al. (1976). Thus, the review of applications which follows must be viewed as only the beginning of a much wider development. The list is clearly not all-inclusive in that many of the more esoteric applications, such as weather prediction, have not been included.

In these applications the following methods are often used:

1. *Regression analysis*: for model building and prediction.
2. *Factor analysis*: to obtain a parsimonious description of a complex data base.
3. *Univariate and multivariate analysis of variance*: to test hypotheses and search for interactions, for example in clinical drug trials.
4. *Discriminant analysis*: to find hyperplanes that optimally separate groups, typically used in disease screens.

5. *Time-series analysis*: particularly the fast Fourier transform (FFT), to demonstrate relationships between serial observations.

6. *Clustering and pattern recognition methods*: to find groups, used not infrequently in image analysis.

DEMOGRAPHY. An application with a great impact on peoples' lives is the use of statistical computing in the 1970 U.S. Census. For the first time in the Census, all data was recorded on magnetic tape, and as a result, tabulations, economic analyses, analyses of migration patterns, housing and population characteristics, etc., have been published in timely fashion. In fact, success with the 1970 Census has encouraged the retrospective encoding of much data from the 1960 Census in computer form so that computer-based comparisons could be made between the results from the two censuses.

Internationally, the United Nations (UN) statistics office has been instrumental in assembling worldwide data. In 1973, a totally computerized census was conducted in Nigeria.

EPIDEMIOLOGY. Computers have been used widely in epidemiological studies of many diseases and implied causes of diseases, such as cancer, smoking, bacterial and viral infections, longevity and aging, and the effects of pollutants. In the United States, much of this work has been carried out by the National Center for Health Statistics (NCHS). Worldwide, the World Health Organization (WHO), a special agency of the UN, has been a foremost propounder of the use of computer statistics in this field.

MORTALITY. Mortality statistics are routinely obtained by means of digital computers, particularly related to various census and other geographic divisions. This, in turn, has led to the recompilation of many actuarial tables. Again, much data produced in this fashion is available through the NCHS and the UN.

PSYCHOLOGICAL TESTING. The evaluation of psychological profiles, educational tests, and similar instruments is performed routinely, and has been made possible by the use of statistical computing. In fact, the classical methods of factor analysis, of which many types have been developed, did not come into the fore until the high-speed, large-scale computer became a fact. Among the more important psychometric and aptitude testing instruments are Cattell's 16 Personality Factors (16 PF), the U.S. Department of Labor's General Aptitude Test Battery (GATB), and the Mayo Clinic's Minnesota Multiphasic Personality Inventory (MMPI). Educational tests appear to be substantially less robust at this point. This seems to be more a problem of norms than technique. Tests of this type have also been used to evaluate various psychiatric or neurotic conditions such as anxiety and depression.

DRUG RESEARCH. One of the major applications of statistics, particularly multivariate statistics, is in the evaluation of the therapeutic and side effects of pharmaceutical compounds. In this area of application the differing viewpoints of different investigators can be compensated by analysis of covariance. Since most humans exhibit a strong placebo response, advanced statistical methods have also permitted the compensation for this effect in experimental designs, particularly double-blind crossover designs.

MEDICAL DIAGNOSTICS AND SCREENING. Diagnostic screens to detect diseases from multivariate data have been developed for thyroid diseases, chronic lung diseases, and pelvic diseases, among others. Computers are also used in reading electrocardiograms, karyotyping chromosomes, classifying leukocytes, screening multiphasic elements, and calculating pulmonary function, blood volume, and similar repetitive tasks.

ADVERTISING AND MARKETING. These related fields have represented a major application of statistical computing in recent years. It is not always clear that the applications are appropriate, since the models used are often not sound. The choice of advertising medium, the areas to be studied, the strategies in marketing, and the demographic characteristics of the population to which one wishes to sell are often parameters in these applications.

ECONOMETRICS. Econometrics, particularly econometric forecasting, has been widely applied since the advent of high-speed digital computers. The applications have ranged from computation of the consumer price index to the allocation of resources and even to the modeling of entire economies. Time-series analysis, particularly the fast Fourier transform, has found wide application in this area. Econometrics, however, is at the mercy of models and is a good example of the ease of computation offset by difficulty with the underlying model structure. In other words, while it is not difficult to build easily computable models and to test their impact analytically, in fact the degree of adequacy with which the model reflects reality often leaves much to be desired. Fully adequate models, however, will likely involve computations beyond the capacity of even the most powerful of today's systems.

IMAGE ANALYSIS AND RECOGNITION. While some practitioners may not consider this an application of statistical computing, the methods used in image analysis and recognition are in fact statistical. Such methods encompass clustering, pattern recognition, and feature detection, and have been applied in aerial surveillance (the famous detection of Soviet missile bases in Cuba), in character recognition on checks and similar documents, as well as in biomedical techniques such as machine reading of chest X-rays to detect enlargement of the heart and similar malformations, and in comparison of perceived image "quality" to objective image parameters. These applications of statistical computing are rapidly expanding.

**Summary.** The discussion here reveals that many applications exist at this writing, though only a small fraction of the possibilities have been explored. While the reader may get the impression that there are virtually no limitations to what computers can do in this field, in fact many applications—particularly those dealing with numerous variables, which includes image analysis—are restricted by the size of the problem, which in turn is reflected in central memory limitations as well as the speed of computation of presently existing machines.

REFERENCES

1976. Enslein, K., A. Ralston, and H. S. Wilf (Eds.). *Statistical Methods for Digital Computers*. Vol. 3. Mathematical Methods for Digital Computers. New York: John Wiley.

K. ENSLEIN

# STOCHASTIC PROCESS

For articles on related subjects *see* MONTE CARLO METHOD; and RANDOM NUMBER GENERATION.

The theory of stochastic processes deals with events that develop in time or space and which cannot be described precisely except in terms of *probability theory*. Formally, a stochastic process is a collection of random variables $X_t$, indexed by the parameter $t$, such that for any finite set of $t$'s, the joint probability distribution of corresponding $X$'s is specified. This definition is so broad that it includes practically all of probability and statistics; in practice, the term *stochastic process* (also *time series* or, particularly in Russia, *random function*) is usually used to describe events that develop in time and whose realizations are curves, either continuous or with jumps. Examples of continuous processes: the barometric pressure at Greenwich Observatory during November 1934, or your blood pressure as you read this article. Examples of processes with jumps: arrivals at an airline counter; the number of mutations in a developing colony of bacteria.

Since chance is involved with measurements we take on most things, or the measured objects are so complicated that we resort to probability arguments to describe them, the theory of stochastic processes pervades virtually all the sciences. Computers play an increasingly important role in development and applications of that theory. For example, they are used for simulation, i.e., in the generation of stochastic processes using random numbers in the computer to verify theory or approximations provided by theory. They are used to suggest experimental lines of investigation for further theory, or to study robustness of existing theory—i.e., how good are the theoretical results when the (often necessarily simple) assumptions on which the theory was developed do not hold precisely. Computers also play an essential role in analyzing data collected on stochastic processes, for many procedures call for complicated and lengthy calculations such as Fourier and Laplace transforms, harmonic and spectral analysis, serial correlation, prediction, and so on.

Finally, computer science itself has led to consideration of new kinds or new levels of stochastic processes, ranging from queueing processes describing user demands in time-sharing systems to the complicated branching processes involved in the study of algorithms and their treatment by compilers and programming languages, as well as descriptions of the electromagnetic signals and associated random "noise" that are the physical bases of all modern computers.

REFERENCES

Extensive references, including development of theory and applications, may be found in numerous books. Those listed here are especially useful.

1964. Hammersley, J. M., and D. C. Handscomb. *Monte Carlo Methods*. London: Methuen.
1965. Cox, D. R., and H. D. Miller. *The Theory of Stochastic Processes*. London: Methuen.

G. MARSAGLIA

# STORAGE ALLOCATION

For articles on related subjects *see* ADDRESSING; ASSOCIATIVE MEMORY; DATA BASE AND DATA BASE MANAGEMENT; MEMORY: Main; OVERLAY; STORAGE HIERARCHY; STORAGE MANAGEMENT STRUCTURES; TIME SHARING; and VIRTUAL MEMORY.

Storage in a digital computer system must be allocated to programs and data that are being executed, just as for any other resource in the system. While the cost of hardware used for storage is rapidly decreasing in the 1970s, the demands for storage generated by increasingly sophisticated software systems and application programs are quickly diluting the benefits from the availability of cheaper, larger storage.

A computer system will normally have several levels of storage, usually referred to as "main" (or primary) storage, "secondary" (or auxiliary) storage, and so on. Main storage is implemented using fast but relatively expensive components. Secondary storage is slower and less expensive. A typical system will have more of secondary than of main storage. The lower levels of storage are intended for storing large amounts of information for relatively long periods of time. When some part of the information is to be referenced during a computation, it is usually transferred to main storage first; i.e., it is *loaded* into main storage.

Sound resource management frequently dictates that programs and data should be allocated only the minimum amount of main storage that is necessary, but additional amounts are often acquired and are released dynamically. Thus, a program may be allocated an initial amount of *static* main storage when it is loaded from secondary storage, which it will use until its execution is completed. During the computation, there may be requests to a supervisory system for additional dynamically allocated main storage, which will receive temporary values for subsequent computation or communication to other *processes*, and which may then be released back to the supervisory system when it is no longer required.

Another use for dynamically acquired storage (as well as the initially acquired storage) is for the introduction of additional segments of programs and/or data, while parts of the program or data which were used and are no longer needed are released or overwritten. When the same storage is used and reused in this way, it is called an "overlay" process. It should be noted that dynamic acquisition of space is not just an alternative to explicit overlay management; for certain types of programs, such as recursive programs, one cannot anticipate in advance the amount of storage that will be necessary. Depending on the depth of the recursion, one might need a very long chain of temporary storage acquisitions, each to be released on return to the next higher level of recursion.

A considerable amount of program and data management is involved in an explicit overlay process. It has been estimated that as much as 50% of a program development effort may be concerned with design and implementation of overlay procedures. For this reason, various software and hardware systems have included features that help to alleviate the overlay burden. For example, the PL/I language provides for the allocation of *static* storage to variables, and also for two modes of dynamic allocation, one of which acquires storage for variables declared at the time of entry to a block (with automatic release of the storage back to the supervisory system on exit from the block), and the other of which gives complete control to the program to request space at any time, with subsequent responsibility for its explicit release.

One concept introduced (at least partly because of the overlay problem) is *virtual storage.* Here, program and data are assigned addresses independent of the amount of physical storage actually available and independent of the location from which the program will actually be executed. Thus, one might use 32 bits to represent an address (thus addressing about four billion items), while the available physical (main) storage might accommodate about a quarter-million items (needing only 18 bits for the representation of a particular address). This large ratio of total virtual storage to total physical storage implies a potentially massive overlay problem, although only occasionally will a program or its data be expected to occupy a very large fraction of the virtual storage.

Given that the program and data are allocated enough addresses in virtual storage to enable them to be accommodated there without any worry about overlay, but also given the expectation that the physical storage will be shared with other programs and data in a typical time-sharing or multiprogramming system, it is quite commonly necessary for the system to invoke an automatic overlay procedure. This is typically accomplished in a virtual storage system by bringing into physical storage from secondary storage only those parts of virtual storage which have been referenced (or can reasonably be expected to be referenced shortly). By recording in a table the mapping (i.e., correspondence between parts of virtual storage and physical storage established when pieces of virtual storage are brought into main memory), addresses may be transplanted dynamically. Those references to virtual addresses that are not already mapped into physical storage can be intercepted by special hardware, and that part of virtual storage now needed, called a "page," can then be brought into main memory. Pages are usually of a fixed size and therefore may be deposited into physical storage wherever a space of that size can be found.

Because the current location is entered into a mapping table whenever a page is introduced into physical storage, dynamic address translation can provide up-to-date interpretation of addresses (see below). This allows the effect of dynamic relocation without the overhead of actually modifying the addresses within instructions. The determination of which pages are to be removed from physical storage to make room for needed incoming pages has itself been the object of research. Also, the question of pages of variable size is being studied, since a fixed size inevitably leads to some wasted space whenever a block of programs or data does not fill exactly a multiple of the page size.

Although it is possible to implement in software the mapping described above, the overhead is considerable, and recent computers that incorporate virtual storage concepts have provided a hardware implementation for dynamic address translation. In addition, several computers have introduced an additional concept, *segmentation*. Here, one views virtual storage as having identifiable regions, called "segments," each containing enough addresses so that programs or data stored in them will not try to assign the same addresses more than once, even if they expand during execution by means of dynamic allocation of additional virtual storage. Segments are thus different from pages in that page boundaries assume a predetermined relationship to blocks of physical storage, whereas segments are viewed as functional subdivisions of virtual storage (and usually contain a number of virtual pages).

An important motivation behind the use of segments is the facility for sharing programs and data. In physical storage systems, one often finds programs written so that all addresses are given as displacements from a *base* address; and this is implemented by maintaining the base address in a hardware register. In this way, different copies of the program (or data) can be placed into storage in different locations while executing. Similarly, by establishing a *convention* that programs and data be *address-free* (i.e., that all addresses be represented as displacements from the expected contents of a base register) and by arranging for base addresses of segments to be maintained in registers during execution, relocation within virtual storage can be accomplished. This is illustrated in Fig. 1. Now individual users of the system may "load" programs or data into different areas of virtual storage (i.e., into different segments), and can arrange to share the copies that are actually loaded into physical storage through the paging mechanism. Fig. 2 illustrates this sharing.

Various hardware devices are being included in some new systems to facilitate the implementation of paging, and—to a lesser extent—segmentation. One example of a hardware implementation of the dynamic address translation described above is given in Fig. 3. The virtual address is separated into three parts. The first, called the "segment number," can be viewed (with an appropriate number of trailing zeroes) as the base address of a segment of virtual storage. In the implementation as shown in Fig. 3, however, it is used as an index into a *segment table* maintained for that user to retrieve the appropriate page table; i.e., a table showing the virtual-to-physical mapping for those pages of the referenced segment for which the mapping exists. Once the page-table base address has been retrieved from the segment table, the page number obtained as the second part of the original virtual address is used as an index into the page table to retrieve the physical

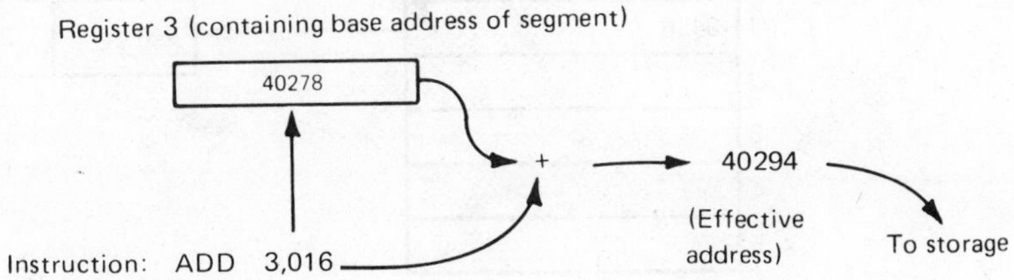


**Fig. 1.** Relocation within virtual storage.

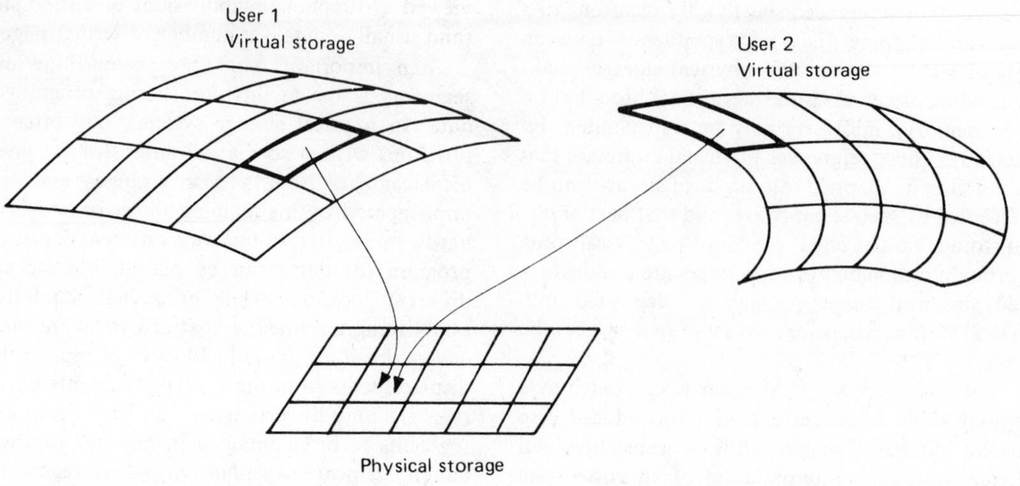


**Fig. 2.** Sharing in physical storage.

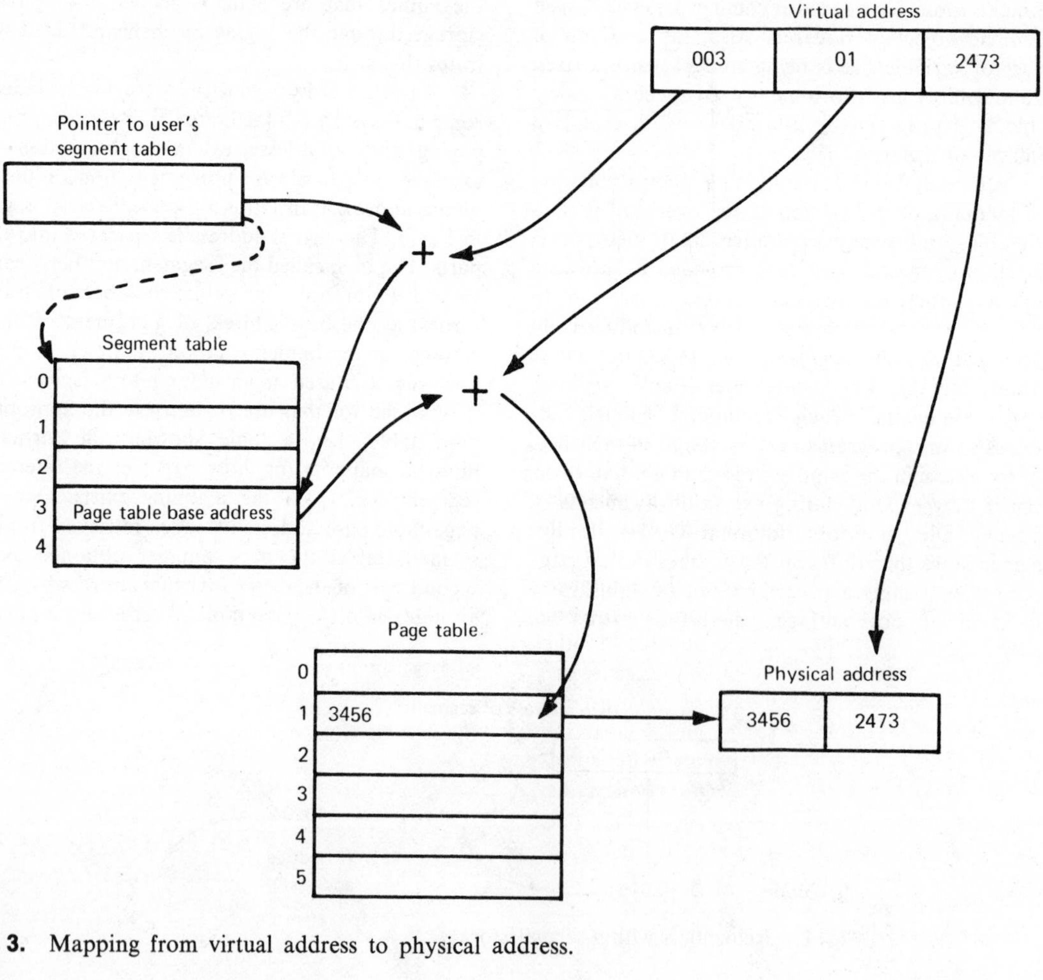


**Fig. 3.** Mapping from virtual address to physical address.

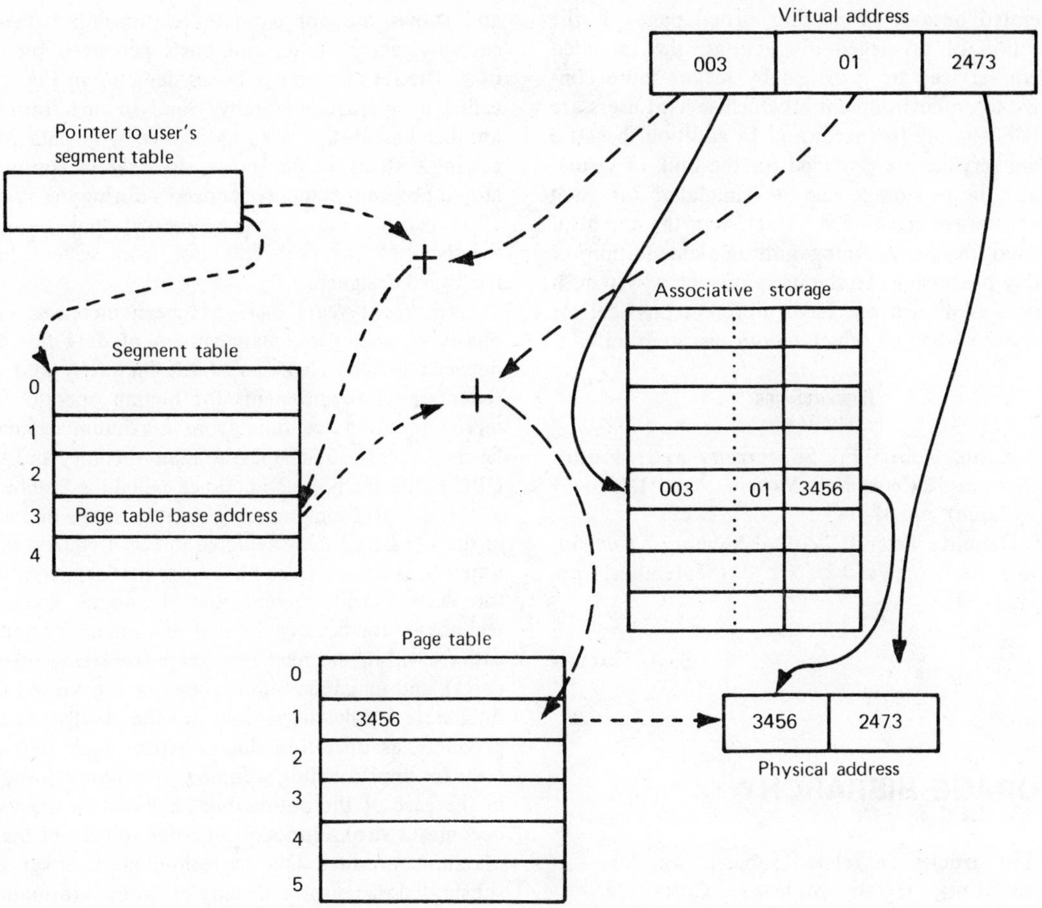


**Fig. 4.** Mapping from virtual address to physical address, showing the use of associative storage.

address corresponding to the base of that page in virtual storage. The third part of the original virtual address is then added (in fact, appended, since trailing zeroes are not included in the page table), and the result—generated in this manner by the hardware—is the desired physical address.

If the virtual page containing the referenced address is not present in physical storage—and only a few will be, depending on the number of other users of the system—an interrupt will be generated, causing a delay in the execution of that program while the desired page is found and loaded into physical storage. (This system service is the substitute for the cumbersome overlay process described earlier.) Of course all tables mentioned above must be protected by the supervisory system from access by programs that are not authorized to do so.

Accessing segment and page tables, as in Fig. 3, does imply additional storage references, thus potentially implying a large overhead. Several hardware systems include a provision for some *associative storage*, which retains several of the most recent mapping results. Thus, around a dozen entries will be maintained, each consisting of a segment and page number pair, together with the corresponding physical page-base address. A subsequent search with the same segment-page pair will quickly produce the physical page-base address without the need for accessing the segment and page tables. This is illustrated in Fig. 4, where the segment table and page table would not be accessed once a match is found in associative storage.

Another interesting application of virtual storage is the implementation of the *virtual machine*. Here a program is written as if it had a segment of virtual storage as its physical storage, and most (nonprivileged) instructions are executed on the hardware at full speed. When interrupts are thus generated because of missing virtual pages or the execution of privileged instructions, the intended system services are provided by means more conducive to an environment in which several users are actually sharing the hardware. In addition, because paging services are provided for the bulk of virtual storage, large storage can be simulated for each virtual storage machine at a fraction of the overhead incurred in the planning and implementation of overlay processing. To the users of such a system, it appears as if each one has a different physical (or software) system on which to run his program.

REFERENCES

1969. Rosin, Robert F. "Supervisory and Monitor Systems," *Computing Surveys*, Vol. 1, No. 1 (March), pp. 37–54.

1970. Denning, Peter J. "Virtual Memory," *Computing Surveys*, Vol. 2, No. 3 (September), pp. 153–190.

B. A. GALLER

## STORAGE HIERARCHY

For articles on related subjects *see* ADDRESSING; CACHE MEMORY; COMPUTER SYSTEMS; MEMORY: Main; MEMORY: Auxiliary; STORAGE ALLOCATION; and VIRTUAL MEMORY.

For articles on related terms *see* BENCHMARK; and BUFFER.

Computing systems designed for a broad range of data processing applications must include a number of memory functions, which are normally provided by a set of data storage subsystems. Each member of this set will have, within the total system, a unique capacity, access time, and cost of manufacture per stored bit. The reason for this is that the economics which govern the manufacture of storage structures is such that a structure with an access time which is close to the cycle time of the central processing unit will have a relatively high cost of manufacture per stored bit, while the storage structure with the lowest cost of manufacture per stored bit will have the longest access time and greatest capacity.

Fig. 1 lists a number of technologies that are currently used to implement data storage structures, and shows the approximate relationship between capacity, access time, and costs perceived by the user. The set of memory boxes depicted in Fig. 1 is called a "storage hierarchy," and in one form or another has always been associated with data processing systems. In particular, since the inception of stored program computer concepts during the 1940–1950 period, the storage hierarchy has become the focus of increasing attention from systems and hardware designers.

In recent years there has been increased emphasis on automatic management of data transfer between various elements of the hierarchy and on reduction of requirements for human operator intervention to move data from maximum capacity levels (i.e., disks and tapes) to main memory and the CPU buffer memory (sometimes called the "cache").

It is worth remembering that the shape and size of the storage systems depicted in Fig. 1 change with time; in particular, it is now clear that semiconductor devices will become the dominant memory technology for both cache and main memory applications within the next few years (replacing ferrite cores), and magnetic bubbles may be introduced for bulk-store applications late in the 1970s. These products, as do automobiles, require high start-up costs for implementing volume manufacture; also, as in the case of the automobile, the cost to the user becomes a strong function of total volume of manufactured product. Due to technological advances, substantial increases in density of stored information in both magnetic and solid-state storage products will take place during the next ten years, thus accelerating the tendency toward lower storage costs and increased use of large memory and bulk-storage capacity.

**Automatic Storage Hierarchies—How They Work.** As previously pointed out, computing systems have always included some form of storage hardware hierarchy, mainly based on the economic imperatives existing at a given time in the evolution of computer technology. As regards the manipulation of the stored data, two distinct but somewhat overlapping approaches have evolved, each changing its form as the technologies improved. The first, historically, has evolved as a data management approach and has come into being mainly as a consequence of the "access gap" depicted in Fig. 1.

DATA MANAGEMENT APPROACH. The separation between access-time capability (and cost per bit) of solid-state storage devices and electromechanical storage devices resulted in system designs of the type shown in Fig. 2. Note that the user has access to a

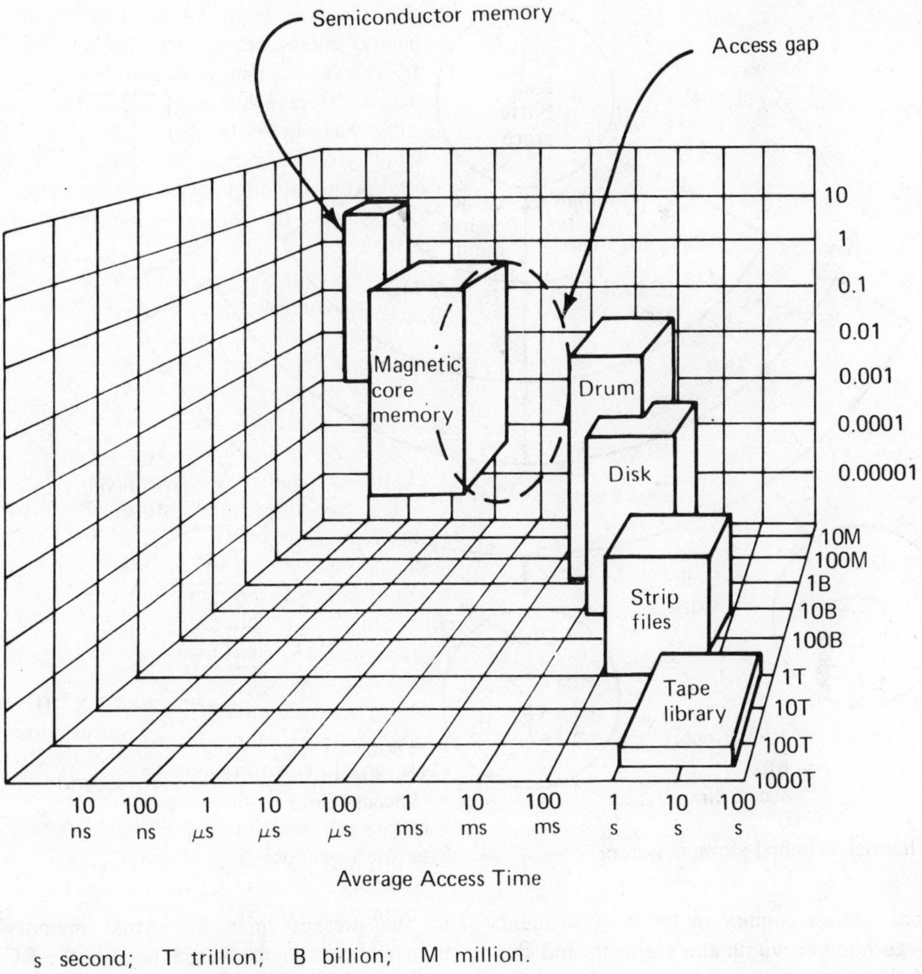


**Fig. 1.** Storage technologies.

limited amount of directly addressable storage of the type shown on the left-hand side of the "access gap" in Fig. 1, while, to gain access to storage units on the right side of the access gap, the user must invoke channel-attached bulk store. More recently, "virtual memory" schemes have been invoked in which the user gives up some direct control in return for the ability to run a program (or more than one program if it is a multiprogramming application) even though total program size exceeds main memory capacity. This is accomplished in practice by treating main memory plus a much larger amount of disk storage as one large main memory and moving portions of data stored on the disk into and out of the real main memory so that the user nearly perceives the rapid access performance of real main memory while using the much greater amounts of storage available on the disks. This is carried out as follows:

When a computer program is placed into a virtual storage system, it is automatically divided into small sections called "pages." These pages are assigned to larger groups called "segments." Initially, a page can occupy real main memory, but as real main memory becomes needed for some other task, the page of data is transferred to external page storage on a disk. When required again by the data processing job, the page is automatically shifted back through the channels into the main memory. The process of shifting pages back and forth between main memory and disk files is called "paging."

On many systems, a hardware unit called a "dynamic address translator" automatically identi-

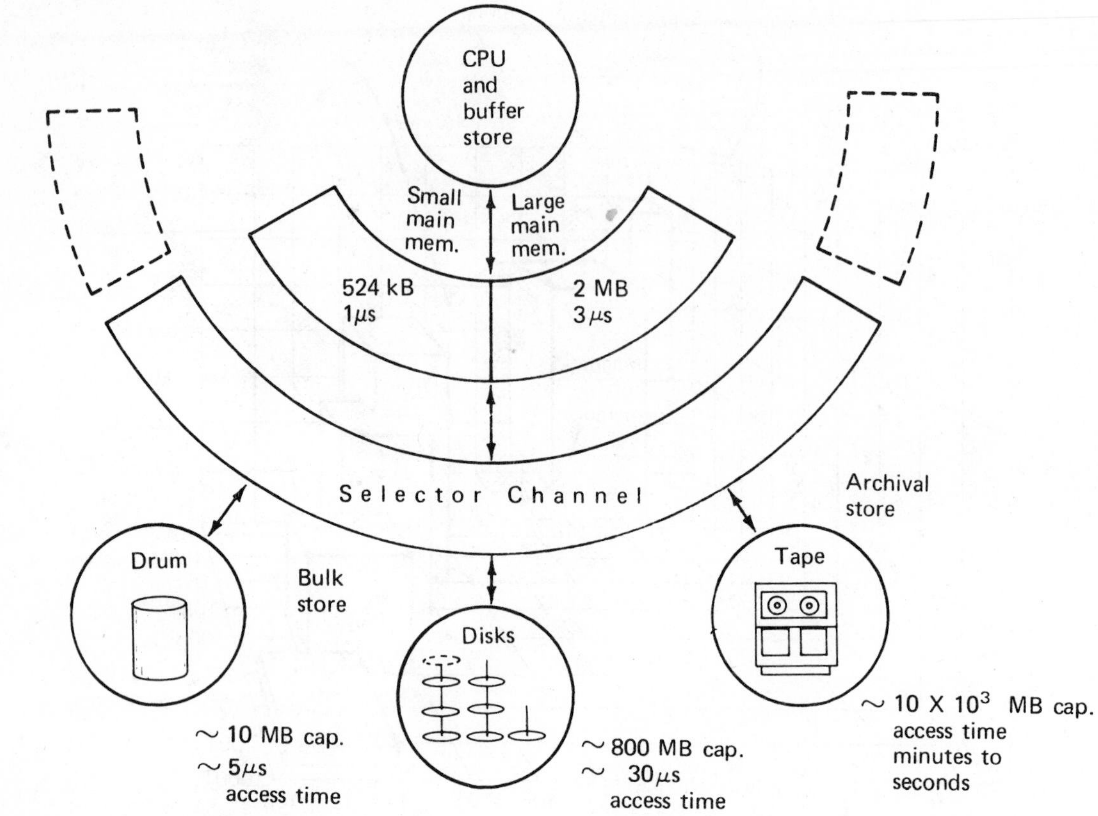


**Fig. 2.** Channel-switched storage system.

fies a virtual address inquiry in terms of segment number, page number within the segment, and the position of the record with reference to the beginning of the page. To speed program execution, the dynamic address-translation unit contains a translation look-aside buffer (small memory), which holds the addresses of previously referenced pages located in real main memory. If a real memory location for a referenced page is found, time need not be spent on a search of previously stored segment and page tables that indicate the locations of all pages in the storage system.

From a historic standpoint it is interesting to observe that data exchange operations (read "virtual memory") of the type just described were used in data processing machines that were in serial production as far back as the early 1960s. In 1962 the Burroughs 5000 series machines swapped variable-length program segments between fixed-head disk files and main memory-core storage. Other pioneers in this area were a number of UNIVAC machines, which as early as 1963 interchanged programs between main memory and fast access drums. Closer to the present time, a "virtual memory" data-management scheme was invoked in the RCA Spectra series of machines, beginning in 1970. Most recently, similar capability has been made available in a number of the IBM System 360 machines. In practice then, the combination of the need to overcome the access time limitations of high-capacity disk technology and the desire to take advantage of fast but relatively expensive medium-capacity main memory has resulted in schemes such as virtual memory, in which the user is gradually removed from direct control of outboard bulk storage.

Direct Hierarchy Control. The second approach, called "direct hierarchy control," assumes that a storage subsystem can be designed so that the entire storage structure is totally transparent to the user/programmer and internal data transfer is completely under control of built-in algorithms. In principle, the user requires no a priori information about the distribution of data among the various levels of the subsystem. A representation of this type of storage system is shown in Fig. 3.

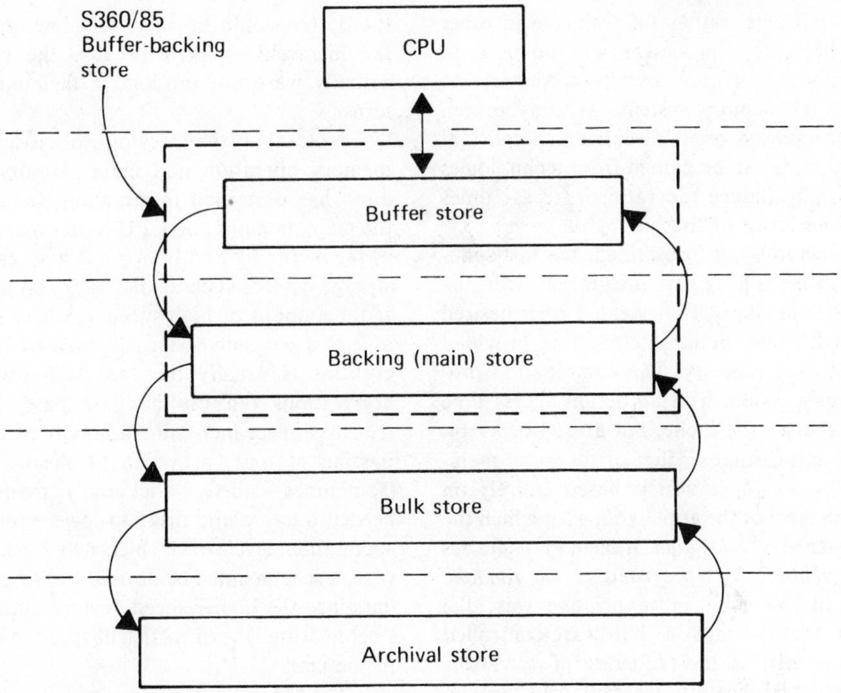


**Fig. 3.** Directly coupled hierarchical storage system.

This concept was successfully implemented in the cache main memories of the IBM/360 models 85 and 195 and, more recently, in the System 370/models 155 and 165 (Liptay, 1968; Lin and Mattson, 1972). In the Model 85, a directly coupled storage hierarchy—consisting of a 16- or 32-kilobyte cache memory with an 80 ns access cycle and a 500-kilobyte to 4 megabyte main store with a 1 $\mu$s cycle time—provided performance approximately equivalent to 80% of that obtainable with a main memory with an 80 ns access cycle.

The logical mechanism for shifting stored data back and forth between the cache and main memory in the Model 85 is as follows: Both the cache and main storage are divided into *logical* sectors, each sector consisting of 16 blocks, each of which contains 64 bytes. Because of the very limited capacity of the cache, there are many fewer cache sectors than main memory sectors. In operation, a matching action takes place in which each cache sector is assigned to a different main memory sector. Clearly, because of the limited number of cache sectors, the large majority of main memory sectors cannot have any cache sectors assigned to them. Each of the cache sectors keeps track of the address of the main storage section to which it is assigned, via its own address register. The assignment of cache sectors is accomplished via a "least recently used algorithm" as follows:

An activity list is maintained to keep track of the time of referral to the cache sectors. The sector at the top of the list is the one most recently referred to; the second one is the next most recently referred to, etc. When it is necessary to reassign a sector to a different main storage location, the one selected is the one at the bottom of the list. This cache sector is always the one that has gone the longest without being referred to. Conversely, when a cache sector is called out, it always moves to the top of the list, and all other sectors fall down one position.

In the Model 85, two CPU cycles are required to extract data from the cache; the first cycle is used to interrogate the sector address registers to determine if the data is in the cache, and the second cycle is then used to read the data out. If the data is not present, additional cycles are required until a data block is loaded into the cache from main memory. In comparison with the previously described virtual memory scheme, the main difference is that the data swapping is directed, to a large extent, by the "wired-in," least recently used algorithm rather than software, and because of the great compression of the access gap the very fast processor can afford to wait a few cycles while data is moved from main memory to the cache, rather than engage in other jobs. More likely, the processor will be used to manage some of the software "overhead" required to operate a virtual memory system. As can be seen from this necessarily brief discussion, important systems advantages can be gained from technologies that economically reduce the ratio of access times between various levels of the hierarchy.

For the hierarchy just described, the fast semiconductor storage physically integrated with the logic structure in the CPU yielded the desired machine speed, while the large core store provided the desired storage capacity. The combination provided a memory system with an actual access time approaching that of the cache, but at a cost per bit and capacity approximating that of the main memory. This successful operation is based entirely on the fact that in most of the applications for which the system is designed, *the location of memory addresses generated by real-life user programs is not random.* Indeed, to put this in a more positive way, the phenomenon that permits a hardware-controlled hierarchy to operate is the *clustering of addressing patterns* in actual application programs run through the machine.

It is interesting and useful to note that during the development of the System/360 Model 85, an alternate system was simulated which was in all respects identical to the proposed Model 85 except that the two-level cache main memory hierarchy was replaced by a single-level store with cache access time and main memory capacity. The performance of such a system would be that achieved by a physically realizable Model 85 if wanted data was always found in the cache. The performance of this (simulated) machine thus represented an upper bound on the performance of the proposed Model 85, and in fact was a benchmark against which the performance of the realizable Model 85 could be measured. By using a very large number of tapes containing about 250,000 instructions, each as input to both a simulation of the "real" machine and the "benchmark" single-level machine operating at cache speed, it was determined that the real machine could operate at an instruction execution rate of between 66% and 96% of the benchmark machine. In addition to this finding, it was also determined (by using the same set of trace tapes as input) that the average probability of finding data wanted for a fetch in CPU buffer memory was 0.968. Looking at this quite remarkable result in another way, the simulation studies indicated that if the location of the addresses derived from the tapes were truly random, the probability of finding data wanted in the buffer would be very, very low indeed. Clearly, the hierarchy worked because the real programs actually were not random in their addressing patterns.

Note that the previous discussion of virtual memory operation and main memory cache operation has described information exchange between the main memory and CPU buffer memory members of the hierarchy and between fast access "outboard" storage devices such as disk files and main memory. If the amount of high-speed auxiliary storage available to a particular user is limited by relatively high cost (as is usually the case with disks), and the applications (an on-line data base, for example) tend to collect increasing amounts of data with the passing of time, a systematic means of migrating (sometimes called "trickling") momentarily unneeded data on the disks to lower cost (and longer access time) levels of the hierarchy is necessary. Likewise, a scheme must be devised to bring back wanted data into the higher-speed devices (sometimes called "percolating") with sufficient speed to be acceptable to the user.

The exact criteria by which data stored in on-line disks or other forms of bulk storage is migrated to very low-cost archival storage, such as unmounted reels of magnetic tape, are of great practical importance. As a brief example, in operations of the storage hierarchy for on-line data base applications managed by TSS/360 (time-sharing system/360), the initial criterion used to govern the distribution of data among various categories of stored data (such as data on disks mounted on drives; data on disk packs, but not mounted; data on tape reels, not mounted) was the date on which a volume of data (disk or reel of tape) was last used. Specifically, a volume of data recorded and stored on a disk was migrated to a lower level, depending only on the length of time since its last use. The details of the scheme have been designed to enable inclusion of other criteria as they are deemed necessary (Lin and Mattson, 1972).

The very important principle of combining storage technologies with significantly different access-time differentials into a *hardware-controlled memory hierarchy* that appears as a single level of storage to the programmer was demonstrated as early as 1962 in the pioneering Manchester University Atlas machine. In 1965 M. V. Wilkes also suggested the use of a slave memory in conjunction with a large store as a scheme to implement dynamic storage allocation. The Model 85 high-speed, buffer-main memory hierarchy is analogous to this scheme and is somewhat related to the combination of small content-addressable memories and large auxiliary stores used in multiprogrammed time-sharing systems. All these systems exploit strong regularities in the statistics of the instruction-addressing patterns in order to achieve success. In the System/360 Model 67, to consider another example, a key factor in performance is the probability of finding a recall address in the associative registers that are used to hold the segment-page map for the system.

In view of the large access-time differential between main memory and available file technology, and between file technology and tape libraries, one can ask a reasonable question: Can the buffer-backing concept also be applied to those levels? The answer is probably yes, assuming that a great deal more is learned about the statistics of data flow in real applications than has been required for earlier system designs.

About the only observation that can be made without some information on actual data flow, particularly between the very high capacity levels, is that the influence of "misses" (unsuccessful accesses) in successively slower levels of the hierarchy becomes more dominant as the capacities of the successive backing stores become very large. That is, a high percentage of "hits" or successful accesses in high-speed buffers (or upper levels) will result in backing-store "misses" with more random statistical properties when viewed through the "aperture" of the high-speed buffer-block size. It seems reasonable to assume that the optimal adjustment of block sizes and replacement sequences within the hierarchy structure in this type of data processing system would proceed, at least initially, by increasing the size of the data block as storage unit capacity increased.

**Technologies for Storage Hierarchies.** Magnetic disk files have been a vital element in data processing systems for the past ten years, and in all likelihood will be important for the next ten years. The best of these devices have high reliability, relatively low access times (in the tens of milliseconds) and medium-to-large storage capacities (the IBM 3330 disk file has a capacity of $800 \times 10^6$ bytes). The user cost per stored bit is attractively low (for rental equipment, this cost is in the vicinity of \$10 per megabyte per month). Storage devices of this type dominate current bulk-storage systems.

Areal densities in magnetic recording have increased by a factor of about 10 every five or six years during the past two decades and, since current areal densities are rather far from theoretical limits, it seems reasonable to assume that densities will continue to increase at a similar rate. This means that further decreases in cost per bit to the customer can be expected. However, because of the need to eliminate (or at least compress) the access gap described earlier, and because applications trend toward extremely large amounts of very rapid access storage, it would be desirable for disk files eventually to be displaced by superior technologies. The key to this accomplishment is the further development of solid-state technologies that can populate as many levels of the storage hierarchy as possible with memory structures whose capacities, access time, modularity, and costs substantially eliminate the access gap characteristic of present data processing systems. The main hopes in this area presently lie with magnetic bubbles and further advances in semiconductor devices.

Magnetic bubbles are very small, highly mobile, cylinder-shaped magnetic domains rather easily formed in certain ferrite and other materials (Bobeck and Scovil, 1971). One of these materials (known as an *orthoferrite*) contains serpentine-shaped magnetic domains in its natural state. Magnetic "bubbles" are formed by applying an external magnetic field to a thin platelet of this material (see Fig. 4) in such a way as to change the shape of the serpentine domains into tiny cylinder-shaped domains in which the axis of the cylinder is oriented along the vertical axis (i.e., in the "thin" direction of the platelet, as shown in Fig. 4). It is important to note that the bubbles, once formed, can be easily moved in any lateral direction by application of extremely small, suitably directed forces created by interaction of the bubble fields with other magnetic fields resulting from electric currents in wiring patterns or other magnetic-field generating structures placed on the platelet (see Fig. 5).

From a device standpoint, the possibility of being able to move information to a sensing station without the need to attach a driving voltage and ground wire to each bit location is an attractive one. Clearly, some of the enormous economic advantages of rotating files and tape drives, in comparison with existing array sructures, are obtained for this reason, and also because we are willing to accept slow sequential access in order to obtain further cost benefits. In the case of bubbles, it is not unreasonable to hope that a combination of relatively small bit-cell size (3 mils or less), and very much higher access rates than are obtainable with mechanical systems, will lead to an acceptable gap-filling technology.

The major impact of the magnetic bubble scheme lies, however, in its potential to achieve

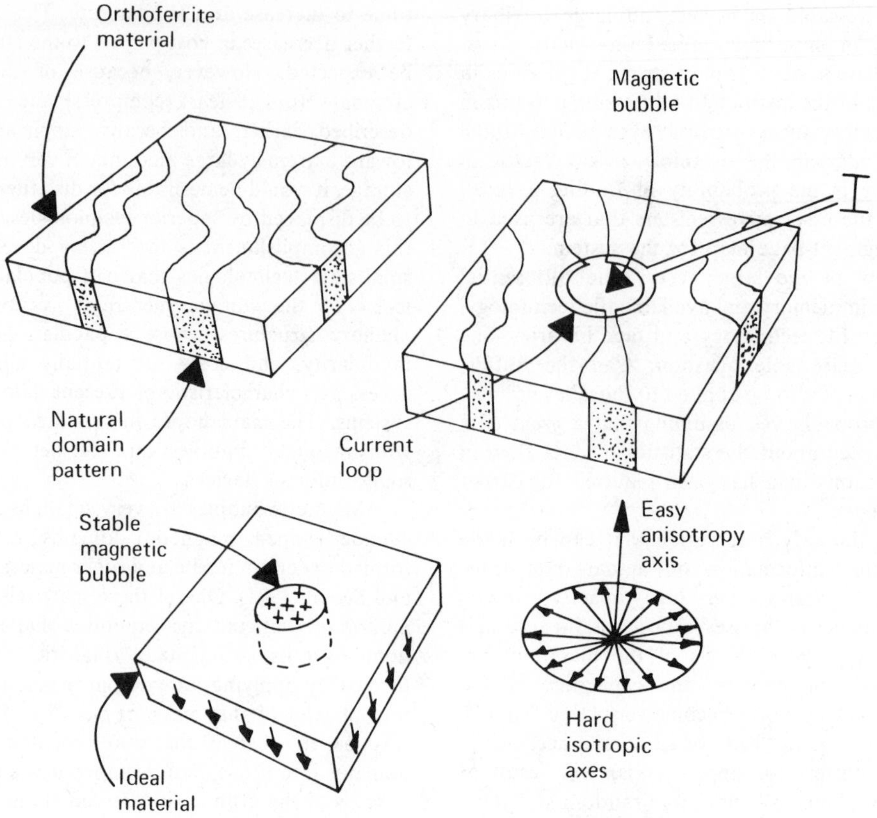


**Fig. 4.** Magnetic bubble formation. Magnetization normal to surface permits bubble motion in any direction normal to direction of magnetization.

significantly lower costs than can semiconductor technology in those storage system applications where access times must be several orders of magnitude shorter than disks are capable of, but which are somewhat longer than the access times that semiconductors can conveniently provide. This lower cost potential is based on simplified photolithography, fewer masking steps, and simpler materials requirements when compared with the manufacture of semiconductor memories. In addition, and again unlike the case for the manufacture of semiconductors, relatively small portions of the mask area are susceptible to defects. These simplifications in the basic manufacturing process imply higher yields, which should result in lower cost to the user. In terms of the current state-of-the-art, experimental registers with storage densities in excess of 2.5 million bits per square inch and bit transfer rates exceeding one million bits per second have been fabricated. These performance figures are certainly comparable to the areal densities achieved in available disk products, and are higher than in most tape products. The magnetic bubble memory is also nonvolatile. The added value of this characteristic to the total storage system requires further study, particularly if competitive low-cost semiconductor memory technologies with controlled volatility can be developed so that they have much shorter access time.

Another approach showing particular promise is a variation of semiconductor technology. The concept is based on the ability of semiconductor structures to store and transfer electric charge (Fig. 6). More precisely, the concept consists of storing charge carriers in sharply defined regions at the surface of metal-insulator-semiconductor (MIS) structures, and applying a technique for transferring these carriers from a particular region to an adjacent region by moving the boundaries of the region (Boyle and Smith, 1971). The boundaries of these

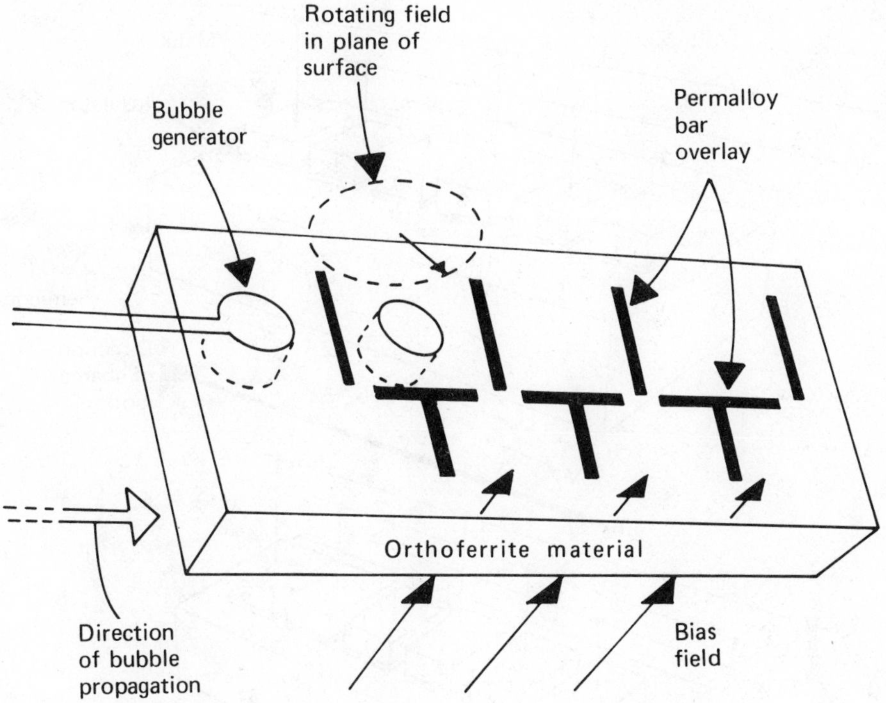


**Fig. 5.** Magnetic bubble shift-register structure.

regions, which form potential wells, are moved by the sequential application of signal voltages to appropriate electrodes on the MIS structure. Stored charge will move to the new location in accordance with the location of the new potential well boundary (Fig. 6).

The action of the charge-coupled device bears some functional resemblance to that of the bubble scheme, where information is stored and transferred in the form of stable magnetic domains. In an analogous manner, the charge-coupled scheme uses the charge-storage and transfer property of an integrated MIS structure to store and transfer information. Various useful logic and memory devices—such as shift registers, delay lines, and electronic analogs of drums and disks—are conceivable and can be realized by constructing a set of these storage "capacitors" on a single substrate with provision for the manipulation of the potentials to be applied to various electrodes. The charge-coupled memory is volatile, and therefore some type of refresh or regenerative action is needed in a practical memory system. On the other hand, since the scheme does not necessarily require separate power and ground wires for each stored bit, and since it is a variation on existing FET (field-effect transistor) production technology, there is some hope in this technology for bulk memory at bit costs approaching current rotating-file costs, but with improved access times in the range of 10 to 100 $\mu$s.

As in the case of magnetic bubbles, the potential cost advantage of charge-coupled semiconductor devices results from simplicity of structure and the associated elimination of a number of sensitive manufacturing steps. Charge-coupled memory structures can also be much smaller than conventional semiconductor structures. For example, a conventional shift register uses about 20 square mils of silicon area per bit, mainly because each bit may need to have as many as six FET devices. In comparison, because of the extreme simplicity of the CCD (charge-coupled device) structure, a bit may need no more than one device for implementation. Reports in the recent literature indicate that one bit per 2 square mils of surface (or less) is well within the limits of available photolithography and other relevant production techniques. Densities of one million bits per square inch and greater are achievable in the foreseeable future.

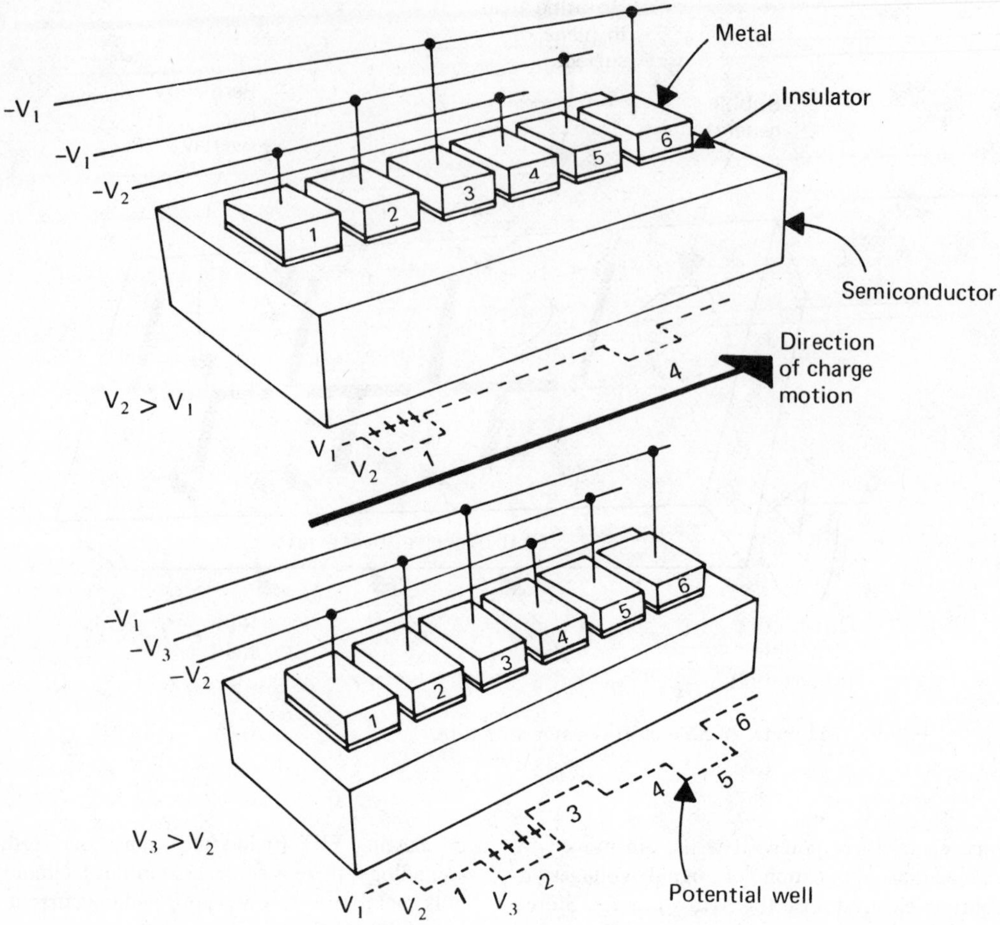


**Fig. 6.** Charge-coupled device shift-register structure.

In addition to low cost, both charge-coupled semiconductor and magnetic bubble devices possess the important property of dissipating far less energy per processed bit than the semiconductor memory cells used to data. A. H. Bobeck and H. E. D. Scovil of the Bell Telephone Laboratories have reported that the energy dissipated in the magnetic bubble material per switched bit may be as small as $4 \times 10^{-14}$ joule (Bobeck and Scovil, 1971). W. S. Boyle and C. E. Smith (1971), also of Bell Labs have reported that calculations based on a highly idealized charge-coupled device, in which charge is transported by a moving sine wave potential well, indicated the same loss per bit in the semiconductor material. This compares with the approximately $10^{-12}$ joule delay product (power times switching delay) characteristic of current semiconductor devices. Whether or not this increase in efficiency can be implemented in practice is really not known at this time. If this advantage can be realized, the decrease in power requirements and heat dissipation in future random-access memory structures will indeed result in increases in memory capacities, reduction in space requirements, and improvements in system performance considerably beyond the levels achieved via current main memory and bulk storage technology.

## References

1965. Scarrott, C. C. "The Efficient Use of Multilevel Storage," *Proc. IFIP Congress,* Vol. VI, pp. 137–141.

1968. Liptay, J. S. "Structural Aspects of the System/360 Model 85-Part II-The Cache," *IBM Systems Journal,* Vol. 7, No. 1, pp. 15–21.

1969. Considine, J. P., and A. H. Weis. "Establishment and Maintenance of a Storage Hierarchy for an On-Line Data Base Under TSS/360," *Proc. of the FJCC, November 1969,* Vol. 35. Washington, D.C.: Thompson Book Co., pp. 433–440.
1971. Bobeck, A. H., and H. E. D. Scovil. "Magnetic Bubbles," *Scientific American* (June), pp. 78–90.
1971. Boyle, W. S., and G. E. Smith. "Charge Coupled Devices," *IEEE Spectrum* (July).
1972. Hodges, D. A. *Semiconductor Memories.* New York: IEEE Press.
1972. Lin, S. Y., and R. L. Mattson. "Cost-Performance Evaluation of Memory Hierarchies," *IEEE Transactions on Magnetics* (September), pp. 390–392.
1975. Chang, S. (Ed.). *Magnetic Bubble Technology —Integrated Circuit Magnetics for Digital Storage and Processing.* New York: IEEE Press.

E. SHAPIRO

## STORAGE MANAGEMENT STRUCTURES

For articles on related subjects *see* BLOCK AND BLOCKING; DATA ACCESS METHODS; DATA STRUCTURES, SET CONCEPTS FOR; FILES; LOGICAL AND PHYSICAL UNITS; and MEMORY, Auxiliary.
For articles on related terms *see* DATA BASE AND DATA BASE MANAGEMENT; RECORD; and VOLUME.

A data base is an organized collection of known data about an enterprise or about a field of endeavor. For example, a given data base may contain data about the curriculum, the teaching personnel and facilities, and the students of a school; about the personnel, the inventory, and the cost/sales figures of a business; or about the authors, the titles, the subjects, the key words, and the abstracts of documents in a library.

Data bases are becoming increasingly complex. Their structuring and management is a tough job, made even more difficult by semantic confusion. This article discusses concepts of storage management and their structural interrelationships. Data structure diagrams are used to illustrate these relationships because they provide both a method of documentation and a basis of comparison between different storage structures of data bases.

Computerized data exists as a sequence of bits residing on storage media. In order to *find* any specific piece of data, its location (i.e., its place in the physical storage structure) must be known or knowable. In order to *understand* the data and glean information from it, its logical structure must be known or knowable. The bridge between physical storage structure and logical structure is the allocation structure, i.e., that element of data base systems which deals with the mapping of logically structured data onto physical storage media. [Bachman (1972) gives a detailed history and analysis of storage structures, and this article is, to a considerable extent, derived from his work.]

**Data Structure Diagrams.** In this article the data structure diagram technique is used for the illustrations. Bachman (1969) describes this technique in detail.

The diagramming technique is based on a notation dealing with classes, specifically with classes of entities and the relationships among them. An "entity" in this context is an object or concept under consideration (e.g., "a school" is an entity); an "entity class" is a group of entities that are sufficiently similar in terms of their attributes to be considered collectively. In data structure diagrams a box is used as a symbol for an entity class; thus [SCHOOL] represents the class of schools under consideration.

The arrow "→" is used to symbolize 1:$n$ relationships among entity classes; specifically, one occurrence of the entity class at the shaft of the arrow is associated with $n$ (zero, one, or many) occurrences of the entity class at the head of the arrow, thus:

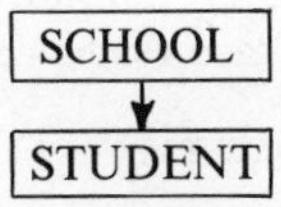


This drawing means:

1. There is a class of entities called "school."
2. There is a class of entities called "student."
3. Any number of students may be associated with a school.
4. Each student is associated with one, and only one, school.

**Concepts.** The following concepts relate to physical, logical, and allocation structures. They are presented together with the terms that have been given to them; generally the italicized term is the preferred one. Definitions of the IFIP-ICC vocabulary (1966) are used whenever appropriate.

PHYSICAL CONCEPTS

1. A *physical record* is a unit of storage on any medium that may be directly and independently read or written (without need to read and rewrite adjacent physical storage space).

2. A *track* is a unit of a storage medium characterized by most rapid serial transfer of consecutively recorded data. (The concept is most often applied to disks.) A track may be divided into one or more physical records.

3. A *cylinder* is a unit of (secondary) storage characterized by the fact that consecutive transfer of data recorded within one cylinder is substantially faster than the consecutive transfer of data recorded on different cylinders. (This concept is primarily disk-oriented.) Cylinders may be subdivided into one or more tracks.

4. A *volume* (file, physical tape reel, physical file, disk pack, drum, tape file, disk file) is a unit of storage capable of having data recorded upon it and being subsequently read. It is usually associated on a 1:1 basis (permanent or temporary) with a storage device. If disk, then it is subdivided into one or more cylinders.

5. A storage *device* is a unit of (secondary) storage hardware capable of permanently or temporarily holding a volume and having read/write (and possibly cylinder selection) mechanisms for the volume.

Storage devices should be differentiated from I/O devices, which are hardware units basically concerned with bringing data into the system from the outside world, or transmitting processed data back out, such as card readers and printers.

LOGICAL CONCEPTS

1. A *field* (data item, item, elementary item, based variable) is a unit of information storage which holds the value associated with some measure. The value may be represented as a character string, a number, a boolean value, or a pointer that will indirectly lead to the value.

2. A *logical record* is a unit of logical storage created by the execution of a WRITE/STORE command, which may subsequently be reaccessed by the execution of a READ/RETRIEVE/FIND command. A logical record may be subdivided into zero, one, or more fields.

3. A *page* is a unit of logical storage, characterized by logically contiguous addressability when resident in main storage. It is capable of holding zero, one, or more logical records.

4. A *logical file* (area, realm, segment) is a named unit of logical storage which serves as a container for logical records. It is subdivided into one or more pages.

ALLOCATION STRUCTURE CONCEPTS

1. A *block* is a unit of media allocation which serves as the data transfer unit between main and secondary storage. One or more (generally consecutively recorded) physical record(s) may be mapped into it.

2. An *extent* is a unit of media allocation, representing a contiguously addressed portion of a volume. It is subdivided into one or more blocks for physical access.

Three hierarchies exist within the concepts established above. They are:

1. Physical storage structure hierarchy (device/volume/cylinder/track/physical record).

2. Logical storage structure hierarchy (logical file/page/logical record/field).

3. Storage allocation structure hierarchy (extent/block).

These three hierarchies may be observed throughout the study of storage structures; the interrelationships between their elements permit the translation of logical READ/WRITE operations into the necessary physical manipulation commands.

**Physical Storage Structure.** Fig. 1 shows a disk volume (removable disk pack) consisting of a number of cylinders, each cylinder consisting of a number of tracks, and each track consisting of a number of physical records; "a number of" should be interpreted here as zero, one, several, or many. The diagram also illustrates a "sometime 1:1" relationship between a volume and a storage device, "sometime" being those times when the volume is mounted. (A "sometime 1:1" relationship is illustrated by a dashed line *without* an arrowhead. A "sometime 1:*n*" relationship, such as a magnetic cartridge storage device with a number of removable cartridges, would be illustrated by a dashed line *with* an arrowhead.)

On a fixed-head magnetic drum there is a "permanent 1:1" relationship between the concepts of storage device and volume, and a "permanent 1:1" relationship between the concepts of volume and cylinder; the three concepts are merged. These

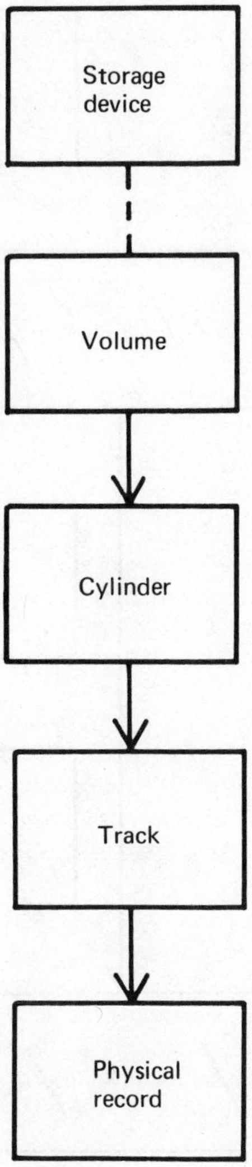


**Fig. 1.** Physical storage structure for removable disk storage.

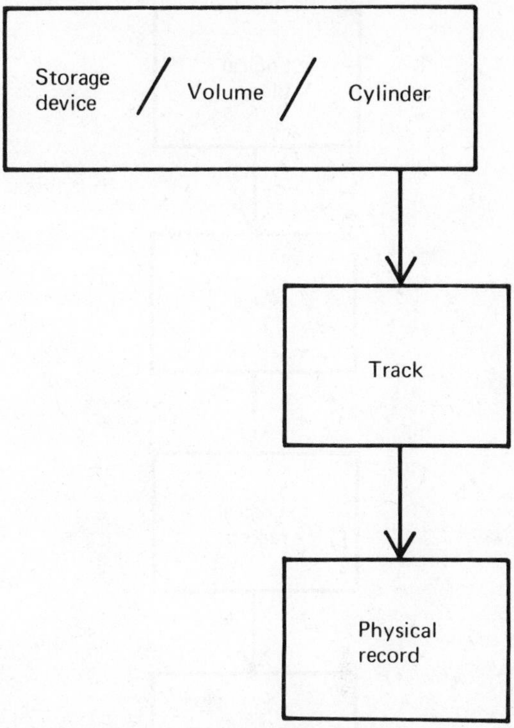


**Fig. 2.** Physical storage structure for drum.

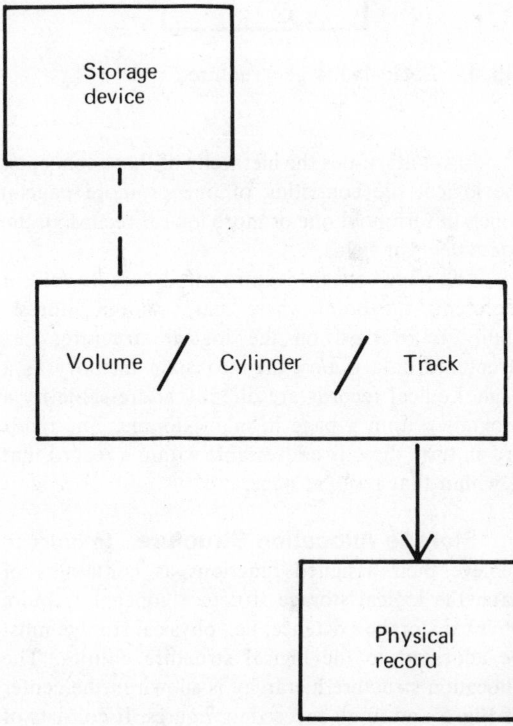


**Fig. 3.** Physical storage structure for magnetic tape.

merged concepts are represented by a single entity class, illustrated at the top of Fig. 2. At the middle and bottom are the entity classes supporting the track and physical record concepts, as before.

On magnetic tape, the concepts of volume, cylinder, and track are merged, thus making the physical storage structure of the tape different. Fig. 3 shows this difference, also illustrating the removability of the magnetic tape volume from the device —i.e., the "sometime 1:1" relationship.

**Logical Storage Structure.** The elements of logical storage structures are logical files, pages, logical records, and fields.

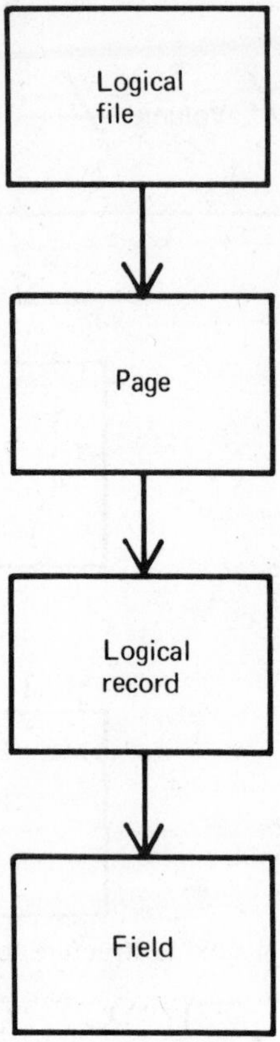


**Fig. 4.** Logical storage structure.

Fig. 4 illustrates the hierarchy of these concepts: the logical file consisting of one or more page(s) which in turn hold one or more logical record(s), the containers for fields.

The page concept is introduced here because it represents the point where main storage addressability is overlaid on the logical structure; i.e., structured data is brought into main memory as a page. Logical records are directly addressable by a program within a page in main storage. The fields are, in turn, directly addressable within a record that is within that resident page.

**Storage Allocation Structure.** In order to achieve their assigned functions as containers of data, the logical storage structure concepts require physical storage existence; i.e., physical storage must be allocated to the logical structure entities. The allocation structure hierarchy is shown in the center of Fig. 5 and in all succeeding figures. It consists of the concepts of *extent* and *block*. The extent is the concept of gross or coarse allocation (i.e., the

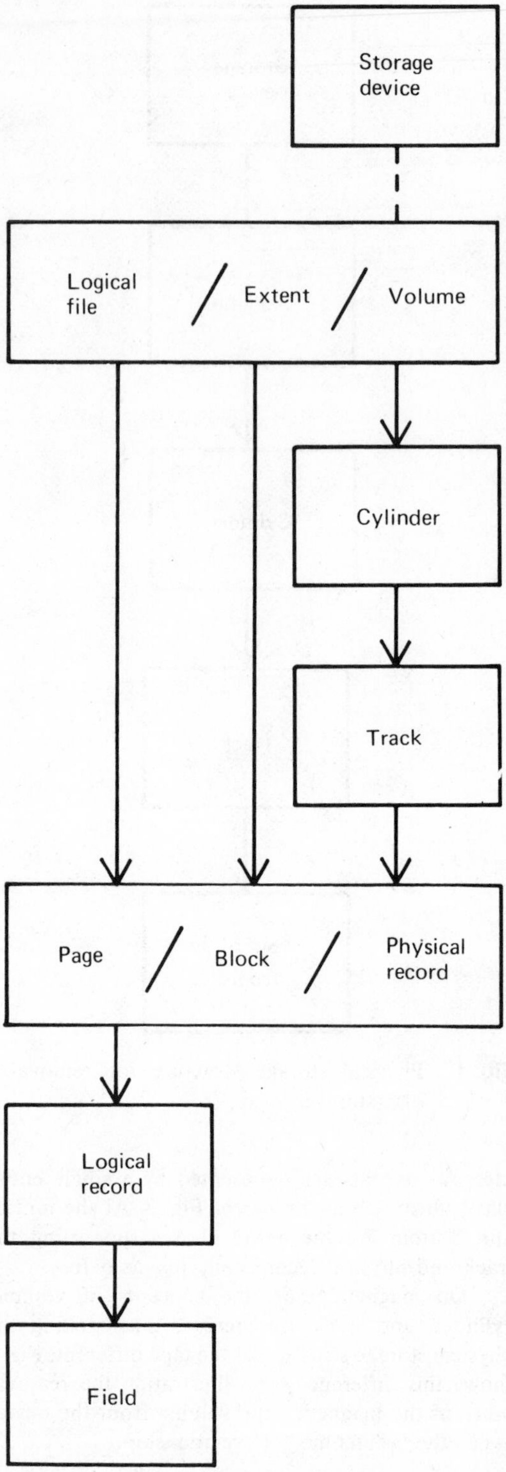


**Fig. 5.** Storage structure for blocked records on removable disk storage.

assignment of a portion, or all, of a volume to physically hold a portion, or all, of a logical file). The block is a finer allocation concept, which relates a page of the logical structure hierarchy to a physical record of the storage structure hierarchy. The role of these allocation concepts (extent and block) is to join the physical and logical storage structure concepts into an integrated whole, allowing the storage-processing algorithms to map logical structures onto the appropriate physical storage structures.

STORAGE STRUCTURE FOR REMOVABLE DISK STORAGE

*Blocked Files.* Fig. 5 uses the allocation concepts of *extent* and *block* to integrate the physical storage structure shown in Fig. 1 with the logical storage structure of Fig. 4. In Fig. 5 the blocked-record logical file is shown, mapped onto removable-disk storage, while maintaining the one logical file to one volume basis. The three storage hierarchies (logical, allocation, and physical) are very clearly seen in this data structure diagram, since the entity classes implementing the concepts are drawn vertically and in parallel. The *physical storage structure* on the right begins with the storage-device concept and descends through the concepts of volume, cylinder, track, and physical record. The *logical storage structure* on the left begins with logical file concept and descends through the concepts of page, logical record, and field. The *allocation structure* hierarchy in the middle begins with the extent concept and descends to the block concept.

An example of such a structure could be the "student file" of a school, residing on a removable disk pack (thus merging the concepts of logical file, extent, and volume). If, say, the disk pack had at least 26 cylinders, then the file could be physically distributed so that each cylinder would contain the data about all students whose last names start with the same letter of the alphabet: $A$ = cylinder 1, $B$ = cylinder 2, . . . , $Z$ = cylinder 26. One physical record of fixed size is read at a time, merging the concepts of page, block, and physical record. Within a given page there could be any number of logical records representing data about individual students.

*Provision for Page Extension; Index Sequential Files.* One of the most important functional changes made possible by disk storage was the opportunity to change from the "update by rewriting (an entire file)" to an "update in place" strategy. But updating in place causes problems when the logical records are to be maintained in some predefined collation sequence (e.g., sorted alphabetically by name) for batch type (i.e., serial) processing: The maintenance of a collation sequence requires that new logical records be physically inserted at the correct point in a page. Therefore, provision must be made for extension to effectively allow the page to grow when new logical records are to be inserted.

Growth potential is provided for by establishing separate entity classes (IFIP, 1966) for the "page" and "block" concepts. At file creation time, one block is allocated to each page, and a group of blocks is reserved for overflow. When an existing page needs to grow to support logical record insertion, an overflow block is allocated and appended to the page. This strategy is typically adopted for index sequential files.

Fig. 6 illustrates this structure. The page and block concepts have now been split into separate entity classes, and there is an "alternative 1:$n$" relationship between them: A page *may* consist of a variable number of blocks, but a block *need not be* associated with a page. Unassociated blocks, which are held in inventory and are available overflow blocks, belong to the extent; the forked arrow designates this alternative relationship, namely, that a given block belongs either to a page or to an extent, but not to both. (The available block inventory is equivalent to the available space list in list processing.)

*Linked Sequential Files.* For handling very dynamic files in a volume, a specialized mapping is desirable. One of these is called "linked sequential" mapping. It has two important features as compared to the example of Fig. 6. The logical file is subordinate to the extent (see Fig. 7) so that many small temporary files can be created and destroyed within the extent; blocks, rather than being appended to a page when allocated to it, are "linked" to it by placing a pointer to the new block in the last block allocated. Fig. 7 also illustrates the relationship between page/extent (respectively) and block, which exists because a block is either assigned to a page or is in the available block inventory, but not both. This structure is exemplified by the case of a small school that needs less than a whole disk pack for its files. Thus, the volume (disk pack) is subdivided into extents, which may in turn contain one or more logical files. One of these could be the "student file." As enrollment grows, more blocks may be assigned to pages from the pool of available blocks initially assigned to extents. If enrollment shrinks, the reverse of the procedure takes place.

*Randomized Files.* A variation of the dynamic allocation structure of Fig. 7 supports direct access to a particular page of a logical file without traversing the links in the preceding pages of the file to find it. This mapping requires that a randomization

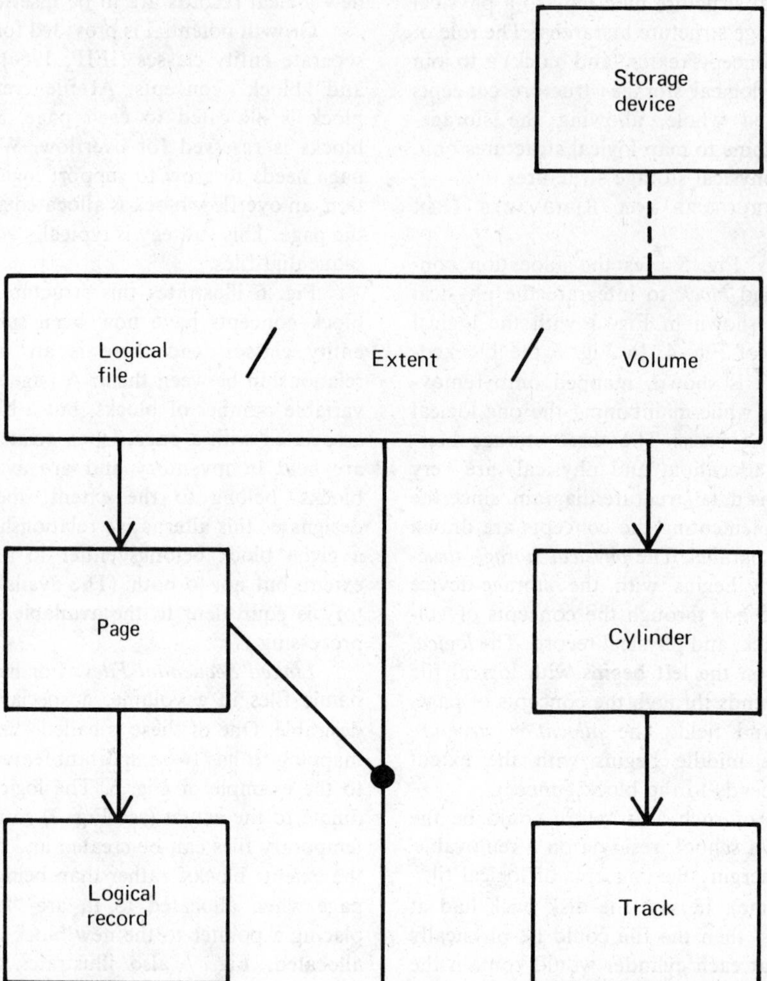

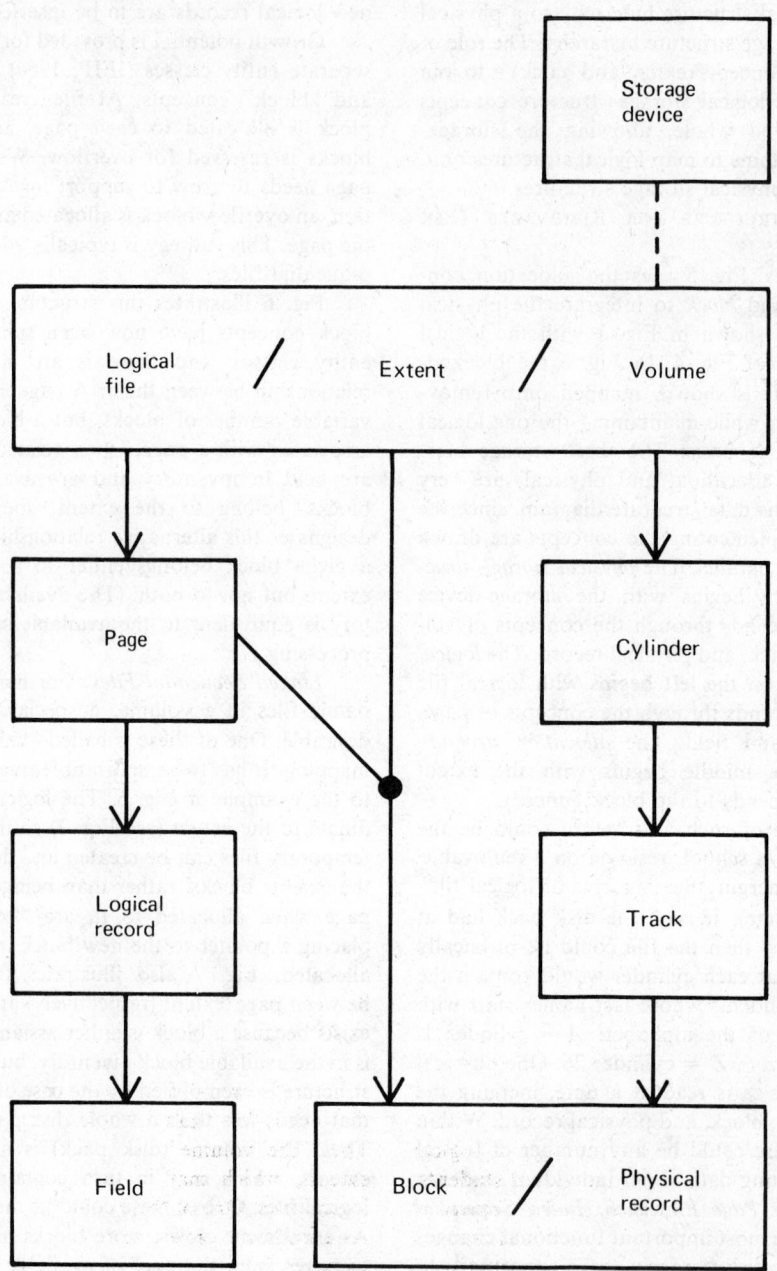


**Fig. 6.** Storage structure for blocked records on removable disk storage with overflow provisions.

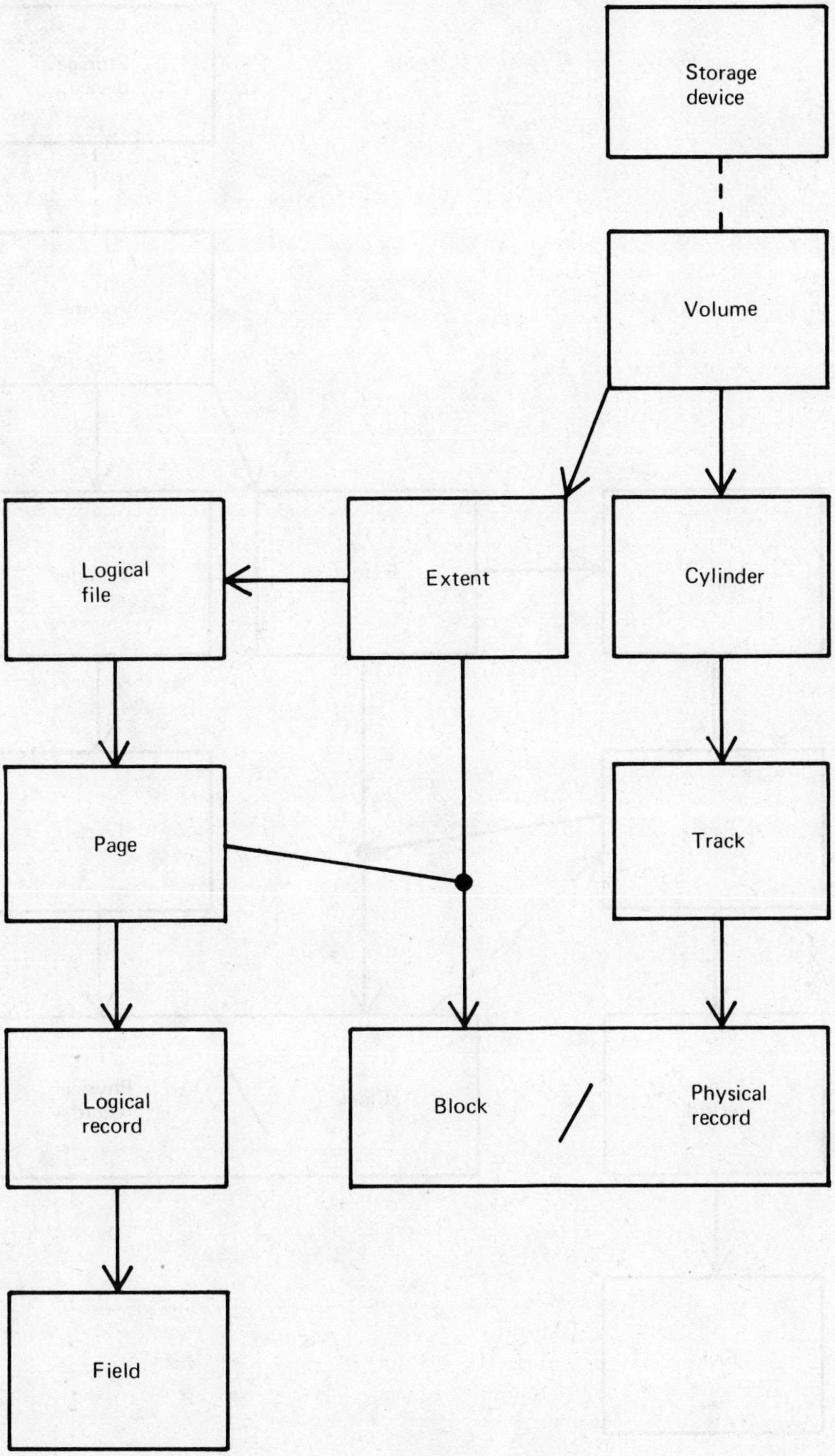


**Fig. 7.** Storage structure for linked sequentially paged files.

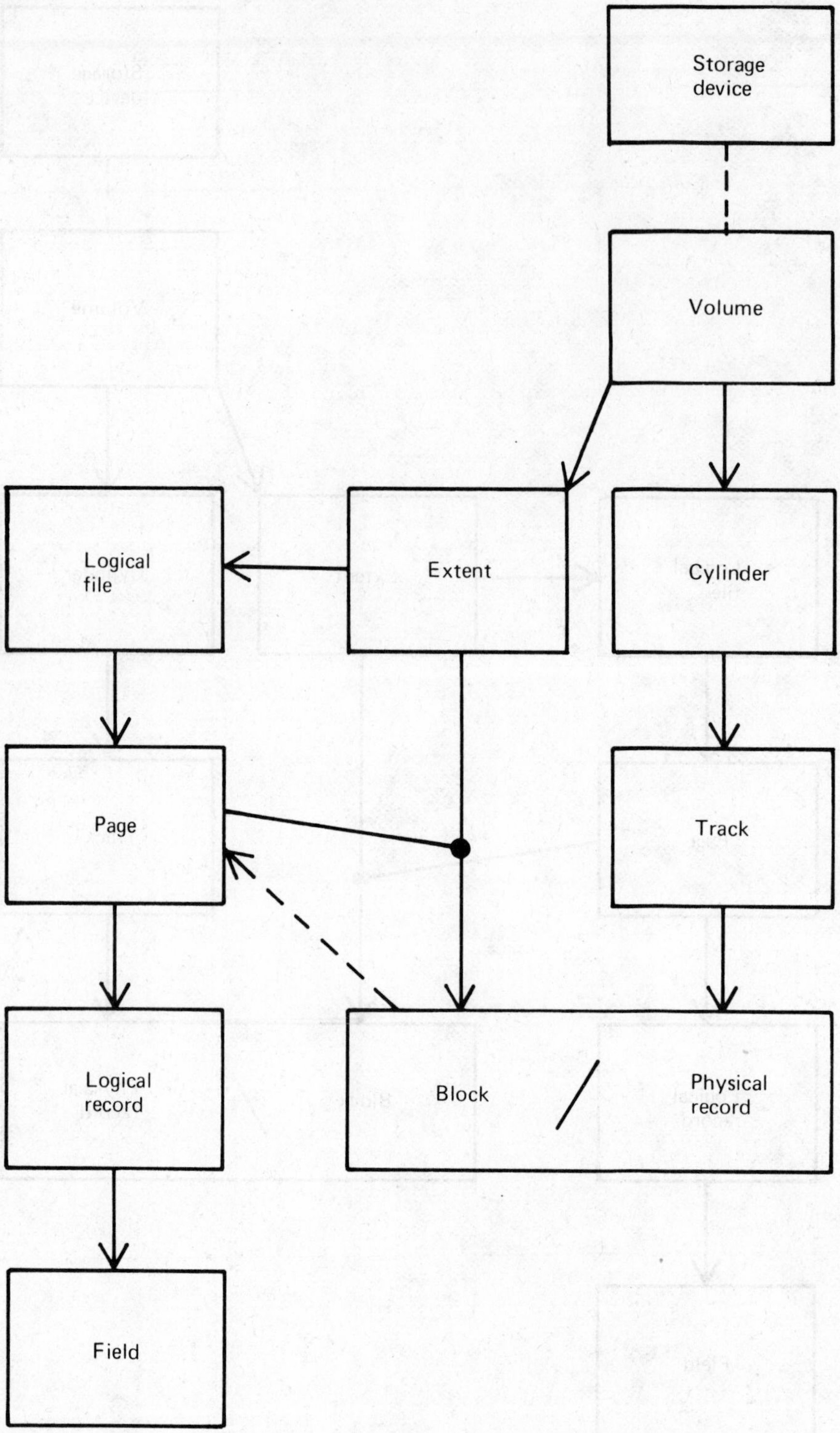


**Fig. 8.** Storage structure for randomized paged files.

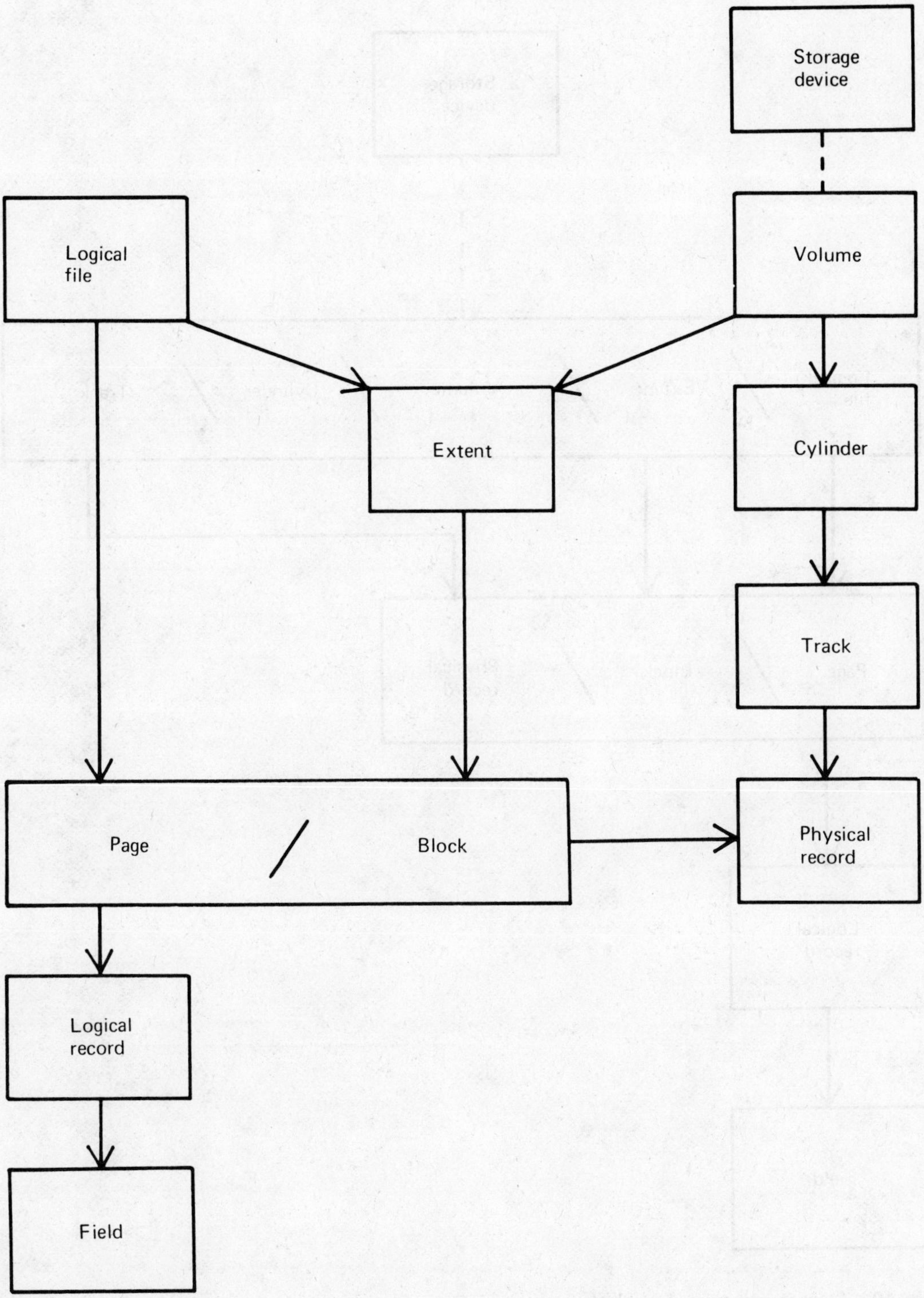


**Fig. 9.** Storage structure for integrated data store (IDS) files.

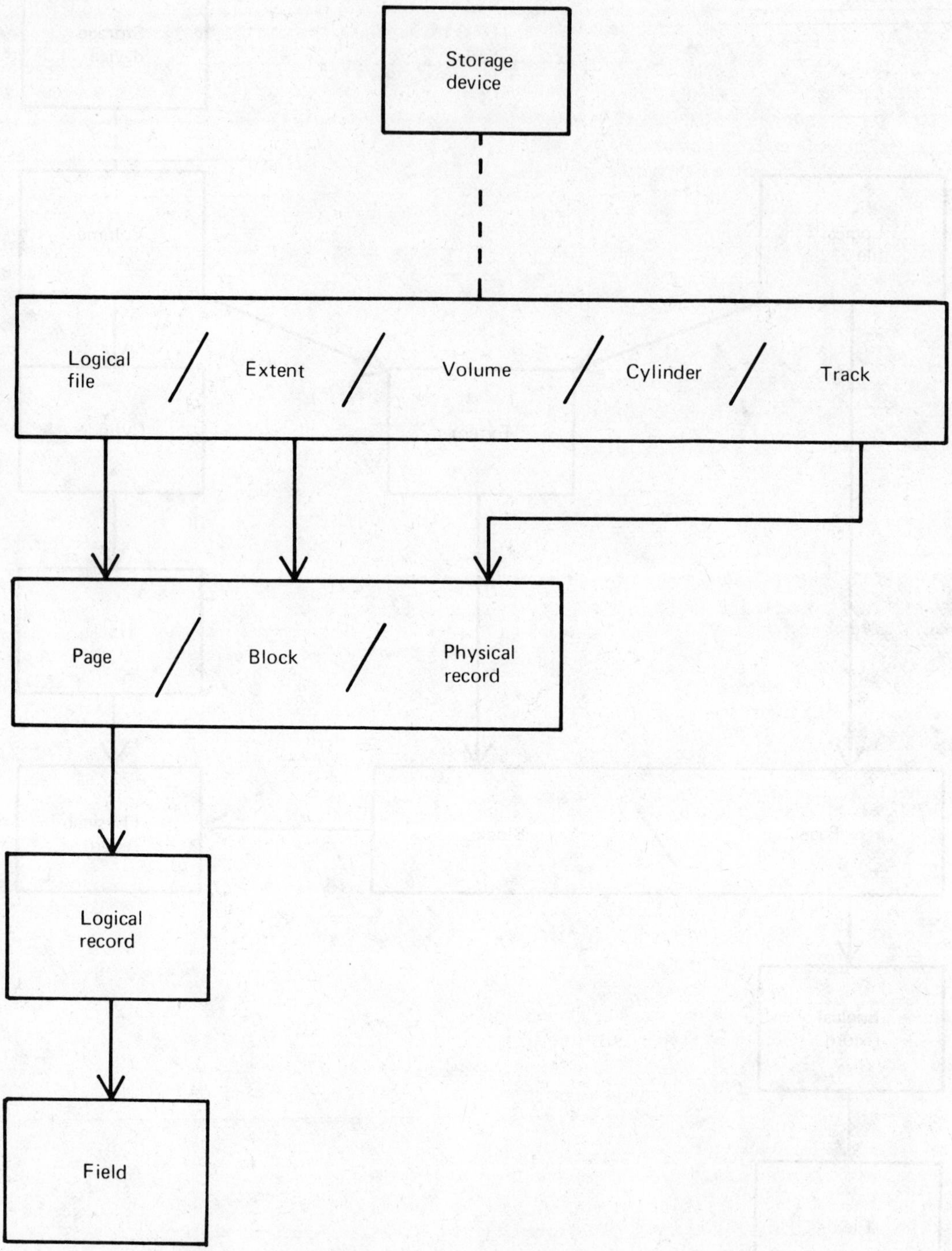


**Fig. 10.** Storage structure for blocked magnetic tape files.

(address calculation) algorithm be used to transform the file name and desired page number into the block number of an extent that is its calculated place of residency, provided the page exists. This storage allocation structure has the well-known "synonym" problem associated with randomization: When more than one page randomizes to the same block number, the extra pages must actually be stored in some other block to be retrieved when requested.

The structure shown in Fig. 8 supports the solution of the synonym problem via the addition of a dashed arrow pointing from the entity class for "block/physical record" to the entity class "page." This specifies the relationship that will exist when a number of created pages all randomize to the same block. The solid lines originating at "page" and "extent," and which join and point to the "block/physical record" entity classes, represent the alternate 1:*n* relationship between page/extent, respectively, and the block.

*Integrated Data Store (IDS) Files.* Through all the examples so far, physical record and block concepts have existed on a 1:1 basis. This is appropriate for the type of secondary storage media on which physical records of any length may be written within the track to create a block of the desired size. However, some disks have a fixed number of standard-sized physical records (sectors) per track. In these cases a block is designated as a container for *n* physical records. Fig. 9 shows how the fixed physical record size has split the entity class of the merged concepts of block and physical record into separate entity classes. It also illustrates the actual storage structure of the Honeywell integrated data store (IDS) data base system.

STORAGE STRUCTURE FOR BLOCKED MAGNETIC TAPE FILES. The discussion so far has centered on disk-resident files. To illustrate that the concepts are equally applicable to other storage media, Fig. 10 uses the allocation concepts of extent and block to integrate the physical storage structure of the magnetic tape (Fig. 3) and the logical storage structure (Fig. 4). It shows a file on magnetic tape where more than one logical record may exist per page. In this case, the concepts of a logical file, extent, volume, cylinder, and track are merged into a single entity class. The concepts of a page, block, and physical record are merged into a second entity class, the occurrences of which exist in a many-to-one relationship with occurrences of the first one. The remaining entity classes represent the concepts of the logical record stored within the page, the field(s) contained within the logical record, and (at the top of the figure) the storage device concept. Note that the dashed line between the storage device and the volume indicates a "sometime 1:1" relationship.

A thoughtfully designed logical structure is a necessity, especially for files that might be moved from one kind of volume to a different one (say, from tape to disk, or vice versa). It is relatively easy to move a blocked logical file for which processing is strictly sequential; tape is a sequential medium and other than sequential access to data contained on it is impractical. As sophistication of processing increases, such files are becoming quite rare; thus, intermedium movement of files in practical terms means tape to disk or disk to disk. The problem in the latter case is that of reconciling differences of potentially different track/physical record sizes with the preexisting logical page size without wasting too much physical storage space.

**Summary.** The discussion in this article has presented a set of concepts that have been defined and used as structural elements in describing storage structures. In many cases, the system objectives permitted two or more concepts to be merged into a single entity class, thus effecting a simplification. However, the need for comparison between data base systems and the need for a general approach to understanding new systems suggest that each of these concepts should be allowed to maintain its own distinct identity, even when merged.

The data-structure diagramming technique used to illustrate the relationships between storage structure concepts should be helpful in filling existing as well as emerging concepts into a solid frame of reference for the study and implementation of present and future, more advanced, data base systems.

REFERENCES

1966. International Federation for Information Processing and International Computation Centre. *IFIP-ICC Vocabulary of Information Processing.* Amsterdam: North-Holland.

1969. Bachman, C. W. "Data Structure Diagrams," *Data Base* (Quarterly News Letter of ACM-SIGBDP), Vol. 1, No. 2 (Summer).

1972. Bachman, C. W. "The Evaluation of Storage Structures," CACM, Vol. 15, No. 7 (July).

S. C. BREWER

# STORAGE ORGANIZATION

For articles on related subjects *see* ADDRESSING; and MACHINE INSTRUCTION SET. For articles on related terms *see* ASCII; and STRING.

If information is to be stored in a computer system, a representation must be chosen to be used internally. The internal representation may be chosen to be quite different from the external form, as long as there are unique transformations from one to the other. In fact, this freedom to use various internal forms has created problems in situations where information generated on one computer system must be processed on another system.

Although there were some early attempts to represent decimal digits directly, such as by selecting one of ten vacuum tubes for each digit, they did not prove to be feasible or economical. It soon became quite standard to use various two-state devices as primitive information-bearing units. Typical two-state devices are punched cards (with the presence or absence of a hole in a particular position on the card being the two states), high or low voltage on a particular electronic circuit, presence or absence of magnetized spots on the surface of a revolving drum or disk (or on a reel of tape), and so on.

Assuming such a two-state representation, one can treat a collection of such devices (or a *string*) as a unit as well. From the early interpretation of such strings as representing numbers with two states in each digit position (i.e., 0 or 1), these digits have become known as binary digits, or *bits*. This interpretation regards a string of zeroes and ones as an integer expressed in *base* 2 form. The term "bits" has now been generalized to include zeroes and ones found in strings that are not interpreted as binary integers.

Information other than binary integers must also be represented in storage. In some computer systems (in particular, those involved with monetary computations), there is a need for representing decimal digits per se and for doing decimal arithmetic on these digits. (This need arises from the different round-off effects generated in binary and decimal arithmetic.) In other situations, it is necessary to represent alphabetic characters and punctuation symbols so as to process ordinary text, names, etc. In such cases, each alphabetic, numeric, or punctuation character is assigned a particular string of bits as its representation. Part of one such assignment, which uses eight-bit strings and has received wide support, is called the American Standard Code for Information Interchange (ASCII). Note that some of the 256 possible strings are not assigned symbols (see table in article on ASCII); these are reserved for later expansion. Others are given symbols that are neither letters, digits, nor punctuation characters; they are control symbols, usually used in communications to signal the beginning and end of a transmitted string, and so on. Earlier computers tended to use six-bit strings to represent symbols, but it became clear that this was too restrictive, and in recent years eight-bit strings have become standard. The term "byte" is used in referring to a bit string which is of the size corresponding to the symbol representation in a particular system. Thus, there are computers with six-bit bytes, but today one expects eight-bit bytes.

We have seen that a string of bits can have more than one interpretation, so that 11000001 can represent the letter A or the binary form of the decimal integer 193. Yet another interpretation of a string of bits may be as a computer instruction. In this case, some of the bits in the string are interpreted in the control unit of the system as a code for the operation to be performed. The remaining bits might be used to indicate registers (either special registers or storage locations), whose contents are to be used as input to the operation, or which are to receive the results of the operation as new contents. Several formats of instructions from typical computers are shown in Fig. 1.

Some early computers had separate storage for instructions and for data, but this did not last long because it proved costly to provide separate arithmetic processors for two kinds of storage, especially when many operations involved with modifying instructions were so similar to ordinary arithmetic operations. However, the development of microprogramming and read-only storage has somewhat restored separation of instructions and data.

Once separate storage for instructions and data was abandoned, it became necessary to find ways to store, and access, any kind of information from any part of storage. Very often, storage was divided into fixed-length strings called "words," usually from 36 to 60 bits long.* Each word would contain one or more instructions as numbers in fixed- or floating-point form or a number of bytes so that the word length was always a multiple of the byte length. Addresses in such computers usually specified in-

* Smaller computers, particularly minicomputers, often intended for applications in which long numbers were not needed, usually have from 12 to 24 bits in a word.

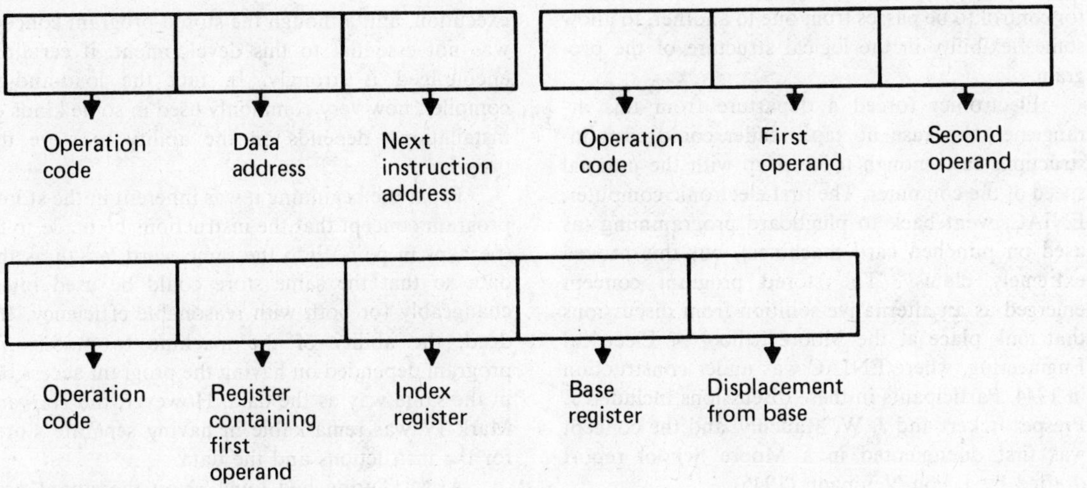


**Fig. 1.** Typical instruction formats.

dividual words, and one could access separate bytes only by shifting or masking operations.

Computers intended for commercial applications, on the other hand, were typically designed to facilitate variable-length strings of characters, since so much of their data exhibited this variability. Thus, one found computers in which both instructions and data were of variable length, with an address specifying the beginning of a string of characters, and a special *word mark* symbol signaling the end of a string.

Recently, computers have been designed to try to reflect both kinds of needs: fixed-length words to represent numbers, and variable-length strings of characters. In these cases, addresses usually specify a particular byte (occasionally even a particular bit) in storage, and a word is treated explicitly as a multiple of the byte length. Instructions may vary in length also, depending on the number of addresses they need to reference. This is to be contrasted with the fixed-word-length machine, where all addresses typically had to fit into the word, but where many bits were wasted if fewer addresses were needed in particular instructions.

REFERENCE

1969. Rosen, S. "Electronic Computers: A Historical Survey," *Computing Reviews,* Vol. 1, No. 1 (March), pp. 7–36.

B. A. GALLER

# STORE.

*See* MEMORY; and READ-ONLY STORE.

# STORED PROGRAM CONCEPT

For articles on related subjects *see* ADDRESS MODIFICATION; ASSEMBLERS: DIGITAL COMPUTERS.

For articles on related terms *see* BABBAGE, CHARLES; ECKERT, J. PRESPER; EDSAC; EDVAC; ENIAC; LOAD-AND-GO COMPILER; MARK I; MAUCHLY, JOHN W.; TURING, ALAN M.; VON NEUMANN, JOHN; and WILKES, MAURICE V.

The key design feature of modern computers, which allows the instructions to be held in the internal store while they are awaiting execution, is known as the "stored program concept." Many computers, beginning with the Analytical Engine of Charles Babbage, and including the Automatic Sequence Controlled Calculator (Harvard Mark I), were designed to perform discrete operations, each specified by a concisely coded instruction. Prior to the use of electronics, however, these instructions were taken by the control unit from a special input device that read a tape or belt. Program loops required a loop of tape to be mounted (and the Harvard Mark I had three readers) with provision for control to be passes from one to another, to allow some flexibility in the logical structure of the program.

Electronics forced a departure from this arrangement because no tape reader could scan instructions fast enough to keep up with the internal speed of the computer. The first electronic computer, ENIAC, went back to plugboard programming (as used on punched card machines), but this proved extremely clumsy. The stored program concept emerged as an alternative solution from discussions that took place at the Moore School of Electrical Engineering, where ENIAC was under construction in 1944. Participants in these discussions included J. Presper Eckert and J. W. Mauchly, and the concept was first documented in a Moore School report drafted by J. von Neumann (1945).

Besides solving the speed problem, the concept had two important effects. First, program jumps could be used liberally without incurring the time penalty required to hunt along the program tape. (Some early machines, especially those based on drum stores, had some residual timing penalties affecting the arrangement of jumps, but these were comparatively unimportant.) Therefore, much more complex program structures could be contemplated. Secondly, the instructions held in the internal store were accessible to be operated upon in the same way as the data during the execution of the program.

Both these possibilities were quickly exploited when the first stored-program computers came into service in 1949. Alteration of programs during execution enormously increased the scope of automatic computing, and was heavily used in the early days. Since then, its use has diminished considerably, for several reasons, the main ones being the introduction of index registers (these achieved more economically the effect of address modification, which had been the commonest purpose of program alteration) and the trend toward time-sharing systems and run-time diagnostic systems (which required programs to be "pure procedures", i.e., unaltered and unalterable during execution, all variations being embodied in sets of parameters held in a working store segment).

Another development, which demanded the abandonment of program alteration during execution, was the use of read-only memories for programs needed very frequently. These, however, have remained special items, it being unusual for more than a small part of a computer's store to be of this type.

The potentialities of program-processing were much more fully exploited later in the preprocessing of programs by assemblers and compilers before execution, and although the stored-program concept was not essential to this development, it certainly encouraged it strongly. In fact the load-and-go compiler, now very commonly used in some kinds of installations, depends on the ability to store the program.

From the beginning it was inherent in the stored program concept that the instructions be made to fit (perhaps in pairs) into the same word length as the data so that the same store could be used interchangeably for both with reasonable efficiency. Indeed, the ability of the machine to modify its program depended on having the program accessible in the same way as the data. However, the Harvard Mark IV was remarkable in having separate stores for the instructions and the data.

A. M. Turing had touched on the stored program concept in a paper on mathematical logic in 1936 (which led to the term "Turing machine"), though not in a form that showed its potential practicality. The first electronic stored-program machine to obey instructions was that built by Williams and Kilburn in Manchester, England, and the first to carry out practical calculations was the EDSAC, built by Wilkes at Cambridge, England, which was operating in May 1949. Both EDSAC and EDVAC, designed at the Moore School by Eckert and Mauchly, embodied many of the ideas incorporated in van Neumann's report (1945), but EDVAC did not become operational until 1951.

In the years that have followed these early implementations, the stored program concept has been elaborated in many ways. Programming techniques and languages of many kinds have been developed, as well as operating systems and all the various components of modern software. Perhaps the most fundamental variation from the original idea has been the introduction of program interrupts, which means that the sequence of execution of the instructions is no longer uniquely determined by the program and its data, but can be affected by external events occurring during the execution.

These, however, are all auxiliary to the stored program concept itself, an essentially simple, but profoundly important, concept that has characterized the main stream of digital computer development since 1945. This concept, together with the practical development of electronics, has made possible the computer revolution as we now know it.

### Reference

1945. von Neumann, John. "First Draft of a Report on the EDVAC," Contract No. W-670-ORD-

4926, U.S. Army Ordnance Department and University of Pennsylvania, Moore School of Electrical Engineering, University of Pennsylvania, Philadelphia, Pa., June 30.

S. GILL

**STRESS.** *See* PROBLEM-ORIENTED LANGUAGES.

## STRETCH

For articles on related subjects *see* DIGITAL COMPUTERS: Early; LIVERMORE AUTOMATIC RESEARCH COMPUTER; and MANUFACTURERS, COMPUTER.

The *Stretch* computer (formally the IBM 7030) was the outcome of a research and development project started in 1955 and aimed at an advance in performance of around two orders of magnitude over the then existing computer technology and organization. It was a joint project between the IBM Corporation and the Los Alamos Scientific Laboratory of the U.S. Atomic Energy Commission.

The first computer (Fig. 1) was delivered to Los Alamos in 1961. Although the machine did not quite "stretch" as far as the ambitious performance goal originally set, at that time it was still the most powerful computer in existence. After ten years of service, the Los Alamos machine was dismantled in 1971. Seven other Stretch machines were built.

**Fig. 1.** The first Stretch computer being tested just prior to its installation at the Los Alamos Scientific Laboratory.

Stretch was the first major solid-state computer developed by IBM, and its transistor, core, and disk storage technologies were applied extensively to other computers of the 7000 series. Its sophisticated internal organization (Buchholz, 1962) departed substantially from that of previous computers. An instruction look-ahead unit, for example, permitted up to six instructions at one time to be in various stages of execution; thus, Stretch became the first pipeline computer. While the sophistication contributed to the high speed of Stretch, the resulting complexity of implementation, in retrospect, also kept the speed somewhat short of the objective.

Other than speed, perhaps the most significant feature was the provision in one computer system of both the parallel floating-point arithmetic then associated with "scientific" computers, and the serial, variable-length, fixed-point arithmetic and character processing functions then found only in "commercial" computers.

The computer had been planned as the largest of a single line of general-purpose compatible machines. However, this concept did not materialize until the later System/360, which also adopted several other basic concepts of Stretch. Some of the terminology from the Stretch project (computer architecture, byte) has since entered general use.

A major nonarithmetical extension to Stretch, referred to as *Harvest*, provided very powerful data streaming and table look-up operations on a byte-by-byte basis (Buchholz, 1962, chap. 17). Only one Harvest machine was built.

REFERENCES

1962. Buchholz, W. (Ed.). *Planning a Computer System (Project Stretch)*. New York: McGraw-Hill.

W. BUCHHOLZ

## STRING

For article on related subject *see* STRING PROCESSING LANGUAGES.

For articles on related terms *see* ASCII; BINARY CODED DECIMAL, NATURAL; CHARACTER SET; COLLATING SEQUENCE; CONCATENATION; EBCDIC; and LISTS AND LIST PROCESSING.

## STRING PROCESSING LANGUAGES

In computer programming, the term "string" usually refers to a sequence of characters. This usage is an analogy to physical objects strung together, one after another, such as a string of beads. While this term can be applied to any type of object, it is usually reserved *for characters*, and the word "list" is usually used *for other objects*.

Strings are typically written from left to right. Thus, ABC is a string of three characters, the first being A and the last being C. Strings may be arbitrarily long, although there are sometimes restrictions in practice. Since a string is a sequence of characters, two strings appended together form another string. Appending strings is called "concatenation" (or sometimes simply "catenation"). An important string is the *null string*, containing no characters, which is important because it is the identity with respect to concatenation; concatenating the null string onto a string does not change that string. A sequence of consecutive characters within a string is a *substring*. Thus, BAT is a substring of BRICKBAT, but BB is not.

Strings are important because almost all computer input and output consists of strings, including programs and data. While this aspect of input and output is often not of direct concern to the user of the computer, in some problem areas, such as language translation, text editing, and artificial intelligence, strings are important per se.

An important aspect of strings is the characters they may contain. This is determined by the *character set* of the computer on which the string is represented. Character sets differ in specific characters, the number of characters, and the order in which they are arranged. There are several more or less standard character sets and a few variants. Most common are BCD (64 characters), ASCII (128 characters) and EBCDIC (256 characters). BCD contains upper-case letters, numbers, some punctuation marks, and a few special symbols. ASCII and EBCDIC contain lower-case letters as well, and more special symbols. Within the computer, a character is represented by a pattern of bits. In BCD, each character is represented by six bits (hence, the 64 characters). In ASCII, there are seven bits; and in EBCDIC, eight. The correspondence between a bit pattern and a specific character is a matter of convention.

The characters arranged in order of their internal numerical representation are said to be in *collating sequence*, or lexical order. For the letters, this order corresponds to ordinary alphabetical order. For other characters, different conventions apply. In ASCII, the digits come before the letters, while in EBCDIC the converse is true. The lexical order of characters extends to strings. Thus, strings may be compared lexically, i.e., for their relative alphabetical order. Such comparison is the basis of sorting. The leftmost character of a string is the most significant one for the purposes of determining lexical order, as is the case in a dictionary, except that characters other than letters must be considered.

The *graphic* is the printed representation of a character. This representation is standard for letters and numbers, but sometimes varies for other characters, depending on the printing device. Not all characters have graphics. The blank, for example, has no graphic and appears as a space when printed. In the larger character sets, there are many characters without graphics, depending somewhat on the specific printing device.

R. GRISWOLD

## STRING PROCESSING LANGUAGES

For articles on related subjects *see* LIST PROCESSING LANGUAGES; LISTS AND LIST PROCESSING; MACROLANGUAGES; PROGRAMMING LANGUAGES; and PROGRAMMING LINGUISTICS.

For articles on related terms *see* CONCATENATION; LOOP; MACROINSTRUCTION; MARKOV ALGORITHM; and STRING.

In programming contexts the term *string* usually refers to a sequence of characters. For example, ABC is a string of three characters. Strings are more prevalent in computer processing than is generally realized. In most cases, input to the computer is in the form of strings. Punched cards provide a typical example. Similarly, output from the computer is in the form of strings; a printed line is no more than a string of characters. In spite of this fact, string processing has received comparatively little attention.

**Strings and String Processing.** The majority of effort and attention has been concentrated on numerical and business data processing, and the most widely used and well-known programming languages are in these areas. However, a substantial amount of string processing is performed. For example, a compiler must accept strings as input, analyze these strings, and produce other strings to be printed. Operating systems must analyze command strings and perform appropriate actions. Because compilers and operating systems are used so heavily, they must be extremely efficient. For this reason, such processors have typically been written in assembly language rather than in higher-level string-processing languages.

Nevertheless, string processing often must be performed in situations in which the complexity of the problem is such that higher-level languages offer many advantages. Examples are language translation, computational linguistics, symbolic mathematics, text editing, and document formatting.

Developers of languages for string processing have been in a less well-defined position than developers of numerical processing languages. While mathematical notation for numerical computation has developed over centuries, and its current form is widely known and fairly well standardized, string processing is a new area. There is no general agreement on what operations should be performed in string processing, nor is there a standard notation. The developers of string-processing languages started largely without conventions. As a result, notation, program structure, and approach to problem formulation are often radically different from those of more conventional programming languages.

**Operations on Strings.** While there were no generally agreed-upon string operations when string-processing languages were first developed, four operations have achieved general acceptance: concatenation, identification of substrings, pattern matching, and transformation of strings to replace identified substrings by other strings.

*Concatenation* (sometimes called "catenation") is the process of appending one string to another to produce a longer string. Thus, the result of concatenating the strings AB and CDE is the string ABCDE. This operation is a natural extension of the concept of a string as a sequence of characters.

*A substring* is a string within another string. For example, BC is a substring of ABCDE. The most important and far-reaching string operation is that of pattern matching.

Stated in general terms, *pattern matching* is the process of examining a string to locate substrings or to determine if a string has certain properties. Examples are the presence of a specific substring, substrings in certain positions, substrings in a specified relationship to each other, and so on.

*Transformation* of strings is typically accomplished in conjunction with pattern matching, using the results of pattern matching to effect a replacement of substrings.

The descriptions of the languages that follow emphasize approaches to string processing and the major facilities that deal with strings. No attempt has been made to describe these languages completely or in detail. Readers interested in the individual languages should refer to the cited reference material.

**Comit.** Comit (Yngve, 1963), designed in 1957–1958, was the first of the string-processing languages. The motivation behind the development of Comit was the need for a tool for mechanical language translation. Comit strongly reflects these origins, and is oriented toward the representation of natural languages.

BASIC CONCEPTS. In Comit, unlike most other string-processing languages, a string is composed of *constituents*, which may consist of more than one character. Thus, a word composed of many characters may be a single constituent in a string. A string is written as a series of constituents separated by + signs. An example is

```
FOURSCORE + AND + SEVEN + YEARS + AGO
```

The character – is used to represent a space (blank). Thus, to include spaces between words, the string becomes

```
FOURSCORE + – + AND + – + SEVEN
                    + – YEARS + – AGO
```

All characters other than letters have syntactic meaning in Comit. A star (asterisk) in front of a character other than a letter indicates that the character is to be taken literally rather than for its syntactic meaning. For example, the sentence

```
33 ARE IN THE TOP 1/2.
```

is written

```
*3*3 + – + ARE + – + IN + – + THE
               + – + TOP + – + *1*/*2*.
```

Attention is focused on a *workspace*, which contains the string currently being processed. There are also 128 *shelves*, any of which may be exchanged with the workspace to change the focus of attention. Thus, there may be at most 129 distinct strings in a program at any one time.

A Comit program consists of a sequence of rules, each of which has five parts:

*name left-half = right-half // routing goto*

The name identifies the rule. The left-half is a pattern applied to the work space. The right-half specifies processing to be performed on the portion of the work space matched by the left-half. The routing, separated from the rest of the rule by two slashes, performs operations other than pattern matching. If a rule has no routing field, the slashes are not required. The goto controls program flow.

PATTERN MATCHING. The most important aspects of Comit are the pattern matching performed in the left-half and the transformation on the workspace produced by the right-half. The left-half may specify full constituents as written in a string, a specific number of constituents of unspecified value, an indefinite number of constituents, an earlier constituent referenced by its position in the left-half, and so on. A full constituent is written as it is in a string. Other left-half constituents are represented by special notations. For example: *$n* matches *n* consecutive constituents, regardless of their value; *$* matches any number of constituents. The integer *n* matches the same string that the *n*th constituent of the left-half matched. An example of a left-half is

```
THE + $1 + $ + 2
```

This left-half, composed of four constituents, specifies a constituent consisting of the characters THE, followed by any single constituent, followed by any number of constituents until a constituent is encountered which is the same as the one matched by the second constituent, namely, $1. Pattern matching is left to right. Left-half constituents must match consecutive constituents in the workspace.

If the work space contains

```
THE + FIRST
└─┘   └───┘
 1      2
+ MAN + IN + LINE + IS + SERVED + FIRST
  └────────────────────────────┘   └───┘
                3                    4
```

the match for each of the constituents is as shown. Note that the fourth constituent of the left-half matches the same constituents of the workspace as the second constituent of the left-half. The third constituent of the left-half consequently matches the intervening five constituents of the workspace. When a match occurs, workspace constituents are associated with the left-half constituents they matched, and are subsequently referenced by the number of the corresponding left-half constituent.

The right-half may contain full constituents and integers that correspond to the constituents of the left-half. The matched portion of the workspace is replaced by constituents specified in the right-half. Continuing the example above, the rule

```
THE + $1 + $ + 2 = 1 + SECOND + 3 + 4
```

transforms the workspace into

```
THE + SECOND + MAN + IN + LINE +
IS + SERVED + FIRST
```

Constituents may have attributes, called "subscripts." Subscripts may be logical or numerical. A slash separates a constituent from its subscripts, which are in turn separated by commas. An example is

```
MORGAN/.36,SEX MALE,
        HOBBIES CHESS PHOTOGRAPHY
```

The period indicates a numerical subscript whose value is 36; SEX and HOBBIES are logical subscripts and have values MALE, and CHESS and PHOTOGRAPHY, respectively. Thus, there are many logical subscripts, each with a number of values. Subscripts associate information with constituents and provide an important facility, which may be used in pattern matching to identify constituents with desired properties. There are a number of operations for manipulating subscripts.

OTHER FACILITIES. The routing part of a rule permits operations that cannot be performed in the right-half. Examples are exchange of the workspace with a shelf, movement of constituents between the workspace and shelves, printing the workspace, reading data into the workspace, and so on. There are a variety of formats for reading and printing.

The goto part of a rule controls program flow. Control may be transferred to a named rule, back to the same statement for execution again, to the next statement, and so on.

Conditional loops may be programmed in a number of ways. One conditional operation is left-half matching, which may fail. For example, the left-half $10 would fail to match the workspace given earlier because the workspace does not contain ten constituents. When a left-half fails to match, the remainder of the rule is not performed, and control passes to the next rule in line. Special notations are used for names and gotos to facilitate the programming of loops. A * may be used for the name of a rule that needs no other specific identification. A * in the goto indicates that control is to be transferred to the next rule in line after the current statement is executed. A / in the goto indicates that control is to be returned to the present rule if it is executed successfully. Thus, the following statement, with a blank right-half and a / in the goto, can be used to remove all occurrences of THE from the work space.

```
* THE = /
```

When the left-half finally fails to match, execution continues with the next rule in line. Arithmetic performed on numerical subscripts can also be used to control loops.

A mechanism called the "dispatcher" facilitates selection of program branches, utilizing logical subscripts corresponding to rule names to select subrules according to corresponding subscript values. The dispatcher can select one of a number of subrules on the basis of a pseudo-random choice. The ability to have program branches selected at random is useful in operations such as the simulation of card shuffling. *List rules* provide for processing searches in alphabetical order to improve running speeds, facilitate dictionary look-up, and sorting.

STATUS. The current version of Comit is Comit II. Comit II contains a number of improvements and features not contained in the original version, and is upward-compatible so that programs written for the original version of Comit will also run on Comit II. Comit II has been implemented on the IBM 7000 series and the IBM 360/370. Because of its early origin, Comit lacks a number of features that are available in more recently developed languages. Comit is still in use, but most programmers have turned to newer languages.

**The Snobol Languages.** The first Snobol (string-oriented symbolic language) language was designed and implemented in 1962–1963. The major motivation behind the development of Snobol was the need for a general-purpose language for processing strings of characters. Manipulation of symbolic mathematical expressions was also an important consideration.

SNOBOL

*Basic Concepts.* In Snobol, unlike Comit, a string is simply a sequence of characters. Enclosing quotation marks delimit the string, but are not part of the string. An example is

```
'FOURSCORE AND SEVEN YEARS AGO'
```

Such a string is said to be specified *literally*. Strings may be assigned to names for subsequent reference. An example is the assignment statement

```
FIRST = 'MORGAN'
```

which assigns the string MORGAN to the name FIRST. There is no specific limit to the number of distinct strings. Storage management is handled automatically without declarations. Concatenation is performed by writing the strings to be concatenated one after another with separating blanks. Such strings can be given literally or as the value of names. For example

```
FULLNAME = FIRST ' SMITH'
```

assigns the string MORGAN SMITH to the name FULLNAME. The blank is simply a character like any other, as illustrated.

A Snobol program consists of a sequence of statements. There are three basic kinds of statements: assignment, pattern matching, and replacement. The respective forms are

*label subject = object* *goto*
*label subject pattern* *goto*
*label subject pattern = object goto*

An optional *label* identifies the statement. The *subject* provides the focus for the statement and is the name on which operations are performed. The *goto* controls program flow and is optional. An assignment statement assigns a value to a name. A pattern-matching statement examines the value of a name for a *pattern*, and a replacement statement modifies that part of the subject matched by the pattern.

*Pattern Matching.* Patterns in Snobol consist of a sequence of components. There are two types of components: specific strings and *string variables*. A specific string may be given literally or referred to by name. A string variable is indicated by delimiting *s which bracket a name. There are several types of string variables. One is the arbitrary string variable, which can match any string. It is similar to the Comit $ notation, except that whatever the string variable matches is assigned to the name between the *s. Pattern matching is left to right, and components of the pattern must match consecutive substrings of the subject. An example is

```
Z  'T' *FILL* 'N'
```

In this statement the value of Z is matched for any string that begins with a T and ends with an N. The substring between the T and N is assigned to the name FILL. If the value of Z is TEEN, the value assigned to FILL is EE. Thus, string variables provide a means of assigning substrings to names.

There are also *balanced string variables* and *fixed-length string* variables. A balanced string variable matches a string that is properly balanced with respect to parentheses like an ordinary mathematical expression. An example is SIN(X+F(3)). A fixed-length string variable matches any string of a specific length.

Balanced string variables are indicated by parentheses bracketing the name between the *s. Thus *(ARG)* represents a balanced string variable. If the value of EXP is the expression given above, the statement

```
EXP  'SIN('  *(ARG)*  ')'
```

matches and assigns the string X+F(3) to the name ARG.

Fixed-length string variables are indicated by a / and a quoted number following the name. The statement

```
TEXT  ','  *C/"1"*
```

examines the value of TEXT for a comma and assigns the character following the comma to the name C.

Replacement is a combination of pattern matching and assignment in which the matched substring is replaced by the object. The statement

```
FULLNAME  'SMITH'  =  'JONES'
```

replaces the substring SMITH by JONES and consequently changes the value of FULLNAME to MORGAN JONES.

*Indirect Referencing.* An interesting and important feature of Snobol is its ability to use any string as a name. A string may be computed and then used as a name by the *indirect reference* operator $. A $ placed in front of a string uses the value of that string as a name. For example, the statements

```
X = 'NUM'
N = '3'
HOLIDAY = X N
$HOLIDAY = 'EASTER'
```

first assigns the value NUM3 to the name HOLIDAY and then assigns the value EASTER to the name NUM3. The indirect referencing operator, similar in concept to indirect addressing in assembly language, thus provides a way of constructing names out of data.

*Other Facilities.* Input and output take place by using specially designated names as subjects. Arithmetic facilities are rudimentary. Integer arithmetic is performed on strings of numerals.

The goto part of a statement controls program flow. Gotos can be unconditional to a labeled statement, or conditional on the success or failure of pattern matching. Loops are programmed using the conditional nature of pattern matching.

*Status.* Snobol was superseded by Snobol3 in 1965. Snobol3 is similar to Snobol, but has several additional features, including a number of built-in functions and a facility for programmer-defined, recursive functions. Snobol3 was in turn superseded by Snobol4 in 1967.

SNOBOL4. Snobol4 (Griswold et al., 1971) is the most recent language in the Snobol series. While Snobol4 is a natural descendant of earlier Snobol languages and is based on many of the same ideas and approaches to string processing, Snobol4 introduced a number of new concepts. The most important, from a string-processing point of view, are those dealing with pattern matching.

*Patterns.* In Comit and the earlier Snobol languages, different types of patterns are indicated by specific notations. In Snobol4, on the other hand, patterns are data objects that are constructed by functions and operations. Consequently, quite complicated patterns can be built up in a series of steps.

There are two basic pattern-construction operations: alternation and concatenation. The alternation of two patterns is a pattern that will match anything either of its two components will match. The concatenation of two patterns is a pattern that will match anything its two components will match consecutively. Alternation is represented by a vertical bar, and concatenation by a blank. An example of pattern construction is

```
PET = 'CAT' | 'DOG'
PETKIND = PET '-LIKE'
```

The pattern PET matches either of the strings CAT or DOG, and PETKIND matches anything PET matches, followed by the string -LIKE (i.e., CAT-LIKE or DOG-LIKE). The pattern-constructing process can be continued, progressively building more complicated patterns.

To generalize the concept of patterns and avoid the need for special notations for each type, there are a number of pattern-valued functions. For example, the value of LEN(*n*) is a pattern that matches *n* characters, and the value of TAB(*n*) is a pattern that matches a substring through the *n*th character of the subject string. An example is given by the statement

```
OPER = TAB(6) 'X'
```

which creates a pattern that will match any string containing an X as its seventh character. Other pattern-valued functions create patterns that match any one of a number of specific characters, search for specific characters, and so on. An example is SPAN('0123456789') which matches a substring consisting only of digits.

As in Snobol, pattern matching is left to right, and components must match consecutive substrings of the subject string. When a component fails to match, alternative matches are attempted. If no alternative is specified, the pattern-matching process backs up to earlier, successfully matched components, seeking other ways in which the entire pattern match can succeed. The pattern-matching process includes the concept of a cursor, which is an imaginary marker in the subject string indicating the current position of the match. Movement of the cursor is implicit, not under direct control of the programmer, although in some patterns there is a direct correlation. Thus LEN(3) moves the cursor to the right three characters. The cursor cannot be moved to the left by a successful match.

Names may be attached to components of patterns so that when the component matches a substring, the substring matched is assigned to the name. Attachment is indicated by the binary $ operator. An example is

```
HEAD = LEN(7) $ LABEL
```

This statement constructs a pattern that matches seven characters. The seven characters, when matched, are assigned to the name LABEL. Thus, the statement

```
CARD HEAD
```

simply assigns the first seven characters of the value of CARD to LABEL. If the match fails (because CARD is less than seven characters long), no assignment is made to LABEL.

Another aspect of pattern matching is the ability to modify the meaning of a component during pattern matching, depending on substrings matched by earlier components. Evaluation of an expression in a pattern may be deferred by prefacing that expression by *. The expression is then left unevaluated until it is encountered in pattern matching. An example of the power of this facility is given by the following pattern:

```
LIT = SPAN('0123456789') $ N 'H' LEN(*N)
```

When LIT is used in pattern matching, the argument of LEN is not evaluated until after the first part of the pattern has matched; SPAN matches a substring of digits and assigns that substring to the name N. The remainder of the pattern matches the letter H and then a number of characters that depends on the value just assigned to N. Thus, this pattern matches Hollerith literal constructions as given in Fortran format specifications. It is also possible to define recursive patterns using unevaluated expressions.

*Other Facilities.* Other string processing facilities include alphabetical comparison of strings, mappings from one set of characters to another, and deletion of trailing blanks. Unlike the earlier Snobol languages, which were purely string processing languages, Snobol4 includes many types of data. In addition to the common types such as integer and real, Snobol4 includes arrays as data objects, tables that provide associative look-up features, and the ability to define new data types during execution. These defined data types provide list-processing facilities. In many cases it is possible to perform data-type conversions between various types of data. It is possible to convert a string into program statements during program execution, and hence to modify or extend the program while it is running. Snobol4 is actually a general-purpose language that strongly emphasizes string processing and contains a number of exotic features.

*Status.* Snobol4 is the most widely used and generally the most available string-processing language. It has been implemented on most large-scale scientific computers, including the IBM 360/370, CDC 3600, CDC 6000 series, UNIVAC 1100 series, DEC-System 10, XDS Sigma 5/6/7, Burroughs 6700, and Atlas 2. There are a number of dialects that differ somewhat from the basic version. An extension of Snobol4, called Snobol4B, incorporates a facility for manipulating three-dimensional character strings called "blocks."

**Other String-Processing Languages.** Ambit (Wolfberg, 1972), developed in 1964, is a string-processing language oriented toward algebraic manipulation. In many respects, Ambit is similar to the Comit and Snobol languages. However, the strings it operates on are parenthesized expressions that correspond to tree structures. In fact, strings are implemented as fully linked trees. In Ambit, unlike most other string-processing languages, two strings are considered equivalent even if they differ in the position and number of blanks they contain. A basic *replacement rule* consists of a *citation*, specifying a pattern, and a *replacement*, which effects a transformation on the string under consideration. The citation may match only one way; the replacement rule must be unambiguous. An important aspect of Ambit pattern matching is the explicit reference to pointers, which identify specific positions in strings. More recently, three versions of Ambit have been distinguished. Ambit/S for manipulation of strings, Ambit/G for manipulating general data structures, and Ambit/L for list processing.

Convert (Guzmán and McIntosh, 1966) is an extension of Lisp, incorporating pattern-matching and transformation operations. There are a number of fundamental patterns and facilities for constructing more complicated ones. The function RESEMBLE applies patterns to strings. The function REPLACE performs transformations using skeletons that specify the structure of the replacement. A rule consists of a pattern and a skeleton. Convert applies the pattern to a string. If a "resemblance" is found, values of relevant parts are identified and substituted into the skeleton to effect the conversion.

Axle (Cohen and Wegstein, 1965), like Comit, has a workspace that is the focus of attention for pattern matching and replacement. Axle has *assertion tables*, which specify patterns. These specifications may be recursive. *Imperative tables* specify patterns to be matched and corresponding replacements. A pattern-matching procedure determines which imperative is applicable. Axle has *markers*, which may be positioned in the work space. These markers may be used to avoid reprocessing previously transformed parts of the workspace.

Panon (Forino, 1968) is a language based on generalized Markov algorithms, and includes a number of pattern-matching facilities and rules for transforming strings. A Panon program is itself a string, and hence susceptable to self-modification.

Not all string-processing languages are high level. EOL (Lukaszewicz and Nievergelt, 1967) is a string-processing language whose operations are low level, being more akin to machine language. In fact, EOL is thought of as the assembly language for a hypothetical EOL machine. EOL programs consist of a sequence of instructions that includes calls to subroutines and macro definitions. Data is processed as *stacks* of *constituents*. A constituent is a string of characters and may be of a number of types. EOL instructions manipulate the stack and constituents on them.

In addition to the languages discussed above, many languages intended for specific areas of application, or which stress other features, also have substantial string-processing facilities. More recently developed general-purpose languages such as PL/I have string-processing facilities, and macro languages form an entire class of important string processing languages.

REFERENCES

1963. Yngve, Victor H. *Computer Programming with COMIT II*. Cambridge, Mass.: M.I.T. Press.

1965. Cohen, Kenneth, and J. H. Wegstein. "AXLE: An Axiomatic Language for String Transformations," *Communications of the ACM*, Vol. 8, No. 11 (November), pp. 657–661.

1966. Guzmán, Adolfo, and Harold V. McIntosh. "CONVERT," *Communications of the ACM*, Vol. 9, No. 8 (August), pp. 604–615.

1967. Lukaszewicz, L., and J. Nievergelt. "EOL Programming Examples: A Primer," Report No. 242. Urbana, Illinois: Dept. of Computer Science, University of Illinois (September).

1968. Forino, A. Caracciolo. "String Processing Languages and Generalized Markov Algorithms," *Symbol Manipulation Languages and Techniques*. Proceedings of the IFIP Working Conference on Symbol Manipulation Languages. Amsterdam: North-Holland, pp. 141–206.

1971. Griswold, R. E., J. F. Poage, and I. P. Polonsky. *The SNOBOL4 Programming Language*, 2d ed. Englewood Cliffs, N.J.: Prentice-Hall.

1972. Wolfberg, Michael S. "Fundamentals of the AMBIT/L List-Processing Language," in Proceedings of a Symposium on Two-Dimensional Man-Machine Communication. *SIGPLAN Notices*, Vol. 7, No. 10 (October), pp. 66–75.

R. E. GRISWOLD

## STRUCTURED PROGRAMMING

For articles on related subjects *see* MODULAR PROGRAMMING; PASCAL; PRO-

CEDURE-ORIENTED LANGUAGES, Programming in; and PROGRAM.
For article on related term *see* BACKTRACKING.

Structured programming (SP) is concerned with improving the programming process through better organization of programs and better programming notation to facilitate correct and clear descriptions of data and control structures.

Improved programming languages and organized programming techniques should result in the production of programs that are:

1. More understandable and therefore more easily modified and documented.
2. More economical to run because good organization and notation makes it easier for an optimizing compiler to "understand" the program's logic.
3. More correct and therefore more easily debugged because general correctness theorems dealing with structures can be applied to proving the correctness of programs.

**Structured Programs.** The physical structure of a well-organized program corresponds to the sequence of steps in the algorithm being implemented. At a lower level, all parts of the implementation of one idea are grouped in a structure that clearly indicates how the various parts are selected and sequenced, and the relation of this idea to neighboring ideas.

The program should be expressed in the most natural and appropriate representation. When, as usually happens, the most approriate notation is not available in the programming language being used, the programmer should, in effect, translate the natural notation (now expressed as comments) into the available notation. If the language being used is a lower-level language (e.g., assembly language), it may be necessary to introduce intermediate levels of notation to guide the reader by stages to understanding the final code.

SP is sometimes confused with **goto**-less programming. A programmer should not use a **goto** when a better representation is available, and he should use a **goto** when the alternatives are worse. If a language includes:

1. a compound statement (as in Algol 60),
2. an **if-then-else** statement,
3. iteration statements such as the **while**, **repeat**, and **for** statements in Pascal (Wirth, 1971b), and
4. an **exit** statement for abnormal exit from a compound structure.

then there should always be a better alternative to a **goto**. The problem with the **goto** is that it is too general a construct to indicate clearly why it is being used. Each **goto** should be accompanied by enough comments to make its purpose perfectly clear.

Some people limit their conception of structured programs to programs with structured control, and ignore the equally important factor of structured data. When the data has to be manipulated to fit the available data structure representations, the program becomes less readable. The programmer is responsible for explaining to the reader how he has performed the mapping. In a "good" language for structured programming, the programmer tells the reader and the computer how to map his representations into the computer's representations, and then goes about using his representations in his program. When he is compelled to use basic (rather than natural) representations in his program, he is obliged to tell the reader (comments, again) what the intentions of the code are in terms of the natural representations.

It is clear that a good language for SP has a carefully thought out assortment of control structures and data-structure definition facilities. If a language provides one kind of iterative control statement for counter-controlled loops, and others for loops controlled by the boolean value of an expression, then the former should be used when the loop is expected to terminate as a result of the counter's reaching its terminal value, and the others should be used when some other condition is expected to terminate the loop. This makes it easier for a reader to discern the "nature" of the control being exercised by the loop.

When a line of code is a continuation of a previous line, or a subsidiary idea (e.g., a statement in a loop is subsidiary to the loop control statement), it should be indented from the left margin established by the principal statement. When indented code might be so long or complex as to obscure the principal level of control, then thought must be given to making this code into a procedure. A good rule of thumb is to try to get each principal idea (at some level) to fit on a single page.

**Structured Programming Techniques.** SP is often associated with a particular programming technique, e.g., "stepwise refinement" (Wirth, 1971a). Although stepwise refinement (also called "top-down" programming) is a useful tool for ex-

```
var    /* DECLARATIONS */
  N      : integer; /* N CUBES IN PROBLEM */

begin
  /* READ CUBE DESCRIPTIONS */
  read(N); for i := 1 to N do read_cube_description(i);

  repeat

        set_up_next_arrangement;

        if solution then print_solution

    until all_arrangements_processed;

  /* NOW WE ARE DONE */
  write( 'ALL ARRANGEMENTS PROCESSED' ) end.
```

**Fig. 1.** Top-level program to solve the "Instant Insanity" problem.

```
var  /* DECLARATIONS */
  N, NCS    :  integer; /* N CUBES IN PROBLEM.
                           NCS CUBES IN CURRENT SOLUTION.
                           (ALSO THE NUMBER OF THE
                           LAST CUBE IN THE SOLUTION.)*/
begin
  /* READ CUBE DESCRIPTIONS */
  read(N); for i := 1 to N do read_cube_description(i);

  NCS := 1;          /* LOOP INITIALIZATION */

  repeat

        set_up_next_arrangement(NCS);

        if solution(NCS) then

              if NCS = N then print_solution

              else NCS := NCS + 1

    until all_arrangements_processed;

  /* NOW WE ARE DONE */
  write( 'ALL ARRANGEMENTS PROCESSED' ) end.
```

**Fig. 2.** Step 2 in solving the Instant Insanity problem

```
var  /* DECLARATIONS */
   N, NCS      :  integer; /* N CUBES IN PROBLEM.
                              NCS CUBES IN CURRENT SOLUTION.
                              (ALSO THE NUMBER OF THE
                              LAST CUBE IN THE SOLUTION.)*/

   POS, P_MAX  :  array [1:N_MAX] of 0..24;

begin
   /* READ CUBE DESCRIPTIONS */
   read(N); for i := 1 to N do read_cube_description(i);

   NCS := 1; POS[1] := 0;      /* LOOP INITIALIZATION */

   repeat

         /* SET UP NEXT ARRANGEMENT */

         POS[NCS] := POS[NCS] + 1;

         if POS[NCS] ≤ P_MAX[NCS] then begin

            fixcube(NCS,POS[NCS]);

            if solution(NCS) then

                 if NCS = N then print_solution

                 else begin NCS := NCS + 1;

                 /* INTRODUCE ANOTHER CUBE */

                            POS[NCS] := 0  end end

         else /* NO SOLUTION WITH NEWEST CUBE. REMOVE IT
                 AND TRY FOR ANOTHER SOLUTION WITH FEWER
                 CUBES. */

              NCS := NCS - 1

   until NCS = 0;

/* NOW WE ARE DONE */
write( 'ALL ARRANGEMENTS PROCESSED' ) end.
```

**Fig. 3.** Step 3 in solving the Instant Insanity problem.

plaining a program, and illustrates how much nicer it is to explain a structured program than a haphazardly written one, it is unlikely that the art of programming can be restricted to the use of a single technique.

BACKGROUND. The concept of SP is due to Dijkstra (Dahl et al., 1972). Pascal, a language developed by N. Wirth (1971b) illustrates many of the trends in the design of languages for SP. A further discussion of SP techniques can be found in his book (1973). An excellent summary of the current status of SP (plus additional references) is to be found in Gries (1974).

*Example.* Figs. 1, 2, and 3 illustrate three steps in the development of a structured program to find all solutions to the "Instant Insanity" problem. In this problem, some number *N* of cubes with sides of various colors are to be arranged in a column so that each side of the column shows *N* different colors (i.e., no color is repeated). This example will illustrate the concepts of "stepwise refinement" and the creation of structured programs. The language used is a dialect of Pascal (Wirth, 1971b). (Wirth (1973) gives other, more detailed examples of structured program development.)

The three steps in the solution of the Instant Insanity problem proceed as follows:

1. Refer to Fig. 1. This program is really just a "plan of attack." The only important decision that has been made is the nature of the loop (**repeat** ... **until**). As the solution develops, it will become clear why this was a good choice.

2. Refer to Fig. 2. In this second step, a decision has been made to use *backtracking* to decrease the number of arrangements to be examined. This approach may be summarized as follows: To begin, set up only one cube. (NCS is the number of cubes in the solution). This is always a "solution" to the one-cube problem. If the current arrangement is a solution and there are fewer than *N* cubes involved, it is necessary to introduce another cube and seek an arrangement of this cube with the previous cubes (keeping these fixed) to form a solution. If the most recently added cube cannot be so arranged, it will be necessary to remove it from the arrangement and seek another arrangement with the smaller number of cubes that will be the solution.

The "backtracking" part of the algorithm has not yet been introduced into this program. Step 2 considers only the idea that another cube must be added when there is a solution with fewer than *N* cubes.

3. Refer to Fig. 3. In this third step, a position vector (POS) is defined. Each position of the cube is assigned a numerical value. The procedure "fixcube" selects a position for a cube depending on the value stored in the corresponding position vector. The P_MAX vector holds the maximum value (number of positions) for each cube. This is used because it is observed that only three positions need to be examined for the first cube, instead of the usual 24. Each position for the first cube conceals a different pair of opposite sides, thus avoiding trivial permutations of a solution. When a new cube is introduced into the arrangement, its entry in the position vector is set to zero. Removing a cube from an arrangement requires only that NCS be decremented.

Subsequent steps in the development of the structured program would involve the coding of each of the procedures—"fixcube," "solution," and "print solution"—in Fig. 3.

REFERENCES


1971a. Wirth, N. "Program Development by Stepwise Refinement," *Communications of the ACM*, Vol. 14 (April), pp. 221–227.

1971b. Wirth, N. "The Programming Language PASCAL," *Acta Informatica*, Vol. 1, pp. 35–63.

1972. Dahl, O-J., E. W. Dijkstra, and C. A. R. Hoare. *Structured Programming*. New York: Academic Press.

1973. Wirth, N. *Systematic Programming: An Introduction*. Englewood Cliffs, N.J.: Prentice-Hall.

1974. Gries, D. (Letter in the *ACM Forum*), *Communications of the ACM*, Vol. 17 (November), pp. 655–657.


G. R. BERGLASS

## SUBPROGRAMS.

*See* PROCEDURE; PROCEDURE, PURE; SUBPROGRAMS, CALLING; and SUBROUTINE.

## SUBPROGRAMS, CALLING

For articles on related subjects *see* ARGUMENT; PROCEDURE; SIDE EFFECT; and SUBROUTINE.

This article is not concerned specifically with the statements and other syntactic means by which subprograms or procedures are called from another part of a program, but rather with the mechanisms used to trasfer arguments from the calling program to the subprogram. For the actual calling itself, there are two basic constructs, as follows:

1. The appearance of the name of a *function* procedure with its actual arguments in an expression; for example, in Fortran,

A = B + FCN1(C,D)*FCN2(2.3 + D,J/K)

2. The use of an explicit statement for calling a procedure; for example,

Fortran: CALL PROC(A,B*C,2.3,D(I))
Algol: proc(A,B*C,2.3,D[I]);

More interesting and subtle are the means by which the arguments are transferred. There are three basic techniques:

1. Call by value.

2. Call by location (sometimes known as call by "reference").

3. Call by name.

**Call by Value.** In the case of call by a value, the subprogram is provided with the value of the argument and no path leads back to the referencing program or to any of its storage elements. Call by value is illustrated in Fig. 1(a) for the argument B*C. The subprogram thus has no control over the referencing program. In this manner, any side effects are "short circuited" and have no effect.

**Call by Location.** In this case the referencing program does not provide to the subprogram the value of the argument but provides instead the address of the memory location at which that value can be found. It is then the responsibility of the subprogram to access the data through this mechanism. This is illustrated in Fig. 1(b) for the argument A. Somewhere in the body of the procedure PROC is a memory location that will store the address of A in the calling program. Thus, with call by

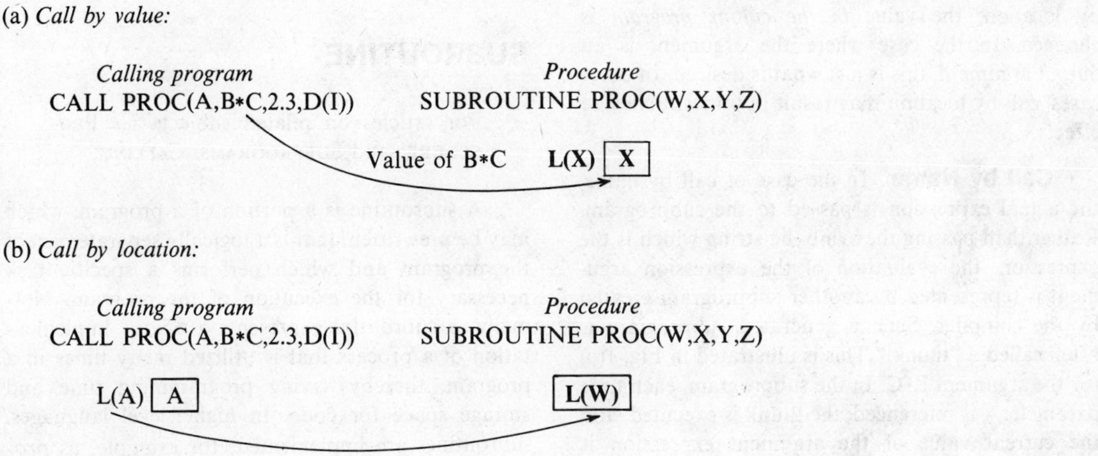

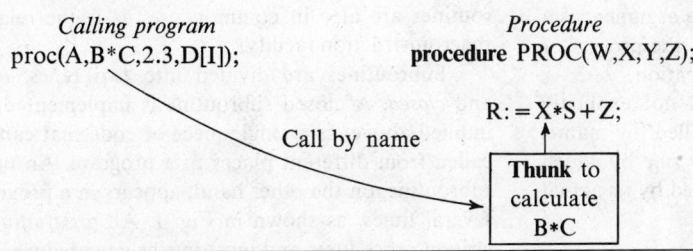


**Fig. 1.** Passing arguments to procedures.

location, the subprogram in effect shares memory with the calling program.

For an argument which itself is an expression rather than a variable name, like B*C in Fig. 1, there is no automatically corresponding address in the calling program. Therefore, if B*C is called by location, the calling program must create a location for the value of B*C, evaluate B*C, and put it in this location, and then transfer the address of this location to the subprogram. This is then essentially the same in effect as calling by value.

But in two other cases, calling by location and calling by value are quite different:

1. If the calling argument is an array, say, of 1,000 elements, then calling by value would require that all 1,000 elements be transferred and that memory space be allocated in both calling program and subprogram for these 1,000 elements. But if the call is by location, then only the address of the first element in the array need be transferred to the subprogram.

2. If the formal argument appears on the left-hand side of an assignment statement in the subprogram, then, if the call is by value, the value of this argument *in the subprogram* is changed when the assignment statement is executed. But, if the call is by location, the value *in the calling program* is changed. In the case where the argument is an output argument, this is just what is desired. In other cases, call by location may result in undesirable side effects.

**Call by Name.** In the case of call by name, the actual expression is passed to the subprogram. Rather than passing the symbolic string which is the expression, the evaluation of the expression argument is represented by another subprogram created by the compiler. Such a generated subprogram is often called a "thunk." This is illustrated in Fig. 1(c) for the argument B*C. In the subprogram, each time parameter X is referenced, the thunk is executed, and the current value of the argument expression is determined and is used as the value of X. Such values may change during the execution of the subprogram as the result of side effects. When the argument is a simple identifier (i.e., unsubscripted), the process of call by name is equivalent to call by location.

In Algol any parameter that is not explicitly stated to be called by value is called by name. Indeed, Algol specifies a formal *copy rule* by which each formal parameter is to be replaced by its actual parameter. Thus, the statement

```
R: = X*S + Z;
```

in Fig. 1(c)—which uses Algol notation for convenience—should actually become

```
R: = (B*C)*S + D[I];
```

when called as shown in the figure. (S is a local variable.) In actual Algol implementations the equivalent mechanism shown in Fig. 1(c) is almost always employed.

Whatever the language used, the programmer must always be aware of how that language implements argument passing. Otherwise, programs may not execute as planned or may cause undesirable side effects.

REFERENCE

1964. Randell, B., and L. J. Russell. *Algol 60 Implementation*. New York: Academic Press.

1971. Ralston, A. *An Introduction to Programming and Computer Science*. New York: McGraw-Hill.

J. A. N. LEE AND A. RALSTON

## SUBROUTINE

For articles on related subjects *see* PROCEDURE; and SUBPROGRAMS, CALLING.

A subroutine is a portion of a program, which may be prewritten, that is a logically separate part of the program and which performs a specific task necessary for the execution of the program. Normally, a subroutine represents a unique implementation of a process that is utilized many times in a program, thereby saving programming time and storage space for code. In higher-level languages, subroutines are implemented, for example, as *procedures* in Algol and as SUBROUTINES and FUNCTIONS in Fortran. In assembly language programs, subroutines are also in common use, as is the related macroinstruction facility.

Subroutines are divided into two types, *open* and *closed*. A closed subroutine is implemented, as implied above, as a single piece of code that can be called from different places in a program. An open subroutine, on the other hand, appears in a program several times, as shown in Fig. 1. All programmer-written procedures and most intrinsic procedures are implemented as closed subroutines in higher-level

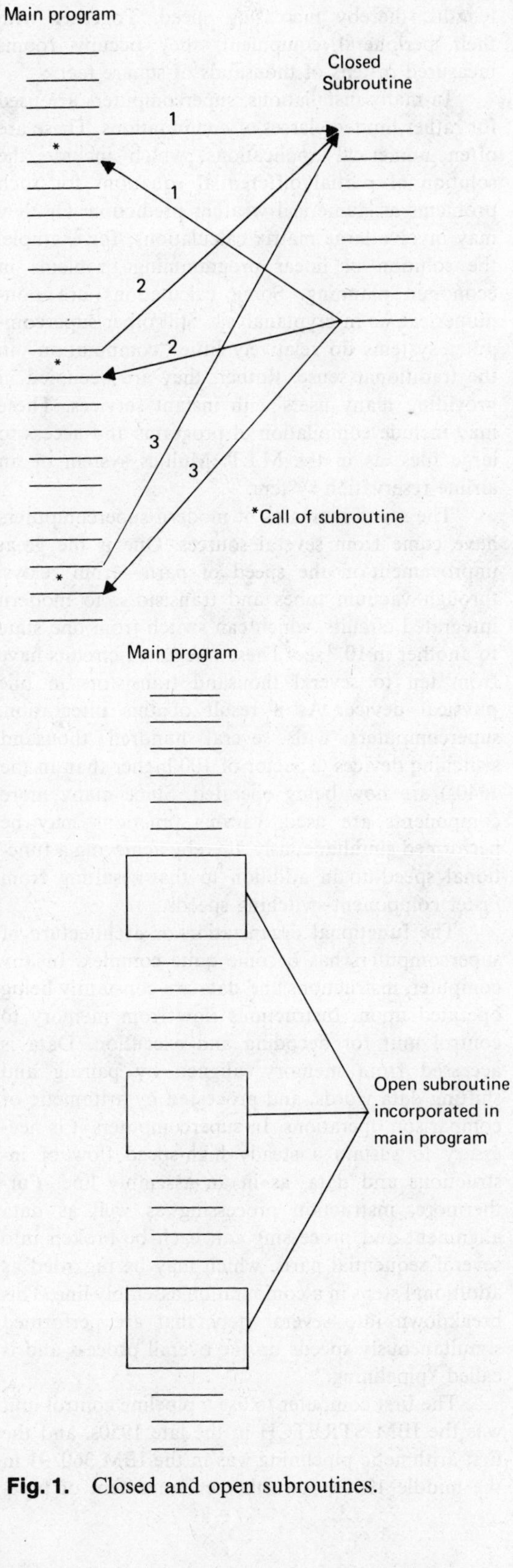


**Fig. 1.** Closed and open subroutines.

languages (see Fig. 1). In some cases, however, it is more economical to copy the subroutine code into the calling program whenever it is called. This happens when the code is so brief that integrating it into the main program is less prodigal of storage space than the instructions needed in the main program to call a closed subroutine.

For example, the Fortran function ABS(X), whose value is the absolute value of the argument X, is normally implemented as an open subroutine because typically it can be implemented with two machine-language instructions:

| | |
|---|---|
| CADD L(X) | Clear the accumulator and add the contents of the location of X into the accumulator |
| SSP | Set sign of accumulator plus |

The contrasting implementation of open and closed subroutines are sometimes called "in line" and "out of line" coding. The subroutine idea dates back to the earliest days of computers (Wilkes et al., 1951). Its invention was of great significance because it brought to computer programming a weapon vital to any intellectual arsenal, namely, the ability to break complex tasks into smaller units and then to treat each smaller unit separately.

### Reference


1951. Wilkes, M. V., D. J. Wheeler, and S. Gill. *The Preparation of Programs for an Electronic Digital Computer*. Reading, Mass.: Addison-Wesley.


J. A. N. Lee and A. Ralston

# SUPERCOMPUTERS

## PRINCIPLES

For articles on related subjects *see* Digital Computers: Contemporary and Future; Performance Measurement and Evaluation; and Performance of Computers. For articles on related terms *see* Aiken, Howard; Eckert, J. Presper; ENIAC; Grosch's Law; Mauchly, John W.; Stretch; and Zuse, Konrad.

The term "supercomputer" adapts to several intuitive definitions. In a given period of time it may be applied to computers of the highest speed, largest functional size, biggest physical dimensions, or greatest monetary cost. Since all these attributes tend to occur in certain computers, such machines are referred to as supercomputers. A more explicit definition is difficult, but the following discussion of these four attributes characterizes supercomputers. The importance of relating characteristics of a machine to its year of introduction leads to a brief historical outline.

The first modern computers began to operate in the early 1940s. These include the Mark I, designed and built by Howard Aiken of Harvard University and IBM engineers, the Bell Telephone Laboratories' series started by George Stibitz, and a series begun in the 1930s by the German computer pioneer Konrad Zuse. These early machines used electrical relays as their basic components. Typically, they contained fewer than 10,000 relays and performed arithmetic operations at a rate of about one per second. Although their complexity and speed were comparable to modern electronic desk calculators, they were the first supercomputers.

The introduction of vacuum-tube components in ENIAC by Eckert and Mauchly at the University of Pennsylvania in the late 1940s led to a speed increase by a factor of about 1,000. Until 1948, computer memory words were accessed serially. At that time, F. C. Williams of Manchester University built a cathode-ray tube memory, each of whose words could be accessed in the same amount of time—the first random-access memory. The machine made by the Manchester group also integrated a rotating magnetic drum for secondary storage, and thus operated a memory hierarchy in 1949. Thus, by 1950, many of the complexities of modern supercomputers had appeared, although in a miniature scale by present standards.

Over the span of the past 30 years, the raw speed of the fastest computers has approximately doubled each year. Thus, we are now approaching speeds of about $10^9$ (i.e., one billion) operations per second. The price of modern supercomputers is in the range of $5 million to $15 million. Early machines had at most 1,000 words of primary memory, whereas modern supercomputers have up to a million words of primary memory together with slower secondary memories arranged in a three- or four-level hierarchy, which may contain a total of from $10^8$ to $10^{10}$ words. The power requirements of such computers is measured in hundreds of kilowatts. They are housed in cabinets that may be 6 ft tall and more than 30 ft long, although some are arranged in the shape of a square or a cross to minimize wire lengths, thereby increasing speed. Together with their peripheral equipment, they occupy rooms measured in tens of thousands of square feet.

In many installations, supercomputers are used for rather limited classes of computations. These are often numerical applications, which include the solution of partial differential equations for such problems as numerical weather prediction. Or they may involve large matrix calculations; for example, the solution of linear programming problems in economic planning. Some calculations are non-numerical, as in cryptanalysis. Still other supercomputer systems do relatively little "computation" in the traditional sense. Rather, they are occupied in providing many users with instant services. These may include compilation of programs and access to large files, as in the M.I.T. Multics system or an airline reservation system.

The speed increases of modern supercomputers have come from several sources. One is the great improvement in the speed of parts—from relays, through vacuum tubes and transistors, to modern integrated circuits, which can switch from one state to another in $10^{-9}$ sec. These integrated circuits have from ten to several thousand transistors in one physical device. As a result of this integration, supercomputers with several hundred thousand switching devices (a factor of 100 higher than in the 1940s) are now being operated. Since many more components are used, various functions may be performed simultaneously, thereby achieving a functional speed-up in addition to that resulting from faster component-switching speeds.

The functional organization or architecture of supercomputers has become quite complex. In any computer, instructions and data are constantly being operated upon. Instructions flow from memory to control unit for decoding and execution. Data is accessed from memory, aligned by pairing and shifting data words, and processed by arithmetic or comparison operations. In supercomputers it is necessary to sustain a steady high-speed flow of instructions and data, as in an assembly line. Furthermore, instruction processing as well as data alignment and processing can each be broken into several sequential parts, which may be regarded as additional steps in a computation assembly line. This breakdown into several steps that are performed simultaneously speeds up the overall process and is called "pipelining."

The first computer to use a pipeline control unit was the IBM STRETCH in the late 1950s, and the first arithmetic pipelining was in the IBM 360/91 in the middle 1960s. A further enhancement of pipelining is found in vector pipeline machines. These machines have instructions whose operands are vectors of data words. Several of the present fastest machine designs use the vector pipeline approach, including the Texas Instruments Advanced Scientific Computer ASC and the Control Data STAR (Fig. 1).

**Fig. 1.** Control Data STAR-100, which can perform 100 million instructions per second.

To deliver instructions and data at very high speed, many random access memories are arranged in parallel in these machines. The first machines to interleave two memories in parallel were the IBM STRETCH and the University of Illinois' ILLIAC II in the late 1950s. These machines used magnetic-core memory units from which a word could be accessed in a few millionths of a second. Present supercomputers use semiconductor memory units from which five or more words can be accessed in one-millionth of a second. Very high effective speeds are obtained by arranging 100 or more such units in parallel.

An alternative to pipeline processing is to operate more than one processor in parallel and arrange several memories in parallel to supply instructions and data. A number of large computer systems introduced variations of this in the early 1960s. The major supercomputers of the 1960s and early 1970s were the Control Data 6600 and 7600 models, which are capable of performing a number of simultaneous processing fuctions.

Another approach to parallel processing is to allow one instruction sequence to control many identical processors as they simultaneously perform a sequence of identical operations. This kind of parallelism, sometimes called "array processing," is incorporated in ILLIAC IV (Fig. 2), which was designed by the University of Illinois and Burroughs in the late 1960s, and came into operation in 1973. For particular applications, machines in which each parallel processor operates on just one binary digit are quite effective. An example is the Goodyear Aerospace STARAN, which is called an "associative processor" because of its ability to search its memory for particular contents to be processed. Thus, while ILLIAC IV has 64 processors of 64-bit words, associative processors such as STARAN may have several hundred (or thousand) processors of one bit each.

One motivation for building faster and faster supercomputers is simply to achieve higher processing speeds. This allows users to complete their computational tasks faster or to engage in new and more complex computations that would have been impractical on slower machines. In fact, various supercomputers at present are becoming more and more specialized for particular classes of computations.

Another motivation for building large computers is the economy of scale which may be achieved. Of course there are large one-time development

**Fig. 2.** The ILLIAC IV with the array of processors on the right. The cabinet at the far left is a laser store with a capacity of one trillion bits.

costs, but for machines that reach the production stage, Grosch's law states that in a fixed period of time, a machine's "performance" is proportional to the square of its price. This price/performance ratio has been validated for each of the past 20 or more years, with various definitions of "performance." Explanations vary: Performance evaluation may simply be the manufacturer's pricing policy or it may reflect engineering and manufacturing costs.

It seems likely that new supercomputers will continue to appear. The supercomputers of 20 years ago were similar to the minicomputers of today —operating on scalar operands. Today's supercomputers operate on vector operands. In the future, supercomputers may operate simultaneously on multidimensional arrays whose elements are parse trees of arithmetic expressions, with many parallel operations being performed, each in a pipelined way. Ultimately, the speed of a supercomputer is a function of the switching speed of its parts and the amount of simultaneity that exists in the computations to be performed. The former constraint arises from the physics of its hardware devices. The latter constraint arises from the logical and numerical structure of the algorithms being executed.

References

1962. Buchholz, W. (Ed.). *Planning A Computer System: Project STRETCH*. New York: McGraw-Hill.

1971. Bell, C. G., and A. Newell. *Computer Structures: Readings and Examples*. New York: McGraw-Hill.

D. J. Kuck

## IMPLEMENTATIONS

For articles on related subjects *see* Control Data Corporation (CDC) 6000 Series; Integrated Circuitry; Multiprocessing; Parallel Processing; and Performance of Computers.

For articles on related terms *see* Arithmetic, Computer; and Arithmetic-Logic Unit.

As noted in the first part of this article, there are physical as well as logical reasons why computers cannot operate arbitrarily fast. The physics of switching devices prevents them from changing states in zero time: presently, fast circuitry switches in about 1 ns (one billionth of a second). Furthermore, electric signals cannot travel faster than the speed of light (about 1 ft/ns), and in fact they usually travel along wires at some speed less than this. The switching and propagation delays are added together to determine minimum times required for various operations. Thus, using the fastest parts they can afford, supercomputer designers must turn to logical design and machine organization techniques to speed up computer operation.

One of the most obvious techniques for making faster computers is to employ some form of parallelism. Thus, memory, central processor, control unit, and input/output devices may all be designed to operate concurrently. Furthermore, each may be organized to perform more than one operation at a time. We focus our attention here on the parallel internal operation of central processors and to a lesser extent on control units.

Consider first the replication of identical arithmetic units (AU). Suppose we wish to add (or multiply, etc.) $n$ pairs of numbers to form $n$ sums: $a_1 + b_1, a_2 + b_2, \ldots, a_n + b_n$. Using $n$ AUs, as shown in Fig. 1, we can form these sums in the same time as required to do one addition with one AU. Thus, $n$ AUs computing this kind of sum would be $n$ times faster than a single AU. Notice, however, that if we needed $m$ sums of $2m$ numbers, the speed-up over one AU using $n$ AUs would be only $m/\lceil m/n \rceil$ instead of $n$, where $\lceil m/n \rceil$ is the smallest integer greater than or equal to $m/n$. For example, if we want $m = 3n/2$ sums, $n$ AUs could do this in two steps, whereas one AU would require $3n/2$ steps, so the speed-up would be $3n/4$ instead of $n$.

Now, however, assume we wish to add $2n$ numbers to produce just one sum: $a_1 + a_2 + a_3 + \cdots a_{2n}$. Again, using $n$ AUs, we first form $n$ sums $a_1 + a_2, a_3 + a_4, \ldots, a_{2n-1} + a_{2n}$. Now we must use $n/2$ AU (or $n - 1)/2$ if $n$ is odd) to reduce these $n$ sums to $n/2$ (or $(n - 1)/2$) sums $(a_1 + a_2) + (a_3 + a_4), (a_5 + a_6) + (a_7 + a_8) \cdots (a_{2n-3} + a_{2n-2}) + (a_{2n-1} + a_{2n})$. We keep repeating this until we have just one sum. This is illustrated in Fig. 2. In general, it requires $\lceil \log_2 2n \rceil$ time steps to reduce $2n$ operands to one sum, where $\lceil \log_2 2n \rceil$ is the smallest integer greater than or equal to $\log_2 2n$. A single AU could have done this same operation in $2n - 1$ steps. Thus, on this kind of computation, $n$ AUs are only $(2n - 1)/\lceil \log_2 2n \rceil$ times faster than a single AU instead of $n$ times faster, as for the previous computation. In general, the effectiveness of replications of AUs is dependent on the number of

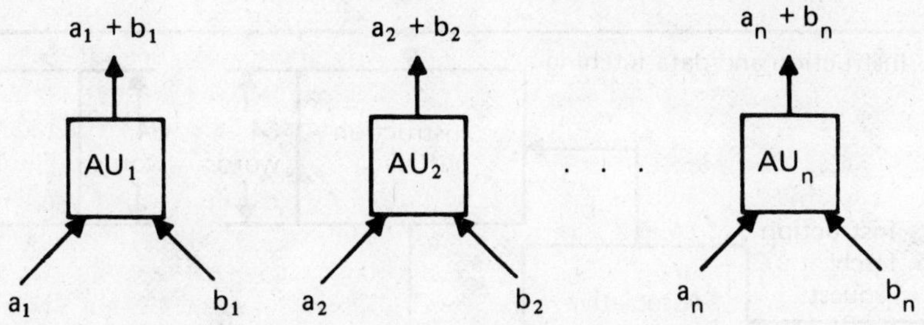


**Fig. 1.** Computation of *n* sums by *n* arithmetic units.

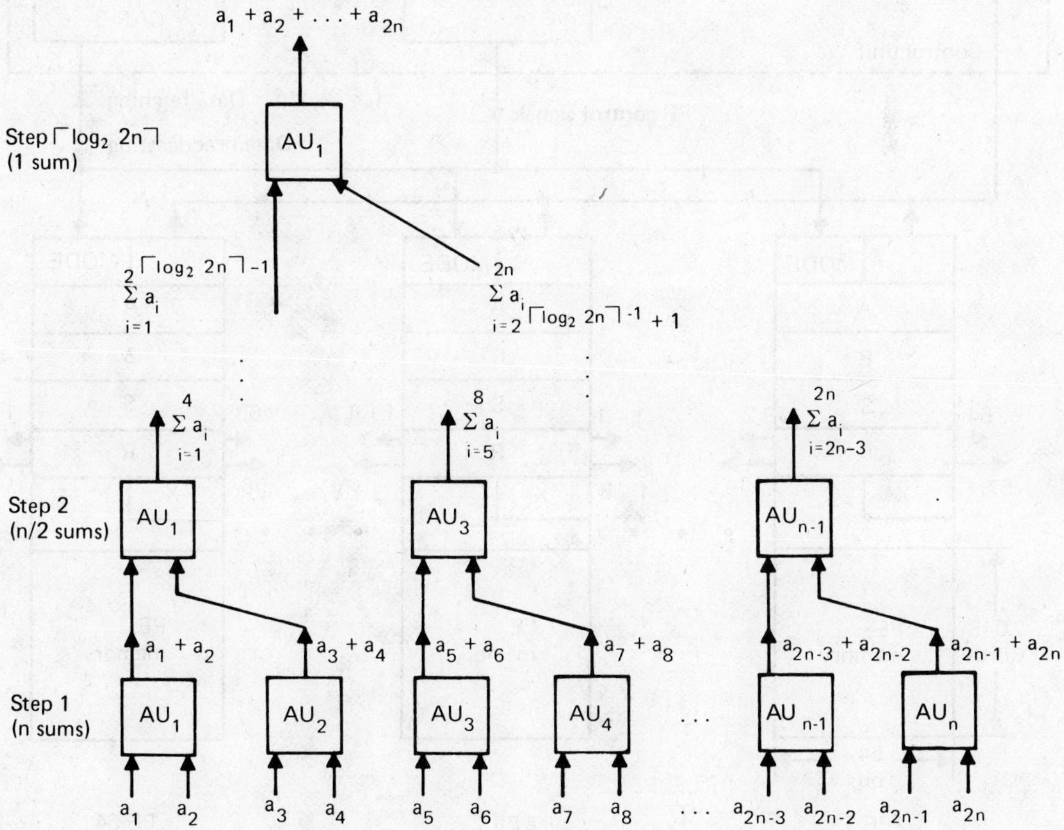


**Fig. 2.** Formation of the sum of 2*n* numbers by *n* AUs.

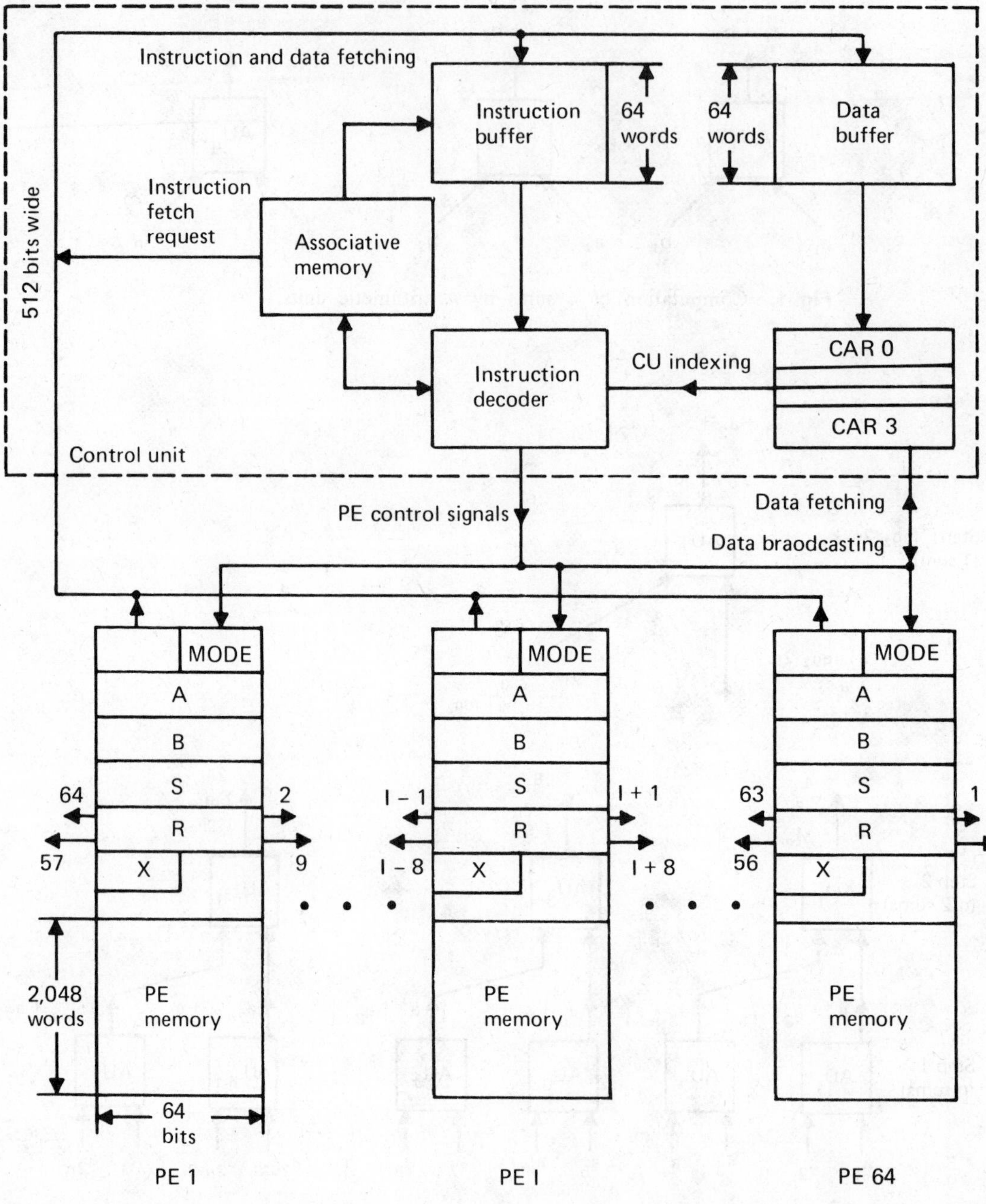


**Fig. 3.** ILLIAC IV organization. (Modified from Ackins and Kuck, "Seismic Signal Processing via the ILLIAC IV Computer," *IEEE Trans. Geoscience Electronics,* Vol. GE-7 (January 1969), pp. 34–41.)

operations that can be done in parallel in a given program, and on the interaction between these operations.

This technique of using parallel units has been employed to a significant degree in several recent computers, including Goodyear's STARAN and Burroughs' ILLIAC IV. We now sketch some details of the organization of ILLIAC IV.

ILLIAC IV consists of 64 identical AUs, called "processing elements" (PE), driven by a control unit (CU) as illustrated in Fig. 3. The primary purpose of the CU is to fetch instructions and direct the PEs to perform some operation. However, the CU may not direct the PEs to perform different operations at the same time. All PEs must perform the same operation at the same time, although some PEs may be turned off if they are not needed. In addition to fetching instructions and directing the PEs, the CU is capable of performing some simple fixed-point arithmetic, indexing, and logical functions, using the four accumulator registers (CAR); it can store data and constants in 64 data buffer registers, and it can fetch and store data in PE memory.

Each PE contains four 64-bit arithmetic registers (A,B,R, and S), a 16-bit index register (X), and several 1-bit registers (MODE) which are used to store results of logical tests and to turn the PE on or off. The PE can do 64-bit floating- or fixed-point operations, two simultaneous 32-bit floating- or fixed-point operations, or eight simultaneous 8-bit fixed-point operations. It can access data either from its own memory, from the CU in common with all other PEs, or from one of the other PEs via the routing network, which is capable of moving data between PEs by basic distances of +1, −1, +8, or −8. Each PE memory consists of 2,048 64-bit words (for a total of 131,072 words), and each PE can index its own memory independently of other PEs.

A PE can perform two simultaneous 32-bit floating-point operations in about 800 ns. Thus, 64 PEs are capable of 128 32-bit operations every 800 ns or 160 million operations per second. However, ILLIAC IV can achieve such speed only on programs that require 128 identical operations at once. On more general programs, the effective speed will

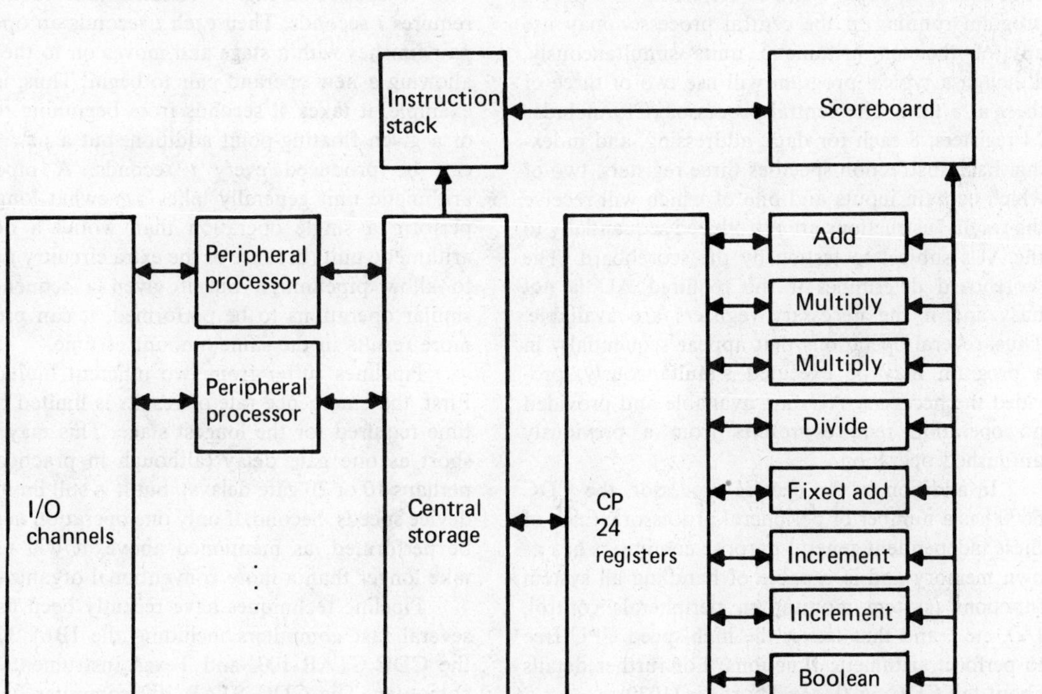


**Fig. 4.** Schematic of the CDC 6600 showing ten AUs.

**Fig. 5.** A CDC 6600 computer installation.

be somewhat less than this. For further details about ILLIAC IV, see Bell and Newell (1971).

While ILLIAC IV uses 64 *identical* arithmetic units and is well suited to a particular class of computation, a slower but somewhat more general technique involves the use of a number of *different* arithmetic units. This is best illustrated by the CDC 6600 shown in Figs. 4 and 5. Referring to Fig. 4 a program running in the central processor may use any of the ten arithmetic units simultaneously, although a typical program will use two or three of these at a time. The central processor (CP) includes 24 registers, 8 each for data, addressing, and indexing. Each instruction specifies three registers, two of which contain inputs and one of which will receive the result. Instructions are introduced sequentially to the AUs subject to testing by the scoreboard. The scoreboard determines if the required AU is not busy and if the necessary registers are available. Thus, several operations that appear sequentially in a program may be executed simultaneously, provided the necessary AUs are available and provided no operation requires results from a previously unfinished operation.

In addition to the central processor, the CDC 6600 has a number of peripheral processors. Each of these independent general-purpose computers has its own memory and is capable of handling all system functions (system monitoring, peripherals control, I/O, etc.), and thus leaves the high-speed CPU free to perform arithmetic functions. For further details about the CDC 6600, see Thornton (1970).

*Pipelining* is another technique used to speed up computers. This involves breaking each basic operation (addition, multiplication, etc.) into a number of independent stages, similar to the way an assembly line is organized. For example, a floating-point addition operation can be divided into four separate

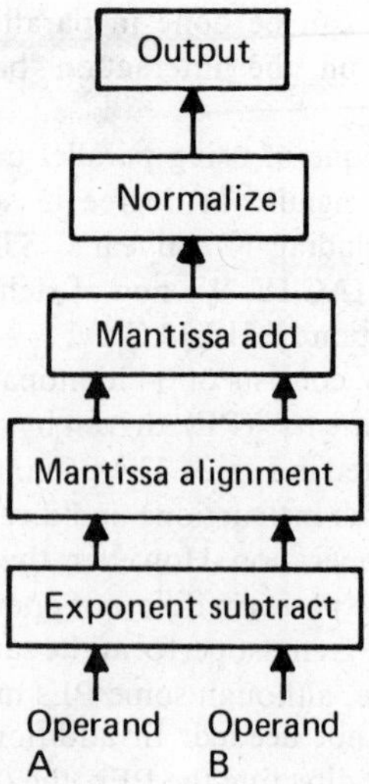


**Fig. 6.** A floating-point addition pipeline.

operations: exponent subtraction, mantissa alignment, mantissa add, and normalization of the result. This is shown in Fig. 6. Assume that each stage requires $t$ seconds. Then each $t$ seconds an operand pair finishes with a stage and moves on to the next, allowing a new operand pair to begin. Thus, in this example, it takes $4t$ seconds from beginning to end of a given floating-point addition, but a new result can be produced every $t$ seconds. A pipelined arithmetic unit generally takes somewhat longer to perform a single operation than would a normal arithmetic unit (because of the extra circuitry needed to allow pipelining), but if given a sequence of similar operations to be performed, it can produce more results in the same amount of time.

Pipelines suffer from two inherent limitations. First, the emergence rate of results is limited by the time required for the longest stage. This may be as short as one gate delay (although in practice it is perhaps 10 or 20 gate delays), but it is still limited by device speeds. Second, if only one operation needs to be performed, as mentioned above, it will usually take longer than a more conventional organization.

Pipeline techniques have recently been used in several fast computers including the IBM 360/91, the CDC STAR-100, and Texas Instruments ASC computer. The CDC STAR-100 computer has two pipeline processors. One processor contains pipelined floating-point addition and multiplication units. The other contains pipelined floating-point addition and multipurpose units (the multipurpose unit can do pipelined addition, multiplication, division, or square root), and a standard, nonpipelined

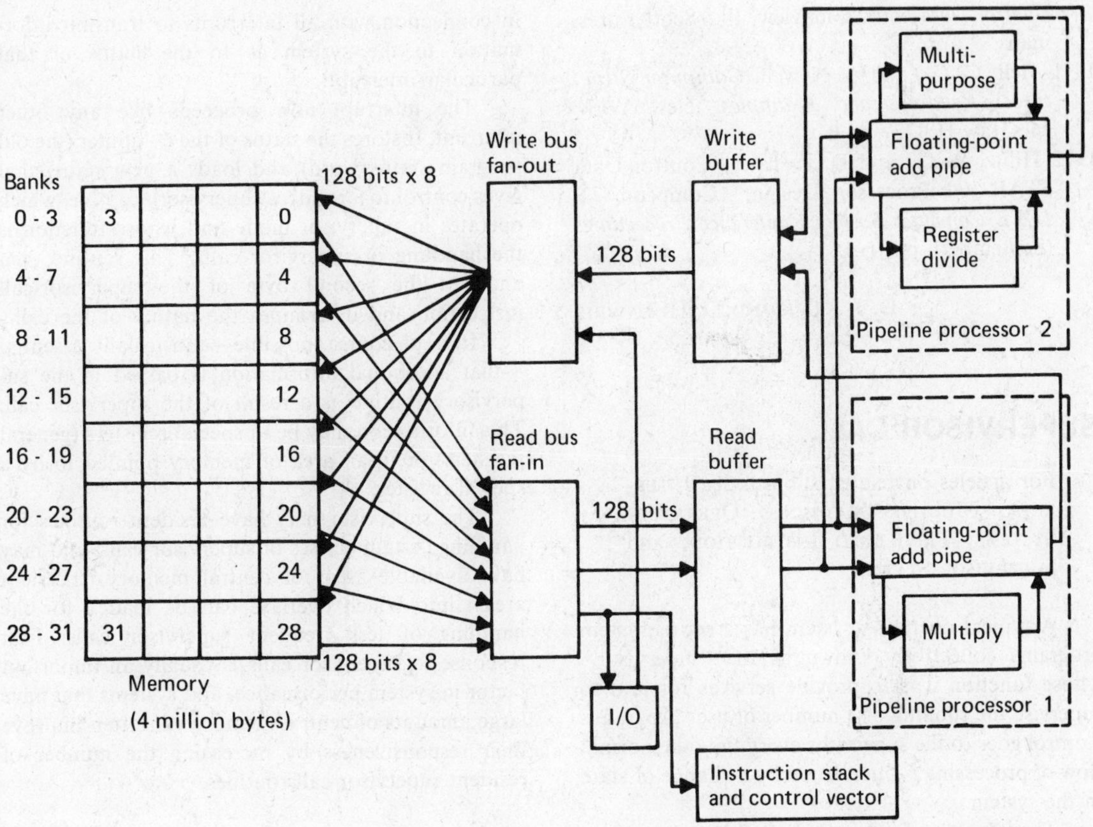


**Fig. 7.** Block diagram of CDC STAR-100. (From Hintz and Tate, "Control Data STAR-100 Processor Design," Compcon 72, *IEEE Computer Society Conference Proceedings* (September), pp. 1–4.

floating-point division unit. In the STAR-100, the pipeline stage delay (*t* in the above example) is approximately 40 ns, and total pipeline delay is 160 ns for addition and 320 ns for multiplication. Each 64-bit pipeline can be split into two 32-bit pipelines. Thus, the STAR-100 can perform four 32-bit operations simultaneously and can achieve a rate of four 32-bit operations every 40 ns, or 100 million operations per second.

Fig. 7 shows these two pipelines, together with memories, memory buffer, and memory selection devices. As shown, memory consists of 32 interleaved memory banks, each consisting of 2,048 512-bit words. (Each memory word can hold eight 64-bit data words or sixteen 32-bit data words.) The memory system can supply 512 bits of data, i.e., sixteen 32-bit words, every 40 ns. The memory buffer units are necessary in order to smooth the flow of data between memories and pipelines, since the pipelines may require as many as twelve 32-bit numbers every 40 ns (eight in and four out), and the memory system may miss a few cycles as a result of access conflicts. More details can be found in Hintz and Tate (1972).

In general, parallel operation and pipeline techniques are employed in varying degrees in today's fastest computers. At the lowest level, arithmetic and word transmissions are performed in digit-parallel fashion. Arithmetic or other functional units are often pipelined, more than one arithmetic unit can be used simultaneously, and there may be a pool of different functional units available for use by one or more programs. The degree to which various techniques are employed depends on the required cost and speed of the final system and the type of programs to be executed.

## References

1970. Thornton, J. E. *Design of a Computer: The*

*Control Data 6600*. Glenview, Ill.: Scott Foresman.

1971. Bell, C. G., and A. Newell. *Computer Structures: Readings and Examples*. New York: McGraw-Hill.

1972. Hintz, R. G., and D. P. Tate. "Control Data STAR-100 Processor Design," Compcon 72, *IEEE Computer Society Conference Proceedings* (September), pp. 1–4.

D. J. KUCK AND D. H. LAWRIE

# SUPERVISOR CALL

For articles on related subjects *see* INTERRUPT; MULTIPROGRAMMING; OPERATING SYSTEMS; PRIVILEGED INSTRUCTION; and SUPERVISOR STATE.

A typical operating system has a set of system programs collectively known as the "supervisor," whose function it is to provide services for and to supervise the running of a number of user programs. Control goes to the supervisor every time the normal flow of processing is interrupted by a change of state in the system.

The purpose of a *supervisor call* is to provide a mechanism whereby a program can interrupt the normal flow of processing and ask the supervisor to perform a function for the program that the program either cannot or is not permitted to perform for itself.

The most typical supervisor calls have to do with input and output. In a multiprogramming system it is essential to have system control of input/output devices, especially those devices shared by a number of programs.

Most computers that were designed for multiprogramming systems have a supervisory mode of operation and hardware interlocks that prevent certain supervisory operations from taking place except when the computer is operating in supervisory mode. This may be handled by means of special privileged instructions that can be executed only in supervisory mode, or only in some other way.

In the IBM 360/370 systems, for example, a supervisor call is made through the execution of an instruction whose effect is to create an interrupt. The instruction is 2 bytes long. The first byte is the supervisor-call instruction code, and the second byte describes the nature of the supervisor call. This second byte goes into a special register which is used in connection with all interrupts to transmit information to the system as to the status of that particular interrupt.

The interrupt now proceeds like any other interrupt. It stores the status of the computer (the old program status word) and loads a new status that gives control to a resident supervisory routine, which operates in supervisor mode and whose function is the handling of supervisor calls. This routine then analyzes the second byte of the supervisor-call instruction and determines the nature of the call.

It is, of course, possible—and usually essential—that additional information is passed to the supervisory routine as a result of the supervisor call. This information may be in special registers (general registers) or in an area of memory pointed to by a special register.

The supervisor may have resident routines for handling certain classes of supervisor calls, and may have available areas of central memory (transient areas) into which overlays can be loaded for the handling of less frequent supervisor calls. Fast response to supervisor calls is usually an important factor in system performance, and systems that have large amounts of central memory can often improve their responsiveness by increasing the number of resident supervisor-call routines.

S. ROSEN

# SWAC

For articles on related subjects *see* DIGITAL COMPUTERS: Early; and SEAC.

SWAC (National Bureau of Standards Western Automatic Computer) was dedicated in August 1950, and at the time of its dedication was the fastest computer in existence. It was begun in January 1949 at the National Bureau of Standard's field station, the Institute for Numerical Analysis at the University of California at Los Angeles, and was designed and constructed under the direction of the author. Originally named the ZEPHYR, due to its modest-sized budget and staff as contrasted with much larger projects being carried on elsewhere, it was later renamed the SWAC.

The SWAC was a parallel computer using Williams' tube (cathode-ray tube, or CRT) memory. The memory cycle was 16 $\mu$s consisting of an 8 $\mu$s action cycle and an 8 $\mu$s restore cycle (where some

**Fig. 1.** The SWAC.

other memory location was restored). An addition of 37-bit operands occurred in 64 μs, and multiplication occurred in 384 μs. Due to technical difficulties with Williams' tube storage, the memory was never increased beyond 256 words. A 4,096-word magnetic drum was added to the system with coordinated addressing so that block transfers of 32 words between the two memories occurred with no latency.

Initial input and output was by typewriter and punched paper tape. These were soon replaced by a card reader (240 cards per minute) and a card punch (80 cards per minute). The SWAC used a four-address command structure. A floating-point interpretive system named SWACPEC was developed, which made it much easier for users to write programs.

In 1953 the SWAC was producing about 53 hr of useful computing time per week. SWAC was used in a research computing environment, and therefore many of the problems tended to be quite large. Solution times from 177 to 453 hr are reported by Huskey et al. (1953). Some of the early problems included the search for Mersenne primes, the Fourier synthesis of X-ray diffraction patterns of crystals, the solution of systems of linear equations, and problems in differential equations.

When the National Bureau of Standards ceased to support the Institute for Numerical Analysis, the SWAC was transferred to the University and moved to the Engineering Building at UCLA. There it continued in useful operation until December 1967. Parts of the SWAC are now on exhibit in the Museum of Science and Industry in Los Angeles.

REFERENCES

1951. Huskey, H. D. "Semiautomatic Instruction on the Zephyr," *Proceedings of a Second Symposium on Large-Scale Digital Computing Machinery*. Cambridge, Mass.: Harvard University Press, pp. 83–90.

1953. Huskey, H. D., R. Thorensen, B. F. Ambrosio, and E. C. Yowell. "The SWAC—Design Features and Operating Experience," *Proceedings of the I.R.E.*, Vol. 41, No. 10 (October), pp. 1294–1299.

H. D. HUSKEY

# SWAPPING

For articles on related subjects *see* MEMORY: AUXILIARY; SCHEDULING ALGORITHM; TIME SHARING; and TIME SLICE.

For articles on related terms *see* ALGORITHM; and WORKING SET.

Swapping is a process found most frequently in time-shared computer operating systems. It is used to move programs between primary storage (usually core memory, but integrated circuit memories have recently become common) and secondary storage (drums or disk files). Swapping is necessary to maximize the efficient use of valuable primary storage where programs must be located in order to be executed, but which cost an order of magnitude more than secondary storage.

When the operating system locates a program in a "waiting" state—i.e., one that can no longer use the CPU normally because it is waiting to complete an I/O operation—it *swaps* the program to secondary storage, replacing it with another program that is ready to use the CPU. In time-sharing systems, the longest waiting state occurs as the program awaits input from the relatively slow typewriter, Teletype, or similar terminal.

The time-sharing systems of the early 1960s at M.I.T., The RAND Corporation, Systems Development Corporation, and Dartmouth College contain examples of the swapping process. In these systems, only one program could reside in core at one time, not because of core size limits but because all programs could execute properly at only one location. This produced an extremely simple cycle: Execute a program for a certain period, swap that program to secondary storage, swap the next program chosen into core, and (coming full circle) execute the program just arrived for its proper period. (Algorithms for selecting the next program for execution and for terminating each execution are discussed elsewhere in the Scheduling Algorithm and Time Slice articles.)

Clearly, throughput of executed programs is progessively increased as swapping time is lowered relative to execution time. A total swap time of 500 ms must be balanced with an execution time of 500 ms to achieve only 50% CPU utilization! This problem, together with the difficulty of actually identifying programs that will execute for long periods of time (many programs unexpectedly give up the CPU in order to do other things, such as terminal I/O), led to the development of scheduling algorithms whose purpose was to increase utilization by identifying long-running programs and allowing them long execution times. In the middle 1960s, new hardware developments (first relocation registers, then base registers, and finally full-memory-mapping hardware) and the development of multiprogrammed operating systems allowed several programs to be resident in core memory at a time. This permitted one program to be executed while two others were changing places in primary and secondary storage. Some systems have permanently resident batch programs, one of which contains and controls all the time-sharing programs that are swapped by that superprogram—not by the operating system.

Recently, more sophisticated forms of swapping have come into use. Demand paging and segmentation allow programs to be only partially resident for execution. When reference to a nonresident page or segment is detected, the operating system "swaps" in the needed page. Systems of this type were first developed in the early 1960s on the Atlas machine in England and on the Burroughs 5000, although their use did not become widespread until the early 1970s. These techniques, called "demand paging," provide more efficiency by reducing the average size of a program resident in primary storage, thus permitting more programs to reside in primary storge. Each increase in the number of resident programs increases the probability that some program can be found to execute simultaneously with swapping I/O. The reduction in size was achieved at the expense of the paging I/O, which, if not properly controlled, could result in an excessive I/O condition known as "thrashing." A concept known as the "working set," in which the system identified a group of most-used pages and arranged to keep then in memory so that paging I/O is held to an acceptably low level, has helped to alleviate this problem.

### References

1962. Corbato, F. J., M. Merwin-Dagget, and R. C. Daley. "An Experimental Time-sharing System," *Proc. Spring Joint Computer Conference*, Vol. 21, pp. 335–344.

1968. Denning, P. J. "The Working Set Model for Program Behavior," *Comm. ACM,* Vol. 11, pp. 323–333.

G. E. Bryan

## SYMBOL MANIPULATION

For articles on related subjects *see* Addressing; Algebraic Manipulation Languages; Associative Languages; Automata Theory; Input-Output Devices; Lists and List Processing; Stored Program Concept; and String Processing Languages.

For articles on related terms *see* Artificial Intelligence; Interpreter; Language Translation; and Simulation.

The power of a modern computer derives from its being more than an arithmetic calculator. It is, in fact, a general-purpose symbol-manipulating system. A symbol *token* is a pattern that can be compared by an information processing system with some other symbol token and judged equal with it or different from it. The basic test for equality of tokens incorporated in an information processing system determines the fundamental alphabet of symbols it is prepared to recognize and distinguish. A symbol, then, is a class of equal tokens with respect to this basic test.

The key characteristic of symbols for an information processing system is their ability to *designate*, i.e., to have referents. This means that an information process can take a symbol token as input and use it to gain access to a referenced object in order to affect it or be affected by it in some way: to read it,

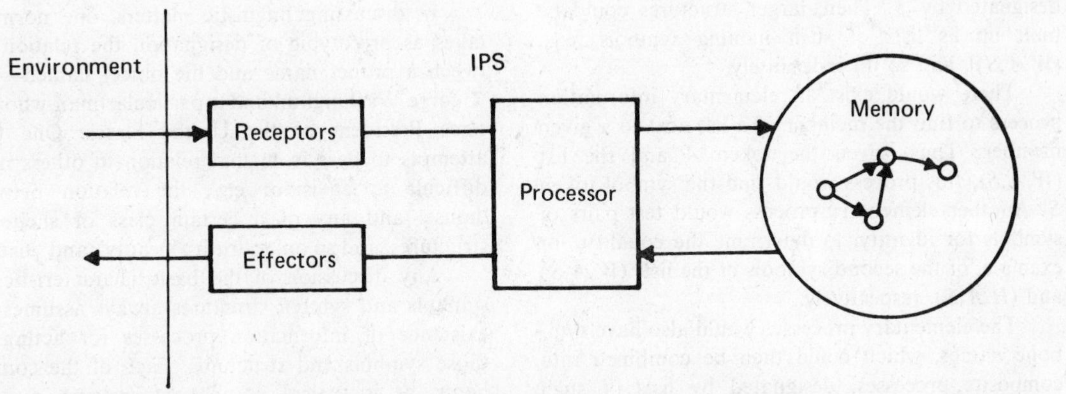


**Fig. 1.** General structure of an information processing system. (From *Human Problem Solving,* Allen Newell and Herbert A. Simon. Englewood Cliffs, N.J.: Prentice-Hall, 1972.)

modify it, build a new structure with it, and so on. Hence, three concepts are central to understanding symbol manipulation: information processing system, symbol structure, and designation.

**Information Processing Systems.** An information processing system (IPS) is a system (Fig. 1) consisting of a memory containing symbol structures, a processor, effectors, and receptors. Leaving out of account the effectors and receptors, we can summarize the characteristics of an IPS in this way:

1. There is a set of elements, called *symbols.*
2. Symbols may be formed into symbol structures by means of a set of *relations.*
3. There is a *memory,* capable of storing and retaining symbol structures.
4. There is a set of *information processes* that take symbol structures as inputs and produce symbol structure outputs.
5. The IPS has a component, the *processor,* that consists of (a) an ability to execute a set of *elementary information processes* (EIP); (b) *short-term memory* (STM) that holds the input and output symbol structures of the EIPs; and (c) an *interpreter* that determines the sequence of EIPs to be executed by the IPS as a function of the symbol structures in STM.

Symbol Structures. We say that a symbol structure *designates* (or *references,* or *points to*) an object if there exist information processes that admit the symbol structure as input, and either: (1) affect the object; or (2) produce, as output, symbol structures that are affected by the object.

A symbol structure serves as a *program* if the object it designates is an information process, and the interpreter, if given the program, can execute the designated process.

A symbol is *primitive* if its designation is fixed by the elementary information processes or by the external environment of the IPS.

The "objects" that symbols designate may include symbol structures stored in the IPS memories (data structures and programs), processes that the IPS is capable of executing, or objects in an external environment of sensible (readable) stimuli. To *read* is to create in memory internal symbol structures (representations) that designate external stimuli; to *write* is to create responses in the external environment that are designated by internal symbol structures.

The relation between a designating symbol and its object may have any degree of directness or indirectness. A structure can point to a structure that points to a structure that points to. . . .

*Example.* The meaning of these concepts can be illustrated by an example. An IPS for receiving Morse Code will have to be able to perceive the basic external stimuli: dots, dashes, letter spaces, and word spaces. These stimuli could be represented internally by two different primitive symbol types, say "•" and "-", together with conventions for representing letters as lists of primitive symbols, and words as lists of letters. Sequences of stimuli could be represented by ordered sets (*lists*) of primitive tokens. Thus, if the external stimulus were a sequence of three dashes followed by a letter space, the read processes might store the symbol structure (-,-,-), the ")" representing the letter space.

In turn, each of these simple symbol structures would be assigned a *name*—i.e., a designating symbol. The structure (-,-,-), for example, might be designated by *S*. Then, larger structures could be built up as lists of such naming symbols [e.g., (*W*,*A*,*S*)], and so on indefinitely.

There would exist an elementary information process to find the member of a list next to a given member. Thus, given the token *A* and the list (*W*,*A*,*S*), this process would find the symbol token *S*. Another elementary process would test pairs of symbols for identity, to determine the equality, for example, of the second symbols of the lists (*W*,*A*,*S*) and (*H*,*A*,*S*), respectively.

The elementary processes would also have symbolic names, which could then be combined into composite processes, designated by lists of such names, thus allowing an arbitrarily complex subroutine structure. For example, the process for testing symbol identity could be combined with the process for finding the next symbol on a list, to test whether two lists are identical.

To execute composite processes, the IPS could use an interpretive process. A symbol structuure (the program) would designate the sequence of elementary processes to be executed. The interpreter would keep track of the current elementary process being executed, and after execution would find the next process to be executed.

Finally, additional information could be associated with the symbol structures. With the list (*W*,*A*,*S*) might be associated the descriptors—part of speech (verb) and tense (past)—the two pairs constituting a description of the list. There would then be additional elementary processes to obtain the descriptions, given the list.

These postulates for an IPS are entirely abstract, making no assertions about how the structures and processes are realized, whether physically or biologically. Digital computers are physical systems that fit this abstraction; some psychologists, though not all, believe that the human cognitive system is also an information processing system in the sense of these postulates. Whether or not this view is correct cannot be settled conclusively on the basis of the evidence now available. Some success has been achieved, however, in modeling a range of human cognitive capabilities by means of appropriately defined information processing systems.

DESIGNATION. It would be more correct to say that symbol *structures* designate than to say that *symbols* designate. For example, if an information process takes as input the symbol structure (color, houseA) and produces the symbol 'white', then the symbol structure (color, houseA) designates *white*, and hence indirectly designates the color of the house in question.

In discussing linguistic matters, one normally takes as prototypic of designation the relation between a proper name and the object named—e.g., 'George Washington' and a particular man who was once President of the United States. One then attempts to pass from that relation to others more difficult to envision: e.g., the relation between 'house' and any of a certain class of sheltering structures, and so on to 'truth', 'beauty', and 'justice'.

Any discussion of the basic characteristics of symbols and symbol structures always assumes the existence of information processes for acting on those symbols and structures. Each of the components, as is typical in abstract systems, remains essentially undefined, except when taken in conjunction with the other parts. Thus, the concept of *list* is inextricably mingled with the concept of a process for finding the *next* item on a list—i.e., for responding to the ordering relation that defines the list.

Some symbols have their meaning fixed by the existence of elementary information processes that treat them in fixed ways. The most important examples are:

1. Symbols that designate specific external events or structures (e.g., internal representations of real characters).
2. Symbols that designate elementary information processes, so that these EIPs can be executed when these symbols call for the execution.

What collection of symbols is primitive for a specific IPS will vary with the particular application. For example, for purposes of visual pattern recognition, the primitive symbols might be set up to correspond, more or less approximately, to the elementary discriminations of which the retina is capable, and it is usual in such applications to describe the sensory input as a two-dimensional array of intensities. Similarly, an information processing theory of speech recognition might take as primitive symbols the elementary features that are postulated to define phonemes. In applications where sensory discrimination is not the central concern, it may be more convenient to omit pattern recognition at this elementary level and to take encodings of familiar configurations of sensory objects as the alphabet of primitive symbols. Thus, for particular applications, letters of the alphabet, or even whole words, might be taken as primitive symbols. An important consequence of taking letters as primitive symbols is that we cannot then speak of one pair of letters as more closely resembling each other than another pair. There is no notion of degree of difference or similarity among them.

REPRESENTATION. A simple example has already shown how primitive symbols can be combined into lists and descriptions. A couple of additional examples will illustrate the wide range of representations that can be accommodated by these means. In storing chess information, the men can be designated by symbols that have descriptions—defining each man's type (King, Queen, Rook, etc.) color, and positions on the board. Squares can also be represented as described symbols, whose descriptions include information about the geometry of the board, i.e., which squares adjoin them. A position, in this representation, is a symbol structure that associates with each square the symbol of the man occupying that square, if any, and which identifies the adjacent squares in various directions.

A somewhat different representation might be suitable for expressions from symbolic logic; e.g., $(P \vee Q) \cdot (Q \supset R)$. This expression can be represented by just this list of symbols, including parentheses. The expression can also be represented by a list structure, whose main list is $(\cdot, A, B)$, where $A$ is the symbol that designates the list $(\vee, P, Q)$, and $B$ the symbol that designates the list $(\supset, Q, R)$. Alternatively, making use of the relations of left (for left subexpression) and right (for right subexpression), the same logic expression could be represented as a tree structure (Fig. 2). Yet another representation of the expression uses descriptions. Take as attributes *term, connective, left*, and *right*, and as symbols a number of nodes, $x1$, $x2$. ... Then the logic expression could be represented as the following set of descriptions:

| | | |
|---|---|---|
| connective($x1$) = $\cdot$ | left($x1$) = $x2$ | right($x1$) = $x3$ |
| connective($x2$) = $\vee$ | left($x2$) = $x4$ | right($x2$) = $x5$ |
| connective($x3$) = $\supset$ | left($x3$) = $x6$ | right($x3$) = $x7$ |
| term($x4$) = $P$ | | |
| term($x5$) = $Q$ | | |
| term($x6$) = $Q$ | | |
| term($x7$) = $R$ | | |

These associations can be represented pictorially, as in Fig. 3. All of these representations are very closely related, as can be observed. That there are many ways of representing something should not be surprising. We could give still others, e.g., Polish prefix notation. All that is needed for a representation is some scheme of associations (relations) together with a set of information processes that can extract the appropriate information about connections. It is not usually possible to tell from its output exactly what internal representation is being used by an IPS, especially when alternate representations are as isomorphic as those presented here. However, in other cases, particularly in representing problems, the choice of representation can have striking observable consequences for external behavior.

If too limited a repertory of symbol structures and designations is provided by an IPS, the encoding of complex information can become an exercise in virtuosity that yields little benefit of any other kind. It appears that the structures essential to provide appropriate direct representation of a very wide

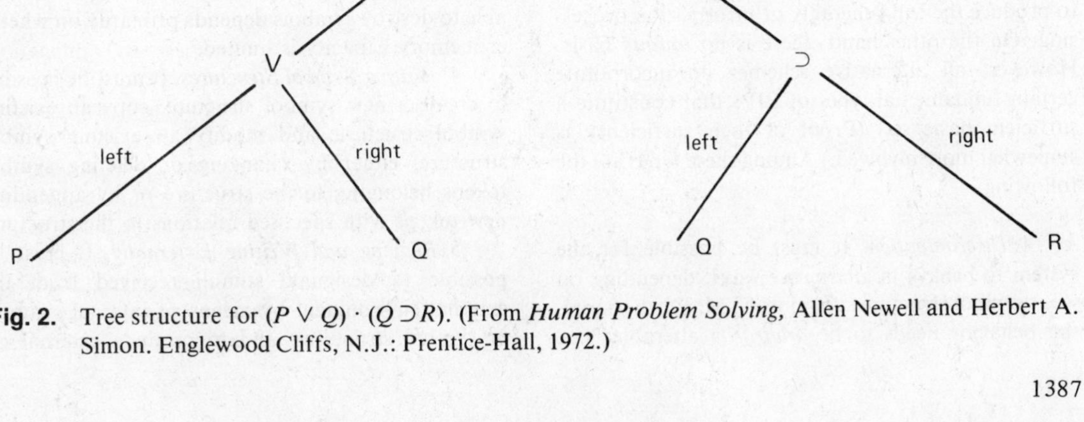

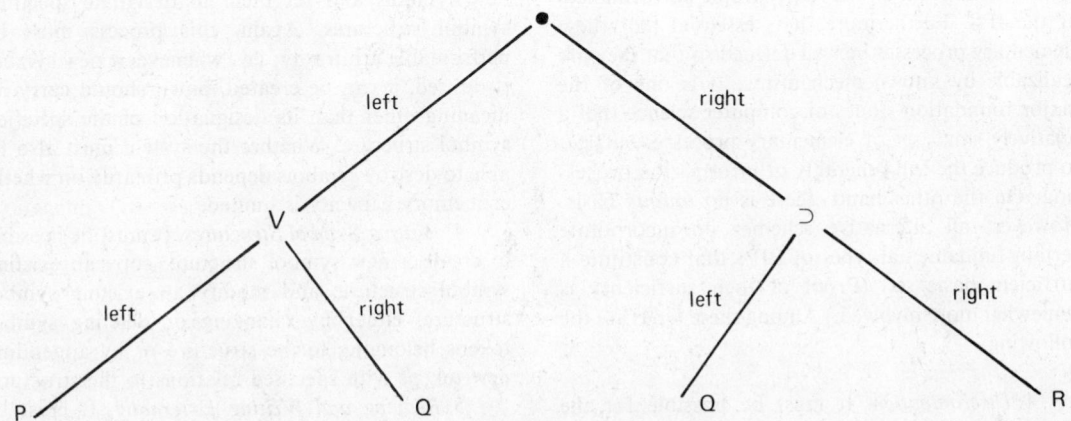

**Fig. 2.** Tree structure for $(P \vee Q) \cdot (Q \supset R)$. (From *Human Problem Solving,* Allen Newell and Herbert A. Simon. Englewood Cliffs, N.J.: Prentice-Hall, 1972.)

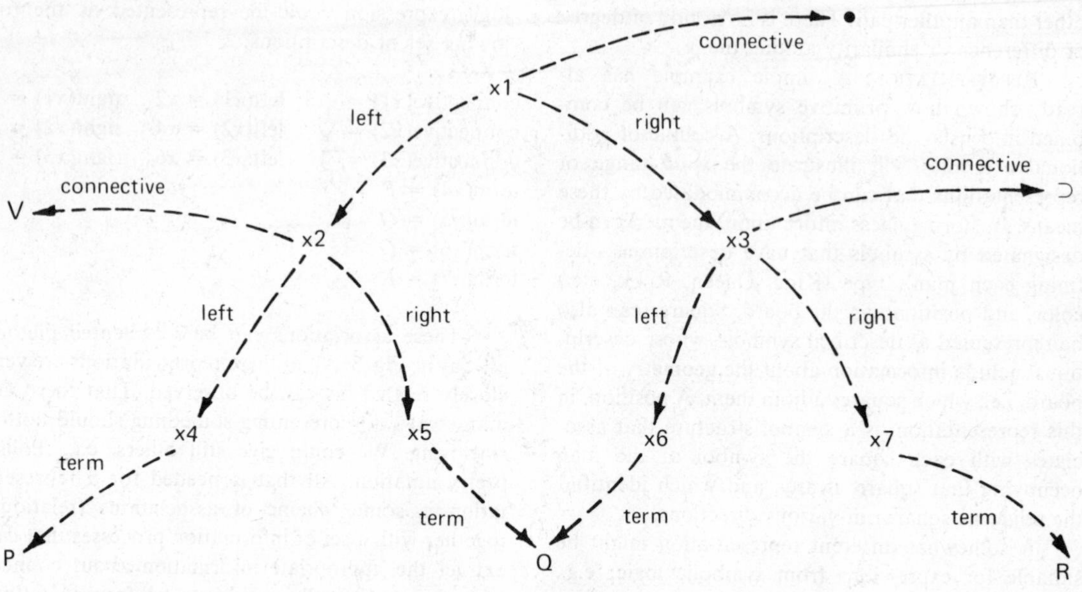


**Fig. 3.** Association structure for $(P \vee Q) \cdot (Q \supset R)$. (From *Human Problem Solving,* Allen Newell and Herbert A. Simon. Englewood Cliffs, N.J.: Prentice-Hall, 1972.)

range of stimuli are list structures and descriptions, the two types of structures we have used extensively in our examples. Other types of structures may be needed occasionally, but these two types are the core of the representational capability used in most information processing systems.

**Elementary Information Processes.** There must be a sufficiently general and powerful collection of elementary information processes to extract from them all the macroscopic performances of the IPS. Furthermore, it is essential that these elementary processes be well defined so that they are realizable by known mechanisms. It is one of the major foundation stones of computer science that a relatively small set of elementary processes suffices to produce the full generality of information processing. On the other hand, there is no *unique* basis. However, all alternative schemes do incorporate certain fundamental types of EIPs that constitute a sufficient basic set. (Proof of their sufficiency is somewhat more involved.) Among these types are the following:

1. *Discrimination.* It must be possible for the system to behave in alternative ways, depending on what symbol structures are in its STM. Furthermore, the behavior needs to be *arbitrarily* alterable; i.e., transfer of control to an independent program must be possible.

2. *Tests and Comparisons.* It must be possible to determine that two symbol tokens do or do not belong to the same symbol type. Comparisons are often directly coupled with conditional behavior, but they may equally well lead to the production of a conventional symbol (e.g., *true* or *false*) that can later be discriminated.

3. *Symbol Creation.* It must be possible to create new symbols and set them to designate specified symbol structures. Again, this process must be performable arbitrarily; i.e., whenever a new symbol is desired, it can be created, but it should carry no meaning other than its designation of the specified symbol structure. Whether the system must also be able to destroy symbols depends primarily on whether memory capacity is limited.

4. *Writing Symbol Structures.* It must be possible to create a new symbol structure, copy an existing symbol structure, and modify an existing symbol structure, either by changing or deleting symbol tokens belonging to the structure or by appending new tokens with specified relations to the structure.

5. *Reading and Writing Externally.* It must be possible to designate stimuli received from the external environment by means of internal symbols or symbol structures, and to produce external re-

sponses as a function of internal symbol structures that designate these responses.

6. *Designating Symbol Structures.* It must be possible to designate various parts of any given symbol structure, and to obtain designations of other parts, as a function of given parts and relations. Again, this may be achieved in many ways, but there must not be any parts of symbol structures that are in principle inaccessible.

7. *Storing Symbol Structures.* It must be possible to remember a symbol structure for later use, by storing it in the memory and retrieving it at any arbitrary time via a symbol structure that designates it. How much memory is available, of course, conditions strongly how complex the totality of stored structures may be. The memory must be highly reliable over time.

Even the earliest stored-program computers essentially met these requirements for an information processing system. The abstract characterization of a system such as that outlined here was developed in close relation with the invention and application of list processing and string manipulation languages, particularly in the domains of artificial intelligence, computer simulation of human cognitive processes, machine translation of language, and the design and construction of compilers. These applications make little use of the computer as a rapid arithmetic calculator, and depend basically upon its generality as a system for manipulating symbols.

**Source Information.** This article is drawn in large part from pages 20 to 30 of Newell and Simon (1972). For a formal approach to symbol manipulation in terms of Markov algorithms, see Chapter 1 of Galler and Perlis (1970), or Chapter 2 of Knuth (1968). Descriptions of two widely used list-processing languages illustrating many of the concepts discussed in this article will be found in Berkeley and Bobrow (1964) and in Griswold, Poage, and Polonsky (1968).

REFERENCES

1964. Berkeley, E. C., and D. G. Bobrow (Eds.). *The Programming Language LISP.* Cambridge, Mass.: Information International, Inc.

1968. Griswold, R. D., J. F. Poage, and I. P. Polonsky. *The SNOBOL4 Programming Language.* Englewood Cliffs, N.J.: Prentice-Hall.

1968. Knuth, Donald E. *The Art of Computer Programming*, Vol. 1. Reading, Mass.: Addison-Wesley.

1970. Galler, B. A., and A. J. Perlis. *A View of Programming Languages.* Reading, Mass.: Addison-Wesley. (Especially Chapters 1 and 3.)

1972. Newell, Allen, and H. A. Simon. *Human Problem Solving.* Englewood Cliffs, N.J.: Prentice-Hall.

A. NEWELL AND H. A. SIMON

## SYNTAX, SEMANTICS, AND PRAGMATICS

For articles on related subjects *see* GRAMMAR; LANGUAGE PROCESSORS; PROGRAMMING LANGUAGES; and PROGRAMMING LINGUISTICS.

For article on related term *see* STRING.

Every language of communication possesses two identifiable properties; the form of the language and the meaning associated with the form. In the case of natural languages (i.e., those languages used for human-to-human communication), the syntax of the language is generally referred to as its *grammar*. The syntax is a set of rules specifying which forms of the language are grammatically acceptable. For example, if a simple English sentence is specified to have the grammar

*noun phrase verb phrase*

and a *noun phrase* is composed of an *article* followed by a *noun*, while a *verb phrase* is defined to be a *verb* followed by a *noun phrase*, we may see that the sentence

"The cat drank the milk"

is a syntactically correct English sentence, provided the word "the" is in the class of *articles*, "cat" and "milk" are *nouns*, and "drank" is a *verb*. However, by the same reasoning, the sentence

"The milk drank the cat"

is equally valid syntactically, but has no valid meaning.

The *meaning* associated with syntactically correct instances of a language can be viewed from two points of view; the meaning intended by the originator of the sentence and the meaning retrieved by a receiver. It is not always the case that these two meanings are identical. The former is called the *semantics* of the language, and the latter its *pragmatic* meaning. Much of modern humor is based on the skillful interplay between these two aspects of meaning, particularly with respect to the pun and the riddle.

Linguistic ambiguity may be caused by syntactic inadequacies or by a confusion between semantic and pragmatic meanings. An example of the former is the sign on a jet airplane:

NO SMOKING AREA
IN REAR CABIN

Does this imply there is a place in the rear cabin where smoking is not allowed (a NO-SMOKING AREA) or that there is no place in the rear cabin where smoking is allowed (NO SMOKING-AREA)? On the other hand, the sentence

"I did not say that he stole the money"

can have a multitude of meanings in the spoken language, depending on such factors as emphasis, articulation, and tone. Each pair of the different meanings is a candidate for ambiguity between its semantic and pragmatic meaning.

In the case of programming languages, the distinctions above also apply, but in addition, there are some relatively subtle differences which have developed between computer languages and their associated formal language theory. When used by a computer linguist, grammar is usually applied to the rules governing the generation of strings in a language, while syntax is usually concerned with the recognition by the computer of whether or not a given string is a legal string in the language. There is, therefore, a complementary relationship between the productions of a grammar and the rules of syntax used by a computer language processor to recognize strings in the language.

The implementation of a computer language on a particular computer automatically removes any syntactic ambiguity that may have been present in the language definition by giving one and only one meaning to any language construct. Semantic and pragmatic ambiguities are still possible; they cause much confusion between what the programmer thought was meant and what the computer takes as the meaning of what the programmer wrote.

REFERENCE

1969. Sammet, J. E. *Programming Languages: History and Fundamentals*. Englewood Cliffs, N.J.: Prentice-Hall.

J. A. N. LEE AND A. RALSTON

## SYNTAX-DIRECTED COMPILER. *See* COMPILER, SYNTAX-DIRECTED.

## SYSTEM CHART

For articles on related subjects *see* DOCUMENTATION; FLOWCHART; and FLOW DIAGRAM.

A system chart is a variety of flowchart. It is distinguished from other varieties of flowchart by its stress on the component operations that in sequence make up a system. Usually, these component operations are programs to be executed by a computer, but they may be operations to be done by other machines or by people. Examples of component operations are "transcribe data from handwritten documents," "sort," and "run program WY-37." System charts are sometimes known as "run diagrams." They can be distinguished from other varieties of flowchart by the dominant use of input/output identifications and the clearly layered structure of input-process-output.

N. CHAPIN

## SYSTEM GENERATION

For articles on related subjects *see* OPERATING SYSTEMS; and UPDATE.

System generation is the process of implementing a basic system at a specific installation. The process is diagrammed in Fig. 1. A program known as the system generator receives as input a description of the basic operating system to be generated and a specification of parameters describing the specific installation (such as the types, quantities, and configuration of the system equipment). The generator processes the description of the basic

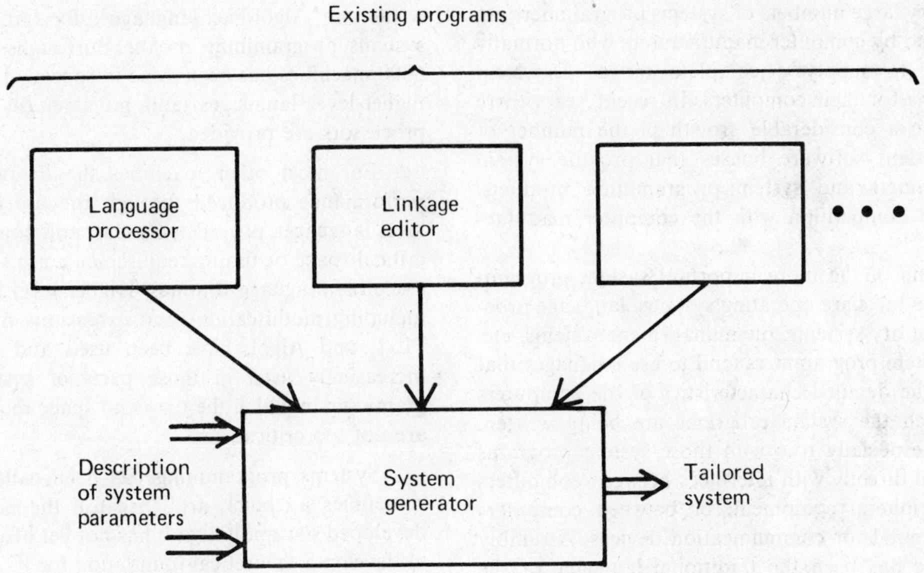


**Fig. 1.** System generation.

system, substituting the parameters for variables in the description, and produces as output a specific system tailored to the installation. The system generator program will use the facilities of the existing basic system while it produces the tailored system; after production the tailored system can be loaded and started, thus bringing it into operation. By this technique a manufacturer need prepare only one version of the updated system for distribution to its customers, who then can produce from it a new system that will run efficiently on the specific equipment at their installations.

The process outlined above is applicable to systems that are language processors (e.g., PL/I) as well as for complete operating systems (e.g., OS/VS2 for IBM System/370). If the basic system is a language processor, the parameters may specify such items as options regarding compile-time and run-time diagnostics, methods of object-code optimization, formats for symbol table listings, and formation of address maps. If the basic system is a complete operating system, the parameters will include the details of the hardware configuration, of the system libraries, the procedures to be used for allocation and control of system resources (e.g., memory and processor management policies, protection mechanism), accounting and billing procedures, and performance monitoring procedures. In some cases, the parameters may specify procedures that are to be integrated into the basic system.

It should be obvious that this description of system generation applies also if the installation already has a running system. It is not at all uncommon to generate a newer version of an operating system using a previous release of the same system or a more primitive version of the same system.

P. J. Denning and D. E. Denning

# SYSTEMS PROGRAMMING

For articles on related subjects *see* Applications Programming; and Machine and Assembly Language Programming.

For articles on related terms *see* Files; Language Processors; Operating Systems; and Utility Program.

Systems programming is concerned with the development and production of programs that have to do with translation, loading, supervision, maintenance, control, and running of computers and computer programs. The distinction is usually made between systems programming and applications programming, although the distinction is not always obvious, especially on small special-purpose or limited-purpose computers.

## SYSTEMS PROGRAMMING

Very large numbers of systems programmers are employed by computer manufacturers who normally attempt to supply a complete range of system programs for their computers. In recent years there has been a considerable growth in the number of independent software houses that provide system programmers and system programming products, often in competition with the computer manufacturers.

Some of the more important system programming products are operating systems, language processors, utility systems, file management systems, etc.

System programmers tend to use languages that reflect the detailed characteristics of the computers for which the system programs are being written. This is especially true with those system programs that deal directly with interfaces between computers and peripheral equipment, or between computers and terminals or communication devices. Assembly language has been the traditional language of the system programmer, and many of the design features of assembly languages reflect the needs of system programmers.

In recent years there has been a concerted effort to develop languages and systems that would permit system programmers to operate in higher-level languages. The problem addressed was the extremely high cost of system programming, and the unreliability and difficulty of maintenance of large systems written in assembly languages.

The most successful effort in this area was made by Burroughs Corporation. The logical design of the larger Burroughs machines has been such as to provide relatively efficient execution of programs written in Algol-like languages. By fiat, then, all systems programming on the Burroughs 5000 and 6000 machines has been done in special Algol-based higher-level languages, and no assembly language processors are provided.

For most other machines the degradation in performance produced through the use of higher-level languages proved too great, and routines with critical space or timing requirements are still mostly assembly language routines. Higher-level languages; including modifications and extensions of Fortran, PL/I, and Algol, have been used and are being increasingly used in those parts of systems programming in which the time and space requirements are not too critical.

Systems programming has been called an art, sometimes a "black art," because the need for it developed so rapidly that it has not yet been possible to develop a theoretical foundation for it, or even to adopt criteria of good practice among practitioners in the field. There have been many textbooks written, many courses offered, and whole curricula devised to train people in the area of systems programming, but these efforts have had only limited success. To this day, there are programmers with little formal education or experience who can perform prodigious feats of systems programming, and others who have successfully completed all relevant courses in the best universities who could not get even a relatively simple programming system to run if their lives depended upon it.

S. Rosen

# T

## TABLE LOOKUP

For articles on related subjects *see* ACCESS METHODS; FILES; and SORTING.
For articles on related terms *see* BINARY SEARCH; HASHING; KEY; and RECORD.

In everyday life, table lookup problems may range from a telephone number to the sine of an angle, to the recipe for pecan pie. Lookup, or searching for some information, in a table is also required in many programming applications, including the writing of compilers and interpreters (Glass, 1969). Table manipulation, search techniques, and routines should be considered, developed, and cataloged at all computer installations because they are so generally useful.

**Definitions.** The definitions promulgated by the American National Standards Institute (ANSI) in *Vocabulary for Information Processing* have been adapted to this article. These include:

*Record.* A logical unit of information that may contain one or more fields.

*Field.* A specific area of a record used for a particular category of data; e.g., a group of card columns used for pay rate.

*File.* A collection or batch of related records that must be processed in some way.

*Table.* A collection or batch of records containing "control" or master information to be used repeatedly in a process; e.g., a collection of records containing employee number versus pay rate fields.

*Key.* The particular field of a record on which the processing is performed; e.g., a lookup process might be performed on the employee number field (the key) to determine the pay rate for that employee.

*Position.* The "place" or logical location of a record in a table; e.g., position 13 of a table contains a particular record.

**General Considerations.** This presentation of lookup techniques is limited to the consideration of tables that can be totally contained in the main memory of the computer and in which all table positions are available in equal access time. The methodology could be complicated by considering techniques for tables that are too large for such storage or for tables on external direct-access devices where access time is not uniform. The table is considered fixed during processing; i.e., it need not be altered or updated (table records added, deleted, or revised) dynamically.

In file processing with a table, both file and table records may exist in computer-readable form on card decks, tape reels, disk packs, etc. or the table may be built into or generated by the program. If built in or generated, the programmer can exercise his judgment on the arrangement of the table. If the table must be read in, the programmer can simply read table items into sequential locations and use the table as it stands, or he can rearrange the table to his preference. He should realize that the rearrangement takes time on the computer and should be justified by time saved in searching the table when his file is processed. When large files or tables are involved, table organization that enables faster lookup is very profitable.

In addition to table arrangement considerations, the matter of key transformation—converting existing logical table- and file-record keys to a different form or arrangement—must be considered because of its speed advantage. This subject will be discussed after some foundation for lookup techniques has been established.

## Search Techniques

THE SEQUENTIAL SEARCH. The sequential search is the most straightforward of table lookups. It consists simply of starting at some table position (usually the beginning) and comparing the file-record key in hand with each table-record key, one at a time, until either a match is found or all table positions have been searched. The sequential search is easily programmed, and lends itself nicely to index-register or address-modification techniques on most computers. Also, it is easy to code in a higher-level language.

If the table is ordered or arranged in sequence on the key, various techniques can be used to speed up the search. For example, the key in every tenth table position could be interrogated, starting with position 1, until a table-record key greater than the current file record is found, at which point a sequential search could be started in reverse on each position until the match is found or a "less than" comparison results. Also, other table characteristics, if known, might be used to advantage.

MERGE SEARCH. The merge search is a sequential search technique requiring that both the table and file records be ordered in the same sequence on the key involved. The keys are compared, starting with the first file record and first table position. If a match is not found, the table is searched sequentially until an equal or greater table-record key is found. If greater, the table does not have that key, and the file must be rolled on to examine the next record; if equal, the record is processed, and the next file record is considered. It is not necessary to start over with table position 1; one simply starts the search for each file record at the table position where the previous search terminated.

This merge technique will often turn out to be the fastest one if the table and file are already ordered in the desired sequence. If the program at hand must justify the required ordering, other techniques may be faster. This method, contrary to others to be discussed, does not require that all table positions be in memory at once; both table and file records could be on magnetic tape, for example. Thus, the merge technique could be very useful when tables are too large for memory.

Fig. 1 presents a flow diagram of the merge technique.

BINARY SEARCH. The term "binary search" comes from the principal feature of this technique, which provides that each "look" into the table either finds the key in question or eliminates *half* of the table positions from further consideration. A binary search requires that the table be ordered on the table keys. Ascending sequence is assumed in this discussion.

The procedure begins by comparing the current file-record key to the table key at the midposition of the table. If the file-record key is greater, the lower half of the table can be ignored, and the next look can be taken at the midposition of the remaining upper half. This process continues until a key match is found or the table "shrinks" to nothing. Fig. 2 should help clarify this technique.

The maximum number of inspections or looks into the table necessary to find the record key being sought, or to ascertain that it is missing, is the smallest integer $L$ satisfying the relation

$$2^L \geq N + 1,$$

where $L$ is the number of looks and $N$ is the number of table positions. This may be rewritten as

$$\log_2(N + 1) + 1 > L \geq \log_2(N + 1).$$

Comparing the binary and sequential techniques in terms of the probable number of looks required to find a file-record key is shown in Table 1. While the saving in number of looks required for large tables proves that the binary search technique has a great advantage, the factor of *time per look* must be considered. If this time were equal for both methods, the binary search would always be best, but more tests are involved in the binary search, so each look takes longer. Thus, if we assume a 5:1 advantage for the sequential technique, the break-even point would be somewhere around a 50-position table, neglecting the table setup time.

Certain techniques may be used to accelerate each look of a binary search when the program is written in machine or assembly language. For example, on computers with a three-way compare

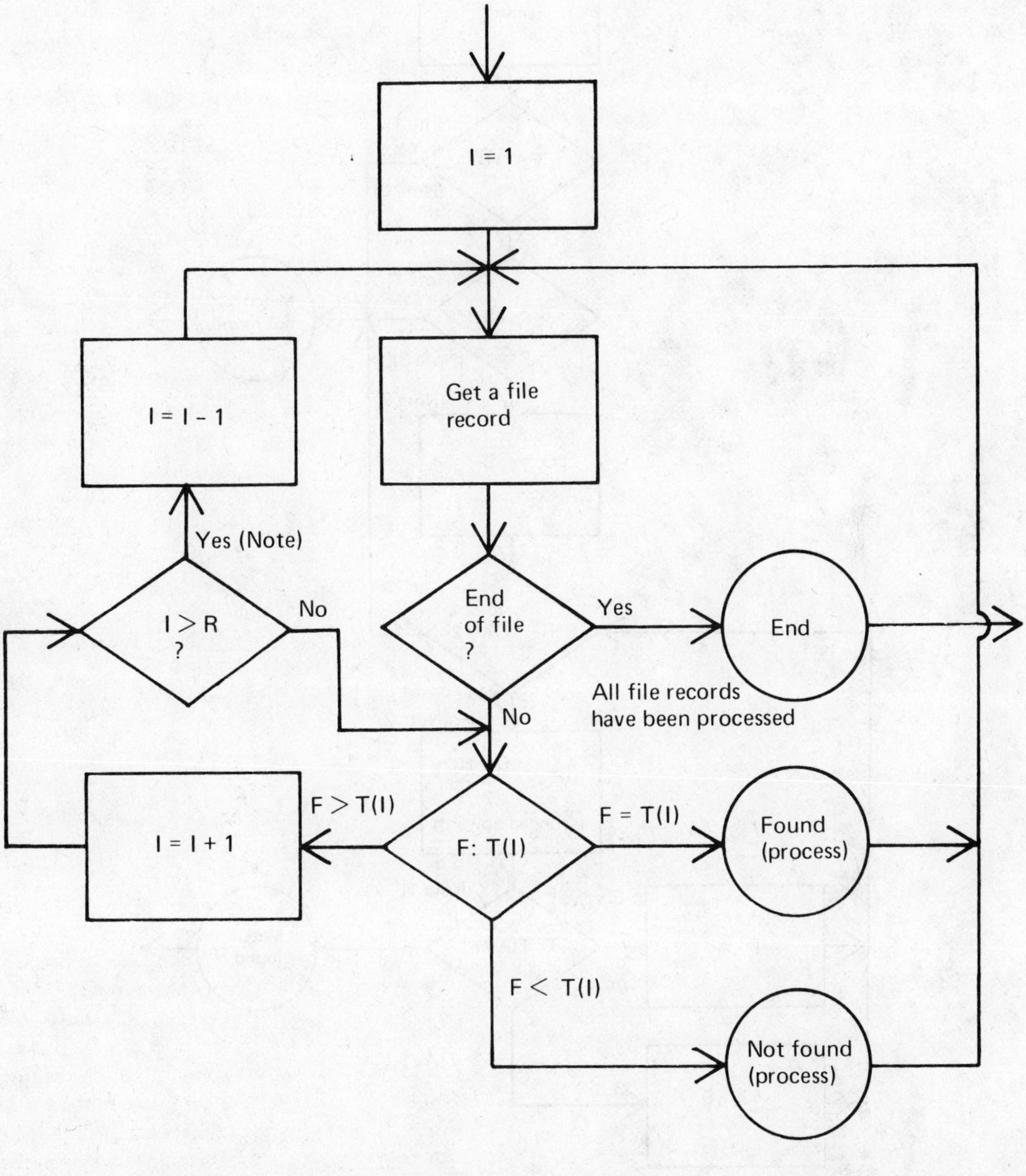


**Fig. 1.** Flow diagram of merge search technique. $R$ = count of records in table; $T(I)$ = key of $I$th table record (in position $I$); $F$ = current file-record key. Table is sorted in ascending order on key $T$, i.e., $T(I)$ = lowest key; $T(R)$ = highest key . File records are sorted in ascending order on key $F$. *Note:* An alternative at "yes" to $I = I - 1$ would be: At the first occurrence of $I > R$, branch to a procedure that simply reads the balance of file records and treats them as "not found."

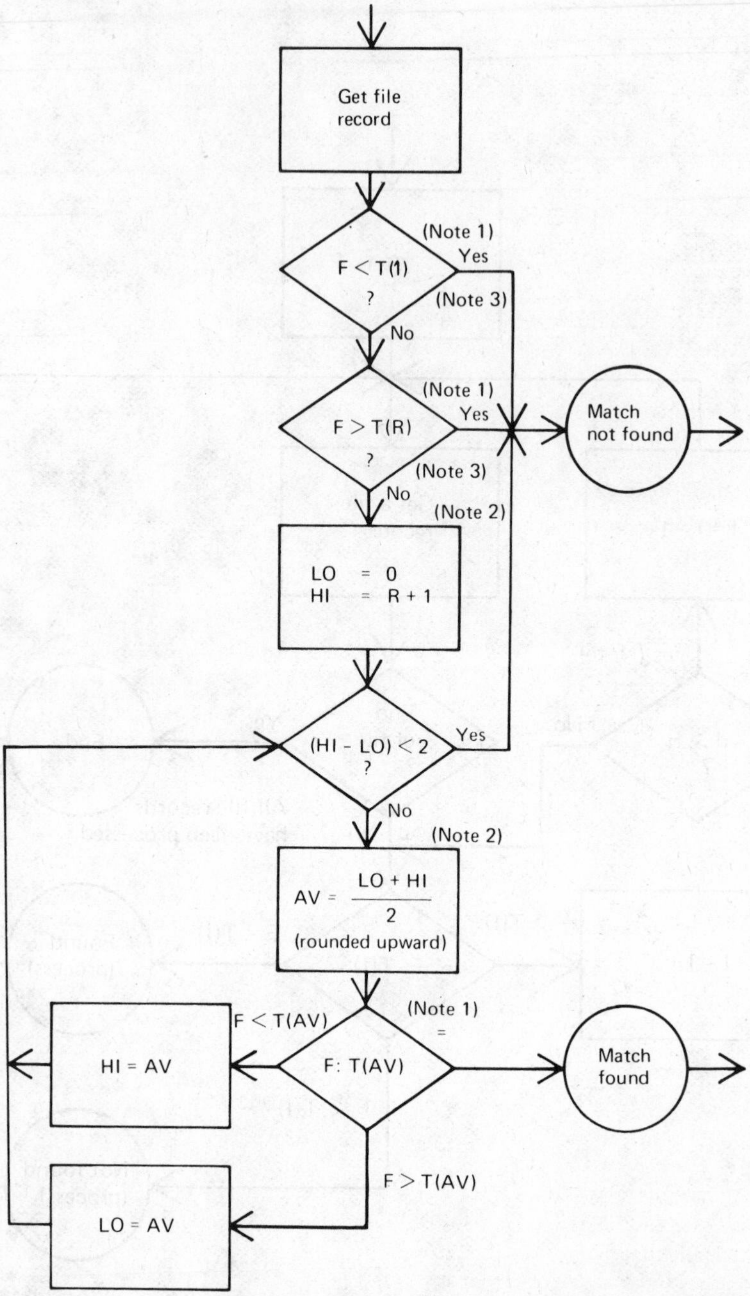


**Fig. 2.** Flow diagram of a general binary search technique. $R$ = count of records in table; $T(I)$ = key of $I$th table record (in position $I$); $F$ = current file-record key. Table is sorted in ascending sequence on keys, i.e., $T(1)$ = lowest key and $T(R)$ = highest. *Note 1:* This test is dependent upon table keys being ascendingly ordered in collating sequence upon which test is based. *Note 2:* LO, HI, and AV are fields (integer) which control the table positions being looked in. *Note 3:* These tests are not necessary, but may save time if many file-record keys will not be found in table.

**Table 1.** Comparison of Table Size Versus Number of Looks Required in Sequential and Binary Searches

| Number of Table Positions | Number of Looks Required: Sequential Maximum | Sequential Average | Binary Maximum | Binary Average |
|---|---|---|---|---|
| 5 | 5 | 3 | 3 | 2 |
| 10 | 10 | 5 | 4 | 3 |
| 50 | 50 | 25 | 6 | 5 |
| 100 | 100 | 50 | 7 | 6 |
| 1,000 | 1,000 | 500 | 10 | 9 |
| 10,000 | 10,000 | 5,000 | 14 | 13 |
| 100,000 | 100,000 | 50,000 | 17 | 16 |
| 1,000,000 | 1,000,000 | 500,000 | 20 | 19 |

instruction, and for applications in which keys can be contained in single machine words and table record keys are stored sequentially in contiguous machine words, binary searches approaching the time-per-look speed of sequential searches can be written.

While not directly a part of the search methodology, a technique for saving table arrangement (sorting) time may be worth considering in some applications. This technique adds indirectness to the lookup, however, and requires more storage space because a pointer is required with each table position. The technique's virtue derives from elimination of the need to rearrange associated (nonkey) fields of the table records. The technique consists of appending a pointer, which represents the position of the ancilliary fields, to the key field. This key/pointer record is then stored in a separate table, and this table—not the one containing the nonkey fields—is sorted. A search on the key will reveal a key hit, but the table record must be retrieved by looking in the "pointed to" position. Fig. 3 illustrates the table setup.

Direct Lookup. This technique is perhaps inherently the fastest, when it can be used. Opposed to other techniques, it involves no trial-and-error searching, but an exact relationship must be established between key and position. This relationship has to be determined or known in advance of table creation because table records must be stored in a position that is a function of the key value. Thus, the table storage allocation must include positions for all possible table records whose keys are in range.

Consider a simple example in which the table-record keys are numeric and are three-digit part numbers varying from legitimate values of 001 to 999. One could allocate a 1,000-position table and, as the table is input, store the records in the position

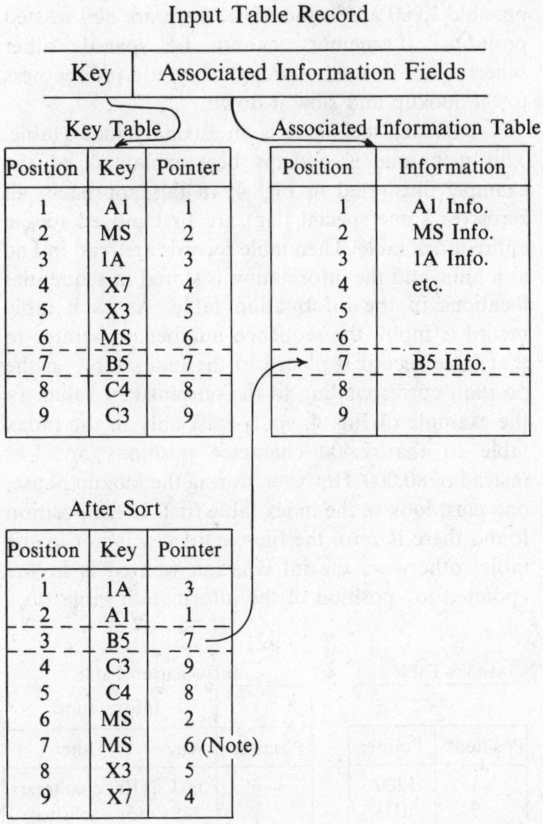


**Fig. 3.** Method for saving sort time in setting up ordered table for binary (or other) search. *Note:* Including the pointer as a low-order part of the key during sort keeps duplicate keys in "as input" order.

indicated by their key (e.g., the table record whose key is part number 123 goes into table position 123). Here there is an exact 1:1 relationship between key and position. The technique cannot directly handle duplicate keys in the table. It is not necessary to store the table-record key in the table because its value is implied by its record position. For example, an input file record with part number 123 could have an associated table record in table position 123. In higher-level language, TP (123) contains the information being sought; the subscript indicates the table position.

The possibility that table position 123 does not have information must be considered. This can be dealt with by storing some flag or special unique character in all invalid table positions. A waste of memory results if the table has many voids (or is sparse). That is, if only 200 part numbers of the possible 1,000 are in the table, there are 800 wasted positions. If memory cannot be spared, other schemes can be used, although they add indirectness to the lookup and slow it down.

One such technique is an auxiliary index table. This technique is perhaps best explained by the example illustrated in Fig. 4. In this approach, all zeros (or some special flag) are first moved to the entire index table. Then table records are read in one at a time, and the information is stored in sequential locations in the information table. As each table record is input, the sequence number or pointer to that table record is placed in the index table in the position corresponding to the current key value. In the example of Fig. 4, voids exist only in the index table so that 2,400 character positions are lost instead of 80,000. However, during the lookup phase, one must look in the index table first. If the position found there is zero, the file-record key is not in the table; otherwise, the information wanted is in the "pointed to" position of the information table.

Index Table

| Position* | Pointer |
|---|---|
| 1 | 200 |
| 2 | 003 |
| 3 | 001 |
| 4 | 000 |
| . | . |
| . | . |
| 123 | 088 |
| . | . |
| . | . |
| 785 | 002 |
| . | . |
| . | . |
| 999 | 000 |

Information Table

| | Information | |
|---|---|---|
| Position* | Key | Other |
| 1 | 003 | (100 characters |
| 2 | 785 | for each item) |
| 3 | 002 | |
| . | . | |
| . | . | |
| 88 | 123 | |
| . | . | |
| . | . | |
| 200 | 001 | |

**Fig. 4.** Memory conservation through use of index table. *Note: These fields are not required to be stored in memory, but are shown to illustrate the technique.

This direct technique, with or without indexing schemes, can be applied to many situations and is quite fast. It is very good in situations where tables are logically multidimensional, assuming again the numeric key restriction.

KEY TRANSFORMATION. An important adjunct to direct table lookup is the subject of key transformation. Often the table keys, even if numeric, cannot be considered table positions because the resulting table would be too sparse. Transforming a key field from its natural form and length to a different representation may be worthwhile in some applications so that a quasi-direct lookup can be made rather than a trial-and-error search. This is done by performing some routine operation on the original key to transform it into a new key. This is often called "hashing," and hash addresses are the transformed keys so created. These hash addresses are then used as direct-entry positions.

For example, suppose there is a table of part numbers that are ten numeric characters in length, but there may be no more than 10,000 unique part numbers. As a direct-entry table would have to allow 10 billion ($10^{10}$) positions to handle only $10^4$ possible keys, a scheme must be contrived to transform the original ten-digit key to an integer that will represent the table position of that part in a much more compact table.

There are many possible schemes. One simple one is the division-remainder method: Choose a number close to the number of table positions needed. Use that number as a divisor to extract a quotient and a remainder from the dividend (which is the original key). The remainder so obtained is the transformed key. Using 10,000 as the divisor, the transformed key becomes the original key modulo 10,000. The following table lists some examples.

| *Original Key (Part Number)* | *Transformed Key* |
|---|---|
| 00 0000 1000 | 1000 |
| 00 0001 0000 | 0 |
| 00 0001 0001 | 1 |
| 00 0001 0099 | 99 |
| 10 0001 0099 | 99 |
| 22 3333 4444 | 4444 |
| 90 0020 0110 | 110 |
| 99 0020 0112 | 112 |

These examples were constructed to illustrate the matter of duplicate transformed keys.

Ideally, the transform scheme would convert the original keys to transformed keys with no duplicates. While schemes can be constructed to minimize "hash clash," its possibility cannot be eliminated completely, and because of this, the original key must be stored in the table. Further, some scheme must be used to handle duplicate transformed keys, and there are many choices to consider. Different divisors should be tried out to minimize the number of duplicate keys generated; for example using 9,999 or some divisor other than 10,000 might result in fewer duplicate keys. Also, different transform schemes should be considered.

The duplicates could be handled simply by an overflow table, which operates as follows: If a transformed key finds a void in the direct-entry table, it is placed there. However, if the place is already occupied by a previously transformed key, then the direct-entry position is flagged to indicate the overflow occurrence, and the overflowed key (original key) is stored in the next sequential position of the overflow table. Thus, in searching such a direct-entry table with an overflow table, the file-record key must be transformed into a direct table position. If the key is found in the direct-entry table with no overflow flag, there is a match. If the position is occupied by either a nonmatching key without an overflow indicator or by a void, there is no match. If, however, there is a nonmatching key with an overflow indication, the overflow table must be searched to see if the record key of interest is there. This overflow table could be searched sequentially or arranged for faster methods.

If the total number of overflow keys is significant, an approach with more finesse can be used to handle the search for overflowed keys from the direct-entry table. The overflow flag in the direct-entry table of the transformed key, if nonzero, may be constructed to be an overflow table position. This would "chain" the lookup directly to the overflow table position containing the overflowed key. Thus, the overflow table itself would become a direct-entry table. Please note, however, that only the first direct-entry overflow can be handled in this way unless the overflow table itself has an overflow indicator. (More than one hash clash in a given transformed key position is possible.) This overflow chaining technique is illustrated by the example in Fig. 5. It should result in faster lookup than a trial-and-error overflow table search. In both approaches, however, enough space (computer memory) must be allocated to provide for all overflows, so the programmer must "know" the table and key transform characteristics quite well.

Some other methods of key transformation are: folding, radix transformation, and digit rearrangement. These key transform techniques per se have nothing special to recommend them over the division-remainder method. They are probably no faster and do not necessarily produce fewer duplicate transformed keys. The digit rearrangement technique has possibilities for reducing duplicates, if careful digit analysis is done on the original keys of a given table in order to determine which digit positions to select. That is, one should select digit positions in the original key in which digit values 0 through 9 are evenly distributed.

*Direct-Entry Table*

| Position (transformed key) | Original* Key | Overflow† Table Key |
|---|---|---|
| 0 | 00 0001 0000 | 0 |
| 1 | 00 0001 0001 | 1 |
| 2 | 0 | 0 |
| 3 | 30 0050 0003 | 0 |
| 4 | 20 0120 0004 | 2 |
| . | | |
| . | | |
| . | | |

*Overflow Table*

| Position | Original Key | Overflow† Table Key |
|---|---|---|
| 1 | 20 0050 0001 | 0 |
| 2 | 30 0017 0004 | 4 |
| 3 | 00 0010 0167 | 0 |
| 4 | 30 0018 0004 | 0 |
| . | | |
| . | | |
| . | | |

**Fig. 5.** Example of an overflow-handling technique. *Note: 0 indicates no keys transform to this position. †Note: 0 indicates an "end of chain" condition (no more keys with this "hash" address).

There are situations in which key transform techniques offer a speed advantage, as the table need not be ordered and the key transform time is probably faster than the time required to sort the table. The lookup time (where the percentage of overflows is small) is probably faster than a binary search if the key transform technique is quick. Thus, some sacrifice in program complexity and additional memory for overflow handling could speed program execution. Compiler and assembler programs use such techniques to advantage for handling symbol tables (Glass, 1969; Morris, 1968) that are dynamic (i.e., need to be searched while they are being built).

**Closing Remarks.** Faced with an application, how does the programmer know which procedure will be best for his situation? There is probably no general solution to this problem because of the many variables involved. Sometimes it is intuitively judged that one technique is the most natural choice in a given application. Often, combinations of techniques can be used to advantage. At times the programmer can carefully plan his program and perhaps test out various techniques to optimize it. At other times, the main consideration is: "Have it running by the first of the month!"

Again, it is important to remember that technique optimization is economically advantageous only for programs that (1) execute often; and/or (2) have a large number of file records; and/or (3) have large tables. An attempt to define "often" and "large" is intentionally avoided.

This article is a condensation of a previous treatment (Price, 1971), based on work performed for the U.S. Atomic Energy Commission.

References

1969. Glass, Robert L. "An Elementary Discussion of Compiler/Interpreter Writing," *Computing Surveys*, Vol. 1, No. 1 (March), p. 55.
This paper mentions use of tables and search techniques in various phases of compiler/interpreter writing.

1968. Morris, Robert. "Scatter Storage Techniques," *Comm. ACM*, Vol. 11, No. 1 (January), pp. 38–43.
Scatter storage techniques applied to processing symbol tables, as in compilers and assemblers. A well-written paper, recommended to anyone interested in dynamic tables and key transforms.

1970. American National Standards Institute. *A Vocabulary for Information Processing*, ANSI X3.12–1970.
Defines and names computer-related words and concepts.

1971. Price, C. E. "Table Lookup Techniques," *Computing Surveys*, Vol. 3, No. 2 (June), p. 49.

C. E. Price

# TAPE LABEL

For article on related subject *see* Memory: Auxiliary.

Magnetic tape labels are special records appearing at the beginning and end of a reel of magnetic tape to provide details about the file of records stored on the tape.

A *header label* is a block of data at the beginning of a magnetic tape file containing descriptive information to identify the file. A header label may be, for example, 80 characters long, with all data recorded in even parity at the same density as the remainder of the data file. Header records would usually be separated from succeeding data records by an interrecord gap. A header label may contain the following fields (with the length in number of characters given in brackets):

1. Density [1] specifies density of recording in file.
2. Header-label identifier [2] identifies record as header label record.
3. Logical unit number [2] specifies logical unit to which file is assigned.
4. Retention period code [3] specifies (in days) retention period of file; only after expiration of this period may the tape be overwritten.
5. File name [14] identifies file, using any combination of characters legal in the specific code used.
6. Reel number [2] identifies sequence of reels for multireel files.
7. Data written [6] expressed in day, month, and last two numerals of the year. Identifies date written and is used with the retention period to determine release date of file.
8. Edition or generation number [2] identifies a single file set. Each time amendment data is applied to a magnetic tape file an entirely new copy of the file is created, containing all the valid data amendments. This new reel will bear the same field name as the original reel that was amended; the two will, however, be different generations of the same file and as such will bear generation numbers.
9. User-supplied information [48] contains any comments the user might find to be useful.

When a file is opened, this data is checked by the program to insure that the correct file is being processed; also, if the tape is to be used for writing, to check that the retention period has been exceeded.

A *trailer label* is a special record appearing at the end of a file stored on magnetic tape. It serves to identify the end of the file and usually provides some control data related to that file. A trailer label may be, for example, 80 characters long, with all data recorded in even parity at the same density as the remainder of the data file. End-of-file marks precede and follow the trailer label. A trailer label usually contains the following fields (with length of characters given in brackets):

1. Trailer label identifier [3] identifies label as EOT (end of tape) or EOS (end of set) or EOF (end of file.

2. Record count [5] provides number of records in the file for controlling purposes.

3. User field [72] contains any comments the user might find to be useful.

The main advantages of tape labels lie in their ability to provide the computing system with means to accept only properly identified input files for each computer run, and to accept input in the correct sequence when more than one reel is used. Labels also make it possible for the operating system to identify the end-of-file (EOF) or end-of-reel (EOR) status. Use of labels, however, complicates the programming task somewhat, and also creates some administrative problems in the assignment of label codes.

The need not uncommonly arises to interchange information recorded on magnetic tape between different users and different computers. This may be made possible by use of common standards for tape labels or by software that allows the system to handle unlabeled tapes as well as tapes with atypical labels.

J. NECAS

## TARGET PROGRAM. *See* OBJECT PROGRAM.

## TASK

For articles on related subjects *see* JOB; OPERATING SYSTEMS: Principles and Theory; and PROGRAM STATUS WORDS AND STATE VECTORS.

A *task* (or *process*) is an atomic unit of activity in a computer system. It is specified in terms of its external characteristics only, its internal structure and operation being unspecified. The external characteristics of a task that must be specified will depend on the context in which a task is being studied or controlled; these include: input and output parameters or variables, resource requirements, and execution time.

If, for example, the context of a discussion is the evaluation of arithmetic expressions, tasks in that discussion will be the arithmetic operations of the computer. Or, if the discussion concerns the determinate operation of a set of tasks on common data, the tasks in that discussion are arbitrary procedures. In discussions where task-resource demands are being considered, some systems adopt the view that a task demand is a function of time; in contrast, others adopt the view that the demand of a task is fixed, and that time-varying demands are modeled by considering appropriate networks of tasks with constant demands.

If a system must preempt resources from a task at a certain point in its execution, a description of the task state with respect to the given resource at the time of preemption will have to be formulated. The *task descriptor* or *state vector* is an example of this when the processor is the preemptible resource.

A task is said to be *uninterpreted* if its function or operation is unspecified. Many systems are set up to control uninterpreted tasks, since (1) there is no way of knowing during the system design what specific tasks will be run, and (2) system behavior should be reproducible to the extent that the computations performed by arbitrary tasks will not depend on their relative speeds.

A *multitask system* is one in which two or more tasks can be in progress (i.e., between their points of initiation and termination) at any given time. The simplest form of multitask system assumes that all the tasks are *independent*; but many systems permit *precedence constraints* to be implemented—i.e., the requirement that the initiation of a certain task must always follow the terminations of other specified tasks.

The term "process" is also used to mean essentially the same as *task*. The literature is filled with so many conflicting definitions of *process* that many people find the term "task" less confusing. The word "process" is most often used to describe programs in execution, a somewhat more restricted context than that suggested above for tasks.

P. J. DENNING AND D. E. DENNING

## TELEPROCESSING SYSTEMS

For articles on related subjects *see* COMMUNICATION CONTROL UNITS; COMMUNICATIONS AND COMPUTERS; COMPUTER NETWORKS; DATA COMMUNICATIONS; PROCESSING MODES; REAL TIME APPLICATIONS; and TIME SHARING.

# TELEPROCESSING SYSTEMS

For articles on related terms *see* ACCESS METHODS; and DATA ACQUISITION COMPUTER.

Remote-terminal processing systems, often called "teleprocessing systems" (a term originally introduced by IBM), refer to a form of information processing in which remote terminals access a computer via some type of communication line. In recent years, the number of such systems has grown very rapidly, and all indications are that this growth will be sustained, for reasons of economics and convenience. These systems can provide various data processing services to many locations simultaneously without the necessity of having a computer at each such location. The six basic types are described in this article.

**Inquiry and Response Systems.** In these systems the computer is used as a mass storage facility which can be accessed by a large number of terminal users via a communication network. The best examples are the various airline or hotel reservation systems, automatic document retrieval, and inventory control systems. The user enters a query at a terminal, causing the computer to search its files and send back the information. The files may be updated automatically or by the user.

Fig. 1 shows, in simplified form, the structure and extent of the SABRE II reservation system for American Airlines. In this system, about 1,900 terminals in various locations of the country are supported by two IBM 360/65 computers, one of which is a backup system. Approximately one million messages are handled daily. The average length of an inquiry message is 15 characters, and the response averages 60 characters.

**Data Collection Systems.** In data collection systems, also called "data acquisition systems,"

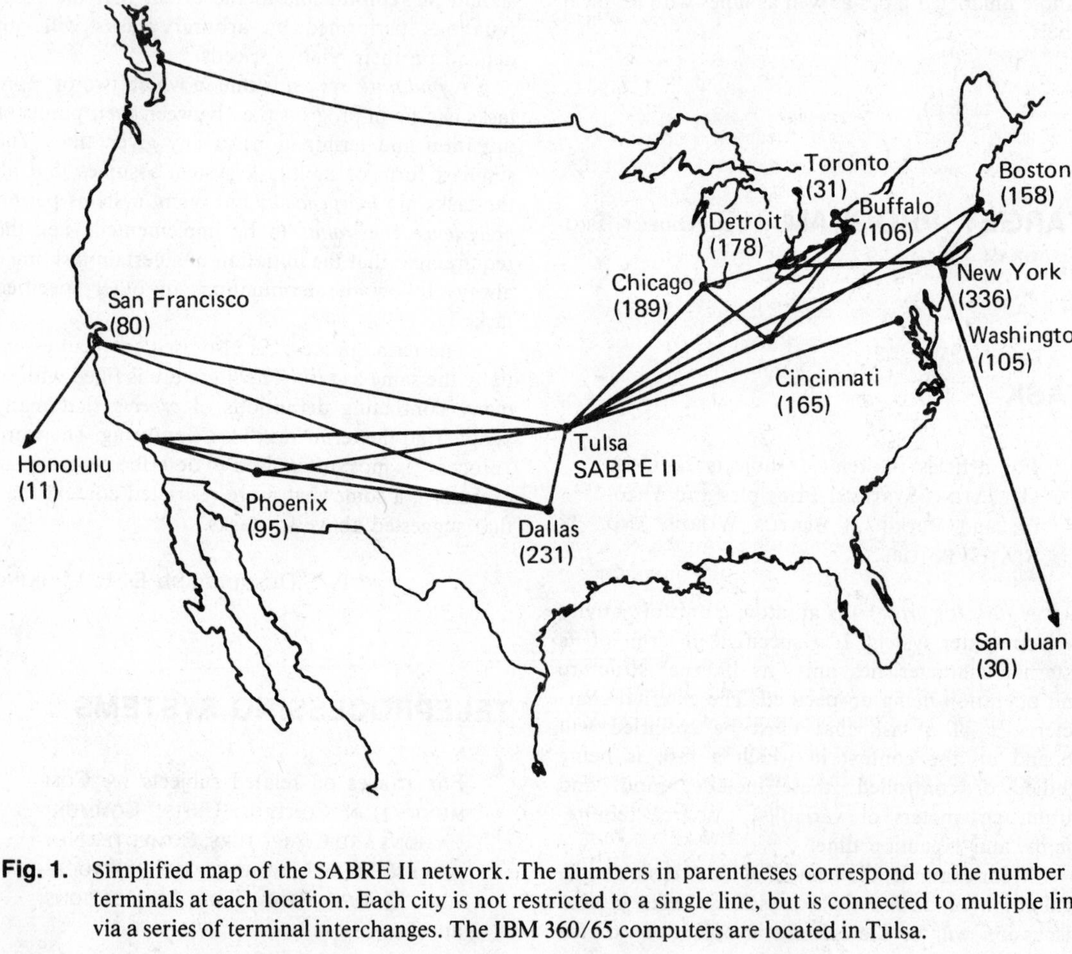


**Fig. 1.** Simplified map of the SABRE II network. The numbers in parentheses correspond to the number of terminals at each location. Each city is not restricted to a single line, but is connected to multiple lines via a series of terminal interchanges. The IBM 360/65 computers are located in Tulsa.

information from various terminals is entered and stored in the central computer. This data may be processed immediately (on-line real-time systems) or at some subsequent time, or it may be just used to update records that may be used for inquiry and response systems or accounting purposes. Examples of such systems are the automatic recording of transactions on the stock exchange or at banks, keeping track of the status of factory output at various stages, and weather recording.

**Data Distribution Systems.** A data distribution system is the converse of a data collection system in the sense that the basic flow of data is in the opposite direction, i.e., from computer to terminal. Dissemination of information such as stock quotations or timetables to a select group of customers are examples of such systems. The transmission of data may be continuous, in batches, or on demand, depending upon the specific application.

**Conversational Systems.** These systems are designed to permit concurrent dialogs between the central computer and many local or remote users. In this mode of operation, each statement or command entered by a user is executed immediately, and a reply is sent back before the next statement or command may be entered. These are usually called "time-sharing" systems, and may be special-purpose (closed) or general-purpose (open) systems. The former allows users to prepare and execute programs in a very limited number of languages. The latter allow access to a large variety of compilers, editing and debugging aids, and special application libraries, and usually include the ability to add additional facilities. The M.I.T. Multics systems is an example of a general-purpose system. In both general and special-purpose designs, however, the emphasis is on rapid response to many users. The potential uses of these systems appear to be almost unlimited.

Included in this category are the interactive graphics systems. Here, computer information is displayed on a cathode-ray tube in response to commands from a keyboard or lightpen. Such systems are widely used in computer-aided design of airplane wings, car bodies, integrated circuit masks and circuit layouts, and other applications.

Another example is computer-aided instruction systems where students at terminals study computer-assigned material, perform assignments, and answer questions. Answers are examined and used to guide future computer-student dialog, depending upon progress made.

**Remote Batch-Processing Systems.** In a remote batch-processing system, the computer waits for a job from a remote terminal. It then places the job in the batch queue along with other jobs currently in the system. After execution, the output is transmitted to the originating terminal. This may take a fraction of a second or several minutes. This is different from a conversational system because an almost immediate response is essential in the latter.

These systems are used widely where the central or host computer has several remote batch stations, which may consist of line printer, card reader, and card punch. The remote terminals may also be other computers.

**Message Switching Systems.** Message switching systems are special cases of data collection and data distribution systems, where very little or no processing is done on the data. The computer merely acts as a switching center, collecting data from, and distributing data to, various terminals. In these systems, it is possible for several terminals to send messages simultaneously to the same destination. Some of these messages must therefore be temporarily stored until the terminal is free to accept them. For this reason, such systems are often called "store and forward" systems.

**Other Types of Teleprocessing Systems.** The categories discussed above serve only to summarize the general characteristics of teleprocessing systems. In many cases the distinction between them is fuzzy. Combinations and variations are possible. Thus, monitoring systems are similar to data collection systems, but the input is usually from some source other than a computer terminal (e.g., a transducer monitoring heartbeat).

Process control systems may be thought of as closed-loop monitoring systems that regulate an ongoing process. Some types of remote batch processing systems support host-to-host computer communication for backup or load sharing. In the former, reliability of the overall network is increased, whereas in the latter the turnaround time on an overloaded computer is decreased by sending jobs to a lightly loaded computer. Type setting or document-production systems can be thought of as a type of data distribution system.

**Hardware and Software Requirements.** The systems described are types of multiprogrammed, time-shared, or real-time systems. They may run from small special-purpose systems servicing several terminals all the way to very large general-purpose systems servicing several hundred or thousand local or remote terminals. The general-purpose systems usually provide simultaneous conversational and remote batch processing as well as the capability to run some of the more specialized systems described in the preceding section.

The desirable hardware features include a computer with independent data channels and flexible interrupt structure, memory protection, relocation hardware, and mass storage. Communication controllers, terminals, and the communication network also must be compatible with the type of application the system must support.

The software includes an executive, a file-management system, a terminal access method, a command processor, and application software packages. The *executive* provides system protection, processor and core allocation, schedules the running of user programs, and handles all interrupts. The *file-management* system provides access and allocation of direct-access storage devices. It also allows users to share, create, change, and delete files. The *access method* handles communication between computer and terminals. The *command processor* provides the interface between the user and the system. It allows him to log in and out, manipulate files, and gain access to application software such as compilers, debugging aids, and other system functions.

**Conclusion.** A combination of appropriate computer hardware and software together with a suitable data communication network can service a large number of remote terminals. Conversely, a terminal user may access a number of computers for special purposes. The uses of these teleprocessing systems are almost unlimited and are growing rapidly. A more thorough review of the hardware and software aspects of such systems may be gained from other articles in this Encyclopedia. Many of the articles on applications of computers relate to uses of teleprocessing systems.

References

1968. Heau, E., and D. McNelis. *Principles of Data Communications for Professional Programmers and System Analysts*. Computer Methods Corporation, pp. 114–132.

1970. Watson, R. W. *Timesharing System Design Concepts*. New York: McGraw-Hill.

1971. Oliver, P. "Design Specifications for a Generalized Teleprocessing System," *IAG Journal*, Vol. 4, No. 4, pp. 350–359.

J. S. Sobolewski

# TERMINALS

For articles on related subjects *see* Audio Response Terminal; Computer Graphics; Data Communications; Input-Output Devices; Intelligent Terminal; Multiplexing; Point-of-Sale Terminal; Processing Modes; Text Editing Systems; and Time Sharing.

For articles on related terms *see* ASCII; EBCDIC; Error Correcting Code; Job; Multiprogramming; Parity; and Record.

A computer terminal is a device that allows users of a data processing system (DPS) to gain access to (i.e., to input programs and data to, and to obtain output from) that system in a more convenient manner than through the input/output (I/O) devices local to that system (e.g., local card readers, card punches, and line printers). Often, computer terminals are located away from the DPS, at locations convenient to the users of that system. Computer terminals fall into two main categories: batch and interactive.

**Batch Terminals.** The primary purpose of a batch terminal is to allow users to access a DPS just as they would via that system's local I/O devices, but to do so from locations remote from that system. Therefore, a batch terminal contains I/O devices that are similar to the devices attached directly to the DPS. The simplest batch terminals usually have a printer and a card reader; more complex terminals may have, in addition, a card punch, one or more magnetic tape drives, one or more disk drives, as well as other I/O devices. In fact, often a small, general-purpose DPS (or even a medium-sized one) is used as a batch terminal to a larger DPS.

Batch terminals are connected to a DPS via communications links. These links operate at speeds that typically range from 120 characters per second to about 6,000 characters per second, although higher speeds are used in some instances. These links may be *dedicated* (i.e., they connect a batch terminal to a DPS in a permanent fashion), or *dial-up* (just like a dial telephone). Dial-up links allow a batch terminal to access a number of DPSs and do not require that a DPS *port* (the DPSs end of a link) be tied up by a particular batch terminal when that terminal is not in use. Typically, dial-up links are not used for high link speeds, primarily because high-speed dial-up links tend to be more error prone, and are not as yet generally available. Links can also be multiplexed; this means that several terminals can simultaneously use a single link, each terminal transmitting and receiving at a speed that is a fraction of the total speed of which the link is capable.

Information is usually transmitted to and from a batch terminal (most often, but not always, in one direction at a time) via a *carrier signal*, which is modulated (i.e., changed in amplitude or frequency) to represent 0 and 1 bits. (This modulation and the corresponding demodulation at the other end of the link are performed by a device known as a modulator-demodulator, or *modem* for short.) Groups of these bits represent text characters (letters, digits, etc.) or control characters. Each such character is represented by a group of from 6 to 11 bits.

The terminal is equipped with a control unit, which decodes the signal from, and encodes signals to the communications link, and controls the operation of the various I/O devices of the terminal. The control unit usually also has provision for checking the validity of the information it receives from the DPS; this checking is done using parity bits on each character, special check characters at the end of each message, and other error-detecting and error-correcting schemes. If the control unit detects a transmission error (i.e., an error usually due to the communications link), it requests the DPS to retransmit the record (i.e., the message) in error. Conversely, it also can retransmit a record, should the DPS request it to do so. The control unit, which is often physically built into one of the I/O devices, also provides the required switches, pushbuttons, and indicators for the operator of the terminal. Fig. 1 is a simplified diagram of the connection between a batch terminal and a DPS.

In actual operation, once the connection between the terminal and the DPS has been established, the operator of the terminal indicates via the control unit whether he or she wishes to transmit programs and data to the DPS, or whether the DPS should send to the terminal any output it has for that terminal. Every time a record is sent to or from the terminal, the receiver of the record (the DPS or the terminal) acknowledges the receipt of that record (or, in the case of an error, requests retransmission); then the next record in sequence is sent. The simpler batch terminals are normally capable of either transmitting or receiving, but cannot perform both functions at the same time (i.e., they cannot operate in the full-duplex mode). Some terminals (which in fact are computers in their own right) can transmit, receive, and perform local data processing, all at the same time. Fig. 2 shows a typical batch terminal.

**Interactive Terminals.** The primary purpose of an interactive (or time-sharing) terminal is to allow the user of a DPS to use that system in a mode (often called "interactive" or "conversational") that is characterized by relatively fast response time to each individual user request—thus the term "interactive."

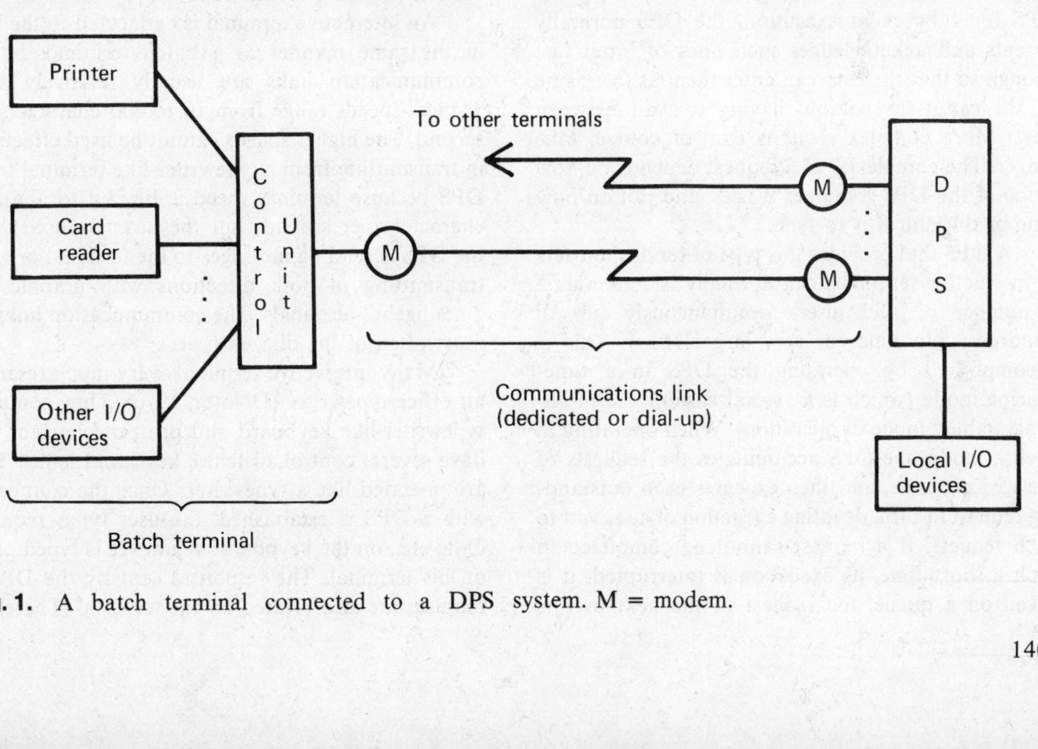


**Fig. 1.** A batch terminal connected to a DPS system. M = modem.

**Fig. 2.** The IBM 2780, a common batch terminal.

In contrast to a batch terminal, the user of an interactive terminal does not submit an entire task (or job) at one time to the DPS, but rather enters requests (program statements or data) one line at a time. The DPS accepts each line and, if it is a request (usually called a "command"), executes it. The time between successive requests is usually measured in seconds or fractions of seconds, and when entering program statements that are to be collected by the DPS for subsequent execution, the DPS normally accepts and acknowledges such lines of input fast enough so that the user can enter them as fast as he or she can type, without having to wait between lines. More complex requests can, of course, take longer. The complexity of a request depends on how much of the DPS resources it uses, and not on how long or difficult it is to type.

A DPS that provides this type of service to users of interactive terminals can normally accommodate a number of such users simultaneously (up to hundreds at a time for very large DPSs). This is accomplished by operating the DPS in a time-sharing mode (which is a special case of the multi-programmed mode of operation). When operating in such a mode, the DPS accumulates the requests of the various users, and then executes each outstanding request in turn, devoting a fraction of a second to each request. If a request cannot be completed in such a short time, its execution is interrupted, it is saved on a queue, the request of the next user is executed, and so on. Because a DPS is a very fast device when compared to the terminal speed with which a user can enter requests and data, each user will normally get the impression that the DPS is devoting all its resources to those current requests, unless, of course, the requests are very complex. As a result, each user can usually work as fast as he can, and generally is unaware of the presence of other concurrent users of the DPS.

An interactive terminal is connected to the DPS in the same manner as a batch terminal, but its communication links are usually relatively slow. Typical speeds range from 10 to 600 characters per second. The higher speeds cannot be used effectively in transmitting from a typewriter-like terminal to the DPS because terminal speed is limited to about 10 characters per second, but they can be used when the DPS is sending messages to the terminal or when transmitting in both directions with graphic and "intelligent" terminals. The communication links are most often of the dial-up type.

Many interactive terminals very much resemble an office typewriter (Dolotta, 1970). They contain a typewriter-like keyboard and print mechanism, and have several control switches, keys, and lights. They are operated like a typewriter: Once the connection with a DPS is established, the user types requests, data, etc., on the keyboard. Whatever is typed prints on his terminal. The responses sent by the DPS to the user are also printed on the terminal. Therefore, what eventually appears on the paper in front of the user is a series of lines of text in the form of a "conversation," some lines having been typed by the user and some by DPS.

Interactive terminals first appeared in the early 1960s. These early terminals are simple adaptations of Teletypewriters, and were used to communicate with a DPS rather than with each other. Fig. 3 shows such a terminal. They were typically quite slow (10 characters per second), had a limited character set (on the order of 50 characters, with 26 upper-case letters, 10 digits, and some punctuation characters), and produced printing of the type seen on telegrams and stock quotation "tickers."

**Fig. 3.** A Model 33 KSR Teletype® with paper tape attachment, a commonly used terminal in early and more current time-sharing systems.

As the popularity of interactive data processing grew, a large variety of terminals specifically designed to be so used appeared on the market. As a result, interactive terminals have become faster, easier to operate, and lighter (and thus somewhat more portable). They are now capable of printing and transmitting larger numbers of distinct characters (typically, on the order of 90 characters, with 52 upper- and lower-case letters, 10 digits, and a number of punctuation and special characters, such as brackets, braces, and arithmetic symbols). Some terminals have interchangeable print elements, which increases the number of available characters considerably.

Many of these newer terminals have additional features not normally found on typewriters or on older terminals, but which are very useful for interacting with a DPS (Dolotta, 1970; Ossanna and Saltzer, 1970). Some of these features are as follows:

1. Print suppression, which allows the DPS to turn off the printing mechanism of the terminal at certain times; e.g., when the user has to type the secret password that authorizes access to the DPS.
2. Forward and backward line and half-line paper feed, which is useful for printing subscripts, superscripts, etc.
3. Tab stops, which can be cleared and set by both the user and the DPS, thus allowing automatic formatting by the DPS of the text to be printed on the terminal.
4. Both forward and reverse vertical tabs.
5. Form feed, which allows the DPS to space the paper to the top of the next page.
6. Plotting capability, which allows the DPS to move the print element and the paper (left and right, forward and backward) in increments as small as a hundredth of an inch. Fig. 4 shows one such terminal.

Also currently on the market are interactive terminals, which display text on a television-like screen rather than print it on paper (hard-copy). Such character display (or soft copy) terminals are capable of higher speeds than printing terminals, and allow the user to enter or receive more than one line of text at a time. On some interactive terminals, the user can alter and correct the text after he has entered it, prior to transmitting it to the DPS. This is possible because such terminals usually have a local memory (buffer) that holds whatever text is displayed on the screen (some hard-copy terminals also have such buffers, but usually they can only store one or two lines of text). Display terminals (Fig. 5) normally do not produce a printed record of the interaction between the user and the DPS.

Some display terminals (graphic terminals) also display characters on their screen or draw arbitrary curves. They are more complex (and more expensive) than simple character display terminals. Fig. 6 shows a graphic terminal.

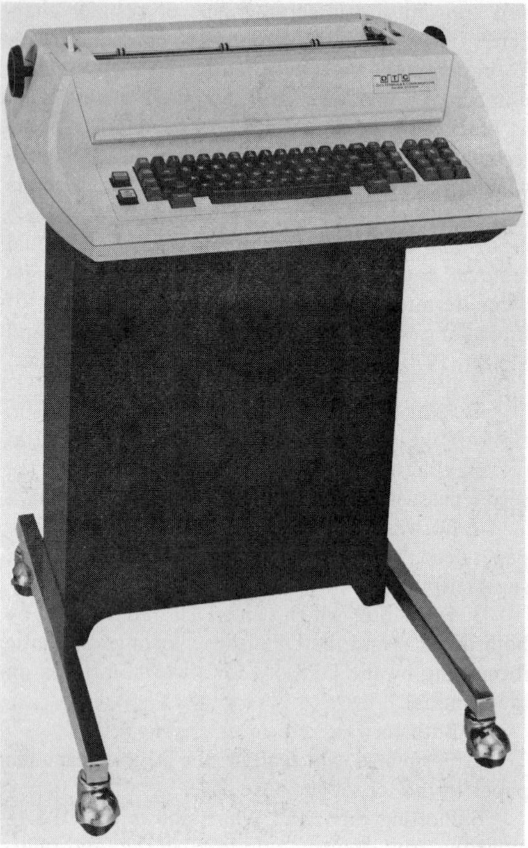

**Fig. 4.** The DTC-300, a contemporary time-sharing terminal.

**Fig. 5.** The Hazeltine 2,000-character display terminal.

**Fig. 6.** The Tektronix 4015 graphic terminal (left) and associated 4610 hard-copy unit (right).

Several of the more sophisticated display and graphic terminals allow the user to enter some of the input with a penlike device that "writes" directly on the terminal screen or on a special "tablet."

Many interactive terminals allow the attachment of paper tape readers and punches, or magnetic cassette recorders, etc. These devices often permit the user to edit and record the input onto tape in a local mode (i.e., without having to connect the terminal to the DPS); and this input is transmitted at a later time to the DPS at a higher speed. Similarly, output from the DPS can be recorded onto a tape, and then examined locally by the user at his or her leisure. The terminal shown in Fig. 8 has this capability; the tape cassette drives can be seen in the upper panel of the illustration.

**Special-Purpose Terminals.** In certain cases, one or more DPS and all the interactive terminals connected to them are devoted to a single task; e.g., airline or hotel reservations, banking operations, supermarket check-out operations [so-called point of sale (PoS) applications], and manufacturing assembly-line reporting. In these instances, the terminals are specifically tailored to allow their operators to perform their tasks as efficiently and conveniently as possible. PoS terminals are usually connected to the DPS via dedicated (and often multiplexed) communications links; they are highly

**Fig. 7.** The NCR 270 financial terminal.

specialized and may contain no general-purpose keyboard or printer, but instead may be equipped with special indicators and other devices (e.g., magnetic badge readers, credit card readers, optical scanners). In some cases, they provide their output in the form of voice response via a telephone (e.g., in giving a bank clerk the current balance in a customer's account). In some cases, a DPS accepts input from regular pushbutton telephones; it is expected that this use of telephones will grow significantly with time. Fig. 7 shows a terminal used by bank tellers.

**Additional Applications.** Terminals can be designed to communicate with a DPS in a variety of ways; e.g., by dial-up or dedicated communications links, and by attachment of several terminals to a single communications link in a multidrop (i.e., like a party-line telephone) fashion rather than point to point. Terminals are generally designed to use one of several methods of encoding characters into sequences of 1 and 0 bits. The most common encoding schemes used in the United States are the American Standard Code for Information Exchange (ASCII) and the Extended Binary-Coded-Decimal Interchange Code (EBCDIC), but other codes are also used, especially with older terminals. Terminals may also use either synchronous or start/stop line disciplines. The former requires that characters be sent on the link at predetermined times that are synchronized between the two ends of the line. The latter, which allows characters to be sent at any time, uses the link less efficiently, and is seldom used at speeds of over 200 characters per second.

There is a current trend to provide more and more data processing capability ("logic," or "intelligence") in terminals, both batch and interactive. This allows terminals to do local editing, text compression, etc., and results in more efficient utilization of communication links and faster response to user requests. The development of more and more "intelligent" terminals is likely to continue for some time to come (Hobbs, 1971). Fig. 8 shows one such terminal.

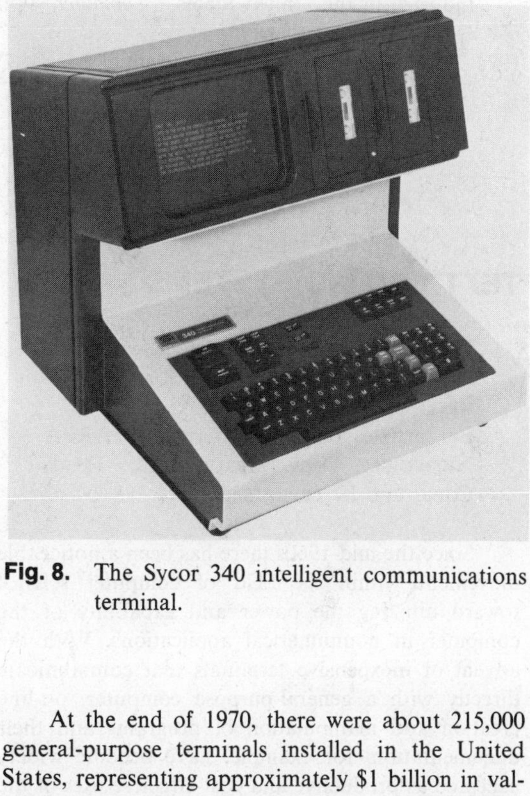

**Fig. 8.** The Sycor 340 intelligent communications terminal.

At the end of 1970, there were about 215,000 general-purpose terminals installed in the United States, representing approximately $1 billion in value. At the end of 1972, there were about 336,000 general-purpose and 139,000 special-purpose terminals. During the year 1972, there were added 91,000 new general-purpose terminals with a market value of $430 million. It is predicted that 800,000 general-purpose terminals will have been installed in the United States by the end of 1975, and that there will be 1.2 million general-purpose and 600,000 special-purpose terminals by 1977, a total of 1.8 million terminals (Salzman, 1971; *Computer Decisions*, 1974). This represents a compound growth of approximately 30% per year.

REFERENCES

1970. Dolotta, T. A. "Functional Specifications for Typewriter-like Time-Sharing Terminals," *Computing Surveys*, Vol. 2, No. 1, pp. 5–31.

1970. Saltzer, J. H., and J. F. Ossanna. "Technical and Human Engineering Problems in Connecting Terminals to a Time-Sharing System," *American Federation of Information Processing Societies (AFIPS) Conference Proceedings*, Vol. 37, pp. 355–362.

1971. Hobbs, L. C. "The Rationale for Smart Terminals," *Computer*, Vol. 4, No. 6, pp. 33–35.

1971. Salzman, R. M. "An Outlook for the Terminal Industry in the United States," *Computer*, Vol. 4, No. 6, pp. 18–25.

1974. *Anon.* "The Shape of the Terminal Market," *Computer Decisions* (September), p. 42.

T. A. DOLOTTA

# TEXT EDITING SYSTEMS

For articles on related subjects *see* COMMAND AND JOB CONTROL LANGUAGES; TERMINALS; and TIME SHARING.
For articles on related terms *see* ARPA NETWORK; DATA STRUCTURES; HARD COPY; and INTERPRETER.

Since the mid-1960s there has been a noticeable movement within the field of computer science toward utilizing the power and capability of the computer in nonnumerical applications. With the advent of inexpensive terminals that communicate directly with a general-purpose computer, on-line creation and manipulation of programs and their documentation, for example, have become widely accepted as productive and cost-effective uses of the computer. Indeed, it has been realized that the facilities provided by the central editing program of a time-sharing system, and its command language, are among the most important determinants of the system's convenience, power, and consequent utility. In addition, special-purpose, computer-assisted text-editing packages have become accepted in industry and government for producing technical manuals, proposals, and other documents that require many updates in a limited period of time.

The purpose of this article is to survey, from the user's point of view, various methods and issues for the on-line creation and editing of computer programs and ordinary text. For additional descriptions of currently available systems see van Dam and Rice (1971); for implementation details, see Rice and van Dam (1971).

The generic design goals of on-line text-editing programs, from the user's point of view, are:

1. Fast response to a large number of terminals (which ideally are designed with good "human factors" for the editing task).
2. A concise, mnemonic command language with informative feedback.
3. Powerful commands, with few restrictions and exceptions, to make possible everything that one can do to hard copy with pencil, scissors, and staples, or anything that one can do to program card decks.
4. Commands that take advantage of computer capabilities, e.g., moving to the first occurrence of a user-specified pattern in the file (also known as pattern, content, or context scanning); "uniform" substitution of one pattern for another every place it occurs, or only in the first instance, or only if the pattern occurs in a certain column-dependent field; automatic renumbering of sections or references after the file is altered; and flexible hard-copy output.

All these goals are to be met using as little as possible of such resources as money, implementation time, CPU cycles, core and disk space. Furthermore, the goals are both interdependent and conflicting, since (for example) increased power in the command repertoire implies greater demand on resources and therefore slower response time (or support of fewer terminals).

In the next section, some characteristics of different types of editors are reviewed. Subsequent sections give several examples of program editors, describe several free-form text editors, and conclude with a brief look at editing terminal hardware.

## General Distinguishing Characteristics

TYPICAL STRUCTURE OF A TEXT EDITOR. The functional block diagram in Fig. 1 is representative of most text-editing systems (*editors* for short), though the overall system in a particular case need not be segmented into the exact set of subprograms shown. (A typical system is shown in Fig. 2.) The user is seated at a typewriter terminal or a cathode-ray tube display console (CRT) on which one or more lines of characters of his file are visible. The terminal

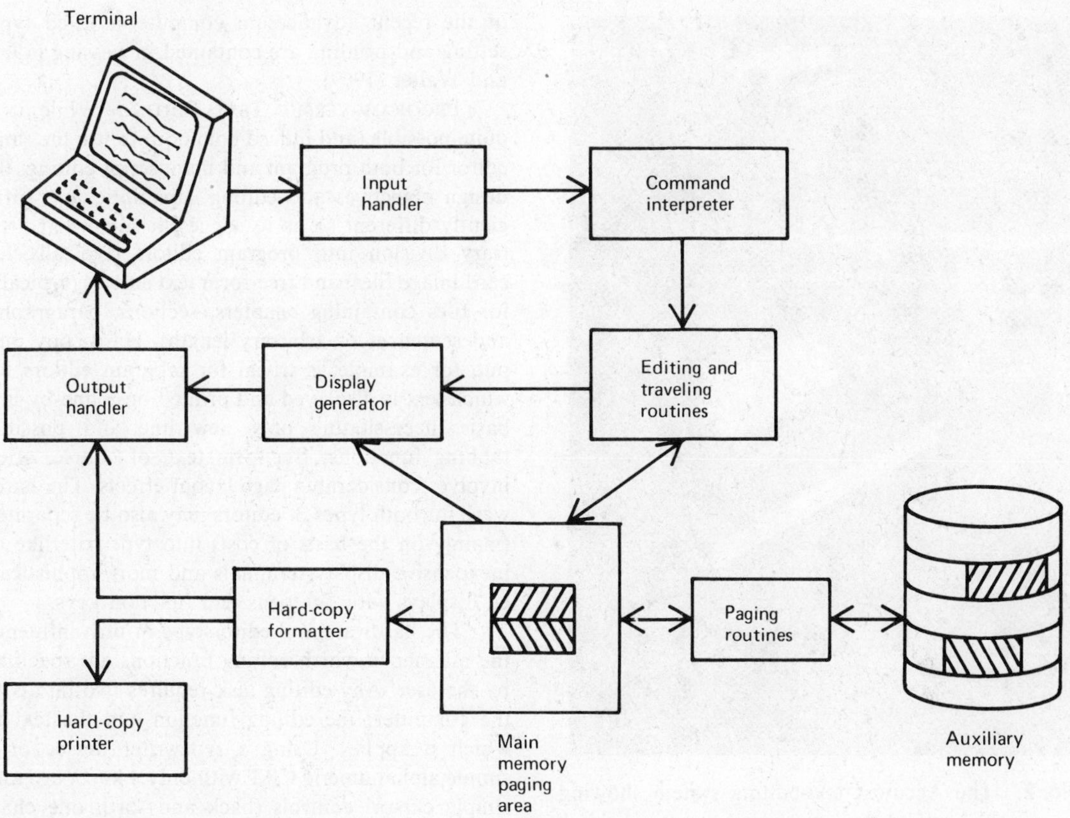


**Fig. 1.** Overview of an on-line editor.

in effect provides the user with a "window" with which he may view a certain part of his file. The user's commands to alter the displayed text are entered via the typewriter keyboard (or function keys, lightpen, or other input device). The physical/logical attention (interrupt) generated when he transmits a command is fielded by the input handler to a command interpreter. This interpreter parses the requested command, typically into an editing operation (insert, delete, substitute, rearrange, etc.) and associated data. The latter consists primarily of positioning information (e.g., at what point in the text an insertion is to be made, or between what two points in the text a deletion is to be made) and literal character string data (e.g., the text to be inserted). In addition to editing, the user may move ("travel") through the text, either to read or to make changes in a different section. The command in this case might be to advance the display window in the file, and the associated data field would indicate the number of display lines to be advanced (scrolled) and the direction (forward or backward).

The parsed (internal) form of the request is passed to whichever editing or traveling routine performs the actual operation. In the case of an editing command, the internal form of the text (the data structure) is altered and the updated text is redisplayed by the display generator for feedback to the user. When the files are large, and traveling or large edits are invoked, the relevant portion of the storage structure may not be resident in core, in which case the paging routines must be called upon to replace some inactive data in core with the data requested from secondary storage.

In the general case, the system supports multiple terminals, and a time-sharing monitor/file-handler is superimposed on the block diagram. It has basic responsibility for supervising the sharing of programs and core among users while guaranteeing the integrity of their files. It may also provide other services, such as user-to-user messaging or even file sharing for cooperative efforts.

The hard-copy formatter (which may in fact be largely merged with the display generator) is used in

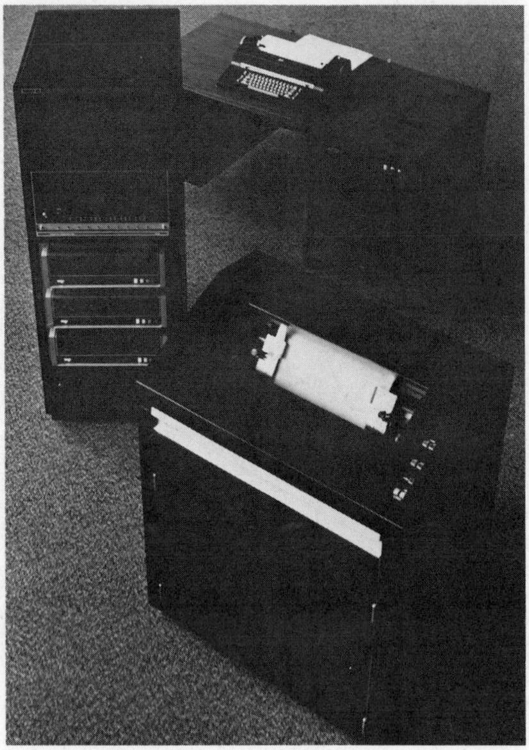

**Fig. 2.** The Accutext text-editing system showing the processor, typewriter terminal, and printer.

the case of free-form text (as opposed to program text) as a post-processor to convert the storage structure of the file to conventional hard copy for output on typewriter terminals, high-speed line printers, or even photocomposition devices. In his text, the user may specify "format codes" (typesetting codes) that determine margins, headings, running heads, paragraphs, left and/or right margin justification, indents, centering, underscores, typeface changes, and other "page layout" effects. Sample codes might be "-s1-" for skip one line, "-p-" for paragraph, or "-t10-" for tab to tenth column position, etc. These codes are frequently stored in line with the text itself and may be treated as indistinguishable from text for editing purposes. When the formatter (also called "printout" or "runoff program") finds a code, it calculates character and line spacings to produce the requested effects, often using justification (right-margin alignment) and hyphenation. Sophisticated formatters may produce other by-products useful for hard copy: footnotes, tables of contents, lists of figures, indexes, spelling checks, etc. Very readable accounts of the recent advances in computer-assisted typesetting and printing are contained in Lessing (1969) and Walter (1969).

PROGRAM VERSUS TEXT EDITING. While it is quite possible (and indeed common) to use the same editor for both program and manuscript editing, the design objectives and editing capabilities are sufficiently different so as to suggest a somewhat arbitrary division into program editors (typically for card image files) and free-form text editors (typically for files containing chapters, sections, paragraphs, and sentences of arbitrary length). Hard-copy output, for example, is trivial for program editors for which text is displayed and printed on a line-by-line basis, necessitating only new line and possibly tabbing functions; free-form text, of course, often involves considerable page layout effects. The hardware for both types of editors may also be separated (mainly on the basis of cost) into typewriterlike or inexpensive display terminals and more sophisticated displays with lightpens and function keys.

The hardware and editor type in turn influence the manner in which editing functions are specified by the user. Any editing task requires two inputs to the computer: the editing function and the text to which it applies. Using a typewriter device or a simple alphanumeric CRT with only a keyboard and simple cursor[1] controls (back and forth one character at a time) requires identification of the text to be acted upon by line numbers and/or specification of the literal character strings involved (context specification). Context specification requires a bit of extra work for the user, since he must type enough characters to identify the location uniquely; otherwise, unintentional ambiguities might be introduced.

On a more general-purpose CRT display, time may be saved by pointing to the exact location with either a lightpen or a data-tablet stylus, or by indirect indication with a cursor driven by keys, a "joystick," or other $X$-$Y$ indicators; identification is accurate and immediate. Other advantages of a CRT are that the user has instantaneous response (unless the CRT is a typewriter replacement connected by voice-grade line to the computer), has a larger viewing area, and is not impacted by the noise of a typewriter. On-line composition is a pleasant contrast to having to mark up hard copy, which is then transcribed by a secretary, essentially requiring that the work be done twice.

[1] A *cursor* is a special symbol, such as a caret or underscore, that points to a character position on the screen, either to identify or to allow specification or replacement of the character at that location.

Program and text editors also differ in terms of the functions they require and the corresponding data structures that facilitate these functions. When editing a program, one typically modifies it "in place," substituting for one small string of text —such as an operation code or an operand address —or inserting a label in a field. In this case it is reasonable to store the text by line in card image or printer line image format. Editing manuscript text, however, typically involves not just typographical error correction, but also insertions and substitution of arbitrarily sized character strings at arbitrary points. With this increased lack of uniformity, the data structure should be more flexible to cope with the unrestricted editing (e.g., allowing text to overflow or contract automatically from line to line within a paragraph). Thus, the unit of storage within which text varies may be several hundred characters, a paragraph, or even an entire section. The data-structure/file-structure issue is discussed in more detail in the next section.

Finally, both program and text editor files may be viewed as more than a collection of lines or literal character strings. For example, the block structure of a procedural-language program or the outline hierarchy of a section-numbered text could be represented by suitable formatting on a display screen. This type of structure must, of course, be specified by indentations or "special codes" by the user as he inputs the text so it may be encoded in the data structure of the file.

EXAMPLES OF FILE STRUCTURES AND CORRESPONDING OPERATIONS. The most definitive distinction between editors is in the type of file segmentation employed (the basic unit of text division). The simplest type is a (fixed length) *line editor*, which stores a file of discrete lines of text to be printed out on the console (or displayed) and manipulated on a line-by-line basis. The editing operations are limited and are specified for lines identified by a specific number. For example, representative editing commands for this type of editor are:

| | |
|---|---|
| e37;42 | erase lines 37–42 |
| 37;abcd;wxyz | substitute wxyz for abcd in line 37 |
| 37;abcd;abcdwxyz | insert wxyz after abcd in line 37 (note the need to duplicate the leading context) |
| m76;37;45 | move lines 37–45 after line 76 |

The commands in this example consist of single character command names (*e* for erase, *m* for move, and no character for the default case of substitute), followed by line number(s) and relevant text strings. Delimiters (the ";" in this case) separate the individual parameters. Since the number of characters allowed per line is limited (usually 80 or 132), any editing done in a line must not result in a greater line length. If the bound is exceeded—e.g., if 12 characters are inserted in a line already containing 122 characters—the remaining characters in the line (those beyond 132), will be lost, although with some editors the user will be informed that this has occurred. This truncation of a line poses no problem for program editing where the file typically consists of card images, one per line, but it is a real nuisance to the user who wants to make arbitrary size inserts within a line.

Also, in most line editors the numbering of these "relative" line numbers is sequential from the top of the file, so that internal renumbering occurs when lines are inserted, deleted, or moved. This is a major hindrance to ease of editing, as the user must either keep track of the changes himself, get an up-to-date printout after every few changes, or edit strictly in one direction from the bottom of the file up. This last technique only allows editing by transcription from hard copy and clearly prevents on-line creation. To obviate this drawback, some line editors have absolute line numbers that serve as fixed points of reference (integer or decimal names for lines, effectively) and do not change as editing is done. This feature, although producing nonsequentially (and therefore nonmnemonically) numbered files, does facilitate editing.

A more sophisticated type of line editor is the *context-driven line editor*. With this system the user need not know and keep track of line numbers, since he can have the computer search for a pattern rather than referencing its line number. The user thus specifies text by line content. Typical commands include:

| | |
|---|---|
| l/pattern/ | locate first line in which pattern occurs |
| c/old/new/ | change the first occurrence of old to new (in less than 132 characters) |
| c/old/new/** | change old to new wherever it occurs |
| d5 | delete 5 lines, beginning with the current one |

The delimiter (/) may be any character not occurring in the pattern.

While editing in context-driven line editors is still restricted to a group of lines or a single string within a line, it is more natural and convenient to specify context than a line number, which may be constantly changing. However, the problem of line truncation still exists in currently available context editors, as does the problem of context strings that are split between two successive lines and cannot, therefore, be located or edited without being split. (These are implementation restrictions, not inherent ones, and are due to the preoccupation of designers with programming rather than text editing.)

The next distinguishing file segmentation is found in the (context driven) *statement editor*. Here the text is divided into "superlines"; a maximum of text in a line greater than 132 characters is allowed, which results in easier editing. Designed with both program and text editing in mind, current statement editors offer the user freedom from truncation problems, and often additional features such as the ability to group statements for purposes of naming, viewing, editing, showing outline hierarchies, etc. These features may not be necessary or even useful in program editors.

Taking the statement editor one step further to allow arbitrary length superlines that expand and contract (flow) as necessary, we come to the final type of segmentation: the *stream*, or *string, editor*. This type of editor, typically context-driven, is inherently the most powerful and is especially designed for free-form text editing, preferably on display consoles.

**Program Editors.** Computer program editors have become increasingly popular in time-sharing environments, where a facility for the on-line modification of programs combined with some form of remote job entry (execution) greatly increase a programmer's productivity. Immediate verification of correct syntax of the program is occasionally provided.

The most common method for editing a program in a non–time-sharing environment is still to insert and delete cards from a punched card source deck, which then has to be read back into the computer through the card reader. The dropping or loss of decks evokes bitter memories for all programmers. Also, backspacing over typographical errors with a keypunch is not recommended! An on-line editing system that stores the programs on disk or tape eliminates the need for hand-carrying card decks to and from the machine, and enables updates to be made quickly and efficiently. When used in conjunction with a time-sharing system under which the source program can be readily compiled, the time required to write and debug a program is greatly reduced.

THE CMS EDITOR. As an example of how a line-oriented program editor might be used, assume that the following section of a program, which computes the sum of two matrices, is to be modified to compute the difference of the two matrices:

```
ADD: FOR ROW = 1 TO N DO;
        FOR COLUMN = 1 TO M DO;
            C(ROW,COLUMN) = A(ROW,COLUMN)
                          + B(ROW,COLUMN);
        END;
     END;
```

The following sequence of interactions with the editor would provide the necessary changes (the user's requests are in lower case and the machine's responses are in capitals):

```
find add:
ADD: FOR ROW = 1 TO N DO;
change /add/subtract/
SUBTRACT: FOR ROW = 1 TO N DO;
next 2
    C(ROW,COLUMN) = A(ROW,COLUMN)
                  + B(ROW,COLUMN);
change /+/-/
    C(ROW,COLUMN) = A(ROW,COLUMN)
                  - B(ROW,COLUMN);
top
change /add/subtract/ * *
```

The routine ADD: is first located by using the column-dependent "find" command, which searches for the string ADD: beginning in the first position of a line; then, the label ADD is changed to SUBTRACT. Then, the line pointer is moved ahead two lines by the command "next 2" to locate the next line to be changed; the addition (+) is changed to subtraction (−). The remaining two commands search the entire program (starting at the "top") to replace all occurrences of ADD with SUBTRACT so that any references to the ADD routine now refer to SUBTRACT.

The typical program editor also provides flexible tabbing facilities that require less typing for the user when column-dependent languages such as Fortran are being used. A tabbing facility also makes the programmer more likely to indicate block structures and nesting levels by suitable indentations, a useful documentation technique. Default (internal) tab settings appropriate to the specific language are automatically applied to the file.

Quick Editor (QED). Although a program editor, QED utilizes variable-length lines. Designed by the University of California, Berkeley, and used commercially by Com-Share, a time-sharing service bureau, QED provides maximum convenience for the user via a simple and mnemonic command language and line-independent access to the text.

QED is internally superline oriented: Text is not stored as a fixed-length record or a variable-length record with an associated length. Instead, the end of the line is delimited by an internal marker. QED can search for labels or an arbitrary string anywhere in the text.

Editing commands include insert, delete, change, and substitute, plus control characters that are used to make more complex (but still minor) editing changes within a line.

An interesting feature of QED is that a sequence of editing operations can be saved by the system as a normal text file. At a later time this set of commands can be re-executed to re-edit the text. This re-editing facility makes it possible to maintain different versions of a file without having to duplicate the main file many times. The text is stored only once; the alternate versions in short files contain only the editing changes. This is useful for testing changes to an operational program without actually modifying the original program until the changes have been checked out.

## Free-Form Text Editors

Advantages. The advantages to any author of having at his fingertips all of his resources for original creation and continued rewriting and updating are tremendous. With the power and memory of a computer, a reduction in document production time is easily achieved, since a manuscript may be perfected without costly delays. The advantages of computer-assisted editing include:

1. Easy access.
2. Immediacy of response.
3. Ease of making hard copy without intermediate stages of typing, proofreading, retyping, reproofing, etc.
4. Reduced turnaround time for any type of file research and writing task.
5. Common access to the same data base (which is useful for a pool of researchers or documenters working in the same area, or for common access to updated project management information).
6. "Constructive plagiarism": the easy modification of previously written materials for present purposes (as in the writing of papers, contracts, proposals, or brochures).
7. Great simplification of document dissemination and storage in a display oriented on-line environment—no hard-copy bulk, but any degree of archival protection desired.
8. Far greater flexibility for browsing and linking text fragments than with manual methods of working with hard copy.
9. Relatively modest cost for all this increase in productivity and efficiency, when compared with all aspects of present systems: writing, retyping, proofreading, typesetting, revision of galley and page proofs, printing, binding, distribution, storage (and subsequent inaccessibility due to distance, lack of shelf space, poor indexing, borrowed or lost copies, etc.). The user cost includes the machine time used and the rental or purchase cost of the terminals employed.

As with any innovation, there are disadvantages to on-line text manipulation. The hardest to overcome is personal reluctance to give up the ingrained habit of using hard copy, especially for those of the "back of the envelope" or "red pencil" schools. Other drawbacks include inability to keep a record of all the editing changes made, and the current (but diminishing) high cost of communications and displays. Acceptance of these techniques will be gradual, increasing as the disadvantages (such as cost) are diminished by technological advances. At the present time, the following sample of free-form text editors, ranging in cost and capability from limited to high, represent the state-of-the-art. The first group are really almost "degenerate" cases of free-form manuscript editors, since most large computer program editors are more powerful; they are quite commonly used for manuscript preparation, however, and therefore deserve mention.

MTST, MCST, ASTROCOMP. These "stand-alone" editing systems are similar in their design and intended use, and do not require the services of a large general-purpose computer. MTST (Magnetic Tape Selectric Typewriter) consists of a single IBM Selectric typewriter connected to a small control/memory unit (two tape drives) and is typically used for printing out neat looking (but unjustified) form letters and manuscripts (e.g., legal contracts). Editing must be done from the top of a tape to the bottom, and must be referenced by line numbers. However, line numbers change as lines are inserted, so that one must recompute line numbers of lines below as one passes through a tape inserting new lines. To perform any change, no matter how trivial, within a line, it is necessary to specify a line number and *retype* the whole line even if the text is being neither expanded nor contracted. The length of a line is not restricted, however.

The editing is implemented by working from an original tape onto a second tape. Thus, in addition to new and modified lines, lines not modified must be copied from the original onto the second tape.

The MCST (Magnetic Card Selectric Typewriter) is much the same as the MTST, except that its storage medium is a magnetic card and retyping of the entire card is necessary for any corrections. Line length is restricted to 100 characters. The MCST has the advantage that it may be directly connected to an on-line system running on a computer.

The ASTROCOMP system consists of up to eight typewriters and memory units connected to one control unit (the DEC PDP-8). Various peripherals (including line printer, paper tape, compatible nine-track IBM tape unit) are available for hard copy and input preparation for phototypesetters.

The editing functions of ASTROCOMP are a bit easier to use than those of MTST/MCST. Text is stored in lines, which are numbered sequentially from the top of the file. As above, line numbers change dynamically as lines are inserted or deleted. The basic editing command is SUBSTITUTE, which is performed by specifying a line number, the old text string, and the new string. Individual lines may be erased or moved by number. Verification is provided by a printout of the affected line before the change is actually made.

SYSTEM/360 ATS, VIPCOM. More viable for text editing than MTST or ASTROCOMP, ATS (Administrative Terminal System) and VIPcom utilize typewriter-like terminals (usually IBM Selectric typewriters or compatible alphanumeric displays) as their interactive device. VIPcom is basically ATS with photocomposition output; both allow various forms of input and formatted output.

As in ASTROCOMP, the kind and amount of editing are limited by the use of dynamically changing line numbers. Deletions and substitutions are easily made, but insertions of new lines require the user to type the new text at the end of the file and then move it to the new location. One may also edit the file from the bottom to the top, but this is not a natural way of working.

HYPERTEXT EDITING SYSTEM (HES) AND FILE RETRIEVAL, AND EDITING SYSTEM (FRESS). These two editors far surpass those previously discussed, in both capability and ease of use; however, they are also more expensive to implement.

HES, although in limited production use, was originally designed as an experimental CRT-based system for studying text-handling techniques. Oriented toward fully formatted typeset output (as well as flexible input and on-line editing), HES uses a lightpen and a set of function keys to select and indicate editing functions of the text. As indicated in the discussion of general editor characteristics, the use of a CRT display, function keys, and lightpen eliminate the need to remember function names, to type extra context, or to work from hard-copy output.

To demonstrate the facility of HES, the following example of a "move" is given: To move a portion of text, the "move" function key is pressed; next the beginning and the end characters of the text string to be moved are pointed at with the lightpen. The system then allows the user to find the location in his file to which the material is to be moved. The point of insertion is indicated with the lightpen, and the text below is moved up or down to accommodate the new text. The user may "return" to the original point of departure to verify that the edit has been completed as he intended.

The data structure (and therefore the editing operation) is completely independent of display or printout lines and pages. Each area of text arbitrarily designated by the user may be visualized as a continuous linear string of text, like a scroll, and represents a single page, a footnote, a complete chapter, or an entire book. This data structure allows interlinking of text areas to form cross-references. The linked text fragments are called a "hypertext". This is defined by Nelson (1967) as "the combination of natural language text with the computer's capacities for interactive, branching, or dynamic display ... a nonlinear text ... which cannot be printed conveniently ... on a conventional page. ... An example of a hypertext would be an encyclopedia like this one, or a set of programming and systems reference manuals with each cross-referenced text fragment instantly viewable when the user lightpens the cross-reference in the original text. Functions are provided in HES to allow the fragments of text to be interpreted and examined in a variety of ways, in particular to have linear paths traced through the hypertext for either on-line browsing purposes or for printing in a conventional manuscript form. The system also remembers the sequences of links the user has taken and allows him to reverse his course.

The commercially available production version of HES is called FRESS and supports a variety of terminals in such a way that all functions are usable, even on the lowest power terminal. The standard terminal supported is the IBM 2741 typewriter, although a CRT alphanumeric display may be used for faster and more convenient editing and on-line browsing.

FRESS is designed for major restructuring of large segments of text. In addition to the insert, delete, substitute, move, and copy functions found in HES, FRESS offers such diverse features as completely arbitrary size string edits; outline section numbering and retrieval of sections by user specified keywords, as in NLS (see next section); and linking and editing of text segments between files.

THE ON-LINE SYSTEM (NLS) OF THE AUGMENTED HUMAN INTELLECT (AHI) RESEARCH CENTER. The work being done by the AHI group embodies far more than just a powerful text editor. Their aim is to utilize the power of the computer in all aspects of their work, forming an "on-line community."

> We are concentrating fully upon reaching the point where we can do all of our work on line—placing in computer store all of our specifications, plans, designs, programs, documentation, reports, memos, bibliography and reference notes, etc., and doing all of our scratch work, planning, designing, debugging, etc., and a good deal of our intercommunication, via the consoles. (Engelbart and English, 1968).

The NLS center has become the information utility for the ARPA network, handling all its documentation, archival storage, and information dissemination. One of the most significant capabilities of NLS is its ability to display a file from many points of view. For instance, the various headings of the hierarchical outline structure of a text may be stored as part of the data structure. One may then request, for example, any section or all sections down to two levels of subsections or the first line of each of the subsections on the fourth level. The text is thus viewed as a collection of segments called "statements," with a tree structure superimposed on this basic data structure. Most of the tree manipulations are allowed at a given level in the tree, e.g., locating or deleting the next statement or the previous one, locating the first substatement, rearranging neighboring statements, etc. Note that this hierarchical approach to files, in contrast to the continuous string approach of HES and FRESS, is useful for documents as well as programs. NLS is an extremely powerful system capable of handling teletypes but also much more powerful displays utilizing standard television monitors equipped with standard alphanumeric keyboards, the SRI (Stanford Research Institute) mouse (an *x-y* transducer for moving a cursor), and the SRI five-button keyset for one-handed input of commands and literal text. The article by Engelbart and English (1968) is highly recommended.

**Editing Features of Typical Terminals.** The most common editing terminals today are still the teletypewriters (Teletype Model ASR33, IBM 2741, and their equivalents), principally because of their relatively modest cost (about $800 for the simplest Teletype model to approximately $3,500 for the 2741). In particular, acoustically coupled teletypewriters running up to 300 baud (15 to 30 characters per second) provide a convenient, portable terminal for original input, program editing, and "minor surgery" on ordinary manuscripts.

The price of alphanumeric CRT terminals has decreased steadily over the past several years, while the available capabilities, in terms of number of displayable characters and editing options, have increased. A continuum of editing power is available in these terminals, starting from a small CRT to replace the hard-copy Teletype (selling for as little as $2,000) and ranging to a $15,000 large-screen terminal that is capable of local interactive text editing. The examples given below are intended to give the reader an idea of the cost/power combinations that are available. (The Teletype replacements have not been considered because they have no editing capabilities to speak of.)

The Harris 1100 consists of a 2,000 character CRT (with single- and double-column formats), 2K bytes of MOS shift-register memory, a 100-symbol character set, and keyboard and function keys. In 1972 it sold for $14,500. Display buffer memory is expandable in 2K-byte increments, to a maximum of 6K bytes, at a cost of $2,000 per increment to provide buffering of and scrolling through a 6,000-character data base. Editing may be accomplished on line via telephone communications lines, with capacities up to 1,200 characters per second, or off line using paper tape for all I/O.

Standard features include a cursor with up/down/left/right/newline/home controls (but, unfortunately, no repeat key), a scroll function that is designed for systems with more than 2K bytes of memory, and a nice range of editing capabilities. In addition to the standard-character editing functions of insert, delete, and overstrike, these include "block" editing commands: By inserting special "define block" symbols in front of and immediately following an arbitrary string of text, a block may be defined and then edited (either deleted or rearranged, i.e., moved to the current cursor position) or outputted (either to paper tape or a computer, depending on the mode of operation). The terminal is oriented toward copy editing, and is used by a number of newspapers and printers in the United States and Europe.

The IMLAC PDS-1 is an example of a device capable of local data-structure editing, and of being tied into a larger host computer on which the data base can be stored. It is a small computer (like a 16-bit PDP-8) with up to 32K 16-bit words of local memory. It is integrated with a CRT that uses the PDS-1 core for a display buffer. It has no character generator, and characters are displayed (approximately 1,300 to 1,400 characters) through the use of character-stroke subroutines, executed by the scope. Cursor manipulation is handled by software in the PDS-1. Rudimentary vector graphics are also provided, and the total package (with 4K bytes of core and a lightpen) can be obtained for approximately $10,000.

**Conclusion.** On-line composition and editing of programs, coupled with interactive debugging, has become an established, cost-effective use of computers. Similarly, minor text editing, such as the correction of typographical errors in memoranda, is cost effective, since only Teletype consoles and minimal service from the CPU are required. In contrast, the imaginative use of computers for on-line composition and extensive manipulation of free-form text are still in the early stages of experimentation and user conversion. This is due partially to the high cost of CRT terminals, which provide the human factors essential to general-purpose editing, partially to the high cost of system resources and implementation time for the sophisticated programs required, and partially to the long time required to wean users from traditional off-line hard-copy processes.

Hardware prices are coming down steadily, however, and as more users switch to on-line thinking, creating, and manipulating, it is hoped that this use of computers will become increasingly accepted (and judged cost-effective) to the same extent that numerical and data processing applications are already considered to be legitimate uses of the computer.

REFERENCES

1967. Nelson, T. H. "Getting It Out of Our System," in George Schecter (Ed.), *Information Retrieval: Critical View.* Washington, D.C.: Thompson Books.

1968. Engelbart, D. C., and W. K. English. "A Research Center for Augmenting Human Intellect," *Proc. FJCC,* Vol. 33, Pt. 1, AFIPS Press, pp. 395–410.

1969. Lessing, L. "The Printed Word Goes Electronic," *Fortune,* (September), pp. 116–119, 188–190.

1969. Walter, G. O. "Typesetting," *Scientific American,* Vol. 220, No. 5 (May), pp. 60–69.

1971. Rice, D. and A. van Dam. "An Introduction to Information Structures and Paging Considerations for Online Text Editing Systems," in J. Tou (Ed.), *Advances in Information Systems Science,* Vol. 4. New York: Plenum Press, pp. 93–159.

1971. van Dam, A. and D. Rice. "On-line Text Editing: A Survey," *ACM Computing Surveys,* Vol. 3, No. 3 (September), pp. 93–114.

A. VAN DAM

## THEOREM PROVING

For articles on related subjects *see* ARTIFICIAL INTELLIGENCE; and PROGRAM CORRECTNESS, PROOF OF.

The two approaches to automated theorem proving are proof finding and consequence finding. A proof-finding program attempts to find a proof for a certain given theorem. A consequence-finding program is given some axioms and then tries to deduce consequences from the axioms and to select "interesting" consequences.

Some of the purposes of programming a computer to prove theorems concern artificial intelligence (Feigenbaum and Feldman, 1963; Slagle, 1971) and deductions. Artificial intelligence researchers point out that proving a nontrivial theorem is an intellectually difficult problem. Most of the theorem-proving programs we mention in this article use mathematical logic or, to be specific, the first-order predicate calculus, which is also called "quantification theory" (Chang and Lee, 1973). In mathematical logic, one can express fairly conveniently almost all kinds of deductive arguments. Writing a theorem-proving program that uses mathematical logic allows the researcher to study deduction in its purest form. Deduction is important because it plays a major role in solving many kinds of problems (not just in mathematics). A program that can prove theorems has what John McCarthy has called *common sense*; i.e., it has the ability to make deductions from given facts. This kind of common sense is an important part of human intelligence. Programs that use mathematical logic to find proofs have been extended to deduce answers to questions.

The other purposes of programming a computer to prove theorems concern mathematics and mathematical logic. Mathematicians point out that a program of the future that could prove new and interesting theorems would be useful in itself. So far, the only new and interesting theorem proved by a program was proved by the program of Guard et al. (1969). It would be a tremendous achievement if some program of the future proved or disproved the famous last theorem of Fermat or the Goldbach conjectures. Mathematical logic is well suited to computers, since logicians have striven for decades to make their inference rules "mechanical." It is an attractive idea to write a program based on mathematical logic, since this is a well-formulated and well-studied branch of mathematics. In addition, programming a computer to prove theorems is a way to study mathematical logic. For example, the programmer may develop powerful, natural, intuitive inference rules to which heuristics can be added easily.

We begin the history of automated theorem proving by mentioning some early programs that have proved theorems in areas other than the first-order predicate calculus. A program called the "Logic Theorist," or simply LT, by Allen Newell, J. C. Shaw, and Herbert Simon in 1957 proves theorems in propositional calculus (also called "sentential calculus," or boolean algebra). It performs at approximately the level of a fair-to-good college student on the same theorems. A 1959 program mainly due to Herbert Gelernter proves geometry theorems at the level of a good high school student. A program called ADEPT proves theorems in group theory. It performs at approximately the level of an intelligent college student proving the same theorems.

P. Gilmore and Hao Wang, as well as Martin Davis and Hilary Putnam were among the first to program a computer to find proofs in the first-order predicate calculus. (Each of these programs substitutes many constant terms for the variables and then checks to see if the theorem has been proved. If not, more constant terms are added and another check is made, etc.) After these programs had been written, J. A. Robinson developed an inference rule, which he called the "resolution principle." Roughly speaking, the resolution principle draws the most general, possible conclusion from two given statements, where the conclusion and the two statements generally contain variables. The resolution principle is more natural, more intuitive, and easier for people to use than are the inference rules used by the previous predicate calculus programs. Furthermore, it is easier to think of heuristics to add to the resolution principle.

A procedure that uses the resolution principle for proof finding tries to show that the negation of the given theorem to be proved is unsatisfiable (contradictory, inconsistent). The resolution principle is complete for proof finding in the sense of the following theorem, first proved by J. A. Robinson: "If a finite set of clauses [statements] is unsatisfiable, a contradiction can be found in a finite number of applications of the resolution principle." This means, in principle, that there is a computer program which, for any true theorem in first-order predicate calculus, can find a proof using the resolution principle. In practice, however, limitations of computer time and memory space prevent programs from finding proofs for many true theorems. However, various people have written proof-finding programs embodying the resolution principle. These programs are more powerful than the previous predicate calculus programs.

The resolution principle is complete for consequence finding in the sense of the following theorem, first proved by R. Lee: "If a clause $C$ is a consequence of a finite non-empty set of clauses, a clause $T$ can be found in a finite number of applications of the resolution principle such that $C$ is an immediate consequence of $T$ alone." Lee wrote a consequence-finding program based on the resolution principle.

Several researchers have strengthened these completeness theorems by showing that certain restricted forms of the resolution principle are still complete. This is of practical importance to automated theorem proving because theoretical considerations and computer experiments indicate that restricted and complete resolution tends to be more efficient than is unrestricted resolution.

Programs using the resolution principle or its restrictions have proved already known theorems (found proofs and found consequences)—e.g., the first theorems in group theory in abstract algebra. Although quite general, these programs have been so slow that they have proved only a few theorems of any interest. In order to speed up the search for proofs of theorems involving the equality predicate, complete, valid, efficient (in time) inference rules, namely, paramodulation and E-resolution, were developed for theories with equality. Each of the new rules replaces the equality axioms and is used in addition to the resolution principle. Partial ordering (Slagle and Norton, 1973) and total ordering (Slagle and Norton, 1974) were built into computer programs, and the experimental results were very favorable. The work of Plotkin (1973) shows ways to build in many equational theories, including theories with commutativity and associativity, which are valuable concepts to build in, since they so frequently occur in important theories—e.g., number theory (plus and times) and set theory (union and intersection).

REFERENCES

1963. Feigenbaum, E., and J. Feldman. (Eds.). *Computers and Thought*. New York: McGraw-Hill.

1969. Guard, J., F. Oglesby, J. Bennett, and L. Settle. "Semiautomated Mathematics," *JACM*, Vol. 16 (January), pp. 49–62.

1971. Slagle, J. *Artificial Intelligence: The Heuristic Programming Approach*. New York: McGraw-Hill.

1973. Chang, C, and R. Lee. *Symbolic Logic and Mechanical Theorem Proving*. New York: Academic Press.

1973. Slagle, J., and L. Norton. "Experiments with an Automatic Theorem Prover Having Partial Ordering Inference Rules," *CACM*, Vol. 16 (November), pp. 682–688.

J. R. SLAGLE

# THRASHING

For articles on related subjects *see* MULTIPROGRAMMING; SCHEDULING ALGORITHM; and TASK.

For article on related term *see* WORKING SET.

Thrashing is the name of a phenomenon observed in some multiprogramming systems in which poorly designed memory management strategies are used; it refers to a collapse of processing efficiency when overcommitment of main memory is attempted. If memory is overcommitted, then at least one task will not have its working set (i.e., the minimum set of instructions and data needed in main memory for efficient processing) present, and therefore the task will be unable to operate efficiently. If, in addition, the memory management policy attempts to acquire space for the pages requested by the inefficient task by preempting them from the working sets of other tasks, then these deprived tasks may also find their working sets incomplete in memory, whereupon they, too, may enter an inefficient mode of operation. This can spread rapidly among all active tasks, so that the net effect is that no task at all can operate efficiently, a condition called "thrashing." There are two causes of thrashing:

1. The total working sets of active tasks exceed available memory.
2. Space is acquired for some active tasks by taking space allocated to the working sets of others.

It should be noted that condition 2 is equivalent to a condition of unstable feedback: The tasks whose totality of working sets are not present are allowed to interfere with the other tasks.

One solution of the thrashing problem is to institute controls that prevent the instability. The simplest form of control operates as follows: A priority list of active tasks is set up; if the total working sets of active tasks exceed memory, space is preempted from the lowest priority tasks having space in memory. In this way the $k$ highest priority tasks at a given time have their working sets in memory (for some of $k$), and the tasks of priority lower than $k$ have at most a portion of their working sets present. If memory is chosen sufficiently large, the mean value of $k$ can be high enough to keep the processing efficiency as high as desired. This control mechanism prevents thrashing by preventing feedback: No task can preempt space held by the working sets of higher priority tasks. (See Wilkes, 1973, for more detail.)

Thrashing is primarily a problem in a system where the ratio of the access time between auxiliary memory (e.g., drum or disk) and main memory is large (e.g., in core/drum systems where the ratio is in excess of $10^4$). In these cases a single missing page or segment fault (i.e., an interrupt indicating that reference to a page or segment missing from main memory has occurred) takes a long time to service and adversely affects efficiency. When the access time ratio is small (e.g., in cache/core systems where it seldom exceeds $10^2$), the effect on efficiency of an additional missing-page fault is comparatively much less significant.

REFERENCE

1973. Wilkes, M. V. "The Dynamics of Paging," *Computer J.* (February).

P. J. DENNING AND D. E. DENNING

# THROUGHPUT

For articles on related subjects *see* JOB; PERFORMANCE OF COMPUTERS; PERFORMANCE MEASUREMENT AND EVALUATION; SCHEDULING ALGORITHM; and TURNAROUND TIME.

The throughput of a computer system during a given interval of time is the average rate at which jobs are completed by the system in that interval. If $n$ jobs are completed in an interval of $t$ seconds, the throughput is taken as $n/t$ jobs per second during that interval.

Throughput is frequently used as a figure of merit for a system: the higher the throughput, the more highly regarded the system. Considered alone, however, throughput can prove to be a most deceptive measure. At least five factors affect throughput: the capacity of the system, the time interval over which throughput is measured, the load on the system, the scheduling method, and the job mix.

*The capacity of the system* is the maximum rate at which the system can process work. It is usually stated with respect to each job class to which the system caters, a job class being the set of jobs whose resource requirements (processor, memory, devices) fall in specified intervals; for example, all jobs whose processor time requirement is between 30 and 60 sec, main memory requirement is between 5K and 10K words, and which uses no devices, might constitute one class.

The precise specifications of job classes in a given system will depend on the objectives of that system. The capacity of a given class is the maximum rate at which the system can complete the jobs in that class. Evidently, the throughput of jobs in a given class cannot exceed the system's capacity in that class; in fact, if the arrival rate of such jobs approaches the capacity of the system to process them, a large backlog will accumulate, making system response time to them unacceptably long. Put another way, whenever throughput is maximized in the sense that it approaches system capacity in each job class, intolerable delays to jobs will be the inevitable result, and throughput in this case clearly gives a deceptive picture of the system's performance.

*The time interval* over which throughput is measured is the second factor of importance. It is well known that, by giving priority to short jobs (i.e., jobs whose residence time in the system, or whose processing time, is short), the system throughput will be high. However, because little attention is being devoted thereby to the long jobs, a backlog of long jobs may accumulate. Assuming that the system management intends to get all submitted work completed eventually, there will necessarily come a time when the long jobs must be processed and the short ones are left as backlog, but during their processing, the throughput will be low. Thus, over a time interval long enough so that all jobs submitted are processed, the throughput will be proportional to $1/S$, where $S$ is the mean service time over all job classes. However, over an interval during which short jobs are favored, the throughput can be considerably higher than $1/S$, whereas during another interval during which the backlog of long jobs is removed, the throughput can be considerably less than $1/S$. Once again, throughput can give a deceptive picture of system performance.

As suggested in the discussion of the first factor, *the load* on the system is a third factor affecting throughput. For job class $i$, let $F_i$ denote the fraction of time during which such a job queue for this class is present in the system demanding processing, and let $S_i$ denote the mean time to service each job. Then, the system capacity in class $i$ is proportional to $1/S_i$ (mean output rate if queue is always full), and the throughput in class $i$ is proportional to $F_i/S_i$. This is illustrated in Fig. 1. Evidently, as the load of class $i$ jobs increases, $F_i$ increases and approaches unity so that the throughput of class $i$ jobs increases correspondingly. However, even as the load increases, the response time within class $i$ may increase sharply (it is usually proportional to $1/(1 - F_i)$), so that once again judging performance merely by throughput can be deceptive.

*The scheduling method* is a fourth factor affecting throughput. It was shown above that giving preference to short jobs during an interval will produce high throughput during that interval. In more general terms, suppose the system devotes a

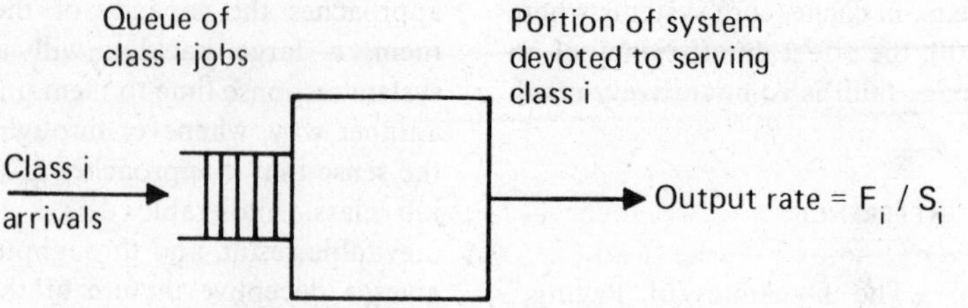


**Fig. 1.** Load on the system.

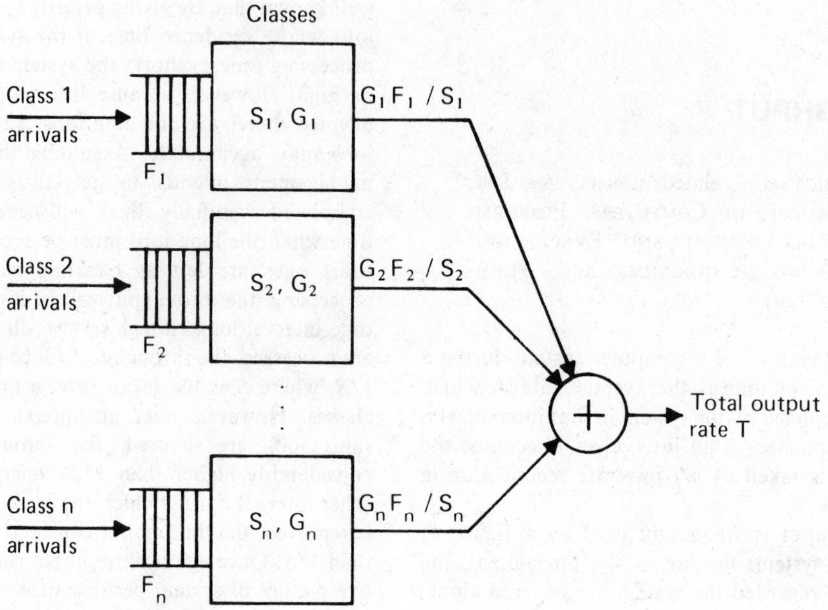


**Fig. 2.** Throughput.

fraction $G_i$ of total capacity to class $i$ jobs; the throughput in class $i$ is then proportional to $G_iF_i/S_i$. Since the values of $G_i$ for each class $i$ are a function of the scheduling method, the throughput in each class depends on the scheduling method, and the total throughput is proportional to $T$, where

$$T = G_1F_1/S_1 + G_2F_2/S_2 + \ldots + G_nF_n/S_n,$$

will also depend on the scheduling method. This is illustrated in Fig. 2. (The reader should observe that there is interaction between $G_i$ and $F_i$, since increasing $G_i$ will reduce the backlog in class $i$ and thus reduce $F_i$; therefore the computation of throughput by the preceding formula cannot be carried out directly.) As noted above, $T$ is also proportional to the constant $1/S$, where $S$ is the mean service time over all job classes. The implication of this is: If the scheduling method increases throughput above $1/S$ for some classes, it will reduce it below $1/S$ for others. Once again, the interpretation of the throughput can be deceptive if the scheduling method is unknown.

The final factor affecting throughput is the *job mix*, i.e., the distribution of jobs among the job classes. The effect of this factor should be clear, in light of the preceding discussion.

It is apparent, therefore, that one needs to conduct a thorough analysis of a system with respect to the five factors before a useful or meaningful interpretation can be attached to throughput. It is also apparent that performance of a single system cannot be judged solely by its throughput, nor can two systems be compared simply by comparing their throughputs. Similarly, if one wishes to improve system throughput, he must consider how this can be done while considering the constraints imposed by the five factors. It is not an easy problem.

P. J. DENNING AND D. E. DENNING

# TIME SHARING

For articles on related subjects *see* COMPUTER ACCOUNTING AND RESOURCE CONTROL; MULTIPROGRAMMING; PROCESSING MODES; SCHEDULING ALGORITHM; SWAPPING; TIME SLICE; and VIRTUAL MEMORY. For articles on related terms *see* FIFO-LIFO; INTERRUPT; and REGISTER.

Time sharing is a method of operating a computer so that two or more users are simultaneously able to present problems to the machine and to receive answers from it. The means usually adopted to perform this service is to do some computation or processing for one user and then, before finishing his task, to lay it aside temporarily and do some computation for a different user. Because time is often divided into relatively small pieces (typically, about ¼ of a second), this technique is sometimes called "time slicing" or "time-division multiplexing." Time sharing is similar in many ways to multiprocessing and has many of the same problems. The major difference between the two is that in time sharing the user is on line to the computer, and hence provision must be made for his need for reasonably rapid response.

Early time-sharing systems include the System Development Corporation program for the USQ-32, Project MAC at M.I.T., the Dartmouth system, and various systems for military use.

Let us try to imagine a very simple form of a time-sharing system (see Fig. 1). There are *n* terminals serving up to *n* users, and there are *n* + 1 blocks of main addressable storage (say, magnetic core) and a central processing unit (CPU). One block of store holds a supervisory control program while the other *n* stores hold programs for the *n* users.

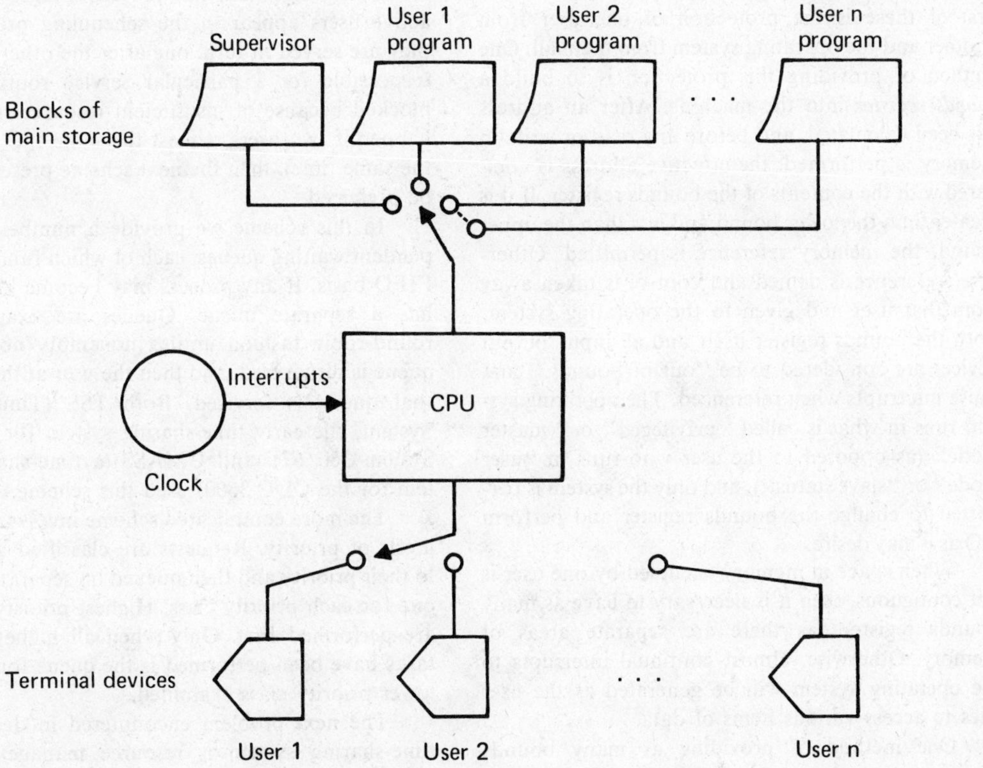


**Fig. 1.** A highly simplified time-sharing system.

The operation is as follows: First terminal 1 is connected to the system and control is given to user program 1. At the end of a fixed period of time (called a "quantum," or time slice), the clock generates an interrupt, which causes control to be given to the supervisory program. This program saves the "context" of program 1 and then transfers control to program 2. The "context" of a program is the information unique to the current state of the program. During the course of execution of the program, this information is to be found in common data areas or in registers of the CPU rather than in the storage area belonging to that program. For example, the program counter contains the address of the next instruction to be executed within the program. Under normal circumstances this must be saved at the end of a quantum so that, when the program is restarted, steps will neither be repeated nor skipped. After *n* quanta have expired, control returns to program 1, which resumes from where it left off. If *n* quanta represents a time period that is short with respect to human reaction time, then one machine satisfies the needs of *n* people by sharing its time among them.

Even with a design as simplistic as this one, there are nontrivial problems to be resolved. The first of these is the protection of one user from another and the operating system from them all. One method of providing this protection is to build a *bounds register* into the machine. After an address has been calculated, and before any read or write in memory is performed, the effective address is compared with the contents of the bounds register. If it is greater than the lower bound and less than the upper bound, the memory reference is permitted. Otherwise, reference is denied and control is taken away from that user and given to the operating system. Both the bounds register itself and all input/output devices are considered to be "out of bounds," and cause interrupts when referenced. The operating system runs in what is called "privileged" or "master mode" (as opposed to the user who runs in "user mode" or "slave status"), and only the system is permitted to change the bounds register and perform I/O as it may desire.

When space in memory occupied by one user is not contiguous, then it is necessary to have as many bounds registers as there are separate areas of memory. Otherwise, almost continual interrupts to the operating system will be generated as the user tries to access various items of data.

One method of providing as many bounds registers as may be needed is called "segmentation," in which all memory references are indirect through a segment table that contains a base address plus an "extent" for each independent segment of code or data. The need for such segmentation can arise when data and programs are shared on a partially exclusive basis among three or more users.

The next problem to be faced in designing a time-sharing system is the scheduling problem. The least sophisticated scheme is the one described above, namely, to give service to user 1, then to user 2, then to user 3, etc. This is called the round-robin scheduling algorithm. The obvious disadvantage of it is that some users may be out to lunch, thinking, or have gone to sleep. However, if the time required to determine whether or not a user needs service is short, the scheme has the merit of simplicity. It is often used for polled I/O devices.

The next simplest scheme of scheduling service is the single first-in/first-out (FIFO) queue. As requests for service are generated, they are entered onto the end of a single FIFO queue. When it is possible to perform a service, the name of the user at the head of the queue is removed from the queue, and the service he requested is performed. If there are sufficient resources available so that it is never impossible to provide a requested service, then this scheduling algorithm has the advantages that only active users appear in the scheduling process and they are served in turn, one after the other. When it *is* possible for a particular service routine to be blocked because of insufficient resources (as might happen if two users request the same I/O device at the same time), then the next scheme presented is to be preferred.

In this scheme we provide a number of independent waiting queues, each of which function on a FIFO basis. If any process may become blocked, it has a separate queue. Queues are examined in round-robin fashion until a nonempty/nonblocked queue is discovered, and then the user at the head of that queue is serviced. Both TSS (Time-Sharing System, the early time-sharing system for the IBM System 360/67) and UMASS (a time-sharing system for the CDC 3600) used this scheme.

The more complicated scheme involves multiple levels of priority. Requests are classified according to their priority and then queued on separate queues, one for each priority class. Highest priority services are performed first. Only when all higher priority tasks have been performed is the queue for the next lower priority class examined.

The next problem encountered in designing a time-sharing system is resource management. As shown in Fig. 1, all users are resident in main store, but this is clearly wasteful of relatively expensive

**Fig. 2.** The DEC-10 system, the central computer of a widely used time-sharing system.

main store. Typically, almost all user programs reside on some form of slow backup storage, such as a drum. Then, when a program is to be executed (given a quantum of CPU time), it is "rolled in" from the drum into core, executed, and then rolled out again. Since most machines that host time-sharing systems have semiautonomous data channels, it is possible to be rolling in the "next" candidate for execution, executing the "present," and rolling out the "previous" candidate all at the same time, thus utilizing effectively the time that would otherwise be wasted waiting for the next program to be rolled in. This presupposes that the next program to be executed is known to the system.

This method of overlapped I/O and computation tries to optimize the use of three different resources, all of which are in limited supply in any time-sharing system. The first resource is space in main storage: If it were unlimited, we would just leave all user programs in main storage and do no swapping in and out of programs. If the I/O transfer rate were unlimited, then we could just wait until a program's turn to execute arrived, whip it into core, execute it and then whip it out again, without bothering with overlap. Finally, if CPU time were an unlimited resource each user could have his own machine.

In a multiprocessing system that is not on line, a program is allowed to continue executing as long as it can profitably do so. Control is taken away only when a program has to wait for an I/O transfer or for some other resource. In a time-sharing system, control is taken away in those cases and also after the expiration of some maximum time. This is done so that every user can get *some* service every few seconds. If the service is sufficient and the seconds between services are few enough, the user has the illusion that he is in control of his own private computer and not just receiving one *n*th of a big machine.

Time sharing arose, in part, because batch turnaround times were so long that they were impeding the solution of problems. The goal was to bring the user back into "contact" with the machine so that he could do on-line debugging and program development. Time sharing presupposes that there is a fast, expensive, central machine and a number of slow peripheral users. If the ratio of speeds comes anywhere near unity, the central processor cannot move fast enough to give the illusion of being in several places at once. If the central processor becomes inexpensive, then every user will be able to afford his own machine and thus eliminate the inevitable overhead involved in switching tasks.

The reader may be interested in some statistics collected about user behavior on one university time-sharing system. In the UMASS system, a typical user signs on for 20 min. During this time, he makes four or five attempts to run his program. Each such attempt consumes 1½ sec of CPU time and generates about 900 characters of output. A typical stored program consists of around 1,500 characters.

An important aspect of multiaccess systems (not discussed above) is that of file management. To be useful, a time-sharing system must retain a user's programs and data between sessions. This implies considerable on-line storage, usually in the form of disks.

When more than one person is connected to a single computer system, it is necessary to determine whether or not the actions of one user have any effect upon another. For example, each user in a typical scientific situation hopes to be completely independent of every other user, but in a commercial on-line reservation system, the sale of a ticket by one agent must be reflected in the availability of that resource at all other points of sale. Both extremes, as well as many intermediate points, exist.

A time-sharing system that is limited to performing one service—be it ticket sales, warehouse management, off-track betting, or whatever—is said to be *dedicated*. This is to be contrasted with a system in which the user can construct programs that will be run or interpreted by the system and will perform calculations or operations unthought of by the original designers.

REFERENCES

1970. Martin, J. and A. R. D. Norman. *The Computerized Society*. Englewood Cliffs, N.J.: Prentice-Hall.

1970. Watson, R. J. *Time Sharing System Design Concepts*. New York: McGraw-Hill.

C. C. FOSTER

# TIME SLICE

For articles on related subjects *see* SCHEDULING ALGORITHM; SWAPPING; and TIME SHARING.

For articles on related terms *see* FRONT END; INTERRUPT; and OPERATING SYSTEMS.

In the late 1950s and early 1960s, computer systems were envisioned that could be used simultaneously by several people, each at a typewriterlike terminal, each appearing to have exclusive use of the computer. The computer was to take advantage of the typing time of one user by turning its attention to another. If the computational tasks requested were short enough, then all users could be serviced, and the illusion of a single-user private computer could be maintained. Early systems served less than a dozen people, whereas modern systems service 10 to 100. But what if there were one or more very long computational tasks?

Time slicing provided a part of the answer. At the end of each time slice (or time quantum of, say, 100 ms), the operating system would interrupt the current user program and turn its attention to other users before returning to the interrupted program for another slice of time. A variety of scheduling algorithms were developed whose general purpose was to maintain high-speed response to terminal requests with reasonable computer efficiency. Multiplexing among compute-bound programs (i.e., ones that require I/O only at relatively long intervals) by time slicing uses the machine less efficiently than serial run-to-completion because a certain amount of time is required to switch from program to program. Also, longer average start-to-finish turnaround times occur: Serially run, two equal jobs finish at time $n$ and $2n$ (for an average turnaround of $3n/2$); with time slicing, both finish in somewhat more than $2n$ for an average of somewhat more than $2n$. But the important characteristics of time sharing and time slicing are high-speed response to many short computational requests and nearly continuous access to the machine; total problem turnaround time is a secondary consideration.

Early systems, which often took care of the low-speed terminal I/O with a separate "front end" computer, were driven exclusively by the time-slice clock and ignored the loss of CPU time incurred by the inability to overlap it with I/O to disk file and tape. The loss became more pronounced as time-sharing system applications became more sophisticated. Explicit interrupt signals from the I/O hardware, together with the later introduction of multiple programs in core storage, combined to give the new operating systems both knowledge of possible overlaps of I/O and CPU execution, and means of making use of these periods of time. Some modern systems can achieve 95% CPU use together with significant concurrent use of swapping and file I/O devices.

The event-driven systems, which required the operating system to make a scheduling decision (not only each time slice, but also for each of many other events such as I/O starts and completes), ran the risk of spending too much time deciding and not enough time doing. To solve this problem, one system, Xerox's UTS and its successor, CP-V, which run on Sigma 6 and Sigma 9 machines, adopted two control quanta in addition to the primary time-slicing quantum. One of these establishes a minimum interval between changes from program to program, regardless of the importance of the intervening events; it thus establishes a lower bound on the system overhead incurred in such changes. The second provides corresponding control and minimums for swapping, allowing a program to execute for a minimum period (if needed) before swapping is permitted.

REFERENCE

1969. Bryan, G. E., and J. E. Shemer. "The UTS Time-Sharing System: Performance Analysis and Instrumentation," *Proc. Second Symposium on Operating Systems Principles,* pp. 147–158. Princeton: Princeton University Press.

G. E. BRYAN

## TRACE

For article on related subject *see* DEBUGGING.

For articles on related subjects *see* COMMAND AND JOB CONTROL LANGUAGES; and ITERATION.

A trace is a debugging aid consisting of a display that chronicles the actions and results of individual steps in a program; the term is sometimes used for a control program that produces this kind of display.

The debugging process precipitates countless problems, whose correction requires stepwise detailed records of a program's execution. A trace is designed to provide this type of information by taking the user's program and placing it under control of a special routine, which monitors the progress of the program. Continuous execution of the user's program is replaced by a process whereby the trace program intercedes between steps of the user's program, displaying a variety of material before permitting execution of the next step. Of course the type of information varies with the particular trace facility; however, the contents of most traces are characterized by such items as a copy of the instruction, its location, and operand and register values before and after execution. In addition, some trace facilities are concerned with the sequence of events in a program, as well as with the history of various data items. In this case the display will include indications as to whether certain branches have been followed, information about cyclic processes, and so on.

Since these facilities are intended specifically for debugging, they are designed so that their insertion and subsequent deletion are straightforward. In some systems a trace is superimposed by explicit specification external to the program itself, in which case the request is communicated via the job control language to the operating system under which the program functions. In other systems, the trace facilities are part of the programming language and can be activated as an intrinsic part of the user's source program. Either form of invocation requires a small amount of highly localized specification, so that it is very easily removed once its purpose has been served.

One such trace facility, provided by the CHECK feature of PL/I, makes it possible to tag selected variable names in a source procedure for automatic tracing. Then, when the program (i.e., its machine language equivalent) executes, each tagged variable name is printed along with its value every time that value changes.

The procedure described below illustrates an aspect of this facility: Its intent is to read successive values of variable $N$. Each $N$ is printed, accompanied by a value $T$, which is computed as

$$N^2/\Sigma_{k=1}^{N}(1 + \sqrt{k}).$$

An $N$ of zero stops the run. (In the program in Fig. 1, $S$ is used to store the value of the denominator.)

Fig. 2 shows sample output produced by the procedure in Fig. 1. Inspection of the results raises

| VALUE OF N | VALUE OF T |
|---|---|
| 3 | 1.25939E+00 |
| 5 | 1.21781E+00 |
| 4 | 5.21600E-01 |
| 6 | 7.57789E-01 |
| 8 | 8.91209E-01 |
| 7 | 5.30934E-01 |
| 9 | 6.71664E-01 |

**Fig. 2**

```
R:  PROCEDURE OPTIONS(MAIN):
    PUT LIST ('VALUE OF N','VALUE OF T'); S=0;
IN: GET LIST(N); IF N=0 THEN STOP;
        DO K=1 TO N;    S=S+1+SQRT(K);    END;
    T=N**2/S;    PUT SKIP LIST(N,T);    GO TO IN;
    END R;
```

**Fig. 1**

```
(CHECK(K,S)): R:  PROCEDURE OPTIONS(MAIN);
                  PUT LIST ('VALUE OF N','VALUE OF T'); S=0
             IN:  GET LIST(N); IF N=0 THEN STOP;
                      DO K=1 TO N;    S=S+1+SQRT(K);    END;
                  T=N**2/S;    PUT SKIP LIST(N,T);    GO TO IN;
                  END R;
```

**Fig. 3**

```
VALUE OF N              VALUE OF T

S= 0.00000E+00;

K=        1;

S= 2.00000E+00;

K=        2;

S= 4.41421E+00;

K=        3;

S= 7.14626E+00;

K=        4;

         3                        1.25939E+00

K=        1;

S= 9.14626E+00;

K=        2;

S= 1.15604E+01;

K=        3;

S= 1.42925E+01;
        .
        .
        .
```

**Fig. 4**

some suspicions: Although the formula for *T* suggests that its value should increase with increasing *N*, its behavior apparently contradicts this.

In an effort to shed some light on this anomaly, the variables *K* and *S* have been tagged for automatic tracing by specifying them as part of the PROCEDURE statement (Fig. 3). The other statements are unchanged. As a result of this addition, *K* and *S* are printed whenever they change. Examination of this augmented output (Fig. 4) for a repeated run now shows what happened: All is well for the first *N*. Then, when the second *N* is read and the summation process is begun again, *S* keeps right on growing from its previous value, indicating that *S* is not being reinitialized for each new *N*.

Because of its iterations, branches, and calls, the execution of even a modest-sized program may involve thousands of individual steps. Consequently, an unfettered trace routine easily can fill several cubic feet of paper with information, most of which is of no interest. Accordingly, all trace facilities include provisions for damping their zeal. For example, the user may limit the trace to a certain section of his program, allowing the rest of it to execute normally. In addition, he may choose to examine certain variables; if he does, the trace output will show only those steps in which the specified variables are affected. Moreover, the user's primary interest may be in the flow of logic, in which case the trace can be restricted to a record of branches, subroutine calls, and other sequence changes.

S. V. Pollack

## TRANSLATION, LANGUAGE. *See* LANGUAGE TRANSLATION.

## TRAP

For article on related subject *see* INTERRUPT.

For article on related term *see* GENERATIONS, COMPUTER.

When the occurrence of an exceptional event in a processor results in an automatic transfer to a special routine for handling that event, this transfer is called a "trap."

Some practitioners consider the trap and interrupt as being synonymous, while others think of a trap in a somewhat narrower context, i.e., the range of exceptional events that occur within the central processor. Whatever the categorization, the point is that when an exceptional condition (such as an attempt to divide by zero) occurs in a processor equipped with trapping facilities, the hardware automatically executes a transfer to a specific storage location that is permanently assigned for that particular contingency. That location is used to store a transfer instruction to the appropriate handling routine.

Although an exceptional condition may produce circumstances that cannot be remedied by a programmed procedure, there are other conditions from which it is possible to recover. (For example, in some contexts it may be appropriate to set an underflow value to zero without undue harm to the process.) Accordingly, pertinent address information automatically is preserved so that a proper return can be made, once the trapping routine has been completed.

Several such locations might be reserved, depending on the types of conditions the processor is designed to recognize. Typically, separate trapping addresses would be provided for overflow, underflow, illegal address, and illegal operation, in addition to division by zero (sometimes called a "divide check"), already mentioned.

Prior to the introduction of trapping facilities (generally associated with so-called "second generation" computers) the programmer had to include explicit test instructions at each point where some exceptional condition might possibly occur. The need to do this is obviated by the trapping facility, since it operates over the entire program. However, software trapping facilities, such as the ON condition in PL/I, still exist to give programmers additional control over exceptional conditions.

Systems equipped with trapping facilities usually include a machine instruction that allows the user to force one of several kinds of traps, thereby giving him the opportunity to simulate a given type of exceptional condition. This capability has been used to considerable advantage in developing a variety of debugging aids and special features in software programs. Certain trapping facilities also may be explicitly turned off (disabled) by the programmer for all or part of a procedure, whereupon the system ignores the precipitating event and refrains from intervention.

S. V. Pollack and T. E. Sterling

# TREE

For articles on related subjects *see* Data Structures; Games on Computers; and Graph Theory.

A tree is a special form of directed graph with the following properties: (1) either it has no vertices or has a distinguished vertex called the "root vertex," which has no predecessors; and (2) every vertex other than the root vertex has a unique predecessor.

Vertices of a tree which have successors are called "nonterminal vertices," while vertices that have no successors are called "terminal vertices" or "leaves." Fig. 1 illustrates a tree with root vertex *a*; two nonterminal vertices *a*, *c*; and three terminal vertices *b*, *d*, *e*.

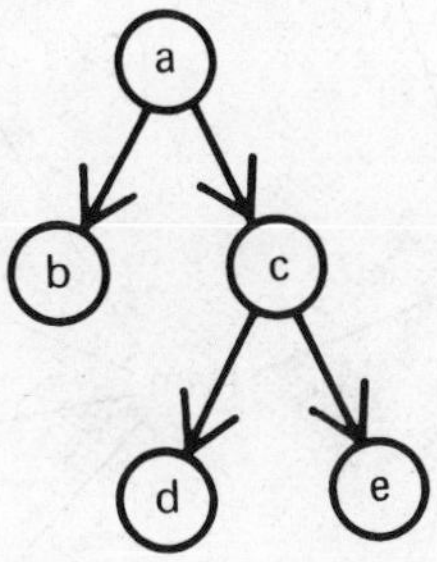


**Fig. 1.** A tree showing terminal and nonterminal vertices.

Trees in which each nonterminal vertex has at most *n* successors are called "*n*-ary" trees. Trees in which each nonterminal vertex has at most two successors are called "binary" trees. The tree in Fig. 1 is an example of a binary tree.

Trees are a natural data structure for expressing the operator-operand structure of arithmetic expressions. The expression $x + y * z$ may be represented by the tree structure in Fig. 2, where the operators are represented by nonterminal vertices and the operands of an operator are represented by successor subtrees of the operator vertex. Thus, the operands

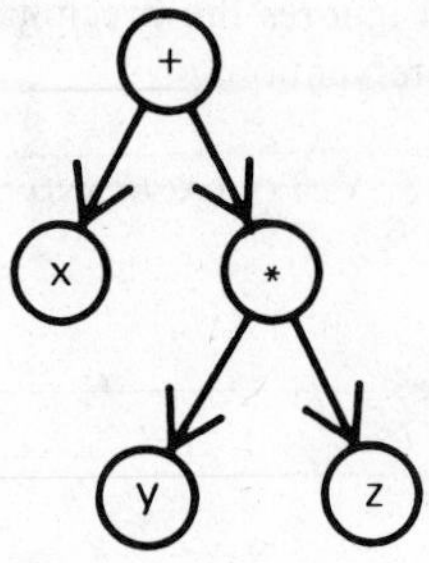


**Fig. 2.** A tree representing an operator-operand structure.

of + are $x$ and $y * z$, and are represented by successor subtrees of the vertex +.

Trees are a natural data structure for any data objects whose components stand in a hierarchical relation to each other. For example, the organization chart of a company may be represented by a tree structure, and family trees are, as their name implies, representable by a tree structure. The biblical family tree in Fig. 3 is taken from Knuth (1968).

Tree structures may be indicated by parentheses, nesting, or indentation, as illustrated in Fig. 4 which shows alternative representations of the tree of Fig. 1.

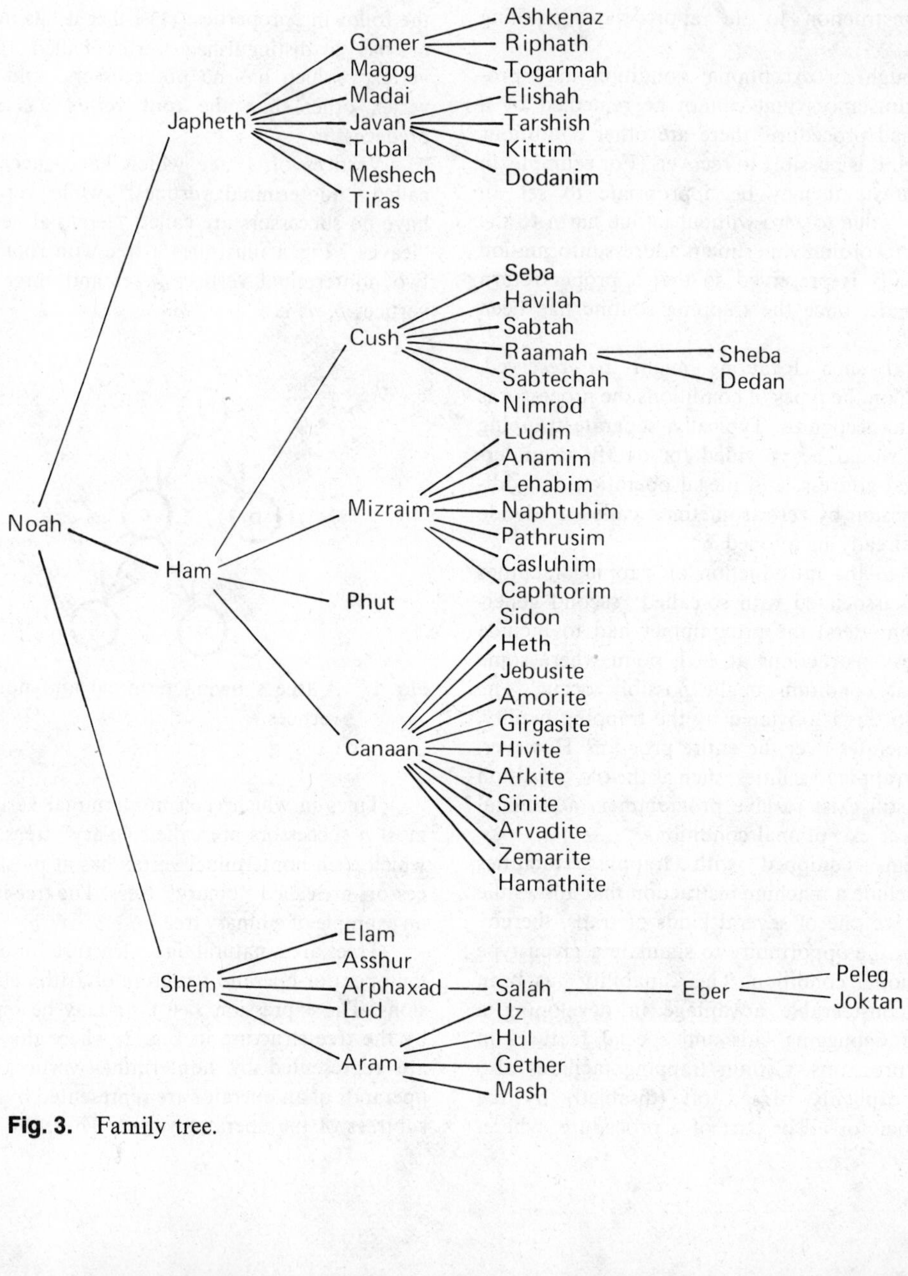


**Fig. 3.** Family tree.

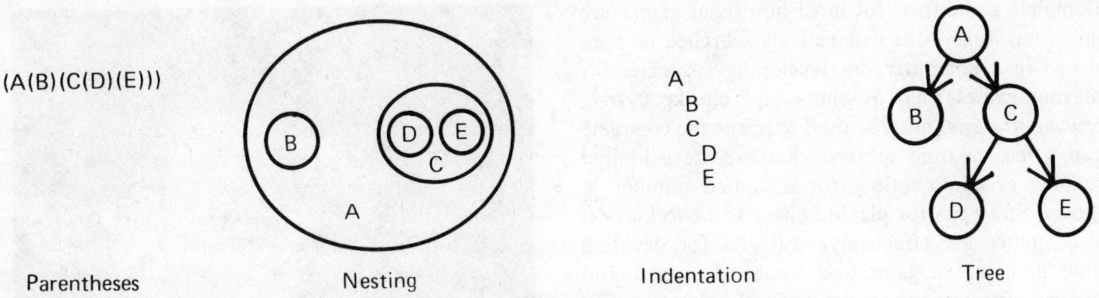


**Fig. 4.** Alternative representations of tree of Fig. 1.

Tree structures may be specified by declarations in programming languages like Cobol and PL/I. For example, the tree structure in Fig. 4 may be specified by the following declaration:

```
DECLARE 1  A
        2  B
        2  C
           3  D
           3  E
```

Tree structures are convenient for storing sets of lexicographically ordered objects for purposes of alphabetically oriented information retrieval. For example, the five words "dog," "cat," "lion," "fox," "tiger" can be stored in the tree structure shown in Fig. 5. A word in this tree structure can be found by comparing it to successive nodes, starting at the root node and taking the left successor if the word occurs earlier in a dictionary ordering or the right successor if it occurs later. Success is reported if the word matches; failure is reported if there is no successor of the kind required for the next step of search. The failure signal may be used to trigger a procedure for adding the new word to the tree as a new successor at the point of failure.

*Example.* (1) Assume that we want to determine if the word "fox" is in the tree. The word "fox" is compared with the word "dog," and since it occurs later in the alphabet, the right branch is taken. Then "fox" is compared with "lion," and since it occurs earlier in the alphabet, the left branch is taken. The third comparison results in a match.

(2) Determine whether the word "chicken" is in the tree; if absent, add it to the tree. First compare "chicken" with "dog" and take the left branch. Then compare "chicken" with "cat" and take the right branch. Then report failure because there is no right successor of "cat." Add "chicken" as the new right successor of "cat."

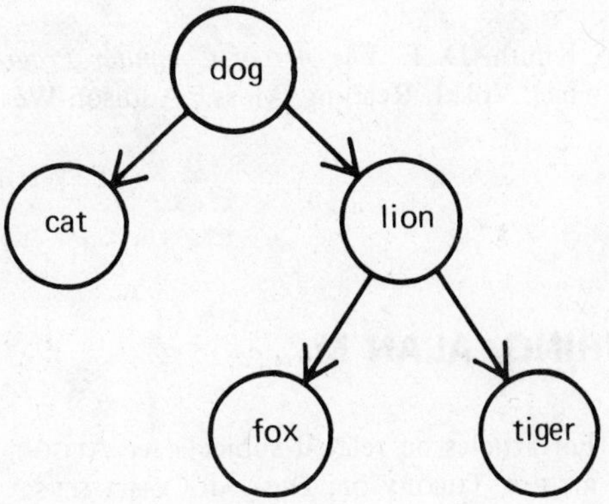


**Fig. 5.** Tree used for information retrieval.

The tree structure representing a given set of sorted words depends on the order in which the words are presented during the construction of the tree. However, the tree representation of the sorted words is convenient, both because of the ease with which new words may be added to the structure and because the number of accesses in general depends on the logarithm of the number of words in the tree.

Trees are used in the analysis of strategies for games such as chess and checkers. In this case, the vertices of the tree represent positions in the game, and a given vertex has as its successors all vertices that can be reached in one move from the given position. The set of all continuations of a game from a given position can be represented by a tree having the given position as its root vertex. The set of all games can be represented by a tree having the initial position as its root vertex. Each path through the tree from the root vertex to a terminal vertex represents a complete game.

It has been estimated that the complete game tree for checkers has about $10^{40}$ vertices, while the complete game tree for chess has about $10^{120}$ vertices.

## TURING, ALAN M.

Complete game trees for most nontrivial games are much too large to be exhaustively searched or even stored in a computer. In developing strategies for playing games such as chess and checkers, *tree-pruning strategies* must be used to prune the complete game tree, creating subtrees that explore a limited number of continuations for a limited number of moves. Strategies for playing chess and checkers on a computer are effectively strategies for deciding how the complete game tree should be pruned, and for choosing a move on the basis of information in the pruned game tree.

REFERENCE

1968. Knuth, D. E. *The Art of Computer Programming,* Vol. 1. Reading, Mass.: Addison-Wesley.

P. WEGNER

**Fig. 1.** Alan Mathison Turing.

# TURING, ALAN M.

For articles on related subjects *see* ALGORITHMS, THEORY OF; DIGITAL COMPUTERS: Early; and TURING MACHINES.

For articles on related terms *see* BABBAGE, CHARLES; EDVAC; and VON NEUMANN, JOHN.

Alan Mathison Turing (1912–1954) was born in London, the son of Julius Mathison Turing of the Indian Civil Service and of Ethel Sara Turing (neé Stoney). The Stoneys were a family of considerable scientific distinction, three of them having been Fellows of the Royal Society.

From an early age, Alan Turing showed an extraordinary aptitude for science and mathematics, and in 1931 he entered King's College Cambridge as a Mathematical Scholar. He was clearly bored with the rather trivial first-year course, and gained only a second class in Part I of the Mathematical Tripos. At the end of the third year, however, he was a Wrangler, and gained a distinction in the advanced papers. He was elected a Fellow of King's in 1935 for a dissertation on the Central Limit Theorem of Probability. Characteristically he rediscovered this, being quite unaware of previous work. The following year he was awarded a Smith's Prize for his thesis on the same topic.

It was in 1935 that he first became interested in mathematical logic, and in 1937 he published his now celebrated paper "On Computable Numbers with an Application to the Entscheidungsproblem," in which he introduced the concept of a Turing machine. This paper attracted immediate attention and led to an invitation to Princeton, where he worked with Alonzo Church. He took his Ph.D. there in 1938, the subject of his thesis being "Systems of Logic based on Ordinals." Turing contemplated staying in the United States and was offered a post as assistant to von Neumann, but in 1938 he decided to return to Cambridge. Until the outbreak of war, he worked on "A Method for the Calculation of the Zeta-Function," a topic to which he was to return in later years.

During World War II, Turing (being of military age) was required to work on government scientific research. He spent 1939–1945 at the British Foreign Office on work of a highly confidential nature, which has not yet been declassified. For his work he was awarded the Officer Order of the British Empire (OBE). It is certain that in this period he gained a detailed knowledge of pulse techniques, and this was to have a decisive influence on his subsequent career. In 1942 he visited the United States on official business. During this visit he had the opportunity to see the latest work on computers and to renew old contacts at Princeton.

In 1945 he declined an offer of a Fellowship at Kings' in favor of joining the newly formed Mathematics Division at the National Physical Laboratory (NPL). His early work on computability, combined with his wartime experience in electronics, had fired him with an enthusiasm for working on the design of an electronic computer. The machine he designed, which was called the Automatic Computing Engine (ACE) in recognition of Babbage's pioneering work, was characteristically original. Although Turing knew something of the von Neumann proposals for EDVAC, he was not unduly influenced by them. The ACE, as Turing conceived it, was too ambitious a project, considering the current state of electronic techniques. Therefore, he left NPL in 1948, dissatisfied with the rate of progress.

While in the Mathematics Division of NPL, Turing became keenly interested in numerical analysis. His paper, "Rounding-off Errors in Matrix Processes," showed that the acute anxiety about the effect of rounding errors in Gaussian elimination was largely unjustified. This paper has been overshadowed to some extent by the von Neumann and Goldstine paper on matrix inversion, but it is a brilliant piece of work and would have repaid a closer study at the time. After Turing left NPL, it was decided to build a pilot model embodying Turing's ideas (the Pilot ACE), and this was completed in 1950. It was a highly successful computer and some 30 engineered versions of it were subsequently constructed by the English Electric Company under the name DEUCE. The original Pilot ACE is in the Science Museum in Kensington, London.

On leaving NPL, Turing was appointed to a Readership at Manchester University, where he worked in close collaboration with F. C. Williams and T. Kilburn, both pioneers in the electronic computer field. He was elected a Fellow of the Royal Society in 1951. Papers published while he was at Manchester include further work on the Riemann zeta-function, a remarkable discussion on computing machinery and intelligence and the impressive chemical basis of morphogenesis. The latter was his main interest at that time, and he left uncompleted another substantial paper on the same topic.

Turing died tragically in 1954 at the age of 41. His publications, impressive though some of them are, give only the merest hint of his extraordinary originality and versatility. In recognition of his outstanding pioneering work, the ACM has named its most prestigious award, The Turing Award. It is awarded annually for contributions to computer science of a technical nature.

REFERENCES

1955. Newman, M. H. A. *The Biographical Memoirs of Fellows of the Royal Society,* Vol. 1. London: The Royal Society, pp. 253–263.

1959. Turing, Sarah. *A. M. Turing.* Cambridge: Heffer & Sons.

1970. Wilkinson, J. H. "Some Comments from a Numerical Analyst" (The 1970 A. M. Turing Lecture), *JACM,* Vol. 18, No. 2, pp. 137–147.

J. H. WILKINSON

# TURING MACHINE

For articles on related subjects *see* ALGORITHMS, THEORY OF; AUTOMATA THEORY; SEQUENTIAL MACHINES; and TURING, ALAN M.

For article on related term *see* PAPER TAPE.

A Turing machine is an abstract computing device invented by Alan M. Turing in 1936. A reprint of his original paper appears in Davis (1965). A Turing machine consists of (1) a *control unit,* which can assume any one of a finite number of possible states; (2) a *tape,* marked off into discrete squares, each of which can store a single symbol, taken from a finite set of possible symbols; and (3) a *read-write head,* which moves along the tape and transmits information to and from the control unit (see Fig. 1).

**The Basic Model.** A Turing machine computes via a sequence of discrete steps. Its behavior at a given point in time is completely determined by the symbol currently being scanned by the read-write head, and by the internal state of the control unit. On a given step, it will write a symbol on the tape, move along the tape at most one square to the left or right, and enter a new internal state. The new symbol is permitted to be the same as the current symbol; similarly, it is permissible to stay on the same tape square on a given step and/or to reenter the same state. Certain symbol-state situations may cause the machine to halt.

For example, on a single step the machine in Fig. 1 could begin in state $q_3$, change the *A* under scan to an *E*, move left one square and enter state $q_5$. It would now be scanning a *T*; its next action would be uniquely determined by the new state $q_5$ and the fact that it was scanning a *T*. It would continue indefinitely in this step-by-step fashion unless it

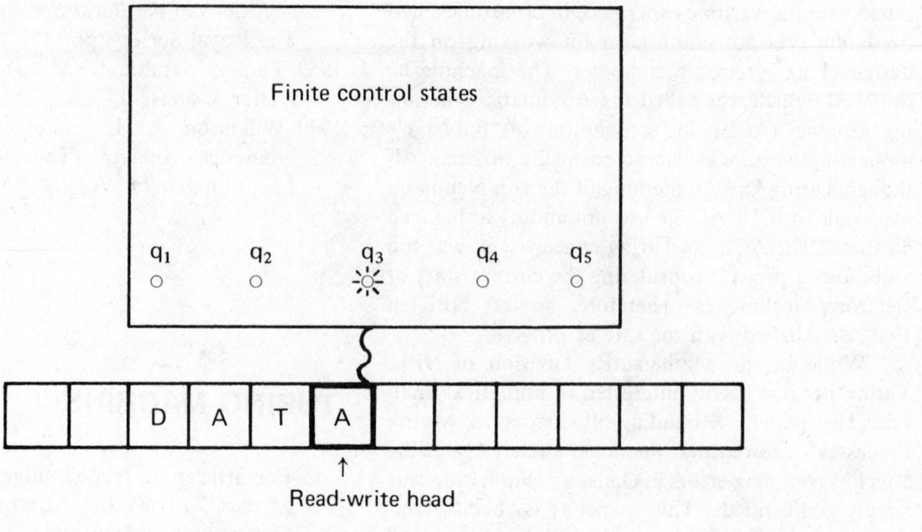


**Fig. 1.** Architecture of a Turing machine.

reached a state-symbol combination, causing it to halt.

The tape of a Turing machine is often depicted as infinite, and some persons view this idealization as hopelessly unrealistic. A better approach is to view the tape as finite but indefinitely extendible; i.e, new blank squares can be attached to either end of the tape at will to prevent the machine from running off the tape. Thus, there is no uniform bound on either the time or space used by a Turing machine; both are allowed to grow indefinitely.

The *program* of a Turing machine defines its action for the various state-symbol combinations that are possible. This program can be presented in a number of different ways, e.g., state transition diagrams, assembly-like languages, etc. The two most common ways are a tabular form and representation as a set of quintuples. Each state-symbol combination is represented by either an entry in the table or a single quintuple in the set. In the quintuple convention, the action described above would have been due to the presence of the quintuple

$$\langle q_3, A, E, L, q_5\rangle$$

where we abbreviate left, right, and no-shift by *L,R,N,* respectively.

An example of a Turing machine in tabular form is now presented. The state set of this machine *M* corresponds to rows in Table 1 and the symbol set (alphabet) to columns. The blank symbol is denoted by *B*. *M* will compute the function $f(x) = 2^x$ according to the following conventions:

1. $x$ and $f(x)$ are written as binary integers.
2. The tape initially contains $x$ and is blank elsewhere.
3. *M* begins in state $q_1$, scanning the leftmost bit of $x$.
4. When it halts, $f(x)$ will be the only nonblank item on the tape.

**Table 1.** Program for *M*

| Present State | B is scanned write/shift/state | 0 is scanned write/shift/state | 1 is scanned write/shift/state | Comment |
|---|---|---|---|---|
| $q_1$ | 1, $L$, $q_7$ | 0, $R$, $q_1$ | 1, $R$, $q_2$ | Is $x$ 0? |
| $q_2$ | $B$, $R$, $q_3$ | 0, $R$, $q_2$ | 1, $R$, $q_2$ | $x \neq 0$ |
| $q_3$ | 0, $L$, $q_4$ | 0, $R$, $q_3$ | Error | Write a new 0 |
| $q_4$ | $B$, $L$, $q_5$ | 0, $L$, $q_4$ | Error | Go back to $x$ |
| $q_5$ | Error | 1, $L$, $q_5$ | 0, $L$, $q_6$ | Decrease $x$ |
| $q_6$ | $B$, $R$, $q_1$ | 0, $L$, $q_6$ | 1, $L$, $q_6$ | Go to starting positio |
| $q_7$ | Halt | $B$, $L$, $q_7$ | Error | Clean up |

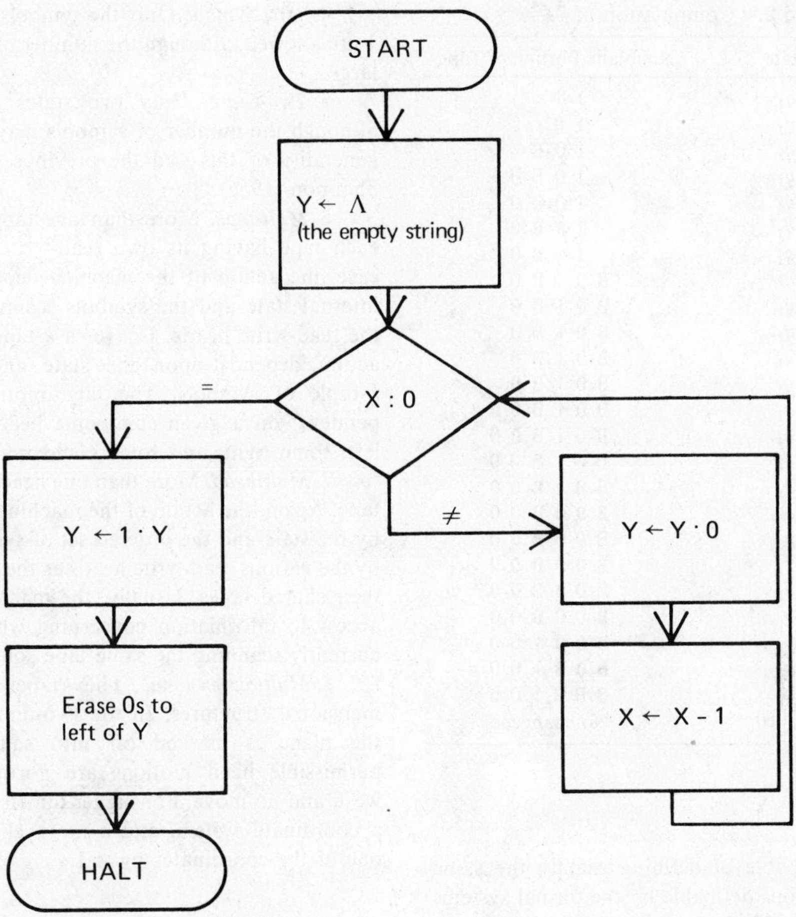


**Fig. 2.** Flowchart for $M$.

The algorithm used is given by the flowchart in Fig. 2. Essentially, each time the string that initially represents $x$ is changed to represent the next smaller integer, a 0 is written on the tape to the right of $x$. When $x$ has been decreased to 0, a 1 is written to the left of the generated string of $x$ zeros. The zeros to the left of the 1 are then erased, and $M$ halts. As is often the case, the algorithm is best thought of as an exercise in symbol manipulation rather than as arithmetic.

The entries in Table 1 labeled "error" cannot occur in a normal computation. By convention, $M$ would halt if started in such state-symbol situations.

An *instantaneous description* (total machine configuration) of a machine consists of the entire set of machine conditions at a given point in a computation, i.e., the contents of the tape, the position of the read-write head on the tape, and the internal state of the machine. A computation, then, is simply an entire history of instantaneous descriptions beginning with the start configuration and ending with a halt configuration. Table 2 gives the computation of the machine $M$ when started in state $q_1$ on the input 10 (binary 2). The symbol scanned is set in boldface type. Note that when $M$ halts, its read-write head is not scanning the leftmost digit of the output 100; the reader is invited to add one more state to $M$ and get it to do this.

**Modified Turing Machines.** Turing's original model has been altered in a number of ways by a number of different authors. In each of the cases discussed below, it has been proved that the altered model and the original model can each compute the same class of functions. This is done by showing that for every machine of a given type, there exists a standard Turing machine which can simulate its behavior, and conversely. Turing machines have also

**Table 2.** Computation of *M*

| Time | State | Nonblank Portion of Tape |
|---|---|---|
| 0 | $q_1$ | **1** 0 |
| 1 | $q_2$ | 1 **0** |
| 2 | $q_2$ | 1 0 **B** |
| 3 | $q_3$ | 1 0 B **B** |
| 4 | $q_4$ | 1 0 **B** 0 |
| 5 | $q_5$ | 1 **0** B 0 |
| 6 | $q_5$ | **1** 1 B 0 |
| 7 | $q_6$ | **B** 0 1 B 0 |
| 8 | $q_1$ | B **0** 1 B 0 |
| 9 | $q_1$ | B 0 **1** B 0 |
| 10 | $q_2$ | B 0 1 **B** 0 |
| 11 | $q_3$ | B 0 1 B **0** |
| 12 | $q_3$ | B 0 1 B 0 **B** |
| 13 | $q_4$ | B 0 1 B **0** 0 |
| 14 | $q_4$ | B 0 1 **B** 0 0 |
| 15 | $q_5$ | B 0 **1** B 0 0 |
| 16 | $q_6$ | B **0** 0 B 0 0 |
| 17 | $q_6$ | **B** 0 0 B 0 0 |
| 18 | $q_1$ | B **0** 0 B 0 0 |
| 19 | $q_1$ | B 0 **0** B 0 0 |
| 20 | $q_1$ | B 0 0 **B** 0 0 |
| 21 | $q_7$ | B 0 **0** 1 0 0 |
| 22 | $q_7$ | B **0** B 1 0 0 |
| 23 | $q_7$ | **B** B B 1 0 0 |
| 24 | Halted | No change |

been shown capable of defining exactly the same classes of functions definable by the formal systems of Kleene, Church, Rosser, Markov, and others. Church's thesis and *Turing's Thesis* assert that their respective models correctly capture the mathematical notion of effective computability, i.e., of explicit algorithmic processes. Since the models are equivalent in the sense given above, the two theses are equivalent.

The following list contains some of the more common variations that do not affect the classes of functions which can be computed (although the efficiency of a computation may change with the model).

1. *Post-Davis*. The machine cannot both change the symbol under scan and move along the tape on the same step (Davis, 1958).
2. *One-ended Tape*. The tape can be extended to the right, but not to the left. Thus, the read-write head could fall off the left end of the tape.
3. *Paper Tape*. A blank square can have a nonblank symbol written on it, but this symbol cannot be changed thereafter.
4. *Two-Symbol*. Only the symbols *B* (blank) and 1 are allowed, although the number of states may be large.
5. *Two-State*. Only two states are permitted, although the number of symbols may be large. The generality of this and the previous case is due to Shannon (1956).
6. *Multitape*. More than one tape is permitted, each tape having its own read-write head. In this case, the action of the machine depends upon the internal state and the symbols scanned by each of the read-write heads; i.e., for a *k*-tape machine, the action depends upon the state and an ordered *k*-tuple of symbols. The tape motions are independent; on a given step some heads could move left, some right, and some could remain in place.
7. *Multihead*. More than one head is allowed per tape. Again, the action of the machine is determined by the state and the ordered set of symbols scanned by the various read-write heads as they crawl around their shared tapes. Usually, the machine is allowed access to information concerning which heads are currently scanning the same tape square.
8. *Multidimensional*. The "tapes" are multidimensional structures. In the two-dimensional case, the plane is marked off into squares and the permissible head motions are north, south, east, west, and no move. For higher dimensions, one uses a coordinate system, and a move changes at most one of the coordinates by $\pm 1$.

**Advantages of Turing's Model.** The usefulness of the Turing model of computation lies in its simplicity, despite which it has all the fundamental properties that a computing system must possess: a finite program, a large data store, and a deterministic step-by-step mode of computation. In particular, one can show that any computer can be simulated (albeit rather slowly) by a Turing machine. The converse is also true, provided provisions are made to handle larger amounts of storage as needed.

For example, it is true that a minicomputer with an accumulator and "sufficiently large" storage can do any computation with only the instructions SUBTRACT, STORE, and TRANSFER ON MINUS, if one assumes the usual conventions of a single-address von Neumann machine. It is much easier to prove this by showing how to simulate a Turing machine on the minicomputer rather than by attempting to simulate all of the instructions of a large-scale computer.

Since a Turing machine can simulate any computing device, it follows that anything that cannot be computed on a Turing machine cannot be computed at all. The fact that there are such unsolvable problems motivated Turing to devise his abstract machine. This has also given rise to the theory of algorithms.

Turing machines can also simulate each other by interpretive procedures. In particular, it is possible to program a Turing machine to accept the description of the program and input data of any other Turing machine computation, and to simulate that computation. Such a machine is called a "universal" Turing machine.

Although Turing machines have probably been studied theoretically more than other abstract computing devices, two other models deserve mention. A *random-access machine* looks much like a single-address computer and stores its data in a finite number of cells. The idealization used here is that each cell can store any integer, and hence must have an unbounded number of bits. An *iterative array* consists of a network of finite-state sequential machines. Again, an unbounded memory is needed; this is achieved by allowing the network to be expanded in the middle of a computation, if necessary. Iterative arrays are useful in studying certain kinds of parallel processes.

**Time Complexity of Turing Machine Computations.** A number of theoretical results have shown that studying the complexity of Turing machine computations can yield insight into the efficiency of computations on real hardware. Within a broad range of conditions, the cost of a computation on a Turing machine (e.g., the number of steps required) is within a polynomial function of the cost of any machine with a finite number of processors. If the real Turing machine has at least two tapes, the relationship to cost on a real machine will often be linear.

On the other hand, Turing machine time studies are insensitive to a constant factor, i.e., computations on a multitape Turing machine can always be sped up by a factor of 2 by increasing the symbol set so as to pack at least two symbols of the original alphabet on a tape square. (Some additional programming is required to make this work in all cases.) Doubling the speed of real machines, on the other hand, cannot be achieved without either a technological breakthrough or increase in the cost of the hardware, and hence the cost per machine hour.

The Post-Davis, one-ended tape, and two-state variants introduced in the preceding section can be made to run as fast as ordinary (one-tape) Turing machines. The two-symbol variant will run within a constant factor of the others, but since the number of symbols is fixed, the speed-up trick may not be employed.

Although the multihead variant appears to be more powerful than the multitape model, P. Fischer, A. Meyer, and A. Rosenberg have shown that the two variants are equivalent in a very strong sense. Any multihead machine can be replaced by an equally fast equivalent multitape machine (but with perhaps a greater total number of heads).

On the other hand, one-tape Turing machines cannot always simulate multitape machines without loss of time. There exist examples for which the time on the one-tape machine must be the square of the multitape machine time. Thus, multitape (and multihead and multidimensional) machines are more efficient than ordinary Turing machines. For this reason, the multitape model is probably the most useful model for efficiency studies, although the one-tape version is better for computability-noncomputability investigations because of its greater simplicity.

The squaring of time to go from a multitape machine to a one-tape machine is never exceeded. In fact, any variant of a Turing machine with a bounded number of processors requiring time $t$ for a computation can be simulated by an ordinary Turing machine in time at most $t^2$.

When considering multitape Turing machines with different numbers of tapes, some interesting questions remain unsolved. Aanderaa has shown that for any $k$, certain problems can be solved faster on a $k$-tape machine than on a $(k-1)$-tape machine. However, the amount of saving cannot be large, since Hennie and Stearns have shown that any multitape machine requiring time $t$ can be simulated by a two-tape Turing machine in time at most $t\,(\log_2 t)$. Whether this bound can be improved is still an open question.

REFERENCES

1956. Shannon, C. E., and J. McCarthy (Eds.). *Automata Studies*. Princeton, N.J.: Princeton University Press.

1958. Davis, Martin. *Computability and Unsolvability*. New York: McGraw-Hill.

1965. Davis, Martin (Ed.). *The Undecidable*. Hewlett: Raven Press.

P. C. FISCHER

# TURNAROUND TIME

For articles on related subjects *see* Job; and Task.

Turnaround time is the elapsed time from the time a job is submitted to be run on a computer until the results are available. From the point of view of the input/output data control clerk, turnaround extends from the time when the job arrives for processing, to the time when the job deck and report(s) are dispatched to the user. From the machine operator's point of view, it lasts only from the time he loads the job deck into the card reader until the last line of the report has been printed.

But from the user's point of view, turnaround time is the period that begins when the job is delivered to the point at which it is dispatched to the computing center, and ends when his output is delivered to the point where he picks it up. These points may be at the computing center itself, in which case the turnaround time for the user is the same as for the data control clerk. But if the user is sufficiently remote from the computing center to require a courier service for pickup and delivery, then his turnaround time is longer, perhaps considerably so, than that of the data control clerk. These various differences often give rise to a great deal of lively discussion about computing center performance between users and the staff of the computing center.

In time-sharing systems, the time elapsed between sending a line of input and the computer acceptance of it (when possibly some acknowledgment is returned) is a form of turnaround time called "response time."

Typical computing center turnaround times vary from a few minutes to a few hours (with most being closer to the latter), while response times should be no more than a few seconds (say 10, at most).

Turnaround time from a communications standpoint is the length of time required to reverse a communication line from the send mode to the receive mode. Since messages in some applications are very short (and must be verified through return of some signal), the turnaround time can be as long or longer than the time required to send the message or return the verification. Therefore it becomes an important consideration in investigation of line efficiency.

C. L. Meek

# TURNKEY

For article on related subject *see* Service Bureaus, Data Processing.

Turnkey preparation of a facility means that a single contractor acquires and sets up all necessary premises, equipment, supplies, and operating personnel. All the customer needs to do is "turn the key" to begin full and effective usage of his new facility. Sometimes the contractor continues to operate the facility for the customer (usually called "facilities management"); in other cases, the customer assumes operational control.

Turnkey facilities are appropriate for customers who are unable to perform (or wish to avoid) their own subcontracting for ordering and testing components acquired from several different vendors. Recruiting, screening, and training a technical staff is also a highly specialized and sensitive task. A turnkey contractor earns his fee by either imposing surcharges on each item or service procured for the facility or committing in advance to a fixed price, from which he disburses funds to procure the items and services, pocketing the difference.

D. N. Freeman

## ULTRASONIC MEMORY

For article on related subject *see* MEMORY; Main.
For articles on related terms *see* EDSAC; EDVAC; and UNIVAC.

Ultrasonic memories played an important role in the early development of digital computers, but are now mainly of historical interest. The report on the EDVAC drafted by von Neumann in June 1945 on behalf of the group at the Moore School of Electrical Engineering, Philadelphia, clearly envisaged this type of memory, although it did not describe the physical principles on which it operated. Of the early machines, the EDSAC, SEAC, Pilot ACE, EDVAC, and UNIVAC all had ultrasonic memories.

The principle is illustrated in Fig. 1. A train of pulses representing the numbers to be stored is

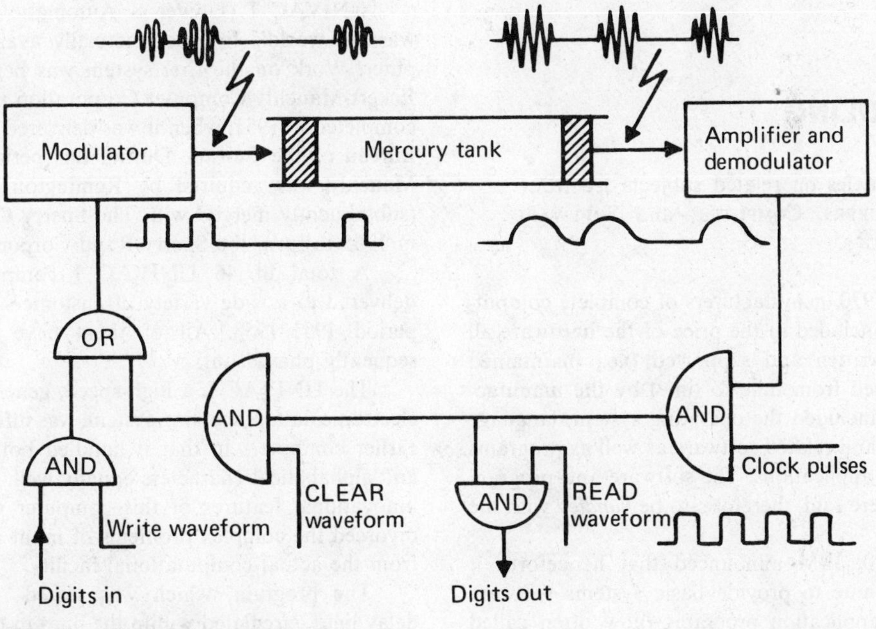


**Fig. 1.** Ultrasonic memory.

modulated onto a carrier and applied to a piezoelectric crystal in contact with a column of mercury. The ultrasonic pulses so generated travel along the column until they reach another crystal at the far end. This converts them back into electric signals, which are amplified and rectified. The resulting pulses are applied to a gate together with pulses from a continuously running clock pulse generator. This gating operation serves the twin purposes of regeneration and synchronization. The emerging pulses, which are exact replicas of the original pulses, are reapplied to the modulator and continue to circulate. The operations of reading, clearing, and writing can be performed by applying to the gates shown suitable waveforms accurately synchronized with the clock. A typical main memory consisted of a group of 32 tanks, as the columns were called, each between 0.5 and 1.5 meters long and giving a delay of between one-third and 1 ms.

In the mid-1950s, ultrasonic memories using a fine nickel wire in the form of a coil as the propagation medium appeared in some low-cost computers. The waves were excited by making use of the magnetostrictive properties of the nickel.

REFERENCE

1956. Wilkes, M. V. *Automatic Digital Computers*. New York: John Wiley.

M. V. WILKES

# UNBUNDLING

For articles on related subjects *see* MANUFACTURERS, COMPUTER; and SOFTWARE PACKAGES.

Until 1970, manufacturers of complete computer systems included in the price of the hardware all programs written and supported (i.e., maintained and improved from time to time) by the manufacturer. This included the operating system, language processors, and related software as well as programs for specific applications. The software and program packages were said, therefore, to be *bundled* with the hardware.

In 1970, IBM announced that henceforth it would continue to provide basic systems software and some application programs (now often called "program packages") with the hardware, but that other packages (and other previously bundled services, such as educational services) would be charged for separately and would thus be *unbundled*. Other manufacturers followed IBM's lead, and today virtually all manufacturers have unbundled significant amounts of their support, although basic systems software continues to be bundled.

Types of programs that are typically unbundled are very large applications packages whose cost of development is substantial (e.g., linear programming packages), and language processors that are expected to be used by only a small number of customers.

A. S. DOUGLAS

# UNIVAC. *See* MANUFACTURERS, COMPUTER.

# UNIVAC I

For articles on related subjects *see* DIGITAL COMPUTERS: Early; ECKERT, J. PRESPER; and MAUCHLY, JOHN W.

UNIVAC I (Universal Automatic Computer) was the world's first commercially available computer. Work on the first system was begun by the Eckert-Mauchly Computer Corporation in 1948 and completed in 1951, when it was delivered to the U.S. Bureau of the Census. During this period, Eckert-Mauchly was acquired by Remington Rand Inc. (subsequently merged with The Sperry Corporation in 1955 to form the Sperry-Rand Corporation).

A total of 46 UNIVAC I computers were delivered to a wide variety of customers during the period 1951–1958. All of them have been subsequently phased out.

The UNIVAC I, a high-speed, general-purpose electronic data processing system, was different from earlier computers in that it handled both numbers and alphabetical characters equally well. One of the innovational features of this computer was that it divorced the complex problems of input and output from the actual computational facility.

The program, which was stored in mercury delay lines, circulated within the lines in the form of acoustical pulses that could be read from the line

Fig. 1. UNIVAC 1.

and written into it. Information could be accessed at a speed of 40 to 400 millionths of a second.

Raw data was transcribed to magnetic tape by a key-to-tape device. Data on punched cards was transcribed to magnetic tape with a card-to-tape converter. Magnetic tape was the principal input medium and was also used for permanent storage of data. Input could also be effected from the keyboard of the control console during the processing of a program.

Output was recorded on magnetic tape. Data on output tapes was transcribed to punched cards by a tape-to-card converter or to printed copy by a printer. Alphabetical, numeric, and symbolic characters were accommodated in any combination in reading, writing, and processing operations.

Buffered storage registers permitted the central computer to continue processing while other data was being read from, or recorded on, magnetic tape. The system featured many automatic self-checking techniques, including duplicate circuits for all computing operations.

The operating characteristics were as follows: circuitry—chiefly serial, 2.25 MHz bit rate; Internal Operating Code—7 bits (four numeric pulses in excess-three notation, two zone pulses, and one parity pulse); word length, 12 characters including sign; block length, 60 words; program code, single address, automatic sequencing; internal storage capacity, 1,000 words or 12,000 characters.

The speed of the basic arithmetic functions were: addition or subtraction, 0.525 ms; multiplication, 2.150 ms; division, 3.890 ms; comparison, 0.365 ms.

M. M. Maynard

# UNIVAC SCIENTIFIC EXCHANGE (USE)

For article on related subject *see* Computer User Groups.

In December 1955, four prospective users of UNIVAC 1103A computers and company representatives met in Los Angeles to organize the user's group for large-scale UNIVAC scientific computers, UNIVAC Scientific Exchange, or USE. Over the succeeding three months, policies and objectives were established and three committees were formed: Standards, Programming, and Publications.

These committees soon achieved a number of significant accomplishments. These included development of a language for communications, known as the USE language; the development of standard formats for coding routines and subroutines; and the definition of a minimum USE 1103A.

Probably the most significant undertaking of the group was the production of a compiler known as the USE compiler. This was in fact an assembler with advanced characteristics for the period in which it was produced. It was used successfully for several years.

During the early years of USE, an extensive library of routines and subroutines were distributed to all members and other interested groups.

As the organization expanded, the working committees became the primary structures for determining the activities of the organization and the areas of mutual interest. When a particular interest outgrew the bounds of an existing committee, a new committee was formed to investigate the subject.

As newer computers entered the Sperry UNIVAC product line, USE membership policies were amended to extend invitations to users of the newer computers. In 1964 it was decided to substitute the term "UNIVAC Large-Scale Scientific Computers" rather than refer to specific computer models. In May 1966, the term "Scientific" was removed.

Over the years, USE has cooperated in many activities in the computer field. For example, a USE representative was a member of the United States delegation to the committee that developed Algol. Subsequently, USE members were involved with Codasyl in the development of Cobol.

Some members of USE also maintain memberships in the other large UNIVAC users' group, known as UUA (UNIVAC Users' Association), an organization open to the user of any UNIVAC computing system. In 1961, a joint committee was formed, composed of three representatives of USE and UUA, to work out methods of closer cooperation. Several joint conferences were held by USE and UUA between 1965 and 1968. The growth of both organizations led to separate meetings after 1968.

The USE governing body today is a seven-member Board of Governors. It consists of a president and vice-president, each elected for a two-year term; three other members, one elected each year, serving for three years; the past president, who serves for a two-year period; and the executive secretary, who is a nonvoting member designated by Sperry-Rand.

The next level of management within USE is the Administrative Committee composed of the working group chairmen, service group chairmen, and special interest group chairmen, together with members of the Board of Governors. This committee is chaired by the vice-president.

At present, USE has a membership of about 200 organizations. Two general meetings attended by over 600 persons are held each year, one in the spring and the other in the fall. Presidents elected in the period 1955–1974 are as follows:

Walter F. Bauer, 1955
Randall E. Porter and Jules Mersel, 1956
R. B. Talmadge, 1956–1957
R. P. Rich, 1957–1958
Donn Combelic, 1958
Jules Mersel, 1959
Dorothy P. Armstrong, 1959–1960
J. H. Dietrich, 1960–1961
Ben Mittman, 1961–1962
J. W. Hanson, 1962–1963
R. P. Castanias, 1963
J. W. Hanson and C. D. Card, 1964
Norman Moraff and E. D. P. Gross, 1965
Earl Boone, 1966–1968
Wayne Youtz, 1968–1970
Wayne Fuhrmann, 1970–1972
Bernard Peters, 1972–1974
Robert Lees, 1974–

M. M. MAYNARD

# UPDATE

For article on related subject *see* FILES.

To update information is to make more current or to bring up to date by adding, changing, or deleting information in a computer file. Examples are: adding in last week's earnings to bring an earnings record up to date; substituting more recent temperature and wind readings in reporting the latest weather; and keeping a class roster current by deleting the names of students who have moved away.

An update run, or simply an "update," is a computer run during which information (most commonly in files) is modified (by adding, deleting, or changing it) to make that information more current. Usually, at the time a tape or disk file is updated, the old file is copied (in the case of tape, transferred from an old reel of tape onto a new one). During the copying operation, additional items are inserted, changes are made to existing items, and deleted items are dropped. The old file is then retained in case an error was made in creating the new one, or in the event the new one might be damaged.

Tables (kept in storage) are also updated by adding, deleting, or changing information. In this case no copy of the old version is typically made; rather it is just altered, and the old version is thereby lost. This means that the superseded table is not reproducible, in contrast to the tape file update, which is reproducible for purposes of auditing or duplication.

C. L. MEEK

**USE.** *See* UNIVAC SCIENTIFIC EXCHANGE.

# UTILITY PROGRAM

For articles on related subjects *see* PROGRAM LIBRARIES; SORT-MERGE PACKAGES; and UPDATE.

A utility program is one provided by a computing center to its users to perform a task required by many or most of its users. The most common group of utility programs are those that copy information from one medium to another. Characteristically, they have names like "card-to-disk," "disk-to-print," "tape-to-tape," etc., and can handle different record lengths, blocking factors, etc. These programs usually do not inspect the information being copied, and therefore they are not used when a selection of records must be made or when records must be altered or deleted. Utility programs are used to streamline an operation. For example, it may be faster to write a file on disk initially (perhaps because the tape drives are tied up) for later copying to tape than to write the file directly onto tape.

These utility programs can be used to great advantage during debugging and testing to assure that the desired information is being written as intended. A programmer will copy a tape file or a disk file to the printer to see what it looks like. Although the output is usually very hard to read (columns will not line up, headings will not be present, and negative numbers may appear as alphabetic characters, all according to the conventions of the machine), it is adequate to check that the file is being written correctly.

Utility programs also include sort-merge programs and certain error-checking programs that locate bad spots on tape or disk, although the latter are more often included with diagnostics or diagnostic programs.

C. L. MEEK

# V

**Variables.** *See* Control Variable; and Global and Local Variables.

## VIENNA DEFINITION LANGUAGE

For articles on related subjects *see* Backus-Naur Form; Meta Language; Programming Linguistics; and Syntax, Semantics, and Pragmatics.

For articles on related terms *see* Tree.

The Vienna definition language (VDL) is a language for defining the syntax and semantics of programming languages. It consists of a *syntactic meta language* for defining the syntax of program and data structures and a *semantic meta language* that specifies programming language semantics "operationally" in terms of the computations to which programs give rise during execution.

Syntactic structures in VDL may be graphically represented by means of unordered trees whose edges are labeled by selectors. For example, the expression $a + b$ might be represented in VDL by any one of a set of equivalent unordered trees such as those in Fig. 1.

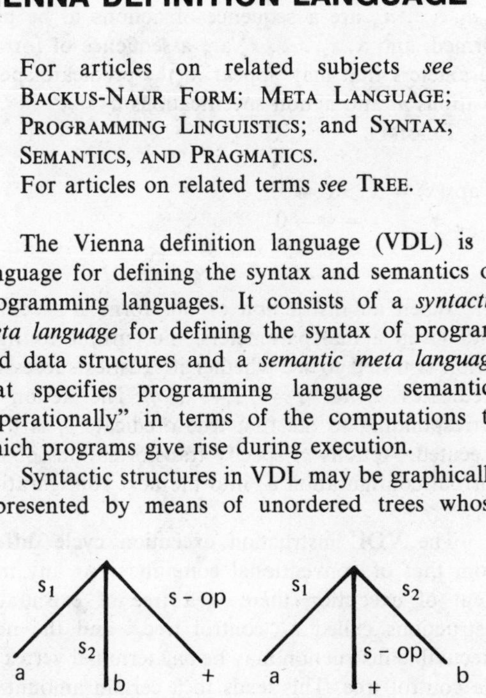


Fig. 1.

These tree ($t$) structures may in turn be represented in linear notation as

$$t = (\langle s_1{:}a\rangle\ \langle s_2{:}b\rangle,\ \langle s - \text{op}{:}+\rangle)$$

or

$$t = (\langle s_1{:}a\rangle,\ \langle s - \text{op}{:}+\rangle,\ \langle s_2{:}b\rangle)$$

Selectors in a VDL syntactic structure serve the same role as pointers in a list structure and may be used to select components of the syntactic structure by "applying" the selector to the syntactic structure. In the preceding example, $s_1(t)$, $s_2(t)$, $s - \text{op}(t)$ yield the respective components $a,b,+$.

Syntactic objects may be either *elementary (atomic) objects* with no components (such as the objects $a,b,+$ above) or *composite objects* (such as the tree $t$ above) whose components may be selected by selectors.

The syntactic meta language of VDL is illustrated by the following definition of a simple class of arithmetic expressions:

$$\text{expr} = \text{const} \vee \text{var} \vee \text{binary}$$
$$\text{binary} = (\langle s_1{:}\text{expr}\rangle,\ \langle s_2{:}\text{expr}\rangle,\ \langle s - \text{op}{:}\ \text{op}\rangle)$$
$$\text{op} = \{+, *\}$$

This definition specifies that an expression can be a constant (const), a variable (var), or a binary, where constants and variables are elementary objects with no components, and a binary is a composite object with two components of the type "expr" selectable by the selectors $s_1$, $s_2$, and a third component of the type "op" selectable by $s$ − op. The expression $a + b * c$ may be represented in terms of the preceding syntax by a tree structure whose edges are labeled by selectors as shown in Fig. 2.

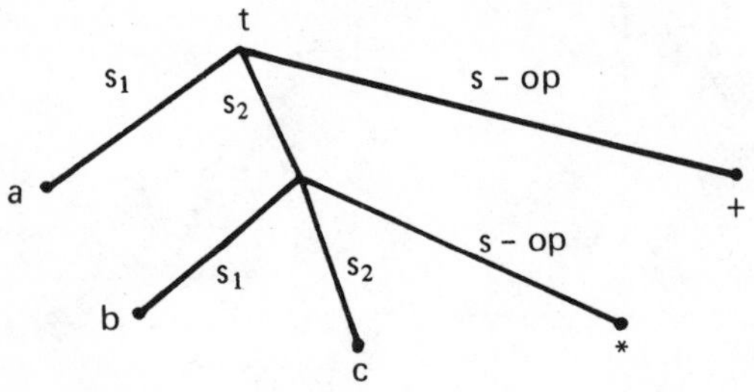


**Fig. 2.**

If the tree structure in Fig. 2 is denoted by $t$, then $s_1(t) = a$, $s_2(t) = b * c$, $s - \text{op}(t) = +$, $s_1 \cdot s_2(t) = b$, $s_2 \cdot s_2(t) = c$, and $s - \text{op} \cdot s_2(t) = *$.

The example illustrates that syntactic objects in VDL are represented by trees whose edges are labeled by selectors, and that components of a tree-structured syntactic object may be selected by specifying the sequence of selectors along the path from the root to the selected subtree.

It is instructive to contrast syntactic specification in VDL with syntactic specification of a corresponding class of expressions in BNF (Backus Naur form). The previously given class of arithmetic expressions could be specified in BNF as follows:

$$\begin{aligned} \langle \text{expr} \rangle &::= \langle \text{const} \rangle \mid \langle \text{var} \rangle \mid \langle \text{binary} \rangle \\ \langle \text{binary} \rangle &::= \langle \text{expr} \rangle \langle \text{op} \rangle \langle \text{expr} \rangle \\ \langle \text{op} \rangle &::= + \mid - \end{aligned}$$

The difference between the BNF and VDL syntactic meta languages is brought out by comparing the two specifications of binary. In BNF a binary is a string consisting of an expression followed by an operator followed by a second expression. In VDL a binary is a structure with three components selectable by the selectors $s_1$, $s_2$ and $s$ − op. If the representation for expressions were changed from infix to prefix notation, so that $a + b * c$ were written as $+a * bc$, then the BNF specification would have to be modified to reflect this change in order, but the VDL representation could remain the same. Because VDL specifies structure independently of the order in which components appear in a specific representation, a VDL syntactic specification is sometimes referred to as an "abstract syntax."

The *semantics* of a programming language is defined in VDL in terms of the sequences of information-structure transformations to which programs give rise during execution. Every computation starts with an initial configuration $\xi_0$, which contains a syntactic representation of both the program structure and the data structure on which the program is to operate. Terminating computations consist of a finite sequence of configurations $\xi_0 \rightarrow \xi_1 \rightarrow \cdots \rightarrow \xi_n$, where $\xi_{j+1}$ is obtained from $\xi_j$ by the execution of an instruction. The configurations $\xi_j$ are referred to as "instantaneous descriptions," "snapshots," or "states." The instructions form the heart of the semantic specification of a programming language and have the following general form of definition:

$$\begin{aligned} \text{instruction-name } (x_1, x_2, \ldots, x_n) = {} & p_1 \rightarrow a_1 \\ & p_2 \rightarrow a_2 \\ & \ldots \\ & p_m \rightarrow a_m \end{aligned}$$

where $p_1, p_2, \ldots, p_m$ are a sequence of predicates, $a_1, a_2, \ldots, a_m$ are a sequence of actions to be performed, and $x_1, x_2, \ldots, x_n$ are a sequence of formal parameters that may appear in the predicate specifications $p_i$ and action specifications $a_i$.

EXAMPLE

$$\begin{aligned} \text{abs}(x) = {} & x > 0 \rightarrow x \\ & x = 0 \rightarrow 0 \\ & x < 0 \rightarrow -x \end{aligned}$$

When an instruction of this form is executed with given actual parameters, the current configuration is tested to see whether it satisfies successive predicates $p_i$ for $i = 1, 2, \ldots, n$. The action $a_i$ corresponding to the first true predicate $p_i$ is then executed. Actions $a_i$ specify transformations of the current configuration $\xi_j$ into the next configuration $\xi_{j+1}$.

The VDL instruction execution cycle differs from that of conventional computers. At any moment of execution there is a tree of executable instructions called a "control tree," and the next executable instruction may be *any* terminal vertex of the control tree. This leads to a certain amount of nondeterminacy in the instruction execution process, which allows VDL to model nondeterminacy in specifying (for example) the order of execution for certain expressions in PL/I, and also to model nondeterminacy of execution in certain kinds of multitasking.

There are two kinds of instructions in VDL:

1. Self-replacing instructions, which when they are executed replace the terminal vertex of the control tree at which they occur by a subtree of instructions.

2. Value-returning instructions, which return a computed value to predecessor vertices of the control tree and delete the executed instruction from the control tree.

A computation in VDL generally starts with a control tree consisting of a single vertex containing an instruction such as interpret-program (*t*), where *t* is the syntactic specification of the program to be executed. The first few executed instructions are generally self-replacing instructions that generate successively larger control trees (determined by the abstract syntax of *t*) until terminal vertices corresponding to value-returning instructions are generated. Execution terminates when an empty control tree is generated.

The Vienna definition language was developed by Peter Lucas, Kurt Walk, and others at the IBM Vienna Laboratory. It has been applied to the definition of PL/I (Lucas and Walk, 1969), Basic (Lee, 1972), and a number of other programming languages. A more detailed introduction to the basic concepts of VDL may be found in Wegner (1972).

### References


1969. Lucas, P., and K. Walk. "On the Formal Description of PL/I," *Annual Review of Automatic Programming* Vol. 6, No. 9.

1972. Lee, J. A. N. *Computer Semantics*. New York: Van Nostrand-Rheinhold.

1972. Wegner, P. "The Vienna Definition Language," *Computing Surveys*, Vol. 4, pp. 5–63.


P. Wegner

## VIM

For articles on related subjects *see* Computer User Groups; and Control Data Corporation (CDC) 6000 Series.

VIM began as the "VIM Users Organization for Control Data Corporation (CDC) 6000 Series Computers." The first meeting was held in 1965 and was attended by representatives of ten organizations. The name "VIM" was suggested by Professor Max Goldstein, New York University, as the pseudo-Roman numeral representation of 6000. The group incorporated as VIM, Inc., in March 1970. The membership has been expanded to include organizations using CDC 6000, CDC 7000, and CDC CYBER series computer systems.

The membership of VIM, Inc., consists (as of October 1973) of 211 member organizations located in 24 countries throughout the world. The membership is almost evenly divided among universities, governmental agencies, and corporations.

The principal purposes of VIM are "to foster the development, free exchange and communication of research data pertaining to VIM computers among the users of VIM computers in the best scientific tradition and to provide a means of communication with the manufacturer of VIM computers."

Committees are the primary elements of communication for achieving the purposes of VIM. There are working committees for operating systems, software evaluation, scientific languages, business information systems, remote computing and graphics, installation management and products, user developments and communications, and documentation. The committees interface with manufacturers in the critical review of hardware and software products available for use in conjunction with VIM computers.

General meetings of VIM are held twice a year. The committees meet more frequently and are primarily responsible for providing the technical program at the general meetings.

VIM maintains a library of programs donated by member organizations. Publications of VIM include a catalog of the VIM library and a regular newsletter that contains copies of letters and other documents of interest to its members.

Past presidents of the VIM Users Organization, in order of service, are Kent K. Curtis, Ben H. Mount, Thomas R. Parkin, and Charles H. Warlick. Past presidents of VIM, Inc., are Dr. Warlick, William L. Evans, and F. William Rambo. The address of VIM is 8100 34th Avenue S, Minneapolis, Minn. 5540.

C. H. Warlick

# VIRTUAL MEMORY

For articles on related subjects *see* ADDRESSING; INTERRUPT; MEMORY: Main; OPERATING SYSTEMS: Principles and Theory; STORAGE ALLOCATION; STORAGE HIERARCHY; and TIME SHARING.

For articles on related terms, *see* BASE REGISTER; CACHE MEMORY; and MEMORY PROTECTION.

The term "virtual memory" (or virtual storage) denotes the main memory of a virtual (i.e., simulated) computer. Virtual memory can be characterized by the following concepts: address (or name) space, memory space, and address translation (or mapping). An address (or name) space $N$ of a program is the set of all addresses that can be generated by the processor as it executes the program (if the processor generates $a$-bit addresses, $N$ contains at most $2^a$ words). The memory space $M$ is the set of all location addresses recognized by the main memory hardware (if this hardware recognizes $b$-bit addresses, $M$ contains $2^b$ addresses).

Address translation is represented at each instant of time by a mapping $f: N \rightarrow M$, such that $f(x)$ gives the location address of virtual address $x$ if $x$ has been allocated space in $M$ and $f(x)$ is otherwise undefined. The physical interpretation of $f$ is that a device (the address-mapping mechanism) is interposed between the processor and memory, as shown in Fig. 1. Whenever the processor generates a reference to an $x$ for which $f(x)$ is defined, the mechanism presents address $f(x)$ to memory and allows the reference to proceed. Otherwise, if $f(x)$ is undefined, the mechanism generates an *addressing interrupt*; the interrupt handler will locate the missing piece of information in the auxiliary memory, move it into main memory (perhaps also moving out other information to make room), and update the representation of $f$ to show the changes. Then, when the interrupted program is resumed, it finds $f(x)$ defined and can proceed.

Two common examples of the system of Fig. 1 are the core/drum configuration, in which $M$ is a core memory and $A$ is a drum; and the cache/core configuration, in which $M$ is a high-speed semiconductor-register memory (called a "cache") and $A$ is a core memory (sometimes a slower speed semiconductor memory).

The name space $N$ implemented by a mechanism such as that mentioned above is frequently referred to as the "virtual address space" or the "virtual memory" within which the processor operates. Frequently, the size of $N$ exceeds the size of $M$, in which case the virtual memory system is given the responsibility of memory management; i.e., it determines which subset of $N$ resides in $M$ at any time. The virtual memory may also be smaller than the real memory; most systems using this alternative place all of $N$ in $M$, using the address translation mechanism to solve the relocation and protection problems. An example of the latter type of system is the CDC 6000 series; although it is not referred to explicitly as "virtual memory" in this case, it is nevertheless an example of the type of mechanism under discussion here.

**Implementation.** Implementing the address translation requires a representation for the mapping

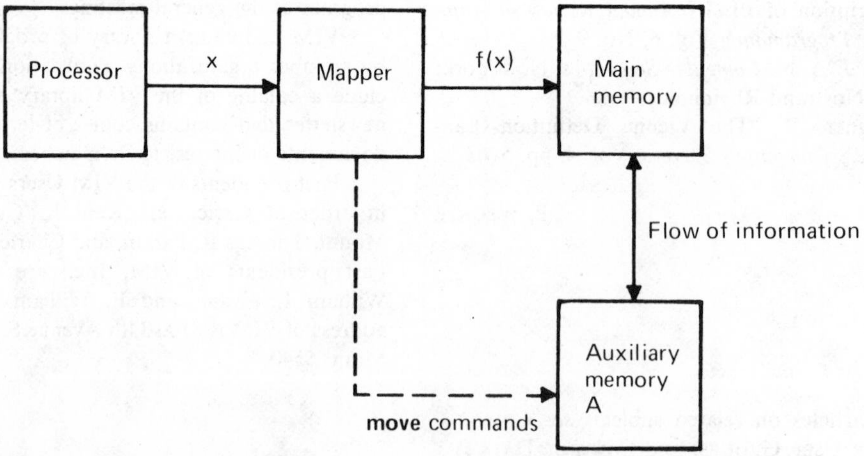


**Fig. 1.** The mapping function.

$f$, done usually in the form of a directly indexed table. However, implementing $f$ to contain one entry for each virtual address would (especially if $N$ is larger than $M$) require the untenable assumption of a storage space for the table $f$ larger than the main memory hardware space of the system.

To keep the number of entries in the table $f$ manageable, block-oriented mappings are used. (This has the added advantage that the blocks can be the same as those normally used as units of auxiliary memory storage and transfer.) In this case, $N$ is regarded as a collection of blocks, each being a set of contiguous addresses characterized by a base address and a length. A virtual address $x$ must be represented (or translated to) the form $(b, w)$, where $b$ is a block address and $w$ is a relative address (offset) in block $b$. The mapping table contains entries showing the correspondence between blocks of $N$ and $M$. The translation process consists of three steps:

$$x \to (b,w) \to (f(b),w) \to f(b) + w,$$

as shown in Fig. 2. The translation of $x$ to $(b,w)$ takes time $T_1$; the translation of $(b,w)$ to $(f(b),w)$ takes time $T_2$ (the time to look up $f(b)$ in the table); and the translation of $(f(b),w)$ to $f(b) + w$ takes time $T_3$ (the time to add two numbers).

The translation function would be considered impractical unless the total translation time $T_1 + T_2 + T_3$ can be made small compared to the memory reference time. Since the time to add two numbers is very small, $T_3$ is not normally an important quantity. Thus, the efficiency of the translation operation depends on $T_1 + T_2$.

The two most common methods of making $T_1$ negligible or zero are *segmentation* and *paging*. Segmentation is a technique used to partition the name space into blocks of various sizes (known as segments), usually corresponding to logical regions. In the Burroughs B5000 and later series, for example, the Algol compiler creates segments corresponding to the block structure of the language and the organization of the data. The Honeywell 6180 (which implements a segmented name space under "Multics") requires the programmer to define the segments and refer to words by symbolic two-part addresses of the form (segment-name, word-name).

In contrast to segmentation, paging is a technique used to partition the name space in blocks of the same size (known as pages). Since the page boundaries bear no prior relation to logical boundaries in the name space, the programmer is not generally apprised of the pagination of his name space; however, the compiler or loader may be designed to reorganize information among pages to improve performance when the cost of such reorganization (which is high) can be justified. As will be discussed below, the principal attraction of paging is the major simplifications it affords in systems design.

Returning to the discussion of Fig. 2, the name space is, under segmentation, partitioned into regions by the programmer or the compiler, and each region becomes a block. In this case all virtual memory references are programmed or compiled in the form of pairs $(b,w)$, whence $T_1 = 0$. In contrast,

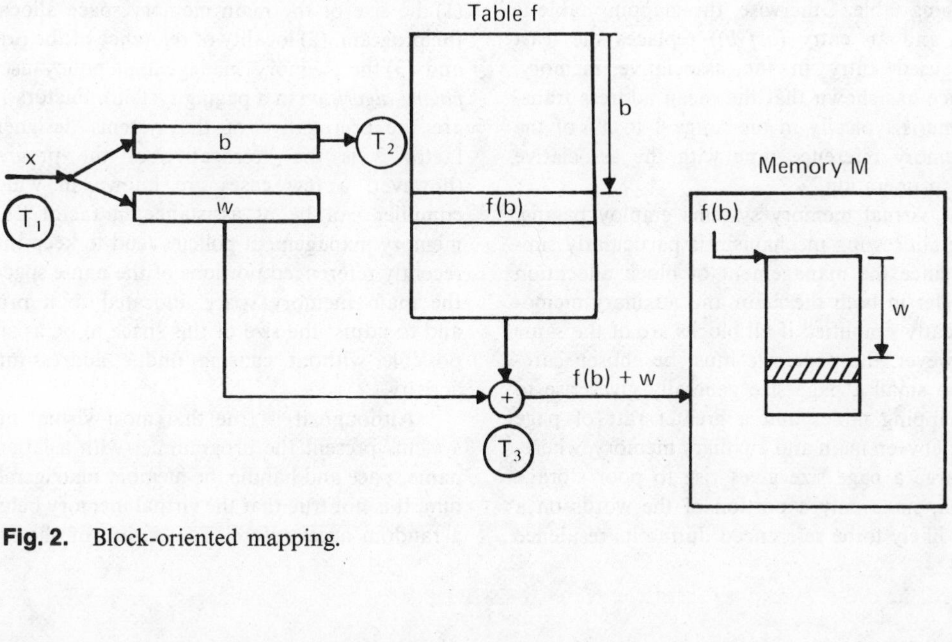


**Fig. 2.** Block-oriented mapping.

the name space is, under paging, partitioned into fixed-size blocks (pages). All addresses compiled in the program are linear offsets relative to the base of the name space. The computation $x \Rrightarrow (b,w)$ when the page size is $s$ words is specified by

$$(b,w) = ([x/s],\ x \bmod s) \tag{1}$$

where the brackets denote "integer part of" and $x \bmod s$ denotes the remainder in dividing $x$ by $s$ ($0 \leq x \bmod s < s$). If $s = 2^q$ (for some $q \geq 0$) and binary arithmetic is used, the computation (1) reduces to a triviality: $w$ is specified by the $q$ low-order bits of the register containing $x$, and $b$ is specified by the remaining bits. Thus, $T_1 = 0$ when paging is used.

Now, $T_2$ is the only time of significance in a paging or segmentation scheme. Most systems (especially multiple task systems) are unwilling to provide special hardware for storing the entire mapping table, the table being therefore relegated to main memory. Accordingly, the time $T_2$ would seem to be comparable with the main memory reference time, and the objective of making $T_1 + T_2 + T_3$ small would seem to be unrealizable. An ingenious solution using an associative memory with a much faster reference time than the main memory has been found. A small associative memory (typically containing at most 16 cells) is included in the mapping mechanism. Each cell contains an entry of the form $(x, f(x))$. When the block number $b$ of an address is determined, all the cells of the associative memory are searched in parallel. If an entry $(b, f(b))$ is found, the base address $f(b)$ of the block is available immediately without having to reference the mapping table. Otherwise, the mapping table is accessed and an entry $(b, f(b))$ replaces the least recently used entry in the associative memory. Experience has shown that the mean address translation time is typically in the range 1 to 3% of the main memory reference time with the associative memory in operation.

Most virtual memory systems employ paging, since the addressing mechanism is particularly simple and since the management of block allocation and transfer in both the main and auxiliary memories is greatly simplified if all blocks are of the same size. However, the page size must be chosen carefully. Too small a page size generally gives rise to larger mapping tables and a greater rate of page transfer between main and auxiliary memory, whereas too large a page size gives rise to poor storage utilization, since only a portion of the words on a page are likely to be referenced during its residence time in main memory. Paging alone, even if properly designed, does not alter the linear appearance of the name space, and thus cannot offer the programmer the significant programming advantages possible in a block-structured name space (such as can be offered with segmentation). A compromise using both segmentation and paging can be implemented for this purpose (see Denning, 1970 and 1971).

Memory protection is easily implemented under a virtual memory mechanism, another reason these mechanisms are so attractive. Clearly, no program can access any information other than what is in its address space, since each and every reference is translated with respect to the mapping table of the currently running program. Also, each entry of the mapping table (Fig. 2) is typically of the form

$$b\colon (d,\ f(b),\ pc,\ L)$$

where $d$ is a single bit set to 1 if and only if $f(b)$ is defined, $pc$ is a protection code indicating which types of access are permitted to block $b$ (e.g., read or write), and $L$ is the length of block $b$ (omitted in paging systems). If the word portion $w$ of the $(b,w)$ pair does not satisfy $0 \leq w < L$, or if the type of access being attempted is not authorized by $pc$, a protection interrupt is generated by the mapping mechanism (see Wilkes, 1973).

**Performance Considerations.** Because of the associative memory technique, address-translation time is not usually an important factor in the efficiency of program execution in a virtual memory. The factors that affect performance are, in decreasing order of their immediate effects on efficiency, (1) the size of the main memory space allocated to the program, (2) locality of reference of the program, and (3) the memory management policy used (the *paging algorithm* in a paging system). Factors 1 and 3 are the prerogative of the systems designer, and factor 2 is the prerogative of the programmer (however, a few cases are known in which the compiler can be of assistance in factor 2). Most memory management policies tend to keep the most recently referenced portions of the name space $N$ in the main memory space allocated to a program, and to adjust the size of this space to be as small as possible without causing undue address-interrupt activity.

Although it is true that most virtual memory systems present the programmer with a large linear name space and handle the memory management for him, it is not true that the virtual memory behaves as a random access store. The nature of the memory management policies causes the access time to an object in virtual memory to be short when the object or a neighbor has been referenced recently, and long otherwise. The programmer, therefore, can be confident of highly efficient operation of his program in a virtual memory only if he has successfully organized his algorithm and data: (1) to concentrate references in small ''localities'' of address space; (2) to avoid scattering references over a wide range of address space in short time intervals; and (3) to avoid sudden shifts in the address space locality into which references are concentrated.

REFERENCES

1970. Denning, P. J. "Virtual Memory," *Computing Surveys 2*, Vol. 3, pp. 153–189.
1971. "Third Generation Computer System," *Computing Surveys*, Vol. 3, pp. 175–216.
1972. Wilkes, M. V. *Time Sharing Computer Systems* (2d ed.). New York: American Elsevier.

P. J. DENNING

## VOLUME

For articles on related subjects *see* DATA SET; FILES; and LABEL.

A volume is a physical unit of a storage medium capable of having data recorded on it and subsequently read. The general meaning of the term is applied to volumes of books as well as to tape reels, drums, disk packs, etc., of the data processing world.

Just as there are single and multivolume books, there are also single and multivolume physical files, or data bases. Volumes consist of extents; each extent contains one or more pages (also called "blocks"). The size of a physical page is generally the function of the physical characteristics of the storage medium, of the computer main store architecture, and of the amount and structure of data.

Corresponding to the title page of a book, the first data element encountered on a volume, called the "data set label," should—and almost always does—identify the data base that (partially or in its entirety) resides on it, the volume number, page size, number of pages, "author," plus whatever additional information (such as read/write authority, available space, etc.) is appropriate to the intelligent perusal of data contained in the volume.

S. C. BREWER

## VON NEUMANN, JOHN

For articles on related subject *see* DIGITAL COMPUTERS, Early; EDVAC; ENIAC; STORED PROGRAM CONCEPT; and VON NEUMANN MACHINE.
For articles of related terms *see* AIKEN, HOWARD; ECKERT, J. PRESPER; MARK I; and MAUCHLY, JOHN W.

John von Neumann (b. Dec. 28, 1903, Budapest, Hungary; d. Feb. 8, 1957, Washington, D.C.) has become one of the major legendary figures of twentieth century mathematics. The stories of his quickness of mind, power of absolute recall, linguistic range, and sense of humor abound in the literature and among his former associates. During his career he made significant contributions to logic, to quantum physics, to the theory of high-speed computing machines, and to economics through the mathematical theory of games and strategy. His work in any one of the fields would have secured him a distinguished position in present-day science.

Von Neumann received his early education at the Lutheran gymnasium in Budapest from 1911

**Fig. 1.** John von Neumann (From the Institute for Advanced Study, Princeton, N.J.)

through 1921. Toward the end of this period he was also privately tutored by M. Fekete, later to become another well-known Hungarian mathematician, with whom von Neumann published his first paper before he reached the age of 18.

There is a story that von Neumann's father opposed his desire to study mathematics. So, although he enrolled in the University of Budapest, he studied chemistry in Berlin (1921–1923) and Zurich (1923–1925), where he received his diploma in chemical engineering. In 1926, however, he received a Budapest Ph.D. in mathematics with a dissertation concerning the axiomatization of set theory.

During the late 1920s he was Privatdozent at Berlin and Hamburg. He quickly established a reputation with publications in set theory, algebra, and quantum mechanics in this period. In 1928 he proved the minimax theorem of game theory. This was later elaborated and applied in his work (with Oskar Morganstern), "The Theory of Games and Economic Behavior" (1944).

In 1930 he was invited to be a visiting lecturer at Princeton University. When the Institute for Advanced Study was founded in 1933, he was appointed one of the original six professors of its School of Mathematics. He kept this position for the rest of his life.

Von Neumann's work in the 1930s firmly established his already highly regarded reputation as a mathematician. In 1931 he published a book on the mathematical foundation of quantum mechanics, and in that same decade he formulated and proved the mean ergodic theorem for unitary operators. He published a series of papers (some with F. J. Murray) in the latter half of the 1930s, on what he called "rings of operators" (now known as von Neumann algebras), which led him to work in what he called "continuous" geometry.

World War II was a watershed mark in von Neumann's career. Prior to 1940, his work fell primarily into the area of theoretical mathematics and physics, but for the remainder of his career he appeared as an applied mathematician. The citation on his honorary D.Sc. from Princeton (1947) identified him as a mathematician, but the encomium described him in terms of his impact as a physicist, engineer, and patriot. His papers from 1940 were mainly on statistics, hydrodynamics, ballistics, problems of detonation, meteorology, the applicability of game theory, and the theory and design of computers.

Although von Neumann had the ability to perform incredible mental calculations, his research led him to examine the possibility for machine assistance. His work on the hydrogen bomb in 1944 and the problem of implosion led him to make use of the computational ability of Howard Aiken's Automatic Sequence Control Calculator (Mark I) at Harvard. During the late summer of 1944, a chance encounter with Herman Goldstine made him aware of the world's first electronic computer being built under the direction of John Mauchly and J. Presper Eckert at the Moore School of Electrical Engineering of the University of Pennsylvania. His first visit to the ENIAC project occurred in August of that year, and this marked the beginning of his role in the theory of electronic computers and automata.

Von Neumann's role in the next level of conception and implementation is difficult to assess. There is evidence that Eckert and Mauchly were involved in discussions that included the development of a mercury delay-line memory with the ability to store both numbers and instructions. Shortly before von Neumann's first visit in 1944, the group had already committed itself to the construction of a successor to ENIAC as soon as time permitted. While von Neumann's authorship of the first EDVAC proposal in mid-1945 may not entitle his admirers to claim for him stored program conceptual priority, it is indicative of the great impact of his presence as a consultant to the group, his probing questions, and his ability to synthesize critical ideas. With the EDVAC paper, the modern era of electronic computers took a major stride forward.

By late 1945, von Neumann had decided to build a high-speed, general-purpose electronic computer at the Institute for Advanced Study. His documents of the period clearly articulate his vision on the ability of the proposed computer to " ... revolutionize the purely mathematical approach to the theory of non-linear differential equations ... extend quantum theory to systems of more particles and more degrees of freedom ... render a computational approach ... to the phenomenon of turbulence ... remove many bottlenecks in the computing approach to ordinary and electron optics. ... Such a machine if intelligently used will completely revolutionize ... the field of approximation mathematics." (Memorandum on the Program of the High Speed Computer, Nov. 8, 1945.) The impact of the IAS computer and its progeny (such as Illiac, Maniac, Johnniac, etc.) is well known. The whole family is still generally referred to as "von Neumann machines."

Von Neumann's clarity and precision of thought had a profound impact in many areas from which we will continue to benefit in the decades ahead. He was clearly one of the major scientific figures of this century.

REFERENCES

1958. Bochner, Salomon. "John von Neumann," in National Academy of Sciences *Biographical Memoirs*, Vol. 32, pp. 438–457.
1972. Goldstine, Herman H. *The Computer from Pascal to von Neumann*. Princeton: Princeton University Press, pp. 167–183.
1973. Halmos, Paul R. "The Legend of John von Neumann," *American Mathematical Monthly*, April, pp. 382–394.

H. S. TROPP

# VON NEUMANN MACHINE

For articles on related subjects *see* PROGRAM COUNTER; STORED PROGRAM CONCEPT; and VON NEUMANN, JOHN.

It can be debated at great length as to what person or persons were the first to put forth any given concept, and this holds true in computer science as much as it does in aviation, political philosophy, etc. However, probably the most influential paper in the history of computer science, whether or not anyone else expressed similar ideas any earlier, was written in 1946 by John von Neumann, then on the staff of the Institute for Advanced Study at Princeton University, in collaboration with Arthur W. Burks and Herman H. Goldstein. Its title is "Preliminary Discussion of the Logical Design of an Electronic Computing Instrument," and the ideas it contains, collectively known as "the von Neumann machine," have provided the foundation for essentially all computer system development since that date.

Central to the von Neumann machine is the concept of the stored program—the principle that instructions and data are to be stored together intermixed in a single, uniform storage medium rather than separately, as was previously the case. Not only can computations proceed at electronic speeds, but instructions as well as data can be read and written under program control. From this basic idea it follows that an element in storage has an ambiguous quality with respect to its interpretation; this ambiguity is resolved only temporarily when it is fetched and either executed as an instruction or operated on as data. One exploitation of this ambiguity results in the technique of instruction modification in which a datum, created as the result of some operations in the arithmetic-logic unit of the computer, is placed in storage as would be any other datum but is then fetched and executed as an instruction. Iteration is realized by refetching the instruction as a datum, modifying it by operating on its address field, and then storing it and refetching and reexecuting it as an instruction. Contemporary programming practice, particularly in a multiprogramming environment, precludes the physical modification of instructions in storage. However, the basic idea of logical instruction modification is still central in computer science, but it is supported by more recent developments as index registers, base registers, and indirect addressing, which provide similar effects but leave instructions unchanged in storage.

Another concept central to the von Neumann machine is the program counter, a register that is used to indicate the location of the next instruction to be executed and which is automatically incremented by each instruction fetch. With the rare exception of machines that use rotating memory devices for main storage, essentially all computers use this technique, since it clearly reduces the storage space that would otherwise be necessary if each instruction contained a field to indicate the address of its successor. The idea of branching, which is often very difficult for a beginning machine language programmer to understand, can in this context become obvious in that it is effected merely by the replacement of the contents of the location counter from some other source, often but not always a field in the current instruction.

No short article can do justice to these and the many other ideas expressed so clearly by von Neumann and his colleagues in 1946. Every computer scientist should read the original report, which fortunately can be found in several sources, among them being those below.

REFERENCES

1963. Traub, A. H., Ed. *The Collected Works of John von Neumann*, Vol. 5. New York: Macmillan, pp. 34–79.
1971. Bell, C. G., and A. Newell. *Computer Structures*. New York: McGraw-Hill, pp. 92–119.

R. F. ROSIN

W

## WATSON, THOMAS J., SR.

For articles on related subjects *see* DIGITAL COMPUTERS: Early; HOLLERITH, HERMAN; and MANUFACTURERS, COMPUTER.

Thomas John Watson was born in East Campbell, Steuben County, New York, on February 17, 1874, of Scots-Irish descent. The son of Thomas and Jane White Watson, he was educated at the Addison Academy and the School of Commerce in Elmira, New York.

He started work in May 1892 as a bookkeeper in Painted Post, New York, at a salary of $6.00 a week. Following this first job, he sold sewing machines and musical instruments in the same village before joining the National Cash Register Company in Buffalo, New York, as a salesman. Four years later, National Cash Register promoted him to manager in Rochester. Promotion to special representative followed, and four and a half years later he was appointed the company's general sales manager.

It was at this time that Watson, bent on inspiring a dispirited NCR sales force, introduced the motto "THINK." He is quoted (*THINK*, 1956) as having told a meeting of salesmen that the phrase "I didn't think" had cost the world millions of dollars. Overnight, framed placards with the single word "THINK" sprouted throughout the offices of the company. Later, when he took the helm at IBM, he reintroduced this motto.

**Fig. 1.** Thomas John Watson.

Watson resigned from NCR in 1913, a few months after his marriage to Jeannette M. Kittridge, to assume the presidency of the ailing Computing-Tabulating-Recording Company, a 1911 merger of the Computing Scale Company of America, the Tabulating Machine Company, and the International Time Recording Company.

From 1913 until his death 43 years later, Thomas J. Watson built the C-T-R Company, which became the International Business Machines Corporation in 1924, into the leading manufacturer first of automatically operated electromechanical business machines and then of electronic computers and business machines. It became one of the largest, most successful corporations in the world. During this time he always placed heavy emphasis on education, research, and engineering in order to insure the growth of the company. Under his leadership IBM's history was a succession of technical innovations and inventions that included new applications of punched cards to business, government, and education, the introduction of the first commercially successful electric typewriter in 1934, opening the electronic computer era commercially in 1948 with the marketing of the 604 programmable electronic calculator, and the top position in the electronic computing and data processing field in the 1950s.

A great deal of Watson's success was due to his understanding of customer's needs, which resulted in steady improvements in IBM's product lines.

One of Watson's lifelong interests was in education, and he sought to put his business acumen at the service of the universities and their faculties, giving equipment for the Columbia University Statistical Bureau (1928); the Astronomical Computing Bureau at Columbia (1934); designing and building as a gift the first large-scale computer, the IBM Automatic Sequence Controlled Calculator (the Mark I) for Harvard (1944); and dedicating the Selective Sequence Electronic Calculator to "assist the scientist in institutions of higher learning, in government, and in industry to explore the consequences of man's thought to the outermost reaches of time, space, and physical conditions" (1948). In the early 1930s he began serving as a trustee of various universities, including Lafayette College, which always remained a sentimental favorite, partly because it was there that he received the first of over 30 honorary degrees he would accumulate before his death. He also served for many years as a trustee of Columbia University.

A month before he died on June 19, 1956, Watson turned over the post of chief executive officer of IBM to his eldest son, Thomas Watson, Jr., who in 1952 succeeded his father as president of the corporation.

### REFERENCES

1956. *Anon. THINK* (July-August-September), pp. 4–48.

1962. Belden, T. and M. Belden. *The Lengthening Shadow*. Boston: Little, Brown.

1969. Rodgers, W. *THINK—A Biography of the Watsons and IBM*. New York: Stein and Day.

J. C. MCPHERSON

## WELL-FORMED FORMULA

For articles on related subjects *see* GRAMMAR, GENERATIVE; PARSING; PRODUCTION; and PROGRAMMING LINGUISTICS.

A well-formed formula (WFF) over a set $G$ of grammatical or syntactical rules is a finite sequence or string of symbols that is grammatically or syntactically correct; i.e., it belongs to the set of all sequences of symbols that can be constructed or formed by using the rules in $G$.

For instance, if $G = \{S \rightarrow aSb, S \rightarrow ab\}$ is the set of grammatical rules in a generative grammar, then a string $x$ is well formed if and only if it is of the form $a^nb^n$ for $n \geq 1$. Other examples of well-formed formulas are arithmetic expressions, well-formed parentheses expressions (Dyck sets)—where each left parenthesis has to be properly matched by a right parenthesis—and well-formed formulas in propositional calculus.

Given an arbitrary grammar $G$, the question whether an arbitrary string is well formed with respect to $G$ is equivalent to the question of whether it belongs to the language generated by $G$. This question is decidable for many important classes of languages or sets; i.e., there exists an algorithm that determines after finitely many steps whether a given string is well formed. Examples of such languages include WFF's in the propositional calculus, syntactically correct PL/I statements, etc.

P. C. FISCHER AND D. WOTSCHKE

## WHIRLWIND I

For article on related subject *see* DIGITAL COMPUTERS: Early.

Project Whirlwind was sponsored at the Massachusetts Institute of Technology by the Special Devices Division of the Office of Research and Inventions, U.S. Navy. It was originally started in 1944 to investigate the solution of aircraft stability and control problems associated with flight simulation by analog methods. By 1946 it had become apparent that the use of an analog computer would lead to excessive complexity, and therefore other computing techniques should be studied. Thus, in 1946, a proposal was made for a 16-bit binary general-purpose computer utilizing electrostatic storage and a 1 MHz pulse rate. Although initially proposed as serial, the requirement for 20,000 multiplications per second led eventually to a parellel machine.

Whirlwind was constructed under the leadership of J. W. Forrester. When first put in service during the third quarter of 1949, the computer had 3,300 tubes and 8,900 crystal diodes (germanium point-contact diodes). By June of 1950, one hour of error-free operation with 256 words of electrostatic storage had been achieved. In March of 1951, it was operational on a routine basis on a 35-hour per week schedule. During 1953 a magnetic tape system and a magnetic drum system were installed and electrostatic storage was replaced by two banks of core memory consisting of 1,024 words of 16 bits each. By December 1954, the computer had grown to 12,500 vacuum tubes and 23,803 crystal diodes.

Whirlwind occupied a two-story building. The CPU, control console, and CRT displays occupied the second floor. One bit of the arithmetic logic unit was a bay of equipment 2 ft wide and 12 ft high. The drum storage system and data communications interface occupied the ground floor. The basement was filled with power supplies, and the roof of the building was covered with air-conditioning equipment to remove the heat generated by a power consumption on the order of 150 kW.

Whirlwind was a 16-bit parallel, single-address, binary computer. Instructions as well as data occupied words of 16 bits in memory. The operation code had 5 bits and the address had 11 bits. Eventually, all 32 possible operation codes were utilized. Multiplication and division were included in the operation codes. The initial program-load problem was solved by the use of a bank of 32 registers of toggle switches. In routine operation, various bootstrap programs were stored in the toggle-switch memory.

Automatic marginal checking was initiated during the fourth quarter of 1949. The computer had the ability to select any section of itself, vary the voltages to that section, and test for failure. By comparing the results from day to day, it was possible to determine if trends toward failure were developing in the components.

Whirlwind used magnetic tape and magnetic drum for auxiliary memory. Input/output equipment included large cathode-ray tubes, photoelectric tape readers, Flexowriters, and, in connection with the Air Force semiautomatic ground-environment air defense system (SAGE), data communication links were established with a number of radar sets and with other computers. One of the cathode-ray tubes had a microfilm camera attached so that large-volume output could be displayed on a CRT and microfilmed. This was a common method of obtaining memory dumps. Prints of the microfilm were available the next morning. With electrostatic storage, the computer was capable of approximately 20,000 operations per second, which increased to 40,000 per second when a magnetic-core memory system was installed.

On the software side, there were pioneering efforts in the development of a symbolic assembler, a comprehensive interpretive system that provided a comprehensive mathematical package including floating-point operations, a batch-operating system, and an off-line printout system that permitted recording the results at high speed on magnetic tape and later printing the results off line without the use of the computer.

Despite its physical size, Whirlwind was, in modern terms, a 16-bit minicomputer. It was, however, a most important project in the development of parallel, binary computers. The Whirlwind project itself and those it spawned (the Memory Test Computer, the TX-0 and TX-2 computers at the Lincoln Laboratory of M.I.T., and the AN/FSQ-7 manufactured by IBM for the SAGE system) led to many hardware and software developments, most notably magnetic-core memories and the first operating systems. Whirlwind influenced the early IBM 700 series computers and the computers developed by the Digital Equipment Corporation, much of whose initial staff came from the Lincoln Laboratory.

Whirlwind operated until 1959. Parts of it are now in the Smithsonian Institution.

J. N. ACKLEY

# WIENER, NORBERT

For articles on related subjects *see* CYBERNETICS; and DIGITAL COMPUTERS: Early.

Norbert Wiener (b. Columbia, Missouri, Nov. 26, 1894; d. Stockholm, Sweden, Mar. 18, 1964) was

**Fig. 1.** Norbert Wiener.

one of America's most important mathematicians, and a controversial scientist who left a rich heritage of accomplishments, not only through his more than one hundred publications, but also through his personal contacts with scientists throughout the world.

Of his boyhood, Wiener said: "I got my classical education from my father, who was professor of Slavic languages at Harvard. My scientific education I got for myself." (*Current Biography,* 1950).

Wiener received his A.B. degree from Tufts College in 1909 and his Ph.D. from Harvard in 1913 with a thesis in mathematical logic. The years 1913 to 1915 were significant ones. Traveling under Harvard's Sheldon Fellowship, he worked under Alfred North Whitehead, Bertrand Russell, G. H. Hardy, and J. E. Littlewood in Cambridge, and David Hilbert and Edmund Landau at Göttingen.

After America's entry into World War I, Wiener joined the facility at Aberdeen Proving Ground, where he worked on designing artillery range tables. In 1919, with the help of Harvard Professor W. F. Osgood, he secured an appointment as an instructor at M.I.T., an association he maintained until his retirement in 1960.

He was a Guggenheim Fellow at Copenhagen and Gottingen in 1926, and he was also a visiting lecturer at Cambridge (1931–1932) and at Tsing Hua University in Peiping, China (1935–1936). Many significant influences occurred during this pre-war era. At Cambridge, Bertrand Russell encouraged him to read Rutherford's work on the theory of the electron and the nature of matter. At M.I.T. he formed a close friendship with Harold Hazen, and was early exposed to the theory of feedback and servomechanisms. It was also during this period that he met Arturo Rosenblueth, who was engaged in neurophysiological research.

Wiener's direct contributions to the early development of electronic digital computers are difficult to determine. His wartime work on prediction theory and the research in radar and fire control were all to have a major impact by the end of the 1940s. By then, however, his name was synonomous with cybernetics (Wiener, 1948). In his writings on cybernetics, Wiener laid the foundation for the philosophical relations between mechanistic and mathematical scientific theories. This work may not have directly contributed to the actual machine developments, but it did much to stimulate research in automata and in attempts to stimulate human thought processes. Wiener was also very conscious of the long-range impact of the computer on man and society. In "The Human Use of Human Beings" (Wiener, 1950), he warned of the dangers that could be caused by selfish exploitation of the computer's potential.

Norbert Wiener was active in professional societies both in the United States and abroad. He also received many honors, such as the Bôcher Prize of the American Mathematical Society (1933). His major publications, in addition to the above, include works on the Fourier integral and its application, Brownian motion, time series, relativity and quantum theory, mathematical foundations, postulational theory, vector and differential spaces, and potential theory.

### References

1948. Wiener, Norbert. *Cybernetics, or Control and Communication in the Animal and Machine.* Cambridge, Mass.: M.I.T. Press.

1950. *Anon. Current Biography,* pp. 615–617.

1950. Wiener, Norbert. *The Human Use of Human Beings; Cybernetics and Society.* Boston: Houghton Mifflin.

1953. Wiener, Norbert. *Ex-Prodigy.* Cambridge, Mass.: M.I.T. Press.

1956. Wiener, Norbert. *I Am A Mathematician.* Cambridge, Mass.: M.I.T. Press.

H. TROPP

## WILKES, MAURICE V.

For articles on related subjects *see* DIGITAL COMPUTERS: Early.

For articles on related terms *see* British Computer Society; EDSAC; Microprogramming; Stored Program Concept.

Maurice Vincent Wilkes (b. 1913) studied mathematics and physics at Cambridge and conducted research on the ionosphere. He worked on radar during World War II, and then directed the Mathematical Laboratory (now the Computer Laboratory) of the University of Cambridge from 1945 onward throughout the whole development of stored program computers. It was here that the first of these to go into service, the Electronic Delay Storage Automatic Calculator (EDSAC), built by Wilkes and his team, began operating in May 1949. He became a Fellow of the Royal Society in 1956, was the first president of the British Computer Society 1957–1960, and the first United Kingdom member of the Council of IFIP 1960–1963. He was the ACM Turing Lecturer in 1967 and received the Harry Goode Award from AFIPS in 1968.

Wilkes led the first practical development of programming for stored program machines, including the first program library. He originated labels (which he called "floating addresses"), an early form of macros (which he called "synthetic orders"), and microprogramming (which was used in the design of the second Cambridge machine, EDSAC II). He later became interested in machine-independent computing, and in this connection developed a simple list-processing language known as Wisp. He was an early advocate of data transmission. He contributed to the development of time sharing systems, both as a visiting member of Project MAC at M.I.T. and through the system developed in his own laboratory during 1965–1970. In particular, he and his colleagues introduced many ideas relating to facilities for filing and editing for the ordinary user.

In addition to numerous papers and articles, he has written the following books: *Oscillations of the Earth's Atmosphere* (1949), *Preparation of Programs for an Electronic Digital Computer* (joint author; 1951, 2d ed. 1958), *Automatic Digital Computers* (1956), *A Short Introduction to Numerical Analysis* (1966), *Time-Sharing Computer Systems* (1966, 2d ed. 1972).

S. Gill

**Fig. 1.** Maurice Vincent Wilkes.

## WILLIAMS' TUBE MEMORY

For articles on related subjects *see* Memory: Main; and Ultrasonic Memory.
For article on related term *see* SWAC.

The first stored-program computers were based on two kinds of memory—ultrasonic delay lines and a cathode-ray tube (CRT) system named after F. C. Williams of Manchester University. Experimentation with both schemes was being carried on in 1947 in England and in the United States, and by 1949–1950 computers of both types were operational. By 1954 magnetic-core memories had superseded both delay line and Williams' tube memories.

Storage of information at a spot on the inside of the face of the CRT was determined by the relative charge level. The secondary emission ratio for phosphors (and for glass) is greater than 1. Thus, if the face is bombarded with a primary electron beam (1,000 to 2,000 volt acceleration), then the spot becomes positively charged because more low-energy secondary electrons are emitted by the surface than arrive in the primary electron beam. Equilibrium is reached when the relatively positive charge of the spot attracts enough electrons to balance the flow. If a spot is charged, then the nearby area is "discharged" by the secondary electrons from the primary spot.

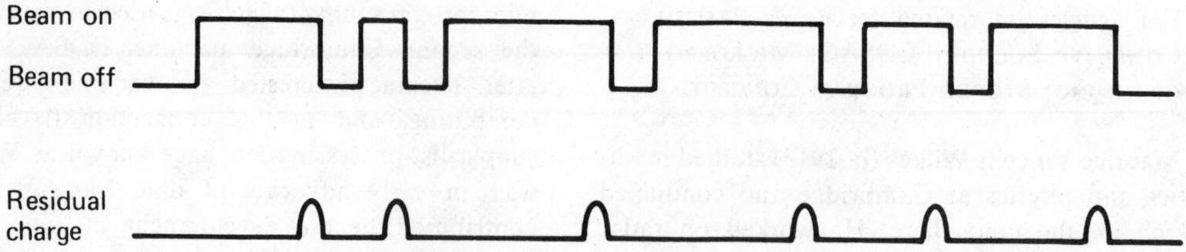


**Fig. 1.** Williams' charge storage pattern.

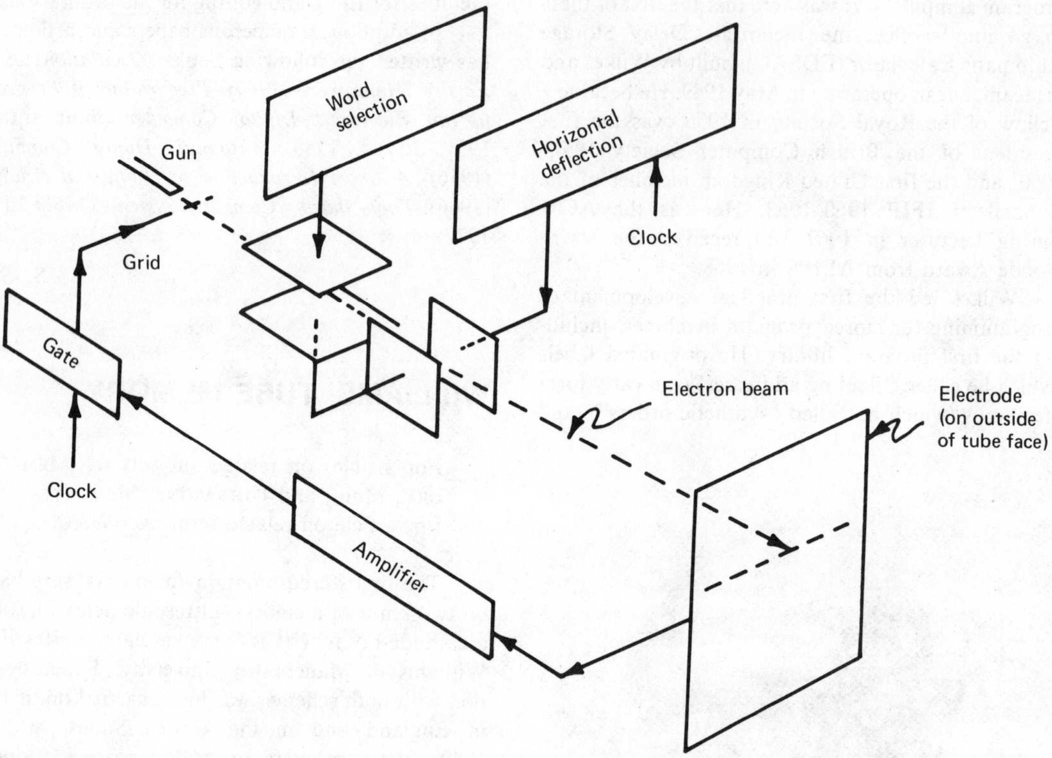


**Fig. 2.** Williams' CRT information storage system.

Williams used the CRTs in a bit-serial mode. To write information on the tube, the electron beam is deflected along a horizontal line, and at each point where the beam is turned off, a residual positive charge remains (Fig. 1). To read the information from the CRT, an electrode is place on the outside of the face of the CRT (Fig. 2). As the beam again sweeps over a line, the change of potential on the inside face is capacitively picked up by the electrode. Since the spots of positive charge occur just before the turn-off points, the resulting signal occurs in time to again turn off the beam at the same place. (Williams called this an "anticipation" pulse.) As the beam sweeps a horizontal line, the induced potential on the electrode is amplified, and via the gating circuits and the control grid of the CRT (Fig. 2), the beam is turned off in a pattern identical to that of the previous sweep. Thus, the line being read is not destroyed by the reading process. However, since reading a given line tended to discharge the neighboring lines, it was necessary to systematically regenerate the whole array. A typical scheme was to regenerate during odd-word times and to access information during even-word times.

The beam, being on or off at a given position (or clock time), can represent the zeros or ones of a binary number. Alternative storage schemes involved using focus/defocused spots, or dots and dashes, at grid points on the face of the cathode-ray tube. By changing the vertical or word deflection (Fig. 2), several different numbers can be stored on one CRT. (Williams stored thirty-two 32-bit numbers.)

The SWAC at the Institute for Numerical Analysis used the Williams' tube in a parallel mode with the *k*th bit of the memory words stored in the *k*th CRT. Williams' tubes in the parallel mode were also used in the computer at the Institute for Advanced Study. Parallel systems stored 256 to 1,024 bits per tube.

Other memory systems (e.g., Whirlwind) used special tubes with a second "flooding gun" to maintain the storage. Rajchman (RCA) designed a special memory tube called the "Selectron," which was originally intended to be used in the computer at the Institute for Advanced Study.

Commercially, Ferranti (England) marketed the Williams' serial scheme, and IBM used the parallel mode in its 701 computers (1953).

REFERENCES

1949. Williams, F. C., and T. Kilburn. "A Storage System for Use With Binary Digital Computing Machines," *J. Inst. Elect. Engrs.*, Vol. 96, part III, pp. 81–100.

H. D. HUSKEY

# WORD LENGTH, VARIABLE

For article on related subject *see* ADDRESSING.
For article on related term *see* IBM 360-370 SERIES.

Word length is an important characteristic of most computers. Most minicomputers use 16-bit words. The IBM 360/370 series and most systems influenced by the IBM design philosophy use a 32-bit word length. The large UNIVAC and Honeywell machines use 36-bit words; Control Data's Cyber systems are 60-bit word machines, and Burroughs' big systems use 48-bit words.

Computers have been built in which there was no preferred or fixed word length. Most of these were data processing machines that operated on character strings. An example is the IBM 1400 series, in which there was a marker bit (called a "word mark" or "flag") associated with each character position in memory. The setting of these marker bits broke up memory into variable-length words or fields. The best known scientifically oriented computer with a variable word length was the IBM 1620, a widely used small computer of the early 1960s.

In more recent computers, the use of count fields in instructions permits the use of variable-length operands. Even though most machines do have a preferred fixed-length word when they are operating on binary operands, they can behave as variable-length word machines when they are dealing with operands that consist of strings of coded decimal digits or coded characters.

S. ROSEN

# WORKING SET

For articles on related subjects *see* OPERATING SYSTEMS: Principles and Theory; and THRASHING.
For articles on related terms *see* TIME SLICE; and VIRTUAL MEMORY.

"Working set" is an abbreviation of a term applied to a concept as old as electronic computing: "set of working information." It specifically refers to the smallest set of instruction and data words of a given program which should be loaded into the main memory of a computer system so that efficient processing is possible. An important connotation of the term is *dynamic:* The working set can change in both content and size from one instant of time to another. It is incorrect to apply the term to a static notion (as, for example, in "the working set is the amount of memory required so that the average processing efficiency over the execution of a given program is some stated percentage.")

The loose definition of working set as given above can be made more precise in specific contexts. For example, the working set of an Algol program (as on Burroughs B5000 and later series machines) is taken as the set of instructions constituting the presently running procedure together with the set of all activation records (i.e., local storage used by activated procedures) of that program. The working set of a program operating in some IBM OS/360 or 370 environments is taken as the set of pages referenced by the program during its most recently completed time slice. Most definitions employ, either implicitly (as in the Burroughs example) or explicitly (as in the IBM example), some past time interval, and take the working set as the collection of blocks of information referenced over that interval. When a fixed time interval (known sometimes as the "working set window") is used, it is possible to specify precisely the relations among working set size, processing efficiency, and probability that the object next referenced is not in the working set (Denning, 1968).

The working set concept is important in dynamic memory management. The working-set principle of dynamic multiprogramming asserts that a task may be active only if its working set is in main memory. A memory management policy that implements this principle will guarantee each active task a minimal level of processing efficiency, and will usually protect a computer system against the possibility of *thrashing*. It is frequently employed in memory management procedures in virtual memory systems.

Closely associated with the concept of working set is *locality*. Locality is the combined property that (1) all blocks of a program are referenced with unequal densities during any interval of time, and (2) references to any given block tend to be heavily clustered in certain time intervals and are sparse in others. The better a program's locality, the more predictable its immediate future memory demand, and the smaller and more stable will its working set be. Since most dynamic memory management policies use some measure of a past working set as a predictor of immediate future memory demand, it is evident that good locality begets good performance under such policies. For this reason, program locality is important in obtaining good performance from virtual memory systems (in which few or no memory management decisions are made by programmers); in fact, improvements in processing efficiency in a given program brought about by semingly minor improvements in its locality frequently range from 300 to 1,000%!

The size of the address space is less important than locality, and there is often a trade-off between the total size of an address space and the locality of the program contained in it. Since locality derives from the way the programmer designs his algorithm and data, it is not true (as is often claimed) that virtual memory systems relieve the programmer *completely* from responsibilities of memory management. However, it *is* true that good locality can be achieved at very little effort; thus, the payoff of virtual memory systems accrues to those who invest in good locality in their programs.

### Reference

1968. Denning, P. J., "The Working Set Model for Program Behavior," *Communications ACM*, Vol. 11, No. 5 (May), pp. 323–333.

P. J. Denning and D. E. Denning

# Z

## ZUSE, KONRAD

For article on related subject *see* DIGITAL COMPUTERS: Origins, and Early.

Konrad Zuse (b. 1910 in Berlin) studied construction engineering at the Technische Hochschule Berlin-Charlottenburg and received the degree in Dipl.Ing. in 1935. In 1934 he had already started development work on program-controlled computing machines with electromechanical and mechanical elements. He felt that the tiresome calculations required in this field should be done by a machine. In 1938 he had completed his first model (Z1). In 1941 his first fully working machine (Z3) was operational; it used the binary number system with floating-point arithmetic. Zuse invented a relay adder in which four relays produced the sum of two binary places and which, in an *n*-place binary adder, yields the *n*-place sum in one switching step.

During the next four years, Zuse built a number of special machines and the all-purpose relay computer Z4. The Z3 was destroyed by bombs (it was reconstructed in the 1960s), but the Z4 was saved, and in 1949 it was installed at the Eidgenössische Technische Hochschule in Zürich. In 1954 it was transferred to a research institute in St. Louis near Basle, where it was operated for five years. Around 1945, when facilities for circuit development were not available to Zuse, he turned to programming and designing an algorithmic language which he called Plankalkül (Bauer and Wössner, 1972). Its notation was in a kind of matrix form, and it could be used for both numerical and nonnumerical problems (Zuse used it to describe a full chess program).

**Fig. 1.** Konrad Zuse.

## ZUSE, KONRAD

In 1949 Zuse formed his own company ZUSE KG, and went into manufacturing. His first successful product was Z11, a relay computer for geodetical and optical applications. His second product was Z22, a vacuum-tube computer (later replaced by its transistorized version Z23); it had an extremely flexible instruction code, achieved by a set of functional bits, an early form of microprogramming. The Z22 was delivered first in 1958, and more than 50 were made. In 1958 Zuse published one of his ideas that was ahead of his time. This was the field computer, a parallel processor, especially suited for differential equations. In the same year, he designed a computer-controlled plotter called Z64, or Graphomat.

After a number of financial difficulties, Zuse left ZUSE KG, which was absorbed by Siemens AG in 1969. Three years before he had become a professor at the University of Göttingen.

In 1957 Zuse received the honorary degree of Dr.techn. in Berlin; in 1964 he received the Werner von Siemens-Ring; in 1965, the Harry Goode Medal from AFIPS; in 1969, the German Diesel Medal; and in the same year the Austrian Exner Medal.

The achievements of Dr. Zuse can be properly evaluated only if his isolation is taken into account. His background was construction engineering, and he knew practically nothing about other computer developments (in Germany or abroad, in his time or earlier) until a very late stage. During all his life, Dr. Zuse received too little understanding and support. The German military had no interest in his work, and while the German Research Council after the war did its best to support him, their efforts were not enough to keep his company alive.

### REFERENCES


1972. Bauer, F. L., and H. Wössner. "The 'Plankalkül of Konrad Zuse: A Forerunner of Today's Programming Languages," *Communications of the ACM*, Vol. 15, pp. 678–685.

1973. Zuse, Konrad. "Der Computer—mein Lebenswerk" (Verlag Moderne Industries, Munich, 1969); "Method for Automatic Execution of Calculations with the Aid of Computers"; "The Outline of a Computer Development from Mechanics to Electronics"; in Brian Randell (Ed.), *The Origins of Digital Computers*. Berlin: Springer Verlag, pp. 155–186.


H. ZEMANEK

# APPENDIX I

## ABBREVIATIONS AND ACRONYMS

This list contains abbreviations and acronyms used in the articles in this Encyclopedia other than those used by authors just for local purposes in their articles. It also contains a few additional abbreviations which are in such common use that they serve a reference purpose here.

| | |
|---|---|
| ABA | American Bankers Association |
| ACC | Accumulator |
| ACE | Automatic Computing Engine |
| ACM | Association for Computing Machinery |
| ADAPSO | Association of Data Processing Service Organizations |
| ADCIS | Association for the Development of Computer-based Instruction Systems |
| ADI | American Documentation Institute |
| ADP | Automatic Data Processing |
| AEDS | Association for Educational Data Systems |
| AESC | American Engineering Standards Committee (now ANSC) |
| AFCET | Association Française pour la Cybernetique, Economique et Technique |
| AFIPS | American Federation of Information Processing Societies |
| AICA | Association Internationale pour le Calcul Analogique |
| AIEE | American Institute of Electronic and Electrical Engineers (now part of IEEE) |
| AIMACO | Air Materiel Command Compiler |
| ALGOL | Algorithmic Language |
| ALU | Arithmetic-Logic Unit |
| AM | Amplitude Modulation |
| ANSC | American National Standards Committee |
| ANSI | American National Standards Institute |
| APEC | Automated Procedures for Engineering Consultants |
| APL | A Programming Language |
| APT | Automatically Programmed Tools |
| ARPA | Advanced Research Projects Agency |
| ARQ | Automatic Repeat Request |
| ASA | American Standards Association (now ANSI) |
| ASC | Advanced Scientific Computer (of Texas Instruments) |
| ASCII | American Standard Code for Information Interchange |
| ASIS | American Society for Information Science |
| ASME | American Society of Mechanical Engineers |
| ASMME | American Society of Mining and Metallurgical Engineers |
| ASTM | American Society of Testing Materials |
| ATDM | Asynchronous Time Division Multiplexing |
| ATS | Administrative Terminal System |
| BASIC | Beginner's All-purpose Symbolic Instruction Code |
| BCD | Binary-Coded Decimal |
| BCS | British Computer Society |
| BDP | Business Data Processing |
| BIMD | Biomedical Series of Computer Programs |
| BINAC | Binary Northrop Aircraft Computer |

| | |
|---|---|
| BLISS | Basic Language for Implementing Systems Software |
| BMD | Biomedical Series of Computer Programs |
| BMEWS | Ballistic Missile Early Warning System |
| BNF | Backus-Naur Form (sometimes Backus-Normal Form) |
| BOSS | Burroughs Operational System Simulator |
| BPL | Business Planning Language |
| CAE | Computer-Assisted Education |
| CAI | Computer-Assisted Instruction |
| CAL | Computer-Assisted Learning |
| CALGO | Collected Algorithms (by ACM) |
| CBE | Computer-Based Education |
| CBEMA | Computer and Business Equipment Manufacturers Association |
| CBMS | Conference Board of the Mathematical Sciences |
| CCITT | Comité Consultatif International Télégraphique et Téléphonique |
| CDC | Control Data Corporation |
| CDP | Certificate in Data Processing |
| CEPA | Civil Engineering Programming Applications |
| CG | Computer Graphics |
| CIB | Cobol Information Bulletin |
| CIM | Computer Input from Microfilm |
| CM | Central Memory |
| CMC | Communications Mode Control |
| CMI | Computer-Managed Instruction |
| CMS | Cambridge Monitor System |
| COBOL | Common Business-Oriented Language |
| CODASYL | Conference on Data Systems Languages |
| COGO | Coordinate Geometry |
| COM | Computer Output on Microfilm |
| COSMIC | Computer Software Management and Information Center |
| CP | Central Processor |
| CPC | Card Programmed Calculator |
| CPM | Critical Path Method |
| CPU | Central Processing Unit |
| CRAM | Card Random Access Memory |
| CRC | Cyclic Redundancy Check |
| CRT | Cathode-Ray Tube |
| CSMP | Continuous System Modeling Program |
| CSSL | Continuous System Simulation Language |
| CTSS | Compatible Time-Sharing System |
| CUBE | Cooperating Users of Burroughs Equipment |
| DAA | Data Access Arrangement |
| DARMS | Digital Alternate Representation of Music Symbols |
| DBMS | Data Base Management System |
| DD | Data Definition (card) |
| DDC | Direct Digital Control |
| DEC | Digital Equipment Corporation |
| DECUS | Digital Equipment Corporation Users Society |
| DETAB | Decision Table Language |
| DFT | Discrete Fourier Transform |
| DLIMP | Descriptive Language Implemented by Macro Processor |
| DLT | Decision Logic Translator |
| DMA | Direct Memory Access |
| DMS | Data Management System |
| DOD | Department of Defense |

| | |
|---|---|
| DOS | Disk Operating System |
| DP | Data Processing |
| DPMA | Data Processing Management Association |
| DPU | Display Processing Unit |
| DRO | Destructive Read Out |
| DTL | Diode-Transistor Logic |
| DYANA | Dynamics Analyzer |
| EAI | Electronic Associates Incorporated |
| EBCDIC | Extended Binary-Coded Decimal Interchange Code |
| ECAP | Electric Circuit Analysis Program |
| ECG | Electrocardiogram |
| ECMA | European Computer Manufacturers Association |
| ECS | Extended Core Storage |
| ECTL | Emitter-Coupled Transistor Logic |
| EDP | Electronic Data Processing |
| EDSAC | Electronic Delay Storage Automatic Calculator |
| EDUCOM | Educational Communications (short name of the Interuniversity Communications Council) |
| EDVAC | Electronic Discrete Variable Automatic Computer |
| EIA | Electronic Industries Association |
| EIN | Educational Information Network |
| ENIAC | Electronic Numerical Integrator and Computer |
| EPAM | Elementary Perceiver and Memorizer |
| EXPLOR | Explicitly-defined Patterns, Local Operations, and Randomness |
| FAP | Fortran Assembly Program |
| FDM | Frequency Division Multiplexing |
| FET | Field-Effect Transistor |
| FFT | Fast Fourier Transform |
| FIACC | Five International Associations Coordinating Committee |
| FIFO | First-In First-Out |
| FIPS | Federal Information Processing Standards |
| FJCC | Fall Joint Computer Conference |
| FM | Frequency Modulation |
| FNU | Federation of NCR Users |
| FOCUS | Forum of Control Data Users |
| FORMAC | Formula Manipulation Compiler |
| FORTRAN | Formula Translation (or Translator) |
| GASP | General Activity Simulation Program |
| GENESYS | General Engineering System |
| GIGO | Garbage-In Garbage-Out |
| GIPSY | General Information Processing System |
| GIS | General Information System |
| GPL | Generalized Programming Language |
| GPM | General-Purpose Macrogenerator |
| GPS | General Problem Solver |
| GPSS | General-Purpose Systems Simulator |
| GRIPHOS | General Retrieval and Information Processing for Humanities-Oriented Studies |
| GUIDE | Guidance for Users of Integrated Data-processing Equipment |
| HASP | Houston Automatic Spooling Program |
| HIS | Hospital Information System |
| HISSG | Hospital Information System Sharing Group |
| HSCF | Health Sciences Computing Facility (at UCLA) |
| HUG | Honeywell Users Group |
| IAG | International Applications Group (of IFIP) |
| IBI-ICC | Intergovernmental Bureau for Informatics–International Computation Centre (now just IBI) |

## APPENDIX

| | |
|---|---|
| IBM | International Business Machines (Corp.) |
| IC | Integrated Circuit |
| ICCP | Institute for Certification of Computer Professionals |
| ICES | Integrated Civil Engineering System |
| ICL | International Computers Limited |
| ICU | Intensive Care Unit |
| IDFT | Inverse Discrete Fourier Transform |
| IFAC | International Federation of Automatic Control |
| IFIP | International Federation for Information Processing |
| IFORS | International Federation of Operations Research Societies |
| ILLIAC | Illinois Automatic Computer |
| IMIS | Integrated Management Information System |
| IMP | Interface Message Processor |
| IMS | Information Management System |
| I/O | Input/Output |
| IOCS | Input/Output Control System |
| IPL/V | Information Processing Language V |
| IPS | Information Processing System |
| IR | Information Retrieval (also, Instruction Register) |
| IRIA | Institute de Récherche d'Informatique et d'Automatique |
| ISAM | Index Sequential Access Method |
| ISO | International Standards Organization |
| ISTAB | International Systems Technical Advisory Board (of ANSI) |
| JCL | Job Control Language |
| JOHNNIAC | John von Neumann's Integrator and Automatic Computer |
| JOSS | Johnniac Open-Shop System |
| JOVIAL | Jules' (Schwartz) Own Version of IAL (International Algebraic Language) |
| JUG | Joint Users Group |
| KWIC | Keyword-in-Context |
| KWOC | Keyword-out-of-Context |
| $L^6$ | (Bell Telephone) Laboratories Low-Level Linked-List Language |
| LARC | Livermore Automatic Research Computer |
| LCS | Large Core Storage |
| LED | Light-Emitting Diode |
| LIFO | Last-In First-Out |
| LISP | List Processing |
| LP | Linear Programming |
| LRC | Longitudinal Redundancy Check |
| LSB | Least Significant Bit |
| LSI | Large-Scale Integration |
| LT | Logic Theorist |
| LU | Logic Unit |
| MANIAC | Mechanical and Numerical Integrator and Computer |
| MBQ | Modified Biquinary Code |
| MCP | Master Control Program |
| MCST | Magnetic Card Selectric Typewriter |
| MDAC | Multiplying Digital-to-Analog Converter |
| MEDLARS | Medical Literature Analysis and Retrieval System |
| MEDLINE | Medlars On-Line System |
| MFT | Multiprogramming with a Fixed Number of Tasks |
| MICR | Magnetic-Ink Character Recognition |
| MIMR | Magnetic-Ink Mark Recognition |
| MIS | Management Information System *or* Metal-Insulator-Semiconductor |
| M.I.T. | Massachusetts Institute of Technology |

| | |
|---|---|
| MLC | Multiline Controller |
| MMPI | Minnesota Multiphase Personality Inventory |
| MOS | Metal-Oxide Semiconductor |
| MOSFET | Metal-Oxide Semiconductor Field-Effect Transistor |
| MQ | Multiplier-Quotient |
| MQR | Multiplier-Quotient Register |
| MSB | Most Significant Bit |
| MSI | Medium-Scale Integration |
| MSM | Message-Switching Multiplexing |
| MSW | Machine Status Word |
| MT | Machine Translation |
| MTBF | Mean Time Between Failures |
| MTS | Michigan Terminal System |
| MTST | Magnetic Tape Selectric Typewriter |
| MULTICS | Multiplexed Information and Computing Service |
| MVT | Multiprogramming with a Variable Number of Tasks |
| NAND | Not AND |
| NASA | National Aeronautics and Space Agency |
| NBCD | Natural Binary-Coded Decimal |
| NBCH | Natural Binary-Coded Hexadecimal |
| NBS | National Bureau of Standards |
| NCC | Network Control Center *or* National Computer Conference |
| NCHS | National Center for Health Statistics |
| NCR | National Cash Register |
| NDRO | Non-Destructive Read Out |
| NIC | Network Information Center |
| NIH | National Institutes of Health |
| NLM | National Library of Medicine |
| NORC | Naval Ordnance Research Calculator |
| NSA | National Security Agency |
| OAO | Orbiting Astronomical Observatory |
| OCR | Optical Character Recognition |
| OEM | Original Equipment Manufacturer |
| OMR | Optical Mark Reader |
| OP | Operation |
| ORDVAC | Ordnance Variable Automatic Computer |
| OS | Operating System |
| PDE | Partial Differential Equation |
| PDP | Programmed Data Processor |
| PECN | Pacific Educational Computer Network |
| PEPR | Precision Encoding and Pattern Recognition |
| PERT | Program Evaluation and Review Technique |
| PL/I | Programming Language I |
| PLATO | Programmed Logic for Automatic Teaching Operations |
| PM | Phase Modulation |
| PMOS | P-Channel Metal Oxide Semiconductor |
| PMS | Processor-Memory-Switch |
| POL | Procedure-Oriented Language *or* Problem-Oriented Language |
| PoS | Point-of-Sale Terminal |
| PP | Peripheral Processor |
| PPL | Polymorphic Programming Language |
| PRT | Program Reference Table |
| PSW | Program Status Word |
| PUFFT | Purdue (University) Fast Fortran |

| | |
|---|---|
| QSAM | Queued Sequential Access Method |
| QUIKTRAN | Quick Fortran |
| RAM | Random Access Memory |
| RAMAC | Random Access Method of Accounting and Control |
| RAND | Research and Development |
| RCA | Radio Corporation of America |
| RILM | Repertoire International de la Littérature Musicale |
| RJE | Remote Job Entry |
| ROM | Read-Only Memory |
| ROS | Read-Only Storage |
| RPG | Report Program Generator |
| RTL | Resistor-Transistor Logic |
| R/W | Read/Write |
| SAGE | Semi-Automatic Ground Environment |
| SAINT | Symbolic Automatic Integrator |
| SAP | Symbolic Assembly Program |
| SCI | Simulation Councils Incorporated (now SCS) |
| SCS | Society for Computer Simulation |
| SDI | Selective Dissemination of Information |
| SEAC | Standards Eastern Automatic Computer |
| SEL | Systems Engineering Laboratories |
| SEPOL | Settlement Problem-Oriented Language |
| SERCUS | Society for the Exchange of Raytheon Computer Users Software |
| SIAM | Society for Industrial and Applied Mathematics |
| SIC | Special Interest Committee (of ACM) |
| SIG | Special Interest Group (of ACM) |
| SIMULA | Simulation Language |
| SIN | Symbolic Integrator |
| SJCC | Spring Joint Computer Conference |
| SMIS | Society for Management Information Systems |
| SNOBOL | String-Oriented Symbolic Language |
| SNR | Signal-to-Noise Ratio |
| SOAP | Symbolic Optimizer and Assembly Program |
| SP | Structured Programming |
| SPARC | Standards Planning and Requirements Committee |
| SPL | Simple Programming Language |
| SPOOLING | Simultaneous Peripheral Operations On Line |
| SPS | Symbolic Programming System |
| SPSS | Statistical Package for the Social Sciences |
| SRI | Stanford Research Institute *or* Systems Research Institute |
| SSC | Standards Steering Committee |
| SSEC | Selective Sequence Electronic Calculator |
| SSI | Small-Scale Integration |
| SSP | Scientific Subroutine Package |
| STAR | Self-Test and Repair (Computer) |
| STDM | Synchronous Time-Division Multiplexing |
| STRESS | Structural Engineering Systems Solver |
| STRUDL | Structural Design Language |
| SWAC | Standards Western Automatic Computer |
| SWAP | Society for Wang Applications and Programs |
| TASI | Time-Assigned Speech Interpolation |
| TAXIR | Taxonomic Information Retrieval |
| TDM | Time-Division Multiplexing |
| TICCIT | Time-Shared Interactive Computer-Controlled Informational Television |

| | |
|---|---|
| TIES | Total Integrated Engineering System |
| TI-MIX | Texas Instruments Minicomputer Information Exchange |
| TIP | Terminal IMP (Interface Message Processor) |
| TMR | Triple Modular Redundancy |
| TRAC | Text Reckoning and Compiler |
| TSS | Time-Sharing System |
| TTL | Transistor-Transistor Logic |
| TUCC | Triangle Universities Computing Center |
| UCLA | University of California at Los Angeles |
| UCSD | University of California at San Diego |
| UCSF | University of California at San Francisco |
| UNCOL | Universal Computer-Oriented Language |
| UNIVAC | Universal Automatic Computer |
| USASCII | United States of America Standard Code for Information Interchange (see ASCII) |
| USASI | United States of America Standards Institute (now ANSI) |
| USC | University of Southern California |
| USE | Univac Scientific Exchange |
| UUA | Univac Users Association |
| VDL | Vienna Definition Language |
| VDU | Visual Display Unit |
| VIM | Name of Control Data Corporation 6000 series users organization [Roman 6 (VI) and Roman 1000 (M)] |
| VM | Virtual Memory |
| VS | Virtual Storage |
| VSAM | Virtual Sequential Access Method |
| WATFIV | Successor to WATFOR |
| WATFOR | University of Waterloo Fortran |
| WFF | Well-formed Formula |
| WHO | World Health Organization |
| XDS | Xerox Data Systems |
| XOR | Exclusive OR |

## MATHEMATICAL NOTATION

| *Symbol* | *Meaning* |
|---|---|
| GENERAL | |
| $\Sigma$ | Summation ($\sum_{i=1}^{n} a_i = a_1 + a_2 + \cdots + a_n$). |
| $\int$ | Integral |
| $\lvert\ \rvert$ | Absolute value ($\lvert a\rvert = a$ if $a \geq 0$, $= -a$ if $a < 0$) |
| [ ] | Greatest integer in ([2.4] = 2, [−2.4] = −3) |
| [ ] | Closed interval ($[a,b]$ includes all $x$ such that $a \leq x \leq b$) |
| ( ) | Open interval [$(a,b)$ includes all $x$ such that $a < x < b$] |
| [ ), ( ] | Half-open (half-closed) interval {$[a, b)$ includes all $x$ such that $a \leq x < b$} |
| $\approx, \simeq$ | Approximately equal |
| $\sim$ | Asymptotic to |
| x | Set product [$A \times B$ consists of all pairs $(a,b)$ where $a \in A$, $b \in B$] |
| modulo (or mod) | Remainder ($x$ mod $y$ is remainder when $x$ is divided by $y$; thus, 8 mod 3 is 2) |
| $\circ$ | Binary operation (i.e., denotes any operation like + which requires two operands) |
| fl | Floating point (fl($x + y$) denotes the floating-point sum of $x$ and $y$) |
| iff | If and only if |

## APPENDIX

| | |
|---|---|
| LOGIC | |
| $\vee$ | Or |
| $\wedge$ | And |
| $\sim$ | Not |
| $\supset$ | Implication |
| $\equiv$ | Equivalence |
| $\not\equiv$ | Inequivalence |

*Notes*

1. For a description of the notation used in describing computer language constructs, *see* BACKUS-NAUR FORM.
2. For symbols used in logical circuitry, *see* COMPUTER CIRCUITRY.

## UNITS OF MEASURE

This list contains abbreviations of units of measure used in the Encyclopedia; these usually appear in their abbreviated form.

| | |
|---|---|
| *General* | |
| K | 1,000 or 1024 ($=2^{10}$); the latter refers mainly to measures of computer storage capacity |
| M | 1,000,000 |
| *Time* | |
| ms | millisecond ($10^{-3}$ sec) |
| $\mu$s | microsecond ($10^{-6}$ sec) |
| ns | nanosecond ($10^{-9}$ sec) |
| ps | picosecond ($10^{-12}$ sec) |
| *Electricity* | |
| Hz | Hertz (cycles/sec) |
| KHz | Kilohertz ($10^3$ cycles/sec) |
| MHz | Megahertz ($10^6$ cycles/sec) |
| Kc | Kilocycle ($10^3$ cycles) |
| Mc | Megacycle ($10^6$ cycles; sometimes, $10^6$ cycles/sec = 1 MHz) |
| mW | Milliwatt ($10^{-3}$ watt) |
| KW | Kilowatt ($10^3$ watts) |
| mv | Millivolt ($10^{-3}$ volt) |
| mA | Milliamp ($10^{-3}$ amp) |
| *Storage* | |
| Kb | Kilobit ($10^3$ bits) |
| Mb | Megabit ($10^6$ bits) |
| KB | Kilobyte ($10^3$ bytes) |
| MB | Megabyte ($10^6$ bytes) |
| L(x) | Location of x (in main memory) |
| C(A) | Contents of location A (in main memory) |
| *I/O* | |
| bps | Bits per second |
| chps | Characters per second |

| | |
|---|---|
| chpi | Characters per inch |
| cps | Cards per second |
| cpm | Cards per minute |
| lpm | Lines per minute |
| rpm | Revolutions per minute |

*Miscellaneous*

| | |
|---|---|
| $\mu$ | Micron ($10^{-6}$ meter) |
| mbar | Millibar ($10^{-3}$ bar [cgs unit of pressure]) |

# APPENDIX II

# USEFUL NUMERICAL TABLES

## POWERS OF TWO TABLE

| $2^n$ | $n$ | $2^{-n}$ |
|---|---|---|
| 1 | 0 | 1.0 |
| 2 | 1 | 0.5 |
| 4 | 2 | 0.25 |
| 8 | 3 | 0.125 |
| 16 | 4 | 0.062 5 |
| 32 | 5 | 0.031 25 |
| 64 | 6 | 0.015 625 |
| 128 | 7 | 0.007 812 5 |
| 256 | 8 | 0.003 906 25 |
| 512 | 9 | 0.001 953 125 |
| 1 024 | 10 | 0.000 976 562 5 |
| 2 048 | 11 | 0.000 488 281 25 |
| 4 096 | 12 | 0.000 244 140 625 |
| 8 192 | 13 | 0.000 122 070 312 5 |
| 16 384 | 14 | 0.000 061 035 156 25 |
| 32 768 | 15 | 0.000 030 517 578 125 |
| 65 536 | 16 | 0.000 015 258 789 062 5 |
| 131 072 | 17 | 0.000 007 629 394 531 25 |
| 262 144 | 18 | 0.000 003 814 697 265 625 |
| 524 288 | 19 | 0.000 001 907 348 632 812 5 |
| 1 048 576 | 20 | 0.000 000 953 674 316 406 25 |
| 2 097 152 | 21 | 0.000 000 476 837 158 203 125 |
| 4 194 304 | 22 | 0.000 000 238 418 579 101 562 5 |
| 8 388 608 | 23 | 0.000 000 119 209 289 550 781 25 |
| 16 777 216 | 24 | 0.000 000 059 604 644 775 390 625 |
| 33 554 432 | 25 | 0.000 000 029 802 322 387 695 312 5 |
| 67 108 864 | 26 | 0.000 000 014 901 161 193 847 656 25 |
| 134 217 728 | 27 | 0.000 000 007 450 580 596 923 828 125 |
| 268 435 456 | 28 | 0.000 000 003 725 290 298 461 914 062 5 |
| 536 870 912 | 29 | 0.000 000 001 862 645 149 230 957 031 25 |
| 1 073 741 824 | 30 | 0.000 000 000 931 322 574 615 478 515 625 |
| 2 147 483 648 | 31 | 0.000 000 000 465 661 287 307 739 257 812 5 |
| 4 294 967 296 | 32 | 0.000 000 000 232 830 643 653 869 628 906 25 |
| 8 589 934 592 | 33 | 0.000 000 000 116 415 321 826 934 814 453 125 |
| 17 179 869 184 | 34 | 0.000 000 000 058 207 660 913 467 407 226 562 5 |
| 34 359 738 368 | 35 | 0.000 000 000 029 103 830 456 733 703 613 281 25 |
| 68 719 476 736 | 36 | 0.000 000 000 014 551 915 228 366 851 806 640 625 |
| 137 438 953 472 | 37 | 0.000 000 000 007 275 957 614 183 425 903 320 312 5 |
| 274 877 906 944 | 38 | 0.000 000 000 003 637 978 807 091 712 951 660 156 25 |
| 549 755 813 888 | 39 | 0.000 000 000 001 818 989 403 545 856 475 830 078 125 |

# OCTAL-DECIMAL INTEGER CONVERSION TABLE

0000 to 0777 (Octal) | 0000 to 0511 (Decimal)

Octal Decimal
10000 - 4096
20000 - 8192
30000 - 12288
40000 - 16384
50000 - 20480
60000 - 24576
70000 - 28672

| | 0 | 1 | 2 | 3 | 4 | 5 | 6 | 7 |
|---|---|---|---|---|---|---|---|---|
| 0000 | 0000 | 0001 | 0002 | 0003 | 0004 | 0005 | 0006 | 0007 |
| 0010 | 0008 | 0009 | 0010 | 0011 | 0012 | 0013 | 0014 | 0015 |
| 0020 | 0016 | 0017 | 0018 | 0019 | 0020 | 0021 | 0022 | 0023 |
| 0030 | 0024 | 0025 | 0026 | 0027 | 0028 | 0029 | 0030 | 0031 |
| 0040 | 0032 | 0033 | 0034 | 0035 | 0036 | 0037 | 0038 | 0039 |
| 0050 | 0040 | 0041 | 0042 | 0043 | 0044 | 0045 | 0046 | 0047 |
| 0060 | 0048 | 0049 | 0050 | 0051 | 0052 | 0053 | 0054 | 0055 |
| 0070 | 0056 | 0057 | 0058 | 0059 | 0060 | 0061 | 0062 | 0063 |
| 0100 | 0064 | 0065 | 0066 | 0067 | 0068 | 0069 | 0070 | 0071 |
| 0110 | 0072 | 0073 | 0074 | 0075 | 0076 | 0077 | 0078 | 0079 |
| 0120 | 0080 | 0081 | 0082 | 0083 | 0084 | 0085 | 0086 | 0087 |
| 0130 | 0088 | 0089 | 0090 | 0091 | 0092 | 0093 | 0094 | 0095 |
| 0140 | 0096 | 0097 | 0098 | 0099 | 0100 | 0101 | 0102 | 0103 |
| 0150 | 0104 | 0105 | 0106 | 0107 | 0108 | 0109 | 0110 | 0111 |
| 0160 | 0112 | 0113 | 0114 | 0115 | 0116 | 0117 | 0118 | 0119 |
| 0170 | 0120 | 0121 | 0122 | 0123 | 0124 | 0125 | 0126 | 0127 |
| 0200 | 0128 | 0129 | 0130 | 0131 | 0132 | 0133 | 0134 | 0135 |
| 0210 | 0136 | 0137 | 0138 | 0139 | 0140 | 0141 | 0142 | 0143 |
| 0220 | 0144 | 0145 | 0146 | 0147 | 0148 | 0149 | 0150 | 0151 |
| 0230 | 0152 | 0153 | 0154 | 0155 | 0156 | 0157 | 0158 | 0159 |
| 0240 | 0160 | 0161 | 0162 | 0163 | 0164 | 0165 | 0166 | 0167 |
| 0250 | 0168 | 0169 | 0170 | 0171 | 0172 | 0173 | 0174 | 0175 |
| 0260 | 0176 | 0177 | 0178 | 0179 | 0180 | 0181 | 0182 | 0183 |
| 0270 | 0184 | 0185 | 0186 | 0187 | 0188 | 0189 | 0190 | 0191 |
| 0300 | 0192 | 0193 | 0194 | 0195 | 0196 | 0197 | 0198 | 0199 |
| 0310 | 0200 | 0201 | 0202 | 0203 | 0204 | 0205 | 0206 | 0207 |
| 0320 | 0208 | 0209 | 0210 | 0211 | 0212 | 0213 | 0214 | 0215 |
| 0330 | 0216 | 0217 | 0218 | 0219 | 0220 | 0221 | 0222 | 0223 |
| 0340 | 0224 | 0225 | 0226 | 0227 | 0228 | 0229 | 0230 | 0231 |
| 0350 | 0232 | 0233 | 0234 | 0235 | 0236 | 0237 | 0238 | 0239 |
| 0360 | 0240 | 0241 | 0242 | 0243 | 0244 | 0245 | 0246 | 0247 |
| 0370 | 0248 | 0249 | 0250 | 0251 | 0252 | 0253 | 0254 | 0255 |

| | 0 | 1 | 2 | 3 | 4 | 5 | 6 | 7 |
|---|---|---|---|---|---|---|---|---|
| 0400 | 0256 | 0257 | 0258 | 0259 | 0260 | 0261 | 0262 | 0263 |
| 0410 | 0264 | 0265 | 0266 | 0267 | 0268 | 0269 | 0270 | 0271 |
| 0420 | 0272 | 0273 | 0274 | 0275 | 0276 | 0277 | 0278 | 0279 |
| 0430 | 0280 | 0281 | 0282 | 0283 | 0284 | 0285 | 0286 | 0287 |
| 0440 | 0288 | 0289 | 0290 | 0291 | 0292 | 0293 | 0294 | 0295 |
| 0450 | 0296 | 0297 | 0298 | 0299 | 0300 | 0301 | 0302 | 0303 |
| 0460 | 0304 | 0305 | 0306 | 0307 | 0308 | 0309 | 0310 | 0311 |
| 0470 | 0312 | 0313 | 0314 | 0315 | 0316 | 0317 | 0318 | 0319 |
| 0500 | 0320 | 0321 | 0322 | 0323 | 0324 | 0325 | 0326 | 0327 |
| 0510 | 0328 | 0329 | 0330 | 0331 | 0332 | 0333 | 0334 | 0335 |
| 0520 | 0336 | 0337 | 0338 | 0339 | 0340 | 0341 | 0342 | 0343 |
| 0530 | 0344 | 0345 | 0346 | 0347 | 0348 | 0349 | 0350 | 0351 |
| 0540 | 0352 | 0353 | 0354 | 0355 | 0356 | 0357 | 0358 | 0359 |
| 0550 | 0360 | 0361 | 0362 | 0363 | 0364 | 0365 | 0366 | 0367 |
| 0560 | 0368 | 0369 | 0370 | 0371 | 0372 | 0373 | 0374 | 0375 |
| 0570 | 0376 | 0377 | 0378 | 0379 | 0380 | 0381 | 0382 | 0383 |
| 0600 | 0384 | 0385 | 0386 | 0387 | 0388 | 0389 | 0390 | 0391 |
| 0610 | 0392 | 0393 | 0394 | 0395 | 0396 | 0397 | 0398 | 0399 |
| 0620 | 0400 | 0401 | 0402 | 0403 | 0404 | 0405 | 0406 | 0407 |
| 0630 | 0408 | 0409 | 0410 | 0411 | 0412 | 0413 | 0414 | 0415 |
| 0640 | 0416 | 0417 | 0418 | 0419 | 0420 | 0421 | 0422 | 0423 |
| 0650 | 0424 | 0425 | 0426 | 0427 | 0428 | 0429 | 0430 | 0431 |
| 0660 | 0432 | 0433 | 0434 | 0435 | 0436 | 0437 | 0438 | 0439 |
| 0670 | 0440 | 0441 | 0442 | 0443 | 0444 | 0445 | 0446 | 0447 |
| 0700 | 0448 | 0449 | 0450 | 0451 | 0452 | 0453 | 0454 | 0455 |
| 0710 | 0456 | 0457 | 0458 | 0459 | 0460 | 0461 | 0462 | 0463 |
| 0720 | 0464 | 0465 | 0466 | 0467 | 0468 | 0469 | 0470 | 0471 |
| 0730 | 0472 | 0473 | 0474 | 0475 | 0476 | 0477 | 0478 | 0479 |
| 0740 | 0480 | 0481 | 0482 | 0483 | 0484 | 0485 | 0486 | 0487 |
| 0750 | 0488 | 0489 | 0490 | 0491 | 0492 | 0493 | 0494 | 0495 |
| 0760 | 0496 | 0497 | 0498 | 0499 | 0500 | 0501 | 0502 | 0503 |
| 0770 | 0504 | 0505 | 0506 | 0507 | 0508 | 0509 | 0510 | 0511 |

1000 to 1777 (Octal) | 0512 to 1023 (Decimal)

| | 0 | 1 | 2 | 3 | 4 | 5 | 6 | 7 |
|---|---|---|---|---|---|---|---|---|
| 1000 | 0512 | 0513 | 0514 | 0515 | 0516 | 0517 | 0518 | 0519 |
| 1010 | 0520 | 0521 | 0522 | 0523 | 0524 | 0525 | 0526 | 0527 |
| 1020 | 0528 | 0529 | 0530 | 0531 | 0532 | 0533 | 0534 | 0535 |
| 1030 | 0536 | 0537 | 0538 | 0539 | 0540 | 0541 | 0542 | 0543 |
| 1040 | 0544 | 0545 | 0546 | 0547 | 0548 | 0549 | 0550 | 0551 |
| 1050 | 0552 | 0553 | 0554 | 0555 | 0556 | 0557 | 0558 | 0559 |
| 1060 | 0560 | 0561 | 0562 | 0563 | 0564 | 0565 | 0566 | 0567 |
| 1070 | 0568 | 0569 | 0570 | 0571 | 0572 | 0573 | 0574 | 0575 |
| 1100 | 0576 | 0577 | 0578 | 0579 | 0580 | 0581 | 0582 | 0583 |
| 1110 | 0584 | 0585 | 0586 | 0587 | 0588 | 0589 | 0590 | 0591 |
| 1120 | 0592 | 0593 | 0594 | 0595 | 0596 | 0597 | 0598 | 0599 |
| 1130 | 0600 | 0601 | 0602 | 0603 | 0604 | 0605 | 0606 | 0607 |
| 1140 | 0608 | 0609 | 0610 | 0611 | 0612 | 0613 | 0614 | 0615 |
| 1150 | 0616 | 0617 | 0618 | 0619 | 0620 | 0621 | 0622 | 0623 |
| 1160 | 0624 | 0625 | 0626 | 0627 | 0628 | 0629 | 0630 | 0631 |
| 1170 | 0632 | 0633 | 0634 | 0635 | 0636 | 0637 | 0638 | 0639 |
| 1200 | 0640 | 0641 | 0642 | 0643 | 0644 | 0645 | 0646 | 0647 |
| 1210 | 0648 | 0649 | 0650 | 0651 | 0652 | 0653 | 0654 | 0655 |
| 1220 | 0656 | 0657 | 0658 | 0659 | 0660 | 0661 | 0662 | 0663 |
| 1230 | 0664 | 0665 | 0666 | 0667 | 0668 | 0669 | 0670 | 0671 |
| 1240 | 0672 | 0673 | 0674 | 0675 | 0676 | 0677 | 0678 | 0679 |
| 1250 | 0680 | 0681 | 0682 | 0683 | 0684 | 0685 | 0686 | 0687 |
| 1260 | 0688 | 0689 | 0690 | 0691 | 0692 | 0693 | 0694 | 0695 |
| 1270 | 0696 | 0697 | 0698 | 0699 | 0700 | 0701 | 0702 | 0703 |
| 1300 | 0704 | 0705 | 0706 | 0707 | 0708 | 0709 | 0710 | 0711 |
| 1310 | 0712 | 0713 | 0714 | 0715 | 0716 | 0717 | 0718 | 0719 |
| 1320 | 0720 | 0721 | 0722 | 0723 | 0724 | 0725 | 0726 | 0727 |
| 1330 | 0728 | 0729 | 0730 | 0731 | 0732 | 0733 | 0734 | 0735 |
| 1340 | 0736 | 0737 | 0738 | 0739 | 0740 | 0741 | 0742 | 0743 |
| 1350 | 0744 | 0745 | 0746 | 0747 | 0748 | 0749 | 0750 | 0751 |
| 1360 | 0752 | 0753 | 0754 | 0755 | 0756 | 0757 | 0758 | 0759 |
| 1370 | 0760 | 0761 | 0762 | 0763 | 0764 | 0765 | 0766 | 0767 |

| | 0 | 1 | 2 | 3 | 4 | 5 | 6 | 7 |
|---|---|---|---|---|---|---|---|---|
| 1400 | 0768 | 0769 | 0770 | 0771 | 0772 | 0773 | 0774 | 0775 |
| 1410 | 0776 | 0777 | 0778 | 0779 | 0780 | 0781 | 0782 | 0783 |
| 1420 | 0784 | 0785 | 0786 | 0787 | 0788 | 0789 | 0790 | 0791 |
| 1430 | 0792 | 0793 | 0794 | 0795 | 0796 | 0797 | 0798 | 0799 |
| 1440 | 0800 | 0801 | 0802 | 0803 | 0804 | 0805 | 0806 | 0807 |
| 1450 | 0808 | 0809 | 0810 | 0811 | 0812 | 0813 | 0814 | 0815 |
| 1460 | 0816 | 0817 | 0818 | 0819 | 0820 | 0821 | 0822 | 0823 |
| 1470 | 0824 | 0825 | 0826 | 0827 | 0828 | 0829 | 0830 | 0831 |
| 1500 | 0832 | 0833 | 0834 | 0835 | 0836 | 0837 | 0838 | 0839 |
| 1510 | 0840 | 0841 | 0842 | 0843 | 0844 | 0845 | 0846 | 0847 |
| 1520 | 0848 | 0849 | 0850 | 0851 | 0852 | 0853 | 0854 | 0855 |
| 1530 | 0856 | 0857 | 0858 | 0859 | 0860 | 0861 | 0862 | 0863 |
| 1540 | 0864 | 0865 | 0866 | 0867 | 0868 | 0869 | 0870 | 0871 |
| 1550 | 0872 | 0873 | 0874 | 0875 | 0876 | 0877 | 0878 | 0879 |
| 1560 | 0880 | 0881 | 0882 | 0883 | 0884 | 0885 | 0886 | 0887 |
| 1570 | 0888 | 0889 | 0890 | 0891 | 0892 | 0893 | 0894 | 0895 |
| 1600 | 0896 | 0897 | 0898 | 0899 | 0900 | 0901 | 0902 | 0903 |
| 1610 | 0904 | 0905 | 0906 | 0907 | 0908 | 0909 | 0910 | 0911 |
| 1620 | 0912 | 0913 | 0914 | 0915 | 0916 | 0917 | 0918 | 0919 |
| 1630 | 0920 | 0921 | 0922 | 0923 | 0924 | 0925 | 0926 | 0927 |
| 1640 | 0928 | 0929 | 0930 | 0931 | 0932 | 0933 | 0934 | 0935 |
| 1650 | 0936 | 0937 | 0938 | 0939 | 0940 | 0941 | 0942 | 0943 |
| 1660 | 0944 | 0945 | 0946 | 0947 | 0948 | 0949 | 0950 | 0951 |
| 1670 | 0952 | 0953 | 0954 | 0955 | 0956 | 0957 | 0958 | 0959 |
| 1700 | 0960 | 0961 | 0962 | 0963 | 0964 | 0965 | 0966 | 0967 |
| 1710 | 0968 | 0969 | 0970 | 0971 | 0972 | 0973 | 0974 | 0975 |
| 1720 | 0976 | 0977 | 0978 | 0979 | 0980 | 0981 | 0982 | 0983 |
| 1730 | 0984 | 0985 | 0986 | 0987 | 0988 | 0989 | 0990 | 0991 |
| 1740 | 0992 | 0993 | 0994 | 0995 | 0996 | 0997 | 0998 | 0999 |
| 1750 | 1000 | 1001 | 1002 | 1003 | 1004 | 1005 | 1006 | 1007 |
| 1760 | 1008 | 1009 | 1010 | 1011 | 1012 | 1013 | 1014 | 1015 |
| 1770 | 1016 | 1017 | 1018 | 1019 | 1020 | 1021 | 1022 | 1023 |

# OCTAL-DECIMAL FRACTION CONVERSION TABLE

| OCTAL | DEC. | OCTAL | DEC. | OCTAL | DEC. | OCTAL | DEC. |
|---|---|---|---|---|---|---|---|
| .000 | .000000 | .100 | .125000 | .200 | .250000 | .300 | .375000 |
| .001 | .001953 | .101 | .126953 | .201 | .251953 | .301 | .376953 |
| .002 | .003906 | .102 | .128906 | .202 | .253906 | .302 | .378906 |
| .003 | .005859 | .103 | .130859 | .203 | .255859 | .303 | .380859 |
| .004 | .007812 | .104 | .132812 | .204 | .257812 | .304 | .382812 |
| .005 | .009765 | .105 | .134765 | .205 | .259765 | .305 | .384765 |
| .006 | .011718 | .106 | .136718 | .206 | .261718 | .306 | .386718 |
| .007 | .013671 | .107 | .138671 | .207 | .263671 | .307 | .388671 |
| .010 | .015625 | .110 | .140625 | .210 | .265625 | .310 | .390625 |
| .011 | .017578 | .111 | .142578 | .211 | .267578 | .311 | .392578 |
| .012 | .019531 | .112 | .144531 | .212 | .269531 | .312 | .394531 |
| .013 | .021484 | .113 | .146484 | .213 | .271484 | .313 | .396484 |
| .014 | .023437 | .114 | .148437 | .214 | .273437 | .314 | .398437 |
| .015 | .025390 | .115 | .150390 | .215 | .275390 | .315 | .400390 |
| .016 | .027343 | .116 | .152343 | .216 | .277343 | .316 | .402343 |
| .017 | .029296 | .117 | .154296 | .217 | .279296 | .317 | .404296 |
| .020 | .031250 | .120 | .156250 | .220 | .281250 | .320 | .406250 |
| .021 | .033203 | .121 | .158203 | .221 | .283203 | .321 | .408203 |
| .022 | .035156 | .122 | .160156 | .222 | .285156 | .322 | .410156 |
| .023 | .037109 | .123 | .162109 | .223 | .287109 | .323 | .412109 |
| .024 | .039062 | .124 | .164062 | .224 | .289062 | .324 | .414062 |
| .025 | .041015 | .125 | .166015 | .225 | .291015 | .325 | .416015 |
| .026 | .042968 | .126 | .167968 | .226 | .292968 | .326 | .417968 |
| .027 | .044921 | .127 | .169921 | .227 | .294921 | .327 | .419921 |
| .030 | .046875 | .130 | .171875 | .230 | .296875 | .330 | .421875 |
| .031 | .048828 | .131 | .173828 | .231 | .298828 | .331 | .423828 |
| .032 | .050781 | .132 | .175781 | .232 | .300781 | .332 | .425781 |
| .033 | .052734 | .133 | .177734 | .233 | .302734 | .333 | .427734 |
| .034 | .054687 | .134 | .179687 | .234 | .304687 | .334 | .429687 |
| .035 | .056640 | .135 | .181640 | .235 | .306640 | .335 | .431640 |
| .036 | .058593 | .136 | .183593 | .236 | .308593 | .336 | .433593 |
| .037 | .060546 | .137 | .185546 | .237 | .310546 | .337 | .435546 |
| .040 | .062500 | .140 | .187500 | .240 | .312500 | .340 | .437500 |
| .041 | .064453 | .141 | .189453 | .241 | .314453 | .341 | .439453 |
| .042 | .066406 | .142 | .191406 | .242 | .316406 | .342 | .441406 |
| .043 | .068359 | .143 | .193359 | .243 | .318359 | .343 | .443359 |
| .044 | .070312 | .144 | .195312 | .244 | .320312 | .344 | .445312 |
| .045 | .072265 | .145 | .197265 | .245 | .322265 | .345 | .447265 |
| .046 | .074218 | .146 | .199218 | .246 | .324218 | .346 | .449218 |
| .047 | .076171 | .147 | .201171 | .247 | .326171 | .347 | .451171 |
| .050 | .078125 | .150 | .203125 | .250 | .328125 | .350 | .453125 |
| .051 | .080078 | .151 | .205078 | .251 | .330078 | .351 | .455078 |
| .052 | .082031 | .152 | .207031 | .252 | .332031 | .352 | .457031 |
| .053 | .083984 | .153 | .208984 | .253 | .333984 | .353 | .458984 |
| .054 | .085937 | .154 | .210937 | .254 | .335937 | .354 | .460937 |
| .055 | .087890 | .155 | .212890 | .255 | .337890 | .355 | .462890 |
| .056 | .089843 | .156 | .214843 | .256 | .339843 | .356 | .464843 |
| .057 | .091796 | .157 | .216796 | .257 | .341796 | .357 | .466796 |
| .060 | .093750 | .160 | .218750 | .260 | .343750 | .360 | .468750 |
| .061 | .095703 | .161 | .220703 | .261 | .345703 | .361 | .470703 |
| .062 | .097656 | .162 | .222656 | .262 | .347656 | .362 | .472656 |
| .063 | .099609 | .163 | .224609 | .263 | .349609 | .363 | .474609 |
| .064 | .101562 | .164 | .226562 | .264 | .351562 | .364 | .476562 |
| .065 | .103515 | .165 | .228515 | .265 | .353515 | .365 | .478515 |
| .066 | .105468 | .166 | .230468 | .266 | .355468 | .366 | .480468 |
| .067 | .107421 | .167 | .232421 | .267 | .357421 | .367 | .482421 |
| .070 | .109375 | .170 | .234375 | .270 | .359375 | .370 | .484375 |
| .071 | .111328 | .171 | .236328 | .271 | .361328 | .371 | .486328 |
| .072 | .113281 | .172 | .238281 | .272 | .363281 | .372 | .488281 |
| .073 | .115234 | .173 | .240234 | .273 | .365234 | .373 | .490234 |
| .074 | .117187 | .174 | .242187 | .274 | .367187 | .374 | .492187 |
| .075 | .119140 | .175 | .244140 | .275 | .369140 | .375 | .494140 |
| .076 | .121093 | .176 | .246093 | .276 | .371093 | .376 | .496093 |
| .077 | .123046 | .177 | .248046 | .277 | .373046 | .377 | .498046 |

# INDEX

The *Encyclopedia of Computer Science* is a comprehensive reference in which a great amount of information is contained in almost 500 articles. In order to help the user locate the subject he is looking for, the entire contents has been analyzed and organized in the index. To find an answer, the reader should look up the *key* word in his question, and the index will guide him to the location of such information. The usefulness of this encyclopedia will be greatly increased if the user becomes familiar with the following basic principles:

*Index headings* in boldface capital letters indicate there is a main article on the subject. The first reference is to *that* article.

*Cross references* in the index refer to index headings.

A *see* cross reference directs you from a heading where there are no references to a heading where you will find all the entries.

A *see also* cross reference directs you to related information.

*Alphabetical arrangement*

All entries are arranged alphabetically by word, up to a comma in an inverted heading. Example:

Computer
Computer, Using a
Computer accounting and resource control
Computers, Multiple address
Computers and society

Abbreviations appear at the beginning of each letter. Acronyms, however, are alphabetized with the regular headings.

A

## INDEX

## INDEX



### B

## INDEX



## C

## INDEX

# INDEX

## INDEX

## INDEX

# I

## INDEX



## L

## N

## S

# INDEX